jubilee, and a deduction shall be made from the valuation. 19And if he who dedicates the field wishes to redeem it, then he shall add a fifth to its valuation price, and it shall remain his. 20But if he does not wish to redeem the field, or if he has sold the field to another man, it shall not be redeemed anymore. 21But the field, when it is released in the jubilee, shall be a holy gift to the LORD, like a field that has been devoted. The priest shall be in possession of it. 22If he dedicates to the LORD a field that he has bought, which is not a part of his possession, 23then the priest shall calculate the amount of the valuation for it up to the year of jubilee, and the man shall give the valuation on that day as a holy gift to the LORD. 24In the year of jubilee the field shall return to him from whom it was bought, to whom the land belongs as a possession. 25Every valuation shall be according to the shekel of the sanctuary: twenty gerahs[1] shall make a shekel.

26"But a firstborn of animals, which as a firstborn belongs to the LORD, no man may dedicate; whether ox or sheep, it is the LORD's. 27And if it is an unclean animal, then he shall buy it back at the valuation, and add a fifth to it; or, if it is not redeemed, it shall be sold at the valuation.

28"But no devoted thing that a man devotes to the LORD, of anything that he has, whether man or beast, or of his inherited field, shall be sold or redeemed; every devoted thing is most holy to the LORD. 29No one devoted, who is to be devoted for destruction[2] from mankind, shall be ransomed; he shall surely be put to death.

30"Every tithe of the land, whether of the seed of the land or of the fruit of the trees, is the LORD's; it is holy to the LORD. 31If a man wishes to redeem some of his tithe, he shall add a fifth to it. 32And every tithe of herds and flocks, every tenth animal of all that pass under the herdsman's staff, shall be holy to the LORD. 33One shall not differentiate between good or bad, neither shall he make a substitute for it; and if he does substitute for it, then both it and the substitute shall be holy; it shall not be redeemed."

34These are the commandments that the LORD commanded Moses for the people of Israel on Mount Sinai.

[1] A *gerah* was about 1/50 ounce or 0.6 gram [2] That is, set apart (devoted) as an offering to the Lord (for destruction)

ENGLISH STANDARD VERSION

The Jesus Bible

sixty-six books. one story. all about one name.

ZONDERVAN®

Published by Zondervan
Grand Rapids, Michigan, USA

www.Zondervan.com

Library of Congress Catalog Card Number 2018948803

Printed in Vietnam

---

26 27 28 29 30 31 32 33 /SEV/ 20 19 18 17 16 15 14 13 12 11

TABLE OF CONTENTS

THE OLD TESTAMENT

THE NEW TESTAMENT

PREFACE

The Bible

"This Book [is] the most valuable thing that this world affords. Here is Wisdom; this is the royal Law; these are the lively Oracles of God." With these words the Moderator of the Church of Scotland hands a Bible to the new monarch in Britain's coronation service. These words echo the King James Bible translators, who wrote in 1611: "God's sacred Word . . . is that inestimable treasure that excelleth all the riches of the earth." This assessment of the Bible is the motivating force behind the publication of the English Standard Version.

Translation Legacy

The English Standard Version (ESV) stands in the classic mainstream of English Bible translations over the past half-millennium. The fountainhead of that stream was William Tyndale's New Testament of 1526; marking its course were the King James Version of 1611 (KJV), the English Revised Version of 1885 (RV), the American Standard Version of 1901 (ASV), and the Revised Standard Version of 1952 and 1971 (RSV). In that stream, faithfulness to the text and vigorous pursuit of precision were combined with simplicity, beauty, and dignity of expression. Our goal has been to carry forward this legacy for this generation and generations to come.

To this end each word and phrase in the ESV has been carefully weighed against the original Hebrew, Aramaic, and Greek, to ensure the fullest accuracy and clarity and to avoid under-translating or overlooking any nuance of the original text. The words and phrases themselves grow out of the Tyndale–King James legacy, and most recently out of the RSV, with the 1971 RSV text providing the starting point for our work. Archaic language has been brought into line with current usage and significant corrections have been made in the translation of key texts. But throughout, our goal has been to retain the depth of meaning and enduring quality of language that have made their indelible mark on the English-speaking world and have defined the life and doctrine of its church over the last five centuries.

Translation Philosophy

The ESV is an "essentially literal" translation that seeks as far as possible to reproduce the precise wording of the original text and the personal style of each Bible writer. As such, its emphasis is on "word-for-word" correspondence, at the same time taking full account of differences in grammar, syntax, and idiom between current literary English and the original languages. Thus it seeks to be transparent to the original text, letting the reader see as directly as possible the structure and exact force of the original.

In contrast to the ESV, some Bible versions have followed a "thought-for-thought" rather than "word-for-word" translation philosophy, emphasizing "dynamic equivalence" rather than the "essentially literal" meaning of the original. A "thought-for-thought" translation is of necessity more inclined to reflect the interpretive views of the translator and the influences of contemporary culture.

Every translation is at many points a trade-off between literal precision and readability, between "formal equivalence" in expression and "functional equivalence" in communication, and the ESV is no exception. Within this framework we have sought to be "as literal as possible" while maintaining clarity of expression and literary excellence. Therefore, to the extent that plain English permits and the meaning in each case allows, we have sought to use the same English word for important recurring words in the original; and, as far as grammar and syntax allow, we have rendered Old Testament passages cited in the New in ways that show their correspondence. Thus in each of these areas, as well as throughout the Bible as a whole, we have sought to capture the echoes and overtones of meaning that are so abundantly present in the original texts.

As an essentially literal translation, taking into account grammar and syntax, the ESV thus seeks to carry over every possible nuance of meaning in the original words of Scripture into our own language. As such, the ESV is ideally suited for in-depth study of the Bible. Indeed, with commitment to literary excellence, the ESV is equally well suited for public reading and preaching, for private reading and reflection, for both academic and devotional study, and for Scripture memorization.

Translation Principles and Style

The ESV also carries forward classic translation principles in its literary style. Accordingly it retains theological terminology—words such as grace, faith, justification, sanctification, redemption, regeneration, reconciliation, propitiation—because of their central importance for Christian doctrine and also because the underlying Greek words were already becoming key words and technical terms among Christians in New Testament times.

The ESV lets the stylistic variety of the biblical writers fully express itself—from the exalted prose that opens Genesis, to the flowing narratives of the historical books, to the rich metaphors and dramatic imagery of the poetic books, to the ringing rhetoric in the prophetic books, to the smooth elegance of Luke, to the profound simplicities of John, and the closely reasoned logic of Paul.

In punctuating, paragraphing, dividing long sentences, and rendering connectives, the ESV follows the path that seems to make the ongoing flow of thought clearest in English. The biblical languages regularly connect sentences by frequent repetition of words such as "and," "but," and "for," in a way that goes beyond the conventions of current literary English. Effective translation, however, requires that these links in the original be reproduced so that the flow of the argument will be transparent to the reader. We have therefore normally translated these connectives, though occasionally we have varied the rendering by using alternatives (such as "also," "however," "now," "so," "then," or "thus") when they better express the linkage in specific instances.

In the area of gender language, the goal of the ESV is to render literally what is in the original. For example, "anyone" replaces "any man" where there is no word corresponding to "man" in the original languages, and "people" rather than "men" is regularly used where the original languages refer to both men and women. But the words "man" and "men" are retained where a male meaning component is part of the original Greek or Hebrew. Likewise, the word "man" has been retained where the original text intends to convey a clear contrast between "God" on the one hand and "man" on the other hand, with "man" being used in the collective sense of the whole human race (see Luke 2:52). Similarly, the English word "brothers" (translating the Greek word *adelphoi*) is retained as an important familial form of address between fellow-Jews and fellow-Christians in the first century. A recurring note is included to indicate that the term "brothers" (*adelphoi*) was often used in Greek to refer to both men and women, and to indicate the specific instances in the text where this is the case. In addition, the English word "sons" (translating the Greek word *huioi*) is retained in specific instances because the underlying Greek term usually includes a male meaning component and it was used as a legal term in the adoption and inheritance laws of first-century Rome. As used by the apostle Paul, this term refers to the status of all Christians, both men and women, who, having been adopted into God's family, now enjoy all the privileges, obligations, and inheritance rights of God's children.

The inclusive use of the generic "he" has also regularly been retained, because this is consistent with similar usage in the original languages and because an essentially literal translation would be impossible without it.

In each case the objective has been transparency to the original text, allowing the reader to understand the original on its own terms rather than in the terms of our present-day Western culture.

The Translation of Specialized Terms

In the translation of biblical terms referring to God, the ESV takes great care to convey the specific nuances of meaning of the original Hebrew and Greek words. First, concerning terms that refer to God in the Old Testament: God, the Maker of heaven and earth, introduced himself to the people of Israel with a special personal name, the consonants for which are YHWH (see Exodus 3:14–15). Scholars call this the "Tetragrammaton," a Greek term referring to the four Hebrew letters YHWH. The exact pronunciation of YHWH is uncertain, because the Jewish people considered the personal name of God to be so holy that it should never be spoken aloud. Instead of reading the word YHWH, they would normally read the Hebrew word *'adonay* ("Lord"), and the ancient translations into Greek, Syriac, and Aramaic also followed this practice. When the vowels of the word *'adonay* are placed with the consonants of YHWH, this results in the familiar word *Jehovah* that was used in some earlier English Bible translations. As is common among English translations today, the ESV usually renders the personal name of God (YHWH) with the word LORD (printed in small capitals). An exception to this is when the Hebrew word *'adonay* appears together with YHWH, in which case the two words are rendered together as "the Lord [in lowercase] GOD [in small capitals]." In contrast to the personal name for God (YHWH), the more general name for God in Old Testament Hebrew is *'elohim* and its related forms of *'el* or *'eloah*, all of which are normally translated "God" (in lowercase letters). The use of these different ways to translate the Hebrew words for God is especially beneficial to English readers, enabling them to see and understand the different ways that the *personal* name and the *general* name for God are both used to refer to the *One True God* of the Old Testament.

Second, in the New Testament, the Greek word *Christos* has been translated consistently as "Christ." Although the term originally meant simply "anointed," among Jews in New Testament times it had specifically come to designate the Messiah, the great Savior that God had promised to raise up. In other New Testament contexts, however, especially among Gentiles, *Christos* ("Christ") was on its way to becoming a proper name. It is important, therefore, to keep the context in mind in understanding the various ways that *Christos* ("Christ") is used in the New Testament. At the same time, in accord with its "essentially literal" translation philosophy, the ESV has retained consistency and concordance in the translation of *Christos* ("Christ") throughout the New Testament.

Third, a particular difficulty is presented when words in biblical Hebrew and Greek refer to ancient practices and institutions that do not correspond directly to those in the modern world. Such is the case in the translation of *'ebed* (Hebrew) and *doulos* (Greek), terms which are often rendered "slave." These terms, however, actually cover a range of relationships that requires a range of renderings—"slave," "bondservant," or "servant"—depending on the context. Further, the word "slave" currently carries associations with the often brutal and dehumanizing institution of slavery particularly in nineteenth-century America. For this reason, the ESV translation of the words *'ebed* and *doulos* has been undertaken with particular attention to their meaning in each specific context. Thus in Old Testament times, one might enter slavery either voluntarily (e.g., to escape poverty or to pay off a debt) or involuntarily (e.g., by birth, by being captured in battle, or by judicial sentence). Protection for all in servitude in ancient Israel was provided by the Mosaic Law, including specific provisions for release from slavery. In New Testament times, a *doulos* is often best described as a "bondservant"—that is, as someone in the Roman Empire officially bound under contract to serve his master for seven years (except for those in Caesar's household in Rome who were contracted for fourteen years). When the contract expired, the person was freed, given his wage that had been saved by the master, and officially declared a freedman. The ESV usage thus seeks to express the most fitting nuance of meaning in each context. Where absolute ownership by a master is envisaged (as in Romans 6), "slave" is used; where a more limited form of servitude is in view, "bondservant" is used (as in 1 Corinthians 7:21–24); where the context indicates a wide range of freedom (as in John 4:51), "servant" is preferred. Footnotes are generally provided to identify the Hebrew or Greek and the range of meaning that these terms may carry in each case. The issues involved in translating the Greek word *doulos* apply also to the Greek word *sundoulos*, translated in the text as "fellow servant."

Fourth, it is sometimes suggested that Bible translations should capitalize pronouns referring to deity. It has seemed best not to capitalize deity pronouns in the ESV, however, for the following reasons: first, there is nothing in the original Hebrew and Greek manuscripts that corresponds to such capitalization; second, the practice of capitalizing deity pronouns in English Bible translations is a recent innovation, which began only in the mid-twentieth century; and, third, such capitalization is absent from the KJV Bible and the whole stream of Bible translations that the ESV carries forward.

A fifth specialized term, the word "behold," usually has been retained as the most common translation for the Hebrew word *hinneh* and the Greek word *idou*. Both of these words mean something like "Pay careful attention to what follows! This is important!" Other than the word "behold," there is no single word in English that fits well in most contexts. Although "Look!" and "See!" and "Listen!" would be workable in some contexts, in many others these words lack sufficient weight and dignity. Given the principles of "essentially literal" translation, it is important not to leave *hinneh* and *idou* completely untranslated, and so to lose the intended emphasis in the original languages. The older and more formal word "behold" has usually been retained, therefore, as the best available option for conveying the original weight of meaning.

Textual Basis and Resources

The ESV is based on the Masoretic text of the Hebrew Bible as found in *Biblia Hebraica Stuttgartensia* (5th ed., 1997), and on the Greek text in the 2014 editions of the *Greek New Testament* (5th corrected ed.), published by the United Bible Societies (UBS), and *Novum Testamentum Graece* (28th ed., 2012), edited by Nestle and Aland. The currently renewed respect among Old Testament scholars for the Masoretic text is reflected in the ESV's attempt, wherever possible, to translate difficult Hebrew passages as they stand in the Masoretic text rather than resorting to emendations or to finding an alternative reading in the ancient versions. In exceptional, difficult cases, the Dead Sea Scrolls, the Septuagint, the Samaritan Pentateuch, the Syriac Peshitta, the Latin Vulgate, and other sources were consulted to shed possible light on the text, or, if necessary, to support a divergence from the Masoretic text. Similarly, in a few difficult cases in the New Testament, the ESV has followed a Greek text different from the text given preference in the UBS/Nestle-Aland 28th edition. Throughout, the translation team has benefited greatly from the massive textual resources that have become readily available recently, from new insights into biblical laws and culture, and from current advances in Hebrew and Greek lexicography and grammatical understanding.

Textual Footnotes

The footnotes that are included in most editions of the ESV are therefore an integral part of the ESV translation, informing the reader of textual variations and difficulties and showing how these have been resolved by the ESV translation team. In addition to this, the footnotes indicate significant alternative readings and occasionally provide an explanation for technical terms or for a difficult reading in the text.

Publishing Team

The ESV publishing team has included more than a hundred people. The fourteen-member Translation Oversight Committee has benefited from the work of more than fifty biblical experts serving as Translation Review Scholars and from the comments of the more than fifty members of the Advisory Council, all of which was carried out under the auspices of the Crossway Board of Directors. This hundred-plus-member team shares a common commitment to the truth of God's Word and to historic Christian orthodoxy and is international in scope, including leaders in many denominations.

To God's Honor and Praise

We know that no Bible translation is perfect; but we also know that God uses imperfect and inadequate things to his honor and praise. So to our triune God and to his people we offer what we have done, with our prayers that it may prove useful, with gratitude for much help given, and with ongoing wonder that our God should ever have entrusted to us so momentous a task.

Soli Deo Gloria!—To God alone be the glory!

The Translation Oversight Committee

CONTRIBUTORS

EDITOR IN CHIEF

Louie Giglio

GENERAL EDITOR

Aaron B. Coe, PhD

FEATURE ARTICLES

Randy Alcorn ("Forever" article, p. 1938)
Aaron B. Coe, PhD ("Savior" article, p. 1518)
Louie Giglio ("Revolt" article, p. 24 and "People" article, p. 256)
Max Lucado ("Church" article, p. 1686)
John Piper, PhD ("Beginnings" article, p. 10)

LEAD WRITER

Matthew A. Rogers, PhD

CONTENT ARCHITECT

John Kramp

LEAD EDITOR

Carol Postma

EDITORIAL TEAM, PASSION PUBLISHING

Aaron B. Coe, PhD
Kevin Marks
Emily Vogeltanz

EDITORIAL TEAM, ZONDERVAN

Melinda Bouma
John Kramp
Daniel Marrs
Carol Postma
Mike Vander Klipp

CONTRIBUTING WRITERS

Jon Akin, PhD
Carmen Coe
Jason Dees, PhD
Kyle Dunn
Jeni Fobart
Lindsay Guerin
Jonathan Hansen
Jake Jelinek
Michael Kelley
John Kramp
Gregg Matte
Pat McCarty
Will McGee
Matt Metzger
Sam Perry
Tobin Perry
Joe Rice
Ben Roberts
Matt Sliger, PhD
Tim Smith
Ben Stuart
Ryan West, PhD
Thomas West
Jonny Wills
Karen Woodall
Don Wooley
Freddy T. Wyatt
Aynsley Younker
Brett Younker

WELCOME

TO THE STORY OF GOD!

—LOUIE GIGLIO

No book on earth has been talked about, debated, revered, or hated more than the one you hold in your hands. This single book has revolutionized cultures and ignited revolutions.

It's not uncommon for people to approach the Bible with preconceived notions about where it came from or what it has to say. Some assert it is fable, created by men. Others view it as just another religious manual, while some see it simply as a helpful roadmap for those seeking spiritual guidance.

But ultimately the Bible defines itself, claiming to be a book like no other. The Bible declares that it is altogether different — the holy, sacred, inspired, alive, and active Word of God. It is the unique story of God from beginning to end, with one central character — Jesus Christ.

From the beginning of time, oral tradition (story) has played a crucial role in human development, serving as the vehicle by which communities bonded, history was understood, and culture was transferred from one generation to the next. In places where the written word has yet to emerge, the singular force of story remains.

Yet everywhere on earth, no matter how advanced the civilization, people are attracted to well-told stories. Every great film, novel, song, video game, and art form — even the recounting of a recent vacation or the marketing muscle of the best corporate brand — is rooted in the power of story.

Why are we so attracted to story? Could it be because we are made in the image of a story-creating God, born into the already-in-motion story of the One who has always been, yet chose to make himself known to you and me? The story is undoubtedly his story, yet miraculously, he weaves us into its pages as those prized and pursued by him.

Theologian N. T. Wright says that Scripture reveals that Christianity is the true story of the whole world. That's a beautiful thought when you consider the idea of story is woven into the fabric of humanity.

Speaking of and for itself, the Bible says, "All Scripture is breathed out by God" (2Ti 3:16). While penned by human writers under the inspiration of the Holy Spirit, the Bible is comprised of God-breathed words. What you are holding is not simply ink on a page. It is breath on a page! It is the revelation of the holiness, mercy, and grace of God to everyone.

Front and center in the story is Jesus. He is the God-man who created everything, yet he entered history to redeem sinful man and raise us by grace to everlasting life. Not only carefully chronicled by eyewitness Gospel accounts, Jesus' life was also acknowledged by the leading historians of his day. His death and resurrection are the defining moments in human history, the latter being one of the most investigated events of all time. As Jesus' death and resurrection are proclaimed, their power brings men and women from spiritual death to life on every continent every single day.

But Jesus' role in the story is not confined to the accounts of Matthew, Mark, Luke, and John. Jesus is as visible on the first page as the last. He is as present in the Garden of Eden as he is in the garden tomb. The entire story points to him. Jesus himself affirms this when he said, "You search the Scriptures because you think that in them you have eternal life; and it is they that bear witness" (Jn 5:39).

That's why we have created *The Jesus Bible*. Filled with relevant notes and pertinent articles, *The Jesus Bible* will help you follow the thread of Jesus from cover to cover to discover a new depth to the Bible's meaning as you see him in every chapter of the story.

You may be asking, "How do I get my head around such a massive story? Where do I start in gaining a better grasp of the full story of the Bible?"

The Bible is best understood when it's viewed as one story in six acts:

As we take a quick look at each act, we see traces of Jesus at every turn.

BEGINNINGS

Every story has a beginning.

Every philosopher, scientist, civilization, poet, religion, and everyday person has a story of beginnings.

As Jesus people, our story begins with a creating God. The text underscores that you are created in the image of God. Thus, your origination was in the mind of a majestic God. Everything beautiful, spiritual, wonderful, and eternal about you is the result of his divine image woven into your spirit from the start.

The triune God ("Let *us* make man in *our* image," Ge 1:26, emphasis added) works through the Son to bring about the creation of everything. "For by him [Jesus] all things were created, in heaven and on earth, visible and invisible, whether thrones or dominions or rulers or authorities — all things were created through him and for him" (Col 1:16).

In the beginning Jesus created everything.

WELCOME

(CONTINUED)

REVOLT

Every story has a problem. The problem for humanity is sin.

Though welcomed into paradise, Adam and Eve had free will. Choosing to attempt to become like God, they fell into physical and spiritual death. The consequences were severe, and humankind was separated from their Creator. Yet, in mercy, God sacrificed an animal and made a covering for the man and woman. This covering was a picture of what was to come — forgiveness and righteousness through the sacrifice of Jesus Christ.

When people revolted, God had already set in motion a plan of salvation through Jesus Christ.

PEOPLE

Every story has participants — those who are going to be impacted by the unfolding drama.

The fall resulted in mankind's struggles with hardship of every kind. But God was not silent. Through Abraham, God commissioned a people to be his — a special, chosen people who would be a witness on earth of his faithfulness. God showered them in blessing, yet they constantly reverted to sinful ways. Time and time again the people rejected God, their decisions *ultimately leading them to oppression* and loss. Invariably, they called out to the God they had forgotten, and God, in turn, always showed mercy.

At each turn of this vicious cycle of death and destruction, God would announce through a prophet a coming Savior, Jesus Christ.

SAVIOR

Every story has a hero. In this story his name is Jesus.

The Bible says that in the fullness of time, God's promised Savior was born in a stable. Jesus did what no other could do, by bringing an end to the system of sacrifice and ritual. Once and for all, Jesus appeased God's wrath through his death on the cross, opening the way for rebels to come home to a peacemaking Father.

A star led the wise men to the place of Christ's birth, but history has been pointing to Jesus since time began. Jesus is God's appointed and God's anointed. He is the way, the truth, and the life. All come to the Father through him (Jn 14:6).

CHURCH

Every story has an effect.

The church is made up of a people who have been redeemed by Jesus and have been formed to live on mission with him.

Once Jesus was raised from the dead and ascended into heaven, he sent the Holy Spirit to give birth to his Church. While churches come in all shapes and sizes, the true Church of Jesus is comprised of all who have confessed him as Savior and Lord. A living organism, his body, the Church, serves to extend his grace and truth on earth. Powered by that same Spirit, the Church exists to proclaim Jesus' glory to all people.

FOREVER

Every story has a resolution.

At a time only the Father knows, everything in heaven and earth will be put right once and for all. Those opposed to Jesus will get what they have asked for — an eternity without his goodness and glory. The redeemed will gather in his presence from every race and nation, singing the song of Jesus who rescued them from death and brought them into unending life.

As you open these pages, you step into the greatest story of all. Rich in historical accuracy, this biblical story, written over thousands of years by dozens of authors, is stunning in its symmetry and cohesiveness. Contrary to what some may think, this story isn't designed to limit mankind. The story of Jesus liberates us in his light, saving us from the perilous paths of our limited understanding and leading us to the most vibrant life imaginable.

Through the Scripture, God makes extraordinary promises to you and me. The Bible claims it can make us wise, bring life to our souls, open our eyes to see who and whose we are, fill our hearts with joy, make us purposeful, give our lives meaning, restore what has been lost, and protect us from a shipwrecked life.

If you approach the Bible with an open mind, I am confident you will be met by the Spirit of God who breathed these words into existence. He promises that "he will guide you into all the truth" (Jn 16:13). Ultimately, you will come face to face with the One who appears on each page and in every act. You will soon discover that it is Jesus whom the story is all about.

And that's the goal. For as precious and enduring as the Bible is, you were not made for information alone, but for a relationship with Jesus. He is the One who helps us see that truth is not simply a thing; rather, truth is a person. Truth is in Jesus and Jesus is truth. He alone is the One who ends death and gives life to all who hope in him.

Welcome to the story of God. More specifically, welcome to the story of how Jesus creates and restores all things.

OLD TESTAMENT

JESUS: OUR GLORIOUS CREATOR

GENESIS

GENESIS

CREATION *Unknown*	ABRAM GOES TO CANAAN *c. 2091 BC*	JACOB AND HIS FAMILY GO TO EGYPT *c. 1876 BC*

The book of beginnings starts with the most significant words of all time: "In the beginning, God." With these words, the story of God's grand and glorious plan for humanity commences. The opening book of the Bible is about God's created design for his world, humankind's fall into sin and rebellion, and God's gracious plan to rescue his beloved people from the terrible implications of their sin. The stories of famous people such as Abram/Abraham, Isaac, Jacob, and Joseph fill the book and trace the story of God's grace toward his chosen people. At the outset of the Bible, right after the first sin, God promised to send One who would defeat Satan and sin forever. Jesus, the creative Word by which God spoke all things into being (Jn 1:1), would one day make his dwelling in a fallen world in order to save sinful humanity.

God, through Moses, prepared these documents to present a unified picture of the nature and character of himself and his work in the world to the second generation of those freed from slavery in Egypt — those who were poised to take the land of promise. This record of God's dealings with humanity, starting with his created design, connected this generation to God's continued grace, mercy, and guidance.

The first few chapters of Genesis introduce the God of creation and his goal for his created image-bearers. Human sin contaminated and marred God's created world, but it has not thwarted his purposes. He will still be known and worshiped, and his glory will fill the earth. In order to demonstrate his holiness and hatred of sin, God acted in judgment (Ge 3:16 – 19). This judgment, however, did not obscure the abundance of grace seen throughout Genesis. He pledged to send a child, an offspring of the woman, who would one day crush Satan forever (Ge 3:15). In this way, God declared that he had a plan to reclaim rebellious image-bearers from their sin. Throughout Genesis, God repeatedly made these promises in the form of a series of covenants in which he pledged his loyalty, faithfulness, and grace to humans, who were then called to respond to this grace with worshipful obedience.

God's created design and mission in the world have not changed. He is still intent on filling the earth with his glory and using his created image-bearers to accomplish that goal. Christ, in his wrath-bearing death and life-giving resurrection, allows people to fulfill the very purpose for which they were created. His death fulfilled the covenant promises of God to make a way for people to have a right relationship with God in spite of human sin. Jesus' perfect obedience demonstrated the values of the kingdom of God and defined the hope that we look for — the coming day when sin and death will be eradicated forever.

IN THE BEGINNING, GOD CREATED THE HEAVENS AND THE EARTH.

Genesis 1:1

GENESIS 1:3

LET THERE BE LIGHT

God brings light into darkness. That is a recurring theme throughout the Bible, and it begins here. In this verse, the spoken words of God create physical light to brighten a dark world. The New Testament records God's sending his Son, Jesus, to be the light of the world (Jn 1:1–14). And Paul wrote to the church in Corinth that salvation occurs when God commands the light of his own glory "in the face of Jesus Christ" to shine on the darkness of sinful hearts (2Co 4:6). Light represents the glory and salvation of God as it is expressed in Jesus Christ. Jesus is the exact representation of God, and he revealed God to a world sitting in darkness. Those who trust in Jesus are brought from the darkness of sin into God's light—where there is joy, peace, and hope forever. In the end, there will be no more darkness, and the light of God's glory will shine brightly in God's eternal kingdom (Rev 21:23).

GENESIS 1:26–27

MADE IN GOD'S IMAGE

Human beings are uniquely created in the image of God. When the rest of creation was being birthed, it was "good." God created the birds, fish, plants, and stars to display his splendor and oh, how amazing they are. God said these creations were good. However, when it came to humans, the tone changed. He

(continued on page 6)

GENESIS

The Creation of the World

1 In the beginning, God created the heavens and the earth. 2 The earth was without form and void, and darkness was over the face of the deep. And the Spirit of God was hovering over the face of the waters.

3 And God said, "Let there be light," and there was light. 4 And God saw that the light was good. And God separated the light from the darkness. 5 God called the light Day, and the darkness he called Night. And there was evening and there was morning, the first day.

6 And God said, "Let there be an expanse[1] in the midst of the waters, and let it separate the waters from the waters." 7 And God made[2] the expanse and separated the waters that were under the expanse from the waters that were above the expanse. And it was so. 8 And God called the expanse Heaven.[3] And there was evening and there was morning, the second day.

9 And God said, "Let the waters under the heavens be gathered together into one place, and let the dry land appear." And it was so. 10 God called the dry land Earth,[4] and the waters that were gathered together he called Seas. And God saw that it was good.

11 And God said, "Let the earth sprout vegetation, plants[5] yielding seed, and fruit trees bearing fruit in which is their seed, each according to its kind, on the earth." And it was so. 12 The earth brought forth vegetation, plants yielding seed according to their own kinds, and trees bearing fruit in which is their seed, each according to its kind. And God saw that it was good. 13 And there was evening and there was morning, the third day.

14 And God said, "Let there be lights in the expanse of the heavens to separate the day from the night. And let them be for signs and for seasons,[6] and for days and years, 15 and let them be lights in the expanse of the heavens to give light upon the earth." And it was so. 16 And God made the two great lights—the greater light to rule the day and the lesser light to rule the night—and the stars. 17 And God set them in the expanse of the heavens to give light on the earth, 18 to rule over the day and over the night, and to separate the light from the darkness. And God saw that it was good. 19 And there was evening and there was morning, the fourth day.

20 And God said, "Let the waters swarm with swarms of living creatures, and let birds[7] fly above the earth across the expanse of the heavens." 21 So God created the great sea creatures and every living creature that moves, with which the waters swarm, according to their kinds, and every winged bird according to its kind. And God saw that it was good. 22 And God blessed them, saying, "Be fruitful and multiply and fill the waters in the seas, and let birds multiply on the earth." 23 And there was evening and there was morning, the fifth day.

24 And God said, "Let the earth bring forth living creatures according to their kinds—livestock and creeping things and beasts of the earth according to their kinds." And it was so. 25 And God made the beasts of the earth according to their kinds and the livestock according to their kinds, and everything that creeps on the ground according to its kind. And God saw that it was good.

26 Then God said, "Let us make man[8] in our image, after our likeness. And let them have dominion over the fish of the sea and over the birds of the heavens and over the livestock and over all the earth and over every creeping thing that creeps on the earth."

[1] Or *a canopy*; also verses 7, 8, 14, 15, 17, 20 [2] Or *fashioned*; also verse 16 [3] Or *Sky*; also verses 9, 14, 15, 17, 20, 26, 28, 30; 2:1 [4] Or *Land*; also verses 11, 12, 22, 24, 25, 26, 28, 30; 2:1 [5] Or *small plants*; also verses 12, 29 [6] Or *appointed times* [7] Or *flying things*; see Leviticus 11:19–20 [8] The Hebrew word for *man* (*adam*) is the generic term for mankind and becomes the proper name *Adam*

JESUS CREATED EVERYTHING AND HOLDS IT ALL TOGETHER

Jesus has been from the beginning. We live in a pluralist society where many people believe in some type of "god." Therefore you probably would not get a whole lot of pushback when you say, "God created the heavens and the earth." However, understanding that Jesus created everything changes how one views the whole of Scripture. Colossians 1:15 – 17 says that "He is the image of the invisible God, the firstborn of all creation. For by him all things were created, in heaven and on earth, visible and invisible, whether thrones or dominions or rulers or authorities — all things were created through him and for him. And he is before all things, and in him all things hold together." Paul writes that all things were created by, through, and for Jesus.

John makes a similar claim at the outset of his Gospel. The New Testament was written in Greek to a largely Greco-Roman audience. The Greeks believed that there was a unifying force that holds the entire world together. They defined that force as the *Logos*. The Gospel of John defines the *Logos* as Jesus. John 1:1 – 2 says, "In the beginning was the Word [*Logos*], and the Word [*Logos*] was with God, and the Word [*Logos*] was God. He was in the beginning with God." The Word of God — the very agent God used to create all things — took on flesh and made his dwelling on earth in the person of Jesus Christ.

John and Paul affirm this is the agent of creation — the eternal Word of God who was used by God to make something out of nothing. Understanding that Jesus created everything and holds everything together should shape how we read the whole of Scripture. Jesus does not make his first appearance in the book of Matthew. God's Trinitarian nature is on display from the outset of the Scriptures. And, in many ways, the various stories found throughout the Old Testament help explain the nature, character, and work of Jesus Christ. Time and time again, God sets the stage for the sending of the Son to fulfill his eternal plan to save those who were dead in their sins.

(Made in God's Image, continued)

said that the creation of humans was "very good." Human beings are an extra-special creation for at least three reasons. First, it is clear that humans have an identity that is rooted in God. When God said, "Let us make man in our image," he reiterated the presence of Jesus and the Holy Spirit in the act of creation (see article on Ge 1:1). Humans are special because Jesus, as a part of the Trinity, created them in his image. Second, humans are special because they were created for a unique purpose. No two humans are the same. Other aspects of creation serve general functions, but only humans have a unique, individual purpose. Third, humans are designed to have a one-on-one relationship with God through Jesus, powered by the Holy Spirit. As a right of being created in the image of their Creator, humans can relate directly to him. It is through Jesus that this relationship is made possible. He came and tore down the dividing wall of hostility that separated his special creation from God (Ro 8:34–39).

GENESIS 1:28

GOD'S CREATED MISSION

Adam and Eve lived on mission. This is seen in a couple of ways. First, they were to multiply and fill the earth. As created image-bearers, were it not for sin, they would naturally multiply and fill the earth with more and more image-bearing worshipers of God. As worshipers spread, the glory of God would be seen throughout the world God had created. Second, people were to exercise dominion over God's world. They were to do more than simply care for

(continued on next page)

27 So God created man in his own image,
in the image of God he created him;
male and female he created them.

28And God blessed them. And God said to them, "Be fruitful and multiply and
fill the earth and subdue it, and have dominion over the fish of the sea and over
the birds of the heavens and over every living thing that moves on the earth."
29And God said, "Behold, I have given you every plant yielding seed that is on the
face of all the earth, and every tree with seed in its fruit. You shall have them for
food. 30And to every beast of the earth and to every bird of the heavens and to
everything that creeps on the earth, everything that has the breath of life, I have
given every green plant for food." And it was so. 31And God saw everything that
he had made, and behold, it was very good. And there was evening and there was
morning, the sixth day.

The Seventh Day, God Rests

2 Thus the heavens and the earth were finished, and all the host of them. 2And
on the seventh day God finished his work that he had done, and he rested on
the seventh day from all his work that he had done. 3So God blessed the seventh
day and made it holy, because on it God rested from all his work that he had done
in creation.

The Creation of Man and Woman

4 These are the generations
of the heavens and the earth when they were created,
in the day that the LORD God made the earth and the heavens.

5When no bush of the field[1] was yet in the land[2] and no small plant of the field
had yet sprung up—for the LORD God had not caused it to rain on the land, and
there was no man to work the ground, 6and a mist[3] was going up from the land
and was watering the whole face of the ground—7then the LORD God formed the
man of dust from the ground and breathed into his nostrils the breath of life, and
the man became a living creature. 8And the LORD God planted a garden in Eden, in
the east, and there he put the man whom he had formed. 9And out of the ground
the LORD God made to spring up every tree that is pleasant to the sight and good
for food. The tree of life was in the midst of the garden, and the tree of the knowledge of good and evil.

10A river flowed out of Eden to water the garden, and there it divided and became four rivers. 11The name of the first is the Pishon. It is the one that flowed
around the whole land of Havilah, where there is gold. 12And the gold of that land
is good; bdellium and onyx stone are there. 13The name of the second river is the
Gihon. It is the one that flowed around the whole land of Cush. 14And the name
of the third river is the Tigris, which flows east of Assyria[4]. And the fourth river
is the Euphrates.

15The LORD God took the man and put him in the garden of Eden to work it and
keep it. 16And the LORD God commanded the man, saying, "You may surely eat of
every tree of the garden, 17but of the tree of the knowledge of good and evil you
shall not eat, for in the day that you eat[5] of it you shall surely die."

18Then the LORD God said, "It is not good that the man should be alone; I
will make him a helper fit for[6] him." 19Now out of the ground the LORD God had
formed[7] every beast of the field and every bird of the heavens and brought them
to the man to see what he would call them. And whatever the man called every
living creature, that was its name. 20The man gave names to all livestock and to
the birds of the heavens and to every beast of the field. But for Adam[8] there was
not found a helper fit for him. 21So the LORD God caused a deep sleep to fall upon

[1]Or *open country* [2]Or *earth*; also verse 6 [3]Or *spring* [4]Or *Asshur* [5]Or *when you eat*
[6]Or *corresponding to*; also verse 20 [7]Or *And out of the ground the LORD God formed* [8]Or *the man*

the man, and while he slept took one of his ribs and closed up its place with flesh.
22And the rib that the LORD God had taken from the man he made[1] into a woman
and brought her to the man. 23Then the man said,

"This at last is bone of my bones
  and flesh of my flesh;
she shall be called Woman,
  because she was taken out of Man."[2]

24Therefore a man shall leave his father and his mother and hold fast to his wife,
and they shall become one flesh. 25And the man and his wife were both naked
and were not ashamed.

The Fall

3 Now the serpent was more crafty than any other beast of the field that the
LORD God had made.
He said to the woman, "Did God actually say, 'You[3] shall not eat of any tree
in the garden'?" 2And the woman said to the serpent, "We may eat of the fruit of
the trees in the garden, 3but God said, 'You shall not eat of the fruit of the tree
that is in the midst of the garden, neither shall you touch it, lest you die.'" 4But
the serpent said to the woman, "You will not surely die. 5For God knows that
when you eat of it your eyes will be opened, and you will be like God, knowing
good and evil." 6So when the woman saw that the tree was good for food, and
that it was a delight to the eyes, and that the tree was to be desired to make one
wise,[4] she took of its fruit and ate, and she also gave some to her husband who
was with her, and he ate. 7Then the eyes of both were opened, and they knew
that they were naked. And they sewed fig leaves together and made themselves
loincloths.
8And they heard the sound of the LORD God walking in the garden in the cool[5]
of the day, and the man and his wife hid themselves from the presence of the LORD
God among the trees of the garden. 9But the LORD God called to the man and said
to him, "Where are you?"[6] 10And he said, "I heard the sound of you in the garden,
and I was afraid, because I was naked, and I hid myself." 11He said, "Who told you
that you were naked? Have you eaten of the tree of which I commanded you not
to eat?" 12The man said, "The woman whom you gave to be with me, she gave
me fruit of the tree, and I ate." 13Then the LORD God said to the woman, "What is
this that you have done?" The woman said, "The serpent deceived me, and I ate."
14The LORD God said to the serpent,

"Because you have done this,
  cursed are you above all livestock
  and above all beasts of the field;
on your belly you shall go,
  and dust you shall eat
  all the days of your life.
15 I will put enmity between you and the woman,
  and between your offspring[7] and her offspring;
he shall bruise your head,
  and you shall bruise his heel."

16To the woman he said,

"I will surely multiply your pain in childbearing;
  in pain you shall bring forth children.
Your desire shall be for[8] your husband,
  and he shall rule over you."

[1]Hebrew *built* [2]The Hebrew words for *woman* (*ishshah*) and *man* (*ish*) sound alike [3]In Hebrew *you* is plural in verses 1–5 [4]Or *to give insight* [5]Hebrew *wind* [6]In Hebrew *you* is singular in verses 9 and 11 [7]Hebrew *seed*; so throughout Genesis [8]Or *to*, or *toward*, or *against* (see 4:7)

(God's Created Mission, continued)

the world—they were to harness the latent potential built into God's very good created design in order to magnify the order, beauty, and capabilities inherent in all things made by God. Sin changed all that God created, but it did not obliterate this mandate. In Christ, men and women can fulfill their God-given mission to fill the earth with worshipers and develop the world in such a way as to bring God great glory.

GENESIS 3:15–17

THE PROMISED ONE

God's judgment of sin is interrupted by a stunning picture of his grace. Because of human sin, there are vast implications—from men and women to the very creation itself. But God promises that sin will not have the final word. This first reference to the plan of God to save fallen sinners, sometimes referred to as the *protoevangelium* (the first gospel), declares God's commitment to his creation. He will not abandon it to destruction but will pursue it in love. His promise is clear—a descendant of the woman will crush the head of the serpent. The heel of this male heir of the first parents will be struck, though the child will emerge victorious by crushing the head of the evil one. The exact nature of the plan is yet to be explained, but the plan is already in place. Jesus, the promised seed of the woman, would leave no doubt as to the fulfillment of this promise. It would appear that Satan had done far more than strike the heel of the Son of God as Jesus hung lifeless on a cross. But God would have the final word. Through Jesus' victorious resurrection, he would crush

(continued on page 9)

THE FIRST ADAM AND THE RUIN OF HUMANITY

Adam and Eve represent a profound paradox. They are simultaneously the crowning achievement of God's creation, created in his very image, and the symbol of mankind's greatest failure. In verse 1 the serpent appeared in Paradise with no introduction. The serpent symbolizes something both fascinating and loathsome. Yet neither Adam nor Eve saw the danger embodied in the serpent. The danger of this creature was quickly realized in verse 8 after Adam and Eve were enticed by its suggestion and drawn into the depth of sin. According to his custom, God came walking through the garden in the cool of the day, and for the first time Adam and Eve hid from him in shame because of their sinful disobedience.

In Romans 5:12–21 Paul takes his readers back to this very moment in history and offers a divinely inspired interpretation. He explains that Adam's sin led to the downfall and death of the entire human race. Through one man (Adam), death came. Yet through one Man (Jesus Christ), grace and the gift of God (eternal life) were given.

The works of these two men, Adam and Jesus, are not merely opposites of one another. Christ's work — the work of redemption accomplished on the cross — is far greater, for it brings God's life and redemption to those who are spiritually dead. The death of Adam spread to all, but the life of Christ overcame it. Through Adam's disobedience, death reigned, and the world stood condemned before God.

In the face of this condemnation, Jesus offered humanity the free gift of salvation by faith that resulted in justification. That is to say, the aim of this gift is to justify (remove condemnation from) those who stood condemned. This glorious promise provides remarkable hope for those who are "in Christ." They have been reborn, by the power of God, and their status is transferred from being "in Adam" to "in Christ." In turn, they receive the inheritance promised to all those who are "in Christ" and avoid the wrath of those who are "in Adam." So much greater is the work of Jesus than the sin of Adam!

(The Promised One, continued)

the head of Satan—permanently declaring victory over sin and death and fulfilling the promise made at the outset of the Bible.

17 And to Adam he said,

"Because you have listened to the voice of your wife
and have eaten of the tree
of which I commanded you,
'You shall not eat of it,'
cursed is the ground because of you;
in pain you shall eat of it all the days of your life;
18 thorns and thistles it shall bring forth for you;
and you shall eat the plants of the field.
19 By the sweat of your face
you shall eat bread,
till you return to the ground,
for out of it you were taken;
for you are dust,
and to dust you shall return."

20 The man called his wife's name Eve, because she was the mother of all living.[1] 21 And the LORD God made for Adam and for his wife garments of skins and
clothed them.

22 Then the LORD God said, "Behold, the man has become like one of us in
knowing good and evil. Now, lest he reach out his hand and take also of the tree
of life and eat, and live forever—" 23 therefore the LORD God sent him out from the
garden of Eden to work the ground from which he was taken. 24 He drove out the
man, and at the east of the garden of Eden he placed the cherubim and a flaming
sword that turned every way to guard the way to the tree of life.

Cain and Abel

4 Now Adam knew Eve his wife, and she conceived and bore Cain, saying, "I
have gotten[2] a man with the help of the LORD." 2 And again, she bore his brother Abel. Now Abel was a keeper of sheep, and Cain a worker of the ground. 3 In the
course of time Cain brought to the LORD an offering of the fruit of the ground,
4 and Abel also brought of the firstborn of his flock and of their fat portions. And
the LORD had regard for Abel and his offering, 5 but for Cain and his offering he
had no regard. So Cain was very angry, and his face fell. 6 The LORD said to Cain,
"Why are you angry, and why has your face fallen? 7 If you do well, will you not be
accepted?[3] And if you do not do well, sin is crouching at the door. Its desire is for[4]
you, and you must rule over it."

8 Cain spoke to Abel his brother.[5] And when they were in the field, Cain rose
up against his brother Abel and killed him. 9 Then the LORD said to Cain, "Where
is Abel your brother?" He said, "I do not know; am I my brother's keeper?" 10 And
the LORD said, "What have you done? The voice of your brother's blood is crying to me from the ground. 11 And now you are cursed from the ground, which
has opened its mouth to receive your brother's blood from your hand. 12 When
you work the ground, it shall no longer yield to you its strength. You shall be a
fugitive and a wanderer on the earth." 13 Cain said to the LORD, "My punishment
is greater than I can bear.[6] 14 Behold, you have driven me today away from the
ground, and from your face I shall be hidden. I shall be a fugitive and a wanderer
on the earth, and whoever finds me will kill me." 15 Then the LORD said to him,
"Not so! If anyone kills Cain, vengeance shall be taken on him sevenfold." And
the LORD put a mark on Cain, lest any who found him should attack him. 16 Then
Cain went away from the presence of the LORD and settled in the land of Nod,[7]
east of Eden.

[1] *Eve* sounds like the Hebrew for *life-giver* and resembles the word for *living* [2] *Cain* sounds like the Hebrew for *gotten* [3] Hebrew *will there not be a lifting up* [of your face]? [4] Or *to*, or *toward*, or *against* (see 3:16) [5] Hebrew; Samaritan, Septuagint, Syriac, Vulgate add *Let us go out to the field* [6] Or *My guilt is too great to bear* [7] *Nod* means *wandering*

BEGINNINGS

JESUS AS THE SUPREME DISPLAY OF THE GLORY OF GOD

GENESIS 1 – 2

After the question "Does God exist?" (to which God answers, "I AM," Ex 3:14), the next question that can shape your life most deeply is "Why did God create the world?"

The short answer that resounds through the whole Bible like rolling thunder is this: *God created the world for his glory*. We'll see what that means below, but first let's establish the fact. "Bring my sons from afar and my daughters from the end of the earth, everyone who is called by my name, whom *I created for my glory,* whom I formed and made" (Isa 43:6 – 7). Even if the narrower meaning here is "I brought Israel into being for my glory," the use of the words "created," "formed," and "made" is pointing us back to the original act of creation. This is why Israel *ultimately* exists. Because this is why *all things* ultimately exist — for the glory of God.

THE BIBLE IS CLEAR

When the first chapter of the Bible says, "God created man *in his own image,* in the *image of God* he created him; male and female he created them" (Ge 1:27), what is the point? The point of an image is to image. Images are erected in public to display the original. Point to the original. Glorify the original.

God made humans in his image so that the world would be filled with reflectors of God. Images of God. Billions of statues of God. So that nobody would miss the point of creation. Nobody (unless spiritually blind) could miss the point of humanity, namely, God! Knowing, loving, showing God.

The angels cry, "Holy, holy, holy is the LORD of hosts; *the whole earth is full of his glory*" (Isa 6:3). It's full of human image-bearers. Glorious ruins. But not only humans. Also nature! Why such a breathtaking world for us to live in? Why such a vast universe? Scientists now say (I can't verify it!) that there are more stars in the universe than there are words and sounds that all humans of all time have ever spoken. Why is it so gigantic?

The Bible is crystal clear about this: "The heavens declare the glory of God" (Ps 19:1). If someone asks, "If earth is the only inhabited planet in the universe, and man the only rational inhabitant among the stars, why is there such a large and empty universe?" The answer is that it's not about us. It's about God. Which means it's not an overstatement; it's an understatement. God created us to know him and love him and show him. And then he gave us a hint of what he is like — the universe.

We can see the purpose of creation even where the apostle Paul describes how we have fallen short of it. He says in Romans 1:20 – 21:

> "For his [God's] invisible attributes, namely, his eternal power and divine nature, have

been clearly perceived, ever since the creation of the world, in the things that have been made. So they are without excuse. For although they knew God, they did not honor him as God or give thanks to him."

The great tragedy of the universe is that, while human beings were made to glorify God, we have all fallen short of this purpose and "exchanged the glory of the immortal God for images resembling mortal man and birds and animals and creeping things" (Ro 1:23).

GOD HELPS US FEEL THIS TRUTH

So, resounding through the whole Bible — from eternity to eternity — like rolling thunder is God's great purpose for all things: *He created the world for his glory*. Besides Isaiah 43:7 ("created for my glory"), Isaiah presses home the reality over and over to help us feel it and make it part of the fabric of our thinking:

> "Every valley shall be lifted up, and every mountain and hill be made low ... And the *glory of the LORD shall be revealed*, and all flesh shall see it together" (Isa 40:4 – 5).
>
> "I am the LORD; that is my name; my glory I give to no other" (Isa 42:8).
>
> "For the LORD has redeemed Jacob, and will be glorified in Israel" (Isa 44:23).
>
> "For my name's sake I defer my anger; for the sake of my praise I restrain it for you ... I have tried you in the furnace of affliction. For my own sake, for my own sake, I do it, for how should my name be profaned? My glory I will not give to another" (Isa 48:9 – 11).
>
> "And he said to me, 'You are my servant, Israel, in whom *I will be glorified*' " (Isa 49:3).
>
> "The Spirit of the Lord GOD is upon me, because the LORD has anointed me to bring good news to the poor ... They may be called oaks of righteousness, the planting of the LORD, *that he may be glorified*" (Isa 61:1 – 3).

GLORIFY IS DIFFERENT FROM BEAUTIFY

This is why God created the world — that he may be glorified. Which does not mean that he may be *made* glorious. Don't take the word *glorify* and treat it like the word *beautify*. To beautify means to take something plain and make it beautiful. We don't take a plain God and make him beautiful. That is not what glorifying God means.

When God created the world, he did not create out of any need or any weakness or any deficiency. He created out of fullness and strength and complete sufficiency. As Jonathan Edwards said, "Tis no argument of the emptiness or deficiency of a fountain that it is inclined to overflow."

BEGINNINGS

(CONTINUED)

GENESIS 1–2

Or switch to the word *magnify*. We magnify his glory like a *telescope*, not a microscope. Microscopes make small things look bigger than they are. Telescopes make unimaginably big things look more like what they really are. Our lives are to be telescopes for the glory of God.

WHY THIS PARTICULAR WORLD?

But we can't leave it here. It's too general. It's too disconnected from the specific persons of the Trinity and from the flow of history the way God is guiding it. The question is not just, "Why did God create the world?" but why *this* world? Why these thousands of years of human history with a glorious beginning, and a horrible fall into sin, and a history of Israel, and the coming of the Son of God into the world, a substitutionary death, a triumphant resurrection, the founding of the church, and the history of global missions to where we are today? Why *this* world? This history?

And the short answer to that question is for the glory of God's grace displayed supremely in the death of Jesus. Or to say it more fully, this world — this history as it is unfolding — was created and is guided and sustained by God so that the grace of God, supremely displayed in the death and resurrection of Jesus for sinners, would be glorified throughout all eternity in the Christ-exalting joys of the redeemed.

Or let's just keep it short: This world exists for the glory of God's grace revealed in the saving work of Jesus. There is an unbreakable connection between the glory of God, the glory of grace, the glory of Christ, the glory of the cross.

THE GLORY OF GOD AND THE CROSS OF CHRIST

Let me show you this from God's Word in five steps.

1. The apex — the highpoint — of God's display of his own glory is the display of his grace.

"He [God] predestined us for adoption to himself as sons through Jesus Christ, according to the purpose of his will, *to the praise of his glorious grace*" (Eph 1:5 – 6). In other words, the glory of God's *grace* — what Paul calls "the immeasurable riches of his grace in kindness toward us in Christ Jesus" (Eph 2:7) — is the highpoint and endpoint in the revelation of God's glory. And the aim of predestination is that we live "to the praise of his glorious grace" forever.

This is the endpoint of his glory, and everything else — even God's wrath — serves this. So Paul said, "Desiring to show his *wrath* and to make known his power, has endured with much patience vessels of wrath ... in order *to make known the riches of his glory for vessels of mercy*" (Ro 9:22 – 23). Wrath is penultimate. The glory of grace on the objects of mercy is ultimate.

2. God planned this—the praise of the glory of his grace—before creation.

God "chose us in him before the foundation of the world … to the praise of his glorious grace" (Eph 1:4,6).

Grace was not an afterthought in response to the fall of man. It was planned before creation. It was the plan, because grace is the summit of the mountain of his glory. And he created the world for his glory. He planned the world for the glory of *his grace*.

3. God's plan was that the praise of the glory of his grace would come about through the Son of God, Jesus Christ.

"He predestined us for adoption to himself as sons *through Jesus Christ* … to the praise of his glorious grace" (Eph 1:5 – 6). This predestination to the praise of the glory of God's grace happened "through Jesus Christ." In the eternal fellowship of the Trinity, the Father and the Son planned that God's grace would be supremely revealed through the saving work of the Son.

4. From eternity, God's plan was that the glory of God's grace would reach its highpoint in the saving work of Jesus on the cross.

We see this in the title that was already on the book of the redeemed before the creation of the world. Before there was any human sin to die for, God planned that his Son would be slain for sinners. We know this because of the name given to the book of life before creation. "And all who dwell on earth will worship it [the beast], everyone whose name has not been written before the foundation of the world in the book of life of the Lamb who was slain" (Rev 13:8).

The name of the book before creation was "the book of life of the Lamb *who was slain.*" The plan was glory. The plan was grace. The plan was Christ. And the plan was *death*. And that death for sinners like us is the heart of the gospel, which is why Paul calls it "the *gospel of the glory of Christ*" (2Co 4:4).

5. Therefore, the ultimate purpose of creating and guiding and sustaining this world—this history—is the praise of the glory of the grace of God in the crucifixion of his Son for sinners.

This is why Revelation 5:9 and 13 show that for all eternity we will sing the song *of the Lamb*. We will say with white-hot admiration and praise, "Worthy are you to take the scroll and to open its seals, *for you were slain,* and by your blood you ransomed people for God from every tribe and language and people and nation" (Rev 5:9).

YOUR BRIGHTEST TREASURE

So we ask again, in conclusion, "Why did God create the world?" And we answer with the

BEGINNINGS

(CONTINUED)

GENESIS 1–2

Scriptures: *God created the world for his glory.* God did not create out of need. He did not create the world out of a deficiency. He was not lonely. He was supremely happy in the fellowship of the Trinity — Father, Son, and Holy Spirit. He created the world to put his glory on display that his people might know him, and enjoy him and show him.

And why did he create a world that would become like this world? A world that fell into sin? A world that exchanged his glory for the glory of images? Why would he permit and guide and sustain such a world? And we answer, for *the praise of the glory of the grace of God displayed supremely in the death of Jesus.*

I ask:

- Is the glory of God the brightest treasure on the horizon of your future? Paul expressed the Christian heart in Romans 5:2, "We rejoice in hope of the glory of God."
- Is the glory of grace the sweetest news to your guilty soul?
- Is the glory of Christ in your life the present, personal embodiment of the grace of God?
- Is the glory of the cross the saddest and happiest beauty to your redeemed soul?

Note: When italics are used in the Scripture quotations above, they have been added by the author to show emphasis.

17Cain knew his wife, and she conceived and bore Enoch. When he built a city,
he called the name of the city after the name of his son, Enoch. 18To Enoch was
born Irad, and Irad fathered Mehujael, and Mehujael fathered Methushael, and
Methushael fathered Lamech. 19And Lamech took two wives. The name of the
one was Adah, and the name of the other Zillah. 20Adah bore Jabal; he was the
father of those who dwell in tents and have livestock. 21His brother's name was
Jubal; he was the father of all those who play the lyre and pipe. 22Zillah also bore
Tubal-cain; he was the forger of all instruments of bronze and iron. The sister of
Tubal-cain was Naamah.

23Lamech said to his wives:

"Adah and Zillah, hear my voice;
 you wives of Lamech, listen to what I say:
I have killed a man for wounding me,
 a young man for striking me.
24 If Cain's revenge is sevenfold,
 then Lamech's is seventy-sevenfold."

25And Adam knew his wife again, and she bore a son and called his name Seth,
for she said, "God has appointed[1] for me another offspring instead of Abel, for
Cain killed him." 26To Seth also a son was born, and he called his name Enosh. At
that time people began to call upon the name of the LORD.

Adam's Descendants to Noah

5 This is the book of the generations of Adam. When God created man, he made
him in the likeness of God. 2Male and female he created them, and he blessed
them and named them Man[2] when they were created. 3When Adam had lived 130
years, he fathered a son in his own likeness, after his image, and named him Seth.
4The days of Adam after he fathered Seth were 800 years; and he had other sons
and daughters. 5Thus all the days that Adam lived were 930 years, and he died.

6When Seth had lived 105 years, he fathered Enosh. 7Seth lived after he fathered Enosh 807 years and had other sons and daughters. 8Thus all the days of
Seth were 912 years, and he died.

9When Enosh had lived 90 years, he fathered Kenan. 10Enosh lived after he
fathered Kenan 815 years and had other sons and daughters. 11Thus all the days of
Enosh were 905 years, and he died.

12When Kenan had lived 70 years, he fathered Mahalalel. 13Kenan lived after
he fathered Mahalalel 840 years and had other sons and daughters. 14Thus all the
days of Kenan were 910 years, and he died.

15When Mahalalel had lived 65 years, he fathered Jared. 16Mahalalel lived after
he fathered Jared 830 years and had other sons and daughters. 17Thus all the days
of Mahalalel were 895 years, and he died.

18When Jared had lived 162 years, he fathered Enoch. 19Jared lived after he fathered Enoch 800 years and had other sons and daughters. 20Thus all the days of
Jared were 962 years, and he died.

21When Enoch had lived 65 years, he fathered Methuselah. 22Enoch walked
with God[3] after he fathered Methuselah 300 years and had other sons and daughters. 23Thus all the days of Enoch were 365 years. 24Enoch walked with God, and
he was not,[4] for God took him.

25When Methuselah had lived 187 years, he fathered Lamech. 26Methuselah
lived after he fathered Lamech 782 years and had other sons and daughters.
27Thus all the days of Methuselah were 969 years, and he died.

28When Lamech had lived 182 years, he fathered a son 29and called his name
Noah, saying, "Out of the ground that the LORD has cursed, this one shall bring us
relief[5] from our work and from the painful toil of our hands." 30Lamech lived after

[1] *Seth* sounds like the Hebrew for *he appointed* [2] Hebrew *adam* [3] Septuagint *pleased God*; also verse 24
[4] Septuagint *was not found* [5] *Noah* sounds like the Hebrew for *rest*

GENESIS 5:5

DEATH REIGNS UNTIL CHRIST

The pace of chapter 5 demonstrates the tragedy of human sin. Person after person appears and then is gone. The repetition of the phrase "and he died" reminds the reader of the implications of the curse. No longer can people live forever; they appear for a moment and then return to the ground (Ge 3:19). There is no escaping this reality. The just and the unjust, the righteous and the unrighteous, all die. From Adam to Noah, death reigns universally. Jesus, knowing and experiencing this reality personally when confronted with the death of his friend Lazarus, makes a remarkable claim. Those who believe in him, even though their physical bodies will die, will be raised to new life forever (Jn 11:25–26). Like Christ, they will pass through death only to emerge victorious. Belief in Christ is the only antidote to the lineage of death recounted in Genesis and seen throughout all subsequent generations.

he fathered Noah 595 years and had other sons and daughters. 31 Thus all the days of Lamech were 777 years, and he died.

32 After Noah was 500 years old, Noah fathered Shem, Ham, and Japheth.

Increasing Corruption on Earth

6 When man began to multiply on the face of the land and daughters were born to them, 2 the sons of God saw that the daughters of man were attractive. And they took as their wives any they chose. 3 Then the LORD said, "My Spirit shall not abide in[1] man forever, for he is flesh: his days shall be 120 years." 4 The Nephilim[2] were on the earth in those days, and also afterward, when the sons of God came in to the daughters of man and they bore children to them. These were the mighty men who were of old, the men of renown.

5 The LORD saw that the wickedness of man was great in the earth, and that every intention of the thoughts of his heart was only evil continually. 6 And the LORD regretted that he had made man on the earth, and it grieved him to his heart. 7 So the LORD said, "I will blot out man whom I have created from the face of the land, man and animals and creeping things and birds of the heavens, for I am sorry that I have made them." 8 But Noah found favor in the eyes of the LORD.

Noah and the Flood

9 These are the generations of Noah. Noah was a righteous man, blameless in his generation. Noah walked with God. 10 And Noah had three sons, Shem, Ham, and Japheth.

11 Now the earth was corrupt in God's sight, and the earth was filled with violence. 12 And God saw the earth, and behold, it was corrupt, for all flesh had corrupted their way on the earth. 13 And God said to Noah, "I have determined to make an end of all flesh,[3] for the earth is filled with violence through them. Behold, I will destroy them with the earth. 14 Make yourself an ark of gopher wood.[4] Make rooms in the ark, and cover it inside and out with pitch. 15 This is how you are to make it: the length of the ark 300 cubits,[5] its breadth 50 cubits, and its height 30 cubits. 16 Make a roof[6] for the ark, and finish it to a cubit above, and set the door of the ark in its side. Make it with lower, second, and third decks. 17 For behold, I will bring a flood of waters upon the earth to destroy all flesh in which is the breath of life under heaven. Everything that is on the earth shall die. 18 But I will establish my covenant with you, and you shall come into the ark, you, your sons, your wife, and your sons' wives with you. 19 And of every living thing of all flesh, you shall bring two of every sort into the ark to keep them alive with you. They shall be male and female. 20 Of the birds according to their kinds, and of the animals according to their kinds, of every creeping thing of the ground, according to its kind, two of every sort shall come in to you to keep them alive. 21 Also take with you every sort of food that is eaten, and store it up. It shall serve as food for you and for them." 22 Noah did this; he did all that God commanded him.

7 Then the LORD said to Noah, "Go into the ark, you and all your household, for I have seen that you are righteous before me in this generation. 2 Take with you seven pairs of all clean animals,[7] the male and his mate, and a pair of the animals that are not clean, the male and his mate, 3 and seven pairs[8] of the birds of the heavens also, male and female, to keep their offspring alive on the face of all the earth. 4 For in seven days I will send rain on the earth forty days and forty nights, and every living thing[9] that I have made I will blot out from the face of the ground." 5 And Noah did all that the LORD had commanded him.

6 Noah was six hundred years old when the flood of waters came upon the earth. 7 And Noah and his sons and his wife and his sons' wives with him went

GENESIS 6:18

NOAH AND THE FLOOD

The story of Noah offers a clear picture of the saving mercy of God. In the midst of humanity's sin and rebellion, God made a way for the salvation of the human race through Noah and the ark. Were there not a man and a family who by God's grace stood out from the wickedness of their day, there would have been a new beginning on the part of God that would have omitted all of us! Mercifully, God provided Noah and his family with the ark to escape the floodwaters. The ark is a powerful picture of Jesus Christ, in whom salvation would come to everyone who believed in him. Jesus, like the ark, would one day be lifted high above the floodwaters of our sin to endure the full wrath of God. By putting our hope in Jesus, we are rescued like Noah and his family.

[1] Or *My Spirit shall not contend with* [2] Or *giants* [3] Hebrew *The end of all flesh has come before me* [4] Transliterated from Hebrew; the identity of this tree is uncertain [5] A *cubit* was about 18 inches or 45 centimeters [6] Or *skylight* [7] Or *seven of each kind of clean animal* [8] Or *seven of each kind* [9] Hebrew *all existence*; also verse 23

SIN

The exact nature of the sin described in these verses is perplexing to most readers. While the actions are somewhat unclear, what is abundantly evident is the fact that God's good, created order has been corrupted by human rebellion. The people have done the very thing God commanded them to do in the garden — they have been fruitful and multiplied and filled the earth (Ge 1:28). Sadly, rather than filling the earth with image-bearers who reflect God's glory, they have instead filled the earth with brokenness.

Interestingly, the sin recounted here describes the people seeing something as beautiful and pursuing that thing in rebellion to God's command, as did Adam and Eve. Rather than submitting to the command of God and trusting the goodness of his dictates, the first couple chose to trust their eyes and follow the lusts of their hearts (Ge 3:1 – 7). At its core, this is the nature of all sin.

God, the Creator of all things, knows best how the human life should be lived. He provides clear guidance on his good and gracious plans for humanity, which are ultimately for good. Sin is rooted in unbelief in the promises of God. Rather than trusting in the ways of God, all people choose to follow the desires of their own hearts and, in so doing, elevate themselves to the position of God. People believe they know better than God; therefore, they run after the lusts of their hearts and the desires of their eyes. John warns, however, that these things are passing away and so are those who live their lives in pursuit of them. Only those who do "the will of God" can live (1Jn 2:16 – 17).

But, how does one do the will of God? The implications of Adam's sin and the fall are not merely that all people make bad decisions, yet if they try hard enough they can keep God's law. Rather, sin renders all people unable to keep God's law and trapped in the shackles of their sin. Jesus perfectly and completely lived the life they could not live, no matter how hard they tried. Those who are aware of their inability to keep God's law can turn to Christ in repentance and faith and be given the free gift of righteousness. By grace, God credits the perfection of Jesus to men and women who could never earn it by their own merit (2Co 5:21).

into the ark to escape the waters of the flood. 8Of clean animals, and of animals
that are not clean, and of birds, and of everything that creeps on the ground, 9two
and two, male and female, went into the ark with Noah, as God had commanded
Noah. 10And after seven days the waters of the flood came upon the earth.

11In the six hundredth year of Noah's life, in the second month, on the seventeenth day of the month, on that day all the fountains of the great deep burst
forth, and the windows of the heavens were opened. 12And rain fell upon the earth
forty days and forty nights. 13On the very same day Noah and his sons, Shem and
Ham and Japheth, and Noah's wife and the three wives of his sons with them
entered the ark, 14they and every beast, according to its kind, and all the livestock
according to their kinds, and every creeping thing that creeps on the earth, according to its kind, and every bird, according to its kind, every winged creature.
15They went into the ark with Noah, two and two of all flesh in which there was
the breath of life. 16And those that entered, male and female of all flesh, went in
as God had commanded him. And the LORD shut him in.

17The flood continued forty days on the earth. The waters increased and bore
up the ark, and it rose high above the earth. 18The waters prevailed and increased
greatly on the earth, and the ark floated on the face of the waters. 19And the waters
prevailed so mightily on the earth that all the high mountains under the whole
heaven were covered. 20The waters prevailed above the mountains, covering
them fifteen cubits[1] deep. 21And all flesh died that moved on the earth, birds, livestock, beasts, all swarming creatures that swarm on the earth, and all mankind.
22Everything on the dry land in whose nostrils was the breath of life died. 23He
blotted out every living thing that was on the face of the ground, man and animals and creeping things and birds of the heavens. They were blotted out from
the earth. Only Noah was left, and those who were with him in the ark. 24And the
waters prevailed on the earth 150 days.

The Flood Subsides

8 But God remembered Noah and all the beasts and all the livestock that were
with him in the ark. And God made a wind blow over the earth, and the waters subsided. 2The fountains of the deep and the windows of the heavens were
closed, the rain from the heavens was restrained, 3and the waters receded from
the earth continually. At the end of 150 days the waters had abated, 4and in the
seventh month, on the seventeenth day of the month, the ark came to rest on the
mountains of Ararat. 5And the waters continued to abate until the tenth month;
in the tenth month, on the first day of the month, the tops of the mountains were
seen.

6At the end of forty days Noah opened the window of the ark that he had made
7and sent forth a raven. It went to and fro until the waters were dried up from
the earth. 8Then he sent forth a dove from him, to see if the waters had subsided
from the face of the ground. 9But the dove found no place to set her foot, and
she returned to him to the ark, for the waters were still on the face of the whole
earth. So he put out his hand and took her and brought her into the ark with him.
10He waited another seven days, and again he sent forth the dove out of the ark.
11And the dove came back to him in the evening, and behold, in her mouth was a
freshly plucked olive leaf. So Noah knew that the waters had subsided from the
earth. 12Then he waited another seven days and sent forth the dove, and she did
not return to him anymore.

13In the six hundred and first year, in the first month, the first day of the
month, the waters were dried from off the earth. And Noah removed the covering of the ark and looked, and behold, the face of the ground was dry. 14In the
second month, on the twenty-seventh day of the month, the earth had dried out.
15Then God said to Noah, 16"Go out from the ark, you and your wife, and your

GENESIS 7:23

THE REALITY OF NOAH AND THE FLOOD

In the days of Noah, the wickedness of mankind had reached a breaking point. The sin that started with Adam and Eve in the garden had spread throughout the entire world and "every intention of the thoughts of his heart was only evil continually" (Ge 6:5). In response to the rebellion of humanity, God sent a flood to destroy every living creature on the earth. People died—old people and young, beautiful and brave along with the grisly and gray. Only Noah and those with him escaped the terrible, universal death of the wicked. Even the survival of Noah and his family was the result of undeserved mercy, because they were broken and sinful like everyone else (Ge 9:20–27). Many people have rejected the story of Noah and the flood as folklore without any historical merit. However, Jesus affirmed the reality of the "days of Noah" when he compared them to the last days (Mt 24:37–38; Lk 17:26–27). Peter also used the story of Noah and the flood as a pattern for the final judgment (1Pe 3:20; 2Pe 2:5; 3:5–6).

[1]A *cubit* was about 18 inches or 45 centimeters

sons and your sons' wives with you. 17Bring out with you every living thing that
is with you of all flesh—birds and animals and every creeping thing that creeps
on the earth—that they may swarm on the earth, and be fruitful and multiply on
the earth." 18So Noah went out, and his sons and his wife and his sons' wives with
him. 19Every beast, every creeping thing, and every bird, everything that moves
on the earth, went out by families from the ark.

God's Covenant with Noah

20Then Noah built an altar to the LORD and took some of every clean animal
and some of every clean bird and offered burnt offerings on the altar. 21And when
the LORD smelled the pleasing aroma, the LORD said in his heart, "I will never
again curse[1] the ground because of man, for the intention of man's heart is evil
from his youth. Neither will I ever again strike down every living creature as I have
done. 22While the earth remains, seedtime and harvest, cold and heat, summer
and winter, day and night, shall not cease."

9 And God blessed Noah and his sons and said to them, "Be fruitful and multiply and fill the earth. 2The fear of you and the dread of you shall be upon
every beast of the earth and upon every bird of the heavens, upon everything that
creeps on the ground and all the fish of the sea. Into your hand they are delivered.
3Every moving thing that lives shall be food for you. And as I gave you the green
plants, I give you everything. 4But you shall not eat flesh with its life, that is, its
blood. 5And for your lifeblood I will require a reckoning: from every beast I will
require it and from man. From his fellow man I will require a reckoning for the
life of man.

6 "Whoever sheds the blood of man,
by man shall his blood be shed,
for God made man in his own image.

7And you,[2] be fruitful and multiply, increase greatly on the earth and multiply
in it."

8Then God said to Noah and to his sons with him, 9"Behold, I establish my
covenant with you and your offspring after you, 10and with every living creature
that is with you, the birds, the livestock, and every beast of the earth with you,
as many as came out of the ark; it is for every beast of the earth. 11I establish my
covenant with you, that never again shall all flesh be cut off by the waters of the
flood, and never again shall there be a flood to destroy the earth." 12And God said,
"This is the sign of the covenant that I make between me and you and every living creature that is with you, for all future generations: 13I have set my bow in the
cloud, and it shall be a sign of the covenant between me and the earth. 14When I
bring clouds over the earth and the bow is seen in the clouds, 15I will remember
my covenant that is between me and you and every living creature of all flesh.
And the waters shall never again become a flood to destroy all flesh. 16When the
bow is in the clouds, I will see it and remember the everlasting covenant between
God and every living creature of all flesh that is on the earth." 17God said to Noah,
"This is the sign of the covenant that I have established between me and all flesh
that is on the earth."

Noah's Descendants

18The sons of Noah who went forth from the ark were Shem, Ham, and Japheth. (Ham was the father of Canaan.) 19These three were the sons of Noah, and
from these the people of the whole earth were dispersed.[3]

20Noah began to be a man of the soil, and he planted a vineyard.[4] 21He drank
of the wine and became drunk and lay uncovered in his tent. 22And Ham, the
father of Canaan, saw the nakedness of his father and told his two brothers

---

[1]Or *dishonor* [2]In Hebrew *you* is plural [3]Or *from these the whole earth was populated* [4]Or *Noah, a man of the soil, was the first to plant a vineyard*

THE BOW IN THE HEAVENS

The rainbow is a symbol of God's promise never to destroy the earth again with a flood. More importantly, it serves as a tangible reminder of the faithfulness of God to fulfill his promises to his people. To modern ears, the notion of God's "remembering" something may sound strange. How can an all-knowing God forget anything? Rather, the text points out that God would consistently call to mind his covenant promises, even when the people's rebellion seemingly knew no end.

These promises stem from the task given to Adam and Eve in the garden (Ge 1:26–31). They were not merely to relax and enjoy their home. They were to represent God by exercising dominion and rule over the world in which they were placed. They were also to multiply and fill the earth with image-bearing worshipers.

Sin holistically altered the nature of this task, but it did not change the mission. The mission continues even after the systemic nature of sin was demonstrated in unthinkable ways, causing God to lament his work of creation (Ge 6:6). God acted in judgment, though he sustained a chosen remnant from the flood. Following their deliverance in the ark, God reinstated his mission with Noah and his family (Ge 9:1). They were called to multiply and fill the earth — a task made possible by the grace of God.

God affirmed his role in their lives and mission through a covenant. Throughout the ancient world, covenants were often used to describe the relationship of a king to his subjects. In it, the nature of the relationship was described along with the subjects' responsibilities for obedience and life in the kingdom. This was certainly the case with Noah.

The foundation of God's covenant with Noah and his family was grace and mercy. He called them, protected them, and pledged his faithfulness to them. The death of Jesus fulfilled God's covenant to Noah. As the pointed spear of a Roman soldier pierced Jesus' side while he hung on a criminal's cross, God's wrath was directed at God's only Son (Jn 19:34). In that climactic moment, the wrath of God and the grace of God met, and all of God's promises found their fulfillment in Jesus (2Co 1:20).

outside. 23 Then Shem and Japheth took a garment, laid it on both their shoulders, and walked backward and covered the nakedness of their father. Their
faces were turned backward, and they did not see their father's nakedness.
24 When Noah awoke from his wine and knew what his youngest son had done
to him, 25 he said,

"Cursed be Canaan;
    a servant of servants shall he be to his brothers."

26 He also said,

"Blessed be the LORD, the God of Shem;
    and let Canaan be his servant.
27 May God enlarge Japheth,[1]
    and let him dwell in the tents of Shem,
    and let Canaan be his servant."

28 After the flood Noah lived 350 years. 29 All the days of Noah were 950 years,
and he died.

Nations Descended from Noah

10 These are the generations of the sons of Noah, Shem, Ham, and Japheth.
Sons were born to them after the flood.
2 The sons of Japheth: Gomer, Magog, Madai, Javan, Tubal, Meshech, and Tiras.
3 The sons of Gomer: Ashkenaz, Riphath, and Togarmah. 4 The sons of Javan: Elishah, Tarshish, Kittim, and Dodanim. 5 From these the coastland peoples spread
in their lands, each with his own language, by their clans, in their nations.
6 The sons of Ham: Cush, Egypt, Put, and Canaan. 7 The sons of Cush: Seba,
Havilah, Sabtah, Raamah, and Sabteca. The sons of Raamah: Sheba and Dedan.
8 Cush fathered Nimrod; he was the first on earth to be a mighty man.[2] 9 He was a
mighty hunter before the LORD. Therefore it is said, "Like Nimrod a mighty hunter
before the LORD." 10 The beginning of his kingdom was Babel, Erech, Accad, and
Calneh, in the land of Shinar. 11 From that land he went into Assyria and built
Nineveh, Rehoboth-Ir, Calah, and 12 Resen between Nineveh and Calah; that is the
great city. 13 Egypt fathered Ludim, Anamim, Lehabim, Naphtuhim, 14 Pathrusim,
Casluhim (from whom[3] the Philistines came), and Caphtorim.
15 Canaan fathered Sidon his firstborn and Heth, 16 and the Jebusites, the Amorites, the Girgashites, 17 the Hivites, the Arkites, the Sinites, 18 the Arvadites, the
Zemarites, and the Hamathites. Afterward the clans of the Canaanites dispersed.
19 And the territory of the Canaanites extended from Sidon in the direction of Gerar as far as Gaza, and in the direction of Sodom, Gomorrah, Admah, and Zeboiim,
as far as Lasha. 20 These are the sons of Ham, by their clans, their languages, their
lands, and their nations.
21 To Shem also, the father of all the children of Eber, the elder brother of Japheth,[4] children were born. 22 The sons of Shem: Elam, Asshur, Arpachshad, Lud,
and Aram. 23 The sons of Aram: Uz, Hul, Gether, and Mash. 24 Arpachshad fathered
Shelah; and Shelah fathered Eber. 25 To Eber were born two sons: the name of the
one was Peleg,[5] for in his days the earth was divided, and his brother's name was
Joktan. 26 Joktan fathered Almodad, Sheleph, Hazarmaveth, Jerah, 27 Hadoram,
Uzal, Diklah, 28 Obal, Abimael, Sheba, 29 Ophir, Havilah, and Jobab; all these were
the sons of Joktan. 30 The territory in which they lived extended from Mesha in the
direction of Sephar to the hill country of the east. 31 These are the sons of Shem,
by their clans, their languages, their lands, and their nations.
32 These are the clans of the sons of Noah, according to their genealogies, in
their nations, and from these the nations spread abroad on the earth after the
flood.

[1] *Japheth* sounds like the Hebrew for *enlarge* [2] Or *he began to be a mighty man on the earth* [3] Or *from where* [4] Or *the brother of Japheth the elder* [5] *Peleg* means *division*

GENESIS 10:1

JESUS FROM THE FAMILY OF NOAH

Though not every ancient people group is listed in this chapter, it is seen here that all of the people of the earth, regardless of locale or language, descended from Noah. From this line Abraham and ultimately Jesus will emerge. It was Abraham with whom God made an everlasting covenant, promising that kings would come from his line (Ge 17:6). In the first line of the New Testament, Jesus is introduced as Messiah and "the son of Abraham" (Mt 1:1). It is clear to see, even this early on in Scripture, that God had a plan that was ultimately revealed in Jesus. The coming of Jesus as the Promised One in the line of Abraham established the continuity of the promise and plan of God from Genesis to Revelation.

The Tower of Babel

11 Now the whole earth had one language and the same words. 2And as people
migrated from the east, they found a plain in the land of Shinar and settled
there. 3And they said to one another, "Come, let us make bricks, and burn them
thoroughly." And they had brick for stone, and bitumen for mortar. 4Then they
said, "Come, let us build ourselves a city and a tower with its top in the heavens,
and let us make a name for ourselves, lest we be dispersed over the face of the
whole earth." 5And the LORD came down to see the city and the tower, which the
children of man had built. 6And the LORD said, "Behold, they are one people, and
they have all one language, and this is only the beginning of what they will do.
And nothing that they propose to do will now be impossible for them. 7Come, let
us go down and there confuse their language, so that they may not understand
one another's speech." 8So the LORD dispersed them from there over the face of all
the earth, and they left off building the city. 9Therefore its name was called Babel,
because there the LORD confused[1] the language of all the earth. And from there
the LORD dispersed them over the face of all the earth.

Shem's Descendants

10These are the generations of Shem. When Shem was 100 years old, he fathered Arpachshad two years after the flood. 11And Shem lived after he fathered
Arpachshad 500 years and had other sons and daughters.
12When Arpachshad had lived 35 years, he fathered Shelah. 13And Arpachshad
lived after he fathered Shelah 403 years and had other sons and daughters.
14When Shelah had lived 30 years, he fathered Eber. 15And Shelah lived after
he fathered Eber 403 years and had other sons and daughters.
16When Eber had lived 34 years, he fathered Peleg. 17And Eber lived after he
fathered Peleg 430 years and had other sons and daughters.
18When Peleg had lived 30 years, he fathered Reu. 19And Peleg lived after he
fathered Reu 209 years and had other sons and daughters.
20When Reu had lived 32 years, he fathered Serug. 21And Reu lived after he
fathered Serug 207 years and had other sons and daughters.
22When Serug had lived 30 years, he fathered Nahor. 23And Serug lived after
he fathered Nahor 200 years and had other sons and daughters.
24When Nahor had lived 29 years, he fathered Terah. 25And Nahor lived after
he fathered Terah 119 years and had other sons and daughters.
26When Terah had lived 70 years, he fathered Abram, Nahor, and Haran.

Terah's Descendants

27Now these are the generations of Terah. Terah fathered Abram, Nahor, and
Haran; and Haran fathered Lot. 28Haran died in the presence of his father Terah
in the land of his kindred, in Ur of the Chaldeans. 29And Abram and Nahor took
wives. The name of Abram's wife was Sarai, and the name of Nahor's wife, Milcah,
the daughter of Haran the father of Milcah and Iscah. 30Now Sarai was barren;
she had no child.
31Terah took Abram his son and Lot the son of Haran, his grandson, and
Sarai his daughter-in-law, his son Abram's wife, and they went forth together
from Ur of the Chaldeans to go into the land of Canaan, but when they came to
Haran, they settled there. 32The days of Terah were 205 years, and Terah died
in Haran.

The Call of Abram

12 Now the LORD said[2] to Abram, "Go from your country[3] and your kindred
and your father's house to the land that I will show you. 2And I will make of
you a great nation, and I will bless you and make your name great, so that you will

[1] *Babel* sounds like the Hebrew for *confused* [2] Or *had said* [3] Or *land*

THE SIN AT BABEL

At the heart of sin is the desire for humanity to believe that they know better than God. In the garden Satan tempted Eve by asking her, "Did God actually say ...?" in regards to his admonition to not eat the fruit from the tree. When it comes to Babel, the same reality is in play; the people believe they have come up with a better way than what God commanded.

After human beings had been wiped from the planet by the flood, God made a covenant with the lone survivors, Noah and his family, to "fill the earth" (Ge 9:1). However, by the time we get to the story of Babel, the people have concocted a plan that would keep them from having to keep this command (Ge 11:4).

In Babel we see a combination of arrogance and insecurity. The tower demonstrates mankind's taking matters into their own hands, in essence showing God that they know better than he does. Their actions show that they are not relying on God for their well-being; they can handle life on their own. The reality is that the people, by seeking to make a name for themselves, were in competition with God.

In not wanting to scatter over the earth, the people again were showing that they did not trust God for their security. They felt that scattering included too many unknowns, thus leading them to believe that they would be better off staying in one place. This insecurity paralyzed them into believing they needed their own plan. Ultimately God came and shattered the selfish plans of the people by confusing their language and scattering them throughout the earth.

In Acts 1:8, Jesus says his followers are to be his witnesses to the "end of the earth." However, once the power of the Holy Spirit came in Acts 2, the result was not a scattering to the ends of the earth, but a staying in one place, Jerusalem. This all changed when Stephen was stoned to death in Acts 7 and persecution came against the church. This tyranny resulted in the church spreading throughout the known world.

Ultimately what Babel and the early church in Jerusalem show us is that God is asking us to trust him. However, in the face of human pride and disobedience, he will choose to allow calamities to occur in order for his plans to move forward.

REVOLT

GENESIS 3–11

Something is wrong with humanity. While we might try to put on our best face for the world, evil lurks deep inside us all. To deny this reality is to close our eyes to history, for the checkered past of humankind is a monument to the fallen nature we all bear.

Should we ever think otherwise, we need only visit the gas chambers of Auschwitz, where haunted walls recount unspeakable murderous acts; the Edmund Pettus Bridge in Selma, Alabama, where blacks were brutalized because of the color of their skin; the jungle of the Congo, where child soldiers were forced to maim or kill their families; or the brothels of Delhi, where innocent young girls are bought and sold to appease twisted cravings. A brief stop in any of these places should jar us back to grim reality again.

We are capable of committing outrageous wrongs. Those sins, both the ones we act out and those we harbor in our thoughts, are equal in the eyes of God.

So it was in the beginning, starting with Adam and Eve in the Garden of Eden.

REBELLIOUS FROM THE START

Since that time, humankind's capacity to rebel against God has not diminished. We are born with a propensity to go our own way. The first humans arrived on earth with a choice: the free will to follow God toward abundant life or to do things their own way and come face-to-face with death. Adam and Eve chose death, and we all bear the consequences of their fall (Ro 5:12).

How easy it is for us to condemn the first couple for their derelict behavior. God himself walked with them in the cool of the day, and everything about their world was perfect. They were naked, yet unashamed; free from sickness, weariness, brokenness, pain, and death. Before them were trees of every kind, gifts of God for their enjoyment. Adam and Eve's purpose was to manage and care for the plants and creatures on the earth. Their very being was fashioned in the image of God. Among the trees of the garden, God placed the tree of life and the tree of the knowledge of good *and* evil in the center. He instructed Adam to steer clear of the fruit of the latter lest he die. One tree to avoid versus countless trees to enjoy, all set in paradise. An easy choice, right?

However, another voice, the voice of a serpent personifying Satan himself, entered God's story and blurred the lines between good and evil. Satan, like humankind, at one time also had a choice. He could have worshiped God in the company of the angels or revolted. Foolishly, Satan chose his own glory and was jolted from heaven like a falling star. In Satan's rebellion, God granted him limited freedom on earth. With that freedom he sold a lie to Adam and Eve, convincing them that God was trying to rob them of a greater joy by keeping them from this one tree.

The serpent called God's trustworthiness into question, undermining God's character and goodwill toward his creation. Adam and Eve took the bait and turned their backs on God, reaching for the heights of God-like status, yet falling to the depths of futility, rebellion, and death.

Immediately, paradise was shattered into a billion tiny pieces. Guilt ended innocence. The couple hid from the presence of God. Judgment fell. Death entered the scene. Adam and Eve's perfectly harmonious tenure in the Garden of Eden was over.

I WILL DO IT MY WAY

What happened in the garden is called sin. But there is no better way to characterize it than using the word *revolt*. Humankind said on that day what we still say every day. I WILL DO IT MY WAY!

It's hard to imagine anyone spitting in the face of a friend, tracking mud through the home of a neighbor on a rainy day, cutting off a funeral procession in traffic, or mocking a person with a disability. Common human decency causes us to recoil at the thought. Yet, we casually ignore the Almighty, rebuff his counsel, laugh at his wisdom, pursue our own pleasure, and straight-up say no when he calls us to his path and plan.

If the word *revolt* sounds too strong, consider that God is the originator and owner of us all. Yet, we attempt to dismiss and belittle the One who formed us from the dust. We spit in God's face and slam the door on his love. Often without a thought or even a twinge of regret, we treat God worse than we treat most of our friends and neighbors. We repeatedly say toward heaven, "No, thanks, I'm doing just fine without you!"

God has graciously invited us into his story, breathed into us the very breath that gives us life, and invited us to know and walk with him. To do less, to choose less, is to shove our will in the face of the Almighty. And every time we do, we turn his best for us upside down.

In God's eyes all people are in the same predicament. That's what Scripture indicates when the New Testament writer Paul says, "All have sinned and fall short of the glory of God" (Ro 3:23). The prophet Isaiah amplified our plight when he wrote, "All we like sheep have gone astray; we have turned — every one — to his own way" (Isa 53:6). The psalmist wrote, "They have all turned aside; together they have become corrupt; there is none who does good, not even one" (Ps 14:3).

Like Adam and Eve, we seek to elevate ourselves to God's status, free ourselves from his authority, and define for ourselves what is wrong and what is right.

Comparing our behavior against someone else's in an attempt to make ourselves look more desirable does us no good. Revolt has never

REVOLT

(CONTINUED)

GENESIS 3 – 11

been about the magnitude of our sin but the fact that we are willing to look into the face of a good and loving God and turn and run the other way.

TRADING TRUTH FOR LIES

Left to ourselves, we will do what Adam and Eve did in the garden. We exchange "the glory of the immortal God for images resembling mortal man and birds and animals and creeping things" (Ro 1:23). God promised life and sought to protect people from destruction and death. The serpent twisted God's words, and the world around us does the same. We often discard what is best for us from God's perspective for what is easiest. We ditch what is good for what is convenient. Our culture scoffs at what is innocent and pure while it celebrates what is perverse and immoral. More and more, honesty, decency, and modesty are marginalized and even vilified.

This exchange of truth for lies does not happen without consequences. Once jettisoned from Eden, humankind did not cease to worship (which we were created to do); humans just exchanged the true worship of holy God for something else. Scripture says, "They exchanged the truth about God for a lie and worshiped and served the creature rather than the Creator" (Ro 1:25).

When we turn our God-intended worship toward a person or pleasure or thing, we break ranks with God and violate the first of his Ten Commandments (Ex 20:3).

Sin shatters God's perfect plan for us and leaves us with powerless idols that soak up our affection while returning nothing of spiritual benefit to our lives.

But that's not all. It gets worse.

As we see in Eden, a holy, righteous, and just God cannot turn a blind eye toward our revolt. He cannot simply wink and magically make it disappear. While we rationalize away our sin, God cannot deny his own character.

Our sin derailed our worship, separated us from God, introduced us to hardship and toil, put hostility between us and others, filled our hearts with selfish intentions, brought pain into childbirth, and spawned a global epidemic of hatred and war and injustice that marches on in full force today.

Even creation itself was rocked by humankind's sinful revolt. Natural disasters continue to mar our world, and nothing in creation on this earth is as it was meant to be (Ro 8:19 – 22). Everything has been broken because of sin. Decay and death now mark every inch of human existence.

Families fracture. Marriages fail. Litigations flourish. Deception darkens. Addiction crushes. Complacency numbs. Violence escalates. Insanity imprisons. Pleasures disappoint. Riches disappear. Prejudice blinds. Insecurity mars. Jealousy rots. Power corrupts.

GOD'S WRATH

Yet, our sin does something more. Our revolt places us in the crosshairs of God's wrath — his righteous indignation that is set on eradicating all wrong from the face of the earth.

While God's wrath gets a bad rap, any of us, if we thought it through, would act in the same way. We want the weight of justice to fall on those who abuse and injure us or others. In the same way, yet on a much grander scale, God's wrath will fall on every rebel heart. Humankind is without excuse, guilty before a holy God and deserving of eternal punishment.

Revolt didn't simply make us bad. It left us spiritually dead (Ro 6:23). But, fortunately this is God's story and not ours. The story does not end in death; rather, the seeds of salvation are sown in Eden's soil. The God of mercy trumped revolt with redemption in an outrageous plan to buy back the rebels at the cost of his one and only Son.

While judgment rained down on Adam and Eve and the earth and the serpent, grace was on the horizon. The first sign of grace was God's banishment of Adam and Eve from the Garden of Eden. In this act of kindness, he prevented those he loved from eating from the tree of life, thus saving them from living forever in their state of death. Outside Eden, a heavenly mission could ensue, one foreshadowed as God made coverings for the man and the woman.

Once sin smashed Eden's innocence, Adam and Eve were filled with shame. No one told them to be ashamed, as if guilt is a human-induced effect meant to give control of the people to religious higher-ups. Adam and Eve were convinced on their own that something was amiss. Their consciences shouted "run and hide" as the Spirit of God brought conviction to their hearts.

GOD'S MERCY AND GRACE

Though God judged their actions, his mercy intervened to cover their shame. Using fig leaves from a nearby tree, Adam and Eve tried to hide their nakedness. But God went a step further by clothing them with animal skin. This was a picture of the sacrifice of the One who would ultimately shed his blood so that all people could have an opportunity to be saved.

This kind of grace is staggering, especially in light of the fact that there is no record of so much as an "I'm sorry" from Adam or Eve. Once their deed was exposed, Adam danced the dance we often dance as well, passing the blame to Eve in a weak attempt to deflect God's attention from his disobedience and the responsibility only he himself bore.

REVOLT

(CONTINUED)

GENESIS 3–11

One would think Adam would have quickly blurted out, "Please forgive me, God! I am a fool and I cannot believe what I've done." But Adam couldn't bring himself to confess, so he blamed someone else.

Yet, God's redemption plan was undeterred.

Not only did he make a covering for their nakedness, but God also promised that a descendant of Adam and Eve would one day crush the serpent's head, though he would be harmed in the process (Ge 3:15). This promise and plan, while far from clear in Genesis 3, would define the story that unfolds in the rest of the Bible. God fulfilled his promise by seeing to it that Jesus Christ, a descendant of the woman, would crush Satan, sin, and death forever.

God wasn't going to turn his back on those who were made to bear his image in the world. While humankind chose their own way, Jesus yielded to the Father's plan. Taking on flesh, Jesus was tempted like every other human, yet Jesus did not sin. Jesus exchanged his life for every rebel who turns to him to accept the price he paid for their sin and trust in him for salvation.

The final sacrifice for sin was made as Jesus took our blows, carried our sin, bore our shame, and was crushed by the wrath of God in our place. In the process, "For our sake he made him to be sin who knew no sin, so that in him we might become the righteousness of God" (2Co 5:21). Rebels could now be forgiven. Sinners could be made clean. And all those who drifted far from their heavenly Father could come home again.

The key to this brand-new life is our willingness to end the revolt. To be forgiven, we must admit our sin. To say that we have no sin is to make God a liar and seal our fate (1Jn 1:10). But to admit our wrongs and raise the white flag of surrender is to truly find freedom and enjoy life in God's presence that will never end.

BEGINNINGS	REVOLT	PEOPLE	INTERTESTAMENTAL PERIOD	SAVIOR	CHURCH	FOREVER
GENESIS 1–2 (pg. 10)	GENESIS 3–11 (pg. 24)	GENESIS 12 to MALACHI (pg. 256)	(pg. 1468)	GOSPELS to ACTS 1 (pg. 1518)	ACTS 2 to REVELATION 20 (pg. 1686)	REVELATION 21–22 (pg. 1938)

be a blessing. 3 I will bless those who bless you, and him who dishonors you I will
curse, and in you all the families of the earth shall be blessed."[1]
4 So Abram went, as the LORD had told him, and Lot went with him. Abram was
seventy-five years old when he departed from Haran. 5 And Abram took Sarai his
wife, and Lot his brother's son, and all their possessions that they had gathered,
and the people that they had acquired in Haran, and they set out to go to the land
of Canaan. When they came to the land of Canaan, 6 Abram passed through the
land to the place at Shechem, to the oak[2] of Moreh. At that time the Canaanites
were in the land. 7 Then the LORD appeared to Abram and said, "To your offspring
I will give this land." So he built there an altar to the LORD, who had appeared to
him. 8 From there he moved to the hill country on the east of Bethel and pitched
his tent, with Bethel on the west and Ai on the east. And there he built an altar to
the LORD and called upon the name of the LORD. 9 And Abram journeyed on, still
going toward the Negeb.

Abram and Sarai in Egypt

10 Now there was a famine in the land. So Abram went down to Egypt to sojourn there, for the famine was severe in the land. 11 When he was about to enter
Egypt, he said to Sarai his wife, "I know that you are a woman beautiful in appearance, 12 and when the Egyptians see you, they will say, 'This is his wife.' Then
they will kill me, but they will let you live. 13 Say you are my sister, that it may
go well with me because of you, and that my life may be spared for your sake."
14 When Abram entered Egypt, the Egyptians saw that the woman was very beautiful. 15 And when the princes of Pharaoh saw her, they praised her to Pharaoh. And
the woman was taken into Pharaoh's house. 16 And for her sake he dealt well with
Abram; and he had sheep, oxen, male donkeys, male servants, female servants,
female donkeys, and camels.
17 But the LORD afflicted Pharaoh and his house with great plagues because of
Sarai, Abram's wife. 18 So Pharaoh called Abram and said, "What is this you have
done to me? Why did you not tell me that she was your wife? 19 Why did you say,
'She is my sister,' so that I took her for my wife? Now then, here is your wife; take
her, and go." 20 And Pharaoh gave men orders concerning him, and they sent him
away with his wife and all that he had.

Abram and Lot Separate

13 So Abram went up from Egypt, he and his wife and all that he had, and Lot
with him, into the Negeb.
2 Now Abram was very rich in livestock, in silver, and in gold. 3 And he journeyed on from the Negeb as far as Bethel to the place where his tent had been at
the beginning, between Bethel and Ai, 4 to the place where he had made an altar at
the first. And there Abram called upon the name of the LORD. 5 And Lot, who went
with Abram, also had flocks and herds and tents, 6 so that the land could not support both of them dwelling together; for their possessions were so great that they
could not dwell together, 7 and there was strife between the herdsmen of Abram's
livestock and the herdsmen of Lot's livestock. At that time the Canaanites and the
Perizzites were dwelling in the land.
8 Then Abram said to Lot, "Let there be no strife between you and me, and
between your herdsmen and my herdsmen, for we are kinsmen.[3] 9 Is not the whole
land before you? Separate yourself from me. If you take the left hand, then I will
go to the right, or if you take the right hand, then I will go to the left." 10 And Lot
lifted up his eyes and saw that the Jordan Valley was well watered everywhere like
the garden of the LORD, like the land of Egypt, in the direction of Zoar. (This was
before the LORD destroyed Sodom and Gomorrah.) 11 So Lot chose for himself all
the Jordan Valley, and Lot journeyed east. Thus they separated from each other.

[1] Or *by you all the families of the earth shall bless themselves* [2] Or *terebinth* [3] Hebrew *we are men, brothers*

ONGOING PROMISES OF A FAITHFUL GOD

The covenant between God and Abraham (often referred to as the Abrahamic covenant) occupies the central focus of the next several chapters of the Bible. Genesis 12 begins with a vital prologue that sets the stage for the promises and ceremonies that would follow. They testify to the irrevocable nature of the promises of God.

The passage begins with a task given to Abram. He was called to leave all that he had known — his home, most of his family, and his country of origin — and travel to an unknown location that God would reveal in due time. While the passage begins with an act of obedience, it is clear that the covenant is based on the promises of God.

Seven promises follow in rapid succession. (1) God promised to make Abram into a great nation — a pledge that would find fulfillment in the birth of the Hebrew nation. (2) God promised to bless Abram, his family and the nation that would emerge with his loving care and continued provision. (3) Abram, later renamed Abraham, would be given a name that would live on long after his earthly life concluded. (4) The nation would be a blessing to other nations as they modeled conformity to God's law and demonstrated proper worship of the awe-inspiring God. (5) God would bless those who blessed the nation. (6) God would stand in judgment against those who oppressed his people. (7) All people would be blessed through Abram and the generations that followed him.

These grand and glorious promises were rooted in the nature and character of God. In spite of the people's unbelief, rebellion, idolatry, and spiritual adultery, God remained faithful to his promises because the covenant was based on grace and not on law. Paul wrote that God gave Abraham these promises long before the law was given on Mount Sinai (Gal 3:16–17).

As one born in the line of Abraham, Jesus was the means by which these promises were fulfilled. All those in Christ, born again by the grace of God, are children of Abraham and recipients of the promises of God that were fulfilled in Jesus. Paul testified to this reality when he claimed that all those who respond in faith to the good news of Jesus are heirs of the promises given to Abraham (Gal 3:28–29).

12Abram settled in the land of Canaan, while Lot settled among the cities of the valley and moved his tent as far as Sodom. 13Now the men of Sodom were wicked, great sinners against the LORD.

14The LORD said to Abram, after Lot had separated from him, "Lift up your eyes and look from the place where you are, northward and southward and eastward and westward, 15for all the land that you see I will give to you and to your offspring forever. 16I will make your offspring as the dust of the earth, so that if one can count the dust of the earth, your offspring also can be counted. 17Arise, walk through the length and the breadth of the land, for I will give it to you." 18So Abram moved his tent and came and settled by the oaks[1] of Mamre, which are at Hebron, and there he built an altar to the LORD.

Abram Rescues Lot

14 In the days of Amraphel king of Shinar, Arioch king of Ellasar, Chedorlaomer king of Elam, and Tidal king of Goiim, 2these kings made war with Bera king of Sodom, Birsha king of Gomorrah, Shinab king of Admah, Shemeber king of Zeboiim, and the king of Bela (that is, Zoar). 3And all these joined forces in the Valley of Siddim (that is, the Salt Sea). 4Twelve years they had served Chedorlaomer, but in the thirteenth year they rebelled. 5In the fourteenth year Chedorlaomer and the kings who were with him came and defeated the Rephaim in Ashteroth-karnaim, the Zuzim in Ham, the Emim in Shaveh-kiriathaim, 6and the Horites in their hill country of Seir as far as El-paran on the border of the wilderness. 7Then they turned back and came to En-mishpat (that is, Kadesh) and defeated all the country of the Amalekites, and also the Amorites who were dwelling in Hazazon-tamar.

8Then the king of Sodom, the king of Gomorrah, the king of Admah, the king of Zeboiim, and the king of Bela (that is, Zoar) went out, and they joined battle in the Valley of Siddim 9with Chedorlaomer king of Elam, Tidal king of Goiim, Amraphel king of Shinar, and Arioch king of Ellasar, four kings against five. 10Now the Valley of Siddim was full of bitumen pits, and as the kings of Sodom and Gomorrah fled, some fell into them, and the rest fled to the hill country. 11So the enemy took all the possessions of Sodom and Gomorrah, and all their provisions, and went their way. 12They also took Lot, the son of Abram's brother, who was dwelling in Sodom, and his possessions, and went their way.

13Then one who had escaped came and told Abram the Hebrew, who was living by the oaks[2] of Mamre the Amorite, brother of Eshcol and of Aner. These were allies of Abram. 14When Abram heard that his kinsman had been taken captive, he led forth his trained men, born in his house, 318 of them, and went in pursuit as far as Dan. 15And he divided his forces against them by night, he and his servants, and defeated them and pursued them to Hobah, north of Damascus. 16Then he brought back all the possessions, and also brought back his kinsman Lot with his possessions, and the women and the people.

Abram Blessed by Melchizedek

17After his return from the defeat of Chedorlaomer and the kings who were with him, the king of Sodom went out to meet him at the Valley of Shaveh (that is, the King's Valley). 18And Melchizedek king of Salem brought out bread and wine. (He was priest of God Most High.) 19And he blessed him and said,

"Blessed be Abram by God Most High,
Possessor[3] of heaven and earth;
20 and blessed be God Most High,
who has delivered your enemies into your hand!"

And Abram gave him a tenth of everything. 21And the king of Sodom said to Abram, "Give me the persons, but take the goods for yourself." 22But Abram said

[1]Or *terebinths* [2]Or *terebinths* [3]Or *Creator*; also verse 22

to the king of Sodom, "I have lifted my hand[1] to the LORD, God Most High, Possessor of heaven and earth, 23 that I would not take a thread or a sandal strap or anything that is yours, lest you should say, 'I have made Abram rich.' 24 I will take nothing but what the young men have eaten, and the share of the men who went with me. Let Aner, Eshcol, and Mamre take their share."

God's Covenant with Abram

15 After these things the word of the LORD came to Abram in a vision: "Fear not, Abram, I am your shield; your reward shall be very great." 2 But Abram said, "O Lord GOD, what will you give me, for I continue[2] childless, and the heir of my house is Eliezer of Damascus?" 3 And Abram said, "Behold, you have given me no offspring, and a member of my household will be my heir." 4 And behold, the word of the LORD came to him: "This man shall not be your heir; your very own son[3] shall be your heir." 5 And he brought him outside and said, "Look toward heaven, and number the stars, if you are able to number them." Then he said to him, "So shall your offspring be." 6 And he believed the LORD, and he counted it to him as righteousness.

7 And he said to him, "I am the LORD who brought you out from Ur of the Chaldeans to give you this land to possess." 8 But he said, "O Lord GOD, how am I to know that I shall possess it?" 9 He said to him, "Bring me a heifer three years old, a female goat three years old, a ram three years old, a turtledove, and a young pigeon." 10 And he brought him all these, cut them in half, and laid each half over against the other. But he did not cut the birds in half. 11 And when birds of prey came down on the carcasses, Abram drove them away.

12 As the sun was going down, a deep sleep fell on Abram. And behold, dreadful and great darkness fell upon him. 13 Then the LORD said to Abram, "Know for certain that your offspring will be sojourners in a land that is not theirs and will be servants there, and they will be afflicted for four hundred years. 14 But I will bring judgment on the nation that they serve, and afterward they shall come out with great possessions. 15 As for you, you shall go to your fathers in peace; you shall be buried in a good old age. 16 And they shall come back here in the fourth generation, for the iniquity of the Amorites is not yet complete."

17 When the sun had gone down and it was dark, behold, a smoking fire pot and a flaming torch passed between these pieces. 18 On that day the LORD made a covenant with Abram, saying, "To your offspring I give[4] this land, from the river of Egypt to the great river, the river Euphrates, 19 the land of the Kenites, the Kenizzites, the Kadmonites, 20 the Hittites, the Perizzites, the Rephaim, 21 the Amorites, the Canaanites, the Girgashites and the Jebusites."

Sarai and Hagar

16 Now Sarai, Abram's wife, had borne him no children. She had a female Egyptian servant whose name was Hagar. 2 And Sarai said to Abram, "Behold now, the LORD has prevented me from bearing children. Go in to my servant; it may be that I shall obtain children[5] by her." And Abram listened to the voice of Sarai. 3 So, after Abram had lived ten years in the land of Canaan, Sarai, Abram's wife, took Hagar the Egyptian, her servant, and gave her to Abram her husband as a wife. 4 And he went in to Hagar, and she conceived. And when she saw that she had conceived, she looked with contempt on her mistress.[6] 5 And Sarai said to Abram, "May the wrong done to me be on you! I gave my servant to your embrace, and when she saw that she had conceived, she looked on me with contempt. May the LORD judge between you and me!" 6 But Abram said to Sarai, "Behold, your servant is in your power; do to her as you please." Then Sarai dealt harshly with her, and she fled from her.

[1] Or *I have taken a solemn oath* [2] Or *I shall die* [3] Hebrew *what will come out of your own loins* [4] Or *have given* [5] Hebrew *be built up*, which sounds like the Hebrew for *children* [6] Hebrew *her mistress was dishonorable in her eyes*; similarly in verse 5

GENESIS 15:6

FAITH AND OBEDIENCE

Faith and obedience were hallmarks of Abram's life (Heb 11:18–19). When God made Abram promises, he believed. And when he was commanded, Abram obeyed (Ge 12:4; 22:3). At times this faith required great risk on Abram's part. Abram left what was known to him in order to step out into what God was calling him to. It is faith like Abram's—faith in the only living God—that saves sinners (Eph 2:8). It was Abram's faith in God's promise to give him many descendants that caused God to count him as righteous (Ge 15:1–6). Abram's faith was well founded in the God who always keeps his promises. It's important to note that it wasn't Abram's own righteous living or good deeds that made him righteous in God's eyes; it was simply faith.

7The angel of the LORD found her by a spring of water in the wilderness, the
spring on the way to Shur. 8And he said, "Hagar, servant of Sarai, where have you
come from and where are you going?" She said, "I am fleeing from my mistress Sarai." 9The angel of the LORD said to her, "Return to your mistress and submit to her."
10The angel of the LORD also said to her, "I will surely multiply your offspring so that
they cannot be numbered for multitude." 11And the angel of the LORD said to her,

"Behold, you are pregnant
   and shall bear a son.
You shall call his name Ishmael,[1]
   because the LORD has listened to your affliction.
12 He shall be a wild donkey of a man,
   his hand against everyone
   and everyone's hand against him,
and he shall dwell over against all his kinsmen."

13So she called the name of the LORD who spoke to her, "You are a God of seeing,"[2]
for she said, "Truly here I have seen him who looks after me."[3] 14Therefore the
well was called Beer-lahai-roi;[4] it lies between Kadesh and Bered.
15And Hagar bore Abram a son, and Abram called the name of his son, whom
Hagar bore, Ishmael. 16Abram was eighty-six years old when Hagar bore Ishmael
to Abram.

Abraham and the Covenant of Circumcision

17 When Abram was ninety-nine years old the LORD appeared to Abram and
said to him, "I am God Almighty;[5] walk before me, and be blameless, 2that
I may make my covenant between me and you, and may multiply you greatly."
3Then Abram fell on his face. And God said to him, 4"Behold, my covenant is with
you, and you shall be the father of a multitude of nations. 5No longer shall your
name be called Abram,[6] but your name shall be Abraham,[7] for I have made you
the father of a multitude of nations. 6I will make you exceedingly fruitful, and I
will make you into nations, and kings shall come from you. 7And I will establish
my covenant between me and you and your offspring after you throughout their
generations for an everlasting covenant, to be God to you and to your offspring
after you. 8And I will give to you and to your offspring after you the land of your
sojournings, all the land of Canaan, for an everlasting possession, and I will be
their God."
9And God said to Abraham, "As for you, you shall keep my covenant, you and
your offspring after you throughout their generations. 10This is my covenant,
which you shall keep, between me and you and your offspring after you: Every
male among you shall be circumcised. 11You shall be circumcised in the flesh of
your foreskins, and it shall be a sign of the covenant between me and you. 12He
who is eight days old among you shall be circumcised. Every male throughout
your generations, whether born in your house or bought with your money from
any foreigner who is not of your offspring, 13both he who is born in your house
and he who is bought with your money, shall surely be circumcised. So shall my
covenant be in your flesh an everlasting covenant. 14Any uncircumcised male
who is not circumcised in the flesh of his foreskin shall be cut off from his people;
he has broken my covenant."

Isaac's Birth Promised

15And God said to Abraham, "As for Sarai your wife, you shall not call her name
Sarai, but Sarah[8] shall be her name. 16I will bless her, and moreover, I will give[9]

[1] *Ishmael* means *God hears* [2] Or *You are a God who sees me* [3] Hebrew *Have I really seen him here who sees me?* or *Would I have looked here for the one who sees me?* [4] *Beer-lahai-roi* means *the well of the Living One who sees me* [5] Hebrew *El Shaddai* [6] *Abram* means *exalted father* [7] *Abraham* means *father of a multitude* [8] *Sarai* and *Sarah* mean *princess* [9] Hebrew *have given*

GENESIS 16:15

VISITATION FROM GOD

Hagar, a slave, got caught up in Abram and Sarai's attempt to bear the son that God had promised them. Though Hagar became pregnant with a son, the conception was not according to the Lord's plan and she grew dismayed (Ge 16:4–5). After being mistreated by Sarai, Hagar ran away and was met by the angel of the Lord. The site and outcome of Hagar's visitation from the angel of the Lord are beautiful. She was found by a spring of water in the desert, which closely represented her situation — pregnant with a child, yet feeling abandoned and hopeless. She was comforted by this visitation (Ge 16:13) despite being told that her son, Ishmael, would not be the son of promise but would experience hostility in all of his relationships and that he would roam the desert like a wild donkey (Ge 16:11–12; Gal 4:22–23).

FATHER OF MANY NATIONS

God's grand mission to restore his rebellious worshipers, as broad as it seems, was as narrow as a single man — Abram. But the scope of that mission was about to become much broader. God told Abram that he was going to make him the father of many nations and accordingly renamed him "Abraham." The Lord would indeed make Abram into Abraham, and he would do it in two ways.

In a purely physical sense, Abraham's sons Ishmael and Isaac would become the fathers of nations. Ishmael, in spite of his shame and rejection, would father a great nation (Ge 17:20). His children would go on to become the Ishmaelites (25:13 – 16; 37:27 – 28). Isaac's two sons, Esau and Jacob, were both the source of nations. Esau would become the father of the Edomites (36:9), who lived on the borders of Canaan. Abraham's grandson Jacob was renamed "Israel" by God — the name of the great nation he would father (35:10 – 11).

In a spiritual sense, Abraham's descendants would form a massive number of individuals from many nations. God used Abraham as a father of many spiritual descendants who, like him, entered into a relationship with God by faith. This cross-national, interracial people group was what God was working to establish through Abraham.

God's promise to make Abraham the father of many nations involved two major campaigns into the hostile territory of the rebellious Gentile nations, drawing worshipers who would place their faith in God. The first campaign to reach the nations occurred as God called Israel to be his witness to the Gentiles (Isa 42:5 – 7). While limited in success, many representatives from other nations were reached during this time; Israel's witness to the Gentiles included unique missionaries like Jonah and memorable converts such as Rahab and Ruth.

God's second campaign to bring his promise to completion involves his new cross-national, interracial people — the church. From its very onset, the church was intended to finish the work of reaching the nations (Ac 2:5 – 11). As the church expands, bringing the message of Abrahamic faith to the nations, God's promise to Abraham is slowly coming to fruition.

you a son by her. I will bless her, and she shall become nations; kings of peoples shall come from her." 17Then Abraham fell on his face and laughed and said to himself, "Shall a child be born to a man who is a hundred years old? Shall Sarah, who is ninety years old, bear a child?" 18And Abraham said to God, "Oh that Ishmael might live before you!" 19God said, "No, but Sarah your wife shall bear you a son, and you shall call his name Isaac.[1] I will establish my covenant with him as an everlasting covenant for his offspring after him. 20As for Ishmael, I have heard you; behold, I have blessed him and will make him fruitful and multiply him greatly. He shall father twelve princes, and I will make him into a great nation. 21But I will establish my covenant with Isaac, whom Sarah shall bear to you at this time next year."

22When he had finished talking with him, God went up from Abraham. 23Then Abraham took Ishmael his son and all those born in his house or bought with his money, every male among the men of Abraham's house, and he circumcised the flesh of their foreskins that very day, as God had said to him. 24Abraham was ninety-nine years old when he was circumcised in the flesh of his foreskin. 25And Ishmael his son was thirteen years old when he was circumcised in the flesh of his foreskin. 26That very day Abraham and his son Ishmael were circumcised. 27And all the men of his house, those born in the house and those bought with money from a foreigner, were circumcised with him.

18 And the LORD appeared to him by the oaks[2] of Mamre, as he sat at the door of his tent in the heat of the day. 2He lifted up his eyes and looked, and behold, three men were standing in front of him. When he saw them, he ran from the tent door to meet them and bowed himself to the earth 3and said, "O Lord,[3] if I have found favor in your sight, do not pass by your servant. 4Let a little water be brought, and wash your feet, and rest yourselves under the tree, 5while I bring a morsel of bread, that you may refresh yourselves, and after that you may pass on—since you have come to your servant." So they said, "Do as you have said." 6And Abraham went quickly into the tent to Sarah and said, "Quick! Three seahs[4] of fine flour! Knead it, and make cakes." 7And Abraham ran to the herd and took a calf, tender and good, and gave it to a young man, who prepared it quickly. 8Then he took curds and milk and the calf that he had prepared, and set it before them. And he stood by them under the tree while they ate.

9They said to him, "Where is Sarah your wife?" And he said, "She is in the tent." 10The LORD said, "I will surely return to you about this time next year, and Sarah your wife shall have a son." And Sarah was listening at the tent door behind him. 11Now Abraham and Sarah were old, advanced in years. The way of women had ceased to be with Sarah. 12So Sarah laughed to herself, saying, "After I am worn out, and my lord is old, shall I have pleasure?" 13The LORD said to Abraham, "Why did Sarah laugh and say, 'Shall I indeed bear a child, now that I am old?' 14Is anything too hard[5] for the LORD? At the appointed time I will return to you, about this time next year, and Sarah shall have a son." 15But Sarah denied it,[6] saying, "I did not laugh," for she was afraid. He said, "No, but you did laugh."

16Then the men set out from there, and they looked down toward Sodom. And Abraham went with them to set them on their way. 17The LORD said, "Shall I hide from Abraham what I am about to do, 18seeing that Abraham shall surely become a great and mighty nation, and all the nations of the earth shall be blessed in him? 19For I have chosen[7] him, that he may command his children and his household after him to keep the way of the LORD by doing righteousness and justice, so that the LORD may bring to Abraham what he has promised him." 20Then the LORD said, "Because the outcry against Sodom and Gomorrah is great and their sin is very grave, 21I will go down to see whether they have done altogether[8] according to the outcry that has come to me. And if not, I will know."

[1] *Isaac* means *he laughs* [2] Or *terebinths* [3] Or *My lord* [4] A *seah* was about 7.7 quarts or 7.3 liters [5] Or *wonderful* [6] Or *acted falsely* [7] Hebrew *known* [8] Or *they deserve destruction*; Hebrew *they have made a complete end*

GENESIS 18:1–2

A KNOWABLE GOD

God's tender affection for his people is shown by his willingness to reveal himself, often through his spoken word, to his people. It is clear that the people of God were stunned that God would even speak to them. They often stood at a distance, in fear and awe, at the revelation of God to his people (Ex 20:21). These appearances in the Old Testament find perfect fulfillment in the incarnation of Jesus Christ. In his birth, Jesus willingly laid aside the glories of heaven to take the form of a servant in order to make a way for sinful people to come to the Father (Php 2:1–11). In his deity, Jesus demonstrated and declared to the world the nature and character of God in a way that allowed humanity to see not only a temporary glimpse of his glory but also the exact imprint of God's glory in a permanent, ongoing fashion (Heb 1:3). Jesus made himself known so that fallen men and women can know God.

Abraham Intercedes for Sodom

22So the men turned from there and went toward Sodom, but Abraham still stood before the LORD. 23Then Abraham drew near and said, "Will you indeed sweep away the righteous with the wicked? 24Suppose there are fifty righteous within the city. Will you then sweep away the place and not spare it for the fifty righteous who are in it? 25Far be it from you to do such a thing, to put the righteous to death with the wicked, so that the righteous fare as the wicked! Far be that from you! Shall not the Judge of all the earth do what is just?" 26And the LORD said, "If I find at Sodom fifty righteous in the city, I will spare the whole place for their sake."

27Abraham answered and said, "Behold, I have undertaken to speak to the Lord, I who am but dust and ashes. 28Suppose five of the fifty righteous are lacking. Will you destroy the whole city for lack of five?" And he said, "I will not destroy it if I find forty-five there." 29Again he spoke to him and said, "Suppose forty are found there." He answered, "For the sake of forty I will not do it." 30Then he said, "Oh let not the Lord be angry, and I will speak. Suppose thirty are found there." He answered, "I will not do it, if I find thirty there." 31He said, "Behold, I have undertaken to speak to the Lord. Suppose twenty are found there." He answered, "For the sake of twenty I will not destroy it." 32Then he said, "Oh let not the Lord be angry, and I will speak again but this once. Suppose ten are found there." He answered, "For the sake of ten I will not destroy it." 33And the LORD went his way, when he had finished speaking to Abraham, and Abraham returned to his place.

God Rescues Lot

19 The two angels came to Sodom in the evening, and Lot was sitting in the gate of Sodom. When Lot saw them, he rose to meet them and bowed himself with his face to the earth 2and said, "My lords, please turn aside to your servant's house and spend the night and wash your feet. Then you may rise up early and go on your way." They said, "No; we will spend the night in the town square." 3But he pressed them strongly; so they turned aside to him and entered his house. And he made them a feast and baked unleavened bread, and they ate.

4But before they lay down, the men of the city, the men of Sodom, both young and old, all the people to the last man, surrounded the house. 5And they called to Lot, "Where are the men who came to you tonight? Bring them out to us, that we may know them." 6Lot went out to the men at the entrance, shut the door after him, 7and said, "I beg you, my brothers, do not act so wickedly. 8Behold, I have two daughters who have not known any man. Let me bring them out to you, and do to them as you please. Only do nothing to these men, for they have come under the shelter of my roof." 9But they said, "Stand back!" And they said, "This fellow came to sojourn, and he has become the judge! Now we will deal worse with you than with them." Then they pressed hard against the man Lot, and drew near to break the door down. 10But the men reached out their hands and brought Lot into the house with them and shut the door. 11And they struck with blindness the men who were at the entrance of the house, both small and great, so that they wore themselves out groping for the door.

12Then the men said to Lot, "Have you anyone else here? Sons-in-law, sons, daughters, or anyone you have in the city, bring them out of the place. 13For we are about to destroy this place, because the outcry against its people has become great before the LORD, and the LORD has sent us to destroy it." 14So Lot went out and said to his sons-in-law, who were to marry his daughters, "Up! Get out of this place, for the LORD is about to destroy the city." But he seemed to his sons-in-law to be jesting.

15As morning dawned, the angels urged Lot, saying, "Up! Take your wife and your two daughters who are here, lest you be swept away in the punishment of the city." 16But he lingered. So the men seized him and his wife and his two daughters

by the hand, the LORD being merciful to him, and they brought him out and set
him outside the city. 17And as they brought them out, one said, "Escape for your
life. Do not look back or stop anywhere in the valley. Escape to the hills, lest you be
swept away." 18And Lot said to them, "Oh, no, my lords. 19Behold, your servant has
found favor in your sight, and you have shown me great kindness in saving my life.
But I cannot escape to the hills, lest the disaster overtake me and I die. 20Behold,
this city is near enough to flee to, and it is a little one. Let me escape there—is
it not a little one?—and my life will be saved!" 21He said to him, "Behold, I grant
you this favor also, that I will not overthrow the city of which you have spoken.
22Escape there quickly, for I can do nothing till you arrive there." Therefore the
name of the city was called Zoar.[1]

God Destroys Sodom

23The sun had risen on the earth when Lot came to Zoar. 24Then the LORD
rained on Sodom and Gomorrah sulfur and fire from the LORD out of heaven.
25And he overthrew those cities, and all the valley, and all the inhabitants of the
cities, and what grew on the ground. 26But Lot's wife, behind him, looked back,
and she became a pillar of salt.

27And Abraham went early in the morning to the place where he had stood
before the LORD. 28And he looked down toward Sodom and Gomorrah and toward
all the land of the valley, and he looked and, behold, the smoke of the land went
up like the smoke of a furnace.

29So it was that, when God destroyed the cities of the valley, God remembered
Abraham and sent Lot out of the midst of the overthrow when he overthrew the
cities in which Lot had lived.

Lot and His Daughters

30Now Lot went up out of Zoar and lived in the hills with his two daughters, for
he was afraid to live in Zoar. So he lived in a cave with his two daughters. 31And the
firstborn said to the younger, "Our father is old, and there is not a man on earth
to come in to us after the manner of all the earth. 32Come, let us make our father
drink wine, and we will lie with him, that we may preserve offspring from our
father." 33So they made their father drink wine that night. And the firstborn went
in and lay with her father. He did not know when she lay down or when she arose.

34The next day, the firstborn said to the younger, "Behold, I lay last night with
my father. Let us make him drink wine tonight also. Then you go in and lie with
him, that we may preserve offspring from our father." 35So they made their father
drink wine that night also. And the younger arose and lay with him, and he did
not know when she lay down or when she arose. 36Thus both the daughters of Lot
became pregnant by their father. 37The firstborn bore a son and called his name
Moab.[2] He is the father of the Moabites to this day. 38The younger also bore a son
and called his name Ben-ammi.[3] He is the father of the Ammonites to this day.

Abraham and Abimelech

20 From there Abraham journeyed toward the territory of the Negeb and lived
between Kadesh and Shur; and he sojourned in Gerar. 2And Abraham said
of Sarah his wife, "She is my sister." And Abimelech king of Gerar sent and took
Sarah. 3But God came to Abimelech in a dream by night and said to him, "Behold,
you are a dead man because of the woman whom you have taken, for she is a man's
wife." 4Now Abimelech had not approached her. So he said, "Lord, will you kill an
innocent people? 5Did he not himself say to me, 'She is my sister'? And she herself
said, 'He is my brother.' In the integrity of my heart and the innocence of my hands
I have done this." 6Then God said to him in the dream, "Yes, I know that you have
done this in the integrity of your heart, and it was I who kept you from sinning
against me. Therefore I did not let you touch her. 7Now then, return the man's wife,

GENESIS 19:24

SODOM AND GOMORRAH

Sodom and Gomorrah stand as testimony to the judgment of God. Though the inhabitants of these cities shared the common depravity that has reigned since Adam, their sin was uniquely and justly condemned by God and judged in a most memorable way. The very names Sodom and Gomorrah are known to this day to be marks of heinous sin and immorality. God's judgment was not the act of a vindictive or capricious deity; rather, it followed his gracious allowance of time and space to repent. Peter wrote that this episode should serve as a warning to all those who rebel against God and fail to repent of their sin (2Pe 2:6,9–10). He will surely and rightly judge those who live in disobedience. But he will do so after granting them space and time to repent, lest they suffer the same fate as Sodom and Gomorrah. Our God is a gracious judge, who will one day perfectly condemn sin.

[1]*Zoar* means *little* [2]*Moab* sounds like the Hebrew for *from father* [3]*Ben-ammi* means *son of my people*

for he is a prophet, so that he will pray for you, and you shall live. But if you do not return her, know that you shall surely die, you and all who are yours."

8So Abimelech rose early in the morning and called all his servants and told them all these things. And the men were very much afraid. 9Then Abimelech called Abraham and said to him, "What have you done to us? And how have I sinned against you, that you have brought on me and my kingdom a great sin? You have done to me things that ought not to be done." 10And Abimelech said to Abraham, "What did you see, that you did this thing?" 11Abraham said, "I did it because I thought, 'There is no fear of God at all in this place, and they will kill me because of my wife.' 12Besides, she is indeed my sister, the daughter of my father though not the daughter of my mother, and she became my wife. 13And when God caused me to wander from my father's house, I said to her, 'This is the kindness you must do me: at every place to which we come, say of me, "He is my brother."'"

14Then Abimelech took sheep and oxen, and male servants and female servants, and gave them to Abraham, and returned Sarah his wife to him. 15And Abimelech said, "Behold, my land is before you; dwell where it pleases you." 16To Sarah he said, "Behold, I have given your brother a thousand pieces of silver. It is a sign of your innocence in the eyes of all[1] who are with you, and before everyone you are vindicated." 17Then Abraham prayed to God, and God healed Abimelech, and also healed his wife and female slaves so that they bore children. 18For the LORD had closed all the wombs of the house of Abimelech because of Sarah, Abraham's wife.

The Birth of Isaac

21 The LORD visited Sarah as he had said, and the LORD did to Sarah as he had promised. 2And Sarah conceived and bore Abraham a son in his old age at the time of which God had spoken to him. 3Abraham called the name of his son who was born to him, whom Sarah bore him, Isaac.[2] 4And Abraham circumcised his son Isaac when he was eight days old, as God had commanded him. 5Abraham was a hundred years old when his son Isaac was born to him. 6And Sarah said, "God has made laughter for me; everyone who hears will laugh over me." 7And she said, "Who would have said to Abraham that Sarah would nurse children? Yet I have borne him a son in his old age."

God Protects Hagar and Ishmael

8And the child grew and was weaned. And Abraham made a great feast on the day that Isaac was weaned. 9But Sarah saw the son of Hagar the Egyptian, whom she had borne to Abraham, laughing.[3] 10So she said to Abraham, "Cast out this slave woman with her son, for the son of this slave woman shall not be heir with my son Isaac." 11And the thing was very displeasing to Abraham on account of his son. 12But God said to Abraham, "Be not displeased because of the boy and because of your slave woman. Whatever Sarah says to you, do as she tells you, for through Isaac shall your offspring be named. 13And I will make a nation of the son of the slave woman also, because he is your offspring." 14So Abraham rose early in the morning and took bread and a skin of water and gave it to Hagar, putting it on her shoulder, along with the child, and sent her away. And she departed and wandered in the wilderness of Beersheba.

15When the water in the skin was gone, she put the child under one of the bushes. 16Then she went and sat down opposite him a good way off, about the distance of a bowshot, for she said, "Let me not look on the death of the child." And as she sat opposite him, she lifted up her voice and wept. 17And God heard the voice of the boy, and the angel of God called to Hagar from heaven and said to her, "What troubles you, Hagar? Fear not, for God has heard the voice of the boy where he is. 18Up! Lift up the boy, and hold him fast with your hand, for I will

GENESIS 21:1–7

GOD IS FAITHFUL

Isaac's birth previews the coming of Jesus. Isaac was born because God is faithful and promised Abraham a son, just as he promised sinners a Savior. The birth of Isaac came as a demonstration of God's grace, just as it was demonstrated at the coming of Christ. Abraham and Sarah were quite elderly when Isaac was born—so far beyond the years of child bearing that Sarah laughed at God's plan (Ge 18:9–12)—yet God often does the humanly impossible to fulfill his purposes. Jesus, after all, was born of a virgin, conceived from the Holy Spirit (Mt 1:18). Though Abraham and Sarah devised what they thought to be a more practical plan to fulfill God's promise by using Hagar as a surrogate (Ge 16:1–4), it was ultimately God's faithfulness—not human effort—that brought forth Isaac. In a similar way, Jesus came to earth because God is faithful and fulfills all of his promises. After Isaac was born, Sarah laughed once again, but this time it was not out of unbelief and mockery but out of astonishment and joy (Ge 21:5–6). Today, believers should also be filled with joy and astonishment at the faithfulness of God to keep his promises.

[1]Hebrew *It is a covering of eyes for all* [2]*Isaac* means *he laughs* [3]Possibly *laughing in mockery*

make him into a great nation." 19Then God opened her eyes, and she saw a well of
water. And she went and filled the skin with water and gave the boy a drink. 20And
God was with the boy, and he grew up. He lived in the wilderness and became an
expert with the bow. 21He lived in the wilderness of Paran, and his mother took a
wife for him from the land of Egypt.

A Treaty with Abimelech

22At that time Abimelech and Phicol the commander of his army said to Abraham, "God is with you in all that you do. 23Now therefore swear to me here by God
that you will not deal falsely with me or with my descendants or with my posterity, but as I have dealt kindly with you, so you will deal with me and with the land
where you have sojourned." 24And Abraham said, "I will swear."

25When Abraham reproved Abimelech about a well of water that Abimelech's
servants had seized, 26Abimelech said, "I do not know who has done this thing;
you did not tell me, and I have not heard of it until today." 27So Abraham took
sheep and oxen and gave them to Abimelech, and the two men made a covenant.
28Abraham set seven ewe lambs of the flock apart. 29And Abimelech said to Abraham, "What is the meaning of these seven ewe lambs that you have set apart?"
30He said, "These seven ewe lambs you will take from my hand, that this[1] may
be a witness for me that I dug this well." 31Therefore that place was called Beersheba,[2] because there both of them swore an oath. 32So they made a covenant
at Beersheba. Then Abimelech and Phicol the commander of his army rose up
and returned to the land of the Philistines. 33Abraham planted a tamarisk tree in
Beersheba and called there on the name of the LORD, the Everlasting God. 34And
Abraham sojourned many days in the land of the Philistines.

The Sacrifice of Isaac

22 After these things God tested Abraham and said to him, "Abraham!" And
he said, "Here I am." 2He said, "Take your son, your only son Isaac, whom
you love, and go to the land of Moriah, and offer him there as a burnt offering
on one of the mountains of which I shall tell you." 3So Abraham rose early in the
morning, saddled his donkey, and took two of his young men with him, and his
son Isaac. And he cut the wood for the burnt offering and arose and went to the
place of which God had told him. 4On the third day Abraham lifted up his eyes
and saw the place from afar. 5Then Abraham said to his young men, "Stay here
with the donkey; I and the boy[3] will go over there and worship and come again to
you." 6And Abraham took the wood of the burnt offering and laid it on Isaac his
son. And he took in his hand the fire and the knife. So they went both of them
together. 7And Isaac said to his father Abraham, "My father!" And he said, "Here I
am, my son." He said, "Behold, the fire and the wood, but where is the lamb for a
burnt offering?" 8Abraham said, "God will provide for himself the lamb for a burnt
offering, my son." So they went both of them together.

9When they came to the place of which God had told him, Abraham built the
altar there and laid the wood in order and bound Isaac his son and laid him on
the altar, on top of the wood. 10Then Abraham reached out his hand and took the
knife to slaughter his son. 11But the angel of the LORD called to him from heaven
and said, "Abraham, Abraham!" And he said, "Here I am." 12He said, "Do not lay
your hand on the boy or do anything to him, for now I know that you fear God,
seeing you have not withheld your son, your only son, from me." 13And Abraham
lifted up his eyes and looked, and behold, behind him was a ram, caught in a
thicket by his horns. And Abraham went and took the ram and offered it up as
a burnt offering instead of his son. 14So Abraham called the name of that place,
"The LORD will provide";[4] as it is said to this day, "On the mount of the LORD it
shall be provided."[5]

[1]Or *you* [2]*Beersheba* means *well of seven* or *well of the oath* [3]Or *young man*; also verse 12 [4]Or *will see*
[5]Or *he will be seen*

GENESIS 22:5

CONFIDENCE IN GOD

Abraham's confidence in light of his impending task testifies to a deeper confidence — his profound confidence in God. Not only had God asked him to do this startling task, but Abraham was also certain that God would provide a means of deliverance. He told his servants to wait while he and Isaac, his son, went to worship God on the mountain. Knowing that God commanded him to sacrifice his son, Abraham told the servants that he and the boy would come back soon. "I and the boy will go over there and worship and come again to you," he said. He knew that God had promised to create a great nation through Isaac (Ge 12:1 – 3; 13:14 – 16; 15:1 – 21; 17:1 – 22; 18:1 – 15). For this reason, Abraham knew that God would either deliver Isaac from death or resurrect him following his death (Heb 11:19). Either way, God would keep his word. Jesus also trusted God in the face of impending death. The ultimate Son of the promise, Jesus asked that God take away the cup of his suffering (Lk 22:42). Yet Jesus knew that God would be faithful — either by providing deliverance from death or through his subsequent, victorious resurrection. Unlike Isaac, Jesus would willingly and confidently walk not only to the brink of death but also through death itself and once again demonstrate the faithfulness of God to his promises.

GENESIS 22:17–18

BLESSED TO BLESS

God promised Abraham that he and his descendants would be a blessing to all people (see also Ge 12:2–3). The obedience of God's people would lead to this blessing of the nations. This promise demonstrated the vast mission of the nation of Israel. They were a chosen nation, not merely for their own blessing, but so that through them God would declare and demonstrate his glory to every other nation as well. God affirmed this promise once again to Abraham and declared the means by which the blessing would happen—the obedience of God's people. Likewise, in God's church, Jew and Gentile alike are called by God to be a blessing to the nations. As God's chosen people, a new and holy nation purchased by Christ's blood, the church serves as a light to the nations by obeying God (1Pe 2:9–10).

GENESIS 24:1–53

FINDING A BRIDE

Abraham's servant was commissioned to undertake a difficult journey to find a bride for Isaac. After a journey of about three weeks, this man arrived with impressive gifts but an unlikely task—find a woman in a distant land, who is of a particular family, and who will respond in faith to leave her land and become Isaac's wife. Despite the seeming impossibility of the mission, the servant cried out to God for help, and God orchestrated the events to ensure that Isaac received a wife and the promise of a descendant who would bring universal blessing to mankind.

(continued on page 42)

[15]And the angel of the LORD called to Abraham a second time from heaven
[16]and said, "By myself I have sworn, declares the LORD, because you have done
this and have not withheld your son, your only son, [17]I will surely bless you, and
I will surely multiply your offspring as the stars of heaven and as the sand that is
on the seashore. And your offspring shall possess the gate of his[1] enemies, [18]and
in your offspring shall all the nations of the earth be blessed, because you have
obeyed my voice." [19]So Abraham returned to his young men, and they arose and
went together to Beersheba. And Abraham lived at Beersheba.

[20]Now after these things it was told to Abraham, "Behold, Milcah also has
borne children to your brother Nahor: [21]Uz his firstborn, Buz his brother, Kemuel
the father of Aram, [22]Chesed, Hazo, Pildash, Jidlaph, and Bethuel." [23](Bethuel fathered
Rebekah.) These eight Milcah bore to Nahor, Abraham's brother. [24]Moreover,
his concubine, whose name was Reumah, bore Tebah, Gaham, Tahash, and
Maacah.

Sarah's Death and Burial

23 Sarah lived 127 years; these were the years of the life of Sarah. [2]And Sarah
died at Kiriath-arba (that is, Hebron) in the land of Canaan, and Abraham
went in to mourn for Sarah and to weep for her. [3]And Abraham rose up from
before his dead and said to the Hittites,[2] [4]"I am a sojourner and foreigner among
you; give me property among you for a burying place, that I may bury my dead
out of my sight." [5]The Hittites answered Abraham, [6]"Hear us, my lord; you are a
prince of God[3] among us. Bury your dead in the choicest of our tombs. None of us
will withhold from you his tomb to hinder you from burying your dead." [7]Abraham
rose and bowed to the Hittites, the people of the land. [8]And he said to them,
"If you are willing that I should bury my dead out of my sight, hear me and entreat
for me Ephron the son of Zohar, [9]that he may give me the cave of Machpelah,
which he owns; it is at the end of his field. For the full price let him give it to me
in your presence as property for a burying place."

[10]Now Ephron was sitting among the Hittites, and Ephron the Hittite answered
Abraham in the hearing of the Hittites, of all who went in at the gate of
his city, [11]"No, my lord, hear me: I give you the field, and I give you the cave that is
in it. In the sight of the sons of my people I give it to you. Bury your dead." [12]Then
Abraham bowed down before the people of the land. [13]And he said to Ephron in
the hearing of the people of the land, "But if you will, hear me: I give the price of
the field. Accept it from me, that I may bury my dead there." [14]Ephron answered
Abraham, [15]"My lord, listen to me: a piece of land worth four hundred shekels[4] of
silver, what is that between you and me? Bury your dead." [16]Abraham listened to
Ephron, and Abraham weighed out for Ephron the silver that he had named in the
hearing of the Hittites, four hundred shekels of silver, according to the weights
current among the merchants.

[17]So the field of Ephron in Machpelah, which was to the east of Mamre, the
field with the cave that was in it and all the trees that were in the field, throughout
its whole area, was made over [18]to Abraham as a possession in the presence
of the Hittites, before all who went in at the gate of his city. [19]After this, Abraham
buried Sarah his wife in the cave of the field of Machpelah east of Mamre (that
is, Hebron) in the land of Canaan. [20]The field and the cave that is in it were made
over to Abraham as property for a burying place by the Hittites.

Isaac and Rebekah

24 Now Abraham was old, well advanced in years. And the LORD had blessed
Abraham in all things. [2]And Abraham said to his servant, the oldest of his
household, who had charge of all that he had, "Put your hand under my thigh,
[3]that I may make you swear by the LORD, the God of heaven and God of the earth,

[1]Or *their* [2]Hebrew *sons of Heth*; also verses 5, 7, 10, 16, 18, 20 [3]Or *a mighty prince* [4]A *shekel* was about 2/5 ounce or 11 grams

GENESIS 22:1 – 18

THE SACRIFICIAL SON

Without question, this story of Abraham and Isaac is one of the most shocking and memorable narratives in all of Scripture. And yet in its outcome, it is one of the greatest stories describing the loyalty of God to his covenant and the foreshadowing of his plan to save the world. In Genesis 3:15, God made a promise to destroy evil and redeem humanity through the offspring of the woman.

In this story God puts Abraham's faithfulness to the test by asking him to do the unthinkable, to sacrifice his son Isaac as a burnt offering. Abraham had another son, Ishmael, but Isaac was the "only son" (Ge 22:2) in which all of God's promises resided because he was born of Sarah. Isaac represented the continuation of God's promise to bless all the nations of the earth through Abraham's descendants (Ge 12:1 – 3), and the ultimate promise to destroy evil in the world (Ge 3:15). Everything about Isaac's life was the result of God's supernatural plan and provision. Against all odds Sarah, Abraham's wife, became pregnant with Isaac, despite being 90 years old (Ge 17:17). And now, in spite of all that Isaac represented, God asked Abraham to surrender his beloved son.

The toll of this command on Abraham and Sarah must have been enormous. What a powerful picture of what God did to his only Son for us! Little is said of Abraham's thoughts, or the thoughts of the boy's mother. All we read is the account of the father's complete obedience to God's command (Ge 22:3). Abraham laid the wood for the offering on his son's back, and Isaac carried it to the altar. Isaac was confused. "Behold, the fire and the wood, but where is the lamb for a burnt offering?" Then Abraham offers a glimpse of his faith in God's provision by saying, "God will provide for *himself* the lamb" (Ge 22:7 – 8, emphasis added). Abraham understood, like the apostle Paul after him, that God must keep his promises in order to uphold his *own* righteousness. The sacrifice of Jesus not only fulfilled God's promise to destroy evil and save the world, but it also proved God's righteousness by providing a punishment for the sin of the whole world. Just as God provided Jesus *himself* to demonstrate *his* righteousness and take the punishment we deserved, so also he provided a ram *himself* to uphold his promise by keeping Isaac alive.

(Finding a Bride, continued)

In a similar sense, Jesus carried out a mission to bring his bride to himself. No distance or cost or improbability would keep him from getting his bride. He came from heaven to earth in order to rescue his church. He paid a price for his bride that exceeded the greatest kingly riches imaginable; his blood secured her as his own. Moreover, the sovereign hand of God orchestrated the events of the gospel and the plans of people's lives so that the improbable — rebels becoming worshipers of God — would become a reality.

that you will not take a wife for my son from the daughters of the Canaanites, among whom I dwell, 4but will go to my country and to my kindred, and take a wife for my son Isaac." 5The servant said to him, "Perhaps the woman may not be willing to follow me to this land. Must I then take your son back to the land from which you came?" 6Abraham said to him, "See to it that you do not take my son back there. 7The LORD, the God of heaven, who took me from my father's house and from the land of my kindred, and who spoke to me and swore to me, 'To your offspring I will give this land,' he will send his angel before you, and you shall take a wife for my son from there. 8But if the woman is not willing to follow you, then you will be free from this oath of mine; only you must not take my son back there." 9So the servant put his hand under the thigh of Abraham his master and swore to him concerning this matter.

10Then the servant took ten of his master's camels and departed, taking all sorts of choice gifts from his master; and he arose and went to Mesopotamia[1] to the city of Nahor. 11And he made the camels kneel down outside the city by the well of water at the time of evening, the time when women go out to draw water. 12And he said, "O LORD, God of my master Abraham, please grant me success today and show steadfast love to my master Abraham. 13Behold, I am standing by the spring of water, and the daughters of the men of the city are coming out to draw water. 14Let the young woman to whom I shall say, 'Please let down your jar that I may drink,' and who shall say, 'Drink, and I will water your camels'—let her be the one whom you have appointed for your servant Isaac. By this[2] I shall know that you have shown steadfast love to my master."

15Before he had finished speaking, behold, Rebekah, who was born to Bethuel the son of Milcah, the wife of Nahor, Abraham's brother, came out with her water jar on her shoulder. 16The young woman was very attractive in appearance, a maiden[3] whom no man had known. She went down to the spring and filled her jar and came up. 17Then the servant ran to meet her and said, "Please give me a little water to drink from your jar." 18She said, "Drink, my lord." And she quickly let down her jar upon her hand and gave him a drink. 19When she had finished giving him a drink, she said, "I will draw water for your camels also, until they have finished drinking." 20So she quickly emptied her jar into the trough and ran again to the well to draw water, and she drew for all his camels. 21The man gazed at her in silence to learn whether the LORD had prospered his journey or not.

22When the camels had finished drinking, the man took a gold ring weighing a half shekel,[4] and two bracelets for her arms weighing ten gold shekels, 23and said, "Please tell me whose daughter you are. Is there room in your father's house for us to spend the night?" 24She said to him, "I am the daughter of Bethuel the son of Milcah, whom she bore to Nahor." 25She added, "We have plenty of both straw and fodder, and room to spend the night." 26The man bowed his head and worshiped the LORD 27and said, "Blessed be the LORD, the God of my master Abraham, who has not forsaken his steadfast love and his faithfulness toward my master. As for me, the LORD has led me in the way to the house of my master's kinsmen." 28Then the young woman ran and told her mother's household about these things.

29Rebekah had a brother whose name was Laban. Laban ran out toward the man, to the spring. 30As soon as he saw the ring and the bracelets on his sister's arms, and heard the words of Rebekah his sister, "Thus the man spoke to me," he went to the man. And behold, he was standing by the camels at the spring. 31He said, "Come in, O blessed of the LORD. Why do you stand outside? For I have prepared the house and a place for the camels." 32So the man came to the house and unharnessed the camels, and gave straw and fodder to the camels, and there was water to wash his feet and the feet of the men who were with him. 33Then food was set before him to eat. But he said, "I will not eat until I have said what I have to say." He said, "Speak on."

[1]Hebrew *Aram-naharaim* [2]Or *By her* [3]Or *a woman of marriageable age* [4]A *shekel* was about 2/5 ounce or 11 grams

34So he said, "I am Abraham's servant. 35The LORD has greatly blessed my master, and he has become great. He has given him flocks and herds, silver and gold,
male servants and female servants, camels and donkeys. 36And Sarah my master's
wife bore a son to my master when she was old, and to him he has given all that
he has. 37My master made me swear, saying, 'You shall not take a wife for my son
from the daughters of the Canaanites, in whose land I dwell, 38but you shall go to
my father's house and to my clan and take a wife for my son.' 39I said to my master,
'Perhaps the woman will not follow me.' 40But he said to me, 'The LORD, before
whom I have walked, will send his angel with you and prosper your way. You shall
take a wife for my son from my clan and from my father's house. 41Then you will
be free from my oath, when you come to my clan. And if they will not give her to
you, you will be free from my oath.'

42"I came today to the spring and said, 'O LORD, the God of my master Abra-
ham, if now you are prospering the way that I go, 43behold, I am standing by the
spring of water. Let the virgin who comes out to draw water, to whom I shall say,
"Please give me a little water from your jar to drink," 44and who will say to me,
"Drink, and I will draw for your camels also," let her be the woman whom the
LORD has appointed for my master's son.'

45"Before I had finished speaking in my heart, behold, Rebekah came out
with her water jar on her shoulder, and she went down to the spring and drew
water. I said to her, 'Please let me drink.' 46She quickly let down her jar from her
shoulder and said, 'Drink, and I will give your camels drink also.' So I drank, and
she gave the camels drink also. 47Then I asked her, 'Whose daughter are you?'
She said, 'The daughter of Bethuel, Nahor's son, whom Milcah bore to him.' So I
put the ring on her nose and the bracelets on her arms. 48Then I bowed my head
and worshiped the LORD and blessed the LORD, the God of my master Abraham,
who had led me by the right way[1] to take the daughter of my master's kinsman
for his son. 49Now then, if you are going to show steadfast love and faithfulness
to my master, tell me; and if not, tell me, that I may turn to the right hand or
to the left."

50Then Laban and Bethuel answered and said, "The thing has come from the
LORD; we cannot speak to you bad or good. 51Behold, Rebekah is before you; take
her and go, and let her be the wife of your master's son, as the LORD has spoken."

52When Abraham's servant heard their words, he bowed himself to the earth
before the LORD. 53And the servant brought out jewelry of silver and of gold,
and garments, and gave them to Rebekah. He also gave to her brother and to her
mother costly ornaments. 54And he and the men who were with him ate and
drank, and they spent the night there. When they arose in the morning, he said,
"Send me away to my master." 55Her brother and her mother said, "Let the young
woman remain with us a while, at least ten days; after that she may go." 56But he
said to them, "Do not delay me, since the LORD has prospered my way. Send me
away that I may go to my master." 57They said, "Let us call the young woman and
ask her." 58And they called Rebekah and said to her, "Will you go with this man?"
She said, "I will go." 59So they sent away Rebekah their sister and her nurse, and
Abraham's servant and his men. 60And they blessed Rebekah and said to her,

"Our sister, may you become
    thousands of ten thousands,
and may your offspring possess
    the gate of those who hate him!"[2]

61Then Rebekah and her young women arose and rode on the camels and followed the man. Thus the servant took Rebekah and went his way.

62Now Isaac had returned from Beer-lahai-roi and was dwelling in the Negeb.
63And Isaac went out to meditate in the field toward evening. And he lifted up his

[1] Or *faithfully* [2] Or *hate them*

eyes and saw, and behold, there were camels coming. [64]And Rebekah lifted up her eyes, and when she saw Isaac, she dismounted from the camel [65]and said to the servant, "Who is that man, walking in the field to meet us?" The servant said, "It is my master." So she took her veil and covered herself. [66]And the servant told Isaac all the things that he had done. [67]Then Isaac brought her into the tent of Sarah his mother and took Rebekah, and she became his wife, and he loved her. So Isaac was comforted after his mother's death.

Abraham's Death and His Descendants

25 Abraham took another wife, whose name was Keturah. [2]She bore him Zimran, Jokshan, Medan, Midian, Ishbak, and Shuah. [3]Jokshan fathered Sheba and Dedan. The sons of Dedan were Asshurim, Letushim, and Leummim. [4]The sons of Midian were Ephah, Epher, Hanoch, Abida, and Eldaah. All these were the children of Keturah. [5]Abraham gave all he had to Isaac. [6]But to the sons of his concubines Abraham gave gifts, and while he was still living he sent them away from his son Isaac, eastward to the east country.

[7]These are the days of the years of Abraham's life, 175 years. [8]Abraham breathed his last and died in a good old age, an old man and full of years, and was gathered to his people. [9]Isaac and Ishmael his sons buried him in the cave of Machpelah, in the field of Ephron the son of Zohar the Hittite, east of Mamre, [10]the field that Abraham purchased from the Hittites. There Abraham was buried, with Sarah his wife. [11]After the death of Abraham, God blessed Isaac his son. And Isaac settled at Beer-lahai-roi.

[12]These are the generations of Ishmael, Abraham's son, whom Hagar the Egyptian, Sarah's servant, bore to Abraham. [13]These are the names of the sons of Ishmael, named in the order of their birth: Nebaioth, the firstborn of Ishmael; and Kedar, Adbeel, Mibsam, [14]Mishma, Dumah, Massa, [15]Hadad, Tema, Jetur, Naphish, and Kedemah. [16]These are the sons of Ishmael and these are their names, by their villages and by their encampments, twelve princes according to their tribes. [17](These are the years of the life of Ishmael: 137 years. He breathed his last and died, and was gathered to his people.) [18]They settled from Havilah to Shur, which is opposite Egypt in the direction of Assyria. He settled[1] over against all his kinsmen.

The Birth of Esau and Jacob

[19]These are the generations of Isaac, Abraham's son: Abraham fathered Isaac, [20]and Isaac was forty years old when he took Rebekah, the daughter of Bethuel the Aramean of Paddan-aram, the sister of Laban the Aramean, to be his wife. [21]And Isaac prayed to the LORD for his wife, because she was barren. And the LORD granted his prayer, and Rebekah his wife conceived. [22]The children struggled together within her, and she said, "If it is thus, why is this happening to me?"[2] So she went to inquire of the LORD. [23]And the LORD said to her,

"Two nations are in your womb,
    and two peoples from within you[3] shall be divided;
the one shall be stronger than the other,
    the older shall serve the younger."

[24]When her days to give birth were completed, behold, there were twins in her womb. [25]The first came out red, all his body like a hairy cloak, so they called his name Esau. [26]Afterward his brother came out with his hand holding Esau's heel, so his name was called Jacob.[4] Isaac was sixty years old when she bore them.

[27]When the boys grew up, Esau was a skillful hunter, a man of the field, while Jacob was a quiet man, dwelling in tents. [28]Isaac loved Esau because he ate of his game, but Rebekah loved Jacob.

[1]Hebrew *fell* [2]Or *why do I live?* [3]Or *from birth* [4]*Jacob* means *He takes by the heel*, or *He cheats*

GENESIS 25:23

FINGERPRINTS OF GRACE

What a scandalous claim! In the original readers' culture, the claim that an older brother would serve a younger brother was outrageous and disgraceful. But in God's dealings with people, this sort of role reversal is just the opposite; it is a work of grace (Ro 9:10 – 13). Grace turns the natural order of things on its head. Time and again throughout the book of Genesis, the headlines to these narratives seemed shocking to their original audience. Perhaps in the mind of the modern reader this wonder is lost, but the implications for Christians are gigantic. God seeks to restore worshipers to himself by graciously pouring out his favor upon them. Consider the following headlines in light of God's scandalous grace:

God gave animal skins to Adam and Eve instead of retribution (Ge 3:21). Adam and Eve deserved death for their rebellion (2:17), but God gave them grace instead.

Abel gained favor with God over Cain (Ge 4:4 – 5). In another example of the younger sibling receiving the grace of God, Abel was granted God's favor because he brought a simple sacrifice out of faith (Heb 11:4), while Cain only revealed his sinful heart in the encounter (Ge 4:5 – 7).

God spared a flawed man and his family by means of an ark. It would be easy to skim over or avoid Genesis 9:20 – 27 due to its awkward and uncomfortable content. It serves as a contradistinction to the man whom the writer first introduced as having "found favor in the eyes of the LORD" (Ge 6:8). The fact remains that Noah's favor with God was not because he was or would always be a perfect man.

Abraham received a unilateral covenant from God. The ramifications of God's pledge to Abram in Genesis 15 are vast. From this fountainhead, the rest of the Scriptures pour out. But the history of this blessed man was far from pristine. Joshua wrote that Abram's father worshiped other gods (Jos 24:2), and Abram lied to protect himself (Ge 12:10 – 20; 20:2). God's grace turns Abram into the father of many nations and a source of everlasting blessing to the whole world.

Every narrative of the book of Genesis is covered in the fingerprints of grace. All of these upheavals and role reversals are the handiwork of a gracious God who pours out his favor in order to bring maximum glory to himself.

Esau Sells His Birthright

29 Once when Jacob was cooking stew, Esau came in from the field, and he was exhausted. 30 And Esau said to Jacob, "Let me eat some of that red stew, for I am exhausted!" (Therefore his name was called Edom.[1]) 31 Jacob said, "Sell me your birthright now." 32 Esau said, "I am about to die; of what use is a birthright to me?" 33 Jacob said, "Swear to me now." So he swore to him and sold his birthright to Jacob. 34 Then Jacob gave Esau bread and lentil stew, and he ate and drank and rose and went his way. Thus Esau despised his birthright.

God's Promise to Isaac

26 Now there was a famine in the land, besides the former famine that was in the days of Abraham. And Isaac went to Gerar to Abimelech king of the Philistines. 2 And the LORD appeared to him and said, "Do not go down to Egypt; dwell in the land of which I shall tell you. 3 Sojourn in this land, and I will be with you and will bless you, for to you and to your offspring I will give all these lands, and I will establish the oath that I swore to Abraham your father. 4 I will multiply your offspring as the stars of heaven and will give to your offspring all these lands. And in your offspring all the nations of the earth shall be blessed, 5 because Abraham obeyed my voice and kept my charge, my commandments, my statutes, and my laws."

GENESIS 26:2–5

HEIR OF THE PROMISE

God designed a world for his created image-bearers to multiply and fill. His covenant with Abraham established the ongoing validity of this goal, even in the face of human sin (Ge 12:1–3). In this passage, God reiterates his promise to Isaac and pledges to be faithful to his promise by multiplying Isaac's descendants, giving them a great land and blessing all the earth through his family. Peter demonstrates that these promises find their fulfillment in the birth of the New Testament church and the sending of God's Spirit (Ac 3:25). In the church, all those who bear Jesus' name, both Jews and Gentiles alike, can be grafted into one heavenly family (Gal 3:8). As Abraham's offspring, the church is now the heir of the promises of God and entrusted with the mission of filling the earth with image-bearing worshipers who are a blessing to the nations.

Isaac and Abimelech

6 So Isaac settled in Gerar. 7 When the men of the place asked him about his wife, he said, "She is my sister," for he feared to say, "My wife," thinking, "lest the men of the place should kill me because of Rebekah," because she was attractive in appearance. 8 When he had been there a long time, Abimelech king of the Philistines looked out of a window and saw Isaac laughing with[2] Rebekah his wife. 9 So Abimelech called Isaac and said, "Behold, she is your wife. How then could you say, 'She is my sister'?" Isaac said to him, "Because I thought, 'Lest I die because of her.'" 10 Abimelech said, "What is this you have done to us? One of the people might easily have lain with your wife, and you would have brought guilt upon us." 11 So Abimelech warned all the people, saying, "Whoever touches this man or his wife shall surely be put to death."

12 And Isaac sowed in that land and reaped in the same year a hundredfold. The LORD blessed him, 13 and the man became rich, and gained more and more until he became very wealthy. 14 He had possessions of flocks and herds and many servants, so that the Philistines envied him. 15 (Now the Philistines had stopped and filled with earth all the wells that his father's servants had dug in the days of Abraham his father.) 16 And Abimelech said to Isaac, "Go away from us, for you are much mightier than we."

17 So Isaac departed from there and encamped in the Valley of Gerar and settled there. 18 And Isaac dug again the wells of water that had been dug in the days of Abraham his father, which the Philistines had stopped after the death of Abraham. And he gave them the names that his father had given them. 19 But when Isaac's servants dug in the valley and found there a well of spring water, 20 the herdsmen of Gerar quarreled with Isaac's herdsmen, saying, "The water is ours." So he called the name of the well Esek,[3] because they contended with him. 21 Then they dug another well, and they quarreled over that also, so he called its name Sitnah.[4] 22 And he moved from there and dug another well, and they did not quarrel over it. So he called its name Rehoboth,[5] saying, "For now the LORD has made room for us, and we shall be fruitful in the land."

23 From there he went up to Beersheba. 24 And the LORD appeared to him the same night and said, "I am the God of Abraham your father. Fear not, for I am

[1] *Edom* sounds like the Hebrew for *red* [2] Hebrew may suggest an intimate relationship [3] *Esek* means *contention* [4] *Sitnah* means *enmity* [5] *Rehoboth* means *broad places*, or *room*

with you and will bless you and multiply your offspring for my servant Abraham's sake." 25So he built an altar there and called upon the name of the LORD and pitched his tent there. And there Isaac's servants dug a well.

26When Abimelech went to him from Gerar with Ahuzzath his adviser and Phicol the commander of his army, 27Isaac said to them, "Why have you come to me, seeing that you hate me and have sent me away from you?" 28They said, "We see plainly that the LORD has been with you. So we said, let there be a sworn pact between us, between you and us, and let us make a covenant with you, 29that you will do us no harm, just as we have not touched you and have done to you nothing but good and have sent you away in peace. You are now the blessed of the LORD." 30So he made them a feast, and they ate and drank. 31In the morning they rose early and exchanged oaths. And Isaac sent them on their way, and they departed from him in peace. 32That same day Isaac's servants came and told him about the well that they had dug and said to him, "We have found water." 33He called it Shibah;[1] therefore the name of the city is Beersheba to this day.

34When Esau was forty years old, he took Judith the daughter of Beeri the Hittite to be his wife, and Basemath the daughter of Elon the Hittite, 35and they made life bitter[2] for Isaac and Rebekah.

Isaac Blesses Jacob

27 When Isaac was old and his eyes were dim so that he could not see, he called Esau his older son and said to him, "My son"; and he answered, "Here I am." 2He said, "Behold, I am old; I do not know the day of my death. 3Now then, take your weapons, your quiver and your bow, and go out to the field and hunt game for me, 4and prepare for me delicious food, such as I love, and bring it to me so that I may eat, that my soul may bless you before I die."

5Now Rebekah was listening when Isaac spoke to his son Esau. So when Esau went to the field to hunt for game and bring it, 6Rebekah said to her son Jacob, "I heard your father speak to your brother Esau, 7'Bring me game and prepare for me delicious food, that I may eat it and bless you before the LORD before I die.' 8Now therefore, my son, obey my voice as I command you. 9Go to the flock and bring me two good young goats, so that I may prepare from them delicious food for your father, such as he loves. 10And you shall bring it to your father to eat, so that he may bless you before he dies." 11But Jacob said to Rebekah his mother, "Behold, my brother Esau is a hairy man, and I am a smooth man. 12Perhaps my father will feel me, and I shall seem to be mocking him and bring a curse upon myself and not a blessing." 13His mother said to him, "Let your curse be on me, my son; only obey my voice, and go, bring them to me."

14So he went and took them and brought them to his mother, and his mother prepared delicious food, such as his father loved. 15Then Rebekah took the best garments of Esau her older son, which were with her in the house, and put them on Jacob her younger son. 16And the skins of the young goats she put on his hands and on the smooth part of his neck. 17And she put the delicious food and the bread, which she had prepared, into the hand of her son Jacob.

18So he went in to his father and said, "My father." And he said, "Here I am. Who are you, my son?" 19Jacob said to his father, "I am Esau your firstborn. I have done as you told me; now sit up and eat of my game, that your soul may bless me." 20But Isaac said to his son, "How is it that you have found it so quickly, my son?" He answered, "Because the LORD your God granted me success." 21Then Isaac said to Jacob, "Please come near, that I may feel you, my son, to know whether you are really my son Esau or not." 22So Jacob went near to Isaac his father, who felt him and said, "The voice is Jacob's voice, but the hands are the hands of Esau." 23And he did not recognize him, because his hands were hairy like his brother Esau's hands. So he blessed him. 24He said, "Are you really my son Esau?" He answered,

[1]*Shibah* sounds like the Hebrew for *oath* [2]Hebrew *they were bitterness of spirit*

"I am." 25 Then he said, "Bring it near to me, that I may eat of my son's game and
bless you." So he brought it near to him, and he ate; and he brought him wine,
and he drank.
26 Then his father Isaac said to him, "Come near and kiss me, my son." 27 So
he came near and kissed him. And Isaac smelled the smell of his garments and
blessed him and said,

"See, the smell of my son
is as the smell of a field that the LORD has blessed!
28 May God give you of the dew of heaven
and of the fatness of the earth
and plenty of grain and wine.
29 Let peoples serve you,
and nations bow down to you.
Be lord over your brothers,
and may your mother's sons bow down to you.
Cursed be everyone who curses you,
and blessed be everyone who blesses you!"

30 As soon as Isaac had finished blessing Jacob, when Jacob had scarcely gone
out from the presence of Isaac his father, Esau his brother came in from his
hunting. 31 He also prepared delicious food and brought it to his father. And he
said to his father, "Let my father arise and eat of his son's game, that you may
bless me." 32 His father Isaac said to him, "Who are you?" He answered, "I am
your son, your firstborn, Esau." 33 Then Isaac trembled very violently and said,
"Who was it then that hunted game and brought it to me, and I ate it all before
you came, and I have blessed him? Yes, and he shall be blessed." 34 As soon as
Esau heard the words of his father, he cried out with an exceedingly great and
bitter cry and said to his father, "Bless me, even me also, O my father!" 35 But
he said, "Your brother came deceitfully, and he has taken away your blessing."
36 Esau said, "Is he not rightly named Jacob?[1] For he has cheated me these two
times. He took away my birthright, and behold, now he has taken away my blessing." Then he said, "Have you not reserved a blessing for me?" 37 Isaac answered
and said to Esau, "Behold, I have made him lord over you, and all his brothers I
have given to him for servants, and with grain and wine I have sustained him.
What then can I do for you, my son?" 38 Esau said to his father, "Have you but
one blessing, my father? Bless me, even me also, O my father." And Esau lifted
up his voice and wept.
39 Then Isaac his father answered and said to him:

"Behold, away from[2] the fatness of the earth shall your dwelling be,
and away from[3] the dew of heaven on high.
40 By your sword you shall live,
and you shall serve your brother;
but when you grow restless
you shall break his yoke from your neck."

41 Now Esau hated Jacob because of the blessing with which his father had
blessed him, and Esau said to himself, "The days of mourning for my father are
approaching; then I will kill my brother Jacob." 42 But the words of Esau her older
son were told to Rebekah. So she sent and called Jacob her younger son and said
to him, "Behold, your brother Esau comforts himself about you by planning to kill
you. 43 Now therefore, my son, obey my voice. Arise, flee to Laban my brother in
Haran 44 and stay with him a while, until your brother's fury turns away— 45 until
your brother's anger turns away from you, and he forgets what you have done to
him. Then I will send and bring you from there. Why should I be bereft of you
both in one day?"

[1] *Jacob* means *He takes by the heel*, or *He cheats* [2] Or *Behold, of* [3] Or *and of*

46Then Rebekah said to Isaac, "I loathe my life because of the Hittite women.[1] If Jacob marries one of the Hittite women like these, one of the women of the land, what good will my life be to me?"

Jacob Sent to Laban

28 Then Isaac called Jacob and blessed him and directed him, "You must not take a wife from the Canaanite women. 2Arise, go to Paddan-aram to the house of Bethuel your mother's father, and take as your wife from there one of the daughters of Laban your mother's brother. 3God Almighty[2] bless you and make you fruitful and multiply you, that you may become a company of peoples. 4May he give the blessing of Abraham to you and to your offspring with you, that you may take possession of the land of your sojournings that God gave to Abraham!" 5Thus Isaac sent Jacob away. And he went to Paddan-aram, to Laban, the son of Bethuel the Aramean, the brother of Rebekah, Jacob's and Esau's mother.

Esau Marries an Ishmaelite

6Now Esau saw that Isaac had blessed Jacob and sent him away to Paddan-aram to take a wife from there, and that as he blessed him he directed him, "You must not take a wife from the Canaanite women," 7and that Jacob had obeyed his father and his mother and gone to Paddan-aram. 8So when Esau saw that the Canaanite women did not please Isaac his father, 9Esau went to Ishmael and took as his wife, besides the wives he had, Mahalath the daughter of Ishmael, Abraham's son, the sister of Nebaioth.

Jacob's Dream

10Jacob left Beersheba and went toward Haran. 11And he came to a certain place and stayed there that night, because the sun had set. Taking one of the stones of the place, he put it under his head and lay down in that place to sleep. 12And he dreamed, and behold, there was a ladder[3] set up on the earth, and the top of it reached to heaven. And behold, the angels of God were ascending and descending on it! 13And behold, the LORD stood above it[4] and said, "I am the LORD, the God of Abraham your father and the God of Isaac. The land on which you lie I will give to you and to your offspring. 14Your offspring shall be like the dust of the earth, and you shall spread abroad to the west and to the east and to the north and to the south, and in you and your offspring shall all the families of the earth be blessed. 15Behold, I am with you and will keep you wherever you go, and will bring you back to this land. For I will not leave you until I have done what I have promised you." 16Then Jacob awoke from his sleep and said, "Surely the LORD is in this place, and I did not know it." 17And he was afraid and said, "How awesome is this place! This is none other than the house of God, and this is the gate of heaven."

18So early in the morning Jacob took the stone that he had put under his head and set it up for a pillar and poured oil on the top of it. 19He called the name of that place Bethel,[5] but the name of the city was Luz at the first. 20Then Jacob made a vow, saying, "If God will be with me and will keep me in this way that I go, and will give me bread to eat and clothing to wear, 21so that I come again to my father's house in peace, then the LORD shall be my God, 22and this stone, which I have set up for a pillar, shall be God's house. And of all that you give me I will give a full tenth to you."

Jacob Marries Leah and Rachel

29 Then Jacob went on his journey and came to the land of the people of the east. 2As he looked, he saw a well in the field, and behold, three flocks of sheep lying beside it, for out of that well the flocks were watered. The stone on the well's mouth was large, 3and when all the flocks were gathered there, the

[1]Hebrew *daughters of Heth* [2]Hebrew *El Shaddai* [3]Or *a flight of steps* [4]Or *beside him* [5]*Bethel* means *the house of God*

GENESIS 28:10–22

A STAIRWAY FROM HEAVEN

Fleeing to Haran to escape his brother's wrath, Jacob stopped for the night. Jacob dreamed that a stairway stretched from heaven to earth, with angels ascending and descending the heavenly staircase. The picture portrayed the grand, cosmic reality of life on this earth. While it may seem that all that is real is that which can be seen, there is an eternal, heavenly world closely connected to this one. The heavenly realm is consistently interacting with this world in ways that lie beyond what the human mind can comprehend and the human eye can see.

Jesus' birth would bring this reality into greater focus. The fully divine and human Son of God would serve as the ladder between heaven and earth (Jn 1:51). At his baptism, the heavens were opened and the Spirit of God descended on the Son of God, indicating his divine status and God-ordained mission (Mt 3:13–17). In Jesus, heaven met earth, and with him came glimpses of the coming kingdom as the lame walked, the blind regained sight, and prisoners gained freedom (Lk 4:18). At the incarnation, the Son of God descended the heavenly staircase in order to usher sinful humanity into the kingdom of God.

shepherds would roll the stone from the mouth of the well and water the sheep, and put the stone back in its place over the mouth of the well.

4Jacob said to them, "My brothers, where do you come from?" They said, "We are from Haran." 5He said to them, "Do you know Laban the son of Nahor?" They said, "We know him." 6He said to them, "Is it well with him?" They said, "It is well; and see, Rachel his daughter is coming with the sheep!" 7He said, "Behold, it is still high day; it is not time for the livestock to be gathered together. Water the sheep and go, pasture them." 8But they said, "We cannot until all the flocks are gathered together and the stone is rolled from the mouth of the well; then we water the sheep."

9While he was still speaking with them, Rachel came with her father's sheep, for she was a shepherdess. 10Now as soon as Jacob saw Rachel the daughter of Laban his mother's brother, and the sheep of Laban his mother's brother, Jacob came near and rolled the stone from the well's mouth and watered the flock of Laban his mother's brother. 11Then Jacob kissed Rachel and wept aloud. 12And Jacob told Rachel that he was her father's kinsman, and that he was Rebekah's son, and she ran and told her father.

13As soon as Laban heard the news about Jacob, his sister's son, he ran to meet him and embraced him and kissed him and brought him to his house. Jacob told Laban all these things, 14and Laban said to him, "Surely you are my bone and my flesh!" And he stayed with him a month.

15Then Laban said to Jacob, "Because you are my kinsman, should you therefore serve me for nothing? Tell me, what shall your wages be?" 16Now Laban had two daughters. The name of the older was Leah, and the name of the younger was Rachel. 17Leah's eyes were weak,[1] but Rachel was beautiful in form and appearance. 18Jacob loved Rachel. And he said, "I will serve you seven years for your younger daughter Rachel." 19Laban said, "It is better that I give her to you than that I should give her to any other man; stay with me." 20So Jacob served seven years for Rachel, and they seemed to him but a few days because of the love he had for her.

21Then Jacob said to Laban, "Give me my wife that I may go in to her, for my time is completed." 22So Laban gathered together all the people of the place and made a feast. 23But in the evening he took his daughter Leah and brought her to Jacob, and he went in to her. 24(Laban gave[2] his female servant Zilpah to his daughter Leah to be her servant.) 25And in the morning, behold, it was Leah! And Jacob said to Laban, "What is this you have done to me? Did I not serve with you for Rachel? Why then have you deceived me?" 26Laban said, "It is not so done in our country, to give the younger before the firstborn. 27Complete the week of this one, and we will give you the other also in return for serving me another seven years." 28Jacob did so, and completed her week. Then Laban gave him his daughter Rachel to be his wife. 29(Laban gave his female servant Bilhah to his daughter Rachel to be her servant.) 30So Jacob went in to Rachel also, and he loved Rachel more than Leah, and served Laban for another seven years.

Jacob's Children

31When the LORD saw that Leah was hated, he opened her womb, but Rachel was barren. 32And Leah conceived and bore a son, and she called his name Reuben,[3] for she said, "Because the LORD has looked upon my affliction; for now my husband will love me." 33She conceived again and bore a son, and said, "Because the LORD has heard that I am hated, he has given me this son also." And she called his name Simeon.[4] 34Again she conceived and bore a son, and said, "Now this time my husband will be attached to me, because I have borne him three sons." Therefore his name was called Levi.[5] 35And she conceived again and bore a son,

---

[1]Or *soft* [2]Or *had given*; also verse 29 [3]*Reuben* means *See, a son* [4]*Simeon* sounds like the Hebrew for *heard* [5]*Levi* sounds like the Hebrew for *attached*

and said, "This time I will praise the LORD." Therefore she called his name Judah.[1] Then she ceased bearing.

30 When Rachel saw that she bore Jacob no children, she envied her sister. She said to Jacob, "Give me children, or I shall die!" 2Jacob's anger was kindled against Rachel, and he said, "Am I in the place of God, who has withheld from you the fruit of the womb?" 3Then she said, "Here is my servant Bilhah; go in to her, so that she may give birth on my behalf,[2] that even I may have children[3] through her." 4So she gave him her servant Bilhah as a wife, and Jacob went in to her. 5And Bilhah conceived and bore Jacob a son. 6Then Rachel said, "God has judged me, and has also heard my voice and given me a son." Therefore she called his name Dan.[4] 7Rachel's servant Bilhah conceived again and bore Jacob a second son. 8Then Rachel said, "With mighty wrestlings[5] I have wrestled with my sister and have prevailed." So she called his name Naphtali.[6]

9When Leah saw that she had ceased bearing children, she took her servant Zilpah and gave her to Jacob as a wife. 10Then Leah's servant Zilpah bore Jacob a son. 11And Leah said, "Good fortune has come!" so she called his name Gad.[7] 12Leah's servant Zilpah bore Jacob a second son. 13And Leah said, "Happy am I! For women have called me happy." So she called his name Asher.[8]

14In the days of wheat harvest Reuben went and found mandrakes in the field and brought them to his mother Leah. Then Rachel said to Leah, "Please give me some of your son's mandrakes." 15But she said to her, "Is it a small matter that you have taken away my husband? Would you take away my son's mandrakes also?" Rachel said, "Then he may lie with you tonight in exchange for your son's mandrakes." 16When Jacob came from the field in the evening, Leah went out to meet him and said, "You must come in to me, for I have hired you with my son's mandrakes." So he lay with her that night. 17And God listened to Leah, and she conceived and bore Jacob a fifth son. 18Leah said, "God has given me my wages because I gave my servant to my husband." So she called his name Issachar.[9]

19And Leah conceived again, and she bore Jacob a sixth son. 20Then Leah said, "God has endowed me with a good endowment; now my husband will honor me, because I have borne him six sons." So she called his name Zebulun.[10] 21Afterward she bore a daughter and called her name Dinah.

22Then God remembered Rachel, and God listened to her and opened her womb. 23She conceived and bore a son and said, "God has taken away my reproach." 24And she called his name Joseph,[11] saying, "May the LORD add to me another son!"

Jacob's Prosperity

25As soon as Rachel had borne Joseph, Jacob said to Laban, "Send me away, that I may go to my own home and country. 26Give me my wives and my children for whom I have served you, that I may go, for you know the service that I have given you." 27But Laban said to him, "If I have found favor in your sight, I have learned by divination that[12] the LORD has blessed me because of you. 28Name your wages, and I will give it." 29Jacob said to him, "You yourself know how I have served you, and how your livestock has fared with me. 30For you had little before I came, and it has increased abundantly, and the LORD has blessed you wherever I turned. But now when shall I provide for my own household also?" 31He said, "What shall I give you?" Jacob said, "You shall not give me anything. If you will do this for me, I will again pasture your flock and keep it: 32let me pass through all your flock today, removing from it every speckled and spotted sheep and every

[1] *Judah* sounds like the Hebrew for *praise* [2] Hebrew *on my knees* [3] Hebrew *be built up*, which sounds like the Hebrew for *children* [4] *Dan* sounds like the Hebrew for *judged* [5] Hebrew *With wrestlings of God* [6] *Naphtali* sounds like the Hebrew for *wrestling* [7] *Gad* sounds like the Hebrew for *good fortune* [8] *Asher* sounds like the Hebrew for *happy* [9] *Issachar* sounds like the Hebrew for *wages*, or *hire* [10] *Zebulun* sounds like the Hebrew for *honor* [11] *Joseph* means *May he add*, and sounds like the Hebrew for *taken away* [12] Or *have become rich and*

black lamb, and the spotted and speckled among the goats, and they shall be my wages. 33 So my honesty will answer for me later, when you come to look into my wages with you. Every one that is not speckled and spotted among the goats and black among the lambs, if found with me, shall be counted stolen." 34 Laban said, "Good! Let it be as you have said." 35 But that day Laban removed the male goats that were striped and spotted, and all the female goats that were speckled and spotted, every one that had white on it, and every lamb that was black, and put them in the charge of his sons. 36 And he set a distance of three days' journey between himself and Jacob, and Jacob pastured the rest of Laban's flock.

37 Then Jacob took fresh sticks of poplar and almond and plane trees, and peeled white streaks in them, exposing the white of the sticks. 38 He set the sticks that he had peeled in front of the flocks in the troughs, that is, the watering places, where the flocks came to drink. And since they bred when they came to drink, 39 the flocks bred in front of the sticks and so the flocks brought forth striped, speckled, and spotted. 40 And Jacob separated the lambs and set the faces of the flocks toward the striped and all the black in the flock of Laban. He put his own droves apart and did not put them with Laban's flock. 41 Whenever the stronger of the flock were breeding, Jacob would lay the sticks in the troughs before the eyes of the flock, that they might breed among the sticks, 42 but for the feebler of the flock he would not lay them there. So the feebler would be Laban's, and the stronger Jacob's. 43 Thus the man increased greatly and had large flocks, female servants and male servants, and camels and donkeys.

Jacob Flees from Laban

31 Now Jacob heard that the sons of Laban were saying, "Jacob has taken all that was our father's, and from what was our father's he has gained all this wealth." 2 And Jacob saw that Laban did not regard him with favor as before. 3 Then the LORD said to Jacob, "Return to the land of your fathers and to your kindred, and I will be with you."

4 So Jacob sent and called Rachel and Leah into the field where his flock was 5 and said to them, "I see that your father does not regard me with favor as he did before. But the God of my father has been with me. 6 You know that I have served your father with all my strength, 7 yet your father has cheated me and changed my wages ten times. But God did not permit him to harm me. 8 If he said, 'The spotted shall be your wages,' then all the flock bore spotted; and if he said, 'The striped shall be your wages,' then all the flock bore striped. 9 Thus God has taken away the livestock of your father and given them to me. 10 In the breeding season of the flock I lifted up my eyes and saw in a dream that the goats that mated with the flock were striped, spotted, and mottled. 11 Then the angel of God said to me in the dream, 'Jacob,' and I said, 'Here I am!' 12 And he said, 'Lift up your eyes and see, all the goats that mate with the flock are striped, spotted, and mottled, for I have seen all that Laban is doing to you. 13 I am the God of Bethel, where you anointed a pillar and made a vow to me. Now arise, go out from this land and return to the land of your kindred.'" 14 Then Rachel and Leah answered and said to him, "Is there any portion or inheritance left to us in our father's house? 15 Are we not regarded by him as foreigners? For he has sold us, and he has indeed devoured our money. 16 All the wealth that God has taken away from our father belongs to us and to our children. Now then, whatever God has said to you, do."

17 So Jacob arose and set his sons and his wives on camels. 18 He drove away all his livestock, all his property that he had gained, the livestock in his possession that he had acquired in Paddan-aram, to go to the land of Canaan to his father Isaac. 19 Laban had gone to shear his sheep, and Rachel stole her father's household gods. 20 And Jacob tricked[1] Laban the Aramean, by not telling him that he

[1] Hebrew *stole the heart of*; also verses 26, 27

intended to flee. [21]He fled with all that he had and arose and crossed the Euphrates,[1] and set his face toward the hill country of Gilead.

[22]When it was told Laban on the third day that Jacob had fled, [23]he took his kinsmen with him and pursued him for seven days and followed close after him into the hill country of Gilead. [24]But God came to Laban the Aramean in a dream by night and said to him, "Be careful not to say anything to Jacob, either good or bad."

[25]And Laban overtook Jacob. Now Jacob had pitched his tent in the hill country, and Laban with his kinsmen pitched tents in the hill country of Gilead. [26]And Laban said to Jacob, "What have you done, that you have tricked me and driven away my daughters like captives of the sword? [27]Why did you flee secretly and trick me, and did not tell me, so that I might have sent you away with mirth and songs, with tambourine and lyre? [28]And why did you not permit me to kiss my sons and my daughters farewell? Now you have done foolishly. [29]It is in my power to do you harm. But the God of your[2] father spoke to me last night, saying, 'Be careful not to say anything to Jacob, either good or bad.' [30]And now you have gone away because you longed greatly for your father's house, but why did you steal my gods?" [31]Jacob answered and said to Laban, "Because I was afraid, for I thought that you would take your daughters from me by force. [32]Anyone with whom you find your gods shall not live. In the presence of our kinsmen point out what I have that is yours, and take it." Now Jacob did not know that Rachel had stolen them.

[33]So Laban went into Jacob's tent and into Leah's tent and into the tent of the two female servants, but he did not find them. And he went out of Leah's tent and entered Rachel's. [34]Now Rachel had taken the household gods and put them in the camel's saddle and sat on them. Laban felt all about the tent, but did not find them. [35]And she said to her father, "Let not my lord be angry that I cannot rise before you, for the way of women is upon me." So he searched but did not find the household gods.

[36]Then Jacob became angry and berated Laban. Jacob said to Laban, "What is my offense? What is my sin, that you have hotly pursued me? [37]For you have felt through all my goods; what have you found of all your household goods? Set it here before my kinsmen and your kinsmen, that they may decide between us two. [38]These twenty years I have been with you. Your ewes and your female goats have not miscarried, and I have not eaten the rams of your flocks. [39]What was torn by wild beasts I did not bring to you. I bore the loss of it myself. From my hand you required it, whether stolen by day or stolen by night. [40]There I was: by day the heat consumed me, and the cold by night, and my sleep fled from my eyes. [41]These twenty years I have been in your house. I served you fourteen years for your two daughters, and six years for your flock, and you have changed my wages ten times. [42]If the God of my father, the God of Abraham and the Fear of Isaac, had not been on my side, surely now you would have sent me away empty-handed. God saw my affliction and the labor of my hands and rebuked you last night."

[43]Then Laban answered and said to Jacob, "The daughters are my daughters, the children are my children, the flocks are my flocks, and all that you see is mine. But what can I do this day for these my daughters or for their children whom they have borne? [44]Come now, let us make a covenant, you and I. And let it be a witness between you and me." [45]So Jacob took a stone and set it up as a pillar. [46]And Jacob said to his kinsmen, "Gather stones." And they took stones and made a heap, and they ate there by the heap. [47]Laban called it Jegar-sahadutha,[3] but Jacob called it Galeed.[4] [48]Laban said, "This heap is a witness between you and me today." Therefore he named it Galeed, [49]and Mizpah,[5] for he said, "The LORD watch between you and me, when we are out of one another's sight. [50]If you oppress my daughters, or if you take wives besides my daughters, although no one is with us, see, God is witness between you and me."

[1]Hebrew *the River* [2]The Hebrew for *your* is plural here [3]Aramaic *the heap of witness* [4]Hebrew *the heap of witness* [5]*Mizpah* means *watchpost*

GENESIS 31:22–24

RESTORING PEACE IN A BROKEN WORLD

God's rescue operation for humanity integrally involved the descendants of Jacob. God had promised to Jacob, as his father and grandfather before him, that his grand plan for restoring *shalom* back to the universe was via a massive blessing in and through his descendants (Ge 28:13–15). Hope for blessing rested in the safety and expansion of this fledgling family. And God would ensure that Jacob would move forward under divine protection and multiplication. In this passage, Jacob risked his life and the Messiah's line. His aggressive business relationship with Laban and ensuing flight from his father-in-law put him in a dangerous spot. God continued to demonstrate his faithfulness to Jacob, in spite of the seeming chaos. Ultimately, the potential risks that threatened to short-circuit God's plan in Jesus were also overcome in his sovereignty and power. This story of the protection and progress of God's plan for the redemptive Messiah plays out again and again in the pages of Scripture.

51 Then Laban said to Jacob, "See this heap and the pillar, which I have set between you and me. 52 This heap is a witness, and the pillar is a witness, that I will
not pass over this heap to you, and you will not pass over this heap and this pillar
to me, to do harm. 53 The God of Abraham and the God of Nahor, the God of their
father, judge between us." So Jacob swore by the Fear of his father Isaac, 54 and
Jacob offered a sacrifice in the hill country and called his kinsmen to eat bread.
They ate bread and spent the night in the hill country.

55 [1]Early in the morning Laban arose and kissed his grandchildren and his
daughters and blessed them. Then Laban departed and returned home.

Jacob Fears Esau

32 Jacob went on his way, and the angels of God met him. 2 And when Jacob
saw them he said, "This is God's camp!" So he called the name of that place
Mahanaim.[2]

3 And Jacob sent[3] messengers before him to Esau his brother in the land of
Seir, the country of Edom, 4 instructing them, "Thus you shall say to my lord Esau:
Thus says your servant Jacob, 'I have sojourned with Laban and stayed until now.
5 I have oxen, donkeys, flocks, male servants, and female servants. I have sent to
tell my lord, in order that I may find favor in your sight.'"

6 And the messengers returned to Jacob, saying, "We came to your brother
Esau, and he is coming to meet you, and there are four hundred men with him."
7 Then Jacob was greatly afraid and distressed. He divided the people who were
with him, and the flocks and herds and camels, into two camps, 8 thinking,
"If Esau comes to the one camp and attacks it, then the camp that is left will
escape."

9 And Jacob said, "O God of my father Abraham and God of my father Isaac,
O LORD who said to me, 'Return to your country and to your kindred, that I may
do you good,' 10 I am not worthy of the least of all the deeds of steadfast love and
all the faithfulness that you have shown to your servant, for with only my staff I
crossed this Jordan, and now I have become two camps. 11 Please deliver me from
the hand of my brother, from the hand of Esau, for I fear him, that he may come
and attack me, the mothers with the children. 12 But you said, 'I will surely do you
good, and make your offspring as the sand of the sea, which cannot be numbered
for multitude.'"

13 So he stayed there that night, and from what he had with him he took a present for his brother Esau, 14 two hundred female goats and twenty male goats, two
hundred ewes and twenty rams, 15 thirty milking camels and their calves, forty
cows and ten bulls, twenty female donkeys and ten male donkeys. 16 These he
handed over to his servants, every drove by itself, and said to his servants, "Pass
on ahead of me and put a space between drove and drove." 17 He instructed the
first, "When Esau my brother meets you and asks you, 'To whom do you belong?
Where are you going? And whose are these ahead of you?' 18 then you shall say,
'They belong to your servant Jacob. They are a present sent to my lord Esau. And
moreover, he is behind us.'" 19 He likewise instructed the second and the third
and all who followed the droves, "You shall say the same thing to Esau when you
find him, 20 and you shall say, 'Moreover, your servant Jacob is behind us.'" For he
thought, "I may appease him[4] with the present that goes ahead of me, and afterward I shall see his face. Perhaps he will accept me."[5] 21 So the present passed on
ahead of him, and he himself stayed that night in the camp.

Jacob Wrestles with God

22 The same night he arose and took his two wives, his two female servants,
and his eleven children,[6] and crossed the ford of the Jabbok. 23 He took them

[1]Ch 32:1 in Hebrew [2]*Mahanaim* means *two camps* [3]Or *had sent* [4]Hebrew *appease his face* [5]Hebrew *he will lift my face* [6]Or *sons*

and sent them across the stream, and everything else that he had. 24And Jacob was left alone. And a man wrestled with him until the breaking of the day.
25When the man saw that he did not prevail against Jacob, he touched his hip
socket, and Jacob's hip was put out of joint as he wrestled with him. 26Then he
said, "Let me go, for the day has broken." But Jacob said, "I will not let you go
unless you bless me." 27And he said to him, "What is your name?" And he said,
"Jacob." 28Then he said, "Your name shall no longer be called Jacob, but Israel,[1]
for you have striven with God and with men, and have prevailed." 29Then Jacob
asked him, "Please tell me your name." But he said, "Why is it that you ask
my name?" And there he blessed him. 30So Jacob called the name of the place
Peniel,[2] saying, "For I have seen God face to face, and yet my life has been delivered." 31The sun rose upon him as he passed Penuel, limping because of his
hip. 32Therefore to this day the people of Israel do not eat the sinew of the thigh
that is on the hip socket, because he touched the socket of Jacob's hip on the
sinew of the thigh.

Jacob Meets Esau

33 And Jacob lifted up his eyes and looked, and behold, Esau was coming,
and four hundred men with him. So he divided the children among Leah
and Rachel and the two female servants. 2And he put the servants with their children in front, then Leah with her children, and Rachel and Joseph last of all. 3He
himself went on before them, bowing himself to the ground seven times, until he
came near to his brother.

4But Esau ran to meet him and embraced him and fell on his neck and kissed
him, and they wept. 5And when Esau lifted up his eyes and saw the women and
children, he said, "Who are these with you?" Jacob said, "The children whom
God has graciously given your servant." 6Then the servants drew near, they
and their children, and bowed down. 7Leah likewise and her children drew
near and bowed down. And last Joseph and Rachel drew near, and they bowed
down. 8Esau said, "What do you mean by all this company[3] that I met?" Jacob
answered, "To find favor in the sight of my lord." 9But Esau said, "I have enough,
my brother; keep what you have for yourself." 10Jacob said, "No, please, if I have
found favor in your sight, then accept my present from my hand. For I have
seen your face, which is like seeing the face of God, and you have accepted
me. 11Please accept my blessing that is brought to you, because God has dealt
graciously with me, and because I have enough." Thus he urged him, and he
took it.

12Then Esau said, "Let us journey on our way, and I will go ahead of[4] you." 13But
Jacob said to him, "My lord knows that the children are frail, and that the nursing
flocks and herds are a care to me. If they are driven hard for one day, all the flocks
will die. 14Let my lord pass on ahead of his servant, and I will lead on slowly, at the
pace of the livestock that are ahead of me and at the pace of the children, until I
come to my lord in Seir."

15So Esau said, "Let me leave with you some of the people who are with me."
But he said, "What need is there? Let me find favor in the sight of my lord." 16So
Esau returned that day on his way to Seir. 17But Jacob journeyed to Succoth, and
built himself a house and made booths for his livestock. Therefore the name of
the place is called Succoth.[5]

18And Jacob came safely[6] to the city of Shechem, which is in the land of Canaan, on his way from Paddan-aram, and he camped before the city. 19And from
the sons of Hamor, Shechem's father, he bought for a hundred pieces of money[7]
the piece of land on which he had pitched his tent. 20There he erected an altar and
called it El-Elohe-Israel.[8]

[1] *Israel* means *He strives with God*, or *God strives* [2] *Peniel* means *the face of God* [3] Hebrew *camp* [4] Or *along with* [5] *Succoth* means *booths* [6] Or *peacefully* [7] Hebrew *a hundred qesitah*; a unit of money of uncertain value [8] *El-Elohe-Israel* means *God, the God of Israel*

A NEW NAME

God gave Jacob a new name. Throughout the Old Testament, a name carried an identity. For example, God changed Abram's name to Abraham to indicate that he would be "the father of a multitude of nations" (Ge 17:5). The new name indicated the favor of God and pointed forward to the coming promise of God.

In a similar fashion, after wrestling with God, Jacob was renamed Israel. This name was then used to refer to the entire nation that derived from his family lineage. This name was not chosen by Jacob but was given to him by God as a gift and a promise. For the rest of his life, this new name reminded Jacob of the favor of God in allowing him to wrestle with God and live, and of his privileged place within God's redemptive plan. God's chosen people throughout the Old Testament would be reminded of their status as God's people when anyone referred to them by the name Israel.

The New Testament church is no longer defined by an ethnic heritage like the nation of Israel. Now, Jews and Gentiles alike are grafted into one diverse family with God as their Father. God grants all those who are saved by faith in Jesus the glorious privilege of being called a child of God (Jn 1:12). As children, they are granted a unique identity given to them by virtue of their relationship with God. In fact, within the church, God's people are called Christians because of their relationship with Jesus Christ. This name denotes far more than mere proximity to Jesus. God's people are those who are "in Christ" — called into relationship with him and given a role to play in his redemptive mission.

This new identity also indicates the changes that are brought by God's Spirit in the life of his children. "Therefore, if anyone is in Christ, he is a new creation. The old has passed away; behold, the new has come" (2Co 5:17). The saving work of God fundamentally changes the identity of those saved by faith. No longer dead in trespasses and sins, God's people are declared holy and blameless and are given a right relationship with God. Like the change of a name, this change of identity should produce radical transformation in the worship, life, and mission of God's children.

ENEMIES MADE FRIENDS

Genesis 33 recounts the unthinkable reconciliation between Jacob and Esau. These estranged brothers had seemingly insurmountable odds stacked against the restoration of their relationship. Their history had been marked by strife, deceit, and mutual harm. The relationship between these two men was ravaged by sin, and they became bitter enemies. But Esau, in an act of love and mercy, pursued his brother and received him back into fellowship with lavish generosity.

Like Jacob, all of humanity is guilty of rebellion and sin against God, thus altering their relationship with their Creator. Image-bearers, created to walk with God in fellowship, find themselves estranged from God and unable to right the relationship by their own choosing. This broken fellowship takes those who were created to be friends of God and makes them his enemies (Ro 5:10). All people, like Jacob, should rightfully cower in fear and shame because of the judgment they surely deserve.

God's mercy is seen in the restorative act that he works on behalf of his enemies. Rather than expecting them to grovel in his presence or clean themselves up through obedience, God pursues his enemies in love. The biblical notion of reconciliation captures this profound image. God takes those who were his enemies and works on their behalf to bring them back into a right relationship with himself (Col 1:21 – 22). Like Esau, God pursues his enemies, recognizes their need, and blesses them with a restored relationship as an act of mercy.

Jesus elaborates on this work of reconciliation in his parable of a loving father and his wayward son (Lk 15:11 – 32). The son requested his inheritance early, only to squander everything and end up longing to eat from the trough of the pigs he fed. Only then did the young man realize his sin. The son expected to meet his father's displeasure and anticipated taking the posture of a hired servant. As the son returned, his dad saw him while he was a long way off and ran to meet him. Rather than shame or condemnation, the son was greeted by his father's loving embrace. The father gave him a hero's welcome — killing the fattened calf in order to throw a party and celebrate the return of his son. Like Esau and the loving father, God is pictured as a merciful heavenly Father who pursues his enemies in love and invites them into a restored relationship made possible through Jesus' death.

The Defiling of Dinah

34 Now Dinah the daughter of Leah, whom she had borne to Jacob, went out to see the women of the land. 2And when Shechem the son of Hamor the Hivite, the prince of the land, saw her, he seized her and lay with her and humiliated her. 3And his soul was drawn to Dinah the daughter of Jacob. He loved the young woman and spoke tenderly to her. 4So Shechem spoke to his father Hamor, saying, "Get me this girl for my wife."

5Now Jacob heard that he had defiled his daughter Dinah. But his sons were with his livestock in the field, so Jacob held his peace until they came. 6And Hamor the father of Shechem went out to Jacob to speak with him. 7The sons of Jacob had come in from the field as soon as they heard of it, and the men were indignant and very angry, because he had done an outrageous thing in Israel by lying with Jacob's daughter, for such a thing must not be done.

8But Hamor spoke with them, saying, "The soul of my son Shechem longs for your[1] daughter. Please give her to him to be his wife. 9Make marriages with us. Give your daughters to us, and take our daughters for yourselves. 10You shall dwell with us, and the land shall be open to you. Dwell and trade in it, and get property in it." 11Shechem also said to her father and to her brothers, "Let me find favor in your eyes, and whatever you say to me I will give. 12Ask me for as great a bride-price[2] and gift as you will, and I will give whatever you say to me. Only give me the young woman to be my wife."

13The sons of Jacob answered Shechem and his father Hamor deceitfully, because he had defiled their sister Dinah. 14They said to them, "We cannot do this thing, to give our sister to one who is uncircumcised, for that would be a disgrace to us. 15Only on this condition will we agree with you—that you will become as we are by every male among you being circumcised. 16Then we will give our daughters to you, and we will take your daughters to ourselves, and we will dwell with you and become one people. 17But if you will not listen to us and be circumcised, then we will take our daughter, and we will be gone."

18Their words pleased Hamor and Hamor's son Shechem. 19And the young man did not delay to do the thing, because he delighted in Jacob's daughter. Now he was the most honored of all his father's house. 20So Hamor and his son Shechem came to the gate of their city and spoke to the men of their city, saying, 21"These men are at peace with us; let them dwell in the land and trade in it, for behold, the land is large enough for them. Let us take their daughters as wives, and let us give them our daughters. 22Only on this condition will the men agree to dwell with us to become one people—when every male among us is circumcised as they are circumcised. 23Will not their livestock, their property and all their beasts be ours? Only let us agree with them, and they will dwell with us." 24And all who went out of the gate of his city listened to Hamor and his son Shechem, and every male was circumcised, all who went out of the gate of his city.

25On the third day, when they were sore, two of the sons of Jacob, Simeon and Levi, Dinah's brothers, took their swords and came against the city while it felt secure and killed all the males. 26They killed Hamor and his son Shechem with the sword and took Dinah out of Shechem's house and went away. 27The sons of Jacob came upon the slain and plundered the city, because they had defiled their sister. 28They took their flocks and their herds, their donkeys, and whatever was in the city and in the field. 29All their wealth, all their little ones and their wives, all that was in the houses, they captured and plundered.

30Then Jacob said to Simeon and Levi, "You have brought trouble on me by making me stink to the inhabitants of the land, the Canaanites and the Perizzites. My numbers are few, and if they gather themselves against me and attack me, I shall be destroyed, both I and my household." 31But they said, "Should he treat our sister like a prostitute?"

[1]The Hebrew for *your* is plural here [2]Or *engagement present*

God Blesses and Renames Jacob

35 God said to Jacob, "Arise, go up to Bethel and dwell there. Make an altar there to the God who appeared to you when you fled from your brother Esau." 2So Jacob said to his household and to all who were with him, "Put away the foreign gods that are among you and purify yourselves and change your garments. 3Then let us arise and go up to Bethel, so that I may make there an altar to the God who answers me in the day of my distress and has been with me wherever I have gone." 4So they gave to Jacob all the foreign gods that they had, and the rings that were in their ears. Jacob hid them under the terebinth tree that was near Shechem.

5And as they journeyed, a terror from God fell upon the cities that were around them, so that they did not pursue the sons of Jacob. 6And Jacob came to Luz (that is, Bethel), which is in the land of Canaan, he and all the people who were with him, 7and there he built an altar and called the place El-bethel,[1] because there God had revealed himself to him when he fled from his brother. 8And Deborah, Rebekah's nurse, died, and she was buried under an oak below Bethel. So he called its name Allon-bacuth.[2]

9God appeared[3] to Jacob again, when he came from Paddan-aram, and blessed him. 10And God said to him, "Your name is Jacob; no longer shall your name be called Jacob, but Israel shall be your name." So he called his name Israel. 11And God said to him, "I am God Almighty:[4] be fruitful and multiply. A nation and a company of nations shall come from you, and kings shall come from your own body.[5] 12The land that I gave to Abraham and Isaac I will give to you, and I will give the land to your offspring after you." 13Then God went up from him in the place where he had spoken with him. 14And Jacob set up a pillar in the place where he had spoken with him, a pillar of stone. He poured out a drink offering on it and poured oil on it. 15So Jacob called the name of the place where God had spoken with him Bethel.

The Deaths of Rachel and Isaac

16Then they journeyed from Bethel. When they were still some distance[6] from Ephrath, Rachel went into labor, and she had hard labor. 17And when her labor was at its hardest, the midwife said to her, "Do not fear, for you have another son." 18And as her soul was departing (for she was dying), she called his name Ben-oni;[7] but his father called him Benjamin.[8] 19So Rachel died, and she was buried on the way to Ephrath (that is, Bethlehem), 20and Jacob set up a pillar over her tomb. It is the pillar of Rachel's tomb, which is there to this day. 21Israel journeyed on and pitched his tent beyond the tower of Eder.

22While Israel lived in that land, Reuben went and lay with Bilhah his father's concubine. And Israel heard of it.

Now the sons of Jacob were twelve. 23The sons of Leah: Reuben (Jacob's firstborn), Simeon, Levi, Judah, Issachar, and Zebulun. 24The sons of Rachel: Joseph and Benjamin. 25The sons of Bilhah, Rachel's servant: Dan and Naphtali. 26The sons of Zilpah, Leah's servant: Gad and Asher. These were the sons of Jacob who were born to him in Paddan-aram.

27And Jacob came to his father Isaac at Mamre, or Kiriath-arba (that is, Hebron), where Abraham and Isaac had sojourned. 28Now the days of Isaac were 180 years. 29And Isaac breathed his last, and he died and was gathered to his people, old and full of days. And his sons Esau and Jacob buried him.

Esau's Descendants

36 These are the generations of Esau (that is, Edom). 2Esau took his wives from the Canaanites: Adah the daughter of Elon the Hittite, Oholibamah the daughter of Anah the daughter[9] of Zibeon the Hivite, 3and Basemath,

[1] *El-bethel* means *God of Bethel* [2] *Allon-bacuth* means *oak of weeping* [3] Or *had appeared* [4] Hebrew *El Shaddai* [5] Hebrew *from your loins* [6] Or *about two hours' distance* [7] *Ben-oni* could mean *son of my sorrow,* or *son of my strength* [8] *Benjamin* means *son of the right hand* [9] Hebrew; Samaritan, Septuagint, Syriac *son*; also verse 14

GENESIS 35:1–7

A PLACE FOR WORSHIP

God told Jacob to return to the place where he first saw God's glory (Ge 28:10–19). The rationale behind this command was unclear at the time. All Jacob knew was that God told him to return to Bethel, and once he arrived, he must worship God at an altar that he must build. Like his grandfather, Abraham, Jacob heard God and obeyed. His actions were predicated on his knowledge of God's past faithfulness and his awareness of the Lord's continued care. Jacob's obedience positioned him to receive the blessing of God.

Like Jacob, Jesus' followers obey the commands of God based on his faithfulness in their lives and their desire to worship him as he deserves (Jn 15:14). Obedience positions God's people to fulfill his purposes for their lives and receive the blessing he has promised—perhaps not in this life, but certainly in the life to come (Jn 10:10).

Ishmael's daughter, the sister of Nebaioth. 4And Adah bore to Esau, Eliphaz; Basemath bore Reuel; 5and Oholibamah bore Jeush, Jalam, and Korah. These are the
sons of Esau who were born to him in the land of Canaan.

6Then Esau took his wives, his sons, his daughters, and all the members of his
household, his livestock, all his beasts, and all his property that he had acquired
in the land of Canaan. He went into a land away from his brother Jacob. 7For their
possessions were too great for them to dwell together. The land of their sojournings could not support them because of their livestock. 8So Esau settled in the hill
country of Seir. (Esau is Edom.)

9These are the generations of Esau the father of the Edomites in the hill country of Seir. 10These are the names of Esau's sons: Eliphaz the son of Adah the wife
of Esau, Reuel the son of Basemath the wife of Esau. 11The sons of Eliphaz were
Teman, Omar, Zepho, Gatam, and Kenaz. 12(Timna was a concubine of Eliphaz,
Esau's son; she bore Amalek to Eliphaz.) These are the sons of Adah, Esau's wife.
13These are the sons of Reuel: Nahath, Zerah, Shammah, and Mizzah. These are
the sons of Basemath, Esau's wife. 14These are the sons of Oholibamah the daughter of Anah the daughter of Zibeon, Esau's wife: she bore to Esau Jeush, Jalam,
and Korah.

15These are the chiefs of the sons of Esau. The sons of Eliphaz the firstborn
of Esau: the chiefs Teman, Omar, Zepho, Kenaz, 16Korah, Gatam, and Amalek;
these are the chiefs of Eliphaz in the land of Edom; these are the sons of Adah.
17These are the sons of Reuel, Esau's son: the chiefs Nahath, Zerah, Shammah, and
Mizzah; these are the chiefs of Reuel in the land of Edom; these are the sons of
Basemath, Esau's wife. 18These are the sons of Oholibamah, Esau's wife: the chiefs
Jeush, Jalam, and Korah; these are the chiefs born of Oholibamah the daughter
of Anah, Esau's wife. 19These are the sons of Esau (that is, Edom), and these are
their chiefs.

20These are the sons of Seir the Horite, the inhabitants of the land: Lotan, Shobal, Zibeon, Anah, 21Dishon, Ezer, and Dishan; these are the chiefs of the Horites,
the sons of Seir in the land of Edom. 22The sons of Lotan were Hori and Hemam;
and Lotan's sister was Timna. 23These are the sons of Shobal: Alvan, Manahath,
Ebal, Shepho, and Onam. 24These are the sons of Zibeon: Aiah and Anah; he is the
Anah who found the hot springs in the wilderness, as he pastured the donkeys
of Zibeon his father. 25These are the children of Anah: Dishon and Oholibamah
the daughter of Anah. 26These are the sons of Dishon: Hemdan, Eshban, Ithran,
and Cheran. 27These are the sons of Ezer: Bilhan, Zaavan, and Akan. 28These are
the sons of Dishan: Uz and Aran. 29These are the chiefs of the Horites: the chiefs
Lotan, Shobal, Zibeon, Anah, 30Dishon, Ezer, and Dishan; these are the chiefs of
the Horites, chief by chief in the land of Seir.

31These are the kings who reigned in the land of Edom, before any king
reigned over the Israelites. 32Bela the son of Beor reigned in Edom, the name
of his city being Dinhabah. 33Bela died, and Jobab the son of Zerah of Bozrah
reigned in his place. 34Jobab died, and Husham of the land of the Temanites
reigned in his place. 35Husham died, and Hadad the son of Bedad, who defeated
Midian in the country of Moab, reigned in his place, the name of his city being
Avith. 36Hadad died, and Samlah of Masrekah reigned in his place. 37Samlah
died, and Shaul of Rehoboth on the Euphrates[1] reigned in his place. 38Shaul
died, and Baal-hanan the son of Achbor reigned in his place. 39Baal-hanan the
son of Achbor died, and Hadar reigned in his place, the name of his city being Pau; his wife's name was Mehetabel, the daughter of Matred, daughter of
Mezahab.

40These are the names of the chiefs of Esau, according to their clans and their
dwelling places, by their names: the chiefs Timna, Alvah, Jetheth, 41Oholibamah,
Elah, Pinon, 42Kenaz, Teman, Mibzar, 43Magdiel, and Iram; these are the chiefs of

[1]Hebrew *the River*

Edom (that is, Esau, the father of Edom), according to their dwelling places in the land of their possession.

Joseph's Dreams

37 Jacob lived in the land of his father's sojournings, in the land of Canaan. 2 These are the generations of Jacob.

Joseph, being seventeen years old, was pasturing the flock with his brothers. He was a boy with the sons of Bilhah and Zilpah, his father's wives. And Joseph brought a bad report of them to their father. 3 Now Israel loved Joseph more than any other of his sons, because he was the son of his old age. And he made him a robe of many colors.[1] 4 But when his brothers saw that their father loved him more than all his brothers, they hated him and could not speak peacefully to him.

5 Now Joseph had a dream, and when he told it to his brothers they hated him even more. 6 He said to them, "Hear this dream that I have dreamed: 7 Behold, we were binding sheaves in the field, and behold, my sheaf arose and stood upright. And behold, your sheaves gathered around it and bowed down to my sheaf." 8 His brothers said to him, "Are you indeed to reign over us? Or are you indeed to rule over us?" So they hated him even more for his dreams and for his words.

9 Then he dreamed another dream and told it to his brothers and said, "Behold, I have dreamed another dream. Behold, the sun, the moon, and eleven stars were bowing down to me." 10 But when he told it to his father and to his brothers, his father rebuked him and said to him, "What is this dream that you have dreamed? Shall I and your mother and your brothers indeed come to bow ourselves to the ground before you?" 11 And his brothers were jealous of him, but his father kept the saying in mind.

Joseph Sold by His Brothers

12 Now his brothers went to pasture their father's flock near Shechem. 13 And Israel said to Joseph, "Are not your brothers pasturing the flock at Shechem? Come, I will send you to them." And he said to him, "Here I am." 14 So he said to him, "Go now, see if it is well with your brothers and with the flock, and bring me word." So he sent him from the Valley of Hebron, and he came to Shechem. 15 And a man found him wandering in the fields. And the man asked him, "What are you seeking?" 16 "I am seeking my brothers," he said. "Tell me, please, where they are pasturing the flock." 17 And the man said, "They have gone away, for I heard them say, 'Let us go to Dothan.'" So Joseph went after his brothers and found them at Dothan.

18 They saw him from afar, and before he came near to them they conspired against him to kill him. 19 They said to one another, "Here comes this dreamer. 20 Come now, let us kill him and throw him into one of the pits.[2] Then we will say that a fierce animal has devoured him, and we will see what will become of his dreams." 21 But when Reuben heard it, he rescued him out of their hands, saying, "Let us not take his life." 22 And Reuben said to them, "Shed no blood; throw him into this pit here in the wilderness, but do not lay a hand on him"—that he might rescue him out of their hand to restore him to his father. 23 So when Joseph came to his brothers, they stripped him of his robe, the robe of many colors that he wore. 24 And they took him and threw him into a pit. The pit was empty; there was no water in it.

25 Then they sat down to eat. And looking up they saw a caravan of Ishmaelites coming from Gilead, with their camels bearing gum, balm, and myrrh, on their way to carry it down to Egypt. 26 Then Judah said to his brothers, "What profit is it if we kill our brother and conceal his blood? 27 Come, let us sell him to the Ishmaelites, and let not our hand be upon him, for he is our brother, our own flesh."

[1] See Septuagint, Vulgate; or (with Syriac) *a robe with long sleeves*. The meaning of the Hebrew is uncertain; also verses 23, 32 [2] Or *cisterns*; also verses 22, 24

And his brothers listened to him. 28 Then Midianite traders passed by. And they drew Joseph up and lifted him out of the pit, and sold him to the Ishmaelites for twenty shekels[1] of silver. They took Joseph to Egypt.

29 When Reuben returned to the pit and saw that Joseph was not in the pit, he tore his clothes 30 and returned to his brothers and said, "The boy is gone, and I, where shall I go?" 31 Then they took Joseph's robe and slaughtered a goat and dipped the robe in the blood. 32 And they sent the robe of many colors and brought it to their father and said, "This we have found; please identify whether it is your son's robe or not." 33 And he identified it and said, "It is my son's robe. A fierce animal has devoured him. Joseph is without doubt torn to pieces." 34 Then Jacob tore his garments and put sackcloth on his loins and mourned for his son many days. 35 All his sons and all his daughters rose up to comfort him, but he refused to be comforted and said, "No, I shall go down to Sheol to my son, mourning." Thus his father wept for him. 36 Meanwhile the Midianites had sold him in Egypt to Potiphar, an officer of Pharaoh, the captain of the guard.

Judah and Tamar

38 It happened at that time that Judah went down from his brothers and turned aside to a certain Adullamite, whose name was Hirah. 2 There Judah saw the daughter of a certain Canaanite whose name was Shua. He took her and went in to her, 3 and she conceived and bore a son, and he called his name Er. 4 She conceived again and bore a son, and she called his name Onan. 5 Yet again she bore a son, and she called his name Shelah. Judah[2] was in Chezib when she bore him.

6 And Judah took a wife for Er his firstborn, and her name was Tamar. 7 But Er, Judah's firstborn, was wicked in the sight of the LORD, and the LORD put him to death. 8 Then Judah said to Onan, "Go in to your brother's wife and perform the duty of a brother-in-law to her, and raise up offspring for your brother." 9 But Onan knew that the offspring would not be his. So whenever he went in to his brother's wife he would waste the semen on the ground, so as not to give offspring to his brother. 10 And what he did was wicked in the sight of the LORD, and he put him to death also. 11 Then Judah said to Tamar his daughter-in-law, "Remain a widow in your father's house, till Shelah my son grows up"—for he feared that he would die, like his brothers. So Tamar went and remained in her father's house.

12 In the course of time the wife of Judah, Shua's daughter, died. When Judah was comforted, he went up to Timnah to his sheepshearers, he and his friend Hirah the Adullamite. 13 And when Tamar was told, "Your father-in-law is going up to Timnah to shear his sheep," 14 she took off her widow's garments and covered herself with a veil, wrapping herself up, and sat at the entrance to Enaim, which is on the road to Timnah. For she saw that Shelah was grown up, and she had not been given to him in marriage. 15 When Judah saw her, he thought she was a prostitute, for she had covered her face. 16 He turned to her at the roadside and said, "Come, let me come in to you," for he did not know that she was his daughter-in-law. She said, "What will you give me, that you may come in to me?" 17 He answered, "I will send you a young goat from the flock." And she said, "If you give me a pledge, until you send it—" 18 He said, "What pledge shall I give you?" She replied, "Your signet and your cord and your staff that is in your hand." So he gave them to her and went in to her, and she conceived by him. 19 Then she arose and went away, and taking off her veil she put on the garments of her widowhood.

20 When Judah sent the young goat by his friend the Adullamite to take back the pledge from the woman's hand, he did not find her. 21 And he asked the men of the place, "Where is the cult prostitute[3] who was at Enaim at the roadside?" And they said, "No cult prostitute has been here." 22 So he returned to Judah and said, "I have not found her. Also, the men of the place said, 'No cult prostitute has been

[1] A *shekel* was about 2/5 ounce or 11 grams [2] Hebrew *He* [3] Hebrew *sacred woman*; a woman who served a pagan deity by prostitution; also verse 22

here.'" 23 And Judah replied, "Let her keep the things as her own, or we shall be
laughed at. You see, I sent this young goat, and you did not find her."
24 About three months later Judah was told, "Tamar your daughter-in-law has
been immoral.[1] Moreover, she is pregnant by immorality."[2] And Judah said, "Bring
her out, and let her be burned." 25 As she was being brought out, she sent word
to her father-in-law, "By the man to whom these belong, I am pregnant." And
she said, "Please identify whose these are, the signet and the cord and the staff."
26 Then Judah identified them and said, "She is more righteous than I, since I did
not give her to my son Shelah." And he did not know her again.
27 When the time of her labor came, there were twins in her womb. 28 And when
she was in labor, one put out a hand, and the midwife took and tied a scarlet
thread on his hand, saying, "This one came out first." 29 But as he drew back his
hand, behold, his brother came out. And she said, "What a breach you have made
for yourself!" Therefore his name was called Perez.[3] 30 Afterward his brother came
out with the scarlet thread on his hand, and his name was called Zerah.

Joseph and Potiphar's Wife

39 Now Joseph had been brought down to Egypt, and Potiphar, an officer of
Pharaoh, the captain of the guard, an Egyptian, had bought him from the
Ishmaelites who had brought him down there. 2 The LORD was with Joseph, and
he became a successful man, and he was in the house of his Egyptian master. 3 His
master saw that the LORD was with him and that the LORD caused all that he did
to succeed in his hands. 4 So Joseph found favor in his sight and attended him, and
he made him overseer of his house and put him in charge of all that he had. 5 From
the time that he made him overseer in his house and over all that he had, the LORD
blessed the Egyptian's house for Joseph's sake; the blessing of the LORD was on all
that he had, in house and field. 6 So he left all that he had in Joseph's charge, and
because of him he had no concern about anything but the food he ate.
Now Joseph was handsome in form and appearance. 7 And after a time his
master's wife cast her eyes on Joseph and said, "Lie with me." 8 But he refused and
said to his master's wife, "Behold, because of me my master has no concern about
anything in the house, and he has put everything that he has in my charge. 9 He is
not greater in this house than I am, nor has he kept back anything from me except
you, because you are his wife. How then can I do this great wickedness and sin
against God?" 10 And as she spoke to Joseph day after day, he would not listen to
her, to lie beside her or to be with her.
11 But one day, when he went into the house to do his work and none of the
men of the house was there in the house, 12 she caught him by his garment, saying, "Lie with me." But he left his garment in her hand and fled and got out of the
house. 13 And as soon as she saw that he had left his garment in her hand and had
fled out of the house, 14 she called to the men of her household and said to them,
"See, he has brought among us a Hebrew to laugh at us. He came in to me to lie
with me, and I cried out with a loud voice. 15 And as soon as he heard that I lifted
up my voice and cried out, he left his garment beside me and fled and got out of
the house." 16 Then she laid up his garment by her until his master came home,
17 and she told him the same story, saying, "The Hebrew servant, whom you have
brought among us, came in to me to laugh at me. 18 But as soon as I lifted up my
voice and cried, he left his garment beside me and fled out of the house."
19 As soon as his master heard the words that his wife spoke to him, "This is
the way your servant treated me," his anger was kindled. 20 And Joseph's master
took him and put him into the prison, the place where the king's prisoners were
confined, and he was there in prison. 21 But the LORD was with Joseph and showed
him steadfast love and gave him favor in the sight of the keeper of the prison.
22 And the keeper of the prison put Joseph in charge of all the prisoners who were

[1] Or *has committed prostitution* [2] Or *by prostitution* [3] Perez means *a breach*

GENESIS 38:30

AN UNLIKELY FAMILY

Perez and Zerah were unexpected recipients of the blessing of God. These twin children of the licentious relationship between Judah and his daughter-in-law Tamar established families within the house of Judah (1Ch 2:3–9). Though Tamar displayed suspicious behavior and was probably a Canaanite, she was grafted into the people of God and became a member of the family of promise (Ru 4:12,18–22). Her name is mentioned again in a most unlikely place—the lineage of Jesus Christ, the Messiah (Mt 1:3).

While recounting the Jewish origins of the Messiah, Matthew included the names of scores of unlikely people who became the recipients of God's grace and were a part of ushering in the birth of the promised Son of God. God's family is defined, not by ethnicity or morality, but by the grace of God. He uses all sorts of people, even those with questionable pasts, to demonstrate the stunning riches of his grace in kindness to all people in Christ Jesus (Eph 2:7).

GENESIS 39:1–23

TRUST AND TEMPTATION

Joseph's resistance to temptation is a testimony to his trust in God's work on his behalf. Not only would giving in to the temptation have catered to his masculine desires, but also it would have surely secured the favor of a powerful woman. Still Joseph rejected the advances of Potiphar's wife and entrusted himself to the care of God.

(continued on next page)

(Trust and Temptation, continued)

In a similar way, at the beginning of his earthly ministry, Jesus faced temptation by Satan himself. Had he capitulated to Satan's ploy, he could have attained glory and power in a moment. However, knowing this was not the plan of God, he rejected Satan and entrusted himself to God's grand purposes (Mt 4:1–11). Like Joseph, Jesus rested in the faithfulness of God. Jesus sets an example for Christians seeking victory over temptation. God's people are to entrust themselves to God, knowing that "for those who love God all things work together for good, for those who are called according to his purpose" (Ro 8:28).

in the prison. Whatever was done there, he was the one who did it. 23The keeper
of the prison paid no attention to anything that was in Joseph's charge, because
the LORD was with him. And whatever he did, the LORD made it succeed.

Joseph Interprets Two Prisoners' Dreams

40 Some time after this, the cupbearer of the king of Egypt and his baker
committed an offense against their lord the king of Egypt. 2And Pharaoh
was angry with his two officers, the chief cupbearer and the chief baker, 3and he
put them in custody in the house of the captain of the guard, in the prison where
Joseph was confined. 4The captain of the guard appointed Joseph to be with them,
and he attended them. They continued for some time in custody.

5And one night they both dreamed—the cupbearer and the baker of the king
of Egypt, who were confined in the prison—each his own dream, and each dream
with its own interpretation. 6When Joseph came to them in the morning, he saw
that they were troubled. 7So he asked Pharaoh's officers who were with him in
custody in his master's house, "Why are your faces downcast today?" 8They said
to him, "We have had dreams, and there is no one to interpret them." And Joseph
said to them, "Do not interpretations belong to God? Please tell them to me."

9So the chief cupbearer told his dream to Joseph and said to him, "In my dream
there was a vine before me, 10and on the vine there were three branches. As soon
as it budded, its blossoms shot forth, and the clusters ripened into grapes. 11Pha-
raoh's cup was in my hand, and I took the grapes and pressed them into Pharaoh's
cup and placed the cup in Pharaoh's hand." 12Then Joseph said to him, "This is its
interpretation: the three branches are three days. 13In three days Pharaoh will lift
up your head and restore you to your office, and you shall place Pharaoh's cup in
his hand as formerly, when you were his cupbearer. 14Only remember me, when it
is well with you, and please do me the kindness to mention me to Pharaoh, and so
get me out of this house. 15For I was indeed stolen out of the land of the Hebrews,
and here also I have done nothing that they should put me into the pit."

16When the chief baker saw that the interpretation was favorable, he said to
Joseph, "I also had a dream: there were three cake baskets on my head, 17and in
the uppermost basket there were all sorts of baked food for Pharaoh, but the birds
were eating it out of the basket on my head." 18And Joseph answered and said,
"This is its interpretation: the three baskets are three days. 19In three days Pharaoh
will lift up your head—from you!—and hang you on a tree. And the birds will eat
the flesh from you."

20On the third day, which was Pharaoh's birthday, he made a feast for all his
servants and lifted up the head of the chief cupbearer and the head of the chief
baker among his servants. 21He restored the chief cupbearer to his position, and
he placed the cup in Pharaoh's hand. 22But he hanged the chief baker, as Joseph
had interpreted to them. 23Yet the chief cupbearer did not remember Joseph, but
forgot him.

Joseph Interprets Pharaoh's Dreams

41 After two whole years, Pharaoh dreamed that he was standing by the Nile,
2and behold, there came up out of the Nile seven cows, attractive and
plump, and they fed in the reed grass. 3And behold, seven other cows, ugly and
thin, came up out of the Nile after them, and stood by the other cows on the
bank of the Nile. 4And the ugly, thin cows ate up the seven attractive, plump cows.
And Pharaoh awoke. 5And he fell asleep and dreamed a second time. And behold,
seven ears of grain, plump and good, were growing on one stalk. 6And behold,
after them sprouted seven ears, thin and blighted by the east wind. 7And the thin
ears swallowed up the seven plump, full ears. And Pharaoh awoke, and behold,
it was a dream. 8So in the morning his spirit was troubled, and he sent and called
for all the magicians of Egypt and all its wise men. Pharaoh told them his dreams,
but there was none who could interpret them to Pharaoh.

9Then the chief cupbearer said to Pharaoh, "I remember my offenses today. 10When Pharaoh was angry with his servants and put me and the chief baker in custody in the house of the captain of the guard, 11we dreamed on the same night, he and I, each having a dream with its own interpretation. 12A young Hebrew was there with us, a servant of the captain of the guard. When we told him, he interpreted our dreams to us, giving an interpretation to each man according to his dream. 13And as he interpreted to us, so it came about. I was restored to my office, and the baker was hanged."

14Then Pharaoh sent and called Joseph, and they quickly brought him out of the pit. And when he had shaved himself and changed his clothes, he came in before Pharaoh. 15And Pharaoh said to Joseph, "I have had a dream, and there is no one who can interpret it. I have heard it said of you that when you hear a dream you can interpret it." 16Joseph answered Pharaoh, "It is not in me; God will give Pharaoh a favorable answer."[1] 17Then Pharaoh said to Joseph, "Behold, in my dream I was standing on the banks of the Nile. 18Seven cows, plump and attractive, came up out of the Nile and fed in the reed grass. 19Seven other cows came up after them, poor and very ugly and thin, such as I had never seen in all the land of Egypt. 20And the thin, ugly cows ate up the first seven plump cows, 21but when they had eaten them no one would have known that they had eaten them, for they were still as ugly as at the beginning. Then I awoke. 22I also saw in my dream seven ears growing on one stalk, full and good. 23Seven ears, withered, thin, and blighted by the east wind, sprouted after them, 24and the thin ears swallowed up the seven good ears. And I told it to the magicians, but there was no one who could explain it to me."

25Then Joseph said to Pharaoh, "The dreams of Pharaoh are one; God has revealed to Pharaoh what he is about to do. 26The seven good cows are seven years, and the seven good ears are seven years; the dreams are one. 27The seven lean and ugly cows that came up after them are seven years, and the seven empty ears blighted by the east wind are also seven years of famine. 28It is as I told Pharaoh; God has shown to Pharaoh what he is about to do. 29There will come seven years of great plenty throughout all the land of Egypt, 30but after them there will arise seven years of famine, and all the plenty will be forgotten in the land of Egypt. The famine will consume the land, 31and the plenty will be unknown in the land by reason of the famine that will follow, for it will be very severe. 32And the doubling of Pharaoh's dream means that the thing is fixed by God, and God will shortly bring it about. 33Now therefore let Pharaoh select a discerning and wise man, and set him over the land of Egypt. 34Let Pharaoh proceed to appoint overseers over the land and take one-fifth of the produce of the land[2] of Egypt during the seven plentiful years. 35And let them gather all the food of these good years that are coming and store up grain under the authority of Pharaoh for food in the cities, and let them keep it. 36That food shall be a reserve for the land against the seven years of famine that are to occur in the land of Egypt, so that the land may not perish through the famine."

Joseph Rises to Power

37This proposal pleased Pharaoh and all his servants. 38And Pharaoh said to his servants, "Can we find a man like this, in whom is the Spirit of God?"[3] 39Then Pharaoh said to Joseph, "Since God has shown you all this, there is none so discerning and wise as you are. 40You shall be over my house, and all my people shall order themselves as you command.[4] Only as regards the throne will I be greater than you." 41And Pharaoh said to Joseph, "See, I have set you over all the land of Egypt." 42Then Pharaoh took his signet ring from his hand and put it on Joseph's hand, and clothed him in garments of fine linen and put a gold chain about his neck.

[1]Or (compare Samaritan, Septuagint) *Without God it is not possible to give Pharaoh an answer about his welfare* [2]Or *over the land and organize the land* [3]Or *of the gods* [4]Hebrew *and according to your command all my people shall kiss the ground*

43And he made him ride in his second chariot. And they called out before him, "Bow the knee!"[1] Thus he set him over all the land of Egypt. 44Moreover, Pharaoh said to Joseph, "I am Pharaoh, and without your consent no one shall lift up hand or foot in all the land of Egypt." 45And Pharaoh called Joseph's name Zaphenath-paneah. And he gave him in marriage Asenath, the daughter of Potiphera priest of On. So Joseph went out over the land of Egypt.

46Joseph was thirty years old when he entered the service of Pharaoh king of Egypt. And Joseph went out from the presence of Pharaoh and went through all the land of Egypt. 47During the seven plentiful years the earth produced abundantly, 48and he gathered up all the food of these seven years, which occurred in the land of Egypt, and put the food in the cities. He put in every city the food from the fields around it. 49And Joseph stored up grain in great abundance, like the sand of the sea, until he ceased to measure it, for it could not be measured.

50Before the year of famine came, two sons were born to Joseph. Asenath, the daughter of Potiphera priest of On, bore them to him. 51Joseph called the name of the firstborn Manasseh. "For," he said, "God has made me forget all my hardship and all my father's house."[2] 52The name of the second he called Ephraim, "For God has made me fruitful in the land of my affliction."[3]

53The seven years of plenty that occurred in the land of Egypt came to an end, 54and the seven years of famine began to come, as Joseph had said. There was famine in all lands, but in all the land of Egypt there was bread. 55When all the land of Egypt was famished, the people cried to Pharaoh for bread. Pharaoh said to all the Egyptians, "Go to Joseph. What he says to you, do."

56So when the famine had spread over all the land, Joseph opened all the storehouses[4] and sold to the Egyptians, for the famine was severe in the land of Egypt. 57Moreover, all the earth came to Egypt to Joseph to buy grain, because the famine was severe over all the earth.

Joseph's Brothers Go to Egypt

42 When Jacob learned that there was grain for sale in Egypt, he said to his sons, "Why do you look at one another?" 2And he said, "Behold, I have heard that there is grain for sale in Egypt. Go down and buy grain for us there, that we may live and not die." 3So ten of Joseph's brothers went down to buy grain in Egypt. 4But Jacob did not send Benjamin, Joseph's brother, with his brothers, for he feared that harm might happen to him. 5Thus the sons of Israel came to buy among the others who came, for the famine was in the land of Canaan.

6Now Joseph was governor over the land. He was the one who sold to all the people of the land. And Joseph's brothers came and bowed themselves before him with their faces to the ground. 7Joseph saw his brothers and recognized them, but he treated them like strangers and spoke roughly to them. "Where do you come from?" he said. They said, "From the land of Canaan, to buy food." 8And Joseph recognized his brothers, but they did not recognize him. 9And Joseph remembered the dreams that he had dreamed of them. And he said to them, "You are spies; you have come to see the nakedness of the land." 10They said to him, "No, my lord, your servants have come to buy food. 11We are all sons of one man. We are honest men. Your servants have never been spies."

12He said to them, "No, it is the nakedness of the land that you have come to see." 13And they said, "We, your servants, are twelve brothers, the sons of one man in the land of Canaan, and behold, the youngest is this day with our father, and one is no more." 14But Joseph said to them, "It is as I said to you. You are spies. 15By this you shall be tested: by the life of Pharaoh, you shall not go from this place unless your youngest brother comes here. 16Send one of you, and let him bring your brother, while you remain confined, that your words may be tested, whether

[1] *Abrek*, probably an Egyptian word, similar in sound to the Hebrew word meaning *to kneel* [2] *Manasseh* sounds like the Hebrew for *making to forget* [3] *Ephraim* sounds like the Hebrew for *making fruitful*
[4] Hebrew *all that was in them*

there is truth in you. Or else, by the life of Pharaoh, surely you are spies." 17And he
put them all together in custody for three days.
18On the third day Joseph said to them, "Do this and you will live, for I fear God:
19if you are honest men, let one of your brothers remain confined where you are
in custody, and let the rest go and carry grain for the famine of your households,
20and bring your youngest brother to me. So your words will be verified, and you
shall not die." And they did so. 21Then they said to one another, "In truth we are
guilty concerning our brother, in that we saw the distress of his soul, when he
begged us and we did not listen. That is why this distress has come upon us."
22And Reuben answered them, "Did I not tell you not to sin against the boy? But
you did not listen. So now there comes a reckoning for his blood." 23They did not
know that Joseph understood them, for there was an interpreter between them.
24Then he turned away from them and wept. And he returned to them and spoke
to them. And he took Simeon from them and bound him before their eyes. 25And
Joseph gave orders to fill their bags with grain, and to replace every man's money
in his sack, and to give them provisions for the journey. This was done for them.
26Then they loaded their donkeys with their grain and departed. 27And as one
of them opened his sack to give his donkey fodder at the lodging place, he saw his
money in the mouth of his sack. 28He said to his brothers, "My money has been
put back; here it is in the mouth of my sack!" At this their hearts failed them, and
they turned trembling to one another, saying, "What is this that God has done
to us?"
29When they came to Jacob their father in the land of Canaan, they told him
all that had happened to them, saying, 30"The man, the lord of the land, spoke
roughly to us and took us to be spies of the land. 31But we said to him, 'We are
honest men; we have never been spies. 32We are twelve brothers, sons of our father. One is no more, and the youngest is this day with our father in the land of
Canaan.' 33Then the man, the lord of the land, said to us, 'By this I shall know that
you are honest men: leave one of your brothers with me, and take grain for the
famine of your households, and go your way. 34Bring your youngest brother to me.
Then I shall know that you are not spies but honest men, and I will deliver your
brother to you, and you shall trade in the land.'"
35As they emptied their sacks, behold, every man's bundle of money was in
his sack. And when they and their father saw their bundles of money, they were
afraid. 36And Jacob their father said to them, "You have bereaved me of my children: Joseph is no more, and Simeon is no more, and now you would take Benjamin. All this has come against me." 37Then Reuben said to his father, "Kill my two
sons if I do not bring him back to you. Put him in my hands, and I will bring him
back to you." 38But he said, "My son shall not go down with you, for his brother
is dead, and he is the only one left. If harm should happen to him on the journey
that you are to make, you would bring down my gray hairs with sorrow to Sheol."

Joseph's Brothers Return to Egypt

43 Now the famine was severe in the land. 2And when they had eaten the
grain that they had brought from Egypt, their father said to them, "Go
again, buy us a little food." 3But Judah said to him, "The man solemnly warned
us, saying, 'You shall not see my face unless your brother is with you.' 4If you will
send our brother with us, we will go down and buy you food. 5But if you will not
send him, we will not go down, for the man said to us, 'You shall not see my face,
unless your brother is with you.'" 6Israel said, "Why did you treat me so badly as to
tell the man that you had another brother?" 7They replied, "The man questioned
us carefully about ourselves and our kindred, saying, 'Is your father still alive? Do
you have another brother?' What we told him was in answer to these questions.
Could we in any way know that he would say, 'Bring your brother down'?" 8And
Judah said to Israel his father, "Send the boy with me, and we will arise and go,
that we may live and not die, both we and you and also our little ones. 9I will be

GENESIS 43:8–9

BECOMING A SLAVE SO A SLAVE COULD GO FREE

Judah makes a risky and bold move in this passage, in complete contrast to his cowardly and unrighteous behavior earlier (Ge 37:26–27; 38:11–26). When Judah was forced to act on this pledge (44:33–34), he remained faithful to his promise, offering himself as a slave so that his brother could avoid a similar fate (44:17). His substitutionary act would have allowed Benjamin to return to his father as a free man.

Centuries later, one of Judah's descendants would offer himself in the place of sinners so that they might be freed from their penalty and slavery. Judah's pledge of his life as the substitute for his younger brother is a striking parallel to Jesus' substitutionary sacrifice of his life for his adopted brothers and sisters—the church (Ro 8:17,29). Unlike Judah, however (Ge 37:26–27), Jesus did not contribute to the slavery of the church. Instead, Jesus graciously pledged himself as a substitute so that he might bring home his redeemed ones, right into the heavenly Father's very presence.

a pledge of his safety. From my hand you shall require him. If I do not bring him back to you and set him before you, then let me bear the blame forever. 10If we had not delayed, we would now have returned twice."

11Then their father Israel said to them, "If it must be so, then do this: take some of the choice fruits of the land in your bags, and carry a present down to the man, a little balm and a little honey, gum, myrrh, pistachio nuts, and almonds. 12Take double the money with you. Carry back with you the money that was returned in the mouth of your sacks. Perhaps it was an oversight. 13Take also your brother, and arise, go again to the man. 14May God Almighty[1] grant you mercy before the man, and may he send back your other brother and Benjamin. And as for me, if I am bereaved of my children, I am bereaved."

15So the men took this present, and they took double the money with them, and Benjamin. They arose and went down to Egypt and stood before Joseph.

16When Joseph saw Benjamin with them, he said to the steward of his house, "Bring the men into the house, and slaughter an animal and make ready, for the men are to dine with me at noon." 17The man did as Joseph told him and brought the men to Joseph's house. 18And the men were afraid because they were brought to Joseph's house, and they said, "It is because of the money, which was replaced in our sacks the first time, that we are brought in, so that he may assault us and fall upon us to make us servants and seize our donkeys." 19So they went up to the steward of Joseph's house and spoke with him at the door of the house, 20and said, "Oh, my lord, we came down the first time to buy food. 21And when we came to the lodging place we opened our sacks, and there was each man's money in the mouth of his sack, our money in full weight. So we have brought it again with us, 22and we have brought other money down with us to buy food. We do not know who put our money in our sacks." 23He replied, "Peace to you, do not be afraid. Your God and the God of your father has put treasure in your sacks for you. I received your money." Then he brought Simeon out to them. 24And when the man had brought the men into Joseph's house and given them water, and they had washed their feet, and when he had given their donkeys fodder, 25they prepared the present for Joseph's coming at noon, for they heard that they should eat bread there.

26When Joseph came home, they brought into the house to him the present that they had with them and bowed down to him to the ground. 27And he inquired about their welfare and said, "Is your father well, the old man of whom you spoke? Is he still alive?" 28They said, "Your servant our father is well; he is still alive." And they bowed their heads and prostrated themselves. 29And he lifted up his eyes and saw his brother Benjamin, his mother's son, and said, "Is this your youngest brother, of whom you spoke to me? God be gracious to you, my son!" 30Then Joseph hurried out, for his compassion grew warm for his brother, and he sought a place to weep. And he entered his chamber and wept there. 31Then he washed his face and came out. And controlling himself he said, "Serve the food." 32They served him by himself, and them by themselves, and the Egyptians who ate with him by themselves, because the Egyptians could not eat with the Hebrews, for that is an abomination to the Egyptians. 33And they sat before him, the firstborn according to his birthright and the youngest according to his youth. And the men looked at one another in amazement. 34Portions were taken to them from Joseph's table, but Benjamin's portion was five times as much as any of theirs. And they drank and were merry[2] with him.

Joseph Tests His Brothers

44 Then he commanded the steward of his house, "Fill the men's sacks with food, as much as they can carry, and put each man's money in the mouth of his sack, 2and put my cup, the silver cup, in the mouth of the sack of the youngest, with his money for the grain." And he did as Joseph told him.

[1]Hebrew *El Shaddai* [2]Hebrew *and became intoxicated*

3As soon as the morning was light, the men were sent away with their donkeys. 4They had gone only a short distance from the city. Now Joseph said to his steward, "Up, follow after the men, and when you overtake them, say to them, 'Why have you repaid evil for good?[1] 5Is it not from this that my lord drinks, and by this that he practices divination? You have done evil in doing this.'"

6When he overtook them, he spoke to them these words. 7They said to him, "Why does my lord speak such words as these? Far be it from your servants to do such a thing! 8Behold, the money that we found in the mouths of our sacks we brought back to you from the land of Canaan. How then could we steal silver or gold from your lord's house? 9Whichever of your servants is found with it shall die, and we also will be my lord's servants." 10He said, "Let it be as you say: he who is found with it shall be my servant, and the rest of you shall be innocent." 11Then each man quickly lowered his sack to the ground, and each man opened his sack. 12And he searched, beginning with the eldest and ending with the youngest. And the cup was found in Benjamin's sack. 13Then they tore their clothes, and every man loaded his donkey, and they returned to the city.

14When Judah and his brothers came to Joseph's house, he was still there. They fell before him to the ground. 15Joseph said to them, "What deed is this that you have done? Do you not know that a man like me can indeed practice divination?" 16And Judah said, "What shall we say to my lord? What shall we speak? Or how can we clear ourselves? God has found out the guilt of your servants; behold, we are my lord's servants, both we and he also in whose hand the cup has been found." 17But he said, "Far be it from me that I should do so! Only the man in whose hand the cup was found shall be my servant. But as for you, go up in peace to your father."

18Then Judah went up to him and said, "Oh, my lord, please let your servant speak a word in my lord's ears, and let not your anger burn against your servant, for you are like Pharaoh himself. 19My lord asked his servants, saying, 'Have you a father, or a brother?' 20And we said to my lord, 'We have a father, an old man, and a young brother, the child of his old age. His brother is dead, and he alone is left of his mother's children, and his father loves him.' 21Then you said to your servants, 'Bring him down to me, that I may set my eyes on him.' 22We said to my lord, 'The boy cannot leave his father, for if he should leave his father, his father would die.' 23Then you said to your servants, 'Unless your youngest brother comes down with you, you shall not see my face again.'

24"When we went back to your servant my father, we told him the words of my lord. 25And when our father said, 'Go again, buy us a little food,' 26we said, 'We cannot go down. If our youngest brother goes with us, then we will go down. For we cannot see the man's face unless our youngest brother is with us.' 27Then your servant my father said to us, 'You know that my wife bore me two sons. 28One left me, and I said, "Surely he has been torn to pieces," and I have never seen him since. 29If you take this one also from me, and harm happens to him, you will bring down my gray hairs in evil to Sheol.'

30"Now therefore, as soon as I come to your servant my father, and the boy is not with us, then, as his life is bound up in the boy's life, 31as soon as he sees that the boy is not with us, he will die, and your servants will bring down the gray hairs of your servant our father with sorrow to Sheol. 32For your servant became a pledge of safety for the boy to my father, saying, 'If I do not bring him back to you, then I shall bear the blame before my father all my life.' 33Now therefore, please let your servant remain instead of the boy as a servant to my lord, and let the boy go back with his brothers. 34For how can I go back to my father if the boy is not with me? I fear to see the evil that would find my father."

[1]Septuagint (compare Vulgate) adds *Why have you stolen my silver cup?*

Joseph Provides for His Brothers and Family

45 Then Joseph could not control himself before all those who stood by him.
He cried, "Make everyone go out from me." So no one stayed with him
when Joseph made himself known to his brothers. 2And he wept aloud, so that
the Egyptians heard it, and the household of Pharaoh heard it. 3And Joseph said
to his brothers, "I am Joseph! Is my father still alive?" But his brothers could not
answer him, for they were dismayed at his presence.
4So Joseph said to his brothers, "Come near to me, please." And they came
near. And he said, "I am your brother, Joseph, whom you sold into Egypt. 5And
now do not be distressed or angry with yourselves because you sold me here, for
God sent me before you to preserve life. 6For the famine has been in the land these
two years, and there are yet five years in which there will be neither plowing nor
harvest. 7And God sent me before you to preserve for you a remnant on earth, and
to keep alive for you many survivors. 8So it was not you who sent me here, but God.
He has made me a father to Pharaoh, and lord of all his house and ruler over all the
land of Egypt. 9Hurry and go up to my father and say to him, 'Thus says your son
Joseph, God has made me lord of all Egypt. Come down to me; do not tarry. 10You
shall dwell in the land of Goshen, and you shall be near me, you and your children
and your children's children, and your flocks, your herds, and all that you have.
11There I will provide for you, for there are yet five years of famine to come, so that
you and your household, and all that you have, do not come to poverty.' 12And now
your eyes see, and the eyes of my brother Benjamin see, that it is my mouth that
speaks to you. 13You must tell my father of all my honor in Egypt, and of all that you
have seen. Hurry and bring my father down here." 14Then he fell upon his brother
Benjamin's neck and wept, and Benjamin wept upon his neck. 15And he kissed all
his brothers and wept upon them. After that his brothers talked with him.
16When the report was heard in Pharaoh's house, "Joseph's brothers have
come," it pleased Pharaoh and his servants. 17And Pharaoh said to Joseph, "Say to
your brothers, 'Do this: load your beasts and go back to the land of Canaan, 18and
take your father and your households, and come to me, and I will give you the
best of the land of Egypt, and you shall eat the fat of the land.' 19And you, Joseph,
are commanded to say, 'Do this: take wagons from the land of Egypt for your little
ones and for your wives, and bring your father, and come. 20Have no concern for[1]
your goods, for the best of all the land of Egypt is yours.'"
21The sons of Israel did so: and Joseph gave them wagons, according to the
command of Pharaoh, and gave them provisions for the journey. 22To each and
all of them he gave a change of clothes, but to Benjamin he gave three hundred
shekels[2] of silver and five changes of clothes. 23To his father he sent as follows:
ten donkeys loaded with the good things of Egypt, and ten female donkeys loaded
with grain, bread, and provision for his father on the journey. 24Then he sent his
brothers away, and as they departed, he said to them, "Do not quarrel on the way."
25So they went up out of Egypt and came to the land of Canaan to their father
Jacob. 26And they told him, "Joseph is still alive, and he is ruler over all the land
of Egypt." And his heart became numb, for he did not believe them. 27But when
they told him all the words of Joseph, which he had said to them, and when he
saw the wagons that Joseph had sent to carry him, the spirit of their father Jacob
revived. 28And Israel said, "It is enough; Joseph my son is still alive. I will go and
see him before I die."

Joseph Brings His Family to Egypt

46 So Israel took his journey with all that he had and came to Beersheba, and
offered sacrifices to the God of his father Isaac. 2And God spoke to Israel
in visions of the night and said, "Jacob, Jacob." And he said, "Here I am." 3Then
he said, "I am God, the God of your father. Do not be afraid to go down to Egypt,

---

GENESIS 45:4–7

AN APPOINTED TIME

Joseph beautifully summed up his experience for his brothers, declaring the providence of God in the face of their evil actions. Joseph stated his confidence in the timing of God, the love of God, and the grace of God. God's timing put Joseph in the right position at the right time to save the lives of his family. The providential care of God was still at work behind all the chaos—providing for his chosen ones in the coming drought. And God's grace gave hope and forgiveness in spite of the hurt and sin that Joseph had experienced through the ordeal.

Similarly, Jesus was sent by the Father at the appointed time (Gal 4:4–5). God precisely ordained the time of Christ's coming so that the events would properly unfold, resulting in the salvation of many lives (Ro 5:10). His love was the grand motive for his coming (Jn 3:16), and his grace even offered hope for those who had put him to death (Lk 23:34; Ac 2:22–24,36–38).

---

[1]Hebrew *Let your eye not pity* [2]A *shekel* was about 2/5 ounce or 11 grams

A DWELLING PLACE FOREVER

While Joseph did not know it, his work in Egypt was preparing a place for a provision for his family. God had seen fit to bring Joseph to Egypt, bestowing wisdom upon him, and positioning him to prepare the nation for the impending famine. Joseph gave himself to the work of developing a strategy, building facilities, and preparing the people to store massive amounts of grain. Though they did not recognize Joseph, his hungry brothers asked for his gracious provision of food. Joseph revealed his identity to his brothers who reported the stunning news to their aging father. Joseph's work through his years in Egypt had prepared a blessing for those in his family.

Jesus also indicates that he is preparing a place of blessing for his people. Like Joseph's, Jesus' path to this position is unexpected. He would suffer and die on a Roman cross, be raised to life by the power of God, and ascend to the right hand of the Father. There he works to prepare a place of blessing for the people of God. God pictures the heavenly dwelling like a house with many rooms (Jn 14:2 – 3). He will work to prepare this place for his people between the resurrection and the coming day when God will make all things new.

It is difficult to fathom the splendor of this dwelling place. In the span of six days, Creator God made all things that exist. The vast mountain ranges, breathtaking beaches, and sprawling forests demonstrate the handiwork of God at the dawn of creation. Now, many years later, God is working to prepare a new dwelling in which his people will live forever. Quoting the prophet Isaiah, Paul exclaimed that no eye has seen, no ear has heard, and no mind has conceived what God has prepared for his people (1Co 2:9).

The biblical images of heaven seem to make people grapple for words to describe the glory of this place. The heavenly dwelling, free from the implications of sin, is described as containing streets made of gold and seas as beautiful as crystal. There, God's people will be given the bountiful provision of God's blessing. Free from sin, they will be able to worship God by enjoying fellowship with God, loving one another, giving of themselves in meaningful work, and feasting on the storehouse of God's good gifts that he has prepared for them to enjoy.

for there I will make you into a great nation. 4I myself will go down with you to Egypt, and I will also bring you up again, and Joseph's hand shall close your eyes."

5Then Jacob set out from Beersheba. The sons of Israel carried Jacob their father, their little ones, and their wives, in the wagons that Pharaoh had sent to carry him. 6They also took their livestock and their goods, which they had gained in the land of Canaan, and came into Egypt, Jacob and all his offspring with him, 7his sons, and his sons' sons with him, his daughters, and his sons' daughters. All his offspring he brought with him into Egypt.

8Now these are the names of the descendants of Israel, who came into Egypt, Jacob and his sons. Reuben, Jacob's firstborn, 9and the sons of Reuben: Hanoch, Pallu, Hezron, and Carmi. 10The sons of Simeon: Jemuel, Jamin, Ohad, Jachin, Zohar, and Shaul, the son of a Canaanite woman. 11The sons of Levi: Gershon, Kohath, and Merari. 12The sons of Judah: Er, Onan, Shelah, Perez, and Zerah (but Er and Onan died in the land of Canaan); and the sons of Perez were Hezron and Hamul. 13The sons of Issachar: Tola, Puvah, Yob, and Shimron. 14The sons of Zebulun: Sered, Elon, and Jahleel. 15These are the sons of Leah, whom she bore to Jacob in Paddan-aram, together with his daughter Dinah; altogether his sons and his daughters numbered thirty-three.

16The sons of Gad: Ziphion, Haggi, Shuni, Ezbon, Eri, Arodi, and Areli. 17The sons of Asher: Imnah, Ishvah, Ishvi, Beriah, with Serah their sister. And the sons of Beriah: Heber and Malchiel. 18These are the sons of Zilpah, whom Laban gave to Leah his daughter; and these she bore to Jacob—sixteen persons.

19The sons of Rachel, Jacob's wife: Joseph and Benjamin. 20And to Joseph in the land of Egypt were born Manasseh and Ephraim, whom Asenath, the daughter of Potiphera the priest of On, bore to him. 21And the sons of Benjamin: Bela, Becher, Ashbel, Gera, Naaman, Ehi, Rosh, Muppim, Huppim, and Ard. 22These are the sons of Rachel, who were born to Jacob—fourteen persons in all.

23The son[1] of Dan: Hushim. 24The sons of Naphtali: Jahzeel, Guni, Jezer, and Shillem. 25These are the sons of Bilhah, whom Laban gave to Rachel his daughter, and these she bore to Jacob—seven persons in all.

26All the persons belonging to Jacob who came into Egypt, who were his own descendants, not including Jacob's sons' wives, were sixty-six persons in all. 27And the sons of Joseph, who were born to him in Egypt, were two. All the persons of the house of Jacob who came into Egypt were seventy.

Jacob and Joseph Reunited

28He had sent Judah ahead of him to Joseph to show the way before him in Goshen, and they came into the land of Goshen. 29Then Joseph prepared his chariot and went up to meet Israel his father in Goshen. He presented himself to him and fell on his neck and wept on his neck a good while. 30Israel said to Joseph, "Now let me die, since I have seen your face and know that you are still alive." 31Joseph said to his brothers and to his father's household, "I will go up and tell Pharaoh and will say to him, 'My brothers and my father's household, who were in the land of Canaan, have come to me. 32And the men are shepherds, for they have been keepers of livestock, and they have brought their flocks and their herds and all that they have.' 33When Pharaoh calls you and says, 'What is your occupation?' 34you shall say, 'Your servants have been keepers of livestock from our youth even until now, both we and our fathers,' in order that you may dwell in the land of Goshen, for every shepherd is an abomination to the Egyptians."

Jacob's Family Settles in Goshen

47 So Joseph went in and told Pharaoh, "My father and my brothers, with their flocks and herds and all that they possess, have come from the land of Canaan. They are now in the land of Goshen." 2And from among his brothers

[1]Hebrew *sons*

he took five men and presented them to Pharaoh. 3 Pharaoh said to his brothers,
"What is your occupation?" And they said to Pharaoh, "Your servants are shepherds, as our fathers were." 4 They said to Pharaoh, "We have come to sojourn in
the land, for there is no pasture for your servants' flocks, for the famine is severe
in the land of Canaan. And now, please let your servants dwell in the land of Goshen." 5 Then Pharaoh said to Joseph, "Your father and your brothers have come to
you. 6 The land of Egypt is before you. Settle your father and your brothers in the
best of the land. Let them settle in the land of Goshen, and if you know any able
men among them, put them in charge of my livestock."

7 Then Joseph brought in Jacob his father and stood him before Pharaoh, and
Jacob blessed Pharaoh. 8 And Pharaoh said to Jacob, "How many are the days of
the years of your life?" 9 And Jacob said to Pharaoh, "The days of the years of my
sojourning are 130 years. Few and evil have been the days of the years of my life,
and they have not attained to the days of the years of the life of my fathers in
the days of their sojourning." 10 And Jacob blessed Pharaoh and went out from
the presence of Pharaoh. 11 Then Joseph settled his father and his brothers and
gave them a possession in the land of Egypt, in the best of the land, in the land
of Rameses, as Pharaoh had commanded. 12 And Joseph provided his father, his
brothers, and all his father's household with food, according to the number of
their dependents.

Joseph and the Famine

13 Now there was no food in all the land, for the famine was very severe, so that
the land of Egypt and the land of Canaan languished by reason of the famine.
14 And Joseph gathered up all the money that was found in the land of Egypt and
in the land of Canaan, in exchange for the grain that they bought. And Joseph
brought the money into Pharaoh's house. 15 And when the money was all spent in
the land of Egypt and in the land of Canaan, all the Egyptians came to Joseph and
said, "Give us food. Why should we die before your eyes? For our money is gone."
16 And Joseph answered, "Give your livestock, and I will give you food in exchange
for your livestock, if your money is gone." 17 So they brought their livestock to
Joseph, and Joseph gave them food in exchange for the horses, the flocks, the
herds, and the donkeys. He supplied them with food in exchange for all their livestock that year. 18 And when that year was ended, they came to him the following
year and said to him, "We will not hide from my lord that our money is all spent.
The herds of livestock are my lord's. There is nothing left in the sight of my lord
but our bodies and our land. 19 Why should we die before your eyes, both we and
our land? Buy us and our land for food, and we with our land will be servants to
Pharaoh. And give us seed that we may live and not die, and that the land may
not be desolate."

20 So Joseph bought all the land of Egypt for Pharaoh, for all the Egyptians sold
their fields, because the famine was severe on them. The land became Pharaoh's.
21 As for the people, he made servants of them[1] from one end of Egypt to the other.
22 Only the land of the priests he did not buy, for the priests had a fixed allowance
from Pharaoh and lived on the allowance that Pharaoh gave them; therefore they
did not sell their land.

23 Then Joseph said to the people, "Behold, I have this day bought you and your
land for Pharaoh. Now here is seed for you, and you shall sow the land. 24 And at
the harvests you shall give a fifth to Pharaoh, and four fifths shall be your own, as
seed for the field and as food for yourselves and your households, and as food for
your little ones." 25 And they said, "You have saved our lives; may it please my lord,
we will be servants to Pharaoh." 26 So Joseph made it a statute concerning the land
of Egypt, and it stands to this day, that Pharaoh should have the fifth; the land of
the priests alone did not become Pharaoh's.

[1] Samaritan, Septuagint, Vulgate; Hebrew *he removed them to the cities*

27 Thus Israel settled in the land of Egypt, in the land of Goshen. And they
gained possessions in it, and were fruitful and multiplied greatly. 28 And Jacob
lived in the land of Egypt seventeen years. So the days of Jacob, the years of his
life, were 147 years.

29 And when the time drew near that Israel must die, he called his son Joseph and said to him, "If now I have found favor in your sight, put your hand
under my thigh and promise to deal kindly and truly with me. Do not bury me
in Egypt, 30 but let me lie with my fathers. Carry me out of Egypt and bury me
in their burying place." He answered, "I will do as you have said." 31 And he said,
"Swear to me"; and he swore to him. Then Israel bowed himself upon the head
of his bed.[1]

Jacob Blesses Ephraim and Manasseh

48 After this, Joseph was told, "Behold, your father is ill." So he took with
him his two sons, Manasseh and Ephraim. 2 And it was told to Jacob, "Your
son Joseph has come to you." Then Israel summoned his strength and sat up in
bed. 3 And Jacob said to Joseph, "God Almighty[2] appeared to me at Luz in the land
of Canaan and blessed me, 4 and said to me, 'Behold, I will make you fruitful and
multiply you, and I will make of you a company of peoples and will give this land
to your offspring after you for an everlasting possession.' 5 And now your two
sons, who were born to you in the land of Egypt before I came to you in Egypt, are
mine; Ephraim and Manasseh shall be mine, as Reuben and Simeon are. 6 And the
children that you fathered after them shall be yours. They shall be called by the
name of their brothers in their inheritance. 7 As for me, when I came from Pad-
dan, to my sorrow Rachel died in the land of Canaan on the way, when there was
still some distance[3] to go to Ephrath, and I buried her there on the way to Ephrath
(that is, Bethlehem)."

8 When Israel saw Joseph's sons, he said, "Who are these?" 9 Joseph said to his
father, "They are my sons, whom God has given me here." And he said, "Bring
them to me, please, that I may bless them." 10 Now the eyes of Israel were dim
with age, so that he could not see. So Joseph brought them near him, and he
kissed them and embraced them. 11 And Israel said to Joseph, "I never expected
to see your face; and behold, God has let me see your offspring also." 12 Then
Joseph removed them from his knees, and he bowed himself with his face to the
earth. 13 And Joseph took them both, Ephraim in his right hand toward Israel's
left hand, and Manasseh in his left hand toward Israel's right hand, and brought
them near him. 14 And Israel stretched out his right hand and laid it on the head
of Ephraim, who was the younger, and his left hand on the head of Manasseh,
crossing his hands (for Manasseh was the firstborn). 15 And he blessed Joseph
and said,

"The God before whom my fathers Abraham and Isaac walked,
the God who has been my shepherd all my life long to
this day,
16 the angel who has redeemed me from all evil, bless the boys;
and in them let my name be carried on, and the name of my
fathers Abraham and Isaac;
and let them grow into a multitude[4] in the midst of the
earth."

17 When Joseph saw that his father laid his right hand on the head of Ephraim,
it displeased him, and he took his father's hand to move it from Ephraim's head to
Manasseh's head. 18 And Joseph said to his father, "Not this way, my father; since
this one is the firstborn, put your right hand on his head." 19 But his father refused
and said, "I know, my son, I know. He also shall become a people, and he also

[1] Hebrew; Septuagint *staff* [2] Hebrew *El Shaddai* [3] Or *about two hours' distance* [4] Or *let them be like fish for multitude*

shall be great. Nevertheless, his younger brother shall be greater than he, and his offspring shall become a multitude[1] of nations." 20So he blessed them that day, saying,

"By you Israel will pronounce blessings, saying,
'God make you as Ephraim and as Manasseh.'"

Thus he put Ephraim before Manasseh. 21Then Israel said to Joseph, "Behold, I am about to die, but God will be with you and will bring you again to the land of your fathers. 22Moreover, I have given to you rather than to your brothers one mountain slope[2] that I took from the hand of the Amorites with my sword and with my bow."

Jacob Blesses His Sons

49 Then Jacob called his sons and said, "Gather yourselves together, that I may tell you what shall happen to you in days to come.

2 "Assemble and listen, O sons of Jacob,
listen to Israel your father.

3 "Reuben, you are my firstborn,
my might, and the firstfruits of my strength,
preeminent in dignity and preeminent in power.
4 Unstable as water, you shall not have preeminence,
because you went up to your father's bed;
then you defiled it—he went up to my couch!

5 "Simeon and Levi are brothers;
weapons of violence are their swords.
6 Let my soul come not into their council;
O my glory, be not joined to their company.
For in their anger they killed men,
and in their willfulness they hamstrung oxen.
7 Cursed be their anger, for it is fierce,
and their wrath, for it is cruel!
I will divide them in Jacob
and scatter them in Israel.

8 "Judah, your brothers shall praise you;
your hand shall be on the neck of your enemies;
your father's sons shall bow down before you.
9 Judah is a lion's cub;
from the prey, my son, you have gone up.
He stooped down; he crouched as a lion
and as a lioness; who dares rouse him?
10 The scepter shall not depart from Judah,
nor the ruler's staff from between his feet,
until tribute comes to him;[3]
and to him shall be the obedience of the peoples.
11 Binding his foal to the vine
and his donkey's colt to the choice vine,
he has washed his garments in wine
and his vesture in the blood of grapes.
12 His eyes are darker than wine,
and his teeth whiter than milk.

GENESIS 49:10

THE RULING KING FROM JUDAH

The royal lineage of Jesus is foreshadowed in the images of this text. The scepter was an ornate rod used by kings to communicate their authoritative dictates. Those in power could grant laws and enact judgment should one fail to submit to their rule. This verse refers to the divine King and Lawgiver who would come from the line of Judah to fulfill the promises of this passage. To this King, all people, not simply those of a certain earthly kingdom, would owe their allegiance.

Jesus, the King from the tribe of Judah, ushers in the kingdom of God and announces the rule and reign of God through his incarnation. One day, all people (in heaven, on earth, and under the earth) will bow at his very name (Php 2:9–11). As the great suffering servant, his earthly ministry and his execution via a criminal's death seem to undermine his cosmic rule. But his victorious resurrection and glorious ascension vindicate his claim to deity and establish him as the King of kings and Lord of lords and the One to whom all people owe their worship (Ro 1:4).

[1]Hebrew *fullness* [2]Or *one portion of the land*; Hebrew *shekem*, which sounds like the town and district called *Shechem* [3]By a slight revocalization; a slight emendation yields (compare Septuagint, Syriac, Targum) *until he comes to whom it belongs*; Hebrew *until Shiloh comes*, or *until he comes to Shiloh*

13 "Zebulun shall dwell at the shore of the sea;
he shall become a haven for ships,
and his border shall be at Sidon.

14 "Issachar is a strong donkey,
crouching between the sheepfolds.[1]
15 He saw that a resting place was good,
and that the land was pleasant,
so he bowed his shoulder to bear,
and became a servant at forced labor.

16 "Dan shall judge his people
as one of the tribes of Israel.
17 Dan shall be a serpent in the way,
a viper by the path,
that bites the horse's heels
so that his rider falls backward.
18 I wait for your salvation, O LORD.

19 "Raiders shall raid Gad,[2]
but he shall raid at their heels.

20 "Asher's food shall be rich,
and he shall yield royal delicacies.

21 "Naphtali is a doe let loose
that bears beautiful fawns.[3]

22 "Joseph is a fruitful bough,
a fruitful bough by a spring;
his branches run over the wall.[4]
23 The archers bitterly attacked him,
shot at him, and harassed him severely,
24 yet his bow remained unmoved;
his arms[5] were made agile
by the hands of the Mighty One of Jacob
(from there is the Shepherd,[6] the Stone of Israel),
25 by the God of your father who will help you,
by the Almighty[7] who will bless you
with blessings of heaven above,
blessings of the deep that crouches beneath,
blessings of the breasts and of the womb.
26 The blessings of your father
are mighty beyond the blessings of my parents,
up to the bounties of the everlasting hills.[8]
May they be on the head of Joseph,
and on the brow of him who was set apart from his brothers.

27 "Benjamin is a ravenous wolf,
in the morning devouring the prey
and at evening dividing the spoil."

Jacob's Death and Burial

28 *All these* are the twelve tribes of Israel. This is what their father said to them
as he blessed them, blessing each with the blessing suitable to him. 29 Then he

[1]Or *between its saddlebags* [2]*Gad* sounds like the Hebrew for *raiders* and *raid* [3]Or *he gives beautiful words*, or *that bears fawns of the fold* [4]Or *Joseph is a wild donkey, a wild donkey beside a spring, his wild colts beside the wall* [5]Hebrew *the arms of his hands* [6]Or *by the name of the Shepherd* [7]Hebrew *Shaddai*
[8]A slight emendation yields (compare Septuagint) *the blessings of the eternal mountains, the bounties of the everlasting hills*

commanded them and said to them, "I am to be gathered to my people; bury me with my fathers in the cave that is in the field of Ephron the Hittite, 30 in the cave that is in the field at Machpelah, to the east of Mamre, in the land of Canaan, which Abraham bought with the field from Ephron the Hittite to possess as a burying place. 31 There they buried Abraham and Sarah his wife. There they buried Isaac and Rebekah his wife, and there I buried Leah— 32 the field and the cave that is in it were bought from the Hittites." 33 When Jacob finished commanding his sons, he drew up his feet into the bed and breathed his last and was gathered to his people.

50 Then Joseph fell on his father's face and wept over him and kissed him. 2 And Joseph commanded his servants the physicians to embalm his father. So the physicians embalmed Israel. 3 Forty days were required for it, for that is how many are required for embalming. And the Egyptians wept for him seventy days.

4 And when the days of weeping for him were past, Joseph spoke to the household of Pharaoh, saying, "If now I have found favor in your eyes, please speak in the ears of Pharaoh, saying, 5 'My father made me swear, saying, "I am about to die: in my tomb that I hewed out for myself in the land of Canaan, there shall you bury me." Now therefore, let me please go up and bury my father. Then I will return.'" 6 And Pharaoh answered, "Go up, and bury your father, as he made you swear." 7 So Joseph went up to bury his father. With him went up all the servants of Pharaoh, the elders of his household, and all the elders of the land of Egypt, 8 as well as all the household of Joseph, his brothers, and his father's household. Only their children, their flocks, and their herds were left in the land of Goshen. 9 And there went up with him both chariots and horsemen. It was a very great company. 10 When they came to the threshing floor of Atad, which is beyond the Jordan, they lamented there with a very great and grievous lamentation, and he made a mourning for his father seven days. 11 When the inhabitants of the land, the Canaanites, saw the mourning on the threshing floor of Atad, they said, "This is a grievous mourning by the Egyptians." Therefore the place was named Abel-mizraim;[1] it is beyond the Jordan. 12 Thus his sons did for him as he had commanded them, 13 for his sons carried him to the land of Canaan and buried him in the cave of the field at Machpelah, to the east of Mamre, which Abraham bought with the field from Ephron the Hittite to possess as a burying place. 14 After he had buried his father, Joseph returned to Egypt with his brothers and all who had gone up with him to bury his father.

God's Good Purposes

15 When Joseph's brothers saw that their father was dead, they said, "It may be that Joseph will hate us and pay us back for all the evil that we did to him." 16 So they sent a message to Joseph, saying, "Your father gave this command before he died: 17 'Say to Joseph, "Please forgive the transgression of your brothers and their sin, because they did evil to you."' And now, please forgive the transgression of the servants of the God of your father." Joseph wept when they spoke to him. 18 His brothers also came and fell down before him and said, "Behold, we are your servants." 19 But Joseph said to them, "Do not fear, for am I in the place of God? 20 As for you, you meant evil against me, but God meant it for good, to bring it about that many people[2] should be kept alive, as they are today. 21 So do not fear; I will provide for you and your little ones." Thus he comforted them and spoke kindly to them.

The Death of Joseph

22 So Joseph remained in Egypt, he and his father's house. Joseph lived 110 years. 23 And Joseph saw Ephraim's children of the third generation. The children

[1] *Abel-mizraim* means *mourning* (or *meadow*) *of Egypt* [2] Or *a numerous people*

MEANT FOR EVIL, USED FOR GOOD

God rules and reigns over all things and orchestrates the events of this world to perfectly fulfill his good intentions for his creation. This hope is magnified in light of the depth of human sin and the systemic evil at work in the world. God is capable of taking every facet of life, even great evil, and working it together to accomplish his will.

This truth is demonstrated profoundly in Joseph's life. The outcast brother, sold into slavery and forgotten in prison, finds himself second in command in all of Egypt. His brothers' actions, though malicious, were used by God in order to position Joseph to save his brothers and his family when they needed food in order to escape the famine. While Joseph may never have chosen the path his life took, he could look back at the course of his life and see the ever-present hand of God. Joseph affirmed the grand scope of the sovereignty of God when he reassured his brothers that the things they meant for evil were ultimately under the authority of God. No evil plan of humans could thwart the purposes of a sovereign God.

God demonstrates his sovereign hand throughout the continued history of his people. He takes all things, even their rebellion, and uses them to accomplish even greater good. The greatest experience of human depravity is seen in the brutal murder of the perfect Son of God. At the cross, it would seem that the religious leaders, Roman authorities, and Satan himself had emerged victorious. Yet, as with the life of Joseph, God was orchestrating these unthinkable acts in order to accomplish the great good of satisfying the wrath of God through the death of his Son.

Believers can find hope to face the complex, and often tumultuous, circumstances of life in a fallen world with the knowledge of the sovereign rule and reign of God. Paul reminds the church in Rome that all things, even suffering and sin, "work together for good, for those who are called according to his purpose" (Ro 8:28). God is not surprised by evil. He is not at a loss for how to respond. His plans cannot be defeated, and he will accomplish everything exactly as he intends.

also of Machir the son of Manasseh were counted as Joseph's own.[1] 24And Joseph
said to his brothers, "I am about to die, but God will visit you and bring you up out
of this land to the land that he swore to Abraham, to Isaac, and to Jacob." 25Then
Joseph made the sons of Israel swear, saying, "God will surely visit you, and you
shall carry up my bones from here." 26So Joseph died, being 110 years old. They
embalmed him, and he was put in a coffin in Egypt.

GENESIS 50:24

THE GOD OF ABRAHAM, ISAAC, AND JACOB

Approaching death, Joseph reassured his family of the covenant faithfulness of God. The threefold repetition of the names Abraham, Isaac, and Jacob is used through the Pentateuch to describe the recipients of the promises God made to Abram in Genesis 12:1–3 (Ge 48:15; 49:29–31; Ex 2:24; 3:16). Joseph recognized that his death was not the culmination of the work of God on behalf of the people of God. This work did not depend on Joseph; rather it rested on the faithfulness of God. Joseph knew that God was always faithful to his promises and would surely bring the nation of Israel into the good land that he had pledged to them as their inheritance. God's covenantal faithfulness led him to send Jesus as the fulfillment of the promises he made to Abraham, Isaac, and Jacob. The hope of Joseph's life found its fulfillment in the sending of the Savior.

[1]Hebrew *were born on Joseph's knees*

JESUS: OUR MIRACULOUS DELIVERER

EXODUS

EXODUS

ISRAELITES ENSLAVED IN EGYPT *c. 1600 BC*	MOSES IS BORN *c. 1526 BC*	EXODUS FROM EGYPT *c. 1446 BC*

The book of Exodus describes a climactic moment in the life of the people of God — their deliverance from slavery in Egypt by the mighty hand of the Lord. The population of Israel in Exodus is the fulfillment of God's promise to Abram/Abraham in Genesis 12:1 – 3; these people, whom God had called as his chosen ones, and their descendants serve as a central focus throughout the remainder of the Old Testament.

God called Moses, the main character in Exodus, to lead the people out of Egypt. In spite of Moses' initial protests to God, Moses approached the hard-hearted Pharaoh and implored him to release God's people from slavery. When Pharaoh refused, God began his process of deliverance, demonstrating the scope of his might and power. Following his work of deliverance, God gave his people the Law so they could understand how they should respond to God's grace and fulfill their calling to be "a kingdom of priests and a holy nation" (19:6).

The first section of Exodus (chs. 1 – 18) describes in glorious detail the way that God prevailed over the greatest world power at that time — the nation of Egypt. Through his miraculous might, God demonstrated his supremacy over the false gods of the nations and the sinful hearts of kings. The Hebrew people continually recounted the wonders of God's might throughout the book of Exodus, and, in fact, still celebrate this deliverance today.

The second section (chs. 19 – 40) outlines the Law of God, given as a benevolent gift of grace by a personal God to his chosen people. They represent his unique nature and character, demonstrating that God is righteous, holy in all things, and rightly deserving of the worship of those whom he has saved. The book ends with the completion of the tabernacle, which stands as the center point of their encampment and the central place of worship for God's people throughout their journey in the wilderness.

The book of Exodus portrays Moses as a God-ordained redeemer of the people of God. For this reason he serves as a type of messiah, a precursor to the One who was to come, Jesus Christ. Like Moses, Jesus would serve in three roles: as a prophet — communicating God's word to the people; as a priest — making it possible for humankind to worship God rightly; and as a king — leading the people from slavery into safety. The historical events of this book, such as the Passover (ch. 12), prefigure the atoning work of Christ for the sins of his people (Jn 1:29,36; 1Co 5:7). Christ is the perfect sacrifice, the fulfillment of the Old Testament law (Mt 5:17), and the One who breaks the shackles of sin and delivers his people forever.

FEAR NOT, STAND FIRM, AND
SEE THE SALVATION OF THE LORD,
WHICH HE WILL WORK FOR YOU TODAY.

Exodus 14:13

EXODUS

Israel Increases Greatly in Egypt

1 These are the names of the sons of Israel who came to Egypt with Jacob, each with his household: 2Reuben, Simeon, Levi, and Judah, 3Issachar, Zebulun, and Benjamin, 4Dan and Naphtali, Gad and Asher. 5All the descendants of Jacob were seventy persons; Joseph was already in Egypt. 6Then Joseph died, and all his brothers and all that generation. 7But the people of Israel were fruitful and increased greatly; they multiplied and grew exceedingly strong, so that the land was filled with them.

Pharaoh Oppresses Israel

8Now there arose a new king over Egypt, who did not know Joseph. 9And he said to his people, "Behold, the people of Israel are too many and too mighty for us. 10Come, let us deal shrewdly with them, lest they multiply, and, if war breaks out, they join our enemies and fight against us and escape from the land." 11Therefore they set taskmasters over them to afflict them with heavy burdens. They built for Pharaoh store cities, Pithom and Raamses. 12But the more they were oppressed, the more they multiplied and the more they spread abroad. And the Egyptians were in dread of the people of Israel. 13So they ruthlessly made the people of Israel work as slaves 14and made their lives bitter with hard service, in mortar and brick, and in all kinds of work in the field. In all their work they ruthlessly made them work as slaves.

15Then the king of Egypt said to the Hebrew midwives, one of whom was named Shiphrah and the other Puah, 16"When you serve as midwife to the Hebrew women and see them on the birthstool, if it is a son, you shall kill him, but if it is a daughter, she shall live." 17But the midwives feared God and did not do as the king of Egypt commanded them, but let the male children live. 18So the king of Egypt called the midwives and said to them, "Why have you done this, and let the male children live?" 19The midwives said to Pharaoh, "Because the Hebrew women are not like the Egyptian women, for they are vigorous and give birth before the midwife comes to them." 20So God dealt well with the midwives. And the people multiplied and grew very strong. 21And because the midwives feared God, he gave them families. 22Then Pharaoh commanded all his people, "Every son that is born to the Hebrews[1] you shall cast into the Nile, but you shall let every daughter live."

The Birth of Moses

2 Now a man from the house of Levi went and took as his wife a Levite woman. 2The woman conceived and bore a son, and when she saw that he was a fine child, she hid him three months. 3When she could hide him no longer, she took for him a basket made of bulrushes[2] and daubed it with bitumen and pitch. She put the child in it and placed it among the reeds by the river bank. 4And his sister stood at a distance to know what would be done to him. 5Now the daughter of Pharaoh came down to bathe at the river, while her young women walked beside the river. She saw the basket among the reeds and sent her servant woman, and she took it. 6When she opened it, she saw the child, and *behold*, the baby was crying. She took pity on him and said, "This is one of the Hebrews' children." 7Then his sister said to Pharaoh's daughter, "Shall I go and call you a nurse from the Hebrew women to nurse the child for you?" 8And Pharaoh's daughter said to her, "Go." So the girl went and called the child's mother. 9And Pharaoh's daughter said to her, "Take this child away and nurse him for

[1]Samaritan, Septuagint, Targum; Hebrew lacks *to the Hebrews* [2]Hebrew *papyrus reeds*

EXODUS 1:6–7

MULTIPLICATION

In spite of the sin of humanity, God was faithful to allow people to fulfill their created design. They were fruitful, multiplied, and filled the earth (Ge 1:26–28). God's promise to Abraham was proven true. His children were as numerous as the stars in the sky (Ge 15:5) and the sand on the shore (Ge 22:17). These promises, made to the patriarch and his barren wife, were seemingly hopeless. But God acted by providing a son for Abraham and Sarah and greatly multiplied subsequent generations in spite of their sin and rebellion.

The abundance of the people of Israel is only a small microcosm of the people whom God would call to himself across the span of the centuries. Paul wrote in Galatians 3:26–29 that all those who place their faith in Christ are heirs of the promise made to Abraham and seen at the outset of the book of Exodus. Now God's people, by virtue of the grace of God, fill the globe testifying to the faithfulness of God to sustain his people forever.

EXODUS 2:1–10

DRAWN OUT OF THE WATER

Moses was born to parents from the house of Levi, which eventually became the priestly family for Israel. After three months, Moses' mother placed him in a basket to protect him from murder at the hands of

(continued on next page)

me, and I will give you your wages." So the woman took the child and nursed him. 10When the child grew older, she brought him to Pharaoh's daughter, and he became her son. She named him Moses, "Because," she said, "I drew him out of the water."[1]

Moses Flees to Midian

11One day, when Moses had grown up, he went out to his people and looked on their burdens, and he saw an Egyptian beating a Hebrew, one of his people.[2] 12He looked this way and that, and seeing no one, he struck down the Egyptian and hid him in the sand. 13When he went out the next day, behold, two Hebrews were struggling together. And he said to the man in the wrong, "Why do you strike your companion?" 14He answered, "Who made you a prince and a judge over us? Do you mean to kill me as you killed the Egyptian?" Then Moses was afraid, and thought, "Surely the thing is known." 15When Pharaoh heard of it, he sought to kill Moses. But Moses fled from Pharaoh and stayed in the land of Midian. And he sat down by a well.

16Now the priest of Midian had seven daughters, and they came and drew water and filled the troughs to water their father's flock. 17The shepherds came and drove them away, but Moses stood up and saved them, and watered their flock. 18When they came home to their father Reuel, he said, "How is it that you have come home so soon today?" 19They said, "An Egyptian delivered us out of the hand of the shepherds and even drew water for us and watered the flock." 20He said to his daughters, "Then where is he? Why have you left the man? Call him, that he may eat bread." 21And Moses was content to dwell with the man, and he gave Moses his daughter Zipporah. 22She gave birth to a son, and he called his name Gershom, for he said, "I have been a sojourner[3] in a foreign land."

God Hears Israel's Groaning

23During those many days the king of Egypt died, and the people of Israel groaned because of their slavery and cried out for help. Their cry for rescue from slavery came up to God. 24And God heard their groaning, and God remembered his covenant with Abraham, with Isaac, and with Jacob. 25God saw the people of Israel—and God knew.

The Burning Bush

3 Now Moses was keeping the flock of his father-in-law, Jethro, the priest of Midian, and he led his flock to the west side of the wilderness and came to Horeb, the mountain of God. 2And the angel of the LORD appeared to him in a flame of fire out of the midst of a bush. He looked, and behold, the bush was burning, yet it was not consumed. 3And Moses said, "I will turn aside to see this great sight, why the bush is not burned." 4When the LORD saw that he turned aside to see, God called to him out of the bush, "Moses, Moses!" And he said, "Here I am." 5Then he said, "Do not come near; take your sandals off your feet, for the place on which you are standing is holy ground." 6And he said, "I am the God of your father, the God of Abraham, the God of Isaac, and the God of Jacob." And Moses hid his face, for he was afraid to look at God.

7Then the LORD said, "I have surely seen the affliction of my people who are in Egypt and have heard their cry because of their taskmasters. I know their sufferings, 8and I have come down to deliver them out of the hand of the Egyptians and to bring them up out of that land to a good and broad land, a land flowing with milk and honey, to the place of the Canaanites, the Hittites, the Amorites, the Perizzites, the Hivites, and the Jebusites. 9And now, behold, the cry of the people of Israel has come to me, and I have also seen the oppression with which

[1]*Moses* sounds like the Hebrew for *draw out* [2]Hebrew *brothers* [3]*Gershom* sounds like the Hebrew for *sojourner*

(Drawn Out of the Water, continued)

Pharaoh. Like the ark that protected Noah, this small basket sustained Moses until Pharaoh's daughter found him. The daughter was ill-equipped to nurse a baby, so she called a Hebrew woman, the mother of Moses, to nurse the child. Miraculously, God provided deliverance for the baby, but he did so through the very one who tried to destroy him. Moses was adopted by Pharaoh's daughter and was raised in Pharaoh's house. Moses' Egyptian name means "is born," which sounds like the Hebrew for "draw out," thus testifying to God's deliverance of his ordained leader from the waters of the Nile.

In a similar fashion, God protected Jesus at the outset of his ministry from the hand of Herod, who wanted to destroy any threat to his throne by killing all Jewish boys two years old and under (Mt 2:13–16). Like Moses, Jesus was delivered by God from the enemy and was positioned to fulfill God's appointed plan for his life.

EXODUS 3:14

"I AM"

God provided his people with a name that denotes his uncaused, independent, and eternal character. Moses, faced with the unenviable task of asking Pharaoh for the freedom of the Israelites, asked God for his name. He knew that the Israelites would ask for the name of the one who gave Moses these instructions. God told Moses to call him, "I AM." He is and will always be. He owes nothing and no one for his existence. Rather, he is the supreme, uncreated, sovereign, and sole God of the universe. All things owe their being to him.

Jesus used this same name to declare his identity during his earthly ministry. While the people argued about the relationship of Jesus to the promises God made to Abraham, Jesus defied their understanding by declaring that he is not merely one in a long line of those whom God uses. Rather, he is the "I am" (Jn 8:58). The immense nature of this claim caused many to attempt to stone Jesus because they knew the implications of this term. By using this term Jesus announced himself to be God, committing the ultimate sin of blasphemy in the minds of his Jewish audience. They simply could not comprehend that this carpenter from Nazareth could be the very Son of God, in human form, to whom all people owe their *allegiance and worship.*

the Egyptians oppress them. 10Come, I will send you to Pharaoh that you may bring my people, the children of Israel, out of Egypt." 11But Moses said to God, "Who am I that I should go to Pharaoh and bring the children of Israel out of Egypt?" 12He said, "But I will be with you, and this shall be the sign for you, that I have sent you: when you have brought the people out of Egypt, you shall serve God on this mountain."

13Then Moses said to God, "If I come to the people of Israel and say to them, 'The God of your fathers has sent me to you,' and they ask me, 'What is his name?' what shall I say to them?" 14God said to Moses, "I AM WHO I AM."[1] And he said, "Say this to the people of Israel: 'I AM has sent me to you.'" 15God also said to Moses, "Say this to the people of Israel: 'The LORD,[2] the God of your fathers, the God of Abraham, the God of Isaac, and the God of Jacob, has sent me to you.' This is my name forever, and thus I am to be remembered throughout all generations. 16Go and gather the elders of Israel together and say to them, 'The LORD, the God of your fathers, the God of Abraham, of Isaac, and of Jacob, has appeared to me, saying, "I have observed you and what has been done to you in Egypt, 17and I promise that I will bring you up out of the affliction of Egypt to the land of the Canaanites, the Hittites, the Amorites, the Perizzites, the Hivites, and the Jebusites, a land flowing with milk and honey."' 18And they will listen to your voice, and you and the elders of Israel shall go to the king of Egypt and say to him, 'The LORD, the God of the Hebrews, has met with us; and now, please let us go a three days' journey into the wilderness, that we may sacrifice to the LORD our God.' 19But I know that the king of Egypt will not let you go unless compelled by a mighty hand.[3] 20So I will stretch out my hand and strike Egypt with all the wonders that I will do in it; after that he will let you go. 21And I will give this people favor in the sight of the Egyptians; and when you go, you shall not go empty, 22but each woman shall ask of her neighbor, and any woman who lives in her house, for silver and gold jewelry, and for clothing. You shall put them on your sons and on your daughters. So you shall plunder the Egyptians."

Moses Given Powerful Signs

4 Then Moses answered, "But behold, they will not believe me or listen to my voice, for they will say, 'The LORD did not appear to you.'" 2The LORD said to him, "What is that in your hand?" He said, "A staff." 3And he said, "Throw it on the ground." So he threw it on the ground, and it became a serpent, and Moses ran from it. 4But the LORD said to Moses, "Put out your hand and catch it by the tail"—so he put out his hand and caught it, and it became a staff in his hand— 5"that they may believe that the LORD, the God of their fathers, the God of Abraham, the God of Isaac, and the God of Jacob, has appeared to you." 6Again, the LORD said to him, "Put your hand inside your cloak."[4] And he put his hand inside his cloak, and when he took it out, behold, his hand was leprous[5] like snow. 7Then God said, "Put your hand back inside your cloak." So he put his hand back inside his cloak, and when he took it out, behold, it was restored like the rest of his flesh. 8"If they will not believe you," God said, "or listen to the first sign, they may believe the latter sign. 9If they will not believe even these two signs or listen to your voice, you shall take some water from the Nile and pour it on the dry ground, and the water that you shall take from the Nile will become blood on the dry ground."

10But Moses said to the LORD, "Oh, my Lord, I am not eloquent, either in the past or since you have spoken to your servant, but I am slow of speech and of tongue." 11Then the LORD said to him, "Who has made man's mouth? Who makes him mute, or deaf, or seeing, or blind? Is it not I, the LORD? 12Now therefore go,

[1]Or *I AM WHAT I AM*, or *I WILL BE WHAT I WILL BE* [2]The word *LORD*, when spelled with capital letters, stands for the divine name, *YHWH*, which is here connected with the verb *hayah*, "to be" in verse 14 [3]Septuagint, Vulgate; Hebrew *go, not by a mighty hand* [4]Hebrew *into your bosom*; also verse 7 [5]*Leprosy* was a term for several skin diseases; see Leviticus 13

and I will be with your mouth and teach you what you shall speak." 13But he said, "Oh, my Lord, please send someone else." 14Then the anger of the LORD was kindled against Moses and he said, "Is there not Aaron, your brother, the Levite? I know that he can speak well. Behold, he is coming out to meet you, and when he sees you, he will be glad in his heart. 15You shall speak to him and put the words in his mouth, and I will be with your mouth and with his mouth and will teach you both what to do. 16He shall speak for you to the people, and he shall be your mouth, and you shall be as God to him. 17And take in your hand this staff, with which you shall do the signs."

Moses Returns to Egypt

18Moses went back to Jethro his father-in-law and said to him, "Please let me go back to my brothers in Egypt to see whether they are still alive." And Jethro said to Moses, "Go in peace." 19And the LORD said to Moses in Midian, "Go back to Egypt, for all the men who were seeking your life are dead." 20So Moses took his wife and his sons and had them ride on a donkey, and went back to the land of Egypt. And Moses took the staff of God in his hand.

21And the LORD said to Moses, "When you go back to Egypt, see that you do before Pharaoh all the miracles that I have put in your power. But I will harden his heart, so that he will not let the people go. 22Then you shall say to Pharaoh, 'Thus says the LORD, Israel is my firstborn son, 23and I say to you, "Let my son go that he may serve me." If you refuse to let him go, behold, I will kill your firstborn son.'"

24At a lodging place on the way the LORD met him and sought to put him to death. 25Then Zipporah took a flint and cut off her son's foreskin and touched Moses'[1] feet with it and said, "Surely you are a bridegroom of blood to me!" 26So he let him alone. It was then that she said, "A bridegroom of blood," because of the circumcision.

27The LORD said to Aaron, "Go into the wilderness to meet Moses." So he went and met him at the mountain of God and kissed him. 28And Moses told Aaron all the words of the LORD with which he had sent him to speak, and all the signs that he had commanded him to do. 29Then Moses and Aaron went and gathered together all the elders of the people of Israel. 30Aaron spoke all the words that the LORD had spoken to Moses and did the signs in the sight of the people. 31And the people believed; and when they heard that the LORD had visited the people of Israel and that he had seen their affliction, they bowed their heads and worshiped.

Making Bricks Without Straw

5 Afterward Moses and Aaron went and said to Pharaoh, "Thus says the LORD, the God of Israel, 'Let my people go, that they may hold a feast to me in the wilderness.'" 2But Pharaoh said, "Who is the LORD, that I should obey his voice and let Israel go? I do not know the LORD, and moreover, I will not let Israel go." 3Then they said, "The God of the Hebrews has met with us. Please let us go a three days' journey into the wilderness that we may sacrifice to the LORD our God, lest he fall upon us with pestilence or with the sword." 4But the king of Egypt said to them, "Moses and Aaron, why do you take the people away from their work? Get back to your burdens." 5And Pharaoh said, "Behold, the people of the land are now many,[2] and you make them rest from their burdens!" 6The same day Pharaoh commanded the taskmasters of the people and their foremen, 7"You shall no longer give the people straw to make bricks, as in the past; let them go and gather straw for themselves. 8But the number of bricks that they made in the past you shall impose on them, you shall by no means reduce it, for they are idle. Therefore they cry, 'Let us go and offer sacrifice to our God.' 9Let heavier work be laid on the men that they may labor at it and pay no regard to lying words."

[1]Hebrew *his* [2]Samaritan *they are now more numerous than the people of the land*

10So the taskmasters and the foremen of the people went out and said to the people, "Thus says Pharaoh, 'I will not give you straw. 11Go and get your straw yourselves wherever you can find it, but your work will not be reduced in the least.' " 12So the people were scattered throughout all the land of Egypt to gather stubble for straw. 13The taskmasters were urgent, saying, "Complete your work, your daily task each day, as when there was straw." 14And the foremen of the people of Israel, whom Pharaoh's taskmasters had set over them, were beaten and were asked, "Why have you not done all your task of making bricks today and yesterday, as in the past?"

15Then the foremen of the people of Israel came and cried to Pharaoh, "Why do you treat your servants like this? 16No straw is given to your servants, yet they say to us, 'Make bricks!' And behold, your servants are beaten; but the fault is in your own people." 17But he said, "You are idle, you are idle; that is why you say, 'Let us go and sacrifice to the LORD.' 18Go now and work. No straw will be given you, but you must still deliver the same number of bricks." 19The foremen of the people of Israel saw that they were in trouble when they said, "You shall by no means reduce your number of bricks, your daily task each day." 20They met Moses and Aaron, who were waiting for them, as they came out from Pharaoh; 21and they said to them, "The LORD look on you and judge, because you have made us stink in the sight of Pharaoh and his servants, and have put a sword in their hand to kill us."

22Then Moses turned to the LORD and said, "O Lord, why have you done evil to this people? Why did you ever send me? 23For since I came to Pharaoh to speak in your name, he has done evil to this people, and you have not delivered your people at all."

God Promises Deliverance

6 But the LORD said to Moses, "Now you shall see what I will do to Pharaoh; for with a strong hand he will send them out, and with a strong hand he will drive them out of his land."

2God spoke to Moses and said to him, "I am the LORD. 3I appeared to Abraham, to Isaac, and to Jacob, as God Almighty,[1] but by my name the LORD I did not make myself known to them. 4I also established my covenant with them to give them the land of Canaan, the land in which they lived as sojourners. 5Moreover, I have heard the groaning of the people of Israel whom the Egyptians hold as slaves, and I have remembered my covenant. 6Say therefore to the people of Israel, 'I am the LORD, and I will bring you out from under the burdens of the Egyptians, and I will deliver you from slavery to them, and I will redeem you with an outstretched arm and with great acts of judgment. 7I will take you to be my people, and I will be your God, and you shall know that I am the LORD your God, who has brought you out from under the burdens of the Egyptians. 8I will bring you into the land that I swore to give to Abraham, to Isaac, and to Jacob. I will give it to you for a possession. I am the LORD.' " 9Moses spoke thus to the people of Israel, but they did not listen to Moses, because of their broken spirit and harsh slavery.

10So the LORD said to Moses, 11"Go in, tell Pharaoh king of Egypt to let the people of Israel go out of his land." 12But Moses said to the LORD, "Behold, the people of Israel have not listened to me. How then shall Pharaoh listen to me, for I am of uncircumcised lips?" 13But the LORD spoke to Moses and Aaron and gave them a charge about the people of Israel and about Pharaoh king of Egypt: to bring the people of Israel out of the land of Egypt.

The Genealogy of Moses and Aaron

14These are the heads of their fathers' houses: the sons of Reuben, the firstborn of Israel: Hanoch, Pallu, Hezron, and Carmi; these are the clans of Reuben.

[1]Hebrew *El Shaddai*

I AM THE LORD

The patriarchs had known God Almighty, but they had never heard the unique name of God. God revealed himself to Moses with intimate clarity, connecting his personal name with the wonders that he had done for the people up to this point in their story. He is the One who called Abraham, initiated a covenant with him, and inaugurated a great nation through a child promised to him and his then-barren wife (Ge 12; 15). He is the God who used what man intended for evil to promote Joseph to second-in-command in Egypt (Ge 50:20). He is the One who led his people to seek refuge in the land of Egypt to escape a dire famine. And he is the One who promised to deliver the people from slavery through Moses' leadership. The people were urged to avoid worry — the God who promised to act on their behalf is the God who had always come through on the behalf of his people.

This personal revelation is distinct to Christians. The God of the Bible is not some disengaged deity, unconcerned with the plight of his people. Rather, he is the God who is both omnipotent and sovereignly in charge of all things and the God who is intimately concerned and engaged with the affairs of his children.

This personal care is best demonstrated in the way Jesus humbled himself, leaving the right hand of the Father and taking the place of a servant on the cross (Php 2:5 – 11). Paul wrote that God was intent on redeeming his people, so Jesus laid aside equality with God and humbled himself to take on human flesh. While, in the age to come, every knee will bow and every tongue will confess that Jesus is Lord, the early ministry of Jesus demonstrated how far God would stoop to show his personal love for his children. Jesus is the perfect Son of God, yet one who loved his enemies and called them his friends (Ro 5:10). He is the radiance of the glory of God, yet willing to love those who show even a childlike faith (Lk 18:16). God is the King of the universe, yet one who allows frail humans to approach him as their father (Ro 8:15). He is *Yahweh,* the Lord God Almighty.

15The sons of Simeon: Jemuel, Jamin, Ohad, Jachin, Zohar, and Shaul, the son of a Canaanite woman; these are the clans of Simeon. 16These are the names of the sons of Levi according to their generations: Gershon, Kohath, and Merari, the years of the life of Levi being 137 years. 17The sons of Gershon: Libni and Shimei, by their clans. 18The sons of Kohath: Amram, Izhar, Hebron, and Uzziel, the years of the life of Kohath being 133 years. 19The sons of Merari: Mahli and Mushi. These are the clans of the Levites according to their generations. 20Amram took as his wife Jochebed his father's sister, and she bore him Aaron and Moses, the years of the life of Amram being 137 years. 21The sons of Izhar: Korah, Nepheg, and Zichri. 22The sons of Uzziel: Mishael, Elzaphan, and Sithri. 23Aaron took as his wife Elisheba, the daughter of Amminadab and the sister of Nahshon, and she bore him Nadab, Abihu, Eleazar, and Ithamar. 24The sons of Korah: Assir, Elkanah, and Abiasaph; these are the clans of the Korahites. 25Eleazar, Aaron's son, took as his wife one of the daughters of Putiel, and she bore him Phinehas. These are the heads of the fathers' houses of the Levites by their clans.

26These are the Aaron and Moses to whom the LORD said: "Bring out the people of Israel from the land of Egypt by their hosts." 27It was they who spoke to Pharaoh king of Egypt about bringing out the people of Israel from Egypt, this Moses and this Aaron.

28On the day when the LORD spoke to Moses in the land of Egypt, 29the LORD said to Moses, "I am the LORD; tell Pharaoh king of Egypt all that I say to you." 30But Moses said to the LORD, "Behold, I am of uncircumcised lips. How will Pharaoh listen to me?"

Moses and Aaron Before Pharaoh

7 And the LORD said to Moses, "See, I have made you like God to Pharaoh, and your brother Aaron shall be your prophet. 2You shall speak all that I command you, and your brother Aaron shall tell Pharaoh to let the people of Israel go out of his land. 3But I will harden Pharaoh's heart, and though I multiply my signs and wonders in the land of Egypt, 4Pharaoh will not listen to you. Then I will lay my hand on Egypt and bring my hosts, my people the children of Israel, out of the land of Egypt by great acts of judgment. 5The Egyptians shall know that I am the LORD, when I stretch out my hand against Egypt and bring out the people of Israel from among them." 6Moses and Aaron did so; they did just as the LORD commanded them. 7Now Moses was eighty years old, and Aaron eighty-three years old, when they spoke to Pharaoh.

8Then the LORD said to Moses and Aaron, 9"When Pharaoh says to you, 'Prove yourselves by working a miracle,' then you shall say to Aaron, 'Take your staff and cast it down before Pharaoh, that it may become a serpent.'" 10So Moses and Aaron went to Pharaoh and did just as the LORD commanded. Aaron cast down his staff before Pharaoh and his servants, and it became a serpent. 11Then Pharaoh summoned the wise men and the sorcerers, and they, the magicians of Egypt, also did the same by their secret arts. 12For each man cast down his staff, and they became serpents. But Aaron's staff swallowed up their staffs. 13Still Pharaoh's heart was hardened, and he would not listen to them, as the LORD had said.

The First Plague: Water Turned to Blood

14Then the LORD said to Moses, "Pharaoh's heart is hardened; he refuses to let the people go. 15Go to Pharaoh in the morning, as he is going out to the water, and stand on the bank of the Nile to meet him. Take in your hand the staff that turned into a serpent. 16And you shall say to him, 'The LORD, the God of the Hebrews, sent me to you, saying, "Let my people go, that they may serve me in the wilderness." But so far, you have not obeyed. 17Thus says the LORD, "By this you shall know that I am the LORD: behold, with the staff that is in my hand I will strike the water that is in the Nile, and it shall turn into blood. 18The fish in the Nile shall die, and the Nile will stink, and the Egyptians will grow weary of drinking water

from the Nile."'" 19And the LORD said to Moses, "Say to Aaron, 'Take your staff
and stretch out your hand over the waters of Egypt, over their rivers, their canals,
and their ponds, and all their pools of water, so that they may become blood, and
there shall be blood throughout all the land of Egypt, even in vessels of wood and
in vessels of stone.'"
20Moses and Aaron did as the LORD commanded. In the sight of Pharaoh and
in the sight of his servants he lifted up the staff and struck the water in the Nile,
and all the water in the Nile turned into blood. 21And the fish in the Nile died,
and the Nile stank, so that the Egyptians could not drink water from the Nile.
There was blood throughout all the land of Egypt. 22But the magicians of Egypt
did the same by their secret arts. So Pharaoh's heart remained hardened, and
he would not listen to them, as the LORD had said. 23Pharaoh turned and went
into his house, and he did not take even this to heart. 24And all the Egyptians
dug along the Nile for water to drink, for they could not drink the water of the
Nile.
25Seven full days passed after the LORD had struck the Nile.

The Second Plague: Frogs

8 [1] Then the LORD said to Moses, "Go in to Pharaoh and say to him, 'Thus says
the LORD, "Let my people go, that they may serve me. 2But if you refuse to
let them go, behold, I will plague all your country with frogs. 3The Nile shall
swarm with frogs that shall come up into your house and into your bedroom and
on your bed and into the houses of your servants and your people,[2] and into your
ovens and your kneading bowls. 4The frogs shall come up on you and on your
people and on all your servants."'" 5[3]And the LORD said to Moses, "Say to Aaron,
'Stretch out your hand with your staff over the rivers, over the canals and over the
pools, and make frogs come up on the land of Egypt!'" 6So Aaron stretched out
his hand over the waters of Egypt, and the frogs came up and covered the land of
Egypt. 7But the magicians did the same by their secret arts and made frogs come
up on the land of Egypt.
8Then Pharaoh called Moses and Aaron and said, "Plead with the LORD to take
away the frogs from me and from my people, and I will let the people go to sacrifice to the LORD." 9Moses said to Pharaoh, "Be pleased to command me when
I am to plead for you and for your servants and for your people, that the frogs
be cut off from you and your houses and be left only in the Nile." 10And he said,
"Tomorrow." Moses said, "Be it as you say, so that you may know that there is no
one like the LORD our God. 11The frogs shall go away from you and your houses
and your servants and your people. They shall be left only in the Nile." 12So Moses and Aaron went out from Pharaoh, and Moses cried to the LORD about the
frogs, as he had agreed with Pharaoh.[4] 13And the LORD did according to the word
of Moses. The frogs died out in the houses, the courtyards, and the fields. 14And
they gathered them together in heaps, and the land stank. 15But when Pharaoh
saw that there was a respite, he hardened his heart and would not listen to them,
as the LORD had said.

The Third Plague: Gnats

16Then the LORD said to Moses, "Say to Aaron, 'Stretch out your staff and strike
the dust of the earth, so that it may become gnats in all the land of Egypt.'" 17And
they did so. Aaron stretched out his hand with his staff and struck the dust of the
earth, and there were gnats on man and beast. All the dust of the earth became
gnats in all the land of Egypt. 18The magicians tried by their secret arts to produce gnats, but they could not. So there were gnats on man and beast. 19Then the
magicians said to Pharaoh, "This is the finger of God." But Pharaoh's heart was
hardened, and he would not listen to them, as the LORD had said.

[1]Ch 7:26 in Hebrew [2]Or *among your people* [3]Ch 8:1 in Hebrew [4]Or *which he had brought upon Pharaoh*

The Fourth Plague: Flies

20Then the LORD said to Moses, "Rise up early in the morning and present
yourself to Pharaoh, as he goes out to the water, and say to him, 'Thus says
the LORD, "Let my people go, that they may serve me. 21Or else, if you will not
let my people go, behold, I will send swarms of flies on you and your servants
and your people, and into your houses. And the houses of the Egyptians shall
be filled with swarms of flies, and also the ground on which they stand. 22But
on that day I will set apart the land of Goshen, where my people dwell, so that
no swarms of flies shall be there, that you may know that I am the LORD in
the midst of the earth.[1] 23Thus I will put a division[2] between my people and
your people. Tomorrow this sign shall happen."'" 24And the LORD did so. There
came great swarms of flies into the house of Pharaoh and into his servants'
houses. Throughout all the land of Egypt the land was ruined by the swarms
of flies.

25Then Pharaoh called Moses and Aaron and said, "Go, sacrifice to your God
within the land." 26But Moses said, "It would not be right to do so, for the offerings we shall sacrifice to the LORD our God are an abomination to the Egyptians.
If we sacrifice offerings abominable to the Egyptians before their eyes, will they
not stone us? 27We must go three days' journey into the wilderness and sacrifice to the LORD our God as he tells us." 28So Pharaoh said, "I will let you go to
sacrifice to the LORD your God in the wilderness; only you must not go very far
away. Plead for me." 29Then Moses said, "Behold, I am going out from you and
I will plead with the LORD that the swarms of flies may depart from Pharaoh,
from his servants, and from his people, tomorrow. Only let not Pharaoh cheat
again by not letting the people go to sacrifice to the LORD." 30So Moses went
out from Pharaoh and prayed to the LORD. 31And the LORD did as Moses asked,
and removed the swarms of flies from Pharaoh, from his servants, and from his
people; not one remained. 32But Pharaoh hardened his heart this time also, and
did not let the people go.

The Fifth Plague: Egyptian Livestock Die

9 Then the LORD said to Moses, "Go in to Pharaoh and say to him, 'Thus says
the LORD, the God of the Hebrews, "Let my people go, that they may serve
me. 2For if you refuse to let them go and still hold them, 3behold, the hand of the
LORD will fall with a very severe plague upon your livestock that are in the field,
the horses, the donkeys, the camels, the herds, and the flocks. 4But the LORD will
make a distinction between the livestock of Israel and the livestock of Egypt, so
that nothing of all that belongs to the people of Israel shall die."'" 5And the LORD
set a time, saying, "Tomorrow the LORD will do this thing in the land." 6And the
next day the LORD did this thing. All the livestock of the Egyptians died, but not
one of the livestock of the people of Israel died. 7And Pharaoh sent, and behold,
not one of the livestock of Israel was dead. But the heart of Pharaoh was hardened, and he did not let the people go.

The Sixth Plague: Boils

8And the LORD said to Moses and Aaron, "Take handfuls of soot from the kiln,
and let Moses throw them in the air in the sight of Pharaoh. 9It shall become fine
dust over all the land of Egypt, and become boils breaking out in sores on man
and beast throughout all the land of Egypt." 10So they took soot from the kiln and
stood before Pharaoh. And Moses threw it in the air, and it became boils breaking
out in sores on man and beast. 11And the magicians could not stand before Moses because of the boils, for the boils came upon the magicians and upon all the
Egyptians. 12But the LORD hardened the heart of Pharaoh, and he did not listen to
them, as the LORD had spoken to Moses.

[1]Or *that I the LORD am in the land* [2]Septuagint, Vulgate; Hebrew *set redemption*

EXODUS 8:22

SET APART

In the fourth plague, God explicitly singled out the land of Goshen, the dwelling place of the Israelites, for protection from his judgment, making his people the recipients of his gracious mercy. God demonstrated his power through his ability to withhold a judgment, such as a swarm of flies, from a certain location while flies wreaked havoc on the rest of the surrounding region. No one could deny that the people of God were uniquely set apart to him.

In a similar fashion, God's people are uniquely set apart from God's judgment and for his use. Authors of the New Testament, such as Paul, used an astounding word to speak of Christians—they called believers "saints" (1Co 1:2; Eph 1:1). This word denotes a special type of person, not by virtue of their perfect conformity to God's law but because of the imputed righteousness provided through Christ's death. God's people are chosen by God to be holy, uniquely set apart for God's purposes and protected from his judgment (Col 3:12). In the coming age, those who trust in Jesus will be protected from the ultimate judgment of God, while many others will face eternal destruction.

The Seventh Plague: Hail

13Then the LORD said to Moses, "Rise up early in the morning and present yourself before Pharaoh and say to him, 'Thus says the LORD, the God of the Hebrews, "Let my people go, that they may serve me. 14For this time I will send all my plagues on you yourself,[1] and on your servants and your people, so that you may know that there is none like me in all the earth. 15For by now I could have put out my hand and struck you and your people with pestilence, and you would have been cut off from the earth. 16But for this purpose I have raised you up, to show you my power, so that my name may be proclaimed in all the earth. 17You are still exalting yourself against my people and will not let them go. 18Behold, about this time tomorrow I will cause very heavy hail to fall, such as never has been in Egypt from the day it was founded until now. 19Now therefore send, get your livestock and all that you have in the field into safe shelter, for every man and beast that is in the field and is not brought home will die when the hail falls on them."'" 20Then whoever feared the word of the LORD among the servants of Pharaoh hurried his slaves and his livestock into the houses, 21but whoever did not pay attention to the word of the LORD left his slaves and his livestock in the field.

22Then the LORD said to Moses, "Stretch out your hand toward heaven, so that there may be hail in all the land of Egypt, on man and beast and every plant of the field, in the land of Egypt." 23Then Moses stretched out his staff toward heaven, and the LORD sent thunder and hail, and fire ran down to the earth. And the LORD rained hail upon the land of Egypt. 24There was hail and fire flashing continually in the midst of the hail, very heavy hail, such as had never been in all the land of Egypt since it became a nation. 25The hail struck down everything that was in the field in all the land of Egypt, both man and beast. And the hail struck down every plant of the field and broke every tree of the field. 26Only in the land of Goshen, where the people of Israel were, was there no hail.

27Then Pharaoh sent and called Moses and Aaron and said to them, "This time I have sinned; the LORD is in the right, and I and my people are in the wrong. 28Plead with the LORD, for there has been enough of God's thunder and hail. I will let you go, and you shall stay no longer." 29Moses said to him, "As soon as I have gone out of the city, I will stretch out my hands to the LORD. The thunder will cease, and there will be no more hail, so that you may know that the earth is the LORD's. 30But as for you and your servants, I know that you do not yet fear the LORD God." 31(The flax and the barley were struck down, for the barley was in the ear and the flax was in bud. 32But the wheat and the emmer[2] were not struck down, for they are late in coming up.) 33So Moses went out of the city from Pharaoh and stretched out his hands to the LORD, and the thunder and the hail ceased, and the rain no longer poured upon the earth. 34But when Pharaoh saw that the rain and the hail and the thunder had ceased, he sinned yet again and hardened his heart, he and his servants. 35So the heart of Pharaoh was hardened, and he did not let the people of Israel go, just as the LORD had spoken through Moses.

The Eighth Plague: Locusts

10 Then the LORD said to Moses, "Go in to Pharaoh, for I have hardened his heart and the heart of his servants, that I may show these signs of mine among them, 2and that you may tell in the hearing of your son and of your grandson how I have dealt harshly with the Egyptians and what signs I have done among them, that you may know that I am the LORD."

3So Moses and Aaron went in to Pharaoh and said to him, "Thus says the LORD, the God of the Hebrews, 'How long will you refuse to humble yourself before me? Let my people go, that they may serve me. 4For if you refuse to let my people go, behold, tomorrow I will bring locusts into your country, 5and they shall cover the face of the land, so that no one can see the land. And they shall eat what is left to

[1]Hebrew *on your heart* [2]A type of wheat

EXODUS 9:13–16

PHARAOH

Pharaoh's vindictive rule contrasted sharply with the goodness of God. Pharaoh was an evil ruler of a powerful nation, setting himself up as the supreme object of his people's worship and obedience. God rightly judged Pharaoh's treachery in order to free his chosen people, demonstrate his power, and declare his glory to the world. God hardened Pharaoh in his sin and demonstrated that he can, and will, use the disobedience of fallen humanity in order to accomplish his sovereign purposes.

Pilate fulfilled the same role in relation to God's mission to reclaim his wayward people. Facing death, Jesus stood before a ruler who failed to act justly. Fearing the wrath of the people, Pilate condemned Jesus to death. Jesus warned Pilate that only God granted him the power to hand down the death sentence. In the death of his Son, God used the hardness of heart of rebellious leaders to accomplish his good purposes (Jn 19:8–11). Though Pilate attempted to rid himself of the guilt of his crime (Mt 27:24–26), God will ultimately hold wayward leaders guilty for their sin. In time, all rulers, no matter how powerful, will face a far greater King who will execute his righteous judgment.

you after the hail, and they shall eat every tree of yours that grows in the field,
6 and they shall fill your houses and the houses of all your servants and of all the
Egyptians, as neither your fathers nor your grandfathers have seen, from the day
they came on earth to this day.'" Then he turned and went out from Pharaoh.
7 Then Pharaoh's servants said to him, "How long shall this man be a snare to
us? Let the men go, that they may serve the LORD their God. Do you not yet understand that Egypt is ruined?" 8 So Moses and Aaron were brought back to Pharaoh.
And he said to them, "Go, serve the LORD your God. But which ones are to go?"
9 Moses said, "We will go with our young and our old. We will go with our sons and
daughters and with our flocks and herds, for we must hold a feast to the LORD."
10 But he said to them, "The LORD be with you, if ever I let you and your little ones
go! Look, you have some evil purpose in mind.[1] 11 No! Go, the men among you, and
serve the LORD, for that is what you are asking." And they were driven out from
Pharaoh's presence.
12 Then the LORD said to Moses, "Stretch out your hand over the land of Egypt
for the locusts, so that they may come upon the land of Egypt and eat every plant
in the land, all that the hail has left." 13 So Moses stretched out his staff over the
land of Egypt, and the LORD brought an east wind upon the land all that day and
all that night. When it was morning, the east wind had brought the locusts. 14 The
locusts came up over all the land of Egypt and settled on the whole country of
Egypt, such a dense swarm of locusts as had never been before, nor ever will be
again. 15 They covered the face of the whole land, so that the land was darkened,
and they ate all the plants in the land and all the fruit of the trees that the hail
had left. Not a green thing remained, neither tree nor plant of the field, through
all the land of Egypt. 16 Then Pharaoh hastily called Moses and Aaron and said, "I
have sinned against the LORD your God, and against you. 17 Now therefore, forgive
my sin, please, only this once, and plead with the LORD your God only to remove
this death from me." 18 So he went out from Pharaoh and pleaded with the LORD.
19 And the LORD turned the wind into a very strong west wind, which lifted the
locusts and drove them into the Red Sea. Not a single locust was left in all the
country of Egypt. 20 But the LORD hardened Pharaoh's heart, and he did not let the
people of Israel go.

The Ninth Plague: Darkness

21 Then the LORD said to Moses, "Stretch out your hand toward heaven, that
there may be darkness over the land of Egypt, a darkness to be felt." 22 So Moses
stretched out his hand toward heaven, and there was pitch darkness in all the
land of Egypt three days. 23 They did not see one another, nor did anyone rise from
his place for three days, but all the people of Israel had light where they lived.
24 Then Pharaoh called Moses and said, "Go, serve the LORD; your little ones also
may go with you; only let your flocks and your herds remain behind." 25 But Moses
said, "You must also let us have sacrifices and burnt offerings, that we may sacrifice to the LORD our God. 26 Our livestock also must go with us; not a hoof shall be
left behind, for we must take of them to serve the LORD our God, and we do not
know with what we must serve the LORD until we arrive there." 27 But the LORD
hardened Pharaoh's heart, and he would not let them go. 28 Then Pharaoh said to
him, "Get away from me; take care never to see my face again, for on the day you
see my face you shall die." 29 Moses said, "As you say! I will not see your face again."

A Final Plague Threatened

11 The LORD said to Moses, "Yet one plague more I will bring upon Pharaoh
and upon Egypt. Afterward he will let you go from here. When he lets you
go, he will drive you away completely. 2 Speak now in the hearing of the people,
that they ask, every man of his neighbor and every woman of her neighbor, for

---

[1] Hebrew *before your face*

silver and gold jewelry." 3And the LORD gave the people favor in the sight of the
Egyptians. Moreover, the man Moses was very great in the land of Egypt, in the
sight of Pharaoh's servants and in the sight of the people.
4So Moses said, "Thus says the LORD: 'About midnight I will go out in the midst
of Egypt, 5and every firstborn in the land of Egypt shall die, from the firstborn
of Pharaoh who sits on his throne, even to the firstborn of the slave girl who is
behind the handmill, and all the firstborn of the cattle. 6There shall be a great cry
throughout all the land of Egypt, such as there has never been, nor ever will be
again. 7But not a dog shall growl against any of the people of Israel, either man or
beast, that you may know that the LORD makes a distinction between Egypt and
Israel.' 8And all these your servants shall come down to me and bow down to me,
saying, 'Get out, you and all the people who follow you.' And after that I will go
out." And he went out from Pharaoh in hot anger. 9Then the LORD said to Moses,
"Pharaoh will not listen to you, that my wonders may be multiplied in the land
of Egypt."
10Moses and Aaron did all these wonders before Pharaoh, and the LORD hardened Pharaoh's heart, and he did not let the people of Israel go out of his land.

The Passover

12 The LORD said to Moses and Aaron in the land of Egypt, 2"This month shall
be for you the beginning of months. It shall be the first month of the year
for you. 3Tell all the congregation of Israel that on the tenth day of this month
every man shall take a lamb according to their fathers' houses, a lamb for a household. 4And if the household is too small for a lamb, then he and his nearest neighbor shall take according to the number of persons; according to what each can eat
you shall make your count for the lamb. 5Your lamb shall be without blemish, a
male a year old. You may take it from the sheep or from the goats, 6and you shall
keep it until the fourteenth day of this month, when the whole assembly of the
congregation of Israel shall kill their lambs at twilight.[1]
7"Then they shall take some of the blood and put it on the two doorposts and
the lintel of the houses in which they eat it. 8They shall eat the flesh that night,
roasted on the fire; with unleavened bread and bitter herbs they shall eat it. 9Do
not eat any of it raw or boiled in water, but roasted, its head with its legs and its
inner parts. 10And you shall let none of it remain until the morning; anything that
remains until the morning you shall burn. 11In this manner you shall eat it: with
your belt fastened, your sandals on your feet, and your staff in your hand. And
you shall eat it in haste. It is the LORD's Passover. 12For I will pass through the land
of Egypt that night, and I will strike all the firstborn in the land of Egypt, both man
and beast; and on all the gods of Egypt I will execute judgments: I am the LORD.
13The blood shall be a sign for you, on the houses where you are. And when I see
the blood, I will pass over you, and no plague will befall you to destroy you, when
I strike the land of Egypt.
14"This day shall be for you a memorial day, and you shall keep it as a feast to
the LORD; throughout your generations, as a statute forever, you shall keep it as
a feast. 15Seven days you shall eat unleavened bread. On the first day you shall
remove leaven out of your houses, for if anyone eats what is leavened, from the
first day until the seventh day, that person shall be cut off from Israel. 16On the
first day you shall hold a holy assembly, and on the seventh day a holy assembly.
No work shall be done on those days. But what everyone needs to eat, that alone
may be prepared by you. 17And you shall observe the Feast of Unleavened Bread,
for on this very day I brought your hosts out of the land of Egypt. Therefore you
shall observe this day, throughout your generations, as a statute forever. 18In the
first month, from the fourteenth day of the month at evening, you shall eat unleavened bread until the twenty-first day of the month at evening. 19For seven

[1]Hebrew *between the two evenings*

THE PASSOVER LAMB

The Passover celebrates God's miraculous deliverance of his people from slavery in Egypt. The focal point of the ceremony was the sacrifice of a Passover lamb whose blood was placed on the doorframes of the houses of the Israelites. While God enacted his final plague, the killing of the firstborn of the nation of Egypt, those living in homes marked by blood were spared death.

God provided clear specifications for the lamb that could be used at Passover — the lamb had to be a young male, without blemish or defect. In order to ensure its purity, the lamb was examined for four days following its selection. Those animals meeting God's requirements were sacrificed in public, and none of the animal's bones could be broken (Ex 12:46). The severity of the coming judgment required that the people of God observe this sacrifice with the utmost care. The annual commemoration of the Passover reminded the people both of the faithfulness of God to provide deliverance for his people and of their ongoing need for a substitute to pay the price their sin deserved.

The Passover sacrifice is one of the clearest pictures in the Old Testament of the coming work of Jesus. At the beginning of his earthly ministry, John the Baptist called Jesus "the Lamb of God, who takes away the sin of the world" (Jn 1:29). His life met the requirements for a Passover sacrifice. He too was a young male, perfect in all ways. He would die a heinous, public death, though none of his bones were broken in the process (Jn 19:36). Because of Jesus' death, those covered by his blood are spared the coming judgment (Ro 5:9; Eph 2:13).

New Testament authors refer to Jesus' work using the imagery of the Passover because of the exact way in which Jesus fulfills the divinely orchestrated image of the Passover lamb (1Pe 1:19). Paul calls Jesus the Passover lamb who was sacrificed for his church (1Co 5:7). His perfect purity and substitutionary death uniquely qualified him to play this role. As the one and only Son of God, he could do what no animal could ever do — he could permanently satisfy the wrath of God on behalf of his people.

days no leaven is to be found in your houses. If anyone eats what is leavened, that
person will be cut off from the congregation of Israel, whether he is a sojourner or
a native of the land. [20]You shall eat nothing leavened; in all your dwelling places
you shall eat unleavened bread."

[21]Then Moses called all the elders of Israel and said to them, "Go and select
lambs for yourselves according to your clans, and kill the Passover lamb. [22]Take
a bunch of hyssop and dip it in the blood that is in the basin, and touch the lintel
and the two doorposts with the blood that is in the basin. None of you shall go
out of the door of his house until the morning. [23]For the LORD will pass through
to strike the Egyptians, and when he sees the blood on the lintel and on the two
doorposts, the LORD will pass over the door and will not allow the destroyer to enter your houses to strike you. [24]You shall observe this rite as a statute for you and
for your sons forever. [25]And when you come to the land that the LORD will give
you, as he has promised, you shall keep this service. [26]And when your children
say to you, 'What do you mean by this service?' [27]you shall say, 'It is the sacrifice
of the LORD's Passover, for he passed over the houses of the people of Israel in
Egypt, when he struck the Egyptians but spared our houses.'" And the people
bowed their heads and worshiped.

[28]Then the people of Israel went and did so; as the LORD had commanded Moses and Aaron, so they did.

The Tenth Plague: Death of the Firstborn

[29]At midnight the LORD struck down all the firstborn in the land of Egypt, from
the firstborn of Pharaoh who sat on his throne to the firstborn of the captive who
was in the dungeon, and all the firstborn of the livestock. [30]And Pharaoh rose up
in the night, he and all his servants and all the Egyptians. And there was a great cry
in Egypt, for there was not a house where someone was not dead. [31]Then he summoned Moses and Aaron by night and said, "Up, go out from among my people,
both you and the people of Israel; and go, serve the LORD, as you have said. [32]Take
your flocks and your herds, as you have said, and be gone, and bless me also!"

The Exodus

[33]The Egyptians were urgent with the people to send them out of the land in
haste. For they said, "We shall all be dead." [34]So the people took their dough before it was leavened, their kneading bowls being bound up in their cloaks on their
shoulders. [35]The people of Israel had also done as Moses told them, for they had
asked the Egyptians for silver and gold jewelry and for clothing. [36]And the LORD
had given the people favor in the sight of the Egyptians, so that they let them have
what they asked. Thus they plundered the Egyptians.

[37]And the people of Israel journeyed from Rameses to Succoth, about six hundred thousand men on foot, besides women and children. [38]A mixed multitude
also went up with them, and very much livestock, both flocks and herds. [39]And
they baked unleavened cakes of the dough that they had brought out of Egypt, for
it was not leavened, because they were thrust out of Egypt and could not wait, nor
had they prepared any provisions for themselves.

[40]The time that the people of Israel lived in Egypt was 430 years. [41]At the end
of 430 years, on that very day, all the hosts of the LORD went out from the land of
Egypt. [42]It was a night of watching by the LORD, to bring them out of the land of
Egypt; so this same night is a night of watching kept to the LORD by all the people
of Israel throughout their generations.

Institution of the Passover

[43]And the LORD said to Moses and Aaron, "This is the statute of the Passover:
no foreigner shall eat of it, [44]but every slave[1] that is bought for money may eat of

[1]Or *servant*; the Hebrew term *'ebed* designates a range of social and economic roles (see Preface)

it after you have circumcised him. 45No foreigner or hired worker may eat of it. 46It
shall be eaten in one house; you shall not take any of the flesh outside the house,
and you shall not break any of its bones. 47All the congregation of Israel shall keep
it. 48If a stranger shall sojourn with you and would keep the Passover to the LORD,
let all his males be circumcised. Then he may come near and keep it; he shall be as
a native of the land. But no uncircumcised person shall eat of it. 49There shall be
one law for the native and for the stranger who sojourns among you."

50All the people of Israel did just as the LORD commanded Moses and Aaron.
51And on that very day the LORD brought the people of Israel out of the land of
Egypt by their hosts.

Consecration of the Firstborn

13 The LORD said to Moses, 2"Consecrate to me all the firstborn. Whatever is
the first to open the womb among the people of Israel, both of man and of
beast, is mine."

The Feast of Unleavened Bread

3Then Moses said to the people, "Remember this day in which you came out
from Egypt, out of the house of slavery, for by a strong hand the LORD brought
you out from this place. No leavened bread shall be eaten. 4Today, in the month
of Abib, you are going out. 5And when the LORD brings you into the land of the
Canaanites, the Hittites, the Amorites, the Hivites, and the Jebusites, which he
swore to your fathers to give you, a land flowing with milk and honey, you shall
keep this service in this month. 6Seven days you shall eat unleavened bread, and
on the seventh day there shall be a feast to the LORD. 7Unleavened bread shall be
eaten for seven days; no leavened bread shall be seen with you, and no leaven
shall be seen with you in all your territory. 8You shall tell your son on that day, 'It
is because of what the LORD did for me when I came out of Egypt.' 9And it shall be
to you as a sign on your hand and as a memorial between your eyes, that the law
of the LORD may be in your mouth. For with a strong hand the LORD has brought
you out of Egypt. 10You shall therefore keep this statute at its appointed time from
year to year.

11"When the LORD brings you into the land of the Canaanites, as he swore to
you and your fathers, and shall give it to you, 12you shall set apart to the LORD all
that first opens the womb. All the firstborn of your animals that are males shall
be the LORD's. 13Every firstborn of a donkey you shall redeem with a lamb, or if
you will not redeem it you shall break its neck. Every firstborn of man among
your sons you shall redeem. 14And when in time to come your son asks you, 'What
does this mean?' you shall say to him, 'By a strong hand the LORD brought us out
of Egypt, from the house of slavery. 15For when Pharaoh stubbornly refused to let
us go, the LORD killed all the firstborn in the land of Egypt, both the firstborn of
man and the firstborn of animals. Therefore I sacrifice to the LORD all the males
that first open the womb, but all the firstborn of my sons I redeem.' 16It shall be
as a mark on your hand or frontlets between your eyes, for by a strong hand the
LORD brought us out of Egypt."

Pillars of Cloud and Fire

17When Pharaoh let the people go, God did not lead them by way of the land
of the Philistines, although that was near. For God said, "Lest the people change
their minds when they see war and return to Egypt." 18But God led the people
around by the way of the wilderness toward the Red Sea. And the people of Israel
went up out of the land of Egypt equipped for battle. 19Moses took the bones of
Joseph with him, for Joseph[1] had made the sons of Israel solemnly swear, saying,
"God will surely visit you, and you shall carry up my bones with you from here."

[1]Samaritan, Septuagint; Hebrew *he*

[20]And they moved on from Succoth and encamped at Etham, on the edge of the wilderness. [21]And the LORD went before them by day in a pillar of cloud to lead them along the way, and by night in a pillar of fire to give them light, that they might travel by day and by night. [22]The pillar of cloud by day and the pillar of fire by night did not depart from before the people.

Crossing the Red Sea

14 Then the LORD said to Moses, [2]"Tell the people of Israel to turn back and encamp in front of Pi-hahiroth, between Migdol and the sea, in front of Baal-zephon; you shall encamp facing it, by the sea. [3]For Pharaoh will say of the people of Israel, 'They are wandering in the land; the wilderness has shut them in.' [4]And I will harden Pharaoh's heart, and he will pursue them, and I will get glory over Pharaoh and all his host, and the Egyptians shall know that I am the LORD." And they did so.

[5]When the king of Egypt was told that the people had fled, the mind of Pharaoh and his servants was changed toward the people, and they said, "What is this we have done, that we have let Israel go from serving us?" [6]So he made ready his chariot and took his army with him, [7]and took six hundred chosen chariots and all the other chariots of Egypt with officers over all of them. [8]And the LORD hardened the heart of Pharaoh king of Egypt, and he pursued the people of Israel while the people of Israel were going out defiantly. [9]The Egyptians pursued them, all Pharaoh's horses and chariots and his horsemen and his army, and overtook them encamped at the sea, by Pi-hahiroth, in front of Baal-zephon.

[10]When Pharaoh drew near, the people of Israel lifted up their eyes, and behold, the Egyptians were marching after them, and they feared greatly. And the people of Israel cried out to the LORD. [11]They said to Moses, "Is it because there are no graves in Egypt that you have taken us away to die in the wilderness? What have you done to us in bringing us out of Egypt? [12]Is not this what we said to you in Egypt: 'Leave us alone that we may serve the Egyptians'? For it would have been better for us to serve the Egyptians than to die in the wilderness." [13]And Moses said to the people, "Fear not, stand firm, and see the salvation of the LORD, which he will work for you today. For the Egyptians whom you see today, you shall never see again. [14]The LORD will fight for you, and you have only to be silent."

[15]The LORD said to Moses, "Why do you cry to me? Tell the people of Israel to go forward. [16]Lift up your staff, and stretch out your hand over the sea and divide it, that the people of Israel may go through the sea on dry ground. [17]And I will harden the hearts of the Egyptians so that they shall go in after them, and I will get glory over Pharaoh and all his host, his chariots, and his horsemen. [18]And the Egyptians shall know that I am the LORD, when I have gotten glory over Pharaoh, his chariots, and his horsemen."

[19]Then the angel of God who was going before the host of Israel moved and went behind them, and the pillar of cloud moved from before them and stood behind them, [20]coming between the host of Egypt and the host of Israel. And there was the cloud and the darkness. And it lit up the night[1] without one coming near the other all night.

[21]Then Moses stretched out his hand over the sea, and the LORD drove the sea back by a strong east wind all night and made the sea dry land, and the waters were divided. [22]And the people of Israel went into the midst of the sea on dry ground, the waters being a wall to them on their right hand and on their left. [23]The Egyptians pursued and went in after them into the midst of the sea, all Pharaoh's horses, his chariots, and his horsemen. [24]And in the morning watch the LORD in the pillar of fire and of cloud looked down on the Egyptian forces and threw the Egyptian forces into a panic, [25]clogging[2] their chariot wheels so that they drove

[1]Septuagint *and the night passed* [2]Or *binding* (compare Samaritan, Septuagint, Syriac); Hebrew *removing*

EXODUS 14:21–31

THE GREAT ONE

The great work of deliverance is attributed to God and God alone. The great power of the Lord acted on behalf of his people and broke the shackles of their slavery. The people clearly understood the might of God displayed in this act because they responded in awestruck fear. The great work of a great God propelled Israel into their subsequent journey toward the promised land.

Throughout human history the strong arm of the Lord has worked on behalf of his people. He gave them victory and delivered them from the dire circumstances caused by their sinful rebellion (Ps 89:13; 118:15–24), foreshadowing the climactic moment when God broke into human history through the person of Jesus Christ. Jesus' perfect life, substitutionary death, and victorious resurrection accomplish a far greater work of deliverance than the exodus from Egypt. Christ's work accomplished a "great" salvation for all his people (Heb 2:3). Like the nation of Israel responded, our proper response to the great work accomplished by this great God is awestruck worship.

THE LIGHT

As night fell, the darkness of the desert made travel virtually impossible. The movement of thousands of people across a rugged terrain was not easy in the day, much less at night. Light was a practical necessity for survival in the wilderness. Without it, the people would be left to stumble in the darkness, face the constant fear of unforeseen attacks by their enemies, and struggle to accomplish the basic actions necessary for living in a harsh land.

Once again, God provided for his people in a unique way. Rather than asking the people to create light, he provided it for them in the form of a pillar of fire. Often a mark of judgment, here the fire of God was a means of his provision. Even more, the fire embodied the presence of God among his people. The Israelites simply looked out at night, saw the pillar of fire, and were reminded that God was their God and they were his people. He had broken into the darkness of human history and chosen them to be his. Even in the wilderness, they were reminded that God had worked mighty deeds of deliverance on their behalf and was leading them to the land of promise.

God's very being is characterized by light. The apostle John wrote, "God is light, and in him is no darkness at all" (1Jn 1:5). His holiness is described as a perfect light, without the darkness of sin. Jesus, as the perfect Son of God, was sent on a mission to a dark world. His birth was the embodiment of God's light (Jn 1:5). He came to a sin-darkened world and overcame that darkness by his all-consuming light.

He lights the path by which all those who know him can follow him. God's children no longer have to cower in the darkness; they can come into the light where they will discover newfound safety, peace, and joy. In fact, a central mark of God's people is that they love the light. Sin festers and grows in the darkness, so those who long to obey God renounce the darkness and drag their sin into the light of God's grace. There they find fellowship with God and fellowship with one another (1Jn 1:6–7). In God's light, sin is hated, repentance is ongoing, and holiness is pursued.

heavily. And the Egyptians said, "Let us flee from before Israel, for the LORD fights
for them against the Egyptians."
26Then the LORD said to Moses, "Stretch out your hand over the sea, that the
water may come back upon the Egyptians, upon their chariots, and upon their
horsemen." 27So Moses stretched out his hand over the sea, and the sea returned
to its normal course when the morning appeared. And as the Egyptians fled into
it, the LORD threw[1] the Egyptians into the midst of the sea. 28The waters returned
and covered the chariots and the horsemen; of all the host of Pharaoh that had
followed them into the sea, not one of them remained. 29But the people of Israel
walked on dry ground through the sea, the waters being a wall to them on their
right hand and on their left.
30Thus the LORD saved Israel that day from the hand of the Egyptians, and Israel saw the Egyptians dead on the seashore. 31Israel saw the great power that the
LORD used against the Egyptians, so the people feared the LORD, and they believed
in the LORD and in his servant Moses.

The Song of Moses

15 Then Moses and the people of Israel sang this song to the LORD, saying,

"I will sing to the LORD, for he has triumphed gloriously;
the horse and his rider[2] he has thrown into the sea.
2 The LORD is my strength and my song,
and he has become my salvation;
this is my God, and I will praise him,
my father's God, and I will exalt him.
3 The LORD is a man of war;
the LORD is his name.

4 "Pharaoh's chariots and his host he cast into the sea,
and his chosen officers were sunk in the Red Sea.
5 The floods covered them;
they went down into the depths like a stone.
6 Your right hand, O LORD, glorious in power,
your right hand, O LORD, shatters the enemy.
7 In the greatness of your majesty you overthrow your
adversaries;
you send out your fury; it consumes them like stubble.
8 At the blast of your nostrils the waters piled up;
the floods stood up in a heap;
the deeps congealed in the heart of the sea.
9 The enemy said, 'I will pursue, I will overtake,
I will divide the spoil, my desire shall have its fill of them.
I will draw my sword; my hand shall destroy them.'
10 You blew with your wind; the sea covered them;
they sank like lead in the mighty waters.

11 "Who is like you, O LORD, among the gods?
Who is like you, majestic in holiness,
awesome in glorious deeds, doing wonders?
12 You stretched out your right hand;
the earth swallowed them.

13 "You have led in your steadfast love the people whom you have
redeemed;
you have guided them by your strength to your holy
abode.

[1]Hebrew *shook off* [2]Or *its chariot*; also verse 21

EXODUS 15:1–21

VICTORY SONG

The juxtaposition of "strength" and "song" portrays the basis for the song found in Exodus 15. This entire passage reflects a victory cry from the people of God recounting the profound strength and power of the Lord shown in their deliverance. They sang as a redeemed people, confidently relishing the powerful kindness God had shown them. The divine, sovereign, and omnipotent God acted to deliver his beloved people. This work was not motivated by the inherent righteousness of the people of God. In fact, the case is just the opposite. God's strength is seen in his action toward a depraved, wayward, and stiff-necked people whom he knew would be unfaithful to their covenant promises.

God continued to act strongly on behalf of his people through Jesus, who defeats Satan, sin, and death forever. As a result, Paul could taunt death in his letter to the church at Corinth, mocking the fact that the sting of sin and death has been revoked through Christ's redemptive work (1Co 15:54–57). The church can sing a strong, victorious, and joyful cry of deliverance to God.

PATH OF DELIVERANCE

Moses' command to not be afraid must have sounded foolish as the Israelites watched as Pharaoh and his army drew near. Yet, the Lord promised to provide salvation by accomplishing a deed so vast, so incredible, and so unheard of that only God could do it.

The people stood on the brink of the Red Sea, unable to cross, with the sound of six hundred chariots barreling down upon them. At best, they would be hauled off to return to slavery in Egypt where they would be forced to work even harder than before. At worst, they would be killed for their insurrection. The hardness of Pharaoh's heart proved that the latter was the more likely outcome.

God promised, however, that he would provide a way of escape — the people must simply trust in him. After commanding Moses to lift up his staff and stretch out his hand, God told him to divide the water and instruct the people to walk forward in God's path of deliverance. The vast Red Sea obeyed the command of the Lord and formed a wall of water on either side of the Israelites, allowing them to walk forward on dry ground. After safely arriving on the other bank, the nation of God turned around to watch the waters consume the army of Pharaoh.

These types of scenes are all too common for the people of God. Their sin places them in situations where, unless God acts and delivers them, they will be crushed and consumed. The angelic announcement on the night of Jesus' birth demonstrated that he had come to deliver his people. "Fear not," the angel said to the shepherds. "I bring you good news of great joy that will be for all the people" (Lk 2:10).

This good news follows a similar blueprint as God's deliverance of his people at the Red Sea. Jesus' work provides a singular way of deliverance (Jn 14:6). He is, in fact, the only way in which sinful mankind can be delivered from the plight of sin. This path is not easy, however. It is a narrow path, and only those who trust God and spurn the ways of this world will be led to safety (Mt 7:13 – 14). Like Israel before, the church today must trust that God will deliver his people, but only through the path that he has made in Christ.

14 The peoples have heard; they tremble;
pangs have seized the inhabitants of Philistia.
15 Now are the chiefs of Edom dismayed;
trembling seizes the leaders of Moab;
all the inhabitants of Canaan have melted away.
16 Terror and dread fall upon them;
because of the greatness of your arm, they are still as a stone,
till your people, O LORD, pass by,
till the people pass by whom you have purchased.
17 You will bring them in and plant them on your own mountain,
the place, O LORD, which you have made for your abode,
the sanctuary, O Lord, which your hands have established.
18 The LORD will reign forever and ever."

19For when the horses of Pharaoh with his chariots and his horsemen went
into the sea, the LORD brought back the waters of the sea upon them, but the
people of Israel walked on dry ground in the midst of the sea. 20Then Miriam
the prophetess, the sister of Aaron, took a tambourine in her hand, and all the
women went out after her with tambourines and dancing. 21And Miriam sang
to them:

"Sing to the LORD, for he has triumphed gloriously;
the horse and his rider he has thrown into the sea."

Bitter Water Made Sweet

22Then Moses made Israel set out from the Red Sea, and they went into
the wilderness of Shur. They went three days in the wilderness and found no
water. 23When they came to Marah, they could not drink the water of Marah
because it was bitter; therefore it was named Marah.[1] 24And the people grumbled against Moses, saying, "What shall we drink?" 25And he cried to the LORD,
and the LORD showed him a log,[2] and he threw it into the water, and the water
became sweet.

There the LORD[3] made for them a statute and a rule, and there he tested them,
26saying, "If you will diligently listen to the voice of the LORD your God, and do
that which is right in his eyes, and give ear to his commandments and keep all his
statutes, I will put none of the diseases on you that I put on the Egyptians, for I
am the LORD, your healer."

27Then they came to Elim, where there were twelve springs of water and seventy palm trees, and they encamped there by the water.

Bread from Heaven

16 They set out from Elim, and all the congregation of the people of Israel
came to the wilderness of Sin, which is between Elim and Sinai, on the
fifteenth day of the second month after they had departed from the land of Egypt.
2And the whole congregation of the people of Israel grumbled against Moses and
Aaron in the wilderness, 3and the people of Israel said to them, "Would that we
had died by the hand of the LORD in the land of Egypt, when we sat by the meat
pots and ate bread to the full, for you have brought us out into this wilderness to
kill this whole assembly with hunger."

4Then the LORD said to Moses, "Behold, I am about to rain bread from heaven
for you, and the people shall go out and gather a day's portion every day, that I
may test them, whether they will walk in my law or not. 5On the sixth day, when
they prepare what they bring in, it will be twice as much as they gather daily." 6So
Moses and Aaron said to all the people of Israel, "At evening you shall know that
it was the LORD who brought you out of the land of Egypt, 7and in the morning

[1] *Marah* means *bitterness* [2] Or *tree* [3] Hebrew *he*

EXODUS 16:4–5

GOD PROVIDES

With the Passover and mighty works of God at the forefront of their minds, Moses led the nation of Israel across a body of water into the wilderness and up to a mountain. Along the way, the massive, hungry gaggle of people had to trust God for the provision of bread from heaven as they divided into their allotted encampments each night, trusting that they could skip collecting bread on the Sabbath and survive the harsh desert conditions.

In John's Gospel, Jesus engaged the people in a similar drama. As the Passover season was immediately at hand and because of the mighty works of God done by Jesus, a large crowd of people followed him across a body of water and up to a mountain in the wilderness (Jn 6:1–4). Jesus then proceeded to sustain them with bread and meat in the wilderness (Jn 6:5–13).

Ultimately, Jesus offered the people the opportunity to participate in a second exodus—a spiritual exodus. In this exodus, he wanted them to do more than eat the physical bread which would sustain them for a day, but to trust in him so that they might eat and live forever (Jn 6:47–51).

you shall see the glory of the LORD, because he has heard your grumbling against
the LORD. For what are we, that you grumble against us?" 8And Moses said, "When
the LORD gives you in the evening meat to eat and in the morning bread to the full,
because the LORD has heard your grumbling that you grumble against him—what
are we? Your grumbling is not against us but against the LORD."

9Then Moses said to Aaron, "Say to the whole congregation of the people of
Israel, 'Come near before the LORD, for he has heard your grumbling.'" 10And
as soon as Aaron spoke to the whole congregation of the people of Israel, they
looked toward the wilderness, and behold, the glory of the LORD appeared in
the cloud. 11And the LORD said to Moses, 12"I have heard the grumbling of the
people of Israel. Say to them, 'At twilight you shall eat meat, and in the morning you shall be filled with bread. Then you shall know that I am the LORD your
God.'"

13In the evening quail came up and covered the camp, and in the morning dew
lay around the camp. 14And when the dew had gone up, there was on the face of
the wilderness a fine, flake-like thing, fine as frost on the ground. 15When the
people of Israel saw it, they said to one another, "What is it?"[1] For they did not
know what it was. And Moses said to them, "It is the bread that the LORD has given
you to eat. 16This is what the LORD has commanded: 'Gather of it, each one of you,
as much as he can eat. You shall each take an omer,[2] according to the number of
the persons that each of you has in his tent.'" 17And the people of Israel did so.
They gathered, some more, some less. 18But when they measured it with an omer,
whoever gathered much had nothing left over, and whoever gathered little had no
lack. Each of them gathered as much as he could eat. 19And Moses said to them,
"Let no one leave any of it over till the morning." 20But they did not listen to Moses. Some left part of it till the morning, and it bred worms and stank. And Moses
was angry with them. 21Morning by morning they gathered it, each as much as he
could eat; but when the sun grew hot, it melted.

22On the sixth day they gathered twice as much bread, two omers each. And
when all the leaders of the congregation came and told Moses, 23he said to them,
"This is what the LORD has commanded: 'Tomorrow is a day of solemn rest, a holy
Sabbath to the LORD; bake what you will bake and boil what you will boil, and all
that is left over lay aside to be kept till the morning.'" 24So they laid it aside till
the morning, as Moses commanded them, and it did not stink, and there were no
worms in it. 25Moses said, "Eat it today, for today is a Sabbath to the LORD; today
you will not find it in the field. 26Six days you shall gather it, but on the seventh
day, which is a Sabbath, there will be none."

27On the seventh day some of the people went out to gather, but they found
none. 28And the LORD said to Moses, "How long will you refuse to keep my commandments and my laws? 29See! The LORD has given you the Sabbath; therefore
on the sixth day he gives you bread for two days. Remain each of you in his place;
let no one go out of his place on the seventh day." 30So the people rested on the
seventh day.

31Now the house of Israel called its name manna. It was like coriander seed,
white, and the taste of it was like wafers made with honey. 32Moses said, "This
is what the LORD has commanded: 'Let an omer of it be kept throughout your
generations, so that they may see the bread with which I fed you in the wilderness, when I brought you out of the land of Egypt.'" 33And Moses said to Aaron,
"Take a jar, and put an omer of manna in it, and place it before the LORD to be kept
throughout your generations." 34As the LORD commanded Moses, so Aaron placed
it before the testimony to be kept. 35The people of Israel ate the manna forty years,
till they came to a habitable land. They ate the manna till they came to the border
of the land of Canaan. 36(An omer is the tenth part of an ephah.)[3]

[1]Or *"It is manna"*; Hebrew *man hu* [2]An *omer* was about 2 quarts or 2 liters [3]An *ephah* was about 3/5 bushel or 22 liters

BREAD FROM HEAVEN

God fed his people with bread from heaven. This act of kindness was magnified by the fact that God's people seemed to be filled with unending complaints against God and the leaders he had appointed. They foolishly longed for the days of slavery in Egypt, where they recalled eating pots of meat and all the food they wanted. Now they feared that they would starve in the wilderness. Only one chapter removed from the miraculous deliverance at the Red Sea and their song of victory, the people now blamed God and mourned their seemingly dire circumstances.

God faithfully feeds his faithless children. His motive for providing this food is clear — God wanted his people to see his glory and remember that he was working on their behalf. Each day, they awakened to fresh evidence of God's generosity. And this blessing was specific, not just to the nation of Israel as a whole, but also to each of the families of the people of God.

Jesus compared his mission on this earth to the provision of manna in the desert. After demonstrating his miraculous power by feeding five thousand on a hillside and walking on water, he describes himself as "the bread of life" (Jn 6:35). Those who know him discover a source of nourishment far greater than any meal can provide. Jesus satisfies the craving of all those longing for a source of satisfaction in life and hope in the life to come. Like manna in the wilderness, Jesus provides food for a hungry soul. His provision is sufficient to meet the needs of all those who, by faith, feast on him. In shocking imagery, Jesus said that those who eat his flesh and drink his blood will have eternal life (Jn 6:53 – 54). Many, upon hearing these words, turned back and no longer followed Jesus (Jn 6:66).

On the night he was betrayed, these startling words would have profound significance. In an upper room, Jesus would celebrate the Passover with his disciples. There he would break a loaf of bread as a picture of his soon-to-be-broken body. From that time on, those who know Jesus celebrate the Lord's Supper by eating the bread as a reminder of the Lord's great sacrifice. They are reminded that true fulfillment, satisfaction, and nourishment are found by feasting on the bread from heaven, broken for his followers.

Water from the Rock

17 All the congregation of the people of Israel moved on from the wilderness
of Sin by stages, according to the commandment of the LORD, and camped
at Rephidim, but there was no water for the people to drink. 2 Therefore the people
quarreled with Moses and said, "Give us water to drink." And Moses said to them,
"Why do you quarrel with me? Why do you test the LORD?" 3 But the people thirst-
ed there for water, and the people grumbled against Moses and said, "Why did you
bring us up out of Egypt, to kill us and our children and our livestock with thirst?"
4 So Moses cried to the LORD, "What shall I do with this people? They are almost
ready to stone me." 5 And the LORD said to Moses, "Pass on before the people,
taking with you some of the elders of Israel, and take in your hand the staff with
which you struck the Nile, and go. 6 Behold, I will stand before you there on the
rock at Horeb, and you shall strike the rock, and water shall come out of it, and
the people will drink." And Moses did so, in the sight of the elders of Israel. 7 And
he called the name of the place Massah[1] and Meribah,[2] because of the quarreling
of the people of Israel, and because they tested the LORD by saying, "Is the LORD
among us or not?"

Israel Defeats Amalek

8 Then Amalek came and fought with Israel at Rephidim. 9 So Moses said to
Joshua, "Choose for us men, and go out and fight with Amalek. Tomorrow I will
stand on the top of the hill with the staff of God in my hand." 10 So Joshua did as
Moses told him, and fought with Amalek, while Moses, Aaron, and Hur went up
to the top of the hill. 11 Whenever Moses held up his hand, Israel prevailed, and
whenever he lowered his hand, Amalek prevailed. 12 But Moses' hands grew weary,
so they took a stone and put it under him, and he sat on it, while Aaron and Hur
held up his hands, one on one side, and the other on the other side. So his hands
were steady until the going down of the sun. 13 And Joshua overwhelmed Amalek
and his people with the sword.

14 Then the LORD said to Moses, "Write this as a memorial in a book and recite
it in the ears of Joshua, that I will utterly blot out the memory of Amalek from
under heaven." 15 And Moses built an altar and called the name of it, The LORD Is
My Banner, 16 saying, "A hand upon the throne[3] of the LORD! The LORD will have
war with Amalek from generation to generation."

Jethro's Advice

18 Jethro, the priest of Midian, Moses' father-in-law, heard of all that God
had done for Moses and for Israel his people, how the LORD had brought
Israel out of Egypt. 2 Now Jethro, Moses' father-in-law, had taken Zipporah, Moses' wife, after he had sent her home, 3 along with her two sons. The name of
the one was Gershom (for he said, "I have been a sojourner[4] in a foreign land"),
4 and the name of the other, Eliezer[5] (for he said, "The God of my father was my
help, and delivered me from the sword of Pharaoh"). 5 Jethro, Moses' father-in-
law, came with his sons and his wife to Moses in the wilderness where he was
encamped at the mountain of God. 6 And when he sent word to Moses, "I,[6] your
father-in-law Jethro, am coming to you with your wife and her two sons with
her," 7 Moses went out to meet his father-in-law and bowed down and kissed
him. And they asked each other of their welfare and went into the tent. 8 Then
Moses told his father-in-law all that the LORD had done to Pharaoh and to the
Egyptians for Israel's sake, all the hardship that had come upon them in the way,
and how the LORD had delivered them. 9 And Jethro rejoiced for all the good that
the LORD had done to Israel, in that he had delivered them out of the hand of
the Egyptians.

[1] *Massah* means *testing* [2] *Meribah* means *quarreling* [3] A slight change would yield *upon the banner*
[4] *Gershom* sounds like the Hebrew for *sojourner* [5] *Eliezer* means *My God is help* [6] Hebrew; Samaritan, Septuagint, Syriac *behold*

EXODUS 17:6

STRIKING THE ROCK

Despite Israel's faithlessness, God continued to provide for his people. In this particular instance, God sustained the people by having Moses strike the rock, from which water miraculously began to flow. While this provision was a startling way to provide water, the water itself was normal. The people of Israel would need water again in the future, and God would certainly provide.

In John 4:13–14, Jesus responded to a request for water by claiming that he could provide water that would cause a person never to be thirsty again. Jesus would indeed provide this water, but he was not speaking of literal water. Instead, Jesus was referencing the way in which God would provide salvation from sin. In the same way that Moses struck the rock to provide the life-saving water, Jesus was stricken and afflicted on the cross in order to provide the life-giving water of salvation. God struck one rock to provide for the temporary, physical needs of his people, but he struck the second Rock to provide for the spiritual needs of his people.

WATER FROM THE ROCK

The people demanded that Moses provide water to satiate their thirst. God provided Moses with instructions for how to provide water for their needs. God told Moses to take the rod and strike a rock. From this unlikely source, God provided water to meet the people's need. The faithless Israelites were reminded that the Lord would take care of them by bringing water from a rock.

The rock of God continues to nourish God's people throughout all of redemptive history. Centuries after God's miraculous provision from a rock in the wilderness, Jesus faced another group of contentious people. This time the Pharisees and the Sadducees asked him to show them a sign to validate his authority. Jesus, knowing their hearts, refused to entertain their demands. Rather, he took his disciples to a remote, mountainous location at Caesarea Philippi and there gave them a vivid object lesson.

He asked his followers to describe the public opinion regarding his identity. Peter, as the outspoken leader of Jesus' inner circle, declared that Jesus is "the Christ, the Son of the living God" (Mt 16:16). These titles were not mere flattery, but demonstrated that Peter understood Jesus to be the long-awaited King in the line of David. Jesus responded to Peter, whose name means "rock," telling him that this confession would be the basis for the foundation of his church. Jesus will build his church on this truth, and nothing, not even the gates of hell, will be able to destroy his church (Mt 16:17 – 18).

This rock will provide water for God's people for days without end. Jesus himself will provide streams of living water to his people in the church. Those who recognize their thirst can come to Jesus and be satisfied. Not only that, but the Spirit of God will fill them with streams of living water to quench their thirst forever (Jn 7:38 – 39).

10Jethro said, "Blessed be the LORD, who has delivered you out of the hand of
the Egyptians and out of the hand of Pharaoh and has delivered the people from
under the hand of the Egyptians. 11Now I know that the LORD is greater than all
gods, because in this affair they dealt arrogantly with the people."[1] 12And Jethro,
Moses' father-in-law, brought a burnt offering and sacrifices to God; and Aaron
came with all the elders of Israel to eat bread with Moses' father-in-law before
God.

13The next day Moses sat to judge the people, and the people stood around
Moses from morning till evening. 14When Moses' father-in-law saw all that he was
doing for the people, he said, "What is this that you are doing for the people? Why
do you sit alone, and all the people stand around you from morning till evening?"
15And Moses said to his father-in-law, "Because the people come to me to inquire
of God; 16when they have a dispute, they come to me and I decide between one
person and another, and I make them know the statutes of God and his laws."
17Moses' father-in-law said to him, "What you are doing is not good. 18You and
the people with you will certainly wear yourselves out, for the thing is too heavy
for you. You are not able to do it alone. 19Now obey my voice; I will give you advice, and God be with you! You shall represent the people before God and bring
their cases to God, 20and you shall warn them about the statutes and the laws,
and make them know the way in which they must walk and what they must do.
21Moreover, look for able men from all the people, men who fear God, who are
trustworthy and hate a bribe, and place such men over the people as chiefs of
thousands, of hundreds, of fifties, and of tens. 22And let them judge the people
at all times. Every great matter they shall bring to you, but any small matter they
shall decide themselves. So it will be easier for you, and they will bear the burden
with you. 23If you do this, God will direct you, you will be able to endure, and all
this people also will go to their place in peace."

24So Moses listened to the voice of his father-in-law and did all that he had
said. 25Moses chose able men out of all Israel and made them heads over the people, chiefs of thousands, of hundreds, of fifties, and of tens. 26And they judged
the people at all times. Any hard case they brought to Moses, but any small matter
they decided themselves. 27Then Moses let his father-in-law depart, and he went
away to his own country.

Israel at Mount Sinai

19 On the third new moon after the people of Israel had gone out of the land
of Egypt, on that day they came into the wilderness of Sinai. 2They set out
from Rephidim and came into the wilderness of Sinai, and they encamped in the
wilderness. There Israel encamped before the mountain, 3while Moses went up to
God. The LORD called to him out of the mountain, saying, "Thus you shall say to
the house of Jacob, and tell the people of Israel: 4'You yourselves have seen what
I did to the Egyptians, and how I bore you on eagles' wings and brought you to
myself. 5Now therefore, if you will indeed obey my voice and keep my covenant,
you shall be my treasured possession among all peoples, for all the earth is mine;
6and you shall be to me a kingdom of priests and a holy nation.' These are the
words that you shall speak to the people of Israel."

7So Moses came and called the elders of the people and set before them all
these words that the LORD had commanded him. 8All the people answered together and said, "All that the LORD has spoken we will do." And Moses reported
the words of the people to the LORD. 9And the LORD said to Moses, "Behold, I am
coming to you in a thick cloud, that the people may hear when I speak with you,
and may also believe you forever."

When Moses told the words of the people to the LORD, 10the LORD said to
Moses, "Go to the people and consecrate them today and tomorrow, and let them

---

[1]Hebrew *with them*

wash their garments 11and be ready for the third day. For on the third day the LORD
will come down on Mount Sinai in the sight of all the people. 12And you shall set
limits for the people all around, saying, 'Take care not to go up into the mountain
or touch the edge of it. Whoever touches the mountain shall be put to death. 13No
hand shall touch him, but he shall be stoned or shot;[1] whether beast or man, he
shall not live.' When the trumpet sounds a long blast, they shall come up to the
mountain." 14So Moses went down from the mountain to the people and consecrated the people; and they washed their garments. 15And he said to the people,
"Be ready for the third day; do not go near a woman."

16On the morning of the third day there were thunders and lightnings and a
thick cloud on the mountain and a very loud trumpet blast, so that all the people
in the camp trembled. 17Then Moses brought the people out of the camp to meet
God, and they took their stand at the foot of the mountain. 18Now Mount Sinai
was wrapped in smoke because the LORD had descended on it in fire. The smoke
of it went up like the smoke of a kiln, and the whole mountain trembled greatly.
19And as the sound of the trumpet grew louder and louder, Moses spoke, and God
answered him in thunder. 20The LORD came down on Mount Sinai, to the top of
the mountain. And the LORD called Moses to the top of the mountain, and Moses
went up.

21And the LORD said to Moses, "Go down and warn the people, lest they break
through to the LORD to look and many of them perish. 22Also let the priests who
come near to the LORD consecrate themselves, lest the LORD break out against
them." 23And Moses said to the LORD, "The people cannot come up to Mount Sinai, for you yourself warned us, saying, 'Set limits around the mountain and consecrate it.'" 24And the LORD said to him, "Go down, and come up bringing Aaron
with you. But do not let the priests and the people break through to come up to
the LORD, lest he break out against them." 25So Moses went down to the people
and told them.

The Ten Commandments

20 And God spoke all these words, saying,
2"I am the LORD your God, who brought you out of the land of Egypt, out
of the house of slavery.

3"You shall have no other gods before[2] me.

4"You shall not make for yourself a carved image, or any likeness of anything
that is in heaven above, or that is in the earth beneath, or that is in the water under the earth. 5You shall not bow down to them or serve them, for I the LORD your
God am a jealous God, visiting the iniquity of the fathers on the children to the
third and fourth generation of those who hate me, 6but showing steadfast love to
thousands[3] of those who love me and keep my commandments.

7"You shall not take the name of the LORD your God in vain, for the LORD will
not hold him guiltless who takes his name in vain.

8"Remember the Sabbath day, to keep it holy. 9Six days you shall labor, and do
all your work, 10but the seventh day is a Sabbath to the LORD your God. On it you
shall not do any work, you, or your son, or your daughter, your male servant, or
your female servant, or your livestock, or the sojourner who is within your gates.
11For in six days the LORD made the heavens and the earth, the sea, and all that is
in them, and rested on the seventh day. Therefore the LORD blessed the Sabbath
day and made it holy.

12"Honor your father and your mother, that your days may be long in the land
that the LORD your God is giving you.

13"You shall not murder.[4]

14"You shall not commit adultery.

[1]That is, shot with an arrow [2]Or *besides* [3]Or *to the thousandth generation* [4]The Hebrew word also covers causing human death through carelessness or negligence

EXODUS 19:12

APPROACHING GOD

God's people were forbidden from approaching God. Graciously, God dwelt among the people at his appointed mountain. This location, however, was protected lest the sinful people came near to a holy God. The all-consuming holiness of God would consume those who came into his presence. Only the priests at certain appointed times and in clearly defined ways could enter the presence of God. God was so concerned about protecting his dwelling that he instructed Moses to set boundaries around the mountain to keep the people at a safe distance. If the people failed to honor the boundaries, they were harshly judged by God.

The book of Hebrews demonstrates a stark transition that occurred as a result of Christ's work. Since Jesus perfectly and finally provided the sacrifice for the sins of his people, the dividing walls between God and man have been removed. A new and living way has now been opened whereby God's people can have confidence to draw near to him through the blood of Christ (Heb 10:19–22). Rather than finding safety by maintaining distance from God, those who know Christ can find safety by drawing near to God.

EXODUS 20:1–17

THE LAW OF GOD

The role of the law is a hotly debated question among Bible scholars. One thing is certain: at the outset, the law was never designed as a means by which people could earn a right relationship with God. The preamble to the law in Exodus 20 bases the

(continued on next page)

15“You shall not steal.
16“You shall not bear false witness against your neighbor.
17“You shall not covet your neighbor’s house; you shall not covet your neighbor’s wife, or his male servant, or his female servant, or his ox, or his donkey, or
anything that is your neighbor’s.”
18Now when all the people saw the thunder and the flashes of lightning and
the sound of the trumpet and the mountain smoking, the people were afraid[1] and
trembled, and they stood far off 19and said to Moses, “You speak to us, and we will
listen; but do not let God speak to us, lest we die.” 20Moses said to the people, “Do
not fear, for God has come to test you, that the fear of him may be before you, that
you may not sin.” 21The people stood far off, while Moses drew near to the thick
darkness where God was.

Laws About Altars

22And the LORD said to Moses, “Thus you shall say to the people of Israel: ‘You
have seen for yourselves that I have talked with you from heaven. 23You shall not
make gods of silver to be with me, nor shall you make for yourselves gods of gold.
24An altar of earth you shall make for me and sacrifice on it your burnt offerings
and your peace offerings, your sheep and your oxen. In every place where I cause
my name to be remembered I will come to you and bless you. 25If you make me an
altar of stone, you shall not build it of hewn stones, for if you wield your tool on it
you profane it. 26And you shall not go up by steps to my altar, that your nakedness
be not exposed on it.’

Laws About Slaves

21 “Now these are the rules that you shall set before them. 2When you buy a
Hebrew slave,[2] he shall serve six years, and in the seventh he shall go out
free, for nothing. 3If he comes in single, he shall go out single; if he comes in married, then his wife shall go out with him. 4If his master gives him a wife and she
bears him sons or daughters, the wife and her children shall be her master’s, and
he shall go out alone. 5But if the slave plainly says, ‘I love my master, my wife, and
my children; I will not go out free,’ 6then his master shall bring him to God, and
he shall bring him to the door or the doorpost. And his master shall bore his ear
through with an awl, and he shall be his slave forever.
7“When a man sells his daughter as a slave, she shall not go out as the male
slaves do. 8If she does not please her master, who has designated her[3] for himself,
then he shall let her be redeemed. He shall have no right to sell her to a foreign
people, since he has broken faith with her. 9If he designates her for his son, he
shall deal with her as with a daughter. 10If he takes another wife to himself, he
shall not diminish her food, her clothing, or her marital rights. 11And if he does
not do these three things for her, she shall go out for nothing, without payment
of money.
12“Whoever strikes a man so that he dies shall be put to death. 13But if he did
not lie in wait for him, but God let him fall into his hand, then I will appoint for
you a place to which he may flee. 14But if a man willfully attacks another to kill
him by cunning, you shall take him from my altar, that he may die.
15“Whoever strikes his father or his mother shall be put to death.
16“Whoever steals a man and sells him, and anyone found in possession of
him, shall be put to death.
17“Whoever curses[4] his father or his mother shall be put to death.
18“When men quarrel and one strikes the other with a stone or with his fist
and the man does not die but takes to his bed, 19then if the man rises again and

[1]Samaritan, Septuagint, Syriac, Vulgate; Masoretic Text *the people saw* [2]Or *servant*; the Hebrew term *'ebed* designates a range of social and economic roles; also verses 5, 6, 7, 20, 21, 26, 27, 32 (see Preface) [3]Or *so that he has not designated her* [4]Or *dishonors*; Septuagint *reviles*

(The Law of God, continued)

dictates of God on his character and work. He is the one who established a relationship with his people and showed his might by delivering them from slavery in Egypt. As a result of God’s gracious initiative, the people were to respond through worshipful obedience.

Though Israel was never able to keep the law perfectly, the law showed the nature of obedience and highlighted the inability of fallen humanity to obey God (Ro 7:7 – 12). Their failure only served to demonstrate their need for a Savior to atone for their sins. God’s work to make propitiation for the sins of his people prompts a desire to obey, not in order to earn his favor, but as a proper response to his unilateral work. A life of obedience is a work of God’s grace by the power of his Spirit in those whom he has already adopted as his children.

EXODUS 21:2 – 4

FREEDOM

The law of Israel contained a provision for granting freedom to fellow Israelites who sold themselves as indentured servants. After a period of six years, indentured servants were set free and allowed to return to their former lives. This process ensured that the ongoing practice of granting freedom was built into the fabric of the people of God.

Jesus taught that this practice modeled a far greater heavenly reality. The nature of sin enslaves all mankind by virtue of their common relationship with Adam’s sin and their ongoing sinful actions (Jn 8:34 – 36). Jesus’ work proclaimed freedom to spiritual slaves (Ro 6:22). Now free from the penalty

(continued on page 112)

THE TWO GREATEST COMMANDMENTS

The law was given as a gift of God's grace. God made a covenant with the entire nation of Israel while they were encamped at Mount Sinai. This covenant, often known as the Mosaic covenant because God gave the law through Moses, formalized the relationship that God would have with his people. In keeping with the form of ancient treaties, the law expounded the type of relationship that a superior (God) would have with his subjects (the nation of Israel). At the outset of the law, God reminded the people of his faithful character and the way he had cared for them.

Through obedience to the law, God's people could live out their identity as a holy people in contrast to their pagan neighbors. They were the object of God's relentless love and had become his special treasure (Ex 19:5–6). Through the law, they were given unique insight into the way God designed his people to function, relate to one another, and approach him. Their distinctive way of life would also serve to expose the surrounding nations to the glory of God. Other nations were meant to look at the nation of Israel and be drawn to know their God.

The instructions given in chapter 20 outline the path of righteousness that God desires for his people to follow. These first ten laws begin with the supremacy of God in all things and the type of worship he is due. From there, the people of God were given instructions on how their love for God should inform their love for other people made in the image of God.

Jesus distilled the law to these two chief pillars as well. When asked what the greatest commandment in the law is, he summarized the law as love for God and love for others. All of the law and the prophets' instructions hang on these two great commands, according to Jesus (Mt 22:37–40). This simplicity need not minimize the grand scope of the law but is meant to demonstrate the intended focus of obedience. A heart filled with love for God and for others will spill over into innumerable actions that embody this love. As God's beloved people, the church is to model the sacrificial work of Jesus himself, give themselves to the good work of loving God and others, and, in so doing, fulfill the law of Christ.

(Freedom, continued)

and power of sin, Christians are free to submit to a far greater Master, one whose yoke is easy and whose burden is light (Mt 11:30).

walks outdoors with his staff, he who struck him shall be clear; only he shall pay for the loss of his time, and shall have him thoroughly healed.

20 "When a man strikes his slave, male or female, with a rod and the slave dies under his hand, he shall be avenged. 21 But if the slave survives a day or two, he is not to be avenged, for the slave is his money.

22 "When men strive together and hit a pregnant woman, so that her children come out, but there is no harm, the one who hit her shall surely be fined, as the woman's husband shall impose on him, and he shall pay as the judges determine. 23 But if there is harm,[1] then you shall pay life for life, 24 eye for eye, tooth for tooth, hand for hand, foot for foot, 25 burn for burn, wound for wound, stripe for stripe.

26 "When a man strikes the eye of his slave, male or female, and destroys it, he shall let the slave go free because of his eye. 27 If he knocks out the tooth of his slave, male or female, he shall let the slave go free because of his tooth.

28 "When an ox gores a man or a woman to death, the ox shall be stoned, and its flesh shall not be eaten, but the owner of the ox shall not be liable. 29 But if the ox has been accustomed to gore in the past, and its owner has been warned but has not kept it in, and it kills a man or a woman, the ox shall be stoned, and its owner also shall be put to death. 30 If a ransom is imposed on him, then he shall give for the redemption of his life whatever is imposed on him. 31 If it gores a man's son or daughter, he shall be dealt with according to this same rule. 32 If the ox gores a slave, male or female, the owner shall give to their master thirty shekels[2] of silver, and the ox shall be stoned.

Laws About Restitution

33 "When a man opens a pit, or when a man digs a pit and does not cover it, and an ox or a donkey falls into it, 34 the owner of the pit shall make restoration. He shall give money to its owner, and the dead beast shall be his.

35 "When one man's ox butts another's, so that it dies, then they shall sell the live ox and share its price, and the dead beast also they shall share. 36 Or if it is known that the ox has been accustomed to gore in the past, and its owner has not kept it in, he shall repay ox for ox, and the dead beast shall be his.

22 [3] "If a man steals an ox or a sheep, and kills it or sells it, he shall repay five oxen for an ox, and four sheep for a sheep. 2[4] If a thief is found breaking in and is struck so that he dies, there shall be no bloodguilt for him, 3 but if the sun has risen on him, there shall be bloodguilt for him. He[5] shall surely pay. If he has nothing, then he shall be sold for his theft. 4 If the stolen beast is found alive in his possession, whether it is an ox or a donkey or a sheep, he shall pay double.

5 "If a man causes a field or vineyard to be grazed over, or lets his beast loose and it feeds in another man's field, he shall make restitution from the best in his own field and in his own vineyard.

6 "If fire breaks out and catches in thorns so that the stacked grain or the standing grain or the field is consumed, he who started the fire shall make full restitution.

7 "If a man gives to his neighbor money or goods to keep safe, and it is stolen from the man's house, then, if the thief is found, he shall pay double. 8 If the thief is not found, the owner of the house shall come near to God to show whether or not he has put his hand to his neighbor's property. 9 For every breach of trust, whether it is for an ox, for a donkey, for a sheep, for a cloak, or for any kind of lost thing, of which one says, 'This is it,' the case of both parties shall come before God. The one whom God condemns shall pay double to his neighbor.

10 "If a man gives to his neighbor a donkey or an ox or a sheep or any beast to keep safe, and it dies or is injured or is driven away, without anyone seeing it, 11 an oath by the LORD shall be between them both to see whether or not he has put

---

[1] *Or so that her children come out and it is clear who was to blame, he shall be fined as the woman's husband shall impose on him, and he alone shall pay.* [23] *If it is unclear who was to blame* [2] A *shekel* was about 2/5 ounce or 11 grams [3] Ch 21:37 in Hebrew [4] Ch 22:1 in Hebrew [5] That is, the thief

his hand to his neighbor's property. The owner shall accept the oath, and he shall not make restitution. [12]But if it is stolen from him, he shall make restitution to its owner. [13]If it is torn by beasts, let him bring it as evidence. He shall not make restitution for what has been torn.

[14]"If a man borrows anything of his neighbor, and it is injured or dies, the owner not being with it, he shall make full restitution. [15]If the owner was with it, he shall not make restitution; if it was hired, it came for its hiring fee.[1]

Laws for a Just Community

[16]"If a man seduces a virgin[2] who is not betrothed and lies with her, he shall give the bride-price[3] for her and make her his wife. [17]If her father utterly refuses to give her to him, he shall pay money equal to the bride-price for virgins.

[18]"You shall not permit a sorceress to live.

[19]"Whoever lies with an animal shall be put to death.

[20]"Whoever sacrifices to any god, other than the LORD alone, shall be devoted to destruction.[4]

[21]"You shall not wrong a sojourner or oppress him, for you were sojourners in the land of Egypt. [22]You shall not mistreat any widow or fatherless child. [23]If you do mistreat them, and they cry out to me, I will surely hear their cry, [24]and my wrath will burn, and I will kill you with the sword, and your wives shall become widows and your children fatherless.

[25]"If you lend money to any of my people with you who is poor, you shall not be like a moneylender to him, and you shall not exact interest from him. [26]If ever you take your neighbor's cloak in pledge, you shall return it to him before the sun goes down, [27]for that is his only covering, and it is his cloak for his body; in what else shall he sleep? And if he cries to me, I will hear, for I am compassionate.

[28]"You shall not revile God, nor curse a ruler of your people.

[29]"You shall not delay to offer from the fullness of your harvest and from the outflow of your presses. The firstborn of your sons you shall give to me. [30]You shall do the same with your oxen and with your sheep: seven days it shall be with its mother; on the eighth day you shall give it to me.

[31]"You shall be consecrated to me. Therefore you shall not eat any flesh that is torn by beasts in the field; you shall throw it to the dogs.

23 "You shall not spread a false report. You shall not join hands with a wicked man to be a malicious witness. [2]You shall not fall in with the many to do evil, nor shall you bear witness in a lawsuit, siding with the many, so as to pervert justice, [3]nor shall you be partial to a poor man in his lawsuit.

[4]"If you meet your enemy's ox or his donkey going astray, you shall bring it back to him. [5]If you see the donkey of one who hates you lying down under its burden, you shall refrain from leaving him with it; you shall rescue it with him.

[6]"You shall not pervert the justice due to your poor in his lawsuit. [7]Keep far from a false charge, and do not kill the innocent and righteous, for I will not acquit the wicked. [8]And you shall take no bribe, for a bribe blinds the clear-sighted and subverts the cause of those who are in the right.

[9]"You shall not oppress a sojourner. You know the heart of a sojourner, for you were sojourners in the land of Egypt.

Laws About the Sabbath and Festivals

[10]"For six years you shall sow your land and gather in its yield, [11]but the seventh year you shall let it rest and lie fallow, that the poor of your people may eat; and what they leave the beasts of the field may eat. You shall do likewise with your vineyard, and with your olive orchard.

---

[1]Or *it is reckoned in* (Hebrew *comes into*) *its hiring fee* [2]Or *a girl of marriageable age*; also verse 17 [3]Or *engagement present*; also verse 17 [4]That is, set apart (devoted) as an offering to the Lord (for destruction)

12 "Six days you shall do your work, but on the seventh day you shall rest; that your ox and your donkey may have rest, and the son of your servant woman, and the alien, may be refreshed.

13 "Pay attention to all that I have said to you, and make no mention of the names of other gods, nor let it be heard on your lips.

14 "Three times in the year you shall keep a feast to me. 15 You shall keep the Feast of Unleavened Bread. As I commanded you, you shall eat unleavened bread for seven days at the appointed time in the month of Abib, for in it you came out of Egypt. None shall appear before me empty-handed. 16 You shall keep the Feast of Harvest, of the firstfruits of your labor, of what you sow in the field. You shall keep the Feast of Ingathering at the end of the year, when you gather in from the field the fruit of your labor. 17 Three times in the year shall all your males appear before the Lord GOD.

18 "You shall not offer the blood of my sacrifice with anything leavened, or let the fat of my feast remain until the morning.

19 "The best of the firstfruits of your ground you shall bring into the house of the LORD your God.

"You shall not boil a young goat in its mother's milk.

Conquest of Canaan Promised

20 "Behold, I send an angel before you to guard you on the way and to bring you to the place that I have prepared. 21 Pay careful attention to him and obey his voice; do not rebel against him, for he will not pardon your transgression, for my name is in him.

22 "But if you carefully obey his voice and do all that I say, then I will be an enemy to your enemies and an adversary to your adversaries.

23 "When my angel goes before you and brings you to the Amorites and the Hittites and the Perizzites and the Canaanites, the Hivites and the Jebusites, and I blot them out, 24 you shall not bow down to their gods nor serve them, nor do as they do, but you shall utterly overthrow them and break their pillars in pieces. 25 You shall serve the LORD your God, and he[1] will bless your bread and your water, and I will take sickness away from among you. 26 None shall miscarry or be barren in your land; I will fulfill the number of your days. 27 I will send my terror before you and will throw into confusion all the people against whom you shall come, and I will make all your enemies turn their backs to you. 28 And I will send hornets[2] before you, which shall drive out the Hivites, the Canaanites, and the Hittites from before you. 29 I will not drive them out from before you in one year, lest the land become desolate and the wild beasts multiply against you. 30 Little by little I will drive them out from before you, until you have increased and possess the land. 31 And I will set your border from the Red Sea to the Sea of the Philistines, and from the wilderness to the Euphrates,[3] for I will give the inhabitants of the land into your hand, and you shall drive them out before you. 32 You shall make no covenant with them and their gods. 33 They shall not dwell in your land, lest they make you sin against me; for if you serve their gods, it will surely be a snare to you."

The Covenant Confirmed

24 Then he said to Moses, "Come up to the LORD, you and Aaron, Nadab, and Abihu, and seventy of the elders of Israel, and worship from afar. 2 Moses alone shall come near to the LORD, but the others shall not come near, and the people shall not come up with him."

3 Moses came and told the people all the words of the LORD and all the rules.[4] And all the people answered with one voice and said, "All the words that the LORD has spoken we will do." 4 And Moses wrote down all the words of the LORD. He rose

[1] Septuagint, Vulgate *I* [2] Or *the hornet* [3] Hebrew *the River* [4] Or *all the just decrees*

GOD'S ANGEL

God, on occasion, tangibly manifested himself among the nation of Israel in the form of an angel. The phrase "my angel" can refer either to a supernatural being or to a God-appointed messenger. For example, the prophet Malachi's name itself means "my messenger." The connection between the angel of the Lord and the messenger of God highlights the focus of these types of appearances of God in the Old Testament. The angel of the Lord was given the assignment to communicate God's word to his people, often at critical junctures in their journey. The angel led the people of God as the cloud and fire did in their wilderness journey (Ex 13:21 – 22; 14:19 – 24; 16:10; 19:9,16; 24:15 – 18; 33:9 – 11; 34:5; 40:34 – 38).

The special role of the angels and their sudden appearances lead some to question whether these angels are the pre-incarnate form of Jesus himself. Theophanies, or appearances of God among his people, occur on rare occasions in the Old Testament. This angel appears to Hagar and Ishmael in the wilderness (Ge 16:7 – 14), to Abraham by the trees of Mamre (Ge 18:1 – 3), to Jacob in a dream (Ge 31:11 – 13), and to Moses in the flame of a burning bush (Ex 3:2 – 4).

In each of these occasions, the angel appears to have unique insight, even personal knowledge, of the nature, character, and plan of God. Some suppose him to be the second member of the Trinity, making a brief appearance on the earth before the God-ordained time of his birth had arrived (Gal 4:4 – 7). The Scriptures do not clearly state that this is the case, so firm conclusions are impossible.

What is clear is that God, in tangible form, consistently breaks into human history in order to care for his people, communicate his message to them, and lead them from harm and to safety. The incarnation of Jesus would represent far more than a mere theophany in the Old Testament. His birth brought with it the in-breaking of the kingdom of God, the revelation of God's eternal plan of redemption, and the process by which humanity could be made right with God through faith in this promise.

early in the morning and built an altar at the foot of the mountain, and twelve pillars, according to the twelve tribes of Israel. 5And he sent young men of the people of Israel, who offered burnt offerings and sacrificed peace offerings of oxen to the LORD. 6And Moses took half of the blood and put it in basins, and half of the blood he threw against the altar. 7Then he took the Book of the Covenant and read it in the hearing of the people. And they said, "All that the LORD has spoken we will do, and we will be obedient." 8And Moses took the blood and threw it on the people and said, "Behold the blood of the covenant that the LORD has made with you in accordance with all these words."

9Then Moses and Aaron, Nadab, and Abihu, and seventy of the elders of Israel went up, 10and they saw the God of Israel. There was under his feet as it were a pavement of sapphire stone, like the very heaven for clearness. 11And he did not lay his hand on the chief men of the people of Israel; they beheld God, and ate and drank.

12The LORD said to Moses, "Come up to me on the mountain and wait there, that I may give you the tablets of stone, with the law and the commandment, which I have written for their instruction." 13So Moses rose with his assistant Joshua, and Moses went up into the mountain of God. 14And he said to the elders, "Wait here for us until we return to you. And behold, Aaron and Hur are with you. Whoever has a dispute, let him go to them."

15Then Moses went up on the mountain, and the cloud covered the mountain. 16The glory of the LORD dwelt on Mount Sinai, and the cloud covered it six days. And on the seventh day he called to Moses out of the midst of the cloud. 17Now the appearance of the glory of the LORD was like a devouring fire on the top of the mountain in the sight of the people of Israel. 18Moses entered the cloud and went up on the mountain. And Moses was on the mountain forty days and forty nights.

Contributions for the Sanctuary

25 The LORD said to Moses, 2"Speak to the people of Israel, that they take for me a contribution. From every man whose heart moves him you shall receive the contribution for me. 3And this is the contribution that you shall receive from them: gold, silver, and bronze, 4blue and purple and scarlet yarns and fine twined linen, goats' hair, 5tanned rams' skins, goatskins,[1] acacia wood, 6oil for the lamps, spices for the anointing oil and for the fragrant incense, 7onyx stones, and stones for setting, for the ephod and for the breastpiece. 8And let them make me a sanctuary, that I may dwell in their midst. 9Exactly as I show you concerning the pattern of the tabernacle, and of all its furniture, so you shall make it.

The Ark of the Covenant

10"They shall make an ark of acacia wood. Two cubits[2] and a half shall be its length, a cubit and a half its breadth, and a cubit and a half its height. 11You shall overlay it with pure gold, inside and outside shall you overlay it, and you shall make on it a molding of gold around it. 12You shall cast four rings of gold for it and put them on its four feet, two rings on the one side of it, and two rings on the other side of it. 13You shall make poles of acacia wood and overlay them with gold. 14And you shall put the poles into the rings on the sides of the ark to carry the ark by them. 15The poles shall remain in the rings of the ark; they shall not be taken from it. 16And you shall put into the ark the testimony that I shall give you.

17"You shall make a mercy seat[3] of pure gold. Two cubits and a half shall be its length, and a cubit and a half its breadth. 18And you shall make two cherubim of gold; of hammered work shall you make them, on the two ends of the mercy seat. 19Make one cherub on the one end, and one cherub on the other end. Of one

[1]Uncertain; possibly *dolphin skins*, or *dugong skins*; compare 26:14 [2]A *cubit* was about 18 inches or 45 centimeters [3]Or *cover*

EXODUS 24:5–8

SPRINKLED WITH BLOOD

God's covenant relationship with his people was made possible by the blood of a sacrifice. At the Passover, the Israelites placed blood over the doors of their houses. Here the individual members of the nation of Israel were sprinkled with the blood of the covenant. The people understood that their relationship with God was predicated on the substitutionary death of something else. The sin of the people was transmitted to the animal, and the animal died the death the people deserved, temporarily restoring their relationship with God.

Whereas the people of God in the Old Testament were marked with the blood of a sacrificial animal, the people of God in the church are permanently covered with the blood of the perfect sacrifice—Jesus Christ. Peter, writing to Christians scattered throughout Asia Minor, noted that they also were sprinkled with the blood of Jesus Christ (1Pe 1:2). Though they are dispersed among the nations, God still marks his people by blood.

EXODUS 25:17–22

ATONEMENT

The atonement cover (mercy seat) was the place for sacrifices within the tabernacle on the Day of Atonement. The title, derived from the verb meaning "to cover over," "to atone *for*," or "to make propitiation," was the place of offering on this day. This symbol refers to the cover placed on top of the ark and was the base on which the cherubim were placed

(continued on page 118)

A HEAVENLY PATTERN

To a modern reader, the exact specifications for the construction of the ark of the testimony may seem like a strange matter to include in God's written Word. Paul reminded the church, however, that there is no portion of the Scriptures which is not profitable for their edification (2Ti 3:16). Not only did God provide these instructions to the nation of Israel, but he also preserved them throughout the centuries for the instruction of his church. Thus, this passage (and the many others like it in the Old Testament) is important for understanding how God dwells among his people.

Creation itself was arranged in a particular order, with rivers marking the outmost boundaries of the Garden of Eden (Ge 2:10 – 14). Though the dimensions are not specified, it is clear there was a pattern for the organization of the dwelling of God among his first created image bearers. Sin exiled the first couple from the garden and banished them from the intimacy of God's presence.

Years later, Moses was shown a pattern for the ongoing dwelling of God among his people. This dwelling would not be in a garden but in an intricately designed tabernacle, filled with furniture designed to symbolize the way in which humanity could again commune with God. Moses was not simply asked to build a dwelling for God, but he was given the exact specifications for the shape, size, and structure of this gathering place and was commanded to follow the exact pattern that he was shown by God. This pattern indicated that there is a heavenly form to which the earthly tabernacle corresponds and reflects (Heb 8:5 – 6). The tabernacle, and later the temple, served as the physical location for the dwelling of God among the people until he would dwell among them perfectly in the form of his incarnate Son, Jesus Christ (Jn 1:1 – 14). Through Christ's work, the dwelling of God would move among the people, no longer confined to a dwelling made by human hands (Ac 17:24).

His second coming will one day usher in a day when the dwelling of God will once again be among his people (Rev 21:1 – 4). The prophet Habakkuk pictures a day when "the earth will be filled with the knowledge of the glory of the LORD as the waters cover the sea" (Hab 2:14). No longer will there be boundaries separating humanity from God, but the entire cosmos will resound with his fame.

(Atonement, continued)

(Heb 9:5). There, sacrificial animals were offered to the Lord and, by God's mercy, peace between God and humanity was established. The mercy seat served as the physical location at which the mercy and judgment of God met, and the sins of mankind were atoned for.

At the cross, God's mercy and judgment met as they did at the mercy seat. There, God's judgment was placed upon his Son, and his mercy was freely given. His death atones, or covers over, the sins of his people, making peace by the blood of the cross (Col 1:20; 1Jn 4:10). The ongoing significance of the cross as a symbol for Christians testifies to the profound way in which this peace with God is possible.

EXODUS 26:31–33

DRAW NEAR

Even within the tabernacle, the priests were separated from God by a curtain. The two chambers of the tabernacle were divided by a beautiful, intricately made curtain, which was hung from posts. The innermost area, the Most Holy Place, was the site of the offering made by the high priest on the annual Day of Atonement to atone for the sins of the people. The high priest could not enter the area behind the curtain into the Most Holy Place whenever he wanted, but only at the God-appointed time and by following a carefully outlined protocol. To transgress this process and enter God's presence in another way would lead to certain death.

The division between man and God was forever obliterated at the cross. In essence, Christ entered the Most Holy Place and offered himself

(continued on next page)

piece with the mercy seat shall you make the cherubim on its two ends. [20]The cherubim shall spread out their wings above, overshadowing the mercy seat with their wings, their faces one to another; toward the mercy seat shall the faces of the cherubim be. [21]And you shall put the mercy seat on the top of the ark, and in the ark you shall put the testimony that I shall give you. [22]There I will meet with you, and from above the mercy seat, from between the two cherubim that are on the ark of the testimony, I will speak with you about all that I will give you in commandment for the people of Israel.

The Table for Bread

[23]"You shall make a table of acacia wood. Two cubits shall be its length, a cubit its breadth, and a cubit and a half its height. [24]You shall overlay it with pure gold and make a molding of gold around it. [25]And you shall make a rim around it a handbreadth[1] wide, and a molding of gold around the rim. [26]And you shall make for it four rings of gold, and fasten the rings to the four corners at its four legs. [27]Close to the frame the rings shall lie, as holders for the poles to carry the table. [28]You shall make the poles of acacia wood, and overlay them with gold, and the table shall be carried with these. [29]And you shall make its plates and dishes for incense, and its flagons and bowls with which to pour drink offerings; you shall make them of pure gold. [30]And you shall set the bread of the Presence on the table before me regularly.

The Golden Lampstand

[31]"You shall make a lampstand of pure gold. The lampstand shall be made of hammered work: its base, its stem, its cups, its calyxes, and its flowers shall be of one piece with it. [32]And there shall be six branches going out of its sides, three branches of the lampstand out of one side of it and three branches of the lampstand out of the other side of it; [33]three cups made like almond blossoms, each with calyx and flower, on one branch, and three cups made like almond blossoms, each with calyx and flower, on the other branch—so for the six branches going out of the lampstand. [34]And on the lampstand itself there shall be four cups made like almond blossoms, with their calyxes and flowers, [35]and a calyx of one piece with it under each pair of the six branches going out from the lampstand. [36]Their calyxes and their branches shall be of one piece with it, the whole of it a single piece of hammered work of pure gold. [37]You shall make seven lamps for it. And the lamps shall be set up so as to give light on the space in front of it. [38]Its tongs and their trays shall be of pure gold. [39]It shall be made, with all these utensils, out of a talent[2] of pure gold. [40]And see that you make them after the pattern for them, which is being shown you on the mountain.

The Tabernacle

26 "Moreover, you shall make the tabernacle with ten curtains of fine twined linen and blue and purple and scarlet yarns; you shall make them with cherubim skillfully worked into them. [2]The length of each curtain shall be twenty-eight cubits,[3] and the breadth of each curtain four cubits; all the curtains shall be the same size. [3]Five curtains shall be coupled to one another, and the other five curtains shall be coupled to one another. [4]And you shall make loops of blue on the edge of the outermost curtain in the first set. Likewise you shall make loops on the edge of the outermost curtain in the second set. [5]Fifty loops you shall make on the one curtain, and fifty loops you shall make on the edge of the curtain that is in the second set; the loops shall be opposite one another. [6]And you shall make fifty clasps of gold, and couple the curtains one to the other with the clasps, so that the tabernacle may be a single whole.

[1]A *handbreadth* was about 3 inches or 7.5 centimeters [2]A *talent* was about 75 pounds or 34 kilograms
[3]A *cubit* was about 18 inches or 45 centimeters

7“You shall also make curtains of goats’ hair for a tent over the tabernacle;
eleven curtains shall you make. 8The length of each curtain shall be thirty cubits,
and the breadth of each curtain four cubits. The eleven curtains shall be the same
size. 9You shall couple five curtains by themselves, and six curtains by themselves, and the sixth curtain you shall double over at the front of the tent. 10You
shall make fifty loops on the edge of the curtain that is outermost in one set, and
fifty loops on the edge of the curtain that is outermost in the second set.
11“You shall make fifty clasps of bronze, and put the clasps into the loops, and
couple the tent together that it may be a single whole. 12And the part that remains
of the curtains of the tent, the half curtain that remains, shall hang over the back
of the tabernacle. 13And the extra that remains in the length of the curtains, the
cubit on the one side, and the cubit on the other side, shall hang over the sides of
the tabernacle, on this side and that side, to cover it. 14And you shall make for the
tent a covering of tanned rams’ skins[1] and a covering of goatskins on top.
15“You shall make upright frames for the tabernacle of acacia wood. 16Ten
cubits shall be the length of a frame, and a cubit and a half the breadth of each
frame. 17There shall be two tenons in each frame, for fitting together. So shall
you do for all the frames of the tabernacle. 18You shall make the frames for the
tabernacle: twenty frames for the south side; 19and forty bases of silver you shall
make under the twenty frames, two bases under one frame for its two tenons,
and two bases under the next frame for its two tenons; 20and for the second side
of the tabernacle, on the north side twenty frames, 21and their forty bases of
silver, two bases under one frame, and two bases under the next frame. 22And
for the rear of the tabernacle westward you shall make six frames. 23And you
shall make two frames for corners of the tabernacle in the rear; 24they shall be
separate beneath, but joined at the top, at the first ring. Thus shall it be with both
of them; they shall form the two corners. 25And there shall be eight frames, with
their bases of silver, sixteen bases; two bases under one frame, and two bases
under another frame.
26“You shall make bars of acacia wood, five for the frames of the one side of the
tabernacle, 27and five bars for the frames of the other side of the tabernacle, and
five bars for the frames of the side of the tabernacle at the rear westward. 28The
middle bar, halfway up the frames, shall run from end to end. 29You shall overlay
the frames with gold and shall make their rings of gold for holders for the bars,
and you shall overlay the bars with gold. 30Then you shall erect the tabernacle
according to the plan for it that you were shown on the mountain.
31“And you shall make a veil of blue and purple and scarlet yarns and fine
twined linen. It shall be made with cherubim skillfully worked into it. 32And you
shall hang it on four pillars of acacia overlaid with gold, with hooks of gold, on
four bases of silver. 33And you shall hang the veil from the clasps, and bring the
ark of the testimony in there within the veil. And the veil shall separate for you
the Holy Place from the Most Holy. 34You shall put the mercy seat on the ark of the
testimony in the Most Holy Place. 35And you shall set the table outside the veil,
and the lampstand on the south side of the tabernacle opposite the table, and you
shall put the table on the north side.
36“You shall make a screen for the entrance of the tent, of blue and purple
and scarlet yarns and fine twined linen, embroidered with needlework. 37And you
shall make for the screen five pillars of acacia, and overlay them with gold. Their
hooks shall be of gold, and you shall cast five bases of bronze for them.

The Bronze Altar

27 “You shall make the altar of acacia wood, five cubits[2] long and five cubits
broad. The altar shall be square, and its height shall be three cubits. 2And
you shall make horns for it on its four corners; its horns shall be of one piece with

(Draw Near, continued)

there as a sacrifice for the sins of the world. He did not enter with the blood of bulls and goats, but rather with his own blood, offering a perfect sacrifice once and for all. The symbolic rending of the temple curtain, from top to bottom, indicated that access to God has been granted because of what Christ has accomplished (Mt 27:51). Those with faith in Jesus can, with confidence, draw near to his presence at any time (Heb 4:16).

[1] Or *of rams’ skins dyed red* [2] A *cubit* was about 18 inches or 45 centimeters

it, and you shall overlay it with bronze. [3]You shall make pots for it to receive its ashes, and shovels and basins and forks and fire pans. You shall make all its utensils of bronze. [4]You shall also make for it a grating, a network of bronze, and on the net you shall make four bronze rings at its four corners. [5]And you shall set it under the ledge of the altar so that the net extends halfway down the altar. [6]And you shall make poles for the altar, poles of acacia wood, and overlay them with bronze. [7]And the poles shall be put through the rings, so that the poles are on the two sides of the altar when it is carried. [8]You shall make it hollow, with boards. As it has been shown you on the mountain, so shall it be made.

The Court of the Tabernacle

[9]"You shall make the court of the tabernacle. On the south side the court shall have hangings of fine twined linen a hundred cubits long for one side. [10]Its twenty pillars and their twenty bases shall be of bronze, but the hooks of the pillars and their fillets shall be of silver. [11]And likewise for its length on the north side there shall be hangings a hundred cubits long, its pillars twenty and their bases twenty, of bronze, but the hooks of the pillars and their fillets shall be of silver. [12]And for the breadth of the court on the west side there shall be hangings for fifty cubits, with ten pillars and ten bases. [13]The breadth of the court on the front to the east shall be fifty cubits. [14]The hangings for the one side of the gate shall be fifteen cubits, with their three pillars and three bases. [15]On the other side the hangings shall be fifteen cubits, with their three pillars and three bases. [16]For the gate of the court there shall be a screen twenty cubits long, of blue and purple and scarlet yarns and fine twined linen, embroidered with needlework. It shall have four pillars and with them four bases. [17]All the pillars around the court shall be filleted with silver. Their hooks shall be of silver, and their bases of bronze. [18]The length of the court shall be a hundred cubits, the breadth fifty, and the height five cubits, with hangings of fine twined linen and bases of bronze. [19]All the utensils of the tabernacle for every use, and all its pegs and all the pegs of the court, shall be of bronze.

Oil for the Lamp

[20]"You shall command the people of Israel that they bring to you pure beaten olive oil for the light, that a lamp may regularly be set up to burn. [21]In the tent of meeting, outside the veil that is before the testimony, Aaron and his sons shall tend it from evening to morning before the LORD. It shall be a statute forever to be observed throughout their generations by the people of Israel.

The Priests' Garments

28 "Then bring near to you Aaron your brother, and his sons with him, from among the people of Israel, to serve me as priests—Aaron and Aaron's sons, Nadab and Abihu, Eleazar and Ithamar. [2]And you shall make holy garments for Aaron your brother, for glory and for beauty. [3]You shall speak to all the skillful, whom I have filled with a spirit of skill, that they make Aaron's garments to consecrate him for my priesthood. [4]These are the garments that they shall make: a breastpiece, an ephod, a robe, a coat of checker work, a turban, and a sash. They shall make holy garments for Aaron your brother and his sons to serve me as priests. [5]They shall receive gold, blue and purple and scarlet yarns, and fine twined linen.

[6]"And they shall make the ephod of gold, of blue and purple and scarlet yarns, and of fine twined linen, skillfully worked. [7]It shall have two shoulder pieces attached to its two edges, so that it may be joined together. [8]And the skillfully woven band on it shall be made like it and be of one piece with it, of gold, blue and purple and scarlet yarns, and fine twined linen. [9]You shall take two onyx stones, and engrave on them the names of the sons of Israel, [10]six of their names on the one stone, and the names of the remaining six on the other stone, in the order of

their birth. 11As a jeweler engraves signets, so shall you engrave the two stones
with the names of the sons of Israel. You shall enclose them in settings of gold
filigree. 12And you shall set the two stones on the shoulder pieces of the ephod, as
stones of remembrance for the sons of Israel. And Aaron shall bear their names
before the LORD on his two shoulders for remembrance. 13You shall make settings
of gold filigree, 14and two chains of pure gold, twisted like cords; and you shall
attach the corded chains to the settings.

15"You shall make a breastpiece of judgment, in skilled work. In the style of
the ephod you shall make it—of gold, blue and purple and scarlet yarns, and fine
twined linen shall you make it. 16It shall be square and doubled, a span[1] its length
and a span its breadth. 17You shall set in it four rows of stones. A row of sardius,[2]
topaz, and carbuncle shall be the first row; 18and the second row an emerald, a
sapphire, and a diamond; 19and the third row a jacinth, an agate, and an amethyst;
20and the fourth row a beryl, an onyx, and a jasper. They shall be set in gold filigree. 21There shall be twelve stones with their names according to the names of
the sons of Israel. They shall be like signets, each engraved with its name, for the
twelve tribes. 22You shall make for the breastpiece twisted chains like cords, of
pure gold. 23And you shall make for the breastpiece two rings of gold, and put the
two rings on the two edges of the breastpiece. 24And you shall put the two cords
of gold in the two rings at the edges of the breastpiece. 25The two ends of the two
cords you shall attach to the two settings of filigree, and so attach it in front to the
shoulder pieces of the ephod. 26You shall make two rings of gold, and put them at
the two ends of the breastpiece, on its inside edge next to the ephod. 27And you
shall make two rings of gold, and attach them in front to the lower part of the two
shoulder pieces of the ephod, at its seam above the skillfully woven band of the
ephod. 28And they shall bind the breastpiece by its rings to the rings of the ephod
with a lace of blue, so that it may lie on the skillfully woven band of the ephod,
so that the breastpiece shall not come loose from the ephod. 29So Aaron shall
bear the names of the sons of Israel in the breastpiece of judgment on his heart,
when he goes into the Holy Place, to bring them to regular remembrance before
the LORD. 30And in the breastpiece of judgment you shall put the Urim and the
Thummim, and they shall be on Aaron's heart, when he goes in before the LORD.
Thus Aaron shall bear the judgment of the people of Israel on his heart before the
LORD regularly.

31"You shall make the robe of the ephod all of blue. 32It shall have an opening
for the head in the middle of it, with a woven binding around the opening, like
the opening in a garment,[3] so that it may not tear. 33On its hem you shall make
pomegranates of blue and purple and scarlet yarns, around its hem, with bells
of gold between them, 34a golden bell and a pomegranate, a golden bell and a
pomegranate, around the hem of the robe. 35And it shall be on Aaron when he
ministers, and its sound shall be heard when he goes into the Holy Place before
the LORD, and when he comes out, so that he does not die.

36"You shall make a plate of pure gold and engrave on it, like the engraving of
a signet, 'Holy to the LORD.' 37And you shall fasten it on the turban by a cord of
blue. It shall be on the front of the turban. 38It shall be on Aaron's forehead, and
Aaron shall bear any guilt from the holy things that the people of Israel consecrate
as their holy gifts. It shall regularly be on his forehead, that they may be accepted
before the LORD.

39"You shall weave the coat in checker work of fine linen, and you shall make
a turban of fine linen, and you shall make a sash embroidered with needlework.

40"For Aaron's sons you shall make coats and sashes and caps. You shall
make them for glory and beauty. 41And you shall put them on Aaron your
brother, and on his sons with him, and shall anoint them and ordain them and

[1]A *span* was about 9 inches or 22 centimeters [2]The identity of some of these stones is uncertain
[3]The meaning of the Hebrew word is uncertain; possibly *coat of mail*

consecrate them, that they may serve me as priests. 42 You shall make for them linen undergarments to cover their naked flesh. They shall reach from the hips to the thighs; 43 and they shall be on Aaron and on his sons when they go into the tent of meeting or when they come near the altar to minister in the Holy Place, lest they bear guilt and die. This shall be a statute forever for him and for his offspring after him.

Consecration of the Priests

29 “Now this is what you shall do to them to consecrate them, that they may serve me as priests. Take one bull of the herd and two rams without blemish, 2 and unleavened bread, unleavened cakes mixed with oil, and unleavened wafers smeared with oil. You shall make them of fine wheat flour. 3 You shall put them in one basket and bring them in the basket, and bring the bull and the two rams. 4 You shall bring Aaron and his sons to the entrance of the tent of meeting and wash them with water. 5 Then you shall take the garments, and put on Aaron the coat and the robe of the ephod, and the ephod, and the breastpiece, and gird him with the skillfully woven band of the ephod. 6 And you shall set the turban on his head and put the holy crown on the turban. 7 You shall take the anointing oil and pour it on his head and anoint him. 8 Then you shall bring his sons and put coats on them, 9 and you shall gird Aaron and his sons with sashes and bind caps on them. And the priesthood shall be theirs by a statute forever. Thus you shall ordain Aaron and his sons.

10 “Then you shall bring the bull before the tent of meeting. Aaron and his sons shall lay their hands on the head of the bull. 11 Then you shall kill the bull before the LORD at the entrance of the tent of meeting, 12 and shall take part of the blood of the bull and put it on the horns of the altar with your finger, and the rest of[1] the blood you shall pour out at the base of the altar. 13 And you shall take all the fat that covers the entrails, and the long lobe of the liver, and the two kidneys with the fat that is on them, and burn them on the altar. 14 But the flesh of the bull and its skin and its dung you shall burn with fire outside the camp; it is a sin offering.

15 “Then you shall take one of the rams, and Aaron and his sons shall lay their hands on the head of the ram, 16 and you shall kill the ram and shall take its blood and throw it against the sides of the altar. 17 Then you shall cut the ram into pieces, and wash its entrails and its legs, and put them with its pieces and its head, 18 and burn the whole ram on the altar. It is a burnt offering to the LORD. It is a pleasing aroma, a food offering[2] to the LORD.

19 “You shall take the other ram, and Aaron and his sons shall lay their hands on the head of the ram, 20 and you shall kill the ram and take part of its blood and put it on the tip of the right ear of Aaron and on the tips of the right ears of his sons, and on the thumbs of their right hands and on the great toes of their right feet, and throw the rest of the blood against the sides of the altar. 21 Then you shall take part of the blood that is on the altar, and of the anointing oil, and sprinkle it on Aaron and his garments, and on his sons and his sons' garments with him. He and his garments shall be holy, and his sons and his sons' garments with him.

22 “You shall also take the fat from the ram and the fat tail and the fat that covers the entrails, and the long lobe of the liver and the two kidneys with the fat that is on them, and the right thigh (for it is a ram of ordination), 23 and one loaf of bread and one cake of bread made with oil, and one wafer out of the basket of unleavened bread that is before the LORD. 24 You shall put all these on the palms of Aaron and on the palms of his sons, and wave them for a wave offering before the LORD. 25 Then you shall take them from their hands and burn them on the altar on top of the burnt offering, as a pleasing aroma before the LORD. It is a food offering to the LORD.

[1] Hebrew *all* [2] Or *an offering by fire*; also verses 25, 41

26"You shall take the breast of the ram of Aaron's ordination and wave it for a wave offering before the LORD, and it shall be your portion. 27And you shall consecrate the breast of the wave offering that is waved and the thigh of the priests' portion that is contributed from the ram of ordination, from what was Aaron's and his sons'. 28It shall be for Aaron and his sons as a perpetual due from the people of Israel, for it is a contribution. It shall be a contribution from the people of Israel from their peace offerings, their contribution to the LORD.

29"The holy garments of Aaron shall be for his sons after him; they shall be anointed in them and ordained in them. 30The son who succeeds him as priest, who comes into the tent of meeting to minister in the Holy Place, shall wear them seven days.

31"You shall take the ram of ordination and boil its flesh in a holy place. 32And Aaron and his sons shall eat the flesh of the ram and the bread that is in the basket in the entrance of the tent of meeting. 33They shall eat those things with which atonement was made at their ordination and consecration, but an outsider shall not eat of them, because they are holy. 34And if any of the flesh for the ordination or of the bread remain until the morning, then you shall burn the remainder with fire. It shall not be eaten, because it is holy.

35"Thus you shall do to Aaron and to his sons, according to all that I have commanded you. Through seven days shall you ordain them, 36and every day you shall offer a bull as a sin offering for atonement. Also you shall purify the altar, when you make atonement for it, and shall anoint it to consecrate it. 37Seven days you shall make atonement for the altar and consecrate it, and the altar shall be most holy. Whatever touches the altar shall become holy.

38"Now this is what you shall offer on the altar: two lambs a year old day by day regularly. 39One lamb you shall offer in the morning, and the other lamb you shall offer at twilight. 40And with the first lamb a tenth measure[1] of fine flour mingled with a fourth of a hin[2] of beaten oil, and a fourth of a hin of wine for a drink offering. 41The other lamb you shall offer at twilight, and shall offer with it a grain offering and its drink offering, as in the morning, for a pleasing aroma, a food offering to the LORD. 42It shall be a regular burnt offering throughout your generations at the entrance of the tent of meeting before the LORD, where I will meet with you, to speak to you there. 43There I will meet with the people of Israel, and it shall be sanctified by my glory. 44I will consecrate the tent of meeting and the altar. Aaron also and his sons I will consecrate to serve me as priests. 45I will dwell among the people of Israel and will be their God. 46And they shall know that I am the LORD their God, who brought them out of the land of Egypt that I might dwell among them. I am the LORD their God.

The Altar of Incense

30 "You shall make an altar on which to burn incense; you shall make it of acacia wood. 2A cubit[3] shall be its length, and a cubit its breadth. It shall be square, and two cubits shall be its height. Its horns shall be of one piece with it. 3You shall overlay it with pure gold, its top and around its sides and its horns. And you shall make a molding of gold around it. 4And you shall make two golden rings for it. Under its molding on two opposite sides of it you shall make them, and they shall be holders for poles with which to carry it. 5You shall make the poles of acacia wood and overlay them with gold. 6And you shall put it in front of the veil that is above the ark of the testimony, in front of the mercy seat that is above the testimony, where I will meet with you. 7And Aaron shall burn fragrant incense on it. Every morning when he dresses the lamps he shall burn it, 8and when Aaron sets up the lamps at twilight, he shall burn it, a regular incense offering before the LORD throughout your generations. 9You shall not offer unauthorized incense on

[1]Possibly an ephah (about 3/5 bushel or 22 liters) [2]A *hin* was about 4 quarts or 3.5 liters [3]A *cubit* was about 18 inches or 45 centimeters

PRIESTS

Aaron and his sons were uniquely set apart by God to serve as priests among the people of God. They played a mediator function between the people and God in that they represented the people before God. They had unique access to God because they oversaw the people's worship of God, making sacrifices on behalf of the people and representing their needs before a holy God. Like Noah and Abraham before them (Ge 8:20; 22:13), the priests were to worship God in the manner and location prescribed by him alone. Their work was not what most might think of when they imagine the holy leaders of the people of God. Rather than sterile worship, the priests gave themselves to the ongoing slaughter of animal after animal on behalf of the sins of the people. Their work was bloody and grotesque. In the desert heat, the ongoing sacrifice of animals would have created a nauseating concoction of animal waste, blood, sweat, and rotting flesh.

The imagery of the priesthood is central to the language the New Testament authors used to describe Jesus' work (Heb 7). Like Aaron and his sons, Jesus is appointed by God to the office of priest. He is given the task of facilitating the worship of God by his people and representing them before God. However, unlike the ancient priests who would offer an animal sacrifice, Jesus offered himself (Heb 7:27). The God-appointed priest and the very Son of God became the lamb of sacrifice on behalf of the sins of his people. His brutal execution embodied the nature of the priest's work. His beaten and bloodied body hung naked on a Roman cross in the heat of the day for all to see. Passersby would turn their faces in revulsion at this repulsive sight. Few would believe that on the cross the great high priest accomplished his greatest priestly work.

His once-for-all sacrifice finally and forever accomplished the work of the priesthood. This act completed, he sits now at the right hand of the Father, knowing that there will never again be the need for another sacrifice for sin (Heb 10:12). Now those who worship God do so, not by means of a human priesthood and an animal sacrifice, but through faith in Jesus, the One who was both the great high priest and the perfect Lamb of God.

it, or a burnt offering, or a grain offering, and you shall not pour a drink offering
on it. 10Aaron shall make atonement on its horns once a year. With the blood of
the sin offering of atonement he shall make atonement for it once in the year
throughout your generations. It is most holy to the LORD."

The Census Tax

11The LORD said to Moses, 12"When you take the census of the people of Israel,
then each shall give a ransom for his life to the LORD when you number them,
that there be no plague among them when you number them. 13Each one who
is numbered in the census shall give this: half a shekel[1] according to the shekel
of the sanctuary (the shekel is twenty gerahs),[2] half a shekel as an offering to
the LORD. 14Everyone who is numbered in the census, from twenty years old and
upward, shall give the LORD's offering. 15The rich shall not give more, and the poor
shall not give less, than the half shekel, when you give the LORD's offering to make
atonement for your lives. 16You shall take the atonement money from the people
of Israel and shall give it for the service of the tent of meeting, that it may bring
the people of Israel to remembrance before the LORD, so as to make atonement
for your lives."

The Bronze Basin

17The LORD said to Moses, 18"You shall also make a basin of bronze, with its
stand of bronze, for washing. You shall put it between the tent of meeting and the
altar, and you shall put water in it, 19with which Aaron and his sons shall wash
their hands and their feet. 20When they go into the tent of meeting, or when they
come near the altar to minister, to burn a food offering[3] to the LORD, they shall
wash with water, so that they may not die. 21They shall wash their hands and their
feet, so that they may not die. It shall be a statute forever to them, even to him and
to his offspring throughout their generations."

The Anointing Oil and Incense

22The LORD said to Moses, 23"Take the finest spices: of liquid myrrh 500 shekels, and of sweet-smelling cinnamon half as much, that is, 250, and 250 of aro-
matic cane, 24and 500 of cassia, according to the shekel of the sanctuary, and a
hin[4] of olive oil. 25And you shall make of these a sacred anointing oil blended as
by the perfumer; it shall be a holy anointing oil. 26With it you shall anoint the
tent of meeting and the ark of the testimony, 27and the table and all its utensils,
and the lampstand and its utensils, and the altar of incense, 28and the altar of
burnt offering with all its utensils and the basin and its stand. 29You shall consecrate them, that they may be most holy. Whatever touches them will become holy.
30You shall anoint Aaron and his sons, and consecrate them, that they may serve
me as priests. 31And you shall say to the people of Israel, 'This shall be my holy
anointing oil throughout your generations. 32It shall not be poured on the body of
an ordinary person, and you shall make no other like it in composition. It is holy,
and it shall be holy to you. 33Whoever compounds any like it or whoever puts any
of it on an outsider shall be cut off from his people.'"

34The LORD said to Moses, "Take sweet spices, stacte, and onycha, and galba-
num, sweet spices with pure frankincense (of each shall there be an equal part),
35and make an incense blended as by the perfumer, seasoned with salt, pure and
holy. 36You shall beat some of it very small, and put part of it before the testimony
in the tent of meeting where I shall meet with you. It shall be most holy for you.
37And the incense that you shall make according to its composition, you shall not
make for yourselves. It shall be for you holy to the LORD. 38Whoever makes any
like it to use as perfume shall be cut off from his people."

[1]A *shekel* was about 2/5 ounce or 11 grams [2]A *gerah* was about 1/50 ounce or 0.6 gram [3]Or *an offering by fire* [4]A *hin* was about 4 quarts or 3.5 liters

Oholiab and Bezalel

31 The LORD said to Moses, 2“See, I have called by name Bezalel the son of Uri, son of Hur, of the tribe of Judah, 3and I have filled him with the Spirit of God, with ability and intelligence, with knowledge and all craftsmanship, 4to devise artistic designs, to work in gold, silver, and bronze, 5in cutting stones for setting, and in carving wood, to work in every craft. 6And behold, I have appointed with him Oholiab, the son of Ahisamach, of the tribe of Dan. And I have given to all able men ability, that they may make all that I have commanded you: 7the tent of meeting, and the ark of the testimony, and the mercy seat that is on it, and all the furnishings of the tent, 8the table and its utensils, and the pure lampstand with all its utensils, and the altar of incense, 9and the altar of burnt offering with all its utensils, and the basin and its stand, 10and the finely worked garments,[1] the holy garments for Aaron the priest and the garments of his sons, for their service as priests, 11and the anointing oil and the fragrant incense for the Holy Place. According to all that I have commanded you, they shall do.”

The Sabbath

12And the LORD said to Moses, 13“You are to speak to the people of Israel and say, ‘Above all you shall keep my Sabbaths, for this is a sign between me and you throughout your generations, that you may know that I, the LORD, sanctify you. 14You shall keep the Sabbath, because it is holy for you. Everyone who profanes it shall be put to death. Whoever does any work on it, that soul shall be cut off from among his people. 15Six days shall work be done, but the seventh day is a Sabbath of solemn rest, holy to the LORD. Whoever does any work on the Sabbath day shall be put to death. 16Therefore the people of Israel shall keep the Sabbath, observing the Sabbath throughout their generations, as a covenant forever. 17It is a sign forever between me and the people of Israel that in six days the LORD made the heavens and the earth, and on the seventh day he rested and was refreshed.’ ”

18And he gave to Moses, when he had finished speaking with him on Mount Sinai, the two tablets of the testimony, tablets of stone, written with the finger of God.

The Golden Calf

32 When the people saw that Moses delayed to come down from the mountain, the people gathered themselves together to Aaron and said to him, “Up, make us gods who shall go before us. As for this Moses, the man who brought us up out of the land of Egypt, we do not know what has become of him.” 2So Aaron said to them, “Take off the rings of gold that are in the ears of your wives, your sons, and your daughters, and bring them to me.” 3So all the people took off the rings of gold that were in their ears and brought them to Aaron. 4And he received the gold from their hand and fashioned it with a graving tool and made a golden[2] calf. And they said, “These are your gods, O Israel, who brought you up out of the land of Egypt!” 5When Aaron saw this, he built an altar before it. And Aaron made a proclamation and said, “Tomorrow shall be a feast to the LORD.” 6And they rose up early the next day and offered burnt offerings and brought peace offerings. And the people sat down to eat and drink and rose up to play.

7And the LORD said to Moses, “Go down, for your people, whom you brought up out of the land of Egypt, have corrupted themselves. 8They have turned aside quickly out of the way that I commanded them. They have made for themselves a golden calf and have worshiped it and sacrificed to it and said, ‘These are your gods, O Israel, who brought you up out of the land of Egypt!’ ” 9And the LORD said to Moses, “I have seen this people, and behold, it is a stiff-necked people. 10Now therefore let me alone, that my wrath may burn hot against them and I may consume them, in order that I may make a great nation of you.”

[1]Or *garments for worship* [2]Hebrew *cast metal*; also verse 8

EXODUS 31:1–11

WORKMANSHIP

Bezalel son of Uri is not a household name for most people. However, at the beginning of the construction of the tabernacle he is singled out as uniquely filled with God's Spirit and instrumental in building a house of worship for the people of God. Bezalel, whose name means "in the shadow of God," reflects God's glory by serving as the lead artisan for the tabernacle. The result of the Spirit's work is seen in Bezalel's wisdom, understanding, knowledge, and workmanship. Bezalel has a multitude of gifts uniquely suited for his calling to build the tabernacle (Ex 31:3; 35:31).

Paul would later use the same concept to speak of all those who are brought from death to life by virtue of Jesus' work. They are then "his workmanship, created in Christ Jesus for good works" (Eph 2:10). Certainly these works will differ from person to person, yet all people are endowed with gifts by the Spirit and given a vital role to play in God's mission in the world (Ro 12:3–8).

[11]But Moses implored the LORD his God and said, "O LORD, why does your wrath
burn hot against your people, whom you have brought out of the land of Egypt
with great power and with a mighty hand? [12]Why should the Egyptians say, 'With
evil intent did he bring them out, to kill them in the mountains and to consume
them from the face of the earth'? Turn from your burning anger and relent from
this disaster against your people. [13]Remember Abraham, Isaac, and Israel, your
servants, to whom you swore by your own self, and said to them, 'I will multiply
your offspring as the stars of heaven, and all this land that I have promised I will
give to your offspring, and they shall inherit it forever.'" [14]And the LORD relented
from the disaster that he had spoken of bringing on his people.
[15]Then Moses turned and went down from the mountain with the two tablets
of the testimony in his hand, tablets that were written on both sides; on the front
and on the back they were written. [16]The tablets were the work of God, and the
writing was the writing of God, engraved on the tablets. [17]When Joshua heard the
noise of the people as they shouted, he said to Moses, "There is a noise of war in
the camp." [18]But he said, "It is not the sound of shouting for victory, or the sound
of the cry of defeat, but the sound of singing that I hear." [19]And as soon as he came
near the camp and saw the calf and the dancing, Moses' anger burned hot, and
he threw the tablets out of his hands and broke them at the foot of the mountain.
[20]He took the calf that they had made and burned it with fire and ground it to
powder and scattered it on the water and made the people of Israel drink it.
[21]And Moses said to Aaron, "What did this people do to you that you have
brought such a great sin upon them?" [22]And Aaron said, "Let not the anger of my
lord burn hot. You know the people, that they are set on evil. [23]For they said to me,
'Make us gods who shall go before us. As for this Moses, the man who brought us
up out of the land of Egypt, we do not know what has become of him.' [24]So I said
to them, 'Let any who have gold take it off.' So they gave it to me, and I threw it
into the fire, and out came this calf."
[25]And when Moses saw that the people had broken loose (for Aaron had let
them break loose, to the derision of their enemies), [26]then Moses stood in the gate
of the camp and said, "Who is on the LORD's side? Come to me." And all the sons
of Levi gathered around him. [27]And he said to them, "Thus says the LORD God of
Israel, 'Put your sword on your side each of you, and go to and fro from gate to gate
throughout the camp, and each of you kill his brother and his companion and his
neighbor.'" [28]And the sons of Levi did according to the word of Moses. And that
day about three thousand men of the people fell. [29]And Moses said, "Today you
have been ordained for the service of the LORD, each one at the cost of his son and
of his brother, so that he might bestow a blessing upon you this day."
[30]The next day Moses said to the people, "You have sinned a great sin. And
now I will go up to the LORD; perhaps I can make atonement for your sin." [31]So
Moses returned to the LORD and said, "Alas, this people has sinned a great sin.
They have made for themselves gods of gold. [32]But now, if you will forgive their
sin—but if not, please blot me out of your book that you have written." [33]But the
LORD said to Moses, "Whoever has sinned against me, I will blot out of my book.
[34]But now go, lead the people to the place about which I have spoken to you; behold, my angel shall go before you. Nevertheless, in the day when I visit, I will visit
their sin upon them."
[35]Then the LORD sent a plague on the people, because they made the calf, the
one that Aaron made.

The Command to Leave Sinai

33 The LORD said to Moses, "Depart; go up from here, you and the people
whom you have brought up out of the land of Egypt, to the land of which I
swore to Abraham, Isaac, and Jacob, saying, 'To your offspring I will give it.' [2]I will
send an angel before you, and I will drive out the Canaanites, the Amorites, the
Hittites, the Perizzites, the Hivites, and the Jebusites. [3]Go up to a land flowing

---

EXODUS 32:11–13

PERFECT INTERCESSION

Moses interceded before God on behalf of the people in a priestly prayer, asking him to relent from destroying the nation based on three factors. First, God had just delivered the nation of Israel from Egypt, and he could not abandon them now. Second, Pharaoh would learn of the destruction of the nation and believe that Egypt had, in fact, been victorious and that God's plan was to bring them out of Egypt in order to kill them. Third, God had promised to uphold his covenant to his people, and he could not turn back on his promises. Moses' prayer demonstrated his understanding of the severity of the sin of the people, his knowledge of the glory of the Lord, and his zeal for his people.

Jesus' intercessory prayer in the garden on the night he was betrayed follows this same pattern (Jn 17). Knowing the reality of life in a fallen world, he asked God to guard his people, protect them from the enemy, demonstrate his love to them, and transform them by means of his Word. The author of Hebrews stated that Jesus, as the sinless intercessor and Son of God, has been resurrected and has ascended to the right hand of the Father so he can plead for the needs of his people (Heb 7:23–25).

EXODUS 32:32

MY LIFE FOR THEIR LIVES

Moses begged God to forgive the sin of the people, offering to give

(continued on next page)

(My Life for Their Lives, continued)

his life as a substitute for theirs should God so desire. The inexcusable sin of making and worshiping the golden calf prompted the righteous judgment of God. How could a people who had so recently been the recipients of the might and power of God decide to do such a thing? The inexplicable nature of this sin highlights the foolishness of all sin and the necessity of God's judgment.

Yet, as always, God's grace shone through. He did not blot Israel from the face of the earth, though he would have been justified in doing so. He was faithful to his covenant and sustained the nation, though he judged those who sinned against him. In his request, Moses recognized that someone must die for these sins, and he asked God to allow a substitute. But what they needed was a perfect substitute—one who was without sin and capable of offering himself to God as an unblemished sacrifice. They needed Jesus, the one who could do what Moses could not—namely, offer himself for sin, not merely for Israel, but for all of God's people forever.

EXODUS 33:18–23

GLORY

Moses made an astounding request. He asked God to show him his glory. The word "glory" conveys the idea of weight, significance, or importance. In short, God's glory is the sum total of all the things that make him God. God, in an act of grace, agreed to Moses' request and provided him a brief and passing glimpse of his eternal worth and majesty, demonstrating his power, his love to his chosen servant, and his calling for Moses to lead Israel into the promised land.

(continued on next page)

with milk and honey; but I will not go up among you, lest I consume you on the
way, for you are a stiff-necked people."
4When the people heard this disastrous word, they mourned, and no one put
on his ornaments. 5For the LORD had said to Moses, "Say to the people of Israel,
'You are a stiff-necked people; if for a single moment I should go up among you,
I would consume you. So now take off your ornaments, that I may know what to
do with you.'" 6Therefore the people of Israel stripped themselves of their ornaments, from Mount Horeb onward.

The Tent of Meeting

7Now Moses used to take the tent and pitch it outside the camp, far off from
the camp, and he called it the tent of meeting. And everyone who sought the LORD
would go out to the tent of meeting, which was outside the camp. 8Whenever
Moses went out to the tent, all the people would rise up, and each would stand
at his tent door, and watch Moses until he had gone into the tent. 9When Moses
entered the tent, the pillar of cloud would descend and stand at the entrance of
the tent, and the LORD[1] would speak with Moses. 10And when all the people saw
the pillar of cloud standing at the entrance of the tent, all the people would rise
up and worship, each at his tent door. 11Thus the LORD used to speak to Moses face
to face, as a man speaks to his friend. When Moses turned again into the camp,
his assistant Joshua the son of Nun, a young man, would not depart from the tent.

Moses' Intercession

12Moses said to the LORD, "See, you say to me, 'Bring up this people,' but you
have not let me know whom you will send with me. Yet you have said, 'I know you
by name, and you have also found favor in my sight.' 13Now therefore, if I have
found favor in your sight, please show me now your ways, that I may know you
in order to find favor in your sight. Consider too that this nation is your people."
14And he said, "My presence will go with you, and I will give you rest." 15And he
said to him, "If your presence will not go with me, do not bring us up from here.
16For how shall it be known that I have found favor in your sight, I and your people? Is it not in your going with us, so that we are distinct, I and your people, from
every other people on the face of the earth?"
17And the LORD said to Moses, "This very thing that you have spoken I will
do, for you have found favor in my sight, and I know you by name." 18Moses said,
"Please show me your glory." 19And he said, "I will make all my goodness pass
before you and will proclaim before you my name 'The LORD.' And I will be gracious to whom I will be gracious, and will show mercy on whom I will show mercy.
20But," he said, "you cannot see my face, for man shall not see me and live." 21And
the LORD said, "Behold, there is a place by me where you shall stand on the rock,
22and while my glory passes by I will put you in a cleft of the rock, and I will cover
you with my hand until I have passed by. 23Then I will take away my hand, and you
shall see my back, but my face shall not be seen."

Moses Makes New Tablets

34 The LORD said to Moses, "Cut for yourself two tablets of stone like the
first, and I will write on the tablets the words that were on the first tablets, which you broke. 2Be ready by the morning, and come up in the morning to
Mount Sinai, and present yourself there to me on the top of the mountain. 3No
one shall come up with you, and let no one be seen throughout all the mountain.
Let no flocks or herds graze opposite that mountain." 4So Moses cut two tablets
of stone like the first. And he rose early in the morning and went up on Mount
Sinai, as the LORD had commanded him, and took in his hand two tablets of stone.
5The LORD descended in the cloud and stood with him there, and proclaimed the

[1] Hebrew *he*

name of the LORD. 6The LORD passed before him and proclaimed, "The LORD, the
LORD, a God merciful and gracious, slow to anger, and abounding in steadfast
love and faithfulness, 7keeping steadfast love for thousands,[1] forgiving iniquity
and transgression and sin, but who will by no means clear the guilty, visiting the
iniquity of the fathers on the children and the children's children, to the third and
the fourth generation." 8And Moses quickly bowed his head toward the earth and
worshiped. 9And he said, "If now I have found favor in your sight, O Lord, please
let the Lord go in the midst of us, for it is a stiff-necked people, and pardon our
iniquity and our sin, and take us for your inheritance."

The Covenant Renewed

10And he said, "Behold, I am making a covenant. Before all your people I will
do marvels, such as have not been created in all the earth or in any nation. And
all the people among whom you are shall see the work of the LORD, for it is an
awesome thing that I will do with you.
11"Observe what I command you this day. Behold, I will drive out before you
the Amorites, the Canaanites, the Hittites, the Perizzites, the Hivites, and the
Jebusites. 12Take care, lest you make a covenant with the inhabitants of the land
to which you go, lest it become a snare in your midst. 13You shall tear down their
altars and break their pillars and cut down their Asherim 14(for you shall worship
no other god, for the LORD, whose name is Jealous, is a jealous God), 15lest you
make a covenant with the inhabitants of the land, and when they whore after
their gods and sacrifice to their gods and you are invited, you eat of his sacrifice,
16and you take of their daughters for your sons, and their daughters whore after
their gods and make your sons whore after their gods.
17"You shall not make for yourself any gods of cast metal.
18"You shall keep the Feast of Unleavened Bread. Seven days you shall eat unleavened bread, as I commanded you, at the time appointed in the month Abib,
for in the month Abib you came out from Egypt. 19All that open the womb are
mine, all your male[2] livestock, the firstborn of cow and sheep. 20The firstborn of
a donkey you shall redeem with a lamb, or if you will not redeem it you shall break
its neck. All the firstborn of your sons you shall redeem. And none shall appear
before me empty-handed.
21"Six days you shall work, but on the seventh day you shall rest. In plowing
time and in harvest you shall rest. 22You shall observe the Feast of Weeks, the
firstfruits of wheat harvest, and the Feast of Ingathering at the year's end. 23Three
times in the year shall all your males appear before the Lord GOD, the God of Israel. 24For I will cast out nations before you and enlarge your borders; no one
shall covet your land, when you go up to appear before the LORD your God three
times in the year.
25"You shall not offer the blood of my sacrifice with anything leavened, or let
the sacrifice of the Feast of the Passover remain until the morning. 26The best of
the firstfruits of your ground you shall bring to the house of the LORD your God.
You shall not boil a young goat in its mother's milk."
27And the LORD said to Moses, "Write these words, for in accordance with
these words I have made a covenant with you and with Israel." 28So he was there
with the LORD forty days and forty nights. He neither ate bread nor drank water.
And he wrote on the tablets the words of the covenant, the Ten Commandments.[3]

The Shining Face of Moses

29When Moses came down from Mount Sinai, with the two tablets of the testimony in his hand as he came down from the mountain, Moses did not know
that the skin of his face shone because he had been talking with God.[4] 30Aaron

[1]Or *to the thousandth generation* [2]Septuagint, Theodotion, Vulgate, Targum; the meaning of the Hebrew is uncertain [3]Hebrew *the ten words* [4]Hebrew *him*

(Glory, continued)

One would think that this type of exposure to the glory of God would be reserved only for the great leaders of the Bible—people like Abraham, Joseph, Moses, or David. Yet God actually provides all Christians with an ever-increasing display of his glory (2Co 4:6). But this glimpse of glory is not physically observable now. Instead, the Spirit of God captivates believers' hearts with the glory of God, flooding them with the light of Christ and allowing them to see the majesty of God demonstrated in the person and work of Jesus Christ. This glimpse of glory is the basis for loving God, renouncing sin, and serving in God's mission in the world.

and all the people of Israel saw Moses, and behold, the skin of his face shone, and they were afraid to come near him. 31 But Moses called to them, and Aaron and all the leaders of the congregation returned to him, and Moses talked with them. 32 Afterward all the people of Israel came near, and he commanded them all that the LORD had spoken with him on Mount Sinai. 33 And when Moses had finished speaking with them, he put a veil over his face.

34 Whenever Moses went in before the LORD to speak with him, he would remove the veil, until he came out. And when he came out and told the people of Israel what he was commanded, 35 the people of Israel would see the face of Moses, that the skin of Moses' face was shining. And Moses would put the veil over his face again, until he went in to speak with him.

Sabbath Regulations

35 Moses assembled all the congregation of the people of Israel and said to them, "These are the things that the LORD has commanded you to do. 2 Six days work shall be done, but on the seventh day you shall have a Sabbath of solemn rest, holy to the LORD. Whoever does any work on it shall be put to death. 3 You shall kindle no fire in all your dwelling places on the Sabbath day."

Contributions for the Tabernacle

4 Moses said to all the congregation of the people of Israel, "This is the thing that the LORD has commanded. 5 Take from among you a contribution to the LORD. Whoever is of a generous heart, let him bring the LORD's contribution: gold, silver, and bronze; 6 blue and purple and scarlet yarns and fine twined linen; goats' hair, 7 tanned rams' skins, and goatskins;[1] acacia wood, 8 oil for the light, spices for the anointing oil and for the fragrant incense, 9 and onyx stones and stones for setting, for the ephod and for the breastpiece.

10 "Let every skillful craftsman among you come and make all that the LORD has commanded: 11 the tabernacle, its tent and its covering, its hooks and its frames, its bars, its pillars, and its bases; 12 the ark with its poles, the mercy seat, and the veil of the screen; 13 the table with its poles and all its utensils, and the bread of the Presence; 14 the lampstand also for the light, with its utensils and its lamps, and the oil for the light; 15 and the altar of incense, with its poles, and the anointing oil and the fragrant incense, and the screen for the door, at the door of the tabernacle; 16 the altar of burnt offering, with its grating of bronze, its poles, and all its utensils, the basin and its stand; 17 the hangings of the court, its pillars and its bases, and the screen for the gate of the court; 18 the pegs of the tabernacle and the pegs of the court, and their cords; 19 the finely worked garments for ministering[2] in the Holy Place, the holy garments for Aaron the priest, and the garments of his sons, for their service as priests."

20 Then all the congregation of the people of Israel departed from the presence of Moses. 21 And they came, everyone whose heart stirred him, and everyone whose spirit moved him, and brought the LORD's contribution to be used for the tent of meeting, and for all its service, and for the holy garments. 22 So they came, both men and women. All who were of a willing heart brought brooches and earrings and signet rings and armlets, all sorts of gold objects, every man dedicating an offering of gold to the LORD. 23 And every one who possessed blue or purple or scarlet yarns or fine linen or goats' hair or tanned rams' skins or goatskins brought them. 24 Everyone who could make a contribution of silver or bronze brought it as the LORD's contribution. And every one who possessed acacia wood of any use in the work brought it. 25 And every skillful woman spun with her hands, and they all brought what they had spun in blue and purple and scarlet yarns and fine twined linen. 26 All the women whose hearts stirred them to use

[1] The meaning of the Hebrew word is uncertain; also verse 23; compare 25:5 [2] Or *garments for worship*; see 31:10

UNVEILED FACES

Moses' proximity to God's glory caused his face to radiate with light. The fact that a sinful man like Moses was allowed to see a glimpse of the glory of God demonstrates the sacrifice of God and his willingness — in fact, his desire — to be known by those whom he has created. As Moses descended from the mountain, the glow on his face proved that he had been in the presence of God.

The veil separating mankind from the glory of God was symbolic of a far greater divide. The holy, blameless God could no longer commune with his broken image-bearers due to their sin. Without a sacrifice, mankind would never again be able to walk with God in the cool of the garden and talk with him as a friend. Instead, all people were cast out of his presence, shown by the distance the people had to maintain between themselves and the mountain on which God dwelled. Even Moses could not partake of the full radiance of the glory of God, nor could he communicate that glory to the people without a veil of separation.

Paul claimed that the entire Old Testament law and sacrificial system functioned as a preventative veil that hindered the ability of the Jewish nation to properly respond to the person and work of Jesus Christ (2Co 3:7–18). Rather than serving as a tutor to show people their need for Christ, the law caused people to stumble and miss their need for Christ's redemptive work. The veil was far more than something they wore on their faces, but it was something that surrounded their hearts and prevented them from faith in Jesus. They wrongly believed that they could be made right with God by keeping the law rather than repenting and trusting in Christ.

Paul pointed out that this type of veil can only be removed by Christ himself. He, by the work of his Spirit, is capable of removing the veil that separates humanity from God. This freedom from the burden of the law allows mankind to see and respond to the glory of God with unveiled faces. And, as people see the glory of God, they are transformed to reflect that glory, from one degree to another, until the great and glorious day when all of his people see him face to face.

A FOREVER REST

Sabbath-rest followed the model God established in creation, when, after creating the world in six days, he rested on the seventh day and called it holy. This rhythm of work and rest was built into the way God designed humanity to function and thrive. All believers are to give themselves to meaningful work that cares for and enhances God's world in order to give him glory. Then, as an act of faith and trust, believers must rest, showing their dependence on God and finding satisfaction in intimacy with their Creator.

The hope of the promised land served as a picture of Sabbath-rest. After enslavement in Egypt and an arduous journey in the wilderness, the people found rest in a land that was free from war and flowing with milk and honey. There they could dwell in safety and worship God rightly — or so they thought. The story of the nation of Israel proves that such rest was short-lived, at best. The people were never willing to drive out the inhabitants of the land completely, thus they were constantly facing the threat of enemy attacks. Their inconsistent obedience meant that the judgment of God was never far off. The hope of rest remained, but it likely seemed like a long-forgotten dream.

The author of Hebrews reminded a scattered church, long after Israel's failure and exile, that the hope of rest still stands (Heb 4). This time, however, the promise of rest is not found in a day of the week or a location on a map. Instead, the promise of rest is found by being united with Christ, free from the tyranny of sin. This rest frees humanity from the laborious and impossible process of trying to secure God's blessing by means of their righteous deeds. Since Christ has fulfilled the law for his people and given them his righteousness through faith, they can rest, knowing that the work is finished and their standing before God is secure. They can find rest at any time and at any place by coming to Christ whose yoke is easy and whose burden is light (Mt 11:30). In him, weary souls can find refreshment, and broken hearts can be made whole.

their skill spun the goats' hair. 27And the leaders brought onyx stones and stones to be set, for the ephod and for the breastpiece, 28and spices and oil for the light, and for the anointing oil, and for the fragrant incense. 29All the men and women, the people of Israel, whose heart moved them to bring anything for the work that the LORD had commanded by Moses to be done brought it as a freewill offering to the LORD.

Construction of the Tabernacle

30Then Moses said to the people of Israel, "See, the LORD has called by name Bezalel the son of Uri, son of Hur, of the tribe of Judah; 31and he has filled him with the Spirit of God, with skill, with intelligence, with knowledge, and with all craftsmanship, 32to devise artistic designs, to work in gold and silver and bronze, 33in cutting stones for setting, and in carving wood, for work in every skilled craft. 34And he has inspired him to teach, both him and Oholiab the son of Ahisamach of the tribe of Dan. 35He has filled them with skill to do every sort of work done by an engraver or by a designer or by an embroiderer in blue and purple and scarlet yarns and fine twined linen, or by a weaver—by any sort of workman or skilled designer.

36 "Bezalel and Oholiab and every craftsman in whom the LORD has put skill and intelligence to know how to do any work in the construction of the sanctuary shall work in accordance with all that the LORD has commanded."

2And Moses called Bezalel and Oholiab and every craftsman in whose mind the LORD had put skill, everyone whose heart stirred him up to come to do the work. 3And they received from Moses all the contribution that the people of Israel had brought for doing the work on the sanctuary. They still kept bringing him freewill offerings every morning, 4so that all the craftsmen who were doing every sort of task on the sanctuary came, each from the task that he was doing, 5and said to Moses, "The people bring much more than enough for doing the work that the LORD has commanded us to do." 6So Moses gave command, and word was proclaimed throughout the camp, "Let no man or woman do anything more for the contribution for the sanctuary." So the people were restrained from bringing, 7for the material they had was sufficient to do all the work, and more.

8And all the craftsmen among the workmen made the tabernacle with ten curtains. They were made of fine twined linen and blue and purple and scarlet yarns, with cherubim skillfully worked. 9The length of each curtain was twenty-eight cubits,[1] and the breadth of each curtain four cubits. All the curtains were the same size.

10He[2] coupled five curtains to one another, and the other five curtains he coupled to one another. 11He made loops of blue on the edge of the outermost curtain of the first set. Likewise he made them on the edge of the outermost curtain of the second set. 12He made fifty loops on the one curtain, and he made fifty loops on the edge of the curtain that was in the second set. The loops were opposite one another. 13And he made fifty clasps of gold, and coupled the curtains one to the other with clasps. So the tabernacle was a single whole.

14He also made curtains of goats' hair for a tent over the tabernacle. He made eleven curtains. 15The length of each curtain was thirty cubits, and the breadth of each curtain four cubits. The eleven curtains were the same size. 16He coupled five curtains by themselves, and six curtains by themselves. 17And he made fifty loops on the edge of the outermost curtain of the one set, and fifty loops on the edge of the other connecting curtain. 18And he made fifty clasps of bronze to couple the tent together that it might be a single whole. 19And he made for the tent a covering of tanned rams' skins and goatskins.

20Then he made the upright frames for the tabernacle of acacia wood. 21Ten cubits was the length of a frame, and a cubit and a half the breadth of each frame.

[1]A *cubit* was about 18 inches or 45 centimeters [2]Probably Bezalel (compare 35:30; 37:1)

[22]Each frame had two tenons for fitting together. He did this for all the frames of the tabernacle. [23]The frames for the tabernacle he made thus: twenty frames for the south side. [24]And he made forty bases of silver under the twenty frames, two bases under one frame for its two tenons, and two bases under the next frame for its two tenons. [25]For the second side of the tabernacle, on the north side, he made twenty frames [26]and their forty bases of silver, two bases under one frame and two bases under the next frame. [27]For the rear of the tabernacle westward he made six frames. [28]He made two frames for corners of the tabernacle in the rear. [29]And they were separate beneath but joined at the top, at the first ring. He made two of them this way for the two corners. [30]There were eight frames with their bases of silver: sixteen bases, under every frame two bases.

[31]He made bars of acacia wood, five for the frames of the one side of the tabernacle, [32]and five bars for the frames of the other side of the tabernacle, and five bars for the frames of the tabernacle at the rear westward. [33]And he made the middle bar to run from end to end halfway up the frames. [34]And he overlaid the frames with gold, and made their rings of gold for holders for the bars, and overlaid the bars with gold.

[35]He made the veil of blue and purple and scarlet yarns and fine twined linen; with cherubim skillfully worked into it he made it. [36]And for it he made four pillars of acacia and overlaid them with gold. Their hooks were of gold, and he cast for them four bases of silver. [37]He also made a screen for the entrance of the tent, of blue and purple and scarlet yarns and fine twined linen, embroidered with needlework, [38]and its five pillars with their hooks. He overlaid their capitals, and their fillets were of gold, but their five bases were of bronze.

Making the Ark

37 Bezalel made the ark of acacia wood. Two cubits[1] and a half was its length, a cubit and a half its breadth, and a cubit and a half its height. [2]And he overlaid it with pure gold inside and outside, and made a molding of gold around it. [3]And he cast for it four rings of gold for its four feet, two rings on its one side and two rings on its other side. [4]And he made poles of acacia wood and overlaid them with gold [5]and put the poles into the rings on the sides of the ark to carry the ark. [6]And he made a mercy seat of pure gold. Two cubits and a half was its length, and a cubit and a half its breadth. [7]And he made two cherubim of gold. He made them of hammered work on the two ends of the mercy seat, [8]one cherub on the one end, and one cherub on the other end. Of one piece with the mercy seat he made the cherubim on its two ends. [9]The cherubim spread out their wings above, overshadowing the mercy seat with their wings, with their faces one to another; toward the mercy seat were the faces of the cherubim.

Making the Table

[10]He also made the table of acacia wood. Two cubits was its length, a cubit its breadth, and a cubit and a half its height. [11]And he overlaid it with pure gold, and made a molding of gold around it. [12]And he made a rim around it a handbreadth[2] wide, and made a molding of gold around the rim. [13]He cast for it four rings of gold and fastened the rings to the four corners at its four legs. [14]Close to the frame were the rings, as holders for the poles to carry the table. [15]He made the poles of acacia wood to carry the table, and overlaid them with gold. [16]And he made the vessels of pure gold that were to be on the table, its plates and dishes for incense, and its bowls and flagons with which to pour drink offerings.

Making the Lampstand

[17]He also made the lampstand of pure gold. He made the lampstand of hammered work. Its base, its stem, its cups, its calyxes, and its flowers were of one

[1]A *cubit* was about 18 inches or 45 centimeters [2]A *handbreadth* was about 3 inches or 7.5 centimeters

piece with it. [18]And there were six branches going out of its sides, three branches
of the lampstand out of one side of it and three branches of the lampstand out
of the other side of it; [19]three cups made like almond blossoms, each with calyx
and flower, on one branch, and three cups made like almond blossoms, each with
calyx and flower, on the other branch—so for the six branches going out of the
lampstand. [20]And on the lampstand itself were four cups made like almond blossoms, with their calyxes and flowers, [21]and a calyx of one piece with it under each
pair of the six branches going out of it. [22]Their calyxes and their branches were
of one piece with it. The whole of it was a single piece of hammered work of pure
gold. [23]And he made its seven lamps and its tongs and its trays of pure gold. [24]He
made it and all its utensils out of a talent[1] of pure gold.

Making the Altar of Incense

[25]He made the altar of incense of acacia wood. Its length was a cubit, and its
breadth was a cubit. It was square, and two cubits was its height. Its horns were
of one piece with it. [26]He overlaid it with pure gold, its top and around its sides
and its horns. And he made a molding of gold around it, [27]and made two rings of
gold on it under its molding, on two opposite sides of it, as holders for the poles
with which to carry it. [28]And he made the poles of acacia wood and overlaid them
with gold.

[29]He made the holy anointing oil also, and the pure fragrant incense, blended
as by the perfumer.

Making the Altar of Burnt Offering

38 He made the altar of burnt offering of acacia wood. Five cubits[2] was its
length, and five cubits its breadth. It was square, and three cubits was its
height. [2]He made horns for it on its four corners. Its horns were of one piece with
it, and he overlaid it with bronze. [3]And he made all the utensils of the altar, the
pots, the shovels, the basins, the forks, and the fire pans. He made all its utensils
of bronze. [4]And he made for the altar a grating, a network of bronze, under its
ledge, extending halfway down. [5]He cast four rings on the four corners of the
bronze grating as holders for the poles. [6]He made the poles of acacia wood and
overlaid them with bronze. [7]And he put the poles through the rings on the sides
of the altar to carry it with them. He made it hollow, with boards.

Making the Bronze Basin

[8]He made the basin of bronze and its stand of bronze, from the mirrors of the
ministering women who ministered in the entrance of the tent of meeting.

Making the Court

[9]And he made the court. For the south side the hangings of the court were of
fine twined linen, a hundred cubits; [10]their twenty pillars and their twenty bases
were of bronze, but the hooks of the pillars and their fillets were of silver. [11]And
for the north side there were hangings of a hundred cubits; their twenty pillars
and their twenty bases were of bronze, but the hooks of the pillars and their fillets were of silver. [12]And for the west side were hangings of fifty cubits, their ten
pillars, and their ten bases; the hooks of the pillars and their fillets were of silver.
[13]And for the front to the east, fifty cubits. [14]The hangings for one side of the gate
were fifteen cubits, with their three pillars and three bases. [15]And so for the other
side. On both sides of the gate of the court were hangings of fifteen cubits, with
their three pillars and their three bases. [16]All the hangings around the court were
of fine twined linen. [17]And the bases for the pillars were of bronze, but the hooks
of the pillars and their fillets were of silver. The overlaying of their capitals was
also of silver, and all the pillars of the court were filleted with silver. [18]And the

[1]A *talent* was about 75 pounds or 34 kilograms [2]A *cubit* was about 18 inches or 45 centimeters

screen for the gate of the court was embroidered with needlework in blue and
purple and scarlet yarns and fine twined linen. It was twenty cubits long and five
cubits high in its breadth, corresponding to the hangings of the court. 19And their
pillars were four in number. Their four bases were of bronze, their hooks of silver,
and the overlaying of their capitals and their fillets of silver. 20And all the pegs for
the tabernacle and for the court all around were of bronze.

Materials for the Tabernacle

21These are the records of the tabernacle, the tabernacle of the testimony,
as they were recorded at the commandment of Moses, the responsibility of the
Levites under the direction of Ithamar the son of Aaron the priest. 22Bezalel the
son of Uri, son of Hur, of the tribe of Judah, made all that the LORD commanded
Moses; 23and with him was Oholiab the son of Ahisamach, of the tribe of Dan, an
engraver and designer and embroiderer in blue and purple and scarlet yarns and
fine twined linen.

24All the gold that was used for the work, in all the construction of the sanctuary, the gold from the offering, was twenty-nine talents and 730 shekels,[1] by the
shekel of the sanctuary. 25The silver from those of the congregation who were
recorded was a hundred talents and 1,775 shekels, by the shekel of the sanctuary:
26a beka[2] a head (that is, half a shekel, by the shekel of the sanctuary), for everyone who was listed in the records, from twenty years old and upward, for 603,550
men. 27The hundred talents of silver were for casting the bases of the sanctuary
and the bases of the veil; a hundred bases for the hundred talents, a talent a base.
28And of the 1,775 shekels he made hooks for the pillars and overlaid their capitals
and made fillets for them. 29The bronze that was offered was seventy talents and
2,400 shekels; 30with it he made the bases for the entrance of the tent of meeting,
the bronze altar and the bronze grating for it and all the utensils of the altar, 31the
bases around the court, and the bases of the gate of the court, all the pegs of the
tabernacle, and all the pegs around the court.

Making the Priestly Garments

39 From the blue and purple and scarlet yarns they made finely woven garments,[3] for ministering in the Holy Place. They made the holy garments for
Aaron, as the LORD had commanded Moses.

2He made the ephod of gold, blue and purple and scarlet yarns, and fine
twined linen. 3And they hammered out gold leaf, and he cut it into threads to
work into the blue and purple and the scarlet yarns, and into the fine twined lin-
en, in skilled design. 4They made for the ephod attaching shoulder pieces, joined
to it at its two edges. 5And the skillfully woven band on it was of one piece with it
and made like it, of gold, blue and purple and scarlet yarns, and fine twined linen,
as the LORD had commanded Moses.

6They made the onyx stones, enclosed in settings of gold filigree, and engraved
like the engravings of a signet, according to the names of the sons of Israel. 7And
he set them on the shoulder pieces of the ephod to be stones of remembrance for
the sons of Israel, as the LORD had commanded Moses.

8He made the breastpiece, in skilled work, in the style of the ephod, of gold,
blue and purple and scarlet yarns, and fine twined linen. 9It was square. They
made the breastpiece doubled, a span[4] its length and a span its breadth when
doubled. 10And they set in it four rows of stones. A row of sardius, topaz, and
carbuncle was the first row; 11and the second row, an emerald, a sapphire, and
a diamond; 12and the third row, a jacinth, an agate, and an amethyst; 13and the
fourth row, a beryl, an onyx, and a jasper. They were enclosed in settings of gold
filigree. 14There were twelve stones with their names according to the names of

[1]A *talent* was about 75 pounds or 34 kilograms; a *shekel* was about 2/5 ounce or 11 grams [2]A *beka* was about 1/5 ounce or 5.5 grams [3]Or *garments for worship* [4]A *span* was about 9 inches or 22 centimeters

the sons of Israel. They were like signets, each engraved with its name, for the
twelve tribes. 15And they made on the breastpiece twisted chains like cords, of
pure gold. 16And they made two settings of gold filigree and two gold rings, and
put the two rings on the two edges of the breastpiece. 17And they put the two
cords of gold in the two rings at the edges of the breastpiece. 18They attached the
two ends of the two cords to the two settings of filigree. Thus they attached it in
front to the shoulder pieces of the ephod. 19Then they made two rings of gold, and
put them at the two ends of the breastpiece, on its inside edge next to the ephod.
20And they made two rings of gold, and attached them in front to the lower part
of the two shoulder pieces of the ephod, at its seam above the skillfully woven
band of the ephod. 21And they bound the breastpiece by its rings to the rings of
the ephod with a lace of blue, so that it should lie on the skillfully woven band of
the ephod, and that the breastpiece should not come loose from the ephod, as the
LORD had commanded Moses.

22He also made the robe of the ephod woven all of blue, 23and the opening of
the robe in it was like the opening in a garment, with a binding around the opening, so that it might not tear. 24On the hem of the robe they made pomegranates
of blue and purple and scarlet yarns and fine twined linen. 25They also made bells
of pure gold, and put the bells between the pomegranates all around the hem of
the robe, between the pomegranates— 26a bell and a pomegranate, a bell and a
pomegranate around the hem of the robe for ministering, as the LORD had commanded Moses.

27They also made the coats, woven of fine linen, for Aaron and his sons, 28and
the turban of fine linen, and the caps of fine linen, and the linen undergarments
of fine twined linen, 29and the sash of fine twined linen and of blue and purple
and scarlet yarns, embroidered with needlework, as the LORD had commanded
Moses.

30They made the plate of the holy crown of pure gold, and wrote on it an inscription, like the engraving of a signet, "Holy to the LORD." 31And they tied to it a
cord of blue to fasten it on the turban above, as the LORD had commanded Moses.

32Thus all the work of the tabernacle of the tent of meeting was finished, and
the people of Israel did according to all that the LORD had commanded Moses;
so they did. 33Then they brought the tabernacle to Moses, the tent and all its
utensils, its hooks, its frames, its bars, its pillars, and its bases; 34the covering of
tanned rams' skins and goatskins, and the veil of the screen; 35the ark of the testimony with its poles and the mercy seat; 36the table with all its utensils, and the
bread of the Presence; 37the lampstand of pure gold and its lamps with the lamps
set and all its utensils, and the oil for the light; 38the golden altar, the anointing oil
and the fragrant incense, and the screen for the entrance of the tent; 39the bronze
altar, and its grating of bronze, its poles, and all its utensils; the basin and its
stand; 40the hangings of the court, its pillars, and its bases, and the screen for the
gate of the court, its cords, and its pegs; and all the utensils for the service of the
tabernacle, for the tent of meeting; 41the finely worked garments for ministering
in the Holy Place, the holy garments for Aaron the priest, and the garments of his
sons for their service as priests. 42According to all that the LORD had commanded
Moses, so the people of Israel had done all the work. 43And Moses saw all the
work, and behold, they had done it; as the LORD had commanded, so had they
done it. Then Moses blessed them.

The Tabernacle Erected

40 The LORD spoke to Moses, saying, 2"On the first day of the first month
you shall erect the tabernacle of the tent of meeting. 3And you shall put
in it the ark of the testimony, and you shall screen the ark with the veil. 4And you
shall bring in the table and arrange it, and you shall bring in the lampstand and
set up its lamps. 5And you shall put the golden altar for incense before the ark of
the testimony, and set up the screen for the door of the tabernacle. 6You shall set

EXODUS 39:32

FINALLY FINISHED

The place of worship was finally finished. After what was surely a grueling process, the Israelites were now able to celebrate the completion of the means by which they could worship God on their journey to the promised land. God's house, though, would not last forever. Once in the promised land, the people of God would construct a stationary dwelling for God—the temple. On its completion, the temple was thought to be a permanent structure (2Ch 8:16). The rebellion of the people and their exile from the land proved that the temple would not last forever either. The people were carried away from the land, and the temple was destroyed. The impermanence of the tabernacle and temple demonstrated the need for a dwelling place for God that would last.

Jesus' incarnation was the means by which God "tabernacled," or dwelt among, his people once again (Jn 1:14). His cry from the cross, "It is finished" was finally true (Jn 19:30). The dwelling of God among people was permanently and irrevocably established through Christ's work. The Holy Spirit has filled his people and will never be taken away.

the altar of burnt offering before the door of the tabernacle of the tent of meeting, [7]and place the basin between the tent of meeting and the altar, and put water in it. [8]And you shall set up the court all around, and hang up the screen for the gate of the court.

[9]"Then you shall take the anointing oil and anoint the tabernacle and all that is in it, and consecrate it and all its furniture, so that it may become holy. [10]You shall also anoint the altar of burnt offering and all its utensils, and consecrate the altar, so that the altar may become most holy. [11]You shall also anoint the basin and its stand, and consecrate it. [12]Then you shall bring Aaron and his sons to the entrance of the tent of meeting and shall wash them with water [13]and put on Aaron the holy garments. And you shall anoint him and consecrate him, that he may serve me as priest. [14]You shall bring his sons also and put coats on them, [15]and anoint them, as you anointed their father, that they may serve me as priests. And their anointing shall admit them to a perpetual priesthood throughout their generations."

[16]This Moses did; according to all that the LORD commanded him, so he did. [17]In the first month in the second year, on the first day of the month, the tabernacle was erected. [18]Moses erected the tabernacle. He laid its bases, and set up its frames, and put in its poles, and raised up its pillars. [19]And he spread the tent over the tabernacle and put the covering of the tent over it, as the LORD had commanded Moses. [20]He took the testimony and put it into the ark, and put the poles on the ark and set the mercy seat above on the ark. [21]And he brought the ark into the tabernacle and set up the veil of the screen, and screened the ark of the testimony, as the LORD had commanded Moses. [22]He put the table in the tent of meeting, on the north side of the tabernacle, outside the veil, [23]and arranged the bread on it before the LORD, as the LORD had commanded Moses. [24]He put the lampstand in the tent of meeting, opposite the table on the south side of the tabernacle, [25]and set up the lamps before the LORD, as the LORD had commanded Moses. [26]He put the golden altar in the tent of meeting before the veil, [27]and burned fragrant incense on it, as the LORD had commanded Moses. [28]He put in place the screen for the door of the tabernacle. [29]And he set the altar of burnt offering at the entrance of the tabernacle of the tent of meeting, and offered on it the burnt offering and the grain offering, as the LORD had commanded Moses. [30]He set the basin between the tent of meeting and the altar, and put water in it for washing, [31]with which Moses and Aaron and his sons washed their hands and their feet. [32]When they went into the tent of meeting, and when they approached the altar, they washed, as the LORD commanded Moses. [33]And he erected the court around the tabernacle and the altar, and set up the screen of the gate of the court. So Moses finished the work.

The Glory of the LORD

[34]Then the cloud covered the tent of meeting, and the glory of the LORD filled the tabernacle. [35]And Moses was not able to enter the tent of meeting because the cloud settled on it, and the glory of the LORD filled the tabernacle. [36]Throughout all their journeys, whenever the cloud was taken up from over the tabernacle, the people of Israel would set out. [37]But if the cloud was not taken up, then they did not set out till the day that it was taken up. [38]For the cloud of the LORD was on the tabernacle by day, and fire was in it by night, in the sight of all the house of Israel throughout all their journeys.

JESUS: OUR SACRIFICIAL SUBSTITUTE

LEVITICUS

LEVITICUS

EXODUS FROM EGYPT *c. 1446 BC*	AARON AND SONS CONSECRATED AS PRIESTS *c. 1445 BC*	FORTY YEARS IN THE WILDERNESS ENDS *c. 1406 BC*

The recently redeemed nation of Israel received instructions on proper worship throughout the book of Leviticus. God's love for his people is demonstrated in his unrelenting drive for fellowship with them. By giving these detailed instructions, God established the way that these fallen people would approach a holy God during their journey from Egypt to their final dwelling in the promised land. These instructions were clearly not a means by which people earned favor with God; rather, they outlined the path of worship for those who had already experienced God's gracious, redemptive work.

This book outlines the nature of that worship and details many of the responsibilities of those who served as priestly mediators between God and the nation itself. The instructions provided in the book describe how impure people can approach a holy God and can be forgiven of their sins. For this reason, Leviticus was not simply a manual for the priests. Its instructions helped all of God's people to understand how to approach God on his terms and offer him the worship he rightly deserves.

The book of Leviticus was written to describe the way that God's people could live in ritual and moral purity in spite of their sin. If they did so, God could dwell among the people and demonstrate his glory to them, and they could fulfill their mission of serving as a light to the surrounding nations. The consistent theme of sacrifice throughout the book demonstrates that sin has drastic implications — someone or something had to die to cover personal and communal sin before people could worship God rightly. The sacrificial death of a substitute was meant to remind the nation that they lived and worshiped under God's gracious permission in spite of their sinfulness. Leviticus, therefore, describes two main themes that are vital to understanding God's great work of salvation: first, the consequence of sin is death; second, the only way for people to avoid death is through the sacrifice of a substitute.

Leviticus, while often thought of as an archaic book filled with outdated rituals, directly foreshadows the work of Christ. Jesus serves as the perfect Lamb of God who takes away the sin of the world (Jn 1:29). In his substitutionary death, Christ fulfills the sacrifices called for throughout the book. He also serves as the great high priest — the one who makes it possible for fallen humanity to have a right relationship with God. Jesus was, and still is, the mediator between God and humanity, making human worship of a holy God possible.

AND THE PRIEST SHALL MAKE ATONEMENT
FOR HIM BEFORE THE LORD, AND HE
SHALL BE FORGIVEN FOR ANY OF THE THINGS
THAT ONE MAY DO AND THEREBY BECOME GUILTY.

Leviticus 6:7

LEVITICUS

Laws for Burnt Offerings

1 The LORD called Moses and spoke to him from the tent of meeting, saying, [2]“Speak to the people of Israel and say to them, When any one of you brings an offering to the LORD, you shall bring your offering of livestock from the herd or from the flock.

[3]“If his offering is a burnt offering from the herd, he shall offer a male without blemish. He shall bring it to the entrance of the tent of meeting, that he may be accepted before the LORD. [4]He shall lay his hand on the head of the burnt offering, and it shall be accepted for him to make atonement for him. [5]Then he shall kill the bull before the LORD, and Aaron’s sons the priests shall bring the blood and throw the blood against the sides of the altar that is at the entrance of the tent of meeting. [6]Then he shall flay the burnt offering and cut it into pieces, [7]and the sons of Aaron the priest shall put fire on the altar and arrange wood on the fire. [8]And Aaron’s sons the priests shall arrange the pieces, the head, and the fat, on the wood that is on the fire on the altar; [9]but its entrails and its legs he shall wash with water. And the priest shall burn all of it on the altar, as a burnt offering, a food offering[1] with a pleasing aroma to the LORD.

[10]“If his gift for a burnt offering is from the flock, from the sheep or goats, he shall bring a male without blemish, [11]and he shall kill it on the north side of the altar before the LORD, and Aaron’s sons the priests shall throw its blood against the sides of the altar. [12]And he shall cut it into pieces, with its head and its fat, and the priest shall arrange them on the wood that is on the fire on the altar, [13]but the entrails and the legs he shall wash with water. And the priest shall offer all of it and burn it on the altar; it is a burnt offering, a food offering with a pleasing aroma to the LORD.

[14]“If his offering to the LORD is a burnt offering of birds, then he shall bring his offering of turtledoves or pigeons. [15]And the priest shall bring it to the altar and wring off its head and burn it on the altar. Its blood shall be drained out on the side of the altar. [16]He shall remove its crop with its contents[2] and cast it beside the altar on the east side, in the place for ashes. [17]He shall tear it open by its wings, but shall not sever it completely. And the priest shall burn it on the altar, on the wood that is on the fire. It is a burnt offering, a food offering with a pleasing aroma to the LORD.

Laws for Grain Offerings

2 “When anyone brings a grain offering as an offering to the LORD, his offering shall be of fine flour. He shall pour oil on it and put frankincense on it [2]and bring it to Aaron’s sons the priests. And he shall take from it a handful of the fine flour and oil, with all of its frankincense, and the priest shall burn this as its memorial portion on the altar, a food offering with a pleasing aroma to the LORD. [3]But the rest of the grain offering shall be for Aaron and his sons; it is a most holy part of the LORD’s food offerings.

[4]“When you bring a grain offering baked in the oven as an offering, it shall be unleavened loaves of fine flour mixed with oil or unleavened wafers smeared with oil. [5]And if your offering is a grain offering baked on a griddle, it shall be of fine flour unleavened, mixed with oil. [6]You shall break it in pieces and pour oil on it; it is a grain offering. [7]And if your offering is a grain offering cooked in a pan, it shall be made of fine flour with oil. [8]And you shall bring the grain offering that is made of these things to the LORD, and when it is presented to the priest, he shall bring it to the altar. [9]And the priest shall take from the grain offering its memorial portion

[1]Or *an offering by fire*; so throughout Leviticus [2]Or *feathers*

LEVITICUS 1:1–2

OFFERINGS OF SACRIFICE

The first offerings recorded in Scripture were made by Cain and Abel. In the book of Leviticus, Israel's priests managed the transaction between God and mankind. They ensured God's instructions for offerings were carefully followed. Blood was splashed on the holy altar, specific parts of the sacrifice were burned, and an aroma pleasing to the Lord rose from the fire. The offerings were not made to the Lord because he had needs. They were careful acts of thanksgiving and repentance, acknowledging Israel's covenant God as Creator and Judge.

Burnt offerings	required the slaughter of an unblemished animal as atonement — a bull, sheep, goat, or bird. Blood and death were offered as substitutionary payment for the person who sinned.
Grain offerings	accompanied all burnt offerings. Raw, roasted, or baked grain was given in gratitude to God for the fruitfulness of the land.
Peace offerings	were given out of gratitude, expressing fellowship between the worshiper and God. Unblemished cattle, sheep, and goats were sacrificed in response to blessings or as unprompted offerings of thanksgiving.
Sin offerings	involved the occasion of sin committed unintentionally, but no restitution was possible since the violation was against God. Different types of sacrifices were prescribed for different people within Israelite society — from high priest down to common citizen.
Guilt offerings	atoned for sins committed unintentionally, where restitution could be made to the one offended. A guilt offering would be made when there was either a mistreatment of the Lord's holy things or an offense against a neighbor. In both cases, the priests calculated restitution.

Atonement was gruesome work — the noise of animals dying, the scene of blood splashed on an altar, the smoky smell of cooked flesh. In Leviticus, we see this was also intensely personal work. When the one who sinned brought an offering, they were required to place a hand on the animal's head as it was killed. The up-close experience reminded the sinner of personal guilt and the cost to regain right standing with God.

At an appointed time, God made a new and final way for dealing with sin. Jesus offered himself as the once-for-all sacrifice for our guilt (Heb 10:10). The cross became a holy altar for Christ's worthy blood. Jesus became our sacrificial lamb. Jesus suffered a terrible death he did not deserve — absorbing wrath we could never withstand, to give us hope for forgiveness. When Jesus died, the Levitical system of sacrifice became obsolete. Jesus, now alive forever, remains the only offering sufficient to cancel sin. The Lord no longer requires or accepts the blood of animals. Now, he only accepts personal faith in the death and resurrection of Jesus (Ro 10:9–10).

and burn this on the altar, a food offering with a pleasing aroma to the LORD. 10But the rest of the grain offering shall be for Aaron and his sons; it is a most holy part of the LORD's food offerings.

11"No grain offering that you bring to the LORD shall be made with leaven, for you shall burn no leaven nor any honey as a food offering to the LORD. 12As an offering of firstfruits you may bring them to the LORD, but they shall not be offered on the altar for a pleasing aroma. 13You shall season all your grain offerings with salt. You shall not let the salt of the covenant with your God be missing from your grain offering; with all your offerings you shall offer salt.

14"If you offer a grain offering of firstfruits to the LORD, you shall offer for the grain offering of your firstfruits fresh ears, roasted with fire, crushed new grain. 15And you shall put oil on it and lay frankincense on it; it is a grain offering. 16And the priest shall burn as its memorial portion some of the crushed grain and some of the oil with all of its frankincense; it is a food offering to the LORD.

Laws for Peace Offerings

3 "If his offering is a sacrifice of peace offering, if he offers an animal from the herd, male or female, he shall offer it without blemish before the LORD. 2And he shall lay his hand on the head of his offering and kill it at the entrance of the tent of meeting, and Aaron's sons the priests shall throw the blood against the sides of the altar. 3And from the sacrifice of the peace offering, as a food offering to the LORD, he shall offer the fat covering the entrails and all the fat that is on the entrails, 4and the two kidneys with the fat that is on them at the loins, and the long lobe of the liver that he shall remove with the kidneys. 5Then Aaron's sons shall burn it on the altar on top of the burnt offering, which is on the wood on the fire; it is a food offering with a pleasing aroma to the LORD.

6"If his offering for a sacrifice of peace offering to the LORD is an animal from the flock, male or female, he shall offer it without blemish. 7If he offers a lamb for his offering, then he shall offer it before the LORD, 8lay his hand on the head of his offering, and kill it in front of the tent of meeting; and Aaron's sons shall throw its blood against the sides of the altar. 9Then from the sacrifice of the peace offering he shall offer as a food offering to the LORD its fat; he shall remove the whole fat tail, cut off close to the backbone, and the fat that covers the entrails and all the fat that is on the entrails 10and the two kidneys with the fat that is on them at the loins and the long lobe of the liver that he shall remove with the kidneys. 11And the priest shall burn it on the altar as a food offering to the LORD.

12"If his offering is a goat, then he shall offer it before the LORD 13and lay his hand on its head and kill it in front of the tent of meeting, and the sons of Aaron shall throw its blood against the sides of the altar. 14Then he shall offer from it, as his offering for a food offering to the LORD, the fat covering the entrails and all the fat that is on the entrails 15and the two kidneys with the fat that is on them at the loins and the long lobe of the liver that he shall remove with the kidneys. 16And the priest shall burn them on the altar as a food offering with a pleasing aroma. All fat is the LORD's. 17It shall be a statute forever throughout your generations, in all your dwelling places, that you eat neither fat nor blood."

Laws for Sin Offerings

4 And the LORD spoke to Moses, saying, 2"Speak to the people of Israel, saying, If anyone sins unintentionally[1] in any of the LORD's commandments about things not to be done, and does any one of them, 3if it is the anointed priest who sins, thus bringing guilt on the people, then he shall offer for the sin that he has committed a bull from the herd without blemish to the LORD for a sin offering. 4He shall bring the bull to the entrance of the tent of meeting before the LORD

[1] Or *by mistake*; so throughout Leviticus

LEVITICUS 3:1

WITHOUT DEFECT

Only the best of flock or herd or crop was fit for sacrifice to God, who is infinitely worthy. Each offering had to be free of anything objectionable—a standard that mattered enormously to the Lord (Mal 1:6–14). The repeated instruction for a sacrifice "without blemish" challenged the giver to consider what best honored God, reflecting a sincere and reverent sacrifice of worship.

When God graced the world with a Savior, he gave us the best—his own Son. Jesus is perfect in every way. In him there is no evil or weakness or fault or flaw. Our redemption has been accomplished through Christ who is precious, a lamb without blemish or spot (1Pe 1:19). The quality of God's offering on the cross shows his great love for people and confirms that only Jesus, who never sinned, could be a sufficient sacrifice. Jesus is worthy and without defect. Faith in him reconciles us to the Lord—making us holy and without blemish, fully acceptable to God (Col 1:22).

LEVITICUS 4:1–12

OFFERINGS

For the people of Israel, an offering was something a person brought to God to secure cleansing from sin or to express thanksgiving and devotion (see article on Lev 1:1–2). The system of exact procedures, though bloody and complex, was a gift of divine mercy. God created ways for sinners to cancel guilt. And he arranged rituals so the people could respond to his many works with gratitude and praise. The sacrificial system ensured that God's people

(continued on next page)

and lay his hand on the head of the bull and kill the bull before the LORD. 5And
the anointed priest shall take some of the blood of the bull and bring it into the
tent of meeting, 6and the priest shall dip his finger in the blood and sprinkle part
of the blood seven times before the LORD in front of the veil of the sanctuary.
7And the priest shall put some of the blood on the horns of the altar of fragrant
incense before the LORD that is in the tent of meeting, and all the rest of the blood
of the bull he shall pour out at the base of the altar of burnt offering that is at the
entrance of the tent of meeting. 8And all the fat of the bull of the sin offering he
shall remove from it, the fat that covers the entrails and all the fat that is on the
entrails 9and the two kidneys with the fat that is on them at the loins and the long
lobe of the liver that he shall remove with the kidneys 10(just as these are taken
from the ox of the sacrifice of the peace offerings); and the priest shall burn them
on the altar of burnt offering. 11But the skin of the bull and all its flesh, with its
head, its legs, its entrails, and its dung— 12all the rest of the bull—he shall carry
outside the camp to a clean place, to the ash heap, and shall burn it up on a fire of
wood. On the ash heap it shall be burned up.

13"If the whole congregation of Israel sins unintentionally[1] and the thing is
hidden from the eyes of the assembly, and they do any one of the things that by
the LORD's commandments ought not to be done, and they realize their guilt,[2]
14when the sin which they have committed becomes known, the assembly shall
offer a bull from the herd for a sin offering and bring it in front of the tent of
meeting. 15And the elders of the congregation shall lay their hands on the head of
the bull before the LORD, and the bull shall be killed before the LORD. 16Then the
anointed priest shall bring some of the blood of the bull into the tent of meeting,
17and the priest shall dip his finger in the blood and sprinkle it seven times before
the LORD in front of the veil. 18And he shall put some of the blood on the horns of
the altar that is in the tent of meeting before the LORD, and the rest of the blood
he shall pour out at the base of the altar of burnt offering that is at the entrance
of the tent of meeting. 19And all its fat he shall take from it and burn on the altar.
20Thus shall he do with the bull. As he did with the bull of the sin offering, so shall
he do with this. And the priest shall make atonement for them, and they shall
be forgiven. 21And he shall carry the bull outside the camp and burn it up as he
burned the first bull; it is the sin offering for the assembly.

22"When a leader sins, doing unintentionally any one of all the things that by
the commandments of the LORD his God ought not to be done, and realizes his
guilt, 23or the sin which he has committed is made known to him, he shall bring as
his offering a goat, a male without blemish, 24and shall lay his hand on the head of
the goat and kill it in the place where they kill the burnt offering before the LORD;
it is a sin offering. 25Then the priest shall take some of the blood of the sin offering
with his finger and put it on the horns of the altar of burnt offering and pour out
the rest of its blood at the base of the altar of burnt offering. 26And all its fat he
shall burn on the altar, like the fat of the sacrifice of peace offerings. So the priest
shall make atonement for him for his sin, and he shall be forgiven.

27"If anyone of the common people sins unintentionally in doing any one of
the things that by the LORD's commandments ought not to be done, and realizes
his guilt, 28or the sin which he has committed is made known to him, he shall
bring for his offering a goat, a female without blemish, for his sin which he has
committed. 29And he shall lay his hand on the head of the sin offering and kill
the sin offering in the place of burnt offering. 30And the priest shall take some of
its blood with his finger and put it on the horns of the altar of burnt offering and
pour out all the rest of its blood at the base of the altar. 31And all its fat he shall
remove, as the fat is removed from the peace offerings, and the priest shall burn
it on the altar for a pleasing aroma to the LORD. And the priest shall make atonement for him, and he shall be forgiven.

[1]Or *makes a mistake* [2]Or *suffer for their guilt*, or *are guilty*; also verses 22, 27, and chapter 5

(Offerings, continued)

could have hope that their sin would be forgiven by a holy God and that they could, in turn, joyfully worship him with all of life.

Jesus' death on the cross was the ultimate offering, a final sacrifice that ended the need for any others. Jesus gave himself up for us all as the perfect sacrifice for sin (Eph 5:2). While offerings for sin are no longer required, the Lord delights in people giving themselves as sacrifices of praise and service to him (Ro 12:1).

32 “If he brings a lamb as his offering for a sin offering, he shall bring a female without blemish 33 and lay his hand on the head of the sin offering and kill it for a sin offering in the place where they kill the burnt offering. 34 Then the priest shall take some of the blood of the sin offering with his finger and put it on the horns of the altar of burnt offering and pour out all the rest of its blood at the base of the altar. 35 And all its fat he shall remove as the fat of the lamb is removed from the sacrifice of peace offerings, and the priest shall burn it on the altar, on top of the LORD’s food offerings. And the priest shall make atonement for him for the sin which he has committed, and he shall be forgiven.

5 “If anyone sins in that he hears a public adjuration to testify, and though he is a witness, whether he has seen or come to know the matter, yet does not speak, he shall bear his iniquity; 2 or if anyone touches an unclean thing, whether a carcass of an unclean wild animal or a carcass of unclean livestock or a carcass of unclean swarming things, and it is hidden from him and he has become unclean, and he realizes his guilt; 3 or if he touches human uncleanness, of whatever sort the uncleanness may be with which one becomes unclean, and it is hidden from him, when he comes to know it, and realizes his guilt; 4 or if anyone utters with his lips a rash oath to do evil or to do good, any sort of rash oath that people swear, and it is hidden from him, when he comes to know it, and he realizes his guilt in any of these; 5 when he realizes his guilt in any of these and confesses the sin he has committed, 6 he shall bring to the LORD as his compensation[1] for the sin that he has committed, a female from the flock, a lamb or a goat, for a sin offering. And the priest shall make atonement for him for his sin.

7 “But if he cannot afford a lamb, then he shall bring to the LORD as his compensation for the sin that he has committed two turtledoves or two pigeons,[2] one for a sin offering and the other for a burnt offering. 8 He shall bring them to the priest, who shall offer first the one for the sin offering. He shall wring its head from its neck but shall not sever it completely, 9 and he shall sprinkle some of the blood of the sin offering on the side of the altar, while the rest of the blood shall be drained out at the base of the altar; it is a sin offering. 10 Then he shall offer the second for a burnt offering according to the rule. And the priest shall make atonement for him for the sin that he has committed, and he shall be forgiven.

11 “But if he cannot afford two turtledoves or two pigeons, then he shall bring as his offering for the sin that he has committed a tenth of an ephah[3] of fine flour for a sin offering. He shall put no oil on it and shall put no frankincense on it, for it is a sin offering. 12 And he shall bring it to the priest, and the priest shall take a handful of it as its memorial portion and burn this on the altar, on the LORD’s food offerings; it is a sin offering. 13 Thus the priest shall make atonement for him for the sin which he has committed in any one of these things, and he shall be forgiven. And the remainder[4] shall be for the priest, as in the grain offering.”

Laws for Guilt Offerings

14 The LORD spoke to Moses, saying, 15 “If anyone commits a breach of faith and sins unintentionally in any of the holy things of the LORD, he shall bring to the LORD as his compensation, a ram without blemish out of the flock, valued[5] in silver shekels,[6] according to the shekel of the sanctuary, for a guilt offering. 16 He shall also make restitution for what he has done amiss in the holy thing and shall add a fifth to it and give it to the priest. And the priest shall make atonement for him with the ram of the guilt offering, and he shall be forgiven.

17 “If anyone sins, doing any of the things that by the LORD’s commandments ought not to be done, though he did not know it, then realizes his guilt, he shall bear his iniquity. 18 He shall bring to the priest a ram without blemish out of the flock, or its equivalent, for a guilt offering, and the priest shall make atonement

[1] Hebrew *his guilt penalty*; so throughout Leviticus [2] Septuagint *two young pigeons*; also verse 11
[3] An *ephah* was about 3/5 bushel or 22 liters [4] Septuagint; Hebrew *it* [5] Or *flock, or its equivalent*
[6] A *shekel* was about 2/5 ounce or 11 grams

for him for the mistake that he made unintentionally, and he shall be forgiven. 19It
is a guilt offering; he has indeed incurred guilt before[1] the LORD."
6 [2] The LORD spoke to Moses, saying, 2"If anyone sins and commits a breach of
faith against the LORD by deceiving his neighbor in a matter of deposit or
security, or through robbery, or if he has oppressed his neighbor 3or has found
something lost and lied about it, swearing falsely—in any of all the things that
people do and sin thereby— 4if he has sinned and has realized his guilt and will
restore what he took by robbery or what he got by oppression or the deposit that
was committed to him or the lost thing that he found 5or anything about which he
has sworn falsely, he shall restore it in full and shall add a fifth to it, and give it to
him to whom it belongs on the day he realizes his guilt. 6And he shall bring to the
priest as his compensation to the LORD a ram without blemish out of the flock, or
its equivalent, for a guilt offering. 7And the priest shall make atonement for him
before the LORD, and he shall be forgiven for any of the things that one may do
and thereby become guilty."

The Priests and the Offerings

8[3]The LORD spoke to Moses, saying, 9"Command Aaron and his sons, saying,
This is the law of the burnt offering. The burnt offering shall be on the hearth on
the altar all night until the morning, and the fire of the altar shall be kept burning
on it. 10And the priest shall put on his linen garment and put his linen undergarment on his body, and he shall take up the ashes to which the fire has reduced the
burnt offering on the altar and put them beside the altar. 11Then he shall take off
his garments and put on other garments and carry the ashes outside the camp to
a clean place. 12The fire on the altar shall be kept burning on it; it shall not go out.
The priest shall burn wood on it every morning, and he shall arrange the burnt
offering on it and shall burn on it the fat of the peace offerings. 13Fire shall be kept
burning on the altar continually; it shall not go out.

14"And this is the law of the grain offering. The sons of Aaron shall offer it before the LORD in front of the altar. 15And one shall take from it a handful of the fine
flour of the grain offering and its oil and all the frankincense that is on the grain
offering and burn this as its memorial portion on the altar, a pleasing aroma to the
LORD. 16And the rest of it Aaron and his sons shall eat. It shall be eaten unleavened
in a holy place. In the court of the tent of meeting they shall eat it. 17It shall not
be baked with leaven. I have given it as their portion of my food offerings. It is a
thing most holy, like the sin offering and the guilt offering. 18Every male among
the children of Aaron may eat of it, as decreed forever throughout your generations, from the LORD's food offerings. Whatever touches them shall become holy."

19The LORD spoke to Moses, saying, 20"This is the offering that Aaron and his
sons shall offer to the LORD on the day when he is anointed: a tenth of an ephah[4]
of fine flour as a regular grain offering, half of it in the morning and half in the
evening. 21It shall be made with oil on a griddle. You shall bring it well mixed, in
baked[5] pieces like a grain offering, and offer it for a pleasing aroma to the LORD.
22The priest from among Aaron's sons, who is anointed to succeed him, shall offer
it to the LORD as decreed forever. The whole of it shall be burned. 23Every grain
offering of a priest shall be wholly burned. It shall not be eaten."

24The LORD spoke to Moses, saying, 25"Speak to Aaron and his sons, saying,
This is the law of the sin offering. In the place where the burnt offering is killed
shall the sin offering be killed before the LORD; it is most holy. 26The priest who
offers it for sin shall eat it. In a holy place it shall be eaten, in the court of the tent
of meeting. 27Whatever touches its flesh shall be holy, and when any of its blood
is splashed on a garment, you shall wash that on which it was splashed in a holy
place. 28And the earthenware vessel in which it is boiled shall be broken. But if it
is boiled in a bronze vessel, that shall be scoured and rinsed in water. 29Every male

[1]Or *he has paid full compensation to* [2]Ch 5:20 in Hebrew [3]Ch 6:1 in Hebrew [4]An *ephah* was about 3/5 bushel or 22 liters [5]The meaning of the Hebrew is uncertain

LEVITICUS 6:8–13

FIRE AND ASH

Maintaining the altar fire was the daily work of Aaron and his sons. Ashes from previous sacrifices had to be removed each day. The priests were instructed to always keep the fire burning on the altar—it must not go out. Perpetual fire symbolized the perpetual worship of God and the continual need for atonement and reconciliation.

Jesus came from heaven to fulfill the Law and to finish, by his death, the work of atonement for sin. He died on the cross, but unlike the sacrifices before, Jesus was not destroyed—becoming like ash. He triumphed over the grave by rising from the dead, and he is alive forever (Ro 6:9–10; Rev 1:18).

Today there is no need for maintaining a connection to God through fire. We have all that we need through Christ. Jesus the Son is our Savior from sin, our access to adoption by the Father, and the one who secured the continual presence of the Spirit in our lives.

among the priests may eat of it; it is most holy. 30But no sin offering shall be eaten from which any blood is brought into the tent of meeting to make atonement in the Holy Place; it shall be burned up with fire.

7 “This is the law of the guilt offering. It is most holy. 2In the place where they kill the burnt offering they shall kill the guilt offering, and its blood shall be thrown against the sides of the altar. 3And all its fat shall be offered, the fat tail, the fat that covers the entrails, 4the two kidneys with the fat that is on them at the loins, and the long lobe of the liver that he shall remove with the kidneys. 5The priest shall burn them on the altar as a food offering to the LORD; it is a guilt offering. 6Every male among the priests may eat of it. It shall be eaten in a holy place. It is most holy. 7The guilt offering is just like the sin offering; there is one law for them. The priest who makes atonement with it shall have it. 8And the priest who offers any man’s burnt offering shall have for himself the skin of the burnt offering that he has offered. 9And every grain offering baked in the oven and all that is prepared on a pan or a griddle shall belong to the priest who offers it. 10And every grain offering, mixed with oil or dry, shall be shared equally among all the sons of Aaron.

11“And this is the law of the sacrifice of peace offerings that one may offer to the LORD. 12If he offers it for a thanksgiving, then he shall offer with the thanksgiving sacrifice unleavened loaves mixed with oil, unleavened wafers smeared with oil, and loaves of fine flour well mixed with oil. 13With the sacrifice of his peace offerings for thanksgiving he shall bring his offering with loaves of leavened bread. 14And from it he shall offer one loaf from each offering, as a gift to the LORD. It shall belong to the priest who throws the blood of the peace offerings. 15And the flesh of the sacrifice of his peace offerings for thanksgiving shall be eaten on the day of his offering. He shall not leave any of it until the morning. 16But if the sacrifice of his offering is a vow offering or a freewill offering, it shall be eaten on the day that he offers his sacrifice, and on the next day what remains of it shall be eaten. 17But what remains of the flesh of the sacrifice on the third day shall be burned up with fire. 18If any of the flesh of the sacrifice of his peace offering is eaten on the third day, he who offers it shall not be accepted, neither shall it be credited to him. It is tainted, and he who eats of it shall bear his iniquity.

19“Flesh that touches any unclean thing shall not be eaten. It shall be burned up with fire. All who are clean may eat flesh, 20but the person who eats of the flesh of the sacrifice of the LORD’s peace offerings while an uncleanness is on him, that person shall be cut off from his people. 21And if anyone touches an unclean thing, whether human uncleanness or an unclean beast or any unclean detestable creature, and then eats some flesh from the sacrifice of the LORD’s peace offerings, that person shall be cut off from his people.”

22The LORD spoke to Moses, saying, 23“Speak to the people of Israel, saying, You shall eat no fat, of ox or sheep or goat. 24The fat of an animal that dies of itself and the fat of one that is torn by beasts may be put to any other use, but on no account shall you eat it. 25For every person who eats of the fat of an animal of which a food offering may be made to the LORD shall be cut off from his people. 26Moreover, you shall eat no blood whatever, whether of fowl or of animal, in any of your dwelling places. 27Whoever eats any blood, that person shall be cut off from his people.”

28The LORD spoke to Moses, saying, 29“Speak to the people of Israel, saying, Whoever offers the sacrifice of his peace offerings to the LORD shall bring his offering to the LORD from the sacrifice of his peace offerings. 30His own hands shall bring the LORD’s food offerings. He shall bring the fat with the breast, that the breast may be waved as a wave offering before the LORD. 31The priest shall burn the fat on the altar, but the breast shall be for Aaron and his sons. 32And the right thigh you shall give to the priest as a contribution from the sacrifice of your peace offerings. 33Whoever among the sons of Aaron offers the blood of the peace offerings and the fat shall have the right thigh for a portion. 34For the breast that is

LEVITICUS 7:13

YEAST

Yeast added to bread dough has an expanding and multiplying effect. The dough rises, often doubling its original size. Yeast is the difference between leavened and unleavened bread—the two types specified for the various offerings and feasts in the Israelite community. Since the bread with yeast mentioned here was not burned on the altar, the prohibition in Leviticus 2:11 and Exodus 23:18 did not apply.

In the New Testament, yeast is usually referenced in a negative connotation as an agent of corruption. Symbolizing evil, yeast is something to get rid of because a small amount can have a big impact. Jesus gave a warning against the leaven of the Pharisees and Sadducees—pointing to the corrupting influence of legalism and hypocrisy (Mt 16:6). Only in Matthew 13:33 is leaven used as a positive symbol of the permeating power of the gospel. Jesus compared the kingdom of heaven to yeast, which once added, changes the entire batch of dough. When a person moves from death to life through the gospel, their entire life is changed by the power of Christ.

waved and the thigh that is contributed I have taken from the people of Israel, out of the sacrifices of their peace offerings, and have given them to Aaron the priest and to his sons, as a perpetual due from the people of Israel. [35]This is the portion of Aaron and of his sons from the LORD's food offerings, from the day they were presented to serve as priests of the LORD. [36]The LORD commanded this to be given them by the people of Israel, from the day that he anointed them. It is a perpetual due throughout their generations."

[37]This is the law of the burnt offering, of the grain offering, of the sin offering, of the guilt offering, of the ordination offering, and of the peace offering, [38]which the LORD commanded Moses on Mount Sinai, on the day that he commanded the people of Israel to bring their offerings to the LORD, in the wilderness of Sinai.

Consecration of Aaron and His Sons

8 The LORD spoke to Moses, saying, [2]"Take Aaron and his sons with him, and the garments and the anointing oil and the bull of the sin offering and the two rams and the basket of unleavened bread. [3]And assemble all the congregation at the entrance of the tent of meeting." [4]And Moses did as the LORD commanded him, and the congregation was assembled at the entrance of the tent of meeting.

[5]And Moses said to the congregation, "This is the thing that the LORD has commanded to be done." [6]And Moses brought Aaron and his sons and washed them with water. [7]And he put the coat on him and tied the sash around his waist and clothed him with the robe and put the ephod on him and tied the skillfully woven band of the ephod around him, binding it to him with the band.[1] [8]And he placed the breastpiece on him, and in the breastpiece he put the Urim and the Thummim. [9]And he set the turban on his head, and on the turban, in front, he set the golden plate, the holy crown, as the LORD commanded Moses.

[10]Then Moses took the anointing oil and anointed the tabernacle and all that was in it, and consecrated them. [11]And he sprinkled some of it on the altar seven times, and anointed the altar and all its utensils and the basin and its stand, to consecrate them. [12]And he poured some of the anointing oil on Aaron's head and anointed him to consecrate him. [13]And Moses brought Aaron's sons and clothed them with coats and tied sashes around their waists and bound caps on them, as the LORD commanded Moses.

[14]Then he brought the bull of the sin offering, and Aaron and his sons laid their hands on the head of the bull of the sin offering. [15]And he[2] killed it, and Moses took the blood, and with his finger put it on the horns of the altar around it and purified the altar and poured out the blood at the base of the altar and consecrated it to make atonement for it. [16]And he took all the fat that was on the entrails and the long lobe of the liver and the two kidneys with their fat, and Moses burned them on the altar. [17]But the bull and its skin and its flesh and its dung he burned up with fire outside the camp, as the LORD commanded Moses.

[18]Then he presented the ram of the burnt offering, and Aaron and his sons laid their hands on the head of the ram. [19]And he killed it, and Moses threw the blood against the sides of the altar. [20]He cut the ram into pieces, and Moses burned the head and the pieces and the fat. [21]He washed the entrails and the legs with water, and Moses burned the whole ram on the altar. It was a burnt offering with a pleasing aroma, a food offering for the LORD, as the LORD commanded Moses.

[22]Then he presented the other ram, the ram of ordination, and Aaron and his sons laid their hands on the head of the ram. [23]And he killed it, and Moses took some of its blood and put it on the lobe of Aaron's right ear and on the thumb of his right hand and on the big toe of his right foot. [24]Then he presented Aaron's sons, and Moses put some of the blood on the lobes of their right ears and on the thumbs of their right hands and on the big toes of their right feet. And Moses threw the blood against the sides of the altar. [25]Then he took the fat and the fat

[1]Hebrew *with it* [2]Probably Aaron or his representative; possibly Moses; also verses 16–23

LEVITICUS 8:12

ANOINTING

God chose and set apart the descendants of Abraham from all the peoples of the earth. They were holy in their identity as the children of God and holy in their vocation as the people of God (Lev 20:26). Among the Israelites, God designated the tribe of Levi to serve in the tabernacle. And within this tribe, Aaron and his sons were appointed priests. They were not perfect men. They were sinful and in need of the same ongoing cleansing and covering which their service facilitated for others.

In Leviticus 8:12, Moses anointed Aaron with oil to consecrate him like the kings of Israel (1Sa 10:1) and some of God's prophets (1Ki 19:16). Aaron was inaugurated as a mediator to instruct and facilitate worship, sacrifices, and the yearly observances God required.

Aaron's position was a foreshadowing of God's permanent high priest, Jesus Christ. Aaron was anointed with oil, but "God anointed Jesus of Nazareth with the Holy Spirit and with power" (Ac 10:38). Jesus combines in his person the offices of high priest, king, and prophet, so he is *the* anointed one, which is the meaning of the names Messiah and Christ.

THE LAW

The Law of God came to the people of Israel through Moses (Ex 21:1). In decrees, commands, instructions, and statutes, the Lord declared how their relationship with him would work. The Law gave glimpses into the nature and character of God — revealing his preferences and methods. It gave boundaries and much-needed clarity for how to approach and relate to God.

Having heard from the Lord in the fire and smoke atop Mount Sinai, Moses went down and told the people all the Lord's words and laws before writing everything down (Ex 24:3 – 4). Eventually, God inscribed his laws on stone tablets and gave them to Moses (Ex 24:12).

It is common to think of the Law as limited to the Ten Commandments. Actually, it was comprised of regulations for worship, instructions on legal matters, principles for society, edicts for sexual conduct, and more. When obeyed, the Law was a path to fruitful life (Lev 18:4 – 5). The Lord made it clear that his laws were not negotiable — he expected unconditional obedience. Those refusing to listen to him and carry out all of his commands would be met with divine terror, overwhelming cost, and the realization that God would always get his way (Lev 26:14 – 39).

The Law is much more than a set of restrictions — it gives guidance about the destructiveness of sin and it highlights habits leading to contentment and joy. The benefits of following God's laws are passionately extolled by the writer of Psalm 119, who learned to take delight in the Lord's commands.

The Law governed the Old Testament system of sacrifices — the mechanisms for maintaining a right standing with God. Yet it was only a shadow of the superior sacrifice Jesus made when he came to earth to redeem us from the guilt of our sins. In his death, Jesus set aside the first way and paved a new way by providing the perfect, ultimate sacrifice of himself once and for all. Men and women are now made holy through faith in his sacrifice and resurrection (Heb 10:1 – 10). This helps us understand Jesus' words when he said that he did not come to abolish the Law but to fulfill it (Mt 5:17).

tail and all the fat that was on the entrails and the long lobe of the liver and the two kidneys with their fat and the right thigh, 26and out of the basket of unleavened bread that was before the LORD he took one unleavened loaf and one loaf of bread with oil and one wafer and placed them on the pieces of fat and on the right thigh. 27And he put all these in the hands of Aaron and in the hands of his sons and waved them as a wave offering before the LORD. 28Then Moses took them from their hands and burned them on the altar with the burnt offering. This was an ordination offering with a pleasing aroma, a food offering to the LORD. 29And Moses took the breast and waved it for a wave offering before the LORD. It was Moses' portion of the ram of ordination, as the LORD commanded Moses.

30Then Moses took some of the anointing oil and of the blood that was on the altar and sprinkled it on Aaron and his garments, and also on his sons and his sons' garments. So he consecrated Aaron and his garments, and his sons and his sons' garments with him.

31And Moses said to Aaron and his sons, "Boil the flesh at the entrance of the tent of meeting, and there eat it and the bread that is in the basket of ordination offerings, as I commanded, saying, 'Aaron and his sons shall eat it.' 32And what remains of the flesh and the bread you shall burn up with fire. 33And you shall not go outside the entrance of the tent of meeting for seven days, until the days of your ordination are completed, for it will take seven days to ordain you. 34As has been done today, the LORD has commanded to be done to make atonement for you. 35At the entrance of the tent of meeting you shall remain day and night for seven days, performing what the LORD has charged, so that you do not die, for so I have been commanded." 36And Aaron and his sons did all the things that the LORD commanded by Moses.

The LORD Accepts Aaron's Offering

9 On the eighth day Moses called Aaron and his sons and the elders of Israel, 2and he said to Aaron, "Take for yourself a bull calf for a sin offering and a ram for a burnt offering, both without blemish, and offer them before the LORD. 3And say to the people of Israel, 'Take a male goat for a sin offering, and a calf and a lamb, both a year old without blemish, for a burnt offering, 4and an ox and a ram for peace offerings, to sacrifice before the LORD, and a grain offering mixed with oil, for today the LORD will appear to you.'" 5And they brought what Moses commanded in front of the tent of meeting, and all the congregation drew near and stood before the LORD. 6And Moses said, "This is the thing that the LORD commanded you to do, that the glory of the LORD may appear to you." 7Then Moses said to Aaron, "Draw near to the altar and offer your sin offering and your burnt offering and make atonement for yourself and for the people, and bring the offering of the people and make atonement for them, as the LORD has commanded."

8So Aaron drew near to the altar and killed the calf of the sin offering, which was for himself. 9And the sons of Aaron presented the blood to him, and he dipped his finger in the blood and put it on the horns of the altar and poured out the blood at the base of the altar. 10But the fat and the kidneys and the long lobe of the liver from the sin offering he burned on the altar, as the LORD commanded Moses. 11The flesh and the skin he burned up with fire outside the camp.

12Then he killed the burnt offering, and Aaron's sons handed him the blood, and he threw it against the sides of the altar. 13And they handed the burnt offering to him, piece by piece, and the head, and he burned them on the altar. 14And he washed the entrails and the legs and burned them with the burnt offering on the altar.

15Then he presented the people's offering and took the goat of the sin offering that was for the people and killed it and offered it as a sin offering, like the first one. 16And he presented the burnt offering and offered it according to the rule. 17And he presented the grain offering, took a handful of it, and burned it on the altar, besides the burnt offering of the morning.

LEVITICUS 9:7

ATONEMENT

In the Scriptures, *atonement* refers to payment for sin. Offerings were made to gain God's favor so that he would remove a worshiper's guilt. The sacrifice was presented as a substitute for the offender. An animal died in the offender's place, and the wrath of God was turned aside. The imagery was clear—because of sin someone had to die. It would either be the sinner or a substitute.

Like the animals offered to atone for the sins of the Israelites, Jesus' life was offered as a substitute for ours. His death satisfied God's wrath and covered our sin (Ro 3:25). This concept is captured in the lyrics of the hymn, "Jesus Paid It All": "Oh praise the one who paid my debt and raised this life up from the dead!" Jesus, as the great substitute, paid the price of death on behalf of his people. The one who paid our penalty is worthy of glory and honor both now and forever.

18 Then he killed the ox and the ram, the sacrifice of peace offerings for the people. And Aaron's sons handed him the blood, and he threw it against the sides of the altar. 19 But the fat pieces of the ox and of the ram, the fat tail and that which covers the entrails and the kidneys and the long lobe of the liver— 20 they put the fat pieces on the breasts, and he burned the fat pieces on the altar, 21 but the breasts and the right thigh Aaron waved for a wave offering before the LORD, as Moses commanded.

22 Then Aaron lifted up his hands toward the people and blessed them, and he came down from offering the sin offering and the burnt offering and the peace offerings. 23 And Moses and Aaron went into the tent of meeting, and when they came out they blessed the people, and the glory of the LORD appeared to all the people. 24 And fire came out from before the LORD and consumed the burnt offering and the pieces of fat on the altar, and when all the people saw it, they shouted and fell on their faces.

The Death of Nadab and Abihu

10 Now Nadab and Abihu, the sons of Aaron, each took his censer and put fire in it and laid incense on it and offered unauthorized[1] fire before the LORD, which he had not commanded them. 2 And fire came out from before the LORD and consumed them, and they died before the LORD. 3 Then Moses said to Aaron, "This is what the LORD has said: 'Among those who are near me I will be sanctified, and before all the people I will be glorified.'" And Aaron held his peace.

4 And Moses called Mishael and Elzaphan, the sons of Uzziel the uncle of Aaron, and said to them, "Come near; carry your brothers away from the front of the sanctuary and out of the camp." 5 So they came near and carried them in their coats out of the camp, as Moses had said. 6 And Moses said to Aaron and to Eleazar and Ithamar his sons, "Do not let the hair of your heads hang loose, and do not tear your clothes, lest you die, and wrath come upon all the congregation; but let your brothers, the whole house of Israel, bewail the burning that the LORD has kindled. 7 And do not go outside the entrance of the tent of meeting, lest you die, for the anointing oil of the LORD is upon you." And they did according to the word of Moses.

8 And the LORD spoke to Aaron, saying, 9 "Drink no wine or strong drink, you or your sons with you, when you go into the tent of meeting, lest you die. It shall be a statute forever throughout your generations. 10 You are to distinguish between the holy and the common, and between the unclean and the clean, 11 and you are to teach the people of Israel all the statutes that the LORD has spoken to them by Moses."

12 Moses spoke to Aaron and to Eleazar and Ithamar, his surviving sons: "Take the grain offering that is left of the LORD's food offerings, and eat it unleavened beside the altar, for it is most holy. 13 You shall eat it in a holy place, because it is your due and your sons' due, from the LORD's food offerings, for so I am commanded. 14 But the breast that is waved and the thigh that is contributed you shall eat in a clean place, you and your sons and your daughters with you, for they are given as your due and your sons' due from the sacrifices of the peace offerings of the people of Israel. 15 The thigh that is contributed and the breast that is waved they shall bring with the food offerings of the fat pieces to wave for a wave offering before the LORD, and it shall be yours and your sons' with you as a due forever, as the LORD has commanded."

16 Now Moses diligently inquired about the goat of the sin offering, and behold, it was burned up! And he was angry with Eleazar and Ithamar, the surviving sons of Aaron, saying, 17 "Why have you not eaten the sin offering in the place of the sanctuary, since it is a thing most holy and has been given to you that you may bear the iniquity of the congregation, to make atonement for them before the LORD? 18 Behold, its blood was not brought into the inner part of the sanctuary. You certainly ought to have eaten it in the sanctuary, as I commanded." 19 And Aaron

[1] Or *strange*

LEVITICUS 10:1–2

APPROACHING GOD

Aaron's sons Nadab and Abihu were sanctuary priests who inappropriately approached God, offering "unauthorized fire before the LORD" in some unspecified way. As a result, they were consumed by fire from the Lord. God gave specific instructions for how priests were to come before him. These instructions were as much for their protection as they were for God's honor (Ex 19:22).

Fire was a daily part of Israel's worship of God—offerings were burned and lamps held a flame. The death of Aaron's sons reveals that access to God's presence required strict adherence to his methods and protocols. Yet God's plan from the beginning was to make a way to draw near to him with confidence and assurance without fear. That method is no longer through careful ritual but through faith in the life, death, and resurrection of Jesus Christ. All are invited to approach him with repentance and faith (Eph 3:12). In John 14:6, Jesus confirms that he is the exclusive way for entering God's presence: "No one comes to the Father except through me."

THE SINFUL PRIEST AND THE SINLESS PRIEST

Aaron (the high priest of Israel) and Jesus (the great high priest) have a few things in common — yet they are profoundly different.

They are the same in the following features:

- Aaron exercised his office by carefully following the Lord's commands (Lev 8:36). Though he was imperfect, his example is noteworthy. Jesus, on the other hand, came to do perfectly what Aaron fell short of. Jesus is the ultimate example of honoring God — as he always yielded to his Father's leadership (Jn 8:28).
- Aaron served so that the glory of the Lord would appear to the people (Lev 9:6). Jesus came to enable mankind to see and know God (Jn 1:18). In fact, anyone who has seen Jesus has seen the Father (Jn 14:8 – 11). Jesus came to earth as the exact image of the invisible God (Col 1:15).

However, they were different in a number of ways:

- Aaron was an appointed mediator between the people and God. Eventually, he and his successors were made obsolete by Jesus. Jesus Christ is the one and only mediator between God and mankind (1Ti 2:5 – 6). And because Christ's work on the cross enabled our righteousness, we are invited to approach God on our own with confidence (Heb 4:16).
- Aaron arranged for atonement for all of Israel (Lev 9:7). Jesus purchased atonement for the whole world, for all who would come to him by faith (1Jn 2:2). Jesus came to Israel as the promised Messiah, but salvation in his name is available for people of every nation (Ro 3:29).
- Aaron needed to make atonement for his own sins (Lev 9:8). Jesus never sinned. He was and is perfect in word, thought, and deed. Jesus died on the cross as an unblemished substitute. His sinless perfection made him a worthy sacrifice and makes him a worthy priest in heaven (Heb 7:26 – 27).
- Aaron was a priest over Israel because he was ordained and anointed by Moses (Lev 8:1 – 12). Jesus the Son is our great high priest, unique and eternal — because God the Father designated him for that honor (Heb 5:1 – 5). While Aaron stood *before* God, Jesus *is* God (Col 1:15 – 17).

said to Moses, “Behold, today they have offered their sin offering and their burnt
offering before the LORD, and yet such things as these have happened to me! If I
had eaten the sin offering today, would the LORD have approved?” 20And when
Moses heard that, he approved.

Clean and Unclean Animals

11 And the LORD spoke to Moses and Aaron, saying to them, 2“Speak to the people of Israel, saying, These are the living things that you may eat among all
the animals that are on the earth. 3Whatever parts the hoof and is cloven-footed
and chews the cud, among the animals, you may eat. 4Nevertheless, among those
that chew the cud or part the hoof, you shall not eat these: The camel, because it
chews the cud but does not part the hoof, is unclean to you. 5And the rock badger,
because it chews the cud but does not part the hoof, is unclean to you. 6And the
hare, because it chews the cud but does not part the hoof, is unclean to you. 7And
the pig, because it parts the hoof and is cloven-footed but does not chew the cud,
is unclean to you. 8You shall not eat any of their flesh, and you shall not touch
their carcasses; they are unclean to you.

9“These you may eat, of all that are in the waters. Everything in the waters that
has fins and scales, whether in the seas or in the rivers, you may eat. 10But anything in the seas or the rivers that does not have fins and scales, of the swarming
creatures in the waters and of the living creatures that are in the waters, is detestable to you. 11You shall regard them as detestable; you shall not eat any of their
flesh, and you shall detest their carcasses. 12Everything in the waters that does not
have fins and scales is detestable to you.

13“And these you shall detest among the birds;[1] they shall not be eaten; they are
detestable: the eagle,[2] the bearded vulture, the black vulture, 14the kite, the falcon
of any kind, 15every raven of any kind, 16the ostrich, the nighthawk, the sea gull,
the hawk of any kind, 17the little owl, the cormorant, the short-eared owl, 18the
barn owl, the tawny owl, the carrion vulture, 19the stork, the heron of any kind,
the hoopoe, and the bat.

20“All winged insects that go on all fours are detestable to you. 21Yet among
the winged insects that go on all fours you may eat those that have jointed legs
above their feet, with which to hop on the ground. 22Of them you may eat: the
locust of any kind, the bald locust of any kind, the cricket of any kind, and the
grasshopper of any kind. 23But all other winged insects that have four feet are
detestable to you.

24“And by these you shall become unclean. Whoever touches their carcass
shall be unclean until the evening, 25and whoever carries any part of their carcass shall wash his clothes and be unclean until the evening. 26Every animal that
parts the hoof but is not cloven-footed or does not chew the cud is unclean to you.
Everyone who touches them shall be unclean. 27And all that walk on their paws,
among the animals that go on all fours, are unclean to you. Whoever touches their
carcass shall be unclean until the evening, 28and he who carries their carcass shall
wash his clothes and be unclean until the evening; they are unclean to you.

29“And these are unclean to you among the swarming things that swarm on
the ground: the mole rat, the mouse, the great lizard of any kind, 30the gecko, the
monitor lizard, the lizard, the sand lizard, and the chameleon. 31These are unclean
to you among all that swarm. Whoever touches them when they are dead shall be
unclean until the evening. 32And anything on which any of them falls when they
are dead shall be unclean, whether it is an article of wood or a garment or a skin
or a sack, any article that is used for any purpose. It must be put into water, and it
shall be unclean until the evening; then it shall be clean. 33And if any of them falls
into any earthenware vessel, all that is in it shall be unclean, and you shall break it.
34Any food in it that could be eaten, on which water comes, shall be unclean. And

[1]Or *things that fly*; compare Genesis 1:20 [2]The identity of many of these birds is uncertain

all drink that could be drunk from every such vessel shall be unclean. 35And everything on which any part of their carcass falls shall be unclean. Whether oven or stove, it shall be broken in pieces. They are unclean and shall remain unclean for you. 36Nevertheless, a spring or a cistern holding water shall be clean, but whoever touches a carcass in them shall be unclean. 37And if any part of their carcass falls upon any seed grain that is to be sown, it is clean, 38but if water is put on the seed and any part of their carcass falls on it, it is unclean to you.

39"And if any animal which you may eat dies, whoever touches its carcass shall be unclean until the evening, 40and whoever eats of its carcass shall wash his clothes and be unclean until the evening. And whoever carries the carcass shall wash his clothes and be unclean until the evening.

41"Every swarming thing that swarms on the ground is detestable; it shall not be eaten. 42Whatever goes on its belly, and whatever goes on all fours, or whatever has many feet, any swarming thing that swarms on the ground, you shall not eat, for they are detestable. 43You shall not make yourselves detestable with any swarming thing that swarms, and you shall not defile yourselves with them, and become unclean through them. 44For I am the LORD your God. Consecrate yourselves therefore, and be holy, for I am holy. You shall not defile yourselves with any swarming thing that crawls on the ground. 45For I am the LORD who brought you up out of the land of Egypt to be your God. You shall therefore be holy, for I am holy."

46This is the law about beast and bird and every living creature that moves through the waters and every creature that swarms on the ground, 47to make a distinction between the unclean and the clean and between the living creature that may be eaten and the living creature that may not be eaten.

Purification After Childbirth

12 The LORD spoke to Moses, saying, 2"Speak to the people of Israel, saying, If a woman conceives and bears a male child, then she shall be unclean seven days. As at the time of her menstruation, she shall be unclean. 3And on the eighth day the flesh of his foreskin shall be circumcised. 4Then she shall continue for thirty-three days in the blood of her purifying. She shall not touch anything holy, nor come into the sanctuary, until the days of her purifying are completed. 5But if she bears a female child, then she shall be unclean two weeks, as in her menstruation. And she shall continue in the blood of her purifying for sixty-six days.

6"And when the days of her purifying are completed, whether for a son or for a daughter, she shall bring to the priest at the entrance of the tent of meeting a lamb a year old for a burnt offering, and a pigeon or a turtledove for a sin offering, 7and he shall offer it before the LORD and make atonement for her. Then she shall be clean from the flow of her blood. This is the law for her who bears a child, either male or female. 8And if she cannot afford a lamb, then she shall take two turtledoves or two pigeons,[1] one for a burnt offering and the other for a sin offering. And the priest shall make atonement for her, and she shall be clean."

Laws About Leprosy

13 The LORD spoke to Moses and Aaron, saying, 2"When a person has on the skin of his body a swelling or an eruption or a spot, and it turns into a case of leprous[2] disease on the skin of his body, then he shall be brought to Aaron the priest or to one of his sons the priests, 3and the priest shall examine the diseased area on the skin of his body. And if the hair in the diseased area has turned white and the disease appears to be deeper than the skin of his body, it is a case of leprous disease. When the priest has examined him, he shall pronounce him unclean. 4But if the spot is white in the skin of his body and appears no deeper than the skin, and the hair in it has not turned white, the priest shall shut up the

[1]Septuagint *two young pigeons* [2]*Leprosy* was a term for several skin diseases

HOLINESS

There is no one like our God. He is holy and perfect in motive and action, the essence of a clean, pure light of love and glory. He is absolutely unique from the lifeless gods of the nations.

God chose to put his greatness and goodness on display through a special relationship with the people of Israel. With the blessings of his care and provision came an expectation that the people would consecrate themselves and be holy as he is — not divine, but separate and unique in the ways of worship and daily conduct. The call to be holy was not simply to make Israel look different from other peoples — they were to be holy by association, because God is holy. In other words, their holiness spoke something about him. The careful life they lived in accordance with God's requirements helped identify them as belonging to him.

God gave laws for appropriate interaction with the people and things around them. His commands were connected to the goal of remaining clean and undefiled. Some laws listed what should not be touched or eaten — these things would render a person unclean. The letter of these laws applied only to ancient Israel, but the spirit of them continues to apply to God's people today. Like the Hebrews, we are called to holiness in every area of life (1Pe 1:14–16).

Jesus brought new clarity to what it means to be clean. He taught that what defiles us comes from the inside — from the heart — not from external things we touch or eat (Mt 15:1–11). Christians live under the covering of God's grace. Our forgiveness is full and permanent — we do not fear defilement leading to a loss of the righteousness given to us by Christ. We touch and eat in a careful freedom built upon the Holy Spirit living in us and our discernment of sin.

We are holy because of Jesus (Heb 10:10) — and yet the Bible calls us to keep growing in holiness as we separate ourselves from sin (1Th 4:1–8). Christians are purchased people. God has every right to expect our obedience to his preferences for how we live out our days on the earth. When we live holy lives, we distinguish ourselves as God's people and honor him through happy obedience.

diseased person for seven days. [5]And the priest shall examine him on the seventh
day, and if in his eyes the disease is checked and the disease has not spread in the
skin, then the priest shall shut him up for another seven days. [6]And the priest
shall examine him again on the seventh day, and if the diseased area has faded
and the disease has not spread in the skin, then the priest shall pronounce him
clean; it is only an eruption. And he shall wash his clothes and be clean. [7]But if
the eruption spreads in the skin, after he has shown himself to the priest for his
cleansing, he shall appear again before the priest. [8]And the priest shall look, and if
the eruption has spread in the skin, then the priest shall pronounce him unclean;
it is a leprous disease.

[9]"When a man is afflicted with a leprous disease, he shall be brought to the
priest, [10]and the priest shall look. And if there is a white swelling in the skin that
has turned the hair white, and there is raw flesh in the swelling, [11]it is a chronic
leprous disease in the skin of his body, and the priest shall pronounce him unclean. He shall not shut him up, for he is unclean. [12]And if the leprous disease
breaks out in the skin, so that the leprous disease covers all the skin of the diseased person from head to foot, so far as the priest can see, [13]then the priest shall
look, and if the leprous disease has covered all his body, he shall pronounce him
clean of the disease; it has all turned white, and he is clean. [14]But when raw flesh
appears on him, he shall be unclean. [15]And the priest shall examine the raw flesh
and pronounce him unclean. Raw flesh is unclean, for it is a leprous disease. [16]But
if the raw flesh recovers and turns white again, then he shall come to the priest,
[17]and the priest shall examine him, and if the disease has turned white, then the
priest shall pronounce the diseased person clean; he is clean.

[18]"If there is in the skin of one's body a boil and it heals, [19]and in the place of
the boil there comes a white swelling or a reddish-white spot, then it shall be
shown to the priest. [20]And the priest shall look, and if it appears deeper than the
skin and its hair has turned white, then the priest shall pronounce him unclean.
It is a case of leprous disease that has broken out in the boil. [21]But if the priest
examines it and there is no white hair in it and it is not deeper than the skin, but
has faded, then the priest shall shut him up seven days. [22]And if it spreads in the
skin, then the priest shall pronounce him unclean; it is a disease. [23]But if the spot
remains in one place and does not spread, it is the scar of the boil, and the priest
shall pronounce him clean.

[24]"Or, when the body has a burn on its skin and the raw flesh of the burn
becomes a spot, reddish-white or white, [25]the priest shall examine it, and if the
hair in the spot has turned white and it appears deeper than the skin, then it is a
leprous disease. It has broken out in the burn, and the priest shall pronounce him
unclean; it is a case of leprous disease. [26]But if the priest examines it and there is
no white hair in the spot and it is no deeper than the skin, but has faded, the priest
shall shut him up seven days, [27]and the priest shall examine him the seventh day.
If it is spreading in the skin, then the priest shall pronounce him unclean; it is a
case of leprous disease. [28]But if the spot remains in one place and does not spread
in the skin, but has faded, it is a swelling from the burn, and the priest shall pronounce him clean, for it is the scar of the burn.

[29]"When a man or woman has a disease on the head or the beard, [30]the priest
shall examine the disease. And if it appears deeper than the skin, and the hair in
it is yellow and thin, then the priest shall pronounce him unclean. It is an itch, a
leprous disease of the head or the beard. [31]And if the priest examines the itching
disease and it appears no deeper than the skin and there is no black hair in it,
then the priest shall shut up the person with the itching disease for seven days,
[32]and on the seventh day the priest shall examine the disease. If the itch has not
spread, and there is in it no yellow hair, and the itch appears to be no deeper than
the skin, [33]then he shall shave himself, but the itch he shall not shave; and the
priest shall shut up the person with the itching disease for another seven days.
[34]And on the seventh day the priest shall examine the itch, and if the itch has not

spread in the skin and it appears to be no deeper than the skin, then the priest shall pronounce him clean. And he shall wash his clothes and be clean. 35But if the itch spreads in the skin after his cleansing, 36then the priest shall examine him, and if the itch has spread in the skin, the priest need not seek for the yellow hair; he is unclean. 37But if in his eyes the itch is unchanged and black hair has grown in it, the itch is healed and he is clean, and the priest shall pronounce him clean.

38"When a man or a woman has spots on the skin of the body, white spots, 39the priest shall look, and if the spots on the skin of the body are of a dull white, it is leukoderma that has broken out in the skin; he is clean.

40"If a man's hair falls out from his head, he is bald; he is clean. 41And if a man's hair falls out from his forehead, he has baldness of the forehead; he is clean. 42But if there is on the bald head or the bald forehead a reddish-white diseased area, it is a leprous disease breaking out on his bald head or his bald forehead. 43Then the priest shall examine him, and if the diseased swelling is reddish-white on his bald head or on his bald forehead, like the appearance of leprous disease in the skin of the body, 44he is a leprous man, he is unclean. The priest must pronounce him unclean; his disease is on his head.

45"The leprous person who has the disease shall wear torn clothes and let the hair of his head hang loose, and he shall cover his upper lip[1] and cry out, 'Unclean, unclean.' 46He shall remain unclean as long as he has the disease. He is unclean. He shall live alone. His dwelling shall be outside the camp.

47"When there is a case of leprous disease in a garment, whether a woolen or a linen garment, 48in warp or woof of linen or wool, or in a skin or in anything made of skin, 49if the disease is greenish or reddish in the garment, or in the skin or in the warp or the woof or in any article made of skin, it is a case of leprous disease, and it shall be shown to the priest. 50And the priest shall examine the disease and shut up that which has the disease for seven days. 51Then he shall examine the disease on the seventh day. If the disease has spread in the garment, in the warp or the woof, or in the skin, whatever be the use of the skin, the disease is a persistent leprous disease; it is unclean. 52And he shall burn the garment, or the warp or the woof, the wool or the linen, or any article made of skin that is diseased, for it is a persistent leprous disease. It shall be burned in the fire.

53"And if the priest examines, and if the disease has not spread in the garment, in the warp or the woof or in any article made of skin, 54then the priest shall command that they wash the thing in which is the disease, and he shall shut it up for another seven days. 55And the priest shall examine the diseased thing after it has been washed. And if the appearance of the diseased area has not changed, though the disease has not spread, it is unclean. You shall burn it in the fire, whether the rot is on the back or on the front.

56"But if the priest examines, and if the diseased area has faded after it has been washed, he shall tear it out of the garment or the skin or the warp or the woof. 57Then if it appears again in the garment, in the warp or the woof, or in any article made of skin, it is spreading. You shall burn with fire whatever has the disease. 58But the garment, or the warp or the woof, or any article made of skin from which the disease departs when you have washed it, shall then be washed a second time, and be clean."

59This is the law for a case of leprous disease in a garment of wool or linen, either in the warp or the woof, or in any article made of skin, to determine whether it is clean or unclean.

Laws for Cleansing Lepers

14 The Lord spoke to Moses, saying, 2"This shall be the law of the leprous person for the day of his cleansing. He shall be brought to the priest, 3and the priest shall go out of the camp, and the priest shall look. Then, if the case of

LEVITICUS 14:1–3

EXAMINATION

To be required to live outside the camp meant removal from the community because something made a person unclean. There, far off from family and friends, an awkward society of the defiled waited for permission to return. For the leper, seeing a priest walk his or her way was an anxious moment. They desperately needed the spiritual leader's pronouncement of "clean." Once a positive determination was made, proper rituals were carried out, giving thanks to God for healing and restoration.

The priest of Leviticus 14:3 prefigures Christ in the act of moving toward untouchables. In Luke 5:12–14, Jesus encounters a leper who falls on the ground begging to be made clean—a plea born of a desperate existence in crushing isolation. Jesus did more than examine the leper. He touched him and spoke a command that instantly made him clean. Jesus is full of compassion and power. He brings near those who were once far off, enabling them to know love and community through his name.

[1]Or *mustache*

leprous disease is healed in the leprous person, 4the priest shall command them
to take for him who is to be cleansed two live[1] clean birds and cedarwood and
scarlet yarn and hyssop. 5And the priest shall command them to kill one of the
birds in an earthenware vessel over fresh[2] water. 6He shall take the live bird with
the cedarwood and the scarlet yarn and the hyssop, and dip them and the live
bird in the blood of the bird that was killed over the fresh water. 7And he shall
sprinkle it seven times on him who is to be cleansed of the leprous disease. Then
he shall pronounce him clean and shall let the living bird go into the open field.
8And he who is to be cleansed shall wash his clothes and shave off all his hair and
bathe himself in water, and he shall be clean. And after that he may come into the
camp, but live outside his tent seven days. 9And on the seventh day he shall shave
off all his hair from his head, his beard, and his eyebrows. He shall shave off all
his hair, and then he shall wash his clothes and bathe his body in water, and he
shall be clean.

10"And on the eighth day he shall take two male lambs without blemish, and
one ewe lamb a year old without blemish, and a grain offering of three tenths of
an ephah[3] of fine flour mixed with oil, and one log[4] of oil. 11And the priest who
cleanses him shall set the man who is to be cleansed and these things before the
LORD, at the entrance of the tent of meeting. 12And the priest shall take one of
the male lambs and offer it for a guilt offering, along with the log of oil, and wave
them for a wave offering before the LORD. 13And he shall kill the lamb in the place
where they kill the sin offering and the burnt offering, in the place of the sanctuary. For the guilt offering, like the sin offering, belongs to the priest; it is most
holy. 14The priest shall take some of the blood of the guilt offering, and the priest
shall put it on the lobe of the right ear of him who is to be cleansed and on the
thumb of his right hand and on the big toe of his right foot. 15Then the priest shall
take some of the log of oil and pour it into the palm of his own left hand 16and
dip his right finger in the oil that is in his left hand and sprinkle some oil with
his finger seven times before the LORD. 17And some of the oil that remains in his
hand the priest shall put on the lobe of the right ear of him who is to be cleansed
and on the thumb of his right hand and on the big toe of his right foot, on top of
the blood of the guilt offering. 18And the rest of the oil that is in the priest's hand
he shall put on the head of him who is to be cleansed. Then the priest shall make
atonement for him before the LORD. 19The priest shall offer the sin offering, to
make atonement for him who is to be cleansed from his uncleanness. And afterward he shall kill the burnt offering. 20And the priest shall offer the burnt offering
and the grain offering on the altar. Thus the priest shall make atonement for him,
and he shall be clean.

21"But if he is poor and cannot afford so much, then he shall take one male
lamb for a guilt offering to be waved, to make atonement for him, and a tenth of
an ephah of fine flour mixed with oil for a grain offering, and a log of oil; 22also
two turtledoves or two pigeons, whichever he can afford. The one shall be a sin
offering and the other a burnt offering. 23And on the eighth day he shall bring
them for his cleansing to the priest, to the entrance of the tent of meeting, before
the LORD. 24And the priest shall take the lamb of the guilt offering and the log
of oil, and the priest shall wave them for a wave offering before the LORD. 25And
he shall kill the lamb of the guilt offering. And the priest shall take some of the
blood of the guilt offering and put it on the lobe of the right ear of him who is to
be cleansed, and on the thumb of his right hand and on the big toe of his right
foot. 26And the priest shall pour some of the oil into the palm of his own left hand,
27and shall sprinkle with his right finger some of the oil that is in his left hand
seven times before the LORD. 28And the priest shall put some of the oil that is in his
hand on the lobe of the right ear of him who is to be cleansed and on the thumb

[1]Or *wild* [2]Or *running*; Hebrew *living*; also verses 6, 50, 51, 52 [3]An *ephah* was about 3/5 bushel or 22 liters
[4]A *log* was about 1/3 quart or 0.3 liter

of his right hand and on the big toe of his right foot, in the place where the blood
of the guilt offering was put. 29And the rest of the oil that is in the priest's hand
he shall put on the head of him who is to be cleansed, to make atonement for him
before the LORD. 30And he shall offer, of the turtledoves or pigeons, whichever he
can afford, 31one[1] for a sin offering and the other for a burnt offering, along with a
grain offering. And the priest shall make atonement before the LORD for him who
is being cleansed. 32This is the law for him in whom is a case of leprous disease,
who cannot afford the offerings for his cleansing."

Laws for Cleansing Houses

33The LORD spoke to Moses and Aaron, saying, 34"When you come into the
land of Canaan, which I give you for a possession, and I put a case of leprous
disease in a house in the land of your possession, 35then he who owns the house
shall come and tell the priest, 'There seems to me to be some case of disease in
my house.' 36Then the priest shall command that they empty the house before
the priest goes to examine the disease, lest all that is in the house be declared
unclean. And afterward the priest shall go in to see the house. 37And he shall
examine the disease. And if the disease is in the walls of the house with greenish
or reddish spots, and if it appears to be deeper than the surface, 38then the priest
shall go out of the house to the door of the house and shut up the house seven
days. 39And the priest shall come again on the seventh day, and look. If the disease
has spread in the walls of the house, 40then the priest shall command that they
take out the stones in which is the disease and throw them into an unclean place
outside the city. 41And he shall have the inside of the house scraped all around,
and the plaster that they scrape off they shall pour out in an unclean place outside
the city. 42Then they shall take other stones and put them in the place of those
stones, and he shall take other plaster and plaster the house.

43"If the disease breaks out again in the house, after he has taken out the
stones and scraped the house and plastered it, 44then the priest shall go and look.
And if the disease has spread in the house, it is a persistent leprous disease in the
house; it is unclean. 45And he shall break down the house, its stones and timber
and all the plaster of the house, and he shall carry them out of the city to an unclean place. 46Moreover, whoever enters the house while it is shut up shall be unclean until the evening, 47and whoever sleeps in the house shall wash his clothes,
and whoever eats in the house shall wash his clothes.

48"But if the priest comes and looks, and if the disease has not spread in the
house after the house was plastered, then the priest shall pronounce the house
clean, for the disease is healed. 49And for the cleansing of the house he shall take
two small birds, with cedarwood and scarlet yarn and hyssop, 50and shall kill one
of the birds in an earthenware vessel over fresh water 51and shall take the cedarwood and the hyssop and the scarlet yarn, along with the live bird, and dip
them in the blood of the bird that was killed and in the fresh water and sprinkle
the house seven times. 52Thus he shall cleanse the house with the blood of the
bird and with the fresh water and with the live bird and with the cedarwood and
hyssop and scarlet yarn. 53And he shall let the live bird go out of the city into the
open country. So he shall make atonement for the house, and it shall be clean."

54This is the law for any case of leprous disease: for an itch, 55for leprous disease in a garment or in a house, 56and for a swelling or an eruption or a spot, 57to
show when it is unclean and when it is clean. This is the law for leprous disease.

Laws About Bodily Discharges

15 The LORD spoke to Moses and Aaron, saying, 2"Speak to the people of Israel
and say to them, When any man has a discharge from his body,[2] his discharge is unclean. 3And this is the law of his uncleanness for a discharge: whether

[1] Septuagint, Syriac; Hebrew *afford, 31such as he can afford, one* [2] Hebrew *flesh*; also verse 3

his body runs with his discharge, or his body is blocked up by his discharge, it is
his uncleanness. 4Every bed on which the one with the discharge lies shall be
unclean, and everything on which he sits shall be unclean. 5And anyone who
touches his bed shall wash his clothes and bathe himself in water and be unclean until the evening. 6And whoever sits on anything on which the one with
the discharge has sat shall wash his clothes and bathe himself in water and be
unclean until the evening. 7And whoever touches the body of the one with the
discharge shall wash his clothes and bathe himself in water and be unclean until
the evening. 8And if the one with the discharge spits on someone who is clean,
then he shall wash his clothes and bathe himself in water and be unclean until
the evening. 9And any saddle on which the one with the discharge rides shall be
unclean. 10And whoever touches anything that was under him shall be unclean
until the evening. And whoever carries such things shall wash his clothes and
bathe himself in water and be unclean until the evening. 11Anyone whom the one
with the discharge touches without having rinsed his hands in water shall wash
his clothes and bathe himself in water and be unclean until the evening. 12And an
earthenware vessel that the one with the discharge touches shall be broken, and
every vessel of wood shall be rinsed in water.

13"And when the one with a discharge is cleansed of his discharge, then he
shall count for himself seven days for his cleansing, and wash his clothes. And
he shall bathe his body in fresh water and shall be clean. 14And on the eighth day
he shall take two turtledoves or two pigeons and come before the LORD to the
entrance of the tent of meeting and give them to the priest. 15And the priest shall
use them, one for a sin offering and the other for a burnt offering. And the priest
shall make atonement for him before the LORD for his discharge.

16"If a man has an emission of semen, he shall bathe his whole body in water
and be unclean until the evening. 17And every garment and every skin on which
the semen comes shall be washed with water and be unclean until the evening.
18If a man lies with a woman and has an emission of semen, both of them shall
bathe themselves in water and be unclean until the evening.

19"When a woman has a discharge, and the discharge in her body is blood,
she shall be in her menstrual impurity for seven days, and whoever touches her
shall be unclean until the evening. 20And everything on which she lies during her
menstrual impurity shall be unclean. Everything also on which she sits shall be
unclean. 21And whoever touches her bed shall wash his clothes and bathe himself
in water and be unclean until the evening. 22And whoever touches anything on
which she sits shall wash his clothes and bathe himself in water and be unclean
until the evening. 23Whether it is the bed or anything on which she sits, when he
touches it he shall be unclean until the evening. 24And if any man lies with her
and her menstrual impurity comes upon him, he shall be unclean seven days, and
every bed on which he lies shall be unclean.

25"If a woman has a discharge of blood for many days, not at the time of her
menstrual impurity, or if she has a discharge beyond the time of her impurity, all
the days of the discharge she shall continue in uncleanness. As in the days of her
impurity, she shall be unclean. 26Every bed on which she lies, all the days of her
discharge, shall be to her as the bed of her impurity. And everything on which
she sits shall be unclean, as in the uncleanness of her menstrual impurity. 27And
whoever touches these things shall be unclean, and shall wash his clothes and
bathe himself in water and be unclean until the evening. 28But if she is cleansed
of her discharge, she shall count for herself seven days, and after that she shall be
clean. 29And on the eighth day she shall take two turtledoves or two pigeons and
bring them to the priest, to the entrance of the tent of meeting. 30And the priest
shall use one for a sin offering and the other for a burnt offering. And the priest
shall make atonement for her before the LORD for her unclean discharge.

31"Thus you shall keep the people of Israel separate from their uncleanness,
lest they die in their uncleanness by defiling my tabernacle that is in their midst."

[32]This is the law for him who has a discharge and for him who has an emission of semen, becoming unclean thereby; [33]also for her who is unwell with her menstrual impurity, that is, for anyone, male or female, who has a discharge, and for the man who lies with a woman who is unclean.

The Day of Atonement

16 The LORD spoke to Moses after the death of the two sons of Aaron, when they drew near before the LORD and died, [2]and the LORD said to Moses, "Tell Aaron your brother not to come at any time into the Holy Place inside the veil, before the mercy seat that is on the ark, so that he may not die. For I will appear in the cloud over the mercy seat. [3]But in this way Aaron shall come into the Holy Place: with a bull from the herd for a sin offering and a ram for a burnt offering. [4]He shall put on the holy linen coat and shall have the linen undergarment on his body, and he shall tie the linen sash around his waist, and wear the linen turban; these are the holy garments. He shall bathe his body in water and then put them on. [5]And he shall take from the congregation of the people of Israel two male goats for a sin offering, and one ram for a burnt offering.

[6]"Aaron shall offer the bull as a sin offering for himself and shall make atonement for himself and for his house. [7]Then he shall take the two goats and set them before the LORD at the entrance of the tent of meeting. [8]And Aaron shall cast lots over the two goats, one lot for the LORD and the other lot for Azazel.[1] [9]And Aaron shall present the goat on which the lot fell for the LORD and use it as a sin offering, [10]but the goat on which the lot fell for Azazel shall be presented alive before the LORD to make atonement over it, that it may be sent away into the wilderness to Azazel.

[11]"Aaron shall present the bull as a sin offering for himself, and shall make atonement for himself and for his house. He shall kill the bull as a sin offering for himself. [12]And he shall take a censer full of coals of fire from the altar before the LORD, and two handfuls of sweet incense beaten small, and he shall bring it inside the veil [13]and put the incense on the fire before the LORD, that the cloud of the incense may cover the mercy seat that is over the testimony, so that he does not die. [14]And he shall take some of the blood of the bull and sprinkle it with his finger on the front of the mercy seat on the east side, and in front of the mercy seat he shall sprinkle some of the blood with his finger seven times.

[15]"Then he shall kill the goat of the sin offering that is for the people and bring its blood inside the veil and do with its blood as he did with the blood of the bull, sprinkling it over the mercy seat and in front of the mercy seat. [16]Thus he shall make atonement for the Holy Place, because of the uncleannesses of the people of Israel and because of their transgressions, all their sins. And so he shall do for the tent of meeting, which dwells with them in the midst of their uncleannesses. [17]No one may be in the tent of meeting from the time he enters to make atonement in the Holy Place until he comes out and has made atonement for himself and for his house and for all the assembly of Israel. [18]Then he shall go out to the altar that is before the LORD and make atonement for it, and shall take some of the blood of the bull and some of the blood of the goat, and put it on the horns of the altar all around. [19]And he shall sprinkle some of the blood on it with his finger seven times, and cleanse it and consecrate it from the uncleannesses of the people of Israel.

[20]"And when he has made an end of atoning for the Holy Place and the tent of meeting and the altar, he shall present the live goat. [21]And Aaron shall lay both his hands on the head of the live goat, and confess over it all the iniquities of the people of Israel, and all their transgressions, all their sins. And he shall put them on the head of the goat and send it away into the wilderness by the hand of a man who is in readiness. [22]The goat shall bear all their iniquities on itself to a remote area, and he shall let the goat go free in the wilderness.

[1]The meaning of *Azazel* is uncertain; possibly the name of a place or a demon, traditionally a scapegoat; also verses 10, 26

LEVITICUS 16:20–22

BEARING OUR SIN

There are two goats in the stages of the Day of Atonement ritual described in Leviticus 16. One goat served its purpose by dying and the other by remaining alive. The first goat was killed as a sacrifice, its blood sprinkled on the mercy seat, tent of meeting, and altar. The second goat bore the sins of the nation on its head. Aaron laid both hands on this beast while confessing all of Israel's sins. This is the origin of the term *scapegoat*. The animal was led away—carrying all of their sins—and was released in a remote place where it could not return to the Israelite camp.

When Jesus made atonement on the cross, he bore the sins of the human race (1Jn 2:2). For the Christian, all guilt has been removed—and it will not return. Jesus died under the weight of our sins and God's righteous wrath so that we might have forgiveness and have new life in him (1Pe 2:24).

JESUS AND THE DAY OF ATONEMENT

Atonement is the process of restoring right standing with God once sin has occurred. In the Old Testament, an elaborate ceremony took place every year to atone for Israel's sins. In accordance with God's instructions, their guilt had to be covered over — their offenses had to be paid for through the shedding of blood.

Before entering the Most Holy Place, the high priest had to carefully wash himself and put on special garments. A bull was killed to cover the sins of the priest and his household. Then the priest cast lots over two goats — one to be sacrificed and one to become the scapegoat, carrying the people's sins away from the community. Incense was burned over the ark so that smoke concealed the holiest place, protecting the priest. The blood of the sacrificed bull and goat were sprinkled on the mercy seat, the tent of meeting, and the altar. Then the scapegoat was sent off with all of Israel's sins on its head. Then the priest washed himself and changed his clothes before exiting the tent to burn portions of the offering on the altar. Finally, the remains of the animals were removed and the attendants who removed them — along with the man who led the scapegoat away — had to wash their clothes and bathe themselves. All of this happened every year so that people could be cleansed from all their sins (Lev 16:1 – 30).

The main feature of the ceremony, the shedding of blood, taught that atonement symbolizes the substitution of life for life. In that way, the Old Testament points forward to the atoning sacrifice of Christ on the cross for our sins. God presented Jesus as a sacrifice of atonement (Ro 3:25 – 26). He gave his only Son as a payment for the sins of the world. Jesus had no guilt of his own, so he was worthy to be our substitute upon the altar of the cross.

God did this to demonstrate his righteousness. Sin was never waved off, disregarded, or left unaccounted for. God upheld his righteousness and the worth of his name by requiring blood atonement for cleansing from sin. Justice shines in the way God kept his word to punish sin. Grace shines in the way God placed all of our sins on Christ. Salvation is a free gift to those with faith (Eph 2:8 – 9), but the gift itself was not free — atonement was purchased with the precious blood of Christ (1Pe 1:18 – 19).

23"Then Aaron shall come into the tent of meeting and shall take off the linen garments that he put on when he went into the Holy Place and shall leave them there. 24And he shall bathe his body in water in a holy place and put on his garments and come out and offer his burnt offering and the burnt offering of the people and make atonement for himself and for the people. 25And the fat of the sin offering he shall burn on the altar. 26And he who lets the goat go to Azazel shall wash his clothes and bathe his body in water, and afterward he may come into the camp. 27And the bull for the sin offering and the goat for the sin offering, whose blood was brought in to make atonement in the Holy Place, shall be carried outside the camp. Their skin and their flesh and their dung shall be burned up with fire. 28And he who burns them shall wash his clothes and bathe his body in water, and afterward he may come into the camp.

29"And it shall be a statute to you forever that in the seventh month, on the tenth day of the month, you shall afflict yourselves[1] and shall do no work, either the native or the stranger who sojourns among you. 30For on this day shall atonement be made for you to cleanse you. You shall be clean before the LORD from all your sins. 31It is a Sabbath of solemn rest to you, and you shall afflict yourselves; it is a statute forever. 32And the priest who is anointed and consecrated as priest in his father's place shall make atonement, wearing the holy linen garments. 33He shall make atonement for the holy sanctuary, and he shall make atonement for the tent of meeting and for the altar, and he shall make atonement for the priests and for all the people of the assembly. 34And this shall be a statute forever for you, that atonement may be made for the people of Israel once in the year because of all their sins." And Aaron[2] did as the LORD commanded Moses.

The Place of Sacrifice

17 And the LORD spoke to Moses, saying, 2"Speak to Aaron and his sons and to all the people of Israel and say to them, This is the thing that the LORD has commanded. 3If any one of the house of Israel kills an ox or a lamb or a goat in the camp, or kills it outside the camp, 4and does not bring it to the entrance of the tent of meeting to offer it as a gift to the LORD in front of the tabernacle of the LORD, bloodguilt shall be imputed to that man. He has shed blood, and that man shall be cut off from among his people. 5This is to the end that the people of Israel may bring their sacrifices that they sacrifice in the open field, that they may bring them to the LORD, to the priest at the entrance of the tent of meeting, and sacrifice them as sacrifices of peace offerings to the LORD. 6And the priest shall throw the blood on the altar of the LORD at the entrance of the tent of meeting and burn the fat for a pleasing aroma to the LORD. 7So they shall no more sacrifice their sacrifices to goat demons, after whom they whore. This shall be a statute forever for them throughout their generations.

8"And you shall say to them, Any one of the house of Israel, or of the strangers who sojourn among them, who offers a burnt offering or sacrifice 9and does not bring it to the entrance of the tent of meeting to offer it to the LORD, that man shall be cut off from his people.

Laws Against Eating Blood

10"If any one of the house of Israel or of the strangers who sojourn among them eats any blood, I will set my face against that person who eats blood and will cut him off from among his people. 11For the life of the flesh is in the blood, and I have given it for you on the altar to make atonement for your souls, for it is the blood that makes atonement by the life. 12Therefore I have said to the people of Israel, No person among you shall eat blood, neither shall any stranger who sojourns among you eat blood.

13"Any one also of the people of Israel, or of the strangers who sojourn among

[1]Or *shall fast*; also verse 31 [2]Hebrew *he*

NOTHING BUT THE BLOOD OF JESUS

Atonement required blood. God explained that the life of a creature is in its blood — so the life-liquid must be treated with respect. It is the blood that effected atonement, but the substance had no power in itself. The power to cancel sin resides in God, who ordained the method.

Jesus did not secure our pardon by simply living a sinless life. He bled so we could be free. Without the shedding of blood there is no forgiveness of sin (Heb 9:22). Take note of the multiple New Testament references to the power of the blood of Jesus:

"This is my blood of the covenant, which is poured out for many" (Mk 14:24).

"Christ Jesus, whom God put forward as a propitiation by his blood, to be received by faith. This was to show God's righteousness, because in his divine forbearance he had passed over former sins" (Ro 3:24 – 25).

"In the same way also he took the cup, after supper, saying, 'This cup is the new covenant in my blood. Do this, as often as you drink it, in remembrance of me.' For as often as you eat this bread and drink the cup, you proclaim the Lord's death until he comes" (1Co 11:25 – 26).

"In him we have redemption through his blood, the forgiveness of our trespasses, according to the riches of his grace" (Eph 1:7).

"But now in Christ Jesus you who once were far off have been brought near by the blood of Christ" (Eph 2:13).

"And through him to reconcile to himself all things, whether on earth or in heaven, making peace by the blood of his cross" (Col 1:20).

"Therefore, brothers, since we have confidence to enter the holy places by the blood of Jesus, by the new and living way that he opened for us through the curtain, that is, through his flesh" (Heb 10:19 – 20).

"[K]nowing that you were ransomed from the futile ways inherited from your forefathers, not with perishable things such as silver or gold, but with the precious blood of Christ, like that of a lamb without blemish or spot" (1Pe 1:18 – 19).

"But if we walk in the light, as he is in the light, we have fellowship with one another, and the blood of Jesus his Son cleanses us from all sin" (1Jn 1:7).

"To him who loves us and has freed us from our sins by his blood" (Rev 1:5).

"These are the ones coming out of the great tribulation. They have washed their robes and made them white in the blood of the Lamb" (Rev 7:14).

"And they have conquered him by the blood of the Lamb" (Rev 12:11).

All who want their sins forgiven must be purified by the blood of Jesus Christ (1Jn 1:7). There is no other way — atonement is in the blood. Good works do not cancel the debt of sin. Great knowledge does not move people from death to life. The only hope for salvation is faith in the shed blood of Jesus.

them, who takes in hunting any beast or bird that may be eaten shall pour out its blood and cover it with earth. 14For the life of every creature[1] is its blood: its blood is its life.[2] Therefore I have said to the people of Israel, You shall not eat the blood of any creature, for the life of every creature is its blood. Whoever eats it shall be cut off. 15And every person who eats what dies of itself or what is torn by beasts, whether he is a native or a sojourner, shall wash his clothes and bathe himself in water and be unclean until the evening; then he shall be clean. 16But if he does not wash them or bathe his flesh, he shall bear his iniquity."

Unlawful Sexual Relations

18 And the LORD spoke to Moses, saying, 2"Speak to the people of Israel and say to them, I am the LORD your God. 3You shall not do as they do in the land of Egypt, where you lived, and you shall not do as they do in the land of Canaan, to which I am bringing you. You shall not walk in their statutes. 4You shall follow my rules[3] and keep my statutes and walk in them. I am the LORD your God. 5You shall therefore keep my statutes and my rules; if a person does them, he shall live by them: I am the LORD.

6"None of you shall approach any one of his close relatives to uncover nakedness. I am the LORD. 7You shall not uncover the nakedness of your father, which is the nakedness of your mother; she is your mother, you shall not uncover her nakedness. 8You shall not uncover the nakedness of your father's wife; it is your father's nakedness. 9You shall not uncover the nakedness of your sister, your father's daughter or your mother's daughter, whether brought up in the family or in another home. 10You shall not uncover the nakedness of your son's daughter or of your daughter's daughter, for their nakedness is your own nakedness. 11You shall not uncover the nakedness of your father's wife's daughter, brought up in your father's family, since she is your sister. 12You shall not uncover the nakedness of your father's sister; she is your father's relative. 13You shall not uncover the nakedness of your mother's sister, for she is your mother's relative. 14You shall not uncover the nakedness of your father's brother, that is, you shall not approach his wife; she is your aunt. 15You shall not uncover the nakedness of your daughter-in-law; she is your son's wife, you shall not uncover her nakedness. 16You shall not uncover the nakedness of your brother's wife; it is your brother's nakedness. 17You shall not uncover the nakedness of a woman and of her daughter, and you shall not take her son's daughter or her daughter's daughter to uncover her nakedness; they are relatives; it is depravity. 18And you shall not take a woman as a rival wife to her sister, uncovering her nakedness while her sister is still alive.

19"You shall not approach a woman to uncover her nakedness while she is in her menstrual uncleanness. 20And you shall not lie sexually with your neighbor's wife and so make yourself unclean with her. 21You shall not give any of your children to offer them[4] to Molech, and so profane the name of your God: I am the LORD. 22You shall not lie with a male as with a woman; it is an abomination. 23And you shall not lie with any animal and so make yourself unclean with it, neither shall any woman give herself to an animal to lie with it: it is perversion.

24"Do not make yourselves unclean by any of these things, for by all these the nations I am driving out before you have become unclean, 25and the land became unclean, so that I punished its iniquity, and the land vomited out its inhabitants. 26But you shall keep my statutes and my rules and do none of these abominations, either the native or the stranger who sojourns among you 27(for the people of the land, who were before you, did all of these abominations, so that the land became unclean), 28lest the land vomit you out when you make it unclean, as it vomited out the nation that was before you. 29For everyone who does any of these abominations, the persons who do them shall be cut off from among their

[1]Hebrew *all flesh* [2]Hebrew *it is in its life* [3]Or *my just decrees*; also verse 5 [4]Hebrew *to make them pass through* [the fire]

LEVITICUS 18:1–5

OBEY AND BE DIFFERENT

Moses relayed God's command to reject the practices of the Egyptians and Canaanites especially in the area of sexual ethics. God's people were to obey his laws and decrees even if the culture gave permission for something different. His commands were more than distinguishing markers for his unique people—they were a means to life. God pointed his people on paths of joy and satisfaction, leading them to avoid paths of regret and destruction.

Jesus calls us to keep his commands just as he obeyed the commands of the Father. Christians seek to obey because we are submitted to the authority of God over all of life—no matter what others around us do. The primacy given to sexual ethics applies to the church, as well. This is a clear distinguishing mark for God's church to this day. Concurrently, we seek to obey because it keeps us close to Jesus and results in great joy (Jn 15:10–11).

people. 30So keep my charge never to practice any of these abominable customs
that were practiced before you, and never to make yourselves unclean by them: I
am the LORD your God."

The LORD Is Holy

19 And the LORD spoke to Moses, saying, 2"Speak to all the congregation of
the people of Israel and say to them, You shall be holy, for I the LORD your
God am holy. 3Every one of you shall revere his mother and his father, and you
shall keep my Sabbaths: I am the LORD your God. 4Do not turn to idols or make for
yourselves any gods of cast metal: I am the LORD your God.
5"When you offer a sacrifice of peace offerings to the LORD, you shall offer it so
that you may be accepted. 6It shall be eaten the same day you offer it or on the day
after, and anything left over until the third day shall be burned up with fire. 7If it
is eaten at all on the third day, it is tainted; it will not be accepted, 8and everyone
who eats it shall bear his iniquity, because he has profaned what is holy to the
LORD, and that person shall be cut off from his people.

Love Your Neighbor as Yourself

9"When you reap the harvest of your land, you shall not reap your field right
up to its edge, neither shall you gather the gleanings after your harvest. 10And
you shall not strip your vineyard bare, neither shall you gather the fallen grapes
of your vineyard. You shall leave them for the poor and for the sojourner: I am the
LORD your God.
11"You shall not steal; you shall not deal falsely; you shall not lie to one another. 12You shall not swear by my name falsely, and so profane the name of your
God: I am the LORD.
13"You shall not oppress your neighbor or rob him. The wages of a hired worker
shall not remain with you all night until the morning. 14You shall not curse the
deaf or put a stumbling block before the blind, but you shall fear your God: I am
the LORD.
15"You shall do no injustice in court. You shall not be partial to the poor or defer to the great, but in righteousness shall you judge your neighbor. 16You shall not
go around as a slanderer among your people, and you shall not stand up against
the life[1] of your neighbor: I am the LORD.
17"You shall not hate your brother in your heart, but you shall reason frankly
with your neighbor, lest you incur sin because of him. 18You shall not take vengeance or bear a grudge against the sons of your own people, but you shall love
your neighbor as yourself: I am the LORD.

You Shall Keep My Statutes

19"You shall keep my statutes. You shall not let your cattle breed with a different kind. You shall not sow your field with two kinds of seed, nor shall you wear
a garment of cloth made of two kinds of material.
20"If a man lies sexually with a woman who is a slave, assigned to another
man and not yet ransomed or given her freedom, a distinction shall be made.
They shall not be put to death, because she was not free; 21but he shall bring his
compensation to the LORD, to the entrance of the tent of meeting, a ram for a
guilt offering. 22And the priest shall make atonement for him with the ram of the
guilt offering before the LORD for his sin that he has committed, and he shall be
forgiven for the sin that he has committed.
23"When you come into the land and plant any kind of tree for food, then you
shall regard its fruit as forbidden.[2] Three years it shall be forbidden to you; it must
not be eaten. 24And in the fourth year all its fruit shall be holy, an offering of praise
to the LORD. 25But in the fifth year you may eat of its fruit, to increase its yield for
you: I am the LORD your God.

[1]Hebrew *blood* [2]Hebrew *as its uncircumcision*

LEVITICUS 19:18

REVENGE

When wronged and wounded by others, Christians face the option to seek revenge or to love as Jesus taught. Someone once asked him about the greatest commandment and his reply was to love God with all your heart, soul, and mind. He then added, "Love your neighbor as yourself," quoting this section of Leviticus (Mt 22:39). Jesus loved fully and freely, showing us how to love others—even those who hurt us.

Bearing a grudge—scheming for the opportunity to strike back—is one of the easiest things to do. Refusing to take revenge is one of the hardest. It is the courageous and God-honoring choice; trusting him to accomplish justice while dispensing mercy and grace.

Revenge-seeking keeps anger fanned into flame and keeps open the wound of offense. Withholding forgiveness supports a sense of self-importance and entitlement, looking to win some invisible competition. Most importantly, it is contrary to the instruction and example of Christ. Facing the cross, a most horrific display of hatred and torture, Jesus did not call down heaven against mankind. His response was, "Father, forgive them" (Lk 23:34). No grudge, no desire for revenge, only love—full and free.

26“You shall not eat any flesh with the blood in it. You shall not interpret omens or tell fortunes. 27You shall not round off the hair on your temples or mar the edges of your beard. 28You shall not make any cuts on your body for the dead or tattoo yourselves: I am the LORD.

29“Do not profane your daughter by making her a prostitute, lest the land fall into prostitution and the land become full of depravity. 30You shall keep my Sabbaths and reverence my sanctuary: I am the LORD.

31“Do not turn to mediums or necromancers; do not seek them out, and so make yourselves unclean by them: I am the LORD your God.

32“You shall stand up before the gray head and honor the face of an old man, and you shall fear your God: I am the LORD.

33“When a stranger sojourns with you in your land, you shall not do him wrong. 34You shall treat the stranger who sojourns with you as the native among you, and you shall love him as yourself, for you were strangers in the land of Egypt: I am the LORD your God.

35“You shall do no wrong in judgment, in measures of length or weight or quantity. 36You shall have just balances, just weights, a just ephah, and a just hin:[1] I am the LORD your God, who brought you out of the land of Egypt. 37And you shall observe all my statutes and all my rules, and do them: I am the LORD.”

Punishment for Child Sacrifice

20 The LORD spoke to Moses, saying, 2“Say to the people of Israel, Any one of the people of Israel or of the strangers who sojourn in Israel who gives any of his children to Molech shall surely be put to death. The people of the land shall stone him with stones. 3I myself will set my face against that man and will cut him off from among his people, because he has given one of his children to Molech, to make my sanctuary unclean and to profane my holy name. 4And if the people of the land do at all close their eyes to that man when he gives one of his children to Molech, and do not put him to death, 5then I will set my face against that man and against his clan and will cut them off from among their people, him and all who follow him in whoring after Molech.

6“If a person turns to mediums and necromancers, whoring after them, I will set my face against that person and will cut him off from among his people. 7Consecrate yourselves, therefore, and be holy, for I am the LORD your God. 8Keep my statutes and do them; I am the LORD who sanctifies you. 9For anyone who curses his father or his mother shall surely be put to death; he has cursed his father or his mother; his blood is upon him.

Punishments for Sexual Immorality

10“If a man commits adultery with the wife of[2] his neighbor, both the adulterer and the adulteress shall surely be put to death. 11If a man lies with his father’s wife, he has uncovered his father’s nakedness; both of them shall surely be put to death; their blood is upon them. 12If a man lies with his daughter-in-law, both of them shall surely be put to death; they have committed perversion; their blood is upon them. 13If a man lies with a male as with a woman, both of them have committed an abomination; they shall surely be put to death; their blood is upon them. 14If a man takes a woman and her mother also, it is depravity; he and they shall be burned with fire, that there may be no depravity among you. 15If a man lies with an animal, he shall surely be put to death, and you shall kill the animal. 16If a woman approaches any animal and lies with it, you shall kill the woman and the animal; they shall surely be put to death; their blood is upon them.

17“If a man takes his sister, a daughter of his father or a daughter of his mother, and sees her nakedness, and she sees his nakedness, it is a disgrace, and they shall

---

[1]An *ephah* was about 3/5 bushel or 22 liters; a *hin* was about 4 quarts or 3.5 liters [2]Hebrew repeats *if a man commits adultery with the wife of*

be cut off in the sight of the children of their people. He has uncovered his sister's nakedness, and he shall bear his iniquity. [18]If a man lies with a woman during her menstrual period and uncovers her nakedness, he has made naked her fountain, and she has uncovered the fountain of her blood. Both of them shall be cut off from among their people. [19]You shall not uncover the nakedness of your mother's sister or of your father's sister, for that is to make naked one's relative; they shall bear their iniquity. [20]If a man lies with his uncle's wife, he has uncovered his uncle's nakedness; they shall bear their sin; they shall die childless. [21]If a man takes his brother's wife, it is impurity.[1] He has uncovered his brother's nakedness; they shall be childless.

You Shall Be Holy

[22]"You shall therefore keep all my statutes and all my rules and do them, that the land where I am bringing you to live may not vomit you out. [23]And you shall not walk in the customs of the nation that I am driving out before you, for they did all these things, and therefore I detested them. [24]But I have said to you, 'You shall inherit their land, and I will give it to you to possess, a land flowing with milk and honey.' I am the LORD your God, who has separated you from the peoples. [25]You shall therefore separate the clean beast from the unclean, and the unclean bird from the clean. You shall not make yourselves detestable by beast or by bird or by anything with which the ground crawls, which I have set apart for you to hold unclean. [26]You shall be holy to me, for I the LORD am holy and have separated you from the peoples, that you should be mine.

[27]"A man or a woman who is a medium or a necromancer shall surely be put to death. They shall be stoned with stones; their blood shall be upon them."

Holiness and the Priests

21 And the LORD said to Moses, "Speak to the priests, the sons of Aaron, and say to them, No one shall make himself unclean for the dead among his people, [2]except for his closest relatives, his mother, his father, his son, his daughter, his brother, [3]or his virgin sister (who is near to him because she has had no husband; for her he may make himself unclean). [4]He shall not make himself unclean as a husband among his people and so profane himself. [5]They shall not make bald patches on their heads, nor shave off the edges of their beards, nor make any cuts on their body. [6]They shall be holy to their God and not profane the name of their God. For they offer the LORD's food offerings, the bread of their God; therefore they shall be holy. [7]They shall not marry a prostitute or a woman who has been defiled, neither shall they marry a woman divorced from her husband, for the priest is holy to his God. [8]You shall sanctify him, for he offers the bread of your God. He shall be holy to you, for I, the LORD, who sanctify you, am holy. [9]And the daughter of any priest, if she profanes herself by whoring, profanes her father; she shall be burned with fire.

[10]"The priest who is chief among his brothers, on whose head the anointing oil is poured and who has been consecrated to wear the garments, shall not let the hair of his head hang loose nor tear his clothes. [11]He shall not go in to any dead bodies nor make himself unclean, even for his father or for his mother. [12]He shall not go out of the sanctuary, lest he profane the sanctuary of his God, for the consecration of the anointing oil of his God is on him: I am the LORD. [13]And he shall take a wife in her virginity.[2] [14]A widow, or a divorced woman, or a woman who has been defiled, or a prostitute, these he shall not marry. But he shall take as his wife a virgin[3] of his own people, [15]that he may not profane his offspring among his people, for I am the LORD who sanctifies him."

[16]And the LORD spoke to Moses, saying, [17]"Speak to Aaron, saying, None of your offspring throughout their generations who has a blemish may approach to

[1]Hebrew *menstrual impurity* [2]Or *a young wife* [3]Hebrew *young woman*

PUNISHMENTS FOR SIN

When parents respond to misbehavior with appropriate and measured discipline, the child is likely to think their parents are cruel and lacking grace. For many readers, God's plan of discipline for sinners — spelled out in Leviticus 20 — seems cruel, harsh, and even extreme. In most cases, all parties in the sinful activity were to be put to death by the community.

The promised punishments were actually generous warnings, shedding light on God's desire that his people live and not die. His explicit commands helped the people know what conduct to avoid. The Lord, who is always just, repeatedly noted that offenders who disregarded his warnings would die — but their blood would be on their own heads (Lev 20:9,11,12,13,16,27).

The list of behaviors and consequences also served to train the Israelites to obey their God while staying away from the dark practices of other nations. God wanted them anchored to his concept of holiness before they entered the new land he was about to give them (Lev 20:22 – 24).

In the New Testament, Jesus gave the community new instructions for responding to friends and family members in sin. He taught that the offender should be pursued with the goal of repentance. Jesus even outlined different scenarios and responses (Mt 18:15 – 17). Paul the apostle instructed that churches should remove sinners claiming to be Christians if they refused to repent from wickedness (1Co 5:9 – 13).

There is evidence that death as a consequence of defiance occurred beyond the Old Testament context. Paul explained to the Corinthian church that some of their people had become sick or died because they mistreated the occasion of the Lord's Supper (1Co 11:27 – 32). Elsewhere in the New Testament we are reminded that the Lord disciplines us as a father disciplines the children he loves (Heb 12:5 – 11).

God requires holiness from his people and promises to assist us in the process. He will, through our obedience and close association with him — together with occasional necessary discipline — make his people holy (Lev 20:7 – 8). He will do this for his glory and for our good.

offer the bread of his God. [18]For no one who has a blemish shall draw near, a man blind or lame, or one who has a mutilated face or a limb too long, [19]or a man who has an injured foot or an injured hand, [20]or a hunchback or a dwarf or a man with a defect in his sight or an itching disease or scabs or crushed testicles. [21]No man of the offspring of Aaron the priest who has a blemish shall come near to offer the LORD's food offerings; since he has a blemish, he shall not come near to offer the bread of his God. [22]He may eat the bread of his God, both of the most holy and of the holy things, [23]but he shall not go through the veil or approach the altar, because he has a blemish, that he may not profane my sanctuaries,[1] for I am the LORD who sanctifies them." [24]So Moses spoke to Aaron and to his sons and to all the people of Israel.

22 And the LORD spoke to Moses, saying, [2]"Speak to Aaron and his sons so that they abstain from the holy things of the people of Israel, which they dedicate to me, so that they do not profane my holy name: I am the LORD. [3]Say to them, 'If any one of all your offspring throughout your generations approaches the holy things that the people of Israel dedicate to the LORD, while he has an uncleanness, that person shall be cut off from my presence: I am the LORD. [4]None of the offspring of Aaron who has a leprous disease or a discharge may eat of the holy things until he is clean. Whoever touches anything that is unclean through contact with the dead or a man who has had an emission of semen, [5]and whoever touches a swarming thing by which he may be made unclean or a person from whom he may take uncleanness, whatever his uncleanness may be— [6]the person who touches such a thing shall be unclean until the evening and shall not eat of the holy things unless he has bathed his body in water. [7]When the sun goes down he shall be clean, and afterward he may eat of the holy things, because they are his food. [8]He shall not eat what dies of itself or is torn by beasts, and so make himself unclean by it: I am the LORD.' [9]They shall therefore keep my charge, lest they bear sin for it and die thereby when they profane it: I am the LORD who sanctifies them.

[10]"A lay person shall not eat of a holy thing; no foreign guest of the priest or hired worker shall eat of a holy thing, [11]but if a priest buys a slave[2] as his property for money, the slave[3] may eat of it, and anyone born in his house may eat of his food. [12]If a priest's daughter marries a layman, she shall not eat of the contribution of the holy things. [13]But if a priest's daughter is widowed or divorced and has no child and returns to her father's house, as in her youth, she may eat of her father's food; yet no lay person shall eat of it. [14]And if anyone eats of a holy thing unintentionally, he shall add the fifth of its value to it and give the holy thing to the priest. [15]They shall not profane the holy things of the people of Israel, which they contribute to the LORD, [16]and so cause them to bear iniquity and guilt, by eating their holy things: for I am the LORD who sanctifies them."

Acceptable Offerings

[17]And the LORD spoke to Moses, saying, [18]"Speak to Aaron and his sons and all the people of Israel and say to them, When any one of the house of Israel or of the sojourners in Israel presents a burnt offering as his offering, for any of their vows or freewill offerings that they offer to the LORD, [19]if it is to be accepted for you it shall be a male without blemish, of the bulls or the sheep or the goats. [20]You shall not offer anything that has a blemish, for it will not be acceptable for you. [21]And when anyone offers a sacrifice of peace offerings to the LORD to fulfill a vow or as a freewill offering from the herd or from the flock, to be accepted it must be perfect; there shall be no blemish in it. [22]Animals blind or disabled or mutilated or having a discharge or an itch or scabs you shall not offer to the LORD or give them to the LORD as a food offering on the altar. [23]You may present a bull or a lamb that has a part too long or too short for a freewill offering, but for a vow offering

[1]Or *my holy precincts* [2]Or *servant*; twice in this verse [3]Hebrew *he*

it cannot be accepted. [24]Any animal that has its testicles bruised or crushed or
torn or cut you shall not offer to the LORD; you shall not do it within your land,
[25]neither shall you offer as the bread of your God any such animals gotten from a
foreigner. Since there is a blemish in them, because of their mutilation, they will
not be accepted for you."

[26]And the LORD spoke to Moses, saying, [27]"When an ox or sheep or goat is
born, it shall remain seven days with its mother, and from the eighth day on it
shall be acceptable as a food offering to the LORD. [28]But you shall not kill an ox or
a sheep and her young in one day. [29]And when you sacrifice a sacrifice of thanksgiving to the LORD, you shall sacrifice it so that you may be accepted. [30]It shall be
eaten on the same day; you shall leave none of it until morning: I am the LORD.

[31]"So you shall keep my commandments and do them: I am the LORD. [32]And
you shall not profane my holy name, that I may be sanctified among the people
of Israel. I am the LORD who sanctifies you, [33]who brought you out of the land of
Egypt to be your God: I am the LORD."

Feasts of the LORD

23 The LORD spoke to Moses, saying, [2]"Speak to the people of Israel and say to
them, These are the appointed feasts of the LORD that you shall proclaim as
holy convocations; they are my appointed feasts.

The Sabbath

[3]"Six days shall work be done, but on the seventh day is a Sabbath of solemn
rest, a holy convocation. You shall do no work. It is a Sabbath to the LORD in all
your dwelling places.

The Passover

[4]"These are the appointed feasts of the LORD, the holy convocations, which
you shall proclaim at the time appointed for them. [5]In the first month, on the
fourteenth day of the month at twilight,[1] is the LORD's Passover. [6]And on the fifteenth day of the same month is the Feast of Unleavened Bread to the LORD; for
seven days you shall eat unleavened bread. [7]On the first day you shall have a holy
convocation; you shall not do any ordinary work. [8]But you shall present a food
offering to the LORD for seven days. On the seventh day is a holy convocation; you
shall not do any ordinary work."

The Feast of Firstfruits

[9]And the LORD spoke to Moses, saying, [10]"Speak to the people of Israel and say
to them, When you come into the land that I give you and reap its harvest, you
shall bring the sheaf of the firstfruits of your harvest to the priest, [11]and he shall
wave the sheaf before the LORD, so that you may be accepted. On the day after
the Sabbath the priest shall wave it. [12]And on the day when you wave the sheaf,
you shall offer a male lamb a year old without blemish as a burnt offering to the
LORD. [13]And the grain offering with it shall be two tenths of an ephah[2] of fine flour
mixed with oil, a food offering to the LORD with a pleasing aroma, and the drink
offering with it shall be of wine, a fourth of a hin.[3] [14]And you shall eat neither
bread nor grain parched or fresh until this same day, until you have brought the
offering of your God: it is a statute forever throughout your generations in all
your dwellings.

The Feast of Weeks

[15]"You shall count seven full weeks from the day after the Sabbath, from the
day that you brought the sheaf of the wave offering. [16]You shall count fifty days to
the day after the seventh Sabbath. Then you shall present a grain offering of new

[1]Hebrew *between the two evenings* [2]An *ephah* was about 3/5 bushel or 22 liters [3]A *hin* was about 4 quarts or 3.5 liters

LEVITICUS 23:5

THE PASSOVER

The Passover is a religious commemoration that all Jewish people are familiar with as they celebrate liberation by God from the tyranny of the Egyptians. The last plague God unleashed upon the Egyptians was one of death—the death of the firstborn in every family. Yet the Lord made a way to go through this judgment untouched by death. Any family who killed a lamb and painted its blood over the doorpost of their home would be *passed over* by the Lord (Ex 12:13). Long after their deliverance, the Israelites understood the significance in the annual day of remembrance: a lamb was sacrificed so that by its death others would be spared.

On the night Jesus was betrayed and handed over for trial and execution, he gathered with his disciples to celebrate the Passover (Mt 26:17–19). But Jesus took this religious ceremony and breathed life into it in a way his disciples never expected. "This is *my* body ... This is *my* blood ... poured out for many" (Mt 26:26–28, emphasis added). Jesus is "the Lamb of God, who takes away the sin of the world" (Jn 1:29). His innocent blood was shed so that by his death and resurrection others could have life (Mt 20:28).

LEVITICUS 23:15–22

THE FEAST OF WEEKS AND PENTECOST

The Lord commanded a summer Feast of Weeks exactly seven Sabbaths after the Feast of Firstfruits, which celebrated the beginning of the barley harvest. Wherever they

(continued on next page)

grain to the LORD. 17You shall bring from your dwelling places two loaves of bread to be waved, made of two tenths of an ephah. They shall be of fine flour, and they shall be baked with leaven, as firstfruits to the LORD. 18And you shall present with the bread seven lambs a year old without blemish, and one bull from the herd and two rams. They shall be a burnt offering to the LORD, with their grain offering and their drink offerings, a food offering with a pleasing aroma to the LORD. 19And you shall offer one male goat for a sin offering, and two male lambs a year old as a sacrifice of peace offerings. 20And the priest shall wave them with the bread of the firstfruits as a wave offering before the LORD, with the two lambs. They shall be holy to the LORD for the priest. 21And you shall make a proclamation on the same day. You shall hold a holy convocation. You shall not do any ordinary work. It is a statute forever in all your dwelling places throughout your generations.

22"And when you reap the harvest of your land, you shall not reap your field right up to its edge, nor shall you gather the gleanings after your harvest. You shall leave them for the poor and for the sojourner: I am the LORD your God."

The Feast of Trumpets

23And the LORD spoke to Moses, saying, 24"Speak to the people of Israel, saying, In the seventh month, on the first day of the month, you shall observe a day of solemn rest, a memorial proclaimed with blast of trumpets, a holy convocation. 25You shall not do any ordinary work, and you shall present a food offering to the LORD."

The Day of Atonement

26And the LORD spoke to Moses, saying, 27"Now on the tenth day of this seventh month is the Day of Atonement. It shall be for you a time of holy convocation, and you shall afflict yourselves[1] and present a food offering to the LORD. 28And you shall not do any work on that very day, for it is a Day of Atonement, to make atonement for you before the LORD your God. 29For whoever is not afflicted[2] on that very day shall be cut off from his people. 30And whoever does any work on that very day, that person I will destroy from among his people. 31You shall not do any work. It is a statute forever throughout your generations in all your dwelling places. 32It shall be to you a Sabbath of solemn rest, and you shall afflict yourselves. On the ninth day of the month beginning at evening, from evening to evening shall you keep your Sabbath."

The Feast of Booths

33And the LORD spoke to Moses, saying, 34"Speak to the people of Israel, saying, On the fifteenth day of this seventh month and for seven days is the Feast of Booths[3] to the LORD. 35On the first day shall be a holy convocation; you shall not do any ordinary work. 36For seven days you shall present food offerings to the LORD. On the eighth day you shall hold a holy convocation and present a food offering to the LORD. It is a solemn assembly; you shall not do any ordinary work.

37"These are the appointed feasts of the LORD, which you shall proclaim as times of holy convocation, for presenting to the LORD food offerings, burnt offerings and grain offerings, sacrifices and drink offerings, each on its proper day, 38besides the LORD's Sabbaths and besides your gifts and besides all your vow offerings and besides all your freewill offerings, which you give to the LORD.

39"On the fifteenth day of the seventh month, when you have gathered in the produce of the land, you shall celebrate the feast of the LORD seven days. On the first day shall be a solemn rest, and on the eighth day shall be a solemn rest. 40And you shall take on the first day the fruit of splendid trees, branches of palm trees and boughs of leafy trees and willows of the brook, and you shall rejoice before the LORD your God seven days. 41You shall celebrate it as a feast to the LORD for

[1]Or *shall fast*; also verse 32 [2]Or *is not fasting* [3]Or *Tabernacles*

(The Feast of Weeks and Pentecost, continued)

were, Israelites were required to come together for a sacred assembly. They rested from work and offered various sacrifices to God, reflecting on his goodness at the onset of the wheat harvest. This national gathering eventually became known as *Pentecost*—a name containing the Greek word for *fifty*, the number of days between the Firstfruits and Weeks celebrations.

Jesus promised his disciples that when he finished his earthly work and ascended to be with the Father, he would send the Holy Spirit (Jn 16:4–14). On the day of Pentecost, the Holy Spirit came with fire and power—giving birth to the church (Ac 2:1–11). The Holy Spirit came to bear witness to Jesus, to outfit the church with gifts, to unite all believers, and to empower Christian ministry. Jews from every nation were gathered in Jerusalem for the feast when the Spirit descended from heaven. God seized this moment to demonstrate that the gospel of Jesus is for people of every tribe and tongue.

seven days in the year. It is a statute forever throughout your generations; you shall celebrate it in the seventh month. 42 You shall dwell in booths for seven days. All native Israelites shall dwell in booths, 43 that your generations may know that I made the people of Israel dwell in booths when I brought them out of the land of Egypt: I am the LORD your God."

44 Thus Moses declared to the people of Israel the appointed feasts of the LORD.

The Lamps

24 The LORD spoke to Moses, saying, 2 "Command the people of Israel to bring you pure oil from beaten olives for the lamp, that a light may be kept burning regularly. 3 Outside the veil of the testimony, in the tent of meeting, Aaron shall arrange it from evening to morning before the LORD regularly. It shall be a statute forever throughout your generations. 4 He shall arrange the lamps on the lampstand of pure gold[1] before the LORD regularly.

Bread for the Tabernacle

5 "You shall take fine flour and bake twelve loaves from it; two tenths of an ephah[2] shall be in each loaf. 6 And you shall set them in two piles, six in a pile, on the table of pure gold[3] before the LORD. 7 And you shall put pure frankincense on each pile, that it may go with the bread as a memorial portion as a food offering to the LORD. 8 Every Sabbath day Aaron shall arrange it before the LORD regularly; it is from the people of Israel as a covenant forever. 9 And it shall be for Aaron and his sons, and they shall eat it in a holy place, since it is for him a most holy portion out of the LORD's food offerings, a perpetual due."

Punishment for Blasphemy

10 Now an Israelite woman's son, whose father was an Egyptian, went out among the people of Israel. And the Israelite woman's son and a man of Israel fought in the camp, 11 and the Israelite woman's son blasphemed the Name, and cursed. Then they brought him to Moses. His mother's name was Shelomith, the daughter of Dibri, of the tribe of Dan. 12 And they put him in custody, till the will of the LORD should be clear to them.

13 Then the LORD spoke to Moses, saying, 14 "Bring out of the camp the one who cursed, and let all who heard him lay their hands on his head, and let all the congregation stone him. 15 And speak to the people of Israel, saying, Whoever curses his God shall bear his sin. 16 Whoever blasphemes the name of the LORD shall surely be put to death. All the congregation shall stone him. The sojourner as well as the native, when he blasphemes the Name, shall be put to death.

An Eye for an Eye

17 "Whoever takes a human life shall surely be put to death. 18 Whoever takes an animal's life shall make it good, life for life. 19 If anyone injures his neighbor, as he has done it shall be done to him, 20 fracture for fracture, eye for eye, tooth for tooth; whatever injury he has given a person shall be given to him. 21 Whoever kills an animal shall make it good, and whoever kills a person shall be put to death. 22 You shall have the same rule for the sojourner and for the native, for I am the LORD your God." 23 So Moses spoke to the people of Israel, and they brought out of the camp the one who had cursed and stoned him with stones. Thus the people of Israel did as the LORD commanded Moses.

The Sabbath Year

25 The LORD spoke to Moses on Mount Sinai, saying, 2 "Speak to the people of Israel and say to them, When you come into the land that I give you, the land shall keep a Sabbath to the LORD. 3 For six years you shall sow your field,

[1] Hebrew *the pure lampstand* [2] An *ephah* was about 3/5 bushel or 22 liters [3] Hebrew *the pure table*

FEASTS

The majority of the laws in Leviticus deal with matters of *worship*: legislation concerning offerings and sacrifices, priests, the Day of Atonement, and the annual religious feasts. God's people followed a calendar of carefully directed observances. Weekly, the *Sabbath* was celebrated as a day of solemn rest from all work. On the first day of each month, the *New Moon* feast featured a day of rest, specific sacrifices, and the blowing of trumpets. A series of special celebrations and rituals occurred once each year:

Passover. On the fourteenth day of the first month, this feast commemorated God's deliverance of Israel from bondage in Egypt.

The Feast of Unleavened Bread. This feast, which marked the beginning of the barley harvest, immediately followed Passover and lasted until the twenty-first day of the month.

The Feast of Firstfruits. This offering was to be a portion, the "firstfruits," of the harvest. In giving this offering, the people demonstrated their dependence and trust in God for their provision.

The Feast of Weeks (Pentecost). This feast took place fifty days after the barley harvest and involved new grain offerings from the wheat harvest to the Lord, together with animal sacrifices and a wave offering of bread.

The Feast of Trumpets (Rosh Hashanah). The first day of the seventh month marked this occasion which involved a Sabbath-rest, the blowing of trumpets, and a holy convocation.

The Day of Atonement (Yom Kippur). Observed on the tenth day of the seventh month, this was a day of fasting and rest for the purpose of atoning for the sins of the past year.

The Feast of Booths (Tabernacles). This seven-day celebration lasted from the fifteenth to the twenty-first day of the seventh month. The people lived in booths for seven days to remember the exodus from Egypt.

Beyond these annual observances, Israelites celebrated the *sabbath year* every seventh year. It was designated as a "year of release" to allow the land to lie fallow.

Every fiftieth year was the *Year of Jubilee*. This followed seven sabbath years, with liberty proclaimed to those who were servants because of debt. It also returned land to the former owners.

and for six years you shall prune your vineyard and gather in its fruits, 4 but in the seventh year there shall be a Sabbath of solemn rest for the land, a Sabbath to the LORD. You shall not sow your field or prune your vineyard. 5 You shall not reap what grows of itself in your harvest, or gather the grapes of your undressed vine. It shall be a year of solemn rest for the land. 6 The Sabbath of the land[1] shall provide food for you, for yourself and for your male and female slaves[2] and for your hired worker and the sojourner who lives with you, 7 and for your cattle and for the wild animals that are in your land: all its yield shall be for food.

The Year of Jubilee

8 "You shall count seven weeks[3] of years, seven times seven years, so that the time of the seven weeks of years shall give you forty-nine years. 9 Then you shall sound the loud trumpet on the tenth day of the seventh month. On the Day of Atonement you shall sound the trumpet throughout all your land. 10 And you shall consecrate the fiftieth year, and proclaim liberty throughout the land to all its inhabitants. It shall be a jubilee for you, when each of you shall return to his property and each of you shall return to his clan. 11 That fiftieth year shall be a jubilee for you; in it you shall neither sow nor reap what grows of itself nor gather the grapes from the undressed vines. 12 For it is a jubilee. It shall be holy to you. You may eat the produce of the field.[4]

13 "In this year of jubilee each of you shall return to his property. 14 And if you make a sale to your neighbor or buy from your neighbor, you shall not wrong one another. 15 You shall pay your neighbor according to the number of years after the jubilee, and he shall sell to you according to the number of years for crops. 16 If the years are many, you shall increase the price, and if the years are few, you shall reduce the price, for it is the number of the crops that he is selling to you. 17 You shall not wrong one another, but you shall fear your God, for I am the LORD your God.

18 "Therefore you shall do my statutes and keep my rules and perform them, and then you will dwell in the land securely. 19 The land will yield its fruit, and you will eat your fill and dwell in it securely. 20 And if you say, 'What shall we eat in the seventh year, if we may not sow or gather in our crop?' 21 I will command my blessing on you in the sixth year, so that it will produce a crop sufficient for three years. 22 When you sow in the eighth year, you will be eating some of the old crop; you shall eat the old until the ninth year, when its crop arrives.

Redemption of Property

23 "The land shall not be sold in perpetuity, for the land is mine. For you are strangers and sojourners with me. 24 And in all the country you possess, you shall allow a redemption of the land.

25 "If your brother becomes poor and sells part of his property, then his nearest redeemer shall come and redeem what his brother has sold. 26 If a man has no one to redeem it and then himself becomes prosperous and finds sufficient means to redeem it, 27 let him calculate the years since he sold it and pay back the balance to the man to whom he sold it, and then return to his property. 28 But if he does not have sufficient means to recover it, then what he sold shall remain in the hand of the buyer until the year of jubilee. In the jubilee it shall be released, and he shall return to his property.

29 "If a man sells a dwelling house in a walled city, he may redeem it within a year of its sale. For a full year he shall have the right of redemption. 30 If it is not redeemed within a full year, then the house in the walled city shall belong in perpetuity to the buyer, throughout his generations; it shall not be released in the jubilee. 31 But the houses of the villages that have no wall around them shall be classified with the fields of the land. They may be redeemed, and they shall be released in the jubilee. 32 As for the cities of the Levites, the Levites may redeem at

LEVITICUS 25:10

JUBILEE

The word *jubilee* means "ram's horn" or "trumpet," but the concept is rooted in liberation. Every fiftieth year, a trumpet would blow throughout the land to announce a special season of God's favor. By decree, each person returned to their family property—even if that property now belonged to another. Ownership reverted to the original family, restoring what had been lost to crop failure, illness, or some other financial hardship. The jubilee reversed the string of events that forced family land-owners to become land-sellers, then people of no land, usually hiring themselves out as servants. The sound of the fiftieth year trumpet was a happy signal of a reset to life and community—debts were canceled, hardships were erased, and families long scattered were reconnected in the land of their fathers and mothers.

Jesus had his own trumpeting moment (Lk 4:16–21). Reading from the scroll of Isaiah, he announced a perpetual jubilee for people, not property. Jesus came into the world to reverse the effects of sin, restore lost things, forgive debts, liberate prisoners, and reconcile people to God.

[1] That is, the Sabbath produce of the land [2] Or *servants* [3] Or *Sabbaths* [4] Or *countryside*

any time the houses in the cities they possess. 33And if one of the Levites exercises his right of redemption, then the house that was sold in a city they possess shall be released in the jubilee. For the houses in the cities of the Levites are their possession among the people of Israel. 34But the fields of pastureland belonging to their cities may not be sold, for that is their possession forever.

Kindness for Poor Brothers

35"If your brother becomes poor and cannot maintain himself with you, you shall support him as though he were a stranger and a sojourner, and he shall live with you. 36Take no interest from him or profit, but fear your God, that your brother may live beside you. 37You shall not lend him your money at interest, nor give him your food for profit. 38I am the LORD your God, who brought you out of the land of Egypt to give you the land of Canaan, and to be your God.

39"If your brother becomes poor beside you and sells himself to you, you shall not make him serve as a slave: 40he shall be with you as a hired worker and as a sojourner. He shall serve with you until the year of the jubilee. 41Then he shall go out from you, he and his children with him, and go back to his own clan and return to the possession of his fathers. 42For they are my servants,[1] whom I brought out of the land of Egypt; they shall not be sold as slaves. 43You shall not rule over him ruthlessly but shall fear your God. 44As for your male and female slaves whom you may have: you may buy male and female slaves from among the nations that are around you. 45You may also buy from among the strangers who sojourn with you and their clans that are with you, who have been born in your land, and they may be your property. 46You may bequeath them to your sons after you to inherit as a possession forever. You may make slaves of them, but over your brothers the people of Israel you shall not rule, one over another ruthlessly.

Redeeming a Poor Man

47"If a stranger or sojourner with you becomes rich, and your brother beside him becomes poor and sells himself to the stranger or sojourner with you or to a member of the stranger's clan, 48then after he is sold he may be redeemed. One of his brothers may redeem him, 49or his uncle or his cousin may redeem him, or a close relative from his clan may redeem him. Or if he grows rich he may redeem himself. 50He shall calculate with his buyer from the year when he sold himself to him until the year of jubilee, and the price of his sale shall vary with the number of years. The time he was with his owner shall be rated as the time of a hired worker. 51If there are still many years left, he shall pay proportionately for his redemption some of his sale price. 52If there remain but a few years until the year of jubilee, he shall calculate and pay for his redemption in proportion to his years of service. 53He shall treat him as a worker hired year by year. He shall not rule ruthlessly over him in your sight. 54And if he is not redeemed by these means, then he and his children with him shall be released in the year of jubilee. 55For it is to me that the people of Israel are servants.[2] They are my servants whom I brought out of the land of Egypt: I am the LORD your God.

Blessings for Obedience

26 "You shall not make idols for yourselves or erect an image or pillar, and you shall not set up a figured stone in your land to bow down to it, for I am the LORD your God. 2You shall keep my Sabbaths and reverence my sanctuary: I am the LORD.

3"If you walk in my statutes and observe my commandments and do them, 4then I will give you your rains in their season, and the land shall yield its increase, and the trees of the field shall yield their fruit. 5Your threshing shall last to the time of the grape harvest, and the grape harvest shall last to the time for

[1]Hebrew *slaves* [2]Or *slaves*

sowing. And you shall eat your bread to the full and dwell in your land securely. 6I will give peace in the land, and you shall lie down, and none shall make you afraid. And I will remove harmful beasts from the land, and the sword shall not go through your land. 7You shall chase your enemies, and they shall fall before you by the sword. 8Five of you shall chase a hundred, and a hundred of you shall chase ten thousand, and your enemies shall fall before you by the sword. 9I will turn to you and make you fruitful and multiply you and will confirm my covenant with you. 10You shall eat old store long kept, and you shall clear out the old to make way for the new. 11I will make my dwelling[1] among you, and my soul shall not abhor you. 12And I will walk among you and will be your God, and you shall be my people. 13I am the LORD your God, who brought you out of the land of Egypt, that you should not be their slaves. And I have broken the bars of your yoke and made you walk erect.

Punishment for Disobedience

14"But if you will not listen to me and will not do all these commandments, 15if you spurn my statutes, and if your soul abhors my rules, so that you will not do all my commandments, but break my covenant, 16then I will do this to you: I will visit you with panic, with wasting disease and fever that consume the eyes and make the heart ache. And you shall sow your seed in vain, for your enemies shall eat it. 17I will set my face against you, and you shall be struck down before your enemies. Those who hate you shall rule over you, and you shall flee when none pursues you. 18And if in spite of this you will not listen to me, then I will discipline you again sevenfold for your sins, 19and I will break the pride of your power, and I will make your heavens like iron and your earth like bronze. 20And your strength shall be spent in vain, for your land shall not yield its increase, and the trees of the land shall not yield their fruit.

21"Then if you walk contrary to me and will not listen to me, I will continue striking you, sevenfold for your sins. 22And I will let loose the wild beasts against you, which shall bereave you of your children and destroy your livestock and make you few in number, so that your roads shall be deserted.

23"And if by this discipline you are not turned to me but walk contrary to me, 24then I also will walk contrary to you, and I myself will strike you sevenfold for your sins. 25And I will bring a sword upon you, that shall execute vengeance for the covenant. And if you gather within your cities, I will send pestilence among you, and you shall be delivered into the hand of the enemy. 26When I break your supply[2] of bread, ten women shall bake your bread in a single oven and shall dole out your bread again by weight, and you shall eat and not be satisfied.

27"But if in spite of this you will not listen to me, but walk contrary to me, 28then I will walk contrary to you in fury, and I myself will discipline you sevenfold for your sins. 29You shall eat the flesh of your sons, and you shall eat the flesh of your daughters. 30And I will destroy your high places and cut down your incense altars and cast your dead bodies upon the dead bodies of your idols, and my soul will abhor you. 31And I will lay your cities waste and will make your sanctuaries desolate, and I will not smell your pleasing aromas. 32And I myself will devastate the land, so that your enemies who settle in it shall be appalled at it. 33And I will scatter you among the nations, and I will unsheathe the sword after you, and your land shall be a desolation, and your cities shall be a waste.

34"Then the land shall enjoy[3] its Sabbaths as long as it lies desolate, while you are in your enemies' land; then the land shall rest, and enjoy its Sabbaths. 35As long as it lies desolate it shall have rest, the rest that it did not have on your Sabbaths when you were dwelling in it. 36And as for those of you who are left, I will send faintness into their hearts in the lands of their enemies. The sound of a driven leaf shall put them to flight, and they shall flee as one flees from the sword,

[1]Hebrew *tabernacle* [2]Hebrew *staff* [3]Or *pay for*; twice in this verse; also verse 43

and they shall fall when none pursues. 37They shall stumble over one another, as if to escape a sword, though none pursues. And you shall have no power to stand before your enemies. 38And you shall perish among the nations, and the land of your enemies shall eat you up. 39And those of you who are left shall rot away in your enemies' lands because of their iniquity, and also because of the iniquities of their fathers they shall rot away like them.

40"But if they confess their iniquity and the iniquity of their fathers in their treachery that they committed against me, and also in walking contrary to me, 41so that I walked contrary to them and brought them into the land of their enemies—if then their uncircumcised heart is humbled and they make amends for their iniquity, 42then I will remember my covenant with Jacob, and I will remember my covenant with Isaac and my covenant with Abraham, and I will remember the land. 43But the land shall be abandoned by them and enjoy its Sabbaths while it lies desolate without them, and they shall make amends for their iniquity, because they spurned my rules and their soul abhorred my statutes. 44Yet for all that, when they are in the land of their enemies, I will not spurn them, neither will I abhor them so as to destroy them utterly and break my covenant with them, for I am the LORD their God. 45But I will for their sake remember the covenant with their forefathers, whom I brought out of the land of Egypt in the sight of the nations, that I might be their God: I am the LORD."

46These are the statutes and rules and laws that the LORD made between himself and the people of Israel through Moses on Mount Sinai.

Laws About Vows

27 The LORD spoke to Moses, saying, 2"Speak to the people of Israel and say to them, If anyone makes a special vow to the LORD involving the valuation of persons, 3then the valuation of a male from twenty years old up to sixty years old shall be fifty shekels[1] of silver, according to the shekel of the sanctuary. 4If the person is a female, the valuation shall be thirty shekels. 5If the person is from five years old up to twenty years old, the valuation shall be for a male twenty shekels, and for a female ten shekels. 6If the person is from a month old up to five years old, the valuation shall be for a male five shekels of silver, and for a female the valuation shall be three shekels of silver. 7And if the person is sixty years old or over, then the valuation for a male shall be fifteen shekels, and for a female ten shekels. 8And if someone is too poor to pay the valuation, then he shall be made to stand before the priest, and the priest shall value him; the priest shall value him according to what the vower can afford.

9"If the vow[2] is an animal that may be offered as an offering to the LORD, all of it that he gives to the LORD is holy. 10He shall not exchange it or make a substitute for it, good for bad, or bad for good; and if he does in fact substitute one animal for another, then both it and the substitute shall be holy. 11And if it is any unclean animal that may not be offered as an offering to the LORD, then he shall stand the animal before the priest, 12and the priest shall value it as either good or bad; as the priest values it, so it shall be. 13But if he wishes to redeem it, he shall add a fifth to the valuation.

14"When a man dedicates his house as a holy gift to the LORD, the priest shall value it as either good or bad; as the priest values it, so it shall stand. 15And if the donor wishes to redeem his house, he shall add a fifth to the valuation price, and it shall be his.

16"If a man dedicates to the LORD part of the land that is his possession, then the valuation shall be in proportion to its seed. A homer[3] of barley seed shall be valued at fifty shekels of silver. 17If he dedicates his field from the year of jubilee, the valuation shall stand, 18but if he dedicates his field after the jubilee, then the priest shall calculate the price according to the years that remain until the year of

[1]A *shekel* was about 2/5 ounce or 11 grams [2]Hebrew *it* [3]A *homer* was about 6 bushels or 220 liters

REDEMPTION THROUGH JESUS

The Israelites occasionally made vows for giving themselves, their animals, their houses, and their land to serve the purposes of the tabernacle. These people and things were dedicated to the Lord. If someone wished to reclaim their devoted object, it had to be *redeemed* — bought back. By redeeming at a certain price that which had been dedicated to the sanctuary, the Israelite gave the value of the gift they had vowed. Leviticus 27 established value amounts for redemption. Some items were given a fixed price. Other items such as houses and property received a value amount only after a priest inspected their worth. In many cases, an additional percentage was added to the redemption value in order to make up for any loss incurred by the sanctuary.

As unsavory as it may seem to modern readers, monetary values were assigned for the redemption of individual people. Amounts were set according to age and gender, in relation to a person's potential for work or child-bearing. The highest values were placed on men between the ages of twenty and sixty. The lowest values were placed on females in the age range of one month to five years. However, when the one making a vow was too poor to pay prescribed amounts, the priest could set a price according to what the person could afford.

Redemption is a treasured concept in our salvation through Jesus Christ. We have been justified by grace — only because Jesus *redeemed* us (Ro 3:24). He bought us back from the curse of the law (Gal 3:13). And through his redemption, we have received adoption as sons and daughters of God (Gal 4:4 – 5). The payment made was neither cheap nor common. We were purchased with the precious blood of Christ — something of infinite value and worth (1Pe 1:18 – 19). Our redemption speaks to the scope of God's outrageous love. And it reveals his desire to liberate us from the law which left us without hope. In the fulfillment of a glorious plan made before the foundation of the world, God both judged sin and paid for sin on the cross. He chose to redeem rebels through the life and blood of his Son.

JESUS: OUR GRACIOUS PROVISION

NUMBERS

NUMBERS

CENSUS, TRIBES, DUTIES GIVEN *c. 1445 BC*	AARON DIES *c. 1407 BC*	ISRAEL ENTERS PROMISED LAND *c. 1406 BC*

The book of Numbers stands as a testimony of God's faithfulness in leading his people through the wilderness to the brink of the promised land. This journey was not a straightforward path toward triumph: the people were both the recipients of God's gracious blessings and the rebellious agents of idolatry. Through discipline and instruction, God trained the hearts of the people to worship him as they prepared to enter the land.

Many of the names and places mentioned throughout this book are unknown to the modern reader, which leads many to assume that the book of Numbers lacks relevance for today. Israel's journey is, however, an ongoing testimony to the faithfulness of God. Each name is a person God had redeemed from slavery in Egypt. Each place is evidence of God's provision. Each movement is an indication of God's military might and his faithfulness to his promises.

The book of Numbers begins in the wilderness of Sinai in the second month of the second year after God rescued Israel from slavery in Egypt. The journey stretched across nearly another 39 years in the wilderness as the people moved toward the promised land. The first census listed the men who were the first generation of those redeemed from Israel and who were prepared to lead the advance of the people of God. Instead of obedience to God, however, this first generation consistently murmured against the Lord, failed to trust his provision, and committed heinous sins of disobedience against his instructions.

The Lord judged this generation by preventing them from entering the promised land; however, he continued to sustain their lives and provide for their needs in the wilderness. He graciously communicated his word to this generation so that they could prepare their sons and daughters to take the land. After 40 years of wandering, Moses and Aaron counted the second generation (Nu 26). They were prepared to enter the land. The question remained: Would this generation succeed where their parents had failed?

This book, like all of the Old Testament, stands as a testimony to God's promise to deliver his people from the consequences of their sin. In Numbers, God demonstrated his divine forbearance and benevolence to a wayward and stubborn people. In spite of their sin, God accomplished his good purposes in their lives and on behalf of the surrounding nations. These good purposes ultimately came to a crescendo in the provision of the Messiah, Jesus Christ, who perfectly and finally dealt with Satan, sin, and death. The book foreshadows God's sovereign intention to accomplish these purposes against the backdrop of human sin. Nothing can stop God's plan — not even human sin. His grace is sufficient to lead his people lovingly into his presence — then, now, and forever.

GOD IS NOT MAN, THAT HE SHOULD LIE,
OR A SON OF MAN, THAT HE SHOULD CHANGE HIS MIND.
HAS HE SAID, AND WILL HE NOT DO IT?
OR HAS HE SPOKEN, AND WILL HE NOT FULFILL IT?

Numbers 23:19

NUMBERS

A Census of Israel's Warriors

1 The Lord spoke to Moses in the wilderness of Sinai, in the tent of meeting, on the first day of the second month, in the second year after they had come out of the land of Egypt, saying, 2"Take a census of all the congregation of the people of Israel, by clans, by fathers' houses, according to the number of names, every male, head by head. 3From twenty years old and upward, all in Israel who are able to go to war, you and Aaron shall list them, company by company. 4And there shall be with you a man from each tribe, each man being the head of the house of his fathers. 5And these are the names of the men who shall assist you. From Reuben, Elizur the son of Shedeur; 6from Simeon, Shelumiel the son of Zurishaddai; 7from Judah, Nahshon the son of Amminadab; 8from Issachar, Nethanel the son of Zuar; 9from Zebulun, Eliab the son of Helon; 10from the sons of Joseph, from Ephraim, Elishama the son of Ammihud, and from Manasseh, Gamaliel the son of Pedahzur; 11from Benjamin, Abidan the son of Gideoni; 12from Dan, Ahiezer the son of Ammishaddai; 13from Asher, Pagiel the son of Ochran; 14from Gad, Eliasaph the son of Deuel; 15from Naphtali, Ahira the son of Enan." 16These were the ones chosen from the congregation, the chiefs of their ancestral tribes, the heads of the clans of Israel.

17Moses and Aaron took these men who had been named, 18and on the first day of the second month, they assembled the whole congregation together, who registered themselves by clans, by fathers' houses, according to the number of names from twenty years old and upward, head by head, 19as the Lord commanded Moses. So he listed them in the wilderness of Sinai.

20The people of Reuben, Israel's firstborn, their generations, by their clans, by their fathers' houses, according to the number of names, head by head, every male from twenty years old and upward, all who were able to go to war: 21those listed of the tribe of Reuben were 46,500.

22Of the people of Simeon, their generations, by their clans, by their fathers' houses, those of them who were listed, according to the number of names, head by head, every male from twenty years old and upward, all who were able to go to war: 23those listed of the tribe of Simeon were 59,300.

24Of the people of Gad, their generations, by their clans, by their fathers' houses, according to the number of the names, from twenty years old and upward, all who were able to go to war: 25those listed of the tribe of Gad were 45,650.

26Of the people of Judah, their generations, by their clans, by their fathers' houses, according to the number of names, from twenty years old and upward, every man able to go to war: 27those listed of the tribe of Judah were 74,600.

28Of the people of Issachar, their generations, by their clans, by their fathers' houses, according to the number of names, from twenty years old and upward, every man able to go to war: 29those listed of the tribe of Issachar were 54,400.

30Of the people of Zebulun, their generations, by their clans, by their fathers' houses, according to the number of names, from twenty years old and upward, every man able to go to war: 31those listed of the tribe of Zebulun were 57,400.

32Of the people of Joseph, namely, of the people of Ephraim, their generations, by their clans, by their fathers' houses, according to the number of names, from twenty years old and upward, every man able to go to war: 33those listed of the tribe of Ephraim were 40,500.

34Of the people of Manasseh, their generations, by their clans, by their fathers' houses, according to the number of names, from twenty years old and upward, every man able to go to war: 35those listed of the tribe of Manasseh were 32,200.

36Of the people of Benjamin, their generations, by their clans, by their fathers'

houses, according to the number of names, from twenty years old and upward,
every man able to go to war: 37those listed of the tribe of Benjamin were 35,400.
38Of the people of Dan, their generations, by their clans, by their fathers' houses, according to the number of names, from twenty years old and upward, every
man able to go to war: 39those listed of the tribe of Dan were 62,700.
40Of the people of Asher, their generations, by their clans, by their fathers'
houses, according to the number of names, from twenty years old and upward,
every man able to go to war: 41those listed of the tribe of Asher were 41,500.
42Of the people of Naphtali, their generations, by their clans, by their fathers'
houses, according to the number of names, from twenty years old and upward,
every man able to go to war: 43those listed of the tribe of Naphtali were 53,400.
44These are those who were listed, whom Moses and Aaron listed with the
help of the chiefs of Israel, twelve men, each representing his fathers' house. 45So
all those listed of the people of Israel, by their fathers' houses, from twenty years
old and upward, every man able to go to war in Israel— 46all those listed were
603,550.

Levites Exempted

47But the Levites were not listed along with them by their ancestral tribe. 48For
the LORD spoke to Moses, saying, 49"Only the tribe of Levi you shall not list, and
you shall not take a census of them among the people of Israel. 50But appoint
the Levites over the tabernacle of the testimony, and over all its furnishings, and
over all that belongs to it. They are to carry the tabernacle and all its furnishings,
and they shall take care of it and shall camp around the tabernacle. 51When the
tabernacle is to set out, the Levites shall take it down, and when the tabernacle is
to be pitched, the Levites shall set it up. And if any outsider comes near, he shall
be put to death. 52The people of Israel shall pitch their tents by their companies,
each man in his own camp and each man by his own standard. 53But the Levites
shall camp around the tabernacle of the testimony, so that there may be no wrath
on the congregation of the people of Israel. And the Levites shall keep guard over
the tabernacle of the testimony." 54Thus did the people of Israel; they did according to all that the LORD commanded Moses.

Arrangement of the Camp

2 The LORD spoke to Moses and Aaron, saying, 2"The people of Israel shall camp
each by his own standard, with the banners of their fathers' houses. They
shall camp facing the tent of meeting on every side. 3Those to camp on the east
side toward the sunrise shall be of the standard of the camp of Judah by their
companies, the chief of the people of Judah being Nahshon the son of Amminadab, 4his company as listed being 74,600. 5Those to camp next to him shall be
the tribe of Issachar, the chief of the people of Issachar being Nethanel the son of
Zuar, 6his company as listed being 54,400. 7Then the tribe of Zebulun, the chief of
the people of Zebulun being Eliab the son of Helon, 8his company as listed being
57,400. 9All those listed of the camp of Judah, by their companies, were 186,400.
They shall set out first on the march.
10"On the south side shall be the standard of the camp of Reuben by their
companies, the chief of the people of Reuben being Elizur the son of Shedeur,
11his company as listed being 46,500. 12And those to camp next to him shall be
the tribe of Simeon, the chief of the people of Simeon being Shelumiel the son
of Zurishaddai, 13his company as listed being 59,300. 14Then the tribe of Gad, the
chief of the people of Gad being Eliasaph the son of Reuel, 15his company as listed
being 45,650. 16All those listed of the camp of Reuben, by their companies, were
151,450. They shall set out second.
17"Then the tent of meeting shall set out, with the camp of the Levites in the
midst of the camps; as they camp, so shall they set out, each in position, standard
by standard.

NUMBERS 2:1–2

DISTANCE

The intricate order and arrangement of the people of God made it clear that they were to maintain a considerable distance between themselves and the presence of God. In his grace, God dwelled among the people via the tent of meeting, or tabernacle. But they camped some distance from the tabernacle, and they were only able to approach the Lord's presence at certain times and in carefully prescribed ways. Due to the sinfulness of the people, they dared not approach the holy dwelling of God in their own way or by their own merit.

In the New Testament, Paul wrote that the substitutionary death of Jesus makes it possible for those who were once far off to be brought near to God (Eph 2:13). They would still not approach him on their own merit, but through faith in Christ's work. Those who are in Christ no longer must stand far off, distant from the presence of God, but they can freely and confidently enter his presence at any time (Eph 3:12).

NUMBERS 2:3–34

ENCAMPMENT

The tribe of Judah, leading Issachar and Zebulun, occupied the preferred position on the east side of the camp. From this position, they marched first when Israel was called by God. Reuben, Simeon, and Gad departed second. God's presence remained at the center of his people—with the Levites as they carried the tent of meeting—as their formation marched through the wilderness. The final six tribes followed behind, so that the nation on the

(continued on next page)

(Encampment, continued)

move directly mirrored the encampment. Judah was uniquely equipped to lead Israel because God provided them with the largest number of military men. The tribe's unique role extended to the coming Messiah. Through them, One came as a ruler, bringing the obedience of the nations and reigning with the eternal scepter (Ge 49:10). The Lord Jesus Christ descended from Judah as the King, a sovereign and great high priest despite not being a Levite. He ushered in a change in the law and offered hope through his death and resurrection (Heb 7:11,14). He is the Judaic leader of his people, and the one his people follow at all times.

18“On the west side shall be the standard of the camp of Ephraim by their companies, the chief of the people of Ephraim being Elishama the son of Ammihud, 19his company as listed being 40,500. 20And next to him shall be the tribe of Manasseh, the chief of the people of Manasseh being Gamaliel the son of Pedahzur, 21his company as listed being 32,200. 22Then the tribe of Benjamin, the chief of the people of Benjamin being Abidan the son of Gideoni, 23his company as listed being 35,400. 24All those listed of the camp of Ephraim, by their companies, were 108,100. They shall set out third on the march.

25“On the north side shall be the standard of the camp of Dan by their companies, the chief of the people of Dan being Ahiezer the son of Ammishaddai, 26his company as listed being 62,700. 27And those to camp next to him shall be the tribe of Asher, the chief of the people of Asher being Pagiel the son of Ochran, 28his company as listed being 41,500. 29Then the tribe of Naphtali, the chief of the people of Naphtali being Ahira the son of Enan, 30his company as listed being 53,400. 31All those listed of the camp of Dan were 157,600. They shall set out last, standard by standard.”

32These are the people of Israel as listed by their fathers' houses. All those listed in the camps by their companies were 603,550. 33But the Levites were not listed among the people of Israel, as the LORD commanded Moses.

34Thus did the people of Israel. According to all that the LORD commanded Moses, so they camped by their standards, and so they set out, each one in his clan, according to his fathers' house.

The Sons of Aaron

3 These are the generations of Aaron and Moses at the time when the LORD spoke with Moses on Mount Sinai. 2These are the names of the sons of Aaron: Nadab the firstborn, and Abihu, Eleazar, and Ithamar. 3These are the names of the sons of Aaron, the anointed priests, whom he ordained to serve as priests. 4But Nadab and Abihu died before the LORD when they offered unauthorized fire before the LORD in the wilderness of Sinai, and they had no children. So Eleazar and Ithamar served as priests in the lifetime of Aaron their father.

Duties of the Levites

5And the LORD spoke to Moses, saying, 6“Bring the tribe of Levi near, and set them before Aaron the priest, that they may minister to him. 7They shall keep guard over him and over the whole congregation before the tent of meeting, as they minister at the tabernacle. 8They shall guard all the furnishings of the tent of meeting, and keep guard over the people of Israel as they minister at the tabernacle. 9And you shall give the Levites to Aaron and his sons; they are wholly given to him from among the people of Israel. 10And you shall appoint Aaron and his sons, and they shall guard their priesthood. But if any outsider comes near, he shall be put to death.”

11And the LORD spoke to Moses, saying, 12“Behold, I have taken the Levites from among the people of Israel instead of every firstborn who opens the womb among the people of Israel. The Levites shall be mine, 13for all the firstborn are mine. On the day that I struck down all the firstborn in the land of Egypt, I consecrated for my own all the firstborn in Israel, both of man and of beast. They shall be mine: I am the LORD.”

14And the LORD spoke to Moses in the wilderness of Sinai, saying, 15“List the sons of Levi, by fathers' houses and by clans; every male from a month old and upward you shall list.” 16So Moses listed them according to the word of the LORD, as he was commanded. 17And these were the sons of Levi by their names: Gershon and Kohath and Merari. 18And these are the names of the sons of Gershon by their clans: Libni and Shimei. 19And the sons of Kohath by their clans: Amram, Izhar, Hebron, and Uzziel. 20And the sons of Merari by their clans: Mahli and Mushi. These are the clans of the Levites, by their fathers' houses.

REVOLVING AROUND WORSHIP

God prescribed a specific arrangement for the people of God as they lived in the wilderness. The central point around which all the people were encamped was the tent of meeting — that is, the tabernacle. In this tent, God dwelled among his people, and they worshiped him by means of the sacrificial system. The members of the tribe of Levi who oversaw Israelite worship encircled the tent. From there, the twelve tribes of the people of God were broken into four groups with three tribes in each group. The tribes of Dan, Asher, and Naphtali camped to the north of the tent; Issachar, Judah, and Zebulun to the east; Gad, Reuben, and Simeon to the south; and Benjamin, Ephraim, and Manasseh to the west. This alignment demonstrated that the focal point for the life of the people of God was the worship of the God of Abraham, Isaac, and Jacob. Worship was not an arbitrary, additional task to which the people of God were required to attend to from time to time. Rather, their whole lives and, in fact, their entire community revolved around worship. Also, any other nation which observed the camp of the people of God immediately understood that God was central to their identity and mission.

John, the author of the book of Revelation, pictured a similar reality in heaven when all things will be made new; however, John wrote, "a great multitude that no one could number, from every nation, from all tribes and peoples and languages" will gather around the throne and declare, "Salvation belongs to our God who sits on the throne, and to the Lamb!" (Rev 7:9 – 10). God's people will one day gather around the presence of God in all-consuming worship.

The Christian life, as a foretaste of this coming reality, is meant to center on the worship of the true and living God. Worship, as described by the New Testament authors, is to be the hub around which all of life revolves. In fact, Paul wrote that Christians are to give their entire lives to God as an act of "spiritual worship" (Ro 12:1). Whole-life worship is made possible through the finished work of Jesus and empowered by the Spirit of God. The beauty of Jesus' work should prompt believers to organize their lives around worship. As they do, others will be able to see the centrality of God among the people of God.

[21]To Gershon belonged the clan of the Libnites and the clan of the Shimeites;
these were the clans of the Gershonites. [22]Their listing according to the number
of all the males from a month old and upward was[1] 7,500. [23]The clans of the Gershonites were to camp behind the tabernacle on the west, [24]with Eliasaph, the son
of Lael as chief of the fathers' house of the Gershonites. [25]And the guard duty of
the sons of Gershon in the tent of meeting involved the tabernacle, the tent with
its covering, the screen for the entrance of the tent of meeting, [26]the hangings of
the court, the screen for the door of the court that is around the tabernacle and
the altar, and its cords—all the service connected with these.

[27]To Kohath belonged the clan of the Amramites and the clan of the Izharites
and the clan of the Hebronites and the clan of the Uzzielites; these are the clans
of the Kohathites. [28]According to the number of all the males, from a month old
and upward, there were 8,600, keeping guard over the sanctuary. [29]The clans of
the sons of Kohath were to camp on the south side of the tabernacle, [30]with Elizaphan the son of Uzziel as chief of the fathers' house of the clans of the Kohathites.
[31]And their guard duty involved the ark, the table, the lampstand, the altars, the
vessels of the sanctuary with which the priests minister, and the screen; all the
service connected with these. [32]And Eleazar the son of Aaron the priest was to be
chief over the chiefs of the Levites, and to have oversight of those who kept guard
over the sanctuary.

[33]To Merari belonged the clan of the Mahlites and the clan of the Mushites:
these are the clans of Merari. [34]Their listing according to the number of all the
males from a month old and upward was 6,200. [35]And the chief of the fathers'
house of the clans of Merari was Zuriel the son of Abihail. They were to camp on
the north side of the tabernacle. [36]And the appointed guard duty of the sons of
Merari involved the frames of the tabernacle, the bars, the pillars, the bases, and
all their accessories; all the service connected with these; [37]also the pillars around
the court, with their bases and pegs and cords.

[38]Those who were to camp before the tabernacle on the east, before the tent
of meeting toward the sunrise, were Moses and Aaron and his sons, guarding the
sanctuary itself, to protect[2] the people of Israel. And any outsider who came near
was to be put to death. [39]All those listed among the Levites, whom Moses and
Aaron listed at the commandment of the LORD, by clans, all the males from a
month old and upward, were 22,000.

Redemption of the Firstborn

[40]And the LORD said to Moses, "List all the firstborn males of the people of
Israel, from a month old and upward, taking the number of their names. [41]And
you shall take the Levites for me—I am the LORD—instead of all the firstborn
among the people of Israel, and the cattle of the Levites instead of all the firstborn
among the cattle of the people of Israel." [42]So Moses listed all the firstborn among
the people of Israel, as the LORD commanded him. [43]And all the firstborn males,
according to the number of names, from a month old and upward as listed were
22,273.

[44]And the LORD spoke to Moses, saying, [45]"Take the Levites instead of all the
firstborn among the people of Israel, and the cattle of the Levites instead of their
cattle. The Levites shall be mine: I am the LORD. [46]And as the redemption price
for the 273 of the firstborn of the people of Israel, over and above the number of
the male Levites, [47]you shall take five shekels[3] per head; you shall take them according to the shekel of the sanctuary (the shekel of twenty gerahs[4]), [48]and give
the money to Aaron and his sons as the redemption price for those who are over."
[49]So Moses took the redemption money from those who were over and above
those redeemed by the Levites. [50]From the firstborn of the people of Israel he
took the money, 1,365 shekels, by the shekel of the sanctuary. [51]And Moses gave

[1]Hebrew *their listing was* [2]Hebrew *guard* [3]A *shekel* was about 2/5 ounce or 11 grams [4]A *gerah* was about 1/50 ounce or 0.6 gram

the redemption money to Aaron and his sons, according to the word of the LORD, as the LORD commanded Moses.

Duties of the Kohathites, Gershonites, and Merarites

4 The LORD spoke to Moses and Aaron, saying, 2"Take a census of the sons of Kohath from among the sons of Levi, by their clans and their fathers' houses, 3from thirty years old up to fifty years old, all who can come on duty, to do the work in the tent of meeting. 4This is the service of the sons of Kohath in the tent of meeting: the most holy things. 5When the camp is to set out, Aaron and his sons shall go in and take down the veil of the screen and cover the ark of the testimony with it. 6Then they shall put on it a covering of goatskin[1] and spread on top of that a cloth all of blue, and shall put in its poles. 7And over the table of the bread of the Presence they shall spread a cloth of blue and put on it the plates, the dishes for incense, the bowls, and the flagons for the drink offering; the regular showbread also shall be on it. 8Then they shall spread over them a cloth of scarlet and cover the same with a covering of goatskin, and shall put in its poles. 9And they shall take a cloth of blue and cover the lampstand for the light, with its lamps, its tongs, its trays, and all the vessels for oil with which it is supplied. 10And they shall put it with all its utensils in a covering of goatskin and put it on the carrying frame. 11And over the golden altar they shall spread a cloth of blue and cover it with a covering of goatskin, and shall put in its poles. 12And they shall take all the vessels of the service that are used in the sanctuary and put them in a cloth of blue and cover them with a covering of goatskin and put them on the carrying frame. 13And they shall take away the ashes from the altar and spread a purple cloth over it. 14And they shall put on it all the utensils of the altar, which are used for the service there, the fire pans, the forks, the shovels, and the basins, all the utensils of the altar; and they shall spread on it a covering of goatskin, and shall put in its poles. 15And when Aaron and his sons have finished covering the sanctuary and all the furnishings of the sanctuary, as the camp sets out, after that the sons of Kohath shall come to carry these, but they must not touch the holy things, lest they die. These are the things of the tent of meeting that the sons of Kohath are to carry.

16"And Eleazar the son of Aaron the priest shall have charge of the oil for the light, the fragrant incense, the regular grain offering, and the anointing oil, with the oversight of the whole tabernacle and all that is in it, of the sanctuary and its vessels."

17The LORD spoke to Moses and Aaron, saying, 18"Let not the tribe of the clans of the Kohathites be destroyed from among the Levites, 19but deal thus with them, that they may live and not die when they come near to the most holy things: Aaron and his sons shall go in and appoint them each to his task and to his burden, 20but they shall not go in to look on the holy things even for a moment, lest they die."

21The LORD spoke to Moses, saying, 22"Take a census of the sons of Gershon also, by their fathers' houses and by their clans. 23From thirty years old up to fifty years old, you shall list them, all who can come to do duty, to do service in the tent of meeting. 24This is the service of the clans of the Gershonites, in serving and bearing burdens: 25they shall carry the curtains of the tabernacle and the tent of meeting with its covering and the covering of goatskin that is on top of it and the screen for the entrance of the tent of meeting 26and the hangings of the court and the screen for the entrance of the gate of the court that is around the tabernacle and the altar, and their cords and all the equipment for their service. And they shall do all that needs to be done with regard to them. 27All the service of the sons of the Gershonites shall be at the command of Aaron and his sons, in all that they are to carry and in all that they have to do. And you shall assign to their charge all that they are to carry. 28This is the service of the clans of the sons

[1]The meaning of the Hebrew word is uncertain; compare Exodus 25:5

SEPARATION

Since Adam and Eve's sin in the garden, the people of God were separated from the presence of God. This division between mankind and God was first marked by "cherubim and a flaming sword" that kept sinful humanity from the tree of life (Ge 3:24).

Subsequently, the presence of God dwelled among the people in the tent of meeting. There, too, God's people had symbolic dividing walls between themselves and the holy things of God. Inside the tabernacle, curtains were used to mark the boundaries past which the people were not allowed to enter. Only certain people were permitted to go past the curtains — and then only in carefully prescribed ways and at designated times. These verses describe the different layers of curtains that marked divisions between the Most Holy Place and everything outside of that. The Gershonites were responsible for carrying these curtains and putting them in place. Once in place, these curtains marked the fact that God was set apart. Furthermore, the curtains represented the fact that there were many different layers that the people had to go through before they were able to come before God, and it was a long process before they were able to experience his presence. The curtains made it clear that God was distinct, holy, and — without a sacrificial offering — altogether unapproachable by fallen humanity.

These divisions were rendered obsolete as a result of Jesus' work on the cross. The moment of Jesus' death was marked by a stunning occurrence. The immense curtain in the temple was torn in two from top to bottom (Mk 15:38), demonstrating that God had opened the way for people to enter God's presence. No longer do God's image-bearers need to stand at a distance, separated by dividing walls, but by virtue of Christ's work they can dwell in God's presence again. In addition, Paul wrote that Christ's work tears down the "dividing wall of hostility" that has separated different types of people from one another (Eph 2:14). Now all people, regardless of gender, race, or other distinguishing marks, can enter the presence of God as one people. There they will find not walls that divide but a Savior who welcomes sinners and invites them to enter his presence in worship.

of the Gershonites in the tent of meeting, and their guard duty is to be under the
direction of Ithamar the son of Aaron the priest.
29"As for the sons of Merari, you shall list them by their clans and their fathers'
houses. 30From thirty years old up to fifty years old, you shall list them, everyone
who can come on duty, to do the service of the tent of meeting. 31And this is what
they are charged to carry, as the whole of their service in the tent of meeting: the
frames of the tabernacle, with its bars, pillars, and bases, 32and the pillars around
the court with their bases, pegs, and cords, with all their equipment and all their
accessories. And you shall list by name the objects that they are required to carry.
33This is the service of the clans of the sons of Merari, the whole of their service
in the tent of meeting, under the direction of Ithamar the son of Aaron the priest."
34And Moses and Aaron and the chiefs of the congregation listed the sons of
the Kohathites, by their clans and their fathers' houses, 35from thirty years old
up to fifty years old, everyone who could come on duty, for service in the tent of
meeting; 36and those listed by clans were 2,750. 37This was the list of the clans of
the Kohathites, all who served in the tent of meeting, whom Moses and Aaron
listed according to the commandment of the LORD by Moses.
38Those listed of the sons of Gershon, by their clans and their fathers' houses,
39from thirty years old up to fifty years old, everyone who could come on duty
for service in the tent of meeting— 40those listed by their clans and their fathers'
houses were 2,630. 41This was the list of the clans of the sons of Gershon, all who
served in the tent of meeting, whom Moses and Aaron listed according to the
commandment of the LORD.
42Those listed of the clans of the sons of Merari, by their clans and their fathers' houses, 43from thirty years old up to fifty years old, everyone who could
come on duty, for service in the tent of meeting— 44those listed by clans were
3,200. 45This was the list of the clans of the sons of Merari, whom Moses and
Aaron listed according to the commandment of the LORD by Moses.
46All those who were listed of the Levites, whom Moses and Aaron and the
chiefs of Israel listed, by their clans and their fathers' houses, 47from thirty years
old up to fifty years old, everyone who could come to do the service of ministry and the service of bearing burdens in the tent of meeting, 48those listed were
8,580. 49According to the commandment of the LORD through Moses they were
listed, each one with his task of serving or carrying. Thus they were listed by him,
as the LORD commanded Moses.

Unclean People

5 The LORD spoke to Moses, saying, 2"Command the people of Israel that they
put out of the camp everyone who is leprous[1] or has a discharge and everyone
who is unclean through contact with the dead. 3You shall put out both male and
female, putting them outside the camp, that they may not defile their camp, in the
midst of which I dwell." 4And the people of Israel did so, and put them outside the
camp; as the LORD said to Moses, so the people of Israel did.

Confession and Restitution

5And the LORD spoke to Moses, saying, 6"Speak to the people of Israel, When
a man or woman commits any of the sins that people commit by breaking faith
with the LORD, and that person realizes his guilt, 7he shall confess his sin that he
has committed.[2] And he shall make full restitution for his wrong, adding a fifth
to it and giving it to him to whom he did the wrong. 8But if the man has no next
of kin to whom restitution may be made for the wrong, the restitution for wrong
shall go to the LORD for the priest, in addition to the ram of atonement with which
atonement is made for him. 9And every contribution, all the holy donations of the
people of Israel, which they bring to the priest, shall be his. 10Each one shall keep
his holy donations: whatever anyone gives to the priest shall be his."

[1] *Leprosy* was a term for several skin diseases; see Leviticus 13 [2] Hebrew *they shall confess their sin that they have committed*

A Test for Adultery

11And the LORD spoke to Moses, saying, 12"Speak to the people of Israel, If any man's wife goes astray and breaks faith with him, 13if a man lies with her sexually, and it is hidden from the eyes of her husband, and she is undetected though she has defiled herself, and there is no witness against her, since she was not taken in the act, 14and if the spirit of jealousy comes over him and he is jealous of his wife who has defiled herself, or if the spirit of jealousy comes over him and he is jealous of his wife, though she has not defiled herself, 15then the man shall bring his wife to the priest and bring the offering required of her, a tenth of an ephah[1] of barley flour. He shall pour no oil on it and put no frankincense on it, for it is a grain offering of jealousy, a grain offering of remembrance, bringing iniquity to remembrance.

16"And the priest shall bring her near and set her before the LORD. 17And the priest shall take holy water in an earthenware vessel and take some of the dust that is on the floor of the tabernacle and put it into the water. 18And the priest shall set the woman before the LORD and unbind the hair of the woman's head and place in her hands the grain offering of remembrance, which is the grain offering of jealousy. And in his hand the priest shall have the water of bitterness that brings the curse. 19Then the priest shall make her take an oath, saying, 'If no man has lain with you, and if you have not turned aside to uncleanness while you were under your husband's authority, be free from this water of bitterness that brings the curse. 20But if you have gone astray, though you are under your husband's authority, and if you have defiled yourself, and some man other than your husband has lain with you, 21then' (let the priest make the woman take the oath of the curse, and say to the woman) 'the LORD make you a curse and an oath among your people, when the LORD makes your thigh fall away and your body swell. 22May this water that brings the curse pass into your bowels and make your womb swell and your thigh fall away.' And the woman shall say, 'Amen, Amen.'

23"Then the priest shall write these curses in a book and wash them off into the water of bitterness. 24And he shall make the woman drink the water of bitterness that brings the curse, and the water that brings the curse shall enter into her and cause bitter pain. 25And the priest shall take the grain offering of jealousy out of the woman's hand and shall wave the grain offering before the LORD and bring it to the altar. 26And the priest shall take a handful of the grain offering, as its memorial portion, and burn it on the altar, and afterward shall make the woman drink the water. 27And when he has made her drink the water, then, if she has defiled herself and has broken faith with her husband, the water that brings the curse shall enter into her and cause bitter pain, and her womb shall swell, and her thigh shall fall away, and the woman shall become a curse among her people. 28But if the woman has not defiled herself and is clean, then she shall be free and shall conceive children.

29"This is the law in cases of jealousy, when a wife, though under her husband's authority, goes astray and defiles herself, 30or when the spirit of jealousy comes over a man and he is jealous of his wife. Then he shall set the woman before the LORD, and the priest shall carry out for her all this law. 31The man shall be free from iniquity, but the woman shall bear her iniquity."

The Nazirite Vow

6 And the LORD spoke to Moses, saying, 2"Speak to the people of Israel and say to them, When either a man or a woman makes a special vow, the vow of a Nazirite,[2] to separate himself to the LORD, 3he shall separate himself from wine and strong drink. He shall drink no vinegar made from wine or strong drink and shall not drink any juice of grapes or eat grapes, fresh or dried. 4All the days of his

NUMBERS 6:2–15

NAZIRITE

Any Israelite who desired to make a special promise or commitment to God would make a Nazirite vow. The vow was intended to mark these individuals as holy—uniquely set apart for God for a prescribed period of time (v. 8). The person who made this vow committed to abstain from eating or drinking anything that comes from the grapevine (vv. 3–4), cutting their hair (v. 5), and going near a dead body (vv. 6–7). If someone died suddenly in a Nazirite's presence, the Nazirite became defiled and had to bring a sacrifice to the priest (vv. 9–15). These procedures were marks of holiness among the people of God.

Jesus, however, did not commit himself to such practices. He was known for touching the diseased and the dead and associating himself with tax collectors and other notorious sinners (Lk 5:13; 7:34). Association with brokenness, not asceticism, marked the way the Son of God demonstrated extreme commitment to the Father. Similarly, the church is meant to live on a mission to the margins of society, caring for the broken and wounded. In doing so, the church models the holiness demonstrated by Jesus himself.

[1]An *ephah* was about 3/5 bushel or 22 liters [2]*Nazirite* means *one separated*, or *one consecrated*

separation[1] he shall eat nothing that is produced by the grapevine, not even the
seeds or the skins.
5“All the days of his vow of separation, no razor shall touch his head. Until the
time is completed for which he separates himself to the LORD, he shall be holy. He
shall let the locks of hair of his head grow long.
6“All the days that he separates himself to the LORD he shall not go near a dead
body. 7Not even for his father or for his mother, for brother or sister, if they die,
shall he make himself unclean, because his separation to God is on his head. 8All
the days of his separation he is holy to the LORD.
9“And if any man dies very suddenly beside him and he defiles his consecrated
head, then he shall shave his head on the day of his cleansing; on the seventh day
he shall shave it. 10On the eighth day he shall bring two turtledoves or two pigeons
to the priest to the entrance of the tent of meeting, 11and the priest shall offer one
for a sin offering and the other for a burnt offering, and make atonement for him,
because he sinned by reason of the dead body. And he shall consecrate his head
that same day 12and separate himself to the LORD for the days of his separation and
bring a male lamb a year old for a guilt offering. But the previous period shall be
void, because his separation was defiled.
13“And this is the law for the Nazirite, when the time of his separation has been
completed: he shall be brought to the entrance of the tent of meeting, 14and he
shall bring his gift to the LORD, one male lamb a year old without blemish for a
burnt offering, and one ewe lamb a year old without blemish as a sin offering, and
one ram without blemish as a peace offering, 15and a basket of unleavened bread,
loaves of fine flour mixed with oil, and unleavened wafers smeared with oil, and
their grain offering and their drink offerings. 16And the priest shall bring them before the LORD and offer his sin offering and his burnt offering, 17and he shall offer
the ram as a sacrifice of peace offering to the LORD, with the basket of unleavened
bread. The priest shall offer also its grain offering and its drink offering. 18And the
Nazirite shall shave his consecrated head at the entrance of the tent of meeting and
shall take the hair from his consecrated head and put it on the fire that is under the
sacrifice of the peace offering. 19And the priest shall take the shoulder of the ram,
when it is boiled, and one unleavened loaf out of the basket and one unleavened
wafer, and shall put them on the hands of the Nazirite, after he has shaved the hair
of his consecration, 20and the priest shall wave them for a wave offering before the
LORD. They are a holy portion for the priest, together with the breast that is waved
and the thigh that is contributed. And after that the Nazirite may drink wine.
21“This is the law of the Nazirite. But if he vows an offering to the LORD above
his Nazirite vow, as he can afford, in exact accordance with the vow that he takes,
then he shall do in addition to the law of the Nazirite.”

Aaron's Blessing

22The LORD spoke to Moses, saying, 23“Speak to Aaron and his sons, saying,
Thus you shall bless the people of Israel: you shall say to them,

24 The LORD bless you and keep you;
25 the LORD make his face to shine upon you and be gracious to you;
26 the LORD lift up his countenance[2] upon you and give you peace.

27“So shall they put my name upon the people of Israel, and I will bless them.”

Offerings at the Tabernacle's Consecration

7 On the day when Moses had finished setting up the tabernacle and had
anointed and consecrated it with all its furnishings and had anointed and
consecrated the altar with all its utensils, 2the chiefs of Israel, heads of their
fathers' houses, who were the chiefs of the tribes, who were over those who were

[1]Or *Naziriteship* [2]Or *face*

NUMBERS 7:1

ANOINTED

The symbolic anointing with oil was a critical, outward mark that indicated God had selected a person or object to fulfill a unique role in his plan for the community. Priests, like Aaron, received this anointing, as did prophets and kings (Ex 30:30; 1Ki 19:16). The anointing usually came from an important leader and was often given to the next-generation leader at the outset of his ministry.

At the opening of Jesus' ministry, he was also anointed by God the Father, who poured out nothing less than the Holy Spirit on Jesus' life and work on earth (Ac 10:37–38). This unique anointing was beyond any anointing witnessed thus far in Scripture. God himself proclaimed the blessing over Jesus (Mt 3:17), emphasizing his pleasure in the Son as Moses alluded to in the Aaronic benediction (Nu 6:22–27). Thus Jesus is the archetypal anointed one—the Christ. This anointing of Christ still has lasting effects for the people of God today. Christians, because of their relationship with Jesus, also receive anointing for their commission to spread the fame of God to the nations. Just as the Holy Spirit descended on Christ, so he dwells within believers today (2Co 1:21–22).

NUMBERS 6:24–26

THREE BLESSINGS

God's people received innumerable blessings from the hand of God. In this passage, the Lord instructed Moses to tell Aaron and his sons to say a blessing on the people. This famous Aaronic benediction declared the blessing that would rest on all of the people by virtue of God's care. This blessing, which immediately followed a lengthy description of the Nazirite vow, made it clear that the people would receive God's blessings through his benevolence and not through outstanding acts of devotion on their part. The recounted actions provide vivid images of God's goodness. He promised to bless and keep his people. He assured them that he would accomplish his good purposes and plans and would make his face shine on them, allowing them to have an intimate sense of the presence of his glory — splendor and beauty akin to what Moses experienced when he talked with God on Mount Sinai (Ex 34:29–35). God would be gracious to the people, allowing them access to his presence (in spite of their sin). His countenance would be lifted up toward the people. Rather than a scornful expression of wrath, God would smile upon the people in love. And he would give them peace with himself and with one another.

Jesus offered a similar priestly prayer in the Garden of Gethsemane prior to his crucifixion (Jn 17:1–26). He first prayed for himself (v. 2). Then he asked the Father to protect his disciples from the evil one and his schemes in the world (vv. 11,15). Jesus prayed that the Father would give them grace to be transformed by God's Word so that they could be sent on a mission into the world (vv. 17–18). He longed for believers to experience the peace found in the perfect unity of the Godhead and to reflect this peace in oneness with those whom God came to save (vv. 22–23). Finally, he asked that they would see the glory of God and find delight in his presence (v. 24). These prayers would come to pass in Christ's death, burial, and resurrection as the great high priest and perfect Lamb of God.

listed, approached 3and brought their offerings before the LORD, six wagons and
twelve oxen, a wagon for every two of the chiefs, and for each one an ox. They
brought them before the tabernacle. 4Then the LORD said to Moses, 5"Accept these
from them, that they may be used in the service of the tent of meeting, and give
them to the Levites, to each man according to his service." 6So Moses took the
wagons and the oxen and gave them to the Levites. 7Two wagons and four oxen
he gave to the sons of Gershon, according to their service. 8And four wagons and
eight oxen he gave to the sons of Merari, according to their service, under the direction of Ithamar the son of Aaron the priest. 9But to the sons of Kohath he gave
none, because they were charged with the service of the holy things that had to
be carried on the shoulder. 10And the chiefs offered offerings for the dedication
of the altar on the day it was anointed; and the chiefs offered their offering before
the altar. 11And the LORD said to Moses, "They shall offer their offerings, one chief
each day, for the dedication of the altar."

12He who offered his offering the first day was Nahshon the son of Amminadab, of the tribe of Judah. 13And his offering was one silver plate whose weight
was 130 shekels,[1] one silver basin of 70 shekels, according to the shekel of the
sanctuary, both of them full of fine flour mixed with oil for a grain offering; 14one
golden dish of 10 shekels, full of incense; 15one bull from the herd, one ram, one
male lamb a year old, for a burnt offering; 16one male goat for a sin offering; 17and
for the sacrifice of peace offerings, two oxen, five rams, five male goats, and five
male lambs a year old. This was the offering of Nahshon the son of Amminadab.

18On the second day Nethanel the son of Zuar, the chief of Issachar, made an
offering. 19He offered for his offering one silver plate whose weight was 130 shekels, one silver basin of 70 shekels, according to the shekel of the sanctuary, both
of them full of fine flour mixed with oil for a grain offering; 20one golden dish of
10 shekels, full of incense; 21one bull from the herd, one ram, one male lamb a year
old, for a burnt offering; 22one male goat for a sin offering; 23and for the sacrifice
of peace offerings, two oxen, five rams, five male goats, and five male lambs a year
old. This was the offering of Nethanel the son of Zuar.

24On the third day Eliab the son of Helon, the chief of the people of Zebulun:
25his offering was one silver plate whose weight was 130 shekels, one silver basin
of 70 shekels, according to the shekel of the sanctuary, both of them full of fine
flour mixed with oil for a grain offering; 26one golden dish of 10 shekels, full of
incense; 27one bull from the herd, one ram, one male lamb a year old, for a burnt
offering; 28one male goat for a sin offering; 29and for the sacrifice of peace offerings, two oxen, five rams, five male goats, and five male lambs a year old. This was
the offering of Eliab the son of Helon.

30On the fourth day Elizur the son of Shedeur, the chief of the people of Reuben: 31his offering was one silver plate whose weight was 130 shekels, one silver
basin of 70 shekels, according to the shekel of the sanctuary, both of them full
of fine flour mixed with oil for a grain offering; 32one golden dish of 10 shekels,
full of incense; 33one bull from the herd, one ram, one male lamb a year old, for a
burnt offering; 34one male goat for a sin offering; 35and for the sacrifice of peace
offerings, two oxen, five rams, five male goats, and five male lambs a year old.
This was the offering of Elizur the son of Shedeur.

36On the fifth day Shelumiel the son of Zurishaddai, the chief of the people
of Simeon: 37his offering was one silver plate whose weight was 130 shekels, one
silver basin of 70 shekels, according to the shekel of the sanctuary, both of them
full of fine flour mixed with oil for a grain offering; 38one golden dish of 10 shekels, full of incense; 39one bull from the herd, one ram, one male lamb a year old,
for a burnt offering; 40one male goat for a sin offering; 41and for the sacrifice of
peace offerings, two oxen, five rams, five male goats, and five male lambs a year
old. This was the offering of Shelumiel the son of Zurishaddai.

---

[1]A *shekel* was about 2/5 ounce or 11 grams

[42]On the sixth day Eliasaph the son of Deuel, the chief of the people of Gad: [43]his offering was one silver plate whose weight was 130 shekels, one silver basin of 70 shekels, according to the shekel of the sanctuary, both of them full of fine flour mixed with oil for a grain offering; [44]one golden dish of 10 shekels, full of incense; [45]one bull from the herd, one ram, one male lamb a year old, for a burnt offering; [46]one male goat for a sin offering; [47]and for the sacrifice of peace offerings, two oxen, five rams, five male goats, and five male lambs a year old. This was the offering of Eliasaph the son of Deuel.

[48]On the seventh day Elishama the son of Ammihud, the chief of the people of Ephraim: [49]his offering was one silver plate whose weight was 130 shekels, one silver basin of 70 shekels, according to the shekel of the sanctuary, both of them full of fine flour mixed with oil for a grain offering; [50]one golden dish of 10 shekels, full of incense; [51]one bull from the herd, one ram, one male lamb a year old, for a burnt offering; [52]one male goat for a sin offering; [53]and for the sacrifice of peace offerings, two oxen, five rams, five male goats, and five male lambs a year old. This was the offering of Elishama the son of Ammihud.

[54]On the eighth day Gamaliel the son of Pedahzur, the chief of the people of Manasseh: [55]his offering was one silver plate whose weight was 130 shekels, one silver basin of 70 shekels, according to the shekel of the sanctuary, both of them full of fine flour mixed with oil for a grain offering; [56]one golden dish of 10 shekels, full of incense; [57]one bull from the herd, one ram, one male lamb a year old, for a burnt offering; [58]one male goat for a sin offering; [59]and for the sacrifice of peace offerings, two oxen, five rams, five male goats, and five male lambs a year old. This was the offering of Gamaliel the son of Pedahzur.

[60]On the ninth day Abidan the son of Gideoni, the chief of the people of Benjamin: [61]his offering was one silver plate whose weight was 130 shekels, one silver basin of 70 shekels, according to the shekel of the sanctuary, both of them full of fine flour mixed with oil for a grain offering; [62]one golden dish of 10 shekels, full of incense; [63]one bull from the herd, one ram, one male lamb a year old, for a burnt offering; [64]one male goat for a sin offering; [65]and for the sacrifice of peace offerings, two oxen, five rams, five male goats, and five male lambs a year old. This was the offering of Abidan the son of Gideoni.

[66]On the tenth day Ahiezer the son of Ammishaddai, the chief of the people of Dan: [67]his offering was one silver plate whose weight was 130 shekels, one silver basin of 70 shekels, according to the shekel of the sanctuary, both of them full of fine flour mixed with oil for a grain offering; [68]one golden dish of 10 shekels, full of incense; [69]one bull from the herd, one ram, one male lamb a year old, for a burnt offering; [70]one male goat for a sin offering; [71]and for the sacrifice of peace offerings, two oxen, five rams, five male goats, and five male lambs a year old. This was the offering of Ahiezer the son of Ammishaddai.

[72]On the eleventh day Pagiel the son of Ochran, the chief of the people of Asher: [73]his offering was one silver plate whose weight was 130 shekels, one silver basin of 70 shekels, according to the shekel of the sanctuary, both of them full of fine flour mixed with oil for a grain offering; [74]one golden dish of 10 shekels, full of incense; [75]one bull from the herd, one ram, one male lamb a year old, for a burnt offering; [76]one male goat for a sin offering; [77]and for the sacrifice of peace offerings, two oxen, five rams, five male goats, and five male lambs a year old. This was the offering of Pagiel the son of Ochran.

[78]On the twelfth day Ahira the son of Enan, the chief of the people of Naphtali: [79]his offering was one silver plate whose weight was 130 shekels, one silver basin of 70 shekels, according to the shekel of the sanctuary, both of them full of fine flour mixed with oil for a grain offering; [80]one golden dish of 10 shekels, full of incense; [81]one bull from the herd, one ram, one male lamb a year old, for a burnt offering; [82]one male goat for a sin offering; [83]and for the sacrifice of peace offerings, two oxen, five rams, five male goats, and five male lambs a year old. This was the offering of Ahira the son of Enan.

[84]This was the dedication offering for the altar on the day when it was anointed, from the chiefs of Israel: twelve silver plates, twelve silver basins, twelve golden dishes, [85]each silver plate weighing 130 shekels and each basin 70, all the silver of the vessels 2,400 shekels according to the shekel of the sanctuary, [86]the twelve golden dishes, full of incense, weighing 10 shekels apiece according to the shekel of the sanctuary, all the gold of the dishes being 120 shekels; [87]all the cattle for the burnt offering twelve bulls, twelve rams, twelve male lambs a year old, with their grain offering; and twelve male goats for a sin offering; [88]and all the cattle for the sacrifice of peace offerings twenty-four bulls, the rams sixty, the male goats sixty, the male lambs a year old sixty. This was the dedication offering for the altar after it was anointed.

[89]And when Moses went into the tent of meeting to speak with the LORD, he heard the voice speaking to him from above the mercy seat that was on the ark of the testimony, from between the two cherubim; and it spoke to him.

The Seven Lamps

8 Now the LORD spoke to Moses, saying, [2]"Speak to Aaron and say to him, When you set up the lamps, the seven lamps shall give light in front of the lampstand." [3]And Aaron did so: he set up its lamps in front of the lampstand, as the LORD commanded Moses. [4]And this was the workmanship of the lampstand, hammered work of gold. From its base to its flowers, it was hammered work; according to the pattern that the LORD had shown Moses, so he made the lampstand.

Cleansing of the Levites

[5]And the LORD spoke to Moses, saying, [6]"Take the Levites from among the people of Israel and cleanse them. [7]Thus you shall do to them to cleanse them: sprinkle the water of purification upon them, and let them go with a razor over all their body, and wash their clothes and cleanse themselves. [8]Then let them take a bull from the herd and its grain offering of fine flour mixed with oil, and you shall take another bull from the herd for a sin offering. [9]And you shall bring the Levites before the tent of meeting and assemble the whole congregation of the people of Israel. [10]When you bring the Levites before the LORD, the people of Israel shall lay their hands on the Levites, [11]and Aaron shall offer the Levites before the LORD as a wave offering from the people of Israel, that they may do the service of the LORD. [12]Then the Levites shall lay their hands on the heads of the bulls, and you shall offer the one for a sin offering and the other for a burnt offering to the LORD to make atonement for the Levites. [13]And you shall set the Levites before Aaron and his sons, and shall offer them as a wave offering to the LORD.

[14]"Thus you shall separate the Levites from among the people of Israel, and the Levites shall be mine. [15]And after that the Levites shall go in to serve at the tent of meeting, when you have cleansed them and offered them as a wave offering. [16]For they are wholly given to me from among the people of Israel. Instead of all who open the womb, the firstborn of all the people of Israel, I have taken them for myself. [17]For all the firstborn among the people of Israel are mine, both of man and of beast. On the day that I struck down all the firstborn in the land of Egypt I consecrated them for myself, [18]and I have taken the Levites instead of all the firstborn among the people of Israel. [19]And I have given the Levites as a gift to Aaron and his sons from among the people of Israel, to do the service for the people of Israel at the tent of meeting and to make atonement for the people of Israel, that there may be no plague among the people of Israel when the people of Israel come near the sanctuary."

[20]Thus did Moses and Aaron and all the congregation of the people of Israel to the Levites. According to all that the LORD commanded Moses concerning the Levites, the people of Israel did to them. [21]And the Levites purified themselves from sin and washed their clothes, and Aaron offered them as a wave offering before the LORD, and Aaron made atonement for them to cleanse them. [22]And

NUMBERS 8:5–22

PURIFICATION OF THE LEVITES

The purification and dedication of the Levites is a drama that acted out the love of the Father and the sacrifice of the Son. First, in order to bring the Levites into God's presence, a sacrifice was necessary (vv. 12–14). In the second act, the Levites were dedicated to God's service as living sacrifices in order to bring the whole nation into fellowship with God (vv. 15–19). They became a firstborn sacrifice—the best the nation had to offer to satisfy the demand of God's Law. As Levites, their lives were to be marked by a distinctive holiness.

In a similar drama, Jesus gave himself as the great sacrifice for sin (Col 1:14,20). He is the one who restores, not just a tribe or nation, but the entire cosmos to a relationship with God. And he is God's firstborn—the best God has to satisfy the demand of his Law (v. 15).

after that the Levites went in to do their service in the tent of meeting before Aaron and his sons; as the LORD had commanded Moses concerning the Levites, so they did to them.

Retirement of the Levites

23 And the LORD spoke to Moses, saying, 24 "This applies to the Levites: from twenty-five years old and upward they[1] shall come to do duty in the service of the tent of meeting. 25 And from the age of fifty years they shall withdraw from the duty of the service and serve no more. 26 They minister[2] to their brothers in the tent of meeting by keeping guard, but they shall do no service. Thus shall you do to the Levites in assigning their duties."

NUMBERS 9:1–14

THE PASSOVER

The Passover was a particularly poignant time in the life of the people of God. It served as an ongoing reminder of the Lord's protection and stood as a lasting reminder that the Lord had delivered his people and that he would surely fulfill his promises on their behalf. Here, at the base of Mount Sinai, the people celebrated the Passover before their journey to the land of Canaan.

In the New Testament, Jesus celebrated the Passover with his disciples before his journey to the cross. The significance of Jesus celebrating the Passover with his disciples is that he acknowledged the Lord's provision both throughout history and through what was about to occur in his crucifixion. Jesus knew that his death on the cross and resurrection from the dead was a fulfillment of God's promises to his people. A feast that had been celebrated throughout Israel's history completely changed when Jesus offered his body as an eternal sacrifice.

The Passover Celebrated

9 And the LORD spoke to Moses in the wilderness of Sinai, in the first month of the second year after they had come out of the land of Egypt, saying, 2 "Let the people of Israel keep the Passover at its appointed time. 3 On the fourteenth day of this month, at twilight, you shall keep it at its appointed time; according to all its statutes and all its rules you shall keep it." 4 So Moses told the people of Israel that they should keep the Passover. 5 And they kept the Passover in the first month, on the fourteenth day of the month, at twilight, in the wilderness of Sinai; according to all that the LORD commanded Moses, so the people of Israel did. 6 And there were certain men who were unclean through touching a dead body, so that they could not keep the Passover on that day, and they came before Moses and Aaron on that day. 7 And those men said to him, "We are unclean through touching a dead body. Why are we kept from bringing the LORD's offering at its appointed time among the people of Israel?" 8 And Moses said to them, "Wait, that I may hear what the LORD will command concerning you."

9 The LORD spoke to Moses, saying, 10 "Speak to the people of Israel, saying, If any one of you or of your descendants is unclean through touching a dead body, or is on a long journey, he shall still keep the Passover to the LORD. 11 In the second month on the fourteenth day at twilight they shall keep it. They shall eat it with unleavened bread and bitter herbs. 12 They shall leave none of it until the morning, nor break any of its bones; according to all the statute for the Passover they shall keep it. 13 But if anyone who is clean and is not on a journey fails to keep the Passover, that person shall be cut off from his people because he did not bring the LORD's offering at its appointed time; that man shall bear his sin. 14 And if a stranger sojourns among you and would keep the Passover to the LORD, according to the statute of the Passover and according to its rule, so shall he do. You shall have one statute, both for the sojourner and for the native."

The Cloud Covering the Tabernacle

15 On the day that the tabernacle was set up, the cloud covered the tabernacle, the tent of the testimony. And at evening it was over the tabernacle like the appearance of fire until morning. 16 So it was always: the cloud covered it by day[3] and the appearance of fire by night. 17 And whenever the cloud lifted from over the tent, after that the people of Israel set out, and in the place where the cloud settled down, there the people of Israel camped. 18 At the command of the LORD the people of Israel set out, and at the command of the LORD they camped. As long as the cloud rested over the tabernacle, they remained in camp. 19 Even when the cloud continued over the tabernacle many days, the people of Israel kept the charge of the LORD and did not set out. 20 Sometimes the cloud was a few days over the tabernacle, and according to the command of the LORD they remained in camp; then according to the command of the LORD they set out. 21 And sometimes the cloud remained from evening until morning. And when

[1] Hebrew *he*; also verses 25, 26 [2] Hebrew *He ministers* [3] Septuagint, Syriac, Vulgate; Hebrew lacks *by day*

FOLLOWING JESUS

God made it clear how the people were to follow him in their journey from the wilderness to the promised land. They would not have to guess as to where God wanted them to dwell and when he wanted them to move. During the day, a cloud covered the dwelling of God in the tabernacle. There, God communed with his people. At night, this cloud turned to fire, and the entire nation saw the all-consuming presence of the Lord. When God was ready for the people to break camp and set out to a new location, the cloud moved, traveling ahead of the people to the place God wanted them to go next. God's instructions were simple: Stay put as long as the cloud and fire are there. When they move, you move. When the people did this, they could rest assured that they were following God and moving in the path he ordained.

The same simple message inaugurates Jesus' earthly ministry. "Follow me," he says to his newly commissioned disciples (Mt 4:19). Over the next three years, they accompanied the Son of God as he boldly proclaimed the availability of the kingdom of God and performed many miraculous signs that demonstrated the dawning of a new age. Following Jesus had much in common with the way in which the nation of Israel followed God in the wilderness. Where Jesus went, the disciples went, and there they received the blessing of his presence and provision.

Following his death and resurrection, Jesus sent the Holy Spirit to provide all subsequent believers with guidance for how they can also follow Jesus. As believers are filled with God's Spirit (Eph 5:18) and refrain from those practices that may quench his Spirit, they can follow the path that God has purposed for their lives. This path may seem less clear than following a cloud and fire in the wilderness or walking the earth following the Son of God. However, believers are now indwelt with God's Spirit — meaning that the power to obey and follow Jesus now comes from within. Rather than following external signs, God's people have the Spirit of God living within them and directing their steps to follow his ways.

the cloud lifted in the morning, they set out, or if it continued for a day and a night, when the cloud lifted they set out. [22]Whether it was two days, or a month, or a longer time, that the cloud continued over the tabernacle, abiding there, the people of Israel remained in camp and did not set out, but when it lifted they set out. [23]At the command of the LORD they camped, and at the command of the LORD they set out. They kept the charge of the LORD, at the command of the LORD by Moses.

NUMBERS 10:1–10

TRUMPET CALLS

The sound of the trumpet served as a rallying call for the people of Israel, as a sign of advancement and as a declaration of military action. This instrument, a straight horn with a flaring hammered silver bell at the end, was used primarily to signal the movement of the nation of Israel. Whenever the trumpet sounded the people began their march to wherever God was leading them. At the sound of the trumpet declaring military action, the people of God broke camp, moved toward the land in their God-ordained arrangement, and fought in the power God supplied.

Jesus secured a greater victory over an oppressive enemy through his death, burial, and resurrection, yet little fanfare accompanied this first victory. However, a day is coming when the "last trumpet" will sound, Jesus will return, and he will declare to the entire world that he is the victor (1Co 15:50–57). Until that day, believers fight a spiritual opponent in the power supplied by God's Spirit (Eph 6:10–17), fully trusting that Jesus has already won the battle on their behalf.

The Silver Trumpets

10 The LORD spoke to Moses, saying, [2]"Make two silver trumpets. Of hammered work you shall make them, and you shall use them for summoning the congregation and for breaking camp. [3]And when both are blown, all the congregation shall gather themselves to you at the entrance of the tent of meeting. [4]But if they blow only one, then the chiefs, the heads of the tribes of Israel, shall gather themselves to you. [5]When you blow an alarm, the camps that are on the east side shall set out. [6]And when you blow an alarm the second time, the camps that are on the south side shall set out. An alarm is to be blown whenever they are to set out. [7]But when the assembly is to be gathered together, you shall blow a long blast, but you shall not sound an alarm. [8]And the sons of Aaron, the priests, shall blow the trumpets. The trumpets shall be to you for a perpetual statute throughout your generations. [9]And when you go to war in your land against the adversary who oppresses you, then you shall sound an alarm with the trumpets, that you may be remembered before the LORD your God, and you shall be saved from your enemies. [10]On the day of your gladness also, and at your appointed feasts and at the beginnings of your months, you shall blow the trumpets over your burnt offerings and over the sacrifices of your peace offerings. They shall be a reminder of you before your God: I am the LORD your God."

Israel Leaves Sinai

[11]In the second year, in the second month, on the twentieth day of the month, the cloud lifted from over the tabernacle of the testimony, [12]and the people of Israel set out by stages from the wilderness of Sinai. And the cloud settled down in the wilderness of Paran. [13]They set out for the first time at the command of the LORD by Moses. [14]The standard of the camp of the people of Judah set out first by their companies, and over their company was Nahshon the son of Amminadab. [15]And over the company of the tribe of the people of Issachar was Nethanel the son of Zuar. [16]And over the company of the tribe of the people of Zebulun was Eliab the son of Helon.

[17]And when the tabernacle was taken down, the sons of Gershon and the sons of Merari, who carried the tabernacle, set out. [18]And the standard of the camp of Reuben set out by their companies, and over their company was Elizur the son of Shedeur. [19]And over the company of the tribe of the people of Simeon was Shelumiel the son of Zurishaddai. [20]And over the company of the tribe of the people of Gad was Eliasaph the son of Deuel.

[21]Then the Kohathites set out, carrying the holy things, and the tabernacle was set up before their arrival. [22]And the standard of the camp of the people of Ephraim set out by their companies, and over their company was Elishama the son of Ammihud. [23]And over the company of the tribe of the people of Manasseh was Gamaliel the son of Pedahzur. [24]And over the company of the tribe of the people of Benjamin was Abidan the son of Gideoni.

[25]Then the standard of the camp of the people of Dan, acting as the rear guard of all the camps, set out by their companies, and over their company was Ahiezer the son of Ammishaddai. [26]And over the company of the tribe of the people of Asher was Pagiel the son of Ochran. [27]And over the company of the tribe of the people of Naphtali was Ahira the son of Enan. [28]This was the order of march of the people of Israel by their companies, when they set out.

29 And Moses said to Hobab the son of Reuel the Midianite, Moses' father-in-
law, "We are setting out for the place of which the LORD said, 'I will give it to you.'
Come with us, and we will do good to you, for the LORD has promised good to
Israel." 30 But he said to him, "I will not go. I will depart to my own land and to my
kindred." 31 And he said, "Please do not leave us, for you know where we should
camp in the wilderness, and you will serve as eyes for us. 32 And if you do go with
us, whatever good the LORD will do to us, the same will we do to you."
33 So they set out from the mount of the LORD three days' journey. And the ark
of the covenant of the LORD went before them three days' journey, to seek out a
resting place for them. 34 And the cloud of the LORD was over them by day, whenever they set out from the camp.
35 And whenever the ark set out, Moses said, "Arise, O LORD, and let your enemies be scattered, and let those who hate you flee before you." 36 And when it
rested, he said, "Return, O LORD, to the ten thousand thousands of Israel."

The People Complain

11 And the people complained in the hearing of the LORD about their misfor-
tunes, and when the LORD heard it, his anger was kindled, and the fire of
the LORD burned among them and consumed some outlying parts of the camp.
2 Then the people cried out to Moses, and Moses prayed to the LORD, and the fire
died down. 3 So the name of that place was called Taberah,[1] because the fire of the
LORD burned among them.
4 Now the rabble that was among them had a strong craving. And the people of
Israel also wept again and said, "Oh that we had meat to eat! 5 We remember the
fish we ate in Egypt that cost nothing, the cucumbers, the melons, the leeks, the
onions, and the garlic. 6 But now our strength is dried up, and there is nothing at
all but this manna to look at."
7 Now the manna was like coriander seed, and its appearance like that of bdellium. 8 The people went about and gathered it and ground it in handmills or beat
it in mortars and boiled it in pots and made cakes of it. And the taste of it was like
the taste of cakes baked with oil. 9 When the dew fell upon the camp in the night,
the manna fell with it.
10 Moses heard the people weeping throughout their clans, everyone at the
door of his tent. And the anger of the LORD blazed hotly, and Moses was displeased. 11 Moses said to the LORD, "Why have you dealt ill with your servant? And
why have I not found favor in your sight, that you lay the burden of all this people
on me? 12 Did I conceive all this people? Did I give them birth, that you should say
to me, 'Carry them in your bosom, as a nurse carries a nursing child,' to the land
that you swore to give their fathers? 13 Where am I to get meat to give to all this
people? For they weep before me and say, 'Give us meat, that we may eat.' 14 I am
not able to carry all this people alone; the burden is too heavy for me. 15 If you will
treat me like this, kill me at once, if I find favor in your sight, that I may not see
my wretchedness."

Elders Appointed to Aid Moses

16 Then the LORD said to Moses, "Gather for me seventy men of the elders of
Israel, whom you know to be the elders of the people and officers over them, and
bring them to the tent of meeting, and let them take their stand there with you.
17 And I will come down and talk with you there. And I will take some of the Spirit
that is on you and put it on them, and they shall bear the burden of the people
with you, so that you may not bear it yourself alone. 18 And say to the people, 'Consecrate yourselves for tomorrow, and you shall eat meat, for you have wept in the
hearing of the LORD, saying, "Who will give us meat to eat? For it was better for
us in Egypt." Therefore the LORD will give you meat, and you shall eat. 19 You shall

[1] *Taberah* means *burning*

THE FIRE FROM THE LORD

The Israelites were prone to complain against the Lord and his anointed leaders. At an earlier stage, only three days after their miraculous deliverance from the Egyptian army at the Red Sea, they murmured against God because they lacked water (Ex 15:22–24). Here, after another three-day journey, they complained again (for unspecified reasons). Their complaints demonstrated a failure to trust God to meet the needs of his people, even though he had always cared for them. This act of rebellion necessitated the judgment of God, which came in the form of fire from the Lord that consumed some of the people. The dual attributes of God's judgment and his mercy are on display. *Some* of the people on the *outskirts* of the camp were destroyed, but not *all* of the people *throughout* the camp. The fire from the Lord is both an act of judgment and a warning to the entire nation.

Fire is symbolic of the judgment of God against the contamination of sin (Ge 19:24). During his earthly ministry, two of Jesus' disciples asked him if they should call down fire from heaven to consume an inhospitable Samaritan village. Jesus, however, rebuked the disciples (Lk 9:51–55).

The coming day of the Lord, at the end of this age, will be marked by the same fire of judgment (2Pe 3:10). This fire will purge the earth and all created things from the contamination brought about by sin. Those who remain hostile to God will be destroyed and thrown into the fiery furnace. "In that place there will be weeping and gnashing of teeth" (Mt 13:49–50).

These dire warnings function like the fire seen in Numbers 11. They demonstrate the unrivaled holiness of God and his utter hatred of the sins that deface his good, created order. However, God in his goodness allows time for those who do not know him to believe. His Word urges people to turn to him while it is still "today" (Heb 3:12–13). Additionally, an urgency is placed on believers to make Jesus known to those who do not know him. The Lord desires that no one on earth would perish (Jn 3:16; 2Pe 3:9).

not eat just one day, or two days, or five days, or ten days, or twenty days, [20]but a whole month, until it comes out at your nostrils and becomes loathsome to you, because you have rejected the LORD who is among you and have wept before him, saying, "Why did we come out of Egypt?"'" [21]But Moses said, "The people among whom I am number six hundred thousand on foot, and you have said, 'I will give them meat, that they may eat a whole month!' [22]Shall flocks and herds be slaughtered for them, and be enough for them? Or shall all the fish of the sea be gathered together for them, and be enough for them?" [23]And the LORD said to Moses, "Is the LORD's hand shortened? Now you shall see whether my word will come true for you or not."

[24]So Moses went out and told the people the words of the LORD. And he gathered seventy men of the elders of the people and placed them around the tent. [25]Then the LORD came down in the cloud and spoke to him, and took some of the Spirit that was on him and put it on the seventy elders. And as soon as the Spirit rested on them, they prophesied. But they did not continue doing it.

[26]Now two men remained in the camp, one named Eldad, and the other named Medad, and the Spirit rested on them. They were among those registered, but they had not gone out to the tent, and so they prophesied in the camp. [27]And a young man ran and told Moses, "Eldad and Medad are prophesying in the camp." [28]And Joshua the son of Nun, the assistant of Moses from his youth, said, "My lord Moses, stop them." [29]But Moses said to him, "Are you jealous for my sake? Would that all the LORD's people were prophets, that the LORD would put his Spirit on them!" [30]And Moses and the elders of Israel returned to the camp.

Quail and a Plague

[31]Then a wind from the LORD sprang up, and it brought quail from the sea and let them fall beside the camp, about a day's journey on this side and a day's journey on the other side, around the camp, and about two cubits[1] above the ground. [32]And the people rose all that day and all night and all the next day, and gathered the quail. Those who gathered least gathered ten homers.[2] And they spread them out for themselves all around the camp. [33]While the meat was yet between their teeth, before it was consumed, the anger of the LORD was kindled against the people, and the LORD struck down the people with a very great plague. [34]Therefore the name of that place was called Kibroth-hattaavah,[3] because there they buried the people who had the craving. [35]From Kibroth-hattaavah the people journeyed to Hazeroth, and they remained at Hazeroth.

Miriam and Aaron Oppose Moses

12 Miriam and Aaron spoke against Moses because of the Cushite woman whom he had married, for he had married a Cushite woman. [2]And they said, "Has the LORD indeed spoken only through Moses? Has he not spoken through us also?" And the LORD heard it. [3]Now the man Moses was very meek, more than all people who were on the face of the earth. [4]And suddenly the LORD said to Moses and to Aaron and Miriam, "Come out, you three, to the tent of meeting." And the three of them came out. [5]And the LORD came down in a pillar of cloud and stood at the entrance of the tent and called Aaron and Miriam, and they both came forward. [6]And he said, "Hear my words: If there is a prophet among you, I the LORD make myself known to him in a vision; I speak with him in a dream. [7]Not so with my servant Moses. He is faithful in all my house. [8]With him I speak mouth to mouth, clearly, and not in riddles, and he beholds the form of the LORD. Why then were you not afraid to speak against my servant Moses?" [9]And the anger of the LORD was kindled against them, and he departed.

[1]A *cubit* was about 18 inches or 45 centimeters [2]A *homer* was about 6 bushels or 220 liters
[3]*Kibroth-hattaavah* means *graves of craving*

NUMBERS 12:3

HUMILITY

Moses' leadership of the people of God was characterized by unrivaled humility. This parenthetical note, added within the story of the conflict between Miriam, Aaron, and Moses, demonstrated the way in which Old Testament leaders exemplified God's character. Much about Moses' life could have resulted in pride—he was chosen by God, called to lead the people, and saw firsthand God's glory. Yet his humility was singled out as a distinctive characteristic that allowed him to faithfully lead God's people. He was not, however, without fault. Like Noah and Abraham before him, his sin clouded his judgment, and this ultimately disqualified him from leading the people into the promised land (Nu 20:12).

All people, like Moses, are mere shadows of the perfection that is Jesus Christ. Jesus' humility was demonstrated by his willingness to leave the glories of heaven, take on the form of a servant, and suffer and die at the hands of the very ones he came to save (Php 2:5–11).

10 When the cloud removed from over the tent, behold, Miriam was leprous,[1] like snow. And Aaron turned toward Miriam, and behold, she was leprous. 11 And Aaron said to Moses, "Oh, my lord, do not punish us[2] because we have done foolishly and have sinned. 12 Let her not be as one dead, whose flesh is half eaten away when he comes out of his mother's womb." 13 And Moses cried to the LORD, "O God, please heal her—please." 14 But the LORD said to Moses, "If her father had but spit in her face, should she not be shamed seven days? Let her be shut outside the camp seven days, and after that she may be brought in again." 15 So Miriam was shut outside the camp seven days, and the people did not set out on the march till Miriam was brought in again. 16 After that the people set out from Hazeroth, and camped in the wilderness of Paran.

Spies Sent into Canaan

13 The LORD spoke to Moses, saying, 2 "Send men to spy out the land of Canaan, which I am giving to the people of Israel. From each tribe of their fathers you shall send a man, every one a chief among them." 3 So Moses sent them from the wilderness of Paran, according to the command of the LORD, all of them men who were heads of the people of Israel. 4 And these were their names: From the tribe of Reuben, Shammua the son of Zaccur; 5 from the tribe of Simeon, Shaphat the son of Hori; 6 from the tribe of Judah, Caleb the son of Jephunneh; 7 from the tribe of Issachar, Igal the son of Joseph; 8 from the tribe of Ephraim, Hoshea the son of Nun; 9 from the tribe of Benjamin, Palti the son of Raphu; 10 from the tribe of Zebulun, Gaddiel the son of Sodi; 11 from the tribe of Joseph (that is, from the tribe of Manasseh), Gaddi the son of Susi; 12 from the tribe of Dan, Ammiel the son of Gemalli; 13 from the tribe of Asher, Sethur the son of Michael; 14 from the tribe of Naphtali, Nahbi the son of Vophsi; 15 from the tribe of Gad, Geuel the son of Machi. 16 These were the names of the men whom Moses sent to spy out the land. And Moses called Hoshea the son of Nun, Joshua.

17 Moses sent them to spy out the land of Canaan and said to them, "Go up into the Negeb and go up into the hill country, 18 and see what the land is, and whether the people who dwell in it are strong or weak, whether they are few or many, 19 and whether the land that they dwell in is good or bad, and whether the cities that they dwell in are camps or strongholds, 20 and whether the land is rich or poor, and whether there are trees in it or not. Be of good courage and bring some of the fruit of the land." Now the time was the season of the first ripe grapes.

21 So they went up and spied out the land from the wilderness of Zin to Rehob, near Lebo-hamath. 22 They went up into the Negeb and came to Hebron. Ahiman, Sheshai, and Talmai, the descendants of Anak, were there. (Hebron was built seven years before Zoan in Egypt.) 23 And they came to the Valley of Eshcol and cut down from there a branch with a single cluster of grapes, and they carried it on a pole between two of them; they also brought some pomegranates and figs. 24 That place was called the Valley of Eshcol,[3] because of the cluster that the people of Israel cut down from there.

Report of the Spies

25 At the end of forty days they returned from spying out the land. 26 And they came to Moses and Aaron and to all the congregation of the people of Israel in the wilderness of Paran, at Kadesh. They brought back word to them and to all the congregation, and showed them the fruit of the land. 27 And they told him, "We came to the land to which you sent us. It flows with milk and honey, and this is its fruit. 28 However, the people who dwell in the land are strong, and the cities are fortified and very large. And besides, we saw the descendants of Anak there. 29 The Amalekites dwell in the land of the Negeb. The Hittites, the Jebusites, and

---

[1] *Leprosy* was a term for several skin diseases; see Leviticus 13 [2] Hebrew *do not lay sin upon us*
[3] *Eshcol* means *cluster*

the Amorites dwell in the hill country. And the Canaanites dwell by the sea, and
along the Jordan."
[30]But Caleb quieted the people before Moses and said, "Let us go up at once
and occupy it, for we are well able to overcome it." [31]Then the men who had gone
up with him said, "We are not able to go up against the people, for they are stronger than we are." [32]So they brought to the people of Israel a bad report of the land
that they had spied out, saying, "The land, through which we have gone to spy it
out, is a land that devours its inhabitants, and all the people that we saw in it are
of great height. [33]And there we saw the Nephilim (the sons of Anak, who come
from the Nephilim), and we seemed to ourselves like grasshoppers, and so we
seemed to them."

The People Rebel

14 Then all the congregation raised a loud cry, and the people wept that night.
[2]And all the people of Israel grumbled against Moses and Aaron. The whole
congregation said to them, "Would that we had died in the land of Egypt! Or
would that we had died in this wilderness! [3]Why is the LORD bringing us into this
land, to fall by the sword? Our wives and our little ones will become a prey. Would
it not be better for us to go back to Egypt?" [4]And they said to one another, "Let us
choose a leader and go back to Egypt."
[5]Then Moses and Aaron fell on their faces before all the assembly of the congregation of the people of Israel. [6]And Joshua the son of Nun and Caleb the son
of Jephunneh, who were among those who had spied out the land, tore their
clothes [7]and said to all the congregation of the people of Israel, "The land, which
we passed through to spy it out, is an exceedingly good land. [8]If the LORD delights
in us, he will bring us into this land and give it to us, a land that flows with milk
and honey. [9]Only do not rebel against the LORD. And do not fear the people of the
land, for they are bread for us. Their protection is removed from them, and the
LORD is with us; do not fear them." [10]Then all the congregation said to stone them
with stones. But the glory of the LORD appeared at the tent of meeting to all the
people of Israel.
[11]And the LORD said to Moses, "How long will this people despise me? And how
long will they not believe in me, in spite of all the signs that I have done among
them? [12]I will strike them with the pestilence and disinherit them, and I will make
of you a nation greater and mightier than they."

Moses Intercedes for the People

[13]But Moses said to the LORD, "Then the Egyptians will hear of it, for you
brought up this people in your might from among them, [14]and they will tell the
inhabitants of this land. They have heard that you, O LORD, are in the midst of
this people. For you, O LORD, are seen face to face, and your cloud stands over
them and you go before them, in a pillar of cloud by day and in a pillar of fire by
night. [15]Now if you kill this people as one man, then the nations who have heard
your fame will say, [16]'It is because the LORD was not able to bring this people into
the land that he swore to give to them that he has killed them in the wilderness.'
[17]And now, please let the power of the Lord be great as you have promised, saying,
[18]'The LORD is slow to anger and abounding in steadfast love, forgiving iniquity
and transgression, but he will by no means clear the guilty, visiting the iniquity
of the fathers on the children, to the third and the fourth generation.' [19]Please
pardon the iniquity of this people, according to the greatness of your steadfast
love, just as you have forgiven this people, from Egypt until now."

God Promises Judgment

[20]Then the LORD said, "I have pardoned, according to your word. [21]But truly,
as I live, and as all the earth shall be filled with the glory of the LORD, [22]none
of the men who have seen my glory and my signs that I did in Egypt and in the

NUMBERS 14:9

THE SIN OF REBELLION

The word *rebel* poignantly describes an aspect of the nature of sin. Rebels are those who willingly disregard and disobey the directives of an established authority. The Israelites were instructed to follow the directives of God and, in so doing, take the land God had promised. However, if the people rebelled, they would face the judgment of the Lord. The stiff-necked people often failed to heed these warnings, choosing to usurp the authority of God and go their own way (Dt 1:26,43; 9:23–24). The consequences for such rebellion often involved physical destruction and divine chastisement. Paul warned the church at Corinth that "these things took place as examples for us, that we might not desire evil as they did" (1Co 10:6). The negative example of the rebellious nature of the people of God is meant to warn all sinful rebels of the implications of such rebellion, both in this life and in the age to come.

CONFIDENCE IN THE LORD

The Israelites were instructed to take a land that was already inhabited. This was surely a daunting challenge for a nation that had been wandering in the wilderness. In order to discern the challenge these inhabitants would present, the Israelites sent twelve spies into the land. These men all acknowledged that the land was indeed a good land — flowing with milk, honey, and other examples of God's exceeding kindness. But rather than being emboldened with courage, the spies shuddered in fear at the power of the people and the fortifications of their cities. As a result, the Israelites were tempted to turn back. Caleb and Joshua were the exception. They recognized the scope of the mission and the obstacles that they would face, but they had confidence in the Lord. They knew that he had always been faithful to his people. He had delivered them from slavery in Egypt and protected them through the treacherous wilderness. He would never abandon them. He is a God who always fulfills his promises, even in the face of seemingly insurmountable odds.

Most onlookers would have assumed that Jesus' victory would be unlikely as well. Few things about his life communicated that he would be the victorious King of the universe. In fact, it seemed quite the opposite. He was born in a lowly stable, was raised in obscurity, ministered as an itinerant teacher, and died the death of a common criminal. The men responsible for his crucifixion, in a grand, cosmic irony, mocked him with a sign declaring him to be the king of the Jews (Mt 27:37). Yet God is always faithful to his promise. He used the sacrifice of his Son, against all odds, to overthrow a far greater enemy than the nation of Israel would ever face — Satan, sin, and death.

Believers today may also find themselves cowering in fear at the power and might of the forces arrayed against them. It may seem that the enemy is powerful and the world is winning. Yet those who know Jesus can take heart knowing that "he who is in you is greater than he who is in the world" (1Jn 4:4). Christians can live with confidence knowing that they are indwelt by an all-powerful God, and this God will always fulfill his good promises.

RESISTING GOD DESPITE HIS WORK

The contemptuous Israelites turned their scorn toward Moses and Aaron. Longing to return to Egypt, they blamed these God-ordained leaders and even talked about stoning them. The irony is stark. Moses and Aaron were the human means by which God accomplished his miraculous deliverance of the people from slavery in Egypt. There, God had enacted signs and wonders to demonstrate his glory and power. No one could deny that this deliverance was from the Lord. Yet not long after observing God's might and being the recipients of his favor, the people of God blamed God for bringing them into the wilderness to die. Moses and Aaron, as the leaders of the people, were the objects of the nation's accusations; however, the people clearly believed that the fault actually lay with God himself (v. 3). In the New Testament, Stephen, in his speech to the Sanhedrin, said that the failure of the people to obey God should be attributed to their rejection of him and their disbelief in his promises (Ac 7:39).

Jesus suffered a similar fate. Throughout his earthly ministry, he provided countless signs and wonders, demonstrating himself to be the Son of God and the one through whom the kingdom of God would come. In spite of these clear manifestations of the power of God, many still did not believe (Jn 12:37).

As a foreshadowing of his own subsequent resurrection, Jesus raised his friend Lazarus from the dead to life in the plain sight of all those watching (Jn 11). This miraculous act was soon reported to the Jewish religious leaders who, rather than believing that he was the Son of God, concocted a plan to kill him for fear that all of the people would follow Jesus. Their sin was evidenced by their disbelief.

Today, people are prone to resist the clear work of God as well. All around are abundant evidences of his goodness, and he still performs mighty signs and wonders to demonstrate his power. Yet many do not believe. Their hard-hearted resistance to these acts of God is evidence of their pride. Like the Israelites before them, many will be judged for their disbelief in God's goodness and grace. Those who recognize God's work can, by the power of his Spirit, humble themselves and believe in him.

wilderness, and yet have put me to the test these ten times and have not obeyed my voice, 23shall see the land that I swore to give to their fathers. And none of those who despised me shall see it. 24But my servant Caleb, because he has a different spirit and has followed me fully, I will bring into the land into which he went, and his descendants shall possess it. 25Now, since the Amalekites and the Canaanites dwell in the valleys, turn tomorrow and set out for the wilderness by the way to the Red Sea."

26And the LORD spoke to Moses and to Aaron, saying, 27"How long shall this wicked congregation grumble against me? I have heard the grumblings of the people of Israel, which they grumble against me. 28Say to them, 'As I live, declares the LORD, what you have said in my hearing I will do to you: 29your dead bodies shall fall in this wilderness, and of all your number, listed in the census from twenty years old and upward, who have grumbled against me, 30not one shall come into the land where I swore that I would make you dwell, except Caleb the son of Jephunneh and Joshua the son of Nun. 31But your little ones, who you said would become a prey, I will bring in, and they shall know the land that you have rejected. 32But as for you, your dead bodies shall fall in this wilderness. 33And your children shall be shepherds in the wilderness forty years and shall suffer for your faithlessness, until the last of your dead bodies lies in the wilderness. 34According to the number of the days in which you spied out the land, forty days, a year for each day, you shall bear your iniquity forty years, and you shall know my displeasure.' 35I, the LORD, have spoken. Surely this will I do to all this wicked congregation who are gathered together against me: in this wilderness they shall come to a full end, and there they shall die."

36And the men whom Moses sent to spy out the land, who returned and made all the congregation grumble against him by bringing up a bad report about the land— 37the men who brought up a bad report of the land—died by plague before the LORD. 38Of those men who went to spy out the land, only Joshua the son of Nun and Caleb the son of Jephunneh remained alive.

Israel Defeated in Battle

39When Moses told these words to all the people of Israel, the people mourned greatly. 40And they rose early in the morning and went up to the heights of the hill country, saying, "Here we are. We will go up to the place that the LORD has promised, for we have sinned." 41But Moses said, "Why now are you transgressing the command of the LORD, when that will not succeed? 42Do not go up, for the LORD is not among you, lest you be struck down before your enemies. 43For there the Amalekites and the Canaanites are facing you, and you shall fall by the sword. Because you have turned back from following the LORD, the LORD will not be with you." 44But they presumed to go up to the heights of the hill country, although neither the ark of the covenant of the LORD nor Moses departed out of the camp. 45Then the Amalekites and the Canaanites who lived in that hill country came down and defeated them and pursued them, even to Hormah.

Laws About Sacrifices

15 The LORD spoke to Moses, saying, 2"Speak to the people of Israel and say to them, When you come into the land you are to inhabit, which I am giving you, 3and you offer to the LORD from the herd or from the flock a food offering[1] or a burnt offering or a sacrifice, to fulfill a vow or as a freewill offering or at your appointed feasts, to make a pleasing aroma to the LORD, 4then he who brings his offering shall offer to the LORD a grain offering of a tenth of an ephah[2] of fine flour, mixed with a quarter of a hin[3] of oil; 5and you shall offer with the burnt offering, or for the sacrifice, a quarter of a hin of wine for the drink offering for

---

[1] Or *an offering by fire*; so throughout Numbers [2] An *ephah* was about 3/5 bushel or 22 liters [3] A *hin* was about 4 quarts or 3.5 liters

each lamb. 6Or for a ram, you shall offer for a grain offering two tenths of an
ephah of fine flour mixed with a third of a hin of oil. 7And for the drink offering
you shall offer a third of a hin of wine, a pleasing aroma to the LORD. 8And when
you offer a bull as a burnt offering or sacrifice, to fulfill a vow or for peace offerings to the LORD, 9then one shall offer with the bull a grain offering of three
tenths of an ephah of fine flour, mixed with half a hin of oil. 10And you shall offer
for the drink offering half a hin of wine, as a food offering, a pleasing aroma to
the LORD.

11"Thus it shall be done for each bull or ram, or for each lamb or young goat.
12As many as you offer, so shall you do with each one, as many as there are. 13Every
native Israelite shall do these things in this way, in offering a food offering, with a
pleasing aroma to the LORD. 14And if a stranger is sojourning with you, or anyone
is living permanently among you, and he wishes to offer a food offering, with a
pleasing aroma to the LORD, he shall do as you do. 15For the assembly, there shall
be one statute for you and for the stranger who sojourns with you, a statute forever throughout your generations. You and the sojourner shall be alike before the
LORD. 16One law and one rule shall be for you and for the stranger who sojourns
with you."

17The LORD spoke to Moses, saying, 18"Speak to the people of Israel and say to
them, When you come into the land to which I bring you 19and when you eat of
the bread of the land, you shall present a contribution to the LORD. 20Of the first
of your dough you shall present a loaf as a contribution; like a contribution from
the threshing floor, so shall you present it. 21Some of the first of your dough you
shall give to the LORD as a contribution throughout your generations.

Laws About Unintentional Sins

22"But if you sin unintentionally,[1] and do not observe all these commandments that the LORD has spoken to Moses, 23all that the LORD has commanded
you by Moses, from the day that the LORD gave commandment, and onward
throughout your generations, 24then if it was done unintentionally without the
knowledge of the congregation, all the congregation shall offer one bull from the
herd for a burnt offering, a pleasing aroma to the LORD, with its grain offering and
its drink offering, according to the rule, and one male goat for a sin offering. 25And
the priest shall make atonement for all the congregation of the people of Israel,
and they shall be forgiven, because it was a mistake, and they have brought their
offering, a food offering to the LORD, and their sin offering before the LORD for
their mistake. 26And all the congregation of the people of Israel shall be forgiven,
and the stranger who sojourns among them, because the whole population was
involved in the mistake.

27"If one person sins unintentionally, he shall offer a female goat a year old
for a sin offering. 28And the priest shall make atonement before the LORD for the
person who makes a mistake, when he sins unintentionally, to make atonement
for him, and he shall be forgiven. 29You shall have one law for him who does anything unintentionally, for him who is native among the people of Israel and for the
stranger who sojourns among them. 30But the person who does anything with a
high hand, whether he is native or a sojourner, reviles the LORD, and that person
shall be cut off from among his people. 31Because he has despised the word of the
LORD and has broken his commandment, that person shall be utterly cut off; his
iniquity shall be on him."

A Sabbathbreaker Executed

32While the people of Israel were in the wilderness, they found a man gathering sticks on the Sabbath day. 33And those who found him gathering sticks
brought him to Moses and Aaron and to all the congregation. 34They put him in

[1] Or *by mistake*; also verses 24, 27, 28, 29

custody, because it had not been made clear what should be done to him. 35 And
the LORD said to Moses, "The man shall be put to death; all the congregation shall
stone him with stones outside the camp." 36 And all the congregation brought him
outside the camp and stoned him to death with stones, as the LORD commanded
Moses.

Tassels on Garments

37 The LORD said to Moses, 38 "Speak to the people of Israel, and tell them to
make tassels on the corners of their garments throughout their generations, and
to put a cord of blue on the tassel of each corner. 39 And it shall be a tassel for you
to look at and remember all the commandments of the LORD, to do them, not to
follow[1] after your own heart and your own eyes, which you are inclined to whore
after. 40 So you shall remember and do all my commandments, and be holy to your
God. 41 I am the LORD your God, who brought you out of the land of Egypt to be
your God: I am the LORD your God."

Korah's Rebellion

16 Now Korah the son of Izhar, son of Kohath, son of Levi, and Dathan and
Abiram the sons of Eliab, and On the son of Peleth, sons of Reuben, took
men. 2 And they rose up before Moses, with a number of the people of Israel, 250
chiefs of the congregation, chosen from the assembly, well-known men. 3 They
assembled themselves together against Moses and against Aaron and said to
them, "You have gone too far! For all in the congregation are holy, every one of
them, and the LORD is among them. Why then do you exalt yourselves above the
assembly of the LORD?" 4 When Moses heard it, he fell on his face, 5 and he said
to Korah and all his company, "In the morning the LORD will show who is his,[2]
and who is holy, and will bring him near to him. The one whom he chooses he
will bring near to him. 6 Do this: take censers, Korah and all his company; 7 put
fire in them and put incense on them before the LORD tomorrow, and the man
whom the LORD chooses shall be the holy one. You have gone too far, sons of
Levi!" 8 And Moses said to Korah, "Hear now, you sons of Levi: 9 is it too small a
thing for you that the God of Israel has separated you from the congregation of
Israel, to bring you near to himself, to do service in the tabernacle of the LORD
and to stand before the congregation to minister to them, 10 and that he has
brought you near him, and all your brothers the sons of Levi with you? And
would you seek the priesthood also? 11 Therefore it is against the LORD that you
and all your company have gathered together. What is Aaron that you grumble
against him?"

12 And Moses sent to call Dathan and Abiram the sons of Eliab, and they said,
"We will not come up. 13 Is it a small thing that you have brought us up out of a land
flowing with milk and honey, to kill us in the wilderness, that you must also make
yourself a prince over us? 14 Moreover, you have not brought us into a land flowing
with milk and honey, nor given us inheritance of fields and vineyards. Will you
put out the eyes of these men? We will not come up." 15 And Moses was very angry
and said to the LORD, "Do not respect their offering. I have not taken one donkey
from them, and I have not harmed one of them."

16 And Moses said to Korah, "Be present, you and all your company, before the
LORD, you and they, and Aaron, tomorrow. 17 And let every one of you take his censer and put incense on it, and every one of you bring before the LORD his censer,
250 censers; you also, and Aaron, each his censer." 18 So every man took his censer
and put fire in them and laid incense on them and stood at the entrance of the
tent of meeting with Moses and Aaron. 19 Then Korah assembled all the congregation against them at the entrance of the tent of meeting. And the glory of the LORD
appeared to all the congregation.

---

[1] Hebrew *to spy out* [2] Septuagint *The LORD knows those who are his*

20And the LORD spoke to Moses and to Aaron, saying, 21"Separate yourselves from among this congregation, that I may consume them in a moment." 22And they fell on their faces and said, "O God, the God of the spirits of all flesh, shall one man sin, and will you be angry with all the congregation?" 23And the LORD spoke to Moses, saying, 24"Say to the congregation, Get away from the dwelling of Korah, Dathan, and Abiram."

25Then Moses rose and went to Dathan and Abiram, and the elders of Israel followed him. 26And he spoke to the congregation, saying, "Depart, please, from the tents of these wicked men, and touch nothing of theirs, lest you be swept away with all their sins." 27So they got away from the dwelling of Korah, Dathan, and Abiram. And Dathan and Abiram came out and stood at the door of their tents, together with their wives, their sons, and their little ones. 28And Moses said, "Hereby you shall know that the LORD has sent me to do all these works, and that it has not been of my own accord. 29If these men die as all men die, or if they are visited by the fate of all mankind, then the LORD has not sent me. 30But if the LORD creates something new, and the ground opens its mouth and swallows them up with all that belongs to them, and they go down alive into Sheol, then you shall know that these men have despised the LORD."

31And as soon as he had finished speaking all these words, the ground under them split apart. 32And the earth opened its mouth and swallowed them up, with their households and all the people who belonged to Korah and all their goods. 33So they and all that belonged to them went down alive into Sheol, and the earth closed over them, and they perished from the midst of the assembly. 34And all Israel who were around them fled at their cry, for they said, "Lest the earth swallow us up!" 35And fire came out from the LORD and consumed the 250 men offering the incense.

36[1]Then the LORD spoke to Moses, saying, 37"Tell Eleazar the son of Aaron the priest to take up the censers out of the blaze. Then scatter the fire far and wide, for they have become holy. 38As for the censers of these men who have sinned at the cost of their lives, let them be made into hammered plates as a covering for the altar, for they offered them before the LORD, and they became holy. Thus they shall be a sign to the people of Israel." 39So Eleazar the priest took the bronze censers, which those who were burned had offered, and they were hammered out as a covering for the altar, 40to be a reminder to the people of Israel, so that no outsider, who is not of the descendants of Aaron, should draw near to burn incense before the LORD, lest he become like Korah and his company—as the LORD said to him through Moses.

41But on the next day all the congregation of the people of Israel grumbled against Moses and against Aaron, saying, "You have killed the people of the LORD." 42And when the congregation had assembled against Moses and against Aaron, they turned toward the tent of meeting. And behold, the cloud covered it, and the glory of the LORD appeared. 43And Moses and Aaron came to the front of the tent of meeting, 44and the LORD spoke to Moses, saying, 45"Get away from the midst of this congregation, that I may consume them in a moment." And they fell on their faces. 46And Moses said to Aaron, "Take your censer, and put fire on it from off the altar and lay incense on it and carry it quickly to the congregation and make atonement for them, for wrath has gone out from the LORD; the plague has begun." 47So Aaron took it as Moses said and ran into the midst of the assembly. And behold, the plague had already begun among the people. And he put on the incense and made atonement for the people. 48And he stood between the dead and the living, and the plague was stopped. 49Now those who died in the plague were 14,700, besides those who died in the affair of Korah. 50And Aaron returned to Moses at the entrance of the tent of meeting, when the plague was stopped.

[1]Ch 17:1 in Hebrew

GRUMBLING INSTEAD OF SERVING

Korah's rebellion stands as a testament to the disastrous results of arrogant leadership. In Numbers 16, Korah asserted that his family deserved just as much privilege as was given to Aaron and his descendants (v. 3). Korah demanded that Moses and Aaron level the playing field for priestly service. Dissatisfied with caring for the mundane aspects of the tabernacle, the upstarts saw the Aaronic priesthood as a position of prestige and unfair advantage (vv. 8 – 11). But as Korah seized the next rung, God brought his efforts to nothing. The rebellion of Korah and those who banded with him against God was quickly brought to a dramatic end (vv. 31 – 35).

The destruction of Korah is so memorable that Jude's critique of the prideful behavior of the false teachers of his day distinctly reminded him of Korah's behavior (Jude 11). Jude underscored the pride of false teachers by combining the stories of Cain, Balaam, and Korah to make his point. The pride of leaders like Korah is just as dangerous and unfulfilling today as it was when the children of Israel were wandering in the desert (vv. 12 – 13).

Jesus and Korah stand in stark contrast. Korah used his influence in his pursuit of authority. Recognizing his status in the community, Korah made a tactical move against Moses and Aaron (Nu 16:1 – 2). In contrast, Paul described the ministry of Jesus as a rejection of significance (Php 2:6 – 8). Jesus could have drawn together the elite of society in order to stage a coup, but he opted to follow the Father's will and serve and die instead.

Korah assumed that roles of service are actually positions of power. Korah's claim that Moses and Aaron had set themselves above the rest of the nation revealed his view of leadership. To Korah, leadership was an opportunity to exert one's power — controlling the weak for self-serving ends. Jesus modeled the opposite view of leadership. Leadership is primarily an opportunity to serve (Jn 13:15 – 16).

Korah saw success also as a path of upward mobility. Moses rebuked Korah's dissatisfaction with menial and mundane service (Nu 16:9 – 11), highlighting his upward ambitions. Jesus served as the opposite example. Korah took up his censer, but Jesus took up a towel (Jn 13:1 – 17). Korah's attempted climb caused many to fall (Nu 16:31 – 35); Jesus' descent caused many to rise (Ro 5:18 – 21).

Aaron's Staff Buds

17[1] The LORD spoke to Moses, saying, 2"Speak to the people of Israel, and
get from them staffs, one for each fathers' house, from all their chiefs
according to their fathers' houses, twelve staffs. Write each man's name on his
staff, 3and write Aaron's name on the staff of Levi. For there shall be one staff
for the head of each fathers' house. 4Then you shall deposit them in the tent of
meeting before the testimony, where I meet with you. 5And the staff of the man
whom I choose shall sprout. Thus I will make to cease from me the grumblings of
the people of Israel, which they grumble against you." 6Moses spoke to the people
of Israel. And all their chiefs gave him staffs, one for each chief, according to their
fathers' houses, twelve staffs. And the staff of Aaron was among their staffs. 7And
Moses deposited the staffs before the LORD in the tent of the testimony.
8On the next day Moses went into the tent of the testimony, and behold, the
staff of Aaron for the house of Levi had sprouted and put forth buds and produced
blossoms, and it bore ripe almonds. 9Then Moses brought out all the staffs from
before the LORD to all the people of Israel. And they looked, and each man took
his staff. 10And the LORD said to Moses, "Put back the staff of Aaron before the
testimony, to be kept as a sign for the rebels, that you may make an end of their
grumblings against me, lest they die." 11Thus did Moses; as the LORD commanded
him, so he did.
12And the people of Israel said to Moses, "Behold, we perish, we are undone,
we are all undone. 13Everyone who comes near, who comes near to the tabernacle
of the LORD, shall die. Are we all to perish?"

Duties of Priests and Levites

18 So the LORD said to Aaron, "You and your sons and your father's house with
you shall bear iniquity connected with the sanctuary, and you and your
sons with you shall bear iniquity connected with your priesthood. 2And with you
bring your brothers also, the tribe of Levi, the tribe of your father, that they may
join you and minister to you while you and your sons with you are before the
tent of the testimony. 3They shall keep guard over you and over the whole tent,
but shall not come near to the vessels of the sanctuary or to the altar lest they,
and you, die. 4They shall join you and keep guard over the tent of meeting for all
the service of the tent, and no outsider shall come near you. 5And you shall keep
guard over the sanctuary and over the altar, that there may never again be wrath
on the people of Israel. 6And behold, I have taken your brothers the Levites from
among the people of Israel. They are a gift to you, given to the LORD, to do the
service of the tent of meeting. 7And you and your sons with you shall guard your
priesthood for all that concerns the altar and that is within the veil; and you shall
serve. I give your priesthood as a gift,[2] and any outsider who comes near shall be
put to death."
8Then the LORD spoke to Aaron, "Behold, I have given you charge of the contributions made to me, all the consecrated things of the people of Israel. I have
given them to you as a portion and to your sons as a perpetual due. 9This shall
be yours of the most holy things, reserved from the fire: every offering of theirs,
every grain offering of theirs and every sin offering of theirs and every guilt offering of theirs, which they render to me, shall be most holy to you and to your
sons. 10In a most holy place shall you eat it. Every male may eat it; it is holy to
you. 11This also is yours: the contribution of their gift, all the wave offerings of
the people of Israel. I have given them to you, and to your sons and daughters
with you, as a perpetual due. Everyone who is clean in your house may eat it.
12All the best of the oil and all the best of the wine and of the grain, the firstfruits
of what they give to the LORD, I give to you. 13The first ripe fruits of all that is in
their land, which they bring to the LORD, shall be yours. Everyone who is clean in

[1]Ch 17:16 in Hebrew [2]Hebrew *service of gift*

your house may eat it. 14Every devoted thing in Israel shall be yours. 15Everything that opens the womb of all flesh, whether man or beast, which they offer to the LORD, shall be yours. Nevertheless, the firstborn of man you shall redeem, and the firstborn of unclean animals you shall redeem. 16And their redemption price (at a month old you shall redeem them) you shall fix at five shekels[1] in silver, according to the shekel of the sanctuary, which is twenty gerahs. 17But the firstborn of a cow, or the firstborn of a sheep, or the firstborn of a goat, you shall not redeem; they are holy. You shall sprinkle their blood on the altar and shall burn their fat as a food offering, with a pleasing aroma to the LORD. 18But their flesh shall be yours, as the breast that is waved and as the right thigh are yours. 19All the holy contributions that the people of Israel present to the LORD I give to you, and to your sons and daughters with you, as a perpetual due. It is a covenant of salt forever before the LORD for you and for your offspring with you." 20And the LORD said to Aaron, "You shall have no inheritance in their land, neither shall you have any portion among them. I am your portion and your inheritance among the people of Israel.

21"To the Levites I have given every tithe in Israel for an inheritance, in return for their service that they do, their service in the tent of meeting, 22so that the people of Israel do not come near the tent of meeting, lest they bear sin and die. 23But the Levites shall do the service of the tent of meeting, and they shall bear their iniquity. It shall be a perpetual statute throughout your generations, and among the people of Israel they shall have no inheritance. 24For the tithe of the people of Israel, which they present as a contribution to the LORD, I have given to the Levites for an inheritance. Therefore I have said of them that they shall have no inheritance among the people of Israel."

25And the LORD spoke to Moses, saying, 26"Moreover, you shall speak and say to the Levites, 'When you take from the people of Israel the tithe that I have given you from them for your inheritance, then you shall present a contribution from it to the LORD, a tithe of the tithe. 27And your contribution shall be counted to you as though it were the grain of the threshing floor, and as the fullness of the winepress. 28So you shall also present a contribution to the LORD from all your tithes, which you receive from the people of Israel. And from it you shall give the LORD's contribution to Aaron the priest. 29Out of all the gifts to you, you shall present every contribution due to the LORD; from each its best part is to be dedicated.' 30Therefore you shall say to them, 'When you have offered from it the best of it, then the rest shall be counted to the Levites as produce of the threshing floor, and as produce of the winepress. 31And you may eat it in any place, you and your households, for it is your reward in return for your service in the tent of meeting. 32And you shall bear no sin by reason of it, when you have contributed the best of it. But you shall not profane the holy things of the people of Israel, lest you die.'"

Laws for Purification

19 Now the LORD spoke to Moses and to Aaron, saying, 2"This is the statute of the law that the LORD has commanded: Tell the people of Israel to bring you a red heifer without defect, in which there is no blemish, and on which a yoke has never come. 3And you shall give it to Eleazar the priest, and it shall be taken outside the camp and slaughtered before him. 4And Eleazar the priest shall take some of its blood with his finger, and sprinkle some of its blood toward the front of the tent of meeting seven times. 5And the heifer shall be burned in his sight. *Its* skin, its flesh, and its blood, with its dung, shall be burned. 6And the priest shall take cedarwood and hyssop and scarlet yarn, and throw them into the fire burning the heifer. 7Then the priest shall wash his clothes and bathe his body in water, and afterward he may come into the camp. But the priest shall be unclean until evening. 8The one who burns the heifer shall wash his clothes in water and

NUMBERS 19:1–6

THE RED HEIFER

The pervasive images of death throughout the Old Testament demonstrate the stark consequences of sin. In grace, God made it possible for the death of a red heifer to be used in the act of ceremonial cleansing. The ashes of the heifer were mixed with water to provide a means of cleansing after contact with dead bodies. The death of the red heifer merely prefigured a much greater substitute, the Lord Jesus Christ. His death did not simply cover the sins of his people; his death bore the wrath of the curse forever. The author of Hebrews used this image to contrast the external cleansing brought about by "the ashes of a heifer" and the internal transformation wrought by "the blood of Christ" (Heb 9:13–14). He bore the wrath of God in order to purge his people from the consequences of sin and empower them to throw off sin and pursue obedience with a clear conscience.

[1]A *shekel* was about 2/5 ounce or 11 grams

bathe his body in water and shall be unclean until evening. 9And a man who is clean shall gather up the ashes of the heifer and deposit them outside the camp in a clean place. And they shall be kept for the water for impurity for the congregation of the people of Israel; it is a sin offering. 10And the one who gathers the ashes of the heifer shall wash his clothes and be unclean until evening. And this shall be a perpetual statute for the people of Israel, and for the stranger who sojourns among them.

11"Whoever touches the dead body of any person shall be unclean seven days. 12He shall cleanse himself with the water on the third day and on the seventh day, and so be clean. But if he does not cleanse himself on the third day and on the seventh day, he will not become clean. 13Whoever touches a dead person, the body of anyone who has died, and does not cleanse himself, defiles the tabernacle of the LORD, and that person shall be cut off from Israel; because the water for impurity was not thrown on him, he shall be unclean. His uncleanness is still on him.

14"This is the law when someone dies in a tent: everyone who comes into the tent and everyone who is in the tent shall be unclean seven days. 15And every open vessel that has no cover fastened on it is unclean. 16Whoever in the open field touches someone who was killed with a sword or who died naturally, or touches a human bone or a grave, shall be unclean seven days. 17For the unclean they shall take some ashes of the burnt sin offering, and fresh[1] water shall be added in a vessel. 18Then a clean person shall take hyssop and dip it in the water and sprinkle it on the tent and on all the furnishings and on the persons who were there and on whoever touched the bone, or the slain or the dead or the grave. 19And the clean person shall sprinkle it on the unclean on the third day and on the seventh day. Thus on the seventh day he shall cleanse him, and he shall wash his clothes and bathe himself in water, and at evening he shall be clean.

20"If the man who is unclean does not cleanse himself, that person shall be cut off from the midst of the assembly, since he has defiled the sanctuary of the LORD. Because the water for impurity has not been thrown on him, he is unclean. 21And it shall be a statute forever for them. The one who sprinkles the water for impurity shall wash his clothes, and the one who touches the water for impurity shall be unclean until evening. 22And whatever the unclean person touches shall be unclean, and anyone who touches it shall be unclean until evening."

The Death of Miriam

20 And the people of Israel, the whole congregation, came into the wilderness of Zin in the first month, and the people stayed in Kadesh. And Miriam died there and was buried there.

The Waters of Meribah

2Now there was no water for the congregation. And they assembled themselves together against Moses and against Aaron. 3And the people quarreled with Moses and said, "Would that we had perished when our brothers perished before the LORD! 4Why have you brought the assembly of the LORD into this wilderness, that we should die here, both we and our cattle? 5And why have you made us come up out of Egypt to bring us to this evil place? It is no place for grain or figs or vines or pomegranates, and there is no water to drink." 6Then Moses and Aaron went from the presence of the assembly to the entrance of the tent of meeting and fell on their faces. And the glory of the LORD appeared to them, 7and the LORD spoke to Moses, saying, 8"Take the staff, and assemble the congregation, you and Aaron your brother, and tell the rock before their eyes to yield its water. So you shall bring water out of the rock for them and give drink to the congregation and their cattle." 9And Moses took the staff from before the LORD, as he commanded him.

[1]Hebrew *living*

NUMBERS 20:1–13

BANISHED FROM THE PROMISED LAND

The sin of ingratitude raised its ugly head again, as it did when the Israelite people first left Egypt forty years earlier (Ex 17). The same issue, a lack of water, provoked the people to blame God and their leaders. God was not angry with the hostile people; instead, he lovingly desired to provide the nurture they needed. In contrast to God's kindness, Moses responded in unrighteous anger and disobeyed by striking the rock (as God had instructed him to in Ex 17) and losing the opportunity to enter into the promised land.

Similarly, Adam and Eve in the garden had a lapse of judgment and ate from the tree of the knowledge of good and evil. This deliberate disobedience caused their ejection from the Garden of Eden. Their sin demanded that someone come and remedy the sinful state in which mankind was entrenched.

God's providence and grace are evident in the gushing of the rock to provide for the people and the livestock in spite of Moses' actions. God demonstrated his benevolent nature to supply the needs of his people. This grace is manifested richly to all mankind, even while they were (and are) still sinners (Ro 5:8), through the death of Christ on the cross.

Moses Strikes the Rock

10Then Moses and Aaron gathered the assembly together before the rock, and he said to them, "Hear now, you rebels: shall we bring water for you out of this rock?" 11And Moses lifted up his hand and struck the rock with his staff twice, and water came out abundantly, and the congregation drank, and their livestock. 12And the LORD said to Moses and Aaron, "Because you did not believe in me, to uphold me as holy in the eyes of the people of Israel, therefore you shall not bring this assembly into the land that I have given them." 13These are the waters of Meribah,[1] where the people of Israel quarreled with the LORD, and through them he showed himself holy.

Edom Refuses Passage

14Moses sent messengers from Kadesh to the king of Edom: "Thus says your brother Israel: You know all the hardship that we have met: 15how our fathers went down to Egypt, and we lived in Egypt a long time. And the Egyptians dealt harshly with us and our fathers. 16And when we cried to the LORD, he heard our voice and sent an angel and brought us out of Egypt. And here we are in Kadesh, a city on the edge of your territory. 17Please let us pass through your land. We will not pass through field or vineyard, or drink water from a well. We will go along the King's Highway. We will not turn aside to the right hand or to the left until we have passed through your territory." 18But Edom said to him, "You shall not pass through, lest I come out with the sword against you." 19And the people of Israel said to him, "We will go up by the highway, and if we drink of your water, I and my livestock, then I will pay for it. Let me only pass through on foot, nothing more." 20But he said, "You shall not pass through." And Edom came out against them with a large army and with a strong force. 21Thus Edom refused to give Israel passage through his territory, so Israel turned away from him.

The Death of Aaron

22And they journeyed from Kadesh, and the people of Israel, the whole congregation, came to Mount Hor. 23And the LORD said to Moses and Aaron at Mount Hor, on the border of the land of Edom, 24"Let Aaron be gathered to his people, for he shall not enter the land that I have given to the people of Israel, because you rebelled against my command at the waters of Meribah. 25Take Aaron and Eleazar his son and bring them up to Mount Hor. 26And strip Aaron of his garments and put them on Eleazar his son. And Aaron shall be gathered to his people and shall die there." 27Moses did as the LORD commanded. And they went up Mount Hor in the sight of all the congregation. 28And Moses stripped Aaron of his garments and put them on Eleazar his son. And Aaron died there on the top of the mountain. Then Moses and Eleazar came down from the mountain. 29And when all the congregation saw that Aaron had perished, all the house of Israel wept for Aaron thirty days.

Arad Destroyed

21 When the Canaanite, the king of Arad, who lived in the Negeb, heard that Israel was coming by the way of Atharim, he fought against Israel, and took some of them captive. 2And Israel vowed a vow to the LORD and said, "If you will indeed give this people into my hand, then I will devote their cities to destruction."[2] 3And the LORD heeded the voice of Israel and gave over the Canaanites, and they devoted them and their cities to destruction. So the name of the place was called Hormah.[3]

The Bronze Serpent

4From Mount Hor they set out by the way to the Red Sea, to go around the land of Edom. And the people became impatient on the way. 5And the people

---

[1] *Meribah* means *quarreling* [2] That is, set apart (devote) as an offering to the Lord (for destruction); also verse 3 [3] *Hormah* means *destruction*

JESUS IS THE LIVING WATER

God's patience and provision for his people is memorably demonstrated in the two passages where the Lord brought water out of a rock to refresh a thirsty nation (Ex 17; Nu 20). On these occasions, God chose to bless his murmuring and rebellious people rather than punish them. He nourished and satisfied them when they were least deserving of his gift. Through the story of redemption found throughout the Bible, this theme surfaces, culminating in the life and ministry of Jesus.

The psalms are full of allusions to God's blessing as water, even directly referencing God's miraculous provision in the wilderness (Ps 78:15; 105:41). In a frequently referenced passage, the psalmist compared passion for God to the desire of an exhausted wild animal for water (Ps 42:1 – 2). The psalmist also recognized that God's blessing is the only drink that will truly satisfy the needy soul (Ps 63:1 – 5).

By Jeremiah's time, the nation had walked away from God, and the exile was rapidly closing in. The impending destruction gave the weeping prophet an opportunity to issue an urgent call for repentance. The Lord wanted to be a fresh fountain of water for the Israelites (Jer 2:13). He desired to flood their souls with blessing, but they wanted to satisfy their own needs, a futile attempt that only resulted in a deeper emptiness than ever before (17:13).

Another prophet, Isaiah, frequently relied upon water imagery to focus the attention of the nation on a coming blessing of God which would bring hydration to their parched souls and desolate land (Isa 12:3; 41:17 – 18; 44:3; 58:11). In an impassioned plea, Isaiah called upon not merely the nation of Israel but everyone who thirsts to partake of the abundance of God's water supply (55:1 – 2).

Jesus' use of water imagery for God's blessing — a blessing that flows out from him — relied heavily upon the Old Testament echoes in the Pentateuch, psalms, and prophets. On two occasions in John's Gospel, Jesus called on people to drink the life-giving supply of blessing that only he can offer. His offer applied to the Samaritan woman who was distant from God (Jn 4:1 – 30) and to the dutifully religious crowd gathered at the Jewish temple (7:37 – 38). The blessing of God in the person of Christ is available free of charge to every thirsty soul who relinquishes their attempts at self-satisfaction and turns to Jesus for living water.

spoke against God and against Moses, "Why have you brought us up out of Egypt to die in the wilderness? For there is no food and no water, and we loathe this worthless food." 6Then the LORD sent fiery serpents among the people, and they bit the people, so that many people of Israel died. 7And the people came to Moses and said, "We have sinned, for we have spoken against the LORD and against you. Pray to the LORD, that he take away the serpents from us." So Moses prayed for the people. 8And the LORD said to Moses, "Make a fiery serpent and set it on a pole, and everyone who is bitten, when he sees it, shall live." 9So Moses made a bronze[1] serpent and set it on a pole. And if a serpent bit anyone, he would look at the bronze serpent and live.

NUMBERS 21:7–9

ALLEVIATION OF THE CURSE

The poisonous snakes (fiery serpents) represented God's judgment of the people for their proclivity to sin. The people cried out to Moses for help. God instructed Moses to craft a unique source of deliverance—an image of a snake placed on a pole and lifted up among the people. Those who looked at this symbol lived. Jesus used this image to instruct Nicodemus about the way he would provide true and lasting healing from the work of the enemy. Jesus said that those who look in faith upon his death on a cross will live (Jn 3:14–15). The Roman cross is a far more grotesque image than a snake, as heinous criminals and scoundrels died horrific deaths in plain view of everyone. Soon, Jesus said, his death on a cross would alleviate the curse brought about by the sin in the garden (Ge 3:15). Those who look to him in repentance and faith will live—in this life and in the age to come.

The Song of the Well

10And the people of Israel set out and camped in Oboth. 11And they set out from Oboth and camped at Iye-abarim, in the wilderness that is opposite Moab, toward the sunrise. 12From there they set out and camped in the Valley of Zered. 13From there they set out and camped on the other side of the Arnon, which is in the wilderness that extends from the border of the Amorites, for the Arnon is the border of Moab, between Moab and the Amorites. 14Therefore it is said in the Book of the Wars of the LORD,

"Waheb in Suphah, and the valleys of the Arnon,
15 and the slope of the valleys
that extends to the seat of Ar,
and leans to the border of Moab."

16And from there they continued to Beer;[2] that is the well of which the LORD said to Moses, "Gather the people together, so that I may give them water." 17Then Israel sang this song:

"Spring up, O well!—Sing to it!—
18 the well that the princes made,
that the nobles of the people dug,
with the scepter and with their staffs."

And from the wilderness they went on to Mattanah, 19and from Mattanah to Nahaliel, and from Nahaliel to Bamoth, 20and from Bamoth to the valley lying in the region of Moab by the top of Pisgah that looks down on the desert.[3]

King Sihon Defeated

21Then Israel sent messengers to Sihon king of the Amorites, saying, 22"Let me pass through your land. We will not turn aside into field or vineyard. We will not drink the water of a well. We will go by the King's Highway until we have passed through your territory." 23But Sihon would not allow Israel to pass through his territory. He gathered all his people together and went out against Israel to the wilderness and came to Jahaz and fought against Israel. 24And Israel defeated him with the edge of the sword and took possession of his land from the Arnon to the Jabbok, as far as to the Ammonites, for the border of the Ammonites was strong. 25And Israel took all these cities, and Israel settled in all the cities of the Amorites, in Heshbon, and in all its villages. 26For Heshbon was the city of Sihon the king of the Amorites, who had fought against the former king of Moab and taken all his land out of his hand, as far as the Arnon. 27Therefore the ballad singers say,

"Come to Heshbon, let it be built;
let the city of Sihon be established.
28 For fire came out from Heshbon,
flame from the city of Sihon.

[1]Or *copper* [2]*Beer* means *well* [3]Or *Jeshimon*

DRAWING ALL PEOPLE

The people of Israel had a tendency to have short memories. When they were hungry or thirsty, they forgot that God had provided food and water in the past. When they learned of their strong enemies, they forgot that God had delivered them from Egypt with no need for an army (Nu 14:1–4). In Numbers 21, the people of Israel began to loathe the miraculous manna and started to complain once again about their food. In previous occurrences, God responded to complaints with miraculous provision (Ex 15:22–27; 16:1–17). However, on this occasion God responded with a miraculous judgment — venomous snakes. This judgment remained even after the people of Israel realized their sin. Rather than removing the venomous snakes, God commanded Moses to fashion a bronze snake. Moses then placed that snake on a pole, and all Israel gathered before the snake to receive healing. Though Israel had a tendency to forget God's provision, the people did not soon forget how they were healed from the snakes.

Sometimes people need examples to remind them that God is faithful. Israel was not unique in this tendency to forget God's past actions and seek comfort elsewhere. Just as Israel's sin in Numbers 21 had consequences, everyone's sin has consequences, and the result is death and separation from God. These consequences do not disappear when people realize their sin, just as God did not simply remove the snakes when Israel repented. However, Jesus stated that he too would be lifted up as Moses lifted up the bronze snake (Jn 3:14–15; 12:32–33). Jesus intercedes on behalf of his people, and he made the payment for their sin on the cross. In order for people to be healed from the sting of sin and death, they must first draw near and look on Jesus in faith, just as the people of Israel drew near and looked upon the snake to be healed.

When life is difficult, people need reminders that God is active and righting the world of the effects of sin. Jesus is that reminder. He has already healed his people from the sting of sin, just as the bronze snake healed the people of Israel from the bites of snakes.

It devoured Ar of Moab,
  and swallowed[1] the heights of the Arnon.
29 Woe to you, O Moab!
  You are undone, O people of Chemosh!
He has made his sons fugitives,
  and his daughters captives,
  to an Amorite king, Sihon.
30 So we overthrew them;
  Heshbon, as far as Dibon, perished;
  and we laid waste as far as Nophah;
  fire spread as far as Medeba."[2]

King Og Defeated

[31]Thus Israel lived in the land of the Amorites. [32]And Moses sent to spy out
Jazer, and they captured its villages and dispossessed the Amorites who were
there. [33]Then they turned and went up by the way to Bashan. And Og the king of
Bashan came out against them, he and all his people, to battle at Edrei. [34]But the
LORD said to Moses, "Do not fear him, for I have given him into your hand, and all
his people, and his land. And you shall do to him as you did to Sihon king of the
Amorites, who lived at Heshbon." [35]So they defeated him and his sons and all his
people, until he had no survivor left. And they possessed his land.

Balak Summons Balaam

22 Then the people of Israel set out and camped in the plains of Moab beyond
the Jordan at Jericho. [2]And Balak the son of Zippor saw all that Israel had
done to the Amorites. [3]And Moab was in great dread of the people, because they
were many. Moab was overcome with fear of the people of Israel. [4]And Moab said
to the elders of Midian, "This horde will now lick up all that is around us, as the ox
licks up the grass of the field." So Balak the son of Zippor, who was king of Moab
at that time, [5]sent messengers to Balaam the son of Beor at Pethor, which is near
the River[3] in the land of the people of Amaw,[4] to call him, saying, "Behold, a people has come out of Egypt. They cover the face of the earth, and they are dwelling
opposite me. [6]Come now, curse this people for me, since they are too mighty for
me. Perhaps I shall be able to defeat them and drive them from the land, for I
know that he whom you bless is blessed, and he whom you curse is cursed."

[7]So the elders of Moab and the elders of Midian departed with the fees for
divination in their hand. And they came to Balaam and gave him Balak's message.
[8]And he said to them, "Lodge here tonight, and I will bring back word to you, as
the LORD speaks to me." So the princes of Moab stayed with Balaam. [9]And God
came to Balaam and said, "Who are these men with you?" [10]And Balaam said to
God, "Balak the son of Zippor, king of Moab, has sent to me, saying, [11]'Behold, a
people has come out of Egypt, and it covers the face of the earth. Now come, curse
them for me. Perhaps I shall be able to fight against them and drive them out.'"
[12]God said to Balaam, "You shall not go with them. You shall not curse the people,
for they are blessed." [13]So Balaam rose in the morning and said to the princes of
Balak, "Go to your own land, for the LORD has refused to let me go with you." [14]So
the princes of Moab rose and went to Balak and said, "Balaam refuses to come
with us."

[15]Once again Balak sent princes, more in number and more honorable than
these. [16]And they came to Balaam and said to him, "Thus says Balak the son of
Zippor: 'Let nothing hinder you from coming to me, [17]for I will surely do you great
honor, and whatever you say to me I will do. Come, curse this people for me.'"
[18]But Balaam answered and said to the servants of Balak, "Though Balak were to

[1]Septuagint; Hebrew *the lords of* [2]Compare Samaritan and Septuagint; Hebrew *and we laid waste as far as Nophah, which is as far as Medeba* [3]That is, the Euphrates [4]Or *the people of his kindred*

NUMBERS 22:1–35

LYING PROPHETS

God used key figures throughout the Old Testament to declare his word to the nation of Israel. Since these individuals spoke on behalf of God himself, it was vital that they rightly represent his message. Lying came with a stark consequence and evoked the divine displeasure of God. He uses any instrument, even a talking donkey, to arrest those who lead God's people astray. This prophetic role was embodied by Jesus during his early ministry. The words he spoke were given to him by the Father and served as a clarion call to his disciples, those whom the Father had called out of the world (Jn 8:28; 12:49; 17:13–18). Because Jesus is God's Son, he can be trusted to only and always speak what is true. These words serve as both a foundation for obedience by God's people and a wall of protection from the assaults of the evil one.

give me his house full of silver and gold, I could not go beyond the command of the LORD my God to do less or more. 19So you, too, please stay here tonight, that I may know what more the LORD will say to me." 20And God came to Balaam at night and said to him, "If the men have come to call you, rise, go with them; but only do what I tell you." 21So Balaam rose in the morning and saddled his donkey and went with the princes of Moab.

Balaam's Donkey and the Angel

22But God's anger was kindled because he went, and the angel of the LORD took his stand in the way as his adversary. Now he was riding on the donkey, and his two servants were with him. 23And the donkey saw the angel of the LORD standing in the road, with a drawn sword in his hand. And the donkey turned aside out of the road and went into the field. And Balaam struck the donkey, to turn her into the road. 24Then the angel of the LORD stood in a narrow path between the vineyards, with a wall on either side. 25And when the donkey saw the angel of the LORD, she pushed against the wall and pressed Balaam's foot against the wall. So he struck her again. 26Then the angel of the LORD went ahead and stood in a narrow place, where there was no way to turn either to the right or to the left. 27When the donkey saw the angel of the LORD, she lay down under Balaam. And Balaam's anger was kindled, and he struck the donkey with his staff. 28Then the LORD opened the mouth of the donkey, and she said to Balaam, "What have I done to you, that you have struck me these three times?" 29And Balaam said to the donkey, "Because you have made a fool of me. I wish I had a sword in my hand, for then I would kill you." 30And the donkey said to Balaam, "Am I not your donkey, on which you have ridden all your life long to this day? Is it my habit to treat you this way?" And he said, "No."

31Then the LORD opened the eyes of Balaam, and he saw the angel of the LORD standing in the way, with his drawn sword in his hand. And he bowed down and fell on his face. 32And the angel of the LORD said to him, "Why have you struck your donkey these three times? Behold, I have come out to oppose you because your way is perverse[1] before me. 33The donkey saw me and turned aside before me these three times. If she had not turned aside from me, surely just now I would have killed you and let her live." 34Then Balaam said to the angel of the LORD, "I have sinned, for I did not know that you stood in the road against me. Now therefore, if it is evil in your sight, I will turn back." 35And the angel of the LORD said to Balaam, "Go with the men, but speak only the word that I tell you." So Balaam went on with the princes of Balak.

36When Balak heard that Balaam had come, he went out to meet him at the city of Moab, on the border formed by the Arnon, at the extremity of the border. 37And Balak said to Balaam, "Did I not send to you to call you? Why did you not come to me? Am I not able to honor you?" 38Balaam said to Balak, "Behold, I have come to you! Have I now any power of my own to speak anything? The word that God puts in my mouth, that must I speak." 39Then Balaam went with Balak, and they came to Kiriath-huzoth. 40And Balak sacrificed oxen and sheep, and sent for Balaam and for the princes who were with him.

41And in the morning Balak took Balaam and brought him up to Bamoth-baal, and from there he saw a fraction of the people.

Balaam's First Oracle

23 And Balaam said to Balak, "Build for me here seven altars, and prepare for me here seven bulls and seven rams." 2Balak did as Balaam had said. And Balak and Balaam offered on each altar a bull and a ram. 3And Balaam said to Balak, "Stand beside your burnt offering, and I will go. Perhaps the LORD will come to meet me, and whatever he shows me I will tell you." And he went to a bare

[1]Or *reckless*

height, 4and God met Balaam. And Balaam said to him, "I have arranged the seven
altars and I have offered on each altar a bull and a ram." 5And the LORD put a word
in Balaam's mouth and said, "Return to Balak, and thus you shall speak." 6And he
returned to him, and behold, he and all the princes of Moab were standing beside
his burnt offering. 7And Balaam took up his discourse and said,

"From Aram Balak has brought me,
the king of Moab from the eastern mountains:
'Come, curse Jacob for me,
and come, denounce Israel!'
8 How can I curse whom God has not cursed?
How can I denounce whom the LORD has not denounced?
9 For from the top of the crags I see him,
from the hills I behold him;
behold, a people dwelling alone,
and not counting itself among the nations!
10 Who can count the dust of Jacob
or number the fourth part[1] of Israel?
Let me die the death of the upright,
and let my end be like his!"

11And Balak said to Balaam, "What have you done to me? I took you to curse
my enemies, and behold, you have done nothing but bless them." 12And he answered and said, "Must I not take care to speak what the LORD puts in my mouth?"

Balaam's Second Oracle

13And Balak said to him, "Please come with me to another place, from which
you may see them. You shall see only a fraction of them and shall not see them
all. Then curse them for me from there." 14And he took him to the field of Zophim,
to the top of Pisgah, and built seven altars and offered a bull and a ram on each
altar. 15Balaam said to Balak, "Stand here beside your burnt offering, while I meet
the LORD over there." 16And the LORD met Balaam and put a word in his mouth
and said, "Return to Balak, and thus shall you speak." 17And he came to him, and
behold, he was standing beside his burnt offering, and the princes of Moab with
him. And Balak said to him, "What has the LORD spoken?" 18And Balaam took up
his discourse and said,

"Rise, Balak, and hear;
give ear to me, O son of Zippor:
19 God is not man, that he should lie,
or a son of man, that he should change his mind.
Has he said, and will he not do it?
Or has he spoken, and will he not fulfill it?
20 Behold, I received a command to bless:
he has blessed, and I cannot revoke it.
21 He has not beheld misfortune in Jacob,
nor has he seen trouble in Israel.
The LORD their God is with them,
and the shout of a king is among them.
22 God brings them out of Egypt
and is for them like the horns of the wild ox.
23 For there is no enchantment against Jacob,
no divination against Israel;
now it shall be said of Jacob and Israel,
'What has God wrought!'

[1] Or *dust clouds*

24 Behold, a people! As a lioness it rises up
and as a lion it lifts itself;
it does not lie down until it has devoured the prey
and drunk the blood of the slain."

25 And Balak said to Balaam, "Do not curse them at all, and do not bless them at
all." 26 But Balaam answered Balak, "Did I not tell you, 'All that the LORD says, that
I must do'?" 27 And Balak said to Balaam, "Come now, I will take you to another
place. Perhaps it will please God that you may curse them for me from there." 28 So
Balak took Balaam to the top of Peor, which overlooks the desert.[1] 29 And Balaam
said to Balak, "Build for me here seven altars and prepare for me here seven bulls
and seven rams." 30 And Balak did as Balaam had said, and offered a bull and a
ram on each altar.

Balaam's Third Oracle

24 When Balaam saw that it pleased the LORD to bless Israel, he did not go, as
at other times, to look for omens, but set his face toward the wilderness.
2 And Balaam lifted up his eyes and saw Israel camping tribe by tribe. And the
Spirit of God came upon him, 3 and he took up his discourse and said,

"The oracle of Balaam the son of Beor,
the oracle of the man whose eye is opened,[2]
4 the oracle of him who hears the words of God,
who sees the vision of the Almighty,
falling down with his eyes uncovered:
5 How lovely are your tents, O Jacob,
your encampments, O Israel!
6 Like palm groves[3] that stretch afar,
like gardens beside a river,
like aloes that the LORD has planted,
like cedar trees beside the waters.
7 Water shall flow from his buckets,
and his seed shall be in many waters;
his king shall be higher than Agag,
and his kingdom shall be exalted.
8 God brings him out of Egypt
and is for him like the horns of the wild ox;
he shall eat up the nations, his adversaries,
and shall break their bones in pieces
and pierce them through with his arrows.
9 He crouched, he lay down like a lion
and like a lioness; who will rouse him up?
Blessed are those who bless you,
and cursed are those who curse you."

10 And Balak's anger was kindled against Balaam, and he struck his hands together. And Balak said to Balaam, "I called you to curse my enemies, and behold,
you have blessed them these three times. 11 Therefore now flee to your own place.
I said, 'I will certainly honor you,' but the LORD has held you back from honor."
12 And Balaam said to Balak, "Did I not tell your messengers whom you sent to me,
13 'If Balak should give me his house full of silver and gold, I would not be able to
go beyond the word of the LORD, to do either good or bad of my own will. What
the LORD speaks, that will I speak'? 14 And now, behold, I am going to my people.
Come, I will let you know what this people will do to your people in the latter
days."

---

[1] Or *Jeshimon* [2] Or *closed*, or *perfect*; also verse 15 [3] Or *valleys*

Balaam's Final Oracle

15 And he took up his discourse and said,

"The oracle of Balaam the son of Beor,
the oracle of the man whose eye is opened,
16 the oracle of him who hears the words of God,
and knows the knowledge of the Most High,
who sees the vision of the Almighty,
falling down with his eyes uncovered:
17 I see him, but not now;
I behold him, but not near:
a star shall come out of Jacob,
and a scepter shall rise out of Israel;
it shall crush the forehead[1] of Moab
and break down all the sons of Sheth.
18 Edom shall be dispossessed;
Seir also, his enemies, shall be dispossessed.
Israel is doing valiantly.
19 And one from Jacob shall exercise dominion
and destroy the survivors of cities!"

20 Then he looked on Amalek and took up his discourse and said,

"Amalek was the first among the nations,
but its end is utter destruction."

21 And he looked on the Kenite, and took up his discourse and said,

"Enduring is your dwelling place,
and your nest is set in the rock.
22 Nevertheless, Kain shall be burned
when Asshur takes you away captive."

23 And he took up his discourse and said,

"Alas, who shall live when God does this?
24 But ships shall come from Kittim
and shall afflict Asshur and Eber;
and he too shall come to utter destruction."

25 Then Balaam rose and went back to his place. And Balak also went his way.

Baal Worship at Peor

25 While Israel lived in Shittim, the people began to whore with the daughters of Moab. 2 These invited the people to the sacrifices of their gods, and the people ate and bowed down to their gods. 3 So Israel yoked himself to Baal of Peor. And the anger of the LORD was kindled against Israel. 4 And the LORD said to Moses, "Take all the chiefs of the people and hang[2] them in the sun before the LORD, that the fierce anger of the LORD may turn away from Israel." 5 And Moses said to the judges of Israel, "Each of you kill those of his men who have yoked themselves to Baal of Peor."

6 And behold, one of the people of Israel came and brought a Midianite woman to his family, in the sight of Moses and in the sight of the whole congregation of the people of Israel, while they were weeping in the entrance of the tent of meeting. 7 When Phinehas the son of Eleazar, son of Aaron the priest, saw it, he rose and left the congregation and took a spear in his hand 8 and went after the man of Israel into the chamber and pierced both of them, the man of Israel and the woman through her belly. Thus the plague on the people of Israel was stopped. 9 Nevertheless, those who died by the plague were twenty-four thousand.

[1] Hebrew *corners* [of the head] [2] Or *impale*

A STAR AND A SCEPTER

This is the fourth message proclaimed by the pagan prophet Balaam. God's use of Balaam, a non-Jewish outsider, proves that God's ways and thoughts are truly above human intentions (Isa 55:8). God used a prophet who was on the payroll of an enemy nation, which was the antithesis of what would have been expected. However, God utilizes whatever and whomever he desires to reveal himself and his plan to his people.

Balaam's poetic prophecy offered a ray of hope to the reader, reminding them of a coming Messiah. The coming of the Messiah had been anticipated since the revolt of Adam (Ge 3:15) and promised through the line of Abraham (22:18). Additionally, Jacob prophesied that his son, Judah, would be heir to the royal lineage of the nation through his offspring (49:10).

Balaam pictured the Messiah-king using imagery of a "star" and a "scepter" (Nu 24:17). The Messiah would be like a star, bright and radiant. Upon the birth of the Messiah, Jesus, there was a star marking the place of his birth (Mt 2:1 – 10). In the book of Revelation, Jesus refers to himself as "the root and the descendant of David, the bright morning star" (Rev 22:16).

The scepter evokes thoughts of royalty. A king would normally hold a scepter as a symbol of his power. The king's responsibility was not solely to rule over his people but also to care for them. Subsequently, the Messiah came not merely to usher in a new kingdom but also to take care of and shepherd the people of that kingdom. This is what sets apart the Messiah-king from the kings of the day.

Balaam's prophecy concluded with the future Messiah bringing victory over the enemies of God (Nu 24:17 – 19). Moab, the nation that hired Balaam, was proclaimed as the one who would be destroyed and become a possession of Israel. Edom denied Israel safe passage (20:14 – 21) and ultimately caused their own destruction. The Messiah, who came from the line of Jacob, will call every created thing to do what they were created to do — worship the God of creation through the power of the Spirit. The Messiah will bid all people to come and worship him (Php 2:10 – 11).

The Zeal of Phinehas

[10]And the LORD said to Moses, [11]"Phinehas the son of Eleazar, son of Aaron the priest, has turned back my wrath from the people of Israel, in that he was jealous with my jealousy among them, so that I did not consume the people of Israel in my jealousy. [12]Therefore say, 'Behold, I give to him my covenant of peace, [13]and it shall be to him and to his descendants after him the covenant of a perpetual priesthood, because he was jealous for his God and made atonement for the people of Israel.'"

[14]The name of the slain man of Israel, who was killed with the Midianite woman, was Zimri the son of Salu, chief of a father's house belonging to the Simeonites. [15]And the name of the Midianite woman who was killed was Cozbi the daughter of Zur, who was the tribal head of a father's house in Midian.

[16]And the LORD spoke to Moses, saying, [17]"Harass the Midianites and strike them down, [18]for they have harassed you with their wiles, with which they beguiled you in the matter of Peor, and in the matter of Cozbi, the daughter of the chief of Midian, their sister, who was killed on the day of the plague on account of Peor."

Census of the New Generation

26 After the plague, the LORD said to Moses and to Eleazar the son of Aaron, the priest, [2]"Take a census of all the congregation of the people of Israel, from twenty years old and upward, by their fathers' houses, all in Israel who are able to go to war." [3]And Moses and Eleazar the priest spoke with them in the plains of Moab by the Jordan at Jericho, saying, [4]"Take a census of the people,[1] from twenty years old and upward," as the LORD commanded Moses. The people of Israel who came out of the land of Egypt were:

[5]Reuben, the firstborn of Israel; the sons of Reuben: of Hanoch, the clan of the Hanochites; of Pallu, the clan of the Palluites; [6]of Hezron, the clan of the Hezronites; of Carmi, the clan of the Carmites. [7]These are the clans of the Reubenites, and those listed were 43,730. [8]And the sons of Pallu: Eliab. [9]The sons of Eliab: Nemuel, Dathan, and Abiram. These are the Dathan and Abiram, chosen from the congregation, who contended against Moses and Aaron in the company of Korah, when they contended against the LORD [10]and the earth opened its mouth and swallowed them up together with Korah, when that company died, when the fire devoured 250 men, and they became a warning. [11]But the sons of Korah did not die.

[12]The sons of Simeon according to their clans: of Nemuel, the clan of the Nemuelites; of Jamin, the clan of the Jaminites; of Jachin, the clan of the Jachinites; [13]of Zerah, the clan of the Zerahites; of Shaul, the clan of the Shaulites. [14]These are the clans of the Simeonites, 22,200.

[15]The sons of Gad according to their clans: of Zephon, the clan of the Zephonites; of Haggi, the clan of the Haggites; of Shuni, the clan of the Shunites; [16]of Ozni, the clan of the Oznites; of Eri, the clan of the Erites; [17]of Arod, the clan of the Arodites; of Areli, the clan of the Arelites. [18]These are the clans of the sons of Gad as they were listed, 40,500.

[19]The sons of Judah were Er and Onan; and Er and Onan died in the land of Canaan. [20]And the sons of Judah according to their clans were: of Shelah, the clan of the Shelanites; of Perez, the clan of the Perezites; of Zerah, the clan of the Zerahites. [21]And the sons of Perez were: of Hezron, the clan of the Hezronites; of Hamul, the clan of the Hamulites. [22]These are the clans of Judah as they were listed, 76,500.

[23]The sons of Issachar according to their clans: of Tola, the clan of the Tolaites; of Puvah, the clan of the Punites; [24]of Jashub, the clan of the Jashubites; of Shimron, the clan of the Shimronites. [25]These are the clans of Issachar as they were listed, 64,300.

---

[1]*Take a census of the people* is implied (compare verse 2)

26The sons of Zebulun, according to their clans: of Sered, the clan of the Seredites; of Elon, the clan of the Elonites; of Jahleel, the clan of the Jahleelites. 27These are the clans of the Zebulunites as they were listed, 60,500.

28The sons of Joseph according to their clans: Manasseh and Ephraim. 29The sons of Manasseh: of Machir, the clan of the Machirites; and Machir was the father of Gilead; of Gilead, the clan of the Gileadites. 30These are the sons of Gilead: of Iezer, the clan of the Iezerites; of Helek, the clan of the Helekites; 31and of Asriel, the clan of the Asrielites; and of Shechem, the clan of the Shechemites; 32and of Shemida, the clan of the Shemidaites; and of Hepher, the clan of the Hepherites. 33Now Zelophehad the son of Hepher had no sons, but daughters. And the names of the daughters of Zelophehad were Mahlah, Noah, Hoglah, Milcah, and Tirzah. 34These are the clans of Manasseh, and those listed were 52,700.

35These are the sons of Ephraim according to their clans: of Shuthelah, the clan of the Shuthelahites; of Becher, the clan of the Becherites; of Tahan, the clan of the Tahanites. 36And these are the sons of Shuthelah: of Eran, the clan of the Eranites. 37These are the clans of the sons of Ephraim as they were listed, 32,500. These are the sons of Joseph according to their clans.

38The sons of Benjamin according to their clans: of Bela, the clan of the Belaites; of Ashbel, the clan of the Ashbelites; of Ahiram, the clan of the Ahiramites; 39of Shephupham, the clan of the Shuphamites; of Hupham, the clan of the Huphamites. 40And the sons of Bela were Ard and Naaman: of Ard, the clan of the Ardites; of Naaman, the clan of the Naamites. 41These are the sons of Benjamin according to their clans, and those listed were 45,600.

42These are the sons of Dan according to their clans: of Shuham, the clan of the Shuhamites. These are the clans of Dan according to their clans. 43All the clans of the Shuhamites, as they were listed, were 64,400.

44The sons of Asher according to their clans: of Imnah, the clan of the Imnites; of Ishvi, the clan of the Ishvites; of Beriah, the clan of the Beriites. 45Of the sons of Beriah: of Heber, the clan of the Heberites; of Malchiel, the clan of the Malchielites. 46And the name of the daughter of Asher was Serah. 47These are the clans of the sons of Asher as they were listed, 53,400.

48The sons of Naphtali according to their clans: of Jahzeel, the clan of the Jahzeelites; of Guni, the clan of the Gunites; 49of Jezer, the clan of the Jezerites; of Shillem, the clan of the Shillemites. 50These are the clans of Naphtali according to their clans, and those listed were 45,400.

51This was the list of the people of Israel, 601,730.

52The LORD spoke to Moses, saying, 53"Among these the land shall be divided for inheritance according to the number of names. 54To a large tribe you shall give a large inheritance, and to a small tribe you shall give a small inheritance; every tribe shall be given its inheritance in proportion to its list. 55But the land shall be divided by lot. According to the names of the tribes of their fathers they shall inherit. 56Their inheritance shall be divided according to lot between the larger and the smaller."

57This was the list of the Levites according to their clans: of Gershon, the clan of the Gershonites; of Kohath, the clan of the Kohathites; of Merari, the clan of the Merarites. 58These are the clans of Levi: the clan of the Libnites, the clan of the Hebronites, the clan of the Mahlites, the clan of the Mushites, the clan of the Korahites. And Kohath was the father of Amram. 59The name of Amram's wife was Jochebed the daughter of Levi, who was born to Levi in Egypt. And she bore to Amram Aaron and Moses and Miriam their sister. 60And to Aaron were born Nadab, Abihu, Eleazar, and Ithamar. 61But Nadab and Abihu died when they offered unauthorized fire before the LORD. 62And those listed were 23,000, every male from a month old and upward. For they were not listed among the people of Israel, because there was no inheritance given to them among the people of Israel.

63These were those listed by Moses and Eleazar the priest, who listed the

NUMBERS 26:53

A NEW LAND

Central to the promises of God was the gift of land. Reminiscent of the Garden of Eden, the people were promised that they would dwell with God in a good land overflowing with the provision of the Lord. The Israelites were not merely inhabitants in this land; they were each given a portion of the land as a bountiful inheritance. They were reminded that God was not merely a God of the nation but a personal God who cared for each of them individually. Jesus demonstrated the same personal care when he promised an inheritance in heaven to all of his children (Jn 14:1–4). He is now preparing this dwelling place for each of those who have trusted in him by faith and repentance. There they will receive the inheritance of those who are in Christ Jesus as they rule and reign forever with him in a new land, the new heaven and new earth (2Pe 3:13; Rev 21:1).

people of Israel in the plains of Moab by the Jordan at Jericho. 64But among these there was not one of those listed by Moses and Aaron the priest, who had listed the people of Israel in the wilderness of Sinai. 65For the LORD had said of them, "They shall die in the wilderness." Not one of them was left, except Caleb the son of Jephunneh and Joshua the son of Nun.

The Daughters of Zelophehad

27 Then drew near the daughters of Zelophehad the son of Hepher, son of Gilead, son of Machir, son of Manasseh, from the clans of Manasseh the son of Joseph. The names of his daughters were: Mahlah, Noah, Hoglah, Milcah, and Tirzah. 2And they stood before Moses and before Eleazar the priest and before the chiefs and all the congregation, at the entrance of the tent of meeting, saying, 3"Our father died in the wilderness. He was not among the company of those who gathered themselves together against the LORD in the company of Korah, but died for his own sin. And he had no sons. 4Why should the name of our father be taken away from his clan because he had no son? Give to us a possession among our father's brothers."

5Moses brought their case before the LORD. 6And the LORD said to Moses, 7"The daughters of Zelophehad are right. You shall give them possession of an inheritance among their father's brothers and transfer the inheritance of their father to them. 8And you shall speak to the people of Israel, saying, 'If a man dies and has no son, then you shall transfer his inheritance to his daughter. 9And if he has no daughter, then you shall give his inheritance to his brothers. 10And if he has no brothers, then you shall give his inheritance to his father's brothers. 11And if his father has no brothers, then you shall give his inheritance to the nearest kinsman of his clan, and he shall possess it. And it shall be for the people of Israel a statute and rule, as the LORD commanded Moses.'"

Joshua to Succeed Moses

12The LORD said to Moses, "Go up into this mountain of Abarim and see the land that I have given to the people of Israel. 13When you have seen it, you also shall be gathered to your people, as your brother Aaron was, 14because you rebelled against my word in the wilderness of Zin when the congregation quarreled, failing to uphold me as holy at the waters before their eyes." (These are the waters of Meribah of Kadesh in the wilderness of Zin.) 15Moses spoke to the LORD, saying, 16"Let the LORD, the God of the spirits of all flesh, appoint a man over the congregation 17who shall go out before them and come in before them, who shall lead them out and bring them in, that the congregation of the LORD may not be as sheep that have no shepherd." 18So the LORD said to Moses, "Take Joshua the son of Nun, a man in whom is the Spirit, and lay your hand on him. 19Make him stand before Eleazar the priest and all the congregation, and you shall commission him in their sight. 20You shall invest him with some of your authority, that all the congregation of the people of Israel may obey. 21And he shall stand before Eleazar the priest, who shall inquire for him by the judgment of the Urim before the LORD. At his word they shall go out, and at his word they shall come in, both he and all the people of Israel with him, the whole congregation." 22And Moses did as the LORD commanded him. He took Joshua and made him stand before Eleazar the priest and the whole congregation, 23and he laid his hands on him and commissioned him as the LORD directed through Moses.

Daily Offerings

28 The LORD spoke to Moses, saying, 2"Command the people of Israel and say to them, 'My offering, my food for my food offerings, my pleasing aroma, you shall be careful to offer to me at its appointed time.' 3And you shall say to them, This is the food offering that you shall offer to the LORD: two male lambs a year old without blemish, day by day, as a regular offering. 4The one lamb you

NUMBERS 27:15–17

SHEEP WITHOUT A SHEPHERD

Moses recognized that sinful people were doomed to destruction without a godly leader. The people of God are pictured here as wayward and helpless sheep without the care of a benevolent shepherd. Knowing of his impending death, Moses interceded on behalf of the people and asked God to provide a shepherd who could lead the people into God's promised land. God anointed Joshua for this role; however, like all subsequent leaders, he proved inadequate to fully provide the leadership and care that the people required.

Israel needed more than any sinful human leader could provide. This need prompted Jesus, like Moses, to lament over the condition of God's flock (Mk 6:34). He knew that they needed a Good Shepherd who would not only lead them to safety but also ultimately lay down his life for the sheep he so dearly loved (Jn 10:1–18). Jesus provided the type of care Moses longed for in this passage—a kind of leadership that is impossible for a fallen person to provide. Only the Son of God could be the Good Shepherd the people so desperately needed.

NUMBERS 28:1–8

ONGOING DAILY OFFERINGS

God commanded his people to carefully make the proper offerings for sin—offerings that took place every day. The frequency of these sacrifices filled the wilderness with the blood of slaughtered animals,

(continued on next page)

shall offer in the morning, and the other lamb you shall offer at twilight; 5also a tenth of an ephah[1] of fine flour for a grain offering, mixed with a quarter of a hin[2] of beaten oil. 6It is a regular burnt offering, which was ordained at Mount Sinai for a pleasing aroma, a food offering to the LORD. 7Its drink offering shall be a quarter of a hin for each lamb. In the Holy Place you shall pour out a drink offering of strong drink to the LORD. 8The other lamb you shall offer at twilight. Like the grain offering of the morning, and like its drink offering, you shall offer it as a food offering, with a pleasing aroma to the LORD.

Sabbath Offerings

9"On the Sabbath day, two male lambs a year old without blemish, and two tenths of an ephah of fine flour for a grain offering, mixed with oil, and its drink offering: 10this is the burnt offering of every Sabbath, besides the regular burnt offering and its drink offering.

Monthly Offerings

11"At the beginnings of your months, you shall offer a burnt offering to the LORD: two bulls from the herd, one ram, seven male lambs a year old without blemish; 12also three tenths of an ephah of fine flour for a grain offering, mixed with oil, for each bull, and two tenths of fine flour for a grain offering, mixed with oil, for the one ram; 13and a tenth of fine flour mixed with oil as a grain offering for every lamb; for a burnt offering with a pleasing aroma, a food offering to the LORD. 14Their drink offerings shall be half a hin of wine for a bull, a third of a hin for a ram, and a quarter of a hin for a lamb. This is the burnt offering of each month throughout the months of the year. 15Also one male goat for a sin offering to the LORD; it shall be offered besides the regular burnt offering and its drink offering.

Passover Offerings

16"On the fourteenth day of the first month is the LORD's Passover, 17and on the fifteenth day of this month is a feast. Seven days shall unleavened bread be eaten. 18On the first day there shall be a holy convocation. You shall not do any ordinary work, 19but offer a food offering, a burnt offering to the LORD: two bulls from the herd, one ram, and seven male lambs a year old; see that they are without blemish; 20also their grain offering of fine flour mixed with oil; three tenths of an ephah shall you offer for a bull, and two tenths for a ram; 21a tenth shall you offer for each of the seven lambs; 22also one male goat for a sin offering, to make atonement for you. 23You shall offer these besides the burnt offering of the morning, which is for a regular burnt offering. 24In the same way you shall offer daily, for seven days, the food of a food offering, with a pleasing aroma to the LORD. It shall be offered besides the regular burnt offering and its drink offering. 25And on the seventh day you shall have a holy convocation. You shall not do any ordinary work.

Offerings for the Feast of Weeks

26"On the day of the firstfruits, when you offer a grain offering of new grain to the LORD at your Feast of Weeks, you shall have a holy convocation. You shall not do any ordinary work, 27but offer a burnt offering, with a pleasing aroma to the LORD: two bulls from the herd, one ram, seven male lambs a year old; 28also their grain offering of fine flour mixed with oil, three tenths of an ephah for each bull, two tenths for one ram, 29a tenth for each of the seven lambs; 30with one male goat, to make atonement for you. 31Besides the regular burnt offering and its grain offering, you shall offer them and their drink offering. See that they are without blemish.

[1]An *ephah* was about 3/5 bushel or 22 liters [2]A *hin* was about 4 quarts or 3.5 liters

(Ongoing Daily Offerings, continued)

vividly reminding Israel that sin demanded a blood sacrifice. The sheer volume of people, combined with the heat of the wilderness, made this a stark reality for all to see. The people longed for the day when these seemingly unending sacrifices would cease and they could permanently and unalterably be made right with God.

Jesus, as the pure and spotless Lamb of God, did just that. The writer of Hebrews demonstrated that Jesus' sacrificial death fully and finally made atonement for the sins of his people. No longer are daily sacrifices necessary because believers "have been sanctified through the offering of the body of Jesus Christ once for all" (Heb 10:1–10).

NUMBERS 29:1–6

OFFERINGS OF JOY

The Old Testament sacrificial system was complex and costly. God provided instructions that required hundreds and hundreds of bulls, rams, lambs, and goats to be killed every year (not to mention the use of massive amounts of grain, oil, and wine). The altar of the tabernacle became messy and bloody—much like the hearts of God's people. But these instructions concerning worship were given to a people who were already in relationship with God—they are his people and he is their God. These sacrifices were never meant to be a means whereby people, by their own merit, could procure a relationship with God. They were meant to be offerings of joy, acts of worship, an outpouring of praise to the God who had already redeemed them. This is true for all of God's people throughout redemptive history. Sacrifices, whether of time, money, obedience, or praise, are not meant to make one right before God. Only Jesus can do that. His death redeemed a people, called them to himself and made them right with God. The response to that grace is seen in the sacrifices of praise offered by the people of God.

Offerings for the Feast of Trumpets

29 "On the first day of the seventh month you shall have a holy convocation. You shall not do any ordinary work. It is a day for you to blow the trumpets, [2]and you shall offer a burnt offering, for a pleasing aroma to the LORD: one bull from the herd, one ram, seven male lambs a year old without blemish; [3]also their grain offering of fine flour mixed with oil, three tenths of an ephah[1] for the bull, two tenths for the ram, [4]and one tenth for each of the seven lambs; [5]with one male goat for a sin offering, to make atonement for you; [6]besides the burnt offering of the new moon, and its grain offering, and the regular burnt offering and its grain offering, and their drink offering, according to the rule for them, for a pleasing aroma, a food offering to the LORD.

Offerings for the Day of Atonement

[7]"On the tenth day of this seventh month you shall have a holy convocation and afflict yourselves.[2] You shall do no work, [8]but you shall offer a burnt offering to the LORD, a pleasing aroma: one bull from the herd, one ram, seven male lambs a year old: see that they are without blemish. [9]And their grain offering shall be of fine flour mixed with oil, three tenths of an ephah for the bull, two tenths for the one ram, [10]a tenth for each of the seven lambs: [11]also one male goat for a sin offering, besides the sin offering of atonement, and the regular burnt offering and its grain offering, and their drink offerings.

Offerings for the Feast of Booths

[12]"On the fifteenth day of the seventh month you shall have a holy convocation. You shall not do any ordinary work, and you shall keep a feast to the LORD seven days. [13]And you shall offer a burnt offering, a food offering, with a pleasing aroma to the LORD, thirteen bulls from the herd, two rams, fourteen male lambs a year old; they shall be without blemish; [14]and their grain offering of fine flour mixed with oil, three tenths of an ephah for each of the thirteen bulls, two tenths for each of the two rams, [15]and a tenth for each of the fourteen lambs; [16]also one male goat for a sin offering, besides the regular burnt offering, its grain offering and its drink offering.

[17]"On the second day twelve bulls from the herd, two rams, fourteen male lambs a year old without blemish, [18]with the grain offering and the drink offerings for the bulls, for the rams, and for the lambs, in the prescribed quantities; [19]also one male goat for a sin offering, besides the regular burnt offering and its grain offering, and their drink offerings.

[20]"On the third day eleven bulls, two rams, fourteen male lambs a year old without blemish, [21]with the grain offering and the drink offerings for the bulls, for the rams, and for the lambs, in the prescribed quantities; [22]also one male goat for a sin offering, besides the regular burnt offering and its grain offering and its drink offering.

[23]"On the fourth day ten bulls, two rams, fourteen male lambs a year old without blemish, [24]with the grain offering and the drink offerings for the bulls, for the rams, and for the lambs, in the prescribed quantities; [25]also one male goat for a sin offering, besides the regular burnt offering, its grain offering and its drink offering.

[26]"On the fifth day nine bulls, two rams, fourteen male lambs a year old without blemish, [27]with the grain offering and the drink offerings for the bulls, for the rams, and for the lambs, in the prescribed quantities; [28]also one male goat for a sin offering; besides the regular burnt offering and its grain offering and its drink offering.

[29]"On the sixth day eight bulls, two rams, fourteen male lambs a year old without blemish, [30]with the grain offering and the drink offerings for the bulls, for

[1]An *ephah* was about 3/5 bushel or 22 liters [2]Or *and fast*

the rams, and for the lambs, in the prescribed quantities; 31also one male goat for
a sin offering; besides the regular burnt offering, its grain offering, and its drink
offerings.
32"On the seventh day seven bulls, two rams, fourteen male lambs a year old
without blemish, 33with the grain offering and the drink offerings for the bulls,
for the rams, and for the lambs, in the prescribed quantities; 34also one male goat
for a sin offering; besides the regular burnt offering, its grain offering, and its
drink offering.
35"On the eighth day you shall have a solemn assembly. You shall not do any
ordinary work, 36but you shall offer a burnt offering, a food offering, with a pleasing aroma to the LORD: one bull, one ram, seven male lambs a year old without
blemish, 37and the grain offering and the drink offerings for the bull, for the ram,
and for the lambs, in the prescribed quantities; 38also one male goat for a sin offering; besides the regular burnt offering and its grain offering and its drink offering.
39"These you shall offer to the LORD at your appointed feasts, in addition to
your vow offerings and your freewill offerings, for your burnt offerings, and for
your grain offerings, and for your drink offerings, and for your peace offerings."
40[1]So Moses told the people of Israel everything just as the LORD had commanded Moses.

Men and Vows

30 Moses spoke to the heads of the tribes of the people of Israel, saying, "This
is what the LORD has commanded. 2If a man vows a vow to the LORD, or
swears an oath to bind himself by a pledge, he shall not break his word. He shall
do according to all that proceeds out of his mouth.

Women and Vows

3"If a woman vows a vow to the LORD and binds herself by a pledge, while
within her father's house in her youth, 4and her father hears of her vow and of her
pledge by which she has bound herself and says nothing to her, then all her vows
shall stand, and every pledge by which she has bound herself shall stand. 5But if
her father opposes her on the day that he hears of it, no vow of hers, no pledge by
which she has bound herself shall stand. And the LORD will forgive her, because
her father opposed her.
6"If she marries a husband, while under her vows or any thoughtless utterance of her lips by which she has bound herself, 7and her husband hears of it and
says nothing to her on the day that he hears, then her vows shall stand, and her
pledges by which she has bound herself shall stand. 8But if, on the day that her
husband comes to hear of it, he opposes her, then he makes void her vow that
was on her, and the thoughtless utterance of her lips by which she bound herself.
And the LORD will forgive her. 9(But any vow of a widow or of a divorced woman,
anything by which she has bound herself, shall stand against her.) 10And if she
vowed in her husband's house or bound herself by a pledge with an oath, 11and
her husband heard of it and said nothing to her and did not oppose her, then all
her vows shall stand, and every pledge by which she bound herself shall stand.
12But if her husband makes them null and void on the day that he hears them,
then whatever proceeds out of her lips concerning her vows or concerning her
pledge of herself shall not stand. Her husband has made them void, and the LORD
will forgive her. 13Any vow and any binding oath to afflict herself,[2] her husband
may establish,[3] or her husband may make void. 14But if her husband says nothing
to her from day to day, then he establishes all her vows or all her pledges that are
upon her. He has established them, because he said nothing to her on the day that
he heard of them. 15But if he makes them null and void after he has heard of them,
then he shall bear her iniquity."

[1]Ch 30:1 in Hebrew [2]Or *to fast* [3]Or *may allow to stand*

16 These are the statutes that the LORD commanded Moses about a man and his wife and about a father and his daughter while she is in her youth within her father's house.

Vengeance on Midian

31 The LORD spoke to Moses, saying, 2 "Avenge the people of Israel on the Midianites. Afterward you shall be gathered to your people." 3 So Moses spoke to the people, saying, "Arm men from among you for the war, that they may go against Midian to execute the LORD's vengeance on Midian. 4 You shall send a thousand from each of the tribes of Israel to the war." 5 So there were provided, out of the thousands of Israel, a thousand from each tribe, twelve thousand armed for war. 6 And Moses sent them to the war, a thousand from each tribe, together with Phinehas the son of Eleazar the priest, with the vessels of the sanctuary and the trumpets for the alarm in his hand. 7 They warred against Midian, as the LORD commanded Moses, and killed every male. 8 They killed the kings of Midian with the rest of their slain, Evi, Rekem, Zur, Hur, and Reba, the five kings of Midian. And they also killed Balaam the son of Beor with the sword. 9 And the people of Israel took captive the women of Midian and their little ones, and they took as plunder all their cattle, their flocks, and all their goods. 10 All their cities in the places where they lived, and all their encampments, they burned with fire, 11 and took all the spoil and all the plunder, both of man and of beast. 12 Then they brought the captives and the plunder and the spoil to Moses, and to Eleazar the priest, and to the congregation of the people of Israel, at the camp on the plains of Moab by the Jordan at Jericho.

13 Moses and Eleazar the priest and all the chiefs of the congregation went to meet them outside the camp. 14 And Moses was angry with the officers of the army, the commanders of thousands and the commanders of hundreds, who had come from service in the war. 15 Moses said to them, "Have you let all the women live? 16 Behold, these, on Balaam's advice, caused the people of Israel to act treacherously against the LORD in the incident of Peor, and so the plague came among the congregation of the LORD. 17 Now therefore, kill every male among the little ones, and kill every woman who has known man by lying with him. 18 But all the young girls who have not known man by lying with him keep alive for yourselves. 19 Encamp outside the camp seven days. Whoever of you has killed any person and whoever has touched any slain, purify yourselves and your captives on the third day and on the seventh day. 20 You shall purify every garment, every article of skin, all work of goats' hair, and every article of wood."

21 Then Eleazar the priest said to the men in the army who had gone to battle: "This is the statute of the law that the LORD has commanded Moses: 22 only the gold, the silver, the bronze, the iron, the tin, and the lead, 23 everything that can stand the fire, you shall pass through the fire, and it shall be clean. Nevertheless, it shall also be purified with the water for impurity. And whatever cannot stand the fire, you shall pass through the water. 24 You must wash your clothes on the seventh day, and you shall be clean. And afterward you may come into the camp."

25 The LORD said to Moses, 26 "Take the count of the plunder that was taken, both of man and of beast, you and Eleazar the priest and the heads of the fathers' houses of the congregation, 27 and divide the plunder into two parts between the warriors who went out to battle and all the congregation. 28 And levy for the LORD a tribute from the men of war who went out to battle, one out of five hundred, of the people and of the oxen and of the donkeys and of the flocks. 29 Take it from their half and give it to Eleazar the priest as a contribution to the LORD. 30 And from the people of Israel's half you shall take one drawn out of every fifty, of the people, of the oxen, of the donkeys, and of the flocks, of all the cattle, and give them to the Levites who keep guard over the tabernacle of the LORD." 31 And Moses and Eleazar the priest did as the LORD commanded Moses.

[32]Now the plunder remaining of the spoil that the army took was 675,000 sheep, [33]72,000 cattle, [34]61,000 donkeys, [35]and 32,000 persons in all, women who had not known man by lying with him. [36]And the half, the portion of those who had gone out in the army, numbered 337,500 sheep, [37]and the LORD's tribute of sheep was 675. [38]The cattle were 36,000, of which the LORD's tribute was 72. [39]The donkeys were 30,500, of which the LORD's tribute was 61. [40]The persons were 16,000, of which the LORD's tribute was 32 persons. [41]And Moses gave the tribute, which was the contribution for the LORD, to Eleazar the priest, as the LORD commanded Moses.

[42]From the people of Israel's half, which Moses separated from that of the men who had served in the army— [43]now the congregation's half was 337,500 sheep, [44]36,000 cattle, [45]and 30,500 donkeys, [46]and 16,000 persons— [47]from the people of Israel's half Moses took one of every 50, both of persons and of beasts, and gave them to the Levites who kept guard over the tabernacle of the LORD, as the LORD commanded Moses.

[48]Then the officers who were over the thousands of the army, the commanders of thousands and the commanders of hundreds, came near to Moses [49]and said to Moses, "Your servants have counted the men of war who are under our command, and there is not a man missing from us. [50]And we have brought the LORD's offering, what each man found, articles of gold, armlets and bracelets, signet rings, earrings, and beads, to make atonement for ourselves before the LORD." [51]And Moses and Eleazar the priest received from them the gold, all crafted articles. [52]And all the gold of the contribution that they presented to the LORD, from the commanders of thousands and the commanders of hundreds, was 16,750 shekels.[1] [53](The men in the army had each taken plunder for himself.) [54]And Moses and Eleazar the priest received the gold from the commanders of thousands and of hundreds, and brought it into the tent of meeting, as a memorial for the people of Israel before the LORD.

Reuben and Gad Settle in Gilead

32 Now the people of Reuben and the people of Gad had a very great number of livestock. And they saw the land of Jazer and the land of Gilead, and behold, the place was a place for livestock. [2]So the people of Gad and the people of Reuben came and said to Moses and to Eleazar the priest and to the chiefs of the congregation, [3]"Ataroth, Dibon, Jazer, Nimrah, Heshbon, Elealeh, Sebam, Nebo, and Beon, [4]the land that the LORD struck down before the congregation of Israel, is a land for livestock, and your servants have livestock." [5]And they said, "If we have found favor in your sight, let this land be given to your servants for a possession. Do not take us across the Jordan."

[6]But Moses said to the people of Gad and to the people of Reuben, "Shall your brothers go to the war while you sit here? [7]Why will you discourage the heart of the people of Israel from going over into the land that the LORD has given them? [8]Your fathers did this, when I sent them from Kadesh-barnea to see the land. [9]For when they went up to the Valley of Eshcol and saw the land, they discouraged the heart of the people of Israel from going into the land that the LORD had given them. [10]And the LORD's anger was kindled on that day, and he swore, saying, [11]'Surely none of the men who came up out of Egypt, from twenty years old and upward, shall see the land that I swore to give to Abraham, to Isaac, and to Jacob, because they have not wholly followed me, [12]none except Caleb the son of Jephunneh the Kenizzite and Joshua the son of Nun, for they have wholly followed the LORD.' [13]And the LORD's anger was kindled against Israel, and he made them wander in the wilderness forty years, until all the generation that had done evil in the sight of the LORD was gone. [14]And behold, you have risen in your fathers' place, a brood of sinful men, to increase still more the fierce anger of the LORD

[1]A *shekel* was about 2/5 ounce or 11 grams

against Israel! 15For if you turn away from following him, he will again abandon
them in the wilderness, and you will destroy all this people."

16Then they came near to him and said, "We will build sheepfolds here for
our livestock, and cities for our little ones, 17but we will take up arms, ready to
go before the people of Israel, until we have brought them to their place. And our
little ones shall live in the fortified cities because of the inhabitants of the land.
18We will not return to our homes until each of the people of Israel has gained his
inheritance. 19For we will not inherit with them on the other side of the Jordan
and beyond, because our inheritance has come to us on this side of the Jordan to
the east." 20So Moses said to them, "If you will do this, if you will take up arms to
go before the LORD for the war, 21and every armed man of you will pass over the
Jordan before the LORD, until he has driven out his enemies from before him 22and
the land is subdued before the LORD; then after that you shall return and be free of
obligation to the LORD and to Israel, and this land shall be your possession before
the LORD. 23But if you will not do so, behold, you have sinned against the LORD,
and be sure your sin will find you out. 24Build cities for your little ones and folds
for your sheep, and do what you have promised." 25And the people of Gad and
the people of Reuben said to Moses, "Your servants will do as my lord commands.
26Our little ones, our wives, our livestock, and all our cattle shall remain there in
the cities of Gilead, 27but your servants will pass over, every man who is armed for
war, before the LORD to battle, as my lord orders."

28So Moses gave command concerning them to Eleazar the priest and to Joshua the son of Nun and to the heads of the fathers' houses of the tribes of the
people of Israel. 29And Moses said to them, "If the people of Gad and the people
of Reuben, every man who is armed to battle before the LORD, will pass with you
over the Jordan and the land shall be subdued before you, then you shall give
them the land of Gilead for a possession. 30However, if they will not pass over
with you armed, they shall have possessions among you in the land of Canaan."
31And the people of Gad and the people of Reuben answered, "What the LORD has
said to your servants, we will do. 32We will pass over armed before the LORD into
the land of Canaan, and the possession of our inheritance shall remain with us
beyond the Jordan."

33And Moses gave to them, to the people of Gad and to the people of Reuben
and to the half-tribe of Manasseh the son of Joseph, the kingdom of Sihon king
of the Amorites and the kingdom of Og king of Bashan, the land and its cities
with their territories, the cities of the land throughout the country. 34And the
people of Gad built Dibon, Ataroth, Aroer, 35Atroth-shophan, Jazer, Jogbehah,
36Beth-nimrah and Beth-haran, fortified cities, and folds for sheep. 37And the
people of Reuben built Heshbon, Elealeh, Kiriathaim, 38Nebo, and Baal-meon
(their names were changed), and Sibmah. And they gave other names to the cities that they built. 39And the sons of Machir the son of Manasseh went to Gilead
and captured it, and dispossessed the Amorites who were in it. 40And Moses gave
Gilead to Machir the son of Manasseh, and he settled in it. 41And Jair the son of
Manasseh went and captured their villages, and called them Havvoth-jair.[1] 42And
Nobah went and captured Kenath and its villages, and called it Nobah, after his
own name.

Recounting Israel's Journey

33 These are the stages of the people of Israel, when they went out of the
land of Egypt by their companies under the leadership of Moses and Aaron. 2Moses wrote down their starting places, stage by stage, by command of the
LORD, and these are their stages according to their starting places. 3They set out
from Rameses in the first month, on the fifteenth day of the first month. On the
day after the Passover, the people of Israel went out triumphantly in the sight of

---

[1] *Havvoth-jair* means *the villages of Jair*

all the Egyptians, 4while the Egyptians were burying all their firstborn, whom
the LORD had struck down among them. On their gods also the LORD executed
judgments.
5So the people of Israel set out from Rameses and camped at Succoth. 6And
they set out from Succoth and camped at Etham, which is on the edge of the wilderness. 7And they set out from Etham and turned back to Pi-hahiroth, which
is east of Baal-zephon, and they camped before Migdol. 8And they set out from
before Hahiroth[1] and passed through the midst of the sea into the wilderness, and
they went a three days' journey in the wilderness of Etham and camped at Marah.
9And they set out from Marah and came to Elim; at Elim there were twelve springs
of water and seventy palm trees, and they camped there. 10And they set out from
Elim and camped by the Red Sea. 11And they set out from the Red Sea and camped
in the wilderness of Sin. 12And they set out from the wilderness of Sin and camped
at Dophkah. 13And they set out from Dophkah and camped at Alush. 14And they set
out from Alush and camped at Rephidim, where there was no water for the people
to drink. 15And they set out from Rephidim and camped in the wilderness of Sinai.
16And they set out from the wilderness of Sinai and camped at Kibroth-hattaavah.
17And they set out from Kibroth-hattaavah and camped at Hazeroth. 18And they set
out from Hazeroth and camped at Rithmah. 19And they set out from Rithmah and
camped at Rimmon-perez. 20And they set out from Rimmon-perez and camped at
Libnah. 21And they set out from Libnah and camped at Rissah. 22And they set out
from Rissah and camped at Kehelathah. 23And they set out from Kehelathah and
camped at Mount Shepher. 24And they set out from Mount Shepher and camped at
Haradah. 25And they set out from Haradah and camped at Makheloth. 26And they
set out from Makheloth and camped at Tahath. 27And they set out from Tahath
and camped at Terah. 28And they set out from Terah and camped at Mithkah.
29And they set out from Mithkah and camped at Hashmonah. 30And they set out
from Hashmonah and camped at Moseroth. 31And they set out from Moseroth
and camped at Bene-jaakan. 32And they set out from Bene-jaakan and camped at
Hor-haggidgad. 33And they set out from Hor-haggidgad and camped at Jotbathah.
34And they set out from Jotbathah and camped at Abronah. 35And they set out
from Abronah and camped at Ezion-geber. 36And they set out from Ezion-geber
and camped in the wilderness of Zin (that is, Kadesh). 37And they set out from
Kadesh and camped at Mount Hor, on the edge of the land of Edom.
38And Aaron the priest went up Mount Hor at the command of the LORD and
died there, in the fortieth year after the people of Israel had come out of the land
of Egypt, on the first day of the fifth month. 39And Aaron was 123 years old when
he died on Mount Hor.
40And the Canaanite, the king of Arad, who lived in the Negeb in the land of
Canaan, heard of the coming of the people of Israel.
41And they set out from Mount Hor and camped at Zalmonah. 42And they set
out from Zalmonah and camped at Punon. 43And they set out from Punon and
camped at Oboth. 44And they set out from Oboth and camped at Iye-abarim, in
the territory of Moab. 45And they set out from Iyim and camped at Dibon-gad.
46And they set out from Dibon-gad and camped at Almon-diblathaim. 47And
they set out from Almon-diblathaim and camped in the mountains of Abarim,
before Nebo. 48And they set out from the mountains of Abarim and camped in
the plains of Moab by the Jordan at Jericho; 49they camped by the Jordan from
Beth-jeshimoth as far as Abel-shittim in the plains of Moab.

Drive Out the Inhabitants

50And the LORD spoke to Moses in the plains of Moab by the Jordan at Jericho,
saying, 51"Speak to the people of Israel and say to them, When you pass over the
Jordan into the land of Canaan, 52then you shall drive out all the inhabitants of

[1] Some manuscripts and versions *Pi-hahiroth*

the land from before you and destroy all their figured stones and destroy all their
metal images and demolish all their high places. [53]And you shall take possession
of the land and settle in it, for I have given the land to you to possess it. [54]You
shall inherit the land by lot according to your clans. To a large tribe you shall
give a large inheritance, and to a small tribe you shall give a small inheritance.
Wherever the lot falls for anyone, that shall be his. According to the tribes of your
fathers you shall inherit. [55]But if you do not drive out the inhabitants of the land
from before you, then those of them whom you let remain shall be as barbs in
your eyes and thorns in your sides, and they shall trouble you in the land where
you dwell. [56]And I will do to you as I thought to do to them."

NUMBERS 34:1–13

INHERITANCE

At the culmination of the book of Numbers, God's people were given a detailed description of where God was leading them after all the years of wandering. There they received the inheritance that God had promised and had been faithful to fulfill. God's people throughout the Bible are promised such an inheritance. Unlike the children of Israel, however, Christians do not receive an inheritance because of a national identity but because of an adoption effected through the blood of the Son of God (Col 1:12). Because of the gift of Jesus, the Father qualifies believers to participate in an inheritance that they could never deserve. In addition, unlike the children of Israel, the church does not receive an earthly inheritance of tangible significance. The earthly inheritance is found in the hope, joy, and peace that comes through knowing they have a right relationship with God and a secure eternal destiny. The church is granted a heavenly and eternal inheritance—Jesus Christ himself.

Boundaries of the Land

34 The LORD spoke to Moses, saying, [2]"Command the people of Israel, and
say to them, When you enter the land of Canaan (this is the land that shall
fall to you for an inheritance, the land of Canaan as defined by its borders), [3]your
south side shall be from the wilderness of Zin alongside Edom, and your southern
border shall run from the end of the Salt Sea on the east. [4]And your border shall
turn south of the ascent of Akrabbim, and cross to Zin, and its limit shall be south
of Kadesh-barnea. Then it shall go on to Hazar-addar, and pass along to Azmon.
[5]And the border shall turn from Azmon to the Brook of Egypt, and its limit shall
be at the sea.

[6]"For the western border, you shall have the Great Sea and its[1] coast. This shall
be your western border.

[7]"This shall be your northern border: from the Great Sea you shall draw a line
to Mount Hor. [8]From Mount Hor you shall draw a line to Lebo-hamath, and the
limit of the border shall be at Zedad. [9]Then the border shall extend to Ziphron,
and its limit shall be at Hazar-enan. This shall be your northern border.

[10]"You shall draw a line for your eastern border from Hazar-enan to Shepham.
[11]And the border shall go down from Shepham to Riblah on the east side of Ain.
And the border shall go down and reach to the shoulder of the Sea of Chinnereth
on the east. [12]And the border shall go down to the Jordan, and its limit shall be at
the Salt Sea. This shall be your land as defined by its borders all around."

[13]Moses commanded the people of Israel, saying, "This is the land that you
shall inherit by lot, which the LORD has commanded to give to the nine tribes and
to the half-tribe. [14]For the tribe of the people of Reuben by fathers' houses and the
tribe of the people of Gad by their fathers' houses have received their inheritance,
and also the half-tribe of Manasseh. [15]The two tribes and the half-tribe have received their inheritance beyond the Jordan east of Jericho, toward the sunrise."

List of Tribal Chiefs

[16]The LORD spoke to Moses, saying, [17]"These are the names of the men who
shall divide the land to you for inheritance: Eleazar the priest and Joshua the son
of Nun. [18]You shall take one chief from every tribe to divide the land for inheritance. [19]These are the names of the men: Of the tribe of Judah, Caleb the son of
Jephunneh. [20]Of the tribe of the people of Simeon, Shemuel the son of Ammihud.
[21]Of the tribe of Benjamin, Elidad the son of Chislon. [22]Of the tribe of the people
of Dan a chief, Bukki the son of Jogli. [23]Of the people of Joseph: of the tribe of the
people of Manasseh a chief, Hanniel the son of Ephod. [24]And of the tribe of the
people of Ephraim a chief, Kemuel the son of Shiphtan. [25]Of the tribe of the people of Zebulun a chief, Elizaphan the son of Parnach. [26]Of the tribe of the people
of Issachar a chief, Paltiel the son of Azzan. [27]And of the tribe of the people of
Asher a chief, Ahihud the son of Shelomi. [28]Of the tribe of the people of Naphtali
a chief, Pedahel the son of Ammihud." [29]These are the men whom the LORD commanded to divide the inheritance for the people of Israel in the land of Canaan.

[1]Syriac; Hebrew lacks *its*

Cities for the Levites

35 The LORD spoke to Moses in the plains of Moab by the Jordan at Jericho, saying, 2"Command the people of Israel to give to the Levites some of the inheritance of their possession as cities for them to dwell in. And you shall give to the Levites pasturelands around the cities. 3The cities shall be theirs to dwell in, and their pasturelands shall be for their cattle and for their livestock and for all their beasts. 4The pasturelands of the cities, which you shall give to the Levites, shall reach from the wall of the city outward a thousand cubits[1] all around. 5And you shall measure, outside the city, on the east side two thousand cubits, and on the south side two thousand cubits, and on the west side two thousand cubits, and on the north side two thousand cubits, the city being in the middle. This shall belong to them as pastureland for their cities.

6"The cities that you give to the Levites shall be the six cities of refuge, where you shall permit the manslayer to flee, and in addition to them you shall give forty-two cities. 7All the cities that you give to the Levites shall be forty-eight, with their pasturelands. 8And as for the cities that you shall give from the possession of the people of Israel, from the larger tribes you shall take many, and from the smaller tribes you shall take few; each, in proportion to the inheritance that it inherits, shall give of its cities to the Levites."

Cities of Refuge

9And the LORD spoke to Moses, saying, 10"Speak to the people of Israel and say to them, When you cross the Jordan into the land of Canaan, 11then you shall select cities to be cities of refuge for you, that the manslayer who kills any person without intent may flee there. 12The cities shall be for you a refuge from the avenger, that the manslayer may not die until he stands before the congregation for judgment. 13And the cities that you give shall be your six cities of refuge. 14You shall give three cities beyond the Jordan, and three cities in the land of Canaan, to be cities of refuge. 15These six cities shall be for refuge for the people of Israel, and for the stranger and for the sojourner among them, that anyone who kills any person without intent may flee there.

16"But if he struck him down with an iron object, so that he died, he is a murderer. The murderer shall be put to death. 17And if he struck him down with a stone tool that could cause death, and he died, he is a murderer. The murderer shall be put to death. 18Or if he struck him down with a wooden tool that could cause death, and he died, he is a murderer. The murderer shall be put to death. 19The avenger of blood shall himself put the murderer to death; when he meets him, he shall put him to death. 20And if he pushed him out of hatred or hurled something at him, lying in wait, so that he died, 21or in enmity struck him down with his hand, so that he died, then he who struck the blow shall be put to death. He is a murderer. The avenger of blood shall put the murderer to death when he meets him.

22"But if he pushed him suddenly without enmity, or hurled anything on him without lying in wait 23or used a stone that could cause death, and without seeing him dropped it on him, so that he died, though he was not his enemy and did not seek his harm, 24then the congregation shall judge between the manslayer and the avenger of blood, in accordance with these rules. 25And the congregation shall rescue the manslayer from the hand of the avenger of blood, and the congregation shall restore him to his city of refuge to which he had fled, and he shall live in it until the death of the high priest who was anointed with the holy oil. 26But if the manslayer shall at any time go beyond the boundaries of his city of refuge to which he fled, 27and the avenger of blood finds him outside the boundaries of his city of refuge, and the avenger of blood kills the manslayer, he shall not be guilty of blood. 28For he must remain in his city of refuge until the death of the

[1]A *cubit* was about 18 inches or 45 centimeters

NUMBERS 35:6–34

CITIES OF REFUGE

As God's people made their final preparations to enter the promised land, God commanded Moses to establish six cities of refuge from the towns given to the tribe of Levi, where both Israelites and foreigners living among them who were accused of murder could seek sanctuary. The Old Testament Law allowed for the closest male relative of a person who was killed to seek vengeance for their deceased family member. But if the death was perhaps accidental, the "manslayer" could flee to a city of refuge where the accused would stand trial and, if found guilty of intentional murder by the judges, would face the death penalty. God refused to allow injustice to go unpunished because it would pollute both the people and their land; God's justice demanded that sin be punished.

But the cities of refuge also pointed forward to Christ, an even better sanctuary and means of dealing with the sins of God's people. All are guilty of sin and, if forced to stand trial before God alone, would be condemned to eternal punishment; however, God's people can take hold of Christ as their refuge. He offers them forgiveness from their sins and escape from the death they all deserve (Jn 8:51).

high priest, but after the death of the high priest the manslayer may return to the land of his possession. [29]And these things shall be for a statute and rule for you throughout your generations in all your dwelling places.

[30]"If anyone kills a person, the murderer shall be put to death on the evidence of witnesses. But no person shall be put to death on the testimony of one witness. [31]Moreover, you shall accept no ransom for the life of a murderer, who is guilty of death, but he shall be put to death. [32]And you shall accept no ransom for him who has fled to his city of refuge, that he may return to dwell in the land before the death of the high priest. [33]You shall not pollute the land in which you live, for blood pollutes the land, and no atonement can be made for the land for the blood that is shed in it, except by the blood of the one who shed it. [34]You shall not defile the land in which you live, in the midst of which I dwell, for I the LORD dwell in the midst of the people of Israel."

Marriage of Female Heirs

36 The heads of the fathers' houses of the clan of the people of Gilead the son of Machir, son of Manasseh, from the clans of the people of Joseph, came near and spoke before Moses and before the chiefs, the heads of the fathers' houses of the people of Israel. [2]They said, "The LORD commanded my lord to give the land for inheritance by lot to the people of Israel, and my lord was commanded by the LORD to give the inheritance of Zelophehad our brother to his daughters. [3]But if they are married to any of the sons of the other tribes of the people of Israel, then their inheritance will be taken from the inheritance of our fathers and added to the inheritance of the tribe into which they marry. So it will be taken away from the lot of our inheritance. [4]And when the jubilee of the people of Israel comes, then their inheritance will be added to the inheritance of the tribe into which they marry, and their inheritance will be taken from the inheritance of the tribe of our fathers."

[5]And Moses commanded the people of Israel according to the word of the LORD, saying, "The tribe of the people of Joseph is right. [6]This is what the LORD commands concerning the daughters of Zelophehad: 'Let them marry whom they think best, only they shall marry within the clan of the tribe of their father. [7]The inheritance of the people of Israel shall not be transferred from one tribe to another, for every one of the people of Israel shall hold on to the inheritance of the tribe of his fathers. [8]And every daughter who possesses an inheritance in any tribe of the people of Israel shall be wife to one of the clan of the tribe of her father, so that every one of the people of Israel may possess the inheritance of his fathers. [9]So no inheritance shall be transferred from one tribe to another, for each of the tribes of the people of Israel shall hold on to its own inheritance.'"

[10]The daughters of Zelophehad did as the LORD commanded Moses, [11]for Mahlah, Tirzah, Hoglah, Milcah, and Noah, the daughters of Zelophehad, were married to sons of their father's brothers. [12]They were married into the clans of the people of Manasseh the son of Joseph, and their inheritance remained in the tribe of their father's clan.

[13]These are the commandments and the rules that the LORD commanded through Moses to the people of Israel in the plains of Moab by the Jordan at Jericho.

JESUS: OUR PROMISED HOPE

DEUTERONOMY

DEUTERONOMY

EXODUS FROM EGYPT *c. 1446 BC*	MOSES ADDRESSES ISRAEL IN MOAB *c. 1406 BC*	ISRAEL ENTERS PROMISED LAND *c. 1406 BC*

The fifth and final book of Moses recounts Moses' last statements to the people of God as they camped on the plains of Moab prior to entering the promised land. Moses, in his old age, knew that he would not enter the land as a result of his sin in the wilderness (Nu 20:1 – 12). But God graciously allowed Moses to see the land and to speak words of hope, grace and encouragement to the nation prior to their crossing the Jordan River and entering the land of promise.

Inspired by God, Deuteronomy serves as a testimony of God's grace written by those who had experienced God's miraculous favor firsthand. In it Moses recounts the national history of God's people — from their deliverance from Egypt, to their rebellion on the brink of the promised land, to their subsequent sojourn in the wilderness for nearly 40 years. He reminds the nation of their sin and rebellion, while consistently affirming God's covenantal faithfulness. Not only had God judged their sin, but he had also protected them in the wilderness and taught them to depend only on him for their daily survival.

This historical backdrop contrasts with the future promises of God to the new generation. The people did not have to wallow in shame and self-pity; rather, they could learn from the lessons of the past and trust God to fulfill his promises to them. The repetition of the word "today" throughout the book testifies to the forward-facing nature of Moses' exhortations (Dt 4:40).

In this way, this book is about grace. God freely gave a stiff-necked people a relationship with him and the gift of the promised land apart from anything they had done — in fact, in *spite* of all that they had done. As Moses looked over the people and toward the promised land on the horizon, he could die knowing that God was, is, and will always be faithful to his promises.

The covenantal structure of the book reminded the people of God's covenant commitments and their subsequent responsibilities. For this reason, Deuteronomy is a foundational document on which the subsequent history of God's people rests.

Moses knew full well that the people would prove incapable once again of keeping their covenant promises. That's why he pledged that God would raise up a future prophet from their midst to lead the people by his Word (Dt 18:15). This future prophet, the Messiah, would declare the new covenant promises whereby God's people, Jew and Gentile alike, could claim the inheritance promised to Abraham long ago. Moses' prophecy was perfectly fulfilled by Jesus (Lk 22:20).

SEE, THE LORD YOUR GOD HAS SET THE LAND BEFORE YOU.
GO UP, TAKE POSSESSION, AS THE LORD,
THE GOD OF YOUR FATHERS, HAS TOLD YOU.
DO NOT FEAR OR BE DISMAYED.

Deuteronomy 1:21

DEUTERONOMY

The Command to Leave Horeb

1 These are the words that Moses spoke to all Israel beyond the Jordan in the wilderness, in the Arabah opposite Suph, between Paran and Tophel, Laban, Hazeroth, and Dizahab. 2 It is eleven days' journey from Horeb by the way of Mount Seir to Kadesh-barnea. 3 In the fortieth year, on the first day of the eleventh month, Moses spoke to the people of Israel according to all that the LORD had given him in commandment to them, 4 after he had defeated Sihon the king of the Amorites, who lived in Heshbon, and Og the king of Bashan, who lived in Ashtaroth and in Edrei. 5 Beyond the Jordan, in the land of Moab, Moses undertook to explain this law, saying, 6 "The LORD our God said to us in Horeb, 'You have stayed long enough at this mountain. 7 Turn and take your journey, and go to the hill country of the Amorites and to all their neighbors in the Arabah, in the hill country and in the lowland and in the Negeb and by the seacoast, the land of the Canaanites, and Lebanon, as far as the great river, the river Euphrates. 8 See, I have set the land before you. Go in and take possession of the land that the LORD swore to your fathers, to Abraham, to Isaac, and to Jacob, to give to them and to their offspring after them.'

Leaders Appointed

9 "At that time I said to you, 'I am not able to bear you by myself. 10 The LORD your God has multiplied you, and behold, you are today as numerous as the stars of heaven. 11 May the LORD, the God of your fathers, make you a thousand times as many as you are and bless you, as he has promised you! 12 How can I bear by myself the weight and burden of you and your strife? 13 Choose for your tribes wise, understanding, and experienced men, and I will appoint them as your heads.' 14 And you answered me, 'The thing that you have spoken is good for us to do.' 15 So I took the heads of your tribes, wise and experienced men, and set them as heads over you, commanders of thousands, commanders of hundreds, commanders of fifties, commanders of tens, and officers, throughout your tribes. 16 And I charged your judges at that time, 'Hear the cases between your brothers, and judge righteously between a man and his brother or the alien who is with him. 17 You shall not be partial in judgment. You shall hear the small and the great alike. You shall not be intimidated by anyone, for the judgment is God's. And the case that is too hard for you, you shall bring to me, and I will hear it.' 18 And I commanded you at that time all the things that you should do.

Israel's Refusal to Enter the Land

19 "Then we set out from Horeb and went through all that great and terrifying wilderness that you saw, on the way to the hill country of the Amorites, as the LORD our God commanded us. And we came to Kadesh-barnea. 20 And I said to you, 'You have come to the hill country of the Amorites, which the LORD our God is giving us. 21 See, the LORD your God has set the land before you. Go up, take possession, as the LORD, the God of your fathers, has told you. Do not fear or be dismayed.' 22 Then all of you came near me and said, 'Let us send men before us, that they may explore the land for us and bring us word again of the way by which we must go up and the cities into which we shall come.' 23 The thing seemed good to me, and I took twelve men from you, one man from each tribe. 24 And they turned and went up into the hill country, and came to the Valley of Eshcol and spied it out. 25 And they took in their hands some of the fruit of the land and brought it down to us, and brought us word again and said, 'It is a good land that the LORD our God is giving us.'

DEUTERONOMY 1:1

LOOK TO THE WORD

In the Jewish tradition, the book of Deuteronomy is called "words" (*debarim*), meaning the words of Moses to the people of God. Moses' goal in this book was to restate and explain the law of God found in Exodus. Therefore, our English title of the book—from the Greek *deuteros* + *nomos*—means "second law" or the second accumulation of God's law for his people. In this book, Moses emphasized the covenant between God and Israel and the requirements God placed on his people to ensure ongoing blessings. Do not overlook the importance of the covenantal requirements of keeping the law throughout the pages of Deuteronomy. The Old Testament reveals a cyclical pattern of Israel being unable to keep the law, falling into sin, and needing to make continuous sacrificial offerings to atone for their failures—thus, the need for Jesus, who kept the law perfectly and went to the cross as a perfect, unblemished sacrifice on our behalf.

26“Yet you would not go up, but rebelled against the command of the LORD
your God. 27And you murmured in your tents and said, ‘Because the LORD hated
us he has brought us out of the land of Egypt, to give us into the hand of the
Amorites, to destroy us. 28Where are we going up? Our brothers have made our
hearts melt, saying, “The people are greater and taller than we. The cities are
great and fortified up to heaven. And besides, we have seen the sons of the Anakim there.”’ 29Then I said to you, ‘Do not be in dread or afraid of them. 30The
LORD your God who goes before you will himself fight for you, just as he did for
you in Egypt before your eyes, 31and in the wilderness, where you have seen how
the LORD your God carried you, as a man carries his son, all the way that you
went until you came to this place.’ 32Yet in spite of this word you did not believe
the LORD your God, 33who went before you in the way to seek you out a place to
pitch your tents, in fire by night and in the cloud by day, to show you by what
way you should go.

The Penalty for Israel’s Rebellion

34“And the LORD heard your words and was angered, and he swore, 35‘Not one
of these men of this evil generation shall see the good land that I swore to give to
your fathers, 36except Caleb the son of Jephunneh. He shall see it, and to him and
to his children I will give the land on which he has trodden, because he has wholly
followed the LORD!’ 37Even with me the LORD was angry on your account and said,
‘You also shall not go in there. 38Joshua the son of Nun, who stands before you, he
shall enter. Encourage him, for he shall cause Israel to inherit it. 39And as for your
little ones, who you said would become a prey, and your children, who today have
no knowledge of good or evil, they shall go in there. And to them I will give it, and
they shall possess it. 40But as for you, turn, and journey into the wilderness in the
direction of the Red Sea.’

41“Then you answered me, ‘We have sinned against the LORD. We ourselves
will go up and fight, just as the LORD our God commanded us.’ And every one
of you fastened on his weapons of war and thought it easy to go up into the hill
country. 42And the LORD said to me, ‘Say to them, Do not go up or fight, for I am
not in your midst, lest you be defeated before your enemies.’ 43So I spoke to you,
and you would not listen; but you rebelled against the command of the LORD and
presumptuously went up into the hill country. 44Then the Amorites who lived in
that hill country came out against you and chased you as bees do and beat you
down in Seir as far as Hormah. 45And you returned and wept before the LORD,
but the LORD did not listen to your voice or give ear to you. 46So you remained at
Kadesh many days, the days that you remained there.

The Wilderness Years

2 “Then we turned and journeyed into the wilderness in the direction of the
Red Sea, as the LORD told me. And for many days we traveled around Mount
Seir. 2Then the LORD said to me, 3‘You have been traveling around this mountain country long enough. Turn northward 4and command the people, “You are
about to pass through the territory of your brothers, the people of Esau, who
live in Seir; and they will be afraid of you. So be very careful. 5Do not contend
with them, for I will not give you any of their land, no, not so much as for the
sole of the foot to tread on, because I have given Mount Seir to Esau as a possession. 6You shall purchase food from them with money, that you may eat,
and you shall also buy water from them with money, that you may drink. 7For
the LORD your God has blessed you in all the work of your hands. He knows
your going through this great wilderness. These forty years the LORD your God
has been with you. You have lacked nothing.”’ 8So we went on, away from our
brothers, the people of Esau, who live in Seir, away from the Arabah road from
Elath and Ezion-geber.

“And we turned and went in the direction of the wilderness of Moab. 9And the LORD said to me, 'Do not harass Moab or contend with them in battle, for I will not give you any of their land for a possession, because I have given Ar to the people of Lot for a possession.' [10](The Emim formerly lived there, a people great and many, and tall as the Anakim. [11]Like the Anakim they are also counted as Rephaim, but the Moabites call them Emim. [12]The Horites also lived in Seir formerly, but the people of Esau dispossessed them and destroyed them from before them and settled in their place, as Israel did to the land of their possession, which the LORD gave to them.) [13]'Now rise up and go over the brook Zered.' So we went over the brook Zered. [14]And the time from our leaving Kadesh-barnea until we crossed the brook Zered was thirty-eight years, until the entire generation, that is, the men of war, had perished from the camp, as the LORD had sworn to them. [15]For indeed the hand of the LORD was against them, to destroy them from the camp, until they had perished.

[16]"So as soon as all the men of war had perished and were dead from among the people, [17]the LORD said to me, [18]'Today you are to cross the border of Moab at Ar. [19]And when you approach the territory of the people of Ammon, do not harass them or contend with them, for I will not give you any of the land of the people of Ammon as a possession, because I have given it to the sons of Lot for a possession.' [20](It is also counted as a land of Rephaim. Rephaim formerly lived there—but the Ammonites call them Zamzummim— [21]a people great and many, and tall as the Anakim; but the LORD destroyed them before the Ammonites,[1] and they dispossessed them and settled in their place, [22]as he did for the people of Esau, who live in Seir, when he destroyed the Horites before them and they dispossessed them and settled in their place even to this day. [23]As for the Avvim, who lived in villages as far as Gaza, the Caphtorim, who came from Caphtor, destroyed them and settled in their place.) [24]'Rise up, set out on your journey and go over the Valley of the Arnon. Behold, I have given into your hand Sihon the Amorite, king of Heshbon, and his land. Begin to take possession, and contend with him in battle. [25]This day I will begin to put the dread and fear of you on the peoples who are under the whole heaven, who shall hear the report of you and shall tremble and be in anguish because of you.'

The Defeat of King Sihon

[26]"So I sent messengers from the wilderness of Kedemoth to Sihon the king of Heshbon, with words of peace, saying, [27]'Let me pass through your land. I will go only by the road; I will turn aside neither to the right nor to the left. [28]You shall sell me food for money, that I may eat, and give me water for money, that I may drink. Only let me pass through on foot, [29]as the sons of Esau who live in Seir and the Moabites who live in Ar did for me, until I go over the Jordan into the land that the LORD our God is giving to us.' [30]But Sihon the king of Heshbon would not let us pass by him, for the LORD your God hardened his spirit and made his heart obstinate, that he might give him into your hand, as he is this day. [31]And the LORD said to me, 'Behold, I have begun to give Sihon and his land over to you. Begin to take possession, that you may occupy his land.' [32]Then Sihon came out against us, he and all his people, to battle at Jahaz. [33]And the LORD our God gave him over to us, and we defeated him and his sons and all his people. [34]And we captured all his cities at that time and devoted to destruction[2] every city, men, women, and children. We left no survivors. [35]Only the livestock we took as spoil for ourselves, with the plunder of the cities that we captured. [36]From Aroer, which is on the edge of the Valley of the Arnon, and from the city that is in the valley, as far as Gilead, there was not a city too high for us. The LORD our God gave all into our hands. [37]Only to the land of the sons of Ammon you did not draw near, that is, to all the banks of the river Jabbok and the cities of the hill country, whatever the LORD our God had forbidden us.

[1]Hebrew *them* [2]That is, set apart (devoted) as an offering to the Lord (for destruction)

DEUTERONOMY 2:24

CHRIST, THE VICTOR OVER SIN

Sihon the Amorite, king of Heshbon, refused Israel peaceful passage through his land during their wilderness wanderings and attacked the vulnerable Israelites (Nu 21:21–26; Dt 2:26–37). As a new generation prepared to enter the land, God spoke through Moses, declaring, "Behold, I have given into your hand Sihon the Amorite, king of Heshbon, and his land." This is likely a subtle reminder that the previous generation had accused God of bringing them from Egypt only to be handed to the Amorites (Dt 1:27). So God extended the same command (and promise) to the new generation that the previous generation had ignored. God made it clear that he would fulfill his promise, and as Israel obeyed they experienced the victory of God who led them into battle and delivered them. Israel's strength was insufficient for the battle, but by placing their faith in God to lead them, they enjoyed the victory by God's saving right hand.

Just as God led Israel through the sea, out of the wilderness, and into the promised land, he delivered them from their chief threat—sin—and continued to act on behalf of his people against the worst enemy. God's ultimate saving activity came through his Son, Jesus. Rather than Jesus rallying Israel together to lead them in battle, he came to seek and save the lost and *to redeem the people of God* by removing the separation sin created. Through Jesus, God won the victory over humanity's chief enemy.

The Defeat of King Og

3 "Then we turned and went up the way to Bashan. And Og the king of Bashan
came out against us, he and all his people, to battle at Edrei. 2But the LORD said
to me, 'Do not fear him, for I have given him and all his people and his land into
your hand. And you shall do to him as you did to Sihon the king of the Amorites,
who lived at Heshbon.' 3So the LORD our God gave into our hand Og also, the king
of Bashan, and all his people, and we struck him down until he had no survivor
left. 4And we took all his cities at that time—there was not a city that we did not
take from them—sixty cities, the whole region of Argob, the kingdom of Og in
Bashan. 5All these were cities fortified with high walls, gates, and bars, besides
very many unwalled villages. 6And we devoted them to destruction,[1] as we did to
Sihon the king of Heshbon, devoting to destruction every city, men, women, and
children. 7But all the livestock and the spoil of the cities we took as our plunder.
8So we took the land at that time out of the hand of the two kings of the Amorites
who were beyond the Jordan, from the Valley of the Arnon to Mount Hermon
9(the Sidonians call Hermon Sirion, while the Amorites call it Senir), 10all the cities of the tableland and all Gilead and all Bashan, as far as Salecah and Edrei, cities
of the kingdom of Og in Bashan. 11(For only Og the king of Bashan was left of the
remnant of the Rephaim. Behold, his bed was a bed of iron. Is it not in Rabbah of
the Ammonites? Nine cubits[2] was its length, and four cubits its breadth, according to the common cubit.[3])

12"When we took possession of this land at that time, I gave to the Reubenites
and the Gadites the territory beginning at Aroer, which is on the edge of the Valley of the Arnon, and half the hill country of Gilead with its cities. 13The rest of
Gilead, and all Bashan, the kingdom of Og, that is, all the region of Argob, I gave
to the half-tribe of Manasseh. (All that portion of Bashan is called the land of
Rephaim. 14Jair the Manassite took all the region of Argob, that is, Bashan, as far
as the border of the Geshurites and the Maacathites, and called the villages after
his own name, Havvoth-jair, as it is to this day.) 15To Machir I gave Gilead, 16and
to the Reubenites and the Gadites I gave the territory from Gilead as far as the
Valley of the Arnon, with the middle of the valley as a border, as far over as the
river Jabbok, the border of the Ammonites; 17the Arabah also, with the Jordan as
the border, from Chinnereth as far as the Sea of the Arabah, the Salt Sea, under
the slopes of Pisgah on the east.

18"And I commanded you at that time, saying, 'The LORD your God has given
you this land to possess. All your men of valor shall cross over armed before your
brothers, the people of Israel. 19Only your wives, your little ones, and your livestock (I know that you have much livestock) shall remain in the cities that I have
given you, 20until the LORD gives rest to your brothers, as to you, and they also
occupy the land that the LORD your God gives them beyond the Jordan. Then each
of you may return to his possession which I have given you.' 21And I commanded
Joshua at that time, 'Your eyes have seen all that the LORD your God has done
to these two kings. So will the LORD do to all the kingdoms into which you are
crossing. 22You shall not fear them, for it is the LORD your God who fights for you.'

Moses Forbidden to Enter the Land

23"And I pleaded with the LORD at that time, saying, 24'O Lord GOD, you have
only begun to show your servant your greatness and your mighty hand. For what
god is there in heaven or on earth who can do such works and mighty acts as
yours? 25Please let me go over and see the good land beyond the Jordan, that
good hill country and Lebanon.' 26But the LORD was angry with me because of
you and would not listen to me. And the LORD said to me, 'Enough from you; do
not speak to me of this matter again. 27Go up to the top of Pisgah and lift up your

[1]That is, set apart (devoted) as an offering to the Lord (for destruction); twice in this verse [2]A *cubit* was about 18 inches or 45 centimeters [3]Hebrew *cubit of a man*

A SURE STANDING AS GOD'S PEOPLE

The history of God's people in the Old Testament shows how unsure their standing was before God. The Israelites were people chosen by God, called to be his people. Additionally, God established clear requirements for the covenant relationship between himself and his people, requirements to atone for their human fallibility in light of his perfect holiness. He even appointed Moses to lead his people out of slavery in Egypt and to serve as a mediator between himself and his people lest their sins cause his displeasure to negate this covenant relationship. Yet these clear requirements, means of atoning for unholiness and an appointed mediator, were not sufficient.

Much like the Israelites, how tremendous are the sins of all people. No person can keep the covenant requirements of relationship with God. As the Israelites' sins and unbelief led to judgment from God, all people's failure to have perfect faith and obedience makes them deserving of his displeasure as well. But Christians have a mediator who is far superior to Moses, one who keeps God's standard of perfection on their behalf (Jer 31:31–34; Heb 9:14–15). Whereas Moses was unable to ensure the Lord's favor as the leader of his people, Jesus enables believers to enter the presence of God with confidence as their numerous sins were cast on him and his perfect righteousness was bestowed to them (Heb 10:19–22).

Believers do not have to live in fear—afraid that one day God's promises will not come to pass—because, in Jesus, God will not condemn those he calls to be his people (Ro 8:1–4). Through Jesus the righteous requirements of the law are fulfilled. Jesus provides a sure standing before God, one that entails unending blessings as his people, now and for all of eternity.

eyes westward and northward and southward and eastward, and look at it with
your eyes, for you shall not go over this Jordan. 28But charge Joshua, and encourage and strengthen him, for he shall go over at the head of this people, and he
shall put them in possession of the land that you shall see.' 29So we remained in
the valley opposite Beth-peor.

Moses Commands Obedience

4 "And now, O Israel, listen to the statutes and the rules[1] that I am teaching you,
and do them, that you may live, and go in and take possession of the land that
the LORD, the God of your fathers, is giving you. 2You shall not add to the word
that I command you, nor take from it, that you may keep the commandments of
the LORD your God that I command you. 3Your eyes have seen what the LORD did
at Baal-peor, for the LORD your God destroyed from among you all the men who
followed the Baal of Peor. 4But you who held fast to the LORD your God are all alive
today. 5See, I have taught you statutes and rules, as the LORD my God commanded
me, that you should do them in the land that you are entering to take possession
of it. 6Keep them and do them, for that will be your wisdom and your understanding in the sight of the peoples, who, when they hear all these statutes, will say,
'Surely this great nation is a wise and understanding people.' 7For what great nation is there that has a god so near to it as the LORD our God is to us, whenever
we call upon him? 8And what great nation is there, that has statutes and rules so
righteous as all this law that I set before you today?

9"Only take care, and keep your soul diligently, lest you forget the things that
your eyes have seen, and lest they depart from your heart all the days of your
life. Make them known to your children and your children's children— 10how on
the day that you stood before the LORD your God at Horeb, the LORD said to me,
'Gather the people to me, that I may let them hear my words, so that they may
learn to fear me all the days that they live on the earth, and that they may teach
their children so.' 11And you came near and stood at the foot of the mountain,
while the mountain burned with fire to the heart of heaven, wrapped in darkness, cloud, and gloom. 12Then the LORD spoke to you out of the midst of the fire.
You heard the sound of words, but saw no form; there was only a voice. 13And he
declared to you his covenant, which he commanded you to perform, that is, the
Ten Commandments,[2] and he wrote them on two tablets of stone. 14And the LORD
commanded me at that time to teach you statutes and rules, that you might do
them in the land that you are going over to possess.

Idolatry Forbidden

15"Therefore watch yourselves very carefully. Since you saw no form on the
day that the LORD spoke to you at Horeb out of the midst of the fire, 16beware lest
you act corruptly by making a carved image for yourselves, in the form of any
figure, the likeness of male or female, 17the likeness of any animal that is on the
earth, the likeness of any winged bird that flies in the air, 18the likeness of anything that creeps on the ground, the likeness of any fish that is in the water under
the earth. 19And beware lest you raise your eyes to heaven, and when you see the
sun and the moon and the stars, all the host of heaven, you be drawn away and
bow down to them and serve them, things that the LORD your God has allotted to
all the peoples under the whole heaven. 20But the LORD has taken you and brought
you out of the iron furnace, out of Egypt, to be a people of his own inheritance, as
you are this day. 21Furthermore, the LORD was angry with me because of you, and
he swore that I should not cross the Jordan, and that I should not enter the good
land that the LORD your God is giving you for an inheritance. 22For I must die in
this land; I must not go over the Jordan. But you shall go over and take possession
of that good land. 23Take care, lest you forget the covenant of the LORD your God,

[1]Or *just decrees*; also verses 5, 8, 14, 45 [2]Hebrew *the ten words*

THE IMPORTANCE OF REMEMBERING

Throughout Scripture, remembering is a major theme. Authors constantly reminded God's people to remember his faithfulness. The nations were admonished to remember the Lord and turn to him (Ps 22:27). In contrast, the Lord was petitioned to not remember sins and show instead his goodness and pour out his blessing (Ps 25:6–7). Among God's people the failure to remember results in cyclical patterns of sin and rebellion (Isa 57:11). When the people forgot God — both his character and his past faithfulness to the nation — they were prone to a host of sins. Most specifically, the people of God pursued the idolatry of the surrounding nations. False gods seemed more tangible, more concrete, and more immediate. One could see and touch these false gods. Ironically, though these gods had a material substance, they could not speak or act on behalf of the people. Yahweh, in contrast, was not made by human hands but could act mightily on behalf of his people. The nation of Israel was reminded, time and time again, not to forget this.

How forgetful God's people are concerning the truths of Scripture, thus finding themselves unable to stand firm on God's promises (1Co 15:1). They forget the goodness of the Lord and his Word. They forget the frailty of human limitations and their propensity to live according to their own way. They forget their former longings for the Lord and the blessed experience of walking closely with him. God knows his people's limitations and sees their forgetfulness as another way in which they need his gracious mercy. Therefore, he reminds them again and again to remember him, and he supplies the means to overcome their human inability to remember the things of God by providing the Spirit of Christ (Jn 14:26).

The Good News of the gospel is that Jesus remembers the covenant that God made with his people and intercedes in the midst of unfaithful moments (Heb 7:24–25). Without fail, Jesus is remembering and reminding the Father of his promises to his children. Jesus remembers and applies his death and resurrection as payment. Jesus remembers and sends the Spirit to strengthen his children during their journey of faith and to remind them of the goodness of God and walking in his ways. The triune God remembers because of Jesus' intercession and oversight of continued sanctification (Ro 8:26–30).

which he made with you, and make a carved image, the form of anything that the
LORD your God has forbidden you. 24For the LORD your God is a consuming fire,
a jealous God.
25"When you father children and children's children, and have grown old in
the land, and you act corruptly by making a carved image in the form of anything,
and by doing what is evil in the sight of the LORD your God, so as to provoke him
to anger, 26I call heaven and earth to witness against you today, that you will soon
utterly perish from the land that you are going over the Jordan to possess. You will
not live long in it, but will be utterly destroyed. 27And the LORD will scatter you
among the peoples, and you will be left few in number among the nations where
the LORD will drive you. 28And there you will serve gods of wood and stone, the
work of human hands, that neither see, nor hear, nor eat, nor smell. 29But from
there you will seek the LORD your God and you will find him, if you search after
him with all your heart and with all your soul. 30When you are in tribulation, and
all these things come upon you in the latter days, you will return to the LORD your
God and obey his voice. 31For the LORD your God is a merciful God. He will not
leave you or destroy you or forget the covenant with your fathers that he swore
to them.

The LORD Alone Is God

32"For ask now of the days that are past, which were before you, since the day
that God created man on the earth, and ask from one end of heaven to the other,
whether such a great thing as this has ever happened or was ever heard of. 33Did
any people ever hear the voice of a god speaking out of the midst of the fire, as you
have heard, and still live? 34Or has any god ever attempted to go and take a nation
for himself from the midst of another nation, by trials, by signs, by wonders, and
by war, by a mighty hand and an outstretched arm, and by great deeds of terror,
all of which the LORD your God did for you in Egypt before your eyes? 35To you it
was shown, that you might know that the LORD is God; there is no other besides
him. 36Out of heaven he let you hear his voice, that he might discipline you. And
on earth he let you see his great fire, and you heard his words out of the midst of
the fire. 37And because he loved your fathers and chose their offspring after them[1]
and brought you out of Egypt with his own presence, by his great power, 38driv-
ing out before you nations greater and mightier than you, to bring you in, to give
you their land for an inheritance, as it is this day, 39know therefore today, and lay
it to your heart, that the LORD is God in heaven above and on the earth beneath;
there is no other. 40Therefore you shall keep his statutes and his commandments,
which I command you today, that it may go well with you and with your children
after you, and that you may prolong your days in the land that the LORD your God
is giving you for all time."

Cities of Refuge

41Then Moses set apart three cities in the east beyond the Jordan, 42that the
manslayer might flee there, anyone who kills his neighbor unintentionally, without being at enmity with him in time past; he may flee to one of these cities and
save his life: 43Bezer in the wilderness on the tableland for the Reubenites, Ramoth in Gilead for the Gadites, and Golan in Bashan for the Manassites.

Introduction to the Law

44This is the law that Moses set before the people of Israel. 45These are the
testimonies, the statutes, and the rules, which Moses spoke to the people of Israel
when they came out of Egypt, 46beyond the Jordan in the valley opposite Beth-
peor, in the land of Sihon the king of the Amorites, who lived at Heshbon, whom
Moses and the people of Israel defeated when they came out of Egypt. 47And they

[1]Hebrew *his offspring after him*

DEUTERONOMY 4:32–40

THE LORD IS GOD

God's approach to establish a relationship with Israel at Sinai represents a significant moment in human history. Until Sinai, gods were considered territorially constrained and without obligation to peoples. However, God chose to deliver Israel from bondage in Egypt in such spectacular fashion in order to demonstrate his love for Israel so they might know God's magnificence over and above the gods of other nations. As highlighted in other texts, the book of Deuteronomy was written to help Israel understand and remember God's power to deliver them, his sovereignty over heaven and earth (not a corner of land), and his love for them over other nations. Toward that end, Moses consistently reminded each generation of what God had done for their ancestors by calling them to remember the story of their deliverance.

John 1 narrates another monumental moment in human history, one that is worthy of being consistently remembered: the incarnation. When God took on human flesh and "dwelt" (literally, "tabernacled"; v. 14) among God's people, they were provided greater access to God throughout Jesus' public ministry. It is through Jesus that God has proven his power to deliver his people from the power of sin, shown us his absolute love, and provided a way for all nations of the earth to have a relationship with the one true God.

DEUTERONOMY 5:4 – 5

A BETTER MEDIATOR

A mediator is a person who seeks to resolve conflicts, bringing about a negotiated peace between two parties who are at odds with one another. The conflict between God and mankind is not one that a mediator can simply negotiate away. Something deep — God's holiness — has been transgressed and the required mediation involves the offending party making it right. The enmity between God and humanity calls for something much more significant than a typical negotiation. Something supernatural needs to occur to bring about a resolution in the conflict between God's holiness and fallen human beings.

Though we see Moses functioning as a mediator in Deuteronomy 5:5, Christians have a mediator who is far superior to him. In fact, this mediator satisfied the terms of the negotiation himself by taking the punishment required to bring about peace and right the wrongs caused by our unrighteousness (Jer 31:31 – 34; Heb 9:14 – 15). Whereas Moses was unable to ensure the Lord's continued favor as the leader of the Israelites, Jesus secured eternal blessing for those who find righteousness in him. Whereas the people of Israel feared the presence of God because of their sin (Dt 5:5), Christians may enter the presence of God boldly because of a perfect standing before the Lord through Jesus (Eph 3:12). In Jesus and through faith in him, believers may approach God with freedom and confidence that they will not be rejected or judged for shortcomings. His righteous perfection covers imperfection and provides admission into the presence of God. What a mediator is Christ Jesus!

took possession of his land and the land of Og, the king of Bashan, the two kings of the Amorites, who lived to the east beyond the Jordan; 48 from Aroer, which is on the edge of the Valley of the Arnon, as far as Mount Sirion[1] (that is, Hermon), 49 together with all the Arabah on the east side of the Jordan as far as the Sea of the Arabah, under the slopes of Pisgah.

The Ten Commandments

5 And Moses summoned all Israel and said to them, "Hear, O Israel, the statutes and the rules that I speak in your hearing today, and you shall learn them and be careful to do them. 2 The LORD our God made a covenant with us in Horeb. 3 Not with our fathers did the LORD make this covenant, but with us, who are all of us here alive today. 4 The LORD spoke with you face to face at the mountain, out of the midst of the fire, 5 while I stood between the LORD and you at that time, to declare to you the word of the LORD. For you were afraid because of the fire, and you did not go up into the mountain. He said:

6 " 'I am the LORD your God, who brought you out of the land of Egypt, out of the house of slavery.

7 " 'You shall have no other gods before[2] me.

8 " 'You shall not make for yourself a carved image, or any likeness of anything that is in heaven above, or that is on the earth beneath, or that is in the water under the earth. 9 You shall not bow down to them or serve them, for I the LORD your God am a jealous God, visiting the iniquity of the fathers on the children to the third and fourth generation of those who hate me, 10 but showing steadfast love to thousands[3] of those who love me and keep my commandments.

11 " 'You shall not take the name of the LORD your God in vain, for the LORD will not hold him guiltless who takes his name in vain.

12 " 'Observe the Sabbath day, to keep it holy, as the LORD your God commanded you. 13 Six days you shall labor and do all your work, 14 but the seventh day is a Sabbath to the LORD your God. On it you shall not do any work, you or your son or your daughter or your male servant or your female servant, or your ox or your donkey or any of your livestock, or the sojourner who is within your gates, that your male servant and your female servant may rest as well as you. 15 You shall remember that you were a slave[4] in the land of Egypt, and the LORD your God brought you out from there with a mighty hand and an outstretched arm. Therefore the LORD your God commanded you to keep the Sabbath day.

16 " 'Honor your father and your mother, as the LORD your God commanded you, that your days may be long, and that it may go well with you in the land that the LORD your God is giving you.

17 " 'You shall not murder.[5]

18 " 'And you shall not commit adultery.

19 " 'And you shall not steal.

20 " 'And you shall not bear false witness against your neighbor.

21 " 'And you shall not covet your neighbor's wife. And you shall not desire your neighbor's house, his field, or his male servant, or his female servant, his ox, or his donkey, or anything that is your neighbor's.'

22 "These words the LORD spoke to all your assembly at the mountain out of the midst of the fire, the cloud, and the thick darkness, with a loud voice; and he added no more. And he wrote them on two tablets of stone and gave them to me. 23 And as soon as you heard the voice out of the midst of the darkness, while the mountain was burning with fire, you came near to me, all the heads of your tribes, and your elders. 24 And you said, 'Behold, the LORD our God has shown us his glory and greatness, and we have heard his voice out of the midst of the fire. This day we have seen God speak with man, and man still live. 25 Now therefore why should we

[1] Syriac; Hebrew *Sion* [2] Or *besides* [3] Or *to the thousandth generation* [4] Or *servant* [5] The Hebrew word also covers causing human death through carelessness or negligence

die? For this great fire will consume us. If we hear the voice of the LORD our God
any more, we shall die. 26For who is there of all flesh, that has heard the voice of
the living God speaking out of the midst of fire as we have, and has still lived? 27Go
near and hear all that the LORD our God will say, and speak to us all that the LORD
our God will speak to you, and we will hear and do it.'

28"And the LORD heard your words, when you spoke to me. And the LORD said
to me, 'I have heard the words of this people, which they have spoken to you.
They are right in all that they have spoken. 29Oh that they had such a heart as this
always, to fear me and to keep all my commandments, that it might go well with
them and with their descendants[1] forever! 30Go and say to them, "Return to your
tents." 31But you, stand here by me, and I will tell you the whole commandment
and the statutes and the rules that you shall teach them, that they may do them
in the land that I am giving them to possess.' 32You shall be careful therefore to do
as the LORD your God has commanded you. You shall not turn aside to the right
hand or to the left. 33You shall walk in all the way that the LORD your God has commanded you, that you may live, and that it may go well with you, and that you may
live long in the land that you shall possess.

The Greatest Commandment

6 "Now this is the commandment—the statutes and the rules[2]—that the LORD
your God commanded me to teach you, that you may do them in the land to
which you are going over, to possess it, 2that you may fear the LORD your God, you
and your son and your son's son, by keeping all his statutes and his commandments, which I command you, all the days of your life, and that your days may be
long. 3Hear therefore, O Israel, and be careful to do them, that it may go well with
you, and that you may multiply greatly, as the LORD, the God of your fathers, has
promised you, in a land flowing with milk and honey.

4"Hear, O Israel: The LORD our God, the LORD is one.[3] 5You shall love the LORD
your God with all your heart and with all your soul and with all your might. 6And
these words that I command you today shall be on your heart. 7You shall teach
them diligently to your children, and shall talk of them when you sit in your
house, and when you walk by the way, and when you lie down, and when you
rise. 8You shall bind them as a sign on your hand, and they shall be as frontlets
between your eyes. 9You shall write them on the doorposts of your house and on
your gates.

10"And when the LORD your God brings you into the land that he swore to your
fathers, to Abraham, to Isaac, and to Jacob, to give you—with great and good cities that you did not build, 11and houses full of all good things that you did not fill,
and cisterns that you did not dig, and vineyards and olive trees that you did not
plant—and when you eat and are full, 12then take care lest you forget the LORD,
who brought you out of the land of Egypt, out of the house of slavery. 13It is the
LORD your God you shall fear. Him you shall serve and by his name you shall
swear. 14You shall not go after other gods, the gods of the peoples who are around
you— 15for the LORD your God in your midst is a jealous God—lest the anger of
the LORD your God be kindled against you, and he destroy you from off the face
of the earth.

16"You shall not put the LORD your God to the test, as you tested him at Massah. 17You shall diligently keep the commandments of the LORD your God, and his
testimonies and his statutes, which he has commanded you. 18And you shall do
what is right and good in the sight of the LORD, that it may go well with you, and
that you may go in and take possession of the good land that the LORD swore to
give to your fathers 19by thrusting out all your enemies from before you, as the
LORD has promised.

[1]Or *sons* [2]Or *just decrees*; also verse 20 [3]Or *The LORD our God is one LORD*; or *The LORD is our God, the LORD is one*; or *The LORD is our God, the LORD alone*

20“When your son asks you in time to come, ‘What is the meaning of the testimonies and the statutes and the rules that the LORD our God has commanded you?’ 21then you shall say to your son, ‘We were Pharaoh’s slaves in Egypt. And the LORD brought us out of Egypt with a mighty hand. 22And the LORD showed signs and wonders, great and grievous, against Egypt and against Pharaoh and all his household, before our eyes. 23And he brought us out from there, that he might bring us in and give us the land that he swore to give to our fathers. 24And the LORD commanded us to do all these statutes, to fear the LORD our God, for our good always, that he might preserve us alive, as we are this day. 25And it will be righteousness for us, if we are careful to do all this commandment before the LORD our God, as he has commanded us.’

A Chosen People

7 “When the LORD your God brings you into the land that you are entering to take possession of it, and clears away many nations before you, the Hittites, the Girgashites, the Amorites, the Canaanites, the Perizzites, the Hivites, and the Jebusites, seven nations more numerous and mightier than you, 2and when the LORD your God gives them over to you, and you defeat them, then you must devote them to complete destruction.[1] You shall make no covenant with them and show no mercy to them. 3You shall not intermarry with them, giving your daughters to their sons or taking their daughters for your sons, 4for they would turn away your sons from following me, to serve other gods. Then the anger of the LORD would be kindled against you, and he would destroy you quickly. 5But thus shall you deal with them: you shall break down their altars and dash in pieces their pillars and chop down their Asherim and burn their carved images with fire.

6“For you are a people holy to the LORD your God. The LORD your God has chosen you to be a people for his treasured possession, out of all the peoples who are on the face of the earth. 7It was not because you were more in number than any other people that the LORD set his love on you and chose you, for you were the fewest of all peoples, 8but it is because the LORD loves you and is keeping the oath that he swore to your fathers, that the LORD has brought you out with a mighty hand and redeemed you from the house of slavery, from the hand of Pharaoh king of Egypt. 9Know therefore that the LORD your God is God, the faithful God who keeps covenant and steadfast love with those who love him and keep his commandments, to a thousand generations, 10and repays to their face those who hate him, by destroying them. He will not be slack with one who hates him. He will repay him to his face. 11You shall therefore be careful to do the commandment and the statutes and the rules that I command you today.

12“And because you listen to these rules and keep and do them, the LORD your God will keep with you the covenant and the steadfast love that he swore to your fathers. 13He will love you, bless you, and multiply you. He will also bless the fruit of your womb and the fruit of your ground, your grain and your wine and your oil, the increase of your herds and the young of your flock, in the land that he swore to your fathers to give you. 14You shall be blessed above all peoples. There shall not be male or female barren among you or among your livestock. 15And the LORD will take away from you all sickness, and none of the evil diseases of Egypt, which you knew, will he inflict on you, but he will lay them on all who hate you. 16And you shall consume all the peoples that the LORD your God will give over to you. Your eye shall not pity them, neither shall you serve their gods, for that would be a snare to you.

17“If you say in your heart, ‘These nations are greater than I. How can I dispossess them?’ 18you shall not be afraid of them but you shall remember what the LORD your God did to Pharaoh and to all Egypt, 19the great trials that your eyes saw, the signs, the wonders, the mighty hand, and the outstretched arm,

[1]That is, set apart (devote) as an offering to the Lord (for destruction)

THE TRIUNE GOD MERCIFULLY BLESSES HIS CHILDREN

Knowing God, keeping the decrees of God, loving God alone without serving other gods — the commands within Deuteronomy can be a bit overwhelming, even to the point of feeling the weight of works-based righteousness. A reader of the Bible must ask why God wanted Moses to emphasize these themes over and over again throughout this book, particularly in chapter 6. As verses 1 – 3 and 6 – 9 teach, the exhortations in this chapter are for the people's own good and the good of their children. Moses calls Israel to love the Lord with all of one's heart, soul, and strength (vv. 4 – 5). Total love is the ideal. Why? It is for his people's good. There is no better place to be than centering one's life around the law — or teachings — of God because they exist to show us the path to blessing and deep joy in knowing the Father. Yet, all people know that they often pursue other things as their ultimate desire. Why is it so impossible to follow God's way if we know that it leads to blessing and not doing so leads to sorrow?

Just as the Israelites were enslaved in Egypt, unable to alter their circumstances, all people are enslaved to sin apart from God interjecting his merciful grace in their lives (Eph 2:1 – 10). As this chapter of Deuteronomy progresses, it is evident that any commands from God to his people are tied closely to the mercy he has shown to them (Dt 6:20 – 25). God's glorious mercy takes human sin, placing it on Jesus as the atonement for humanity's inability to love God completely as commanded in Deuteronomy 6:5. Jesus has kept the law — a requirement to be righteous before God according to Deuteronomy 6:25 — and given us the righteousness of Jesus himself (Ro 3:21 – 22). This is true because the Father draws believers to himself (Jn 6:44), Jesus offers the perfect life and sacrifice for sin, and the Spirit guides believers in truth (Jn 16:13). The triune God works mercifully on Christians' behalf to ensure that they will experience the blessed experience of living in his favor. They do not follow the law of God in order to earn his favor but because he has shown favor in his mercy. God's children are freed by God's gracious mercy through Christ to experience the blessing of following God's desires for us found in the Bible.

PEOPLE

GENESIS 12 TO MALACHI

All of us constantly find ourselves in a vicious cycle with God, a pattern we see clearly throughout this act of Scripture. The stages are familiar: God initiates a relationship and blesses us, God calls us to honor him, and we promise to serve and worship him alone, yet we soon drift into complacency. We are easily enticed by the flickering lights of temptation, so we wander and stray. Ultimately, we defy our Creator, falling into dark pits of sin with dreadful consequences. We hit rock bottom, we get fed up, we long for change, we cry out for mercy, God hears and restores, we promise to never leave him again ... but, in time the cycle begins again.

Yet, even when we are faithless, God remains faithful.

The consequence of the *revolt* in Eden was that mankind eventually scattered across the earth. And as they spread far and wide, their sin followed them. When they moved on, the fruit of their brokenness went with them. Relationships were torn apart. Hope dimmed and the earth was filled with rebellion as God's people continued to cultivate their fallen nature and direct their sin into ever-increasing forms of disobedience (Ge 11:1 – 9).

Yet in the midst of unrest and devastation, God chose a people — a people who would be set apart and "holy to the LORD." Out of all the people groups on earth, God chose Israel "to be a people for his treasured possession" (Dt 7:6). God chose Abram to be the ancestor and leader of this people, promising to make him "a great nation." And ultimately, all people of the world would be blessed through him (Ge 12:2 – 3). God was on a mission for all of humanity. He would redeem people, through a *people!*

God's plan was to bless, prosper, and guide his people as a demonstration of his goodness in a self-destructing world where people worshiped everything but the one true God. But God's chosen people were incessantly rebellious, constantly doing things their own way.

However, God's mission never changed. God was not caught off-guard by humanity's decision. Because he is sovereign (ruling over all things) and omniscient (knowing all things) God had already factored humanity's revolt into the equation. God ordained a rescue mission to restore fallen people to his original intention for their lives. Though one mission had stalled (humankind's opportunity to purely reflect God's glory), God's supreme mission (exalting his love, grace, and mercy by the renewal of all things through the gift of his Son) was now underway.

Where people were (and are) unable to invent sufficient ways to draw near to a perfect God (through religion), God was building a bridge by which the Almighty could span the gap from heaven to mankind (through grace). Thus, grace reverses normal thinking — that we have to find a way to God — and ushers in the inconceivable: God makes a way to us.

So, you might be asking, if salvation is coming in the next act of the story, why don't we just skip this act called *people* and get right to the life and times of Jesus? Why not just get straight to his salvation work on the cross? Why keep re-reading the sin-filled cycle of God's chosen people? The answer is because the section called *people* is in fact about one *person,* and in studying the Old Testament account of God's relationship with his chosen people we see at least seven key things about God:

1. The Old Testament gives us a glimpse into God's glory.

God is not like mankind. Though he created us in his image, God alone is holy. He is *other.* He is altogether on an entirely different plane than humans — not just a little bigger. Mankind does not look at God eye-to-eye. God stoops from the heights of heaven to make himself known to humanity. And when he reaches down to show us who he is, he leads with his glory.

The Hebrew word for *glory* in much of the Old Testament can be translated as *weight.* To put it mildly and a bit figuratively, God is *heavy.* His righteousness, perfection, brilliance, and radiant beauty span galaxies and cause the earth to shudder. Lightning and thunder proceed from his throne. To see him in full would be the end of any mortal.

Thus, God reveals glimpses of himself to fallen mankind. Knowing sinful people could never find God on their own, God initiates a relationship and reveals himself to his created ones. And when God shows up to engage mankind, his glory follows. Whether a burning bush through which he spoke to Moses, a cloud by day and a fiery pillar at night to lead them, or a cloud that descended from heaven to envelop the place where Moses encountered God on behalf of the people, God displayed his glory to the Israelites.

Even as God gave the law, he did it through his glory. As Moses was on Mount Sinai receiving the stone tablets containing the Ten Commandments, he asked to see God's glory (Ex 33:18). God tucked him into a craggy place. Then God covered Moses with his hand and only allowed him to see his back after he had passed by (Ex 33:18 – 23). Moses' face shone in the aftermath as he came down from the mountain, and the Israelites were "afraid to come near him" (Ex 34). God's glory is no small thing. It is not something to be taken lightly.

The people failed to grasp the *weight,* but God could not disregard his glory. He dwells in unapproachable light (1Ti 6:16). And, he fiercely defends his glory — his name (Isa 42:8).

2. The Old Testament gives us a glimpse into God's mercy.

God would have been without fault if he had simply said "goodbye and good luck" to

PEOPLE

(CONTINUED)

GENESIS 12 TO MALACHI

Adam and Eve when he expelled them from the garden. Instead, he watched over his people and later came to Abram with a blessing and a promise.

God's call of Abram was a decisive juncture in the story (Ge 12:1 – 3). Were it not for God's initiative, humans would have been lost in sin forever and doomed to destruction. Yet God made a covenant with Abram in which he promised that his children would be the recipients of God's gracious salvation. Establishing covenants was a common practice in the ancient Near East, a means by which a king would establish a relationship between himself and his subjects. In these agreements, the parties would initiate the terms of the relationship, the responsibilities of both parties, the blessings that would come to those who kept the covenant, and the curses that would result from disobedience. God, in a breathtaking act of love, entered into this kind of relationship with his sin-stained people.

God selected Abram and called him to leave his pagan city and to travel to the land of God's choosing where he would receive God's blessing and become the father of a great nation. Abram believed God and was counted righteous as a result (Ge 15:6). God pledged his covenant faithfulness and bountiful love to Abram and his heirs (Ge 17). More astounding is the fact that God's promises were not predicated on Abram's obedience; rather, the covenant promises were based solely on the character and generosity of God. God made promises to Abram, even changing his name to "Abraham," which means "father of a multitude" (Ge 17:5). God does not break his promises, since "his steadfast love endures forever" (Ps 136:3).

From Abraham onward, God began gathering his people. Abraham's descendants, the Israelites, were the recipients of a multitude of blessings from God. God delivered them from slavery in Egypt in a miraculous demonstration of his power. And God made an extraordinary offer to them: You will be my people and I will be your God. Through you I will show all the inhabitants of the earth that I am the One true God (Ge 17:7 – 8; Ex 6:7).

3. The Old Testament gives us a glimpse into God's provision.

Once God delivered his people from Egyptian bondage, he led them by an arduous route toward the promised land. He did this to protect and lead them through salvation's waters at the Red Sea and into a desert land that would teach them that God provides no matter what circumstances his people face.

In the desert he showed them his provision by giving them manna to eat (Ex 16:31); he showed his protecting presence by giving them a cloud by day and fire by night to guide their way (Ex 13:21); and he showed them his faithfulness as a promise-keeping God by never leaving or forsaking them (Ex 13 – 17).

4. The Old Testament gives us a glimpse into the fact that religion is not enough.

In the wilderness, God gave the people of Israel his law, which was never intended to institute a means by which people could merit their own salvation. Rather, God gave them the law to expose their sinful nature.

The sacrificial system God established made it clear that sin required punishment (Ge 3:21). The people brought a sacrificial substitute — an animal that bore the sin of the people in their place. The wrath of God for sin was ceremonially placed on the substitute; in turn, the people were able to avoid God's wrath for their rebellion and sin. The ongoing practice of sacrifice ensured that the people would never forget that the only way to placate God's fury over sin was through the blood sacrifice of a substitute.

This system pointed the way to a promised hope — a Messiah — who would fulfill the intent of the sacrificial system once and for all (Mt 5:17).

5. The Old Testament gives us a glimpse into God's eternal plan.

God ultimately led his people to the promised land. Like the garden of old, the promised land was a place of God's choosing where the people were to live while they enjoyed God's bountiful provision.

God used forty years in the wilderness to humble his people and teach them to depend on him. He then allowed them to conquer the pagan inhabitants of the land, and he set them there to reflect his glory to the world once more. More astounding, God lived among his people in the tabernacle. There his presence would reside, and his people could continually worship him through their sacrifices. Yet this land of promise was only a preview of *forever* — the final act in God's story — in which his people will permanently live with him and enjoy eternal freedom from sin, death, and shame in heaven.

6. The Old Testament gives us a glimpse into the dreadful state of humanity apart from God.

God's people had so much going for them. Not only did they have a relationship with God (though partial), they also had the law, which told them how to obey God; the sacrificial system that allowed them to worship God; the tabernacle where they could experience the presence of God; and the land where they could enjoy the provision of God. These gifts of grace should have allowed them to fill the earth with the knowledge of God's glory. His fame was not meant to be limited to the nation of Israel; through them, all nations would hear about the One true God and see his glory reflected in his people.

The people, however, proved to be utter failures in this mission. They embraced

PEOPLE

(CONTINUED)

GENESIS 12 TO MALACHI

the idolatrous practices of the surrounding nations rather than living a distinctive, holy life as God had required. They looked toward human leaders — like Saul, David, and Solomon — to usher in God's promised blessings while they turned away from God himself. As a result, God's people began to unravel at the seams, splintering into two separate nations and facing continual threats of war.

God had no choice but to judge his rebellious people. As a result, God's people were defeated by their pagan enemies and exiled from their land to become servants of ruthless masters who mocked and hated Jehovah God. Through the prophets, God called the people back home again, and the cycle continued.

For centuries Israel's defiance led to collapse, and collapse led to contrition. Contrition always birthed a cry for mercy, and that cry was always heard by a merciful God. Enemies, whom God used as instruments of judgment for his people, were dispatched and defeated in one heavenly gesture. Even when his rebellious people were helpless, God would seek them out and draw them to himself.

But every generation seemed to take Israel further from Eden's paradise. The scene at the end of the Old Testament is bleak. God's remnant people were broken and in need of deliverance from their cycle of death. Thankfully, God's mission never changed. The prophets continued to remind God's people of the coming promised One — the Messiah who would fulfill God's promises, reclaim God's people as worshipers, and establish his rule and reign forever. He would give his people a new heart, pulsating with the new life of his Spirit (Eze 36:26). God would not abandon his people; rather, he would save them in his time and in his way.

7. The Old Testament gives us a glimpse into God's invitation to know him as sons and daughters.

Where people proved to be faithless, God was faithful, never once denying his own character. So while it might be tempting to skim over the Old Testament account and get to the good news of the New Testament, we find in the Old Testament a helpful mirror for ourselves. We are challenged to take seriously our inclination towards the deceptive but deadly spiral of sin's cycle. It is a picture of our depravity that keeps us humbly dependent on his Spirit's leading every step of the way, and it contains the promise of heaven's beauty and our true home. We also find a constant reminder of God's mercy, mercies that are new every day (La 3:22 – 23). We are encouraged by his provision as we see over and over a God who is able to be more than we need in every situation. While the Old Testament serves as a reminder that our effort will never be enough to make us acceptable to God, it still invites us to draw near to God.

In the end, through a relationship made possible by the death and resurrection of Jesus Christ, we not only become God's people but are actually born again as God's adopted sons and daughters, made alive by faith to become all that he always dreamed we would be. His Spirit dwells within us, affording us a fellowship (relationship) with God that the people living in the time of the Old Testament could only dream of. In Christ, the Almighty God becomes our perfect Father, and we humbly walk with him forever.

BEGINNINGS	REVOLT	PEOPLE	INTERTESTAMENTAL PERIOD	SAVIOR	CHURCH	FOREVER
GENESIS 1–2 (pg. 10)	GENESIS 3–11 (pg. 24)	GENESIS 12 to MALACHI (pg. 256)	(pg. 1468)	GOSPELS to ACTS 1 (pg. 1518)	ACTS 2 to REVELATION 20 (pg. 1686)	REVELATION 21–22 (pg. 1938)

THE BLESSINGS AND RESPONSIBILITY OF THE ELECT

These verses show the wondrous grace of God toward his people. Having done nothing of note nor being special in any way, the Israelites were selected by God out of all the existing nations to be a chosen people upon whom he would bestow his covenant blessings (vv. 7 – 8). The history of Israel is full of examples of their continuous inability to remain faithful to the Lord and keep his law — yet God was faithful to keep his oath to the nation (v. 9). This text contains what theologians call the doctrine of election: God choosing people upon whom he bestows his unmerited favor without end, even when those people prove to be unfaithful to him.

Moses was referring to the covenant that God made with Abraham in Genesis 12. In the establishment of this covenant between God and the descendants of Abraham, being God's chosen people was a great privilege for the Israelites. But there were also tremendous implications associated with that privilege that benefited other nations (Ge 12:3). In the first few chapters of Scripture, God took action on behalf of his image-bearers as he refused to abandon humanity to live in the effects of the fall brought about by Adam and Eve. He began a plan of redemption by making a sacrifice to cover their sin and nakedness, an animal sacrifice that prefigured the killing of Jesus to cover sin and shame (Ge 3:21). In Genesis 12, God unfolded another aspect of his plan of redemption hinted at in Genesis 3:15. By redeeming Israel to be his people, God chose them to be a holy nation set apart as a picture of humanity restored to a right relationship with its Creator, the one true and living God. They, in turn, would be the vehicle through which he would bring about redemption and restoration from sin, sorrow, and death to their fellow human beings — to be a blessing to the nations. Ultimately, through the lineage of the Hebrew nation the Christ came, extending God's chosen race beyond ethnic lines.

To this day, God's story of redemption continues. He continues to elect people, bringing them from sin and darkness to himself (Jn 6:44; Eph 2:1 – 10). The means that God uses to spread his story of redemption is through his people sharing the gospel (Ro 10:14). Truly, believers receive tremendous blessing as God's children, as he knows our every need and will never leave us or forsake us (Dt 31:6; Heb 13:5). This blessing, however, is not simply one in which privileges associated with being a child of the King are received, but rather a privileged status of being set apart for service is declared (Mt 28:19 – 20).

by which the LORD your God brought you out. So will the LORD your God do to all the peoples of whom you are afraid. 20Moreover, the LORD your God will send hornets among them, until those who are left and hide themselves from you are destroyed. 21You shall not be in dread of them, for the LORD your God is in your midst, a great and awesome God. 22The LORD your God will clear away these nations before you little by little. You may not make an end of them at once,[1] lest the wild beasts grow too numerous for you. 23But the LORD your God will give them over to you and throw them into great confusion, until they are destroyed. 24And he will give their kings into your hand, and you shall make their name perish from under heaven. No one shall be able to stand against you until you have destroyed them. 25The carved images of their gods you shall burn with fire. You shall not covet the silver or the gold that is on them or take it for yourselves, lest you be ensnared by it, for it is an abomination to the LORD your God. 26And you shall not bring an abominable thing into your house and become devoted to destruction[2] like it. You shall utterly detest and abhor it, for it is devoted to destruction.

Remember the LORD Your God

8 "The whole commandment that I command you today you shall be careful to do, that you may live and multiply, and go in and possess the land that the LORD swore to give to your fathers. 2And you shall remember the whole way that the LORD your God has led you these forty years in the wilderness, that he might humble you, testing you to know what was in your heart, whether you would keep his commandments or not. 3And he humbled you and let you hunger and fed you with manna, which you did not know, nor did your fathers know, that he might make you know that man does not live by bread alone, but man lives by every word[3] that comes from the mouth of the LORD. 4Your clothing did not wear out on you and your foot did not swell these forty years. 5Know then in your heart that, as a man disciplines his son, the LORD your God disciplines you. 6So you shall keep the commandments of the LORD your God by walking in his ways and by fearing him. 7For the LORD your God is bringing you into a good land, a land of brooks of water, of fountains and springs, flowing out in the valleys and hills, 8a land of wheat and barley, of vines and fig trees and pomegranates, a land of olive trees and honey, 9a land in which you will eat bread without scarcity, in which you will lack nothing, a land whose stones are iron, and out of whose hills you can dig copper. 10And you shall eat and be full, and you shall bless the LORD your God for the good land he has given you.

11"Take care lest you forget the LORD your God by not keeping his commandments and his rules and his statutes, which I command you today, 12lest, when you have eaten and are full and have built good houses and live in them, 13and when your herds and flocks multiply and your silver and gold is multiplied and all that you have is multiplied, 14then your heart be lifted up, and you forget the LORD your God, who brought you out of the land of Egypt, out of the house of slavery, 15who led you through the great and terrifying wilderness, with its fiery serpents and scorpions and thirsty ground where there was no water, who brought you water out of the flinty rock, 16who fed you in the wilderness with manna that your fathers did not know, that he might humble you and test you, to do you good in the end. 17Beware lest you say in your heart, 'My power and the might of my hand have gotten me this wealth.' 18You shall remember the LORD your God, for it is he who gives you power to get wealth, that he may confirm his covenant that he swore to your fathers, as it is this day. 19And if you forget the LORD your God and go after other gods and serve them and worship them, I solemnly warn you today that you shall surely perish. 20Like the nations that the LORD makes to perish before you, so shall you perish, because you would not obey the voice of the LORD your God.

[1]Or *quickly* [2]That is, set apart (devoted) as an offering to the Lord (for destruction); twice in this verse
[3]Hebrew *by all*

DEUTERONOMY 8:2–3

TRUE SATISFACTION FOR HUNGER AND THIRST

As Israel wandered through the wilderness, they were humbled and tested by God in order to reveal the true condition of their hearts, especially whether or not they trusted the Lord's promise when provisions were lacking and they grew hungry. God saw their need and responded to it, using the occasion to refine his people's faith in him yet again. His proclamation reminded them that life is not supported by physical sustenance alone—people require more than bread and water to live and thrive on earth. In this incident, God taught the Israelites that their spiritual life was sustained in the same way their physical bodies were sustained: with daily faith.

During his temptation in the wilderness Jesus referenced this verse when Satan enticed him to "command these stones to become loaves of bread" to prove himself to be the Son of God (Mt 4:3). But Jesus trusted that God would supply all that he needed physically, spiritually, emotionally, and otherwise. Also, by drawing upon this text, Jesus linked himself to the Lord God of Israel and strengthened his self-identification as the living bread of heaven (Jn 6:33–51). By contrasting himself with the manna given to Israel, which only met temporary physical needs, he revealed the superiority of the eternal nourishment found in him as opposed to physical sustenance alone.

DEUTERONOMY 9:25–29

THE NEED FOR ONE TO INTERCEDE

After Israel sinned against God by making a golden calf and worshiping it while Moses was in the presence of God on Mount Sinai, God approached Moses to disown his people and begin again with Moses. The book of Deuteronomy intensifies the nature of Israel's sin in the incident with the golden calf by putting it in the context of Israel's recent reception of the Ten Commandments and the saving activity of God who brought them out of bondage in Egypt "with a mighty hand" (v. 26). However, Moses countered God's plan to disassociate from Israel by interceding on their behalf. He pleaded with God to remember his promises to the patriarchs and overlook the people's sin. He also argued that by destroying the people of God's own inheritance, God's saving power and the authenticity of God's love for his treasured possession would be called into question.

Just as Moses interceded on behalf of Israel, so also Jesus Christ intercedes on behalf of believers who approach God through him. The salvation Jesus offers through the new covenant is a complete salvation that endures for all time and extends to all of life. Those who place their faith in the finished work of Jesus are saved by virtue of his sinless life, sacrificial death, and glorious resurrection.

Not Because of Righteousness

9 "Hear, O Israel: you are to cross over the Jordan today, to go in to dispossess nations greater and mightier than you, cities great and fortified up to heaven, [2]a people great and tall, the sons of the Anakim, whom you know, and of whom you have heard it said, 'Who can stand before the sons of Anak?' [3]Know therefore today that he who goes over before you as a consuming fire is the LORD your God. He will destroy them and subdue them before you. So you shall drive them out and make them perish quickly, as the LORD has promised you.

[4]"Do not say in your heart, after the LORD your God has thrust them out before you, 'It is because of my righteousness that the LORD has brought me in to possess this land,' whereas it is because of the wickedness of these nations that the LORD is driving them out before you. [5]Not because of your righteousness or the uprightness of your heart are you going in to possess their land, but because of the wickedness of these nations the LORD your God is driving them out from before you, and that he may confirm the word that the LORD swore to your fathers, to Abraham, to Isaac, and to Jacob.

[6]"Know, therefore, that the LORD your God is not giving you this good land to possess because of your righteousness, for you are a stubborn people. [7]Remember and do not forget how you provoked the LORD your God to wrath in the wilderness. From the day you came out of the land of Egypt until you came to this place, you have been rebellious against the LORD. [8]Even at Horeb you provoked the LORD to wrath, and the LORD was so angry with you that he was ready to destroy you. [9]When I went up the mountain to receive the tablets of stone, the tablets of the covenant that the LORD made with you, I remained on the mountain forty days and forty nights. I neither ate bread nor drank water. [10]And the LORD gave me the two tablets of stone written with the finger of God, and on them were all the words that the LORD had spoken with you on the mountain out of the midst of the fire on the day of the assembly. [11]And at the end of forty days and forty nights the LORD gave me the two tablets of stone, the tablets of the covenant. [12]Then the LORD said to me, 'Arise, go down quickly from here, for your people whom you have brought from Egypt have acted corruptly. They have turned aside quickly out of the way that I commanded them; they have made themselves a metal image.'

The Golden Calf

[13]"Furthermore, the LORD said to me, 'I have seen this people, and behold, it is a stubborn people. [14]Let me alone, that I may destroy them and blot out their name from under heaven. And I will make of you a nation mightier and greater than they.' [15]So I turned and came down from the mountain, and the mountain was burning with fire. And the two tablets of the covenant were in my two hands. [16]And I looked, and behold, you had sinned against the LORD your God. You had made yourselves a golden[1] calf. You had turned aside quickly from the way that the LORD had commanded you. [17]So I took hold of the two tablets and threw them out of my two hands and broke them before your eyes. [18]Then I lay prostrate before the LORD as before, forty days and forty nights. I neither ate bread nor drank water, because of all the sin that you had committed, in doing what was evil in the sight of the LORD to provoke him to anger. [19]For I was afraid of the anger and hot displeasure that the LORD bore against you, so that he was ready to destroy you. But the LORD listened to me that time also. [20]And the LORD was so angry with Aaron that he was ready to destroy him. And I prayed for Aaron also at the same time. [21]Then I took the sinful thing, the calf that you had made, and burned it with fire and crushed it, grinding it very small, until it was as fine as dust. And I threw the dust of it into the brook that ran down from the mountain.

[22]"At Taberah also, and at Massah and at Kibroth-hattaavah you provoked the

[1]Hebrew *cast metal*

LORD to wrath. 23And when the LORD sent you from Kadesh-barnea, saying, 'Go up
and take possession of the land that I have given you,' then you rebelled against
the commandment of the LORD your God and did not believe him or obey his
voice. 24You have been rebellious against the LORD from the day that I knew you.
25"So I lay prostrate before the LORD for these forty days and forty nights, because the LORD had said he would destroy you. 26And I prayed to the LORD, 'O Lord
GOD, do not destroy your people and your heritage, whom you have redeemed
through your greatness, whom you have brought out of Egypt with a mighty
hand. 27Remember your servants, Abraham, Isaac, and Jacob. Do not regard the
stubbornness of this people, or their wickedness or their sin, 28lest the land from
which you brought us say, "Because the LORD was not able to bring them into the
land that he promised them, and because he hated them, he has brought them out
to put them to death in the wilderness." 29For they are your people and your heritage, whom you brought out by your great power and by your outstretched arm.'

New Tablets of Stone

10 "At that time the LORD said to me, 'Cut for yourself two tablets of stone like
the first, and come up to me on the mountain and make an ark of wood.
2And I will write on the tablets the words that were on the first tablets that you
broke, and you shall put them in the ark.' 3So I made an ark of acacia wood, and
cut two tablets of stone like the first, and went up the mountain with the two
tablets in my hand. 4And he wrote on the tablets, in the same writing as before,
the Ten Commandments[1] that the LORD had spoken to you on the mountain out
of the midst of the fire on the day of the assembly. And the LORD gave them to me.
5Then I turned and came down from the mountain and put the tablets in the ark
that I had made. And there they are, as the LORD commanded me."
6(The people of Israel journeyed from Beeroth Bene-jaakan[2] to Moserah. There
Aaron died, and there he was buried. And his son Eleazar ministered as priest
in his place. 7From there they journeyed to Gudgodah, and from Gudgodah to
Jotbathah, a land with brooks of water. 8At that time the LORD set apart the tribe
of Levi to carry the ark of the covenant of the LORD to stand before the LORD to
minister to him and to bless in his name, to this day. 9Therefore Levi has no portion or inheritance with his brothers. The LORD is his inheritance, as the LORD
your God said to him.)
10"I myself stayed on the mountain, as at the first time, forty days and forty
nights, and the LORD listened to me that time also. The LORD was unwilling to
destroy you. 11And the LORD said to me, 'Arise, go on your journey at the head of
the people, so that they may go in and possess the land, which I swore to their
fathers to give them.'

Circumcise Your Heart

12"And now, Israel, what does the LORD your God require of you, but to fear
the LORD your God, to walk in all his ways, to love him, to serve the LORD your
God with all your heart and with all your soul, 13and to keep the commandments
and statutes of the LORD, which I am commanding you today for your good? 14Be-
hold, to the LORD your God belong heaven and the heaven of heavens, the earth
with all that is in it. 15Yet the LORD set his heart in love on your fathers and chose
their offspring after them, you above all peoples, as you are this day. 16Circumcise
therefore the foreskin of your heart, and be no longer stubborn. 17For the LORD
your God is God of gods and Lord of lords, the great, the mighty, and the awesome
God, who is not partial and takes no bribe. 18He executes justice for the fatherless
and the widow, and loves the sojourner, giving him food and clothing. 19Love the
sojourner, therefore, for you were sojourners in the land of Egypt. 20You shall fear
the LORD your God. You shall serve him and hold fast to him, and by his name you

[1]Hebrew *the ten words* [2]Or *the wells of the Bene-jaakan*

DEUTERONOMY 10:16

SPIRITUAL RENEWAL THROUGH JESUS ALONE

Moses commanded the Israelites to circumcise their hearts rather than being rebellious. Circumcision carried tremendous significance in the minds of the Israelites as it was a physical sign of the covenant between them and God. Living in close proximity to the Canaanites whose worship system involved sexual promiscuity, circumcision of a Hebrew male was a reminder to avoid such cultural rituals. But circumcision was much more than a physical act. A person's heart must reflect the physical sign. God is concerned not merely with the outward marks of holiness but with the posture of the human heart. The covenant of God required a spiritual change to love God as he desires: with all of one's heart and soul (Dt 10:12–13; 30:6). Such a necessary change only comes through Jesus (Col 2:11–12). In Christ our debt was canceled; our flesh which ruled us was buried, and we were raised from death to life.

shall swear. 21 He is your praise. He is your God, who has done for you these great and terrifying things that your eyes have seen. 22 Your fathers went down to Egypt seventy persons, and now the LORD your God has made you as numerous as the stars of heaven.

Love and Serve the LORD

11 "You shall therefore love the LORD your God and keep his charge, his statutes, his rules, and his commandments always. 2 And consider today (since I am not speaking to your children who have not known or seen it), consider the discipline[1] of the LORD your God, his greatness, his mighty hand and his outstretched arm, 3 his signs and his deeds that he did in Egypt to Pharaoh the king of Egypt and to all his land, 4 and what he did to the army of Egypt, to their horses and to their chariots, how he made the water of the Red Sea flow over them as they pursued after you, and how the LORD has destroyed them to this day, 5 and what he did to you in the wilderness, until you came to this place, 6 and what he did to Dathan and Abiram the sons of Eliab, son of Reuben, how the earth opened its mouth and swallowed them up, with their households, their tents, and every living thing that followed them, in the midst of all Israel. 7 For your eyes have seen all the great work of the LORD that he did.

8 "You shall therefore keep the whole commandment that I command you today, that you may be strong, and go in and take possession of the land that you are going over to possess, 9 and that you may live long in the land that the LORD swore to your fathers to give to them and to their offspring, a land flowing with milk and honey. 10 For the land that you are entering to take possession of it is not like the land of Egypt, from which you have come, where you sowed your seed and irrigated it,[2] like a garden of vegetables. 11 But the land that you are going over to possess is a land of hills and valleys, which drinks water by the rain from heaven, 12 a land that the LORD your God cares for. The eyes of the LORD your God are always upon it, from the beginning of the year to the end of the year.

13 "And if you will indeed obey my commandments that I command you today, to love the LORD your God, and to serve him with all your heart and with all your soul, 14 he[3] will give the rain for your land in its season, the early rain and the later rain, that you may gather in your grain and your wine and your oil. 15 And he will give grass in your fields for your livestock, and you shall eat and be full. 16 Take care lest your heart be deceived, and you turn aside and serve other gods and worship them; 17 then the anger of the LORD will be kindled against you, and he will shut up the heavens, so that there will be no rain, and the land will yield no fruit, and you will perish quickly off the good land that the LORD is giving you.

18 "You shall therefore lay up these words of mine in your heart and in your soul, and you shall bind them as a sign on your hand, and they shall be as frontlets between your eyes. 19 You shall teach them to your children, talking of them when you are sitting in your house, and when you are walking by the way, and when you lie down, and when you rise. 20 You shall write them on the doorposts of your house and on your gates, 21 that your days and the days of your children may be multiplied in the land that the LORD swore to your fathers to give them, as long as the heavens are above the earth. 22 For if you will be careful to do all this commandment that I command you to do, loving the LORD your God, walking in all his ways, and holding fast to him, 23 then the LORD will drive out all these nations before you, and you will dispossess nations greater and mightier than you. 24 Every place on which the sole of your foot treads shall be yours. Your territory shall be from the wilderness to[4] the Lebanon, and from the River, the river Euphrates, to the western sea. 25 No one shall be able to stand against you. The LORD your God will lay the fear of you and the dread of you on all the land that you shall tread, as he promised you.

[1] Or *instruction* [2] Hebrew *watered it with your feet* [3] Samaritan, Septuagint, Vulgate; Hebrew *I*; also verse 15 [4] Hebrew *and*

THE PURPOSE OF THE LAW

Moses addressed the heart of the moral law given by God to the nation of Israel (v. 12). Incidentally, the heart of the law is intended to address the hearts of sinful men and women. Based on God's majestic work of redemption, a feat that proved him to be the one true God, the people were to respond in wholehearted worship. This worship would spring from a deep love for God and a desire to please him.

Moses revealed another motive for keeping the law. Not only is the law a response to the grace of God, but it is also the best way to live life. As Moses said here in the text, the law is for the good of the people (v. 13). Many times people are prone to assume that God's laws are foolish or a barrier to human joy and fulfillment.

This could not be further from the truth. The law of God is true because it is based on the nature of God who made all things. Who else would know how best to live than the one who created all things in the first place? The law of God is wise — it counteracts human folly and instructs men and women on the mind of God. Finally, obedience to the law is the path to human joy and flourishing. Sin, not God's law, is the barrier to joy.

The pages of Scripture repeatedly attest to this reality. They demonstrate that God is all-wise and his law is the path to true life (Ps 19:7 – 9; 119:1 – 176). But time and time again, the people demonstrated that they were incapable of keeping the law (Ro 7:7 – 12). Moses pointed forward to the need for heart transformation rather than mere external obedience to the law (Dt 10:16). He knew that their obedience would be short-lived. What they needed was circumcised hearts instead of hearts of stone. God, through the prophet Ezekiel, declared that a day would come when God would remove the heart of stone and put a heart of flesh in its place (Eze 36:26). This new heart is a gift of God's grace given to those who place their faith in Jesus Christ and are reborn by his Spirit (Jn 3:3 – 5).

DEUTERONOMY 12:1–7

JESUS EXPANDS THE PLACE OF TRUE WORSHIP

The place of worship in the Old Testament was extremely important. The presence of God rested on the place he chose. Unlike the false places of worship—that were creations of cultures surrounding the Israelites—God commanded that true worship would occur only in the place he designated. In these verses, Moses contrasted the false places of worship so prevalent at that time with the place of true worship chosen by God. The preeminent means of access to God was found in the tabernacle while Israel wandered in the wilderness and for many years after settling in the promised land, and later in the temple in Jerusalem.

The place of true worship is just as important today as it was at that time, but God has expanded the reality of "place." In Jesus, the place of worship is no longer limited to a specific physical location (Jn 2:18–22). Now the Spirit of God dwells within believers, and our bodies serve as the temple of God (1Co 6:19). This is why Christians are able to "pray without ceasing," meaning, worship God wherever they are, at all times (1Th 5:17).

26"See, I am setting before you today a blessing and a curse: 27the blessing, if you obey the commandments of the LORD your God, which I command you today, 28and the curse, if you do not obey the commandments of the LORD your God, but turn aside from the way that I am commanding you today, to go after other gods that you have not known. 29And when the LORD your God brings you into the land that you are entering to take possession of it, you shall set the blessing on Mount Gerizim and the curse on Mount Ebal. 30Are they not beyond the Jordan, west of the road, toward the going down of the sun, in the land of the Canaanites who live in the Arabah, opposite Gilgal, beside the oak[1] of Moreh? 31For you are to cross over the Jordan to go in to take possession of the land that the LORD your God is giving you. And when you possess it and live in it, 32you shall be careful to do all the statutes and the rules that I am setting before you today.

The LORD's Chosen Place of Worship

12 "These are the statutes and rules that you shall be careful to do in the land that the LORD, the God of your fathers, has given you to possess, all the days that you live on the earth. 2You shall surely destroy all the places where the nations whom you shall dispossess served their gods, on the high mountains and on the hills and under every green tree. 3You shall tear down their altars and dash in pieces their pillars and burn their Asherim with fire. You shall chop down the carved images of their gods and destroy their name out of that place. 4You shall not worship the LORD your God in that way. 5But you shall seek the place that the LORD your God will choose out of all your tribes to put his name and make his habitation[2] there. There you shall go, 6and there you shall bring your burnt offerings and your sacrifices, your tithes and the contribution that you present, your vow offerings, your freewill offerings, and the firstborn of your herd and of your flock. 7And there you shall eat before the LORD your God, and you shall rejoice, you and your households, in all that you undertake, in which the LORD your God has blessed you.

8"You shall not do according to all that we are doing here today, everyone doing whatever is right in his own eyes, 9for you have not as yet come to the rest and to the inheritance that the LORD your God is giving you. 10But when you go over the Jordan and live in the land that the LORD your God is giving you to inherit, and when he gives you rest from all your enemies around, so that you live in safety, 11then to the place that the LORD your God will choose, to make his name dwell there, there you shall bring all that I command you: your burnt offerings and your sacrifices, your tithes and the contribution that you present, and all your finest vow offerings that you vow to the LORD. 12And you shall rejoice before the LORD your God, you and your sons and your daughters, your male servants and your female servants, and the Levite that is within your towns, since he has no portion or inheritance with you. 13Take care that you do not offer your burnt offerings at any place that you see, 14but at the place that the LORD will choose in one of your tribes, there you shall offer your burnt offerings, and there you shall do all that I am commanding you.

15"However, you may slaughter and eat meat within any of your towns, as much as you desire, according to the blessing of the LORD your God that he has given you. The unclean and the clean may eat of it, as of the gazelle and as of the deer. 16Only you shall not eat the blood; you shall pour it out on the earth like water. 17You may not eat within your towns the tithe of your grain or of your wine or of your oil, or the firstborn of your herd or of your flock, or any of your vow offerings that you vow, or your freewill offerings or the contribution that you present, 18but you shall eat them before the LORD your God in the place that the LORD your God will choose, you and your son and your daughter, your male servant and your female servant, and the Levite who is within your towns. And

[1]Septuagint, Syriac; see Genesis 12:6. Hebrew *oaks, or terebinths* [2]Or *name as its habitation*

you shall rejoice before the LORD your God in all that you undertake. 19Take care
that you do not neglect the Levite as long as you live in your land.
20"When the LORD your God enlarges your territory, as he has promised you,
and you say, 'I will eat meat,' because you crave meat, you may eat meat whenever you desire. 21If the place that the LORD your God will choose to put his name
there is too far from you, then you may kill any of your herd or your flock, which
the LORD has given you, as I have commanded you, and you may eat within your
towns whenever you desire. 22Just as the gazelle or the deer is eaten, so you may
eat of it. The unclean and the clean alike may eat of it. 23Only be sure that you do
not eat the blood, for the blood is the life, and you shall not eat the life with the
flesh. 24You shall not eat it; you shall pour it out on the earth like water. 25You shall
not eat it, that all may go well with you and with your children after you, when
you do what is right in the sight of the LORD. 26But the holy things that are due
from you, and your vow offerings, you shall take, and you shall go to the place that
the LORD will choose, 27and offer your burnt offerings, the flesh and the blood, on
the altar of the LORD your God. The blood of your sacrifices shall be poured out
on the altar of the LORD your God, but the flesh you may eat. 28Be careful to obey
all these words that I command you, that it may go well with you and with your
children after you forever, when you do what is good and right in the sight of the
LORD your God.

Warning Against Idolatry

29"When the LORD your God cuts off before you the nations whom you go in
to dispossess, and you dispossess them and dwell in their land, 30take care that
you be not ensnared to follow them, after they have been destroyed before you,
and that you do not inquire about their gods, saying, 'How did these nations serve
their gods?—that I also may do the same.' 31You shall not worship the LORD your
God in that way, for every abominable thing that the LORD hates they have done
for their gods, for they even burn their sons and their daughters in the fire to
their gods.
32[1]"Everything that I command you, you shall be careful to do. You shall not
add to it or take from it.

13 "If a prophet or a dreamer of dreams arises among you and gives you a sign
or a wonder, 2and the sign or wonder that he tells you comes to pass, and
if he says, 'Let us go after other gods,' which you have not known, 'and let us
serve them,' 3you shall not listen to the words of that prophet or that dreamer of
dreams. For the LORD your God is testing you, to know whether you love the LORD
your God with all your heart and with all your soul. 4You shall walk after the LORD
your God and fear him and keep his commandments and obey his voice, and you
shall serve him and hold fast to him. 5But that prophet or that dreamer of dreams
shall be put to death, because he has taught rebellion against the LORD your God,
who brought you out of the land of Egypt and redeemed you out of the house of
slavery, to make you leave the way in which the LORD your God commanded you
to walk. So you shall purge the evil[2] from your midst.
6"If your brother, the son of your mother, or your son or your daughter or the
wife you embrace[3] or your friend who is as your own soul entices you secretly,
saying, 'Let us go and serve other gods,' which neither you nor your fathers have
known, 7some of the gods of the peoples who are around you, whether near you
or far off from you, from the one end of the earth to the other, 8you shall not yield
to him or listen to him, nor shall your eye pity him, nor shall you spare him, nor
shall you conceal him. 9But you shall kill him. Your hand shall be first against him
to put him to death, and afterward the hand of all the people. 10You shall stone
him to death with stones, because he sought to draw you away from the LORD
your God, who brought you out of the land of Egypt, out of the house of slavery.

[1]Ch 13:1 in Hebrew [2]Or *evil person* [3]Hebrew *the wife of your bosom*

11 And all Israel shall hear and fear and never again do any such wickedness as this among you.

12 "If you hear in one of your cities, which the LORD your God is giving you to dwell there, 13 that certain worthless fellows have gone out among you and have drawn away the inhabitants of their city, saying, 'Let us go and serve other gods,' which you have not known, 14 then you shall inquire and make search and ask diligently. And behold, if it be true and certain that such an abomination has been done among you, 15 you shall surely put the inhabitants of that city to the sword, devoting it to destruction,[1] all who are in it and its cattle, with the edge of the sword. 16 You shall gather all its spoil into the midst of its open square and burn the city and all its spoil with fire, as a whole burnt offering to the LORD your God. It shall be a heap forever. It shall not be built again. 17 None of the devoted things shall stick to your hand, that the LORD may turn from the fierceness of his anger and show you mercy and have compassion on you and multiply you, as he swore to your fathers, 18 if you obey the voice of the LORD your God, keeping all his commandments that I am commanding you today, and doing what is right in the sight of the LORD your God.

Clean and Unclean Food

14 "You are the sons of the LORD your God. You shall not cut yourselves or make any baldness on your foreheads for the dead. 2 For you are a people holy to the LORD your God, and the LORD has chosen you to be a people for his treasured possession, out of all the peoples who are on the face of the earth.

3 "You shall not eat any abomination. 4 These are the animals you may eat: the ox, the sheep, the goat, 5 the deer, the gazelle, the roebuck, the wild goat, the ibex,[2] the antelope, and the mountain sheep. 6 Every animal that parts the hoof and has the hoof cloven in two and chews the cud, among the animals, you may eat. 7 Yet of those that chew the cud or have the hoof cloven you shall not eat these: the camel, the hare, and the rock badger, because they chew the cud but do not part the hoof, are unclean for you. 8 And the pig, because it parts the hoof but does not chew the cud, is unclean for you. Their flesh you shall not eat, and their carcasses you shall not touch.

9 "Of all that are in the waters you may eat these: whatever has fins and scales you may eat. 10 And whatever does not have fins and scales you shall not eat; it is unclean for you.

11 "You may eat all clean birds. 12 But these are the ones that you shall not eat: the eagle,[3] the bearded vulture, the black vulture, 13 the kite, the falcon of any kind; 14 every raven of any kind; 15 the ostrich, the nighthawk, the sea gull, the hawk of any kind; 16 the little owl and the short-eared owl, the barn owl 17 and the tawny owl, the carrion vulture and the cormorant, 18 the stork, the heron of any kind; the hoopoe and the bat. 19 And all winged insects are unclean for you; they shall not be eaten. 20 All clean winged things you may eat.

21 "You shall not eat anything that has died naturally. You may give it to the sojourner who is within your towns, that he may eat it, or you may sell it to a foreigner. For you are a people holy to the LORD your God.

"You shall not boil a young goat in its mother's milk.

Tithes

22 "You shall tithe all the yield of your seed that comes from the field year by year. 23 And before the LORD your God, in the place that he will choose, to make his name dwell there, you shall eat the tithe of your grain, of your wine, and of your oil, and the firstborn of your herd and flock, that you may learn to fear the LORD your God always. 24 And if the way is too long for you, so that you are not able to carry the tithe, when the LORD your God blesses you, because the place

[1] That is, setting apart (devoting) as an offering to the Lord (for destruction) [2] Or *addax* [3] The identity of many of these birds is uncertain

is too far from you, which the LORD your God chooses, to set his name there,
25then you shall turn it into money and bind up the money in your hand and go
to the place that the LORD your God chooses 26and spend the money for whatever you desire—oxen or sheep or wine or strong drink, whatever your appetite
craves. And you shall eat there before the LORD your God and rejoice, you and
your household. 27And you shall not neglect the Levite who is within your towns,
for he has no portion or inheritance with you.

28"At the end of every three years you shall bring out all the tithe of your produce in the same year and lay it up within your towns. 29And the Levite, because
he has no portion or inheritance with you, and the sojourner, the fatherless, and
the widow, who are within your towns, shall come and eat and be filled, that the
LORD your God may bless you in all the work of your hands that you do.

The Sabbatical Year

15 "At the end of every seven years you shall grant a release. 2And this is the
manner of the release: every creditor shall release what he has lent to his
neighbor. He shall not exact it of his neighbor, his brother, because the LORD's release has been proclaimed. 3Of a foreigner you may exact it, but whatever of yours
is with your brother your hand shall release. 4But there will be no poor among
you; for the LORD will bless you in the land that the LORD your God is giving you
for an inheritance to possess— 5if only you will strictly obey the voice of the LORD
your God, being careful to do all this commandment that I command you today.
6For the LORD your God will bless you, as he promised you, and you shall lend to
many nations, but you shall not borrow, and you shall rule over many nations, but
they shall not rule over you.

7"If among you, one of your brothers should become poor, in any of your
towns within your land that the LORD your God is giving you, you shall not harden
your heart or shut your hand against your poor brother, 8but you shall open your
hand to him and lend him sufficient for his need, whatever it may be. 9Take care
lest there be an unworthy thought in your heart and you say, 'The seventh year,
the year of release is near,' and your eye look grudgingly[1] on your poor brother,
and you give him nothing, and he cry to the LORD against you, and you be guilty
of sin. 10You shall give to him freely, and your heart shall not be grudging when
you give to him, because for this the LORD your God will bless you in all your work
and in all that you undertake. 11For there will never cease to be poor in the land.
Therefore I command you, 'You shall open wide your hand to your brother, to the
needy and to the poor, in your land.'

12"If your brother, a Hebrew man or a Hebrew woman, is sold[2] to you, he shall
serve you six years, and in the seventh year you shall let him go free from you.
13And when you let him go free from you, you shall not let him go empty-handed.
14You shall furnish him liberally out of your flock, out of your threshing floor, and
out of your winepress. As the LORD your God has blessed you, you shall give to
him. 15You shall remember that you were a slave in the land of Egypt, and the LORD
your God redeemed you; therefore I command you this today. 16But if he says to
you, 'I will not go out from you,' because he loves you and your household, since
he is well-off with you, 17then you shall take an awl, and put it through his ear into
the door, and he shall be your slave[3] forever. And to your female slave[4] you shall
do the same. 18It shall not seem hard to you when you let him go free from you,
for at half the cost of a hired worker he has served you six years. So the LORD your
God will bless you in all that you do.

19"All the firstborn males that are born of your herd and flock you shall dedicate to the LORD your God. You shall do no work with the firstborn of your herd,
nor shear the firstborn of your flock. 20You shall eat it, you and your household,

[1]Or *be evil*; also verse 10 [2]Or *sells himself* [3]Or *servant*; the Hebrew term *'ebed* designates a range of social and economic roles (see Preface) [4]Or *servant*

DEUTERONOMY 15:1–6

RELIEF FROM MISERY

Financial poverty and debt is a crushing experience, making the indebted person or family feel that there is little to no hope for escape. So binding is financial poverty that the Lord inspired the authors of Scripture to include instructions on how to properly handle finances (Lev 25:25–28; Ps 37:21; Pr 28:8; Mt 25:27; Ro 13:8). In cases where Israelites owed a debt to a fellow countryman, Moses commanded that the creditor release the debtor after seven years, offering relief to the oppressive realities of being in debt. How great was this news to those crushed by unending financial obligations!

This financial relief points to the proclamation of Jesus bringing good news to the poor, offering freedom from various forms of intense suffering (Lk 4:18–19). While we do not have the same legal statutes in place to offer freedom from debt every seven years, Jesus offers the Lord's favor in the midst of human sorrow. Our physical circumstances may not change, but Jesus provides relief and comfort to those struggling under oppression or crushing experiences. He offers the kingdom of God to his followers: a sure blessing that will include a wonderful and worshipful exchange of our current suffering for blessing without end in the eternal presence of God.

JESUS, OUR JUBILEE

To be released from an overwhelming debt is a tremendous experience. In this chapter, the Lord wanted his people to see this concept within the larger framework of his mercy to them. The primary theme in this chapter is Jubilee, which started on the Day of Atonement to symbolize that Israel's sin had been paid for (Lev 25). This celebratory concept was intended to remind the Israelites of God's act to rescue them from Egyptian bondage (Dt 15:15) with applications for contemporary considerations such as releasing people from their debts (vv. 1 – 6) and being generous to the poor (vv. 7 – 11). Ultimately, the Israelites were expected to cancel various bondages — indentured servants, debts, or liens on land — based on God's gracious mercy toward them as a people.

This practice prefigured the ultimate jubilee offered by God through Christ's atonement for our debt to sin (Ro 6:17 – 18). In the same way that the Israelites were enslaved to the Egyptians and were unable to free themselves, all people are hopelessly bound to sin apart from Christ's act on their behalf to offer them freedom (Ro 5:6 – 8). His death and resurrection, as payment for the debt of sin, is the only means that God the Father has provided for people to be reconciled to God (Jn 14:6). He gives people the credit needed to be free from sin and death. He became the benefactor, willing to make a payment and release them from a line of credit that proved to be beyond their capability to pay for (Dt 15:2). Whereas all people were dead through Adam, Christ has brought life to all who believe the gospel and are redeemed by the Lord (Ro 5:12 – 21).

Theologians refer to this transaction as the "great exchange," meaning what was due to mankind — because of our sin — was transferred to Jesus, and what was due to him — because of his perfection — was transferred to believers. He took the wrath of God on our behalf and transferred to us the blessings of the Father which we had absolutely no right to claim. Indeed, Christians have a reason to shout to the nations that we have "jubilee" in Jesus!

before the LORD your God year by year at the place that the LORD will choose. [21]But if it has any blemish, if it is lame or blind or has any serious blemish whatever, you shall not sacrifice it to the LORD your God. [22]You shall eat it within your towns. The unclean and the clean alike may eat it, as though it were a gazelle or a deer. [23]Only you shall not eat its blood; you shall pour it out on the ground like water.

Passover

16 "Observe the month of Abib and keep the Passover to the LORD your God, for in the month of Abib the LORD your God brought you out of Egypt by night. [2]And you shall offer the Passover sacrifice to the LORD your God, from the flock or the herd, at the place that the LORD will choose, to make his name dwell there. [3]You shall eat no leavened bread with it. Seven days you shall eat it with unleavened bread, the bread of affliction—for you came out of the land of Egypt in haste—that all the days of your life you may remember the day when you came out of the land of Egypt. [4]No leaven shall be seen with you in all your territory for seven days, nor shall any of the flesh that you sacrifice on the evening of the first day remain all night until morning. [5]You may not offer the Passover sacrifice within any of your towns that the LORD your God is giving you, [6]but at the place that the LORD your God will choose, to make his name dwell in it, there you shall offer the Passover sacrifice, in the evening at sunset, at the time you came out of Egypt. [7]And you shall cook it and eat it at the place that the LORD your God will choose. And in the morning you shall turn and go to your tents. [8]For six days you shall eat unleavened bread, and on the seventh day there shall be a solemn assembly to the LORD your God. You shall do no work on it.

The Feast of Weeks

[9]"You shall count seven weeks. Begin to count the seven weeks from the time the sickle is first put to the standing grain. [10]Then you shall keep the Feast of Weeks to the LORD your God with the tribute of a freewill offering from your hand, which you shall give as the LORD your God blesses you. [11]And you shall rejoice before the LORD your God, you and your son and your daughter, your male servant and your female servant, the Levite who is within your towns, the sojourner, the fatherless, and the widow who are among you, at the place that the LORD your God will choose, to make his name dwell there. [12]You shall remember that you were a slave in Egypt; and you shall be careful to observe these statutes.

The Feast of Booths

[13]"You shall keep the Feast of Booths seven days, when you have gathered in the produce from your threshing floor and your winepress. [14]You shall rejoice in your feast, you and your son and your daughter, your male servant and your female servant, the Levite, the sojourner, the fatherless, and the widow who are within your towns. [15]For seven days you shall keep the feast to the LORD your God at the place that the LORD will choose, because the LORD your God will bless you in all your produce and in all the work of your hands, so that you will be altogether joyful.

[16]"Three times a year all your males shall appear before the LORD your God at the place that he will choose: at the Feast of Unleavened Bread, at the Feast of Weeks, and at the Feast of Booths. They shall not appear before the LORD empty-handed. [17]Every man shall give as he is able, according to the blessing of the LORD your God that he has given you.

Justice

[18]"You shall appoint judges and officers in all your towns that the LORD your God is giving you, according to your tribes, and they shall judge the people with righteous judgment. [19]You shall not pervert justice. You shall not show partiality, and you shall not accept a bribe, for a bribe blinds the eyes of the wise and

DEUTERONOMY 16:21—17:7

JESUS, THE CENTER OF SCRIPTURE AND TRUE RELIGION

There are so many options, so many ways that people try to worship God. From Eastern meditation and yoga to other world religions, mankind seeks to communicate with a higher being and satisfy the requirements of various religious systems. Yet we must ask the question, what does all of this activity actually accomplish? According to this passage, it does not accomplish anything more than stir up God's anger when his people carry out religious practices that are not aligned with Scripture. Jesus taught us that not all religious activity is equal or even valid and that God expects his creatures to worship him in specific ways (Jn 4:22–24). God's people, however, often drift to religious practices that are not satisfying to God, reflecting pagan values or the imaginations of religious leaders rather than Scripture. Valid religion is found in Jesus alone (Jn 14:6–7). He is the capstone of God's revelation in the Bible and through him we worship God according to his standard. All of Scripture points to Jesus as the perfect revelation of God, his ideals, and his desires for us as his created beings (Heb 1:1–3).

DEUTERONOMY 17:14–20

JESUS, THE PERFECT KING

Here are instructions from the Lord to Israel concerning their desire to have a king reign over them. God

(continued on next page)

subverts the cause of the righteous. 20 Justice, and only justice, you shall follow,
that you may live and inherit the land that the LORD your God is giving you.

Forbidden Forms of Worship

21 "You shall not plant any tree as an Asherah beside the altar of the LORD your
God that you shall make. 22 And you shall not set up a pillar, which the LORD your
God hates.

17 "You shall not sacrifice to the LORD your God an ox or a sheep in which is a
blemish, any defect whatever, for that is an abomination to the LORD your
God.

2 "If there is found among you, within any of your towns that the LORD your
God is giving you, a man or woman who does what is evil in the sight of the LORD
your God, in transgressing his covenant, 3 and has gone and served other gods
and worshiped them, or the sun or the moon or any of the host of heaven, which
I have forbidden, 4 and it is told you and you hear of it, then you shall inquire
diligently, and if it is true and certain that such an abomination has been done in
Israel, 5 then you shall bring out to your gates that man or woman who has done
this evil thing, and you shall stone that man or woman to death with stones. 6 On
the evidence of two witnesses or of three witnesses the one who is to die shall be
put to death; a person shall not be put to death on the evidence of one witness.
7 The hand of the witnesses shall be first against him to put him to death, and
afterward the hand of all the people. So you shall purge[1] the evil[2] from your midst.

Legal Decisions by Priests and Judges

8 "If any case arises requiring decision between one kind of homicide and another, one kind of legal right and another, or one kind of assault and another, any
case within your towns that is too difficult for you, then you shall arise and go up
to the place that the LORD your God will choose. 9 And you shall come to the Levitical priests and to the judge who is in office in those days, and you shall consult
them, and they shall declare to you the decision. 10 Then you shall do according to
what they declare to you from that place that the LORD will choose. And you shall
be careful to do according to all that they direct you. 11 According to the instructions that they give you, and according to the decision which they pronounce to
you, you shall do. You shall not turn aside from the verdict that they declare to
you, either to the right hand or to the left. 12 The man who acts presumptuously by
not obeying the priest who stands to minister there before the LORD your God, or
the judge, that man shall die. So you shall purge the evil from Israel. 13 And all the
people shall hear and fear and not act presumptuously again.

Laws Concerning Israel's Kings

14 "When you come to the land that the LORD your God is giving you, and you
possess it and dwell in it and then say, 'I will set a king over me, like all the nations
that are around me,' 15 you may indeed set a king over you whom the LORD your
God will choose. One from among your brothers you shall set as king over you.
You may not put a foreigner over you, who is not your brother. 16 Only he must not
acquire many horses for himself or cause the people to return to Egypt in order to
acquire many horses, since the LORD has said to you, 'You shall never return that
way again.' 17 And he shall not acquire many wives for himself, lest his heart turn
away, nor shall he acquire for himself excessive silver and gold.

18 "And when he sits on the throne of his kingdom, he shall write for himself in
a book a copy of this law, approved by[3] the Levitical priests. 19 And it shall be with
him, and he shall read in it all the days of his life, that he may learn to fear the
LORD his God by keeping all the words of this law and these statutes, and doing
them, 20 that his heart may not be lifted up above his brothers, and that he may not

[1]Septuagint *drive out*; also verse 12 [2]Or *evil person*; also verse 12 [3]Hebrew *from before*

turn aside from the commandment, either to the right hand or to the left, so that he may continue long in his kingdom, he and his children, in Israel.

Provision for Priests and Levites

18 "The Levitical priests, all the tribe of Levi, shall have no portion or inheritance with Israel. They shall eat the LORD's food offerings[1] as their[2] inheritance. 2They shall have no inheritance among their brothers; the LORD is their inheritance, as he promised them. 3And this shall be the priests' due from the people, from those offering a sacrifice, whether an ox or a sheep: they shall give to the priest the shoulder and the two cheeks and the stomach. 4The firstfruits of your grain, of your wine and of your oil, and the first fleece of your sheep, you shall give him. 5For the LORD your God has chosen him out of all your tribes to stand and minister in the name of the LORD, him and his sons for all time.

6"And if a Levite comes from any of your towns out of all Israel, where he lives—and he may come when he desires[3]—to the place that the LORD will choose, 7and ministers in the name of the LORD his God, like all his fellow Levites who stand to minister there before the LORD, 8then he may have equal portions to eat, besides what he receives from the sale of his patrimony.[4]

Abominable Practices

9"When you come into the land that the LORD your God is giving you, you shall not learn to follow the abominable practices of those nations. 10There shall not be found among you anyone who burns his son or his daughter as an offering,[5] anyone who practices divination or tells fortunes or interprets omens, or a sorcerer 11or a charmer or a medium or a necromancer or one who inquires of the dead, 12for whoever does these things is an abomination to the LORD. And because of these abominations the LORD your God is driving them out before you. 13You shall be blameless before the LORD your God, 14for these nations, which you are about to dispossess, listen to fortune-tellers and to diviners. But as for you, the LORD your God has not allowed you to do this.

A New Prophet like Moses

15"The LORD your God will raise up for you a prophet like me from among you, from your brothers—it is to him you shall listen— 16just as you desired of the LORD your God at Horeb on the day of the assembly, when you said, 'Let me not hear again the voice of the LORD my God or see this great fire any more, lest I die.' 17And the LORD said to me, 'They are right in what they have spoken. 18I will raise up for them a prophet like you from among their brothers. And I will put my words in his mouth, and he shall speak to them all that I command him. 19And whoever will not listen to my words that he shall speak in my name, I myself will require it of him. 20But the prophet who presumes to speak a word in my name that I have not commanded him to speak, or[6] who speaks in the name of other gods, that same prophet shall die.' 21And if you say in your heart, 'How may we know the word that the LORD has not spoken?'— 22when a prophet speaks in the name of the LORD, if the word does not come to pass or come true, that is a word that the LORD has not spoken; the prophet has spoken it presumptuously. You need not be afraid of him.

Laws Concerning Cities of Refuge

19 "When the LORD your God cuts off the nations whose land the LORD your God is giving you, and you dispossess them and dwell in their cities and in their houses, 2you shall set apart three cities for yourselves in the land that the LORD your God is giving you to possess. 3You shall measure the distances[7] and

[1]Or *the offerings by fire to the LORD* [2]Hebrew *his* [3]Or *lives—if he comes enthusiastically* [4]The meaning of the Hebrew is uncertain [5]Hebrew *makes his son or his daughter pass through the fire* [6]Or *and* [7]Hebrew *road*

(Jesus, the Perfect King, continued)

laid out in detail (through Moses) the type of person who should be their king, setting a standard for the leader of the Israelites. Throughout the remainder of the Old Testament, however, the kings of Israel proved to be lacking in major ways—although Moses clearly stated the requirements. Saul turned out to be an evil man, seeking ungodly pursuits rather than the way of the Lord. David committed murder and adultery, operating as a scandalous and selfish leader. Although he was considered extremely wise, Solomon had numerous wives and concubines, thus violating God's instructions for a king (v. 17). As great as these men were, they were fallible human beings and left much to be desired. Ultimately, Jesus proved to be the King that Israel always wanted (Isa 9:6–7). Jesus fulfilled the ideals expressed in these verses of Deuteronomy 17, without blemish, moral failure, or selfish ambition. He is a stark contrast to the imperfect kings of Israel in the Old Testament.

CHRIST, THE PROMISED PROPHET

Throughout the first five books of the Bible (the Pentateuch), Moses served the people of Israel in three primary offices or ways: prophet (Dt 34:10 – 12), priest (Ex 32:31 – 35), and as a type of king or ruler (Ex 18:24 – 26). The people of God relied on Moses to lead them as a forming nation and in religious practices according to God's Word, as well as petitioning the Lord on their behalf. Moses foretold of another prophet that God would raise up to serve Israel in the same vein. Deuteronomy 18:15 states, "The LORD your God will raise up for you a prophet like me from among you, from your brothers — it is to him you shall listen." This verse established a culture of anticipation that went unfulfilled for hundreds of years. The people of Israel longed for the next great leader, one who would lead them as a king, priest, and prophet. Moses foreshadowed the one for whom Israel waited. He was a type of Christ, looking forward to the Messiah who was yet to come.

Jesus proved to be the long-anticipated prophet, following in the offices of Moses and fulfilling the anticipation of Israel recorded in the Old Testament (Mt 4:12 – 17; Lk 4:16 – 21). Although many Israelites looked for a military leader, Jesus came as a humble servant, even willing to face the most humiliating form of execution within the Roman Empire (Php 2:5 – 8). He is a king — whose kingdom is not of this world — who came to serve his people by atoning for their sin on a cross to rescue them from the judgment of God. He is a prophet who proclaimed the commands of God and showed his followers the right path to please the Lord (Jn 14:15,23). Finally, he is a priest, going before the Father on behalf of the people of God, an office he currently fulfills at the right hand of the Father without ceasing (Heb 7:23 – 25).

Ultimately, all of the Old Testament authors — from Moses to David and the other prophets — looked forward to the day when the Messiah would come and bring finality to their anticipation, a day when they would see their ultimate Prophet, Priest, and King.

divide into three parts the area of the land that the LORD your God gives you as a possession, so that any manslayer can flee to them.

4“This is the provision for the manslayer, who by fleeing there may save his life. If anyone kills his neighbor unintentionally without having hated him in the past— 5as when someone goes into the forest with his neighbor to cut wood, and his hand swings the axe to cut down a tree, and the head slips from the handle and strikes his neighbor so that he dies—he may flee to one of these cities and live, 6lest the avenger of blood in hot anger pursue the manslayer and overtake him, because the way is long, and strike him fatally, though the man did not deserve to die, since he had not hated his neighbor in the past. 7Therefore I command you, You shall set apart three cities. 8And if the LORD your God enlarges your territory, as he has sworn to your fathers, and gives you all the land that he promised to give to your fathers— 9provided you are careful to keep all this commandment, which I command you today, by loving the LORD your God and by walking ever in his ways—then you shall add three other cities to these three, 10lest innocent blood be shed in your land that the LORD your God is giving you for an inheritance, and so the guilt of bloodshed be upon you.

11“But if anyone hates his neighbor and lies in wait for him and attacks him and strikes him fatally so that he dies, and he flees into one of these cities, 12then the elders of his city shall send and take him from there, and hand him over to the avenger of blood, so that he may die. 13Your eye shall not pity him, but you shall purge the guilt of innocent blood[1] from Israel, so that it may be well with you.

Property Boundaries

14“You shall not move your neighbor’s landmark, which the men of old have set, in the inheritance that you will hold in the land that the LORD your God is giving you to possess.

Laws Concerning Witnesses

15“A single witness shall not suffice against a person for any crime or for any wrong in connection with any offense that he has committed. Only on the evidence of two witnesses or of three witnesses shall a charge be established. 16If a malicious witness arises to accuse a person of wrongdoing, 17then both parties to the dispute shall appear before the LORD, before the priests and the judges who are in office in those days. 18The judges shall inquire diligently, and if the witness is a false witness and has accused his brother falsely, 19then you shall do to him as he had meant to do to his brother. So you shall purge the evil[2] from your midst. 20And the rest shall hear and fear, and shall never again commit any such evil among you. 21Your eye shall not pity. It shall be life for life, eye for eye, tooth for tooth, hand for hand, foot for foot.

Laws Concerning Warfare

20 “When you go out to war against your enemies, and see horses and chariots and an army larger than your own, you shall not be afraid of them, for the LORD your God is with you, who brought you up out of the land of Egypt. 2And when you draw near to the battle, the priest shall come forward and speak to the people 3and shall say to them, ‘Hear, O Israel, today you are drawing near for battle against your enemies: let not your heart faint. Do not fear or panic or be in dread of them, 4for the LORD your God is he who goes with you to fight for you against your enemies, to give you the victory.’ 5Then the officers shall speak to the people, saying, ‘Is there any man who has built a new house and has not dedicated it? Let him go back to his house, lest he die in the battle and another man dedicate it. 6And is there any man who has planted a vineyard and has not enjoyed its fruit? Let him go back to his house, lest he die in the battle

[1]Or *the blood of the innocent* [2]Or *evil person*

and another man enjoy its fruit. 7And is there any man who has betrothed a wife
and has not taken her? Let him go back to his house, lest he die in the battle and
another man take her.' 8And the officers shall speak further to the people, and
say, 'Is there any man who is fearful and fainthearted? Let him go back to his
house, lest he make the heart of his fellows melt like his own.' 9And when the officers have finished speaking to the people, then commanders shall be appointed
at the head of the people.

10"When you draw near to a city to fight against it, offer terms of peace to it.
11And if it responds to you peaceably and it opens to you, then all the people who
are found in it shall do forced labor for you and shall serve you. 12But if it makes no
peace with you, but makes war against you, then you shall besiege it. 13And when
the LORD your God gives it into your hand, you shall put all its males to the sword,
14but the women and the little ones, the livestock, and everything else in the city,
all its spoil, you shall take as plunder for yourselves. And you shall enjoy the spoil
of your enemies, which the LORD your God has given you. 15Thus you shall do to
all the cities that are very far from you, which are not cities of the nations here.
16But in the cities of these peoples that the LORD your God is giving you for an inheritance, you shall save alive nothing that breathes, 17but you shall devote them
to complete destruction,[1] the Hittites and the Amorites, the Canaanites and the
Perizzites, the Hivites and the Jebusites, as the LORD your God has commanded,
18that they may not teach you to do according to all their abominable practices
that they have done for their gods, and so you sin against the LORD your God.

19"When you besiege a city for a long time, making war against it in order to
take it, you shall not destroy its trees by wielding an axe against them. You may
eat from them, but you shall not cut them down. Are the trees in the field human,
that they should be besieged by you? 20Only the trees that you know are not trees
for food you may destroy and cut down, that you may build siegeworks against
the city that makes war with you, until it falls.

Atonement for Unsolved Murders

21 "If in the land that the LORD your God is giving you to possess someone is
found slain, lying in the open country, and it is not known who killed him,
2then your elders and your judges shall come out, and they shall measure the
distance to the surrounding cities. 3And the elders of the city that is nearest to the
slain man shall take a heifer that has never been worked and that has not pulled in
a yoke. 4And the elders of that city shall bring the heifer down to a valley with running water, which is neither plowed nor sown, and shall break the heifer's neck
there in the valley. 5Then the priests, the sons of Levi, shall come forward, for the
LORD your God has chosen them to minister to him and to bless in the name of
the LORD, and by their word every dispute and every assault shall be settled. 6And
all the elders of that city nearest to the slain man shall wash their hands over the
heifer whose neck was broken in the valley, 7and they shall testify, 'Our hands did
not shed this blood, nor did our eyes see it shed. 8Accept atonement, O LORD, for
your people Israel, whom you have redeemed, and do not set the guilt of innocent
blood in the midst of your people Israel, so that their blood guilt be atoned for.'
9So you shall purge the guilt of innocent blood from your midst, when you do
what is right in the sight of the LORD.

Marrying Female Captives

10"When you go out to war against your enemies, and the LORD your God gives
them into your hand and you take them captive, 11and you see among the captives
a beautiful woman, and you desire to take her to be your wife, 12and you bring her
home to your house, she shall shave her head and pare her nails. 13And she shall
take off the clothes in which she was captured and shall remain in your house

[1]That is, set apart (devote) as an offering to the Lord (for destruction)

and lament her father and her mother a full month. After that you may go in to
her and be her husband, and she shall be your wife. 14But if you no longer delight
in her, you shall let her go where she wants. But you shall not sell her for money,
nor shall you treat her as a slave, since you have humiliated her.

Inheritance Rights of the Firstborn

15"If a man has two wives, the one loved and the other unloved, and both the
loved and the unloved have borne him children, and if the firstborn son belongs
to the unloved,[1] 16then on the day when he assigns his possessions as an inheritance to his sons, he may not treat the son of the loved as the firstborn in preference to the son of the unloved, who is the firstborn, 17but he shall acknowledge
the firstborn, the son of the unloved, by giving him a double portion of all that he
has, for he is the firstfruits of his strength. The right of the firstborn is his.

A Rebellious Son

18"If a man has a stubborn and rebellious son who will not obey the voice of
his father or the voice of his mother, and, though they discipline him, will not
listen to them, 19then his father and his mother shall take hold of him and bring
him out to the elders of his city at the gate of the place where he lives, 20and they
shall say to the elders of his city, 'This our son is stubborn and rebellious; he will
not obey our voice; he is a glutton and a drunkard.' 21Then all the men of the city
shall stone him to death with stones. So you shall purge the evil from your midst,
and all Israel shall hear, and fear.

A Man Hanged on a Tree Is Cursed

22"And if a man has committed a crime punishable by death and he is put to
death, and you hang him on a tree, 23his body shall not remain all night on the
tree, but you shall bury him the same day, for a hanged man is cursed by God. You
shall not defile your land that the LORD your God is giving you for an inheritance.

Various Laws

22 "You shall not see your brother's ox or his sheep going astray and ignore
them. You shall take them back to your brother. 2And if he does not live
near you and you do not know who he is, you shall bring it home to your house,
and it shall stay with you until your brother seeks it. Then you shall restore it to
him. 3And you shall do the same with his donkey or with his garment, or with
any lost thing of your brother's, which he loses and you find; you may not ignore
it. 4You shall not see your brother's donkey or his ox fallen down by the way and
ignore them. You shall help him to lift them up again.

5"A woman shall not wear a man's garment, nor shall a man put on a woman's
cloak, for whoever does these things is an abomination to the LORD your God.

6"If you come across a bird's nest in any tree or on the ground, with young ones
or eggs and the mother sitting on the young or on the eggs, you shall not take the
mother with the young. 7You shall let the mother go, but the young you may take
for yourself, that it may go well with you, and that you may live long.

8"When you build a new house, you shall make a parapet for your roof, that
you may not bring the guilt of blood upon your house, if anyone should fall
from it.

9"You shall not sow your vineyard with two kinds of seed, lest the whole yield
be forfeited,[2] the crop that you have sown and the yield of the vineyard. 10You
shall not plow with an ox and a donkey together. 11You shall not wear cloth of wool
and linen mixed together.

12"You shall make yourself tassels on the four corners of the garment with
which you cover yourself.

[1]Or *hated*; also verses 16, 17 [2]Hebrew *become holy*

A CURSED MAN

The promised land was of such value that God made provisions to ensure that its splendor was protected. God knew that his people would rebel from his law and kill one another, as the story of Cain and Abel demonstrates (Ge 4:8). This sin, and others like it, tarnished the people of God and the land itself. God instructed the people to punish the evildoer with death, as a sign of God's divine judgment against sins of this magnitude. At times those who were put to death by stoning, the ordinary form of capital punishment prescribed by the law, would be impaled on a pole as a testimony to all bystanders of the implications of sin. God, however, instructed the nation to take down those bodies which were exposed in this fashion and bury them right away. They were cursed by God, and the bodies should not remain overnight.

Centuries later the Romans invented a far more notorious form of exposure. Rather than executing criminals first, they would nail them to a wooden cross. This punishment was reserved for the worst of the worst, particularly those who undermined the Roman government. The Romans wanted to teach onlookers a lesson, and crucifixion on a wooden cross was a sure sign that they had better not offend Rome. They killed in the most excruciating way and made sure everyone saw the agony.

The Romans intended Jesus' crucifixion to make this same point. Not only had he supposedly usurped the rule of Rome, but also he had claimed to be God—a claim the Jews thought was blasphemous since Jesus was a Jewish carpenter from Nazareth (Jn 10:30–33). His brutal torture and execution were designed to show that he was not a king and certainly not God.

God used Jesus' crucifixion to communicate a far greater message, one rooted in Deuteronomy 21. As he hung on the cross, Jesus was cursed by God. His curse was not based on his sin, however. He was the pure and spotless Son of God. He was cursed by God for the sin of his people. Jesus willingly became a cursed man, submitting himself to death on a cross in order to save men and women from having to bear the wrath of God themselves (Gal 3:10–14). He was cursed so that his people could be blessed.

Laws Concerning Sexual Immorality

13“If any man takes a wife and goes in to her and then hates her 14and accuses
her of misconduct and brings a bad name upon her, saying, ‘I took this woman,
and when I came near her, I did not find in her evidence of virginity,’ 15then the
father of the young woman and her mother shall take and bring out the evidence
of her virginity to the elders of the city in the gate. 16And the father of the young
woman shall say to the elders, ‘I gave my daughter to this man to marry, and he
hates her; 17and behold, he has accused her of misconduct, saying, “I did not
find in your daughter evidence of virginity.” And yet this is the evidence of my
daughter’s virginity.’ And they shall spread the cloak before the elders of the city.
18Then the elders of that city shall take the man and whip[1] him, 19and they shall
fine him a hundred shekels[2] of silver and give them to the father of the young
woman, because he has brought a bad name upon a virgin[3] of Israel. And she
shall be his wife. He may not divorce her all his days. 20But if the thing is true,
that evidence of virginity was not found in the young woman, 21then they shall
bring out the young woman to the door of her father’s house, and the men of her
city shall stone her to death with stones, because she has done an outrageous
thing in Israel by whoring in her father’s house. So you shall purge the evil from
your midst.

22“If a man is found lying with the wife of another man, both of them shall
die, the man who lay with the woman, and the woman. So you shall purge the
evil from Israel.

23“If there is a betrothed virgin, and a man meets her in the city and lies with
her, 24then you shall bring them both out to the gate of that city, and you shall
stone them to death with stones, the young woman because she did not cry for
help though she was in the city, and the man because he violated his neighbor’s
wife. So you shall purge the evil from your midst.

25“But if in the open country a man meets a young woman who is betrothed,
and the man seizes her and lies with her, then only the man who lay with her
shall die. 26But you shall do nothing to the young woman; she has committed no offense punishable by death. For this case is like that of a man attacking and murdering his neighbor, 27because he met her in the open country, and
though the betrothed young woman cried for help there was no one to rescue
her.

28“If a man meets a virgin who is not betrothed, and seizes her and lies with
her, and they are found, 29then the man who lay with her shall give to the father
of the young woman fifty shekels of silver, and she shall be his wife, because he
has violated her. He may not divorce her all his days.

30[4]“A man shall not take his father’s wife, so that he does not uncover his father’s nakedness.[5]

Those Excluded from the Assembly

23 “No one whose testicles are crushed or whose male organ is cut off shall
enter the assembly of the Lord.

2“No one born of a forbidden union may enter the assembly of the Lord. Even
to the tenth generation, none of his descendants may enter the assembly of the
Lord.

3“No Ammonite or Moabite may enter the assembly of the Lord. Even to the
tenth generation, none of them may enter the assembly of the Lord forever, 4be-
cause they did not meet you with bread and with water on the way, when you
came out of Egypt, and because they hired against you Balaam the son of Beor
from Pethor of Mesopotamia, to curse you. 5But the Lord your God would not
listen to Balaam; instead the Lord your God turned the curse into a blessing for

[1]Or *discipline* [2]A *shekel* was about 2/5 ounce or 11 grams [3]Or *girl of marriageable age* [4]Ch 23:1 in Hebrew [5]Hebrew *uncover his father’s skirt*

you, because the LORD your God loved you. 6 You shall not seek their peace or their prosperity all your days forever.

7 "You shall not abhor an Edomite, for he is your brother. You shall not abhor an Egyptian, because you were a sojourner in his land. 8 Children born to them in the third generation may enter the assembly of the LORD.

Uncleanness in the Camp

9 "When you are encamped against your enemies, then you shall keep yourself from every evil thing.

10 "If any man among you becomes unclean because of a nocturnal emission, then he shall go outside the camp. He shall not come inside the camp, 11 but when evening comes, he shall bathe himself in water, and as the sun sets, he may come inside the camp.

12 "You shall have a place outside the camp, and you shall go out to it. 13 And you shall have a trowel with your tools, and when you sit down outside, you shall dig a hole with it and turn back and cover up your excrement. 14 Because the LORD your God walks in the midst of your camp, to deliver you and to give up your enemies before you, therefore your camp must be holy, so that he may not see anything indecent among you and turn away from you.

Miscellaneous Laws

15 "You shall not give up to his master a slave[1] who has escaped from his master to you. 16 He shall dwell with you, in your midst, in the place that he shall choose within one of your towns, wherever it suits him. You shall not wrong him.

17 "None of the daughters of Israel shall be a cult prostitute, and none of the sons of Israel shall be a cult prostitute. 18 You shall not bring the fee of a prostitute or the wages of a dog[2] into the house of the LORD your God in payment for any vow, for both of these are an abomination to the LORD your God.

19 "You shall not charge interest on loans to your brother, interest on money, interest on food, interest on anything that is lent for interest. 20 You may charge a foreigner interest, but you may not charge your brother interest, that the LORD your God may bless you in all that you undertake in the land that you are entering to take possession of it.

21 "If you make a vow to the LORD your God, you shall not delay fulfilling it, for the LORD your God will surely require it of you, and you will be guilty of sin. 22 But if you refrain from vowing, you will not be guilty of sin. 23 You shall be careful to do what has passed your lips, for you have voluntarily vowed to the LORD your God what you have promised with your mouth.

24 "If you go into your neighbor's vineyard, you may eat your fill of grapes, as many as you wish, but you shall not put any in your bag. 25 If you go into your neighbor's standing grain, you may pluck the ears with your hand, but you shall not put a sickle to your neighbor's standing grain.

Laws Concerning Divorce

24 "When a man takes a wife and marries her, if then she finds no favor in his eyes because he has found some indecency in her, and he writes her a certificate of divorce and puts it in her hand and sends her out of his house, and she departs out of his house, 2 and if she goes and becomes another man's wife, 3 and the latter man hates her and writes her a certificate of divorce and puts it in her hand and sends her out of his house, or if the latter man dies, who took her to be his wife, 4 then her former husband, who sent her away, may not take her again to be his wife, after she has been defiled, for that is an abomination before the LORD. And you shall not bring sin upon the land that the LORD your God is giving you for an inheritance.

[1]Or *servant*; the Hebrew term *'ebed* designates a range of social and economic roles (see Preface)
[2]Or *male prostitute*

DEUTERONOMY 24:1–4

GOD'S COVENANT AND DIVORCE

Divorce among the people of God was never advocated or promoted, though it was granted on occasion as a concession to human sin. Jesus said that it was because of the hardness of the human heart that Moses permitted divorce (Mk 10:2–5). Jesus then pointed to God's created design in the beginning, while warning people not to tear apart that which God had joined together (Mk 10:6–9). The covenantal nature of marriage is meant to model the way in which God loves, pursues, and sacrifices on behalf of adulterous people (Eph 5:22–33). Therefore any act, especially divorce, which violates the marriage covenant fails to model the faithfulness of God demonstrated throughout redemptive history. While scholars may debate whether or not Jesus grants exceptions for divorce, one thing is clear—divorce is a result of human sin and fails to model the covenant faithfulness of God to his people.

Miscellaneous Laws

5"When a man is newly married, he shall not go out with the army or be liable for any other public duty. He shall be free at home one year to be happy with his wife[1] whom he has taken.

6"No one shall take a mill or an upper millstone in pledge, for that would be taking a life in pledge.

7"If a man is found stealing one of his brothers of the people of Israel, and if he treats him as a slave or sells him, then that thief shall die. So you shall purge the evil from your midst.

8"Take care, in a case of leprous[2] disease, to be very careful to do according to all that the Levitical priests shall direct you. As I commanded them, so you shall be careful to do. 9Remember what the LORD your God did to Miriam on the way as you came out of Egypt.

10"When you make your neighbor a loan of any sort, you shall not go into his house to collect his pledge. 11You shall stand outside, and the man to whom you make the loan shall bring the pledge out to you. 12And if he is a poor man, you shall not sleep in his pledge. 13You shall restore to him the pledge as the sun sets, that he may sleep in his cloak and bless you. And it shall be righteousness for you before the LORD your God.

14"You shall not oppress a hired worker who is poor and needy, whether he is one of your brothers or one of the sojourners who are in your land within your towns. 15You shall give him his wages on the same day, before the sun sets (for he is poor and counts on it), lest he cry against you to the LORD, and you be guilty of sin.

16"Fathers shall not be put to death because of their children, nor shall children be put to death because of their fathers. Each one shall be put to death for his own sin.

17"You shall not pervert the justice due to the sojourner or to the fatherless, or take a widow's garment in pledge, 18but you shall remember that you were a slave in Egypt and the LORD your God redeemed you from there; therefore I command you to do this.

19"When you reap your harvest in your field and forget a sheaf in the field, you shall not go back to get it. It shall be for the sojourner, the fatherless, and the widow, that the LORD your God may bless you in all the work of your hands. 20When you beat your olive trees, you shall not go over them again. It shall be for the sojourner, the fatherless, and the widow. 21When you gather the grapes of your vineyard, you shall not strip it afterward. It shall be for the sojourner, the fatherless, and the widow. 22You shall remember that you were a slave in the land of Egypt; therefore I command you to do this.

25 "If there is a dispute between men and they come into court and the judges decide between them, acquitting the innocent and condemning the guilty, 2then if the guilty man deserves to be beaten, the judge shall cause him to lie down and be beaten in his presence with a number of stripes in proportion to his offense. 3Forty stripes may be given him, but not more, lest, if one should go on to beat him with more stripes than these, your brother be degraded in your sight.

4"You shall not muzzle an ox when it is treading out the grain.

Laws Concerning Levirate Marriage

5"If brothers dwell together, and one of them dies and has no son, the wife of the dead man shall not be married outside the family to a stranger. Her husband's brother shall go in to her and take her as his wife and perform the duty of a husband's brother to her. 6And the first son whom she bears shall succeed to the name of his dead brother, that his name may not be blotted out of Israel. 7And if the man does not wish to take his brother's wife, then his brother's wife shall go up to the gate to the elders and say, 'My husband's brother refuses to perpetuate

---

[1]Or *to make happy his wife* [2]*Leprosy* was a term for several skin diseases; see Leviticus 13

his brother's name in Israel; he will not perform the duty of a husband's brother to me.' 8Then the elders of his city shall call him and speak to him, and if he persists, saying, 'I do not wish to take her,' 9then his brother's wife shall go up to him in the presence of the elders and pull his sandal off his foot and spit in his face. And she shall answer and say, 'So shall it be done to the man who does not build up his brother's house.' 10And the name of his house[1] shall be called in Israel, 'The house of him who had his sandal pulled off.'

Miscellaneous Laws

11"When men fight with one another and the wife of the one draws near to rescue her husband from the hand of him who is beating him and puts out her hand and seizes him by the private parts, 12then you shall cut off her hand. Your eye shall have no pity.

13"You shall not have in your bag two kinds of weights, a large and a small. 14You shall not have in your house two kinds of measures, a large and a small. 15A full and fair[2] weight you shall have, a full and fair measure you shall have, that your days may be long in the land that the LORD your God is giving you. 16For all who do such things, all who act dishonestly, are an abomination to the LORD your God.

17"Remember what Amalek did to you on the way as you came out of Egypt, 18how he attacked you on the way when you were faint and weary, and cut off your tail, those who were lagging behind you, and he did not fear God. 19Therefore when the LORD your God has given you rest from all your enemies around you, in the land that the LORD your God is giving you for an inheritance to possess, you shall blot out the memory of Amalek from under heaven; you shall not forget.

Offerings of Firstfruits and Tithes

26 "When you come into the land that the LORD your God is giving you for an inheritance and have taken possession of it and live in it, 2you shall take some of the first of all the fruit of the ground, which you harvest from your land that the LORD your God is giving you, and you shall put it in a basket, and you shall go to the place that the LORD your God will choose, to make his name to dwell there. 3And you shall go to the priest who is in office at that time and say to him, 'I declare today to the LORD your God that I have come into the land that the LORD swore to our fathers to give us.' 4Then the priest shall take the basket from your hand and set it down before the altar of the LORD your God.

5"And you shall make response before the LORD your God, 'A wandering Aramean was my father. And he went down into Egypt and sojourned there, few in number, and there he became a nation, great, mighty, and populous. 6And the Egyptians treated us harshly and humiliated us and laid on us hard labor. 7Then we cried to the LORD, the God of our fathers, and the LORD heard our voice and saw our affliction, our toil, and our oppression. 8And the LORD brought us out of Egypt with a mighty hand and an outstretched arm, with great deeds of terror,[3] with signs and wonders. 9And he brought us into this place and gave us this land, a land flowing with milk and honey. 10And behold, now I bring the first of the fruit of the ground, which you, O LORD, have given me.' And you shall set it down before the LORD your God and worship before the LORD your God. 11And you shall rejoice in all the good that the LORD your God has given to you and to your house, you, and the Levite, and the sojourner who is among you.

12"When you have finished paying all the tithe of your produce in the third year, which is the year of tithing, giving it to the Levite, the sojourner, the fatherless, and the widow, so that they may eat within your towns and be filled, 13then you shall say before the LORD your God, 'I have removed the sacred portion

[1] Hebrew *its name* [2] Or *just*, or *righteous*; twice in this verse [3] Hebrew *with great terror*

DEUTERONOMY 26:1–11

FIRSTFRUITS OFFERING

When God's people entered the promised land, they were instructed to give an offering of the firstfruits of their harvest to God. This first portion was placed in a basket, brought to the tabernacle, and offered to God as an act of worship. The offering demonstrated that the people remembered that God had graciously given them a good land and that all things were a gift from his hand. Though the offering described here only occurred once, the Israelites were also instructed to offer their firstfruits annually (Lev 23:10–11).

Paul spoke of Jesus as a firstfruits offering. His victory over death served as a precursor to the resurrection of all those who are in Christ Jesus (1Co 15:20–23). Christians celebrate the firstfruits offering when they reflect upon and trust in the finished work of Jesus Christ. They also offer their lives as a living sacrifice to God—knowing that all good things they are given are a gift from God and a testimony to his faithfulness (Ro 12:1–2; Heb 13:15).

out of my house, and moreover, I have given it to the Levite, the sojourner, the fatherless, and the widow, according to all your commandment that you have commanded me. I have not transgressed any of your commandments, nor have I forgotten them. [14]I have not eaten of the tithe while I was mourning, or removed any of it while I was unclean, or offered any of it to the dead. I have obeyed the voice of the LORD my God. I have done according to all that you have commanded me. [15]Look down from your holy habitation, from heaven, and bless your people Israel and the ground that you have given us, as you swore to our fathers, a land flowing with milk and honey.'

[16]"This day the LORD your God commands you to do these statutes and rules. You shall therefore be careful to do them with all your heart and with all your soul. [17]You have declared today that the LORD is your God, and that you will walk in his ways, and keep his statutes and his commandments and his rules, and will obey his voice. [18]And the LORD has declared today that you are a people for his treasured possession, as he has promised you, and that you are to keep all his commandments, [19]and that he will set you in praise and in fame and in honor high above all nations that he has made, and that you shall be a people holy to the LORD your God, as he promised."

The Altar on Mount Ebal

27 Now Moses and the elders of Israel commanded the people, saying, "Keep the whole commandment that I command you today. [2]And on the day you cross over the Jordan to the land that the LORD your God is giving you, you shall set up large stones and plaster them with plaster. [3]And you shall write on them all the words of this law, when you cross over to enter the land that the LORD your God is giving you, a land flowing with milk and honey, as the LORD, the God of your fathers, has promised you. [4]And when you have crossed over the Jordan, you shall set up these stones, concerning which I command you today, on Mount Ebal, and you shall plaster them with plaster. [5]And there you shall build an altar to the LORD your God, an altar of stones. You shall wield no iron tool on them; [6]you shall build an altar to the LORD your God of uncut[1] stones. And you shall offer burnt offerings on it to the LORD your God, [7]and you shall sacrifice peace offerings and shall eat there, and you shall rejoice before the LORD your God. [8]And you shall write on the stones all the words of this law very plainly."

Curses from Mount Ebal

[9]Then Moses and the Levitical priests said to all Israel, "Keep silence and hear, O Israel: this day you have become the people of the LORD your God. [10]You shall therefore obey the voice of the LORD your God, keeping his commandments and his statutes, which I command you today."

[11]That day Moses charged the people, saying, [12]"When you have crossed over the Jordan, these shall stand on Mount Gerizim to bless the people: Simeon, Levi, Judah, Issachar, Joseph, and Benjamin. [13]And these shall stand on Mount Ebal for the curse: Reuben, Gad, Asher, Zebulun, Dan, and Naphtali. [14]And the Levites shall declare to all the men of Israel in a loud voice:

[15]" 'Cursed be the man who makes a carved or cast metal image, an abomination to the LORD, a thing made by the hands of a craftsman, and sets it up in secret.' And all the people shall answer and say, 'Amen.'

[16]" 'Cursed be anyone who dishonors his father or his mother.' And all the people shall say, 'Amen.'

[17]" 'Cursed be anyone who moves his neighbor's landmark.' And all the people shall say, 'Amen.'

[18]" 'Cursed be anyone who misleads a blind man on the road.' And all the people shall say, 'Amen.'

---

[1]Hebrew *whole*

JESUS, HIS FOLLOWERS, AND THE POOR

A trend in evangelical circles is the emphasis on being socially conscious, which includes caring for the weak and vulnerable. This trend, however, is nothing new.

The Old Testament leaves little room to doubt God's perspective on this issue: he cares about human suffering and calls his people to do the same. In these verses, Moses tied an Israelite's holiness before the Lord to a faithful tithe and providing for the foreigner, fatherless, and widow (along with the Levite) according to the command of God (v. 13). Without doubt, the Hebrews could not claim to live a satisfactory life according to God's Word without caring for the vulnerable people around them. The consistent theme evident throughout Deuteronomy is this: righteousness is not the result of works performed, but rather works are an expected outcome of the faith of persons within the covenant community. God expected his people to care about the hurting and disadvantaged among them because renewed and circumcised hearts gave them a love for such people.

The New Testament, much like the Old Testament, is straightforward in teaching that God cares about human suffering and calls his people to do the same. The life and teachings of Jesus, the ministry of the early church in Acts (Ac 4:34 – 35), and the exhortations of Paul (Ro 12:13) all point to this fact: God wants his people to care for the weak and vulnerable around them.

Christ taught his followers to be compassionate and merciful to those who are weary and heavy laden. There is a clear connection between righteousness and good works in caring for the weak and vulnerable (Lk 10:29 – 37). Christ assumed that his followers would assist the needy in meeting their physical needs (Mt 6:2 – 3). In the vein of Jesus' teachings and actions, believers are to clothe and feed the homeless, care for the neglected, and love all people. Jesus made an obvious connection that should propel all Christians to action — that is, those who have true righteousness in Christ will care for the "least of these" among us (Mt 25:34 – 40).

19“ ‘Cursed be anyone who perverts the justice due to the sojourner, the fatherless, and the widow.’ And all the people shall say, ‘Amen.’

20“ ‘Cursed be anyone who lies with his father’s wife, because he has uncovered his father’s nakedness.’[1] And all the people shall say, ‘Amen.’

21“ ‘Cursed be anyone who lies with any kind of animal.’ And all the people shall say, ‘Amen.’

22“ ‘Cursed be anyone who lies with his sister, whether the daughter of his father or the daughter of his mother.’ And all the people shall say, ‘Amen.’

23“ ‘Cursed be anyone who lies with his mother-in-law.’ And all the people shall say, ‘Amen.’

24“ ‘Cursed be anyone who strikes down his neighbor in secret.’ And all the people shall say, ‘Amen.’

25“ ‘Cursed be anyone who takes a bribe to shed innocent blood.’ And all the people shall say, ‘Amen.’

26“ ‘Cursed be anyone who does not confirm the words of this law by doing them.’ And all the people shall say, ‘Amen.’

Blessings for Obedience

28 “And if you faithfully obey the voice of the LORD your God, being careful to do all his commandments that I command you today, the LORD your God will set you high above all the nations of the earth. 2And all these blessings shall come upon you and overtake you, if you obey the voice of the LORD your God.
3Blessed shall you be in the city, and blessed shall you be in the field. 4Blessed shall be the fruit of your womb and the fruit of your ground and the fruit of your cattle, the increase of your herds and the young of your flock. 5Blessed shall be your basket and your kneading bowl. 6Blessed shall you be when you come in, and blessed shall you be when you go out.

7“The LORD will cause your enemies who rise against you to be defeated before you. They shall come out against you one way and flee before you seven ways.
8The LORD will command the blessing on you in your barns and in all that you undertake. And he will bless you in the land that the LORD your God is giving you. 9The LORD will establish you as a people holy to himself, as he has sworn to you, if you keep the commandments of the LORD your God and walk in his ways.
10And all the peoples of the earth shall see that you are called by the name of the LORD, and they shall be afraid of you. 11And the LORD will make you abound in prosperity, in the fruit of your womb and in the fruit of your livestock and in the fruit of your ground, within the land that the LORD swore to your fathers to give you. 12The LORD will open to you his good treasury, the heavens, to give the rain to your land in its season and to bless all the work of your hands. And you shall lend to many nations, but you shall not borrow. 13And the LORD will make you the head and not the tail, and you shall only go up and not down, if you obey the commandments of the LORD your God, which I command you today, being careful to do them, 14and if you do not turn aside from any of the words that I command you today, to the right hand or to the left, to go after other gods to serve them.

Curses for Disobedience

15“But if you will not obey the voice of the LORD your God or be careful to do all his commandments and his statutes that I command you today, then all these curses shall come upon you and overtake you. 16Cursed shall you be in the city, and cursed shall you be in the field. 17Cursed shall be your basket and your kneading bowl. 18Cursed shall be the fruit of your womb and the fruit of your ground, the increase of your herds and the young of your flock. 19Cursed shall you be when you come in, and cursed shall you be when you go out.

20“The LORD will send on you curses, confusion, and frustration in all that you

[1]Hebrew *uncovered his father’s skirt*

DEUTERONOMY 28:1–19

PERFECTION ENSURES BLESSING, IMPERFECTION BRINGS CURSES

Who can be perfect? Who can keep the rules all the time without failing, even one little bit? No one! Yet the book of Deuteronomy clearly shows the connection between covenant blessings and the requirement to keep the law of God carefully. There is no room for negotiation. God established his covenant requirements—if Israel wanted to be a holy nation, set apart as the blessed people of the one true God, they had to do what he wanted. What he demanded of them was to be “careful to do all his commandments” (v. 1). And Moses stated clearly the consequences of not keeping all his commands: curses come to those who do not keep all of God’s commands perfectly (v. 15). What an overwhelming predicament! Keep the commands of God and be blessed. Fail to do so and you, your family, your land, and your work will be cursed. It seems cruel because of the impossibility to meet God’s mandatory flawlessness. The Israelites knew their deficiencies and need for intercession and sacrifices to atone for their imperfections.

The people of God are no different today. No one is able to perfectly keep God’s requirements to be in a covenant relationship with him; therefore, all are in danger of receiving a curse from the Lord. But God, in a gracious act of mercy, sent Jesus to bear the curse, redeeming the elect from the consequences of unrighteousness (Gal 3:10–14).

undertake to do, until you are destroyed and perish quickly on account of the evil of your deeds, because you have forsaken me. [21]The LORD will make the pestilence stick to you until he has consumed you off the land that you are entering to take possession of it. [22]The LORD will strike you with wasting disease and with fever, inflammation and fiery heat, and with drought[1] and with blight and with mildew. They shall pursue you until you perish. [23]And the heavens over your head shall be bronze, and the earth under you shall be iron. [24]The LORD will make the rain of your land powder. From heaven dust shall come down on you until you are destroyed.

[25]"The LORD will cause you to be defeated before your enemies. You shall go out one way against them and flee seven ways before them. And you shall be a horror to all the kingdoms of the earth. [26]And your dead body shall be food for all birds of the air and for the beasts of the earth, and there shall be no one to frighten them away. [27]The LORD will strike you with the boils of Egypt, and with tumors and scabs and itch, of which you cannot be healed. [28]The LORD will strike you with madness and blindness and confusion of mind, [29]and you shall grope at noonday, as the blind grope in darkness, and you shall not prosper in your ways.[2] And you shall be only oppressed and robbed continually, and there shall be no one to help you. [30]You shall betroth a wife, but another man shall ravish her. You shall build a house, but you shall not dwell in it. You shall plant a vineyard, but you shall not enjoy its fruit. [31]Your ox shall be slaughtered before your eyes, but you shall not eat any of it. Your donkey shall be seized before your face, but shall not be restored to you. Your sheep shall be given to your enemies, but there shall be no one to help you. [32]Your sons and your daughters shall be given to another people, while your eyes look on and fail with longing for them all day long, but you shall be helpless. [33]A nation that you have not known shall eat up the fruit of your ground and of all your labors, and you shall be only oppressed and crushed continually, [34]so that you are driven mad by the sights that your eyes see. [35]The LORD will strike you on the knees and on the legs with grievous boils of which you cannot be healed, from the sole of your foot to the crown of your head.

[36]"The LORD will bring you and your king whom you set over you to a nation that neither you nor your fathers have known. And there you shall serve other gods of wood and stone. [37]And you shall become a horror, a proverb, and a byword among all the peoples where the LORD will lead you away. [38]You shall carry much seed into the field and shall gather in little, for the locust shall consume it. [39]You shall plant vineyards and dress them, but you shall neither drink of the wine nor gather the grapes, for the worm shall eat them. [40]You shall have olive trees throughout all your territory, but you shall not anoint yourself with the oil, for your olives shall drop off. [41]You shall father sons and daughters, but they shall not be yours, for they shall go into captivity. [42]The cricket[3] shall possess all your trees and the fruit of your ground. [43]The sojourner who is among you shall rise higher and higher above you, and you shall come down lower and lower. [44]He shall lend to you, and you shall not lend to him. He shall be the head, and you shall be the tail.

[45]"All these curses shall come upon you and pursue you and overtake you till you are destroyed, because you did not obey the voice of the LORD your God, to keep his commandments and his statutes that he commanded you. [46]They shall be a sign and a wonder against you and your offspring forever. [47]Because you did not serve the LORD your God with joyfulness and gladness of heart, because of the abundance of all things, [48]therefore you shall serve your enemies whom the LORD will send against you, in hunger and thirst, in nakedness, and lacking everything. And he will put a yoke of iron on your neck until he has destroyed you. [49]The LORD will bring a nation against you from far away, from the end of the earth, swooping down like the eagle, a nation whose language you do not understand,

[1]Or *sword* [2]Or *shall not succeed in finding your ways* [3]Identity uncertain

50a hard-faced nation who shall not respect the old or show mercy to the young.
51It shall eat the offspring of your cattle and the fruit of your ground, until you are
destroyed; it also shall not leave you grain, wine, or oil, the increase of your herds
or the young of your flock, until they have caused you to perish.

52"They shall besiege you in all your towns, until your high and fortified walls,
in which you trusted, come down throughout all your land. And they shall besiege you in all your towns throughout all your land, which the LORD your God has
given you. 53And you shall eat the fruit of your womb, the flesh of your sons and
daughters, whom the LORD your God has given you, in the siege and in the distress
with which your enemies shall distress you. 54The man who is the most tender
and refined among you will begrudge food to his brother, to the wife he embraces,[1]
and to the last of the children whom he has left, 55so that he will not give to any of
them any of the flesh of his children whom he is eating, because he has nothing
else left, in the siege and in the distress with which your enemy shall distress you
in all your towns. 56The most tender and refined woman among you, who would
not venture to set the sole of her foot on the ground because she is so delicate and
tender, will begrudge to the husband she embraces,[2] to her son and to her daughter, 57her afterbirth that comes out from between her feet and her children whom
she bears, because lacking everything she will eat them secretly, in the siege and in
the distress with which your enemy shall distress you in your towns.

58"If you are not careful to do all the words of this law that are written in this
book, that you may fear this glorious and awesome name, the LORD your God,
59then the LORD will bring on you and your offspring extraordinary afflictions,
afflictions severe and lasting, and sicknesses grievous and lasting. 60And he will
bring upon you again all the diseases of Egypt, of which you were afraid, and they
shall cling to you. 61Every sickness also and every affliction that is not recorded
in the book of this law, the LORD will bring upon you, until you are destroyed.
62Whereas you were as numerous as the stars of heaven, you shall be left few in
number, because you did not obey the voice of the LORD your God. 63And as the
LORD took delight in doing you good and multiplying you, so the LORD will take
delight in bringing ruin upon you and destroying you. And you shall be plucked
off the land that you are entering to take possession of it.

64"And the LORD will scatter you among all peoples, from one end of the earth
to the other, and there you shall serve other gods of wood and stone, which neither you nor your fathers have known. 65And among these nations you shall find
no respite, and there shall be no resting place for the sole of your foot, but the
LORD will give you there a trembling heart and failing eyes and a languishing soul.
66Your life shall hang in doubt before you. Night and day you shall be in dread and
have no assurance of your life. 67In the morning you shall say, 'If only it were evening!' and at evening you shall say, 'If only it were morning!' because of the dread
that your heart shall feel, and the sights that your eyes shall see. 68And the LORD
will bring you back in ships to Egypt, a journey that I promised that you should
never make again; and there you shall offer yourselves for sale to your enemies as
male and female slaves, but there will be no buyer."

The Covenant Renewed in Moab

29[3] These are the words of the covenant that the LORD commanded Moses to
make with the people of Israel in the land of Moab, besides the covenant
that he had made with them at Horeb.

2[4]And Moses summoned all Israel and said to them: "You have seen all that
the LORD did before your eyes in the land of Egypt, to Pharaoh and to all his servants and to all his land, 3the great trials that your eyes saw, the signs, and those
great wonders. 4But to this day the LORD has not given you a heart to understand

[1]Hebrew *the wife of his bosom* [2]Hebrew *the husband of her bosom* [3]Ch 28:69 in Hebrew [4]Ch 29:1 in Hebrew

DEUTERONOMY 29:1–6

THE NEED FOR A NEW HEART

Moses traced the Israelites' inability to keep the terms of the covenant of God to a root problem. According to verse 4, the Lord had not given them the ability to understand, see, and hear. Immediately following chapter 28, which contrasts the blessings for keeping God's covenant commands with curses for not doing so, Moses connected their potential inability to uphold their end of the covenant requirements with the fact that they were unable to appreciate all the Lord had done for them. Elsewhere, it is clear that their inadequacies are connected to needing a new or changed heart (Dt 10:16; 30:6; Eze 36:26). Being an ethnic Israelite had limitations. Physical connection to a genealogical line did not equate to blessings from the Lord. Therefore, the Old Testament authors offered a consistent message: the people of God were unable to keep God's law, thus they needed spiritual renewal. This message prefigured the new heart to come in Christ (Jer 31:31–34). Apart from renewal in Christ Jesus, no one can come to God by pleasing him and keeping all his commands (Ro 3:10–12,21–26).

or eyes to see or ears to hear. 5I have led you forty years in the wilderness. Your
clothes have not worn out on you, and your sandals have not worn off your feet.
6You have not eaten bread, and you have not drunk wine or strong drink, that you
may know that I am the LORD your God. 7And when you came to this place, Sihon
the king of Heshbon and Og the king of Bashan came out against us to battle,
but we defeated them. 8We took their land and gave it for an inheritance to the
Reubenites, the Gadites, and the half-tribe of the Manassites. 9Therefore keep
the words of this covenant and do them, that you may prosper[1] in all that you do.

10"You are standing today, all of you, before the LORD your God: the heads of
your tribes,[2] your elders, and your officers, all the men of Israel, 11your little ones,
your wives, and the sojourner who is in your camp, from the one who chops your
wood to the one who draws your water, 12so that you may enter into the sworn
covenant of the LORD your God, which the LORD your God is making with you
today, 13that he may establish you today as his people, and that he may be your
God, as he promised you, and as he swore to your fathers, to Abraham, to Isaac,
and to Jacob. 14It is not with you alone that I am making this sworn covenant, 15but
with whoever is standing here with us today before the LORD our God, and with
whoever is not here with us today.

16"You know how we lived in the land of Egypt, and how we came through
the midst of the nations through which you passed. 17And you have seen their
detestable things, their idols of wood and stone, of silver and gold, which were
among them. 18Beware lest there be among you a man or woman or clan or tribe
whose heart is turning away today from the LORD our God to go and serve the gods
of those nations. Beware lest there be among you a root bearing poisonous and
bitter fruit, 19one who, when he hears the words of this sworn covenant, blesses
himself in his heart, saying, 'I shall be safe, though I walk in the stubbornness of
my heart.' This will lead to the sweeping away of moist and dry alike. 20The LORD
will not be willing to forgive him, but rather the anger of the LORD and his jealousy
will smoke against that man, and the curses written in this book will settle upon
him, and the LORD will blot out his name from under heaven. 21And the LORD will
single him out from all the tribes of Israel for calamity, in accordance with all the
curses of the covenant written in this Book of the Law. 22And the next generation, your children who rise up after you, and the foreigner who comes from a far
land, will say, when they see the afflictions of that land and the sicknesses with
which the LORD has made it sick— 23the whole land burned out with brimstone
and salt, nothing sown and nothing growing, where no plant can sprout, an overthrow like that of Sodom and Gomorrah, Admah, and Zeboiim, which the LORD
overthrew in his anger and wrath— 24all the nations will say, 'Why has the LORD
done thus to this land? What caused the heat of this great anger?' 25Then people
will say, 'It is because they abandoned the covenant of the LORD, the God of their
fathers, which he made with them when he brought them out of the land of Egypt,
26and went and served other gods and worshiped them, gods whom they had not
known and whom he had not allotted to them. 27Therefore the anger of the LORD
was kindled against this land, bringing upon it all the curses written in this book,
28and the LORD uprooted them from their land in anger and fury and great wrath,
and cast them into another land, as they are this day.'

29"The secret things belong to the LORD our God, but the things that are revealed belong to us and to our children forever, that we may do all the words of
this law.

Repentance and Forgiveness

30 "And when all these things come upon you, the blessing and the curse,
which I have set before you, and you call them to mind among all the nations where the LORD your God has driven you, 2and return to the LORD your God,

[1]Or *deal wisely* [2]Septuagint, Syriac; Hebrew *your heads, your tribes*

you and your children, and obey his voice in all that I command you today, with
all your heart and with all your soul, 3then the LORD your God will restore your
fortunes and have mercy on you, and he will gather you again from all the peoples
where the LORD your God has scattered you. 4If your outcasts are in the uttermost
parts of heaven, from there the LORD your God will gather you, and from there
he will take you. 5And the LORD your God will bring you into the land that your
fathers possessed, that you may possess it. And he will make you more prosperous and numerous than your fathers. 6And the LORD your God will circumcise
your heart and the heart of your offspring, so that you will love the LORD your
God with all your heart and with all your soul, that you may live. 7And the LORD
your God will put all these curses on your foes and enemies who persecuted you.
8And you shall again obey the voice of the LORD and keep all his commandments
that I command you today. 9The LORD your God will make you abundantly prosperous in all the work of your hand, in the fruit of your womb and in the fruit of
your cattle and in the fruit of your ground. For the LORD will again take delight in
prospering you, as he took delight in your fathers, 10when you obey the voice of
the LORD your God, to keep his commandments and his statutes that are written
in this Book of the Law, when you turn to the LORD your God with all your heart
and with all your soul.

The Choice of Life and Death

11"For this commandment that I command you today is not too hard for you,
neither is it far off. 12It is not in heaven, that you should say, 'Who will ascend
to heaven for us and bring it to us, that we may hear it and do it?' 13Neither is it
beyond the sea, that you should say, 'Who will go over the sea for us and bring it
to us, that we may hear it and do it?' 14But the word is very near you. It is in your
mouth and in your heart, so that you can do it.

15"See, I have set before you today life and good, death and evil. 16If you obey
the commandments of the LORD your God[1] that I command you today, by loving
the LORD your God, by walking in his ways, and by keeping his commandments
and his statutes and his rules,[2] then you shall live and multiply, and the LORD
your God will bless you in the land that you are entering to take possession of
it. 17But if your heart turns away, and you will not hear, but are drawn away to
worship other gods and serve them, 18I declare to you today, that you shall surely
perish. You shall not live long in the land that you are going over the Jordan to
enter and possess. 19I call heaven and earth to witness against you today, that
I have set before you life and death, blessing and curse. Therefore choose life,
that you and your offspring may live, 20loving the LORD your God, obeying his
voice and holding fast to him, for he is your life and length of days, that you may
dwell in the land that the LORD swore to your fathers, to Abraham, to Isaac, and
to Jacob, to give them."

Joshua to Succeed Moses

31 So Moses continued to speak these words to all Israel. 2And he said to
them, "I am 120 years old today. I am no longer able to go out and come in.
The LORD has said to me, 'You shall not go over this Jordan.' 3The LORD your God
himself will go over before you. He will destroy these nations before you, so that
you shall dispossess them, and Joshua will go over at your head, as the LORD has
spoken. 4And the LORD will do to them as he did to Sihon and Og, the kings of the
Amorites, and to their land, when he destroyed them. 5And the LORD will give
them over to you, and you shall do to them according to the whole commandment that I have commanded you. 6Be strong and courageous. Do not fear or be
in dread of them, for it is the LORD your God who goes with you. He will not leave
you or forsake you."

[1]Septuagint; Hebrew lacks *If you obey the commandments of the LORD your God* [2]Or *his just decrees*

DEUTERONOMY 30:11–14

THE NEAR WORD

Moses did not claim that God's word, or message, is easy to obey but that his word is near. No one has traveled to the heavens or to a remote part of the world, but God has given his law to his people in a form they can understand. Like God himself, his word is near to the people (Ro 10:6–8). They could hear it, memorize it, and talk about it with others. God does not stand far off and require that humans come to him through their own moral efforts or that they wander in darkness trying to discern his plan and purpose for life. Instead, he comes near—first in the form of his revealed Word given to Moses and then in the form of God's Son, Jesus, who would dwell among the people in the flesh (Jn 1:1–14). The nearness of God demonstrates the great length that God goes to to save his people from their sins.

DEUTERONOMY 31:1–6

AN EVER-PRESENT GOD

Moses commanded the people to take heart, be courageous, and take the land God had promised to give them as an inheritance. The basis for their courage was found in the fact that God would surely go before them into the land. His ever-present protection and guidance was meant to bolster the confidence of the people as they ventured into a land filled with imposing nations and idolatrous worship. As with the pillar of fire and the cloud in the wilderness, God pledged to go before the people on this journey, and if they would simply trust him, he would

(continued on page 293)

CHOOSE LIFE

At the end of his life, knowing that he would die without ever entering the promised land, Moses once again held out the covenant promises of God to the nation of Israel. In many ways, the challenge to "choose life, that you and your offspring may live" (v. 19) is as old as mankind. In the garden, God held out the same promise to Adam and Eve (Ge 2:15–17), though they made the foolish choice and pursued death. Ever since, all people have been trapped in a cycle of sin. Certainly there have been times when people returned to God, but these seasons have been short-lived.

Moses, at this point the leader of God's people for forty years, knew full well the inability of the people to choose life that they could live. Throughout their journey, they had consistently murmured against God, doubted Moses' leadership, and been given over to death and destruction. Moses began his final sermons to the people of God on the plains of Moab with a vivid recounting of the gory details of their rebellion in chapter 1 of this very book. Even Moses, the great deliverer, had been unable to consistently choose life; therefore he died without ever stepping foot on the ground that he had been pursuing for forty years (3:21–29).

Yet, he again reminded the people of their need to choose life. By this point, the entire generation that scorned the promises of God and were forced to wander in the wilderness had died. This new generation could vividly remember the death of their parents in these wilderness years. They now were faced with a decision: Would they follow in the path of their ancestors, disobey God, and die — or would they be a new generation who trusted God, walked in his ways, and lived bountifully in the land of promise?

Jesus' life and ministry ushered in hope for all those trapped in the cyclical pattern of sin and death. He fulfilled God's promises to the people by giving them a path to life. John wrote that Jesus claimed to be "the way, and the truth, and the life" (Jn 14:6). By coming to him, people can find the path to life, not through conformity to a system of rules, but by submission to the person of Christ. In him is life and life to the full (Jn 10:10).

7 Then Moses summoned Joshua and said to him in the sight of all Israel, "Be strong and courageous, for you shall go with this people into the land that the LORD has sworn to their fathers to give them, and you shall put them in possession of it. 8 It is the LORD who goes before you. He will be with you; he will not leave you or forsake you. Do not fear or be dismayed."

The Reading of the Law

9 Then Moses wrote this law and gave it to the priests, the sons of Levi, who carried the ark of the covenant of the LORD, and to all the elders of Israel. 10 And Moses commanded them, "At the end of every seven years, at the set time in the year of release, at the Feast of Booths, 11 when all Israel comes to appear before the LORD your God at the place that he will choose, you shall read this law before all Israel in their hearing. 12 Assemble the people, men, women, and little ones, and the sojourner within your towns, that they may hear and learn to fear the LORD your God, and be careful to do all the words of this law, 13 and that their children, who have not known it, may hear and learn to fear the LORD your God, as long as you live in the land that you are going over the Jordan to possess."

Joshua Commissioned to Lead Israel

14 And the LORD said to Moses, "Behold, the days approach when you must die. Call Joshua and present yourselves in the tent of meeting, that I may commission him." And Moses and Joshua went and presented themselves in the tent of meeting. 15 And the LORD appeared in the tent in a pillar of cloud. And the pillar of cloud stood over the entrance of the tent.

16 And the LORD said to Moses, "Behold, you are about to lie down with your fathers. Then this people will rise and whore after the foreign gods among them in the land that they are entering, and they will forsake me and break my covenant that I have made with them. 17 Then my anger will be kindled against them in that day, and I will forsake them and hide my face from them, and they will be devoured. And many evils and troubles will come upon them, so that they will say in that day, 'Have not these evils come upon us because our God is not among us?' 18 And I will surely hide my face in that day because of all the evil that they have done, because they have turned to other gods.

19 "Now therefore write this song and teach it to the people of Israel. Put it in their mouths, that this song may be a witness for me against the people of Israel. 20 For when I have brought them into the land flowing with milk and honey, which I swore to give to their fathers, and they have eaten and are full and grown fat, they will turn to other gods and serve them, and despise me and break my covenant. 21 And when many evils and troubles have come upon them, this song shall confront them as a witness (for it will live unforgotten in the mouths of their offspring). For I know what they are inclined to do even today, before I have brought them into the land that I swore to give." 22 So Moses wrote this song the same day and taught it to the people of Israel.

23 And the LORD[1] commissioned Joshua the son of Nun and said, "Be strong and courageous, for you shall bring the people of Israel into the land that I swore to give them. I will be with you."

24 When Moses had finished writing the words of this law in a book to the very end, 25 Moses commanded the Levites who carried the ark of the covenant of the LORD, 26 "Take this Book of the Law and put it by the side of the ark of the covenant of the LORD your God, that it may be there for a witness against you. 27 For I know how rebellious and stubborn you are. Behold, even today while I am yet alive with you, you have been rebellious against the LORD. How much more after my death! 28 Assemble to me all the elders of your tribes and your officers, that I may speak these words in their ears and call heaven and earth to witness against them.

(An Ever-Present God, continued)

grant them victory and bountiful blessing in the land.

In much the same way, Jesus gave his followers a mission grand in scope. Go into all the world, he said, and declare and demonstrate the hope of the gospel and call people to repentance and faith. This mission would be impossible were it not for the promise of God to go with his church and supply it with all the power, protection, and provision needed to accomplish the mission to which it is entrusted (Mt 28:20). The presence of God, going both before and with the church, should provide it with confidence and encouragement to embark on the mission of filling the earth "with the knowledge of the glory of the LORD" (Hab 2:14).

[1] Hebrew *he*

29 For I know that after my death you will surely act corruptly and turn aside from
the way that I have commanded you. And in the days to come evil will befall you,
because you will do what is evil in the sight of the LORD, provoking him to anger
through the work of your hands."

The Song of Moses

30 Then Moses spoke the words of this song until they were finished, in the
ears of all the assembly of Israel:

32 "Give ear, O heavens, and I will speak,
and let the earth hear the words of my mouth.
2 May my teaching drop as the rain,
my speech distill as the dew,
like gentle rain upon the tender grass,
and like showers upon the herb.
3 For I will proclaim the name of the LORD;
ascribe greatness to our God!

4 "The Rock, his work is perfect,
for all his ways are justice.
A God of faithfulness and without iniquity,
just and upright is he.
5 They have dealt corruptly with him;
they are no longer his children because they are blemished;
they are a crooked and twisted generation.
6 Do you thus repay the LORD,
you foolish and senseless people?
Is not he your father, who created you,
who made you and established you?
7 Remember the days of old;
consider the years of many generations;
ask your father, and he will show you,
your elders, and they will tell you.
8 When the Most High gave to the nations their inheritance,
when he divided mankind,
he fixed the borders[1] of the peoples
according to the number of the sons of God.[2]
9 But the LORD's portion is his people,
Jacob his allotted heritage.

10 "He found him in a desert land,
and in the howling waste of the wilderness;
he encircled him, he cared for him,
he kept him as the apple of his eye.
11 Like an eagle that stirs up its nest,
that flutters over its young,
spreading out its wings, catching them,
bearing them on its pinions,
12 the LORD alone guided him,
no foreign god was with him.
13 He made him ride on the high places of the land,
and he ate the produce of the field,
and he suckled him with honey out of the rock,
and oil out of the flinty rock.
14 Curds from the herd, and milk from the flock,
with fat[3] of lambs,

[1]Or *territories* [2]Compare Dead Sea Scroll, Septuagint; Masoretic Text *sons of Israel* [3]That is, with the best

rams of Bashan and goats,
with the very finest[1] of the wheat—
and you drank foaming wine made from the blood of the grape.

15 "But Jeshurun grew fat, and kicked;
you grew fat, stout, and sleek;
then he forsook God who made him
and scoffed at the Rock of his salvation.
16 They stirred him to jealousy with strange gods;
with abominations they provoked him to anger.
17 They sacrificed to demons that were not God,
to gods they had never known,
to new gods that had come recently,
whom your fathers had never dreaded.
18 You were unmindful of the Rock that bore[2] you,
and you forgot the God who gave you birth.

19 "The LORD saw it and spurned them,
because of the provocation of his sons and his daughters.
20 And he said, 'I will hide my face from them;
I will see what their end will be,
for they are a perverse generation,
children in whom is no faithfulness.
21 They have made me jealous with what is no god;
they have provoked me to anger with their idols.
So I will make them jealous with those who are no people;
I will provoke them to anger with a foolish nation.
22 For a fire is kindled by my anger,
and it burns to the depths of Sheol,
devours the earth and its increase,
and sets on fire the foundations of the mountains.

23 " 'And I will heap disasters upon them;
I will spend my arrows on them;
24 they shall be wasted with hunger,
and devoured by plague
and poisonous pestilence;
I will send the teeth of beasts against them,
with the venom of things that crawl in the dust.
25 Outdoors the sword shall bereave,
and indoors terror,
for young man and woman alike,
the nursing child with the man of gray hairs.
26 I would have said, "I will cut them to pieces;
I will wipe them from human memory,"
27 had I not feared provocation by the enemy,
lest their adversaries should misunderstand,
lest they should say, "Our hand is triumphant,
it was not the LORD who did all this." '

28 "For they are a nation void of counsel,
and there is no understanding in them.
29 If they were wise, they would understand this;
they would discern their latter end!
30 How could one have chased a thousand,
and two have put ten thousand to flight,
unless their Rock had sold them,
and the LORD had given them up?

[1]Hebrew *with the kidney fat* [2]Or *fathered*

DEUTERONOMY 32:48–52

THE GOD OF SECOND CHANCES

God's grace is evident in Moses' death. Moses had experienced the highs and lows of the universal human experience. But he also had been the mouthpiece of God before Pharaoh, led the miraculous deliverance of the people from Egypt, seen the glory of God firsthand, and received the very law of God. Yet he had rebelled against God, "broke faith" with God, and failed to "treat [God] as holy" (Nu 20:24; Dt 32:51). His sinful choice resulted in his inability to go into the land of promise; but God, in his kindness, did allow him to see the land. It is as if God was saying, "Moses, have a look. See my faithfulness. I told you that I would bring my people here. There was never a reason to doubt me. I always keep my promises."

At the end of his life, Moses could die with the assurance that God would lead his people into the land and his work had not been in vain. In a similar fashion, God provides grace-filled second chances to all those who, like Moses, David, Paul, and a host of others, have a questionable past. Jesus' work assures believers that, no matter what mistakes they have made, God will surely keep his promises and lead them into the eternal rest he has secured for his people (Heb 4:1–11).

31 For their rock is not as our Rock;
our enemies are by themselves.
32 For their vine comes from the vine of Sodom
and from the fields of Gomorrah;
their grapes are grapes of poison;
their clusters are bitter;
33 their wine is the poison of serpents
and the cruel venom of asps.

34 "'Is not this laid up in store with me,
sealed up in my treasuries?
35 Vengeance is mine, and recompense,[1]
for the time when their foot shall slip;
for the day of their calamity is at hand,
and their doom comes swiftly.'
36 For the LORD will vindicate[2] his people
and have compassion on his servants,
when he sees that their power is gone
and there is none remaining, bond or free.
37 Then he will say, 'Where are their gods,
the rock in which they took refuge,
38 who ate the fat of their sacrifices
and drank the wine of their drink offering?
Let them rise up and help you;
let them be your protection!

39 "'See now that I, even I, am he,
and there is no god beside me;
I kill and I make alive;
I wound and I heal;
and there is none that can deliver out of my hand.
40 For I lift up my hand to heaven
and swear, As I live forever,
41 if I sharpen my flashing sword[3]
and my hand takes hold on judgment,
I will take vengeance on my adversaries
and will repay those who hate me.
42 I will make my arrows drunk with blood,
and my sword shall devour flesh—
with the blood of the slain and the captives,
from the long-haired heads of the enemy.'

43 "Rejoice with him, O heavens;[4]
bow down to him, all gods,[5]
for he avenges the blood of his children[6]
and takes vengeance on his adversaries.
He repays those who hate him[7]
and cleanses[8] his people's land."[9]

44 Moses came and recited all the words of this song in the hearing of the people, he and Joshua[10] the son of Nun. 45 And when Moses had finished speaking all
these words to all Israel, 46 he said to them, "Take to heart all the words by which
I am warning you today, that you may command them to your children, that they

[1] Septuagint *and I will repay* [2] Septuagint *judge* [3] Hebrew *the lightning of my sword* [4] Dead Sea Scroll, Septuagint; Masoretic Text *Rejoice his people, O nations* [5] Masoretic Text lacks *bow down to him, all gods* [6] Dead Sea Scroll, Septuagint; Masoretic Text *servants* [7] Dead Sea Scroll, Septuagint; Masoretic Text lacks *He repays those who hate him* [8] Or *atones for* [9] Septuagint, Vulgate; Hebrew *his land his people* [10] Septuagint, Syriac, Vulgate; Hebrew *Hoshea*

may be careful to do all the words of this law. 47For it is no empty word for you, but
your very life, and by this word you shall live long in the land that you are going
over the Jordan to possess."

Moses' Death Foretold

48That very day the LORD spoke to Moses, 49"Go up this mountain of the
Abarim, Mount Nebo, which is in the land of Moab, opposite Jericho, and view the
land of Canaan, which I am giving to the people of Israel for a possession. 50And
die on the mountain which you go up, and be gathered to your people, as Aaron
your brother died in Mount Hor and was gathered to his people, 51because you
broke faith with me in the midst of the people of Israel at the waters of Meribah-
kadesh, in the wilderness of Zin, and because you did not treat me as holy in the
midst of the people of Israel. 52For you shall see the land before you, but you shall
not go there, into the land that I am giving to the people of Israel."

Moses' Final Blessing on Israel

33 This is the blessing with which Moses the man of God blessed the people
of Israel before his death. 2He said,

"The LORD came from Sinai
  and dawned from Seir upon us;[1]
  he shone forth from Mount Paran;
he came from the ten thousands of holy ones,
  with flaming fire[2] at his right hand.
3 Yes, he loved his people,[3]
  all his holy ones were in his[4] hand;
so they followed[5] in your steps,
  receiving direction from you,
4 when Moses commanded us a law,
  as a possession for the assembly of Jacob.
5 Thus the LORD[6] became king in Jeshurun,
  when the heads of the people were gathered,
  all the tribes of Israel together.

6 "Let Reuben live, and not die,
  but let his men be few."

7And this he said of Judah:

"Hear, O LORD, the voice of Judah,
  and bring him in to his people.
With your hands contend[7] for him,
  and be a help against his adversaries."

8And of Levi he said,

"Give to Levi[8] your Thummim,
  and your Urim to your godly one,
whom you tested at Massah,
  with whom you quarreled at the waters of Meribah;
9 who said of his father and mother,
  'I regard them not';
he disowned his brothers
  and ignored his children.
For they observed your word
  and kept your covenant.

[1]Septuagint, Syriac, Vulgate; Hebrew *them* [2]The meaning of the Hebrew word is uncertain
[3]Septuagint; Hebrew *peoples* [4]Hebrew *your* [5]The meaning of the Hebrew word is uncertain
[6]Hebrew *Thus he* [7]Probable reading; Hebrew *With his hands he contended* [8]Dead Sea Scroll, Septuagint; Masoretic Text lacks *Give to Levi*

10 They shall teach Jacob your rules
and Israel your law;
they shall put incense before you
and whole burnt offerings on your altar.
11 Bless, O LORD, his substance,
and accept the work of his hands;
crush the loins of his adversaries,
of those who hate him, that they rise not again."

12Of Benjamin he said,

"The beloved of the LORD dwells in safety.
The High God[1] surrounds him all day long,
and dwells between his shoulders."

13And of Joseph he said,

"Blessed by the LORD be his land,
with the choicest gifts of heaven above,[2]
and of the deep that crouches beneath,
14 with the choicest fruits of the sun
and the rich yield of the months,
15 with the finest produce of the ancient mountains
and the abundance of the everlasting hills,
16 with the best gifts of the earth and its fullness
and the favor of him who dwells in the bush.
May these rest on the head of Joseph,
on the pate of him who is prince among his brothers.
17 A firstborn bull[3]—he has majesty,
and his horns are the horns of a wild ox;
with them he shall gore the peoples,
all of them, to the ends of the earth;
they are the ten thousands of Ephraim,
and they are the thousands of Manasseh."

18And of Zebulun he said,

"Rejoice, Zebulun, in your going out,
and Issachar, in your tents.
19 They shall call peoples to their mountain;
there they offer right sacrifices;
for they draw from the abundance of the seas
and the hidden treasures of the sand."

20And of Gad he said,

"Blessed be he who enlarges Gad!
Gad crouches like a lion;
he tears off arm and scalp.
21 He chose the best of the land for himself,
for there a commander's portion was reserved;
and he came with the heads of the people,
with Israel he executed the justice of the LORD,
and his judgments for Israel."

22And of Dan he said,

"Dan is a lion's cub
that leaps from Bashan."

---

[1]Septuagint; Hebrew *dwells in safety by him. He* [2]Two Hebrew manuscripts and Targum; Hebrew *with the dew* [3]Dead Sea Scroll, Septuagint, Samaritan; Masoretic Text *His firstborn bull*

[23]And of Naphtali he said,

"O Naphtali, sated with favor,
and full of the blessing of the LORD,
possess the lake[1] and the south."

[24]And of Asher he said,

"Most blessed of sons be Asher;
let him be the favorite of his brothers,
and let him dip his foot in oil.
25 Your bars shall be iron and bronze,
and as your days, so shall your strength be.

26 "There is none like God, O Jeshurun,
who rides through the heavens to your help,
through the skies in his majesty.
27 The eternal God is your dwelling place,[2]
and underneath are the everlasting arms.[3]
And he thrust out the enemy before you
and said, 'Destroy.'
28 So Israel lived in safety,
Jacob lived alone,[4]
in a land of grain and wine,
whose heavens drop down dew.
29 Happy are you, O Israel! Who is like you,
a people saved by the LORD,
the shield of your help,
and the sword of your triumph!
Your enemies shall come fawning to you,
and you shall tread upon their backs."

The Death of Moses

34 Then Moses went up from the plains of Moab to Mount Nebo, to the top of
Pisgah, which is opposite Jericho. And the LORD showed him all the land,
Gilead as far as Dan, [2]all Naphtali, the land of Ephraim and Manasseh, all the land
of Judah as far as the western sea, [3]the Negeb, and the Plain, that is, the Valley of
Jericho the city of palm trees, as far as Zoar. [4]And the LORD said to him, "This is
the land of which I swore to Abraham, to Isaac, and to Jacob, 'I will give it to your
offspring.' I have let you see it with your eyes, but you shall not go over there."
[5]So Moses the servant of the LORD died there in the land of Moab, according to the
word of the LORD, [6]and he buried him in the valley in the land of Moab opposite
Beth-peor; but no one knows the place of his burial to this day. [7]Moses was 120
years old when he died. His eye was undimmed, and his vigor unabated. [8]And the
people of Israel wept for Moses in the plains of Moab thirty days. Then the days
of weeping and mourning for Moses were ended.

[9]And Joshua the son of Nun was full of the spirit of wisdom, for Moses had
laid his hands on him. So the people of Israel obeyed him and did as the LORD
had commanded Moses. [10]And there has not arisen a prophet since in Israel like
Moses, whom the LORD knew face to face, [11]none like him for all the signs and the
wonders that the LORD sent him to do in the land of Egypt, to Pharaoh and to all
his servants and to all his land, [12]and for all the mighty power and all the great
deeds of terror that Moses did in the sight of all Israel.

[1]Or *west* [2]Or *a dwelling place* [3]Revocalization of verse 27 yields *He subdues the ancient gods, and shatters the forces of old* [4]Hebrew *the abode of Jacob was alone*

DEUTERONOMY 34:10–12

A PROPHET LIKE MOSES

Interestingly, Deuteronomy ends with three verses that express an extreme void within the nation of Israel. After the death of Moses, there was no one like him to fill his leadership position at the same level of quality that the Israelites came to expect from him. There is a felt emptiness created by the death of Moses. During his time as the leader of this people, he interacted with God face to face, led a nation out of Egyptian slavery, performed miracles, and exhibited unrivaled wisdom. While Moses was not without fault, it is clear that he was a gift of God to the people of God. The people looked to him as a mediator between them and God and as a leader who helped them to follow God's ways. Following his death, the people of Israel continued to anticipate a prophet who would be like Moses, a longing that was left unfulfilled until the birth of Jesus (Ac 3:22–26).

JESUS: OUR PERFECT LEADER

JOSHUA

JOSHUA

EXODUS FROM EGYPT *c. 1446 BC*	CONQUEST OF CANAAN *c. 1406 – 1400 BC*	PERIOD OF JUDGES BEGINS *c. 1375 BC*

The book of Joshua describes Israel's conquest of the promised land from the initial invasion across the Jordan River to the final division of the land among the twelve tribes. This historical narrative highlights God's might, power, and faithfulness as Israel's commander-in-chief. He is the one who fulfills his promises, wins the victories, and gives good land as a gift to his children. This reality is seen clearly in the battle of Jericho (Jos 6), in which God unequivocally demonstrates that he is the One who fights on behalf of his people.

The events in the book of Joshua recount the various tactics God used to give Israel victory over the inhabitants of Canaan. The descriptions do not suggest that Israel advanced due to their superior strength or military savvy. In fact, when they acted apart from God's will, three thousand of Israel's troops were routed by a small contingent of enemy soldiers (Jos 7:2 – 5). Throughout the book, God demonstrates that Israel's victories were because of his power at work in the people and not because of their skill.

Though the book describes the possession of the land, the focus is on the fact that this land is a fulfillment of God's covenant promises to Abraham (Ge 12:7; 13:14 – 17; 15:18 – 21; 17:8; 22:17), to Isaac (Ge 26:3 – 4), to Jacob (Ge 28:4,13; 35:12), and to the succeeding generations (Ge 48:4 – 22; 50:24). The land they receive is a good and fertile land, flowing with milk and honey; but more importantly it is the promised land — the fulfillment of God's promises and a concrete demonstration of his covenant faithfulness.

The book is named for the human leader who takes center stage throughout the book. Joshua's name, which means "the LORD saves" or "the LORD gives victory," demonstrates that his leadership was representative of God's guidance. God's strength and might, seen throughout the book of Joshua, are emblematic of a far greater victory won by Jesus Christ. Joshua's name, in fact, is the Hebrew equivalent of the name "Jesus" (which is a Greek name). When Joshua led God's people into the land, he foreshadowed the One who would ultimately bring "many sons to glory" (Heb 2:10) and who "gives us the victory" through his own work on the cross (1Co 15:57).

Though Joshua proved to be a good and worthy leader, every human leader pales in comparison to Jesus. While on earth, Jesus was the perfect embodiment of humility and action. He confronted the injustices of corrupt religious leaders and government officials, yet led with gentleness when interacting with society's most vulnerable people. Though we can learn much from looking at the lives of great leaders like Joshua, we must always judge each one in light of Jesus, who was and remains our perfect leader (Rev 21:1 – 7).

HAVE I NOT COMMANDED YOU? BE STRONG AND COURAGEOUS. DO NOT BE FRIGHTENED, AND DO NOT BE DISMAYED, FOR THE LORD YOUR GOD IS WITH YOU WHEREVER YOU GO.

Joshua 1:9

JOSHUA

God Commissions Joshua

1 After the death of Moses the servant of the LORD, the LORD said to Joshua the son of Nun, Moses' assistant, 2 "Moses my servant is dead. Now therefore arise, go over this Jordan, you and all this people, into the land that I am giving to them, to the people of Israel. 3 Every place that the sole of your foot will tread upon I have given to you, just as I promised to Moses. 4 From the wilderness and this Lebanon as far as the great river, the river Euphrates, all the land of the Hittites to the Great Sea toward the going down of the sun shall be your territory. 5 No man shall be able to stand before you all the days of your life. Just as I was with Moses, so I will be with you. I will not leave you or forsake you. 6 Be strong and courageous, for you shall cause this people to inherit the land that I swore to their fathers to give them. 7 Only be strong and very courageous, being careful to do according to all the law that Moses my servant commanded you. Do not turn from it to the right hand or to the left, that you may have good success[1] wherever you go. 8 This Book of the Law shall not depart from your mouth, but you shall meditate on it day and night, so that you may be careful to do according to all that is written in it. For then you will make your way prosperous, and then you will have good success. 9 Have I not commanded you? Be strong and courageous. Do not be frightened, and do not be dismayed, for the LORD your God is with you wherever you go."

Joshua Assumes Command

10 And Joshua commanded the officers of the people, 11 "Pass through the midst of the camp and command the people, 'Prepare your provisions, for within three days you are to pass over this Jordan to go in to take possession of the land that the LORD your God is giving you to possess.'"

12 And to the Reubenites, the Gadites, and the half-tribe of Manasseh Joshua said, 13 "Remember the word that Moses the servant of the LORD commanded you, saying, 'The LORD your God is providing you a place of rest and will give you this land.' 14 Your wives, your little ones, and your livestock shall remain in the land that Moses gave you beyond the Jordan, but all the men of valor among you shall pass over armed before your brothers and shall help them, 15 until the LORD gives rest to your brothers as he has to you, and they also take possession of the land that the LORD your God is giving them. Then you shall return to the land of your possession and shall possess it, the land that Moses the servant of the LORD gave you beyond the Jordan toward the sunrise."

16 And they answered Joshua, "All that you have commanded us we will do, and wherever you send us we will go. 17 Just as we obeyed Moses in all things, so we will obey you. Only may the LORD your God be with you, as he was with Moses! 18 Whoever rebels against your commandment and disobeys your words, whatever you command him, shall be put to death. Only be strong and courageous."

Rahab Hides the Spies

2 And Joshua the son of Nun sent[2] two men secretly from Shittim as spies, saying, "Go, view the land, especially Jericho." And they went and came into the house of a prostitute whose name was Rahab and lodged there. 2 And it was told to the king of Jericho, "Behold, men of Israel have come here tonight to search out the land." 3 Then the king of Jericho sent to Rahab, saying, "Bring out the men who have come to you, who entered your house, for they have come to search out all the land." 4 But the woman had taken the two men and hidden them. And she said, "True, the men came to me, but I did not know where they were from.

[1] Or *may act wisely* [2] Or *had sent*

JOSHUA 1:6–7,9,18

COURAGE

Strength and courage are not found naturally in fallen humanity. Sin renders people frail, broken, shameful, and fearful—though they may mask these feelings with all sorts of actions. Joshua demonstrated the basis for true strength and courage both for the nation of Israel and for all Christians throughout history. Joshua reminded the people of the ever-present faithfulness of God. God keeps his word, so people can have confidence that God will do what he promises regardless of the odds. God has given the Bible, which provides authoritative guidance into the plans and purposes of God. When people conform their lives to God's standards by the power of his Spirit, they can have boldness, courage, and strength, knowing they are walking faithfully with God. The faithfulness of God and the Word of God were the God-ordained means of providing strength and courage to the people as they entered the promised land. In the same way, today's church is a testimony of God's faithfulness and his written Word. As Christians reflect on the faithfulness of God and the Word of God, they will develop the strength and courage that they could never find in themselves.

THE BEAUTY OF THE LAW

The Lord called Joshua to be strong and courageous as Joshua replaced Moses as Israel's leader and led the people into the promised land. This calling was based on his obedience and submission to the Word of God. As the Creator, God knows how life is meant to be lived and the way for people to experience life to the full (Jn 10:10). The gift of the law was a gracious act of God to instruct his people in his ways. It was never intended to be a moralistic plan to earn God's favor. Rather, the law was given to those who had already experienced God's redeeming grace. In the law, God provided instructions for how his children can love him and other people. This law is not a collection of arbitrary dictates from a malevolent deity, but instead it is the wisdom of God distilled in human language. It is a path to joy and life — the way people were meant to live.

The Bible continually portrays the law of God in this fashion. For example, in the longest psalm in the Bible, Psalm 119, the author says that he loves, treasures, delights in, and longs for the law. It is a source of hope, peace, joy, and direction. In Psalm 19, the psalmist says the law revives the soul, makes wise the simple, gives joy to the heart, and gives light to the eyes (Ps 19:7–8). The law is a beautiful gift from a gracious God.

Jesus testified to the lasting value of the law when he said that he did not come to abolish the law (Mt 5:17). Instead, Jesus amplified the law, explaining the transformation that should result as a proper response to his work. In his masterful Sermon on the Mount in Matthew 5 through 7, Jesus called people to a far greater standard of obedience than mere conformity to external regulations. Instead of simply condemning murder, Jesus unmasked the anger that fueled this act. Adultery is not the prime culprit, but lust rooted in the human heart is the real problem. Jesus methodically outlined the heart-level change that the law relied upon. Rather than rendering the law obsolete, Jesus showed that the law continued to provide an authoritative standard and guidance for God's people. Now, because of the finished work of Christ, believers have hope that the price for their disobedience to the law has been paid and that they have God's Spirit dwelling within them, providing them the power to live the life God intends.

5And when the gate was about to be closed at dark, the men went out. I do not know where the men went. Pursue them quickly, for you will overtake them." 6But she had brought them up to the roof and hid them with the stalks of flax that she had laid in order on the roof. 7So the men pursued after them on the way to the Jordan as far as the fords. And the gate was shut as soon as the pursuers had gone out.

8Before the men[1] lay down, she came up to them on the roof 9and said to the men, "I know that the LORD has given you the land, and that the fear of you has fallen upon us, and that all the inhabitants of the land melt away before you. 10For we have heard how the LORD dried up the water of the Red Sea before you when you came out of Egypt, and what you did to the two kings of the Amorites who were beyond the Jordan, to Sihon and Og, whom you devoted to destruction.[2] 11And as soon as we heard it, our hearts melted, and there was no spirit left in any man because of you, for the LORD your God, he is God in the heavens above and on the earth beneath. 12Now then, please swear to me by the LORD that, as I have dealt kindly with you, you also will deal kindly with my father's house, and give me a sure sign 13that you will save alive my father and mother, my brothers and sisters, and all who belong to them, and deliver our lives from death." 14And the men said to her, "Our life for yours even to death! If you do not tell this business of ours, then when the LORD gives us the land we will deal kindly and faithfully with you."

15Then she let them down by a rope through the window, for her house was built into the city wall, so that she lived in the wall. 16And she said[3] to them, "Go into the hills, or the pursuers will encounter you, and hide there three days until the pursuers have returned. Then afterward you may go your way." 17The men said to her, "We will be guiltless with respect to this oath of yours that you have made us swear. 18Behold, when we come into the land, you shall tie this scarlet cord in the window through which you let us down, and you shall gather into your house your father and mother, your brothers, and all your father's household. 19Then if anyone goes out of the doors of your house into the street, his blood shall be on his own head, and we shall be guiltless. But if a hand is laid on anyone who is with you in the house, his blood shall be on our head. 20But if you tell this business of ours, then we shall be guiltless with respect to your oath that you have made us swear." 21And she said, "According to your words, so be it." Then she sent them away, and they departed. And she tied the scarlet cord in the window.

22They departed and went into the hills and remained there three days until the pursuers returned, and the pursuers searched all along the way and found nothing. 23Then the two men returned. They came down from the hills and passed over and came to Joshua the son of Nun, and they told him all that had happened to them. 24And they said to Joshua, "Truly the LORD has given all the land into our hands. And also, all the inhabitants of the land melt away because of us."

Israel Crosses the Jordan

3 Then Joshua rose early in the morning and they set out from Shittim. And they came to the Jordan, he and all the people of Israel, and lodged there before they passed over. 2At the end of three days the officers went through the camp 3and commanded the people, "As soon as you see the ark of the covenant of the LORD your God being carried by the Levitical priests, then you shall set out from your place and follow it. 4Yet there shall be a distance between you and it, about 2,000 cubits[4] in length. Do not come near it, in order that you may know the way you shall go, for you have not passed this way before." 5Then Joshua said to the people, "Consecrate yourselves, for tomorrow the LORD will do wonders among you." 6And Joshua said to the priests, "Take up the ark of the covenant

JOSHUA 2:8–11

RAHAB AND FAITH

Rahab's claim was an amazing expression of faith from the lips of a Gentile prostitute. Not only had she heard of the God of Israel—the one true and living God—but she also believed the power and promises of God. She affirmed that God would indeed give the land in which she lived to the nation of Israel. This affirmation of faith was a life-altering claim for Rahab. With it, she set herself apart from her people, her land, and the pagan gods her people worshiped. Her faith radically changed her future, and within a short period, her faith was confirmed as she witnessed the destruction of her people and her city. Rahab was saved by faith. This truth sets the paradigm for God's saving work throughout all history. Down through the ages believers are saved not based on their righteous deeds but by their faith in God's faithfulness. Faith has the power to save God's people from life in a fallen world and from the judgment of God.

[1]Hebrew *they* [2]That is, set apart (devoted) as an offering to the Lord (for destruction) [3]Or *had said*
[4]A *cubit* was about 18 inches or 45 centimeters

and pass on before the people." So they took up the ark of the covenant and went before the people.

7The LORD said to Joshua, "Today I will begin to exalt you in the sight of all Israel, that they may know that, as I was with Moses, so I will be with you. 8And as for you, command the priests who bear the ark of the covenant, 'When you come to the brink of the waters of the Jordan, you shall stand still in the Jordan.'" 9And Joshua said to the people of Israel, "Come here and listen to the words of the LORD your God." 10And Joshua said, "Here is how you shall know that the living God is among you and that he will without fail drive out from before you the Canaanites, the Hittites, the Hivites, the Perizzites, the Girgashites, the Amorites, and the Jebusites. 11Behold, the ark of the covenant of the Lord of all the earth[1] is passing over before you into the Jordan. 12Now therefore take twelve men from the tribes of Israel, from each tribe a man. 13And when the soles of the feet of the priests bearing the ark of the LORD, the Lord of all the earth, shall rest in the waters of the Jordan, the waters of the Jordan shall be cut off from flowing, and the waters coming down from above shall stand in one heap."

14So when the people set out from their tents to pass over the Jordan with the priests bearing the ark of the covenant before the people, 15and as soon as those bearing the ark had come as far as the Jordan, and the feet of the priests bearing the ark were dipped in the brink of the water (now the Jordan overflows all its banks throughout the time of harvest), 16the waters coming down from above stood and rose up in a heap very far away, at Adam, the city that is beside Zarethan, and those flowing down toward the Sea of the Arabah, the Salt Sea, were completely cut off. And the people passed over opposite Jericho. 17Now the priests bearing the ark of the covenant of the LORD stood firmly on dry ground in the midst of the Jordan, and all Israel was passing over on dry ground until all the nation finished passing over the Jordan.

Twelve Memorial Stones from the Jordan

4 When all the nation had finished passing over the Jordan, the LORD said to Joshua, 2"Take twelve men from the people, from each tribe a man, 3and command them, saying, 'Take twelve stones from here out of the midst of the Jordan, from the very place where the priests' feet stood firmly, and bring them over with you and lay them down in the place where you lodge tonight.'" 4Then Joshua called the twelve men from the people of Israel, whom he had appointed, a man from each tribe. 5And Joshua said to them, "Pass on before the ark of the LORD your God into the midst of the Jordan, and take up each of you a stone upon his shoulder, according to the number of the tribes of the people of Israel, 6that this may be a sign among you. When your children ask in time to come, 'What do those stones mean to you?' 7then you shall tell them that the waters of the Jordan were cut off before the ark of the covenant of the LORD. When it passed over the Jordan, the waters of the Jordan were cut off. So these stones shall be to the people of Israel a memorial forever."

8And the people of Israel did just as Joshua commanded and took up twelve stones out of the midst of the Jordan, according to the number of the tribes of the people of Israel, just as the LORD told Joshua. And they carried them over with them to the place where they lodged and laid them down[2] there. 9And Joshua set up[3] twelve stones in the midst of the Jordan, in the place where the feet of the priests bearing the ark of the covenant had stood; and they are there to this day. 10For the priests bearing the ark stood in the midst of the Jordan until everything was finished that the LORD commanded Joshua to tell the people, according to all that Moses had commanded Joshua.

The people passed over in haste. 11And when all the people had finished passing over, the ark of the LORD and the priests passed over before the people. 12The

[1]Hebrew *the ark of the covenant, the Lord of all the earth* [2]Or *to rest* [3]Or *Joshua had set up*

SEEN AND UNSEEN

Joshua had a memorial built to remind the people of God's faithfulness in giving them the land of promise. This external marker served to remind the nation of God's power to do the unthinkable — lead a band of former slaves to obtain a good land inhabited by giants in walled cities. The presence of two and a half tribes on the eastern side of the Jordan meant that the people would continue to traverse the Jordan and see these memorial stones. As early as Noah in Genesis 8:20, God's people built such visible altars or memorials to remind them to worship God for his character and actions.

Sadly, these external markers often became a source of idolatrous worship for the people. For example, the Samaritan woman in John 4 asked Jesus for the location where true worship was to happen (Jn 4:20). Would it be on the mountain where her ancestors worshiped or would it be in Jerusalem? Jesus, knowing the deep-seated brokenness of this woman, beckoned her to a deeper form of worship — one that would not be marked by an external location but one that would happen by the Spirit of God dwelling within a person.

The radical grace shown by Jesus to this woman demonstrated the ongoing faithfulness of God to his promises. He gives an inheritance far greater than physical land to all those who trust in him. This woman, in spite of her checkered past, could inherit the great and glorious promises made to Abraham. One wonders whether that well in Samaria continued to function as a memorial for her in the days, weeks, months, and years to follow. Like the memorial stones in the Jordan, every time this woman saw the ordinary well — one she likely visited every day — she was reminded of the day that her life changed forever. Certainly an old well was not meant to be an object of worship, but it could have served as a valuable memorial of God's grace and kindness. Even more, John recorded that many in the city believed in the good news of Jesus because of this woman's testimony (Jn 4:39).

sons of Reuben and the sons of Gad and the half-tribe of Manasseh passed over armed before the people of Israel, as Moses had told them. 13About 40,000 ready for war passed over before the LORD for battle, to the plains of Jericho. 14On that day the LORD exalted Joshua in the sight of all Israel, and they stood in awe of him just as they had stood in awe of Moses, all the days of his life.

15And the LORD said to Joshua, 16"Command the priests bearing the ark of the testimony to come up out of the Jordan." 17So Joshua commanded the priests, "Come up out of the Jordan." 18And when the priests bearing the ark of the covenant of the LORD came up from the midst of the Jordan, and the soles of the priests' feet were lifted up on dry ground, the waters of the Jordan returned to their place and overflowed all its banks, as before.

19The people came up out of the Jordan on the tenth day of the first month, and they encamped at Gilgal on the east border of Jericho. 20And those twelve stones, which they took out of the Jordan, Joshua set up at Gilgal. 21And he said to the people of Israel, "When your children ask their fathers in times to come, 'What do these stones mean?' 22then you shall let your children know, 'Israel passed over this Jordan on dry ground.' 23For the LORD your God dried up the waters of the Jordan for you until you passed over, as the LORD your God did to the Red Sea, which he dried up for us until we passed over, 24so that all the peoples of the earth may know that the hand of the LORD is mighty, that you may fear the LORD your God forever."[1]

The New Generation Circumcised

5 As soon as all the kings of the Amorites who were beyond the Jordan to the west, and all the kings of the Canaanites who were by the sea, heard that the LORD had dried up the waters of the Jordan for the people of Israel until they had crossed over, their hearts melted and there was no longer any spirit in them because of the people of Israel.

2At that time the LORD said to Joshua, "Make flint knives and circumcise the sons of Israel a second time." 3So Joshua made flint knives and circumcised the sons of Israel at Gibeath-haaraloth.[2] 4And this is the reason why Joshua circumcised them: all the males of the people who came out of Egypt, all the men of war, had died in the wilderness on the way after they had come out of Egypt. 5Though all the people who came out had been circumcised, yet all the people who were born on the way in the wilderness after they had come out of Egypt had not been circumcised. 6For the people of Israel walked forty years in the wilderness, until all the nation, the men of war who came out of Egypt, perished, because they did not obey the voice of the LORD; the LORD swore to them that he would not let them see the land that the LORD had sworn to their fathers to give to us, a land flowing with milk and honey. 7So it was their children, whom he raised up in their place, that Joshua circumcised. For they were uncircumcised, because they had not been circumcised on the way.

8When the circumcising of the whole nation was finished, they remained in their places in the camp until they were healed. 9And the LORD said to Joshua, "Today I have rolled away the reproach of Egypt from you." And so the name of that place is called Gilgal[3] to this day.

First Passover in Canaan

10While the people of Israel were encamped at Gilgal, they kept the Passover on the fourteenth day of the month in the evening on the plains of Jericho. 11And the day after the Passover, on that very day, they ate of the produce of the land, unleavened cakes and parched grain. 12And the manna ceased the day after they ate of the produce of the land. And there was no longer manna for the people of Israel, but they ate of the fruit of the land of Canaan that year.

[1]Or *all the days* [2]*Gibeath-haaraloth* means *the hill of the foreskins* [3]*Gilgal* sounds like the Hebrew for *to roll*

A FRESH START

The scene at Gilgal is far from pleasant to the modern reader. The mass circumcision undertaken in this passage was a stunning, public testimony of both the failure and the future hope of the people of God. The Israelites had abandoned the practice of circumcision during their wilderness wanderings. The absence of circumcision seemed to be a mark of shame on the nation.

Now, on the brink of the promised land, the people made a bold statement that was meant to signify their commitment to keep the covenant once again. The external mark of circumcision was meant to communicate a heart change to allow the new generation to inherit the land and remain faithful to God in it. The Lord blessed this act, saying that the mark of shame had been taken away.

The continued hard-heartedness and rebellion of the people necessitated something far greater to take away the shame of sin. The author of Hebrews wrote that Jesus despised the cross — though he endured it and completely overcame it through his victorious resurrection (Heb 12:2). The inglorious nature of his brutal death was a public means by which God took on himself the shame of sin. In this act, the full wrath of God toward sin was poured out on Jesus and, as a result, believers are forever forgiven, clean, holy, and pure.

For those who know him, Christ removes the shamefulness that sin brings. Like Adam and Eve in the garden, all people are prone to hide in shame because of the foolish choices they have made (Ge 3:7). Shame causes people to try to cover their sin with all sorts of flimsy fig leaves such as good behavior, community service, or religious performance. Jesus offers a better way. By accepting his free gift of salvation, men and women can embrace the good news that he has taken away their shame forever. In spite of sin, they are loved, accepted, and declared holy, and this declaration is based on the work of God on their behalf and not their moral goodness. Christians experience a far greater act of circumcision, one not done with human hands to the external body but one done by God to the heart (Ro 2:28 – 29).

The Commander of the LORD's Army

[13]When Joshua was by Jericho, he lifted up his eyes and looked, and behold, a man was standing before him with his drawn sword in his hand. And Joshua went to him and said to him, "Are you for us, or for our adversaries?" [14]And he said, "No; but I am the commander of the army of the LORD. Now I have come." And Joshua fell on his face to the earth and worshiped[1] and said to him, "What does my lord say to his servant?" [15]And the commander of the LORD's army said to Joshua, "Take off your sandals from your feet, for the place where you are standing is holy." And Joshua did so.

The Fall of Jericho

6 Now Jericho was shut up inside and outside because of the people of Israel. None went out, and none came in. [2]And the LORD said to Joshua, "See, I have given Jericho into your hand, with its king and mighty men of valor. [3]You shall march around the city, all the men of war going around the city once. Thus shall you do for six days. [4]Seven priests shall bear seven trumpets of rams' horns before the ark. On the seventh day you shall march around the city seven times, and the priests shall blow the trumpets. [5]And when they make a long blast with the ram's horn, when you hear the sound of the trumpet, then all the people shall shout with a great shout, and the wall of the city will fall down flat,[2] and the people shall go up, everyone straight before him." [6]So Joshua the son of Nun called the priests and said to them, "Take up the ark of the covenant and let seven priests bear seven trumpets of rams' horns before the ark of the LORD." [7]And he said to the people, "Go forward. March around the city and let the armed men pass on before the ark of the LORD."

[8]And just as Joshua had commanded the people, the seven priests bearing the seven trumpets of rams' horns before the LORD went forward, blowing the trumpets, with the ark of the covenant of the LORD following them. [9]The armed men were walking before the priests who were blowing the trumpets, and the rear guard was walking after the ark, while the trumpets blew continually. [10]But Joshua commanded the people, "You shall not shout or make your voice heard, neither shall any word go out of your mouth, until the day I tell you to shout. Then you shall shout." [11]So he caused the ark of the LORD to circle the city, going about it once. And they came into the camp and spent the night in the camp.

[12]Then Joshua rose early in the morning, and the priests took up the ark of the LORD. [13]And the seven priests bearing the seven trumpets of rams' horns before the ark of the LORD walked on, and they blew the trumpets continually. And the armed men were walking before them, and the rear guard was walking after the ark of the LORD, while the trumpets blew continually. [14]And the second day they marched around the city once, and returned into the camp. So they did for six days.

[15]On the seventh day they rose early, at the dawn of day, and marched around the city in the same manner seven times. It was only on that day that they marched around the city seven times. [16]And at the seventh time, when the priests had blown the trumpets, Joshua said to the people, "Shout, for the LORD has given you the city. [17]And the city and all that is within it shall be devoted to the LORD for destruction.[3] Only Rahab the prostitute and all who are with her in her house shall live, because she hid the messengers whom we sent. [18]But you, keep yourselves from the things devoted to destruction, lest when you have devoted them you take any of the devoted things and make the camp of Israel a thing for destruction and bring trouble upon it. [19]But all silver and gold, and every vessel of bronze and iron, are holy to the LORD; they shall go into the treasury of the LORD." [20]So the people shouted, and the trumpets were blown. As soon as the people

[1]Or *and paid homage* [2]Hebrew *under itself*; also verse 20 [3]That is, set apart (devoted) as an offering to the Lord (for destruction); also verses 18, 21

JOSHUA 5:13–14

WORTHY OF WORSHIP

People behave differently when they are in the presence of someone they truly believe to be significant or important. Joshua's response to the man in this passage demonstrated the significance of this enigmatic figure, who some scholars believe to be the pre-incarnate Christ. Joshua did what many will one day do when they meet Jesus—he fell on his face in reverence. Much about the figure in this passage is unclear—his name, his background, and the way in which he appeared. He disclosed his identity in a similar cryptic form by saying that he was the commander of the Lord's army. Joshua's subsequent response also affirmed the greatness of this man. He humbled himself and awaited the instructions of one to whom honor is clearly due. Joshua demonstrated his submission and faithfulness to the appearance of God here near Jericho. One day, all people will give similar honor to God, as every knee will bow and every tongue will acknowledge that Jesus is Lord (Php 2:10–11). Some will bow in judgment and be cast away from God's presence forever. Others will bow in worship of the one true King forever (Rev 1:17; 4:10; 7:11; 11:16).

heard the sound of the trumpet, the people shouted a great shout, and the wall fell down flat, so that the people went up into the city, every man straight before him, and they captured the city. [21]Then they devoted all in the city to destruction, both men and women, young and old, oxen, sheep, and donkeys, with the edge of the sword.

[22]But to the two men who had spied out the land, Joshua said, "Go into the prostitute's house and bring out from there the woman and all who belong to her, as you swore to her." [23]So the young men who had been spies went in and brought out Rahab and her father and mother and brothers and all who belonged to her. And they brought all her relatives and put them outside the camp of Israel. [24]And they burned the city with fire, and everything in it. Only the silver and gold, and the vessels of bronze and of iron, they put into the treasury of the house of the LORD. [25]But Rahab the prostitute and her father's household and all who belonged to her, Joshua saved alive. And she has lived in Israel to this day, because she hid the messengers whom Joshua sent to spy out Jericho.

[26]Joshua laid an oath on them at that time, saying, "Cursed before the LORD be the man who rises up and rebuilds this city, Jericho.

"At the cost of his firstborn
shall he lay its foundation,
and at the cost of his youngest son
shall he set up its gates."

[27]So the LORD was with Joshua, and his fame was in all the land.

Israel Defeated at Ai

7 But the people of Israel broke faith in regard to the devoted things, for Achan the son of Carmi, son of Zabdi, son of Zerah, of the tribe of Judah, took some of the devoted things. And the anger of the LORD burned against the people of Israel.

[2]Joshua sent men from Jericho to Ai, which is near Beth-aven, east of Bethel, and said to them, "Go up and spy out the land." And the men went up and spied out Ai. [3]And they returned to Joshua and said to him, "Do not have all the people go up, but let about two or three thousand men go up and attack Ai. Do not make the whole people toil up there, for they are few." [4]So about three thousand men went up there from the people. And they fled before the men of Ai, [5]and the men of Ai killed about thirty-six of their men and chased them before the gate as far as Shebarim and struck them at the descent. And the hearts of the people melted and became as water.

[6]Then Joshua tore his clothes and fell to the earth on his face before the ark of the LORD until the evening, he and the elders of Israel. And they put dust on their heads. [7]And Joshua said, "Alas, O Lord GOD, why have you brought this people over the Jordan at all, to give us into the hands of the Amorites, to destroy us? Would that we had been content to dwell beyond the Jordan! [8]O Lord, what can I say, when Israel has turned their backs before their enemies! [9]For the Canaanites and all the inhabitants of the land will hear of it and will surround us and cut off our name from the earth. And what will you do for your great name?"

The Sin of Achan

[10]The LORD said to Joshua, "Get up! Why have you fallen on your face? [11]Israel has sinned; they have transgressed my covenant that I commanded them; they have taken some of the devoted things; they have stolen and lied and put them among their own belongings. [12]Therefore the people of Israel cannot stand before their enemies. They turn their backs before their enemies, because they have become devoted for destruction.[1] I will be with you no more, unless you

[1]That is, set apart (devoted) as an offering to the Lord (for destruction)

AN UNLIKELY ANCESTOR OF JESUS

The story of Rahab serves as a glimmer of hope in the midst of the destruction of the pagan nations who inhabited the land God had promised to give his children. News of God's might and power had long ago reached the nations, though they continued to harden their hearts in unbelief. As a result, God's judgment was poured out on the people for their sin. At this point in redemptive history, that judgment was enacted primarily through God's people, the nation of Israel, who were told to destroy these pagan nations.

Rahab proved to be an exception. Although a pagan and a prostitute, this woman had protected the Hebrew spies as they entered the land and, as a result, was given the promise of protection. Now that the people were finally laying claim to the land, the spies remained true to their promise and allowed Rahab and all of her family to escape the destruction that fell on the city.

Rahab stands in a long line of unlikely recipients of God's mercy. Matthew, in his Gospel account, begins with a lengthy genealogy, which was meant to demonstrate to his Jewish audience that Jesus Christ was the long-awaited, promised descendant of Abraham and David. This genealogy is not what one might expect, however. Matthew did not simply list the fathers of the faith — such as Abraham or David. The list prominently included a wide assortment of unlikely or unheard-of characters, such as Tamar, Bathsheba, Ahaz, Eliud, Mary, and Rahab. Some of these are only mentioned briefly in the annals of Scripture; some are not mentioned at all. Others such as Bathsheba and Rahab are known for their sin. But there they are listed, called by name and linked to the coming of Jesus.

The ancestry of Jesus may be one of the greatest testaments to the grace of God recorded in all of the Scripture. Not only was Rahab spared from death, but she was also brought into the family of God and given a share of the inheritance promised to his people. Her story serves as a great encouragement to all subsequent generations of outcasts, no-names, and sinners of all sorts. God's grace extends to all types of people. In fact, the grace of God is seen most clearly when he saves and transforms those, like Rahab, who otherwise have no hope.

destroy the devoted things from among you. 13Get up! Consecrate the people and say, 'Consecrate yourselves for tomorrow; for thus says the LORD, God of Israel, "There are devoted things in your midst, O Israel. You cannot stand before your enemies until you take away the devoted things from among you." 14In the morning therefore you shall be brought near by your tribes. And the tribe that the LORD takes by lot shall come near by clans. And the clan that the LORD takes shall come near by households. And the household that the LORD takes shall come near man by man. 15And he who is taken with the devoted things shall be burned with fire, he and all that he has, because he has transgressed the covenant of the LORD, and because he has done an outrageous thing in Israel.'"

16So Joshua rose early in the morning and brought Israel near tribe by tribe, and the tribe of Judah was taken. 17And he brought near the clans of Judah, and the clan of the Zerahites was taken. And he brought near the clan of the Zerahites man by man, and Zabdi was taken. 18And he brought near his household man by man, and Achan the son of Carmi, son of Zabdi, son of Zerah, of the tribe of Judah, was taken. 19Then Joshua said to Achan, "My son, give glory to the LORD God of Israel and give praise[1] to him. And tell me now what you have done; do not hide it from me." 20And Achan answered Joshua, "Truly I have sinned against the LORD God of Israel, and this is what I did: 21when I saw among the spoil a beautiful cloak from Shinar, and 200 shekels of silver, and a bar of gold weighing 50 shekels,[2] then I coveted them and took them. And see, they are hidden in the earth inside my tent, with the silver underneath."

22So Joshua sent messengers, and they ran to the tent; and behold, it was hidden in his tent with the silver underneath. 23And they took them out of the tent and brought them to Joshua and to all the people of Israel. And they laid them down before the LORD. 24And Joshua and all Israel with him took Achan the son of Zerah, and the silver and the cloak and the bar of gold, and his sons and daughters and his oxen and donkeys and sheep and his tent and all that he had. And they brought them up to the Valley of Achor. 25And Joshua said, "Why did you bring trouble on us? The LORD brings trouble on you today." And all Israel stoned him with stones. They burned them with fire and stoned them with stones. 26And they raised over him a great heap of stones that remains to this day. Then the LORD turned from his burning anger. Therefore, to this day the name of that place is called the Valley of Achor.[3]

The Fall of Ai

8 And the LORD said to Joshua, "Do not fear and do not be dismayed. Take all the fighting men with you, and arise, go up to Ai. See, I have given into your hand the king of Ai, and his people, his city, and his land. 2And you shall do to Ai and its king as you did to Jericho and its king. Only its spoil and its livestock you shall take as plunder for yourselves. Lay an ambush against the city, behind it."

3So Joshua and all the fighting men arose to go up to Ai. And Joshua chose 30,000 mighty men of valor and sent them out by night. 4And he commanded them, "Behold, you shall lie in ambush against the city, behind it. Do not go very far from the city, but all of you remain ready. 5And I and all the people who are with me will approach the city. And when they come out against us just as before, we shall flee before them. 6And they will come out after us, until we have drawn them away from the city. For they will say, 'They are fleeing from us, just as before.' So we will flee before them. 7Then you shall rise up from the ambush and seize the city, for the LORD your God will give it into your hand. 8And as soon as you have taken the city, you shall set the city on fire. You shall do according to the word of the LORD. See, I have commanded you." 9So Joshua sent them out. And they went to the place of ambush and lay between Bethel and Ai, to the west of Ai, but Joshua spent that night among the people.

[1]Or *and make confession* [2]A *shekel* was about 2/5 ounce or 11 grams [3]*Achor* means *trouble*

DISOBEDIENCE: THE DESTRUCTIVE PATTERN

The book of Joshua began on a high note. Finally, after years of wandering in the wilderness, the people took the land. The fall of Jericho, recorded in chapter 6, served as a foreshadowing of the way God would grant the nation victory over the pagan nations. They would prevail, not because of military might, political shrewdness, or sheer force, but simply because God would demonstrate his power and give them the land as a gift of grace. He intended to teach them that these battles and, in fact, all the challenges of life, are not won by human might or power, but by the Spirit of God (Zec 4:6).

The juxtaposition of Joshua 7 against the extraordinary story of God's power in chapter 6 demonstrates the folly of the human heart and the diabolical implication of sin. Achan, a random Israelite in the tribe of Judah, sinned in secret — or so he thought. He took some of the spoils of war, which were meant to be devoted to God, and kept them for himself. The result of Achan's sin was disastrous, both for Achan and for the entire nation.

Like Achan, all people are prone to harbor secret sin in their hearts even in the face of the amazing faithfulness and power of God actively at work in their lives. Secret sin is never secret in the presence of an all-knowing God. And, like Achan's sin, those hidden actions have far-reaching implications for families, communities, and even nations. Therefore, Paul implored people to relinquish those sins done in secret and bring them out into the light of Christ, where true and lasting transformation can be found (Eph 5:8 – 16). His counsel is driven by a stark reality: time is fleeting, and the judgment of God is imminent. The judgment of sin, seen acutely in the story of Achan, will fall on all those who fail to repent and trust in Christ. God will ultimately bring into the light all things that are done in secret (1Co 4:5). Christians, having placed their faith in Christ, can bring their sin out from the shadows and into the light. They, of all people, know the catastrophic implications of hidden sin and the freedom found by bringing sin into the light.

10 Joshua arose early in the morning and mustered the people and went up, he and the elders of Israel, before the people to Ai. 11 And all the fighting men who were with him went up and drew near before the city and encamped on the north side of Ai, with a ravine between them and Ai. 12 He took about 5,000 men and set them in ambush between Bethel and Ai, to the west of the city. 13 So they stationed the forces, the main encampment that was north of the city and its rear guard west of the city. But Joshua spent that night in the valley. 14 And as soon as the king of Ai saw this, he and all his people, the men of the city, hurried and went out early to the appointed place[1] toward the Arabah to meet Israel in battle. But he did not know that there was an ambush against him behind the city. 15 And Joshua and all Israel pretended to be beaten before them and fled in the direction of the wilderness. 16 So all the people who were in the city were called together to pursue them, and as they pursued Joshua they were drawn away from the city. 17 Not a man was left in Ai or Bethel who did not go out after Israel. They left the city open and pursued Israel.

18 Then the LORD said to Joshua, "Stretch out the javelin that is in your hand toward Ai, for I will give it into your hand." And Joshua stretched out the javelin that was in his hand toward the city. 19 And the men in the ambush rose quickly out of their place, and as soon as he had stretched out his hand, they ran and entered the city and captured it. And they hurried to set the city on fire. 20 So when the men of Ai looked back, behold, the smoke of the city went up to heaven, and they had no power to flee this way or that, for the people who fled to the wilderness turned back against the pursuers. 21 And when Joshua and all Israel saw that the ambush had captured the city, and that the smoke of the city went up, then they turned back and struck down the men of Ai. 22 And the others came out from the city against them, so they were in the midst of Israel, some on this side, and some on that side. And Israel struck them down, until there was left none that survived or escaped. 23 But the king of Ai they took alive, and brought him near to Joshua.

24 When Israel had finished killing all the inhabitants of Ai in the open wilderness where they pursued them, and all of them to the very last had fallen by the edge of the sword, all Israel returned to Ai and struck it down with the edge of the sword. 25 And all who fell that day, both men and women, were 12,000, all the people of Ai. 26 But Joshua did not draw back his hand with which he stretched out the javelin until he had devoted all the inhabitants of Ai to destruction.[2] 27 Only the livestock and the spoil of that city Israel took as their plunder, according to the word of the LORD that he commanded Joshua. 28 So Joshua burned Ai and made it forever a heap of ruins, as it is to this day. 29 And he hanged the king of Ai on a tree until evening. And at sunset Joshua commanded, and they took his body down from the tree and threw it at the entrance of the gate of the city and raised over it a great heap of stones, which stands there to this day.

Joshua Renews the Covenant

30 At that time Joshua built an altar to the LORD, the God of Israel, on Mount Ebal, 31 just as Moses the servant of the LORD had commanded the people of Israel, as it is written in the Book of the Law of Moses, "an altar of uncut stones, upon which no man has wielded an iron tool." And they offered on it burnt offerings to the LORD and sacrificed peace offerings. 32 And there, in the presence of the people of Israel, he wrote on the stones a copy of the law of Moses, which he had written. 33 And all Israel, sojourner as well as native born, with their elders and officers and their judges, stood on opposite sides of the ark before the Levitical priests who carried the ark of the covenant of the LORD, half of them in front of Mount Gerizim and half of them in front of Mount Ebal, just as Moses the servant of the LORD had commanded at the first, to bless the people of Israel. 34 And afterward he read all the words of the law, the blessing and the curse, according to all that

---

JOSHUA 8:30–35

OLD AND NEW COVENANTS

Joshua recounted the law of God given to Moses and established it as the ongoing standard response of God's people to his grace as they entered the land. This law, written on tablets of stone, was a God-given gift of grace to provide former slaves with the keys to the blessing and freedom found in obedience to God.

Paul later said that something far more incredible happened through the gift of salvation. The law is no longer contained on tablets of stone—now it is written on the human heart (2Co 3:3). The transformation brought about by God's saving grace should be demonstrated by those who claim to follow Jesus. This change is not the result of following an abstract set of external, moral principles but the working of the Spirit of God dwelling in the hearts of God's people. God, through the work of salvation, takes out a person's heart of stone and puts in its place a heart of flesh that pulsates with new life. On this new heart is written God's law—a miracle far greater than the Law given at Mount Sinai.

---

[1] Hebrew *appointed time* [2] That is, set apart (devoted) as an offering to the Lord (for destruction)

is written in the Book of the Law. 35There was not a word of all that Moses commanded that Joshua did not read before all the assembly of Israel, and the women, and the little ones, and the sojourners who lived[1] among them.

The Gibeonite Deception

9 As soon as all the kings who were beyond the Jordan in the hill country and in the lowland all along the coast of the Great Sea toward Lebanon, the Hittites, the Amorites, the Canaanites, the Perizzites, the Hivites, and the Jebusites, heard of this, 2they gathered together as one to fight against Joshua and Israel.

3But when the inhabitants of Gibeon heard what Joshua had done to Jericho and to Ai, 4they on their part acted with cunning and went and made ready provisions and took worn-out sacks for their donkeys, and wineskins, worn-out and torn and mended, 5with worn-out, patched sandals on their feet, and worn-out clothes. And all their provisions were dry and crumbly. 6And they went to Joshua in the camp at Gilgal and said to him and to the men of Israel, "We have come from a distant country, so now make a covenant with us." 7But the men of Israel said to the Hivites, "Perhaps you live among us; then how can we make a covenant with you?" 8They said to Joshua, "We are your servants." And Joshua said to them, "Who are you? And where do you come from?" 9They said to him, "From a very distant country your servants have come, because of the name of the LORD your God. For we have heard a report of him, and all that he did in Egypt, 10and all that he did to the two kings of the Amorites who were beyond the Jordan, to Sihon the king of Heshbon, and to Og king of Bashan, who lived in Ashtaroth. 11So our elders and all the inhabitants of our country said to us, 'Take provisions in your hand for the journey and go to meet them and say to them, "We are your servants. Come now, make a covenant with us."' 12Here is our bread. It was still warm when we took it from our houses as our food for the journey on the day we set out to come to you, but now, behold, it is dry and crumbly. 13These wineskins were new when we filled them, and behold, they have burst. And these garments and sandals of ours are worn out from the very long journey." 14So the men took some of their provisions, but did not ask counsel from the LORD. 15And Joshua made peace with them and made a covenant with them, to let them live, and the leaders of the congregation swore to them.

16At the end of three days after they had made a covenant with them, they heard that they were their neighbors and that they lived among them. 17And the people of Israel set out and reached their cities on the third day. Now their cities were Gibeon, Chephirah, Beeroth, and Kiriath-jearim. 18But the people of Israel did not attack them, because the leaders of the congregation had sworn to them by the LORD, the God of Israel. Then all the congregation murmured against the leaders. 19But all the leaders said to all the congregation, "We have sworn to them by the LORD, the God of Israel, and now we may not touch them. 20This we will do to them: let them live, lest wrath be upon us, because of the oath that we swore to them." 21And the leaders said to them, "Let them live." So they became cutters of wood and drawers of water for all the congregation, just as the leaders had said of them.

22Joshua summoned them, and he said to them, "Why did you deceive us, saying, 'We are very far from you,' when you dwell among us? 23Now therefore you are cursed, and some of you shall never be anything but servants, cutters of wood and drawers of water for the house of my God." 24They answered Joshua, "Because it was told to your servants for a certainty that the LORD your God had commanded his servant Moses to give you all the land and to destroy all the inhabitants of the land from before you—so we feared greatly for our lives because of you and did this thing. 25And now, behold, we are in your hand. Whatever seems good and right in your sight to do to us, do it." 26So he did this to them and delivered them

[1]Or *traveled*

out of the hand of the people of Israel, and they did not kill them. 27But Joshua made them that day cutters of wood and drawers of water for the congregation and for the altar of the LORD, to this day, in the place that he should choose.

The Sun Stands Still

10 As soon as Adoni-zedek, king of Jerusalem, heard how Joshua had captured Ai and had devoted it to destruction,[1] doing to Ai and its king as he had done to Jericho and its king, and how the inhabitants of Gibeon had made peace with Israel and were among them, 2he[2] feared greatly, because Gibeon was a great city, like one of the royal cities, and because it was greater than Ai, and all its men were warriors. 3So Adoni-zedek king of Jerusalem sent to Hoham king of Hebron, to Piram king of Jarmuth, to Japhia king of Lachish, and to Debir king of Eglon, saying, 4"Come up to me and help me, and let us strike Gibeon. For it has made peace with Joshua and with the people of Israel." 5Then the five kings of the Amorites, the king of Jerusalem, the king of Hebron, the king of Jarmuth, the king of Lachish, and the king of Eglon, gathered their forces and went up with all their armies and encamped against Gibeon and made war against it.

6And the men of Gibeon sent to Joshua at the camp in Gilgal, saying, "Do not relax your hand from your servants. Come up to us quickly and save us and help us, for all the kings of the Amorites who dwell in the hill country are gathered against us." 7So Joshua went up from Gilgal, he and all the people of war with him, and all the mighty men of valor. 8And the LORD said to Joshua, "Do not fear them, for I have given them into your hands. Not a man of them shall stand before you." 9So Joshua came upon them suddenly, having marched up all night from Gilgal. 10And the LORD threw them into a panic before Israel, who[3] struck them with a great blow at Gibeon and chased them by the way of the ascent of Beth-horon and struck them as far as Azekah and Makkedah. 11And as they fled before Israel, while they were going down the ascent of Beth-horon, the LORD threw down large stones from heaven on them as far as Azekah, and they died. There were more who died because of the hailstones than the sons of Israel killed with the sword.

12At that time Joshua spoke to the LORD in the day when the LORD gave the Amorites over to the sons of Israel, and he said in the sight of Israel,

"Sun, stand still at Gibeon,
  and moon, in the Valley of Aijalon."
13 And the sun stood still, and the moon stopped,
  until the nation took vengeance on their enemies.

Is this not written in the Book of Jashar? The sun stopped in the midst of heaven and did not hurry to set for about a whole day. 14There has been no day like it before or since, when the LORD heeded the voice of a man, for the LORD fought for Israel.

15So Joshua returned, and all Israel with him, to the camp at Gilgal.

Five Amorite Kings Executed

16These five kings fled and hid themselves in the cave at Makkedah. 17And it was told to Joshua, "The five kings have been found, hidden in the cave at Makkedah." 18And Joshua said, "Roll large stones against the mouth of the cave and set men by it to guard them, 19but do not stay there yourselves. Pursue your enemies; attack their rear guard. Do not let them enter their cities, for the LORD your God has given them into your hand." 20When Joshua and the sons of Israel had finished striking them with a great blow until they were wiped out, and when the remnant that remained of them had entered into the fortified cities, 21then all the people returned safe to Joshua in the camp at Makkedah. Not a man moved his tongue against any of the people of Israel.

[1]That is, set apart (devoted) as an offering to the Lord (for destruction); also verses 28, 35, 37, 39, 40
[2]One Hebrew manuscript, Vulgate (compare Syriac); most Hebrew manuscripts *they* [3]Or *and he*

THE SUN AND THE SON

God's continued control over creation was demonstrated by his ability to make the sun stand still. At Joshua's request, God showed his continued control over creation by extending daylight in order to aid Israel's victory in battle. Though we don't know exactly what happened, these miraculous events displayed God's ability to overcome darkness.

Not only can God overcome darkness in his created order, but he also has the power to banish the darkness of sin from the human heart (Eph 1:18). God overcame human blindness and grants his children the ability to see the light of his glory, seen most clearly in the person of Jesus (2Co 4:4). Those who see Jesus and respond in faith are transformed to reflect his image before the world.

John began his Gospel by claiming that Jesus was the light of God in human form — a light that came to push back the darkness of a world blinded by sin (Jn 1:1 – 14). John wrote, however, that people — because of sin — are unable or unwilling to see the light of Jesus; as a result, they choose to remain in the darkness.

So what did Jesus do? He entered the darkness and experienced it in order to overcome it. The scene at the cross testified to this reality. For three hours in the middle of the day while Jesus hung beaten and naked on a Roman cross, darkness filled the land (Mt 27:45; Lk 23:44). The entire cosmos testified to the fact that the wrath of God against human sin was being poured out on Jesus. At this point, few would have thought that this work was a means of ushering in the light of the glory of the kingdom of God as a crucified Savior hung on a Roman cross in darkness. But God knew that this was the only way to bring those trapped in darkness into the light. The Son of God had to endure darkness for them so that they could come with him into his kingdom of light (Col 1:13). After three days in a dark tomb, Jesus emerged into the light demonstrating that he overcame the darkness of sin. His resurrection was the firstfruits of all those who, like Jesus, will experience the joy of life in the light and the glory of the resurrection (1Co 15:20).

22Then Joshua said, "Open the mouth of the cave and bring those five kings out to me from the cave." 23And they did so, and brought those five kings out to him from the cave, the king of Jerusalem, the king of Hebron, the king of Jarmuth, the king of Lachish, and the king of Eglon. 24And when they brought those kings out to Joshua, Joshua summoned all the men of Israel and said to the chiefs of the men of war who had gone with him, "Come near; put your feet on the necks of these kings." Then they came near and put their feet on their necks. 25And Joshua said to them, "Do not be afraid or dismayed; be strong and courageous. For thus the LORD will do to all your enemies against whom you fight." 26And afterward Joshua struck them and put them to death, and he hanged them on five trees. And they hung on the trees until evening. 27But at the time of the going down of the sun, Joshua commanded, and they took them down from the trees and threw them into the cave where they had hidden themselves, and they set large stones against the mouth of the cave, which remain to this very day.

28As for Makkedah, Joshua captured it on that day and struck it, and its king, with the edge of the sword. He devoted to destruction every person in it; he left none remaining. And he did to the king of Makkedah just as he had done to the king of Jericho.

Conquest of Southern Canaan

29Then Joshua and all Israel with him passed on from Makkedah to Libnah and fought against Libnah. 30And the LORD gave it also and its king into the hand of Israel. And he struck it with the edge of the sword, and every person in it; he left none remaining in it. And he did to its king as he had done to the king of Jericho.

31Then Joshua and all Israel with him passed on from Libnah to Lachish and laid siege to it and fought against it. 32And the LORD gave Lachish into the hand of Israel, and he captured it on the second day and struck it with the edge of the sword, and every person in it, as he had done to Libnah.

33Then Horam king of Gezer came up to help Lachish. And Joshua struck him and his people, until he left none remaining.

34Then Joshua and all Israel with him passed on from Lachish to Eglon. And they laid siege to it and fought against it. 35And they captured it on that day, and struck it with the edge of the sword. And he devoted every person in it to destruction that day, as he had done to Lachish.

36Then Joshua and all Israel with him went up from Eglon to Hebron. And they fought against it 37and captured it and struck it with the edge of the sword, and its king and its towns, and every person in it. He left none remaining, as he had done to Eglon, and devoted it to destruction and every person in it.

38Then Joshua and all Israel with him turned back to Debir and fought against it 39and he captured it with its king and all its towns. And they struck them with the edge of the sword and devoted to destruction every person in it; he left none remaining. Just as he had done to Hebron and to Libnah and its king, so he did to Debir and to its king.

40So Joshua struck the whole land, the hill country and the Negeb and the lowland and the slopes, and all their kings. He left none remaining, but devoted to destruction all that breathed, just as the LORD God of Israel commanded. 41And Joshua struck them from Kadesh-barnea as far as Gaza, and all the country of Goshen, as far as Gibeon. 42And Joshua captured all these kings and their land at one time, because the LORD God of Israel fought for Israel. 43Then Joshua returned, and all Israel with him, to the camp at Gilgal.

Conquests in Northern Canaan

11 When Jabin, king of Hazor, heard of this, he sent to Jobab king of Madon, and to the king of Shimron, and to the king of Achshaph, 2and to the kings who were in the northern hill country, and in the Arabah south of Chinneroth, and in the lowland, and in Naphoth-dor on the west, 3to the Canaanites in the east

and the west, the Amorites, the Hittites, the Perizzites, and the Jebusites in the hill
country, and the Hivites under Hermon in the land of Mizpah. 4And they came
out with all their troops, a great horde, in number like the sand that is on the seashore, with very many horses and chariots. 5And all these kings joined their forces
and came and encamped together at the waters of Merom to fight against Israel.
6And the LORD said to Joshua, "Do not be afraid of them, for tomorrow at this
time I will give over all of them, slain, to Israel. You shall hamstring their horses
and burn their chariots with fire." 7So Joshua and all his warriors came suddenly
against them by the waters of Merom and fell upon them. 8And the LORD gave
them into the hand of Israel, who struck them and chased them as far as Great
Sidon and Misrephoth-maim, and eastward as far as the Valley of Mizpeh. And
they struck them until he left none remaining. 9And Joshua did to them just as the
LORD said to him: he hamstrung their horses and burned their chariots with fire.
10And Joshua turned back at that time and captured Hazor and struck its king
with the sword, for Hazor formerly was the head of all those kingdoms. 11And they
struck with the sword all who were in it, devoting them to destruction;[1] there was
none left that breathed. And he burned Hazor with fire. 12And all the cities of
those kings, and all their kings, Joshua captured, and struck them with the edge
of the sword, devoting them to destruction, just as Moses the servant of the LORD
had commanded. 13But none of the cities that stood on mounds did Israel burn,
except Hazor alone; that Joshua burned. 14And all the spoil of these cities and the
livestock, the people of Israel took for their plunder. But every person they struck
with the edge of the sword until they had destroyed them, and they did not leave
any who breathed. 15Just as the LORD had commanded Moses his servant, so Moses commanded Joshua, and so Joshua did. He left nothing undone of all that the
LORD had commanded Moses.
16So Joshua took all that land, the hill country and all the Negeb and all the
land of Goshen and the lowland and the Arabah and the hill country of Israel
and its lowland 17from Mount Halak, which rises toward Seir, as far as Baal-gad in
the Valley of Lebanon below Mount Hermon. And he captured all their kings and
struck them and put them to death. 18Joshua made war a long time with all those
kings. 19There was not a city that made peace with the people of Israel except the
Hivites, the inhabitants of Gibeon. They took them all in battle. 20For it was the
LORD's doing to harden their hearts that they should come against Israel in battle,
in order that they should be devoted to destruction and should receive no mercy
but be destroyed, just as the LORD commanded Moses.
21And Joshua came at that time and cut off the Anakim from the hill country,
from Hebron, from Debir, from Anab, and from all the hill country of Judah, and
from all the hill country of Israel. Joshua devoted them to destruction with their
cities. 22There was none of the Anakim left in the land of the people of Israel. Only
in Gaza, in Gath, and in Ashdod did some remain. 23So Joshua took the whole
land, according to all that the LORD had spoken to Moses. And Joshua gave it for
an inheritance to Israel according to their tribal allotments. And the land had rest
from war.

Kings Defeated by Moses

12 Now these are the kings of the land whom the people of Israel defeated
and took possession of their land beyond the Jordan toward the sunrise,
from the Valley of the Arnon to Mount Hermon, with all the Arabah eastward:
2Sihon king of the Amorites who lived at Heshbon and ruled from Aroer, which
is on the edge of the Valley of the Arnon, and from the middle of the valley as
far as the river Jabbok, the boundary of the Ammonites, that is, half of Gilead,
3and the Arabah to the Sea of Chinneroth eastward, and in the direction of Beth-
jeshimoth, to the Sea of the Arabah, the Salt Sea, southward to the foot of the

[1]That is, setting apart (devoting) as an offering to the Lord (for destruction); also verses 12, 20, 21

JOSHUA 12:1–24

TRIUMPH

Joshua 12 recounts a list of kings that Israel has defeated. The list goes into great detail by not only giving the names of the defeated kings, but also going to great length to describe the land over which the defeated kings previously ruled. The vast size of this territory is a testament to God's ability to conquer great kings and great lands.

These victories are minor in comparison to the far greater victory won by Jesus himself. He did not simply win a battle against a pagan king, but he defeated Satan, sin, and the principalities of darkness. He did not merely conquer a portion of land, but he secured his rule and reign over all the earth (Eph 1:21–22). While the list of kings and land in Joshua 12 may appear large and valuable to people, Jesus was not inclined to accept temporal kingdoms as his victory (Mt 4:8–10). By virtue of Jesus' work, he is worthy of all honor, fame, and glory forever. All things, both in heaven and on earth, both temporal and cosmic, both now and forever, are placed under his kingly rule. This list of victories may be "great," but it pales in comparison to the ultimate victory of Jesus.

slopes of Pisgah; 4 and Og[1] king of Bashan, one of the remnant of the Rephaim, who lived at Ashtaroth and at Edrei 5 and ruled over Mount Hermon and Salecah and all Bashan to the boundary of the Geshurites and the Maacathites, and over half of Gilead to the boundary of Sihon king of Heshbon. 6 Moses, the servant of the LORD, and the people of Israel defeated them. And Moses the servant of the LORD gave their land for a possession to the Reubenites and the Gadites and the half-tribe of Manasseh.

Kings Defeated by Joshua

7 And these are the kings of the land whom Joshua and the people of Israel defeated on the west side of the Jordan, from Baal-gad in the Valley of Lebanon to Mount Halak, that rises toward Seir (and Joshua gave their land to the tribes of Israel as a possession according to their allotments, 8 in the hill country, in the lowland, in the Arabah, in the slopes, in the wilderness, and in the Negeb, the land of the Hittites, the Amorites, the Canaanites, the Perizzites, the Hivites, and the Jebusites): 9 the king of Jericho, one; the king of Ai, which is beside Bethel, one; 10 the king of Jerusalem, one; the king of Hebron, one; 11 the king of Jarmuth, one; the king of Lachish, one; 12 the king of Eglon, one; the king of Gezer, one; 13 the king of Debir, one; the king of Geder, one; 14 the king of Hormah, one; the king of Arad, one; 15 the king of Libnah, one; the king of Adullam, one; 16 the king of Makkedah, one; the king of Bethel, one; 17 the king of Tappuah, one; the king of Hepher, one; 18 the king of Aphek, one; the king of Lasharon, one; 19 the king of Madon, one; the king of Hazor, one; 20 the king of Shimron-meron, one; the king of Achshaph, one; 21 the king of Taanach, one; the king of Megiddo, one; 22 the king of Kedesh, one; the king of Jokneam in Carmel, one; 23 the king of Dor in Naphath-dor, one; the king of Goiim in Galilee,[2] one; 24 the king of Tirzah, one: in all, thirty-one kings.

Land Still to Be Conquered

13 Now Joshua was old and advanced in years, and the LORD said to him, "You are old and advanced in years, and there remains yet very much land to possess. 2 This is the land that yet remains: all the regions of the Philistines, and all those of the Geshurites 3 (from the Shihor, which is east of Egypt, northward to the boundary of Ekron, it is counted as Canaanite; there are five rulers of the Philistines, those of Gaza, Ashdod, Ashkelon, Gath, and Ekron), and those of the Avvim, 4 in the south, all the land of the Canaanites, and Mearah that belongs to the Sidonians, to Aphek, to the boundary of the Amorites, 5 and the land of the Gebalites, and all Lebanon, toward the sunrise, from Baal-gad below Mount Hermon to Lebo-hamath, 6 all the inhabitants of the hill country from Lebanon to Misrephoth-maim, even all the Sidonians. I myself will drive them out from before the people of Israel. Only allot the land to Israel for an inheritance, as I have commanded you. 7 Now therefore divide this land for an inheritance to the nine tribes and half the tribe of Manasseh."

The Inheritance East of the Jordan

8 With the other half of the tribe of Manasseh[3] the Reubenites and the Gadites received their inheritance, which Moses gave them, beyond the Jordan eastward, as Moses the servant of the LORD gave them: 9 from Aroer, which is on the edge of the Valley of the Arnon, and the city that is in the middle of the valley, and all the tableland of Medeba as far as Dibon; 10 and all the cities of Sihon king of the Amorites, who reigned in Heshbon, as far as the boundary of the Ammonites; 11 and Gilead, and the region of the Geshurites and Maacathites, and all Mount Hermon, and all Bashan to Salecah; 12 all the kingdom of Og in Bashan, who reigned in Ashtaroth and in Edrei (he alone was left of the remnant of the Rephaim); these Moses had struck and driven out. 13 Yet the people of Israel did

JOSHUA 13:8

INHERITANCE

The word *inheritance* refers to a possession or property that is given to an heir. Throughout the Old Testament, the word was linked to God's faithfulness to give the people the things he had promised them. Specifically here, Joshua referred to the giving of a parcel of land that God had long ago pledged to the descendants of Abraham. God, as the owner of all things, can bequeath anything he desires to his children as a gift of his grace.

The nature of the promised inheritance extends far beyond a piece of land. The inheritance of God is most clearly seen in him giving of himself to his people (Ps 16:5–6; Jer 10:16). He is the real gift of grace. In his kindness, God allows his people to know him and fellowship with him in spite of their sin. The gift of God makes every gift the fallen world can offer pale in comparison. Those who know the nature of the glorious inheritance in Christ (Col 1:12; 2:3) can relinquish the promises of a fallen world and treasure the far greater gift of knowing God (1Pe 1:4).

[1] Septuagint; Hebrew *the boundary of Og* [2] Septuagint; Hebrew *Gilgal* [3] Hebrew *With it*

not drive out the Geshurites or the Maacathites, but Geshur and Maacath dwell in the midst of Israel to this day.

14To the tribe of Levi alone Moses gave no inheritance. The offerings by fire to the LORD God of Israel are their inheritance, as he said to him.

15And Moses gave an inheritance to the tribe of the people of Reuben according to their clans. 16So their territory was from Aroer, which is on the edge of the Valley of the Arnon, and the city that is in the middle of the valley, and all the tableland by Medeba; 17with Heshbon, and all its cities that are in the tableland; Dibon, and Bamoth-baal, and Beth-baal-meon, 18and Jahaz, and Kedemoth, and Mephaath, 19and Kiriathaim, and Sibmah, and Zereth-shahar on the hill of the valley, 20and Beth-peor, and the slopes of Pisgah, and Beth-jeshimoth, 21that is, all the cities of the tableland, and all the kingdom of Sihon king of the Amorites, who reigned in Heshbon, whom Moses defeated with the leaders of Midian, Evi and Rekem and Zur and Hur and Reba, the princes of Sihon, who lived in the land. 22Balaam also, the son of Beor, the one who practiced divination, was killed with the sword by the people of Israel among the rest of their slain. 23And the border of the people of Reuben was the Jordan as a boundary. This was the inheritance of the people of Reuben, according to their clans with their cities and villages.

24Moses gave an inheritance also to the tribe of Gad, to the people of Gad, according to their clans. 25Their territory was Jazer, and all the cities of Gilead, and half the land of the Ammonites, to Aroer, which is east of Rabbah, 26and from Heshbon to Ramath-mizpeh and Betonim, and from Mahanaim to the territory of Debir,[1] 27and in the valley Beth-haram, Beth-nimrah, Succoth, and Zaphon, the rest of the kingdom of Sihon king of Heshbon, having the Jordan as a boundary, to the lower end of the Sea of Chinnereth, eastward beyond the Jordan. 28This is the inheritance of the people of Gad according to their clans, with their cities and villages.

29And Moses gave an inheritance to the half-tribe of Manasseh. It was allotted to the half-tribe of the people of Manasseh according to their clans. 30Their region extended from Mahanaim, through all Bashan, the whole kingdom of Og king of Bashan, and all the towns of Jair, which are in Bashan, sixty cities, 31and half Gilead, and Ashtaroth, and Edrei, the cities of the kingdom of Og in Bashan. These were allotted to the people of Machir the son of Manasseh for the half of the people of Machir according to their clans.

32These are the inheritances that Moses distributed in the plains of Moab, beyond the Jordan east of Jericho. 33But to the tribe of Levi Moses gave no inheritance; the LORD God of Israel is their inheritance, just as he said to them.

The Inheritance West of the Jordan

14 These are the inheritances that the people of Israel received in the land of Canaan, which Eleazar the priest and Joshua the son of Nun and the heads of the fathers' houses of the tribes of the people of Israel gave them to inherit. 2Their inheritance was by lot, just as the LORD had commanded by the hand of Moses for the nine and one-half tribes. 3For Moses had given an inheritance to the two and one-half tribes beyond the Jordan, but to the Levites he gave no inheritance among them. 4For the people of Joseph were two tribes, Manasseh and Ephraim. And no portion was given to the Levites in the land, but only cities to dwell in, with their pasturelands for their livestock and their substance. 5The people of Israel did as the LORD commanded Moses; they allotted the land.

Caleb's Request and Inheritance

6Then the people of Judah came to Joshua at Gilgal. And Caleb the son of Jephunneh the Kenizzite said to him, "You know what the LORD said to Moses the man of God in Kadesh-barnea concerning you and me. 7I was forty years old when

[1]Septuagint, Syriac, Vulgate; Hebrew *Lidebir*

JOSHUA 14:6–9

CALEB

Caleb, because of his faithfulness and obedience to God, was given entrance into the land and the glorious inheritance God pledged to his people—a gift that was squandered by those of Caleb's generation. Over the ensuing decades, Caleb watched as all of his contemporaries died in the wilderness. Surely Caleb doubted the promise of God as he wandered in the wilderness, observed the hard-heartedness of the people, and watched person after person die under the judgment of God. Would God be faithful to give the people this long-awaited land? If so, would he remember Caleb and grant him an inheritance among the people?

Like Caleb, Christians today await the fulfillment of God's promises. In a fallen world, it can be easy to question whether God's plan is unfolding as intended, whether Christ will return, and whether he will remember his children when he does. The faithfulness of God to remember Caleb serves as an encouragement of God's care for every person who longs for his coming (2Pe 3:11–13).

CANAAN

The biblical authors portrayed the land of Canaan with a vast array of imagery. The land flowed "with milk and honey," symbolic of the lavish provision of God for his people (Ex 33:3). The land was also a land of peace (*shalom*). In the land of the promise and in contrast to the effects of the curse of sin, the people were meant to live free from the destruction caused by war. Finally, the land allowed the people to worship God, live under his rule, and experience fellowship with him. Whereas Adam and Eve walked with God in the cool of the day in the garden, now God's people could walk with him and experience his grace once again. For these reasons the land of Canaan served as a type of Garden of Eden.

Not only did Canaan point backward to the Garden of Eden, but it also pointed forward to a far greater reality. The blessing, peace, and fellowship meant to be experienced in the land would be a fleeting reality. Sin hampered Israel's experience of the land's beauty and ultimately caused the people to be banished from the land at the hands of the Assyrians and Babylonians. The people were forced to look forward to a better day, a day when these realities could be experienced fully and finally.

John's vision in Revelation 21 points forward to the hope of the coming kingdom of God for those who have experienced the grace of God. John pictured "a new heaven and a new earth" using similar themes. The blessings of God will be experienced in previously unknown ways. The greatest images the human mind can conjure — streets made of gold and walls made of precious stones — were used by John to describe this coming reality. In addition, the peace of God will also reign over all. No longer will war and disease contaminate God's world. There will be lasting peace, and, as a result, there will be no more tears, no more division, and no more pain. Finally, God's rule and reign will be perfectly experienced on earth as it is in heaven. Christians today cry, "Come, Lord Jesus," knowing that this is the only hope for experiencing God's blessing, peace, and presence perfectly and forever (Rev 22:20).

Moses the servant of the LORD sent me from Kadesh-barnea to spy out the land, and I brought him word again as it was in my heart. 8But my brothers who went up with me made the heart of the people melt; yet I wholly followed the LORD my God. 9And Moses swore on that day, saying, 'Surely the land on which your foot has trodden shall be an inheritance for you and your children forever, because you have wholly followed the LORD my God.' 10And now, behold, the LORD has kept me alive, just as he said, these forty-five years since the time that the LORD spoke this word to Moses, while Israel walked in the wilderness. And now, behold, I am this day eighty-five years old. 11I am still as strong today as I was in the day that Moses sent me; my strength now is as my strength was then, for war and for going and coming. 12So now give me this hill country of which the LORD spoke on that day, for you heard on that day how the Anakim were there, with great fortified cities. It may be that the LORD will be with me, and I shall drive them out just as the LORD said."

13Then Joshua blessed him, and he gave Hebron to Caleb the son of Jephunneh for an inheritance. 14Therefore Hebron became the inheritance of Caleb the son of Jephunneh the Kenizzite to this day, because he wholly followed the LORD, the God of Israel. 15Now the name of Hebron formerly was Kiriath-arba.[1] (Arba[2] was the greatest man among the Anakim.) And the land had rest from war.

The Allotment for Judah

15 The allotment for the tribe of the people of Judah according to their clans reached southward to the boundary of Edom, to the wilderness of Zin at the farthest south. 2And their south boundary ran from the end of the Salt Sea, from the bay that faces southward. 3It goes out southward of the ascent of Akrabbim, passes along to Zin, and goes up south of Kadesh-barnea, along by Hezron, up to Addar, turns about to Karka, 4passes along to Azmon, goes out by the Brook of Egypt, and comes to its end at the sea. This shall be your south boundary. 5And the east boundary is the Salt Sea, to the mouth of the Jordan. And the boundary on the north side runs from the bay of the sea at the mouth of the Jordan. 6And the boundary goes up to Beth-hoglah and passes along north of Beth-arabah. And the boundary goes up to the stone of Bohan the son of Reuben. 7And the boundary goes up to Debir from the Valley of Achor, and so northward, turning toward Gilgal, which is opposite the ascent of Adummim, which is on the south side of the valley. And the boundary passes along to the waters of En-shemesh and ends at En-rogel. 8Then the boundary goes up by the Valley of the Son of Hinnom at the southern shoulder of the Jebusite (that is, Jerusalem). And the boundary goes up to the top of the mountain that lies over against the Valley of Hinnom, on the west, at the northern end of the Valley of Rephaim. 9Then the boundary extends from the top of the mountain to the spring of the waters of Nephtoah, and from there to the cities of Mount Ephron. Then the boundary bends around to Baalah (that is, Kiriath-jearim). 10And the boundary circles west of Baalah to Mount Seir, passes along to the northern shoulder of Mount Jearim (that is, Chesalon), and goes down to Beth-shemesh and passes along by Timnah. 11The boundary goes out to the shoulder of the hill north of Ekron, then the boundary bends around to Shikkeron and passes along to Mount Baalah and goes out to Jabneel. Then the boundary comes to an end at the sea. 12And the west boundary was the Great Sea with its coastline. This is the boundary around the people of Judah according to their clans.

13According to the commandment of the LORD to Joshua, he gave to Caleb the son of Jephunneh a portion among the people of Judah, Kiriath-arba, that is, Hebron (Arba was the father of Anak). 14And Caleb drove out from there the three sons of Anak, Sheshai and Ahiman and Talmai, the descendants of Anak. 15And he went up from there against the inhabitants of Debir. Now the name of Debir

[1] *Kiriath-arba* means *the city of Arba* [2] Hebrew *He*

formerly was Kiriath-sepher. [16]And Caleb said, “He who attacks Kiriath-sepher and captures it, I will give him Achsah my daughter as wife.” [17]And Othniel the son of Kenaz, the brother of Caleb, captured it. And he gave him Achsah his daughter as wife. [18]When she came to him, she urged him to ask her father for a field. And she dismounted from her donkey, and Caleb said to her, “What do you want?” [19]She said to him, “Give me a blessing. Since you have given me the land of the Negeb, give me also springs of water.” And he gave her the upper springs and the lower springs.

[20]This is the inheritance of the tribe of the people of Judah according to their clans. [21]The cities belonging to the tribe of the people of Judah in the extreme south, toward the boundary of Edom, were Kabzeel, Eder, Jagur, [22]Kinah, Dimonah, Adadah, [23]Kedesh, Hazor, Ithnan, [24]Ziph, Telem, Bealoth, [25]Hazor-hadattah, Kerioth-hezron (that is, Hazor), [26]Amam, Shema, Moladah, [27]Hazar-gaddah, Heshmon, Beth-pelet, [28]Hazar-shual, Beersheba, Biziothiah, [29]Baalah, Iim, Ezem, [30]Eltolad, Chesil, Hormah, [31]Ziklag, Madmannah, Sansannah, [32]Lebaoth, Shilhim, Ain, and Rimmon: in all, twenty-nine cities with their villages.

[33]And in the lowland, Eshtaol, Zorah, Ashnah, [34]Zanoah, En-gannim, Tappuah, Enam, [35]Jarmuth, Adullam, Socoh, Azekah, [36]Shaaraim, Adithaim, Gederah, Gederothaim: fourteen cities with their villages.

[37]Zenan, Hadashah, Migdal-gad, [38]Dilean, Mizpeh, Joktheel, [39]Lachish, Bozkath, Eglon, [40]Cabbon, Lahmam, Chitlish, [41]Gederoth, Beth-dagon, Naamah, and Makkedah: sixteen cities with their villages.

[42]Libnah, Ether, Ashan, [43]Iphtah, Ashnah, Nezib, [44]Keilah, Achzib, and Mareshah: nine cities with their villages.

[45]Ekron, with its towns and its villages; [46]from Ekron to the sea, all that were by the side of Ashdod, with their villages.

[47]Ashdod, its towns and its villages; Gaza, its towns and its villages; to the Brook of Egypt, and the Great Sea with its coastline.

[48]And in the hill country, Shamir, Jattir, Socoh, [49]Dannah, Kiriath-sannah (that is, Debir), [50]Anab, Eshtemoh, Anim, [51]Goshen, Holon, and Giloh: eleven cities with their villages.

[52]Arab, Dumah, Eshan, [53]Janim, Beth-tappuah, Aphekah, [54]Humtah, Kiriath-arba (that is, Hebron), and Zior: nine cities with their villages.

[55]Maon, Carmel, Ziph, Juttah, [56]Jezreel, Jokdeam, Zanoah, [57]Kain, Gibeah, and Timnah: ten cities with their villages.

[58]Halhul, Beth-zur, Gedor, [59]Maarath, Beth-anoth, and Eltekon: six cities with their villages.

[60]Kiriath-baal (that is, Kiriath-jearim), and Rabbah: two cities with their villages.

[61]In the wilderness, Beth-arabah, Middin, Secacah, [62]Nibshan, the City of Salt, and Engedi: six cities with their villages.

[63]But the Jebusites, the inhabitants of Jerusalem, the people of Judah could not drive out, so the Jebusites dwell with the people of Judah at Jerusalem to this day.

The Allotment for Ephraim and Manasseh

16 The allotment of the people of Joseph went from the Jordan by Jericho, east of the waters of Jericho, into the wilderness, going up from Jericho into the hill country to Bethel. [2]Then going from Bethel to Luz, it passes along to Ataroth, the territory of the Archites. [3]Then it goes down westward to the territory of the Japhletites, as far as the territory of Lower Beth-horon, then to Gezer, and it ends at the sea.

[4]The people of Joseph, Manasseh and Ephraim, received their inheritance.

[5]The territory of the people of Ephraim by their clans was as follows: the boundary of their inheritance on the east was Ataroth-addar as far as Upper Beth-horon, [6]and the boundary goes from there to the sea. On the north is Michmethath. Then on the east the boundary turns around toward Taanath-shiloh

---

JOSHUA 16:1–4

PROVISION FOR THE TRIBES

God fulfilled his promise by giving an allotment of the land to each of the tribes of Israel (Nu 33:54). Among a huge mass of humanity, God took care to provide for each of the tribes and, consequently, each of the families making up these tribes. The sovereign King of the universe takes personal care of each person who is the recipient of his promise. Two and a half tribes were given land on the east side of the Jordan, while the remaining nine and a half tribes were given territory west of the Jordan.

Jesus also made a remarkable claim recorded in John’s Gospel. He compared himself to a Good Shepherd who would ultimately lay down his life to demonstrate his love and care for his sheep. This shepherding care is seen in the personal attention he gives to each of his sheep. The sheep’s ability to hear and respond to the shepherd’s voice demonstrates their knowledge of him. He calls his sheep, not as a group, but individually — by name. God also keeps those whom he calls, and he will not let any enemy snatch them from his hand (Jn 10:1–29).

and passes along beyond it on the east to Janoah, 7then it goes down from Janoah
to Ataroth and to Naarah, and touches Jericho, ending at the Jordan. 8From Tappuah the boundary goes westward to the brook Kanah and ends at the sea. Such is
the inheritance of the tribe of the people of Ephraim by their clans, 9together with
the towns that were set apart for the people of Ephraim within the inheritance of
the Manassites, all those towns with their villages. 10However, they did not drive
out the Canaanites who lived in Gezer, so the Canaanites have lived in the midst
of Ephraim to this day but have been made to do forced labor.

17 Then allotment was made to the people of Manasseh, for he was the firstborn of Joseph. To Machir the firstborn of Manasseh, the father of Gilead,
were allotted Gilead and Bashan, because he was a man of war. 2And allotments
were made to the rest of the people of Manasseh by their clans, Abiezer, Helek,
Asriel, Shechem, Hepher, and Shemida. These were the male descendants of
Manasseh the son of Joseph, by their clans.

3Now Zelophehad the son of Hepher, son of Gilead, son of Machir, son of
Manasseh, had no sons, but only daughters, and these are the names of his
daughters: Mahlah, Noah, Hoglah, Milcah, and Tirzah. 4They approached Eleazar
the priest and Joshua the son of Nun and the leaders and said, "The LORD commanded Moses to give us an inheritance along with our brothers." So according
to the mouth of the LORD he gave them an inheritance among the brothers of
their father. 5Thus there fell to Manasseh ten portions, besides the land of Gilead
and Bashan, which is on the other side of the Jordan, 6because the daughters of
Manasseh received an inheritance along with his sons. The land of Gilead was
allotted to the rest of the people of Manasseh.

7The territory of Manasseh reached from Asher to Michmethath, which is
east of Shechem. Then the boundary goes along southward to the inhabitants of
En-tappuah. 8The land of Tappuah belonged to Manasseh, but the town of Tappuah on the boundary of Manasseh belonged to the people of Ephraim. 9Then
the boundary went down to the brook Kanah. These cities, to the south of the
brook, among the cities of Manasseh, belong to Ephraim. Then the boundary
of Manasseh goes on the north side of the brook and ends at the sea, 10the land
to the south being Ephraim's and that to the north being Manasseh's, with the
sea forming its boundary. On the north Asher is reached, and on the east Issachar. 11Also in Issachar and in Asher Manasseh had Beth-shean and its villages,
and Ibleam and its villages, and the inhabitants of Dor and its villages, and the
inhabitants of En-dor and its villages, and the inhabitants of Taanach and its
villages, and the inhabitants of Megiddo and its villages; the third is Naphath.[1]
12Yet the people of Manasseh could not take possession of those cities, but the
Canaanites persisted in dwelling in that land. 13Now when the people of Israel
grew strong, they put the Canaanites to forced labor, but did not utterly drive
them out.

14Then the people of Joseph spoke to Joshua, saying, "Why have you given me
but one lot and one portion as an inheritance, although I am a numerous people,
since all along the LORD has blessed me?" 15And Joshua said to them, "If you are
a numerous people, go up by yourselves to the forest, and there clear ground for
yourselves in the land of the Perizzites and the Rephaim, since the hill country of
Ephraim is too narrow for you." 16The people of Joseph said, "The hill country is
not enough for us. Yet all the Canaanites who dwell in the plain have chariots of
iron, both those in Beth-shean and its villages and those in the Valley of Jezreel."
17Then Joshua said to the house of Joseph, to Ephraim and Manasseh, "You are a
numerous people and have great power. You shall not have one allotment only,
18but the hill country shall be yours, for though it is a forest, you shall clear it and
possess it to its farthest borders. For you shall drive out the Canaanites, though
they have chariots of iron, and though they are strong."

[1]The meaning of the Hebrew is uncertain

Allotment of the Remaining Land

18 Then the whole congregation of the people of Israel assembled at Shiloh
and set up the tent of meeting there. The land lay subdued before them.
2There remained among the people of Israel seven tribes whose inheritance
had not yet been apportioned. 3So Joshua said to the people of Israel, "How long
will you put off going in to take possession of the land, which the LORD, the God
of your fathers, has given you? 4Provide three men from each tribe, and I will
send them out that they may set out and go up and down the land. They shall
write a description of it with a view to their inheritances, and then come to me.
5They shall divide it into seven portions. Judah shall continue in his territory
on the south, and the house of Joseph shall continue in their territory on the
north. 6And you shall describe the land in seven divisions and bring the description here to me. And I will cast lots for you here before the LORD our God.
7The Levites have no portion among you, for the priesthood of the LORD is their
heritage. And Gad and Reuben and half the tribe of Manasseh have received
their inheritance beyond the Jordan eastward, which Moses the servant of the
LORD gave them."
8So the men arose and went, and Joshua charged those who went to write
the description of the land, saying, "Go up and down in the land and write a
description and return to me. And I will cast lots for you here before the LORD
in Shiloh." 9So the men went and passed up and down in the land and wrote
in a book a description of it by towns in seven divisions. Then they came to
Joshua to the camp at Shiloh, 10and Joshua cast lots for them in Shiloh before
the LORD. And there Joshua apportioned the land to the people of Israel, to each
his portion.

The Inheritance for Benjamin

11The lot of the tribe of the people of Benjamin according to its clans came up,
and the territory allotted to it fell between the people of Judah and the people of
Joseph. 12On the north side their boundary began at the Jordan. Then the boundary goes up to the shoulder north of Jericho, then up through the hill country
westward, and it ends at the wilderness of Beth-aven. 13From there the boundary
passes along southward in the direction of Luz, to the shoulder of Luz (that is,
Bethel), then the boundary goes down to Ataroth-addar, on the mountain that
lies south of Lower Beth-horon. 14Then the boundary goes in another direction,
turning on the western side southward from the mountain that lies to the south,
opposite Beth-horon, and it ends at Kiriath-baal (that is, Kiriath-jearim), a city
belonging to the people of Judah. This forms the western side. 15And the southern
side begins at the outskirts of Kiriath-jearim. And the boundary goes from there
to Ephron,[1] to the spring of the waters of Nephtoah. 16Then the boundary goes
down to the border of the mountain that overlooks the Valley of the Son of Hinnom, which is at the north end of the Valley of Rephaim. And it then goes down
the Valley of Hinnom, south of the shoulder of the Jebusites, and downward to
En-rogel. 17Then it bends in a northerly direction going on to En-shemesh, and
from there goes to Geliloth, which is opposite the ascent of Adummim. Then it
goes down to the stone of Bohan the son of Reuben, 18and passing on to the north
of the shoulder of Beth-arabah[2] it goes down to the Arabah. 19Then the boundary passes on to the north of the shoulder of Beth-hoglah. And the boundary
ends at the northern bay of the Salt Sea, at the south end of the Jordan: this is
the southern border. 20The Jordan forms its boundary on the eastern side. This is
the inheritance of the people of Benjamin, according to their clans, boundary by
boundary all around.
21Now the cities of the tribe of the people of Benjamin according to their
clans were Jericho, Beth-hoglah, Emek-keziz, 22Beth-arabah, Zemaraim, Bethel,

[1]See 15:9; Hebrew *westward* [2]Septuagint; Hebrew *to the shoulder over against the Arabah*

JOSHUA 18:1–10

BLESSINGS OF FAITHFULNESS

This scene was eerily reminiscent of the sending of the spies in Numbers 13, except this time the result was more favorable. This time emissaries of the nation went throughout the promised land to map out the territory allotted to the seven tribes who had not yet received their land. There they saw the glorious inheritance that God would give to the nation. The land would testify to the faithfulness of God and demonstrate that he was continuing to accomplish his mission.

The church functions in the same way today. As believers gather in local churches around the world, they see a tangible picture of the grace of God. He is still at work, granting salvation to the lost and uniting them together into his family. Local churches, filled with believers, put the manifold wisdom of God on display for a watching world. The mystery of his grace, hidden for generations yet revealed in the person of Jesus, is evident for all to see (Eph 3:8–11). He is indeed faithful to bless his people, on earth and ultimately in heaven.

23 Avvim, Parah, Ophrah, 24 Chephar-ammoni, Ophni, Geba—twelve cities with
their villages: 25 Gibeon, Ramah, Beeroth, 26 Mizpeh, Chephirah, Mozah, 27 Rekem,
Irpeel, Taralah, 28 Zela, Haeleph, Jebus[1] (that is, Jerusalem), Gibeah[2] and Kiriath-
jearim[3]—fourteen cities with their villages. This is the inheritance of the people
of Benjamin according to its clans.

The Inheritance for Simeon

19 The second lot came out for Simeon, for the tribe of the people of Simeon,
according to their clans, and their inheritance was in the midst of the inheritance of the people of Judah. 2 And they had for their inheritance Beersheba,
Sheba, Moladah, 3 Hazar-shual, Balah, Ezem, 4 Eltolad, Bethul, Hormah, 5 Ziklag,
Beth-marcaboth, Hazar-susah, 6 Beth-lebaoth, and Sharuhen—thirteen cities
with their villages; 7 Ain, Rimmon, Ether, and Ashan—four cities with their villages, 8 together with all the villages around these cities as far as Baalath-beer,
Ramah of the Negeb. This was the inheritance of the tribe of the people of Simeon
according to their clans. 9 The inheritance of the people of Simeon formed part of
the territory of the people of Judah. Because the portion of the people of Judah
was too large for them, the people of Simeon obtained an inheritance in the midst
of their inheritance.

The Inheritance for Zebulun

10 The third lot came up for the people of Zebulun, according to their clans.
And the territory of their inheritance reached as far as Sarid. 11 Then their boundary goes up westward and on to Mareal and touches Dabbesheth, then the brook
that is east of Jokneam. 12 From Sarid it goes in the other direction eastward toward
the sunrise to the boundary of Chisloth-tabor. From there it goes to Daberath,
then up to Japhia. 13 From there it passes along on the east toward the sunrise to
Gath-hepher, to Eth-kazin, and going on to Rimmon it bends toward Neah, 14 then
on the north the boundary turns about to Hannathon, and it ends at the Valley of
Iphtahel; 15 and Kattath, Nahalal, Shimron, Idalah, and Bethlehem—twelve cities
with their villages. 16 This is the inheritance of the people of Zebulun, according
to their clans—these cities with their villages.

The Inheritance for Issachar

17 The fourth lot came out for Issachar, for the people of Issachar, according to
their clans. 18 Their territory included Jezreel, Chesulloth, Shunem, 19 Hapharaim,
Shion, Anaharath, 20 Rabbith, Kishion, Ebez, 21 Remeth, En-gannim, En-haddah,
Beth-pazzez. 22 The boundary also touches Tabor, Shahazumah, and Beth-
shemesh, and its boundary ends at the Jordan—sixteen cities with their villages.
23 This is the inheritance of the tribe of the people of Issachar, according to their
clans—the cities with their villages.

The Inheritance for Asher

24 The fifth lot came out for the tribe of the people of Asher according to their
clans. 25 Their territory included Helkath, Hali, Beten, Achshaph, 26 Allammelech,
Amad, and Mishal. On the west it touches Carmel and Shihor-libnath, 27 then it
turns eastward, it goes to Beth-dagon, and touches Zebulun and the Valley of Iphtahel northward to Beth-emek and Neiel. Then it continues in the north to Cabul,
28 Ebron, Rehob, Hammon, Kanah, as far as Sidon the Great. 29 Then the boundary
turns to Ramah, reaching to the fortified city of Tyre. Then the boundary turns to
Hosah, and it ends at the sea; Mahalab,[4] Achzib, 30 Ummah, Aphek and Rehob—
twenty-two cities with their villages. 31 This is the inheritance of the tribe of the
people of Asher according to their clans—these cities with their villages.

---

[1] Septuagint, Syriac, Vulgate; Hebrew *the Jebusite* [2] Hebrew *Gibeath* [3] Septuagint; Hebrew *Kiriath*
[4] Compare Septuagint; Hebrew *Mehebel*

The Inheritance for Naphtali

32The sixth lot came out for the people of Naphtali, for the people of Naphtali, according to their clans. 33And their boundary ran from Heleph, from the oak in Zaanannim, and Adami-nekeb, and Jabneel, as far as Lakkum, and it ended at the Jordan. 34Then the boundary turns westward to Aznoth-tabor and goes from there to Hukkok, touching Zebulun at the south and Asher on the west and Judah on the east at the Jordan. 35The fortified cities are Ziddim, Zer, Hammath, Rakkath, Chinnereth, 36Adamah, Ramah, Hazor, 37Kedesh, Edrei, En-hazor, 38Yiron, Migdal-el, Horem, Beth-anath, and Beth-shemesh—nineteen cities with their villages. 39This is the inheritance of the tribe of the people of Naphtali according to their clans—the cities with their villages.

The Inheritance for Dan

40The seventh lot came out for the tribe of the people of Dan, according to their clans. 41And the territory of its inheritance included Zorah, Eshtaol, Ir-shemesh, 42Shaalabbin, Aijalon, Ithlah, 43Elon, Timnah, Ekron, 44Eltekeh, Gibbethon, Baalath, 45Jehud, Bene-berak, Gath-rimmon, 46and Me-jarkon and Rakkon with the territory over against Joppa. 47When the territory of the people of Dan was lost to them, the people of Dan went up and fought against Leshem, and after capturing it and striking it with the sword they took possession of it and settled in it, calling Leshem, Dan, after the name of Dan their ancestor. 48This is the inheritance of the tribe of the people of Dan, according to their clans—these cities with their villages.

The Inheritance for Joshua

49When they had finished distributing the several territories of the land as inheritances, the people of Israel gave an inheritance among them to Joshua the son of Nun. 50By command of the LORD they gave him the city that he asked, Timnath-serah in the hill country of Ephraim. And he rebuilt the city and settled in it.

51These are the inheritances that Eleazar the priest and Joshua the son of Nun and the heads of the fathers' houses of the tribes of the people of Israel distributed by lot at Shiloh before the LORD, at the entrance of the tent of meeting. So they finished dividing the land.

The Cities of Refuge

20 Then the LORD said to Joshua, 2"Say to the people of Israel, 'Appoint the cities of refuge, of which I spoke to you through Moses, 3that the manslayer who strikes any person without intent or unknowingly may flee there. They shall be for you a refuge from the avenger of blood. 4He shall flee to one of these cities and shall stand at the entrance of the gate of the city and explain his case to the elders of that city. Then they shall take him into the city and give him a place, and he shall remain with them. 5And if the avenger of blood pursues him, they shall not give up the manslayer into his hand, because he struck his neighbor unknowingly, and did not hate him in the past. 6And he shall remain in that city until he has stood before the congregation for judgment, until the death of him who is high priest at the time. Then the manslayer may return to his own town and his own home, to the town from which he fled.'"

7So they set apart Kedesh in Galilee in the hill country of Naphtali, and Shechem in the hill country of Ephraim, and Kiriath-arba (that is, Hebron) in the hill country of Judah. 8And beyond the Jordan east of Jericho, they appointed Bezer in the wilderness on the tableland, from the tribe of Reuben, and Ramoth in Gilead, from the tribe of Gad, and Golan in Bashan, from the tribe of Manasseh. 9These were the cities designated for all the people of Israel and for the stranger sojourning among them, that anyone who killed a person without intent could

JOSHUA 20:1–3

CITIES OF REFUGE

The first three verses of Joshua 20 provide a description of cities intended as safe zones for people who had accidentally killed someone. If someone was killed, that person's family and loved ones were likely to seek out the killer and avenge the dead person. The goal of these cities was to provide a place of refuge for people who had unintentionally killed someone, and the cities were also to provide a place for the cases of both sides to be heard.

These cities typify Christ and the refuge that he is for believers. Every person has sinned against another person in one way or another, and though this sin may not be murder, everyone needs a place of refuge. For believers, Christ is that refuge. He provides a place for people to come when they are guilty, and he acts as a representative before the judgment of God to all who come to him. However, when the trial is held and the sins of believers are to be accounted for, Jesus has already taken all punishment on behalf of those who trust in him. These cities of refuge were meant to temporarily keep people safe while they waited for a fair trial, but Jesus provides believers with an eternal refuge and a fair trial in which their guilt has already been accounted for.

flee there, so that he might not die by the hand of the avenger of blood, till he stood before the congregation.

Cities and Pasturelands Allotted to Levi

21 Then the heads of the fathers' houses of the Levites came to Eleazar the priest and to Joshua the son of Nun and to the heads of the fathers' houses of the tribes of the people of Israel. 2And they said to them at Shiloh in the land of Canaan, "The LORD commanded through Moses that we be given cities to dwell in, along with their pasturelands for our livestock." 3So by command of the LORD the people of Israel gave to the Levites the following cities and pasturelands out of their inheritance.

4The lot came out for the clans of the Kohathites. So those Levites who were descendants of Aaron the priest received by lot from the tribes of Judah, Simeon, and Benjamin, thirteen cities.

5And the rest of the Kohathites received by lot from the clans of the tribe of Ephraim, from the tribe of Dan and the half-tribe of Manasseh, ten cities.

6The Gershonites received by lot from the clans of the tribe of Issachar, from the tribe of Asher, from the tribe of Naphtali, and from the half-tribe of Manasseh in Bashan, thirteen cities.

7The Merarites according to their clans received from the tribe of Reuben, the tribe of Gad, and the tribe of Zebulun, twelve cities.

8These cities and their pasturelands the people of Israel gave by lot to the Levites, as the LORD had commanded through Moses.

9Out of the tribe of the people of Judah and the tribe of the people of Simeon they gave the following cities mentioned by name, 10which went to the descendants of Aaron, one of the clans of the Kohathites who belonged to the people of Levi; since the lot fell to them first. 11They gave them Kiriath-arba (Arba being the father of Anak), that is Hebron, in the hill country of Judah, along with the pasturelands around it. 12But the fields of the city and its villages had been given to Caleb the son of Jephunneh as his possession.

13And to the descendants of Aaron the priest they gave Hebron, the city of refuge for the manslayer, with its pasturelands, Libnah with its pasturelands, 14Jattir with its pasturelands, Eshtemoa with its pasturelands, 15Holon with its pasturelands, Debir with its pasturelands, 16Ain with its pasturelands, Juttah with its pasturelands, Beth-shemesh with its pasturelands—nine cities out of these two tribes; 17then out of the tribe of Benjamin, Gibeon with its pasturelands, Geba with its pasturelands, 18Anathoth with its pasturelands, and Almon with its pasturelands—four cities. 19The cities of the descendants of Aaron, the priests, were in all thirteen cities with their pasturelands.

20As to the rest of the Kohathites belonging to the Kohathite clans of the Levites, the cities allotted to them were out of the tribe of Ephraim. 21To them were given Shechem, the city of refuge for the manslayer, with its pasturelands in the hill country of Ephraim, Gezer with its pasturelands, 22Kibzaim with its pasturelands, Beth-horon with its pasturelands—four cities; 23and out of the tribe of Dan, Elteke with its pasturelands, Gibbethon with its pasturelands, 24Aijalon with its pasturelands, Gath-rimmon with its pasturelands—four cities; 25and out of the half-tribe of Manasseh, Taanach with its pasturelands, and Gath-rimmon with its pasturelands—two cities. 26The cities of the clans of the rest of the Kohathites were ten in all with their pasturelands.

27And to the Gershonites, one of the clans of the Levites, were given out of the half-tribe of Manasseh, Golan in Bashan with its pasturelands, the city of refuge for the manslayer, and Beeshterah with its pasturelands—two cities; 28and out of the tribe of Issachar, Kishion with its pasturelands, Daberath with its pasturelands, 29Jarmuth with its pasturelands, En-gannim with its pasturelands—four cities; 30and out of the tribe of Asher, Mishal with its pasturelands, Abdon with its pasturelands, 31Helkath with its pasturelands, and Rehob with its

pasturelands—four cities; [32]and out of the tribe of Naphtali, Kedesh in Galilee
with its pasturelands, the city of refuge for the manslayer, Hammoth-dor with
its pasturelands, and Kartan with its pasturelands—three cities. [33]The cities of
the several clans of the Gershonites were in all thirteen cities with their pasturelands.

[34]And to the rest of the Levites, the Merarite clans, were given out of the tribe
of Zebulun, Jokneam with its pasturelands, Kartah with its pasturelands, [35]Dim-
nah with its pasturelands, Nahalal with its pasturelands—four cities; [36]and out
of the tribe of Reuben, Bezer with its pasturelands, Jahaz with its pasturelands,
[37]Kedemoth with its pasturelands, and Mephaath with its pasturelands—four cities; [38]and out of the tribe of Gad, Ramoth in Gilead with its pasturelands, the city
of refuge for the manslayer, Mahanaim with its pasturelands, [39]Heshbon with its
pasturelands, Jazer with its pasturelands—four cities in all. [40]As for the cities of
the several Merarite clans, that is, the remainder of the clans of the Levites, those
allotted to them were in all twelve cities.

[41]The cities of the Levites in the midst of the possession of the people of Israel
were in all forty-eight cities with their pasturelands. [42]These cities each had its
pasturelands around it. So it was with all these cities.

[43]Thus the LORD gave to Israel all the land that he swore to give to their fathers. And they took possession of it, and they settled there. [44]And the LORD gave
them rest on every side just as he had sworn to their fathers. Not one of all their
enemies had withstood them, for the LORD had given all their enemies into their
hands. [45]Not one word of all the good promises that the LORD had made to the
house of Israel had failed; all came to pass.

The Eastern Tribes Return Home

22 At that time Joshua summoned the Reubenites and the Gadites and the
half-tribe of Manasseh, [2]and said to them, "You have kept all that Moses
the servant of the LORD commanded you and have obeyed my voice in all that I
have commanded you. [3]You have not forsaken your brothers these many days,
down to this day, but have been careful to keep the charge of the LORD your God.
[4]And now the LORD your God has given rest to your brothers, as he promised
them. Therefore turn and go to your tents in the land where your possession lies,
which Moses the servant of the LORD gave you on the other side of the Jordan.
[5]Only be very careful to observe the commandment and the law that Moses the
servant of the LORD commanded you, to love the LORD your God, and to walk in
all his ways and to keep his commandments and to cling to him and to serve him
with all your heart and with all your soul." [6]So Joshua blessed them and sent them
away, and they went to their tents.

[7]Now to the one half of the tribe of Manasseh Moses had given a possession in
Bashan, but to the other half Joshua had given a possession beside their brothers
in the land west of the Jordan. And when Joshua sent them away to their homes
and blessed them, [8]he said to them, "Go back to your tents with much wealth
and with very much livestock, with silver, gold, bronze, and iron, and with much
clothing. Divide the spoil of your enemies with your brothers." [9]So the people of
Reuben and the people of Gad and the half-tribe of Manasseh returned home,
parting from the people of Israel at Shiloh, which is in the land of Canaan, to go
to the land of Gilead, their own land of which they had possessed themselves by
command of the LORD through Moses.

The Eastern Tribes' Altar of Witness

[10]And when they came to the region of the Jordan that is in the land of Canaan,
the people of Reuben and the people of Gad and the half-tribe of Manasseh built
there an altar by the Jordan, an altar of imposing size. [11]And the people of Israel
heard it said, "Behold, the people of Reuben and the people of Gad and the half-
tribe of Manasseh have built the altar at the frontier of the land of Canaan, in the

---

JOSHUA 22:10–34

TRIBES ON THE OTHER SIDE OF THE JORDAN

The tribes of Reuben, Gad, and half of the tribe of Manasseh were allotted an inheritance on the east side of the Jordan River. There they constructed an imposing altar to declare their faithfulness to God and to demonstrate their ongoing loyalty to the other tribes who crossed the Jordan and settled in Canaan. In fact, they went with these tribes into the land and fought to secure and rid it of its pagan inhabitants before returning back to their portion of the land on the other side of the Jordan. The tribes to the west of the Jordan questioned this altar because they wrongly assumed that the people intended to worship at that altar and not with the rest of the nation at the altar in the tabernacle. The rest of the nation relented of their questioning after learning that the altar—rather than being a location for aberrant worship—was meant to be a witness to future generations of the commitment of the Transjordan tribes to remain faithful to the Lord. John, in the book of Revelation, pictures Jesus as "the faithful witness" who, like this altar, would prove to be a faithful and credible witness throughout all generations (Rev 1:5).

region about the Jordan, on the side that belongs to the people of Israel." [12]And
when the people of Israel heard of it, the whole assembly of the people of Israel
gathered at Shiloh to make war against them.

[13]Then the people of Israel sent to the people of Reuben and the people of
Gad and the half-tribe of Manasseh, in the land of Gilead, Phinehas the son of
Eleazar the priest, [14]and with him ten chiefs, one from each of the tribal families of Israel, every one of them the head of a family among the clans of Israel.
[15]And they came to the people of Reuben, the people of Gad, and the half-tribe
of Manasseh, in the land of Gilead, and they said to them, [16]"Thus says the whole
congregation of the LORD, 'What is this breach of faith that you have committed
against the God of Israel in turning away this day from following the LORD by
building yourselves an altar this day in rebellion against the LORD? [17]Have we
not had enough of the sin at Peor from which even yet we have not cleansed
ourselves, and for which there came a plague upon the congregation of the LORD,
[18]that you too must turn away this day from following the LORD? And if you too
rebel against the LORD today then tomorrow he will be angry with the whole
congregation of Israel. [19]But now, if the land of your possession is unclean, pass
over into the LORD's land where the LORD's tabernacle stands, and take for yourselves a possession among us. Only do not rebel against the LORD or make us as
rebels by building for yourselves an altar other than the altar of the LORD our
God. [20]Did not Achan the son of Zerah break faith in the matter of the devoted
things, and wrath fell upon all the congregation of Israel? And he did not perish
alone for his iniquity.'"

[21]Then the people of Reuben, the people of Gad, and the half-tribe of Manasseh
said in answer to the heads of the families of Israel, [22]"The Mighty One, God, the
LORD! The Mighty One, God, the LORD! He knows; and let Israel itself know! If it
was in rebellion or in breach of faith against the LORD, do not spare us today [23]for
building an altar to turn away from following the LORD. Or if we did so to offer
burnt offerings or grain offerings or peace offerings on it, may the LORD himself
take vengeance. [24]No, but we did it from fear that in time to come your children
might say to our children, 'What have you to do with the LORD, the God of Israel?
[25]For the LORD has made the Jordan a boundary between us and you, you people
of Reuben and people of Gad. You have no portion in the LORD.' So your children
might make our children cease to worship the LORD. [26]Therefore we said, 'Let us
now build an altar, not for burnt offering, nor for sacrifice, [27]but to be a witness
between us and you, and between our generations after us, that we do perform
the service of the LORD in his presence with our burnt offerings and sacrifices and
peace offerings, so your children will not say to our children in time to come, "You
have no portion in the LORD."' [28]And we thought, 'If this should be said to us or to
our descendants in time to come, we should say, "Behold, the copy of the altar of
the LORD, which our fathers made, not for burnt offerings, nor for sacrifice, but to
be a witness between us and you."' [29]Far be it from us that we should rebel against
the LORD and turn away this day from following the LORD by building an altar for
burnt offering, grain offering, or sacrifice, other than the altar of the LORD our
God that stands before his tabernacle!"

[30]When Phinehas the priest and the chiefs of the congregation, the heads
of the families of Israel who were with him, heard the words that the people of
Reuben and the people of Gad and the people of Manasseh spoke, it was good
in their eyes. [31]And Phinehas the son of Eleazar the priest said to the people of
Reuben and the people of Gad and the people of Manasseh, "Today we know that
the LORD is in our midst, because you have not committed this breach of faith
against the LORD. Now you have delivered the people of Israel from the hand of
the LORD."

[32]Then Phinehas the son of Eleazar the priest, and the chiefs, returned from
the people of Reuben and the people of Gad in the land of Gilead to the land of
Canaan, to the people of Israel, and brought back word to them. [33]And the report

was good in the eyes of the people of Israel. And the people of Israel blessed God and spoke no more of making war against them to destroy the land where the people of Reuben and the people of Gad were settled. [34]The people of Reuben and the people of Gad called the altar Witness, "For," they said, "it is a witness between us that the LORD is God."

Joshua's Charge to Israel's Leaders

23 A long time afterward, when the LORD had given rest to Israel from all their surrounding enemies, and Joshua was old and well advanced in years, [2]Joshua summoned all Israel, its elders and heads, its judges and officers, and said to them, "I am now old and well advanced in years. [3]And you have seen all that the LORD your God has done to all these nations for your sake, for it is the LORD your God who has fought for you. [4]Behold, I have allotted to you as an inheritance for your tribes those nations that remain, along with all the nations that I have already cut off, from the Jordan to the Great Sea in the west. [5]The LORD your God will push them back before you and drive them out of your sight. And you shall possess their land, just as the LORD your God promised you. [6]Therefore, be very strong to keep and to do all that is written in the Book of the Law of Moses, turning aside from it neither to the right hand nor to the left, [7]that you may not mix with these nations remaining among you or make mention of the names of their gods or swear by them or serve them or bow down to them, [8]but you shall cling to the LORD your God just as you have done to this day. [9]For the LORD has driven out before you great and strong nations. And as for you, no man has been able to stand before you to this day. [10]One man of you puts to flight a thousand, since it is the LORD your God who fights for you, just as he promised you. [11]Be very careful, therefore, to love the LORD your God. [12]For if you turn back and cling to the remnant of these nations remaining among you and make marriages with them, so that you associate with them and they with you, [13]know for certain that the LORD your God will no longer drive out these nations before you, but they shall be a snare and a trap for you, a whip on your sides and thorns in your eyes, until you perish from off this good ground that the LORD your God has given you.

[14]"And now I am about to go the way of all the earth, and you know in your hearts and souls, all of you, that not one word has failed of all the good things[1] that the LORD your God promised concerning you. All have come to pass for you; not one of them has failed. [15]But just as all the good things that the LORD your God promised concerning you have been fulfilled for you, so the LORD will bring upon you all the evil things, until he has destroyed you from off this good land that the LORD your God has given you, [16]if you transgress the covenant of the LORD your God, which he commanded you, and go and serve other gods and bow down to them. Then the anger of the LORD will be kindled against you, and you shall perish quickly from off the good land that he has given to you."

The Covenant Renewal at Shechem

24 Joshua gathered all the tribes of Israel to Shechem and summoned the elders, the heads, the judges, and the officers of Israel. And they presented themselves before God. [2]And Joshua said to all the people, "Thus says the LORD, the God of Israel, 'Long ago, your fathers lived beyond the Euphrates,[2] Terah, the father of Abraham and of Nahor; and they served other gods. [3]Then I took your father Abraham from beyond the River[3] and led him through all the land of Canaan, and made his offspring many. I gave him Isaac. [4]And to Isaac I gave Jacob and Esau. And I gave Esau the hill country of Seir to possess, but Jacob and his children went down to Egypt. [5]And I sent Moses and Aaron, and I plagued Egypt with what I did in the midst of it, and afterward I brought you out.

[1]Or *words*; also twice in verse 15 [2]Hebrew *the River* [3]That is, the Euphrates; also verses 14, 15

JOSHUA 23:6–8

JOSHUA'S CHALLENGE

Joshua reminded the people of the necessity of obedience as they fully possessed the land. Faithful obedience serves two key functions both now and then. First, it demonstrates that a person has experienced the grace of God. The fact of God's faithfulness fuels the fires of obedience. Second, it allows people to realize the blessings of God. The Israelites would live long in the land that God had given them if they obeyed his law and shunned the worship of the idols of the land.

The New Testament authors exhorted the church to obedience based on the same foundations. The love of God, seen in the grace of God, empowers the people of God to obey the Word of God. Jesus said that those who love him will demonstrate this love through their obedience to his commands (Jn 14:15). Because God knows the best way to live, obedience to his commands is a path to life, freedom, joy, and peace (Ps 119:105).

JESUS: THE PROMISE OF GOD

Joshua finished his life with an astounding observation about God's work. He claimed that God had been faithful to fulfill every one of his promises to the nation of Israel. In spite of the sin of the people and the vast scope of God's redemptive work, God had proven the covenant-keeping nature of his character. He is always faithful to his promises. He always keeps his word. He will never break a promise.

While this claim comes at the culmination of Joshua's life and mission, it continues throughout all subsequent generations. In fact, God's promises were meant to extend throughout all generations. His promise in Genesis 3:15, that one would come who would defeat Satan forever, was not merely a promise to the nation of Israel but to all those who would suffer under the implications of life in a sin-drenched world. His promises to the nation of Israel, fulfilled in their taking of the land, represent only a portion of the great and glorious promises made by God throughout all history.

Paul, at the beginning of his letter to the church at Rome, claimed that Jesus was the pinnacle of the fulfillment of the promises of God (Ro 1:1 – 4). Jesus' sacrificial death was not a knee-jerk reaction by God to address human sin but was the plan of God before the foundation of the world. Paul traced the details of the coming of Christ — from his lineage, to the timing of his birth, to the manner of his death — and identified them as a fulfillment of God's plan. The writings of the prophets validate this claim, as they make repeated promises about intricate details of Jesus' life that are ultimately fulfilled hundreds of years later. This confidence led Paul to conclude, in 2 Corinthians 1:18 – 20, that all of God's promises are answered in Christ. Both the specific promises regarding the Messiah and the general promises regarding God's plan for dealing with human sin are fulfilled by Jesus.

God's faithfulness to his promises provides hope for his people. Not only has he done what he said he would do, but he will continue to perfectly execute his plan. In spite of the seeming chaos of life in a fallen world, Christians can take heart that he has overcome the world and will perfectly accomplish all he set out to do (Jn 16:33).

[6]“ ‘Then I brought your fathers out of Egypt, and you came to the sea. And the Egyptians pursued your fathers with chariots and horsemen to the Red Sea. [7]And when they cried to the Lord, he put darkness between you and the Egyptians and made the sea come upon them and cover them; and your eyes saw what I did in Egypt. And you lived in the wilderness a long time. [8]Then I brought you to the land of the Amorites, who lived on the other side of the Jordan. They fought with you, and I gave them into your hand, and you took possession of their land, and I destroyed them before you. [9]Then Balak the son of Zippor, king of Moab, arose and fought against Israel. And he sent and invited Balaam the son of Beor to curse you, [10]but I would not listen to Balaam. Indeed, he blessed you. So I delivered you out of his hand. [11]And you went over the Jordan and came to Jericho, and the leaders of Jericho fought against you, and also the Amorites, the Perizzites, the Canaanites, the Hittites, the Girgashites, the Hivites, and the Jebusites. And I gave them into your hand. [12]And I sent the hornet before you, which drove them out before you, the two kings of the Amorites; it was not by your sword or by your bow. [13]I gave you a land on which you had not labored and cities that you had not built, and you dwell in them. You eat the fruit of vineyards and olive orchards that you did not plant.’

Choose Whom You Will Serve

[14]“Now therefore fear the Lord and serve him in sincerity and in faithfulness. Put away the gods that your fathers served beyond the River and in Egypt, and serve the Lord. [15]And if it is evil in your eyes to serve the Lord, choose this day whom you will serve, whether the gods your fathers served in the region beyond the River, or the gods of the Amorites in whose land you dwell. But as for me and my house, we will serve the Lord.”

[16]Then the people answered, “Far be it from us that we should forsake the Lord to serve other gods, [17]for it is the Lord our God who brought us and our fathers up from the land of Egypt, out of the house of slavery, and who did those great signs in our sight and preserved us in all the way that we went, and among all the peoples through whom we passed. [18]And the Lord drove out before us all the peoples, the Amorites who lived in the land. Therefore we also will serve the Lord, for he is our God.”

[19]But Joshua said to the people, “You are not able to serve the Lord, for he is a holy God. He is a jealous God; he will not forgive your transgressions or your sins. [20]If you forsake the Lord and serve foreign gods, then he will turn and do you harm and consume you, after having done you good.” [21]And the people said to Joshua, “No, but we will serve the Lord.” [22]Then Joshua said to the people, “You are witnesses against yourselves that you have chosen the Lord, to serve him.” And they said, “We are witnesses.” [23]He said, “Then put away the foreign gods that are among you, and incline your heart to the Lord, the God of Israel.” [24]And the people said to Joshua, “The Lord our God we will serve, and his voice we will obey.” [25]So Joshua made a covenant with the people that day, and put in place statutes and rules for them at Shechem. [26]And Joshua wrote these words in the Book of the Law of God. And he took a large stone and set it up there under the terebinth that was by the sanctuary of the Lord. [27]And Joshua said to all the people, “Behold, this stone shall be a witness against us, for it has heard all the words of the Lord that he spoke to us. Therefore it shall be a witness against you, lest you deal falsely with your God.” [28]So Joshua sent the people away, every man to his inheritance.

Joshua’s Death and Burial

[29]After these things Joshua the son of Nun, the servant of the Lord, died, being 110 years old. [30]And they buried him in his own inheritance at Timnath-serah, which is in the hill country of Ephraim, north of the mountain of Gaash.

JOSHUA 24:14–15

MAKE A CHOICE

Joshua continued to remind the nation of the life-altering choice that each person must make. Either they would serve the false gods worshiped by their ancestors and the pagan people in the land, or they would fear the one true God and serve him alone. Joshua then publicly made his choice: he and his household would serve the Lord. Like Joshua and the nation of Israel, all people today face a similar choice—a decision of what to do with Jesus Christ.

Jesus continually held out the divisive nature of his claim to be God and the only path to salvation (Ac 4:12). Not only would those who worship him as the one true God have to flee the idolatry of the world, but they may also have to choose loyalty to God over loyalty to their family, friends, or any other thing or person that hindered their walk with God. This choice, for all God’s people, is a path of self-denial and self-sacrifice. But those who choose this path have been promised to ultimately find life in God’s kingdom forever.

31Israel served the LORD all the days of Joshua, and all the days of the elders
who outlived Joshua and had known all the work that the LORD did for Israel.
32As for the bones of Joseph, which the people of Israel brought up from Egypt,
they buried them at Shechem, in the piece of land that Jacob bought from the sons
of Hamor the father of Shechem for a hundred pieces of money.[1] It became an
inheritance of the descendants of Joseph.
33And Eleazar the son of Aaron died, and they buried him at Gibeah, the town
of Phinehas his son, which had been given him in the hill country of Ephraim.

[1]Hebrew *for a hundred qesitah*; a unit of money of uncertain value

JESUS: OUR RIGHTEOUS RULER

JUDGES

JUDGES

DEBORAH, BARAK DEFEAT CANAANITES	GIDEON DEFEATS MIDIANITES	SAMSON OPPOSES THE PHILISTINES
c. 1209 – 1169 BC	*c. 1162 BC*	*c. 1075 – 1055 BC*

The book of Judges demonstrates God's continued faithfulness to his persistently wayward people. The cyclical pattern of the people's sin and God's rescue is the steady refrain throughout the book. Often God demonstrated his love through judgment, purging the filth of sin from among the people and teaching them to fear him alone. Yet despite their sin, God continued to send human deliverers — namely, the judges — whom he empowered to remind the people of God's ways and call them to repentance and obedience.

Judges demonstrates the depravity of humankind and the necessity of God's judgment. God did not turn his back to Israel's sin; rather, he turned toward his beloved people in loving pursuit. God's redemptive mission necessitated that he allow Israel to feel the weight of their choices because sin has earthly consequences as well as heavenly ones. Israel suffered consistent internal strife and external turmoil with foreign nations. Through it all, God was always faithful to the covenant promises he made to Abraham and his descendants. Then as now, salvation happens by God's sheer grace: there is no question that the people don't merit God's mercy through their own moral uprightness or their willingness to turn from their sin. God acts because he is faithful. This same covenant faithfulness provides the only hope of God's people throughout time and eternity.

The pattern of rebellion, judgment, and deliverance dominates each subsequent event in Israel's life. Over time, this pattern devolved as the Israelites found increasingly heinous ways to rebel against God's decrees and their faithlessness necessitated God's judgment. The book consistently demonstrates Israel's corrupt nature throughout the time of the judges, beginning with the generation that followed Joshua's (2:6 – 15). In contrast to the preceding book of Joshua, this book sounds a depressing, hopeless tone that indicates just how far and how quickly the people of God had fallen.

By the end of the book, there is no question as to whether a human leader would ever be capable of delivering the people from their sin. As we see from the cycles in Judges, only God is capable of rescuing such a wayward people.

Today, all believers understand this reality. Broken and battered by sin, people long for the true deliverer, the One of whom the judges were a mere shadow. Jesus, the incarnate Son of God, has provided this deliverance by taking God's judgment on himself and fulfilling for all time God's promise to always be faithful to his people.

THE LORD SENT A PROPHET TO THE PEOPLE OF ISRAEL.
AND HE SAID TO THEM, "THUS SAYS THE LORD,
THE GOD OF ISRAEL: I LED YOU UP FROM EGYPT
AND BROUGHT YOU OUT OF THE HOUSE OF SLAVERY."

Judges 6:8

JUDGES

The Continuing Conquest of Canaan

1 After the death of Joshua, the people of Israel inquired of the LORD, "Who shall go up first for us against the Canaanites, to fight against them?" [2]The LORD said, "Judah shall go up; behold, I have given the land into his hand." [3]And Judah said to Simeon his brother, "Come up with me into the territory allotted to me, that we may fight against the Canaanites. And I likewise will go with you into the territory allotted to you." So Simeon went with him. [4]Then Judah went up and the LORD gave the Canaanites and the Perizzites into their hand, and they defeated 10,000 of them at Bezek. [5]They found Adoni-bezek at Bezek and fought against him and defeated the Canaanites and the Perizzites. [6]Adoni-bezek fled, but they pursued him and caught him and cut off his thumbs and his big toes. [7]And Adoni-bezek said, "Seventy kings with their thumbs and their big toes cut off used to pick up scraps under my table. As I have done, so God has repaid me." And they brought him to Jerusalem, and he died there.

[8]And the men of Judah fought against Jerusalem and captured it and struck it with the edge of the sword and set the city on fire. [9]And afterward the men of Judah went down to fight against the Canaanites who lived in the hill country, in the Negeb, and in the lowland. [10]And Judah went against the Canaanites who lived in Hebron (now the name of Hebron was formerly Kiriath-arba), and they defeated Sheshai and Ahiman and Talmai.

[11]From there they went against the inhabitants of Debir. The name of Debir was formerly Kiriath-sepher. [12]And Caleb said, "He who attacks Kiriath-sepher and captures it, I will give him Achsah my daughter as wife." [13]And Othniel the son of Kenaz, Caleb's younger brother, captured it. And he gave him Achsah his daughter as wife. [14]When she came to him, she urged him to ask her father for a field. And she dismounted from her donkey, and Caleb said to her, "What do you want?" [15]She said to him, "Give me a blessing. Since you have given me the land of the Negeb, give me also springs of water." And Caleb gave her the upper springs and the lower springs.

[16]And the descendants of the Kenite, Moses' father-in-law, went up with the people of Judah from the city of palms into the wilderness of Judah, which lies in the Negeb near Arad, and they went and settled with the people. [17]And Judah went with Simeon his brother, and they defeated the Canaanites who inhabited Zephath and devoted it to destruction. So the name of the city was called Hormah.[1] [18]Judah also captured Gaza with its territory, and Ashkelon with its territory, and Ekron with its territory. [19]And the LORD was with Judah, and he took possession of the hill country, but he could not drive out the inhabitants of the plain because they had chariots of iron. [20]And Hebron was given to Caleb, as Moses had said. And he drove out from it the three sons of Anak. [21]But the people of Benjamin did not drive out the Jebusites who lived in Jerusalem, so the Jebusites have lived with the people of Benjamin in Jerusalem to this day.

[22]The house of Joseph also went up against Bethel, and the LORD was with them. [23]And the house of Joseph scouted out Bethel. (Now the name of the city was formerly Luz.) [24]And the spies saw a man coming out of the city, and they said to him, "Please show us the way into the city, and we will deal kindly with you." [25]And he showed them the way into the city. And they struck the city with the edge of the sword, but they let the man and all his family go. [26]And the man went to the land of the Hittites and built a city and called its name Luz. That is its name to this day.

JUDGES 1:1–2

NEEDING A LEADER

Joshua had just passed away, leaving Israel's leadership role vacant. The main question for the Israelites was inescapable: Who was going to lead them into battle? God had promised Israel a land that was inhabited by the Canaanites, but with the death of Joshua and the lack of a king, no clear military leader existed to conquer the land. The Lord himself boldly proclaimed that Judah would lead the people into the land. Previously, the scepter and ruler's staff were promised to never depart from Judah, revealing the line of kings to come (Ge 49:10). The first true king of Judah and the great king of Israel came in the form of a shepherd boy, King David, with the final culmination of the line of Judah being a carpenter, Jesus, the promised Messiah and everlasting King (Mt 1:1–16).

[1] *Hormah* means *utter destruction*

LEADERS IN MISSION

God was faithful to his promise to give the descendants of Abraham a land overflowing with his blessing and provision. Since the time when Adam lived in the garden, God gave his image-bearers a significant role in leading his people. Abraham, Isaac, Jacob, Joseph, Moses, and Joshua are examples of individuals God used. These leaders, though fallen and marred by the consequences of sin, were instrumental in stewarding God's work in the world. Yet as children of the curse, these leaders all died.

The book of Judges opens with the death of a great leader of Israel. Joshua mobilized the people of God to conquer the land of Canaan following Moses' death. He exhorted the people to be obedient, emboldened them with confidence, and led them to take the land God had provided. This land, however, was still littered with God's enemies. God commanded his people to rid the land of any nation who stood opposed to the one true God and his people. At the time of Joshua's death, much work remained undone and the mission needed to be completed.

Now the God-ordained leaders — the tribe of Judah — needed to take up the mantle of leadership. Empowered by God's Spirit, they led God's people to face their bitter opponents. God's promise was clear — he would go before them and remain with them so they had nothing to fear. It was God, and God alone, who would win the victory and give the opponents over to destruction. All the nation of Israel needed to do was trust and obey.

God's faithfulness to his mission continues today. Leaders come and go, but God remains sovereign to work according to his good purposes. This work will continue based on the power and presence of God — not the ingenuity or strength of human leaders.

Jesus demonstrated this reality following his resurrection. He told his followers to wait on the power of the Holy Spirit before they moved out in mission with him (Ac 1:4). For them, the task would not be occupying a territory by military might but filling the entire earth with the knowledge and glory of God. This mission is one that will happen "not by might, nor by power, but by my Spirit, says the LORD of hosts" (Zec 4:6).

Failure to Complete the Conquest

[27]Manasseh did not drive out the inhabitants of Beth-shean and its villages, or Taanach and its villages, or the inhabitants of Dor and its villages, or the inhabitants of Ibleam and its villages, or the inhabitants of Megiddo and its villages, for the Canaanites persisted in dwelling in that land. [28]When Israel grew strong, they put the Canaanites to forced labor, but did not drive them out completely.

[29]And Ephraim did not drive out the Canaanites who lived in Gezer, so the Canaanites lived in Gezer among them.

[30]Zebulun did not drive out the inhabitants of Kitron, or the inhabitants of Nahalol, so the Canaanites lived among them, but became subject to forced labor.

[31]Asher did not drive out the inhabitants of Acco, or the inhabitants of Sidon or of Ahlab or of Achzib or of Helbah or of Aphik or of Rehob, [32]so the Asherites lived among the Canaanites, the inhabitants of the land, for they did not drive them out.

[33]Naphtali did not drive out the inhabitants of Beth-shemesh, or the inhabitants of Beth-anath, so they lived among the Canaanites, the inhabitants of the land. Nevertheless, the inhabitants of Beth-shemesh and of Beth-anath became subject to forced labor for them.

[34]The Amorites pressed the people of Dan back into the hill country, for they did not allow them to come down to the plain. [35]The Amorites persisted in dwelling in Mount Heres, in Aijalon, and in Shaalbim, but the hand of the house of Joseph rested heavily on them, and they became subject to forced labor. [36]And the border of the Amorites ran from the ascent of Akrabbim, from Sela and upward.

Israel's Disobedience

2 Now the angel of the LORD went up from Gilgal to Bochim. And he said, "I brought you up from Egypt and brought you into the land that I swore to give to your fathers. I said, 'I will never break my covenant with you, [2]and you shall make no covenant with the inhabitants of this land; you shall break down their altars.' But you have not obeyed my voice. What is this you have done? [3]So now I say, I will not drive them out before you, but they shall become thorns in your sides, and their gods shall be a snare to you." [4]As soon as the angel of the LORD spoke these words to all the people of Israel, the people lifted up their voices and wept. [5]And they called the name of that place Bochim.[1] And they sacrificed there to the LORD.

The Death of Joshua

[6]When Joshua dismissed the people, the people of Israel went each to his inheritance to take possession of the land. [7]And the people served the LORD all the days of Joshua, and all the days of the elders who outlived Joshua, who had seen all the great work that the LORD had done for Israel. [8]And Joshua the son of Nun, the servant of the LORD, died at the age of 110 years. [9]And they buried him within the boundaries of his inheritance in Timnath-heres, in the hill country of Ephraim, north of the mountain of Gaash. [10]And all that generation also were gathered to their fathers. And there arose another generation after them who did not know the LORD or the work that he had done for Israel.

Israel's Unfaithfulness

[11]And the people of Israel did what was evil in the sight of the LORD and served the Baals. [12]And they abandoned the LORD, the God of their fathers, who had brought them out of the land of Egypt. They went after other gods, from among the gods of the peoples who were around them, and bowed down to them. And they provoked the LORD to anger. [13]They abandoned the LORD and served the Baals and the Ashtaroth. [14]So the anger of the LORD was kindled against Israel,

JUDGES 2:1–3

WARNINGS TO A WAYWARD PEOPLE

God in his grace gives all people an opportunity to turn from their sin and follow him. In the Old Testament, God appeared to his people in visible form. The "angel of the LORD" is not specifically named, though it is clear that the angel represents God by declaring a message of warning and impending judgment. Sadly, the cyclical pattern of rebellion continued until Jesus' birth.

Jesus, in similar fashion, inaugurated his earthly ministry by proclaiming, "Repent, for the kingdom of heaven is at hand" (Mt 4:17). Like the angel, he warned the people to turn from their sin lest they face the wrath of God. Little did they know that the very One who spoke these words would soon bear the weight of the wrath and judgment of God to deliver God's people from the consequences of their sin forever. In Jesus, God not only warns people about the effects of their sin, but he gives them an opportunity for everlasting atonement for those sins.

[1] *Bochim* means *weepers*

and he gave them over to plunderers, who plundered them. And he sold them into
the hand of their surrounding enemies, so that they could no longer withstand
their enemies. [15]Whenever they marched out, the hand of the LORD was against
them for harm, as the LORD had warned, and as the LORD had sworn to them. And
they were in terrible distress.

The LORD Raises Up Judges

[16]Then the LORD raised up judges, who saved them out of the hand of those
who plundered them. [17]Yet they did not listen to their judges, for they whored
after other gods and bowed down to them. They soon turned aside from the way
in which their fathers had walked, who had obeyed the commandments of the
LORD, and they did not do so. [18]Whenever the LORD raised up judges for them, the
LORD was with the judge, and he saved them from the hand of their enemies all
the days of the judge. For the LORD was moved to pity by their groaning because
of those who afflicted and oppressed them. [19]But whenever the judge died, they
turned back and were more corrupt than their fathers, going after other gods,
serving them and bowing down to them. They did not drop any of their practices
or their stubborn ways. [20]So the anger of the LORD was kindled against Israel, and
he said, "Because this people have transgressed my covenant that I commanded
their fathers and have not obeyed my voice, [21]I will no longer drive out before
them any of the nations that Joshua left when he died, [22]in order to test Israel by
them, whether they will take care to walk in the way of the LORD as their fathers
did, or not." [23]So the LORD left those nations, not driving them out quickly, and he
did not give them into the hand of Joshua.

3 Now these are the nations that the LORD left, to test Israel by them, that is,
all in Israel who had not experienced all the wars in Canaan. [2]It was only in
order that the generations of the people of Israel might know war, to teach war to
those who had not known it before. [3]These are the nations: the five lords of the
Philistines and all the Canaanites and the Sidonians and the Hivites who lived on
Mount Lebanon, from Mount Baal-hermon as far as Lebo-hamath. [4]They were
for the testing of Israel, to know whether Israel would obey the commandments
of the LORD, which he commanded their fathers by the hand of Moses. [5]So the
people of Israel lived among the Canaanites, the Hittites, the Amorites, the Perizzites, the Hivites, and the Jebusites. [6]And their daughters they took to themselves for wives, and their own daughters they gave to their sons, and they served
their gods.

Othniel

[7]And the people of Israel did what was evil in the sight of the LORD. They forgot
the LORD their God and served the Baals and the Asheroth. [8]Therefore the anger
of the LORD was kindled against Israel, and he sold them into the hand of Cushan-
rishathaim king of Mesopotamia. And the people of Israel served Cushan-
rishathaim eight years. [9]But when the people of Israel cried out to the LORD, the
LORD raised up a deliverer for the people of Israel, who saved them, Othniel the
son of Kenaz, Caleb's younger brother. [10]The Spirit of the LORD was upon him, and
he judged Israel. He went out to war, and the LORD gave Cushan-rishathaim king
of Mesopotamia into his hand. And his hand prevailed over Cushan-rishathaim.
[11]So the land had rest for forty years. Then Othniel the son of Kenaz died.

Ehud

[12]And the people of Israel again did what was evil in the sight of the LORD, and
the LORD strengthened Eglon the king of Moab against Israel, because they had
done what was evil in the sight of the LORD. [13]He gathered to himself the Ammonites and the Amalekites, and went and defeated Israel. And they took possession
of the city of palms. [14]And the people of Israel served Eglon the king of Moab
eighteen years.

JUDGES 2:16–19

A TUTOR TO THE GOSPEL

Even at the beginning, the author made it clear that the judges failed to produce lasting change in the people. In fact, the death of a judge seemingly fueled the rebellion of the people. With each successive judge, the people's rebellion continued to escalate. The leadership of the judges functioned to expose the nation to the depravity of their sin and inability to keep God's righteous law. Paul, in the New Testament, wrote that this is a primary function of the Old Testament law and sacrificial system. It was meant to serve as a "guardian" to teach the people what God commands and to show them that they were altogether unable to obey his law (Gal 3:24). This inability is meant to cause people to long for a true and lasting deliverer who will accomplish what the judges could not. Jesus' work provides hope for people who, acknowledging their inability to keep God's law, place their faith in his finished work on their behalf.

A FAITHFUL GOD AND AN UNFAITHFUL PEOPLE

The book of Judges presents a stark contrast between the faithfulness of God and the unfaithfulness of his people. It is astounding to consider that so soon after their miraculous deliverance from Egypt, a generation arrived on the scene that knew neither the Lord nor the works that he had done for them. The very same nation who was an eyewitness to the stunning might of God had now forgotten him altogether. Their forgetfulness is seen in their ever-increasing propensity toward rebellion.

One would anticipate that their sin would prompt God to abandon his people forever. Yet, time and time again, an avalanche of God's grace meets the faithlessness of the people. In fact, the text records God's pity on the people and his attentiveness to their cries. Previously, Moses recounted how the people of God groaned because of their slavery and cried out to the Lord (Ex 2:23 – 25). These cries for deliverance were met by responses from the Lord. He heard their cries. He remembered the promises he had made in his covenant with them. He saw their need, and he knew their pain. This is the nature of the faithfulness of God — he hears, remembers, sees, and knows.

Generations later, God heard the cries of his people and provided judges to lead them to victory. He did this despite the fact that they had demonstrated a perpetual inability to obey, even for a generation. God's faithfulness is clearly not predicated on the goodness of his people. Rather, God's faithfulness is founded on his character. He is a faithful God who always keeps his promises.

The faithfulness of God is the hope on which the Christian life is built. Those who know Jesus through repentance and faith can rest assured that God is faithful to his promises (1Co 1:9). He will not abandon his people, nor will he turn his back on them when they are unfaithful. Instead he hears, remembers, sees, and knows. He hears the cry for mercy from those who know they are broken. He remembers his covenant, made long ago to Abraham, to save his people. He knows the needs of his people and, by virtue of Christ's work, has made provision to meet those needs and restore them to a right relationship with him forever.

15Then the people of Israel cried out to the LORD, and the LORD raised up for them a deliverer, Ehud, the son of Gera, the Benjaminite, a left-handed man. The people of Israel sent tribute by him to Eglon the king of Moab. 16And Ehud made for himself a sword with two edges, a cubit[1] in length, and he bound it on his right thigh under his clothes. 17And he presented the tribute to Eglon king of Moab. Now Eglon was a very fat man. 18And when Ehud had finished presenting the tribute, he sent away the people who carried the tribute. 19But he himself turned back at the idols near Gilgal and said, "I have a secret message for you, O king." And he commanded, "Silence." And all his attendants went out from his presence. 20And Ehud came to him as he was sitting alone in his cool roof chamber. And Ehud said, "I have a message from God for you." And he arose from his seat. 21And Ehud reached with his left hand, took the sword from his right thigh, and thrust it into his belly. 22And the hilt also went in after the blade, and the fat closed over the blade, for he did not pull the sword out of his belly; and the dung came out. 23Then Ehud went out into the porch[2] and closed the doors of the roof chamber behind him and locked them.

24When he had gone, the servants came, and when they saw that the doors of the roof chamber were locked, they thought, "Surely he is relieving himself in the closet of the cool chamber." 25And they waited till they were embarrassed. But when he still did not open the doors of the roof chamber, they took the key and opened them, and there lay their lord dead on the floor.

26Ehud escaped while they delayed, and he passed beyond the idols and escaped to Seirah. 27When he arrived, he sounded the trumpet in the hill country of Ephraim. Then the people of Israel went down with him from the hill country, and he was their leader. 28And he said to them, "Follow after me, for the LORD has given your enemies the Moabites into your hand." So they went down after him and seized the fords of the Jordan against the Moabites and did not allow anyone to pass over. 29And they killed at that time about 10,000 of the Moabites, all strong, able-bodied men; not a man escaped. 30So Moab was subdued that day under the hand of Israel. And the land had rest for eighty years.

Shamgar

31After him was Shamgar the son of Anath, who killed 600 of the Philistines with an oxgoad, and he also saved Israel.

Deborah and Barak

4 And the people of Israel again did what was evil in the sight of the LORD after Ehud died. 2And the LORD sold them into the hand of Jabin king of Canaan, who reigned in Hazor. The commander of his army was Sisera, who lived in Harosheth-hagoyim. 3Then the people of Israel cried out to the LORD for help, for he had 900 chariots of iron and he oppressed the people of Israel cruelly for twenty years.

4Now Deborah, a prophetess, the wife of Lappidoth, was judging Israel at that time. 5She used to sit under the palm of Deborah between Ramah and Bethel in the hill country of Ephraim, and the people of Israel came up to her for judgment. 6She sent and summoned Barak the son of Abinoam from Kedesh-naphtali and said to him, "Has not the LORD, the God of Israel, commanded you, 'Go, gather your men at Mount Tabor, taking 10,000 from the people of Naphtali and the people of Zebulun. 7And I will draw out Sisera, the general of Jabin's army, to meet you by the river Kishon with his chariots and his troops, and I will give him into your hand'?" 8Barak said to her, "If you will go with me, I will go, but if you will not go with me, I will not go." 9And she said, "I will surely go with you. Nevertheless, the road on which you are going will not lead to your glory, for the LORD will sell Sisera into the hand of a woman." Then Deborah arose and went with Barak to

[1]A *cubit* was about 18 inches or 45 centimeters [2]The meaning of the Hebrew word is uncertain

JUDGES 4:1–10

A BRIEF RAY OF HOPE

The story of Deborah and Barak provides a brief respite in an otherwise depressing decline of the nation of Israel. Their faithfulness is seen in their willingness to hear the Lord and obey his commands. Their responsiveness to God stands in stark contrast to the stiff-necked rebellion and hard-heartedness demonstrated by God's people throughout most of the remainder of the book.

These glimmers of hope are short-lived throughout the Old Testament. The brief faithfulness of certain individuals or leaders was rapidly followed by the onslaught of rebellion and sin. This pattern continued until the time of Christ. Jesus obeyed where all others fell, not just once, but through the entirety of his life. Peter wrote that Jesus never sinned, completely obeying the law of God down to the very last detail (1Pe 2:22). This perfect righteousness demonstrated that he is the Son of God who was given as a gift to those who place their faith in his work on the cross. Those who are in Christ can look forward to a coming day when a permanent break from sin will take place and the earth itself will be forever purified from the impediments of sin.

Kedesh. [10]And Barak called out Zebulun and Naphtali to Kedesh. And 10,000 men went up at his heels, and Deborah went up with him.

[11]Now Heber the Kenite had separated from the Kenites, the descendants of Hobab the father-in-law of Moses, and had pitched his tent as far away as the oak in Zaanannim, which is near Kedesh.

[12]When Sisera was told that Barak the son of Abinoam had gone up to Mount Tabor, [13]Sisera called out all his chariots, 900 chariots of iron, and all the men who were with him, from Harosheth-hagoyim to the river Kishon. [14]And Deborah said to Barak, "Up! For this is the day in which the LORD has given Sisera into your hand. Does not the LORD go out before you?" So Barak went down from Mount Tabor with 10,000 men following him. [15]And the LORD routed Sisera and all his chariots and all his army before Barak by the edge of the sword. And Sisera got down from his chariot and fled away on foot. [16]And Barak pursued the chariots and the army to Harosheth-hagoyim, and all the army of Sisera fell by the edge of the sword; not a man was left.

[17]But Sisera fled away on foot to the tent of Jael, the wife of Heber the Kenite, for there was peace between Jabin the king of Hazor and the house of Heber the Kenite. [18]And Jael came out to meet Sisera and said to him, "Turn aside, my lord; turn aside to me; do not be afraid." So he turned aside to her into the tent, and she covered him with a rug. [19]And he said to her, "Please give me a little water to drink, for I am thirsty." So she opened a skin of milk and gave him a drink and covered him. [20]And he said to her, "Stand at the opening of the tent, and if any man comes and asks you, 'Is anyone here?' say, 'No.'" [21]But Jael the wife of Heber took a tent peg, and took a hammer in her hand. Then she went softly to him and drove the peg into his temple until it went down into the ground while he was lying fast asleep from weariness. So he died. [22]And behold, as Barak was pursuing Sisera, Jael went out to meet him and said to him, "Come, and I will show you the man whom you are seeking." So he went in to her tent, and there lay Sisera dead, with the tent peg in his temple.

[23]So on that day God subdued Jabin the king of Canaan before the people of Israel. [24]And the hand of the people of Israel pressed harder and harder against Jabin the king of Canaan, until they destroyed Jabin king of Canaan.

The Song of Deborah and Barak

5 Then sang Deborah and Barak the son of Abinoam on that day:

2 "That the leaders took the lead in Israel,
that the people offered themselves willingly,
bless the LORD!

3 "Hear, O kings; give ear, O princes;
to the LORD I will sing;
I will make melody to the LORD, the God
of Israel.

4 "LORD, when you went out from Seir,
when you marched from the region of Edom,
the earth trembled
and the heavens dropped,
yes, the clouds dropped water.
5 The mountains quaked before the LORD,
even Sinai before the LORD,[1] the God of Israel.

6 "In the days of Shamgar, son of Anath,
in the days of Jael, the highways were abandoned,
and travelers kept to the byways.

[1]Or *before the LORD, the One of Sinai, before the LORD*

JUDGES 5:1–31

SONGS OF DELIVERANCE

Singing was a distinctive feature of worship for the nation of Israel. This musical praise, sometimes accompanied by an instrument, was meant to be a way for the people to exalt God and his faithfulness throughout all generations. Following their miraculous deliverance from the hand of Pharaoh, Moses and the children of God sang praise declaring, "The LORD will reign forever and ever" (Ex 15:18). Years later and living in the land of promise, Deborah and Barak sang a song to bless the Lord for his mighty work. Songs are found throughout the pages of Scripture and are often a means by which people declare praise to God for something he has done for the worshiper (Ps 98:5; 101:1; 149:3) or for his faithful character (Ps 9:11; 105:2). Often the singing of praise was accompanied by a call to worship, in which the people were summoned to offer their praise to God (Jdg 5:3; Isa 12:5). The singing of praise to God continues to be a distinctive feature in the life of the church (Col 3:16). The church is to declare God's wondrous deeds in providing salvation through Christ and his faithful character throughout all generations.

7 The villagers ceased in Israel;
they ceased to be until I arose;
I, Deborah, arose as a mother in Israel.
8 When new gods were chosen,
then war was in the gates.
Was shield or spear to be seen
among forty thousand in Israel?
9 My heart goes out to the commanders of Israel
who offered themselves willingly among the people.
Bless the LORD.

10 "Tell of it, you who ride on white donkeys,
you who sit on rich carpets[1]
and you who walk by the way.
11 To the sound of musicians[2] at the watering places,
there they repeat the righteous triumphs of the LORD,
the righteous triumphs of his villagers in Israel.

"Then down to the gates marched the people of the LORD.

12 "Awake, awake, Deborah!
Awake, awake, break out in a song!
Arise, Barak, lead away your captives,
O son of Abinoam.
13 Then down marched the remnant of the noble;
the people of the LORD marched down for me against the mighty.
14 From Ephraim their root they marched down into the valley,[3]
following you, Benjamin, with your kinsmen;
from Machir marched down the commanders,
and from Zebulun those who bear the lieutenant's[4] staff;
15 the princes of Issachar came with Deborah,
and Issachar faithful to Barak;
into the valley they rushed at his heels.
Among the clans of Reuben
there were great searchings of heart.
16 Why did you sit still among the sheepfolds,
to hear the whistling for the flocks?
Among the clans of Reuben
there were great searchings of heart.
17 Gilead stayed beyond the Jordan;
and Dan, why did he stay with the ships?
Asher sat still at the coast of the sea,
staying by his landings.
18 Zebulun is a people who risked their lives to the death;
Naphtali, too, on the heights of the field.

19 "The kings came, they fought;
then fought the kings of Canaan,
at Taanach, by the waters of Megiddo;
they got no spoils of silver.
20 From heaven the stars fought,
from their courses they fought against Sisera.
21 The torrent Kishon swept them away,
the ancient torrent, the torrent Kishon.
March on, my soul, with might!

[1]The meaning of the Hebrew word is uncertain; it may connote *saddle blankets* [2]Or *archers*; the meaning of the Hebrew word is uncertain [3]Septuagint; Hebrew *in Amalek* [4]Hebrew *commander's*

22 “Then loud beat the horses’ hoofs
with the galloping, galloping of his steeds.

23 “Curse Meroz, says the angel of the LORD,
curse its inhabitants thoroughly,
because they did not come to the help of the LORD,
to the help of the LORD against the mighty.

24 “Most blessed of women be Jael,
the wife of Heber the Kenite,
of tent-dwelling women most blessed.
25 He asked for water and she gave him milk;
she brought him curds in a noble’s bowl.
26 She sent her hand to the tent peg
and her right hand to the workmen’s mallet;
she struck Sisera;
she crushed his head;
she shattered and pierced his temple.
27 Between her feet
he sank, he fell, he lay still;
between her feet
he sank, he fell;
where he sank,
there he fell—dead.

28 “Out of the window she peered,
the mother of Sisera wailed through the lattice:
‘Why is his chariot so long in coming?
Why tarry the hoofbeats of his chariots?’
29 Her wisest princesses answer,
indeed, she answers herself,
30 ‘Have they not found and divided the spoil?—
A womb or two for every man;
spoil of dyed materials for Sisera,
spoil of dyed materials embroidered,
two pieces of dyed work embroidered for the neck as spoil?’

31 “So may all your enemies perish, O LORD!
But your friends be like the sun as he rises in his might.”

And the land had rest for forty years.

Midian Oppresses Israel

6 The people of Israel did what was evil in the sight of the LORD, and the LORD
gave them into the hand of Midian seven years. 2And the hand of Midian
overpowered Israel, and because of Midian the people of Israel made for themselves the dens that are in the mountains and the caves and the strongholds. 3For
whenever the Israelites planted crops, the Midianites and the Amalekites and the
people of the East would come up against them. 4They would encamp against
them and devour the produce of the land, as far as Gaza, and leave no sustenance
in Israel and no sheep or ox or donkey. 5For they would come up with their livestock and their tents; they would come like locusts in number—both they and
their camels could not be counted—so that they laid waste the land as they came
in. 6And Israel was brought very low because of Midian. And the people of Israel
cried out for help to the LORD.

7When the people of Israel cried out to the LORD on account of the Midianites,
8the LORD sent a prophet to the people of Israel. And he said to them, “Thus says
the LORD, the God of Israel: I led you up from Egypt and brought you out of the
house of slavery. 9And I delivered you from the hand of the Egyptians and from

the hand of all who oppressed you, and drove them out before you and gave you their land. 10And I said to you, 'I am the LORD your God; you shall not fear the gods of the Amorites in whose land you dwell.' But you have not obeyed my voice."

The Call of Gideon

11Now the angel of the LORD came and sat under the terebinth at Ophrah, which belonged to Joash the Abiezrite, while his son Gideon was beating out wheat in the winepress to hide it from the Midianites. 12And the angel of the LORD appeared to him and said to him, "The LORD is with you, O mighty man of valor." 13And Gideon said to him, "Please, my lord, if the LORD is with us, why then has all this happened to us? And where are all his wonderful deeds that our fathers recounted to us, saying, 'Did not the LORD bring us up from Egypt?' But now the LORD has forsaken us and given us into the hand of Midian." 14And the LORD[1] turned to him and said, "Go in this might of yours and save Israel from the hand of Midian; do not I send you?" 15And he said to him, "Please, Lord, how can I save Israel? Behold, my clan is the weakest in Manasseh, and I am the least in my father's house." 16And the LORD said to him, "But I will be with you, and you shall strike the Midianites as one man." 17And he said to him, "If now I have found favor in your eyes, then show me a sign that it is you who speak with me. 18Please do not depart from here until I come to you and bring out my present and set it before you." And he said, "I will stay till you return."

19So Gideon went into his house and prepared a young goat and unleavened cakes from an ephah[2] of flour. The meat he put in a basket, and the broth he put in a pot, and brought them to him under the terebinth and presented them. 20And the angel of God said to him, "Take the meat and the unleavened cakes, and put them on this rock, and pour the broth over them." And he did so. 21Then the angel of the LORD reached out the tip of the staff that was in his hand and touched the meat and the unleavened cakes. And fire sprang up from the rock and consumed the meat and the unleavened cakes. And the angel of the LORD vanished from his sight. 22Then Gideon perceived that he was the angel of the LORD. And Gideon said, "Alas, O Lord GOD! For now I have seen the angel of the LORD face to face." 23But the LORD said to him, "Peace be to you. Do not fear; you shall not die." 24Then Gideon built an altar there to the LORD and called it, The LORD Is Peace. To this day it still stands at Ophrah, which belongs to the Abiezrites.

25That night the LORD said to him, "Take your father's bull, and the second bull seven years old, and pull down the altar of Baal that your father has, and cut down the Asherah that is beside it 26and build an altar to the LORD your God on the top of the stronghold here, with stones laid in due order. Then take the second bull and offer it as a burnt offering with the wood of the Asherah that you shall cut down." 27So Gideon took ten men of his servants and did as the LORD had told him. But because he was too afraid of his family and the men of the town to do it by day, he did it by night.

Gideon Destroys the Altar of Baal

28When the men of the town rose early in the morning, behold, the altar of Baal was broken down, and the Asherah beside it was cut down, and the second bull was offered on the altar that had been built. 29And they said to one another, "Who has done this thing?" And after they had searched and inquired, they said, "Gideon the son of Joash has done this thing." 30Then the men of the town said to Joash, "Bring out your son, that he may die, for he has broken down the altar of Baal and cut down the Asherah beside it." 31But Joash said to all who stood against him, "Will you contend for Baal? Or will you save him? Whoever contends for him shall be put to death by morning. If he is a god, let him contend for himself, because his altar has been broken down." 32Therefore on that day Gideon[3] was

[1]Septuagint *the angel of the LORD*; also verse 16 [2]An *ephah* was about 3/5 bushel or 22 liters [3]Hebrew *he*

JUDGES 6:13

THE LORD

The two uses of the word "lord" in this passage are illustrative of the supreme worth of God alone. Gideon first referred to the angel of God as "my lord." This usage indicates a polite address to a person worthy of respect. When Gideon spoke of God, however, he referred to him as "the LORD." This title declares the personal name of God (Yahweh), which was the name God used when speaking to Moses at Mount Horeb at the burning bush (Ex 3:13–16; 6:2–8). When the Israelites spoke of "Yahweh," they were referring to the nature and character of the One who had called them to himself and executed marvelous acts to deliver them and give them a land. Much more, he was the God whom they had sinned against, yet he had provided them with a means of fellowship with him. God is not merely a person worthy of respect, but he is the One to whom all people owe their ultimate allegiance.

Jesus embodied the title of "Lord" during his earthly ministry, substitutionary death, and victorious resurrection. As the ruler of all creation, he is to be preeminent in all things—including every facet of the lives of his children (Col 1:15–20).

called Jerubbaal, that is to say, "Let Baal contend against him," because he broke down his altar.

[33]Now all the Midianites and the Amalekites and the people of the East came together, and they crossed the Jordan and encamped in the Valley of Jezreel. [34]But the Spirit of the LORD clothed Gideon, and he sounded the trumpet, and the Abiezrites were called out to follow him. [35]And he sent messengers throughout all Manasseh, and they too were called out to follow him. And he sent messengers to Asher, Zebulun, and Naphtali, and they went up to meet them.

The Sign of the Fleece

[36]Then Gideon said to God, "If you will save Israel by my hand, as you have said, [37]behold, I am laying a fleece of wool on the threshing floor. If there is dew on the fleece alone, and it is dry on all the ground, then I shall know that you will save Israel by my hand, as you have said." [38]And it was so. When he rose early next morning and squeezed the fleece, he wrung enough dew from the fleece to fill a bowl with water. [39]Then Gideon said to God, "Let not your anger burn against me; let me speak just once more. Please let me test just once more with the fleece. Please let it be dry on the fleece only, and on all the ground let there be dew." [40]And God did so that night; and it was dry on the fleece only, and on all the ground there was dew.

Gideon's Three Hundred Men

7 Then Jerubbaal (that is, Gideon) and all the people who were with him rose early and encamped beside the spring of Harod. And the camp of Midian was north of them, by the hill of Moreh, in the valley.

[2]The LORD said to Gideon, "The people with you are too many for me to give the Midianites into their hand, lest Israel boast over me, saying, 'My own hand has saved me.' [3]Now therefore proclaim in the ears of the people, saying, 'Whoever is fearful and trembling, let him return home and hurry away from Mount Gilead.'" Then 22,000 of the people returned, and 10,000 remained.

[4]And the LORD said to Gideon, "The people are still too many. Take them down to the water, and I will test them for you there, and anyone of whom I say to you, 'This one shall go with you,' shall go with you, and anyone of whom I say to you, 'This one shall not go with you,' shall not go." [5]So he brought the people down to the water. And the LORD said to Gideon, "Every one who laps the water with his tongue, as a dog laps, you shall set by himself. Likewise, every one who kneels down to drink." [6]And the number of those who lapped, putting their hands to their mouths, was 300 men, but all the rest of the people knelt down to drink water. [7]And the LORD said to Gideon, "With the 300 men who lapped I will save you and give the Midianites into your hand, and let all the others go every man to his home." [8]So the people took provisions in their hands, and their trumpets. And he sent all the rest of Israel every man to his tent, but retained the 300 men. And the camp of Midian was below him in the valley.

[9]That same night the LORD said to him, "Arise, go down against the camp, for I have given it into your hand. [10]But if you are afraid to go down, go down to the camp with Purah your servant. [11]And you shall hear what they say, and afterward your hands shall be strengthened to go down against the camp." Then he went down with Purah his servant to the outposts of the armed men who were in the camp. [12]And the Midianites and the Amalekites and all the people of the East lay along the valley like locusts in abundance, and their camels were without number, as the sand that is on the seashore in abundance. [13]When Gideon came, behold, a man was telling a dream to his comrade. And he said, "Behold, I dreamed a dream, and behold, a cake of barley bread tumbled into the camp of Midian and came to the tent and struck it so that it fell and turned it upside down, so that the tent lay flat." [14]And his comrade answered, "This is no other than the sword of Gideon the son of Joash, a man of Israel; God has given into his hand Midian and all the camp."

PUTTING GOD TO THE TEST

Gideon put God to the test. Gideon, by placing a fleece on the floor, took matters into his own hands and showed that he did not fully trust God. God had already told him that he would fight on behalf of his people. Gideon's practice, however, confirmed that he was reluctant to simply take God at his word. The tangible symbol of the wet fleece was a secondary sign of God's faithfulness to confirm his word to the leader he had chosen.

Faced with a far more daunting challenge, Jesus, at the beginning of his earthly ministry, was placed in a situation in which his trust in God's word was challenged (Mt 4:1–11). Satan tempted Jesus to circumvent God's plan and take matters into his own hands. First, after fasting for forty days, Jesus was challenged to turn stones into bread. Jesus, who would soon multiply a meager amount of fish and bread to feed the multitudes, surely had the ability to turn a stone into a piece of bread. But this action would have amounted to a failure to trust that God the Father, in his time and ways, would supply Jesus' needs. Second, Satan tempted Jesus to throw himself off the highest point of the temple, citing that angels would protect him. This temptation would have bypassed the God-ordained path for his life, death, and victorious resurrection. Third, the King of the universe was tempted to doubt God's word and procure his own path to power and glory.

At each juncture, Jesus refused to test God's word and faithfulness. Instead, relying on the power of God's promises, he rejected Satan and continued to walk in confidence that God would provide. Throughout Jesus' earthly ministry, religious leaders continued to place tests before Jesus in an effort to discount his claims to being the Son of God (Mt 16:1; Mk 10:2). Jesus refused to cater to their demands, while indicating that his public words and deeds were more than enough to show them who he was.

God's Word and his proven faithfulness are a strong foundation for the faith of his people today. Met with the challenges of life in a fallen world, the church need not test God with trivial exercises like Gideon did here. God's people, following the pattern set by Jesus, can stand securely on his Word and his character even in an uncertain future.

[15]As soon as Gideon heard the telling of the dream and its interpretation, he worshiped. And he returned to the camp of Israel and said, "Arise, for the LORD has given the host of Midian into your hand." [16]And he divided the 300 men into three companies and put trumpets into the hands of all of them and empty jars, with torches inside the jars. [17]And he said to them, "Look at me, and do likewise. When I come to the outskirts of the camp, do as I do. [18]When I blow the trumpet, I and all who are with me, then blow the trumpets also on every side of all the camp and shout, 'For the LORD and for Gideon.'"

Gideon Defeats Midian

[19]So Gideon and the hundred men who were with him came to the outskirts of the camp at the beginning of the middle watch, when they had just set the watch. And they blew the trumpets and smashed the jars that were in their hands. [20]Then the three companies blew the trumpets and broke the jars. They held in their left hands the torches, and in their right hands the trumpets to blow. And they cried out, "A sword for the LORD and for Gideon!" [21]Every man stood in his place around the camp, and all the army ran. They cried out and fled. [22]When they blew the 300 trumpets, the LORD set every man's sword against his comrade and against all the army. And the army fled as far as Beth-shittah toward Zererah,[1] as far as the border of Abel-meholah, by Tabbath. [23]And the men of Israel were called out from Naphtali and from Asher and from all Manasseh, and they pursued after Midian.

[24]Gideon sent messengers throughout all the hill country of Ephraim, saying, "Come down against the Midianites and capture the waters against them, as far as Beth-barah, and also the Jordan." So all the men of Ephraim were called out, and they captured the waters as far as Beth-barah, and also the Jordan. [25]And they captured the two princes of Midian, Oreb and Zeeb. They killed Oreb at the rock of Oreb, and Zeeb they killed at the winepress of Zeeb. Then they pursued Midian, and they brought the heads of Oreb and Zeeb to Gideon across the Jordan.

Gideon Defeats Zebah and Zalmunna

8 Then the men of Ephraim said to him, "What is this that you have done to us, not to call us when you went to fight against Midian?" And they accused him fiercely. [2]And he said to them, "What have I done now in comparison with you? Is not the gleaning of the grapes of Ephraim better than the grape harvest of Abiezer? [3]God has given into your hands the princes of Midian, Oreb and Zeeb. What have I been able to do in comparison with you?" Then their anger[2] against him subsided when he said this.

[4]And Gideon came to the Jordan and crossed over, he and the 300 men who were with him, exhausted yet pursuing. [5]So he said to the men of Succoth, "Please give loaves of bread to the people who follow me, for they are exhausted, and I am pursuing after Zebah and Zalmunna, the kings of Midian." [6]And the officials of Succoth said, "Are the hands of Zebah and Zalmunna already in your hand, that we should give bread to your army?" [7]So Gideon said, "Well then, when the LORD has given Zebah and Zalmunna into my hand, I will flail your flesh with the thorns of the wilderness and with briers." [8]And from there he went up to Penuel, and spoke to them in the same way, and the men of Penuel answered him as the men of Succoth had answered. [9]And he said to the men of Penuel, "When I come again in peace, I will break down this tower."

[10]Now Zebah and Zalmunna were in Karkor with their army, about 15,000 men, all who were left of all the army of the people of the East, for there had fallen 120,000 men who drew the sword. [11]And Gideon went up by the way of the tent dwellers east of Nobah and Jogbehah and attacked the army, for the army felt secure. [12]And Zebah and Zalmunna fled, and he pursued them and captured the two kings of Midian, Zebah and Zalmunna, and he threw all the army into a panic.

[1]Some Hebrew manuscripts *Zeredah* [2]Hebrew *their spirit*

13Then Gideon the son of Joash returned from the battle by the ascent of
Heres. 14And he captured a young man of Succoth and questioned him. And he
wrote down for him the officials and elders of Succoth, seventy-seven men. 15And
he came to the men of Succoth and said, "Behold Zebah and Zalmunna, about
whom you taunted me, saying, 'Are the hands of Zebah and Zalmunna already in
your hand, that we should give bread to your men who are exhausted?' " 16And he
took the elders of the city, and he took thorns of the wilderness and briers and
with them taught the men of Succoth a lesson. 17And he broke down the tower of
Penuel and killed the men of the city.
18Then he said to Zebah and Zalmunna, "Where are the men whom you killed
at Tabor?" They answered, "As you are, so were they. Every one of them resembled
the son of a king." 19And he said, "They were my brothers, the sons of my mother.
As the LORD lives, if you had saved them alive, I would not kill you." 20So he said
to Jether his firstborn, "Rise and kill them!" But the young man did not draw his
sword, for he was afraid, because he was still a young man. 21Then Zebah and Zalmunna said, "Rise yourself and fall upon us, for as the man is, so is his strength."
And Gideon arose and killed Zebah and Zalmunna, and he took the crescent ornaments that were on the necks of their camels.

Gideon's Ephod

22Then the men of Israel said to Gideon, "Rule over us, you and your son and
your grandson also, for you have saved us from the hand of Midian." 23Gideon said
to them, "I will not rule over you, and my son will not rule over you; the LORD will
rule over you." 24And Gideon said to them, "Let me make a request of you: every
one of you give me the earrings from his spoil." (For they had golden earrings, because they were Ishmaelites.) 25And they answered, "We will willingly give them."
And they spread a cloak, and every man threw in it the earrings of his spoil. 26And
the weight of the golden earrings that he requested was 1,700 shekels[1] of gold,
besides the crescent ornaments and the pendants and the purple garments worn
by the kings of Midian, and besides the collars that were around the necks of their
camels. 27And Gideon made an ephod of it and put it in his city, in Ophrah. And
all Israel whored after it there, and it became a snare to Gideon and to his family.
28So Midian was subdued before the people of Israel, and they raised their heads
no more. And the land had rest for forty years in the days of Gideon.

The Death of Gideon

29Jerubbaal the son of Joash went and lived in his own house. 30Now Gideon
had seventy sons, his own offspring,[2] for he had many wives. 31And his concubine
who was in Shechem also bore him a son, and he called his name Abimelech.
32And Gideon the son of Joash died in a good old age and was buried in the tomb
of Joash his father, at Ophrah of the Abiezrites.
33As soon as Gideon died, the people of Israel turned again and whored after
the Baals and made Baal-berith their god. 34And the people of Israel did not remember the LORD their God, who had delivered them from the hand of all their
enemies on every side, 35and they did not show steadfast love to the family of
Jerubbaal (that is, Gideon) in return for all the good that he had done to Israel.

Abimelech's Conspiracy

9 Now Abimelech the son of Jerubbaal went to Shechem to his mother's relatives and said to them and to the whole clan of his mother's family, 2"Say in
the ears of all the leaders of Shechem, 'Which is better for you, that all seventy
of the sons of Jerubbaal rule over you, or that one rule over you?' Remember also
that I am your bone and your flesh."
3And his mother's relatives spoke all these words on his behalf in the ears of

[1]A *shekel* was about 2/5 ounce or 11 grams [2]Hebrew *who came from his own loins*

all the leaders of Shechem, and their hearts inclined to follow Abimelech, for they said, "He is our brother." 4And they gave him seventy pieces of silver out of the house of Baal-berith with which Abimelech hired worthless and reckless fellows, who followed him. 5And he went to his father's house at Ophrah and killed his brothers the sons of Jerubbaal, seventy men, on one stone. But Jotham the youngest son of Jerubbaal was left, for he hid himself. 6And all the leaders of Shechem came together, and all Beth-millo, and they went and made Abimelech king, by the oak of the pillar at Shechem.

7When it was told to Jotham, he went and stood on top of Mount Gerizim and cried aloud and said to them, "Listen to me, you leaders of Shechem, that God may listen to you. 8The trees once went out to anoint a king over them, and they said to the olive tree, 'Reign over us.' 9But the olive tree said to them, 'Shall I leave my abundance, by which gods and men are honored, and go hold sway over the trees?' 10And the trees said to the fig tree, 'You come and reign over us.' 11But the fig tree said to them, 'Shall I leave my sweetness and my good fruit and go hold sway over the trees?' 12And the trees said to the vine, 'You come and reign over us.' 13But the vine said to them, 'Shall I leave my wine that cheers God and men and go hold sway over the trees?' 14Then all the trees said to the bramble, 'You come and reign over us.' 15And the bramble said to the trees, 'If in good faith you are anointing me king over you, then come and take refuge in my shade, but if not, let fire come out of the bramble and devour the cedars of Lebanon.'

16"Now therefore, if you acted in good faith and integrity when you made Abimelech king, and if you have dealt well with Jerubbaal and his house and have done to him as his deeds deserved— 17for my father fought for you and risked his life and delivered you from the hand of Midian, 18and you have risen up against my father's house this day and have killed his sons, seventy men on one stone, and have made Abimelech, the son of his female servant, king over the leaders of Shechem, because he is your relative— 19if you then have acted in good faith and integrity with Jerubbaal and with his house this day, then rejoice in Abimelech, and let him also rejoice in you. 20But if not, let fire come out from Abimelech and devour the leaders of Shechem and Beth-millo; and let fire come out from the leaders of Shechem and from Beth-millo and devour Abimelech." 21And Jotham ran away and fled and went to Beer and lived there, because of Abimelech his brother.

The Downfall of Abimelech

22Abimelech ruled over Israel three years. 23And God sent an evil spirit between Abimelech and the leaders of Shechem, and the leaders of Shechem dealt treacherously with Abimelech, 24that the violence done to the seventy sons of Jerubbaal might come, and their blood be laid on Abimelech their brother, who killed them, and on the men of Shechem, who strengthened his hands to kill his brothers. 25And the leaders of Shechem put men in ambush against him on the mountaintops, and they robbed all who passed by them along that way. And it was told to Abimelech.

26And Gaal the son of Ebed moved into Shechem with his relatives, and the leaders of Shechem put confidence in him. 27And they went out into the field and gathered the grapes from their vineyards and trod them and held a festival; and they went into the house of their god and ate and drank and reviled Abimelech. 28And Gaal the son of Ebed said, "Who is Abimelech, and who are we of Shechem, that we should serve him? Is he not the son of Jerubbaal, and is not Zebul his officer? Serve the men of Hamor the father of Shechem; but why should we serve him? 29Would that this people were under my hand! Then I would remove Abimelech. I would say[1] to Abimelech, 'Increase your army, and come out.'"

30When Zebul the ruler of the city heard the words of Gaal the son of Ebed,

[1]Septuagint; Hebrew *and he said*

JUDGES 9:1 – 20

HUMAN LEADERSHIP AFTER THE FALL

The nation of Israel was meant to be a theocracy — a people living under the sovereign rule and reign of God. The story of the people of God demonstrated their consistent desire to elevate human leaders to dignified, and often aberrant, positions of power. The people of God never seemed to be satisfied with what God had established for them.

Human government is the locus of the cumulative power of people, which has been entrusted to leaders in unique ways throughout the history of God's people. At times, human leaders walk faithfully with God and lead the people to repentance and obedience. These leaders can be valuable means of restraining evil, judging wickedness, and instructing the nation in the ways of God.

More often, human government provides an outlet for pride and rebellion. The book of Judges details the destruction that resulted from human leaders who were unwilling to submit to God and who were absorbed with their own authority. Not only were these leaders prone to lead people to rebel, but they also persecuted those seeking to walk faithfully with God.

The failure of human leaders and the persecution of God's people were addressed by Jesus in what is referred to as the Sermon on the Mount (Mt 5 – 7). Jesus cautioned his followers against defensiveness or retaliation for persecution. Instead, he said that people are blessed when they are persecuted by virtue of their association with him. Those who are persecuted can rest assured that they will receive a reward in heaven.

Broken human government is an ongoing reality of life in a fallen world, and it can drive the church to either cower in fear or persevere through God-honoring submission to human leaders, praying on their behalf, and honoring the office these leaders hold (Ro 13:1 – 7). God, in his grand sovereignty, holds the destiny of the world and the hearts of the leaders in his ever-capable hands. Even in the midst of the rebellion of leaders, God's people can trust that he is working all things together for their good and his glory.

his anger was kindled. 31And he sent messengers to Abimelech secretly,[1] saying, "Behold, Gaal the son of Ebed and his relatives have come to Shechem, and they are stirring up[2] the city against you. 32Now therefore, go by night, you and the people who are with you, and set an ambush in the field. 33Then in the morning, as soon as the sun is up, rise early and rush upon the city. And when he and the people who are with him come out against you, you may do to them as your hand finds to do."

34So Abimelech and all the men who were with him rose up by night and set an ambush against Shechem in four companies. 35And Gaal the son of Ebed went out and stood in the entrance of the gate of the city, and Abimelech and the people who were with him rose from the ambush. 36And when Gaal saw the people, he said to Zebul, "Look, people are coming down from the mountaintops!" And Zebul said to him, "You mistake[3] the shadow of the mountains for men." 37Gaal spoke again and said, "Look, people are coming down from the center of the land, and one company is coming from the direction of the Diviners' Oak." 38Then Zebul said to him, "Where is your mouth now, you who said, 'Who is Abimelech, that we should serve him?' Are not these the people whom you despised? Go out now and fight with them." 39And Gaal went out at the head of the leaders of Shechem and fought with Abimelech. 40And Abimelech chased him, and he fled before him. And many fell wounded, up to the entrance of the gate. 41And Abimelech lived at Arumah, and Zebul drove out Gaal and his relatives, so that they could not dwell at Shechem.

42On the following day, the people went out into the field, and Abimelech was told. 43He took his people and divided them into three companies and set an ambush in the fields. And he looked and saw the people coming out of the city. So he rose against them and killed them. 44Abimelech and the company that was with him rushed forward and stood at the entrance of the gate of the city, while the two companies rushed upon all who were in the field and killed them. 45And Abimelech fought against the city all that day. He captured the city and killed the people who were in it, and he razed the city and sowed it with salt.

46When all the leaders of the Tower of Shechem heard of it, they entered the stronghold of the house of El-berith. 47Abimelech was told that all the leaders of the Tower of Shechem were gathered together. 48And Abimelech went up to Mount Zalmon, he and all the people who were with him. And Abimelech took an axe in his hand and cut down a bundle of brushwood and took it up and laid it on his shoulder. And he said to the men who were with him, "What you have seen me do, hurry and do as I have done." 49So every one of the people cut down his bundle and following Abimelech put it against the stronghold, and they set the stronghold on fire over them, so that all the people of the Tower of Shechem also died, about 1,000 men and women.

50Then Abimelech went to Thebez and encamped against Thebez and captured it. 51But there was a strong tower within the city, and all the men and women and all the leaders of the city fled to it and shut themselves in, and they went up to the roof of the tower. 52And Abimelech came to the tower and fought against it and drew near to the door of the tower to burn it with fire. 53And a certain woman threw an upper millstone on Abimelech's head and crushed his skull. 54Then he called quickly to the young man his armor-bearer and said to him, "Draw your sword and kill me, lest they say of me, 'A woman killed him.'" And his young man thrust him through, and he died. 55And when the men of Israel saw that Abimelech was dead, everyone departed to his home. 56Thus God returned the evil of Abimelech, which he committed against his father in killing his seventy brothers. 57And God also made all the evil of the men of Shechem return on their heads, and upon them came the curse of Jotham the son of Jerubbaal.

JUDGES 9:50–56

LONGING FOR A KING

Abimelech, who was the son of Gideon by his Shechemite slave woman turned concubine (Jdg 8:11; 9:18), suffered the just consequences for his sin. The actions of the woman and Abimelech's armor-bearer are clearly the execution of the judgment of God. Though Abimelech schemed to have himself crowned king, it quickly became evident that his kingdom would only harness the violent depravity of humanity (9:1–6,42–49). People need leaders to lead them, but human kings, like Abimelech, are incapable of ushering people into the *shalom* of God. The Israelites' deep-seated longing for a king and the constant disappointment in human kings left a void, which King Jesus eventually filled. His life demonstrated that only the sinless Son of God would be capable of leading people to follow God rightly. John, in his apocalyptic visions in the book of Revelation, declares Jesus to be the "Lord of lords and King of kings" (Rev 17:14; 19:16). All human leadership pales in comparison to the majesty of Jesus' rule and reign. By submitting to him, men and women can be led into a true and lasting kingdom not marked by death and depravity, but filled with love, peace, and joy. And his great kingdom will have no end.

[1]Or *at Tormah* [2]Hebrew *besieging*, or *closing up* [3]Hebrew *You see*

Tola and Jair

10 After Abimelech there arose to save Israel Tola the son of Puah, son of
Dodo, a man of Issachar, and he lived at Shamir in the hill country of
Ephraim. 2And he judged Israel twenty-three years. Then he died and was buried
at Shamir.
3After him arose Jair the Gileadite, who judged Israel twenty-two years. 4And
he had thirty sons who rode on thirty donkeys, and they had thirty cities, called
Havvoth-jair to this day, which are in the land of Gilead. 5And Jair died and was
buried in Kamon.

Further Disobedience and Oppression

6The people of Israel again did what was evil in the sight of the LORD and
served the Baals and the Ashtaroth, the gods of Syria, the gods of Sidon, the gods
of Moab, the gods of the Ammonites, and the gods of the Philistines. And they
forsook the LORD and did not serve him. 7So the anger of the LORD was kindled
against Israel, and he sold them into the hand of the Philistines and into the hand
of the Ammonites, 8and they crushed and oppressed the people of Israel that
year. For eighteen years they oppressed all the people of Israel who were beyond
the Jordan in the land of the Amorites, which is in Gilead. 9And the Ammonites
crossed the Jordan to fight also against Judah and against Benjamin and against
the house of Ephraim, so that Israel was severely distressed.
10And the people of Israel cried out to the LORD, saying, "We have sinned
against you, because we have forsaken our God and have served the Baals." 11And
the LORD said to the people of Israel, "Did I not save you from the Egyptians and
from the Amorites, from the Ammonites and from the Philistines? 12The Sidonians also, and the Amalekites and the Maonites oppressed you, and you cried out
to me, and I saved you out of their hand. 13Yet you have forsaken me and served
other gods; therefore I will save you no more. 14Go and cry out to the gods whom
you have chosen; let them save you in the time of your distress." 15And the people
of Israel said to the LORD, "We have sinned; do to us whatever seems good to you.
Only please deliver us this day." 16So they put away the foreign gods from among
them and served the LORD, and he became impatient over the misery of Israel.
17Then the Ammonites were called to arms, and they encamped in Gilead. And
the people of Israel came together, and they encamped at Mizpah. 18And the people, the leaders of Gilead, said one to another, "Who is the man who will begin to
fight against the Ammonites? He shall be head over all the inhabitants of Gilead."

Jephthah Delivers Israel

11 Now Jephthah the Gileadite was a mighty warrior, but he was the son of a
prostitute. Gilead was the father of Jephthah. 2And Gilead's wife also bore
him sons. And when his wife's sons grew up, they drove Jephthah out and said to
him, "You shall not have an inheritance in our father's house, for you are the son
of another woman." 3Then Jephthah fled from his brothers and lived in the land
of Tob, and worthless fellows collected around Jephthah and went out with him.
4After a time the Ammonites made war against Israel. 5And when the Ammonites made war against Israel, the elders of Gilead went to bring Jephthah from
the land of Tob. 6And they said to Jephthah, "Come and be our leader, that we may
fight against the Ammonites." 7But Jephthah said to the elders of Gilead, "Did you
not hate me and drive me out of my father's house? Why have you come to me
now when you are in distress?" 8And the elders of Gilead said to Jephthah, "That
is why we have turned to you now, that you may go with us and fight against the
Ammonites and be our head over all the inhabitants of Gilead." 9Jephthah said to
the elders of Gilead, "If you bring me home again to fight against the Ammonites,
and the LORD gives them over to me, I will be your head." 10And the elders of
Gilead said to Jephthah, "The LORD will be witness between us, if we do not do as
you say." 11So Jephthah went with the elders of Gilead, and the people made him

---

JUDGES 11:1–3

MIGHTY IN FAITH

The author of Judges refers to Jephthah, who became one of Israel's judges, as "a mighty warrior." Jephthah was from Gilead, located east of the Jordan River. Jephthah's might distinguished him from other men. Because he was the son of an illegitimate relationship, his half brothers expelled him from the family. As a result, he fled to the land of Tob, and there he became the leader of a group of "worthless fellows"—likely roaming mercenaries. Centuries later, in the book of Hebrews, Jephthah appeared in another list. This time he is singled out, not for his might, his illegitimate birth, or his wayward relationships, but for his faith (Heb 11:32). He is listed alongside greats such as Abraham, Moses, and David as one who modeled the type of faith that all Christians should possess. Jephthah demonstrated that faith is the distinguishing mark of greatness in the economy of the kingdom of God.

head and leader over them. And Jephthah spoke all his words before the LORD at Mizpah.

[12]Then Jephthah sent messengers to the king of the Ammonites and said, "What do you have against me, that you have come to me to fight against my land?" [13]And the king of the Ammonites answered the messengers of Jephthah, "Because Israel on coming up from Egypt took away my land, from the Arnon to the Jabbok and to the Jordan; now therefore restore it peaceably." [14]Jephthah again sent messengers to the king of the Ammonites [15]and said to him, "Thus says Jephthah: Israel did not take away the land of Moab or the land of the Ammonites, [16]but when they came up from Egypt, Israel went through the wilderness to the Red Sea and came to Kadesh. [17]Israel then sent messengers to the king of Edom, saying, 'Please let us pass through your land,' but the king of Edom would not listen. And they sent also to the king of Moab, but he would not consent. So Israel remained at Kadesh.

[18]"Then they journeyed through the wilderness and went around the land of Edom and the land of Moab and arrived on the east side of the land of Moab and camped on the other side of the Arnon. But they did not enter the territory of Moab, for the Arnon was the boundary of Moab. [19]Israel then sent messengers to Sihon king of the Amorites, king of Heshbon, and Israel said to him, 'Please let us pass through your land to our country,' [20]but Sihon did not trust Israel to pass through his territory, so Sihon gathered all his people together and encamped at Jahaz and fought with Israel. [21]And the LORD, the God of Israel, gave Sihon and all his people into the hand of Israel, and they defeated them. So Israel took possession of all the land of the Amorites, who inhabited that country. [22]And they took possession of all the territory of the Amorites from the Arnon to the Jabbok and from the wilderness to the Jordan. [23]So then the LORD, the God of Israel, dispossessed the Amorites from before his people Israel; and are you to take possession of them? [24]Will you not possess what Chemosh your god gives you to possess? And all that the LORD our God has dispossessed before us, we will possess. [25]Now are you any better than Balak the son of Zippor, king of Moab? Did he ever contend against Israel, or did he ever go to war with them? [26]While Israel lived in Heshbon and its villages, and in Aroer and its villages, and in all the cities that are on the banks of the Arnon, 300 years, why did you not deliver them within that time? [27]I therefore have not sinned against you, and you do me wrong by making war on me. The LORD, the Judge, decide this day between the people of Israel and the people of Ammon." [28]But the king of the Ammonites did not listen to the words of Jephthah that he sent to him.

Jephthah's Tragic Vow

[29]Then the Spirit of the LORD was upon Jephthah, and he passed through Gilead and Manasseh and passed on to Mizpah of Gilead, and from Mizpah of Gilead he passed on to the Ammonites. [30]And Jephthah made a vow to the LORD and said, "If you will give the Ammonites into my hand, [31]then whatever[1] comes out from the doors of my house to meet me when I return in peace from the Ammonites shall be the LORD's, and I will offer it[2] up for a burnt offering." [32]So Jephthah crossed over to the Ammonites to fight against them, and the LORD gave them into his hand. [33]And he struck them from Aroer to the neighborhood of Minnith, twenty cities, and as far as Abel-keramim, with a great blow. So the Ammonites were subdued before the people of Israel.

[34]Then Jephthah came to his home at Mizpah. And behold, his daughter came out to meet him with tambourines and with dances. She was his only child; besides her he had neither son nor daughter. [35]And as soon as he saw her, he tore his clothes and said, "Alas, my daughter! You have brought me very low, and you have become the cause of great trouble to me. For I have opened my mouth to

[1]Or *whoever* [2]Or *him*

the LORD, and I cannot take back my vow." [36]And she said to him, "My father,
you have opened your mouth to the LORD; do to me according to what has gone
out of your mouth, now that the LORD has avenged you on your enemies, on the
Ammonites." [37]So she said to her father, "Let this thing be done for me: leave me
alone two months, that I may go up and down on the mountains and weep for my
virginity, I and my companions." [38]So he said, "Go." Then he sent her away for two
months, and she departed, she and her companions, and wept for her virginity on
the mountains. [39]And at the end of two months, she returned to her father, who
did with her according to his vow that he had made. She had never known a man,
and it became a custom in Israel [40]that the daughters of Israel went year by year
to lament the daughter of Jephthah the Gileadite four days in the year.

Jephthah's Conflict with Ephraim

12 The men of Ephraim were called to arms, and they crossed to Zaphon and
said to Jephthah, "Why did you cross over to fight against the Ammonites
and did not call us to go with you? We will burn your house over you with fire."
[2]And Jephthah said to them, "I and my people had a great dispute with the Ammonites, and when I called you, you did not save me from their hand. [3]And when
I saw that you would not save me, I took my life in my hand and crossed over
against the Ammonites, and the LORD gave them into my hand. Why then have
you come up to me this day to fight against me?" [4]Then Jephthah gathered all the
men of Gilead and fought with Ephraim. And the men of Gilead struck Ephraim,
because they said, "You are fugitives of Ephraim, you Gileadites, in the midst of
Ephraim and Manasseh." [5]And the Gileadites captured the fords of the Jordan
against the Ephraimites. And when any of the fugitives of Ephraim said, "Let me
go over," the men of Gilead said to him, "Are you an Ephraimite?" When he said,
"No," [6]they said to him, "Then say Shibboleth," and he said, "Sibboleth," for he
could not pronounce it right. Then they seized him and slaughtered him at the
fords of the Jordan. At that time 42,000 of the Ephraimites fell.
[7]Jephthah judged Israel six years. Then Jephthah the Gileadite died and was
buried in his city in Gilead.[1]

Ibzan, Elon, and Abdon

[8]After him Ibzan of Bethlehem judged Israel. [9]He had thirty sons, and thirty
daughters he gave in marriage outside his clan, and thirty daughters he brought
in from outside for his sons. And he judged Israel seven years. [10]Then Ibzan died
and was buried at Bethlehem.
[11]After him Elon the Zebulunite judged Israel, and he judged Israel ten years.
[12]Then Elon the Zebulunite died and was buried at Aijalon in the land of Zebulun.
[13]After him Abdon the son of Hillel the Pirathonite judged Israel. [14]He had
forty sons and thirty grandsons, who rode on seventy donkeys, and he judged
Israel eight years. [15]Then Abdon the son of Hillel the Pirathonite died and was
buried at Pirathon in the land of Ephraim, in the hill country of the Amalekites.

The Birth of Samson

13 And the people of Israel again did what was evil in the sight of the LORD, so
the LORD gave them into the hand of the Philistines for forty years.
[2]There was a certain man of Zorah, of the tribe of the Danites, whose name
was Manoah. And his wife was barren and had no children. [3]And the angel of the
LORD appeared to the woman and said to her, "Behold, you are barren and have
not borne children, but you shall conceive and bear a son. [4]Therefore be careful
and drink no wine or strong drink, and eat nothing unclean, [5]for behold, you shall
conceive and bear a son. No razor shall come upon his head, for the child shall be
a Nazirite to God from the womb, and he shall begin to save Israel from the hand

[1]Septuagint; Hebrew *in the cities of Gilead*

of the Philistines." 6Then the woman came and told her husband, "A man of God
came to me, and his appearance was like the appearance of the angel of God, very
awesome. I did not ask him where he was from, and he did not tell me his name,
7but he said to me, 'Behold, you shall conceive and bear a son. So then drink no
wine or strong drink, and eat nothing unclean, for the child shall be a Nazirite to
God from the womb to the day of his death.'"

8Then Manoah prayed to the LORD and said, "O Lord, please let the man of
God whom you sent come again to us and teach us what we are to do with the
child who will be born." 9And God listened to the voice of Manoah, and the angel
of God came again to the woman as she sat in the field. But Manoah her husband
was not with her. 10So the woman ran quickly and told her husband, "Behold, the
man who came to me the other day has appeared to me." 11And Manoah arose and
went after his wife and came to the man and said to him, "Are you the man who
spoke to this woman?" And he said, "I am." 12And Manoah said, "Now when your
words come true, what is to be the child's manner of life, and what is his mission?"
13And the angel of the LORD said to Manoah, "Of all that I said to the woman let
her be careful. 14She may not eat of anything that comes from the vine, neither let
her drink wine or strong drink, or eat any unclean thing. All that I commanded
her let her observe."

15Manoah said to the angel of the LORD, "Please let us detain you and prepare
a young goat for you." 16And the angel of the LORD said to Manoah, "If you detain
me, I will not eat of your food. But if you prepare a burnt offering, then offer it to
the LORD." (For Manoah did not know that he was the angel of the LORD.) 17And
Manoah said to the angel of the LORD, "What is your name, so that, when your
words come true, we may honor you?" 18And the angel of the LORD said to him,
"Why do you ask my name, seeing it is wonderful?" 19So Manoah took the young
goat with the grain offering, and offered it on the rock to the LORD, to the one who
works[1] wonders, and Manoah and his wife were watching. 20And when the flame
went up toward heaven from the altar, the angel of the LORD went up in the flame
of the altar. Now Manoah and his wife were watching, and they fell on their faces
to the ground.

21The angel of the LORD appeared no more to Manoah and to his wife. Then
Manoah knew that he was the angel of the LORD. 22And Manoah said to his wife,
"We shall surely die, for we have seen God." 23But his wife said to him, "If the
LORD had meant to kill us, he would not have accepted a burnt offering and a
grain offering at our hands, or shown us all these things, or now announced to us
such things as these." 24And the woman bore a son and called his name Samson.
And the young man grew, and the LORD blessed him. 25And the Spirit of the LORD
began to stir him in Mahaneh-dan, between Zorah and Eshtaol.

Samson's Marriage

14 Samson went down to Timnah, and at Timnah he saw one of the daughters of the Philistines. 2Then he came up and told his father and mother, "I
saw one of the daughters of the Philistines at Timnah. Now get her for me as my
wife." 3But his father and mother said to him, "Is there not a woman among the
daughters of your relatives, or among all our people, that you must go to take a
wife from the uncircumcised Philistines?" But Samson said to his father, "Get her
for me, for she is right in my eyes."

4His father and mother did not know that it was from the LORD, for he was
seeking an opportunity against the Philistines. At that time the Philistines ruled
over Israel.

5Then Samson went down with his father and mother to Timnah, and they
came to the vineyards of Timnah. And behold, a young lion came toward him
roaring. 6Then the Spirit of the LORD rushed upon him, and although he had

[1] Septuagint, Vulgate; Hebrew *LORD, and working*

JUDGES 14:6–19

THE SPIRIT'S POWER

The Holy Spirit played an active role in the Old Testament. In the book of Judges, the Holy Spirit empowered numerous individuals. The Holy Spirit "clothed Gideon" when Gideon fought against the Midianites and Amalekites (Jdg 6:34); the Spirit "was upon Jephthah" (11:29) when he went to fight against the Ammonites; the Spirit also "rushed upon" Samson and enabled him to defeat his adversary (14:6). When the Holy Spirit moved, amazing things happened.

While the Holy Spirit used people in the Old Testament to perform mighty deeds, the Spirit is still doing great things today. Jesus told his disciples that it was to their benefit that he would leave them, for after he left, "the Helper" would come (Jn 16:5–15). Jesus promised that the Holy Spirit would convict the world of sin and guide the disciples into all truth. Though Christians today may not have the physical strength to tear apart a lion like Samson did, they have an even greater power to stand against sin and take the gospel to the nations.

A COMING REDEEMER

Samson and Jesus brought Spirit-empowered redemption to God's people in remarkably similar ways. Just consider the contours of Samson's life. Even before his miraculous birth, an angel appeared to Samson's parents, preparing them for his ministry (Jdg 13:2 – 3; Lk 1:26 – 27,34) and explaining that their child would act as a savior of his people (Jdg 13:5; Mt 1:21). Samson was consecrated to live a life of marked devotion to God by following the Nazirite vow, underscoring the importance of fulfilling the Law (Jdg 13:7; Mt 5:17). Samson's mission in life was uniquely empowered by the Spirit (Jdg 14:6,19; Mt 3:16). During this mission, Samson served as the sole agent of God's work to redeem his people. While Deborah had Barak, and Gideon had his soldiers, Samson bore God-given responsibilities alone. In the course of Samson's work, God ordained that he be handed over to the Gentile occupiers by his fellow Israelites (Jdg 15:9 – 13; Mt 27:1 – 2), ultimately experiencing painful betrayal at the hands of one whom he loved (Jdg 16:15,18 – 21; Mt 26:47 – 50) and mockery from his oppressors (Jdg 16:23 – 27; Mt 26:67 – 68; 27:27 – 31). At the end of all this, the epitaph of Samson was that he achieved more in his death than he did in his life (Jdg 16:30; Jn 12:31 – 32; Heb 2:14; 1Jn 3:8). These shocking parallels between Samson and Jesus are no accident!

In spite of the similarity in their life narratives, Jesus and Samson stand in stark contrast. Samson caved to the morals of his society while Jesus confronted the norms of his culture. One slept with a prostitute (Jdg 16:1), while the other brings life-change to prostitutes and sinners (Lk 7:36 – 39; Jn 8:11). They evidence vastly different levels of commitment to the plan of God. Samson risked his mission in the arms of a prostitute, but Jesus remained committed even when faced with a cross. When Jesus could have asserted his own will or sought his own comfort, he chose the Father's will instead (Lk 22:42). Samson pursued a physical deliverance of God's people through the slaughter of their enemies on the battlefield. Jesus secured the spiritual deliverance of God's people through his own slaughter on the cross.

nothing in his hand, he tore the lion in pieces as one tears a young goat. But he
did not tell his father or his mother what he had done. 7 Then he went down and
talked with the woman, and she was right in Samson's eyes.

8 After some days he returned to take her. And he turned aside to see the carcass of the lion, and behold, there was a swarm of bees in the body of the lion, and
honey. 9 He scraped it out into his hands and went on, eating as he went. And he
came to his father and mother and gave some to them, and they ate. But he did not
tell them that he had scraped the honey from the carcass of the lion.

10 His father went down to the woman, and Samson prepared a feast there, for
so the young men used to do. 11 As soon as the people saw him, they brought thirty
companions to be with him. 12 And Samson said to them, "Let me now put a riddle
to you. If you can tell me what it is, within the seven days of the feast, and find it
out, then I will give you thirty linen garments and thirty changes of clothes, 13 but
if you cannot tell me what it is, then you shall give me thirty linen garments and
thirty changes of clothes." And they said to him, "Put your riddle, that we may
hear it." 14 And he said to them,

"Out of the eater came something to eat.
Out of the strong came something sweet."

And in three days they could not solve the riddle.

15 On the fourth[1] day they said to Samson's wife, "Entice your husband to tell
us what the riddle is, lest we burn you and your father's house with fire. Have you
invited us here to impoverish us?" 16 And Samson's wife wept over him and said,
"You only hate me; you do not love me. You have put a riddle to my people, and
you have not told me what it is." And he said to her, "Behold, I have not told my
father nor my mother, and shall I tell you?" 17 She wept before him the seven days
that their feast lasted, and on the seventh day he told her, because she pressed
him hard. Then she told the riddle to her people. 18 And the men of the city said to
him on the seventh day before the sun went down,

"What is sweeter than honey?
What is stronger than a lion?"

And he said to them,

"If you had not plowed with my heifer,
you would not have found out my riddle."

19 And the Spirit of the LORD rushed upon him, and he went down to Ashkelon and
struck down thirty men of the town and took their spoil and gave the garments
to those who had told the riddle. In hot anger he went back to his father's house.
20 And Samson's wife was given to his companion, who had been his best man.

Samson Defeats the Philistines

15 After some days, at the time of wheat harvest, Samson went to visit his wife
with a young goat. And he said, "I will go in to my wife in the chamber." But
her father would not allow him to go in. 2 And her father said, "I really thought that
you utterly hated her, so I gave her to your companion. Is not her younger sister
more beautiful than she? Please take her instead." 3 And Samson said to them,
"This time I shall be innocent in regard to the Philistines, when I do them harm."
4 So Samson went and caught 300 foxes and took torches. And he turned them tail
to tail and put a torch between each pair of tails. 5 And when he had set fire to the
torches, he let the foxes go into the standing grain of the Philistines and set fire to
the stacked grain and the standing grain, as well as the olive orchards. 6 Then the
Philistines said, "Who has done this?" And they said, "Samson, the son-in-law of
the Timnite, because he has taken his wife and given her to his companion." And
the Philistines came up and burned her and her father with fire. 7 And Samson

[1] Septuagint, Syriac; Hebrew *seventh*

said to them, "If this is what you do, I swear I will be avenged on you, and after that I will quit." 8And he struck them hip and thigh with a great blow, and he went down and stayed in the cleft of the rock of Etam.

9Then the Philistines came up and encamped in Judah and made a raid on Lehi. 10And the men of Judah said, "Why have you come up against us?" They said, "We have come up to bind Samson, to do to him as he did to us." 11Then 3,000 men of Judah went down to the cleft of the rock of Etam, and said to Samson, "Do you not know that the Philistines are rulers over us? What then is this that you have done to us?" And he said to them, "As they did to me, so have I done to them." 12And they said to him, "We have come down to bind you, that we may give you into the hands of the Philistines." And Samson said to them, "Swear to me that you will not attack me yourselves." 13They said to him, "No; we will only bind you and give you into their hands. We will surely not kill you." So they bound him with two new ropes and brought him up from the rock.

14When he came to Lehi, the Philistines came shouting to meet him. Then the Spirit of the LORD rushed upon him, and the ropes that were on his arms became as flax that has caught fire, and his bonds melted off his hands. 15And he found a fresh jawbone of a donkey, and put out his hand and took it, and with it he struck 1,000 men. 16And Samson said,

"With the jawbone of a donkey,
    heaps upon heaps,
with the jawbone of a donkey
    have I struck down a thousand men."

17As soon as he had finished speaking, he threw away the jawbone out of his hand. And that place was called Ramath-lehi.[1]

18And he was very thirsty, and he called upon the LORD and said, "You have granted this great salvation by the hand of your servant, and shall I now die of thirst and fall into the hands of the uncircumcised?" 19And God split open the hollow place that is at Lehi, and water came out from it. And when he drank, his spirit returned, and he revived. Therefore the name of it was called En-hakkore;[2] it is at Lehi to this day. 20And he judged Israel in the days of the Philistines twenty years.

Samson and Delilah

16 Samson went to Gaza, and there he saw a prostitute, and he went in to her. 2The Gazites were told, "Samson has come here." And they surrounded the place and set an ambush for him all night at the gate of the city. They kept quiet all night, saying, "Let us wait till the light of the morning; then we will kill him." 3But Samson lay till midnight, and at midnight he arose and took hold of the doors of the gate of the city and the two posts, and pulled them up, bar and all, and put them on his shoulders and carried them to the top of the hill that is in front of Hebron.

4After this he loved a woman in the Valley of Sorek, whose name was Delilah. 5And the lords of the Philistines came up to her and said to her, "Seduce him, and see where his great strength lies, and by what means we may overpower him, that we may bind him to humble him. And we will each give you 1,100 pieces of silver." 6So Delilah said to Samson, "Please tell me where your great strength lies, and how you might be bound, that one could subdue you."

7Samson said to her, "If they bind me with seven fresh bowstrings that have not been dried, then I shall become weak and be like any other man." 8Then the lords of the Philistines brought up to her seven fresh bowstrings that had not been dried, and she bound him with them. 9Now she had men lying in ambush in an inner chamber. And she said to him, "The Philistines are upon you, Samson!" But he snapped the bowstrings, as a thread of flax snaps when it touches the fire. So the secret of his strength was not known.

---

[1] *Ramath-lehi* means *the hill of the jawbone* [2] *En-hakkore* means *the spring of him who called*

10 Then Delilah said to Samson, "Behold, you have mocked me and told me lies. Please tell me how you might be bound." 11 And he said to her, "If they bind me with new ropes that have not been used, then I shall become weak and be like any other man." 12 So Delilah took new ropes and bound him with them and said to him, "The Philistines are upon you, Samson!" And the men lying in ambush were in an inner chamber. But he snapped the ropes off his arms like a thread.

13 Then Delilah said to Samson, "Until now you have mocked me and told me lies. Tell me how you might be bound." And he said to her, "If you weave the seven locks of my head with the web and fasten it tight with the pin, then I shall become weak and be like any other man." 14 So while he slept, Delilah took the seven locks of his head and wove them into the web.[1] And she made them tight with the pin and said to him, "The Philistines are upon you, Samson!" But he awoke from his sleep and pulled away the pin, the loom, and the web.

15 And she said to him, "How can you say, 'I love you,' when your heart is not with me? You have mocked me these three times, and you have not told me where your great strength lies." 16 And when she pressed him hard with her words day after day, and urged him, his soul was vexed to death. 17 And he told her all his heart, and said to her, "A razor has never come upon my head, for I have been a Nazirite to God from my mother's womb. If my head is shaved, then my strength will leave me, and I shall become weak and be like any other man."

18 When Delilah saw that he had told her all his heart, she sent and called the lords of the Philistines, saying, "Come up again, for he has told me all his heart." Then the lords of the Philistines came up to her and brought the money in their hands. 19 She made him sleep on her knees. And she called a man and had him shave off the seven locks of his head. Then she began to torment him, and his strength left him. 20 And she said, "The Philistines are upon you, Samson!" And he awoke from his sleep and said, "I will go out as at other times and shake myself free." But he did not know that the LORD had left him. 21 And the Philistines seized him and gouged out his eyes and brought him down to Gaza and bound him with bronze shackles. And he ground at the mill in the prison. 22 But the hair of his head began to grow again after it had been shaved.

The Death of Samson

23 Now the lords of the Philistines gathered to offer a great sacrifice to Dagon their god and to rejoice, and they said, "Our god has given Samson our enemy into our hand." 24 And when the people saw him, they praised their god. For they said, "Our god has given our enemy into our hand, the ravager of our country, who has killed many of us."[2] 25 And when their hearts were merry, they said, "Call Samson, that he may entertain us." So they called Samson out of the prison, and he entertained them. They made him stand between the pillars. 26 And Samson said to the young man who held him by the hand, "Let me feel the pillars on which the house rests, that I may lean against them." 27 Now the house was full of men and women. All the lords of the Philistines were there, and on the roof there were about 3,000 men and women, who looked on while Samson entertained.

28 Then Samson called to the LORD and said, "O Lord GOD, please remember me and please strengthen me only this once, O God, that I may be avenged on the Philistines for my two eyes." 29 And Samson grasped the two middle pillars on which the house rested, and he leaned his weight against them, his right hand on the one and his left hand on the other. 30 And Samson said, "Let me die with the Philistines." Then he bowed with all his strength, and the house fell upon the lords and upon all the people who were in it. So the dead whom he killed at his death were more than those whom he had killed during his life. 31 Then his brothers and all his family came down and took him and brought him up and buried him between Zorah and Eshtaol in the tomb of Manoah his father. He had judged Israel twenty years.

[1] Compare Septuagint; Hebrew lacks *and fasten it tight . . . into the web* [2] Or *who has multiplied our slain*

Micah and the Levite

17 There was a man of the hill country of Ephraim, whose name was Micah.
2And he said to his mother, "The 1,100 pieces of silver that were taken
from you, about which you uttered a curse, and also spoke it in my ears, behold, the silver is with me; I took it." And his mother said, "Blessed be my son
by the LORD." 3And he restored the 1,100 pieces of silver to his mother. And his
mother said, "I dedicate the silver to the LORD from my hand for my son, to make
a carved image and a metal image. Now therefore I will restore it to you." 4So
when he restored the money to his mother, his mother took 200 pieces of silver
and gave it to the silversmith, who made it into a carved image and a metal image. And it was in the house of Micah. 5And the man Micah had a shrine, and he
made an ephod and household gods, and ordained[1] one of his sons, who became
his priest. 6In those days there was no king in Israel. Everyone did what was right
in his own eyes.
7Now there was a young man of Bethlehem in Judah, of the family of Judah,
who was a Levite, and he sojourned there. 8And the man departed from the town
of Bethlehem in Judah to sojourn where he could find a place. And as he journeyed, he came to the hill country of Ephraim to the house of Micah. 9And Micah
said to him, "Where do you come from?" And he said to him, "I am a Levite of
Bethlehem in Judah, and I am going to sojourn where I may find a place." 10And
Micah said to him, "Stay with me, and be to me a father and a priest, and I will
give you ten pieces of silver a year and a suit of clothes and your living." And the
Levite went in. 11And the Levite was content to dwell with the man, and the young
man became to him like one of his sons. 12And Micah ordained the Levite, and the
young man became his priest, and was in the house of Micah. 13Then Micah said,
"Now I know that the LORD will prosper me, because I have a Levite as priest."

Danites Take the Levite and the Idol

18 In those days there was no king in Israel. And in those days the tribe of the
people of Dan was seeking for itself an inheritance to dwell in, for until
then no inheritance among the tribes of Israel had fallen to them. 2So the people
of Dan sent five able men from the whole number of their tribe, from Zorah and
from Eshtaol, to spy out the land and to explore it. And they said to them, "Go and
explore the land." And they came to the hill country of Ephraim, to the house of
Micah, and lodged there. 3When they were by the house of Micah, they recognized the voice of the young Levite. And they turned aside and said to him, "Who
brought you here? What are you doing in this place? What is your business here?"
4And he said to them, "This is how Micah dealt with me: he has hired me, and I
have become his priest." 5And they said to him, "Inquire of God, please, that we
may know whether the journey on which we are setting out will succeed." 6And
the priest said to them, "Go in peace. The journey on which you go is under the
eye of the LORD."
7Then the five men departed and came to Laish and saw the people who were
there, how they lived in security, after the manner of the Sidonians, quiet and unsuspecting, lacking[2] nothing that is in the earth and possessing wealth, and how
they were far from the Sidonians and had no dealings with anyone. 8And when
they came to their brothers at Zorah and Eshtaol, their brothers said to them,
"What do you report?" 9They said, "Arise, and let us go up against them, for we
have seen the land, and behold, it is very good. And will you do nothing? Do not
be slow to go, to enter in and possess the land. 10As soon as you go, you will come
to an unsuspecting people. The land is spacious, for God has given it into your
hands, a place where there is no lack of anything that is in the earth."
11So 600 men of the tribe of Dan, armed with weapons of war, set out from
Zorah and Eshtaol, 12and went up and encamped at Kiriath-jearim in Judah. On

[1]Hebrew *filled the hand of*; also verse 12 [2]Compare 18:10; the meaning of the Hebrew word is uncertain

this account that place is called Mahaneh-dan[1] to this day; behold, it is west of Kiriath-jearim. 13And they passed on from there to the hill country of Ephraim, and came to the house of Micah.

14Then the five men who had gone to scout out the country of Laish said to their brothers, "Do you know that in these houses there are an ephod, household gods, a carved image, and a metal image? Now therefore consider what you will do." 15And they turned aside there and came to the house of the young Levite, at the home of Micah, and asked him about his welfare. 16Now the 600 men of the Danites, armed with their weapons of war, stood by the entrance of the gate. 17And the five men who had gone to scout out the land went up and entered and took the carved image, the ephod, the household gods, and the metal image, while the priest stood by the entrance of the gate with the 600 men armed with weapons of war. 18And when these went into Micah's house and took the carved image, the ephod, the household gods, and the metal image, the priest said to them, "What are you doing?" 19And they said to him, "Keep quiet; put your hand on your mouth and come with us and be to us a father and a priest. Is it better for you to be priest to the house of one man, or to be priest to a tribe and clan in Israel?" 20And the priest's heart was glad. He took the ephod and the household gods and the carved image and went along with the people.

21So they turned and departed, putting the little ones and the livestock and the goods in front of them. 22When they had gone a distance from the home of Micah, the men who were in the houses near Micah's house were called out, and they overtook the people of Dan. 23And they shouted to the people of Dan, who turned around and said to Micah, "What is the matter with you, that you come with such a company?" 24And he said, "You take my gods that I made and the priest, and go away, and what have I left? How then do you ask me, 'What is the matter with you?'" 25And the people of Dan said to him, "Do not let your voice be heard among us, lest angry fellows fall upon you, and you lose your life with the lives of your household." 26Then the people of Dan went their way. And when Micah saw that they were too strong for him, he turned and went back to his home.

27But the people of Dan took what Micah had made, and the priest who belonged to him, and they came to Laish, to a people quiet and unsuspecting, and struck them with the edge of the sword and burned the city with fire. 28And there was no deliverer because it was far from Sidon, and they had no dealings with anyone. It was in the valley that belongs to Beth-rehob. Then they rebuilt the city and lived in it. 29And they named the city Dan, after the name of Dan their ancestor, who was born to Israel; but the name of the city was Laish at the first. 30And the people of Dan set up the carved image for themselves, and Jonathan the son of Gershom, son of Moses,[2] and his sons were priests to the tribe of the Danites until the day of the captivity of the land. 31So they set up Micah's carved image that he made, as long as the house of God was at Shiloh.

A Levite and His Concubine

19 In those days, when there was no king in Israel, a certain Levite was sojourning in the remote parts of the hill country of Ephraim, who took to himself a concubine from Bethlehem in Judah. 2And his concubine was unfaithful to[3] him, and she went away from him to her father's house at Bethlehem in Judah, and was there some four months. 3Then her husband arose and went after her, to speak kindly to her and bring her back. He had with him his servant and a couple of donkeys. And she brought him into her father's house. And when the girl's father saw him, he came with joy to meet him. 4And his father-in-law, the girl's father, made him stay, and he remained with him three days. So they ate and drank and spent the night there. 5And on the fourth day they arose early in the morning, and he prepared to go, but the girl's father said to his son-in-law,

JUDGES 19:1–30

THE CYCLE OF SIN

Sin is never satisfied—it festers, grows, spreads, and destroys all things in its path. The unnamed Levite and the people of Gibeah illustrate the depth of depravity of which humans are capable. There seemed to be no end to the self-centeredness of mankind apart from God's gracious intervention. This reality was compounded in the seasons when the nation was without human leaders; though, even when they had leaders, they proved to be incapable of consistent obedience. They needed a deliverer, a Savior, to break the cycle of sin, condemnation, and death.

Paul declared that Jesus' once-for-all sacrifice breaks the death-grip of sin and sets believers free to live a righteous life (Ro 6:15–23). Whereas the just outcome of sin is death, the fruit of Jesus' work is freedom, joy, and holiness. Jesus' victory is the only power great enough to break the power of sin within the nation of Israel and all of humanity.

[1]*Mahaneh-dan* means *camp of Dan* [2]Or *Manasseh* [3]Septuagint, Old Latin *became angry with*

"Strengthen your heart with a morsel of bread, and after that you may go." 6So the two of them sat and ate and drank together. And the girl's father said to the man, "Be pleased to spend the night, and let your heart be merry." 7And when the man rose up to go, his father-in-law pressed him, till he spent the night there again. 8And on the fifth day he arose early in the morning to depart. And the girl's father said, "Strengthen your heart and wait until the day declines." So they ate, both of them. 9And when the man and his concubine and his servant rose up to depart, his father-in-law, the girl's father, said to him, "Behold, now the day has waned toward evening. Please, spend the night. Behold, the day draws to its close. Lodge here and let your heart be merry, and tomorrow you shall arise early in the morning for your journey, and go home."

10But the man would not spend the night. He rose up and departed and arrived opposite Jebus (that is, Jerusalem). He had with him a couple of saddled donkeys, and his concubine was with him. 11When they were near Jebus, the day was nearly over, and the servant said to his master, "Come now, let us turn aside to this city of the Jebusites and spend the night in it." 12And his master said to him, "We will not turn aside into the city of foreigners, who do not belong to the people of Israel, but we will pass on to Gibeah." 13And he said to his young man, "Come and let us draw near to one of these places and spend the night at Gibeah or at Ramah." 14So they passed on and went their way. And the sun went down on them near Gibeah, which belongs to Benjamin, 15and they turned aside there, to go in and spend the night at Gibeah. And he went in and sat down in the open square of the city, for no one took them into his house to spend the night.

16And behold, an old man was coming from his work in the field at evening. The man was from the hill country of Ephraim, and he was sojourning in Gibeah. The men of the place were Benjaminites. 17And he lifted up his eyes and saw the traveler in the open square of the city. And the old man said, "Where are you going? And where do you come from?" 18And he said to him, "We are passing from Bethlehem in Judah to the remote parts of the hill country of Ephraim, from which I come. I went to Bethlehem in Judah, and I am going to the house of the LORD,[1] but no one has taken me into his house. 19We have straw and feed for our donkeys, with bread and wine for me and your female servant and the young man with your servants. There is no lack of anything." 20And the old man said, "Peace be to you; I will care for all your wants. Only, do not spend the night in the square." 21So he brought him into his house and gave the donkeys feed. And they washed their feet, and ate and drank.

Gibeah's Crime

22As they were making their hearts merry, behold, the men of the city, worthless fellows, surrounded the house, beating on the door. And they said to the old man, the master of the house, "Bring out the man who came into your house, that we may know him." 23And the man, the master of the house, went out to them and said to them, "No, my brothers, do not act so wickedly; since this man has come into my house, do not do this vile thing. 24Behold, here are my virgin daughter and his concubine. Let me bring them out now. Violate them and do with them what seems good to you, but against this man do not do this outrageous thing." 25But the men would not listen to him. So the man seized his concubine and made her go out to them. And they knew her and abused her all night until the morning. And as the dawn began to break, they let her go. 26And as morning appeared, the woman came and fell down at the door of the man's house where her master was, until it was light.

27And her master rose up in the morning, and when he opened the doors of the house and went out to go on his way, behold, there was his concubine lying at the door of the house, with her hands on the threshold. 28He said to her, "Get

[1]Septuagint *my home*; compare verse 29

up, let us be going." But there was no answer. Then he put her on the donkey, and the man rose up and went away to his home. [29]And when he entered his house, he took a knife, and taking hold of his concubine he divided her, limb by limb, into twelve pieces, and sent her throughout all the territory of Israel. [30]And all who saw it said, "Such a thing has never happened or been seen from the day that the people of Israel came up out of the land of Egypt until this day; consider it, take counsel, and speak."

Israel's War with the Tribe of Benjamin

20 Then all the people of Israel came out, from Dan to Beersheba, including the land of Gilead, and the congregation assembled as one man to the LORD at Mizpah. [2]And the chiefs of all the people, of all the tribes of Israel, presented themselves in the assembly of the people of God, 400,000 men on foot that drew the sword. [3](Now the people of Benjamin heard that the people of Israel had gone up to Mizpah.) And the people of Israel said, "Tell us, how did this evil happen?" [4]And the Levite, the husband of the woman who was murdered, answered and said, "I came to Gibeah that belongs to Benjamin, I and my concubine, to spend the night. [5]And the leaders of Gibeah rose against me and surrounded the house against me by night. They meant to kill me, and they violated my concubine, and she is dead. [6]So I took hold of my concubine and cut her in pieces and sent her throughout all the country of the inheritance of Israel, for they have committed abomination and outrage in Israel. [7]Behold, you people of Israel, all of you, give your advice and counsel here."

[8]And all the people arose as one man, saying, "None of us will go to his tent, and none of us will return to his house. [9]But now this is what we will do to Gibeah: we will go up against it by lot, [10]and we will take ten men of a hundred throughout all the tribes of Israel, and a hundred of a thousand, and a thousand of ten thousand, to bring provisions for the people, that when they come they may repay Gibeah of Benjamin for all the outrage that they have committed in Israel." [11]So all the men of Israel gathered against the city, united as one man.

[12]And the tribes of Israel sent men through all the tribe of Benjamin, saying, "What evil is this that has taken place among you? [13]Now therefore give up the men, the worthless fellows in Gibeah, that we may put them to death and purge evil from Israel." But the Benjaminites would not listen to the voice of their brothers, the people of Israel. [14]Then the people of Benjamin came together out of the cities to Gibeah to go out to battle against the people of Israel. [15]And the people of Benjamin mustered out of their cities on that day 26,000 men who drew the sword, besides the inhabitants of Gibeah, who mustered 700 chosen men. [16]Among all these were 700 chosen men who were left-handed; every one could sling a stone at a hair and not miss. [17]And the men of Israel, apart from Benjamin, mustered 400,000 men who drew the sword; all these were men of war.

[18]The people of Israel arose and went up to Bethel and inquired of God, "Who shall go up first for us to fight against the people of Benjamin?" And the LORD said, "Judah shall go up first."

[19]Then the people of Israel rose in the morning and encamped against Gibeah. [20]And the men of Israel went out to fight against Benjamin, and the men of Israel drew up the battle line against them at Gibeah. [21]The people of Benjamin came out of Gibeah and destroyed on that day 22,000 men of the Israelites. [22]But the people, the men of Israel, took courage, and again formed the battle line in the same place where they had formed it on the first day. [23]And the people of Israel went up and wept before the LORD until the evening. And they inquired of the LORD, "Shall we again draw near to fight against our brothers, the people of Benjamin?" And the LORD said, "Go up against them."

[24]So the people of Israel came near against the people of Benjamin the second day. [25]And Benjamin went against them out of Gibeah the second day, and destroyed 18,000 men of the people of Israel. All these were men who drew the

sword. 26 Then all the people of Israel, the whole army, went up and came to Bethel
and wept. They sat there before the LORD and fasted that day until evening, and
offered burnt offerings and peace offerings before the LORD. 27 And the people of
Israel inquired of the LORD (for the ark of the covenant of God was there in those
days, 28 and Phinehas the son of Eleazar, son of Aaron, ministered before it in
those days), saying, "Shall we go out once more to battle against our brothers, the
people of Benjamin, or shall we cease?" And the LORD said, "Go up, for tomorrow
I will give them into your hand."

29 So Israel set men in ambush around Gibeah. 30 And the people of Israel went
up against the people of Benjamin on the third day and set themselves in array
against Gibeah, as at other times. 31 And the people of Benjamin went out against
the people and were drawn away from the city. And as at other times they began
to strike and kill some of the people in the highways, one of which goes up to
Bethel and the other to Gibeah, and in the open country, about thirty men of
Israel. 32 And the people of Benjamin said, "They are routed before us, as at the
first." But the people of Israel said, "Let us flee and draw them away from the
city to the highways." 33 And all the men of Israel rose up out of their place and
set themselves in array at Baal-tamar, and the men of Israel who were in ambush
rushed out of their place from Maareh-geba.[1] 34 And there came against Gibeah
10,000 chosen men out of all Israel, and the battle was hard, but the Benjaminites
did not know that disaster was close upon them. 35 And the LORD defeated Benjamin before Israel, and the people of Israel destroyed 25,100 men of Benjamin that
day. All these were men who drew the sword. 36 So the people of Benjamin saw
that they were defeated.

The men of Israel gave ground to Benjamin, because they trusted the men in
ambush whom they had set against Gibeah. 37 Then the men in ambush hurried
and rushed against Gibeah; the men in ambush moved out and struck all the city
with the edge of the sword. 38 Now the appointed signal between the men of Israel
and the men in the main ambush was that when they made a great cloud of smoke
rise up out of the city 39 the men of Israel should turn in battle. Now Benjamin
had begun to strike and kill about thirty men of Israel. They said, "Surely they
are defeated before us, as in the first battle." 40 But when the signal began to rise
out of the city in a column of smoke, the Benjaminites looked behind them, and
behold, the whole of the city went up in smoke to heaven. 41 Then the men of Israel
turned, and the men of Benjamin were dismayed, for they saw that disaster was
close upon them. 42 Therefore they turned their backs before the men of Israel
in the direction of the wilderness, but the battle overtook them. And those who
came out of the cities were destroying them in their midst. 43 Surrounding the
Benjaminites, they pursued them and trod them down from Nohah[2] as far as opposite Gibeah on the east. 44 Eighteen thousand men of Benjamin fell, all of them
men of valor. 45 And they turned and fled toward the wilderness to the rock of
Rimmon. Five thousand men of them were cut down in the highways. And they
were pursued hard to Gidom, and 2,000 men of them were struck down. 46 So all
who fell that day of Benjamin were 25,000 men who drew the sword, all of them
men of valor. 47 But 600 men turned and fled toward the wilderness to the rock
of Rimmon and remained at the rock of Rimmon four months. 48 And the men of
Israel turned back against the people of Benjamin and struck them with the edge
of the sword, the city, men and beasts and all that they found. And all the towns
that they found they set on fire.

Wives Provided for the Tribe of Benjamin

21 Now the men of Israel had sworn at Mizpah, "No one of us shall give his
daughter in marriage to Benjamin." 2 And the people came to Bethel and
sat there till evening before God, and they lifted up their voices and wept bitterly.

[1] Some Septuagint manuscripts *place west of Geba* [2] Septuagint; Hebrew [at their] *resting place*

NOT JUST ANY KING

The anticlimactic ending of the book of Judges portrays a hopeless nation. Throughout the book, the author noted a correlation between the evil of the people and the absence of a king (17:6; 18:1; 19:1; 21:25). Each time, though, it appears that the sin of the people advanced in terms of its scope and destructive impact. Here the people who were meant to dwell in an amazing land and delight in fellowship with God are presented as a divided people living in constant fear.

The blame is placed squarely on the shoulders of the people. They did what was right in their own eyes and, in so doing, failed to do what was right in the eyes of God. Like Adam and Eve in the garden, they disregarded the wisdom of God and trusted in their own discernment.

Over and over again, God's people fall prey to the temptation of Satan to trust in themselves and follow after their own desires. The apostle John explained that "all that is in the world — the desires of the flesh and the desires of the eyes and pride of life" comes from the world and is doomed for destruction (1Jn 2:16). Time after time people chase after desires that were never meant to fully satisfy their soul.

The path to life is found through a king. Not just any king, but *the* King. King Jesus invites people to follow a better leader who both models a life of total obedience to God and invites others to follow this path. Jesus, as the truer and better Adam, would do what Adam could not do. Jesus obeyed where Adam failed. Jesus led his people to obey God (Ro 5:12 – 21). He did far more than any earthly human king could ever do — he took the judgment of God. Through his death and resurrection, he grants his people the gift of a perfect, righteous standing before God. In his presence, they find acceptance, love, and forgiveness. Jesus' perfect kingship is the type of leadership that the people at the conclusion of the book of Judges — and people today — desperately need.

[3]And they said, "O LORD, the God of Israel, why has this happened in Israel, that
today there should be one tribe lacking in Israel?" [4]And the next day the people
rose early and built there an altar and offered burnt offerings and peace offerings.
[5]And the people of Israel said, "Which of all the tribes of Israel did not come up in
the assembly to the LORD?" For they had taken a great oath concerning him who
did not come up to the LORD to Mizpah, saying, "He shall surely be put to death."
[6]And the people of Israel had compassion for Benjamin their brother and said,
"One tribe is cut off from Israel this day. [7]What shall we do for wives for those
who are left, since we have sworn by the LORD that we will not give them any of
our daughters for wives?"

[8]And they said, "What one is there of the tribes of Israel that did not come up
to the LORD to Mizpah?" And behold, no one had come to the camp from Jabesh-
gilead, to the assembly. [9]For when the people were mustered, behold, not one of
the inhabitants of Jabesh-gilead was there. [10]So the congregation sent 12,000 of
their bravest men there and commanded them, "Go and strike the inhabitants
of Jabesh-gilead with the edge of the sword; also the women and the little ones.
[11]This is what you shall do: every male and every woman that has lain with a
male you shall devote to destruction." [12]And they found among the inhabitants
of Jabesh-gilead 400 young virgins who had not known a man by lying with him,
and they brought them to the camp at Shiloh, which is in the land of Canaan.

[13]Then the whole congregation sent word to the people of Benjamin who were
at the rock of Rimmon and proclaimed peace to them. [14]And Benjamin returned
at that time. And they gave them the women whom they had saved alive of the
women of Jabesh-gilead, but they were not enough for them. [15]And the people
had compassion on Benjamin because the LORD had made a breach in the tribes
of Israel.

[16]Then the elders of the congregation said, "What shall we do for wives for
those who are left, since the women are destroyed out of Benjamin?" [17]And they
said, "There must be an inheritance for the survivors of Benjamin, that a tribe not
be blotted out from Israel. [18]Yet we cannot give them wives from our daughters."
For the people of Israel had sworn, "Cursed be he who gives a wife to Benjamin."
[19]So they said, "Behold, there is the yearly feast of the LORD at Shiloh, which is
north of Bethel, on the east of the highway that goes up from Bethel to Shechem,
and south of Lebonah." [20]And they commanded the people of Benjamin, saying,
"Go and lie in ambush in the vineyards [21]and watch. If the daughters of Shiloh
come out to dance in the dances, then come out of the vineyards and snatch each
man his wife from the daughters of Shiloh, and go to the land of Benjamin. [22]And
when their fathers or their brothers come to complain to us, we will say to them,
'Grant them graciously to us, because we did not take for each man of them his
wife in battle, neither did you give them to them, else you would now be guilty.'"
[23]And the people of Benjamin did so and took their wives, according to their number, from the dancers whom they carried off. Then they went and returned to
their inheritance and rebuilt the towns and lived in them. [24]And the people of
Israel departed from there at that time, every man to his tribe and family, and they
went out from there every man to his inheritance.

[25]In those days there was no king in Israel. Everyone did what was right in his
own eyes.

JESUS: OUR REDEEMER

RUTH

RUTH

PERIOD OF THE JUDGES *c. 1375 – 1050 BC*	SAUL BECOMES KING OF ISRAEL *c. 1050 BC*	DAVID'S REIGN BEGINS *c. 1010 BC*

The book of Ruth poignantly describes a story of redemption and love. Ruth, a Moabite woman and one of the main characters of the book, was saved by the sovereign care of God. Through her relationship with her late husband and her mother-in-law, Naomi, Ruth learned about the God of Israel, became his devoted follower, and faithfully followed his leading. Undoubtedly this decision did not come without cost for Ruth, though through obedience to Yahweh she found greater blessing — both the provision she needed to survive and a central role in the family line of Jesus Christ (Ru 4:18 – 22; Mt 1:5).

The story of Ruth takes place during the time when a series of judges led the people of God. This period is known to have been a time of extreme moral decline and spiritual poverty. The story of Ruth and Boaz provides a glimpse of the hope of redemption that can come even in the midst of overwhelming cultural chaos and immorality.

The loyalty that Ruth demonstrates toward Naomi throughout the book is emblematic of the type of covenant love that God shows to his people. Even though Ruth was originally unfamiliar with the Law of God, she was a recipient of God's gracious blessings to his people.

God's sovereign work is seen throughout the story of Ruth and Boaz. The odds seemed stacked against their relationship from the outset — Ruth was an outsider who, after suffering great loss, followed her mother-in-law to Bethlehem. She had every reason to feel discouraged and defeated. Without a husband or a family, Ruth's future prospects were dim. She was a poverty-stricken widow scraping out a meager existence by gleaning what the harvesters left in the wheat fields. What she could not see is clear to the modern reader — God was orchestrating all the seemingly isolated events of her life to bring her to the knowledge of the one true and living God and into the blessing that he had promised to his children.

A central concept of the book, and the role played by Boaz, Ruth's eventual husband, is that of a redeemer. In ancient Israel, a man's nearest relative was expected to marry a widow and provide for her needs to fulfill the obligations of her husband, including providing an heir. Boaz claimed that responsibility for Naomi's deceased husband and sons, dramatically changing the lives and the futures of both Ruth and Naomi. Like Boaz, Jesus was a redeemer. He paid the ultimate price for humanity's redemption — his own blood — and claimed his people by the power of his love, changing their eternal futures. Boaz's love for Ruth is a picture of the way that God loves his church. He takes notice of her, redeems her, lavishes grace upon her, and places her within the community of faith as her redeemer. God blessed the marriage of Ruth and Boaz with a child who would become an ancestor to King David and later a part of the earthly line of the promised Messiah.

THE LORD REPAY YOU FOR WHAT YOU HAVE DONE,
AND A FULL REWARD BE GIVEN YOU BY THE LORD,
THE GOD OF ISRAEL, UNDER WHOSE WINGS
YOU HAVE COME TO TAKE REFUGE!

Ruth 2:12

RUTH

RUTH 1:1 – 2

BETHLEHEM AND THE STORY OF RUTH

Even the smallest details in Scripture matter. Bethlehem means "house of food" or "house of bread" and is the place where the Messiah was prophesied to come from (Mic 5:2). When the Israelites were wandering in the desert, God gave them manna from heaven (Ex 16:31). He provided for his people, foreshadowing the ultimate and final provision they would have in Jesus Christ. Jesus called himself the bread of life (Jn 6:35). Through the story of Ruth, God preserved and protected the line of David, thus protecting the lineage of Jesus (Mt 1:1 – 17). The symbolism of food found in the story of Ruth is a reminder that even the smallest details matter in the story of God.

RUTH 1:14 – 17

RUTH'S CHOICE

As the story unfolds, the character of Ruth takes shape as she swears an oath to stay with her mother-in-law after her husband's untimely death. She had to choose between her old life and the gods of her people or her husband's family and their God. She chose the latter. Ruth must have seen something different in her mother-in-law, and Ruth began to serve the one true God. Throughout the book of Ruth, God honored that choice in many ways, with the most incredible one being that Ruth, a woman and foreigner from humble beginnings, ultimately became part of the lineage

(continued on page 380)

Naomi Widowed

1 In the days when the judges ruled there was a famine in the land, and a man
of Bethlehem in Judah went to sojourn in the country of Moab, he and his
wife and his two sons. [2]The name of the man was Elimelech and the name of his
wife Naomi, and the names of his two sons were Mahlon and Chilion. They were
Ephrathites from Bethlehem in Judah. They went into the country of Moab and
remained there. [3]But Elimelech, the husband of Naomi, died, and she was left
with her two sons. [4]These took Moabite wives; the name of the one was Orpah
and the name of the other Ruth. They lived there about ten years, [5]and both
Mahlon and Chilion died, so that the woman was left without her two sons and
her husband.

Ruth's Loyalty to Naomi

[6]Then she arose with her daughters-in-law to return from the country of
Moab, for she had heard in the fields of Moab that the LORD had visited his people
and given them food. [7]So she set out from the place where she was with her two
daughters-in-law, and they went on the way to return to the land of Judah. [8]But
Naomi said to her two daughters-in-law, "Go, return each of you to her mother's
house. May the LORD deal kindly with you, as you have dealt with the dead and
with me. [9]The LORD grant that you may find rest, each of you in the house of her
husband!" Then she kissed them, and they lifted up their voices and wept. [10]And
they said to her, "No, we will return with you to your people." [11]But Naomi said,
"Turn back, my daughters; why will you go with me? Have I yet sons in my womb
that they may become your husbands? [12]Turn back, my daughters; go your way,
for I am too old to have a husband. If I should say I have hope, even if I should have
a husband this night and should bear sons, [13]would you therefore wait till they
were grown? Would you therefore refrain from marrying? No, my daughters, for
it is exceedingly bitter to me for your sake that the hand of the LORD has gone out
against me." [14]Then they lifted up their voices and wept again. And Orpah kissed
her mother-in-law, but Ruth clung to her.

[15]And she said, "See, your sister-in-law has gone back to her people and to her
gods; return after your sister-in-law." [16]But Ruth said, "Do not urge me to leave
you or to return from following you. For where you go I will go, and where you
lodge I will lodge. Your people shall be my people, and your God my God. [17]Where
you die I will die, and there will I be buried. May the LORD do so to me and more
also if anything but death parts me from you." [18]And when Naomi saw that she
was determined to go with her, she said no more.

Naomi and Ruth Return

[19]So the two of them went on until they came to Bethlehem. And when they
came to Bethlehem, the whole town was stirred because of them. And the women
said, "Is this Naomi?" [20]She said to them, "Do not call me Naomi;[1] call me Mara,[2]
for the Almighty has dealt very bitterly with me. [21]I went away full, and the LORD
has brought me back empty. Why call me Naomi, when the LORD has testified
against me and the Almighty has brought calamity upon me?"

[22]So Naomi returned, and Ruth the Moabite her daughter-in-law with her,
who returned from the country of Moab. And they came to Bethlehem at the beginning of barley harvest.

---

[1] *Naomi* means *pleasant* [2] *Mara* means *bitter*

GOD AND THE WORLD

Ruth was determined to remain by her mother-in-law's side. This was important since her assertion that Naomi's God would be her God is an affirmation of her faith in the one true God of Israel. She was choosing to cling to God, to Naomi, and to Naomi's people, forsaking all that she had ever known to follow God. Ruth had an opportunity to choose between making a new life with God or returning to her old way of life and the idols of her people. She decided to remain fervently and stubbornly by her mother-in-law's side to serve God and stay true to the faith she had come to know.

It is amazing that God chose someone (a woman no less) outside of the Jewish faith to not only follow the God of Israel but also to become a part of the lineage of the Messiah (Mt 1:5). This was a shadow of the reality that would be the redemption of the entire world, first for the Jew and then for the Gentile (Ro 1:16). Jesus would not only be the Savior of the Jews but of the whole world. He actually had Gentile (non-Jewish) blood running through his human veins, thanks to "outsiders" in his family line such as Ruth. When he came to earth, he made it abundantly clear that salvation was offered for the whole world.

Similar to Ruth, who was brought into the family of God through her Jewish family and her faith, followers of Jesus are brought into the family of God through faith in Christ and grace given by God. "So then you are no longer strangers and aliens, but you are fellow citizens with the saints and members of the household of God, built on the foundation of the apostles and prophets, Christ Jesus himself being the cornerstone" (Eph 2:19 – 20). John writes in John 3:16, which has become an epic anthem for the worldwide church epitomizing the gospel message, "For God so loved the world, that he gave his only Son, that whoever believes in him should not perish but have eternal life."

(Ruth's Choice, continued)

of the Messiah (4:18–22; Mt 1:5). She walked with the wise (Naomi) and became wise (Pr 13:20). She honored God and he brought her into his story. Similarly, those who follow Christ can choose to honor God with their choices and draw near to him, and he will, in turn, draw near to them (Jas 4:8).

RUTH 2:8–12

KINDNESS TO A FOREIGNER

Kindness and family are strong themes throughout the book of Ruth. The word "kindly" in Ruth 1:8 means "loyal love" and refers to the loyalty of God to the covenant of his people. Naomi expressed the hope that the Lord's love would extend to her daughters-in-law, who were not Jewish. It is mentioned repeatedly that Ruth was a Moabite, a foreigner, but she was brought into the family of God through her earthly family.

Boaz reached out to Ruth with great kindness and respect. He allowed her to gather barley in his field and eat with the harvesters, providing protection and provision for her needs. Boaz showed his great faith and integrity in this small act. Based upon Levitical law, harvesting was to be done with only one pass, leaving behind some for the poor and foreigners (of which Ruth was both) to gather for their needs. The heart of this law was to allow God's people to respond to his provision by being generous to those with less.

Ruth Meets Boaz

2 Now Naomi had a relative of her husband's, a worthy man of the clan of Elimelech, whose name was Boaz. 2And Ruth the Moabite said to Naomi, "Let me go to the field and glean among the ears of grain after him in whose sight I shall find favor." And she said to her, "Go, my daughter." 3So she set out and went and gleaned in the field after the reapers, and she happened to come to the part of the field belonging to Boaz, who was of the clan of Elimelech. 4And behold, Boaz came from Bethlehem. And he said to the reapers, "The LORD be with you!" And they answered, "The LORD bless you." 5Then Boaz said to his young man who was in charge of the reapers, "Whose young woman is this?" 6And the servant who was in charge of the reapers answered, "She is the young Moabite woman, who came back with Naomi from the country of Moab. 7She said, 'Please let me glean and gather among the sheaves after the reapers.' So she came, and she has continued from early morning until now, except for a short rest."[1]

8Then Boaz said to Ruth, "Now, listen, my daughter, do not go to glean in another field or leave this one, but keep close to my young women. 9Let your eyes be on the field that they are reaping, and go after them. Have I not charged the young men not to touch you? And when you are thirsty, go to the vessels and drink what the young men have drawn." 10Then she fell on her face, bowing to the ground, and said to him, "Why have I found favor in your eyes, that you should take notice of me, since I am a foreigner?" 11But Boaz answered her, "All that you have done for your mother-in-law since the death of your husband has been fully told to me, and how you left your father and mother and your native land and came to a people that you did not know before. 12The LORD repay you for what you have done, and a full reward be given you by the LORD, the God of Israel, under whose wings you have come to take refuge!" 13Then she said, "I have found favor in your eyes, my lord, for you have comforted me and spoken kindly to your servant, though I am not one of your servants."

14And at mealtime Boaz said to her, "Come here and eat some bread and dip your morsel in the wine." So she sat beside the reapers, and he passed to her roasted grain. And she ate until she was satisfied, and she had some left over. 15When she rose to glean, Boaz instructed his young men, saying, "Let her glean even among the sheaves, and do not reproach her. 16And also pull out some from the bundles for her and leave it for her to glean, and do not rebuke her."

17So she gleaned in the field until evening. Then she beat out what she had gleaned, and it was about an ephah[2] of barley. 18And she took it up and went into the city. Her mother-in-law saw what she had gleaned. She also brought out and gave her what food she had left over after being satisfied. 19And her mother-in-law said to her, "Where did you glean today? And where have you worked? Blessed be the man who took notice of you." So she told her mother-in-law with whom she had worked and said, "The man's name with whom I worked today is Boaz." 20And Naomi said to her daughter-in-law, "May he be blessed by the LORD, whose kindness has not forsaken the living or the dead!" Naomi also said to her, "The man is a close relative of ours, one of our redeemers." 21And Ruth the Moabite said, "Besides, he said to me, 'You shall keep close by my young men until they have finished all my harvest.'" 22And Naomi said to Ruth, her daughter-in-law, "It is good, my daughter, that you go out with his young women, lest in another field you be assaulted." 23So she kept close to the young women of Boaz, gleaning until the end of the barley and wheat harvests. And she lived with her mother-in-law.

Ruth and Boaz at the Threshing Floor

3 Then Naomi her mother-in-law said to her, "My daughter, should I not seek rest for you, that it may be well with you? 2Is not Boaz our relative, with whose young women you were? See, he is winnowing barley tonight at the threshing

---

[1]Compare Septuagint, Vulgate; the meaning of the Hebrew phrase is uncertain [2]An *ephah* was about 3/5 bushel or 22 liters

floor. 3Wash therefore and anoint yourself, and put on your cloak and go down to the threshing floor, but do not make yourself known to the man until he has finished eating and drinking. 4But when he lies down, observe the place where he lies. Then go and uncover his feet and lie down, and he will tell you what to do." 5And she replied, "All that you say I will do."

6So she went down to the threshing floor and did just as her mother-in-law had commanded her. 7And when Boaz had eaten and drunk, and his heart was merry, he went to lie down at the end of the heap of grain. Then she came softly and uncovered his feet and lay down. 8At midnight the man was startled and turned over, and behold, a woman lay at his feet! 9He said, "Who are you?" And she answered, "I am Ruth, your servant. Spread your wings[1] over your servant, for you are a redeemer." 10And he said, "May you be blessed by the LORD, my daughter. You have made this last kindness greater than the first in that you have not gone after young men, whether poor or rich. 11And now, my daughter, do not fear. I will do for you all that you ask, for all my fellow townsmen know that you are a worthy woman. 12And now it is true that I am a redeemer. Yet there is a redeemer nearer than I. 13Remain tonight, and in the morning, if he will redeem you, good; let him do it. But if he is not willing to redeem you, then, as the LORD lives, I will redeem you. Lie down until the morning."

14So she lay at his feet until the morning, but arose before one could recognize another. And he said, "Let it not be known that the woman came to the threshing floor." 15And he said, "Bring the garment you are wearing and hold it out." So she held it, and he measured out six measures of barley and put it on her. Then she went into the city. 16And when she came to her mother-in-law, she said, "How did you fare, my daughter?" Then she told her all that the man had done for her, 17saying, "These six measures of barley he gave to me, for he said to me, 'You must not go back empty-handed to your mother-in-law.'" 18She replied, "Wait, my daughter, until you learn how the matter turns out, for the man will not rest but will settle the matter today."

Boaz Redeems Ruth

4 Now Boaz had gone up to the gate and sat down there. And behold, the redeemer, of whom Boaz had spoken, came by. So Boaz said, "Turn aside, friend; sit down here." And he turned aside and sat down. 2And he took ten men of the elders of the city and said, "Sit down here." So they sat down. 3Then he said to the redeemer, "Naomi, who has come back from the country of Moab, is selling the parcel of land that belonged to our relative Elimelech. 4So I thought I would tell you of it and say, 'Buy it in the presence of those sitting here and in the presence of the elders of my people.' If you will redeem it, redeem it. But if you[2] will not, tell me, that I may know, for there is no one besides you to redeem it, and I come after you." And he said, "I will redeem it." 5Then Boaz said, "The day you buy the field from the hand of Naomi, you also acquire Ruth[3] the Moabite, the widow of the dead, in order to perpetuate the name of the dead in his inheritance." 6Then the redeemer said, "I cannot redeem it for myself, lest I impair my own inheritance. Take my right of redemption yourself, for I cannot redeem it."

7Now this was the custom in former times in Israel concerning redeeming and exchanging: to confirm a transaction, the one drew off his sandal and gave it to the other, and this was the manner of attesting in Israel. 8So when the redeemer said to Boaz, "Buy it for yourself," he drew off his sandal. 9Then Boaz said to the elders and all the people, "You are witnesses this day that I have bought from the hand of Naomi all that belonged to Elimelech and all that belonged to Chilion and to Mahlon. 10Also Ruth the Moabite, the widow of Mahlon, I have bought to be my wife, to perpetuate the name of the dead in his inheritance, that the name of the

[1]Compare 2:12; the word for *wings* can also mean *corners of a garment* [2]Hebrew *he* [3]Masoretic Text *you also buy it from Ruth*

RUTH 3:11

RUTH: AN UNLIKELY CHOICE

When Boaz acknowledged that Ruth was a "worthy woman," he used the same Hebrew phrase as is found in Proverbs 31:10. In this time period, it would be considered outrageous, even absurd, that a woman who was not of Jewish descent would be the star of a book situated in the original Hebrew Bible. The Jewish audience reading Ruth would immediately recognize this embodiment of a noble woman as that used in Proverbs 31. The same Hebrew phrasing is used in both places, and it is astounding that words famously written to depict a highly honored, godly woman would also be used to describe Ruth. God chose an unlikely person to show his love and mercy to his people. In the same way, God has chosen to show his love to his people through what Jesus has done, choosing them in him before the foundation of the world (Eph 1:4), thus enabling them to choose a new life with him despite their sin and rebellion.

JESUS: OUR REDEEMER

The book of Ruth is a beautiful picture of God's plan for redemption that was ultimately realized in Jesus. A clear picture of Jesus can be seen through Boaz's relationship with Ruth as her "redeemer." Upon the death of her husband, Ruth had only her mother-in-law, Naomi. Both were poor and dependent on the kindness of others for their well-being. Naomi sent Ruth to gather grain in a nearby field, and a series of events led to Boaz acting as a possible "redeemer" and eventually a marriage, ultimately redeeming Ruth's family name and securing her place in the lineage of Jesus.

A redeemer, or *ga'al* (*go'el*) in the Hebrew, refers to a close relative who acts as a protector of the family rights. He could be called upon to perform a number of duties including buying back property the family had sold, providing an heir for a deceased relative, releasing a family member from slavery, or avenging a relative's murder. God calls himself the "Redeemer" or close relative of Israel in Isaiah 60:16.

By becoming human, Jesus became humanity's own Redeemer. He came from heaven and walked the earth, bringing with him restoration and making it available to all people through the cross and a relationship with him. Just as Boaz made it possible for Naomi and Ruth's lineage to live on, now through Christ all believers are made holy, invited into the family of God (Heb 2:11), and become heirs of God and co-heirs with Christ (Ro 8:17). Just as Boaz preserved and protected Ruth's family and their future, in the most perfect way Christ preserves his people, restores dignity, and gives hope for the future. Reading and studying Ruth in light of what has now been revealed in Jesus shows not only the glorious stamp of God and his work in Ruth's day, but also the undeniable way that redemption in Christ was being prepared before the foundation of time. Jesus was then and is now the true Redeemer, always the ultimate protector, the One who continues to preserve the very lives of his people today, as they continue to follow him day by day.

dead may not be cut off from among his brothers and from the gate of his native
place. You are witnesses this day." [11]Then all the people who were at the gate and
the elders said, "We are witnesses. May the LORD make the woman, who is coming
into your house, like Rachel and Leah, who together built up the house of Israel.
May you act worthily in Ephrathah and be renowned in Bethlehem, [12]and may
your house be like the house of Perez, whom Tamar bore to Judah, because of the
offspring that the LORD will give you by this young woman."

Ruth and Boaz Marry

[13]So Boaz took Ruth, and she became his wife. And he went in to her, and the
LORD gave her conception, and she bore a son. [14]Then the women said to Naomi,
"Blessed be the LORD, who has not left you this day without a redeemer, and may
his name be renowned in Israel! [15]He shall be to you a restorer of life and a nour-
isher of your old age, for your daughter-in-law who loves you, who is more to you
than seven sons, has given birth to him." [16]Then Naomi took the child and laid
him on her lap and became his nurse. [17]And the women of the neighborhood gave
him a name, saying, "A son has been born to Naomi." They named him Obed. He
was the father of Jesse, the father of David.

The Genealogy of David

[18]Now these are the generations of Perez: Perez fathered Hezron, [19]Hezron
fathered Ram, Ram fathered Amminadab, [20]Amminadab fathered Nahshon,
Nahshon fathered Salmon, [21]Salmon fathered Boaz, Boaz fathered Obed, [22]Obed
fathered Jesse, and Jesse fathered David.

RUTH 4:13–17

A GOD OF ABUNDANCE

At the beginning of the book of Ruth, Naomi said the Lord had "dealt very bitterly with" her and "brought calamity" on her. By the end of the book of Ruth, God had not only restored Ruth through her redeemer Boaz, but he had also provided for Naomi. This is a beautiful restoration of her life. God took Naomi's emptiness and bitterness (1:20–21) and replaced it with abundance and blessing through Ruth and Boaz and their child Obed.

Fullness can be experienced when people come to know Jesus and become part of the church. They go from emptiness to abundance in Christ. Boaz gave Ruth an overabundance of food to take back to Naomi, and Naomi immediately blessed Boaz for his kindness (2:14–20). Her emptiness began to turn into fullness. God provided for Ruth and her mother-in-law through Boaz, and in the same way, he has provided for all of our needs through Christ.

JESUS: OUR TRUE KING

1 SAMUEL

1 SAMUEL

SAMUEL IS BORN *c. 1105 BC*	SAMUEL ANOINTS DAVID *c. 1025 BC*	REIGN OF DAVID BEGINS *c. 1010 BC*

The book of 1 Samuel opens at a spiritual low point in the nation of Israel. The judges were still ruling over Israel, and the people had continued to fall prey to idolatry. Even some of the priests had been corrupted by heinous sin. The failure of Israel's leaders accentuated the people's moral perversion; they showed open disdain for God and his word. In the face of such rebellion, however, God protected a remnant of faithful Israelites who loved God and kept his word.

The moral chaos prompted infighting among the people of God and rebellion against the rule of the judges. The nation longed for a king to lead them — a desire they developed through watching the surrounding nations. They were under constant threat and harassment by neighboring powers, and they wanted a king to unify them so that they could protect themselves. Despite Samuel's warnings (1Sa 8:6 – 20) the people persisted in their request, and God granted it. He called a man who seemed to possess all of the marks of a king — he was handsome, tall, and early on in his reign showed signs of strong military prowess. The people appointed Saul by lot, and he led God's people for forty years (1Sa 10). His ultimately fatal flaw was his repeated disregard for God's commands late in his reign. His rebellion incurred God's judgment; God rejected him as king and allowed him to suffer the consequences of his folly.

God prompted Samuel to anoint David as king over Israel while Saul was still in power. As young David's reputation for following God's direction with courage and conviction grew, Saul even brought him on as a leader in the Israelite military. David's fame grew and Saul quickly lost heart, became jealous of David's victories, and eventually tried to kill David. In the wake of Saul's failure to obey him, God raised up King David, who obeyed God's commands and led Israel in a way Saul never could.

The united monarchy in Israel demonstrated how God led his people through human agents. These leaders were entrusted with the task of speaking God's word and modeling God's character to lead the people of Israel to obey him in all things. Sin effectively hamstrung these men in their attempt to provide the type of leadership God desired, exposing the fact that no human leader can provide perfect leadership for his people. Only the true King, Jesus Christ, can ever provide the kind of leadership that faithfully represents God and his will for humanity.

THERE IS NONE HOLY LIKE THE LORD:
FOR THERE IS NONE BESIDES YOU;
THERE IS NO ROCK LIKE OUR GOD.

---

1 Samuel 2:2

1 SAMUEL

The Birth of Samuel

1 There was a certain man of Ramathaim-zophim of the hill country of Ephraim
whose name was Elkanah the son of Jeroham, son of Elihu, son of Tohu, son
of Zuph, an Ephrathite. 2He had two wives. The name of the one was Hannah,
and the name of the other, Peninnah. And Peninnah had children, but Hannah
had no children.
3Now this man used to go up year by year from his city to worship and to sacrifice to the LORD of hosts at Shiloh, where the two sons of Eli, Hophni and Phinehas, were priests of the LORD. 4On the day when Elkanah sacrificed, he would give
portions to Peninnah his wife and to all her sons and daughters. 5But to Hannah
he gave a double portion, because he loved her, though the LORD had closed her
womb.[1] 6And her rival used to provoke her grievously to irritate her, because the
LORD had closed her womb. 7So it went on year by year. As often as she went up
to the house of the LORD, she used to provoke her. Therefore Hannah wept and
would not eat. 8And Elkanah, her husband, said to her, "Hannah, why do you
weep? And why do you not eat? And why is your heart sad? Am I not more to you
than ten sons?"
9After they had eaten and drunk in Shiloh, Hannah rose. Now Eli the priest
was sitting on the seat beside the doorpost of the temple of the LORD. 10She was
deeply distressed and prayed to the LORD and wept bitterly. 11And she vowed a vow
and said, "O LORD of hosts, if you will indeed look on the affliction of your servant
and remember me and not forget your servant, but will give to your servant a son,
then I will give him to the LORD all the days of his life, and no razor shall touch
his head."
12As she continued praying before the LORD, Eli observed her mouth. 13Han-
nah was speaking in her heart; only her lips moved, and her voice was not heard.
Therefore Eli took her to be a drunken woman. 14And Eli said to her, "How long
will you go on being drunk? Put your wine away from you." 15But Hannah answered, "No, my lord, I am a woman troubled in spirit. I have drunk neither wine
nor strong drink, but I have been pouring out my soul before the LORD. 16Do not
regard your servant as a worthless woman, for all along I have been speaking out
of my great anxiety and vexation." 17Then Eli answered, "Go in peace, and the God
of Israel grant your petition that you have made to him." 18And she said, "Let your
servant find favor in your eyes." Then the woman went her way and ate, and her
face was no longer sad.
19They rose early in the morning and worshiped before the LORD; then they
went back to their house at Ramah. And Elkanah knew Hannah his wife, and
the LORD remembered her. 20And in due time Hannah conceived and bore a
son, and she called his name Samuel, for she said, "I have asked for him from
the LORD."[2]

Samuel Given to the LORD

21The man Elkanah and all his house went up to offer to the LORD the yearly
sacrifice and to pay his vow. 22But Hannah did not go up, for she said to her husband, "As soon as the child is weaned, I will bring him, so that he may appear in
the presence of the LORD and dwell there forever." 23Elkanah her husband said to
her, "Do what seems best to you; wait until you have weaned him; only, may the
LORD establish his word." So the woman remained and nursed her son until she

[1]Syriac; the meaning of the Hebrew is uncertain. Septuagint *And, although he loved Hannah, he would give Hannah only one portion, because the LORD had closed her womb* [2]*Samuel* sounds like the Hebrew for *heard of God*

weaned him. 24And when she had weaned him, she took him up with her, along
with a three-year-old bull,[1] an ephah[2] of flour, and a skin of wine, and she brought
him to the house of the LORD at Shiloh. And the child was young. 25Then they
slaughtered the bull, and they brought the child to Eli. 26And she said, "Oh, my
lord! As you live, my lord, I am the woman who was standing here in your presence, praying to the LORD. 27For this child I prayed, and the LORD has granted me
my petition that I made to him. 28Therefore I have lent him to the LORD. As long as
he lives, he is lent to the LORD."

And he worshiped the LORD there.

Hannah's Prayer

2 And Hannah prayed and said,

"My heart exults in the LORD;
my horn is exalted in the LORD.
My mouth derides my enemies,
because I rejoice in your salvation.

2 "There is none holy like the LORD:
for there is none besides you;
there is no rock like our God.
3 Talk no more so very proudly,
let not arrogance come from your mouth;
for the LORD is a God of knowledge,
and by him actions are weighed.
4 The bows of the mighty are broken,
but the feeble bind on strength.
5 Those who were full have hired themselves out for
bread,
but those who were hungry have ceased to hunger.
The barren has borne seven,
but she who has many children is forlorn.
6 The LORD kills and brings to life;
he brings down to Sheol and raises up.
7 The LORD makes poor and makes rich;
he brings low and he exalts.
8 He raises up the poor from the dust;
he lifts the needy from the ash heap
to make them sit with princes
and inherit a seat of honor.
For the pillars of the earth are the LORD's,
and on them he has set the world.

9 "He will guard the feet of his faithful ones,
but the wicked shall be cut off in darkness,
for not by might shall a man prevail.
10 The adversaries of the LORD shall be broken to pieces;
against them he will thunder in heaven.
The LORD will judge the ends of the earth;
he will give strength to his king
and exalt the horn of his anointed."

11Then Elkanah went home to Ramah. And the boy[3] was ministering to the
LORD in the presence of Eli the priest.

[1]Dead Sea Scroll, Septuagint, Syriac; Masoretic Text *three bulls* [2]An *ephah* was about 3/5 bushel or 22 liters [3]Hebrew *na'ar* can be rendered *boy* (2:11, 18, 21, 26; 3:1, 8), *servant* (2:13, 15), or *young man* (2:17), depending on the context

1 SAMUEL 2:9–10

HANNAH'S PRAYER

Hannah's prayer echoed the longing of God's people. They were waiting for a king who would reign with power and bring stability and safety to Israel. Hannah's prayer demonstrated the characteristics of a world under the rule and reign of God. It will be a world where God delivers his people, silences his enemies, and brings justice to the entire world. The longing for a king like this is expressed in the final words of Hannah's prayer. She prayed with anticipation for a king that would be strengthened and anointed by God. Hannah directed the reader toward a messianic figure, a savior of God's people, who would bring justice and peace to the world.

Years later, Mary, the mother of Jesus, offered a prayer similar to Hannah's (Lk 1:46–55). Mary's prayer anticipated the arrival of a far greater King who would do what no Old Testament king could do—usher in the rule and reign of God.

Eli's Worthless Sons

12Now the sons of Eli were worthless men. They did not know the LORD. 13The custom of the priests with the people was that when any man offered sacrifice, the priest's servant would come, while the meat was boiling, with a three-pronged fork in his hand, 14and he would thrust it into the pan or kettle or cauldron or pot. All that the fork brought up the priest would take for himself. This is what they did at Shiloh to all the Israelites who came there. 15Moreover, before the fat was burned, the priest's servant would come and say to the man who was sacrificing, "Give meat for the priest to roast, for he will not accept boiled meat from you but only raw." 16And if the man said to him, "Let them burn the fat first, and then take as much as you wish," he would say, "No, you must give it now, and if not, I will take it by force." 17Thus the sin of the young men was very great in the sight of the LORD, for the men treated the offering of the LORD with contempt.

18Samuel was ministering before the LORD, a boy clothed with a linen ephod. 19And his mother used to make for him a little robe and take it to him each year when she went up with her husband to offer the yearly sacrifice. 20Then Eli would bless Elkanah and his wife, and say, "May the LORD give you children by this woman for the petition she asked of the LORD." So then they would return to their home.

21Indeed the LORD visited Hannah, and she conceived and bore three sons and two daughters. And the boy Samuel grew in the presence of the LORD.

Eli Rebukes His Sons

22Now Eli was very old, and he kept hearing all that his sons were doing to all Israel, and how they lay with the women who were serving at the entrance to the tent of meeting. 23And he said to them, "Why do you do such things? For I hear of your evil dealings from all these people. 24No, my sons; it is no good report that I hear the people of the LORD spreading abroad. 25If someone sins against a man, God will mediate for him, but if someone sins against the LORD, who can intercede for him?" But they would not listen to the voice of their father, for it was the will of the LORD to put them to death.

26Now the boy Samuel continued to grow both in stature and in favor with the LORD and also with man.

The LORD Rejects Eli's Household

27And there came a man of God to Eli and said to him, "Thus says the LORD, 'Did I indeed reveal myself to the house of your father when they were in Egypt subject to the house of Pharaoh? 28Did I choose him out of all the tribes of Israel to be my priest, to go up to my altar, to burn incense, to wear an ephod before me? I gave to the house of your father all my offerings by fire from the people of Israel. 29Why then do you scorn[1] my sacrifices and my offerings that I commanded for my dwelling, and honor your sons above me by fattening yourselves on the choicest parts of every offering of my people Israel?' 30Therefore the LORD, the God of Israel, declares: 'I promised that your house and the house of your father should go in and out before me forever,' but now the LORD declares: 'Far be it from me, for those who honor me I will honor, and those who despise me shall be lightly esteemed. 31Behold, the days are coming when I will cut off your strength and the strength of your father's house, so that there will not be an old man in your house. 32Then in distress you will look with envious eye on all the prosperity that shall be bestowed on Israel, and there shall not be an old man in your house forever. 33The only one of you whom I shall not cut off from my altar shall be spared to weep his[2] eyes out to grieve his heart, and all the descendants[3] of your house shall die by the sword of men.[4] 34And this that shall come upon

[1]Hebrew *kick at* [2]Septuagint; Hebrew *your*; twice in this verse [3]Hebrew *increase* [4]Septuagint; Hebrew *die as men*

your two sons, Hophni and Phinehas, shall be the sign to you: both of them shall die on the same day. [35]And I will raise up for myself a faithful priest, who shall do according to what is in my heart and in my mind. And I will build him a sure house, and he shall go in and out before my anointed forever. [36]And everyone who is left in your house shall come to implore him for a piece of silver or a loaf of bread and shall say, "Please put me in one of the priests' places, that I may eat a morsel of bread."'"

The Lord Calls Samuel

3 Now the boy Samuel was ministering to the LORD in the presence of Eli. And the word of the LORD was rare in those days; there was no frequent vision.

[2]At that time Eli, whose eyesight had begun to grow dim so that he could not see, was lying down in his own place. [3]The lamp of God had not yet gone out, and Samuel was lying down in the temple of the LORD, where the ark of God was.

[4]Then the LORD called Samuel, and he said, "Here I am!" [5]and ran to Eli and said, "Here I am, for you called me." But he said, "I did not call; lie down again." So he went and lay down.

[6]And the LORD called again, "Samuel!" and Samuel arose and went to Eli and said, "Here I am, for you called me." But he said, "I did not call, my son; lie down again." [7]Now Samuel did not yet know the LORD, and the word of the LORD had not yet been revealed to him.

[8]And the LORD called Samuel again the third time. And he arose and went to Eli and said, "Here I am, for you called me." Then Eli perceived that the LORD was calling the boy. [9]Therefore Eli said to Samuel, "Go, lie down, and if he calls you, you shall say, 'Speak, LORD, for your servant hears.'" So Samuel went and lay down in his place.

[10]And the LORD came and stood, calling as at other times, "Samuel! Samuel!" And Samuel said, "Speak, for your servant hears." [11]Then the LORD said to Samuel, "Behold, I am about to do a thing in Israel at which the two ears of everyone who hears it will tingle. [12]On that day I will fulfill against Eli all that I have spoken concerning his house, from beginning to end. [13]And I declare to him that I am about to punish his house forever, for the iniquity that he knew, because his sons were blaspheming God,[1] and he did not restrain them. [14]Therefore I swear to the house of Eli that the iniquity of Eli's house shall not be atoned for by sacrifice or offering forever."

[15]Samuel lay until morning; then he opened the doors of the house of the LORD. And Samuel was afraid to tell the vision to Eli. [16]But Eli called Samuel and said, "Samuel, my son." And he said, "Here I am." [17]And Eli said, "What was it that he told you? Do not hide it from me. May God do so to you and more also if you hide anything from me of all that he told you." [18]So Samuel told him everything and hid nothing from him. And he said, "It is the LORD. Let him do what seems good to him."

[19]And Samuel grew, and the LORD was with him and let none of his words fall to the ground. [20]And all Israel from Dan to Beersheba knew that Samuel was established as a prophet of the LORD. [21]And the LORD appeared again at Shiloh, for the LORD revealed himself to Samuel at Shiloh by the word of the LORD.

The Philistines Capture the Ark

4 And the word of Samuel came to all Israel.
Now Israel went out to battle against the Philistines. They encamped at Ebenezer, and the Philistines encamped at Aphek. [2]The Philistines drew up in line against Israel, and when the battle spread, Israel was defeated before the Philistines, who killed about four thousand men on the field of battle. [3]And when the people came to the camp, the elders of Israel said, "Why has the LORD defeated

[1]Or *blaspheming for themselves*

1 SAMUEL 3:19–21

THE CALL OF SAMUEL

Israel was in a desperate time in history. Their priests were tarnished and doomed by the wickedness of Eli's sons and Eli's failure to restrain or remove them (1Sa 2:12–36), and Israel was without a prophet because no one was speaking the word of the Lord (1Sa 3:1). They were experiencing moral anarchy, as "everyone did what was right in his own eyes" (Jdg 21:25). It was a time when Israel was in dire need of a priest to serve the people faithfully, a prophet to speak the word of the Lord, and a judge to lead the people in the pursuit of justice and righteousness. God called Samuel to fill these roles. The Lord was with Samuel as he grew up, and Samuel fulfilled these roles for the sake of Israel.

Samuel's faithfulness directs attention to the One who would serve as an even greater prophet, priest, and judge. Jesus would be the ultimate prophet, preaching with authority (Mk 1:27). He would be the ultimate priest, offering himself as the atoning sacrifice for the sins of the world (Heb 9:11–14). He would stand before his Father, the ultimate judge (Jn 5:27–30), completely innocent but offering himself in the place of sinners.

SPEAK, FOR YOUR SERVANT HEARS

Samuel served as the assistant to the high priest Eli. One evening Samuel heard a voice calling to him. Assuming it was Eli calling, he asked what the high priest wanted from him. But Eli had not called. This happened three times when Eli realized that it must be God calling out to Samuel. Eli instructed Samuel to answer, "Speak, LORD, for your servant hears" (v. 9). Eli realized that when God speaks, one must take the time to listen. God was calling Samuel to become his prophet at a time when Israel desperately needed someone to speak the word of the Lord. Samuel was the one whom God would use to move his people from leadership by judges to rule by a king. Samuel would become a great prophet and priest for his people and would ultimately anoint Israel's first two kings, Saul and David. The Bible says that "Samuel grew, and the LORD was with him and let none of his words fall to the ground" (v. 19). God called Samuel to a great task, but it had to begin with Samuel listening to God's voice.

This is a theme that runs throughout the Scriptures. When God calls someone to lead his people, he often calls them first to a time of hearing his voice. David was anointed to be king, but before taking the throne, he first spent many years as a shepherd listening to God. The apostle Paul was called by God to become a great missionary, but before going to work, he spent three years listening to God (Gal 1:16–17). Likewise, Jesus taught that he did nothing without first hearing from the Father (Jn 5:19; 8:28; 12:49). Jesus would go on to tell his disciples that they could hear from God through the Holy Spirit and that he would guide them in the way that they should live (Lk 12:12; Jn 16:13). When a person becomes a disciple of Jesus, they are given the Spirit as a gift that takes up residence in their heart. Then the process of learning to identify the Spirit's voice begins, to become attuned to the call of God. The task of the Christian is to listen to God's voice through the Spirit and the Word and like Samuel to confess, "Speak, LORD, for your servant hears."

us today before the Philistines? Let us bring the ark of the covenant of the LORD
here from Shiloh, that it[1] may come among us and save us from the power of
our enemies." [4]So the people sent to Shiloh and brought from there the ark of
the covenant of the LORD of hosts, who is enthroned on the cherubim. And the
two sons of Eli, Hophni and Phinehas, were there with the ark of the covenant
of God.

[5]As soon as the ark of the covenant of the LORD came into the camp, all Israel gave a mighty shout, so that the earth resounded. [6]And when the Philistines
heard the noise of the shouting, they said, "What does this great shouting in the
camp of the Hebrews mean?" And when they learned that the ark of the LORD had
come to the camp, [7]the Philistines were afraid, for they said, "A god has come into
the camp." And they said, "Woe to us! For nothing like this has happened before.
[8]Woe to us! Who can deliver us from the power of these mighty gods? These are
the gods who struck the Egyptians with every sort of plague in the wilderness.
[9]Take courage, and be men, O Philistines, lest you become slaves to the Hebrews
as they have been to you; be men and fight."

[10]So the Philistines fought, and Israel was defeated, and they fled, every man
to his home. And there was a very great slaughter, for thirty thousand foot soldiers of Israel fell. [11]And the ark of God was captured, and the two sons of Eli,
Hophni and Phinehas, died.

The Death of Eli

[12]A man of Benjamin ran from the battle line and came to Shiloh the same day,
with his clothes torn and with dirt on his head. [13]When he arrived, Eli was sitting
on his seat by the road watching, for his heart trembled for the ark of God. And
when the man came into the city and told the news, all the city cried out. [14]When
Eli heard the sound of the outcry, he said, "What is this uproar?" Then the man
hurried and came and told Eli. [15]Now Eli was ninety-eight years old and his eyes
were set so that he could not see. [16]And the man said to Eli, "I am he who has
come from the battle; I fled from the battle today." And he said, "How did it go,
my son?" [17]He who brought the news answered and said, "Israel has fled before
the Philistines, and there has also been a great defeat among the people. Your two
sons also, Hophni and Phinehas, are dead, and the ark of God has been captured."
[18]As soon as he mentioned the ark of God, Eli fell over backward from his seat by
the side of the gate, and his neck was broken and he died, for the man was old and
heavy. He had judged Israel forty years.

[19]Now his daughter-in-law, the wife of Phinehas, was pregnant, about to give
birth. And when she heard the news that the ark of God was captured, and that
her father-in-law and her husband were dead, she bowed and gave birth, for her
pains came upon her. [20]And about the time of her death the women attending
her said to her, "Do not be afraid, for you have borne a son." But she did not answer or pay attention. [21]And she named the child Ichabod, saying, "The glory has
departed[2] from Israel!" because the ark of God had been captured and because of
her father-in-law and her husband. [22]And she said, "The glory has departed from
Israel, for the ark of God has been captured."

The Philistines and the Ark

5 When the Philistines captured the ark of God, they brought it from Ebenezer
to Ashdod. [2]Then the Philistines took the ark of God and brought it into the
house of Dagon and set it up beside Dagon. [3]And when the people of Ashdod rose
early the next day, behold, Dagon had fallen face downward on the ground before
the ark of the LORD. So they took Dagon and put him back in his place. [4]But when
they rose early on the next morning, behold, Dagon had fallen face downward on
the ground before the ark of the LORD, and the head of Dagon and both his hands

[1]Or *he* [2]Or *gone into exile*; also verse 22

1 SAMUEL 5:1–5

VICTORY OVER FALSE GODS

Dagon was the chief god of the Philistines and was thought to control the weather and the fertility of the land. Worship of Dagon was thought to ensure a good crop and bring blessing. The Philistines placed their hope for a blessing and a secure future in the hands of Dagon. But in the presence of the ark of God, Dagon fell on his face — as if he were worshiping the one true God — and was ultimately left in broken pieces.

This story shows that before the true God, all false gods are exposed for the frauds that they are. When people place their hope for the future in the hands of something other than God, they have created an idol. People often make idols out of success, popularity, or wealth, hoping that these things will provide ultimate joy and security. But it is only God who offers complete joy. The apostle John explained that there is coming a day when all people will be exposed as they are judged before the throne of the one true God (Rev 20:11–15).

were lying cut off on the threshold. Only the trunk of Dagon was left to him. 5This is why the priests of Dagon and all who enter the house of Dagon do not tread on the threshold of Dagon in Ashdod to this day.

6The hand of the LORD was heavy against the people of Ashdod, and he terrified and afflicted them with tumors, both Ashdod and its territory. 7And when the men of Ashdod saw how things were, they said, "The ark of the God of Israel must not remain with us, for his hand is hard against us and against Dagon our god." 8So they sent and gathered together all the lords of the Philistines and said, "What shall we do with the ark of the God of Israel?" They answered, "Let the ark of the God of Israel be brought around to Gath." So they brought the ark of the God of Israel there. 9But after they had brought it around, the hand of the LORD was against the city, causing a very great panic, and he afflicted the men of the city, both young and old, so that tumors broke out on them. 10So they sent the ark of God to Ekron. But as soon as the ark of God came to Ekron, the people of Ekron cried out, "They have brought around to us the ark of the God of Israel to kill us and our people." 11They sent therefore and gathered together all the lords of the Philistines and said, "Send away the ark of the God of Israel, and let it return to its own place, that it may not kill us and our people." For there was a deathly panic throughout the whole city. The hand of God was very heavy there. 12The men who did not die were struck with tumors, and the cry of the city went up to heaven.

The Ark Returned to Israel

6 The ark of the LORD was in the country of the Philistines seven months. 2And the Philistines called for the priests and the diviners and said, "What shall we do with the ark of the LORD? Tell us with what we shall send it to its place." 3They said, "If you send away the ark of the God of Israel, do not send it empty, but by all means return him a guilt offering. Then you will be healed, and it will be known to you why his hand does not turn away from you." 4And they said, "What is the guilt offering that we shall return to him?" They answered, "Five golden tumors and five golden mice, according to the number of the lords of the Philistines, for the same plague was on all of you and on your lords. 5So you must make images of your tumors and images of your mice that ravage the land, and give glory to the God of Israel. Perhaps he will lighten his hand from off you and your gods and your land. 6Why should you harden your hearts as the Egyptians and Pharaoh hardened their hearts? After he had dealt severely with them, did they not send the people away, and they departed? 7Now then, take and prepare a new cart and two milk cows on which there has never come a yoke, and yoke the cows to the cart, but take their calves home, away from them. 8And take the ark of the LORD and place it on the cart and put in a box at its side the figures of gold, which you are returning to him as a guilt offering. Then send it off and let it go its way 9and watch. If it goes up on the way to its own land, to Beth-shemesh, then it is he who has done us this great harm, but if not, then we shall know that it is not his hand that struck us; it happened to us by coincidence."

10The men did so, and took two milk cows and yoked them to the cart and shut up their calves at home. 11And they put the ark of the LORD on the cart and the box with the golden mice and the images of their tumors. 12And the cows went straight in the direction of Beth-shemesh along one highway, lowing as they went. They turned neither to the right nor to the left, and the lords of the Philistines went after them as far as the border of Beth-shemesh. 13Now the people of Beth-shemesh were reaping their wheat harvest in the valley. And when they lifted up their eyes and saw the ark, they rejoiced to see it. 14The cart came into the field of Joshua of Beth-shemesh and stopped there. A great stone was there. And they split up the wood of the cart and offered the cows as a burnt offering to the LORD. 15And the Levites took down the ark of the LORD and the box that was beside it, in which were the golden figures, and set them upon the great stone. And the men of Beth-

---

1 SAMUEL 6:1–12

RELIGION: MAKING UP A RESPONSE TO GOD

After taking possession of the ark of the Lord, the Philistines began experiencing trouble. Their possession of the ark caused the god Dagon to topple and brought about a plague of tumors on the Philistines. It was clear that God's judgment was on them. They assumed the solution was to simply return the ark along with a guilt offering. This proved to be more difficult than imagined because they did not know the proper requirements for such a task.

Often, when people experience guilt they attempt to conjure up ways to appease God's judgment. They do this because they don't have a clear understanding of God's pathways of forgiveness. But Jesus came to make God's way and requirements clear. Jesus is the ultimate sacrifice for sins, and his death is the only offering that is acceptable to God (Jn 3:16; Ro 3:25). The way to forgiveness and grace is not through empty sacrifices but only through belief in Jesus.

shemesh offered burnt offerings and sacrificed sacrifices on that day to the LORD. 16 And when the five lords of the Philistines saw it, they returned that day to Ekron.

17 These are the golden tumors that the Philistines returned as a guilt offering to the LORD: one for Ashdod, one for Gaza, one for Ashkelon, one for Gath, one for Ekron, 18 and the golden mice, according to the number of all the cities of the Philistines belonging to the five lords, both fortified cities and unwalled villages. The great stone beside which they set down the ark of the LORD is a witness to this day in the field of Joshua of Beth-shemesh.

19 And he struck some of the men of Beth-shemesh, because they looked upon the ark of the LORD. He struck seventy men of them,[1] and the people mourned because the LORD had struck the people with a great blow. 20 Then the men of Beth-shemesh said, "Who is able to stand before the LORD, this holy God? And to whom shall he go up away from us?" 21 So they sent messengers to the inhabitants of Kiriath-jearim, saying, "The Philistines have returned the ark of the LORD. Come down and take it up to you."

7 And the men of Kiriath-jearim came and took up the ark of the LORD and brought it to the house of Abinadab on the hill. And they consecrated his son Eleazar to have charge of the ark of the LORD. 2 From the day that the ark was lodged at Kiriath-jearim, a long time passed, some twenty years, and all the house of Israel lamented after the LORD.

Samuel Judges Israel

3 And Samuel said to all the house of Israel, "If you are returning to the LORD with all your heart, then put away the foreign gods and the Ashtaroth from among you and direct your heart to the LORD and serve him only, and he will deliver you out of the hand of the Philistines." 4 So the people of Israel put away the Baals and the Ashtaroth, and they served the LORD only.

5 Then Samuel said, "Gather all Israel at Mizpah, and I will pray to the LORD for you." 6 So they gathered at Mizpah and drew water and poured it out before the LORD and fasted on that day and said there, "We have sinned against the LORD." And Samuel judged the people of Israel at Mizpah. 7 Now when the Philistines heard that the people of Israel had gathered at Mizpah, the lords of the Philistines went up against Israel. And when the people of Israel heard of it, they were afraid of the Philistines. 8 And the people of Israel said to Samuel, "Do not cease to cry out to the LORD our God for us, that he may save us from the hand of the Philistines." 9 So Samuel took a nursing lamb and offered it as a whole burnt offering to the LORD. And Samuel cried out to the LORD for Israel, and the LORD answered him. 10 As Samuel was offering up the burnt offering, the Philistines drew near to attack Israel. But the LORD thundered with a mighty sound that day against the Philistines and threw them into confusion, and they were defeated before Israel. 11 And the men of Israel went out from Mizpah and pursued the Philistines and struck them, as far as below Beth-car.

12 Then Samuel took a stone and set it up between Mizpah and Shen[2] and called its name Ebenezer;[3] for he said, "Till now the LORD has helped us." 13 So the Philistines were subdued and did not again enter the territory of Israel. And the hand of the LORD was against the Philistines all the days of Samuel. 14 The cities that the Philistines had taken from Israel were restored to Israel, from Ekron to Gath, and Israel delivered their territory from the hand of the Philistines. There was peace also between Israel and the Amorites.

15 Samuel judged Israel all the days of his life. 16 And he went on a circuit year by year to Bethel, Gilgal, and Mizpah. And he judged Israel in all these places. 17 Then he would return to Ramah, for his home was there, and there also he judged Israel. And he built there an altar to the LORD.

---

[1] Most Hebrew manuscripts *struck of the people seventy men, fifty thousand men* [2] Hebrew; Septuagint, Syriac *Jeshanah* [3] *Ebenezer* means *stone of help*

FAITHFUL LEADERSHIP

Samuel was a faithful leader. At a time when Israel lacked trustworthy leadership, Samuel proved himself to be an honorable prophet, priest, and judge. In this passage, he demonstrated his leadership in each of these roles. He used his prophetic voice to call the people to repent of their idolatry (v. 3). He acted as a priest and interceded on behalf of the nation (v. 9). He was declared as a faithful judge (or leader) over Israel all the days of his life (v. 15). Samuel lived in obedience to the Lord and called his nation to turn from their idols and seek God. This God-centered leadership brought great blessing for the people. But in spite of this, the Israelites wanted to go their own way.

This is the last story about Samuel in the Bible before the people ask for a king. God had been faithful to Israel under Samuel's leadership because he feared the Lord and recognized that the Lord alone was the true king of the people. But the people wanted to be like other nations and have an earthly king they could see. Under Samuel's leadership and God's rule, the people were protected from the Philistines (v. 13). God kept them safe because Samuel was faithful to the Lord. But under the rule of Saul, they lived in fear of their enemies. Faithful leadership is crucial for the prospering of God's people.

Samuel's faithfulness pointed the people of Israel toward what they truly needed. They needed a savior who would stand as a prophet, priest, and king — one who would call people to repentance, intercede for them on behalf of their sins, and rule and reign with justice and grace. Samuel's life prefigures Jesus. In the past, God spoke through prophets but now has spoken through his Son Jesus — creator and heir of all things (Heb 1:1–3). He is hailed as the great high priest who provides purification for sins. He sits at the throne of God and reigns as the true king that God's people have always longed for. God's people experienced peace and safety under the leadership of Samuel, but under the rule and reign of Jesus, believers will experience the fullness of the kingdom of God where all things will be made right for all of eternity.

Israel Demands a King

8 When Samuel became old, he made his sons judges over Israel. 2The name
of his firstborn son was Joel, and the name of his second, Abijah; they were
judges in Beersheba. 3Yet his sons did not walk in his ways but turned aside after
gain. They took bribes and perverted justice.
4Then all the elders of Israel gathered together and came to Samuel at Ramah
5and said to him, "Behold, you are old and your sons do not walk in your ways.
Now appoint for us a king to judge us like all the nations." 6But the thing displeased Samuel when they said, "Give us a king to judge us." And Samuel prayed
to the LORD. 7And the LORD said to Samuel, "Obey the voice of the people in all
that they say to you, for they have not rejected you, but they have rejected me
from being king over them. 8According to all the deeds that they have done, from
the day I brought them up out of Egypt even to this day, forsaking me and serving
other gods, so they are also doing to you. 9Now then, obey their voice; only you
shall solemnly warn them and show them the ways of the king who shall reign
over them."

Samuel's Warning Against Kings

10So Samuel told all the words of the LORD to the people who were asking for
a king from him. 11He said, "These will be the ways of the king who will reign over
you: he will take your sons and appoint them to his chariots and to be his horsemen and to run before his chariots. 12And he will appoint for himself commanders
of thousands and commanders of fifties, and some to plow his ground and to reap
his harvest, and to make his implements of war and the equipment of his chariots.
13He will take your daughters to be perfumers and cooks and bakers. 14He will take
the best of your fields and vineyards and olive orchards and give them to his servants. 15He will take the tenth of your grain and of your vineyards and give it to his
officers and to his servants. 16He will take your male servants and female servants
and the best of your young men[1] and your donkeys, and put them to his work. 17He
will take the tenth of your flocks, and you shall be his slaves. 18And in that day you
will cry out because of your king, whom you have chosen for yourselves, but the
LORD will not answer you in that day."

The LORD Grants Israel's Request

19But the people refused to obey the voice of Samuel. And they said, "No! But
there shall be a king over us, 20that we also may be like all the nations, and that
our king may judge us and go out before us and fight our battles." 21And when
Samuel had heard all the words of the people, he repeated them in the ears of the
LORD. 22And the LORD said to Samuel, "Obey their voice and make them a king."
Samuel then said to the men of Israel, "Go every man to his city."

Saul Chosen to Be King

9 There was a man of Benjamin whose name was Kish, the son of Abiel, son of
Zeror, son of Becorath, son of Aphiah, a Benjaminite, a man of wealth. 2And
he had a son whose name was Saul, a handsome young man. There was not a man
among the people of Israel more handsome than he. From his shoulders upward
he was taller than any of the people.
3Now the donkeys of Kish, Saul's father, were lost. So Kish said to Saul his son,
"Take one of the young men with you, and arise, go and look for the donkeys."
4And he passed through the hill country of Ephraim and passed through the land
of Shalishah, but they did not find them. And they passed through the land of
Shaalim, but they were not there. Then they passed through the land of Benjamin,
but did not find them.

---

[1]Septuagint *cattle*

CHANGING KINGS

The Israelites' request that Samuel establish a king to rule over Israel was an act of faithlessness that led to serious negative consequences. Kingship itself is not necessarily an evil institution. However, for the Israelites it demonstrated a lack of trust in God to provide for their needs. Deuteronomy 17:14 – 20 anticipates a kingship by outlining God's rules for a king of Israel. So why is Israel's request for a king an act of faithlessness?

Israel's request was a desire to be like "all the nations" (1Sa 8:5,20). God had chosen and redeemed Israel so that they would be different from the nations around them. What differentiated Israel from other nations was the fact that God was their king. This eliminated the need for a human king. Their desire to be like everyone else was an act of disobedience to what God had called them to be — set apart. By deciding to become more like the cultures around them, Israel was denying the purposes for which God had created and saved them. Samuel warned the people that this sinful act would cause all kinds of grief to the nation. The Israelites opened themselves up to a king who would exploit and suppress them rather than love and protect them. This king would be far from the picture God outlined for Israel in Deuteronomy 17. There would indeed be serious consequences to Israel's rebellion. What they thought would bring them peace and security would instead bring them destruction and harm.

But even in spite of their disobedience, God honored their request for a king. He told Samuel to surrender to their evil desire. God even demonstrated his grace in their request. Israel's first king, Saul, would be a disappointment and would do exactly what Samuel warned. But their second king, David, would lead them well, and through his offspring would come Jesus, the Messiah. Jesus would ultimately remove the guilt of the people by dying on the cross for their sins. While Israel would still have to suffer for the consequences of their decision, God would be gracious to provide for them even in their disobedience.

In Jesus, God's provision is not conditional. His gift of grace is not based on humanity's righteousness or unrighteousness, but solely on his mercy for people. The heart of the gospel is that "God shows his love for us in that while we were still sinners, Christ died for us" (Ro 5:8).

5When they came to the land of Zuph, Saul said to his servant[1] who was with
him, "Come, let us go back, lest my father cease to care about the donkeys and
become anxious about us." 6But he said to him, "Behold, there is a man of God
in this city, and he is a man who is held in honor; all that he says comes true. So
now let us go there. Perhaps he can tell us the way we should go." 7Then Saul
said to his servant, "But if we go, what can we bring the man? For the bread in
our sacks is gone, and there is no present to bring to the man of God. What do
we have?" 8The servant answered Saul again, "Here, I have with me a quarter
of a shekel[2] of silver, and I will give it to the man of God to tell us our way."
9(Formerly in Israel, when a man went to inquire of God, he said, "Come, let
us go to the seer," for today's "prophet" was formerly called a seer.) 10And Saul
said to his servant, "Well said; come, let us go." So they went to the city where
the man of God was.

11As they went up the hill to the city, they met young women coming out to
draw water and said to them, "Is the seer here?" 12They answered, "He is; behold,
he is just ahead of you. Hurry. He has come just now to the city, because the people have a sacrifice today on the high place. 13As soon as you enter the city you will
find him, before he goes up to the high place to eat. For the people will not eat till
he comes, since he must bless the sacrifice; afterward those who are invited will
eat. Now go up, for you will meet him immediately." 14So they went up to the city.
As they were entering the city, they saw Samuel coming out toward them on his
way up to the high place.

15Now the day before Saul came, the LORD had revealed to Samuel: 16"Tomorrow about this time I will send to you a man from the land of Benjamin, and you
shall anoint him to be prince[3] over my people Israel. He shall save my people from
the hand of the Philistines. For I have seen[4] my people, because their cry has come
to me." 17When Samuel saw Saul, the LORD told him, "Here is the man of whom
I spoke to you! He it is who shall restrain my people." 18Then Saul approached
Samuel in the gate and said, "Tell me where is the house of the seer?" 19Samuel
answered Saul, "I am the seer. Go up before me to the high place, for today you
shall eat with me, and in the morning I will let you go and will tell you all that is
on your mind. 20As for your donkeys that were lost three days ago, do not set your
mind on them, for they have been found. And for whom is all that is desirable
in Israel? Is it not for you and for all your father's house?" 21Saul answered, "Am
I not a Benjaminite, from the least of the tribes of Israel? And is not my clan the
humblest of all the clans of the tribe of Benjamin? Why then have you spoken to
me in this way?"

22Then Samuel took Saul and his young man and brought them into the hall
and gave them a place at the head of those who had been invited, who were about
thirty persons. 23And Samuel said to the cook, "Bring the portion I gave you, of
which I said to you, 'Put it aside.'" 24So the cook took up the leg and what was on
it and set them before Saul. And Samuel said, "See, what was kept is set before
you. Eat, because it was kept for you until the hour appointed, that you might eat
with the guests."[5]

So Saul ate with Samuel that day. 25And when they came down from the high
place into the city, a bed was spread for Saul on the roof, and he lay down to sleep.[6]
26Then at the break of dawn[7] Samuel called to Saul on the roof, "Up, that I may
send you on your way." So Saul arose, and both he and Samuel went out into the
street.

27As they were going down to the outskirts of the city, Samuel said to Saul,
"Tell the servant to pass on before us, and when he has passed on, stop here yourself for a while, that I may make known to you the word of God."

---

[1]Hebrew *young man*; also verses 7, 8, 10, 27 [2]A *shekel* was about 2/5 ounce or 11 grams [3]Or *leader*
[4]Septuagint adds *the affliction of* [5]Hebrew *appointed, saying, 'I have invited the people'* [6]Septuagint;
Hebrew *city, he spoke with Saul on the roof* [7]Septuagint; Hebrew *And they arose early, and at the break
of dawn*

1 SAMUEL 10:1–10

CHANGE OF HEART

In this account, God changed Saul's heart. In Hebrew this expression literally reads, "God changed him for another heart." It may seem that Saul's subsequent attitudes and behavior did not reflect a genuine spiritual life. Yet, Saul seemed to have struggled with his sin and experienced times where he desired to worship God (14:34–35; 15:24–31). Nevertheless, for Saul to embrace the life God was calling him to live, he needed God to change his heart.

This theme of a need for inner transformation and a new heart runs throughout the Scriptures (Eze 36:26). The New Testament demonstrates that complete inner transformation comes through Jesus and is empowered by the Holy Spirit (Jn 3:5). Jesus' transforming work changes lives from the inside out (2Co 5:17). Therefore, believers can receive the same heart that David asked for in Psalm 51. God works to change the hearts of those who follow him, and Saul and David are examples of what believers today can experience.

Saul Anointed King

10 Then Samuel took a flask of oil and poured it on his head and kissed him and said, "Has not the LORD anointed you to be prince[1] over his people Israel? And you shall reign over the people of the LORD and you will save them from the hand of their surrounding enemies. And this shall be the sign to you that the LORD has anointed you to be prince[2] over his heritage. 2When you depart from me today, you will meet two men by Rachel's tomb in the territory of Benjamin at Zelzah, and they will say to you, 'The donkeys that you went to seek are found, and now your father has ceased to care about the donkeys and is anxious about you, saying, "What shall I do about my son?"' 3Then you shall go on from there farther and come to the oak of Tabor. Three men going up to God at Bethel will meet you there, one carrying three young goats, another carrying three loaves of bread, and another carrying a skin of wine. 4And they will greet you and give you two loaves of bread, which you shall accept from their hand. 5After that you shall come to Gibeath-elohim,[3] where there is a garrison of the Philistines. And there, as soon as you come to the city, you will meet a group of prophets coming down from the high place with harp, tambourine, flute, and lyre before them, prophesying. 6Then the Spirit of the LORD will rush upon you, and you will prophesy with them and be turned into another man. 7Now when these signs meet you, do what your hand finds to do, for God is with you. 8Then go down before me to Gilgal. And behold, I am coming down to you to offer burnt offerings and to sacrifice peace offerings. Seven days you shall wait, until I come to you and show you what you shall do."

9When he turned his back to leave Samuel, God gave him another heart. And all these signs came to pass that day. 10When they came to Gibeah,[4] behold, a group of prophets met him, and the Spirit of God rushed upon him, and he prophesied among them. 11And when all who knew him previously saw how he prophesied with the prophets, the people said to one another, "What has come over the son of Kish? Is Saul also among the prophets?" 12And a man of the place answered, "And who is their father?" Therefore it became a proverb, "Is Saul also among the prophets?" 13When he had finished prophesying, he came to the high place.

14Saul's uncle said to him and to his servant, "Where did you go?" And he said, "To seek the donkeys. And when we saw they were not to be found, we went to Samuel." 15And Saul's uncle said, "Please tell me what Samuel said to you." 16And Saul said to his uncle, "He told us plainly that the donkeys had been found." But about the matter of the kingdom, of which Samuel had spoken, he did not tell him anything.

Saul Proclaimed King

17Now Samuel called the people together to the LORD at Mizpah. 18And he said to the people of Israel, "Thus says the LORD, the God of Israel, 'I brought up Israel out of Egypt, and I delivered you from the hand of the Egyptians and from the hand of all the kingdoms that were oppressing you.' 19But today you have rejected your God, who saves you from all your calamities and your distresses, and you have said to him, 'Set a king over us.' Now therefore present yourselves before the LORD by your tribes and by your thousands."

20Then Samuel brought all the tribes of Israel near, and the tribe of Benjamin was taken by lot. 21He brought the tribe of Benjamin near by its clans, and the clan of the Matrites was taken by lot;[5] and Saul the son of Kish was taken by lot. But when they sought him, he could not be found. 22So they inquired again of the LORD, "Is there a man still to come?" and the LORD said, "Behold, he has hidden

---

[1] Or *leader* [2] Septuagint; Hebrew lacks *over his people Israel? And you shall. . . . to be prince* [3] *Gibeath-elohim* means *the hill of God* [4] *Gibeah* means *the hill* [5] Septuagint adds *finally he brought the family of the Matrites near, man by man*

himself among the baggage." 23Then they ran and took him from there. And when he stood among the people, he was taller than any of the people from his shoulders upward. 24And Samuel said to all the people, "Do you see him whom the LORD has chosen? There is none like him among all the people." And all the people shouted, "Long live the king!"

25Then Samuel told the people the rights and duties of the kingship, and he wrote them in a book and laid it up before the LORD. Then Samuel sent all the people away, each one to his home. 26Saul also went to his home at Gibeah, and with him went men of valor whose hearts God had touched. 27But some worthless fellows said, "How can this man save us?" And they despised him and brought him no present. But he held his peace.

Saul Defeats the Ammonites

11 Then Nahash the Ammonite went up and besieged Jabesh-gilead, and all the men of Jabesh said to Nahash, "Make a treaty with us, and we will serve you." 2But Nahash the Ammonite said to them, "On this condition I will make a treaty with you, that I gouge out all your right eyes, and thus bring disgrace on all Israel." 3The elders of Jabesh said to him, "Give us seven days' respite that we may send messengers through all the territory of Israel. Then, if there is no one to save us, we will give ourselves up to you." 4When the messengers came to Gibeah of Saul, they reported the matter in the ears of the people, and all the people wept aloud.

5Now, behold, Saul was coming from the field behind the oxen. And Saul said, "What is wrong with the people, that they are weeping?" So they told him the news of the men of Jabesh. 6And the Spirit of God rushed upon Saul when he heard these words, and his anger was greatly kindled. 7He took a yoke of oxen and cut them in pieces and sent them throughout all the territory of Israel by the hand of the messengers, saying, "Whoever does not come out after Saul and Samuel, so shall it be done to his oxen!" Then the dread of the LORD fell upon the people, and they came out as one man. 8When he mustered them at Bezek, the people of Israel were three hundred thousand, and the men of Judah thirty thousand. 9And they said to the messengers who had come, "Thus shall you say to the men of Jabesh-gilead: 'Tomorrow, by the time the sun is hot, you shall have salvation.'" When the messengers came and told the men of Jabesh, they were glad. 10Therefore the men of Jabesh said, "Tomorrow we will give ourselves up to you, and you may do to us whatever seems good to you." 11And the next day Saul put the people in three companies. And they came into the midst of the camp in the morning watch and struck down the Ammonites until the heat of the day. And those who survived were scattered, so that no two of them were left together.

The Kingdom Is Renewed

12Then the people said to Samuel, "Who is it that said, 'Shall Saul reign over us?' Bring the men, that we may put them to death." 13But Saul said, "Not a man shall be put to death this day, for today the LORD has worked salvation in Israel." 14Then Samuel said to the people, "Come, let us go to Gilgal and there renew the kingdom." 15So all the people went to Gilgal, and there they made Saul king before the LORD in Gilgal. There they sacrificed peace offerings before the LORD, and there Saul and all the men of Israel rejoiced greatly.

Samuel's Farewell Address

12 And Samuel said to all Israel, "Behold, I have obeyed your voice in all that you have said to me and have made a king over you. 2And now, behold, the king walks before you, and I am old and gray; and behold, my sons are with you. I have walked before you from my youth until this day. 3Here I am; testify against me before the LORD and before his anointed. Whose ox have I taken? Or whose donkey have I taken? Or whom have I defrauded? Whom have I oppressed? Or

1 SAMUEL 12:22

HIS NAME'S SAKE

In this chapter, Samuel delivered his farewell speech to the Israelites and reminded the people of God's faithfulness to them throughout history. He retold their journey from deliverance in Egypt to the promised land (vv. 6–8). But he also reminded them of their faithlessness and the times they turned their backs on God (vv. 9–10). He explained that because they had now asked for a human king, they were once again demonstrating their lack of trust in God to provide for their needs. As they began to wise up about what they had done, they became afraid. But Samuel encouraged them by telling them that while they may have been faithless, God was still faithful. God would continue to love and accept them "for his great name's sake."

In ancient times, one's name stood for one's character. The name of God speaks of his reputation and attributes. For God to abandon his people would be inconsistent with his reputation for faithfulness. He would remain faithful to them by delivering on his promise to send a Messiah to redeem and restore his people. In the New Testament, the apostle Paul writes of Jesus, "If we are faithless, he remains faithful—for he cannot deny himself" (2Ti 2:13). By sending Jesus, God the Father demonstrated that he never gives up on those he *loves because* he *cannot* disown his own character.

from whose hand have I taken a bribe to blind my eyes with it? Testify against me[1] and I will restore it to you." 4They said, "You have not defrauded us or oppressed us or taken anything from any man's hand." 5And he said to them, "The LORD is witness against you, and his anointed is witness this day, that you have not found anything in my hand." And they said, "He is witness."

6And Samuel said to the people, "The LORD is witness,[2] who appointed Moses and Aaron and brought your fathers up out of the land of Egypt. 7Now therefore stand still that I may plead with you before the LORD concerning all the righteous deeds of the LORD that he performed for you and for your fathers. 8When Jacob went into Egypt, and the Egyptians oppressed them,[3] then your fathers cried out to the LORD and the LORD sent Moses and Aaron, who brought your fathers out of Egypt and made them dwell in this place. 9But they forgot the LORD their God. And he sold them into the hand of Sisera, commander of the army of Hazor,[4] and into the hand of the Philistines, and into the hand of the king of Moab. And they fought against them. 10And they cried out to the LORD and said, 'We have sinned, because we have forsaken the LORD and have served the Baals and the Ashtaroth. But now deliver us out of the hand of our enemies, that we may serve you.' 11And the LORD sent Jerubbaal and Barak[5] and Jephthah and Samuel and delivered you out of the hand of your enemies on every side, and you lived in safety. 12And when you saw that Nahash the king of the Ammonites came against you, you said to me, 'No, but a king shall reign over us,' when the LORD your God was your king. 13And now behold the king whom you have chosen, for whom you have asked; behold, the LORD has set a king over you. 14If you will fear the LORD and serve him and obey his voice and not rebel against the commandment of the LORD, and if both you and the king who reigns over you will follow the LORD your God, it will be well. 15But if you will not obey the voice of the LORD, but rebel against the commandment of the LORD, then the hand of the LORD will be against you and your king.[6] 16Now therefore stand still and see this great thing that the LORD will do before your eyes. 17Is it not wheat harvest today? I will call upon the LORD, that he may send thunder and rain. And you shall know and see that your wickedness is great, which you have done in the sight of the LORD, in asking for yourselves a king." 18So Samuel called upon the LORD, and the LORD sent thunder and rain that day, and all the people greatly feared the LORD and Samuel.

19And all the people said to Samuel, "Pray for your servants to the LORD your God, that we may not die, for we have added to all our sins this evil, to ask for ourselves a king." 20And Samuel said to the people, "Do not be afraid; you have done all this evil. Yet do not turn aside from following the LORD, but serve the LORD with all your heart. 21And do not turn aside after empty things that cannot profit or deliver, for they are empty. 22For the LORD will not forsake his people, for his great name's sake, because it has pleased the LORD to make you a people for himself. 23Moreover, as for me, far be it from me that I should sin against the LORD by ceasing to pray for you, and I will instruct you in the good and the right way. 24Only fear the LORD and serve him faithfully with all your heart. For consider what great things he has done for you. 25But if you still do wickedly, you shall be swept away, both you and your king."

Saul Fights the Philistines

13 Saul lived for one year and then became king, and when he had reigned for two years over Israel,[7] 2Saul chose three thousand men of Israel. Two thousand were with Saul in Michmash and the hill country of Bethel, and a thousand

[1]Septuagint; Hebrew lacks *Testify against me* [2]Septuagint; Hebrew lacks *is witness* [3]Septuagint; Hebrew lacks *and the Egyptians oppressed them* [4]Septuagint *the army of Jabin king of Hazor* [5]Septuagint, Syriac; Hebrew *Bedan* [6]Septuagint; Hebrew *fathers* [7]Hebrew *Saul was one year old when he became king, and he reigned two years over Israel*; some Greek manuscripts give Saul's age when he began to reign as thirty years

OBEDIENCE AND BLESSING

First Samuel demonstrates the blessing that comes when one is obedient to God versus the destruction that comes when one chooses to live one's own way. This is a key biblical theme that runs throughout the Old Testament. This principle is seen very clearly in 1 Samuel 12:14 – 15: obedience to God leads one into a blessed life while disobedience to God's ways often brings one troubles. The examples are numerous: the disobedience of Eli's sons disqualified them from becoming judges in Israel. The same was true of Samuel's sons.

The life of Saul demonstrates this principle even more clearly. Saul disobeyed God on a number of occasions. Saul was impatient with God's timing when he offered a sacrifice before the Lord's commanded time (13:7 – 14). He was rash and foolish when he made an oath he was unable to honor (14:24 – 44). He disobeyed the Lord's instructions to totally destroy the Amalekites and their possessions (15:1 – 34). He was greatly jealous when the people praised David for his heroics and virtue (18:8). On many occasions he sought to kill David (18:10 – 11,20 – 25; 19:7 – 10; 22:6 – 19; 23:7 – 8; 24:1 – 2; 26:1 – 3; 27:1). He dishonored the Lord by consulting with a medium (28:3 – 25). Saul's kingship was marked by disobedience to God, and the consequences were serious: God's Spirit departed from Saul and left him to his own destruction. As a result, Saul would lose the approval of his people and forfeit his kingship.

David, on the other hand, showed himself to be obedient to God. God looked beyond his appearance and named him the king of Israel. David was a man after God's own heart (13:14), and God blessed him for it. However, even David would fail to be fully obedient to God's commands (2Sa 11:1 – 27). His life was not without flaws, and there were consequences. Israel's greatest hope was in a king who would never let them down and would always obey God's ways.

Jesus' life was marked by full obedience to the will of the Father. Even when obedience cost him his life, Jesus never took the path of disobedience. He proclaimed, "Not my will, but yours, be done" (Lk 22:42). Jesus' obedience would bring the ultimate blessing. Although he would be crucified, he made a way for all of God's people to experience ultimate blessing and access to the kingdom of God by removing sins.

were with Jonathan in Gibeah of Benjamin. The rest of the people he sent home, every man to his tent. 3Jonathan defeated the garrison of the Philistines that was at Geba, and the Philistines heard of it. And Saul blew the trumpet throughout all the land, saying, "Let the Hebrews hear." 4And all Israel heard it said that Saul had defeated the garrison of the Philistines, and also that Israel had become a stench to the Philistines. And the people were called out to join Saul at Gilgal.

5And the Philistines mustered to fight with Israel, thirty thousand chariots and six thousand horsemen and troops like the sand on the seashore in multitude. They came up and encamped in Michmash, to the east of Beth-aven. 6When the men of Israel saw that they were in trouble (for the people were hard pressed), the people hid themselves in caves and in holes and in rocks and in tombs and in cisterns, 7and some Hebrews crossed the fords of the Jordan to the land of Gad and Gilead. Saul was still at Gilgal, and all the people followed him trembling.

Saul's Unlawful Sacrifice

8He waited seven days, the time appointed by Samuel. But Samuel did not come to Gilgal, and the people were scattering from him. 9So Saul said, "Bring the burnt offering here to me, and the peace offerings." And he offered the burnt offering. 10As soon as he had finished offering the burnt offering, behold, Samuel came. And Saul went out to meet him and greet him. 11Samuel said, "What have you done?" And Saul said, "When I saw that the people were scattering from me, and that you did not come within the days appointed, and that the Philistines had mustered at Michmash, 12I said, 'Now the Philistines will come down against me at Gilgal, and I have not sought the favor of the LORD.' So I forced myself, and offered the burnt offering." 13And Samuel said to Saul, "You have done foolishly. You have not kept the command of the LORD your God, with which he commanded you. For then the LORD would have established your kingdom over Israel forever. 14But now your kingdom shall not continue. The LORD has sought out a man after his own heart, and the LORD has commanded him to be prince[1] over his people, because you have not kept what the LORD commanded you." 15And Samuel arose and went up from Gilgal. The rest of the people went up after Saul to meet the army; they went up from Gilgal[2] to Gibeah of Benjamin.

And Saul numbered the people who were present with him, about six hundred men. 16And Saul and Jonathan his son and the people who were present with them stayed in Geba of Benjamin, but the Philistines encamped in Michmash. 17And raiders came out of the camp of the Philistines in three companies. One company turned toward Ophrah, to the land of Shual; 18another company turned toward Beth-horon; and another company turned toward the border that looks down on the Valley of Zeboim toward the wilderness.

19Now there was no blacksmith to be found throughout all the land of Israel, for the Philistines said, "Lest the Hebrews make themselves swords or spears." 20But every one of the Israelites went down to the Philistines to sharpen his plowshare, his mattock, his axe, or his sickle,[3] 21and the charge was two-thirds of a shekel[4] for the plowshares and for the mattocks, and a third of a shekel[5] for sharpening the axes and for setting the goads.[6] 22So on the day of the battle there was neither sword nor spear found in the hand of any of the people with Saul and Jonathan, but Saul and Jonathan his son had them. 23And the garrison of the Philistines went out to the pass of Michmash.

Jonathan Defeats the Philistines

14 One day Jonathan the son of Saul said to the young man who carried his armor, "Come, let us go over to the Philistine garrison on the other side." But he did not tell his father. 2Saul was staying in the outskirts of Gibeah in the

[1]Or *leader* [2]Septuagint; Hebrew lacks *The rest of the people . . . from Gilgal* [3]Septuagint; Hebrew *plowshare* [4]Hebrew *was a pim* [5]A *shekel* was about 2/5 ounce or 11 grams [6]The meaning of the Hebrew verse is uncertain

pomegranate cave[1] at Migron. The people who were with him were about six hundred men, 3including Ahijah the son of Ahitub, Ichabod's brother, son of Phinehas, son of Eli, the priest of the LORD in Shiloh, wearing an ephod. And the people
did not know that Jonathan had gone. 4Within the passes, by which Jonathan
sought to go over to the Philistine garrison, there was a rocky crag on the one side
and a rocky crag on the other side. The name of the one was Bozez, and the name
of the other Seneh. 5The one crag rose on the north in front of Michmash, and the
other on the south in front of Geba.

6Jonathan said to the young man who carried his armor, "Come, let us go
over to the garrison of these uncircumcised. It may be that the LORD will work
for us, for nothing can hinder the LORD from saving by many or by few." 7And
his armor-bearer said to him, "Do all that is in your heart. Do as you wish.[2]
Behold, I am with you heart and soul." 8Then Jonathan said, "Behold, we will
cross over to the men, and we will show ourselves to them. 9If they say to us,
'Wait until we come to you,' then we will stand still in our place, and we will
not go up to them. 10But if they say, 'Come up to us,' then we will go up, for the
LORD has given them into our hand. And this shall be the sign to us." 11So both of
them showed themselves to the garrison of the Philistines. And the Philistines
said, "Look, Hebrews are coming out of the holes where they have hidden themselves." 12And the men of the garrison hailed Jonathan and his armor-bearer
and said, "Come up to us, and we will show you a thing." And Jonathan said to
his armor-bearer, "Come up after me, for the LORD has given them into the hand
of Israel." 13Then Jonathan climbed up on his hands and feet, and his armor-
bearer after him. And they fell before Jonathan, and his armor-bearer killed
them after him. 14And that first strike, which Jonathan and his armor-bearer
made, killed about twenty men within as it were half a furrow's length in an
acre[3] of land. 15And there was a panic in the camp, in the field, and among all
the people. The garrison and even the raiders trembled, the earth quaked, and
it became a very great panic.[4]

16And the watchmen of Saul in Gibeah of Benjamin looked, and behold, the
multitude was dispersing here and there.[5] 17Then Saul said to the people who were
with him, "Count and see who has gone from us." And when they had counted,
behold, Jonathan and his armor-bearer were not there. 18So Saul said to Ahijah,
"Bring the ark of God here." For the ark of God went at that time with the people[6]
of Israel. 19Now while Saul was talking to the priest, the tumult in the camp of
the Philistines increased more and more. So Saul said to the priest, "Withdraw
your hand." 20Then Saul and all the people who were with him rallied and went
into the battle. And behold, every Philistine's sword was against his fellow, and
there was very great confusion. 21Now the Hebrews who had been with the Philistines before that time and who had gone up with them into the camp, even they
also turned to be with the Israelites who were with Saul and Jonathan. 22Like-
wise, when all the men of Israel who had hidden themselves in the hill country
of Ephraim heard that the Philistines were fleeing, they too followed hard after
them in the battle. 23So the LORD saved Israel that day. And the battle passed beyond Beth-aven.

Saul's Rash Vow

24And the men of Israel had been hard pressed that day, so Saul had laid an
oath on the people, saying, "Cursed be the man who eats food until it is evening
and I am avenged on my enemies." So none of the people had tasted food. 25Now
when all the people[7] came to the forest, behold, there was honey on the ground.
26And when the people entered the forest, behold, the honey was dropping, but
no one put his hand to his mouth, for the people feared the oath. 27But Jonathan

[1]Or *under the pomegranate* [tree] [2]Septuagint *Do all that your mind inclines to* [3]Hebrew *a yoke*
[4]Or *became a panic from God* [5]Septuagint; Hebrew *they went here and there* [6]Hebrew; Septuagint
"Bring the ephod." For at that time he wore the ephod before the people [7]Hebrew *land*

1 SAMUEL 14:24–46

FOOLISH OATHS

By declaring, "Cursed be the man who eats food until it is evening," Saul foolishly ordered that none of his soldiers should eat until he had taken vengeance on his enemies (v. 24). Unlike Jonathan, Saul did not view the battle as the Lord's (v. 12). Saul made another foolish oath (v. 39) when he proclaimed that whoever was guilty must die. The recklessness with which Saul made these oaths placed him in a situation in which his credibility as a leader was called into question. By failing to honor his oaths, Saul proved himself to be rash and unworthy of trust.

In contrast, Jesus told his disciples in the Sermon on the Mount to avoid making oaths. He said, "Let what you say be simply 'Yes' or 'No'; anything more than this comes from evil" (Mt 5:37). Saul's inability to keep his word showed that ultimately he was not the king that Israel hoped for. Only Jesus, the true King of Israel, would keep his word to the end. He is the King who can be trusted and worshiped.

had not heard his father charge the people with the oath, so he put out the tip of the staff that was in his hand and dipped it in the honeycomb and put his hand to his mouth, and his eyes became bright. 28Then one of the people said, "Your father strictly charged the people with an oath, saying, 'Cursed be the man who eats food this day.'" And the people were faint. 29Then Jonathan said, "My father has troubled the land. See how my eyes have become bright because I tasted a little of this honey. 30How much better if the people had eaten freely today of the spoil of their enemies that they found. For now the defeat among the Philistines has not been great."

31They struck down the Philistines that day from Michmash to Aijalon. And the people were very faint. 32The people pounced on the spoil and took sheep and oxen and calves and slaughtered them on the ground. And the people ate them with the blood. 33Then they told Saul, "Behold, the people are sinning against the LORD by eating with the blood." And he said, "You have dealt treacherously; roll a great stone to me here."[1] 34And Saul said, "Disperse yourselves among the people and say to them, 'Let every man bring his ox or his sheep and slaughter them here and eat, and do not sin against the LORD by eating with the blood.'" So every one of the people brought his ox with him that night and they slaughtered them there. 35And Saul built an altar to the LORD; it was the first altar that he built to the LORD.

36Then Saul said, "Let us go down after the Philistines by night and plunder them until the morning light; let us not leave a man of them." And they said, "Do whatever seems good to you." But the priest said, "Let us draw near to God here." 37And Saul inquired of God, "Shall I go down after the Philistines? Will you give them into the hand of Israel?" But he did not answer him that day. 38And Saul said, "Come here, all you leaders of the people, and know and see how this sin has arisen today. 39For as the LORD lives who saves Israel, though it be in Jonathan my son, he shall surely die." But there was not a man among all the people who answered him. 40Then he said to all Israel, "You shall be on one side, and I and Jonathan my son will be on the other side." And the people said to Saul, "Do what seems good to you." 41Therefore Saul said, "O LORD God of Israel, why have you not answered your servant this day? If this guilt is in me or in Jonathan my son, O LORD, God of Israel, give Urim. But if this guilt is in your people Israel, give Thummim."[2] And Jonathan and Saul were taken, but the people escaped. 42Then Saul said, "Cast the lot between me and my son Jonathan." And Jonathan was taken.

43Then Saul said to Jonathan, "Tell me what you have done." And Jonathan told him, "I tasted a little honey with the tip of the staff that was in my hand. Here I am; I will die." 44And Saul said, "God do so to me and more also; you shall surely die, Jonathan." 45Then the people said to Saul, "Shall Jonathan die, who has worked this great salvation in Israel? Far from it! As the LORD lives, there shall not one hair of his head fall to the ground, for he has worked with God this day." So the people ransomed Jonathan, so that he did not die. 46Then Saul went up from pursuing the Philistines, and the Philistines went to their own place.

Saul Fights Israel's Enemies

47When Saul had taken the kingship over Israel, he fought against all his enemies on every side, against Moab, against the Ammonites, against Edom, against the kings of Zobah, and against the Philistines. Wherever he turned he routed them. 48And he did valiantly and struck the Amalekites and delivered Israel out of the hands of those who plundered them.

49Now the sons of Saul were Jonathan, Ishvi, and Malchi-shua. And the names

[1]Septuagint; Hebrew *this day* [2]Vulgate and Septuagint; Hebrew *Therefore Saul said to the LORD, the God of Israel, "Give Thummim."*

of his two daughters were these: the name of the firstborn was Merab, and the name of the younger Michal. 50And the name of Saul's wife was Ahinoam the daughter of Ahimaaz. And the name of the commander of his army was Abner the son of Ner, Saul's uncle. 51Kish was the father of Saul, and Ner the father of Abner was the son of Abiel.

52There was hard fighting against the Philistines all the days of Saul. And when Saul saw any strong man, or any valiant man, he attached him to himself.

The LORD Rejects Saul

15 And Samuel said to Saul, "The LORD sent me to anoint you king over his people Israel; now therefore listen to the words of the LORD. 2Thus says the LORD of hosts, 'I have noted what Amalek did to Israel in opposing them on the way when they came up out of Egypt. 3Now go and strike Amalek and devote to destruction[1] all that they have. Do not spare them, but kill both man and woman, child and infant, ox and sheep, camel and donkey.'"

4So Saul summoned the people and numbered them in Telaim, two hundred thousand men on foot, and ten thousand men of Judah. 5And Saul came to the city of Amalek and lay in wait in the valley. 6Then Saul said to the Kenites, "Go, depart; go down from among the Amalekites, lest I destroy you with them. For you showed kindness to all the people of Israel when they came up out of Egypt." So the Kenites departed from among the Amalekites. 7And Saul defeated the Amalekites from Havilah as far as Shur, which is east of Egypt. 8And he took Agag the king of the Amalekites alive and devoted to destruction all the people with the edge of the sword. 9But Saul and the people spared Agag and the best of the sheep and of the oxen and of the fattened calves[2] and the lambs, and all that was good, and would not utterly destroy them. All that was despised and worthless they devoted to destruction.

10The word of the LORD came to Samuel: 11"I regret[3] that I have made Saul king, for he has turned back from following me and has not performed my commandments." And Samuel was angry, and he cried to the LORD all night. 12And Samuel rose early to meet Saul in the morning. And it was told Samuel, "Saul came to Carmel, and behold, he set up a monument for himself and turned and passed on and went down to Gilgal." 13And Samuel came to Saul, and Saul said to him, "Blessed be you to the LORD. I have performed the commandment of the LORD." 14And Samuel said, "What then is this bleating of the sheep in my ears and the lowing of the oxen that I hear?" 15Saul said, "They have brought them from the Amalekites, for the people spared the best of the sheep and of the oxen to sacrifice to the LORD your God, and the rest we have devoted to destruction." 16Then Samuel said to Saul, "Stop! I will tell you what the LORD said to me this night." And he said to him, "Speak."

17And Samuel said, "Though you are little in your own eyes, are you not the head of the tribes of Israel? The LORD anointed you king over Israel. 18And the LORD sent you on a mission and said, 'Go, devote to destruction the sinners, the Amalekites, and fight against them until they are consumed.' 19Why then did you not obey the voice of the LORD? Why did you pounce on the spoil and do what was evil in the sight of the LORD?" 20And Saul said to Samuel, "I have obeyed the voice of the LORD. I have gone on the mission on which the LORD sent me. I have brought Agag the king of Amalek, and I have devoted the Amalekites to destruction. 21But the people took of the spoil, sheep and oxen, the best of the things devoted to destruction, to sacrifice to the LORD your God in Gilgal." 22And Samuel said,

"Has the LORD as great delight in burnt offerings and sacrifices,
as in obeying the voice of the LORD?

---

[1]That is, set apart (devote) as an offering to the Lord (for destruction); also verses 8, 9, 15, 18, 20, 21
[2]The meaning of the Hebrew term is uncertain [3]See also verses 29, 35

OBEDIENCE AND SACRIFICE

First Samuel 15 tells the tragic story of the Lord rejecting Saul as Israel's king. This account serves as a warning that the Lord values obedience to his commands over religious practices. Saul and his army were commanded by the Lord to destroy the Amalekites and to leave nothing behind. But when Saul returned from the battle, the Lord was displeased. By bringing the Amalekites' king and the best of their cattle home from the battle, rather than destroying them, Saul had failed to honor the entirety of the Lord's command. God spoke to Samuel and expressed his regret for making Saul king (v. 11). Samuel was upset, and he cried out to God all that night. The next morning he brought a message to Saul. "Why then did you not obey the voice of the LORD?" he asked (v. 19). Saul replied, "I have obeyed the voice of the LORD," explaining that his men brought home the cattle for offering a sacrifice to the Lord (vv. 20 – 21). Then Samuel explained a core principle: "To obey is better than sacrifice" (v. 22). This assertion runs throughout the Old Testament, that God desires our obedience more than our religious rituals (Ps 40:6 – 8; 50:8 – 15; 51:16 – 17; Pr 15:8; 21:3; 28:9; Isa 1:11 – 15; Jer 6:19 – 20; Hos 6:6; Am 5:21).

This is a puzzling principle because on the surface it seems that Saul was doing an honorable thing to please the Lord. But the Lord showed Samuel and Saul that formal religious worship is no substitute for an obedient life. God was offering a glimpse of what was to come in the anointing of David as Israel's new king — God is concerned with the heart rather than the external appearance (1Sa 16:7). In the lives of believers today, the principle still applies. Church attendance, Bible studies, and Christian conferences are great, but they are no substitute for genuine obedience to God.

In the New Testament, Jesus demonstrated what a life of obedience to the Father looked like in practice. Jesus upset the religious leaders of the day because he disobeyed the external religious laws and customs. But Jesus was not concerned with impressing those around him. He was only concerned with pleasing his Father. Jesus' obedience was what God wanted — for him to lay down his life for sinners. Jesus demonstrated costly obedience to the Father throughout his life (Jn 10:18; Ro 5:19; Heb 5:8; 1Jn 3:16). Ultimately, Jesus was obedient to death on a cross (Php 2:8). Jesus' obedience was the most pleasing sacrifice to the Lord. By his obedience, sinners can now be free from sin.

Behold, to obey is better than sacrifice,
and to listen than the fat of rams.
23 For rebellion is as the sin of divination,
and presumption is as iniquity and idolatry.
Because you have rejected the word of the LORD,
he has also rejected you from being king."

24 Saul said to Samuel, "I have sinned, for I have transgressed the commandment of the LORD and your words, because I feared the people and obeyed their voice. 25 Now therefore, please pardon my sin and return with me that I may bow before the LORD." 26 And Samuel said to Saul, "I will not return with you. For you have rejected the word of the LORD, and the LORD has rejected you from being king over Israel." 27 As Samuel turned to go away, Saul seized the skirt of his robe, and it tore. 28 And Samuel said to him, "The LORD has torn the kingdom of Israel from you this day and has given it to a neighbor of yours, who is better than you. 29 And also the Glory of Israel will not lie or have regret, for he is not a man, that he should have regret." 30 Then he said, "I have sinned; yet honor me now before the elders of my people and before Israel, and return with me, that I may bow before the LORD your God." 31 So Samuel turned back after Saul, and Saul bowed before the LORD.

32 Then Samuel said, "Bring here to me Agag the king of the Amalekites." And Agag came to him cheerfully.[1] Agag said, "Surely the bitterness of death is past." 33 And Samuel said, "As your sword has made women childless, so shall your mother be childless among women." And Samuel hacked Agag to pieces before the LORD in Gilgal.

34 Then Samuel went to Ramah, and Saul went up to his house in Gibeah of Saul. 35 And Samuel did not see Saul again until the day of his death, but Samuel grieved over Saul. And the LORD regretted that he had made Saul king over Israel.

David Anointed King

16 The LORD said to Samuel, "How long will you grieve over Saul, since I have rejected him from being king over Israel? Fill your horn with oil, and go. I will send you to Jesse the Bethlehemite, for I have provided for myself a king among his sons." 2 And Samuel said, "How can I go? If Saul hears it, he will kill me." And the LORD said, "Take a heifer with you and say, 'I have come to sacrifice to the LORD.' 3 And invite Jesse to the sacrifice, and I will show you what you shall do. And you shall anoint for me him whom I declare to you." 4 Samuel did what the LORD commanded and came to Bethlehem. The elders of the city came to meet him trembling and said, "Do you come peaceably?" 5 And he said, "Peaceably; I have come to sacrifice to the LORD. Consecrate yourselves, and come with me to the sacrifice." And he consecrated Jesse and his sons and invited them to the sacrifice.

6 When they came, he looked on Eliab and thought, "Surely the LORD's anointed is before him." 7 But the LORD said to Samuel, "Do not look on his appearance or on the height of his stature, because I have rejected him. For the LORD sees not as man sees: man looks on the outward appearance, but the LORD looks on the heart." 8 Then Jesse called Abinadab and made him pass before Samuel. And he said, "Neither has the LORD chosen this one." 9 Then Jesse made Shammah pass by. And he said, "Neither has the LORD chosen this one." 10 And Jesse made seven of his sons pass before Samuel. And Samuel said to Jesse, "The LORD has not chosen these." 11 Then Samuel said to Jesse, "Are all your sons here?" And he said, "There remains yet the youngest,[2] but behold, he is keeping the sheep." And Samuel said to Jesse, "Send and get him, for we will not sit down till he comes here." 12 And he sent and brought him in. Now he was ruddy and had beautiful eyes and was handsome. And the LORD said, "Arise, anoint him, for this is he."

[1] Or *haltingly* (compare Septuagint); the Hebrew is uncertain [2] Or *smallest*

1 SAMUEL 16:1–13

ANOINTED ONE

Anointing with oil signified the act of placing a person into a special office or setting them apart for sacred rites. The word *messiah* means "anointed one" and refers to a king or priest set apart by God for a high position of service. This passage tells how God chose David to be Israel's king after Saul's refusal to remain true to God. David was anointed to become the king that Israel needed — one who would be faithful to God. While Saul and David both served as an "anointed one," they were ultimately paving the way for Jesus, the true Messiah and the ultimate anointed one.

In the Old Testament, the Messiah is referred to as David's son (Isa 9:6–7), the "root of Jesse" (Isa 11:10), and the servant of the Lord (Isa 42:1–4). God's people have always been in need of the salvation that the Messiah would bring through his personal suffering and death, and it is clear that he would eventually rule over the nations (Zec 9:9–10; Ro 15:12). In the New Testament, Jesus is clearly recognized as that Messiah, and he himself claimed to be God's anointed one (Mt 3:17; Jn 4:25–26).

LOOKING AT THE HEART

With all the drama of an "unlikely hero" story, 1 Samuel 16 introduces the reader to David, a shepherd boy from Bethlehem. King Saul had just recently been stripped of his kingship because of his disobedience, and Samuel went on the search for Israel's next king. God sent Samuel to meet Jesse in Bethlehem, where God instructed him to anoint one of Jesse's sons.

When Jesse's sons arrived, Samuel had an immediate assumption about whom God had in mind for king. Samuel remembered Saul's impressive appearance (9:1 – 2) as he saw Eliab, Jesse's oldest son. But God reminded Samuel that he is not concerned with one's appearance but rather their heart. In the end, God instructed Samuel to anoint David, the youngest of Jesse's sons. Samuel failed to see David's potential because he was only looking at his outward appearance. But God knew David's heart. He knew that David was different from Saul and that David was a man who desired the heart of God (1Sa 13:14; Ac 13:22). David may not have been impressive to those around him, but God knew what was inside him and saw that he would lead Israel in a way that glorified God.

David was an unlikely king. He was not the king that Israel expected, but he was the king that God wanted for them. Similarly, Jesus was not what many of the religious leaders expected the Messiah to be. Jesus — born in Bethlehem to a virgin mother and an earthly family of humble means — seemed nothing like the savior Israel imagined. They expected a warrior king, but God gave them a suffering servant who humbly gave himself for the sake of others (Isa 53:2 – 6; Php 2:1 – 11). Many people failed to recognize him for who he was, and in the end they put him to death (Isa 52:14; 53:2). They imagined a messiah who would destroy their enemies, but God gave them Jesus, who came to save their enemies by inviting them into his kingdom. Jesus was God in the flesh; his heart was completely pure. He may not have been externally impressive, but he embodied the perfect love and grace of God here on this earth.

13 Then Samuel took the horn of oil and anointed him in the midst of his brothers.
And the Spirit of the LORD rushed upon David from that day forward. And Samuel
rose up and went to Ramah.

David in Saul's Service

14 Now the Spirit of the LORD departed from Saul, and a harmful spirit from the
LORD tormented him. 15 And Saul's servants said to him, "Behold now, a harmful
spirit from God is tormenting you. 16 Let our lord now command your servants
who are before you to seek out a man who is skillful in playing the lyre, and when
the harmful spirit from God is upon you, he will play it, and you will be well." 17 So
Saul said to his servants, "Provide for me a man who can play well and bring him
to me." 18 One of the young men answered, "Behold, I have seen a son of Jesse the
Bethlehemite, who is skillful in playing, a man of valor, a man of war, prudent
in speech, and a man of good presence, and the LORD is with him." 19 Therefore
Saul sent messengers to Jesse and said, "Send me David your son, who is with
the sheep." 20 And Jesse took a donkey laden with bread and a skin of wine and a
young goat and sent them by David his son to Saul. 21 And David came to Saul and
entered his service. And Saul loved him greatly, and he became his armor-bearer.
22 And Saul sent to Jesse, saying, "Let David remain in my service, for he has found
favor in my sight." 23 And whenever the harmful spirit from God was upon Saul,
David took the lyre and played it with his hand. So Saul was refreshed and was
well, and the harmful spirit departed from him.

David and Goliath

17 Now the Philistines gathered their armies for battle. And they were gathered at Socoh, which belongs to Judah, and encamped between Socoh and
Azekah, in Ephes-dammim. 2 And Saul and the men of Israel were gathered, and
encamped in the Valley of Elah, and drew up in line of battle against the Philistines. 3 And the Philistines stood on the mountain on the one side, and Israel stood
on the mountain on the other side, with a valley between them. 4 And there came
out from the camp of the Philistines a champion named Goliath of Gath, whose
height was six[1] cubits[2] and a span. 5 He had a helmet of bronze on his head, and
he was armed with a coat of mail, and the weight of the coat was five thousand
shekels[3] of bronze. 6 And he had bronze armor on his legs, and a javelin of bronze
slung between his shoulders. 7 The shaft of his spear was like a weaver's beam, and
his spear's head weighed six hundred shekels of iron. And his shield-bearer went
before him. 8 He stood and shouted to the ranks of Israel, "Why have you come
out to draw up for battle? Am I not a Philistine, and are you not servants of Saul?
Choose a man for yourselves, and let him come down to me. 9 If he is able to fight
with me and kill me, then we will be your servants. But if I prevail against him and
kill him, then you shall be our servants and serve us." 10 And the Philistine said,
"I defy the ranks of Israel this day. Give me a man, that we may fight together."
11 When Saul and all Israel heard these words of the Philistine, they were dismayed
and greatly afraid.

12 Now David was the son of an Ephrathite of Bethlehem in Judah, named Jesse,
who had eight sons. In the days of Saul the man was already old and advanced in
years.[4] 13 The three oldest sons of Jesse had followed Saul to the battle. And the
names of his three sons who went to the battle were Eliab the firstborn, and next
to him Abinadab, and the third Shammah. 14 David was the youngest. The three
eldest followed Saul, 15 but David went back and forth from Saul to feed his father's
sheep at Bethlehem. 16 For forty days the Philistine came forward and took his
stand, morning and evening.

17 And Jesse said to David his son, "Take for your brothers an ephah[5] of this

---

[1]Hebrew; Septuagint, Dead Sea Scroll and Josephus *four* [2]A *cubit* was about 18 inches or 45 centimeters
[3]A *shekel* was about 2/5 ounce or 11 grams [4]Septuagint, Syriac; Hebrew *advanced among men* [5]An
ephah was about 3/5 bushel or 22 liters

parched grain, and these ten loaves, and carry them quickly to the camp to your brothers. [18]Also take these ten cheeses to the commander of their thousand. See if your brothers are well, and bring some token from them."

[19]Now Saul and they and all the men of Israel were in the Valley of Elah, fighting with the Philistines. [20]And David rose early in the morning and left the sheep with a keeper and took the provisions and went, as Jesse had commanded him. And he came to the encampment as the host was going out to the battle line, shouting the war cry. [21]And Israel and the Philistines drew up for battle, army against army. [22]And David left the things in charge of the keeper of the baggage and ran to the ranks and went and greeted his brothers. [23]As he talked with them, behold, the champion, the Philistine of Gath, Goliath by name, came up out of the ranks of the Philistines and spoke the same words as before. And David heard him.

[24]All the men of Israel, when they saw the man, fled from him and were much afraid. [25]And the men of Israel said, "Have you seen this man who has come up? Surely he has come up to defy Israel. And the king will enrich the man who kills him with great riches and will give him his daughter and make his father's house free in Israel." [26]And David said to the men who stood by him, "What shall be done for the man who kills this Philistine and takes away the reproach from Israel? For who is this uncircumcised Philistine, that he should defy the armies of the living God?" [27]And the people answered him in the same way, "So shall it be done to the man who kills him."

[28]Now Eliab his eldest brother heard when he spoke to the men. And Eliab's anger was kindled against David, and he said, "Why have you come down? And with whom have you left those few sheep in the wilderness? I know your presumption and the evil of your heart, for you have come down to see the battle." [29]And David said, "What have I done now? Was it not but a word?" [30]And he turned away from him toward another, and spoke in the same way, and the people answered him again as before.

[31]When the words that David spoke were heard, they repeated them before Saul, and he sent for him. [32]And David said to Saul, "Let no man's heart fail because of him. Your servant will go and fight with this Philistine." [33]And Saul said to David, "You are not able to go against this Philistine to fight with him, for you are but a youth, and he has been a man of war from his youth." [34]But David said to Saul, "Your servant used to keep sheep for his father. And when there came a lion, or a bear, and took a lamb from the flock, [35]I went after him and struck him and delivered it out of his mouth. And if he arose against me, I caught him by his beard and struck him and killed him. [36]Your servant has struck down both lions and bears, and this uncircumcised Philistine shall be like one of them, for he has defied the armies of the living God." [37]And David said, "The LORD who delivered me from the paw of the lion and from the paw of the bear will deliver me from the hand of this Philistine." And Saul said to David, "Go, and the LORD be with you!"

[38]Then Saul clothed David with his armor. He put a helmet of bronze on his head and clothed him with a coat of mail, [39]and David strapped his sword over his armor. And he tried in vain to go, for he had not tested them. Then David said to Saul, "I cannot go with these, for I have not tested them." So David put them off. [40]Then he took his staff in his hand and chose five smooth stones from the brook and put them in his shepherd's pouch. His sling was in his hand, and he approached the Philistine.

[41]And the Philistine moved forward and came near to David, with his shield-bearer in front of him. [42]And when the Philistine looked and saw David, he disdained him, for he was but a youth, ruddy and handsome in appearance. [43]And the Philistine said to David, "Am I a dog, that you come to me with sticks?" And the Philistine cursed David by his gods. [44]The Philistine said to David, "Come to me, and I will give your flesh to the birds of the air and to the beasts of the

field." 45Then David said to the Philistine, "You come to me with a sword and
with a spear and with a javelin, but I come to you in the name of the LORD of
hosts, the God of the armies of Israel, whom you have defied. 46This day the
LORD will deliver you into my hand, and I will strike you down and cut off your
head. And I will give the dead bodies of the host of the Philistines this day to
the birds of the air and to the wild beasts of the earth, that all the earth may
know that there is a God in Israel, 47and that all this assembly may know that
the LORD saves not with sword and spear. For the battle is the LORD's, and he will
give you into our hand."

48When the Philistine arose and came and drew near to meet David, David ran
quickly toward the battle line to meet the Philistine. 49And David put his hand in
his bag and took out a stone and slung it and struck the Philistine on his forehead.
The stone sank into his forehead, and he fell on his face to the ground.

50So David prevailed over the Philistine with a sling and with a stone, and
struck the Philistine and killed him. There was no sword in the hand of David.
51Then David ran and stood over the Philistine and took his sword and drew it out
of its sheath and killed him and cut off his head with it. When the Philistines saw
that their champion was dead, they fled. 52And the men of Israel and Judah rose
with a shout and pursued the Philistines as far as Gath[1] and the gates of Ekron,
so that the wounded Philistines fell on the way from Shaaraim as far as Gath
and Ekron. 53And the people of Israel came back from chasing the Philistines,
and they plundered their camp. 54And David took the head of the Philistine and
brought it to Jerusalem, but he put his armor in his tent.

55As soon as Saul saw David go out against the Philistine, he said to Abner, the
commander of the army, "Abner, whose son is this youth?" And Abner said, "As
your soul lives, O king, I do not know." 56And the king said, "Inquire whose son
the boy is." 57And as soon as David returned from the striking down of the Philistine, Abner took him, and brought him before Saul with the head of the Philistine
in his hand. 58And Saul said to him, "Whose son are you, young man?" And David
answered, "I am the son of your servant Jesse the Bethlehemite."

David and Jonathan's Friendship

18 As soon as he had finished speaking to Saul, the soul of Jonathan was knit
to the soul of David, and Jonathan loved him as his own soul. 2And Saul
took him that day and would not let him return to his father's house. 3Then Jonathan made a covenant with David, because he loved him as his own soul. 4And
Jonathan stripped himself of the robe that was on him and gave it to David, and
his armor, and even his sword and his bow and his belt. 5And David went out
and was successful wherever Saul sent him, so that Saul set him over the men of
war. And this was good in the sight of all the people and also in the sight of Saul's
servants.

Saul's Jealousy of David

6As they were coming home, when David returned from striking down the
Philistine, the women came out of all the cities of Israel, singing and dancing, to
meet King Saul, with tambourines, with songs of joy, and with musical instruments.[2] 7And the women sang to one another as they celebrated,

"Saul has struck down his thousands,
and David his ten thousands."

8And Saul was very angry, and this saying displeased him. He said, "They have
ascribed to David ten thousands, and to me they have ascribed thousands, and
what more can he have but the kingdom?" 9And Saul eyed David from that day on.

10The next day a harmful spirit from God rushed upon Saul, and he raved

[1]Septuagint; Hebrew *Gai* [2]Or *triangles*, or *three-stringed instruments*

1 SAMUEL 18:1–4

SACRIFICIAL FRIENDSHIP

This covenant between Jonathan and David was a mutual agreement in which the two men were bound to care for the needs and attend to the interests of each other. This is a beautiful picture of friendship. Jonathan had little to gain by entering into a covenant with David. As Saul's son, Jonathan was next in line to the throne. Instead, Jonathan took off his robe, armor, and sword (symbols of his kingly authority) and gave them to David. He honored David by giving up his rights. This is a great picture of friendship.

Jesus later told his disciples, "Greater love has no one than this, that someone lay down his life for his friends" (Jn 15:13). Like Jonathan gave up his rights to enter into a covenant with David, Jesus gave up his rights by laying down his life for sinners so that they could be called his friends. He laid aside his kingly robes and died the death of a sinner, so that sinners could have eternal life.

within his house while David was playing the lyre, as he did day by day. Saul had his spear in his hand. 11And Saul hurled the spear, for he thought, "I will pin David to the wall." But David evaded him twice.

12Saul was afraid of David because the LORD was with him but had departed from Saul. 13So Saul removed him from his presence and made him a commander of a thousand. And he went out and came in before the people. 14And David had success in all his undertakings, for the LORD was with him. 15And when Saul saw that he had great success, he stood in fearful awe of him. 16But all Israel and Judah loved David, for he went out and came in before them.

David Marries Michal

17Then Saul said to David, "Here is my elder daughter Merab. I will give her to you for a wife. Only be valiant for me and fight the LORD's battles." For Saul thought, "Let not my hand be against him, but let the hand of the Philistines be against him." 18And David said to Saul, "Who am I, and who are my relatives, my father's clan in Israel, that I should be son-in-law to the king?" 19But at the time when Merab, Saul's daughter, should have been given to David, she was given to Adriel the Meholathite for a wife.

20Now Saul's daughter Michal loved David. And they told Saul, and the thing pleased him. 21Saul thought, "Let me give her to him, that she may be a snare for him and that the hand of the Philistines may be against him." Therefore Saul said to David a second time,[1] "You shall now be my son-in-law." 22And Saul commanded his servants, "Speak to David in private and say, 'Behold, the king has delight in you, and all his servants love you. Now then become the king's son-in-law.'" 23And Saul's servants spoke those words in the ears of David. And David said, "Does it seem to you a little thing to become the king's son-in-law, since I am a poor man and have no reputation?" 24And the servants of Saul told him, "Thus and so did David speak." 25Then Saul said, "Thus shall you say to David, 'The king desires no bride-price except a hundred foreskins of the Philistines, that he may be avenged of the king's enemies.'" Now Saul thought to make David fall by the hand of the Philistines. 26And when his servants told David these words, it pleased David well to be the king's son-in-law. Before the time had expired, 27David arose and went, along with his men, and killed two hundred of the Philistines. And David brought their foreskins, which were given in full number to the king, that he might become the king's son-in-law. And Saul gave him his daughter Michal for a wife. 28But when Saul saw and knew that the LORD was with David, and that Michal, Saul's daughter, loved him, 29Saul was even more afraid of David. So Saul was David's enemy continually.

30Then the commanders of the Philistines came out to battle, and as often as they came out David had more success than all the servants of Saul, so that his name was highly esteemed.

Saul Tries to Kill David

19 And Saul spoke to Jonathan his son and to all his servants, that they should kill David. But Jonathan, Saul's son, delighted much in David. 2And Jonathan told David, "Saul my father seeks to kill you. Therefore be on your guard in the morning. Stay in a secret place and hide yourself. 3And I will go out and stand beside my father in the field where you are, and I will speak to my father about you. And if I learn anything I will tell you." 4And Jonathan spoke well of David to Saul his father and said to him, "Let not the king sin against his servant David, because he has not sinned against you, and because his deeds have brought good to you. 5For he took his life in his hand and he struck down the Philistine, and the LORD worked a great salvation for all Israel. You saw it, and rejoiced. Why then will you sin against innocent blood by killing David without cause?" 6And Saul

[1]Hebrew *by two*

1 SAMUEL 19:1

PERSECUTING AN INNOCENT ONE

Saul realized that the people loved David more than him. He became enraged and jealous and began plotting to kill David. When his more indirect plans to ensnare David crumbled (18:17–30), he clearly announced his plans to kill David. David was completely innocent according to the law, yet Saul wanted to kill him because he was a threat to Saul's power and control.

Jesus also posed a threat to the religious leaders of his day—so much so that they wanted him killed (Mt 12:14; Mk 3:6; Jn 11:53). Before Jesus' crucifixion, Pontius Pilate could not find any fault in Jesus but still sent him to be crucified because he feared losing his own power (Jn 19:1–16). If Jesus is indeed the King of kings, then only he is worthy to lead. In order to follow Jesus, control must be surrendered to him. Many people reject Jesus because they fear losing their own sense of power and control over their lives. But Jesus is a good king and can be trusted. Instead of trying to silence him, believers are invited to walk in faith and know that he is trustworthy to follow.

listened to the voice of Jonathan. Saul swore, "As the LORD lives, he shall not be
put to death." 7And Jonathan called David, and Jonathan reported to him all these
things. And Jonathan brought David to Saul, and he was in his presence as before.
8And there was war again. And David went out and fought with the Philistines
and struck them with a great blow, so that they fled before him. 9Then a harmful
spirit from the LORD came upon Saul, as he sat in his house with his spear in his
hand. And David was playing the lyre. 10And Saul sought to pin David to the wall
with the spear, but he eluded Saul, so that he struck the spear into the wall. And
David fled and escaped that night.
11Saul sent messengers to David's house to watch him, that he might kill him in
the morning. But Michal, David's wife, told him, "If you do not escape with your
life tonight, tomorrow you will be killed." 12So Michal let David down through
the window, and he fled away and escaped. 13Michal took an image[1] and laid it on
the bed and put a pillow of goats' hair at its head and covered it with the clothes.
14And when Saul sent messengers to take David, she said, "He is sick." 15Then Saul
sent the messengers to see David, saying, "Bring him up to me in the bed, that I
may kill him." 16And when the messengers came in, behold, the image was in the
bed, with the pillow of goats' hair at its head. 17Saul said to Michal, "Why have
you deceived me thus and let my enemy go, so that he has escaped?" And Michal
answered Saul, "He said to me, 'Let me go. Why should I kill you?'"
18Now David fled and escaped, and he came to Samuel at Ramah and told him
all that Saul had done to him. And he and Samuel went and lived at Naioth. 19And
it was told Saul, "Behold, David is at Naioth in Ramah." 20Then Saul sent messengers to take David, and when they saw the company of the prophets prophesying,
and Samuel standing as head over them, the Spirit of God came upon the messengers of Saul, and they also prophesied. 21When it was told Saul, he sent other
messengers, and they also prophesied. And Saul sent messengers again the third
time, and they also prophesied. 22Then he himself went to Ramah and came to
the great well that is in Secu. And he asked, "Where are Samuel and David?" And
one said, "Behold, they are at Naioth in Ramah." 23And he went there to Naioth in
Ramah. And the Spirit of God came upon him also, and as he went he prophesied
until he came to Naioth in Ramah. 24And he too stripped off his clothes, and he
too prophesied before Samuel and lay naked all that day and all that night. Thus
it is said, "Is Saul also among the prophets?"

Jonathan Warns David

20 Then David fled from Naioth in Ramah and came and said before Jonathan, "What have I done? What is my guilt? And what is my sin before
your father, that he seeks my life?" 2And he said to him, "Far from it! You shall
not die. Behold, my father does nothing either great or small without disclosing
it to me. And why should my father hide this from me? It is not so." 3But David
vowed again, saying, "Your father knows well that I have found favor in your eyes,
and he thinks, 'Do not let Jonathan know this, lest he be grieved.' But truly, as
the LORD lives and as your soul lives, there is but a step between me and death."
4Then Jonathan said to David, "Whatever you say, I will do for you." 5David said to
Jonathan, "Behold, tomorrow is the new moon, and I should not fail to sit at table
with the king. But let me go, that I may hide myself in the field till the third day at
evening. 6If your father misses me at all, then say, 'David earnestly asked leave of
me to run to Bethlehem his city, for there is a yearly sacrifice there for all the clan.'
7If he says, 'Good!' it will be well with your servant, but if he is angry, then know
that harm is determined by him. 8Therefore deal kindly with your servant, for you
have brought your servant into a covenant of the LORD with you. But if there is
guilt in me, kill me yourself, for why should you bring me to your father?" 9And
Jonathan said, "Far be it from you! If I knew that it was determined by my father

[1]Or *a household god*

that harm should come to you, would I not tell you?" 10Then David said to Jonathan, "Who will tell me if your father answers you roughly?" 11And Jonathan said
to David, "Come, let us go out into the field." So they both went out into the field.
12And Jonathan said to David, "The LORD, the God of Israel, be witness![1] When I
have sounded out my father, about this time tomorrow, or the third day, behold, if
he is well disposed toward David, shall I not then send and disclose it to you? 13But
should it please my father to do you harm, the LORD do so to Jonathan and more
also if I do not disclose it to you and send you away, that you may go in safety.
May the LORD be with you, as he has been with my father. 14If I am still alive, show
me the steadfast love of the LORD, that I may not die; 15and do not cut off[2] your
steadfast love from my house forever, when the LORD cuts off every one of the enemies of David from the face of the earth." 16And Jonathan made a covenant with
the house of David, saying, "May[3] the LORD take vengeance on David's enemies."
17And Jonathan made David swear again by his love for him, for he loved him as
he loved his own soul.
18Then Jonathan said to him, "Tomorrow is the new moon, and you will be
missed, because your seat will be empty. 19On the third day go down quickly to
the place where you hid yourself when the matter was in hand, and remain beside
the stone heap.[4] 20And I will shoot three arrows to the side of it, as though I shot
at a mark. 21And behold, I will send the boy, saying, 'Go, find the arrows.' If I say
to the boy, 'Look, the arrows are on this side of you, take them,' then you are to
come, for, as the LORD lives, it is safe for you and there is no danger. 22But if I say
to the youth, 'Look, the arrows are beyond you,' then go, for the LORD has sent you
away. 23And as for the matter of which you and I have spoken, behold, the LORD is
between you and me forever."
24So David hid himself in the field. And when the new moon came, the king
sat down to eat food. 25The king sat on his seat, as at other times, on the seat by
the wall. Jonathan sat opposite,[5] and Abner sat by Saul's side, but David's place
was empty.
26Yet Saul did not say anything that day, for he thought, "Something has happened to him. He is not clean; surely he is not clean." 27But on the second day, the
day after the new moon, David's place was empty. And Saul said to Jonathan his
son, "Why has not the son of Jesse come to the meal, either yesterday or today?"
28Jonathan answered Saul, "David earnestly asked leave of me to go to Bethlehem.
29He said, 'Let me go, for our clan holds a sacrifice in the city, and my brother has
commanded me to be there. So now, if I have found favor in your eyes, let me get
away and see my brothers.' For this reason he has not come to the king's table."
30Then Saul's anger was kindled against Jonathan, and he said to him, "You
son of a perverse, rebellious woman, do I not know that you have chosen the
son of Jesse to your own shame, and to the shame of your mother's nakedness?
31For as long as the son of Jesse lives on the earth, neither you nor your kingdom
shall be established. Therefore send and bring him to me, for he shall surely die."
32Then Jonathan answered Saul his father, "Why should he be put to death? What
has he done?" 33But Saul hurled his spear at him to strike him. So Jonathan knew
that his father was determined to put David to death. 34And Jonathan rose from
the table in fierce anger and ate no food the second day of the month, for he was
grieved for David, because his father had disgraced him.
35In the morning Jonathan went out into the field to the appointment with
David, and with him a little boy. 36And he said to his boy, "Run and find the arrows that I shoot." As the boy ran, he shot an arrow beyond him. 37And when the
boy came to the place of the arrow that Jonathan had shot, Jonathan called after
the boy and said, "Is not the arrow beyond you?" 38And Jonathan called after the
boy, "Hurry! Be quick! Do not stay!" So Jonathan's boy gathered up the arrows and

[1]Hebrew lacks *be witness* [2]Or *but if I die, do not cut off* [3]Septuagint *earth,* [16]*let not the name of Jonathan be cut off from the house of David. And may* [4]Septuagint; Hebrew *the stone Ezel* [5]Compare Septuagint; Hebrew *stood up*

came to his master. 39 But the boy knew nothing. Only Jonathan and David knew
the matter. 40 And Jonathan gave his weapons to his boy and said to him, "Go and
carry them to the city." 41 And as soon as the boy had gone, David rose from beside
the stone heap[1] and fell on his face to the ground and bowed three times. And they
kissed one another and wept with one another, David weeping the most. 42 Then
Jonathan said to David, "Go in peace, because we have sworn both of us in the
name of the LORD, saying, 'The LORD shall be between me and you, and between
my offspring and your offspring, forever.'" And he rose and departed, and Jonathan went into the city.[2]

David and the Holy Bread

21 [3] Then David came to Nob, to Ahimelech the priest. And Ahimelech came
to meet David, trembling, and said to him, "Why are you alone, and no
one with you?" 2 And David said to Ahimelech the priest, "The king has charged
me with a matter and said to me, 'Let no one know anything of the matter about
which I send you, and with which I have charged you.' I have made an appointment with the young men for such and such a place. 3 Now then, what do you
have on hand? Give me five loaves of bread, or whatever is here." 4 And the priest
answered David, "I have no common bread on hand, but there is holy bread—if
the young men have kept themselves from women." 5 And David answered the
priest, "Truly women have been kept from us as always when I go on an expedition. The vessels of the young men are holy even when it is an ordinary journey.
How much more today will their vessels be holy?" 6 So the priest gave him the
holy bread, for there was no bread there but the bread of the Presence, which
is removed from before the LORD, to be replaced by hot bread on the day it is
taken away.
7 Now a certain man of the servants of Saul was there that day, detained before
the LORD. His name was Doeg the Edomite, the chief of Saul's herdsmen.
8 Then David said to Ahimelech, "Then have you not here a spear or a sword at
hand? For I have brought neither my sword nor my weapons with me, because the
king's business required haste." 9 And the priest said, "The sword of Goliath the
Philistine, whom you struck down in the Valley of Elah, behold, it is here wrapped
in a cloth behind the ephod. If you will take that, take it, for there is none but that
here." And David said, "There is none like that; give it to me."

David Flees to Gath

10 And David rose and fled that day from Saul and went to Achish the king of
Gath. 11 And the servants of Achish said to him, "Is not this David the king of the
land? Did they not sing to one another of him in dances,

'Saul has struck down his thousands,
  and David his ten thousands'?"

12 And David took these words to heart and was much afraid of Achish the king
of Gath. 13 So he changed his behavior before them and pretended to be insane
in their hands and made marks on the doors of the gate and let his spittle run
down his beard. 14 Then Achish said to his servants, "Behold, you see the man is
mad. Why then have you brought him to me? 15 Do I lack madmen, that you have
brought this fellow to behave as a madman in my presence? Shall this fellow come
into my house?"

David at the Cave of Adullam

22 David departed from there and escaped to the cave of Adullam. And when
his brothers and all his father's house heard it, they went down there to
him. 2 And everyone who was in distress, and everyone who was in debt, and

[1] Septuagint; Hebrew *from beside the south* [2] This sentence is 21:1 in Hebrew [3] Ch 21:2 in Hebrew

1 SAMUEL 21:3–6

HOLY BREAD

In response to David's request for provisions, Ahimelech explained that there was no ordinary bread. The only bread available was the sacred or consecrated bread, sometimes called the "bread of the Presence," which had been displayed before the Lord in the tabernacle (v. 6; Ex 25:30; Lev 24:5–9). According to God's law, this bread could be eaten only by priests. David explained to Ahimelech that his men had avoided ritual impurity, having had no recent sexual contact with women (Ex 19:15; Lev 15:16–18). And this consecrated bread had been replaced with new bread before the Lord.

The Talmud, the Jewish collection of laws and doctrines, explains this apparent breach of the law on the basis that the preservation of life takes precedence over nearly all other commandments in the law. Jesus referred to this incident in his discussion with the Pharisees concerning the Sabbath (Mt 12:2–4; Mk 2:25–26). The spirit of the law was kept by Ahimelech's compassionate act.

1 SAMUEL 22:1–2

AN UNIMPRESSIVE TEAM

While David was on the run from Saul, many men began to form around him offering protection, and he rose to become their commander. What a ragtag crowd assembled around David! These were primarily men who were oppressed and discontented with Saul's rule. Many were distressed. Others were in considerable debt—meaning they

(continued on next page)

(An Unimpressive Team, continued)

were in danger of being sold into slavery by their creditors (2Ki 4:1). The four hundred men soon grew to six hundred (1Sa 23:13). They were a group of drifters and debtors, troublemakers and those who were troubled. But many of them would ultimately become David's "mighty men" (2Sa 23:8–39).

In the New Testament, Jesus assembled a team consisting of tax collectors, fishermen, and zealots. Jesus' group of disciples would not be impressive, but the apostle Paul would say, "Not many of you were wise according to worldly standards ... But God chose what is foolish in the world to shame the wise; God chose what is weak in the world to shame the strong" (1Co 1:26–27).

everyone who was bitter in soul,[1] gathered to him. And he became commander over them. And there were with him about four hundred men.

3 And David went from there to Mizpeh of Moab. And he said to the king of Moab, "Please let my father and my mother stay[2] with you, till I know what God will do for me." 4 And he left them with the king of Moab, and they stayed with him all the time that David was in the stronghold. 5 Then the prophet Gad said to David, "Do not remain in the stronghold; depart, and go into the land of Judah." So David departed and went into the forest of Hereth.

Saul Kills the Priests at Nob

6 Now Saul heard that David was discovered, and the men who were with him. Saul was sitting at Gibeah under the tamarisk tree on the height with his spear in his hand, and all his servants were standing about him. 7 And Saul said to his servants who stood about him, "Hear now, people of Benjamin; will the son of Jesse give every one of you fields and vineyards, will he make you all commanders of thousands and commanders of hundreds, 8 that all of you have conspired against me? No one discloses to me when my son makes a covenant with the son of Jesse. None of you is sorry for me or discloses to me that my son has stirred up my servant against me, to lie in wait, as at this day." 9 Then answered Doeg the Edomite, who stood by the servants of Saul, "I saw the son of Jesse coming to Nob, to Ahimelech the son of Ahitub, 10 and he inquired of the LORD for him and gave him provisions and gave him the sword of Goliath the Philistine."

11 Then the king sent to summon Ahimelech the priest, the son of Ahitub, and all his father's house, the priests who were at Nob, and all of them came to the king. 12 And Saul said, "Hear now, son of Ahitub." And he answered, "Here I am, my lord." 13 And Saul said to him, "Why have you conspired against me, you and the son of Jesse, in that you have given him bread and a sword and have inquired of God for him, so that he has risen against me, to lie in wait, as at this day?" 14 Then Ahimelech answered the king, "And who among all your servants is so faithful as David, who is the king's son-in-law, and captain over[3] your bodyguard, and honored in your house? 15 Is today the first time that I have inquired of God for him? No! Let not the king impute anything to his servant or to all the house of my father, for your servant has known nothing of all this, much or little." 16 And the king said, "You shall surely die, Ahimelech, you and all your father's house." 17 And the king said to the guard who stood about him, "Turn and kill the priests of the LORD, because their hand also is with David, and they knew that he fled and did not disclose it to me." But the servants of the king would not put out their hand to strike the priests of the LORD. 18 Then the king said to Doeg, "You turn and strike the priests." And Doeg the Edomite turned and struck down the priests, and he killed on that day eighty-five persons who wore the linen ephod. 19 And Nob, the city of the priests, he put to the sword; both man and woman, child and infant, ox, donkey and sheep, he put to the sword.

20 But one of the sons of Ahimelech the son of Ahitub, named Abiathar, escaped and fled after David. 21 And Abiathar told David that Saul had killed the priests of the LORD. 22 And David said to Abiathar, "I knew on that day, when Doeg the Edomite was there, that he would surely tell Saul. I have occasioned the death of all the persons of your father's house. 23 Stay with me; do not be afraid, for he who seeks my life seeks your life. With me you shall be in safekeeping."

David Saves the City of Keilah

23 Now they told David, "Behold, the Philistines are fighting against Keilah and are robbing the threshing floors." 2 Therefore David inquired of the LORD, "Shall I go and attack these Philistines?" And the LORD said to David, "Go

[1] Or *discontented* [2] Syriac, Vulgate; Hebrew *go out* [3] Septuagint, Targum; Hebrew *and has turned aside to*

and attack the Philistines and save Keilah." 3But David's men said to him, "Behold,
we are afraid here in Judah; how much more then if we go to Keilah against the
armies of the Philistines?" 4Then David inquired of the LORD again. And the LORD
answered him, "Arise, go down to Keilah, for I will give the Philistines into your
hand." 5And David and his men went to Keilah and fought with the Philistines and
brought away their livestock and struck them with a great blow. So David saved
the inhabitants of Keilah.

6When Abiathar the son of Ahimelech had fled to David to Keilah, he had come
down with an ephod in his hand. 7Now it was told Saul that David had come to
Keilah. And Saul said, "God has given him into my hand, for he has shut himself in
by entering a town that has gates and bars." 8And Saul summoned all the people to
war, to go down to Keilah, to besiege David and his men. 9David knew that Saul was
plotting harm against him. And he said to Abiathar the priest, "Bring the ephod
here." 10Then David said, "O LORD, the God of Israel, your servant has surely heard
that Saul seeks to come to Keilah, to destroy the city on my account. 11Will the men
of Keilah surrender me into his hand? Will Saul come down, as your servant has
heard? O LORD, the God of Israel, please tell your servant." And the LORD said, "He
will come down." 12Then David said, "Will the men of Keilah surrender me and my
men into the hand of Saul?" And the LORD said, "They will surrender you." 13Then
David and his men, who were about six hundred, arose and departed from Keilah,
and they went wherever they could go. When Saul was told that David had escaped
from Keilah, he gave up the expedition. 14And David remained in the strongholds in
the wilderness, in the hill country of the wilderness of Ziph. And Saul sought him
every day, but God did not give him into his hand.

Saul Pursues David

15David saw that Saul had come out to seek his life. David was in the wilderness of Ziph at Horesh. 16And Jonathan, Saul's son, rose and went to David at
Horesh, and strengthened his hand in God. 17And he said to him, "Do not fear,
for the hand of Saul my father shall not find you. You shall be king over Israel,
and I shall be next to you. Saul my father also knows this." 18And the two of them
made a covenant before the LORD. David remained at Horesh, and Jonathan went
home.

19Then the Ziphites went up to Saul at Gibeah, saying, "Is not David hiding
among us in the strongholds at Horesh, on the hill of Hachilah, which is south of
Jeshimon? 20Now come down, O king, according to all your heart's desire to come
down, and our part shall be to surrender him into the king's hand." 21And Saul
said, "May you be blessed by the LORD, for you have had compassion on me. 22Go,
make yet more sure. Know and see the place where his foot is, and who has seen
him there, for it is told me that he is very cunning. 23See therefore and take note of
all the lurking places where he hides, and come back to me with sure information.
Then I will go with you. And if he is in the land, I will search him out among all the
thousands of Judah." 24And they arose and went to Ziph ahead of Saul.

Now David and his men were in the wilderness of Maon, in the Arabah to the
south of Jeshimon. 25And Saul and his men went to seek him. And David was told,
so he went down to the rock and lived in the wilderness of Maon. And when Saul
heard that, he pursued after David in the wilderness of Maon. 26Saul went on one
side of the mountain, and David and his men on the other side of the mountain.
And David was hurrying to get away from Saul. As Saul and his men were closing
in on David and his men to capture them, 27a messenger came to Saul, saying,
"Hurry and come, for the Philistines have made a raid against the land." 28So Saul
returned from pursuing after David and went against the Philistines. Therefore
that place was called the Rock of Escape.[1] 29[2]And David went up from there and
lived in the strongholds of Engedi.

---

[1]Or *Rock of Divisions* [2]Ch 24:1 in Hebrew

David Spares Saul's Life

24 [1] When Saul returned from following the Philistines, he was told, "Behold,
David is in the wilderness of Engedi." 2Then Saul took three thousand
chosen men out of all Israel and went to seek David and his men in front of the
Wildgoats' Rocks. 3And he came to the sheepfolds by the way, where there was
a cave, and Saul went in to relieve himself.[2] Now David and his men were sitting
in the innermost parts of the cave. 4And the men of David said to him, "Here is
the day of which the LORD said to you, 'Behold, I will give your enemy into your
hand, and you shall do to him as it shall seem good to you.'" Then David arose
and stealthily cut off a corner of Saul's robe. 5And afterward David's heart struck
him, because he had cut off a corner of Saul's robe. 6He said to his men, "The LORD
forbid that I should do this thing to my lord, the LORD's anointed, to put out my
hand against him, seeing he is the LORD's anointed." 7So David persuaded his men
with these words and did not permit them to attack Saul. And Saul rose up and
left the cave and went on his way.

8Afterward David also arose and went out of the cave, and called after Saul,
"My lord the king!" And when Saul looked behind him, David bowed with his face
to the earth and paid homage. 9And David said to Saul, "Why do you listen to the
words of men who say, 'Behold, David seeks your harm'? 10Behold, this day your
eyes have seen how the LORD gave you today into my hand in the cave. And some
told me to kill you, but I spared you.[3] I said, 'I will not put out my hand against my
lord, for he is the LORD's anointed.' 11See, my father, see the corner of your robe
in my hand. For by the fact that I cut off the corner of your robe and did not kill
you, you may know and see that there is no wrong or treason in my hands. I have
not sinned against you, though you hunt my life to take it. 12May the LORD judge
between me and you, may the LORD avenge me against you, but my hand shall not
be against you. 13As the proverb of the ancients says, 'Out of the wicked comes
wickedness.' But my hand shall not be against you. 14After whom has the king of
Israel come out? After whom do you pursue? After a dead dog! After a flea! 15May
the LORD therefore be judge and give sentence between me and you, and see to it
and plead my cause and deliver me from your hand."

16As soon as David had finished speaking these words to Saul, Saul said, "Is
this your voice, my son David?" And Saul lifted up his voice and wept. 17He said
to David, "You are more righteous than I, for you have repaid me good, whereas
I have repaid you evil. 18And you have declared this day how you have dealt well
with me, in that you did not kill me when the LORD put me into your hands. 19For
if a man finds his enemy, will he let him go away safe? So may the LORD reward
you with good for what you have done to me this day. 20And now, behold, I know
that you shall surely be king, and that the kingdom of Israel shall be established
in your hand. 21Swear to me therefore by the LORD that you will not cut off my offspring after me, and that you will not destroy my name out of my father's house."
22And David swore this to Saul. Then Saul went home, but David and his men
went up to the stronghold.

The Death of Samuel

25 Now Samuel died. And all Israel assembled and mourned for him, and
they buried him in his house at Ramah.

David and Abigail

Then David rose and went down to the wilderness of Paran. 2And there was a
man in Maon whose business was in Carmel. The man was very rich; he had three
thousand sheep and a thousand goats. He was shearing his sheep in Carmel. 3Now
the name of the man was Nabal, and the name of his wife Abigail. The woman
was discerning and beautiful, but the man was harsh and badly behaved; he was

[1]Ch 24:2 in Hebrew [2]Hebrew *cover his feet* [3]Septuagint, Syriac, Targum; Hebrew *it* [my eye] *spared you*

---

1 SAMUEL 25:1–31

ABIGAIL INTERCEDES

When Abigail discovered that her husband, Nabal, had foolishly rejected David's request for food and water, she realized that her entire household was in danger. She collected and brought a large amount of food for David and his men, and she begged David for mercy. David was so affected by Abigail's words and actions that he extended mercy on her household and sent her home in peace.

This story offers an interesting parallel for understanding the work of Jesus. Mankind is like Nabal by foolishly rejecting God's goodness and consequently deserving his judgment. Like David, God holds all accountable for their disobedience. The only hope for humanity is someone to intercede like Abigail interceded for Nabal. She demonstrated how Jesus bridges the gap between sinful humanity and a holy God. Jesus intercedes on behalf of people and accepts the penalty for our sin so that we can receive mercy.

THE LORD'S ANOINTED

At this point in Israel's history, a civil war threatened to divide the nation as Saul was trying to kill David. David had ascended to great popularity while Saul had fallen out of favor with the people. While David was out slaying giants and winning battles, Saul's jealousy eroded the health of the kingdom. Blinded by his own insecurities, Saul lost the support of his people. Saul tried to kill David on numerous occasions until David finally fled to the wilderness.

For years, David had been running from Saul and his men. But something unexpected happened inside this cave. Saul found himself in a vulnerable position and at the mercy of David. Of course, David's men encouraged him to take advantage of the situation and end Saul's life. In this moment, David had the chance to end Saul's terror over his life and take the throne that God had ordained for him years earlier. David had the political power, the public's support, and the right from God to the throne, but he used this opportunity to reinforce Saul and his kingship instead of destroying him.

To cut off a piece of Saul's robe (vv. 4,11) would have been a symbolic act that discredited Saul's authority as king. It may have looked as if David was going to listen to the encouragements of his friends and kill Saul. Despite the fact that killing Saul would have seemed like the logical thing to do, David knew he could not kill God's anointed king no matter the circumstances. David refused to touch Saul because he was showing his allegiance to "the LORD's anointed" (vv. 6,10). David realized that all of his popularity and status had been given to him by God. Therefore, David trusted that God would protect him and give him the throne at the right time.

In the New Testament, Jesus demonstrated that he was truly the anointed Son of God. Yet the people used opportunities to disobey God's ways — and they struck the anointed one. Still, Jesus demonstrated great mercy. He did not strike back but instead forgave them and prayed for them (Lk 23:34). After his crucifixion, death, and burial, Jesus rose from the dead and took his rightful place on the throne in heaven, establishing his kingdom once and forever.

a Calebite. 4 David heard in the wilderness that Nabal was shearing his sheep. 5 So David sent ten young men. And David said to the young men, "Go up to Carmel, and go to Nabal and greet him in my name. 6 And thus you shall greet him:[1] 'Peace be to you, and peace be to your house, and peace be to all that you have. 7 I hear that you have shearers. Now your shepherds have been with us, and we did them no harm, and they missed nothing all the time they were in Carmel. 8 Ask your young men, and they will tell you. Therefore let my young men find favor in your eyes, for we come on a feast day. Please give whatever you have at hand to your servants and to your son David.' "

9 When David's young men came, they said all this to Nabal in the name of David, and then they waited. 10 And Nabal answered David's servants, "Who is David? Who is the son of Jesse? There are many servants these days who are breaking away from their masters. 11 Shall I take my bread and my water and my meat that I have killed for my shearers and give it to men who come from I do not know where?" 12 So David's young men turned away and came back and told him all this. 13 And David said to his men, "Every man strap on his sword!" And every man of them strapped on his sword. David also strapped on his sword. And about four hundred men went up after David, while two hundred remained with the baggage.

14 But one of the young men told Abigail, Nabal's wife, "Behold, David sent messengers out of the wilderness to greet our master, and he railed at them. 15 Yet the men were very good to us, and we suffered no harm, and we did not miss anything when we were in the fields, as long as we went with them. 16 They were a wall to us both by night and by day, all the while we were with them keeping the sheep. 17 Now therefore know this and consider what you should do, for harm is determined against our master and against all his house, and he is such a worthless man that one cannot speak to him."

18 Then Abigail made haste and took two hundred loaves and two skins of wine and five sheep already prepared and five seahs[2] of parched grain and a hundred clusters of raisins and two hundred cakes of figs, and laid them on donkeys. 19 And she said to her young men, "Go on before me; behold, I come after you." But she did not tell her husband Nabal. 20 And as she rode on the donkey and came down under cover of the mountain, behold, David and his men came down toward her, and she met them. 21 Now David had said, "Surely in vain have I guarded all that this fellow has in the wilderness, so that nothing was missed of all that belonged to him, and he has returned me evil for good. 22 God do so to the enemies of David[3] and more also, if by morning I leave so much as one male of all who belong to him."

23 When Abigail saw David, she hurried and got down from the donkey and fell before David on her face and bowed to the ground. 24 She fell at his feet and said, "On me alone, my lord, be the guilt. Please let your servant speak in your ears, and hear the words of your servant. 25 Let not my lord regard this worthless fellow, Nabal, for as his name is, so is he. Nabal[4] is his name, and folly is with him. But I your servant did not see the young men of my lord, whom you sent. 26 Now then, my lord, as the LORD lives, and as your soul lives, because the LORD has restrained you from bloodguilt and from saving with your own hand, now then let your enemies and those who seek to do evil to my lord be as Nabal. 27 And now let this present that your servant has brought to my lord be given to the young men who follow my lord. 28 Please forgive the trespass of your servant. For the LORD will certainly make my lord a sure house, because my lord is fighting the battles of the LORD, and evil shall not be found in you so long as you live. 29 If men rise up to pursue you and to seek your life, the life of my lord shall be bound in the bundle of the living in the care of the LORD your God. And the lives of your enemies he shall sling out as from the hollow of a sling. 30 And when the LORD has done to

---

[1] or *shall say to him who lives* [2] A *seah* was about 7.7 quarts or 7.3 liters [3] Septuagint *to David* [4] *Nabal* means *fool*

my lord according to all the good that he has spoken concerning you and has appointed you prince[1] over Israel, [31]my lord shall have no cause of grief or pangs of conscience for having shed blood without cause or for my lord working salvation himself. And when the LORD has dealt well with my lord, then remember your servant."

[32]And David said to Abigail, "Blessed be the LORD, the God of Israel, who sent you this day to meet me! [33]Blessed be your discretion, and blessed be you, who have kept me this day from bloodguilt and from working salvation with my own hand! [34]For as surely as the LORD, the God of Israel, lives, who has restrained me from hurting you, unless you had hurried and come to meet me, truly by morning there had not been left to Nabal so much as one male." [35]Then David received from her hand what she had brought him. And he said to her, "Go up in peace to your house. See, I have obeyed your voice, and I have granted your petition."

[36]And Abigail came to Nabal, and behold, he was holding a feast in his house, like the feast of a king. And Nabal's heart was merry within him, for he was very drunk. So she told him nothing at all until the morning light. [37]In the morning, when the wine had gone out of Nabal, his wife told him these things, and his heart died within him, and he became as a stone. [38]And about ten days later the LORD struck Nabal, and he died.

[39]When David heard that Nabal was dead, he said, "Blessed be the LORD who has avenged the insult I received at the hand of Nabal, and has kept back his servant from wrongdoing. The LORD has returned the evil of Nabal on his own head." Then David sent and spoke to Abigail, to take her as his wife. [40]When the servants of David came to Abigail at Carmel, they said to her, "David has sent us to you to take you to him as his wife." [41]And she rose and bowed with her face to the ground and said, "Behold, your handmaid is a servant to wash the feet of the servants of my lord." [42]And Abigail hurried and rose and mounted a donkey, and her five young women attended her. She followed the messengers of David and became his wife.

[43]David also took Ahinoam of Jezreel, and both of them became his wives. [44]Saul had given Michal his daughter, David's wife, to Palti the son of Laish, who was of Gallim.

David Spares Saul Again

26 Then the Ziphites came to Saul at Gibeah, saying, "Is not David hiding himself on the hill of Hachilah, which is on the east of Jeshimon?" [2]So Saul arose and went down to the wilderness of Ziph with three thousand chosen men of Israel to seek David in the wilderness of Ziph. [3]And Saul encamped on the hill of Hachilah, which is beside the road on the east of Jeshimon. But David remained in the wilderness. When he saw that Saul came after him into the wilderness, [4]David sent out spies and learned that Saul had indeed come. [5]Then David rose and came to the place where Saul had encamped. And David saw the place where Saul lay, with Abner the son of Ner, the commander of his army. Saul was lying within the encampment, while the army was encamped around him.

[6]Then David said to Ahimelech the Hittite, and to Joab's brother Abishai the son of Zeruiah, "Who will go down with me into the camp to Saul?" And Abishai said, "I will go down with you." [7]So David and Abishai went to the army by night. And there lay Saul sleeping within the encampment, with his spear stuck in the ground at his head, and Abner and the army lay around him. [8]Then Abishai said to David, "God has given your enemy into your hand this day. Now please let me pin him to the earth with one stroke of the spear, and I will not strike him twice." [9]But David said to Abishai, "Do not destroy him, for who can put out his hand against the LORD's anointed and be guiltless?" [10]And David said, "As the LORD lives,

[1]Or *leader*

1 SAMUEL 26:17–25

REPENTANCE AND ACTION

Saul considered David's popularity to be a threat to his power and authority. He wanted nothing more than for David to be out of the picture. For years, Saul pursued David hoping to kill him. David was understandably distressed as he constantly feared for his life, but God always protected him. On this particular occasion, David found Saul in a vulnerable position and had the opportunity to kill him—which would have ended David's struggle and gained him the kingship. When Saul realized his situation, he admitted that he had acted like a fool and even promised David that he would never again try to harm him. David was skeptical—he sensed that Saul had not truly repented or experienced a real change in character (27:1).

In the New Testament, when Jesus spoke of repentance he was speaking about something more than a mere apology. Repentance is a change in character, a turning and walking the other direction. Jesus began his ministry by proclaiming, "Repent, for the kingdom of heaven is at hand" (Mt 4:17). Turning to God and following Jesus are the genuine demonstrations of a new life.

1 SAMUEL 27:1

FEAR OF THE FUTURE

David confessed his greatest fear: "Now I shall perish one day by the *hand of Saul." He had been running* for his life from Saul for so long that he felt uncertain of his future. Perhaps David dreamed of his life before God had anointed him. Being

(continued on next page)

the LORD will strike him, or his day will come to die, or he will go down into battle and perish. 11The LORD forbid that I should put out my hand against the LORD's anointed. But take now the spear that is at his head and the jar of water, and let us go." 12So David took the spear and the jar of water from Saul's head, and they went away. No man saw it or knew it, nor did any awake, for they were all asleep, because a deep sleep from the LORD had fallen upon them.

13Then David went over to the other side and stood far off on the top of the hill, with a great space between them. 14And David called to the army, and to Abner the son of Ner, saying, "Will you not answer, Abner?" Then Abner answered, "Who are you who calls to the king?" 15And David said to Abner, "Are you not a man? Who is like you in Israel? Why then have you not kept watch over your lord the king? For one of the people came in to destroy the king your lord. 16This thing that you have done is not good. As the LORD lives, you deserve to die, because you have not kept watch over your lord, the LORD's anointed. And now see where the king's spear is and the jar of water that was at his head."

17Saul recognized David's voice and said, "Is this your voice, my son David?" And David said, "It is my voice, my lord, O king." 18And he said, "Why does my lord pursue after his servant? For what have I done? What evil is on my hands? 19Now therefore let my lord the king hear the words of his servant. If it is the LORD who has stirred you up against me, may he accept an offering, but if it is men, may they be cursed before the LORD, for they have driven me out this day that I should have no share in the heritage of the LORD, saying, 'Go, serve other gods.' 20Now therefore, let not my blood fall to the earth away from the presence of the LORD, for the king of Israel has come out to seek a single flea like one who hunts a partridge in the mountains."

21Then Saul said, "I have sinned. Return, my son David, for I will no more do you harm, because my life was precious in your eyes this day. Behold, I have acted foolishly, and have made a great mistake." 22And David answered and said, "Here is the spear, O king! Let one of the young men come over and take it. 23The LORD rewards every man for his righteousness and his faithfulness, for the LORD gave you into my hand today, and I would not put out my hand against the LORD's anointed. 24Behold, as your life was precious this day in my sight, so may my life be precious in the sight of the LORD, and may he deliver me out of all tribulation." 25Then Saul said to David, "Blessed be you, my son David! You will do many things and will succeed in them." So David went his way, and Saul returned to his place.

David Flees to the Philistines

27 Then David said in his heart, "Now I shall perish one day by the hand of Saul. There is nothing better for me than that I should escape to the land of the Philistines. Then Saul will despair of seeking me any longer within the borders of Israel, and I shall escape out of his hand." 2So David arose and went over, he and the six hundred men who were with him, to Achish the son of Maoch, king of Gath. 3And David lived with Achish at Gath, he and his men, every man with his household, and David with his two wives, Ahinoam of Jezreel, and Abigail of Carmel, Nabal's widow. 4And when it was told Saul that David had fled to Gath, he no longer sought him.

5Then David said to Achish, "If I have found favor in your eyes, let a place be given me in one of the country towns, that I may dwell there. For why should your servant dwell in the royal city with you?" 6So that day Achish gave him Ziklag. Therefore Ziklag has belonged to the kings of Judah to this day. 7And the number of the days that David lived in the country of the Philistines was a year and four months.

8Now David and his men went up and made raids against the Geshurites, the Girzites, and the Amalekites, for these were the inhabitants of the land from of old, as far as Shur, to the land of Egypt. 9And David would strike the land and

would leave neither man nor woman alive, but would take away the sheep, the
oxen, the donkeys, the camels, and the garments, and come back to Achish.
10When Achish asked, "Where have you made a raid today?" David would say,
"Against the Negeb of Judah," or, "Against the Negeb of the Jerahmeelites," or,
"Against the Negeb of the Kenites." 11And David would leave neither man nor
woman alive to bring news to Gath, thinking, "lest they should tell about us
and say, 'So David has done.'" Such was his custom all the while he lived in
the country of the Philistines. 12And Achish trusted David, thinking, "He has
made himself an utter stench to his people Israel; therefore he shall always be
my servant."

Saul and the Medium of En-dor

28 In those days the Philistines gathered their forces for war, to fight against
Israel. And Achish said to David, "Understand that you and your men are
to go out with me in the army." 2David said to Achish, "Very well, you shall know
what your servant can do." And Achish said to David, "Very well, I will make you
my bodyguard for life."
3Now Samuel had died, and all Israel had mourned for him and buried him in
Ramah, his own city. And Saul had put the mediums and the necromancers out
of the land. 4The Philistines assembled and came and encamped at Shunem. And
Saul gathered all Israel, and they encamped at Gilboa. 5When Saul saw the army
of the Philistines, he was afraid, and his heart trembled greatly. 6And when Saul
inquired of the LORD, the LORD did not answer him, either by dreams, or by Urim,
or by prophets. 7Then Saul said to his servants, "Seek out for me a woman who is
a medium, that I may go to her and inquire of her." And his servants said to him,
"Behold, there is a medium at En-dor."
8So Saul disguised himself and put on other garments and went, he and two
men with him. And they came to the woman by night. And he said, "Divine for me
by a spirit and bring up for me whomever I shall name to you." 9The woman said
to him, "Surely you know what Saul has done, how he has cut off the mediums
and the necromancers from the land. Why then are you laying a trap for my life to
bring about my death?" 10But Saul swore to her by the LORD, "As the LORD lives, no
punishment shall come upon you for this thing." 11Then the woman said, "Whom
shall I bring up for you?" He said, "Bring up Samuel for me." 12When the woman
saw Samuel, she cried out with a loud voice. And the woman said to Saul, "Why
have you deceived me? You are Saul." 13The king said to her, "Do not be afraid.
What do you see?" And the woman said to Saul, "I see a god coming up out of the
earth." 14He said to her, "What is his appearance?" And she said, "An old man is
coming up, and he is wrapped in a robe." And Saul knew that it was Samuel, and
he bowed with his face to the ground and paid homage.
15Then Samuel said to Saul, "Why have you disturbed me by bringing me up?"
Saul answered, "I am in great distress, for the Philistines are warring against me,
and God has turned away from me and answers me no more, either by prophets
or by dreams. Therefore I have summoned you to tell me what I shall do." 16And
Samuel said, "Why then do you ask me, since the LORD has turned from you and
become your enemy? 17The LORD has done to you as he spoke by me, for the LORD
has torn the kingdom out of your hand and given it to your neighbor, David. 18Be-
cause you did not obey the voice of the LORD and did not carry out his fierce
wrath against Amalek, therefore the LORD has done this thing to you this day.
19Moreover, the LORD will give Israel also with you into the hand of the Philistines,
and tomorrow you and your sons shall be with me. The LORD will give the army of
Israel also into the hand of the Philistines."
20Then Saul fell at once full length on the ground, filled with fear because of
the words of Samuel. And there was no strength in him, for he had eaten nothing all day and all night. 21And the woman came to Saul, and when she saw that
he was terrified, she said to him, "Behold, your servant has obeyed you. I have

(Fear of the Future, continued)

a shepherd was hard work, but as a keeper of sheep he would not have to live in constant fear for his life. As it was, it seemed like following God's will for his life was the scariest possible future.

In the New Testament, Jesus' disciples must have felt the same fear. Thomas said, "Let us also go, that we may die with him" (Jn 11:16). The disciples did not know the future, but they knew Jesus was trustworthy; they had seen him perform signs and wonders and had sat under his teaching. As Peter said, "Lord, to whom shall we go? You have the words of eternal life" (Jn 6:68). We do not know what the future holds, but we do know the one who holds the future: Jesus.

taken my life in my hand and have listened to what you have said to me. 22Now
therefore, you also obey your servant. Let me set a morsel of bread before you;
and eat, that you may have strength when you go on your way." 23He refused and
said, "I will not eat." But his servants, together with the woman, urged him, and
he listened to their words. So he arose from the earth and sat on the bed. 24Now
the woman had a fattened calf in the house, and she quickly killed it, and she took
flour and kneaded it and baked unleavened bread of it, 25and she put it before Saul
and his servants, and they ate. Then they rose and went away that night.

The Philistines Reject David

29 Now the Philistines had gathered all their forces at Aphek. And the Israelites were encamped by the spring that is in Jezreel. 2As the lords of the
Philistines were passing on by hundreds and by thousands, and David and his
men were passing on in the rear with Achish, 3the commanders of the Philistines
said, "What are these Hebrews doing here?" And Achish said to the commanders
of the Philistines, "Is this not David, the servant of Saul, king of Israel, who has
been with me now for days and years, and since he deserted to me I have found no
fault in him to this day." 4But the commanders of the Philistines were angry with
him. And the commanders of the Philistines said to him, "Send the man back,
that he may return to the place to which you have assigned him. He shall not go
down with us to battle, lest in the battle he become an adversary to us. For how
could this fellow reconcile himself to his lord? Would it not be with the heads of
the men here? 5Is not this David, of whom they sing to one another in dances,

'Saul has struck down his thousands,
and David his ten thousands'?"

6Then Achish called David and said to him, "As the LORD lives, you have been
honest, and to me it seems right that you should march out and in with me in the
campaign. For I have found nothing wrong in you from the day of your coming
to me to this day. Nevertheless, the lords do not approve of you. 7So go back now;
and go peaceably, that you may not displease the lords of the Philistines." 8And
David said to Achish, "But what have I done? What have you found in your servant
from the day I entered your service until now, that I may not go and fight against
the enemies of my lord the king?" 9And Achish answered David and said, "I know
that you are as blameless in my sight as an angel of God. Nevertheless, the commanders of the Philistines have said, 'He shall not go up with us to the battle.'
10Now then rise early in the morning with the servants of your lord who came
with you, and start early in the morning, and depart as soon as you have light."
11So David set out with his men early in the morning to return to the land of the
Philistines. But the Philistines went up to Jezreel.

David's Wives Are Captured

30 Now when David and his men came to Ziklag on the third day, the Amalekites had made a raid against the Negeb and against Ziklag. They had
overcome Ziklag and burned it with fire 2and taken captive the women and all[1]
who were in it, both small and great. They killed no one, but carried them off
and went their way. 3And when David and his men came to the city, they found
it burned with fire, and their wives and sons and daughters taken captive. 4Then
David and the people who were with him raised their voices and wept until they
had no more strength to weep. 5David's two wives also had been taken captive,
Ahinoam of Jezreel and Abigail the widow of Nabal of Carmel. 6And David was
greatly distressed, for the people spoke of stoning him, because all the people
were bitter in soul,[2] each for his sons and daughters. But David strengthened himself in the LORD his God.

7And David said to Abiathar the priest, the son of Ahimelech, "Bring me the

[1]Septuagint; Hebrew lacks *and all* [2]Compare 22:2

1 SAMUEL 30:3–6

FINDING STRENGTH THROUGH PRAYER

David found himself in a difficult situation. He was greatly distressed because he was grieving the capture of his family. He also feared for his life because his men wanted to stone him to death. They were angry and felt that David, as their leader, was the one responsible for the situation they were in. David felt hopeless, so he turned to the giver of hope and "strengthened himself in the LORD his God" (v. 6). David served as an example of how to respond in the midst of fear.

Likewise, Jesus demonstrated where our true source of strength is found. When Jesus felt the pressures of life, he would take time to pull away from his public ministry and seek solitude with God. When the crowds became too large, he would retreat to spend time with his Father (Mk 1:35). When the fear of the future was painful to bear, he communed with the Father to find the strength to continue (Mt 26:36). If even Jesus himself needed time alone with God to find strength, how much more so do we need to find strength in him? "Draw near to God, and he will draw near to you" (Jas 4:8).

SAUL AND THE MEDIUM AT EN-DOR

First Samuel 28 tells the story of Saul's final disobedience to the Lord. On the eve of the battle with the Philistines, Saul knew the outcome. When God refused to speak to him, Saul sought advice from a medium at En-dor. A "medium" was one who consulted the dead on behalf of the living. It was a form of witchcraft that was prevalent in the nations surrounding Israel. God, however, had condemned all forms of witchcraft (Ex 22:18; Lev 19:31; 20:6,27; Dt 18:10 – 12,14). The Israelites were not to associate with mediums as it would have been in direct disobedience to God. Once again, Saul went his own way rather than submitting to the way of the Lord.

The medium was aware of God's commands and was skeptical of Saul inquiring of her, thinking it was a trap. Saul assured her of her safety, and she obliged, bringing up Samuel. Samuel informed Saul that his days were numbered. Saul, the once-anointed king of Israel, was seeing the result of his disobedient life.

The story of Saul's disobedience should serve as a warning to all people; there are consequences to blatant and continued sin. Saul had gotten to the point where he felt as if he was above God's commands. He assumed the rules did not apply to him. By God's grace, the Holy Spirit is given to believers to help lead in God's ways (Jn 14:26 – 27). The Spirit illuminates the truth of the Scriptures in our lives and helps us apply God's Word. God has also provided the church to help when seeking counsel. When looking for wisdom, the Scriptures encourage people to seek counsel from godly friends who will help us live obedient to the ways of the Lord (Pr 11:14). Saul's life is a cautionary tale of trying to find wisdom apart from the Holy Spirit and godly counsel. Saul's attempt at wisdom apart from God led him on a downward slope into spiritual darkness. The wisdom of the Spirit, on the other hand, leads us into all truth (Jn 16:13).

ephod." So Abiathar brought the ephod to David. 8And David inquired of the LORD, "Shall I pursue after this band? Shall I overtake them?" He answered him, "Pursue, for you shall surely overtake and shall surely rescue." 9So David set out, and the six hundred men who were with him, and they came to the brook Besor, where those who were left behind stayed. 10But David pursued, he and four hundred men. Two hundred stayed behind, who were too exhausted to cross the brook Besor.

11They found an Egyptian in the open country and brought him to David. And they gave him bread and he ate. They gave him water to drink, 12and they gave him a piece of a cake of figs and two clusters of raisins. And when he had eaten, his spirit revived, for he had not eaten bread or drunk water for three days and three nights. 13And David said to him, "To whom do you belong? And where are you from?" He said, "I am a young man of Egypt, servant to an Amalekite, and my master left me behind because I fell sick three days ago. 14We had made a raid against the Negeb of the Cherethites and against that which belongs to Judah and against the Negeb of Caleb, and we burned Ziklag with fire." 15And David said to him, "Will you take me down to this band?" And he said, "Swear to me by God that you will not kill me or deliver me into the hands of my master, and I will take you down to this band."

David Defeats the Amalekites

16And when he had taken him down, behold, they were spread abroad over all the land, eating and drinking and dancing, because of all the great spoil they had taken from the land of the Philistines and from the land of Judah. 17And David struck them down from twilight until the evening of the next day, and not a man of them escaped, except four hundred young men, who mounted camels and fled. 18David recovered all that the Amalekites had taken, and David rescued his two wives. 19Nothing was missing, whether small or great, sons or daughters, spoil or anything that had been taken. David brought back all. 20David also captured all the flocks and herds, and the people drove the livestock before him,[1] and said, "This is David's spoil."

21Then David came to the two hundred men who had been too exhausted to follow David, and who had been left at the brook Besor. And they went out to meet David and to meet the people who were with him. And when David came near to the people he greeted them. 22Then all the wicked and worthless fellows among the men who had gone with David said, "Because they did not go with us, we will not give them any of the spoil that we have recovered, except that each man may lead away his wife and children, and depart." 23But David said, "You shall not do so, my brothers, with what the LORD has given us. He has preserved us and given into our hand the band that came against us. 24Who would listen to you in this matter? For as his share is who goes down into the battle, so shall his share be who stays by the baggage. They shall share alike." 25And he made it a statute and a rule for Israel from that day forward to this day.

26When David came to Ziklag, he sent part of the spoil to his friends, the elders of Judah, saying, "Here is a present for you from the spoil of the enemies of the LORD." 27It was for those in Bethel, in Ramoth of the Negeb, in Jattir, 28in Aroer, in Siphmoth, in Eshtemoa, 29in Racal, in the cities of the Jerahmeelites, in the cities of the Kenites, 30in Hormah, in Bor-ashan, in Athach, 31in Hebron, for all the places where David and his men had roamed.

The Death of Saul

31 Now the Philistines were fighting against Israel, and the men of Israel fled before the Philistines and fell slain on Mount Gilboa. 2And the Philistines overtook Saul and his sons, and the Philistines struck down Jonathan and

[1]The meaning of the Hebrew clause is uncertain

Abinadab and Malchi-shua, the sons of Saul. 3The battle pressed hard against
Saul, and the archers found him, and he was badly wounded by the archers. 4Then
Saul said to his armor-bearer, "Draw your sword, and thrust me through with it,
lest these uncircumcised come and thrust me through, and mistreat me." But his
armor-bearer would not, for he feared greatly. Therefore Saul took his own sword
and fell upon it. 5And when his armor-bearer saw that Saul was dead, he also fell
upon his sword and died with him. 6Thus Saul died, and his three sons, and his
armor-bearer, and all his men, on the same day together. 7And when the men of
Israel who were on the other side of the valley and those beyond the Jordan saw
that the men of Israel had fled and that Saul and his sons were dead, they abandoned their cities and fled. And the Philistines came and lived in them.

8The next day, when the Philistines came to strip the slain, they found Saul
and his three sons fallen on Mount Gilboa. 9So they cut off his head and stripped
off his armor and sent messengers throughout the land of the Philistines, to carry
the good news to the house of their idols and to the people. 10They put his armor
in the temple of Ashtaroth, and they fastened his body to the wall of Beth-shan.
11But when the inhabitants of Jabesh-gilead heard what the Philistines had done
to Saul, 12all the valiant men arose and went all night and took the body of Saul
and the bodies of his sons from the wall of Beth-shan, and they came to Jabesh
and burned them there. 13And they took their bones and buried them under the
tamarisk tree in Jabesh and fasted seven days.

JESUS: OUR ETERNAL ONE

2 SAMUEL

2 SAMUEL

REIGN OF DAVID BEGINS	ABSALOM REVOLTS AGAINST DAVID	DAVID DIES/SOLOMON BECOMES KING
c. 1010 BC	*c. 980 BC*	*c. 970 BC*

Second Samuel provides a biography of the life of one of history's greatest human leaders. God called and appointed King David, a man of unremarkable pedigree, to lead the nation of Israel following Saul's extended, but ultimately failed, reign. David inherited a fractured nation that, under God's direction, he built into a prominent, powerful, united nation. The book of 2 Samuel, like most political biographies, describes the character traits that enabled David to lead the people — traits such as his courage, faith, daily reliance on God, and wisdom. David's failures are also chronicled throughout the book, as his lust and pride ultimately hindered his leadership and resulted in tragic consequences for David, his family, and the nation.

Second Samuel describes the time from the death of Saul to the latter part of David's reign. With God's leading, David united the people and led this young nation to become a military power able to dominate the other, much more established nations of his day. After capturing the Jebusite fortress of Jerusalem, David made this fortified city the capital of the nation and organized Israel's worship of God at this key location. From there, David led the people to drive out the inhabitants of the land in all of the surrounding region. Israel's burgeoning military power combined with the waning influence of the pagan nations allowed David to eventually control territory from the border of Egypt to the Euphrates River. God's leadership over Israel and their submission to his rule allowed them to appropriate the blessings found in the promised land. God had not only proven faithful to give them the land, but he also was faithful to provide his promised blessings for their obedience.

The account of David's reign maintains a consistently hopeful tone in contrast to the failure seen at the end of Saul's rule. Even after his well-publicized personal failures, David's humility and leadership served as the embodiment of God's leadership among the people. Yet David himself would not be the eternal king; that king would come through David's line and would rule in a way far superior to David — without the sin that ultimately hampered David's reign. God reiterated his covenant commitment to his people and provided David with a unique glimpse into the way in which he would ultimately fulfill his promises in the Davidic covenant, where God promised David an eternal throne, an eternal reign, and an eternal dynasty (2Sa 7:12 – 16). God fulfilled this threefold promise to David by sending Jesus, the Messiah who had been promised for centuries. This perfect King would perfectly establish God's eternal throne, reign, and dynasty (Lk 1:32 – 33). It's this perfect reign that believers both enjoy today through the power of the Holy Spirit and look forward to in the future, when Jesus will return on the clouds to bring justice to the nations and to restore all of creation (Mt 24:30; 26:64).

THIS GOD — HIS WAY IS PERFECT;
THE WORD OF THE LORD PROVES TRUE;
HE IS A SHIELD FOR ALL THOSE WHO TAKE REFUGE IN HIM.

---

2 Samuel 22:31

2 SAMUEL

David Hears of Saul's Death

1 After the death of Saul, when David had returned from striking down the Amalekites, David remained two days in Ziklag. 2 And on the third day, behold, a man
came from Saul's camp, with his clothes torn and dirt on his head. And when he
came to David, he fell to the ground and paid homage. 3 David said to him, "Where
do you come from?" And he said to him, "I have escaped from the camp of Israel."
4 And David said to him, "How did it go? Tell me." And he answered, "The people fled
from the battle, and also many of the people have fallen and are dead, and Saul and
his son Jonathan are also dead." 5 Then David said to the young man who told him,
"How do you know that Saul and his son Jonathan are dead?" 6 And the young man
who told him said, "By chance I happened to be on Mount Gilboa, and there was
Saul leaning on his spear, and behold, the chariots and the horsemen were close
upon him. 7 And when he looked behind him, he saw me, and called to me. And I
answered, 'Here I am.' 8 And he said to me, 'Who are you?' I answered him, 'I am an
Amalekite.' 9 And he said to me, 'Stand beside me and kill me, for anguish has seized
me, and yet my life still lingers.' 10 So I stood beside him and killed him, because I was
sure that he could not live after he had fallen. And I took the crown that was on his
head and the armlet that was on his arm, and I have brought them here to my lord."

11 Then David took hold of his clothes and tore them, and so did all the men
who were with him. 12 And they mourned and wept and fasted until evening for
Saul and for Jonathan his son and for the people of the LORD and for the house of
Israel, because they had fallen by the sword. 13 And David said to the young man
who told him, "Where do you come from?" And he answered, "I am the son of a
sojourner, an Amalekite." 14 David said to him, "How is it you were not afraid to
put out your hand to destroy the LORD's anointed?" 15 Then David called one of the
young men and said, "Go, execute him." And he struck him down so that he died.
16 And David said to him, "Your blood be on your head, for your own mouth has
testified against you, saying, 'I have killed the LORD's anointed.'"

David's Lament for Saul and Jonathan

17 And David lamented with this lamentation over Saul and Jonathan his son,
18 and he said it[1] should be taught to the people of Judah; behold, it is written in
the Book of Jashar.[2] He said:

19 "Your glory, O Israel, is slain on your high places!
  How the mighty have fallen!
20 Tell it not in Gath,
  publish it not in the streets of Ashkelon,
lest the daughters of the Philistines rejoice,
  lest the daughters of the uncircumcised exult.

21 "You mountains of Gilboa,
  let there be no dew or rain upon you,
  nor fields of offerings![3]
For there the shield of the mighty was defiled,
  the shield of Saul, not anointed with oil.

22 "From the blood of the slain,
  from the fat of the mighty,
the bow of Jonathan turned not back,
  and the sword of Saul returned not empty.

[1] Septuagint; Hebrew *the Bow*, which may be the name of the lament's tune [2] Or *of the upright*
[3] Septuagint *firstfruits*

2 SAMUEL 1:17–27

GRACE AND FORGIVENESS

Some of the most amazing storylines throughout Scripture involve grace and forgiveness. Typically, when human reasoning would say that bitterness is warranted, God shows that his grace is enough. In this passage, David was extremely gracious regarding Saul. Rather than recount Saul's shortcomings, David chose to honor him in this song. In spite of all that Saul had done to harm David, he did not hold these things against him following his death.

Likewise, through Jesus, God does not hold the sins of believers against them. When he sees them, he does not see the sin, but he sees Jesus. "As far as the east is from the west, so far does he remove our transgressions from us" (Ps 103:12). In many respects, David prefigured the grace and forgiveness of Christ, foreshadowing Jesus' gracious response to people through all time. Even while suffering under the hands of his oppressors, Jesus responded with grace and forgiveness rather than employing the powerful wrath of God (Mt 26:53).

23 “Saul and Jonathan, beloved and lovely!
    In life and in death they were not divided;
  they were swifter than eagles;
    they were stronger than lions.

24 “You daughters of Israel, weep over Saul,
    who clothed you luxuriously in scarlet,
    who put ornaments of gold on your apparel.

25 “How the mighty have fallen
    in the midst of the battle!

  “Jonathan lies slain on your high places.
26   I am distressed for you, my brother Jonathan;
  very pleasant have you been to me;
    your love to me was extraordinary,
    surpassing the love of women.

27 “How the mighty have fallen,
    and the weapons of war perished!”

David Anointed King of Judah

2 After this David inquired of the Lord, “Shall I go up into any of the cities of Judah?” And the Lord said to him, “Go up.” David said, “To which shall I go up?”
And he said, “To Hebron.” 2So David went up there, and his two wives also, Ahinoam of Jezreel and Abigail the widow of Nabal of Carmel. 3And David brought up
his men who were with him, everyone with his household, and they lived in the
towns of Hebron. 4And the men of Judah came, and there they anointed David
king over the house of Judah.
When they told David, “It was the men of Jabesh-gilead who buried Saul,”
5David sent messengers to the men of Jabesh-gilead and said to them, “May you be
blessed by the Lord, because you showed this loyalty to Saul your lord and buried
him. 6Now may the Lord show steadfast love and faithfulness to you. And I will
do good to you because you have done this thing. 7Now therefore let your hands
be strong, and be valiant, for Saul your lord is dead, and the house of Judah has
anointed me king over them.”

Ish-bosheth Made King of Israel

8But Abner the son of Ner, commander of Saul’s army, took Ish-bosheth the
son of Saul and brought him over to Mahanaim, 9and he made him king over Gilead and the Ashurites and Jezreel and Ephraim and Benjamin and all Israel. 10Ish-
bosheth, Saul’s son, was forty years old when he began to reign over Israel, and
he reigned two years. But the house of Judah followed David. 11And the time that
David was king in Hebron over the house of Judah was seven years and six months.

The Battle of Gibeon

12Abner the son of Ner, and the servants of Ish-bosheth the son of Saul, went
out from Mahanaim to Gibeon. 13And Joab the son of Zeruiah and the servants of
David went out and met them at the pool of Gibeon. And they sat down, the one
on the one side of the pool, and the other on the other side of the pool. 14And Abner said to Joab, “Let the young men arise and compete before us.” And Joab said,
“Let them arise.” 15Then they arose and passed over by number, twelve for Benjamin and Ish-bosheth the son of Saul, and twelve of the servants of David. 16And
each caught his opponent by the head and thrust his sword in his opponent’s side,
so they fell down together. Therefore that place was called Helkath-hazzurim,[1]
which is at Gibeon. 17And the battle was very fierce that day. And Abner and the
men of Israel were beaten before the servants of David.

[1] *Helkath-hazzurim* means *the field of sword-edges*

2 SAMUEL 2:8–17

A GUARANTEED KINGDOM

David’s security, as king over the people of Israel, proved to be in question throughout this book. In the natural order of things, it would not be uncommon for the son of the deceased king to ascend to the throne. However, that was not God’s plan. David’s kingdom was guaranteed and never in question from the perspective of God’s sovereign oversight of his life.

Jesus was born as a proclaimed king, one whose reign would be without end, the one for whom Israel longed. Zechariah 9:9 states, “Rejoice greatly, O daughter of Zion! Shout aloud, O daughter of Jerusalem! Behold, your king is coming to you; righteous and having salvation is he, humble and mounted on a donkey, on a colt, the foal of a donkey.” Although it seemed that his rule was insecure to his disciples at times, Jesus’ kingdom was promised. Even today, when believers look around them and feel that the world has gone awry, God’s plan of final redemption has not changed. He is working all things to his glory and moving all things toward a final conclusion when Jesus will have final victory over all ungodliness (Rev 21:6–8). His is a kingdom that is guaranteed.

18And the three sons of Zeruiah were there, Joab, Abishai, and Asahel. Now Asahel was as swift of foot as a wild gazelle. 19And Asahel pursued Abner, and as he went, he turned neither to the right hand nor to the left from following Abner. 20Then Abner looked behind him and said, "Is it you, Asahel?" And he answered, "It is I." 21Abner said to him, "Turn aside to your right hand or to your left, and seize one of the young men and take his spoil." But Asahel would not turn aside from following him. 22And Abner said again to Asahel, "Turn aside from following me. Why should I strike you to the ground? How then could I lift up my face to your brother Joab?" 23But he refused to turn aside. Therefore Abner struck him in the stomach with the butt of his spear, so that the spear came out at his back. And he fell there and died where he was. And all who came to the place where Asahel had fallen and died, stood still.

24But Joab and Abishai pursued Abner. And as the sun was going down they came to the hill of Ammah, which lies before Giah on the way to the wilderness of Gibeon. 25And the people of Benjamin gathered themselves together behind Abner and became one group and took their stand on the top of a hill. 26Then Abner called to Joab, "Shall the sword devour forever? Do you not know that the end will be bitter? How long will it be before you tell your people to turn from the pursuit of their brothers?" 27And Joab said, "As God lives, if you had not spoken, surely the men would not have given up the pursuit of their brothers until the morning." 28So Joab blew the trumpet, and all the men stopped and pursued Israel no more, nor did they fight anymore.

29And Abner and his men went all that night through the Arabah. They crossed the Jordan, and marching the whole morning, they came to Mahanaim. 30Joab returned from the pursuit of Abner. And when he had gathered all the people together, there were missing from David's servants nineteen men besides Asahel. 31But the servants of David had struck down of Benjamin 360 of Abner's men. 32And they took up Asahel and buried him in the tomb of his father, which was at Bethlehem. And Joab and his men marched all night, and the day broke upon them at Hebron.

Abner Joins David

3 There was a long war between the house of Saul and the house of David. And David grew stronger and stronger, while the house of Saul became weaker and weaker.

2And sons were born to David at Hebron: his firstborn was Amnon, of Ahinoam of Jezreel; 3and his second, Chileab, of Abigail the widow of Nabal of Carmel; and the third, Absalom the son of Maacah the daughter of Talmai king of Geshur; 4and the fourth, Adonijah the son of Haggith; and the fifth, Shephatiah the son of Abital; 5and the sixth, Ithream, of Eglah, David's wife. These were born to David in Hebron.

6While there was war between the house of Saul and the house of David, Abner was making himself strong in the house of Saul. 7Now Saul had a concubine whose name was Rizpah, the daughter of Aiah. And Ish-bosheth said to Abner, "Why have you gone in to my father's concubine?" 8Then Abner was very angry over the words of Ish-bosheth and said, "Am I a dog's head of Judah? To this day I keep showing steadfast love to the house of Saul your father, to his brothers, and to his friends, and have not given you into the hand of David. And yet you charge me today with a fault concerning a woman. 9God do so to Abner and more also, if I do not accomplish for David what the Lord has sworn to him, 10to transfer the kingdom from the house of Saul and set up the throne of David over Israel and over Judah, from Dan to Beersheba." 11And Ish-bosheth could not answer Abner another word, because he feared him.

12And Abner sent messengers to David on his behalf,[1] saying, "To whom does

[1] Or *where he was*; Septuagint *at Hebron*

the land belong? Make your covenant with me, and behold, my hand shall be with
you to bring over all Israel to you." 13And he said, "Good; I will make a covenant
with you. But one thing I require of you; that is, you shall not see my face unless
you first bring Michal, Saul's daughter, when you come to see my face." 14Then
David sent messengers to Ish-bosheth, Saul's son, saying, "Give me my wife Michal, for whom I paid the bridal price of a hundred foreskins of the Philistines."
15And Ish-bosheth sent and took her from her husband Paltiel the son of Laish.
16But her husband went with her, weeping after her all the way to Bahurim. Then
Abner said to him, "Go, return." And he returned.

17And Abner conferred with the elders of Israel, saying, "For some time past
you have been seeking David as king over you. 18Now then bring it about, for the
LORD has promised David, saying, 'By the hand of my servant David I will save
my people Israel from the hand of the Philistines, and from the hand of all their
enemies.'" 19Abner also spoke to Benjamin. And then Abner went to tell David at
Hebron all that Israel and the whole house of Benjamin thought good to do.

20When Abner came with twenty men to David at Hebron, David made a feast
for Abner and the men who were with him. 21And Abner said to David, "I will
arise and go and will gather all Israel to my lord the king, that they may make a
covenant with you, and that you may reign over all that your heart desires." So
David sent Abner away, and he went in peace.

22Just then the servants of David arrived with Joab from a raid, bringing much
spoil with them. But Abner was not with David at Hebron, for he had sent him
away, and he had gone in peace. 23When Joab and all the army that was with him
came, it was told Joab, "Abner the son of Ner came to the king, and he has let him
go, and he has gone in peace." 24Then Joab went to the king and said, "What have
you done? Behold, Abner came to you. Why is it that you have sent him away, so
that he is gone? 25You know that Abner the son of Ner came to deceive you and
to know your going out and your coming in, and to know all that you are doing."

Joab Murders Abner

26When Joab came out from David's presence, he sent messengers after Abner,
and they brought him back from the cistern of Sirah. But David did not know
about it. 27And when Abner returned to Hebron, Joab took him aside into the
midst of the gate to speak with him privately, and there he struck him in the stomach, so that he died, for the blood of Asahel his brother. 28Afterward, when David
heard of it, he said, "I and my kingdom are forever guiltless before the LORD for
the blood of Abner the son of Ner. 29May it fall upon the head of Joab and upon
all his father's house, and may the house of Joab never be without one who has a
discharge or who is leprous or who holds a spindle or who falls by the sword or
who lacks bread!" 30So Joab and Abishai his brother killed Abner, because he had
put their brother Asahel to death in the battle at Gibeon.

David Mourns Abner

31Then David said to Joab and to all the people who were with him, "Tear your
clothes and put on sackcloth and mourn before Abner." And King David followed
the bier. 32They buried Abner at Hebron. And the king lifted up his voice and
wept at the grave of Abner, and all the people wept. 33And the king lamented for
Abner, saying,

"Should Abner die as a fool dies?
34 Your hands were not bound;
  your feet were not fettered;
as one falls before the wicked
  you have fallen."

And all the people wept again over him. 35Then all the people came to persuade
David to eat bread while it was yet day. But David swore, saying, "God do so to me

and more also, if I taste bread or anything else till the sun goes down!" 36And all the people took notice of it, and it pleased them, as everything that the king did pleased all the people. 37So all the people and all Israel understood that day that it had not been the king's will to put to death Abner the son of Ner. 38And the king said to his servants, "Do you not know that a prince and a great man has fallen this day in Israel? 39And I was gentle today, though anointed king. These men, the sons of Zeruiah, are more severe than I. The LORD repay the evildoer according to his wickedness!"

Ish-bosheth Murdered

4 When Ish-bosheth, Saul's son, heard that Abner had died at Hebron, his courage failed, and all Israel was dismayed. 2Now Saul's son had two men who were captains of raiding bands; the name of the one was Baanah, and the name of the other Rechab, sons of Rimmon a man of Benjamin from Beeroth (for Beeroth also is counted part of Benjamin; 3the Beerothites fled to Gittaim and have been sojourners there to this day).

4Jonathan, the son of Saul, had a son who was crippled in his feet. He was five years old when the news about Saul and Jonathan came from Jezreel, and his nurse took him up and fled, and as she fled in her haste, he fell and became lame. And his name was Mephibosheth.

5Now the sons of Rimmon the Beerothite, Rechab and Baanah, set out, and about the heat of the day they came to the house of Ish-bosheth as he was taking his noonday rest. 6And they came into the midst of the house as if to get wheat, and they stabbed him in the stomach. Then Rechab and Baanah his brother escaped.[1] 7When they came into the house, as he lay on his bed in his bedroom, they struck him and put him to death and beheaded him. They took his head and went by the way of the Arabah all night, 8and brought the head of Ish-bosheth to David at Hebron. And they said to the king, "Here is the head of Ish-bosheth, the son of Saul, your enemy, who sought your life. The LORD has avenged my lord the king this day on Saul and on his offspring." 9But David answered Rechab and Baanah his brother, the sons of Rimmon the Beerothite, "As the LORD lives, who has redeemed my life out of every adversity, 10when one told me, 'Behold, Saul is dead,' and thought he was bringing good news, I seized him and killed him at Ziklag, which was the reward I gave him for his news. 11How much more, when wicked men have killed a righteous man in his own house on his bed, shall I not now require his blood at your hand and destroy you from the earth?" 12And David commanded his young men, and they killed them and cut off their hands and feet and hanged them beside the pool at Hebron. But they took the head of Ish-bosheth and buried it in the tomb of Abner at Hebron.

David Anointed King of Israel

5 Then all the tribes of Israel came to David at Hebron and said, "Behold, we are your bone and flesh. 2In times past, when Saul was king over us, it was you who led out and brought in Israel. And the LORD said to you, 'You shall be shepherd of my people Israel, and you shall be prince[2] over Israel.'" 3So all the elders of Israel came to the king at Hebron, and King David made a covenant with them at Hebron before the LORD, and they anointed David king over Israel. 4David was thirty years old when he began to reign, and he reigned forty years. 5At Hebron he reigned over Judah seven years and six months, and at Jerusalem he reigned over all Israel and Judah thirty-three years.[3]

6And the king and his men went to Jerusalem against the Jebusites, the inhabitants of the land, who said to David, "You will not come in here, but the blind and the lame will ward you off"—thinking, "David cannot come in here." 7Nevertheless, David took the stronghold of Zion, that is, the city of David. 8And David said

[1] Septuagint *And behold, the doorkeeper of the house had been cleaning wheat, but she grew drowsy and slept. So Rechab and Baanah his brother slipped in* [2] Or *leader* [3] Dead Sea Scroll lacks verses 4–5

2 SAMUEL 4:1–12

RETRIBUTION AND GRACE

The deaths of Saul, Abner, and Ish-bosheth removed major obstacles from David's path to be king over Israel. David secured power in both the northern and southern territories as a result of Rimmon's two merciless sons, Baanah and Rechab. After murdering Ish-bosheth, these men expected a reward because they believed themselves to be agents acting on David's behalf and the Lord's. But they misread the situation, revealing that they did not know David's values as king and were mistaken concerning the judgment and purposes of God. Ultimately, David understood that men like Baanah and Rechab could not grasp that the Lord redeems life and brings judgment on the wrongdoer.

Another example of this is found in Luke 9:51–56. Jesus was on his way to Jerusalem and opted to go through Samaria, where he did not receive a warm reception. The disciples were incensed, particularly James and John, so they asked Jesus if they should call down fire from heaven to consume the Samaritans. Jesus rebuked the disciples, whose understanding of retribution was mistaken. Jesus, like David, embraced even bitter rivals in love and forgiveness—an embrace that he continues to offer to this day to those who deserve *nothing* other than retribution.

FORGIVENESS VERSUS RETALIATION

As Saul's chief military leader and head of his protection unit, Abner had no doubt made David's life miserable, seeking to kill him as Saul directed and desired. Yet David forgave Abner and formed a constructive alliance with him. In contrast, Joab hated Abner because Abner had killed his brother. As a result, Joab killed Abner. While Joab's desire to avenge his brother's death might be understandable, David too had reason to seek revenge. But he didn't. Instead he wept because of Abner's death. David, in a sign of mourning, put on sackcloth and wept at Abner's grave (vv. 31–32). The people of Israel were stunned by David's response and urged him to eat (v. 35). Instead, David reminded the people that a great man had died, and they too should honor him (vv. 36–39). In spite of Abner's sin, David did not treat him as his sin deserved but chose to esteem his life.

How much more astounding is the grace of God in the face of human sin. God knows all things — every aspect of the rebellious hearts of all people. Nothing is hidden from God (Heb 4:13). All sins that people try to hide are known fully by God. Yet God willingly forgives sin — blotting it out forever for those who place their faith in Jesus (Isa 43:25). This forgiveness does not mean that God turns a blind eye to human failures. He knows full well the treachery of his people, yet he forgives anyway. He removes sin as far as the east is from the west as an intentional act of his grace (Ps 103:12). How can a just God forgive in this way? Paul answered this in Romans 3:25–26. God is just because he did not simply ignore sin, but he placed the penalty for sin on his Son, Jesus. Because Jesus satisfied the wrath of God, those who know Jesus can be made right with God. In this way, God does not treat his children as their sin deserves but instead lavishes mercy and grace on them.

on that day, "Whoever would strike the Jebusites, let him get up the water shaft to attack 'the lame and the blind,' who are hated by David's soul." Therefore it is said, "The blind and the lame shall not come into the house." 9And David lived in the stronghold and called it the city of David. And David built the city all around from the Millo inward. 10And David became greater and greater, for the LORD, the God of hosts, was with him.

11And Hiram king of Tyre sent messengers to David, and cedar trees, also carpenters and masons who built David a house. 12And David knew that the LORD had established him king over Israel, and that he had exalted his kingdom for the sake of his people Israel.

13And David took more concubines and wives from Jerusalem, after he came from Hebron, and more sons and daughters were born to David. 14And these are the names of those who were born to him in Jerusalem: Shammua, Shobab, Nathan, Solomon, 15Ibhar, Elishua, Nepheg, Japhia, 16Elishama, Eliada, and Eliphelet.

David Defeats the Philistines

17When the Philistines heard that David had been anointed king over Israel, all the Philistines went up to search for David. But David heard of it and went down to the stronghold. 18Now the Philistines had come and spread out in the Valley of Rephaim. 19And David inquired of the LORD, "Shall I go up against the Philistines? Will you give them into my hand?" And the LORD said to David, "Go up, for I will certainly give the Philistines into your hand." 20And David came to Baal-perazim, and David defeated them there. And he said, "The LORD has broken through my enemies before me like a breaking flood." Therefore the name of that place is called Baal-perazim.[1] 21And the Philistines left their idols there, and David and his men carried them away.

22And the Philistines came up yet again and spread out in the Valley of Rephaim. 23And when David inquired of the LORD, he said, "You shall not go up; go around to their rear, and come against them opposite the balsam trees. 24And when you hear the sound of marching in the tops of the balsam trees, then rouse yourself, for then the LORD has gone out before you to strike down the army of the Philistines." 25And David did as the LORD commanded him, and struck down the Philistines from Geba to Gezer.

The Ark Brought to Jerusalem

6 David again gathered all the chosen men of Israel, thirty thousand. 2And David arose and went with all the people who were with him from Baale-judah to bring up from there the ark of God, which is called by the name of the LORD of hosts who sits enthroned on the cherubim. 3And they carried the ark of God on a new cart and brought it out of the house of Abinadab, which was on the hill. And Uzzah and Ahio,[2] the sons of Abinadab, were driving the new cart, 4with the ark of God,[3] and Ahio went before the ark.

Uzzah and the Ark

5And David and all the house of Israel were celebrating before the LORD, with songs[4] and lyres and harps and tambourines and castanets and cymbals. 6And when they came to the threshing floor of Nacon, Uzzah put out his hand to the ark of God and took hold of it, for the oxen stumbled. 7And the anger of the LORD was kindled against Uzzah, and God struck him down there because of his error, and he died there beside the ark of God. 8And David was angry because the LORD had broken out against Uzzah. And that place is called Perez-uzzah[5] to this day. 9And David was afraid of the LORD that day, and he said, "How can the ark of the LORD come to me?" 10So David was not willing to take the ark of the LORD into

[1] *Baal-perazim* means *Lord of breaking through* [2] Or *and his brother*; also verse 4 [3] Compare Septuagint; Hebrew *the new cart, 4and brought it out of the house of Abinadab, which was on the hill, with the ark of God* [4] Septuagint, 1 Chronicles 13:8; Hebrew *fir trees* [5] *Perez-uzzah* means *the breaking out against Uzzah*

---

2 SAMUEL 6:1–10

VIOLATING THE HOLINESS OF GOD

For Israel, the ark represented God's awe-inspiring presence, and it unified the twelve tribes as one people. For this pilgrimage David had men set the ark on a new cart pulled by oxen. When the oxen stumbled, Uzzah reached out to stabilize it. Immediately, the anger of the Lord burned against him and he died.

The Lord had given strict instructions concerning the transportation of the ark (Ex 25:13–14; Nu 4:15; 7:7–9; 2Ch 15:13–15). It was only to be transported by poles carried on the shoulders of Levites. When these commands were violated, the Lord defended his holiness. This zeal frightened David. All in the procession were reminded that when the fear of the Lord fades, the community is at risk. When sinful man encroaches upon the holiness of God, a price must be paid.

Because of Christ's atoning death and resurrection, believers now have access to boldly approach God in prayer with confidence and a clean conscience (Heb 10:19–22). Jesus paid the price for encroaching upon the holiness of God. On the cross, Jesus died in our place as payment. Therefore, Jesus opened a new and living way to enter the holy sanctuary of God.

JERUSALEM, THE CITY OF GOD

The city of Jerusalem has held a place of significance in Scripture for thousands of years. In one of his first acts as king over all the tribes of Israel, David assailed the Jebusites in Jerusalem, taking the city as his royal seat. He was able to do these things not by his own might but rather by the power of almighty God (v. 10). David and his army were mocked as weak (v. 6), but God enabled them to overpower the Jebusite warriors and gain control of the city. God established David's city as a physical manifestation of his goodness to his people. For years to come, it was described in Scripture with the utmost regard: the city of God (Ps 87:1 – 3), the place where God put his name (2Ki 21:4), a place of salvation (Isa 46:13), "the throne of the LORD" (Jer 3:17), and the holy city (Isa 52:1). This city, however, fell from prominence as the people of God faced hardships and exile at the hands of neighboring nations in the days to come.

Many years later, Jerusalem would again become central to the redemptive story of God. It was outside of this city where Jesus' sacrifice took place, establishing the promise of a future forever in the presence of God for those who repent of their sins while believing and calling on the name of Jesus for forgiveness. The promise of salvation from God was established through David at a physical location, and that location became the central place in which Jesus expanded God's kingdom through another victory — a victory over death.

In Christ, believers also look to Jerusalem with historical and spiritual significance as well as with hope of a beautiful promise associated with salvation. Revelation 21:1 – 5 reads, "Then I saw a new heaven and a new earth . . . And I saw the holy city, new Jerusalem, coming down out of heaven from God, prepared as a bride adorned for her husband. And I heard a loud voice from the throne saying, 'Behold, the dwelling place of God is with man. He will dwell with them, and they will be his people, and God himself will be with them as their God. He will wipe away every tear from their eyes, and death shall be no more, neither shall there be mourning, nor crying, nor pain anymore, for the former things have passed away.' And he who was seated on the throne said, 'Behold, I am making all things new.' "

the city of David. But David took it aside to the house of Obed-edom the Gittite. 11And the ark of the LORD remained in the house of Obed-edom the Gittite three months, and the LORD blessed Obed-edom and all his household.

12And it was told King David, "The LORD has blessed the household of Obed-edom and all that belongs to him, because of the ark of God." So David went and brought up the ark of God from the house of Obed-edom to the city of David with rejoicing. 13And when those who bore the ark of the LORD had gone six steps, he sacrificed an ox and a fattened animal. 14And David danced before the LORD with all his might. And David was wearing a linen ephod. 15So David and all the house of Israel brought up the ark of the LORD with shouting and with the sound of the horn.

David and Michal

16As the ark of the LORD came into the city of David, Michal the daughter of Saul looked out of the window and saw King David leaping and dancing before the LORD, and she despised him in her heart. 17And they brought in the ark of the LORD and set it in its place, inside the tent that David had pitched for it. And David offered burnt offerings and peace offerings before the LORD. 18And when David had finished offering the burnt offerings and the peace offerings, he blessed the people in the name of the LORD of hosts 19and distributed among all the people, the whole multitude of Israel, both men and women, a cake of bread, a portion of meat,[1] and a cake of raisins to each one. Then all the people departed, each to his house.

20And David returned to bless his household. But Michal the daughter of Saul came out to meet David and said, "How the king of Israel honored himself today, uncovering himself today before the eyes of his servants' female servants, as one of the vulgar fellows shamelessly uncovers himself!" 21And David said to Michal, "It was before the LORD, who chose me above your father and above all his house, to appoint me as prince[2] over Israel, the people of the LORD—and I will celebrate before the LORD. 22I will make myself yet more contemptible than this, and I will be abased in your[3] eyes. But by the female servants of whom you have spoken, by them I shall be held in honor." 23And Michal the daughter of Saul had no child to the day of her death.

The LORD's Covenant with David

7 Now when the king lived in his house and the LORD had given him rest from all his surrounding enemies, 2the king said to Nathan the prophet, "See now, I dwell in a house of cedar, but the ark of God dwells in a tent." 3And Nathan said to the king, "Go, do all that is in your heart, for the LORD is with you."

4But that same night the word of the LORD came to Nathan, 5"Go and tell my servant David, 'Thus says the LORD: Would you build me a house to dwell in? 6I have not lived in a house since the day I brought up the people of Israel from Egypt to this day, but I have been moving about in a tent for my dwelling. 7In all places where I have moved with all the people of Israel, did I speak a word with any of the judges[4] of Israel, whom I commanded to shepherd my people Israel, saying, "Why have you not built me a house of cedar?"' 8Now, therefore, thus you shall say to my servant David, 'Thus says the LORD of hosts, I took you from the pasture, from following the sheep, that you should be prince[5] over my people Israel. 9And I have been with you wherever you went and have cut off all your enemies from before you. And I will make for you a great name, like the name of the great ones of the earth. 10And I will appoint a place for my people Israel and will plant them, so that they may dwell in their own place and be disturbed no more. And violent men shall afflict them no more, as formerly, 11from the time that I appointed judges over my people Israel. And I will give you rest from all your

2 SAMUEL 7:8

THE GOOD SHEPHERD

From David's childhood, he was tasked with watching over a flock, playing an important role in his family's source of income. He was to guard the livestock from predators and thieves alike. Taking David from his humble beginnings as a lowly shepherd, God gave him the responsibility to rule over God's chosen nation. The skills David learned during his early years translated into his oversight of God's people as he led and protected them throughout his time as king.

Jesus, in turn, would prove to be the chosen shepherd of God's people. It is significant how often Jesus used this same imagery as he taught about his life and ministry when he called himself the good shepherd and his followers his sheep (Jn 10:11,14). Jesus saw himself as one designated to protect and lead the people of God and—as a faithful shepherd—give his own life for the sake of the sheep.

[1]Vulgate; the meaning of the Hebrew term is uncertain [2]Or *leader* [3]Septuagint; Hebrew *my*
[4]Compare 1 Chronicles 17:6; Hebrew *tribes* [5]Or *leader*

enemies. Moreover, the LORD declares to you that the LORD will make you a house.
12When your days are fulfilled and you lie down with your fathers, I will raise up
your offspring after you, who shall come from your body,[1] and I will establish his
kingdom. 13He shall build a house for my name, and I will establish the throne of
his kingdom forever. 14I will be to him a father, and he shall be to me a son. When
he commits iniquity, I will discipline him with the rod of men, with the stripes of
the sons of men, 15but my steadfast love will not depart from him, as I took it from
Saul, whom I put away from before you. 16And your house and your kingdom shall
be made sure forever before me.[2] Your throne shall be established forever.' " 17In
accordance with all these words, and in accordance with all this vision, Nathan
spoke to David.

David's Prayer of Gratitude

18Then King David went in and sat before the LORD and said, "Who am I, O Lord
GOD, and what is my house, that you have brought me thus far? 19And yet this was
a small thing in your eyes, O Lord GOD. You have spoken also of your servant's
house for a great while to come, and this is instruction for mankind, O Lord GOD!
20And what more can David say to you? For you know your servant, O Lord GOD!
21Because of your promise, and according to your own heart, you have brought
about all this greatness, to make your servant know it. 22Therefore you are great,
O Lord GOD. For there is none like you, and there is no God besides you, according
to all that we have heard with our ears. 23And who is like your people Israel, the
one nation on earth whom God went to redeem to be his people, making himself a name and doing for them[3] great and awesome things by driving out before
your people,[4] whom you redeemed for yourself from Egypt, a nation and its gods?
24And you established for yourself your people Israel to be your people forever.
And you, O LORD, became their God. 25And now, O LORD God, confirm forever the
word that you have spoken concerning your servant and concerning his house,
and do as you have spoken. 26And your name will be magnified forever, saying,
'The LORD of hosts is God over Israel,' and the house of your servant David will be
established before you. 27For you, O LORD of hosts, the God of Israel, have made
this revelation to your servant, saying, 'I will build you a house.' Therefore your
servant has found courage to pray this prayer to you. 28And now, O Lord GOD, you
are God, and your words are true, and you have promised this good thing to your
servant. 29Now therefore may it please you to bless the house of your servant, so
that it may continue forever before you. For you, O Lord GOD, have spoken, and
with your blessing shall the house of your servant be blessed forever."

David's Victories

8 After this David defeated the Philistines and subdued them, and David took
Metheg-ammah out of the hand of the Philistines.
2And he defeated Moab and he measured them with a line, making them lie
down on the ground. Two lines he measured to be put to death, and one full line
to be spared. And the Moabites became servants to David and brought tribute.
3David also defeated Hadadezer the son of Rehob, king of Zobah, as he went to
restore his power at the river Euphrates. 4And David took from him 1,700 horsemen, and 20,000 foot soldiers. And David hamstrung all the chariot horses but
left enough for 100 chariots. 5And when the Syrians of Damascus came to help
Hadadezer king of Zobah, David struck down 22,000 men of the Syrians. 6Then
David put garrisons in Aram of Damascus, and the Syrians became servants to
David and brought tribute. And the LORD gave victory to David wherever he went.
7And David took the shields of gold that were carried by the servants of Hadadezer and brought them to Jerusalem. 8And from Betah and from Berothai, cities
of Hadadezer, King David took very much bronze.

[1]Hebrew *loins* [2]Septuagint; Hebrew *you* [3]With a few Targums, Vulgate, Syriac; Hebrew *you*
[4]Septuagint (compare 1 Chronicles 17:21); Hebrew *awesome things for your land, before your people*

JESUS, THE PROMISED KING

David's life is one of great triumphs mixed with personal failures, reoccurring political and military uncertainty, and betrayal by his son Absalom (2Sa 15:1 – 37). All of these aspects of his life were events and developments within the larger narrative of God's grace. The Lord established David's kingdom, using him to band together God's people to form the strongest military power in the Middle East at that time. It was through David that God settled his people as a nation among the Middle Eastern nations, spreading the Israelites' territory from Egypt to the Euphrates River. Eventually God gave David rest from his military conquests (2Sa 7:1), affording the war-hardened king the opportunity to look to the future. David's desire was to build a temple for the Lord, yet this was not God's plan (vv. 2 – 7).

Rather than implementing David's good intentions, God made it clear to Nathan that his desire was much larger. He had positioned his people, through David's leadership, to be established forever. God's vision was to establish and fulfill promises that he had made to his people as they came out of Egypt through a covenant with David's heirs (vv. 8 – 17). David's son Solomon would solidify the Jewish nation forever, as well as build a house for God's Name (v. 13).

David's prayer in verses 18 – 29 concludes by showing his response to the Lord. David expressed his humble response to God's promises to David — which ultimately unfolded fully in the New Testament through the birth, life, death, and resurrection of Jesus. These promises revealed God's larger acts of redemption as recounted by David (vv. 22 – 24). It was here that David realized his significant contribution to the Lord's grander scheme. God had used David's life and work as a piece of a much larger puzzle that is revealed over the course of the entirety of Scripture: God's story of redemption.

God enabled David to see his glorious plan to establish a kingdom for himself that, through David's heirs, would be unending. Those promises were fulfilled initially during Jesus' earthly ministry and established finally when Jesus was crucified and defeated death (Lk 2:4; 20:41; Rev 3:7; 5:5; 22:16). Jesus was called the Son of the Most High, given the throne of his forefather David and promised a kingdom with no end (Lk 1:32 – 33). Clearly, Jesus was the One through whom God finalized his covenant promises to David. Whereas other heirs of David sinned, failed, and eventually died, Jesus proved to be the ultimate Heir — living a perfect life and defeating sin and death.

9When Toi king of Hamath heard that David had defeated the whole army of Hadadezer, 10Toi sent his son Joram to King David, to ask about his health and to bless him because he had fought against Hadadezer and defeated him, for Hadadezer had often been at war with Toi. And Joram brought with him articles of silver, of gold, and of bronze. 11These also King David dedicated to the LORD, together with the silver and gold that he dedicated from all the nations he subdued, 12from Edom, Moab, the Ammonites, the Philistines, Amalek, and from the spoil of Hadadezer the son of Rehob, king of Zobah.

13And David made a name for himself when he returned from striking down 18,000 Edomites in the Valley of Salt. 14Then he put garrisons in Edom; throughout all Edom he put garrisons, and all the Edomites became David's servants. And the LORD gave victory to David wherever he went.

David's Officials

15So David reigned over all Israel. And David administered justice and equity to all his people. 16Joab the son of Zeruiah was over the army, and Jehoshaphat the son of Ahilud was recorder, 17and Zadok the son of Ahitub and Ahimelech the son of Abiathar were priests, and Seraiah was secretary, 18and Benaiah the son of Jehoiada was over[1] the Cherethites and the Pelethites, and David's sons were priests.

David's Kindness to Mephibosheth

9 And David said, "Is there still anyone left of the house of Saul, that I may show him kindness for Jonathan's sake?" 2Now there was a servant of the house of Saul whose name was Ziba, and they called him to David. And the king said to him, "Are you Ziba?" And he said, "I am your servant." 3And the king said, "Is there not still someone of the house of Saul, that I may show the kindness of God to him?" Ziba said to the king, "There is still a son of Jonathan; he is crippled in his feet." 4The king said to him, "Where is he?" And Ziba said to the king, "He is in the house of Machir the son of Ammiel, at Lo-debar." 5Then King David sent and brought him from the house of Machir the son of Ammiel, at Lo-debar. 6And Mephibosheth the son of Jonathan, son of Saul, came to David and fell on his face and paid homage. And David said, "Mephibosheth!" And he answered, "Behold, I am your servant." 7And David said to him, "Do not fear, for I will show you kindness for the sake of your father Jonathan, and I will restore to you all the land of Saul your father, and you shall eat at my table always." 8And he paid homage and said, "What is your servant, that you should show regard for a dead dog such as I?"

9Then the king called Ziba, Saul's servant, and said to him, "All that belonged to Saul and to all his house I have given to your master's grandson. 10And you and your sons and your servants shall till the land for him and shall bring in the produce, that your master's grandson may have bread to eat. But Mephibosheth your master's grandson shall always eat at my table." Now Ziba had fifteen sons and twenty servants. 11Then Ziba said to the king, "According to all that my lord the king commands his servant, so will your servant do." So Mephibosheth ate at David's[2] table, like one of the king's sons. 12And Mephibosheth had a young son, whose name was Mica. And all who lived in Ziba's house became Mephibosheth's servants. 13So Mephibosheth lived in Jerusalem, for he ate always at the king's table. Now he was lame in both his feet.

David Defeats Ammon and Syria

10 After this the king of the Ammonites died, and Hanun his son reigned in his place. 2And David said, "I will deal loyally[3] with Hanun the son of Nahash, as his father dealt loyally with me." So David sent by his servants to console him concerning his father. And David's servants came into the land of the Ammonites. 3But the princes of the Ammonites said to Hanun their lord, "Do you think,

[1]Compare 20:23, 1 Chronicles 18:17, Syriac, Targum, Vulgate; Hebrew lacks *was over* [2]Septuagint; Hebrew *my* [3]Or *kindly*; twice in this verse

2 SAMUEL 8:15

THE JUST KING

David is described as administering justice and equality which are two of the primary attributes of the character of God (Ps 33:5; Jer 9:24) and virtues of people that pleased the Lord (Ps 106:3; Eze 18:5). By executing justice and promoting equality, one could expect to continue in the covenant promises and blessings between God and his people. As king, David's godly leadership brought blessing upon the land and people. His administration enforced and fostered authentic worship, and he led military campaigns according to the word of the Lord. He kept records and commands with such competency that future generations could remember all the wonders that the Lord had done.

As great as David's reign was, a greater king would come. Isaiah 9:6–7 pointed to an expected king whose reign would be much greater than David's glorious rule. It drew upon David's kingship and pointed Israel toward the hope of a future ideal king who would rule as God himself, over all the earth and in righteousness and peace for all time. In this way, Isaiah applied 2 Samuel 8:15 to Jesus, the Son of God. The connection offered by Isaiah shows that Jesus is the Davidic King, the Messiah for whom all of Israel longed!

2 SAMUEL 9:7–11

UNMERITED MERCY

Mephibosheth had a justified reason to fear King David. Typically when founding a new dynasty, kings in the Middle East killed all surviving heirs of a deposed monarch to keep

(continued on next page)

(Unmerited Mercy, continued)

them from trying to regain power. David's response to Mephibosheth is a picture of God's work in Christ: no longer considering people his enemies, but considering them his friends and making them "the king's sons." For example, the apostle Paul wrote, "For while we were still weak, at the right time Christ died for the ungodly. For one will scarcely die for a righteous person — though perhaps for a good person one would dare even to die — but God shows his love for us in that while we were still sinners, Christ died for us" (Ro 5:6 – 8). Whereas those without Christ were once children of darkness — deserving the displeasure of the King of light — they have now received unmerited mercy from God through Jesus' sacrifice (Eph 5:8). Like David, God chose to not vanquish humanity, as was deserved for being children of his great enemy, but rather gave mercy and favor to people, making them his very own children. Like Mephibosheth, people who are followers of Jesus have no reason to fear because God has adopted them into his forever family.

2 SAMUEL 10:1 – 4

REJECTING A GRACIOUS OFFER

After David had established Israel's supremacy in the region, he was determined to demonstrate covenant faithfulness, or "kindness," to one inside the covenant nation (Mephibosheth; 2Sa 9:7) and to one outside the covenantal people of God (Hanun; 2Sa 10:2). David was a king willing to put self-interest at risk in order to uphold justice and righteousness with friend and rival alike. He sent a delegation to the new Ammonite king, Hanun, in order

(continued on next page)

because David has sent comforters to you, that he is honoring your father? Has not David sent his servants to you to search the city and to spy it out and to overthrow it?" 4 So Hanun took David's servants and shaved off half the beard of each and cut off their garments in the middle, at their hips, and sent them away. 5 When it was told David, he sent to meet them, for the men were greatly ashamed. And the king said, "Remain at Jericho until your beards have grown and then return."

6 When the Ammonites saw that they had become a stench to David, the Ammonites sent and hired the Syrians of Beth-rehob, and the Syrians of Zobah, 20,000 foot soldiers, and the king of Maacah with 1,000 men, and the men of Tob, 12,000 men. 7 And when David heard of it, he sent Joab and all the host of the mighty men. 8 And the Ammonites came out and drew up in battle array at the entrance of the gate, and the Syrians of Zobah and of Rehob and the men of Tob and Maacah were by themselves in the open country.

9 When Joab saw that the battle was set against him both in front and in the rear, he chose some of the best men of Israel and arrayed them against the Syrians. 10 The rest of his men he put in the charge of Abishai his brother, and he arrayed them against the Ammonites. 11 And he said, "If the Syrians are too strong for me, then you shall help me, but if the Ammonites are too strong for you, then I will come and help you. 12 Be of good courage, and let us be courageous for our people, and for the cities of our God, and may the LORD do what seems good to him." 13 So Joab and the people who were with him drew near to battle against the Syrians, and they fled before him. 14 And when the Ammonites saw that the Syrians fled, they likewise fled before Abishai and entered the city. Then Joab returned from fighting against the Ammonites and came to Jerusalem.

15 But when the Syrians saw that they had been defeated by Israel, they gathered themselves together. 16 And Hadadezer sent and brought out the Syrians who were beyond the Euphrates.[1] They came to Helam, with Shobach the commander of the army of Hadadezer at their head. 17 And when it was told David, he gathered all Israel together and crossed the Jordan and came to Helam. The Syrians arrayed themselves against David and fought with him. 18 And the Syrians fled before Israel, and David killed of the Syrians the men of 700 chariots, and 40,000 horsemen, and wounded Shobach the commander of their army, so that he died there. 19 And when all the kings who were servants of Hadadezer saw that they had been defeated by Israel, they made peace with Israel and became subject to them. So the Syrians were afraid to save the Ammonites anymore.

David and Bathsheba

11 In the spring of the year, the time when kings go out to battle, David sent Joab, and his servants with him, and all Israel. And they ravaged the Ammonites and besieged Rabbah. But David remained at Jerusalem.

2 It happened, late one afternoon, when David arose from his couch and was walking on the roof of the king's house, that he saw from the roof a woman bathing; and the woman was very beautiful. 3 And David sent and inquired about the woman. And one said, "Is not this Bathsheba, the daughter of Eliam, the wife of Uriah the Hittite?" 4 So David sent messengers and took her, and she came to him, and he lay with her. (Now she had been purifying herself from her uncleanness.) Then she returned to her house. 5 And the woman conceived, and she sent and told David, "I am pregnant."

6 So David sent word to Joab, "Send me Uriah the Hittite." And Joab sent Uriah to David. 7 When Uriah came to him, David asked how Joab was doing and how the people were doing and how the war was going. 8 Then David said to Uriah, "Go down to your house and wash your feet." And Uriah went out of the king's house, and there followed him a present from the king. 9 But Uriah slept at the door of the king's house with all the servants of his lord, and did not go down to

[1] Hebrew *the River*

his house. [10]When they told David, "Uriah did not go down to his house," David
said to Uriah, "Have you not come from a journey? Why did you not go down to
your house?" [11]Uriah said to David, "The ark and Israel and Judah dwell in booths,
and my lord Joab and the servants of my lord are camping in the open field. Shall
I then go to my house, to eat and to drink and to lie with my wife? As you live, and
as your soul lives, I will not do this thing." [12]Then David said to Uriah, "Remain
here today also, and tomorrow I will send you back." So Uriah remained in Jerusalem that day and the next. [13]And David invited him, and he ate in his presence
and drank, so that he made him drunk. And in the evening he went out to lie on
his couch with the servants of his lord, but he did not go down to his house.

[14]In the morning David wrote a letter to Joab and sent it by the hand of Uriah. [15]In the letter he wrote, "Set Uriah in the forefront of the hardest fighting,
and then draw back from him, that he may be struck down, and die." [16]And as
Joab was besieging the city, he assigned Uriah to the place where he knew there
were valiant men. [17]And the men of the city came out and fought with Joab,
and some of the servants of David among the people fell. Uriah the Hittite also
died. [18]Then Joab sent and told David all the news about the fighting. [19]And he
instructed the messenger, "When you have finished telling all the news about
the fighting to the king, [20]then, if the king's anger rises, and if he says to you,
'Why did you go so near the city to fight? Did you not know that they would
shoot from the wall? [21]Who killed Abimelech the son of Jerubbesheth? Did not
a woman cast an upper millstone on him from the wall, so that he died at Thebez? Why did you go so near the wall?' then you shall say, 'Your servant Uriah
the Hittite is dead also.'"

[22]So the messenger went and came and told David all that Joab had sent him
to tell. [23]The messenger said to David, "The men gained an advantage over us and
came out against us in the field, but we drove them back to the entrance of the
gate. [24]Then the archers shot at your servants from the wall. Some of the king's
servants are dead, and your servant Uriah the Hittite is dead also." [25]David said to
the messenger, "Thus shall you say to Joab, 'Do not let this matter displease you,
for the sword devours now one and now another. Strengthen your attack against
the city and overthrow it.' And encourage him."

[26]When the wife of Uriah heard that Uriah her husband was dead, she lamented over her husband. [27]And when the mourning was over, David sent and brought
her to his house, and she became his wife and bore him a son. But the thing that
David had done displeased the LORD.

Nathan Rebukes David

12 And the LORD sent Nathan to David. He came to him and said to him,
"There were two men in a certain city, the one rich and the other poor.
[2]The rich man had very many flocks and herds, [3]but the poor man had nothing
but one little ewe lamb, which he had bought. And he brought it up, and it grew
up with him and with his children. It used to eat of his morsel and drink from his
cup and lie in his arms,[1] and it was like a daughter to him. [4]Now there came a traveler to the rich man, and he was unwilling to take one of his own flock or herd to
prepare for the guest who had come to him, but he took the poor man's lamb and
prepared it for the man who had come to him." [5]Then David's anger was greatly
kindled against the man, and he said to Nathan, "As the LORD lives, the man who
has done this deserves to die, [6]and he shall restore the lamb fourfold, because he
did this thing, and because he had no pity."

[7]Nathan said to David, "You are the man! Thus says the LORD, the God of Israel,
'I anointed you king over Israel, and I delivered you out of the hand of Saul. [8]And
I gave you your master's house and your master's wives into your arms and gave
you the house of Israel and of Judah. And if this were too little, I would add to you

[1]Hebrew *bosom*; also verse 8

(Rejecting a Gracious Offer, continued)

to offer condolences on the death of his father. Rather than receive the men graciously, Hanun shaved off half their beards and cut off their garments to utterly humiliate David's messengers.

In response to humanity's propensity to repeat the patterns established by Hanun and the Israelites, God sent his only Son in order to save the people. He came preaching, performing miracles and signs, and proclaiming the good news that God's kingdom had come. How did Israel receive Jesus? The Jewish leaders responded by advocating the beating, stripping, and crucifying of him on the cross.

BETRAYAL LEADING TO DEATH

Decisions matter. David's sin with Bathsheba was preceded by a decision he made to stay at home versus going off to war with his men. This choice afforded him the circumstances to take what was not his, having sex with a woman whose husband was off at war. Committing adultery with Bathsheba clearly violated God's standard for righteous sexuality in passages such as Genesis 2:22 – 24 and Exodus 20:14. Both of these decisions led to a truly terrible decision: David trying to hide his actions through the murder of an innocent man. Bathsheba's husband, Uriah, was one of David's mighty warriors and a purely innocent victim of David's horrible choices (2Sa 11:15). David betrayed Uriah, an act that led to the death of his faithful comrade.

In this account of David's betrayal of Uriah, there is a parallel to the life of Jesus. Like Uriah, Jesus was betrayed by a friend — Judas — and sent to his death because of Judas' actions. But, more importantly, this story of David's act reflects all of humankind's betrayal of Jesus. Through our personal sin, each person has contributed to the collective sin for which Jesus died. First Peter 2:22 – 24 demonstrates that Jesus, who was completely innocent of any wrongdoing, suffered a wrongful death: "He committed no sin, neither was deceit found in his mouth. When he was reviled, he did not revile in return; when he suffered, he did not threaten, but continued entrusting himself to him who judges justly. He himself bore our sins in his body on the tree, that we might die to sin and live to righteousness. By his wounds you have been healed." Quoting Isaiah 53, Peter tells his readers that Jesus was betrayed and sentenced to death unjustly for the sake of taking away the sins of believers. In the same way that Uriah was an innocent party in David's deceptive schemes, Jesus was an innocent recipient of the penalty due for mankind's sins.

as much more. [9]Why have you despised the word of the LORD, to do what is evil in his sight? You have struck down Uriah the Hittite with the sword and have taken his wife to be your wife and have killed him with the sword of the Ammonites. [10]Now therefore the sword shall never depart from your house, because you have despised me and have taken the wife of Uriah the Hittite to be your wife.' [11]Thus says the LORD, 'Behold, I will raise up evil against you out of your own house. And I will take your wives before your eyes and give them to your neighbor, and he shall lie with your wives in the sight of this sun. [12]For you did it secretly, but I will do this thing before all Israel and before the sun.'" [13]David said to Nathan, "I have sinned against the LORD." And Nathan said to David, "The LORD also has put away your sin; you shall not die. [14]Nevertheless, because by this deed you have utterly scorned the LORD,[1] the child who is born to you shall die." [15]Then Nathan went to his house.

David's Child Dies

And the LORD afflicted the child that Uriah's wife bore to David, and he became sick. [16]David therefore sought God on behalf of the child. And David fasted and went in and lay all night on the ground. [17]And the elders of his house stood beside him, to raise him from the ground, but he would not, nor did he eat food with them. [18]On the seventh day the child died. And the servants of David were afraid to tell him that the child was dead, for they said, "Behold, while the child was yet alive, we spoke to him, and he did not listen to us. How then can we say to him the child is dead? He may do himself some harm." [19]But when David saw that his servants were whispering together, David understood that the child was dead. And David said to his servants, "Is the child dead?" They said, "He is dead." [20]Then David arose from the earth and washed and anointed himself and changed his clothes. And he went into the house of the LORD and worshiped. He then went to his own house. And when he asked, they set food before him, and he ate. [21]Then his servants said to him, "What is this thing that you have done? You fasted and wept for the child while he was alive; but when the child died, you arose and ate food." [22]He said, "While the child was still alive, I fasted and wept, for I said, 'Who knows whether the LORD will be gracious to me, that the child may live?' [23]But now he is dead. Why should I fast? Can I bring him back again? I shall go to him, but he will not return to me."

Solomon's Birth

[24]Then David comforted his wife, Bathsheba, and went in to her and lay with her, and she bore a son, and he called his name Solomon. And the LORD loved him [25]and sent a message by Nathan the prophet. So he called his name Jedidiah,[2] because of the LORD.

Rabbah Is Captured

[26]Now Joab fought against Rabbah of the Ammonites and took the royal city. [27]And Joab sent messengers to David and said, "I have fought against Rabbah; moreover, I have taken the city of waters. [28]Now then gather the rest of the people together and encamp against the city and take it, lest I take the city and it be called by my name." [29]So David gathered all the people together and went to Rabbah and fought against it and took it. [30]And he took the crown of their king from his head. The weight of it was a talent[3] of gold, and in it was a precious stone, and it was placed on David's head. And he brought out the spoil of the city, a very great amount. [31]And he brought out the people who were in it and set them to labor with saws and iron picks and iron axes and made them toil at[4] the brick kilns. And thus he did to all the cities of the Ammonites. Then David and all the people returned to Jerusalem.

---

[1]Masoretic Text *the enemies of the LORD*; Dead Sea Scroll *the word of the LORD* [2]*Jedidiah* means *beloved of the LORD* [3]A *talent* was about 75 pounds or 34 kilograms [4]Hebrew *pass through*

2 SAMUEL 12:15–23

HOPE OF THE RESURRECTION

The death of a child is a terribly tragic experience. Indeed, anytime a loved one or a close friend dies, deep anguish follows—as is the case here with the death of David's son. In the midst of sorrow associated with death, Christians have complete confidence to believe they will be reunited with a deceased loved one. The story of the death of David's son suggests that David believed he and his child would be reunited. David said, "I shall go to him, but he will not return to me." Christian believers can hold to the same hope that Old Testament believers understood faintly—that death is inevitable, but God's people will have life after death. Jesus said: "I am the resurrection and the life. Whoever believes in me, though he die, yet shall he live, and everyone who lives and believes in me shall never die" (Jn 11:25–26). Jesus' words were not empty but rather were validated through his own resurrection. Truly, Jesus has power over death—the greatest and most feared inevitability in the human experience—and has promised to apply that power to his followers (1Pe 1:3–7).

Amnon and Tamar

13 Now Absalom, David's son, had a beautiful sister, whose name was Tamar.
And after a time Amnon, David's son, loved her. 2And Amnon was so tormented that he made himself ill because of his sister Tamar, for she was a virgin,
and it seemed impossible to Amnon to do anything to her. 3But Amnon had a
friend, whose name was Jonadab, the son of Shimeah, David's brother. And Jonadab was a very crafty man. 4And he said to him, "O son of the king, why are you
so haggard morning after morning? Will you not tell me?" Amnon said to him,
"I love Tamar, my brother Absalom's sister." 5Jonadab said to him, "Lie down on
your bed and pretend to be ill. And when your father comes to see you, say to
him, 'Let my sister Tamar come and give me bread to eat, and prepare the food in
my sight, that I may see it and eat it from her hand.'" 6So Amnon lay down and
pretended to be ill. And when the king came to see him, Amnon said to the king,
"Please let my sister Tamar come and make a couple of cakes in my sight, that I
may eat from her hand."

7Then David sent home to Tamar, saying, "Go to your brother Amnon's house
and prepare food for him." 8So Tamar went to her brother Amnon's house, where
he was lying down. And she took dough and kneaded it and made cakes in his
sight and baked the cakes. 9And she took the pan and emptied it out before him,
but he refused to eat. And Amnon said, "Send out everyone from me." So everyone went out from him. 10Then Amnon said to Tamar, "Bring the food into
the chamber, that I may eat from your hand." And Tamar took the cakes she had
made and brought them into the chamber to Amnon her brother. 11But when she
brought them near him to eat, he took hold of her and said to her, "Come, lie with
me, my sister." 12She answered him, "No, my brother, do not violate[1] me, for such
a thing is not done in Israel; do not do this outrageous thing. 13As for me, where
could I carry my shame? And as for you, you would be as one of the outrageous
fools in Israel. Now therefore, please speak to the king, for he will not withhold
me from you." 14But he would not listen to her, and being stronger than she, he
violated her and lay with her.

15Then Amnon hated her with very great hatred, so that the hatred with which
he hated her was greater than the love with which he had loved her. And Amnon
said to her, "Get up! Go!" 16But she said to him, "No, my brother, for this wrong
in sending me away is greater than the other that you did to me."[2] But he would
not listen to her. 17He called the young man who served him and said, "Put this
woman out of my presence and bolt the door after her." 18Now she was wearing a
long robe with sleeves,[3] for thus were the virgin daughters of the king dressed. So
his servant put her out and bolted the door after her. 19And Tamar put ashes on
her head and tore the long robe that she wore. And she laid her hand on her head
and went away, crying aloud as she went.

20And her brother Absalom said to her, "Has Amnon your brother been with
you? Now hold your peace, my sister. He is your brother; do not take this to heart."
So Tamar lived, a desolate woman, in her brother Absalom's house. 21When King
David heard of all these things, he was very angry.[4] 22But Absalom spoke to Amnon neither good nor bad, for Absalom hated Amnon, because he had violated
his sister Tamar.

Absalom Murders Amnon

23After two full years Absalom had sheepshearers at Baal-hazor, which is near
Ephraim, and Absalom invited all the king's sons. 24And Absalom came to the
king and said, "Behold, your servant has sheepshearers. Please let the king and
his servants go with your servant." 25But the king said to Absalom, "No, my son,
let us not all go, lest we be burdensome to you." He pressed him, but he would not

---

2 SAMUEL 13:1–15

THE CORROSIVE NATURE OF SIN

The story of Amnon and Tamar is the first in a trilogy of narratives (the other two relating to Absalom's murder of Amnon and Absalom's return from exile) that take the book of Samuel in a dark direction. They also correspond to David's adultery with Bathsheba and the murder of Uriah the Hittite. The nature of sin was on full display here, especially 2 Samuel 13:15, where the false promises of sin that fueled Amnon's lust led him toward destruction. "The hatred with which he hated her was greater than the love with which he had loved her." Here is a powerful description of the destructive nature of sin and the expected consequences when sin is brought into the light.

The question becomes how to overcome the power of sin that leads to death. "All have sinned and fall short of the glory of God, and are justified by his grace as a gift, through the redemption that is in Christ Jesus" (Ro 3:23–24). Sin is a human condition that is universal and terminal. But God provided Jesus, whose death accomplished the redemption of all who believe in him. Sin is corrosive, creating sorrow and bitterness that permeates all of life apart from the grace and redemption of God through Christ Jesus.

---

[1]Or *humiliate*; also verses 14, 22, 32 [2]Compare Septuagint, Vulgate; the meaning of the Hebrew is uncertain [3]Or *a robe of many colors* (compare Genesis 37:3); compare *long robe*, verse 19 [4]Dead Sea Scroll, Septuagint add *But he would not punish his son Amnon, because he loved him, since he was his firstborn*

go but gave him his blessing. 26Then Absalom said, "If not, please let my brother Amnon go with us." And the king said to him, "Why should he go with you?" 27But Absalom pressed him until he let Amnon and all the king's sons go with him. 28Then Absalom commanded his servants, "Mark when Amnon's heart is merry with wine, and when I say to you, 'Strike Amnon,' then kill him. Do not fear; have I not commanded you? Be courageous and be valiant." 29So the servants of Absalom did to Amnon as Absalom had commanded. Then all the king's sons arose, and each mounted his mule and fled.

30While they were on the way, news came to David, "Absalom has struck down all the king's sons, and not one of them is left." 31Then the king arose and tore his garments and lay on the earth. And all his servants who were standing by tore their garments. 32But Jonadab the son of Shimeah, David's brother, said, "Let not my lord suppose that they have killed all the young men, the king's sons, for Amnon alone is dead. For by the command of Absalom this has been determined from the day he violated his sister Tamar. 33Now therefore let not my lord the king so take it to heart as to suppose that all the king's sons are dead, for Amnon alone is dead."

Absalom Flees to Geshur

34But Absalom fled. And the young man who kept the watch lifted up his eyes and looked, and behold, many people were coming from the road behind him[1] by the side of the mountain. 35And Jonadab said to the king, "Behold, the king's sons have come; as your servant said, so it has come about." 36And as soon as he had finished speaking, behold, the king's sons came and lifted up their voice and wept. And the king also and all his servants wept very bitterly.

37But Absalom fled and went to Talmai the son of Ammihud, king of Geshur. And David mourned for his son day after day. 38So Absalom fled and went to Geshur, and was there three years. 39And the spirit of the king[2] longed to go out[3] to Absalom, because he was comforted about Amnon, since he was dead.

Absalom Returns to Jerusalem

14 Now Joab the son of Zeruiah knew that the king's heart went out to Absalom. 2And Joab sent to Tekoa and brought from there a wise woman and said to her, "Pretend to be a mourner and put on mourning garments. Do not anoint yourself with oil, but behave like a woman who has been mourning many days for the dead. 3Go to the king and speak thus to him." So Joab put the words in her mouth.

4When the woman of Tekoa came to the king, she fell on her face to the ground and paid homage and said, "Save me, O king." 5And the king said to her, "What is your trouble?" She answered, "Alas, I am a widow; my husband is dead. 6And your servant had two sons, and they quarreled with one another in the field. There was no one to separate them, and one struck the other and killed him. 7And now the whole clan has risen against your servant, and they say, 'Give up the man who struck his brother, that we may put him to death for the life of his brother whom he killed.' And so they would destroy the heir also. Thus they would quench my coal that is left and leave to my husband neither name nor remnant on the face of the earth."

8Then the king said to the woman, "Go to your house, and I will give orders concerning you." 9And the woman of Tekoa said to the king, "On me be the guilt, my lord the king, and on my father's house; let the king and his throne be guiltless." 10The king said, "If anyone says anything to you, bring him to me, and he shall never touch you again." 11Then she said, "Please let the king invoke the Lord your God, that the avenger of blood kill no more, and my son be not destroyed." He said, "As the Lord lives, not one hair of your son shall fall to the ground."

[1]Septuagint *the Horonaim Road* [2]Dead Sea Scroll, Septuagint; Hebrew *David* [3]Compare Vulgate *ceased to go out*

2 SAMUEL 14:1,23–33

LOVE AND JUSTICE

David's love for Absalom, his son, was admirable, but in his love, he set aside justice. Absalom had murdered his half brother Amnon, a sin that required consequences. David's actions, as the king of Israel tasked with protecting the people and ensuring that godliness permeated the land, thus fell far short of God's standards in the case of his son. By focusing on love at the expense of justice, David failed to deal adequately with either justice or love. The law made it clear that murder deserved death (Nu 35:31–34). Yet David allowed his love for his son to become paramount, causing him to overlook a clear biblical precedent in this case.

In contrast, God the Father loved his Son, Jesus, but allowed his wrath against sin to fall on Jesus to provide a way for people to come to God. The Trinitarian God—Father, Son, and Holy Spirit—carried out the ultimate act of love in order to uphold justice and extend the love of forgiveness to all who believe. God would not, like David, simply overlook sin. Rather, he required the consequence of death for mankind's sin. This was a payment initiated by the Father, made by Jesus, and applied by the Holy Spirit (Jn 14:16–17; Ro 3:21–26). Truly, God has offered love, while upholding justice, to his chosen children.

12 Then the woman said, "Please let your servant speak a word to my lord the
king." He said, "Speak." 13 And the woman said, "Why then have you planned such
a thing against the people of God? For in giving this decision the king convicts
himself, inasmuch as the king does not bring his banished one home again. 14 We
must all die; we are like water spilled on the ground, which cannot be gathered up
again. But God will not take away life, and he devises means so that the banished
one will not remain an outcast. 15 Now I have come to say this to my lord the king
because the people have made me afraid, and your servant thought, 'I will speak
to the king; it may be that the king will perform the request of his servant. 16 For
the king will hear and deliver his servant from the hand of the man who would
destroy me and my son together from the heritage of God.' 17 And your servant
thought, 'The word of my lord the king will set me at rest,' for my lord the king is
like the angel of God to discern good and evil. The LORD your God be with you!"

18 Then the king answered the woman, "Do not hide from me anything I ask
you." And the woman said, "Let my lord the king speak." 19 The king said, "Is the
hand of Joab with you in all this?" The woman answered and said, "As surely as
you live, my lord the king, one cannot turn to the right hand or to the left from
anything that my lord the king has said. It was your servant Joab who commanded
me; it was he who put all these words in the mouth of your servant. 20 In order to
change the course of things your servant Joab did this. But my lord has wisdom
like the wisdom of the angel of God to know all things that are on the earth."

21 Then the king said to Joab, "Behold now, I grant this; go, bring back the young
man Absalom." 22 And Joab fell on his face to the ground and paid homage and
blessed the king. And Joab said, "Today your servant knows that I have found
favor in your sight, my lord the king, in that the king has granted the request of his
servant." 23 So Joab arose and went to Geshur and brought Absalom to Jerusalem.
24 And the king said, "Let him dwell apart in his own house; he is not to come into
my presence." So Absalom lived apart in his own house and did not come into the
king's presence.

25 Now in all Israel there was no one so much to be praised for his handsome
appearance as Absalom. From the sole of his foot to the crown of his head there
was no blemish in him. 26 And when he cut the hair of his head (for at the end of
every year he used to cut it; when it was heavy on him, he cut it), he weighed the
hair of his head, two hundred shekels[1] by the king's weight. 27 There were born to
Absalom three sons, and one daughter whose name was Tamar. She was a beautiful woman.

28 So Absalom lived two full years in Jerusalem, without coming into the king's
presence. 29 Then Absalom sent for Joab, to send him to the king, but Joab would
not come to him. And he sent a second time, but Joab would not come. 30 Then he
said to his servants, "See, Joab's field is next to mine, and he has barley there; go
and set it on fire." So Absalom's servants set the field on fire.[2] 31 Then Joab arose
and went to Absalom at his house and said to him, "Why have your servants set
my field on fire?" 32 Absalom answered Joab, "Behold, I sent word to you, 'Come
here, that I may send you to the king, to ask, "Why have I come from Geshur? It
would be better for me to be there still." Now therefore let me go into the presence of the king, and if there is guilt in me, let him put me to death.'" 33 Then Joab
went to the king and told him, and he summoned Absalom. So he came to the
king and bowed himself on his face to the ground before the king, and the king
kissed Absalom.

Absalom's Conspiracy

15 After this Absalom got himself a chariot and horses, and fifty men to run
before him. 2 And Absalom used to rise early and stand beside the way of
the gate. And when any man had a dispute to come before the king for judgment,

[1] A *shekel* was about 2/5 ounce or 11 grams [2] Septuagint, Dead Sea Scroll add *So Joab's servants came to him with their clothes torn, and they said to him, "The servants of Absalom have set your field on fire."*

Absalom would call to him and say, "From what city are you?" And when he said,
"Your servant is of such and such a tribe in Israel," 3Absalom would say to him,
"See, your claims are good and right, but there is no man designated by the king
to hear you." 4Then Absalom would say, "Oh that I were judge in the land! Then
every man with a dispute or cause might come to me, and I would give him justice." 5And whenever a man came near to pay homage to him, he would put out
his hand and take hold of him and kiss him. 6Thus Absalom did to all of Israel who
came to the king for judgment. So Absalom stole the hearts of the men of Israel.

7And at the end of four[1] years Absalom said to the king, "Please let me go and
pay my vow, which I have vowed to the LORD, in Hebron. 8For your servant vowed
a vow while I lived at Geshur in Aram, saying, 'If the LORD will indeed bring me
back to Jerusalem, then I will offer worship to[2] the LORD.'" 9The king said to him,
"Go in peace." So he arose and went to Hebron. 10But Absalom sent secret messengers throughout all the tribes of Israel, saying, "As soon as you hear the sound
of the trumpet, then say, 'Absalom is king at Hebron!'" 11With Absalom went two
hundred men from Jerusalem who were invited guests, and they went in their innocence and knew nothing. 12And while Absalom was offering the sacrifices, he
sent for[3] Ahithophel the Gilonite, David's counselor, from his city Giloh. And the
conspiracy grew strong, and the people with Absalom kept increasing.

David Flees Jerusalem

13And a messenger came to David, saying, "The hearts of the men of Israel
have gone after Absalom." 14Then David said to all his servants who were with
him at Jerusalem, "Arise, and let us flee, or else there will be no escape for us from
Absalom. Go quickly, lest he overtake us quickly and bring down ruin on us and
strike the city with the edge of the sword." 15And the king's servants said to the
king, "Behold, your servants are ready to do whatever my lord the king decides."
16So the king went out, and all his household after him. And the king left ten concubines to keep the house. 17And the king went out, and all the people after him.
And they halted at the last house.

18And all his servants passed by him, and all the Cherethites, and all the Pelethites, and all the six hundred Gittites who had followed him from Gath, passed
on before the king. 19Then the king said to Ittai the Gittite, "Why do you also go
with us? Go back and stay with the king, for you are a foreigner and also an exile
from your home. 20You came only yesterday, and shall I today make you wander
about with us, since I go I know not where? Go back and take your brothers with
you, and may the LORD show[4] steadfast love and faithfulness to you." 21But Ittai
answered the king, "As the LORD lives, and as my lord the king lives, wherever my
lord the king shall be, whether for death or for life, there also will your servant
be." 22And David said to Ittai, "Go then, pass on." So Ittai the Gittite passed on
with all his men and all the little ones who were with him. 23And all the land wept
aloud as all the people passed by, and the king crossed the brook Kidron, and all
the people passed on toward the wilderness.

24And Abiathar came up, and behold, Zadok came also with all the Levites,
bearing the ark of the covenant of God. And they set down the ark of God until
the people had all passed out of the city. 25Then the king said to Zadok, "Carry the
ark of God back into the city. If I find favor in the eyes of the LORD, he will bring
me back and let me see both it and his dwelling place. 26But if he says, 'I have no
pleasure in you,' behold, here I am, let him do to me what seems good to him."
27The king also said to Zadok the priest, "Are you not a seer? Go back[5] to the city
in peace, with your two sons, Ahimaaz your son, and Jonathan the son of Abiathar. 28See, I will wait at the fords of the wilderness until word comes from you to
inform me." 29So Zadok and Abiathar carried the ark of God back to Jerusalem,
and they remained there.

[1]Septuagint, Syriac; Hebrew *forty* [2]Or *will serve* [3]Or *sent* [4]Septuagint; Hebrew lacks *may the LORD show* [5]Septuagint *The king also said to Zadok the priest, "Look, go back*

2 SAMUEL 15:30–32

THE MOUNT OF OLIVES

David and Jesus each had a unique connection with the Mount of Olives. When Absalom rose up as usurper of his father, David fled Jerusalem via the Mount of Olives. It was David's chosen path away from his son, perhaps so that he could worship God as he left the safety of his palace to an unknown future and the wilderness before him. Second Samuel 15:32 notes that the Mount of Olives was a well-known place of worship for the people of God. After celebrating the Passover feast with his disciples and instituting the Lord's Supper, Jesus and his disciples went out to the Mount of Olives (Mt 26:30). At a particular spot on the mountain—Gethsemane—Jesus prayed to the Father in a way that David would not. Unlike David, Jesus made it clear that he would not seek to escape the hand of his oppressor. Rather, he accepted the Father's will (Mt 26:39).

2 SAMUEL 16:5–14

GODLY RESPONSE TO FALSE ACCUSATION

With the threat of Absalom's coup budding, David fled Jerusalem for his life, encountering an enduring threat on his way out of town. During this vulnerable flight, David was assaulted by stones and *curses from Shimei, who vocalized* an undercurrent of thought in Israel—that David was reaping what he had sown by replacing the house of Saul. David did not express his

(continued on next page)

30But David went up the ascent of the Mount of Olives, weeping as he went,
barefoot and with his head covered. And all the people who were with him covered their heads, and they went up, weeping as they went. 31And it was told David,
"Ahithophel is among the conspirators with Absalom." And David said, "O LORD,
please turn the counsel of Ahithophel into foolishness."
32While David was coming to the summit, where God was worshiped, behold,
Hushai the Archite came to meet him with his coat torn and dirt on his head.
33David said to him, "If you go on with me, you will be a burden to me. 34But if
you return to the city and say to Absalom, 'I will be your servant, O king; as I
have been your father's servant in time past, so now I will be your servant,' then
you will defeat for me the counsel of Ahithophel. 35Are not Zadok and Abiathar
the priests with you there? So whatever you hear from the king's house, tell it to
Zadok and Abiathar the priests. 36Behold, their two sons are with them there,
Ahimaaz, Zadok's son, and Jonathan, Abiathar's son, and by them you shall send
to me everything you hear." 37So Hushai, David's friend, came into the city, just as
Absalom was entering Jerusalem.

David and Ziba

16 When David had passed a little beyond the summit, Ziba the servant of
Mephibosheth met him, with a couple of donkeys saddled, bearing two
hundred loaves of bread, a hundred bunches of raisins, a hundred of summer
fruits, and a skin of wine. 2And the king said to Ziba, "Why have you brought
these?" Ziba answered, "The donkeys are for the king's household to ride on, the
bread and summer fruit for the young men to eat, and the wine for those who
faint in the wilderness to drink." 3And the king said, "And where is your master's
son?" Ziba said to the king, "Behold, he remains in Jerusalem, for he said, 'Today
the house of Israel will give me back the kingdom of my father.'" 4Then the king
said to Ziba, "Behold, all that belonged to Mephibosheth is now yours." And Ziba
said, "I pay homage; let me ever find favor in your sight, my lord the king."

Shimei Curses David

5When King David came to Bahurim, there came out a man of the family of the
house of Saul, whose name was Shimei, the son of Gera, and as he came he cursed
continually. 6And he threw stones at David and at all the servants of King David,
and all the people and all the mighty men were on his right hand and on his left.
7And Shimei said as he cursed, "Get out, get out, you man of blood, you worthless
man! 8The LORD has avenged on you all the blood of the house of Saul, in whose
place you have reigned, and the LORD has given the kingdom into the hand of your
son Absalom. See, your evil is on you, for you are a man of blood."
9Then Abishai the son of Zeruiah said to the king, "Why should this dead dog
curse my lord the king? Let me go over and take off his head." 10But the king said,
"What have I to do with you, you sons of Zeruiah? If he is cursing because the
LORD has said to him, 'Curse David,' who then shall say, 'Why have you done so?'"
11And David said to Abishai and to all his servants, "Behold, my own son seeks
my life; how much more now may this Benjaminite! Leave him alone, and let him
curse, for the LORD has told him to. 12It may be that the LORD will look on the
wrong done to me,[1] and that the LORD will repay me with good for his cursing
today." 13So David and his men went on the road, while Shimei went along on the
hillside opposite him and cursed as he went and threw stones at him and flung
dust. 14And the king, and all the people who were with him, arrived weary at the
Jordan.[2] And there he refreshed himself.

Absalom Enters Jerusalem

15Now Absalom and all the people, the men of Israel, came to Jerusalem, and
Ahithophel with him. 16And when Hushai the Archite, David's friend, came to

[1]Septuagint, Vulgate *will look upon my affliction* [2]Septuagint; Hebrew lacks *at the Jordan*

Absalom, Hushai said to Absalom, "Long live the king! Long live the king!" 17And
Absalom said to Hushai, "Is this your loyalty to your friend? Why did you not go
with your friend?" 18And Hushai said to Absalom, "No, for whom the LORD and
this people and all the men of Israel have chosen, his I will be, and with him I will
remain. 19And again, whom should I serve? Should it not be his son? As I have
served your father, so I will serve you."
20Then Absalom said to Ahithophel, "Give your counsel. What shall we do?"
21Ahithophel said to Absalom, "Go in to your father's concubines, whom he has
left to keep the house, and all Israel will hear that you have made yourself a stench
to your father, and the hands of all who are with you will be strengthened." 22So
they pitched a tent for Absalom on the roof. And Absalom went in to his father's concubines in the sight of all Israel. 23Now in those days the counsel that
Ahithophel gave was as if one consulted the word of God; so was all the counsel
of Ahithophel esteemed, both by David and by Absalom.

Hushai Saves David

17 Moreover, Ahithophel said to Absalom, "Let me choose twelve thousand
men, and I will arise and pursue David tonight. 2I will come upon him while
he is weary and discouraged and throw him into a panic, and all the people who
are with him will flee. I will strike down only the king, 3and I will bring all the
people back to you as a bride comes home to her husband. You seek the life of
only one man,[1] and all the people will be at peace." 4And the advice seemed right
in the eyes of Absalom and all the elders of Israel.
5Then Absalom said, "Call Hushai the Archite also, and let us hear what he
has to say." 6And when Hushai came to Absalom, Absalom said to him, "Thus
has Ahithophel spoken; shall we do as he says? If not, you speak." 7Then Hushai
said to Absalom, "This time the counsel that Ahithophel has given is not good."
8Hushai said, "You know that your father and his men are mighty men, and that
they are enraged,[2] like a bear robbed of her cubs in the field. Besides, your father
is expert in war; he will not spend the night with the people. 9Behold, even now
he has hidden himself in one of the pits or in some other place. And as soon as
some of the people fall[3] at the first attack, whoever hears it will say, 'There has
been a slaughter among the people who follow Absalom.' 10Then even the valiant
man, whose heart is like the heart of a lion, will utterly melt with fear, for all
Israel knows that your father is a mighty man, and that those who are with him
are valiant men. 11But my counsel is that all Israel be gathered to you, from Dan
to Beersheba, as the sand by the sea for multitude, and that you go to battle in
person. 12So we shall come upon him in some place where he is to be found, and
we shall light upon him as the dew falls on the ground, and of him and all the
men with him not one will be left. 13If he withdraws into a city, then all Israel will
bring ropes to that city, and we shall drag it into the valley, until not even a pebble
is to be found there." 14And Absalom and all the men of Israel said, "The counsel
of Hushai the Archite is better than the counsel of Ahithophel." For the LORD had
ordained[4] to defeat the good counsel of Ahithophel, so that the LORD might bring
harm upon Absalom.
15Then Hushai said to Zadok and Abiathar the priests, "Thus and so did
Ahithophel counsel Absalom and the elders of Israel, and thus and so have I
counseled. 16Now therefore send quickly and tell David, 'Do not stay tonight at
the fords of the wilderness, but by all means pass over, lest the king and all the
people who are with him be swallowed up.'" 17Now Jonathan and Ahimaaz were
waiting at En-rogel. A female servant was to go and tell them, and they were to go
and tell King David, for they were not to be seen entering the city. 18But a young
man saw them and told Absalom. So both of them went away quickly and came

[1]Septuagint; Hebrew *back to you. Like the return of the whole is the man whom you seek* [2]Hebrew *bitter of soul* [3]Or *And as he falls on them* [4]Hebrew *commanded*

(Godly Response to False Accusation, continued)

own innocence, engage Shimei, or ask God to interfere, but rather he waited on God's vindication.

Jesus reacted in a similar way: "When he was reviled, he did not revile in return; when he suffered, he did not threaten, but continued entrusting himself to him who judges justly" (1Pe 2:23). Like David, Jesus did not retreat in the face of intimidation, but he trusted God in the midst of his trials. Jesus' example shows believers how they should respond to difficulties even when facing false accusations: "Consider him who endured from sinners such hostility against himself, so that you may not grow weary or fainthearted" (Heb 12:3). Believers can draw courage from Jesus' faithful and enduring example of glorifying God by trusting him to provide justification and vindication at the right time.

2 SAMUEL 16:15–22

THE CHAIN OF SIN'S CONSEQUENCES

Absalom's behavior fulfilled God's prophecy to David in 2 Samuel 12:11–12. David understood his exile, the acts of Absalom, and the curses heaped on him by Shimei as punishment from the Lord (2Sa 16:10–12). This passage illustrates the foundational principle of sin that humanity reaps what is sown and what is sown has long-term, unanticipated negative consequences. David believed he had fallen out of favor with the Lord and expected nothing other than a future of consequences for his sins. After all, he had seen his predecessor Saul suffer the same fate.

(continued on next page)

(The Chain of Sin's Consequences, continued)

One should expect a growing chain of consequences for previous poor decisions and ungodly actions. Sin can spread over a lifetime, and even over generations, before we appreciate fully the "good news" of the gospel about Jesus' life, death, and resurrection. While there are certainly consequences to sin, Jesus unconditionally loves all of humanity in spite of their offenses toward him. Unlike David, who had an insecure hope that God would restore favor on him, all people who follow Jesus have an assurance that God will never leave nor forsake his own (Heb 13:5–6). Even the seemingly worst of sins, such as Peter's denial of Jesus, do not warrant an insecure standing before God.

2 SAMUEL 17:1–14

VANQUISHING SIN'S CONSEQUENCES

As Absalom was plotting to attack and kill David, counterforces were already coming into place to block his progress. God used the "advice" of Hushai to give David and his men an advantage and an opportunity to prevail over Absalom's wicked schemes. Although Absalom thought he was in control of the situation, God was already working against him to fulfill his promises to David and to David's other descendants. In the same way, those who resist God and pursue sin are laying up trouble for themselves (Ro 2:4–9). This life is filled with events shaped by sinful human actions. For believers, Jesus *has applied his grace to cover sin.* Yet, Christians still experience the implications of the wrong actions of others. Part of the "good news" of the gospel is that eventually the

(continued on next page)

to the house of a man at Bahurim, who had a well in his courtyard. And they
went down into it. 19And the woman took and spread a covering over the well's
mouth and scattered grain on it, and nothing was known of it. 20When Absalom's
servants came to the woman at the house, they said, "Where are Ahimaaz and
Jonathan?" And the woman said to them, "They have gone over the brook[1] of
water." And when they had sought and could not find them, they returned to
Jerusalem.

21After they had gone, the men came up out of the well, and went and told
King David. They said to David, "Arise, and go quickly over the water, for thus and
so has Ahithophel counseled against you." 22Then David arose, and all the people
who were with him, and they crossed the Jordan. By daybreak not one was left
who had not crossed the Jordan.

23When Ahithophel saw that his counsel was not followed, he saddled his
donkey and went off home to his own city. He set his house in order and hanged
himself, and he died and was buried in the tomb of his father.

24Then David came to Mahanaim. And Absalom crossed the Jordan with all
the men of Israel. 25Now Absalom had set Amasa over the army instead of Joab.
Amasa was the son of a man named Ithra the Ishmaelite,[2] who had married Abigal
the daughter of Nahash, sister of Zeruiah, Joab's mother. 26And Israel and Absalom encamped in the land of Gilead.

27When David came to Mahanaim, Shobi the son of Nahash from Rabbah of
the Ammonites, and Machir the son of Ammiel from Lo-debar, and Barzillai the
Gileadite from Rogelim, 28brought beds, basins, and earthen vessels, wheat, barley, flour, parched grain, beans and lentils,[3] 29honey and curds and sheep and
cheese from the herd, for David and the people with him to eat, for they said, "The
people are hungry and weary and thirsty in the wilderness."

Absalom Killed

18 Then David mustered the men who were with him and set over them commanders of thousands and commanders of hundreds. 2And David sent out
the army, one third under the command of Joab, one third under the command of
Abishai the son of Zeruiah, Joab's brother, and one third under the command of
Ittai the Gittite. And the king said to the men, "I myself will also go out with you."
3But the men said, "You shall not go out. For if we flee, they will not care about
us. If half of us die, they will not care about us. But you are worth ten thousand
of us. Therefore it is better that you send us help from the city." 4The king said to
them, "Whatever seems best to you I will do." So the king stood at the side of the
gate, while all the army marched out by hundreds and by thousands. 5And the
king ordered Joab and Abishai and Ittai, "Deal gently for my sake with the young
man Absalom." And all the people heard when the king gave orders to all the commanders about Absalom.

6So the army went out into the field against Israel, and the battle was fought in
the forest of Ephraim. 7And the men of Israel were defeated there by the servants
of David, and the loss there was great on that day, twenty thousand men. 8The
battle spread over the face of all the country, and the forest devoured more people
that day than the sword.

9And Absalom happened to meet the servants of David. Absalom was riding
on his mule, and the mule went under the thick branches of a great oak,[4] and his
head caught fast in the oak, and he was suspended between heaven and earth,
while the mule that was under him went on. 10And a certain man saw it and told
Joab, "Behold, I saw Absalom hanging in an oak." 11Joab said to the man who told
him, "What, you saw him! Why then did you not strike him there to the ground?
I would have been glad to give you ten pieces of silver and a belt." 12But the man

[1]The meaning of the Hebrew word is uncertain [2]Compare 1 Chronicles 2:17; Hebrew *Israelite* [3]Hebrew adds *and parched grain* [4]Or *terebinth*; also verses 10, 14

said to Joab, "Even if I felt in my hand the weight of a thousand pieces of silver, I would not reach out my hand against the king's son, for in our hearing the king commanded you and Abishai and Ittai, 'For my sake protect the young man Absalom.' 13On the other hand, if I had dealt treacherously against his life[1] (and there is nothing hidden from the king), then you yourself would have stood aloof." 14Joab said, "I will not waste time like this with you." And he took three javelins in his hand and thrust them into the heart of Absalom while he was still alive in the oak. 15And ten young men, Joab's armor-bearers, surrounded Absalom and struck him and killed him.

16Then Joab blew the trumpet, and the troops came back from pursuing Israel, for Joab restrained them. 17And they took Absalom and threw him into a great pit in the forest and raised over him a very great heap of stones. And all Israel fled every one to his own home. 18Now Absalom in his lifetime had taken and set up for himself the pillar that is in the King's Valley, for he said, "I have no son to keep my name in remembrance." He called the pillar after his own name, and it is called Absalom's monument[2] to this day.

David Hears of Absalom's Death

19Then Ahimaaz the son of Zadok said, "Let me run and carry news to the king that the LORD has delivered him from the hand of his enemies." 20And Joab said to him, "You are not to carry news today. You may carry news another day, but today you shall carry no news, because the king's son is dead." 21Then Joab said to the Cushite, "Go, tell the king what you have seen." The Cushite bowed before Joab, and ran. 22Then Ahimaaz the son of Zadok said again to Joab, "Come what may, let me also run after the Cushite." And Joab said, "Why will you run, my son, seeing that you will have no reward for the news?" 23"Come what may," he said, "I will run." So he said to him, "Run." Then Ahimaaz ran by the way of the plain, and outran the Cushite.

24Now David was sitting between the two gates, and the watchman went up to the roof of the gate by the wall, and when he lifted up his eyes and looked, he saw a man running alone. 25The watchman called out and told the king. And the king said, "If he is alone, there is news in his mouth." And he drew nearer and nearer. 26The watchman saw another man running. And the watchman called to the gate and said, "See, another man running alone!" The king said, "He also brings news." 27The watchman said, "I think the running of the first is like the running of Ahimaaz the son of Zadok." And the king said, "He is a good man and comes with good news."

28Then Ahimaaz cried out to the king, "All is well." And he bowed before the king with his face to the earth and said, "Blessed be the LORD your God, who has delivered up the men who raised their hand against my lord the king." 29And the king said, "Is it well with the young man Absalom?" Ahimaaz answered, "When Joab sent the king's servant, your servant, I saw a great commotion, but I do not know what it was." 30And the king said, "Turn aside and stand here." So he turned aside and stood still.

David's Grief

31And behold, the Cushite came, and the Cushite said, "Good news for my lord the king! For the LORD has delivered you this day from the hand of all who rose up against you." 32The king said to the Cushite, "Is it well with the young man Absalom?" And the Cushite answered, "May the enemies of my lord the king and all who rise up against you for evil be like that young man." 33[3]And the king was deeply moved and went up to the chamber over the gate and wept. And as he went, he said, "O my son Absalom, my son, my son Absalom! Would I had died instead of you, O Absalom, my son, my son!"

[1]Or *at the risk of my life* [2]Or *Absalom's hand* [3]Ch 19:1 in Hebrew

(Vanquishing Sin's Consequences, continued)

world will see how God has conquered sin's effects in our world once and for all. One day, believers will experience the beautiful reality expressed in Revelation 21:4: "He will wipe away every tear from their eyes, and death shall be no more, neither shall there be mourning, nor crying, nor pain anymore, for the former things have passed away." Even now, God is at work to set things right, to work against evil and bring peace through Christ. And there is a much greater day in the future, one that is no longer marred by sin's consequences.

A BROKEN HEART

In spite of Absalom's treachery, David grieved at the death of his son. Absalom's conspiracy, beginning in chapter 15, led to greater divisiveness and suffering among the nation. Not only did David suffer harm at the hands of these enemies, but he also continually wept because of the situation they found themselves in (15:30). It surely broke his heart to consider that his son Absalom had abandoned him. David also understood that this rebellion would lead to harm for those who remained loyal to him. In spite of these factors, David urged his men to be gentle with Absalom — not because he deserved it but because of David's deep love for him (18:5).

News of Absalom's death was overwhelming for King David. Upon hearing the news, David mourned for his loss and wept bitter tears (18:33). His heartfelt desire was that he would have died in Absalom's place.

Many years later, Jesus would also weep over the people whom he loved. Jesus, looking over the city of Jerusalem, repeated his longing for the people to turn to him (Mt 23:37; Lk 19:41 – 44). His desire was to care for them as a hen does baby chicks, but the people chose to disregard his care and run into their own destruction. Jesus demonstrated his tender love for his enemies, which would be shown fully by his sacrificial death on their behalf (Ro 5:8).

The great apostle Paul also modeled this heart of compassion for enemies of God. Writing to the church in Rome, Paul made a bold claim. He said that he wished that he were cut off from the mercy of God if that meant that God's people would understand and respond to the grace offered through Christ (Ro 9:3).

God's people, moved by love for those who do not know Jesus, should long for them to be reconciled to God. This longing should produce a broken heart, passionate prayer, and bold witness.

2 SAMUEL 20:1–2

UNFAITHFUL DESERTION AND UNCOMPROMISING LOYALTY

In the midst of difficult times, loyalty is at a premium. Those who are loyal to a leader, despite the current circumstances or potential outcomes, are worth their weight in gold. The majority of David's reign over the Hebrews required great loyalty from his followers. In the incident recorded here, the king interacts with men who have been disloyal and those who stayed faithful. The ones who remained faithful did so in spite of the overarching uncertainty of the situation. This incident very much resembles the experience of Jesus several centuries later. Not only did one of his inner circle betray him to the authorities (Mt 26:46–47), leading to his death, but all of his followers left him out of fear for their own lives (Mt 26:56). Jesus suffered the awful experience of a Roman crucifixion with none of his closest followers being willing to suffer with him. Denial and fear were the responses of his close disciples. Yet even they experienced forgiveness from the resurrected Jesus (Jn 21:17). Although we may prove disloyal to the Lord at times, he always proves faithful. Jesus is loyal without compromise.

24And Mephibosheth the son of Saul came down to meet the king. He had neither taken care of his feet nor trimmed his beard nor washed his clothes, from the day the king departed until the day he came back in safety. 25And when he came to Jerusalem to meet the king, the king said to him, "Why did you not go with me, Mephibosheth?" 26He answered, "My lord, O king, my servant deceived me, for your servant said to him, 'I will saddle a donkey for myself,[1] that I may ride on it and go with the king.' For your servant is lame. 27He has slandered your servant to my lord the king. But my lord the king is like the angel of God; do therefore what seems good to you. 28For all my father's house were but men doomed to death before my lord the king, but you set your servant among those who eat at your table. What further right have I, then, to cry to the king?" 29And the king said to him, "Why speak any more of your affairs? I have decided: you and Ziba shall divide the land." 30And Mephibosheth said to the king, "Oh, let him take it all, since my lord the king has come safely home."

31Now Barzillai the Gileadite had come down from Rogelim, and he went on with the king to the Jordan, to escort him over the Jordan. 32Barzillai was a very aged man, eighty years old. He had provided the king with food while he stayed at Mahanaim, for he was a very wealthy man. 33And the king said to Barzillai, "Come over with me, and I will provide for you with me in Jerusalem." 34But Barzillai said to the king, "How many years have I still to live, that I should go up with the king to Jerusalem? 35I am this day eighty years old. Can I discern what is pleasant and what is not? Can your servant taste what he eats or what he drinks? Can I still listen to the voice of singing men and singing women? Why then should your servant be an added burden to my lord the king? 36Your servant will go a little way over the Jordan with the king. Why should the king repay me with such a reward? 37Please let your servant return, that I may die in my own city near the grave of my father and my mother. But here is your servant Chimham. Let him go over with my lord the king, and do for him whatever seems good to you." 38And the king answered, "Chimham shall go over with me, and I will do for him whatever seems good to you, and all that you desire of me I will do for you." 39Then all the people went over the Jordan, and the king went over. And the king kissed Barzillai and blessed him, and he returned to his own home. 40The king went on to Gilgal, and Chimham went on with him. All the people of Judah, and also half the people of Israel, brought the king on his way.

41Then all the men of Israel came to the king and said to the king, "Why have our brothers the men of Judah stolen you away and brought the king and his household over the Jordan, and all David's men with him?" 42All the men of Judah answered the men of Israel, "Because the king is our close relative. Why then are you angry over this matter? Have we eaten at all at the king's expense? Or has he given us any gift?" 43And the men of Israel answered the men of Judah, "We have ten shares in the king, and in David also we have more than you. Why then did you despise us? Were we not the first to speak of bringing back our king?" But the words of the men of Judah were fiercer than the words of the men of Israel.

The Rebellion of Sheba

20 Now there happened to be there a worthless man, whose name was Sheba, the son of Bichri, a Benjaminite. And he blew the trumpet and said,

"We have no portion in David,
and we have no inheritance in the son of Jesse;
every man to his tents, O Israel!"

2So all the men of Israel withdrew from David and followed Sheba the son of Bichri. But the men of Judah followed their king steadfastly from the Jordan to Jerusalem.

[1]Septuagint, Syriac, Vulgate *Saddle a donkey for me*

Joab Rebukes David

19 It was told Joab, "Behold, the king is weeping and mourning for Absalom."
[2]So the victory that day was turned into mourning for all the people, for the
people heard that day, "The king is grieving for his son." [3]And the people stole into
the city that day as people steal in who are ashamed when they flee in battle. [4]The
king covered his face, and the king cried with a loud voice, "O my son Absalom,
O Absalom, my son, my son!" [5]Then Joab came into the house to the king and said,
"You have today covered with shame the faces of all your servants, who have this
day saved your life and the lives of your sons and your daughters and the lives
of your wives and your concubines, [6]because you love those who hate you and
hate those who love you. For you have made it clear today that commanders and
servants are nothing to you, for today I know that if Absalom were alive and all of
us were dead today, then you would be pleased. [7]Now therefore arise, go out and
speak kindly to your servants, for I swear by the LORD, if you do not go, not a man
will stay with you this night, and this will be worse for you than all the evil that
has come upon you from your youth until now." [8]Then the king arose and took
his seat in the gate. And the people were all told, "Behold, the king is sitting in the
gate." And all the people came before the king.

David Returns to Jerusalem

Now Israel had fled every man to his own home. [9]And all the people were
arguing throughout all the tribes of Israel, saying, "The king delivered us from
the hand of our enemies and saved us from the hand of the Philistines, and now
he has fled out of the land from Absalom. [10]But Absalom, whom we anointed
over us, is dead in battle. Now therefore why do you say nothing about bringing
the king back?"

[11]And King David sent this message to Zadok and Abiathar the priests: "Say
to the elders of Judah, 'Why should you be the last to bring the king back to his
house, when the word of all Israel has come to the king?[1] [12]You are my brothers;
you are my bone and my flesh. Why then should you be the last to bring back
the king?' [13]And say to Amasa, 'Are you not my bone and my flesh? God do so to
me and more also, if you are not commander of my army from now on in place
of Joab.'" [14]And he swayed the heart of all the men of Judah as one man, so that
they sent word to the king, "Return, both you and all your servants." [15]So the king
came back to the Jordan, and Judah came to Gilgal to meet the king and to bring
the king over the Jordan.

David Pardons His Enemies

[16]And Shimei the son of Gera, the Benjaminite, from Bahurim, hurried to come
down with the men of Judah to meet King David. [17]And with him were a thousand
men from Benjamin. And Ziba the servant of the house of Saul, with his fifteen
sons and his twenty servants, rushed down to the Jordan before the king, [18]and
they crossed the ford to bring over the king's household and to do his pleasure.
And Shimei the son of Gera fell down before the king, as he was about to cross
the Jordan, [19]and said to the king, "Let not my lord hold me guilty or remember
how your servant did wrong on the day my lord the king left Jerusalem. Do not let
the king take it to heart. [20]For your servant knows that I have sinned. Therefore,
behold, I have come this day, the first of all the house of Joseph to come down to
meet my lord the king." [21]Abishai the son of Zeruiah answered, "Shall not Shimei
be put to death for this, because he cursed the LORD's anointed?" [22]But David said,
"What have I to do with you, you sons of Zeruiah, that you should this day be as
an adversary to me? Shall anyone be put to death in Israel this day? For do I not
know that I am this day king over Israel?" [23]And the king said to Shimei, "You shall
not die." And the king gave him his oath.

[1]Septuagint; Hebrew *to the king, to his house*

David's Song of Deliverance

22 And David spoke to the LORD the words of this song on the day when the
LORD delivered him from the hand of all his enemies, and from the hand
of Saul. 2 He said,

"The LORD is my rock and my fortress and my deliverer,
3 my[1] God, my rock, in whom I take refuge,
my shield, and the horn of my salvation,
my stronghold and my refuge,
my savior; you save me from violence.
4 I call upon the LORD, who is worthy to be praised,
and I am saved from my enemies.

5 "For the waves of death encompassed me,
the torrents of destruction assailed me;[2]
6 the cords of Sheol entangled me;
the snares of death confronted me.

7 "In my distress I called upon the LORD;
to my God I called.
From his temple he heard my voice,
and my cry came to his ears.

8 "Then the earth reeled and rocked;
the foundations of the heavens trembled
and quaked, because he was angry.
9 Smoke went up from his nostrils,[3]
and devouring fire from his mouth;
glowing coals flamed forth from him.
10 He bowed the heavens and came down;
thick darkness was under his feet.
11 He rode on a cherub and flew;
he was seen on the wings of the wind.
12 He made darkness around him his canopy,
thick clouds, a gathering of water.
13 Out of the brightness before him
coals of fire flamed forth.
14 The LORD thundered from heaven,
and the Most High uttered his voice.
15 And he sent out arrows and scattered them;
lightning, and routed them.
16 Then the channels of the sea were seen;
the foundations of the world were laid bare,
at the rebuke of the LORD,
at the blast of the breath of his nostrils.

17 "He sent from on high, he took me;
he drew me out of many waters.
18 He rescued me from my strong enemy,
from those who hated me,
for they were too mighty for me.
19 They confronted me in the day of my calamity,
but the LORD was my support.
20 He brought me out into a broad place;
he rescued me, because he delighted in me.

21 "The LORD dealt with me according to my righteousness;
according to the cleanness of my hands he rewarded me.

[1]Septuagint (compare Psalm 18:2); Hebrew lacks *my* [2]Or *terrified me* [3]Or *in his wrath*

2 SAMUEL 22:1–51

HEAD OF NATIONS

According to verse 1 of this chapter, David wrote this song of praise as he reflected on how God had delivered him from his enemies. After years of hardship at the hands of various enemies—whether it was the unjust envy of Saul (1Sa 18:8–9) or the warring Philistines—David now experienced peace and authored this song, having seen the evidence that God was his rock, fortress, and deliverer (2Sa 22:2). Although generated out of the personal deliverance experience of David, this song was included in the book of Psalms (Ps 18) because it has broader applications for those who experience God's love and protection. Also noteworthy are the parts of this song that speak of David as the "head of the nations" (2Sa 22:44; Ps 18:43). In a limited sense, this applied to David in his day, but it would apply ultimately to Jesus as discussed in 2 Samuel 7. David closed his song of praise by highlighting God's faithfulness to him and his descendants forever. Clearly, God had faithfully honored his promise to David by preserving his place as the head of nations, a promise that David remembered and that was applied to Jesus in Luke 1:32–33.

22 For I have kept the ways of the LORD
and have not wickedly departed from my God.
23 For all his rules were before me,
and from his statutes I did not turn aside.
24 I was blameless before him,
and I kept myself from guilt.
25 And the LORD has rewarded me according to my righteousness,
according to my cleanness in his sight.

26 "With the merciful you show yourself merciful;
with the blameless man you show yourself blameless;
27 with the purified you deal purely,
and with the crooked you make yourself seem tortuous.
28 You save a humble people,
but your eyes are on the haughty to bring them down.
29 For you are my lamp, O LORD,
and my God lightens my darkness.
30 For by you I can run against a troop,
and by my God I can leap over a wall.
31 This God—his way is perfect;
the word of the LORD proves true;
he is a shield for all those who take refuge in him.

32 "For who is God, but the LORD?
And who is a rock, except our God?
33 This God is my strong refuge
and has made my[1] way blameless.[2]
34 He made my feet like the feet of a deer
and set me secure on the heights.
35 He trains my hands for war,
so that my arms can bend a bow of bronze.
36 You have given me the shield of your salvation,
and your gentleness made me great.
37 You gave a wide place for my steps under me,
and my feet[3] did not slip;
38 I pursued my enemies and destroyed them,
and did not turn back until they were consumed.
39 I consumed them; I thrust them through, so that they did not rise;
they fell under my feet.
40 For you equipped me with strength for the battle;
you made those who rise against me sink under me.
41 You made my enemies turn their backs to me,[4]
those who hated me, and I destroyed them.
42 They looked, but there was none to save;
they cried to the LORD, but he did not answer them.
43 I beat them fine as the dust of the earth;
I crushed them and stamped them down like the mire of the streets.

44 "You delivered me from strife with my people;[5]
you kept me as the head of the nations;
people whom I had not known served me.
45 Foreigners came cringing to me;
as soon as they heard of me, they obeyed me.
46 Foreigners lost heart
and came trembling[6] out of their fortresses.

[1]Or *his*; also verse 34 [2]Compare Psalm 18:32; Hebrew *he has blamelessly set my way free*, or *he has made my way spring up blamelessly* [3]Hebrew *ankles* [4]Or *You gave me my enemies' necks* [5]Septuagint *with the peoples* [6]Compare Psalm 18:45; Hebrew *equipped themselves*

47 "The LORD lives, and blessed be my rock,
and exalted be my God, the rock of my salvation,
48 the God who gave me vengeance
and brought down peoples under me,
49 who brought me out from my enemies;
you exalted me above those who rose against me;
you delivered me from men of violence.

50 "For this I will praise you, O LORD, among the nations,
and sing praises to your name.
51 Great salvation he brings[1] to his king,
and shows steadfast love to his anointed,
to David and his offspring forever."

The Last Words of David

23 Now these are the last words of David:

The oracle of David, the son of Jesse,
the oracle of the man who was raised on high,
the anointed of the God of Jacob,
the sweet psalmist of Israel:[2]

2 "The Spirit of the LORD speaks by me;
his word is on my tongue.
3 The God of Israel has spoken;
the Rock of Israel has said to me:
When one rules justly over men,
ruling in the fear of God,
4 he dawns on them like the morning light,
like the sun shining forth on a cloudless morning,
like rain[3] that makes grass to sprout from the earth.

5 "For does not my house stand so with God?
For he has made with me an everlasting covenant,
ordered in all things and secure.
For will he not cause to prosper
all my help and my desire?
6 But worthless men[4] are all like thorns that are thrown away,
for they cannot be taken with the hand;
7 but the man who touches them
arms himself with iron and the shaft of a spear,
and they are utterly consumed with fire."[5]

David's Mighty Men

8These are the names of the mighty men whom David had: Josheb-basshebeth
a Tahchemonite; he was chief of the three.[6] He wielded his spear[7] against eight
hundred whom he killed at one time.
9And next to him among the three mighty men was Eleazar the son of Dodo,
son of Ahohi. He was with David when they defied the Philistines who were gathered there for battle, and the men of Israel withdrew. 10He rose and struck down
the Philistines until his hand was weary, and his hand clung to the sword. And
the LORD brought about a great victory that day, and the men returned after him
only to strip the slain.
11And next to him was Shammah, the son of Agee the Hararite. The Philistines
gathered together at Lehi,[8] where there was a plot of ground full of lentils, and the

[1]Or *He is a tower of salvation* [2]Or *the favorite of the songs of Israel* [3]Hebrew *from rain* [4]Hebrew *worthlessness* [5]Hebrew *consumed with fire in the sitting* [6]Or *of the captains* [7]Compare 1 Chronicles 11:11; the meaning of the Hebrew expression is uncertain [8]Or *gathered together as a camp*

COVENANTS MADE AND RENEWED

David's final poetic words revealed the supreme trust he had in God's faithfulness to fulfill his promises. He reaffirmed the "everlasting covenant" God made with David long ago (v. 5). These promises, first made in 2 Samuel 7:12 – 16, were a firm foundation for David's trust, even in the face of his impending death. God's covenant pledged that someone from David's lineage would reign as God's anointed king. In the short term, this promise was fulfilled in David's son, Solomon, who built the temple and established the worship of God among the people. But this would not be the end of God's covenant promises. David reminded Solomon that if he walked faithfully before God, he would not lack a successor on the throne of Israel (1Ki 2:4). Solomon knew the promise of God's anointed king was still to come. Neither David nor Solomon could fully understand or comprehend the person of Jesus Christ, but their hope was clearly set on a coming king who would, unlike them, be able to usher in the rule and reign of God over his people. The prophet Isaiah looked forward to this day when he wrote:

> "For to us a child is born,
> to us a son is given;
> and the government shall be upon his shoulder,
> and his name shall be called
> Wonderful Counselor, Mighty God,
> Everlasting Father, Prince of Peace.
> Of the increase of his government and of peace
> there will be no end,
> on the throne of David and over his kingdom,
> to establish it and to uphold it
> with justice and with righteousness
> from this time forth and forevermore.
> The zeal of the LORD of hosts will do this" (Isa 9:6 – 7).

God would fulfill his promises, just as David believed. Though the people would continue to turn from God, God would not abandon his people. The zeal of God and not the faithfulness of humanity would establish the throne of David. And this throne, unlike David's, will have no end.

men fled from the Philistines. 12But he took his stand in the midst of the plot and
defended it and struck down the Philistines, and the LORD worked a great victory.
13And three of the thirty chief men went down and came about harvest time
to David at the cave of Adullam, when a band of Philistines was encamped in the
Valley of Rephaim. 14David was then in the stronghold, and the garrison of the
Philistines was then at Bethlehem. 15And David said longingly, "Oh, that someone
would give me water to drink from the well of Bethlehem that is by the gate!"
16Then the three mighty men broke through the camp of the Philistines and drew
water out of the well of Bethlehem that was by the gate and carried and brought
it to David. But he would not drink of it. He poured it out to the LORD 17and said,
"Far be it from me, O LORD, that I should do this. Shall I drink the blood of the men
who went at the risk of their lives?" Therefore he would not drink it. These things
the three mighty men did.

18Now Abishai, the brother of Joab, the son of Zeruiah, was chief of the thirty.[1]
And he wielded his spear against three hundred men[2] and killed them and won
a name beside the three. 19He was the most renowned of the thirty[3] and became
their commander, but he did not attain to the three.

20And Benaiah the son of Jehoiada was a valiant man[4] of Kabzeel, a doer of
great deeds. He struck down two ariels[5] of Moab. He also went down and struck
down a lion in a pit on a day when snow had fallen. 21And he struck down an
Egyptian, a handsome man. The Egyptian had a spear in his hand, but Benaiah
went down to him with a staff and snatched the spear out of the Egyptian's
hand and killed him with his own spear. 22These things did Benaiah the son of
Jehoiada, and won a name beside the three mighty men. 23He was renowned
among the thirty, but he did not attain to the three. And David set him over his
bodyguard.

24Asahel the brother of Joab was one of the thirty; Elhanan the son of Dodo of
Bethlehem, 25Shammah of Harod, Elika of Harod, 26Helez the Paltite, Ira the son
of Ikkesh of Tekoa, 27Abiezer of Anathoth, Mebunnai the Hushathite, 28Zalmon
the Ahohite, Maharai of Netophah, 29Heleb the son of Baanah of Netophah, Ittai the son of Ribai of Gibeah of the people of Benjamin, 30Benaiah of Pirathon,
Hiddai of the brooks of Gaash, 31Abi-albon the Arbathite, Azmaveth of Bahurim,
32Eliahba the Shaalbonite, the sons of Jashen, Jonathan, 33Shammah the Hararite,
Ahiam the son of Sharar the Hararite, 34Eliphelet the son of Ahasbai of Maacah,
Eliam the son of Ahithophel the Gilonite, 35Hezro[6] of Carmel, Paarai the Arbite,
36Igal the son of Nathan of Zobah, Bani the Gadite, 37Zelek the Ammonite, Naharai of Beeroth, the armor-bearer of Joab the son of Zeruiah, 38Ira the Ithrite, Gareb
the Ithrite, 39Uriah the Hittite: thirty-seven in all.

David's Census

24 Again the anger of the LORD was kindled against Israel, and he incited
David against them, saying, "Go, number Israel and Judah." 2So the king
said to Joab, the commander of the army,[7] who was with him, "Go through all the
tribes of Israel, from Dan to Beersheba, and number the people, that I may know
the number of the people." 3But Joab said to the king, "May the LORD your God
add to the people a hundred times as many as they are, while the eyes of my lord
the king still see it, but why does my lord the king delight in this thing?" 4But the
king's word prevailed against Joab and the commanders of the army. So Joab and
the commanders of the army went out from the presence of the king to number
the people of Israel. 5They crossed the Jordan and began from Aroer,[8] and from
the city that is in the middle of the valley, toward Gad and on to Jazer. 6Then they
came to Gilead, and to Kadesh in the land of the Hittites;[9] and they came to Dan,

[1] Two Hebrew manuscripts, Syriac; most Hebrew manuscripts *three* [2] Or *slain ones* [3] Compare 1 Chronicles 11:21; Hebrew *Was he the most renowned of the three?* [4] Or *the son of Ishhai* [5] The meaning of the word *ariel* is uncertain [6] Or *Hezrai* [7] Septuagint *to Joab and the commanders of the army* [8] Septuagint; Hebrew *encamped in Aroer* [9] Septuagint; Hebrew *to the land of Tahtim-hodshi*

THE NEED FOR ATONEMENT

There are consequences for sin. This has been the overarching story in the life of David. David's saga entails acts of disobedience and then moments of repentance and reconciliation with God. However, the impact of his sin was evident. In this episode, the result of David's sin was that over seventy thousand people lost their lives in a plague (24:15). Again, the consequences of sin are real!

Ultimately, David found atonement for his sin by God's grace and mercy. Out of this tragic scene comes the site for the future temple of Solomon, which became a central location for the future of the Jewish people (1Ch 21:28 — 22:1). God's promises of grace to his people thus come together in this instance of David atoning for his sin (2Sa 24:18 – 25). God is able to take the ugliness of a person's disobedience and turn it into a beautiful picture of his redeeming grace.

This location and the future temple point to a much greater atonement, offered by the grace and mercy of God through a much greater temple. This entire narrative of worship that develops through the stories of David and Solomon prefigures Christ as the final temple where atonement was accomplished once for all believers (Jn 2:19 – 21). The atonement for sin required a perfect sacrifice. Jesus was that sacrifice. According to 1 Peter 1:18 – 21, Jesus was the perfect, spotless Lamb of God, who offered himself as a payment to God for the offenses of believers. The Jewish people could inherit eternal salvation, not by their ethnic heritage, but by believing in the gospel secured by the atonement of Jesus, the spotless Lamb. As Luke wrote, "And beginning with Moses and all the Prophets, he interpreted to them in all the Scriptures the things concerning himself" (Lk 24:27). These authors had a rich understanding of who Jesus is. He is the atonement. He is the temple. He is what David needed as well as what we need: the once-for-all offering for sins.

and from Dan[1] they went around to Sidon, 7and came to the fortress of Tyre and to all the cities of the Hivites and Canaanites; and they went out to the Negeb of Judah at Beersheba. 8So when they had gone through all the land, they came to Jerusalem at the end of nine months and twenty days. 9And Joab gave the sum of the numbering of the people to the king: in Israel there were 800,000 valiant men who drew the sword, and the men of Judah were 500,000.

The Lord's Judgment of David's Sin

10But David's heart struck him after he had numbered the people. And David said to the Lord, "I have sinned greatly in what I have done. But now, O Lord, please take away the iniquity of your servant, for I have done very foolishly." 11And when David arose in the morning, the word of the Lord came to the prophet Gad, David's seer, saying, 12"Go and say to David, 'Thus says the Lord, Three things I offer[2] you. Choose one of them, that I may do it to you.'" 13So Gad came to David and told him, and said to him, "Shall three[3] years of famine come to you in your land? Or will you flee three months before your foes while they pursue you? Or shall there be three days' pestilence in your land? Now consider, and decide what answer I shall return to him who sent me." 14Then David said to Gad, "I am in great distress. Let us fall into the hand of the Lord, for his mercy is great; but let me not fall into the hand of man."

15So the Lord sent a pestilence on Israel from the morning until the appointed time. And there died of the people from Dan to Beersheba 70,000 men. 16And when the angel stretched out his hand toward Jerusalem to destroy it, the Lord relented from the calamity and said to the angel who was working destruction among the people, "It is enough; now stay your hand." And the angel of the Lord was by the threshing floor of Araunah the Jebusite. 17Then David spoke to the Lord when he saw the angel who was striking the people, and said, "Behold, I have sinned, and I have done wickedly. But these sheep, what have they done? Please let your hand be against me and against my father's house."

David Builds an Altar

18And Gad came that day to David and said to him, "Go up, raise an altar to the Lord on the threshing floor of Araunah the Jebusite." 19So David went up at Gad's word, as the Lord commanded. 20And when Araunah looked down, he saw the king and his servants coming on toward him. And Araunah went out and paid homage to the king with his face to the ground. 21And Araunah said, "Why has my lord the king come to his servant?" David said, "To buy the threshing floor from you, in order to build an altar to the Lord, that the plague may be averted from the people." 22Then Araunah said to David, "Let my lord the king take and offer up what seems good to him. Here are the oxen for the burnt offering and the threshing sledges and the yokes of the oxen for the wood. 23All this, O king, Araunah gives to the king." And Araunah said to the king, "May the Lord your God accept you." 24But the king said to Araunah, "No, but I will buy it from you for a price. I will not offer burnt offerings to the Lord my God that cost me nothing." So David bought the threshing floor and the oxen for fifty shekels[4] of silver. 25And David built there an altar to the Lord and offered burnt offerings and peace offerings. So the Lord responded to the plea for the land, and the plague was averted from Israel.

---

[1]Septuagint; Hebrew *they came to Dan-jaan and* [2]Or *hold over* [3]Compare 1 Chronicles 21:12, Septuagint; Hebrew *seven* [4]A *shekel* was about 2/5 ounce or 11 grams

JESUS: OUR ONLY HOPE

1 KINGS

1 KINGS

REIGN OF SOLOMON *c. 970 – 930 BC*	ISRAEL DIVIDED *c. 930 BC*	ELIJAH BEGINS MINISTRY *c. 875 BC*

The book of 1 Kings portrays the lives of both godly and ungodly individuals during a defining period in the life of the nation of Israel. People such as King David (1Ki 1:24 – 30), King Solomon (1Ki 3:1 – 15), and the Queen of Sheba (1Ki 10:1 – 13) sought after God, though they were far from perfect in this quest. Others such as Ahab and Jezebel notoriously rebelled against God's commands and suffered the just consequences for their actions (2Ki 9:30 – 37; 10:1 – 10). As a whole, the book demonstrates the implications of choosing between these two paths through the lives of good and bad kings, true and false prophets, and an assortment of others whose lives shaped Israel's spiritual odyssey. The ever-present backdrop of God's unchanging faithfulness provides hope and confidence to those who seek him.

The unknown author of this book recounts Israel's history beginning with the death of the great King David in the tenth century and concluding in 2 Kings, nearly 400 years later, with Jerusalem's destruction and the bitter exile of God's divided people. The author highlights the spiritual successes and failures that defined the nation, including Solomon's demise and the nation's successive, nearly immediate splintering — with ten tribes in the north aligning under Jeroboam and two tribes in the south under the rule of Solomon's son Rehoboam. From that time forward, the author juxtaposes the spiritual apostasy of the two kingdoms against the small glimmers of faithfulness still seen among the people.

Though 1 Kings is a historical narrative, it is much more than a mere recounting of factual events. Rather, the author's purpose was theological — he wanted to demonstrate that obedience to God was, and is, the proper response to God's consistent and grace-filled faithfulness. The people had been warned — both before they entered the promised land and throughout their time in the land — that those who failed to honor God and obey his word would face stark consequences. And, time and again, the people of Israel learned the truth of this lesson the hard way. The continued inability of the people to obey points forward to humanity's need for the long-awaited Messiah.

Jesus Christ would do what the nation of Israel was unable to do — he would perfectly obey the law of God. His wisdom, miracles and faithfulness are foreshadowed, though imperfectly, through exemplary figures such as Solomon, Elijah, and Elisha. The stories of God's grace seen in these godly individuals provide believers today with a model of the worshipful obedience that should still be seen among God's people today.

O LORD, GOD OF ISRAEL, THERE IS NO GOD LIKE YOU,
IN HEAVEN ABOVE OR ON EARTH BENEATH,
KEEPING COVENANT AND SHOWING STEADFAST LOVE
TO YOUR SERVANTS WHO WALK BEFORE YOU
WITH ALL THEIR HEART.

---

1 Kings 8:23

1 KINGS

David in His Old Age

1 Now King David was old and advanced in years. And although they covered
him with clothes, he could not get warm. 2Therefore his servants said to
him, "Let a young woman be sought for my lord the king, and let her wait on the
king and be in his service. Let her lie in your arms,[1] that my lord the king may be
warm." 3So they sought for a beautiful young woman throughout all the territory
of Israel, and found Abishag the Shunammite, and brought her to the king. 4The
young woman was very beautiful, and she was of service to the king and attended
to him, but the king knew her not.

Adonijah Sets Himself Up as King

5Now Adonijah the son of Haggith exalted himself, saying, "I will be king."
And he prepared for himself chariots and horsemen, and fifty men to run before
him. 6His father had never at any time displeased him by asking, "Why have you
done thus and so?" He was also a very handsome man, and he was born next
after Absalom. 7He conferred with Joab the son of Zeruiah and with Abiathar the
priest. And they followed Adonijah and helped him. 8But Zadok the priest and Benaiah the son of Jehoiada and Nathan the prophet and Shimei and Rei and David's
mighty men were not with Adonijah.

9Adonijah sacrificed sheep, oxen, and fattened cattle by the Serpent's Stone,
which is beside En-rogel, and he invited all his brothers, the king's sons, and all
the royal officials of Judah, 10but he did not invite Nathan the prophet or Benaiah
or the mighty men or Solomon his brother.

Nathan and Bathsheba Before David

11Then Nathan said to Bathsheba the mother of Solomon, "Have you not heard
that Adonijah the son of Haggith has become king and David our lord does not
know it? 12Now therefore come, let me give you advice, that you may save your
own life and the life of your son Solomon. 13Go in at once to King David, and say to
him, 'Did you not, my lord the king, swear to your servant, saying, "Solomon your
son shall reign after me, and he shall sit on my throne"? Why then is Adonijah
king?' 14Then while you are still speaking with the king, I also will come in after
you and confirm[2] your words."

15So Bathsheba went to the king in his chamber (now the king was very old,
and Abishag the Shunammite was attending to the king). 16Bathsheba bowed and
paid homage to the king, and the king said, "What do you desire?" 17She said to
him, "My lord, you swore to your servant by the LORD your God, saying, 'Solomon
your son shall reign after me, and he shall sit on my throne.' 18And now, behold,
Adonijah is king, although you, my lord the king, do not know it. 19He has sacrificed oxen, fattened cattle, and sheep in abundance, and has invited all the sons of
the king, Abiathar the priest, and Joab the commander of the army, but Solomon
your servant he has not invited. 20And now, my lord the king, the eyes of all Israel
are on you, to tell them who shall sit on the throne of my lord the king after him.
21Otherwise it will come to pass, when my lord the king sleeps with his fathers,
that I and my son Solomon will be counted offenders."

22While she was still speaking with the king, Nathan the prophet came in.
23And they told the king, "Here is Nathan the prophet." And when he came in
before the king, he bowed before the king, with his face to the ground. 24And Nathan said, "My lord the king, have you said, 'Adonijah shall reign after me, and he
shall sit on my throne'? 25For he has gone down this day and has sacrificed oxen,

---

[1]Or *in your bosom* [2]Or *expand on*

fattened cattle, and sheep in abundance, and has invited all the king's sons, the commanders[1] of the army, and Abiathar the priest. And behold, they are eating and drinking before him, and saying, 'Long live King Adonijah!' 26But me, your servant, and Zadok the priest, and Benaiah the son of Jehoiada, and your servant Solomon he has not invited. 27Has this thing been brought about by my lord the king and you have not told your servants who should sit on the throne of my lord the king after him?"

Solomon Anointed King

28Then King David answered, "Call Bathsheba to me." So she came into the king's presence and stood before the king. 29And the king swore, saying, "As the LORD lives, who has redeemed my soul out of every adversity, 30as I swore to you by the LORD, the God of Israel, saying, 'Solomon your son shall reign after me, and he shall sit on my throne in my place,' even so will I do this day." 31Then Bathsheba bowed with her face to the ground and paid homage to the king and said, "May my lord King David live forever!"

32King David said, "Call to me Zadok the priest, Nathan the prophet, and Benaiah the son of Jehoiada." So they came before the king. 33And the king said to them, "Take with you the servants of your lord and have Solomon my son ride on my own mule, and bring him down to Gihon. 34And let Zadok the priest and Nathan the prophet there anoint him king over Israel. Then blow the trumpet and say, 'Long live King Solomon!' 35You shall then come up after him, and he shall come and sit on my throne, for he shall be king in my place. And I have appointed him to be ruler over Israel and over Judah." 36And Benaiah the son of Jehoiada answered the king, "Amen! May the LORD, the God of my lord the king, say so. 37As the LORD has been with my lord the king, even so may he be with Solomon, and make his throne greater than the throne of my lord King David."

38So Zadok the priest, Nathan the prophet, and Benaiah the son of Jehoiada, and the Cherethites and the Pelethites went down and had Solomon ride on King David's mule and brought him to Gihon. 39There Zadok the priest took the horn of oil from the tent and anointed Solomon. Then they blew the trumpet, and all the people said, "Long live King Solomon!" 40And all the people went up after him, playing on pipes, and rejoicing with great joy, so that the earth was split by their noise.

41Adonijah and all the guests who were with him heard it as they finished feasting. And when Joab heard the sound of the trumpet, he said, "What does this uproar in the city mean?" 42While he was still speaking, behold, Jonathan the son of Abiathar the priest came. And Adonijah said, "Come in, for you are a worthy man and bring good news." 43Jonathan answered Adonijah, "No, for our lord King David has made Solomon king, 44and the king has sent with him Zadok the priest, Nathan the prophet, and Benaiah the son of Jehoiada, and the Cherethites and the Pelethites. And they had him ride on the king's mule. 45And Zadok the priest and Nathan the prophet have anointed him king at Gihon, and they have gone up from there rejoicing, so that the city is in an uproar. This is the noise that you have heard. 46Solomon sits on the royal throne. 47Moreover, the king's servants came to congratulate our lord King David, saying, 'May your God make the name of Solomon more famous than yours, and make his throne greater than your throne.' And the king bowed himself on the bed. 48And the king also said, 'Blessed be the LORD, the God of Israel, who has granted someone[2] to sit on my throne this day, my own eyes seeing it.'"

49Then all the guests of Adonijah trembled and rose, and each went his own way. 50And Adonijah feared Solomon. So he arose and went and took hold of the horns of the altar. 51Then it was told Solomon, "Behold, Adonijah fears King

[1]Hebrew; Septuagint *Joab the commander* [2]Septuagint *one of my offspring*

1 KINGS 1:28–39

PROTECTING THE LINE OF DAVID

Throughout the reign of the Davidic dynasty, God faithfully preserved the promises he had made to David. Adonijah, Solomon's older brother, vied to sit on the throne of his father David. As Bathsheba pointed out, had Adonijah gained the throne, she and Solomon would have been counted as criminals (v. 21). God's promises, however, were stronger than Adonijah's schemes. The line of David would be carried on through Solomon, not Adonijah, because the Lord had appointed Solomon ruler over Israel and Judah. God's faithfulness to protect the kingly line of David would usher in the birth of the King of kings, Jesus Christ, a descendant of David and the one to whom the promises pointed (Mt 1:1). Through Christ, the Davidic throne was perfectly established and was secured forever.

Solomon, for behold, he has laid hold of the horns of the altar, saying, 'Let King
Solomon swear to me first that he will not put his servant to death with the
sword.'" 52And Solomon said, "If he will show himself a worthy man, not one
of his hairs shall fall to the earth, but if wickedness is found in him, he shall
die." 53So King Solomon sent, and they brought him down from the altar. And
he came and paid homage to King Solomon, and Solomon said to him, "Go to
your house."

David's Instructions to Solomon

2 When David's time to die drew near, he commanded Solomon his son, saying,
2"I am about to go the way of all the earth. Be strong, and show yourself a man,
3and keep the charge of the LORD your God, walking in his ways and keeping his
statutes, his commandments, his rules, and his testimonies, as it is written in the
Law of Moses, that you may prosper in all that you do and wherever you turn,
4that the LORD may establish his word that he spoke concerning me, saying, 'If
your sons pay close attention to their way, to walk before me in faithfulness with
all their heart and with all their soul, you shall not lack[1] a man on the throne of
Israel.'

5"Moreover, you also know what Joab the son of Zeruiah did to me, how he
dealt with the two commanders of the armies of Israel, Abner the son of Ner, and
Amasa the son of Jether, whom he killed, avenging[2] in time of peace for blood
that had been shed in war, and putting the blood of war[3] on the belt around his[4]
waist and on the sandals on his feet. 6Act therefore according to your wisdom,
but do not let his gray head go down to Sheol in peace. 7But deal loyally with the
sons of Barzillai the Gileadite, and let them be among those who eat at your table,
for with such loyalty[5] they met me when I fled from Absalom your brother. 8And
there is also with you Shimei the son of Gera, the Benjaminite from Bahurim, who
cursed me with a grievous curse on the day when I went to Mahanaim. But when
he came down to meet me at the Jordan, I swore to him by the LORD, saying, 'I will
not put you to death with the sword.' 9Now therefore do not hold him guiltless,
for you are a wise man. You will know what you ought to do to him, and you shall
bring his gray head down with blood to Sheol."

The Death of David

10Then David slept with his fathers and was buried in the city of David. 11And
the time that David reigned over Israel was forty years. He reigned seven years in
Hebron and thirty-three years in Jerusalem. 12So Solomon sat on the throne of
David his father, and his kingdom was firmly established.

Solomon's Reign Established

13Then Adonijah the son of Haggith came to Bathsheba the mother of Solomon. And she said, "Do you come peacefully?" He said, "Peacefully." 14Then he
said, "I have something to say to you." She said, "Speak." 15He said, "You know that
the kingdom was mine, and that all Israel fully expected me to reign. However, the
kingdom has turned about and become my brother's, for it was his from the LORD.
16And now I have one request to make of you; do not refuse me." She said to him,
"Speak." 17And he said, "Please ask King Solomon—he will not refuse you—to
give me Abishag the Shunammite as my wife." 18Bathsheba said, "Very well; I will
speak for you to the king."

19So Bathsheba went to King Solomon to speak to him on behalf of Adonijah.
And the king rose to meet her and bowed down to her. Then he sat on his throne
and had a seat brought for the king's mother, and she sat on his right. 20Then
she said, "I have one small request to make of you; do not refuse me." And the
king said to her, "Make your request, my mother, for I will not refuse you." 21She

[1]Hebrew *there shall not be cut off for you* [2]Septuagint; Hebrew *placing* [3]Septuagint *innocent blood*
[4]Septuagint *my*; twice in this verse [5]Or *steadfast love*

---

1 KINGS 2:1–4

A LESS-THAN-PERFECT KING

It seems that David's charge to Solomon required him to do the impossible—perfectly keep the law of God. In similar fashion, often the nation of Israel was given the command to walk in God's ways, and, in so doing, enjoy the favor and blessing of God. But here that command was uniquely directed at King Solomon alone. As God's chosen king, he was to exemplify godliness for the nation. The subsequent cycle of failure in Solomon's life soon demonstrated that he, like the nation as a whole, was incapable of keeping these lofty instructions. No one, not even the wise king, could keep the law without faltering.

Jesus accomplished what Solomon and every other figure in the Old Testament could not. Jesus perfectly fulfilled the law of God. Peter said that Jesus "committed no sin, neither was deceit found in his mouth" (1Pe 2:22). As the perfect king, Jesus did what Solomon could not do and secured the blessing of God for those who place their faith in his completed work.

said, "Let Abishag the Shunammite be given to Adonijah your brother as his
wife." 22King Solomon answered his mother, "And why do you ask Abishag the
Shunammite for Adonijah? Ask for him the kingdom also, for he is my older
brother, and on his side are Abiathar[1] the priest and Joab the son of Zeruiah."
23Then King Solomon swore by the LORD, saying, "God do so to me and more
also if this word does not cost Adonijah his life! 24Now therefore as the LORD
lives, who has established me and placed me on the throne of David my father,
and who has made me a house, as he promised, Adonijah shall be put to death
today." 25So King Solomon sent Benaiah the son of Jehoiada, and he struck him
down, and he died.

26And to Abiathar the priest the king said, "Go to Anathoth, to your estate,
for you deserve death. But I will not at this time put you to death, because you
carried the ark of the Lord GOD before David my father, and because you shared
in all my father's affliction." 27So Solomon expelled Abiathar from being priest to
the LORD, thus fulfilling the word of the LORD that he had spoken concerning the
house of Eli in Shiloh.

28When the news came to Joab—for Joab had supported Adonijah although
he had not supported Absalom—Joab fled to the tent of the LORD and caught
hold of the horns of the altar. 29And when it was told King Solomon, "Joab has
fled to the tent of the LORD, and behold, he is beside the altar," Solomon sent
Benaiah the son of Jehoiada, saying, "Go, strike him down." 30So Benaiah came
to the tent of the LORD and said to him, "The king commands, 'Come out.'" But
he said, "No, I will die here." Then Benaiah brought the king word again, saying,
"Thus said Joab, and thus he answered me." 31The king replied to him, "Do as he
has said, strike him down and bury him, and thus take away from me and from
my father's house the guilt for the blood that Joab shed without cause. 32The
LORD will bring back his bloody deeds on his own head, because, without the
knowledge of my father David, he attacked and killed with the sword two men
more righteous and better than himself, Abner the son of Ner, commander of the
army of Israel, and Amasa the son of Jether, commander of the army of Judah.
33So shall their blood come back on the head of Joab and on the head of his descendants forever. But for David and for his descendants and for his house and
for his throne there shall be peace from the LORD forevermore." 34Then Benaiah
the son of Jehoiada went up and struck him down and put him to death. And he
was buried in his own house in the wilderness. 35The king put Benaiah the son
of Jehoiada over the army in place of Joab, and the king put Zadok the priest in
the place of Abiathar.

36Then the king sent and summoned Shimei and said to him, "Build yourself
a house in Jerusalem and dwell there, and do not go out from there to any place
whatever. 37For on the day you go out and cross the brook Kidron, know for certain that you shall die. Your blood shall be on your own head." 38And Shimei said
to the king, "What you say is good; as my lord the king has said, so will your servant do." So Shimei lived in Jerusalem many days.

39But it happened at the end of three years that two of Shimei's servants ran
away to Achish, son of Maacah, king of Gath. And when it was told Shimei, "Behold, your servants are in Gath," 40Shimei arose and saddled a donkey and went
to Gath to Achish to seek his servants. Shimei went and brought his servants from
Gath. 41And when Solomon was told that Shimei had gone from Jerusalem to Gath
and returned, 42the king sent and summoned Shimei and said to him, "Did I not
make you swear by the LORD and solemnly warn you, saying, 'Know for certain
that on the day you go out and go to any place whatever, you shall die'? And you
said to me, 'What you say is good; I will obey.' 43Why then have you not kept your
oath to the LORD and the commandment with which I commanded you?" 44The
king also said to Shimei, "You know in your own heart all the harm that you did to

[1]Septuagint, Syriac, Vulgate; Hebrew *and for him and for Abiathar*

David my father. So the LORD will bring back your harm on your own head. 45But
King Solomon shall be blessed, and the throne of David shall be established before the LORD forever." 46Then the king commanded Benaiah the son of Jehoiada,
and he went out and struck him down, and he died.

So the kingdom was established in the hand of Solomon.

Solomon's Prayer for Wisdom

3 Solomon made a marriage alliance with Pharaoh king of Egypt. He took Pharaoh's daughter and brought her into the city of David until he had finished
building his own house and the house of the LORD and the wall around Jerusalem.
2The people were sacrificing at the high places, however, because no house had
yet been built for the name of the LORD.

3Solomon loved the LORD, walking in the statutes of David his father, only he
sacrificed and made offerings at the high places. 4And the king went to Gibeon to
sacrifice there, for that was the great high place. Solomon used to offer a thousand burnt offerings on that altar. 5At Gibeon the LORD appeared to Solomon in
a dream by night, and God said, "Ask what I shall give you." 6And Solomon said,
"You have shown great and steadfast love to your servant David my father, because he walked before you in faithfulness, in righteousness, and in uprightness
of heart toward you. And you have kept for him this great and steadfast love and
have given him a son to sit on his throne this day. 7And now, O LORD my God, you
have made your servant king in place of David my father, although I am but a little
child. I do not know how to go out or come in. 8And your servant is in the midst
of your people whom you have chosen, a great people, too many to be numbered
or counted for multitude. 9Give your servant therefore an understanding mind to
govern your people, that I may discern between good and evil, for who is able to
govern this your great people?"

10It pleased the Lord that Solomon had asked this. 11And God said to him, "Because you have asked this, and have not asked for yourself long life or riches or
the life of your enemies, but have asked for yourself understanding to discern
what is right, 12behold, I now do according to your word. Behold, I give you a wise
and discerning mind, so that none like you has been before you and none like you
shall arise after you. 13I give you also what you have not asked, both riches and
honor, so that no other king shall compare with you, all your days. 14And if you
will walk in my ways, keeping my statutes and my commandments, as your father
David walked, then I will lengthen your days."

15And Solomon awoke, and behold, it was a dream. Then he came to Jerusalem
and stood before the ark of the covenant of the Lord, and offered up burnt offerings and peace offerings, and made a feast for all his servants.

Solomon's Wisdom

16Then two prostitutes came to the king and stood before him. 17The one woman said, "Oh, my lord, this woman and I live in the same house, and I gave birth to
a child while she was in the house. 18Then on the third day after I gave birth, this
woman also gave birth. And we were alone. There was no one else with us in the
house; only we two were in the house. 19And this woman's son died in the night,
because she lay on him. 20And she arose at midnight and took my son from beside
me, while your servant slept, and laid him at her breast, and laid her dead son at
my breast. 21When I rose in the morning to nurse my child, behold, he was dead.
But when I looked at him closely in the morning, behold, he was not the child
that I had borne." 22But the other woman said, "No, the living child is mine, and
the dead child is yours." The first said, "No, the dead child is yours, and the living
child is mine." Thus they spoke before the king.

23Then the king said, "The one says, 'This is my son that is alive, and your
son is dead'; and the other says, 'No; but your son is dead, and my son is the
living one.'" 24And the king said, "Bring me a sword." So a sword was brought

THE VALUE OF WISDOM

God made Solomon an offer that anyone would envy. Solomon could ask God for anything — wealth, honor, a long life (v. 5). The God of all creation and owner of everything extended an offer for any provision Solomon desired. Solomon's request was both unexpected and remarkable. He asked for an understanding mind to distinguish right from wrong, which uniquely equipped him to lead the people of God (v. 9). God responded by granting this request, but he also gave Solomon the wealth and honor he had not requested (v. 13). Solomon is credited with more than 3,000 proverbs and 1,000 songs, and his wisdom eventually made him the most famous man of his day (1Ki 4:33–34).

Wisdom serves as a valuable precursor to wealth and power. Either of these gifts, when given to a fool, leads to great harm; however, wisdom allows a person to utilize God's provision of wealth or power in a manner that causes God's people to thrive. This is why Solomon claimed that wisdom is "better than gain from silver" and yields "profit better than gold" (Pr 3:13–14).

Jesus knew the profitability of wisdom. As the incarnate Son of God, he did not merely possess insight into the mind of God; rather, he actually possessed the mind of God. Wisdom was not personified in Christ; it was perfected in Christ.

God's people continue to find wisdom in Jesus. Solomon's counsel in the book of Proverbs to seek wisdom (Pr 4:7) finds its fulfillment in seeking after Christ. As Christians abide in Christ, they are given insight into the very wisdom of God. For example, the apostles, following Christ's death, burial, and resurrection, began to speak the words given to them by Christ concerning his kingdom. This courageous teaching and perseverance in the face of suffering demonstrated that Peter and John had, in fact, been with Jesus (Ac 4:13). God's Spirit allows Christians today to ascertain the wisdom of God through Jesus. God's children are graciously given "the mind of Christ," allowing them to have Solomon-like insight into God's will and ways (1Co 2:16).

before the king. 25And the king said, "Divide the living child in two, and give half to the one and half to the other." 26Then the woman whose son was alive said to the king, because her heart yearned for her son, "Oh, my lord, give her the living child, and by no means put him to death." But the other said, "He shall be neither mine nor yours; divide him." 27Then the king answered and said, "Give the living child to the first woman, and by no means put him to death; she is his mother." 28And all Israel heard of the judgment that the king had rendered, and they stood in awe of the king, because they perceived that the wisdom of God was in him to do justice.

Solomon's Officials

4 King Solomon was king over all Israel, 2and these were his high officials: Azariah the son of Zadok was the priest; 3Elihoreph and Ahijah the sons of Shisha were secretaries; Jehoshaphat the son of Ahilud was recorder; 4Benaiah the son of Jehoiada was in command of the army; Zadok and Abiathar were priests; 5Azariah the son of Nathan was over the officers; Zabud the son of Nathan was priest and king's friend; 6Ahishar was in charge of the palace; and Adoniram the son of Abda was in charge of the forced labor.

7Solomon had twelve officers over all Israel, who provided food for the king and his household. Each man had to make provision for one month in the year. 8These were their names: Ben-hur, in the hill country of Ephraim; 9Ben-deker, in Makaz, Shaalbim, Beth-shemesh, and Elonbeth-hanan; 10Ben-hesed, in Arubboth (to him belonged Socoh and all the land of Hepher); 11Ben-abinadab, in all Naphath-dor (he had Taphath the daughter of Solomon as his wife); 12Baana the son of Ahilud, in Taanach, Megiddo, and all Beth-shean that is beside Zarethan below Jezreel, and from Beth-shean to Abel-meholah, as far as the other side of Jokmeam; 13Ben-geber, in Ramoth-gilead (he had the villages of Jair the son of Manasseh, which are in Gilead, and he had the region of Argob, which is in Bashan, sixty great cities with walls and bronze bars); 14Ahinadab the son of Iddo, in Mahanaim; 15Ahimaaz, in Naphtali (he had taken Basemath the daughter of Solomon as his wife); 16Baana the son of Hushai, in Asher and Bealoth; 17Jehoshaphat the son of Paruah, in Issachar; 18Shimei the son of Ela, in Benjamin; 19Geber the son of Uri, in the land of Gilead, the country of Sihon king of the Amorites and of Og king of Bashan. And there was one governor who was over the land.

Solomon's Wealth and Wisdom

20Judah and Israel were as many as the sand by the sea. They ate and drank and were happy. 21[1]Solomon ruled over all the kingdoms from the Euphrates[2] to the land of the Philistines and to the border of Egypt. They brought tribute and served Solomon all the days of his life.

22Solomon's provision for one day was thirty cors[3] of fine flour and sixty cors of meal, 23ten fat oxen, and twenty pasture-fed cattle, a hundred sheep, besides deer, gazelles, roebucks, and fattened fowl. 24For he had dominion over all the region west of the Euphrates[4] from Tiphsah to Gaza, over all the kings west of the Euphrates. And he had peace on all sides around him. 25And Judah and Israel lived in safety, from Dan even to Beersheba, every man under his vine and under his fig tree, all the days of Solomon. 26Solomon also had 40,000[5] stalls of horses for his chariots, and 12,000 horsemen. 27And those officers supplied provisions for King Solomon, and for all who came to King Solomon's table, each one in his month. They let nothing be lacking. 28Barley also and straw for the horses and swift steeds they brought to the place where it was required, each according to his duty.

---

[1]Ch 5:1 in Hebrew [2]Hebrew *the River* [3]A *cor* was about 6 bushels or 220 liters [4]Hebrew *the River*; twice in this verse [5]Hebrew; one Hebrew manuscript (see 2 Chronicles 9:25 and Septuagint of 1 Kings 10:26) *4,000*

29And God gave Solomon wisdom and understanding beyond measure, and
breadth of mind like the sand on the seashore, 30so that Solomon's wisdom surpassed the wisdom of all the people of the east and all the wisdom of Egypt. 31For
he was wiser than all other men, wiser than Ethan the Ezrahite, and Heman,
Calcol, and Darda, the sons of Mahol, and his fame was in all the surrounding
nations. 32He also spoke 3,000 proverbs, and his songs were 1,005. 33He spoke of
trees, from the cedar that is in Lebanon to the hyssop that grows out of the wall.
He spoke also of beasts, and of birds, and of reptiles, and of fish. 34And people of
all nations came to hear the wisdom of Solomon, and from all the kings of the
earth, who had heard of his wisdom.

Preparations for Building the Temple

5 [1] Now Hiram king of Tyre sent his servants to Solomon when he heard that
they had anointed him king in place of his father, for Hiram always loved
David. 2And Solomon sent word to Hiram, 3"You know that David my father could
not build a house for the name of the LORD his God because of the warfare with
which his enemies surrounded him, until the LORD put them under the soles of
his feet. 4But now the LORD my God has given me rest on every side. There is neither adversary nor misfortune. 5And so I intend to build a house for the name of
the LORD my God, as the LORD said to David my father, 'Your son, whom I will set
on your throne in your place, shall build the house for my name.' 6Now therefore
command that cedars of Lebanon be cut for me. And my servants will join your
servants, and I will pay you for your servants such wages as you set, for you know
that there is no one among us who knows how to cut timber like the Sidonians."
7As soon as Hiram heard the words of Solomon, he rejoiced greatly and said,
"Blessed be the LORD this day, who has given to David a wise son to be over this
great people." 8And Hiram sent to Solomon, saying, "I have heard the message
that you have sent to me. I am ready to do all you desire in the matter of cedar and
cypress timber. 9My servants shall bring it down to the sea from Lebanon, and I
will make it into rafts to go by sea to the place you direct. And I will have them
broken up there, and you shall receive it. And you shall meet my wishes by providing food for my household." 10So Hiram supplied Solomon with all the timber
of cedar and cypress that he desired, 11while Solomon gave Hiram 20,000 cors[2]
of wheat as food for his household, and 20,000[3] cors of beaten oil. Solomon gave
this to Hiram year by year. 12And the LORD gave Solomon wisdom, as he promised
him. And there was peace between Hiram and Solomon, and the two of them
made a treaty.
13King Solomon drafted forced labor out of all Israel, and the draft numbered
30,000 men. 14And he sent them to Lebanon, 10,000 a month in shifts. They
would be a month in Lebanon and two months at home. Adoniram was in charge
of the draft. 15Solomon also had 70,000 burden-bearers and 80,000 stonecutters in the hill country, 16besides Solomon's 3,300 chief officers who were over
the work, who had charge of the people who carried on the work. 17At the king's
command they quarried out great, costly stones in order to lay the foundation of
the house with dressed stones. 18So Solomon's builders and Hiram's builders and
the men of Gebal did the cutting and prepared the timber and the stone to build
the house.

Solomon Builds the Temple

6 In the four hundred and eightieth year after the people of Israel came out
of the land of Egypt, in the fourth year of Solomon's reign over Israel, in the
month of Ziv, which is the second month, he began to build the house of the
LORD. 2The house that King Solomon built for the LORD was sixty cubits[4] long,

[1]Ch 5:15 in Hebrew [2]A *cor* was about 6 bushels or 220 liters [3]Septuagint; Hebrew *twenty* [4]A *cubit* was about 18 inches or 45 centimeters

1 KINGS 4:29–34

A WISE LEADER

The attribute of wisdom allows worldly rulers to discern critical military strategy and apply the appropriate leadership principles required to rule rightly. History records that the wisdom of Solomon surpassed the wisdom of all his contemporaries — among those known for their wisdom, none could match him. Even pagan kings were attracted to the wisdom of Solomon and traveled from far and wide to learn from his God-given insight. Jesus also was known for his unique wisdom. The crowds and his disciples marveled at his teaching and insight (Mt 7:28). His words were words of life, which provided people with knowledge of the mind of God and the nature of his kingdom. The drastic nature of his teaching prompted many to turn back and no longer follow him (Jn 6:66). Peter, however, demonstrated that some recognized that Jesus possessed unparalleled wisdom. There was no one else, Peter said, who had the words of life; therefore, the disciples would continue to follow even when the teaching they received was hard (Jn 6:68–69). As the unique Son of God, Jesus had the mind of God. And his followers, both then and now, draw near to him in order to understand God's character, will, and ways.

1 KINGS 5:5

FULFILLING A PROMISE

The construction of the temple fulfilled the long-awaited promise of a permanent dwelling place for God among the people (2Sa 7:13).

(continued on next page)

(Fulfilling a Promise, continued)

During their wilderness sojourn, the tabernacle served as a temporary residence for God. Long after the people had taken the land of promise, God pledged to allow Solomon to build a long-term location for the worship of God among his sinful people. In spite of the intimate care God took in establishing the temple, the subsequent failure of the people would lead to its destruction.

Jesus, however, claimed that his resurrection body serves as the true and lasting temple (Jn 2:19–22). No longer would God confine his place of worship to a geographic locale. Rather, he would free people everywhere to live a life of worship before their Creator (Jn 4:20–24). In Christ, God would dwell among his people and then send his Spirit to build those people—his church—into a lasting dwelling place for himself (1Pe 2:4–5).

twenty cubits wide, and thirty cubits high. 3The vestibule in front of the nave of
the house was twenty cubits long, equal to the width of the house, and ten cubits
deep in front of the house. 4And he made for the house windows with recessed
frames.[1] 5He also built a structure[2] against the wall of the house, running around
the walls of the house, both the nave and the inner sanctuary. And he made side
chambers all around. 6The lowest story[3] was five cubits broad, the middle one was
six cubits broad, and the third was seven cubits broad. For around the outside of
the house he made offsets on the wall in order that the supporting beams should
not be inserted into the walls of the house.

7When the house was built, it was with stone prepared at the quarry, so that
neither hammer nor axe nor any tool of iron was heard in the house while it was
being built.

8The entrance for the lowest[4] story was on the south side of the house, and
one went up by stairs to the middle story, and from the middle story to the third.
9So he built the house and finished it, and he made the ceiling of the house of
beams and planks of cedar. 10He built the structure against the whole house, five
cubits high, and it was joined to the house with timbers of cedar.

11Now the word of the LORD came to Solomon, 12"Concerning this house that
you are building, if you will walk in my statutes and obey my rules and keep all my
commandments and walk in them, then I will establish my word with you, which
I spoke to David your father. 13And I will dwell among the children of Israel and
will not forsake my people Israel."

14So Solomon built the house and finished it. 15He lined the walls of the house
on the inside with boards of cedar. From the floor of the house to the walls of the
ceiling, he covered them on the inside with wood, and he covered the floor of the
house with boards of cypress. 16He built twenty cubits of the rear of the house
with boards of cedar from the floor to the walls, and he built this within as an inner sanctuary, as the Most Holy Place. 17The house, that is, the nave in front of the
inner sanctuary, was forty cubits long. 18The cedar within the house was carved
in the form of gourds and open flowers. All was cedar; no stone was seen. 19The
inner sanctuary he prepared in the innermost part of the house, to set there the
ark of the covenant of the LORD. 20The inner sanctuary[5] was twenty cubits long,
twenty cubits wide, and twenty cubits high, and he overlaid it with pure gold. He
also overlaid[6] an altar of cedar. 21And Solomon overlaid the inside of the house
with pure gold, and he drew chains of gold across, in front of the inner sanctuary,
and overlaid it with gold. 22And he overlaid the whole house with gold, until all
the house was finished. Also the whole altar that belonged to the inner sanctuary
he overlaid with gold.

23In the inner sanctuary he made two cherubim of olivewood, each ten cubits high. 24Five cubits was the length of one wing of the cherub, and five cubits
the length of the other wing of the cherub; it was ten cubits from the tip of one
wing to the tip of the other. 25The other cherub also measured ten cubits; both
cherubim had the same measure and the same form. 26The height of one cherub
was ten cubits, and so was that of the other cherub. 27He put the cherubim in the
innermost part of the house. And the wings of the cherubim were spread out so
that a wing of one touched the one wall, and a wing of the other cherub touched
the other wall; their other wings touched each other in the middle of the house.
28And he overlaid the cherubim with gold.

29Around all the walls of the house he carved engraved figures of cherubim
and palm trees and open flowers, in the inner and outer rooms. 30The floor of the
house he overlaid with gold in the inner and outer rooms.

31For the entrance to the inner sanctuary he made doors of olivewood; the lintel and the doorposts were five-sided.[7] 32He covered the two doors of olivewood

[1]Or *blocked lattice windows* [2]Or *platform*; also verse 10 [3]Septuagint; Hebrew *structure, or platform* [4]Septuagint, Targum; Hebrew *middle* [5]Vulgate; Hebrew *And before the inner sanctuary* [6]Septuagint *made* [7]The meaning of the Hebrew phrase is uncertain

GOD AMONG HIS PEOPLE

The intricate physical layout of the temple contained spiritual significance. It revealed a pattern for the worship practices of God's people — from the nation of Israel to the church today. The temple consisted of three main sections: the outer courtyard, the Holy Place and the Most Holy Place (Ex 26:33). In the Most Holy Place, God dwelled among his people and made it possible for their sins to be forgiven.

Since the fall, the fellowship between God and his created image-bearers had been broken. Following their sin, Adam and Eve were banished from the Garden of Eden, and angels guarded the way back into the presence of God. No longer could they simply walk with God in the cool of the day. They were now outsiders, barred from communion with their Creator.

God graciously intervened in humanity's sinful predicament. Rather than requiring the people to prove themselves pure and capable of communing with their holy Creator, God determined to invade their sin-drenched world with his glorious presence. First, he dwelled in a tabernacle that moved with the people throughout their time in the wilderness. Later, God dwelled in the temple, where he communed with people through the sacrifice of substitutionary animals. The temple modeled the original garden, with the entrance to the Most Holy Place guarded by imposing angelic figures carved in olive wood and overlaid with gold, just as angels had once blocked reentry into God's presence (Ge 3:24; 1Ki 6:23 – 28).

Then the dwelling of God among his people took a startling turn. The very Son of God, Jesus Christ, came to dwell among his people (Jn 1:1 – 14). The glory of God became flesh and blood. All people — including tax collectors, prostitutes, Pharisees — could see the glory of God, hear him speak, and see him work wonders. The physical proximity to the glory of God did not mean that all people understood or worshiped God. Many people had eyes but failed to see; they had ears but did not hear (Mk 8:18). However, true worshipers coming to God in faith and repentance see and respond to the glory of God in the person of Christ — a reality that the tabernacle and temple could merely foreshadow.

with carvings of cherubim, palm trees, and open flowers. He overlaid them with gold and spread gold on the cherubim and on the palm trees.

33 So also he made for the entrance to the nave doorposts of olivewood, in the form of a square, 34 and two doors of cypress wood. The two leaves of the one door were folding, and the two leaves of the other door were folding. 35 On them he carved cherubim and palm trees and open flowers, and he overlaid them with gold evenly applied on the carved work. 36 He built the inner court with three courses of cut stone and one course of cedar beams.

37 In the fourth year the foundation of the house of the LORD was laid, in the month of Ziv. 38 And in the eleventh year, in the month of Bul, which is the eighth month, the house was finished in all its parts, and according to all its specifications. He was seven years in building it.

Solomon Builds His Palace

7 Solomon was building his own house thirteen years, and he finished his entire house.

2 He built the House of the Forest of Lebanon. Its length was a hundred cubits[1] and its breadth fifty cubits and its height thirty cubits, and it was built on four[2] rows of cedar pillars, with cedar beams on the pillars. 3 And it was covered with cedar above the chambers that were on the forty-five pillars, fifteen in each row. 4 There were window frames in three rows, and window opposite window in three tiers. 5 All the doorways and windows[3] had square frames, and window was opposite window in three tiers.

6 And he made the Hall of Pillars; its length was fifty cubits, and its breadth thirty cubits. There was a porch in front with pillars, and a canopy in front of them.

7 And he made the Hall of the Throne where he was to pronounce judgment, even the Hall of Judgment. It was finished with cedar from floor to rafters.[4]

8 His own house where he was to dwell, in the other court at the back of the hall, was of like workmanship. Solomon also made a house like this hall for Pharaoh's daughter whom he had taken in marriage.

9 All these were made of costly stones, cut according to measure, sawed with saws, back and front, even from the foundation to the coping, and from the outside to the great court. 10 The foundation was of costly stones, huge stones, stones of eight and ten cubits. 11 And above were costly stones, cut according to measurement, and cedar. 12 The great court had three courses of cut stone all around, and a course of cedar beams; so had the inner court of the house of the LORD and the vestibule of the house.

The Temple Furnishings

13 And King Solomon sent and brought Hiram from Tyre. 14 He was the son of a widow of the tribe of Naphtali, and his father was a man of Tyre, a worker in bronze. And he was full of wisdom, understanding, and skill for making any work in bronze. He came to King Solomon and did all his work.

15 He cast two pillars of bronze. Eighteen cubits was the height of one pillar, and a line of twelve cubits measured its circumference. It was hollow, and its thickness was four fingers. The second pillar was the same.[5] 16 He also made two capitals of cast bronze to set on the tops of the pillars. The height of the one capital was five cubits, and the height of the other capital was five cubits. 17 There were lattices of checker work with wreaths of chain work for the capitals on the tops of the pillars, a lattice[6] for the one capital and a lattice for the other capital. 18 Likewise he made pomegranates[7] in two rows around the one latticework

[1] A *cubit* was about 18 inches or 45 centimeters [2] Septuagint *three* [3] Septuagint; Hebrew *posts* [4] Syriac, Vulgate; Hebrew *floor* [5] Targum, Syriac (compare Septuagint and Jeremiah 52:21); Hebrew *and a line of twelve cubits measured the circumference of the second pillar* [6] Septuagint; Hebrew *seven*; twice in this verse [7] Two manuscripts (compare Septuagint); Hebrew *pillars*

1 KINGS 7:13–51

THE TEMPLE

Solomon's temple had much in common with its precursor—the tabernacle. Both contained a host of ornate furnishings and implements that allowed sinful people to worship a holy God. The slaughter of animals to atone for the sins of the people was the ongoing routine in each. However, the temple differed from the tabernacle in terms of its permanence and its size. The temporary tabernacle was replaced with a building meant to communicate the grandeur of God's glory. This progressive development of God's dwelling is amplified by the prophet Ezekiel's vision of a heavenly temple that would eclipse both the tabernacle and the temple (Eze 40–43).

The church, God's new temple built with the living stones of those who place their faith in Christ, expands the scope of the dwelling of God all the more. Christians now take the dwelling of God with them to the ends of the earth (Mt 28:18–20). Finally, the coming dwelling of God with humanity, pictured by the apostle John, will one day fill the entire cosmos with the presence of God (Rev 21:3; 22:5).

to cover the capital that was on the top of the pillar, and he did the same with
the other capital. 19Now the capitals that were on the tops of the pillars in the
vestibule were of lily-work, four cubits. 20The capitals were on the two pillars and
also above the rounded projection which was beside the latticework. There were
two hundred pomegranates in two rows all around, and so with the other capital.
21He set up the pillars at the vestibule of the temple. He set up the pillar on the
south and called its name Jachin, and he set up the pillar on the north and called
its name Boaz. 22And on the tops of the pillars was lily-work. Thus the work of
the pillars was finished.

23Then he made the sea of cast metal. It was round, ten cubits from brim to
brim, and five cubits high, and a line of thirty cubits measured its circumference.
24Under its brim were gourds, for ten cubits, compassing the sea all around. The
gourds were in two rows, cast with it when it was cast. 25It stood on twelve oxen,
three facing north, three facing west, three facing south, and three facing east.
The sea was set on them, and all their rear parts were inward. 26Its thickness was
a handbreadth,[1] and its brim was made like the brim of a cup, like the flower of a
lily. It held two thousand baths.[2]

27He also made the ten stands of bronze. Each stand was four cubits long, four
cubits wide, and three cubits high. 28This was the construction of the stands: they
had panels, and the panels were set in the frames, 29and on the panels that were
set in the frames were lions, oxen, and cherubim. On the frames, both above and
below the lions and oxen, there were wreaths of beveled work. 30Moreover, each
stand had four bronze wheels and axles of bronze, and at the four corners were
supports for a basin. The supports were cast with wreaths at the side of each.
31Its opening was within a crown that projected upward one cubit. Its opening
was round, as a pedestal is made, a cubit and a half deep. At its opening there
were carvings, and its panels were square, not round. 32And the four wheels were
underneath the panels. The axles of the wheels were of one piece with the stands,
and the height of a wheel was a cubit and a half. 33The wheels were made like a
chariot wheel; their axles, their rims, their spokes, and their hubs were all cast.
34There were four supports at the four corners of each stand. The supports were
of one piece with the stands. 35And on the top of the stand there was a round
band half a cubit high; and on the top of the stand its stays and its panels were of
one piece with it. 36And on the surfaces of its stays and on its panels, he carved
cherubim, lions, and palm trees, according to the space of each, with wreaths all
around. 37After this manner he made the ten stands. All of them were cast alike,
of the same measure and the same form.

38And he made ten basins of bronze. Each basin held forty baths, each basin
measured four cubits, and there was a basin for each of the ten stands. 39And he
set the stands, five on the south side of the house, and five on the north side of
the house. And he set the sea at the southeast corner of the house.

40Hiram also made the pots, the shovels, and the basins. So Hiram finished
all the work that he did for King Solomon on the house of the LORD: 41the two pillars, the two bowls of the capitals that were on the tops of the pillars, and the two
latticeworks to cover the two bowls of the capitals that were on the tops of the
pillars; 42and the four hundred pomegranates for the two latticeworks, two rows
of pomegranates for each latticework, to cover the two bowls of the capitals that
were on the pillars; 43the ten stands, and the ten basins on the stands; 44and the
one sea, and the twelve oxen underneath the sea.

45Now the pots, the shovels, and the basins, all these vessels in the house of
the LORD, which Hiram made for King Solomon, were of burnished bronze. 46In
the plain of the Jordan the king cast them, in the clay ground between Succoth
and Zarethan. 47And Solomon left all the vessels unweighed, because there were
so many of them; the weight of the bronze was not ascertained.

---

[1]A *handbreadth* was about 3 inches or 7.5 centimeters [2]A *bath* was about 6 gallons or 22 liters

48So Solomon made all the vessels that were in the house of the LORD: the golden altar, the golden table for the bread of the Presence, 49the lampstands of pure gold, five on the south side and five on the north, before the inner sanctuary; the flowers, the lamps, and the tongs, of gold; 50the cups, snuffers, basins, dishes for incense, and fire pans, of pure gold; and the sockets of gold, for the doors of the innermost part of the house, the Most Holy Place, and for the doors of the nave of the temple.

51Thus all the work that King Solomon did on the house of the LORD was finished. And Solomon brought in the things that David his father had dedicated, the silver, the gold, and the vessels, and stored them in the treasuries of the house of the LORD.

The Ark Brought into the Temple

8 Then Solomon assembled the elders of Israel and all the heads of the tribes, the leaders of the fathers' houses of the people of Israel, before King Solomon in Jerusalem, to bring up the ark of the covenant of the LORD out of the city of David, which is Zion. 2And all the men of Israel assembled to King Solomon at the feast in the month Ethanim, which is the seventh month. 3And all the elders of Israel came, and the priests took up the ark. 4And they brought up the ark of the LORD, the tent of meeting, and all the holy vessels that were in the tent; the priests and the Levites brought them up. 5And King Solomon and all the congregation of Israel, who had assembled before him, were with him before the ark, sacrificing so many sheep and oxen that they could not be counted or numbered. 6Then the priests brought the ark of the covenant of the LORD to its place in the inner sanctuary of the house, in the Most Holy Place, underneath the wings of the cherubim. 7For the cherubim spread out their wings over the place of the ark, so that the cherubim overshadowed the ark and its poles. 8And the poles were so long that the ends of the poles were seen from the Holy Place before the inner sanctuary; but they could not be seen from outside. And they are there to this day. 9There was nothing in the ark except the two tablets of stone that Moses put there at Horeb, where the LORD made a covenant with the people of Israel, when they came out of the land of Egypt. 10And when the priests came out of the Holy Place, a cloud filled the house of the LORD, 11so that the priests could not stand to minister because of the cloud, for the glory of the LORD filled the house of the LORD.

Solomon Blesses the LORD

12Then Solomon said, "The LORD[1] has said that he would dwell in thick darkness. 13I have indeed built you an exalted house, a place for you to dwell in forever." 14Then the king turned around and blessed all the assembly of Israel, while all the assembly of Israel stood. 15And he said, "Blessed be the LORD, the God of Israel, who with his hand has fulfilled what he promised with his mouth to David my father, saying, 16'Since the day that I brought my people Israel out of Egypt, I chose no city out of all the tribes of Israel in which to build a house, that my name might be there. But I chose David to be over my people Israel.' 17Now it was in the heart of David my father to build a house for the name of the LORD, the God of Israel. 18But the LORD said to David my father, 'Whereas it was in your heart to build a house for my name, you did well that it was in your heart. 19Nevertheless, you shall not build the house, but your son who shall be born to you shall build the house for my name.' 20Now the LORD has fulfilled his promise that he made. For I have risen in the place of David my father, and sit on the throne of Israel, as the LORD promised, and I have built the house for the name of the LORD, the God of Israel. 21And there I have provided a place for the ark, in which is the covenant of the LORD that he made with our fathers, when he brought them out of the land of Egypt."

1Septuagint *The LORD has set the sun in the heavens, but*

THE GLORY OF GOD IN THE TEMPLE

The completion of the temple culminated in the glory of God filling the newly constructed dwelling. It is astounding to consider that the sum total of God's attributes could be located in a structure made with human hands. Yet, this is the nature of God's humility — he stooped to earth to be known by his people. The tangible sign of a cloud, sometimes referred to as the "shekinah glory," signified God's presence within the nation of Israel. With God among them, the people of God had a motive for worship and obedience.

Long before Jesus' day, this first temple, built by Solomon, was destroyed. The second temple, built by the returning Babylonian exiles, was undergoing a massive rebuilding project that had begun under Herod's direction. Jesus stunned his Jewish audience when he claimed that this ever-expanding temple — which by then had been under construction for nearly 50 years and displayed astonishing levels of beauty and opulence — would be destroyed and rebuilt in three days. They failed to discern that Jesus was not talking about a physical structure made by human hands, but about his very body, which would be destroyed on a Roman cross only to be resurrected three days later (Jn 2:19–22).

Paul added to Jesus' identification of his physical body as the true temple where God dwelled among his people. Writing to the church in Corinth which was made up of people saved by Christ, Paul reminded them that they were God's temple (1Co 3:16). The Spirit of God, which once filled the temple, now fills believers with the power and presence of the glory of God.

As with the ancient temple, the awareness of the glory of God dwelling within Christians should prompt worship and obedience. In the church, God's people should be reminded of the holiness of God every time they see one another — fellow image-bearers in whom the Spirit of God dwells. The gathering of the church — whether in small groups, Bible study classes, or in corporate worship — should prompt reverential awe at the fact that God dwells in his people. Not only that, but the ongoing reality of the dwelling of God within his people should cause them to desire to use their bodies in a holy manner. Paul used this logic to urge sexual purity on the part of those indwelled by God's Spirit (1Co 6:19). Since God dwells in his people in all of his glory, sin should be shunned and holiness pursued as an act of worship in the new temple of God.

Solomon's Prayer of Dedication

[22]Then Solomon stood before the altar of the LORD in the presence of all the assembly of Israel and spread out his hands toward heaven, [23]and said, "O LORD, God of Israel, there is no God like you, in heaven above or on earth beneath, keeping covenant and showing steadfast love to your servants who walk before you with all their heart; [24]you have kept with your servant David my father what you declared to him. You spoke with your mouth, and with your hand have fulfilled it this day. [25]Now therefore, O LORD, God of Israel, keep for your servant David my father what you have promised him, saying, 'You shall not lack a man to sit before me on the throne of Israel, if only your sons pay close attention to their way, to walk before me as you have walked before me.' [26]Now therefore, O God of Israel, let your word be confirmed, which you have spoken to your servant David my father.

[27]"But will God indeed dwell on the earth? Behold, heaven and the highest heaven cannot contain you; how much less this house that I have built! [28]Yet have regard to the prayer of your servant and to his plea, O LORD my God, listening to the cry and to the prayer that your servant prays before you this day, [29]that your eyes may be open night and day toward this house, the place of which you have said, 'My name shall be there,' that you may listen to the prayer that your servant offers toward this place. [30]And listen to the plea of your servant and of your people Israel, when they pray toward this place. And listen in heaven your dwelling place, and when you hear, forgive.

[31]"If a man sins against his neighbor and is made to take an oath and comes and swears his oath before your altar in this house, [32]then hear in heaven and act and judge your servants, condemning the guilty by bringing his conduct on his own head, and vindicating the righteous by rewarding him according to his righteousness.

[33]"When your people Israel are defeated before the enemy because they have sinned against you, and if they turn again to you and acknowledge your name and pray and plead with you in this house, [34]then hear in heaven and forgive the sin of your people Israel and bring them again to the land that you gave to their fathers.

[35]"When heaven is shut up and there is no rain because they have sinned against you, if they pray toward this place and acknowledge your name and turn from their sin, when you afflict them, [36]then hear in heaven and forgive the sin of your servants, your people Israel, when you teach them the good way in which they should walk, and grant rain upon your land, which you have given to your people as an inheritance.

[37]"If there is famine in the land, if there is pestilence or blight or mildew or locust or caterpillar, if their enemy besieges them in the land at their gates,[1] whatever plague, whatever sickness there is, [38]whatever prayer, whatever plea is made by any man or by all your people Israel, each knowing the affliction of his own heart and stretching out his hands toward this house, [39]then hear in heaven your dwelling place and forgive and act and render to each whose heart you know, according to all his ways (for you, you only, know the hearts of all the children of mankind), [40]that they may fear you all the days that they live in the land that you gave to our fathers.

[41]"Likewise, when a foreigner, who is not of your people Israel, comes from a far country for your name's sake [42](for they shall hear of your great name and your mighty hand, and of your outstretched arm), when he comes and prays toward this house, [43]hear in heaven your dwelling place and do according to all for which the foreigner calls to you, in order that all the peoples of the earth may know your name and fear you, as do your people Israel, and that they may know that this house that I have built is called by your name.

[44]"If your people go out to battle against their enemy, by whatever way you

---

[1]Septuagint, Syriac *in any of their cities*

shall send them, and they pray to the LORD toward the city that you have chosen and the house that I have built for your name, [45]then hear in heaven their prayer and their plea, and maintain their cause.

[46]"If they sin against you—for there is no one who does not sin—and you are angry with them and give them to an enemy, so that they are carried away captive to the land of the enemy, far off or near, [47]yet if they turn their heart in the land to which they have been carried captive, and repent and plead with you in the land of their captors, saying, 'We have sinned and have acted perversely and wickedly,' [48]if they repent with all their heart and with all their soul in the land of their enemies, who carried them captive, and pray to you toward their land, which you gave to their fathers, the city that you have chosen, and the house that I have built for your name, [49]then hear in heaven your dwelling place their prayer and their plea, and maintain their cause [50]and forgive your people who have sinned against you, and all their transgressions that they have committed against you, and grant them compassion in the sight of those who carried them captive, that they may have compassion on them [51](for they are your people, and your heritage, which you brought out of Egypt, from the midst of the iron furnace). [52]Let your eyes be open to the plea of your servant and to the plea of your people Israel, giving ear to them whenever they call to you. [53]For you separated them from among all the peoples of the earth to be your heritage, as you declared through Moses your servant, when you brought our fathers out of Egypt, O Lord GOD."

Solomon's Benediction

[54]Now as Solomon finished offering all this prayer and plea to the LORD, he arose from before the altar of the LORD, where he had knelt with hands outstretched toward heaven. [55]And he stood and blessed all the assembly of Israel with a loud voice, saying, [56]"Blessed be the LORD who has given rest to his people Israel, according to all that he promised. Not one word has failed of all his good promise, which he spoke by Moses his servant. [57]The LORD our God be with us, as he was with our fathers. May he not leave us or forsake us, [58]that he may incline our hearts to him, to walk in all his ways and to keep his commandments, his statutes, and his rules, which he commanded our fathers. [59]Let these words of mine, with which I have pleaded before the LORD, be near to the LORD our God day and night, and may he maintain the cause of his servant and the cause of his people Israel, as each day requires, [60]that all the peoples of the earth may know that the LORD is God; there is no other. [61]Let your heart therefore be wholly true to the LORD our God, walking in his statutes and keeping his commandments, as at this day."

Solomon's Sacrifices

[62]Then the king, and all Israel with him, offered sacrifice before the LORD. [63]Solomon offered as peace offerings to the LORD 22,000 oxen and 120,000 sheep. So the king and all the people of Israel dedicated the house of the LORD. [64]The same day the king consecrated the middle of the court that was before the house of the LORD, for there he offered the burnt offering and the grain offering and the fat pieces of the peace offerings, because the bronze altar that was before the LORD was too small to receive the burnt offering and the grain offering and the fat pieces of the peace offerings.

[65]So Solomon held the feast at that time, and all Israel with him, a great assembly, from Lebo-hamath to the Brook of Egypt, before the LORD our God, seven days.[1] [66]On the eighth day he sent the people away, and they blessed the king and went to their homes joyful and glad of heart for all the goodness that the LORD had shown to David his servant and to Israel his people.

---

[1]Septuagint; Hebrew *seven days and seven days, fourteen days*

The LORD Appears to Solomon

9 As soon as Solomon had finished building the house of the LORD and the king's house and all that Solomon desired to build, 2the LORD appeared to Solomon a second time, as he had appeared to him at Gibeon. 3And the LORD said to him, "I have heard your prayer and your plea, which you have made before me. I have consecrated this house that you have built, by putting my name there forever. My eyes and my heart will be there for all time. 4And as for you, if you will walk before me, as David your father walked, with integrity of heart and uprightness, doing according to all that I have commanded you, and keeping my statutes and my rules, 5then I will establish your royal throne over Israel forever, as I promised David your father, saying, 'You shall not lack a man on the throne of Israel.' 6But if you turn aside from following me, you or your children, and do not keep my commandments and my statutes that I have set before you, but go and serve other gods and worship them, 7then I will cut off Israel from the land that I have given them, and the house that I have consecrated for my name I will cast out of my sight, and Israel will become a proverb and a byword among all peoples. 8And this house will become a heap of ruins.[1] Everyone passing by it will be astonished and will hiss, and they will say, 'Why has the LORD done thus to this land and to this house?' 9Then they will say, 'Because they abandoned the LORD their God who brought their fathers out of the land of Egypt and laid hold on other gods and worshiped them and served them. Therefore the LORD has brought all this disaster on them.'"

Solomon's Other Acts

10At the end of twenty years, in which Solomon had built the two houses, the house of the LORD and the king's house, 11and Hiram king of Tyre had supplied Solomon with cedar and cypress timber and gold, as much as he desired, King Solomon gave to Hiram twenty cities in the land of Galilee. 12But when Hiram came from Tyre to see the cities that Solomon had given him, they did not please him. 13Therefore he said, "What kind of cities are these that you have given me, my brother?" So they are called the land of Cabul to this day. 14Hiram had sent to the king 120 talents[2] of gold.

15And this is the account of the forced labor that King Solomon drafted to build the house of the LORD and his own house and the Millo and the wall of Jerusalem and Hazor and Megiddo and Gezer 16(Pharaoh king of Egypt had gone up and captured Gezer and burned it with fire, and had killed the Canaanites who lived in the city, and had given it as dowry to his daughter, Solomon's wife; 17so Solomon rebuilt Gezer) and Lower Beth-horon 18and Baalath and Tamar in the wilderness, in the land of Judah,[3] 19and all the store cities that Solomon had, and the cities for his chariots, and the cities for his horsemen, and whatever Solomon desired to build in Jerusalem, in Lebanon, and in all the land of his dominion. 20All the people who were left of the Amorites, the Hittites, the Perizzites, the Hivites, and the Jebusites, who were not of the people of Israel— 21their descendants who were left after them in the land, whom the people of Israel were unable to devote to destruction[4]—these Solomon drafted to be slaves, and so they are to this day. 22But of the people of Israel Solomon made no slaves. They were the soldiers, they were his officials, his commanders, his captains, his chariot commanders and his horsemen.

23These were the chief officers who were over Solomon's work: 550 who had charge of the people who carried on the work.

24But Pharaoh's daughter went up from the city of David to her own house that Solomon had built for her. Then he built the Millo.

25Three times a year Solomon used to offer up burnt offerings and peace

[1] Syriac, Old Latin; Hebrew *will become high* [2] A *talent* was about 75 pounds or 34 kilograms [3] Hebrew lacks *of Judah* [4] That is, set apart (devote) as an offering to the Lord (for destruction)

1 KINGS 9:10–13

CAN ANYTHING GOOD COME FROM THERE?

Solomon gave King Hiram twenty towns in the northern region of the promised land in return for his provision for the people of God. Though the nation surely resented losing a portion of the promised land, it is clear that this region was less than desirable. Even King Hiram, upon seeing the land, named it the land of Cabul, which sounds like the Hebrew for "good-for-nothing." This area around the Sea of Galilee was still considered undesirable at the time of Jesus' life. Many refused to acknowledge that Jesus could be the Messiah because he was from this region (Jn 1:46; 7:41). It was thought that nothing good could come from this worthless land—certainly not the Messiah. God, however, specializes in taking that which is deemed undesirable and using it for his purposes. The epicenter of Jesus' ministry took place in this "good-for-nothing" land, and he would prove that something of little value can be transformed by God into an object of great worth. Jesus' great act of salvation transforms fallen, broken, and undesirable people into trophies of his grace (Eph 2:4–7).

THE CLEAR CHOICES OF DISCIPLESHIP

God's charge to Solomon, though it came at a critical juncture in the national identity of the nation of Israel, was far from original. Moses had ended his instructions to the nation on the brink of the promised land with a similar challenge (Dt 30:11 – 20). Joshua, after leading the people to possess the land and nearing his death, had repeated these instructions (Jos 24:14 – 28). The message was simple: God had given the people his presence and his promises and the people should respond with worship and obedience. In each case, the great leaders explained that the people must make a critical choice between living a life of obedience to God and experiencing his blessings or following the path of disobedience and idolatry and facing pain, discipline, and destruction. The choice between life and death was not a means of securing God's love; rather, the decision to pursue life is the proper response of those who have experienced the love of God in their salvation.

Echoing the leaders before him, Jesus ended his Sermon on the Mount by presenting two ways to live (Mt 7:13 – 14). On the one hand, there is the wide gate that opens to an easy path that Jesus said many will take. Those who choose this path, following the ways of the world and rebelling against God, will find death and destruction. On the other hand, there is the path leading to life and blessing. This path is hard and its entrance narrow. As a result, few find it. These two paths demonstrate the choice confronting all people, both in the nation of Israel and in the world today.

The consistent pattern of the Old Testament people of God reveals that people naturally choose the path to destruction. Jesus is the only one who has ever walked through the narrow gate and perfectly followed the path to life. Through faith, his followers can receive the gift of the righteous life of Christ — meaning that God sees them living the life they could not live, consistently choosing the path to life (2Co 5:16 – 21). He then sent his Spirit to empower his children to walk the narrow path that leads to fullness of life now and an eternal life of glory with God forever (Jn 16:13 – 15).

offerings on the altar that he built to the LORD, making offerings with it[1] before the
LORD. So he finished the house.
26 King Solomon built a fleet of ships at Ezion-geber, which is near Eloth on
the shore of the Red Sea, in the land of Edom. 27 And Hiram sent with the fleet his
servants, seamen who were familiar with the sea, together with the servants of
Solomon. 28 And they went to Ophir and brought from there gold, 420 talents, and
they brought it to King Solomon.

The Queen of Sheba

10 Now when the queen of Sheba heard of the fame of Solomon concerning
the name of the LORD, she came to test him with hard questions. 2 She came
to Jerusalem with a very great retinue, with camels bearing spices and very much
gold and precious stones. And when she came to Solomon, she told him all that
was on her mind. 3 And Solomon answered all her questions; there was nothing
hidden from the king that he could not explain to her. 4 And when the queen of
Sheba had seen all the wisdom of Solomon, the house that he had built, 5 the food
of his table, the seating of his officials, and the attendance of his servants, their
clothing, his cupbearers, and his burnt offerings that he offered at the house of
the LORD, there was no more breath in her.
6 And she said to the king, "The report was true that I heard in my own land
of your words and of your wisdom, 7 but I did not believe the reports until I came
and my own eyes had seen it. And behold, the half was not told me. Your wisdom
and prosperity surpass the report that I heard. 8 Happy are your men! Happy are
your servants, who continually stand before you and hear your wisdom! 9 Blessed
be the LORD your God, who has delighted in you and set you on the throne of
Israel! Because the LORD loved Israel forever, he has made you king, that you may
execute justice and righteousness." 10 Then she gave the king 120 talents[2] of gold,
and a very great quantity of spices and precious stones. Never again came such
an abundance of spices as these that the queen of Sheba gave to King Solomon.
11 Moreover, the fleet of Hiram, which brought gold from Ophir, brought from
Ophir a very great amount of almug wood and precious stones. 12 And the king
made of the almug wood supports for the house of the LORD and for the king's
house, also lyres and harps for the singers. No such almug wood has come or
been seen to this day.
13 And King Solomon gave to the queen of Sheba all that she desired, whatever
she asked besides what was given her by the bounty of King Solomon. So she
turned and went back to her own land with her servants.

Solomon's Great Wealth

14 Now the weight of gold that came to Solomon in one year was 666 talents
of gold, 15 besides that which came from the explorers and from the business of
the merchants, and from all the kings of the west and from the governors of the
land. 16 King Solomon made 200 large shields of beaten gold; 600 shekels[3] of gold
went into each shield. 17 And he made 300 shields of beaten gold; three minas[4] of
gold went into each shield. And the king put them in the House of the Forest of
Lebanon. 18 The king also made a great ivory throne and overlaid it with the finest
gold. 19 The throne had six steps, and the throne had a round top,[5] and on each
side of the seat were armrests and two lions standing beside the armrests, 20 while
twelve lions stood there, one on each end of a step on the six steps. The like of
it was never made in any kingdom. 21 All King Solomon's drinking vessels were of
gold, and all the vessels of the House of the Forest of Lebanon were of pure gold.
None were of silver; silver was not considered as anything in the days of Solomon.
22 For the king had a fleet of ships of Tarshish at sea with the fleet of Hiram. Once

[1] Septuagint lacks *with it* [2] A *talent* was about 75 pounds or 34 kilograms [3] A *shekel* was about 2/5 ounce or 11 grams [4] A *mina* was about 1 1/4 pounds or 0.6 kilogram [5] Or *and at the back of the throne was a calf's head*

every three years the fleet of ships of Tarshish used to come bringing gold, silver, ivory, apes, and peacocks.[1]

[23]Thus King Solomon excelled all the kings of the earth in riches and in wisdom. [24]And the whole earth sought the presence of Solomon to hear his wisdom, which God had put into his mind. [25]Every one of them brought his present, articles of silver and gold, garments, myrrh,[2] spices, horses, and mules, so much year by year.

[26]And Solomon gathered together chariots and horsemen. He had 1,400 chariots and 12,000 horsemen, whom he stationed in the chariot cities and with the king in Jerusalem. [27]And the king made silver as common in Jerusalem as stone, and he made cedar as plentiful as the sycamore of the Shephelah. [28]And Solomon's import of horses was from Egypt and Kue, and the king's traders received them from Kue at a price. [29]A chariot could be imported from Egypt for 600 shekels of silver and a horse for 150, and so through the king's traders they were exported to all the kings of the Hittites and the kings of Syria.

Solomon Turns from the LORD

11 Now King Solomon loved many foreign women, along with the daughter of Pharaoh: Moabite, Ammonite, Edomite, Sidonian, and Hittite women, [2]from the nations concerning which the LORD had said to the people of Israel, "You shall not enter into marriage with them, neither shall they with you, for surely they will turn away your heart after their gods." Solomon clung to these in love. [3]He had 700 wives, who were princesses, and 300 concubines. And his wives turned away his heart. [4]For when Solomon was old his wives turned away his heart after other gods, and his heart was not wholly true to the LORD his God, as was the heart of David his father. [5]For Solomon went after Ashtoreth the goddess of the Sidonians, and after Milcom the abomination of the Ammonites. [6]So Solomon did what was evil in the sight of the LORD and did not wholly follow the LORD, as David his father had done. [7]Then Solomon built a high place for Chemosh the abomination of Moab, and for Molech the abomination of the Ammonites, on the mountain east of Jerusalem. [8]And so he did for all his foreign wives, who made offerings and sacrificed to their gods.

The LORD Raises Adversaries

[9]And the LORD was angry with Solomon, because his heart had turned away from the LORD, the God of Israel, who had appeared to him twice [10]and had commanded him concerning this thing, that he should not go after other gods. But he did not keep what the LORD commanded. [11]Therefore the LORD said to Solomon, "Since this has been your practice and you have not kept my covenant and my statutes that I have commanded you, I will surely tear the kingdom from you and will give it to your servant. [12]Yet for the sake of David your father I will not do it in your days, but I will tear it out of the hand of your son. [13]However, I will not tear away all the kingdom, but I will give one tribe to your son, for the sake of David my servant and for the sake of Jerusalem that I have chosen."

[14]And the LORD raised up an adversary against Solomon, Hadad the Edomite. He was of the royal house in Edom. [15]For when David was in Edom, and Joab the commander of the army went up to bury the slain, he struck down every male in Edom [16](for Joab and all Israel remained there six months, until he had cut off every male in Edom). [17]But Hadad fled to Egypt, together with certain Edomites of his father's servants, Hadad still being a little child. [18]They set out from Midian and came to Paran and took men with them from Paran and came to Egypt, to Pharaoh king of Egypt, who gave him a house and assigned him an allowance of food and gave him land. [19]And Hadad found great favor in the sight of Pharaoh, so that he gave him in marriage the sister of his own wife, the sister of Tahpenes the

[1]Or *baboons* [2]Or *armor*

THE WISE FOOL VERSUS THE WISE SAVIOR

Solomon's wisdom was legendary. God granted his request, bestowing upon him the ability to perfectly distinguish right from wrong, and this unique ability garnered him the attention of the nations of his day (1Ki 4:29 – 34). Throughout history, the name of Solomon has been associated with unparalleled wisdom.

In spite of his great wisdom, Solomon's life testifies to the nature of human sin. He proved repeatedly to be incapable of living in conformity with the wisdom he was given. Though he was unrivaled in his wisdom, he lived like a fool. For example, in the book of Proverbs, Solomon discussed the folly of sexual immorality (Pr 5:1 – 14). He showed that the path of the adulterer was the path to destruction (Pr 7:21 – 23). He exhorted each husband to find satisfaction in his wife and to be captivated by her love (Pr 5:18 – 19). These wise instructions and warnings demonstrate the God-given insight Solomon possessed.

However, Solomon did not live up to his words. During his life, he had 700 wives and 300 concubines. These women led his heart away from the one true God, causing him to build altars to pagan gods on a hill outside of Jerusalem. He lived his life in opposition to the things he knew to be true and, in so doing, demonstrated that he was the wisest fool who has ever lived.

Solomon's life highlights the contrast between great leaders in the Bible and Jesus Christ. Jesus possessed perfect insight into the wisdom of God. He consistently demonstrated that this wisdom was far deeper than mere outward obedience. For example, he commanded people not only to avoid adultery but to flee from lust as well (Mt 5:27 – 30). What makes Jesus' wisdom astounding is not that he said these things, but also that he could live a life that conformed to these standards. Unlike Solomon, the Son of God was always able to live up to his message. He spoke not only of the wisdom of God but also modeled a life of conformity to that very message. The consistency between the wisdom and actions of Jesus proves, once again, that he is who he says he is — the perfect Son of God.

queen. 20And the sister of Tahpenes bore him Genubath his son, whom Tahpenes weaned in Pharaoh's house. And Genubath was in Pharaoh's house among the sons of Pharaoh. 21But when Hadad heard in Egypt that David slept with his fathers and that Joab the commander of the army was dead, Hadad said to Pharaoh, "Let me depart, that I may go to my own country." 22But Pharaoh said to him, "What have you lacked with me that you are now seeking to go to your own country?" And he said to him, "Only let me depart."

23God also raised up as an adversary to him, Rezon the son of Eliada, who had fled from his master Hadadezer king of Zobah. 24And he gathered men about him and became leader of a marauding band, after the killing by David. And they went to Damascus and lived there and made him king in Damascus. 25He was an adversary of Israel all the days of Solomon, doing harm as Hadad did. And he loathed Israel and reigned over Syria.

26Jeroboam the son of Nebat, an Ephraimite of Zeredah, a servant of Solomon, whose mother's name was Zeruah, a widow, also lifted up his hand against the king. 27And this was the reason why he lifted up his hand against the king. Solomon built the Millo, and closed up the breach of the city of David his father. 28The man Jeroboam was very able, and when Solomon saw that the young man was industrious he gave him charge over all the forced labor of the house of Joseph. 29And at that time, when Jeroboam went out of Jerusalem, the prophet Ahijah the Shilonite found him on the road. Now Ahijah had dressed himself in a new garment, and the two of them were alone in the open country. 30Then Ahijah laid hold of the new garment that was on him, and tore it into twelve pieces. 31And he said to Jeroboam, "Take for yourself ten pieces, for thus says the LORD, the God of Israel, 'Behold, I am about to tear the kingdom from the hand of Solomon and will give you ten tribes 32(but he shall have one tribe, for the sake of my servant David and for the sake of Jerusalem, the city that I have chosen out of all the tribes of Israel), 33because they have[1] forsaken me and worshiped Ashtoreth the goddess of the Sidonians, Chemosh the god of Moab, and Milcom the god of the Ammonites, and they have not walked in my ways, doing what is right in my sight and keeping my statutes and my rules, as David his father did. 34Nevertheless, I will not take the whole kingdom out of his hand, but I will make him ruler all the days of his life, for the sake of David my servant whom I chose, who kept my commandments and my statutes. 35But I will take the kingdom out of his son's hand and will give it to you, ten tribes. 36Yet to his son I will give one tribe, that David my servant may always have a lamp before me in Jerusalem, the city where I have chosen to put my name. 37And I will take you, and you shall reign over all that your soul desires, and you shall be king over Israel. 38And if you will listen to all that I command you, and will walk in my ways, and do what is right in my eyes by keeping my statutes and my commandments, as David my servant did, I will be with you and will build you a sure house, as I built for David, and I will give Israel to you. 39And I will afflict the offspring of David because of this, but not forever.'" 40Solomon sought therefore to kill Jeroboam. But Jeroboam arose and fled into Egypt, to Shishak king of Egypt, and was in Egypt until the death of Solomon.

41Now the rest of the acts of Solomon, and all that he did, and his wisdom, are they not written in the Book of the Acts of Solomon? 42And the time that Solomon reigned in Jerusalem over all Israel was forty years. 43And Solomon slept with his fathers and was buried in the city of David his father. And Rehoboam his son reigned in his place.

Rehoboam's Folly

12 Rehoboam went to Shechem, for all Israel had come to Shechem to make him king. 2And as soon as Jeroboam the son of Nebat heard of it (for he was still in Egypt, where he had fled from King Solomon), then Jeroboam returned

[1]Septuagint, Syriac, Vulgate *he has*; twice in this verse

1 KINGS 12:1–17

LASTING REPERCUSSIONS OF DIVISION

The arrogance and harshness of Solomon's son Rehoboam sparked the division of the nation of God's people. The northern kingdom, called Israel, consisted of ten tribes led by Jeroboam, formerly in charge of the labor force under Solomon. The southern kingdom, called Judah, retained Rehoboam as their king. The prophecy of 1 Kings 11:29–33 was fulfilled, and the unified monarchy was ripped apart. Infighting, division, turmoil, and strife henceforth marked the people who were established to be a light to the nations and a testimony to the glory of God. No earthly king would be able to unite the people of God ever again. The people needed a better king to fix the problems created by their sin.

The great unifier of the people of God eventually came in the person of Christ. He broke down the dividing walls separating humankind from one another and formed in himself one new, united people of God (Eph 2:11–22; 4:1–6). This new people, including both Jews and Gentiles, would be grafted together as God's church, a community uniquely marked by unity and sacrificial love.

from[1] Egypt. 3And they sent and called him, and Jeroboam and all the assembly of Israel came and said to Rehoboam, 4"Your father made our yoke heavy. Now therefore lighten the hard service of your father and his heavy yoke on us, and we will serve you." 5He said to them, "Go away for three days, then come again to me." So the people went away.

6Then King Rehoboam took counsel with the old men, who had stood before Solomon his father while he was yet alive, saying, "How do you advise me to answer this people?" 7And they said to him, "If you will be a servant to this people today and serve them, and speak good words to them when you answer them, then they will be your servants forever." 8But he abandoned the counsel that the old men gave him and took counsel with the young men who had grown up with him and stood before him. 9And he said to them, "What do you advise that we answer this people who have said to me, 'Lighten the yoke that your father put on us'?" 10And the young men who had grown up with him said to him, "Thus shall you speak to this people who said to you, 'Your father made our yoke heavy, but you lighten it for us,' thus shall you say to them, 'My little finger is thicker than my father's thighs. 11And now, whereas my father laid on you a heavy yoke, I will add to your yoke. My father disciplined you with whips, but I will discipline you with scorpions.'"

12So Jeroboam and all the people came to Rehoboam the third day, as the king said, "Come to me again the third day." 13And the king answered the people harshly, and forsaking the counsel that the old men had given him, 14he spoke to them according to the counsel of the young men, saying, "My father made your yoke heavy, but I will add to your yoke. My father disciplined you with whips, but I will discipline you with scorpions." 15So the king did not listen to the people, for it was a turn of affairs brought about by the LORD that he might fulfill his word, which the LORD spoke by Ahijah the Shilonite to Jeroboam the son of Nebat.

The Kingdom Divided

16And when all Israel saw that the king did not listen to them, the people answered the king, "What portion do we have in David? We have no inheritance in the son of Jesse. To your tents, O Israel! Look now to your own house, David." So Israel went to their tents. 17But Rehoboam reigned over the people of Israel who lived in the cities of Judah. 18Then King Rehoboam sent Adoram, who was taskmaster over the forced labor, and all Israel stoned him to death with stones. And King Rehoboam hurried to mount his chariot to flee to Jerusalem. 19So Israel has been in rebellion against the house of David to this day. 20And when all Israel heard that Jeroboam had returned, they sent and called him to the assembly and made him king over all Israel. There was none that followed the house of David but the tribe of Judah only.

21When Rehoboam came to Jerusalem, he assembled all the house of Judah and the tribe of Benjamin, 180,000 chosen warriors, to fight against the house of Israel, to restore the kingdom to Rehoboam the son of Solomon. 22But the word of God came to Shemaiah the man of God: 23"Say to Rehoboam the son of Solomon, king of Judah, and to all the house of Judah and Benjamin, and to the rest of the people, 24'Thus says the LORD, You shall not go up or fight against your relatives the people of Israel. Every man return to his home, for this thing is from me.'" So they listened to the word of the LORD and went home again, according to the word of the LORD.

Jeroboam's Golden Calves

25Then Jeroboam built Shechem in the hill country of Ephraim and lived there. And he went out from there and built Penuel. 26And Jeroboam said in his heart, "Now the kingdom will turn back to the house of David. 27If this people go up

[1]Septuagint, Vulgate (compare 2 Chronicles 10:2); Hebrew *lived in*

to offer sacrifices in the temple of the LORD at Jerusalem, then the heart of this
people will turn again to their lord, to Rehoboam king of Judah, and they will kill
me and return to Rehoboam king of Judah." 28 So the king took counsel and made
two calves of gold. And he said to the people, "You have gone up to Jerusalem long
enough. Behold your gods, O Israel, who brought you up out of the land of Egypt."
29 And he set one in Bethel, and the other he put in Dan. 30 Then this thing became
a sin, for the people went as far as Dan to be before one.[1] 31 He also made temples
on high places and appointed priests from among all the people, who were not of
the Levites. 32 And Jeroboam appointed a feast on the fifteenth day of the eighth
month like the feast that was in Judah, and he offered sacrifices on the altar. So he
did in Bethel, sacrificing to the calves that he made. And he placed in Bethel the
priests of the high places that he had made. 33 He went up to the altar that he had
made in Bethel on the fifteenth day in the eighth month, in the month that he had
devised from his own heart. And he instituted a feast for the people of Israel and
went up to the altar to make offerings.

A Man of God Confronts Jeroboam

13 And behold, a man of God came out of Judah by the word of the LORD to
Bethel. Jeroboam was standing by the altar to make offerings. 2 And the man
cried against the altar by the word of the LORD and said, "O altar, altar, thus says
the LORD: 'Behold, a son shall be born to the house of David, Josiah by name, and
he shall sacrifice on you the priests of the high places who make offerings on you,
and human bones shall be burned on you.'" 3 And he gave a sign the same day,
saying, "This is the sign that the LORD has spoken: 'Behold, the altar shall be torn
down, and the ashes that are on it shall be poured out.'" 4 And when the king heard
the saying of the man of God, which he cried against the altar at Bethel, Jeroboam
stretched out his hand from the altar, saying, "Seize him." And his hand, which he
stretched out against him, dried up, so that he could not draw it back to himself.
5 The altar also was torn down, and the ashes poured out from the altar, according
to the sign that the man of God had given by the word of the LORD. 6 And the king
said to the man of God, "Entreat now the favor of the LORD your God, and pray
for me, that my hand may be restored to me." And the man of God entreated the
LORD, and the king's hand was restored to him and became as it was before. 7 And
the king said to the man of God, "Come home with me, and refresh yourself, and
I will give you a reward." 8 And the man of God said to the king, "If you give me
half your house, I will not go in with you. And I will not eat bread or drink water
in this place, 9 for so was it commanded me by the word of the LORD, saying, 'You
shall neither eat bread nor drink water nor return by the way that you came.'"
10 So he went another way and did not return by the way that he came to Bethel.

The Prophet's Disobedience

11 Now an old prophet lived in Bethel. And his sons[2] came and told him all that
the man of God had done that day in Bethel. They also told to their father the
words that he had spoken to the king. 12 And their father said to them, "Which way
did he go?" And his sons showed him the way that the man of God who came from
Judah had gone. 13 And he said to his sons, "Saddle the donkey for me." So they
saddled the donkey for him and he mounted it. 14 And he went after the man of God
and found him sitting under an oak. And he said to him, "Are you the man of God
who came from Judah?" And he said, "I am." 15 Then he said to him, "Come home
with me and eat bread." 16 And he said, "I may not return with you, or go in with
you, neither will I eat bread nor drink water with you in this place, 17 for it was said
to me by the word of the LORD, 'You shall neither eat bread nor drink water there,
nor return by the way that you came.'" 18 And he said to him, "I also am a prophet

---

[1] Septuagint *went to the one at Bethel and to the other as far as Dan* [2] Septuagint, Syriac, Vulgate; Hebrew *son*

THE DIVIDED KINGDOM (930 – 586 BC)

God's people fractured into northern and southern kingdoms following the reign of King Solomon. At one level, the division of the kingdom was a judgment on the Davidic line for specific failures (1Ki 11:9 – 11; 12:12 – 15). Additionally, the northern tribes found their center of politics and trade facing Phoenicia and underwent massive rifts as indicated toward the end of the book of Judges. All of these changes made it easy for them to reject the kingdom and the religion that had once drawn them to the distant, higher elevation of Jerusalem.

While the northern kingdom valued their trade routes to the north, their greatest enemy crouched to the north as well. Syria could wreak havoc on Israel by surging down the trade routes that bisected the nation. Implementing the siege warfare tactics of Tiglath-pileser III, the Assyrians were able to place the northern kingdom under tribute by 732 BC and brought the capital city of Samaria to ruins in 722/721 BC. As typical for the Assyrian campaigns, the remaining people of the northern kingdom were deported, and new inhabitants were brought in.

The rift between the northern and southern kingdoms resulted in a number of territorial conflicts between the two brother nations. This border region south of Bethel was established following clashes between Asa and Baasha. The northern kingdom was often militarily superior and suited to fighting on the plains with many chariots. Their impressive array of chariots is even referenced in the Assyrian records. But Judah, by contrast, needed a substantially smaller force due to its elevation and natural fortification.

Judah's primary source of conflict lay to the west — the land of the Philistines. The artery of trade and the avenue for conquering armies flowed north from Lachish to Hebron and then to Jerusalem. Both the Assyrians (in 701 BC) and the Babylonians (in 597 and 586 BC) laid siege to the city, ultimately turning the city and temple to rubble and bringing a seeming end to the Messianic line of David.

While the northern and southern kingdoms were the same in terms of where they began (descendants of the same man — Abraham) and where they ended up (destroyed and deported), they also exhibited vast differences. The south, despite oscillating between idolatry and faithfulness, remained committed to the line of David. The north descended into idolatry without reprieve under a series of capricious and bloodthirsty dynasties.

GOD'S WORD IN THE MIDST OF SIN

The nation of Israel was prone to idolatry. The worship of pagan gods practiced by the surrounding nations was a regular source of temptation for God's people. The kings of the people of God even set up altars to these foreign gods, thus fostering further sin on the part of the people.

God promised to destroy the pagan altar constructed by Jeroboam, reducing it to rubble and thereby demonstrating its futility. Josiah, a descendant of David, fulfilled this prophecy in 2 Kings 23:15 – 18 when he pulled down the altar and the associated implements of worship and burned them all.

This action proves that, in spite of the sin of the people, God graciously protected them from their folly. Rather than letting their idolatry run amok, he raised up godly leaders who destroyed the altars and hindered the idolatrous worship of the nation. In many ways, the history of the people of God proves the depths of sin that people are capable of practicing. Yet, it could have been far worse without God's ongoing intervention.

God's goal was not simply to destroy the altar of pagan worship but to arrest the people in their sin. The dust heap of an altar was meant to expose the impotence of the pagan gods and the foolishness of the people in worshiping them.

God has always acted to expose the folly of people trapped in cycles of idolatry. Whether their false gods are represented by carved images or embodied in the misdirected pursuits of sex or power, God shatters those gods' illusory attraction. In his grace, God thwarts the worship of these gods by exposing them as false. The goal is the same as that found here in 1 Kings — to prove that false gods are not deserving of worship and to point people to the one true and living God who does deserve that worship. God is the only proper object of worship, and God will use any means necessary — including the destruction of false gods — to cause people to see their need for him.

as you are, and an angel spoke to me by the word of the LORD, saying, 'Bring him back with you into your house that he may eat bread and drink water.'" But he lied to him. 19So he went back with him and ate bread in his house and drank water.

20And as they sat at the table, the word of the LORD came to the prophet who had brought him back. 21And he cried to the man of God who came from Judah, "Thus says the LORD, 'Because you have disobeyed the word of the LORD and have not kept the command that the LORD your God commanded you, 22but have come back and have eaten bread and drunk water in the place of which he said to you, "Eat no bread and drink no water," your body shall not come to the tomb of your fathers.'" 23And after he had eaten bread and drunk, he saddled the donkey for the prophet whom he had brought back. 24And as he went away a lion met him on the road and killed him. And his body was thrown in the road, and the donkey stood beside it; the lion also stood beside the body. 25And behold, men passed by and saw the body thrown in the road and the lion standing by the body. And they came and told it in the city where the old prophet lived.

26And when the prophet who had brought him back from the way heard of it, he said, "It is the man of God who disobeyed the word of the LORD; therefore the LORD has given him to the lion, which has torn him and killed him, according to the word that the LORD spoke to him." 27And he said to his sons, "Saddle the donkey for me." And they saddled it. 28And he went and found his body thrown in the road, and the donkey and the lion standing beside the body. The lion had not eaten the body or torn the donkey. 29And the prophet took up the body of the man of God and laid it on the donkey and brought it back to the city[1] to mourn and to bury him. 30And he laid the body in his own grave. And they mourned over him, saying, "Alas, my brother!" 31And after he had buried him, he said to his sons, "When I die, bury me in the grave in which the man of God is buried; lay my bones beside his bones. 32For the saying that he called out by the word of the LORD against the altar in Bethel and against all the houses of the high places that are in the cities of Samaria shall surely come to pass."

33After this thing Jeroboam did not turn from his evil way, but made priests for the high places again from among all the people. Any who would, he ordained to be priests of the high places. 34And this thing became sin to the house of Jeroboam, so as to cut it off and to destroy it from the face of the earth.

Prophecy Against Jeroboam

14 At that time Abijah the son of Jeroboam fell sick. 2And Jeroboam said to his wife, "Arise, and disguise yourself, that it not be known that you are the wife of Jeroboam, and go to Shiloh. Behold, Ahijah the prophet is there, who said of me that I should be king over this people. 3Take with you ten loaves, some cakes, and a jar of honey, and go to him. He will tell you what shall happen to the child."

4Jeroboam's wife did so. She arose and went to Shiloh and came to the house of Ahijah. Now Ahijah could not see, for his eyes were dim because of his age. 5And the LORD said to Ahijah, "Behold, the wife of Jeroboam is coming to inquire of you concerning her son, for he is sick. Thus and thus shall you say to her."

When she came, she pretended to be another woman. 6But when Ahijah heard the sound of her feet, as she came in at the door, he said, "Come in, wife of Jeroboam. Why do you pretend to be another? For I am charged with unbearable news for you. 7Go, tell Jeroboam, 'Thus says the LORD, the God of Israel: "Because I exalted you from among the people and made you leader over my people Israel 8and tore the kingdom away from the house of David and gave it to you, and yet you have not been like my servant David, who kept my commandments and followed me with all his heart, doing only that which was right in my eyes, 9but you have done evil above all who were before you and have gone and made for yourself other gods and metal images, provoking me to anger, and have cast me behind

[1]Septuagint; Hebrew *he came to the city of the old prophet*

---

1 KINGS 14:1–18

PROPHECY FULFILLED

The sin of Jeroboam caused God to stir the prophet Ahijah to prophesy Jeroboam's impending destruction, the collapse of his kingdom, and the extermination of his household. A short time later, these promises were fulfilled with exacting precision (1Ki 14:17–18; 15:29–30). He and his entire family were destroyed because he provoked the Lord to anger by fostering the rebellion of the nation against God. The immediate fulfillment of God's promises demonstrated that he was faithful to his word and would not leave the guilty unpunished. In this and similar cases, God promised to act and fulfilled his promise in that generation. This quick fulfillment allowed the same people who heard the promise to see it fulfilled before their very eyes, providing a clear confirmation of God's word. However, on other occasions, the fulfillment of biblical prophecy happened following a lengthy span of time. The consistency of God's promises across generations attests to his faithfulness. Prophecy proves that God is faithful, in both the short term and long term, to fulfill his promises to save his people from their sin.

your back, 10therefore behold, I will bring harm upon the house of Jeroboam and
will cut off from Jeroboam every male, both bond and free in Israel, and will burn
up the house of Jeroboam, as a man burns up dung until it is all gone. 11Anyone
belonging to Jeroboam who dies in the city the dogs shall eat, and anyone who
dies in the open country the birds of the heavens shall eat, for the LORD has spoken it."' 12Arise therefore, go to your house. When your feet enter the city, the
child shall die. 13And all Israel shall mourn for him and bury him, for he only of
Jeroboam shall come to the grave, because in him there is found something pleasing to the LORD, the God of Israel, in the house of Jeroboam. 14Moreover, the LORD
will raise up for himself a king over Israel who shall cut off the house of Jeroboam
today. And henceforth, 15the LORD will strike Israel as a reed is shaken in the water,
and root up Israel out of this good land that he gave to their fathers and scatter
them beyond the Euphrates,[1] because they have made their Asherim, provoking
the LORD to anger. 16And he will give Israel up because of the sins of Jeroboam,
which he sinned and made Israel to sin."

17Then Jeroboam's wife arose and departed and came to Tirzah. And as she
came to the threshold of the house, the child died. 18And all Israel buried him
and mourned for him, according to the word of the LORD, which he spoke by his
servant Ahijah the prophet.

The Death of Jeroboam

19Now the rest of the acts of Jeroboam, how he warred and how he reigned,
behold, they are written in the Book of the Chronicles of the Kings of Israel. 20And
the time that Jeroboam reigned was twenty-two years. And he slept with his fathers, and Nadab his son reigned in his place.

Rehoboam Reigns in Judah

21Now Rehoboam the son of Solomon reigned in Judah. Rehoboam was forty-
one years old when he began to reign, and he reigned seventeen years in Jerusalem, the city that the LORD had chosen out of all the tribes of Israel, to put his
name there. His mother's name was Naamah the Ammonite. 22And Judah did
what was evil in the sight of the LORD, and they provoked him to jealousy with
their sins that they committed, more than all that their fathers had done. 23For
they also built for themselves high places and pillars and Asherim on every high
hill and under every green tree, 24and there were also male cult prostitutes in the
land. They did according to all the abominations of the nations that the LORD
drove out before the people of Israel.

25In the fifth year of King Rehoboam, Shishak king of Egypt came up against
Jerusalem. 26He took away the treasures of the house of the LORD and the treasures
of the king's house. He took away everything. He also took away all the shields of
gold that Solomon had made, 27and King Rehoboam made in their place shields of
bronze, and committed them to the hands of the officers of the guard, who kept
the door of the king's house. 28And as often as the king went into the house of the
LORD, the guard carried them and brought them back to the guardroom.

29Now the rest of the acts of Rehoboam and all that he did, are they not written
in the Book of the Chronicles of the Kings of Judah? 30And there was war between
Rehoboam and Jeroboam continually. 31And Rehoboam slept with his fathers and
was buried with his fathers in the city of David. His mother's name was Naamah
the Ammonite. And Abijam his son reigned in his place.

Abijam Reigns in Judah

15 Now in the eighteenth year of King Jeroboam the son of Nebat, Abijam
began to reign over Judah. 2He reigned for three years in Jerusalem. His
mother's name was Maacah the daughter of Abishalom. 3And he walked in all the

---

[1] Hebrew *the River*

sins that his father did before him, and his heart was not wholly true to the LORD his God, as the heart of David his father. [4]Nevertheless, for David's sake the LORD his God gave him a lamp in Jerusalem, setting up his son after him, and establishing Jerusalem, [5]because David did what was right in the eyes of the LORD and did not turn aside from anything that he commanded him all the days of his life, except in the matter of Uriah the Hittite. [6]Now there was war between Rehoboam and Jeroboam all the days of his life. [7]The rest of the acts of Abijam and all that he did, are they not written in the Book of the Chronicles of the Kings of Judah? And there was war between Abijam and Jeroboam. [8]And Abijam slept with his fathers, and they buried him in the city of David. And Asa his son reigned in his place.

Asa Reigns in Judah

[9]In the twentieth year of Jeroboam king of Israel, Asa began to reign over Judah, [10]and he reigned forty-one years in Jerusalem. His mother's name was Maacah the daughter of Abishalom. [11]And Asa did what was right in the eyes of the LORD, as David his father had done. [12]He put away the male cult prostitutes out of the land and removed all the idols that his fathers had made. [13]He also removed Maacah his mother from being queen mother because she had made an abominable image for Asherah. And Asa cut down her image and burned it at the brook Kidron. [14]But the high places were not taken away. Nevertheless, the heart of Asa was wholly true to the LORD all his days. [15]And he brought into the house of the LORD the sacred gifts of his father and his own sacred gifts, silver, and gold, and vessels.

[16]And there was war between Asa and Baasha king of Israel all their days. [17]Baasha king of Israel went up against Judah and built Ramah, that he might permit no one to go out or come in to Asa king of Judah. [18]Then Asa took all the silver and the gold that were left in the treasures of the house of the LORD and the treasures of the king's house and gave them into the hands of his servants. And King Asa sent them to Ben-hadad the son of Tabrimmon, the son of Hezion, king of Syria, who lived in Damascus, saying, [19]"Let there be a covenant[1] between me and you, as there was between my father and your father. Behold, I am sending to you a present of silver and gold. Go, break your covenant with Baasha king of Israel, that he may withdraw from me." [20]And Ben-hadad listened to King Asa and sent the commanders of his armies against the cities of Israel and conquered Ijon, Dan, Abel-beth-maacah, and all Chinneroth, with all the land of Naphtali. [21]And when Baasha heard of it, he stopped building Ramah, and he lived in Tirzah. [22]Then King Asa made a proclamation to all Judah, none was exempt, and they carried away the stones of Ramah and its timber, with which Baasha had been building, and with them King Asa built Geba of Benjamin and Mizpah. [23]Now the rest of all the acts of Asa, all his might, and all that he did, and the cities that he built, are they not written in the Book of the Chronicles of the Kings of Judah? But in his old age he was diseased in his feet. [24]And Asa slept with his fathers and was buried with his fathers in the city of David his father, and Jehoshaphat his son reigned in his place.

Nadab Reigns in Israel

[25]Nadab the son of Jeroboam began to reign over Israel in the second year of Asa king of Judah, and he reigned over Israel two years. [26]He did what was evil in the sight of the LORD and walked in the way of his father, and in his sin which he made Israel to sin.

[27]Baasha the son of Ahijah, of the house of Issachar, conspired against him. And Baasha struck him down at Gibbethon, which belonged to the Philistines, for Nadab and all Israel were laying siege to Gibbethon. [28]So Baasha killed him in the third year of Asa king of Judah and reigned in his place. [29]And as soon as he was

[1]Or *treaty*; twice in this verse

king, he killed all the house of Jeroboam. He left to the house of Jeroboam not one
that breathed, until he had destroyed it, according to the word of the LORD that he
spoke by his servant Ahijah the Shilonite. 30 It was for the sins of Jeroboam that
he sinned and that he made Israel to sin, and because of the anger to which he
provoked the LORD, the God of Israel.
31 Now the rest of the acts of Nadab and all that he did, are they not written in
the Book of the Chronicles of the Kings of Israel? 32 And there was war between
Asa and Baasha king of Israel all their days.

Baasha Reigns in Israel

33 In the third year of Asa king of Judah, Baasha the son of Ahijah began to reign
over all Israel at Tirzah, and he reigned twenty-four years. 34 He did what was evil
in the sight of the LORD and walked in the way of Jeroboam and in his sin which
he made Israel to sin.

16 And the word of the LORD came to Jehu the son of Hanani against Baasha,
saying, 2 "Since I exalted you out of the dust and made you leader over my
people Israel, and you have walked in the way of Jeroboam and have made my
people Israel to sin, provoking me to anger with their sins, 3 behold, I will utterly
sweep away Baasha and his house, and I will make your house like the house of
Jeroboam the son of Nebat. 4 Anyone belonging to Baasha who dies in the city the
dogs shall eat, and anyone of his who dies in the field the birds of the heavens
shall eat."
5 Now the rest of the acts of Baasha and what he did, and his might, are they
not written in the Book of the Chronicles of the Kings of Israel? 6 And Baasha slept
with his fathers and was buried at Tirzah, and Elah his son reigned in his place.
7 Moreover, the word of the LORD came by the prophet Jehu the son of Hanani
against Baasha and his house, both because of all the evil that he did in the sight
of the LORD, provoking him to anger with the work of his hands, in being like the
house of Jeroboam, and also because he destroyed it.

Elah Reigns in Israel

8 In the twenty-sixth year of Asa king of Judah, Elah the son of Baasha began to
reign over Israel in Tirzah, and he reigned two years. 9 But his servant Zimri, commander of half his chariots, conspired against him. When he was at Tirzah, drinking himself drunk in the house of Arza, who was over the household in Tirzah,
10 Zimri came in and struck him down and killed him, in the twenty-seventh year
of Asa king of Judah, and reigned in his place.
11 When he began to reign, as soon as he had seated himself on his throne, he
struck down all the house of Baasha. He did not leave him a single male of his
relatives or his friends. 12 Thus Zimri destroyed all the house of Baasha, according
to the word of the LORD, which he spoke against Baasha by Jehu the prophet, 13 for
all the sins of Baasha and the sins of Elah his son, which they sinned and which
they made Israel to sin, provoking the LORD God of Israel to anger with their idols.
14 Now the rest of the acts of Elah and all that he did, are they not written in the
Book of the Chronicles of the Kings of Israel?

Zimri Reigns in Israel

15 In the twenty-seventh year of Asa king of Judah, Zimri reigned seven days
in Tirzah. Now the troops were encamped against Gibbethon, which belonged
to the Philistines, 16 and the troops who were encamped heard it said, "Zimri has
conspired, and he has killed the king." Therefore all Israel made Omri, the commander of the army, king over Israel that day in the camp. 17 So Omri went up
from Gibbethon, and all Israel with him, and they besieged Tirzah. 18 And when
Zimri saw that the city was taken, he went into the citadel of the king's house and
burned the king's house over him with fire and died, 19 because of his sins that he
committed, doing evil in the sight of the LORD, walking in the way of Jeroboam,

and for his sin which he committed, making Israel to sin. [20]Now the rest of the acts of Zimri, and the conspiracy that he made, are they not written in the Book of the Chronicles of the Kings of Israel?

Omri Reigns in Israel

[21]Then the people of Israel were divided into two parts. Half of the people followed Tibni the son of Ginath, to make him king, and half followed Omri. [22]But the people who followed Omri overcame the people who followed Tibni the son of Ginath. So Tibni died, and Omri became king. [23]In the thirty-first year of Asa king of Judah, Omri began to reign over Israel, and he reigned for twelve years; six years he reigned in Tirzah. [24]He bought the hill of Samaria from Shemer for two talents[1] of silver, and he fortified the hill and called the name of the city that he built Samaria, after the name of Shemer, the owner of the hill.

[25]Omri did what was evil in the sight of the LORD, and did more evil than all who were before him. [26]For he walked in all the way of Jeroboam the son of Nebat, and in the sins that he made Israel to sin, provoking the LORD, the God of Israel, to anger by their idols. [27]Now the rest of the acts of Omri that he did, and the might that he showed, are they not written in the Book of the Chronicles of the Kings of Israel? [28]And Omri slept with his fathers and was buried in Samaria, and Ahab his son reigned in his place.

Ahab Reigns in Israel

[29]In the thirty-eighth year of Asa king of Judah, Ahab the son of Omri began to reign over Israel, and Ahab the son of Omri reigned over Israel in Samaria twenty-two years. [30]And Ahab the son of Omri did evil in the sight of the LORD, more than all who were before him. [31]And as if it had been a light thing for him to walk in the sins of Jeroboam the son of Nebat, he took for his wife Jezebel the daughter of Ethbaal king of the Sidonians, and went and served Baal and worshiped him. [32]He erected an altar for Baal in the house of Baal, which he built in Samaria. [33]And Ahab made an Asherah. Ahab did more to provoke the LORD, the God of Israel, to anger than all the kings of Israel who were before him. [34]In his days Hiel of Bethel built Jericho. He laid its foundation at the cost of Abiram his firstborn, and set up its gates at the cost of his youngest son Segub, according to the word of the LORD, which he spoke by Joshua the son of Nun.

Elijah Predicts a Drought

17 Now Elijah the Tishbite, of Tishbe[2] in Gilead, said to Ahab, "As the LORD, the God of Israel, lives, before whom I stand, there shall be neither dew nor rain these years, except by my word." [2]And the word of the LORD came to him: [3]"Depart from here and turn eastward and hide yourself by the brook Cherith, which is east of the Jordan. [4]You shall drink from the brook, and I have commanded the ravens to feed you there." [5]So he went and did according to the word of the LORD. He went and lived by the brook Cherith that is east of the Jordan. [6]And the ravens brought him bread and meat in the morning, and bread and meat in the evening, and he drank from the brook. [7]And after a while the brook dried up, because there was no rain in the land.

The Widow of Zarephath

[8]Then the word of the LORD came to him, [9]"Arise, go to Zarephath, which belongs to Sidon, and dwell there. Behold, I have commanded a widow there to feed you." [10]So he arose and went to Zarephath. And when he came to the gate of the city, behold, a widow was there gathering sticks. And he called to her and said, "Bring me a little water in a vessel, that I may drink." [11]And as she was going to bring it, he called to her and said, "Bring me a morsel of bread in your hand."

1 KINGS 16:29–33

THE BAD ROAD DOWNWARD

The downward trajectory of the northern kingdom reached new depths in the appointment of Ahab as king over Israel. While the list of sins recounted here is far from unique to Ahab, the extent of his rebellion eclipsed all of those who ruled prior to him. The unraveling of the nation and the continued spread of sin among the people reveal a simple fact—sin is never static. It grows, expands, and contaminates all that it touches. No person or nation, even the nation of Israel, is immune to its destructive nature.

Jesus entered a culture that continued to bear the marks of the impact and spread of sin. Human government is unable to rid itself from the effects of sin and the implications of the fall. Into this broken world, Jesus ushered a new kingdom marked by his perfect rule and reign (Mt 3:2). Submission to Jesus breaks the cycle of sin and provides the hope and peace no human king could ever bring.

[1]A *talent* was about 75 pounds or 34 kilograms [2]Septuagint; Hebrew *of the settlers*

[12]And she said, "As the LORD your God lives, I have nothing baked, only a handful
of flour in a jar and a little oil in a jug. And now I am gathering a couple of sticks
that I may go in and prepare it for myself and my son, that we may eat it and die."
[13]And Elijah said to her, "Do not fear; go and do as you have said. But first make
me a little cake of it and bring it to me, and afterward make something for yourself
and your son. [14]For thus says the LORD, the God of Israel, 'The jar of flour shall not
be spent, and the jug of oil shall not be empty, until the day that the LORD sends
rain upon the earth.'" [15]And she went and did as Elijah said. And she and he and
her household ate for many days. [16]The jar of flour was not spent, neither did the
jug of oil become empty, according to the word of the LORD that he spoke by Elijah.

Elijah Raises the Widow's Son

[17]After this the son of the woman, the mistress of the house, became ill. And
his illness was so severe that there was no breath left in him. [18]And she said to
Elijah, "What have you against me, O man of God? You have come to me to bring
my sin to remembrance and to cause the death of my son!" [19]And he said to her,
"Give me your son." And he took him from her arms and carried him up into the
upper chamber where he lodged, and laid him on his own bed. [20]And he cried to
the LORD, "O LORD my God, have you brought calamity even upon the widow with
whom I sojourn, by killing her son?" [21]Then he stretched himself upon the child
three times and cried to the LORD, "O LORD my God, let this child's life[1] come into
him again." [22]And the LORD listened to the voice of Elijah. And the life of the child
came into him again, and he revived. [23]And Elijah took the child and brought him
down from the upper chamber into the house and delivered him to his mother.
And Elijah said, "See, your son lives." [24]And the woman said to Elijah, "Now I
know that you are a man of God, and that the word of the LORD in your mouth is
truth."

Elijah Confronts Ahab

18 After many days the word of the LORD came to Elijah, in the third year,
saying, "Go, show yourself to Ahab, and I will send rain upon the earth."
[2]So Elijah went to show himself to Ahab. Now the famine was severe in Samaria.
[3]And Ahab called Obadiah, who was over the household. (Now Obadiah feared
the LORD greatly, [4]and when Jezebel cut off the prophets of the LORD, Obadiah
took a hundred prophets and hid them by fifties in a cave and fed them with bread
and water.) [5]And Ahab said to Obadiah, "Go through the land to all the springs of
water and to all the valleys. Perhaps we may find grass and save the horses and
mules alive, and not lose some of the animals." [6]So they divided the land between
them to pass through it. Ahab went in one direction by himself, and Obadiah went
in another direction by himself.

[7]And as Obadiah was on the way, behold, Elijah met him. And Obadiah recognized him and fell on his face and said, "Is it you, my lord Elijah?" [8]And he answered him, "It is I. Go, tell your lord, 'Behold, Elijah is here.'" [9]And he said, "How
have I sinned, that you would give your servant into the hand of Ahab, to kill me?
[10]As the LORD your God lives, there is no nation or kingdom where my lord has not
sent to seek you. And when they would say, 'He is not here,' he would take an oath
of the kingdom or nation, that they had not found you. [11]And now you say, 'Go,
tell your lord, "Behold, Elijah is here."' [12]And as soon as I have gone from you, the
Spirit of the LORD will carry you I know not where. And so, when I come and tell
Ahab and he cannot find you, he will kill me, although I your servant have feared
the LORD from my youth. [13]Has it not been told my lord what I did when Jezebel
killed the prophets of the LORD, how I hid a hundred men of the LORD's prophets
by fifties in a cave and fed them with bread and water? [14]And now you say, 'Go, tell
your lord, "Behold, Elijah is here"'; and he will kill me." [15]And Elijah said, "As the

[1]Or *soul*; also verse 22

THE BREAD OF LIFE

Elijah's actions in chapter 17 are a demonstration of the power of God to provide for people and overcome the disastrous effects of sin and death. Through power given to him by God, Elijah multiplied a small amount of flour and oil in order to provide bread for the widow and her son for many days. God also worked through Elijah to bring the widow's son back to life after he became sick and died. These miracles marked Elijah as God's appointed messenger at that stage in history.

However, Elijah's two miracles recounted in this text have additional significance: they prefigure the person and work of Jesus Christ. Jesus, as God's Son and appointed messenger, was personally able to turn a meager meal into a feast for multitudes (Mt 14:13–21). The feeding of the 5,000 boldly proclaimed that Jesus was capable of abundantly providing for people. Jesus' provision was not limited to mere physical bread, though. He claimed to be the true bread from heaven, sent to provide for all those who would feast on him (Jn 6:26–51).

Jesus also performed other miracles, proving him to be God in the flesh and one who possessed ultimate power over sin and death. Like Elijah, Jesus brought the dead son of a widow back to life. Seeing the woman and having compassion on her, Jesus spoke to the son and he sat up and began to speak (Lk 7:11–15). Jesus said that acts like these demonstrated that he was the Messiah who would bring healing and restoration to those broken by sin's consequences (Lk 7:18–23).

The death of Jesus' friend Lazarus provided another opportunity for him to demonstrate the power he possessed. Unlike the widow's son, Lazarus had been dead for several days and his body had been wrapped in funeral linens and placed in a tomb. Jesus prayed to the Father and then spoke to the corpse, calling it to life. Jesus attested to the fact that raising Lazarus served as a testimony to the glory of God (Jn 11:1–44).

Soon this glory was seen in a far greater resurrection — that of Jesus himself. The power of God over Satan, sin, and death was fully demonstrated by Christ's victorious emergence from the grave. His resurrected life would serve as a firstfruits of the resurrection promised to all those who place their faith in him. By God's power, all those longing for provision and broken by death can be restored to new life, now and forevermore.

Lord of hosts lives, before whom I stand, I will surely show myself to him today."
[16]So Obadiah went to meet Ahab, and told him. And Ahab went to meet Elijah.
[17]When Ahab saw Elijah, Ahab said to him, "Is it you, you troubler of Israel?"
[18]And he answered, "I have not troubled Israel, but you have, and your father's
house, because you have abandoned the commandments of the Lord and followed the Baals. [19]Now therefore send and gather all Israel to me at Mount Carmel, and the 450 prophets of Baal and the 400 prophets of Asherah, who eat at
Jezebel's table."

The Prophets of Baal Defeated

[20]So Ahab sent to all the people of Israel and gathered the prophets together
at Mount Carmel. [21]And Elijah came near to all the people and said, "How long
will you go limping between two different opinions? If the Lord is God, follow
him; but if Baal, then follow him." And the people did not answer him a word.
[22]Then Elijah said to the people, "I, even I only, am left a prophet of the Lord, but
Baal's prophets are 450 men. [23]Let two bulls be given to us, and let them choose
one bull for themselves and cut it in pieces and lay it on the wood, but put no fire
to it. And I will prepare the other bull and lay it on the wood and put no fire to it.
[24]And you call upon the name of your god, and I will call upon the name of the
Lord, and the God who answers by fire, he is God." And all the people answered,
"It is well spoken." [25]Then Elijah said to the prophets of Baal, "Choose for yourselves one bull and prepare it first, for you are many, and call upon the name of
your god, but put no fire to it." [26]And they took the bull that was given them, and
they prepared it and called upon the name of Baal from morning until noon, saying, "O Baal, answer us!" But there was no voice, and no one answered. And they
limped around the altar that they had made. [27]And at noon Elijah mocked them,
saying, "Cry aloud, for he is a god. Either he is musing, or he is relieving himself,
or he is on a journey, or perhaps he is asleep and must be awakened." [28]And they
cried aloud and cut themselves after their custom with swords and lances, until
the blood gushed out upon them. [29]And as midday passed, they raved on until the
time of the offering of the oblation, but there was no voice. No one answered; no
one paid attention.

[30]Then Elijah said to all the people, "Come near to me." And all the people
came near to him. And he repaired the altar of the Lord that had been thrown
down. [31]Elijah took twelve stones, according to the number of the tribes of the
sons of Jacob, to whom the word of the Lord came, saying, "Israel shall be your
name," [32]and with the stones he built an altar in the name of the Lord. And he
made a trench about the altar, as great as would contain two seahs[1] of seed. [33]And
he put the wood in order and cut the bull in pieces and laid it on the wood. And he
said, "Fill four jars with water and pour it on the burnt offering and on the wood."
[34]And he said, "Do it a second time." And they did it a second time. And he said,
"Do it a third time." And they did it a third time. [35]And the water ran around the
altar and filled the trench also with water.

[36]And at the time of the offering of the oblation, Elijah the prophet came near
and said, "O Lord, God of Abraham, Isaac, and Israel, let it be known this day that
you are God in Israel, and that I am your servant, and that I have done all these
things at your word. [37]Answer me, O Lord, answer me, that this people may know
that you, O Lord, are God, and that you have turned their hearts back." [38]Then
the fire of the Lord fell and consumed the burnt offering and the wood and the
stones and the dust, and licked up the water that was in the trench. [39]And when
all the people saw it, they fell on their faces and said, "The Lord, he is God; the
Lord, he is God." [40]And Elijah said to them, "Seize the prophets of Baal; let not
one of them escape." And they seized them. And Elijah brought them down to the
brook Kishon and slaughtered them there.

---

[1]A *seah* was about 7.7 quarts or 7.3 liters

The LORD Sends Rain

41And Elijah said to Ahab, “Go up, eat and drink, for there is a sound of the rushing of rain.” 42So Ahab went up to eat and to drink. And Elijah went up to the top of Mount Carmel. And he bowed himself down on the earth and put his face between his knees. 43And he said to his servant, “Go up now, look toward the sea.” And he went up and looked and said, “There is nothing.” And he said, “Go again,” seven times. 44And at the seventh time he said, “Behold, a little cloud like a man’s hand is rising from the sea.” And he said, “Go up, say to Ahab, ‘Prepare your chariot and go down, lest the rain stop you.’” 45And in a little while the heavens grew black with clouds and wind, and there was a great rain. And Ahab rode and went to Jezreel. 46And the hand of the LORD was on Elijah, and he gathered up his garment and ran before Ahab to the entrance of Jezreel.

1 KINGS 19:1–18

GOD’S PROVISION FOR HIS SERVANTS

God provided for Elijah by meeting his needs, protecting his life, and speaking to him in a gentle whisper. Although Elijah was running for his life and lacked the basic provisions required to survive, God provided for his messenger. In a similar way, when Jesus sent out his new messengers, the disciples, to declare and demonstrate the Good News message, he ensured that they had the necessary resources. Jesus instructed them not to worry about carrying sufficient provision for their journey. They were not to take a staff, a bag, bread, money, or even a change of clothes (Lk 9:1–6). God would provide for these needs as he had for the nation of Israel in the wilderness and for messengers like Elijah. They only needed to trust him.

Christians today can live with the same bold confidence in the care of God, who promises to go with them as they go to make disciples of all nations (Mt 28:19–20). Though they may face suffering, encounter harm, or even be put to death, God’s children can trust that he will allow them to accomplish the mission he has placed before them and will forever meet their needs according to the glorious riches of his grace toward them in Christ Jesus (Php 4:19).

Elijah Flees Jezebel

19 Ahab told Jezebel all that Elijah had done, and how he had killed all the prophets with the sword. 2Then Jezebel sent a messenger to Elijah, saying, “So may the gods do to me and more also, if I do not make your life as the life of one of them by this time tomorrow.” 3Then he was afraid, and he arose and ran for his life and came to Beersheba, which belongs to Judah, and left his servant there.

4But he himself went a day’s journey into the wilderness and came and sat down under a broom tree. And he asked that he might die, saying, “It is enough; now, O LORD, take away my life, for I am no better than my fathers.” 5And he lay down and slept under a broom tree. And behold, an angel touched him and said to him, “Arise and eat.” 6And he looked, and behold, there was at his head a cake baked on hot stones and a jar of water. And he ate and drank and lay down again. 7And the angel of the LORD came again a second time and touched him and said, “Arise and eat, for the journey is too great for you.” 8And he arose and ate and drank, and went in the strength of that food forty days and forty nights to Horeb, the mount of God.

The LORD Speaks to Elijah

9There he came to a cave and lodged in it. And behold, the word of the LORD came to him, and he said to him, “What are you doing here, Elijah?” 10He said, “I have been very jealous for the LORD, the God of hosts. For the people of Israel have forsaken your covenant, thrown down your altars, and killed your prophets with the sword, and I, even I only, am left, and they seek my life, to take it away.” 11And he said, “Go out and stand on the mount before the LORD.” And behold, the LORD passed by, and a great and strong wind tore the mountains and broke in pieces the rocks before the LORD, but the LORD was not in the wind. And after the wind an earthquake, but the LORD was not in the earthquake. 12And after the earthquake a fire, but the LORD was not in the fire. And after the fire the sound of a low whisper.[1] 13And when Elijah heard it, he wrapped his face in his cloak and went out and stood at the entrance of the cave. And behold, there came a voice to him and said, “What are you doing here, Elijah?” 14He said, “I have been very jealous for the LORD, the God of hosts. For the people of Israel have forsaken your covenant, thrown down your altars, and killed your prophets with the sword, and I, even I only, am left, and they seek my life, to take it away.” 15And the LORD said to him, “Go, return on your way to the wilderness of Damascus. And when you arrive, you shall anoint Hazael to be king over Syria. 16And Jehu the son of Nimshi you shall anoint to be king over Israel, and Elisha the son of Shaphat of Abel-meholah you shall anoint to be prophet in your place. 17And the one who escapes from the sword of Hazael shall Jehu put to death, and the one who escapes from the sword of Jehu shall Elisha put to death. 18Yet I will leave seven thousand in Israel, all the knees that have not bowed to Baal, and every mouth that has not kissed him.”

[1]Or *a sound, a thin silence*

TURNING HEARTS TO GOD

The confrontation between Elijah and the prophets of Baal on Mount Carmel is one of the most well-known stories in the book of 1 Kings. As God's messenger, Elijah boldly confronted the pagan worship that not only filled the surrounding nations but also had become rampant among the people of God. Elijah mocked the inability of the pagan gods to prove their power by consuming the offering on the altar. Elijah seemingly stacked the odds against his God; however, in a mighty display of power, the Lord consumed not only the sacrificial offering but also the wood, the stones, and the water Elijah had poured on the altar.

After this miraculous episode, threatened by Jezebel and fearing for his life, Elijah ran into the desert, wanting to end it all (1Ki 19:4). His mountaintop testimony to the glory of God had not turned the hearts of the people back to God or halted the nation's headlong course toward destruction — a course that even the greatest leaders in the nation's history had seemed powerless to stop.

In spite of the nation's failure to return to God in a meaningful way, God continued to display his glorious might through history. At each juncture, the goal was not merely to correct the behavior of people but to redirect their hearts toward proper worship. His glory was meant to turn the hearts of people. This work was necessary due to the fact that sin positions all human hearts in opposition to God, leading them to turn their backs on him and harden their hearts in rebellion. Like Pharaoh in Egypt, no matter what mighty acts humans observe, they staunchly refuse to acknowledge the truthfulness of the claims of Christ and the depravity of their own hearts. God could rightly give people over to their sin and let them run from him forever. But in his grace he continues to demonstrate his glory in order to turn their hearts back to him in worship.

When humans turn from their sin and turn to Christ, they display the fact that God has replaced their hearts of stone with soft and pliable hearts (Eze 36:26). These new hearts, pulsating with life given by the power of God, are drawn to the awe-inspiring glory of God.

The Call of Elisha

19So he departed from there and found Elisha the son of Shaphat, who was plowing with twelve yoke of oxen in front of him, and he was with the twelfth. Elijah passed by him and cast his cloak upon him. 20And he left the oxen and ran after Elijah and said, "Let me kiss my father and my mother, and then I will follow you." And he said to him, "Go back again, for what have I done to you?" 21And he returned from following him and took the yoke of oxen and sacrificed them and boiled their flesh with the yokes of the oxen and gave it to the people, and they ate. Then he arose and went after Elijah and assisted him.

Ahab's Wars with Syria

20 Ben-hadad the king of Syria gathered all his army together. Thirty-two kings were with him, and horses and chariots. And he went up and closed in on Samaria and fought against it. 2And he sent messengers into the city to Ahab king of Israel and said to him, "Thus says Ben-hadad: 3'Your silver and your gold are mine; your best wives and children also are mine.'" 4And the king of Israel answered, "As you say, my lord, O king, I am yours, and all that I have." 5The messengers came again and said, "Thus says Ben-hadad: 'I sent to you, saying, "Deliver to me your silver and your gold, your wives and your children." 6Nevertheless I will send my servants to you tomorrow about this time, and they shall search your house and the houses of your servants and lay hands on whatever pleases you and take it away.'"

7Then the king of Israel called all the elders of the land and said, "Mark, now, and see how this man is seeking trouble, for he sent to me for my wives and my children, and for my silver and my gold, and I did not refuse him." 8And all the elders and all the people said to him, "Do not listen or consent." 9So he said to the messengers of Ben-hadad, "Tell my lord the king, 'All that you first demanded of your servant I will do, but this thing I cannot do.'" And the messengers departed and brought him word again. 10Ben-hadad sent to him and said, "The gods do so to me and more also, if the dust of Samaria shall suffice for handfuls for all the people who follow me." 11And the king of Israel answered, "Tell him, 'Let not him who straps on his armor boast himself as he who takes it off.'" 12When Ben-hadad heard this message as he was drinking with the kings in the booths, he said to his men, "Take your positions." And they took their positions against the city.

Ahab Defeats Ben-hadad

13And behold, a prophet came near to Ahab king of Israel and said, "Thus says the Lord, Have you seen all this great multitude? Behold, I will give it into your hand this day, and you shall know that I am the Lord." 14And Ahab said, "By whom?" He said, "Thus says the Lord, By the servants of the governors of the districts." Then he said, "Who shall begin the battle?" He answered, "You." 15Then he mustered the servants of the governors of the districts, and they were 232. And after them he mustered all the people of Israel, seven thousand.

16And they went out at noon, while Ben-hadad was drinking himself drunk in the booths, he and the thirty-two kings who helped him. 17The servants of the governors of the districts went out first. And Ben-hadad sent out scouts, and they reported to him, "Men are coming out from Samaria." 18He said, "If they have come out for peace, take them alive. Or if they have come out for war, take them alive."

19So these went out of the city, the servants of the governors of the districts and the army that followed them. 20And each struck down his man. The Syrians fled, and Israel pursued them, but Ben-hadad king of Syria escaped on a horse with horsemen. 21And the king of Israel went out and struck the horses and chariots, and struck the Syrians with a great blow.

[22]Then the prophet came near to the king of Israel and said to him, "Come,
strengthen yourself, and consider well what you have to do, for in the spring the
king of Syria will come up against you."
[23]And the servants of the king of Syria said to him, "Their gods are gods of the
hills, and so they were stronger than we. But let us fight against them in the plain,
and surely we shall be stronger than they. [24]And do this: remove the kings, each
from his post, and put commanders in their places, [25]and muster an army like the
army that you have lost, horse for horse, and chariot for chariot. Then we will
fight against them in the plain, and surely we shall be stronger than they." And he
listened to their voice and did so.

Ahab Defeats Ben-hadad Again

[26]In the spring, Ben-hadad mustered the Syrians and went up to Aphek to fight
against Israel. [27]And the people of Israel were mustered and were provisioned
and went against them. The people of Israel encamped before them like two little
flocks of goats, but the Syrians filled the country. [28]And a man of God came near
and said to the king of Israel, "Thus says the LORD, 'Because the Syrians have said,
"The LORD is a god of the hills but he is not a god of the valleys," therefore I will
give all this great multitude into your hand, and you shall know that I am the
LORD.'" [29]And they encamped opposite one another seven days. Then on the seventh day the battle was joined. And the people of Israel struck down of the Syrians
100,000 foot soldiers in one day. [30]And the rest fled into the city of Aphek, and the
wall fell upon 27,000 men who were left.
Ben-hadad also fled and entered an inner chamber in the city. [31]And his servants said to him, "Behold now, we have heard that the kings of the house of Israel
are merciful kings. Let us put sackcloth around our waists and ropes on our heads
and go out to the king of Israel. Perhaps he will spare your life." [32]So they tied
sackcloth around their waists and put ropes on their heads and went to the king of
Israel and said, "Your servant Ben-hadad says, 'Please, let me live.'" And he said,
"Does he still live? He is my brother." [33]Now the men were watching for a sign, and
they quickly took it up from him and said, "Yes, your brother Ben-hadad." Then
he said, "Go and bring him." Then Ben-hadad came out to him, and he caused
him to come up into the chariot. [34]And Ben-hadad said to him, "The cities that
my father took from your father I will restore, and you may establish bazaars for
yourself in Damascus, as my father did in Samaria." And Ahab said, "I will let you
go on these terms." So he made a covenant with him and let him go.

A Prophet Condemns Ben-hadad's Release

[35]And a certain man of the sons of the prophets said to his fellow at the command of the LORD, "Strike me, please." But the man refused to strike him. [36]Then
he said to him, "Because you have not obeyed the voice of the LORD, behold, as
soon as you have gone from me, a lion shall strike you down." And as soon as he
had departed from him, a lion met him and struck him down. [37]Then he found
another man and said, "Strike me, please." And the man struck him—struck him
and wounded him. [38]So the prophet departed and waited for the king by the way,
disguising himself with a bandage over his eyes. [39]And as the king passed, he cried
to the king and said, "Your servant went out into the midst of the battle, and behold, a soldier turned and brought a man to me and said, 'Guard this man; if by
any means he is missing, your life shall be for his life, or else you shall pay a talent[1] of silver.' [40]And as your servant was busy here and there, he was gone." The
king of Israel said to him, "So shall your judgment be; you yourself have decided
it." [41]Then he hurried to take the bandage away from his eyes, and the king of
Israel recognized him as one of the prophets. [42]And he said to him, "Thus says
the LORD, 'Because you have let go out of your hand the man whom I had devoted

[1]A *talent* was about 75 pounds or 34 kilograms

1 KINGS 20:28

GOD OF THE HILLS AND THE VALLEYS

The Syrians embarked on their second campaign in the Jordan Valley from Aphek, a city east of the Sea of Galilee. The hills had long provided a prime advantage for the military of the northern kingdom of Israel. The Syrians assumed the reason the Israelites had been victorious in the past was that their god held power in the hill country. They would soon learn, however, that the Lord was not merely "a god of the hills" but also the God of the valleys. Israel's military position was not what allowed them to be victorious; rather, it was the power of God at work, both in the hills and in the valleys, or plains (1Ki 20:23–25). The same is true for every aspect of the lives of God's people. Whether in the high places of life or in the valleys, God is faithful to his people. As the well-loved psalm recounts, "Even though I walk through the valley of the shadow of death, I will fear no evil, for you are with me" (Ps 23:4). The ever-present reality of God's Spirit allows believers to have hope, even in the deepest valleys of life.

to destruction,[1] therefore your life shall be for his life, and your people for his people.'" [43]And the king of Israel went to his house vexed and sullen and came to Samaria.

Naboth's Vineyard

21 Now Naboth the Jezreelite had a vineyard in Jezreel, beside the palace of Ahab king of Samaria. [2]And after this Ahab said to Naboth, "Give me your vineyard, that I may have it for a vegetable garden, because it is near my house, and I will give you a better vineyard for it; or, if it seems good to you, I will give you its value in money." [3]But Naboth said to Ahab, "The LORD forbid that I should give you the inheritance of my fathers." [4]And Ahab went into his house vexed and sullen because of what Naboth the Jezreelite had said to him, for he had said, "I will not give you the inheritance of my fathers." And he lay down on his bed and turned away his face and would eat no food.

[5]But Jezebel his wife came to him and said to him, "Why is your spirit so vexed that you eat no food?" [6]And he said to her, "Because I spoke to Naboth the Jezreelite and said to him, 'Give me your vineyard for money, or else, if it please you, I will give you another vineyard for it.' And he answered, 'I will not give you my vineyard.'" [7]And Jezebel his wife said to him, "Do you now govern Israel? Arise and eat bread and let your heart be cheerful; I will give you the vineyard of Naboth the Jezreelite."

[8]So she wrote letters in Ahab's name and sealed them with his seal, and she sent the letters to the elders and the leaders who lived with Naboth in his city. [9]And she wrote in the letters, "Proclaim a fast, and set Naboth at the head of the people. [10]And set two worthless men opposite him, and let them bring a charge against him, saying, 'You have cursed[2] God and the king.' Then take him out and stone him to death." [11]And the men of his city, the elders and the leaders who lived in his city, did as Jezebel had sent word to them. As it was written in the letters that she had sent to them, [12]they proclaimed a fast and set Naboth at the head of the people. [13]And the two worthless men came in and sat opposite him. And the worthless men brought a charge against Naboth in the presence of the people, saying, "Naboth cursed God and the king." So they took him outside the city and stoned him to death with stones. [14]Then they sent to Jezebel, saying, "Naboth has been stoned; he is dead."

[15]As soon as Jezebel heard that Naboth had been stoned and was dead, Jezebel said to Ahab, "Arise, take possession of the vineyard of Naboth the Jezreelite, which he refused to give you for money, for Naboth is not alive, but dead." [16]And as soon as Ahab heard that Naboth was dead, Ahab arose to go down to the vineyard of Naboth the Jezreelite, to take possession of it.

The LORD Condemns Ahab

[17]Then the word of the LORD came to Elijah the Tishbite, saying, [18]"Arise, go down to meet Ahab king of Israel, who is in Samaria; behold, he is in the vineyard of Naboth, where he has gone to take possession. [19]And you shall say to him, 'Thus says the LORD, "Have you killed and also taken possession?"' And you shall say to him, 'Thus says the LORD: "In the place where dogs licked up the blood of Naboth shall dogs lick your own blood."'"

[20]Ahab said to Elijah, "Have you found me, O my enemy?" He answered, "I have found you, because you have sold yourself to do what is evil in the sight of the LORD. [21]Behold, I will bring disaster upon you. I will utterly burn you up, and will cut off from Ahab every male, bond or free, in Israel. [22]And I will make your house like the house of Jeroboam the son of Nebat, and like the house of Baasha the son of Ahijah, for the anger to which you have provoked me, and because you have made Israel to sin. [23]And of Jezebel the LORD also said, 'The dogs shall eat

1 KINGS 21:17–19

BLOOD POURED OUT

The Lord's graphic and decisive judgment on King Ahab corresponded to the king's blatant disregard for the commandments of God. Dogs licked up the blood of this once-mighty king by the pool in Samaria (22:37–38). Ahab's death stands as a stark testimony to the dire consequences of abandoning God's law. In taking Naboth's vineyard (cf. Dt 19:14), Ahab revealed that he loved neither God nor his neighbor—the totality of the law of God.

King Jesus lived and died for rebels who fail to love God and their neighbor. His blood was poured out, like King Ahab, as a result of human sin. Jesus, however, was not guilty of sin himself. Rather, he willingly gave his life so that his blood would satisfy the wrath of God, which all of humanity deserved. By faith and repentance, sinful rebels like Ahab can avoid the terrible fate that they deserve.

[1]That is, set apart (devoted) as an offering to the Lord (for destruction) [2]Hebrew *blessed*; also verse 13

Jezebel within the walls of Jezreel.' [24]Anyone belonging to Ahab who dies in the city the dogs shall eat, and anyone of his who dies in the open country the birds of the heavens shall eat."

Ahab's Repentance

[25](There was none who sold himself to do what was evil in the sight of the LORD like Ahab, whom Jezebel his wife incited. [26]He acted very abominably in going after idols, as the Amorites had done, whom the LORD cast out before the people of Israel.)

[27]And when Ahab heard those words, he tore his clothes and put sackcloth on his flesh and fasted and lay in sackcloth and went about dejectedly. [28]And the word of the LORD came to Elijah the Tishbite, saying, [29]"Have you seen how Ahab has humbled himself before me? Because he has humbled himself before me, I will not bring the disaster in his days; but in his son's days I will bring the disaster upon his house."

Ahab and the False Prophets

22 For three years Syria and Israel continued without war. [2]But in the third year Jehoshaphat the king of Judah came down to the king of Israel. [3]And the king of Israel said to his servants, "Do you know that Ramoth-gilead belongs to us, and we keep quiet and do not take it out of the hand of the king of Syria?" [4]And he said to Jehoshaphat, "Will you go with me to battle at Ramoth-gilead?" And Jehoshaphat said to the king of Israel, "I am as you are, my people as your people, my horses as your horses."

[5]And Jehoshaphat said to the king of Israel, "Inquire first for the word of the LORD." [6]Then the king of Israel gathered the prophets together, about four hundred men, and said to them, "Shall I go to battle against Ramoth-gilead, or shall I refrain?" And they said, "Go up, for the Lord will give it into the hand of the king." [7]But Jehoshaphat said, "Is there not here another prophet of the LORD of whom we may inquire?" [8]And the king of Israel said to Jehoshaphat, "There is yet one man by whom we may inquire of the LORD, Micaiah the son of Imlah, but I hate him, for he never prophesies good concerning me, but evil." And Jehoshaphat said, "Let not the king say so." [9]Then the king of Israel summoned an officer and said, "Bring quickly Micaiah the son of Imlah." [10]Now the king of Israel and Jehoshaphat the king of Judah were sitting on their thrones, arrayed in their robes, at the threshing floor at the entrance of the gate of Samaria, and all the prophets were prophesying before them. [11]And Zedekiah the son of Chenaanah made for himself horns of iron and said, "Thus says the LORD, 'With these you shall push the Syrians until they are destroyed.'" [12]And all the prophets prophesied so and said, "Go up to Ramoth-gilead and triumph; the LORD will give it into the hand of the king."

Micaiah Prophesies Against Ahab

[13]And the messenger who went to summon Micaiah said to him, "Behold, the words of the prophets with one accord are favorable to the king. Let your word be like the word of one of them, and speak favorably." [14]But Micaiah said, "As the LORD lives, what the LORD says to me, that I will speak." [15]And when he had come to the king, the king said to him, "Micaiah, shall we go to Ramoth-gilead to battle, or shall we refrain?" And he answered him, "Go up and triumph; the LORD will give it into the hand of the king." [16]But the king said to him, "How many times shall I make you swear that you speak to me nothing but the truth in the name of the LORD?" [17]And he said, "I saw all Israel scattered on the mountains, as sheep that have no shepherd. And the LORD said, 'These have no master; let each return to his home in peace.'" [18]And the king of Israel said to Jehoshaphat, "Did I not tell you that he would not prophesy good concerning me, but evil?" [19]And Micaiah said, "Therefore hear the word of the LORD: I saw the LORD sitting on his throne,

and all the host of heaven standing beside him on his right hand and on his left;
[20]and the LORD said, 'Who will entice Ahab, that he may go up and fall at Ramoth-gilead?' And one said one thing, and another said another. [21]Then a spirit came
forward and stood before the LORD, saying, 'I will entice him.' [22]And the LORD said
to him, 'By what means?' And he said, 'I will go out, and will be a lying spirit in
the mouth of all his prophets.' And he said, 'You are to entice him, and you shall
succeed; go out and do so.' [23]Now therefore behold, the LORD has put a lying spirit
in the mouth of all these your prophets; the LORD has declared disaster for you."
[24]Then Zedekiah the son of Chenaanah came near and struck Micaiah on the
cheek and said, "How did the Spirit of the LORD go from me to speak to you?"
[25]And Micaiah said, "Behold, you shall see on that day when you go into an inner chamber to hide yourself." [26]And the king of Israel said, "Seize Micaiah, and
take him back to Amon the governor of the city and to Joash the king's son, [27]and
say, 'Thus says the king, "Put this fellow in prison and feed him meager rations
of bread and water, until I come in peace."'" [28]And Micaiah said, "If you return
in peace, the LORD has not spoken by me." And he said, "Hear, all you peoples!"

Ahab Killed in Battle

[29]So the king of Israel and Jehoshaphat the king of Judah went up to Ramoth-gilead. [30]And the king of Israel said to Jehoshaphat, "I will disguise myself and go
into battle, but you wear your robes." And the king of Israel disguised himself and
went into battle. [31]Now the king of Syria had commanded the thirty-two captains
of his chariots, "Fight with neither small nor great, but only with the king of Israel." [32]And when the captains of the chariots saw Jehoshaphat, they said, "It is
surely the king of Israel." So they turned to fight against him. And Jehoshaphat
cried out. [33]And when the captains of the chariots saw that it was not the king of
Israel, they turned back from pursuing him. [34]But a certain man drew his bow at
random[1] and struck the king of Israel between the scale armor and the breastplate. Therefore he said to the driver of his chariot, "Turn around and carry me
out of the battle, for I am wounded." [35]And the battle continued that day, and the
king was propped up in his chariot facing the Syrians, until at evening he died.
And the blood of the wound flowed into the bottom of the chariot. [36]And about
sunset a cry went through the army, "Every man to his city, and every man to his
country!"
[37]So the king died, and was brought to Samaria. And they buried the king in
Samaria. [38]And they washed the chariot by the pool of Samaria, and the dogs
licked up his blood, and the prostitutes washed themselves in it, according to the
word of the LORD that he had spoken. [39]Now the rest of the acts of Ahab and all
that he did, and the ivory house that he built and all the cities that he built, are
they not written in the Book of the Chronicles of the Kings of Israel? [40]So Ahab
slept with his fathers, and Ahaziah his son reigned in his place.

Jehoshaphat Reigns in Judah

[41]Jehoshaphat the son of Asa began to reign over Judah in the fourth year of
Ahab king of Israel. [42]Jehoshaphat was thirty-five years old when he began to
reign, and he reigned twenty-five years in Jerusalem. His mother's name was
Azubah the daughter of Shilhi. [43]He walked in all the way of Asa his father. He did
not turn aside from it, doing what was right in the sight of the LORD. Yet the high
places were not taken away, and the people still sacrificed and made offerings on
the high places. [44]Jehoshaphat also made peace with the king of Israel.
[45]Now the rest of the acts of Jehoshaphat, and his might that he showed, and
how he warred, are they not written in the Book of the Chronicles of the Kings of
Judah? [46]And from the land he exterminated the remnant of the male cult prostitutes who remained in the days of his father Asa.

[1]Hebrew *in his innocence*

A PROPHET'S WARNING

Jehoshaphat, the good king of Judah, and Ahab, the wicked king of Israel, agreed to work together to fight the king of Syria and take back Ramoth-gilead. Jehoshaphat sought counsel from the Lord before going into battle. Ahab, desiring to secure military victory, was willing to seek God's direction as well, so long as that direction corresponded with what he wanted to hear. The 400 prophets Ahab gathered did just that — they told Ahab to go into battle and that God would give the land into his hand.

At Jehoshaphat's urging, Ahab sent for the prophet Micaiah. Complaining that Micaiah never prophesied anything good concerning him, Ahab assumed that Micaiah's words would contradict that of the other prophets. At first, it appeared as if God's prophet agreed with the pagan prophets who had spoken beforehand. Ahab continued his inquiry, suspecting that the prophet had more to reveal. His second message, though cryptic, sounded a clear note of warning. The Lord, in fact, had decreed disaster against the armies of Israel and Judah, which would result in the death of King Ahab. In spite of the warning, Jehoshaphat and Ahab rode off into battle and were soundly defeated. The seemingly random death of Ahab was a sure testimony to the truthfulness of God's message through the prophet Micaiah.

Throughout history, the Word of God has elicited a wide range of reactions. Some people, seeking to honor God and walk in his ways, respond to the Word of God with humility, repentance, and obedience. Others, like the religious leaders of Jesus' day, demonstrate their hardness of heart by turning a deaf ear to the commands and warnings of God. Jesus continually denounced the leadership of these "blind guides." He claimed that not only were they deceived but they were also leading others into rebellion (Mt 15:14; 23:16,24). Like the 400 false prophets, the religious leaders of Jesus' day were leading people to follow a system that would result in their condemnation and ultimate death. Jesus, as the truer and better prophet, declared to them the futility of their behavior and pointed them to the path to life. But like King Ahab before them, many turned a deaf ear to these words.

[47]There was no king in Edom; a deputy was king. [48]Jehoshaphat made ships of
Tarshish to go to Ophir for gold, but they did not go, for the ships were wrecked
at Ezion-geber. [49]Then Ahaziah the son of Ahab said to Jehoshaphat, "Let my ser-
vants go with your servants in the ships," but Jehoshaphat was not willing. [50]And
Jehoshaphat slept with his fathers and was buried with his fathers in the city of
David his father, and Jehoram his son reigned in his place.

Ahaziah Reigns in Israel

[51]Ahaziah the son of Ahab began to reign over Israel in Samaria in the seventeenth year of Jehoshaphat king of Judah, and he reigned two years over Israel.
[52]He did what was evil in the sight of the LORD and walked in the way of his father
and in the way of his mother and in the way of Jeroboam the son of Nebat, who
made Israel to sin. [53]He served Baal and worshiped him and provoked the LORD,
the God of Israel, to anger in every way that his father had done.

JESUS: OUR PERFECT PROPHET

2 KINGS

2 KINGS

ELISHA SUCCEEDS ELIJAH *c. 848 BC*	FALL OF ISRAEL *c. 722 BC*	FALL OF JUDAH *c. 586 BC*

The book of 2 Kings continues the narrative of the people of God as they divide into a northern and a southern kingdom. It follows a timeline from the ascension of the prophet Elijah until the ultimate destruction and exile of the divided nations of Israel (722 BC) and Judah (586 BC). This story of the people of God emphasizes the cyclical pattern of sin — both among the leaders of the two nations and the people themselves. The leaders and the people rebelled against God, incurred his judgment, repented, and promised to be faithful, only to fall into greater and greater forms of evil.

The book continues the chronological outline of the leaders of the two nations found in 1 Kings, beginning with the reigns of Ahaziah in the northern kingdom (853 – 852 BC) and Jehoshaphat in the southern kingdom (872 – 848 BC). The narrative follows two vibrant prophetic voices of the time — Elijah and Elisha — and recounts the stories of those shaped by their extended ministries (Elijah ministered for 27 years; Elisha for 51). These prophets provide insight into the role of Jesus, who would invade a spiritually dark world and call people to return to the one true and living God, to live under his rule and reign forever.

At one critical juncture in Israel's history, Jehu, the king of the northern kingdom, *purged the rampant* Baal worship that consistently plagued Israel (2Ki 10:18 – 28). Unfortunately, rather than leading the people to worship the one true God, Jehu continued to allow the worship of the golden calves set up by Jeroboam I (2Ki 10:29). During this time the southern kingdom did not fare much better, languishing under the leadership of the idolatrous king Ahaziah and his wicked mother, Queen Athaliah (2Ki 8:25 – 27; 11:1 – 3).

The death of King Zechariah in 752 BC marked the beginning of a period of rapid decline in the northern kingdom, mirroring its spiritual status. Foolish military and political alliances, combined with the people's spiritual lethargy and moral debauchery, led to their defeat at the hands of the Assyrians in 722 BC. Meanwhile, King Ahaz led the southern kingdom to a similar fate due to his idolatry and rebellion. A large portion of the book of 2 Kings describes the devolution of the nation from the righteous king Hezekiah to the wicked sons and grandsons of Josiah. Under their leadership, the nation faced three invasions and deportations — the last of which happened in 586 BC. Though the book ends tragically with each kingdom cast out of the land, Jehoiachin's release from prison at the end of the book provides a glimmer of hope (25:27 – 30). The Lord would remain faithful to his people and once again restore them to the land.

Throughout the Old Testament, Israel's experience serves as a template for the larger group of people of God throughout history. God's steadfast faithfulness never fails; those who follow him experience his blessing, and those who rebel against him experience trouble (Jn 3:36). The hopeful passages at the end of this book point forward to a time when all peoples will recognize Jesus' just and perfect reign and rule (Php 2:9 – 11) and when his followers will enjoy being in his presence forever.

SO NOW, O LORD OUR GOD, SAVE US, PLEASE,
FROM HIS HAND, THAT ALL THE KINGDOMS OF THE EARTH
MAY KNOW THAT YOU, O LORD, ARE GOD ALONE.

---

2 Kings 19:19

2 KINGS

Elijah Denounces Ahaziah

1 After the death of Ahab, Moab rebelled against Israel.
2Now Ahaziah fell through the lattice in his upper chamber in Samaria, and
lay sick; so he sent messengers, telling them, "Go, inquire of Baal-zebub, the god
of Ekron, whether I shall recover from this sickness." 3But the angel of the LORD
said to Elijah the Tishbite, "Arise, go up to meet the messengers of the king of
Samaria, and say to them, 'Is it because there is no God in Israel that you are going
to inquire of Baal-zebub, the god of Ekron? 4Now therefore thus says the LORD,
You shall not come down from the bed to which you have gone up, but you shall
surely die.'" So Elijah went.
5The messengers returned to the king, and he said to them, "Why have you
returned?" 6And they said to him, "There came a man to meet us, and said to
us, 'Go back to the king who sent you, and say to him, Thus says the LORD, Is it
because there is no God in Israel that you are sending to inquire of Baal-zebub,
the god of Ekron? Therefore you shall not come down from the bed to which you
have gone up, but you shall surely die.'" 7He said to them, "What kind of man was
he who came to meet you and told you these things?" 8They answered him, "He
wore a garment of hair, with a belt of leather about his waist." And he said, "It is
Elijah the Tishbite."
9Then the king sent to him a captain of fifty men with his fifty. He went up to
Elijah, who was sitting on the top of a hill, and said to him, "O man of God, the
king says, 'Come down.'" 10But Elijah answered the captain of fifty, "If I am a man
of God, let fire come down from heaven and consume you and your fifty." Then
fire came down from heaven and consumed him and his fifty.
11Again the king sent to him another captain of fifty men with his fifty. And
he answered and said to him, "O man of God, this is the king's order, 'Come down
quickly!'" 12But Elijah answered them, "If I am a man of God, let fire come down
from heaven and consume you and your fifty." Then the fire of God came down
from heaven and consumed him and his fifty.
13Again the king sent the captain of a third fifty with his fifty. And the third
captain of fifty went up and came and fell on his knees before Elijah and entreated
him, "O man of God, please let my life, and the life of these fifty servants of yours,
be precious in your sight. 14Behold, fire came down from heaven and consumed
the two former captains of fifty men with their fifties, but now let my life be precious in your sight." 15Then the angel of the LORD said to Elijah, "Go down with
him; do not be afraid of him." So he arose and went down with him to the king
16and said to him, "Thus says the LORD, 'Because you have sent messengers to
inquire of Baal-zebub, the god of Ekron—is it because there is no God in Israel to
inquire of his word?—therefore you shall not come down from the bed to which
you have gone up, but you shall surely die.'"
17So he died according to the word of the LORD that Elijah had spoken. Jehoram
became king in his place in the second year of Jehoram the son of Jehoshaphat,
king of Judah, because Ahaziah had no son. 18Now the rest of the acts of Ahaziah
that he did, are they not written in the Book of the Chronicles of the Kings of
Israel?

Elijah Taken to Heaven

2 Now when the LORD was about to take Elijah up to heaven by a whirlwind,
Elijah and Elisha were on their way from Gilgal. 2And Elijah said to Elisha,
"Please stay here, for the LORD has sent me as far as Bethel." But Elisha said, "As
the LORD lives, and as you yourself live, I will not leave you." So they went down to

---

2 KINGS 2:1–16

DIVIDING THE WATERS

The parting of the waters of the Jordan confirmed the succession of the prophets from Elijah to Elisha. This was certainly not the first time that a God-ordained leader had miraculously parted water—Moses did it at the Red Sea (Ex 14:21–22), and Joshua did it at the Jordan (Jos 3:7–17). In the minds of the original readers, water was a symbol of death and chaos due to its seemingly uncontrollable and unexplainable power. The parting of the waters on each occasion not only allowed the people to pass safely, but it also symbolized that God had the power over death and destruction. Chaos was rendered impotent by the all-surpassing greatness and might of God. In its place, the almighty God of Israel provided safety and a sure passage for his people. In a far greater way, Jesus' baptism (Mt 3:13–17) and his miraculous resurrection from the dead (Lk 24:1–8) demonstrate that he has overcome the powers of this broken world and provides his people with a way of escape.

Bethel. 3And the sons of the prophets who were in Bethel came out to Elisha and said to him, "Do you know that today the LORD will take away your master from over you?" And he said, "Yes, I know it; keep quiet."

4Elijah said to him, "Elisha, please stay here, for the LORD has sent me to Jericho." But he said, "As the LORD lives, and as you yourself live, I will not leave you." So they came to Jericho. 5The sons of the prophets who were at Jericho drew near to Elisha and said to him, "Do you know that today the LORD will take away your master from over you?" And he answered, "Yes, I know it; keep quiet."

6Then Elijah said to him, "Please stay here, for the LORD has sent me to the Jordan." But he said, "As the LORD lives, and as you yourself live, I will not leave you." So the two of them went on. 7Fifty men of the sons of the prophets also went and stood at some distance from them, as they both were standing by the Jordan. 8Then Elijah took his cloak and rolled it up and struck the water, and the water was parted to the one side and to the other, till the two of them could go over on dry ground.

9When they had crossed, Elijah said to Elisha, "Ask what I shall do for you, before I am taken from you." And Elisha said, "Please let there be a double portion of your spirit on me." 10And he said, "You have asked a hard thing; yet, if you see me as I am being taken from you, it shall be so for you, but if you do not see me, it shall not be so." 11And as they still went on and talked, behold, chariots of fire and horses of fire separated the two of them. And Elijah went up by a whirlwind into heaven. 12And Elisha saw it and he cried, "My father, my father! The chariots of Israel and its horsemen!" And he saw him no more.

Then he took hold of his own clothes and tore them in two pieces. 13And he took up the cloak of Elijah that had fallen from him and went back and stood on the bank of the Jordan. 14Then he took the cloak of Elijah that had fallen from him and struck the water, saying, "Where is the LORD, the God of Elijah?" And when he had struck the water, the water was parted to the one side and to the other, and Elisha went over.

Elisha Succeeds Elijah

15Now when the sons of the prophets who were at Jericho saw him opposite them, they said, "The spirit of Elijah rests on Elisha." And they came to meet him and bowed to the ground before him. 16And they said to him, "Behold now, there are with your servants fifty strong men. Please let them go and seek your master. It may be that the Spirit of the LORD has caught him up and cast him upon some mountain or into some valley." And he said, "You shall not send." 17But when they urged him till he was ashamed, he said, "Send." They sent therefore fifty men. And for three days they sought him but did not find him. 18And they came back to him while he was staying at Jericho, and he said to them, "Did I not say to you, 'Do not go'?"

19Now the men of the city said to Elisha, "Behold, the situation of this city is pleasant, as my lord sees, but the water is bad, and the land is unfruitful." 20He said, "Bring me a new bowl, and put salt in it." So they brought it to him. 21Then he went to the spring of water and threw salt in it and said, "Thus says the LORD, I have healed this water; from now on neither death nor miscarriage shall come from it." 22So the water has been healed to this day, according to the word that Elisha spoke.

23He went up from there to Bethel, and while he was going up on the way, some small boys came out of the city and jeered at him, saying, "Go up, you baldhead! Go up, you baldhead!" 24And he turned around, and when he saw them, he cursed them in the name of the LORD. And two she-bears came out of the woods and tore forty-two of the boys. 25From there he went on to Mount Carmel, and from there he returned to Samaria.

AN ASCENSION PREVIEW

Elijah's unique ascension into heaven testified to his vital role as a prophet to the people of God at a very critical stage in their history. Elijah shared many similarities with John the Baptist, who would come later to help prepare the way for Jesus. Both John and Elijah lived in the desert, confronted the sinfulness of their day, and urged the people to turn back to God. Jesus himself even pointed out the close association between these two mighty prophets (Mt 17:9 – 13). By his ascension into heaven, Elijah foreshadowed what Jesus would one day do (Lk 24:51). Luke records that those who witnessed Jesus' ascension reacted in worship. Surely, those who witnessed Elijah's miraculous ascension had a similar feeling of awe, fear, and worship — not on account of Elijah, but on account of the glory of God.

Paul encouraged the church at Thessalonica as people raised questions about Jesus' return. Believers at that time expected Jesus to return during their lifetime. As some of the believers died, other believers began to question what would happen to those who died before the second coming of Jesus. Paul told the church to encourage each other with reminders of their future with Christ (1Th 4:17 – 18). The ascension of Jesus is a precursor to what will happen to all who trust in Christ's finished work. Jesus will return, and the dead will rise, join with those who are alive physically and in Christ, and be called up to the Lord (1Th 4:13 – 18). The ascensions of Elijah and Jesus provide a preview for what will happen to all those who have placed their faith in Jesus.

This hope and promise gives all followers of Jesus confidence and strength to endure life in this fallen and broken world. Following Elijah's ascension, Elisha demonstrated the power of God on earth by working a host of miracles (2Ki 2:13 – 22; 4:1 — 6:23). Jesus' disciples, following his ascension and the outpouring of the Holy Spirit at Pentecost, also performed miracles which demonstrated the power of God (Ac 2:43). Today, believers know the power of God and the future hope that awaits all who are in Christ, and they can fully trust that God can and will use them to accomplish great things as well. Since believers know that they *will one day join with* Jesus, they can live out their days without fear. By the power of God's Spirit, believers can live confidently and courageously, trusting that death does not have the final say.

Moab Rebels Against Israel

3 In the eighteenth year of Jehoshaphat king of Judah, Jehoram the son of Ahab became king over Israel in Samaria, and he reigned twelve years. 2He did what was evil in the sight of the LORD, though not like his father and mother, for he put away the pillar of Baal that his father had made. 3Nevertheless, he clung to the sin of Jeroboam the son of Nebat, which he made Israel to sin; he did not depart from it.

4Now Mesha king of Moab was a sheep breeder, and he had to deliver to the king of Israel 100,000 lambs and the wool of 100,000 rams. 5But when Ahab died, the king of Moab rebelled against the king of Israel. 6So King Jehoram marched out of Samaria at that time and mustered all Israel. 7And he went and sent word to Jehoshaphat king of Judah: "The king of Moab has rebelled against me. Will you go with me to battle against Moab?" And he said, "I will go. I am as you are, my people as your people, my horses as your horses." 8Then he said, "By which way shall we march?" Jehoram answered, "By the way of the wilderness of Edom."

9So the king of Israel went with the king of Judah and the king of Edom. And when they had made a circuitous march of seven days, there was no water for the army or for the animals that followed them. 10Then the king of Israel said, "Alas! The LORD has called these three kings to give them into the hand of Moab." 11And Jehoshaphat said, "Is there no prophet of the LORD here, through whom we may inquire of the LORD?" Then one of the king of Israel's servants answered, "Elisha the son of Shaphat is here, who poured water on the hands of Elijah." 12And Jehoshaphat said, "The word of the LORD is with him." So the king of Israel and Jehoshaphat and the king of Edom went down to him.

13And Elisha said to the king of Israel, "What have I to do with you? Go to the prophets of your father and to the prophets of your mother." But the king of Israel said to him, "No; it is the LORD who has called these three kings to give them into the hand of Moab." 14And Elisha said, "As the LORD of hosts lives, before whom I stand, were it not that I have regard for Jehoshaphat the king of Judah, I would neither look at you nor see you. 15But now bring me a musician." And when the musician played, the hand of the LORD came upon him. 16And he said, "Thus says the LORD, 'I will make this dry streambed full of pools.' 17For thus says the LORD, 'You shall not see wind or rain, but that streambed shall be filled with water, so that you shall drink, you, your livestock, and your animals.' 18This is a light thing in the sight of the LORD. He will also give the Moabites into your hand, 19and you shall attack every fortified city and every choice city, and shall fell every good tree and stop up all springs of water and ruin every good piece of land with stones." 20The next morning, about the time of offering the sacrifice, behold, water came from the direction of Edom, till the country was filled with water.

21When all the Moabites heard that the kings had come up to fight against them, all who were able to put on armor, from the youngest to the oldest, were called out and were drawn up at the border. 22And when they rose early in the morning and the sun shone on the water, the Moabites saw the water opposite them as red as blood. 23And they said, "This is blood; the kings have surely fought together and struck one another down. Now then, Moab, to the spoil!" 24But when they came to the camp of Israel, the Israelites rose and struck the Moabites, till they fled before them. And they went forward, striking the Moabites as they went.[1] 25And they overthrew the cities, and on every good piece of land every man threw a stone until it was covered. They stopped every spring of water and felled all the good trees, till only its stones were left in Kir-hareseth, and the slingers surrounded and attacked it. 26When the king of Moab saw that the battle was going against him, he took with him 700 swordsmen to break through,

[1]Septuagint; the meaning of the Hebrew is uncertain

2 KINGS 3:1–20

THE GIFT OF WATER

Jehoram was the king of Israel in Samaria, and though he did not worship the false god Baal like his father, Ahab, he was still an evil king. Jehoram went to war with Moab over lambs and wool, and to bolster his chances of military success he organized an alliance with Judah and Edom. Despite Jehoram's reputation, Jehoshaphat, king of Judah, still joined the alliance without seeking God's wisdom or consulting with the prophet Elisha. Only after the coalition wandered lost in the wilderness of Edom for seven days and almost died of thirst did they seek God's help through the prophet. Elisha told them that God would miraculously provide. Overnight, without wind or rain, God filled the dry valley with water and brought confusion and ultimately defeat to the Moabites. This provision echoed an earlier incident in the wilderness at Horeb when God had miraculously rescued his people by causing water to flow where there was none (Ex 17:6).

Many years later, he provided life-sustaining water of an even better kind through his Son. Jesus offers living water to God's people. In Christ, thirsty souls can be satisfied and sins can be cleansed (Jn 4:7–14). In him, a wellspring forever flows with life (Rev 22:1).

opposite the king of Edom, but they could not. 27Then he took his oldest son who was to reign in his place and offered him for a burnt offering on the wall. And there came great wrath against Israel. And they withdrew from him and returned to their own land.

Elisha and the Widow's Oil

4 Now the wife of one of the sons of the prophets cried to Elisha, "Your servant my husband is dead, and you know that your servant feared the LORD, but the creditor has come to take my two children to be his slaves." 2And Elisha said to her, "What shall I do for you? Tell me; what have you in the house?" And she said, "Your servant has nothing in the house except a jar of oil." 3Then he said, "Go outside, borrow vessels from all your neighbors, empty vessels and not too few. 4Then go in and shut the door behind yourself and your sons and pour into all these vessels. And when one is full, set it aside." 5So she went from him and shut the door behind herself and her sons. And as she poured they brought the vessels to her. 6When the vessels were full, she said to her son, "Bring me another vessel." And he said to her, "There is not another." Then the oil stopped flowing. 7She came and told the man of God, and he said, "Go, sell the oil and pay your debts, and you and your sons can live on the rest."

Elisha and the Shunammite Woman

8One day Elisha went on to Shunem, where a wealthy woman lived, who urged him to eat some food. So whenever he passed that way, he would turn in there to eat food. 9And she said to her husband, "Behold now, I know that this is a holy man of God who is continually passing our way. 10Let us make a small room on the roof with walls and put there for him a bed, a table, a chair, and a lamp, so that whenever he comes to us, he can go in there."

11One day he came there, and he turned into the chamber and rested there. 12And he said to Gehazi his servant, "Call this Shunammite." When he had called her, she stood before him. 13And he said to him, "Say now to her, 'See, you have taken all this trouble for us; what is to be done for you? Would you have a word spoken on your behalf to the king or to the commander of the army?' " She answered, "I dwell among my own people." 14And he said, "What then is to be done for her?" Gehazi answered, "Well, she has no son, and her husband is old." 15He said, "Call her." And when he had called her, she stood in the doorway. 16And he said, "At this season, about this time next year, you shall embrace a son." And she said, "No, my lord, O man of God; do not lie to your servant." 17But the woman conceived, and she bore a son about that time the following spring, as Elisha had said to her.

Elisha Raises the Shunammite's Son

18When the child had grown, he went out one day to his father among the reapers. 19And he said to his father, "Oh, my head, my head!" The father said to his servant, "Carry him to his mother." 20And when he had lifted him and brought him to his mother, the child sat on her lap till noon, and then he died. 21And she went up and laid him on the bed of the man of God and shut the door behind him and went out. 22Then she called to her husband and said, "Send me one of the servants and one of the donkeys, that I may quickly go to the man of God and come back again." 23And he said, "Why will you go to him today? It is neither new moon nor Sabbath." She said, "All is well." 24Then she saddled the donkey, and she said to her servant, "Urge the animal on; do not slacken the pace for me unless I tell you." 25So she set out and came to the man of God at Mount Carmel.

When the man of God saw her coming, he said to Gehazi his servant, "Look, there is the Shunammite. 26Run at once to meet her and say to her, 'Is all well with you? Is all well with your husband? Is all well with the child?' " And she answered,

"All is well." 27And when she came to the mountain to the man of God, she caught hold of his feet. And Gehazi came to push her away. But the man of God said, "Leave her alone, for she is in bitter distress, and the LORD has hidden it from me and has not told me." 28Then she said, "Did I ask my lord for a son? Did I not say, 'Do not deceive me?'" 29He said to Gehazi, "Tie up your garment and take my staff in your hand and go. If you meet anyone, do not greet him, and if anyone greets you, do not reply. And lay my staff on the face of the child." 30Then the mother of the child said, "As the LORD lives and as you yourself live, I will not leave you." So he arose and followed her. 31Gehazi went on ahead and laid the staff on the face of the child, but there was no sound or sign of life. Therefore he returned to meet him and told him, "The child has not awakened."

32When Elisha came into the house, he saw the child lying dead on his bed. 33So he went in and shut the door behind the two of them and prayed to the LORD. 34Then he went up and lay on the child, putting his mouth on his mouth, his eyes on his eyes, and his hands on his hands. And as he stretched himself upon him, the flesh of the child became warm. 35Then he got up again and walked once back and forth in the house, and went up and stretched himself upon him. The child sneezed seven times, and the child opened his eyes. 36Then he summoned Gehazi and said, "Call this Shunammite." So he called her. And when she came to him, he said, "Pick up your son." 37She came and fell at his feet, bowing to the ground. Then she picked up her son and went out.

Elisha Purifies the Deadly Stew

38And Elisha came again to Gilgal when there was a famine in the land. And as the sons of the prophets were sitting before him, he said to his servant, "Set on the large pot, and boil stew for the sons of the prophets." 39One of them went out into the field to gather herbs, and found a wild vine and gathered from it his lap full of wild gourds, and came and cut them up into the pot of stew, not knowing what they were. 40And they poured out some for the men to eat. But while they were eating of the stew, they cried out, "O man of God, there is death in the pot!" And they could not eat it. 41He said, "Then bring flour." And he threw it into the pot and said, "Pour some out for the men, that they may eat." And there was no harm in the pot.

42A man came from Baal-shalishah, bringing the man of God bread of the firstfruits, twenty loaves of barley and fresh ears of grain in his sack. And Elisha said, "Give to the men, that they may eat." 43But his servant said, "How can I set this before a hundred men?" So he repeated, "Give them to the men, that they may eat, for thus says the LORD, 'They shall eat and have some left.'" 44So he set it before them. And they ate and had some left, according to the word of the LORD.

Naaman Healed of Leprosy

5 Naaman, commander of the army of the king of Syria, was a great man with his master and in high favor, because by him the LORD had given victory to Syria. He was a mighty man of valor, but he was a leper.[1] 2Now the Syrians on one of their raids had carried off a little girl from the land of Israel, and she worked in the service of Naaman's wife. 3She said to her mistress, "Would that my lord were with the prophet who is in Samaria! He would cure him of his leprosy." 4So Naaman went in and told his lord, "Thus and so spoke the girl from the land of Israel." 5And the king of Syria said, "Go now, and I will send a letter to the king of Israel."

So he went, taking with him ten talents of silver, six thousand shekels[2] of gold, and ten changes of clothing. 6And he brought the letter to the king of Israel, which

[1] *Leprosy* was a term for several skin diseases; see Leviticus 13 [2] A *talent* was about 75 pounds or 34 kilograms; a *shekel* was about 2/5 ounce or 11 grams

2 KINGS 5:1–3

FAITH IN GOD'S CLEANSING POWER

The young servant girl displayed astounding trust in the power of God to heal her master, a Syrian commander named Naaman. She boldly declared that Elisha could heal Naaman and urged him to seek the prophet's help. Her faith was well founded, as the leprous Naaman was cleansed by the power of God through the prophet's words.

This cleansing prefigured the far greater cleansing that Jesus brings to those who place their trust and faith in him. The cleansing that Christ offers washes away the guilt of sin and ultimately provides a new body, freed from the brokenness of sin. Just as God's gracious healing power extended to Naaman, a non-Israelite, the cleansing power of Christ extends to those of the nation of Israel and beyond—to all tribes, tongues, and nations. The hope of salvation is founded not upon an abstract wish but upon the person of Christ himself. The object of believers' faith, the same God who the servant girl believed could heal Naaman, is worthy of supreme trust.

THE LIMITED POWER OF A MIRACLE

Elisha, like his predecessor Elijah (1Ki 17:17 – 24), performed the miracle of raising a child from death to life by the power of God. The mother was rightly distraught about the loss of her loved one. She had begged God for a child for many years, and now the boy that God had given to her had died. Upon arriving at the home, Elisha stretched himself over the lifeless boy's body, bringing him back to life and restoring him back to his grieving mother. Overwhelming joy must have flooded the mother at the sight of her son alive and breathing.

But sometimes even the most astonishing signs and wonders are not sufficient to turn hearts toward God. One day Jesus told the parable of the rich man and Lazarus. The rich man begged Abraham to send Lazarus back to his family so that his own brothers might avoid the torment that he was facing. Abraham reminded the rich man that the Law and the Prophets should be sufficient; if they rejected those, they would reject a man raised from the dead as well (Lk 16:19 – 31). Those listening to Jesus' parable that day needed to understand that witnessing a miracle — even a resurrection — does not create faith in God. Even when Jesus raised Mary and Martha's brother (who happened to be named Lazarus) from the dead, some of those who watched the miracle immediately left and told the Jewish religious leaders what Jesus had done, and they began plotting ways to kill Jesus (Jn 11).

These miracles and parables foreshadowed the day when Jesus forever defeated death. Without Jesus' resurrection, there would be no purpose for his death. His resurrection is what differentiates Jesus from every other prophet, teacher, or so-called god. Jesus is the resurrected Messiah. The miracles performed in Scripture all relied on God to intervene, thereby providing evidence for his power. But in Jesus, death itself was overcome.

The miracles and resurrection of Jesus display God's power over the grave and his care for the lost and the hurting. These signs and wonders also teach that God's people are to be ambassadors of mercy and compassion to those in need. Most importantly, each miracle and parable ultimately points people to Jesus — and the hope of sharing in Jesus' resurrection. That hope is offered freely to anyone who places their trust in him (Ro 6:4,8 – 11; 8:10 – 11; Col 3:1 – 4).

read, "When this letter reaches you, know that I have sent to you Naaman my
servant, that you may cure him of his leprosy." 7And when the king of Israel read
the letter, he tore his clothes and said, "Am I God, to kill and to make alive, that
this man sends word to me to cure a man of his leprosy? Only consider, and see
how he is seeking a quarrel with me."

8But when Elisha the man of God heard that the king of Israel had torn his
clothes, he sent to the king, saying, "Why have you torn your clothes? Let him
come now to me, that he may know that there is a prophet in Israel." 9So Naaman came with his horses and chariots and stood at the door of Elisha's house.
10And Elisha sent a messenger to him, saying, "Go and wash in the Jordan seven
times, and your flesh shall be restored, and you shall be clean." 11But Naaman
was angry and went away, saying, "Behold, I thought that he would surely come
out to me and stand and call upon the name of the LORD his God, and wave his
hand over the place and cure the leper. 12Are not Abana[1] and Pharpar, the rivers of Damascus, better than all the waters of Israel? Could I not wash in them
and be clean?" So he turned and went away in a rage. 13But his servants came
near and said to him, "My father, it is a great word the prophet has spoken to
you; will you not do it? Has he actually said to you, 'Wash, and be clean'?" 14So
he went down and dipped himself seven times in the Jordan, according to the
word of the man of God, and his flesh was restored like the flesh of a little child,
and he was clean.

Gehazi's Greed and Punishment

15Then he returned to the man of God, he and all his company, and he came
and stood before him. And he said, "Behold, I know that there is no God in all the
earth but in Israel; so accept now a present from your servant." 16But he said, "As
the LORD lives, before whom I stand, I will receive none." And he urged him to
take it, but he refused. 17Then Naaman said, "If not, please let there be given to
your servant two mule loads of earth, for from now on your servant will not offer
burnt offering or sacrifice to any god but the LORD. 18In this matter may the LORD
pardon your servant: when my master goes into the house of Rimmon to worship
there, leaning on my arm, and I bow myself in the house of Rimmon, when I bow
myself in the house of Rimmon, the LORD pardon your servant in this matter."
19He said to him, "Go in peace."

But when Naaman had gone from him a short distance, 20Gehazi, the servant
of Elisha the man of God, said, "See, my master has spared this Naaman the
Syrian, in not accepting from his hand what he brought. As the LORD lives, I will
run after him and get something from him." 21So Gehazi followed Naaman. And
when Naaman saw someone running after him, he got down from the chariot to
meet him and said, "Is all well?" 22And he said, "All is well. My master has sent
me to say, 'There have just now come to me from the hill country of Ephraim
two young men of the sons of the prophets. Please give them a talent of silver
and two changes of clothing.'" 23And Naaman said, "Be pleased to accept two
talents." And he urged him and tied up two talents of silver in two bags, with two
changes of clothing, and laid them on two of his servants. And they carried them
before Gehazi. 24And when he came to the hill, he took them from their hand
and put them in the house, and he sent the men away, and they departed. 25He
went in and stood before his master, and Elisha said to him, "Where have you
been, Gehazi?" And he said, "Your servant went nowhere." 26But he said to him,
"Did not my heart go when the man turned from his chariot to meet you? Was it
a time to accept money and garments, olive orchards and vineyards, sheep and
oxen, male servants and female servants? 27Therefore the leprosy of Naaman
shall cling to you and to your descendants forever." So he went out from his
presence a leper, like snow.

---

[1]Or *Amana*

The Axe Head Recovered

6 Now the sons of the prophets said to Elisha, "See, the place where we dwell
under your charge is too small for us. 2Let us go to the Jordan and each of us
get there a log, and let us make a place for us to dwell there." And he answered,
"Go." 3Then one of them said, "Be pleased to go with your servants." And he answered, "I will go." 4So he went with them. And when they came to the Jordan,
they cut down trees. 5But as one was felling a log, his axe head fell into the water,
and he cried out, "Alas, my master! It was borrowed." 6Then the man of God said,
"Where did it fall?" When he showed him the place, he cut off a stick and threw
it in there and made the iron float. 7And he said, "Take it up." So he reached out
his hand and took it.

Horses and Chariots of Fire

8Once when the king of Syria was warring against Israel, he took counsel with
his servants, saying, "At such and such a place shall be my camp." 9But the man
of God sent word to the king of Israel, "Beware that you do not pass this place,
for the Syrians are going down there." 10And the king of Israel sent to the place
about which the man of God told him. Thus he used to warn him, so that he saved
himself there more than once or twice.

11And the mind of the king of Syria was greatly troubled because of this thing,
and he called his servants and said to them, "Will you not show me who of us
is for the king of Israel?" 12And one of his servants said, "None, my lord, O king;
but Elisha, the prophet who is in Israel, tells the king of Israel the words that you
speak in your bedroom." 13And he said, "Go and see where he is, that I may send
and seize him." It was told him, "Behold, he is in Dothan." 14So he sent there
horses and chariots and a great army, and they came by night and surrounded
the city.

15When the servant of the man of God rose early in the morning and went out,
behold, an army with horses and chariots was all around the city. And the servant
said, "Alas, my master! What shall we do?" 16He said, "Do not be afraid, for those
who are with us are more than those who are with them." 17Then Elisha prayed
and said, "O LORD, please open his eyes that he may see." So the LORD opened the
eyes of the young man, and he saw, and behold, the mountain was full of horses
and chariots of fire all around Elisha. 18And when the Syrians came down against
him, Elisha prayed to the LORD and said, "Please strike this people with blindness." So he struck them with blindness in accordance with the prayer of Elisha.
19And Elisha said to them, "This is not the way, and this is not the city. Follow me,
and I will bring you to the man whom you seek." And he led them to Samaria.

20As soon as they entered Samaria, Elisha said, "O LORD, open the eyes of these
men, that they may see." So the LORD opened their eyes and they saw, and behold,
they were in the midst of Samaria. 21As soon as the king of Israel saw them, he said
to Elisha, "My father, shall I strike them down? Shall I strike them down?" 22He
answered, "You shall not strike them down. Would you strike down those whom
you have taken captive with your sword and with your bow? Set bread and water
before them, that they may eat and drink and go to their master." 23So he prepared
for them a great feast, and when they had eaten and drunk, he sent them away,
and they went to their master. And the Syrians did not come again on raids into
the land of Israel.

Ben-hadad's Siege of Samaria

24Afterward Ben-hadad king of Syria mustered his entire army and went up
and besieged Samaria. 25And there was a great famine in Samaria, as they besieged it, until a donkey's head was sold for eighty shekels of silver, and the fourth
part of a kab[1] of dove's dung for five shekels of silver. 26Now as the king of Israel

[1]A *shekel* was about 2/5 ounce or 11 grams; a *kab* was about 1 quart or 1 liter

GREATER ARE THOSE WITH US

Naaman was a valiant soldier, but his strength could not save him from the disease of leprosy. His miraculous healing demonstrated God's power to overcome physical sickness and suffering. The healing of Naaman's physical leprosy is a fitting picture of the work of Jesus to heal those afflicted by the far greater leprosy of a sin-sick heart.

This miracle revealed at a personal level that God is constantly at work. The story told in 2 Kings 6 broadens this claim. Israel was once again embroiled in conflict with a rival nation — this time with the king of Syria — but the Israelite army had a secret weapon. Elisha, the prophet of God, warned Israel and their king of the movements of their enemy. Every time Syria devised a new tactic, Elisha's warning allowed them to take preemptive measures and avoid defeat. After discovering Israel's secret, the king of Syria sought to capture Elisha. In the dead of night, his forces surrounded the city in which Elisha was staying.

The next morning, Elisha's servant observed the strong force encamped around the city. Answering his servant's alarm, Elisha answered with a word of encouragement: "Those who are with us are more than those who are with them" (6:16). Considering the size of each side's army, Elisha's encouraging words seemed to make no sense. Then Elisha prayed that the servant would see what he saw. Lifting up his eyes, the servant could then see the stunning spiritual reality — the hills were teeming with horses and chariots of fire ready to fight on Israel's behalf.

God still fights for his people, even when they cannot see the full picture. In the book of Revelation, John described Jesus as the Warrior King who will one day return to fight for his people and defeat Satan, sin, and death once and for all (Rev 19:11 – 21). This coming reality provides hope for the people of God: Christ alone is the victorious King who will rid the world of all suffering and pain. In the meantime, this same Warrior King is with his people by the power of the Spirit. Jesus promises that he will go with his people as they seek to take the gospel to the ends of the world (Mt 28:18 – 20). As John reminded the church, "he who is in you is greater than he who is in the world" (1Jn 4:4). Though Satan is taking aim at the people of God, believers can have full confidence. God is at work in ways they cannot see or comprehend, preparing them spiritually for every challenge (Eph 6:10 – 17).

was passing by on the wall, a woman cried out to him, saying, "Help, my lord,
O king!" 27And he said, "If the LORD will not help you, how shall I help you? From
the threshing floor, or from the winepress?" 28And the king asked her, "What is
your trouble?" She answered, "This woman said to me, 'Give your son, that we
may eat him today, and we will eat my son tomorrow.' 29So we boiled my son and
ate him. And on the next day I said to her, 'Give your son, that we may eat him.'
But she has hidden her son." 30When the king heard the words of the woman, he
tore his clothes—now he was passing by on the wall—and the people looked,
and behold, he had sackcloth beneath on his body— 31and he said, "May God do
so to me and more also, if the head of Elisha the son of Shaphat remains on his
shoulders today."

32Elisha was sitting in his house, and the elders were sitting with him. Now the
king had dispatched a man from his presence, but before the messenger arrived
Elisha said to the elders, "Do you see how this murderer has sent to take off my
head? Look, when the messenger comes, shut the door and hold the door fast
against him. Is not the sound of his master's feet behind him?" 33And while he was
still speaking with them, the messenger came down to him and said, "This trouble
is from the LORD! Why should I wait for the LORD any longer?"

Elisha Promises Food

7 But Elisha said, "Hear the word of the LORD: thus says the LORD, Tomorrow
about this time a seah[1] of fine flour shall be sold for a shekel,[2] and two seahs of
barley for a shekel, at the gate of Samaria." 2Then the captain on whose hand the
king leaned said to the man of God, "If the LORD himself should make windows
in heaven, could this thing be?" But he said, "You shall see it with your own eyes,
but you shall not eat of it."

The Syrians Flee

3Now there were four men who were lepers[3] at the entrance to the gate. And
they said to one another, "Why are we sitting here until we die? 4If we say, 'Let
us enter the city,' the famine is in the city, and we shall die there. And if we sit
here, we die also. So now come, let us go over to the camp of the Syrians. If they
spare our lives we shall live, and if they kill us we shall but die." 5So they arose
at twilight to go to the camp of the Syrians. But when they came to the edge of
the camp of the Syrians, behold, there was no one there. 6For the Lord had made
the army of the Syrians hear the sound of chariots and of horses, the sound of a
great army, so that they said to one another, "Behold, the king of Israel has hired
against us the kings of the Hittites and the kings of Egypt to come against us." 7So
they fled away in the twilight and abandoned their tents, their horses, and their
donkeys, leaving the camp as it was, and fled for their lives. 8And when these
lepers came to the edge of the camp, they went into a tent and ate and drank,
and they carried off silver and gold and clothing and went and hid them. Then
they came back and entered another tent and carried off things from it and went
and hid them.

9Then they said to one another, "We are not doing right. This day is a day
of good news. If we are silent and wait until the morning light, punishment will
overtake us. Now therefore come; let us go and tell the king's household." 10So
they came and called to the gatekeepers of the city and told them, "We came to
the camp of the Syrians, and behold, there was no one to be seen or heard there,
nothing but the horses tied and the donkeys tied and the tents as they were."
11Then the gatekeepers called out, and it was told within the king's household.
12And the king rose in the night and said to his servants, "I will tell you what the
Syrians have done to us. They know that we are hungry. Therefore they have gone

[1]A *seah* was about 7.7 quarts or 7.3 liters [2]A *shekel* was about 2/5 ounce or 11 grams [3]*Leprosy* was a term for several skin diseases; see Leviticus 13

2 KINGS 7:3–9

SHARING GOOD NEWS

Syria's siege of Samaria in Israel resulted in economic disaster and famine, but hope was not lost. God was still in control. Elisha prophesied a message of hope: God would reverse his people's suffering (2Ki 7:1). And that is exactly what happened. Four lepers who sat outside the city's gates, knowing that Samaria had nothing to offer them but famine and death, decided to take their chances with the Syrians. At twilight, they made their way to the Syrian camp, but God caused the sound of their approach to be as loud as a great army, and the entire Syrian camp fled in fear. The lepers entered a tent and filled their stomachs with food and their pockets with food, silver, and gold. They entered another tent, taking more and hiding it. Then they were convicted about not sharing the good news, food, and wealth with the rest of Samaria.

God's Son, Jesus, once visited a man ostracized and pushed to the fringes of society and gave him something far more valuable than silver or gold. Like the Israelites in the Old Testament story, this man lived under siege—the spiritual siege of demonic possession—but Jesus saved him. Despite the man's pleas to go with his Savior, Jesus refused. Instead, Jesus sent this man back to his home to tell his family and friends what had happened. *Even more than silver and gold,* the good news of salvation is a treasure meant to be shared (Mk 5:1–20).

out of the camp to hide themselves in the open country, thinking, 'When they come out of the city, we shall take them alive and get into the city.' " 13And one of his servants said, "Let some men take five of the remaining horses, seeing that those who are left here will fare like the whole multitude of Israel who have already perished. Let us send and see." 14So they took two horsemen, and the king sent them after the army of the Syrians, saying, "Go and see." 15So they went after them as far as the Jordan, and behold, all the way was littered with garments and equipment that the Syrians had thrown away in their haste. And the messengers returned and told the king.

16Then the people went out and plundered the camp of the Syrians. So a seah of fine flour was sold for a shekel, and two seahs of barley for a shekel, according to the word of the LORD. 17Now the king had appointed the captain on whose hand he leaned to have charge of the gate. And the people trampled him in the gate, so that he died, as the man of God had said when the king came down to him. 18For when the man of God had said to the king, "Two seahs of barley shall be sold for a shekel, and a seah of fine flour for a shekel, about this time tomorrow in the gate of Samaria," 19the captain had answered the man of God, "If the LORD himself should make windows in heaven, could such a thing be?" And he had said, "You shall see it with your own eyes, but you shall not eat of it." 20And so it happened to him, for the people trampled him in the gate and he died.

The Shunammite's Land Restored

8 Now Elisha had said to the woman whose son he had restored to life, "Arise, and depart with your household, and sojourn wherever you can, for the LORD has called for a famine, and it will come upon the land for seven years." 2So the woman arose and did according to the word of the man of God. She went with her household and sojourned in the land of the Philistines seven years. 3And at the end of the seven years, when the woman returned from the land of the Philistines, she went to appeal to the king for her house and her land. 4Now the king was talking with Gehazi the servant of the man of God, saying, "Tell me all the great things that Elisha has done." 5And while he was telling the king how Elisha had restored the dead to life, behold, the woman whose son he had restored to life appealed to the king for her house and her land. And Gehazi said, "My lord, O king, here is the woman, and here is her son whom Elisha restored to life." 6And when the king asked the woman, she told him. So the king appointed an official for her, saying, "Restore all that was hers, together with all the produce of the fields from the day that she left the land until now."

Hazael Murders Ben-hadad

7Now Elisha came to Damascus. Ben-hadad the king of Syria was sick. And when it was told him, "The man of God has come here," 8the king said to Hazael, "Take a present with you and go to meet the man of God, and inquire of the LORD through him, saying, 'Shall I recover from this sickness?' " 9So Hazael went to meet him, and took a present with him, all kinds of goods of Damascus, forty camels' loads. When he came and stood before him, he said, "Your son Ben-hadad king of Syria has sent me to you, saying, 'Shall I recover from this sickness?' " 10And Elisha said to him, "Go, say to him, 'You shall certainly recover,' but[1] the LORD has shown me that he shall certainly die." 11And he fixed his gaze and stared at him, until he was embarrassed. And the man of God wept. 12And Hazael said, "Why does my lord weep?" He answered, "Because I know the evil that you will do to the people of Israel. You will set on fire their fortresses, and you will kill their young men with the sword and dash in pieces their little ones and rip open their pregnant women." 13And Hazael said, "What is your servant, who is but a dog, that he should do this great thing?" Elisha answered, "The LORD has shown

[1]Some manuscripts *say, 'You shall certainly not recover,' for*

2 KINGS 8:7–15

FULFILLING THE PROPHETIC WORD

The king of Syria, Ben-hadad, was ill and uncertain if he would survive. Word reached him that the prophet Elisha had come to Damascus, so he sent his servant Hazael with forty camels loaded with gifts and asked the prophet whether he would live or die. Hazael did as he was instructed, but he could have never imagined what Elisha would tell him. According to Elisha, God decreed that the king would die and that Hazael would rule over Syria. Earlier God had told this same truth to Elijah, Elisha's predecessor (1Ki 19:15). God's words create and shape reality; they can topple empires and replace kings with servants. At one time, God chose to speak his reality-shaping words through the prophets, people like Elisha and Elijah. Now he has chosen to speak uniquely through his Son, Jesus (Heb 1:1–2). And with ultimate authority and power, Jesus' words pierce the innermost parts of people, revealing their secret thoughts and intentions (Heb 4:12–13). By his word, judgment falls upon the unrepentant and mercy comes to those with a contrite heart.

me that you are to be king over Syria." 14Then he departed from Elisha and came to his master, who said to him, "What did Elisha say to you?" And he answered, "He told me that you would certainly recover." 15But the next day he took the bed cloth[1] and dipped it in water and spread it over his face, till he died. And Hazael became king in his place.

Jehoram Reigns in Judah

16In the fifth year of Joram the son of Ahab, king of Israel, when Jehoshaphat was king of Judah,[2] Jehoram the son of Jehoshaphat, king of Judah, began to reign. 17He was thirty-two years old when he became king, and he reigned eight years in Jerusalem. 18And he walked in the way of the kings of Israel, as the house of Ahab had done, for the daughter of Ahab was his wife. And he did what was evil in the sight of the LORD. 19Yet the LORD was not willing to destroy Judah, for the sake of David his servant, since he promised to give a lamp to him and to his sons forever.

20In his days Edom revolted from the rule of Judah and set up a king of their own. 21Then Joram[3] passed over to Zair with all his chariots and rose by night, and he and his chariot commanders struck the Edomites who had surrounded him, but his army fled home. 22So Edom revolted from the rule of Judah to this day. Then Libnah revolted at the same time. 23Now the rest of the acts of Joram, and all that he did, are they not written in the Book of the Chronicles of the Kings of Judah? 24So Joram slept with his fathers and was buried with his fathers in the city of David, and Ahaziah his son reigned in his place.

Ahaziah Reigns in Judah

25In the twelfth year of Joram the son of Ahab, king of Israel, Ahaziah the son of Jehoram, king of Judah, began to reign. 26Ahaziah was twenty-two years old when he began to reign, and he reigned one year in Jerusalem. His mother's name was Athaliah; she was a granddaughter of Omri king of Israel. 27He also walked in the way of the house of Ahab and did what was evil in the sight of the LORD, as the house of Ahab had done, for he was son-in-law to the house of Ahab.

28He went with Joram the son of Ahab to make war against Hazael king of Syria at Ramoth-gilead, and the Syrians wounded Joram. 29And King Joram returned to be healed in Jezreel of the wounds that the Syrians had given him at Ramah, when he fought against Hazael king of Syria. And Ahaziah the son of Jehoram king of Judah went down to see Joram the son of Ahab in Jezreel, because he was sick.

Jehu Anointed King of Israel

9 Then Elisha the prophet called one of the sons of the prophets and said to him, "Tie up your garments, and take this flask of oil in your hand, and go to Ramoth-gilead. 2And when you arrive, look there for Jehu the son of Jehoshaphat, son of Nimshi. And go in and have him rise from among his fellows, and lead him to an inner chamber. 3Then take the flask of oil and pour it on his head and say, 'Thus says the LORD, I anoint you king over Israel.' Then open the door and flee; do not linger."

4So the young man, the servant of the prophet, went to Ramoth-gilead. 5And when he came, behold, the commanders of the army were in council. And he said, "I have a word for you, O commander." And Jehu said, "To which of us all?" And he said, "To you, O commander." 6So he arose and went into the house. And the young man poured the oil on his head, saying to him, "Thus says the LORD, the God of Israel, I anoint you king over the people of the LORD, over Israel. 7And you shall strike down the house of Ahab your master, so that I may avenge on Jezebel the blood of my servants the prophets, and the blood of all the servants

[1]The meaning of the Hebrew is uncertain [2]Septuagint, Syriac lack *when Jehoshaphat was king of Judah*
[3]*Joram* (also verses 23, 24) is an alternate spelling of *Jehoram* (the son of Jehoshaphat), mentioned in verses 16, 25, 29

of the LORD. 8For the whole house of Ahab shall perish, and I will cut off from
Ahab every male, bond or free, in Israel. 9And I will make the house of Ahab like
the house of Jeroboam the son of Nebat, and like the house of Baasha the son of
Ahijah. 10And the dogs shall eat Jezebel in the territory of Jezreel, and none shall
bury her." Then he opened the door and fled.
11When Jehu came out to the servants of his master, they said to him, "Is all
well? Why did this mad fellow come to you?" And he said to them, "You know the
fellow and his talk." 12And they said, "That is not true; tell us now." And he said,
"Thus and so he spoke to me, saying, 'Thus says the LORD, I anoint you king over
Israel.'" 13Then in haste every man of them took his garment and put it under
him on the bare[1] steps, and they blew the trumpet and proclaimed, "Jehu is king."

Jehu Assassinates Joram and Ahaziah

14Thus Jehu the son of Jehoshaphat the son of Nimshi conspired against
Joram. (Now Joram with all Israel had been on guard at Ramoth-gilead against
Hazael king of Syria, 15but King Joram had returned to be healed in Jezreel of
the wounds that the Syrians had given him, when he fought with Hazael king of
Syria.) So Jehu said, "If this is your decision, then let no one slip out of the city
to go and tell the news in Jezreel." 16Then Jehu mounted his chariot and went to
Jezreel, for Joram lay there. And Ahaziah king of Judah had come down to visit
Joram.
17Now the watchman was standing on the tower in Jezreel, and he saw the
company of Jehu as he came and said, "I see a company." And Joram said, "Take
a horseman and send to meet them, and let him say, 'Is it peace?'" 18So a man on
horseback went to meet him and said, "Thus says the king, 'Is it peace?'" And
Jehu said, "What do you have to do with peace? Turn around and ride behind
me." And the watchman reported, saying, "The messenger reached them, but he
is not coming back." 19Then he sent out a second horseman, who came to them
and said, "Thus the king has said, 'Is it peace?'" And Jehu answered, "What do you
have to do with peace? Turn around and ride behind me." 20Again the watchman
reported, "He reached them, but he is not coming back. And the driving is like the
driving of Jehu the son of Nimshi, for he drives furiously."
21Joram said, "Make ready." And they made ready his chariot. Then Joram
king of Israel and Ahaziah king of Judah set out, each in his chariot, and went
to meet Jehu, and met him at the property of Naboth the Jezreelite. 22And when
Joram saw Jehu, he said, "Is it peace, Jehu?" He answered, "What peace can
there be, so long as the whorings and the sorceries of your mother Jezebel are
so many?" 23Then Joram reined about and fled, saying to Ahaziah, "Treachery,
O Ahaziah!" 24And Jehu drew his bow with his full strength, and shot Joram
between the shoulders, so that the arrow pierced his heart, and he sank in his
chariot. 25Jehu said to Bidkar his aide, "Take him up and throw him on the plot of
ground belonging to Naboth the Jezreelite. For remember, when you and I rode
side by side behind Ahab his father, how the LORD made this pronouncement
against him: 26'As surely as I saw yesterday the blood of Naboth and the blood
of his sons—declares the LORD—I will repay you on this plot of ground.' Now
therefore take him up and throw him on the plot of ground, in accordance with
the word of the LORD."
27When Ahaziah the king of Judah saw this, he fled in the direction of Beth-
haggan. And Jehu pursued him and said, "Shoot him also." And they shot him[2] in
the chariot at the ascent of Gur, which is by Ibleam. And he fled to Megiddo and
died there. 28His servants carried him in a chariot to Jerusalem, and buried him in
his tomb with his fathers in the city of David.
29In the eleventh year of Joram the son of Ahab, Ahaziah began to reign over
Judah.

[1]The meaning of the Hebrew word is uncertain [2]Syriac, Vulgate (compare Septuagint); Hebrew lacks *and they shot him*

Jehu Executes Jezebel

30 When Jehu came to Jezreel, Jezebel heard of it. And she painted her eyes and adorned her head and looked out of the window. 31 And as Jehu entered the gate, she said, "Is it peace, you Zimri, murderer of your master?" 32 And he lifted up his face to the window and said, "Who is on my side? Who?" Two or three eunuchs looked out at him. 33 He said, "Throw her down." So they threw her down. And some of her blood spattered on the wall and on the horses, and they trampled on her. 34 Then he went in and ate and drank. And he said, "See now to this cursed woman and bury her, for she is a king's daughter." 35 But when they went to bury her, they found no more of her than the skull and the feet and the palms of her hands. 36 When they came back and told him, he said, "This is the word of the LORD, which he spoke by his servant Elijah the Tishbite: 'In the territory of Jezreel the dogs shall eat the flesh of Jezebel, 37 and the corpse of Jezebel shall be as dung on the face of the field in the territory of Jezreel, so that no one can say, This is Jezebel.'"

Jehu Slaughters Ahab's Descendants

10 Now Ahab had seventy sons in Samaria. So Jehu wrote letters and sent them to Samaria, to the rulers of the city,[1] to the elders, and to the guardians of the sons[2] of Ahab, saying, 2 "Now then, as soon as this letter comes to you, seeing your master's sons are with you, and there are with you chariots and horses, fortified cities also, and weapons, 3 select the best and fittest of your master's sons and set him on his father's throne and fight for your master's house." 4 But they were exceedingly afraid and said, "Behold, the two kings could not stand before him. How then can we stand?" 5 So he who was over the palace, and he who was over the city, together with the elders and the guardians, sent to Jehu, saying, "We are your servants, and we will do all that you tell us. We will not make anyone king. Do whatever is good in your eyes." 6 Then he wrote to them a second letter, saying, "If you are on my side, and if you are ready to obey me, take the heads of your master's sons and come to me at Jezreel tomorrow at this time." Now the king's sons, seventy persons, were with the great men of the city, who were bringing them up. 7 And as soon as the letter came to them, they took the king's sons and slaughtered them, seventy persons, and put their heads in baskets and sent them to him at Jezreel. 8 When the messenger came and told him, "They have brought the heads of the king's sons," he said, "Lay them in two heaps at the entrance of the gate until the morning." 9 Then in the morning, when he went out, he stood and said to all the people, "You are innocent. It was I who conspired against my master and killed him, but who struck down all these? 10 Know then that there shall fall to the earth nothing of the word of the LORD, which the LORD spoke concerning the house of Ahab, for the LORD has done what he said by his servant Elijah." 11 So Jehu struck down all who remained of the house of Ahab in Jezreel, all his great men and his close friends and his priests, until he left him none remaining.

12 Then he set out and went to Samaria. On the way, when he was at Beth-eked of the Shepherds, 13 Jehu met the relatives of Ahaziah king of Judah, and he said, "Who are you?" And they answered, "We are the relatives of Ahaziah, and we came down to visit the royal princes and the sons of the queen mother." 14 He said, "Take them alive." And they took them alive and slaughtered them at the pit of Beth-eked, forty-two persons, and he spared none of them.

15 And when he departed from there, he met Jehonadab the son of Rechab coming to meet him. And he greeted him and said to him, "Is your heart true to my heart as mine is to yours?" And Jehonadab answered, "It is." Jehu said,[3] "If it is, give me your hand." So he gave him his hand. And Jehu took him up with him

[1] Septuagint, Vulgate; Hebrew *rulers of Jezreel* [2] Hebrew lacks *of the sons* [3] Septuagint; Hebrew lacks *Jehu said*

2 KINGS 10:1–17

JUDGMENT ON FALSE WORSHIP

The destruction of the house of Ahab fulfilled God's prophetic words of judgment (1Ki 21:21–22). God hates idolatry because it distorts human worship and causes people to direct their passions, sacrifices, affections, and loyalties to created things instead of to God. Ahab and Jezebel were guilty not only of personal idolatry but also of leading others to sin against God in this fashion, and their lives illustrate idolatry's destructive effects. Years of pursuing false gods eventually warped Ahab's very identity as king. Instead of caring for his people, he used his position of power to take advantage of them, eventually murdering one of his own subjects and stealing his vineyard (1Ki 21). This sin finally prompted God's terrible punishment. God's judgment comes against all those who exchange the glory of God for worship of created things (Ro 1:18–32).

Throughout Jesus' earthly ministry, he issued similarly strong warnings about the destruction that will surely come to those who fail to worship God. Ironically, Jesus often reserved this condemnation for religious leaders who had turned their religious performance into a source of false worship. Jesus warned these leaders of the temporal judgment they would face as well as the fact *that they would one day be judged by* the one to whom all worship is due (Mt 23:13–39; Rev 20:11–15).

into the chariot. 16And he said, "Come with me, and see my zeal for the LORD." So
he[1] had him ride in his chariot. 17And when he came to Samaria, he struck down
all who remained to Ahab in Samaria, till he had wiped them out, according to the
word of the LORD that he spoke to Elijah.

Jehu Strikes Down the Prophets of Baal

18Then Jehu assembled all the people and said to them, "Ahab served Baal a
little, but Jehu will serve him much. 19Now therefore call to me all the prophets of
Baal, all his worshipers and all his priests. Let none be missing, for I have a great
sacrifice to offer to Baal. Whoever is missing shall not live." But Jehu did it with
cunning in order to destroy the worshipers of Baal. 20And Jehu ordered, "Sanctify
a solemn assembly for Baal." So they proclaimed it. 21And Jehu sent throughout all
Israel, and all the worshipers of Baal came, so that there was not a man left who
did not come. And they entered the house of Baal, and the house of Baal was filled
from one end to the other. 22He said to him who was in charge of the wardrobe,
"Bring out the vestments for all the worshipers of Baal." So he brought out the
vestments for them. 23Then Jehu went into the house of Baal with Jehonadab the
son of Rechab, and he said to the worshipers of Baal, "Search, and see that there is
no servant of the LORD here among you, but only the worshipers of Baal." 24Then
they[2] went in to offer sacrifices and burnt offerings.

Now Jehu had stationed eighty men outside and said, "The man who allows
any of those whom I give into your hands to escape shall forfeit his life." 25So as
soon as he had made an end of offering the burnt offering, Jehu said to the guard
and to the officers, "Go in and strike them down; let not a man escape." So when
they put them to the sword, the guard and the officers cast them out and went
into the inner room of the house of Baal, 26and they brought out the pillar that
was in the house of Baal and burned it. 27And they demolished the pillar of Baal,
and demolished the house of Baal, and made it a latrine to this day.

Jehu Reigns in Israel

28Thus Jehu wiped out Baal from Israel. 29But Jehu did not turn aside from
the sins of Jeroboam the son of Nebat, which he made Israel to sin—that is, the
golden calves that were in Bethel and in Dan. 30And the LORD said to Jehu, "Because you have done well in carrying out what is right in my eyes, and have done
to the house of Ahab according to all that was in my heart, your sons of the fourth
generation shall sit on the throne of Israel." 31But Jehu was not careful to walk in
the law of the LORD, the God of Israel, with all his heart. He did not turn from the
sins of Jeroboam, which he made Israel to sin.

32In those days the LORD began to cut off parts of Israel. Hazael defeated them
throughout the territory of Israel: 33from the Jordan eastward, all the land of Gilead, the Gadites, and the Reubenites, and the Manassites, from Aroer, which is by
the Valley of the Arnon, that is, Gilead and Bashan. 34Now the rest of the acts of
Jehu and all that he did, and all his might, are they not written in the Book of the
Chronicles of the Kings of Israel? 35So Jehu slept with his fathers, and they buried
him in Samaria. And Jehoahaz his son reigned in his place. 36The time that Jehu
reigned over Israel in Samaria was twenty-eight years.

Athaliah Reigns in Judah

11 Now when Athaliah the mother of Ahaziah saw that her son was dead, she
arose and destroyed all the royal family. 2But Jehosheba, the daughter of
King Joram, sister of Ahaziah, took Joash the son of Ahaziah and stole him away
from among the king's sons who were being put to death, and she put[3] him and
his nurse in a bedroom. Thus they[4] hid him from Athaliah, so that he was not put

[1]Septuagint, Syriac, Targum; Hebrew *they* [2]Septuagint *he* (compare verse 25) [3]Compare 2 Chronicles 22:11; Hebrew lacks *and she put* [4]Septuagint, Syriac, Vulgate (compare 2 Chronicles 22:11) *she*

---

2 KINGS 11:1–3

GUARD THE KING

Athaliah, whose name means "the LORD is exalted," did not live up to her name. As the nation unraveled, she continued the murderous pattern of many of the previous pagan leaders. When her son (King Ahaziah) died, she murdered every remaining royal heir and took the throne for herself. But she missed one heir: young Joash, her grandson and the son of Ahaziah. Jehosheba, Ahaziah's half sister, was married to the high priest and stood in a perfect location to rescue and hide Joash. Athaliah may not have even known of Joash's existence, which protected him from her rampage. The Lord protected Joash, ensuring that he would inherit the promises God made to David. Once again, David's royal line endured against all human odds through God's covenant faithfulness (2Sa 7:16).

In the same way, God protected the infant Jesus from death at the hands of King Herod and allowed him to secure the Davidic throne forever (Mt 2:13–20). The entire story of the Bible testifies to God's faithfulness to fulfill his promises and establish his rule and reign.

to death. 3And he remained with her six years, hidden in the house of the LORD,
while Athaliah reigned over the land.

Joash Anointed King in Judah

4But in the seventh year Jehoiada sent and brought the captains of the Carites
and of the guards, and had them come to him in the house of the LORD. And he
made a covenant with them and put them under oath in the house of the LORD,
and he showed them the king's son. 5And he commanded them, "This is the thing
that you shall do: one third of you, those who come off duty on the Sabbath and
guard the king's house 6(another third being at the gate Sur and a third at the gate
behind the guards) shall guard the palace.[1] 7And the two divisions of you, which
come on duty in force on the Sabbath and guard the house of the LORD on behalf
of the king, 8shall surround the king, each with his weapons in his hand. And
whoever approaches the ranks is to be put to death. Be with the king when he goes
out and when he comes in."

9The captains did according to all that Jehoiada the priest commanded, and
they each brought his men who were to go off duty on the Sabbath, with those
who were to come on duty on the Sabbath, and came to Jehoiada the priest. 10And
the priest gave to the captains the spears and shields that had been King David's,
which were in the house of the LORD. 11And the guards stood, every man with his
weapons in his hand, from the south side of the house to the north side of the
house, around the altar and the house on behalf of the king. 12Then he brought
out the king's son and put the crown on him and gave him the testimony. And they
proclaimed him king and anointed him, and they clapped their hands and said,
"Long live the king!"

13When Athaliah heard the noise of the guard and of the people, she went into
the house of the LORD to the people. 14And when she looked, there was the king
standing by the pillar, according to the custom, and the captains and the trumpeters beside the king, and all the people of the land rejoicing and blowing trumpets.
And Athaliah tore her clothes and cried, "Treason! Treason!" 15Then Jehoiada the
priest commanded the captains who were set over the army, "Bring her out between the ranks, and put to death with the sword anyone who follows her." For
the priest said, "Let her not be put to death in the house of the LORD." 16So they
laid hands on her; and she went through the horses' entrance to the king's house,
and there she was put to death.

17And Jehoiada made a covenant between the LORD and the king and people,
that they should be the LORD's people, and also between the king and the people.
18Then all the people of the land went to the house of Baal and tore it down; his altars and his images they broke in pieces, and they killed Mattan the priest of Baal
before the altars. And the priest posted watchmen over the house of the LORD.
19And he took the captains, the Carites, the guards, and all the people of the land,
and they brought the king down from the house of the LORD, marching through
the gate of the guards to the king's house. And he took his seat on the throne of
the kings. 20So all the people of the land rejoiced, and the city was quiet after
Athaliah had been put to death with the sword at the king's house.

Jehoash Reigns in Judah

21[2]Jehoash[3] was seven years old when he began to reign.

12 In the seventh year of Jehu, Jehoash[4] began to reign, and he reigned forty
years in Jerusalem. His mother's name was Zibiah of Beersheba. 2And Jehoash did what was right in the eyes of the LORD all his days, because Jehoiada
the priest instructed him. 3Nevertheless, the high places were not taken away; the
people continued to sacrifice and make offerings on the high places.

[1]The meaning of the Hebrew word is uncertain [2]Ch 12:1 in Hebrew [3]*Jehoash* is an alternate spelling of *Joash* (son of Ahaziah) as in verse 2 [4]*Jehoash* is an alternate spelling of *Joash* (son of Ahaziah) as in 11:2; also verses 2, 4, 6, 7, 18

2 KINGS 12:1–16

THE TEMPLE IN DISREPAIR

The Old Testament records a number of leaders who, like a ray of light breaking through the clouds, did right in the eyes of the Lord. Although Joash's reforms were only partial, he did seek to repair the dilapidated temple. The broken condition of the temple mirrored the people's broken spiritual condition. Joash led the people once again to prioritize the temple and bring about much needed repairs.

In Jesus' day, the disciples were enamored by the beautiful majesty of Herod's temple. While the outward appearance suggested commitment to God, Jesus warned that God's judgment was coming and that the temple would be demolished (Mt 24:1–2). That prophesied destruction occurred in AD 70, when the Romans sacked Jerusalem. Throughout his ministry, Jesus warned against assuming that outward appearances—of people or structures—provide a trustworthy indication of the spiritual state within.

Jehoash Repairs the Temple

[4]Jehoash said to the priests, "All the money of the holy things that is brought
into the house of the LORD, the money for which each man is assessed—the money from the assessment of persons—and the money that a man's heart prompts
him to bring into the house of the LORD, [5]let the priests take, each from his donor, and let them repair the house wherever any need of repairs is discovered."
[6]But by the twenty-third year of King Jehoash, the priests had made no repairs
on the house. [7]Therefore King Jehoash summoned Jehoiada the priest and the
other priests and said to them, "Why are you not repairing the house? Now therefore take no more money from your donors, but hand it over for the repair of the
house." [8]So the priests agreed that they should take no more money from the
people, and that they should not repair the house.
[9]Then Jehoiada the priest took a chest and bored a hole in the lid of it and
set it beside the altar on the right side as one entered the house of the LORD.
And the priests who guarded the threshold put in it all the money that was
brought into the house of the LORD. [10]And whenever they saw that there was
much money in the chest, the king's secretary and the high priest came up and
they bagged and counted the money that was found in the house of the LORD.
[11]Then they would give the money that was weighed out into the hands of the
workmen who had the oversight of the house of the LORD. And they paid it out
to the carpenters and the builders who worked on the house of the LORD, [12]and
to the masons and the stonecutters, as well as to buy timber and quarried stone
for making repairs on the house of the LORD, and for any outlay for the repairs
of the house. [13]But there were not made for the house of the LORD basins of
silver, snuffers, bowls, trumpets, or any vessels of gold, or of silver, from the
money that was brought into the house of the LORD, [14]for that was given to the
workmen who were repairing the house of the LORD with it. [15]And they did not
ask for an accounting from the men into whose hand they delivered the money
to pay out to the workmen, for they dealt honestly. [16]The money from the guilt
offerings and the money from the sin offerings was not brought into the house
of the LORD; it belonged to the priests.
[17]At that time Hazael king of Syria went up and fought against Gath and took
it. But when Hazael set his face to go up against Jerusalem, [18]Jehoash king of
Judah took all the sacred gifts that Jehoshaphat and Jehoram and Ahaziah his
fathers, the kings of Judah, had dedicated, and his own sacred gifts, and all the
gold that was found in the treasuries of the house of the LORD and of the king's
house, and sent these to Hazael king of Syria. Then Hazael went away from
Jerusalem.

The Death of Joash

[19]Now the rest of the acts of Joash and all that he did, are they not written
in the Book of the Chronicles of the Kings of Judah? [20]His servants arose and
made a conspiracy and struck down Joash in the house of Millo, on the way that
goes down to Silla. [21]It was Jozacar the son of Shimeath and Jehozabad the son
of Shomer, his servants, who struck him down, so that he died. And they buried
him with his fathers in the city of David, and Amaziah his son reigned in his
place.

Jehoahaz Reigns in Israel

13 In the twenty-third year of Joash the son of Ahaziah, king of Judah, Jehoahaz the son of Jehu began to reign over Israel in Samaria, and he reigned
seventeen years. [2]He did what was evil in the sight of the LORD and followed the
sins of Jeroboam the son of Nebat, which he made Israel to sin; he did not depart
from them. [3]And the anger of the LORD was kindled against Israel, and he gave
them continually into the hand of Hazael king of Syria and into the hand of Ben-
hadad the son of Hazael. [4]Then Jehoahaz sought the favor of the LORD, and the

Lord listened to him, for he saw the oppression of Israel, how the king of Syria oppressed them. [5](Therefore the Lord gave Israel a savior, so that they escaped from the hand of the Syrians, and the people of Israel lived in their homes as formerly. [6]Nevertheless, they did not depart from the sins of the house of Jeroboam, which he made Israel to sin, but walked[1] in them; and the Asherah also remained in Samaria.) [7]For there was not left to Jehoahaz an army of more than fifty horsemen and ten chariots and ten thousand footmen, for the king of Syria had destroyed them and made them like the dust at threshing. [8]Now the rest of the acts of Jehoahaz and all that he did, and his might, are they not written in the Book of the Chronicles of the Kings of Israel? [9]So Jehoahaz slept with his fathers, and they buried him in Samaria, and Joash his son reigned in his place.

Jehoash Reigns in Israel

[10]In the thirty-seventh year of Joash king of Judah, Jehoash[2] the son of Jehoahaz began to reign over Israel in Samaria, and he reigned sixteen years. [11]He also did what was evil in the sight of the Lord. He did not depart from all the sins of Jeroboam the son of Nebat, which he made Israel to sin, but he walked in them. [12]Now the rest of the acts of Joash and all that he did, and the might with which he fought against Amaziah king of Judah, are they not written in the Book of the Chronicles of the Kings of Israel? [13]So Joash slept with his fathers, and Jeroboam sat on his throne. And Joash was buried in Samaria with the kings of Israel.

The Death of Elisha

[14]Now when Elisha had fallen sick with the illness of which he was to die, Joash king of Israel went down to him and wept before him, crying, "My father, my father! The chariots of Israel and its horsemen!" [15]And Elisha said to him, "Take a bow and arrows." So he took a bow and arrows. [16]Then he said to the king of Israel, "Draw the bow," and he drew it. And Elisha laid his hands on the king's hands. [17]And he said, "Open the window eastward," and he opened it. Then Elisha said, "Shoot," and he shot. And he said, "The Lord's arrow of victory, the arrow of victory over Syria! For you shall fight the Syrians in Aphek until you have made an end of them." [18]And he said, "Take the arrows," and he took them. And he said to the king of Israel, "Strike the ground with them." And he struck three times and stopped. [19]Then the man of God was angry with him and said, "You should have struck five or six times; then you would have struck down Syria until you had made an end of it, but now you will strike down Syria only three times."

[20]So Elisha died, and they buried him. Now bands of Moabites used to invade the land in the spring of the year. [21]And as a man was being buried, behold, a marauding band was seen and the man was thrown into the grave of Elisha, and as soon as the man touched the bones of Elisha, he revived and stood on his feet.

[22]Now Hazael king of Syria oppressed Israel all the days of Jehoahaz. [23]But the Lord was gracious to them and had compassion on them, and he turned toward them, because of his covenant with Abraham, Isaac, and Jacob, and would not destroy them, nor has he cast them from his presence until now.

[24]When Hazael king of Syria died, Ben-hadad his son became king in his place. [25]Then Jehoash the son of Jehoahaz took again from Ben-hadad the son of Hazael the cities that he had taken from Jehoahaz his father in war. Three times Joash defeated him and recovered the cities of Israel.

Amaziah Reigns in Judah

14 In the second year of Joash the son of Joahaz, king of Israel, Amaziah the son of Joash, king of Judah, began to reign. [2]He was twenty-five years old when he began to reign, and he reigned twenty-nine years in Jerusalem. His

[1]Septuagint, Syriac, Targum, Vulgate; Hebrew *he walked* [2]*Jehoash* is an alternate spelling of *Joash* (son of Jehoahaz) as in verses 9, 12–14; also verse 25

2 KINGS 13:22–23

GLIMMERS OF GRACE

The kings and people of Israel continued to walk in sin (2Ki 13:2,11). Yet God provided a glimmer of grace and compassion to his elect by turning toward them and not destroying them—all because of his loyalty to his covenant promises with Abraham, Isaac, and Jacob. God's covenants are indissoluble and eternal. His love pours out on his people even in the midst of their sin. God shows his faithfulness to his people by reminding them of the promises he made and fulfilled in the past.

When Jesus came, he made his relationship to past covenants crystal clear: he had come to fulfill the Law and the Prophets (Mt 5:17). Jesus told Zacchaeus that salvation had come to Zacchaeus' house due to him being a true "son of Abraham" and, thus, a recipient of the covenant promises. And Jesus proclaimed that he came for the lost—those, who like the Old Testament Israelites, live in sin and need salvation (Lk 19:9–10). God always keeps his promises, ultimately offering grace and mercy to those who turn from their sin and put their faith in Jesus.

mother's name was Jehoaddin of Jerusalem. [3]And he did what was right in the eyes of the LORD, yet not like David his father. He did in all things as Joash his father had done. [4]But the high places were not removed; the people still sacrificed and made offerings on the high places. [5]And as soon as the royal power was firmly in his hand, he struck down his servants who had struck down the king his father. [6]But he did not put to death the children of the murderers, according to what is written in the Book of the Law of Moses, where the LORD commanded, "Fathers shall not be put to death because of their children, nor shall children be put to death because of their fathers. But each one shall die for his own sin."

[7]He struck down ten thousand Edomites in the Valley of Salt and took Sela by storm, and called it Joktheel, which is its name to this day.

[8]Then Amaziah sent messengers to Jehoash[1] the son of Jehoahaz, son of Jehu, king of Israel, saying, "Come, let us look one another in the face." [9]And Jehoash king of Israel sent word to Amaziah king of Judah, "A thistle on Lebanon sent to a cedar on Lebanon, saying, 'Give your daughter to my son for a wife,' and a wild beast of Lebanon passed by and trampled down the thistle. [10]You have indeed struck down Edom, and your heart has lifted you up. Be content with your glory, and stay at home, for why should you provoke trouble so that you fall, you and Judah with you?"

[11]But Amaziah would not listen. So Jehoash king of Israel went up, and he and Amaziah king of Judah faced one another in battle at Beth-shemesh, which belongs to Judah. [12]And Judah was defeated by Israel, and every man fled to his home. [13]And Jehoash king of Israel captured Amaziah king of Judah, the son of Jehoash, son of Ahaziah, at Beth-shemesh, and came to Jerusalem and broke down the wall of Jerusalem for four hundred cubits,[2] from the Ephraim Gate to the Corner Gate. [14]And he seized all the gold and silver, and all the vessels that were found in the house of the LORD and in the treasuries of the king's house, also hostages, and he returned to Samaria.

[15]Now the rest of the acts of Jehoash that he did, and his might, and how he fought with Amaziah king of Judah, are they not written in the Book of the Chronicles of the Kings of Israel? [16]And Jehoash slept with his fathers and was buried in Samaria with the kings of Israel, and Jeroboam his son reigned in his place.

[17]Amaziah the son of Joash, king of Judah, lived fifteen years after the death of Jehoash son of Jehoahaz, king of Israel. [18]Now the rest of the deeds of Amaziah, are they not written in the Book of the Chronicles of the Kings of Judah? [19]And they made a conspiracy against him in Jerusalem, and he fled to Lachish. But they sent after him to Lachish and put him to death there. [20]And they brought him on horses; and he was buried in Jerusalem with his fathers in the city of David. [21]And all the people of Judah took Azariah, who was sixteen years old, and made him king instead of his father Amaziah. [22]He built Elath and restored it to Judah, after the king slept with his fathers.

Jeroboam II Reigns in Israel

[23]In the fifteenth year of Amaziah the son of Joash, king of Judah, Jeroboam the son of Joash, king of Israel, began to reign in Samaria, and he reigned forty-one years. [24]And he did what was evil in the sight of the LORD. He did not depart from all the sins of Jeroboam the son of Nebat, which he made Israel to sin. [25]He restored the border of Israel from Lebo-hamath as far as the Sea of the Arabah, according to the word of the LORD, the God of Israel, which he spoke by his servant Jonah the son of Amittai, the prophet, who was from Gath-hepher. [26]For the LORD saw that the affliction of Israel was very bitter, for there was none left, bond or

[1]*Jehoash* is an alternate spelling of *Joash* (son of Jehoahaz) as in 13:9, 12–14; also verses 9, 11–16 [2]A *cubit* was about 18 inches or 45 centimeters

A FALSE VISION OF GREATNESS

The people of Judah, under King Amaziah, walked more faithfully with God than the people of Israel did under their king, Jehoash. God allowed Judah and King Amaziah to conquer a rival nation, but this victory fostered pride in the heart of the king. His pride caused him to think more highly of himself and his actions than he ought, which led him to take reckless action that resulted in devastating consequences for him and his nation. Amaziah challenged Jehoash to battle, and Jehoash replied to him in the form of a fable. By comparing King Amaziah to a thistle in contrast to the cedars of Lebanon, King Jehoash attempted to help him have a more realistic picture of his status and accomplishments. Blinded by pride, Amaziah would not listen. He was soundly defeated in battle by Jehoash's army.

Pride is an ever-present temptation for all people, including those who have received the gift of God's grace. Scripture notes that even Jesus' disciples struggled with pride. For example, immediately following the Lord's Supper, the disciples debated over which one of them was the greatest. They, like Amaziah, had witnessed God doing amazing things in and through their lives. This success fueled their pride. Jesus redirected them, teaching them that his followers would be marked by humility and service (Lk 22:24 – 30). Greatness in the kingdom of God is not found in elevating oneself, but in lowering oneself and modeling the servant-nature of Christ (Php 2:1 – 11).

Jesus also warned his followers about the danger of approaching God with a spirit of pride and self-righteousness. He told the parable of two people, a notorious sinner and a noted religious leader (Lk 18:9 – 14). The religious leader, confident in himself, came to God and thanked him that he was not like the sinful man. The notorious sinner, in contrast, stood at a distance, bowed his head and begged God to be merciful to him in spite of his sin.

Jesus' followers should be marked by a dependence on God for his mercy and grace, knowing that in and of themselves they have nothing to offer. Pride will ultimately lead to destruction, while humility leads to the mercy of God.

free, and there was none to help Israel. 27But the LORD had not said that he would blot out the name of Israel from under heaven, so he saved them by the hand of Jeroboam the son of Joash.

28Now the rest of the acts of Jeroboam and all that he did, and his might, how he fought, and how he restored Damascus and Hamath to Judah in Israel, are they not written in the Book of the Chronicles of the Kings of Israel? 29And Jeroboam slept with his fathers, the kings of Israel, and Zechariah his son reigned in his place.

Azariah Reigns in Judah

15 In the twenty-seventh year of Jeroboam king of Israel, Azariah the son of Amaziah, king of Judah, began to reign. 2He was sixteen years old when he began to reign, and he reigned fifty-two years in Jerusalem. His mother's name was Jecoliah of Jerusalem. 3And he did what was right in the eyes of the LORD, according to all that his father Amaziah had done. 4Nevertheless, the high places were not taken away. The people still sacrificed and made offerings on the high places. 5And the LORD touched the king, so that he was a leper[1] to the day of his death, and he lived in a separate house.[2] And Jotham the king's son was over the household, governing the people of the land. 6Now the rest of the acts of Azariah, and all that he did, are they not written in the Book of the Chronicles of the Kings of Judah? 7And Azariah slept with his fathers, and they buried him with his fathers in the city of David, and Jotham his son reigned in his place.

Zechariah Reigns in Israel

8In the thirty-eighth year of Azariah king of Judah, Zechariah the son of Jeroboam reigned over Israel in Samaria six months. 9And he did what was evil in the sight of the LORD, as his fathers had done. He did not depart from the sins of Jeroboam the son of Nebat, which he made Israel to sin. 10Shallum the son of Jabesh conspired against him and struck him down at Ibleam and put him to death and reigned in his place. 11Now the rest of the deeds of Zechariah, behold, they are written in the Book of the Chronicles of the Kings of Israel. 12(This was the promise of the LORD that he gave to Jehu, "Your sons shall sit on the throne of Israel to the fourth generation." And so it came to pass.)

Shallum Reigns in Israel

13Shallum the son of Jabesh began to reign in the thirty-ninth year of Uzziah[3] king of Judah, and he reigned one month in Samaria. 14Then Menahem the son of Gadi came up from Tirzah and came to Samaria, and he struck down Shallum the son of Jabesh in Samaria and put him to death and reigned in his place. 15Now the rest of the deeds of Shallum, and the conspiracy that he made, behold, they are written in the Book of the Chronicles of the Kings of Israel. 16At that time Menahem sacked Tiphsah and all who were in it and its territory from Tirzah on, because they did not open it to him. Therefore he sacked it, and he ripped open all the women in it who were pregnant.

Menahem Reigns in Israel

17In the thirty-ninth year of Azariah king of Judah, Menahem the son of Gadi began to reign over Israel, and he reigned ten years in Samaria. 18And he did what was evil in the sight of the LORD. He did not depart all his days from all the sins of Jeroboam the son of Nebat, which he made Israel to sin. 19Pul[4] the king of Assyria came against the land, and Menahem gave Pul a thousand talents[5] of silver, that he might help him to confirm his hold on the royal power. 20Menahem exacted the money from Israel, that is, from all the wealthy men, fifty shekels[6] of silver

[1]*Leprosy* was a term for several skin diseases; see Leviticus 13 [2]The meaning of the Hebrew word is uncertain [3]Another name for *Azariah* [4]Another name for *Tiglath-pileser III* (compare verse 29)
[5]A *talent* was about 75 pounds or 34 kilograms [6]A *shekel* was about 2/5 ounce or 11 grams

2 KINGS 15:8–31

THE DOWNWARD SLOPE

Israel's freedom from foreign oppression was short-lived because the leadership of the northern kingdom continued to spiral downward into ungodliness. Israel suffered through a progression of weak kings who largely came to power through conspiracy and assassination. God was at work judging the previous 200 years of rebellion against him. This pattern of wickedness in the kings of Israel was one of the ways by which the judgment of God came upon his people.

Jesus came to the remnant of this nation under the oppression of Rome. They lived in fear of the capricious government and under a deafening silence from their God. There had been no prophets to call them back to God in a long time. Jesus arrived into this world and proclaimed that God's kingdom had come. Liberation and freedom were now available for his people. The wickedness of the religious leaders drove him to call them to repentance (Mt 9:13; Mk 2:17; Lk 5:32). God displays his love for his people in his judgment and his calls for them to repent. It is in this call to repentance that people have the opportunity to cease following wicked leadership and acknowledge God's leadership in their lives.

from every man, to give to the king of Assyria. So the king of Assyria turned back and did not stay there in the land. [21]Now the rest of the deeds of Menahem and all that he did, are they not written in the Book of the Chronicles of the Kings of Israel? [22]And Menahem slept with his fathers, and Pekahiah his son reigned in his place.

Pekahiah Reigns in Israel

[23]In the fiftieth year of Azariah king of Judah, Pekahiah the son of Menahem began to reign over Israel in Samaria, and he reigned two years. [24]And he did what was evil in the sight of the LORD. He did not turn away from the sins of Jeroboam the son of Nebat, which he made Israel to sin. [25]And Pekah the son of Remaliah, his captain, conspired against him with fifty men of the people of Gilead, and struck him down in Samaria, in the citadel of the king's house with Argob and Arieh; he put him to death and reigned in his place. [26]Now the rest of the deeds of Pekahiah and all that he did, behold, they are written in the Book of the Chronicles of the Kings of Israel.

Pekah Reigns in Israel

[27]In the fifty-second year of Azariah king of Judah, Pekah the son of Remaliah began to reign over Israel in Samaria, and he reigned twenty years. [28]And he did what was evil in the sight of the LORD. He did not depart from the sins of Jeroboam the son of Nebat, which he made Israel to sin.

[29]In the days of Pekah king of Israel, Tiglath-pileser king of Assyria came and captured Ijon, Abel-beth-maacah, Janoah, Kedesh, Hazor, Gilead, and Galilee, all the land of Naphtali, and he carried the people captive to Assyria. [30]Then Hoshea the son of Elah made a conspiracy against Pekah the son of Remaliah and struck him down and put him to death and reigned in his place, in the twentieth year of Jotham the son of Uzziah. [31]Now the rest of the acts of Pekah and all that he did, behold, they are written in the Book of the Chronicles of the Kings of Israel.

Jotham Reigns in Judah

[32]In the second year of Pekah the son of Remaliah, king of Israel, Jotham the son of Uzziah, king of Judah, began to reign. [33]He was twenty-five years old when he began to reign, and he reigned sixteen years in Jerusalem. His mother's name was Jerusha the daughter of Zadok. [34]And he did what was right in the eyes of the LORD, according to all that his father Uzziah had done. [35]Nevertheless, the high places were not removed. The people still sacrificed and made offerings on the high places. He built the upper gate of the house of the LORD. [36]Now the rest of the acts of Jotham and all that he did, are they not written in the Book of the Chronicles of the Kings of Judah? [37]In those days the LORD began to send Rezin the king of Syria and Pekah the son of Remaliah against Judah. [38]Jotham slept with his fathers and was buried with his fathers in the city of David his father, and Ahaz his son reigned in his place.

Ahaz Reigns in Judah

16 In the seventeenth year of Pekah the son of Remaliah, Ahaz the son of Jotham, king of Judah, began to reign. [2]Ahaz was twenty years old when he began to reign, and he reigned sixteen years in Jerusalem. And he did not do what was right in the eyes of the LORD his God, as his father David had done, [3]but he walked in the way of the kings of Israel. He even burned his son as an offering,[1] according to the despicable practices of the nations whom the LORD drove out before the people of Israel. [4]And he sacrificed and made offerings on the high places and on the hills and under every green tree.

[5]Then Rezin king of Syria and Pekah the son of Remaliah, king of Israel, came up to wage war on Jerusalem, and they besieged Ahaz but could not conquer him.

[1]Or *made his son pass through the fire*

[6]At that time Rezin the king of Syria recovered Elath for Syria and drove the men
of Judah from Elath, and the Edomites came to Elath, where they dwell to this day.
[7]So Ahaz sent messengers to Tiglath-pileser king of Assyria, saying, "I am your
servant and your son. Come up and rescue me from the hand of the king of Syria
and from the hand of the king of Israel, who are attacking me." [8]Ahaz also took
the silver and gold that was found in the house of the LORD and in the treasures of
the king's house and sent a present to the king of Assyria. [9]And the king of Assyria
listened to him. The king of Assyria marched up against Damascus and took it,
carrying its people captive to Kir, and he killed Rezin.
[10]When King Ahaz went to Damascus to meet Tiglath-pileser king of Assyria,
he saw the altar that was at Damascus. And King Ahaz sent to Uriah the priest a
model of the altar, and its pattern, exact in all its details. [11]And Uriah the priest
built the altar; in accordance with all that King Ahaz had sent from Damascus, so
Uriah the priest made it, before King Ahaz arrived from Damascus. [12]And when
the king came from Damascus, the king viewed the altar. Then the king drew
near to the altar and went up on it [13]and burned his burnt offering and his grain
offering and poured his drink offering and threw the blood of his peace offerings
on the altar. [14]And the bronze altar that was before the LORD he removed from the
front of the house, from the place between his altar and the house of the LORD,
and put it on the north side of his altar. [15]And King Ahaz commanded Uriah the
priest, saying, "On the great altar burn the morning burnt offering and the evening grain offering and the king's burnt offering and his grain offering, with the
burnt offering of all the people of the land, and their grain offering and their drink
offering. And throw on it all the blood of the burnt offering and all the blood of
the sacrifice, but the bronze altar shall be for me to inquire by." [16]Uriah the priest
did all this, as King Ahaz commanded.
[17]And King Ahaz cut off the frames of the stands and removed the basin from
them, and he took down the sea[1] from off the bronze oxen that were under it and
put it on a stone pedestal. [18]And the covered way for the Sabbath that had been
built inside the house and the outer entrance for the king he caused to go around
the house of the LORD, because of the king of Assyria. [19]Now the rest of the acts of
Ahaz that he did, are they not written in the Book of the Chronicles of the Kings
of Judah? [20]And Ahaz slept with his fathers and was buried with his fathers in the
city of David, and Hezekiah his son reigned in his place.

Hoshea Reigns in Israel

17 In the twelfth year of Ahaz king of Judah, Hoshea the son of Elah began to
reign in Samaria over Israel, and he reigned nine years. [2]And he did what
was evil in the sight of the LORD, yet not as the kings of Israel who were before
him. [3]Against him came up Shalmaneser king of Assyria. And Hoshea became his
vassal and paid him tribute. [4]But the king of Assyria found treachery in Hoshea,
for he had sent messengers to So, king of Egypt, and offered no tribute to the king
of Assyria, as he had done year by year. Therefore the king of Assyria shut him up
and bound him in prison. [5]Then the king of Assyria invaded all the land and came
to Samaria, and for three years he besieged it.

The Fall of Israel

[6]In the ninth year of Hoshea, the king of Assyria captured Samaria, and he
carried the Israelites away to Assyria and placed them in Halah, and on the Habor,
the river of Gozan, and in the cities of the Medes.

Exile Because of Idolatry

[7]And this occurred because the people of Israel had sinned against the LORD
their God, who had brought them up out of the land of Egypt from under the

[1]Compare 1 Kings 7:23

2 KINGS 16:10–16

FALSE WORSHIP IN THE TEMPLE

King Ahaz observed a pagan altar while visiting Damascus and purposed to construct a similar altar in the temple of God in Jerusalem, which would have been a further sign of submission to the Assyrians. After he commanded Uriah to construct an altar following the pattern of the one in Damascus, Ahaz offered worship upon the pagan altar in the temple of God. This act demonstrated the profound moral perversion of the nation of Judah. The king himself, who functioned as the people's leader and representative, offered false worship on the site where God was meant to be worshiped.

Jesus faced a similar situation when he observed the money changers and merchants in the temple of God. Jesus drove the people from the temple because he was angered that his house was turned into a den of robbers (Mt 21:12–13). Judah's moral decline did not stop with King Ahaz. Repeatedly the people demonstrated an impoverished view of God by practicing false worship.

The church throughout all generations must guard itself at all costs against twisting God's good gifts into a means of false worship. They must work to protect God's church from those who would lead them to worship something other than God.

2 KINGS 17:7–20

THE CONSEQUENCES OF SIN

The Israelites were often referred to as "stubborn," or stiff-necked

(continued on next page)

(The Consequences of Sin, continued)

(2Ki 17:14). This title is an apt description of the consistent, deep-seated rebellion that plagued the people at every turn. Like an animal stiffens its neck in protest rather than submitting to its master's guidance, so the nations of Israel and Judah refused to submit to God. They had been warned repeatedly that such insubordination would incur the judgment of God. Specifically, they had been told that if they would not obey, God would kick them out of the land in order to protect the honor of his name. God saw their continued rebellion, and he enacted his just judgment.

John the Baptist warned of the impending doom the people in his day too were sure to face. "Repent," he cried (Mt 3:2). Jesus' consistent call was for people to turn from their sin and to turn to him in faith. Those who are unwilling to turn from sin and toward him will face the sure judgment of God that sin deserves. The good news is that all who do repent will be spared the wrath of God, and by his grace they will be granted fellowship with him forever.

hand of Pharaoh king of Egypt, and had feared other gods 8and walked in the customs of the nations whom the LORD drove out before the people of Israel, and in the customs that the kings of Israel had practiced. 9And the people of Israel did secretly against the LORD their God things that were not right. They built for themselves high places in all their towns, from watchtower to fortified city. 10They set up for themselves pillars and Asherim on every high hill and under every green tree, 11and there they made offerings on all the high places, as the nations did whom the LORD carried away before them. And they did wicked things, provoking the LORD to anger, 12and they served idols, of which the LORD had said to them, "You shall not do this." 13Yet the LORD warned Israel and Judah by every prophet and every seer, saying, "Turn from your evil ways and keep my commandments and my statutes, in accordance with all the Law that I commanded your fathers, and that I sent to you by my servants the prophets."

14But they would not listen, but were stubborn, as their fathers had been, who did not believe in the LORD their God. 15They despised his statutes and his covenant that he made with their fathers and the warnings that he gave them. They went after false idols and became false, and they followed the nations that were around them, concerning whom the LORD had commanded them that they should not do like them. 16And they abandoned all the commandments of the LORD their God, and made for themselves metal images of two calves; and they made an Asherah and worshiped all the host of heaven and served Baal. 17And they burned their sons and their daughters as offerings[1] and used divination and omens and sold themselves to do evil in the sight of the LORD, provoking him to anger. 18Therefore the LORD was very angry with Israel and removed them out of his sight. None was left but the tribe of Judah only.

19Judah also did not keep the commandments of the LORD their God, but walked in the customs that Israel had introduced. 20And the LORD rejected all the descendants of Israel and afflicted them and gave them into the hand of plunderers, until he had cast them out of his sight.

21When he had torn Israel from the house of David, they made Jeroboam the son of Nebat king. And Jeroboam drove Israel from following the LORD and made them commit great sin. 22The people of Israel walked in all the sins that Jeroboam did. They did not depart from them, 23until the LORD removed Israel out of his sight, as he had spoken by all his servants the prophets. So Israel was exiled from their own land to Assyria until this day.

Assyria Resettles Samaria

24And the king of Assyria brought people from Babylon, Cuthah, Avva, Hamath, and Sepharvaim, and placed them in the cities of Samaria instead of the people of Israel. And they took possession of Samaria and lived in its cities. 25And at the beginning of their dwelling there, they did not fear the LORD. Therefore the LORD sent lions among them, which killed some of them. 26So the king of Assyria was told, "The nations that you have carried away and placed in the cities of Samaria do not know the law of the god of the land. Therefore he has sent lions among them, and behold, they are killing them, because they do not know the law of the god of the land." 27Then the king of Assyria commanded, "Send there one of the priests whom you carried away from there, and let him[2] go and dwell there and teach them the law of the god of the land." 28So one of the priests whom they had carried away from Samaria came and lived in Bethel and taught them how they should fear the LORD.

29But every nation still made gods of its own and put them in the shrines of the high places that the Samaritans had made, every nation in the cities in which they lived. 30The men of Babylon made Succoth-benoth, the men of Cuth made

[1] Or *made their sons and their daughters pass through the fire* [2] Syriac, Vulgate; Hebrew *them*

Nergal, the men of Hamath made Ashima, 31and the Avvites made Nibhaz and
Tartak; and the Sepharvites burned their children in the fire to Adrammelech and
Anammelech, the gods of Sepharvaim. 32They also feared the LORD and appointed
from among themselves all sorts of people as priests of the high places, who sacrificed for them in the shrines of the high places. 33So they feared the LORD but
also served their own gods, after the manner of the nations from among whom
they had been carried away.

34To this day they do according to the former manner. They do not fear the
LORD, and they do not follow the statutes or the rules or the law or the commandment that the LORD commanded the children of Jacob, whom he named Israel.
35The LORD made a covenant with them and commanded them, "You shall not
fear other gods or bow yourselves to them or serve them or sacrifice to them,
36but you shall fear the LORD, who brought you out of the land of Egypt with great
power and with an outstretched arm. You shall bow yourselves to him, and to
him you shall sacrifice. 37And the statutes and the rules and the law and the commandment that he wrote for you, you shall always be careful to do. You shall not
fear other gods, 38and you shall not forget the covenant that I have made with
you. You shall not fear other gods, 39but you shall fear the LORD your God, and he
will deliver you out of the hand of all your enemies." 40However, they would not
listen, but they did according to their former manner.

41So these nations feared the LORD and also served their carved images. Their
children did likewise, and their children's children—as their fathers did, so they
do to this day.

Hezekiah Reigns in Judah

18 In the third year of Hoshea son of Elah, king of Israel, Hezekiah the son of
Ahaz, king of Judah, began to reign. 2He was twenty-five years old when
he began to reign, and he reigned twenty-nine years in Jerusalem. His mother's
name was Abi the daughter of Zechariah. 3And he did what was right in the eyes
of the LORD, according to all that David his father had done. 4He removed the
high places and broke the pillars and cut down the Asherah. And he broke in
pieces the bronze serpent that Moses had made, for until those days the people
of Israel had made offerings to it (it was called Nehushtan).[1] 5He trusted in the
LORD, the God of Israel, so that there was none like him among all the kings of
Judah after him, nor among those who were before him. 6For he held fast to the
LORD. He did not depart from following him, but kept the commandments that
the LORD commanded Moses. 7And the LORD was with him; wherever he went
out, he prospered. He rebelled against the king of Assyria and would not serve
him. 8He struck down the Philistines as far as Gaza and its territory, from watchtower to fortified city.

9In the fourth year of King Hezekiah, which was the seventh year of Hoshea
son of Elah, king of Israel, Shalmaneser king of Assyria came up against Samaria
and besieged it, 10and at the end of three years he took it. In the sixth year of
Hezekiah, which was the ninth year of Hoshea king of Israel, Samaria was taken.
11The king of Assyria carried the Israelites away to Assyria and put them in Halah,
and on the Habor, the river of Gozan, and in the cities of the Medes, 12because
they did not obey the voice of the LORD their God but transgressed his covenant,
even all that Moses the servant of the LORD commanded. They neither listened
nor obeyed.

Sennacherib Attacks Judah

13In the fourteenth year of King Hezekiah, Sennacherib king of Assyria came
up against all the fortified cities of Judah and took them. 14And Hezekiah king
of Judah sent to the king of Assyria at Lachish, saying, "I have done wrong;

[1] *Nehushtan* sounds like the Hebrew for both *bronze* and *serpent*

THE RELICS OF WORSHIP

Throughout the Old Testament, God gave specific commands to his people regarding the high places on which pagans worshiped a host of false gods. Knowing that the presence of these high places would provide a steady temptation for his people, God commanded them to destroy entirely the worship sites (Nu 33:52; Dt 12:2). Ironically, Israelites who worshiped at these locations sometimes maintained traditions of worship of the one true God while also integrating the perverse worship of a wide array of gods including Baal and Asherah.

King Hezekiah knew that the removal of these locations would not render idolatry obsolete, but it would aid in the return of the people to the worship of the one true God. He also destroyed the objects of worship used by the pagan cults — many of which had been introduced during the reign of his apostate father, Ahaz. One such object of false worship was the bronze snake that had been preserved since the time of Moses (2Ki 18:4). This bronze snake was originally intended by God to provide a tangible symbol of salvation. At some point, however, this God-ordained object became venerated in and of itself — an example of the gift overshadowing the Giver. The snake was never meant to be an object of worship, but, like many symbols, it became something different from what God intended it to be.

Paul argued in the book of Romans that misdirected worship is at the heart of all human sin. People, by virtue of their sin nature, take God's created handiwork and elevate it to a place of worship (Ro 1:23). As a result, the worship of the one true God is overshadowed, devalued, or excluded completely. All things created by God are good, yet they can be turned into a source of sin when given a more prominent place in the human heart than they deserve. Even objects used in worship, such as a church building, style of music, or various programmatic structures in the church can become idolatrous if they cause the people of God to stumble and turn from the worship of the true God. Like the bronze snake, these objects often have great spiritual significance; however, they can become packed with idolatrous potential. All people must guard their hearts from the worship of relics and redirect their hearts, by the power of the Spirit, to worship the only one worthy of all worship: Jesus.

withdraw from me. Whatever you impose on me I will bear." And the king of Assyria required of Hezekiah king of Judah three hundred talents[1] of silver and thirty talents of gold. 15And Hezekiah gave him all the silver that was found in the house of the LORD and in the treasuries of the king's house. 16At that time Hezekiah stripped the gold from the doors of the temple of the LORD and from the doorposts that Hezekiah king of Judah had overlaid and gave it to the king of Assyria. 17And the king of Assyria sent the Tartan, the Rab-saris, and the Rabshakeh with a great army from Lachish to King Hezekiah at Jerusalem. And they went up and came to Jerusalem. When they arrived, they came and stood by the conduit of the upper pool, which is on the highway to the Washer's Field. 18And when they called for the king, there came out to them Eliakim the son of Hilkiah, who was over the household, and Shebnah the secretary, and Joah the son of Asaph, the recorder.

19And the Rabshakeh said to them, "Say to Hezekiah, 'Thus says the great king, the king of Assyria: On what do you rest this trust of yours? 20Do you think that mere words are strategy and power for war? In whom do you now trust, that you have rebelled against me? 21Behold, you are trusting now in Egypt, that broken reed of a staff, which will pierce the hand of any man who leans on it. Such is Pharaoh king of Egypt to all who trust in him. 22But if you say to me, "We trust in the LORD our God," is it not he whose high places and altars Hezekiah has removed, saying to Judah and to Jerusalem, "You shall worship before this altar in Jerusalem"? 23Come now, make a wager with my master the king of Assyria: I will give you two thousand horses, if you are able on your part to set riders on them. 24How then can you repulse a single captain among the least of my master's servants, when you trust in Egypt for chariots and for horsemen? 25Moreover, is it without the LORD that I have come up against this place to destroy it? The LORD said to me, "Go up against this land and destroy it."'"

26Then Eliakim the son of Hilkiah, and Shebnah, and Joah, said to the Rabshakeh, "Please speak to your servants in Aramaic, for we understand it. Do not speak to us in the language of Judah within the hearing of the people who are on the wall." 27But the Rabshakeh said to them, "Has my master sent me to speak these words to your master and to you, and not to the men sitting on the wall, who are doomed with you to eat their own dung and to drink their own urine?"

28Then the Rabshakeh stood and called out in a loud voice in the language of Judah: "Hear the word of the great king, the king of Assyria! 29Thus says the king: 'Do not let Hezekiah deceive you, for he will not be able to deliver you out of my[2] hand. 30Do not let Hezekiah make you trust in the LORD by saying, The LORD will surely deliver us, and this city will not be given into the hand of the king of Assyria.' 31Do not listen to Hezekiah, for thus says the king of Assyria: 'Make your peace with me[3] and come out to me. Then each one of you will eat of his own vine, and each one of his own fig tree, and each one of you will drink the water of his own cistern, 32until I come and take you away to a land like your own land, a land of grain and wine, a land of bread and vineyards, a land of olive trees and honey, that you may live, and not die. And do not listen to Hezekiah when he misleads you by saying, "The LORD will deliver us." 33Has any of the gods of the nations ever delivered his land out of the hand of the king of Assyria? 34Where are the gods of Hamath and Arpad? Where are the gods of Sepharvaim, Hena, and Ivvah? Have they delivered Samaria out of my hand? 35Who among all the gods of the lands have delivered their lands out of my hand, that the LORD should deliver Jerusalem out of my hand?'"

36But the people were silent and answered him not a word, for the king's command was, "Do not answer him." 37Then Eliakim the son of Hilkiah, who was over the household, and Shebna the secretary, and Joah the son of Asaph, the

[1]A *talent* was about 75 pounds or 34 kilograms [2]Hebrew *his* [3]Hebrew *Make a blessing with me*

2 KINGS 18:28–37

GOD'S VINDICATION

Many of the greatest failures in history seemed like prudent decisions at the time. King Sennacherib's mockery of Judah and their God, delivered by his field commander, seemed appropriate based on the situation. God's chosen people had diminished as Assyria sacked the northern kingdom during Hezekiah's reign. Now the remainder of God's special nation was holed up in cities, besieged and starving. The evidence seemed to support Sennacherib's assertion: the God of Judah was powerless in the face of the massive Assyrian army. But despite the military odds, the Lord of armies brought mighty Assyria to its knees. God vindicated his name against the mockers.

At Jesus' trial and execution, many mocked him. The soldiers shamed him (Mt 27:31). Passersby, religious leaders, and even one of those executed alongside him demonstrated their contempt for Jesus by deriding him as he died (Mt 27:38–44). But in the end it was God who emerged victorious (Ps 2:1–4). Jesus rose from the dead and defeated the plans of the religious and political rulers of his day as well as the spiritual powers of darkness that drove them to their wicked schemes (Col 2:15).

recorder, came to Hezekiah with their clothes torn and told him the words of the Rabshakeh.

Isaiah Reassures Hezekiah

19 As soon as King Hezekiah heard it, he tore his clothes and covered himself with sackcloth and went into the house of the LORD. 2And he sent Eliakim, who was over the household, and Shebna the secretary, and the senior priests, covered with sackcloth, to the prophet Isaiah the son of Amoz. 3They said to him, "Thus says Hezekiah, This day is a day of distress, of rebuke, and of disgrace; children have come to the point of birth, and there is no strength to bring them forth. 4It may be that the LORD your God heard all the words of the Rabshakeh, whom his master the king of Assyria has sent to mock the living God, and will rebuke the words that the LORD your God has heard; therefore lift up your prayer for the remnant that is left." 5When the servants of King Hezekiah came to Isaiah, 6Isaiah said to them, "Say to your master, 'Thus says the LORD: Do not be afraid because of the words that you have heard, with which the servants of the king of Assyria have reviled me. 7Behold, I will put a spirit in him, so that he shall hear a rumor and return to his own land, and I will make him fall by the sword in his own land.'"

Sennacherib Defies the LORD

8The Rabshakeh returned, and found the king of Assyria fighting against Libnah, for he heard that the king had left Lachish. 9Now the king heard concerning Tirhakah king of Cush, "Behold, he has set out to fight against you." So he sent messengers again to Hezekiah, saying, 10"Thus shall you speak to Hezekiah king of Judah: 'Do not let your God in whom you trust deceive you by promising that Jerusalem will not be given into the hand of the king of Assyria. 11Behold, you have heard what the kings of Assyria have done to all lands, devoting them to destruction. And shall you be delivered? 12Have the gods of the nations delivered them, the nations that my fathers destroyed, Gozan, Haran, Rezeph, and the people of Eden who were in Telassar? 13Where is the king of Hamath, the king of Arpad, the king of the city of Sepharvaim, the king of Hena, or the king of Ivvah?'"

Hezekiah's Prayer

14Hezekiah received the letter from the hand of the messengers and read it; and Hezekiah went up to the house of the LORD and spread it before the LORD. 15And Hezekiah prayed before the LORD and said: "O LORD, the God of Israel, enthroned above the cherubim, you are the God, you alone, of all the kingdoms of the earth; you have made the heavens and the earth. 16Incline your ear, O LORD, and hear; open your eyes, O LORD, and see; and hear the words of Sennacherib, which he has sent to mock the living God. 17Truly, O LORD, the kings of Assyria have laid waste the nations and their lands 18and have cast their gods into the fire, for they were not gods, but the work of men's hands, wood and stone. Therefore they were destroyed. 19So now, O LORD our God, save us, please, from his hand, that all the kingdoms of the earth may know that you, O LORD, are God alone."

Isaiah Prophesies Sennacherib's Fall

20Then Isaiah the son of Amoz sent to Hezekiah, saying, "Thus says the LORD, the God of Israel: Your prayer to me about Sennacherib king of Assyria I have heard. 21This is the word that the LORD has spoken concerning him:

"She despises you, she scorns you—
    the virgin daughter of Zion;
she wags her head behind you—
    the daughter of Jerusalem.

22 "Whom have you mocked and reviled?
Against whom have you raised your voice
and lifted your eyes to the heights?
Against the Holy One of Israel!
23 By your messengers you have mocked the Lord,
and you have said, 'With my many chariots
I have gone up the heights of the mountains,
to the far recesses of Lebanon;
I felled its tallest cedars,
its choicest cypresses;
I entered its farthest lodging place,
its most fruitful forest.
24 I dug wells
and drank foreign waters,
and I dried up with the sole of my foot
all the streams of Egypt.'

25 "Have you not heard
that I determined it long ago?
I planned from days of old
what now I bring to pass,
that you should turn fortified cities
into heaps of ruins,
26 while their inhabitants, shorn of strength,
are dismayed and confounded,
and have become like plants of the field
and like tender grass,
like grass on the housetops,
blighted before it is grown.

27 "But I know your sitting down
and your going out and coming in,
and your raging against me.
28 Because you have raged against me
and your complacency has come into my ears,
I will put my hook in your nose
and my bit in your mouth,
and I will turn you back on the way
by which you came.

29"And this shall be the sign for you: this year eat what grows of itself, and in
the second year what springs of the same. Then in the third year sow and reap and
plant vineyards, and eat their fruit. 30And the surviving remnant of the house of
Judah shall again take root downward and bear fruit upward. 31For out of Jerusalem shall go a remnant, and out of Mount Zion a band of survivors. The zeal of
the LORD will do this.

32"Therefore thus says the LORD concerning the king of Assyria: He shall not
come into this city or shoot an arrow there, or come before it with a shield or
cast up a siege mound against it. 33By the way that he came, by the same he shall
return, and he shall not come into this city, declares the LORD. 34For I will defend
this city to save it, for my own sake and for the sake of my servant David."

35And that night the angel of the LORD went out and struck down 185,000 in
the camp of the Assyrians. And when people arose early in the morning, behold,
these were all dead bodies. 36Then Sennacherib king of Assyria departed and
went home and lived at Nineveh. 37And as he was worshiping in the house of
Nisroch his god, Adrammelech and Sharezer, his sons, struck him down with
the sword and escaped into the land of Ararat. And Esarhaddon his son reigned
in his place.

Hezekiah's Illness and Recovery

20 In those days Hezekiah became sick and was at the point of death. And Isaiah the prophet the son of Amoz came to him and said to him, "Thus says the LORD, 'Set your house in order, for you shall die; you shall not recover.'" 2Then Hezekiah turned his face to the wall and prayed to the LORD, saying, 3"Now, O LORD, please remember how I have walked before you in faithfulness and with a whole heart, and have done what is good in your sight." And Hezekiah wept bitterly. 4And before Isaiah had gone out of the middle court, the word of the LORD came to him: 5"Turn back, and say to Hezekiah the leader of my people, Thus says the LORD, the God of David your father: I have heard your prayer; I have seen your tears. Behold, I will heal you. On the third day you shall go up to the house of the LORD, 6and I will add fifteen years to your life. I will deliver you and this city out of the hand of the king of Assyria, and I will defend this city for my own sake and for my servant David's sake." 7And Isaiah said, "Bring a cake of figs. And let them take and lay it on the boil, that he may recover."

8And Hezekiah said to Isaiah, "What shall be the sign that the LORD will heal me, and that I shall go up to the house of the LORD on the third day?" 9And Isaiah said, "This shall be the sign to you from the LORD, that the LORD will do the thing that he has promised: shall the shadow go forward ten steps, or go back ten steps?" 10And Hezekiah answered, "It is an easy thing for the shadow to lengthen ten steps. Rather let the shadow go back ten steps." 11And Isaiah the prophet called to the LORD, and he brought the shadow back ten steps, by which it had gone down on the steps of Ahaz.

Hezekiah and the Babylonian Envoys

12At that time Merodach-baladan the son of Baladan, king of Babylon, sent envoys with letters and a present to Hezekiah, for he heard that Hezekiah had been sick. 13And Hezekiah welcomed them, and he showed them all his treasure house, the silver, the gold, the spices, the precious oil, his armory, all that was found in his storehouses. There was nothing in his house or in all his realm that Hezekiah did not show them. 14Then Isaiah the prophet came to King Hezekiah, and said to him, "What did these men say? And from where did they come to you?" And Hezekiah said, "They have come from a far country, from Babylon." 15He said, "What have they seen in your house?" And Hezekiah answered, "They have seen all that is in my house; there is nothing in my storehouses that I did not show them."

16Then Isaiah said to Hezekiah, "Hear the word of the LORD: 17Behold, the days are coming, when all that is in your house, and that which your fathers have stored up till this day, shall be carried to Babylon. Nothing shall be left, says the LORD. 18And some of your own sons, who will come from you, whom you will father, shall be taken away, and they shall be eunuchs in the palace of the king of Babylon." 19Then Hezekiah said to Isaiah, "The word of the LORD that you have spoken is good." For he thought, "Why not, if there will be peace and security in my days?"

20The rest of the deeds of Hezekiah and all his might and how he made the pool and the conduit and brought water into the city, are they not written in the Book of the Chronicles of the Kings of Judah? 21And Hezekiah slept with his fathers, and Manasseh his son reigned in his place.

Manasseh Reigns in Judah

21 Manasseh was twelve years old when he began to reign, and he reigned fifty-five years in Jerusalem. His mother's name was Hephzibah. 2And he did what was evil in the sight of the LORD, according to the despicable practices of the nations whom the LORD drove out before the people of Israel. 3For he rebuilt the high places that Hezekiah his father had destroyed, and he erected altars for Baal and made an Asherah, as Ahab king of Israel had done, and worshiped all

FAITHFULNESS REWARDED

In contrast to many of the kings in ancient Judah, Hezekiah was a great and faithful king. He trusted God and held fast to his commandments (2Ki 18:5 – 6). Faced with his impending death, Hezekiah wept before the Lord and asked that God would extend his life. God, in kindness, granted Hezekiah's request and added fifteen years to his life. While Hezekiah could have easily used this extra fifteen years to his own selfish advantage, he remained faithful to God by living in obedience. However, the verses following Hezekiah's healing describe a rare, unwise decision made by Hezekiah. He hosted envoys from the king of Babylon and revealed to them the vast provision that the Lord had entrusted to him and to the nation.

Isaiah responded to Hezekiah's actions by warning him of a day when invaders from Babylon would return to the land of the people of God only to steal the very riches Hezekiah had shown off. The silver, gold, and even some of Hezekiah's own descendants would be hauled off to that foreign land. Isaiah told Hezekiah that, in the final analysis, nothing would be left of his vast riches. It is easy to read Hezekiah's reaction as selfish and smug. He appeared to be grateful that any negative consequences for his actions would be experienced after his death, so he would not have to deal with his own mistake. However, a more accurate interpretation that is in line with Hezekiah's character is that he humbly accepted the word of the prophet. Hezekiah seemed to resign himself to the consequences of his mistake, and he may have been relieved that what Isaiah said would not happen during his lifetime.

In contrast, Jesus willingly took on the consequences of everyone's mistakes. Jesus knew that, like Hezekiah, everyone has made bad decisions that will one day have consequences — consequences like death and separation from God (Ro 6:23). However, Jesus' death frees believers from these consequences and gives them eternal life with God. Believers should respond to this news with Hezekiah-like humility and gratefulness, knowing that the Word of God is true. It is now the responsibility of Christians to share the great news that Jesus came and paid for everyone's sins.

the host of heaven and served them. 4And he built altars in the house of the LORD, of which the LORD had said, "In Jerusalem will I put my name." 5And he built altars for all the host of heaven in the two courts of the house of the LORD. 6And he burned his son as an offering[1] and used fortune-telling and omens and dealt with mediums and with necromancers. He did much evil in the sight of the LORD, provoking him to anger. 7And the carved image of Asherah that he had made he set in the house of which the LORD said to David and to Solomon his son, "In this house, and in Jerusalem, which I have chosen out of all the tribes of Israel, I will put my name forever. 8And I will not cause the feet of Israel to wander anymore out of the land that I gave to their fathers, if only they will be careful to do according to all that I have commanded them, and according to all the Law that my servant Moses commanded them." 9But they did not listen, and Manasseh led them astray to do more evil than the nations had done whom the LORD destroyed before the people of Israel.

Manasseh's Idolatry Denounced

10And the LORD said by his servants the prophets, 11"Because Manasseh king of Judah has committed these abominations and has done things more evil than all that the Amorites did, who were before him, and has made Judah also to sin with his idols, 12therefore thus says the LORD, the God of Israel: Behold, I am bringing upon Jerusalem and Judah such disaster[2] that the ears of everyone who hears of it will tingle. 13And I will stretch over Jerusalem the measuring line of Samaria, and the plumb line of the house of Ahab, and I will wipe Jerusalem as one wipes a dish, wiping it and turning it upside down. 14And I will forsake the remnant of my heritage and give them into the hand of their enemies, and they shall become a prey and a spoil to all their enemies, 15because they have done what is evil in my sight and have provoked me to anger, since the day their fathers came out of Egypt, even to this day."

16Moreover, Manasseh shed very much innocent blood, till he had filled Jerusalem from one end to another, besides the sin that he made Judah to sin so that they did what was evil in the sight of the LORD.

17Now the rest of the acts of Manasseh and all that he did, and the sin that he committed, are they not written in the Book of the Chronicles of the Kings of Judah? 18And Manasseh slept with his fathers and was buried in the garden of his house, in the garden of Uzza, and Amon his son reigned in his place.

Amon Reigns in Judah

19Amon was twenty-two years old when he began to reign, and he reigned two years in Jerusalem. His mother's name was Meshullemeth the daughter of Haruz of Jotbah. 20And he did what was evil in the sight of the LORD, as Manasseh his father had done. 21He walked in all the way in which his father walked and served the idols that his father served and worshiped them. 22He abandoned the LORD, the God of his fathers, and did not walk in the way of the LORD. 23And the servants of Amon conspired against him and put the king to death in his house. 24But the people of the land struck down all those who had conspired against King Amon, and the people of the land made Josiah his son king in his place. 25Now the rest of the acts of Amon that he did, are they not written in the Book of the Chronicles of the Kings of Judah? 26And he was buried in his tomb in the garden of Uzza, and Josiah his son reigned in his place.

Josiah Reigns in Judah

22 Josiah was eight years old when he began to reign, and he reigned thirty-one years in Jerusalem. His mother's name was Jedidah the daughter of Adaiah of Bozkath. 2And he did what was right in the eyes of the LORD and walked

[1]Hebrew *made his son pass through the fire* [2]Or *evil*

in all the way of David his father, and he did not turn aside to the right or to the left.

Josiah Repairs the Temple

[3]In the eighteenth year of King Josiah, the king sent Shaphan the son of Azaliah, son of Meshullam, the secretary, to the house of the LORD, saying, [4]"Go up to Hilkiah the high priest, that he may count the money that has been brought into the house of the LORD, which the keepers of the threshold have collected from the people. [5]And let it be given into the hand of the workmen who have the oversight of the house of the LORD, and let them give it to the workmen who are at the house of the LORD, repairing the house [6](that is, to the carpenters, and to the builders, and to the masons), and let them use it for buying timber and quarried stone to repair the house. [7]But no accounting shall be asked from them for the money that is delivered into their hand, for they deal honestly."

Hilkiah Finds the Book of the Law

[8]And Hilkiah the high priest said to Shaphan the secretary, "I have found the Book of the Law in the house of the LORD." And Hilkiah gave the book to Shaphan, and he read it. [9]And Shaphan the secretary came to the king, and reported to the king, "Your servants have emptied out the money that was found in the house and have delivered it into the hand of the workmen who have the oversight of the house of the LORD." [10]Then Shaphan the secretary told the king, "Hilkiah the priest has given me a book." And Shaphan read it before the king.

[11]When the king heard the words of the Book of the Law, he tore his clothes. [12]And the king commanded Hilkiah the priest, and Ahikam the son of Shaphan, and Achbor the son of Micaiah, and Shaphan the secretary, and Asaiah the king's servant, saying, [13]"Go, inquire of the LORD for me, and for the people, and for all Judah, concerning the words of this book that has been found. For great is the wrath of the LORD that is kindled against us, because our fathers have not obeyed the words of this book, to do according to all that is written concerning us."

[14]So Hilkiah the priest, and Ahikam, and Achbor, and Shaphan, and Asaiah went to Huldah the prophetess, the wife of Shallum the son of Tikvah, son of Harhas, keeper of the wardrobe (now she lived in Jerusalem in the Second Quarter), and they talked with her. [15]And she said to them, "Thus says the LORD, the God of Israel: 'Tell the man who sent you to me, [16]Thus says the LORD, Behold, I will bring disaster upon this place and upon its inhabitants, all the words of the book that the king of Judah has read. [17]Because they have forsaken me and have made offerings to other gods, that they might provoke me to anger with all the work of their hands, therefore my wrath will be kindled against this place, and it will not be quenched. [18]But to the king of Judah, who sent you to inquire of the LORD, thus shall you say to him, Thus says the LORD, the God of Israel: Regarding the words that you have heard, [19]because your heart was penitent, and you humbled yourself before the LORD, when you heard how I spoke against this place and against its inhabitants, that they should become a desolation and a curse, and you have torn your clothes and wept before me, I also have heard you, declares the LORD. [20]Therefore, behold, I will gather you to your fathers, and you shall be gathered to your grave in peace, and your eyes shall not see all the disaster that I will bring upon this place.'" And they brought back word to the king.

Josiah's Reforms

23 Then the king sent, and all the elders of Judah and Jerusalem were gathered to him. [2]And the king went up to the house of the LORD, and with him all the men of Judah and all the inhabitants of Jerusalem and the priests

MARKS OF REVIVAL

The physical and spiritual reforms under King Josiah marked a critical time of revival among the people of God. Josiah was only eight years old when he began his reign, which lasted 31 years. During that time, he played a central role in the recovery of the spiritual vitality of God's people and, in doing so, provided a lasting testimony to the marks of revival among the people of God.

First, revival begins with a personal commitment to worship and obedience. From an early age, Josiah displayed this commitment, resolving to do what was right in the eyes of God rather than following in the ways of his pagan predecessors. Scripture records that Josiah walked with God and did not turn aside to the right or to the left (v. 2). Like Josiah, God's people must commit to follow him regardless of the cost.

Second, for revival to happen, God's people must prioritize the Word of God. Hilkiah made a remarkable discovery in 2 Kings 22; he found the Book of the Law (some or all of the Pentateuch) in the temple. One would think that there would be no way that the Word of God could be lost in the very dwelling place of God, but this is just what had happened. Once discovered, the king listened to the book being read and came to understand the purposes and plans of God for his people. Believers today must be careful not to lose the Word of God through neglect or apathy. Instead, they must meditate on the Word day and night so that they can be careful to do all that is written in it. The Word is a light and compass.

Third, when God's people long for revival, they must recognize and confess their sins and plead with God for mercy. During the revival under Josiah, the reading of God's Word prompted repentance, first in Josiah's life, and then within the nation. They quickly realized that they had not acted in accordance with the law. Josiah wept at this revelation and tore his clothes as a sign of mourning. He confessed his sins and the sins of the nation before God and vowed to live obediently from that time forward.

Finally, those hoping for revival must decisively turn away from everything that competes with God for their worship. Josiah began an aggressive campaign to rid the land of idols (2Ki 23:4–25). He knew that if idolatry was left unchecked, the people would soon be drawn back into their former patterns of life. Like Josiah, God's people must ruthlessly eliminate anything that would draw their hearts away from God — particularly those things that shaped their former lives of sin (Eph 4:20–24).

and the prophets, all the people, both small and great. And he read in their hearing all the words of the Book of the Covenant that had been found in the
house of the LORD. [3]And the king stood by the pillar and made a covenant be-
fore the LORD, to walk after the LORD and to keep his commandments and his testimonies and his statutes with all his heart and all his soul, to perform the words of this covenant that were written in this book. And all the people joined in the covenant.

[4]And the king commanded Hilkiah the high priest and the priests of the sec-
ond order and the keepers of the threshold to bring out of the temple of the LORD all the vessels made for Baal, for Asherah, and for all the host of heaven. He burned them outside Jerusalem in the fields of the Kidron and carried their ashes
to Bethel. [5]And he deposed the priests whom the kings of Judah had ordained
to make offerings in the high places at the cities of Judah and around Jerusalem; those also who burned incense to Baal, to the sun and the moon and the constellations and all the host of the heavens. [6]And he brought out the Asherah from
the house of the LORD, outside Jerusalem, to the brook Kidron, and burned it at the brook Kidron and beat it to dust and cast the dust of it upon the graves of the
common people. [7]And he broke down the houses of the male cult prostitutes
who were in the house of the LORD, where the women wove hangings for the
Asherah. [8]And he brought all the priests out of the cities of Judah, and defiled
the high places where the priests had made offerings, from Geba to Beersheba. And he broke down the high places of the gates that were at the entrance of the gate of Joshua the governor of the city, which were on one's left at the gate of the
city. [9]However, the priests of the high places did not come up to the altar of the
LORD in Jerusalem, but they ate unleavened bread among their brothers. [10]And
he defiled Topheth, which is in the Valley of the Son of Hinnom, that no one
might burn his son or his daughter as an offering to Molech.[1] [11]And he removed
the horses that the kings of Judah had dedicated to the sun, at the entrance to the house of the LORD, by the chamber of Nathan-melech the chamberlain, which
was in the precincts.[2] And he burned the chariots of the sun with fire. [12]And the
altars on the roof of the upper chamber of Ahaz, which the kings of Judah had made, and the altars that Manasseh had made in the two courts of the house of the LORD, he pulled down and broke in pieces[3] and cast the dust of them into the
brook Kidron. [13]And the king defiled the high places that were east of Jerusa-
lem, to the south of the mount of corruption, which Solomon the king of Israel had built for Ashtoreth the abomination of the Sidonians, and for Chemosh the
abomination of Moab, and for Milcom the abomination of the Ammonites. [14]And
he broke in pieces the pillars and cut down the Asherim and filled their places with the bones of men.

[15]Moreover, the altar at Bethel, the high place erected by Jeroboam the son
of Nebat, who made Israel to sin, that altar with the high place he pulled down
and burned,[4] reducing it to dust. He also burned the Asherah. [16]And as Josiah
turned, he saw the tombs there on the mount. And he sent and took the bones out of the tombs and burned them on the altar and defiled it, according to the word of the LORD that the man of God proclaimed, who had predicted these
things. [17]Then he said, "What is that monument that I see?" And the men of
the city told him, "It is the tomb of the man of God who came from Judah and
predicted[5] these things that you have done against the altar at Bethel." [18]And
he said, "Let him be; let no man move his bones." So they let his bones alone,
with the bones of the prophet who came out of Samaria. [19]And Josiah removed
all the shrines also of the high places that were in the cities of Samaria, which kings of Israel had made, provoking the LORD to anger. He did to them according
to all that he had done at Bethel. [20]And he sacrificed all the priests of the high

[1]Hebrew *might cause his son or daughter to pass through the fire for Molech* [2]The meaning of the Hebrew word is uncertain [3]Hebrew *pieces from there* [4]Septuagint *broke in pieces its stones* [5]Hebrew *called*

2 KINGS 23:21–25

TURNING TO GOD

Josiah turned his affections toward God. He attempted to restore a nation that had lost its foundation and roots back to its covenant fellowship with God. Josiah was a king who followed after the Lord with all his heart, soul, and strength (v. 25). Similar to Moses, whose covenant he was trying to uphold, Josiah served God even though the nation was doomed. Moses and Josiah attempted to display to their people that God was worthy of their service, regardless of the circumstances.

Josiah's rediscovery of the Book of the Law (2Ki 22:8–13) was instrumental in calling the nation to follow the Lord with all of their hearts, souls, and strength. Similarly, in Luke 10:25–28, Jesus questioned an expert in the law regarding a summation of the Law. The expert responded by saying he believed it could be summed up this way: "You shall love the Lord your God with all your heart and with all your soul and with all your strength and with all your mind, and your neighbor as yourself" (Lk 10:27). Jesus agreed, and in Matthew 22:35–40 he identified these two commandments as the first and second most important laws, upon which "depend all the Law and the Prophets" (Mt 22:40). The life of Josiah displayed his unwavering allegiance to the Law—an allegiance grounded in his love for God.

places who were there, on the altars, and burned human bones on them. Then he returned to Jerusalem.

Josiah Restores the Passover

[21]And the king commanded all the people, "Keep the Passover to the LORD your God, as it is written in this Book of the Covenant." [22]For no such Passover had been kept since the days of the judges who judged Israel, or during all the days of the kings of Israel or of the kings of Judah. [23]But in the eighteenth year of King Josiah this Passover was kept to the LORD in Jerusalem.

[24]Moreover, Josiah put away the mediums and the necromancers and the household gods and the idols and all the abominations that were seen in the land of Judah and in Jerusalem, that he might establish the words of the law that were written in the book that Hilkiah the priest found in the house of the LORD. [25]Before him there was no king like him, who turned to the LORD with all his heart and with all his soul and with all his might, according to all the Law of Moses, nor did any like him arise after him.

[26]Still the LORD did not turn from the burning of his great wrath, by which his anger was kindled against Judah, because of all the provocations with which Manasseh had provoked him. [27]And the LORD said, "I will remove Judah also out of my sight, as I have removed Israel, and I will cast off this city that I have chosen, Jerusalem, and the house of which I said, My name shall be there."

Josiah's Death in Battle

[28]Now the rest of the acts of Josiah and all that he did, are they not written in the Book of the Chronicles of the Kings of Judah? [29]In his days Pharaoh Neco king of Egypt went up to the king of Assyria to the river Euphrates. King Josiah went to meet him, and Pharaoh Neco killed him at Megiddo, as soon as he saw him. [30]And his servants carried him dead in a chariot from Megiddo and brought him to Jerusalem and buried him in his own tomb. And the people of the land took Jehoahaz the son of Josiah, and anointed him, and made him king in his father's place.

Jehoahaz's Reign and Captivity

[31]Jehoahaz was twenty-three years old when he began to reign, and he reigned three months in Jerusalem. His mother's name was Hamutal the daughter of Jeremiah of Libnah. [32]And he did what was evil in the sight of the LORD, according to all that his fathers had done. [33]And Pharaoh Neco put him in bonds at Riblah in the land of Hamath, that he might not reign in Jerusalem, and laid on the land a tribute of a hundred talents[1] of silver and a talent of gold. [34]And Pharaoh Neco made Eliakim the son of Josiah king in the place of Josiah his father, and changed his name to Jehoiakim. But he took Jehoahaz away, and he came to Egypt and died there. [35]And Jehoiakim gave the silver and the gold to Pharaoh, but he taxed the land to give the money according to the command of Pharaoh. He exacted the silver and the gold of the people of the land, from everyone according to his assessment, to give it to Pharaoh Neco.

Jehoiakim Reigns in Judah

[36]Jehoiakim was twenty-five years old when he began to reign, and he reigned eleven years in Jerusalem. His mother's name was Zebidah the daughter of Pedaiah of Rumah. [37]And he did what was evil in the sight of the LORD, according to all that his fathers had done.

24 In his days, Nebuchadnezzar king of Babylon came up, and Jehoiakim became his servant for three years. Then he turned and rebelled against him. [2]And the LORD sent against him bands of the Chaldeans and bands of the Syrians and bands of the Moabites and bands of the Ammonites, and sent them

[1]A *talent* was about 75 pounds or 34 kilograms

against Judah to destroy it, according to the word of the Lord that he spoke by
his servants the prophets. 3Surely this came upon Judah at the command of the
Lord, to remove them out of his sight, for the sins of Manasseh, according to all
that he had done, 4and also for the innocent blood that he had shed. For he filled
Jerusalem with innocent blood, and the Lord would not pardon. 5Now the rest
of the deeds of Jehoiakim and all that he did, are they not written in the Book of
the Chronicles of the Kings of Judah? 6So Jehoiakim slept with his fathers, and
Jehoiachin his son reigned in his place. 7And the king of Egypt did not come again
out of his land, for the king of Babylon had taken all that belonged to the king of
Egypt from the Brook of Egypt to the river Euphrates.

Jehoiachin Reigns in Judah

8Jehoiachin was eighteen years old when he became king, and he reigned
three months in Jerusalem. His mother's name was Nehushta the daughter of Elnathan of Jerusalem. 9And he did what was evil in the sight of the Lord, according
to all that his father had done.

Jerusalem Captured

10At that time the servants of Nebuchadnezzar king of Babylon came up to Jerusalem, and the city was besieged. 11And Nebuchadnezzar king of Babylon came
to the city while his servants were besieging it, 12and Jehoiachin the king of Judah
gave himself up to the king of Babylon, himself and his mother and his servants
and his officials and his palace officials. The king of Babylon took him prisoner
in the eighth year of his reign 13and carried off all the treasures of the house of
the Lord and the treasures of the king's house, and cut in pieces all the vessels
of gold in the temple of the Lord, which Solomon king of Israel had made, as the
Lord had foretold. 14He carried away all Jerusalem and all the officials and all the
mighty men of valor, 10,000 captives, and all the craftsmen and the smiths. None
remained, except the poorest people of the land. 15And he carried away Jehoiachin
to Babylon. The king's mother, the king's wives, his officials, and the chief men
of the land he took into captivity from Jerusalem to Babylon. 16And the king of
Babylon brought captive to Babylon all the men of valor, 7,000, and the craftsmen
and the metal workers, 1,000, all of them strong and fit for war. 17And the king of
Babylon made Mattaniah, Jehoiachin's uncle, king in his place, and changed his
name to Zedekiah.

Zedekiah Reigns in Judah

18Zedekiah was twenty-one years old when he became king, and he reigned
eleven years in Jerusalem. His mother's name was Hamutal the daughter of Jeremiah of Libnah. 19And he did what was evil in the sight of the Lord, according to
all that Jehoiakim had done. 20For because of the anger of the Lord it came to the
point in Jerusalem and Judah that he cast them out from his presence.

And Zedekiah rebelled against the king of Babylon.

Fall and Captivity of Judah

25 And in the ninth year of his reign, in the tenth month, on the tenth day
of the month, Nebuchadnezzar king of Babylon came with all his army
against Jerusalem and laid siege to it. And they built siegeworks all around it. 2So
the city was besieged till the eleventh year of King Zedekiah. 3On the ninth day
of the fourth month the famine was so severe in the city that there was no food
for the people of the land. 4Then a breach was made in the city, and all the men
of war fled by night by the way of the gate between the two walls, by the king's
garden, and the Chaldeans were around the city. And they went in the direction
of the Arabah. 5But the army of the Chaldeans pursued the king and overtook
him in the plains of Jericho, and all his army was scattered from him. 6Then they
captured the king and brought him up to the king of Babylon at Riblah, and they

2 KINGS 25:27–30

PRESERVING THE LINE TO JESUS

God used kings like Hezekiah and Josiah to prompt revival in Judah. The revivals were short-lived, however, and the kings following Josiah led the nation toward spiritual unfaithfulness once again. Zedekiah, Judah's last king, dismissed the prophet Jeremiah's warning and rebelled against Nebuchadnezzar, king of Babylon (Jer 38:17–18; 52:3). This prompted a sequence of events that culminated with the Babylonians destroying Jerusalem and the temple in 586 BC. The people of Judah were carried into captivity and their homes were destroyed. It seemed as if the people had finally gone too far—forever and irrevocably severing any hope of a relationship with God. In the midst of this destruction, Jehoiachin, Zedekiah's nephew and the former king of Judah, survived. The line of the Messiah was protected, even as the people of God suffered the just consequences for their idolatry. Once again, God proved that he would be faithful to the promises he made long ago, protecting the Davidic line from which his Son, Jesus Christ, would one day come.

passed sentence on him. 7They slaughtered the sons of Zedekiah before his eyes,
and put out the eyes of Zedekiah and bound him in chains and took him to Babylon.

8In the fifth month, on the seventh day of the month—that was the nineteenth year of King Nebuchadnezzar, king of Babylon—Nebuzaradan, the captain of the bodyguard, a servant of the king of Babylon, came to Jerusalem.
9And he burned the house of the LORD and the king's house and all the houses of Jerusalem; every great house he burned down.
10And all the army of the Chaldeans, who were with the captain of the guard, broke down the walls around Jerusalem.
11And the rest of the people who were left in the city and the deserters who had deserted to the king of Babylon, together with the rest of the multitude, Nebuzaradan the captain of the guard carried into exile.
12But the captain of the guard left some of the poorest of the land to be vinedressers and plowmen.

13And the pillars of bronze that were in the house of the LORD, and the stands and the bronze sea that were in the house of the LORD, the Chaldeans broke in pieces and carried the bronze to Babylon.
14And they took away the pots and the shovels and the snuffers and the dishes for incense and all the vessels of bronze used in the temple service,
15the fire pans also and the bowls. What was of gold the captain of the guard took away as gold, and what was of silver, as silver.
16As for the two pillars, the one sea, and the stands that Solomon had made for the house of the LORD, the bronze of all these vessels was beyond weight.
17The height of the one pillar was eighteen cubits,[1] and on it was a capital of bronze. The height of the capital was three cubits. A latticework and pomegranates, all of bronze, were all around the capital. And the second pillar had the same, with the latticework.

18And the captain of the guard took Seraiah the chief priest and Zephaniah the second priest and the three keepers of the threshold;
19and from the city he took an officer who had been in command of the men of war, and five men of the king's council who were found in the city; and the secretary of the commander of the army, who mustered the people of the land; and sixty men of the people of the land, who were found in the city.
20And Nebuzaradan the captain of the guard took them and brought them to the king of Babylon at Riblah.
21And the king of Babylon struck them down and put them to death at Riblah in the land of Hamath. So Judah was taken into exile out of its land.

Gedaliah Made Governor of Judah

22And over the people who remained in the land of Judah, whom Nebuchadnezzar king of Babylon had left, he appointed Gedaliah the son of Ahikam, son of Shaphan, governor.
23Now when all the captains and their men heard that the king of Babylon had appointed Gedaliah governor, they came with their men to Gedaliah at Mizpah, namely, Ishmael the son of Nethaniah, and Johanan the son of Kareah, and Seraiah the son of Tanhumeth the Netophathite, and Jaazaniah the son of the Maacathite.
24And Gedaliah swore to them and their men, saying, "Do not be afraid because of the Chaldean officials. Live in the land and serve the king of Babylon, and it shall be well with you."
25But in the seventh month, Ishmael the son of Nethaniah, son of Elishama, of the royal family, came with ten men and struck down Gedaliah and put him to death along with the Jews and the Chaldeans who were with him at Mizpah.
26Then all the people, both small and great, and the captains of the forces arose and went to Egypt, for they were afraid of the Chaldeans.

Jehoiachin Released from Prison

27And in the thirty-seventh year of the exile of Jehoiachin king of Judah, in the twelfth month, on the twenty-seventh day of the month, Evil-merodach king

[1]A *cubit* was about 18 inches or 45 centimeters

GOD'S CLEAR WARNING

God used the prophets to warn the people of their moral bankruptcy and their need to repent and return to God. The exile of the people of Judah, recounted in 2 Kings 24 – 25, had long ago been prophesied to the people (Dt 28:49 – 52). Even before the Israelites inherited the land, they were warned that they would be driven from the land if they did not obey God and keep his commands. Interestingly, the Israelites' fate was foreshadowed by their own conquest of the promised land. God told his people to drive out the nations in order to inherit the land, warning that Israel would face a similar fate themselves if they disobeyed (Dt 4:25 – 27).

Prophets such as Isaiah and Jeremiah foresaw the disaster that awaited the people of God due to their sin. Years earlier, Isaiah prophesied that God would use the Babylonian nation to purge his people from the land (Isa 39:5 – 8). Likewise, Jeremiah warned the nation of their impending time in captivity and later summarized the process by which the people were carried into exile (Jer 25:8 – 14; 52:1 – 30).

These prophetic warnings served two purposes. First, they demonstrated that God was providentially in control of all things. As an all-knowing and all-powerful God, he gave the prophets insight into the exact details that would not be fulfilled until much later. Second, they showed that God had left his people clear warnings. God did not simply let his people pursue the wayward longings of their hearts, but he continually raised up individuals who would urge them to return to him before it was too late. Sadly, they did not listen.

The same is true today. God is still perfectly in charge of all things and will accomplish his good purpose in this world (Ro 8:28). This purpose will include the judgment of God against sin. However, God has not left people without warning or without hope. The Word of God, the people of God, and the Spirit of God are all at work in the world, reminding people to turn to God before they have to face his judgment (Mt 3:2; Lk 5:32; Jn 16:8; 1Jn 1:8 – 9).

of Babylon, in the year that he began to reign, graciously freed[1] Jehoiachin king
of Judah from prison. 28And he spoke kindly to him and gave him a seat above
the seats of the kings who were with him in Babylon. 29So Jehoiachin put off his
prison garments. And every day of his life he dined regularly at the king's table,
30and for his allowance, a regular allowance was given him by the king, according
to his daily needs, as long as he lived.

[1]Hebrew *reign, lifted up the head of*

JESUS: OUR PERFECT RESTORER

1 CHRONICLES

1 CHRONICLES

DAVID'S REIGN OVER JUDAH BEGINS *c. 1010 BC*	DAVID'S REIGN OVER ALL ISRAEL BEGINS *c. 1003 BC*	ARK BROUGHT TO JERUSALEM *c. 997 BC*

About a century after God's people were allowed to return home from exile, the author of 1 and 2 Chronicles (perhaps Ezra) sought to inspire the Jews living in Judah to remain faithful to their covenant-keeping God. He did this by reminding them of their unique spiritual heritage and the faithfulness of God, which spanned generations.

The book focuses on the spiritual highlights of the nation's history, thus detailing in great length the reign of King David. As king, David sought to restore the worship of God to the epicenter of Israel's life. He brought the ark of the covenant into Jerusalem amidst great celebration and appointed priests and Levites to lead the people to worship God in the God-ordained pattern. David longed for the people to give God the glory he rightly deserves (1Ch 16:29) — a desire echoed by the Chronicler to the postexilic people.

The book of 1 Chronicles also reminded the restored community of their familial heritage, substantiated by the lengthy genealogy at the outset of this book. The initial audience for the book understood from the genealogy that they were connected to the great heroes of the faith; specifically, the genealogy connected them to King David through the line of Judah's son Perez.

The remnant had returned and sought to rebuild the temple, which had been ravaged by the pagan Babylonians who took Judah into exile. But God would still be faithful to fulfill the promises he made to Abraham, Isaac, and Jacob — and most recently to King David. Through these men, God would carry forth his plan to redeem his people by the establishment of the Davidic kingdom and the eternal royal reign that he had promised to David. The focus on the great triumphs of David's life — such as his conquest of Jerusalem (11:4 – 9), his relocation of the ark to Jerusalem (15:25 – 29), and his victories over Israel's enemies (18:1 – 12) — emboldened the people with strength and hope in the promises they were sure to inherit.

The promises were meant to prompt the people to worship God. David, during his reign, had done just that. His focus on the tabernacle and temple underscored his desire to see the people worship an ever-faithful God. First Chronicles, in a similar fashion, sought to remind the postexilic people of the central importance of proper worship.

God's covenant promises to David were a prelude to what the Messiah would one day bring about. King Jesus walked with God, like David, and now draws the hearts of his people to the proper worship of God. In so doing, he is fulfilling the promises made to David and establishing his royal throne forever.

SING TO THE LORD, ALL THE EARTH!
TELL OF HIS SALVATION FROM DAY TO DAY.
DECLARE HIS GLORY AMONG THE NATIONS,
HIS MARVELOUS WORKS AMONG ALL THE PEOPLES!

---

1 Chronicles 16:23 – 24

1 CHRONICLES

From Adam to Abraham

1 [1] Adam, Seth, Enosh; 2Kenan, Mahalalel, Jared; 3Enoch, Methuselah, Lamech;
4Noah, Shem, Ham, and Japheth.
5The sons of Japheth: Gomer, Magog, Madai, Javan, Tubal, Meshech, and Tiras. 6The sons of Gomer: Ashkenaz, Riphath,[2] and Togarmah. 7The sons of Javan:
Elishah, Tarshish, Kittim, and Rodanim.
8The sons of Ham: Cush, Egypt, Put, and Canaan. 9The sons of Cush: Seba,
Havilah, Sabta, Raamah, and Sabteca. The sons of Raamah: Sheba and Dedan.
10Cush fathered Nimrod. He was the first on earth to be a mighty man.[3]
11Egypt fathered Ludim, Anamim, Lehabim, Naphtuhim, 12Pathrusim,
Casluhim (from whom the Philistines came), and Caphtorim.
13Canaan fathered Sidon his firstborn and Heth, 14and the Jebusites, the Amorites, the Girgashites, 15the Hivites, the Arkites, the Sinites, 16the Arvadites, the
Zemarites, and the Hamathites.
17The sons of Shem: Elam, Asshur, Arpachshad, Lud, and Aram. And the sons
of Aram:[4] Uz, Hul, Gether, and Meshech. 18Arpachshad fathered Shelah, and
Shelah fathered Eber. 19To Eber were born two sons: the name of the one was
Peleg[5] (for in his days the earth was divided), and his brother's name was Joktan. 20Joktan fathered Almodad, Sheleph, Hazarmaveth, Jerah, 21Hadoram, Uzal,
Diklah, 22Obal,[6] Abimael, Sheba, 23Ophir, Havilah, and Jobab; all these were the
sons of Joktan.
24Shem, Arpachshad, Shelah; 25Eber, Peleg, Reu; 26Serug, Nahor, Terah;
27Abram, that is, Abraham.

From Abraham to Jacob

28The sons of Abraham: Isaac and Ishmael. 29These are their genealogies: the
firstborn of Ishmael, Nebaioth, and Kedar, Adbeel, Mibsam, 30Mishma, Dumah,
Massa, Hadad, Tema, 31Jetur, Naphish, and Kedemah. These are the sons of Ishmael. 32The sons of Keturah, Abraham's concubine: she bore Zimran, Jokshan,
Medan, Midian, Ishbak, and Shuah. The sons of Jokshan: Sheba and Dedan. 33The
sons of Midian: Ephah, Epher, Hanoch, Abida, and Eldaah. All these were the descendants of Keturah.
34Abraham fathered Isaac. The sons of Isaac: Esau and Israel. 35The sons of
Esau: Eliphaz, Reuel, Jeush, Jalam, and Korah. 36The sons of Eliphaz: Teman,
Omar, Zepho, Gatam, Kenaz, and of Timna,[7] Amalek. 37The sons of Reuel: Nahath,
Zerah, Shammah, and Mizzah.
38The sons of Seir: Lotan, Shobal, Zibeon, Anah, Dishon, Ezer, and Dishan.
39The sons of Lotan: Hori and Hemam;[8] and Lotan's sister was Timna. 40The sons
of Shobal: Alvan,[9] Manahath, Ebal, Shepho,[10] and Onam. The sons of Zibeon: Aiah
and Anah. 41The son[11] of Anah: Dishon. The sons of Dishon: Hemdan,[12] Eshban,
Ithran, and Cheran. 42The sons of Ezer: Bilhan, Zaavan, and Akan.[13] The sons of
Dishan: Uz and Aran.
43These are the kings who reigned in the land of Edom before any king reigned
over the people of Israel: Bela the son of Beor, the name of his city being Dinhabah. 44Bela died, and Jobab the son of Zerah of Bozrah reigned in his place. 45Jobab

[1]Many names in these genealogies are spelled differently in other biblical books [2]Septuagint; Hebrew *Diphath* [3]Or *He began to be a mighty man on the earth* [4]Septuagint; Hebrew lacks *And the sons of Aram* [5]*Peleg* means *division* [6]Septuagint, Syriac (compare Genesis 10:28); Hebrew *Ebal* [7]Septuagint (compare Genesis 36:12); Hebrew lacks *and of* [8]Septuagint (compare Genesis 36:22); Hebrew *Homam* [9]Septuagint (compare Genesis 36:23); Hebrew *Alian* [10]Septuagint (compare Genesis 36:23); Hebrew *Shephi* [11]Hebrew *sons* [12]Septuagint (compare Genesis 36:26); Hebrew *Hamran* [13]Septuagint (compare Genesis 36:27); Hebrew *Jaakan*

died, and Husham of the land of the Temanites reigned in his place. [46]Husham
died, and Hadad the son of Bedad, who defeated Midian in the country of Moab,
reigned in his place, the name of his city being Avith. [47]Hadad died, and Samlah
of Masrekah reigned in his place. [48]Samlah died, and Shaul of Rehoboth on the
Euphrates[1] reigned in his place. [49]Shaul died, and Baal-hanan, the son of Achbor,
reigned in his place. [50]Baal-hanan died, and Hadad reigned in his place, the name
of his city being Pai; and his wife's name was Mehetabel, the daughter of Matred,
the daughter of Mezahab. [51]And Hadad died.

The chiefs of Edom were: chiefs Timna, Alvah, Jetheth, [52]Oholibamah, Elah,
Pinon, [53]Kenaz, Teman, Mibzar, [54]Magdiel, and Iram; these are the chiefs of Edom.

A Genealogy of David

2 These are the sons of Israel: Reuben, Simeon, Levi, Judah, Issachar, Zebulun, [2]Dan, Joseph, Benjamin, Naphtali, Gad, and Asher. [3]The sons of Judah:
Er, Onan and Shelah; these three Bath-shua the Canaanite bore to him. Now Er,
Judah's firstborn, was evil in the sight of the LORD, and he put him to death. [4]His
daughter-in-law Tamar also bore him Perez and Zerah. Judah had five sons in all.

[5]The sons of Perez: Hezron and Hamul. [6]The sons of Zerah: Zimri, Ethan,
Heman, Calcol, and Dara, five in all. [7]The son[2] of Carmi: Achan, the troubler of
Israel, who broke faith in the matter of the devoted thing; [8]and Ethan's son was
Azariah.

[9]The sons of Hezron that were born to him: Jerahmeel, Ram, and Chelubai.
[10]Ram fathered Amminadab, and Amminadab fathered Nahshon, prince of the
sons of Judah. [11]Nahshon fathered Salmon,[3] Salmon fathered Boaz, [12]Boaz fathered Obed, Obed fathered Jesse. [13]Jesse fathered Eliab his firstborn, Abinadab
the second, Shimea the third, [14]Nethanel the fourth, Raddai the fifth, [15]Ozem the
sixth, David the seventh. [16]And their sisters were Zeruiah and Abigail. The sons
of Zeruiah: Abishai, Joab, and Asahel, three. [17]Abigail bore Amasa, and the father
of Amasa was Jether the Ishmaelite.

[18]Caleb the son of Hezron fathered children by his wife Azubah, and by Jer-
ioth; and these were her sons: Jesher, Shobab, and Ardon. [19]When Azubah died,
Caleb married Ephrath, who bore him Hur. [20]Hur fathered Uri, and Uri fathered
Bezalel.

[21]Afterward Hezron went in to the daughter of Machir the father of Gilead,
whom he married when he was sixty years old, and she bore him Segub. [22]And
Segub fathered Jair, who had twenty-three cities in the land of Gilead. [23]But Geshur and Aram took from them Havvoth-jair, Kenath, and its villages, sixty towns.
All these were descendants of Machir, the father of Gilead. [24]After the death of
Hezron, Caleb went in to Ephrathah,[4] the wife of Hezron his father, and she bore
him Ashhur, the father of Tekoa.

[25]The sons of Jerahmeel, the firstborn of Hezron: Ram, his firstborn, Bunah,
Oren, Ozem, and Ahijah. [26]Jerahmeel also had another wife, whose name was
Atarah; she was the mother of Onam. [27]The sons of Ram, the firstborn of Jerahmeel: Maaz, Jamin, and Eker. [28]The sons of Onam: Shammai and Jada. The sons
of Shammai: Nadab and Abishur. [29]The name of Abishur's wife was Abihail, and
she bore him Ahban and Molid. [30]The sons of Nadab: Seled and Appaim; and
Seled died childless. [31]The son[5] of Appaim: Ishi. The son of Ishi: Sheshan. The
son of Sheshan: Ahlai. [32]The sons of Jada, Shammai's brother: Jether and Jonathan; and Jether died childless. [33]The sons of Jonathan: Peleth and Zaza. These
were the descendants of Jerahmeel. [34]Now Sheshan had no sons, only daughters,
but Sheshan had an Egyptian slave whose name was Jarha. [35]So Sheshan gave his
daughter in marriage to Jarha his slave, and she bore him Attai. [36]Attai fathered
Nathan, and Nathan fathered Zabad. [37]Zabad fathered Ephlal, and Ephlal fathered
Obed. [38]Obed fathered Jehu, and Jehu fathered Azariah. [39]Azariah fathered Helez,

[1]Hebrew *the River* [2]Hebrew *sons* [3]Septuagint (compare Ruth 4:21); Hebrew *Salma* [4]Septuagint, Vulgate; Hebrew *in Caleb Ephrathah* [5]Hebrew *sons*; three times in this verse

and Helez fathered Eleasah. [40]Eleasah fathered Sismai, and Sismai fathered Shallum. [41]Shallum fathered Jekamiah, and Jekamiah fathered Elishama.

[42]The sons of Caleb the brother of Jerahmeel: Mareshah[1] his firstborn, who fathered Ziph. The son[2] of Mareshah: Hebron.[3] [43]The sons of Hebron: Korah, Tappuah, Rekem and Shema. [44]Shema fathered Raham, the father of Jorkeam; and Rekem fathered Shammai. [45]The son of Shammai: Maon; and Maon fathered Beth-zur. [46]Ephah also, Caleb's concubine, bore Haran, Moza, and Gazez; and Haran fathered Gazez. [47]The sons of Jahdai: Regem, Jotham, Geshan, Pelet, Ephah, and Shaaph. [48]Maacah, Caleb's concubine, bore Sheber and Tirhanah. [49]She also bore Shaaph the father of Madmannah, Sheva the father of Machbenah and the father of Gibea; and the daughter of Caleb was Achsah. [50]These were the descendants of Caleb.

The sons[4] of Hur the firstborn of Ephrathah: Shobal the father of Kiriath-jearim, [51]Salma, the father of Bethlehem, and Hareph the father of Beth-gader. [52]Shobal the father of Kiriath-jearim had other sons: Haroeh, half of the Menuhoth. [53]And the clans of Kiriath-jearim: the Ithrites, the Puthites, the Shumathites, and the Mishraites; from these came the Zorathites and the Eshtaolites. [54]The sons of Salma: Bethlehem, the Netophathites, Atroth-beth-joab and half of the Manahathites, the Zorites. [55]The clans also of the scribes who lived at Jabez: the Tirathites, the Shimeathites and the Sucathites. These are the Kenites who came from Hammath, the father of the house of Rechab.

Descendants of David

3 These are the sons of David who were born to him in Hebron: the firstborn, Amnon, by Ahinoam the Jezreelite; the second, Daniel, by Abigail the Carmelite, [2]the third, Absalom, whose mother was Maacah, the daughter of Talmai, king of Geshur; the fourth, Adonijah, whose mother was Haggith; [3]the fifth, Shephatiah, by Abital; the sixth, Ithream, by his wife Eglah; [4]six were born to him in Hebron, where he reigned for seven years and six months. And he reigned thirty-three years in Jerusalem. [5]These were born to him in Jerusalem: Shimea, Shobab, Nathan and Solomon, four by Bath-shua, the daughter of Ammiel; [6]then Ibhar, Elishama, Eliphelet, [7]Nogah, Nepheg, Japhia, [8]Elishama, Eliada, and Eliphelet, nine. [9]All these were David's sons, besides the sons of the concubines, and Tamar was their sister.

[10]The son of Solomon was Rehoboam, Abijah his son, Asa his son, Jehoshaphat his son, [11]Joram his son, Ahaziah his son, Joash his son, [12]Amaziah his son, Azariah his son, Jotham his son, [13]Ahaz his son, Hezekiah his son, Manasseh his son, [14]Amon his son, Josiah his son. [15]The sons of Josiah: Johanan the firstborn, the second Jehoiakim, the third Zedekiah, the fourth Shallum. [16]The descendants of Jehoiakim: Jeconiah his son, Zedekiah his son; [17]and the sons of Jeconiah, the captive: Shealtiel his son, [18]Malchiram, Pedaiah, Shenazzar, Jekamiah, Hoshama and Nedabiah; [19]and the sons of Pedaiah: Zerubbabel and Shimei; and the sons of Zerubbabel: Meshullam and Hananiah, and Shelomith was their sister; [20]and Hashubah, Ohel, Berechiah, Hasadiah, and Jushab-hesed, five. [21]The sons of Hananiah: Pelatiah and Jeshaiah, his son[5] Rephaiah, his son Arnan, his son Obadiah, his son Shecaniah. [22]The son[6] of Shecaniah: Shemaiah. And the sons of Shemaiah: Hattush, Igal, Bariah, Neariah, and Shaphat, six. [23]The sons of Neariah: Elioenai, Hizkiah, and Azrikam, three. [24]The sons of Elioenai: Hodaviah, Eliashib, Pelaiah, Akkub, Johanan, Delaiah, and Anani, seven.

Descendants of Judah

4 The sons of Judah: Perez, Hezron, Carmi, Hur, and Shobal. [2]Reaiah the son of Shobal fathered Jahath, and Jahath fathered Ahumai and Lahad. These were the clans of the Zorathites. [3]These were the sons[7] of Etam: Jezreel, Ishma,

1 CHRONICLES 3:1–9

COMPARE AND CONTRAST

The two books of Chronicles repeat much of the information found in the two books of Kings. Yet there are several ways the two histories differ. The books of Kings had a purpose of *indictment*—documenting the failures of God's people. The books of Chronicles had a purpose of *incitement*—encouraging the Jews returning from captivity. In terms of focus, the two books of Kings give attention to both the northern and southern kingdoms of Israel, including all of their kings whether good or evil. The two books of Chronicles focus on the southern kingdom of Judah—highlighting King David, King Solomon, and their godly successors. On matters of the temple and worship, a sharp contrast is evident—1 and 2 Kings devote only five chapters to these details while 1 and 2 Chronicles devote twenty chapters. In general, the books of Kings offer a civil and political perspective while the books of Chronicles were written from a moral and spiritual point of view.

[1]Septuagint; Hebrew *Mesha* [2]Hebrew *sons* [3]Hebrew *the father of Hebron* [4]Septuagint, Vulgate; Hebrew *son* [5]Septuagint (compare Syriac, Vulgate); Hebrew *sons of*; four times in this verse [6]Hebrew *sons* [7]Septuagint (compare Vulgate); Hebrew *father*

WHY GENEALOGIES?

First Chronicles comprises a history of God's people from Adam through the time of King David. It demonstrates how God had plans for his people from the beginning of human history.

The genealogies remind the church that the Bible is about *real* people in *real* places facing *real* circumstances — some of triumph and some of tragedy. Noah was a real man who built an ark under God's direction so he and his family could be delivered from the flood (Ge 6:13 – 18). Job actually endured the loss of all of his children when a storm caused his oldest son's house to collapse (Job 1:18 – 21). Joseph found himself abandoned at the bottom of a literal pit (Ge 37:24). Deborah was a real prophetess who sang a real song after the defeat of a Canaanite king (Jdg 4:23 — 5:31). Peter actually walked on the Sea of Galilee (Mt 14:22 – 33). Jesus literally died on a cross and actually came back to life again (Mt 27:32 — 28:10).

Some of those named in the genealogical record of 1 Chronicles are people about whom very little is known — people such as Onam, Shammai, Jada, Nadab, Abishur, and Molid. While the details of their stories remain unknown to succeeding generations, they hold a significant place in the line of faith and each of them matters to God. This should be an encouragement to the majority of Christians who will never be famous — the details of their stories will likely dissolve into history. But during their years on earth they play a necessary part in the grand epic of God. One day, when they stand before the Lord at the consummation of all things, they will know the impact of their less-than-famous lives. By faith, God's people live now for the purpose of magnifying Christ, bearing fruit to his eternal glory — caring more about his fame than their own.

The New Testament begins with a beautiful and impressive genealogy in the book of Matthew, following Jesus' lineage back to Abraham (Mt 1:1 – 16). The book of Luke follows the trail all the way back to Adam (Lk 3:23 – 38). The family trees trace Jesus' ancestral line, confirming that he is God's promised Messiah.

Those with saving faith in Jesus stand in a line of spiritual genealogy — a heritage of the gospel passed down from person to person. Believers today have a responsibility. Someone in their past explained the gospel to them, and they now have the privilege to add to that genealogy by helping others respond to Jesus with faith.

and Idbash; and the name of their sister was Hazzelelponi, 4and Penuel fathered Gedor, and Ezer fathered Hushah. These were the sons of Hur, the firstborn of Ephrathah, the father of Bethlehem. 5Ashhur, the father of Tekoa, had two wives, Helah and Naarah; 6Naarah bore him Ahuzzam, Hepher, Temeni, and Haahashtari. These were the sons of Naarah. 7The sons of Helah: Zereth, Izhar, and Ethnan. 8Koz fathered Anub, Zobebah, and the clans of Aharhel, the son of Harum. 9Jabez was more honorable than his brothers; and his mother called his name Jabez, saying, "Because I bore him in pain."[1] 10Jabez called upon the God of Israel, saying, "Oh that you would bless me and enlarge my border, and that your hand might be with me, and that you would keep me from harm[2] so that it might not bring me pain!" And God granted what he asked. 11Chelub, the brother of Shuhah, fathered Mehir, who fathered Eshton. 12Eshton fathered Beth-rapha, Paseah, and Tehinnah, the father of Ir-nahash. These are the men of Recah. 13The sons of Kenaz: Othniel and Seraiah; and the sons of Othniel: Hathath and Meonothai.[3] 14Meonothai fathered Ophrah; and Seraiah fathered Joab, the father of Ge-harashim,[4] so-called because they were craftsmen. 15The sons of Caleb the son of Jephunneh: Iru, Elah, and Naam; and the son[5] of Elah: Kenaz. 16The sons of Jehallelel: Ziph, Ziphah, Tiria, and Asarel. 17The sons of Ezrah: Jether, Mered, Epher, and Jalon. These are the sons of Bithiah, the daughter of Pharaoh, whom Mered married;[6] and she conceived and bore[7] Miriam, Shammai, and Ishbah, the father of Eshtemoa. 18And his Judahite wife bore Jered the father of Gedor, Heber the father of Soco, and Jekuthiel the father of Zanoah. 19The sons of the wife of Hodiah, the sister of Naham, were the fathers of Keilah the Garmite and Eshtemoa the Maacathite. 20The sons of Shimon: Amnon, Rinnah, Ben-hanan, and Tilon. The sons of Ishi: Zoheth and Ben-zoheth. 21The sons of Shelah the son of Judah: Er the father of Lecah, Laadah the father of Mareshah, and the clans of the house of linen workers at Beth-ashbea; 22and Jokim, and the men of Cozeba, and Joash, and Saraph, who ruled in Moab and returned to Lehem[8] (now the records[9] are ancient). 23These were the potters who were inhabitants of Netaim and Gederah. They lived there in the king's service.

Descendants of Simeon

24The sons of Simeon: Nemuel, Jamin, Jarib, Zerah, Shaul; 25Shallum was his son, Mibsam his son, Mishma his son. 26The sons of Mishma: Hammuel his son, Zaccur his son, Shimei his son. 27Shimei had sixteen sons and six daughters; but his brothers did not have many children, nor did all their clan multiply like the men of Judah. 28They lived in Beersheba, Moladah, Hazar-shual, 29Bilhah, Ezem, Tolad, 30Bethuel, Hormah, Ziklag, 31Beth-marcaboth, Hazar-susim, Beth-biri, and Shaaraim. These were their cities until David reigned. 32And their villages were Etam, Ain, Rimmon, Tochen, and Ashan, five cities, 33along with all their villages that were around these cities as far as Baal. These were their settlements, and they kept a genealogical record.

34Meshobab, Jamlech, Joshah the son of Amaziah, 35Joel, Jehu the son of Joshibiah, son of Seraiah, son of Asiel, 36Elioenai, Jaakobah, Jeshohaiah, Asaiah, Adiel, Jesimiel, Benaiah, 37Ziza the son of Shiphi, son of Allon, son of Jedaiah, son of Shimri, son of Shemaiah— 38these mentioned by name were princes in their clans, and their fathers' houses increased greatly. 39They journeyed to the entrance of Gedor, to the east side of the valley, to seek pasture for their flocks, 40where they found rich, good pasture, and the land was very broad, quiet, and *peaceful*, for the former inhabitants there belonged to Ham. 41These, registered by name, came in the days of Hezekiah, king of Judah, and destroyed their tents and the Meunites who were found there, and marked them for destruction to this

[1] *Jabez* sounds like the Hebrew for *pain* [2] Or *evil* [3] Septuagint, Vulgate; Hebrew lacks *Meonothai* [4] *Ge-harashim* means *valley of craftsmen* [5] Hebrew *sons* [6] The clause *These are . . . married* is transposed from verse 18 [7] Hebrew lacks *and bore* [8] Vulgate (compare Septuagint); Hebrew *and Jashubi-lahem* [9] Or *matters*

1 CHRONICLES 4:24–43

HIGHLIGHTING HISTORY

The Chronicles were written to provide the most important elements of Israel's history to those who lived in Judah in the era after the exile. The books provide a selective history of God's people, omitting many of the unsavory incidents recorded in the books of Samuel and Kings—such as those involving Bathsheba, Absalom, and Tamar.

The New Testament presents a different sort of history than the one offered in Chronicles. It openly describes the weaknesses and failures of men and women—pointing out the need all people have for God's grace. Luke revealed Zacchaeus to be a corrupt tax collector, exploiting his own people for profit (Lk 19:1–10). Jesus encountered a woman who had been caught in the act of adultery (Jn 8:1–11). Peter, a key disciple who had many great moments with the Savior, also had episodes of arrogance and even denied knowing Jesus. Nor did Luke sanitize the apostle Paul's history: before meeting Christ on the road to Damascus, Paul was a fierce opponent of the church (Ac 8:1–3).

Every person found by Christ was at one time lost. And after a person follows Jesus they will occasionally stumble in sin. Reading about the failures of ancient disciples gives encouragement to modern followers and connects believers in a kind of camaraderie of grace. Because God preserved these and other accounts of the flawed, God's people today glimpse portraits of themselves—ordinary people in desperate need of salvation that comes through Jesus Christ (Titus 2:11–14).

day, and settled in their place, because there was pasture there for their flocks.
42And some of them, five hundred men of the Simeonites, went to Mount Seir,
having as their leaders Pelatiah, Neariah, Rephaiah, and Uzziel, the sons of Ishi.
43And they defeated the remnant of the Amalekites who had escaped, and they
have lived there to this day.

Descendants of Reuben

5 The sons of Reuben the firstborn of Israel (for he was the firstborn, but
because he defiled his father's couch, his birthright was given to the sons
of Joseph the son of Israel, so that he could not be enrolled as the oldest son;
2though Judah became strong among his brothers and a chief came from him, yet
the birthright belonged to Joseph), 3the sons of Reuben, the firstborn of Israel:
Hanoch, Pallu, Hezron, and Carmi. 4The sons of Joel: Shemaiah his son, Gog his
son, Shimei his son, 5Micah his son, Reaiah his son, Baal his son, 6Beerah his son,
whom Tiglath-pileser[1] king of Assyria carried away into exile; he was a chief of the
Reubenites. 7And his kinsmen by their clans, when the genealogy of their generations was recorded: the chief, Jeiel, and Zechariah, 8and Bela the son of Azaz, son
of Shema, son of Joel, who lived in Aroer, as far as Nebo and Baal-meon. 9He also
lived to the east as far as the entrance of the desert this side of the Euphrates,
because their livestock had multiplied in the land of Gilead. 10And in the days of
Saul they waged war against the Hagrites, who fell into their hand. And they lived
in their tents throughout all the region east of Gilead.

Descendants of Gad

11The sons of Gad lived over against them in the land of Bashan as far as
Salecah: 12Joel the chief, Shapham the second, Janai, and Shaphat in Bashan.
13And their kinsmen according to their fathers' houses: Michael, Meshullam,
Sheba, Jorai, Jacan, Zia and Eber, seven. 14These were the sons of Abihail the son
of Huri, son of Jaroah, son of Gilead, son of Michael, son of Jeshishai, son of Jahdo,
son of Buz. 15Ahi the son of Abdiel, son of Guni, was chief in their fathers' houses,
16and they lived in Gilead, in Bashan and in its towns, and in all the pasturelands
of Sharon to their limits. 17All of these were recorded in genealogies in the days of
Jotham king of Judah, and in the days of Jeroboam king of Israel.

18The Reubenites, the Gadites, and the half-tribe of Manasseh had valiant
men who carried shield and sword, and drew the bow, expert in war, 44,760,
able to go to war. 19They waged war against the Hagrites, Jetur, Naphish, and
Nodab. 20And when they prevailed[2] over them, the Hagrites and all who were
with them were given into their hands, for they cried out to God in the battle, and
he granted their urgent plea because they trusted in him. 21They carried off their
livestock: 50,000 of their camels, 250,000 sheep, 2,000 donkeys, and 100,000
men alive. 22For many fell, because the war was of God. And they lived in their
place until the exile.

The Half-Tribe of Manasseh

23The members of the half-tribe of Manasseh lived in the land. They were very
numerous from Bashan to Baal-hermon, Senir, and Mount Hermon. 24These were
the heads of their fathers' houses: Epher,[3] Ishi, Eliel, Azriel, Jeremiah, Hodaviah,
and Jahdiel, mighty warriors, famous men, heads of their fathers' houses. 25But
they broke faith with the God of their fathers, and whored after the gods of the
peoples of the land, whom God had destroyed before them. 26So the God of Israel
stirred up the spirit of Pul king of Assyria, the spirit of Tiglath-pileser king of Assyria, and he took them into exile, namely, the Reubenites, the Gadites, and the
half-tribe of Manasseh, and brought them to Halah, Habor, Hara, and the river
Gozan, to this day.

[1]Hebrew *Tilgath-pilneser*; also verse 26 [2]Or *they were helped to prevail* [3]Septuagint, Vulgate; Hebrew *and Epher*

1 CHRONICLES 5:1–26

GENERATIONS

Ancient Hebrew culture depended on detailed genealogical lists to determine questions of inheritance and land-use rights. After the conquest of Canaan, each tribe received its portion of the promised land (Jos 13–21). Ownership and land rights were passed from father to oldest son, or daughter if there was no son (Nu 27:1–11). Other matters such as service in the temple and royal succession were also determined by genealogy. Old Testament genealogies attest to God's faithfulness—across generations—in honoring his promise to make Israel a great nation (Ge 12:1–3).

The genealogy of Jesus (Mt 1:1–17) reflects the promises of God kept since the days of Abraham, Isaac, and Jacob (Ac 13:32–33). It shows Christ as the legitimate heir in the line of David. In Jesus, God fulfilled his promise to establish the ultimate King on David's throne (Isa 9:6–7; Ro 1:2–3).

Descendants of Levi

6 [1] The sons of Levi: Gershon, Kohath, and Merari. 2The sons of Kohath: Amram, Izhar, Hebron, and Uzziel. 3The children of Amram: Aaron, Moses, and
Miriam. The sons of Aaron: Nadab, Abihu, Eleazar, and Ithamar. 4Eleazar fathered Phinehas, Phinehas fathered Abishua, 5Abishua fathered Bukki, Bukki
fathered Uzzi, 6Uzzi fathered Zerahiah, Zerahiah fathered Meraioth, 7Meraioth
fathered Amariah, Amariah fathered Ahitub, 8Ahitub fathered Zadok, Zadok fathered Ahimaaz, 9Ahimaaz fathered Azariah, Azariah fathered Johanan, 10and
Johanan fathered Azariah (it was he who served as priest in the house that Solomon built in Jerusalem). 11Azariah fathered Amariah, Amariah fathered Ahitub,
12Ahitub fathered Zadok, Zadok fathered Shallum, 13Shallum fathered Hilkiah,
Hilkiah fathered Azariah, 14Azariah fathered Seraiah, Seraiah fathered Jehozadak; 15and Jehozadak went into exile when the LORD sent Judah and Jerusalem
into exile by the hand of Nebuchadnezzar.

16[2]The sons of Levi: Gershom, Kohath, and Merari. 17And these are the names
of the sons of Gershom: Libni and Shimei. 18The sons of Kohath: Amram, Izhar,
Hebron and Uzziel. 19The sons of Merari: Mahli and Mushi. These are the clans
of the Levites according to their fathers. 20Of Gershom: Libni his son, Jahath his
son, Zimmah his son, 21Joah his son, Iddo his son, Zerah his son, Jeatherai his son.
22The sons of Kohath: Amminadab his son, Korah his son, Assir his son, 23Elkanah
his son, Ebiasaph his son, Assir his son, 24Tahath his son, Uriel his son, Uzziah his
son, and Shaul his son. 25The sons of Elkanah: Amasai and Ahimoth, 26Elkanah
his son, Zophai his son, Nahath his son, 27Eliab his son, Jeroham his son, Elkanah
his son. 28The sons of Samuel: Joel[3] his firstborn, the second Abijah.[4] 29The sons
of Merari: Mahli, Libni his son, Shimei his son, Uzzah his son, 30Shimea his son,
Haggiah his son, and Asaiah his son.

31These are the men whom David put in charge of the service of song in the
house of the LORD after the ark rested there. 32They ministered with song before
the tabernacle of the tent of meeting until Solomon built the house of the LORD
in Jerusalem, and they performed their service according to their order. 33These
are the men who served and their sons. Of the sons of the Kohathites: Heman the
singer the son of Joel, son of Samuel, 34son of Elkanah, son of Jeroham, son of
Eliel, son of Toah, 35son of Zuph, son of Elkanah, son of Mahath, son of Amasai,
36son of Elkanah, son of Joel, son of Azariah, son of Zephaniah, 37son of Tahath,
son of Assir, son of Ebiasaph, son of Korah, 38son of Izhar, son of Kohath, son of
Levi, son of Israel; 39and his brother Asaph, who stood on his right hand, namely,
Asaph the son of Berechiah, son of Shimea, 40son of Michael, son of Baaseiah,
son of Malchijah, 41son of Ethni, son of Zerah, son of Adaiah, 42son of Ethan, son
of Zimmah, son of Shimei, 43son of Jahath, son of Gershom, son of Levi. 44On the
left hand were their brothers, the sons of Merari: Ethan the son of Kishi, son of
Abdi, son of Malluch, 45son of Hashabiah, son of Amaziah, son of Hilkiah, 46son
of Amzi, son of Bani, son of Shemer, 47son of Mahli, son of Mushi, son of Merari,
son of Levi. 48And their brothers the Levites were appointed for all the service of
the tabernacle of the house of God.

49But Aaron and his sons made offerings on the altar of burnt offering and on
the altar of incense for all the work of the Most Holy Place, and to make atonement for Israel, according to all that Moses the servant of God had commanded.
50These are the sons of Aaron: Eleazar his son, Phinehas his son, Abishua his son,
51Bukki his son, Uzzi his son, Zerahiah his son, 52Meraioth his son, Amariah his
son, Ahitub his son, 53Zadok his son, Ahimaaz his son.

54These are their dwelling places according to their settlements within their
borders: to the sons of Aaron of the clans of Kohathites, for theirs was the first
lot, 55to them they gave Hebron in the land of Judah and its surrounding pasturelands, 56but the fields of the city and its villages they gave to Caleb the son

[1]Ch 5:27 in Hebrew [2]Ch 6:1 in Hebrew [3]Septuagint, Syriac (compare verse 33 and 1 Samuel 8:2); Hebrew lacks *Joel* [4]Hebrew *and Abijah*

of Jephunneh. 57 To the sons of Aaron they gave the cities of refuge: Hebron, Libnah with its pasturelands, Jattir, Eshtemoa with its pasturelands, 58 Hilen with
its pasturelands, Debir with its pasturelands, 59 Ashan with its pasturelands, and
Beth-shemesh with its pasturelands; 60 and from the tribe of Benjamin, Gibeon,[1]
Geba with its pasturelands, Alemeth with its pasturelands, and Anathoth with its
pasturelands. All their cities throughout their clans were thirteen.

61 To the rest of the Kohathites were given by lot out of the clan of the tribe,
out of the half-tribe, the half of Manasseh, ten cities. 62 To the Gershomites according to their clans were allotted thirteen cities out of the tribes of Issachar,
Asher, Naphtali and Manasseh in Bashan. 63 To the Merarites according to their
clans were allotted twelve cities out of the tribes of Reuben, Gad, and Zebulun.
64 So the people of Israel gave the Levites the cities with their pasturelands. 65 They
gave by lot out of the tribes of Judah, Simeon, and Benjamin these cities that are
mentioned by name.

66 And some of the clans of the sons of Kohath had cities of their territory out
of the tribe of Ephraim. 67 They were given the cities of refuge: Shechem with its
pasturelands in the hill country of Ephraim, Gezer with its pasturelands, 68 Jokmeam with its pasturelands, Beth-horon with its pasturelands, 69 Aijalon with its
pasturelands, Gath-rimmon with its pasturelands, 70 and out of the half-tribe of
Manasseh, Aner with its pasturelands, and Bileam with its pasturelands, for the
rest of the clans of the Kohathites.

71 To the Gershomites were given out of the clan of the half-tribe of Manasseh:
Golan in Bashan with its pasturelands and Ashtaroth with its pasturelands; 72 and
out of the tribe of Issachar: Kedesh with its pasturelands, Daberath with its pasturelands, 73 Ramoth with its pasturelands, and Anem with its pasturelands; 74 out
of the tribe of Asher: Mashal with its pasturelands, Abdon with its pasturelands,
75 Hukok with its pasturelands, and Rehob with its pasturelands; 76 and out of
the tribe of Naphtali: Kedesh in Galilee with its pasturelands, Hammon with its
pasturelands, and Kiriathaim with its pasturelands. 77 To the rest of the Merarites
were allotted out of the tribe of Zebulun: Rimmono with its pasturelands, Tabor
with its pasturelands, 78 and beyond the Jordan at Jericho, on the east side of the
Jordan, out of the tribe of Reuben: Bezer in the wilderness with its pasturelands,
Jahzah with its pasturelands, 79 Kedemoth with its pasturelands, and Mephaath
with its pasturelands; 80 and out of the tribe of Gad: Ramoth in Gilead with its
pasturelands, Mahanaim with its pasturelands, 81 Heshbon with its pasturelands,
and Jazer with its pasturelands.

Descendants of Issachar

7 The sons[2] of Issachar: Tola, Puah, Jashub, and Shimron, four. 2 The sons of
Tola: Uzzi, Rephaiah, Jeriel, Jahmai, Ibsam, and Shemuel, heads of their fathers' houses, namely of Tola, mighty warriors of their generations, their number
in the days of David being 22,600. 3 The son[3] of Uzzi: Izrahiah. And the sons of
Izrahiah: Michael, Obadiah, Joel, and Isshiah, all five of them were chief men.
4 And along with them, by their generations, according to their fathers' houses,
were units of the army for war, 36,000, for they had many wives and sons. 5 Their
kinsmen belonging to all the clans of Issachar were in all 87,000 mighty warriors,
enrolled by genealogy.

Descendants of Benjamin

6 The sons of Benjamin: Bela, Becher, and Jediael, three. 7 The sons of Bela: Ezbon, Uzzi, Uzziel, Jerimoth, and Iri, five, heads of fathers' houses, mighty warriors.
And their enrollment by genealogies was 22,034. 8 The sons of Becher: Zemirah,
Joash, Eliezer, Elioenai, Omri, Jeremoth, Abijah, Anathoth, and Alemeth. All these
were the sons of Becher. 9 And their enrollment by genealogies, according to their

[1] Septuagint, Syriac (compare Joshua 21:17); Hebrew lacks *Gibeon* [2] Syriac (compare Vulgate); Hebrew *And to the sons* [3] Hebrew *sons*; also verses 10, 12, 17

THE CENTRAL ROLE OF MUSIC IN WORSHIP

Music is a marvelous gift from God — a rhythmic and melodic combination of beauty, art, and emotion. Without a doubt, music enhances the worship experience for God's people. Moses and the Israelites played instruments and sang a song of worship after God ended the pursuit of Pharaoh and his army (Ex 15:1–21). King David composed and commissioned many songs for the Lord — the book of Psalms is full of prayers set to music to be utilized on various occasions of worship. Here, David assigned three men — Heman, Asaph, and Ethan — to lead music at the tabernacle until the completion of Solomon's temple. Many years after the exile, instrumentalists and singers celebrated the rebuilding of Jerusalem's wall with joyful songs of thanksgiving (Ne 12:27). Affection, praise, and gratitude — music carries these from the human soul to the heart of God.

Many of the best-loved songs sung in churches everywhere direct the attention of God's people to Jesus — celebrating his divinity, his power, his love, his sacrifice, and his promised return. Music was evidently meaningful to Christ in the last days before going to the cross. Following the solemn occasion of the Last Supper, Jesus and his disciples crowned the evening with the singing of a hymn before going out to the Mount of Olives (Mt 26:26–30). Worship is a response to God where his "worth" is declared. When Jesus and his followers sang on that night, they were declaring that God was worthy in the midst of trial. Underneath their worship was a belief that God was going to come through in the end.

Scholars believe some New Testament Scripture passages were actually hymns sung by the early church. One example is a section of Paul's letter to the Philippians. Imagine the first-century believers gathered to sing of Jesus with reverence and joy: "Therefore God has highly exalted him and bestowed on him the name that is above every name, so that at the name of Jesus every knee should bow, in heaven and on earth and under the earth, and every tongue confess that Jesus Christ is Lord, to the glory of God the Father" (Php 2:9–11).

14 Of the Levites: Shemaiah the son of Hasshub, son of Azrikam, son of Hashabiah, of the sons of Merari; 15 and Bakbakkar, Heresh, Galal and Mattaniah the son of Mica, son of Zichri, son of Asaph; 16 and Obadiah the son of Shemaiah, son of Galal, son of Jeduthun, and Berechiah the son of Asa, son of Elkanah, who lived in the villages of the Netophathites.

17 The gatekeepers were Shallum, Akkub, Talmon, Ahiman, and their kinsmen (Shallum was the chief); 18 until then they were in the king's gate on the east side as the gatekeepers of the camps of the Levites. 19 Shallum the son of Kore, son of Ebiasaph, son of Korah, and his kinsmen of his fathers' house, the Korahites, were in charge of the work of the service, keepers of the thresholds of the tent, as their fathers had been in charge of the camp of the LORD, keepers of the entrance. 20 And Phinehas the son of Eleazar was the chief officer over them in time past; the LORD was with him. 21 Zechariah the son of Meshelemiah was gatekeeper at the entrance of the tent of meeting. 22 All these, who were chosen as gatekeepers at the thresholds, were 212. They were enrolled by genealogies in their villages. David and Samuel the seer established them in their office of trust. 23 So they and their sons were in charge of the gates of the house of the LORD, that is, the house of the tent, as guards. 24 The gatekeepers were on the four sides, east, west, north, and south. 25 And their kinsmen who were in their villages were obligated to come in every seven days, in turn, to be with these, 26 for the four chief gatekeepers, who were Levites, were entrusted to be over the chambers and the treasures of the house of God. 27 And they lodged around the house of God, for on them lay the duty of watching, and they had charge of opening it every morning.

28 Some of them had charge of the utensils of service, for they were required to count them when they were brought in and taken out. 29 Others of them were appointed over the furniture and over all the holy utensils, also over the fine flour, the wine, the oil, the incense, and the spices. 30 Others, of the sons of the priests, prepared the mixing of the spices, 31 and Mattithiah, one of the Levites, the firstborn of Shallum the Korahite, was entrusted with making the flat cakes. 32 Also some of their kinsmen of the Kohathites had charge of the showbread, to prepare it every Sabbath.

33 Now these, the singers, the heads of fathers' houses of the Levites, were in the chambers of the temple free from other service, for they were on duty day and night. 34 These were heads of fathers' houses of the Levites, according to their generations, leaders. These lived in Jerusalem.

Saul's Genealogy Repeated

35 In Gibeon lived the father of Gibeon, Jeiel, and the name of his wife was Maacah, 36 and his firstborn son Abdon, then Zur, Kish, Baal, Ner, Nadab, 37 Gedor, Ahio, Zechariah, and Mikloth; 38 and Mikloth was the father of Shimeam; and these also lived opposite their kinsmen in Jerusalem, with their kinsmen. 39 Ner fathered Kish, Kish fathered Saul, Saul fathered Jonathan, Malchi-shua, Abinadab, and Eshbaal. 40 And the son of Jonathan was Merib-baal, and Merib-baal fathered Micah. 41 The sons of Micah: Pithon, Melech, Tahrea, and Ahaz.[1] 42 And Ahaz fathered Jarah, and Jarah fathered Alemeth, Azmaveth, and Zimri. And Zimri fathered Moza. 43 Moza fathered Binea, and Rephaiah was his son, Eleasah his son, Azel his son. 44 Azel had six sons and these are their names: Azrikam, Bocheru, Ishmael, Sheariah, Obadiah, and Hanan; these were the sons of Azel.

The Death of Saul and His Sons

10 Now the Philistines fought against Israel, and the men of Israel fled before the Philistines and fell slain on Mount Gilboa. 2 And the Philistines overtook Saul and his sons, and the Philistines struck down Jonathan and Abinadab and Malchi-shua, the sons of Saul. 3 The battle pressed hard against Saul, and the

[1] Compare 8:35; Hebrew lacks *and Ahaz*

1 CHRONICLES 11:1–9

JERUSALEM

One of David's first acts as king was to march to and capture the city of Jerusalem, making it his national capital. This marked the beginning of Jerusalem's significant role in history. About a thousand years later, Jesus rode into the same city astride a donkey, welcomed with cheers: "Hosanna to the Son of David! Blessed is he who comes in the name of the Lord!" (Mt 21:1–11). King David entered Jerusalem with force, determined to conquer the city and its people. Jesus, the King of kings, entered Jerusalem with humility as the Messiah, intent on offering salvation to the whole world. This city has witnessed astounding, world-changing events in its tumultuous history. The book of Revelation hints at significant events in Jerusalem's future, in the time leading up to the consummation of all things (Rev 11:2,8). Ultimately, God will establish a "new Jerusalem" on the earth as a place where his people will dwell in peace forever (Rev 21:1—22:5).

1 CHRONICLES 11:10–47

TRANSFORMATION

The group known as David's mighty men first joined his ranks at the cave of Adullam—where David hid to evade Saul (1Sa 22:1–2). The men, numbered among the distressed, indebted, and discontented, were nothing like the fierce warriors they would become. But when they put themselves under David's command they soon accumulated impressive victories and legendary reputations.

When the group destined to become the twelve disciples first followed

(continued on page 578)

archers found him, and he was wounded by the archers. 4Then Saul said to his armor-bearer, "Draw your sword and thrust me through with it, lest these uncircumcised come and mistreat me." But his armor-bearer would not, for he feared greatly. Therefore Saul took his own sword and fell upon it. 5And when his armor-bearer saw that Saul was dead, he also fell upon his sword and died. 6Thus Saul died; he and his three sons and all his house died together. 7And when all the men of Israel who were in the valley saw that the army[1] had fled and that Saul and his sons were dead, they abandoned their cities and fled, and the Philistines came and lived in them.

8The next day, when the Philistines came to strip the slain, they found Saul and his sons fallen on Mount Gilboa. 9And they stripped him and took his head and his armor, and sent messengers throughout the land of the Philistines to carry the good news to their idols and to the people. 10And they put his armor in the temple of their gods and fastened his head in the temple of Dagon. 11But when all Jabesh-gilead heard all that the Philistines had done to Saul, 12all the valiant men arose and took away the body of Saul and the bodies of his sons, and brought them to Jabesh. And they buried their bones under the oak in Jabesh and fasted seven days.

13So Saul died for his breach of faith. He broke faith with the LORD in that he did not keep the command of the LORD, and also consulted a medium, seeking guidance. 14He did not seek guidance from the LORD. Therefore the LORD put him to death and turned the kingdom over to David the son of Jesse.

David Anointed King

11 Then all Israel gathered together to David at Hebron and said, "Behold, we are your bone and flesh. 2In times past, even when Saul was king, it was you who led out and brought in Israel. And the LORD your God said to you, 'You shall be shepherd of my people Israel, and you shall be prince over my people Israel.'" 3So all the elders of Israel came to the king at Hebron, and David made a covenant with them at Hebron before the LORD. And they anointed David king over Israel, according to the word of the LORD by Samuel.

David Takes Jerusalem

4And David and all Israel went to Jerusalem, that is, Jebus, where the Jebusites were, the inhabitants of the land. 5The inhabitants of Jebus said to David, "You will not come in here." Nevertheless, David took the stronghold of Zion, that is, the city of David. 6David said, "Whoever strikes the Jebusites first shall be chief and commander." And Joab the son of Zeruiah went up first, so he became chief. 7And David lived in the stronghold; therefore it was called the city of David. 8And he built the city all around from the Millo in complete circuit, and Joab repaired the rest of the city. 9And David became greater and greater, for the LORD of hosts was with him.

David's Mighty Men

10Now these are the chiefs of David's mighty men, who gave him strong support in his kingdom, together with all Israel, to make him king, according to the word of the LORD concerning Israel. 11This is an account of David's mighty men: Jashobeam, a Hachmonite, was chief of the three.[2] He wielded his spear against 300 whom he killed at one time.

12And next to him among the three mighty men was Eleazar the son of Dodo, the Ahohite. 13He was with David at Pas-dammim when the Philistines were gathered there for battle. There was a plot of ground full of barley, and the men fled from the Philistines. 14But he took his[3] stand in the midst of the plot and defended it and killed the Philistines. And the LORD saved them by a great victory.

[1]Hebrew *they* [2]Compare 2 Samuel 23:8; Hebrew *thirty*, or *captains* [3]Compare 2 Samuel 23:12; Hebrew *they . . . their*

SAUL, DAVID, AND JESUS

Saul had the throne of all Israel and the blessing of God, but turning away from the Lord resulted in the loss of everything. Following Saul's death, God gave Israel's throne to David.

Saul faltered in obedience when he failed to destroy the Amalekites completely (1Sa 15:1–23). God had instructed that none of the Amalekites — including their livestock — were to survive the attack. God rejected Saul as king because Saul disregarded the instructions in favor of sparing the Amalekite king and keeping the best animals for himself. On another occasion, he chose to disobey God and consulted a medium before going into his final battle with the Philistines (1Sa 28:3–20). Even though Saul sought wisdom, he did so in a manner that was clearly forbidden. In his early days, Saul had walked with God and listened to his words. But by the end of his life, he habitually ignored God and tried to forge his own path through the situations he faced.

Before Saul, Israel had been led by judges raised up by God to guide and protect the people. God alone was their King. When Israel demanded that Samuel give them a human king like the other nations, God allowed it. But God also warned that the monarchy would be a mixed blessing, resulting eventually in hardship for the people (1Sa 8:10–18). Israel's first two kings illustrate both the blessings and the limits of human kingship. They also provide an object lesson on the relationship between divine and human authority. Only when human leaders submit in faith and obedience to God can they provide genuine leadership for God's people. As Saul's failures mounted, God chose to put the kingdom in the hands of David. David outshone Saul in leadership, wisdom, and fidelity to the ways of the Lord. He prospered during his reign — conquering Jerusalem, constructing a palace in the newly named "City of David," and earning the respect of neighboring nations. But for all of David's good qualities, he was a sinner like every other mere human.

Jesus, the King of kings, lived an earthly life far above the examples of Saul and David. Jesus never sinned. He treated all people with compassion and fairness. He exercised authority with humility while standing for justice with unwavering conviction. At all times, he honored God, living in perfect obedience. In love, he gave his life on the cross as a sacrifice for the world's sin. This selfless act — taking on a penalty he did not deserve (2Co 5:21) — is history's greatest act of a King serving the people he loves.

(Transformation, continued)

Jesus, they were ordinary people untrained for the adventures ahead. Several of them were simple fishermen and one was a tax collector. Under Christ's leadership, they became partners in his ministry and eventually leaders of the church. God can use anyone in his kingdom work. Things such as talent, family connections, wealth, or experience are not prerequisites for serving the Lord. Jesus has the power to transform ordinary men and women for accomplishing extraordinary, even eternal things. When average, everyday people follow Jesus, he will accomplish unimaginable things through them!

15Three of the thirty chief men went down to the rock to David at the cave of Adullam, when the army of Philistines was encamped in the Valley of Rephaim. 16David was then in the stronghold, and the garrison of the Philistines was then at Bethlehem. 17And David said longingly, "Oh that someone would give me water to drink from the well of Bethlehem that is by the gate!" 18Then the three mighty men broke through the camp of the Philistines and drew water out of the well of Bethlehem that was by the gate and took it and brought it to David. But David would not drink it. He poured it out to the LORD 19and said, "Far be it from me before my God that I should do this. Shall I drink the lifeblood of these men? For at the risk of their lives they brought it." Therefore he would not drink it. These things did the three mighty men.

20Now Abishai, the brother of Joab, was chief of the thirty.[1] And he wielded his spear against 300 men and killed them and won a name beside the three. 21He was the most renowned[2] of the thirty[3] and became their commander, but he did not attain to the three.

22And Benaiah the son of Jehoiada was a valiant man[4] of Kabzeel, a doer of great deeds. He struck down two heroes of Moab. He also went down and struck down a lion in a pit on a day when snow had fallen. 23And he struck down an Egyptian, a man of great stature, five cubits[5] tall. The Egyptian had in his hand a spear like a weaver's beam, but Benaiah went down to him with a staff and snatched the spear out of the Egyptian's hand and killed him with his own spear. 24These things did Benaiah the son of Jehoiada and won a name beside the three mighty men. 25He was renowned among the thirty, but he did not attain to the three. And David set him over his bodyguard.

26The mighty men were Asahel the brother of Joab, Elhanan the son of Dodo of Bethlehem, 27Shammoth of Harod,[6] Helez the Pelonite, 28Ira the son of Ikkesh of Tekoa, Abiezer of Anathoth, 29Sibbecai the Hushathite, Ilai the Ahohite, 30Maharai of Netophah, Heled the son of Baanah of Netophah, 31Ithai the son of Ribai of Gibeah of the people of Benjamin, Benaiah of Pirathon, 32Hurai of the brooks of Gaash, Abiel the Arbathite, 33Azmaveth of Baharum, Eliahba the Shaalbonite, 34Hashem[7] the Gizonite, Jonathan the son of Shagee the Hararite, 35Ahiam the son of Sachar the Hararite, Eliphal the son of Ur, 36Hepher the Mecherathite, Ahijah the Pelonite, 37Hezro of Carmel, Naarai the son of Ezbai, 38Joel the brother of Nathan, Mibhar the son of Hagri, 39Zelek the Ammonite, Naharai of Beeroth, the armor-bearer of Joab the son of Zeruiah, 40Ira the Ithrite, Gareb the Ithrite, 41Uriah the Hittite, Zabad the son of Ahlai, 42Adina the son of Shiza the Reubenite, a leader of the Reubenites, and thirty with him, 43Hanan the son of Maacah, and Joshaphat the Mithnite, 44Uzzia the Ashterathite, Shama and Jeiel the sons of Hotham the Aroerite, 45Jediael the son of Shimri, and Joha his brother, the Tizite, 46Eliel the Mahavite, and Jeribai, and Joshaviah, the sons of Elnaam, and Ithmah the Moabite, 47Eliel, and Obed, and Jaasiel the Mezobaite.

The Mighty Men Join David

12 Now these are the men who came to David at Ziklag, while he could not move about freely because of Saul the son of Kish. And they were among the mighty men who helped him in war. 2They were bowmen and could shoot arrows and sling stones with either the right or the left hand; they were Benjaminites, Saul's kinsmen. 3The chief was Ahiezer, then Joash, both sons of Shemaah of Gibeah; also Jeziel and Pelet, the sons of Azmaveth; Beracah, Jehu of Anathoth, 4Ishmaiah of Gibeon, a mighty man among the thirty and a leader over the thirty; Jeremiah,[8] Jahaziel, Johanan, Jozabad of Gederah, 5Eluzai,[9] Jerimoth, Bealiah, Shemariah, Shephatiah the Haruphite; 6Elkanah, Isshiah, Azarel, Joezer,

---

[1]Syriac; Hebrew *three* [2]Compare 2 Samuel 23:19; Hebrew *more renowned among the two* [3]Syriac; Hebrew *three* [4]Syriac; Hebrew *the son of a valiant man* [5]*A cubit* was about 18 inches or 45 centimeters [6]Compare 2 Samuel 23:25; Hebrew *the Harorite* [7]Compare Septuagint and 2 Samuel 23:32; Hebrew *the sons of Hashem* [8]Hebrew verse 5 [9]Hebrew verse 6

generations, as heads of their fathers' houses, mighty warriors, was 20,200. 10The
son of Jediael: Bilhan. And the sons of Bilhan: Jeush, Benjamin, Ehud, Chenaanah,
Zethan, Tarshish, and Ahishahar. 11All these were the sons of Jediael according to
the heads of their fathers' houses, mighty warriors, 17,200, able to go to war. 12And
Shuppim and Huppim were the sons of Ir, Hushim the son of Aher.

Descendants of Naphtali

13The sons of Naphtali: Jahziel, Guni, Jezer and Shallum, the descendants of
Bilhah.

Descendants of Manasseh

14The sons of Manasseh: Asriel, whom his Aramean concubine bore; she
bore Machir the father of Gilead. 15And Machir took a wife for Huppim and for
Shuppim. The name of his sister was Maacah. And the name of the second was
Zelophehad, and Zelophehad had daughters. 16And Maacah the wife of Machir
bore a son, and she called his name Peresh; and the name of his brother was
Sheresh; and his sons were Ulam and Rakem. 17The son of Ulam: Bedan. These
were the sons of Gilead the son of Machir, son of Manasseh. 18And his sister Hammolecheth bore Ishhod, Abiezer, and Mahlah. 19The sons of Shemida were Ahian,
Shechem, Likhi, and Aniam.

Descendants of Ephraim

20The sons of Ephraim: Shuthelah, and Bered his son, Tahath his son, Eleadah
his son, Tahath his son, 21Zabad his son, Shuthelah his son, and Ezer and Elead,
whom the men of Gath who were born in the land killed, because they came down
to raid their livestock. 22And Ephraim their father mourned many days, and his
brothers came to comfort him. 23And Ephraim went in to his wife, and she conceived and bore a son. And he called his name Beriah, because disaster had befallen his house.[1] 24His daughter was Sheerah, who built both Lower and Upper
Beth-horon, and Uzzen-sheerah. 25Rephah was his son, Resheph his son, Telah his
son, Tahan his son, 26Ladan his son, Ammihud his son, Elishama his son, 27Nun[2]
his son, Joshua his son. 28Their possessions and settlements were Bethel and its
towns, and to the east Naaran, and to the west Gezer and its towns, Shechem and
its towns, and Ayyah and its towns; 29also in possession of the Manassites, Beth-shean and its towns, Taanach and its towns, Megiddo and its towns, Dor and its
towns. In these lived the sons of Joseph the son of Israel.

Descendants of Asher

30The sons of Asher: Imnah, Ishvah, Ishvi, Beriah, and their sister Serah. 31The
sons of Beriah: Heber, and Malchiel, who fathered Birzaith. 32Heber fathered
Japhlet, Shomer, Hotham, and their sister Shua. 33The sons of Japhlet: Pasach,
Bimhal, and Ashvath. These are the sons of Japhlet. 34The sons of Shemer his
brother: Rohgah, Jehubbah, and Aram. 35The sons of Helem his brother: Zophah,
Imna, Shelesh, and Amal. 36The sons of Zophah: Suah, Harnepher, Shual, Beri,
Imrah. 37Bezer, Hod, Shamma, Shilshah, Ithran, and Beera. 38The sons of Jether:
Jephunneh, Pispa, and Ara. 39The sons of Ulla: Arah, Hanniel, and Rizia. 40All of
these were men of Asher, heads of fathers' houses, approved, mighty warriors,
chiefs of the princes. Their number enrolled by genealogies, for service in war,
was 26,000 men.

A Genealogy of Saul

8 Benjamin fathered Bela his firstborn, Ashbel the second, Aharah the third,
2Nohah the fourth, and Rapha the fifth. 3And Bela had sons: Addar, Gera,
Abihud, 4Abishua, Naaman, Ahoah, 5Gera, Shephuphan, and Huram. 6These are

[1] *Beriah* sounds like the Hebrew for *disaster* [2] Hebrew *Non*

1 CHRONICLES 8:1–40

CHOOSING SAUL RATHER THAN GOD

The book of 1 Chronicles includes the genealogy of Saul, Israel's first king. Saul came to power when the elders of Israel demanded that Samuel, the Lord's man in leadership, appoint a king to lead them like the other nations. Samuel resisted, but the Lord instructed him to carry out their request—noting that asking for a national king was a rejection of God, not of Samuel (1Sa 8:1–9). From the nation's founding, the people had the opportunity to serve God as their true king. Yet arrogance, impatience and envy caused Israel to believe the Lord's kingship was insufficient. Saul reigned forty-two years (1Sa 13:1), but his eventual rebellion against God led to a bitter end (1Ch 10:13–14).

With the appearance of Jesus, Israel and the world once again have the opportunity to serve God as their king. Humankind is limited and corrupt, but God knows all things and always does what is right. He is the ultimate, all-sufficient King. Those who believe in Jesus become more than subjects in God's kingdom—they become his sons and daughters (Jn 1:12).

the sons of Ehud (they were heads of fathers' houses of the inhabitants of Geba, and they were carried into exile to Manahath): 7Naaman,[1] Ahijah, and Gera, that is, Heglam, who fathered[2] Uzza and Ahihud. 8And Shaharaim fathered sons in the country of Moab after he had sent away Hushim and Baara his wives. 9He fathered sons by Hodesh his wife: Jobab, Zibia, Mesha, Malcam, 10Jeuz, Sachia, and Mirmah. These were his sons, heads of fathers' houses. 11He also fathered sons by Hushim: Abitub and Elpaal. 12The sons of Elpaal: Eber, Misham, and Shemed, who built Ono and Lod with its towns, 13and Beriah and Shema (they were heads of fathers' houses of the inhabitants of Aijalon, who caused the inhabitants of Gath to flee); 14and Ahio, Shashak, and Jeremoth. 15Zebadiah, Arad, Eder, 16Michael, Ishpah, and Joha were sons of Beriah. 17Zebadiah, Meshullam, Hizki, Heber, 18Ishmerai, Izliah, and Jobab were the sons of Elpaal. 19Jakim, Zichri, Zabdi, 20Elienai, Zillethai, Eliel, 21Adaiah, Beraiah, and Shimrath were the sons of Shimei. 22Ishpan, Eber, Eliel, 23Abdon, Zichri, Hanan, 24Hananiah, Elam, Anthothijah, 25Iphdeiah, and Penuel were the sons of Shashak. 26Shamsherai, Shehariah, Athaliah, 27Jaareshiah, Elijah, and Zichri were the sons of Jeroham. 28These were the heads of fathers' houses, according to their generations, chief men. These lived in Jerusalem.

29Jeiel[3] the father of Gibeon lived in Gibeon, and the name of his wife was Maacah. 30His firstborn son: Abdon, then Zur, Kish, Baal, Nadab, 31Gedor, Ahio, Zecher, 32and Mikloth (he fathered Shimeah). Now these also lived opposite their kinsmen in Jerusalem, with their kinsmen. 33Ner was the father of Kish, Kish of Saul, Saul of Jonathan, Malchi-shua, Abinadab and Eshbaal; 34and the son of Jonathan was Merib-baal; and Merib-baal was the father of Micah. 35The sons of Micah: Pithon, Melech, Tarea, and Ahaz. 36Ahaz fathered Jehoaddah, and Jehoaddah fathered Alemeth, Azmaveth, and Zimri. Zimri fathered Moza. 37Moza fathered Binea; Raphah was his son, Eleasah his son, Azel his son. 38Azel had six sons, and these are their names: Azrikam, Bocheru, Ishmael, Sheariah, Obadiah, and Hanan. All these were the sons of Azel. 39The sons of Eshek his brother: Ulam his firstborn, Jeush the second, and Eliphelet the third. 40The sons of Ulam were men who were mighty warriors, bowmen, having many sons and grandsons, 150. All these were Benjaminites.

A Genealogy of the Returned Exiles

9 So all Israel was recorded in genealogies, and these are written in the Book of the Kings of Israel. And Judah was taken into exile in Babylon because of their breach of faith. 2Now the first to dwell again in their possessions in their cities were Israel, the priests, the Levites, and the temple servants. 3And some of the people of Judah, Benjamin, Ephraim, and Manasseh lived in Jerusalem: 4Uthai the son of Ammihud, son of Omri, son of Imri, son of Bani, from the sons of Perez the son of Judah. 5And of the Shilonites: Asaiah the firstborn, and his sons. 6Of the sons of Zerah: Jeuel and their kinsmen, 690. 7Of the Benjaminites: Sallu the son of Meshullam, son of Hodaviah, son of Hassenuah, 8Ibneiah the son of Jeroham, Elah the son of Uzzi, son of Michri, and Meshullam the son of Shephatiah, son of Reuel, son of Ibnijah; 9and their kinsmen according to their generations, 956. All these were heads of fathers' houses according to their fathers' houses.

10Of the priests: Jedaiah, Jehoiarib, Jachin, 11and Azariah the son of Hilkiah, son of Meshullam, son of Zadok, son of Meraioth, son of Ahitub, the chief officer of the house of God; 12and Adaiah the son of Jeroham, son of Pashhur, son of Malchijah, and Maasai the son of Adiel, son of Jahzerah, son of Meshullam, son of Meshillemith, son of Immer; 13besides their kinsmen, heads of their fathers' houses, 1,760, mighty men for the work of the service of the house of God.

---

[1]Hebrew *and Naaman* [2]Or *Gera; he carried them into exile and fathered* [3]Compare 9:35; Hebrew lacks *Jeiel*

king called the Gibeonites and spoke to them. Now the Gibeonites were not of the
people of Israel but of the remnant of the Amorites. Although the people of Israel
had sworn to spare them, Saul had sought to strike them down in his zeal for the
people of Israel and Judah. 3And David said to the Gibeonites, "What shall I do
for you? And how shall I make atonement, that you may bless the heritage of the
LORD?" 4The Gibeonites said to him, "It is not a matter of silver or gold between us
and Saul or his house; neither is it for us to put any man to death in Israel." And he
said, "What do you say that I shall do for you?" 5They said to the king, "The man
who consumed us and planned to destroy us, so that we should have no place in
all the territory of Israel, 6let seven of his sons be given to us, so that we may hang
them before the LORD at Gibeah of Saul, the chosen of the LORD." And the king
said, "I will give them."

7But the king spared Mephibosheth, the son of Saul's son Jonathan, because of
the oath of the LORD that was between them, between David and Jonathan the son
of Saul. 8The king took the two sons of Rizpah the daughter of Aiah, whom she
bore to Saul, Armoni and Mephibosheth; and the five sons of Merab[1] the daughter
of Saul, whom she bore to Adriel the son of Barzillai the Meholathite; 9and he gave
them into the hands of the Gibeonites, and they hanged them on the mountain
before the LORD, and the seven of them perished together. They were put to death
in the first days of harvest, at the beginning of barley harvest.

10Then Rizpah the daughter of Aiah took sackcloth and spread it for herself
on the rock, from the beginning of harvest until rain fell upon them from the
heavens. And she did not allow the birds of the air to come upon them by day, or
the beasts of the field by night. 11When David was told what Rizpah the daughter
of Aiah, the concubine of Saul, had done, 12David went and took the bones of Saul
and the bones of his son Jonathan from the men of Jabesh-gilead, who had stolen them from the public square of Beth-shan, where the Philistines had hanged
them, on the day the Philistines killed Saul on Gilboa. 13And he brought up from
there the bones of Saul and the bones of his son Jonathan; and they gathered the
bones of those who were hanged. 14And they buried the bones of Saul and his
son Jonathan in the land of Benjamin in Zela, in the tomb of Kish his father. And
they did all that the king commanded. And after that God responded to the plea
for the land.

War with the Philistines

15There was war again between the Philistines and Israel, and David went
down together with his servants, and they fought against the Philistines. And
David grew weary. 16And Ishbi-benob, one of the descendants of the giants,
whose spear weighed three hundred shekels[2] of bronze, and who was armed
with a new sword, thought to kill David. 17But Abishai the son of Zeruiah came
to his aid and attacked the Philistine and killed him. Then David's men swore to
him, "You shall no longer go out with us to battle, lest you quench the lamp of
Israel."

18After this there was again war with the Philistines at Gob. Then Sibbecai
the Hushathite struck down Saph, who was one of the descendants of the giants. 19And there was again war with the Philistines at Gob, and Elhanan the
son of Jaare-oregim, the Bethlehemite, struck down Goliath the Gittite, the
shaft of whose spear was like a weaver's beam.[3] 20And there was again war
at Gath, where there was a man of great stature, who had six fingers on each
hand, and six toes on each foot, twenty-four in number, and he also was descended from the giants. 21And when he taunted Israel, Jonathan the son of
Shimei, David's brother, struck him down. 22These four were descended from
the giants in Gath, and they fell by the hand of David and by the hand of his
servants.

[1]Two Hebrew manuscripts, Septuagint; most Hebrew manuscripts *Michal* [2]A *shekel* was about 2/5 ounce or 11 grams [3]Contrast 1 Chronicles 20:5, which may preserve the original reading

[3]And David came to his house at Jerusalem. And the king took the ten concubines whom he had left to care for the house and put them in a house under guard and provided for them, but did not go in to them. So they were shut up until the day of their death, living as if in widowhood.

[4]Then the king said to Amasa, "Call the men of Judah together to me within three days, and be here yourself." [5]So Amasa went to summon Judah, but he delayed beyond the set time that had been appointed him. [6]And David said to Abishai, "Now Sheba the son of Bichri will do us more harm than Absalom. Take your lord's servants and pursue him, lest he get himself to fortified cities and escape from us."[1] [7]And there went out after him Joab's men and the Cherethites and the Pelethites, and all the mighty men. They went out from Jerusalem to pursue Sheba the son of Bichri. [8]When they were at the great stone that is in Gibeon, Amasa came to meet them. Now Joab was wearing a soldier's garment, and over it was a belt with a sword in its sheath fastened on his thigh, and as he went forward it fell out. [9]And Joab said to Amasa, "Is it well with you, my brother?" And Joab took Amasa by the beard with his right hand to kiss him. [10]But Amasa did not observe the sword that was in Joab's hand. So Joab struck him with it in the stomach and spilled his entrails to the ground without striking a second blow, and he died.

Then Joab and Abishai his brother pursued Sheba the son of Bichri. [11]And one of Joab's young men took his stand by Amasa and said, "Whoever favors Joab, and whoever is for David, let him follow Joab." [12]And Amasa lay wallowing in his blood in the highway. And anyone who came by, seeing him, stopped. And when the man saw that all the people stopped, he carried Amasa out of the highway into the field and threw a garment over him. [13]When he was taken out of the highway, all the people went on after Joab to pursue Sheba the son of Bichri.

[14]And Sheba passed through all the tribes of Israel to Abel of Beth-maacah,[2] and all the Bichrites[3] assembled and followed him in. [15]And all the men who were with Joab came and besieged him in Abel of Beth-maacah. They cast up a mound against the city, and it stood against the rampart, and they were battering the wall to throw it down. [16]Then a wise woman called from the city, "Listen! Listen! Tell Joab, 'Come here, that I may speak to you.'" [17]And he came near her, and the woman said, "Are you Joab?" He answered, "I am." Then she said to him, "Listen to the words of your servant." And he answered, "I am listening." [18]Then she said, "They used to say in former times, 'Let them but ask counsel at Abel,' and so they settled a matter. [19]I am one of those who are peaceable and faithful in Israel. You seek to destroy a city that is a mother in Israel. Why will you swallow up the heritage of the LORD?" [20]Joab answered, "Far be it from me, far be it, that I should swallow up or destroy! [21]That is not true. But a man of the hill country of Ephraim, called Sheba the son of Bichri, has lifted up his hand against King David. Give up him alone, and I will withdraw from the city." And the woman said to Joab, "Behold, his head shall be thrown to you over the wall." [22]Then the woman went to all the people in her wisdom. And they cut off the head of Sheba the son of Bichri and threw it out to Joab. So he blew the trumpet, and they dispersed from the city, every man to his home. And Joab returned to Jerusalem to the king.

[23]Now Joab was in command of all the army of Israel; and Benaiah the son of Jehoiada was in command of the Cherethites and the Pelethites; [24]and Adoram was in charge of the forced labor; and Jehoshaphat the son of Ahilud was the recorder; [25]and Sheva was secretary; and Zadok and Abiathar were priests; [26]and Ira the Jairite was also David's priest.

David Avenges the Gibeonites

21 Now there was a famine in the days of David for three years, year after year. And David sought the face of the LORD. And the LORD said, "There is bloodguilt on Saul and on his house, because he put the Gibeonites to death." [2]So the

[1]Hebrew *and snatch away our eyes* [2]Compare 20:15; Hebrew *and Beth-maacah* [3]Hebrew *Berites*

2 SAMUEL 21:1–14

ATONEMENT: DEATH IS REQUIRED

Oftentimes the life of a follower of Jesus demands something radical. God's standard for his people is perfection (Mt 5:48). He requires absolute surrender. However, no one is able to live up to that standard, which is what makes God's restorative work throughout Scripture such a miracle. When God restores people to a right relationship with him, he removes the barrier that sin creates between him and humanity. This is a radical thought!

God's standard — perfection — is not just overwhelming; it is impossible. In this passage, the Gibeonites asked for an outrageous payment from David to atone for Saul's sins against them. But in the New Testament, Jesus becomes the once and for all payment for the sin of humanity. No longer would individual sin require individual and unique sacrifices, but Jesus covers all sin — past, present, and future. There is nothing more radical than a perfect man dying once and for all for humanity's indiscretions and failures.

and Jashobeam, the Korahites; 7And Joelah and Zebadiah, the sons of Jeroham
of Gedor.

8From the Gadites there went over to David at the stronghold in the wilderness
mighty and experienced warriors, expert with shield and spear, whose faces were
like the faces of lions and who were swift as gazelles upon the mountains: 9Ezer
the chief, Obadiah second, Eliab third, 10Mishmannah fourth, Jeremiah fifth,
11Attai sixth, Eliel seventh, 12Johanan eighth, Elzabad ninth, 13Jeremiah tenth,
Machbannai eleventh. 14These Gadites were officers of the army; the least was
a match for a hundred men and the greatest for a thousand. 15These are the men
who crossed the Jordan in the first month, when it was overflowing all its banks,
and put to flight all those in the valleys, to the east and to the west.

16And some of the men of Benjamin and Judah came to the stronghold to David. 17David went out to meet them and said to them, "If you have come to me in
friendship to help me, my heart will be joined to you; but if to betray me to my
adversaries, although there is no wrong in my hands, then may the God of our
fathers see and rebuke you." 18Then the Spirit clothed Amasai, chief of the thirty,
and he said,

"We are yours, O David,
and with you, O son of Jesse!
Peace, peace to you,
and peace to your helpers!
For your God helps you."

Then David received them and made them officers of his troops.

19Some of the men of Manasseh deserted to David when he came with the
Philistines for the battle against Saul. (Yet he did not help them, for the rulers of
the Philistines took counsel and sent him away, saying, "At peril to our heads he
will desert to his master Saul.") 20As he went to Ziklag, these men of Manasseh
deserted to him: Adnah, Jozabad, Jediael, Michael, Jozabad, Elihu, and Zillethai,
chiefs of thousands in Manasseh. 21They helped David against the band of raiders,
for they were all mighty men of valor and were commanders in the army. 22For
from day to day men came to David to help him, until there was a great army, like
an army of God.

23These are the numbers of the divisions of the armed troops who came to
David in Hebron to turn the kingdom of Saul over to him, according to the word of
the LORD. 24The men of Judah bearing shield and spear were 6,800 armed troops.
25Of the Simeonites, mighty men of valor for war, 7,100. 26Of the Levites 4,600.
27The prince Jehoiada, of the house of Aaron, and with him 3,700. 28Zadok, a
young man mighty in valor, and twenty-two commanders from his own fathers'
house. 29Of the Benjaminites, the kinsmen of Saul, 3,000, of whom the majority
had to that point kept their allegiance to the house of Saul. 30Of the Ephraimites
20,800, mighty men of valor, famous men in their fathers' houses. 31Of the half-
tribe of Manasseh 18,000, who were expressly named to come and make David
king. 32Of Issachar, men who had understanding of the times, to know what Israel
ought to do, 200 chiefs, and all their kinsmen under their command. 33Of Zebulun 50,000 seasoned troops, equipped for battle with all the weapons of war, to
help David[1] with singleness of purpose. 34Of Naphtali 1,000 commanders with
whom were 37,000 men armed with shield and spear. 35Of the Danites 28,600
men equipped for battle. 36Of Asher 40,000 seasoned troops ready for battle. 37Of
the Reubenites and Gadites and the half-tribe of Manasseh from beyond the Jordan, 120,000 men armed with all the weapons of war.

38All these, men of war, arrayed in battle order, came to Hebron with a whole
heart to make David king over all Israel. Likewise, all the rest of Israel were of a
single mind to make David king. 39And they were there with David for three days,
eating and drinking, for their brothers had made preparation for them. 40And also

[1]Septuagint; Hebrew lacks *David*

THE ISSACHAR MINDSET

The men of Issachar joined with David, offering their swords and unique set of skills. They understood the times and they knew what the Israelites should do. These talents would give a strong advantage to any king.

Knowing details about history and profiles of past leaders can only help to a point — a historian is not as valuable as one who understands the current times and circumstances. The chiefs of Issachar operated in wisdom and discernment, perceiving things such as national momentum, community morale, and the people's capacity for religious and military endeavors. David may well have taken advantage of their counsel when he conferred with his officers before bringing the ark to Jerusalem (1Ch 13:1).

In Jesus' day, he engaged people with a perfect version of the Issachar mindset. Jesus understood the times perfectly, having complete knowledge of all things political, social, and religious. He considered discernment of the times an important ability — even chastising those lacking it (Lk 12:54 – 56). More importantly, he knew what people needed to do. For that reason, Jesus spoke the truth with authority (Mk 1:21 – 22).

Discernment is a valuable skill for followers of Christ. Some situations call for bold action while others require patient observation. At times, a fight must be engaged to preserve old ways, and at other times a fight is needed to revolutionize systems that have become stagnant or corrupt. Knowing what is called for in a given season and identifying the best steps of response is a significant discipleship challenge. It is made more difficult because of humanity's limited knowledge and tendencies toward sin.

As a source of help, Jesus gave the Holy Spirit to counsel the hearts of his people in wisdom and truth. The Holy Spirit reminds them of what Jesus said, guides them away from sin and enables them to glorify Christ (Jn 16:7 – 15). The power that comes through the Holy Spirit gives believers the power to live with strength and conviction. Jesus does not ask his followers to make their way through life on their own; he provides the source for living!

their relatives, from as far as Issachar and Zebulun and Naphtali, came bringing food on donkeys and on camels and on mules and on oxen, abundant provisions of flour, cakes of figs, clusters of raisins, and wine and oil, oxen and sheep, for there was joy in Israel.

The Ark Brought from Kiriath-Jearim

13 David consulted with the commanders of thousands and of hundreds, with every leader. 2 And David said to all the assembly of Israel, "If it seems good to you and from the LORD our God, let us send abroad to our brothers who remain in all the lands of Israel, as well as to the priests and Levites in the cities that have pasturelands, that they may be gathered to us. 3 Then let us bring again the ark of our God to us, for we did not seek it[1] in the days of Saul." 4 All the assembly agreed to do so, for the thing was right in the eyes of all the people.

Uzzah and the Ark

5 So David assembled all Israel from the Nile[2] of Egypt to Lebo-hamath, to bring the ark of God from Kiriath-jearim. 6 And David and all Israel went up to Baalah, that is, to Kiriath-jearim that belongs to Judah, to bring up from there the ark of God, which is called by the name of the LORD who sits enthroned above the cherubim. 7 And they carried the ark of God on a new cart, from the house of Abinadab, and Uzzah and Ahio[3] were driving the cart. 8 And David and all Israel were celebrating before God with all their might, with song and lyres and harps and tambourines and cymbals and trumpets.

9 And when they came to the threshing floor of Chidon, Uzzah put out his hand to take hold of the ark, for the oxen stumbled. 10 And the anger of the LORD was kindled against Uzzah, and he struck him down because he put out his hand to the ark, and he died there before God. 11 And David was angry because the LORD had broken out against Uzzah. And that place is called Perez-uzza[4] to this day. 12 And David was afraid of God that day, and he said, "How can I bring the ark of God home to me?" 13 So David did not take the ark home into the city of David, but took it aside to the house of Obed-edom the Gittite. 14 And the ark of God remained with the household of Obed-edom in his house three months. And the LORD blessed the household of Obed-edom and all that he had.

David's Wives and Children

14 And Hiram king of Tyre sent messengers to David, and cedar trees, also masons and carpenters to build a house for him. 2 And David knew that the LORD had established him as king over Israel, and that his kingdom was highly exalted for the sake of his people Israel.

3 And David took more wives in Jerusalem, and David fathered more sons and daughters. 4 These are the names of the children born to him in Jerusalem: Shammua, Shobab, Nathan, Solomon, 5 Ibhar, Elishua, Elpelet, 6 Nogah, Nepheg, Japhia, 7 Elishama, Beeliada and Eliphelet.

Philistines Defeated

8 When the Philistines heard that David had been anointed king over all Israel, all the Philistines went up to search for David. But David heard of it and went out against them. 9 Now the Philistines had come and made a raid in the Valley of Rephaim. 10 And David inquired of God, "Shall I go up against the Philistines? Will you give them into my hand?" And the LORD said to him, "Go up, and I will give them into your hand." 11 And he went up to Baal-perazim, and David struck them down there. And David said, "God has broken through[5] my enemies by my hand, like a bursting flood." Therefore the name of that place is

[1] Or *him* [2] Hebrew *Shihor* [3] Or *and his brother* [4] *Perez-uzza* means *the breaking out against Uzzah*
[5] *Baal-perazim* means *Lord of breaking through*

1 CHRONICLES 13:1–11

CONFRONTING HOLINESS

David was angry about the death of Uzzah. It seemed harsh that the man should lose his life for reaching to steady and protect the ark of God. Yet the Lord had been clear about protocols for handling holy things (Nu 4:15). The only way to transfer the ark was by using long poles (Ex 25:13–15) and only the Levites were authorized to carry it (1Ch 15:13–15). Despite Uzzah's good intentions, his actions still violated God's law.

In Jesus' ministry, he often confronted religious leaders who assumed they knew how to approach God. In their self-confidence, they missed the gracious nature of Jesus' confrontations with them about their error and their sin. Jesus' stern words for the religious leaders were gracious because God in the flesh did not take their lives—rather, he invited them to change, to go a better way. Just as Uzzah could not touch the ark, so people cannot approach God apart from the way that was established through Christ (Heb 10:19–22). Jesus invites all men and women—no matter what they've done—to find life and forgiveness through faith in him (Jn 14:6).

1 CHRONICLES 14:8–17

WHEN GOD JOINS THE FIGHT

David's army defeated the Philistines in two phases of battle. In both confrontations, the deciding factor was God's intervention—not Israel's military might. David

(continued on next page)

(When God Joins the Fight, continued)

inquired of the Lord both times, yielding to his divine pleasure and will. God accomplished victory for his people and increased his fame among the nations. Even then, God was on a mission to redeem his people and set a precedent for what he would do in the future.

Often, the physical battles of the Old Testament illustrate the spiritual battles between the forces of good and evil. In overview, the life and ministry of Jesus outline the cosmic fight in which Christ defeats Satan and his hosts. Jesus drove out demons (Mt 12:22) and gave his disciples the authority to overcome Satan's power (Lk 10:18–19). The enemy was disarmed and defeated on the cross (Col 2:15), but Satan's ultimate demise won't come until the consummation of history (Rev 20:7–10).

1 CHRONICLES 15:1–29

A DAY OF GLORY

The ark of the covenant's arrival in Jerusalem was a joyous spectacle. All Israel assembled to witness the moment. The Levites appointed singers and musicians to make jubilant sounds with all kinds of instruments—adding to the dancing and shouts of celebration. The people and their king were elated to have the symbol of God's presence at home in their city. And the glory that rested on the ark was God's way of making himself visibly present to his people. The day David brought the ark to Jerusalem was the day when God's glory—his presence and power—was manifest in the city in a new way.

In the beginning of Luke's Gospel we read of Simeon, a faithful son of

(continued on next page)

called Baal-perazim. [12]And they left their gods there, and David gave command, and they were burned.

[13]And the Philistines yet again made a raid in the valley. [14]And when David again inquired of God, God said to him, "You shall not go up after them; go around and come against them opposite the balsam trees. [15]And when you hear the sound of marching in the tops of the balsam trees, then go out to battle, for God has gone out before you to strike down the army of the Philistines." [16]And David did as God commanded him, and they struck down the Philistine army from Gibeon to Gezer. [17]And the fame of David went out into all lands, and the LORD brought the fear of him upon all nations.

The Ark Brought to Jerusalem

15 David[1] built houses for himself in the city of David. And he prepared a place for the ark of God and pitched a tent for it. [2]Then David said that no one but the Levites may carry the ark of God, for the LORD had chosen them to carry the ark of the LORD and to minister to him forever. [3]And David assembled all Israel at Jerusalem to bring up the ark of the LORD to its place, which he had prepared for it. [4]And David gathered together the sons of Aaron and the Levites: [5]of the sons of Kohath, Uriel the chief, with 120 of his brothers; [6]of the sons of Merari, Asaiah the chief, with 220 of his brothers; [7]of the sons of Gershom, Joel the chief, with 130 of his brothers; [8]of the sons of Elizaphan, Shemaiah the chief, with 200 of his brothers; [9]of the sons of Hebron, Eliel the chief, with 80 of his brothers; [10]of the sons of Uzziel, Amminadab the chief, with 112 of his brothers. [11]Then David summoned the priests Zadok and Abiathar, and the Levites Uriel, Asaiah, Joel, Shemaiah, Eliel, and Amminadab, [12]and said to them, "You are the heads of the fathers' houses of the Levites. Consecrate yourselves, you and your brothers, so that you may bring up the ark of the LORD, the God of Israel, to the place that I have prepared for it. [13]Because you did not carry it the first time, the LORD our God broke out against us, because we did not seek him according to the rule." [14]So the priests and the Levites consecrated themselves to bring up the ark of the LORD, the God of Israel. [15]And the Levites carried the ark of God on their shoulders with the poles, as Moses had commanded according to the word of the LORD.

[16]David also commanded the chiefs of the Levites to appoint their brothers as the singers who should play loudly on musical instruments, on harps and lyres and cymbals, to raise sounds of joy. [17]So the Levites appointed Heman the son of Joel; and of his brothers Asaph the son of Berechiah; and of the sons of Merari, their brothers, Ethan the son of Kushaiah; [18]and with them their brothers of the second order, Zechariah, Jaaziel, Shemiramoth, Jehiel, Unni, Eliab, Benaiah, Maaseiah, Mattithiah, Eliphelehu, and Mikneiah, and the gatekeepers Obed-edom and Jeiel. [19]The singers, Heman, Asaph, and Ethan, were to sound bronze cymbals; [20]Zechariah, Aziel, Shemiramoth, Jehiel, Unni, Eliab, Maaseiah, and Benaiah were to play harps according to Alamoth; [21]but Mattithiah, Eliphelehu, Mikneiah, Obed-edom, Jeiel, and Azaziah were to lead with lyres according to the Sheminith. [22]Chenaniah, leader of the Levites in music, should direct the music, for he understood it. [23]Berechiah and Elkanah were to be gatekeepers for the ark. [24]Shebaniah, Joshaphat, Nethanel, Amasai, Zechariah, Benaiah, and Eliezer, the priests, should blow the trumpets before the ark of God. Obed-edom and Jehiah were to be gatekeepers for the ark.

[25]So David and the elders of Israel and the commanders of thousands went to bring up the ark of the covenant of the LORD from the house of Obed-edom with rejoicing. [26]And because God helped the Levites who were carrying the ark of the covenant of the LORD, they sacrificed seven bulls and seven rams. [27]David was clothed with a robe of fine linen, as also were all the Levites who were carrying

[1]Hebrew *He*

the ark, and the singers and Chenaniah the leader of the music of the singers. And
David wore a linen ephod. 28So all Israel brought up the ark of the covenant of the
LORD with shouting, to the sound of the horn, trumpets, and cymbals, and made
loud music on harps and lyres.
29And as the ark of the covenant of the LORD came to the city of David, Michal
the daughter of Saul looked out of the window and saw King David dancing and
celebrating, and she despised him in her heart.

The Ark Placed in a Tent

16 And they brought in the ark of God and set it inside the tent that David had
pitched for it, and they offered burnt offerings and peace offerings before
God. 2And when David had finished offering the burnt offerings and the peace
offerings, he blessed the people in the name of the LORD 3and distributed to all
Israel, both men and women, to each a loaf of bread, a portion of meat,[1] and a
cake of raisins.
4Then he appointed some of the Levites as ministers before the ark of the
LORD, to invoke, to thank, and to praise the LORD, the God of Israel. 5Asaph was
the chief, and second to him were Zechariah, Jeiel, Shemiramoth, Jehiel, Mattithiah, Eliab, Benaiah, Obed-edom, and Jeiel, who were to play harps and lyres;
Asaph was to sound the cymbals, 6and Benaiah and Jahaziel the priests were to
blow trumpets regularly before the ark of the covenant of God. 7Then on that
day David first appointed that thanksgiving be sung to the LORD by Asaph and
his brothers.

David's Song of Thanks

8 Oh give thanks to the LORD; call upon his name;
make known his deeds among the peoples!
9 Sing to him, sing praises to him;
tell of all his wondrous works!
10 Glory in his holy name;
let the hearts of those who seek the LORD rejoice!
11 Seek the LORD and his strength;
seek his presence continually!
12 Remember the wondrous works that he has done,
his miracles and the judgments he uttered,
13 O offspring of Israel his servant,
children of Jacob, his chosen ones!

14 He is the LORD our God;
his judgments are in all the earth.
15 Remember his covenant forever,
the word that he commanded, for a thousand generations,
16 the covenant that he made with Abraham,
his sworn promise to Isaac,
17 which he confirmed to Jacob as a statute,
to Israel as an everlasting covenant,
18 saying, "To you I will give the land of Canaan,
as your portion for an inheritance."
19 When you were few in number,
of little account, and sojourners in it,
20 wandering from nation to nation,
from one kingdom to another people,
21 he allowed no one to oppress them;
he rebuked kings on their account,

[1]Compare Septuagint, Syriac, Vulgate; the meaning of the Hebrew is uncertain

(A Day of Glory, continued)

Israel, who longed for the appearance of God's promised Messiah. Simeon encountered Mary, Joseph, and the Christ-child in the temple and burst into praise for God—salvation for the world had finally come (Lk 2:22–32)! With far less fanfare than the arrival of the ark, Jesus entered the world planning to make his home in the hearts of men and women. When Jesus was born, God's glory came to humanity once again—this time as more than a symbol. When the beloved Son of God took on human nature and was born in Bethlehem, God himself entered history (Jn 1:14).

1 CHRONICLES 16:1

WHERE TO WORSHIP

For a number of years, Israel had, in effect, *two* tabernacles: David constructed a new tent for the ark of the covenant when he moved it to Jerusalem (1Ch 16:1), and in the meantime the old tabernacle remained at Gibeon (1Ch 16:39–40). During David's reign, priests were assigned to both locations. Then, during Solomon's reign, the temple was built on Mount Moriah in Jerusalem (2Ch 3:1—5:1). Throughout Israel's history, various rival locations emerged for the worship of God, including sites in Dan, Bethel, and Samaria.

In Jesus' conversation with a Samaritan woman—many generations after the time of David—she expressed confusion about this issue (Jn 4:19–24). Jesus clarified that the location of worship is less important than the inward dispositions of those worshiping him—the Father seeks those who worship "in spirit and truth" (Jn 4:24). Because God is Spirit, he is not confined to any

(continued on next page)

(Where to Worship, continued)

particular place of worship. God's people can worship the Father in the name of the Son, in the power of the Spirit with reverence and joy—at any time and in any place.

22 saying, "Touch not my anointed ones,
do my prophets no harm!"
23 Sing to the LORD, all the earth!
Tell of his salvation from day to day.
24 Declare his glory among the nations,
his marvelous works among all the peoples!
25 For great is the LORD, and greatly to be praised,
and he is to be feared above all gods.
26 For all the gods of the peoples are worthless idols,
but the LORD made the heavens.
27 Splendor and majesty are before him;
strength and joy are in his place.

28 Ascribe to the LORD, O families of the peoples,
ascribe to the LORD glory and strength!
29 Ascribe to the LORD the glory due his name;
bring an offering and come before him!
Worship the LORD in the splendor of holiness;[1]
30 tremble before him, all the earth;
yes, the world is established; it shall never be moved.
31 Let the heavens be glad, and let the earth rejoice,
and let them say among the nations, "The LORD
reigns!"
32 Let the sea roar, and all that fills it;
let the field exult, and everything in it!
33 Then shall the trees of the forest sing for joy
before the LORD, for he comes to judge the earth.
34 Oh give thanks to the LORD, for he is good;
for his steadfast love endures forever!

35 Say also:

"Save us, O God of our salvation,
and gather and deliver us from among the nations,
that we may give thanks to your holy name
and glory in your praise.
36 Blessed be the LORD, the God of Israel,
from everlasting to everlasting!"

Then all the people said, "Amen!" and praised the LORD.

Worship Before the Ark

37 So David left Asaph and his brothers there before the ark of the covenant
of the LORD to minister regularly before the ark as each day required, 38 and also
Obed-edom and his[2] sixty-eight brothers, while Obed-edom, the son of Jeduthun, and Hosah were to be gatekeepers. 39 And he left Zadok the priest and his
brothers the priests before the tabernacle of the LORD in the high place that was
at Gibeon 40 to offer burnt offerings to the LORD on the altar of burnt offering
regularly morning and evening, to do all that is written in the Law of the LORD
that he commanded Israel. 41 With them were Heman and Jeduthun and the rest
of those chosen and expressly named to give thanks to the LORD, for his steadfast
love endures forever. 42 Heman and Jeduthun had trumpets and cymbals for the
music and instruments for sacred song. The sons of Jeduthun were appointed to
the gate.

43 Then all the people departed each to his house, and David went home to
bless his household.

---

[1] Or *in holy attire* [2] Hebrew *their*

The LORD's Covenant with David

17 Now when David lived in his house, David said to Nathan the prophet, "Behold, I dwell in a house of cedar, but the ark of the covenant of the LORD is under a tent." 2And Nathan said to David, "Do all that is in your heart, for God is with you."

3But that same night the word of the LORD came to Nathan, 4"Go and tell my servant David, 'Thus says the LORD: It is not you who will build me a house to dwell in. 5For I have not lived in a house since the day I brought up Israel to this day, but I have gone from tent to tent and from dwelling to dwelling. 6In all places where I have moved with all Israel, did I speak a word with any of the judges of Israel, whom I commanded to shepherd my people, saying, "Why have you not built me a house of cedar?"' 7Now, therefore, thus shall you say to my servant David, 'Thus says the LORD of hosts, I took you from the pasture, from following the sheep, to be prince over my people Israel, 8and I have been with you wherever you have gone and have cut off all your enemies from before you. And I will make for you a name, like the name of the great ones of the earth. 9And I will appoint a place for my people Israel and will plant them, that they may dwell in their own place and be disturbed no more. And violent men shall waste them no more, as formerly, 10from the time that I appointed judges over my people Israel. And I will subdue all your enemies. Moreover, I declare to you that the LORD will build you a house. 11When your days are fulfilled to walk with your fathers, I will raise up your offspring after you, one of your own sons, and I will establish his kingdom. 12He shall build a house for me, and I will establish his throne forever. 13I will be to him a father, and he shall be to me a son. I will not take my steadfast love from him, as I took it from him who was before you, 14but I will confirm him in my house and in my kingdom forever, and his throne shall be established forever.'" 15In accordance with all these words, and in accordance with all this vision, Nathan spoke to David.

David's Prayer

16Then King David went in and sat before the LORD and said, "Who am I, O LORD God, and what is my house, that you have brought me thus far? 17And this was a small thing in your eyes, O God. You have also spoken of your servant's house for a great while to come, and have shown me future generations,[1] O LORD God! 18And what more can David say to you for honoring your servant? For you know your servant. 19For your servant's sake, O LORD, and according to your own heart, you have done all this greatness, in making known all these great things. 20There is none like you, O LORD, and there is no God besides you, according to all that we have heard with our ears. 21And who is like your people Israel, the one[2] nation on earth whom God went to redeem to be his people, making for yourself a name for great and awesome things, in driving out nations before your people whom you redeemed from Egypt? 22And you made your people Israel to be your people forever, and you, O LORD, became their God. 23And now, O LORD, let the word that you have spoken concerning your servant and concerning his house be established forever, and do as you have spoken, 24and your name will be established and magnified forever, saying, 'The LORD of hosts, the God of Israel, is Israel's God,' and the house of your servant David will be established before you. 25For you, my God, have revealed to your servant that you will build a house for him. Therefore your servant has found courage to pray before you. 26And now, O LORD, you are God, and you have promised this good thing to your servant. 27Now you have been pleased to bless the house of your servant, that it may continue forever before you, for it is you, O LORD, who have blessed, and it is blessed forever."

[1]Or *and you look upon me as a man of high rank* [2]Septuagint, Vulgate *other*

1 CHRONICLES 17:16–27

SUBMITTING TO GOD'S WILL

Despite David's success as a warrior, he was truly humble. He never forgot his modest background as a shepherd and credited his victories to God rather than his own military prowess. In David's heart, there lived a strong desire to build a house for the Lord—a temple for his presence and name (1Ch 22:6–10; Ac 7:45–46). When God told David he would not get to build the temple but that the honor would fall to one of his sons, David remained humble and yielded to God's will. David trusted God's plan even though his dream was denied.

Jesus' human will remained perfectly submitted to the Father's will (Jn 6:38). When faced with drinking the cup of God's wrath—taking on the world's sin at the cross—Jesus remained surrendered, trusting the Father's plan. Though he could have claimed his right as God at any time, he "did not count equality with God a thing to be grasped" (Php 2:6).

CHRONICLING DAVID'S LIFE

The name of King David stirs so many dramatic associations — a shepherd boy tending flocks while singing songs in the night, a young man anointed by Samuel, a stone launched from a sling to kill the giant Goliath, an enviable friendship with Jonathan, the capture of Jerusalem, a half-dressed king dancing for joy over the ark of the covenant, lust-driven adultery and a murder to cover it up, confrontation from the prophet Nathan, the death of an infant while the king begged God for mercy, Absalom's revolt and efforts to kill his own father, preparations for the temple of the Lord and the rise of an heir named Solomon. David's story in Scripture is without rival, apart from that of Jesus.

First Chronicles focuses primarily on David's active leadership — his public administration, planning for the temple, and military victories. The book does not include David's sin with Bathsheba and the many family problems documented so thoroughly in the books of Samuel and the first two chapters of 1 Kings. First Chronicles attends instead to the highlights of David's forty-year reign. David came to the throne only after Saul's unfaithfulness led to his death (1Ch 10:13 — 11:3). The newly crowned king then took Jerusalem as his capital (1Ch 11:4 – 9). Soon after, warriors from all over Israel rallied to join David's army (1Ch 11:10 — 12:38). The middle chapters of the book record David's many royal accomplishments. And the book ends with the report that David "died at a good age, full of days, riches, and honor" (1Ch 29:28).

But no highlight from David's highly impressive biography is more important than the covenant God made with him. The Lord promised David a descendant who would reign forever over an eternal kingdom (1Ch 17:11 – 14). God fulfilled this promise in Christ. "And when he had removed him [Saul], he raised up David to be their king, of whom he testified and said, 'I have found in David the son of Jesse a man after my heart, who will do all my will.' Of this man's offspring God has brought to Israel a Savior, Jesus, as he promised" (Ac 13:22 – 23). In the book of Revelation, Jesus identifies himself as "the root and the descendant of David" (Rev 22:16).

David Defeats His Enemies

18 After this David defeated the Philistines and subdued them, and he took
Gath and its villages out of the hand of the Philistines.
[2]And he defeated Moab, and the Moabites became servants to David and
brought tribute.
[3]David also defeated Hadadezer king of Zobah-Hamath, as he went to set up
his monument[1] at the river Euphrates. [4]And David took from him 1,000 chariots,
7,000 horsemen, and 20,000 foot soldiers. And David hamstrung all the chariot
horses, but left enough for 100 chariots. [5]And when the Syrians of Damascus
came to help Hadadezer king of Zobah, David struck down 22,000 men of the
Syrians. [6]Then David put garrisons[2] in Syria of Damascus, and the Syrians became servants to David and brought tribute. And the LORD gave victory to David[3]
wherever he went. [7]And David took the shields of gold that were carried by the
servants of Hadadezer and brought them to Jerusalem. [8]And from Tibhath and
from Cun, cities of Hadadezer, David took a large amount of bronze. With it Solomon made the bronze sea and the pillars and the vessels of bronze.
[9]When Tou king of Hamath heard that David had defeated the whole army
of Hadadezer, king of Zobah, [10]he sent his son Hadoram to King David, to ask
about his health and to bless him because he had fought against Hadadezer and
defeated him; for Hadadezer had often been at war with Tou. And he sent all sorts
of articles of gold, of silver, and of bronze. [11]These also King David dedicated to
the LORD, together with the silver and gold that he had carried off from all the nations, from Edom, Moab, the Ammonites, the Philistines, and Amalek.
[12]And Abishai, the son of Zeruiah, killed 18,000 Edomites in the Valley of Salt.
[13]Then he put garrisons in Edom, and all the Edomites became David's servants.
And the LORD gave victory to David wherever he went.

David's Administration

[14]So David reigned over all Israel, and he administered justice and equity to
all his people. [15]And Joab the son of Zeruiah was over the army; and Jehoshaphat
the son of Ahilud was recorder; [16]and Zadok the son of Ahitub and Ahimelech the
son of Abiathar were priests; and Shavsha was secretary; [17]and Benaiah the son of
Jehoiada was over the Cherethites and the Pelethites; and David's sons were the
chief officials in the service of the king.

The Ammonites Disgrace David's Men

19 Now after this Nahash the king of the Ammonites died, and his son reigned
in his place. [2]And David said, "I will deal kindly with Hanun the son of Nahash, for his father dealt kindly with me." So David sent messengers to console
him concerning his father. And David's servants came to the land of the Ammonites to Hanun to console him. [3]But the princes of the Ammonites said to Hanun,
"Do you think, because David has sent comforters to you, that he is honoring your
father? Have not his servants come to you to search and to overthrow and to spy
out the land?" [4]So Hanun took David's servants and shaved them and cut off their
garments in the middle, at their hips, and sent them away; [5]and they departed.
When David was told concerning the men, he sent messengers to meet them, for
the men were greatly ashamed. And the king said, "Remain at Jericho until your
beards have grown and then return."
[6]When the Ammonites saw that they had become a stench to David, Hanun
and the Ammonites sent 1,000 talents[4] of silver to hire chariots and horsemen
from Mesopotamia, from Aram-maacah, and from Zobah. [7]They hired 32,000
chariots and the king of Maacah with his army, who came and encamped before
Medeba. And the Ammonites were mustered from their cities and came to battle.

[1]Hebrew *hand* [2]Septuagint, Vulgate, 2 Samuel 8:6 (compare Syriac); Hebrew lacks *garrisons* [3]Hebrew *the LORD saved David*; also verse 13 [4]A *talent* was about 75 pounds or 34 kilograms

1 CHRONICLES 18:14

ADMINISTERING JUSTICE

King David led many military campaigns to protect and serve his people in the course of securing the kingdom's borders. Once the borders were established, he led and served his people in a different way—he dispensed justice. Ruling on disputes and punishing crimes is a necessary function within any nation. People will sin. The weak are violated or exploited. David administered justice for all his people with both firmness and fairness. It is no wonder Israel looked upon him as the ideal king.

The prophet Isaiah foretold of Jesus, the perfect king—who would bring justice to all nations (Isa 42:1–4). Jesus lived on the earth with compassion for the weak and appropriate rebuke for hypocrites and oppressors. When he returns, Jesus will judge all people according to what they have done. Anyone whose name is in his book of life will be saved (Rev 20:11–15). His desire is that all people would have eternal life, which is found only in himself.

1 CHRONICLES 19:1–18

BECOMING ENEMIES

David sent a delegation to the Ammonites, a people who were grieving the death of their king. Paranoia and terrible advice led the new Ammonite king to reject the show of sympathy—resulting in a severe offense against David. Israel, like a disturbed hornet's nest, assembled for battle and won a lopsided victory over the Ammonites and their allies. It is astonishing to observe

(continued on next page)

(Becoming Enemies, continued)

how quickly the Ammonites reverted from friendship with Israel to renewing longtime hostilities.

All people have sinned, making themselves enemies of God. But Jesus gave his life to reconcile rebels. Through faith in Christ's death and resurrection, believers are transferred from the domain of darkness into the kingdom of the Son (Col 1:13). Believing in Jesus—in an instant of awakening—moves a person from death to life, from being God's enemy to being God's child (Ro 5:10). The gift of salvation that comes through Jesus is a miracle and sign of his mercy.

1 CHRONICLES 20:1–3

THE FRUIT OF FORGIVENESS

First Chronicles 20:1–3 differs from its companion passage in 2 Samuel 11. This account, written after the exile, omits mention of David's sin with Bathsheba, the low point of his life. This omission provides a beautiful illustration of full forgiveness through Jesus Christ. While sin always has consequences, God's grace ensures his people are not permanently marked by the worst days of their lives or the worst thing they have done.

In Christ, the guilt of sin is not simply waved off or disregarded. Jesus purchased forgiveness on the cross. Redemption and pardon are never free—they are bought with the precious blood of Christ and then offered to men and women as gifts of grace (Eph 1:7). One of the great benefits of salvation through Jesus is that his people become new creations in him—the old life disappears and a new one begins

(continued on next page)

8 When David heard of it, he sent Joab and all the army of the mighty men. 9 And the Ammonites came out and drew up in battle array at the entrance of the city, and the kings who had come were by themselves in the open country.

Ammonites and Syrians Defeated

10 When Joab saw that the battle was set against him both in front and in the rear, he chose some of the best men of Israel and arrayed them against the Syrians. 11 The rest of his men he put in the charge of Abishai his brother, and they were arrayed against the Ammonites. 12 And he said, "If the Syrians are too strong for me, then you shall help me, but if the Ammonites are too strong for you, then I will help you. 13 Be strong, and let us use our strength for our people and for the cities of our God, and may the LORD do what seems good to him." 14 So Joab and the people who were with him drew near before the Syrians for battle, and they fled before him. 15 And when the Ammonites saw that the Syrians fled, they likewise fled before Abishai, Joab's brother, and entered the city. Then Joab came to Jerusalem.

16 But when the Syrians saw that they had been defeated by Israel, they sent messengers and brought out the Syrians who were beyond the Euphrates,[1] with Shophach the commander of the army of Hadadezer at their head. 17 And when it was told to David, he gathered all Israel together and crossed the Jordan and came to them and drew up his forces against them. And when David set the battle in array against the Syrians, they fought with him. 18 And the Syrians fled before Israel, and David killed of the Syrians the men of 7,000 chariots and 40,000 foot soldiers, and put to death also Shophach the commander of their army. 19 And when the servants of Hadadezer saw that they had been defeated by Israel, they made peace with David and became subject to him. So the Syrians were not willing to save the Ammonites anymore.

The Capture of Rabbah

20 In the spring of the year, the time when kings go out to battle, Joab led out the army and ravaged the country of the Ammonites and came and besieged Rabbah. But David remained at Jerusalem. And Joab struck down Rabbah and overthrew it. 2 And David took the crown of their king from his head. He found that it weighed a talent[2] of gold, and in it was a precious stone. And it was placed on David's head. And he brought out the spoil of the city, a very great amount. 3 And he brought out the people who were in it and set them to labor[3] with saws and iron picks and axes.[4] And thus David did to all the cities of the Ammonites. Then David and all the people returned to Jerusalem.

Philistine Giants Killed

4 And after this there arose war with the Philistines at Gezer. Then Sibbecai the Hushathite struck down Sippai, who was one of the descendants of the giants, and the Philistines were subdued. 5 And there was again war with the Philistines, and Elhanan the son of Jair struck down Lahmi the brother of Goliath the Gittite, the shaft of whose spear was like a weaver's beam. 6 And there was again war at Gath, where there was a man of great stature, who had six fingers on each hand and six toes on each foot, twenty-four in number, and he also was descended from the giants. 7 And when he taunted Israel, Jonathan the son of Shimea, David's brother, struck him down. 8 These were descended from the giants in Gath, and they fell by the hand of David and by the hand of his servants.

David's Census Brings Pestilence

21 Then Satan stood against Israel and incited David to number Israel. 2 So David said to Joab and the commanders of the army, "Go, number Israel, from Beersheba to Dan, and bring me a report, that I may know their number."

[1] Hebrew *the River* [2] A *talent* was about 75 pounds or 34 kilograms [3] Compare 2 Samuel 12:31; Hebrew *he sawed* [4] Compare 2 Samuel 12:31; Hebrew *saws*

[3]But Joab said, "May the LORD add to his people a hundred times as many as they are! Are they not, my lord the king, all of them my lord's servants? Why then should my lord require this? Why should it be a cause of guilt for Israel?" [4]But the king's word prevailed against Joab. So Joab departed and went throughout all Israel and came back to Jerusalem. [5]And Joab gave the sum of the numbering of the people to David. In all Israel there were 1,100,000 men who drew the sword, and in Judah 470,000 who drew the sword. [6]But he did not include Levi and Benjamin in the numbering, for the king's command was abhorrent to Joab.

[7]But God was displeased with this thing, and he struck Israel. [8]And David said to God, "I have sinned greatly in that I have done this thing. But now, please take away the iniquity of your servant, for I have acted very foolishly." [9]And the LORD spoke to Gad, David's seer, saying, [10]"Go and say to David, 'Thus says the LORD, Three things I offer you; choose one of them, that I may do it to you.'" [11]So Gad came to David and said to him, "Thus says the LORD, 'Choose what you will: [12]either three years of famine, or three months of devastation by your foes while the sword of your enemies overtakes you, or else three days of the sword of the LORD, pestilence on the land, with the angel of the LORD destroying throughout all the territory of Israel.' Now decide what answer I shall return to him who sent me." [13]Then David said to Gad, "I am in great distress. Let me fall into the hand of the LORD, for his mercy is very great, but do not let me fall into the hand of man."

[14]So the LORD sent a pestilence on Israel, and 70,000 men of Israel fell. [15]And God sent the angel to Jerusalem to destroy it, but as he was about to destroy it, the LORD saw, and he relented from the calamity. And he said to the angel who was working destruction, "It is enough; now stay your hand." And the angel of the LORD was standing by the threshing floor of Ornan the Jebusite. [16]And David lifted his eyes and saw the angel of the LORD standing between earth and heaven, and in his hand a drawn sword stretched out over Jerusalem. Then David and the elders, clothed in sackcloth, fell upon their faces. [17]And David said to God, "Was it not I who gave command to number the people? It is I who have sinned and done great evil. But these sheep, what have they done? Please let your hand, O LORD my God, be against me and against my father's house. But do not let the plague be on your people."

David Builds an Altar

[18]Now the angel of the LORD had commanded Gad to say to David that David should go up and raise an altar to the LORD on the threshing floor of Ornan the Jebusite. [19]So David went up at Gad's word, which he had spoken in the name of the LORD. [20]Now Ornan was threshing wheat. He turned and saw the angel, and his four sons who were with him hid themselves. [21]As David came to Ornan, Ornan looked and saw David and went out from the threshing floor and paid homage to David with his face to the ground. [22]And David said to Ornan, "Give me the site of the threshing floor that I may build on it an altar to the LORD—give it to me at its full price—that the plague may be averted from the people." [23]Then Ornan said to David, "Take it, and let my lord the king do what seems good to him. See, I give the oxen for burnt offerings and the threshing sledges for the wood and the wheat for a grain offering; I give it all." [24]But King David said to Ornan, "No, but I will buy them for the full price. I will not take for the LORD what is yours, nor offer burnt offerings that cost me nothing." [25]So David paid Ornan 600 shekels[1] of gold by weight for the site. [26]And David built there an altar to the LORD and presented burnt offerings and peace offerings and called on the LORD, and the LORD[2] answered him with fire from heaven upon the altar of burnt offering. [27]Then the LORD commanded the angel, and he put his sword back into its sheath.

[1]A *shekel* was about 2/5 ounce or 11 grams [2]Hebrew *he*

(The Fruit of Forgiveness, continued)

(2Co 5:17). The stains from old sins and the regrets from ungodly choices—marks of disgrace on the lives of those adopted into his family—are erased forever, thanks to Christ's work on the cross (Isa 1:18).

THE PLACE OF SACRIFICE

The site King David purchased from Ornan is a sacred piece of real estate in the history of Israel — significant in both the Old and New Testaments. Known as Mount Moriah (2Ch 3:1), it was there that Abraham brought Isaac with the intention of sacrificing him to the Lord (Ge 22:2). At the last moment, God intervened in the test of faith and provided a ram as a substitute. Abraham called the place "The LORD will provide" (Ge 22:14). David needed Ornan's threshing floor for the site of a sacrificial altar. The Lord's angel instructed the king to make offerings following his sin, repentance, and punishment. God accepted David's burnt offerings and fellowship offerings — compelling him to add more offerings in thanksgiving (1Ch 21:28). This location was so meaningful to David that he declared it to be the location for the house of the Lord, the much anticipated temple of Solomon (1Ch 22:1).

When Jesus died on the cross at the hill called Golgotha, Mount Moriah was involved once again. He was crucified outside of the city gates across the valley from the temple. At the moment of Jesus' death, the veil of the temple — the curtain separating the Most Holy Place from the common areas — ripped in two from top to bottom (Mk 15:37 – 38). This signified that God's presence was finally open to all people. The book of Hebrews describes the access Jesus created by giving himself to ransom mankind: "Therefore, brothers, since we have confidence to enter the holy places by the blood of Jesus, by the new and living way that he opened for us through the curtain, that is, through his flesh, and since we have a great priest over the house of God, let us draw near with a true heart in full assurance of faith, with our hearts sprinkled clean from an evil conscience and our bodies washed with pure water" (Heb 10:19 – 22).

The area around Mount Moriah has been marked by incredible events. The greatest of these is the sacrifice of Jesus as the substitute payment for humanity's sin. Just as God was pleased with Abraham's act of faith and David's offerings, God accepted the death of Jesus as complete atonement. The Father then offered the world the opportunity to be made righteous through faith in the Son (Ro 5:18 – 19).

The location of these sacrifices did not make them special or powerful. They were effective because they were offered in humility to the one true God — and he found them pleasing and acceptable.

[28]At that time, when David saw that the LORD had answered him at the threshing floor of Ornan the Jebusite, he sacrificed there. [29]For the tabernacle of the LORD, which Moses had made in the wilderness, and the altar of burnt offering were at that time in the high place at Gibeon, [30]but David could not go before it to inquire of God, for he was afraid of the sword of the angel of the LORD.

22 Then David said, "Here shall be the house of the LORD God and here the altar of burnt offering for Israel."

David Prepares for Temple Building

[2]David commanded to gather together the resident aliens who were in the land of Israel, and he set stonecutters to prepare dressed stones for building the house of God. [3]David also provided great quantities of iron for nails for the doors of the gates and for clamps, as well as bronze in quantities beyond weighing, [4]and cedar timbers without number, for the Sidonians and Tyrians brought great quantities of cedar to David. [5]For David said, "Solomon my son is young and inexperienced, and the house that is to be built for the LORD must be exceedingly magnificent, of fame and glory throughout all lands. I will therefore make preparation for it." So David provided materials in great quantity before his death.

Solomon Charged to Build the Temple

[6]Then he called for Solomon his son and charged him to build a house for the LORD, the God of Israel. [7]David said to Solomon, "My son, I had it in my heart to build a house to the name of the LORD my God. [8]But the word of the LORD came to me, saying, 'You have shed much blood and have waged great wars. You shall not build a house to my name, because you have shed so much blood before me on the earth. [9]Behold, a son shall be born to you who shall be a man of rest. I will give him rest from all his surrounding enemies. For his name shall be Solomon, and I will give peace and quiet to Israel in his days. [10]He shall build a house for my name. He shall be my son, and I will be his father, and I will establish his royal throne in Israel forever.'

[11]"Now, my son, the LORD be with you, so that you may succeed in building the house of the LORD your God, as he has spoken concerning you. [12]Only, may the LORD grant you discretion and understanding, that when he gives you charge over Israel you may keep the law of the LORD your God. [13]Then you will prosper if you are careful to observe the statutes and the rules that the LORD commanded Moses for Israel. Be strong and courageous. Fear not; do not be dismayed. [14]With great pains I have provided for the house of the LORD 100,000 talents[1] of gold, a million talents of silver, and bronze and iron beyond weighing, for there is so much of it; timber and stone, too, I have provided. To these you must add. [15]You have an abundance of workmen: stonecutters, masons, carpenters, and all kinds of craftsmen without number, skilled in working [16]gold, silver, bronze, and iron. Arise and work! The LORD be with you!"

[17]David also commanded all the leaders of Israel to help Solomon his son, saying, [18]"Is not the LORD your God with you? And has he not given you peace[2] on every side? For he has delivered the inhabitants of the land into my hand, and the land is subdued before the LORD and his people. [19]Now set your mind and heart to seek the LORD your God. Arise and build the sanctuary of the LORD God, so that the ark of the covenant of the LORD and the holy vessels of God may be brought into a house built for the name of the LORD."

David Organizes the Levites

23 When David was old and full of days, he made Solomon his son king over Israel.

[2]David[3] assembled all the leaders of Israel and the priests and the Levites. [3]The

[1]A *talent* was about 75 pounds or 34 kilograms [2]Or *rest* (see 22:9) [3]Hebrew *He*

PREPARING A TEMPLE

King David longed to build the temple, but the Lord chose Solomon to oversee its completion (vv. 7 – 10). God was glad about this house for his Name — it was not merely some human indulgence. The temple would be magnificent and massive and impressive, because God is all of those things (v. 5).

David took care to ready his young and inexperienced son for the daunting task of leading the temple project. He did this by making extensive preparations for finances, materials, and manpower (v. 5). Many thousand talents of gold — along with silver, bronze, iron, wood, and stone — were stockpiled for construction (v. 14). Stonecutters, masons, carpenters, and other skilled craftsmen were recruited for Solomon's use (vv. 15 – 16). And King David ordered all the leaders of Israel to help in the monumental effort (v. 17).

Beyond these material provisions, David issued a charge and spoke a blessing to his son — wishing him success and praying to God for the future leader's discretion and understanding. He also admonished Solomon to observe the laws of the Lord at all times and to go forward in the work without fear: "Be strong and courageous. Fear not; do not be dismayed" (vv. 11 – 13). This blessing is reminiscent of Moses transferring leadership and authority to Joshua near the time of the great deliverer's death (Dt 31:1 – 8).

David spent several years strategizing for the building of the temple. These preparations seem impressive until one considers that God established his plan to reconcile sinful humankind through Jesus before the creation of the world (1Pe 1:19 – 20). Before there was earth or sky or day or night, God chose his future people in Christ to be made holy and to become adopted members of his family (Eph 1:3 – 5).

God's plans are higher and more intricate than finite human plans. His purposes are far beyond anything that the human mind can conceive: "For as the heavens are higher than the earth, so are my ways higher than your ways and my thoughts than your thoughts" (Isa 55:9).

Levites, thirty years old and upward, were numbered, and the total was 38,000 men. 4"Twenty-four thousand of these," David said,[1] "shall have charge of the work in the house of the LORD, 6,000 shall be officers and judges, 54,000 gatekeepers, and 4,000 shall offer praises to the LORD with the instruments that I have made for praise." 6And David organized them in divisions corresponding to the sons of Levi: Gershon, Kohath, and Merari.

7The sons of Gershon[2] were Ladan and Shimei. 8The sons of Ladan: Jehiel the chief, and Zetham, and Joel, three. 9The sons of Shimei: Shelomoth, Haziel, and Haran, three. These were the heads of the fathers' houses of Ladan. 10And the sons of Shimei: Jahath, Zina, and Jeush and Beriah. These four were the sons of Shimei. 11Jahath was the chief, and Zizah the second; but Jeush and Beriah did not have many sons, therefore they became counted as a single father's house.

12The sons of Kohath: Amram, Izhar, Hebron, and Uzziel, four. 13The sons of Amram: Aaron and Moses. Aaron was set apart to dedicate the most holy things, that he and his sons forever should make offerings before the LORD and minister to him and pronounce blessings in his name forever. 14But the sons of Moses the man of God were named among the tribe of Levi. 15The sons of Moses: Gershom and Eliezer. 16The sons of Gershom: Shebuel the chief. 17The sons of Eliezer: Rehabiah the chief. Eliezer had no other sons, but the sons of Rehabiah were very many. 18The sons of Izhar: Shelomith the chief. 19The sons of Hebron: Jeriah the chief, Amariah the second, Jahaziel the third, and Jekameam the fourth. 20The sons of Uzziel: Micah the chief and Isshiah the second.

21The sons of Merari: Mahli and Mushi. The sons of Mahli: Eleazar and Kish. 22Eleazar died having no sons, but only daughters; their kinsmen, the sons of Kish, married them. 23The sons of Mushi: Mahli, Eder, and Jeremoth, three.

24These were the sons of Levi by their fathers' houses, the heads of fathers' houses as they were listed according to the number of the names of the individuals from twenty years old and upward who were to do the work for the service of the house of the LORD. 25For David said, "The LORD, the God of Israel, has given rest to his people, and he dwells in Jerusalem forever. 26And so the Levites no longer need to carry the tabernacle or any of the things for its service." 27For by the last words of David the sons of Levi were numbered from twenty years old and upward. 28For their duty was to assist the sons of Aaron for the service of the house of the LORD, having the care of the courts and the chambers, the cleansing of all that is holy, and any work for the service of the house of God. 29Their duty was also to assist with the showbread, the flour for the grain offering, the wafers of unleavened bread, the baked offering, the offering mixed with oil, and all measures of quantity or size. 30And they were to stand every morning, thanking and praising the LORD, and likewise at evening, 31and whenever burnt offerings were offered to the LORD on Sabbaths, new moons, and feast days, according to the number required of them, regularly before the LORD. 32Thus they were to keep charge of the tent of meeting and the sanctuary, and to attend the sons of Aaron, their brothers, for the service of the house of the LORD.

David Organizes the Priests

24 The divisions of the sons of Aaron were these. The sons of Aaron: Nadab, Abihu, Eleazar, and Ithamar. 2But Nadab and Abihu died before their father and had no children, so Eleazar and Ithamar became the priests. 3With the help of Zadok of the sons of Eleazar, and Ahimelech of the sons of Ithamar, David organized them according to the appointed duties in their service. 4Since more chief men were found among the sons of Eleazar than among the sons of Ithamar, they organized them under sixteen heads of fathers' houses of the sons of Eleazar, and eight of the sons of Ithamar. 5They divided them by lot, all alike, for there were sacred officers and officers of God among both the sons of Eleazar

[1]Hebrew lacks *David said* [2]Vulgate (compare Septuagint, Syriac); Hebrew *to the Gershonite*

1 CHRONICLES 23:24–32

ASSIGNED FOR SERVICE

For centuries, the Levites served in and around the tabernacle—the portable tent of meeting that housed the ark of the covenant and the many accessories used in worship (Nu 4:5–15). Israel's priests managed the sacrificial system and took responsibility for disassembling and reassembling the tent each time the camp relocated. When the Lord arranged for Israel to rest from the threat of war in the last years of David's reign, the king seized the opportunity to reassign the Levites to new responsibilities. This coincided with plans for building a permanent temple in Jerusalem—the portable tent would no longer be necessary. With forethought and care, David managed Israel's leaders for optimum effectiveness in service to the Lord (1Ch 23:2–6).

This is similar to how Jesus loves and serves the church. He assigns various spiritual gifts as needed, for the good of the body of Christ (Ro 12:4–8). Just as national changes in the era of King David called for adjustments in the use of leaders, so Christ manages the church's changing needs—assigning specific gifts to empower ministry. Spiritual gifts are meant to serve the church body, enable it to perform its mission to the world, and glorify God through Jesus (1Pe 4:10–11).

and the sons of Ithamar. 6And the scribe Shemaiah, the son of Nethanel, a Levite, recorded them in the presence of the king and the princes and Zadok the priest and Ahimelech the son of Abiathar and the heads of the fathers' houses of the priests and of the Levites, one father's house being chosen for Eleazar and one chosen for Ithamar.

7The first lot fell to Jehoiarib, the second to Jedaiah, 8the third to Harim, the fourth to Seorim, 9the fifth to Malchijah, the sixth to Mijamin, 10the seventh to Hakkoz, the eighth to Abijah, 11the ninth to Jeshua, the tenth to Shecaniah, 12the eleventh to Eliashib, the twelfth to Jakim, 13the thirteenth to Huppah, the fourteenth to Jeshebeab, 14the fifteenth to Bilgah, the sixteenth to Immer, 15the seventeenth to Hezir, the eighteenth to Happizzez, 16the nineteenth to Pethahiah, the twentieth to Jehezkel, 17the twenty-first to Jachin, the twenty-second to Gamul, 18the twenty-third to Delaiah, the twenty-fourth to Maaziah. 19These had as their appointed duty in their service to come into the house of the LORD according to the procedure established for them by Aaron their father, as the LORD God of Israel had commanded him.

20And of the rest of the sons of Levi: of the sons of Amram, Shubael; of the sons of Shubael, Jehdeiah. 21Of Rehabiah: of the sons of Rehabiah, Isshiah the chief. 22Of the Izharites, Shelomoth; of the sons of Shelomoth, Jahath. 23The sons of Hebron:[1] Jeriah the chief,[2] Amariah the second, Jahaziel the third, Jekameam the fourth. 24The sons of Uzziel, Micah; of the sons of Micah, Shamir. 25The brother of Micah, Isshiah; of the sons of Isshiah, Zechariah. 26The sons of Merari: Mahli and Mushi. The sons of Jaaziah: Beno.[3] 27The sons of Merari: of Jaaziah, Beno, Shoham, Zaccur, and Ibri. 28Of Mahli: Eleazar, who had no sons. 29Of Kish, the sons of Kish: Jerahmeel. 30The sons of Mushi: Mahli, Eder, and Jerimoth. These were the sons of the Levites according to their fathers' houses. 31These also, the head of each father's house and his younger brother alike, cast lots, just as their brothers the sons of Aaron, in the presence of King David, Zadok, Ahimelech, and the heads of fathers' houses of the priests and of the Levites.

David Organizes the Musicians

25 David and the chiefs of the service also set apart for the service the sons of Asaph, and of Heman, and of Jeduthun, who prophesied with lyres, with harps, and with cymbals. The list of those who did the work and of their duties was: 2Of the sons of Asaph: Zaccur, Joseph, Nethaniah, and Asharelah, sons of Asaph, under the direction of Asaph, who prophesied under the direction of the king. 3Of Jeduthun, the sons of Jeduthun: Gedaliah, Zeri, Jeshaiah, Shimei,[4] Hashabiah, and Mattithiah, six, under the direction of their father Jeduthun, who prophesied with the lyre in thanksgiving and praise to the LORD. 4Of Heman, the sons of Heman: Bukkiah, Mattaniah, Uzziel, Shebuel and Jerimoth, Hananiah, Hanani, Eliathah, Giddalti, and Romamti-ezer, Joshbekashah, Mallothi, Hothir, Mahazioth. 5All these were the sons of Heman the king's seer, according to the promise of God to exalt him, for God had given Heman fourteen sons and three daughters. 6They were all under the direction of their father in the music in the house of the LORD with cymbals, harps, and lyres for the service of the house of God. Asaph, Jeduthun, and Heman were under the order of the king. 7The number of them along with their brothers, who were trained in singing to the LORD, all who were skillful, was 288. 8And they cast lots for their duties, small and great, teacher and pupil alike.

9The first lot fell for Asaph to Joseph; the second to Gedaliah, to him and his brothers and his sons, twelve; 10the third to Zaccur, his sons and his brothers, twelve; 11the fourth to Izri, his sons and his brothers, twelve; 12the fifth to Nethaniah, his sons and his brothers, twelve; 13the sixth to Bukkiah, his sons

[1]Compare 23:19; Hebrew lacks *Hebron* [2]Compare 23:19; Hebrew lacks *the chief* [3]Or *his son*; also verse 27
[4]One Hebrew manuscript, Septuagint; most Hebrew manuscripts lack *Shimei*

1 CHRONICLES 25:1–31

PROCLAMATION THROUGH MUSIC

King David knew the importance of proclaiming the wonders of God to increase the Lord's fame on the earth. He assigned 288 people the task of recounting God's works through singing and playing instruments. It was their full-time job to praise the Lord and to prophesy—to proclaim truths about who God is, what he had done, and what he could do. Their music possessed weight; it was much more than a pleasant fanfare or simple song. It was intended to be heard, contemplated, and absorbed. David's music leaders crafted anthems that carried the name of the Lord—creatively reminding people about their God and his care for them.

While Scripture does not depict Jesus using music for creative truth-speaking during his earthly ministry, he acted in ways similar to David as he taught the crowds—often telling parables to connect people to God. These stories spoke of God's character, addressed issues of the day, and illustrated the Father in accessible, easily remembered ways. Christ's parables are full of truth about God and truth about people. They were difficult to ignore, often leaving listeners questioning and thinking about what they had heard. Jesus used as many as forty creative and poignant parables to *paint pictures of the kingdom and* its King (e.g., Mt 13:1–52).

and his brothers, twelve; 14the seventh to Jesharelah, his sons and his brothers,
twelve; 15the eighth to Jeshaiah, his sons and his brothers, twelve; 16the ninth
to Mattaniah, his sons and his brothers, twelve; 17the tenth to Shimei, his sons
and his brothers, twelve; 18the eleventh to Azarel, his sons and his brothers,
twelve; 19the twelfth to Hashabiah, his sons and his brothers, twelve; 20to the
thirteenth, Shubael, his sons and his brothers, twelve; 21to the fourteenth, Mattithiah, his sons and his brothers, twelve; 22to the fifteenth, to Jeremoth, his
sons and his brothers, twelve; 23to the sixteenth, to Hananiah, his sons and his
brothers, twelve; 24to the seventeenth, to Joshbekashah, his sons and his brothers, twelve; 25to the eighteenth, to Hanani, his sons and his brothers, twelve;
26to the nineteenth, to Mallothi, his sons and his brothers, twelve; 27to the
twentieth, to Eliathah, his sons and his brothers, twelve; 28to the twenty-first,
to Hothir, his sons and his brothers, twelve; 29to the twenty-second, to Giddalti,
his sons and his brothers, twelve; 30to the twenty-third, to Mahazioth, his sons
and his brothers, twelve; 31to the twenty-fourth, to Romamti-ezer, his sons and
his brothers, twelve.

Divisions of the Gatekeepers

26 As for the divisions of the gatekeepers: of the Korahites, Meshelemiah the
son of Kore, of the sons of Asaph. 2And Meshelemiah had sons: Zechariah
the firstborn, Jediael the second, Zebadiah the third, Jathniel the fourth, 3Elam
the fifth, Jehohanan the sixth, Eliehoenai the seventh. 4And Obed-edom had
sons: Shemaiah the firstborn, Jehozabad the second, Joah the third, Sachar the
fourth, Nethanel the fifth, 5Ammiel the sixth, Issachar the seventh, Peullethai
the eighth, for God blessed him. 6Also to his son Shemaiah were sons born who
were rulers in their fathers' houses, for they were men of great ability. 7The sons
of Shemaiah: Othni, Rephael, Obed and Elzabad, whose brothers were able men,
Elihu and Semachiah. 8All these were of the sons of Obed-edom with their sons
and brothers, able men qualified for the service; sixty-two of Obed-edom. 9And
Meshelemiah had sons and brothers, able men, eighteen. 10And Hosah, of the
sons of Merari, had sons: Shimri the chief (for though he was not the firstborn,
his father made him chief), 11Hilkiah the second, Tebaliah the third, Zechariah the
fourth: all the sons and brothers of Hosah were thirteen.

12These divisions of the gatekeepers, corresponding to their chief men, had
duties, just as their brothers did, ministering in the house of the Lord. 13And they
cast lots by fathers' houses, small and great alike, for their gates. 14The lot for the
east fell to Shelemiah. They cast lots also for his son Zechariah, a shrewd counsel-
or, and his lot came out for the north. 15Obed-edom's came out for the south, and
to his sons was allotted the gatehouse. 16For Shuppim and Hosah it came out for
the west, at the gate of Shallecheth on the road that goes up. Watch corresponded
to watch. 17On the east there were six each day,[1] on the north four each day, on the
south four each day, as well as two and two at the gatehouse. 18And for the colonnade[2] on the west there were four at the road and two at the colonnade. 19These
were the divisions of the gatekeepers among the Korahites and the sons of Merari.

Treasurers and Other Officials

20And of the Levites, Ahijah had charge of the treasuries of the house of God
and the treasuries of the dedicated gifts. 21The sons of Ladan, the sons of the Gershonites belonging to Ladan, the heads of the fathers' houses belonging to Ladan
the Gershonite: Jehieli.[3]

22The sons of Jehieli, Zetham, and Joel his brother, were in charge of the treasuries of the house of the Lord. 23Of the Amramites, the Izharites, the Hebronites,
and the Uzzielites— 24and Shebuel the son of Gershom, son of Moses, was chief

[1]Septuagint; Hebrew *six Levites* [2]Or *court*; Hebrew *parbar* (meaning uncertain); twice in this verse
[3]The Hebrew of verse 21 is uncertain

1 CHRONICLES 26:20–32

DEDICATED TO THE LORD

The Levites in charge of the treasury were responsible for receiving, storing, and protecting the people's offerings and the plunder accumulated from war victories. Over time, the storehouse acquired large amounts of gold, silver, and other valuables. When civil war broke out between Israel and Judah, the kingdom was divided. Eventually both Israel and Judah were overthrown by other nations, the storehouse was destroyed, and objects of worship were hauled off by foreigners.

In what has been called Jesus' Sermon on the Mount, Jesus taught people the ultimate value of storing up treasures in heaven—such spiritual treasures cannot be stolen or ruined (Mt 6:19–21). All material things treasured by this world will one day meet destruction. But the love God's people show in Christ's name and the works they do to serve his kingdom will endure forever. Those who labor for the Lord will someday receive an eternal reward from him (Col 3:23–24).

officer in charge of the treasuries. 25 His brothers: from Eliezer were his son Rehabiah, and his son Jeshaiah, and his son Joram, and his son Zichri, and his son
Shelomoth. 26 This Shelomoth and his brothers were in charge of all the treasuries
of the dedicated gifts that David the king and the heads of the fathers' houses and
the officers of the thousands and the hundreds and the commanders of the army
had dedicated. 27 From spoil won in battles they dedicated gifts for the maintenance of the house of the LORD. 28 Also all that Samuel the seer and Saul the son
of Kish and Abner the son of Ner and Joab the son of Zeruiah had dedicated—all
dedicated gifts were in the care of Shelomoth[1] and his brothers.

29 Of the Izharites, Chenaniah and his sons were appointed to external duties
for Israel, as officers and judges. 30 Of the Hebronites, Hashabiah and his brothers,
1,700 men of ability, had the oversight of Israel westward of the Jordan for all the
work of the LORD and for the service of the king. 31 Of the Hebronites, Jerijah was
chief of the Hebronites of whatever genealogy or fathers' houses. (In the fortieth
year of David's reign search was made and men of great ability among them were
found at Jazer in Gilead.) 32 King David appointed him and his brothers, 2,700 men
of ability, heads of fathers' houses, to have the oversight of the Reubenites, the
Gadites and the half-tribe of the Manassites for everything pertaining to God and
for the affairs of the king.

Military Divisions

27 This is the number of the people of Israel, the heads of fathers' houses, the
commanders of thousands and hundreds, and their officers who served
the king in all matters concerning the divisions that came and went, month after
month throughout the year, each division numbering 24,000:

2 Jashobeam the son of Zabdiel was in charge of the first division in the first
month; in his division were 24,000. 3 He was a descendant of Perez and was chief
of all the commanders. He served for the first month. 4 Dodai the Ahohite[2] was
in charge of the division of the second month; in his division were 24,000. 5 The
third commander, for the third month, was Benaiah, the son of Jehoiada the chief
priest; in his division were 24,000. 6 This is the Benaiah who was a mighty man of
the thirty and in command of the thirty; Ammizabad his son was in charge of his
division.[3] 7 Asahel the brother of Joab was fourth, for the fourth month, and his
son Zebadiah after him; in his division were 24,000. 8 The fifth commander, for
the fifth month, was Shamhuth the Izrahite; in his division were 24,000. 9 Sixth,
for the sixth month, was Ira, the son of Ikkesh the Tekoite; in his division were
24,000. 10 Seventh, for the seventh month, was Helez the Pelonite, of the sons of
Ephraim; in his division were 24,000. 11 Eighth, for the eighth month, was Sibbecai the Hushathite, of the Zerahites; in his division were 24,000. 12 Ninth, for
the ninth month, was Abiezer of Anathoth, a Benjaminite; in his division were
24,000. 13 Tenth, for the tenth month, was Maharai of Netophah, of the Zerahites;
in his division were 24,000. 14 Eleventh, for the eleventh month, was Benaiah of
Pirathon, of the sons of Ephraim; in his division were 24,000. 15 Twelfth, for the
twelfth month, was Heldai the Netophathite, of Othniel; in his division were
24,000.

Leaders of Tribes

16 Over the tribes of Israel, for the Reubenites, Eliezer the son of Zichri was
chief officer; for the Simeonites, Shephatiah the son of Maacah; 17 for Levi, Hashabiah the son of Kemuel; for Aaron, Zadok; 18 for Judah, Elihu, one of David's brothers; for Issachar, Omri the son of Michael; 19 for Zebulun, Ishmaiah the son of Obadiah; for Naphtali, Jeremoth the son of Azriel; 20 for the Ephraimites, Hoshea the
son of Azaziah; for the half-tribe of Manasseh, Joel the son of Pedaiah; 21 for the

[1] Hebrew *Shelomith* [2] Septuagint; Hebrew *Ahohite and his division and Mikloth the chief officer*
[3] Septuagint, Vulgate; Hebrew *was his division*

half-tribe of Manasseh in Gilead, Iddo the son of Zechariah; for Benjamin, Jaasiel the son of Abner; [22]for Dan, Azarel the son of Jeroham. These were the leaders of the tribes of Israel. [23]David did not count those below twenty years of age, for the LORD had promised to make Israel as many as the stars of heaven. [24]Joab the son of Zeruiah began to count, but did not finish. Yet wrath came upon Israel for this, and the number was not entered in the chronicles of King David.

[25]Over the king's treasuries was Azmaveth the son of Adiel; and over the treasuries in the country, in the cities, in the villages, and in the towers, was Jonathan the son of Uzziah; [26]and over those who did the work of the field for tilling the soil was Ezri the son of Chelub; [27]and over the vineyards was Shimei the Ramathite; and over the produce of the vineyards for the wine cellars was Zabdi the Shiphmite. [28]Over the olive and sycamore trees in the Shephelah was Baal-hanan the Gederite; and over the stores of oil was Joash. [29]Over the herds that pastured in Sharon was Shitrai the Sharonite; over the herds in the valleys was Shaphat the son of Adlai. [30]Over the camels was Obil the Ishmaelite; and over the donkeys was Jehdeiah the Meronothite. [31]Over the flocks was Jaziz the Hagrite. All these were stewards of King David's property.

[32]Jonathan, David's uncle, was a counselor, being a man of understanding and a scribe. He and Jehiel the son of Hachmoni attended the king's sons. [33]Ahithophel was the king's counselor, and Hushai the Archite was the king's friend. [34]Ahithophel was succeeded by Jehoiada the son of Benaiah, and Abiathar. Joab was commander of the king's army.

David's Charge to Israel

28 David assembled at Jerusalem all the officials of Israel, the officials of the tribes, the officers of the divisions that served the king, the commanders of thousands, the commanders of hundreds, the stewards of all the property and livestock of the king and his sons, together with the palace officials, the mighty men and all the seasoned warriors. [2]Then King David rose to his feet and said: "Hear me, my brothers and my people. I had it in my heart to build a house of rest for the ark of the covenant of the LORD and for the footstool of our God, and I made preparations for building. [3]But God said to me, 'You may not build a house for my name, for you are a man of war and have shed blood.' [4]Yet the LORD God of Israel chose me from all my father's house to be king over Israel forever. For he chose Judah as leader, and in the house of Judah my father's house, and among my father's sons he took pleasure in me to make me king over all Israel. [5]And of all my sons (for the LORD has given me many sons) he has chosen Solomon my son to sit on the throne of the kingdom of the LORD over Israel. [6]He said to me, 'It is Solomon your son who shall build my house and my courts, for I have chosen him to be my son, and I will be his father. [7]I will establish his kingdom forever if he continues strong in keeping my commandments and my rules, as he is today.' [8]Now therefore in the sight of all Israel, the assembly of the LORD, and in the hearing of our God, observe and seek out all the commandments of the LORD your God, that you may possess this good land and leave it for an inheritance to your children after you forever.

David's Charge to Solomon

[9]"And you, Solomon my son, know the God of your father and serve him with a whole heart and with a willing mind, for the LORD searches all hearts and understands every plan and thought. If you seek him, he will be found by you, but if you forsake him, he will cast you off forever. [10]Be careful now, for the LORD has chosen you to build a house for the sanctuary; be strong and do it."

[11]Then David gave Solomon his son the plan of the vestibule of the temple,[1] and of its houses, its treasuries, its upper rooms, and its inner chambers, and

[1] Hebrew lacks *of the temple*

1 CHRONICLES 28:2

GOD'S FOOTSTOOL

David realized that a mere building could never house the eternal, all-powerful God of the universe. He planned to construct the temple as the Lord's footstool — a metaphor describing the earthly base of activity for God, who sits enthroned in heaven, high above all things. Elsewhere in Scripture, the whole earth is depicted as God's footstool (Isa 66:1). No physical place of worship — even Solomon's temple — could capture the grandeur and glory of God. He cannot be contained (Ac 7:48–50).

In kindness to the people of the earth, God sent Jesus to disclose his character and power (Jn 1:18). God came down to us from on high — to dwell in hearts, not religious buildings (Eph 3:16–17). God's people do not need to go into a church to be with God — he is Spirit, simultaneously inhabiting all places. Jesus, in whom the fullness of God dwells, is ever-present in the life of the believer (Col 1:19–27).

of the room for the mercy seat; 12 and the plan of all that he had in mind for the courts of the house of the LORD, all the surrounding chambers, the treasuries of the house of God, and the treasuries for dedicated gifts; 13 for the divisions of the priests and of the Levites, and all the work of the service in the house of the LORD; for all the vessels for the service in the house of the LORD, 14 the weight of gold for all golden vessels for each service, the weight of silver vessels for each service, 15 the weight of the golden lampstands and their lamps, the weight of gold for each lampstand and its lamps, the weight of silver for a lampstand and its lamps, according to the use of each lampstand in the service, 16 the weight of gold for each table for the showbread, the silver for the silver tables, 17 and pure gold for the forks, the basins and the cups; for the golden bowls and the weight of each; for the silver bowls and the weight of each; 18 for the altar of incense made of refined gold, and its weight; also his plan for the golden chariot of the cherubim that spread their wings and covered the ark of the covenant of the LORD. 19 "All this he made clear to me in writing from the hand of the LORD, all the work to be done according to the plan."

20 Then David said to Solomon his son, "Be strong and courageous and do it. Do not be afraid and do not be dismayed, for the LORD God, even my God, is with you. He will not leave you or forsake you, until all the work for the service of the house of the LORD is finished. 21 And behold the divisions of the priests and the Levites for all the service of the house of God; and with you in all the work will be every willing man who has skill for any kind of service; also the officers and all the people will be wholly at your command."

Offerings for the Temple

29 And David the king said to all the assembly, "Solomon my son, whom alone God has chosen, is young and inexperienced, and the work is great, for the palace will not be for man but for the LORD God. 2 So I have provided for the house of my God, so far as I was able, the gold for the things of gold, the silver for the things of silver, and the bronze for the things of bronze, the iron for the things of iron, and wood for the things of wood, besides great quantities of onyx and stones for setting, antimony, colored stones, all sorts of precious stones and marble. 3 Moreover, in addition to all that I have provided for the holy house, I have a treasure of my own of gold and silver, and because of my devotion to the house of my God I give it to the house of my God: 4 3,000 talents[1] of gold, of the gold of Ophir, and 7,000 talents of refined silver, for overlaying the walls of the house,[2] 5 and for all the work to be done by craftsmen, gold for the things of gold and silver for the things of silver. Who then will offer willingly, consecrating himself[3] today to the LORD?"

6 Then the leaders of fathers' houses made their freewill offerings, as did also the leaders of the tribes, the commanders of thousands and of hundreds, and the officers over the king's work. 7 They gave for the service of the house of God 5,000 talents and 10,000 darics[4] of gold, 10,000 talents of silver, 18,000 talents of bronze and 100,000 talents of iron. 8 And whoever had precious stones gave them to the treasury of the house of the LORD, in the care of Jehiel the Gershonite. 9 Then the people rejoiced because they had given willingly, for with a whole heart they had offered freely to the LORD. David the king also rejoiced greatly.

David Prays in the Assembly

10 Therefore David blessed the LORD in the presence of all the assembly. And David said: "Blessed are you, O LORD, the God of Israel our father, forever and ever. 11 Yours, O LORD, is the greatness and the power and the glory and the victory and the majesty, for all that is in the heavens and in the earth is yours. Yours is the

[1] A *talent* was about 75 pounds or 34 kilograms [2] Septuagint; Hebrew *houses* [3] Or *ordaining himself*; Hebrew *filling his hand* [4] A *daric* was a coin weighing about 1/4 ounce or 8.5 grams

THE QUEST FOR TRUE WORSHIP

Worship can be thought of as affection, attention, obedience, awe, or credit given to God — inwardly or outwardly — in recognition of his worth or works. This practice has always been central to the people of God. When King David neared death, he called the Israelites together and reminded them of the implications of their status as God's people. They were a people formed around a specific purpose: praising the Lord (1Ch 29:10 – 20). What does it really mean to worship God?

Worship is first and foremost a response. When God's people glimpse the majesty and beauty of God's supreme worth, they do not pause to calculate whether the lyrics or melody fit the sight — they just respond. True worship bursts from a heart that has seen the Lord (Isa 6:1 – 5). He is surrounded by praise at all times. The creatures surrounding him react and respond to his glory — the radiance of his collective perfections — and they never stop speaking praise (Rev 4:8 – 11). Of all the people and things that humans treasure, God is infinitely greater and infinitely more satisfying. He is the ultimate object of awe.

Worship involves much more than music — it includes how God's people live every day. Recognizing God's glorious nature has an impact on the choices made. God desires a lifestyle of worship integrity — a *wholeness,* a seamless quality between what his people profess to believe and the way they live (1Ch 29:17). Obedience is the fruit of true worship. God's people attend church services on Sundays and sing with enthusiasm and intensity. Yet it is Monday that will prove whether or not it was worship. If the end of the songs on Sunday marks the end of their worship, something is wrong. In the New Testament, Paul reminded the church in Rome that offering their very bodies to the service of Jesus constituted their spiritual service of worship (Ro 12:1 – 2).

True worship expresses gratitude for God's provisions and works. Who is faithful like God? His kindness can be seen in the memory of last year, last month, and last night. He is good to his people! He gives breath today. He provided for every need in the past. He answered prayers. For his name's sake and for the good of his people, he has unlocked, opened, diverted, thwarted, arranged, rearranged, and removed — all as blessings to his beloved daughters and sons. "Sing praises to the LORD, O you his saints, and give thanks to his holy name" (Ps 30:4).

kingdom, O LORD, and you are exalted as head above all. 12Both riches and honor come from you, and you rule over all. In your hand are power and might, and in your hand it is to make great and to give strength to all. 13And now we thank you, our God, and praise your glorious name.

14"But who am I, and what is my people, that we should be able thus to offer willingly? For all things come from you, and of your own have we given you. 15For we are strangers before you and sojourners, as all our fathers were. Our days on the earth are like a shadow, and there is no abiding.[1] 16O LORD our God, all this abundance that we have provided for building you a house for your holy name comes from your hand and is all your own. 17I know, my God, that you test the heart and have pleasure in uprightness. In the uprightness of my heart I have freely offered all these things, and now I have seen your people, who are present here, offering freely and joyously to you. 18O LORD, the God of Abraham, Isaac, and Israel, our fathers, keep forever such purposes and thoughts in the hearts of your people, and direct their hearts toward you. 19Grant to Solomon my son a whole heart that he may keep your commandments, your testimonies, and your statutes, performing all, and that he may build the palace for which I have made provision."

20Then David said to all the assembly, "Bless the LORD your God." And all the assembly blessed the LORD, the God of their fathers, and bowed their heads and paid homage to the LORD and to the king. 21And they offered sacrifices to the LORD, and on the next day offered burnt offerings to the LORD, 1,000 bulls, 1,000 rams, and 1,000 lambs, with their drink offerings, and sacrifices in abundance for all Israel. 22And they ate and drank before the LORD on that day with great gladness.

Solomon Anointed King

And they made Solomon the son of David king the second time, and they anointed him as prince for the LORD, and Zadok as priest.

23Then Solomon sat on the throne of the LORD as king in place of David his father. And he prospered, and all Israel obeyed him. 24All the leaders and the mighty men, and also all the sons of King David, pledged their allegiance to King Solomon. 25And the LORD made Solomon very great in the sight of all Israel and bestowed on him such royal majesty as had not been on any king before him in Israel.

The Death of David

26Thus David the son of Jesse reigned over all Israel. 27The time that he reigned over Israel was forty years. He reigned seven years in Hebron and thirty-three years in Jerusalem. 28Then he died at a good age, full of days, riches, and honor. And Solomon his son reigned in his place. 29Now the acts of King David, from first to last, are written in the Chronicles of Samuel the seer, and in the Chronicles of Nathan the prophet, and in the Chronicles of Gad the seer, 30with accounts of all his rule and his might and of the circumstances that came upon him and upon Israel and upon all the kingdoms of the countries.

---

[1] Septuagint, Vulgate; Hebrew *hope*, or *prospect*

JESUS: OUR TRUE WORSHIP

2 CHRONICLES

2 CHRONICLES

SOLOMON BEGINS TEMPLE CONSTRUCTION	ISRAEL DIVIDED	FALL OF JUDAH
c. 966 BC	*c. 930 BC*	*c. 586 BC*

The book of 2 Chronicles follows the pattern established in 1 Chronicles. The author wrote to remind a people in need of encouragement that God had not revoked his promises or forgotten his people. Even though the Israelites had demonstrated their consistent inability to remain faithful, God would do what he had always done—show himself faithful to his gracious promises to his people.

The storied history of the nations of Israel and Judah demonstrates the remarkable power of God's grace to redeem a sinful people. Second Chronicles traces the theme of redemption from David's death (at the end of 1 Chronicles) through the reign of his son Solomon and his successors. Though rulers would come and go, the focus of the book is on how God's actions are consistent with his promises to King David.

Solomon fulfilled David's longing to build a temple for the worship of God. Second Chronicles describes the construction of the temple and the worship that it facilitated for the nation.

This book focuses nearly all of its attention on Judah's history rather than on Israel's. Since the nation divided into two kingdoms, Judah had inherited the promises of the Davidic kingdom. Though David's successors who led Judah ruled only a portion of the overall nation, God remained faithful to his promises to this small remnant. Judah became the core population through which God would accomplish his work of redemption and send the Messiah.

David commissioned and gathered materials so that Solomon could build the temple as God's dwelling place among his people (1Ch 22:5–13). Since the first sin in the garden, humanity had been incapable of coming into the presence of a holy God. God, in his grace, provided a way for the people to approach him in the tabernacle and the temple through the sacrificial system. Solomon himself recognized that this temple was incapable of containing God (2Ch 6:18). While God would humble himself to meet with the people in the temple, there was a resounding need for a far greater dwelling of God among his people.

Jesus' incarnation did what the temple could never do — it invaded the cosmos with the dwelling of God in human form. Jesus came as Immanuel, "God with us" (Mt 1:23), and lived among fallen humanity in a sin-darkened world (Jn 1:1 – 14). Jesus likened his body to the temple, showing that, while it would be destroyed on the cross, God would rebuild it again through his glorious resurrection (Jn 2:19). Ultimately, in God's eternal kingdom, there will be no need for the temple because the presence of God will pervade the new Jerusalem and his worship will fill the Holy City once more (Rev 21:22).

(... IT WAS THE DUTY OF THE TRUMPETERS AND SINGERS TO MAKE THEMSELVES HEARD IN UNISON IN PRAISE AND THANKSGIVING TO THE LORD), AND WHEN THE SONG WAS RAISED, WITH TRUMPETS AND CYMBALS AND OTHER MUSICAL INSTRUMENTS, IN PRAISE TO THE LORD, "FOR HE IS GOOD, FOR HIS STEADFAST LOVE ENDURES FOREVER," THE HOUSE, THE HOUSE OF THE LORD, WAS FILLED WITH A CLOUD.

---

2 Chronicles 5:13

2 CHRONICLES

2 CHRONICLES 1:7–12

ONE GREATER THAN SOLOMON

Solomon was exalted to the throne of Israel in Jerusalem, and that night God appeared and said to him, "Ask what I shall give you." Solomon knew the promise to David his father—that he would never fail to have a son on the throne of Israel (cf. 2Sa 7:4–16). But Solomon also recognized that God had fulfilled his promise to Abraham by making the nation "as numerous as the dust of the earth" (2Ch 1:9; cf. Ge 13:16). Therefore, in order for Solomon to rule well over such a great people, he requested wisdom and knowledge from God to govern the people (2Ch 1:10). God granted Solomon's request.

While Solomon started his reign well, ruling in wisdom, his reign ended in colossal failure (1Ki 11:1–13). Israel needed a truly wise king who not only understood the wisdom that Solomon laid out in the Proverbs but who lived in accord with that wisdom to the end. Isaiah 11:1–3 promised such a king, and the New Testament revealed that this promise was fulfilled in Jesus. He is the Son of David who "increased in wisdom and in stature and in favor with God and man" (Lk 2:52). And he is the one who is "greater than Solomon" (Mt 12:42).

2 CHRONICLES 2:1

JESUS IS THE TRUE TEMPLE

The temple, like the tabernacle, was the place where God lived with his

(continued on page 606)

Solomon Worships at Gibeon

1 Solomon the son of David established himself in his kingdom, and the LORD
his God was with him and made him exceedingly great.
2Solomon spoke to all Israel, to the commanders of thousands and of hundreds, to the judges, and to all the leaders in all Israel, the heads of fathers' houses.
3And Solomon, and all the assembly with him, went to the high place that was at
Gibeon, for the tent of meeting of God, which Moses the servant of the LORD had
made in the wilderness, was there. 4(But David had brought up the ark of God
from Kiriath-jearim to the place that David had prepared for it, for he had pitched
a tent for it in Jerusalem.) 5Moreover, the bronze altar that Bezalel the son of Uri,
son of Hur, had made, was there before the tabernacle of the LORD. And Solomon
and the assembly sought it[1] out. 6And Solomon went up there to the bronze altar
before the LORD, which was at the tent of meeting, and offered a thousand burnt
offerings on it.

Solomon Prays for Wisdom

7In that night God appeared to Solomon, and said to him, "Ask what I shall
give you." 8And Solomon said to God, "You have shown great and steadfast love
to David my father, and have made me king in his place. 9O LORD God, let your
word to David my father be now fulfilled, for you have made me king over a people
as numerous as the dust of the earth. 10Give me now wisdom and knowledge to
go out and come in before this people, for who can govern this people of yours,
which is so great?" 11God answered Solomon, "Because this was in your heart,
and you have not asked for possessions, wealth, honor, or the life of those who
hate you, and have not even asked for long life, but have asked for wisdom and
knowledge for yourself that you may govern my people over whom I have made
you king, 12wisdom and knowledge are granted to you. I will also give you riches,
possessions, and honor, such as none of the kings had who were before you, and
none after you shall have the like." 13So Solomon came from[2] the high place at
Gibeon, from before the tent of meeting, to Jerusalem. And he reigned over Israel.

Solomon Given Wealth

14Solomon gathered together chariots and horsemen. He had 1,400 chariots
and 12,000 horsemen, whom he stationed in the chariot cities and with the king
in Jerusalem. 15And the king made silver and gold as common in Jerusalem as
stone, and he made cedar as plentiful as the sycamore of the Shephelah. 16And
Solomon's import of horses was from Egypt and Kue, and the king's traders would
buy them from Kue for a price. 17They imported a chariot from Egypt for 600 shekels[3] of silver, and a horse for 150. Likewise through them these were exported to
all the kings of the Hittites and the kings of Syria.

Preparing to Build the Temple

2 [4] Now Solomon purposed to build a temple for the name of the LORD, and
a royal palace for himself. 2[5]And Solomon assigned 70,000 men to bear
burdens and 80,000 to quarry in the hill country, and 3,600 to oversee them. 3And
Solomon sent word to Hiram the king of Tyre: "As you dealt with David my father
and sent him cedar to build himself a house to dwell in, so deal with me. 4Behold,
I am about to build a house for the name of the LORD my God and dedicate it to
him for the burning of incense of sweet spices before him, and for the regular

[1]Or *him* [2]Septuagint, Vulgate; Hebrew *to* [3]A *shekel* was about 2/5 ounce or 11 grams [4]Ch 1:18 in Hebrew [5]Ch 2:1 in Hebrew

THE PURPOSE OF THE CHRONICLER

The purpose of those who recorded the books of 1 and 2 Chronicles was different from the purpose of the author of 1 and 2 Kings. The author of 1 and 2 Kings arranged the historical material in those books for the purpose of showing Israel why they had been carried off into exile. The books of Kings were an indictment on Israel for their sin and their breach of the covenant with the Lord. On the other hand, the historical material in the books of Chronicles was arranged with the purpose of showing Israel that God would keep his promises to David. Of all the historical material which could have been included in these books, the writer selected and arranged historical episodes that reaffirmed particular promises: a descendant of David would ultimately reign on the throne forever and a new temple would be built.

So, the author of Kings had an essentially pessimistic purpose while the author of Chronicles had an optimistic purpose. Therefore, Chronicles passes over certain negative events from that time period. It passes over David's sin with Bathsheba and Solomon's sin with his foreign wives. The purpose was not to produce a revisionist history but rather to assure the returned remnant after the Babylonian exile that God would fulfill his promises to David. Chronicles revealed to them that despite the fact that David and all of his sons failed in the past, God would remain merciful and faithful to his promises that a Messiah — specifically a descendant of David — would come to establish an eternal kingdom on earth. These promises would ultimately be fulfilled in Jesus of Nazareth. He is the Son of David who received the promises made to his ancestor. That is why Paul preached, "And as for the fact that he raised him from the dead, no more to return to corruption, he has spoken in this way, 'I will give you the holy and sure blessings of David.' Therefore he says also in another psalm, 'You will not let your Holy One see corruption.' For David, after he had served the purpose of God in his own generation, fell asleep and was laid with his fathers and saw corruption, but he whom God raised up did not see corruption" (Ac 13:34 – 37).

(Jesus Is the True Temple, continued)

people. The temple was the place where God's people could draw near to worship him. The problem was that it was located in Jerusalem, and many had to travel great distances in order to come before God. The New Testament reveals something far greater. Yes, kings — like Solomon — are the ones who build temples. But, King Jesus built a different kind of temple. He said that the true temple was his body (Jn 2:21). With the coming of that temple, worship is no longer relegated to one place (Jn 4:21–23). People can come near to God wherever they are. Jesus is the true temple because he is God in human flesh, living among his people (Jn 1:14).

Believers can draw near to God through Jesus because he has torn down the curtain in the old temple that separated them from God — a feat he accomplished by means of his death on the cross (Mt 27:51). Additionally, God's people are now the temple of God — the church is Christ's body, and the Spirit of God dwells in them (1Co 3:16–17; Eph 2:19–22). King Jesus is building a temple made of living stones (1Pe 2:5). And someday the true temple will be "the Lord God the Almighty and the Lamb" (Rev 21:22). Then, God will forever live among his people with no barriers separating us!

---

2 CHRONICLES 3:1

THE SUBSTITUTE SACRIFICE

Solomon built the temple in Jerusalem on Mount Moriah, a location that had great significance for the people of Israel. God had commanded Abraham to take his son Isaac

(continued on next page)

arrangement of the showbread, and for burnt offerings morning and evening, on
the Sabbaths and the new moons and the appointed feasts of the LORD our God,
as ordained forever for Israel. 5The house that I am to build will be great, for our
God is greater than all gods. 6But who is able to build him a house, since heaven,
even highest heaven, cannot contain him? Who am I to build a house for him,
except as a place to make offerings before him? 7So now send me a man skilled
to work in gold, silver, bronze, and iron, and in purple, crimson, and blue fabrics,
trained also in engraving, to be with the skilled workers who are with me in Judah
and Jerusalem, whom David my father provided. 8Send me also cedar, cypress, and
algum timber from Lebanon, for I know that your servants know how to cut timber
in Lebanon. And my servants will be with your servants, 9to prepare timber for me
in abundance, for the house I am to build will be great and wonderful. 10I will give
for your servants, the woodsmen who cut timber, 20,000 cors[1] of crushed wheat,
20,000 cors of barley, 20,000 baths[2] of wine, and 20,000 baths of oil."

11Then Hiram the king of Tyre answered in a letter that he sent to Solomon,
"Because the LORD loves his people, he has made you king over them." 12Hiram
also said, "Blessed be the LORD God of Israel, who made heaven and earth, who
has given King David a wise son, who has discretion and understanding, who will
build a temple for the LORD and a royal palace for himself.

13"Now I have sent a skilled man, who has understanding, Huram-abi, 14the
son of a woman of the daughters of Dan, and his father was a man of Tyre. He is
trained to work in gold, silver, bronze, iron, stone, and wood, and in purple, blue,
and crimson fabrics and fine linen, and to do all sorts of engraving and execute
any design that may be assigned him, with your craftsmen, the craftsmen of my
lord, David your father. 15Now therefore the wheat and barley, oil and wine, of
which my lord has spoken, let him send to his servants. 16And we will cut whatever timber you need from Lebanon and bring it to you in rafts by sea to Joppa, so
that you may take it up to Jerusalem."

17Then Solomon counted all the resident aliens who were in the land of Israel, after the census of them that David his father had taken, and there were
found 153,600. 18Seventy thousand of them he assigned to bear burdens, 80,000
to quarry in the hill country, and 3,600 as overseers to make the people work.

Solomon Builds the Temple

3 Then Solomon began to build the house of the LORD in Jerusalem on Mount
Moriah, where the LORD[3] had appeared to David his father, at the place that
David had appointed, on the threshing floor of Ornan the Jebusite. 2He began to
build in the second month of the fourth year of his reign. 3These are Solomon's
measurements[4] for building the house of God: the length, in cubits[5] of the old
standard, was sixty cubits, and the breadth twenty cubits. 4The vestibule in front
of the nave of the house was twenty cubits long, equal to the width of the house,[6]
and its height was 120 cubits. He overlaid it on the inside with pure gold. 5The
nave he lined with cypress and covered it with fine gold and made palms and
chains on it. 6He adorned the house with settings of precious stones. The gold
was gold of Parvaim. 7So he lined the house with gold—its beams, its thresholds,
its walls, and its doors—and he carved cherubim on the walls.

8And he made the Most Holy Place. Its length, corresponding to the breadth
of the house, was twenty cubits, and its breadth was twenty cubits. He overlaid it
with 600 talents[7] of fine gold. 9The weight of gold for the nails was fifty shekels.[8]
And he overlaid the upper chambers with gold.

10In the Most Holy Place he made two cherubim of wood[9] and overlaid[10] them

---

[1]A *cor* was about 6 bushels or 220 liters [2]A *bath* was about 6 gallons or 22 liters [3]Septuagint; Hebrew lacks *the LORD* [4]Syriac; Hebrew *foundations* [5]A *cubit* was about 18 inches or 45 centimeters [6]Compare 1 Kings 6:3; the meaning of the Hebrew is uncertain [7]A *talent* was about 75 pounds or 34 kilograms [8]A *shekel* was about 2/5 ounce or 11 grams [9]Septuagint; the meaning of the Hebrew is uncertain [10]Hebrew *they overlaid*

with gold. 11The wings of the cherubim together extended twenty cubits: one wing
of the one, of five cubits, touched the wall of the house, and its other wing, of
five cubits, touched the wing of the other cherub; 12and of this cherub, one wing,
of five cubits, touched the wall of the house, and the other wing, also of five cubits, was joined to the wing of the first cherub. 13The wings of these cherubim
extended twenty cubits. The cherubim[1] stood on their feet, facing the nave. 14And
he made the veil of blue and purple and crimson fabrics and fine linen, and he
worked cherubim on it.
15In front of the house he made two pillars thirty-five cubits high, with a capital of five cubits on the top of each. 16He made chains like a necklace[2] and put
them on the tops of the pillars, and he made a hundred pomegranates and put
them on the chains. 17He set up the pillars in front of the temple, one on the south,
the other on the north; that on the south he called Jachin, and that on the north
Boaz.

The Temple's Furnishings

4 He made an altar of bronze, twenty cubits[3] long and twenty cubits wide and
ten cubits high. 2Then he made the sea of cast metal. It was round, ten cubits
from brim to brim, and five cubits high, and a line of thirty cubits measured its
circumference. 3Under it were figures of gourds,[4] for ten cubits, compassing the
sea all around. The gourds were in two rows, cast with it when it was cast. 4It
stood on twelve oxen, three facing north, three facing west, three facing south,
and three facing east. The sea was set on them, and all their rear parts were inward. 5Its thickness was a handbreadth.[5] And its brim was made like the brim of
a cup, like the flower of a lily. It held 3,000 baths.[6] 6He also made ten basins in
which to wash, and set five on the south side, and five on the north side. In these
they were to rinse off what was used for the burnt offering, and the sea was for
the priests to wash in.
7And he made ten golden lampstands as prescribed, and set them in the temple, five on the south side and five on the north. 8He also made ten tables and
placed them in the temple, five on the south side and five on the north. And he
made a hundred basins of gold. 9He made the court of the priests and the great
court and doors for the court and overlaid their doors with bronze. 10And he set
the sea at the southeast corner of the house.
11Hiram also made the pots, the shovels, and the basins. So Hiram finished
the work that he did for King Solomon on the house of God: 12the two pillars, the
bowls, and the two capitals on the top of the pillars; and the two latticeworks to
cover the two bowls of the capitals that were on the top of the pillars; 13and the
400 pomegranates for the two latticeworks, two rows of pomegranates for each
latticework, to cover the two bowls of the capitals that were on the pillars. 14He
made the stands also, and the basins on the stands, 15and the one sea, and the
twelve oxen underneath it. 16The pots, the shovels, the forks, and all the equipment for these Huram-abi made of burnished bronze for King Solomon for the
house of the LORD. 17In the plain of the Jordan the king cast them, in the clay
ground between Succoth and Zeredah.[7] 18Solomon made all these things in great
quantities, for the weight of the bronze was not sought.
19So Solomon made all the vessels that were in the house of God: the golden
altar, the tables for the bread of the Presence, 20the lampstands and their lamps
of pure gold to burn before the inner sanctuary, as prescribed; 21the flowers, the
lamps, and the tongs, of purest gold; 22the snuffers, basins, dishes for incense, and
fire pans, of pure gold, and the sockets[8] of the temple, for the inner doors to the
Most Holy Place and for the doors of the nave of the temple were of gold.

[1]Hebrew *they* [2]Hebrew *chains in the inner sanctuary* [3]A *cubit* was about 18 inches or 45 centimeters
[4]Hebrew *oxen*; twice in this verse; compare 1 Kings 7:24 [5]A *handbreadth* was about 3 inches or
7.5 centimeters [6]A *bath* was about 6 gallons or 22 liters [7]Spelled *Zarethan* in 1 Kings 7:46 [8]Compare
1 Kings 7:50; Hebrew *the entrance of the house*

(The Substitute Sacrifice, continued)

to Mount Moriah and sacrifice him there (Ge 22:2). Abraham trusted and obeyed God—reasoning that God could raise Isaac from the dead (Heb 11:19). However, God provided a substitute for Isaac, Abraham's only son of the promise. Instead of Isaac, Abraham sacrificed the ram that was caught by its horns in a nearby thicket (Ge 22:13). Solomon built the temple on the same spot, and in the temple animals were offered up as sacrifices in the place of the people to bring forgiveness for their sins. God graciously poured out his judgment on the substitute instead of the sinner.

Years later, God would offer up the ultimate sacrifice—his only Son whom he loved. Jesus is the Lamb of God who takes away the sin of the world (Jn 1:29). Jesus is the sacrifice who took humanity's place on the cross. The story of Isaac and the location of the temple point forward to the offering of God's one and only Son who offers eternal life (Jn 3:16).

ACCESS TO GOD

The Most Holy Place was the inner room of the temple where God dwelled among his people. A veil separated the inner room from mankind, and sinful humanity could not approach a holy God in that inner room without dying. Only the high priest could enter the room without dying, and only once a year under very special conditions on the Day of Atonement. The veil covering the entrance to the Most Holy Place had cherubim woven into it, recalling the events of Genesis 3. When Adam and Eve sinned against God, they were exiled east of the garden so that they could not eat from the tree of life and live forever in their sinful state. Cherubim were placed outside the garden with a flaming sword to keep people out. The Most Holy Place was like a new Garden of Eden — a place of communion with God with an entrance symbolically blocked by cherubim. When the high priest entered the Most Holy Place once a year, it was like a brief return to Paradise, made temporarily possible through a blood sacrifice (Heb 9:7). An animal died so that the priest did not.

When Jesus breathed his last breath on the cross, the veil in the temple was torn in two from top to bottom (Mt 27:51). Jesus' death reopened humankind's access to God. People are no longer separated from him because of their sin. They can be reconciled to God and live with him forever by virtue of Christ's death on the cross. They can now come boldly into his presence in worship. As Scripture says, "Therefore, brothers, since we have confidence to enter the holy places by the blood of Jesus, by the new and living way that he opened for us through the curtain, that is, through his flesh, and since we have a great priest over the house of God, let us draw near with a true heart in full assurance of faith" (Heb 10:19–22). Better yet, Christ's work of reconciliation not only creates fellowship with God now, but grants believers the hope of heaven, where God will live in perfect, unbroken communion with his people forever (Rev 21:3).

5 Thus all the work that Solomon did for the house of the LORD was finished. And Solomon brought in the things that David his father had dedicated, and stored the silver, the gold, and all the vessels in the treasuries of the house of God.

The Ark Brought to the Temple

[2]Then Solomon assembled the elders of Israel and all the heads of the tribes, the leaders of the fathers' houses of the people of Israel, in Jerusalem, to bring up the ark of the covenant of the LORD out of the city of David, which is Zion. [3]And all the men of Israel assembled before the king at the feast that is in the seventh month. [4]And all the elders of Israel came, and the Levites took up the ark. [5]And they brought up the ark, the tent of meeting, and all the holy vessels that were in the tent; the Levitical priests brought them up. [6]And King Solomon and all the congregation of Israel, who had assembled before him, were before the ark, sacrificing so many sheep and oxen that they could not be counted or numbered. [7]Then the priests brought the ark of the covenant of the LORD to its place, in the inner sanctuary of the house, in the Most Holy Place, underneath the wings of the cherubim. [8]The cherubim spread out their wings over the place of the ark, so that the cherubim made a covering above the ark and its poles. [9]And the poles were so long that the ends of the poles were seen from the Holy Place before the inner sanctuary, but they could not be seen from outside. And they are[1] there to this day. [10]There was nothing in the ark except the two tablets that Moses put there at Horeb, where the LORD made a covenant with the people of Israel, when they came out of Egypt. [11]And when the priests came out of the Holy Place (for all the priests who were present had consecrated themselves, without regard to their divisions, [12]and all the Levitical singers, Asaph, Heman, and Jeduthun, their sons and kinsmen, arrayed in fine linen, with cymbals, harps, and lyres, stood east of the altar with 120 priests who were trumpeters; [13]and it was the duty of the trumpeters and singers to make themselves heard in unison in praise and thanksgiving to the LORD), and when the song was raised, with trumpets and cymbals and other musical instruments, in praise to the LORD,

"For he is good,
for his steadfast love endures forever,"

the house, the house of the LORD, was filled with a cloud, [14]so that the priests could not stand to minister because of the cloud, for the glory of the LORD filled the house of God.

Solomon Blesses the People

6 Then Solomon said, "The LORD has said that he would dwell in thick darkness. [2]But I have built you an exalted house, a place for you to dwell in forever." [3]Then the king turned around and blessed all the assembly of Israel, while all the assembly of Israel stood. [4]And he said, "Blessed be the LORD, the God of Israel, who with his hand has fulfilled what he promised with his mouth to David my father, saying, [5]'Since the day that I brought my people out of the land of Egypt, I chose no city out of all the tribes of Israel in which to build a house, that my name might be there, and I chose no man as prince over my people Israel; [6]but I have chosen Jerusalem that my name may be there, and I have chosen David to be over my people Israel.' [7]Now it was in the heart of David my father to build a house for the name of the LORD, the God of Israel. [8]But the LORD said to David my father, 'Whereas it was in your heart to build a house for my name, you did well that it was in your heart. [9]Nevertheless, it is not you who shall build the house, but your son who shall be born to you shall build the house for my name.' [10]Now the LORD has fulfilled his promise that he made. For I have risen in the place of David my father and sit on the throne of Israel, as the LORD promised, and I have built the house for the name of the LORD, the God of Israel. [11]And there

[1]Hebrew *it is*

2 CHRONICLES 5:2–10

GOD LIVES WITH HIS PEOPLE

Once the temple was finished, Solomon had the ark of the covenant brought in and placed in the Most Holy Place. The ark symbolized the presence of God, and its position in the Most Holy Place represented the fact that God lived among his people.

The ark was only temporary though, because God's intention from the beginning was to eventually live among his people as one of them. God took on human flesh in the incarnation of Jesus Christ and "dwelt among us" (Jn 1:14). In fact, all of history is leading up to the moment when God makes his dwelling permanently with his people in the new Jerusalem. Revelation 21:3–4 describes that day: "And I heard a loud voice from the throne saying, 'Behold, the dwelling place of God is with man. He will dwell with them, and they will be his people, and God himself will be with them as their God. He will wipe away every tear from their eyes, and death shall be no more, neither shall there be mourning, nor crying, nor pain anymore, for the former things have passed away.'"

2 CHRONICLES 5:13–14

THE GLORY OF THE LORD

Once the temple was finished and the ark of the covenant was in the Most Holy Place, the glory cloud of the Lord filled the temple, showing that God lived among his people. His very presence was with them.

(continued on next page)

I have set the ark, in which is the covenant of the LORD that he made with the
people of Israel."

Solomon's Prayer of Dedication

12Then Solomon stood before the altar of the LORD in the presence of all the
assembly of Israel and spread out his hands. 13Solomon had made a bronze platform five cubits[1] long, five cubits wide, and three cubits high, and had set it
in the court, and he stood on it. Then he knelt on his knees in the presence of
all the assembly of Israel, and spread out his hands toward heaven, 14and said,
"O LORD, God of Israel, there is no God like you, in heaven or on earth, keeping
covenant and showing steadfast love to your servants who walk before you with
all their heart, 15who have kept with your servant David my father what you
declared to him. You spoke with your mouth, and with your hand have fulfilled
it this day. 16Now therefore, O LORD, God of Israel, keep for your servant David
my father what you have promised him, saying, 'You shall not lack a man to sit
before me on the throne of Israel, if only your sons pay close attention to their
way, to walk in my law as you have walked before me.' 17Now therefore, O LORD,
God of Israel, let your word be confirmed, which you have spoken to your servant David.
18"But will God indeed dwell with man on the earth? Behold, heaven and the
highest heaven cannot contain you, how much less this house that I have built!
19Yet have regard to the prayer of your servant and to his plea, O LORD my God,
listening to the cry and to the prayer that your servant prays before you, 20that
your eyes may be open day and night toward this house, the place where you have
promised to set your name, that you may listen to the prayer that your servant offers toward this place. 21And listen to the pleas of your servant and of your people
Israel, when they pray toward this place. And listen from heaven your dwelling
place, and when you hear, forgive.
22"If a man sins against his neighbor and is made to take an oath and comes
and swears his oath before your altar in this house, 23then hear from heaven and
act and judge your servants, repaying the guilty by bringing his conduct on his
own head, and vindicating the righteous by rewarding him according to his righteousness.
24"If your people Israel are defeated before the enemy because they have
sinned against you, and they turn again and acknowledge your name and pray
and plead with you in this house, 25then hear from heaven and forgive the sin of
your people Israel and bring them again to the land that you gave to them and to
their fathers.
26"When heaven is shut up and there is no rain because they have sinned
against you, if they pray toward this place and acknowledge your name and turn
from their sin, when you afflict[2] them, 27then hear in heaven and forgive the sin
of your servants, your people Israel, when you teach them the good way[3] in which
they should walk, and grant rain upon your land, which you have given to your
people as an inheritance.
28"If there is famine in the land, if there is pestilence or blight or mildew or
locust or caterpillar, if their enemies besiege them in the land at their gates, whatever plague, whatever sickness there is, 29whatever prayer, whatever plea is made
by any man or by all your people Israel, each knowing his own affliction and his
own sorrow and stretching out his hands toward this house, 30then hear from
heaven your dwelling place and forgive and render to each whose heart you know,
according to all his ways, for you, you only, know the hearts of the children of
mankind, 31that they may fear you and walk in your ways all the days that they
live in the land that you gave to our fathers.

[1]A *cubit* was about 18 inches or 45 centimeters [2]Septuagint, Vulgate; Hebrew *answer* [3]Septuagint, Syriac, Vulgate (compare 1 Kings 8:36); Hebrew *toward the good way*

(The Glory of the Lord, continued)

Despite God's presence, Israel's sin and unfaithfulness toward God continued. When the people of Judah were exiled to Babylon for their sin, the glory of God departed from the temple and the temple was destroyed. In fact, Ezekiel saw a vision of the glory of God leaving the temple (Eze 10:3–19). Once the people returned to the land after the exile, they began to rebuild the temple. Yet, as Haggai revealed, the rebuilt temple did not come close to the glory of the previous temple (Hag 2:3). Isaiah prophesied that the Lord's return to Zion would be visible (Isa 52:8)—Israel would visibly see the glory of God return to the land. It is in this context that God's people read the words of John 1:14: "And the Word became flesh and dwelt among us, and we have seen his glory." God's glory lived among his people as one of them. And in the new Jerusalem there will be no temple building or sun because Jesus will be the temple and his glory will shine brightly (Rev 21:22–23).

2 CHRONICLES 6:19–40

PRAYER AND FORGIVENESS

Solomon made a prayer of dedication after he completed the temple. In the prayer, he asked God to keep his eyes continually open toward the temple. The idea was that the temple was a place where God's people could meet with him in prayer—he would see them and hear their requests when they faced the temple. *Solomon's main request was that* when Israel sinned and fell into judgment, they could pray toward the temple, and God would hear their prayers and forgive them. In fact,

(continued on next page)

32"Likewise, when a foreigner, who is not of your people Israel, comes from a
far country for the sake of your great name and your mighty hand and your outstretched arm, when he comes and prays toward this house, 33hear from heaven
your dwelling place and do according to all for which the foreigner calls to you,
in order that all the peoples of the earth may know your name and fear you, as
do your people Israel, and that they may know that this house that I have built is
called by your name.
34"If your people go out to battle against their enemies, by whatever way you
shall send them, and they pray to you toward this city that you have chosen and
the house that I have built for your name, 35then hear from heaven their prayer
and their plea, and maintain their cause.
36"If they sin against you—for there is no one who does not sin—and you are
angry with them and give them to an enemy, so that they are carried away captive
to a land far or near, 37yet if they turn their heart in the land to which they have
been carried captive, and repent and plead with you in the land of their captivity,
saying, 'We have sinned and have acted perversely and wickedly,' 38if they repent
with all their heart and with all their soul in the land of their captivity to which
they were carried captive, and pray toward their land, which you gave to their
fathers, the city that you have chosen and the house that I have built for your
name, 39then hear from heaven your dwelling place their prayer and their pleas,
and maintain their cause and forgive your people who have sinned against you.
40Now, O my God, let your eyes be open and your ears attentive to the prayer of
this place.

41 "And now arise, O LORD God, and go to your resting place,
you and the ark of your might.
Let your priests, O LORD God, be clothed with salvation,
and let your saints rejoice in your goodness.
42 O LORD God, do not turn away the face of your anointed one!
Remember your steadfast love for David your servant."

Fire from Heaven

7 As soon as Solomon finished his prayer, fire came down from heaven and consumed the burnt offering and the sacrifices, and the glory of the LORD filled
the temple. 2And the priests could not enter the house of the LORD, because the
glory of the LORD filled the LORD's house. 3When all the people of Israel saw the
fire come down and the glory of the LORD on the temple, they bowed down with
their faces to the ground on the pavement and worshiped and gave thanks to the
LORD, saying, "For he is good, for his steadfast love endures forever."

The Dedication of the Temple

4Then the king and all the people offered sacrifice before the LORD. 5King Solomon offered as a sacrifice 22,000 oxen and 120,000 sheep. So the king and all the
people dedicated the house of God. 6The priests stood at their posts; the Levites
also, with the instruments for music to the LORD that King David had made for giving thanks to the LORD—for his steadfast love endures forever—whenever David
offered praises by their ministry;[1] opposite them the priests sounded trumpets,
and all Israel stood.
7And Solomon consecrated the middle of the court that was before the house
of the LORD, for there he offered the burnt offering and the fat of the peace offerings, because the bronze altar Solomon had made could not hold the burnt
offering and the grain offering and the fat.
8At that time Solomon held the feast for seven days, and all Israel with him, a
very great assembly, from Lebo-hamath to the Brook of Egypt. 9And on the eighth
day they held a solemn assembly, for they had kept the dedication of the altar

[1]Hebrew *by their hand*

(Prayer and Forgiveness, continued)

Solomon prayed that even foreigners who were not part of Israel could pray toward the temple and have their prayers heard (vv. 32–33). He prayed that in exile the people could pray toward the temple and that God would hear them, forgive them, and return them to the land (vv. 24–25). These verses, written after the exile, would have been incredibly encouraging to the returned exiles because they show that God keeps his promises!

In the New Testament, Jesus is the temple. Anyone, no matter their circumstances or national identity, can pray to him for forgiveness (1Jn 1:9). Solomon confessed, "There is no one who does not sin" (2Ch 6:36). The good news is that there is no one whose sins Jesus will not forgive if they repent.

seven days and the feast seven days. 10On the twenty-third day of the seventh
month he sent the people away to their homes, joyful and glad of heart for the
prosperity[1] that the LORD had granted to David and to Solomon and to Israel his
people.

If My People Pray

11Thus Solomon finished the house of the LORD and the king's house. All that
Solomon had planned to do in the house of the LORD and in his own house he suc-
cessfully accomplished. 12Then the LORD appeared to Solomon in the night and
said to him: "I have heard your prayer and have chosen this place for myself as a
house of sacrifice. 13When I shut up the heavens so that there is no rain, or command the locust to devour the land, or send pestilence among my people, 14if my
people who are called by my name humble themselves, and pray and seek my face
and turn from their wicked ways, then I will hear from heaven and will forgive
their sin and heal their land. 15Now my eyes will be open and my ears attentive to
the prayer that is made in this place. 16For now I have chosen and consecrated this
house that my name may be there forever. My eyes and my heart will be there for
all time. 17And as for you, if you will walk before me as David your father walked,
doing according to all that I have commanded you and keeping my statutes and
my rules, 18then I will establish your royal throne, as I covenanted with David your
father, saying, 'You shall not lack a man to rule Israel.'

19"But if you[2] turn aside and forsake my statutes and my commandments that
I have set before you, and go and serve other gods and worship them, 20then I will
pluck you[3] up from my land that I have given you, and this house that I have consecrated for my name, I will cast out of my sight, and I will make it a proverb and
a byword among all peoples. 21And at this house, which was exalted, everyone
passing by will be astonished and say, 'Why has the LORD done thus to this land
and to this house?' 22Then they will say, 'Because they abandoned the LORD, the
God of their fathers who brought them out of the land of Egypt, and laid hold on
other gods and worshiped them and served them. Therefore he has brought all
this disaster on them.'"

Solomon's Accomplishments

8 At the end of twenty years, in which Solomon had built the house of the LORD
and his own house, 2Solomon rebuilt the cities that Hiram had given to him,
and settled the people of Israel in them.

3And Solomon went to Hamath-zobah and took it. 4He built Tadmor in the
wilderness and all the store cities that he built in Hamath. 5He also built Upper
Beth-horon and Lower Beth-horon, fortified cities with walls, gates, and bars,
6and Baalath, and all the store cities that Solomon had and all the cities for his
chariots and the cities for his horsemen, and whatever Solomon desired to build
in Jerusalem, in Lebanon, and in all the land of his dominion. 7All the people who
were left of the Hittites, the Amorites, the Perizzites, the Hivites, and the Jebusites, who were not of Israel, 8from their descendants who were left after them in
the land, whom the people of Israel had not destroyed—these Solomon drafted as
forced labor, and so they are to this day. 9But of the people of Israel Solomon made
no slaves for his work; they were soldiers, and his officers, the commanders of his
chariots, and his horsemen. 10And these were the chief officers of King Solomon,
250, who exercised authority over the people.

11Solomon brought Pharaoh's daughter up from the city of David to the house
that he had built for her, for he said, "My wife shall not live in the house of David
king of Israel, for the places to which the ark of the LORD has come are holy."

12Then Solomon offered up burnt offerings to the LORD on the altar of the LORD
that he had built before the vestibule, 13as the duty of each day required, offering

---

[1]Or *good* [2]The Hebrew for *you* is plural here [3]Hebrew *them*; twice in this verse

2 CHRONICLES 7:13 – 14

PRAYER FOR REVIVAL

One of the challenges in approaching Scripture is the temptation to allow one's own biases to drive interpretation. It can be tempting, particularly in this specific text, to see a formula of revival for one's own place and time. However, as with any portion of Scripture, it is important to understand the context before attempting to apply it.

A careful reading of 2 Chronicles 7:14 reveals that it is part of a larger sequence that starts in verse 13. This sequence is, in turn, a part of the larger narrative of chapters 6 and 7. Solomon completed building the temple and prayed a grand prayer of dedication (2Ch 6:14 – 42). Solomon specifically prayed that when Israel faced divine judgment for particular sins, they could pray toward the temple in repentance and receive restoration (2Ch 6:36 – 39). Then God appeared to Solomon and granted his earlier request, assuring Solomon that when the people of Israel rebelled, a prayer of repentance would "heal their land" (2Ch 7:11 – 14). Linguistic similarities between Solomon's prayer in chapter 6 and God's words to Solomon in chapter 7 signal a connection between the two passages (e.g., 2Ch 6:26; 7:13). God's promises in 2 Chronicles 7:13 – 14 applied specifically to the people and situations addressed in Solomon's prayer.

Although this passage is not a particular prescription for today, believers can find joy in knowing that the promises of forgiveness and restoration given here have been fulfilled in Jesus Christ — in a manner that far exceeds the scope of the original promises to Solomon. Those who believe in Jesus find true revival. When people come to faith in Christ, they are moving from death to life (Eph 2:1 – 5). They are moving from a state of spiritual blindness to a state of seeing life the way that God intended. Therefore, when people today long for revival in their land, they should ultimately be longing for people to see Jesus for who he really is. Rather than relying on a formula based on a promise made to Solomon, believers should pray that people find new life in Christ. Those individual transformations have the power to change the trajectory of any nation.

according to the commandment of Moses for the Sabbaths, the new moons, and
the three annual feasts—the Feast of Unleavened Bread, the Feast of Weeks, and
the Feast of Booths. [14]According to the ruling of David his father, he appointed the
divisions of the priests for their service, and the Levites for their offices of praise
and ministry before the priests as the duty of each day required, and the gatekeepers in their divisions at each gate, for so David the man of God had commanded.
[15]And they did not turn aside from what the king had commanded the priests and
Levites concerning any matter and concerning the treasuries.

[16]Thus was accomplished all the work of Solomon from[1] the day the foundation of the house of the LORD was laid until it was finished. So the house of the
LORD was completed.

[17]Then Solomon went to Ezion-geber and Eloth on the shore of the sea, in
the land of Edom. [18]And Hiram sent to him by the hand of his servants ships and
servants familiar with the sea, and they went to Ophir together with the servants
of Solomon and brought from there 450 talents[2] of gold and brought it to King
Solomon.

The Queen of Sheba

9 Now when the queen of Sheba heard of the fame of Solomon, she came to
Jerusalem to test him with hard questions, having a very great retinue and
camels bearing spices and very much gold and precious stones. And when she
came to Solomon, she told him all that was on her mind. [2]And Solomon answered
all her questions. There was nothing hidden from Solomon that he could not explain to her. [3]And when the queen of Sheba had seen the wisdom of Solomon, the
house that he had built, [4]the food of his table, the seating of his officials, and the
attendance of his servants, and their clothing, his cupbearers, and their clothing,
and his burnt offerings that he offered at the house of the LORD, there was no
more breath in her.

[5]And she said to the king, "The report was true that I heard in my own land of
your words and of your wisdom, [6]but I did not believe the[3] reports until I came
and my own eyes had seen it. And behold, half the greatness of your wisdom was
not told me; you surpass the report that I heard. [7]Happy are your men! Happy
are these your servants, who continually stand before you and hear your wisdom! [8]Blessed be the LORD your God, who has delighted in you and set you on his
throne as king for the LORD your God! Because your God loved Israel and would
establish them forever, he has made you king over them, that you may execute
justice and righteousness." [9]Then she gave the king 120 talents[4] of gold, and a
very great quantity of spices, and precious stones. There were no spices such as
those that the queen of Sheba gave to King Solomon.

[10]Moreover, the servants of Hiram and the servants of Solomon, who brought
gold from Ophir, brought algum wood and precious stones. [11]And the king made
from the algum wood supports for the house of the LORD and for the king's house,
lyres also and harps for the singers. There never was seen the like of them before
in the land of Judah.

[12]And King Solomon gave to the queen of Sheba all that she desired, whatever
she asked besides what she had brought to the king. So she turned and went back
to her own land with her servants.

Solomon's Wealth

[13]Now the weight of gold that came to Solomon in one year was 666 talents
of gold, [14]besides that which the explorers and merchants brought. And all the
kings of Arabia and the governors of the land brought gold and silver to Solomon.
[15]King Solomon made 200 large shields of beaten gold; 600 shekels[5] of beaten

2 CHRONICLES 9:1–4

THE NATIONS COME TO JESUS

When the queen of Sheba visited Solomon to be blessed by his wisdom, she brought gifts for him. The theme of the nations streaming to Israel and bringing gifts to the king is repeated often in Scripture, and it is fulfilled in Jesus Christ. Isaiah prophesied that the nations would stream to Zion, and that they would bring gifts like gold and frankincense (Isa 2:3–4; 60:6).

In Matthew 2, the wise men came to Israel bringing these very gifts to the newborn King. Throughout Jesus' ministry, people from the nations came to him, such as the Canaanite woman from the region of Tyre and Sidon (Mt 15:21–22) and the centurion whose servant was paralyzed (Mt 8:5–6). This pattern continues with the church. A partial fulfillment of the theme occurred when Gentile churches took up a collection to send to the church in Jerusalem (Ro 15:25–27; 1Co 16:1–4; 2Co 8:1–15). And the pattern will be fulfilled completely when the kings of the earth bring their "glory" to the new Jerusalem (Rev 21:24).

[1]Septuagint, Syriac, Vulgate; Hebrew *to* [2]A *talent* was about 75 pounds or 34 kilograms [3]Hebrew *their* [4]A *talent* was about 75 pounds or 34 kilograms [5]A *shekel* was about 2/5 ounce or 11 grams

gold went into each shield. 16And he made 300 shields of beaten gold; 300 shekels of gold went into each shield; and the king put them in the House of the Forest of Lebanon. 17The king also made a great ivory throne and overlaid it with pure gold. 18The throne had six steps and a footstool of gold, which were attached to the throne, and on each side of the seat were armrests and two lions standing beside the armrests, 19while twelve lions stood there, one on each end of a step on the six steps. Nothing like it was ever made for any kingdom. 20All King Solomon's drinking vessels were of gold, and all the vessels of the House of the Forest of Lebanon were of pure gold. Silver was not considered as anything in the days of Solomon. 21For the king's ships went to Tarshish with the servants of Hiram. Once every three years the ships of Tarshish used to come bringing gold, silver, ivory, apes, and peacocks.[1]

22Thus King Solomon excelled all the kings of the earth in riches and in wisdom. 23And all the kings of the earth sought the presence of Solomon to hear his wisdom, which God had put into his mind. 24Every one of them brought his present, articles of silver and of gold, garments, myrrh,[2] spices, horses, and mules, so much year by year. 25And Solomon had 4,000 stalls for horses and chariots, and 12,000 horsemen, whom he stationed in the chariot cities and with the king in Jerusalem. 26And he ruled over all the kings from the Euphrates[3] to the land of the Philistines and to the border of Egypt. 27And the king made silver as common in Jerusalem as stone, and he made cedar as plentiful as the sycamore of the Shephelah. 28And horses were imported for Solomon from Egypt and from all lands.

Solomon's Death

29Now the rest of the acts of Solomon, from first to last, are they not written in the history of Nathan the prophet, and in the prophecy of Ahijah the Shilonite, and in the visions of Iddo the seer concerning Jeroboam the son of Nebat? 30Solomon reigned in Jerusalem over all Israel forty years. 31And Solomon slept with his fathers and was buried in the city of David his father, and Rehoboam his son reigned in his place.

The Revolt Against Rehoboam

10 Rehoboam went to Shechem, for all Israel had come to Shechem to make him king. 2And as soon as Jeroboam the son of Nebat heard of it (for he was in Egypt, where he had fled from King Solomon), then Jeroboam returned from Egypt. 3And they sent and called him. And Jeroboam and all Israel came and said to Rehoboam, 4"Your father made our yoke heavy. Now therefore lighten the hard service of your father and his heavy yoke on us, and we will serve you." 5He said to them, "Come to me again in three days." So the people went away.

6Then King Rehoboam took counsel with the old men,[4] who had stood before Solomon his father while he was yet alive, saying, "How do you advise me to answer this people?" 7And they said to him, "If you will be good to this people and please them and speak good words to them, then they will be your servants forever." 8But he abandoned the counsel that the old men gave him, and took counsel with the young men who had grown up with him and stood before him. 9And he said to them, "What do you advise that we answer this people who have said to me, 'Lighten the yoke that your father put on us'?" 10And the young men who had grown up with him said to him, "Thus shall you speak to the people who said to you, 'Your father made our yoke heavy, but you lighten it for us'; thus shall you say to them, 'My little finger is thicker than my father's thighs. 11And now, whereas my father laid on you a heavy yoke, I will add to your yoke. My father disciplined you with whips, but I will discipline you with scorpions.'"

12So Jeroboam and all the people came to Rehoboam the third day, as the king

[1]Or *baboons* [2]Or *armor* [3]Hebrew *the River* [4]Or *the elders*; also verses 8, 13

2 CHRONICLES 9:17–19

THE LION OF THE TRIBE OF JUDAH

Perhaps the most stunning features of Solomon's magnificent throne were the statues of lions that surrounded it—located beside each armrest and flanking each of the six steps leading up to the golden footstool. Lions were a fitting symbol for Solomon's kingship. Not only were lions commonly thought of as the kings of the beasts, but Solomon was a king from the tribe of Judah. The lions surrounding the throne recalled the prophecy that God made through Jacob concerning Judah. Jacob called Judah a "lion" who would rule as a king with a scepter, prophesying that he would rule over the nations (Ge 49:9–10). The lions surrounding Solomon's throne called back to Jacob's prophecy about Judah and pointed forward to "the Lion of the tribe of Judah"—Jesus Christ (Rev 5:5). Due to this King's victory on the cross, he "ransomed people for God from every tribe and language and people and nation" (Rev 5:9).

said, “Come to me again the third day.” 13 And the king answered them harshly; and forsaking the counsel of the old men, 14 King Rehoboam spoke to them according to the counsel of the young men, saying, “My father made your yoke heavy, but I will add to it. My father disciplined you with whips, but I will discipline you with scorpions.” 15 So the king did not listen to the people, for it was a turn of affairs brought about by God that the LORD might fulfill his word, which he spoke by Ahijah the Shilonite to Jeroboam the son of Nebat.

16 And when all Israel saw that the king did not listen to them, the people answered the king, “What portion have we in David? We have no inheritance in the son of Jesse. Each of you to your tents, O Israel! Look now to your own house, David.” So all Israel went to their tents. 17 But Rehoboam reigned over the people of Israel who lived in the cities of Judah. 18 Then King Rehoboam sent Hadoram,[1] who was taskmaster over the forced labor, and the people of Israel stoned him to death with stones. And King Rehoboam quickly mounted his chariot to flee to Jerusalem. 19 So Israel has been in rebellion against the house of David to this day.

Rehoboam Secures His Kingdom

11 When Rehoboam came to Jerusalem, he assembled the house of Judah and Benjamin, 180,000 chosen warriors, to fight against Israel, to restore the kingdom to Rehoboam. 2 But the word of the LORD came to Shemaiah the man of God: 3 “Say to Rehoboam the son of Solomon, king of Judah, and to all Israel in Judah and Benjamin, 4 ‘Thus says the LORD, You shall not go up or fight against your relatives. Return every man to his home, for this thing is from me.’ ” So they listened to the word of the LORD and returned and did not go against Jeroboam.

5 Rehoboam lived in Jerusalem, and he built cities for defense in Judah. 6 He built Bethlehem, Etam, Tekoa, 7 Beth-zur, Soco, Adullam, 8 Gath, Mareshah, Ziph, 9 Adoraim, Lachish, Azekah, 10 Zorah, Aijalon, and Hebron, fortified cities that are in Judah and in Benjamin. 11 He made the fortresses strong, and put commanders in them, and stores of food, oil, and wine. 12 And he put shields and spears in all the cities and made them very strong. So he held Judah and Benjamin.

Priests and Levites Come to Jerusalem

13 And the priests and the Levites who were in all Israel presented themselves to him from all places where they lived. 14 For the Levites left their common lands and their holdings and came to Judah and Jerusalem, because Jeroboam and his sons cast them out from serving as priests of the LORD, 15 and he appointed his own priests for the high places and for the goat idols and for the calves that he had made. 16 And those who had set their hearts to seek the LORD God of Israel came after them from all the tribes of Israel to Jerusalem to sacrifice to the LORD, the God of their fathers. 17 They strengthened the kingdom of Judah, and for three years they made Rehoboam the son of Solomon secure, for they walked for three years in the way of David and Solomon.

Rehoboam's Family

18 Rehoboam took as wife Mahalath the daughter of Jerimoth the son of David, and of Abihail the daughter of Eliab the son of Jesse, 19 and she bore him sons, Jeush, Shemariah, and Zaham. 20 After her he took Maacah the daughter of Absalom, who bore him Abijah, Attai, Ziza, and Shelomith. 21 Rehoboam loved Maacah the daughter of Absalom above all his wives and concubines (he took eighteen wives and sixty concubines, and fathered twenty-eight sons and sixty daughters). 22 And Rehoboam appointed Abijah the son of Maacah as chief prince among his brothers, for he intended to make him king. 23 And he dealt wisely and distributed some of his sons through all the districts of Judah and Benjamin, in all the fortified cities, and he gave them abundant provisions and procured wives for them.[2]

[1] Spelled *Adoram* in 1 Kings 12:18 [2] Hebrew *and sought a multitude of wives*

2 CHRONICLES 11:13–17

CORRUPTED RELIGIOUS SYSTEMS

Jeroboam, the newly appointed king of the northern tribes of Israel, refused to allow the priests and Levites who lived in the north to fulfill their ministry. This act was clearly a violation of the law that gave the priests and Levites their duties in Israel (Nu 18:1–7). Instead, Jeroboam constructed goat and calf idols. Jeroboam also set up his own priests. Therefore, the priests and Levites, along with all the people of the northern kingdom who had set their hearts to seek the Lord, returned to Judah and Jerusalem to worship the true God, Yahweh, in the temple.

During the time of Jesus, the religious system had become so corrupted that the leaders of the Pharisees and other groups had, in effect, stopped worshiping the true God. They elevated their traditions above the truth God had revealed in his law. Jesus highlighted the religious leaders' prioritization of human tradition over obedience to God's law, noting that they neglected caring for their elderly parents in favor of donating funds to the temple (Mk 7:9–13). However, there were leaders whose hearts God stirred, such as Nicodemus who came to seek truth from Jesus (Jn 3:1–2). In order to understand Jesus' person and work, it is vital to recognize that part of Jesus' mission included confronting a religious system that had been completely corrupted.

LISTENING TO WRONG VOICES

The people of Israel asked King Rehoboam to lighten the burden of harsh labor that his father Solomon had placed on them. Rehoboam said he would take three days to come up with an answer. The elders counseled Rehoboam to do as the people requested and thereby win their support. Instead, Rehoboam listened to the counsel of his peers who had grown up with him. They told him to make the labor even harsher and bring the people to their knees. They even used an inappropriate euphemism to suggest that Rehoboam was a bigger and mightier man than his father Solomon. Rehoboam listened to the wrong voices and made a foolish decision. His decision led to the division of Israel into two separate kingdoms — the southern kingdom of Judah and the northern kingdom of Israel.

Rehoboam was the son of the wisest man who had ever lived in Israel, and yet he foolishly listened to his peers rather than his elders. His foolishness not only led to a divided nation but would ultimately lead to the exile itself. Solomon had sought throughout his life to instruct his son in wisdom in Proverbs (Pr 5:1,7; 7:1,24). Solomon wanted to set his son up to rule wisely, but Rehoboam was a fool.

This tragedy points to the need for a new king — a better king — who would rule in wisdom and reunite Israel. That king's name is Jesus of Nazareth. He is the Messiah who is the embodiment of all the wisdom of Proverbs (Pr 1:1 – 7; Isa 11:1 – 3). His wisdom is greater than Solomon's (Mt 12:42). He is the Son who grew in wisdom and stature and favor with God and man (Lk 2:52). And as Ezekiel prophesied, God will someday reunite his scattered and divided people as one nation under one King — a new David who shepherds the people of God (Eze 37:15 – 28). These prophecies form the context for Jesus' words: "I am the good shepherd. The good shepherd lays down his life for the sheep"; and "Holy Father, keep them in your name, which you have given me, that they may be one, even as we are one" (Jn 10:11; 17:11).

Egypt Plunders Jerusalem

12 When the rule of Rehoboam was established and he was strong, he abandoned the law of the LORD, and all Israel with him. 2In the fifth year of King Rehoboam, because they had been unfaithful to the LORD, Shishak king of Egypt came up against Jerusalem 3with 1,200 chariots and 60,000 horsemen. And the people were without number who came with him from Egypt—Libyans, Sukkiim, and Ethiopians. 4And he took the fortified cities of Judah and came as far as Jerusalem. 5Then Shemaiah the prophet came to Rehoboam and to the princes of Judah, who had gathered at Jerusalem because of Shishak, and said to them, "Thus says the LORD, 'You abandoned me, so I have abandoned you to the hand of Shishak.'" 6Then the princes of Israel and the king humbled themselves and said, "The LORD is righteous." 7When the LORD saw that they humbled themselves, the word of the LORD came to Shemaiah: "They have humbled themselves. I will not destroy them, but I will grant them some deliverance, and my wrath shall not be poured out on Jerusalem by the hand of Shishak. 8Nevertheless, they shall be servants to him, that they may know my service and the service of the kingdoms of the countries."

9So Shishak king of Egypt came up against Jerusalem. He took away the treasures of the house of the LORD and the treasures of the king's house. He took away everything. He also took away the shields of gold that Solomon had made, 10and King Rehoboam made in their place shields of bronze and committed them to the hands of the officers of the guard, who kept the door of the king's house. 11And as often as the king went into the house of the LORD, the guard came and carried them and brought them back to the guardroom. 12And when he humbled himself the wrath of the LORD turned from him, so as not to make a complete destruction. Moreover, conditions were good[1] in Judah.

13So King Rehoboam grew strong in Jerusalem and reigned. Rehoboam was forty-one years old when he began to reign, and he reigned seventeen years in Jerusalem, the city that the LORD had chosen out of all the tribes of Israel to put his name there. His mother's name was Naamah the Ammonite. 14And he did evil, for he did not set his heart to seek the LORD.

15Now the acts of Rehoboam, from first to last, are they not written in the chronicles of Shemaiah the prophet and of Iddo the seer?[2] There were continual wars between Rehoboam and Jeroboam. 16And Rehoboam slept with his fathers and was buried in the city of David, and Abijah[3] his son reigned in his place.

Abijah Reigns in Judah

13 In the eighteenth year of King Jeroboam, Abijah began to reign over Judah. 2He reigned for three years in Jerusalem. His mother's name was Micaiah[4] the daughter of Uriel of Gibeah.

Now there was war between Abijah and Jeroboam. 3Abijah went out to battle, having an army of valiant men of war, 400,000 chosen men. And Jeroboam drew up his line of battle against him with 800,000 chosen mighty warriors. 4Then Abijah stood up on Mount Zemaraim that is in the hill country of Ephraim and said, "Hear me, O Jeroboam and all Israel! 5Ought you not to know that the LORD God of Israel gave the kingship over Israel forever to David and his sons by a covenant of salt? 6Yet Jeroboam the son of Nebat, a servant of Solomon the son of David, rose up and rebelled against his lord, 7and certain worthless scoundrels[5] gathered about him and defied Rehoboam the son of Solomon, when Rehoboam was young and irresolute[6] and could not withstand them.

8"And now you think to withstand the kingdom of the LORD in the hand of the sons of David, because you are a great multitude and have with you the golden

2 CHRONICLES 12:1–8

NATIONS AS JUDGMENT

Solomon's son Rehoboam abandoned the laws of God, and in response, God raised up a foreign enemy against him—Shishak, the king of Egypt. Rehoboam and his fellow leaders humbled themselves before the Lord. He gave them a measure of relief but they still faced the consequences of their disobedience: servitude to Egypt. God often used foreign armies to judge his people for their sin: Egypt, Assyria, Babylon, Persia, and more. Deuteronomy made clear that the punishment for forsaking the Lord would be captivity to a foreign army and exile (Dt 28:49–68). The exile would end when the people sought the Lord with their whole hearts (Dt 30:1–3).

In the time of Jesus, Israel was captive to Rome. God used Rome in his plan for Jesus to die for the sins of Israel and the sins of the whole world (Jn 11:49–53). Jesus took humanity's place on the cross. It is only through Jesus that people's hearts can be cleansed of sins and be turned wholly toward the Lord.

[1]Hebrew *good things were found* [2]After *seer*, Hebrew adds *according to genealogy* [3]Spelled *Abijam* in 1 Kings 14:31 [4]Spelled *Maacah* in 1 Kings 15:2 [5]Hebrew *worthless men, sons of Belial* [6]Hebrew *soft of heart*

calves that Jeroboam made you for gods. 9Have you not driven out the priests of
the LORD, the sons of Aaron, and the Levites, and made priests for yourselves like
the peoples of other lands? Whoever comes for ordination[1] with a young bull or
seven rams becomes a priest of what are not gods. 10But as for us, the LORD is our
God, and we have not forsaken him. We have priests ministering to the LORD who
are sons of Aaron, and Levites for their service. 11They offer to the LORD every
morning and every evening burnt offerings and incense of sweet spices, set out
the showbread on the table of pure gold, and care for the golden lampstand that
its lamps may burn every evening. For we keep the charge of the LORD our God,
but you have forsaken him. 12Behold, God is with us at our head, and his priests
with their battle trumpets to sound the call to battle against you. O sons of Israel,
do not fight against the LORD, the God of your fathers, for you cannot succeed."

13Jeroboam had sent an ambush around to come upon them from behind.
Thus his troops[2] were in front of Judah, and the ambush was behind them. 14And
when Judah looked, behold, the battle was in front of and behind them. And
they cried to the LORD, and the priests blew the trumpets. 15Then the men of
Judah raised the battle shout. And when the men of Judah shouted, God defeated
Jeroboam and all Israel before Abijah and Judah. 16The men of Israel fled before
Judah, and God gave them into their hand. 17Abijah and his people struck them
with great force, so there fell slain of Israel 500,000 chosen men. 18Thus the men
of Israel were subdued at that time, and the men of Judah prevailed, because they
relied on the LORD, the God of their fathers. 19And Abijah pursued Jeroboam and
took cities from him, Bethel with its villages and Jeshanah with its villages and
Ephron[3] with its villages. 20Jeroboam did not recover his power in the days of
Abijah. And the LORD struck him down, and he died. 21But Abijah grew mighty.
And he took fourteen wives and had twenty-two sons and sixteen daughters.
22The rest of the acts of Abijah, his ways and his sayings, are written in the story
of the prophet Iddo.

Asa Reigns in Judah

14 [4] Abijah slept with his fathers, and they buried him in the city of David.
And Asa his son reigned in his place. In his days the land had rest for ten
years. 2[5]And Asa did what was good and right in the eyes of the LORD his God. 3He
took away the foreign altars and the high places and broke down the pillars and
cut down the Asherim 4and commanded Judah to seek the LORD, the God of their
fathers, and to keep the law and the commandment. 5He also took out of all the
cities of Judah the high places and the incense altars. And the kingdom had rest
under him. 6He built fortified cities in Judah, for the land had rest. He had no war
in those years, for the LORD gave him peace. 7And he said to Judah, "Let us build
these cities and surround them with walls and towers, gates and bars. The land is
still ours, because we have sought the LORD our God. We have sought him, and he
has given us peace on every side." So they built and prospered. 8And Asa had an
army of 300,000 from Judah, armed with large shields and spears, and 280,000
men from Benjamin that carried shields and drew bows. All these were mighty
men of valor.

9Zerah the Ethiopian came out against them with an army of a million men
and 300 chariots, and came as far as Mareshah. 10And Asa went out to meet him,
and they drew up their lines of battle in the Valley of Zephathah at Mareshah.
11And Asa cried to the LORD his God, "O LORD, there is none like you to help, between the mighty and the weak. Help us, O LORD our God, for we rely on you, and
in your name we have come against this multitude. O LORD, you are our God; let
not man prevail against you." 12So the LORD defeated the Ethiopians before Asa
and before Judah, and the Ethiopians fled. 13Asa and the people who were with
him pursued them as far as Gerar, and the Ethiopians fell until none remained

[1]Hebrew *to fill his hand* [2]Hebrew *they* [3]Or *Ephrain* [4]Ch 13:23 in Hebrew [5]Ch 14:1 in Hebrew

2 CHRONICLES 14:2–15

THE SAVING KING

The background to the life and reign of King Asa is the covenant that God made with David. God promised David an eternal dynasty with rest and peace from his enemies (2Sa 7:8–16). But, there was a condition to the covenant. If David's sons would be faithful, then they would be blessed, but if they were unfaithful, then God would punish them (2Sa 7:14). Because Asa walked in the ways of the Lord, the Lord blessed him. Asa began his reign by ridding the land of idolatry, so the Lord granted him victory over his enemies and many years of peace. Zerah the Ethiopian marched against King Asa and Judah with "an army of a million men" (2Ch 14:9). But even though they were outnumbered, Asa humbly relied upon the Lord, and the Lord granted them victory. The Lord used Asa as a warrior-king to save his people from a marauding enemy. The Bible presents Jesus as the Warrior-King who defeats his people's enemies—Satan, sin, and death—and rescues them (cf. Ge 3:15; Rev 19:11–21).

alive, for they were broken before the LORD and his army. The men of Judah[1] carried away very much spoil. 14 And they attacked all the cities around Gerar, for the
fear of the LORD was upon them. They plundered all the cities, for there was much
plunder in them. 15 And they struck down the tents of those who had livestock and
carried away sheep in abundance and camels. Then they returned to Jerusalem.

Asa's Religious Reforms

15 The Spirit of God came[2] upon Azariah the son of Oded, 2 and he went out
to meet Asa and said to him, "Hear me, Asa, and all Judah and Benjamin:
The LORD is with you while you are with him. If you seek him, he will be found by
you, but if you forsake him, he will forsake you. 3 For a long time Israel was without
the true God, and without a teaching priest and without law, 4 but when in their
distress they turned to the LORD, the God of Israel, and sought him, he was found
by them. 5 In those times there was no peace to him who went out or to him who
came in, for great disturbances afflicted all the inhabitants of the lands. 6 They
were broken in pieces. Nation was crushed by nation and city by city, for God
troubled them with every sort of distress. 7 But you, take courage! Do not let your
hands be weak, for your work shall be rewarded."

8 As soon as Asa heard these words, the prophecy of Azariah the son of Oded,
he took courage and put away the detestable idols from all the land of Judah and
Benjamin and from the cities that he had taken in the hill country of Ephraim,
and he repaired the altar of the LORD that was in front of the vestibule of the
house of the LORD.[3] 9 And he gathered all Judah and Benjamin, and those from
Ephraim, Manasseh, and Simeon who were residing with them, for great numbers
had deserted to him from Israel when they saw that the LORD his God was with
him. 10 They were gathered at Jerusalem in the third month of the fifteenth year
of the reign of Asa. 11 They sacrificed to the LORD on that day from the spoil that
they had brought 700 oxen and 7,000 sheep. 12 And they entered into a covenant
to seek the LORD, the God of their fathers, with all their heart and with all their
soul, 13 but that whoever would not seek the LORD, the God of Israel, should be
put to death, whether young or old, man or woman. 14 They swore an oath to the
LORD with a loud voice and with shouting and with trumpets and with horns.
15 And all Judah rejoiced over the oath, for they had sworn with all their heart and
had sought him with their whole desire, and he was found by them, and the LORD
gave them rest all around.

16 Even Maacah, his mother, King Asa removed from being queen mother because she had made a detestable image for Asherah. Asa cut down her image,
crushed it, and burned it at the brook Kidron. 17 But the high places were not taken
out of Israel. Nevertheless, the heart of Asa was wholly true all his days. 18 And he
brought into the house of God the sacred gifts of his father and his own sacred
gifts, silver, and gold, and vessels. 19 And there was no more war until the thirty-
fifth year of the reign of Asa.

2 CHRONICLES 15:1–19

REVIVAL AND THE WORD

The Spirit of God came upon the prophet Azariah, and he preached the word of God to King Asa. Asa applied the preaching of God's prophet, and it led to an incredible revival. Asa implemented everything the prophet said. He put away the idols and he renewed the covenant with the Lord. He also began to reunify Israel: many people from the northern tribes came down to join with Judah because they saw that God was with Asa (15:9). As a part of this spiritual renewal, Asa even removed his mother "from being queen mother because she had made a detestable image for Asherah" (v. 16).

All of this points to Jesus. Jesus was the one anointed by the Spirit of God (Mt 3:16). Jesus was the final prophet and the final word from God (Heb 1:1–2). Jesus inaugurated the new covenant (Jer 31:31–33; Mt 26:28). And renewal by Jesus may mean severing ties with family members. Jesus said, "If anyone comes to me and does not hate his own father and mother and wife and children and brothers and sisters, yes, and even his own life, he cannot be my disciple" (Lk 14:26).

Asa's Last Years

16 In the thirty-sixth year of the reign of Asa, Baasha king of Israel went up
against Judah and built Ramah, that he might permit no one to go out or
come in to Asa king of Judah. 2 Then Asa took silver and gold from the treasures
of the house of the LORD and the king's house and sent them to Ben-hadad king
of Syria, who lived in Damascus, saying, 3 "There is a covenant[4] between me and
you, as there was between my father and your father. Behold, I am sending to
you silver and gold. Go, break your covenant with Baasha king of Israel, that he
may withdraw from me." 4 And Ben-hadad listened to King Asa and sent the commanders of his armies against the cities of Israel, and they conquered Ijon, Dan,
Abel-maim, and all the store cities of Naphtali. 5 And when Baasha heard of it, he

[1]Hebrew *They* [2]Or *was* [3]Hebrew *the vestibule of the LORD* [4]Or *treaty*; twice in this verse

stopped building Ramah and let his work cease. 6Then King Asa took all Judah,
and they carried away the stones of Ramah and its timber, with which Baasha had
been building, and with them he built Geba and Mizpah.
7At that time Hanani the seer came to Asa king of Judah and said to him, "Because you relied on the king of Syria, and did not rely on the LORD your God,
the army of the king of Syria has escaped you. 8Were not the Ethiopians and the
Libyans a huge army with very many chariots and horsemen? Yet because you
relied on the LORD, he gave them into your hand. 9For the eyes of the LORD run to
and fro throughout the whole earth, to give strong support to those whose heart
is blameless[1] toward him. You have done foolishly in this, for from now on you
will have wars." 10Then Asa was angry with the seer and put him in the stocks in
prison, for he was in a rage with him because of this. And Asa inflicted cruelties
upon some of the people at the same time.
11The acts of Asa, from first to last, are written in the Book of the Kings of
Judah and Israel. 12In the thirty-ninth year of his reign Asa was diseased in his
feet, and his disease became severe. Yet even in his disease he did not seek the
LORD, but sought help from physicians. 13And Asa slept with his fathers, dying
in the forty-first year of his reign. 14They buried him in the tomb that he had cut
for himself in the city of David. They laid him on a bier that had been filled with
various kinds of spices prepared by the perfumer's art, and they made a very great
fire in his honor.

Jehoshaphat Reigns in Judah

17 Jehoshaphat his son reigned in his place and strengthened himself against
Israel. 2He placed forces in all the fortified cities of Judah and set garrisons
in the land of Judah, and in the cities of Ephraim that Asa his father had captured. 3The LORD was with Jehoshaphat, because he walked in the earlier ways
of his father David. He did not seek the Baals, 4but sought the God of his father
and walked in his commandments, and not according to the practices of Israel.
5Therefore the LORD established the kingdom in his hand. And all Judah brought
tribute to Jehoshaphat, and he had great riches and honor. 6His heart was courageous in the ways of the LORD. And furthermore, he took the high places and the
Asherim out of Judah.
7In the third year of his reign he sent his officials, Ben-hail, Obadiah, Zechariah, Nethanel, and Micaiah, to teach in the cities of Judah; 8and with them the
Levites, Shemaiah, Nethaniah, Zebadiah, Asahel, Shemiramoth, Jehonathan,
Adonijah, Tobijah, and Tobadonijah; and with these Levites, the priests Elishama
and Jehoram. 9And they taught in Judah, having the Book of the Law of the LORD
with them. They went about through all the cities of Judah and taught among
the people.
10And the fear of the LORD fell upon all the kingdoms of the lands that were
around Judah, and they made no war against Jehoshaphat. 11Some of the Philistines brought Jehoshaphat presents and silver for tribute, and the Arabians also
brought him 7,700 rams and 7,700 goats. 12And Jehoshaphat grew steadily greater.
He built in Judah fortresses and store cities, 13and he had large supplies in the
cities of Judah. He had soldiers, mighty men of valor, in Jerusalem. 14This was
the muster of them by fathers' houses: Of Judah, the commanders of thousands:
Adnah the commander, with 300,000 mighty men of valor; 15and next to him
Jehohanan the commander, with 280,000; 16and next to him Amasiah the son of
Zichri, a volunteer for the service of the LORD, with 200,000 mighty men of valor.
17Of Benjamin: Eliada, a mighty man of valor, with 200,000 men armed with bow
and shield; 18and next to him Jehozabad with 180,000 armed for war. 19These were
in the service of the king, besides those whom the king had placed in the fortified
cities throughout all Judah.

[1] Or *whole*

2 CHRONICLES 16:9

HEARTS FULLY COMMITTED TO GOD

King Asa began his reign fully relying on God, and God granted him victory over his enemies as a result. However, Asa ended his reign relying on humans instead of God. That sad fact ultimately ruined his kingdom. King Baasha of Israel (the northern kingdom) came against Asa and Judah (the southern kingdom). Instead of relying on God for the victory, Asa made a treaty with Syria — giving the treasures of the temple to King Ben-hadad. Hanani the prophet condemned Asa for his actions, pointing out that when Asa had relied on the Lord, Asa had defeated a much mightier Ethiopian army. Hanani, after reminding Asa that the all-seeing God looks for those who rely fully on him and strengthens them, gave this judgment: "You have done foolishly in this, for from now on you will have wars" (v. 9). Because of Asa's sin, he would no longer have rest and peace. Believers today, no less than ancient Israel, need a King whose heart is fully reliant on God and thus brings lasting peace. In contrast to Asa and every other person, Jesus lived on earth as a man fully committed to God, remaining obedient at every point. As a result, he is the King who is the Prince of Peace (Isa 9:6).

2 CHRONICLES 16:11–14

A BETTER KING

Because Asa had rejected God, his reign ended with disease and death. His reign began with such promise, but ended in failure. Every descendant of David failed at some point, but that strengthened the hope

(continued on page 623)

THE STREAMING NATIONS

King Jehoshaphat began his reign by ridding the land of idolatry and reestablishing instruction in God's Word. As a result, the fear of the Lord fell on the nations that surrounded Judah so that they did not make war with Jehoshaphat. These foreign peoples came bringing treasure to King Jehoshaphat. Philistines and Arabs brought tribute gifts to him. Something similar had happened during the reign of Solomon. The nations were in awe of Solomon's wisdom and wanted to be associated with God's blessings in Solomon's life, so they brought tribute gifts to him (1Ki 10:23–25).

The Old Testament promised that what happened with Solomon and Jehoshaphat would happen in a greater way in the future. Isaiah prophesied that the nations would stream to Zion in order to learn the ways of God (Isa 2:2–3). Psalm 72:10–11 foretold that foreign kings would bring gifts to the Messiah and bow down before him, and Isaiah said those gifts would include incense and gold (Isa 60:6). According to Zechariah 8:23, "In those days ten men from the nations of every tongue shall take hold of the robe of a Jew, saying, 'Let us go with you, for we have heard that God is with you.'"

Matthew 2:11 shows the fulfillment of these prophecies when the wise men brought gold, frankincense, and myrrh to the young king. Matthew 8:5–13 also shows the fulfillment of these prophecies when Jesus blessed a Gentile centurion because of his faith. And Revelation 21:24 predicts the final fulfillment of these promises when the kings of the earth bring their splendor into the new Jerusalem. What happened in the reign of King Jehoshaphat was just a preview—a glimpse—of what will happen when Jesus reigns once and for all! Right now nations are streaming to King Jesus as the gospel is preached among the previously unreached through the church's obedience to the Great Commission (Mt 28:18–20). The nations bow to Jesus, and they offer more than just their gifts—they offer their lives (Ro 12:1).

Jehoshaphat Allies with Ahab

18 Now Jehoshaphat had great riches and honor, and he made a marriage alliance with Ahab. 2After some years he went down to Ahab in Samaria. And Ahab killed an abundance of sheep and oxen for him and for the people who were with him, and induced him to go up against Ramoth-gilead. 3Ahab king of Israel said to Jehoshaphat king of Judah, "Will you go with me to Ramoth-gilead?" He answered him, "I am as you are, my people as your people. We will be with you in the war."

4And Jehoshaphat said to the king of Israel, "Inquire first for the word of the LORD." 5Then the king of Israel gathered the prophets together, four hundred men, and said to them, "Shall we go to battle against Ramoth-gilead, or shall I refrain?" And they said, "Go up, for God will give it into the hand of the king." 6But Jehoshaphat said, "Is there not here another prophet of the LORD of whom we may inquire?" 7And the king of Israel said to Jehoshaphat, "There is yet one man by whom we may inquire of the LORD, Micaiah the son of Imlah; but I hate him, for he never prophesies good concerning me, but always evil." And Jehoshaphat said, "Let not the king say so." 8Then the king of Israel summoned an officer and said, "Bring quickly Micaiah the son of Imlah." 9Now the king of Israel and Jehoshaphat the king of Judah were sitting on their thrones, arrayed in their robes. And they were sitting at the threshing floor at the entrance of the gate of Samaria, and all the prophets were prophesying before them. 10And Zedekiah the son of Chenaanah made for himself horns of iron and said, "Thus says the LORD, 'With these you shall push the Syrians until they are destroyed.'" 11And all the prophets prophesied so and said, "Go up to Ramoth-gilead and triumph. The LORD will give it into the hand of the king."

12And the messenger who went to summon Micaiah said to him, "Behold, the words of the prophets with one accord are favorable to the king. Let your word be like the word of one of them, and speak favorably." 13But Micaiah said, "As the LORD lives, what my God says, that I will speak." 14And when he had come to the king, the king said to him, "Micaiah, shall we go to Ramoth-gilead to battle, or shall I refrain?" And he answered, "Go up and triumph; they will be given into your hand." 15But the king said to him, "How many times shall I make you swear that you speak to me nothing but the truth in the name of the LORD?" 16And he said, "I saw all Israel scattered on the mountains, as sheep that have no shepherd. And the LORD said, 'These have no master; let each return to his home in peace.'" 17And the king of Israel said to Jehoshaphat, "Did I not tell you that he would not prophesy good concerning me, but evil?" 18And Micaiah said, "Therefore hear the word of the LORD: I saw the LORD sitting on his throne, and all the host of heaven standing on his right hand and on his left. 19And the LORD said, 'Who will entice Ahab the king of Israel, that he may go up and fall at Ramoth-gilead?' And one said one thing, and another said another. 20Then a spirit came forward and stood before the LORD, saying, 'I will entice him.' And the LORD said to him, 'By what means?' 21And he said, 'I will go out, and will be a lying spirit in the mouth of all his prophets.' And he said, 'You are to entice him, and you shall succeed; go out and do so.' 22Now therefore behold, the LORD has put a lying spirit in the mouth of these your prophets. The LORD has declared disaster concerning you."

23Then Zedekiah the son of Chenaanah came near and struck Micaiah on the cheek and said, "Which way did the Spirit of the LORD go from me to speak to you?" 24And Micaiah said, "Behold, you shall see on that day when you go into an inner chamber to hide yourself." 25And the king of Israel said, "Seize Micaiah and take him back to Amon the governor of the city and to Joash the king's son, 26and say, 'Thus says the king, Put this fellow in prison and feed him with meager rations of bread and water until I return in peace.'" 27And Micaiah said, "If you return in peace, the LORD has not spoken by me." And he said, "Hear, all you peoples!"

(A Better King, continued)

for a King who did not end up rotting in a tomb under the curse of sin (cf. Ps 16:9–11). When Asa's life ended, he was buried, along with spices and perfumes, "in the tomb that he had cut for himself" (2Ch 16:14). However, one Son of David did not need to prepare a tomb for himself; he merely borrowed one for three days. When women came to anoint him with spices as had been done with previous kings, they found only his grave clothes.

Jesus could have relied on the flesh when he was tempted to eat in the wilderness after forty days of fasting or to escape the cross's suffering. But he fully relied on God, and three days later he walked away from death as David's descendant who reigns eternally. So Peter preached, "I may say to you with confidence about the patriarch David that he both died and was buried, and his tomb is with us to this day. Being therefore a prophet, and knowing that God had sworn with an oath to him that he would set one of his descendants on his throne, he foresaw and spoke about the resurrection of the Christ, that he was not abandoned to Hades, nor did his flesh see corruption" (Ac 2:29–31).

2 CHRONICLES 17:7–9

THE WORD PREACHED

The Lord was with King Jehoshaphat because he followed the example of his father David (v. 3). Not only did Jehoshaphat refuse to follow the Baals, but he was also a man of the law — the Word of God. The ideal king — like David early on — was a man who committed himself to God's law (cf. Dt 17:18–19). One of the ways that Jehoshaphat ordered and established his kingdom was by

(continued on next page)

(The Word Preached, continued)

sending out officials, Levites, and priests to every town in Judah to teach the law of God. King Jesus did the same thing in his ministry. Luke 10:1 says, "After this the Lord appointed seventy-two others and sent them on ahead of him, two by two, into every town and place where he himself was about to go." They were sent out to teach about the kingdom of God (Lk 10:9). The teaching of the Word of God is critical to the kingdom of Christ and its advancement. As the Word spreads, the church grows (Ac 6:7; 12:24; 19:20).

2 CHRONICLES 18:1–27

THE REJECTED PROPHET

It could be easy to get caught up in the details of this passage, confused about the mention of an enticing spirit, and miss the point. King Jehoshaphat entered an unholy alliance with the wicked King Ahab of Israel, and they decided to go to battle against the Syrians. However, Jehoshaphat at least had enough sense to request counsel from a true prophet of Yahweh before they went to war. Ahab didn't like the prophet Micaiah because Micaiah always spoke against Ahab. True to form, Micaiah prophesied for God that Ahab would die in battle. In response, Zedekiah, one of Ahab's four hundred prophets, struck Micaiah on the cheek and mocked him. Finally, Ahab had Micaiah thrown in jail.

Micaiah's ministry points to Jesus' ministry as the true but rejected *prophet of the Lord. Like Micaiah*, Jesus was struck on the cheek and mocked (Mt 26:67–68). Like Micaiah, Jesus was seized for his message and put in captivity. And yet,

(continued on next page)

The Defeat and Death of Ahab

28So the king of Israel and Jehoshaphat the king of Judah went up to Ramoth-gilead. 29And the king of Israel said to Jehoshaphat, "I will disguise myself and go into battle, but you wear your robes." And the king of Israel disguised himself, and they went into battle. 30Now the king of Syria had commanded the captains of his chariots, "Fight with neither small nor great, but only with the king of Israel." 31As soon as the captains of the chariots saw Jehoshaphat, they said, "It is the king of Israel." So they turned to fight against him. And Jehoshaphat cried out, and the LORD helped him; God drew them away from him. 32For as soon as the captains of the chariots saw that it was not the king of Israel, they turned back from pursuing him. 33But a certain man drew his bow at random[1] and struck the king of Israel between the scale armor and the breastplate. Therefore he said to the driver of his chariot, "Turn around and carry me out of the battle, for I am wounded." 34And the battle continued that day, and the king of Israel was propped up in his chariot facing the Syrians until evening. Then at sunset he died.

Jehoshaphat's Reforms

19 Jehoshaphat the king of Judah returned in safety to his house in Jerusalem. 2But Jehu the son of Hanani the seer went out to meet him and said to King Jehoshaphat, "Should you help the wicked and love those who hate the LORD? Because of this, wrath has gone out against you from the LORD. 3Nevertheless, some good is found in you, for you destroyed the Asheroth out of the land, and have set your heart to seek God."

4Jehoshaphat lived at Jerusalem. And he went out again among the people, from Beersheba to the hill country of Ephraim, and brought them back to the LORD, the God of their fathers. 5He appointed judges in the land in all the fortified cities of Judah, city by city, 6and said to the judges, "Consider what you do, for you judge not for man but for the LORD. He is with you in giving judgment. 7Now then, let the fear of the LORD be upon you. Be careful what you do, for there is no injustice with the LORD our God, or partiality or taking bribes."

8Moreover, in Jerusalem Jehoshaphat appointed certain Levites and priests and heads of families of Israel, to give judgment for the LORD and to decide disputed cases. They had their seat at Jerusalem. 9And he charged them: "Thus you shall do in the fear of the LORD, in faithfulness, and with your whole heart: 10whenever a case comes to you from your brothers who live in their cities, concerning bloodshed, law or commandment, statutes or rules, then you shall warn them, that they may not incur guilt before the LORD and wrath may not come upon you and your brothers. Thus you shall do, and you will not incur guilt. 11And behold, Amariah the chief priest is over you in all matters of the LORD; and Zebadiah the son of Ishmael, the governor of the house of Judah, in all the king's matters, and the Levites will serve you as officers. Deal courageously, and may the LORD be with the upright!"[2]

Jehoshaphat's Prayer

20 After this the Moabites and Ammonites, and with them some of the Meunites,[3] came against Jehoshaphat for battle. 2Some men came and told Jehoshaphat, "A great multitude is coming against you from Edom,[4] from beyond the sea; and, behold, they are in Hazazon-tamar" (that is, Engedi). 3Then Jehoshaphat was afraid and set his face to seek the LORD, and proclaimed a fast throughout all Judah. 4And Judah assembled to seek help from the LORD; from all the cities of Judah they came to seek the LORD.

5And Jehoshaphat stood in the assembly of Judah and Jerusalem, in the house of the LORD, before the new court, 6and said, "O LORD, God of our fathers, are you not God in heaven? You rule over all the kingdoms of the nations. In your hand

[1] Hebrew *in his innocence* [2] Hebrew *the good* [3] Compare 26:7; Hebrew *Ammonites* [4] One Hebrew manuscript; most Hebrew manuscripts *Aram* (Syria)

are power and might, so that none is able to withstand you. 7Did you not, our
God, drive out the inhabitants of this land before your people Israel, and give it
forever to the descendants of Abraham your friend? 8And they have lived in it
and have built for you in it a sanctuary for your name, saying, 9'If disaster comes
upon us, the sword, judgment,[1] or pestilence, or famine, we will stand before this
house and before you—for your name is in this house—and cry out to you in our
affliction, and you will hear and save.' 10And now behold, the men of Ammon
and Moab and Mount Seir, whom you would not let Israel invade when they came
from the land of Egypt, and whom they avoided and did not destroy— 11behold,
they reward us by coming to drive us out of your possession, which you have
given us to inherit. 12O our God, will you not execute judgment on them? For we
are powerless against this great horde that is coming against us. We do not know
what to do, but our eyes are on you."

13Meanwhile all Judah stood before the LORD, with their little ones, their wives,
and their children. 14And the Spirit of the LORD came[2] upon Jahaziel the son of
Zechariah, son of Benaiah, son of Jeiel, son of Mattaniah, a Levite of the sons of
Asaph, in the midst of the assembly. 15And he said, "Listen, all Judah and inhabitants of Jerusalem and King Jehoshaphat: Thus says the LORD to you, 'Do not be
afraid and do not be dismayed at this great horde, for the battle is not yours but
God's. 16Tomorrow go down against them. Behold, they will come up by the ascent
of Ziz. You will find them at the end of the valley, east of the wilderness of Jeruel.
17You will not need to fight in this battle. Stand firm, hold your position, and see the
salvation of the LORD on your behalf, O Judah and Jerusalem.' Do not be afraid and
do not be dismayed. Tomorrow go out against them, and the LORD will be with you."

18Then Jehoshaphat bowed his head with his face to the ground, and all Judah and the inhabitants of Jerusalem fell down before the LORD, worshiping the
LORD. 19And the Levites, of the Kohathites and the Korahites, stood up to praise
the LORD, the God of Israel, with a very loud voice.

20And they rose early in the morning and went out into the wilderness of
Tekoa. And when they went out, Jehoshaphat stood and said, "Hear me, Judah
and inhabitants of Jerusalem! Believe in the LORD your God, and you will be established; believe his prophets, and you will succeed." 21And when he had taken
counsel with the people, he appointed those who were to sing to the LORD and
praise him in holy attire, as they went before the army, and say,

"Give thanks to the LORD,
for his steadfast love endures forever."

22And when they began to sing and praise, the LORD set an ambush against the
men of Ammon, Moab, and Mount Seir, who had come against Judah, so that they
were routed. 23For the men of Ammon and Moab rose against the inhabitants of
Mount Seir, devoting them to destruction, and when they had made an end of the
inhabitants of Seir, they all helped to destroy one another.

The LORD Delivers Judah

24When Judah came to the watchtower of the wilderness, they looked toward
the horde, and behold, there[3] were dead bodies lying on the ground; none had
escaped. 25When Jehoshaphat and his people came to take their spoil, they found
among them, in great numbers, goods, clothing, and precious things, which they
took for themselves until they could carry no more. They were three days in taking the spoil, it was so much. 26On the fourth day they assembled in the Valley of
Beracah,[4] for there they blessed the LORD. Therefore the name of that place has
been called the Valley of Beracah to this day. 27Then they returned, every man
of Judah and Jerusalem, and Jehoshaphat at their head, returning to Jerusalem
with joy, for the LORD had made them rejoice over their enemies. 28They came to

[1]Or *the sword of judgment* [2]Or *was* [3]Hebrew *they* [4]*Beracah* means *blessing*

(The Rejected Prophet, continued)

God's rejected prophets are always vindicated. Micaiah was vindicated when Ahab fell on the battlefield. And Jesus' words that his opponents would see him coming on the clouds of heaven will be vindicated at his second coming—with power and glory (Mt 24:30; 26:64).

2 CHRONICLES 20:5–12

PRAYER FOR DELIVERANCE

When the Moabites and the Ammonites came against Judah, the people gathered for prayer. This action displayed trust in promises God had given to Solomon in response to Solomon's temple dedication prayer (2Ch 7:11–16). In that prayer, Solomon had prayed that God would hear the cries of his people when they faced the temple (2Ch 6:14–42). In fact, Solomon had specifically prayed that whenever disaster or a foreign army came against Israel, the people should stand before God at the temple and cry to him for salvation.

In his prayer (known as the Lord's Prayer), Jesus similarly trained his disciples to pray that they would be "deliver[ed] ... from evil" (Mt 6:9–13). The New Testament reminds believers that the enemy is not "flesh and blood" (Eph 6:12) and that they can place their hope in Christ since he is in control and has placed all enemies under his feet (1Co 15:25; Eph 1:22).

Jerusalem with harps and lyres and trumpets, to the house of the LORD. 29And the fear of God came on all the kingdoms of the countries when they heard that the LORD had fought against the enemies of Israel. 30So the realm of Jehoshaphat was quiet, for his God gave him rest all around.

31Thus Jehoshaphat reigned over Judah. He was thirty-five years old when he began to reign, and he reigned twenty-five years in Jerusalem. His mother's name was Azubah the daughter of Shilhi. 32He walked in the way of Asa his father and did not turn aside from it, doing what was right in the sight of the LORD. 33The high places, however, were not taken away; the people had not yet set their hearts upon the God of their fathers.

34Now the rest of the acts of Jehoshaphat, from first to last, are written in the chronicles of Jehu the son of Hanani, which are recorded in the Book of the Kings of Israel.

The End of Jehoshaphat's Reign

35After this Jehoshaphat king of Judah joined with Ahaziah king of Israel, who acted wickedly. 36He joined him in building ships to go to Tarshish, and they built the ships in Ezion-geber. 37Then Eliezer the son of Dodavahu of Mareshah prophesied against Jehoshaphat, saying, "Because you have joined with Ahaziah, the LORD will destroy what you have made." And the ships were wrecked and were not able to go to Tarshish.

Jehoram Reigns in Judah

21 Jehoshaphat slept with his fathers and was buried with his fathers in the city of David, and Jehoram his son reigned in his place. 2He had brothers, the sons of Jehoshaphat: Azariah, Jehiel, Zechariah, Azariah, Michael, and Shephatiah; all these were the sons of Jehoshaphat king of Israel.[1] 3Their father gave them great gifts of silver, gold, and valuable possessions, together with fortified cities in Judah, but he gave the kingdom to Jehoram, because he was the firstborn. 4When Jehoram had ascended the throne of his father and was established, he killed all his brothers with the sword, and also some of the princes of Israel. 5Jehoram was thirty-two years old when he became king, and he reigned eight years in Jerusalem. 6And he walked in the way of the kings of Israel, as the house of Ahab had done, for the daughter of Ahab was his wife. And he did what was evil in the sight of the LORD. 7Yet the LORD was not willing to destroy the house of David, because of the covenant that he had made with David, and since he had promised to give a lamp to him and to his sons forever.

8In his days Edom revolted from the rule of Judah and set up a king of their own. 9Then Jehoram passed over with his commanders and all his chariots, and he rose by night and struck the Edomites who had surrounded him and his chariot commanders. 10So Edom revolted from the rule of Judah to this day. At that time Libnah also revolted from his rule, because he had forsaken the LORD, the God of his fathers.

11Moreover, he made high places in the hill country of Judah and led the inhabitants of Jerusalem into whoredom and made Judah go astray. 12And a letter came to him from Elijah the prophet, saying, "Thus says the LORD, the God of David your father, 'Because you have not walked in the ways of Jehoshaphat your father, or in the ways of Asa king of Judah, 13but have walked in the way of the kings of Israel and have enticed Judah and the inhabitants of Jerusalem into whoredom, as the house of Ahab led Israel into whoredom, and also you have killed your brothers, of your father's house, who were better than you, 14behold, the LORD will bring a great plague on your people, your children, your wives, and all your possessions, 15and you yourself will have a severe sickness with a disease of your bowels, until your bowels come out because of the disease, day by day.'"

[1]That is, Judah

WORSHIP AS WARFARE

Armies from Moab and Ammon came against King Jehoshaphat and Judah. The Spirit came on a Levite named Jahaziel. He told the people not to be afraid because the Lord would deliver them in battle, and the people would not have to lift a weapon. Instead, they were to stand still and watch God save them. Then, something amazing happened. The army held a worship service where singers went out in front of the army praising God for the splendor of his holiness. As they sang praises, God destroyed the enemy army! When Judah's army finally got to the spot, they found only dead bodies, and it took three days to carry away all of the plunder.

This victory pointed forward to Jesus Christ. Jesus defeated his people's enemies on their behalf (Heb 2:14 – 15; 10:13). And, like the Old Testament saints, believers today engage in worship as warfare against the enemies — not against "flesh and blood, but against the rulers, against the authorities, against the cosmic powers over this present darkness, against the spiritual forces of evil in the heavenly places" (Eph 6:12). Worship was seen as warfare throughout the Bible. Worship is described in the Old Testament as "appearing before God," which gave the imagery of an army assembling for inspection by the commanding officer. After all, God responded to the prayers of his people by defeating Egypt (Ex 3:7 – 10). And, the trumpet-led worship service at Jericho caused the walls to fall down (Jos 6:20).

In worship gatherings today, the people do not gather at Mount Sinai, but rather they gather spiritually at Mount Zion, surrounded by innumerable angels and the redeemed of all the ages (Heb 12:22 – 23). And as they worship the Lord he thunders from heaven, promising that he is in the process of establishing a kingdom that cannot be shaken. When God talked about his judgment at the end of the age, he pointed to the story of Jehoshaphat (Joel 3:1 – 2,12 – 13). The book of Hebrews further confirms the connection between worship and that day of judgment. God — a consuming fire who devours the enemy and rescues his people — will someday go to war in the final judgment in response to the church's worship (Heb 12:25 – 29; cf. Rev 8:3 – 5).

16 And the LORD stirred up against Jehoram the anger[1] of the Philistines and of the Arabians who are near the Ethiopians. 17 And they came up against Judah and invaded it and carried away all the possessions they found that belonged to the king's house, and also his sons and his wives, so that no son was left to him except Jehoahaz, his youngest son.

18 And after all this the LORD struck him in his bowels with an incurable disease. 19 In the course of time, at the end of two years, his bowels came out because of the disease, and he died in great agony. His people made no fire in his honor, like the fires made for his fathers. 20 He was thirty-two years old when he began to reign, and he reigned eight years in Jerusalem. And he departed with no one's regret. They buried him in the city of David, but not in the tombs of the kings.

Ahaziah Reigns in Judah

22 And the inhabitants of Jerusalem made Ahaziah, his youngest son, king in his place, for the band of men that came with the Arabians to the camp had killed all the older sons. So Ahaziah the son of Jehoram king of Judah reigned. 2 Ahaziah was twenty-two[2] years old when he began to reign, and he reigned one year in Jerusalem. His mother's name was Athaliah, the granddaughter of Omri. 3 He also walked in the ways of the house of Ahab, for his mother was his counselor in doing wickedly. 4 He did what was evil in the sight of the LORD, as the house of Ahab had done. For after the death of his father they were his counselors, to his undoing. 5 He even followed their counsel and went with Jehoram the son of Ahab king of Israel to make war against Hazael king of Syria at Ramoth-gilead. And the Syrians wounded Joram, 6 and he returned to be healed in Jezreel of the wounds that he had received at Ramah, when he fought against Hazael king of Syria. And Ahaziah the son of Jehoram king of Judah went down to see Joram the son of Ahab in Jezreel, because he was wounded.

7 But it was ordained by[3] God that the downfall of Ahaziah should come about through his going to visit Joram. For when he came there, he went out with Jehoram to meet Jehu the son of Nimshi, whom the LORD had anointed to destroy the house of Ahab. 8 And when Jehu was executing judgment on the house of Ahab, he met the princes of Judah and the sons of Ahaziah's brothers, who attended Ahaziah, and he killed them. 9 He searched for Ahaziah, and he was captured while hiding in Samaria, and he was brought to Jehu and put to death. They buried him, for they said, "He is the grandson of Jehoshaphat, who sought the LORD with all his heart." And the house of Ahaziah had no one able to rule the kingdom.

Athaliah Reigns in Judah

10 Now when Athaliah the mother of Ahaziah saw that her son was dead, she arose and destroyed all the royal family of the house of Judah. 11 But Jehoshabeath,[4] the daughter of the king, took Joash the son of Ahaziah and stole him away from among the king's sons who were about to be put to death, and she put him and his nurse in a bedroom. Thus Jehoshabeath, the daughter of King Jehoram and wife of Jehoiada the priest, because she was a sister of Ahaziah, hid him[5] from Athaliah, so that she did not put him to death. 12 And he remained with them six years, hidden in the house of God, while Athaliah reigned over the land.

Joash Made King

23 But in the seventh year Jehoiada took courage and entered into a covenant with the commanders of hundreds, Azariah the son of Jeroham, Ishmael the son of Jehohanan, Azariah the son of Obed, Maaseiah the son of Adaiah, and Elishaphat the son of Zichri. 2 And they went about through Judah and gathered the Levites from all the cities of Judah, and the heads of fathers' houses of Israel, and they came to Jerusalem. 3 And all the assembly made a covenant with the king

[1] Hebrew *spirit* [2] See 2 Kings 8:26; Hebrew *forty-two*; Septuagint *twenty* [3] Hebrew *was from* [4] Spelled *Jehosheba* in 2 Kings 11:2 [5] That is, Joash

THE HIDDEN SAVIOR

When the wicked Athaliah saw that her son Ahaziah was dead, she attempted to murder all of his sons, but Joash was hidden away. The background to this story was the promise of offspring. In Genesis 3:15, God promised a war between the serpent's offspring and the woman's offspring. That meant there would be a great cosmic war throughout history where Satan would attempt to wipe out the line of the Messiah before the Savior came. He moved Cain to murder Abel (Ge 4:1 – 16), Pharaoh to kill the Hebrew males (Ex 1:8 – 22), Haman to attempt to exterminate the Jews in the book of Esther, and Herod to attempt to kill Jesus (Mt 2:13 – 18). This passage in 2 Chronicles would have seemed familiar to the post-exilic Jews. The account of a wicked tyrant attempting to kill many sons, one of whom was hidden and preserved, reminded the text's original audience of the ongoing war between the serpent's offspring and the woman's. And it pointed forward to Jesus who was hidden from Herod and who later saved the world from its sin.

Athaliah attempted to kill all of David's royal descendants, which would have put an end to God's promise that a descendant of David would establish an eternal kingdom (2Sa 7:4 – 17). Her attempt seemed successful, and the promises to David looked dead in Jerusalem tombs. But God has a way of resurrecting seemingly dead promises. When Joash was finally revealed as alive, a coup was staged, Athaliah was killed, and David's offspring once again assumed the throne. The Lord brought life out of what seemed like death.

God so loved the world that he would not allow the line of the Messiah to be wiped out — and when the time was right, he brought forth a son of David who brings everlasting life to all who believe in him. Joash's story points forward to Christ in yet another way. The number seven is highly significant in the Bible. It is the number of the Sabbath — the number of rest. Joash, the son of David, was hidden from a murderous tyrant, assumed the throne, and brought Sabbath-rest to the land after six years under Athaliah's burdensome rule. Jesus, the son of David, would be hidden from a murderous tyrant. Jesus would defeat the enemies. Jesus would assume the throne. And one day, Jesus will bring his people the final rest (Heb 4:3).

in the house of God. And Jehoiada[1] said to them, "Behold, the king's son! Let him reign, as the LORD spoke concerning the sons of David. [4]This is the thing that you shall do: of you priests and Levites who come off duty on the Sabbath, one third shall be gatekeepers, [5]and one third shall be at the king's house and one third at the Gate of the Foundation. And all the people shall be in the courts of the house of the LORD. [6]Let no one enter the house of the LORD except the priests and ministering Levites. They may enter, for they are holy, but all the people shall keep the charge of the LORD. [7]The Levites shall surround the king, each with his weapons in his hand. And whoever enters the house shall be put to death. Be with the king when he comes in and when he goes out."

[8]The Levites and all Judah did according to all that Jehoiada the priest commanded, and they each brought his men, who were to go off duty on the Sabbath, with those who were to come on duty on the Sabbath, for Jehoiada the priest did not dismiss the divisions. [9]And Jehoiada the priest gave to the captains the spears and the large and small shields that had been King David's, which were in the house of God. [10]And he set all the people as a guard for the king, every man with his weapon in his hand, from the south side of the house to the north side of the house, around the altar and the house. [11]Then they brought out the king's son and put the crown on him and gave him the testimony. And they proclaimed him king, and Jehoiada and his sons anointed him, and they said, "Long live the king."

Athaliah Executed

[12]When Athaliah heard the noise of the people running and praising the king, she went into the house of the LORD to the people. [13]And when she looked, there was the king standing by his pillar at the entrance, and the captains and the trumpeters beside the king, and all the people of the land rejoicing and blowing trumpets, and the singers with their musical instruments leading in the celebration. And Athaliah tore her clothes and cried, "Treason! Treason!" [14]Then Jehoiada the priest brought out the captains who were set over the army, saying to them, "Bring her out between the ranks, and anyone who follows her is to be put to death with the sword." For the priest said, "Do not put her to death in the house of the LORD." [15]So they laid hands on her,[2] and she went into the entrance of the horse gate of the king's house, and they put her to death there.

Jehoiada's Reforms

[16]And Jehoiada made a covenant between himself and all the people and the king that they should be the LORD's people. [17]Then all the people went to the house of Baal and tore it down; his altars and his images they broke in pieces, and they killed Mattan the priest of Baal before the altars. [18]And Jehoiada posted watchmen for the house of the LORD under the direction of the Levitical priests and the Levites whom David had organized to be in charge of the house of the LORD, to offer burnt offerings to the LORD, as it is written in the Law of Moses, with rejoicing and with singing, according to the order of David. [19]He stationed the gatekeepers at the gates of the house of the LORD so that no one should enter who was in any way unclean. [20]And he took the captains, the nobles, the governors of the people, and all the people of the land, and they brought the king down from the house of the LORD, marching through the upper gate to the king's house. And they set the king on the royal throne. [21]So all the people of the land rejoiced, and the city was quiet after Athaliah had been put to death with the sword.

Joash Repairs the Temple

24 Joash[3] was seven years old when he began to reign, and he reigned forty years in Jerusalem. His mother's name was Zibiah of Beersheba. [2]And Joash did what was right in the eyes of the LORD all the days of Jehoiada the priest. [3]Jehoiada got for him two wives, and he had sons and daughters.

---

[1]Hebrew *he* [2]Or *they made a passage for her* [3]Spelled *Jehoash* in 2 Kings 12:1

4After this Joash decided to restore the house of the LORD. 5And he gathered the priests and the Levites and said to them, "Go out to the cities of Judah and gather from all Israel money to repair the house of your God from year to year, and see that you act quickly." But the Levites did not act quickly. 6So the king summoned Jehoiada the chief and said to him, "Why have you not required the Levites to bring in from Judah and Jerusalem the tax levied by Moses, the servant of the LORD, and the congregation of Israel for the tent of testimony?" 7For the sons of Athaliah, that wicked woman, had broken into the house of God, and had also used all the dedicated things of the house of the LORD for the Baals.

8So the king commanded, and they made a chest and set it outside the gate of the house of the LORD. 9And proclamation was made throughout Judah and Jerusalem to bring in for the LORD the tax that Moses the servant of God laid on Israel in the wilderness. 10And all the princes and all the people rejoiced and brought their tax and dropped it into the chest until they had finished.[1] 11And whenever the chest was brought to the king's officers by the Levites, when they saw that there was much money in it, the king's secretary and the officer of the chief priest would come and empty the chest and take it and return it to its place. Thus they did day after day, and collected money in abundance. 12And the king and Jehoiada gave it to those who had charge of the work of the house of the LORD, and they hired masons and carpenters to restore the house of the LORD, and also workers in iron and bronze to repair the house of the LORD. 13So those who were engaged in the work labored, and the repairing went forward in their hands, and they restored the house of God to its proper condition and strengthened it. 14And when they had finished, they brought the rest of the money before the king and Jehoiada, and with it were made utensils for the house of the LORD, both for the service and for the burnt offerings, and dishes for incense and vessels of gold and silver. And they offered burnt offerings in the house of the LORD regularly all the days of Jehoiada.

15But Jehoiada grew old and full of days, and died. He was 130 years old at his death. 16And they buried him in the city of David among the kings, because he had done good in Israel, and toward God and his house.

17Now after the death of Jehoiada the princes of Judah came and paid homage to the king. Then the king listened to them. 18And they abandoned the house of the LORD, the God of their fathers, and served the Asherim and the idols. And wrath came upon Judah and Jerusalem for this guilt of theirs. 19Yet he sent prophets among them to bring them back to the LORD. These testified against them, but they would not pay attention.

Joash's Treachery

20Then the Spirit of God clothed Zechariah the son of Jehoiada the priest, and he stood above the people, and said to them, "Thus says God, 'Why do you break the commandments of the LORD, so that you cannot prosper? Because you have forsaken the LORD, he has forsaken you.'" 21But they conspired against him, and by command of the king they stoned him with stones in the court of the house of the LORD. 22Thus Joash the king did not remember the kindness that Jehoiada, Zechariah's father, had shown him, but killed his son. And when he was dying, he said, "May the LORD see and avenge!"[2]

Joash Assassinated

23At the end of the year the army of the Syrians came up against Joash. They came to Judah and Jerusalem and destroyed all the princes of the people from among the people and sent all their spoil to the king of Damascus. 24Though the army of the Syrians had come with few men, the LORD delivered into their hand a very great army, because Judah[3] had forsaken the LORD, the God of their fathers. Thus they executed judgment on Joash.

[1]Or *until it was full* [2]Or *and require it* [3]Hebrew *they*

2 CHRONICLES 24:17–22

KILLING GOD'S MESSENGER

King Joash only did good things as long as he was under the authority of God's priest Jehoiada. As soon as Jehoiada died, Joash failed. He began to listen to the wrong advisers and became an idolater. God empowered Jehoiada's son Zechariah with the Spirit to prophesy against Joash for his evil. However, Joash rejected Zechariah's words and had him killed. Worse yet, Zechariah was stoned to death in the temple courtyard.

This scene points forward to a parable that Jesus told about tenants who were renting a vineyard (Mt 21:33–46). When the landowner sent servants to collect the harvest from the tenants, the tenants killed the servants and eventually murdered the owner's son. One of the servants was stoned to death. Jesus told that parable to indict the nation of Israel and its leaders for the way they treated God's messengers, and he predicted that this habit of murdering God's prophets would culminate in the murder of God's Son. Jesus again referenced that sweep of Old Testament history in Matthew 23:35 when he said they would be held responsible for all the righteous blood shed on earth, from Abel to Zechariah. Jesus' murder on the cross was the climax of Israel's bloody history of rejecting and killing the messengers that God sent to them.

THE NEW TEMPLE

Joash was a good king who did what was right as long as he was under the authority of God's priest. He decided to repair and rebuild the temple because its sacred objects had been used blasphemously to worship Baal. Therefore, Joash commanded the Levites to take up a collection to fund the repairs. When they resisted, Joash had a chest made and called on the people to put money in that chest to fund the repairs. The people joyfully brought their gifts, and the temple was restored.

Many have looked to passages like this to justify giving campaigns for their churches. They might even put together a "Chest of Joash" that people can fill with money dedicated to repairing the roof of the church. But that is not how to apply this passage to our times. Today, the temple is not a building made with bricks and mortar; it is the body of Christ. Joash repaired the temple because kings were temple-builders. The original temple built by King Solomon was torn down by the Babylonians, and the rebuilt temple of Jesus' day was destroyed by the Romans. But the prophets prophesied that a greater temple would be built by a king (Zec 6:12 – 15).

In the New Testament, King Jesus identified his own body as the temple when he equated the rebuilding of the temple with his resurrection from the dead: "Destroy this temple, and in three days I will raise it up" (Jn 2:19). The new temple is Christ's body, and God's people are incorporated into the body of Christ through the unifying work of the Spirit. The church, as the body of Christ, is the new temple where God dwells (Eph 2:19 – 22). The Spirit of God which fell on the tabernacle and later fell on Solomon's temple and which descended on Jesus like a dove has now fallen on the church of God (Ac 2:1 – 21). Money donated for a construction project does not build the new temple. Rather, the spiritually gifted people of the church build it up in Christ Jesus (Eph 4:11 – 16).

25When they had departed from him, leaving him severely wounded, his
servants conspired against him because of the blood of the son[1] of Jehoiada the
priest, and killed him on his bed. So he died, and they buried him in the city of
David, but they did not bury him in the tombs of the kings. 26Those who conspired against him were Zabad the son of Shimeath the Ammonite, and Jehozabad
the son of Shimrith the Moabite. 27Accounts of his sons and of the many oracles
against him and of the rebuilding[2] of the house of God are written in the Story[3] of
the Book of the Kings. And Amaziah his son reigned in his place.

Amaziah Reigns in Judah

25 Amaziah was twenty-five years old when he began to reign, and he reigned
twenty-nine years in Jerusalem. His mother's name was Jehoaddan of Jerusalem. 2And he did what was right in the eyes of the LORD, yet not with a whole
heart. 3And as soon as the royal power was firmly his, he killed his servants who
had struck down the king his father. 4But he did not put their children to death,
according to what is written in the Law, in the Book of Moses, where the LORD
commanded, "Fathers shall not die because of their children, nor children die
because of their fathers, but each one shall die for his own sin."

Amaziah's Victories

5Then Amaziah assembled the men of Judah and set them by fathers' houses
under commanders of thousands and of hundreds for all Judah and Benjamin. He
mustered those twenty years old and upward, and found that they were 300,000
choice men, fit for war, able to handle spear and shield. 6He hired also 100,000
mighty men of valor from Israel for 100 talents[4] of silver. 7But a man of God came
to him and said, "O king, do not let the army of Israel go with you, for the LORD is
not with Israel, with all these Ephraimites. 8But go, act, be strong for the battle.
Why should you suppose that God will cast you down before the enemy? For God
has power to help or to cast down." 9And Amaziah said to the man of God, "But
what shall we do about the hundred talents that I have given to the army of Israel?" The man of God answered, "The LORD is able to give you much more than
this." 10Then Amaziah discharged the army that had come to him from Ephraim
to go home again. And they became very angry with Judah and returned home in
fierce anger. 11But Amaziah took courage and led out his people and went to the
Valley of Salt and struck down 10,000 men of Seir. 12The men of Judah captured
another 10,000 alive and took them to the top of a rock and threw them down
from the top of the rock, and they were all dashed to pieces. 13But the men of the
army whom Amaziah sent back, not letting them go with him to battle, raided
the cities of Judah, from Samaria to Beth-horon, and struck down 3,000 people
in them and took much spoil.

Amaziah's Idolatry

14After Amaziah came from striking down the Edomites, he brought the gods
of the men of Seir and set them up as his gods and worshiped them, making offerings to them. 15Therefore the LORD was angry with Amaziah and sent to him a
prophet, who said to him, "Why have you sought the gods of a people who did not
deliver their own people from your hand?" 16But as he was speaking, the king said
to him, "Have we made you a royal counselor? Stop! Why should you be struck
down?" So the prophet stopped, but said, "I know that God has determined to
destroy you, because you have done this and have not listened to my counsel."

Israel Defeats Amaziah

17Then Amaziah king of Judah took counsel and sent to Joash the son of Jehoahaz, son of Jehu, king of Israel, saying, "Come, let us look one another in the

---

[1]Septuagint, Vulgate; Hebrew *sons* [2]Hebrew *founding* [3]Or *Exposition* [4]A *talent* was about 75 pounds or 34 kilograms

face." 18 And Joash the king of Israel sent word to Amaziah king of Judah, "A thistle
on Lebanon sent to a cedar on Lebanon, saying, 'Give your daughter to my son
for a wife,' and a wild beast of Lebanon passed by and trampled down the thistle.
19 You say, 'See, I[1] have struck down Edom,' and your heart has lifted you up in
boastfulness. But now stay at home. Why should you provoke trouble so that you
fall, you and Judah with you?"

20 But Amaziah would not listen, for it was of God, in order that he might give
them into the hand of their enemies, because they had sought the gods of Edom.
21 So Joash king of Israel went up, and he and Amaziah king of Judah faced one another in battle at Beth-shemesh, which belongs to Judah. 22 And Judah was defeated by Israel, and every man fled to his home. 23 And Joash king of Israel captured
Amaziah king of Judah, the son of Joash, son of Ahaziah, at Beth-shemesh, and
brought him to Jerusalem and broke down the wall of Jerusalem for 400 cubits,[2]
from the Ephraim Gate to the Corner Gate. 24 And he seized all the gold and silver,
and all the vessels that were found in the house of God, in the care of Obed-edom.
He seized also the treasuries of the king's house, also hostages, and he returned
to Samaria.

25 Amaziah the son of Joash, king of Judah, lived fifteen years after the death of
Joash the son of Jehoahaz, king of Israel. 26 Now the rest of the deeds of Amaziah,
from first to last, are they not written in the Book of the Kings of Judah and Israel?
27 From the time when he turned away from the LORD they made a conspiracy
against him in Jerusalem, and he fled to Lachish. But they sent after him to Lachish and put him to death there. 28 And they brought him upon horses, and he
was buried with his fathers in the city of David.[3]

Uzziah Reigns in Judah

26 And all the people of Judah took Uzziah, who was sixteen years old, and
made him king instead of his father Amaziah. 2 He built Eloth and restored
it to Judah, after the king slept with his fathers. 3 Uzziah was sixteen years old
when he began to reign, and he reigned fifty-two years in Jerusalem. His mother's
name was Jecoliah of Jerusalem. 4 And he did what was right in the eyes of the
LORD, according to all that his father Amaziah had done. 5 He set himself to seek
God in the days of Zechariah, who instructed him in the fear of God, and as long
as he sought the LORD, God made him prosper.

6 He went out and made war against the Philistines and broke through the
wall of Gath and the wall of Jabneh and the wall of Ashdod, and he built cities in
the territory of Ashdod and elsewhere among the Philistines. 7 God helped him
against the Philistines and against the Arabians who lived in Gurbaal and against
the Meunites. 8 The Ammonites paid tribute to Uzziah, and his fame spread even
to the border of Egypt, for he became very strong. 9 Moreover, Uzziah built towers
in Jerusalem at the Corner Gate and at the Valley Gate and at the Angle, and fortified them. 10 And he built towers in the wilderness and cut out many cisterns, for
he had large herds, both in the Shephelah and in the plain, and he had farmers
and vinedressers in the hills and in the fertile lands, for he loved the soil. 11 Moreover, Uzziah had an army of soldiers, fit for war, in divisions according to the
numbers in the muster made by Jeiel the secretary and Maaseiah the officer, under the direction of Hananiah, one of the king's commanders. 12 The whole number of the heads of fathers' houses of mighty men of valor was 2,600. 13 Under
their command was an army of 307,500, who could make war with mighty power,
to help the king against the enemy. 14 And Uzziah prepared for all the army shields,
spears, helmets, coats of mail, bows, and stones for slinging. 15 In Jerusalem he
made machines, invented by skillful men, to be on the towers and the corners, to
shoot arrows and great stones. And his fame spread far, for he was marvelously
helped, till he was strong.

[1] Hebrew *you* [2] A *cubit* was about 18 inches or 45 centimeters [3] Hebrew *of Judah*

Uzziah's Pride and Punishment

16But when he was strong, he grew proud, to his destruction. For he was unfaithful to the LORD his God and entered the temple of the LORD to burn incense
on the altar of incense. 17But Azariah the priest went in after him, with eighty
priests of the LORD who were men of valor, 18and they withstood King Uzziah and
said to him, "It is not for you, Uzziah, to burn incense to the LORD, but for the
priests, the sons of Aaron, who are consecrated to burn incense. Go out of the
sanctuary, for you have done wrong, and it will bring you no honor from the LORD
God." 19Then Uzziah was angry. Now he had a censer in his hand to burn incense,
and when he became angry with the priests, leprosy[1] broke out on his forehead in
the presence of the priests in the house of the LORD, by the altar of incense. 20And
Azariah the chief priest and all the priests looked at him, and behold, he was
leprous in his forehead! And they rushed him out quickly, and he himself hurried
to go out, because the LORD had struck him. 21And King Uzziah was a leper to the
day of his death, and being a leper lived in a separate house, for he was excluded
from the house of the LORD. And Jotham his son was over the king's household,
governing the people of the land.

22Now the rest of the acts of Uzziah, from first to last, Isaiah the prophet the
son of Amoz wrote. 23And Uzziah slept with his fathers, and they buried him with
his fathers in the burial field that belonged to the kings, for they said, "He is a
leper." And Jotham his son reigned in his place.

Jotham Reigns in Judah

27 Jotham was twenty-five years old when he began to reign, and he reigned
sixteen years in Jerusalem. His mother's name was Jerushah the daughter
of Zadok. 2And he did what was right in the eyes of the LORD according to all that
his father Uzziah had done, except he did not enter the temple of the LORD. But
the people still followed corrupt practices. 3He built the upper gate of the house
of the LORD and did much building on the wall of Ophel. 4Moreover, he built cities
in the hill country of Judah, and forts and towers on the wooded hills. 5He fought
with the king of the Ammonites and prevailed against them. And the Ammonites
gave him that year 100 talents[2] of silver, and 10,000 cors[3] of wheat and 10,000 of
barley. The Ammonites paid him the same amount in the second and the third
years. 6So Jotham became mighty, because he ordered his ways before the LORD
his God. 7Now the rest of the acts of Jotham, and all his wars and his ways, behold,
they are written in the Book of the Kings of Israel and Judah. 8He was twenty-five
years old when he began to reign, and he reigned sixteen years in Jerusalem. 9And
Jotham slept with his fathers, and they buried him in the city of David, and Ahaz
his son reigned in his place.

Ahaz Reigns in Judah

28 Ahaz was twenty years old when he began to reign, and he reigned sixteen
years in Jerusalem. And he did not do what was right in the eyes of the
LORD, as his father David had done, 2but he walked in the ways of the kings of
Israel. He even made metal images for the Baals, 3and he made offerings in the
Valley of the Son of Hinnom and burned his sons as an offering,[4] according to
the abominations of the nations whom the LORD drove out before the people of
Israel. 4And he sacrificed and made offerings on the high places and on the hills
and under every green tree.

Judah Defeated

5Therefore the LORD his God gave him into the hand of the king of Syria, who
defeated him and took captive a great number of his people and brought them to

2 CHRONICLES 26:16–21

UZZIAH'S PRIDE

Uzziah was a good king who had started out his reign well (v. 5), and as a result he experienced God's blessing. But his successes caused him to swell up with pride, and he began to take prerogatives that did not belong to him. He usurped the authority of the priests and attempted to burn incense in the temple. God judged Uzziah's pride and presumptuousness by striking him with leprosy. His reign ended in great failure, but it revealed that God's people needed a humble king.

Jesus is the antithesis of Uzziah. Jesus did not get struck with leprosy; he went around healing lepers (Lk 17:11–19). Jesus did not pridefully take privileges that did not belong to him; rather he humbly and voluntarily gave up privileges and rights that did belong to him (Php 2:5–11). Jesus is equal with God, and yet he laid aside the free exercise of his rights by humbling himself in becoming a man and dying on the cross. Therefore, God has exalted him to the throne!

[1] *Leprosy* was a term for several skin diseases; see Leviticus 13 [2] A *talent* was about 75 pounds or 34 kilograms [3] A *cor* was about 6 bushels or 220 liters [4] Hebrew *made his sons pass through the fire*

Damascus. He was also given into the hand of the king of Israel, who struck him
with great force. 6For Pekah the son of Remaliah killed 120,000 from Judah in
one day, all of them men of valor, because they had forsaken the LORD, the God
of their fathers. 7And Zichri, a mighty man of Ephraim, killed Maaseiah the king's
son and Azrikam the commander of the palace and Elkanah the next in authority
to the king.

8The men of Israel took captive 200,000 of their relatives, women, sons, and
daughters. They also took much spoil from them and brought the spoil to Samaria. 9But a prophet of the LORD was there, whose name was Oded, and he went
out to meet the army that came to Samaria and said to them, "Behold, because
the LORD, the God of your fathers, was angry with Judah, he gave them into your
hand, but you have killed them in a rage that has reached up to heaven. 10And now
you intend to subjugate the people of Judah and Jerusalem, male and female, as
your slaves. Have you not sins of your own against the LORD your God? 11Now hear
me, and send back the captives from your relatives whom you have taken, for the
fierce wrath of the LORD is upon you."

12Certain chiefs also of the men of Ephraim, Azariah the son of Johanan,
Berechiah the son of Meshillemoth, Jehizkiah the son of Shallum, and Amasa
the son of Hadlai, stood up against those who were coming from the war 13and
said to them, "You shall not bring the captives in here, for you propose to bring
upon us guilt against the LORD in addition to our present sins and guilt. For our
guilt is already great, and there is fierce wrath against Israel." 14So the armed
men left the captives and the spoil before the princes and all the assembly.
15And the men who have been mentioned by name rose and took the captives,
and with the spoil they clothed all who were naked among them. They clothed
them, gave them sandals, provided them with food and drink, and anointed
them, and carrying all the feeble among them on donkeys, they brought them
to their kinsfolk at Jericho, the city of palm trees. Then they returned to Samaria.

16At that time King Ahaz sent to the king[1] of Assyria for help. 17For the Edomites
had again invaded and defeated Judah and carried away captives. 18And the Philistines had made raids on the cities in the Shephelah and the Negeb of Judah, and
had taken Beth-shemesh, Aijalon, Gederoth, Soco with its villages, Timnah with
its villages, and Gimzo with its villages. And they settled there. 19For the LORD
humbled Judah because of Ahaz king of Israel, for he had made Judah act sinfully[2]
and had been very unfaithful to the LORD. 20So Tiglath-pileser[3] king of Assyria
came against him and afflicted him instead of strengthening him. 21For Ahaz took
a portion from the house of the LORD and the house of the king and of the princes,
and gave tribute to the king of Assyria, but it did not help him.

Ahaz's Idolatry

22In the time of his distress he became yet more faithless to the LORD—this
same King Ahaz. 23For he sacrificed to the gods of Damascus that had defeated
him and said, "Because the gods of the kings of Syria helped them, I will sacrifice
to them that they may help me." But they were the ruin of him and of all Israel.
24And Ahaz gathered together the vessels of the house of God and cut in pieces
the vessels of the house of God, and he shut up the doors of the house of the
LORD, and he made himself altars in every corner of Jerusalem. 25In every city of
Judah he made high places to make offerings to other gods, provoking to anger
the LORD, the God of his fathers. 26Now the rest of his acts and all his ways, from
first to last, behold, they are written in the Book of the Kings of Judah and Israel.
27And Ahaz slept with his fathers, and they buried him in the city, in Jerusalem,
for they did not bring him into the tombs of the kings of Israel. And Hezekiah his
son reigned in his place.

[1]Septuagint, Syriac, Vulgate (compare 2 Kings 16:7); Hebrew *kings* [2]Or *wildly* [3]Hebrew *Tilgath-pilneser*

Hezekiah Reigns in Judah

29 Hezekiah began to reign when he was twenty-five years old, and he reigned twenty-nine years in Jerusalem. His mother's name was Abijah[1] the daughter of Zechariah. 2And he did what was right in the eyes of the LORD, according to all that David his father had done.

Hezekiah Cleanses the Temple

3In the first year of his reign, in the first month, he opened the doors of the house of the LORD and repaired them. 4He brought in the priests and the Levites and assembled them in the square on the east 5and said to them, "Hear me, Levites! Now consecrate yourselves, and consecrate the house of the LORD, the God of your fathers, and carry out the filth[2] from the Holy Place. 6For our fathers have been unfaithful and have done what was evil in the sight of the LORD our God. They have forsaken him and have turned away their faces from the habitation of the LORD and turned their backs. 7They also shut the doors of the vestibule and put out the lamps and have not burned incense or offered burnt offerings in the Holy Place to the God of Israel. 8Therefore the wrath of the LORD came on Judah and Jerusalem, and he has made them an object of horror, of astonishment, and of hissing, as you see with your own eyes. 9For behold, our fathers have fallen by the sword, and our sons and our daughters and our wives are in captivity for this. 10Now it is in my heart to make a covenant with the LORD, the God of Israel, in order that his fierce anger may turn away from us. 11My sons, do not now be negligent, for the LORD has chosen you to stand in his presence, to minister to him and to be his ministers and make offerings to him."

12Then the Levites arose, Mahath the son of Amasai, and Joel the son of Azariah, of the sons of the Kohathites; and of the sons of Merari, Kish the son of Abdi, and Azariah the son of Jehallelel; and of the Gershonites, Joah the son of Zimmah, and Eden the son of Joah; 13and of the sons of Elizaphan, Shimri and Jeuel; and of the sons of Asaph, Zechariah and Mattaniah; 14and of the sons of Heman, Jehuel and Shimei; and of the sons of Jeduthun, Shemaiah and Uzziel. 15They gathered their brothers and consecrated themselves and went in as the king had commanded, by the words of the LORD, to cleanse the house of the LORD. 16The priests went into the inner part of the house of the LORD to cleanse it, and they brought out all the uncleanness that they found in the temple of the LORD into the court of the house of the LORD. And the Levites took it and carried it out to the brook Kidron. 17They began to consecrate on the first day of the first month, and on the eighth day of the month they came to the vestibule of the LORD. Then for eight days they consecrated the house of the LORD, and on the sixteenth day of the first month they finished. 18Then they went in to Hezekiah the king and said, "We have cleansed all the house of the LORD, the altar of burnt offering and all its utensils, and the table for the showbread and all its utensils. 19All the utensils that King Ahaz discarded in his reign when he was faithless, we have made ready and consecrated, and behold, they are before the altar of the LORD."

Hezekiah Restores Temple Worship

20Then Hezekiah the king rose early and gathered the officials of the city and went up to the house of the LORD. 21And they brought seven bulls, seven rams, seven lambs, and seven male goats for a sin offering for the kingdom and for the sanctuary and for Judah. And he commanded the priests, the sons of Aaron, to offer them on the altar of the LORD. 22So they slaughtered the bulls, and the priests received the blood and threw it against the altar. And they slaughtered the rams, and their blood was thrown against the altar. And they slaughtered the lambs, and their blood was thrown against the altar. 23Then the goats for the sin offering were brought to the king and the assembly, and they laid their hands on them,

[1]Spelled *Abi* in 2 Kings 18:2 [2]Hebrew *impurity*

---

2 CHRONICLES 29:3–19

THE KING CLEANSES THE TEMPLE

King Hezekiah ordered that the priests and Levites should enter the temple and cleanse it from its defilements. The temple had been greatly defiled under King Ahaz (2Ki 16:10–16), but now King Hezekiah took measures to dedicate it to the Lord once again. The priests and Levites removed all the unholy objects of pagan worship and carried them to the Kidron Valley. Then, the ritually purified priests and Levites led the nation in renewed worship, offering hundreds of sacrifices and singing praises to God in the temple (2Ch 29:20–36).

Many years later, a descendant of Hezekiah walked into the temple and saw it defiled by the money changers. Jesus drove them out and cleansed the temple (Mt 21:12–13; Jn 2:13–17). He told them that the temple was to be a house of prayer, but they had turned it into a den of robbers. Like King Hezekiah, King Jesus cleaned out the temple, which was the house of God, so that people could rightly and appropriately worship the one true God. Now Jesus is the new temple—and believers can worship God in spirit and in truth wherever they are if they come to God through Jesus.

[24]and the priests slaughtered them and made a sin offering with their blood on the altar, to make atonement for all Israel. For the king commanded that the burnt offering and the sin offering should be made for all Israel.

[25]And he stationed the Levites in the house of the LORD with cymbals, harps, and lyres, according to the commandment of David and of Gad the king's seer and of Nathan the prophet, for the commandment was from the LORD through his prophets. [26]The Levites stood with the instruments of David, and the priests with the trumpets. [27]Then Hezekiah commanded that the burnt offering be offered on the altar. And when the burnt offering began, the song to the LORD began also, and the trumpets, accompanied by the instruments of David king of Israel. [28]The whole assembly worshiped, and the singers sang, and the trumpeters sounded. All this continued until the burnt offering was finished. [29]When the offering was finished, the king and all who were present with him bowed themselves and worshiped. [30]And Hezekiah the king and the officials commanded the Levites to sing praises to the LORD with the words of David and of Asaph the seer. And they sang praises with gladness, and they bowed down and worshiped.

[31]Then Hezekiah said, "You have now consecrated yourselves to[1] the LORD. Come near; bring sacrifices and thank offerings to the house of the LORD." And the assembly brought sacrifices and thank offerings, and all who were of a willing heart brought burnt offerings. [32]The number of the burnt offerings that the assembly brought was 70 bulls, 100 rams, and 200 lambs; all these were for a burnt offering to the LORD. [33]And the consecrated offerings were 600 bulls and 3,000 sheep. [34]But the priests were too few and could not flay all the burnt offerings, so until other priests had consecrated themselves, their brothers the Levites helped them, until the work was finished—for the Levites were more upright in heart than the priests in consecrating themselves. [35]Besides the great number of burnt offerings, there was the fat of the peace offerings, and there were the drink offerings for the burnt offerings. Thus the service of the house of the LORD was restored. [36]And Hezekiah and all the people rejoiced because God had provided for the people, for the thing came about suddenly.

Passover Celebrated

30 Hezekiah sent to all Israel and Judah, and wrote letters also to Ephraim and Manasseh, that they should come to the house of the LORD at Jerusalem to keep the Passover to the LORD, the God of Israel. [2]For the king and his princes and all the assembly in Jerusalem had taken counsel to keep the Passover in the second month— [3]for they could not keep it at that time because the priests had not consecrated themselves in sufficient number, nor had the people assembled in Jerusalem— [4]and the plan seemed right to the king and all the assembly. [5]So they decreed to make a proclamation throughout all Israel, from Beersheba to Dan, that the people should come and keep the Passover to the LORD, the God of Israel, at Jerusalem, for they had not kept it as often as prescribed. [6]So couriers went throughout all Israel and Judah with letters from the king and his princes, as the king had commanded, saying, "O people of Israel, return to the LORD, the God of Abraham, Isaac, and Israel, that he may turn again to the remnant of you who have escaped from the hand of the kings of Assyria. [7]Do not be like your fathers and your brothers, who were faithless to the LORD God of their fathers, so that he made them a desolation, as you see. [8]Do not now be stiff-necked as your fathers were, but yield yourselves to the LORD and come to his sanctuary, which he has consecrated forever, and serve the LORD your God, that his fierce anger may turn away from you. [9]For if you return to the LORD, your brothers and your children will find compassion with their captors and return to this land. For the LORD your God is gracious and merciful and will not turn away his face from you, if you return to him."

2 CHRONICLES 30:1–20

HEZEKIAH AND THE PASSOVER

King Hezekiah arranged for the people to celebrate the Passover because they had not always observed it as they should have. Not only did he arrange for the southern tribes to eat the meal, but he also brought a degree of unity by arranging for the northern tribes to be involved if they desired. The Passover celebrated how God had saved the people of Israel while they were slaves in Egypt (Ex 11:1—12:42). God defeated the Egyptians and rescued his people from slavery. The Hebrews were saved from the plague because they killed a lamb and smeared its blood on the doorposts of their houses. The lamb substituted for the firstborn of the house. When the Lord saw the blood on the doorpost he passed over it.

This meal pointed forward to the full and final salvation of God's people through Jesus—the Lamb who takes away the sin of the world (Jn 1:29). He is the Passover Lamb for all God's people (1Co 5:7). He died in humanity's place so that eternal death will pass by.

[1]Hebrew *filled your hand for*

10 So the couriers went from city to city through the country of Ephraim and
Manasseh, and as far as Zebulun, but they laughed them to scorn and mocked
them. 11 However, some men of Asher, of Manasseh, and of Zebulun humbled
themselves and came to Jerusalem. 12 The hand of God was also on Judah to give
them one heart to do what the king and the princes commanded by the word of
the LORD.
13 And many people came together in Jerusalem to keep the Feast of Unleavened Bread in the second month, a very great assembly. 14 They set to work and
removed the altars that were in Jerusalem, and all the altars for burning incense
they took away and threw into the brook Kidron. 15 And they slaughtered the Passover lamb on the fourteenth day of the second month. And the priests and the
Levites were ashamed, so that they consecrated themselves and brought burnt
offerings into the house of the LORD. 16 They took their accustomed posts according to the Law of Moses the man of God. The priests threw the blood that they
received from the hand of the Levites. 17 For there were many in the assembly who
had not consecrated themselves. Therefore the Levites had to slaughter the Passover lamb for everyone who was not clean, to consecrate it to the LORD. 18 For a
majority of the people, many of them from Ephraim, Manasseh, Issachar, and
Zebulun, had not cleansed themselves, yet they ate the Passover otherwise than
as prescribed. For Hezekiah had prayed for them, saying, "May the good LORD
pardon everyone 19 who sets his heart to seek God, the LORD, the God of his fathers, even though not according to the sanctuary's rules of cleanness."[1] 20 And
the LORD heard Hezekiah and healed the people. 21 And the people of Israel who
were present at Jerusalem kept the Feast of Unleavened Bread seven days with
great gladness, and the Levites and the priests praised the LORD day by day, singing with all their might[2] to the LORD. 22 And Hezekiah spoke encouragingly to all
the Levites who showed good skill in the service of the LORD. So they ate the food
of the festival for seven days, sacrificing peace offerings and giving thanks to the
LORD, the God of their fathers.
23 Then the whole assembly agreed together to keep the feast for another
seven days. So they kept it for another seven days with gladness. 24 For Hezekiah
king of Judah gave the assembly 1,000 bulls and 7,000 sheep for offerings, and
the princes gave the assembly 1,000 bulls and 10,000 sheep. And the priests consecrated themselves in great numbers. 25 The whole assembly of Judah, and the
priests and the Levites, and the whole assembly that came out of Israel, and the
sojourners who came out of the land of Israel, and the sojourners who lived in
Judah, rejoiced. 26 So there was great joy in Jerusalem, for since the time of Solomon the son of David king of Israel there had been nothing like this in Jerusalem.
27 Then the priests and the Levites arose and blessed the people, and their voice
was heard, and their prayer came to his holy habitation in heaven.

Hezekiah Organizes the Priests

31 Now when all this was finished, all Israel who were present went out to the
cities of Judah and broke in pieces the pillars and cut down the Asherim
and broke down the high places and the altars throughout all Judah and Benjamin, and in Ephraim and Manasseh, until they had destroyed them all. Then all
the people of Israel returned to their cities, every man to his possession.
2 And Hezekiah appointed the divisions of the priests and of the Levites, division by division, each according to his service, the priests and the Levites, for
burnt offerings and peace offerings, to minister in the gates of the camp of the
LORD and to give thanks and praise. 3 The contribution of the king from his own
possessions was for the burnt offerings: the burnt offerings of morning and evening, and the burnt offerings for the Sabbaths, the new moons, and the appointed

[1] Hebrew *not according to the cleanness of holiness* [2] Compare 1 Chronicles 13:8; Hebrew *with instruments of might*

feasts, as it is written in the Law of the LORD. [4]And he commanded the people
who lived in Jerusalem to give the portion due to the priests and the Levites, that
they might give themselves to the Law of the LORD. [5]As soon as the command
was spread abroad, the people of Israel gave in abundance the firstfruits of grain,
wine, oil, honey, and of all the produce of the field. And they brought in abundantly the tithe of everything. [6]And the people of Israel and Judah who lived in
the cities of Judah also brought in the tithe of cattle and sheep, and the tithe of
the dedicated things that had been dedicated to the LORD their God, and laid them
in heaps. [7]In the third month they began to pile up the heaps, and finished them
in the seventh month. [8]When Hezekiah and the princes came and saw the heaps,
they blessed the LORD and his people Israel. [9]And Hezekiah questioned the priests
and the Levites about the heaps. [10]Azariah the chief priest, who was of the house
of Zadok, answered him, "Since they began to bring the contributions into the
house of the LORD, we have eaten and had enough and have plenty left, for the
LORD has blessed his people, so that we have this large amount left."

[11]Then Hezekiah commanded them to prepare chambers in the house of the
LORD, and they prepared them. [12]And they faithfully brought in the contributions, the tithes, and the dedicated things. The chief officer in charge of them was
Conaniah the Levite, with Shimei his brother as second, [13]while Jehiel, Azaziah,
Nahath, Asahel, Jerimoth, Jozabad, Eliel, Ismachiah, Mahath, and Benaiah were
overseers assisting Conaniah and Shimei his brother, by the appointment of
Hezekiah the king and Azariah the chief officer of the house of God. [14]And Kore
the son of Imnah the Levite, keeper of the east gate, was over the freewill offerings
to God, to apportion the contribution reserved for the LORD and the most holy offerings. [15]Eden, Miniamin, Jeshua, Shemaiah, Amariah, and Shecaniah were faithfully assisting him in the cities of the priests, to distribute the portions to their
brothers, old and young alike, by divisions, [16]except those enrolled by genealogy,
males from three years old and upward—all who entered the house of the LORD as
the duty of each day required—for their service according to their offices, by their
divisions. [17]The enrollment of the priests was according to their fathers' houses;
that of the Levites from twenty years old and upward was according to their offices, by their divisions. [18]They were enrolled with all their little children, their
wives, their sons, and their daughters, the whole assembly, for they were faithful
in keeping themselves holy. [19]And for the sons of Aaron, the priests, who were in
the fields of common land belonging to their cities, there were men in the several
cities who were designated by name to distribute portions to every male among
the priests and to everyone among the Levites who was enrolled.

[20]Thus Hezekiah did throughout all Judah, and he did what was good and right
and faithful before the LORD his God. [21]And every work that he undertook in the
service of the house of God and in accordance with the law and the commandments, seeking his God, he did with all his heart, and prospered.

Sennacherib Invades Judah

32 After these things and these acts of faithfulness, Sennacherib king of Assyria came and invaded Judah and encamped against the fortified cities,
thinking to win them for himself. [2]And when Hezekiah saw that Sennacherib
had come and intended to fight against Jerusalem, [3]he planned with his officers
and his mighty men to stop the water of the springs that were outside the city;
and they helped him. [4]A great many people were gathered, and they stopped all
the springs and the brook that flowed through the land, saying, "Why should the
kings of Assyria come and find much water?" [5]He set to work resolutely and built
up all the wall that was broken down and raised towers upon it,[1] and outside it
he built another wall, and he strengthened the Millo in the city of David. He also
made weapons and shields in abundance. [6]And he set combat commanders over

[1]Vulgate; Hebrew *and raised upon the towers*

the people and gathered them together to him in the square at the gate of the city and spoke encouragingly to them, saying, 7“Be strong and courageous. Do not be afraid or dismayed before the king of Assyria and all the horde that is with him, for there are more with us than with him. 8With him is an arm of flesh, but with us is the LORD our God, to help us and to fight our battles.” And the people took confidence from the words of Hezekiah king of Judah.

Sennacherib Blasphemes

9After this, Sennacherib king of Assyria, who was besieging Lachish with all his forces, sent his servants to Jerusalem to Hezekiah king of Judah and to all the people of Judah who were in Jerusalem, saying, 10“Thus says Sennacherib king of Assyria, ‘On what are you trusting, that you endure the siege in Jerusalem? 11Is not Hezekiah misleading you, that he may give you over to die by famine and by thirst, when he tells you, “The LORD our God will deliver us from the hand of the king of Assyria”? 12Has not this same Hezekiah taken away his high places and his altars and commanded Judah and Jerusalem, “Before one altar you shall worship, and on it you shall burn your sacrifices”? 13Do you not know what I and my fathers have done to all the peoples of other lands? Were the gods of the nations of those lands at all able to deliver their lands out of my hand? 14Who among all the gods of those nations that my fathers devoted to destruction was able to deliver his people from my hand, that your God should be able to deliver you from my hand? 15Now, therefore, do not let Hezekiah deceive you or mislead you in this fashion, and do not believe him, for no god of any nation or kingdom has been able to deliver his people from my hand or from the hand of my fathers. How much less will your God deliver you out of my hand!’ ”

16And his servants said still more against the LORD God and against his servant Hezekiah. 17And he wrote letters to cast contempt on the LORD, the God of Israel, and to speak against him, saying, “Like the gods of the nations of the lands who have not delivered their people from my hands, so the God of Hezekiah will not deliver his people from my hand.” 18And they shouted it with a loud voice in the language of Judah to the people of Jerusalem who were on the wall, to frighten and terrify them, in order that they might take the city. 19And they spoke of the God of Jerusalem as they spoke of the gods of the peoples of the earth, which are the work of men’s hands.

The LORD Delivers Jerusalem

20Then Hezekiah the king and Isaiah the prophet, the son of Amoz, prayed because of this and cried to heaven. 21And the LORD sent an angel, who cut off all the mighty warriors and commanders and officers in the camp of the king of Assyria. So he returned with shame of face to his own land. And when he came into the house of his god, some of his own sons struck him down there with the sword. 22So the LORD saved Hezekiah and the inhabitants of Jerusalem from the hand of Sennacherib king of Assyria and from the hand of all his enemies, and he provided for them on every side. 23And many brought gifts to the LORD to Jerusalem and precious things to Hezekiah king of Judah, so that he was exalted in the sight of all nations from that time onward.

Hezekiah’s Pride and Achievements

24In those days Hezekiah became sick and was at the point of death, and he prayed to the LORD, and he answered him and gave him a sign. 25But Hezekiah did not make return according to the benefit done to him, for his heart was proud. Therefore wrath came upon him and Judah and Jerusalem. 26But Hezekiah humbled himself for the pride of his heart, both he and the inhabitants of Jerusalem, so that the wrath of the LORD did not come upon them in the days of Hezekiah.

27And Hezekiah had very great riches and honor, and he made for himself treasuries for silver, for gold, for precious stones, for spices, for shields, and for all kinds of costly vessels; 28storehouses also for the yield of grain, wine, and oil; and stalls for all kinds of cattle, and sheepfolds. 29He likewise provided cities for himself, and flocks and herds in abundance, for God had given him very great possessions. 30This same Hezekiah closed the upper outlet of the waters of Gihon and directed them down to the west side of the city of David. And Hezekiah prospered in all his works. 31And so in the matter of the envoys of the princes of Babylon, who had been sent to him to inquire about the sign that had been done in the land, God left him to himself, in order to test him and to know all that was in his heart.

32Now the rest of the acts of Hezekiah and his good deeds, behold, they are written in the vision of Isaiah the prophet, the son of Amoz, in the Book of the Kings of Judah and Israel. 33And Hezekiah slept with his fathers, and they buried him in the upper part of the tombs of the sons of David, and all Judah and the inhabitants of Jerusalem did him honor at his death. And Manasseh his son reigned in his place.

Manasseh Reigns in Judah

33 Manasseh was twelve years old when he began to reign, and he reigned fifty-five years in Jerusalem. 2And he did what was evil in the sight of the LORD, according to the abominations of the nations whom the LORD drove out before the people of Israel. 3For he rebuilt the high places that his father Hezekiah had broken down, and he erected altars to the Baals, and made Asheroth, and worshiped all the host of heaven and served them. 4And he built altars in the house of the LORD, of which the LORD had said, "In Jerusalem shall my name be forever." 5And he built altars for all the host of heaven in the two courts of the house of the LORD. 6And he burned his sons as an offering in the Valley of the Son of Hinnom, and used fortune-telling and omens and sorcery, and dealt with mediums and with necromancers. He did much evil in the sight of the LORD, provoking him to anger. 7And the carved image of the idol that he had made he set in the house of God, of which God said to David and to Solomon his son, "In this house, and in Jerusalem, which I have chosen out of all the tribes of Israel, I will put my name forever, 8and I will no more remove the foot of Israel from the land that I appointed for your fathers, if only they will be careful to do all that I have commanded them, all the law, the statutes, and the rules given through Moses." 9Manasseh led Judah and the inhabitants of Jerusalem astray, to do more evil than the nations whom the LORD destroyed before the people of Israel.

Manasseh's Repentance

10The LORD spoke to Manasseh and to his people, but they paid no attention. 11Therefore the LORD brought upon them the commanders of the army of the king of Assyria, who captured Manasseh with hooks and bound him with chains of bronze and brought him to Babylon. 12And when he was in distress, he entreated the favor of the LORD his God and humbled himself greatly before the God of his fathers. 13He prayed to him, and God was moved by his entreaty and heard his plea and brought him again to Jerusalem into his kingdom. Then Manasseh knew that the LORD was God.

14Afterward he built an outer wall for the city of David west of Gihon, in the valley, and for the entrance into the Fish Gate, and carried it around Ophel, and raised it to a very great height. He also put commanders of the army in all the fortified cities in Judah. 15And he took away the foreign gods and the idol from the house of the LORD, and all the altars that he had built on the mountain of the house of the LORD and in Jerusalem, and he threw them outside of the city. 16He also restored the altar of the LORD and offered on it sacrifices of peace offerings and of thanksgiving, and he commanded Judah to serve the LORD, the God of Israel. 17Nevertheless, the people still sacrificed at the high places, but only to the LORD their God.

18Now the rest of the acts of Manasseh, and his prayer to his God, and the words of the seers who spoke to him in the name of the LORD, the God of Israel, behold, they are in the Chronicles of the Kings of Israel. 19 And his prayer, and how God was moved by his entreaty, and all his sin and his faithlessness, and the sites on which he built high places and set up the Asherim and the images, before he humbled himself, behold, they are written in the Chronicles of the Seers.[1] 20 So Manasseh slept with his fathers, and they buried him in his house, and Amon his son reigned in his place.

Amon's Reign and Death

21 Amon was twenty-two years old when he began to reign, and he reigned two years in Jerusalem. 22 And he did what was evil in the sight of the LORD, as Manasseh his father had done. Amon sacrificed to all the images that Manasseh his father had made, and served them. 23 And he did not humble himself before the LORD, as Manasseh his father had humbled himself, but this Amon incurred guilt more and more. 24 And his servants conspired against him and put him to death in his house. 25 But the people of the land struck down all those who had conspired against King Amon. And the people of the land made Josiah his son king in his place.

Josiah Reigns in Judah

34 Josiah was eight years old when he began to reign, and he reigned thirty-one years in Jerusalem. 2 And he did what was right in the eyes of the LORD, and walked in the ways of David his father; and he did not turn aside to the right hand or to the left. 3 For in the eighth year of his reign, while he was yet a boy, he began to seek the God of David his father, and in the twelfth year he began to purge Judah and Jerusalem of the high places, the Asherim, and the carved and the metal images. 4 And they chopped down the altars of the Baals in his presence, and he cut down the incense altars that stood above them. And he broke in pieces the Asherim and the carved and the metal images, and he made dust of them and scattered it over the graves of those who had sacrificed to them. 5 He also burned the bones of the priests on their altars and cleansed Judah and Jerusalem. 6 And in the cities of Manasseh, Ephraim, and Simeon, and as far as Naphtali, in their ruins[2] all around, 7 he broke down the altars and beat the Asherim and the images into powder and cut down all the incense altars throughout all the land of Israel. Then he returned to Jerusalem.

The Book of the Law Found

8 Now in the eighteenth year of his reign, when he had cleansed the land and the house, he sent Shaphan the son of Azaliah, and Maaseiah the governor of the city, and Joah the son of Joahaz, the recorder, to repair the house of the LORD his God. 9 They came to Hilkiah the high priest and gave him the money that had been brought into the house of God, which the Levites, the keepers of the threshold, had collected from Manasseh and Ephraim and from all the remnant of Israel and from all Judah and Benjamin and from the inhabitants of Jerusalem. 10 And they gave it to the workmen who were working in the house of the LORD. And the workmen who were working in the house of the LORD gave it for repairing and restoring the house. 11 They gave it to the carpenters and the builders to buy quarried stone, and timber for binders and beams for the buildings that the kings of Judah had let go to ruin. 12 And the men did the work faithfully. Over them were set Jahath and Obadiah the Levites, of the sons of Merari, and Zechariah and Meshullam, of the sons of the Kohathites, to have oversight. The Levites, all who were skillful with instruments of music, 13 were over the burden-bearers and directed all who did work in every kind of service, and some of the Levites were scribes and officials and gatekeepers.

14 While they were bringing out the money that had been brought into the house of the LORD, Hilkiah the priest found the Book of the Law of the LORD given

[1] One Hebrew manuscript, Septuagint; most Hebrew manuscripts *of Hozai* [2] The meaning of the Hebrew is uncertain

2 CHRONICLES 34:14–33

JOSIAH'S REFORMS

During King Josiah's reign, the high priest found the Book of the Law in the temple. A messenger took it and read it to the king, and Josiah ripped his robes because he was convicted about his nation's disobedience to God's Word. He repented and cried out in confession to the Lord. The Lord indicated that all of the curses of Deuteronomy 28:15–68 would come upon the people, but because of their repentance, God would not exile them during Josiah's reign.

The first readers of this passage in Chronicles were the Jews who lived in Judah some years after the exile. While this account may seem like bad news, it was actually good news to the restored community. If God kept his word by exiling the people, and if God kept his word by bringing them back to the land, then God would certainly keep his word to circumcise their hearts so that they could wholeheartedly follow him. Daniel and Jeremiah prophesied about the complete fulfillment of this promise of inner transformation and salvation, which would come when the Messiah was put to death (Jer 31:31–34; Da 9:24–27). Jesus, in his death, inaugurated a new covenant and brought full and lasting transformation to his people.

EXILE AND RESTORATION

The inclusion of the story of Manasseh's sin, exile in Babylon, repentance, and return to the land fits perfectly with Chronicles' purpose. Unlike 1 and 2 Kings which justified the exile, the books of Chronicles were intended to highlight the reality of the Lord's faithfulness to his covenant with David so as to strengthen the people's hope that a descendant of David would reign and the promises would be fulfilled. Manasseh's story is a great example of God's mercy and faithfulness to those who had returned from exile. If the worst king in David's line could be restored to the throne before the exile, then surely the Lord would be gracious and restore the Davidic line after the exile.

Manasseh's story strengthened the hope of the post-exilic Jews that God would one day establish David's dynasty, defeat their enemies, and finally save them. In fact, Manasseh's story was a picture in miniature of God's dealings with his people. Manasseh had sinned, been taken in exile to Babylon, repented while in Babylon, and then returned to the land. Just as God restored the king when he repented in exile, so God also restored the nation itself after its exile to Babylon. God was faithful to his promise to David and to the nation, despite all that had happened.

The inadequacy of David's sons as described in Chronicles anticipated David's great Son who would come — Jesus Christ. None of the sons had lived up to the ideal, and yet despite their failings, God remained faithful to his promise that one day a son of David would establish an eternal kingdom. Long after the restoration from exile, Jesus sits on the throne forever with all of his enemies under his feet. He fulfills all of the good qualities of David, Solomon, and the others with none of their bad qualities. Chronicles began with a genealogy, and it ended with exile and an invitation to return. Chronicles was the last book of the Hebrew canon, and the very next words in the Bible after the end of Chronicles are these: "The book of the genealogy of Jesus Christ, the son of David" (Mt 1:1).

through[1] Moses. 15Then Hilkiah answered and said to Shaphan the secretary, "I have found the Book of the Law in the house of the LORD." And Hilkiah gave the book to Shaphan. 16Shaphan brought the book to the king, and further reported to the king, "All that was committed to your servants they are doing. 17They have emptied out the money that was found in the house of the LORD and have given it into the hand of the overseers and the workmen." 18Then Shaphan the secretary told the king, "Hilkiah the priest has given me a book." And Shaphan read from it before the king.

19And when the king heard the words of the Law, he tore his clothes. 20And the king commanded Hilkiah, Ahikam the son of Shaphan, Abdon the son of Micah, Shaphan the secretary, and Asaiah the king's servant, saying, 21"Go, inquire of the LORD for me and for those who are left in Israel and in Judah, concerning the words of the book that has been found. For great is the wrath of the LORD that is poured out on us, because our fathers have not kept the word of the LORD, to do according to all that is written in this book."

Huldah Prophesies Disaster

22So Hilkiah and those whom the king had sent[2] went to Huldah the prophetess, the wife of Shallum the son of Tokhath, son of Hasrah, keeper of the wardrobe (now she lived in Jerusalem in the Second Quarter) and spoke to her to that effect. 23And she said to them, "Thus says the LORD, the God of Israel: 'Tell the man who sent you to me, 24Thus says the LORD, Behold, I will bring disaster upon this place and upon its inhabitants, all the curses that are written in the book that was read before the king of Judah. 25Because they have forsaken me and have made offerings to other gods, that they might provoke me to anger with all the works of their hands, therefore my wrath will be poured out on this place and will not be quenched. 26But to the king of Judah, who sent you to inquire of the LORD, thus shall you say to him, Thus says the LORD, the God of Israel: Regarding the words that you have heard, 27because your heart was tender and you humbled yourself before God when you heard his words against this place and its inhabitants, and you have humbled yourself before me and have torn your clothes and wept before me, I also have heard you, declares the LORD. 28Behold, I will gather you to your fathers, and you shall be gathered to your grave in peace, and your eyes shall not see all the disaster that I will bring upon this place and its inhabitants.'" And they brought back word to the king.

29Then the king sent and gathered together all the elders of Judah and Jerusalem. 30And the king went up to the house of the LORD, with all the men of Judah and the inhabitants of Jerusalem and the priests and the Levites, all the people both great and small. And he read in their hearing all the words of the Book of the Covenant that had been found in the house of the LORD. 31And the king stood in his place and made a covenant before the LORD, to walk after the LORD and to keep his commandments and his testimonies and his statutes, with all his heart and all his soul, to perform the words of the covenant that were written in this book. 32Then he made all who were present in Jerusalem and in Benjamin join in it. And the inhabitants of Jerusalem did according to the covenant of God, the God of their fathers. 33And Josiah took away all the abominations from all the territory that belonged to the people of Israel and made all who were present in Israel serve the LORD their God. All his days they did not turn away from following the LORD, the God of their fathers.

Josiah Keeps the Passover

35 Josiah kept a Passover to the LORD in Jerusalem. And they slaughtered the Passover lamb on the fourteenth day of the first month. 2He appointed the priests to their offices and encouraged them in the service of the house of the

[1]Hebrew *by the hand of* [2]Syriac, Vulgate; Hebrew lacks *had sent*

Lord. [3]And he said to the Levites who taught all Israel and who were holy to the
Lord, "Put the holy ark in the house that Solomon the son of David, king of Israel,
built. You need not carry it on your shoulders. Now serve the Lord your God and
his people Israel. [4]Prepare yourselves according to your fathers' houses by your
divisions, as prescribed in the writing of David king of Israel and the document
of Solomon his son. [5]And stand in the Holy Place according to the groupings of
the fathers' houses of your brothers the lay people, and according to the division
of the Levites by fathers' household. [6]And slaughter the Passover lamb, and consecrate yourselves, and prepare for your brothers, to do according to the word of
the Lord by[1] Moses."

[7]Then Josiah contributed to the lay people, as Passover offerings for all who
were present, lambs and young goats from the flock to the number of 30,000, and
3,000 bulls; these were from the king's possessions. [8]And his officials contributed
willingly to the people, to the priests, and to the Levites. Hilkiah, Zechariah, and
Jehiel, the chief officers of the house of God, gave to the priests for the Passover
offerings 2,600 Passover lambs and 300 bulls. [9]Conaniah also, and Shemaiah and
Nethanel his brothers, and Hashabiah and Jeiel and Jozabad, the chiefs of the Levites, gave to the Levites for the Passover offerings 5,000 lambs and young goats
and 500 bulls.

[10]When the service had been prepared for, the priests stood in their place,
and the Levites in their divisions according to the king's command. [11]And they
slaughtered the Passover lamb, and the priests threw the blood that they received
from them while the Levites flayed the sacrifices. [12]And they set aside the burnt
offerings that they might distribute them according to the groupings of the fathers' houses of the lay people, to offer to the Lord, as it is written in the Book
of Moses. And so they did with the bulls. [13]And they roasted the Passover lamb
with fire according to the rule; and they boiled the holy offerings in pots, in caul-
drons, and in pans, and carried them quickly to all the lay people. [14]And afterward
they prepared for themselves and for the priests, because the priests, the sons
of Aaron, were offering the burnt offerings and the fat parts until night; so the
Levites prepared for themselves and for the priests, the sons of Aaron. [15]The singers, the sons of Asaph, were in their place according to the command of David,
and Asaph, and Heman, and Jeduthun the king's seer; and the gatekeepers were
at each gate. They did not need to depart from their service, for their brothers the
Levites prepared for them.

[16]So all the service of the Lord was prepared that day, to keep the Passover and
to offer burnt offerings on the altar of the Lord, according to the command of
King Josiah. [17]And the people of Israel who were present kept the Passover at that
time, and the Feast of Unleavened Bread seven days. [18]No Passover like it had been
kept in Israel since the days of Samuel the prophet. None of the kings of Israel had
kept such a Passover as was kept by Josiah, and the priests and the Levites, and
all Judah and Israel who were present, and the inhabitants of Jerusalem. [19]In the
eighteenth year of the reign of Josiah this Passover was kept.

Josiah Killed in Battle

[20]After all this, when Josiah had prepared the temple, Neco king of Egypt went
up to fight at Carchemish on the Euphrates, and Josiah went out to meet him.
[21]But he sent envoys to him, saying, "What have we to do with each other, king
of Judah? I am not coming against you this day, but against the house with which
I am at war. And God has commanded me to hurry. Cease opposing God, who is
with me, lest he destroy you." [22]Nevertheless, Josiah did not turn away from him,
but disguised himself in order to fight with him. He did not listen to the words of
Neco from the mouth of God, but came to fight in the plain of Megiddo. [23]And the
archers shot King Josiah. And the king said to his servants, "Take me away, for I am

[1]Hebrew *by the hand of*

badly wounded." 24So his servants took him out of the chariot and carried him in
his second chariot and brought him to Jerusalem. And he died and was buried in
the tombs of his fathers. All Judah and Jerusalem mourned for Josiah. 25Jeremiah
also uttered a lament for Josiah; and all the singing men and singing women have
spoken of Josiah in their laments to this day. They made these a rule in Israel;
behold, they are written in the Laments. 26Now the rest of the acts of Josiah, and
his good deeds according to what is written in the Law of the LORD, 27and his acts,
first and last, behold, they are written in the Book of the Kings of Israel and Judah.

Judah's Decline

36 The people of the land took Jehoahaz the son of Josiah and made him king
in his father's place in Jerusalem. 2Jehoahaz was twenty-three years old
when he began to reign, and he reigned three months in Jerusalem. 3Then the
king of Egypt deposed him in Jerusalem and laid on the land a tribute of a hundred talents of silver and a talent[1] of gold. 4And the king of Egypt made Eliakim
his brother king over Judah and Jerusalem, and changed his name to Jehoiakim.
But Neco took Jehoahaz his brother and carried him to Egypt.

5Jehoiakim was twenty-five years old when he began to reign, and he reigned
eleven years in Jerusalem. He did what was evil in the sight of the LORD his God.
6Against him came up Nebuchadnezzar king of Babylon and bound him in chains
to take him to Babylon. 7Nebuchadnezzar also carried part of the vessels of the
house of the LORD to Babylon and put them in his palace in Babylon. 8Now the rest
of the acts of Jehoiakim, and the abominations that he did, and what was found
against him, behold, they are written in the Book of the Kings of Israel and Judah.
And Jehoiachin his son reigned in his place.

9Jehoiachin was eighteen[2] years old when he became king, and he reigned
three months and ten days in Jerusalem. He did what was evil in the sight of the
LORD. 10In the spring of the year King Nebuchadnezzar sent and brought him to
Babylon, with the precious vessels of the house of the LORD, and made his brother
Zedekiah king over Judah and Jerusalem.

11Zedekiah was twenty-one years old when he began to reign, and he reigned
eleven years in Jerusalem. 12He did what was evil in the sight of the LORD his God.
He did not humble himself before Jeremiah the prophet, who spoke from the
mouth of the LORD. 13He also rebelled against King Nebuchadnezzar, who had
made him swear by God. He stiffened his neck and hardened his heart against
turning to the LORD, the God of Israel. 14All the officers of the priests and the
people likewise were exceedingly unfaithful, following all the abominations of
the nations. And they polluted the house of the LORD that he had made holy in
Jerusalem.

15The LORD, the God of their fathers, sent persistently to them by his messengers, because he had compassion on his people and on his dwelling place. 16But
they kept mocking the messengers of God, despising his words and scoffing at
his prophets, until the wrath of the LORD rose against his people, until there was
no remedy.

Jerusalem Captured and Burned

17Therefore he brought up against them the king of the Chaldeans, who killed
their young men with the sword in the house of their sanctuary and had no compassion on young man or virgin, old man or aged. He gave them all into his hand.
18And all the vessels of the house of God, great and small, and the treasures of
the house of the LORD, and the treasures of the king and of his princes, all these
he brought to Babylon. 19And they burned the house of God and broke down the
wall of Jerusalem and burned all its palaces with fire and destroyed all its precious
vessels. 20He took into exile in Babylon those who had escaped from the sword,

---

[1]A *talent* was about 75 pounds or 34 kilograms [2]Septuagint (compare 2 Kings 24:8); most Hebrew manuscripts *eight*

and they became servants to him and to his sons until the establishment of the
kingdom of Persia, 21to fulfill the word of the LORD by the mouth of Jeremiah, until
the land had enjoyed its Sabbaths. All the days that it lay desolate it kept Sabbath,
to fulfill seventy years.

The Proclamation of Cyrus

22Now in the first year of Cyrus king of Persia, that the word of the LORD by the
mouth of Jeremiah might be fulfilled, the LORD stirred up the spirit of Cyrus king
of Persia, so that he made a proclamation throughout all his kingdom and also
put it in writing: 23"Thus says Cyrus king of Persia, 'The LORD, the God of heaven,
has given me all the kingdoms of the earth, and he has charged me to build him
a house at Jerusalem, which is in Judah. Whoever is among you of all his people,
may the LORD his God be with him. Let him go up.'"

JESUS: OUR HOPE FOR RETURN

EZRA

TEMPLE DESTROYED	TEMPLE REBUILT	EZRA ARRIVES IN JERUSALEM
c. 586 BC	*c. 536 – 516 BC*	*c. 458 BC*

The book of Ezra tells the story of the return of the remnant of Jews back to the promised land from captivity in Babylon. There this remnant sought to rebuild the temple and reestablish themselves as a community marked by God as his treasured possession. This small band of Jews faced a host of obstacles and impediments along the way, but through it all God once again showed that he was faithful to his promises.

In 539 BC, King Cyrus of Persia defeated the once-mighty Babylonian Empire. Once in power, Cyrus did what the Babylonian kings had been unwilling to do — he allowed the captive peoples to return to their homelands and to worship their respective gods. Among those exiles was this small band of Israelites who were allowed to return to Jerusalem while remaining subject to the Persian emperor.

The return took place in two stages, the first of which was led by Zerubbabel in about 538 BC. He led a group back to the promised land and began the work of rebuilding the temple (chs. 1 – 6). This daunting work took two decades to complete — the people finally finished in the sixth year of the reign of Darius (c. 516 BC). Ezra led a second group back in 458 BC and instituted a number of reforms during that time, calling the people to account for their practice of intermarriage with their pagan neighbors and leading them to confess their sins.

The story told in Ezra portrays the grand scope of the task of rebuilding the temple as well as rebuilding the nation as a worshiping people of God. Through his gracious acts on their behalf, God fulfilled his promise to the people to allow them to dwell in the land of promise and worship him in the temple. The words of earlier prophets rang in the people's ears as they faced the overwhelming task of rebuilding the life of the people of God in the land of God. Their hope was not simply that God would rebuild the temple; they trusted that God could rebuild their hearts as well.

Zerubbabel, as a descendant of David, is found in the genealogy of Jesus Christ at the outset of Matthew's Gospel (Mt 1:12 – 13). Perhaps more important, when God returned his people to the land of promise, he took another step toward setting the stage for the advent of Jesus Christ, who was to be born in this land in the city of Bethlehem (Mic 5:2). Through Christ, God now calls his people to repent and return to him, and grants them forgiveness and restoration when they do.

NOW THEN MAKE CONFESSION TO THE LORD,
THE GOD OF YOUR FATHERS
AND DO HIS WILL.

Ezra 10:11

EZRA

The Proclamation of Cyrus

1 In the first year of Cyrus king of Persia, that the word of the LORD by the mouth of Jeremiah might be fulfilled, the LORD stirred up the spirit of Cyrus king of Persia, so that he made a proclamation throughout all his kingdom and also put it in writing:

2"Thus says Cyrus king of Persia: The LORD, the God of heaven, has given me all the kingdoms of the earth, and he has charged me to build him a house at Jerusalem, which is in Judah. 3Whoever is among you of all his people, may his God be with him, and let him go up to Jerusalem, which is in Judah, and rebuild the house of the LORD, the God of Israel—he is the God who is in Jerusalem. 4And let each survivor, in whatever place he sojourns, be assisted by the men of his place with silver and gold, with goods and with beasts, besides freewill offerings for the house of God that is in Jerusalem."

5Then rose up the heads of the fathers' houses of Judah and Benjamin, and the priests and the Levites, everyone whose spirit God had stirred to go up to rebuild the house of the LORD that is in Jerusalem. 6And all who were about them aided them with vessels of silver, with gold, with goods, with beasts, and with costly wares, besides all that was freely offered. 7Cyrus the king also brought out the vessels of the house of the LORD that Nebuchadnezzar had carried away from Jerusalem and placed in the house of his gods. 8Cyrus king of Persia brought these out in the charge of Mithredath the treasurer, who counted them out to Sheshbazzar the prince of Judah. 9And this was the number of them: 30 basins of gold, 1,000 basins of silver, 29 censers, 10 30 bowls of gold, 410 bowls of silver, and 1,000 other vessels; 11all the vessels of gold and of silver were 5,400. All these did Sheshbazzar bring up, when the exiles were brought up from Babylonia to Jerusalem.

The Exiles Return

2 Now these were the people of the province who came up out of the captivity of those exiles whom Nebuchadnezzar the king of Babylon had carried captive to Babylonia. They returned to Jerusalem and Judah, each to his own town. 2They came with Zerubbabel, Jeshua, Nehemiah, Seraiah, Reelaiah, Mordecai, Bilshan, Mispar, Bigvai, Rehum, and Baanah.

The number of the men of the people of Israel: 3the sons of Parosh, 2,172. 4The sons of Shephatiah, 372. 5The sons of Arah, 775. 6The sons of Pahath-moab, namely the sons of Jeshua and Joab, 2,812. 7The sons of Elam, 1,254. 8The sons of Zattu, 945. 9The sons of Zaccai, 760. 10The sons of Bani, 642. 11The sons of Bebai, 623. 12The sons of Azgad, 1,222. 13The sons of Adonikam, 666. 14The sons of Bigvai, 2,056. 15The sons of Adin, 454. 16The sons of Ater, namely of Hezekiah, 98. 17The sons of Bezai, 323. 18The sons of Jorah, 112. 19The sons of Hashum, 223. 20The sons of Gibbar, 95. 21The sons of Bethlehem, 123. 22The men of Netophah, 56. 23The men of Anathoth, 128. 24The sons of Azmaveth, 42. 25The sons of Kiriath-arim, Chephirah, and Beeroth, 743. 26The sons of Ramah and Geba, 621. 27The men of Michmas, 122. 28The men of Bethel and Ai, 223. 29The sons of Nebo, 52. 30The sons of Magbish, 156. 31The sons of the other Elam, 1,254. 32The sons of Harim, 320. 33The sons of Lod, Hadid, and Ono, 725. 34The sons of Jericho, 345. 35The sons of Senaah, 3,630.

36The priests: the sons of Jedaiah, of the house of Jeshua, 973. 37The sons of Immer, 1,052. 38The sons of Pashhur, 1,247. 39The sons of Harim, 1,017.

40The Levites: the sons of Jeshua and Kadmiel, of the sons of Hodaviah, 74. 41The singers: the sons of Asaph, 128. 42The sons of the gatekeepers: the sons of Shallum, the sons of Ater, the sons of Talmon, the sons of Akkub, the sons of Hatita, and the sons of Shobai, in all 139.

EZRA 1:2–4

CYRUS POINTS TO THE MESSIAH

About 150 years beforehand, Isaiah prophesied the events described in the book of Ezra. He foretold that Cyrus would be the Lord's "shepherd" and would rebuild Jerusalem and its temple (Isa 44:28). This prophecy was fulfilled in Ezra 1:2–4 when Cyrus proclaimed that he would rebuild the Lord's temple and he released the Israelites to return to their homeland for the construction project. This pagan king can be viewed as a foreshadowing of the Messiah.

Like Cyrus but much better, the true Messiah is a king-shepherd who rules with the Lord's authority (Eze 34:23–24; 37:24–25; Jn 10:11). Like Cyrus, Jesus Christ would build God's house. Jesus said that his body was the temple, which would be destroyed and then raised up again in three days (Jn 2:19–22). Also, the church is the new "holy temple in the Lord" which Jesus built by his death and resurrection (Eph 2:19–22). Finally, like Cyrus, the Messiah would bring about a new exodus. The original exodus—when the Lord saved his people from slavery in Egypt—was the premier salvation event in the Old Testament. However, a promise was made that a new exodus would occur in the future, with the Lord freeing his people from slavery forever and living among them. Passages like *Isaiah 11 and Ezekiel 37* prophesied that the Messiah would accomplish this new and final salvation, and the New Testament describes the fulfillment of these prophecies in Jesus of Nazareth (cf. Rev 21:1–5).

43The temple servants: the sons of Ziha, the sons of Hasupha, the sons of Tabbaoth, 44the sons of Keros, the sons of Siaha, the sons of Padon, 45the sons of Lebanah, the sons of Hagabah, the sons of Akkub, 46the sons of Hagab, the sons of Shamlai, the sons of Hanan, 47the sons of Giddel, the sons of Gahar, the sons of Reaiah, 48the sons of Rezin, the sons of Nekoda, the sons of Gazzam, 49the sons of Uzza, the sons of Paseah, the sons of Besai, 50the sons of Asnah, the sons of Meunim, the sons of Nephisim, 51the sons of Bakbuk, the sons of Hakupha, the sons of Harhur, 52the sons of Bazluth, the sons of Mehida, the sons of Harsha, 53the sons of Barkos, the sons of Sisera, the sons of Temah, 54the sons of Neziah, and the sons of Hatipha.

55The sons of Solomon's servants: the sons of Sotai, the sons of Hassophereth, the sons of Peruda, 56the sons of Jaalah, the sons of Darkon, the sons of Giddel, 57the sons of Shephatiah, the sons of Hattil, the sons of Pochereth-hazzebaim, and the sons of Ami.

58All the temple servants and the sons of Solomon's servants were 392.

59The following were those who came up from Tel-melah, Tel-harsha, Cherub, Addan, and Immer, though they could not prove their fathers' houses or their descent, whether they belonged to Israel: 60the sons of Delaiah, the sons of Tobiah, and the sons of Nekoda, 652. 61Also, of the sons of the priests: the sons of Habaiah, the sons of Hakkoz, and the sons of Barzillai (who had taken a wife from the daughters of Barzillai the Gileadite, and was called by their name). 62These sought their registration among those enrolled in the genealogies, but they were not found there, and so they were excluded from the priesthood as unclean. 63The governor told them that they were not to partake of the most holy food, until there should be a priest to consult Urim and Thummim.

64The whole assembly together was 42,360, 65besides their male and female servants, of whom there were 7,337, and they had 200 male and female singers. 66Their horses were 736, their mules were 245, 67their camels were 435, and their donkeys were 6,720.

68Some of the heads of families, when they came to the house of the LORD that is in Jerusalem, made freewill offerings for the house of God, to erect it on its site. 69According to their ability they gave to the treasury of the work 61,000 darics[1] of gold, 5,000 minas[2] of silver, and 100 priests' garments.

70Now the priests, the Levites, some of the people, the singers, the gatekeepers, and the temple servants lived in their towns, and all the rest of Israel[3] in their towns.

Rebuilding the Altar

3 When the seventh month came, and the children of Israel were in the towns, the people gathered as one man to Jerusalem. 2Then arose Jeshua the son of Jozadak, with his fellow priests, and Zerubbabel the son of Shealtiel with his kinsmen, and they built the altar of the God of Israel, to offer burnt offerings on it, as it is written in the Law of Moses the man of God. 3They set the altar in its place, for fear was on them because of the peoples of the lands, and they offered burnt offerings on it to the LORD, burnt offerings morning and evening. 4And they kept the Feast of Booths, as it is written, and offered the daily burnt offerings by number according to the rule, as each day required, 5and after that the regular burnt offerings, the offerings at the new moon and at all the appointed feasts of the LORD, and the offerings of everyone who made a freewill offering to the LORD. 6From the first day of the seventh month they began to offer burnt offerings to the LORD. But the foundation of the temple of the LORD was not yet laid. 7So they gave money to the masons and the carpenters, and food, drink, and oil to the Sidonians and the Tyrians to bring cedar trees from Lebanon to the sea, to Joppa, according to the grant that they had from Cyrus king of Persia.

[1]A *daric* was a coin weighing about 1/4 ounce or 8.5 grams [2]A *mina* was about 1 1/4 pounds or 0.6 kilogram [3]Hebrew *all Israel*

EZRA 2:1–2

THE DAVIDIC PROMISE

Ezra 2 lists those that returned to Israel from captivity. What is most important about this passage is that David's family returned from captivity through his descendant Zerubbabel. In 2 Samuel 7:16, God promised an eternal dynasty to David—David would never fail to have a son on the throne of Israel. The keeping of that promise looked bleak when Nebuchadnezzar razed Jerusalem to the ground and took David's descendants as captives to Babylon. However, Amos foretold that the fallen house of David would be restored (Am 9:11). This prophecy began to be realized in Ezra 2 when Zerubbabel returned to Jerusalem. God would finally fulfill this prophecy by raising David's descendant—Jesus of Nazareth—from the dead and seating him on an eternal throne (Ac 2:29–36; 13:32–37). The fact that Zerubbabel, from the royal line of David, was one of the returning exiles must have given great hope to the restored community that God keeps his promises no matter the situation. This truth should give God's people hope today as well.

Rebuilding the Temple

8Now in the second year after their coming to the house of God at Jerusalem, in the second month, Zerubbabel the son of Shealtiel and Jeshua the son of Jozadak made a beginning, together with the rest of their kinsmen, the priests and the Levites and all who had come to Jerusalem from the captivity. They appointed the Levites, from twenty years old and upward, to supervise the work of the house of the LORD. 9And Jeshua with his sons and his brothers, and Kadmiel and his sons, the sons of Judah, together supervised the workmen in the house of God, along with the sons of Henadad and the Levites, their sons and brothers.

10And when the builders laid the foundation of the temple of the LORD, the priests in their vestments came forward with trumpets, and the Levites, the sons of Asaph, with cymbals, to praise the LORD, according to the directions of David king of Israel. 11And they sang responsively, praising and giving thanks to the LORD,

"For he is good,
for his steadfast love endures forever toward Israel."

And all the people shouted with a great shout when they praised the LORD, because the foundation of the house of the LORD was laid. 12But many of the priests and Levites and heads of fathers' houses, old men who had seen the first house, wept with a loud voice when they saw the foundation of this house being laid, though many shouted aloud for joy, 13so that the people could not distinguish the sound of the joyful shout from the sound of the people's weeping, for the people shouted with a great shout, and the sound was heard far away.

Adversaries Oppose the Rebuilding

4 Now when the adversaries of Judah and Benjamin heard that the returned exiles were building a temple to the LORD, the God of Israel, 2they approached Zerubbabel and the heads of fathers' houses and said to them, "Let us build with you, for we worship your God as you do, and we have been sacrificing to him ever since the days of Esarhaddon king of Assyria who brought us here." 3But Zerubbabel, Jeshua, and the rest of the heads of fathers' houses in Israel said to them, "You have nothing to do with us in building a house to our God; but we alone will build to the LORD, the God of Israel, as King Cyrus the king of Persia has commanded us."

4Then the people of the land discouraged the people of Judah and made them afraid to build 5and bribed counselors against them to frustrate their purpose, all the days of Cyrus king of Persia, even until the reign of Darius king of Persia.

6And in the reign of Ahasuerus, in the beginning of his reign, they wrote an accusation against the inhabitants of Judah and Jerusalem.

The Letter to King Artaxerxes

7In the days of Artaxerxes, Bishlam and Mithredath and Tabeel and the rest of their associates wrote to Artaxerxes king of Persia. The letter was written in Aramaic and translated.[1] 8Rehum the commander and Shimshai the scribe wrote a letter against Jerusalem to Artaxerxes the king as follows: 9Rehum the commander, Shimshai the scribe, and the rest of their associates, the judges, the governors, the officials, the Persians, the men of Erech, the Babylonians, the men of Susa, that is, the Elamites, 10and the rest of the nations whom the great and noble Osnappar deported and settled in the cities of Samaria and in the rest of the province Beyond the River. 11(This is a copy of the letter that they sent.) "To Artaxerxes the king: Your servants, the men of the province Beyond the River, send greeting. And now 12be it known to the king that the Jews who came up from you to us have

EZRA 3:8

KINGS, PRIESTS, AND TEMPLES

Ezra 3:8 notified its readers that Zerubbabel and Joshua oversaw the building of the new temple. This was significant because Zerubbabel was a descendant of King David and Joshua was the high priest. It makes good sense that these two men would oversee the project since kings are temple-builders and priests are temple-workers. After all, King David wanted to build the original temple (2Sa 7:1–13), and his son Solomon ended up building it (1Ki 5–8). It was fitting that for the second temple, David's offspring, Zerubbabel, oversaw its construction. And it was also fitting that Joshua the high priest took up the priestly duty of interceding for the people by offering sacrifices to the Lord in the temple for the people's sins (Ezr 6:15–18; cf. Lev 1–9; 16).

Both of these roles — king and priest — point forward to Jesus Christ, who is both the greater King and the greater Priest. He built God's temple — the church (Eph 2:19–22). He offered the final sacrifice to God that once and for all dealt with humanity's sin problem (Heb 10:11–14). And Jesus is the risen high priest who "is able to save to the uttermost those who draw near to God through him, since he always lives to make intercession for them" (Heb 7:25). He is the one who gives true and lasting access to God and his house!

[1]Hebrew *written in Aramaic and translated in Aramaic*, indicating that 4:8–6:18 is in Aramaic; another interpretation is *The letter was written in the Aramaic script and set forth in the Aramaic language*

gone to Jerusalem. They are rebuilding that rebellious and wicked city. They are finishing the walls and repairing the foundations. 13Now be it known to the king that if this city is rebuilt and the walls finished, they will not pay tribute, custom, or toll, and the royal revenue will be impaired. 14Now because we eat the salt of the palace[1] and it is not fitting for us to witness the king's dishonor, therefore we send and inform the king, 15in order that search may be made in the book of the records of your fathers. You will find in the book of the records and learn that this city is a rebellious city, hurtful to kings and provinces, and that sedition was stirred up in it from of old. That was why this city was laid waste. 16We make known to the king that if this city is rebuilt and its walls finished, you will then have no possession in the province Beyond the River."

The King Orders the Work to Cease

17The king sent an answer: "To Rehum the commander and Shimshai the scribe and the rest of their associates who live in Samaria and in the rest of the province Beyond the River, greeting. And now 18the letter that you sent to us has been plainly read before me. 19And I made a decree, and search has been made, and it has been found that this city from of old has risen against kings, and that rebellion and sedition have been made in it. 20And mighty kings have been over Jerusalem, who ruled over the whole province Beyond the River, to whom tribute, custom, and toll were paid. 21Therefore make a decree that these men be made to cease, and that this city be not rebuilt, until a decree is made by me. 22And take care not to be slack in this matter. Why should damage grow to the hurt of the king?"

23Then, when the copy of King Artaxerxes' letter was read before Rehum and Shimshai the scribe and their associates, they went in haste to the Jews at Jerusalem and by force and power made them cease. 24Then the work on the house of God that is in Jerusalem stopped, and it ceased until the second year of the reign of Darius king of Persia.

Rebuilding Begins Anew

5 Now the prophets, Haggai and Zechariah the son of Iddo, prophesied to the Jews who were in Judah and Jerusalem, in the name of the God of Israel who was over them. 2Then Zerubbabel the son of Shealtiel and Jeshua the son of Jozadak arose and began to rebuild the house of God that is in Jerusalem, and the prophets of God were with them, supporting them.

3At the same time Tattenai the governor of the province Beyond the River and Shethar-bozenai and their associates came to them and spoke to them thus: "Who gave you a decree to build this house and to finish this structure?" 4They also asked them this:[2] "What are the names of the men who are building this building?" 5But the eye of their God was on the elders of the Jews, and they did not stop them until the report should reach Darius and then an answer be returned by letter concerning it.

Tattenai's Letter to King Darius

6This is a copy of the letter that Tattenai the governor of the province Beyond the River and Shethar-bozenai and his associates, the governors who were in the province Beyond the River, sent to Darius the king. 7They sent him a report, in which was written as follows: "To Darius the king, all peace. 8Be it known to the king that we went to the province of Judah, to the house of the great God. It is being built with huge stones, and timber is laid in the walls. This work goes on diligently and prospers in their hands. 9Then we asked those elders and spoke to them thus: 'Who gave you a decree to build this house and to finish this structure?' 10We also asked them their names, for your information, that we might

[1]Aramaic *because the salt of the palace is our salt* [2]Septuagint, Syriac; Aramaic *Then we said to them,*

EZRA 3:12–13

THE GREATER, MORE GLORIOUS TEMPLE

When the workers laid the foundation of the new temple, the older people who had seen Solomon's temple wept loudly—apparently realizing from the outset that the second temple was not going to be as glorious as the first. Yet, several years later the Lord promised, through the prophet Haggai, that the future glory of this temple would far outshine the glory of Solomon's temple, and the Lord would fill the new temple with his glory (Hag 2:7–9). The first temple had occasionally been enveloped by the glory of God in a way that all Israel could see that God was with them (1Ki 8:10–11), just as the tabernacle had been previously (Ex 40:34). Just before the exile, God gave Ezekiel a vision, in chapter 10, of his glory departing from the temple. However, Ezekiel also received a vision, in chapter 43, promising that the glory of the Lord would return to a perfect new temple.

John's Gospel describes, in part, the fulfillment of that prophecy: the Word (Jesus) became flesh and "dwelt among us, and we have seen his glory" (Jn 1:14). Revelation says there will be no temple in the new Jerusalem because "the Lord God the Almighty and the Lamb" are its temple, and no sun will be needed there because God's glory will provide the light (Rev 21:22–23). The rebuilt temple in Ezra's day did not hold a candle to the glory of the future temple—where God himself will live with his people forever as their God (Rev 21:3).

write down the names of their leaders.[1] 11And this was their reply to us: 'We are the
servants of the God of heaven and earth, and we are rebuilding the house that was
built many years ago, which a great king of Israel built and finished. 12But because
our fathers had angered the God of heaven, he gave them into the hand of Nebuchadnezzar king of Babylon, the Chaldean, who destroyed this house and carried
away the people to Babylonia. 13However, in the first year of Cyrus king of Babylon, Cyrus the king made a decree that this house of God should be rebuilt. 14And
the gold and silver vessels of the house of God, which Nebuchadnezzar had taken
out of the temple that was in Jerusalem and brought into the temple of Babylon,
these Cyrus the king took out of the temple of Babylon, and they were delivered
to one whose name was Sheshbazzar, whom he had made governor; 15and he said
to him, "Take these vessels, go and put them in the temple that is in Jerusalem,
and let the house of God be rebuilt on its site." 16Then this Sheshbazzar came and
laid the foundations of the house of God that is in Jerusalem, and from that time
until now it has been in building, and it is not yet finished.' 17Therefore, if it seems
good to the king, let search be made in the royal archives there in Babylon, to see
whether a decree was issued by Cyrus the king for the rebuilding of this house of
God in Jerusalem. And let the king send us his pleasure in this matter."

The Decree of Darius

6 Then Darius the king made a decree, and search was made in Babylonia, in
the house of the archives where the documents were stored. 2And in Ecbata-
na, the citadel that is in the province of Media, a scroll was found on which this
was written: "A record. 3In the first year of Cyrus the king, Cyrus the king issued
a decree: Concerning the house of God at Jerusalem, let the house be rebuilt, the
place where sacrifices were offered, and let its foundations be retained. Its height
shall be sixty cubits[2] and its breadth sixty cubits, 4with three layers of great stones
and one layer of timber. Let the cost be paid from the royal treasury. 5And also
let the gold and silver vessels of the house of God, which Nebuchadnezzar took
out of the temple that is in Jerusalem and brought to Babylon, be restored and
brought back to the temple that is in Jerusalem, each to its place. You shall put
them in the house of God."

6"Now therefore, Tattenai, governor of the province Beyond the River,
Shethar-bozenai, and your[3] associates the governors who are in the province
Beyond the River, keep away. 7Let the work on this house of God alone. Let the
governor of the Jews and the elders of the Jews rebuild this house of God on its
site. 8Moreover, I make a decree regarding what you shall do for these elders of
the Jews for the rebuilding of this house of God. The cost is to be paid to these
men in full and without delay from the royal revenue, the tribute of the province
from Beyond the River. 9And whatever is needed—bulls, rams, or sheep for burnt
offerings to the God of heaven, wheat, salt, wine, or oil, as the priests at Jerusalem
require—let that be given to them day by day without fail, 10that they may offer
pleasing sacrifices to the God of heaven and pray for the life of the king and his
sons. 11Also I make a decree that if anyone alters this edict, a beam shall be pulled
out of his house, and he shall be impaled on it, and his house shall be made a
dunghill. 12May the God who has caused his name to dwell there overthrow any
king or people who shall put out a hand to alter this, or to destroy this house of
God that is in Jerusalem. I Darius make a decree; let it be done with all diligence."

The Temple Finished and Dedicated

13Then, according to the word sent by Darius the king, Tattenai, the governor
of the province Beyond the River, Shethar-bozenai, and their associates did with
all diligence what Darius the king had ordered. 14And the elders of the Jews built
and prospered through the prophesying of Haggai the prophet and Zechariah the

[1] Aramaic *of the men at their heads* [2] A *cubit* was about 18 inches or 45 centimeters [3] Aramaic *their*

son of Iddo. They finished their building by decree of the God of Israel and by decree of Cyrus and Darius and Artaxerxes king of Persia; 15and this house was finished on the third day of the month of Adar, in the sixth year of the reign of Darius the king.

16And the people of Israel, the priests and the Levites, and the rest of the returned exiles, celebrated the dedication of this house of God with joy. 17They offered at the dedication of this house of God 100 bulls, 200 rams, 400 lambs, and as a sin offering for all Israel 12 male goats, according to the number of the tribes of Israel. 18And they set the priests in their divisions and the Levites in their divisions, for the service of God at Jerusalem, as it is written in the Book of Moses.

Passover Celebrated

19On the fourteenth day of the first month, the returned exiles kept the Passover. 20For the priests and the Levites had purified themselves together; all of them were clean. So they slaughtered the Passover lamb for all the returned exiles, for their fellow priests, and for themselves. 21It was eaten by the people of Israel who had returned from exile, and also by every one who had joined them and separated himself from the uncleanness of the peoples of the land to worship the LORD, the God of Israel. 22And they kept the Feast of Unleavened Bread seven days with joy, for the LORD had made them joyful and had turned the heart of the king of Assyria to them, so that he aided them in the work of the house of God, the God of Israel.

Ezra Sent to Teach the People

7 Now after this, in the reign of Artaxerxes king of Persia, Ezra the son of Seraiah, son of Azariah, son of Hilkiah, 2son of Shallum, son of Zadok, son of Ahitub, 3son of Amariah, son of Azariah, son of Meraioth, 4son of Zerahiah, son of Uzzi, son of Bukki, 5son of Abishua, son of Phinehas, son of Eleazar, son of Aaron the chief priest— 6this Ezra went up from Babylonia. He was a scribe skilled in the Law of Moses that the LORD, the God of Israel, had given, and the king granted him all that he asked, for the hand of the LORD his God was on him.

7And there went up also to Jerusalem, in the seventh year of Artaxerxes the king, some of the people of Israel, and some of the priests and Levites, the singers and gatekeepers, and the temple servants. 8And Ezra[1] came to Jerusalem in the fifth month, which was in the seventh year of the king. 9For on the first day of the first month he began to go up from Babylonia, and on the first day of the fifth month he came to Jerusalem, for the good hand of his God was on him. 10For Ezra had set his heart to study the Law of the LORD, and to do it and to teach his statutes and rules in Israel.

11This is a copy of the letter that King Artaxerxes gave to Ezra the priest, the scribe, a man learned in matters of the commandments of the LORD and his statutes for Israel:[2] 12"Artaxerxes, king of kings, to Ezra the priest, the scribe of the Law of the God of heaven. Peace.[3] And now 13I make a decree that anyone of the people of Israel or their priests or Levites in my kingdom, who freely offers to go to Jerusalem, may go with you. 14For you are sent by the king and his seven counselors to make inquiries about Judah and Jerusalem according to the Law of your God, which is in your hand, 15and also to carry the silver and gold that the king and his counselors have freely offered to the God of Israel, whose dwelling is in Jerusalem, 16with all the silver and gold that you shall find in the whole province of Babylonia, and with the freewill offerings of the people and the priests, vowed willingly for the house of their God that is in Jerusalem. 17With this money, then, you shall with all diligence buy bulls, rams, and lambs, with their grain offerings and their drink offerings, and you shall offer them on the altar of the house of your God that is in Jerusalem. 18Whatever seems good to you and your brothers

[1]Hebrew *he* [2]The text of Ezra 7:12-26 is in Aramaic [3]Aramaic *Perfect* (probably a greeting)

EZRA 6:16–20

THE LAMB WHO REMOVES THE WORLD'S SIN

At the dedication of the new temple, the Israelites offered hundreds of sin offerings to atone for their sins, including twelve goats to atone for each of the twelve tribes. Atonement means that these sacrifices received the judgment of God that the people of Israel deserved because of their sin. Then, in connection with the dedication of the new temple, the returned exiles celebrated the Passover. The Passover recalled how the Lord passed over the Israelite houses in Egypt and did not kill their firstborn. Death had already happened in that house when a lamb was killed in the firstborn's place (Ex 12). However, these activities—sacrifice and Passover—were merely provisional because they could not deal with the people's sin problem once for all. All of these slaughtered animals pointed forward to the final Passover Lamb—Jesus Christ—who takes away the sin of the world (Jn 1:29; 1Co 5:7).

to do with the rest of the silver and gold, you may do, according to the will of
your God. 19The vessels that have been given you for the service of the house of
your God, you shall deliver before the God of Jerusalem. 20And whatever else is
required for the house of your God, which it falls to you to provide, you may provide it out of the king's treasury.

21"And I, Artaxerxes the king, make a decree to all the treasurers in the province Beyond the River: Whatever Ezra the priest, the scribe of the Law of the God
of heaven, requires of you, let it be done with all diligence, 22up to 100 talents[1] of
silver, 100 cors[2] of wheat, 100 baths[3] of wine, 100 baths of oil, and salt without
prescribing how much. 23Whatever is decreed by the God of heaven, let it be done
in full for the house of the God of heaven, lest his wrath be against the realm of
the king and his sons. 24We also notify you that it shall not be lawful to impose
tribute, custom, or toll on anyone of the priests, the Levites, the singers, the door-
keepers, the temple servants, or other servants of this house of God.

25"And you, Ezra, according to the wisdom of your God that is in your hand,
appoint magistrates and judges who may judge all the people in the province Beyond the River, all such as know the laws of your God. And those who do not
know them, you shall teach. 26Whoever will not obey the law of your God and the
law of the king, let judgment be strictly executed on him, whether for death or for
banishment or for confiscation of his goods or for imprisonment."

27Blessed be the LORD, the God of our fathers, who put such a thing as this into
the heart of the king, to beautify the house of the LORD that is in Jerusalem, 28and
who extended to me his steadfast love before the king and his counselors, and
before all the king's mighty officers. I took courage, for the hand of the LORD my
God was on me, and I gathered leading men from Israel to go up with me.

Genealogy of Those Who Returned with Ezra

8 These are the heads of their fathers' houses, and this is the genealogy of
those who went up with me from Babylonia, in the reign of Artaxerxes the
king: 2Of the sons of Phinehas, Gershom. Of the sons of Ithamar, Daniel. Of the
sons of David, Hattush. 3Of the sons of Shecaniah, who was of the sons of Parosh,
Zechariah, with whom were registered 150 men. 4Of the sons of Pahath-moab,
Eliehoenai the son of Zerahiah, and with him 200 men. 5Of the sons of Zattu,[4]
Shecaniah the son of Jahaziel, and with him 300 men. 6Of the sons of Adin, Ebed
the son of Jonathan, and with him 50 men. 7Of the sons of Elam, Jeshaiah the son
of Athaliah, and with him 70 men. 8Of the sons of Shephatiah, Zebadiah the son
of Michael, and with him 80 men. 9Of the sons of Joab, Obadiah the son of Jehiel,
and with him 218 men. 10Of the sons of Bani,[5] Shelomith the son of Josiphiah, and
with him 160 men. 11Of the sons of Bebai, Zechariah, the son of Bebai, and with
him 28 men. 12Of the sons of Azgad, Johanan the son of Hakkatan, and with him
110 men. 13Of the sons of Adonikam, those who came later, their names being
Eliphelet, Jeuel, and Shemaiah, and with them 60 men. 14Of the sons of Bigvai,
Uthai and Zaccur, and with them 70 men.

Ezra Sends for Levites

15I gathered them to the river that runs to Ahava, and there we camped three
days. As I reviewed the people and the priests, I found there none of the sons of
Levi. 16Then I sent for Eliezer, Ariel, Shemaiah, Elnathan, Jarib, Elnathan, Nathan,
Zechariah, and Meshullam, leading men, and for Joiarib and Elnathan, who were
men of insight, 17and sent them to Iddo, the leading man at the place Casiphia,
telling them what to say to Iddo and his brothers and[6] the temple servants at the
place Casiphia, namely, to send us ministers for the house of our God. 18And by
the good hand of our God on us, they brought us a man of discretion, of the sons

[1] A *talent* was about 75 pounds or 34 kilograms [2] A *cor* was about 6 bushels or 220 liters [3] A *bath* was about 6 gallons or 22 liters [4] Septuagint; Hebrew lacks *of Zattu* [5] Septuagint; Hebrew lacks *Bani* [6] Hebrew lacks *and*

of Mahli the son of Levi, son of Israel, namely Sherebiah with his sons and kinsmen, 18; 19also Hashabiah, and with him Jeshaiah of the sons of Merari, with his kinsmen and their sons, 20; 20besides 220 of the temple servants, whom David and his officials had set apart to attend the Levites. These were all mentioned by name.

Fasting and Prayer for Protection

21Then I proclaimed a fast there, at the river Ahava, that we might humble ourselves before our God, to seek from him a safe journey for ourselves, our children, and all our goods. 22For I was ashamed to ask the king for a band of soldiers and horsemen to protect us against the enemy on our way, since we had told the king, "The hand of our God is for good on all who seek him, and the power of his wrath is against all who forsake him." 23So we fasted and implored our God for this, and he listened to our entreaty.

Priests to Guard Offerings

24Then I set apart twelve of the leading priests: Sherebiah, Hashabiah, and ten of their kinsmen with them. 25And I weighed out to them the silver and the gold and the vessels, the offering for the house of our God that the king and his counselors and his lords and all Israel there present had offered. 26I weighed out into their hand 650 talents[1] of silver, and silver vessels worth 200 talents,[2] and 100 talents of gold, 2720 bowls of gold worth 1,000 darics,[3] and two vessels of fine bright bronze as precious as gold. 28And I said to them, "You are holy to the LORD, and the vessels are holy, and the silver and the gold are a freewill offering to the LORD, the God of your fathers. 29Guard them and keep them until you weigh them before the chief priests and the Levites and the heads of fathers' houses in Israel at Jerusalem, within the chambers of the house of the LORD." 30So the priests and the Levites took over the weight of the silver and the gold and the vessels, to bring them to Jerusalem, to the house of our God.

31Then we departed from the river Ahava on the twelfth day of the first month, to go to Jerusalem. The hand of our God was on us, and he delivered us from the hand of the enemy and from ambushes by the way. 32We came to Jerusalem, and there we remained three days. 33On the fourth day, within the house of our God, the silver and the gold and the vessels were weighed into the hands of Meremoth the priest, son of Uriah, and with him was Eleazar the son of Phinehas, and with them were the Levites, Jozabad the son of Jeshua and Noadiah the son of Binnui. 34The whole was counted and weighed, and the weight of everything was recorded.

35At that time those who had come from captivity, the returned exiles, offered burnt offerings to the God of Israel, twelve bulls for all Israel, ninety-six rams, seventy-seven lambs, and as a sin offering twelve male goats. All this was a burnt offering to the LORD. 36They also delivered the king's commissions to the king's satraps[4] and to the governors of the province Beyond the River, and they aided the people and the house of God.

Ezra Prays About Intermarriage

9 After these things had been done, the officials approached me and said, "The people of Israel and the priests and the Levites have not separated themselves from the peoples of the lands with their abominations, from the Canaanites, the Hittites, the Perizzites, the Jebusites, the Ammonites, the Moabites, the Egyptians, and the Amorites. 2For they have taken some of their daughters to be wives for themselves and for their sons, so that the holy race[5] has mixed itself with the peoples of the lands. And in this faithlessness the hand of the officials and chief

---

[1]A *talent* was about 75 pounds or 34 kilograms [2]Revocalization; the number is missing in the Masoretic Text [3]A *daric* was a coin weighing about 1/4 ounce or 8.5 grams [4]A *satrap* was a Persian official [5]Hebrew *offspring*

THE BACKDROP OF EZRA

God, in Deuteronomy 30, had prophesied that Israel would disobey God's law and go into exile. Once in exile, they would seek the Lord with all their hearts and the Lord would restore them to the land. God also promised that he would one day circumcise the hearts of his people so that they would be fully devoted to him (Dt 30:1–6). At first glance, Ezra might seem to depict the fulfillment of this prophecy. After all, the people had forsaken the Lord, gone into exile, and then returned to the land. But while God's promises to Israel were starting to come true, they were not fully realized. The people's hearts had not been transformed, which was evident in the fact that they intermarried with the pagans in the land just as they had done when they entered the land after the exodus from Egypt (Jdg 3:5–6; Ezr 9:1–2). The Israelites did not separate themselves from the neighboring peoples and their sinful practices. The issue was one of religion, not race — being unequally yoked to unbelievers.

To understand what happened in Ezra, one must realize that Daniel's prayer in Daniel 9 forms the backdrop to the two books known as Ezra and Nehemiah. As Daniel read Jeremiah's prophecy in Jeremiah 29:10–14, he realized that the exile in Babylon would last seventy years (Da 9:2). So, in accordance with Deuteronomy and 1 Kings 8, Daniel prayed to the Lord confessing the sins of Israel in order to prepare them for the return to the land. He understood that repentance had to precede the return. Ezra reveals that God stirred up King Cyrus to return the Israelites to their land in order to fulfill God's word spoken through Jeremiah (Ezr 1:1).

However, the angel Gabriel came to Daniel at the end of his prayer and prophesied that the exile would not just last seventy years. Rather, the exile would last seventy times seven years (weeks) — not truly coming to an end until the anointed one, the Messiah, was put to death (Da 9:20–27).

So Ezra is an "already but not yet" book. God's promises were already partially coming true but had not yet fully come true. God kept his promise to bring them back to the land, but the transformation promised in Deuteronomy and other places had not happened. They were, in a sense, exiles in their own land (a situation that remained in effect at the time of Jesus, at which point Judea was under Roman rule). Therefore, Ezra pointed to the need for Israel to be truly rescued from exile and truly transformed. Ezra pointed forward to the need for the Messiah. Not until Jesus was separated from God the Father as he hung on the cross (Da 9:26) would the people's separation from God truly end and their transformation be fully accomplished.

men has been foremost." 3As soon as I heard this, I tore my garment and my cloak and pulled hair from my head and beard and sat appalled. 4Then all who trembled at the words of the God of Israel, because of the faithlessness of the returned exiles, gathered around me while I sat appalled until the evening sacrifice. 5And at the evening sacrifice I rose from my fasting, with my garment and my cloak torn, and fell upon my knees and spread out my hands to the LORD my God, 6saying:

"O my God, I am ashamed and blush to lift my face to you, my God, for our iniquities have risen higher than our heads, and our guilt has mounted up to the heavens. 7From the days of our fathers to this day we have been in great guilt. And for our iniquities we, our kings, and our priests have been given into the hand of the kings of the lands, to the sword, to captivity, to plundering, and to utter shame, as it is today. 8But now for a brief moment favor has been shown by the LORD our God, to leave us a remnant and to give us a secure hold[1] within his holy place, that our God may brighten our eyes and grant us a little reviving in our slavery. 9For we are slaves. Yet our God has not forsaken us in our slavery, but has extended to us his steadfast love before the kings of Persia, to grant us some reviving to set up the house of our God, to repair its ruins, and to give us protection[2] in Judea and Jerusalem.

10"And now, O our God, what shall we say after this? For we have forsaken your commandments, 11which you commanded by your servants the prophets, saying, 'The land that you are entering, to take possession of it, is a land impure with the impurity of the peoples of the lands, with their abominations that have filled it from end to end with their uncleanness. 12Therefore do not give your daughters to their sons, neither take their daughters for your sons, and never seek their peace or prosperity, that you may be strong and eat the good of the land and leave it for an inheritance to your children forever.' 13And after all that has come upon us for our evil deeds and for our great guilt, seeing that you, our God, have punished us less than our iniquities deserved and have given us such a remnant as this, 14shall we break your commandments again and intermarry with the peoples who practice these abominations? Would you not be angry with us until you consumed us, so that there should be no remnant, nor any to escape? 15O LORD, the God of Israel, you are just, for we are left a remnant that has escaped, as it is today. Behold, we are before you in our guilt, for none can stand before you because of this."

The People Confess Their Sin

10 While Ezra prayed and made confession, weeping and casting himself down before the house of God, a very great assembly of men, women, and children, gathered to him out of Israel, for the people wept bitterly. 2And Shecaniah the son of Jehiel, of the sons of Elam, addressed Ezra: "We have broken faith with our God and have married foreign women from the peoples of the land, but even now there is hope for Israel in spite of this. 3Therefore let us make a covenant with our God to put away all these wives and their children, according to the counsel of my lord[3] and of those who tremble at the commandment of our God, and let it be done according to the Law. 4Arise, for it is your task, and we are with you; be strong and do it." 5Then Ezra arose and made the leading priests and Levites and all Israel take an oath that they would do as had been said. So they took the oath.

6Then Ezra withdrew from before the house of God and went to the chamber of Jehohanan the son of Eliashib, where he spent the night,[4] neither eating bread nor drinking water, for he was mourning over the faithlessness of the exiles. 7And a proclamation was made throughout Judah and Jerusalem to all the returned exiles that they should assemble at Jerusalem, 8and that if anyone did not come within three days, by order of the officials and the elders all his property should be forfeited, and he himself banned from the congregation of the exiles.

[1]Hebrew *nail, or tent-pin* [2]Hebrew *a wall* [3]Or *of the Lord* [4]Probable reading; Hebrew *where he went*

EZRA 9:13

THE REMNANT

The Lord promised Abraham that his offspring would be an uncountable multitude as numerous as the stars in the heaven and the sand on the seashore (Ge 22:17). After Israel's rebellion against the Lord and his judgment on them in the Babylonian exile, only a remnant—a small number of people—returned to the land. But as Isaiah had prophesied—using the example of a tree that is cut down to a stump but sprouts new growth—from the broken stump of the returned exiles the Messiah would sprout and bring forth new life (Isa 6:11–13; 11:1). During the time of Ezra, Israel was a small stump, but in the future it would once again sprout into an uncountable multitude. God would keep his promise that the offspring of Abraham would be as numerous as the stars and the sand. How did God keep his promise? Through the offspring of Abraham who is Jesus Christ (Gal 3:16). All who believe in Jesus—regardless of ethnicity—are the offspring of Abraham (Gal 3:28–29), and no one will be able to count that multitude on the last day (Rev 7:9).

EZRA 10:1

THE MERCY OF GOD

Ezra gave an outward sign of repentance by tearing his clothes and pulling hair from his head and beard (Ezr 9:3). He then offered a prayer of repentance by recounting the faithless history of Israel. But he also acknowledged that despite their sin, God had shown favor in more recent events, particularly the return of the remnant and the reconstruction of

(continued on next page)

(The Mercy of God, continued)

the temple. Despite God's favor, the returned exiles sinned by intermarrying with the inhabitants of the land, just as the people of Israel had done when they first entered the promised land after the exodus from Egypt (Ezr 9:1–2; Jdg 3:5–6). Even some of the priests had married foreign women (Ezr 10:18). The problem with the marriages was not race; it was religion. God's chosen people had married idolaters who did not worship the true God. And yet, following Ezra's prayer of confession, the people followed Ezra's lead and began to confess their sins in front of the temple (10:1).

This scene of repentance reflected a request Solomon had made of God long ago: that God would be merciful and forgive his rebellious, exiled people if they turned toward the temple and confessed their sins (1Ki 8:46–51). Despite the Israelites' continual disobedience, God remained incredibly merciful to them. The situation for believers today is different from ancient Israel. The church does not pray toward a temple made with bricks and mortar. Rather, God's people pray to the new temple—Jesus of Nazareth (Jn 2:21). And when they do, he is faithful to forgive their sins (1Jn 1:9).

9Then all the men of Judah and Benjamin assembled at Jerusalem within the
three days. It was the ninth month, on the twentieth day of the month. And all the
people sat in the open square before the house of God, trembling because of this
matter and because of the heavy rain. 10And Ezra the priest stood up and said to
them, "You have broken faith and married foreign women, and so increased the
guilt of Israel. 11Now then make confession to the LORD, the God of your fathers
and do his will. Separate yourselves from the peoples of the land and from the
foreign wives." 12Then all the assembly answered with a loud voice, "It is so; we
must do as you have said. 13But the people are many, and it is a time of heavy rain;
we cannot stand in the open. Nor is this a task for one day or for two, for we have
greatly transgressed in this matter. 14Let our officials stand for the whole assembly. Let all in our cities who have taken foreign wives come at appointed times,
and with them the elders and judges of every city, until the fierce wrath of our
God over this matter is turned away from us." 15Only Jonathan the son of Asahel
and Jahzeiah the son of Tikvah opposed this, and Meshullam and Shabbethai the
Levite supported them.

16Then the returned exiles did so. Ezra the priest selected men,[1] heads of
fathers' houses, according to their fathers' houses, each of them designated by
name. On the first day of the tenth month they sat down to examine the matter;
17and by the first day of the first month they had come to the end of all the men
who had married foreign women.

Those Guilty of Intermarriage

18Now there were found some of the sons of the priests who had married foreign women: Maaseiah, Eliezer, Jarib, and Gedaliah, some of the sons of Jeshua
the son of Jozadak and his brothers. 19They pledged themselves to put away their
wives, and their guilt offering was a ram of the flock for their guilt.[2] 20Of the sons
of Immer: Hanani and Zebadiah. 21Of the sons of Harim: Maaseiah, Elijah, Shemaiah, Jehiel, and Uzziah. 22Of the sons of Pashhur: Elioenai, Maaseiah, Ishmael,
Nethanel, Jozabad, and Elasah.

23Of the Levites: Jozabad, Shimei, Kelaiah (that is, Kelita), Pethahiah, Judah,
and Eliezer. 24Of the singers: Eliashib. Of the gatekeepers: Shallum, Telem, and
Uri.

25And of Israel: of the sons of Parosh: Ramiah, Izziah, Malchijah, Mijamin,
Eleazar, Hashabiah,[3] and Benaiah. 26Of the sons of Elam: Mattaniah, Zechariah, Jehiel, Abdi, Jeremoth, and Elijah. 27Of the sons of Zattu: Elioenai, Eliashib,
Mattaniah, Jeremoth, Zabad, and Aziza. 28Of the sons of Bebai were Jehohanan,
Hananiah, Zabbai, and Athlai. 29Of the sons of Bani were Meshullam, Malluch,
Adaiah, Jashub, Sheal, and Jeremoth. 30Of the sons of Pahath-moab: Adna, Che-
lal, Benaiah, Maaseiah, Mattaniah, Bezalel, Binnui, and Manasseh. 31Of the sons
of Harim: Eliezer, Isshijah, Malchijah, Shemaiah, Shimeon, 32Benjamin, Malluch,
and Shemariah. 33Of the sons of Hashum: Mattenai, Mattattah, Zabad, Eliphelet,
Jeremai, Manasseh, and Shimei. 34Of the sons of Bani: Maadai, Amram, Uel, 35Be-
naiah, Bedeiah, Cheluhi, 36Vaniah, Meremoth, Eliashib, 37Mattaniah, Mattenai,
Jaasu. 38Of the sons of Binnui:[4] Shimei, 39Shelemiah, Nathan, Adaiah, 40Mach-
nadebai, Shashai, Sharai, 41Azarel, Shelemiah, Shemariah, 42Shallum, Amariah,
and Joseph. 43Of the sons of Nebo: Jeiel, Mattithiah, Zabad, Zebina, Jaddai, Joel,
and Benaiah. 44All these had married foreign women, and some of the women
had even borne children.[5]

[1]Syriac; Hebrew *And there were selected Ezra . . .* [2]Or *as their reparation* [3]Septuagint; Hebrew *Malchijah*
[4]Septuagint; Hebrew *Bani, Binnui* [5]Or *and they put them away with their children*

JESUS: OUR REBUILDER OF THE BROKEN

NEHEMIAH

NEHEMIAH

EZRA ARRIVES IN JERUSALEM	NEHEMIAH ARRIVES IN JERUSALEM	NEHEMIAH REBUILDS THE WALL
c. 458 BC	*c. 444 BC*	*c. 444 BC*

The book of Nehemiah tells the story of a God-ordained leader and his work to aid the restored community to rebuild the wall around the city of Jerusalem. But, more than that, the book recounts God's faithfulness to his promise to restore the fortunes of his people and grant them the joy that comes through worshiping him.

In 444 BC, the Persian emperor Artaxerxes granted Nehemiah the freedom to relocate to the Jewish homeland, even appointing him to be the governor of Judah. Once there, Nehemiah led the people, descendants of the remnant that had returned from exile a century earlier, to rebuild the wall around Jerusalem. Under his direction, this task took only 52 days. In about 432 BC, Nehemiah was recalled to Persia for approximately a year before returning to Judah for a second term (5:14; 13:6 – 7).

Nehemiah's inclusion of Ezra's spiritual reforms in this book makes clear that his goal was to restore the spiritual health of the people along with rebuilding the wall. The earlier exile to Babylon and the temple's destruction vividly portrayed the consequences of sin. The fact that Jerusalem was in shambles was a picture of the spiritual state of the people, and God would not allow his people to tarnish his name and make a mockery of his dwelling place. Rebuilding the temple (which happened a century before Nehemiah's return) and the wall around the city demonstrated that God had not forgotten his people; he would help his people rebuild, and would be worshiped once again.

The people that Nehemiah came back to, however, continued in their lackadaisical spiritual stupor, even after having been in the land for many years. They had faced ongoing opposition since their return, which exposed their spiritual lethargy and coldhearted indifference to the Lord. In light of God's mercies, God anointed leaders like Nehemiah and prophets like Malachi to continue to remind the people of their need to repent. The latter half of the book of Nehemiah portrays the spiritual revival that followed their rebuilding of the wall around the city. Not only was the city rebuilt, but the people were rebuilt as well.

One theme of the book is clear — God will see to it that his name is glorified. In spite of the people's sin and the brokenness of life in a fallen world, he would, time and time again, see to it that his people were restored so that the world would know the greatness of his name. The spiritual restoration led by Nehemiah is a picture of the hope offered by the good news of Jesus. To those broken and destroyed by sin, Jesus' work offers the ever-present hope of restoration.

YOU ARE A GOD READY TO FORGIVE, GRACIOUS AND MERCIFUL, SLOW TO ANGER AND ABOUNDING IN STEADFAST LOVE.

Nehemiah 9:17

NEHEMIAH

Report from Jerusalem

1 The words of Nehemiah the son of Hacaliah.
Now it happened in the month of Chislev, in the twentieth year, as I was in
Susa the citadel, 2that Hanani, one of my brothers, came with certain men from
Judah. And I asked them concerning the Jews who escaped, who had survived the
exile, and concerning Jerusalem. 3And they said to me, "The remnant there in the
province who had survived the exile is in great trouble and shame. The wall of
Jerusalem is broken down, and its gates are destroyed by fire."

Nehemiah's Prayer

4As soon as I heard these words I sat down and wept and mourned for days,
and I continued fasting and praying before the God of heaven. 5And I said,
"O LORD God of heaven, the great and awesome God who keeps covenant and
steadfast love with those who love him and keep his commandments, 6let your
ear be attentive and your eyes open, to hear the prayer of your servant that I
now pray before you day and night for the people of Israel your servants, confessing the sins of the people of Israel, which we have sinned against you. Even
I and my father's house have sinned. 7We have acted very corruptly against you
and have not kept the commandments, the statutes, and the rules that you commanded your servant Moses. 8Remember the word that you commanded your
servant Moses, saying, 'If you are unfaithful, I will scatter you among the peoples, 9but if you return to me and keep my commandments and do them, though
your outcasts are in the uttermost parts of heaven, from there I will gather them
and bring them to the place that I have chosen, to make my name dwell there.'
10They are your servants and your people, whom you have redeemed by your
great power and by your strong hand. 11O Lord, let your ear be attentive to the
prayer of your servant, and to the prayer of your servants who delight to fear
your name, and give success to your servant today, and grant him mercy in the
sight of this man."

Now I was cupbearer to the king.

Nehemiah Sent to Judah

2 In the month of Nisan, in the twentieth year of King Artaxerxes, when wine
was before him, I took up the wine and gave it to the king. Now I had not been
sad in his presence. 2And the king said to me, "Why is your face sad, seeing you
are not sick? This is nothing but sadness of the heart." Then I was very much
afraid. 3I said to the king, "Let the king live forever! Why should not my face be
sad, when the city, the place of my fathers' graves, lies in ruins, and its gates have
been destroyed by fire?" 4Then the king said to me, "What are you requesting?"
So I prayed to the God of heaven. 5And I said to the king, "If it pleases the king,
and if your servant has found favor in your sight, that you send me to Judah, to
the city of my fathers' graves, that I may rebuild it." 6And the king said to me (the
queen sitting beside him), "How long will you be gone, and when will you return?"
So it pleased the king to send me when I had given him a time. 7And I said to the
king, "If it pleases the king, let letters be given me to the governors of the province
Beyond the River, that they may let me pass through until I come to Judah, 8and a
letter to Asaph, the keeper of the king's forest, that he may give me timber to make
beams for the gates of the fortress of the temple, and for the wall of the city, and
for the house that I shall occupy." And the king granted me what I asked, for the
good hand of my God was upon me.

NEHEMIAH 2:4–5

WHAT ARE YOU REQUESTING?

Four months after Nehemiah heard of the conditions in Jerusalem, the king asked him a blunt question: "What are you requesting?" It was within the king's power to grant Nehemiah almost anything or to punish him as he wished. The moment was ripe with potential and danger. Nehemiah prayed to God, then answered with an extravagant request. He desired to leave the service of the king, the most powerful person in the world, to go and rebuild the wall of Jerusalem. The king could have received this as an insult and responded accordingly, but God answered Nehemiah's prayers and the audacious request was granted.

In the New Testament, Jesus asked two blind men, "What do you want me to do for you?" (Mt 20:32). Full of faith, the men asked for the impossible—that their eyes might be opened. Jesus, full of power, granted the request and gave them sight. A contrasting story appears in Acts 3:1–10. A man lame from birth asked Peter and John for money. His request was much too small. Instead of giving him silver or gold, Peter healed him "in the name of Jesus Christ of Nazareth." The man stood, walked, then leaped into the air praising God. Jesus reminded his followers that all authority in heaven and on earth had been given to him (Mt 28:18). Jesus is the King of all kings, and, by his grace, believers can boldly ask for blessings that accord with his will and bring glory to his name.

REALITY-CHANGING PRAYER

The gap between "what was" and "what should be" led Nehemiah to many days of tearful mourning. The first Israelites had returned from exile to the holy city of Jerusalem nearly a century earlier. In spite of these years and all that *should* have been accomplished, God's people remained "in great trouble and shame" (v. 3). The personal condition of its inhabitants mirrored the physical condition of Jerusalem. Collectively, they were broken, humiliated, vulnerable to their enemies, and seemingly incapable of moving into the future God intended. Though a thousand miles away and living in great luxury, Nehemiah was shattered by the news. His response was to take action, and his first action was prayer. The remainder of the book of Nehemiah is really the record of history-changing events set in motion by one man's prayer.

Nehemiah offers a practical case study of God-honoring prayer. He began by declaring the greatness of God and God's faithfulness to his covenant. Nehemiah understood that the current conditions in Jerusalem were not God's will. He also understood the conditions in Jerusalem to be the result of sin. Nehemiah openly confessed the collective sins of Israel, and also his own. Though he had never been to Jerusalem himself, he shared an identity as one of the "children of Israel," and likewise shared in their guilt. Though God's people had broken covenant with God, he had not left them without hope. Nehemiah did not wallow helplessly in despair but declared his belief in God's promise of restoration for those who would return to him. Nehemiah's prayer of confession and declaration marked such a returning to God. It was a pivotal moment of change that decisively transformed the trajectory of Nehemiah's life and the life of all Israel.

The idea of "confession," or "declaration," is central to the gospel. In Romans 10:9 – 10, the apostle Paul wrote, "If you confess with your mouth that Jesus is Lord and believe in your heart that God raised him from the dead, you will be saved. For with the heart one believes and is justified, and with the mouth one confesses and is saved." The greatest change any human being can experience is that of salvation. This change is marked by confessing Jesus as Lord (the one to whom every aspect of our lives is to be submitted) and believing the truth of his resurrection (a demonstration of God's love and God's power even over death). Such a confession dramatically alters the course of one's life. Moreover, as Jesus lives in the believer and accomplishes his will through those who obey him, the world is transformed as well.

Nehemiah Inspects Jerusalem's Walls

9Then I came to the governors of the province Beyond the River and gave them the king's letters. Now the king had sent with me officers of the army and horsemen. 10But when Sanballat the Horonite and Tobiah the Ammonite servant heard this, it displeased them greatly that someone had come to seek the welfare of the people of Israel.

11So I went to Jerusalem and was there three days. 12Then I arose in the night, I and a few men with me. And I told no one what my God had put into my heart to do for Jerusalem. There was no animal with me but the one on which I rode. 13I went out by night by the Valley Gate to the Dragon Spring and to the Dung Gate, and I inspected the walls of Jerusalem that were broken down and its gates that had been destroyed by fire. 14Then I went on to the Fountain Gate and to the King's Pool, but there was no room for the animal that was under me to pass. 15Then I went up in the night by the valley and inspected the wall, and I turned back and entered by the Valley Gate, and so returned. 16And the officials did not know where I had gone or what I was doing, and I had not yet told the Jews, the priests, the nobles, the officials, and the rest who were to do the work.

17Then I said to them, "You see the trouble we are in, how Jerusalem lies in ruins with its gates burned. Come, let us build the wall of Jerusalem, that we may no longer suffer derision." 18And I told them of the hand of my God that had been upon me for good, and also of the words that the king had spoken to me. And they said, "Let us rise up and build." So they strengthened their hands for the good work. 19But when Sanballat the Horonite and Tobiah the Ammonite servant and Geshem the Arab heard of it, they jeered at us and despised us and said, "What is this thing that you are doing? Are you rebelling against the king?" 20Then I replied to them, "The God of heaven will make us prosper, and we his servants will arise and build, but you have no portion or right or claim[1] in Jerusalem."

Rebuilding the Wall

3 Then Eliashib the high priest rose up with his brothers the priests, and they built the Sheep Gate. They consecrated it and set its doors. They consecrated it as far as the Tower of the Hundred, as far as the Tower of Hananel. 2And next to him the men of Jericho built. And next to them[2] Zaccur the son of Imri built.

3The sons of Hassenaah built the Fish Gate. They laid its beams and set its doors, its bolts, and its bars. 4And next to them Meremoth the son of Uriah, son of Hakkoz repaired. And next to them Meshullam the son of Berechiah, son of Meshezabel repaired. And next to them Zadok the son of Baana repaired. 5And next to them the Tekoites repaired, but their nobles would not stoop to serve their Lord.[3]

6Joiada the son of Paseah and Meshullam the son of Besodeiah repaired the Gate of Yeshanah.[4] They laid its beams and set its doors, its bolts, and its bars. 7And next to them repaired Melatiah the Gibeonite and Jadon the Meronothite, the men of Gibeon and of Mizpah, the seat of the governor of the province Beyond the River. 8Next to them Uzziel the son of Harhaiah, goldsmiths, repaired. Next to him Hananiah, one of the perfumers, repaired, and they restored Jerusalem as far as the Broad Wall. 9Next to them Rephaiah the son of Hur, ruler of half the district of[5] Jerusalem, repaired. 10Next to them Jedaiah the son of Harumaph repaired opposite his house. And next to him Hattush the son of Hashabneiah repaired. 11Malchijah the son of Harim and Hasshub the son of Pahath-moab repaired another section and the Tower of the Ovens. 12Next to him Shallum the son of Hallohesh, ruler of half the district of Jerusalem, repaired, he and his daughters.

[1]Or *memorial* [2]Hebrew *him* [3]Or *lords* [4]Or *of the old city* [5]Or *foreman of half the portion assigned to*; also verses 12, 14, 15, 16, 17, 18

13Hanun and the inhabitants of Zanoah repaired the Valley Gate. They rebuilt
it and set its doors, its bolts, and its bars, and repaired a thousand cubits[1] of the
wall, as far as the Dung Gate.
14Malchijah the son of Rechab, ruler of the district of Beth-haccherem, repaired the Dung Gate. He rebuilt it and set its doors, its bolts, and its bars.
15And Shallum the son of Col-hozeh, ruler of the district of Mizpah, repaired
the Fountain Gate. He rebuilt it and covered it and set its doors, its bolts, and
its bars. And he built the wall of the Pool of Shelah of the king's garden, as far
as the stairs that go down from the city of David. 16After him Nehemiah the
son of Azbuk, ruler of half the district of Beth-zur, repaired to a point opposite the tombs of David, as far as the artificial pool, and as far as the house of
the mighty men. 17After him the Levites repaired: Rehum the son of Bani. Next
to him Hashabiah, ruler of half the district of Keilah, repaired for his district.
18After him their brothers repaired: Bavvai the son of Henadad, ruler of half the
district of Keilah. 19Next to him Ezer the son of Jeshua, ruler of Mizpah, repaired
another section opposite the ascent to the armory at the buttress.[2] 20After him
Baruch the son of Zabbai repaired[3] another section from the buttress to the
door of the house of Eliashib the high priest. 21After him Meremoth the son of
Uriah, son of Hakkoz repaired another section from the door of the house of
Eliashib to the end of the house of Eliashib. 22After him the priests, the men of
the surrounding area, repaired. 23After them Benjamin and Hasshub repaired
opposite their house. After them Azariah the son of Maaseiah, son of Ananiah
repaired beside his own house. 24After him Binnui the son of Henadad repaired
another section, from the house of Azariah to the buttress and to the corner.
25Palal the son of Uzai repaired opposite the buttress and the tower projecting
from the upper house of the king at the court of the guard. After him Pedaiah
the son of Parosh 26and the temple servants living on Ophel repaired to a point
opposite the Water Gate on the east and the projecting tower. 27After him the
Tekoites repaired another section opposite the great projecting tower as far as
the wall of Ophel.
28Above the Horse Gate the priests repaired, each one opposite his own
house. 29After them Zadok the son of Immer repaired opposite his own house.
After him Shemaiah the son of Shecaniah, the keeper of the East Gate, repaired. 30After him Hananiah the son of Shelemiah and Hanun the sixth son
of Zalaph repaired another section. After him Meshullam the son of Berechiah
repaired opposite his chamber. 31After him Malchijah, one of the goldsmiths,
repaired as far as the house of the temple servants and of the merchants, opposite the Muster Gate,[4] and to the upper chamber of the corner. 32And between
the upper chamber of the corner and the Sheep Gate the goldsmiths and the
merchants repaired.

Opposition to the Work

4 [5] Now when Sanballat heard that we were building the wall, he was angry
and greatly enraged, and he jeered at the Jews. 2And he said in the presence
of his brothers and of the army of Samaria, "What are these feeble Jews doing?
Will they restore it for themselves?[6] Will they sacrifice? Will they finish up in a
day? Will they revive the stones out of the heaps of rubbish, and burned ones at
that?" 3Tobiah the Ammonite was beside him, and he said, "Yes, what they are
building—if a fox goes up on it he will break down their stone wall!" 4Hear, O our
God, for we are despised. Turn back their taunt on their own heads and give them
up to be plundered in a land where they are captives. 5Do not cover their guilt,
and let not their sin be blotted out from your sight, for they have provoked you to
anger in the presence of the builders.

[1]A *cubit* was about 18 inches or 45 centimeters [2]Or *corner*; also verses 20, 24, 25 [3]Some manuscripts *vigorously repaired* [4]Or *Hammiphkad Gate* [5]Ch 3:33 in Hebrew [6]Or *Will they commit themselves to God?*

NEHEMIAH 4:1–18

ESCALATING OPPOSITION

The rebuilding of the wall of Jerusalem was met with opposition from the beginning. Others had a vested interest in keeping the restored community weak. They were protecting their own power and influence in the area, and they saw the rise of Jerusalem as a threat. As the work of rebuilding continued, the threats against the people of Judah multiplied. In the first verses of chapter 4, the opposition consisted of mocking words from Sanballat and Tobiah. By the seventh verse, the list of enemies had grown to include the Arabs, the Ammonites, and the Ashdodites, all of whom threatened violence. Nehemiah's response? He prayed, took preventive measures, and continued working. Once again, he urged the people not to be afraid, but to "remember the Lord, who is great and awesome" (v. 14).

Opposition to Jesus' ministry followed a similar pattern. Initially, the religious and national leaders were eager to hear Jesus and to witness his miracles. They soon realized, however, that Jesus represented a threat to every power structure and political agenda. The more Jesus was embraced by the general population, the more he was opposed by the leaders of Israel's factions. The more he accomplished God's will, the more his enemies conspired to kill him. Like Nehemiah, Jesus responded with prayer and perseverance.

BUILDING TOGETHER

Jerusalem's wall had lain in disrepair for more than 140 years, since its destruction by the Babylonians in 586 BC. Eventually, Cyrus of Persia, who had conquered Babylon in 539 BC, allowed the Jews to return to their homeland shortly thereafter. Nehemiah's party, with the permission of King Artaxerxes, arrived in Jerusalem approximately 94 years after the first returnees. Through all the prior years, the rubble of the city's walls and the burned timbers of its gates had been a constant reminder of Judah's shame and weakness. The Jews had attempted to rebuild the walls earlier in the reign of Artaxerxes I; but after some protests, the king ordered the Jews to stop the work (Ezr 4:21 – 23). This likely led to the report made to Nehemiah (Ne 1:3) and his efforts to once again rebuild the walls.

Nehemiah did not encourage them to trust in themselves for this work. Instead, Nehemiah told them how *God* had already acted for their good (2:18). With this news, they accepted the invitation. Rather than briefly summarizing the construction work, chapter 3 offers a remarkably detailed account of how many different people — from different families, of different cities, with different vocations, both men and women — came together to restore Jerusalem's walls and reset its gates. They were an unlikely team, but they shared a common purpose. As each did his or her part, the work was completed.

Centuries later, Jesus invited an even more disparate group to the all-encompassing task of rebuilding Israel spiritually. The twelve disciples included fishermen, a tax collector, and likely an anti-government zealot. As Jesus' followers grew in number, the level of diversity only increased. They had little in common except Jesus himself, and he was enough. Through these first believers, Jesus established and spread his church. As was true with the rebuilding of the wall in Nehemiah's time, the church is built only as believers fulfill their individual roles in humble cooperation with others. The apostle Paul refers to the church as the body of Christ (Ro 12:3 – 8; 1Co 12; Eph 4:1 – 16). The body is made up of many parts. While each part is different, all are critically important. Each believer possesses different spiritual gifts, but the body is only complete when each is present to share those gifts. Every believer has a function, but the mission of the church can only be completed when each is faithful to fulfill that function.

6So we built the wall. And all the wall was joined together to half its height, for
the people had a mind to work.
7[1]But when Sanballat and Tobiah and the Arabs and the Ammonites and the
Ashdodites heard that the repairing of the walls of Jerusalem was going forward
and that the breaches were beginning to be closed, they were very angry. 8And
they all plotted together to come and fight against Jerusalem and to cause confusion in it. 9And we prayed to our God and set a guard as a protection against them
day and night.
10In Judah it was said,[2] "The strength of those who bear the burdens is failing. There is too much rubble. By ourselves we will not be able to rebuild the
wall." 11And our enemies said, "They will not know or see till we come among
them and kill them and stop the work." 12At that time the Jews who lived near
them came from all directions and said to us ten times, "You must return to us."[3]
13So in the lowest parts of the space behind the wall, in open places, I stationed
the people by their clans, with their swords, their spears, and their bows. 14And
I looked and arose and said to the nobles and to the officials and to the rest of
the people, "Do not be afraid of them. Remember the Lord, who is great and
awesome, and fight for your brothers, your sons, your daughters, your wives,
and your homes."

The Work Resumes

15When our enemies heard that it was known to us and that God had frustrated their plan, we all returned to the wall, each to his work. 16From that day on,
half of my servants worked on construction, and half held the spears, shields,
bows, and coats of mail. And the leaders stood behind the whole house of Judah,
17who were building on the wall. Those who carried burdens were loaded in such
a way that each labored on the work with one hand and held his weapon with
the other. 18And each of the builders had his sword strapped at his side while
he built. The man who sounded the trumpet was beside me. 19And I said to the
nobles and to the officials and to the rest of the people, "The work is great and
widely spread, and we are separated on the wall, far from one another. 20In the
place where you hear the sound of the trumpet, rally to us there. Our God will
fight for us."
21So we labored at the work, and half of them held the spears from the break
of dawn until the stars came out. 22I also said to the people at that time, "Let every
man and his servant pass the night within Jerusalem, that they may be a guard for
us by night and may labor by day." 23So neither I nor my brothers nor my servants
nor the men of the guard who followed me, none of us took off our clothes; each
kept his weapon at his right hand.[4]

Nehemiah Stops Oppression of the Poor

5 Now there arose a great outcry of the people and of their wives against their
Jewish brothers. 2For there were those who said, "With our sons and our
daughters, we are many. So let us get grain, that we may eat and keep alive." 3There
were also those who said, "We are mortgaging our fields, our vineyards, and our
houses to get grain because of the famine." 4And there were those who said, "We
have borrowed money for the king's tax on our fields and our vineyards. 5Now our
flesh is as the flesh of our brothers, our children are as their children. Yet we are
forcing our sons and our daughters to be slaves, and some of our daughters have
already been enslaved, but it is not in our power to help it, for other men have our
fields and our vineyards."
6I was very angry when I heard their outcry and these words. 7I took counsel
with myself, and I brought charges against the nobles and the officials. I said to

[1]Ch 4:1 in Hebrew [2]Hebrew *Judah said* [3]The meaning of the Hebrew is uncertain [4]Or *his weapon when drinking*

them, "You are exacting interest, each from his brother." And I held a great assembly against them 8and said to them, "We, as far as we are able, have bought back
our Jewish brothers who have been sold to the nations, but you even sell your
brothers that they may be sold to us!" They were silent and could not find a word
to say. 9So I said, "The thing that you are doing is not good. Ought you not to walk
in the fear of our God to prevent the taunts of the nations our enemies? 10More-
over, I and my brothers and my servants are lending them money and grain. Let us
abandon this exacting of interest. 11Return to them this very day their fields, their
vineyards, their olive orchards, and their houses, and the percentage of money,
grain, wine, and oil that you have been exacting from them." 12Then they said,
"We will restore these and require nothing from them. We will do as you say."
And I called the priests and made them swear to do as they had promised. 13I also
shook out the fold[1] of my garment and said, "So may God shake out every man
from his house and from his labor who does not keep this promise. So may he be
shaken out and emptied." And all the assembly said "Amen" and praised the LORD.
And the people did as they had promised.

Nehemiah's Generosity

14Moreover, from the time that I was appointed to be their governor in the
land of Judah, from the twentieth year to the thirty-second year of Artaxerxes
the king, twelve years, neither I nor my brothers ate the food allowance of the
governor. 15The former governors who were before me laid heavy burdens on the
people and took from them for their daily ration[2] forty shekels[3] of silver. Even
their servants lorded it over the people. But I did not do so, because of the fear of
God. 16I also persevered in the work on this wall, and we acquired no land, and all
my servants were gathered there for the work. 17Moreover, there were at my table
150 men, Jews and officials, besides those who came to us from the nations that
were around us. 18Now what was prepared at my expense[4] for each day was one ox
and six choice sheep and birds, and every ten days all kinds of wine in abundance.
Yet for all this I did not demand the food allowance of the governor, because the
service was too heavy on this people. 19Remember for my good, O my God, all that
I have done for this people.

Conspiracy Against Nehemiah

6 Now when Sanballat and Tobiah and Geshem the Arab and the rest of our
enemies heard that I had built the wall and that there was no breach left in it
(although up to that time I had not set up the doors in the gates), 2Sanballat and
Geshem sent to me, saying, "Come and let us meet together at Hakkephirim in the
plain of Ono." But they intended to do me harm. 3And I sent messengers to them,
saying, "I am doing a great work and I cannot come down. Why should the work
stop while I leave it and come down to you?" 4And they sent to me four times in
this way, and I answered them in the same manner. 5In the same way Sanballat
for the fifth time sent his servant to me with an open letter in his hand. 6In it was
written, "It is reported among the nations, and Geshem[5] also says it, that you and
the Jews intend to rebel; that is why you are building the wall. And according to
these reports you wish to become their king. 7And you have also set up prophets
to proclaim concerning you in Jerusalem, 'There is a king in Judah.' And now the
king will hear of these reports. So now come and let us take counsel together."
8Then I sent to him, saying, "No such things as you say have been done, for you
are inventing them out of your own mind." 9For they all wanted to frighten us,
thinking, "Their hands will drop from the work, and it will not be done." But now,
O God,[6] strengthen my hands.
10Now when I went into the house of Shemaiah the son of Delaiah, son of

[1]Hebrew *bosom* [2]Compare Vulgate; Hebrew *took from them for food and wine after* [3]A *shekel* was about 2/5 ounce or 11 grams [4]Or *prepared for me* [5]Hebrew *Gashmu* [6]Hebrew lacks *O God*

NEHEMIAH 6:1–19

DEVIOUS CRITICS

Having failed to stop Nehemiah from rebuilding the wall by open opposition, his enemies changed tactics. They attempted to distract him with invitations for dialogue. To provoke fear, they said Nehemiah intended to have himself declared king of Judah—an act that would have represented revolt against Artaxerxes and would likely lead to the destruction of all they had built. Finally, they tried to trick Nehemiah into discrediting himself by cowardly seeking safety in the Holy Place inside the temple, a place where only priests were allowed. In this last ploy, Shemaiah, a fellow Israelite, was a coconspirator. Nehemiah maintained his righteousness in the face of these temptations and kept his focus on the work of God.

The enemies of Jesus, even Satan himself, used many of these same tactics. In the wilderness the devil tempted Jesus to betray God for his own gain (Mt 4:1–11). Jesus remained steadfast. Throughout Jesus' ministry, religious leaders tried to trick him in order to discredit him. Their attempts to trap Jesus with politically and religiously charged riddles met with failure every time. In the end, as was the case with Nehemiah, the enemies of Jesus engaged someone on the inside, Judas, in their efforts. Even this, however, served God's purpose of salvation. In spite of the most severe temptations, and in spite of having the power to spare himself, Jesus remained faithful to the end. "He humbled himself by becoming obedient to the point of death, even death on a cross" (Php 2:8).

GOOD NEWS FOR THE POOR

In Nehemiah 5, the focus shifts from external opposition to internal strife. The wealthy of Judah had taken advantage of the poor, whose needs had reached a critical level. Without adequate food and money to pay their taxes, the poor had mortgaged their land, borrowed money at interest, and had even been reduced to selling their children to their fellow Jews as slaves. Loaning money at interest and enslaving a fellow Jew were both violations of Jewish law and an egregious failure to love and care for one's neighbor. Upon learning of these travesties, Nehemiah confronted the guilty. True to form, his actions were grounded in his understanding of God and God's will. The behavior of the wealthy indicated a lack of reverence for God and an indifference to how their actions against the poor dishonored God.

Nehemiah's own conduct toward those in need was exemplary. It was within his legal rights as governor to tax the people to cover his own expenses. It was also customary for a man in his position to burden those under his rule for his own benefit. Like other members of the wealthy class, Nehemiah could have enriched himself through acquiring and selling real estate or loaning money at interest. But he did none of these things. He understood that true reverence for God requires treating others with compassion, confronting oppressors, and caring for the poor.

Jesus, teaching in a synagogue many years later, read from the book of Isaiah: "The Spirit of the Lord is upon me, because he has anointed me to proclaim good news to the poor. He has sent me to proclaim liberty to the captives and recovering of sight to the blind, to set at liberty those who are oppressed" (Lk 4:18). Jesus then made clear to his listeners that he was the fulfillment of Isaiah's prophecy. Jesus' ministry centered on the gospel, the ultimate expression of which is Jesus' atoning death on the cross and his defeat of death in the resurrection. His sacrifice makes salvation possible for all who repent and believe. But Jesus also made it clear that repentance and belief lead a true follower of Christ to genuine concern and action on behalf of the poor, the suffering, and the oppressed. Jesus did not mince words when it came to those who profited at the expense of others or who were indifferent to their needs. He warned his disciples to beware of the teachers of the law who *appeared* pious but loved privilege and money and cheated widows of their property in pursuit of these things. Though these religious leaders enjoyed an elevated status in Jewish culture, Jesus said they would receive especially severe punishment (Lk 20:46 – 47).

NEHEMIAH 7:1–3

BUILDING PEOPLE AND A CITY

The rebuilding of Jerusalem was primarily a venture of spiritual restoration. This spiritual goal was achieved, however, with physical work. Likewise, the ongoing spiritual vitality of this rebuilt city would require the never-ending work of meeting practical needs. To that end, Nehemiah appointed gatekeepers to guard the city gates, as well as the temple, and musicians to lead worship in the temple (v. 1). To ensure the city's security, Nehemiah appointed two officials, each with responsibility for half of Jerusalem (v. 2; cf. 3:9,12). Additionally, citizens were to take turns standing guard near their own homes. Nehemiah, managing the details, ordered that the gates remain closed until well into the day (7:3). This would prevent sneak attacks at sunrise, the normal time for a city's gates to be opened.

Jesus promised to build his church (Mt 16:18). Whereas the walls and gates of Jerusalem represented a defense against enemies, Jesus depicts his church as on offense, storming enemy territory. In this spiritual venture of building the church, Jesus' strategy was to send his disciples out in pairs. The spiritual ministry of preaching and healing required dirty, well-traveled feet, as well as considering the physical necessities of food and lodging. Addressing these practical details, Jesus instructed them to stay in a home where they were welcomed and to eat and drink whatever was offered (Lk 10:1–12). Jesus' practical strategy was used by the apostles and the early church as well, resulting in the expansion of the Christian faith throughout the known world.

Mehetabel, who was confined to his home, he said, "Let us meet together in the house of God, within the temple. Let us close the doors of the temple, for they are coming to kill you. They are coming to kill you by night." 11But I said, "Should such a man as I run away? And what man such as I could go into the temple and live?[1] I will not go in." 12And I understood and saw that God had not sent him, but he had pronounced the prophecy against me because Tobiah and Sanballat had hired him. 13For this purpose he was hired, that I should be afraid and act in this way and sin, and so they could give me a bad name in order to taunt me. 14Remember Tobiah and Sanballat, O my God, according to these things that they did, and also the prophetess Noadiah and the rest of the prophets who wanted to make me afraid.

The Wall Is Finished

15So the wall was finished on the twenty-fifth day of the month Elul, in fifty-two days. 16And when all our enemies heard of it, all the nations around us were afraid and fell greatly in their own esteem, for they perceived that this work had been accomplished with the help of our God. 17Moreover, in those days the nobles of Judah sent many letters to Tobiah, and Tobiah's letters came to them. 18For many in Judah were bound by oath to him, because he was the son-in-law of Shecaniah the son of Arah: and his son Jehohanan had taken the daughter of Meshullam the son of Berechiah as his wife. 19Also they spoke of his good deeds in my presence and reported my words to him. And Tobiah sent letters to make me afraid.

7 Now when the wall had been built and I had set up the doors, and the gatekeepers, the singers, and the Levites had been appointed, 2I gave my brother Hanani and Hananiah the governor of the castle charge over Jerusalem, for he was a more faithful and God-fearing man than many. 3And I said to them, "Let not the gates of Jerusalem be opened until the sun is hot. And while they are still standing guard, let them shut and bar the doors. Appoint guards from among the inhabitants of Jerusalem, some at their guard posts and some in front of their own homes." 4The city was wide and large, but the people within it were few, and no houses had been rebuilt.

Lists of Returned Exiles

5Then my God put it into my heart to assemble the nobles and the officials and the people to be enrolled by genealogy. And I found the book of the genealogy of those who came up at the first, and I found written in it:

6These were the people of the province who came up out of the captivity of those exiles whom Nebuchadnezzar the king of Babylon had carried into exile. They returned to Jerusalem and Judah, each to his town. 7They came with Zerubbabel, Jeshua, Nehemiah, Azariah, Raamiah, Nahamani, Mordecai, Bilshan, Mispereth, Bigvai, Nehum, Baanah.

The number of the men of the people of Israel: 8the sons of Parosh, 2,172. 9The sons of Shephatiah, 372. 10The sons of Arah, 652. 11The sons of Pahath-moab, namely the sons of Jeshua and Joab, 2,818. 12The sons of Elam, 1,254. 13The sons of Zattu, 845. 14The sons of Zaccai, 760. 15The sons of Binnui, 648. 16The sons of Bebai, 628. 17The sons of Azgad, 2,322. 18The sons of Adonikam, 667. 19The sons of Bigvai, 2,067. 20The sons of Adin, 655. 21The sons of Ater, namely of Hezekiah, 98. 22The sons of Hashum, 328. 23The sons of Bezai, 324. 24The sons of Hariph, 112. 25The sons of Gibeon, 95. 26The men of Bethlehem and Netophah, 188. 27The men of Anathoth, 128. 28The men of Beth-azmaveth, 42. 29The men of Kiriath-jearim, Chephirah, and Beeroth, 743. 30The men of Ramah and Geba, 621. 31The men of Michmas, 122. 32The men of Bethel and Ai, 123. 33The men of the other Nebo, 52. 34The sons of the other Elam, 1,254. 35The sons of Harim, 320.

[1]Or *would go into the temple to save his life*

36The sons of Jericho, 345. 37The sons of Lod, Hadid, and Ono, 721. 38The sons of
Senaah, 3,930.
39The priests: the sons of Jedaiah, namely the house of Jeshua, 973. 40The sons
of Immer, 1,052. 41The sons of Pashhur, 1,247. 42The sons of Harim, 1,017.
43The Levites: the sons of Jeshua, namely of Kadmiel of the sons of Hodevah,
74. 44The singers: the sons of Asaph, 148. 45The gatekeepers: the sons of Shallum,
the sons of Ater, the sons of Talmon, the sons of Akkub, the sons of Hatita, the
sons of Shobai, 138.
46The temple servants: the sons of Ziha, the sons of Hasupha, the sons of Tabbaoth, 47the sons of Keros, the sons of Sia, the sons of Padon, 48the sons of Lebana,
the sons of Hagaba, the sons of Shalmai, 49the sons of Hanan, the sons of Giddel,
the sons of Gahar, 50the sons of Reaiah, the sons of Rezin, the sons of Nekoda,
51the sons of Gazzam, the sons of Uzza, the sons of Paseah, 52the sons of Besai,
the sons of Meunim, the sons of Nephushesim, 53the sons of Bakbuk, the sons of
Hakupha, the sons of Harhur, 54the sons of Bazlith, the sons of Mehida, the sons
of Harsha, 55the sons of Barkos, the sons of Sisera, the sons of Temah, 56the sons
of Neziah, the sons of Hatipha.
57The sons of Solomon's servants: the sons of Sotai, the sons of Sophereth,
the sons of Perida, 58the sons of Jaala, the sons of Darkon, the sons of Giddel,
59the sons of Shephatiah, the sons of Hattil, the sons of Pochereth-hazzebaim,
the sons of Amon.
60All the temple servants and the sons of Solomon's servants were 392.
61The following were those who came up from Tel-melah, Tel-harsha, Cherub,
Addon, and Immer, but they could not prove their fathers' houses nor their descent, whether they belonged to Israel: 62the sons of Delaiah, the sons of Tobiah,
the sons of Nekoda, 642. 63Also, of the priests: the sons of Hobaiah, the sons of
Hakkoz, the sons of Barzillai (who had taken a wife of the daughters of Barzillai the Gileadite and was called by their name). 64These sought their registration
among those enrolled in the genealogies, but it was not found there, so they were
excluded from the priesthood as unclean. 65The governor told them that they
were not to partake of the most holy food until a priest with Urim and Thummim
should arise.

Totals of People and Gifts

66The whole assembly together was 42,360, 67besides their male and female
servants, of whom there were 7,337. And they had 245 singers, male and female.
68Their horses were 736, their mules 245,[1] 69their camels 435, and their donkeys
6,720.
70Now some of the heads of fathers' houses gave to the work. The governor
gave to the treasury 1,000 darics[2] of gold, 50 basins, 30 priests' garments and
500 minas[3] of silver.[4] 71And some of the heads of fathers' houses gave into the
treasury of the work 20,000 darics of gold and 2,200 minas of silver. 72And what
the rest of the people gave was 20,000 darics of gold, 2,000 minas of silver, and
67 priests' garments.
73So the priests, the Levites, the gatekeepers, the singers, some of the people,
the temple servants, and all Israel, lived in their towns.

And when the seventh month had come, the people of Israel were in their towns.

Ezra Reads the Law

8 And all the people gathered as one man into the square before the Water
Gate. And they told Ezra the scribe to bring the Book of the Law of Moses that
the LORD had commanded Israel. 2So Ezra the priest brought the Law before the

[1]Compare Ezra 2:66 and the margins of some Hebrew manuscripts; Hebrew lacks *Their horses . . . 245*
[2]A *daric* was a coin weighing about 1/4 ounce or 8.5 grams [3]A *mina* was about 1 1/4 pounds or 0.6 kilogram [4]Probable reading; Hebrew lacks *minas of silver*

assembly, both men and women and all who could understand what they heard, on the first day of the seventh month. 3 And he read from it facing the square before the Water Gate from early morning until midday, in the presence of the men and the women and those who could understand. And the ears of all the people were attentive to the Book of the Law. 4 And Ezra the scribe stood on a wooden platform that they had made for the purpose. And beside him stood Mattithiah, Shema, Anaiah, Uriah, Hilkiah, and Maaseiah on his right hand, and Pedaiah, Mishael, Malchijah, Hashum, Hashbaddanah, Zechariah, and Meshullam on his left hand. 5 And Ezra opened the book in the sight of all the people, for he was above all the people, and as he opened it all the people stood. 6 And Ezra blessed the LORD, the great God, and all the people answered, "Amen, Amen," lifting up their hands. And they bowed their heads and worshiped the LORD with their faces to the ground. 7 Also Jeshua, Bani, Sherebiah, Jamin, Akkub, Shabbethai, Hodiah, Maaseiah, Kelita, Azariah, Jozabad, Hanan, Pelaiah, the Levites,[1] helped the people to understand the Law, while the people remained in their places. 8 They read from the book, from the Law of God, clearly,[2] and they gave the sense, so that the people understood the reading.

This Day Is Holy

9 And Nehemiah, who was the governor, and Ezra the priest and scribe, and the Levites who taught the people said to all the people, "This day is holy to the LORD your God; do not mourn or weep." For all the people wept as they heard the words of the Law. 10 Then he said to them, "Go your way. Eat the fat and drink sweet wine and send portions to anyone who has nothing ready, for this day is holy to our Lord. And do not be grieved, for the joy of the LORD is your strength." 11 So the Levites calmed all the people, saying, "Be quiet, for this day is holy; do not be grieved." 12 And all the people went their way to eat and drink and to send portions and to make great rejoicing, because they had understood the words that were declared to them.

Feast of Booths Celebrated

13 On the second day the heads of fathers' houses of all the people, with the priests and the Levites, came together to Ezra the scribe in order to study the words of the Law. 14 And they found it written in the Law that the LORD had commanded by Moses that the people of Israel should dwell in booths[3] during the feast of the seventh month, 15 and that they should proclaim it and publish it in all their towns and in Jerusalem, "Go out to the hills and bring branches of olive, wild olive, myrtle, palm, and other leafy trees to make booths, as it is written." 16 So the people went out and brought them and made booths for themselves, each on his roof, and in their courts and in the courts of the house of God, and in the square at the Water Gate and in the square at the Gate of Ephraim. 17 And all the assembly of those who had returned from the captivity made booths and lived in the booths, for from the days of Jeshua the son of Nun to that day the people of Israel had not done so. And there was very great rejoicing. 18 And day by day, from the first day to the last day, he read from the Book of the Law of God. They kept the feast seven days, and on the eighth day there was a solemn assembly, according to the rule.

The People of Israel Confess Their Sin

9 Now on the twenty-fourth day of this month the people of Israel were assembled with fasting and in sackcloth, and with earth on their heads. 2 And the Israelites[4] separated themselves from all foreigners and stood and confessed their sins and the iniquities of their fathers. 3 And they stood up in their place and read from the Book of the Law of the LORD their God for a quarter of the

[1] Vulgate; Hebrew *and the Levites* [2] Or *with interpretation*, or *paragraph by paragraph* [3] Or *temporary shelters* [4] Hebrew *the offspring of Israel*

GRACE THROUGH THE WORD

In Nehemiah 8, physical rebuilding and the practicalities of sustaining a city gave way to the greater work of spiritual revival. Importantly, this revival was launched by the reading of God's Word. The priest Ezra had brought the Book of the Law to Jerusalem some 14 years earlier. Now, just six days after the completion of the wall, the Book of the Law was being made public to everyone. It was a remarkable scene. Everyone was included — men, women, and children. For five or six hours, they heard words written to the people of Israel in an era long-since forgotten. As they listened, they were overwhelmed by how far they had fallen short of who they were meant to be. As Nehemiah had grieved the conditions of Jerusalem (1:3 – 4), they grieved over their sins and those of their ancestors. They mourned and wept, evidence of conviction and sorrow. This was a natural response, but the reaction of Nehemiah and the Levites is instructive. This was not a time to dwell on the mistakes of the past, but to embrace a new reality marked by obedience and faithfulness. The reading of the Law was not to produce mourning for what was, but to celebrate the victory of the present and a joyful hope for the future.

The Gospels recount the story of Jesus. His perfect love and unblemished faithfulness stand in stark contrast to our sinfulness. In reading about and hearing of Jesus, people are confronted with the magnitude of their failures. Humans have become so much less than they were created to be. Yet, Jesus did not die so that sinful humans would wallow in their sinful past. The writings of the New Testament are not given to produce mourning but repentance which leads to rejoicing. Conviction *is* overwhelming apart from the grace of Christ.

Among New Testament writers, the apostle Paul was unparalleled in his recognition of sin's terrible power. But this recognition fueled his appreciation for the beauty and power of grace. Writing to the church at Corinth, Paul said, "Therefore, if anyone is in Christ, he is a new creation. The old has passed away; behold, the new has come" (2Co 5:17). As one who had violently persecuted Christians only to become the faith's greatest evangelist, Paul had seen the reality of these words in his own life. Since the time of Paul, for two thousand years, these words have been passed down from generation to generation. Like all of Scripture, they are an invitation to celebrate what Christ has done and to embrace with confidence a future filled with hope.

day; for another quarter of it they made confession and worshiped the LORD their God. 4On the stairs of the Levites stood Jeshua, Bani, Kadmiel, Shebaniah, Bunni, Sherebiah, Bani, and Chenani; and they cried with a loud voice to the LORD their God. 5Then the Levites, Jeshua, Kadmiel, Bani, Hashabneiah, Sherebiah, Hodiah, Shebaniah, and Pethahiah, said, “Stand up and bless the LORD your God from everlasting to everlasting. Blessed be your glorious name, which is exalted above all blessing and praise.

6[1]“You are the LORD, you alone. You have made heaven, the heaven of heavens, with all their host, the earth and all that is on it, the seas and all that is in them; and you preserve all of them; and the host of heaven worships you. 7You are the LORD, the God who chose Abram and brought him out of Ur of the Chaldeans and gave him the name Abraham. 8You found his heart faithful before you, and made with him the covenant to give to his offspring the land of the Canaanite, the Hittite, the Amorite, the Perizzite, the Jebusite, and the Girgashite. And you have kept your promise, for you are righteous.

9“And you saw the affliction of our fathers in Egypt and heard their cry at the Red Sea, 10and performed signs and wonders against Pharaoh and all his servants and all the people of his land, for you knew that they acted arrogantly against our fathers. And you made a name for yourself, as it is to this day. 11And you divided the sea before them, so that they went through the midst of the sea on dry land, and you cast their pursuers into the depths, as a stone into mighty waters. 12By a pillar of cloud you led them in the day, and by a pillar of fire in the night to light for them the way in which they should go. 13You came down on Mount Sinai and spoke with them from heaven and gave them right rules and true laws, good statutes and commandments, 14and you made known to them your holy Sabbath and commanded them commandments and statutes and a law by Moses your servant. 15You gave them bread from heaven for their hunger and brought water for them out of the rock for their thirst, and you told them to go in to possess the land that you had sworn to give them.

16“But they and our fathers acted presumptuously and stiffened their neck and did not obey your commandments. 17They refused to obey and were not mindful of the wonders that you performed among them, but they stiffened their neck and appointed a leader to return to their slavery in Egypt.[2] But you are a God ready to forgive, gracious and merciful, slow to anger and abounding in steadfast love, and did not forsake them. 18Even when they had made for themselves a golden[3] calf and said, ‘This is your God who brought you up out of Egypt,’ and had committed great blasphemies, 19you in your great mercies did not forsake them in the wilderness. The pillar of cloud to lead them in the way did not depart from them by day, nor the pillar of fire by night to light for them the way by which they should go. 20You gave your good Spirit to instruct them and did not withhold your manna from their mouth and gave them water for their thirst. 21Forty years you sustained them in the wilderness, and they lacked nothing. Their clothes did not wear out and their feet did not swell.

22“And you gave them kingdoms and peoples and allotted to them every corner. So they took possession of the land of Sihon king of Heshbon and the land of Og king of Bashan. 23You multiplied their children as the stars of heaven, and you brought them into the land that you had told their fathers to enter and possess. 24So the descendants went in and possessed the land, and you subdued before them the inhabitants of the land, the Canaanites, and gave them into their hand, with their kings and the peoples of the land, that they might do with them as they would. 25And they captured fortified cities and a rich land, and took possession of houses full of all good things, cisterns already hewn, vineyards, olive orchards and fruit trees in abundance. So they ate and were filled and became fat and delighted themselves in your great goodness.

[1]Septuagint adds *And Ezra said* [2]Some Hebrew manuscripts; many Hebrew manuscripts *and in their rebellion appointed a leader to return to their slavery* [3]Hebrew *metal*

26“Nevertheless, they were disobedient and rebelled against you and cast your law behind their back and killed your prophets, who had warned them in order to turn them back to you, and they committed great blasphemies. 27Therefore you gave them into the hand of their enemies, who made them suffer. And in the time of their suffering they cried out to you and you heard them from heaven, and according to your great mercies you gave them saviors who saved them from the hand of their enemies. 28But after they had rest they did evil again before you, and you abandoned them to the hand of their enemies, so that they had dominion over them. Yet when they turned and cried to you, you heard from heaven, and many times you delivered them according to your mercies. 29And you warned them in order to turn them back to your law. Yet they acted presumptuously and did not obey your commandments, but sinned against your rules, which if a person does them, he shall live by them, and they turned a stubborn shoulder and stiffened their neck and would not obey. 30Many years you bore with them and warned them by your Spirit through your prophets. Yet they would not give ear. Therefore you gave them into the hand of the peoples of the lands. 31Nevertheless, in your great mercies you did not make an end of them or forsake them, for you are a gracious and merciful God.

32“Now, therefore, our God, the great, the mighty, and the awesome God, who keeps covenant and steadfast love, let not all the hardship seem little to you that has come upon us, upon our kings, our princes, our priests, our prophets, our fathers, and all your people, since the time of the kings of Assyria until this day. 33Yet you have been righteous in all that has come upon us, for you have dealt faithfully and we have acted wickedly. 34Our kings, our princes, our priests, and our fathers have not kept your law or paid attention to your commandments and your warnings that you gave them. 35Even in their own kingdom, and amid your great goodness that you gave them, and in the large and rich land that you set before them, they did not serve you or turn from their wicked works. 36Behold, we are slaves this day; in the land that you gave to our fathers to enjoy its fruit and its good gifts, behold, we are slaves. 37And its rich yield goes to the kings whom you have set over us because of our sins. They rule over our bodies and over our livestock as they please, and we are in great distress.

38[1]“Because of all this we make a firm covenant in writing; on the sealed document are the names of[2] our princes, our Levites, and our priests.

The People Who Sealed the Covenant

10[3] “On the seals are the names of[4] Nehemiah the governor, the son of Hacaliah, Zedekiah, 2Seraiah, Azariah, Jeremiah, 3Pashhur, Amariah, Malchijah, 4Hattush, Shebaniah, Malluch, 5Harim, Meremoth, Obadiah, 6Daniel, Ginnethon, Baruch, 7Meshullam, Abijah, Mijamin, 8Maaziah, Bilgai, Shemaiah; these are the priests. 9And the Levites: Jeshua the son of Azaniah, Binnui of the sons of Henadad, Kadmiel; 10and their brothers, Shebaniah, Hodiah, Kelita, Pelaiah, Hanan, 11Mica, Rehob, Hashabiah, 12Zaccur, Sherebiah, Shebaniah, 13Hodiah, Bani, Beninu. 14The chiefs of the people: Parosh, Pahath-moab, Elam, Zattu, Bani, 15Bunni, Azgad, Bebai, 16Adonijah, Bigvai, Adin, 17Ater, Hezekiah, Azzur, 18Hodiah, Hashum, Bezai, 19Hariph, Anathoth, Nebai, 20Magpiash, Meshullam, Hezir, 21Meshezabel, Zadok, Jaddua, 22Pelatiah, Hanan, Anaiah, 23Hoshea, Hananiah, Hasshub, 24Hallohesh, Pilha, Shobek, 25Rehum, Hashabnah, Maaseiah, 26Ahiah, Hanan, Anan, 27Malluch, Harim, Baanah.

The Obligations of the Covenant

28“The rest of the people, the priests, the Levites, the gatekeepers, the singers, the temple servants, and all who have separated themselves from the peoples of the lands to the Law of God, their wives, their sons, their daughters, all who have

[1]Ch 10:1 in Hebrew [2]Hebrew lacks *the names of* [3]Ch 10:2 in Hebrew [4]Hebrew lacks *the names of*

NEHEMIAH 10:28–39

GOOD INTENTIONS TO OBEY

In this passage, the people collectively entered into a covenant to keep God's law. This involved the practical move of taxing themselves to ensure the temple's activities were sufficiently funded. Additionally, they made laws that required giving of their "firstfruits" to the house of the Lord, including their sons, livestock, produce, wine, and oil. Their enthusiasm for the things of God is awe-inspiring, their self-sacrificing intentions laudable. Good intentions, however, were not sufficient to ensure obedience. Like their ancestors and their descendants, they failed to keep their covenant with God.

In the early church, a dispute arose about what parts of the Jewish law were binding on Christians. Some insisted that new believers had to be circumcised in order to be saved and should be required to keep the Law of Moses (Ac 15:5). As the leaders of the church gathered to resolve this conflict, the apostle Peter stood and reminded them that in spite of their best intentions neither they nor their ancestors had proven capable of obedience to the law. Then, he pointed them to Christianity's central, life-changing truths. God purifies hearts through *faith.* The hope of a Christian is founded in *grace.* In their fallen state, human beings are simply unable to obey God and are unable to save themselves. But Peter's conclusion is reassuring and confident: "But we believe that we will be saved through the grace of the Lord Jesus, just as they will" (Ac 15:11).

REMEMBERING WITH A PURPOSE

The story of Israel is marked by critical moments of transition. In these moments, the leader of Israel sometimes gathered the people to hear and remember together their collective history. Both Moses (Dt 32:1 – 43) and Joshua (Jos 24:1 – 28) initiated such gatherings just before their deaths. Similarly, upon finding the Book of the Law, King Josiah gathered all the people of Judah and read it to them (2Ki 23:1 – 3). Remembering the past gave them a focus for the future. Having heard their own story, God's people faced a decision. They could renew their covenant and continue on with God, or choose a different future, dedicated to other "gods."

In Nehemiah 9, the people had been engaged in public worship for more than three weeks. Their days were filled with listening to the Book of the Law, followed by confession and worship. Spiritually they were being prepared to renew their covenant with God. This covenant was not defined by a code of behavior or a list of intellectual truths. The covenant was framed by the narrative of God's gracious acts toward a rebellious people. After praising the greatness of God and acknowledging him as the Creator and Sustainer of all things, the Levites retold the story. Beginning with the Lord's call of Abraham and covenant with him, they remembered God's faithfulness and lamented their ancestors' sins. These sins had ultimately led to the punishment of exile. In spite of having returned physically to their homeland, it is clear that the people understood they were still under God's judgment. They recognized that they were not fully restored — a truth made painfully clear in the fact that they lived as "slaves" in their own land, under the rule of the pagan Persian Empire (vv. 36 – 37). From Abraham to their present moment, all was remembered. And this remembering had the desired result.

In the New Testament, Stephen followed the tradition of his ancestors in publicly recounting Israel's history (Ac 7:2 – 53). His purpose was to confront his persecutors with God's goodness and the fact of their sin. Though they imagined themselves to be the most righteous of their kinsmen, Stephen painted a very different picture. They were actually *guilty of opposing* God. They had rejected the new covenant established by Christ, betraying and murdering him instead. Throughout Israel's history, when the story of Israel was retold, the people of Israel had renewed their commitment to God. Stephen's speech proved to be an exception; the leaders of Israel tragically chose a different path.

knowledge and understanding, [29]join with their brothers, their nobles, and enter into a curse and an oath to walk in God's Law that was given by Moses the servant of God, and to observe and do all the commandments of the LORD our Lord and his rules and his statutes. [30]We will not give our daughters to the peoples of the land or take their daughters for our sons. [31]And if the peoples of the land bring in goods or any grain on the Sabbath day to sell, we will not buy from them on the Sabbath or on a holy day. And we will forgo the crops of the seventh year and the exaction of every debt.

[32]"We also take on ourselves the obligation to give yearly a third part of a shekel[1] for the service of the house of our God: [33]for the showbread, the regular grain offering, the regular burnt offering, the Sabbaths, the new moons, the appointed feasts, the holy things, and the sin offerings to make atonement for Israel, and for all the work of the house of our God. [34]We, the priests, the Levites, and the people, have likewise cast lots for the wood offering, to bring it into the house of our God, according to our fathers' houses, at times appointed, year by year, to burn on the altar of the LORD our God, as it is written in the Law. [35]We obligate ourselves to bring the firstfruits of our ground and the firstfruits of all fruit of every tree, year by year, to the house of the LORD; [36]also to bring to the house of our God, to the priests who minister in the house of our God, the firstborn of our sons and of our cattle, as it is written in the Law, and the firstborn of our herds and of our flocks; [37]and to bring the first of our dough, and our contributions, the fruit of every tree, the wine and the oil, to the priests, to the chambers of the house of our God; and to bring to the Levites the tithes from our ground, for it is the Levites who collect the tithes in all our towns where we labor. [38]And the priest, the son of Aaron, shall be with the Levites when the Levites receive the tithes. And the Levites shall bring up the tithe of the tithes to the house of our God, to the chambers of the storehouse. [39]For the people of Israel and the sons of Levi shall bring the contribution of grain, wine, and oil to the chambers, where the vessels of the sanctuary are, as well as the priests who minister, and the gatekeepers and the singers. We will not neglect the house of our God."

The Leaders in Jerusalem

11 Now the leaders of the people lived in Jerusalem. And the rest of the people cast lots to bring one out of ten to live in Jerusalem the holy city, while nine out of ten[2] remained in the other towns. [2]And the people blessed all the men who willingly offered to live in Jerusalem.

[3]These are the chiefs of the province who lived in Jerusalem; but in the towns of Judah everyone lived on his property in their towns: Israel, the priests, the Levites, the temple servants, and the descendants of Solomon's servants. [4]And in Jerusalem lived certain of the sons of Judah and of the sons of Benjamin. Of the sons of Judah: Athaiah the son of Uzziah, son of Zechariah, son of Amariah, son of Shephatiah, son of Mahalalel, of the sons of Perez; [5]and Maaseiah the son of Baruch, son of Col-hozeh, son of Hazaiah, son of Adaiah, son of Joiarib, son of Zechariah, son of the Shilonite. [6]All the sons of Perez who lived in Jerusalem were 468 valiant men.

[7]And these are the sons of Benjamin: Sallu the son of Meshullam, son of Joed, son of Pedaiah, son of Kolaiah, son of Maaseiah, son of Ithiel, son of Jeshaiah, [8]and his brothers, men of valor, 928.[3] [9]Joel the son of Zichri was their overseer; and Judah the son of Hassenuah was second over the city.

[10]Of the priests: Jedaiah the son of Joiarib, Jachin, [11]Seraiah the son of Hilkiah, son of Meshullam, son of Zadok, son of Meraioth, son of Ahitub, ruler of the house of God, [12]and their brothers who did the work of the house, 822; and Adaiah the son of Jeroham, son of Pelaliah, son of Amzi, son of Zechariah, son of

[1]A *shekel* was about 2/5 ounce or 11 grams [2]Hebrew *nine hands* [3]Compare Septuagint; Hebrew *Jeshaiah, and after him Gabbai, Sallai, 928*

Pashhur, son of Malchijah, 13and his brothers, heads of fathers' houses, 242; and
Amashsai, the son of Azarel, son of Ahzai, son of Meshillemoth, son of Immer,
14and their brothers, mighty men of valor, 128; their overseer was Zabdiel the son
of Haggedolim.
15And of the Levites: Shemaiah the son of Hasshub, son of Azrikam, son of
Hashabiah, son of Bunni; 16and Shabbethai and Jozabad, of the chiefs of the Levites, who were over the outside work of the house of God; 17and Mattaniah the
son of Mica, son of Zabdi, son of Asaph, who was the leader of the praise,[1] who
gave thanks, and Bakbukiah, the second among his brothers; and Abda the son
of Shammua, son of Galal, son of Jeduthun. 18All the Levites in the holy city were
284.
19The gatekeepers, Akkub, Talmon and their brothers, who kept watch at the
gates, were 172. 20And the rest of Israel, and of the priests and the Levites, were
in all the towns of Judah, every one in his inheritance. 21But the temple servants
lived on Ophel; and Ziha and Gishpa were over the temple servants.
22The overseer of the Levites in Jerusalem was Uzzi the son of Bani, son of
Hashabiah, son of Mattaniah, son of Mica, of the sons of Asaph, the singers, over
the work of the house of God. 23For there was a command from the king concerning them, and a fixed provision for the singers, as every day required. 24And
Pethahiah the son of Meshezabel, of the sons of Zerah the son of Judah, was at
the king's side[2] in all matters concerning the people.

Villages Outside Jerusalem

25And as for the villages, with their fields, some of the people of Judah lived in
Kiriath-arba and its villages, and in Dibon and its villages, and in Jekabzeel and its
villages, 26and in Jeshua and in Moladah and Beth-pelet, 27in Hazar-shual, in Beersheba and its villages, 28in Ziklag, in Meconah and its villages, 29in En-rimmon, in
Zorah, in Jarmuth, 30Zanoah, Adullam, and their villages, Lachish and its fields,
and Azekah and its villages. So they encamped from Beersheba to the Valley of
Hinnom. 31The people of Benjamin also lived from Geba onward, at Michmash,
Aija, Bethel and its villages, 32Anathoth, Nob, Ananiah, 33Hazor, Ramah, Gittaim,
34Hadid, Zeboim, Neballat, 35Lod, and Ono, the valley of craftsmen. 36And certain
divisions of the Levites in Judah were assigned to Benjamin.

Priests and Levites

12 These are the priests and the Levites who came up with Zerubbabel the son
of Shealtiel, and Jeshua: Seraiah, Jeremiah, Ezra, 2Amariah, Malluch, Hattush, 3Shecaniah, Rehum, Meremoth, 4Iddo, Ginnethoi, Abijah, 5Mijamin, Maa-
diah, Bilgah, 6Shemaiah, Joiarib, Jedaiah, 7Sallu, Amok, Hilkiah, Jedaiah. These
were the chiefs of the priests and of their brothers in the days of Jeshua.
8And the Levites: Jeshua, Binnui, Kadmiel, Sherebiah, Judah, and Mattaniah,
who with his brothers was in charge of the songs of thanksgiving. 9And Bakbukiah and Unni and their brothers stood opposite them in the service. 10And Jeshua
was the father of Joiakim, Joiakim the father of Eliashib, Eliashib the father of
Joiada, 11Joiada the father of Jonathan, and Jonathan the father of Jaddua.
12And in the days of Joiakim were priests, heads of fathers' houses: of Seraiah,
Meraiah; of Jeremiah, Hananiah; 13of Ezra, Meshullam; of Amariah, Jehohanan;
14of Malluchi, Jonathan; of Shebaniah, Joseph; 15of Harim, Adna; of Meraioth,
Helkai; 16of Iddo, Zechariah; of Ginnethon, Meshullam; 17of Abijah, Zichri; of Miniamin, of Moadiah, Piltai; 18of Bilgah, Shammua; of Shemaiah, Jehonathan; 19of
Joiarib, Mattenai; of Jedaiah, Uzzi; 20of Sallai, Kallai; of Amok, Eber; 21of Hilkiah,
Hashabiah; of Jedaiah, Nethanel.
22In the days of Eliashib, Joiada, Johanan, and Jaddua, the Levites were recorded as heads of fathers' houses; so too were the priests in the reign of Darius the

[1]Compare Septuagint, Vulgate; Hebrew *beginning* [2]Hebrew *hand*

Persian. [23]As for the sons of Levi, their heads of fathers' houses were written in the Book of the Chronicles until the days of Johanan the son of Eliashib. [24]And the chiefs of the Levites: Hashabiah, Sherebiah, and Jeshua the son of Kadmiel, with their brothers who stood opposite them, to praise and to give thanks, according to the commandment of David the man of God, watch by watch. [25]Mattaniah, Bakbukiah, Obadiah, Meshullam, Talmon, and Akkub were gatekeepers standing guard at the storehouses of the gates. [26]These were in the days of Joiakim the son of Jeshua son of Jozadak, and in the days of Nehemiah the governor and of Ezra, the priest and scribe.

Dedication of the Wall

[27]And at the dedication of the wall of Jerusalem they sought the Levites in all their places, to bring them to Jerusalem to celebrate the dedication with gladness, with thanksgivings and with singing, with cymbals, harps, and lyres. [28]And the sons of the singers gathered together from the district surrounding Jerusalem and from the villages of the Netophathites; [29]also from Beth-gilgal and from the region of Geba and Azmaveth, for the singers had built for themselves villages around Jerusalem. [30]And the priests and the Levites purified themselves, and they purified the people and the gates and the wall.

[31]Then I brought the leaders of Judah up onto the wall and appointed two great choirs that gave thanks. One went to the south on the wall to the Dung Gate. [32]And after them went Hoshaiah and half of the leaders of Judah, [33]and Azariah, Ezra, Meshullam, [34]Judah, Benjamin, Shemaiah, and Jeremiah, [35]and certain of the priests' sons with trumpets: Zechariah the son of Jonathan, son of Shemaiah, son of Mattaniah, son of Micaiah, son of Zaccur, son of Asaph; [36]and his relatives, Shemaiah, Azarel, Milalai, Gilalai, Maai, Nethanel, Judah, and Hanani, with the musical instruments of David the man of God. And Ezra the scribe went before them. [37]At the Fountain Gate they went up straight before them by the stairs of the city of David, at the ascent of the wall, above the house of David, to the Water Gate on the east.

[38]The other choir of those who gave thanks went to the north, and I followed them with half of the people, on the wall, above the Tower of the Ovens, to the Broad Wall, [39]and above the Gate of Ephraim, and by the Gate of Yeshanah,[1] and by the Fish Gate and the Tower of Hananel and the Tower of the Hundred, to the Sheep Gate; and they came to a halt at the Gate of the Guard. [40]So both choirs of those who gave thanks stood in the house of God, and I and half of the officials with me; [41]and the priests Eliakim, Maaseiah, Miniamin, Micaiah, Elioenai, Zechariah, and Hananiah, with trumpets; [42]and Maaseiah, Shemaiah, Eleazar, Uzzi, Jehohanan, Malchijah, Elam, and Ezer. And the singers sang with Jezrahiah as their leader. [43]And they offered great sacrifices that day and rejoiced, for God had made them rejoice with great joy; the women and children also rejoiced. And the joy of Jerusalem was heard far away.

Service at the Temple

[44]On that day men were appointed over the storerooms, the contributions, the firstfruits, and the tithes, to gather into them the portions required by the Law for the priests and for the Levites according to the fields of the towns, for Judah rejoiced over the priests and the Levites who ministered. [45]And they performed the service of their God and the service of purification, as did the singers and the gatekeepers, according to the command of David and his son Solomon. [46]For long ago in the days of David and Asaph there were directors of the singers, and there were songs[2] of praise and thanksgiving to God. [47]And all Israel in the days of Zerubbabel and in the days of Nehemiah gave the daily portions for the singers and the gatekeepers; and they set apart that which was for the Levites; and the Levites set apart that which was for the sons of Aaron.

[1]Or *of the old city* [2]Or *leaders*

NEHEMIAH 12:27–43

JOYFUL PRAISE AND WORSHIP

Conditions in Jerusalem were dramatically better than when Nehemiah had arrived. Separated individuals had become a true people who, by God's grace, had achieved what had seemed impossible. Strong walls and protective gates had replaced rubble and burned timbers. Encouragement had overcome despair. It was a time to celebrate what God had accomplished through their faithfulness. Tobiah the Ammonite had mocked them, saying even the weight of a fox would cause their wall to crumble (Ne 4:3). Now the leaders of the people and two large choirs, accompanied by musicians, stood atop the walls playing instruments, singing loudly, and offering thanksgiving. It was an incredible time of rejoicing. Such joy-filled celebration honors God and encourages even greater faith.

This celebration, like the book of Psalms, underscores the importance of worship, singing, and praise in the Old Testament, but these were no less important in the New Testament. One example is found in Philippians 2:5–11, seen by many as an early Christian hymn. These poetic words recounted and celebrated the example of Jesus' humility and obedience, even to the point of dying on the cross. Paul makes clear his purpose in sharing the hymn. It is not just remembrance but a call to action. The celebration of Jesus is also a call to follow Jesus' example. God-honoring celebration has the effect of encouraging greater obedience and a deeper faith.

Nehemiah's Final Reforms

13 On that day they read from the Book of Moses in the hearing of the people.
And in it was found written that no Ammonite or Moabite should ever enter the assembly of God, 2for they did not meet the people of Israel with bread
and water, but hired Balaam against them to curse them—yet our God turned the
curse into a blessing. 3As soon as the people heard the law, they separated from
Israel all those of foreign descent.

4Now before this, Eliashib the priest, who was appointed over the chambers of
the house of our God, and who was related to Tobiah, 5prepared for Tobiah a large
chamber where they had previously put the grain offering, the frankincense, the
vessels, and the tithes of grain, wine, and oil, which were given by commandment
to the Levites, singers, and gatekeepers, and the contributions for the priests.
6While this was taking place, I was not in Jerusalem, for in the thirty-second year
of Artaxerxes king of Babylon I went to the king. And after some time I asked leave
of the king 7and came to Jerusalem, and I then discovered the evil that Eliashib
had done for Tobiah, preparing for him a chamber in the courts of the house of
God. 8And I was very angry, and I threw all the household furniture of Tobiah
out of the chamber. 9Then I gave orders, and they cleansed the chambers, and I
brought back there the vessels of the house of God, with the grain offering and
the frankincense.

10I also found out that the portions of the Levites had not been given to them,
so that the Levites and the singers, who did the work, had fled each to his field.
11So I confronted the officials and said, "Why is the house of God forsaken?" And
I gathered them together and set them in their stations. 12Then all Judah brought
the tithe of the grain, wine, and oil into the storehouses. 13And I appointed as treasurers over the storehouses Shelemiah the priest, Zadok the scribe, and Pedaiah
of the Levites, and as their assistant Hanan the son of Zaccur, son of Mattaniah,
for they were considered reliable, and their duty was to distribute to their brothers. 14Remember me, O my God, concerning this, and do not wipe out my good
deeds that I have done for the house of my God and for his service.

15In those days I saw in Judah people treading winepresses on the Sabbath, and
bringing in heaps of grain and loading them on donkeys, and also wine, grapes,
figs, and all kinds of loads, which they brought into Jerusalem on the Sabbath day.
And I warned them on the day when they sold food. 16Tyrians also, who lived in
the city, brought in fish and all kinds of goods and sold them on the Sabbath to
the people of Judah, in Jerusalem itself! 17Then I confronted the nobles of Judah
and said to them, "What is this evil thing that you are doing, profaning the Sabbath day? 18Did not your fathers act in this way, and did not our God bring all this
disaster[1] on us and on this city? Now you are bringing more wrath on Israel by
profaning the Sabbath."

19As soon as it began to grow dark at the gates of Jerusalem before the Sabbath,
I commanded that the doors should be shut and gave orders that they should not
be opened until after the Sabbath. And I stationed some of my servants at the
gates, that no load might be brought in on the Sabbath day. 20Then the merchants
and sellers of all kinds of wares lodged outside Jerusalem once or twice. 21But I
warned them and said to them, "Why do you lodge outside the wall? If you do so
again, I will lay hands on you." From that time on they did not come on the Sabbath. 22Then I commanded the Levites that they should purify themselves and
come and guard the gates, to keep the Sabbath day holy. Remember this also in my
favor, O my God, and spare me according to the greatness of your steadfast love.

23In those days also I saw the Jews who had married women of Ashdod, Ammon, and Moab. 24And half of their children spoke the language of Ashdod, and
they could not speak the language of Judah, but only the language of each people.
25And I confronted them and cursed them and beat some of them and pulled out

[1]The Hebrew word can mean *evil*, *harm*, or *disaster*, depending on the context

NEHEMIAH 13:4–28

CORRUPTION THROUGH COMPROMISE

Sometime after the dedication of the wall, Nehemiah returned to Persia. Arriving again in Jerusalem, he found the walls intact but the spiritual health of its inhabitants in ruin. Evidence of their compromised faith was everywhere. Tobiah the Ammonite, with the help of Jewish allies, had taken up residence in one of the temple's storerooms. The Levites and musicians had returned to their fields because the people had not honored their pledge to support them. The Sabbath had been utterly defiled, in spite of the people's agreement to keep it holy. Instead of a day of rest dedicated to God, work and commerce continued as if it were any other day. The people's compromise had driven them further from God, which angered Nehemiah.

Over 400 years later, Jesus, too, was angry at the spiritual corruption of God's people. The most vivid displays of this anger are Jesus' cleansing of the temple—apparently once at the beginning of his ministry (Jn 2:13–17) and once at the end of his ministry (Mt 21:12–13). The temple was meant to be a place of prayer. Instead God's house had become a place where the poor were defrauded, as merchants sold animals for sacrifice, and money-changers charged a fee for converting currency. Jesus' response to their compromise and corruption is much like Nehemiah's in that it is not limited to words of admonition. Jesus flipped over the tables of the money-changers and drove both them and the merchants out of the temple.

their hair. And I made them take an oath in the name of God, saying, "You shall
not give your daughters to their sons, or take their daughters for your sons or
for yourselves. [26]Did not Solomon king of Israel sin on account of such women?
Among the many nations there was no king like him, and he was beloved by his
God, and God made him king over all Israel. Nevertheless, foreign women made
even him to sin. [27]Shall we then listen to you and do all this great evil and act
treacherously against our God by marrying foreign women?"

[28]And one of the sons of Jehoiada, the son of Eliashib the high priest, was
the son-in-law of Sanballat the Horonite. Therefore I chased him from me. [29]Re-
member them, O my God, because they have desecrated the priesthood and the
covenant of the priesthood and the Levites.

[30]Thus I cleansed them from everything foreign, and I established the duties
of the priests and Levites, each in his work; [31]and I provided for the wood offering
at appointed times, and for the firstfruits.

Remember me, O my God, for good.

JESUS: OUR DIVINE ADVOCATE

ESTHER

ESTHER

FIRST JEWS RETURN TO JUDAH FROM EXILE	AHASUERUS REIGNS IN PERSIA	THE JEWS TRIUMPH OVER THEIR ENEMIES (PURIM)
c. 538 BC	*c. 486 – 465 BC*	*c. 473 BC*

The book of Esther, one of only two books in the Bible named after a woman, recounts the story of the rise of a beautiful young orphan girl from obscurity to royalty. The story has all of the action, romance, power, and deceit often found in a great novel. Through it all, the main character of the book is never actually mentioned; God himself is at work to protect his people and save them from clear destruction, yet we never hear any of the characters, even the Jewish ones, mention him.

The events described in Esther span the years in which Ahasuerus ruled over Persia. He continued his father Darius's campaign against Greece, and around 483 BC he threw a magnificent feast to celebrate his accomplishments and to prepare the population for further military incursions.

Esther is not mentioned in historical writings outside of the Bible, so little is known about her background or position. The word "queen" may refer merely to a principal wife rather than to someone who ruled alongside the king. Esther was a Jew, though she originally hid this fact from her Persian rulers. She even chose to use her Persian name, Esther, instead of her Jewish name, Hadassah, even in the final, climactic moment in the book when she revealed her true identity.

God's sovereign work is seen throughout the book of Esther. Though some people balk at admitting this book's significance, noting that the name of God is never mentioned, it is clear that the unnamed author was well aware of God's providence from start to finish. As God has always done, he proves that no situation, no matter how broken, is beyond his reach or his influence. God is always at work, orchestrating with his providential hand and turning hopelessness into hopefulness.

At a time when God seemed distant, even absent, from his people, the author reveals that God was still at work. Even in the very center of the Persian kingdom, he protected a remnant of people whom he would use to accomplish his purpose of bringing glory to his name. God did not forget those Israelites who remained in foreign lands. They too knew God's gracious protection, experienced his mercy, and testified to his greatness among the nations.

God sent Jesus, like Esther, at a particular point in history to accomplish his sovereign plan. Paul revealed that God sent Jesus at just the right time to redeem fallen humanity (Gal 4:4 – 5). Though both Esther and Jesus were put in harm's way, God used them both to fulfill his masterful plan in spite of opposition and danger. Esther's boldness and courage are emblematic of the faith that comes to those who trust in Jesus and rest in the sure fact that God will always accomplish his mission.

AND WHO KNOWS WHETHER YOU
HAVE NOT COME TO THE KINGDOM
FOR SUCH A TIME AS THIS?

Esther 4:14

ESTHER

The King's Banquets

1 Now in the days of Ahasuerus, the Ahasuerus who reigned from India to Ethiopia over 127 provinces, 2in those days when King Ahasuerus sat on his royal
throne in Susa, the citadel, 3in the third year of his reign he gave a feast for all his
officials and servants. The army of Persia and Media and the nobles and governors of the provinces were before him, 4while he showed the riches of his royal
glory and the splendor and pomp of his greatness for many days, 180 days. 5And
when these days were completed, the king gave for all the people present in Susa
the citadel, both great and small, a feast lasting for seven days in the court of the
garden of the king's palace. 6There were white cotton curtains and violet hangings fastened with cords of fine linen and purple to silver rods[1] and marble pillars,
and also couches of gold and silver on a mosaic pavement of porphyry, marble,
mother-of-pearl, and precious stones. 7Drinks were served in golden vessels, vessels of different kinds, and the royal wine was lavished according to the bounty of
the king. 8And drinking was according to this edict: "There is no compulsion." For
the king had given orders to all the staff of his palace to do as each man desired.
9Queen Vashti also gave a feast for the women in the palace that belonged to King
Ahasuerus.

Queen Vashti's Refusal

10On the seventh day, when the heart of the king was merry with wine, he
commanded Mehuman, Biztha, Harbona, Bigtha and Abagtha, Zethar and Car-
kas, the seven eunuchs who served in the presence of King Ahasuerus, 11to bring
Queen Vashti before the king with her royal crown,[2] in order to show the peoples
and the princes her beauty, for she was lovely to look at. 12But Queen Vashti refused to come at the king's command delivered by the eunuchs. At this the king
became enraged, and his anger burned within him.

13Then the king said to the wise men who knew the times (for this was the
king's procedure toward all who were versed in law and judgment, 14the men
next to him being Carshena, Shethar, Admatha, Tarshish, Meres, Marsena, and
Memucan, the seven princes of Persia and Media, who saw the king's face, and
sat first in the kingdom): 15"According to the law, what is to be done to Queen
Vashti, because she has not performed the command of King Ahasuerus delivered by the eunuchs?" 16Then Memucan said in the presence of the king and
the officials, "Not only against the king has Queen Vashti done wrong, but also
against all the officials and all the peoples who are in all the provinces of King
Ahasuerus. 17For the queen's behavior will be made known to all women, causing them to look at their husbands with contempt,[3] since they will say, 'King
Ahasuerus commanded Queen Vashti to be brought before him, and she did
not come.' 18This very day the noble women of Persia and Media who have
heard of the queen's behavior will say the same to all the king's officials, and
there will be contempt and wrath in plenty. 19If it please the king, let a royal
order go out from him, and let it be written among the laws of the Persians and
the Medes so that it may not be repealed, that Vashti is never again to come before King Ahasuerus. And let the king give her royal position to another who is
better than she. 20So when the decree made by the king is proclaimed throughout all his kingdom, for it is vast, all women will give honor to their husbands,
high and low alike." 21This advice pleased the king and the princes, and the king
did as Memucan proposed. 22He sent letters to all the royal provinces, to every
province in its own script and to every people in its own language, that every

[1]Or *rings* [2]Or *headdress* [3]Hebrew *to disdain their husbands in their eyes*

THE IMPOSSIBLE MADE POSSIBLE

The book of Esther records a terrifying situation for the chosen people of God. King Ahasuerus had a vast kingdom. He had amassed 127 provinces stretching from India to Ethiopia. People of numerous ethnicities, languages, customs, and religions were under his command. The Jews were one of many minorities immersed in Persian daily life. But even though they had been exiled from their homeland many years earlier, God still had his hand of protection on them. At the climax of this story, an irrevocable law was passed legalizing the genocide of the Jewish people. This seemed like an impossible situation, but God proved to be in control the whole time.

The book of Esther opens with six months of festivities, likely a war council held to plan the Persian invasion of Greece. After that, everyone in Susa — from the greatest to the least — was invited to an opulent garden party that lasted a week. Sadly, at the end of this feast, when the king and all his guests were intoxicated and irrational, he called for his queen to parade around for the pleasure of everyone to see. However, the queen refused. When she didn't expose herself to all the partiers, the king asked his advisers what should be done. It was decided that her royal position was to be given to another who was more worthy. In the midst of this challenging set of circumstances, the door was opened for Esther to step into the story. One queen had to be removed so that another could step in to what God had planned. Esther stepped in so that ultimately her people could be saved.

Jesus said in Matthew 5:48, "You therefore must be perfect, as your heavenly Father is perfect." That is an impossible standard! Thank goodness Jesus makes believers worthy. Jesus stepped into the story of humanity so that the will of God could be accomplished. No one is worthy to carry out the story of God on their own, but Jesus makes the way "to walk in a manner worthy of the Lord, fully pleasing to him: bearing fruit in every good work and increasing in the knowledge of God" (Col 1:10).

Even though King Ahasuerus's feast ended with the dismissal of a queen, it provided an open door for God to put someone in place who would have influence over the king and save God's people — a provision so dramatic that the Jewish people still celebrate it today.

man be master in his own household and speak according to the language of his people.

Esther Chosen Queen

2 After these things, when the anger of King Ahasuerus had abated, he remembered Vashti and what she had done and what had been decreed against her. [2]Then the king's young men who attended him said, "Let beautiful young virgins be sought out for the king. [3]And let the king appoint officers in all the provinces of his kingdom to gather all the beautiful young virgins to the harem in Susa the citadel, under custody of Hegai, the king's eunuch, who is in charge of the women. Let their cosmetics be given them. [4]And let the young woman who pleases the king[1] be queen instead of Vashti." This pleased the king, and he did so.

[5]Now there was a Jew in Susa the citadel whose name was Mordecai, the son of Jair, son of Shimei, son of Kish, a Benjaminite, [6]who had been carried away from Jerusalem among the captives carried away with Jeconiah king of Judah, whom Nebuchadnezzar king of Babylon had carried away. [7]He was bringing up Hadassah, that is Esther, the daughter of his uncle, for she had neither father nor mother. The young woman had a beautiful figure and was lovely to look at, and when her father and her mother died, Mordecai took her as his own daughter. [8]So when the king's order and his edict were proclaimed, and when many young women were gathered in Susa the citadel in custody of Hegai, Esther also was taken into the king's palace and put in custody of Hegai, who had charge of the women. [9]And the young woman pleased him and won his favor. And he quickly provided her with her cosmetics and her portion of food, and with seven chosen young women from the king's palace, and advanced her and her young women to the best place in the harem. [10]Esther had not made known her people or kindred, for Mordecai had commanded her not to make it known. [11]And every day Mordecai walked in front of the court of the harem to learn how Esther was and what was happening to her.

[12]Now when the turn came for each young woman to go in to King Ahasuerus, after being twelve months under the regulations for the women, since this was the regular period of their beautifying, six months with oil of myrrh and six months with spices and ointments for women— [13]when the young woman went in to the king in this way, she was given whatever she desired to take with her from the harem to the king's palace. [14]In the evening she would go in, and in the morning she would return to the second harem in custody of Shaashgaz, the king's eunuch, who was in charge of the concubines. She would not go in to the king again, unless the king delighted in her and she was summoned by name.

[15]When the turn came for Esther the daughter of Abihail the uncle of Mordecai, who had taken her as his own daughter, to go in to the king, she asked for nothing except what Hegai the king's eunuch, who had charge of the women, advised. Now Esther was winning favor in the eyes of all who saw her. [16]And when Esther was taken to King Ahasuerus, into his royal palace, in the tenth month, which is the month of Tebeth, in the seventh year of his reign, [17]the king loved Esther more than all the women, and she won grace and favor in his sight more than all the virgins, so that he set the royal crown[2] on her head and made her queen instead of Vashti. [18]Then the king gave a great feast for all his officials and servants; it was Esther's feast. He also granted a remission of taxes to the provinces and gave gifts with royal generosity.

Mordecai Discovers a Plot

[19]Now when the virgins were gathered together the second time, Mordecai was sitting at the king's gate. [20]Esther had not made known her kindred or her people, as Mordecai had commanded her, for Esther obeyed Mordecai just as when she was brought up by him. [21]In those days, as Mordecai was sitting at

ESTHER 2:8–9

THE SEARCH

A search was made across all of the Persian Empire for a new queen. Esther was gathered with many other young women in the palace. The competition was fierce, and Esther probably felt inadequate. However, out of all of the potential choices, she was the one chosen by the king!

Jesus told several parables demonstrating how God the Father will search for his loved ones. The lost sheep in Luke 15:4–6 and the lost coin in Luke 15:8–9 both tell of a great search. Each child of God is valuable to him. Esther was searched for and chosen out of all the young women of a massive kingdom. What were the odds?! The same search will be made for each believer. Out of all the people on earth, God the Father won't stop till his chosen know and walk in the love of their Savior.

[1]Hebrew *who is good in the eyes of the king* [2]Or *headdress*

the king's gate, Bigthan and Teresh, two of the king's eunuchs, who guarded the threshold, became angry and sought to lay hands on King Ahasuerus. 22And this came to the knowledge of Mordecai, and he told it to Queen Esther, and Esther told the king in the name of Mordecai. 23When the affair was investigated and found to be so, the men were both hanged on the gallows.[1] And it was recorded in the book of the chronicles in the presence of the king.

Haman Plots Against the Jews

3 After these things King Ahasuerus promoted Haman the Agagite, the son of Hammedatha, and advanced him and set his throne above all the officials who were with him. 2And all the king's servants who were at the king's gate bowed down and paid homage to Haman, for the king had so commanded concerning him. But Mordecai did not bow down or pay homage. 3Then the king's servants who were at the king's gate said to Mordecai, "Why do you transgress the king's command?" 4And when they spoke to him day after day and he would not listen to them, they told Haman, in order to see whether Mordecai's words would stand, for he had told them that he was a Jew. 5And when Haman saw that Mordecai did not bow down or pay homage to him, Haman was filled with fury. 6But he disdained[2] to lay hands on Mordecai alone. So, as they had made known to him the people of Mordecai, Haman sought to destroy[3] all the Jews, the people of Mordecai, throughout the whole kingdom of Ahasuerus.

7In the first month, which is the month of Nisan, in the twelfth year of King Ahasuerus, they cast Pur (that is, they cast lots) before Haman day after day; and they cast it month after month till the twelfth month, which is the month of Adar. 8Then Haman said to King Ahasuerus, "There is a certain people scattered abroad and dispersed among the peoples in all the provinces of your kingdom. Their laws are different from those of every other people, and they do not keep the king's laws, so that it is not to the king's profit to tolerate them. 9If it please the king, let it be decreed that they be destroyed, and I will pay 10,000 talents[4] of silver into the hands of those who have charge of the king's business, that they may put it into the king's treasuries." 10So the king took his signet ring from his hand and gave it to Haman the Agagite, the son of Hammedatha, the enemy of the Jews. 11And the king said to Haman, "The money is given to you, the people also, to do with them as it seems good to you."

12Then the king's scribes were summoned on the thirteenth day of the first month, and an edict, according to all that Haman commanded, was written to the king's satraps and to the governors over all the provinces and to the officials of all the peoples, to every province in its own script and every people in its own language. It was written in the name of King Ahasuerus and sealed with the king's signet ring. 13Letters were sent by couriers to all the king's provinces with instruction to destroy, to kill, and to annihilate all Jews, young and old, women and children, in one day, the thirteenth day of the twelfth month, which is the month of Adar, and to plunder their goods. 14A copy of the document was to be issued as a decree in every province by proclamation to all the peoples to be ready for that day. 15The couriers went out hurriedly by order of the king, and the decree was issued in Susa the citadel. And the king and Haman sat down to drink, but the city of Susa was thrown into confusion.

Esther Agrees to Help the Jews

4 When Mordecai learned all that had been done, Mordecai tore his clothes and put on sackcloth and ashes, and went out into the midst of the city, and he cried out with a loud and bitter cry. 2He went up to the entrance of the king's gate, for no one was allowed to enter the king's gate clothed in sackcloth. 3And in every

[1]Or *wooden beam* or *stake*; Hebrew *tree* or *wood*. This Persian execution practice involved affixing or impaling a person on a stake or pole (compare Ezra 6:11) [2]Hebrew *disdained in his eyes* [3]Or *annihilate*
[4]A *talent* was about 75 pounds or 34 kilograms

ESTHER 3:5–6

HATRED

At the close of chapter 2, Mordecai saved King Ahasuerus's life by exposing a plot to take his life. But nothing was done to reward Mordecai for his good deed (2:21–23; 6:3). The next recorded events are the rise and promotion of Haman. Haman was no friend of Mordecai. "When Haman saw that Mordecai did not bow down or pay homage to him, Haman was filled with fury" (3:5). His rage consumed him so much that he not only wanted to kill Mordecai, but all of his people too (3:6).

Jesus felt the same sting of hatred. Luke 6:11 says that the Pharisees and the religious teachers "were filled with fury and discussed with one another what they might do to Jesus." There is a striking parallel between Haman's directive to "destroy, to kill, and to annihilate all Jews" (Est 3:13) and Jesus' description of the thief who "comes only to steal and kill and destroy" (Jn 10:10).

province, wherever the king's command and his decree reached, there was great mourning among the Jews, with fasting and weeping and lamenting, and many of them lay in sackcloth and ashes.

4When Esther's young women and her eunuchs came and told her, the queen was deeply distressed. She sent garments to clothe Mordecai, so that he might take off his sackcloth, but he would not accept them. 5Then Esther called for Hathach, one of the king's eunuchs, who had been appointed to attend her, and ordered him to go to Mordecai to learn what this was and why it was. 6Hathach went out to Mordecai in the open square of the city in front of the king's gate, 7and Mordecai told him all that had happened to him, and the exact sum of money that Haman had promised to pay into the king's treasuries for the destruction of the Jews. 8Mordecai also gave him a copy of the written decree issued in Susa for their destruction,[1] that he might show it to Esther and explain it to her and command her to go to the king to beg his favor and plead with him[2] on behalf of her people. 9And Hathach went and told Esther what Mordecai had said. 10Then Esther spoke to Hathach and commanded him to go to Mordecai and say, 11"All the king's servants and the people of the king's provinces know that if any man or woman goes to the king inside the inner court without being called, there is but one law—to be put to death, except the one to whom the king holds out the golden scepter so that he may live. But as for me, I have not been called to come in to the king these thirty days."

12And they told Mordecai what Esther had said. 13Then Mordecai told them to reply to Esther, "Do not think to yourself that in the king's palace you will escape any more than all the other Jews. 14For if you keep silent at this time, relief and deliverance will rise for the Jews from another place, but you and your father's house will perish. And who knows whether you have not come to the kingdom for such a time as this?" 15Then Esther told them to reply to Mordecai, 16"Go, gather all the Jews to be found in Susa, and hold a fast on my behalf, and do not eat or drink for three days, night or day. I and my young women will also fast as you do. Then I will go to the king, though it is against the law, and if I perish, I perish."[3] 17Mordecai then went away and did everything as Esther had ordered him.

Esther Prepares a Banquet

5 On the third day Esther put on her royal robes and stood in the inner court of the king's palace, in front of the king's quarters, while the king was sitting on his royal throne inside the throne room opposite the entrance to the palace. 2And when the king saw Queen Esther standing in the court, she won favor in his sight, and he held out to Esther the golden scepter that was in his hand. Then Esther approached and touched the tip of the scepter. 3And the king said to her, "What is it, Queen Esther? What is your request? It shall be given you, even to the half of my kingdom." 4And Esther said, "If it please the king,[4] let the king and Haman come today to a feast that I have prepared for the king." 5Then the king said, "Bring Haman quickly, so that we may do as Esther has asked." So the king and Haman came to the feast that Esther had prepared. 6And as they were drinking wine after the feast, the king said to Esther, "What is your wish? It shall be granted you. And what is your request? Even to the half of my kingdom, it shall be fulfilled."[5] 7Then Esther answered, "My wish and my request is: 8If I have found favor in the sight of the king, and if it please the king[6] to grant my wish and fulfill my request, let the king and Haman come to the feast that I will prepare for them, and tomorrow I will do as the king has said."

Haman Plans to Hang Mordecai

9And Haman went out that day joyful and glad of heart. But when Haman saw Mordecai in the king's gate, that he neither rose nor trembled before him, he

[1]Or *annihilation* [2]Hebrew *and seek from before his face* [3]Hebrew *if I am destroyed, then I will be destroyed*
[4]Hebrew *If it is good to the king* [5]Or *done* [6]Hebrew *if it is good to the king*

ESTHER 5:1–2

CLOSING THE GAP

The walk toward the king's hall in the inner court must have been terrifying for Queen Esther. Approaching the king without being summoned could easily be punishable by death. In this moment there is a "gap" created — where action is taken in obedience before the result is known. Believers can find courage in Esther's actions. When steps are taken in obedience, this can leave a gap for the Holy Spirit to move and even exceed expectations.

Before Jesus' sacrifice, access to God was not available to everyone. Paul connected the pieces in Ephesians 2:18: "For through him we both have access in one Spirit to the Father." In this gap, the Holy Spirit meets the believer's obedience and delivers God-sized results.

Ultimately the king replied to Esther, "And what is your request? Even to the half of my kingdom, it shall be fulfilled" (Est 5:6). Our heavenly Father has given us an even better response, "If you ask me anything in my name, I will do it" (Jn 14:14). Jesus stands in the gap for those who believe in him and follow him.

GOD PROTECTS HIS PEOPLE

Mordecai trusted God to protect his people. Since Mordecai was a devout Jew, we can be sure that his faith and resolve stood on the firm foundation of what the prophets of God proclaimed. God had previously said through the prophet Isaiah, "Because you are precious in my eyes, and honored, and I love you, I give men in return for you, peoples in exchange for your life. Fear not, for I am with you" (Isa 43:4 – 5). Mordecai could see how God had allowed Esther to become queen so she could be used by God to save her people and fulfill the promises of God.

As her adoptive father, Mordecai would have taught Esther how to put her trust in God, take a step of faith, and believe God would give her favor. Mordecai advised Queen Esther to "go to the king to beg his favor and plead with him on behalf of her people" (Est 4:8). Likewise, in each struggle, trial, and pain, believers "have an advocate with the Father, Jesus Christ the righteous" (1Jn 2:1). Every presented request is an opportunity for Jesus to intercede.

Believers can be sure that God wants to use his children to do great things. The words of the prophet Isaiah are a rallying cry: "For Zion's sake I will not keep silent, and for Jerusalem's sake I will not be quiet, until her righteousness goes forth as brightness, and her salvation as a burning torch" (Isa 62:1). If Esther kept silent, Mordecai was sure that deliverance would "rise for the Jews from another place" (Est 4:14).

Queen Esther undoubtedly found courage in the promises of God. Her faith became greater than her doubt. "Then I will go to the king, though it is against the law, and if I perish, I perish" (4:16). Ultimately, she was willing to sacrifice her own life, foreshadowing the willingness of Jesus to die for us (Lk 22:42; Ro 5:6 – 11). As the body of Christ, the church has the assurance that whatever the circumstances, no matter how awful it seems, nothing will be able to separate us from God's love (Ro 8:38 – 39).

was filled with wrath against Mordecai. 10Nevertheless, Haman restrained himself and went home, and he sent and brought his friends and his wife Zeresh. 11And Haman recounted to them the splendor of his riches, the number of his sons, all the promotions with which the king had honored him, and how he had advanced him above the officials and the servants of the king. 12Then Haman said, "Even Queen Esther let no one but me come with the king to the feast she prepared. And tomorrow also I am invited by her together with the king. 13Yet all this is worth nothing to me, so long as I see Mordecai the Jew sitting at the king's gate." 14Then his wife Zeresh and all his friends said to him, "Let a gallows[1] fifty cubits[2] high be made, and in the morning tell the king to have Mordecai hanged upon it. Then go joyfully with the king to the feast." This idea pleased Haman, and he had the gallows made.

The King Honors Mordecai

6 On that night the king could not sleep. And he gave orders to bring the book of memorable deeds, the chronicles, and they were read before the king. 2And it was found written how Mordecai had told about Bigthana[3] and Teresh, two of the king's eunuchs, who guarded the threshold, and who had sought to lay hands on King Ahasuerus. 3And the king said, "What honor or distinction has been bestowed on Mordecai for this?" The king's young men who attended him said, "Nothing has been done for him." 4And the king said, "Who is in the court?" Now Haman had just entered the outer court of the king's palace to speak to the king about having Mordecai hanged on the gallows[4] that he had prepared for him. 5And the king's young men told him, "Haman is there, standing in the court." And the king said, "Let him come in." 6So Haman came in, and the king said to him, "What should be done to the man whom the king delights to honor?" And Haman said to himself, "Whom would the king delight to honor more than me?" 7And Haman said to the king, "For the man whom the king delights to honor, 8let royal robes be brought, which the king has worn, and the horse that the king has ridden, and on whose head a royal crown[5] is set. 9And let the robes and the horse be handed over to one of the king's most noble officials. Let them dress the man whom the king delights to honor, and let them lead him on the horse through the square of the city, proclaiming before him: 'Thus shall it be done to the man whom the king delights to honor.'" 10Then the king said to Haman, "Hurry; take the robes and the horse, as you have said, and do so to Mordecai the Jew, who sits at the king's gate. Leave out nothing that you have mentioned." 11So Haman took the robes and the horse, and he dressed Mordecai and led him through the square of the city, proclaiming before him, "Thus shall it be done to the man whom the king delights to honor."

12Then Mordecai returned to the king's gate. But Haman hurried to his house, mourning and with his head covered. 13And Haman told his wife Zeresh and all his friends everything that had happened to him. Then his wise men and his wife Zeresh said to him, "If Mordecai, before whom you have begun to fall, is of the Jewish people, you will not overcome him but will surely fall before him."

Esther Reveals Haman's Plot

14While they were yet talking with him, the king's eunuchs arrived and hurried to bring Haman to the feast that Esther had prepared.

7 So the king and Haman went in to feast with Queen Esther. 2And on the second day, as they were drinking wine after the feast, the king again said to Esther, "What is your wish, Queen Esther? It shall be granted you. And what is your request? Even to the half of my kingdom, it shall be fulfilled." 3Then Queen Esther answered, "If I have found favor in your sight, O king, and if it please the king, let

ESTHER 6:4–10

PRIDE VERSUS HUMILITY

It's not hard to see the irony in this turn of events. Haman was on his way to recommend that Mordecai be hanged, yet he unknowingly is recommending that Mordecai be honored and given the royal treatment. "Pride goes before destruction, and a haughty spirit before a fall" (Pr 16:18). Exhibit A: Haman.

Even after Mordecai saved the king's life, Mordecai was humble enough not to demand recognition or a reward. Jesus said, "Whoever exalts himself will be humbled, and whoever humbles himself will be exalted" (Mt 23:12).

God's timing is perfect, and he knows where to find his followers when he is ready to honor them. Believers don't have to manipulate or force their position anywhere . . . at work . . . in the church . . . among friends and family. But "your Father who sees in secret will reward you" (Mt 6:18).

Jesus is the ultimate model and inspiration. Not only did Jesus model humility (Php 2:8), his followers also are to be marked by humility. Christians should live "with all humility and gentleness, with patience, bearing with one another in love, eager to maintain the unity of the Spirit in the bond of peace" (Eph 4:2–3).

[1]Or *wooden beam*; twice in this verse (see note on 2:23) [2]A *cubit* was about 18 inches or 45 centimeters
[3]*Bigthana* is an alternate spelling of *Bigthan* (see 2:21) [4]Or *wooden beam* (see note on 2:23)
[5]Or *headdress*

my life be granted me for my wish, and my people for my request. 4For we have been sold, I and my people, to be destroyed, to be killed, and to be annihilated. If we had been sold merely as slaves, men and women, I would have been silent, for our affliction is not to be compared with the loss to the king." 5Then King Ahasuerus said to Queen Esther, "Who is he, and where is he, who has dared[1] to do this?" 6And Esther said, "A foe and enemy! This wicked Haman!" Then Haman was terrified before the king and the queen.

Haman Is Hanged

7And the king arose in his wrath from the wine-drinking and went into the palace garden, but Haman stayed to beg for his life from Queen Esther, for he saw that harm was determined against him by the king. 8And the king returned from the palace garden to the place where they were drinking wine, as Haman was falling on the couch where Esther was. And the king said, "Will he even assault the queen in my presence, in my own house?" As the word left the mouth of the king, they covered Haman's face. 9Then Harbona, one of the eunuchs in attendance on the king, said, "Moreover, the gallows[2] that Haman has prepared for Mordecai, whose word saved the king, is standing at Haman's house, fifty cubits[3] high." And the king said, "Hang him on that." 10So they hanged Haman on the gallows that he had prepared for Mordecai. Then the wrath of the king abated.

Esther Saves the Jews

8 On that day King Ahasuerus gave to Queen Esther the house of Haman, the enemy of the Jews. And Mordecai came before the king, for Esther had told what he was to her. 2And the king took off his signet ring, which he had taken from Haman, and gave it to Mordecai. And Esther set Mordecai over the house of Haman.

3Then Esther spoke again to the king. She fell at his feet and wept and pleaded with him to avert the evil plan of Haman the Agagite and the plot that he had devised against the Jews. 4When the king held out the golden scepter to Esther, Esther rose and stood before the king. 5And she said, "If it please the king, and if I have found favor in his sight, and if the thing seems right before the king, and I am pleasing in his eyes, let an order be written to revoke the letters devised by Haman the Agagite, the son of Hammedatha, which he wrote to destroy the Jews who are in all the provinces of the king. 6For how can I bear to see the calamity that is coming to my people? Or how can I bear to see the destruction of my kindred?" 7Then King Ahasuerus said to Queen Esther and to Mordecai the Jew, "Behold, I have given Esther the house of Haman, and they have hanged him on the gallows,[4] because he intended to lay hands on the Jews. 8But you may write as you please with regard to the Jews, in the name of the king, and seal it with the king's ring, for an edict written in the name of the king and sealed with the king's ring cannot be revoked."

9The king's scribes were summoned at that time, in the third month, which is the month of Sivan, on the twenty-third day. And an edict was written, according to all that Mordecai commanded concerning the Jews, to the satraps and the governors and the officials of the provinces from India to Ethiopia, 127 provinces, to each province in its own script and to each people in its own language, and also to the Jews in their script and their language. 10And he wrote in the name of King Ahasuerus and sealed it with the king's signet ring. Then he sent the letters by mounted couriers riding on swift horses that were used in the king's service, bred from the royal stud, 11saying that the king allowed the Jews who were in every city to gather and defend their lives, to destroy, to kill, and to annihilate any armed force of any people or province that might attack

[1]Hebrew *whose heart has filled him* [2]Or *wooden beam*; also verse 10 (see note on 2:23) [3]A *cubit* was about 18 inches or 45 centimeters [4]Or *wooden beam* (see note on 2:23)

ESTHER 7:10

PARADOX

Haman gave full vent to his anger, and it made him a fool (Pr 29:11). He listened to the advice of his wife and friends, and in a great paradox, Haman was impaled on the very pole they had advised him to set up for Mordecai. Jesus said, "Nothing is hidden that will not be made manifest, nor is anything secret that will not be known and come to light" (Lk 8:17).

Believers also wrestle with the paradox of Paul's great proclamation, "For to me to live is Christ, and to die is gain" (Php 1:21). Paul reasoned that if he survived his imprisonment, he would be able to continue preaching the gospel and see lives transformed. But he also knew that if he died, God could also use his death to further the kingdom, *and* he would be with Jesus! Paul clearly saw the advantages of both life and death. Jesus' death gave us life. Because of Jesus' death and resurrection, death is swallowed up in victory (1Co 15:54).

ESTHER 8:1–8

WRITE A NEW CHAPTER

Up until this point, Queen Esther had to approach the king and confront Haman alone. The closest Mordecai had gotten was the king's gate. But finally Mordecai had an audience with the king after the queen revealed they were related. Mordecai was given Haman's position as second in rank to the king (10:3) and the king's signet ring. The same ring King Ahasuerus had given to Haman, he now placed on Mordecai's

(continued on next page)

(Write a New Chapter, continued)

finger. The ring on Haman's hand brought great mourning, fasting, and tears (4:3). But on Mordecai's hand, it brought happiness, joy, and honor (8:16).

Because of his newfound favor with the king, Mordecai and Queen Esther were asked to write a new decree that would allow the Jews to defend themselves. Mordecai could have requested an audience with the king after he saved his life or later when he was publicly honored for doing so. But he waited for God to move on his behalf. "Both riches and honor come from you, and you rule over all. In your hand are power and might, and in your hand it is to make great and to give strength to all" (1Ch 29:12).

them, children and women included, and to plunder their goods, 12on one day throughout all the provinces of King Ahasuerus, on the thirteenth day of the twelfth month, which is the month of Adar. 13A copy of what was written was to be issued as a decree in every province, being publicly displayed to all peoples, and the Jews were to be ready on that day to take vengeance on their enemies. 14So the couriers, mounted on their swift horses that were used in the king's service, rode out hurriedly, urged by the king's command. And the decree was issued in Susa the citadel.

15Then Mordecai went out from the presence of the king in royal robes of blue and white, with a great golden crown[1] and a robe of fine linen and purple, and the city of Susa shouted and rejoiced. 16The Jews had light and gladness and joy and honor. 17And in every province and in every city, wherever the king's command and his edict reached, there was gladness and joy among the Jews, a feast and a holiday. And many from the peoples of the country declared themselves Jews, for fear of the Jews had fallen on them.

The Jews Destroy Their Enemies

9 Now in the twelfth month, which is the month of Adar, on the thirteenth day of the same, when the king's command and edict were about to be carried out, on the very day when the enemies of the Jews hoped to gain the mastery over them, the reverse occurred: the Jews gained mastery over those who hated them. 2The Jews gathered in their cities throughout all the provinces of King Ahasuerus to lay hands on those who sought their harm. And no one could stand against them, for the fear of them had fallen on all peoples. 3All the officials of the provinces and the satraps and the governors and the royal agents also helped the Jews, for the fear of Mordecai had fallen on them. 4For Mordecai was great in the king's house, and his fame spread throughout all the provinces, for the man Mordecai grew more and more powerful. 5The Jews struck all their enemies with the sword, killing and destroying them, and did as they pleased to those who hated them. 6In Susa the citadel itself the Jews killed and destroyed 500 men, 7and also killed Parshandatha and Dalphon and Aspatha 8and Poratha and Adalia and Aridatha 9and Parmashta and Arisai and Aridai and Vaizatha, 10the ten sons of Haman the son of Hammedatha, the enemy of the Jews, but they laid no hand on the plunder.

11That very day the number of those killed in Susa the citadel was reported to the king. 12And the king said to Queen Esther, "In Susa the citadel the Jews have killed and destroyed 500 men and also the ten sons of Haman. What then have they done in the rest of the king's provinces! Now what is your wish? It shall be granted you. And what further is your request? It shall be fulfilled." 13And Esther said, "If it please the king, let the Jews who are in Susa be allowed tomorrow also to do according to this day's edict. And let the ten sons of Haman be hanged on the gallows."[2] 14So the king commanded this to be done. A decree was issued in Susa, and the ten sons of Haman were hanged. 15The Jews who were in Susa gathered also on the fourteenth day of the month of Adar and they killed 300 men in Susa, but they laid no hands on the plunder.

16Now the rest of the Jews who were in the king's provinces also gathered to defend their lives, and got relief from their enemies and killed 75,000 of those who hated them, but they laid no hands on the plunder. 17This was on the thirteenth day of the month of Adar, and on the fourteenth day they rested and made that a day of feasting and gladness. 18But the Jews who were in Susa gathered on the thirteenth day and on the fourteenth, and rested on the fifteenth day, making that a day of feasting and gladness. 19Therefore the Jews of the villages, who live in the rural towns, hold the fourteenth day of the month of Adar as a day for gladness and feasting, as a holiday, and as a day on which they send gifts of food to one another.

[1]Or *headdress* [2]Or *wooden beam*; also verse 25 (see note on 2:23)

THE PRINCIPLE OF THE SEED

Almost 12 months had passed since the couriers had taken Haman's edict throughout the Persian Empire (3:7–14). On the day God's people were to be annihilated, they were given the right to defend themselves and overpowered their enemies instead. God's people had seen deliverance from the hands of their enemies many times before, but memories are short.

God established the principle of the seed. He governs over the rules and economy of sowing, planting, feeding, producing, pruning, reaping, harvesting, and gleaning. As his people, all believers are led through each of these phases with the utmost love and care. Lean in. Keep in close conversation with the heavenly Father. Esther used several occasions to plant a seed and implore her king's favor, and his response was always, "What is your wish? It shall be granted you. And what further is your request? It shall be fulfilled" (9:12).

Esther was even willing for her seed to die so others would live. In John 12:24 and 27 Jesus said about his own life, "Truly, truly, I say to you, unless a grain of wheat falls into the earth and dies, it remains alone; but if it dies, it bears much fruit ... Now is my soul troubled. And what shall I say? 'Father, save me from this hour'? But for this purpose I have come to this hour." The hopes and dreams and treasures of a Christ follower are counted as loss and sown in the ground to ultimately produce a harvest greater than one can imagine. Whatever is given up in trust to Jesus, God uses as seed to produce a large crop.

Jesus longs for us to see his overarching story. In the midst of tragedy, there is purpose. Suffering offers a closeness and intimacy with Jesus. As his beloved, we are in a position to ask and keep asking to see his name glorified. "Ask, and it will be given to you; seek, and you will find; knock, and it will be opened to you" (Mt 7:7).

Jesus' followers can rest in the promise of God that in all things — including present suffering — "we know that for those who love God all things work together for good, for those who are called according to his purpose" (Ro 8:28). God is writing an overarching story of redemption across all time until Christ's return. Believers can entrust their "seed" — families, businesses, dreams, health, and their very lives — into the hands of God. There is assurance that with the planting of a seed, a great harvest is coming when Jesus returns.

The Feast of Purim Inaugurated

[20]And Mordecai recorded these things and sent letters to all the Jews who
were in all the provinces of King Ahasuerus, both near and far, [21]obliging them
to keep the fourteenth day of the month Adar and also the fifteenth day of
the same, year by year, [22]as the days on which the Jews got relief from their
enemies, and as the month that had been turned for them from sorrow into
gladness and from mourning into a holiday; that they should make them days
of feasting and gladness, days for sending gifts of food to one another and gifts
to the poor.

[23]So the Jews accepted what they had started to do, and what Mordecai had
written to them. [24]For Haman the Agagite, the son of Hammedatha, the enemy of
all the Jews, had plotted against the Jews to destroy them, and had cast Pur (that
is, cast lots), to crush and to destroy them. [25]But when it came before the king,
he gave orders in writing that his evil plan that he had devised against the Jews
should return on his own head, and that he and his sons should be hanged on
the gallows. [26]Therefore they called these days Purim, after the term Pur. Therefore, because of all that was written in this letter, and of what they had faced in
this matter, and of what had happened to them, [27]the Jews firmly obligated themselves and their offspring and all who joined them, that without fail they would
keep these two days according to what was written and at the time appointed
every year, [28]that these days should be remembered and kept throughout every
generation, in every clan, province, and city, and that these days of Purim should
never fall into disuse among the Jews, nor should the commemoration of these
days cease among their descendants.

[29]Then Queen Esther, the daughter of Abihail, and Mordecai the Jew gave full
written authority, confirming this second letter about Purim. [30]Letters were sent
to all the Jews, to the 127 provinces of the kingdom of Ahasuerus, in words of
peace and truth, [31]that these days of Purim should be observed at their appointed
seasons, as Mordecai the Jew and Queen Esther obligated them, and as they had
obligated themselves and their offspring, with regard to their fasts and their lamenting. [32]The command of Esther confirmed these practices of Purim, and it
was recorded in writing.

The Greatness of Mordecai

10 King Ahasuerus imposed tax on the land and on the coastlands of the sea.
[2]And all the acts of his power and might, and the full account of the high
honor of Mordecai, to which the king advanced him, are they not written in the
Book of the Chronicles of the kings of Media and Persia? [3]For Mordecai the Jew
was second in rank to King Ahasuerus, and he was great among the Jews and
popular with the multitude of his brothers, for he sought the welfare of his people
and spoke peace to all his people.

ESTHER 10:1–3

A DAY TO REMEMBER

Mordecai left a legacy. For the rest of his life, Mordecai was well known and respected by his people for his greatness. He was known for seeking good for the Jewish people. Purim is still celebrated among the Jewish people today in remembrance of how God delivered the Jews from a day marked for their destruction. Nothing would thwart the plans of God for the promised Messiah. Throughout Scripture, God has always had a purpose to reconcile the world to him (2Co 5:19). Believers should remember these days and God's ways so "that the next generation might know them, the children yet unborn, and arise and tell them to their children, so that they should set their hope in God and not forget the works of God, but keep his commandments" (Ps 78:6–7).

JESUS: OUR SUFFERING SAVIOR

JOB

JOB

ABRAHAM IS BORN	ISAAC IS BORN	ABRAHAM DIES
c. 2166 BC	*c. 2066 BC*	*c. 1991 BC*

Job probably lived in the second millennium BC (2000 – 1000), and his story is one of the most famous stories in all the Bible. Christians and non-Christians alike are likely to know this tale of suffering and pain. The book begins and ends with a prose description of Job's life, comparing the suffering Satan inflicted on him over against God's care, protection, and ultimate blessing (chs. 1 – 2; 42:7 – 17). The majority of the book is made up of a series of speeches, spoken by men who were Job's early supporters (2:13), but quickly became his greatest critics (chs. 3 – 37).

This book tackles massive questions that have loomed in the minds of sufferers throughout all time. How can a good God allow righteous people to suffer? Doesn't this either make God unloving or unjust? Why doesn't God stop human suffering, and the suffering of all creation, if he is in control of all things?

These questions are posed throughout the book, though the answers seem to evade the grasp of Job, his wife, and his friends. Ultimately, God speaks and reminds Job that his knowledge is very limited when compared to the inexplicable wisdom of God. God is good and he is in control — though his people may wonder where he is at certain times. God cautions Job, and the readers of this book, against trying to make a simplistic correlation between their blessing or suffering on this earth and God's goodness, care, or control. God is always at work and is capable of using great pain and suffering to fulfill his good purposes for this world.

Jesus' death on the cross is the ultimate example of God's control over evil. On the surface, it seems like the cross was the greatest evil that could have been perpetrated against God's Son. Jesus' body, beaten and broken, hung on a Roman cross — to the horror of his followers. It seemed that Jesus' battle against evil was lost. Yet all the while, God was working to perfectly accomplish his glorious mission to save fallen sinners. His mission required that his Son go *through* suffering, not around it. Three days later, Jesus' empty tomb shouted victory to all creation. Jesus Christ, the promised Messiah, had defeated Satan, sin, and death through the most unlikely path: by experiencing death himself.

Christians today can take heart in the fact that, while they will surely suffer, God is at work and he can be trusted. He has already won the war.

THE LORD GAVE, AND THE LORD HAS TAKEN AWAY;
BLESSED BE THE NAME OF THE LORD.

Job 1:21

JOB

Job's Character and Wealth

1 There was a man in the land of Uz whose name was Job, and that man was blameless and upright, one who feared God and turned away from evil. 2There were born to him seven sons and three daughters. 3He possessed 7,000 sheep, 3,000 camels, 500 yoke of oxen, and 500 female donkeys, and very many servants, so that this man was the greatest of all the people of the east. 4His sons used to go and hold a feast in the house of each one on his day, and they would send and invite their three sisters to eat and drink with them. 5And when the days of the feast had run their course, Job would send and consecrate them, and he would rise early in the morning and offer burnt offerings according to the number of them all. For Job said, "It may be that my children have sinned, and cursed[1] God in their hearts." Thus Job did continually.

Satan Allowed to Test Job

6Now there was a day when the sons of God came to present themselves before the LORD, and Satan[2] also came among them. 7The LORD said to Satan, "From where have you come?" Satan answered the LORD and said, "From going to and fro on the earth, and from walking up and down on it." 8And the LORD said to Satan, "Have you considered my servant Job, that there is none like him on the earth, a blameless and upright man, who fears God and turns away from evil?" 9Then Satan answered the LORD and said, "Does Job fear God for no reason? 10Have you not put a hedge around him and his house and all that he has, on every side? You have blessed the work of his hands, and his possessions have increased in the land. 11But stretch out your hand and touch all that he has, and he will curse you to your face." 12And the LORD said to Satan, "Behold, all that he has is in your hand. Only against him do not stretch out your hand." So Satan went out from the presence of the LORD.

Satan Takes Job's Property and Children

13Now there was a day when his sons and daughters were eating and drinking wine in their oldest brother's house, 14and there came a messenger to Job and said, "The oxen were plowing and the donkeys feeding beside them, 15and the Sabeans fell upon them and took them and struck down the servants[3] with the edge of the sword, and I alone have escaped to tell you." 16While he was yet speaking, there came another and said, "The fire of God fell from heaven and burned up the sheep and the servants and consumed them, and I alone have escaped to tell you." 17While he was yet speaking, there came another and said, "The Chaldeans formed three groups and made a raid on the camels and took them and struck down the servants with the edge of the sword, and I alone have escaped to tell you." 18While he was yet speaking, there came another and said, "Your sons and daughters were eating and drinking wine in their oldest brother's house, 19and behold, a great wind came across the wilderness and struck the four corners of the house, and it fell upon the young people, and they are dead, and I alone have escaped to tell you."

20Then Job arose and tore his robe and shaved his head and fell on the ground and worshiped. 21And he said, "Naked I came from my mother's womb, and naked shall I return. The LORD gave, and the LORD has taken away; blessed be the name of the LORD."

22In all this Job did not sin or charge God with wrong.

[1]The Hebrew word *bless* is used euphemistically for *curse* in 1:5, 11; 2:5, 9 [2]Hebrew *the Accuser* or *the Adversary*; so throughout chapters 1–2 [3]Hebrew *the young men*; also verses 16, 17

JOB 1:6–12

GOD HAS NO EQUAL

The first two chapters of Job provide a rare glimpse into the activity in heaven. The living God, the ruling and reigning sovereign Lord, sits at the center of the divine throne room, surrounded and served by celestial "sons of God," or angels (1Ki 22:19; Ps 89:5–7). Satan, numbered among these created beings, is in no way the Lord's equal in power, majesty, or knowledge. Though he has some degree of control over the earth at the present time (1Jn 5:19), he remains a subservient creature subject to the authority of the one supreme ruler (Rev 17:14). The book of Job teaches that God is sovereign over all of life's activities and circumstances. The New Testament reveals that Jesus himself is this incomparable God, without equal: Jesus is "far above all rule and authority and power and dominion, and above every name that is named, not only in this age but also in the one to come" (Eph 1:21). All of Scripture—including the difficult book of Job—demonstrates that even in the difficult times, Jesus remains the sovereign God.

Satan Attacks Job's Health

2 Again there was a day when the sons of God came to present themselves before the LORD, and Satan also came among them to present himself before the LORD. 2 And the LORD said to Satan, "From where have you come?" Satan answered the LORD and said, "From going to and fro on the earth, and from walking up and down on it." 3 And the LORD said to Satan, "Have you considered my servant Job, that there is none like him on the earth, a blameless and upright man, who fears God and turns away from evil? He still holds fast his integrity, although you incited me against him to destroy him without reason." 4 Then Satan answered the LORD and said, "Skin for skin! All that a man has he will give for his life. 5 But stretch out your hand and touch his bone and his flesh, and he will curse you to your face." 6 And the LORD said to Satan, "Behold, he is in your hand; only spare his life."

7 So Satan went out from the presence of the LORD and struck Job with loathsome sores from the sole of his foot to the crown of his head. 8 And he took a piece of broken pottery with which to scrape himself while he sat in the ashes.

9 Then his wife said to him, "Do you still hold fast your integrity? Curse God and die." 10 But he said to her, "You speak as one of the foolish women would speak. Shall we receive good from God, and shall we not receive evil?"[1] In all this Job did not sin with his lips.

Job's Three Friends

11 Now when Job's three friends heard of all this evil that had come upon him, they came each from his own place, Eliphaz the Temanite, Bildad the Shuhite, and Zophar the Naamathite. They made an appointment together to come to show him sympathy and comfort him. 12 And when they saw him from a distance, they did not recognize him. And they raised their voices and wept, and they tore their robes and sprinkled dust on their heads toward heaven. 13 And they sat with him on the ground seven days and seven nights, and no one spoke a word to him, for they saw that his suffering was very great.

Job Laments His Birth

3 After this Job opened his mouth and cursed the day of his birth. 2 And Job said:

3 "Let the day perish on which I was born,
and the night that said,
'A man is conceived.'
4 Let that day be darkness!
May God above not seek it,
nor light shine upon it.
5 Let gloom and deep darkness claim it.
Let clouds dwell upon it;
let the blackness of the day terrify it.
6 That night—let thick darkness seize it!
Let it not rejoice among the days of the year;
let it not come into the number of the
months.
7 Behold, let that night be barren;
let no joyful cry enter it.
8 Let those curse it who curse the day,
who are ready to rouse up Leviathan.
9 Let the stars of its dawn be dark;
let it hope for light, but have none,
nor see the eyelids of the morning,

[1] Or *disaster*; also verse 11

JOB 2:11–13

TRUSTING GOD THROUGH PAIN

Satan's malicious work brought about a perfect storm of calamity in Job's life. Gone were his children and his property, and his physical suffering had left him barely recognizable. In the void of God's silence concerning his situation, Job sought solace in the company of his companions. For a time, they sat in silence with him, sharing in his sufferings. But in subsequent chapters, Job only found more agony as his friends speculated aloud that all these terrible events were the fruit of Job's unfaithfulness and sin. Adversity often leaves people asking why. When answers do not come, believers should not necessarily assume God is ignoring or punishing them for wrongdoing. Scripture promises that God hears prayers (Pr 15:29) and actively works in the most desperate situations to bring about good (Ro 8:28).

The Gospels record the incredible torment Jesus endured as the supreme example of trusting God in the midst of suffering. Blinded by his pain but quoting Psalm 22, Jesus exclaimed, "My God, my God, why have you forsaken me?" (Mt 27:46). Though he could not sense his Father's presence through the unimaginable anguish, Jesus trusted enough to place his life into the Almighty's hands (Lk 23:46). His model graphically reminds believers that faith in God's unseen work is possible—and profitable—even when they do not feel anything but agony and sorrow.

JOB 4:7–9

SUFFERING AS PUNISHMENT?

Strength to endure affliction often comes through the company of supporting and encouraging companions (1Th 5:11). However, when Eliphaz spoke, his distorted beliefs only added to Job's suffering. His counsel echoed the persistent human conviction that God brings blessing to the righteous and only allows tragedy to fall on sinners, thus concluding that Job must have received just punishment for his sin. Jesus soundly refuted this kind of thinking in the New Testament. In one instance, citing two separate events that resulted in the deaths of a number of innocent citizens, Christ made it clear that unrighteousness does not always result in personal calamity. "Do you think that these Galileans were worse sinners than all the other Galileans, because they suffered in this way?" Jesus asked; then he quickly responded to his own question with an emphatic, "No, I tell you" (Lk 13:1–5; cf. Jn 9:1–3). His concluding remark—"unless you repent, you will all likewise perish"—warned that all people are sinful from birth, and in need of repentance and forgiveness (Lk 13:3,5; Ac 2:38; Ro 3:10,23). Such salvation—the kind that saves us from the wrath of God—comes only through a relationship *with Christ (Jn 3:36).*

10 because it did not shut the doors of my mother's womb,
nor hide trouble from my eyes.

11 "Why did I not die at birth,
come out from the womb and expire?
12 Why did the knees receive me?
Or why the breasts, that I should nurse?
13 For then I would have lain down and been quiet;
I would have slept; then I would have been at rest,
14 with kings and counselors of the earth
who rebuilt ruins for themselves,
15 or with princes who had gold,
who filled their houses with silver.
16 Or why was I not as a hidden stillborn child,
as infants who never see the light?
17 There the wicked cease from troubling,
and there the weary are at rest.
18 There the prisoners are at ease together;
they hear not the voice of the taskmaster.
19 The small and the great are there,
and the slave is free from his master.

20 "Why is light given to him who is in misery,
and life to the bitter in soul,
21 who long for death, but it comes not,
and dig for it more than for hidden treasures,
22 who rejoice exceedingly
and are glad when they find the grave?
23 Why is light given to a man whose way is hidden,
whom God has hedged in?
24 For my sighing comes instead of[1] my bread,
and my groanings are poured out like water.
25 For the thing that I fear comes upon me,
and what I dread befalls me.
26 I am not at ease, nor am I quiet;
I have no rest, but trouble comes."

Eliphaz Speaks: The Innocent Prosper

4 Then Eliphaz the Temanite answered and said:

2 "If one ventures a word with you, will you be impatient?
Yet who can keep from speaking?
3 Behold, you have instructed many,
and you have strengthened the weak hands.
4 Your words have upheld him who was stumbling,
and you have made firm the feeble knees.
5 But now it has come to you, and you are impatient;
it touches you, and you are dismayed.
6 Is not your fear of God[2] your confidence,
and the integrity of your ways your hope?

7 "Remember: who that was innocent ever perished?
Or where were the upright cut off?
8 As I have seen, those who plow iniquity
and sow trouble reap the same.

[1]Or *like*; Hebrew *before* [2]Hebrew lacks *of God*

9 By the breath of God they perish,
and by the blast of his anger they are consumed.
10 The roar of the lion, the voice of the fierce lion,
the teeth of the young lions are broken.
11 The strong lion perishes for lack of prey,
and the cubs of the lioness are scattered.

12 "Now a word was brought to me stealthily;
my ear received the whisper of it.
13 Amid thoughts from visions of the night,
when deep sleep falls on men,
14 dread came upon me, and trembling,
which made all my bones shake.
15 A spirit glided past my face;
the hair of my flesh stood up.
16 It stood still,
but I could not discern its appearance.
A form was before my eyes;
there was silence, then I heard a voice:
17 'Can mortal man be in the right before[1] God?
Can a man be pure before his Maker?
18 Even in his servants he puts no trust,
and his angels he charges with error;
19 how much more those who dwell in houses of clay,
whose foundation is in the dust,
who are crushed like[2] the moth.
20 Between morning and evening they are beaten to pieces;
they perish forever without anyone regarding it.
21 Is not their tent-cord plucked up within them,
do they not die, and that without wisdom?'

5 "Call now; is there anyone who will answer you?
To which of the holy ones will you turn?
2 Surely vexation kills the fool,
and jealousy slays the simple.
3 I have seen the fool taking root,
but suddenly I cursed his dwelling.
4 His children are far from safety;
they are crushed in the gate,
and there is no one to deliver them.
5 The hungry eat his harvest,
and he takes it even out of thorns,[3]
and the thirsty pant[4] after his[5] wealth.
6 For affliction does not come from the dust,
nor does trouble sprout from the ground,
7 but man is born to trouble
as the sparks fly upward.

8 "As for me, I would seek God,
and to God would I commit my cause,
9 who does great things and unsearchable,
marvelous things without number:
10 he gives rain on the earth
and sends waters on the fields;

[1]Or *more than*; twice in this verse [2]Or *before* [3]The meaning of the Hebrew is uncertain [4]Aquila, Symmachus, Syriac, Vulgate; Hebrew could be read as *and the snare pants* [5]Hebrew *their*

JOB 5:1–8

TO JUDGE OR NOT TO JUDGE

Eliphaz made broad and sweeping judgments about Job's character based chiefly on the intensity of his friend's suffering. He also insinuated that the demise of Job's children was due to Job's foolishness (vv. 2–4), questioned the depth of Job's faith (v. 8), and since "affliction does not come from the dust" (v. 6), implied that Job was essentially the cause of his own suffering. These flawed accusations were based solely in Eliphaz's own assumptions (vv. 3,8) and served only to intensify Job's anguish.

While Jesus warned against passing judgments like this (Mt 7:1), Scripture still charges believers to "test [or judge] the spirits" of those who claim to have a word from God (1Jn 4:1) and to make wise judgments about all things (1Co 2:15). The surface contradiction between these verses and the Matthew passage can be resolved by looking at the Greek terms. The words *dokimazô* (1Jn 4:1) and *anakrinô* (1Co 2:15) carry subtle differences in meaning from the word *krinô* (Mt 7:1), which Jesus used when he warned against judging other people. The first two words encourage believers to evaluate all things carefully and wisely and to exercise spiritual discernment. The word in Matthew 7:1, *krinô*, indicates a type of legal judgment that pronounces condemnation. Jesus went on to warn that "the measure you use" to judge others will be "measured to you" (Mt 7:2). This should stand as a powerful reminder to remain generous at all times, extending great grace, mercy, and forgiveness.

11 he sets on high those who are lowly,
and those who mourn are lifted to safety.
12 He frustrates the devices of the crafty,
so that their hands achieve no success.
13 He catches the wise in their own craftiness,
and the schemes of the wily are brought to a quick end.
14 They meet with darkness in the daytime
and grope at noonday as in the night.
15 But he saves the needy from the sword of their mouth
and from the hand of the mighty.
16 So the poor have hope,
and injustice shuts her mouth.

17 "Behold, blessed is the one whom God reproves;
therefore despise not the discipline of the Almighty.
18 For he wounds, but he binds up;
he shatters, but his hands heal.
19 He will deliver you from six troubles;
in seven no evil[1] shall touch you.
20 In famine he will redeem you from death,
and in war from the power of the sword.
21 You shall be hidden from the lash of the tongue,
and shall not fear destruction when it comes.
22 At destruction and famine you shall laugh,
and shall not fear the beasts of the earth.
23 For you shall be in league with the stones of the field,
and the beasts of the field shall be at peace with you.
24 You shall know that your tent is at peace,
and you shall inspect your fold and miss nothing.
25 You shall know also that your offspring shall be many,
and your descendants as the grass of the earth.
26 You shall come to your grave in ripe old age,
like a sheaf gathered up in its season.
27 Behold, this we have searched out; it is true.
Hear, and know it for your good."[2]

Job Replies: My Complaint Is Just

6 Then Job answered and said:

2 "Oh that my vexation were weighed,
and all my calamity laid in the balances!
3 For then it would be heavier than the sand of the sea;
therefore my words have been rash.
4 For the arrows of the Almighty are in me;
my spirit drinks their poison;
the terrors of God are arrayed against me.
5 Does the wild donkey bray when he has grass,
or the ox low over his fodder?
6 Can that which is tasteless be eaten without salt,
or is there any taste in the juice of the mallow?[3]
7 My appetite refuses to touch them;
they are as food that is loathsome to me.[4]

8 "Oh that I might have my request,
and that God would fulfill my hope,

[1]Or *disaster* [2]Hebrew *for yourself* [3]The meaning of the Hebrew word is uncertain [4]The meaning of the Hebrew is uncertain

9 that it would please God to crush me,
that he would let loose his hand and cut me off!
10 This would be my comfort;
I would even exult[1] in pain unsparing,
for I have not denied the words of the Holy One.
11 What is my strength, that I should wait?
And what is my end, that I should be patient?
12 Is my strength the strength of stones, or is my flesh bronze?
13 Have I any help in me,
when resource is driven from me?

14 "He who withholds[2] kindness from a friend
forsakes the fear of the Almighty.
15 My brothers are treacherous as a torrent-bed,
as torrential streams that pass away,
16 which are dark with ice,
and where the snow hides itself.
17 When they melt, they disappear;
when it is hot, they vanish from their place.
18 The caravans turn aside from their course;
they go up into the waste and perish.
19 The caravans of Tema look,
the travelers of Sheba hope.
20 They are ashamed because they were confident;
they come there and are disappointed.
21 For you have now become nothing;
you see my calamity and are afraid.
22 Have I said, 'Make me a gift'?
Or, 'From your wealth offer a bribe for me'?
23 Or, 'Deliver me from the adversary's hand'?
Or, 'Redeem me from the hand of the ruthless'?

24 "Teach me, and I will be silent;
make me understand how I have gone astray.
25 How forceful are upright words!
But what does reproof from you reprove?
26 Do you think that you can reprove words,
when the speech of a despairing man is wind?
27 You would even cast lots over the fatherless,
and bargain over your friend.

28 "But now, be pleased to look at me,
for I will not lie to your face.
29 Please turn; let no injustice be done.
Turn now; my vindication is at stake.
30 Is there any injustice on my tongue?
Cannot my palate discern the cause of calamity?

Job Continues: My Life Has No Hope

7 "Has not man a hard service on earth,
and are not his days like the days of a hired hand?
2 Like a slave who longs for the shadow,
and like a hired hand who looks for his wages,
3 so I am allotted months of emptiness,
and nights of misery are apportioned to me.

---

[1]The meaning of the Hebrew word is uncertain [2]Syriac, Vulgate (compare Targum); the meaning of the Hebrew word is uncertain

JOB 7:17–21

GOD, WHERE ARE YOU?

"God, where are you?" It would seem reasonable and normal for a person in Job's situation to ask that very common question. However, despite his intense level of suffering and lack of knowledge regarding the divine purpose for his adversity, Job never questioned God's presence or activity. Certain of God's involvement, he instead uttered a desperate plea for the Lord to simply leave him alone. But these sputtering statements from the lips of a man pressed by unrelenting despair remind readers that everything that touches their lives is ultimately under the watchful eye of God (Ps 33:18; 34:15; 139:7–12; Pr 15:3).

Centuries later, David's poetic writing gave new meaning to Job's anguished plea. Overwhelmed by the vastness and majesty of the heavens compared to humankind, David was humbled and awed by God's constant presence and care (Ps 8:3–4). Much of the glory and honor ascribed to humanity by the Lord at creation was lost when Adam chose to disobey (Ro 5:12–18), but what was obscured by sin has been restored through the power of the death and resurrection of Jesus (Ro 6:23). Christ was willing to be "made lower than the angels" in his incarnation (Heb 2:9), so that through faith, it became possible for believers to be once again "crowned ... with glory and honor" (Ps 8:5).

4 When I lie down I say, 'When shall I arise?'
But the night is long,
and I toss and turn till the dawn.
5 My flesh is clothed with worms and dirt;
my skin hardens, then breaks out afresh.
6 My days are swifter than a weaver's shuttle
and come to their end without hope.

7 "Remember that my life is a breath;
my eye will never again see good.
8 The eye of him who sees me will behold me no more;
while your eyes are on me, I shall be gone.
9 As the cloud fades and vanishes,
so he who goes down to Sheol does not come up;
10 he returns no more to his house,
nor does his place know him anymore.

11 "Therefore I will not restrain my mouth;
I will speak in the anguish of my spirit;
I will complain in the bitterness of my soul.
12 Am I the sea, or a sea monster,
that you set a guard over me?
13 When I say, 'My bed will comfort me,
my couch will ease my complaint,'
14 then you scare me with dreams
and terrify me with visions,
15 so that I would choose strangling
and death rather than my bones.
16 I loathe my life; I would not live forever.
Leave me alone, for my days are a breath.
17 What is man, that you make so much of him,
and that you set your heart on him,
18 visit him every morning
and test him every moment?
19 How long will you not look away from me,
nor leave me alone till I swallow my spit?
20 If I sin, what do I do to you, you watcher of mankind?
Why have you made me your mark?
Why have I become a burden to you?
21 Why do you not pardon my transgression
and take away my iniquity?
For now I shall lie in the earth;
you will seek me, but I shall not be."

Bildad Speaks: Job Should Repent

8 Then Bildad the Shuhite answered and said:

2 "How long will you say these things,
and the words of your mouth be a great wind?
3 Does God pervert justice?
Or does the Almighty pervert the right?
4 If your children have sinned against him,
he has delivered them into the hand of their transgression.
5 If you will seek God
and plead with the Almighty for mercy,
6 if you are pure and upright,
surely then he will rouse himself for you

and restore your rightful habitation.
7 And though your beginning was small,
your latter days will be very great.

8 "For inquire, please, of bygone ages,
and consider what the fathers have searched out.
9 For we are but of yesterday and know nothing,
for our days on earth are a shadow.
10 Will they not teach you and tell you
and utter words out of their understanding?

11 "Can papyrus grow where there is no marsh?
Can reeds flourish where there is no water?
12 While yet in flower and not cut down,
they wither before any other plant.
13 Such are the paths of all who forget God;
the hope of the godless shall perish.
14 His confidence is severed,
and his trust is a spider's web.[1]
15 He leans against his house, but it does not stand;
he lays hold of it, but it does not endure.
16 He is a lush plant before the sun,
and his shoots spread over his garden.
17 His roots entwine the stone heap;
he looks upon a house of stones.
18 If he is destroyed from his place,
then it will deny him, saying, 'I have never seen you.'
19 Behold, this is the joy of his way,
and out of the soil others will spring.

20 "Behold, God will not reject a blameless man,
nor take the hand of evildoers.
21 He will yet fill your mouth with laughter,
and your lips with shouting.
22 Those who hate you will be clothed with shame,
and the tent of the wicked will be no more."

Job Replies: There Is No Arbiter

9 Then Job answered and said:

2 "Truly I know that it is so:
But how can a man be in the right before God?
3 If one wished to contend with him,
one could not answer him once in a thousand times.
4 He is wise in heart and mighty in strength—
who has hardened himself against him, and succeeded?—
5 he who removes mountains, and they know it not,
when he overturns them in his anger,
6 who shakes the earth out of its place,
and its pillars tremble;
7 who commands the sun, and it does not rise;
who seals up the stars;
8 who alone stretched out the heavens
and trampled the waves of the sea;
9 who made the Bear and Orion,
the Pleiades and the chambers of the south;

[1] Hebrew *house*

10 who does great things beyond searching out,
and marvelous things beyond number.
11 Behold, he passes by me, and I see him not;
he moves on, but I do not perceive him.
12 Behold, he snatches away; who can turn him back?
Who will say to him, 'What are you doing?'

13 "God will not turn back his anger;
beneath him bowed the helpers of Rahab.
14 How then can I answer him,
choosing my words with him?
15 Though I am in the right, I cannot answer him;
I must appeal for mercy to my accuser.[1]
16 If I summoned him and he answered me,
I would not believe that he was listening to my voice.
17 For he crushes me with a tempest
and multiplies my wounds without cause;
18 he will not let me get my breath,
but fills me with bitterness.
19 If it is a contest of strength, behold, he is mighty!
If it is a matter of justice, who can summon him?[2]
20 Though I am in the right, my own mouth would condemn me;
though I am blameless, he would prove me perverse.
21 I am blameless; I regard not myself;
I loathe my life.
22 It is all one; therefore I say,
'He destroys both the blameless and the wicked.'
23 When disaster brings sudden death,
he mocks at the calamity[3] of the innocent.
24 The earth is given into the hand of the wicked;
he covers the faces of its judges—
if it is not he, who then is it?

25 "My days are swifter than a runner;
they flee away; they see no good.
26 They go by like skiffs of reed,
like an eagle swooping on the prey.
27 If I say, 'I will forget my complaint,
I will put off my sad face, and be of good cheer,'
28 I become afraid of all my suffering,
for I know you will not hold me innocent.
29 I shall be condemned;
why then do I labor in vain?
30 If I wash myself with snow
and cleanse my hands with lye,
31 yet you will plunge me into a pit,
and my own clothes will abhor me.
32 For he is not a man, as I am, that I might answer him,
that we should come to trial together.
33 There is no[4] arbiter between us,
who might lay his hand on us both.
34 Let him take his rod away from me,
and let not dread of him terrify me.
35 Then I would speak without fear of him,
for I am not so in myself.

[1]Or *to my judge* [2]Or *who can grant me a hearing?* [3]The meaning of the Hebrew word is uncertain
[4]Or *Would that there were an*

Job Continues: A Plea to God

10 "I loathe my life;
I will give free utterance to my complaint;
I will speak in the bitterness of my soul.
2 I will say to God, Do not condemn me;
let me know why you contend against me.
3 Does it seem good to you to oppress,
to despise the work of your hands
and favor the designs of the wicked?
4 Have you eyes of flesh?
Do you see as man sees?
5 Are your days as the days of man,
or your years as a man's years,
6 that you seek out my iniquity
and search for my sin,
7 although you know that I am not guilty,
and there is none to deliver out of your hand?
8 Your hands fashioned and made me,
and now you have destroyed me altogether.
9 Remember that you have made me like clay;
and will you return me to the dust?
10 Did you not pour me out like milk
and curdle me like cheese?
11 You clothed me with skin and flesh,
and knit me together with bones and sinews.
12 You have granted me life and steadfast love,
and your care has preserved my spirit.
13 Yet these things you hid in your heart;
I know that this was your purpose.
14 If I sin, you watch me
and do not acquit me of my iniquity.
15 If I am guilty, woe to me!
If I am in the right, I cannot lift up my head,
for I am filled with disgrace
and look on my affliction.
16 And were my head lifted up,[1] you would hunt me like
a lion
and again work wonders against me.
17 You renew your witnesses against me
and increase your vexation toward me;
you bring fresh troops against me.

18 "Why did you bring me out from the womb?
Would that I had died before any eye had seen me
19 and were as though I had not been,
carried from the womb to the grave.
20 Are not my days few?
Then cease, and leave me alone, that I may find a little
cheer
21 before I go—and I shall not return—
to the land of darkness and deep shadow,
22 the land of gloom like thick darkness,
like deep shadow without any order,
where light is as thick darkness."

[1]Hebrew lacks *my head*

JOB 11:1–11

BLIND ADVICE

People often make the mistake of giving simplistic answers to those who are in difficult situations. Such was the case with Job's friend Zophar. Regardless of Job's insistence that he was innocent of wrongdoing (6:24; 9:21; 10:2,7), this third companion began his analysis of Job's situation based on the flawed assumption that his friend's great torment was clear evidence of his hidden moral guilt. Citing God's infinite wisdom, he insinuated that not only was Job receiving his due penalty, but that if the full depth of Job's sin were revealed, it would be just for him to receive even greater punishment than he had thus far experienced (11:5–6). However, this insensitive friend evidently missed his own hypocrisy. Since no one can be judged faultless compared to the perfection of God, Zophar also merited the same penalty he thought Job deserved.

In the Sermon on the Mount, Jesus used an exaggerated contrast to warn his followers of well-intentioned but damaging double standards. "Why do you see the speck that is in your brother's eye, but do not notice the log that is in your own eye?... You hypocrite, first take the log out of your own eye, and then you will see clearly to take the speck out of your brother's eye" (Mt 7:3,5). Scripture encourages believers to help and guide others as they deal with wrongdoing (Gal 6:2; Col 3:13,16), but not before serious self-examination and dealing honestly with personal failures.

Zophar Speaks: You Deserve Worse

11 Then Zophar the Naamathite answered and said:

2 "Should a multitude of words go unanswered,
and a man full of talk be judged right?
3 Should your babble silence men,
and when you mock, shall no one shame you?
4 For you say, 'My doctrine is pure,
and I am clean in God's[1] eyes.'
5 But oh, that God would speak
and open his lips to you,
6 and that he would tell you the secrets of wisdom!
For he is manifold in understanding.[2]
Know then that God exacts of you less than your guilt
deserves.

7 "Can you find out the deep things of God?
Can you find out the limit of the Almighty?
8 It is higher than heaven[3]—what can you do?
Deeper than Sheol—what can you know?
9 Its measure is longer than the earth
and broader than the sea.
10 If he passes through and imprisons
and summons the court, who can turn him back?
11 For he knows worthless men;
when he sees iniquity, will he not consider it?
12 But a stupid man will get understanding
when a wild donkey's colt is born a man!

13 "If you prepare your heart,
you will stretch out your hands toward him.
14 If iniquity is in your hand, put it far away,
and let not injustice dwell in your tents.
15 Surely then you will lift up your face without blemish;
you will be secure and will not fear.
16 You will forget your misery;
you will remember it as waters that have passed away.
17 And your life will be brighter than the noonday;
its darkness will be like the morning.
18 And you will feel secure, because there is hope;
you will look around and take your rest in security.
19 You will lie down, and none will make you afraid;
many will court your favor.
20 But the eyes of the wicked will fail;
all way of escape will be lost to them,
and their hope is to breathe their last."

Job Replies: The LORD Has Done This

12 Then Job answered and said:

2 "No doubt you are the people,
and wisdom will die with you.
3 But I have understanding as well as you;
I am not inferior to you.
Who does not know such things as these?

[1]Hebrew *your* [2]The meaning of the Hebrew is uncertain [3]Hebrew *The heights of heaven*

4 I am a laughingstock to my friends;
I, who called to God and he answered me,
a just and blameless man, am a laughingstock.
5 In the thought of one who is at ease there is contempt for misfortune;
it is ready for those whose feet slip.
6 The tents of robbers are at peace,
and those who provoke God are secure,
who bring their god in their hand.[1]

7 "But ask the beasts, and they will teach you;
the birds of the heavens, and they will tell you;
8 or the bushes of the earth, and they will teach you;[2]
and the fish of the sea will declare to you.
9 Who among all these does not know
that the hand of the LORD has done this?
10 In his hand is the life of every living thing
and the breath of all mankind.
11 Does not the ear test words
as the palate tastes food?
12 Wisdom is with the aged,
and understanding in length of days.

13 "With God[3] are wisdom and might;
he has counsel and understanding.
14 If he tears down, none can rebuild;
if he shuts a man in, none can open.
15 If he withholds the waters, they dry up;
if he sends them out, they overwhelm the land.
16 With him are strength and sound wisdom;
the deceived and the deceiver are his.
17 He leads counselors away stripped,
and judges he makes fools.
18 He looses the bonds of kings
and binds a waistcloth on their hips.
19 He leads priests away stripped
and overthrows the mighty.
20 He deprives of speech those who are trusted
and takes away the discernment of the elders.
21 He pours contempt on princes
and loosens the belt of the strong.
22 He uncovers the deeps out of darkness
and brings deep darkness to light.
23 He makes nations great, and he destroys them;
he enlarges nations, and leads them away.
24 He takes away understanding from the chiefs of the people
of the earth
and makes them wander in a trackless waste.
25 They grope in the dark without light,
and he makes them stagger like a drunken man.

Job Continues: Still I Will Hope in God

13 "Behold, my eye has seen all this,
my ear has heard and understood it.
2 What you know, I also know;
I am not inferior to you.

[1]The meaning of the Hebrew is uncertain [2]Or *or speak to the earth, and it will teach you* [3]Hebrew *him*

JOB 12:7–10

OBVIOUSLY

In his longest response to the criticism of his friends, Job continued to reject allegations that his sin was to blame for his suffering. Instead, he reminded them that their self-righteous analysis failed to account for calamities that befall faithful followers of God (Job 12:4) as well as for the prosperity of those who purposefully carry out evil (v. 6). With biting sarcasm, Job challenged his tactless companions to consult the creatures of the earth who were obviously more aware than they are that the Lord ultimately rules over all that transpires on the earth (vv. 7–10; Ps 103:19).

In Romans, Paul agreed with Job's supposition about creation's ability to reveal God, reminding New Testament readers that the truth about God's "eternal power and divine nature" can be understood from nature (Ro 1:20). The complexity and arrangement of each component in the cosmos as well as the order and intricacy of the smallest atom attest to the controlling hand of a purposeful and loving Creator. So clear are his fingerprints that those who claim ignorance of God are "without excuse." With this knowledge also comes the certainty that no one can approach the Lord since humanity's flawed nature is starkly inferior to the one whose glory is declared by the heavens (Ps 19:1). While everyone can learn about God's characteristics from the natural world, the separation caused by sin necessitated the sacrifice of Christ to build the foundational bridge which makes knowing God possible at all (Jn 1:18; 3:16; 10:30; 14:6–10).

3 But I would speak to the Almighty,
and I desire to argue my case with God.
4 As for you, you whitewash with lies;
worthless physicians are you all.
5 Oh that you would keep silent,
and it would be your wisdom!
6 Hear now my argument
and listen to the pleadings of my lips.
7 Will you speak falsely for God
and speak deceitfully for him?
8 Will you show partiality toward him?
Will you plead the case for God?
9 Will it be well with you when he searches you out?
Or can you deceive him, as one deceives a man?
10 He will surely rebuke you
if in secret you show partiality.
11 Will not his majesty terrify you,
and the dread of him fall upon you?
12 Your maxims are proverbs of ashes;
your defenses are defenses of clay.

13 "Let me have silence, and I will speak,
and let come on me what may.
14 Why should I take my flesh in my teeth
and put my life in my hand?
15 Though he slay me, I will hope in him;[1]
yet I will argue my ways to his face.
16 This will be my salvation,
that the godless shall not come before him.
17 Keep listening to my words,
and let my declaration be in your ears.
18 Behold, I have prepared my case;
I know that I shall be in the right.
19 Who is there who will contend with me?
For then I would be silent and die.
20 Only grant me two things,
then I will not hide myself from your face:
21 withdraw your hand far from me,
and let not dread of you terrify me.
22 Then call, and I will answer;
or let me speak, and you reply to me.
23 How many are my iniquities and my sins?
Make me know my transgression and my sin.
24 Why do you hide your face
and count me as your enemy?
25 Will you frighten a driven leaf
and pursue dry chaff?
26 For you write bitter things against me
and make me inherit the iniquities of my
youth.
27 You put my feet in the stocks
and watch all my paths;
you set a limit for[2] the soles of my feet.
28 Man[3] wastes away like a rotten thing,
like a garment that is moth-eaten.

[1]Or *Behold, he will slay me; I have no hope* [2]Or *you marked* [3]Hebrew *He*

Job Continues: Death Comes Soon to All

14 "Man who is born of a woman
is few of days and full of trouble.
2 He comes out like a flower and withers;
he flees like a shadow and continues not.
3 And do you open your eyes on such a one
and bring me into judgment with you?
4 Who can bring a clean thing out of an unclean?
There is not one.
5 Since his days are determined,
and the number of his months is with you,
and you have appointed his limits that he cannot
pass,
6 look away from him and leave him alone,[1]
that he may enjoy, like a hired hand, his day.

7 "For there is hope for a tree,
if it be cut down, that it will sprout again,
and that its shoots will not cease.
8 Though its root grow old in the earth,
and its stump die in the soil,
9 yet at the scent of water it will bud
and put out branches like a young plant.
10 But a man dies and is laid low;
man breathes his last, and where is he?
11 As waters fail from a lake
and a river wastes away and dries up,
12 so a man lies down and rises not again;
till the heavens are no more he will not awake
or be roused out of his sleep.
13 Oh that you would hide me in Sheol,
that you would conceal me until your wrath be past,
that you would appoint me a set time, and
remember me!
14 If a man dies, shall he live again?
All the days of my service I would wait,
till my renewal[2] should come.
15 You would call, and I would answer you;
you would long for the work of your hands.
16 For then you would number my steps;
you would not keep watch over my sin;
17 my transgression would be sealed up in a bag,
and you would cover over my iniquity.

18 "But the mountain falls and crumbles away,
and the rock is removed from its place;
19 the waters wear away the stones;
the torrents wash away the soil of the earth;
so you destroy the hope of man.
20 You prevail forever against him, and he passes;
you change his countenance, and send him away.
21 His sons come to honor, and he does not know it;
they are brought low, and he perceives it not.
22 He feels only the pain of his own body,
and he mourns only for himself."

---

[1] Probable reading; Hebrew *look away from him, that he may cease* [2] Or *relief*

THE CONDITION OF HUMANITY

Job described life's misery and brevity through two vivid metaphors: a fading flower and a fleeing shadow. In the midst of suffering, the fragility and temporariness of life comes to the forefront. The sufferer's life sometimes feels like a cut flower whose petals are beginning to wilt, or like a shadow at sunset growing dimmer by the moment until it slips away.

If all anyone had was Job's sad assessment of reality, then life would be hopeless. But there is a perfect sufferer, who graciously entered into humanity's suffering! The Son of God, a heaven-dwelling member of the Trinity, chose to enter the lives and pain of people.

Suffering taught Job to understand the reality of this sin-marred world: it can be fleeting, painful, and brutal. Knowing this reality, it is incredible that Jesus humbled himself to enter into humankind's condition. Scripture says, "Have this mind among yourselves, which is yours in Christ Jesus, who, though he was in the form of God, did not count equality with God a thing to be grasped, but emptied himself, by taking the form of a servant, being born in the likeness of men" (Php 2:5–7).

Jesus knows what people face on a daily basis, and he entered into it—because of his great love. Jesus' life was not easy. He faced the same hardships and temptations that everyone faces. He endured this life with perfect humility and never once questioned the greatness and goodness of God. His commitment to live for God led him all the way to the cross: "And being found in human form, he humbled himself by becoming obedient to the point of death, even death on a cross" (Php 2:8).

In the midst of suffering, humans can lean on Jesus. Although lamenting and complaining when life is hard is natural for humans, Jesus provides an opportunity to rise above suffering and trust that his ways are perfect. Not only has Jesus joined humanity in their suffering, providing comfort through his presence, but he also brings hope of the final defeat of sin and suffering. Scripture shows that because of the life, death, and resurrection of Christ, the difficulties of life are temporary: "For while we are still in this tent, we groan, being burdened—not that we would be unclothed, but that we would be further clothed, so that what is mortal may be swallowed up by life" (2Co 5:4). In his return, Jesus will make a new creation where the flowers never fade and the shadows never grow dim.

Eliphaz Accuses: Job Does Not Fear God

15 Then Eliphaz the Temanite answered and said:
2 "Should a wise man answer with windy knowledge,
and fill his belly with the east wind?
3 Should he argue in unprofitable talk,
or in words with which he can do no good?
4 But you are doing away with the fear of God[1]
and hindering meditation before God.
5 For your iniquity teaches your mouth,
and you choose the tongue of the crafty.
6 Your own mouth condemns you, and not I;
your own lips testify against you.

7 "Are you the first man who was born?
Or were you brought forth before the hills?
8 Have you listened in the council of God?
And do you limit wisdom to yourself?
9 What do you know that we do not know?
What do you understand that is not clear to us?
10 Both the gray-haired and the aged are among us,
older than your father.
11 Are the comforts of God too small for you,
or the word that deals gently with you?
12 Why does your heart carry you away,
and why do your eyes flash,
13 that you turn your spirit against God
and bring such words out of your mouth?
14 What is man, that he can be pure?
Or he who is born of a woman, that he can be righteous?
15 Behold, God[2] puts no trust in his holy ones,
and the heavens are not pure in his sight;
16 how much less one who is abominable and corrupt,
a man who drinks injustice like water!

17 "I will show you; hear me,
and what I have seen I will declare
18 (what wise men have told,
without hiding it from their fathers,
19 to whom alone the land was given,
and no stranger passed among them).
20 The wicked man writhes in pain all his days,
through all the years that are laid up for the ruthless.
21 Dreadful sounds are in his ears;
in prosperity the destroyer will come upon him.
22 He does not believe that he will return out of darkness,
and he is marked for the sword.
23 He wanders abroad for bread, saying, 'Where is it?'
He knows that a day of darkness is ready at his hand;
24 distress and anguish terrify him;
they prevail against him, like a king ready for battle.
25 Because he has stretched out his hand against God
and defies the Almighty,
26 running stubbornly against him
with a thickly bossed shield;

[1]Hebrew lacks *of God* [2]Hebrew *he*

JOB 15:4–6

IN YOUR OWN WORDS

The second phase of the conversation between Job and his three friends opened with Eliphaz disputing Job's claim of innocence before God. Twisting Job's words, this companion rejected his desire for a rightful "day in court" by insisting that his own words testified against him (v. 6). While his conclusions seemed plausible from his own flawed point of view, Eliphaz lacked the proper spiritual vantage point to identify the true source of Job's suffering (1:6–12; 2:1–7).

The Jewish leaders expressed a similar lack of spiritual understanding when they attempted to use Jesus' own words to incriminate him. Searching for a credible reason to indict him of treason, they demanded Jesus publicly validate or deny his claim to be the Messiah (Lk 22:67). Refusing to be manipulated, Jesus instead laid claim to sovereignty over a more wide-ranging kingdom than they could comprehend (Mk 14:62). At this, the teachers of the Law believed they had sufficient grounds to condemn Jesus of blasphemy. However, being more concerned about advancing their own agenda than discovering the truth, the accusing leaders missed the crucial spiritual reality: Jesus truly is God.

While people may believe they are pursuing God, like Job's friends or the Jewish council, it is possible they are missing the most obvious truths. Though God loves everyone immensely, he often has priorities that are not easily understood. Sometimes the finite sufferings of God's people fall within a much larger divine plan.

27 because he has covered his face with his fat
and gathered fat upon his waist
28 and has lived in desolate cities,
in houses that none should inhabit,
which were ready to become heaps of ruins;
29 he will not be rich, and his wealth will not endure,
nor will his possessions spread over the earth;[1]
30 he will not depart from darkness;
the flame will dry up his shoots,
and by the breath of his mouth he will depart.
31 Let him not trust in emptiness, deceiving himself,
for emptiness will be his payment.
32 It will be paid in full before his time,
and his branch will not be green.
33 He will shake off his unripe grape like the vine,
and cast off his blossom like the olive tree.
34 For the company of the godless is barren,
and fire consumes the tents of bribery.
35 They conceive trouble and give birth to evil,
and their womb prepares deceit."

Job Replies: Miserable Comforters Are You

16 Then Job answered and said:

2 "I have heard many such things;
miserable comforters are you all.
3 Shall windy words have an end?
Or what provokes you that you answer?
4 I also could speak as you do,
if you were in my place;
I could join words together against you
and shake my head at you.
5 I could strengthen you with my mouth,
and the solace of my lips would assuage your pain.

6 "If I speak, my pain is not assuaged,
and if I forbear, how much of it leaves me?
7 Surely now God has worn me out;
he has[2] made desolate all my company.
8 And he has shriveled me up,
which is a witness against me,
and my leanness has risen up against me;
it testifies to my face.
9 He has torn me in his wrath and hated me;
he has gnashed his teeth at me;
my adversary sharpens his eyes against me.
10 Men have gaped at me with their mouth;
they have struck me insolently on the cheek;
they mass themselves together against me.
11 God gives me up to the ungodly
and casts me into the hands of the wicked.
12 I was at ease, and he broke me apart;
he seized me by the neck and dashed me to pieces;
he set me up as his target;
13 his archers surround me.

[1]Or *nor will his produce bend down to the earth* [2]Hebrew *you have*; also verse 8

JOB 16:6–14

ASSESSING GOD'S LOVE

When put into difficult situations, even committed believers understandably question God's actions. Job was no exception. Though he was certain he was guilty of no wrongdoing, he still wondered if God was angry at him or seeking some kind of vengeance. Often, as in the case of Job, external circumstances fail as reliable indicators of God's attitude toward us.

Romans 5:8 says, "God shows his love for us in that while we were still sinners, Christ died for us." This verse states plainly that Christ's death ultimately *proved* God's love. Believers do not have to depend on comfortable circumstances as a barometer indicating right standing with the Lord. All that was necessary to demonstrate God's unwavering love has already been done. While questions about the purpose for adversity and pain persist, the New Testament points to the crucifixion and resurrection of Jesus Christ as the ultimate, objective, steadfast, and concrete proof of the love of God.

He slashes open my kidneys and does not spare;
he pours out my gall on the ground.
14 He breaks me with breach upon breach;
he runs upon me like a warrior.
15 I have sewed sackcloth upon my skin
and have laid my strength in the dust.
16 My face is red with weeping,
and on my eyelids is deep darkness,
17 although there is no violence in my hands,
and my prayer is pure.

18 "O earth, cover not my blood,
and let my cry find no resting place.
19 Even now, behold, my witness is in heaven,
and he who testifies for me is on high.
20 My friends scorn me;
my eye pours out tears to God,
21 that he would argue the case of a man with God,
as[1] a son of man does with his neighbor.
22 For when a few years have come
I shall go the way from which I shall not return.

Job Continues: Where Then Is My Hope?

17 "My spirit is broken; my days are extinct;
the graveyard is ready for me.
2 Surely there are mockers about me,
and my eye dwells on their provocation.

3 "Lay down a pledge for me with you;
who is there who will put up security for me?
4 Since you have closed their hearts to understanding,
therefore you will not let them triumph.
5 He who informs against his friends to get a share of their property—
the eyes of his children will fail.

6 "He has made me a byword of the peoples,
and I am one before whom men spit.
7 My eye has grown dim from vexation,
and all my members are like a shadow.
8 The upright are appalled at this,
and the innocent stirs himself up against the godless.
9 Yet the righteous holds to his way,
and he who has clean hands grows stronger and stronger.
10 But you, come on again, all of you,
and I shall not find a wise man among you.
11 My days are past; my plans are broken off,
the desires of my heart.
12 They make night into day:
'The light,' they say, 'is near to the darkness.'[2]
13 If I hope for Sheol as my house,
if I make my bed in darkness,
14 if I say to the pit, 'You are my father,'
and to the worm, 'My mother,' or 'My sister,'
15 where then is my hope?
Who will see my hope?

---

[1]Hebrew *and* [2]The meaning of the Hebrew is uncertain

16 Will it go down to the bars of Sheol?
Shall we descend together into the dust?"[1]

Bildad Speaks: God Punishes the Wicked

18 Then Bildad the Shuhite answered and said:

2 "How long will you hunt for words?
Consider, and then we will speak.
3 Why are we counted as cattle?
Why are we stupid in your sight?
4 You who tear yourself in your anger,
shall the earth be forsaken for you,
or the rock be removed out of its place?

5 "Indeed, the light of the wicked is put out,
and the flame of his fire does not shine.
6 The light is dark in his tent,
and his lamp above him is put out.
7 His strong steps are shortened,
and his own schemes throw him down.
8 For he is cast into a net by his own feet,
and he walks on its mesh.
9 A trap seizes him by the heel;
a snare lays hold of him.
10 A rope is hidden for him in the ground,
a trap for him in the path.
11 Terrors frighten him on every side,
and chase him at his heels.
12 His strength is famished,
and calamity is ready for his stumbling.
13 It consumes the parts of his skin;
the firstborn of death consumes his limbs.
14 He is torn from the tent in which he trusted
and is brought to the king of terrors.
15 In his tent dwells that which is none of his;
sulfur is scattered over his habitation.
16 His roots dry up beneath,
and his branches wither above.
17 His memory perishes from the earth,
and he has no name in the street.
18 He is thrust from light into darkness,
and driven out of the world.
19 He has no posterity or progeny among his people,
and no survivor where he used to live.
20 They of the west are appalled at his day,
and horror seizes them of the east.
21 Surely such are the dwellings of the unrighteous,
such is the place of him who knows not God."

Job Replies: My Redeemer Lives

19 Then Job answered and said:

2 "How long will you torment me
and break me in pieces with words?
3 These ten times you have cast reproach upon me;
are you not ashamed to wrong me?

[1] Or *Will they go down to the bars of Sheol? Is rest to be found together in the dust?*

THE MYSTERY OF HUMAN SUFFERING

Job's friends were harsh toward Job. Bildad's speech can be summed up in five searing words: "You got what you deserved." Bildad, along with Job's other two friends, concluded that Job's suffering was evidence of sin in his life (Job 4:7 – 9; 8:1 – 19).

Job's friends' theology was not entirely incorrect, but their perspective was limited. They were right to think that Scripture, especially parts like Deuteronomy 27 and 28, teaches that the righteous person can expect God's blessing and the wicked can expect God's curse. Both Eliphaz (Job 15:27 – 35) and Zophar (Job 20:4 – 29) mentioned that sometimes the wicked will enjoy temporary prosperity as Job had. They believed that the wicked would be punished eventually, as the book of Proverbs teaches (Pr 1:17 – 19; 6:12 – 15). Their theology was an oversimplified combination of multiple truths: bad things are going to happen to bad people, good things are going to happen to good people, and everyone will get what they deserve in the end.

The problem with their theology was that it was too narrow in its scope — and therefore it was not flexible enough to accommodate real life experiences. The three friends made a mistake in how they applied abstract truths to real life experiences. They were right to believe that in the end God rewards the righteous and punishes the wicked. But Job's friends did not have God's perspective on the situation.

Good theology accounts for the complexities of Scripture and the huge range of life experiences. The truth is this: human suffering or happiness in this life is not proportional to people's sins or good works. Sometimes the wicked seem to get away with wrongs; sometimes the righteous experience terrible things that they do not deserve.

The author of Hebrews offered a reminder that God does good things in unexpected ways: "For it was fitting that he, for whom and by whom all things exist, in bringing many sons to glory, should make the founder of their salvation perfect through suffering" (Heb 2:10). God used Jesus' sufferings to bring about the ultimate blessing. He is always at work in the suffering of his people. The exact manner in which God is working may remain a mystery for now. Yet, eternity will show that he was always good, he was always in control, and he was always working to show his glory.

4 And even if it be true that I have erred,
my error remains with myself.
5 If indeed you magnify yourselves against me
and make my disgrace an argument against me,
6 know then that God has put me in the wrong
and closed his net about me.
7 Behold, I cry out, 'Violence!' but I am not answered;
I call for help, but there is no justice.
8 He has walled up my way, so that I cannot pass,
and he has set darkness upon my paths.
9 He has stripped from me my glory
and taken the crown from my head.
10 He breaks me down on every side, and I am gone,
and my hope has he pulled up like a tree.
11 He has kindled his wrath against me
and counts me as his adversary.
12 His troops come on together;
they have cast up their siege ramp[1] against me
and encamp around my tent.

13 "He has put my brothers far from me,
and those who knew me are wholly estranged from me.
14 My relatives have failed me,
my close friends have forgotten me.
15 The guests in my house and my maidservants count me as
a stranger;
I have become a foreigner in their eyes.
16 I call to my servant, but he gives me no answer;
I must plead with him with my mouth for mercy.
17 My breath is strange to my wife,
and I am a stench to the children of my own mother.
18 Even young children despise me;
when I rise they talk against me.
19 All my intimate friends abhor me,
and those whom I loved have turned against me.
20 My bones stick to my skin and to my flesh,
and I have escaped by the skin of my teeth.
21 Have mercy on me, have mercy on me, O you my friends,
for the hand of God has touched me!
22 Why do you, like God, pursue me?
Why are you not satisfied with my flesh?

23 "Oh that my words were written!
Oh that they were inscribed in a book!
24 Oh that with an iron pen and lead
they were engraved in the rock forever!
25 For I know that my Redeemer lives,
and at the last he will stand upon the earth.[2]
26 And after my skin has been thus destroyed,
yet in[3] my flesh I shall see God,
27 whom I shall see for myself,
and my eyes shall behold, and not another.
My heart faints within me!
28 If you say, 'How we will pursue him!'
and, 'The root of the matter is found in him,'[4]

[1]Hebrew *their way* [2]Hebrew *dust* [3]Or *without* [4]Many Hebrew manuscripts *in me*

MY REDEEMER LIVES

Job's belief in God is amazing. Even more striking is how God allowed Job to get to the place where he could trust in God, even though his circumstances looked hopeless. God delivered Job not *from* his sufferings, but *through* his sufferings. In the midst of battling his ignorant friends, something clicked. Through his resistance against bad advice from friends and through his persistent battle for belief, a new insight emerged. Job was able to confess and believe that God was with him.

When faced with intense pain, God's people may not learn "why" as much as they come to know "Who." Job never received answers to all of his questions. What he really needed to learn was that God is the "Who" he could depend on. In life there is so much that happens that cannot be explained. In the midst of life's uncertainties, God knows what people need (La 3:55–57). Jesus is holding on to his people, and this relationship allows them to endure to the end (Jn 10:28).

God was not risking Job's faith; God was refining his faith. Only when everything is stripped away can a person evaluate what truly matters. After suffering unimaginable loss, Job was able to confess, "After my skin has been thus destroyed, yet in my flesh I shall see God, whom I shall see for myself, and my eyes shall behold, and not another. My heart faints within me!" (Job 19:26–27). Oftentimes God's people do not learn that God is all they need until God is all they have.

Without God, this life and the eternity that follows will be full of pain. But when someone trusts in Jesus Christ, God promises that all the sad things will one day be healed and redeemed: "We know that for those who love God all things work together for good, for those who are called according to his purpose" (Ro 8:28).

Job's faith in the midst of the fight is a model for life. "Without faith it is impossible to please him, for whoever would draw near to God must believe that he exists and that he rewards those who seek him" (Heb 11:6). When people put their faith in Jesus, they can have hope that the way things are in the world is not the way they will always be. Suffering and pain can be seen as temporary in light of eternity with Jesus!

29 be afraid of the sword,
for wrath brings the punishment of the sword,
that you may know there is a judgment."

Zophar Speaks: The Wicked Will Suffer

20 Then Zophar the Naamathite answered and said:

2 "Therefore my thoughts answer me,
because of my haste within me.
3 I hear censure that insults me,
and out of my understanding a spirit answers me.
4 Do you not know this from of old,
since man was placed on earth,
5 that the exulting of the wicked is short,
and the joy of the godless but for a moment?
6 Though his height mount up to the heavens,
and his head reach to the clouds,
7 he will perish forever like his own dung;
those who have seen him will say, 'Where is he?'
8 He will fly away like a dream and not be found;
he will be chased away like a vision of the night.
9 The eye that saw him will see him no more,
nor will his place any more behold him.
10 His children will seek the favor of the poor,
and his hands will give back his wealth.
11 His bones are full of his youthful vigor,
but it will lie down with him in the dust.

12 "Though evil is sweet in his mouth,
though he hides it under his tongue,
13 though he is loath to let it go
and holds it in his mouth,
14 yet his food is turned in his stomach;
it is the venom of cobras within him.
15 He swallows down riches and vomits them up again;
God casts them out of his belly.
16 He will suck the poison of cobras;
the tongue of a viper will kill him.
17 He will not look upon the rivers,
the streams flowing with honey and curds.
18 He will give back the fruit of his toil
and will not swallow it down;
from the profit of his trading
he will get no enjoyment.
19 For he has crushed and abandoned the poor;
he has seized a house that he did not build.

20 "Because he knew no contentment in his belly,
he will not let anything in which he delights escape him.
21 There was nothing left after he had eaten;
therefore his prosperity will not endure.
22 In the fullness of his sufficiency he will be in distress;
the hand of everyone in misery will come against him.
23 To fill his belly to the full,
God[1] will send his burning anger against him
and rain it upon him into his body.

[1]Hebrew *he*

JOB 20:3–9

WHEN THE WICKED THRIVE

Zophar attempted to sidestep Job's rebuke with a caustic reminder that evil people only thrive and succeed for a little while. His skewed perspective led him to the conclusion that Job's suffering was the natural consequence of a wicked life exposed at last. Jesus presented a contrasting view that reminds believers to keep an eternal perspective on reward and judgment (Mt 13:24–30). While Scripture assures that the wicked will receive a just punishment for their defiance and rejection of the Lord (Ps 145:20; Jn 3:36; Gal 6:7–8), often that verdict does not come until the end of this earthly life. God's judgment is not hasty, but he promises an eventual day when he will separate good from evil (Mt 25:31–46). While waiting for justice to be served, it is tempting to suppose that the abundance of the unrighteous person is a sign of God's lack of justice. In reality, the delay in judgment is an expression of God's abundant patience and grace, granting unbelievers more time to respond to the mercy and forgiveness extended to them through Jesus Christ (2Pe 3:9).

24 He will flee from an iron weapon;
a bronze arrow will strike him through.
25 It is drawn forth and comes out of his body;
the glittering point comes out of his gallbladder;
terrors come upon him.
26 Utter darkness is laid up for his treasures;
a fire not fanned will devour him;
what is left in his tent will be consumed.
27 The heavens will reveal his iniquity,
and the earth will rise up against him.
28 The possessions of his house will be carried away,
dragged off in the day of God's[1] wrath.
29 This is the wicked man's portion from God,
the heritage decreed for him by God."

Job Replies: The Wicked Do Prosper

21 Then Job answered and said:

2 "Keep listening to my words,
and let this be your comfort.
3 Bear with me, and I will speak,
and after I have spoken, mock on.
4 As for me, is my complaint against man?
Why should I not be impatient?
5 Look at me and be appalled,
and lay your hand over your mouth.
6 When I remember, I am dismayed,
and shuddering seizes my flesh.
7 Why do the wicked live,
reach old age, and grow mighty in power?
8 Their offspring are established in their presence,
and their descendants before their eyes.
9 Their houses are safe from fear,
and no rod of God is upon them.
10 Their bull breeds without fail;
their cow calves and does not miscarry.
11 They send out their little boys like a flock,
and their children dance.
12 They sing to the tambourine and the lyre
and rejoice to the sound of the pipe.
13 They spend their days in prosperity,
and in peace they go down to Sheol.
14 They say to God, 'Depart from us!
We do not desire the knowledge of your ways.
15 What is the Almighty, that we should serve him?
And what profit do we get if we pray to him?'
16 Behold, is not their prosperity in their hand?
The counsel of the wicked is far from me.

17 "How often is it that the lamp of the wicked is put out?
That their calamity comes upon them?
That God[2] distributes pains in his anger?
18 That they are like straw before the wind,
and like chaff that the storm carries away?

[1]Hebrew *his* [2]Hebrew *he*

19 You say, 'God stores up their iniquity for their children.'
Let him pay it out to them, that they may know it.
20 Let their own eyes see their destruction,
and let them drink of the wrath of the Almighty.
21 For what do they care for their houses after them,
when the number of their months is cut off?
22 Will any teach God knowledge,
seeing that he judges those who are on high?
23 One dies in his full vigor,
being wholly at ease and secure,
24 his pails[1] full of milk
and the marrow of his bones moist.
25 Another dies in bitterness of soul,
never having tasted of prosperity.
26 They lie down alike in the dust,
and the worms cover them.

27 "Behold, I know your thoughts
and your schemes to wrong me.
28 For you say, 'Where is the house of the prince?
Where is the tent in which the wicked lived?'
29 Have you not asked those who travel the roads,
and do you not accept their testimony
30 that the evil man is spared in the day of calamity,
that he is rescued in the day of wrath?
31 Who declares his way to his face,
and who repays him for what he has done?
32 When he is carried to the grave,
watch is kept over his tomb.
33 The clods of the valley are sweet to him;
all mankind follows after him,
and those who go before him are innumerable.
34 How then will you comfort me with empty nothings?
There is nothing left of your answers but falsehood."

Eliphaz Speaks: Job's Wickedness Is Great

22 Then Eliphaz the Temanite answered and said:
2 "Can a man be profitable to God?
Surely he who is wise is profitable to himself.
3 Is it any pleasure to the Almighty if you are in the right,
or is it gain to him if you make your ways blameless?
4 Is it for your fear of him that he reproves you
and enters into judgment with you?
5 Is not your evil abundant?
There is no end to your iniquities.
6 For you have exacted pledges of your brothers for
nothing
and stripped the naked of their clothing.
7 You have given no water to the weary to drink,
and you have withheld bread from the hungry.
8 The man with power possessed the land,
and the favored man lived in it.
9 You have sent widows away empty,
and the arms of the fatherless were crushed.

[1]The meaning of the Hebrew word is uncertain

JOB 22:6–11

JUDGED FALSELY BY OTHERS

It is impossible to know everything. But that does not stop many people from entering into conversations or casting accusations as if they do. That is exactly what Eliphaz did to Job. Eliphaz assumed that Job was suffering because Job was wicked—even though Job was suffering because God was in a contest with Satan. The Bible teaches as a general principle that the righteous will always experience God's blessing and the wicked will always experience God's judgment—the life of Job proves that this principle does not always hold true within the limited context of earthly life. Eliphaz accused Job of acquiring his wealth through greed and exploitation of the poor. Yet God's own witness to Satan reveals to the reader that these charges were false (Job 1:8; 2:3). Eliphaz's accusations were baseless; his only proof for Job's alleged wickedness was Job's suffering (22:10–11).

All of this is a great reminder that people should hesitate to cast accusations—they may not have all the pertinent facts. Eliphaz's approach to Job's innocent sufferings foreshadows the manner in which the Pharisees would look at Jesus' actions, even his miracles, and attribute them to Satan (Mt 12:22–28). On the surface, it looked like Eliphaz and the religious leaders could be right—but they did not know all the *information. They judged*, and they judged falsely. Jesus gave a warning that remains relevant today: "Judge not, that you be not judged" (Mt 7:1).

THE NARROW PATH

Job's response to his friends' foolish words and accusations was simple: the facts did not support their theology. The facts showed that many wicked people live a life that looks fairly comfortable. They seem not to suffer. They seem free from struggles. They actually seem to enjoy themselves. At the same time, many righteous people struggle in this world. They try to live for God, but life remains difficult. They give generously but experience seasons when they do not have as much as they need.

The theology of Job's friends broke under the weight of reality. The facts did not add up to their simplistic theological outlook. Many wicked people are not punished in this life, while many righteous people suffer from the cradle to the grave. It did not make sense to accuse Job of secret sin while so many other people who were clearly more wicked than Job did not suffer for their sins.

The world is unfair. Often, the righteous suffer and the wicked prosper. When people fail to realize this reality, they become rigid and uptight in every way. Their counsel sounds much like the words of "comfort" that Job received. They fail to grasp the harsh reality of life in a fallen world, accusing innocent people of harboring hidden sin.

Jesus' life and ministry revealed how mixed up the world is. Contrary to the way of the world, Jesus demonstrated that the heights of true glory can be found only in the depths of humility (Php 2:5 – 11). He taught that the way to attain a full and meaningful life is to give one's life over entirely to Christ and the gospel (Mk 8:34 – 38).

Many people reject the way of Jesus. Jesus contrasted the two ways people look at life by talking about a broad and a narrow path: "Enter by the narrow gate. For the gate is wide and the way is easy that leads to destruction, and those who enter by it are many. For the gate is narrow and the way is hard that leads to life, and those who find it are few" (Mt 7:13 – 14). Many people think that the meaning of life is found here and now. They desperately avoid all difficulties and focus entirely on getting as much pleasure or happiness as possible before they die. But there is another way — the way of Jesus. This world is not all there is. This life is only the prelude to a glorious, divine reality that will be fully revealed in eternity.

10 Therefore snares are all around you,
and sudden terror overwhelms you,
11 or darkness, so that you cannot see,
and a flood of water covers you.

12 "Is not God high in the heavens?
See the highest stars, how lofty they are!
13 But you say, 'What does God know?
Can he judge through the deep darkness?
14 Thick clouds veil him, so that he does not see,
and he walks on the vault of heaven.'
15 Will you keep to the old way
that wicked men have trod?
16 They were snatched away before their time;
their foundation was washed away.[1]
17 They said to God, 'Depart from us,'
and 'What can the Almighty do to us?'[2]
18 Yet he filled their houses with good things—
but the counsel of the wicked is far from me.
19 The righteous see it and are glad;
the innocent one mocks at them,
20 saying, 'Surely our adversaries are cut off,
and what they left the fire has consumed.'

21 "Agree with God, and be at peace;
thereby good will come to you.
22 Receive instruction from his mouth,
and lay up his words in your heart.
23 If you return to the Almighty you will be built up;
if you remove injustice far from your tents,
24 if you lay gold in the dust,
and gold of Ophir among the stones of the torrent-bed,
25 then the Almighty will be your gold
and your precious silver.
26 For then you will delight yourself in the Almighty
and lift up your face to God.
27 You will make your prayer to him, and he will hear you,
and you will pay your vows.
28 You will decide on a matter, and it will be established for you,
and light will shine on your ways.
29 For when they are humbled you say, 'It is because of pride';[3]
but he saves the lowly.
30 He delivers even the one who is not innocent,
who will be delivered through the cleanness of your hands."

JOB 23:1–12

THE DEPTHS OF DESPAIR

Job was honest about his pain and frustration. He cried out to God from the depths of his heart. He felt abandoned, he felt like he did not have the answers to his questions, but he kept holding on to God. Even though God did not seem to be near to Job at all, Job still expressed an unshaken confidence in God. Job knew that God was refining him through this process. Gold must be heated to 1,063 degrees Celsius in order to melt. The impurities in the gold only come out when the gold melts down. Job trusted God when life was hard. He trusted that God was purifying him (v. 10).

Job's sufferings foreshadow the experience of Jesus on the cross as he cried out, "My God, my God, why have you forsaken me?" (Mt 27:46). Job's sufferings were terrible, but they do not compare to the depth of agony that Jesus experienced on the cross as he died for us. God's best for the world is not going around pain and suffering, but through it. Job went through these unthinkable circumstances in order to be refined. Jesus went through the ordeal of the cross in order to create the only way to God.

Job Replies: Where Is God?

23 Then Job answered and said:

2 "Today also my complaint is bitter;[4]
my hand is heavy on account of my groaning.
3 Oh, that I knew where I might find him,
that I might come even to his seat!
4 I would lay my case before him
and fill my mouth with arguments.

[1]Or *their foundation was poured out as a stream* (or *river*) [2]Hebrew *them* [3]Or *you say, 'It is exaltation'*
[4]Or *defiant*

5 I would know what he would answer me
and understand what he would say to me.
6 Would he contend with me in the greatness of his power?
No; he would pay attention to me.
7 There an upright man could argue with him,
and I would be acquitted forever by my judge.

8 "Behold, I go forward, but he is not there,
and backward, but I do not perceive him;
9 on the left hand when he is working, I do not behold him;
he turns to the right hand, but I do not see him.
10 But he knows the way that I take;
when he has tried me, I shall come out as gold.
11 My foot has held fast to his steps;
I have kept his way and have not turned aside.
12 I have not departed from the commandment of his lips;
I have treasured the words of his mouth more than my portion
of food.
13 But he is unchangeable,[1] and who can turn him back?
What he desires, that he does.
14 For he will complete what he appoints for me,
and many such things are in his mind.
15 Therefore I am terrified at his presence;
when I consider, I am in dread of him.
16 God has made my heart faint;
the Almighty has terrified me;
17 yet I am not silenced because of the darkness,
nor because thick darkness covers my face.

24 "Why are not times of judgment kept by the Almighty,
and why do those who know him never see his days?
2 Some move landmarks;
they seize flocks and pasture them.
3 They drive away the donkey of the fatherless;
they take the widow's ox for a pledge.
4 They thrust the poor off the road;
the poor of the earth all hide themselves.
5 Behold, like wild donkeys in the desert
the poor[2] go out to their toil, seeking game;
the wasteland yields food for their children.
6 They gather their[3] fodder in the field,
and they glean the vineyard of the wicked man.
7 They lie all night naked, without clothing,
and have no covering in the cold.
8 They are wet with the rain of the mountains
and cling to the rock for lack of shelter.
9 (There are those who snatch the fatherless child from the breast,
and they take a pledge against the poor.)
10 They go about naked, without clothing;
hungry, they carry the sheaves;
11 among the olive rows of the wicked[4] they make oil;
they tread the winepresses, but suffer thirst.
12 From out of the city the dying[5] groan,
and the soul of the wounded cries for help;
yet God charges no one with wrong.

[1]Or *one* [2]Hebrew *they* [3]Hebrew *his* [4]Hebrew *their olive rows* [5]Or *the men*

JOB 24:1

WHEN GOD IS SILENT

Sometimes God's people feel he is nowhere to be found in their moments of greatest need. Jesus' own disciples felt this way while they were with him. In the midst of a terrible storm, they woke Jesus with the complaint, "Teacher, do you not care that we are perishing?" (Mk 4:38). Job felt this way, too. In the darkest times, no amount of human companionship is sufficient. The soul was made for God, and humans need divine revelation more than philosophical arguments when facing suffering. God has a plan for the good of his people, even though they cannot always see or understand how it is all coming together.

At the heart of God's plan is Jesus — Jesus is how people come to know God and how everything can be made right. Jesus took the worst of humanity's sufferings upon himself. Job wished that someone would step in to mediate between him and God (Job 9:33). Praise God that he has provided the best mediator for us: "For there is one God, and there is one mediator between God and men, the man Christ Jesus, who gave himself as a ransom for all, which is the testimony given at the proper time" (1Ti 2:5 – 6). God sent Jesus at the proper time to defeat sin and make humans right with God; God's people can trust his timing and his provision.

13 "There are those who rebel against the light,
who are not acquainted with its ways,
and do not stay in its paths.
14 The murderer rises before it is light,
that he may kill the poor and needy,
and in the night he is like a thief.
15 The eye of the adulterer also waits for the twilight,
saying, 'No eye will see me';
and he veils his face.
16 In the dark they dig through houses;
by day they shut themselves up;
they do not know the light.
17 For deep darkness is morning to all of them;
for they are friends with the terrors of deep darkness.

18 "You say, 'Swift are they on the face of the waters;
their portion is cursed in the land;
no treader turns toward their vineyards.
19 Drought and heat snatch away the snow waters;
so does Sheol those who have sinned.
20 The womb forgets them;
the worm finds them sweet;
they are no longer remembered,
so wickedness is broken like a tree.'

21 "They wrong the barren, childless woman,
and do no good to the widow.
22 Yet God[1] prolongs the life of the mighty by his power;
they rise up when they despair of life.
23 He gives them security, and they are supported,
and his eyes are upon their ways.
24 They are exalted a little while, and then are gone;
they are brought low and gathered up like all others;
they are cut off like the heads of grain.
25 If it is not so, who will prove me a liar
and show that there is nothing in what I say?"

Bildad Speaks: Man Cannot Be Righteous

25 Then Bildad the Shuhite answered and said:

2 "Dominion and fear are with God;[2]
he makes peace in his high heaven.
3 Is there any number to his armies?
Upon whom does his light not arise?
4 How then can man be in the right before God?
How can he who is born of woman be pure?
5 Behold, even the moon is not bright,
and the stars are not pure in his eyes;
6 how much less man, who is a maggot,
and the son of man, who is a worm!"

Job Replies: God's Majesty Is Unsearchable

26 Then Job answered and said:

2 "How you have helped him who has no power!
How you have saved the arm that has no strength!

[1]Hebrew *he* [2]Hebrew *him*

14 If his children are multiplied, it is for the sword,
and his descendants have not enough bread.
15 Those who survive him the pestilence buries,
and his widows do not weep.
16 Though he heap up silver like dust,
and pile up clothing like clay,
17 he may pile it up, but the righteous will wear it,
and the innocent will divide the silver.
18 He builds his house like a moth's,
like a booth that a watchman makes.
19 He goes to bed rich, but will do so no more;
he opens his eyes, and his wealth is gone.
20 Terrors overtake him like a flood;
in the night a whirlwind carries him off.
21 The east wind lifts him up and he is gone;
it sweeps him out of his place.
22 It[1] hurls at him without pity;
he flees from its[2] power in headlong flight.
23 It claps its hands at him
and hisses at him from its place.

Job Continues: Where Is Wisdom?

28 "Surely there is a mine for silver,
and a place for gold that they refine.
2 Iron is taken out of the earth,
and copper is smelted from the ore.
3 Man puts an end to darkness
and searches out to the farthest limit
the ore in gloom and deep darkness.
4 He opens shafts in a valley away from where anyone lives;
they are forgotten by travelers;
they hang in the air, far away from mankind; they swing
to and fro.
5 As for the earth, out of it comes bread,
but underneath it is turned up as by fire.
6 Its stones are the place of sapphires,[3]
and it has dust of gold.

7 "That path no bird of prey knows,
and the falcon's eye has not seen it.
8 The proud beasts have not trodden it;
the lion has not passed over it.

9 "Man puts his hand to the flinty rock
and overturns mountains by the roots.
10 He cuts out channels in the rocks,
and his eye sees every precious thing.
11 He dams up the streams so that they do not trickle,
and the thing that is hidden he brings out to light.

12 "But where shall wisdom be found?
And where is the place of understanding?
13 Man does not know its worth,
and it is not found in the land of the living.
14 The deep says, 'It is not in me,'
and the sea says, 'It is not with me.'

[1]Or *He* (that is, God); also verse 23 [2]Or *his*; also verse 23 [3]Or *lapis lazuli*; also verse 16

(Righteousness, continued)

displaying his glory to Satan and the entire world by sustaining Job's faith in the midst of suffering. Yet, through the process of enduring suffering, Job was tempted to sin; he was tempted to justify himself (Job 32:2). It seems that Job revealed some pride and self-righteousness. Righteousness means being right with God. Righteousness is not something people can earn or claim for themselves; it is a title and name that God grants through his grace. Deep down inside, Job knew that his trial was not the result of some specific sin he committed. But he could easily drift into the thinking that he had no sin at all — and that would be a terrible mistake.

The Bible is clear that Jesus is the only person who ever lived who can claim a perfect life (Heb 4:15). Jesus is the standard, and from God's perspective, everyone has fallen short of the standard (Ro 3:9 – 18). Becoming right with God is never based on what people do, or how good or kind they are, or how they compare with others. Becoming righteous begins by agreeing with God in his assessment of humanity's sinful nature and looking to the only perfect person, Jesus Christ, to be the perfect One on behalf of sinful humanity. Jesus' righteousness is credited to his people when they call upon him in faith (1Co 1:30).

JOB 28:1 – 28

TRUE WISDOM

The search for wisdom is like a search for hidden treasure. Job 28, a poetic interlude in the book, compares the one who searches for wisdom to a miner searching for something valuable that is buried and hidden in the dark. People will

(continued on next page)

(True Wisdom, continued)

take great risks, brave great depths and heights, and push back darkness in order to find treasure; the search for wisdom is no less strenuous. Simply put, wisdom is knowing and doing the will of God—which is a hard thing to do in the midst of suffering. The book of Proverbs is all about wisdom, and it begins with a thesis statement of sorts about wisdom: "The fear of the LORD is the beginning of knowledge; fools despise wisdom and instruction" (Pr 1:7).

All people fit into one of two categories: those who pursue wisdom, and those who despise wisdom. Jesus taught that true wisdom was to obey his words (Mt 7:24). Jesus also thanked his Father for hiding spiritual truths from people who were wise in their own eyes (Mt 11:25). Wisdom is about seeing that this world does not get it right all the time. Sometimes bad things happen to people who do not deserve it. Sometimes the wicked thrive while the righteous struggle. Wisdom teaches that the way up to glory is to go low in humility; the way to save one's life is to lose it following Jesus. Jesus came to turn the values of the world upside down, through divine wisdom.

15 It cannot be bought for gold,
and silver cannot be weighed as its price.
16 It cannot be valued in the gold of Ophir,
in precious onyx or sapphire.
17 Gold and glass cannot equal it,
nor can it be exchanged for jewels of fine gold.
18 No mention shall be made of coral or of crystal;
the price of wisdom is above pearls.
19 The topaz of Ethiopia cannot equal it,
nor can it be valued in pure gold.

20 "From where, then, does wisdom come?
And where is the place of understanding?
21 It is hidden from the eyes of all living
and concealed from the birds of the air.
22 Abaddon and Death say,
'We have heard a rumor of it with our ears.'

23 "God understands the way to it,
and he knows its place.
24 For he looks to the ends of the earth
and sees everything under the heavens.
25 When he gave to the wind its weight
and apportioned the waters by measure,
26 when he made a decree for the rain
and a way for the lightning of the thunder,
27 then he saw it and declared it;
he established it, and searched it out.
28 And he said to man,
'Behold, the fear of the Lord, that is wisdom,
and to turn away from evil is understanding.'"

Job's Summary Defense

29 And Job again took up his discourse, and said:

2 "Oh, that I were as in the months of old,
as in the days when God watched over me,
3 when his lamp shone upon my head,
and by his light I walked through darkness,
4 as I was in my prime,[1]
when the friendship of God was upon my tent,
5 when the Almighty was yet with me,
when my children were all around me,
6 when my steps were washed with butter,
and the rock poured out for me streams of oil!
7 When I went out to the gate of the city,
when I prepared my seat in the square,
8 the young men saw me and withdrew,
and the aged rose and stood;
9 the princes refrained from talking
and laid their hand on their mouth;
10 the voice of the nobles was hushed,
and their tongue stuck to the roof of their mouth.
11 When the ear heard, it called me blessed,
and when the eye saw, it approved,

[1] Hebrew *my autumn days*

LONGING FOR FORMER GLORY

The Christian life contains mountains and valleys. There are moments when the experience of God feels so high, real, and tangible. Then there are moments in which God feels distant and far away. Expecting only mountaintop experiences with God reveals a misunderstanding of the Christian life. The God whom people worship on the mountain is the same one who walks with them through the valleys (Ps 23:4).

Job found himself in a low valley. A death valley. God seemed so far away. The times that he had spent on the mountain with God seemed like another lifetime. Job longed for past glory, a time when he had experienced good things. He was tired of his present condition and simply wanted to move on. He was heartbroken as he remembered how good his life had been.

God's people can always trust that he is with them. God has promised never to leave or forsake his people (Heb 13:5). When Jesus' followers find themselves at a low point in their journey with God, they need not lose heart. God is with them on the mountains and in the valleys.

Job's longing for the past foreshadows Jesus' prayer to the Father the night before he was betrayed and killed. Jesus expressed his longing for the glory he had experienced in eternity (Jn 17:5). Jesus found himself in a valley lower than Job's. Jesus had known a glory that was much greater than Job's. His heart truly broke as he faced suffering. But Jesus died to make the glory of eternity past into the future hope of everyone who would trust him in faith.

Philippians 2:5 – 11 teaches that Jesus had true glory with God. The Son was sent by the Father to come down off the mountain of glory and to suffer in the valley. God's way of bringing Jesus out of the valley was not *around* suffering, but *through* suffering. God sent Jesus up the hill of Golgotha where Jesus experienced the ultimate loss — loss of the love of his Father. In that moment, God made Jesus to be sin so that his people could become the righteousness of God (2Co 5:21). Jesus endured all this for his glory and for the good of his people. Remembering Christ in the low valleys of life provides sustenance and comfort for the journey back up the mountain.

12 because I delivered the poor who cried for help,
and the fatherless who had none to help him.
13 The blessing of him who was about to perish came upon me,
and I caused the widow's heart to sing for joy.
14 I put on righteousness, and it clothed me;
my justice was like a robe and a turban.
15 I was eyes to the blind
and feet to the lame.
16 I was a father to the needy,
and I searched out the cause of him whom I did not know.
17 I broke the fangs of the unrighteous
and made him drop his prey from his teeth.
18 Then I thought, 'I shall die in my nest,
and I shall multiply my days as the sand,
19 my roots spread out to the waters,
with the dew all night on my branches,
20 my glory fresh with me,
and my bow ever new in my hand.'

21 "Men listened to me and waited
and kept silence for my counsel.
22 After I spoke they did not speak again,
and my word dropped upon them.
23 They waited for me as for the rain,
and they opened their mouths as for the spring rain.
24 I smiled on them when they had no confidence,
and the light of my face they did not cast down.
25 I chose their way and sat as chief,
and I lived like a king among his troops,
like one who comforts mourners.

30 "But now they laugh at me,
men who are younger than I,
whose fathers I would have disdained
to set with the dogs of my flock.
2 What could I gain from the strength of their hands,
men whose vigor is gone?
3 Through want and hard hunger
they gnaw the dry ground by night in waste and desolation;
4 they pick saltwort and the leaves of bushes,
and the roots of the broom tree for their food.[1]
5 They are driven out from human company;
they shout after them as after a thief.
6 In the gullies of the torrents they must dwell,
in holes of the earth and of the rocks.
7 Among the bushes they bray;
under the nettles they huddle together.
8 A senseless, a nameless brood,
they have been whipped out of the land.

9 "And now I have become their song;
I am a byword to them.
10 They abhor me; they keep aloof from me;
they do not hesitate to spit at the sight of me.
11 Because God has loosed my cord and humbled me,
they have cast off restraint[2] in my presence.

[1]Or *warmth* [2]Hebrew *the bridle*

JOB 30:1–31

DAYS OF SUFFERING

Affliction is a terrible thing—just ask Job. The word carries nuances of misery and poverty. It contains the idea of being trapped under a heavy burden. It means suffering. The Bible teaches that God cares about our afflictions. He hears the cries of his people (Ex 2:23–25). The notion of affliction in the Old Testament appears again in the New Testament: Peter tells the suffering Christian to cast "all your anxieties on him, because he cares for you" (1Pe 5:7). The God who controls the universe is the God who cares for you—that is a real comfort. Since he controls all things, we can be assured that he is working in every situation to bring about what is good for his people (Ro 8:28). This is true in our stories, and it is true for Job as well.

Jesus encouraged people to give him their burdens and receive the blessing of being his followers; in doing this, they would find that his burdens were completely different than the afflictions and suffering they carried (Mt 11:28–30). The apostle Paul, who knew suffering all too well, was able to conclude, "For the sake of Christ, then, I am content with weaknesses, insults, hardships, persecutions, and calamities. For when I am weak, then I am strong" (2Co 12:10; see also Ro 12:12).

12 On my right hand the rabble rise;
they push away my feet;
they cast up against me their ways of destruction.
13 They break up my path;
they promote my calamity;
they need no one to help them.
14 As through a wide breach they come;
amid the crash they roll on.
15 Terrors are turned upon me;
my honor is pursued as by the wind,
and my prosperity has passed away like a cloud.

16 "And now my soul is poured out within me;
days of affliction have taken hold of me.
17 The night racks my bones,
and the pain that gnaws me takes no rest.
18 With great force my garment is disfigured;
it binds me about like the collar of my tunic.
19 God[1] has cast me into the mire,
and I have become like dust and ashes.
20 I cry to you for help and you do not answer me;
I stand, and you only look at me.
21 You have turned cruel to me;
with the might of your hand you persecute me.
22 You lift me up on the wind; you make me ride on it,
and you toss me about in the roar of the storm.
23 For I know that you will bring me to death
and to the house appointed for all living.

24 "Yet does not one in a heap of ruins stretch out his hand,
and in his disaster cry for help?[2]
25 Did not I weep for him whose day was hard?
Was not my soul grieved for the needy?
26 But when I hoped for good, evil came,
and when I waited for light, darkness came.
27 My inward parts are in turmoil and never still;
days of affliction come to meet me.
28 I go about darkened, but not by the sun;
I stand up in the assembly and cry for help.
29 I am a brother of jackals
and a companion of ostriches.
30 My skin turns black and falls from me,
and my bones burn with heat.
31 My lyre is turned to mourning,
and my pipe to the voice of those who weep.

Job's Final Appeal

31 "I have made a covenant with my eyes;
how then could I gaze at a virgin?
2 What would be my portion from God above
and my heritage from the Almighty on high?
3 Is not calamity for the unrighteous,
and disaster for the workers of iniquity?
4 Does not he see my ways
and number all my steps?

[1]Hebrew *He* [2]The meaning of the Hebrew is uncertain

JOB 31:1–8

THE HEART BEHIND THE ACTION

Job believed that he was innocent. Innocent is a strong word because it means sinless. Yet the Bible is clear that no mere human is sinless: "Surely there is not a righteous man on earth who does good and never sins" (Ecc 7:20). Job claimed not only that he had done the right things, but that he had acted from a right heart. The heart functions like the throne of our lives—whatever lives and rules in the heart will eventually reign in our lives. Jesus said, "The good person out of the good treasure of his heart produces good, and the evil person out of his evil treasure produces evil, for out of the abundance of the heart his mouth speaks" (Lk 6:45).

Amazingly, Job responded by focusing on the outward actions and the inward motivations he had in his heart (Job 31:5–8). Jesus would come along and highlight the important connection between actions and heart motives in the Sermon on the Mount (Mt 5–7). Yet, it is impossible for people to justify themselves completely before God. Isaiah teaches that all people are ultimately unclean; their best works are like a polluted garment (Isa 64:6). By the conclusion of the book, Job saw and understood his helpless state before a sovereign God and repented in dust and ashes (Job 42:6).

5 “If I have walked with falsehood
and my foot has hastened to deceit;
6 (Let me be weighed in a just balance,
and let God know my integrity!)
7 if my step has turned aside from the way
and my heart has gone after my eyes,
and if any spot has stuck to my hands,
8 then let me sow, and another eat,
and let what grows for me[1] be rooted out.

9 “If my heart has been enticed toward a woman,
and I have lain in wait at my neighbor’s door,
10 then let my wife grind for another,
and let others bow down on her.
11 For that would be a heinous crime;
that would be an iniquity to be punished by the judges;
12 for that would be a fire that consumes as far as Abaddon,
and it would burn to the root all my increase.

13 “If I have rejected the cause of my manservant or my maidservant,
when they brought a complaint against me,
14 what then shall I do when God rises up?
When he makes inquiry, what shall I answer him?
15 Did not he who made me in the womb make him?
And did not one fashion us in the womb?

16 “If I have withheld anything that the poor desired,
or have caused the eyes of the widow to fail,
17 or have eaten my morsel alone,
and the fatherless has not eaten of it
18 (for from my youth the fatherless[2] grew up with me as with a father,
and from my mother’s womb I guided the widow[3]),
19 if I have seen anyone perish for lack of clothing,
or the needy without covering,
20 if his body has not blessed me,[4]
and if he was not warmed with the fleece of my sheep,
21 if I have raised my hand against the fatherless,
because I saw my help in the gate,
22 then let my shoulder blade fall from my shoulder,
and let my arm be broken from its socket.
23 For I was in terror of calamity from God,
and I could not have faced his majesty.

24 “If I have made gold my trust
or called fine gold my confidence,
25 if I have rejoiced because my wealth was abundant
or because my hand had found much,
26 if I have looked at the sun[5] when it shone,
or the moon moving in splendor,
27 and my heart has been secretly enticed,
and my mouth has kissed my hand,
28 this also would be an iniquity to be punished by the judges,
for I would have been false to God above.

29 “If I have rejoiced at the ruin of him who hated me,
or exulted when evil overtook him

[1]Or *let my descendants* [2]Hebrew *he* [3]Hebrew *her* [4]Hebrew *if his loins have not blessed me*
[5]Hebrew *the light*

30 (I have not let my mouth sin
by asking for his life with a curse),
31 if the men of my tent have not said,
'Who is there that has not been filled with his meat?'
32 (the sojourner has not lodged in the street;
I have opened my doors to the traveler),
33 if I have concealed my transgressions as others do[1]
by hiding my iniquity in my heart,
34 because I stood in great fear of the multitude,
and the contempt of families terrified me,
so that I kept silence, and did not go out of doors—
35 Oh, that I had one to hear me!
(Here is my signature! Let the Almighty answer me!)
Oh, that I had the indictment written by my adversary!
36 Surely I would carry it on my shoulder;
I would bind it on me as a crown;
37 I would give him an account of all my steps;
like a prince I would approach him.

38 "If my land has cried out against me
and its furrows have wept together,
39 if I have eaten its yield without payment
and made its owners breathe their last,
40 let thorns grow instead of wheat,
and foul weeds instead of barley."

The words of Job are ended.

Elihu Rebukes Job's Three Friends

32 So these three men ceased to answer Job, because he was righteous in his
own eyes. 2Then Elihu the son of Barachel the Buzite, of the family of Ram,
burned with anger. He burned with anger at Job because he justified himself rather than God. 3He burned with anger also at Job's three friends because they had
found no answer, although they had declared Job to be in the wrong. 4Now Elihu
had waited to speak to Job because they were older than he. 5And when Elihu saw
that there was no answer in the mouth of these three men, he burned with anger.
6And Elihu the son of Barachel the Buzite answered and said:

"I am young in years,
and you are aged;
therefore I was timid and afraid
to declare my opinion to you.
7 I said, 'Let days speak,
and many years teach wisdom.'
8 But it is the spirit in man,
the breath of the Almighty, that makes him understand.
9 It is not the old[2] who are wise,
nor the aged who understand what is right.
10 Therefore I say, 'Listen to me;
let me also declare my opinion.'

11 "Behold, I waited for your words,
I listened for your wise sayings,
while you searched out what to say.
12 I gave you my attention,
and, behold, there was none among you who refuted Job
or who answered his words.

[1]Or *as Adam did* [2]Hebrew *many* [in years]

JOB 32:2

JUSTIFICATION

Self-justification. The theme is faint but present nonetheless in Job's reasoning in the previous chapters. Clearly, God did not allow these things to happen to Job because Job was proud. Instead, God allowed these things to happen in order to bring transformation to Job's life. God wanted Job. In Job's suffering, God proved himself to be extremely kind. It is a kind God who causes a cold to fall upon a person in order to get the person to a doctor—a doctor who then discovers a hidden cancer in time to cure it. In a similar sense, God was good to allow Job's suffering, which exposed that hint of dangerous pride in order to deal with it. Job was more righteous than most of the people of his day were, but he was still far below God's standard of righteousness. God does not save people because they are good, but in order to make them good. Salvation comes before good works. Consider what God said to his people after the exodus: "For I am the LORD who brought you up out of the land of Egypt to be your God. You shall therefore be holy, for I am holy" (Lev 11:45). No matter how "good" people can be, they still fall short of God's standard of holiness and remain in need of a Savior.

13 Beware lest you say, 'We have found wisdom;
God may vanquish him, not a man.'
14 He has not directed his words against me,
and I will not answer him with your speeches.

15 "They are dismayed; they answer no more;
they have not a word to say.
16 And shall I wait, because they do not speak,
because they stand there, and answer no more?
17 I also will answer with my share;
I also will declare my opinion.
18 For I am full of words;
the spirit within me constrains me.
19 Behold, my belly is like wine that has no vent;
like new wineskins ready to burst.
20 I must speak, that I may find relief;
I must open my lips and answer.
21 I will not show partiality to any man
or use flattery toward any person.
22 For I do not know how to flatter,
else my Maker would soon take me away.

Elihu Rebukes Job

33 "But now, hear my speech, O Job,
and listen to all my words.
2 Behold, I open my mouth;
the tongue in my mouth speaks.
3 My words declare the uprightness of my heart,
and what my lips know they speak sincerely.
4 The Spirit of God has made me,
and the breath of the Almighty gives me life.
5 Answer me, if you can;
set your words in order before me; take your stand.
6 Behold, I am toward God as you are;
I too was pinched off from a piece of clay.
7 Behold, no fear of me need terrify you;
my pressure will not be heavy upon you.

8 "Surely you have spoken in my ears,
and I have heard the sound of your words.
9 You say, 'I am pure, without transgression;
I am clean, and there is no iniquity in me.
10 Behold, he finds occasions against me,
he counts me as his enemy,
11 he puts my feet in the stocks
and watches all my paths.'

12 "Behold, in this you are not right. I will answer you,
for God is greater than man.
13 Why do you contend against him,
saying, 'He will answer none of man's[1] words'?[2]
14 For God speaks in one way,
and in two, though man does not perceive it.
15 In a dream, in a vision of the night,
when deep sleep falls on men,
while they slumber on their beds,

[1]Hebrew *his* [2]Or *He will not answer for any of his own words*

TRICKED BY PRIDE?

Job's suffering was not due to his sin. The reader can understand the greater things that are at stake. Job was not being punished. Rather, Job's life was the battleground on which God's glory was being proven supreme against the threats of the enemy.

Even so, sinful attitudes in Job's heart were exposed through the trials he experienced. Elihu's words pierced right to the heart of the problem: Job had been acting as if he was God's equal. Job was wrong to think of God as a mere human who could be held accountable. Elihu later concluded that Job had become proud, even though he sat dejected in ashes (Job 36:8–9; 37:14–24). It is prideful to demand an audience with God to present one's own case: it implies that a mere human can judge whether God has been just (35:2).

The consistent humility of Jesus stands in stark contrast to the pride of Job. Job presumed upon God's kindness and blessings. Jesus knew that all people ultimately deserved to suffer and that everything outside of hell was grace. Jesus was humble at all points in spite of the fact that he is God. Job grew proud and sought to question God even though he was sinful.

Grace is receiving something undeserved. God gives grace to help people in their many struggles. James, the half brother of Jesus, said it like this: "But he gives more grace. Therefore it says, 'God opposes the proud but gives grace to the humble'" (Jas 4:6; cf. Pr 3:34). Pursuing a life of humility begins with a clear picture of God's glory. The humble realize their place is low in comparison to God's majesty. When God comes into focus, everything in their lives is seen for what it really is. Focusing on the glory of God is the only anchor that will keep a heart humble — and God loves the humble in heart. God loves the humble, the meek, and the lowly so much that he promises they will inherit the earth (Mt 5:5).

16 then he opens the ears of men
and terrifies[1] them with warnings,
17 that he may turn man aside from his deed
and conceal pride from a man;
18 he keeps back his soul from the pit,
his life from perishing by the sword.

19 "Man is also rebuked with pain on his bed
and with continual strife in his bones,
20 so that his life loathes bread,
and his appetite the choicest food.
21 His flesh is so wasted away that it cannot be seen,
and his bones that were not seen stick out.
22 His soul draws near the pit,
and his life to those who bring death.
23 If there be for him an angel,
a mediator, one of the thousand,
to declare to man what is right for him,
24 and he is merciful to him, and says,
'Deliver him from going down into the pit;
I have found a ransom;
25 let his flesh become fresh with youth;
let him return to the days of his youthful vigor';
26 then man[2] prays to God, and he accepts him;
he sees his face with a shout of joy,
and he restores to man his righteousness.
27 He sings before men and says:
'I sinned and perverted what was right,
and it was not repaid to me.
28 He has redeemed my soul from going down into the pit,
and my life shall look upon the light.'

29 "Behold, God does all these things,
twice, three times, with a man,
30 to bring back his soul from the pit,
that he may be lighted with the light of life.
31 Pay attention, O Job, listen to me;
be silent, and I will speak.
32 If you have any words, answer me;
speak, for I desire to justify you.
33 If not, listen to me;
be silent, and I will teach you wisdom."

Elihu Asserts God's Justice

34 Then Elihu answered and said:

2 "Hear my words, you wise men,
and give ear to me, you who know;
3 for the ear tests words
as the palate tastes food.
4 Let us choose what is right;
let us know among ourselves what is good.
5 For Job has said, 'I am in the right,
and God has taken away my right;
6 in spite of my right I am counted a liar;
my wound is incurable, though I am without transgression.'

[1]Or *seals* [2]Hebrew *he*

JOB 34:5

BETTER THAN WHAT WE DESERVE

Job had overstated his case. Yes, Job was more righteous than his friends and many people of his day. Yet Elihu, whose words serve as a transition between the speeches of the three friends and God's upcoming speech, was different from Job's three friends. He was young, yet wise. He was patient, yet passionate. And he was truthful, but caring. Elihu spoke with incredible wisdom about the situation. Job had claimed that he was innocent and had not done anything wrong, suggesting that God had denied him justice. People get this distorted view of God when they come to God for what they can get from God, instead of coming to God for God himself. Elihu explained that this kind of thinking is foolishness (34:31–37). God later confirmed that Job spoke without knowledge (38:2). It is dangerous to come to God seeking only the blessings he can give. During Jesus' ministry, his disciples sacrificed much to follow him. Yet Peter asked the question in Matthew 19:27, "We have left everything and followed you. What then will we have?" Jesus confirmed that his disciples would receive rewards upon his return, but Peter's question revealed questionable motives and a misunderstanding about the relationship between God and his people. That relationship, thankfully, is not based on a calculation of behaviors meriting rewards or punishments. Instead, God rewards his people for what Christ has done.

7 What man is like Job,
who drinks up scoffing like water,
8 who travels in company with evildoers
and walks with wicked men?
9 For he has said, 'It profits a man nothing
that he should take delight in God.'

10 "Therefore, hear me, you men of understanding:
far be it from God that he should do wickedness,
and from the Almighty that he should do wrong.
11 For according to the work of a man he will repay him,
and according to his ways he will make it befall
him.
12 Of a truth, God will not do wickedly,
and the Almighty will not pervert justice.
13 Who gave him charge over the earth,
and who laid on him[1] the whole world?
14 If he should set his heart to it
and gather to himself his spirit and his breath,
15 all flesh would perish together,
and man would return to dust.

16 "If you have understanding, hear this;
listen to what I say.
17 Shall one who hates justice govern?
Will you condemn him who is righteous and mighty,
18 who says to a king, 'Worthless one,'
and to nobles, 'Wicked man,'
19 who shows no partiality to princes,
nor regards the rich more than the poor,
for they are all the work of his hands?
20 In a moment they die;
at midnight the people are shaken and pass away,
and the mighty are taken away by no human
hand.

21 "For his eyes are on the ways of a man,
and he sees all his steps.
22 There is no gloom or deep darkness
where evildoers may hide themselves.
23 For God[2] has no need to consider a man further,
that he should go before God in judgment.
24 He shatters the mighty without investigation
and sets others in their place.
25 Thus, knowing their works,
he overturns them in the night, and they are
crushed.
26 He strikes them for their wickedness
in a place for all to see,
27 because they turned aside from following him
and had no regard for any of his ways,
28 so that they caused the cry of the poor to come to him,
and he heard the cry of the afflicted—
29 When he is quiet, who can condemn?
When he hides his face, who can behold him,
whether it be a nation or a man?—

[1]Hebrew lacks *on him* [2]Hebrew *he*

30 that a godless man should not reign,
that he should not ensnare the people.

31 "For has anyone said to God,
'I have borne punishment; I will not offend any more;
32 teach me what I do not see;
if I have done iniquity, I will do it no more'?
33 Will he then make repayment to suit you,
because you reject it?
For you must choose, and not I;
therefore declare what you know.[1]
34 Men of understanding will say to me,
and the wise man who hears me will say:
35 'Job speaks without knowledge;
his words are without insight.'
36 Would that Job were tried to the end,
because he answers like wicked men.
37 For he adds rebellion to his sin;
he claps his hands among us
and multiplies his words against God."

Elihu Condemns Job

35 And Elihu answered and said:
2 "Do you think this to be just?
Do you say, 'It is my right before God,'
3 that you ask, 'What advantage have I?
How am I better off than if I had sinned?'
4 I will answer you
and your friends with you.
5 Look at the heavens, and see;
and behold the clouds, which are higher than you.
6 If you have sinned, what do you accomplish against him?
And if your transgressions are multiplied, what do you do to him?
7 If you are righteous, what do you give to him?
Or what does he receive from your hand?
8 Your wickedness concerns a man like yourself,
and your righteousness a son of man.

9 "Because of the multitude of oppressions people cry out;
they call for help because of the arm of the mighty.[2]
10 But none says, 'Where is God my Maker,
who gives songs in the night,
11 who teaches us more than the beasts of the earth
and makes us wiser than the birds of the heavens?'
12 There they cry out, but he does not answer,
because of the pride of evil men.
13 Surely God does not hear an empty cry,
nor does the Almighty regard it.
14 How much less when you say that you do not see him,
that the case is before him, and you are waiting for him!
15 And now, because his anger does not punish,
and he does not take much note of transgression,[3]
16 Job opens his mouth in empty talk;
he multiplies words without knowledge."

JOB 35:1–3

MISUNDERSTANDING GOD

Job's story is challenging to many who assume that God rewards those who live a righteous life by allowing them to avoid suffering. But that is not how God works. God does not treat his people on the basis of their own lives, but on the basis of the life that Jesus lived for them. God does not have to do this. He chooses to do this—that is why it is called grace. It is undeserved and unearned. God did not owe Job an explanation for anything that had taken place. Furthermore, God had not wronged Job in any way through all of this. And yet, Job asked to argue his case before God in court. Job misunderstood God because God was not under obligation to Job for anything. God does not need people, but he loves them. He is not in debt to people; they are in debt to him. Therefore, the foundational attitude of people in a relationship with God ought to be worship: knowing God and making him known through their lives.

Jesus drove home this point in his own life. In John 17:5, he prayed that God would glorify himself in all that Jesus did. Likewise, God's people should not serve God in order to attain a reward. Rather they should seek to please God with their lives because God is worthy of all honor. And those who devote their lives to God in this way discover that the *very act of worshiping God is the* greatest reward imaginable.

---

[1]The meaning of the Hebrew in verses 29–33 is uncertain [2]Or *the many* [3]Theodotion, Symmachus (compare Vulgate); the meaning of the Hebrew word is uncertain

Elihu Extols God's Greatness

36 And Elihu continued, and said:
2 "Bear with me a little, and I will show you,
for I have yet something to say on God's behalf.
3 I will get my knowledge from afar
and ascribe righteousness to my Maker.
4 For truly my words are not false;
one who is perfect in knowledge is with you.

5 "Behold, God is mighty, and does not despise any;
he is mighty in strength of understanding.
6 He does not keep the wicked alive,
but gives the afflicted their right.
7 He does not withdraw his eyes from the righteous,
but with kings on the throne
he sets them forever, and they are exalted.
8 And if they are bound in chains
and caught in the cords of affliction,
9 then he declares to them their work
and their transgressions, that they are behaving arrogantly.
10 He opens their ears to instruction
and commands that they return from iniquity.
11 If they listen and serve him,
they complete their days in prosperity,
and their years in pleasantness.
12 But if they do not listen, they perish by the sword
and die without knowledge.

13 "The godless in heart cherish anger;
they do not cry for help when he binds them.
14 They die in youth,
and their life ends among the cult prostitutes.
15 He delivers the afflicted by their affliction
and opens their ear by adversity.
16 He also allured you out of distress
into a broad place where there was no cramping,
and what was set on your table was full of fatness.

17 "But you are full of the judgment on the wicked;
judgment and justice seize you.
18 Beware lest wrath entice you into scoffing,
and let not the greatness of the ransom turn you aside.
19 Will your cry for help avail to keep you from distress,
or all the force of your strength?
20 Do not long for the night,
when peoples vanish in their place.
21 Take care; do not turn to iniquity,
for this you have chosen rather than affliction.
22 Behold, God is exalted in his power;
who is a teacher like him?
23 Who has prescribed for him his way,
or who can say, 'You have done wrong'?

24 "Remember to extol his work,
of which men have sung.
25 All mankind has looked on it;
man beholds it from afar.

JOB 36:22–33

PROCLAIMING GOD'S MAJESTY

Warning labels are helpful—they communicate the right way to handle something that is powerful. Elihu gave Job a word of warning and caution. He told Job the right way to make sense of what had taken place. According to Elihu, God intended to teach Job something through his affliction. Rather than trying to correct the teacher, Job was to remember and magnify God as the maker of all things. God's best for Job did not mean going around a tough season of life, but going through it. God's ways are higher than humanity can understand. They cannot know all the reasons God has for doing what he does. God is majestic in all of his ways. He is holy, high above and so much wiser than humans. And yet, God has come near to people in Jesus. Jesus lived as an ordinary man, and yet with majesty (2Pe 1:16). God has thousands of reasons for doing what he does. If he acts in a way that seems unexplainable, it must be remembered that he is always acting for his glory and in a way that is consistent with his majestic character.

26 Behold, God is great, and we know him not;
the number of his years is unsearchable.
27 For he draws up the drops of water;
they distill his mist in rain,
28 which the skies pour down
and drop on mankind abundantly.
29 Can anyone understand the spreading of the clouds,
the thunderings of his pavilion?
30 Behold, he scatters his lightning about him
and covers the roots of the sea.
31 For by these he judges peoples;
he gives food in abundance.
32 He covers his hands with the lightning
and commands it to strike the mark.
33 Its crashing declares his presence;[1]
the cattle also declare that he rises.

Elihu Proclaims God's Majesty

37 "At this also my heart trembles
and leaps out of its place.
2 Keep listening to the thunder of his voice
and the rumbling that comes from his mouth.
3 Under the whole heaven he lets it go,
and his lightning to the corners of the earth.
4 After it his voice roars;
he thunders with his majestic voice,
and he does not restrain the lightnings[2] when his voice is heard.
5 God thunders wondrously with his voice;
he does great things that we cannot comprehend.
6 For to the snow he says, 'Fall on the earth,'
likewise to the downpour, his mighty downpour.
7 He seals up the hand of every man,
that all men whom he made may know it.
8 Then the beasts go into their lairs,
and remain in their dens.
9 From its chamber comes the whirlwind,
and cold from the scattering winds.
10 By the breath of God ice is given,
and the broad waters are frozen fast.
11 He loads the thick cloud with moisture;
the clouds scatter his lightning.
12 They turn around and around by his guidance,
to accomplish all that he commands them
on the face of the habitable world.
13 Whether for correction or for his land
or for love, he causes it to happen.

14 "Hear this, O Job;
stop and consider the wondrous works of God.
15 Do you know how God lays his command upon them
and causes the lightning of his cloud to shine?
16 Do you know the balancings[3] of the clouds,
the wondrous works of him who is perfect in knowledge,
17 you whose garments are hot
when the earth is still because of the south wind?

[1]Hebrew *declares concerning him* [2]Hebrew *them* [3]Or *hoverings*

JOB 37:1–24

AWESOME GOD

Thinking about God should always lead to worship. God has revealed himself in his Word so that people may know him and worship him. Conversations about God should have the ultimate goal of pointing people to God and helping them love God. Elihu's speech ends with praise for God. Elihu points out that no human can control the weather, the storm, or the lightning, but God does. God puts the sky in place and sets the clouds wherever he likes. No human can look into the sun without becoming blurry-eyed for a few minutes, but God's golden splendor is brighter than the sun. He is exalted. He is glorious. He has great power and many other attributes too numerous to name. He could rule over people as a tyrant with power and might, and yet, he chooses to rule with love.

Jesus left the people he encountered with a sense of awe as he exercised his authority humbly (Mt 9:8). His actions inspired people to praise God (Lk 5:26). He lived in such a way that people recognized him as a great prophet and helper sent by God (Lk 7:16). Jesus is majestic. He is the gift that can never be taken away and that leads to a life of worship that never ends. "Therefore let us be grateful for receiving a kingdom that cannot be shaken, and thus let us offer to God acceptable worship, with reverence and awe" (Heb 12:28).

18 Can you, like him, spread out the skies,
hard as a cast metal mirror?
19 Teach us what we shall say to him;
we cannot draw up our case because of darkness.
20 Shall it be told him that I would speak?
Did a man ever wish that he would be swallowed up?

21 "And now no one looks on the light
when it is bright in the skies,
when the wind has passed and cleared them.
22 Out of the north comes golden splendor;
God is clothed with awesome majesty.
23 The Almighty—we cannot find him;
he is great in power;
justice and abundant righteousness he will not violate.
24 Therefore men fear him;
he does not regard any who are wise in their own conceit."[1]

The Lord Answers Job

38 Then the Lord answered Job out of the whirlwind and said:
2 "Who is this that darkens counsel by words without knowledge?
3 Dress for action[2] like a man;
I will question you, and you make it known to me.

4 "Where were you when I laid the foundation of the earth?
Tell me, if you have understanding.
5 Who determined its measurements—surely you know!
Or who stretched the line upon it?
6 On what were its bases sunk,
or who laid its cornerstone,
7 when the morning stars sang together
and all the sons of God shouted for joy?

8 "Or who shut in the sea with doors
when it burst out from the womb,
9 when I made clouds its garment
and thick darkness its swaddling band,
10 and prescribed limits for it
and set bars and doors,
11 and said, 'Thus far shall you come, and no farther,
and here shall your proud waves be stayed'?

12 "Have you commanded the morning since your days began,
and caused the dawn to know its place,
13 that it might take hold of the skirts of the earth,
and the wicked be shaken out of it?
14 It is changed like clay under the seal,
and its features stand out like a garment.
15 From the wicked their light is withheld,
and their uplifted arm is broken.

16 "Have you entered into the springs of the sea,
or walked in the recesses of the deep?
17 Have the gates of death been revealed to you,
or have you seen the gates of deep darkness?
18 Have you comprehended the expanse of the earth?
Declare, if you know all this.

[1]Hebrew *in heart* [2]Hebrew *Gird up your loins*

19 "Where is the way to the dwelling of light,
and where is the place of darkness,
20 that you may take it to its territory
and that you may discern the paths to its home?
21 You know, for you were born then,
and the number of your days is great!

22 "Have you entered the storehouses of the snow,
or have you seen the storehouses of the hail,
23 which I have reserved for the time of trouble,
for the day of battle and war?
24 What is the way to the place where the light is distributed,
or where the east wind is scattered upon the earth?

25 "Who has cleft a channel for the torrents of rain
and a way for the thunderbolt,
26 to bring rain on a land where no man is,
on the desert in which there is no man,
27 to satisfy the waste and desolate land,
and to make the ground sprout with grass?

28 "Has the rain a father,
or who has begotten the drops of dew?
29 From whose womb did the ice come forth,
and who has given birth to the frost of heaven?
30 The waters become hard like stone,
and the face of the deep is frozen.

31 "Can you bind the chains of the Pleiades
or loose the cords of Orion?
32 Can you lead forth the Mazzaroth[1] in their season,
or can you guide the Bear with its children?
33 Do you know the ordinances of the heavens?
Can you establish their rule on the earth?

34 "Can you lift up your voice to the clouds,
that a flood of waters may cover you?
35 Can you send forth lightnings, that they may go
and say to you, 'Here we are'?
36 Who has put wisdom in the inward parts[2]
or given understanding to the mind?[3]
37 Who can number the clouds by wisdom?
Or who can tilt the waterskins of the heavens,
38 when the dust runs into a mass
and the clods stick fast together?

39 "Can you hunt the prey for the lion,
or satisfy the appetite of the young lions,
40 when they crouch in their dens
or lie in wait in their thicket?
41 Who provides for the raven its prey,
when its young ones cry to God for help,
and wander about for lack of food?

39 "Do you know when the mountain goats give birth?
Do you observe the calving of the does?
2 Can you number the months that they fulfill,
and do you know the time when they give birth,

[1]Probably the name of a constellation [2]Or *in the ibis* [3]Or *rooster*

GOD'S POSITION AND OURS

People do not need answers to their questions and arguments as much as they need to be overwhelmed by the fact that they do not understand everything as well as they think they do. This is precisely what Job 38 (and 39) teaches. Job was full of questions and concerns. God's response was not to provide answers, but instead to point Job to everything that he did not understand. God knows people infinitely better than they know themselves.

God's questions to Job are focused on the world in which Job lived. These questions reveal Job's presumption in expecting God to line up with his understanding, when he did not even understand the world around him. As the questions continue throughout Job 38 and 39, it becomes more and more apparent that God is so much higher and wiser than humanity. His words point to the magnitude of his works in creation. When humans open their eyes to those works, they are humbled before God.

This is God's world, and God can and will do what he wants. God has used the weather to bless his people and even help his people in battle. God has also used the weather to judge his people by sending a flood or withholding rain (Ge 7:4; 1Ki 17:1). God's ability to use the weather however he likes proves that he is in control of the weather. In reminding Job of this truth, God also illustrated his character through the weather. Thunder and lightning symbolize God's power and majesty. The falling of rain and snow on the earth, which results in the watering of the ground and nurturing of vegetation, pictures the way the Word works on the hearts of his people and points to the gracious God who gives life. God compares his judgment to raging storms and likens his blessings to refreshing showers.

God contrasts Job's feeble questions with his infinite power to create and manage the world. The way that God questions Job points back to Genesis 1:1 – 10 and John 1:1 – 13 as Jesus, the Word of God, participated in the act of creation. Jesus' power, strength, purpose, and oversight in creation should be the overarching framework that Christians use when viewing or experiencing suffering. This is who Jesus is — the Creator. All thanks be to Jesus. In his grace and mercy he has chosen to be the Savior. All people are utterly dependent on him for life in this world and eternal life with him in the world to come.

3 when they crouch, bring forth their offspring,
and are delivered of their young?
4 Their young ones become strong; they grow up in the open;
they go out and do not return to them.

5 "Who has let the wild donkey go free?
Who has loosed the bonds of the swift donkey,
6 to whom I have given the arid plain for his home
and the salt land for his dwelling place?
7 He scorns the tumult of the city;
he hears not the shouts of the driver.
8 He ranges the mountains as his pasture,
and he searches after every green thing.

9 "Is the wild ox willing to serve you?
Will he spend the night at your manger?
10 Can you bind him in the furrow with ropes,
or will he harrow the valleys after you?
11 Will you depend on him because his strength is great,
and will you leave to him your labor?
12 Do you have faith in him that he will return your grain
and gather it to your threshing floor?

13 "The wings of the ostrich wave proudly,
but are they the pinions and plumage of love?[1]
14 For she leaves her eggs to the earth
and lets them be warmed on the ground,
15 forgetting that a foot may crush them
and that the wild beast may trample them.
16 She deals cruelly with her young, as if they were not hers;
though her labor be in vain, yet she has no fear,
17 because God has made her forget wisdom
and given her no share in understanding.
18 When she rouses herself to flee,[2]
she laughs at the horse and his rider.

19 "Do you give the horse his might?
Do you clothe his neck with a mane?
20 Do you make him leap like the locust?
His majestic snorting is terrifying.
21 He paws[3] in the valley and exults in his strength;
he goes out to meet the weapons.
22 He laughs at fear and is not dismayed;
he does not turn back from the sword.
23 Upon him rattle the quiver,
the flashing spear, and the javelin.
24 With fierceness and rage he swallows the ground;
he cannot stand still at the sound of the trumpet.
25 When the trumpet sounds, he says 'Aha!'
He smells the battle from afar,
the thunder of the captains, and the shouting.

26 "Is it by your understanding that the hawk soars
and spreads his wings toward the south?
27 Is it at your command that the eagle mounts up
and makes his nest on high?

[1]The meaning of the Hebrew is uncertain [2]The meaning of the Hebrew is uncertain [3]Hebrew *They paw*

28 On the rock he dwells and makes his home,
on the rocky crag and stronghold.
29 From there he spies out the prey;
his eyes behold it from far away.
30 His young ones suck up blood,
and where the slain are, there is he."

40 And the LORD said to Job:
2 "Shall a faultfinder contend with the Almighty?
He who argues with God, let him answer it."

Job Promises Silence

3Then Job answered the LORD and said:

4 "Behold, I am of small account; what shall I answer you?
I lay my hand on my mouth.
5 I have spoken once, and I will not answer;
twice, but I will proceed no further."

The LORD Challenges Job

6Then the LORD answered Job out of the whirlwind and said:

7 "Dress for action[1] like a man;
I will question you, and you make it known to me.
8 Will you even put me in the wrong?
Will you condemn me that you may be in the right?
9 Have you an arm like God,
and can you thunder with a voice like his?
10 "Adorn yourself with majesty and dignity;
clothe yourself with glory and splendor.
11 Pour out the overflowings of your anger,
and look on everyone who is proud and abase him.
12 Look on everyone who is proud and bring him low
and tread down the wicked where they stand.
13 Hide them all in the dust together;
bind their faces in the world below.[2]
14 Then will I also acknowledge to you
that your own right hand can save you.

15 "Behold, Behemoth,[3]
which I made as I made you;
he eats grass like an ox.
16 Behold, his strength in his loins,
and his power in the muscles of his belly.
17 He makes his tail stiff like a cedar;
the *sinews of his thighs* are knit together.
18 His bones are tubes of bronze,
his limbs like bars of iron.

19 "He is the first of the works[4] of God;
let him who made him bring near his sword!
20 For the mountains yield food for him
where all the wild beasts play.
21 Under the lotus plants he lies,
in the shelter of the reeds and in the marsh.

[1]Hebrew *Gird up your loins* [2]Hebrew *in the hidden place* [3]A large animal, exact identity uncertain
[4]Hebrew *ways*

JOB 40:8

REAP WHAT YOU SOW?

God asked Job questions that were intended to overwhelm Job — in a good way. The questions all point to God's goodness, power, and freedom. The freedom of God might not seem like good news at first, but as the idea makes itself at home in the hearts of God's people, it becomes more and more beautiful. God's freedom means that God is under no obligation to do anything for anyone. God is only responsible to do what he says he will do.

Job's four friends maintained a general principle that can be found in various forms throughout Scripture: "Whatever one sows, that will he also reap" (Gal 6:7). That is a true statement; people generally receive what they put out. One of the many reasons Job is in the Bible is to show that God may choose to bypass this general rule from time to time and not communicate why — because God is not accountable to people. There may be some comfort in knowing that despite short-term variations, the "law of the harvest" applies in the long term (Gal 6:8 – 10). But at an even more fundamental level, God has transformed the general "you reap what you sow" principle in Jesus Christ. Sinless and undeserving of death, Jesus was crucified on a cross so that sinful humans might have life. In Jesus' death and resurrection, God transformed the standard system of retribution and reward. God is free to do whatever he wills; God decided to send Jesus to save us.

22 For his shade the lotus trees cover him;
the willows of the brook surround him.
23 Behold, if the river is turbulent he is not frightened;
he is confident though Jordan rushes against his mouth.
24 Can one take him by his eyes,[1]
or pierce his nose with a snare?

41 [2] "Can you draw out Leviathan[3] with a fishhook
or press down his tongue with a cord?
2 Can you put a rope in his nose
or pierce his jaw with a hook?
3 Will he make many pleas to you?
Will he speak to you soft words?
4 Will he make a covenant with you
to take him for your servant forever?
5 Will you play with him as with a bird,
or will you put him on a leash for your girls?
6 Will traders bargain over him?
Will they divide him up among the merchants?
7 Can you fill his skin with harpoons
or his head with fishing spears?
8 Lay your hands on him;
remember the battle—you will not do it again!
9[4] Behold, the hope of a man is false;
he is laid low even at the sight of him.
10 No one is so fierce that he dares to stir him up.
Who then is he who can stand before me?
11 Who has first given to me, that I should repay him?
Whatever is under the whole heaven is mine.

12 "I will not keep silence concerning his limbs,
or his mighty strength, or his goodly frame.
13 Who can strip off his outer garment?
Who would come near him with a bridle?
14 Who can open the doors of his face?
Around his teeth is terror.
15 His back is made of[5] rows of shields,
shut up closely as with a seal.
16 One is so near to another
that no air can come between them.
17 They are joined one to another;
they clasp each other and cannot be separated.
18 His sneezings flash forth light,
and his eyes are like the eyelids of the dawn.
19 Out of his mouth go flaming torches;
sparks of fire leap forth.
20 Out of his nostrils comes forth smoke,
as from a boiling pot and burning rushes.
21 His breath kindles coals,
and a flame comes forth from his mouth.
22 In his neck abides strength,
and terror dances before him.
23 The folds of his flesh stick together,
firmly cast on him and immovable.

[1]Or *in his sight* [2]Ch 40:25 in Hebrew [3]A large sea animal, exact identity uncertain [4]Ch 41:1 in Hebrew
[5]Or *His pride is in his*

24 His heart is hard as a stone,
hard as the lower millstone.
25 When he raises himself up, the mighty[1] are afraid;
at the crashing they are beside themselves.
26 Though the sword reaches him, it does not avail,
nor the spear, the dart, or the javelin.
27 He counts iron as straw,
and bronze as rotten wood.
28 The arrow cannot make him flee;
for him, sling stones are turned to stubble.
29 Clubs are counted as stubble;
he laughs at the rattle of javelins.
30 His underparts are like sharp potsherds;
he spreads himself like a threshing sledge on the mire.
31 He makes the deep boil like a pot;
he makes the sea like a pot of ointment.
32 Behind him he leaves a shining wake;
one would think the deep to be white-haired.
33 On earth there is not his like,
a creature without fear.
34 He sees everything that is high;
he is king over all the sons of pride."

Job's Confession and Repentance

42 Then Job answered the LORD and said:

2 "I know that you can do all things,
and that no purpose of yours can be thwarted.
3 'Who is this that hides counsel without knowledge?'
Therefore I have uttered what I did not understand,
things too wonderful for me, which I did not know.
4 'Hear, and I will speak;
I will question you, and you make it known to me.'
5 I had heard of you by the hearing of the ear,
but now my eye sees you;
6 therefore I despise myself,
and repent[2] in dust and ashes."

The LORD Rebukes Job's Friends

7After the LORD had spoken these words to Job, the LORD said to Eliphaz the
Temanite: "My anger burns against you and against your two friends, for you have
not spoken of me what is right, as my servant Job has. 8Now therefore take seven
bulls and seven rams and go to my servant Job and offer up a burnt offering for
yourselves. And my servant Job shall pray for you, for I will accept his prayer not
to deal with you according to your folly. For you have not spoken of me what is
right, as my servant Job has." 9So Eliphaz the Temanite and Bildad the Shuhite
and Zophar the Naamathite went and did what the LORD had told them, and the
LORD accepted Job's prayer.

The LORD Restores Job's Fortunes

10And the LORD restored the fortunes of Job, when he had prayed for his
friends. And the LORD gave Job twice as much as he had before. 11Then came to
him all his brothers and sisters and all who had known him before, and ate bread
with him in his house. And they showed him sympathy and comforted him for all

---

[1]Or *gods* [2]Or *and am comforted upon*

RESTORED BY GRACE ALONE

God treats people in ways they do not deserve — and this is a good thing. All people deserve punishment from God for the sins they have committed against him. Instead of punishment, God decided to draw near to humanity in grace. His grace is a gift that people do not deserve to receive — and it can only be received with the surrendered hands of faith.

God had already displayed grace throughout Job's sufferings. When Satan wanted to tempt and test Job, it was God who limited the extent of Satan's attacks. That was grace. And Job's past fortunes and eventual restoration were all by grace alone. His prosperity was not a reward for his integrity but a gift from God, who "restored the fortunes of Job" and "gave Job twice as much as he had before" so that "the LORD blessed the latter days of Job more than his beginning" (Job 42:10,12).

Job encountered God. It was only after the intense season of suffering, prayer, and waiting that a transformed Job got to see God for who he really is (42:5). Job's response of humility and repentance should serve as an example for every person who encounters God (42:1 – 6). After all of Job's questions and frustrations, he was left with the one phrase that he could confess in confidence: "I know that you can do all things" (42:2).

When Job saw God more clearly, he also began to see himself more clearly. When people discover the reality of God, they find the reality of themselves. Job only discovered these things through an intense season that seemed unbearable at times. But God knows from the beginning what he intends in the end. God knew the journey that he needed to take Job through, so God did it. And for Job to arrive at the destination of a transformed view of God was sheer grace.

The ultimate way God has shown his grace is by sending Jesus Christ to die for sinners. The cross leaves people with limitless reasons for repenting of their rebellion against God, and it should lead them to walk, live, and love more like Jesus.

the evil[1] that the LORD had brought upon him. And each of them gave him a piece
of money[2] and a ring of gold.

12 And the LORD blessed the latter days of Job more than his beginning. And he
had 14,000 sheep, 6,000 camels, 1,000 yoke of oxen, and 1,000 female donkeys.
13 He had also seven sons and three daughters. 14 And he called the name of the
first daughter Jemimah, and the name of the second Keziah, and the name of the
third Keren-happuch. 15 And in all the land there were no women so beautiful as
Job's daughters. And their father gave them an inheritance among their brothers.
16 And after this Job lived 140 years, and saw his sons, and his sons' sons, four
generations. 17 And Job died, an old man, and full of days.

[1] Or *disaster* [2] Hebrew *a qesitah*; a unit of money of uncertain value

THE QUESTION OF RIGHTEOUSNESS

One of Job's friends, Bildad, asked a penetrating question: "How then can man be in the right before God?" (Job 25:4). This vital question operates at several levels, cutting to the heart of the human condition and pointing to the great hope God's people have in Christ.

The question also looks for a solution. Here, Job's friend simply wondered whether righteousness before God was a possibility. From cover to cover, the Bible is absolutely clear that no human being can ever be righteous before God on his or her own. But in Christ, it is possible for sinful people to be made right with God.

The question reveals the complex relationship between sin and suffering. Bildad was clinging to the false idea that Job was suffering because he had unconfessed sin in his life. Job was not sinless, but he was forgiven. He confessed his sins (Job 7:21) and made the sacrifices God demanded (Job 1:5) — and those sacrifices pointed to the ultimate sacrifice of Jesus on the cross.

Lastly, the question highlights a common misunderstanding. No one is righteous before God; this is certain. But Bildad inferred that human beings cannot be righteous because they are the equivalent of a "maggot" or "worm" — and this is entirely misleading (Job 25:6). God never belittles humans like this. God sees people as creatures of worth and value, made in his image and precious enough to send Jesus to die for — even when they are in the depths of sin and rebellion.

Righteousness cannot be attained, but it can be received. Jesus pointed out that it is a mistake to try to justify oneself before God like the Pharisees (Mt 5:20). Only God is righteous (Ps 119:142; cf. Ro 3:10). For humans to be righteous, they need God to give his righteousness to them. This is why people need Jesus! Jesus' perfect life made his sacrificial death a means of righteousness for those who respond to him in faith (Ro 1:17).

All throughout Scripture, righteousness before God is found in trusting God's promises — that is what it means to have faith. This pattern is seen with Abraham, who believed God and it was credited to him as righteousness (Ge 15:6; cf. Ro 4:3). The only way for a person to be right before God is for God to give that person right standing based on Jesus' perfection. What Abraham believed, Jesus accomplished.

JOB 26:7

A NEW EARTH

Job's universe seemed broken beyond repair, and he must have longed for a fresh start, a complete fix, or even an all-new earth. The longing for a new earth is actually a good longing to have, and a longing that all followers of Jesus should experience. God created the earth (Ac 14:15), but the earth has been cursed because of humanity's rebellion, beginning with Adam and Eve's sin in the Garden of Eden. Jesus died to reconcile not only people, but the very world back to him (Col 1:20). Followers of Jesus have now been given the ministry of spreading that reconciliation (2Co 5:11–21). God's people are his ambassadors on this earth, and God is making his appeal through them for the world to be reconciled with the Creator. Christians personally participate by fighting sin, pursuing holiness, doing their jobs in a distinctly Christian way, and most importantly, telling people the good news about what God has done. A day is coming when the new heavens and new earth will descend from heaven and God will live with his people forever (Rev 21:1–5). Life is not about going "up" to heaven as much as it is about heaven coming "down" to earth. Jesus already came as a glimpse of what it will be like when his people live with him forever.

JOB 27:6

RIGHTEOUSNESS

Job's three friends were convinced that Job's sufferings were the result of some sin he must have committed. They were wrong. God was not punishing Job—instead, God was

(continued on next page)

3 How you have counseled him who has no wisdom,
and plentifully declared sound knowledge!
4 With whose help have you uttered words,
and whose breath has come out from you?
5 The dead tremble
under the waters and their inhabitants.
6 Sheol is naked before God,[1]
and Abaddon has no covering.
7 He stretches out the north over the void
and hangs the earth on nothing.
8 He binds up the waters in his thick clouds,
and the cloud is not split open under them.
9 He covers the face of the full moon[2]
and spreads over it his cloud.
10 He has inscribed a circle on the face of the waters
at the boundary between light and darkness.
11 The pillars of heaven tremble
and are astounded at his rebuke.
12 By his power he stilled the sea;
by his understanding he shattered Rahab.
13 By his wind the heavens were made fair;
his hand pierced the fleeing serpent.
14 Behold, these are but the outskirts of his ways,
and how small a whisper do we hear of him!
But the thunder of his power who can understand?"

Job Continues: I Will Maintain My Integrity

27 And Job again took up his discourse, and said:

2 "As God lives, who has taken away my right,
and the Almighty, who has made my soul bitter,
3 as long as my breath is in me,
and the spirit of God is in my nostrils,
4 my lips will not speak falsehood,
and my tongue will not utter deceit.
5 Far be it from me to say that you are right;
till I die I will not put away my integrity from me.
6 I hold fast my righteousness and will not let it go;
my heart does not reproach me for any of my days.

7 "Let my enemy be as the wicked,
and let him who rises up against me be as the unrighteous.
8 For what is the hope of the godless when God cuts him off,
when God takes away his life?
9 Will God hear his cry
when distress comes upon him?
10 Will he take delight in the Almighty?
Will he call upon God at all times?
11 I will teach you concerning the hand of God;
what is with the Almighty I will not conceal.
12 Behold, all of you have seen it yourselves;
why then have you become altogether vain?

13 "This is the portion of a wicked man with God,
and the heritage that oppressors receive from the Almighty:

[1] Hebrew *him* [2] Or *his throne*

JESUS: OUR PRAISE-WORTHY KING

PSALMS

PSALMS

DEATH OF MOSES, TO WHOM PSALM 90 IS ASCRIBED *c. 1406 BC*	DEATH OF DAVID, TO WHOM MANY PSALMS ARE ASCRIBED *c. 970 BC*	BOOK OF PSALMS COMPILED IN FINAL FORM *c. 400 – 300 BC*

God's people are a worshiping people. The psalms are a collection of praise songs written by King David and many of Israel's other worship leaders. Often referred to as Wisdom Literature, the books of Job, Psalms, Proverbs, Ecclesiastes, and Song of Solomon provide insight into God's plans and purposes for his people. While other portions of Scripture include praise to God, the 150 psalms reflect a worshipful, poetic tone that is unique among the books of the Bible. The hope-filled, worship-fueled writings found in Psalms provide a wide array of memorable passages that have inspired the praise of God's people throughout history.

The psalms describe the highs and lows of humanity's plight in a fallen world. At times the psalmists languish under the burden of their sin and the sin of others (Ps 51). The writers cry out to God for deliverance and plead with him for forgiveness. They profess their deep belief that God does indeed hear their prayers, respond to their brokenness, and meet their needs (43:5). In the face of the depths of human pain, God is ever-present to provide a source of refuge for those who love him (46:1).

At other times, the writers of the psalms declare their unceasing joy and praise to God. They sing of his greatness and shout for joy at his works (100:1). He is the God of history who has shown his might and power; he is the God of the people who has graciously given himself to them in covenant relationship (105:8 – 11). The people's repeated refrain of praise to God serves as the psalmists' hope and the ultimate goal of humankind (Ps 103).

Behind the joy and sadness, brokenness and blessedness of the book of Psalms is the future hope of the coming of God's promised One (Ps 2; 22; 110). This One, pictured throughout the book as God's anointed Messiah, will be a true King who will usher in God's kingdom (Ps 89). Numerous psalms point forward to a day when God will answer the longing of his people by sending the One who will deliver his people from the burden of their sin. Many of these psalms are quoted by the Gospel writers or by Jesus himself to show the ways in which Jesus' life, death, and resurrection fulfill God's promise. Jesus declares that God's kingdom is near, and he invites broken sinners to find hope, joy, and love in his kingdom. Unlike earthly kingdoms, however, the coming kingdom of God will have no end.

BLESS THE LORD, O MY SOUL,
AND ALL THAT IS WITHIN ME,
BLESS HIS HOLY NAME!

Psalm 103:1

THE PSALMS

BOOK ONE

Psalm 1

The Way of the Righteous and the Wicked

1 Blessed is the man[1]
who walks not in the counsel of the wicked,
nor stands in the way of sinners,
nor sits in the seat of scoffers;
2 but his delight is in the law[2] of the LORD,
and on his law he meditates day and night.

3 He is like a tree
planted by streams of water
that yields its fruit in its season,
and its leaf does not wither.
In all that he does, he prospers.
4 The wicked are not so,
but are like chaff that the wind drives away.

5 Therefore the wicked will not stand in the judgment,
nor sinners in the congregation of the righteous;
6 for the LORD knows the way of the righteous,
but the way of the wicked will perish.

Psalm 2

The Reign of the LORD's Anointed

1 Why do the nations rage[3]
and the peoples plot in vain?
2 The kings of the earth set themselves,
and the rulers take counsel together,
against the LORD and against his Anointed, saying,
3 "Let us burst their bonds apart
and cast away their cords from us."

4 He who sits in the heavens laughs;
the Lord holds them in derision.
5 Then he will speak to them in his wrath,
and terrify them in his fury, saying,
6 "As for me, I have set my King
on Zion, my holy hill."

7 I will tell of the decree:
The LORD said to me, "You are my Son;
today I have begotten you.
8 Ask of me, and I will make the nations your heritage,
and the ends of the earth your possession.
9 You shall break[4] them with a rod of iron
and dash them in pieces like a potter's vessel."

PSALM 2:6

THE HOLY MOUNTAIN

Generally speaking, "Zion" refers to the city of Jerusalem and, on occasion, serves as a metaphor for God's people (e.g., Isa 3:16; La 4:2). In this case, Zion is pictured as the prominent mountain or hill in Jerusalem, an image that suggests the supremacy and kingship of God as well as the meeting of God with his people. In the ancient Near East, making contact with a deity was widely thought to occur in the highest places of a region, since that's where a heavenly deity could easily reach down to earthly humans. Thus, for the people of Israel and their surrounding neighbors, a mountain was an understandable and expected place to meet with a god. High up in Zion (Jerusalem) the one true God consistently condescended from his throne to reach out to his people (Isa 8:18). In the sacrificial offering of his own Son (Mt 27:45–56), God did not just reach down to a mountaintop. He reached down into the very depths of human existence—to the point of suffering and death—to bring his people back to him.

[1]The singular Hebrew word for *man* (*ish*) is used here to portray a representative example of a godly person; see Preface [2]Or *instruction* [3]Or *nations noisily assemble* [4]Revocalization yields (compare Septuagint) *You shall rule*

MEDITATING ON GOD'S WORD

Psalm 1 serves as a significant foundation for the entire book and encourages its readers to live a life that finds its pleasures solely in God. Here it becomes clear that there are two paths — or rather, two types of people: the wicked and the righteous. This dichotomy is found throughout the Wisdom Literature of the Bible. According to the psalmist, in order to be counted among the "righteous" one must love God's Word (i.e., Hebrew *torah,* or law), meditate on God's instruction, and follow in the way of the Lord.

Learning the way of the Lord is one of the chief priorities of the Christian life, and this can be accomplished only through Christ and through Scripture. In the Gospel of John, Jesus told his listeners that *he* is "the way, and the truth, and the life" (Jn 14:6). *He* is the image of the invisible God (Col 1:15) and in him humanity sees the ultimate picture of righteousness. Knowing Jesus is of first importance as believers move toward becoming "the righteous" men or women described by the psalmist. Following Jesus' example is the next step.

Jesus knew God's words through and through. He knew them well enough to quote Scripture with ease, to speak with surety about his Father's heart, and to live the perfect life. Christians must likewise find their way, truth, and life in the person of Christ and in the breadth of God's words. To that end, they must spend time reading and listening to Scripture so that they can get to know God, understand his likes and dislikes, discern the difference between God's voice and that of the world, and become like deep-rooted trees that yield fruit (Ps 1:3).

Psalm 1 points to one practical way to start and continue on the path of righteousness: "meditate" on God's Word. Interestingly, the Hebrew word used for *meditate* here in Psalm 1 actually means "to utter, to speak, to soliloquize." Meditating on Scripture thus can be thought of as making God's words one's own — either by reading Scripture or recalling it from memory. This is worth noting since the idea of meditation can feel a bit foreign (and somewhat impractical) to many people. It is simply a practical way for Christians to let Scripture permeate their minds, hearts, and lives as they seek to follow the way of Christ.

GOD'S ADDRESS TO HIS SON

Psalm 2 was likely used in the coronation ceremonies of Israel's kings in which the Davidic ruler was declared to be God's son through God's initiative to adopt him as such (2Sa 7:12 – 16). Other songs that served as coronation anthems can be found in Psalms 18, 20, 45, 72, 89, and 110. Each time one of David's descendants was crowned, the words like those found in Psalm 2:7 affirmed both the king's adoption and his authority.

The king's adoption meant that he now looked to God as his "Father" and it signified an intimate, familial relationship. His task was thus to honor his Father by caring for God's people — a task that would be enabled by God himself and would bring glory to his name (2Sa 7:23). Furthermore, the king would be installed as an authoritative mediator of God's promise to make Israel into God's covenant people (2Sa 7:24) who are called to be a blessing to all the nations (Ge 12:1 – 3) — a relevant reflection that must still inform the lives of God's people today.

Finally, the divine decree of "you are my Son" foreshadowed the coming of God's only begotten Son, Jesus — the ultimate mediator and King. The New Testament acknowledges Jesus as the dearly loved Son of God (Mt 3:17), the long-anticipated Davidic Messiah (Mt 16:15 – 17; Mk 8:29; Jn 4:25 – 26; 7:28 – 42), and the eternal King (Rev 3:20 – 21; 11:15). Jesus was declared to be King at his birth (Mt 2:1 – 2), and his coronation, as Paul says in Acts 13:33, was accomplished at his resurrection.

Because of Jesus, people can be adopted into the family of God. Paul quoted Psalm 2:7 in Acts 13:33, assuring those who believe in and follow Jesus that Jesus is still alive and able to offer both the forgiveness of and freedom from sin (Ac 13:28,34,39). Above all, and as previously noted, adoption into God's kingdom means that Christians, like their King, are now set apart to worship God and to be a blessing to all the nations.

10 Now therefore, O kings, be wise;
be warned, O rulers of the earth.
11 Serve the LORD with fear,
and rejoice with trembling.
12 Kiss the Son,
lest he be angry, and you perish in the way,
for his wrath is quickly kindled.
Blessed are all who take refuge in him.

Psalm 3

Save Me, O My God

A Psalm of David, when he fled from Absalom his son.

1 O LORD, how many are my foes!
Many are rising against me;
2 many are saying of my soul,
"There is no salvation for him in God." *Selah*[1]
3 But you, O LORD, are a shield about me,
my glory, and the lifter of my head.
4 I cried aloud to the LORD,
and he answered me from his holy hill. *Selah*
5 I lay down and slept;
I woke again, for the LORD sustained me.
6 I will not be afraid of many thousands of people
who have set themselves against me all around.
7 Arise, O LORD!
Save me, O my God!
For you strike all my enemies on the cheek;
you break the teeth of the wicked.
8 Salvation belongs to the LORD;
your blessing be on your people! *Selah*

Psalm 4

Answer Me When I Call

To the choirmaster: with stringed instruments. A Psalm of David.

1 Answer me when I call, O God of my righteousness!
You have given me relief when I was in distress.
Be gracious to me and hear my prayer!
2 O men,[2] how long shall my honor be turned into shame?
How long will you love vain words and seek after lies? *Selah*
3 But know that the LORD has set apart the godly for himself;
the LORD hears when I call to him.
4 Be angry,[3] and do not sin;
ponder in your own hearts on your beds, and be silent. *Selah*
5 Offer right sacrifices,
and put your trust in the LORD.
6 There are many who say, "Who will show us some good?
Lift up the light of your face upon us, O LORD!"

[1]The meaning of the Hebrew word *Selah*, used frequently in the Psalms, is uncertain. It may be a musical or liturgical direction [2]Or *O men of rank* [3]Or *Be agitated*

PSALM 3:1–8

FINDING JUSTICE IN THE MIDST OF INJUSTICE

The superscription of Psalm 3 establishes the context for David's words — a context of desperation. David's own son had stolen his kingdom and now sought to kill him. While most readers probably cannot relate to the exact circumstances described, they can recall events in their own lives when people have wounded them deeply. They can identify with David's request for divine justice. Although David's words may appear harsh since he compared his enemies to wild animals (i.e., "break the teeth of the wicked" in v. 7), they are the heartfelt pleas of a man who has been hurt. Further, his words must be understood in light of the cross. The punishment requested by David pales in comparison to the ultimate punishment for sin — a punishment that Jesus bore when he took humanity's sins upon himself and died a gruesome death of torture and crucifixion. Psalms like this remind readers that God does not turn a blind eye to injustice and sweep it under the cosmic carpet. Instead, he chose to unleash his wrath against sin on his own Son and, in so doing, make right all wrongs, pay all debts, and free all captives. This psalm shows that God is the one people should cry out to in the midst of unfair pain, because it is God who makes war on sin in order to make peace for all humankind.

PSALM 4:4

BE ANGRY, AND DO NOT SIN

David described circumstances here that warrant feelings of anger. He

(continued on next page)

(Be Angry, and Do Not Sin, continued)

had been personally injured because of wicked people who had actively sought to hear and tell lies. His angst is thus a natural, understandable, and even commendable response to malice and slander. Jesus himself expressed appropriate anger when he made a whip and cleared out the temple courts in order to protect the true purpose of his Father's house (Mt 21:12 – 13; Jn 2:13 – 17). Therefore, God's people must learn to express anger over the things that anger God, yet do so in a manner that does not give an "opportunity to the devil" or give way to prolonged bitterness (Eph 4:26 – 27). Too often, the balances are tipped, and anger is either dishonestly suppressed or abusively expressed. Very rarely do people strike the balance that exemplifies David's command not to sin despite the injustice he felt. Perhaps God's people would do well to follow David's example: to be quiet and ponder the reason for feeling angry. Then, having trusted that vengeance is the Lord's and that his approval is sufficient, speak openly to God about the offense instead of looking for personal revenge.

PSALM 6:1 – 10

LAMENTS AND THE JUDGMENT THAT BRINGS HOPE

David's lament in Psalm 6 expresses extreme discomfort and concern about his circumstances. Though the exact nature of David's situation is unclear, David nevertheless called out to God, pleading for mercy and for deliverance from both his pain and his enemies. The Gospel accounts similarly describe

(continued on next page)

7 You have put more joy in my heart
than they have when their grain and wine abound.

8 In peace I will both lie down and sleep;
for you alone, O LORD, make me dwell in safety.

Psalm 5

Lead Me in Your Righteousness

To the choirmaster: for the flutes. A Psalm of David.

1 Give ear to my words, O LORD;
consider my groaning.
2 Give attention to the sound of my cry,
my King and my God,
for to you do I pray.
3 O LORD, in the morning you hear my voice;
in the morning I prepare a sacrifice for you[1] and watch.

4 For you are not a God who delights in wickedness;
evil may not dwell with you.
5 The boastful shall not stand before your eyes;
you hate all evildoers.
6 You destroy those who speak lies;
the LORD abhors the bloodthirsty and deceitful man.

7 But I, through the abundance of your steadfast love,
will enter your house.
I will bow down toward your holy temple
in the fear of you.
8 Lead me, O LORD, in your righteousness
because of my enemies;
make your way straight before me.

9 For there is no truth in their mouth;
their inmost self is destruction;
their throat is an open grave;
they flatter with their tongue.
10 Make them bear their guilt, O God;
let them fall by their own counsels;
because of the abundance of their transgressions cast them out,
for they have rebelled against you.

11 But let all who take refuge in you rejoice;
let them ever sing for joy,
and spread your protection over them,
that those who love your name may exult in you.
12 For you bless the righteous, O LORD;
you cover him with favor as with a shield.

Psalm 6

O LORD, Deliver My Life

To the choirmaster: with stringed instruments; according to The Sheminith.[2] A Psalm of David.

1 O LORD, rebuke me not in your anger,
nor discipline me in your wrath.

[1]Or *I direct my prayer to you* [2]Probably a musical or liturgical term

2 Be gracious to me, O LORD, for I am languishing;
heal me, O LORD, for my bones are troubled.
3 My soul also is greatly troubled.
But you, O LORD—how long?

4 Turn, O LORD, deliver my life;
save me for the sake of your steadfast love.
5 For in death there is no remembrance of you;
in Sheol who will give you praise?

6 I am weary with my moaning;
every night I flood my bed with tears;
I drench my couch with my weeping.
7 My eye wastes away because of grief;
it grows weak because of all my foes.

8 Depart from me, all you workers of evil,
for the LORD has heard the sound of my weeping.
9 The LORD has heard my plea;
the LORD accepts my prayer.
10 All my enemies shall be ashamed and greatly troubled;
they shall turn back and be put to shame in a moment.

Psalm 7

In You Do I Take Refuge

A Shiggaion[1] of David, which he sang to the LORD concerning the words of Cush, a Benjaminite.

1 O LORD my God, in you do I take refuge;
save me from all my pursuers and deliver me,
2 lest like a lion they tear my soul apart,
rending it in pieces, with none to deliver.

3 O LORD my God, if I have done this,
if there is wrong in my hands,
4 if I have repaid my friend[2] with evil
or plundered my enemy without cause,
5 let the enemy pursue my soul and overtake it,
and let him trample my life to the ground
and lay my glory in the dust. *Selah*

6 Arise, O LORD, in your anger;
lift yourself up against the fury of my enemies;
awake for me; you have appointed a judgment.
7 Let the assembly of the peoples be gathered about you;
over it return on high.

8 The LORD judges the peoples;
judge me, O LORD, according to my righteousness
and according to the integrity that is in me.
9 Oh, let the evil of the wicked come to an end,
and may you establish the righteous—
you who test the minds and hearts,[3]
O righteous God!
10 My shield is with God,
who saves the upright in heart.

[1]Probably a musical or liturgical term [2]Hebrew *the one at peace with me* [3]Hebrew *the hearts and kidneys*

(Laments and the Judgment That Brings Hope, continued)

Jesus as one who suffered at the hands of his enemies, as one who lamented, and as one who prayed (e.g., Mk 14:32–35; Lk 23:20–25). Moreover, Luke was keen to point out that Jesus himself will deal with the problem of suffering as well as with the problem of evildoers. Hence, David's words in Psalm 6:8 are reasserted in Jesus' declaration, "Depart from me, all you workers of evil!" (Lk 13:27). These words appear in a context where Jesus promised to bring judgment to those who persist in their evil actions. Thus, as God's people read this psalm and, at times, resonate with David's plea for mercy and judgment in verses 9–10, they are reminded that Jesus has come in response to their laments and will bring mercy and judgment (Lk 17:26–30).

11 God is a righteous judge,
and a God who feels indignation every day.

12 If a man[1] does not repent, God[2] will whet his sword;
he has bent and readied his bow;
13 he has prepared for him his deadly weapons,
making his arrows fiery shafts.
14 Behold, the wicked man conceives evil
and is pregnant with mischief
and gives birth to lies.
15 He makes a pit, digging it out,
and falls into the hole that he has made.
16 His mischief returns upon his own head,
and on his own skull his violence descends.

17 I will give to the LORD the thanks due to his righteousness,
and I will sing praise to the name of the LORD, the Most High.

Psalm 8

How Majestic Is Your Name

To the choirmaster: according to The Gittith.[3] A Psalm of David.

1 O LORD, our Lord,
how majestic is your name in all the earth!
You have set your glory above the heavens.
2 Out of the mouth of babies and infants,
you have established strength because of your foes,
to still the enemy and the avenger.

3 When I look at your heavens, the work of your fingers,
the moon and the stars, which you have set in place,
4 what is man that you are mindful of him,
and the son of man that you care for him?

5 Yet you have made him a little lower than the heavenly beings[4]
and crowned him with glory and honor.
6 You have given him dominion over the works of your hands;
you have put all things under his feet,
7 all sheep and oxen,
and also the beasts of the field,
8 the birds of the heavens, and the fish of the sea,
whatever passes along the paths of the seas.

9 O LORD, our Lord,
how majestic is your name in all the earth!

Psalm 9[5]

I Will Recount Your Wonderful Deeds

To the choirmaster: according to Muth-labben.[6] A Psalm of David.

1 I will give thanks to the LORD with my whole heart;
I will recount all of your wonderful deeds.
2 I will be glad and exult in you;
I will sing praise to your name, O Most High.

---

[1]Hebrew *he* [2]Hebrew *he* [3]Probably a musical or liturgical term [4]Or *than God*; Septuagint *than the angels* [5]Psalms 9 and 10 together follow an acrostic pattern, each stanza beginning with the successive letters of the Hebrew alphabet. In the Septuagint they form one psalm [6]Probably a musical or liturgical term

GOD USES THE WEAK TO DISPLAY HIS STRENGTH

One reason why God is worthy of praise is because of *how* he accomplishes his will. He uses the weakest voices of the earth — "babies and infants" — to show off his glory and to prevail. Surely this is good news for any and all who have ever felt weak, unsure, or afraid.

The New Testament follows this counterintuitive thread and teaches that weakness is the way of the Christian life. God's people are called "children of God" (1Jn 3:1). Jesus himself invites the little children to come to him (Lk 18:16), and Christians are affectionately referred to as "beloved children" and "little children" (Eph 5:1; 1Jn 2:1). All of this "children" language simply reaffirms the truth that the kingdom of God is upside down. It is the weak whom God uses to shame the strong; it is the children who are able to enter into his presence; it is the lowly who will be raised up (Ps 18:27; 1Co 1:27).

Jesus highlighted the choice to embrace the role of God's child when he said, "Truly, I say to you, unless you turn and become like children, you will never enter the kingdom of heaven. Whoever humbles himself like this child is the greatest in the kingdom of heaven" (Mt 18:3 – 4). To become like a child, then, one must do what children do: ask for help, think highly of others, express wonder and awe, submit to the Father's authority, and so on. After all, God is committed to caring for his children, and he is ever mindful of their needs (Mt 6:26; 7:11).

This psalm reveals that God's mindfulness is unmerited. He *chooses* to see his people, to think about them, to give them the good gift of glory, and to empower them when they are weak. God knows that humanity is frail, yet he delights to pour out his grace by giving his people a position of honor in his creation (Ps 8:5). And he does this because he is truly majestic and worthy of acclaim. That God would work in such a manner makes him easy to worship and praise. This is why David ended with the refrain "O LORD, our Lord, how majestic is your name in all the earth!" (v. 9). God is happy to use those who are weak, and he is doing it for the glory of his name.

PSALM 9:7–10

THE THRONE FOR JUDGMENT

In society today, the idea of judgment is widely misunderstood and really quite unpopular. Yet the Bible talks about God's judgment as the means for making all things right. In God's economy, judgment is what it costs to bring about *restoration*, which is the central hope of all humanity. The "whole creation has been groaning" to be redeemed (Ro 8:22–23). Thus when David celebrated God's "throne for justice," he was picturing the end goals of justice meted out: refuge for the oppressed, remembrance of the needy, and hopes fulfilled for the afflicted (Ps 9:7,9,18).

The longing for judgment and the cry for justice are dealt with at God's throne, and it is Jesus who will act as judge. The New Testament speaks frequently about Jesus' rightful role as judge (Mt 19:28; Jn 5:22–30; Ac 10:42; Ro 2:16). For those who are in Christ, the day that Jesus judges the world is a day to pray for and a day to give thanks for, (2Ti 4:8; 1Jn 4:17; Rev 19–21)—just like David. This is the day when all debts will be paid, tears will be wiped away, and death will be forever conquered because Jesus has assumed the throne!

PSALM 10:1–18

GOD IS IN CONTROL

In light of the brazen abuses committed by wicked people, the psalmist wondered aloud, "Why, O LORD, do you stand far away?" (v. 1). At first glance, it would seem that the perennial question of the problem of evil has again stolen the spotlight and remained unanswered. Yet, the

(continued on next page)

3 When my enemies turn back,
they stumble and perish before[1] your presence.
4 For you have maintained my just cause;
you have sat on the throne, giving righteous judgment.

5 You have rebuked the nations; you have made the wicked perish;
you have blotted out their name forever and ever.
6 The enemy came to an end in everlasting ruins;
their cities you rooted out;
the very memory of them has perished.

7 But the LORD sits enthroned forever;
he has established his throne for justice,
8 and he judges the world with righteousness;
he judges the peoples with uprightness.

9 The LORD is a stronghold for the oppressed,
a stronghold in times of trouble.
10 And those who know your name put their trust in you,
for you, O LORD, have not forsaken those who seek you.

11 Sing praises to the LORD, who sits enthroned in Zion!
Tell among the peoples his deeds!
12 For he who avenges blood is mindful of them;
he does not forget the cry of the afflicted.

13 Be gracious to me, O LORD!
See my affliction from those who hate me,
O you who lift me up from the gates of death,
14 that I may recount all your praises,
that in the gates of the daughter of Zion
I may rejoice in your salvation.

15 The nations have sunk in the pit that they made;
in the net that they hid, their own foot has been caught.
16 The LORD has made himself known; he has executed judgment;
the wicked are snared in the work of their own hands. *Higgaion.[2] Selah*

17 The wicked shall return to Sheol,
all the nations that forget God.

18 For the needy shall not always be forgotten,
and the hope of the poor shall not perish forever.

19 Arise, O LORD! Let not man prevail;
let the nations be judged before you!
20 Put them in fear, O LORD!
Let the nations know that they are but men! *Selah*

Psalm 10

Why Do You Hide Yourself?

1 Why, O LORD, do you stand far away?
Why do you hide yourself in times of trouble?

2 In arrogance the wicked hotly pursue the poor;
let them be caught in the schemes that they have devised.
3 For the wicked boasts of the desires of his soul,
and the one greedy for gain curses[3] and renounces the LORD.

[1]Or *because of* [2]Probably a musical or liturgical term [3]Or *and he blesses the one greedy for gain*

4 In the pride of his face[1] the wicked does not seek him;[2]
all his thoughts are, "There is no God."
5 His ways prosper at all times;
your judgments are on high, out of his sight;
as for all his foes, he puffs at them.
6 He says in his heart, "I shall not be moved;
throughout all generations I shall not meet adversity."
7 His mouth is filled with cursing and deceit and oppression;
under his tongue are mischief and iniquity.
8 He sits in ambush in the villages;
in hiding places he murders the innocent.
His eyes stealthily watch for the helpless;
9 he lurks in ambush like a lion in his thicket;
he lurks that he may seize the poor;
he seizes the poor when he draws him into his net.
10 The helpless are crushed, sink down,
and fall by his might.
11 He says in his heart, "God has forgotten,
he has hidden his face, he will never see it."

12 Arise, O LORD; O God, lift up your hand;
forget not the afflicted.
13 Why does the wicked renounce God
and say in his heart, "You will not call to account"?
14 But you do see, for you note mischief and vexation,
that you may take it into your hands;
to you the helpless commits himself;
you have been the helper of the fatherless.
15 Break the arm of the wicked and evildoer;
call his wickedness to account till you find none.

16 The LORD is king forever and ever;
the nations perish from his land.
17 O LORD, you hear the desire of the afflicted;
you will strengthen their heart; you will incline your ear
18 to do justice to the fatherless and the oppressed,
so that man who is of the earth may strike terror no more.

Psalm 11

The LORD Is in His Holy Temple

To the choirmaster. Of David.

1 In the LORD I take refuge;
how can you say to my soul,
Flee like a bird to your mountain,
2 for behold, the wicked bend the bow;
they have fitted their arrow to the string
to shoot in the dark at the upright in heart;
3 if the foundations are destroyed,
what can the righteous do?[3]

4 The LORD is in his holy temple;
the LORD's throne is in heaven;
his eyes see, his eyelids test the children of man.

[1]Or *of his anger* [2]Or *the wicked says, "He will not call to account"* [3]Or *for the foundations will be destroyed; what has the righteous done?*

(God Is in Control, continued)

psalmist's conclusion suggests not only an answer, but also an entirely different emphasis—*a faith-filled focus on the trustworthiness and action of God.* Consider the psalmist's proclamation that "the LORD is king forever and ever" (v. 16)! Clearly he believed that God hears, God sees, God acts, and God defends "the fatherless and the oppressed"; and God promises that the wicked, ultimately, "strike terror no more" (v. 18). The truth is that God *is* in control. God's kingdom is now, and it is coming. God will reign as King. The bottom line is that the reality of God's authority and actions come to bear on today's injustices—if not now, then in the future. Because of this, God's people can take heart in the good news that Jesus is coming, and he is "coming soon" (Rev 22:20).

PSALM 11:3–4

IF THE FOUNDATIONS ARE DESTROYED

Sometimes it looks like the battle is being lost. Evil appears to triumph daily and the moorings of societal morality are further undone. No matter how impossible the circumstances may seem, the truth is that God is still in control. Knowing that "the LORD is in his holy temple" (v. 4) gave David confidence as he looked forward to the day when the upright would "behold his face" (v. 7). That same knowledge continues to give God's people confidence today. Even though it may feel as though nothing can be done and that "the foundations are destroyed" (v. 3), the truth is that there is always a proven course of action: *trust.* Because God refuses to forsake his people and because he is still in charge, the foundations are *never* truly destroyed. Yes,

(continued on next page)

(If the Foundations Are Destroyed, continued)

the foundations may shake, but the shaking itself is an opportunity for the upright to have their faith tested and proven (v. 5). So when the ground feels like it is giving way, believers must seize the moment to put their confidence in God—the One who is on the throne and whose face they shall very soon see (Rev 22:3–4).

PSALM 12:1–8

THE FLAWLESS WORD OF GOD

Faithlessness. Flattery. Lies. Deception. In this psalm, David lamented the dishonest words of the wicked and contrasted them with the trustworthy words of the Lord. Not only are God's words portrayed as truthful, but also they are described as completely flawless—signified by the number seven (v. 6), which indicates completion in Hebrew. So what does it mean for God's words to be completely flawless? It means that he speaks at the right time in the right way with the right words for the right reason. Imagining this type of perfection is difficult to do in the midst of the world's dishonest and unkind language. Yet, the idea of God's words being flawless is significant. It means that what he says is trustworthy and is worth believing and affirming. As for the world's words, on the other hand, David reminds readers to identify the lies they hear and to reject them, choosing to hold on to God's promises instead. After all, Jesus himself is the guarantee. Paul said, "For all the promises of God find their Yes in him. That is why it is through him that we utter our Amen to God for his glory. And it is God who establishes us with you in Christ, and has anointed us, and who has also put his seal on us and

(continued on next page)

5 The LORD tests the righteous,
but his soul hates the wicked and the one who loves violence.
6 Let him rain coals on the wicked;
fire and sulfur and a scorching wind shall be the portion
of their cup.
7 For the LORD is righteous;
he loves righteous deeds;
the upright shall behold his face.

Psalm 12

The Faithful Have Vanished

To the choirmaster: according to The Sheminith.[1]
A Psalm of David.

1 Save, O LORD, for the godly one is gone;
for the faithful have vanished from among the children
of man.
2 Everyone utters lies to his neighbor;
with flattering lips and a double heart they speak.

3 May the LORD cut off all flattering lips,
the tongue that makes great boasts,
4 those who say, "With our tongue we will prevail,
our lips are with us; who is master over us?"

5 "Because the poor are plundered, because the needy groan,
I will now arise," says the LORD;
"I will place him in the safety for which he longs."
6 The words of the LORD are pure words,
like silver refined in a furnace on the ground,
purified seven times.

7 You, O LORD, will keep them;
you will guard us[2] from this generation forever.
8 On every side the wicked prowl,
as vileness is exalted among the children of man.

Psalm 13

How Long, O LORD?

To the choirmaster. A Psalm of David.

1 How long, O LORD? Will you forget me forever?
How long will you hide your face from me?
2 How long must I take counsel in my soul
and have sorrow in my heart all the day?
How long shall my enemy be exalted over me?

3 Consider and answer me, O LORD my God;
light up my eyes, lest I sleep the sleep of death,
4 lest my enemy say, "I have prevailed over him,"
lest my foes rejoice because I am shaken.

5 But I have trusted in your steadfast love;
my heart shall rejoice in your salvation.
6 I will sing to the LORD,
because he has dealt bountifully with me.

[1]Probably a musical or liturgical term [2]Or *guard him*

Psalm 14

The Fool Says, There Is No God

To the choirmaster. Of David.

1 The fool says in his heart, "There is no God."
They are corrupt, they do abominable deeds;
there is none who does good.

2 The LORD looks down from heaven on the children of man,
to see if there are any who understand,[1]
who seek after God.

3 They have all turned aside; together they have become corrupt;
there is none who does good,
not even one.

4 Have they no knowledge, all the evildoers
who eat up my people as they eat bread
and do not call upon the LORD?

5 There they are in great terror,
for God is with the generation of the righteous.
6 You would shame the plans of the poor,
but[2] the LORD is his refuge.

7 Oh, that salvation for Israel would come out of Zion!
When the LORD restores the fortunes of his people,
let Jacob rejoice, let Israel be glad.

Psalm 15

Who Shall Dwell on Your Holy Hill?

A Psalm of David.

1 O LORD, who shall sojourn in your tent?
Who shall dwell on your holy hill?

2 He who walks blamelessly and does what is right
and speaks truth in his heart;
3 who does not slander with his tongue
and does no evil to his neighbor,
nor takes up a reproach against his friend;
4 in whose eyes a vile person is despised,
but who honors those who fear the LORD;
who swears to his own hurt and does not change;
5 who does not put out his money at interest
and does not take a bribe against the innocent.
He who does these things shall never be moved.

Psalm 16

You Will Not Abandon My Soul

A Miktam[3] of David.

1 Preserve me, O God, for in you I take refuge.
2 I say to the LORD, "You are my Lord;
I have no good apart from you."

[1]Or *that act wisely* [2]Or *for* [3]Probably a musical or liturgical term

(The Flawless Word of God, continued)

given us his Spirit in our hearts as a guarantee" (2Co 1:20–22).

PSALM 13:1–6

HOW LONG?

The psalms are songs, not theological essays, and they express the psalmists' honest thoughts and heartfelt emotions. In this song, David expressed his anguish to God as he repeatedly asked, "How long?" Exhausted and weary, David's questions represent more of a tearful plea than a search for informational answers. Similarly, Jesus called out to God in his desperation. After telling his disciples that his soul was "very sorrowful, even to death," he went away to pray alone: "My Father, if it be possible, let this cup pass from me; nevertheless, not as I will, but as you will" (Mt 26:38–39). These historic accounts not only validate the human need to express oneself openly to God, but also they teach an important lesson. *Both David and Jesus did more than lament.* They asked God for help and they declared their willingness to trust in him. David spoke of God's love and works while Jesus readily surrendered to his Father's will. How often are God's people guilty of lamenting without trusting or, conversely, of declaring faith without honest expressions of the heart? The holistic expression of this psalm—lament, ask, and trust—is a model worth emulating.

PSALM 15:1–5

RELATIVE RIGHTEOUSNESS

Books such as Psalms and Proverbs refer frequently to righteousness in

(continued on next page)

(Relative Righteousness, continued)

order to draw a contrast between the righteous and the wicked, while much of the New Testament speaks of righteousness in a different sense: perfection. This distinction is important to note as the former expresses "relative righteousness" which compares humans to humans, whereas the latter expresses "absolute righteousness" which compares humans to God. When David asked, "Who shall dwell on your holy hill?" he was describing what the people of God should look like (v. 1). "Relative righteousness" looks like doing good, telling the truth, keeping oaths, ethical lending, and more (vv. 2–5). Of course, the expression of relative righteousness (in comparison with those who are not God's people) is an outworking of the imputed "absolute righteousness" of Christ. Romans 10:4 says, "Christ is the end of the law for righteousness to everyone who believes." For those who are in Christ then, God's righteousness has been freely given to them through faith and can now be joyfully manifested by living a righteous life that looks like David's description in Psalm 15 and is empowered by God himself (Eph 3:20; Php 1:6).

PSALM 16:9–11

TODAY'S LIFE AND THE AFTERLIFE

Although the concept of an afterlife was largely undeveloped in ancient Israel, the idea of *Sheol* was loosely equated with death (49:15; Job 11:8; Pr 15:24), from which the righteous could be delivered. David thus expressed his trust in God to protect him from this place of death as he celebrated the joy of finding lasting

(continued on next page)

3 As for the saints in the land, they are the excellent ones,
in whom is all my delight.[1]

4 The sorrows of those who run after[2] another god shall multiply;
their drink offerings of blood I will not pour out
or take their names on my lips.

5 The LORD is my chosen portion and my cup;
you hold my lot.
6 The lines have fallen for me in pleasant places;
indeed, I have a beautiful inheritance.

7 I bless the LORD who gives me counsel;
in the night also my heart instructs me.[3]
8 I have set the LORD always before me;
because he is at my right hand, I shall not be shaken.

9 Therefore my heart is glad, and my whole being[4] rejoices;
my flesh also dwells secure.
10 For you will not abandon my soul to Sheol,
or let your holy one see corruption.[5]

11 You make known to me the path of life;
in your presence there is fullness of joy;
at your right hand are pleasures forevermore.

Psalm 17

In the Shadow of Your Wings

A Prayer of David.

1 Hear a just cause, O LORD; attend to my cry!
Give ear to my prayer from lips free of deceit!
2 From your presence let my vindication come!
Let your eyes behold the right!

3 You have tried my heart, you have visited me by night,
you have tested me, and you will find nothing;
I have purposed that my mouth will not transgress.
4 With regard to the works of man, by the word of your lips
I have avoided the ways of the violent.
5 My steps have held fast to your paths;
my feet have not slipped.

6 I call upon you, for you will answer me, O God;
incline your ear to me; hear my words.
7 Wondrously show[6] your steadfast love,
O Savior of those who seek refuge
from their adversaries at your right hand.

8 Keep me as the apple of your eye;
hide me in the shadow of your wings,
9 from the wicked who do me violence,
my deadly enemies who surround me.

10 They close their hearts to pity;
with their mouths they speak arrogantly.
11 They have now surrounded our steps;
they set their eyes to cast us to the ground.

[1]Or *To the saints in the land, the excellent in whom is all my delight, I say:* [2]Or *who acquire* [3]Hebrew *my kidneys instruct me* [4]Hebrew *my glory* [5]Or *see the pit* [6]Or *Distinguish me by*

12 He is like a lion eager to tear,
as a young lion lurking in ambush.

13 Arise, O LORD! Confront him, subdue him!
Deliver my soul from the wicked by your sword,
14 from men by your hand, O LORD,
from men of the world whose portion is in this life.[1]
You fill their womb with treasure;[2]
they are satisfied with children,
and they leave their abundance to their infants.

15 As for me, I shall behold your face in righteousness;
when I awake, I shall be satisfied with your likeness.

Psalm 18

The LORD Is My Rock and My Fortress

To the choirmaster. A Psalm of David, the servant of the LORD, who addressed the words of this song to the LORD on the day when the LORD delivered him from the hand of all his enemies, and from the hand of Saul. He said:

1 I love you, O LORD, my strength.
2 The LORD is my rock and my fortress and my deliverer,
my God, my rock, in whom I take refuge,
my shield, and the horn of my salvation, my stronghold.
3 I call upon the LORD, who is worthy to be praised,
and I am saved from my enemies.

4 The cords of death encompassed me;
the torrents of destruction assailed me;[3]
5 the cords of Sheol entangled me;
the snares of death confronted me.

6 In my distress I called upon the LORD;
to my God I cried for help.
From his temple he heard my voice,
and my cry to him reached his ears.

7 Then the earth reeled and rocked;
the foundations also of the mountains trembled
and quaked, because he was angry.
8 Smoke went up from his nostrils,[4]
and devouring fire from his mouth;
glowing coals flamed forth from him.
9 He bowed the heavens and came down;
thick darkness was under his feet.
10 He rode on a cherub and flew;
he came swiftly on the wings of the wind.
11 He made darkness his covering, his canopy around him,
thick clouds dark with water.
12 Out of the brightness before him
hailstones and coals of fire broke through his clouds.

13 The LORD also thundered in the heavens,
and the Most High uttered his voice,
hailstones and coals of fire.
14 And he sent out his arrows and scattered them;
he flashed forth lightnings and routed them.

[1]Or *from men whose portion in life is of the world* [2]Or *As for your treasured ones, you fill their womb*
[3]Or *terrified me* [4]Or *in his wrath*

(Today's Life and the Afterlife, continued)

pleasures in God's presence. This initial aspect of David's view offers a practical counter to today's propensity to think too much about the promise of heaven and not enough about the reality of God's transformative presence. Thus David's psalm, in part, encourages God's people to become well acquainted with the goodness of God now, not later!

It was not until Peter's speech at Pentecost, in Acts 2, that people were encouraged to see the wider application of this psalm — the hope of the resurrection. While on the surface of things it seems as though David primarily pointed out the immediate benefits of knowing God, Peter explained that David *also* envisaged the coming Messiah. After quoting Psalm 16:8–11 in Acts 2:25–28, Peter declared, "he [David] foresaw and spoke about the resurrection of the Christ, that he was not abandoned to Hades [the realm of the dead], nor did his flesh see corruption. This Jesus God raised up" (Ac 2:31–32). This psalm celebrates the life-changing nature of God's current presence as well as the future hope of eternal life because of the resurrection of Jesus.

PSALM 17:1–15

SAFE IN THE MIDST OF SLANDER

Desperate for vindication, David cried out to God in this prayer. The repeated references to "lips" and "mouths" suggest David was suffering because of the words of his enemies, possibly through false accusations. Regardless of the exact situation, this psalm presents a particular mindset to employ when facing unfair circumstances, especially

(continued on next page)

(Safe in the Midst of Slander, continued)

when the nature of the challenge is slander or misrepresentation. It's amazing how other people's words can cut to the very heart of a person, leaving them feeling maligned, misunderstood, and destroyed. Yet David—one who knew the infuriating unfairness of slander—chose to focus on more than just vindication. This "something more" had to do with seeing God's face (v. 15); it had to do with his love (v. 7); and it had to do with perspective. God already knows the truth about his people, the truth about the times when they have been wronged and chosen the high road, the truth that their enemies' claims were false. The relief of looking into God's eyes and seeing that *he already knows* will be more satisfying than a certified retraction from an accuser published for all to see. It is God's opinion that counts. It is God's love that matters. It is God's face that makes everyone else's pale in comparison. This is the perspective David brought to bear to be freed from falsehood and lies.

15 Then the channels of the sea were seen,
and the foundations of the world were laid bare
at your rebuke, O LORD,
at the blast of the breath of your nostrils.

16 He sent from on high, he took me;
he drew me out of many waters.
17 He rescued me from my strong enemy
and from those who hated me,
for they were too mighty for me.
18 They confronted me in the day of my calamity,
but the LORD was my support.
19 He brought me out into a broad place;
he rescued me, because he delighted in me.

20 The LORD dealt with me according to my righteousness;
according to the cleanness of my hands he rewarded me.
21 For I have kept the ways of the LORD,
and have not wickedly departed from my God.
22 For all his rules[1] were before me,
and his statutes I did not put away from me.
23 I was blameless before him,
and I kept myself from my guilt.
24 So the LORD has rewarded me according to my righteousness,
according to the cleanness of my hands in his sight.

25 With the merciful you show yourself merciful;
with the blameless man you show yourself blameless;
26 with the purified you show yourself pure;
and with the crooked you make yourself seem tortuous.
27 For you save a humble people,
but the haughty eyes you bring down.
28 For it is you who light my lamp;
the LORD my God lightens my darkness.
29 For by you I can run against a troop,
and by my God I can leap over a wall.
30 This God—his way is perfect;[2]
the word of the LORD proves true;
he is a shield for all those who take refuge in him.

31 For who is God, but the LORD?
And who is a rock, except our God?—
32 the God who equipped me with strength
and made my way blameless.
33 He made my feet like the feet of a deer
and set me secure on the heights.
34 He trains my hands for war,
so that my arms can bend a bow of bronze.
35 You have given me the shield of your salvation,
and your right hand supported me,
and your gentleness made me great.
36 You gave a wide place for my steps under me,
and my feet did not slip.
37 I pursued my enemies and overtook them,
and did not turn back till they were consumed.
38 I thrust them through, so that they were not able to rise;
they fell under my feet.

[1]Or *just decrees* [2]Or *blameless*

39 For you equipped me with strength for the battle;
you made those who rise against me sink under me.
40 You made my enemies turn their backs to me,[1]
and those who hated me I destroyed.
41 They cried for help, but there was none to save;
they cried to the LORD, but he did not answer
them.
42 I beat them fine as dust before the wind;
I cast them out like the mire of the streets.

43 You delivered me from strife with the people;
you made me the head of the nations;
people whom I had not known served me.
44 As soon as they heard of me they obeyed me;
foreigners came cringing to me.
45 Foreigners lost heart
and came trembling out of their fortresses.

46 The LORD lives, and blessed be my rock,
and exalted be the God of my salvation—
47 the God who gave me vengeance
and subdued peoples under me,
48 who rescued me from my enemies;
yes, you exalted me above those who rose against me;
you delivered me from the man of violence.

49 For this I will praise you, O LORD, among the nations,
and sing to your name.
50 Great salvation he brings to his king,
and shows steadfast love to his anointed,
to David and his offspring forever.

Psalm 19

The Law of the LORD Is Perfect

To the choirmaster. A Psalm of David.

1 The heavens declare the glory of God,
and the sky above[2] proclaims his handiwork.
2 Day to day pours out speech,
and night to night reveals knowledge.
3 There is no speech, nor are there words,
whose voice is not heard.
4 Their voice[3] goes out through all the earth,
and their words to the end of the world.
In them he has set a tent for the sun,
5 which comes out like a bridegroom leaving his
chamber,
and, like a strong man, runs its course with joy.
6 Its rising is from the end of the heavens,
and its circuit to the end of them,
and there is nothing hidden from its heat.

7 The law of the LORD is perfect,[4]
reviving the soul;

PSALM 18:43

THE HEAD OF THE NATIONS

Much of the text of this psalm is also found in 2 Samuel 22, as David recounted how the Lord delivered him from Saul and many other enemies so that he could reign as king and, in turn, sing praises to God (Ps 18:49). David even went so far as to say that God had made him "the head of the nations" (v. 43). There is a prophetic expectation in this psalm of the coming Messiah and King, an expectation that Paul highlighted in Romans 15. Paul alluded to the backdrop of Psalm 18 and even quoted directly from verse 49: "Therefore I will praise you among the Gentiles, and sing to your name" (Ro 15:9). In reminding his audience of David's song, of David's deliverance from his enemies so that he could reign for the purpose of making known the glory of God to the nations, Paul effectively set up the argument that Jesus is the fulfillment of the "promises given to the patriarchs" (Ro 15:8), that he is the Messiah, that he will include the Gentiles so that they can "glorify God for his mercy" (Ro 15:9) and that he is, ultimately, the "head of the nations."

[1]Or *You gave me my enemies' necks* [2]Hebrew *the expanse*; compare Genesis 1:6–8 [3]Or *Their measuring line* [4]Or *blameless*

PSALM 20:1–9

WELL-PLACED TRUST

Horse-drawn chariots were one of the primary weapons of warfare in the ancient Near East. Yet David knew that the determining factor of victory was not military might, but rather the name of God (Ps 20:7). Having God on his side meant that the Israelites could "set up [their] banners," signifying triumph over their enemies (v. 5). This is the kind of confidence David had in God's commitment to save "his anointed" (v. 6). Similarly, Jesus trusted in his Father to bring victory over sin and death by giving "his life as a ransom for many" (Mt 20:28). Consider Jesus' admonishment of the disciples as they drew their swords to prevent his arrest: "Do you think that I cannot appeal to my Father, and he will at once send me more than twelve legions of angels?" (Mt 26:53). Jesus showed perfect confidence in his Father's power when he forewarned his disciples of his death while encouraging them that "he will be raised on the third day" (Mt 20:19). Scripture teaches that God is able and willing to save (Zep 3:17). It is the reason why so much of his Word reminds his people that they need not fear, for the battle belongs to the Lord (Dt 31:6; Isa 41:10; Ro 8:15; Heb 13:5–6).

the testimony of the LORD is sure,
making wise the simple;
8 the precepts of the LORD are right,
rejoicing the heart;
the commandment of the LORD is pure,
enlightening the eyes;
9 the fear of the LORD is clean,
enduring forever;
the rules[1] of the LORD are true,
and righteous altogether.
10 More to be desired are they than gold,
even much fine gold;
sweeter also than honey
and drippings of the honeycomb.
11 Moreover, by them is your servant warned;
in keeping them there is great reward.

12 Who can discern his errors?
Declare me innocent from hidden faults.
13 Keep back your servant also from presumptuous sins;
let them not have dominion over me!
Then I shall be blameless,
and innocent of great transgression.

14 Let the words of my mouth and the meditation of my heart
be acceptable in your sight,
O LORD, my rock and my redeemer.

Psalm 20

Trust in the Name of the LORD Our God

To the choirmaster. A Psalm of David.

1 May the LORD answer you in the day of trouble!
May the name of the God of Jacob protect you!
2 May he send you help from the sanctuary
and give you support from Zion!
3 May he remember all your offerings
and regard with favor your burnt sacrifices! *Selah*

4 May he grant you your heart's desire
and fulfill all your plans!
5 May we shout for joy over your salvation,
and in the name of our God set up our banners!
May the LORD fulfill all your petitions!

6 Now I know that the LORD saves his anointed;
he will answer him from his holy heaven
with the saving might of his right hand.
7 Some trust in chariots and some in horses,
but we trust in the name of the LORD our God.
8 They collapse and fall,
but we rise and stand upright.

9 O LORD, save the king!
May he answer us when we call.

[1]Or *just decrees*

Psalm 21

The King Rejoices in the Lord's Strength

To the choirmaster. A Psalm of David.

1 O Lord, in your strength the king rejoices,
and in your salvation how greatly he exults!
2 You have given him his heart's desire
and have not withheld the request of his lips. *Selah*
3 For you meet him with rich blessings;
you set a crown of fine gold upon his head.
4 He asked life of you; you gave it to him,
length of days forever and ever.
5 His glory is great through your salvation;
splendor and majesty you bestow on him.
6 For you make him most blessed forever;[1]
you make him glad with the joy of your presence.
7 For the king trusts in the Lord,
and through the steadfast love of the Most High he shall not be moved.

8 Your hand will find out all your enemies;
your right hand will find out those who hate you.
9 You will make them as a blazing oven
when you appear.
The Lord will swallow them up in his wrath,
and fire will consume them.
10 You will destroy their descendants from the earth,
and their offspring from among the children of man.
11 Though they plan evil against you,
though they devise mischief, they will not succeed.
12 For you will put them to flight;
you will aim at their faces with your bows.

13 Be exalted, O Lord, in your strength!
We will sing and praise your power.

Psalm 22

Why Have You Forsaken Me?

To the choirmaster: according to The Doe of the Dawn.
A Psalm of David.

1 My God, my God, why have you forsaken me?
Why are you so far from saving me, from the words of my groaning?
2 O my God, I cry by day, but you do not answer,
and by night, but I find no rest.

3 Yet you are holy,
enthroned on the praises[2] of Israel.
4 In you our fathers trusted;
they trusted, and you delivered them.
5 To you they cried and were rescued;
in you they trusted and were not put to shame.

6 But I am a worm and not a man,
scorned by mankind and despised by the people.
7 All who see me mock me;
they make mouths at me; they wag their heads;

PSALM 21:1–7

GOD BLESS THE KING

Psalm 21 is a royal psalm, meaning that it focuses on the king and his reign. While the subject matter may feel a bit foreign to today's readers, it is yet a crucial concept within the Christian faith. God's people were ruled by a king during Israel's monarchical period, and the king was responsible for bringing God's will to pass. The king held the highest calling of bringing justice and righteousness to bear in a way that blessed his people and the surrounding nations. Looking forward to Christ's coming reign then, God's people can relate to the expression of eager anticipation found in verse 6—anticipation that the king will be "blessed forever." Indeed, the deepest longing of humanity is for the perfect leader, the discerning judge, the ultimate provider, the champion of peace, and the king of love. Thus, the church today likewise must pray for Christ to come as King over all. After all, "He [God] put all things under his [Jesus] feet and gave him as head over all things to the church, which is his body, the fullness of him who fills all in all" (Eph 1:22–23).

[1]Or *make him a source of blessing forever* [2]Or *dwelling in the praises*

FORSAKEN BY GOD?

Historically, Psalm 22 is attributed to David and is an individual lament of his suffering. He described the utmost feelings of forsakenness and despair yet chose to proclaim God's faithfulness and to believe that deliverance was forthcoming. In its immediate context, this psalm brings perspective to life, particularly to the dark nights of the soul. It reflects the common human experience of suffering and crying out to God, only to be met with God's apparent silence. Reflecting on the stories of God's faithfulness in the past, however, gives God's people reason to believe that he will speak again, he will come through, and he will again rescue his children. In these moments, God's children may cry out in pain while fully expecting to be vindicated. They can choose to worship in the midst of waiting.

The New Testament Gospel writers make use of Psalm 22 in another manner. Alluding to and quoting directly from this psalm, the writers focused on the Messianic concept of the innocent sufferer, one who experiences affliction and scorn only to be vindicated for the purposes of atonement and praise. This expectation of redemption must have couched the cries of Jesus in the context of hope as the first-century audience recalled the psalmist's triumphant conclusion. After the resurrection, it became clear that Jesus' cry of despair had not been the end.

What did Jesus experience in his anguished moments? While the precise details remain unknown, Scripture speaks about Jesus' suffering, crucifixion, and death as something that brought him deep sorrow that he hoped to avoid if at all possible (Mt 26:38 – 39). No one, not even the Savior himself, wants to endure the dark nights of the soul, much less be tortured to death. Furthermore, Christ became "a curse for us" (Gal 3:13) and "bore our sins in his body on the tree" (1Pe 2:24). This type of suffering is interpreted by many evangelical theologians to mean that Jesus endured the very wrath of God to its end, and with it his terrible hatred for sin. Such relational trauma, physical pain, and spiritual torment is beyond our imagination and experience, yet Jesus managed to choose to endure all this for the "joy that was set before him" (Heb 12:2). This is why Christ quoted Psalm 22 (Mt 27:46; Mk 15:34), because he knew that God *would* deliver him from death, just as David believed and as Isaiah prophesied: "Out of the anguish of his soul he shall see and be satisfied" (Isa 53:11). Forsaken for a moment, yes, but only for a short time and for the greater good that God had promised.

8 "He trusts in the LORD; let him deliver him;
let him rescue him, for he delights in him!"

9 Yet you are he who took me from the womb;
you made me trust you at my mother's breasts.
10 On you was I cast from my birth,
and from my mother's womb you have been my God.
11 Be not far from me,
for trouble is near,
and there is none to help.

12 Many bulls encompass me;
strong bulls of Bashan surround me;
13 they open wide their mouths at me,
like a ravening and roaring lion.

14 I am poured out like water,
and all my bones are out of joint;
my heart is like wax;
it is melted within my breast;
15 my strength is dried up like a potsherd,
and my tongue sticks to my jaws;
you lay me in the dust of death.

16 For dogs encompass me;
a company of evildoers encircles me;
they have pierced my hands and feet[1]—
17 I can count all my bones—
they stare and gloat over me;
18 they divide my garments among them,
and for my clothing they cast lots.

19 But you, O LORD, do not be far off!
O you my help, come quickly to my aid!
20 Deliver my soul from the sword,
my precious life from the power of the dog!
21 Save me from the mouth of the lion!
You have rescued[2] me from the horns of the wild oxen!

22 I will tell of your name to my brothers;
in the midst of the congregation I will praise you:
23 You who fear the LORD, praise him!
All you offspring of Jacob, glorify him,
and stand in awe of him, all you offspring of Israel!
24 For he has not despised or abhorred
the affliction of the afflicted,
and he has not hidden his face from him,
but has heard, when he cried to him.

25 From you comes my praise in the great congregation;
my vows I will perform before those who fear him.
26 The afflicted[3] shall eat and be satisfied;
those who seek him shall praise the LORD!
May your hearts live forever!

27 All the ends of the earth shall remember
and turn to the LORD,
and all the families of the nations
shall worship before you.

---

[1]Some Hebrew manuscripts, Septuagint, Vulgate, Syriac; most Hebrew manuscripts *like a lion* [they are at] *my hands and feet* [2]Hebrew *answered* [3]Or *The meek*

28 For kingship belongs to the LORD,
and he rules over the nations.

29 All the prosperous of the earth eat and worship;
before him shall bow all who go down to the dust,
even the one who could not keep himself alive.
30 Posterity shall serve him;
it shall be told of the Lord to the coming generation;
31 they shall come and proclaim his righteousness to a people yet unborn,
that he has done it.

PSALM 24:1–10

GATES OF ZION

While the exact event is not specified, some scholars theorize that a procession involving the ark of the covenant was the occasion for writing Psalm 24. The superscription indicates that it was composed by David, and it may have been written when he first brought the ark into Jerusalem (2Sa 6). It's easy to imagine the ark being carried high as David called out to the people gathered near one of Jerusalem's gates. The very presence of God had come to Israel's capital city, and the people responded with an energetic chorus of praises about his glory. Regardless of the exact circumstance, this psalm clearly celebrated God's presence and might!

The New Testament carries on the themes of Psalm 24 as it describes Jesus as the "King of kings and Lord of lords" (Rev 19:16) who will return to rule his kingdom (Ac 1:11). Jesus will come "on the clouds of heaven with power and great glory" (Mt 24:30) and will gather his people to himself. Christians look forward to his coming: "For the Lord himself will descend from heaven with a cry of command, with the voice of an archangel, and with the sound of the trumpet of God. And the dead in Christ will rise first. Then we who are alive, who are left, will be caught up together with them in the clouds to meet the Lord in the air, and so we will always be with the Lord" (1Th 4:16–17).

Psalm 23

The LORD Is My Shepherd

A Psalm of David.

1 The LORD is my shepherd; I shall not want.
2 He makes me lie down in green pastures.
He leads me beside still waters.[1]
3 He restores my soul.
He leads me in paths of righteousness[2]
for his name's sake.

4 Even though I walk through the valley of the shadow of death,[3]
I will fear no evil,
for you are with me;
your rod and your staff,
they comfort me.

5 You prepare a table before me
in the presence of my enemies;
you anoint my head with oil;
my cup overflows.
6 Surely[4] goodness and mercy[5] shall follow me
all the days of my life,
and I shall dwell[6] in the house of the LORD
forever.[7]

Psalm 24

The King of Glory

A Psalm of David.

1 The earth is the LORD's and the fullness thereof,[8]
the world and those who dwell therein,
2 for he has founded it upon the seas
and established it upon the rivers.

3 Who shall ascend the hill of the LORD?
And who shall stand in his holy place?
4 He who has clean hands and a pure heart,
who does not lift up his soul to what is false
and does not swear deceitfully.
5 He will receive blessing from the LORD
and righteousness from the God of his salvation.
6 Such is the generation of those who seek him,
who seek the face of the God of Jacob.[9] *Selah*

[1]Hebrew *beside waters of rest* [2]Or *in right paths* [3]Or *the valley of deep darkness* [4]Or *Only* [5]Or *steadfast love* [6]Or *shall return to dwell* [7]Hebrew *for length of days* [8]Or *and all that fills it* [9]Septuagint, Syriac, and two Hebrew manuscripts; Masoretic Text *who seek your face, Jacob*

OUR SHEPHERD

Psalm 23 describes God as a caring shepherd. Yet the job of "shepherd" is relatively unknown to the average person today. What exactly does a shepherd do? Why is God depicted as such? A cursory study of shepherds and sheep seems necessary to unpack the riches of the imagery in Psalm 23 as well as the psalm's relevance to the New Testament's depiction of Christ as the "good shepherd" (Jn 10:1 – 18).

One of the primary responsibilities of a shepherd is guarding his flock. Thieves, wild animals, and the wandering inclinations of the sheep themselves mean that a shepherd must actively work to keep his sheep safe from harm (1Sa 17:34 – 35). Every night, a shepherd counts his sheep to ensure none have strayed or been stolen (Jer 33:13). If any of the sheep are missing, he goes out to look for them, discontent to lose any of those under his care (Eze 34:11). Not only does the shepherd tend to their wounds when they have been attacked, but he will also "bind up the injured, and . . . strengthen the weak" even when their injuries or weaknesses are of their own doing (Eze 34:16).

A shepherd also meets his flock's basic needs for food and water by traveling far and wide to locate viable sources. What may appear to be a simple provision is, in actuality, a strenuous undertaking. Leading masses of sheep to food and water often involves trekking across difficult terrain and enduring harsh climates (Ge 31:40). Shepherding requires fortitude, endurance, and skill.

God is depicted in Scripture as the kind of shepherd who does more than provide food, shelter, and safety; he even goes so far as to *bless* his flock. The entire thirty-fourth chapter of Ezekiel describes God as a good shepherd who will "send down the showers in their season; they shall be showers of blessing" (Eze 34:26). Truly the "cup overflows" for those who are shepherded by God himself (Ps 23:5).

Likewise, Jesus refers to himself as the "good shepherd" who "lays down his life for the sheep" (Jn 10:11). He is the Messianic shepherd hoped for by God's people, foreshadowed by the psalmist David, and foretold by the prophets. Jesus is the Good Shepherd worth listening to and worth following (Jn 10:3 – 5), the Good Shepherd who knows the name of every sheep and who died to give them life "abundantly" (vv. 10 – 11).

7 Lift up your heads, O gates!
And be lifted up, O ancient doors,
that the King of glory may come in.
8 Who is this King of glory?
The LORD, strong and mighty,
the LORD, mighty in battle!
9 Lift up your heads, O gates!
And lift them up, O ancient doors,
that the King of glory may come in.
10 Who is this King of glory?
The LORD of hosts,
he is the King of glory! *Selah*

PSALM 25:1–3

UNASHAMED

Honor and shame were of the utmost consequence in ancient Near Eastern culture. It is no surprise then that David felt strongly about avoiding shame (vv. 1–3,20). What is unexpected, however, particularly in a cultural context that bilaterally contrasts honor with shame, is David's choice to bring trust into the equation. Psalm 25 thus highlights the truth that putting one's hopes and trust in God is the only effective deterrent to shame. After all, God promises to guide "the humble in what is right" (v. 9), and a righteous life, trusting in the Lord, is worthy of honor. Trusting God, quite simply, brings honor and spurns shame.

Jesus expanded on this idea when he warned his disciples of his imminent death and of Peter's denial. In light of this, Jesus urged them to trust in him: "Let not your hearts be troubled. Believe in God; believe also in me" (Jn 14:1). He even went so far as to say, "whoever is ashamed of me and of my words, of him will the Son of Man be ashamed when he comes in his glory and the glory of the Father and of the holy angels" (Lk 9:26). Jesus unequivocally calls his followers to trust in him and, in doing so, they will be unashamed and bring honor to God.

Psalm 25[1]

Teach Me Your Paths

Of David.

1 To you, O LORD, I lift up my soul.
2 O my God, in you I trust;
let me not be put to shame;
let not my enemies exult over me.
3 Indeed, none who wait for you shall be put to shame;
they shall be ashamed who are wantonly treacherous.

4 Make me to know your ways, O LORD;
teach me your paths.
5 Lead me in your truth and teach me,
for you are the God of my salvation;
for you I wait all the day long.

6 Remember your mercy, O LORD, and your steadfast love,
for they have been from of old.
7 Remember not the sins of my youth or my transgressions;
according to your steadfast love remember me,
for the sake of your goodness, O LORD!

8 Good and upright is the LORD;
therefore he instructs sinners in the way.
9 He leads the humble in what is right,
and teaches the humble his way.
10 All the paths of the LORD are steadfast love and faithfulness,
for those who keep his covenant and his testimonies.

11 For your name's sake, O LORD,
pardon my guilt, for it is great.
12 Who is the man who fears the LORD?
Him will he instruct in the way that he should choose.
13 His soul shall abide in well-being,
and his offspring shall inherit the land.
14 The friendship[2] of the LORD is for those who fear him,
and he makes known to them his covenant.
15 My eyes are ever toward the LORD,
for he will pluck my feet out of the net.

16 Turn to me and be gracious to me,
for I am lonely and afflicted.

[1]This psalm is an acrostic poem, each verse beginning with the successive letters of the Hebrew alphabet
[2]Or *The secret counsel*

WHO IS THIS KING OF GLORY?

Psalm 24 is a song about the glory of God. But what exactly *is* God's glory? David asked the question, "Who is this King of glory?" and answered with a resounding declaration about God's strength and might. Psalm 96 likewise describes strength as an aspect of God's glory; however, the list goes on to include his "marvelous works" (96:3), his "majesty" (96:6), his "holiness" (96:9), his "righteousness," and his "faithfulness" (96:13). When Moses asked to see God's glory, God said that that he would allow his "goodness" to pass before him (Ex 33:18–19). The point is that just a sampling of the texts about God's glory confirms that it is the sum of every amazing attribute God possesses and every perfect action he does. All of these things comprise its weight, its essence, its brightness and light!

God's glory is further revealed to the world in the person of Christ. He claimed to possess this glory when he prayed, "Father, glorify me in your own presence with the glory that I had with you before the world existed" (Jn 17:5). John likewise attested to Christ's glory when he wrote, "The Word became flesh and dwelt among us, and we have seen his glory, glory as of the only Son from the Father, full of grace and truth" (Jn 1:14). Matthew describes Jesus' glory in his account of the transfiguration, saying, "[Jesus'] face shone like the sun, and his clothes became white as light" (Mt 17:2). And Peter wrote, "We were eyewitnesses of his majesty. For when he received honor and glory form God the Father, and the voice was borne to him by the Majestic Glory, 'This is my beloved Son, with whom I am well pleased,' we ourselves heard this very voice borne from heaven, for we were with him on the holy mountain" (2Pe 1:16–18).

In summary, Jesus is "the Lord of glory" (1Co 2:8). And, since he is continually being revealed to the church through Scripture and by the Holy Spirit, Christians have the unbelievable privilege of seeing the very glory of God through "the face of Jesus Christ" (2Co 4:6). Furthermore, God's people were made to reflect his glory to the world as they grow in their relationship with Christ. There should be a certain radiance about the people who claim to know him, for, as Paul says, they "are being transformed into the same image from one degree of glory to another. For this comes from the Lord who is the Spirit" (2Co 3:18).

PSALM 26:1

VINDICATION

David used the word "vindicate" to ask God for a declaration of righteousness. Claiming to have "walked in my integrity" and to have "trusted in the LORD," David requested that God bring justice and deliverance. Interestingly, the remainder of the psalm reveals that this declaration of vindication is not meant for David's own psychological satisfaction, but rather as a qualification for praising God with integrity. David said, "I wash my hands in innocence and go around your altar, O LORD, proclaiming thanksgiving aloud, and telling all your wondrous deeds" (vv. 6–7). What greater testimony to the character of God than the righteousness of those who have been transformed by him? Their righteousness comes by reflecting on his "steadfast love" and walking "in your faithfulness" (v. 3). It comes by trusting in the Lord (v. 1) and by avoiding evil (vv. 4–5). Through faith, a life of righteousness is possible, and it is meant to legitimate one's testimony about and praises to God through the person of Jesus Christ!

PSALM 27:1

FEAR NO MORE

Fear has no place in the heart of God's children. Even if "evildoers assail me" or an "army encamp[s] against me" or "war arise[s] against me," the people of God can remain confident and unafraid (vv. 2–3). While this mentality is much easier said than done, it is possible. David outlined the way forward in the face of such fearsome trials: "Wait for the LORD; be strong, and let your heart

(continued on next page)

17 The troubles of my heart are enlarged;
bring me out of my distresses.
18 Consider my affliction and my trouble,
and forgive all my sins.

19 Consider how many are my foes,
and with what violent hatred they hate me.
20 Oh, guard my soul, and deliver me!
Let me not be put to shame, for I take refuge
in you.
21 May integrity and uprightness preserve me,
for I wait for you.

22 Redeem Israel, O God,
out of all his troubles.

Psalm 26

I Will Bless the LORD

Of David.

1 Vindicate me, O LORD,
for I have walked in my integrity,
and I have trusted in the LORD without wavering.
2 Prove me, O LORD, and try me;
test my heart and my mind.[1]
3 For your steadfast love is before my eyes,
and I walk in your faithfulness.

4 I do not sit with men of falsehood,
nor do I consort with hypocrites.
5 I hate the assembly of evildoers,
and I will not sit with the wicked.

6 I wash my hands in innocence
and go around your altar, O LORD,
7 proclaiming thanksgiving aloud,
and telling all your wondrous deeds.

8 O LORD, I love the habitation of your house
and the place where your glory dwells.
9 Do not sweep my soul away with sinners,
nor my life with bloodthirsty men,
10 in whose hands are evil devices,
and whose right hands are full of bribes.

11 But as for me, I shall walk in my integrity;
redeem me, and be gracious to me.
12 My foot stands on level ground;
in the great assembly I will bless the LORD.

Psalm 27

The LORD Is My Light and My Salvation

Of David.

1 The LORD is my light and my salvation;
whom shall I fear?

[1]Hebrew *test my kidneys and my heart*

The LORD is the stronghold[1] of my life;
of whom shall I be afraid?

2 When evildoers assail me
to eat up my flesh,
my adversaries and foes,
it is they who stumble and fall.

3 Though an army encamp against me,
my heart shall not fear;
though war arise against me,
yet[2] I will be confident.

4 One thing have I asked of the LORD,
that will I seek after:
that I may dwell in the house of the LORD
all the days of my life,
to gaze upon the beauty of the LORD
and to inquire[3] in his temple.

5 For he will hide me in his shelter
in the day of trouble;
he will conceal me under the cover of his tent;
he will lift me high upon a rock.

6 And now my head shall be lifted up
above my enemies all around me,
and I will offer in his tent
sacrifices with shouts of joy;
I will sing and make melody to the LORD.

7 Hear, O LORD, when I cry aloud;
be gracious to me and answer me!
8 You have said, "Seek[4] my face."
My heart says to you,
"Your face, LORD, do I seek."[5]
9 Hide not your face from me.
Turn not your servant away in anger,
O you who have been my help.
Cast me not off; forsake me not,
O God of my salvation!
10 For my father and my mother have forsaken me,
but the LORD will take me in.

11 Teach me your way, O LORD,
and lead me on a level path
because of my enemies.
12 Give me not up to the will of my adversaries;
for false witnesses have risen against me,
and they breathe out violence.

13 I believe that I shall look[6] upon the goodness of
the LORD
in the land of the living!
14 Wait for the LORD;
be strong, and let your heart take courage;
wait for the LORD!

[1]Or *refuge* [2]Or *in this* [3]Or *meditate* [4]The command (*seek*) is addressed to more than one person
[5]The meaning of the Hebrew verse is uncertain [6]Other Hebrew manuscripts *Oh! Had I not believed that I would look*

(Fear No More, continued)

take courage; wait for the LORD!" (v. 14). Sometimes fighting for faith looks like waiting on God to come through, standing in the strength he has provided for that moment. Jesus offered this reasoning for fighting fear when he said, "And do not fear those who kill the body but cannot kill the soul. Rather fear him who can destroy both soul and body in hell. Are not two sparrows sold for a penny? And not one of them will fall to the ground apart from your Father. But even the hairs of your head are all numbered. Fear not, therefore; you are of more value than many sparrows" (Mt 10:28–31). Jesus promises his presence and with it his peace: "I have said these things to you, that in me you may have peace. In the world you will have tribulation. But take heart; I have overcome the world" (Jn 16:33).

PSALM 28:6–9

GOD HEARS

In his hour of need, the psalmist prayed to God for help because he believed that God listens and responds. The psalmist's hope was not disappointed. The psalmist thanked the Lord with praises in the remainder of his song. Jesus likewise expressed confidence in the truth that God hears when he raised Lazarus from the dead: "And Jesus lifted up his eyes and said, 'Father, I thank you that you have heard me. I knew that you always hear me, but I said this on account of the people standing around, that they may believe that you sent me.' When he had said these things, he cried out with a loud voice, 'Lazarus, come out.' The man who had died came out" (Jn 11:41–44). Notice that Jesus expressed thanks to God *before* God had even answered because he was so sure that his Father would hear and respond. Throughout the Bible, God urges his people to pray with confidence that he will listen and respond (Pr 15:29; Jer 29:12; Mk 11:24; 1Jn 5:14). Once they ask, he faithfully answers, and their appropriate response (like that of the psalmist and of Christ) should be thankful praise!

PSALM 29:1–11

THE GLORY DUE HIS NAME

Psalm 29 calls upon the "heavenly beings" (presumably angels) to acknowledge and attest to the awesomeness of God (vv. 1–2). This style was common among the Canaanites who envisioned heavenly beings as a council of gods worshiping Baal. It is likely that the

(continued on next page)

Psalm 28

The LORD Is My Strength and My Shield

Of David.

1 To you, O LORD, I call;
my rock, be not deaf to me,
lest, if you be silent to me,
I become like those who go down to the pit.
2 Hear the voice of my pleas for mercy,
when I cry to you for help,
when I lift up my hands
toward your most holy sanctuary.[1]

3 Do not drag me off with the wicked,
with the workers of evil,
who speak peace with their neighbors
while evil is in their hearts.
4 Give to them according to their work
and according to the evil of their deeds;
give to them according to the work of their hands;
render them their due reward.
5 Because they do not regard the works of the LORD
or the work of his hands,
he will tear them down and build them up no more.

6 Blessed be the LORD!
For he has heard the voice of my pleas for mercy.
7 The LORD is my strength and my shield;
in him my heart trusts, and I am helped;
my heart exults,
and with my song I give thanks to him.

8 The LORD is the strength of his people;[2]
he is the saving refuge of his anointed.
9 Oh, save your people and bless your heritage!
Be their shepherd and carry them forever.

Psalm 29

Ascribe to the LORD Glory

A Psalm of David.

1 Ascribe to the LORD, O heavenly beings,[3]
ascribe to the LORD glory and strength.
2 Ascribe to the LORD the glory due his name;
worship the LORD in the splendor of holiness.[4]

3 The voice of the LORD is over the waters;
the God of glory thunders,
the LORD, over many waters.
4 The voice of the LORD is powerful;
the voice of the LORD is full of majesty.

5 The voice of the LORD breaks the cedars;
the LORD breaks the cedars of Lebanon.
6 He makes Lebanon to skip like a calf,
and Sirion like a young wild ox.

[1] Hebrew *your innermost sanctuary* [2] Some Hebrew manuscripts, Septuagint, Syriac; most Hebrew manuscripts *is their strength* [3] Hebrew *sons of God*, or *sons of might* [4] Or *in holy attire*

7 The voice of the LORD flashes forth flames of fire.
8 The voice of the LORD shakes the wilderness;
the LORD shakes the wilderness of Kadesh.

9 The voice of the LORD makes the deer give birth[1]
and strips the forests bare,
and in his temple all cry, "Glory!"

10 The LORD sits enthroned over the flood;
the LORD sits enthroned as king forever.
11 May the LORD give strength to his people!
May the LORD bless[2] his people with peace!

Psalm 30

Joy Comes with the Morning

A Psalm of David. A song at the dedication of the temple.

1 I will extol you, O LORD, for you have drawn me up
and have not let my foes rejoice over me.
2 O LORD my God, I cried to you for help,
and you have healed me.
3 O LORD, you have brought up my soul from Sheol;
you restored me to life from among those who go
down to the pit.[3]

4 Sing praises to the LORD, O you his saints,
and give thanks to his holy name.[4]
5 For his anger is but for a moment,
and his favor is for a lifetime.[5]
Weeping may tarry for the night,
but joy comes with the morning.

6 As for me, I said in my prosperity,
"I shall never be moved."
7 By your favor, O LORD,
you made my mountain stand strong;
you hid your face;
I was dismayed.

8 To you, O LORD, I cry,
and to the Lord I plead for mercy:
9 "What profit is there in my death,[6]
if I go down to the pit?[7]
Will the dust praise you?
Will it tell of your faithfulness?
10 Hear, O LORD, and be merciful to me!
O LORD, be my helper!"

11 You have turned for me my mourning into dancing;
you have loosed my sackcloth
and clothed me with gladness,
12 that my glory may sing your praise and not be silent.
O LORD my God, I will give thanks to you
forever!

(The Glory Due His Name, continued)

psalmist used this form in order to subvert the pagan concept and thus set the Lord apart from all other gods. The Lord, as the psalmist declared, is worthy of praise because of his power and majesty, and no other god is like him (v. 4). Ascribing glory to God involves reveling in his many attributes and actions, admiring them and agreeing with the truths about God. Here the psalmist focused on "the voice of the LORD" and used the refrain seven times to paint a complete picture of God's power (vv. 3–9). Furthermore, he proclaimed the unique omnipotence of the Lord who created the flood and who is King of the world (v. 10). This is the God who alone is able to give strength to his people and bless them with peace (v. 11), a God to whom the ascription of glory is surely due!

The New Testament paints a similar picture of Jesus commanding angels and receiving honor and glory and power (Mt 24:31; Rev 5:13). Jesus is the one to whom the final glory is given as he is seated at God's "right hand in the heavenly places, far above all rule and authority and power and dominion" (Eph 1:20–21). It is to Jesus that the church now cries, "Glory!"

[1]Revocalization yields *makes the oaks to shake* [2]Or *The LORD will give . . . The LORD will bless* [3]Or *to life, that I should not go down to the pit* [4]Hebrew *to the memorial of his holiness* (see Exodus 3:15) [5]Or *and in his favor is life* [6]Hebrew *in my blood* [7]Or *to corruption*

JOY IN THE STORM

When people encounter unexpected hardship or difficulty, they often respond with a familiar list of questions: Why is this happening? Who's responsible? What happens now? Though loved by the Father, believers are not exempted from terrible tragedies or the messy situations and consequences of living in a sin-contaminated world. Nor are they freed from the questions that naturally follow distressing events. However, those who know Christ as Savior need to redirect how they respond to their circumstances and move away from demanding answers or pointing fingers. They need to be intentional about seeking God's perspective and trusting him in times of adversity.

In Psalm 30, David's encounter with an undisclosed difficulty left him feeling as if he was in the depths and oppressed by his enemies. But instead of surrendering to the intense emotional pain, he deliberately chose to exalt the Lord (v. 1). That purposeful shift in focus helped David to experience God's presence with him in his circumstances and to rest in the surety of the Lord's control.

Jesus demonstrated this principle to his disciples in a tangible way as they struggled mightily through a fierce storm as their boat was battered by unrelenting wind and waves, and Jesus was asleep in the stern. As the storm raged and anxiety and fear seemed to be winning, the disciples woke Jesus. He calmed the wind and the waves and then asked the disciples, "Why are you so afraid? Have you still no faith?" (Mk 4:40). Instead of simply removing his followers from the raging gale, Christ was with the disciples in the midst of the storm, teaching the disciples a deeper truth than they were expecting: that he is Lord over all things. As his resurrection from the dead later proved, not even death could overpower him (1Co 15:55–57). Through his sacrifice and triumph over sin, he imparts to believers the certain hope of resurrection and eternal life.

Though this life may be filled with the pain of loss, the confusion of disappointment, and the sting of rejection, Christians can be assured that through faith in Jesus, God is always present in their current difficulties. They can faithfully trust in the certainty of their eternal destination, knowing that "weeping may tarry for the night, but joy comes with the morning" (Ps 30:5).

Psalm 31

Into Your Hand I Commit My Spirit

To the choirmaster. A Psalm of David.

1 In you, O LORD, do I take refuge;
let me never be put to shame;
in your righteousness deliver me!
2 Incline your ear to me;
rescue me speedily!
Be a rock of refuge for me,
a strong fortress to save me!

3 For you are my rock and my fortress;
and for your name's sake you lead me and guide me;
4 you take me out of the net they have hidden for me,
for you are my refuge.
5 Into your hand I commit my spirit;
you have redeemed me, O LORD, faithful God.

6 I hate[1] those who pay regard to worthless idols,
but I trust in the LORD.
7 I will rejoice and be glad in your steadfast love,
because you have seen my affliction;
you have known the distress of my soul,
8 and you have not delivered me into the hand of the enemy;
you have set my feet in a broad place.

9 Be gracious to me, O LORD, for I am in distress;
my eye is wasted from grief;
my soul and my body also.
10 For my life is spent with sorrow,
and my years with sighing;
my strength fails because of my iniquity,
and my bones waste away.

11 Because of all my adversaries I have become a reproach,
especially to my neighbors,
and an object of dread to my acquaintances;
those who see me in the street flee from me.
12 I have been forgotten like one who is dead;
I have become like a broken vessel.
13 For I hear the whispering of many—
terror on every side!—
as they scheme together against me,
as they plot to take my life.

14 But I trust in you, O LORD;
I say, "You are my God."
15 My times are in your hand;
rescue me from the hand of my enemies and from my
persecutors!
16 Make your face shine on your servant;
save me in your steadfast love!
17 O LORD, let me not be put to shame,
for I call upon you;
let the wicked be put to shame;
let them go silently to Sheol.

[1]Masoretic Text; one Hebrew manuscript, Septuagint, Syriac, Jerome *You hate*

INTO YOUR HAND

It is not hard to imagine that, in the first century, many Jewish families would practice giving thanks to God at the end of each day. The father might pray Psalm 31:5 with his family as the curtain of night closed over the household: "Into your hand I commit my spirit." These words spoken then are the same words that Jesus spoke as his death drew near on the cross. The knowledge that this was also a prayer that a Hebrew child might have offered up deepens the meaning of these words, subtly but dramatically. And with the addition of one word, Christ shifted his cry from simply an Old Testament quotation to a personal statement: "Father, into your hands I commit my spirit!" (Lk 23:46).

Only moments before, Christ had expressed his inability to feel the presence of the Almighty as the weight of the world's sin pressed down on him. "My God, my God, why have you forsaken me?" he exclaimed (Mt 27:46). Yet, in those final seconds as his physical agony likely reached its peak, Jesus called out to his Father with no formality. It was personal, a desperate plea that only a father would understand from his son. Though unimaginable pain racked his body, this intimate connection was the basis of his trust and gave him the ability to place his life in his Father's hands.

In this, Christ modeled the kind of relationship believers need to cultivate if they are to dispel the fear of the unknown and push back the frightening specter of death. It begins with faith in Jesus (Ro 10:9 – 10) and over time (through Scripture, prayer, worship, and other disciplines) can develop into a relationship that slowly alters a person's core being, providing a sure foundation that will give sustenance through the worst of life's storms.

But until Christ-followers understand the fundamental difference between truly knowing the Father and just obeying a set of religious rules, they will always sense something missing in their lives and struggle with anxiety about the future. Knowing the Lord in a deep, life-altering way is attainable for those who seek him (Jas 4:8).

18 Let the lying lips be mute,
which speak insolently against the righteous
in pride and contempt.

19 Oh, how abundant is your goodness,
which you have stored up for those who fear you
and worked for those who take refuge in you,
in the sight of the children of mankind!
20 In the cover of your presence you hide them
from the plots of men;
you store them in your shelter
from the strife of tongues.

21 Blessed be the LORD,
for he has wondrously shown his steadfast love to me
when I was in a besieged city.
22 I had said in my alarm,[1]
"I am cut off from your sight."
But you heard the voice of my pleas for mercy
when I cried to you for help.

23 Love the LORD, all you his saints!
The LORD preserves the faithful
but abundantly repays the one who acts in pride.
24 Be strong, and let your heart take courage,
all you who wait for the LORD!

Psalm 32

Blessed Are the Forgiven

A Maskil[2] of David.

1 Blessed is the one whose transgression is forgiven,
whose sin is covered.
2 Blessed is the man against whom the LORD counts no iniquity,
and in whose spirit there is no deceit.

3 For when I kept silent, my bones wasted away
through my groaning all day long.
4 For day and night your hand was heavy upon me;
my strength was dried up[3] as by the heat of summer. *Selah*

5 I acknowledged my sin to you,
and I did not cover my iniquity;
I said, "I will confess my transgressions to the LORD,"
and you forgave the iniquity of my sin. *Selah*

6 Therefore let everyone who is godly
offer prayer to you at a time when you may be found;
surely in the rush of great waters,
they shall not reach him.
7 You are a hiding place for me;
you preserve me from trouble;
you surround me with shouts of deliverance. *Selah*

8 I will instruct you and teach you in the way you should go;
I will counsel you with my eye upon you.
9 Be not like a horse or a mule, without understanding,
which must be curbed with bit and bridle,
or it will not stay near you.

[1]Or *in my haste* [2]Probably a musical or liturgical term [3]Hebrew *my vitality was changed*

PSALM 32:1–2

COVERED

Throughout Scripture, David is hailed as the greatest king in the history of Israel. After rescuing the army of Saul from the tyranny of Goliath and the Philistine army, this simple shepherd boy rocketed from obscurity to national celebrity in an instant (1Sa 17–18). Years later, after ascending to the throne, he drew unparalleled loyalty as the collective hopes and aspirations of the people rested on him (2Sa 5:1–5). Though David exhibited supreme devotion to the Lord and led the nation well, he monumentally failed as well. The sordid details of his adultery with Bathsheba, the elaborate but failed attempt to cover it up, and the premeditated murder of her husband Uriah were exposed when God sent Nathan the prophet to confront the king with his wrongdoing (2Sa 11–12). Realizing his transgression was fundamentally against God, David responded with mournful brokenness and genuine repentance (Ps 51). Some commentators believe that the forgiveness and restoration David received from the Lord (2Sa 12:13) prompted him to pen Psalm 32, which extols the magnitude of God's pardon and the resulting freedom received by the one "whose sins is covered" (Ps 32:1). Centuries later, Paul quoted verses 1 and 2 as he explained the total forgiveness and perfect righteousness believers receive from God as a result of Christ's sacrifice on the cross (Ro 4:6–8). The perfection he offers in exchange for sin is not deserved and cannot be earned by good works or right behavior but is imparted solely to God's followers by grace through faith (Eph 2:8).

THE GREATEST NEED

Poverty, disease, and oppression are just a few of the issues that plague the world's population. But none of those can supersede humanity's most basic need: the forgiveness of sin. When Adam and Eve disobeyed their Creator in the Garden of Eden, sin tainted the entire human race, and Adam's legacy of spiritual death was passed on to all of his descendants (Ro 5:12). Since then, all people have been born with a corrupted nature and cannot please God. Ephesians 2:1 describes this condition as being dead in "trespasses and sins." People are not just sick. A little help or a little more effort will not suffice. The undeniable fact is that without Christ, a person's spirit is dead, and no person can pass from death back to life alone. Because of God's compassion for the helpless state of the world, he sent Jesus Christ to pay the price for sin (Ro 4:25; 6:23 – 24). Second Corinthians 5:21 explains the purpose of Christ's death: "For our sake he made him to be sin who knew no sin, so that in him we might become the righteousness of God." He stood in the place of those who were dead in sin so that they could be made spiritually alive.

The apostle Paul helped Christians understand the radical change that takes place at the time of their salvation and grasp the enormity of their new standing with God by reminding them of verses from Psalm 32 (Ro 4:6 – 8). Through faith, sin is removed and righteousness is credited to all those "who believe in him who raised from the dead Jesus our Lord" (Ro 4:23 – 25). Simply put, that means Jesus received the just punishment for the sins of humanity, and as a result, those who believe in him receive the righteousness of Christ and are reconciled to God.

This great exchange is offered to all people through God's grace and mercy and is received through faith (Eph 2:8 – 9). Once a person acknowledges his or her desperate need for a savior (Ro 10:9 – 10), God delights in forgiving that person's guilt (Ps 32:5) and in so doing, meeting humanity's greatest need through the person of Jesus Christ.

10 Many are the sorrows of the wicked,
but steadfast love surrounds the one who trusts
in the LORD.
11 Be glad in the LORD, and rejoice, O righteous,
and shout for joy, all you upright in heart!

Psalm 33

The Steadfast Love of the LORD

1 Shout for joy in the LORD, O you righteous!
Praise befits the upright.
2 Give thanks to the LORD with the lyre;
make melody to him with the harp of ten strings!
3 Sing to him a new song;
play skillfully on the strings, with loud shouts.

4 For the word of the LORD is upright,
and all his work is done in faithfulness.
5 He loves righteousness and justice;
the earth is full of the steadfast love of the LORD.

6 By the word of the LORD the heavens were made,
and by the breath of his mouth all their host.
7 He gathers the waters of the sea as a heap;
he puts the deeps in storehouses.

8 Let all the earth fear the LORD;
let all the inhabitants of the world stand in awe of him!
9 For he spoke, and it came to be;
he commanded, and it stood firm.

10 The LORD brings the counsel of the nations to nothing;
he frustrates the plans of the peoples.
11 The counsel of the LORD stands forever,
the plans of his heart to all generations.
12 Blessed is the nation whose God is the LORD,
the people whom he has chosen as his heritage!

13 The LORD looks down from heaven;
he sees all the children of man;
14 from where he sits enthroned he looks out
on all the inhabitants of the earth,
15 he who fashions the hearts of them all
and observes all their deeds.
16 The king is not saved by his great army;
a warrior is not delivered by his great strength.
17 The war horse is a false hope for salvation,
and by its great might it cannot rescue.

18 Behold, the eye of the LORD is on those who fear him,
on those who hope in his steadfast love,
19 that he may deliver their soul from death
and keep them alive in famine.

20 Our soul waits for the LORD;
he is our help and our shield.
21 For our heart is glad in him,
because we trust in his holy name.
22 Let your steadfast love, O LORD, be upon us,
even as we hope in you.

PSALM 33:1–9

SING AND MAKE MUSIC

The first biblical reference to music appears in Genesis 4 where Jubal, a descendant of Cain, is identified as "the father of all those who play the lyre and pipe" (v. 21). By the time music is specifically mentioned again in the story of Jacob and Laban, it had become an integral part of societal and family activity (Ge 31:27). Scripture indicates that Moses, Miriam, and Joshua employed songs and instruments to commemorate great victories and interventions by God (Ex 15:1; Nu 21:17; Jos 6:4). Women were active in celebratory praise, often leading in dancing, singing, and the playing of melodies to mark important occasions (Ex 15:20–21; Jdg 5:1–3; 11:34; 1Sa 18:6). Music was woven so tightly into the fabric of Hebrew culture that even when the text does not mention it explicitly, readers can rightly assume that it accompanied virtually every significant occasion in public and private activity. However, it was not until the time of King David that instrumental music became a decreed part of worship in the tabernacle and temple (1Ch 15:22; 16:4; 25:1–3). And as an accomplished musician himself (1Sa 16:15–23), David actively encouraged, endorsed, and participated in public worship celebrations (1Ch 15:15–29; 16:1–6). Indeed, he wrote many of the psalms in the book of Psalms. Following this rich heritage guides modern believers to embrace music as an indispensable means of honoring the Lord, celebrating his attributes, and exalting him as the only trustworthy King (Ps 33:4–5,8).

PSALM 34:20

NO BROKEN BONES

Provision was made in the Law of Moses for a variety of forms of capital punishment for persons found guilty of a rather lengthy list of crimes (Ex 21:12–36; Lev 20; 24:10–23). The method of execution was stoning, except for burning in the case of grave sexual sins (Lev 20:14; 21:9). Included in these regulations were also some directions about the proper treatment of the bodies of the executed. Though it was acceptable to display the bodies of deceased criminals on a pole, the Law forbade the exposure of dead bodies overnight (Dt 21:22–23). However, with the Romans' introduction of crucifixion, it became difficult to adhere to this stipulation. The gruesome process often required several days, so if a victim ended up dying on the Sabbath, Jewish people faced a dilemma: either break the Sabbath to perform the work of removing and burying the body, or break the law forbidding the overnight suspension of dead bodies. In cases where such an untenable outcome seemed likely, Jewish leaders endorsed the practice of breaking the criminal's legs, which increased pain but hastened death because the victim then could not put any weight on his legs and breathing would be difficult (Jn 19:31).

With the Passover Sabbath approaching, the Jewish leaders asked for this practice to be applied to Jesus, yet found it to be unnecessary; Christ had already died (Jn 19:33). Keeping his bones intact fulfilled the prophecy of Psalm 34:20, quoted in John 19:36, and identified Jesus with the sacrificial Passover lamb (Ex 12:46). He vividly demonstrated his overwhelming love by voluntarily surrendering his life for the world's sins (Jn 10:18; 15:13; 19:30).

Psalm 34[1]

Taste and See That the Lord Is Good

Of David, when he changed his behavior before Abimelech, so that he drove him out, and he went away.

1 I will bless the Lord at all times;
his praise shall continually be in my mouth.
2 My soul makes its boast in the Lord;
let the humble hear and be glad.
3 Oh, magnify the Lord with me,
and let us exalt his name together!

4 I sought the Lord, and he answered me
and delivered me from all my fears.
5 Those who look to him are radiant,
and their faces shall never be ashamed.
6 This poor man cried, and the Lord heard him
and saved him out of all his troubles.
7 The angel of the Lord encamps
around those who fear him, and delivers them.

8 Oh, taste and see that the Lord is good!
Blessed is the man who takes refuge in him!
9 Oh, fear the Lord, you his saints,
for those who fear him have no lack!
10 The young lions suffer want and hunger;
but those who seek the Lord lack no good thing.

11 Come, O children, listen to me;
I will teach you the fear of the Lord.
12 What man is there who desires life
and loves many days, that he may see good?
13 Keep your tongue from evil
and your lips from speaking deceit.
14 Turn away from evil and do good;
seek peace and pursue it.

15 The eyes of the Lord are toward the righteous
and his ears toward their cry.
16 The face of the Lord is against those who do evil,
to cut off the memory of them from the earth.
17 When the righteous cry for help, the Lord hears
and delivers them out of all their troubles.
18 The Lord is near to the brokenhearted
and saves the crushed in spirit.

19 Many are the afflictions of the righteous,
but the Lord delivers him out of them all.
20 He keeps all his bones;
not one of them is broken.
21 Affliction will slay the wicked,
and those who hate the righteous will be
condemned.
22 The Lord redeems the life of his servants;
none of those who take refuge in him will be
condemned.

[1]This psalm is an acrostic poem, each verse beginning with the successive letters of the Hebrew alphabet

Psalm 35

Great Is the LORD

Of David.

1 Contend, O LORD, with those who contend with me;
fight against those who fight against me!
2 Take hold of shield and buckler
and rise for my help!
3 Draw the spear and javelin[1]
against my pursuers!
Say to my soul,
"I am your salvation!"

4 Let them be put to shame and dishonor
who seek after my life!
Let them be turned back and disappointed
who devise evil against me!
5 Let them be like chaff before the wind,
with the angel of the LORD driving them away!
6 Let their way be dark and slippery,
with the angel of the LORD pursuing them!

7 For without cause they hid their net for me;
without cause they dug a pit for my life.[2]
8 Let destruction come upon him when he does not know it!
And let the net that he hid ensnare him;
let him fall into it—to his destruction!

9 Then my soul will rejoice in the LORD,
exulting in his salvation.
10 All my bones shall say,
"O LORD, who is like you,
delivering the poor
from him who is too strong for him,
the poor and needy from him who robs him?"

11 Malicious[3] witnesses rise up;
they ask me of things that I do not know.
12 They repay me evil for good;
my soul is bereft.[4]
13 But I, when they were sick—
I wore sackcloth;
I afflicted myself with fasting;
I prayed with head bowed[5] on my chest.
14 I went about as though I grieved for my friend or my
brother;
as one who laments his mother,
I bowed down in mourning.

15 But at my stumbling they rejoiced and gathered;
they gathered together against me;
wretches whom I did not know
tore at me without ceasing;
16 like profane mockers at a feast,[6]
they gnash at me with their teeth.

---

[1]Or *and close the way* [2]The word *pit* is transposed from the preceding line; Hebrew *For without cause they hid the pit of their net for me; without cause they dug for my life* [3]Or *Violent* [4]Hebrew *it is bereavement to my soul* [5]Or *my prayer shall turn back* [6]The meaning of the Hebrew phrase is uncertain

17 How long, O Lord, will you look on?
Rescue me from their destruction,
my precious life from the lions!
18 I will thank you in the great congregation;
in the mighty throng I will praise you.

19 Let not those rejoice over me
who are wrongfully my foes,
and let not those wink the eye
who hate me without cause.
20 For they do not speak peace,
but against those who are quiet in the land
they devise words of deceit.
21 They open wide their mouths against me;
they say, "Aha, Aha!
Our eyes have seen it!"

22 You have seen, O LORD; be not silent!
O Lord, be not far from me!
23 Awake and rouse yourself for my vindication,
for my cause, my God and my Lord!
24 Vindicate me, O LORD, my God,
according to your righteousness,
and let them not rejoice over me!
25 Let them not say in their hearts,
"Aha, our heart's desire!"
Let them not say, "We have swallowed him up."

26 Let them be put to shame and disappointed altogether
who rejoice at my calamity!
Let them be clothed with shame and dishonor
who magnify themselves against me!

27 Let those who delight in my righteousness
shout for joy and be glad
and say evermore,
"Great is the LORD,
who delights in the welfare of his servant!"
28 Then my tongue shall tell of your righteousness
and of your praise all the day long.

Psalm 36

How Precious Is Your Steadfast Love

To the choirmaster. Of David, the servant of the LORD.

1 Transgression speaks to the wicked
deep in his heart;[1]
there is no fear of God
before his eyes.
2 For he flatters himself in his own eyes
that his iniquity cannot be found out and hated.
3 The words of his mouth are trouble and deceit;
he has ceased to act wisely and do good.
4 He plots trouble while on his bed;
he sets himself in a way that is not good;
he does not reject evil.

[1]Some Hebrew manuscripts, Syriac, Jerome (compare Septuagint); most Hebrew manuscripts *in my heart*

PSALM 36:1–12

LOVE DEMONSTRATED

In the midst of decrying Judah's sin, the prophet Jeremiah made this observation: "The heart is deceitful above all things, and desperately sick" (Jer 17:9). The opening section of Psalm 36 helps readers further understand this universal condition with a blunt description of the wickedness that resides in the hearts of unbelievers and the subsequent sin that results from rejecting their Creator. Left to themselves, people gravitate away from the Lord and toward an arrogant and destructive sense of ambivalence toward spiritual truth, which leads to self-deceit, evil and, ultimately, the willful rejection of all that is good (vv. 1–4).

Contrast this desperate state with the righteousness, purity, and faithfulness of God. Struggling to describe divine justice and mercy adequately, the psalmist pointed to the vastness of the heavens, the height of the mountains, and the depths of the sea as mere hints of the overwhelming goodness and love of the Almighty (vv. 5–7). In light of his grasp of God's holiness and its vast difference from humanity's fallen condition, the psalmist made an impassioned plea to the Lord to "continue your steadfast love to those who know you" (v. 10). Jesus, who is the very image of God (2Co 4:4; Col 1:15), definitively answered the psalmist's request on behalf of all people by giving his life as a "ransom for many" (Mt 20:28) so that all who believe "might live through him" (1Jn 4:9).

A PRAYER FOR VINDICATION

When difficulty comes in the form of personal attacks, it is easy to feel alone and forgotten, and as if enemies have the upper hand. Such was David's attitude when he opened Psalm 35 with an earnest plea for God to come to his aid and vindicate him (vv. 1 – 3). Blind-sided by the hatred of his adversaries, Israel's king proclaimed his innocence, insisting he had done nothing to incur their wrath. Despite David's sincere prayers for their well-being, his foes continued to slander and attack him at every turn (vv. 11 – 16).

While it is often difficult to understand the motives behind the actions of those who deliberately plot the demise of God-fearing people, some insight comes by understanding that residing in the hearts of unbelievers is a fundamental opposition to the supremacy of God. Those who do not acknowledge Jesus as Lord not only reject their Creator, but in prideful arrogance set themselves up as ultimate arbiters of what is good and right (Pr 16:25; 21:2). This often subconscious (and always futile) struggle with the Lord for control makes them hostile to anything that suggests that they are not "god" in their own lives.

Against this backdrop, it becomes understandable how the Pharisees would oppose Jesus despite his many miracles and obvious good works. All the deeds of the Son of God pointed to a higher authority: his Father in heaven (Jn 5:19; 12:49). But because the Pharisees had rejected God's authority in favor of their own, Jesus' activities became a threat to their political and religious power and personal control of their own lives. Even though they outwardly appeared to follow God through legalistic adherence to the law, their attitudes betrayed their fundamental rejection of him as their head. Jesus' presence and uncompromising devotion to the truth reminded them that they were then and would always be subject to the Lord's authority.

Encounters with those who resist and reject God's message are not uncommon. Jesus reminded his followers that they should expect to receive the same kind of treatment that he himself received (Mt 10:24 – 25). More specifically, he warned that in this world, his followers would have trouble (Jn 16:33). Because Christ's presence and teachings are reflected in the lives of believers (Lk 6:43 – 49; Jn 16:13), their actions will always remind the unbelieving world that there is a God above all gods to whom everyone is accountable regardless of race, nationality, religion, or worldview (Ro 14:11 – 12; Php 2:10; Heb 4:13).

5 Your steadfast love, O LORD, extends to the heavens,
your faithfulness to the clouds.
6 Your righteousness is like the mountains of God;
your judgments are like the great deep;
man and beast you save, O LORD.

7 How precious is your steadfast love, O God!
The children of mankind take refuge in the shadow of your wings.
8 They feast on the abundance of your house,
and you give them drink from the river of your delights.
9 For with you is the fountain of life;
in your light do we see light.

10 Oh, continue your steadfast love to those who know you,
and your righteousness to the upright of heart!
11 Let not the foot of arrogance come upon me,
nor the hand of the wicked drive me away.
12 There the evildoers lie fallen;
they are thrust down, unable to rise.

Psalm 37[1]

He Will Not Forsake His Saints

Of David.

1 Fret not yourself because of evildoers;
be not envious of wrongdoers!
2 For they will soon fade like the grass
and wither like the green herb.

3 Trust in the LORD, and do good;
dwell in the land and befriend faithfulness.[2]
4 Delight yourself in the LORD,
and he will give you the desires of your heart.

5 Commit your way to the LORD;
trust in him, and he will act.
6 He will bring forth your righteousness as the light,
and your justice as the noonday.

7 Be still before the LORD and wait patiently for him;
fret not yourself over the one who prospers in his way,
over the man who carries out evil devices!

8 Refrain from anger, and forsake wrath!
Fret not yourself; it tends only to evil.
9 For the evildoers shall be cut off,
but those who wait for the LORD shall inherit the land.

10 In just a little while, the wicked will be no more;
though you look carefully at his place, he will not be there.
11 But the meek shall inherit the land
and delight themselves in abundant peace.

12 The wicked plots against the righteous
and gnashes his teeth at him,
13 but the Lord laughs at the wicked,
for he sees that his day is coming.

[1]This psalm is an acrostic poem, each stanza beginning with the successive letters of the Hebrew alphabet
[2]Or *and feed on faithfulness*, or *and find safe pasture*

PSALM 37:4

DESIRES OF YOUR HEART

Hopes, aspirations, and desires often push people to excel and be their best. But when longings remain unfulfilled, people tend to become frustrated, bewildered, and disappointed. Christians grappling with deep and unsatisfied yearnings are comforted often by the promise recorded in Psalm 37:4: "Delight yourself in the LORD, and he will give you the desires of your heart." Unfortunately, when the reader's attention is solely focused on how to receive things from the Lord, the important context of this verse is missed. While Scripture does identify God as the source of all that is good (Jas 1:17), his primary intent is not to dole out a limitless supply of gifts or to fulfill self-centered and worldly dreams. Prayers that are focused on the object of desire fail to include the fundamental key to fulfillment of this promise: delighting oneself in the Lord. When a person shifts his or her affection away from objects and to God (and knowing him through Christ), he or she finds that the Almighty supplants that which is less worthy of pursuit and becomes the only true goal and source of satisfaction. Then the Lord is pleased to bestow upon his children their heart's deepest longing—which turns out to be God himself!

14 The wicked draw the sword and bend their bows
to bring down the poor and needy,
to slay those whose way is upright;
15 their sword shall enter their own heart,
and their bows shall be broken.

16 Better is the little that the righteous has
than the abundance of many wicked.
17 For the arms of the wicked shall be broken,
but the LORD upholds the righteous.

18 The LORD knows the days of the blameless,
and their heritage will remain forever;
19 they are not put to shame in evil times;
in the days of famine they have abundance.

20 But the wicked will perish;
the enemies of the LORD are like the glory of the pastures;
they vanish—like smoke they vanish away.

21 The wicked borrows but does not pay back,
but the righteous is generous and gives;
22 for those blessed by the LORD[1] shall inherit the land,
but those cursed by him shall be cut off.

23 The steps of a man are established by the LORD,
when he delights in his way;
24 though he fall, he shall not be cast headlong,
for the LORD upholds his hand.

25 I have been young, and now am old,
yet I have not seen the righteous forsaken
or his children begging for bread.
26 He is ever lending generously,
and his children become a blessing.

27 Turn away from evil and do good;
so shall you dwell forever.
28 For the LORD loves justice;
he will not forsake his saints.
They are preserved forever,
but the children of the wicked shall be cut off.
29 The righteous shall inherit the land
and dwell upon it forever.

30 The mouth of the righteous utters wisdom,
and his tongue speaks justice.
31 The law of his God is in his heart;
his steps do not slip.

32 The wicked watches for the righteous
and seeks to put him to death.
33 The LORD will not abandon him to his power
or let him be condemned when he is brought to trial.

34 Wait for the LORD and keep his way,
and he will exalt you to inherit the land;
you will look on when the wicked are cut off.

35 I have seen a wicked, ruthless man,
spreading himself like a green laurel tree.[2]

[1]Hebrew *by him* [2]The identity of this tree is uncertain

36 But he passed away,[1] and behold, he was no more;
though I sought him, he could not be found.

37 Mark the blameless and behold the upright,
for there is a future for the man of peace.
38 But transgressors shall be altogether destroyed;
the future of the wicked shall be cut off.

39 The salvation of the righteous is from the LORD;
he is their stronghold in the time of trouble.
40 The LORD helps them and delivers them;
he delivers them from the wicked and saves them,
because they take refuge in him.

PSALM 38:1–22

THE IMPACT OF SIN

Psalm 38 begins with David's jarring words penned as he confessed the overwhelming guilt he experienced as a result of sin (vv. 1–4). It is difficult to reconcile the confident assertion of his familiar pastoral psalm that "the LORD is my shepherd" (Ps 23:1) with this lament over wrongdoing that caused wounds that "stink and fester" (38:5) and left him "feeble and crushed" (v. 8). Such language causes some to suggest the psalm was inspired by a life-threatening illness. However, verse 18 clearly reveals this passage to be a depiction of the destruction sin inflicts upon a person's body, mind, soul, and spirit. Realizing his guilt, David's only recourse was to acknowledge his helpless condition and cry out, "Make haste to help me, O Lord, my salvation!" (v. 22).

The New Testament declares this repentant attitude to be critical for receiving the only remedy for humanity's sinful condition: salvation through Jesus Christ. While all parts of salvation, including repentance, faith, belief, and desire, find their source in God (Jn 6:44), one cannot express faith without first realizing personal need and acknowledging Christ as the only One capable of delivering humanity from sin's grip (Ac 16:31; Ro 10:9–10). Then, believers can be confident they have bypassed God's wrath and entered into his grace (Ro 8:1–2). Though consequences of sin may remain, the Lord even uses those to his children's benefit and for his glory (Ro 8:28; Heb 12:4–10).

Psalm 38

Do Not Forsake Me, O LORD

A Psalm of David, for the memorial offering.

1 O LORD, rebuke me not in your anger,
nor discipline me in your wrath!
2 For your arrows have sunk into me,
and your hand has come down on me.

3 There is no soundness in my flesh
because of your indignation;
there is no health in my bones
because of my sin.
4 For my iniquities have gone over my head;
like a heavy burden, they are too heavy for me.

5 My wounds stink and fester
because of my foolishness,
6 I am utterly bowed down and prostrate;
all the day I go about mourning.
7 For my sides are filled with burning,
and there is no soundness in my flesh.
8 I am feeble and crushed;
I groan because of the tumult of my heart.

9 O Lord, all my longing is before you;
my sighing is not hidden from you.
10 My heart throbs; my strength fails me,
and the light of my eyes—it also has gone from me.
11 My friends and companions stand aloof from my plague,
and my nearest kin stand far off.

12 Those who seek my life lay their snares;
those who seek my hurt speak of ruin
and meditate treachery all day long.

13 But I am like a deaf man; I do not hear,
like a mute man who does not open his mouth.
14 I have become like a man who does not hear,
and in whose mouth are no rebukes.

15 But for you, O LORD, do I wait;
it is you, O Lord my God, who will answer.
16 For I said, "Only let them not rejoice over me,
who boast against me when my foot slips!"

[1]Or *But one passed by*

PROMISES TO THE MEEK

History is filled with stories where it appears that those who do evil prosper while righteous and God-loving people suffer without cause. In Psalm 37, troubled people find the encouraging reminder that wrongdoers will not endure forever, and that "the meek shall inherit the land and delight themselves in abundant peace" (v. 11). Hundreds of years later, Jesus made a similar statement in the Sermon on the Mount, reassuring his disciples that regardless of their present situation, the meek "shall inherit the earth" (Mt 5:5). Often, the meaning of both verses is unclear to present-day readers because of an incomplete understanding of the word "meek." Modern dictionaries often add to its generally negative connotation by equating it with words like "timid," "tame," "submissive," and "docile." But since Jesus used the same Greek term to describe himself (Mt 11:28 – 29; translated "gentle"), the better definition of meekness is a more accurate characterization of the biblical meaning.

Scripture declares Christ to be unequaled in power and authority (Mt 26:53; 28:18; Jn 1:1 – 4; Col 1:16; Heb 1:3). Yet despite his rightful position as the Son of God, he willingly submitted himself to his Father (Jn 8:28; 12:49 – 50; 14:10; Php 2:6 – 8). In his interactions with people on earth, he was confident, firm, and spoke fearlessly to those who opposed or misrepresented God (Mt 23:13 – 39); at the same time, to those in need he was approachable, compassionate, and gentle (Mt 9:36; 14:14; 20:34; Mk 6:34; Lk 7:13; Jn 11:34 – 38).

Jesus used the agricultural analogy of two oxen joined by a yoke to invite his followers to embrace an attitude of meekness as they enter into relationship with him (Mt 11:28 – 29). A yoke is a wooden crosspiece fastened over the neck of two or more animals to unite them in pulling a plow or cart. As believers voluntarily yield their rights and submit to Christ, he promises to replace their futile efforts to make themselves right with God (Ro 3:20) with divine "rest for [their] souls" (Mt 11:29). In a world where so many things leave people depleted and empty, Jesus promises restoration, nurture, and rekindled strength to the spiritually meek. He grants them the power to face whatever life brings with a confident assurance that God is "their stronghold in the time of trouble" (Ps 37:39) and that "the righteous shall inherit the land and dwell upon it forever" (v. 29).

17 For I am ready to fall,
and my pain is ever before me.
18 I confess my iniquity;
I am sorry for my sin.
19 But my foes are vigorous, they are mighty,
and many are those who hate me wrongfully.
20 Those who render me evil for good
accuse me because I follow after good.

21 Do not forsake me, O LORD!
O my God, be not far from me!
22 Make haste to help me,
O Lord, my salvation!

Psalm 39

What Is the Measure of My Days?

To the choirmaster: to Jeduthun. A Psalm of David.

1 I said, "I will guard my ways,
that I may not sin with my tongue;
I will guard my mouth with a muzzle,
so long as the wicked are in my presence."
2 I was mute and silent;
I held my peace to no avail,
and my distress grew worse.
3 My heart became hot within me.
As I mused, the fire burned;
then I spoke with my tongue:

4 "O LORD, make me know my end
and what is the measure of my days;
let me know how fleeting I am!
5 Behold, you have made my days a few handbreadths,
and my lifetime is as nothing before you.
Surely all mankind stands as a mere breath! *Selah*
6 Surely a man goes about as a shadow!
Surely for nothing[1] they are in turmoil;
man heaps up wealth and does not know who
will gather!

7 "And now, O Lord, for what do I wait?
My hope is in you.
8 Deliver me from all my transgressions.
Do not make me the scorn of the fool!
9 I am mute; I do not open my mouth,
for it is you who have done it.
10 Remove your stroke from me;
I am spent by the hostility of your hand.
11 When you discipline a man
with rebukes for sin,
you consume like a moth what is dear to him;
surely all mankind is a mere breath! *Selah*

12 "Hear my prayer, O LORD,
and give ear to my cry;
hold not your peace at my tears!

[1]Hebrew *Surely as a breath*

PSALM 39:4–7

BREVITY

It often feels as though the older one gets, the shorter life seems. David seemed to grasp this irony when he wrote of the fleeting nature of life (vv. 4–5). Pointing to the vanity of worldly pursuits that promise fulfillment through fading things such as wealth, power, and prestige, he illustrated how such things are meaningless against the backdrop of the brevity of life on earth (vv. 6,11). Understanding this ultimate futility led him to cry out to the Lord as his only hope (vv. 7,12).

Jesus also derided the senselessness of worrying over temporary things such as food, clothing, and length of life (Mt 6:25–27). He exhorted his followers to make an essential shift to storing up treasure in heaven. Since wealth and possessions can be threatened by theft, destruction, and decay and will ultimately pass away (Lk 21:33), the only true security can be found by investing in things that last for eternity (Mt 6:19–21).

Like worldly possessions, the physical bodies of people are also subject to destruction and decay. However, the New Testament reminds those who believe in Jesus that they have experienced a fundamental change in their lives (2Co 5:17; Col 2:13), and though their bodies waste away, inwardly they are continually renewed (2Co 4:16). Since being born of eternal seed which never perishes through faith in Christ (1Pe 1:23), they can trust God to continue his good work in them until the day of Jesus Christ (Php 1:6).

For I am a sojourner with you,
a guest, like all my fathers.
13 Look away from me, that I may smile again,
before I depart and am no more!"

Psalm 40

My Help and My Deliverer

To the choirmaster. A Psalm of David.

1 I waited patiently for the LORD;
he inclined to me and heard my cry.
2 He drew me up from the pit of destruction,
out of the miry bog,
and set my feet upon a rock,
making my steps secure.
3 He put a new song in my mouth,
a song of praise to our God.
Many will see and fear,
and put their trust in the LORD.

4 Blessed is the man who makes
the LORD his trust,
who does not turn to the proud,
to those who go astray after a lie!
5 You have multiplied, O LORD my God,
your wondrous deeds and your thoughts toward us;
none can compare with you!
I will proclaim and tell of them,
yet they are more than can be told.

6 In sacrifice and offering you have not delighted,
but you have given me an open ear.[1]
Burnt offering and sin offering
you have not required.
7 Then I said, "Behold, I have come;
in the scroll of the book it is written of me:
8 I delight to do your will, O my God;
your law is within my heart."

9 I have told the glad news of deliverance[2]
in the great congregation;
behold, I have not restrained my lips,
as you know, O LORD.
10 I have not hidden your deliverance within my heart;
I have spoken of your faithfulness and your salvation;
I have not concealed your steadfast love and your faithfulness
from the great congregation.

11 As for you, O LORD, you will not restrain
your mercy from me;
your steadfast love and your faithfulness will
ever preserve me!
12 For evils have encompassed me
beyond number;
my iniquities have overtaken me,
and I cannot see;

[1]Hebrew *ears you have dug for me* [2]Hebrew *righteousness*; also verse 10

DESIRING TO DO GOD'S WILL

In Psalm 40, David showed a remarkable example of obedience through troubled and difficult times. These troubles brought him to continual dependence on the Lord, trusting the Lord's plan and strength over his own. In verses 6 – 8, perhaps David had brought a sacrifice and offering. But his focus was on presenting his life to the Lord. He stated, "Behold, I have come; in the scroll of the book it is written of me: I delight to do your will, O my God; your law is within my heart." According to Hebrews 10:5 – 7, Christ spoke these same words to express his obedient submission to the Father in coming to earth. Both Christ and David showed delight in doing God's will over their own.

Although important, the sacrifices themselves were not pleasing to God. He desired obedience. In David's time, sacrifices were a ritual delivering temporary atonement for sin. "Every priest stands daily at his service, offering repeatedly the same sacrifices, which can never take away sins" (Heb 10:11). But through Jesus' obedience to his Father's plan, God provided a sacrifice made perfect forever (Php 2:8). "And by that will we have been sanctified through the offering of the body of Jesus Christ once for all" (Heb 10:10).

In the same way that Jesus offered himself in obedience to God's will, his followers are called to do the same. "Present yourselves to God as those who have been brought from death to life, and your members to God as instruments for righteousness" (Ro 6:13). God's Word presents the human body as a sacred place, the place the Holy Spirit dwells. God paid a high price, the sacrifice of Jesus' body, and in doing so asks his people to honor him through total obedience to God's will. "You are not your own, for you were bought with a price. So glorify God in your body" (1Co 6:19 – 20).

Doing God's will is a practical act of discipleship, a reflection of a heart obedient to God. God asks for the sacrifice of an obedient life, and he sends the Spirit to live in the hearts of his followers in order to empower them to accomplish his purposes. This requires daily surrendering one's own will, allowing the body to die to self and conform to God's will (Ro 12:1 – 2). Throughout his life on earth, Jesus was the ultimate model of this way of life.

they are more than the hairs of my head;
my heart fails me.
13 Be pleased, O LORD, to deliver me!
O LORD, make haste to help me!
14 Let those be put to shame and disappointed altogether
who seek to snatch away my life;
let those be turned back and brought to dishonor
who delight in my hurt!
15 Let those be appalled because of their shame
who say to me, "Aha, Aha!"
16 But may all who seek you
rejoice and be glad in you;
may those who love your salvation
say continually, "Great is the LORD!"
17 As for me, I am poor and needy,
but the Lord takes thought for me.
You are my help and my deliverer;
do not delay, O my God!

Psalm 41

O LORD, Be Gracious to Me

To the choirmaster. A Psalm of David.

1 Blessed is the one who considers the poor![1]
In the day of trouble the LORD delivers him;
2 the LORD protects him and keeps him alive;
he is called blessed in the land;
you do not give him up to the will of his enemies.
3 The LORD sustains him on his sickbed;
in his illness you restore him to full health.[2]
4 As for me, I said, "O LORD, be gracious to me;
heal me,[3] for I have sinned against you!"
5 My enemies say of me in malice,
"When will he die, and his name perish?"
6 And when one comes to see me, he utters empty words,
while his heart gathers iniquity;
when he goes out, he tells it abroad.
7 All who hate me whisper together about me;
they imagine the worst for me.[4]
8 They say, "A deadly thing is poured out[5] on him;
he will not rise again from where he lies."
9 Even my close friend in whom I trusted,
who ate my bread, has lifted his heel against me.
10 But you, O LORD, be gracious to me,
and raise me up, that I may repay them!
11 By this I know that you delight in me:
my enemy will not shout in triumph over me.
12 But you have upheld me because of my integrity,
and set me in your presence forever.
13 Blessed be the LORD, the God of Israel,
from everlasting to everlasting!
Amen and Amen.

[1]Or *weak* [2]Hebrew *you turn all his bed* [3]Hebrew *my soul* [4]Or *they devise evil against me* [5]Or *has fastened*

PSALM 41:9

DOUBLE-CROSSED

Wounds from a friend cut deep. David and Jesus had both felt this pain. In the midst of the Last Supper with his beloved disciples, shortly after Jesus washed their feet, he quoted David's words: "He who ate my bread has lifted his heel against me" (Jn 13:18). Jesus knew Judas would soon betray him. As the perfect Son of God, Jesus intimately knows all people—including their sin and shame—yet he loves them anyway. Jesus' followers are commanded to love like this. Love is a choice, and in times of hurt and betrayal, it will not be easy. Yet through this act of love for others, Jesus says that the watching world will recognize his followers (Jn 13:35). People know that even their closest friends might abandon them if they knew the truth about their sin. But not Jesus. Jesus loves with a perfect, unconditional love. He never gives up on his people. And through this great love, his followers are redeemed (Eph 1:7).

NO MORE HATRED

This psalm was written by David at a time when he found himself betrayed by someone he once trusted (v. 9). It is a prayer asking God, the source of all blessings, to deliver, protect, sustain, and restore him from his undeserved suffering (vv. 1 – 3). His enemies spread lies about him, wanted the worst for him, and tarnished his reputation by spreading gossip (vv. 6 – 8), all the while preferring him dead and forgotten (v. 5).

In the midst of this trial, instead of hating his enemies, David turned to God. He prayerfully pleaded for mercy, knowing God would raise him up and repay his enemies in due time (v. 10). David claimed victory over his enemies and looked to God for his affirmation and praise (v. 11). Through intense pain and hardship, David kept his integrity, knowing that God would uphold him (v. 12). And he called for praise of the one true God, "from everlasting to everlasting" (v. 13).

Jesus Christ, the very Son of God, became flesh and knew the pain of betrayal and hatred. One of his closest associates, enticed by a monetary reward, turned him over to the authorities. Judas approached Jesus in the garden and kissed him on the cheek, signaling to Jesus' enemies that he was the one for whom they were looking (Lk 22:48). Jesus did not allow hate in his heart, but he showed only compassion and gentleness to his friend who betrayed him and to those who arrested him (Lk 22:49 – 51).

The wisdom of Proverbs teaches the consequences of love versus hate — "hatred stirs up strife, but love covers all offenses" (Pr 10:12). Jesus' life modeled perfect love, and the church is called to love "because he first loved us" (1Jn 4:19). For "if anyone says, 'I love God,' and hates his brother, he is a liar" (1Jn 4:20). Followers of Christ who do not love those they do life with, those they can see, are told they cannot love God, whom they have not seen (1Jn 4:20). Jesus commands believers to love even their enemies and those who persecute them (Mt 5:44).

BOOK TWO

Psalm 42

Why Are You Cast Down, O My Soul?

To the choirmaster. A Maskil[1]
of the Sons of Korah.

1 As a deer pants for flowing streams,
so pants my soul for you, O God.
2 My soul thirsts for God,
for the living God.
When shall I come and appear before God?[2]
3 My tears have been my food
day and night,
while they say to me all the day long,
"Where is your God?"
4 These things I remember,
as I pour out my soul:
how I would go with the throng
and lead them in procession to the house
of God
with glad shouts and songs of praise,
a multitude keeping festival.

5 Why are you cast down, O my soul,
and why are you in turmoil within me?
Hope in God; for I shall again praise him,
my salvation[3] 6 and my God.

My soul is cast down within me;
therefore I remember you
from the land of Jordan and of Hermon,
from Mount Mizar.
7 Deep calls to deep
at the roar of your waterfalls;
all your breakers and your waves
have gone over me.
8 By day the LORD commands his steadfast love,
and at night his song is with me,
a prayer to the God of my life.
9 I say to God, my rock:
"Why have you forgotten me?
Why do I go mourning
because of the oppression of the enemy?"
10 As with a deadly wound in my bones,
my adversaries taunt me,
while they say to me all the day long,
"Where is your God?"

11 Why are you cast down, O my soul,
and why are you in turmoil within me?
Hope in God; for I shall again praise him,
my salvation and my God.

[1]Probably a musical or liturgical term [2]Revocalization yields *and see the face of God* [3]Hebrew *the salvation of my face*; also verse 11 and 43:5

PSALM 42:5–11

THE DOWNCAST SOUL

Feelings of sadness and discouragement are inevitable. This life has times of dancing and praising, but also times of deep anguish and despair. The psalmist cried out to God, declaring his downcast soul. Jesus understands. In Luke 22, preceding his impending crucifixion, Jesus cried out to his Father, "'Remove this cup from me' ... And being in agony he prayed more earnestly; and his sweat became like great drops of blood falling down to the ground" (Lk 22:42,44). This passage shows Jesus' very real and deep despair. However, in the midst of crying out to God, he declared his longing for the Father's will to be accomplished, not his own. In the same way, God hears and answers prayer, even when it may seem he has forgotten his people. And because God the Son left his throne in heaven to walk the earth in human flesh, he knows and understands the human experience on every level—physical, spiritual, and emotional. Therefore, God's people can confidently praise him and put their hope in him (Ps 42:11), knowing that one day, through Jesus' costly sacrifice, they will experience anew the presence of God and his goodness.

Psalm 43

Send Out Your Light and Your Truth

1 Vindicate me, O God, and defend my cause
against an ungodly people,
from the deceitful and unjust man
deliver me!
2 For you are the God in whom I take refuge;
why have you rejected me?
Why do I go about mourning
because of the oppression of the enemy?

3 Send out your light and your truth;
let them lead me;
let them bring me to your holy hill
and to your dwelling!
4 Then I will go to the altar of God,
to God my exceeding joy,
and I will praise you with the lyre,
O God, my God.

5 Why are you cast down, O my soul,
and why are you in turmoil within me?
Hope in God; for I shall again praise him,
my salvation and my God.

PSALM 43:5

HOPE IN GOD

Psalm 43 is a prayer to God in a time of trouble. Through doubt and stress, the psalmist urged his inner being, by the power of God, to keep believing. "Why are you cast down, O my soul, and why are you in turmoil within me?" he questioned himself (Ps 43:5). Yet he stood firm, keeping his hope in God and praising him through his distress. Hope in God, through Jesus, is one of the central messages of the New Testament. Without Christ, people have no hope. However, the shed blood of Christ brings believers back to their Creator and gives them the hope they once lacked (Eph 2:12–13). He then prayed that God would give spiritual understanding to his people, opening the eyes of their hearts, allowing them to know the hope to which he has called them—"the riches of his glorious inheritance in the saints" (Eph 1:18). People may hope in many things, but there is one hope that all Christians have in common, the Lord Jesus Christ. It is in him alone that believers find true hope and eternal riches.

Psalm 44

Come to Our Help

To the choirmaster. A Maskil[1] of the Sons of Korah.

1 O God, we have heard with our ears,
our fathers have told us,
what deeds you performed in their days,
in the days of old:
2 you with your own hand drove out the nations,
but them you planted;
you afflicted the peoples,
but them you set free;
3 for not by their own sword did they win the land,
nor did their own arm save them,
but your right hand and your arm,
and the light of your face,
for you delighted in them.

4 You are my King, O God;
ordain salvation for Jacob!
5 Through you we push down our foes;
through your name we tread down those who rise up
against us.
6 For not in my bow do I trust,
nor can my sword save me.
7 But you have saved us from our foes
and have put to shame those who hate us.
8 In God we have boasted continually,
and we will give thanks to your name forever. *Selah*

[1] Probably a musical or liturgical term

9 But you have rejected us and disgraced us
and have not gone out with our armies.
10 You have made us turn back from the foe,
and those who hate us have gotten spoil.
11 You have made us like sheep for slaughter
and have scattered us among the nations.
12 You have sold your people for a trifle,
demanding no high price for them.
13 You have made us the taunt of our neighbors,
the derision and scorn of those around us.
14 You have made us a byword among the nations,
a laughingstock[1] among the peoples.
15 All day long my disgrace is before me,
and shame has covered my face
16 at the sound of the taunter and reviler,
at the sight of the enemy and the avenger.

17 All this has come upon us,
though we have not forgotten you,
and we have not been false to your covenant.
18 Our heart has not turned back,
nor have our steps departed from your way;
19 yet you have broken us in the place of jackals
and covered us with the shadow of death.
20 If we had forgotten the name of our God
or spread out our hands to a foreign god,
21 would not God discover this?
For he knows the secrets of the heart.
22 Yet for your sake we are killed all the day long;
we are regarded as sheep to be slaughtered.

23 Awake! Why are you sleeping, O Lord?
Rouse yourself! Do not reject us forever!
24 Why do you hide your face?
Why do you forget our affliction and
oppression?
25 For our soul is bowed down to the dust;
our belly clings to the ground.
26 Rise up; come to our help!
Redeem us for the sake of your steadfast love!

Psalm 45

Your Throne, O God, Is Forever

To the choirmaster: according to Lilies. A Maskil[2] of the Sons of Korah; a love song.

1 My heart overflows with a pleasing theme;
I address my verses to the king;
my tongue is like the pen of a ready scribe.

2 You are the most handsome of the sons of men;
grace is poured upon your lips;
therefore God has blessed you forever.
3 Gird your sword on your thigh, O mighty one,
in your splendor and majesty!

[1]Hebrew *a shaking of the head* [2]Probably a musical or liturgical term

PSALM 44:24

THE FACE OF CHRIST

Why does God look the other way? The psalmist asked this, thinking God had forgotten the people of Israel in their misery and oppression. The Israelites were conquered by their enemies, scattered, and dishonored, yet they had not fallen away from God. They had remained faithful and obedient to his covenant (Ps 44:17). Yet, God chose to allow afflictions on his people, as if he were hiding his face from them (v. 24). They sought God in their darkness, asking him to reveal himself and his glory.

The New Testament affirms that Jesus came to reveal God to all people, displaying the glory of God in the face of Jesus. "For God, who said, 'Let light shine out of darkness,' has shone in our hearts to give the light of the knowledge of the glory of God in the face of Jesus Christ" (2Co 4:6). No one has seen the Father (Ex 33:20; Jn 6:46), yet through the face of Christ, God's people see his glory revealed. And keeping hearts focused on eternity, Jesus' followers long for Christ's return—when "they will see his face, and his name will be on their foreheads ... They will need no light of lamp or sun, for the Lord God will be their light, and they will reign forever and ever" (Rev 22:4–5).

4 In your majesty ride out victoriously
for the cause of truth and meekness and righteousness;
let your right hand teach you awesome deeds!
5 Your arrows are sharp
in the heart of the king's enemies;
the peoples fall under you.

6 Your throne, O God, is forever and ever.
The scepter of your kingdom is a scepter of uprightness;
7 you have loved righteousness and hated wickedness.
Therefore God, your God, has anointed you
with the oil of gladness beyond your companions;
8 your robes are all fragrant with myrrh and aloes and cassia.
From ivory palaces stringed instruments make you glad;
9 daughters of kings are among your ladies of honor;
at your right hand stands the queen in gold of Ophir.

10 Hear, O daughter, and consider, and incline your ear:
forget your people and your father's house,
11 and the king will desire your beauty.
Since he is your lord, bow to him.
12 The people[1] of Tyre will seek your favor with gifts,
the richest of the people.[2]

13 All glorious is the princess in her chamber, with robes interwoven
with gold.
14 In many-colored robes she is led to the king,
with her virgin companions following behind her.
15 With joy and gladness they are led along
as they enter the palace of the king.

16 In place of your fathers shall be your sons;
you will make them princes in all the earth.
17 I will cause your name to be remembered in all generations;
therefore nations will praise you forever and ever.

Psalm 46

God Is Our Fortress

To the choirmaster. Of the Sons of Korah.
According to Alamoth.[3] A Song.

1 God is our refuge and strength,
a very present[4] help in trouble.
2 Therefore we will not fear though the earth give way,
though the mountains be moved into the heart of the sea,
3 though its waters roar and foam,
though the mountains tremble at its swelling. *Selah*

4 There is a river whose streams make glad the city of God,
the holy habitation of the Most High.
5 God is in the midst of her; she shall not be moved;
God will help her when morning dawns.
6 The nations rage, the kingdoms totter;
he utters his voice, the earth melts.
7 The LORD of hosts is with us;
the God of Jacob is our fortress. *Selah*

[1]Hebrew *daughter* [2]Or *The daughter of Tyre is here with gifts, the richest of people seek your favor*
[3]Probably a musical or liturgical term [4]Or *well proved*

THE KING AND HIS BRIDE

The Israelite king described in this psalm is a king above many kings. He is well respected by the people and by God. He is described as the "most handsome of the sons of men" (v. 2) — one who makes his cause "truth and meekness and righteousness" (v. 4), who always defeats his enemies (v. 5), and who establishes a throne that lasts forever (v. 6). All these qualities point directly to Jesus. He is the King of all kings, "highly exalted" by God (Php 2:7 – 9). Jesus is truth (Jn 14:6), the humblest man to walk the earth (Php 2:8), and his ministry and life constantly challenged people to live for God and pursue righteousness (Mt 5:6). God gives his people "victory through our Lord Jesus Christ" (1Co 15:57). Jesus sits at the right hand of God and his throne "is forever and ever" (Heb 1:8).

Psalm 45 is a song of love — a royal wedding song that celebrates marriage in a grand manner — a wedding between a king and his beloved. The king is completely in love with his bride, and she is asked to honor and adore him (v. 11). This psalm prophetically portrays the glorious reign of Jesus — God's promised Messiah and the final and ultimate King (vv. 6 – 7) — and how his church is his holy bride.

In his great and unfailing love, Jesus, the King over all, invites his church to become his holy bride, asking them to be ready for his return (Rev 19:7). The anticipation of a bride awaiting her groom as the wedding approaches is immeasurable. Months and months of preparation are spent on this one day. The bride is at her very best, with the best of intentions and expectations. Her heart overflows with joy, longing for her groom. This is an exact representation of how the church should be longing, preparing, and eagerly anticipating the coming of King Jesus — singing and praying, "Come, Lord Jesus!" (Rev 22:20).

8 Come, behold the works of the LORD,
how he has brought desolations on the earth.
9 He makes wars cease to the end of the earth;
he breaks the bow and shatters the spear;
he burns the chariots with fire.
10 "Be still, and know that I am God.
I will be exalted among the nations,
I will be exalted in the earth!"
11 The LORD of hosts is with us;
the God of Jacob is our fortress. *Selah*

PSALM 47:1–9

KING OF ALL

All kings have derived authority; only one King, the great God of heaven, is absolute in power and righteousness. This psalm not only exalts and worships God as King, but foreshadows Jesus as the coming King. Jesus is "the blessed and only Sovereign, the King of kings and Lord of lords" (1Ti 6:15) who reigns over the people (Lk 1:33), chooses an inheritance for them (Eph 1:11), was exalted by God (Php 2:9), and ascended into heaven, where he is seated once again on his holy throne (Ac 2:33).

Through King Jesus, victory is promised for God's people, determined long ago by God when "he subdued peoples under us, and nations under our feet" (Ps 47:3). The church longs for the day when Jesus will return—a day when he will display all his glory. He will sit on his throne in all heavenly glory with all the nations gathered before him. And he will say to his people, "Come, you who are blessed by my Father, inherit the kingdom prepared for you from the foundation of the world" (Mt 25:34).

Psalm 47

God Is King over All the Earth

To the choirmaster. A Psalm of the Sons of Korah.

1 Clap your hands, all peoples!
Shout to God with loud songs of joy!
2 For the LORD, the Most High, is to be feared,
a great king over all the earth.
3 He subdued peoples under us,
and nations under our feet.
4 He chose our heritage for us,
the pride of Jacob whom he loves. *Selah*

5 God has gone up with a shout,
the LORD with the sound of a trumpet.
6 Sing praises to God, sing praises!
Sing praises to our King, sing praises!
7 For God is the King of all the earth;
sing praises with a psalm![1]

8 God reigns over the nations;
God sits on his holy throne.
9 The princes of the peoples gather
as the people of the God of Abraham.
For the shields of the earth belong to God;
he is highly exalted!

Psalm 48

Zion, the City of Our God

A Song. A Psalm of the Sons of Korah.

1 Great is the LORD and greatly to be praised
in the city of our God!
His holy mountain, [2]beautiful in elevation,
is the joy of all the earth,
Mount Zion, in the far north,
the city of the great King.
3 Within her citadels God
has made himself known as a fortress.

4 For behold, the kings assembled;
they came on together.
5 As soon as they saw it, they were astounded;
they were in panic; they took to flight.

[1]Hebrew *maskil*

OUR GOD REIGNS

God reigns — over his city, over the earth, and over all the nations (vv. 4 – 5,10). Jerusalem is God's chosen city. And God is the strength and refuge of his city (v. 1). He is within her — not just watching over or in control of, but present and in the midst of the people (v. 7). And he promises that, as long as the people stay faithful to him, the city will not fall (vv. 5,7). Surrounding nations are in turmoil, but the city of God is not to fear, for he is in control; just the sound of his voice can destroy the earth (v. 6). God's people must fix their eyes on what he can do (v. 8), be still and wait on him — allowing him to be exalted on high among the nations (v. 10).

The people of Israel had God as their king, but that didn't satisfy them. They wanted a king they could see. A military king — one who would come and rescue them from their surrounding enemies. God promised his people a king, although the plan was nothing like what they expected or wanted. Jesus, God's Son, came to earth to lead the people and be their Savior — not from their enemies, but from their sins (Mt 1:21). He reigned in a new way — set apart from all other kings. He reigned in humility, not from an earthly throne (Php 2:7). His message was "good news of peace" (Ac 10:36). He came to serve, not to be served (Mt 20:28). And paradoxically, the glory of Jesus' reign is the result of his humble service, gentleness, and self-sacrifice. Jesus did not seek his own glory. Instead, he sought the glory of his Father alone — which resulted in the Father glorifying him (Jn 8:54; Php 2:9 – 11).

Jesus, the King of the Jews, conquered death and now lives within the heart of every believer (Gal 2:20). He is with his believers at all times, never changing (Ps 46:7; Heb 13:8). "Therefore we will not fear" (Ps 46:2) because he is "a very present help in trouble" (Ps 46:1). Thus those who accept Jesus as Savior and believe in him will experience firsthand the comfort of his strength, his power, his protection, and his counsel. He is the one true King, the Savior of all humankind, who is seated at the right hand of God, reigning over the whole earth in all majesty and glory. He is Immanuel — God with us.

6 Trembling took hold of them there,
anguish as of a woman in labor.
7 By the east wind you shattered
the ships of Tarshish.
8 As we have heard, so have we seen
in the city of the LORD of hosts,
in the city of our God,
which God will establish forever. *Selah*

9 We have thought on your steadfast love, O God,
in the midst of your temple.
10 As your name, O God,
so your praise reaches to the ends of the earth.
Your right hand is filled with righteousness.
11 Let Mount Zion be glad!
Let the daughters of Judah rejoice
because of your judgments!

12 Walk about Zion, go around her,
number her towers,
13 consider well her ramparts,
go through her citadels,
that you may tell the next generation
14 that this is God,
our God forever and ever.
He will guide us forever.[1]

Psalm 49

Why Should I Fear in Times of Trouble?

To the choirmaster. A Psalm of the Sons of Korah.

1 Hear this, all peoples!
Give ear, all inhabitants of the world,
2 both low and high,
rich and poor together!
3 My mouth shall speak wisdom;
the meditation of my heart shall be understanding.
4 I will incline my ear to a proverb;
I will solve my riddle to the music of the lyre.

5 Why should I fear in times of trouble,
when the iniquity of those who cheat me surrounds me,
6 those who trust in their wealth
and boast of the abundance of their riches?
7 Truly no man can ransom another,
or give to God the price of his life,
8 for the ransom of their life is costly
and can never suffice,
9 that he should live on forever
and never see the pit.

10 For he sees that even the wise die;
the fool and the stupid alike must perish
and leave their wealth to others.

[1] Septuagint; another reading is (compare Jerome, Syriac) *He will guide us beyond death*

11 Their graves are their homes forever,[1]
their dwelling places to all generations,
though they called lands by their own names.
12 Man in his pomp will not remain;
he is like the beasts that perish.

13 This is the path of those who have foolish confidence;
yet after them people approve of their boasts.[2] *Selah*
14 Like sheep they are appointed for Sheol;
death shall be their shepherd,
and the upright shall rule over them in the morning.
Their form shall be consumed in Sheol, with no place to dwell.
15 But God will ransom my soul from the power of Sheol,
for he will receive me. *Selah*

16 Be not afraid when a man becomes rich,
when the glory of his house increases.
17 For when he dies he will carry nothing away;
his glory will not go down after him.
18 For though, while he lives, he counts himself blessed—
and though you get praise when you do well for yourself—
19 his soul will go to the generation of his fathers,
who will never again see light.
20 Man in his pomp yet without understanding is like the beasts
that perish.

Psalm 50

God Himself Is Judge

A Psalm of Asaph.

1 The Mighty One, God the LORD,
speaks and summons the earth
from the rising of the sun to its setting.
2 Out of Zion, the perfection of beauty,
God shines forth.

3 Our God comes; he does not keep silence;[3]
before him is a devouring fire,
around him a mighty tempest.
4 He calls to the heavens above
and to the earth, that he may judge his people:
5 "Gather to me my faithful ones,
who made a covenant with me by sacrifice!"
6 The heavens declare his righteousness,
for God himself is judge! *Selah*

7 "Hear, O my people, and I will speak;
O Israel, I will testify against you.
I am God, your God.
8 Not for your sacrifices do I rebuke you;
your burnt offerings are continually before me.
9 I will not accept a bull from your house
or goats from your folds.
10 For every beast of the forest is mine,
the cattle on a thousand hills.

[1]Septuagint, Syriac, Targum; Hebrew *Their inward thought was that their homes were forever* [2]Or *and of those after them who approve of their boasts* [3]Or *May our God come, and not keep silence*

PSALM 49:15

RANSOMED

God is a perfect God. His creation was perfect and humankind was created in his perfect image. Yet God's people fell away. They chose sin. They chose their own way, a way that led to death. But God promised to redeem his people, knowing the only way to life was by purchasing their freedom. "You were bought with a price" (1Co 6:20). Christ went ahead of God's people, preparing a place for them and making a way for them, ultimately giving "his life as a ransom for many" (Mt 20:28). Through the blood of his Son, God redeemed humankind. They were once dead in their transgressions, but now are promised to be alive with Christ once again. The psalmist foreshadowed this, stating, "He will receive me" (Ps 49:15). Although risen from the dead and reunited with God (Mk 16:6), Christ showed himself to his disciples and those who loved him. After Christ's resurrection, the disciples were told, "He is going before you to Galilee. There you will see him, just as he told you" (Mk 16:7). In the same way as for his first disciples, Christ has gone ahead of all believers, redeeming them to their Father and giving them hope of eternal life, which was "promised before the ages began" (Titus 1:2).

11 I know all the birds of the hills,
and all that moves in the field is mine.

12 "If I were hungry, I would not tell you,
for the world and its fullness are mine.
13 Do I eat the flesh of bulls
or drink the blood of goats?
14 Offer to God a sacrifice of thanksgiving,[1]
and perform your vows to the Most High,
15 and call upon me in the day of trouble;
I will deliver you, and you shall glorify me."

16 But to the wicked God says:
"What right have you to recite my statutes
or take my covenant on your lips?
17 For you hate discipline,
and you cast my words behind you.
18 If you see a thief, you are pleased with him,
and you keep company with adulterers.

19 "You give your mouth free rein for evil,
and your tongue frames deceit.
20 You sit and speak against your brother;
you slander your own mother's son.
21 These things you have done, and I have been silent;
you thought that I[2] was one like yourself.
But now I rebuke you and lay the charge before you.

22 "Mark this, then, you who forget God,
lest I tear you apart, and there be none to deliver!
23 The one who offers thanksgiving as his sacrifice glorifies me;
to one who orders his way rightly
I will show the salvation of God!"

Psalm 51

Create in Me a Clean Heart, O God

To the choirmaster. A Psalm of David, when Nathan the prophet went to him, after he had gone in to Bathsheba.

1 Have mercy on me,[3] O God,
according to your steadfast love;
according to your abundant mercy
blot out my transgressions.
2 Wash me thoroughly from my iniquity,
and cleanse me from my sin!

3 For I know my transgressions,
and my sin is ever before me.
4 Against you, you only, have I sinned
and done what is evil in your sight,
so that you may be justified in your words
and blameless in your judgment.
5 Behold, I was brought forth in iniquity,
and in sin did my mother conceive me.
6 Behold, you delight in truth in the inward being,
and you teach me wisdom in the secret heart.

[1]Or *Make thanksgiving your sacrifice to God* [2]Or *that the* I AM [3]Or *Be gracious to me*

7 Purge me with hyssop, and I shall be clean;
wash me, and I shall be whiter than snow.
8 Let me hear joy and gladness;
let the bones that you have broken rejoice.
9 Hide your face from my sins,
and blot out all my iniquities.
10 Create in me a clean heart, O God,
and renew a right[1] spirit within me.
11 Cast me not away from your presence,
and take not your Holy Spirit from me.
12 Restore to me the joy of your salvation,
and uphold me with a willing spirit.

13 Then I will teach transgressors your ways,
and sinners will return to you.
14 Deliver me from bloodguiltiness, O God,
O God of my salvation,
and my tongue will sing aloud of your righteousness.
15 O Lord, open my lips,
and my mouth will declare your praise.
16 For you will not delight in sacrifice, or I would give it;
you will not be pleased with a burnt offering.
17 The sacrifices of God are a broken spirit;
a broken and contrite heart, O God, you will not despise.

18 Do good to Zion in your good pleasure;
build up the walls of Jerusalem;
19 then will you delight in right sacrifices,
in burnt offerings and whole burnt offerings;
then bulls will be offered on your altar.

Psalm 52

The Steadfast Love of God Endures

To the choirmaster. A Maskil[2] of David, when Doeg, the Edomite, came and told Saul, "David has come to the house of Ahimelech."

1 Why do you boast of evil, O mighty man?
The steadfast love of God endures all the day.
2 Your tongue plots destruction,
like a sharp razor, you worker of deceit.
3 You love evil more than good,
and lying more than speaking what is right. *Selah*
4 You love all words that devour,
O deceitful tongue.

5 But God will break you down forever;
he will snatch and tear you from your tent;
he will uproot you from the land of the living. *Selah*
6 The righteous shall see and fear,
and shall laugh at him, saying,
7 "See the man who would not make
God his refuge,
but trusted in the abundance of his riches
and sought refuge in his own destruction!"[3]

[1]Or *steadfast* [2]Probably a musical or liturgical term [3]Or *in his work of destruction*

SECOND CHANCES

David sinned against God and his own people. Because of his great sin, people's lives were forever impacted (2Sa 11). When confronted with his failure, David cried out to God with a repentant heart and asked for a second chance. He asked for a chance to choose God's way over his sinful ways. He asked for mercy (Ps 51:1), a pure heart and steadfast spirit (v. 10), a restored relationship with God (v. 12), and deliverance from his guilt (v. 14). David knew he deserved punishment and judgment for his wrongdoings, recognizing that his sin was against God and God alone (v. 4), yet he also knew that God is a God of forgiveness, mercy, and compassion (v. 1).

Even though David, a man after God's own heart, fell into sin, God didn't give up on him. God took David's sin and used it to display his goodness and his glory. Solomon, son of David and Bathsheba, grew up to be the wisest man on earth (1Ki 4:30 – 31). And about a thousand years later, Jesus would come from that same lineage. The Savior of the world was born into a lineage tainted by sin.

God is a God of second chances. He is in every detail and is sovereign over all. Although sin is never a part of his plan, he makes "light shine out of darkness" (2Co 4:6) and "for those who love God all things work together for good, for those who are called according to his purpose" (Ro 8:28). This was Jesus' ultimate mission during his time on earth — to restore God's people, giving them the gift of life instead of death (Jn 10:10). His blood covered over all the sins of humankind, washing them whiter than snow (Ps 51:7; Rev 7:14) — not because they deserved such a gift, but because of God's great love for them (Jn 3:16; Eph 2:4). God promises "that neither death nor life, nor angels nor rulers, nor things present nor things to come, nor powers, nor height nor depth, nor anything else in all creation, will be able to separate us from the love of God in Christ Jesus our Lord" (Ro 8:38 – 39).

8 But I am like a green olive tree
in the house of God.
I trust in the steadfast love of God
forever and ever.
9 I will thank you forever,
because you have done it.
I will wait for your name, for it is good,
in the presence of the godly.

Psalm 53

There Is None Who Does Good

To the choirmaster: according to Mahalath. A Maskil[1] *of David.*

1 The fool says in his heart, "There is no God."
They are corrupt, doing abominable iniquity;
there is none who does good.

2 God looks down from heaven
on the children of man
to see if there are any who understand,[2]
who seek after God.

3 They have all fallen away;
together they have become corrupt;
there is none who does good,
not even one.

4 Have those who work evil no knowledge,
who eat up my people as they eat bread,
and do not call upon God?

5 There they are, in great terror,
where there is no terror!
For God scatters the bones of him who encamps against you;
you put them to shame, for God has rejected them.

6 Oh, that salvation for Israel would come out of Zion!
When God restores the fortunes of his people,
let Jacob rejoice, let Israel be glad.

Psalm 54

The Lord Upholds My Life

To the choirmaster: with stringed instruments.
A Maskil[3] *of David, when the Ziphites went and told Saul,*
"Is not David hiding among us?"

1 O God, save me by your name,
and vindicate me by your might.
2 O God, hear my prayer;
give ear to the words of my mouth.

3 For strangers[4] have risen against me;
ruthless men seek my life;
they do not set God before themselves. *Selah*

4 Behold, God is my helper;
the Lord is the upholder of my life.

[1]Probably musical or liturgical terms [2]Or *who act wisely* [3]Probably a musical or liturgical term [4]Some Hebrew manuscripts and Targum *insolent men* (compare Psalm 86:14)

PSALM 53:1–3

NO GOOD

Everyone—that means all people, believers and unbelievers alike—has sinned. Sin is universal and inescapable. If this concept is not understood, one misses a foundational aspect of the gospel message. No one can live up to what God created humans to be. "For all have sinned and fall short of the glory of God" (Ro 3:23). Knowing people couldn't save themselves, God made a way through his Son. God's people are "justified by his grace as a gift, through the redemption that is in Christ Jesus" (Ro 3:24). Jesus, the only perfect human to walk the earth, was presented as a sacrifice of atonement for the sins of his people. "But he was pierced for our transgressions; he was crushed for our iniquities; upon him was the chastisement that brought us peace, and with his wounds we are healed" (Isa 53:5). And because "there is none who does good" (Ps 53:3; quoted in Ro 3:12), Jesus paid the ultimate sacrifice, suffering in the place of sinners. It is the people's sin that Jesus bore on the cross. And through this act of immeasurable love, he gives hope and life to all who believe.

5 He will return the evil to my enemies;
in your faithfulness put an end to them.

6 With a freewill offering I will sacrifice to you;
I will give thanks to your name, O LORD, for it
is good.
7 For he has delivered me from every trouble,
and my eye has looked in triumph on my enemies.

Psalm 55

Cast Your Burden on the LORD

To the choirmaster: with stringed instruments. A Maskil[1] of David.

1 Give ear to my prayer, O God,
and hide not yourself from my plea for mercy!
2 Attend to me, and answer me;
I am restless in my complaint and I moan,
3 because of the noise of the enemy,
because of the oppression of the wicked.
For they drop trouble upon me,
and in anger they bear a grudge against me.

4 My heart is in anguish within me;
the terrors of death have fallen upon me.
5 Fear and trembling come upon me,
and horror overwhelms me.
6 And I say, "Oh, that I had wings like a dove!
I would fly away and be at rest;
7 yes, I would wander far away;
I would lodge in the wilderness; *Selah*
8 I would hurry to find a shelter
from the raging wind and tempest."

9 Destroy, O Lord, divide their tongues;
for I see violence and strife in the city.
10 Day and night they go around it
on its walls,
and iniquity and trouble are within it;
11 ruin is in its midst;
oppression and fraud
do not depart from its marketplace.

12 For it is not an enemy who taunts me—
then I could bear it;
it is not an adversary who deals insolently with me—
then I could hide from him.
13 But it is you, a man, my equal,
my companion, my familiar friend.
14 We used to take sweet counsel together;
within God's house we walked in the throng.
15 Let death steal over them;
let them go down to Sheol alive;
for evil is in their dwelling place and in their
heart.

16 But I call to God,
and the LORD will save me.

[1]Probably a musical or liturgical term

17 Evening and morning and at noon
I utter my complaint and moan,
and he hears my voice.
18 He redeems my soul in safety
from the battle that I wage,
for many are arrayed against me.
19 God will give ear and humble them,
he who is enthroned from of old, *Selah*
because they do not change
and do not fear God.

20 My companion[1] stretched out his hand against his
friends;
he violated his covenant.
21 His speech was smooth as butter,
yet war was in his heart;
his words were softer than oil,
yet they were drawn swords.

22 Cast your burden on the LORD,
and he will sustain you;
he will never permit
the righteous to be moved.

23 But you, O God, will cast them down
into the pit of destruction;
men of blood and treachery
shall not live out half their days.
But I will trust in you.

Psalm 56

In God I Trust

To the choirmaster: according to The Dove on Far-off Terebinths. A Miktam[2] of David, when the Philistines seized him in Gath.

1 Be gracious to me, O God, for man tramples on me;
all day long an attacker oppresses me;
2 my enemies trample on me all day long,
for many attack me proudly.
3 When I am afraid,
I put my trust in you.
4 In God, whose word I praise,
in God I trust; I shall not be afraid.
What can flesh do to me?

5 All day long they injure my cause;[3]
all their thoughts are against me for evil.
6 They stir up strife, they lurk;
they watch my steps,
as they have waited for my life.
7 For their crime will they escape?
In wrath cast down the peoples, O God!

8 You have kept count of my tossings;[4]
put my tears in your bottle.
Are they not in your book?

[1]Hebrew *He* [2]Probably a musical or liturgical term [3]Or *they twist my words* [4]Or *wanderings*

9 Then my enemies will turn back
in the day when I call.
This I know, that[1] God is for me.
10 In God, whose word I praise,
in the LORD, whose word I praise,
11 in God I trust; I shall not be afraid.
What can man do to me?

12 I must perform my vows to you, O God;
I will render thank offerings to you.
13 For you have delivered my soul from death,
yes, my feet from falling,
that I may walk before God
in the light of life.

Psalm 57

Let Your Glory Be over All the Earth

To the choirmaster: according to Do Not Destroy. A Miktam[2] of David, when he fled from Saul, in the cave.

1 Be merciful to me, O God, be merciful to me,
for in you my soul takes refuge;
in the shadow of your wings I will take refuge,
till the storms of destruction pass by.
2 I cry out to God Most High,
to God who fulfills his purpose for me.
3 He will send from heaven and save me;
he will put to shame him who tramples on me. *Selah*
God will send out his steadfast love and his faithfulness!

4 My soul is in the midst of lions;
I lie down amid fiery beasts—
the children of man, whose teeth are spears and arrows,
whose tongues are sharp swords.

5 Be exalted, O God, above the heavens!
Let your glory be over all the earth!

6 They set a net for my steps;
my soul was bowed down.
They dug a pit in my way,
but they have fallen into it themselves. *Selah*
7 My heart is steadfast, O God,
my heart is steadfast!
I will sing and make melody!
8 Awake, my glory![3]
Awake, O harp and lyre!
I will awake the dawn!
9 I will give thanks to you, O Lord, among the peoples;
I will sing praises to you among the nations.
10 For your steadfast love is great to the heavens,
your faithfulness to the clouds.

11 Be exalted, O God, above the heavens!
Let your glory be over all the earth!

[1]Or *because* [2]Probably a musical or liturgical term [3]Or *my whole being*

PSALM 57:1 – 11

SOVEREIGN OVER ALL

This psalm was David's response to a desperate situation. David was fleeing for his life from King Saul, and he had hidden in a cave. In this moment of distress and uncertainty, David put his dependence and trust in God. He cried out to God, certain that God would send down his mercy and rescue him (Ps 57:1 – 3). He found refuge "in the shadow of [God's] wings," knowing God was with him in the midst of this disaster (v. 1). Although all the circumstances of his life seemed to indicate that God had forgotten him, David knew that God was still sovereign over all. And in the midst of men "whose teeth are spears and arrows, whose tongues are sharp swords" (v. 4), his primary desire was for God to be exalted over all (vv. 5,11).

How difficult it is, in the middle of a storm, through all the deep emotions and uncertainty, to have a steadfast heart, singing and praising God (v. 7). Yet this was exactly David's response. He sang, "I will give thanks to you, O Lord, among the peoples; I will sing praises to you among the nations. For your steadfast love is great to the heavens, your faithfulness to the clouds" (vv. 9 – 10). Without knowing the outcome — whether he would live or die — David chose God's glory.

Jesus showed that same steadfast heart. On the hardest day of his life, knowing he was about to walk a difficult road of suffering and death, he chose to trust God's sovereignty. Praying to God, he knelt down and asked, "Father, if you are willing, remove this cup from me. Nevertheless, not my will, but yours, be done" (Lk 22:42). God's will required Jesus to lay down his life. However, God knew every detail, orchestrating all things, bringing forth a much bigger plan. God had a plan that defeated death, not only for Jesus, but for every believer — "for an hour is coming when all who are in the tombs will hear his voice and come out, those who have done good to the resurrection of life" (Jn 5:28 – 29). So in difficult times, through the fog of uncertainty, God's people can confidently trust him. They can fix their eyes on Jesus and hold on tight knowing victory is coming!

Psalm 58

God Who Judges the Earth

To the choirmaster: according to Do Not Destroy. A Miktam[1] of David.

1 Do you indeed decree what is right, you gods?[2]
  Do you judge the children of man uprightly?
2 No, in your hearts you devise wrongs;
  your hands deal out violence on earth.

3 The wicked are estranged from the womb;
  they go astray from birth, speaking lies.
4 They have venom like the venom of a serpent,
  like the deaf adder that stops its ear,
5 so that it does not hear the voice of charmers
  or of the cunning enchanter.

6 O God, break the teeth in their mouths;
  tear out the fangs of the young lions, O LORD!
7 Let them vanish like water that runs away;
  when he aims his arrows, let them be blunted.
8 Let them be like the snail that dissolves into slime,
  like the stillborn child who never sees the sun.
9 Sooner than your pots can feel the heat of thorns,
  whether green or ablaze, may he sweep them away![3]

10 The righteous will rejoice when he sees the vengeance;
  he will bathe his feet in the blood of the wicked.
11 Mankind will say, "Surely there is a reward for the righteous;
  surely there is a God who judges on earth."

PSALM 58:1–11

JUSTICE

The psalmist knew that the God he served is a God of justice. He is a "God who judges on earth" (v. 11). The judges on earth were ruling unjustly. They were merely humans but acting as if they had divine power (vv. 1–2). Yet, the psalmist prayed to God, asking him to provide justice for his people and for sudden judgment to come upon the unrighteous (vv. 9–11). The psalmist was confident in God and his mighty power to bring divine justice upon these evil judges. Jesus echoed the admonition to rule with justice when he spoke to the Pharisees. He scolded them because they had "neglected the weightier matters of the law: justice and mercy and faithfulness" (Mt 23:23). In the end, Jesus Christ will judge the living and the dead (2Ti 4:1). God's justice will be final and established forever. And the righteous, confident in their future reward (Ps 58:11), wait with great joy, recognizing that their Savior King has already won the victory (Rev 19:11–21).

Psalm 59

Deliver Me from My Enemies

To the choirmaster: according to Do Not Destroy. A Miktam[4] of David, when Saul sent men to watch his house in order to kill him.

1 Deliver me from my enemies, O my God;
  protect me from those who rise up against me;
2 deliver me from those who work evil,
  and save me from bloodthirsty men.

3 For behold, they lie in wait for my life;
  fierce men stir up strife against me.
For no transgression or sin of mine, O LORD,
4 for no fault of mine, they run and make ready.
Awake, come to meet me, and see!
5 You, LORD God of hosts, are God of Israel.
Rouse yourself to punish all the nations;
  spare none of those who treacherously plot evil. *Selah*

6 Each evening they come back,
  howling like dogs
  and prowling about the city.
7 There they are, bellowing with their mouths
  with swords in their lips—
  for "Who," they think,[5] "will hear us?"

[1]Probably a musical or liturgical term [2]Or *you mighty lords* (by revocalization; Hebrew *in silence*) [3]The meaning of the Hebrew verse is uncertain [4]Probably a musical or liturgical term [5]Hebrew lacks *they think*

8 But you, O LORD, laugh at them;
you hold all the nations in derision.
9 O my Strength, I will watch for you,
for you, O God, are my fortress.
10 My God in his steadfast love[1] will meet me;
God will let me look in triumph on my enemies.

11 Kill them not, lest my people forget;
make them totter[2] by your power and bring them down,
O Lord, our shield!
12 For the sin of their mouths, the words of their lips,
let them be trapped in their pride.
For the cursing and lies that they utter,
13 consume them in wrath;
consume them till they are no more,
that they may know that God rules over Jacob
to the ends of the earth. *Selah*

14 Each evening they come back,
howling like dogs
and prowling about the city.
15 They wander about for food
and growl if they do not get their fill.

16 But I will sing of your strength;
I will sing aloud of your steadfast love in the morning.
For you have been to me a fortress
and a refuge in the day of my distress.
17 O my Strength, I will sing praises to you,
for you, O God, are my fortress,
the God who shows me steadfast love.

Psalm 60

He Will Tread Down Our Foes

To the choirmaster: according to Shushan Eduth. A Miktam[3] of David; for instruction; when he strove with Aram-naharaim and with Aram-zobah, and when Joab on his return struck down twelve thousand of Edom in the Valley of Salt.

1 O God, you have rejected us, broken our defenses;
you have been angry; oh, restore us.
2 You have made the land to quake; you have torn it open;
repair its breaches, for it totters.
3 You have made your people see hard things;
you have given us wine to drink that made us stagger.

4 You have set up a banner for those who fear you,
that they may flee to it from the bow.[4] *Selah*
5 That your beloved ones may be delivered,
give salvation by your right hand and answer us!

6 God has spoken in his holiness:[5]
"With exultation I will divide up Shechem
and portion out the Vale of Succoth.
7 Gilead is mine; Manasseh is mine;
Ephraim is my helmet;
Judah is my scepter.

[1]Or *The God who shows me steadfast love* [2]Or *wander* [3]Probably musical or liturgical terms [4]Or *that it may be displayed because of truth* [5]Or *sanctuary*

8 Moab is my washbasin;
upon Edom I cast my shoe;
over Philistia I shout in triumph."[1]

9 Who will bring me to the fortified city?
Who will lead me to Edom?
10 Have you not rejected us, O God?
You do not go forth, O God, with our armies.
11 Oh, grant us help against the foe,
for vain is the salvation of man!
12 With God we shall do valiantly;
it is he who will tread down our foes.

PSALM 61:2

THE ROCK HIGHER THAN I

Aware of his own fragility, the psalmist longed for the stability and security he could find in God—his rock of strength. God is unshakable. He is unalterable in his purposes—not at all fazed by opposition or resistance. Nothing can challenge his strength. The psalmist was wise to recognize his own vulnerability, turning to lean on someone whose position is forever fixed—trusting in his immovable God.

The New Testament compares Jesus to a spiritual rock—identifying him as the source that once sustained Moses and the Israelites liberated from Egypt (1Co 10:4). From this rock, they enjoyed a miraculous supply of desperately needed water (Nu 20:6–11). Jesus provides life for people without hope. All who call on him and believe in his name will be saved (Ro 10:13). Jesus is also referred to as a rock that makes people stumble (1Pe 2:8). Even today his uncompromising call to repentance causes some people to reject him because they love sin and the stuff of earth. Jesus' clear message of salvation through his name alone is too much for many people to accept—they refuse to put faith in him as the long-awaited Messiah.

Psalm 61

Lead Me to the Rock

To the choirmaster: with stringed instruments. Of David.

1 Hear my cry, O God,
listen to my prayer;
2 from the end of the earth I call to you
when my heart is faint.
Lead me to the rock
that is higher than I,
3 for you have been my refuge,
a strong tower against the enemy.

4 Let me dwell in your tent forever!
Let me take refuge under the shelter of your wings! *Selah*
5 For you, O God, have heard my vows;
you have given me the heritage of those who fear your name.

6 Prolong the life of the king;
may his years endure to all generations!
7 May he be enthroned forever before God;
appoint steadfast love and faithfulness to watch over him!
8 So will I ever sing praises to your name,
as I perform my vows day after day.

Psalm 62

My Soul Waits for God Alone

To the choirmaster: according to Jeduthun. A Psalm of David.

1 For God alone my soul waits in silence;
from him comes my salvation.
2 He alone is my rock and my salvation,
my fortress; I shall not be greatly shaken.

3 How long will all of you attack a man
to batter him,
like a leaning wall, a tottering fence?
4 They only plan to thrust him down from his high position.
They take pleasure in falsehood.
They bless with their mouths,
but inwardly they curse. *Selah*

[1]Revocalization (compare Psalm 108:10); Masoretic Text *over me, O Philistia, shout in triumph*

5 For God alone, O my soul, wait in silence,
for my hope is from him.
6 He only is my rock and my salvation,
my fortress; I shall not be shaken.
7 On God rests my salvation and my glory;
my mighty rock, my refuge is God.

8 Trust in him at all times, O people;
pour out your heart before him;
God is a refuge for us. *Selah*

9 Those of low estate are but a breath;
those of high estate are a delusion;
in the balances they go up;
they are together lighter than a breath.
10 Put no trust in extortion;
set no vain hopes on robbery;
if riches increase, set not your heart on them.

11 Once God has spoken;
twice have I heard this:
that power belongs to God,
12 and that to you, O Lord, belongs steadfast love.
For you will render to a man
according to his work.

Psalm 63

My Soul Thirsts for You

A Psalm of David, when he was in the wilderness of Judah.

1 O God, you are my God; earnestly I seek you;
my soul thirsts for you;
my flesh faints for you,
as in a dry and weary land where there is no
water.
2 So I have looked upon you in the sanctuary,
beholding your power and glory.
3 Because your steadfast love is better than life,
my lips will praise you.
4 So I will bless you as long as I live;
in your name I will lift up my hands.

5 My soul will be satisfied as with fat and rich food,
and my mouth will praise you with joyful lips,
6 when I remember you upon my bed,
and meditate on you in the watches of the night;
7 for you have been my help,
and in the shadow of your wings I will sing for joy.
8 My soul clings to you;
your right hand upholds me.

9 But those who seek to destroy my life
shall go down into the depths of the earth;
10 they shall be given over to the power of the sword;
they shall be a portion for jackals.
11 But the king shall rejoice in God;
all who swear by him shall exult,
for the mouths of liars will be stopped.

PSALM 63:1–8

PERSONAL WORSHIP

The psalmist's affection for God and his great need of God's help combined to become a beautiful example of personal worship. The psalmist approached God, savoring his goodness and power as the answers to his heart's hunger and thirst (Ps 63:5). All through the night, the psalmist privately contemplated and remembered God as his help, protector, advocate, and provider (vv. 6–8).

In a similar way, Jesus had a habit of private prayer. He regularly withdrew from others to commune with God (Mk 1:35). In the theological mystery of the Trinity, God the Son desired behind-the-scenes time with God the Father. He got up very early in the morning to secure intimate moments of worshipful gratitude and submission to the Father's will. In this way, Jesus modeled the importance of approaching God as an individual—above and beyond corporate gatherings of worship. Private prayer, intimate thanksgiving, and nonpublic praise are essential disciplines of the Christian life.

PSALM 64:1–10

PLOTTING EVIL

David was familiar with the reality of having enemies who plotted to end his life. He cried out for God to show his strength in these moments in order that God would ultimately receive glory and recognition as the one who holds all power.

In reading this psalm, believers can detect a foreshadowing of Jesus and his dealings with the religious Jewish leaders who plotted to end his life because of who he claimed to be—the Son of God (Mt 26:3–4). Though the religious leaders, like David's enemies, had devised a plan, God showed his power and ultimately received glory. Yet, God's glory came in a way that no one at that time expected. In Psalm 64, God was glorified through the prolonged life of David whom he protected and spared. In the New Testament, God was glorified through the death of his Son sent as a sacrifice for humankind's sin. The attempted destruction of Jesus—his arrest, trial, and crucifixion—actually accomplished the defeat of sin for all who put faith in Jesus for salvation.

PSALM 65:1–13

SALVATION AND GOD'S PROVIDENCE

The psalmist considered a debt of praise still owed to God, remembering the dramatic ways God showed his might through the creation of the world (vv. 6–7). The psalmist also thanked God for the forgiveness of sins—mindful that in the time before God intervened, the people had been overwhelmed (v. 3). In addition, Psalm 65 celebrates God's

(continued on next page)

Psalm 64

Hide Me from the Wicked

To the choirmaster. A Psalm of David.

1 Hear my voice, O God, in my complaint;
preserve my life from dread of the enemy.
2 Hide me from the secret plots of the wicked,
from the throng of evildoers,
3 who whet their tongues like swords,
who aim bitter words like arrows,
4 shooting from ambush at the blameless,
shooting at him suddenly and without fear.

5 They hold fast to their evil purpose;
they talk of laying snares secretly,
thinking, "Who can see them?"
6 They search out injustice,
saying, "We have accomplished a diligent search."
For the inward mind and heart of a man are deep.

7 But God shoots his arrow at them;
they are wounded suddenly.
8 They are brought to ruin, with their own tongues turned against them;
all who see them will wag their heads.
9 Then all mankind fears;
they tell what God has brought about
and ponder what he has done.

10 Let the righteous one rejoice in the LORD
and take refuge in him!
Let all the upright in heart exult!

Psalm 65

O God of Our Salvation

To the choirmaster. A Psalm of David. A Song.

1 Praise is due to you,[1] O God, in Zion,
and to you shall vows be performed.
2 O you who hear prayer,
to you shall all flesh come.
3 When iniquities prevail against me,
you atone for our transgressions.
4 Blessed is the one you choose and bring near,
to dwell in your courts!
We shall be satisfied with the goodness of your house,
the holiness of your temple!

5 By awesome deeds you answer us with righteousness,
O God of our salvation,
the hope of all the ends of the earth
and of the farthest seas;
6 the one who by his strength established the mountains,
being girded with might;
7 who stills the roaring of the seas,
the roaring of their waves,
the tumult of the peoples,

[1] Or *Praise waits for you in silence*

8 so that those who dwell at the ends of the earth are in awe at your signs.
You make the going out of the morning and the evening to shout for joy.
9 You visit the earth and water it;[1]
you greatly enrich it;
the river of God is full of water;
you provide their grain,
for so you have prepared it.
10 You water its furrows abundantly,
settling its ridges,
softening it with showers,
and blessing its growth.
11 You crown the year with your bounty;
your wagon tracks overflow with abundance.
12 The pastures of the wilderness overflow,
the hills gird themselves with joy,
13 the meadows clothe themselves with flocks,
the valleys deck themselves with grain,
they shout and sing together for joy.

Psalm 66

How Awesome Are Your Deeds

To the choirmaster. A Song. A Psalm.

1 Shout for joy to God, all the earth;
2 sing the glory of his name;
give to him glorious praise!
3 Say to God, "How awesome are your deeds!
So great is your power that your enemies come cringing to you.
4 All the earth worships you
and sings praises to you;
they sing praises to your name." *Selah*
5 Come and see what God has done:
he is awesome in his deeds toward the children of man.
6 He turned the sea into dry land;
they passed through the river on foot.
There did we rejoice in him,
7 who rules by his might forever,
whose eyes keep watch on the nations—
let not the rebellious exalt themselves. *Selah*
8 Bless our God, O peoples;
let the sound of his praise be heard,
9 who has kept our soul among the living
and has not let our feet slip.
10 For you, O God, have tested us;
you have tried us as silver is tried.
11 You brought us into the net;
you laid a crushing burden on our backs;
12 you let men ride over our heads;
we went through fire and through water;
yet you have brought us out to a place of abundance.
13 I will come into your house with burnt offerings;
I will perform my vows to you,

[1]Or *and make it overflow*

(Salvation and God's Providence, continued)

providence over all of the blessings people enjoy (vv. 9–13). All good things that happen on the earth are the result of God's intentional works of love, faithfulness, and care.

When Jesus entered the world, people were still helpless under the guilt of sin. Yet Christ died and rose again for the ungodly as a demonstration of God's love for sinners (Ro 5:6–8). Jesus' sacrifice enabled everyone who will trust Jesus to have a relationship with God through faith. This relationship provides access to the providential benefits of God's power. Those who believe in Jesus enjoy the blessings that accompany God's favor. He is a good Father to his adopted sons and daughters.

PSALM 66:16–20

CHERISHING SIN HINDERS PRAYER

The psalmist invited all to hear about the opportunity for securing God's favor (v. 16). He was full of joy because the Lord had heard his prayers. He knew this was only possible because of his genuine humility and distaste for the sins present in his life. "If I had cherished iniquity in my heart, the Lord would not have listened" (v. 18).

Jesus taught that if someone is holding a grudge against someone, they must forgive them in order to receive forgiveness themselves from the Lord (Mk 11:25). This is not a contradiction to grace—adding some formula of work before one can receive pardon. Jesus wants people to go to God with integrity, refusing to make requests while harboring things God hates. It puts people into a position of humility—yielded to God's authority and aligned with his Word.

PSALM 67:1–7

LET ALL PEOPLES PRAISE YOU

The psalmist desired the blessings of God so that he could bring fame to God among the nations. The hope was that all people would see the benefits of following the Lord. From the beginning, God's plan was expansive, involving all the peoples of the earth (Ge 12:3). The evangelistic perspective of this psalm points toward the New Testament focus on sharing the gospel.

Before ascending to heaven, Jesus gave a clear mission to the disciples.

(continued on next page)

14 that which my lips uttered
and my mouth promised when I was in trouble.
15 I will offer to you burnt offerings of fattened animals,
with the smoke of the sacrifice of rams;
I will make an offering of bulls and goats. *Selah*

16 Come and hear, all you who fear God,
and I will tell what he has done for my soul.
17 I cried to him with my mouth,
and high praise was on[1] my tongue.[2]
18 If I had cherished iniquity in my heart,
the Lord would not have listened.
19 But truly God has listened;
he has attended to the voice of my prayer.

20 Blessed be God,
because he has not rejected my prayer
or removed his steadfast love from me!

Psalm 67

Make Your Face Shine upon Us

To the choirmaster: with stringed instruments. A Psalm. A Song.

1 May God be gracious to us and bless us
and make his face to shine upon us, *Selah*
2 that your way may be known on earth,
your saving power among all nations.
3 Let the peoples praise you, O God;
let all the peoples praise you!
4 Let the nations be glad and sing for joy,
for you judge the peoples with equity
and guide the nations upon earth. *Selah*
5 Let the peoples praise you, O God;
let all the peoples praise you!

6 The earth has yielded its increase;
God, our God, shall bless us.
7 God shall bless us;
let all the ends of the earth fear him!

Psalm 68

God Shall Scatter His Enemies

To the choirmaster. A Psalm of David. A Song.

1 God shall arise, his enemies shall be scattered;
and those who hate him shall flee before him!
2 As smoke is driven away, so you shall drive them away;
as wax melts before fire,
so the wicked shall perish before God!
3 But the righteous shall be glad;
they shall exult before God;
they shall be jubilant with joy!

4 Sing to God, sing praises to his name;
lift up a song to him who rides through the deserts;

[1]Hebrew *under* [2]Or *and he was exalted with my tongue*

his name is the LORD;
exult before him!
5 Father of the fatherless and protector of widows
is God in his holy habitation.
6 God settles the solitary in a home;
he leads out the prisoners to prosperity,
but the rebellious dwell in a parched land.

7 O God, when you went out before your people,
when you marched through the wilderness, *Selah*
8 the earth quaked, the heavens poured down rain,
before God, the One of Sinai,
before God,[1] the God of Israel.
9 Rain in abundance, O God, you shed abroad;
you restored your inheritance as it languished;
10 your flock[2] found a dwelling in it;
in your goodness, O God, you provided for the needy.

11 The Lord gives the word;
the women who announce the news are a great host:
12 "The kings of the armies—they flee, they flee!"
The women at home divide the spoil—
13 though you men lie among the sheepfolds—
the wings of a dove covered with silver,
its pinions with shimmering gold.
14 When the Almighty scatters kings there,
let snow fall on Zalmon.

15 O mountain of God, mountain of Bashan;
O many-peaked[3] mountain, mountain of Bashan!
16 Why do you look with hatred, O many-peaked mountain,
at the mount that God desired for his abode,
yes, where the LORD will dwell forever?
17 The chariots of God are twice ten thousand,
thousands upon thousands;
the Lord is among them; Sinai is now in the sanctuary.
18 You ascended on high,
leading a host of captives in your train
and receiving gifts among men,
even among the rebellious, that the LORD God may dwell there.

19 Blessed be the Lord,
who daily bears us up;
God is our salvation. *Selah*
20 Our God is a God of salvation,
and to GOD, the Lord, belong deliverances from death.
21 But God will strike the heads of his enemies,
the hairy crown of him who walks in his guilty ways.
22 The Lord said,
"I will bring them back from Bashan,
I will bring them back from the depths of the sea,
23 that you may strike your feet in their blood,
that the tongues of your dogs may have their portion from the foe."

24 Your procession is[4] seen, O God,
the procession of my God, my King, into the sanctuary—

[1]Or *before God, even Sinai before God* [2]Or *your congregation* [3]Or *hunch-backed*; also verse 16
[4]Or *has been*

(Let All Peoples Praise You, continued)

They were to make new disciples of people from all nations—teaching and baptizing in his name (Mt 28:18–20). The primary way of making disciples is speaking the good news of the gospel—spelling out God's grace, Christ's sacrifice, the defeat of sin, and the hope of eternal life.

When people experience life change through Jesus, he transforms them so that they bring light to the world. Satisfaction in Jesus turns into a living announcement about the sufficiency of Jesus. Christians shine their joyous light in the world—all for the glory of God (Mt 5:14–16).

25 the singers in front, the musicians last,
between them virgins playing tambourines:
26 "Bless God in the great congregation,
the LORD, O you[1] who are of Israel's fountain!"
27 There is Benjamin, the least of them, in the lead,
the princes of Judah in their throng,
the princes of Zebulun, the princes of Naphtali.

28 Summon your power, O God,[2]
the power, O God, by which you have worked for us.
29 Because of your temple at Jerusalem
kings shall bear gifts to you.
30 Rebuke the beasts that dwell among the reeds,
the herd of bulls with the calves of the peoples.
Trample underfoot those who lust after tribute;
scatter the peoples who delight in war.[3]
31 Nobles shall come from Egypt;
Cush shall hasten to stretch out her hands to God.

32 O kingdoms of the earth, sing to God;
sing praises to the Lord, *Selah*
33 to him who rides in the heavens, the ancient heavens;
behold, he sends out his voice, his mighty voice.
34 Ascribe power to God,
whose majesty is over Israel,
and whose power is in the skies.
35 Awesome is God from his[4] sanctuary;
the God of Israel—he is the one who gives power and strength to his people.
Blessed be God!

Psalm 69

Save Me, O God

To the choirmaster: according to Lilies. Of David.

1 Save me, O God!
For the waters have come up to my neck.[5]
2 I sink in deep mire,
where there is no foothold;
I have come into deep waters,
and the flood sweeps over me.
3 I am weary with my crying out;
my throat is parched.
My eyes grow dim
with waiting for my God.

4 More in number than the hairs of my head
are those who hate me without cause;
mighty are those who would destroy me,
those who attack me with lies.
What I did not steal
must I now restore?
5 O God, you know my folly;
the wrongs I have done are not hidden from you.

[1]The Hebrew for *you* is plural here [2]By revocalization (compare Septuagint); Hebrew *Your God has summoned your power* [3]The meaning of the Hebrew verse is uncertain [4]Septuagint; Hebrew *your* [5]Or *waters threaten my life*

6 Let not those who hope in you be put to shame through me,
O Lord GOD of hosts;
let not those who seek you be brought to dishonor through me,
O God of Israel.
7 For it is for your sake that I have borne reproach,
that dishonor has covered my face.
8 I have become a stranger to my brothers,
an alien to my mother's sons.

9 For zeal for your house has consumed me,
and the reproaches of those who reproach you have fallen on me.
10 When I wept and humbled[1] my soul with fasting,
it became my reproach.
11 When I made sackcloth my clothing,
I became a byword to them.
12 I am the talk of those who sit in the gate,
and the drunkards make songs about me.

13 But as for me, my prayer is to you, O LORD.
At an acceptable time, O God,
in the abundance of your steadfast love answer me in your saving faithfulness.
14 Deliver me
from sinking in the mire;
let me be delivered from my enemies
and from the deep waters.
15 Let not the flood sweep over me,
or the deep swallow me up,
or the pit close its mouth over me.

16 Answer me, O LORD, for your steadfast love is good;
according to your abundant mercy, turn to me.
17 Hide not your face from your servant,
for I am in distress; make haste to answer me.
18 Draw near to my soul, redeem me;
ransom me because of my enemies!

19 You know my reproach,
and my shame and my dishonor;
my foes are all known to you.
20 Reproaches have broken my heart,
so that I am in despair.
I looked for pity, but there was none,
and for comforters, but I found none.
21 They gave me poison for food,
and for my thirst they gave me sour wine to drink.

22 Let their own table before them become a snare;
and when they are at peace, let it become a trap.[2]
23 Let their eyes be darkened, so that they cannot see,
and make their loins tremble continually.
24 Pour out your indignation upon them,
and let your burning anger overtake them.
25 May their camp be a desolation;
let no one dwell in their tents.
26 For they persecute him whom you have struck down,
and they recount the pain of those you have wounded.

[1]Hebrew lacks *and humbled* [2]Hebrew; a slight revocalization yields (compare Septuagint, Syriac, Jerome) *a snare, and retribution and a trap*

PSALM 70:1–5

SAVE ME: YES OR NO?

In Psalm 70, David asked God to deliver him from the oppression and suffering brought about by his enemies. He sought refuge in God, expecting the result to include great glory for the Lord (v. 4).

Jesus voiced a prayer in the Gospel of John that includes some similarity to David's prayer (Jn 12:27–28). Laboring under the weight of the task before him, Jesus considered the depth of what he was about to suffer on the cross. He contemplated a request for God to deliver him, but quickly changed direction — affirming that what he was about to endure was the very reason why he came to earth.

In David's words, God is glorified by delivering him from the hands of his enemies. In Jesus' words, God the Father is glorified not by sparing the Son but through the Son's death. If Jesus had avoided the cross, there would be no way for people to have access to God. Through the willing sacrifice of Jesus, God made possible the deliverance of all people who place their faith in Jesus for salvation.

27 Add to them punishment upon punishment;
may they have no acquittal from you.[1]
28 Let them be blotted out of the book of the living;
let them not be enrolled among the righteous.

29 But I am afflicted and in pain;
let your salvation, O God, set me on high!

30 I will praise the name of God with a song;
I will magnify him with thanksgiving.
31 This will please the LORD more than an ox
or a bull with horns and hoofs.
32 When the humble see it they will be glad;
you who seek God, let your hearts revive.
33 For the LORD hears the needy
and does not despise his own people who are prisoners.

34 Let heaven and earth praise him,
the seas and everything that moves in them.
35 For God will save Zion
and build up the cities of Judah,
and people shall dwell there and possess it;
36 the offspring of his servants shall inherit it,
and those who love his name shall dwell in it.

Psalm 70

O LORD, Do Not Delay

To the choirmaster. Of David, for the memorial offering.

1 Make haste, O God, to deliver me!
O LORD, make haste to help me!
2 Let them be put to shame and confusion
who seek my life!
Let them be turned back and brought to dishonor
who delight in my hurt!
3 Let them turn back because of their shame
who say, "Aha, Aha!"

4 May all who seek you
rejoice and be glad in you!
May those who love your salvation
say evermore, "God is great!"
5 But I am poor and needy;
hasten to me, O God!
You are my help and my deliverer;
O LORD, do not delay!

Psalm 71

Forsake Me Not When My Strength Is Spent

1 In you, O LORD, do I take refuge;
let me never be put to shame!
2 In your righteousness deliver me and rescue me;
incline your ear to me, and save me!
3 Be to me a rock of refuge,
to which I may continually come;

[1]Hebrew *may they not come into your righteousness*

you have given the command to save me,
for you are my rock and my fortress.

4 Rescue me, O my God, from the hand of the wicked,
from the grasp of the unjust and cruel man.
5 For you, O Lord, are my hope,
my trust, O LORD, from my youth.
6 Upon you I have leaned from before my birth;
you are he who took me from my mother's womb.
My praise is continually of you.

7 I have been as a portent to many,
but you are my strong refuge.
8 My mouth is filled with your praise,
and with your glory all the day.
9 Do not cast me off in the time of old age;
forsake me not when my strength is spent.
10 For my enemies speak concerning me;
those who watch for my life consult together
11 and say, "God has forsaken him;
pursue and seize him,
for there is none to deliver him."

12 O God, be not far from me;
O my God, make haste to help me!
13 May my accusers be put to shame and consumed;
with scorn and disgrace may they be covered
who seek my hurt.
14 But I will hope continually
and will praise you yet more and more.
15 My mouth will tell of your righteous acts,
of your deeds of salvation all the day,
for their number is past my knowledge.
16 With the mighty deeds of the Lord GOD I will come;
I will remind them of your righteousness, yours alone.

17 O God, from my youth you have taught me,
and I still proclaim your wondrous deeds.
18 So even to old age and gray hairs,
O God, do not forsake me,
until I proclaim your might to another generation,
your power to all those to come.
19 Your righteousness, O God,
reaches the high heavens.
You who have done great things,
O God, who is like you?
20 You who have made me see many troubles and calamities
will revive me again;
from the depths of the earth
you will bring me up again.
21 You will increase my greatness
and comfort me again.

22 I will also praise you with the harp
for your faithfulness, O my God;
I will sing praises to you with the lyre,
O Holy One of Israel.
23 My lips will shout for joy,
when I sing praises to you;
my soul also, which you have redeemed.

PSALM 71:14–18

DECLARING GOD'S GREATNESS AT EVERY AGE

There are many reasons people want to live long lives. Some want to enjoy the fruits of careers — savoring the rewards of retirement. Others want to witness the successes of children and grandchildren. This psalmist had a God-centered reason for wanting to continue to live, and thrive, in his old age. He desired more time to declare the greatness of God's power — to tell the stories of God's faithfulness to the younger people around him.

Jesus encouraged Peter that, though he had sinned, his life would testify to the greatness of God — and he would continue to be used by God in powerful ways (Jn 21:18–19). Even at the end of his life, Peter would faithfully serve Christ. His very death would glorify God. Christians do not reach an age of discharge from the mission — a threshold of years beyond which they can rest from kingdom labors. Believers have the privilege and responsibility to tell the succeeding generations about the goodness and greatness of God. Stories of God's faithfulness inspire the young to trust God — to live boldly, refusing to waste any days of life.

24 And my tongue will talk of your righteous help all the day long,
for they have been put to shame and disappointed
who sought to do me hurt.

Psalm 72

Give the King Your Justice

Of Solomon.

1 Give the king your justice, O God,
and your righteousness to the royal son!
2 May he judge your people with righteousness,
and your poor with justice!
3 Let the mountains bear prosperity for the people,
and the hills, in righteousness!
4 May he defend the cause of the poor of the people,
give deliverance to the children of the needy,
and crush the oppressor!

5 May they fear you[1] while the sun endures,
and as long as the moon, throughout all generations!
6 May he be like rain that falls on the mown grass,
like showers that water the earth!
7 In his days may the righteous flourish,
and peace abound, till the moon be no more!

8 May he have dominion from sea to sea,
and from the River[2] to the ends of the earth!
9 May desert tribes bow down before him,
and his enemies lick the dust!
10 May the kings of Tarshish and of the coastlands
render him tribute;
may the kings of Sheba and Seba
bring gifts!
11 May all kings fall down before him,
all nations serve him!

12 For he delivers the needy when he calls,
the poor and him who has no helper.
13 He has pity on the weak and the needy,
and saves the lives of the needy.
14 From oppression and violence he redeems their life,
and precious is their blood in his sight.

15 Long may he live;
may gold of Sheba be given to him!
May prayer be made for him continually,
and blessings invoked for him all the day!
16 May there be abundance of grain in the land;
on the tops of the mountains may it wave;
may its fruit be like Lebanon;
and may people blossom in the cities
like the grass of the field!
17 May his name endure forever,
his fame continue as long as the sun!
May people be blessed in him,
all nations call him blessed!

[1]Septuagint *He shall endure* [2]That is, the Euphrates

18 Blessed be the LORD, the God of Israel,
who alone does wondrous things.
19 Blessed be his glorious name forever;
may the whole earth be filled with his glory!
Amen and Amen!

20 The prayers of David, the son of Jesse, are ended.

BOOK THREE

Psalm 73

God Is My Strength and Portion Forever

A Psalm of Asaph.

1 Truly God is good to Israel,
to those who are pure in heart.
2 But as for me, my feet had almost stumbled,
my steps had nearly slipped.
3 For I was envious of the arrogant
when I saw the prosperity of the wicked.

4 For they have no pangs until death;
their bodies are fat and sleek.
5 They are not in trouble as others are;
they are not stricken like the rest of mankind.
6 Therefore pride is their necklace;
violence covers them as a garment.
7 Their eyes swell out through fatness;
their hearts overflow with follies.
8 They scoff and speak with malice;
loftily they threaten oppression.
9 They set their mouths against the heavens,
and their tongue struts through the earth.
10 Therefore his people turn back to them,
and find no fault in them.[1]
11 And they say, "How can God know?
Is there knowledge in the Most High?"
12 Behold, these are the wicked;
always at ease, they increase in riches.
13 All in vain have I kept my heart clean
and washed my hands in innocence.
14 For all the day long I have been stricken
and rebuked every morning.
15 If I had said, "I will speak thus,"
I would have betrayed the generation of your children.

16 But when I thought how to understand this,
it seemed to me a wearisome task,
17 until I went into the sanctuary of God;
then I discerned their end.

18 Truly you set them in slippery places;
you make them fall to ruin.
19 How they are destroyed in a moment,
swept away utterly by terrors!

[1]Probable reading; Hebrew *the waters of a full cup are drained by them*

20 Like a dream when one awakes,
O Lord, when you rouse yourself, you despise them as phantoms.
21 When my soul was embittered,
when I was pricked in heart,
22 I was brutish and ignorant;
I was like a beast toward you.

23 Nevertheless, I am continually with you;
you hold my right hand.
24 You guide me with your counsel,
and afterward you will receive me to glory.
25 Whom have I in heaven but you?
And there is nothing on earth that I desire besides you.
26 My flesh and my heart may fail,
but God is the strength[1] of my heart and my portion forever.

27 For behold, those who are far from you shall perish;
you put an end to everyone who is unfaithful to you.
28 But for me it is good to be near God;
I have made the Lord GOD my refuge,
that I may tell of all your works.

Psalm 74

Arise, O God, Defend Your Cause

A Maskil[2] of Asaph.

1 O God, why do you cast us off forever?
Why does your anger smoke against the sheep of your pasture?
2 Remember your congregation, which you have purchased of old,
which you have redeemed to be the tribe of your heritage!
Remember Mount Zion, where you have dwelt.
3 Direct your steps to the perpetual ruins;
the enemy has destroyed everything in the sanctuary!

4 Your foes have roared in the midst of your meeting place;
they set up their own signs for signs.
5 They were like those who swing axes
in a forest of trees.[3]
6 And all its carved wood
they broke down with hatchets and hammers.
7 They set your sanctuary on fire;
they profaned the dwelling place of your name,
bringing it down to the ground.
8 They said to themselves, "We will utterly subdue them";
they burned all the meeting places of God in the land.

9 We do not see our signs;
there is no longer any prophet,
and there is none among us who knows how long.
10 How long, O God, is the foe to scoff?
Is the enemy to revile your name forever?
11 Why do you hold back your hand, your right hand?
Take it from the fold of your garment[4] and destroy them!

12 Yet God my King is from of old,
working salvation in the midst of the earth.

[1]Hebrew *rock* [2]Probably a musical or liturgical term [3]The meaning of the Hebrew is uncertain
[4]Hebrew *from your bosom*

PSALM 73:25–26

TREASURE IN HEAVEN

The writer of this psalm likely encountered many beautiful and impressive things while serving in the temple. Yet the confession of his heart was that God in heaven was his greatest treasure. Nothing on earth could compete with the glories of God. Nothing stirred his affections like the Sovereign Lord.

Jesus taught people to pull back from pursuing the treasures of earth—to stop storing them away for status and security. Money and possessions are temporary bits of wealth, and all of it can be stolen or ruined (Mt 6:19). As the psalmist's greatest prize was in heaven, so Jesus encouraged his listeners to invest in things that would last forever (Mt 6:20). On another occasion, Jesus used a parable to compare the kingdom of heaven to a "treasure hidden in a field, which a man found and covered up. Then in his joy he goes and sells all that he has and buys that field" (Mt 13:44). Life on earth features many luxuries and objects of worth. Jesus teaches people to resist the temptation to chase after things that will not last. Rather, those who believe in Jesus should spend their years investing in their relationship with God and the people he loves—dispensing grace, making disciples, and loving unconditionally. These treasures of heaven will endure forever and bring much glory to God.

PSALM 74:1–12

PAIN

Pain in life is a universal experience—it falls on the righteous and the unrighteous. People often search

(continued on next page)

13 You divided the sea by your might;
you broke the heads of the sea monsters[1] on the waters.
14 You crushed the heads of Leviathan;
you gave him as food for the creatures of the wilderness.
15 You split open springs and brooks;
you dried up ever-flowing streams.
16 Yours is the day, yours also the night;
you have established the heavenly lights and the sun.
17 You have fixed all the boundaries of the earth;
you have made summer and winter.

18 Remember this, O LORD, how the enemy scoffs,
and a foolish people reviles your name.
19 Do not deliver the soul of your dove to the wild beasts;
do not forget the life of your poor forever.

20 Have regard for the covenant,
for the dark places of the land are full of the habitations of violence.
21 Let not the downtrodden turn back in shame;
let the poor and needy praise your name.

22 Arise, O God, defend your cause;
remember how the foolish scoff at you all the day!
23 Do not forget the clamor of your foes,
the uproar of those who rise against you, which goes up continually!

Psalm 75

God Will Judge with Equity

To the choirmaster: according to Do Not Destroy. A Psalm of Asaph. A Song.

1 We give thanks to you, O God;
we give thanks, for your name is near.
We[2] recount your wondrous deeds.

2 "At the set time that I appoint
I will judge with equity.
3 When the earth totters, and all its inhabitants,
it is I who keep steady its pillars. *Selah*
4 I say to the boastful, 'Do not boast,'
and to the wicked, 'Do not lift up your horn;
5 do not lift up your horn on high,
or speak with haughty neck.'"

6 For not from the east or from the west
and not from the wilderness comes lifting up,
7 but it is God who executes judgment,
putting down one and lifting up another.
8 For in the hand of the LORD there is a cup
with foaming wine, well mixed,
and he pours out from it,
and all the wicked of the earth
shall drain it down to the dregs.

9 But I will declare it forever;
I will sing praises to the God of Jacob.
10 All the horns of the wicked I will cut off,
but the horns of the righteous shall be lifted up.

[1]Or *the great sea creatures* [2]Hebrew *They*

(Pain, continued)

for a reason behind trials and tragedies, but answers are elusive since humans cannot fully know the purposes of God. The Bible suggests that in some instances, pain might be punishment for specific sins, a test of faith, fatherly discipline, or a means to drive people to repentance. Usually clear meaning is absent, especially in situations of ongoing suffering. From the pit of pain, the psalmist reached for confidence in God—the one who had been his faithful King for a long time (v. 12). He knew of God's capabilities, yet wondered when relief would come.

Jesus frequently stepped into people's lives during a point of great pain. He performed a miracle for a grieving mother at a funeral (Lk 7:13–15). He touched and healed a man with leprosy (Mt 8:2–3). He changed the lives of a bleeding woman and a worried father over the course of just a few minutes (Mk 5:22–42). Jesus is full of compassion for the pain caused by this world. He is eager for people to know that he cares deeply about their trouble. Jesus is a dependable source of comfort in the face of suffering (2Co 1:3–6).

Psalm 76

Who Can Stand Before You?

To the choirmaster: with stringed instruments. A Psalm of Asaph. A Song.

1 In Judah God is known;
his name is great in Israel.
2 His abode has been established in Salem,
his dwelling place in Zion.
3 There he broke the flashing arrows,
the shield, the sword, and the weapons of war. *Selah*

4 Glorious are you, more majestic
than the mountains full of prey.
5 The stouthearted were stripped of their spoil;
they sank into sleep;
all the men of war
were unable to use their hands.
6 At your rebuke, O God of Jacob,
both rider and horse lay stunned.

7 But you, you are to be feared!
Who can stand before you
when once your anger is roused?
8 From the heavens you uttered judgment;
the earth feared and was still,
9 when God arose to establish judgment,
to save all the humble of the earth. *Selah*

10 Surely the wrath of man shall praise you;
the remnant[1] of wrath you will put on like a belt.
11 Make your vows to the LORD your God and perform them;
let all around him bring gifts
to him who is to be feared,
12 who cuts off the spirit of princes,
who is to be feared by the kings of the earth.

PSALM 77:1–20

OUR HELP IN AGES PAST

This is one psalm, but it reads like two distinct chapters. In the first nine verses, the author bared his soul. He cried out for help, but remained uncomforted (v. 2). The difficulties he faced kept his eyes open at night and his mouth shut during the day (v. 4). In the midst of trouble, he asked the honest questions many in this broken world ask: Does God still love me? Are God's promises still true? (vv. 7–8). That is the first "chapter" of this psalm.

Then the psalmist remembered something else, namely, the character of the God he cried out to. In this second "chapter," he meditated upon the deeds of his God (vv. 10–12), the character of his God (v. 13), and the power of his God (vv. 14–20). Long before the psalmist's sufferings, the people of God were in bondage in Egypt. God heard their cry, redeeming them with a mighty arm (vv. 15–19). In the midst of trouble, the psalmist's only hope was the character of his God.

Jesus instructed his disciples along the same lines in John 14. Though he never promised them a life of ease, he encouraged them to believe *in the midst* of trouble (Jn 14:1). Their only hope, too, was the character of the God who spoke to them. This Jesus — God incarnate — heard their cries and put his power on display by redeeming them.

Psalm 77

In the Day of Trouble I Seek the Lord

To the choirmaster: according to Jeduthun. A Psalm of Asaph.

1 I cry aloud to God,
aloud to God, and he will hear me.
2 In the day of my trouble I seek the Lord;
in the night my hand is stretched out without wearying;
my soul refuses to be comforted.
3 When I remember God, I moan;
when I meditate, my spirit faints. *Selah*

4 You hold my eyelids open;
I am so troubled that I cannot speak.
5 I consider the days of old,
the years long ago.
6 I said,[2] "Let me remember my song in the night;
let me meditate in my heart."
Then my spirit made a diligent search:

[1]Or *extremity* [2]Hebrew lacks *I said*

7 "Will the Lord spurn forever,
and never again be favorable?
8 Has his steadfast love forever ceased?
Are his promises at an end for all time?
9 Has God forgotten to be gracious?
Has he in anger shut up his compassion?" *Selah*

10 Then I said, "I will appeal to this,
to the years of the right hand of the Most High."[1]

11 I will remember the deeds of the LORD;
yes, I will remember your wonders of old.
12 I will ponder all your work,
and meditate on your mighty deeds.
13 Your way, O God, is holy.
What god is great like our God?
14 You are the God who works wonders;
you have made known your might among the peoples.
15 You with your arm redeemed your people,
the children of Jacob and Joseph. *Selah*

16 When the waters saw you, O God,
when the waters saw you, they were afraid;
indeed, the deep trembled.
17 The clouds poured out water;
the skies gave forth thunder;
your arrows flashed on every side.
18 The crash of your thunder was in the whirlwind;
your lightnings lighted up the world;
the earth trembled and shook.
19 Your way was through the sea,
your path through the great waters;
yet your footprints were unseen.[2]
20 You led your people like a flock
by the hand of Moses and Aaron.

Psalm 78

Tell the Coming Generation

A Maskil[3] of Asaph.

1 Give ear, O my people, to my teaching;
incline your ears to the words of my mouth!
2 I will open my mouth in a parable;
I will utter dark sayings from of old,
3 things that we have heard and known,
that our fathers have told us.
4 We will not hide them from their children,
but tell to the coming generation
the glorious deeds of the LORD, and his might,
and the wonders that he has done.

5 He established a testimony in Jacob
and appointed a law in Israel,
which he commanded our fathers
to teach to their children,

[1]Or *This is my grief: that the right hand of the Most High has changed* [2]Hebrew *unknown* [3]Probably a musical or liturgical term

6 that the next generation might know them,
the children yet unborn,
and arise and tell them to their children,
7 so that they should set their hope in God
and not forget the works of God,
but keep his commandments;
8 and that they should not be like their fathers,
a stubborn and rebellious generation,
a generation whose heart was not steadfast,
whose spirit was not faithful to God.

9 The Ephraimites, armed with[1] the bow,
turned back on the day of battle.
10 They did not keep God's covenant,
but refused to walk according to his law.
11 They forgot his works
and the wonders that he had shown them.
12 In the sight of their fathers he performed wonders
in the land of Egypt, in the fields of Zoan.
13 He divided the sea and let them pass through it,
and made the waters stand like a heap.
14 In the daytime he led them with a cloud,
and all the night with a fiery light.
15 He split rocks in the wilderness
and gave them drink abundantly as from the deep.
16 He made streams come out of the rock
and caused waters to flow down like rivers.

17 Yet they sinned still more against him,
rebelling against the Most High in the desert.
18 They tested God in their heart
by demanding the food they craved.
19 They spoke against God, saying,
"Can God spread a table in the wilderness?
20 He struck the rock so that water gushed out
and streams overflowed.
Can he also give bread
or provide meat for his people?"

21 Therefore, when the LORD heard, he was full of wrath;
a fire was kindled against Jacob;
his anger rose against Israel,
22 because they did not believe in God
and did not trust his saving power.
23 Yet he commanded the skies above
and opened the doors of heaven,
24 and he rained down on them manna to eat
and gave them the grain of heaven.
25 Man ate of the bread of the angels;
he sent them food in abundance.
26 He caused the east wind to blow in the heavens,
and by his power he led out the south wind;
27 he rained meat on them like dust,
winged birds like the sand of the seas;
28 he let them fall in the midst of their camp,
all around their dwellings.

[1]Hebrew *armed and shooting*

TEACHING IN PARABLES

In Matthew 13, Jesus used parables to explain the kingdom of God. In fact, he chose not to say much of anything to the gathered crowds in that passage *without* using parables. Though the purposes behind Jesus' teaching style are more than can be enumerated here, it certainly fulfilled the psalmist's words in Psalm 78:2: "I will open my mouth in a parable; I will utter dark sayings from of old" (paraphrased in Mt 13:35).

The parables Jesus taught — the Good Samaritan, the Lost Son, and so on — rank as some of the best-known passages in all of Scripture. Rather than giving complicated teachings wrapped in theologically dense language, Jesus usually used simple, everyday realities to teach the intended truth. For example, he used a lost coin in Luke 15 and differing kinds of soil in Matthew 13.

A few times Jesus applied the parable to his audience by asking the crowd a question, as in the parable of the Good Samaritan: "Which of these three, do you think, proved to be a neighbor to the man who fell among the robbers?" (Lk 10:36). Other times he interpreted the parable himself (Mt 13:18–23). There were also times when the parable was told only to confirm unbelievers in their rejection of him (Mk 4:11–12). In such cases, the simplicity of the parable only highlighted their blindness.

While there might be a few characters in a parable that need to be interpreted, parables are not necessarily strict allegories where every detail demands an attached spiritual symbolism. In the parable of the Lost Son, for example, spiritual significance might wrongly be attached to details of the ring the father gives. Even so, parables do not need to be limited to only one application point. For example, the father in that parable represents God, but it is also clear that the older brother represents the self-righteous Pharisees to whom Jesus spoke.

Jesus' teaching style shared many of the same aims of Psalm 78. Like the psalmist's words long before, Jesus' parables taught "the coming generation the glorious deeds of the LORD, and his might, and the wonders that he has done" (Ps 78:4).

29 And they ate and were well filled,
for he gave them what they craved.
30 But before they had satisfied their craving,
while the food was still in their mouths,
31 the anger of God rose against them,
and he killed the strongest of them
and laid low the young men of Israel.

32 In spite of all this, they still sinned;
despite his wonders, they did not believe.
33 So he made their days vanish like[1] a breath,[2]
and their years in terror.
34 When he killed them, they sought him;
they repented and sought God earnestly.
35 They remembered that God was their rock,
the Most High God their redeemer.
36 But they flattered him with their mouths;
they lied to him with their tongues.
37 Their heart was not steadfast toward him;
they were not faithful to his covenant.
38 Yet he, being compassionate,
atoned for their iniquity
and did not destroy them;
he restrained his anger often
and did not stir up all his wrath.
39 He remembered that they were but flesh,
a wind that passes and comes not again.
40 How often they rebelled against him in the wilderness
and grieved him in the desert!
41 They tested God again and again
and provoked the Holy One of Israel.
42 They did not remember his power[3]
or the day when he redeemed them from the foe,
43 when he performed his signs in Egypt
and his marvels in the fields of Zoan.
44 He turned their rivers to blood,
so that they could not drink of their streams.
45 He sent among them swarms of flies, which devoured them,
and frogs, which destroyed them.
46 He gave their crops to the destroying locust
and the fruit of their labor to the locust.
47 He destroyed their vines with hail
and their sycamores with frost.
48 He gave over their cattle to the hail
and their flocks to thunderbolts.
49 He let loose on them his burning anger,
wrath, indignation, and distress,
a company of destroying angels.
50 He made a path for his anger;
he did not spare them from death,
but gave their lives over to the plague.
51 He struck down every firstborn in Egypt,
the firstfruits of their strength in the tents of Ham.
52 Then he led out his people like sheep
and guided them in the wilderness like a flock.

[1]Hebrew *in* [2]Or *vapor* [3]Hebrew *hand*

53 He led them in safety, so that they were not afraid,
but the sea overwhelmed their enemies.
54 And he brought them to his holy land,
to the mountain which his right hand had won.
55 He drove out nations before them;
he apportioned them for a possession
and settled the tribes of Israel in their tents.

56 Yet they tested and rebelled against the Most High God
and did not keep his testimonies,
57 but turned away and acted treacherously like their
fathers;
they twisted like a deceitful bow.
58 For they provoked him to anger with their high places;
they moved him to jealousy with their idols.
59 When God heard, he was full of wrath,
and he utterly rejected Israel.
60 He forsook his dwelling at Shiloh,
the tent where he dwelt among mankind,
61 and delivered his power to captivity,
his glory to the hand of the foe.
62 He gave his people over to the sword
and vented his wrath on his heritage.
63 Fire devoured their young men,
and their young women had no marriage song.
64 Their priests fell by the sword,
and their widows made no lamentation.
65 Then the Lord awoke as from sleep,
like a strong man shouting because of wine.
66 And he put his adversaries to rout;
he put them to everlasting shame.

67 He rejected the tent of Joseph;
he did not choose the tribe of Ephraim,
68 but he chose the tribe of Judah,
Mount Zion, which he loves.
69 He built his sanctuary like the high heavens,
like the earth, which he has founded forever.
70 He chose David his servant
and took him from the sheepfolds;
71 from following the nursing ewes he brought him
to shepherd Jacob his people,
Israel his inheritance.
72 With upright heart he shepherded them
and guided them with his skillful hand.

Psalm 79

How Long, O Lord?

A Psalm of Asaph.

1 O God, the nations have come into your inheritance;
they have defiled your holy temple;
they have laid Jerusalem in ruins.
2 They have given the bodies of your servants
to the birds of the heavens for food,
the flesh of your faithful to the beasts of the earth.

3 They have poured out their blood like water
all around Jerusalem,
and there was no one to bury them.
4 We have become a taunt to our neighbors,
mocked and derided by those around us.

5 How long, O LORD? Will you be angry forever?
Will your jealousy burn like fire?
6 Pour out your anger on the nations
that do not know you,
and on the kingdoms
that do not call upon your name!
7 For they have devoured Jacob
and laid waste his habitation.

8 Do not remember against us our former iniquities;[1]
let your compassion come speedily to meet us,
for we are brought very low.
9 Help us, O God of our salvation,
for the glory of your name;
deliver us, and atone for our sins,
for your name's sake!
10 Why should the nations say,
"Where is their God?"
Let the avenging of the outpoured blood of your servants
be known among the nations before our eyes!

11 Let the groans of the prisoners come before you;
according to your great power, preserve those doomed to die!
12 Return sevenfold into the lap of our neighbors
the taunts with which they have taunted you, O Lord!
13 But we your people, the sheep of your pasture,
will give thanks to you forever;
from generation to generation we will recount your praise.

PSALM 79:8–10

JUDAH'S REPENTANCE

In this psalm, the reader gets a glimpse into the horror that followed Nebuchadnezzar's invasion of Judah. The birds and wild animals feasted upon bodies left unburied. The temple of God—the locus of the Lord's worship—was defiled. Furthermore, the pagan nations mocked the people of God.

In their recent history, the people of God had stiffened their necks a thousand times too many. They were stubbornly disobedient. But in this psalm, after seeing and experiencing the judgment of God, the psalmist was brought low. He asked the Lord to be compassionate and to remember their sins no longer.

But this was not for Judah's sake alone. Instead, the pleas for help centered upon God's reputation (vv. 9–10). The psalmist lamented the pagan nations' taunt: "Where is their God?" (v. 10). True repentance not only turns away from sin, but turns toward God's honor.

Psalm 80

Restore Us, O God

To the choirmaster: according to Lilies. A Testimony. Of Asaph, a Psalm.

1 Give ear, O Shepherd of Israel,
you who lead Joseph like a flock.
You who are enthroned upon the cherubim, shine forth.
2 Before Ephraim and Benjamin and Manasseh,
stir up your might
and come to save us!

3 Restore us,[2] O God;
let your face shine, that we may be saved!

4 O LORD God of hosts,
how long will you be angry with your people's prayers?
5 You have fed them with the bread of tears
and given them tears to drink in full measure.
6 You make us an object of contention for our neighbors,
and our enemies laugh among themselves.

[1]Or *the iniquities of former generations* [2]Or *Turn us again*; also verses 7, 19

7 Restore us, O God of hosts;
let your face shine, that we may be saved!

8 You brought a vine out of Egypt;
you drove out the nations and planted it.
9 You cleared the ground for it;
it took deep root and filled the land.
10 The mountains were covered with its shade,
the mighty cedars with its branches.
11 It sent out its branches to the sea
and its shoots to the River.[1]
12 Why then have you broken down its walls,
so that all who pass along the way pluck its fruit?
13 The boar from the forest ravages it,
and all that move in the field feed on it.

14 Turn again, O God of hosts!
Look down from heaven, and see;
have regard for this vine,
15 the stock that your right hand planted,
and for the son whom you made strong for yourself.
16 They have burned it with fire; they have cut it down;
may they perish at the rebuke of your face!
17 But let your hand be on the man of your right hand,
the son of man whom you have made strong for yourself!
18 Then we shall not turn back from you;
give us life, and we will call upon your name!

19 Restore us, O LORD God of hosts!
Let your face shine, that we may be saved!

Psalm 81

Oh, That My People Would Listen to Me

To the choirmaster: according to The Gittith.[2] *Of Asaph.*

1 Sing aloud to God our strength;
shout for joy to the God of Jacob!
2 Raise a song; sound the tambourine,
the sweet lyre with the harp.
3 Blow the trumpet at the new moon,
at the full moon, on our feast day.

4 For it is a statute for Israel,
a rule[3] of the God of Jacob.
5 He made it a decree in Joseph
when he went out over[4] the land of Egypt.
I hear a language I had not known:
6 "I relieved your[5] shoulder of the burden;
your hands were freed from the basket.
7 In distress you called, and I delivered you;
I answered you in the secret place of thunder;
I tested you at the waters of Meribah. *Selah*
8 Hear, O my people, while I admonish you!
O Israel, if you would but listen to me!
9 There shall be no strange god among you;
you shall not bow down to a foreign god.

[1]That is, the Euphrates [2]Probably a musical or liturgical term [3]Or *just decree* [4]Or *against*
[5]Hebrew *his*; also next line

PLACE OF HONOR

While the "man of your right hand" (Ps 80:17) originally referred to Israel, Jesus — the "Son of Man" — ultimately fulfills Israel's calling as the Scriptures unfold. Jesus now sits in the place of honor described in this psalm.

Having been raised from the dead, Jesus ascended to the right hand of the Father. Paul spoke of God's power, which "he worked in Christ when he raised him from the dead and seated him at his right hand in the heavenly places" (Eph 1:20). At Pentecost, Peter proclaimed that Jesus had been "exalted at the right hand of God" (Ac 2:33). Though the ascension is sometimes treated as something of an afterthought to the life, death, and resurrection of Jesus, the Scriptures reveal its importance. The ascension marks a decisive moment when God the Father placed honor squarely on his Son.

What is Jesus doing, seated in the place of honor? He reigns as King. The ascension and the kingdom of God are connected. Jesus ascended to be coronated; he ascended to rule. Peter wrote that Jesus "has gone into heaven and is at the right hand of God, with angels, authorities, and powers having been subjected to him" (1Pe 3:22). There is a present kingdom because there is a present, living King. Sitting in the place of honor, ruling as King, Jesus intercedes for his people (Ro 8:34).

In the Scriptures, being seated signifies a completed work. For Old Testament believers, a "seated priest" would likely have seemed like a contradiction in terms. Priests never sat in the tabernacle, reflecting the fact that their priestly work was never complete or final. Every sacrifice and offering was provisional and would need to be repeated. But all this changed with the coming of a true and better priest: "But when Christ had offered for all time a single sacrifice for sins, he sat down at the right hand of God" (Heb 10:12). Those who trust in the man at God's right hand will never be put to shame (1Pe 2:6).

10 I am the LORD your God,
who brought you up out of the land of Egypt.
Open your mouth wide, and I will fill it.

11 "But my people did not listen to my voice;
Israel would not submit to me.
12 So I gave them over to their stubborn hearts,
to follow their own counsels.
13 Oh, that my people would listen to me,
that Israel would walk in my ways!
14 I would soon subdue their enemies
and turn my hand against their foes.
15 Those who hate the LORD would cringe toward him,
and their fate would last forever.
16 But he would feed you[1] with the finest of the wheat,
and with honey from the rock I would satisfy you."

Psalm 82

Rescue the Weak and Needy

A Psalm of Asaph.

1 God has taken his place in the divine council;
in the midst of the gods he holds judgment:
2 "How long will you judge unjustly
and show partiality to the wicked? *Selah*
3 Give justice to the weak and the fatherless;
maintain the right of the afflicted and the destitute.
4 Rescue the weak and the needy;
deliver them from the hand of the wicked."

5 They have neither knowledge nor understanding,
they walk about in darkness;
all the foundations of the earth are shaken.

6 I said, "You are gods,
sons of the Most High, all of you;
7 nevertheless, like men you shall die,
and fall like any prince."[2]

8 Arise, O God, judge the earth;
for you shall inherit all the nations!

Psalm 83

O God, Do Not Keep Silence

A Song. A Psalm of Asaph.

1 O God, do not keep silence;
do not hold your peace or be still, O God!
2 For behold, your enemies make an uproar;
those who hate you have raised their heads.
3 They lay crafty plans against your people;
they consult together against your treasured ones.
4 They say, "Come, let us wipe them out as a nation;
let the name of Israel be remembered no more!"
5 For they conspire with one accord;
against you they make a covenant—

[1]That is, Israel; Hebrew *him* [2]Or *fall as one man, O princes*

SON OF THE MOST HIGH

In the Gospel of John, men holding stones told Jesus that they intended to kill him for blasphemy. This was because he, merely a man in their minds, claimed to be God (Jn 10:33).

In response, Jesus reasoned with them, quoting from Psalm 82:6: "Is it not written in your Law, 'I said, you are gods'?" (Jn 10:34). Jesus used the word *Law* in more general terms, referring to the entire Old Testament. Jesus offered the following argument to his would-be murderers: If Scripture can apply the word *gods* to mere humans, how much more should it be applied to the One whom the Father sent into the world (Jn 10:35–36)? Jesus appealed to the Word of God to address the charge of blasphemy.

A few verses prior in the Gospel of John, Jesus made clear that he and the Father are one (Jn 10:30). Though some had argued that Jesus never claimed to be God, here was his golden opportunity to assert something different. To keep these men from stoning him, all he needed to do was deny this oneness. But Jesus would not.

While children often bear a resemblance to their father, the Son of the Most High shows the world *exactly* what God is like. The author of Hebrews made this point explicit, telling readers that Jesus is "the exact imprint of [God's] nature" (Heb 1:3). Paul expressed the same point in different language: "He [the Son] is the image of the invisible God" (Col 1:15).

Jesus did not cease to be God when he became human. In John's Gospel, these men's Creator and Sustainer stood in the flesh before them. Such was their blindness that they had no idea who he was. If only they could have seen that Jesus was their ultimate source of salvation. He wanted to connect them to God, yet they wanted to stone him.

6 the tents of Edom and the Ishmaelites,
Moab and the Hagrites,
7 Gebal and Ammon and Amalek,
Philistia with the inhabitants of Tyre;
8 Asshur also has joined them;
they are the strong arm of the children of Lot. *Selah*

9 Do to them as you did to Midian,
as to Sisera and Jabin at the river Kishon,
10 who were destroyed at En-dor,
who became dung for the ground.
11 Make their nobles like Oreb and Zeeb,
all their princes like Zebah and Zalmunna,
12 who said, "Let us take possession for ourselves
of the pastures of God."

13 O my God, make them like whirling dust,[1]
like chaff before the wind.
14 As fire consumes the forest,
as the flame sets the mountains ablaze,
15 so may you pursue them with your tempest
and terrify them with your hurricane!
16 Fill their faces with shame,
that they may seek your name, O LORD.
17 Let them be put to shame and dismayed forever;
let them perish in disgrace,
18 that they may know that you alone,
whose name is the LORD,
are the Most High over all the earth.

Psalm 84

My Soul Longs for the Courts of the LORD

To the choirmaster: according to The Gittith.[2] A Psalm of the Sons of Korah.

1 How lovely is your dwelling place,
O LORD of hosts!
2 My soul longs, yes, faints
for the courts of the LORD;
my heart and flesh sing for joy
to the living God.

3 Even the sparrow finds a home,
and the swallow a nest for herself,
where she may lay her young,
at your altars, O LORD of hosts,
my King and my God.
4 Blessed are those who dwell in your house,
ever singing your praise! *Selah*

5 Blessed are those whose strength is in you,
in whose heart are the highways to Zion.[3]
6 As they go through the Valley of Baca
they make it a place of springs;
the early rain also covers it with pools.
7 They go from strength to strength;
each one appears before God in Zion.

[1]Or *like a tumbleweed* [2]Probably a musical or liturgical term [3]Hebrew lacks *to Zion*

PSALM 84:1–12

SPARROWS AND SWALLOWS

The psalmist desired nothing more than to be with God. This psalm seems to indicate that—at that moment—the psalmist, likely a Levite who normally served in the temple, did not have the physical access his soul desired. In the first stanza, he gave the readers an illustration. While the psalmist found himself away from the temple, nothing hindered the birds from staying as long as they desired (v. 3). The psalmist would go on to pen that one day in the temple courts was better than a thousand elsewhere (v. 10). He would sing that the blessed dwell in that temple (v. 4). These sparrows and swallows enjoyed the highest of privileges: never having to leave God's house.

Since the fall, humanity suffers from this separation. The Gospel of John says that Jesus came and made his dwelling among humans (Jn 1:14). He bridged the gulf caused by human sin and made a way for mankind to be made right with God once more. God's people, like the birds in this psalm, enjoy unfettered access to God through this Christ.

8 O LORD God of hosts, hear my prayer;
give ear, O God of Jacob! *Selah*
9 Behold our shield, O God;
look on the face of your anointed!
10 For a day in your courts is better
than a thousand elsewhere.
I would rather be a doorkeeper in the house of my God
than dwell in the tents of wickedness.
11 For the LORD God is a sun and shield;
the LORD bestows favor and honor.
No good thing does he withhold
from those who walk uprightly.
12 O LORD of hosts,
blessed is the one who trusts in you!

Psalm 85

Revive Us Again

To the choirmaster. A Psalm of the Sons of Korah.

1 LORD, you were favorable to your land;
you restored the fortunes of Jacob.
2 You forgave the iniquity of your people;
you covered all their sin. *Selah*
3 You withdrew all your wrath;
you turned from your hot anger.

4 Restore us again, O God of our salvation,
and put away your indignation toward us!
5 Will you be angry with us forever?
Will you prolong your anger to all generations?
6 Will you not revive us again,
that your people may rejoice in you?
7 Show us your steadfast love, O LORD,
and grant us your salvation.

8 Let me hear what God the LORD will speak,
for he will speak peace to his people, to his saints;
but let them not turn back to folly.
9 Surely his salvation is near to those who fear him,
that glory may dwell in our land.

10 Steadfast love and faithfulness meet;
righteousness and peace kiss each other.
11 Faithfulness springs up from the ground,
and righteousness looks down from the sky.
12 Yes, the LORD will give what is good,
and our land will yield its increase.
13 Righteousness will go before him
and make his footsteps a way.

Psalm 86

Great Is Your Steadfast Love

A Prayer of David.

1 Incline your ear, O LORD, and answer me,
for I am poor and needy.

PSALM 85:10–11

RIGHTEOUSNESS AND PEACE

Righteousness and peace demonstrate God's favor toward his people. The things the prophet longed for—peace, justice, and hope—are found in the Lord. Only God can be both just in his judgment of sin and bring about peace through the forgiveness of sin. The blessing the psalmist seeks here will be given to those who fear God and submit to him. The apostle Paul put this coming together on display most explicitly in the letter to the Romans. He wrote that a righteousness that comes from God has been made known through faith in Jesus Christ (Ro 3:21–22). This righteousness embraces peace: "Therefore, since we have been justified by faith, we have peace with God through our Lord Jesus Christ" (Ro 5:1). God has judged sin in Jesus' death and, through that death, granted peace to his children. Mercy and truth meet in Jesus, and in the end, true peace is found in that convergence.

PSALM 86:1–17

HEART CONDITION

This psalm holds the distinction of being one of the few psalms labeled "A Prayer of David." Without question, David lifted his heart to the Lord in these verses. The introduction makes clear his poverty of spirit (v. 1). His cries for mercy continued throughout the day (v. 3). As men sought his life (v. 14), David *sought the Lord. In the middle* of this prayer—comparing his God to the gods of the world—he erupted in praise: "There is none like you among the gods, O Lord,

(continued on next page)

2 Preserve my life, for I am godly;
save your servant, who trusts in you—you are my God.
3 Be gracious to me, O Lord,
for to you do I cry all the day.
4 Gladden the soul of your servant,
for to you, O Lord, do I lift up my soul.
5 For you, O Lord, are good and forgiving,
abounding in steadfast love to all who call upon you.
6 Give ear, O LORD, to my prayer;
listen to my plea for grace.
7 In the day of my trouble I call upon you,
for you answer me.

8 There is none like you among the gods, O Lord,
nor are there any works like yours.
9 All the nations you have made shall come
and worship before you, O Lord,
and shall glorify your name.
10 For you are great and do wondrous things;
you alone are God.
11 Teach me your way, O LORD,
that I may walk in your truth;
unite my heart to fear your name.
12 I give thanks to you, O Lord my God, with my whole heart,
and I will glorify your name forever.
13 For great is your steadfast love toward me;
you have delivered my soul from the depths of Sheol.

14 O God, insolent men have risen up against me;
a band of ruthless men seeks my life,
and they do not set you before them.
15 But you, O Lord, are a God merciful and gracious,
slow to anger and abounding in steadfast love and faithfulness.
16 Turn to me and be gracious to me;
give your strength to your servant,
and save the son of your maidservant.
17 Show me a sign of your favor,
that those who hate me may see and be put to shame
because you, LORD, have helped me and comforted me.

Psalm 87

Glorious Things of You Are Spoken

A Psalm of the Sons of Korah. A Song.

1 On the holy mount stands the city he founded;
2 the LORD loves the gates of Zion
more than all the dwelling places of Jacob.
3 Glorious things of you are spoken,
O city of God. *Selah*

4 Among those who know me I mention Rahab and Babylon;
behold, Philistia and Tyre, with Cush[1]—
"This one was born there," they say.
5 And of Zion it shall be said,
"This one and that one were born in her";
for the Most High himself will establish her.

[1]Probably *Nubia*

(Heart Condition, continued)

nor are there any works like yours" (v. 8). However, he still confessed to having a *divided* heart, a heart not solely focused upon God. David believed it would take nothing less than a work of God to change him. So he prayed: "Teach me your way, O LORD, that I may walk in your truth; *unite* my heart to fear your name. I give thanks to you, O Lord my God, with my *whole* heart, and I will glorify your name forever" (vv. 11–12, emphasis added).

6 The LORD records as he registers the peoples,
"This one was born there." *Selah*

7 Singers and dancers alike say,
"All my springs are in you."

Psalm 88

I Cry Out Day and Night Before You

A Song. A Psalm of the Sons of Korah. To the choirmaster: according to Mahalath Leannoth. A Maskil[1] of Heman the Ezrahite.

1 O LORD, God of my salvation,
I cry out day and night before you.
2 Let my prayer come before you;
incline your ear to my cry!

3 For my soul is full of troubles,
and my life draws near to Sheol.
4 I am counted among those who go down to the pit;
I am a man who has no strength,
5 like one set loose among the dead,
like the slain that lie in the grave,
like those whom you remember no more,
for they are cut off from your hand.
6 You have put me in the depths of the pit,
in the regions dark and deep.
7 Your wrath lies heavy upon me,
and you overwhelm me with all your waves. *Selah*

8 You have caused my companions to shun me;
you have made me a horror[2] to them.
I am shut in so that I cannot escape;
9 my eye grows dim through sorrow.
Every day I call upon you, O LORD;
I spread out my hands to you.
10 Do you work wonders for the dead?
Do the departed rise up to praise you? *Selah*
11 Is your steadfast love declared in the grave,
or your faithfulness in Abaddon?
12 Are your wonders known in the darkness,
or your righteousness in the land of forgetfulness?

13 But I, O LORD, cry to you;
in the morning my prayer comes before you.
14 O LORD, why do you cast my soul away?
Why do you hide your face from me?
15 Afflicted and close to death from my youth up,
I suffer your terrors; I am helpless.[3]
16 Your wrath has swept over me;
your dreadful assaults destroy me.
17 They surround me like a flood all day long;
they close in on me together.
18 You have caused my beloved and my friend to shun me;
my companions have become darkness.[4]

PSALM 88:1–18

THE AGONY OF SEPARATION

No one would accuse this songwriter of holding back how he really felt. He described his life as if he were in the grave. Some of the psalmist's phrasing recalls Job's story: "You have caused my companions to shun me; you have made me a horror to them. I am shut in so that I cannot escape" (v. 8). The psalmist was experiencing separation from the blessing and favor of God. "You have put me in the depths of the pit, in the regions dark and deep," he complains to the Lord (v. 6). However, while most of this psalm speaks to the writer's isolation, he still addressed God as the one who saves him (v. 1).

The silence of God must not be mistaken for the absence of God. Jesus felt abandoned by God at his crucifixion. This abandoned One would cry out, in darkness, on a wooden cross: "My God, my God, why have you forsaken me?" (Mt 27:46). Because of this, nothing in all of creation can separate God's people from his love (Ro 8:39). Jesus experienced separation from God so that his people would never have to.

[1]Probably musical or liturgical terms [2]Or *an abomination* [3]The meaning of the Hebrew word is uncertain [4]Or *darkness has become my only companion*

Psalm 89

I Will Sing of the Steadfast Love of the LORD

A Maskil[1] *of Ethan the Ezrahite.*

1 I will sing of the steadfast love of the LORD forever;
with my mouth I will make known your faithfulness to all generations.
2 For I said, "Steadfast love will be built up forever;
in the heavens you will establish your faithfulness."
3 You have said, "I have made a covenant with my chosen one;
I have sworn to David my servant:
4 'I will establish your offspring forever,
and build your throne for all generations.'" *Selah*

5 Let the heavens praise your wonders, O LORD,
your faithfulness in the assembly of the holy ones!
6 For who in the skies can be compared to the LORD?
Who among the heavenly beings[2] is like the LORD,
7 a God greatly to be feared in the council of the holy ones,
and awesome above all who are around him?
8 O LORD God of hosts,
who is mighty as you are, O LORD,
with your faithfulness all around you?
9 You rule the raging of the sea;
when its waves rise, you still them.
10 You crushed Rahab like a carcass;
you scattered your enemies with your mighty arm.
11 The heavens are yours; the earth also is yours;
the world and all that is in it, you have founded them.
12 The north and the south, you have created them;
Tabor and Hermon joyously praise your name.
13 You have a mighty arm;
strong is your hand, high your right hand.
14 Righteousness and justice are the foundation of your throne;
steadfast love and faithfulness go before you.
15 Blessed are the people who know the festal shout,
who walk, O LORD, in the light of your face,
16 who exult in your name all the day
and in your righteousness are exalted.
17 For you are the glory of their strength;
by your favor our horn is exalted.
18 For our shield belongs to the LORD,
our king to the Holy One of Israel.

19 Of old you spoke in a vision to your godly one,[3] and said:
"I have granted help to one who is mighty;
I have exalted one chosen from the people.
20 I have found David, my servant;
with my holy oil I have anointed him,
21 so that my hand shall be established with him;
my arm also shall strengthen him.
22 The enemy shall not outwit him;
the wicked shall not humble him.
23 I will crush his foes before him
and strike down those who hate him.

[1]Probably a musical or liturgical term [2]Hebrew *the sons of God*, or *the sons of might* [3]Some Hebrew manuscripts *godly ones*

24 My faithfulness and my steadfast love shall be with him,
and in my name shall his horn be exalted.
25 I will set his hand on the sea
and his right hand on the rivers.
26 He shall cry to me, 'You are my Father,
my God, and the Rock of my salvation.'
27 And I will make him the firstborn,
the highest of the kings of the earth.
28 My steadfast love I will keep for him forever,
and my covenant will stand firm[1] for him.
29 I will establish his offspring forever
and his throne as the days of the heavens.
30 If his children forsake my law
and do not walk according to my rules,[2]
31 if they violate my statutes
and do not keep my commandments,
32 then I will punish their transgression with the rod
and their iniquity with stripes,
33 but I will not remove from him my steadfast love
or be false to my faithfulness.
34 I will not violate my covenant
or alter the word that went forth from my lips.
35 Once for all I have sworn by my holiness;
I will not lie to David.
36 His offspring shall endure forever,
his throne as long as the sun before me.
37 Like the moon it shall be established forever,
a faithful witness in the skies." *Selah*

38 But now you have cast off and rejected;
you are full of wrath against your anointed.
39 You have renounced the covenant with your servant;
you have defiled his crown in the dust.
40 You have breached all his walls;
you have laid his strongholds in ruins.
41 All who pass by plunder him;
he has become the scorn of his neighbors.
42 You have exalted the right hand of his foes;
you have made all his enemies rejoice.
43 You have also turned back the edge of his sword,
and you have not made him stand in battle.
44 You have made his splendor to cease
and cast his throne to the ground.
45 You have cut short the days of his youth;
you have covered him with shame. *Selah*

46 How long, O LORD? Will you hide yourself forever?
How long will your wrath burn like fire?
47 Remember how short my time is!
For what vanity you have created all the children
of man!
48 What man can live and never see death?
Who can deliver his soul from the power of Sheol? *Selah*

49 Lord, where is your steadfast love of old,
which by your faithfulness you swore to David?

[1]Or *will remain faithful* [2]Or *my just decrees*

WAITING PATIENTLY

"How long, O Lord?" The psalmist — having likely just seen the destruction of Jerusalem — asked the God of heaven this honest question.

In the first verse, the psalmist declared that his song concerning God's love would never end. His mouth would forever declare the faithfulness of God. However, though he kept singing, the song changed key. God's people no longer enjoyed the Lord's favor, it seemed. Though God had promised to David a throne throughout all generations (v. 4), the splendor of Israel's king was no longer on display (v. 44). The throne having been cast to the ground, the psalmist wondered where God's love had hidden (v. 49).

No matter what God had said, to the psalmist the promises *felt* as if they were false. This is not uncommon, because God spoke regularly to the saints waiting on the deliverance of the Lord. To the Israelites exiled in Babylon, God promised to bring them out of captivity (Jer 29:14). To the New Testament exiles undergoing persecution in 1 Peter, God promised an inheritance that neither spoils nor fades. But that inheritance is not yet fully revealed — it is being kept in heaven "through faith for a salvation ready to be revealed in the last time" (1Pe 1:5).

Hebrews 11 sings a waiting song. After mentioning Abel's, Enoch's, Noah's, Abraham's, and Sarah's lives of faith, the author wrote, "These all died in faith, not having received the things promised, but having seen them and greeted them from afar, and having acknowledged that they were strangers and exiles on the earth" (Heb 11:13). They were certain of what they hoped for, but it remained unseen. They waited, believing.

The psalmist did the same. He waited patiently, remembering the promises of God. In fact, after baring his soul in questioning the Lord's purposes, he still ended the psalm in praise.

The promises never seemed as false as when the promised One took a spear in the side on a Roman cross. Yet three days later when Jesus rose from the dead, the promises were never truer.

50 Remember, O Lord, how your servants are mocked,
and how I bear in my heart the insults[1] of all the many nations,
51 with which your enemies mock, O LORD,
with which they mock the footsteps of your anointed.

52 Blessed be the LORD forever!
Amen and Amen.

BOOK FOUR

Psalm 90

From Everlasting to Everlasting

A Prayer of Moses, the man of God.

1 Lord, you have been our dwelling place[2]
in all generations.
2 Before the mountains were brought forth,
or ever you had formed the earth and the world,
from everlasting to everlasting you are God.

3 You return man to dust
and say, "Return, O children of man!"[3]
4 For a thousand years in your sight
are but as yesterday when it is past,
or as a watch in the night.

5 You sweep them away as with a flood; they are like a dream,
like grass that is renewed in the morning:
6 in the morning it flourishes and is renewed;
in the evening it fades and withers.

7 For we are brought to an end by your anger;
by your wrath we are dismayed.
8 You have set our iniquities before you,
our secret sins in the light of your presence.

9 For all our days pass away under your wrath;
we bring our years to an end like a sigh.
10 The years of our life are seventy,
or even by reason of strength eighty;
yet their span[4] is but toil and trouble;
they are soon gone, and we fly away.
11 Who considers the power of your anger,
and your wrath according to the fear of you?

12 So teach us to number our days
that we may get a heart of wisdom.
13 Return, O LORD! How long?
Have pity on your servants!
14 Satisfy us in the morning with your steadfast love,
that we may rejoice and be glad all our days.
15 Make us glad for as many days as you have afflicted us,
and for as many years as we have seen evil.
16 Let your work be shown to your servants,
and your glorious power to their children.

[1]Hebrew lacks *the insults* [2]Some Hebrew manuscripts (compare Septuagint) *our refuge* [3]Or *of Adam*
[4]Or *pride*

PSALM 90:1–12

THE ETERNAL GOD

Before Genesis 1:1, God was. The eternal God knows no beginning, nor will he know an end. A thousand years are as a day to him (v. 4). While the mountain peaks were born one day, God was not (v. 2). In fact, creation exists because of this eternal God.

Psalm 90 includes multiple reminders that humankind is not by nature eternal. The psalmist, identified as Moses in the superscription, noted that it generally takes 70 or 80 years for humans to turn back to dust (vv. 3,10). In light of this, he prayed that God would help his people to number their days (v. 12).

God is eternal. Humans are not, due to their fallen nature. A merciful Jesus interrupts the ordinary nature of things, declaring, "This is eternal life, that they know you, the only true God, and Jesus Christ whom you have sent" (Jn 17:3). Only an eternal God could give eternal life. Only an eternal and merciful God would.

17 Let the favor[1] of the Lord our God be upon us,
and establish the work of our hands upon us;
yes, establish the work of our hands!

Psalm 91

My Refuge and My Fortress

1 He who dwells in the shelter of the Most High
will abide in the shadow of the Almighty.
2 I will say[2] to the LORD, "My refuge and my fortress,
my God, in whom I trust."

3 For he will deliver you from the snare of the fowler
and from the deadly pestilence.
4 He will cover you with his pinions,
and under his wings you will find refuge;
his faithfulness is a shield and buckler.
5 You will not fear the terror of the night,
nor the arrow that flies by day,
6 nor the pestilence that stalks in darkness,
nor the destruction that wastes at noonday.

7 A thousand may fall at your side,
ten thousand at your right hand,
but it will not come near you.
8 You will only look with your eyes
and see the recompense of the wicked.

9 Because you have made the LORD your dwelling place—
the Most High, who is my refuge[3]—
10 no evil shall be allowed to befall you,
no plague come near your tent.

11 For he will command his angels concerning you
to guard you in all your ways.
12 On their hands they will bear you up,
lest you strike your foot against a stone.
13 You will tread on the lion and the adder;
the young lion and the serpent you will trample underfoot.

14 "Because he holds fast to me in love, I will deliver him;
I will protect him, because he knows my name.
15 When he calls to me, I will answer him;
I will be with him in trouble;
I will rescue him and honor him.
16 With long life I will satisfy him
and show him my salvation."

Psalm 92

How Great Are Your Works

A Psalm. A Song for the Sabbath.

1 It is good to give thanks to the LORD,
to sing praises to your name, O Most High;
2 to declare your steadfast love in the morning,
and your faithfulness by night,

[1]Or *beauty* [2]Septuagint *He will say* [3]Or *For you, O LORD, are my refuge! You have made the Most High your dwelling place*

ANGELS

Scripture seems to indicate that there are tens of thousands of angels. Though angels do not have physical bodies, God created them with both moral discernment and high intelligence. In fact, Hebrews suggests that angels are pervasive enough that believers occasionally show hospitality to angels without knowing it (Heb 13:2).

The psalmist notes here that God "will command his angels concerning you to guard you in all your ways. On their hands they will bear you up, lest you strike your foot against a stone" (Ps 91:11 – 12). Satan would use this text while speaking with Jesus, imploring him to put God to the test (Mt 4:6). Jesus refused to misapply this text, interpreting Psalm 91 in light of the rest of God's Word.

Angels function as examples for believers, as they obey and worship the Lord without ceasing (Isa 6:3). Paul referred to angelic beings as powers, rulers, dominions, and authorities (Eph 1:21; Col 1:16). Though a post-Enlightenment world pushes the nonphysical to the margins, the Bible's descriptions of angels remind the believer that the spiritual world is real.

However, some angels fell from grace and became demonic forces in our world. Unlike humans, who are made in the image of God, God did not show these angels mercy. Peter wrote, "God did not spare angels when they sinned, but cast them into hell and committed them to chains of gloomy darkness to be kept until the judgment" (2Pe 2:4). This reminds the believer of the grace God showed in sending Jesus for the salvation of sinners. In no way was God obligated to save.

The author of Hebrews began his letter by making clear the supremacy of Jesus over the angels. Alluding to Psalm 2, the author noted that God never called any of the angels his Son (Heb 1:5). Quoting from the Old Testament, the author further pointed out that God calls upon all the angels to worship Jesus (Heb 1:6). Finally, the author asked, "To which of the angels has he ever said, 'Sit at my right hand until I make your enemies a footstool for your feet'?" (Heb 1:13). Jesus is supremely better than anything. He alone is the source of a life of joy and contentment.

3 to the music of the lute and the harp,
to the melody of the lyre.
4 For you, O LORD, have made me glad by your work;
at the works of your hands I sing for joy.

5 How great are your works, O LORD!
Your thoughts are very deep!
6 The stupid man cannot know;
the fool cannot understand this:
7 that though the wicked sprout like grass
and all evildoers flourish,
they are doomed to destruction forever;
8 but you, O LORD, are on high forever.
9 For behold, your enemies, O LORD,
for behold, your enemies shall perish;
all evildoers shall be scattered.

10 But you have exalted my horn like that of the wild ox;
you have poured over me[1] fresh oil.
11 My eyes have seen the downfall of my enemies;
my ears have heard the doom of my evil assailants.

12 The righteous flourish like the palm tree
and grow like a cedar in Lebanon.
13 They are planted in the house of the LORD;
they flourish in the courts of our God.
14 They still bear fruit in old age;
they are ever full of sap and green,
15 to declare that the LORD is upright;
he is my rock, and there is no unrighteousness in him.

Psalm 93

The LORD Reigns

1 The LORD reigns; he is robed in majesty;
the LORD is robed; he has put on strength as his belt.
Yes, the world is established; it shall never be moved.
2 Your throne is established from of old;
you are from everlasting.

3 The floods have lifted up, O LORD,
the floods have lifted up their voice;
the floods lift up their roaring.
4 Mightier than the thunders of many waters,
mightier than the waves of the sea,
the LORD on high is mighty!

5 Your decrees are very trustworthy;
holiness befits your house,
O LORD, forevermore.

Psalm 94

The LORD Will Not Forsake His People

1 O LORD, God of vengeance,
O God of vengeance, shine forth!

[1]Compare Syriac; the meaning of the Hebrew is uncertain

2 Rise up, O judge of the earth;
repay to the proud what they deserve!
3 O LORD, how long shall the wicked,
how long shall the wicked exult?
4 They pour out their arrogant words;
all the evildoers boast.
5 They crush your people, O LORD,
and afflict your heritage.
6 They kill the widow and the sojourner,
and murder the fatherless;
7 and they say, "The LORD does not see;
the God of Jacob does not perceive."

8 Understand, O dullest of the people!
Fools, when will you be wise?
9 He who planted the ear, does he not hear?
He who formed the eye, does he not see?
10 He who disciplines the nations, does he not rebuke?
He who teaches man knowledge—
11 the LORD—knows the thoughts of man,
that they are but a breath.[1]

12 Blessed is the man whom you discipline, O LORD,
and whom you teach out of your law,
13 to give him rest from days of trouble,
until a pit is dug for the wicked.
14 For the LORD will not forsake his people;
he will not abandon his heritage;
15 for justice will return to the righteous,
and all the upright in heart will follow it.

16 Who rises up for me against the wicked?
Who stands up for me against evildoers?
17 If the LORD had not been my help,
my soul would soon have lived in the land of silence.
18 When I thought, "My foot slips,"
your steadfast love, O LORD, held me up.
19 When the cares of my heart are many,
your consolations cheer my soul.
20 Can wicked rulers be allied with you,
those who frame[2] injustice by statute?
21 They band together against the life of the righteous
and condemn the innocent to death.[3]
22 But the LORD has become my stronghold,
and my God the rock of my refuge.
23 He will bring back on them their iniquity
and wipe them out for their wickedness;
the LORD our God will wipe them out.

PSALM 95:1–11

A PLACE OF REST

God speaks in verses 8 through 11 of this psalm, taking a few verses to remind the readers of the disobedience of the generation of the exodus. Though the ancestors of the original readers had seen the wonders God performed in their deliverance from slavery, they still hardened their hearts and tested the Lord. In fact, the name "Massah" means "testing" (v. 8). Because of this, God declared that they would never enter his rest (v. 11). The Israelite narrative teaches that seeing God's works does not necessarily lead to knowing his ways (v. 10).

Hebrews 3 and 4 make clear that the "rest" referred to in this psalm points beyond Canaan. "For we who have believed enter that rest" (Heb 4:3). While the exodus generation failed to obey, the author of Hebrews holds out the promise that his readers might enter God's rest "today" (Heb 4:7). Therefore, they were to make every effort to enter (Heb 4:11).

Psalm 95

Let Us Sing Songs of Praise

1 Oh come, let us sing to the LORD;
let us make a joyful noise to the rock of our salvation!
2 Let us come into his presence with thanksgiving;
let us make a joyful noise to him with songs of praise!

[1] Septuagint *they are futile* [2] Or *fashion* [3] Hebrew *condemn innocent blood*

3 For the LORD is a great God,
and a great King above all gods.
4 In his hand are the depths of the earth;
the heights of the mountains are his also.
5 The sea is his, for he made it,
and his hands formed the dry land.

6 Oh come, let us worship and bow down;
let us kneel before the LORD, our Maker!
7 For he is our God,
and we are the people of his pasture,
and the sheep of his hand.
Today, if you hear his voice,
8 do not harden your hearts, as at Meribah,
as on the day at Massah in the wilderness,
9 when your fathers put me to the test
and put me to the proof, though they had seen my work.
10 For forty years I loathed that generation
and said, "They are a people who go astray in their heart,
and they have not known my ways."
11 Therefore I swore in my wrath,
"They shall not enter my rest."

Psalm 96

Worship in the Splendor of Holiness

1 Oh sing to the LORD a new song;
sing to the LORD, all the earth!
2 Sing to the LORD, bless his name;
tell of his salvation from day to day.
3 Declare his glory among the nations,
his marvelous works among all the peoples!
4 For great is the LORD, and greatly to be praised;
he is to be feared above all gods.
5 For all the gods of the peoples are worthless idols,
but the LORD made the heavens.
6 Splendor and majesty are before him;
strength and beauty are in his sanctuary.

7 Ascribe to the LORD, O families of the peoples,
ascribe to the LORD glory and strength!
8 Ascribe to the LORD the glory due his name;
bring an offering, and come into his courts!
9 Worship the LORD in the splendor of holiness;[1]
tremble before him, all the earth!

10 Say among the nations, "The LORD reigns!
Yes, the world is established; it shall never be moved;
he will judge the peoples with equity."

11 Let the heavens be glad, and let the earth rejoice;
let the sea roar, and all that fills it;
12 let the field exult, and everything in it!
Then shall all the trees of the forest sing for joy
13 before the LORD, for he comes,
for he comes to judge the earth.

[1]Or *in holy attire*

PSALM 96:1–13

THE MISSION OF GOD

Everyone worships. The question is not *whether* humans worship, but *whom or what* they worship. In this psalm, the reader finds the Old Testament rationale for joining in God's mission to make himself known. Although the pagan nations were worshiping idols they made, God made the entire world, including these pagans and the materials they used to carve idols (v. 5). Nevertheless, the first verse of this psalm calls upon *all* the earth to sing to God—including idolaters who have turned away from him. Since the creation of the world, God intended to fill the earth with true worshipers. Seeking that which God desires, the people of God declare his glory among pagan nations (v. 3). The apostle John's vision in the book of Revelation gave the reader a peek into God's eternal purposes. John wrote, "And they sang a new song, saying, 'Worthy are you to take the scroll and to open its seals, for you were slain, and by your blood you ransomed people for God from every tribe and language and people and nation'" (Rev 5:9). False gods make false promises. However, the true God, in sending his Son, brought glory to himself by redeeming worshipers from every nation on earth. Let the earth rejoice (Ps 96:11).

SALVATION IS HERE!

God is a God of salvation! By his holy arm, God worked salvation, making it known to his people (Ps 98:1 – 2). Therefore, accompanied by a host of instruments, the people of God were to sing and shout to the Lord (vv. 4 – 6). This psalm makes clear that God did great things for Israel, reminding the people of all his promises to them. But his blessing did not terminate at the nation's borders, nor was it intended to. This salvation that God made known was seen by all the ends of the earth (v. 3).

The salvation that God has brought to his people is to be shouted about with joy, and the people are to burst into jubilant song (v. 4). It cannot be celebrated in somber tones but must be celebrated in exuberant chorus. The sea and all who live in the earth will "roar" in this chorus (v. 7).

The psalmist wrote that the Lord has revealed his righteousness to the nations (v. 2). Certainly God did this in part through the law, but in Jesus righteousness was revealed apart from the law (Ro 3:21). In the New Testament, Paul wrote that in in the gospel "the righteousness of God is revealed from faith for faith" (Ro 1:17). In Jesus, God sent his righteous Savior. The people that he came to save did not earn salvation on their own merit, but it was given by the grace and righteousness of God. This fact gives all people something to celebrate and shout about!

4 Enter his gates with thanksgiving,
and his courts with praise!
Give thanks to him; bless his name!

5 For the LORD is good;
his steadfast love endures forever,
and his faithfulness to all generations.

Psalm 101

I Will Walk with Integrity

A Psalm of David.

1 I will sing of steadfast love and justice;
to you, O LORD, I will make music.
2 I will ponder the way that is blameless.
Oh when will you come to me?
I will walk with integrity of heart
within my house;
3 I will not set before my eyes
anything that is worthless.
I hate the work of those who fall away;
it shall not cling to me.
4 A perverse heart shall be far from me;
I will know nothing of evil.

5 Whoever slanders his neighbor secretly
I will destroy.
Whoever has a haughty look and an arrogant heart
I will not endure.

6 I will look with favor on the faithful in the land,
that they may dwell with me;
he who walks in the way that is blameless
shall minister to me.

7 No one who practices deceit
shall dwell in my house;
no one who utters lies
shall continue before my eyes.

8 Morning by morning I will destroy
all the wicked in the land,
cutting off all the evildoers
from the city of the LORD.

Psalm 102

Do Not Hide Your Face from Me

A Prayer of one afflicted, when he is faint and pours out his complaint before the LORD.

1 Hear my prayer, O LORD;
let my cry come to you!
2 Do not hide your face from me
in the day of my distress!
Incline your ear to me;
answer me speedily in the day when I call!

3 For my days pass away like smoke,
and my bones burn like a furnace.

(Give Thanks, continued)

to the Lord and subsequently reminded them why they should. The psalmist then instructed the people of God to give thanks to the Lord. Then, in similar fashion, readers are given a solid, lasting rationale for why their thanksgiving should be unceasing. This psalm prompts worship with the truths of God's person and deeds.

So, why should they give thanks? The God to whom these readers gave thanks is the unchanging standard for goodness. Furthermore, this good God never ceased to love his people. In the book of Psalms, the Hebrew word *hesed*, translated "steadfast love" in Psalm 100:5, appears as a characteristic of God over 120 times. The book makes its point. Not only is God both good and loving, but no generation has known God to be unfaithful (v. 5). The New Testament equivalent to Old Testament love and faithfulness is grace and truth, seen most clearly in Jesus Christ (Jn 1:17).

4 My heart is struck down like grass and has withered;
I forget to eat my bread.
5 Because of my loud groaning
my bones cling to my flesh.
6 I am like a desert owl of the wilderness,
like an owl[1] of the waste places;
7 I lie awake;
I am like a lonely sparrow on the housetop.
8 All the day my enemies taunt me;
those who deride me use my name for a curse.
9 For I eat ashes like bread
and mingle tears with my drink,
10 because of your indignation and anger;
for you have taken me up and thrown me down.
11 My days are like an evening shadow;
I wither away like grass.

12 But you, O LORD, are enthroned forever;
you are remembered throughout all generations.
13 You will arise and have pity on Zion;
it is the time to favor her;
the appointed time has come.
14 For your servants hold her stones dear
and have pity on her dust.
15 Nations will fear the name of the LORD,
and all the kings of the earth will fear your glory.
16 For the LORD builds up Zion;
he appears in his glory;
17 he regards the prayer of the destitute
and does not despise their prayer.

18 Let this be recorded for a generation to come,
so that a people yet to be created may praise the LORD:
19 that he looked down from his holy height;
from heaven the LORD looked at the earth,
20 to hear the groans of the prisoners,
to set free those who were doomed to die,
21 that they may declare in Zion the name of the LORD,
and in Jerusalem his praise,
22 when peoples gather together,
and kingdoms, to worship the LORD.

23 He has broken my strength in midcourse;
he has shortened my days.
24 "O my God," I say, "take me not away
in the midst of my days—
you whose years endure
throughout all generations!"

25 Of old you laid the foundation of the earth,
and the heavens are the work of your hands.
26 They will perish, but you will remain;
they will all wear out like a garment.
You will change them like a robe, and they will pass away,
27 but you are the same, and your years have no end.
28 The children of your servants shall dwell secure;
their offspring shall be established before you.

[1]The precise identity of these birds is uncertain

PSALM 102:25–27

GOD NEVER CHANGES

The psalmist contrasted, in these few verses, that which perishes with that which is imperishable. In the beginning, God made the heavens and the earth. The rationale follows that if the uncreated God preceded and made the heavens, then clearly he need not perish or change as they do.

All the promises of God depend upon the truth that God is unchanging. The apostle Peter used language similar to the psalmist to assure believers of the finality of God's Word. Quoting the prophet Isaiah, he wrote, "The grass withers, and the flower falls, but the word of the Lord remains forever" (1Pe 1:24–25).

Each autumn, yards are covered with the evidence of the world's perishable nature. Yet, in the midst of this earthly fading, God does not change. The author of Hebrews quoted Ps 102:25–27 and applied it specifically to the Son of God (Heb 1:10–12), going on to argue that Jesus remains the same yesterday, today, and forever (Heb 13:8). Because of this—an unchanging God making unchanging promises—an imperishable inheritance awaits God's people (1Pe 1:4).

Psalm 103

Bless the LORD, O My Soul

Of David.

1 Bless the LORD, O my soul,
and all that is within me,
bless his holy name!
2 Bless the LORD, O my soul,
and forget not all his benefits,
3 who forgives all your iniquity,
who heals all your diseases,
4 who redeems your life from the pit,
who crowns you with steadfast love and mercy,
5 who satisfies you with good
so that your youth is renewed like the eagle's.

6 The LORD works righteousness
and justice for all who are oppressed.
7 He made known his ways to Moses,
his acts to the people of Israel.
8 The LORD is merciful and gracious,
slow to anger and abounding in steadfast love.
9 He will not always chide,
nor will he keep his anger forever.
10 He does not deal with us according to our sins,
nor repay us according to our iniquities.
11 For as high as the heavens are above the earth,
so great is his steadfast love toward those who fear him;
12 as far as the east is from the west,
so far does he remove our transgressions from us.
13 As a father shows compassion to his children,
so the LORD shows compassion to those who fear him.
14 For he knows our frame;[1]
he remembers that we are dust.

15 As for man, his days are like grass;
he flourishes like a flower of the field;
16 for the wind passes over it, and it is gone,
and its place knows it no more.
17 But the steadfast love of the LORD is from everlasting to everlasting
on those who fear him,
and his righteousness to children's children,
18 to those who keep his covenant
and remember to do his commandments.
19 The LORD has established his throne in the heavens,
and his kingdom rules over all.

20 Bless the LORD, O you his angels,
you mighty ones who do his word,
obeying the voice of his word!
21 Bless the LORD, all his hosts,
his ministers, who do his will!
22 Bless the LORD, all his works,
in all places of his dominion.
Bless the LORD, O my soul!

[1]Or *knows how we are formed*

PSALM 103:3

HEALING

The psalmist, in this single verse, spoke of both healing and forgiveness of sins. During one instance in Jesus' ministry, he used a single miracle to prove his authority to accomplish both physical healing and spiritual forgiveness. In the Gospel of Mark, while Jesus was teaching, a crowd pressed in on him. Unable to reach Jesus through the crowd, a group of people lowered their paralyzed friend through the roof of the house to be healed by Jesus. This man's need was obvious — he needed physical healing. Jesus, seemingly insensitive, said, "Son, your sins are forgiven" (Mk 2:5). The teachers of the law nearby thought Jesus blasphemed by claiming to do something only God could do. So Jesus, knowing their innermost thoughts, asked which would be easier: to heal someone or to *say* he forgave his sins? The idea was that it would be easier to *say* his sins were forgiven, since no one could verify that kind of spiritual transformation.

Jesus chose the harder thing to prove his authority. He said, "But that you may know that the Son of Man has authority on earth to forgive sins ... I say to you, rise, pick up your bed, and go home" (Mk 2:10–11). The man stood up, proving what Psalm 103:3 says: Jesus can both heal and forgive.

GUILT IS GONE

Psalm 103 focuses on how God dealt with his people with compassion and grace (v. 8), not treating them as their sins deserved (v. 10). He will not harbor his anger forever (v. 9).

Sin is not only defined by commission, but also by omission. James makes clear that anyone who "knows the right thing to do and fails to do it, for him it is sin" (Jas 4:17). With the greatest commandment demanding the devotion of the entirety of our hearts, minds, and strength to loving God (Mk 12:29 – 30), the biblical case for humanity's guilt is clear. Furthermore, James told his readers that one violation of God's law makes a person guilty of breaking the entirety of it (Jas 2:10).

The apostle Paul made plain humanity's guilt in his letter to the Romans. Regarding the Gentile without God's law, he wrote, "All who have sinned without the law will also perish without the law" (Ro 2:12). Regarding the Jew devoted to God's law, Paul added, "All who have sinned under the law will be judged by the law" (Ro 2:12). To summarize Paul's argument in the first three chapters of Romans: all mouths are stopped; no one is righteous (Ro 3:10). Humankind stands guilty before a holy God.

But psalms like this one reveal to the people of God that the Lord is "merciful and gracious, slow to anger and abounding in steadfast love" (Ps 103:8). This psalm reveals that God's love is immeasurable in human terms. Using terms like "as high as the heavens are above the earth" (v. 11) and "as far as the east is from the west" (v. 12), the author describes the love of God.

The righteous Lord must also be a compassionate Lord (v. 13). This psalm reveals him, pointing the reader to the God-man who would one day look at people with compassion (Mt 9:36). Jesus, the embodiment of grace and love, came to set people free and offer a new way to have a relationship with God the Father.

Psalm 104

O LORD My God, You Are Very Great

1 Bless the LORD, O my soul!
O LORD my God, you are very great!
You are clothed with splendor and majesty,
2 covering yourself with light as with a garment,
stretching out the heavens like a tent.
3 He lays the beams of his chambers on the waters;
he makes the clouds his chariot;
he rides on the wings of the wind;
4 he makes his messengers winds,
his ministers a flaming fire.

5 He set the earth on its foundations,
so that it should never be moved.
6 You covered it with the deep as with a garment;
the waters stood above the mountains.
7 At your rebuke they fled;
at the sound of your thunder they took to flight.
8 The mountains rose, the valleys sank down
to the place that you appointed for them.
9 You set a boundary that they may not pass,
so that they might not again cover the earth.

10 You make springs gush forth in the valleys;
they flow between the hills;
11 they give drink to every beast of the field;
the wild donkeys quench their thirst.
12 Beside them the birds of the heavens dwell;
they sing among the branches.
13 From your lofty abode you water the mountains;
the earth is satisfied with the fruit of your work.

14 You cause the grass to grow for the livestock
and plants for man to cultivate,
that he may bring forth food from the earth
15 and wine to gladden the heart of man,
oil to make his face shine
and bread to strengthen man's heart.

16 The trees of the LORD are watered abundantly,
the cedars of Lebanon that he planted.
17 In them the birds build their nests;
the stork has her home in the fir trees.
18 The high mountains are for the wild goats;
the rocks are a refuge for the rock badgers.

19 He made the moon to mark the seasons;[1]
the sun knows its time for setting.
20 You make darkness, and it is night,
when all the beasts of the forest creep about.
21 The young lions roar for their prey,
seeking their food from God.
22 When the sun rises, they steal away
and lie down in their dens.
23 Man goes out to his work
and to his labor until the evening.

[1]Or *the appointed times* (compare Genesis 1:14)

PSALM 104:10–28

GOD'S CARE

Psalm 104 spells out the details of God's care for the world. The beasts of the field get their water from a spring, but ultimately that water comes from the hand of God (vv. 10–11). God planted the trees that the birds nest in (vv. 16–17). The teeming creatures of the sea look to the Lord for provision (vv. 25–27).

The psalmist made clear God's care for his creation. Jesus would much later take this truth and apply it to his hearers, saying, "Look at the birds of the air: they neither sow nor reap nor gather into barns, and yet your heavenly Father feeds them. Are you not of more value than they?" (Mt 6:26). Peter, who surely heard these words, would later invite Christians to cast, "all your anxieties on him, because he cares for you" (1Pe 5:7).

24 O LORD, how manifold are your works!
In wisdom have you made them all;
the earth is full of your creatures.
25 Here is the sea, great and wide,
which teems with creatures innumerable,
living things both small and great.
26 There go the ships,
and Leviathan, which you formed to play in it.[1]
27 These all look to you,
to give them their food in due season.
28 When you give it to them, they gather it up;
when you open your hand, they are filled with good things.
29 When you hide your face, they are dismayed;
when you take away their breath, they die
and return to their dust.
30 When you send forth your Spirit,[2] they are created,
and you renew the face of the ground.
31 May the glory of the LORD endure forever;
may the LORD rejoice in his works,
32 who looks on the earth and it trembles,
who touches the mountains and they smoke!
33 I will sing to the LORD as long as I live;
I will sing praise to my God while I have being.
34 May my meditation be pleasing to him,
for I rejoice in the LORD.
35 Let sinners be consumed from the earth,
and let the wicked be no more!
Bless the LORD, O my soul!
Praise the LORD!

PSALM 105:1–45

A HISTORY OF FAITHFULNESS

The audience for this psalm is clear: "offspring of Abraham, his servant, children of Jacob" (v. 6). The people of God were to hear and heed these words.

The people of Israel seemed to have suffered from spiritual amnesia. So, beginning with Abraham, the psalmist recounted the faithfulness of God over the span of 40 verses. The God of Israel allowed no one to oppress them (vv. 14–15). The word of the Lord was fulfilled in the rise of Joseph (vv. 17–22). The Lord made his people fruitful, more numerous than their foes (v. 24). When they were enslaved, God sent Moses (v. 26).

While the psalm lists various names, God proves to be the main character. It was God who powerfully delivered them from Pharaoh (vv. 27–38). Though this psalm includes only highlights from Israel's history, the point is clear: nothing God purposed has failed.

The psalmist began with Abraham. Yet, Jesus would assert plainly in the Gospel of John, "Before Abraham was, I am" (Jn 8:58). The epicenter of God's faithfulness not only preceded the father of Israel, but also, all God's promises eventually find their "Yes" in him (2Co 1:20). God remembers his covenant; *God's people remember his wonders* (Ps 105:5–11).

Psalm 105

Tell of All His Wondrous Works

1 Oh give thanks to the LORD; call upon his name;
make known his deeds among the peoples!
2 Sing to him, sing praises to him;
tell of all his wondrous works!
3 Glory in his holy name;
let the hearts of those who seek the LORD rejoice!
4 Seek the LORD and his strength;
seek his presence continually!
5 Remember the wondrous works that he has done,
his miracles, and the judgments he uttered,
6 O offspring of Abraham, his servant,
children of Jacob, his chosen ones!
7 He is the LORD our God;
his judgments are in all the earth.
8 He remembers his covenant forever,
the word that he commanded, for a thousand generations,
9 the covenant that he made with Abraham,
his sworn promise to Isaac,
10 which he confirmed to Jacob as a statute,
to Israel as an everlasting covenant,

[1]Or *you formed to play with* [2]Or *breath*

11 saying, "To you I will give the land of Canaan
as your portion for an inheritance."

12 When they were few in number,
of little account, and sojourners in it,
13 wandering from nation to nation,
from one kingdom to another people,
14 he allowed no one to oppress them;
he rebuked kings on their account,
15 saying, "Touch not my anointed ones,
do my prophets no harm!"

16 When he summoned a famine on the land
and broke all supply[1] of bread,
17 he had sent a man ahead of them,
Joseph, who was sold as a slave.
18 His feet were hurt with fetters;
his neck was put in a collar of iron;
19 until what he had said came to pass,
the word of the LORD tested him.
20 The king sent and released him;
the ruler of the peoples set him free;
21 he made him lord of his house
and ruler of all his possessions,
22 to bind[2] his princes at his pleasure
and to teach his elders wisdom.

23 Then Israel came to Egypt;
Jacob sojourned in the land of Ham.
24 And the LORD made his people very fruitful
and made them stronger than their foes.
25 He turned their hearts to hate his people,
to deal craftily with his servants.

26 He sent Moses, his servant,
and Aaron, whom he had chosen.
27 They performed his signs among them
and miracles in the land of Ham.
28 He sent darkness, and made the land dark;
they did not rebel[3] against his words.
29 He turned their waters into blood
and caused their fish to die.
30 Their land swarmed with frogs,
even in the chambers of their kings.
31 He spoke, and there came swarms of flies,
and gnats throughout their country.
32 He gave them hail for rain,
and fiery lightning bolts through their land.
33 He struck down their vines and fig trees,
and shattered the trees of their country.
34 He spoke, and the locusts came,
young locusts without number,
35 which devoured all the vegetation in their land
and ate up the fruit of their ground.
36 He struck down all the firstborn in their land,
the firstfruits of all their strength.

[1]Hebrew *staff* [2]Septuagint, Syriac, Jerome *instruct* [3]Septuagint, Syriac omit *not*

37 Then he brought out Israel with silver and gold,
and there was none among his tribes who stumbled.
38 Egypt was glad when they departed,
for dread of them had fallen upon it.

39 He spread a cloud for a covering,
and fire to give light by night.
40 They asked, and he brought quail,
and gave them bread from heaven in abundance.
41 He opened the rock, and water gushed out;
it flowed through the desert like a river.
42 For he remembered his holy promise,
and Abraham, his servant.

43 So he brought his people out with joy,
his chosen ones with singing.
44 And he gave them the lands of the nations,
and they took possession of the fruit of the peoples' toil,
45 that they might keep his statutes
and observe his laws.
Praise the LORD!

Psalm 106

Give Thanks to the LORD, for He Is Good

1 Praise the LORD!
Oh give thanks to the LORD, for he is good,
for his steadfast love endures forever!
2 Who can utter the mighty deeds of the LORD,
or declare all his praise?
3 Blessed are they who observe justice,
who do righteousness at all times!

4 Remember me, O LORD, when you show favor to your people;
help me when you save them,[1]
5 that I may look upon the prosperity of your chosen ones,
that I may rejoice in the gladness of your nation,
that I may glory with your inheritance.

6 Both we and our fathers have sinned;
we have committed iniquity; we have done wickedness.
7 Our fathers, when they were in Egypt,
did not consider your wondrous works;
they did not remember the abundance of your steadfast love,
but rebelled by the sea, at the Red Sea.
8 Yet he saved them for his name's sake,
that he might make known his mighty power.
9 He rebuked the Red Sea, and it became dry,
and he led them through the deep as through a desert.
10 So he saved them from the hand of the foe
and redeemed them from the power of the enemy.
11 And the waters covered their adversaries;
not one of them was left.
12 Then they believed his words;
they sang his praise.

13 But they soon forgot his works;
they did not wait for his counsel.

[1]Or *Remember me, O LORD, with the favor you show to your people; help me with your salvation*

14 But they had a wanton craving in the wilderness,
and put God to the test in the desert;
15 he gave them what they asked,
but sent a wasting disease among them.

16 When men in the camp were jealous of Moses
and Aaron, the holy one of the LORD,
17 the earth opened and swallowed up Dathan,
and covered the company of Abiram.
18 Fire also broke out in their company;
the flame burned up the wicked.

19 They made a calf in Horeb
and worshiped a metal image.
20 They exchanged the glory of God[1]
for the image of an ox that eats grass.
21 They forgot God, their Savior,
who had done great things in Egypt,
22 wondrous works in the land of Ham,
and awesome deeds by the Red Sea.
23 Therefore he said he would destroy them—
had not Moses, his chosen one,
stood in the breach before him,
to turn away his wrath from destroying them.

24 Then they despised the pleasant land,
having no faith in his promise.
25 They murmured in their tents,
and did not obey the voice of the LORD.
26 Therefore he raised his hand and swore to them
that he would make them fall in the wilderness,
27 and would make their offspring fall among the nations,
scattering them among the lands.

28 Then they yoked themselves to the Baal of Peor,
and ate sacrifices offered to the dead;
29 they provoked the LORD to anger with their deeds,
and a plague broke out among them.
30 Then Phinehas stood up and intervened,
and the plague was stayed.
31 And that was counted to him as righteousness
from generation to generation forever.

32 They angered him at the waters of Meribah,
and it went ill with Moses on their account,
33 for they made his spirit bitter,[2]
and he spoke rashly with his lips.

34 They did not destroy the peoples,
as the LORD commanded them,
35 but they mixed with the nations
and learned to do as they did.
36 They served their idols,
which became a snare to them.
37 They sacrificed their sons
and their daughters to the demons;
38 they poured out innocent blood,
the blood of their sons and daughters,

---

[1]Hebrew *exchanged their glory* [2]Or *they rebelled against God's Spirit*

PSALM 107:1–32

MERCY ENDURES

The fifth and final book of Psalms begins with a call for the redeemed to give thanks to the Lord, in light of his enduring love (vv. 1–3). Then, using four particular narratives, it illustrates this enduring love of God.

The first narrative tells of a group that suffered from hunger out in the desert, their lives fading away. Then (with the first appearance of a common denominator in all four stories), they cried out to the Lord (vv. 6,13,19,28). The Lord answered, leading them from the desert to a city where their hunger might be satisfied (vv. 6–7). The second group suffered from the punishment of slavery to foreign oppressors. They cried to the Lord and he delivered them (vv. 13–14). The third group suffered from the punishment of wasting disease; however, when they cried to the Lord he showed nothing but mercy (vv. 19–20). The fourth group suffered from fear of the sea's power, their lives being threatened. They too cried to the Lord and the storm was stilled (vv. 28–29).

Not only does each scene show someone crying to the Lord and subsequently being delivered by the Lord's mercy, each one includes the response that should follow: "Let them thank the LORD for his steadfast love, for his wondrous works to the children of man!" (vv. 8,15,21,31). The height of the demonstration of this mercy was in the sending of Jesus, who would die a substitutionary death on behalf of his people. The only response to an enduring love like this is a thankfulness that knows no end.

whom they sacrificed to the idols of Canaan,
and the land was polluted with blood.
39 Thus they became unclean by their acts,
and played the whore in their deeds.

40 Then the anger of the LORD was kindled against his people,
and he abhorred his heritage;
41 he gave them into the hand of the nations,
so that those who hated them ruled over them.
42 Their enemies oppressed them,
and they were brought into subjection under their power.
43 Many times he delivered them,
but they were rebellious in their purposes
and were brought low through their iniquity.

44 Nevertheless, he looked upon their distress,
when he heard their cry.
45 For their sake he remembered his covenant,
and relented according to the abundance of his steadfast love.
46 He caused them to be pitied
by all those who held them captive.

47 Save us, O LORD our God,
and gather us from among the nations,
that we may give thanks to your holy name
and glory in your praise.

48 Blessed be the LORD, the God of Israel,
from everlasting to everlasting!
And let all the people say, "Amen!"
Praise the LORD!

BOOK FIVE

Psalm 107

Let the Redeemed of the LORD Say So

1 Oh give thanks to the LORD, for he is good,
for his steadfast love endures forever!
2 Let the redeemed of the LORD say so,
whom he has redeemed from trouble[1]
3 and gathered in from the lands,
from the east and from the west,
from the north and from the south.

4 Some wandered in desert wastes,
finding no way to a city to dwell in;
5 hungry and thirsty,
their soul fainted within them.
6 Then they cried to the LORD in their trouble,
and he delivered them from their distress.
7 He led them by a straight way
till they reached a city to dwell in.
8 Let them thank the LORD for his steadfast love,
for his wondrous works to the children of man!

[1]Or *from the hand of the foe*

DELIVERED BUT ENSLAVED

This psalm details the Israelites' harrowing deliverance from captivity in Egypt. As just one example, the Red Sea transformed into dry land long enough for the people of God to pass. Then, in a matter of moments, that dry land became a watery graveyard for Israel's adversaries. God saved his people, not for their sake primarily, but to make his power known (v. 8).

Although the people were delivered miraculously from their physical slavery, the rest of the psalm speaks to their continuing slavery to sin. Though they sang of God's promises on the shores of the sea, they soon forgot that melody (v. 13). They no longer trusted the leaders God gave them (v. 16). At the height of their rebellion, they crafted and worshiped idols (vv. 19–20). Rather than standing in contrast to the pagan nations as God commanded them, they assimilated, even to the point of sacrificing their own children to false gods (vv. 34–38). This is not what God delivered them for.

The people of God forgot more than the song of God's deliverance; they forgot their God (v. 21). Therefore, God allowed the pagan nations to overrun them (vv. 40–42). Their enslavement to sin led once again to physical enslavement.

Throughout this psalm, two themes emerge. The people of God forget. God remembers. In fact, these two themes fill the pages of Scripture. The unfaithfulness of God's people does not rub off on their God; he continues to deliver. As Paul would later say, "If we are faithless, he remains faithful — for he cannot deny himself" (2Ti 2:13).

In his letter to the church at Rome, Paul described an act of God more miraculous than the parting of the Red Sea: "Having been set free from sin, [you] have become slaves of righteousness" (Ro 6:18). The chains of the pagan nations could not enslave believers' hearts. Through the work of the resurrection, God destroyed the shackles of sin, making Jesus the new master of all who put their faith in him.

9 For he satisfies the longing soul,
and the hungry soul he fills with good things.

10 Some sat in darkness and in the shadow of death,
prisoners in affliction and in irons,
11 for they had rebelled against the words of God,
and spurned the counsel of the Most High.
12 So he bowed their hearts down with hard labor;
they fell down, with none to help.
13 Then they cried to the LORD in their trouble,
and he delivered them from their distress.
14 He brought them out of darkness and the shadow of death,
and burst their bonds apart.
15 Let them thank the LORD for his steadfast love,
for his wondrous works to the children of man!
16 For he shatters the doors of bronze
and cuts in two the bars of iron.

17 Some were fools through their sinful ways,
and because of their iniquities suffered affliction;
18 they loathed any kind of food,
and they drew near to the gates of death.
19 Then they cried to the LORD in their trouble,
and he delivered them from their distress.
20 He sent out his word and healed them,
and delivered them from their destruction.
21 Let them thank the LORD for his steadfast love,
for his wondrous works to the children of man!
22 And let them offer sacrifices of thanksgiving,
and tell of his deeds in songs of joy!

23 Some went down to the sea in ships,
doing business on the great waters;
24 they saw the deeds of the LORD,
his wondrous works in the deep.
25 For he commanded and raised the stormy wind,
which lifted up the waves of the sea.
26 They mounted up to heaven; they went down to the
depths;
their courage melted away in their evil plight;
27 they reeled and staggered like drunken men
and were at their wits' end.[1]
28 Then they cried to the LORD in their trouble,
and he delivered them from their distress.
29 He made the storm be still,
and the waves of the sea were hushed.
30 Then they were glad that the waters[2] were quiet,
and he brought them to their desired haven.
31 Let them thank the LORD for his steadfast love,
for his wondrous works to the children of man!
32 Let them extol him in the congregation of the people,
and praise him in the assembly of the elders.

33 He turns rivers into a desert,
springs of water into thirsty ground,
34 a fruitful land into a salty waste,
because of the evil of its inhabitants.

[1]Hebrew *and all their wisdom was swallowed up* [2]Hebrew *they*

35 He turns a desert into pools of water,
a parched land into springs of water.
36 And there he lets the hungry dwell,
and they establish a city to live in;
37 they sow fields and plant vineyards
and get a fruitful yield.
38 By his blessing they multiply greatly,
and he does not let their livestock diminish.

39 When they are diminished and brought low
through oppression, evil, and sorrow,
40 he pours contempt on princes
and makes them wander in trackless wastes;
41 but he raises up the needy out of affliction
and makes their families like flocks.
42 The upright see it and are glad,
and all wickedness shuts its mouth.

43 Whoever is wise, let him attend to these things;
let them consider the steadfast love of the LORD.

Psalm 108

With God We Shall Do Valiantly

A Song. A Psalm of David.

1 My heart is steadfast, O God!
I will sing and make melody with all my being![1]
2 Awake, O harp and lyre!
I will awake the dawn!
3 I will give thanks to you, O LORD, among the peoples;
I will sing praises to you among the nations.
4 For your steadfast love is great above the heavens;
your faithfulness reaches to the clouds.

5 Be exalted, O God, above the heavens!
Let your glory be over all the earth!
6 That your beloved ones may be delivered,
give salvation by your right hand and answer me!

7 God has promised in his holiness:[2]
"With exultation I will divide up Shechem
and portion out the Valley of Succoth.
8 Gilead is mine; Manasseh is mine;
Ephraim is my helmet,
Judah my scepter.
9 Moab is my washbasin;
upon Edom I cast my shoe;
over Philistia I shout in triumph."

10 Who will bring me to the fortified city?
Who will lead me to Edom?
11 Have you not rejected us, O God?
You do not go out, O God, with our armies.
12 Oh grant us help against the foe,
for vain is the salvation of man!
13 With God we shall do valiantly;
it is he who will tread down our foes.

[1]Hebrew *with my glory* [2]Or *sanctuary*

Psalm 109

Help Me, O Lord My God

To the choirmaster. A Psalm of David.

1 Be not silent, O God of my praise!
2 For wicked and deceitful mouths are opened against me,
speaking against me with lying tongues.
3 They encircle me with words of hate,
and attack me without cause.
4 In return for my love they accuse me,
but I give myself to prayer.[1]
5 So they reward me evil for good,
and hatred for my love.

6 Appoint a wicked man against him;
let an accuser stand at his right hand.
7 When he is tried, let him come forth guilty;
let his prayer be counted as sin!
8 May his days be few;
may another take his office!
9 May his children be fatherless
and his wife a widow!
10 May his children wander about and beg,
seeking food far from the ruins they inhabit!
11 May the creditor seize all that he has;
may strangers plunder the fruits of his toil!
12 Let there be none to extend kindness to him,
nor any to pity his fatherless children!
13 May his posterity be cut off;
may his name be blotted out in the second generation!
14 May the iniquity of his fathers be remembered before the Lord,
and let not the sin of his mother be blotted out!
15 Let them be before the Lord continually,
that he may cut off the memory of them from the earth!

16 For he did not remember to show kindness,
but pursued the poor and needy
and the brokenhearted, to put them to death.
17 He loved to curse; let curses come[2] upon him!
He did not delight in blessing; may it be far[3] from him!
18 He clothed himself with cursing as his coat;
may it soak[4] into his body like water,
like oil into his bones!
19 May it be like a garment that he wraps around him,
like a belt that he puts on every day!
20 May this be the reward of my accusers from the Lord,
of those who speak evil against my life!

21 But you, O God my Lord,
deal on my behalf for your name's sake;
because your steadfast love is good, deliver me!
22 For I am poor and needy,
and my heart is stricken within me.
23 I am gone like a shadow at evening;
I am shaken off like a locust.

[1]Hebrew *but I am prayer* [2]Revocalization; Masoretic Text *curses have come* [3]Revocalization; Masoretic Text *it is far* [4]Revocalization; Masoretic Text *it has soaked*

PSALM 109:1–5

PERSECUTED UNJUSTLY

"'A servant is not greater than his master.' If they persecuted me, they will also persecute you," Jesus told his disciples (Jn 15:20). Immediately preceding a section of prayers for deliverance, here David detailed the persecution he faced. Wicked men spoke dishonestly against him (Ps 109:2). Without cause they spoke words of hate (v. 3). He showed them friendship; they attacked him (v. 4). He did good toward them; they returned evil (v. 5).

Jesus would tell his kingdom citizens to receive this kind of treatment as a blessing: "Blessed are you when others revile you and persecute you and utter all kinds of evil against you falsely on my account" (Mt 5:11). The world's ire often means the Father's blessing. Anyone who desires to live a godly life should expect persecution (2Ti 3:12). Jesus epitomized this type of reality. Though he never sinned, he was consistently harassed by people. If they persecuted him, certainly they will persecute his followers. A servant is not greater than his master.

24 My knees are weak through fasting;
my body has become gaunt, with no fat.
25 I am an object of scorn to my accusers;
when they see me, they wag their heads.

26 Help me, O LORD my God!
Save me according to your steadfast love!
27 Let them know that this is your hand;
you, O LORD, have done it!
28 Let them curse, but you will bless!
They arise and are put to shame, but your servant will be glad!
29 May my accusers be clothed with dishonor;
may they be wrapped in their own shame as in a cloak!

30 With my mouth I will give great thanks to the LORD;
I will praise him in the midst of the throng.
31 For he stands at the right hand of the needy one,
to save him from those who condemn his soul to death.

Psalm 110

Sit at My Right Hand

A Psalm of David.

1 The LORD says to my Lord:
"Sit at my right hand,
until I make your enemies your footstool."

2 The LORD sends forth from Zion
your mighty scepter.
Rule in the midst of your enemies!
3 Your people will offer themselves freely
on the day of your power,[1]
in holy garments;[2]
from the womb of the morning,
the dew of your youth will be yours.[3]
4 The LORD has sworn
and will not change his mind,
"You are a priest forever
after the order of Melchizedek."

5 The Lord is at your right hand;
he will shatter kings on the day of his wrath.
6 He will execute judgment among the nations,
filling them with corpses;
he will shatter chiefs[4]
over the wide earth.
7 He will drink from the brook by the way;
therefore he will lift up his head.

Psalm 111[5]

Great Are the LORD's Works

1 Praise the LORD!
I will give thanks to the LORD with my whole heart,
in the company of the upright, in the congregation.

[1]Or *on the day you lead your forces* [2]Masoretic Text; some Hebrew manuscripts and Jerome *on the holy mountains* [3]The meaning of the Hebrew is uncertain [4]Or *the head* [5]This psalm is an acrostic poem, each line beginning with the successive letters of the Hebrew alphabet

PSALM 110:1

WHOSE SON IS HE?

No psalm is quoted more frequently in the New Testament than this one. While the same English word (*lord*) is used twice in verse 1, the Hebrew uses two different words. The question for the interpreter centers on the identity of this second "lord."

Jesus posed a form of this question to the Pharisees in Matthew's Gospel. Speaking of the long-expected Messiah, he asked, "Whose son is he?" (Mt 22:42). When the Pharisees responded "the son of David," Jesus quoted Psalm 110:1. In essence, Jesus asked them how, if David wrote this psalm, he can call his son "Lord" (Mt 22:45). Jesus asserted that this Messiah must be more than just the son of David.

Surely Peter was in the audience that day. Not long afterward, at Pentecost, he also quoted Psalm 110:1. Peter made plain to that crowd that David did not ascend to the heavens, though he wrote that this "Lord" would sit at God's right hand (Ac 2:29–35). Though Jesus made the case that this "Lord" could not be *just* the son of David, Peter stated clearly his identity: "Let all the house of Israel therefore know for certain that God has made him both Lord and Christ" (Ac 2:36). Jesus was not just the son of David; he is the Son of God. He is both David's descendant and his Lord.

JESUS, THE PRIEST-KING

In Genesis 14, Moses wrote about a mysterious priest named Melchizedek. He served as priest in Salem, the place later known as Jerusalem. His symbolically rich name means "king of righteousness." Interestingly, Melchizedek not only served as priest of Salem, he ruled as king.

The New Testament makes clear that Melchizedek was a representation of the Messiah who was to come. Psalm 110 speaks of the One whom the New Testament makes clear is Jesus Christ (Ac 2:22–36). God exalted him, seating him at his right hand to rule and reign (Ps 110:1; Eph 1:20).

During the Old Testament era, in every case other than in the person of Melchizedek, the kingly and priestly offices remained separate. One person could not fulfill both roles. The king represented God to humanity; the priest represented humanity to God. However, the role of the Old Testament priest was not the full realization of the plans of God.

In the Old Testament priests had limited authority and ultimately died. Jesus, on the other hand, has ultimate authority and ever lives to make intercession for his people (Heb 7:23–25). Melchizedek did not reign forever, but the Old Testament timeline gives no end to his reign or priesthood. It seemed to continue on, pointing readers to a priest-king who would reign forever: Jesus, in the order of Melchizedek (Ps 110:4).

Not only did Jesus' priesthood surpass the Levitical priesthood, but his sacrifice surpassed the priestly sacrifice. With no need to make atonement for his own sin, Jesus sacrificed himself as a pure and spotless lamb (1Pe 1:19). Not only did he *make* the perfect offering, he *was* that offering.

In Jesus, that which Melchizedek pointed to is perfectly fulfilled. Both offices come together in one person. Only one who was both God and human could represent both God and humanity. Jesus rules as King until all his enemies become his footstool, while interceding as priest for those being reconciled to God.

2 Great are the works of the LORD,
studied by all who delight in them.
3 Full of splendor and majesty is his work,
and his righteousness endures forever.
4 He has caused his wondrous works to be remembered;
the LORD is gracious and merciful.
5 He provides food for those who fear him;
he remembers his covenant forever.
6 He has shown his people the power of his works,
in giving them the inheritance of the nations.
7 The works of his hands are faithful and just;
all his precepts are trustworthy;
8 they are established forever and ever,
to be performed with faithfulness and uprightness.
9 He sent redemption to his people;
he has commanded his covenant forever.
Holy and awesome is his name!
10 The fear of the LORD is the beginning of wisdom;
all those who practice it have a good understanding.
His praise endures forever!

Psalm 112[1]

The Righteous Will Never Be Moved

1 Praise the LORD!
Blessed is the man who fears the LORD,
who greatly delights in his commandments!
2 His offspring will be mighty in the land;
the generation of the upright will be blessed.
3 Wealth and riches are in his house,
and his righteousness endures forever.
4 Light dawns in the darkness for the upright;
he is gracious, merciful, and righteous.
5 It is well with the man who deals generously and lends;
who conducts his affairs with justice.
6 For the righteous will never be moved;
he will be remembered forever.
7 He is not afraid of bad news;
his heart is firm, trusting in the LORD.
8 His heart is steady;[2] he will not be afraid,
until he looks in triumph on his adversaries.
9 He has distributed freely; he has given to the poor;
his righteousness endures forever;
his horn is exalted in honor.
10 The wicked man sees it and is angry;
he gnashes his teeth and melts away;
the desire of the wicked will perish!

Psalm 113

Who Is like the LORD Our God?

1 Praise the LORD!
Praise, O servants of the LORD,
praise the name of the LORD!

PSALMS 113–118

LAST MEAL

Psalms 113–118, called the *Egyptian Hallel*, came to be sung at the yearly Passover. *Hallel* means "praise." Generally, the first two psalms were sung prior to the meal, with the final four being sung after the meal.

While only one of them clearly references the exodus (Ps 114), other appropriate themes emerge. Psalm 113 speaks of the Lord raising the poor and needy from the dust, not unlike the Hebrew slaves. The same themes of the Old Testament Passover meal would eventually be seen in the New Testament Lord's Supper—a meal of remembrance and thanks. Psalm 116 addresses thanksgiving based on God's gracious action. Since these psalms usually accompanied the Passover, it is likely that these were the final songs Jesus sang before going to Gethsemane (Mt 26:30). Though he knew a terrible fate awaited, he was able to give thanks to God for his ongoing faithfulness to his redemptive work.

[1]This psalm is an acrostic poem, each line beginning with the successive letters of the Hebrew alphabet
[2]Or *established* (compare 111:8)

2 Blessed be the name of the LORD
from this time forth and forevermore!
3 From the rising of the sun to its setting,
the name of the LORD is to be praised!

4 The LORD is high above all nations,
and his glory above the heavens!
5 Who is like the LORD our God,
who is seated on high,
6 who looks far down
on the heavens and the earth?
7 He raises the poor from the dust
and lifts the needy from the ash heap,
8 to make them sit with princes,
with the princes of his people.
9 He gives the barren woman a home,
making her the joyous mother of children.
Praise the LORD!

Psalm 114

Tremble at the Presence of the Lord

1 When Israel went out from Egypt,
the house of Jacob from a people of strange language,
2 Judah became his sanctuary,
Israel his dominion.

3 The sea looked and fled;
Jordan turned back.
4 The mountains skipped like rams,
the hills like lambs.

5 What ails you, O sea, that you flee?
O Jordan, that you turn back?
6 O mountains, that you skip like rams?
O hills, like lambs?

7 Tremble, O earth, at the presence of the Lord,
at the presence of the God of Jacob,
8 who turns the rock into a pool of water,
the flint into a spring of water.

Psalm 115

To Your Name Give Glory

1 Not to us, O LORD, not to us, but to your name give glory,
for the sake of your steadfast love and your faithfulness!

2 Why should the nations say,
"Where is their God?"
3 Our God is in the heavens;
he does all that he pleases.

4 Their idols are silver and gold,
the work of human hands.
5 They have mouths, but do not speak;
eyes, but do not see.
6 They have ears, but do not hear;
noses, but do not smell.

7 They have hands, but do not feel;
feet, but do not walk;
and they do not make a sound in their throat.
8 Those who make them become like them;
so do all who trust in them.

9 O Israel,[1] trust in the LORD!
He is their help and their shield.
10 O house of Aaron, trust in the LORD!
He is their help and their shield.
11 You who fear the LORD, trust in the LORD!
He is their help and their shield.

12 The LORD has remembered us; he will bless us;
he will bless the house of Israel;
he will bless the house of Aaron;
13 he will bless those who fear the LORD,
both the small and the great.

14 May the LORD give you increase,
you and your children!
15 May you be blessed by the LORD,
who made heaven and earth!

16 The heavens are the LORD's heavens,
but the earth he has given to the children of man.
17 The dead do not praise the LORD,
nor do any who go down into silence.
18 But we will bless the LORD
from this time forth and forevermore.
Praise the LORD!

Psalm 116

I Love the LORD

1 I love the LORD, because he has heard
my voice and my pleas for mercy.
2 Because he inclined his ear to me,
therefore I will call on him as long as I live.
3 The snares of death encompassed me;
the pangs of Sheol laid hold on me;
I suffered distress and anguish.
4 Then I called on the name of the LORD:
"O LORD, I pray, deliver my soul!"

5 Gracious is the LORD, and righteous;
our God is merciful.
6 The LORD preserves the simple;
when I was brought low, he saved me.
7 Return, O my soul, to your rest;
for the LORD has dealt bountifully with you.

8 For you have delivered my soul from death,
my eyes from tears,
my feet from stumbling;
9 I will walk before the LORD
in the land of the living.

10 I believed, even when[2] I spoke:
"I am greatly afflicted";

[1]Masoretic Text; many Hebrew manuscripts, Septuagint, Syriac *O house of Israel* [2]Or *believed, indeed*; Septuagint *believed, therefore*

11 I said in my alarm,
"All mankind are liars."

12 What shall I render to the LORD
for all his benefits to me?
13 I will lift up the cup of salvation
and call on the name of the LORD,
14 I will pay my vows to the LORD
in the presence of all his people.

15 Precious in the sight of the LORD
is the death of his saints.
16 O LORD, I am your servant;
I am your servant, the son of your maidservant.
You have loosed my bonds.
17 I will offer to you the sacrifice of thanksgiving
and call on the name of the LORD.
18 I will pay my vows to the LORD
in the presence of all his people,
19 in the courts of the house of the LORD,
in your midst, O Jerusalem.
Praise the LORD!

PSALM 116:15

DEATH

The psalmist mentioned here an enemy of humankind: death (Ps 116:3), though he referred to it in verse 15 as "precious"—an overwhelmingly positive term. According to Paul, death came to humanity because of sin: in Adam all die (Ro 5:12). While the scientific advances of the last century—even the last ten years—preserve and extend life in amazing ways, no one evades death forever.

Psalm 110 speaks of Jesus reigning until all his enemies become a footstool for his feet (v. 1). Building upon that truth, Paul wrote, "The last enemy to be destroyed is death" (1Co 15:26). Paul went on to argue in that letter that the resurrection of Jesus makes possible the resurrection of his followers: "For as by a man came death, by a man has come also the resurrection of the dead. For as in Adam all die, so also in Christ shall all be made alive" (1Co 15:21–22). Only through the work of Christ can his followers taunt death: "O death, where is your sting?" (1Co 15:55). Though no one evades death, it need not have the final word.

Psalm 117

The LORD's Faithfulness Endures Forever

1 Praise the LORD, all nations!
Extol him, all peoples!
2 For great is his steadfast love toward us,
and the faithfulness of the LORD endures forever.
Praise the LORD!

Psalm 118

His Steadfast Love Endures Forever

1 Oh give thanks to the LORD, for he is good;
for his steadfast love endures forever!

2 Let Israel say,
"His steadfast love endures forever."
3 Let the house of Aaron say,
"His steadfast love endures forever."
4 Let those who fear the LORD say,
"His steadfast love endures forever."

5 Out of my distress I called on the LORD;
the LORD answered me and set me free.
6 The LORD is on my side; I will not fear.
What can man do to me?
7 The LORD is on my side as my helper;
I shall look in triumph on those who hate me.

8 It is better to take refuge in the LORD
than to trust in man.
9 It is better to take refuge in the LORD
than to trust in princes.

10 All nations surrounded me;
in the name of the LORD I cut them off!
11 They surrounded me, surrounded me on every side;
in the name of the LORD I cut them off!

THE NATIONS PRAISE THE LORD

This is the shortest psalm. However, its brevity should not be confused for insignificance. The psalmist calls upon all the earth — each and every nation — to praise the Lord of the nations (v. 1).

Though many of the psalms speak of God's work among the Israelites, God called Israel to himself for the sake of the world. Genesis 1 – 11 portrays the sinful descent of humanity culminating in the scattering of the people at Babel, but Genesis 12 indicates a brand new start for humanity through God's covenant with Abraham: "In you all the families of the earth shall be blessed" (Ge 12:3). God promised that *all the nations* would be blessed through Abraham. In fact, God blessed Abraham *so that* he might be a blessing.

Then at the exodus, God orchestrated events to assert his unrivaled authority over all the nations, including the enemies of Israel. Even after being conquered by their enemies and forced into exile hundreds of years later, the Israelites continued to claim that their God rules sovereignly over all (Eze 36:16 – 38). God chose Israel to make himself known to all the world.

The Gospel of Luke — by going back beyond Abraham to Adam in its genealogy — hints at the global scope of the gospel's intent (Lk 3:37). At the end of Luke's Gospel, Jesus' commission states that repentance for the forgiveness of sins should be proclaimed *to all nations* (Lk 24:47). In Acts 1:8, Luke picks up on this movement of God from Jerusalem to the ends of the earth, corroborated by the conversion of Gentiles, beginning with Cornelius and others in Acts 10. Erasing any doubt about the global reach of the gospel, Jesus commanded his disciples to make disciples *of every nation* (Mt 28:16 – 20).

In the context of calling believers to welcome one another as Christ welcomed them, Paul quoted from Psalm 117, making clear that the Gentiles were to glorify God for his mercy (Ro 15:11). God's plan has always been that all the nations praise him. The book of Revelation confirms that he will certainly bring this to pass (Rev 7:9 – 10). This is a global God, deserving and desiring global praise.

PSALM 119:1–176

THE WORD

The structure of Psalm 119, the longest psalm (and the longest chapter) in Scripture, is fascinating. The 22 stanzas follow in order the 22 letters of the Hebrew alphabet. Within each eight-verse stanza, the first letter of each line corresponds to the same Hebrew letter. So, in English, this would be eight verses beginning with "A" followed by eight verses beginning with "B," eight verses beginning with "C," and so on.

But the focus of this psalm is not Hebrew letters. The focus of Psalm 119 is the Word. As the most extended treatment of this topic in Scripture, Psalm 119 uses various terms (precepts, law, decrees, statutes, commands) to speak about the Word of God. God's Word is eternal (v. 89). His commands are wise (v. 98). Those who walk in God's commands, God considers blessed (vv. 1–2). If one wants to be pure, the Word of God needs to be his or her guide (v. 9).

The psalm is arranged in an acrostic fashion to help facilitate memorization, likely among children. Memorization of the Word leads to meditation upon the Word, producing the strength the psalmist described: "Make me understand the way of your precepts, and I will meditate on your wondrous works ... strengthen me according to your word!" (vv. 27–28). As the Word made flesh, Jesus would exemplify God's ways and guide God's people.

3 who also do no wrong,
but walk in his ways!
4 You have commanded your precepts
to be kept diligently.
5 Oh that my ways may be steadfast
in keeping your statutes!
6 Then I shall not be put to shame,
having my eyes fixed on all your commandments.
7 I will praise you with an upright heart,
when I learn your righteous rules.[1]
8 I will keep your statutes;
do not utterly forsake me!

Beth

9 How can a young man keep his way pure?
By guarding it according to your word.
10 With my whole heart I seek you;
let me not wander from your commandments!
11 I have stored up your word in my heart,
that I might not sin against you.
12 Blessed are you, O LORD;
teach me your statutes!
13 With my lips I declare
all the rules[2] of your mouth.
14 In the way of your testimonies I delight
as much as in all riches.
15 I will meditate on your precepts
and fix my eyes on your ways.
16 I will delight in your statutes;
I will not forget your word.

Gimel

17 Deal bountifully with your servant,
that I may live and keep your word.
18 Open my eyes, that I may behold
wondrous things out of your law.
19 I am a sojourner on the earth;
hide not your commandments from me!
20 My soul is consumed with longing
for your rules[3] at all times.
21 You rebuke the insolent, accursed ones,
who wander from your commandments.
22 Take away from me scorn and contempt,
for I have kept your testimonies.
23 Even though princes sit plotting against me,
your servant will meditate on your statutes.
24 Your testimonies are my delight;
they are my counselors.

Daleth

25 My soul clings to the dust;
give me life according to your word!

[1]Or *your just and righteous decrees*; also verses 62, 106, 160, 164 [2]Or *all the just decrees* [3]Or *your just decrees*; also verses 30, 39, 43, 52, 75, 102, 108, 137, 156, 175

26 When I told of my ways, you answered me;
teach me your statutes!
27 Make me understand the way of your precepts,
and I will meditate on your wondrous works.
28 My soul melts away for sorrow;
strengthen me according to your word!
29 Put false ways far from me
and graciously teach me your law!
30 I have chosen the way of faithfulness;
I set your rules before me.
31 I cling to your testimonies, O LORD;
let me not be put to shame!
32 I will run in the way of your commandments
when you enlarge my heart![1]

He

33 Teach me, O LORD, the way of your statutes;
and I will keep it to the end.[2]
34 Give me understanding, that I may keep your law
and observe it with my whole heart.
35 Lead me in the path of your commandments,
for I delight in it.
36 Incline my heart to your testimonies,
and not to selfish gain!
37 Turn my eyes from looking at worthless things;
and give me life in your ways.
38 Confirm to your servant your promise,
that you may be feared.
39 Turn away the reproach that I dread,
for your rules are good.
40 Behold, I long for your precepts;
in your righteousness give me life!

Waw

41 Let your steadfast love come to me, O LORD,
your salvation according to your promise;
42 then shall I have an answer for him who taunts me,
for I trust in your word.
43 And take not the word of truth utterly out of my mouth,
for my hope is in your rules.
44 I will keep your law continually,
forever and ever,
45 and I shall walk in a wide place,
for I have sought your precepts.
46 I will also speak of your testimonies before kings
and shall not be put to shame,
47 for I find my delight in your commandments,
which I love.
48 I will lift up my hands toward your commandments, which I love,
and I will meditate on your statutes.

Zayin

49 Remember your word to your servant,
in which you have made me hope.

---

[1]Or *for you set my heart free* [2]Or *keep it as my reward*

50 This is my comfort in my affliction,
that your promise gives me life.
51 The insolent utterly deride me,
but I do not turn away from your law.
52 When I think of your rules from of old,
I take comfort, O LORD.
53 Hot indignation seizes me because of the wicked,
who forsake your law.
54 Your statutes have been my songs
in the house of my sojourning.
55 I remember your name in the night, O LORD,
and keep your law.
56 This blessing has fallen to me,
that I have kept your precepts.

Heth

57 The LORD is my portion;
I promise to keep your words.
58 I entreat your favor with all my heart;
be gracious to me according to your promise.
59 When I think on my ways,
I turn my feet to your testimonies;
60 I hasten and do not delay
to keep your commandments.
61 Though the cords of the wicked ensnare me,
I do not forget your law.
62 At midnight I rise to praise you,
because of your righteous rules.
63 I am a companion of all who fear you,
of those who keep your precepts.
64 The earth, O LORD, is full of your steadfast love;
teach me your statutes!

Teth

65 You have dealt well with your servant,
O LORD, according to your word.
66 Teach me good judgment and knowledge,
for I believe in your commandments.
67 Before I was afflicted I went astray,
but now I keep your word.
68 You are good and do good;
teach me your statutes.
69 The insolent smear me with lies,
but with my whole heart I keep your precepts;
70 their heart is unfeeling like fat,
but I delight in your law.
71 It is good for me that I was afflicted,
that I might learn your statutes.
72 The law of your mouth is better to me
than thousands of gold and silver pieces.

Yodh

73 Your hands have made and fashioned me;
give me understanding that I may learn your commandments.

74 Those who fear you shall see me and rejoice,
because I have hoped in your word.
75 I know, O LORD, that your rules are righteous,
and that in faithfulness you have afflicted me.
76 Let your steadfast love comfort me
according to your promise to your servant.
77 Let your mercy come to me, that I may live;
for your law is my delight.
78 Let the insolent be put to shame,
because they have wronged me with falsehood;
as for me, I will meditate on your precepts.
79 Let those who fear you turn to me,
that they may know your testimonies.
80 May my heart be blameless in your statutes,
that I may not be put to shame!

Kaph

81 My soul longs for your salvation;
I hope in your word.
82 My eyes long for your promise;
I ask, "When will you comfort me?"
83 For I have become like a wineskin in the smoke,
yet I have not forgotten your statutes.
84 How long must your servant endure?[1]
When will you judge those who persecute me?
85 The insolent have dug pitfalls for me;
they do not live according to your law.
86 All your commandments are sure;
they persecute me with falsehood; help me!
87 They have almost made an end of me on earth,
but I have not forsaken your precepts.
88 In your steadfast love give me life,
that I may keep the testimonies of your mouth.

Lamedh

89 Forever, O LORD, your word
is firmly fixed in the heavens.
90 Your faithfulness endures to all generations;
you have established the earth, and it stands
fast.
91 By your appointment they stand this day,
for all things are your servants.
92 If your law had not been my delight,
I would have perished in my affliction.
93 I will never forget your precepts,
for by them you have given me life.
94 I am yours; save me,
for I have sought your precepts.
95 The wicked lie in wait to destroy me,
but I consider your testimonies.
96 I have seen a limit to all perfection,
but your commandment is exceedingly
broad.

[1]Hebrew *How many are the days of your servant?*

Mem

97 Oh how I love your law!
It is my meditation all the day.
98 Your commandment makes me wiser than my enemies,
for it is ever with me.
99 I have more understanding than all my teachers,
for your testimonies are my meditation.
100 I understand more than the aged,[1]
for I keep your precepts.
101 I hold back my feet from every evil way,
in order to keep your word.
102 I do not turn aside from your rules,
for you have taught me.
103 How sweet are your words to my taste,
sweeter than honey to my mouth!
104 Through your precepts I get understanding;
therefore I hate every false way.

Nun

105 Your word is a lamp to my feet
and a light to my path.
106 I have sworn an oath and confirmed it,
to keep your righteous rules.
107 I am severely afflicted;
give me life, O LORD, according to your word!
108 Accept my freewill offerings of praise, O LORD,
and teach me your rules.
109 I hold my life in my hand continually,
but I do not forget your law.
110 The wicked have laid a snare for me,
but I do not stray from your precepts.
111 Your testimonies are my heritage forever,
for they are the joy of my heart.
112 I incline my heart to perform your statutes
forever, to the end.[2]

Samekh

113 I hate the double-minded,
but I love your law.
114 You are my hiding place and my shield;
I hope in your word.
115 Depart from me, you evildoers,
that I may keep the commandments of my God.
116 Uphold me according to your promise, that I may live,
and let me not be put to shame in my hope!
117 Hold me up, that I may be safe
and have regard for your statutes continually!
118 You spurn all who go astray from your statutes,
for their cunning is in vain.
119 All the wicked of the earth you discard like dross,
therefore I love your testimonies.
120 My flesh trembles for fear of you,
and I am afraid of your judgments.

---

[1]Or *the elders* [2]Or *statutes; the reward is eternal*

Ayin

121 I have done what is just and right;
do not leave me to my oppressors.
122 Give your servant a pledge of good;
let not the insolent oppress me.
123 My eyes long for your salvation
and for the fulfillment of your righteous promise.
124 Deal with your servant according to your steadfast
love,
and teach me your statutes.
125 I am your servant; give me understanding,
that I may know your testimonies!
126 It is time for the LORD to act,
for your law has been broken.
127 Therefore I love your commandments
above gold, above fine gold.
128 Therefore I consider all your precepts to be right;
I hate every false way.

Pe

129 Your testimonies are wonderful;
therefore my soul keeps them.
130 The unfolding of your words gives light;
it imparts understanding to the simple.
131 I open my mouth and pant,
because I long for your commandments.
132 Turn to me and be gracious to me,
as is your way with those who love your name.
133 Keep steady my steps according to your promise,
and let no iniquity get dominion over me.
134 Redeem me from man's oppression,
that I may keep your precepts.
135 Make your face shine upon your servant,
and teach me your statutes.
136 My eyes shed streams of tears,
because people do not keep your law.

Tsadhe

137 Righteous are you, O LORD,
and right are your rules.
138 You have appointed your testimonies in righteousness
and in all faithfulness.
139 My zeal consumes me,
because my foes forget your words.
140 Your promise is well tried,
and your servant loves it.
141 I am small and despised,
yet I do not forget your precepts.
142 Your righteousness is righteous forever,
and your law is true.
143 Trouble and anguish have found me out,
but your commandments are my delight.
144 Your testimonies are righteous forever;
give me understanding that I may live.

Qoph

145 With my whole heart I cry; answer me, O LORD!
I will keep your statutes.
146 I call to you; save me,
that I may observe your testimonies.
147 I rise before dawn and cry for help;
I hope in your words.
148 My eyes are awake before the watches of the night,
that I may meditate on your promise.
149 Hear my voice according to your steadfast love;
O LORD, according to your justice give me life.
150 They draw near who persecute me with evil purpose;
they are far from your law.
151 But you are near, O LORD,
and all your commandments are true.
152 Long have I known from your testimonies
that you have founded them forever.

Resh

153 Look on my affliction and deliver me,
for I do not forget your law.
154 Plead my cause and redeem me;
give me life according to your promise!
155 Salvation is far from the wicked,
for they do not seek your statutes.
156 Great is your mercy, O LORD;
give me life according to your rules.
157 Many are my persecutors and my adversaries,
but I do not swerve from your testimonies.
158 I look at the faithless with disgust,
because they do not keep your commands.
159 Consider how I love your precepts!
Give me life, O LORD, according to your steadfast love.
160 The sum of your word is truth,
and every one of your righteous rules endures
forever.

Sin and Shin

161 Princes persecute me without cause,
but my heart stands in awe of your words.
162 I rejoice at your word
like one who finds great spoil.
163 I hate and abhor falsehood,
but I love your law.
164 Seven times a day I praise you
for your righteous rules.
165 Great peace have those who love your law;
nothing can make them stumble.
166 I hope for your salvation, O LORD,
and I do your commandments.
167 My soul keeps your testimonies;
I love them exceedingly.
168 I keep your precepts and testimonies,
for all my ways are before you.

Taw

169 Let my cry come before you, O LORD;
give me understanding according to your word!
170 Let my plea come before you;
deliver me according to your word.
171 My lips will pour forth praise,
for you teach me your statutes.
172 My tongue will sing of your word,
for all your commandments are right.
173 Let your hand be ready to help me,
for I have chosen your precepts.
174 I long for your salvation, O LORD,
and your law is my delight.
175 Let my soul live and praise you,
and let your rules help me.
176 I have gone astray like a lost sheep; seek your servant,
for I do not forget your commandments.

Psalm 120

Deliver Me, O LORD

A Song of Ascents.

1 In my distress I called to the LORD,
and he answered me.
2 Deliver me, O LORD,
from lying lips,
from a deceitful tongue.

3 What shall be given to you,
and what more shall be done to you,
you deceitful tongue?
4 A warrior's sharp arrows,
with glowing coals of the broom tree!

5 Woe to me, that I sojourn in Meshech,
that I dwell among the tents of Kedar!
6 Too long have I had my dwelling
among those who hate peace.
7 I am for peace,
but when I speak, they are for war!

Psalm 121

My Help Comes from the LORD

A Song of Ascents.

1 I lift up my eyes to the hills.
From where does my help come?
2 My help comes from the LORD,
who made heaven and earth.

3 He will not let your foot be moved;
he who keeps you will not slumber.
4 Behold, he who keeps Israel
will neither slumber nor sleep.

5 The LORD is your keeper;
the LORD is your shade on your right hand.

6 The sun shall not strike you by day,
nor the moon by night.
7 The LORD will keep you from all evil;
he will keep your life.
8 The LORD will keep
your going out and your coming in
from this time forth and forevermore.

Psalm 122

Let Us Go to the House of the LORD

A Song of Ascents. Of David.

1 I was glad when they said to me,
"Let us go to the house of the LORD!"
2 Our feet have been standing
within your gates, O Jerusalem!

3 Jerusalem—built as a city
that is bound firmly together,
4 to which the tribes go up,
the tribes of the LORD,
as was decreed for[1] Israel,
to give thanks to the name of the LORD.
5 There thrones for judgment were set,
the thrones of the house of David.

6 Pray for the peace of Jerusalem!
"May they be secure who love you!
7 Peace be within your walls
and security within your towers!"
8 For my brothers and companions' sake
I will say, "Peace be within you!"
9 For the sake of the house of the LORD our God,
I will seek your good.

Psalm 123

Our Eyes Look to the LORD Our God

A Song of Ascents.

1 To you I lift up my eyes,
O you who are enthroned in the heavens!
2 Behold, as the eyes of servants
look to the hand of their master,
as the eyes of a maidservant
to the hand of her mistress,
so our eyes look to the LORD our God,
till he has mercy upon us.

3 Have mercy upon us, O LORD, have mercy upon us,
for we have had more than enough of contempt.
4 Our soul has had more than enough
of the scorn of those who are at ease,
of the contempt of the proud.

[1]Or *as a testimony for*

PSALM 122:1–9

PRAYING FOR PEACE

The Israelites sang this "Song of Ascents" as they journeyed toward Jerusalem. This long, difficult pilgrimage was not simply a matter of duty. After a few details about the city, the psalm points out the reason for this trip: the Israelites went to Jerusalem for the purpose of praise (v. 4). At the very mention of worshiping the Lord in the Lord's city—at the Lord's house—the psalmist rejoiced (v. 1).

However, if Jerusalem were to become dangerous—or if war were to break out—it would make it more difficult for families to venture out. So, the psalmist prayed for peace. The peace he desired certainly brought him benefit, but the psalmist prayed for his fellow pilgrims as well (v. 8). For the sake of the temple of God, he asked for strife to cease (v. 9). War would hinder worship; peace would facilitate praise. Ultimately this peace was only possible through the finished work of Jesus Christ, who came to bring peace between fallen humans and God and peace between his created people (Ro 5:1).

PSALM 123:1–4

PLEADING FOR MERCY

The people of God sang songs and prayers in the hopes that God would *vindicate them and foil the contempt* of the proud. These songs bolstered their hope through years of oppression and pain—when it looked as if God had forgotten them and the

(continued on page 902)

HELP

While looking at the mountains, the psalmist asked a question. Because the psalmist immediately answered his own question, the reader knows this question was rhetorical. There was no doubt in the psalmist's mind: the one who made the mountains is also the one who helps.

The psalmist placed his confidence in the Creator God. The "Songs of Ascents" (beginning at Ps 120) were likely sung as Israelite pilgrims traveled toward Jerusalem. It seems that this psalm narrates the experience of the journey itself, as the pilgrims looked toward the mountains that surrounded their destination. Rather than wasting this moment, the psalmist chose to use the sight as an object lesson. The mountains were impressive. So was their Creator. And, most significant for the people making their way to Jerusalem, that Creator was the traveling pilgrim's helper.

The rest of the psalm speaks of the specifics of God's help. As the people journeyed, the Maker of heaven and earth would keep their feet from slipping. To a crowd likely traveling in rough terrain, this would be a comfort. Furthermore, to a crowd sleeping seemingly in dangerous conditions, the psalmist said, "Behold, he who keeps Israel will neither slumber nor sleep" (v. 4). As they rested, maybe restlessly, God watched over them. The word "keep" indicates that he guarded and protected them. Filling these pilgrims with peace was this truth: the Maker of heaven and earth was their guardian.

The psalm ends with an overview of the aspects of life the Lord watches over. "Your going out and your coming in" points to everything in the pilgrim's life, even hinting at the beginning and ending of one's days (v. 8). Nothing is outside the purview of God's watch and keep. The duration of this promise makes this apparent: the Lord watches over his people now and forevermore.

When the psalmist wrote that they would be kept from all harm, he did not contradict those passages that refer to the persecution that follows those who follow the Lord (Jn 15:20). Instead, the Lord protects his people in the midst of difficulty. Jesus prayed along these lines in his high priestly prayer: "Holy Father, keep them in your name" (Jn 17:11). Followers of Christ will not be kept from difficulty, but they will be kept.

(Pleading for Mercy, continued)

arrogant were winning. Later, these songs would become the anthems sung by the people as they journeyed to Jerusalem.

The psalmist pled for mercy, but not for him alone (v. 3). He sang for his fellow people. While the proud and those at ease heaped insults, he asked that God might show favor to his people.

The psalmist pled patiently. Rather than attempting to strong-arm the hand of God, the people of God submit. A picture gives readers insight into how they should plead with the Lord. Slaves live under the authority of their master, watching the hand of the master until an order comes. So how long will these people continue to look and ask for mercy? The end of verse 2 says, "till he has mercy upon us."

In this same city, years later, the people of Jerusalem were hostile to God and his appointed One. The very radiance of God walked among them, endured the scorn of those at ease, and received the contempt of the proud. In the end, they nailed him to a cross. In stark irony, however, this great act of violence proved the beauty of the mercy of God.

PSALM 124:1–8

IF GOD IS FOR HIS PEOPLE

The Old Testament narrative gives example after example of the Lord's protection of his people. Though the details of each story differ and feature a variety of people used by God—Moses, Joshua, David, and others—the main character remains the same: God himself. Apart from the Lord's intervention, the

(continued on next page)

Psalm 124

Our Help Is in the Name of the LORD

A Song of Ascents. Of David.

1 If it had not been the LORD who was on our side—
let Israel now say—
2 if it had not been the LORD who was on our side
when people rose up against us,
3 then they would have swallowed us up alive,
when their anger was kindled against us;
4 then the flood would have swept us away,
the torrent would have gone over us;
5 then over us would have gone
the raging waters.

6 Blessed be the LORD,
who has not given us
as prey to their teeth!
7 We have escaped like a bird
from the snare of the fowlers;
the snare is broken,
and we have escaped!

8 Our help is in the name of the LORD,
who made heaven and earth.

Psalm 125

The LORD Surrounds His People

A Song of Ascents.

1 Those who trust in the LORD are like Mount Zion,
which cannot be moved, but abides forever.
2 As the mountains surround Jerusalem,
so the LORD surrounds his people,
from this time forth and forevermore.
3 For the scepter of wickedness shall not rest
on the land allotted to the righteous,
lest the righteous stretch out
their hands to do wrong.
4 Do good, O LORD, to those who are good,
and to those who are upright in their hearts!
5 But those who turn aside to their crooked ways
the LORD will lead away with evildoers!
Peace be upon Israel!

Psalm 126

Restore Our Fortunes, O LORD

A Song of Ascents.

1 When the LORD restored the fortunes of Zion,
we were like those who dream.
2 Then our mouth was filled with laughter,
and our tongue with shouts of joy;
then they said among the nations,
"The LORD has done great things for them."

3 The LORD has done great things for us;
we are glad.
4 Restore our fortunes, O LORD,
like streams in the Negeb!
5 Those who sow in tears
shall reap with shouts of joy!
6 He who goes out weeping,
bearing the seed for sowing,
shall come home with shouts of joy,
bringing his sheaves with him.

Psalm 127

Unless the LORD Builds the House

A Song of Ascents. Of Solomon.

1 Unless the LORD builds the house,
those who build it labor in vain.
Unless the LORD watches over the city,
the watchman stays awake in vain.
2 It is in vain that you rise up early
and go late to rest,
eating the bread of anxious toil;
for he gives to his beloved sleep.
3 Behold, children are a heritage from the LORD,
the fruit of the womb a reward.
4 Like arrows in the hand of a warrior
are the children[1] of one's youth.
5 Blessed is the man
who fills his quiver with them!
He shall not be put to shame
when he speaks with his enemies in the gate.[2]

Psalm 128

Blessed Is Everyone Who Fears the LORD

A Song of Ascents.

1 Blessed is everyone who fears the LORD,
who walks in his ways!
2 You shall eat the fruit of the labor of your hands;
you shall be blessed, and it shall be well with you.
3 Your wife will be like a fruitful vine
within your house;
your children will be like olive shoots
around your table.
4 Behold, thus shall the man be blessed
who fears the LORD.
5 The LORD bless you from Zion!
May you see the prosperity of Jerusalem
all the days of your life!
6 May you see your children's children!
Peace be upon Israel!

[1]Or *sons* [2]Or *They shall not be put to shame when they speak with their enemies in the gate*

(If God Is for His People, continued)

people of God would have long ago been swept away by the flood's raging waters (v. 5).

Though it seems obvious, the psalmist endeavored to point out the side the Lord chose in the ongoing conflict between God's people and their enemies. This psalm looks back—reviewing the battles—to clarify beyond any doubt that the people of God overcame only by the power of the Lord.

The apostle Paul made this same point in his letter to the Romans, though he did not only look at past deliverances. Believers root their assurance in the work of Christ. In Christ, condemnation no longer has any teeth (Ro 8:1). God will conform those he calls to the image of his Son (Ro 8:29). Furthermore, those whom he justified freely, he will most certainly glorify in the future (Ro 8:30). Paul looked *back* to the work of Christ while also looking *forward* to a future hope. In light of these truths he wrote, "If God is for us, who can be against us?" (Ro 8:31). Though people have tried, no one has yet come up with a worthy opponent.

PSALM 125:2

SURROUNDED

The issue for the believer is not the intensity of their faith, but the object of it. The enemies of God sought to conquer the city of Jerusalem. To overrun Jerusalem, however, would mean traversing the mountains that surrounded it. So the mountains protected the city, making it more difficult to attack.

When these songs were sung by traveling pilgrims after their ascent,

(continued on page 905)

PAST, PRESENT, AND FUTURE GRACE

The first half of this psalm (vv. 1 – 3) looks back at an event in Israel's past when the Lord displayed his greatness, restoring the fortunes of the people of God. The writer indicated that the people of God were not calloused and dull to the fortunes of God's grace. They responded appropriately, with laughter and songs of joy. In fact, the Lord's greatness on their behalf increased their gladness (v. 3). Furthermore, this was a publicized joy. Even the pagan nations observed, looking on as bystanders and marveling at the Lord's goodness (v. 2).

The second half of this song (vv. 4 – 6) finds the people of God further from fortune. What the psalmist remembered the Lord doing, he prayed for, appealing to God's grace in the past for grace in the present. For the arid Negeb, he prayed for flourishing streams. For those sowing with tears, he prayed for restoration. It seems that the Israelites' grief was so unending that it accompanied them in the mundane acts of their day, even the sowing of seeds (v. 6). As they cast seed, they shed their tears.

For God's people, present difficulties need not dissuade them from trusting in future grace. The psalmist wrote, "Those who sow in tears shall reap with shouts of joy!" (v. 5). God's grace remains inevitable, though full restoration might be paused. In the end, suffering will not triumph. Paul considered present sufferings unworthy to be compared to future glory (Ro 8:18). Elsewhere he wrote that "light momentary affliction" achieves for God's people a surpassing future glory (2Co 4:17).

However, God's certain deliverance does not negate the reality of present suffering. Jesus, with more certainty than anyone, knew Lazarus would rise. Yet, he wept (Jn 11:35). Additionally, the inevitability of God's future grace does not negate the obligation of God's people to pray. Jesus prayed to the Father upon Lazarus's death (Jn 11:41). God's goodness in the past (remembered by the people of God) and promises for the future (trusted by the people of God) compel prayer in the present.

THE MISSING RECORD OF OUR SIN

If God kept a record of every human's past sins, then no one would be able to stand before him when their turn came to give an account for their life. But Psalm 130:3 explains that the Lord does not keep a record of all the times each believer sins. He will not have everyone come before him so that he can scold them for every single sin they committed since they were born. Hebrews 10:17 says, "I will remember their sins and their lawless deeds no more."

God is not looking to discover the faults of man, but instead he is gracious. His memory is short when it comes to humanity's wrongdoing. God's grace is evident. He does not keep score in the midst of mankind's propensity toward waywardness.

This forgiveness, grace, and mercy that God is so eager to give his followers comes through the sinless life, death, and resurrection of Jesus. He is the only way in which humans can receive God's forgiveness (Mt 26:28; Eph 1:7; 1Jn 1:9; 2:12). First John 4:10 explains that Jesus is the "propitiation" for all sins, which means he is the sacrifice that can repair every person's relationship with God, bringing about perfect reconciliation between God and sinners. God no longer has to keep track of everyone's sins because he placed all sin on Jesus when he was on the cross (2Co 5:21). With the sacrifice of Jesus, God provided a remedy for the guilt and shame of all humankind, offering them a clean slate. With the resurrection of Jesus, sin and death have been defeated, and God is now solely focused on bringing everyone to himself through the forgiveness, grace, and mercy that can be found through belief in Jesus and what he did on the cross (Jn 3:16).

Psalm 129

They Have Afflicted Me from My Youth

A Song of Ascents.

1 "Greatly[1] have they afflicted me from my youth"—
let Israel now say—
2 "Greatly have they afflicted me from my youth,
yet they have not prevailed against me.
3 The plowers plowed upon my back;
they made long their furrows."
4 The LORD is righteous;
he has cut the cords of the wicked.
5 May all who hate Zion
be put to shame and turned backward!
6 Let them be like the grass on the housetops,
which withers before it grows up,
7 with which the reaper does not fill his hand
nor the binder of sheaves his arms,
8 nor do those who pass by say,
"The blessing of the LORD be upon you!
We bless you in the name of the LORD!"

Psalm 130

My Soul Waits for the Lord

A Song of Ascents.

1 Out of the depths I cry to you, O LORD!
2 O Lord, hear my voice!
Let your ears be attentive
to the voice of my pleas for mercy!
3 If you, O LORD, should mark iniquities,
O Lord, who could stand?
4 But with you there is forgiveness,
that you may be feared.

5 I wait for the LORD, my soul waits,
and in his word I hope;
6 my soul waits for the Lord
more than watchmen for the morning,
more than watchmen for the morning.

7 O Israel, hope in the LORD!
For with the LORD there is steadfast love,
and with him is plentiful redemption.
8 And he will redeem Israel
from all his iniquities.

Psalm 131

I Have Calmed and Quieted My Soul

A Song of Ascents. Of David.

1 O LORD, my heart is not lifted up;
my eyes are not raised too high;

[1]Or *Often*; also verse 2

(Surrounded, continued)

the people would see the mountains which surrounded them every day. The psalmist takes that reality and points them to the Lord's protection. As the mountains surround Jerusalem, so the Lord surrounds his people. The Lord, in much more significant but unseen ways, protects his people from attack.

Peter described the Lord's protection via salvation by stating that God's people "by God's power are being guarded through faith" (1Pe 1:5). The word "guard" indicates protection — probably from sin, suffering, or Satan. Peter makes the point, however, that God also protects the inheritance awaiting the people of God. God purchased it by the death of his Son; he guards it by his power, as surely as the mountains surround Jerusalem.

PSALM 127:1–5

DEPENDING ON GOD

Many accomplished people have come face to face with their weaknesses and sin while raising children. Though a parent might be able to control countless dynamics at work, at the gym, in school, or elsewhere, a screaming newborn is a different matter. This psalm, which includes some of the most cherished verses on children in Scripture, points the reader to dependence upon the Lord.

Using a series of metaphors, the psalmist (identified as Solomon in the superscription) asserted that the builders of a house profit nothing if they do not recognize who the builder is; the guards might as well drop their swords if they think they ultimately protect. In the same way, believers toil in vain if they fail to depend upon their God (vv. 1–2).

(continued on page 907)

I do not occupy myself with things
too great and too marvelous for me.
2 But I have calmed and quieted my soul,
like a weaned child with its mother;
like a weaned child is my soul within me.

3 O Israel, hope in the LORD
from this time forth and forevermore.

Psalm 132

The LORD Has Chosen Zion

A Song of Ascents.

1 Remember, O LORD, in David's favor,
all the hardships he endured,
2 how he swore to the LORD
and vowed to the Mighty One of Jacob,
3 "I will not enter my house
or get into my bed,
4 I will not give sleep to my eyes
or slumber to my eyelids,
5 until I find a place for the LORD,
a dwelling place for the Mighty One of Jacob."
6 Behold, we heard of it in Ephrathah;
we found it in the fields of Jaar.
7 "Let us go to his dwelling place;
let us worship at his footstool!"

8 Arise, O LORD, and go to your resting place,
you and the ark of your might.
9 Let your priests be clothed with righteousness,
and let your saints shout for joy.
10 For the sake of your servant David,
do not turn away the face of your anointed one.

11 The LORD swore to David a sure oath
from which he will not turn back:
"One of the sons of your body[1]
I will set on your throne.
12 If your sons keep my covenant
and my testimonies that I shall teach them,
their sons also forever
shall sit on your throne."

13 For the LORD has chosen Zion;
he has desired it for his dwelling place:
14 "This is my resting place forever;
here I will dwell, for I have desired it.
15 I will abundantly bless her provisions;
I will satisfy her poor with bread.
16 Her priests I will clothe with salvation,
and her saints will shout for joy.
17 There I will make a horn to sprout for David;
I have prepared a lamp for my anointed.
18 His enemies I will clothe with shame,
but on him his crown will shine."

[1]Hebrew *of your fruit of the womb*

(Depending on God, continued)

Jesus said something similar to the disciples. Without equivocation, he stated: "Apart from me you can do nothing" (Jn 15:5). As branches separated from the vine cannot bear fruit, so humans separated from Christ invariably discover that even their best efforts yield zero results. But if the Lord builds something, nothing can tear it down. Furthermore, if the Lord protects something, nothing can harm it.

PSALM 128:1–6

THE BLESSED LIFE

Psalm 128 focuses on the man who receives blessings. Humanity generally thinks of "blessing" in terms of material abundance or a certain degree of health. If one is healthy or enjoys some measure of familial/financial prosperity, he or she is blessed.

In the introduction of his Sermon on the Mount, Jesus used blessing language to describe citizens of his kingdom. Each beatitude begins with this phrase: "Blessed are ..." (Mt 5:3–11). In a counterintuitive reversal, Jesus taught that those who are poor in spirit, meek, and persecuted all fit this description. Jesus used the term "blessed" not to describe material abundance, mere happiness, or some other trite application. Instead, he used it to describe someone approved or favored by God. The circumstances might not smile upon them, but the God of the circumstances did. How can God smile upon, and approve of, a people so broken? Jesus took upon himself a curse—the antithesis of blessing—so that broken people might enjoy the blessing of reconciliation with God (Gal 3:13–14).

JESUS GIVES REST FOR OUR SOUL

Psalm 131 is one of the shortest psalms in the Bible. It provides a simple and easy-to-understand message, which is that God provides rest for the soul that follows him. In the first verse, the psalmist showed that he was aware that there are heavenly things that are outside his knowledge and unattainable for his own understanding. Instead of choosing to try to understand everything that God was doing, he decided not to occupy himself with "things too great and too marvelous for me." Instead, the psalmist compared himself to a weaned child that is at ultimate peace with its mother. Young children are not worried about getting a job, making money, providing for a family, or any other stresses that may come with being a parent. A child trusts that its mother is going to care for him or her. The psalmist was saying that his relationship with God was similar. There may have been a lot of events going on in the world that God was involved in, but all the psalmist concerned himself with was his personal relationship with God.

A right relationship with God is intended to be a high priority for the believer. Once someone is able to grasp an understanding of that concept, the natural result is a calm and quiet soul. The psalmist understood that if everything was fine between him and God, he did not need to concern himself with whatever was going on outside of that.

Believers can be confident in knowing that a healthy relationship with Jesus produces peace that "surpasses all understanding" (Php 4:7). Practicing the disciplines of the spiritual life will ultimately bring an unshakable confidence. When one regularly prays and meditates on Scripture, one builds a foundation for one's life that will stand strong when the torrents hit. A believer will be at peace knowing that their life is anchored in an unmovable Savior, Jesus Christ.

FULFILLING A ROYAL PSALM

Covenant-grounded worship centers on the promise of the covenant keeper. The psalmist asks God to remember all that David endured in bringing the ark to Jerusalem. Prior to arriving in Jerusalem, the ark had lain in obscurity in Kiriath-jearim for many years.

As the king, David could afford to live at ease. Yet at a significant cost to himself, David desired God to be honored by his people. David made a vow to find a dwelling place for the Mighty One of Jacob (vv. 1 – 5). In 2 Samuel 6, David fulfilled that promise. After a difficult journey that included the sudden death of Uzzah, the ark arrived in Jerusalem. When the ark arrived, great celebration ensued. This psalm asks the Lord to remember this in David's favor.

The psalmist (perhaps Solomon) asked: "For the sake of your servant David, do not turn away the face of your anointed one" (Ps 132:10). This is covenantal language. David's promise to God fills the first half of this psalm. The second half of the text reveals God's promise to David.

True to character, God gave much more than even the psalmist asked for. When the Lord makes an oath, he always stands by it. God promised that he would place one of David's descendants on his throne (v. 11). And if David's sons kept God's covenant and statutes, their sons would reign forever and ever (v. 12).

However, a man from the lineage of David is not sitting on a literal throne in literal Israel today. So what of this promise from God? Have any of David's sons kept the covenant without fail?

Yes, one Son of David kept the covenant and is worthy to sit on the throne for all eternity. And right now, at this moment, he rules and reigns. God kept his promise in the person of Jesus. Jesus today sits at the right hand of God the Father, interceding on behalf of his children.

PSALM 133:1

UNITY

Psalm 133 exclaims the wonderful experience of God's people living and worshiping together as one. If David was the author, he may have written the psalm to commemorate when all Israel joined together at Hebron to make him king (2Sa 5:1–3). Jesus shared the psalmist's sentiment and gave an exhortation in John 13:34 when he said, "As I have loved you, you also are to love one another." He went on to say that everyone should know who God's people are by the way they love each other, and that believers should be identified by the way they live and treat each other. Paul expanded even further upon the idea of unity among believers in Ephesians 4:3: "Maintain the unity of the Spirit in the bond of peace." Unity among believers is clearly important since the psalmist, Jesus, and Paul all thought it to be something worth writing about. Here in Psalms, the psalmist rejoiced about "how good and pleasant it is," and it is clear that he was currently experiencing unity with God's people. By the time Jesus and Paul taught the importance of unity in the New Testament, it came in the form of a command. If God's people listen to the exhortations of Paul and Jesus and live in love and unity, then they too will be able to experience the joy that the psalmist experienced and wrote about in Psalm 133.

Psalm 133

When Brothers Dwell in Unity

A Song of Ascents. Of David.

1 Behold, how good and pleasant it is
when brothers dwell in unity![1]
2 It is like the precious oil on the head,
running down on the beard,
on the beard of Aaron,
running down on the collar of his robes!
3 It is like the dew of Hermon,
which falls on the mountains of Zion!
For there the LORD has commanded the blessing,
life forevermore.

Psalm 134

Come, Bless the LORD

A Song of Ascents.

1 Come, bless the LORD, all you servants of the LORD,
who stand by night in the house of the LORD!
2 Lift up your hands to the holy place
and bless the LORD!

3 May the LORD bless you from Zion,
he who made heaven and earth!

Psalm 135

Your Name, O LORD, Endures Forever

1 Praise the LORD!
Praise the name of the LORD,
give praise, O servants of the LORD,
2 who stand in the house of the LORD,
in the courts of the house of our God!
3 Praise the LORD, for the LORD is good;
sing to his name, for it is pleasant![2]
4 For the LORD has chosen Jacob for himself,
Israel as his own possession.

5 For I know that the LORD is great,
and that our Lord is above all gods.
6 Whatever the LORD pleases, he does,
in heaven and on earth,
in the seas and all deeps.
7 He it is who makes the clouds rise at the end of the earth,
who makes lightnings for the rain
and brings forth the wind from his storehouses.

8 He it was who struck down the firstborn of Egypt,
both of man and of beast;
9 who in your midst, O Egypt,
sent signs and wonders
against Pharaoh and all his servants;

[1]Or *dwell together* [2]Or *for he is beautiful*

10 who struck down many nations
and killed mighty kings,
11 Sihon, king of the Amorites,
and Og, king of Bashan,
and all the kingdoms of Canaan,
12 and gave their land as a heritage,
a heritage to his people Israel.

13 Your name, O LORD, endures forever,
your renown,[1] O LORD, throughout all ages.
14 For the LORD will vindicate his people
and have compassion on his servants.

15 The idols of the nations are silver and gold,
the work of human hands.
16 They have mouths, but do not speak;
they have eyes, but do not see;
17 they have ears, but do not hear,
nor is there any breath in their mouths.
18 Those who make them become like them;
so do all who trust in them.

19 O house of Israel, bless the LORD!
O house of Aaron, bless the LORD!
20 O house of Levi, bless the LORD!
You who fear the LORD, bless the LORD!
21 Blessed be the LORD from Zion,
he who dwells in Jerusalem!
Praise the LORD!

Psalm 136

His Steadfast Love Endures Forever

1 Give thanks to the LORD, for he is good,
for his steadfast love endures forever.
2 Give thanks to the God of gods,
for his steadfast love endures forever.
3 Give thanks to the Lord of lords,
for his steadfast love endures forever;

4 to him who alone does great wonders,
for his steadfast love endures forever;
5 to him who by understanding made the heavens,
for his steadfast love endures forever;
6 to him who spread out the earth above the waters,
for his steadfast love endures forever;
7 to him who made the great lights,
for his steadfast love endures forever;
8 the sun to rule over the day,
for his steadfast love endures forever;
9 the moon and stars to rule over the night,
for his steadfast love endures forever;

10 to him who struck down the firstborn of Egypt,
for his steadfast love endures forever;
11 and brought Israel out from among them,
for his steadfast love endures forever;

[1]Or *remembrance*

PSALM 135:13

YOUR NAME, YOUR FAME

In Psalm 135, the psalmist urged the people of God to praise the Lord because of all the things he had done for them. The psalm lists several historical events that have brought God glory and show how he is worthy of praise. In verse 13, the author changes from focusing on what God has done in the past to deserve praise, and says that the name and renown of the Lord will endure forever and last "throughout all ages." The glory of God is not limited to past historical experiences, but it is something that will continue to increase as time moves on. In Acts, the words of Psalm 135:13 came true as the name of Jesus grew and spread throughout all the nations. Throughout the beginning of Acts, the church was growing, the disciples were doing everything to spread the name of Jesus, and those who accepted him were "walking and leaping and praising God" (Ac 3:8). God's renown did not stop when he rescued the Israelites from Egypt or when he struck down the enemies of the Israelites, as is written in Psalm 135:8 – 12. Instead, those events were merely the beginning of his glory and his renown. Jesus came and God's glory became apparent to all who saw him and heard of him. Today his name continues to endure.

12 with a strong hand and an outstretched arm,
for his steadfast love endures forever;
13 to him who divided the Red Sea in two,
for his steadfast love endures forever;
14 and made Israel pass through the midst of it,
for his steadfast love endures forever;
15 but overthrew[1] Pharaoh and his host in the Red Sea,
for his steadfast love endures forever;
16 to him who led his people through the wilderness,
for his steadfast love endures forever;

17 to him who struck down great kings,
for his steadfast love endures forever;
18 and killed mighty kings,
for his steadfast love endures forever;
19 Sihon, king of the Amorites,
for his steadfast love endures forever;
20 and Og, king of Bashan,
for his steadfast love endures forever;
21 and gave their land as a heritage,
for his steadfast love endures forever;
22 a heritage to Israel his servant,
for his steadfast love endures forever.

23 It is he who remembered us in our low estate,
for his steadfast love endures forever;
24 and rescued us from our foes,
for his steadfast love endures forever;
25 he who gives food to all flesh,
for his steadfast love endures forever.

26 Give thanks to the God of heaven,
for his steadfast love endures forever.

Psalm 137

How Shall We Sing the Lord's Song?

1 By the waters of Babylon,
there we sat down and wept,
when we remembered Zion.
2 On the willows[2] there
we hung up our lyres.
3 For there our captors
required of us songs,
and our tormentors, mirth, saying,
"Sing us one of the songs of Zion!"

4 How shall we sing the Lord's song
in a foreign land?
5 If I forget you, O Jerusalem,
let my right hand forget its skill!
6 Let my tongue stick to the roof of my mouth,
if I do not remember you,
if I do not set Jerusalem
above my highest joy!

[1]Hebrew *shook off* [2]Or *poplars*

A SONG OF PRAISE IN DIFFICULT TIMES

Psalm 137 was written about the difficulties of praising God in hard circumstances. Though the author had recently returned home from captivity in Babylon, he describes how nothing could remove the pain and sorrow that he and his fellow Israelites experienced while living in exile. Despite their captors asking them to "sing us one of the songs of Zion," the Israelites were unable to do so in a foreign land. All the blessings of the Lord had been taken from them, and they did not see how they could offer praise to God at a time of great sadness.

Jesus promised his disciples that they would one day face persecution and hard times (Mt 5:10 – 11; Lk 21:12; Jn 15:20). In Acts, there are descriptions of the violence that the early church initially faced. Perhaps like the Israelite captives in Babylon, the early Christians did not feel like singing songs of praise.

However, the story of Paul shows how it is possible for the people of God to sing songs in a strange land. In Acts 8:1 – 3, he was one of the people bent on destroying the church. But in Acts 9 he had an encounter with Jesus that completely changed his life. Paul became one of the greatest missionaries ever to live, and he did amazing things to spread the name of Jesus. As a leader of the church, Paul was constantly in and out of prison and facing hard persecution, yet he never ceased to praise God. Acts 16:25 tells the story of Paul and Silas in prison singing hymns to God. The reason they were in prison in the first place was because of their ministry on behalf of Jesus, but rather than sulking silently in their cell, they sang praises to God.

While the Israelites in exile had a difficult time singing songs of praise, God shows that he desires his people to praise him constantly, regardless of their circumstances. In Philippians 4, Paul charged the believers to "rejoice in the Lord always" (v. 4), and he made it clear that he had learned to be content whatever the circumstances (v. 11). Paul did not base his ability to praise God on his current situation, but rather he showed that circumstances do not change the fact that it is important to praise God always.

7 Remember, O LORD, against the Edomites
the day of Jerusalem,
how they said, "Lay it bare, lay it bare,
down to its foundations!"
8 O daughter of Babylon, doomed to be destroyed,
blessed shall he be who repays you
with what you have done to us!
9 Blessed shall he be who takes your little ones
and dashes them against the rock!

Psalm 138

Give Thanks to the LORD

Of David.

1 I give you thanks, O LORD, with my whole heart;
before the gods I sing your praise;
2 I bow down toward your holy temple
and give thanks to your name for your steadfast love and your
faithfulness,
for you have exalted above all things
your name and your word.[1]
3 On the day I called, you answered me;
my strength of soul you increased.[2]

4 All the kings of the earth shall give you thanks, O LORD,
for they have heard the words of your mouth,
5 and they shall sing of the ways of the LORD,
for great is the glory of the LORD.
6 For though the LORD is high, he regards the lowly,
but the haughty he knows from afar.

7 Though I walk in the midst of trouble,
you preserve my life;
you stretch out your hand against the wrath of my enemies,
and your right hand delivers me.
8 The LORD will fulfill his purpose for me;
your steadfast love, O LORD, endures forever.
Do not forsake the work of your hands.

Psalm 139

Search Me, O God, and Know My Heart

To the choirmaster. A Psalm of David.

1 O LORD, you have searched me and known me!
2 You know when I sit down and when I rise up;
you discern my thoughts from afar.
3 You search out my path and my lying down
and are acquainted with all my ways.
4 Even before a word is on my tongue,
behold, O LORD, you know it altogether.
5 You hem me in, behind and before,
and lay your hand upon me.
6 Such knowledge is too wonderful for me;
it is high; I cannot attain it.

[1]Or *you have exalted your word above all your name* [2]Hebrew *you made me bold in my soul with strength*

7 Where shall I go from your Spirit?
Or where shall I flee from your presence?
8 If I ascend to heaven, you are there!
If I make my bed in Sheol, you are there!
9 If I take the wings of the morning
and dwell in the uttermost parts of the sea,
10 even there your hand shall lead me,
and your right hand shall hold me.
11 If I say, "Surely the darkness shall cover me,
and the light about me be night,"
12 even the darkness is not dark to you;
the night is bright as the day,
for darkness is as light with you.

13 For you formed my inward parts;
you knitted me together in my mother's womb.
14 I praise you, for I am fearfully and wonderfully made.[1]
Wonderful are your works;
my soul knows it very well.
15 My frame was not hidden from you,
when I was being made in secret,
intricately woven in the depths of the earth.
16 Your eyes saw my unformed substance;
in your book were written, every one of them,
the days that were formed for me,
when as yet there was none of them.

17 How precious to me are your thoughts, O God!
How vast is the sum of them!
18 If I would count them, they are more than the sand.
I awake, and I am still with you.

19 Oh that you would slay the wicked, O God!
O men of blood, depart from me!
20 They speak against you with malicious intent;
your enemies take your name in vain.[2]
21 Do I not hate those who hate you, O LORD?
And do I not loathe those who rise up against you?
22 I hate them with complete hatred;
I count them my enemies.

23 Search me, O God, and know my heart!
Try me and know my thoughts![3]
24 And see if there be any grievous way in me,
and lead me in the way everlasting![4]

Psalm 140

Deliver Me, O LORD, from Evil Men

To the choirmaster. A Psalm of David.

1 Deliver me, O LORD, from evil men;
preserve me from violent men,
2 who plan evil things in their heart
and stir up wars continually.
3 They make their tongue sharp as a serpent's,
and under their lips is the venom of asps. *Selah*

[1]Or *for I am fearfully set apart* [2]Hebrew lacks *your name* [3]Or *cares* [4]Or *in the ancient way* (compare Jeremiah 6:16)

PSALM 139:13–14

THE UNBORN

Psalm 139 is a beautiful picture of how God is involved in every single aspect of every person's life. The first 12 verses discuss how, no matter where David went, God was always with him. God knew his thoughts (v. 2), God knew his ways (v. 3), and God knew his words (v. 4). Furthermore, God knew David when he was in his mother's womb, long before he had thoughts, ways, or words (vv. 13–14). The same holds true for every person in the world. God is involved in every aspect of a human's life. While some think a person's life, as well as God's involvement in it, starts the day they are born, it is clear that God is involved well before the day of birth: "You formed my inward parts; you knitted me together in my mother's womb" (v. 13). In Luke 1:26–38, the angel Gabriel explained to Mary that she would give birth to the Son of God. She was understandably confused because she was a virgin. However, the angel explained that the Holy Spirit would conceive a child in her. Just as Psalm 139 describes, that child would be formed and knit by the hand of God. While Jesus is the only human ever to have been conceived by the Holy Spirit, all children are formed by the Creator.

PSALM 140:12

JUSTICE FOR THE POOR

Jesus is the justice for the poor that the psalmist, possibly David, wrote about here. Throughout Jesus' teachings there is constant mention of the poor and Jesus' intention of saving them. Luke 4:18 says, "He has anointed me to proclaim good news to the poor." Jesus told the rich young man that if he wanted to inherit eternal life, he had to "go, sell all that you have and give to the poor" (Mk 10:21). And in the parable of the Good Samaritan, Jesus showed how, in order to be obedient to God and a good neighbor, one must help those in need (Lk 10:25–37). Indeed, what the psalmist wrote in Psalm 140 was confirmed through Jesus and is continuing to come true today. Jesus used his ministry to show how important the poor are to God, and he encouraged believers to treat the poor as he treated them—with love and care.

PSALM 141:1–2

PRAYER AS INCENSE

In Psalm 141, the psalmist asked God to hear his voice and to accept his prayer "as incense," which is to say, a sweet-smelling fragrance. Today, believers can pray with confidence, knowing that God hears their prayers. Hebrews 7:25 says that Jesus "always lives to make intercession for them." Jesus serves as the intermediary between believers and God, and he takes the requests *of believers and presents them be-*fore God. First John 2:1 adds, "We have an advocate with the Father, Jesus Christ the righteous." While the psalmist begged God to hear

(continued on next page)

4 Guard me, O LORD, from the hands of the wicked;
preserve me from violent men,
who have planned to trip up my feet.
5 The arrogant have hidden a trap for me,
and with cords they have spread a net;[1]
beside the way they have set snares for me. *Selah*

6 I say to the LORD, You are my God;
give ear to the voice of my pleas for mercy, O LORD!
7 O LORD, my Lord, the strength of my salvation,
you have covered my head in the day of battle.
8 Grant not, O LORD, the desires of the wicked;
do not further their[2] evil plot, or they will be exalted! *Selah*

9 As for the head of those who surround me,
let the mischief of their lips overwhelm them!
10 Let burning coals fall upon them!
Let them be cast into fire,
into miry pits, no more to rise!
11 Let not the slanderer be established in the land;
let evil hunt down the violent man speedily!

12 I know that the LORD will maintain the cause of the afflicted,
and will execute justice for the needy.
13 Surely the righteous shall give thanks to your name;
the upright shall dwell in your presence.

Psalm 141

Give Ear to My Voice

A Psalm of David.

1 O LORD, I call upon you; hasten to me!
Give ear to my voice when I call to you!
2 Let my prayer be counted as incense before you,
and the lifting up of my hands as the evening sacrifice!

3 Set a guard, O LORD, over my mouth;
keep watch over the door of my lips!
4 Do not let my heart incline to any evil,
to busy myself with wicked deeds
in company with men who work iniquity,
and let me not eat of their delicacies!

5 Let a righteous man strike me—it is a kindness;
let him rebuke me—it is oil for my head;
let my head not refuse it.
Yet my prayer is continually against their evil deeds.
6 When their judges are thrown over the cliff,[3]
then they shall hear my words, for they are pleasant.
7 As when one plows and breaks up the earth,
so shall our bones be scattered at the mouth of Sheol.[4]

8 But my eyes are toward you, O GOD, my Lord;
in you I seek refuge; leave me not defenseless![5]
9 Keep me from the trap that they have laid for me
and from the snares of evildoers!

[1]Or *they have spread cords as a net* [2]Hebrew *his* [3]Or *When their judges fall into the hands of the Rock*
[4]The meaning of the Hebrew in verses 6, 7 is uncertain [5]Hebrew *refuge; do not pour out my life!*

10 Let the wicked fall into their own nets,
while I pass by safely.

Psalm 142

You Are My Refuge

A Maskil[1] of David, when he was in the cave. A Prayer.

1 With my voice I cry out to the LORD;
with my voice I plead for mercy to the LORD.
2 I pour out my complaint before him;
I tell my trouble before him.

3 When my spirit faints within me,
you know my way!
In the path where I walk
they have hidden a trap for me.
4 Look to the right and see:
there is none who takes notice of me;
no refuge remains to me;
no one cares for my soul.

5 I cry to you, O LORD;
I say, "You are my refuge,
my portion in the land of the living."
6 Attend to my cry,
for I am brought very low!
Deliver me from my persecutors,
for they are too strong for me!
7 Bring me out of prison,
that I may give thanks to your name!
The righteous will surround me,
for you will deal bountifully with me.

Psalm 143

My Soul Thirsts for You

A Psalm of David.

1 Hear my prayer, O LORD;
give ear to my pleas for mercy!
In your faithfulness answer me, in your righteousness!
2 Enter not into judgment with your servant,
for no one living is righteous before you.

3 For the enemy has pursued my soul;
he has crushed my life to the ground;
he has made me sit in darkness like those long dead.
4 Therefore my spirit faints within me;
my heart within me is appalled.

5 I remember the days of old;
I meditate on all that you have done;
I ponder the work of your hands.
6 I stretch out my hands to you;
my soul thirsts for you like a parched land. *Selah*

[1]Probably a musical or liturgical term

(Prayer as Incense, continued)

and accept his prayers, believers today can pray confidently knowing that Jesus will take their prayers to God on their behalf. There is no uncertainty about whether or not God hears the prayers of those who follow him. Jesus made it possible for believers to present their requests to God "in everything by prayer and supplication" (Php 4:6). The prayers of believers are like incense to God who hears them.

OUR REFUGE

According to the superscription attached to Psalm 142, David wrote this psalm when he was hiding in a cave — no doubt because Saul was trying to kill him. In his dire circumstances, he sought refuge in the Lord. David had been anointed to be Israel's next king, and that was why Saul was jealous of him. Yet even though David knew Saul was wrong for trying to kill him, he stayed faithful and refused to act violently toward the king appointed by God. However, it is clear in Psalm 142 that it was not easy for David to sit quietly in a cave and wait for redemption. He cried out to God and offered his complaints, but amidst all of his words, he never gave up faith and he continually recognized that the Lord was his "refuge" and his "portion" (v. 5).

Jesus prayed a similar prayer in John 17:1 – 5. In the hours before his arrest and crucifixion, Jesus cried out to God and prayed for God to be glorified in what he was about to do. Jesus showed incredible resolve and selflessness as he spent only five verses praying for himself, but fourteen verses praying for his disciples and another seven for all future believers. Jesus was about to begin the hardest trial of his life, and his reaction was to seek refuge in his Father and to pray for others.

In praying for future believers, Jesus provided encouragement for believers today to seek refuge in God as he himself did. David and Jesus both knew how important it was to seek refuge and safety in the Father through prayer, and believers are able to do the same amidst their own hardships. Even in the hardest situation of his life, Jesus remembered his followers. While it would have been easy for him to pray solely for himself, he took the time to pray for those around him and for those he knew would one day need his prayers. The examples of David and Jesus are worth emulating, and they each show exactly what prayer should look like in times of crisis and need.

7 Answer me quickly, O LORD!
My spirit fails!
Hide not your face from me,
lest I be like those who go down to the pit.
8 Let me hear in the morning of your steadfast love,
for in you I trust.
Make me know the way I should go,
for to you I lift up my soul.

9 Deliver me from my enemies, O LORD!
I have fled to you for refuge.[1]
10 Teach me to do your will,
for you are my God!
Let your good Spirit lead me
on level ground!

11 For your name's sake, O LORD, preserve my life!
In your righteousness bring my soul out of trouble!
12 And in your steadfast love you will cut off my enemies,
and you will destroy all the adversaries of my soul,
for I am your servant.

Psalm 144

My Rock and My Fortress

Of David.

1 Blessed be the LORD, my rock,
who trains my hands for war,
and my fingers for battle;
2 he is my steadfast love and my fortress,
my stronghold and my deliverer,
my shield and he in whom I take refuge,
who subdues peoples[2] under me.

3 O LORD, what is man that you regard him,
or the son of man that you think of him?
4 Man is like a breath;
his days are like a passing shadow.

5 Bow your heavens, O LORD, and come down!
Touch the mountains so that they smoke!
6 Flash forth the lightning and scatter them;
send out your arrows and rout them!
7 Stretch out your hand from on high;
rescue me and deliver me from the many waters,
from the hand of foreigners,
8 whose mouths speak lies
and whose right hand is a right hand of falsehood.

9 I will sing a new song to you, O God;
upon a ten-stringed harp I will play to you,
10 who gives victory to kings,
who rescues David his servant from the cruel sword.
11 Rescue me and deliver me
from the hand of foreigners,
whose mouths speak lies
and whose right hand is a right hand of falsehood.

---

[1]One Hebrew manuscript, Septuagint; most Hebrew manuscripts *To you I have covered* [2]Many Hebrew manuscripts, Dead Sea Scroll, Jerome, Syriac, Aquila; most Hebrew manuscripts *subdues my people*

GOD'S AMAZING LOVE FOR US

Psalm 144:3 shows David's deep appreciation and amazement at God's ability to care for humanity. Despite everything that God has control over, David wondered at the fact that God takes time to think of humans. This verse is one of those moments for David when he thought over the vastness of creation and realized how small he was in comparison to all that God has made. And it is at that moment that he was struck by how deeply profound God's love for him was. God has created everything on the earth and in the rest of the universe, yet he is able to care deeply for the beating heart of an individual person. David compared human life to a breath and a passing shadow (v. 4), both things that are present one moment and gone the next. In the vastness of eternity, the life of one person is incredibly small, yet God cares for each and every life.

John 3:16 explains how much God loved the world and how he was willing to sacrifice his only Son for the sake of mortal humans. David wrote of his amazement at God's ability to give thought to human beings, yet God does infinitely more than simply give thought. He gives life. To a God who lives forever, a human life is fleeting. However, God not only pays attention to each and every human life, he also gave an ultimate sacrifice in his Son Jesus, so that every human life can have value and purpose. God created a way for fleeting human lives one day to join him in the vastness of eternity through Jesus. He promises humans that "whoever believes in him should not perish but have eternal life" (Jn 3:16).

David was right to be amazed at God's ability to regard humans, yet believers today know that God does so much more than simply regard them. A response of shock and amazement is entirely appropriate when one realizes how extraordinary the sacrifice of Jesus was for the life of each individual human. God did not stop at merely giving thought to humanity. He saved humanity.

12 May our sons in their youth
be like plants full grown,
our daughters like corner pillars
cut for the structure of a palace;
13 may our granaries be full,
providing all kinds of produce;
may our sheep bring forth thousands
and ten thousands in our fields;
14 may our cattle be heavy with young,
suffering no mishap or failure in bearing;[1]
may there be no cry of distress in our streets!
15 Blessed are the people to whom such blessings fall!
Blessed are the people whose God is the LORD!

Psalm 145[2]

Great Is the LORD

A Song of Praise. Of David.

1 I will extol you, my God and King,
and bless your name forever and ever.
2 Every day I will bless you
and praise your name forever and ever.
3 Great is the LORD, and greatly to be praised,
and his greatness is unsearchable.

4 One generation shall commend your works to another,
and shall declare your mighty acts.
5 On the glorious splendor of your majesty,
and on your wondrous works, I will meditate.
6 They shall speak of the might of your awesome deeds,
and I will declare your greatness.
7 They shall pour forth the fame of your abundant goodness
and shall sing aloud of your righteousness.

8 The LORD is gracious and merciful,
slow to anger and abounding in steadfast love.
9 The LORD is good to all,
and his mercy is over all that he has made.
10 All your works shall give thanks to you, O LORD,
and all your saints shall bless you!
11 They shall speak of the glory of your kingdom
and tell of your power,
12 to make known to the children of man your[3] mighty deeds,
and the glorious splendor of your kingdom.
13 Your kingdom is an everlasting kingdom,
and your dominion endures throughout all generations.

[The LORD is faithful in all his words
and kind in all his works.[4]]
14 The LORD upholds all who are falling
and raises up all who are bowed down.
15 The eyes of all look to you,
and you give them their food in due season.

[1]Hebrew *with no breaking in or going out* [2]This psalm is an acrostic poem, each verse beginning with the successive letters of the Hebrew alphabet [3]Hebrew *his*; also next line [4]These two lines are supplied by one Hebrew manuscript, Septuagint, Syriac (compare Dead Sea Scroll)

PSALM 145:1–7

THE GLORY OF GOD

The superscription added to Psalm 145 credits David with authorship of this psalm. Traditionally referred to as "the sweet psalmist of Israel," David was intimately aware of "the glorious splendor of [God's] majesty" (v. 5). He wrote countless verses praising and glorifying God. Psalm 145 shows how God-followers like David come to understand God so well: "Every day I will bless you . . . on your wondrous works, I will meditate" (vv. 2,5). The idea of spending time with God daily is also mentioned in Psalm 1:2, which describes a blessed person as one who meditates on God's law "day and night." David consistently spent quality time with the Lord, and it was because he spent so much time conversing with God that he was able to praise him so readily for his goodness and glory.

In the Gospels there are many instances where Jesus went away to pray and be alone with God (Mt 14:23; Mk 1:35; Lk 6:12; 22:41), so it is clear that Jesus highly valued time spent with his Father. To better understand the glory of God, it is crucial to spend time talking with God and meditating on his Word.

PSALM 146:1–10

REIGN FOREVER

The first nine verses of Psalm 146 offer praise to God for all that he does and is doing. The psalm ends with a declaration that "the LORD will reign forever." First Corinthians 15:24–26 echoes the idea that God will reign forever, and Revelation 11:15 says, "The kingdom of the world has become the kingdom of our Lord and of his Christ, and he shall reign forever and ever." In biblical times, kings struggled to hold their reign over their kingdom for as long as they could, and they placed a high priority on having sons to continue the lineage of their rule after their death. Unlike these kings, God does not have to fight to maintain his rule. In Psalms, 1 Corinthians, and Revelation, it is written that God's reign will never come to an end. And he only needed one Son to confirm his reign here on earth. Jesus reminded people that his Father is the one true Ruler. It is the responsibility of Jesus' followers to continue to follow their King and to bring others along to do the same.

PSALM 147:1–20

SEE WHAT GOD HAS DONE

Throughout the psalms, the psalmists constantly praised God for all of the works that he had done. These works proved God's faithfulness to his people. In Psalm 147, the psalmist listed promises that God had upheld and would continue to uphold, all of which are a testament to his faithfulness. The psalmist praised God for his wondrous deeds to the nation of Israel, likely at a time when they rebuilt

(continued on next page)

16 You open your hand;
you satisfy the desire of every living thing.
17 The LORD is righteous in all his ways
and kind in all his works.
18 The LORD is near to all who call on him,
to all who call on him in truth.
19 He fulfills the desire of those who fear him;
he also hears their cry and saves them.
20 The LORD preserves all who love him,
but all the wicked he will destroy.

21 My mouth will speak the praise of the LORD,
and let all flesh bless his holy name forever and ever.

Psalm 146

Put Not Your Trust in Princes

1 Praise the LORD!
Praise the LORD, O my soul!
2 I will praise the LORD as long as I live;
I will sing praises to my God while I have my being.

3 Put not your trust in princes,
in a son of man, in whom there is no salvation.
4 When his breath departs, he returns to the earth;
on that very day his plans perish.

5 Blessed is he whose help is the God of Jacob,
whose hope is in the LORD his God,
6 who made heaven and earth,
the sea, and all that is in them,
who keeps faith forever;
7 who executes justice for the oppressed,
who gives food to the hungry.

The LORD sets the prisoners free;
8 the LORD opens the eyes of the blind.
The LORD lifts up those who are bowed down;
the LORD loves the righteous.
9 The LORD watches over the sojourners;
he upholds the widow and the fatherless,
but the way of the wicked he brings to ruin.

10 The LORD will reign forever,
your God, O Zion, to all generations.
Praise the LORD!

Psalm 147

He Heals the Brokenhearted

1 Praise the LORD!
For it is good to sing praises to our God;
for it is pleasant,[1] and a song of praise is fitting.
2 The LORD builds up Jerusalem;
he gathers the outcasts of Israel.
3 He heals the brokenhearted
and binds up their wounds.

[1] Or *for he is beautiful*

4 He determines the number of the stars;
he gives to all of them their names.
5 Great is our Lord, and abundant in power;
his understanding is beyond measure.
6 The LORD lifts up the humble;[1]
he casts the wicked to the ground.

7 Sing to the LORD with thanksgiving;
make melody to our God on the lyre!
8 He covers the heavens with clouds;
he prepares rain for the earth;
he makes grass grow on the hills.
9 He gives to the beasts their food,
and to the young ravens that cry.
10 His delight is not in the strength of the horse,
nor his pleasure in the legs of a man,
11 but the LORD takes pleasure in those who fear him,
in those who hope in his steadfast love.

12 Praise the LORD, O Jerusalem!
Praise your God, O Zion!
13 For he strengthens the bars of your gates;
he blesses your children within you.
14 He makes peace in your borders;
he fills you with the finest of the wheat.
15 He sends out his command to the earth;
his word runs swiftly.
16 He gives snow like wool;
he scatters frost like ashes.
17 He hurls down his crystals of ice like crumbs;
who can stand before his cold?
18 He sends out his word, and melts them;
he makes his wind blow and the waters flow.
19 He declares his word to Jacob,
his statutes and rules[2] to Israel.
20 He has not dealt thus with any other nation;
they do not know his rules.[3]
Praise the LORD!

Psalm 148

Praise the Name of the LORD

1 Praise the LORD!
Praise the LORD from the heavens;
praise him in the heights!
2 Praise him, all his angels;
praise him, all his hosts!

3 Praise him, sun and moon,
praise him, all you shining stars!
4 Praise him, you highest heavens,
and you waters above the heavens!

5 Let them praise the name of the LORD!
For he commanded and they were created.
6 And he established them forever and ever;
he gave a decree, and it shall not pass away.[4]

[1]Or *afflicted* [2]Or *and just decrees* [3]Or *his just decrees* [4]Or *it shall not be transgressed*

(See What God Has Done, continued)

the walls around the city of Jerusalem (Ne 2:17–20; 4:1–23). These mighty acts of the Lord demonstrate that he had not forgotten his exilic people and would, once again, give them reason for great praise. Believers will never run out of things to be amazed by as they see all that God has done for them. Like Israel, God always provides for his people. His provision culminated in sending his Son Jesus to provide believers with ultimate salvation, which is in itself everything they could ever need.

PSALM 148:1–14

PRAISE: OUR SPONTANEOUS RESPONSE

Psalm 148 provides an appropriate response to everything that was written in Psalm 147. The word *praise* is used 13 times in 14 verses, which shows just how important it is to praise God for who he is and what he has done. Praising God is mentioned many times in the New Testament, including in the greetings of many of Paul's letters (2Co 1:3; Eph 1:3; Php 1:11). Clearly, it was a priority to Paul to start his letters by offering praise to God. In Hebrews 13:15, believers are encouraged to praise God: "Let us continually offer up a sacrifice of praise." First Peter 1:7 talks about how everything that believers experience is intended to "result in praise and glory and honor" to God. And in 1 Peter 4:11 the apostle Peter wrote that believers should use their spiritual gifts "in order that in everything God may be glorified through Jesus Christ." Today, God has given countless blessings to his people,

(continued on next page)

(Praise: Our Spontaneous Response, continued)

including the blessing of Jesus. The natural response of everyone who knows of these blessings and who knows Jesus should be thanksgiving and praise.

7 Praise the LORD from the earth,
you great sea creatures and all deeps,
8 fire and hail, snow and mist,
stormy wind fulfilling his word!

9 Mountains and all hills,
fruit trees and all cedars!
10 Beasts and all livestock,
creeping things and flying birds!

11 Kings of the earth and all peoples,
princes and all rulers of the earth!
12 Young men and maidens together,
old men and children!

13 Let them praise the name of the LORD,
for his name alone is exalted;
his majesty is above earth and heaven.
14 He has raised up a horn for his people,
praise for all his saints,
for the people of Israel who are near to him.
Praise the LORD!

Psalm 149

Sing to the LORD a New Song

1 Praise the LORD!
Sing to the LORD a new song,
his praise in the assembly of the godly!
2 Let Israel be glad in his Maker;
let the children of Zion rejoice in their King!
3 Let them praise his name with dancing,
making melody to him with tambourine and lyre!
4 For the LORD takes pleasure in his people;
he adorns the humble with salvation.
5 Let the godly exult in glory;
let them sing for joy on their beds.
6 Let the high praises of God be in their throats
and two-edged swords in their hands,
7 to execute vengeance on the nations
and punishments on the peoples,
8 to bind their kings with chains
and their nobles with fetters of iron,
9 to execute on them the judgment written!
This is honor for all his godly ones.
Praise the LORD!

Psalm 150

Let Everything Praise the LORD

1 Praise the LORD!
Praise God in his sanctuary;
praise him in his mighty heavens![1]
2 Praise him for his mighty deeds;
praise him according to his excellent greatness!

[1]Hebrew *expanse* (compare Genesis 1:6–8)

GIVING OUR BEST PRAISE

Psalm 149 gives a great summary of every psalm that comes before it, and it also provides a charge to believers going forward. Throughout the book of Psalms, there are a multitude of different praises given to God, and Psalm 149 reminds the people who are singing the praises to continue to do so because of the great pleasure it brings God (v. 4). There is no greater purpose for a human than to praise the Creator, and that is exactly what the book of Psalms is intended for. The psalms provide reasons for praising God, as well as examples of how to praise God. In Psalm 149, the psalmist pauses to make sure everyone is aware of why they sing praises to God. The people of God sing because "the LORD takes pleasure in his people" (v. 4). It is important to remember that believers are not only supposed to sing praises because God deserves them, but also because God enjoys them.

Also, Psalm 149 serves as a challenge to God's people to give God their best effort when praising him. Believers are not called to recite praises mundanely to God with little to no care about the actual words they are saying, but rather they are to enter into praise with great joy and with heartfelt emotion. The psalmist encourages people to sing "a new song," to "praise [God's] name with dancing," and to "sing for joy on their beds" (vv. 1,3,5). There is a reason that Psalms has the most chapters of any book in the Bible; there are so many ways to sing to God and to bring him praise!

When believers realize all that God has done for them through his Son Jesus, it is natural to respond with joy and praise. It is also important for that praise to be the best possible praise that each person can muster. It is the heart behind the praise that matters more than the words themselves, and that is what the psalmist was trying to say here. Continue to worship God in the ways that he has always been worshiped, but also sing new songs and dance new dances. God is deserving of nothing less than the best praise.

3 Praise him with trumpet sound;
praise him with lute and harp!
4 Praise him with tambourine and dance;
praise him with strings and pipe!
5 Praise him with sounding cymbals;
praise him with loud clashing cymbals!
6 Let everything that has breath praise the LORD!
Praise the LORD!

PSALM 150:6

LET EVERYTHING THAT HAS BREATH PRAISE HIM

Psalm 150 provides a summation of the entire book of Psalms in its final verse: "Let everything that has breath praise the LORD!" Everyone who reads Psalms is exhorted to praise God in all that they do, and Paul encourages believers to do the same (1Th 5:18). While there have been many blessings from God to his people, Jesus and the salvation and grace that come with knowing him are the ultimate blessings from God. Jesus is enough reason to give God praise, and someday all those who are in Christ will give God praise because of Christ and his work. One day "every knee shall bow to me, and every tongue shall confess to God" (Ro 14:11)—those who have failed to trust in Christ will acknowledge this in shame and remorse, while Christians will do so in overwhelming praise. Jesus echoed the fact that everything will eventually give praise to God in Luke 19:40 when he said, "I tell you, if these [people] were silent, the very stones would cry out." It is the responsibility of believers to begin and encourage the praise of God. They are at the forefront of a movement toward a day when every believer and everything will fully embrace the God who created them and give him the praise that only he is worthy of.

JESUS: OUR DIVINE WISDOM

PROVERBS

PROVERBS

BIRTH OF SOLOMON, TO WHOM MOST PROVERBS ARE ASCRIBED	DEATH OF SOLOMON	REIGN OF HEZEKIAH, DURING WHICH SOME OR ALL OF PROVERBS WAS COMPILED
c. 991 BC	*c. 930 BC*	*c. 715 – 686 BC*

The writers of the book of Proverbs distill God's divine wisdom to provide insight for obedient worship in a world wrecked by sin. As a collection of practical wisdom sayings inspired by God, this book provides specific insight into the wisdom that God graciously offers throughout history. Solomon, Lemuel, Agur, and others communicated their wealth of God-given insight to the nation of Israel and to all subsequent readers of Proverbs.

The range of topics throughout the book demonstrates the complexity of human existence. From money to marriage, power to possessions, Proverbs presents practical wisdom for those seeking to follow God faithfully. These subjects are addressed throughout Proverbs in repeated and memorable sayings that were meant to be shared by God's people.

The main contrast in the book is between wisdom and foolishness (1:1 – 7). Foolishness is presented as humanity's natural propensity and, without God's intervention, a dangerous and destructive path for life, ultimately culminating in death and destruction in this life and the next (3:35).

Wisdom, on the other hand, is a gift from God and is the path to the life he intends (2:6). Because all people are born dead in sin and enslaved to foolishness, only God can deliver people from their impending doom. God graciously gives wisdom to those who, through faith, fear him and seek after him with all of their hearts. Wisdom fosters a love for God, fulfillment in life, and intimacy with God — in this life and the next (2:1 – 6).

Sin renders all humankind incapable of following the path of wisdom described in the book of Proverbs. Jesus, however, could and did follow that perfect path. He is the embodiment of the divine wisdom spoken of throughout the book. In his life and sacrificial death, he perfectly obeyed God's commands at great cost to himself. By looking at the life of Jesus, all people can see the One who perfectly followed the path wisdom affords. Jesus, who is the wisdom of God, lived the life humankind was meant to live but could not due to sin. By faith, believers can receive the gift of Jesus' righteous life and perfect standing before God. God gives his children the gift of his Spirit, which empowers them to follow his perfect path of wisdom.

THE FEAR OF THE LORD IS THE BEGINNING OF WISDOM, AND THE KNOWLEDGE OF THE HOLY ONE IS INSIGHT.

Proverbs 9:10

PROVERBS

PROVERBS 1:8–19

AMONG THE CRIMINALS

In this passage Solomon warned his son against the temptation to use illicit means of gaining wealth. Through the voice of a gang that kills and robs people, Solomon presented the enticing prospect of filling one's house with plunder taken from the unsuspecting and innocent. His warning focused on the destructive effects such a lifestyle has—not only on the victims but on the perpetrators of the crimes. Solomon knew where the path of violence and theft leads—to death. The wisdom principle is clear both here and throughout Proverbs: Those who gain money the wrong way bring about their own destruction (Pr 10:2; 15:27).

But what about apparent exceptions to this principle? After all, many people enrich themselves in the wrong ways and seem to get away with it. Consider how this story points to the life of Jesus, the One who will someday rectify all injustice. Judas joined forces with a gang to set a trap for an innocent man. The gang set the trap, the innocent man was executed among criminals, and Judas became richer by thirty pieces of silver. At first blush, this story seems to disprove the proverb. The innocent man died the death that criminals deserved to die, and the guilty man lined his pockets. *But on Sunday morning, Judas was in the grave and Jesus walked out of his,* proving that "treasures gained by wickedness do not profit, but righteousness delivers from death" (Pr 10:2).

The Beginning of Knowledge

1 The proverbs of Solomon, son of David, king of Israel:

2 To know wisdom and instruction,
to understand words of insight,
3 to receive instruction in wise dealing,
in righteousness, justice, and equity;
4 to give prudence to the simple,
knowledge and discretion to the youth—
5 Let the wise hear and increase in learning,
and the one who understands obtain guidance,
6 to understand a proverb and a saying,
the words of the wise and their riddles.

7 The fear of the LORD is the beginning of knowledge;
fools despise wisdom and instruction.

The Enticement of Sinners

8 Hear, my son, your father's instruction,
and forsake not your mother's teaching,
9 for they are a graceful garland for your head
and pendants for your neck.
10 My son, if sinners entice you,
do not consent.
11 If they say, "Come with us, let us lie in wait for blood;
let us ambush the innocent without reason;
12 like Sheol let us swallow them alive,
and whole, like those who go down to the pit;
13 we shall find all precious goods,
we shall fill our houses with plunder;
14 throw in your lot among us;
we will all have one purse"—
15 my son, do not walk in the way with them;
hold back your foot from their paths,
16 for their feet run to evil,
and they make haste to shed blood.
17 For in vain is a net spread
in the sight of any bird,
18 but these men lie in wait for their own blood;
they set an ambush for their own lives.
19 Such are the ways of everyone who is greedy for unjust
gain;
it takes away the life of its possessors.

The Call of Wisdom

20 Wisdom cries aloud in the street,
in the markets she raises her voice;
21 at the head of the noisy streets she cries out;
at the entrance of the city gates she speaks:
22 "How long, O simple ones, will you love being simple?
How long will scoffers delight in their scoffing
and fools hate knowledge?

THE WISE KING

King Solomon was the wisest man in ancient Israel, and he sought to impart that wisdom to the nation by speaking and writing proverbs (1Ki 4:32). Proverbs opens with an introduction that describes the purpose of the book. The wise king, desiring to produce wisdom in the people of Israel, asserted that wisdom begins with the fear of the Lord (Pr 1:7). Thus, wisdom is more than intellect — it is a spiritual attitude.

The problem for the Israelites was that not only were they not wise, but their kings were fools, too. Solomon repeatedly warned his sons not to fall for immoral women, but Solomon fell for foreign women (1Ki 11:1 – 13). Solomon attempted to train his son in wisdom, but his son foolishly split the nation in two by listening to his peers rather than the wise counsel of the elders (1Ki 12:1 – 20). Israel's kings' failures led to the development of a hope for a future king who would be truly wise.

Eventually, Isaiah described the Messiah as one who would embody the kind of wisdom described in the introduction of Proverbs. Drawing upon the language of Proverbs 1:1 – 7, Isaiah wrote, "There shall come forth a shoot from the stump of Jesse, and a branch from his roots shall bear fruit. And the Spirit of the LORD shall rest upon him, the Spirit of wisdom and understanding, the Spirit of counsel and might, the Spirit of knowledge and the fear of the LORD. And his delight shall be in the fear of the LORD" (Isa 11:1 – 3).

The fulfillment of this promise can be found in Jesus Christ. He was given the throne of David (Lk 1:32). He was anointed with the Holy Spirit at his baptism (Mt 3:16). And, Jesus himself said, "The queen of the South will rise up at the judgment with this generation and condemn it, for she came from the ends of the earth to hear the wisdom of Solomon, and behold, something greater than Solomon is here" (Mt 12:42). Jesus is the Spirit-anointed King who is wiser than Solomon. Not only does he teach wisdom, but he also actually lives it out and enables his followers to do so as well.

23 If you turn at my reproof,[1]
behold, I will pour out my spirit to you;
I will make my words known to you.
24 Because I have called and you refused to listen,
have stretched out my hand and no one has heeded,
25 because you have ignored all my counsel
and would have none of my reproof,
26 I also will laugh at your calamity;
I will mock when terror strikes you,
27 when terror strikes you like a storm
and your calamity comes like a whirlwind,
when distress and anguish come upon you.
28 Then they will call upon me, but I will not answer;
they will seek me diligently but will not find me.
29 Because they hated knowledge
and did not choose the fear of the LORD,
30 would have none of my counsel
and despised all my reproof,
31 therefore they shall eat the fruit of their way,
and have their fill of their own devices.
32 For the simple are killed by their turning away,
and the complacency of fools destroys them;
33 but whoever listens to me will dwell secure
and will be at ease, without dread of disaster."

The Value of Wisdom

2 My son, if you receive my words
and treasure up my commandments with you,
2 making your ear attentive to wisdom
and inclining your heart to understanding;
3 yes, if you call out for insight
and raise your voice for understanding,
4 if you seek it like silver
and search for it as for hidden treasures,
5 then you will understand the fear of the LORD
and find the knowledge of God.
6 For the LORD gives wisdom;
from his mouth come knowledge and understanding;
7 he stores up sound wisdom for the upright;
he is a shield to those who walk in integrity,
8 guarding the paths of justice
and watching over the way of his saints.
9 Then you will understand righteousness and justice
and equity, every good path;
10 for wisdom will come into your heart,
and knowledge will be pleasant to your soul;
11 discretion will watch over you,
understanding will guard you,
12 delivering you from the way of evil,
from men of perverted speech,
13 who forsake the paths of uprightness
to walk in the ways of darkness,
14 who rejoice in doing evil
and delight in the perverseness of evil,

[1]Or *Will you turn away at my reproof?*

15 men whose paths are crooked,
and who are devious in their ways.

16 So you will be delivered from the forbidden[1] woman,
from the adulteress[2] with her smooth words,
17 who forsakes the companion of her youth
and forgets the covenant of her God;
18 for her house sinks down to death,
and her paths to the departed;[3]
19 none who go to her come back,
nor do they regain the paths of life.

20 So you will walk in the way of the good
and keep to the paths of the righteous.
21 For the upright will inhabit the land,
and those with integrity will remain in it,
22 but the wicked will be cut off from the land,
and the treacherous will be rooted out of it.

Trust in the LORD with All Your Heart

3 My son, do not forget my teaching,
but let your heart keep my commandments,
2 for length of days and years of life
and peace they will add to you.

3 Let not steadfast love and faithfulness forsake you;
bind them around your neck;
write them on the tablet of your heart.
4 So you will find favor and good success[4]
in the sight of God and man.

5 Trust in the LORD with all your heart,
and do not lean on your own understanding.
6 In all your ways acknowledge him,
and he will make straight your paths.
7 Be not wise in your own eyes;
fear the LORD, and turn away from evil.
8 It will be healing to your flesh[5]
and refreshment[6] to your bones.

9 Honor the LORD with your wealth
and with the firstfruits of all your produce;
10 then your barns will be filled with plenty,
and your vats will be bursting with wine.

11 My son, do not despise the LORD's discipline
or be weary of his reproof,
12 for the LORD reproves him whom he loves,
as a father the son in whom he delights.

Blessed Is the One Who Finds Wisdom

13 Blessed is the one who finds wisdom,
and the one who gets understanding,
14 for the gain from her is better than gain from silver
and her profit better than gold.
15 She is more precious than jewels,
and nothing you desire can compare with her.

[1]Hebrew *strange* [2]Hebrew *foreign woman* [3]Hebrew *to the Rephaim* [4]Or *repute* [5]Hebrew *navel* [6]Or *medicine*

PROVERBS 2:20–22

INHERITING THE EARTH

Solomon urged his son to listen to his wisdom: avoid sexual sin with the adulterous woman. And he clearly outlined the judgment for those who fall for the temptation and the reward for those who avoid it—the upright will dwell in the land, and the wicked will be exiled. To ancient Israel, these promises and warnings were part of the fabric of the nation. If they were unfaithful to God, then they would be exiled from the land, but if they remained faithful to God, then they would remain in the land. To those of us on the other side of the New Testament, these words take on a different meaning. The New Testament expanded the land promise to include the entire earth. As Jesus said, "Blessed are the meek, for they shall inherit the earth" (Mt 5:5). There is only one who was perfectly faithful to God and entirely meek—Jesus of Nazareth. He inherits the whole world, and those who believe in him are his co-heirs who inherit a new creation with him (Ro 8:17). But those who reject Christ will be exiled from the Lord's presence forever.

PROVERBS 3:13–18

THE PEARL OF GREAT VALUE

In this poem about the supreme value of wisdom, Solomon personified wisdom as a woman, telling his readers to seek her above everything else. In the fullness of time, the New Testament revealed that this personification pointed to a real person—Jesus of Nazareth—who should be pursued and treasured above all

(continued on page 935)

FAVOR WITH GOD AND MAN

This passage is about being in a faithful covenant relationship with God where each partner has obligations to uphold. The odd verses here seem to be about the obligation of the human partner in the covenant, and the even verses are about the obligations of the divine partner. Verses 1, 3, 5, 7, 9, and 11 describe expectations on readers to keep God the Father's commands, to bind steadfast love around their necks, to trust in the Lord with all their hearts, not to be wise in their own eyes, to give generously, and to welcome the Lord's discipline. Verses 2, 4, 6, 8, 10, and 12 tell readers what the Lord will do in return, such as granting longer life, favor with God and man, guidance, health, provision, and loving discipline. Those who meet the obligations of being faithful to the Lord and walking in wisdom will experience the Lord meeting his obligations to bless and grow them.

The question that must be asked is, "Who has ever kept the covenant and received these rewards?" The answer is clearly Jesus Christ. Luke 2:52 alludes directly to Proverbs 3:4 to show its fulfillment in Jesus: "And Jesus increased in wisdom and in stature and in favor with God and man." Now, the good news is that he represents his people before the Father in this covenant relationship. He lived up to humanity's obligations on their behalf, and then he took the curses of humanity's covenant breaking in their place. He experienced sickness, sorrows, enemies, and a premature death. Because of who Jesus is and all he has done, he is able to offer full pardon to every covenant breaker who believes in him. His righteous record of keeping the covenant is credited to the account of all who are united to him by faith, and as a result, they will experience the blessings of covenant faithfulness by his merits, not their own. For all those who are in Christ, God will do the work by the power of the Spirit to conform them into the image of his covenant-keeping Son — sometimes through discipline (Pr 3:11 – 12; Heb 12:5 – 6).

16 Long life is in her right hand;
in her left hand are riches and honor.
17 Her ways are ways of pleasantness,
and all her paths are peace.
18 She is a tree of life to those who lay hold of her;
those who hold her fast are called blessed.

19 The LORD by wisdom founded the earth;
by understanding he established the heavens;
20 by his knowledge the deeps broke open,
and the clouds drop down the dew.

21 My son, do not lose sight of these—
keep sound wisdom and discretion,
22 and they will be life for your soul
and adornment for your neck.
23 Then you will walk on your way securely,
and your foot will not stumble.
24 If you lie down, you will not be afraid;
when you lie down, your sleep will be sweet.
25 Do not be afraid of sudden terror
or of the ruin[1] of the wicked, when it comes,
26 for the LORD will be your confidence
and will keep your foot from being caught.
27 Do not withhold good from those to whom it is due,[2]
when it is in your power to do it.

28 Do not say to your neighbor, "Go, and come again,
tomorrow I will give it"—when you have it with you.
29 Do not plan evil against your neighbor,
who dwells trustingly beside you.
30 Do not contend with a man for no reason,
when he has done you no harm.
31 Do not envy a man of violence
and do not choose any of his ways,
32 for the devious person is an abomination to the LORD,
but the upright are in his confidence.
33 The LORD's curse is on the house of the wicked,
but he blesses the dwelling of the righteous.
34 Toward the scorners he is scornful,
but to the humble he gives favor.[3]
35 The wise will inherit honor,
but fools get[4] disgrace.

A Father's Wise Instruction

4 Hear, O sons, a father's instruction,
and be attentive, that you may gain[5] insight,
2 for I give you good precepts;
do not forsake my teaching.
3 When I was a son with my father,
tender, the only one in the sight of my mother,
4 he taught me and said to me,
"Let your heart hold fast my words;
keep my commandments, and live.
5 Get wisdom; get insight;
do not forget, and do not turn away from the words of my mouth.

[1]Hebrew *storm* [2]Hebrew *Do not withhold good from its owners* [3]Or *grace* [4]The meaning of the Hebrew word is uncertain [5]Hebrew *know*

(The Pearl of Great Value, continued)

else (1Co 1:24,30). Wisdom's profits are better than silver, gold, or jewels, so people should seek Jesus at any cost. No other object of desire compares with him. Jesus—like the kingdom of God, the pearl of great value, the treasure hidden in a field (Mt 13:44–46)—is worth selling everything in order to acquire. When people seek Jesus—the wisdom of God—above all else, other things will be added (Pr 3:16–18; Mt 6:33). Solomon knew the value of wisdom from God. In 1 Kings 3, God told Solomon he would grant whatever Solomon asked for. Solomon could have asked for riches, long life, victory over his enemies, or the most glorious empire any king has ever ruled, but instead he asked for wisdom above all else. So God gave him supreme wisdom, and God added to it long life, wealth, and great honor. Jesus is worth more than anything anyone could ever desire, and to those who seek him first he adds many additional blessings.

PROVERBS 3:18

TREE OF LIFE

The term "tree of life" is only found in three books of Scripture: Genesis, Proverbs, and Revelation. In the Garden of Eden, eating from the tree of life granted immortality (Ge 3:22). Proverbs says that wisdom is a tree of life, and the New Testament reveals not only that Jesus is the wisdom of God (1Co 1:24) but also that he grants access to the tree of life (Rev 2:7). Proverbs 3:18, along with the rest of Proverbs, calls humanity back to Paradise. Indeed, in the garden, humankind reached for knowledge apart from God and his Word. Humans sought to determine

(continued on next page)

(Tree of Life, continued)

right and wrong for themselves. As a result, humans became unwise and inherited death—cut off from access to the tree of life. Proverbs reveals the path back to life—wisdom. But only in Christ, who is the wisdom of God, does that path become a reality for finite humans. If they will humble themselves and take hold of Jesus in faith, they will receive back what was lost in Eden.

PROVERBS 5:3–6

THE ADULTEROUS WOMAN

Not only did Solomon personify wisdom, but he also personified foolishness (Pr 9:13–18). Foolishness is a predator hunting people down and trying to kill them, often through sexual temptation. Just like Satan is tracking people down and attempting to ensnare them in sexual sin (1Co 7:5), so foolishness wants to trap and kill (Pr 7:22–23; 23:26–28). Solomon illustrates the lure of foolishness with the smooth words of the adulterous woman (Pr 5:3), which mirror and rival the father's words to the son (Pr 5:1–2). There is both a vertical means of rescue from this predator and a horizontal means. Vertically, a person can be rescued by having a personal relationship with wisdom—who is Jesus Christ (Pr 2:1–22; 7:4–5; 1Co 1:24,30). Horizontally, a person can be rescued by having an intimate relationship with a spouse (Pr 5:15–20). Paul employed this same strategy in 1 Corinthians. He warned his readers to flee sexual immorality (1Co 6:12–18), and encouraged them by reminding them of redemption in Christ (1Co 6:19–20) and calling them to preserve intimacy with their spouses (1Co 7:1–5).

6 Do not forsake her, and she will keep you;
love her, and she will guard you.
7 The beginning of wisdom is this: Get wisdom,
and whatever you get, get insight.
8 Prize her highly, and she will exalt you;
she will honor you if you embrace her.
9 She will place on your head a graceful garland;
she will bestow on you a beautiful crown."

10 Hear, my son, and accept my words,
that the years of your life may be many.
11 I have taught you the way of wisdom;
I have led you in the paths of uprightness.
12 When you walk, your step will not be hampered,
and if you run, you will not stumble.
13 Keep hold of instruction; do not let go;
guard her, for she is your life.
14 Do not enter the path of the wicked,
and do not walk in the way of the evil.
15 Avoid it; do not go on it;
turn away from it and pass on.
16 For they cannot sleep unless they have done wrong;
they are robbed of sleep unless they have made someone stumble.
17 For they eat the bread of wickedness
and drink the wine of violence.
18 But the path of the righteous is like the light of dawn,
which shines brighter and brighter until full day.
19 The way of the wicked is like deep darkness;
they do not know over what they stumble.

20 My son, be attentive to my words;
incline your ear to my sayings.
21 Let them not escape from your sight;
keep them within your heart.
22 For they are life to those who find them,
and healing to all their[1] flesh.
23 Keep your heart with all vigilance,
for from it flow the springs of life.
24 Put away from you crooked speech,
and put devious talk far from you.
25 Let your eyes look directly forward,
and your gaze be straight before you.
26 Ponder[2] the path of your feet;
then all your ways will be sure.
27 Do not swerve to the right or to the left;
turn your foot away from evil.

Warning Against Adultery

5 My son, be attentive to my wisdom;
incline your ear to my understanding,
2 that you may keep discretion,
and your lips may guard knowledge.
3 For the lips of a forbidden[3] woman drip honey,
and her speech[4] is smoother than oil,
4 but in the end she is bitter as wormwood,
sharp as a two-edged sword.

[1]Hebrew *his* [2]Or *Make level* [3]Hebrew *strange*; also verse 20 [4]Hebrew *palate*

THE HEART

This verse is one of the keys to understanding Proverbs. The human heart is the source of each person's actions, words, and thoughts. People have a problem though; their hearts are broken and sinful. Proverbs makes this clear when it says, "Who can say, 'I have made my heart pure; I am clean from my sin'?" (Pr 20:9; cf. 22:15). The reason why people behave badly is because of their hearts. Jesus observed this reality when he said that evil words proceed from an evil heart (Mt 12:33 – 37), and that deceit, sexual immorality, murder, theft, and other sins flow from the heart (Mk 7:20 – 23).

Since humans have heart issues, they need new hearts for real and lasting change. Deuteronomy said that people fail to obey the law when their hearts are not turned toward God (cf. Dt 5:29; 30:1 – 20). It promised that one day the Lord would perform an inner transformation of the heart that would enable obedience (Dt 30:6). This promise was repeated in Ezekiel when the Lord said he would someday give his followers a new heart (Eze 36:26) and in Jeremiah when the Lord said of the new covenant, "I will put my law within them, and I will write it on their hearts" (Jer 31:33).

Proverbs refers to the same hope — the hope for a heart that has God's wisdom and ways written on it (Pr 3:3; 7:3). Foolishness is described in the Hebrew of Proverbs as literally "lacking a heart" or "lacking sense" (Pr 6:32; 7:7; 9:4; 10:13; 11:12; 12:11; 17:18; 24:30; cf. Dt 5:29). The adulterer "lacks sense" (Pr 6:32; 7:7). Both wisdom and folly seek the affection of the one who "lacks sense" (9:4,16). The one who "lacks sense" will die (10:21). And the lazy fool is one who is "lacking sense" (24:30). But, the wise person who listens to wisdom "gains intelligence" (15:32; cf. Eze 36:26).

People need to be born again with a new heart through faith in Jesus Christ, who inaugurated the new covenant with his blood. Jesus said, "This is my blood of the covenant, which is poured out for many for the forgiveness of sins" (Mt 26:28). Only through renewal in Christ can people walk in wisdom.

5 Her feet go down to death;
her steps follow the path to[1] Sheol;
6 she does not ponder the path of life;
her ways wander, and she does not know it.

7 And now, O sons, listen to me,
and do not depart from the words of my mouth.
8 Keep your way far from her,
and do not go near the door of her house,
9 lest you give your honor to others
and your years to the merciless,
10 lest strangers take their fill of your strength,
and your labors go to the house of a foreigner,
11 and at the end of your life you groan,
when your flesh and body are consumed,
12 and you say, "How I hated discipline,
and my heart despised reproof!
13 I did not listen to the voice of my teachers
or incline my ear to my instructors.
14 I am at the brink of utter ruin
in the assembled congregation."

15 Drink water from your own cistern,
flowing water from your own well.
16 Should your springs be scattered abroad,
streams of water in the streets?
17 Let them be for yourself alone,
and not for strangers with you.
18 Let your fountain be blessed,
and rejoice in the wife of your youth,
19 a lovely deer, a graceful doe.
Let her breasts fill you at all times with delight;
be intoxicated[2] always in her love.
20 Why should you be intoxicated, my son, with a forbidden
woman
and embrace the bosom of an adulteress?[3]
21 For a man's ways are before the eyes of the LORD,
and he ponders[4] all his paths.
22 The iniquities of the wicked ensnare him,
and he is held fast in the cords of his sin.
23 He dies for lack of discipline,
and because of his great folly he is led astray.

Practical Warnings

6 My son, if you have put up security for your neighbor,
have given your pledge for a stranger,
2 if you are snared in the words of your mouth,
caught in the words of your mouth,
3 then do this, my son, and save yourself,
for you have come into the hand of your neighbor:
go, hasten,[5] and plead urgently with your neighbor.
4 Give your eyes no sleep
and your eyelids no slumber;
5 save yourself like a gazelle from the hand of the hunter,[6]
like a bird from the hand of the fowler.

[1]Hebrew *lay hold of* [2]Hebrew *be led astray*; also verse 20 [3]Hebrew *a foreign woman* [4]Or *makes level*
[5]Or *humble yourself* [6]Hebrew lacks *of the hunter*

6 Go to the ant, O sluggard;
consider her ways, and be wise.
7 Without having any chief,
officer, or ruler,
8 she prepares her bread in summer
and gathers her food in harvest.
9 How long will you lie there, O sluggard?
When will you arise from your sleep?
10 A little sleep, a little slumber,
a little folding of the hands to rest,
11 and poverty will come upon you like a robber,
and want like an armed man.

12 A worthless person, a wicked man,
goes about with crooked speech,
13 winks with his eyes, signals[1] with his feet,
points with his finger,
14 with perverted heart devises evil,
continually sowing discord;
15 therefore calamity will come upon him suddenly;
in a moment he will be broken beyond healing.

16 There are six things that the LORD hates,
seven that are an abomination to him:
17 haughty eyes, a lying tongue,
and hands that shed innocent blood,
18 a heart that devises wicked plans,
feet that make haste to run to evil,
19 a false witness who breathes out lies,
and one who sows discord among brothers.

Warnings Against Adultery

20 My son, keep your father's commandment,
and forsake not your mother's teaching.
21 Bind them on your heart always;
tie them around your neck.
22 When you walk, they[2] will lead you;
when you lie down, they will watch over you;
and when you awake, they will talk with you.
23 For the commandment is a lamp and the teaching
a light,
and the reproofs of discipline are the way of life,
24 to preserve you from the evil woman,[3]
from the smooth tongue of the adulteress.[4]
25 Do not desire her beauty in your heart,
and do not let her capture you with her eyelashes;
26 for the price of a prostitute is only a loaf of bread,[5]
but a married woman[6] hunts down a precious life.
27 Can a man carry fire next to his chest
and his clothes not be burned?
28 Or can one walk on hot coals
and his feet not be scorched?
29 So is he who goes in to his neighbor's wife;
none who touches her will go unpunished.

[1]Hebrew *scrapes* [2]Hebrew *it*; three times in this verse [3]Revocalization (compare Septuagint) yields *from the wife of a neighbor* [4]Hebrew *the foreign woman* [5]Or (compare Septuagint, Syriac, Vulgate) *for a prostitute leaves a man with nothing but a loaf of bread* [6]Hebrew *a man's wife*

30 People do not despise a thief if he steals
to satisfy his appetite when he is hungry,
31 but if he is caught, he will pay sevenfold;
he will give all the goods of his house.
32 He who commits adultery lacks sense;
he who does it destroys himself.
33 He will get wounds and dishonor,
and his disgrace will not be wiped away.
34 For jealousy makes a man furious,
and he will not spare when he takes revenge.
35 He will accept no compensation;
he will refuse though you multiply gifts.

Warning Against the Adulteress

7 My son, keep my words
and treasure up my commandments with you;
2 keep my commandments and live;
keep my teaching as the apple of your eye;
3 bind them on your fingers;
write them on the tablet of your heart.
4 Say to wisdom, "You are my sister,"
and call insight your intimate friend,
5 to keep you from the forbidden[1] woman,
from the adulteress[2] with her smooth words.

6 For at the window of my house
I have looked out through my lattice,
7 and I have seen among the simple,
I have perceived among the youths,
a young man lacking sense,
8 passing along the street near her corner,
taking the road to her house
9 in the twilight, in the evening,
at the time of night and darkness.

10 And behold, the woman meets him,
dressed as a prostitute, wily of heart.[3]
11 She is loud and wayward;
her feet do not stay at home;
12 now in the street, now in the market,
and at every corner she lies in wait.
13 She seizes him and kisses him,
and with bold face she says to him,
14 "I had to offer sacrifices,[4]
and today I have paid my vows;
15 so now I have come out to meet you,
to seek you eagerly, and I have found you.
16 I have spread my couch with coverings,
colored linens from Egyptian linen;
17 I have perfumed my bed with myrrh,
aloes, and cinnamon.
18 Come, let us take our fill of love till morning;
let us delight ourselves with love.
19 For my husband is not at home;
he has gone on a long journey;

[1]Hebrew *strange* [2]Hebrew *the foreign woman* [3]Hebrew *guarded in heart* [4]Hebrew *peace offerings*

20 he took a bag of money with him;
at full moon he will come home."

21 With much seductive speech she persuades him;
with her smooth talk she compels him.
22 All at once he follows her,
as an ox goes to the slaughter,
or as a stag is caught fast[1]
23 till an arrow pierces its liver;
as a bird rushes into a snare;
he does not know that it will cost him his life.

24 And now, O sons, listen to me,
and be attentive to the words of my mouth.
25 Let not your heart turn aside to her ways;
do not stray into her paths,
26 for many a victim has she laid low,
and all her slain are a mighty throng.
27 Her house is the way to Sheol,
going down to the chambers of death.

The Blessings of Wisdom

8 Does not wisdom call?
Does not understanding raise her voice?
2 On the heights beside the way,
at the crossroads she takes her stand;
3 beside the gates in front of the town,
at the entrance of the portals she cries aloud:
4 "To you, O men, I call,
and my cry is to the children of man.
5 O simple ones, learn prudence;
O fools, learn sense.
6 Hear, for I will speak noble things,
and from my lips will come what is right,
7 for my mouth will utter truth;
wickedness is an abomination to my lips.
8 All the words of my mouth are righteous;
there is nothing twisted or crooked in them.
9 They are all straight to him who understands,
and right to those who find knowledge.
10 Take my instruction instead of silver,
and knowledge rather than choice gold,
11 for wisdom is better than jewels,
and all that you may desire cannot compare with her.

12 "I, wisdom, dwell with prudence,
and I find knowledge and discretion.
13 The fear of the LORD is hatred of evil.
Pride and arrogance and the way of evil
and perverted speech I hate.
14 I have counsel and sound wisdom;
I have insight; I have strength.
15 By me kings reign,
and rulers decree what is just;
16 by me princes rule,
and nobles, all who govern justly.[2]

[1]Probable reading (compare Septuagint, Vulgate, Syriac); Hebrew *as a chain to discipline a fool* [2]Most Hebrew manuscripts; many Hebrew manuscripts, Septuagint *govern the earth*

17 I love those who love me,
and those who seek me diligently find me.
18 Riches and honor are with me,
enduring wealth and righteousness.
19 My fruit is better than gold, even fine gold,
and my yield than choice silver.
20 I walk in the way of righteousness,
in the paths of justice,
21 granting an inheritance to those who love me,
and filling their treasuries.

22 "The LORD possessed[1] me at the beginning of his work,[2]
the first of his acts of old.
23 Ages ago I was set up,
at the first, before the beginning of the earth.
24 When there were no depths I was brought forth,
when there were no springs abounding with water.
25 Before the mountains had been shaped,
before the hills, I was brought forth,
26 before he had made the earth with its fields,
or the first of the dust of the world.
27 When he established the heavens, I was there;
when he drew a circle on the face of the deep,
28 when he made firm the skies above,
when he established[3] the fountains of the deep,
29 when he assigned to the sea its limit,
so that the waters might not transgress his command,
when he marked out the foundations of the earth,
30 then I was beside him, like a master workman,
and I was daily his[4] delight,
rejoicing before him always,
31 rejoicing in his inhabited world
and delighting in the children of man.

32 "And now, O sons, listen to me:
blessed are those who keep my ways.
33 Hear instruction and be wise,
and do not neglect it.
34 Blessed is the one who listens to me,
watching daily at my gates,
waiting beside my doors.
35 For whoever finds me finds life
and obtains favor from the LORD,
36 but he who fails to find me injures himself;
all who hate me love death."

The Way of Wisdom

9 Wisdom has built her house;
she has hewn her seven pillars.
2 She has slaughtered her beasts; she has mixed her wine;
she has also set her table.
3 She has sent out her young women to call
from the highest places in the town,
4 "Whoever is simple, let him turn in here!"
To him who lacks sense she says,

[1]Or *fathered*; Septuagint *created* [2]Hebrew *way* [3]The meaning of the Hebrew is uncertain [4]Or *daily filled with*

THE WISDOM OF GOD

Throughout the first nine chapters of Proverbs, Solomon personified wisdom as a woman. Personification gives human characteristics to an abstract idea. For example, the phrase "Lady Justice is blind" personifies justice as someone who does not look at appearances, thus highlighting the ideal of objectivity in the justice system. Solomon presented wisdom as a woman for at least two reasons. First, wisdom is a feminine noun in Hebrew, and so the personification takes on the gender of the word. Second, Solomon appealed to his son to embrace the wisdom of Proverbs, and what would be more appealing to a young man than an alluring woman?

However, there are several indications that Solomon's personification of wisdom was more than merely a literary device. In Proverbs 8:22 – 31, Solomon heightened wisdom's status beyond his own knowledge or understanding. All true wisdom, he taught, is God's wisdom. Wisdom comes from God and accompanies him in all his works. The New Testament further reveals that Jesus is the wisdom of God (1Co 1:24,30). Consider the following facts:

First, Solomon describes wisdom as the first thing brought forth from God (Pr 8:22). Revelation 3:14 alludes to this exact phrasing in Proverbs 8:22 and applies it to Jesus. This statement does not mean that Jesus was created, but rather that he is supreme over the creation (Jn 1:1 – 3; Col 1:15). After all, he is God's one and only Son (Jn 3:16). He is the wisdom of God.

Second, wisdom existed prior to the creation of the world (Pr 8:23 – 26). The New Testament discloses the same thing about Jesus. The night of his betrayal, Jesus prayed, "And now, Father, glorify me in your own presence with the glory that I had with you before the world existed" (Jn 17:5). Jesus existed before the creation — he is the wisdom of God.

Finally, Proverbs 8 says that not only did wisdom exist prior to the creation, but wisdom seems to have assisted in creating the world (vv. 27 – 31). The New Testament said the same thing about Jesus. Colossians 1:15 – 16 says, "He [the Son] is the image of the invisible God, the firstborn of all creation. For by him all things were created." Like a firstborn son in the biblical world, Jesus had certain rights over creation since Jesus is the wisdom of God who assisted him in creating the world.

5 "Come, eat of my bread
and drink of the wine I have mixed.
6 Leave your simple ways,[1] and live,
and walk in the way of insight."

7 Whoever corrects a scoffer gets himself abuse,
and he who reproves a wicked man incurs injury.
8 Do not reprove a scoffer, or he will hate you;
reprove a wise man, and he will love you.
9 Give instruction[2] to a wise man, and he will be still wiser;
teach a righteous man, and he will increase in learning.
10 The fear of the LORD is the beginning of wisdom,
and the knowledge of the Holy One is insight.
11 For by me your days will be multiplied,
and years will be added to your life.
12 If you are wise, you are wise for yourself;
if you scoff, you alone will bear it.

The Way of Folly

13 The woman Folly is loud;
she is seductive[3] and knows nothing.
14 She sits at the door of her house;
she takes a seat on the highest places of the town,
15 calling to those who pass by,
who are going straight on their way,
16 "Whoever is simple, let him turn in here!"
And to him who lacks sense she says,
17 "Stolen water is sweet,
and bread eaten in secret is pleasant."
18 But he does not know that the dead[4] are there,
that her guests are in the depths of Sheol.

The Proverbs of Solomon

10 The proverbs of Solomon.

A wise son makes a glad father,
but a foolish son is a sorrow to his mother.
2 Treasures gained by wickedness do not profit,
but righteousness delivers from death.
3 The LORD does not let the righteous go hungry,
but he thwarts the craving of the wicked.
4 A slack hand causes poverty,
but the hand of the diligent makes rich.
5 He who gathers in summer is a prudent son,
but he who sleeps in harvest is a son who brings shame.
6 Blessings are on the head of the righteous,
but the mouth of the wicked conceals violence.[5]
7 The memory of the righteous is a blessing,
but the name of the wicked will rot.
8 The wise of heart will receive commandments,
but a babbling fool will come to ruin.
9 Whoever walks in integrity walks securely,
but he who makes his ways crooked will be found out.
10 Whoever winks the eye causes trouble,
and a babbling fool will come to ruin.

[1]Or *Leave the company of the simple* [2]Hebrew lacks *instruction* [3]Or *full of simpleness* [4]Hebrew *Rephaim*
[5]Or *but violence covers the mouth of the wicked*; also verse 11

PROVERBS 9:10

THE FEAR OF THE LORD

According to Solomon, wisdom is based on the fear of the Lord. Proverbs opens with a similar refrain (1:7), demonstrating that the ability to obey all of the practical guidance found throughout Solomon's writings derives from the same source—the fear of the Lord. Often attempts are made to soften or minimize the nature of this fear, leading some to conclude that Solomon was merely referring to awe or reverence for God. Yet, the biblical notion of fearing God is far more holistic (Ecc 12:13–14). The power and judgment of God should cause frail and fallen humans to have a profound sense of fear and submission to the rightful Ruler of all things because it is a fearful thing to fall into the hands of the living God (Heb 10:31). Christians should live in fear of God (Mt 10:28), and this fear is manifest in a life of obedience to God's commands (2Co 7:1). People like Joseph, who are marked by such wisdom, are often referred to as God-fearing individuals (Ge 42:18). Ultimately, however, it is only Jesus whose entire life was lived in the fear of God. Even as he faced death, Jesus willingly laid down his life in obedience to the Father's plan, demonstrating that his desire to obey God was greater than the fear of a brutal death (Lk 22:42). Empowered by the Spirit, Christians are transformed to fear God, and in so doing, find true wisdom.

PROVERBS 10:9

LIVING GOD'S WAY

Solomon described the human life as a walk. All people move through life like a walk, yet not all people walk through life in the same way. Some do so in crooked and perverse ways, while others walk uprightly. The way in which they walk is influenced, not by their aptitude or ability, but by their companions along life's journey. Those who walk with God follow him into paths of righteousness; those who do not walk with him follow "the course of this world ... the prince of the power of the air, the spirit that is now at work in the sons of disobedience" (Eph 2:2).

Godly men and women of faith are singled out as those who walk with God. For example, the enigmatic figure Enoch "walked with God" and was taken by God directly to his presence at the end of his life (Ge 5:22 – 24; Heb 11:5). Noah, who was spared the destruction brought about by the flood, "was a righteous man, blameless in his generation. Noah walked with God" (Ge 6:9; Heb 11:7). Likewise, Abraham trusted God and walked with him, though he did not know where he was going (Ge 12:1 – 3; Heb 11:8). In Jesus' day, his disciples literally walked with him as they followed him to fish for people (Mt 4:19). As the Good Shepherd, God knows how best to lead his people to green pastures and still waters (Ps 23:1 – 2). His children know his voice and follow his leadership because they know that he guides them in the path of life (Jn 10:1 – 6).

It is impossible to walk with God apart from Jesus. All people, by virtue of their inborn sin natures, live counter to God's wisdom and are unwilling to follow his leadership. Jesus was the only man who ever followed God's path perfectly. He walked with God — each day and each moment of each day. He earned a righteous standing before the Father, more than sinners could ever produce on their own. By grace, he gives his righteous standing to his followers, who are seen by God as having lived the upright life God demands (2Co 5:17 – 21). This gift of righteousness then motivates and mobilizes God's people to walk in a manner worthy of their calling, with God as their constant companion through life's journey (Eph 4:1).

11 The mouth of the righteous is a fountain of life,
but the mouth of the wicked conceals violence.
12 Hatred stirs up strife,
but love covers all offenses.
13 On the lips of him who has understanding, wisdom is found,
but a rod is for the back of him who lacks sense.
14 The wise lay up knowledge,
but the mouth of a fool brings ruin near.
15 A rich man's wealth is his strong city;
the poverty of the poor is their ruin.
16 The wage of the righteous leads to life,
the gain of the wicked to sin.
17 Whoever heeds instruction is on the path to life,
but he who rejects reproof leads others astray.
18 The one who conceals hatred has lying lips,
and whoever utters slander is a fool.
19 When words are many, transgression is not lacking,
but whoever restrains his lips is prudent.
20 The tongue of the righteous is choice silver;
the heart of the wicked is of little worth.
21 The lips of the righteous feed many,
but fools die for lack of sense.
22 The blessing of the LORD makes rich,
and he adds no sorrow with it.[1]
23 Doing wrong is like a joke to a fool,
but wisdom is pleasure to a man of understanding.
24 What the wicked dreads will come upon him,
but the desire of the righteous will be granted.
25 When the tempest passes, the wicked is no more,
but the righteous is established forever.
26 Like vinegar to the teeth and smoke to the eyes,
so is the sluggard to those who send him.
27 The fear of the LORD prolongs life,
but the years of the wicked will be short.
28 The hope of the righteous brings joy,
but the expectation of the wicked will perish.
29 The way of the LORD is a stronghold to the blameless,
but destruction to evildoers.
30 The righteous will never be removed,
but the wicked will not dwell in the land.
31 The mouth of the righteous brings forth wisdom,
but the perverse tongue will be cut off.
32 The lips of the righteous know what is acceptable,
but the mouth of the wicked, what is perverse.

11 A false balance is an abomination to the LORD,
but a just weight is his delight.
2 When pride comes, then comes disgrace,
but with the humble is wisdom.
3 The integrity of the upright guides them,
but the crookedness of the treacherous destroys them.
4 Riches do not profit in the day of wrath,
but righteousness delivers from death.
5 The righteousness of the blameless keeps his way straight,
but the wicked falls by his own wickedness.

PROVERBS 11:2

ATTITUDE

Pride and humility are defining traits of the human heart. No one can see either characteristic, but the manifestations of both pride and humility are seen in the actions of all humans. Throughout the proverbs, Solomon connected pride with foolishness and ultimate destruction (Pr 16:18). In contrast, he linked humility with wisdom and the fear of the Lord, leading to life and blessing (Pr 22:4; 29:23). Pride vaunts the person to the supreme arbitrator of life and demonstrates a lack of submission to God as the One who knows how best life should be lived. Discounting God's wisdom through human pride invariably leads to destruction in this life and the next. Humility, in contrast, affirms God is sovereign, omnipotent, and omniscient. He knows how life should be lived far better than humans, whose vision is always limited in this life (1Co 13:12). God stands in opposition to the proud, but promises his faithfulness and grace to the humble in heart (Jas 4:6).

[1]Or *and toil adds nothing to it*

6 The righteousness of the upright delivers them,
but the treacherous are taken captive by their lust.
7 When the wicked dies, his hope will perish,
and the expectation of wealth[1] perishes too.
8 The righteous is delivered from trouble,
and the wicked walks into it instead.
9 With his mouth the godless man would destroy his neighbor,
but by knowledge the righteous are delivered.
10 When it goes well with the righteous, the city rejoices,
and when the wicked perish there are shouts of gladness.
11 By the blessing of the upright a city is exalted,
but by the mouth of the wicked it is overthrown.
12 Whoever belittles his neighbor lacks sense,
but a man of understanding remains silent.
13 Whoever goes about slandering reveals secrets,
but he who is trustworthy in spirit keeps a thing covered.
14 Where there is no guidance, a people falls,
but in an abundance of counselors there is safety.
15 Whoever puts up security for a stranger will surely suffer
harm,
but he who hates striking hands in pledge is secure.
16 A gracious woman gets honor,
and violent men get riches.
17 A man who is kind benefits himself,
but a cruel man hurts himself.
18 The wicked earns deceptive wages,
but one who sows righteousness gets a sure reward.
19 Whoever is steadfast in righteousness will live,
but he who pursues evil will die.
20 Those of crooked heart are an abomination to the LORD,
but those of blameless ways are his delight.
21 Be assured, an evil person will not go unpunished,
but the offspring of the righteous will be delivered.
22 Like a gold ring in a pig's snout
is a beautiful woman without discretion.
23 The desire of the righteous ends only in good,
the expectation of the wicked in wrath.
24 One gives freely, yet grows all the richer;
another withholds what he should give, and only suffers
want.
25 Whoever brings blessing will be enriched,
and one who waters will himself be watered.
26 The people curse him who holds back grain,
but a blessing is on the head of him who sells it.
27 *Whoever diligently seeks good seeks favor,*[2]
but evil comes to him who searches for it.
28 Whoever trusts in his riches will fall,
but the righteous will flourish like a green leaf.
29 Whoever troubles his own household will inherit the wind,
and the fool will be servant to the wise of heart.
30 The fruit of the righteous is a tree of life,
and whoever captures souls is wise.
31 If the righteous is repaid on earth,
how much more the wicked and the sinner!

[1]Or *of his strength*, or *of iniquity* [2]Or *acceptance*

12 Whoever loves discipline loves knowledge,
but he who hates reproof is stupid.
2 A good man obtains favor from the LORD,
but a man of evil devices he condemns.
3 No one is established by wickedness,
but the root of the righteous will never be moved.
4 An excellent wife is the crown of her husband,
but she who brings shame is like rottenness in his bones.
5 The thoughts of the righteous are just;
the counsels of the wicked are deceitful.
6 The words of the wicked lie in wait for blood,
but the mouth of the upright delivers them.
7 The wicked are overthrown and are no more,
but the house of the righteous will stand.
8 A man is commended according to his good sense,
but one of twisted mind is despised.
9 Better to be lowly and have a servant
than to play the great man and lack bread.
10 Whoever is righteous has regard for the life of his beast,
but the mercy of the wicked is cruel.
11 Whoever works his land will have plenty of bread,
but he who follows worthless pursuits lacks sense.
12 Whoever is wicked covets the spoil of evildoers,
but the root of the righteous bears fruit.
13 An evil man is ensnared by the transgression of his lips,[1]
but the righteous escapes from trouble.
14 From the fruit of his mouth a man is satisfied with good,
and the work of a man's hand comes back to him.
15 The way of a fool is right in his own eyes,
but a wise man listens to advice.
16 The vexation of a fool is known at once,
but the prudent ignores an insult.
17 Whoever speaks[2] the truth gives honest evidence,
but a false witness utters deceit.
18 There is one whose rash words are like sword thrusts,
but the tongue of the wise brings healing.
19 Truthful lips endure forever,
but a lying tongue is but for a moment.
20 Deceit is in the heart of those who devise evil,
but those who plan peace have joy.
21 No ill befalls the righteous,
but the wicked are filled with trouble.
22 Lying lips are an abomination to the LORD,
but those who act faithfully are his delight.
23 A prudent man conceals knowledge,
but the heart of fools proclaims folly.
24 The hand of the diligent will rule,
while the slothful will be put to forced labor.
25 Anxiety in a man's heart weighs him down,
but a good word makes him glad.
26 One who is righteous is a guide to his neighbor,[3]
but the way of the wicked leads them astray.
27 Whoever is slothful will not roast his game,
but the diligent man will get precious wealth.[4]

[1]Or *In the transgression of the lips, there is an evil snare* [2]Hebrew *breathes out* [3]Or *The righteous chooses his friends carefully* [4]Or *but diligence is precious wealth*

28 In the path of righteousness is life,
and in its pathway there is no death.

13 A wise son hears his father's instruction,
but a scoffer does not listen to rebuke.
2 From the fruit of his mouth a man eats what is good,
but the desire of the treacherous is for violence.
3 Whoever guards his mouth preserves his life;
he who opens wide his lips comes to ruin.
4 The soul of the sluggard craves and gets nothing,
while the soul of the diligent is richly supplied.
5 The righteous hates falsehood,
but the wicked brings shame[1] and disgrace.
6 Righteousness guards him whose way is blameless,
but sin overthrows the wicked.
7 One pretends to be rich,[2] yet has nothing;
another pretends to be poor,[3] yet has great wealth.
8 The ransom of a man's life is his wealth,
but a poor man hears no threat.
9 The light of the righteous rejoices,
but the lamp of the wicked will be put out.
10 By insolence comes nothing but strife,
but with those who take advice is wisdom.
11 Wealth gained hastily[4] will dwindle,
but whoever gathers little by little will increase it.
12 Hope deferred makes the heart sick,
but a desire fulfilled is a tree of life.
13 Whoever despises the word[5] brings destruction on himself,
but he who reveres the commandment[6] will be rewarded.
14 The teaching of the wise is a fountain of life,
that one may turn away from the snares of death.
15 Good sense wins favor,
but the way of the treacherous is their ruin.[7]
16 Every prudent man acts with knowledge,
but a fool flaunts his folly.
17 A wicked messenger falls into trouble,
but a faithful envoy brings healing.
18 Poverty and disgrace come to him who ignores instruction,
but whoever heeds reproof is honored.
19 A desire fulfilled is sweet to the soul,
but to turn away from evil is an abomination to fools.
20 Whoever walks with the wise becomes wise,
but the companion of fools will suffer harm.
21 Disaster[8] pursues sinners,
but the righteous are rewarded with good.
22 A good man leaves an inheritance to his children's children,
but the sinner's wealth is laid up for the righteous.
23 The fallow ground of the poor would yield much food,
but it is swept away through injustice.
24 Whoever spares the rod hates his son,
but he who loves him is diligent to discipline him.[9]
25 The righteous has enough to satisfy his appetite,
but the belly of the wicked suffers want.

PROVERBS 12:28

ETERNAL LIFE

When read apart from the context of the whole Scripture, this verse may lead readers to believe a false gospel. It seems to say that if anyone lives a righteous life, then that person will inherit eternal life. And this hints that a person's good works can secure a place in heaven after death. The problem is that absolutely no one is righteous (Ro 3:10). Taken within the full context of Scripture, Proverbs 12:28 is actually bad news for sinful humanity. The only righteous one in history is Jesus of Nazareth. Second Corinthians 5:21 describes the Good News: "For our sake he made him to be sin who knew no sin, so that in him we might become the righteousness of God." Christ has brought "life and immortality to light through the gospel" (2Ti 1:10). So, for those who believe in Christ, Proverbs 12:28 is the best news in the entire world because believers are counted as righteous in Christ and will receive eternal life.

[1]Or *stench* [2]Or *One makes himself rich* [3]Or *another makes himself poor* [4]Or *by fraud* [5]Or *a word* [6]Or *a commandment* [7]Probable reading (compare Septuagint, Syriac, Vulgate); Hebrew *is rugged*, or *is an enduring rut* [8]Or *Evil* [9]Or *who loves him disciplines him early*

14 The wisest of women builds her house,
but folly with her own hands tears it down.
2 Whoever walks in uprightness fears the LORD,
but he who is devious in his ways despises him.
3 By the mouth of a fool comes a rod for his back,[1]
but the lips of the wise will preserve them.
4 Where there are no oxen, the manger is clean,
but abundant crops come by the strength of the ox.
5 A faithful witness does not lie,
but a false witness breathes out lies.
6 A scoffer seeks wisdom in vain,
but knowledge is easy for a man of understanding.
7 Leave the presence of a fool,
for there you do not meet words of knowledge.
8 The wisdom of the prudent is to discern his way,
but the folly of fools is deceiving.
9 Fools mock at the guilt offering,
but the upright enjoy acceptance.[2]
10 The heart knows its own bitterness,
and no stranger shares its joy.
11 The house of the wicked will be destroyed,
but the tent of the upright will flourish.
12 There is a way that seems right to a man,
but its end is the way to death.[3]
13 Even in laughter the heart may ache,
and the end of joy may be grief.
14 The backslider in heart will be filled with the fruit of his ways,
and a good man will be filled with the fruit of his ways.
15 The simple believes everything,
but the prudent gives thought to his steps.
16 One who is wise is cautious[4] and turns away from evil,
but a fool is reckless and careless.
17 A man of quick temper acts foolishly,
and a man of evil devices is hated.
18 The simple inherit folly,
but the prudent are crowned with knowledge.
19 The evil bow down before the good,
the wicked at the gates of the righteous.
20 The poor is disliked even by his neighbor,
but the rich has many friends.
21 Whoever despises his neighbor is a sinner,
but blessed is he who is generous to the poor.
22 Do they not go astray who devise evil?
Those who devise good meet[5] steadfast love and faithfulness.
23 In all toil there is profit,
but mere talk tends only to poverty.
24 The crown of the wise is their wealth,
but the folly of fools brings folly.
25 A truthful witness saves lives,
but one who breathes out lies is deceitful.
26 In the fear of the LORD one has strong confidence,
and his children will have a refuge.
27 The fear of the LORD is a fountain of life,
that one may turn away from the snares of death.

[1]Or *In the mouth of a fool is a rod of pride* [2]Hebrew *but among the upright is acceptance* [3]Hebrew *ways of death* [4]Or *fears* [the LORD] [5]Or *show*

28 In a multitude of people is the glory of a king,
but without people a prince is ruined.
29 Whoever is slow to anger has great understanding,
but he who has a hasty temper exalts folly.
30 A tranquil[1] heart gives life to the flesh,
but envy[2] makes the bones rot.
31 Whoever oppresses a poor man insults his Maker,
but he who is generous to the needy honors him.
32 The wicked is overthrown through his evildoing,
but the righteous finds refuge in his death.
33 Wisdom rests in the heart of a man of understanding,
but it makes itself known even in the midst of fools.[3]
34 Righteousness exalts a nation,
but sin is a reproach to any people.
35 A servant who deals wisely has the king's favor,
but his wrath falls on one who acts shamefully.

15 A soft answer turns away wrath,
but a harsh word stirs up anger.
2 The tongue of the wise commends knowledge,
but the mouths of fools pour out folly.
3 The eyes of the LORD are in every place,
keeping watch on the evil and the good.
4 A gentle[4] tongue is a tree of life,
but perverseness in it breaks the spirit.
5 A fool despises his father's instruction,
but whoever heeds reproof is prudent.
6 In the house of the righteous there is much treasure,
but trouble befalls the income of the wicked.
7 The lips of the wise spread knowledge;
not so the hearts of fools.[5]
8 The sacrifice of the wicked is an abomination to the LORD,
but the prayer of the upright is acceptable to him.
9 The way of the wicked is an abomination to the LORD,
but he loves him who pursues righteousness.
10 There is severe discipline for him who forsakes the way;
whoever hates reproof will die.
11 Sheol and Abaddon lie open before the LORD;
how much more the hearts of the children of man!
12 A scoffer does not like to be reproved;
he will not go to the wise.
13 A glad heart makes a cheerful face,
but by sorrow of heart the spirit is crushed.
14 The heart of him who has understanding seeks knowledge,
but the mouths of fools feed on folly.
15 All the days of the afflicted are evil,
but the cheerful of heart has a continual feast.
16 Better is a little with the fear of the LORD
than great treasure and trouble with it.
17 Better is a dinner of herbs where love is
than a fattened ox and hatred with it.
18 A hot-tempered man stirs up strife,
but he who is slow to anger quiets contention.
19 The way of a sluggard is like a hedge of thorns,
but the path of the upright is a level highway.

[1]Or *healing* [2]Or *jealousy* [3]Or *Wisdom rests quietly in the heart of a man of understanding, but makes itself known in the midst of fools* [4]Or *healing* [5]Or *the hearts of fools are not steadfast*

PROVERBS 15:29

PRAYER

While God is aware of every prayer, this verse says that in a certain sense, he does not "hear" every prayer. The righteous can pray to God and be heard, but God is far from the wicked. That does not mean that God does not have any awareness of the prayers of the wicked, but rather that he does not respond to them. Isaiah 59:2 says something very similar: "But your iniquities have made a separation between you and your God, and your sins have hidden his face from you so that he does not hear." Most people do not think they are wicked, but Proverbs says that the prayers of those who ignore God's law are detestable to him (28:9). All people have sinned and broken God's law. So can anyone hope to be heard by God? Jesus Christ—the righteous one—died for people so that they could be accounted righteous before God, and then he entered into the heavenly sanctuary as their mediator before God (2Co 5:21; 1Ti 2:5; Heb 7:25; 9:24). That's why people pray in Jesus' name: it is only through Jesus that the prayers of sinful humans can be heard and answered!

PROVERBS 16:4–6

BY LOVE AND FAITHFULNESS

Solomon affirmed that God is ultimately in control and his good purposes will prevail, even in spite of human sin. Even the wicked, who seem to avoid destruction in this life, will surely face the judgment of God. The prideful person will not escape the coming day of disaster, and the folly of pride will be exposed

(continued on next page)

20 A wise son makes a glad father,
but a foolish man despises his mother.
21 Folly is a joy to him who lacks sense,
but a man of understanding walks straight ahead.
22 Without counsel plans fail,
but with many advisers they succeed.
23 To make an apt answer is a joy to a man,
and a word in season, how good it is!
24 The path of life leads upward for the prudent,
that he may turn away from Sheol beneath.
25 The LORD tears down the house of the proud
but maintains the widow's boundaries.
26 The thoughts of the wicked are an abomination to the LORD,
but gracious words are pure.
27 Whoever is greedy for unjust gain troubles his own household,
but he who hates bribes will live.
28 The heart of the righteous ponders how to answer,
but the mouth of the wicked pours out evil things.
29 The LORD is far from the wicked,
but he hears the prayer of the righteous.
30 The light of the eyes rejoices the heart,
and good news refreshes[1] the bones.
31 The ear that listens to life-giving reproof
will dwell among the wise.
32 Whoever ignores instruction despises himself,
but he who listens to reproof gains intelligence.
33 The fear of the LORD is instruction in wisdom,
and humility comes before honor.

16 The plans of the heart belong to man,
but the answer of the tongue is from the LORD.
2 All the ways of a man are pure in his own eyes,
but the LORD weighs the spirit.[2]
3 Commit your work to the LORD,
and your plans will be established.
4 The LORD has made everything for its purpose,
even the wicked for the day of trouble.
5 Everyone who is arrogant in heart is an abomination to the LORD;
be assured, he will not go unpunished.
6 By steadfast love and faithfulness iniquity is atoned for,
and by the fear of the LORD one turns away from evil.
7 When a man's ways please the LORD,
he makes even his enemies to be at peace with him.
8 Better is a little with righteousness
than great revenues with injustice.
9 The heart of man plans his way,
but the LORD establishes his steps.
10 An oracle is on the lips of a king;
his mouth does not sin in judgment.
11 A just balance and scales are the LORD's;
all the weights in the bag are his work.
12 It is an abomination to kings to do evil,
for the throne is established by righteousness.
13 Righteous lips are the delight of a king,
and he loves him who speaks what is right.

[1]Hebrew *makes fat* [2]Or *spirits*

14 A king's wrath is a messenger of death,
and a wise man will appease it.
15 In the light of a king's face there is life,
and his favor is like the clouds that bring the spring rain.
16 How much better to get wisdom than gold!
To get understanding is to be chosen rather than silver.
17 The highway of the upright turns aside from evil;
whoever guards his way preserves his life.
18 Pride goes before destruction,
and a haughty spirit before a fall.
19 It is better to be of a lowly spirit with the poor
than to divide the spoil with the proud.
20 Whoever gives thought to the word[1] will discover good,
and blessed is he who trusts in the LORD.
21 The wise of heart is called discerning,
and sweetness of speech increases persuasiveness.
22 Good sense is a fountain of life to him who has it,
but the instruction of fools is folly.
23 The heart of the wise makes his speech judicious
and adds persuasiveness to his lips.
24 Gracious words are like a honeycomb,
sweetness to the soul and health to the body.
25 There is a way that seems right to a man,
but its end is the way to death.[2]
26 A worker's appetite works for him;
his mouth urges him on.
27 A worthless man plots evil,
and his speech[3] is like a scorching fire.
28 A dishonest man spreads strife,
and a whisperer separates close friends.
29 A man of violence entices his neighbor
and leads him in a way that is not good.
30 Whoever winks his eyes plans[4] dishonest things;
he who purses his lips brings evil to pass.
31 Gray hair is a crown of glory;
it is gained in a righteous life.
32 Whoever is slow to anger is better than the mighty,
and he who rules his spirit than he who takes a city.
33 The lot is cast into the lap,
but its every decision is from the LORD.

17 Better is a dry morsel with quiet
than a house full of feasting[5] with strife.
2 A servant who deals wisely will rule over a son who acts shamefully
and will share the inheritance as one of the brothers.
3 The crucible is for silver, and the furnace is for gold,
and the LORD tests hearts.
4 An evildoer listens to wicked lips,
and a liar gives ear to a mischievous tongue.
5 Whoever mocks the poor insults his Maker;
he who is glad at calamity will not go unpunished.
6 Grandchildren are the crown of the aged,
and the glory of children is their fathers.
7 Fine speech is not becoming to a fool;
still less is false speech to a prince.

[1]Or *to a matter* [2]Hebrew *ways of death* [3]Hebrew *what is on his lips* [4]Hebrew *to plan* [5]Hebrew *sacrifices*

(By Love and Faithfulness, continued)

on that day. In contrast, those whose lives are marked by humility—who understand the fear of the Lord—they will experience the love and faithfulness of God and in turn love God and walk faithfully with him. This is the glorious truth about the character of God. Though he is holy and pure, he is not quick to anger, nor is he vindictive or capricious in his wrath. He is "the LORD, the LORD, a God merciful and gracious, slow to anger, and abounding in steadfast love and faithfulness" (Ex 34:6). God extends mercy in allowing prideful rebels time to confess their sins and humble themselves before the mighty hand of God. As Peter says, "The Lord is not slow to fulfill his promise as some count slowness, but is patient toward you, not wishing that any should perish, but that all should reach repentance" (2Pe 3:9). Each day God gives is evidence of his love, and those who hear his voice should turn to him in faith as long as today is called today (Heb 3:12–15).

PROVERBS 16:25

NO ALTERNATE ROUTE

The wisdom of man is folly in the eyes of God. Solomon proclaimed a reality that fallen sinners know all too well. The pseudo-wisdom that guides life, more often than not, leads to destruction and disaster. Sinners who presume to know the best way to life often leave a wake of shattered dreams, broken promises, and failure when they pursue their own plans.

What is true with minor decisions is also true on a grand scale. The path that many choose to follow leads to eternal destruction. There is a broad way that seems right to humans, but it ends in eternal separation from God. Jesus warns that many take this way of death (Mt 7:13). Few are those who walk the narrow path — the path to life — and find the joy and salvation that God offers (Mt 7:14). In fact, Jesus is the only one who perfectly walked the narrow way, faithfully obeying God at every turn. By walking this narrow path, Jesus did more than call sinners to follow his example. He gives those who trust him in faith the gift of eternal life. This is why Jesus is the only means of salvation. No one else walked the narrow path in the place of sinners. No one else earned a perfect standing before the Father. And no one else offered his perfect righteousness to sinners as a gift. For this reason Peter proclaimed, "There is salvation in no one else, for there is no other name under heaven given among men by which we must be saved (Ac 4:12).

The path of faith and repentance seems counterintuitive to many. Why not simply try harder to obey God, live a good life in comparison to the world's standards, and seek to avoid major sins? Many try to follow this path that "seems right" only to find that it leads to disaster because, despite the best efforts of sinners, no one can obey God perfectly. Those who choose this path may hear the startling words from the Father on the last day: "I never knew you; depart from me" (Mt 7:23). God will only grant salvation to those who know they cannot walk the narrow way, but cling to the One who has, knowing that "in Christ Jesus" they, too, can avoid the way that leads to death and find the way that leads to life (Ro 8:1; Gal 3:26 – 28).

8 A bribe is like a magic[1] stone in the eyes of the one who gives it;
wherever he turns he prospers.
9 Whoever covers an offense seeks love,
but he who repeats a matter separates close friends.
10 A rebuke goes deeper into a man of understanding
than a hundred blows into a fool.
11 An evil man seeks only rebellion,
and a cruel messenger will be sent against him.
12 Let a man meet a she-bear robbed of her cubs
rather than a fool in his folly.
13 If anyone returns evil for good,
evil will not depart from his house.
14 The beginning of strife is like letting out water,
so quit before the quarrel breaks out.
15 He who justifies the wicked and he who condemns the righteous
are both alike an abomination to the LORD.
16 Why should a fool have money in his hand to buy wisdom
when he has no sense?
17 A friend loves at all times,
and a brother is born for adversity.
18 One who lacks sense gives a pledge
and puts up security in the presence of his neighbor.
19 Whoever loves transgression loves strife;
he who makes his door high seeks destruction.
20 A man of crooked heart does not discover good,
and one with a dishonest tongue falls into calamity.
21 He who sires a fool gets himself sorrow,
and the father of a fool has no joy.
22 A joyful heart is good medicine,
but a crushed spirit dries up the bones.
23 The wicked accepts a bribe in secret[2]
to pervert the ways of justice.
24 The discerning sets his face toward wisdom,
but the eyes of a fool are on the ends of the earth.
25 A foolish son is a grief to his father
and bitterness to her who bore him.
26 To impose a fine on a righteous man is not good,
nor to strike the noble for their uprightness.
27 Whoever restrains his words has knowledge,
and he who has a cool spirit is a man of understanding.
28 Even a fool who keeps silent is considered wise;
when he closes his lips, he is deemed intelligent.

18 Whoever isolates himself seeks his own desire;
he breaks out against all sound judgment.
2 A fool takes no pleasure in understanding,
but only in expressing his opinion.
3 When wickedness comes, contempt comes also,
and with dishonor comes disgrace.
4 The words of a man's mouth are deep waters;
the fountain of wisdom is a bubbling brook.
5 It is not good to be partial to[3] the wicked
or to deprive the righteous of justice.
6 A fool's lips walk into a fight,
and his mouth invites a beating.

[1]Or *precious* [2]Hebrew *a bribe from the bosom* [3]Hebrew *to lift the face of*

PROVERBS 18:24

FRIENDSHIP

Everyone has experienced to some extent the force of the first line in this verse: "A man of many companions may come to ruin." Unfortunately, no one is exempt from being let down and letting others down. This proverb is a reminder that everyone needs a friend who is more than just a casual association—and each person needs to be that kind of friend to others. People need true friends who will be closer and more loyal than even blood relatives. This proverb clearly points to Jesus Christ, who is a friend that is better than family. Jesus described what true friendship is: "Greater love has no one than this, that someone lay down his life for his friends" (Jn 15:13). Jesus displayed the greatest love and friendship to us through his death on the cross. In Christ, we have the friend we need (Jn 15:15), and we can become the kind of friend that others need.

7 A fool's mouth is his ruin,
and his lips are a snare to his soul.
8 The words of a whisperer are like delicious morsels;
they go down into the inner parts of the body.
9 Whoever is slack in his work
is a brother to him who destroys.
10 The name of the LORD is a strong tower;
the righteous man runs into it and is safe.
11 A rich man's wealth is his strong city,
and like a high wall in his imagination.
12 Before destruction a man's heart is haughty,
but humility comes before honor.
13 If one gives an answer before he hears,
it is his folly and shame.
14 A man's spirit will endure sickness,
but a crushed spirit who can bear?
15 An intelligent heart acquires knowledge,
and the ear of the wise seeks knowledge.
16 A man's gift makes room for him
and brings him before the great.
17 The one who states his case first seems right,
until the other comes and examines him.
18 The lot puts an end to quarrels
and decides between powerful contenders.
19 A brother offended is more unyielding than a strong city,
and quarreling is like the bars of a castle.
20 From the fruit of a man's mouth his stomach is satisfied;
he is satisfied by the yield of his lips.
21 Death and life are in the power of the tongue,
and those who love it will eat its fruits.
22 He who finds a wife finds a good thing
and obtains favor from the LORD.
23 The poor use entreaties,
but the rich answer roughly.
24 A man of many companions may come to ruin,
but there is a friend who sticks closer than a brother.

19 Better is a poor person who walks in his integrity
than one who is crooked in speech and is a fool.
2 Desire[1] without knowledge is not good,
and whoever makes haste with his feet misses his way.
3 When a man's folly brings his way to ruin,
his heart rages against the LORD.
4 Wealth brings many new friends,
but a poor man is deserted by his friend.
5 A false witness will not go unpunished,
and he who breathes out lies will not escape.
6 Many seek the favor of a generous man,[2]
and everyone is a friend to a man who gives gifts.
7 All a poor man's brothers hate him;
how much more do his friends go far from him!
He pursues them with words, but does not have them.[3]
8 Whoever gets sense loves his own soul;
he who keeps understanding will discover good.
9 A false witness will not go unpunished,
and he who breathes out lies will perish.

[1] Or *A soul* [2] Or *of a noble* [3] The meaning of the Hebrew sentence is uncertain

10 It is not fitting for a fool to live in luxury,
much less for a slave to rule over princes.
11 Good sense makes one slow to anger,
and it is his glory to overlook an offense.
12 A king's wrath is like the growling of a lion,
but his favor is like dew on the grass.
13 A foolish son is ruin to his father,
and a wife's quarreling is a continual dripping of rain.
14 House and wealth are inherited from fathers,
but a prudent wife is from the LORD.
15 Slothfulness casts into a deep sleep,
and an idle person will suffer hunger.
16 Whoever keeps the commandment keeps his life;
he who despises his ways will die.
17 Whoever is generous to the poor lends to the LORD,
and he will repay him for his deed.
18 Discipline your son, for there is hope;
do not set your heart on putting him to death.
19 A man of great wrath will pay the penalty,
for if you deliver him, you will only have to do it again.
20 Listen to advice and accept instruction,
that you may gain wisdom in the future.
21 Many are the plans in the mind of a man,
but it is the purpose of the LORD that will stand.
22 What is desired in a man is steadfast love,
and a poor man is better than a liar.
23 The fear of the LORD leads to life,
and whoever has it rests satisfied;
he will not be visited by harm.
24 The sluggard buries his hand in the dish
and will not even bring it back to his mouth.
25 Strike a scoffer, and the simple will learn prudence;
reprove a man of understanding, and he will gain knowledge.
26 He who does violence to his father and chases away his mother
is a son who brings shame and reproach.
27 Cease to hear instruction, my son,
and you will stray from the words of knowledge.
28 A worthless witness mocks at justice,
and the mouth of the wicked devours iniquity.
29 Condemnation is ready for scoffers,
and beating for the backs of fools.

20 Wine is a mocker, strong drink a brawler,
and whoever is led astray by it is not wise.[1]
2 The terror of a king is like the growling of a lion;
whoever provokes him to anger forfeits his life.
3 It is an honor for a man to keep aloof from strife,
but every fool will be quarreling.
4 The sluggard does not plow in the autumn;
he will seek at harvest and have nothing.
5 The purpose in a man's heart is like deep water,
but a man of understanding will draw it out.
6 Many a man proclaims his own steadfast love,
but a faithful man who can find?
7 The righteous who walks in his integrity—
blessed are his children after him!

[1]Or *will not become wise*

PROVERBS 20:1

ALCOHOL

Drunkenness is condemned throughout the Bible. Here, Solomon noted the outcome of drunkenness — it produces sin in one's actions and speech. These sinful actions stem from the control alcohol exercises over the one who overindulges. Because this person is controlled by alcohol, he or she acts in foolish and sinful ways. In contrast, God's people are to be controlled by his Spirit, who dwells within them (Eph 5:18). Those who are filled with the Spirit and led according to his wishes are guided into all truth and protected from the type of sin that results from drunkenness (Jn 16:13). What makes alcohol so destructive is that it controls a person, whereas God's Spirit desires to have complete control. Those controlled by the Spirit are empowered to produce godly characteristics such as love, joy, peace, kindness, gentleness, and self-control (Gal 5:22–23). These godly fruits are only produced in the heart of one who is controlled by God's Spirit.

KINDNESS TO THE POOR

Compassion for the poor is an unmistakable mark of God's people. Throughout the Old Testament, the nation of Israel was consistently reminded of their responsibility to care for the poor, the outcast, and the sojourner in their midst. This care was to begin with their own people, as they were to see to it that there were no poor among them (Dt 15:7 – 8). Yet, it was also to extend beyond the ranks of the Israelites, to all those to whom they came in contact (Lev 19:34).

The pattern continues in the New Testament. In Luke 10 an expert in religious law asked Jesus what he must do in order to inherit eternal life. The scholar, attempting to justify himself, tried to prove that he had, in fact, loved God and his neighbor. But he asked Jesus to identify his neighbor. Jesus answered by telling a parable of a man who was robbed, beaten, and left for dead. Two men, who should have known their responsibility to meet this man's needs, passed by on the other side of the road. But the third man, a hated Samaritan, modeled neighbor-love by caring for the beaten man and seeing to it that his needs were met. The last one, the most unlikely of all characters in the story, was the one followers of Jesus should emulate. Such compassion and love is only possible as God's people come to understand that they are, ultimately, the man left for dead on the side of the road. God, like the Samaritan, came to their aid and saved them when they could do nothing to save themselves. Paul reminded the church in Corinth that their love and generosity should be motivated by a deep reflection on this gospel truth: "For you know the grace of our Lord Jesus Christ, that though he was rich, yet for your sake he became poor, so that you by his poverty might become rich" (2Co 8:9).

The New Testament church is marked by this type of gospel understanding through their care for one another. Luke documents the nature of the early church, pointing out that they were "selling their possessions and belongings and distributing the proceeds to all, as any had need" (Ac 2:45). In so doing they proved to know and follow God. As John writes, "If anyone has the world's goods and sees his brother in need, yet closes his heart against him, how does God's love abide in him? Little children, let us not love in word or talk but in deed and in truth" (1Jn 3:17 – 18).

8 A king who sits on the throne of judgment
winnows all evil with his eyes.
9 Who can say, "I have made my heart pure;
I am clean from my sin"?
10 Unequal[1] weights and unequal measures
are both alike an abomination to the LORD.
11 Even a child makes himself known by his acts,
by whether his conduct is pure and upright.[2]
12 The hearing ear and the seeing eye,
the LORD has made them both.
13 Love not sleep, lest you come to poverty;
open your eyes, and you will have plenty of bread.
14 "Bad, bad," says the buyer,
but when he goes away, then he boasts.
15 There is gold and abundance of costly stones,
but the lips of knowledge are a precious jewel.
16 Take a man's garment when he has put up security for a
stranger,
and hold it in pledge when he puts up security for foreigners.[3]
17 Bread gained by deceit is sweet to a man,
but afterward his mouth will be full of gravel.
18 Plans are established by counsel;
by wise guidance wage war.
19 Whoever goes about slandering reveals secrets;
therefore do not associate with a simple babbler.[4]
20 If one curses his father or his mother,
his lamp will be put out in utter darkness.
21 An inheritance gained hastily in the beginning
will not be blessed in the end.
22 Do not say, "I will repay evil";
wait for the LORD, and he will deliver you.
23 Unequal weights are an abomination to the LORD,
and false scales are not good.
24 A man's steps are from the LORD;
how then can man understand his way?
25 It is a snare to say rashly, "It is holy,"
and to reflect only after making vows.
26 A wise king winnows the wicked
and drives the wheel over them.
27 The spirit[5] of man is the lamp of the LORD,
searching all his innermost parts.
28 Steadfast love and faithfulness preserve the king,
and by steadfast love his throne is upheld.
29 The glory of young men is their strength,
but the splendor of old men is their gray hair.
30 Blows that wound cleanse away evil;
strokes make clean the innermost parts.

21 The king's heart is a stream of water in the hand of the LORD;
he turns it wherever he will.
2 Every way of a man is right in his own eyes,
but the LORD weighs the heart.
3 To do righteousness and justice
is more acceptable to the LORD than sacrifice.

[1]Or *Two kinds of*; also verse 23 [2]Or *Even a child can dissemble in his actions, though his conduct seems pure and upright* [3]Or *for an adulteress* (compare 27:13) [4]Hebrew *with one who is simple in his lips* [5]Hebrew *breath*

4 Haughty eyes and a proud heart,
the lamp[1] of the wicked, are sin.
5 The plans of the diligent lead surely to abundance,
but everyone who is hasty comes only to poverty.
6 The getting of treasures by a lying tongue
is a fleeting vapor and a snare of death.[2]
7 The violence of the wicked will sweep them away,
because they refuse to do what is just.
8 The way of the guilty is crooked,
but the conduct of the pure is upright.
9 It is better to live in a corner of the housetop
than in a house shared with a quarrelsome wife.
10 The soul of the wicked desires evil;
his neighbor finds no mercy in his eyes.
11 When a scoffer is punished, the simple becomes wise;
when a wise man is instructed, he gains knowledge.
12 The Righteous One observes the house of the wicked;
he throws the wicked down to ruin.
13 Whoever closes his ear to the cry of the poor
will himself call out and not be answered.
14 A gift in secret averts anger,
and a concealed bribe,[3] strong wrath.
15 When justice is done, it is a joy to the righteous
but terror to evildoers.
16 One who wanders from the way of good sense
will rest in the assembly of the dead.
17 Whoever loves pleasure will be a poor man;
he who loves wine and oil will not be rich.
18 The wicked is a ransom for the righteous,
and the traitor for the upright.
19 It is better to live in a desert land
than with a quarrelsome and fretful woman.
20 Precious treasure and oil are in a wise man's dwelling,
but a foolish man devours it.
21 Whoever pursues righteousness and kindness
will find life, righteousness, and honor.
22 A wise man scales the city of the mighty
and brings down the stronghold in which they trust.
23 Whoever keeps his mouth and his tongue
keeps himself out of trouble.
24 "Scoffer" is the name of the arrogant, haughty man
who acts with arrogant pride.
25 The desire of the sluggard kills him,
for his hands refuse to labor.
26 All day long he craves and craves,
but the righteous gives and does not hold back.
27 The sacrifice of the wicked is an abomination;
how much more when he brings it with evil intent.
28 A false witness will perish,
but the word of a man who hears will endure.
29 A wicked man puts on a bold face,
but the upright gives thought to[4] his ways.
30 No wisdom, no understanding, no counsel
can avail against the LORD.

[1]Or *the plowing* [2]Some Hebrew manuscripts, Septuagint, Latin; most Hebrew manuscripts *vapor for those who seek death* [3]Hebrew *a bribe in the bosom* [4]Or *establishes*

PROVERBS 21:12

THE RIGHTEOUS ONE

Though Solomon was the wisest man who ever lived (until Jesus came), there is a Righteous One who is beyond compare. Solomon portrayed this one as sovereign over all human history and watching the actions of all those whom he made. This same Righteous One looks over the earth seeking "to give strong support to those whose heart is blameless toward him" (2Ch 16:9). Here, the same One notices the rebellion of the wicked and promises to bring them to ruin. The psalmist lamented the reality that, in this life, it may often seem that the wicked prosper and suffer no harm for their sin (Ps 73:3). But God is not blind to their sin. He sees. He knows. And he will judge. Should they fail to repent, God will cast them away from his presence forever (Mt 25:30). The Righteous One will not allow sin to go unpunished. Thankfully, God provided a way to maintain his righteousness and yet punish sin by pouring out his wrath on his Son (Ro 3:21–26). Faith in Jesus' finished work is the only hope all sinners have for escaping sure ruin from the hand of the Righteous One.

31 The horse is made ready for the day of battle,
but the victory belongs to the LORD.

22 A good name is to be chosen rather than great riches,
and favor is better than silver or gold.
2 The rich and the poor meet together;
the LORD is the Maker of them all.
3 The prudent sees danger and hides himself,
but the simple go on and suffer for it.
4 The reward for humility and fear of the LORD
is riches and honor and life.[1]
5 Thorns and snares are in the way of the crooked;
whoever guards his soul will keep far from them.
6 Train up a child in the way he should go;
even when he is old he will not depart from it.
7 The rich rules over the poor,
and the borrower is the slave of the lender.
8 Whoever sows injustice will reap calamity,
and the rod of his fury will fail.
9 Whoever has a bountiful[2] eye will be blessed,
for he shares his bread with the poor.
10 Drive out a scoffer, and strife will go out,
and quarreling and abuse will cease.
11 He who loves purity of heart,
and whose speech is gracious, will have the king as his friend.
12 The eyes of the LORD keep watch over knowledge,
but he overthrows the words of the traitor.
13 The sluggard says, "There is a lion outside!
I shall be killed in the streets!"
14 The mouth of forbidden[3] women is a deep pit;
he with whom the LORD is angry will fall into it.
15 Folly is bound up in the heart of a child,
but the rod of discipline drives it far from him.
16 Whoever oppresses the poor to increase his own wealth,
or gives to the rich, will only come to poverty.

Words of the Wise

17 Incline your ear, and hear the words of the wise,
and apply your heart to my knowledge,
18 for it will be pleasant if you keep them within you,
if all of them are ready on your lips.
19 That your trust may be in the LORD,
I have made them known to you today, even to you.
20 Have I not written for you thirty sayings
of counsel and knowledge,
21 to make you know what is right and true,
that you may give a true answer to those who sent you?

22 Do not rob the poor, because he is poor,
or crush the afflicted at the gate,
23 for the LORD will plead their cause
and rob of life those who rob them.
24 Make no friendship with a man given to anger,
nor go with a wrathful man,
25 lest you learn his ways
and entangle yourself in a snare.

[1]Or *The reward for humility is the fear of the LORD, riches and honor and life* [2]Hebrew *good*
[3]Hebrew *strange*

PROVERBS 22:6

TRAIN UP A CHILD

Many Christian parents feel guilty when their children do not "turn out right," and some of that guilt finds its root in this verse (traditionally rendered, "Train up a child in the way he should go; and when he is old, he will not depart from it"). The logic seems straightforward: If a parent has children who rebel, then that parent must not have raised them right. Yet, a proverb is not a prophecy or a promise. It is a general principle that God will use the discipline and instruction of the parents to start their children off in the way they should go, and the children will continue on that path, or return to it, when they are old. As such, it is a message of hope, even if the child seems to be rebelling from God at any given time. Children will, as a general rule, take what they've learned and integrate it into their personal walks with God as they age. Fallen sinners can find confidence that, though their parenting may seem inadequate and flawed, God will often use this instruction to point children to the way of life everlasting. Also, parents can find hope that God can convict the rebellious and bring them to repentance in his time.

26 Be not one of those who give pledges,
who put up security for debts.
27 If you have nothing with which to pay,
why should your bed be taken from under you?
28 Do not move the ancient landmark
that your fathers have set.
29 Do you see a man skillful in his work?
He will stand before kings;
he will not stand before obscure men.

23 When you sit down to eat with a ruler,
observe carefully what[1] is before you,
2 and put a knife to your throat
if you are given to appetite.
3 Do not desire his delicacies,
for they are deceptive food.
4 Do not toil to acquire wealth;
be discerning enough to desist.
5 When your eyes light on it, it is gone,
for suddenly it sprouts wings,
flying like an eagle toward heaven.
6 Do not eat the bread of a man who is stingy;[2]
do not desire his delicacies,
7 for he is like one who is inwardly calculating.[3]
"Eat and drink!" he says to you,
but his heart is not with you.
8 You will vomit up the morsels that you have eaten,
and waste your pleasant words.
9 Do not speak in the hearing of a fool,
for he will despise the good sense of your words.
10 Do not move an ancient landmark
or enter the fields of the fatherless,
11 for their Redeemer is strong;
he will plead their cause against you.
12 Apply your heart to instruction
and your ear to words of knowledge.
13 Do not withhold discipline from a child;
if you strike him with a rod, he will not die.
14 If you strike him with the rod,
you will save his soul from Sheol.
15 My son, if your heart is wise,
my heart too will be glad.
16 My inmost being[4] will exult
when your lips speak what is right.
17 Let not your heart envy sinners,
but continue in the fear of the LORD all the day.
18 Surely there is a future,
and your hope will not be cut off.

19 Hear, my son, and be wise,
and direct your heart in the way.
20 Be not among drunkards[5]
or among gluttonous eaters of meat,
21 for the drunkard and the glutton will come to poverty,
and slumber will clothe them with rags.

[1]Or *who* [2]Hebrew *whose eye is evil* [3]Or *for as he calculates in his soul, so is he* [4]Hebrew *My kidneys*
[5]Hebrew *those who drink too much wine*

PROVERBS 23:4–5

CONTENTMENT

This passage joins a chorus of verses in Proverbs that urge a balance of diligence and contentment in life with what one has—rather than laziness or a workaholic craving for things that will not last. Jesus told a parable about a rich fool who focused entirely on acquiring and preserving his possessions, only to lose everything he had worked so hard for when he died (Lk 12:15–21). Hebrews gives a good perspective on the kind of contentment Proverbs urges: "Keep your life free from love of money, and be content with what you have, for he has said, 'I will never leave you nor forsake you.' So we can confidently say, 'The Lord is my helper; I will not fear; what can man do to me?'" (Heb 13:5–6). Believers do not ultimately look to money for help but to God. Trust Jesus and be content with what he has provided.

PROVERBS 23:19–21

GLUTTONS AND DRUNKARDS

Overindulgence in food and drink, a sin which runs rampant today, brings terrible consequences. These verses recall the law commanding that rebellious sons who were gluttons and drunkards were to be executed outside the city gates (Dt 21:18–21). Interestingly, Jesus' opponents accused him of violating this principle because he spent time with a disreputable crowd. Jesus said, "The Son of Man has come eating and drinking, and you say, 'Look at him! A glutton and a drunkard, a friend of tax collectors and sinners!'" (Lk 7:34). Jesus not only associated with gluttons and

(continued on next page)

22 Listen to your father who gave you life,
and do not despise your mother when she is old.
23 Buy truth, and do not sell it;
buy wisdom, instruction, and understanding.
24 The father of the righteous will greatly rejoice;
he who fathers a wise son will be glad in him.
25 Let your father and mother be glad;
let her who bore you rejoice.

26 My son, give me your heart,
and let your eyes observe[1] my ways.
27 For a prostitute is a deep pit;
an adulteress[2] is a narrow well.
28 She lies in wait like a robber
and increases the traitors among mankind.

29 Who has woe? Who has sorrow?
Who has strife? Who has complaining?
Who has wounds without cause?
Who has redness of eyes?
30 Those who tarry long over wine;
those who go to try mixed wine.
31 Do not look at wine when it is red,
when it sparkles in the cup
and goes down smoothly.
32 In the end it bites like a serpent
and stings like an adder.
33 Your eyes will see strange things,
and your heart utter perverse things.
34 You will be like one who lies down in the midst of the sea,
like one who lies on the top of a mast.[3]
35 "They struck me," you will say,[4] "but I was not hurt;
they beat me, but I did not feel it.
When shall I awake?
I must have another drink."

24 Be not envious of evil men,
nor desire to be with them,
2 for their hearts devise violence,
and their lips talk of trouble.

3 By wisdom a house is built,
and by understanding it is established;
4 by knowledge the rooms are filled
with all precious and pleasant riches.
5 A wise man is full of strength,
and a man of knowledge enhances his might,
6 for by wise guidance you can wage your war,
and in abundance of counselors there is victory.
7 Wisdom is too high for a fool;
in the gate he does not open his mouth.

8 Whoever plans to do evil
will be called a schemer.
9 The devising[5] of folly is sin,
and the scoffer is an abomination to mankind.

[1]Or *delight in* [2]Hebrew *a foreign woman* [3]Or *of the rigging* [4]Hebrew lacks *you will say*
[5]Or *scheming*

(Gluttons and Drunkards, continued)

drunkards, but he died the death that they should have suffered for sin. Jesus was executed outside the city gates (Heb 13:12)—condemned by the elders and hung on a pole, or tree, under the curse of God (Gal 3:13). His death provides forgiveness for all who lack self-control, and he gives his Spirit to produce fruit (including self-control) in the lives of his followers (Gal 5:22–23).

PROVERBS 24:30–34

LAZINESS AND SIN'S CURSE

Proverbs clearly says that laziness will lead to poverty, but laziness is not just a character defect that makes life a little more difficult. Laziness is a sin according to Proverbs. The lazy man has his field overgrown with thorns, which is a result of the curse on the ground because of Adam and Eve's sin (Ge 3:18). Paul also connected laziness with sin in 1 Timothy 5:8: "But if anyone does not provide for his relatives, and especially for members of his household, he has denied the faith and is worse than an unbeliever." The lack of a work ethic may be evidence of an insincere faith.

The good news is that Proverbs points to Jesus—the wisdom of God. During his time on earth, Jesus was a hard worker. Not only was he a carpenter, but he was supremely concerned with finishing the work the Father sent him to do. "My food," said Jesus, "is to do the will of him who sent me and to accomplish his work" (Jn 4:34). As Jesus was praying to his Father he said, "I glorified you on earth, having accomplished the work that you gave me to do" (Jn 17:4). Also, Hebrews 1:3 states that Jesus is at work right now sustaining the world. In addition to being an example of a wise man who works hard, Jesus also transforms those who believe in him into his image—which includes overcoming the sin of laziness and becoming diligent in doing good (Gal 6:9).

10 If you faint in the day of adversity,
your strength is small.
11 Rescue those who are being taken away to death;
hold back those who are stumbling to the slaughter.
12 If you say, "Behold, we did not know this,"
does not he who weighs the heart perceive it?
Does not he who keeps watch over your soul know it,
and will he not repay man according to his work?

13 My son, eat honey, for it is good,
and the drippings of the honeycomb are sweet to your taste.
14 Know that wisdom is such to your soul;
if you find it, there will be a future,
and your hope will not be cut off.

15 Lie not in wait as a wicked man against the dwelling of the righteous;
do no violence to his home;
16 for the righteous falls seven times and rises again,
but the wicked stumble in times of calamity.

17 Do not rejoice when your enemy falls,
and let not your heart be glad when he stumbles,
18 lest the LORD see it and be displeased,
and turn away his anger from him.

19 Fret not yourself because of evildoers,
and be not envious of the wicked,
20 for the evil man has no future;
the lamp of the wicked will be put out.

21 My son, fear the LORD and the king,
and do not join with those who do otherwise,
22 for disaster will arise suddenly from them,
and who knows the ruin that will come from them both?

More Sayings of the Wise

23 These also are sayings of the wise.

Partiality in judging is not good.
24 Whoever says to the wicked, "You are in the right,"
will be cursed by peoples, abhorred by nations,
25 but those who rebuke the wicked will have delight,
and a good blessing will come upon them.
26 Whoever gives an honest answer
kisses the lips.

27 Prepare your work outside;
get everything ready for yourself in the field,
and after that build your house.

28 Be not a witness against your neighbor without cause,
and do not deceive with your lips.
29 Do not say, "I will do to him as he has done to me;
I will pay the man back for what he has done."

30 I passed by the field of a sluggard,
by the vineyard of a man lacking sense,
31 and behold, it was all overgrown with thorns;
the ground was covered with nettles,
and its stone wall was broken down.
32 Then I saw and considered it;
I looked and received instruction.

33 A little sleep, a little slumber,
a little folding of the hands to rest,
34 and poverty will come upon you like a robber,
and want like an armed man.

More Proverbs of Solomon

25 These also are proverbs of Solomon which the men of Hezekiah king of Judah copied.

2 It is the glory of God to conceal things,
but the glory of kings is to search things out.
3 As the heavens for height, and the earth for depth,
so the heart of kings is unsearchable.
4 Take away the dross from the silver,
and the smith has material for a vessel;
5 take away the wicked from the presence of the king,
and his throne will be established in righteousness.
6 Do not put yourself forward in the king's presence
or stand in the place of the great,
7 for it is better to be told, "Come up here,"
than to be put lower in the presence of a noble.

What your eyes have seen
8 do not hastily bring into court,[1]
for[2] what will you do in the end,
when your neighbor puts you to shame?
9 Argue your case with your neighbor himself,
and do not reveal another's secret,
10 lest he who hears you bring shame upon you,
and your ill repute have no end.

11 A word fitly spoken
is like apples of gold in a setting of silver.
12 Like a gold ring or an ornament of gold
is a wise reprover to a listening ear.
13 Like the cold of snow in the time of harvest
is a faithful messenger to those who send him;
he refreshes the soul of his masters.
14 Like clouds and wind without rain
is a man who boasts of a gift he does not give.

15 With patience a ruler may be persuaded,
and a soft tongue will break a bone.
16 If you have found honey, eat only enough for you,
lest you have your fill of it and vomit it.
17 Let your foot be seldom in your neighbor's house,
lest he have his fill of you and hate you.
18 A man who bears false witness against his neighbor
is like a war club, or a sword, or a sharp arrow.
19 Trusting in a treacherous man in time of trouble
is like a bad tooth or a foot that slips.
20 Whoever sings songs to a heavy heart
is like one who takes off a garment on a cold day,
and like vinegar on soda.
21 If your enemy is hungry, give him bread to eat,
and if he is thirsty, give him water to drink,

[1]Or *presence of a noble, as your eyes have seen.* [8]*Do not go hastily out to court* [2]Hebrew *or else*

PROVERBS 25:21–22

DO GOOD TO ENEMIES

Paul quotes these verses in the context of teaching that the key to doing good to one's enemies is trusting God's justice (Ro 12:17–21). Often the biggest obstacle to releasing a grudge is the fear that it will unjustly discount how bad or hurtful certain actions were. Proverbs and Paul say that the way to let grudges go is by trusting that God will take care of it. Burning coals represent the pricking of the conscience of the wrongdoer, rather than responding in violence. Failing to forgive enemies indicates a lack of trust in the gospel. In effect, holding a grudge says, "The cross of Jesus Christ is enough to forgive the sins I commit against God, but it is not enough to forgive the sins committed against me."

God's people can experience freedom from grudges and do good toward their enemies for two reasons. First, there is a possibility that responding with goodness will open an enemy's heart to the gospel and bring about reconciliation. Second, believers can afford to suffer injustices temporarily knowing that God will someday judge the unrepentant. Trusting in the justice of God enabled Jesus to endure his suffering. The apostle Peter told believers, "To this you have been called, because Christ also suffered for you, leaving you an example, so that you might follow in his steps ... When he was reviled, he did not revile in return; when he suffered, he did not threaten, but continued entrusting himself to him who judges justly" (1Pe 2:21,23).

PROVERBS 26:4–5

ANSWERING A FOOL

These verses do not contradict one another. They should be read together. The point is to teach discernment. In some cases, fools are not worth correcting if answering them requires stooping to their level. In other cases, fools should be corrected, particularly if there is a possibility that answering them will clarify for them the difference between wisdom and their folly. Wisdom is the discernment to know when to answer and when not to answer.

Jesus amazed people with this ability. He knew when a reply would do no good, and in those situations he chose to stay silent. And he knew when to offer correction. He knew exactly how to respond or not respond. Jesus answered the Pharisees' challenge about the disciples not washing their hands (Mt 15:1–9), and he rebuked Peter's assertion that the notion of Jesus suffering and dying was inconceivable and wrong (Mt 16:23). But he also refused to play the chief priests' game about where Jesus' authority came from (Mt 21:23–27), and he remained silent at his trial (Mk 15:5). Jesus grew in wisdom (Lk 2:52), which involved developing the ability to read people and situations. And the Spirit produces this Christ-like wisdom in Jesus' followers.

22 for you will heap burning coals on his head,
and the LORD will reward you.
23 The north wind brings forth rain,
and a backbiting tongue, angry looks.
24 It is better to live in a corner of the housetop
than in a house shared with a quarrelsome wife.
25 Like cold water to a thirsty soul,
so is good news from a far country.
26 Like a muddied spring or a polluted fountain
is a righteous man who gives way before the wicked.
27 It is not good to eat much honey,
nor is it glorious to seek one's own glory.[1]
28 A man without self-control
is like a city broken into and left without walls.

26 Like snow in summer or rain in harvest,
so honor is not fitting for a fool.
2 Like a sparrow in its flitting, like a swallow in its flying,
a curse that is causeless does not alight.
3 A whip for the horse, a bridle for the donkey,
and a rod for the back of fools.
4 Answer not a fool according to his folly,
lest you be like him yourself.
5 Answer a fool according to his folly,
lest he be wise in his own eyes.
6 Whoever sends a message by the hand of a fool
cuts off his own feet and drinks violence.
7 Like a lame man's legs, which hang useless,
is a proverb in the mouth of fools.
8 Like one who binds the stone in the sling
is one who gives honor to a fool.
9 Like a thorn that goes up into the hand of a drunkard
is a proverb in the mouth of fools.
10 Like an archer who wounds everyone
is one who hires a passing fool or drunkard.[2]
11 Like a dog that returns to his vomit
is a fool who repeats his folly.
12 Do you see a man who is wise in his own eyes?
There is more hope for a fool than for him.
13 The sluggard says, "There is a lion in the road!
There is a lion in the streets!"
14 As a door turns on its hinges,
so does a sluggard on his bed.
15 The sluggard buries his hand in the dish;
it wears him out to bring it back to his mouth.
16 The sluggard is wiser in his own eyes
than seven men who can answer sensibly.
17 Whoever meddles in a quarrel not his own
is like one who takes a passing dog by the ears.
18 Like a madman who throws firebrands, arrows, and death
19 is the man who deceives his neighbor
and says, "I am only joking!"
20 For lack of wood the fire goes out,
and where there is no whisperer, quarreling ceases.
21 As charcoal to hot embers and wood to fire,
so is a quarrelsome man for kindling strife.

[1]The meaning of the Hebrew line is uncertain [2]Or *hires a fool or passersby*

22 The words of a whisperer are like delicious morsels;
they go down into the inner parts of the body.
23 Like the glaze[1] covering an earthen vessel
are fervent lips with an evil heart.
24 Whoever hates disguises himself with his lips
and harbors deceit in his heart;
25 when he speaks graciously, believe him not,
for there are seven abominations in his heart;
26 though his hatred be covered with deception,
his wickedness will be exposed in the assembly.
27 Whoever digs a pit will fall into it,
and a stone will come back on him who starts it rolling.
28 A lying tongue hates its victims,
and a flattering mouth works ruin.

27 Do not boast about tomorrow,
for you do not know what a day may bring.
2 Let another praise you, and not your own mouth;
a stranger, and not your own lips.
3 A stone is heavy, and sand is weighty,
but a fool's provocation is heavier than both.
4 Wrath is cruel, anger is overwhelming,
but who can stand before jealousy?
5 Better is open rebuke
than hidden love.
6 Faithful are the wounds of a friend;
profuse are the kisses of an enemy.
7 One who is full loathes honey,
but to one who is hungry everything bitter is sweet.
8 Like a bird that strays from its nest
is a man who strays from his home.
9 Oil and perfume make the heart glad,
and the sweetness of a friend comes from his earnest counsel.[2]
10 Do not forsake your friend and your father's friend,
and do not go to your brother's house in the day of your calamity.
Better is a neighbor who is near
than a brother who is far away.
11 Be wise, my son, and make my heart glad,
that I may answer him who reproaches me.
12 The prudent sees danger and hides himself,
but the simple go on and suffer for it.
13 Take a man's garment when he has put up security for a stranger,
and hold it in pledge when he puts up security for an adulteress.[3]
14 Whoever blesses his neighbor with a loud voice,
rising early in the morning,
will be counted as cursing.
15 A continual dripping on a rainy day
and a quarrelsome wife are alike;
16 to restrain her is to restrain the wind
or to grasp[4] oil in one's right hand.
17 Iron sharpens iron,
and one man sharpens another.[5]
18 Whoever tends a fig tree will eat its fruit,
and he who guards his master will be honored.

[1]By revocalization; Hebrew *silver of dross* [2]Or *and so does the sweetness of a friend that comes from his earnest counsel* [3]Hebrew *a foreign woman*; a slight emendation yields (compare Vulgate; see also 20:16) *foreigners* [4]Hebrew *to meet with* [5]Hebrew *sharpens the face of another*

PROVERBS 27:5–6

OPEN REBUKE

Pushing against the grain of modern culture's "can't we all just get along" mentality, these verses say that having a friend who will tell the truth is valuable—even when that truth is difficult or unwelcome. In fact, people who only tell their acquaintances what they want to hear are not friends but enemies. These verses point to the gospel of Jesus Christ, not only because Jesus was kissed by an enemy masquerading as a friend (Mt 26:49), but also because the cross of Christ is meant to transform the daily lives of believers. If God's people really believe what Scripture says about the cross, then they can both give and receive a rebuke without getting angry. The cross reveals that all people are sinners, so believers should be able to accept a friend's correction. Believers in the cross find comfort not in delusional self-righteousness but in the knowledge that Christ paid the penalty for their sins!

19 As in water face reflects face,
so the heart of man reflects the man.
20 Sheol and Abaddon are never satisfied,
and never satisfied are the eyes of man.
21 The crucible is for silver, and the furnace is for gold,
and a man is tested by his praise.
22 Crush a fool in a mortar with a pestle
along with crushed grain,
yet his folly will not depart from him.

23 Know well the condition of your flocks,
and give attention to your herds,
24 for riches do not last forever;
and does a crown endure to all generations?
25 When the grass is gone and the new growth appears
and the vegetation of the mountains is gathered,
26 the lambs will provide your clothing,
and the goats the price of a field.
27 There will be enough goats' milk for your food,
for the food of your household
and maintenance for your girls.

28 The wicked flee when no one pursues,
but the righteous are bold as a lion.
2 When a land transgresses, it has many rulers,
but with a man of understanding and knowledge,
its stability will long continue.
3 A poor man who oppresses the poor
is a beating rain that leaves no food.
4 Those who forsake the law praise the wicked,
but those who keep the law strive against them.
5 Evil men do not understand justice,
but those who seek the LORD understand it completely.
6 Better is a poor man who walks in his integrity
than a rich man who is crooked in his ways.
7 The one who keeps the law is a son with understanding,
but a companion of gluttons shames his father.
8 Whoever multiplies his wealth by interest and profit[1]
gathers it for him who is generous to the poor.
9 If one turns away his ear from hearing the law,
even his prayer is an abomination.
10 Whoever misleads the upright into an evil way
will fall into his own pit,
but the blameless will have a goodly inheritance.
11 A rich man is wise in his own eyes,
but a poor man who has understanding will find him out.
12 When the righteous triumph, there is great glory,
but when the wicked rise, people hide themselves.
13 Whoever conceals his transgressions will not prosper,
but he who confesses and forsakes them will obtain mercy.
14 Blessed is the one who fears the LORD[2] always,
but whoever hardens his heart will fall into calamity.
15 Like a roaring lion or a charging bear
is a wicked ruler over a poor people.
16 A ruler who lacks understanding is a cruel oppressor,
but he who hates unjust gain will prolong his days.

[1]That is, profit that comes from charging interest to the poor [2]Hebrew lacks *the LORD*

17 If one is burdened with the blood of another,
he will be a fugitive until death;[1]
let no one help him.
18 Whoever walks in integrity will be delivered,
but he who is crooked in his ways will suddenly fall.
19 Whoever works his land will have plenty of bread,
but he who follows worthless pursuits will have plenty of poverty.
20 A faithful man will abound with blessings,
but whoever hastens to be rich will not go unpunished.
21 To show partiality is not good,
but for a piece of bread a man will do wrong.
22 A stingy man[2] hastens after wealth
and does not know that poverty will come upon him.
23 Whoever rebukes a man will afterward find more favor
than he who flatters with his tongue.
24 Whoever robs his father or his mother
and says, "That is no transgression,"
is a companion to a man who destroys.
25 A greedy man stirs up strife,
but the one who trusts in the LORD will be enriched.
26 Whoever trusts in his own mind is a fool,
but he who walks in wisdom will be delivered.
27 Whoever gives to the poor will not want,
but he who hides his eyes will get many a curse.
28 When the wicked rise, people hide themselves,
but when they perish, the righteous increase.

29 He who is often reproved, yet stiffens his neck,
will suddenly be broken beyond healing.
2 When the righteous increase, the people rejoice,
but when the wicked rule, the people groan.
3 He who loves wisdom makes his father glad,
but a companion of prostitutes squanders his wealth.
4 By justice a king builds up the land,
but he who exacts gifts[3] tears it down.
5 A man who flatters his neighbor
spreads a net for his feet.
6 An evil man is ensnared in his transgression,
but a righteous man sings and rejoices.
7 A righteous man knows the rights of the poor;
a wicked man does not understand such knowledge.
8 Scoffers set a city aflame,
but the wise turn away wrath.
9 If a wise man has an argument with a fool,
the fool only rages and laughs, and there is no quiet.
10 Bloodthirsty men hate one who is blameless
and seek the life of the upright.[4]
11 A fool gives full vent to his spirit,
but a wise man quietly holds it back.
12 If a ruler listens to falsehood,
all his officials will be wicked.
13 The poor man and the oppressor meet together;
the LORD gives light to the eyes of both.
14 If a king faithfully judges the poor,
his throne will be established forever.

[1]Hebrew *until the pit* [2]Hebrew *A man whose eye is evil* [3]Or *who taxes heavily* [4]Or *but the upright seek his soul*

PROVERBS 28:27

GENEROSITY TO THE POOR

Generosity to the poor is a central concern of the book of Proverbs. Strikingly, this verse asserts that giving money away leads not to poverty but rather ensures that the giver "will not want." The wisdom of God goes against the grain of human wisdom, which often promotes hoarding as the only way to guarantee sufficient resources. The Lord will bless a lifestyle of generosity, but he will curse those who ignore the poor.

The wisdom of Proverbs finds its fulfillment in Jesus of Nazareth, who at the outset of his ministry said, "The Spirit of the Lord is upon me, because he has anointed me to proclaim good news to the poor" (Lk 4:18). Jesus modeled for believers a generous lifestyle and also grants them the ability to be generous in sharing the gospel, which is true spiritual wealth. Paul wrote, "For you know the grace of our Lord Jesus Christ, that though he was rich, yet for your sake he became poor, so that you by his poverty might become rich" (2Co 8:9). When people believe the good news that Christ gave up everything for them so that they could be co-heirs and receive everything with him, they are enabled to hold loosely to their possessions and give them away to others.

PROVERBS 29:14

ETERNAL KINGDOM

The proverbs of Solomon referred to a faithful king who would establish an eternal kingdom. A key characteristic of this ideal king was fair treatment of the poor. This principle

(continued on next page)

(Eternal Kingdom, continued)

connects up with God's promise to David that one of his descendants would establish a kingdom that lasts forever (2Sa 7:12–16). The problem was that Solomon and the rest of David's descendants leading up to the time of Christ failed. Not one of them was the ideal king. Yet these disappointments only increased the expectation that someday a son of David would be the ideal king and establish an eternal kingdom. Isaiah 11:1–5 described that future king as the embodiment of Proverbs who is anointed with the Spirit of wisdom. The New Testament presents Jesus of Nazareth as that King. He is the Son of David who came ministering to the poor, and he was given the kingdom of David (Lk 1:32).

15 The rod and reproof give wisdom,
but a child left to himself brings shame to his mother.
16 When the wicked increase, transgression increases,
but the righteous will look upon their downfall.
17 Discipline your son, and he will give you rest;
he will give delight to your heart.
18 Where there is no prophetic vision the people cast off restraint,[1]
but blessed is he who keeps the law.
19 By mere words a servant is not disciplined,
for though he understands, he will not respond.
20 Do you see a man who is hasty in his words?
There is more hope for a fool than for him.
21 Whoever pampers his servant from childhood
will in the end find him his heir.[2]
22 A man of wrath stirs up strife,
and one given to anger causes much transgression.
23 One's pride will bring him low,
but he who is lowly in spirit will obtain honor.
24 The partner of a thief hates his own life;
he hears the curse, but discloses nothing.
25 The fear of man lays a snare,
but whoever trusts in the LORD is safe.
26 Many seek the face of a ruler,
but it is from the LORD that a man gets justice.
27 An unjust man is an abomination to the righteous,
but one whose way is straight is an abomination to the wicked.

The Words of Agur

30 The words of Agur son of Jakeh. The oracle.[3]

The man declares, I am weary, O God;
I am weary, O God, and worn out.[4]
2 Surely I am too stupid to be a man.
I have not the understanding of a man.
3 I have not learned wisdom,
nor have I knowledge of the Holy One.
4 Who has ascended to heaven and come down?
Who has gathered the wind in his fists?
Who has wrapped up the waters in a garment?
Who has established all the ends of the earth?
What is his name, and what is his son's name?
Surely you know!

5 Every word of God proves true;
he is a shield to those who take refuge in him.
6 Do not add to his words,
lest he rebuke you and you be found a liar.

7 Two things I ask of you;
deny them not to me before I die:
8 Remove far from me falsehood and lying;
give me neither poverty nor riches;
feed me with the food that is needful for me,
9 lest I be full and deny you
and say, "Who is the LORD?"

[1]Or *the people are discouraged* [2]The meaning of the Hebrew word rendered *his heir* is uncertain
[3]Or *Jakeh, the man of Massa* [4]Revocalization; Hebrew *The man declares to Ithiel, to Ithiel and Ucal*

THE WISE SON OF GOD

The author of this passage was Agur, the son of Jakeh. This man's exact identity remains unknown because this is the only place he is mentioned in the Bible, but clearly he was a follower of God. He started the passage by claiming to be ignorant and unwise (vv. 2 – 3). He confessed that he was limited in terms of his wisdom. Wisdom begins with God, and Agur's problem was that he did not have access to God in heaven. Humanity is limited because they cannot go up to heaven and come down. No human has the wisdom to create the world or hold the wind, so they have no access to true wisdom. Agur asked a series of rhetorical questions to indicate that humanity's wisdom is limited; Agur implies that true wisdom belongs to the Almighty Creator — and *his son* (v. 4).

No human has gone up to heaven and come back down. No human can gather the wind in his fist. No human created the world. However, we read this passage from a different vantage point than Agur. Agur asked the name of the son, but he did not know what it was. We know it — Jesus Christ. We know that Jesus is the God-Man who came down from heaven as wisdom for us. In a roundabout way, Jesus answered Agur's question in his conversation with Nicodemus. He said, "No one has ascended into heaven except he who descended from heaven, the Son of Man" (Jn 3:13). So, God's Son has access to God's wisdom, and in the goodness of God, he sent his Son to earth to make people wise!

Where should people look for that wisdom? Agur answered that question in the next two verses. They should look to the Word of God and refrain from adding to it or taking away from it because "every word of God proves true" (Pr 30:5). Jesus is not just the Son of God; Jesus is the Word of God made flesh (Jn 1:1 – 14). Look to Jesus and his Word for the wisdom of God.

or lest I be poor and steal
and profane the name of my God.

10 Do not slander a servant to his master,
lest he curse you, and you be held guilty.

11 There are those[1] who curse their fathers
and do not bless their mothers.
12 There are those who are clean in their own eyes
but are not washed of their filth.
13 There are those—how lofty are their eyes,
how high their eyelids lift!
14 There are those whose teeth are swords,
whose fangs are knives,
to devour the poor from off the earth,
the needy from among mankind.

15 The leech has two daughters:
Give and Give.[2]
Three things are never satisfied;
four never say, "Enough":
16 Sheol, the barren womb,
the land never satisfied with water,
and the fire that never says, "Enough."

17 The eye that mocks a father
and scorns to obey a mother
will be picked out by the ravens of the valley
and eaten by the vultures.

18 Three things are too wonderful for me;
four I do not understand:
19 the way of an eagle in the sky,
the way of a serpent on a rock,
the way of a ship on the high seas,
and the way of a man with a virgin.

20 This is the way of an adulteress:
she eats and wipes her mouth
and says, "I have done no wrong."

21 Under three things the earth trembles;
under four it cannot bear up:
22 a slave when he becomes king,
and a fool when he is filled with food;
23 an unloved woman when she gets a husband,
and a maidservant when she displaces her mistress.

24 Four things on earth are small,
but they are exceedingly wise:
25 the ants are a people not strong,
yet they provide their food in the summer;
26 the rock badgers are a people not mighty,
yet they make their homes in the cliffs;
27 the locusts have no king,
yet all of them march in rank;
28 the lizard you can take in your hands,
yet it is in kings' palaces.

29 Three things are stately in their tread;
four are stately in their stride:

[1]Hebrew *There is a generation*; also verses 12, 13, 14 [2]Or *"Give, give," they cry*

30 the lion, which is mightiest among beasts
and does not turn back before any;
31 the strutting rooster,[1] the he-goat,
and a king whose army is with him.[2]

32 If you have been foolish, exalting yourself,
or if you have been devising evil,
put your hand on your mouth.
33 For pressing milk produces curds,
pressing the nose produces blood,
and pressing anger produces strife.

The Words of King Lemuel

31 The words of King Lemuel. An oracle that his mother taught him:

2 What are you doing, my son?[3] What are you doing, son of my womb?
What are you doing, son of my vows?
3 Do not give your strength to women,
your ways to those who destroy kings.
4 It is not for kings, O Lemuel,
it is not for kings to drink wine,
or for rulers to take strong drink,
5 lest they drink and forget what has been decreed
and pervert the rights of all the afflicted.
6 Give strong drink to the one who is perishing,
and wine to those in bitter distress;[4]
7 let them drink and forget their poverty
and remember their misery no more.
8 Open your mouth for the mute,
for the rights of all who are destitute.[5]
9 Open your mouth, judge righteously,
defend the rights of the poor and needy.

The Woman Who Fears the Lord

10[6] An excellent wife who can find?
She is far more precious than jewels.
11 The heart of her husband trusts in her,
and he will have no lack of gain.
12 She does him good, and not harm,
all the days of her life.
13 She seeks wool and flax,
and works with willing hands.
14 She is like the ships of the merchant;
she brings her food from afar.
15 She rises while it is yet night
and provides food for her household
and portions for her maidens.
16 She considers a field and buys it;
with the fruit of her hands she plants a vineyard.
17 She dresses herself[7] with strength
and makes her arms strong.
18 She perceives that her merchandise is profitable.
Her lamp does not go out at night.

[1] Or *the magpie*, or *the greyhound*; Hebrew *girt-of-loins* [2] Or *against whom there is no rising up* [3] Hebrew *What, my son?* [4] Hebrew *those bitter in soul* [5] Hebrew *are sons of passing away* [6] Verses 10–31 are an acrostic poem, each verse beginning with the successive letters of the Hebrew alphabet [7] Hebrew *She girds her loins*

19 She puts her hands to the distaff,
and her hands hold the spindle.
20 She opens her hand to the poor
and reaches out her hands to the needy.
21 She is not afraid of snow for her household,
for all her household are clothed in scarlet.[1]
22 She makes bed coverings for herself;
her clothing is fine linen and purple.
23 Her husband is known in the gates
when he sits among the elders of the land.
24 She makes linen garments and sells them;
she delivers sashes to the merchant.
25 Strength and dignity are her clothing,
and she laughs at the time to come.
26 She opens her mouth with wisdom,
and the teaching of kindness is on her tongue.
27 She looks well to the ways of her household
and does not eat the bread of idleness.
28 Her children rise up and call her blessed;
her husband also, and he praises her:
29 "Many women have done excellently,
but you surpass them all."
30 Charm is deceitful, and beauty is vain,
but a woman who fears the LORD is to be praised.
31 Give her of the fruit of her hands,
and let her works praise her in the gates.

[1]Or *in double thickness*

JESUS: OUR TRUE HOPE

ECCLESIASTES

ECCLESIASTES

REIGN OF DAVID	REIGN OF SOLOMON	FALL OF JUDAH
c. 1010 – 970 BC	*c. 970 – 930 BC*	*c. 586 BC*

Meaningless. This is the conclusion of Solomon, traditionally assumed to be the author of Ecclesiastes, regarding life in this world. Everything is meaningless.

Solomon could make this claim because he *had* everything. First, Solomon considered the outcome of pursuing wisdom (1:12 – 18). Having received wisdom as a gift from God, Solomon was uniquely able to assess the result of searching for knowledge apart from God. He described it as madness and folly, "a striving after wind" (1:17). His assessment was that no matter how much wisdom humankind possesses, it is ultimately futile compared to God's wisdom and his plans.

Up next was the pursuit of pleasure (2:1 – 11). Though Solomon could have had anything his heart desired, and pursued these pleasures with perfect wisdom, nothing that he found satisfied his heart for the long term. Pleasures, too, were meaningless. Solomon also assessed the work of his hands (2:17 – 26). This toil, although a good and meaningful aspect of human existence, led to frustration and failure, grief and pain. Even his youthful aspirations for advancement were meaningless for Solomon (4:13 – 16). A man renowned throughout the world for his wealth, Solomon determined that riches were futile as well (5:8 – 20).

The meaninglessness and brevity of life forced Solomon to conclude that life under the sun, no matter how well lived, is not enough. The best humankind can do is eat, drink, and find enjoyment in life with those they love (2:24 – 25). Throughout the book, Solomon shares proverbial wisdom for how to honor God and obey him in this life. These exhortations, no matter how true, can sound hollow for modern readers in light of the overall depressive tone of the book.

Solomon's conclusion forces readers of Ecclesiastes to look beyond this life for the ultimate hope for human existence. No human experience — not wealth, power, success, wisdom, or relationships — will ever satisfy the longing of the human heart. Only Jesus can provide what nothing on this earth can deliver. Those saved by Jesus' work are then sent back into the world with newfound vitality. Life remains toilsome, frustrating, and fraught with failure, but Jesus gives meaning and mission to those who will believe and trust in him for their salvation. These people can have hope in the midst of a broken world, knowing they are loved by God and secure for all eternity. They do not have to follow the path of this world and seek fulfillment in things that will always leave them empty. Instead, God's children can find meaning in worshiping God and in giving their lives away to his mission in the world.

FOR EVERYTHING THERE IS A SEASON,
AND A TIME FOR EVERY MATTER
UNDER HEAVEN.

Ecclesiastes 3:1

ECCLESIASTES

All Is Vanity

1 The words of the Preacher,[1] the son of David, king in Jerusalem.

2 Vanity[2] of vanities, says the Preacher,
vanity of vanities! All is vanity.
3 What does man gain by all the toil
at which he toils under the sun?
4 A generation goes, and a generation comes,
but the earth remains forever.
5 The sun rises, and the sun goes down,
and hastens[3] to the place where it rises.
6 The wind blows to the south
and goes around to the north;
around and around goes the wind,
and on its circuits the wind returns.
7 All streams run to the sea,
but the sea is not full;
to the place where the streams flow,
there they flow again.
8 All things are full of weariness;
a man cannot utter it;
the eye is not satisfied with seeing,
nor the ear filled with hearing.
9 What has been is what will be,
and what has been done is what will be done,
and there is nothing new under the sun.
10 Is there a thing of which it is said,
"See, this is new"?
It has been already
in the ages before us.
11 There is no remembrance of former things,[4]
nor will there be any remembrance
of later things[5] yet to be
among those who come after.

The Vanity of Wisdom

12 I the Preacher have been king over Israel in Jerusalem. 13 And I applied my
heart[6] to seek and to search out by wisdom all that is done under heaven. It is an
unhappy business that God has given to the children of man to be busy with. 14 I
have seen everything that is done under the sun, and behold, all is vanity[7] and a
striving after wind.[8]

15 What is crooked cannot be made straight,
and what is lacking cannot be counted.

16 I said in my heart, "I have acquired great wisdom, surpassing all who were

---

[1]Or *Convener*, or *Collector*; Hebrew *Qoheleth* (so throughout Ecclesiastes) [2]The Hebrew term *hebel*, translated *vanity* or *vain*, refers concretely to a "mist," "vapor," or "mere breath," and metaphorically to something that is fleeting or elusive (with different nuances depending on the context). It appears five times in this verse and in 29 other verses in Ecclesiastes [3]Or *and returns panting* [4]Or *former people* [5]Or *later people* [6]The Hebrew term denotes the center of one's inner life, including mind, will, and emotions [7]The Hebrew term *hebel* can refer to a "vapor" or "mere breath" (see note on 1:2) [8]Or *a feeding on wind*; compare Hosea 12:1 (also in Ecclesiastes 1:17; 2:11, 17, 26; 4:4, 6, 16; 6:9)

THE SEARCH FOR MEANING

In Hebrew, repeating the same word makes that word a superlative — it indicates incomparability. For example, doubling the word "holy" to describe the inner chamber of the tabernacle or temple emphasizes that this room was the "Most Holy " Place (Ex 26:33). In the same way, when Solomon, traditionally assumed to be the author of Ecclesiastes, wrote that everything is "vanity" he was claiming that life is utterly futile, without purpose or worth. Why would he make such a terrible claim?

The Hebrew word *hebel,* translated as "vanity" in this passage, literally means "vapor" or "breath." It resonates with other Scripture passages that emphasize the inherent worthlessness of things that do not last, from the temporary lives of mortals, to idols and false worship practices (1Ki 16:13; Job 7:16; Ps 35:5; Isa 57:13). As James 4:14 says, "You are a mist that appears for a little time and then vanishes." Sin transformed human life into suffering and death. And it was in the course of wrestling with this reality that Solomon cried out, "Everything is vanity"!

Yet, Scripture does not teach that human lives are without meaning. Despite its dark tone, this book presses toward hope by asking readers to ponder where meaning could come from. If death is the final destination for every human regardless of how one has lived, does any of it really matter (Ecc 9:2 – 6)? What can bring true, lasting value to a human's short, vapor-like existence?

Thankfully, Jesus came and gave everyone the opportunity to seek fulfillment beyond his or her own life. While life here on earth would be meaningless in and of itself, Jesus says that humans are made for more than this sinful world (Jn 15:19). Jesus calls everyone to seek eternal life, as opposed to the meaninglessness of an earthly life disconnected from God. First John 2:25 says, "And this is the promise that he made to us — eternal life." The meaninglessness that Solomon referred to is life under the burdensome limits of sin and death. But those who follow Jesus will receive the resurrection of the body and eternal life. This new life in Christ brings genuine meaning — and every Christian's hope of eternity infuses temporal life with renewed purpose.

No one has to look for fulfillment in this broken, fleeting world. Jesus reaches out to mortal humans — whose lives are like vapor — and offers them eternal life with him. Believers today can be encouraged by the knowledge that an eternity with Jesus is anything but meaningless.

over Jerusalem before me, and my heart has had great experience of wisdom and
knowledge." 17 And I applied my heart to know wisdom and to know madness and
folly. I perceived that this also is but a striving after wind.

18 For in much wisdom is much vexation,
and he who increases knowledge increases sorrow.

The Vanity of Self-Indulgence

2 I said in my heart, "Come now, I will test you with pleasure; enjoy yourself."
But behold, this also was vanity.[1] 2 I said of laughter, "It is mad," and of pleasure, "What use is it?" 3 I searched with my heart how to cheer my body with
wine—my heart still guiding me with wisdom—and how to lay hold on folly, till
I might see what was good for the children of man to do under heaven during the
few days of their life. 4 I made great works. I built houses and planted vineyards
for myself. 5 I made myself gardens and parks, and planted in them all kinds of
fruit trees. 6 I made myself pools from which to water the forest of growing trees. 7 I
bought male and female slaves, and had slaves who were born in my house. I had
also great possessions of herds and flocks, more than any who had been before
me in Jerusalem. 8 I also gathered for myself silver and gold and the treasure of
kings and provinces. I got singers, both men and women, and many concubines,[2]
the delight of the sons of man.

9 So I became great and surpassed all who were before me in Jerusalem. Also
my wisdom remained with me. 10 And whatever my eyes desired I did not keep
from them. I kept my heart from no pleasure, for my heart found pleasure in all my
toil, and this was my reward for all my toil. 11 Then I considered all that my hands
had done and the toil I had expended in doing it, and behold, all was vanity and a
striving after wind, and there was nothing to be gained under the sun.

The Vanity of Living Wisely

12 So I turned to consider wisdom and madness and folly. For what can the man
do who comes after the king? Only what has already been done. 13 Then I saw that
there is more gain in wisdom than in folly, as there is more gain in light than in
darkness. 14 The wise person has his eyes in his head, but the fool walks in darkness. And yet I perceived that the same event happens to all of them. 15 Then I said
in my heart, "What happens to the fool will happen to me also. Why then have I
been so very wise?" And I said in my heart that this also is vanity. 16 For of the wise
as of the fool there is no enduring remembrance, seeing that in the days to come
all will have been long forgotten. How the wise dies just like the fool! 17 So I hated
life, because what is done under the sun was grievous to me, for all is vanity and
a striving after wind.

The Vanity of Toil

18 I hated all my toil in which I toil under the sun, seeing that I must leave it to
the man who will come after me, 19 and who knows whether he will be wise or a
fool? Yet he will be master of all for which I toiled and used my wisdom under the
sun. This also is vanity. 20 So I turned about and gave my heart up to despair over
all the toil of my labors under the sun, 21 because sometimes a person who has
toiled with wisdom and knowledge and skill must leave everything to be enjoyed
by someone who did not toil for it. This also is vanity and a great evil. 22 What has
a man from all the toil and striving of heart with which he toils beneath the sun?
23 For all his days are full of sorrow, and his work is a vexation. Even in the night
his heart does not rest. This also is vanity.

24 There is nothing better for a person than that he should eat and drink and
find enjoyment[3] in his toil. This also, I saw, is from the hand of God, 25 for apart

[1] The Hebrew term *hebel* can refer to a "vapor" or "mere breath"; also verses 11, 15, 17, 19, 21, 23, 26 (see note on 1:2) [2] The meaning of the Hebrew word is uncertain [3] Or *and make his soul see good*

ECCLESIASTES 1:18

WITH MUCH WISDOM COMES MUCH SORROW

In verse 18, Solomon lamented the fact that his great wisdom and knowledge had brought him great sorrow and grief. He was not alone in this feeling. In Matthew 26:38, Jesus talked about his soul being deeply grieved. That sorrow was rooted in the knowledge that God had given him. Jesus knew what it was going to take to save humankind. He knew the price of sin would be his own life, and this knowledge weighed heavily on his heart. Yet, Jesus did not let sorrow overtake him. He stayed the course, remaining obedient to the point of death on the cross (Php 2:8). Even though his knowledge and wisdom brought him grief—about the world's sin and the price he would pay on the cross to overcome sin—he gave his life so that believers could experience the joy of a relationship with him. Though wisdom may bring sorrow, knowing Jesus brings ultimate joy.

from him[1] who can eat or who can have enjoyment? 26For to the one who pleases
him God has given wisdom and knowledge and joy, but to the sinner he has given
the business of gathering and collecting, only to give to one who pleases God. This
also is vanity and a striving after wind.

A Time for Everything

3 For everything there is a season, and a time for every matter under heaven:

2 a time to be born, and a time to die;
a time to plant, and a time to pluck up what is planted;
3 a time to kill, and a time to heal;
a time to break down, and a time to build up;
4 a time to weep, and a time to laugh;
a time to mourn, and a time to dance;
5 a time to cast away stones, and a time to gather stones together;
a time to embrace, and a time to refrain from embracing;
6 a time to seek, and a time to lose;
a time to keep, and a time to cast away;
7 a time to tear, and a time to sew;
a time to keep silence, and a time to speak;
8 a time to love, and a time to hate;
a time for war, and a time for peace.

The God-Given Task

9What gain has the worker from his toil? 10I have seen the business that God
has given to the children of man to be busy with. 11He has made everything beautiful in its time. Also, he has put eternity into man's heart, yet so that he cannot
find out what God has done from the beginning to the end. 12I perceived that there
is nothing better for them than to be joyful and to do good as long as they live;
13also that everyone should eat and drink and take pleasure in all his toil—this is
God's gift to man.
14I perceived that whatever God does endures forever; nothing can be added
to it, nor anything taken from it. God has done it, so that people fear before him.
15That which is, already has been; that which is to be, already has been; and God
seeks what has been driven away.[2]

From Dust to Dust

16Moreover, I saw under the sun that in the place of justice, even there was
wickedness, and in the place of righteousness, even there was wickedness. 17I said
in my heart, God will judge the righteous and the wicked, for there is a time for
every matter and for every work. 18I said in my heart with regard to the children
of man that God is testing them that they may see that they themselves are but
beasts. 19For what happens to the children of man and what happens to the beasts
is the same; as one dies, so dies the other. They all have the same breath, and
man has no advantage over the beasts, for all is vanity.[3] 20All go to one place. All
are from the dust, and to dust all return. 21Who knows whether the spirit of man
goes upward and the spirit of the beast goes down into the earth? 22So I saw that
there is nothing better than that a man should rejoice in his work, for that is his
lot. Who can bring him to see what will be after him?

Evil Under the Sun

4 Again I saw all the oppressions that are done under the sun. And behold, the
tears of the oppressed, and they had no one to comfort them! On the side of
their oppressors there was power, and there was no one to comfort them. 2And

ECCLESIASTES 3:11

ETERNAL LIFE

Ecclesiastes tells us that God has "put eternity into man's heart." Humans are created in the image of God (Ge 1:27), and God lives in eternity (Rev 1:8). Solomon poses the idea that humans have an innate desire in their hearts for something beyond their earthly lives. Humans were not made to live, die, and cease existing. Something about how God designed humans makes them stretch toward the eternal God. Scripture eventually reveals that humans were made to live eternally with God. It is natural for our hearts to feel as if there has to be something more—because there *is* something more. John 3:16 and 1 John 2:25 both confirm that God promises eternal life to those who believe. The reason eternity is so appealing to humans is because that is exactly what God created humans for in the first place—to live in relationship with eternal God himself.

[1]Some Hebrew manuscripts, Septuagint, Syriac; most Hebrew manuscripts *apart from me* [2]Hebrew *what has been pursued* [3]The Hebrew term *hebel* can refer to a "vapor" or "mere breath" (see note on 1:2)

TIME

Ecclesiastes 3 starts with the reassurance that there is a time for everything. If there was anything that Solomon was sure of, it was that God is the sovereign ruler over everything. Birth and death, love and hate, war and peace all have their own time under God's control. Amidst chapters that seem to question the meaningfulness of the universe itself, Solomon assured his readers that God remains completely sovereign over everything that happens under the sun.

Jesus was also aware of the truth that there is a time for everything. Early in Jesus' ministry, he attended a wedding in Cana. As the celebration progressed, the host ran out of wine. Jesus' mother asked him to help, but he responded by saying, "My hour has not yet come" (Jn 2:4). Jesus ended up turning water into wine, his first miracle recorded in Scripture. But it is interesting to note that he was not eager to perform a miracle and draw attention to himself. The wedding in Cana was not the only instance where Jesus tried to maintain a low profile. On multiple occasions Jesus performed a miracle and then instructed people not to spread the word about him (Mt 8:2 – 4; 9:29 – 30; Mk 1:40 – 45; 5:21 – 43; Lk 5:13 – 16). Jesus understood that after he performed miracles for people they would want to tell everyone about him — but he also knew that there was a specific time for his name to spread, and he was keen to wait until that time.

Jesus was not trying to hide. Rather, he wanted to reveal his glory in the right place and at the right time. He knew his works and words would lead to the cross, in keeping with God's plan to bring salvation to sinful humanity. But Jesus also wanted to spend sufficient time teaching his disciples in order to prepare them for the task of building the church after his resurrection and ascension. Believers today know that Jesus' time came on the cross, and his name has been spread far and wide since the miracle of his resurrection. God is sovereign over everything that happens under the sun, and God's people can be sure that now is the time to share the Good News about Jesus with all who will listen.

I thought the dead who are already dead more fortunate than the living who are still alive. 3But better than both is he who has not yet been and has not seen the evil deeds that are done under the sun.

4Then I saw that all toil and all skill in work come from a man's envy of his neighbor. This also is vanity[1] and a striving after wind.

5The fool folds his hands and eats his own flesh.

6Better is a handful of quietness than two hands full of toil and a striving after wind.

7Again, I saw vanity under the sun: 8one person who has no other, either son or brother, yet there is no end to all his toil, and his eyes are never satisfied with riches, so that he never asks, "For whom am I toiling and depriving myself of pleasure?" This also is vanity and an unhappy business.

9Two are better than one, because they have a good reward for their toil. 10For if they fall, one will lift up his fellow. But woe to him who is alone when he falls and has not another to lift him up! 11Again, if two lie together, they keep warm, but how can one keep warm alone? 12And though a man might prevail against one who is alone, two will withstand him—a threefold cord is not quickly broken.

13Better was a poor and wise youth than an old and foolish king who no longer knew how to take advice. 14For he went from prison to the throne, though in his own kingdom he had been born poor. 15I saw all the living who move about under the sun, along with that[2] youth who was to stand in the king's[3] place. 16There was no end of all the people, all of whom he led. Yet those who come later will not rejoice in him. Surely this also is vanity and a striving after wind.

Fear God

5 [4] Guard your steps when you go to the house of God. To draw near to listen is better than to offer the sacrifice of fools, for they do not know that they are doing evil. 2[5]Be not rash with your mouth, nor let your heart be hasty to utter a word before God, for God is in heaven and you are on earth. Therefore let your words be few. 3For a dream comes with much business, and a fool's voice with many words.

4When you vow a vow to God, do not delay paying it, for he has no pleasure in fools. Pay what you vow. 5It is better that you should not vow than that you should vow and not pay. 6Let not your mouth lead you[6] into sin, and do not say before the messenger[7] that it was a mistake. Why should God be angry at your voice and destroy the work of your hands? 7For when dreams increase and words grow many, there is vanity;[8] but[9] God is the one you must fear.

The Vanity of Wealth and Honor

8If you see in a province the oppression of the poor and the violation of justice and righteousness, do not be amazed at the matter, for the high official is watched by a higher, and there are yet higher ones over them. 9But this is gain for a land in every way: a king committed to cultivated fields.[10]

10He who loves money will not be satisfied with money, nor he who loves wealth with his income; this also is vanity. 11When goods increase, they increase who eat them, and what advantage has their owner but to see them with his eyes? 12Sweet is the sleep of a laborer, whether he eats little or much, but the full stomach of the rich will not let him sleep.

13There is a grievous evil that I have seen under the sun: riches were kept by their owner to his hurt, 14and those riches were lost in a bad venture. And he is father of a son, but he has nothing in his hand. 15As he came from his mother's

[1]The Hebrew term *hebel* can refer to a "vapor" or "mere breath"; also verses 7, 8, 16 (see note on 1:2)
[2]Hebrew *the second* [3]Hebrew *his* [4]Ch 4:17 in Hebrew [5]Ch 5:1 in Hebrew [6]Hebrew *your flesh*
[7]Or *angel* [8]The Hebrew term *hebel* can refer to a "vapor" or "mere breath"; also verse 10 (see note on 1:2)
[9]Or *For when dreams and vanities increase, words also grow many; but* [10]The meaning of the Hebrew verse is uncertain

ECCLESIASTES 5:10

LOVE OF MONEY

In addition to being the wisest man ever to live (until Jesus), Solomon was arguably one of the richest men in history (1Ki 10:14–25). So when he wrote about wealth, he did so from his own experience. Despite all that Solomon was able to accumulate through his lifetime, he came to the ultimate conclusion that money is ultimately futile and fails to satisfy. Jesus taught about money in Matthew 19:16–24 in his encounter with the rich young ruler, and he concluded by saying, "It is easier for a camel to go through the eye of a needle than for a rich person to enter the kingdom of God." While money is important for survival, love of money is a detriment to one's spiritual health. Combining Solomon's and Jesus' teachings about money, it becomes clear that money fails to satisfy while on earth, and it can be a stumbling block that keeps people from finding ultimate satisfaction in Jesus. However, when people give away their money and possessions to the poor in the name of Jesus, they store up for themselves treasure in heaven (Mt 19:21). Such lasting, heavenly treasure is much more valuable and beneficial than any possession gained on earth (Mt 6:19–21).

womb he shall go again, naked as he came, and shall take nothing for his toil that
he may carry away in his hand. 16 This also is a grievous evil: just as he came, so
shall he go, and what gain is there to him who toils for the wind? 17 Moreover, all
his days he eats in darkness in much vexation and sickness and anger.

18 Behold, what I have seen to be good and fitting is to eat and drink and find
enjoyment[1] in all the toil with which one toils under the sun the few days of his life
that God has given him, for this is his lot. 19 Everyone also to whom God has given
wealth and possessions and power to enjoy them, and to accept his lot and rejoice
in his toil—this is the gift of God. 20 For he will not much remember the days of his
life because God keeps him occupied with joy in his heart.

6 There is an evil that I have seen under the sun, and it lies heavy on mankind:
2 a man to whom God gives wealth, possessions, and honor, so that he lacks
nothing of all that he desires, yet God does not give him power to enjoy them,
but a stranger enjoys them. This is vanity;[2] it is a grievous evil. 3 If a man fathers a
hundred children and lives many years, so that the days of his years are many, but
his soul is not satisfied with life's good things, and he also has no burial, I say that
a stillborn child is better off than he. 4 For it comes in vanity and goes in darkness,
and in darkness its name is covered. 5 Moreover, it has not seen the sun or known
anything, yet it finds rest rather than he. 6 Even though he should live a thousand
years twice over, yet enjoy[3] no good—do not all go to the one place?

7 All the toil of man is for his mouth, yet his appetite is not satisfied.[4] 8 For what
advantage has the wise man over the fool? And what does the poor man have who
knows how to conduct himself before the living? 9 Better is the sight of the eyes
than the wandering of the appetite: this also is vanity and a striving after wind.

10 Whatever has come to be has already been named, and it is known what
man is, and that he is not able to dispute with one stronger than he. 11 The more
words, the more vanity, and what is the advantage to man? 12 For who knows what
is good for man while he lives the few days of his vain[5] life, which he passes like a
shadow? For who can tell man what will be after him under the sun?

The Contrast of Wisdom and Folly

7 A good name is better than precious ointment,
and the day of death than the day of birth.
2 It is better to go to the house of mourning
than to go to the house of feasting,
for this is the end of all mankind,
and the living will lay it to heart.
3 Sorrow is better than laughter,
for by sadness of face the heart is made glad.
4 The heart of the wise is in the house of mourning,
but the heart of fools is in the house of mirth.
5 It is better for a man to hear the rebuke of the wise
than to hear the song of fools.
6 For as the crackling of thorns under a pot,
so is the laughter of the fools;
this also is vanity.[6]
7 Surely oppression drives the wise into madness,
and a bribe corrupts the heart.
8 Better is the end of a thing than its beginning,
and the patient in spirit is better than the proud in spirit.
9 Be not quick in your spirit to become angry,
for anger lodges in the heart[7] of fools.

[1] Or *and see good* [2] The Hebrew term *hebel* can refer to a "vapor" or "mere breath"; also verses 4, 9, 11 (see note on 1:2) [3] Or *see* [4] Hebrew *filled* [5] The Hebrew term *hebel* can refer to a "vapor" or "mere breath" (see note on 1:2) [6] The Hebrew term *hebel* can refer to a "vapor" or "mere breath" (see note on 1:2) [7] Hebrew *in the bosom*

10 Say not, "Why were the former days better than these?"
For it is not from wisdom that you ask this.
11 Wisdom is good with an inheritance,
an advantage to those who see the sun.
12 For the protection of wisdom is like the protection of money,
and the advantage of knowledge is that wisdom preserves the life
of him who has it.
13 Consider the work of God:
who can make straight what he has made crooked?

14In the day of prosperity be joyful, and in the day of adversity consider: God
has made the one as well as the other, so that man may not find out anything that
will be after him.
15In my vain[1] life I have seen everything. There is a righteous man who perishes in his righteousness, and there is a wicked man who prolongs his life in his evildoing. 16Be not overly righteous, and do not make yourself too wise. Why should
you destroy yourself? 17Be not overly wicked, neither be a fool. Why should you
die before your time? 18It is good that you should take hold of this, and from that
withhold not your hand, for the one who fears God shall come out from both of
them.
19Wisdom gives strength to the wise man more than ten rulers who are in a
city.
20Surely there is not a righteous man on earth who does good and never sins.
21Do not take to heart all the things that people say, lest you hear your servant
cursing you. 22Your heart knows that many times you yourself have cursed others.
23All this I have tested by wisdom. I said, "I will be wise," but it was far from
me. 24That which has been is far off, and deep, very deep; who can find it out?
25I turned my heart to know and to search out and to seek wisdom and the
scheme of things, and to know the wickedness of folly and the foolishness that is
madness. 26And I find something more bitter than death: the woman whose heart
is snares and nets, and whose hands are fetters. He who pleases God escapes her,
but the sinner is taken by her. 27Behold, this is what I found, says the Preacher,
while adding one thing to another to find the scheme of things— 28which my soul
has sought repeatedly, but I have not found. One man among a thousand I found,
but a woman among all these I have not found. 29See, this alone I found, that God
made man upright, but they have sought out many schemes.

Keep the King's Command

8 Who is like the wise?
And who knows the interpretation of a thing?
A man's wisdom makes his face shine,
and the hardness of his face is changed.

2I say:[2] Keep the king's command, because of God's oath to him.[3] 3Be not hasty
to go from his presence. Do not take your stand in an evil cause, for he does whatever he pleases. 4For the word of the king is supreme, and who may say to him,
"What are you doing?" 5Whoever keeps a command will know no evil thing, and
the wise heart will know the proper time and the just way.[4] 6For there is a time
and a way for everything, although man's trouble[5] lies heavy on him. 7For he does
not know what is to be, for who can tell him how it will be? 8No man has power to
retain the spirit, or power over the day of death. There is no discharge from war,
nor will wickedness deliver those who are given to it. 9All this I observed while
applying my heart to all that is done under the sun, when man had power over
man to his hurt.

[1]The Hebrew term *hebel* can refer to a "vapor" or "mere breath" (see note on 1:2) [2]Hebrew lacks *say*
[3]Or *because of your oath to God* [4]Or *and judgment* [5]Or *evil*

ECCLESIASTES 7:16–18

AVOID EXTREMES

Ecclesiastes 7:18 balances the statements in the preceding two verses. It is important to be neither a wicked fool, nor an over-righteous zealot. Solomon advised finding a balance between wearing oneself out in the pursuit of perfection and abandoning oneself to sinful excess. That place of moderation and balance is found in the knowledge and fear of God. In Matthew 23, Jesus harshly criticized the Pharisees for being exactly like the people Solomon mentioned in verse 16. He said that the Pharisees were hypocrites. They thought they were living the right way, but they were actually worshiping religion itself and not God, upon whom the religion was founded. Jesus must be the focus of Christianity. Believers are responsible for avoiding extremes and living a balanced life in pursuit of him and him alone. Perfection is unattainable, and sin is unavoidable this side of heaven. In light of this, Jesus simply asks his people to be faithful and follow him.

Those Who Fear God Will Do Well

10Then I saw the wicked buried. They used to go in and out of the holy place and were praised[1] in the city where they had done such things. This also is vanity.[2] 11Because the sentence against an evil deed is not executed speedily, the heart of the children of man is fully set to do evil. 12Though a sinner does evil a hundred times and prolongs his life, yet I know that it will be well with those who fear God, because they fear before him. 13But it will not be well with the wicked, neither will he prolong his days like a shadow, because he does not fear before God.

Man Cannot Know God's Ways

14There is a vanity that takes place on earth, that there are righteous people to whom it happens according to the deeds of the wicked, and there are wicked people to whom it happens according to the deeds of the righteous. I said that this also is vanity. 15And I commend joy, for man has nothing better under the sun but to eat and drink and be joyful, for this will go with him in his toil through the days of his life that God has given him under the sun.

16When I applied my heart to know wisdom, and to see the business that is done on earth, how neither day nor night do one's eyes see sleep, 17then I saw all the work of God, that man cannot find out the work that is done under the sun. However much man may toil in seeking, he will not find it out. Even though a wise man claims to know, he cannot find it out.

Death Comes to All

9 But all this I laid to heart, examining it all, how the righteous and the wise and their deeds are in the hand of God. Whether it is love or hate, man does not know; both are before him. 2It is the same for all, since the same event happens to the righteous and the wicked, to the good and the evil,[3] to the clean and the unclean, to him who sacrifices and him who does not sacrifice. As the good one is, so is the sinner, and he who swears is as he who shuns an oath. 3This is an evil in all that is done under the sun, that the same event happens to all. Also, the hearts of the children of man are full of evil, and madness is in their hearts while they live, and after that they go to the dead. 4But he who is joined with all the living has hope, for a living dog is better than a dead lion. 5For the living know that they will die, but the dead know nothing, and they have no more reward, for the memory of them is forgotten. 6Their love and their hate and their envy have already perished, and forever they have no more share in all that is done under the sun.

Enjoy Life with the One You Love

7Go, eat your bread with joy, and drink your wine with a merry heart, for God has already approved what you do.

8Let your garments be always white. Let not oil be lacking on your head.

9Enjoy life with the wife whom you love, all the days of your vain[4] life that he has given you under the sun, because that is your portion in life and in your toil at which you toil under the sun. 10Whatever your hand finds to do, do it with your might,[5] for there is no work or thought or knowledge or wisdom in Sheol, to which you are going.

Wisdom Better Than Folly

11Again I saw that under the sun the race is not to the swift, nor the battle to the strong, nor bread to the wise, nor riches to the intelligent, nor favor to those with knowledge, but time and chance happen to them all. 12For man does not know his time. Like fish that are taken in an evil net, and like birds that are caught in

---

[1]Some Hebrew manuscripts, Septuagint, Vulgate; most Hebrew manuscripts *forgotten* [2]The Hebrew term *hebel* can refer to a "vapor" or "mere breath"; also twice in verse 14 (see note on 1:2) [3]Septuagint, Syriac, Vulgate; Hebrew lacks *and the evil* [4]The Hebrew term *hebel* can refer to a "vapor" or "mere breath" (see note on 1:2) [5]Or *finds to do with your might, do it*

LIFE IS UNFAIR

Ecclesiastes wrestles with the fact that life is unfair. The fastest person does not always win the race; the best warrior does not always win the battle; wisdom, intelligence, and knowledge do not always result in wealth, prestige, or favor. Solomon understood that sometimes life simply does not work out the way people want it to. People are like fish or birds that get caught in nets and traps — despite their best efforts, people's lives are surrounded by things that remain outside their control. Sometimes young people die. Sometimes evil people experience temporary success. Life is not fair.

However, while the unfairness of life may seem like something to be upset about, consider this: If life were fair, then everyone would receive the just reward for his or her actions. Everyone has sinned, and the just consequence for every sinful action is immediate, eternal separation from God. Thankfully, Jesus came to earth, lived a perfect life, died on the cross for humanity's sins, rose from the grave, and made life completely unfair. Now, everyone who has ever sinned has the opportunity to go to heaven through belief in Jesus. In a fair life, no such opportunity for grace would exist. Everyone would have to receive punishment for their actions. Instead God gives out grace and mercy unconditionally.

Sin made life on earth unfair — but God, in his grace, allows this sinful, unfair world to continue, creating time for sinners to accept his gracious offer of reconciliation through Christ. It is still hard to understand why bad things happen to good people or why good things happen to bad people. Even so, readers of Scripture know that those kinds of injustices are the result of sin, and Solomon does not avoid pointing out the negative consequences of living in a world marked by sin. But when faced with the world's injustices, believers today can celebrate the fact that Jesus' offer of eternal life is an altogether unfair and undeserved gift. All the sinful unfairness of this broken world pales in comparison to the gracious unfairness of salvation, which God lovingly makes available through Christ's death and resurrection.

a snare, so the children of man are snared at an evil time, when it suddenly falls upon them.

13 I have also seen this example of wisdom under the sun, and it seemed great to me. 14 There was a little city with few men in it, and a great king came against it and besieged it, building great siegeworks against it. 15 But there was found in it a poor, wise man, and he by his wisdom delivered the city. Yet no one remembered that poor man. 16 But I say that wisdom is better than might, though the poor man's wisdom is despised and his words are not heard.

17 The words of the wise heard in quiet are better than the shouting of a ruler among fools. 18 Wisdom is better than weapons of war, but one sinner destroys much good.

10 Dead flies make the perfumer's ointment give off a stench;
so a little folly outweighs wisdom and honor.
2 A wise man's heart inclines him to the right,
but a fool's heart to the left.
3 Even when the fool walks on the road, he lacks sense,
and he says to everyone that he is a fool.
4 If the anger of the ruler rises against you, do not leave your place,
for calmness[1] will lay great offenses to rest.

5 There is an evil that I have seen under the sun, as it were an error proceeding
from the ruler: 6 folly is set in many high places, and the rich sit in a low place. 7 I
have seen slaves on horses, and princes walking on the ground like slaves.

8 He who digs a pit will fall into it,
and a serpent will bite him who breaks through a wall.
9 He who quarries stones is hurt by them,
and he who splits logs is endangered by them.
10 If the iron is blunt, and one does not sharpen the edge,
he must use more strength,
but wisdom helps one to succeed.[2]
11 If the serpent bites before it is charmed,
there is no advantage to the charmer.

12 The words of a wise man's mouth win him favor,[3]
but the lips of a fool consume him.
13 The beginning of the words of his mouth is foolishness,
and the end of his talk is evil madness.
14 A fool multiplies words,
though no man knows what is to be,
and who can tell him what will be after him?
15 The toil of a fool wearies him,
for he does not know the way to the city.

16 Woe to you, O land, when your king is a child,
and your princes feast in the morning!
17 Happy are you, O land, when your king is the son of the nobility,
and your princes feast at the proper time,
for strength, and not for drunkenness!
18 Through sloth the roof sinks in,
and through indolence the house leaks.
19 Bread is made for laughter,
and wine gladdens life,
and money answers everything.
20 Even in your thoughts, do not curse the king,
nor in your bedroom curse the rich,

[1]Hebrew *healing* [2]Or *wisdom is an advantage for success* [3]Or *are gracious*

ECCLESIASTES 10:2

JESUS AT GOD'S RIGHT HAND

Solomon's statement about the wise inclining toward the right while the foolish turn toward the left reflects a tendency common in several ancient cultures to associate "the right" or "the right hand" with strength, wisdom, or favor. For example, various Scripture passages refer to God's right hand as a source of deliverance and safety (Ps 17:7; Isa 62:8). Similarly, those who have God at their right hand or side are favored by God and receive his help (Ps 109:31; Isa 63:12). In Ecclesiastes, Solomon extended the "right" motif to describe how wise people set themselves apart by choosing paths that lead to life. The notion that "right" signifies wisdom and power is reflected again in the New Testament. After Jesus had reappeared to the disciples following his death and resurrection, he was taken up into heaven, where he is seated at the right hand of God (Lk 22:69; 24:51). Paul tells believers that this crucified and risen Christ, sitting in authority at God's right hand, is the very power and wisdom of God (1Co 1:22–24; Eph 1:20; Col 3:1). For believers today, inclining their hearts toward the right means turning toward the One who sits at the right hand of God—for Jesus is God's power and wisdom, and the only path to life (Jn 14:6).

for a bird of the air will carry your voice,
or some winged creature tell the matter.

Cast Your Bread upon the Waters

11 Cast your bread upon the waters,
for you will find it after many days.
2 Give a portion to seven, or even to eight,
for you know not what disaster may happen on earth.
3 If the clouds are full of rain,
they empty themselves on the earth,
and if a tree falls to the south or to the north,
in the place where the tree falls, there it will lie.
4 He who observes the wind will not sow,
and he who regards the clouds will not reap.

5As you do not know the way the spirit comes to the bones in the womb[1] of a
woman with child, so you do not know the work of God who makes everything.
6In the morning sow your seed, and at evening withhold not your hand, for
you do not know which will prosper, this or that, or whether both alike will be
good.
7Light is sweet, and it is pleasant for the eyes to see the sun.
8So if a person lives many years, let him rejoice in them all; but let him remember that the days of darkness will be many. All that comes is vanity.[2]
9Rejoice, O young man, in your youth, and let your heart cheer you in the days
of your youth. Walk in the ways of your heart and the sight of your eyes. But know
that for all these things God will bring you into judgment.
10Remove vexation from your heart, and put away pain[3] from your body, for
youth and the dawn of life are vanity.

Remember Your Creator in Your Youth

12 Remember also your Creator in the days of your youth, before the evil days
come and the years draw near of which you will say, "I have no pleasure
in them"; 2before the sun and the light and the moon and the stars are darkened
and the clouds return after the rain, 3in the day when the keepers of the house
tremble, and the strong men are bent, and the grinders cease because they are
few, and those who look through the windows are dimmed, 4and the doors on
the street are shut—when the sound of the grinding is low, and one rises up at
the sound of a bird, and all the daughters of song are brought low— 5they are
afraid also of what is high, and terrors are in the way; the almond tree blossoms,
the grasshopper drags itself along,[4] and desire fails, because man is going to his
eternal home, and the mourners go about the streets— 6before the silver cord is
snapped, or the golden bowl is broken, or the pitcher is shattered at the fountain,
or the wheel broken at the cistern, 7and the dust returns to the earth as it was,
and the spirit returns to God who gave it. 8Vanity[5] of vanities, says the Preacher;
all is vanity.

Fear God and Keep His Commandments

9Besides being wise, the Preacher also taught the people knowledge, weighing
and studying and arranging many proverbs with great care. 10The Preacher sought
to find words of delight, and uprightly he wrote words of truth.
11The words of the wise are like goads, and like nails firmly fixed are the collected sayings; they are given by one Shepherd. 12My son, beware of anything

[1]Some Hebrew manuscripts, Targum; most Hebrew manuscripts *As you do not know the way of the wind, or how the bones grow in the womb* [2]The Hebrew term *hebel* can refer to a "vapor" or "mere breath"; also verse 10 (see note on 1:2) [3]Or *evil* [4]Or *is a burden* [5]The Hebrew term *hebel* can refer to a "vapor" or "mere breath" (three times in this verse); see note on 1:2

ECCLESIASTES 11:9–10

ANXIETY AND HAPPINESS

Solomon almost certainly experienced anxiety and worry as he built for himself an incredible kingdom on earth. But by the time Solomon wrote Ecclesiastes, he had realized the futility of worrying. Drawing from his own experience that worry never brings anything positive in life, he advised his readers to be happy and enjoy the life that God had given them. Solomon's teaching on anxiety is similar to Paul's teaching in Philippians 4:6, where he exhorted believers to combat anxiety with prayer in order to experience the fullness of the peace of God. This emphasis on contentment rooted in Christ reflects Jesus' own teachings about the folly of anxiety (Lk 12:22–31). Worrying indicates a lack of faith in the God who provides for his creatures. As Jesus pointed out, the birds neither sow nor reap, yet they are fed; the wild flowers do not toil to make clothes, yet "even Solomon in all his glory was not arrayed like one of these" (Lk 12:27). Through faith, believers can experience freedom from anxiety and true happiness with the life God has given them. They can cast their anxiety on the God who offers "eternal glory in Christ" (1Pe 5:7,10; cf. Ps 55:22).

JESUS AND LIFE BEYOND DEATH

Solomon closes Ecclesiastes the same way he began: "Vanity of vanities, says the Preacher; all is vanity." However, Solomon adds an important observation at the end of the book: he differentiates the mere human body, which returns to dust, and the human spirit, which returns to God. Solomon's claim that the body will return to the ground echoes the affirmation in Genesis that creatures are mortal; unlike the eternal, living God, humanity's life is a gift, granted and sustained by the breath of God (Ge 2:7). Every human life ends with the burial of a body, and that body returns to the dust from which it was made.

Life is meaningless if a decomposing body in the grave marks the end of the story. But Solomon asserted that in some sense God keeps and preserves human life beyond the grave. While the body of every human turns back into dust after death, "the spirit returns to God who gave it" (Ecc 12:7). There is more to the human body than flesh, blood, and bones.

In Genesis, God made the first human out of dust, but this human did not become a living being until God breathed "into his nostrils the breath of life" (Ge 2:7). The breath of God is in each and every human being. That is what Solomon was referring to when he said that the spirit will return to God. He understood that God's gift of life somehow extended beyond bodily death.

The New Testament affirms and expands the insight that death is not the end. Jesus warned his disciples not to fear those who can only kill the body, but to fear the One who can kill both the body and the soul. God is the only One who has power over the human soul, and his final judgment will answer all the temporary injustices of this sinful world (Mt 10:28; Rev 21:1 – 8). Each soul is of infinite value (Mt 16:26), and believers should devote their souls fully to God (Mt 22:37). Ultimately, the hope found in Christ provides the decisive answer to the troubling questions Solomon raised in Ecclesiastes. Solomon found some solace in the knowledge that the spirit would return to God. But God's people today know that everything is transformed by the hope of heaven: "For you have died, and your life is hidden with Christ in God. When Christ who is your life appears, then you also will appear with him in glory" (Col 3:3 – 4).

beyond these. Of making many books there is no end, and much study is a weariness of the flesh.
[13]The end of the matter; all has been heard. Fear God and keep his commandments, for this is the whole duty of man.[1] [14]For God will bring every deed into
judgment, with[2] every secret thing, whether good or evil.

ECCLESIASTES 12:13

FEAR GOD AND KEEP HIS COMMANDMENTS

After all of his teaching and exhortation, Solomon closed the book of Ecclesiastes with a simple command: "Fear God and keep his commandments." Solomon wrote from an incredibly unique perspective. He had experienced the best that life has to offer in terms of fortune, fame, and pleasure, yet he boiled all of life down into this one simple phrase. Jesus was asked to define the single most important commandment in all the law. He responded with a simple, twofold command: love God and love your neighbor (Mt 22:37–39). The final counsel of Solomon's great wisdom combines with Christ's clarification of the law to reveal an amazing connection between wisdom, obedience, and love. The pinnacle of wisdom is respecting and obeying God—and the heart of obedience to God's law consists of loving God and other people. Amidst all the wisdom and counsel within the book of Ecclesiastes, this insight is something that anyone should be able to apply to their life. Solomon's words of wisdom connect directly to Christ's way of obedience and love.

[1]Or *the duty of all mankind* [2]Or *into the judgment on*

JESUS: OUR DEEPEST COMPANION

SONG OF SOLOMON

SONG OF SOLOMON

REIGN OF DAVID	REIGN OF SOLOMON	ISRAEL DIVIDED
c. 1010 – 970 BC	*c. 970 – 930 BC*	*c. 930 BC*

The Song of Solomon, traditionally assumed to be written by Solomon, provides lyrical insight into the depth of human love and desire. Like the other areas of wisdom discussed in the books of Proverbs, Ecclesiastes, Job, and Psalms, Song of Solomon is meant to describe practical aspects of God's intentions for his people. In this book, the emphasis is on the marriage relationship between a man and a woman: the beauty of the marriage union seen in the passionate pursuit of the lover and his beloved. While human relationships are described in other places in the Wisdom Literature, the Song of Solomon stands alone in its portrayal of human love and sexuality.

Allegorical interpretations of the book seek to compare God's love for his people, epitomized in the work of Jesus Christ, to the bridegroom in Song of Solomon and the church to the bride. The pursuit, love, and faithfulness seen in the book are certainly emblematic of the way God loves his people; however, the main focus of the book centers on the God-ordained priority of marriage and sexual intimacy.

As part of his "very good" creation, God gave away the first bride, Eve, to her husband, Adam. Since that time, God has used marriage to provide love and companionship to his image-bearers and to allow them, together, to accomplish his good purposes on this earth. Together, a married couple models the love God has for his church.

Song of Solomon provides wisdom for lovers on how to pursue one another and love each other well. Using poetic imagery, the book models how couples can speak words of affirmation, seek the fulfillment of their spouse, and find delight in sexual intimacy. This book reveals the practical nature of the Scripture and shows that God cares about all aspects of human existence.

However, as with all other aspects of life in the fallen world, marriage is not intended to be the ultimate pursuit of God's children. While these relationships are a source of great joy and fulfillment, they are a mere shadow of the love found in Christ. Ultimately, marriage is a temporary relationship that embodies the love of Christ through sacrificial service and selfless love. In heaven there will no longer be marriage (Mt 22:30); there God's followers will revel in their beloved Savior, Jesus Christ. Until then, God's people see in the beauty of God-honoring human relationships a picture of the divine companion, Jesus Christ, who will always love us with a never-ending, ever-pursuing love.

MY BELOVED IS MINE, AND I AM HIS.

Song of Solomon 2:16

THE SONG OF SOLOMON

SONG OF SOLOMON 1:7

LOVE SONG

The Song of Solomon portrays the height of human love. Here, the woman asks Solomon where he leads his flocks so that she can arrange to be near him. Her heart is captivated by innocent desire for this man. She does not waste time with emotional innuendo, merely hinting at her affections. She is unashamed and unafraid, freely expressing her interest in the king.

Between a husband and a wife, fear of rejection often veils actual affection. This exists because sin has corrupted human relationships. Jesus—who conquered sin—liberates men and women to live freely in love with a spouse, secure in their marriage commitment. Those who believe in him have right standing with God by faith—trusting grace to cover all aspects of life, including love relationships. The two lovers in this passage illustrate God's delight in joyful marriage marked by unfiltered desire. Perfect love, ultimately realized in the person of Jesus, drives out all fear (1Jn 4:18).

1 The Song of Songs, which is Solomon's.

The Bride Confesses Her Love

She[1]

2 Let him kiss me with the kisses of his mouth!
For your love is better than wine;
3 your anointing oils are fragrant;
your name is oil poured out;
therefore virgins love you.
4 Draw me after you; let us run.
The king has brought me into his chambers.

Others

We will exult and rejoice in you;
we will extol your love more than wine;
rightly do they love you.

She

5 I am very dark, but lovely,
O daughters of Jerusalem,
like the tents of Kedar,
like the curtains of Solomon.
6 Do not gaze at me because I am dark,
because the sun has looked upon me.
My mother's sons were angry with me;
they made me keeper of the vineyards,
but my own vineyard I have not kept!
7 Tell me, you whom my soul loves,
where you pasture your flock,
where you make it lie down at noon;
for why should I be like one who veils herself
beside the flocks of your companions?

Solomon and His Bride Delight in Each Other

He

8 If you do not know,
O most beautiful among women,
follow in the tracks of the flock,
and pasture your young goats
beside the shepherds' tents.

9 I compare you, my love,
to a mare among Pharaoh's chariots.
10 Your cheeks are lovely with ornaments,
your neck with strings of jewels.

Others

11 We will make for you[2] ornaments of gold,
studded with silver.

[1]The translators have added speaker identifications based on the gender and number of the Hebrew words [2]The Hebrew for *you* is feminine singular

She

12 While the king was on his couch,
my nard gave forth its fragrance.
13 My beloved is to me a sachet of myrrh
that lies between my breasts.
14 My beloved is to me a cluster of henna blossoms
in the vineyards of Engedi.

He

15 Behold, you are beautiful, my love;
behold, you are beautiful;
your eyes are doves.

She

16 Behold, you are beautiful, my beloved, truly delightful.
Our couch is green;
17 the beams of our house are cedar;
our rafters are pine.

2 I am a rose[1] of Sharon,
a lily of the valleys.

He

2 As a lily among brambles,
so is my love among the young women.

She

3 As an apple tree among the trees of the forest,
so is my beloved among the young men.
With great delight I sat in his shadow,
and his fruit was sweet to my taste.
4 He brought me to the banqueting house,[2]
and his banner over me was love.
5 Sustain me with raisins;
refresh me with apples,
for I am sick with love.
6 His left hand is under my head,
and his right hand embraces me!
7 I adjure you,[3] O daughters of Jerusalem,
by the gazelles or the does of the field,
that you not stir up or awaken love
until it pleases.

The Bride Adores Her Beloved

8 The voice of my beloved!
Behold, he comes,
leaping over the mountains,
bounding over the hills.
9 My beloved is like a gazelle
or a young stag.
Behold, there he stands
behind our wall,
gazing through the windows,
looking through the lattice.

[1]Probably a bulb, such as a crocus, asphodel, or narcissus [2]Hebrew *the house of wine* [3]That is, I put you on oath; so throughout the Song

SONG OF SOLOMON 2:4

JESUS IS OUR ETERNAL BANNER OF LOVE

King Solomon's banquet hall was a place of splendor, utilized for occasions of great joy. It was furnished with the finest things so that celebrations were extravagant and luxurious. The woman looked forward to joining the king there, aware that the privilege of being in such a place happened only because she was with him. His *banner* over her was a symbol of the permanence of his commitment to his beloved. More than just association, she was chosen—claimed not by force but with love.

When Jesus completed his mission on earth, he ascended to the Father to prepare a place for his bride, the church (Jn 14:2–3). Men and women in Christ are chosen and claimed by love. They are saved by grace—a priceless gift from God (Eph 2:8–9). Their future in the extravagance of heaven is established and guaranteed because they belong to the King. At life's end, those who believe in Jesus will enjoy an everlasting banquet. They will delight in the pleasures of heaven—the greatest of these is the presence of the One who *is* love (1Jn 4:8).

10 My beloved speaks and says to me:
"Arise, my love, my beautiful one,
and come away,
11 for behold, the winter is past;
the rain is over and gone.
12 The flowers appear on the earth,
the time of singing[1] has come,
and the voice of the turtledove
is heard in our land.
13 The fig tree ripens its figs,
and the vines are in blossom;
they give forth fragrance.
Arise, my love, my beautiful one,
and come away.
14 O my dove, in the clefts of the rock,
in the crannies of the cliff,
let me see your face,
let me hear your voice,
for your voice is sweet,
and your face is lovely.
15 Catch the foxes[2] for us,
the little foxes
that spoil the vineyards,
for our vineyards are in blossom."

16 My beloved is mine, and I am his;
he grazes[3] among the lilies.
17 Until the day breathes
and the shadows flee,
turn, my beloved, be like a gazelle
or a young stag on cleft mountains.[4]

The Bride's Dream

3 On my bed by night
I sought him whom my soul loves;
I sought him, but found him not.
2 I will rise now and go about the city,
in the streets and in the squares;
I will seek him whom my soul loves.
I sought him, but found him not.
3 The watchmen found me
as they went about in the city.
"Have you seen him whom my soul loves?"
4 Scarcely had I passed them
when I found him whom my soul loves.
I held him, and would not let him go
until I had brought him into my mother's house,
and into the chamber of her who conceived me.
5 I adjure you, O daughters of Jerusalem,
by the gazelles or the does of the field,
that you not stir up or awaken love
until it pleases.

Solomon Arrives for the Wedding

6 What is that coming up from the wilderness
like columns of smoke,

[1]Or *pruning* [2]Or *jackals* [3]Or *he pastures his flock* [4]Or *mountains of Bether*

perfumed with myrrh and frankincense,
with all the fragrant powders of a merchant?
7 Behold, it is the litter[1] of Solomon!
Around it are sixty mighty men,
some of the mighty men of Israel,
8 all of them wearing swords
and expert in war,
each with his sword at his thigh,
against terror by night.
9 King Solomon made himself a carriage[2]
from the wood of Lebanon.
10 He made its posts of silver,
its back of gold, its seat of purple;
its interior was inlaid with love
by the daughters of Jerusalem.
11 Go out, O daughters of Zion,
and look upon King Solomon,
with the crown with which his mother crowned him
on the day of his wedding,
on the day of the gladness of his heart.

Solomon Admires His Bride's Beauty

He

4 Behold, you are beautiful, my love,
behold, you are beautiful!
Your eyes are doves
behind your veil.
Your hair is like a flock of goats
leaping down the slopes of Gilead.
2 Your teeth are like a flock of shorn ewes
that have come up from the washing,
all of which bear twins,
and not one among them has lost its young.
3 Your lips are like a scarlet thread,
and your mouth is lovely.
Your cheeks are like halves of a pomegranate
behind your veil.
4 Your neck is like the tower of David,
built in rows of stone;[3]
on it hang a thousand shields,
all of them shields of warriors.
5 Your two breasts are like two fawns,
twins of a gazelle,
that graze among the lilies.
6 Until the day breathes
and the shadows flee,
I will go away to the mountain of myrrh
and the hill of frankincense.
7 You are altogether beautiful, my love;
there is no flaw in you.
8 Come with me from Lebanon, my bride;
come with me from Lebanon.
Depart[4] from the peak of Amana,
from the peak of Senir and Hermon,

[1]That is, the couch on which servants carry a king [2]Or *sedan chair* [3]The meaning of the Hebrew word is uncertain [4]Or *Look*

THE WEDDING

Chapter 3 of Song of Solomon depicts the wedding between the two lovers. Verse 6 starts with Solomon's entrance to the wedding ceremony. The king and his escorts arrive to meet the woman, creating a dramatic spectacle. The procession is extravagant. Solomon has spared no expense in presenting himself to his bride. In verses 9 through 11, the text describes two objects connected with the king's arrival: a carriage and a crown.

The carriage was made of wood from Lebanon, some of the most prized material in the world. Its posts were crafted from silver, its base fashioned with gold, and the seat upholstered with purple cloth. Solomon's carriage was unmistakably royal — luxurious and impressive. The other object of note is a crown placed on his head by his mother. This was likely a special wedding wreath, distinguishing him as the day's honored hero and celebrated victor.

The New Testament describes two major entrances by Jesus the Son of God. The first is his birth in a Bethlehem manger (Lk 2:7). This quiet arrival is marked by chosen humility. He could have arrived with fanfare befitting the King of the universe. Yet Jesus chose to take on the nature of a servant (Php 2:7) in order to call his eventual followers to faith. Jesus is worthy of all honor and glory, but his earthly ministry began in near obscurity, celebrated by only a few observers. His other entrance — his future coming from heaven to gather his own and to end sin's reign — will be exponentially more dramatic (1Th 4:14 – 17). The entire population of earth will stop to give stunned attention. Those who believe will rejoice and celebrate. Those who reject salvation in Christ's name will tremble and weep. Jesus will come as a conqueror and King (Titus 2:13).

Solomon's kingship, though significant, is miniscule in comparison to the power and authority of the Son of God. Jesus is not simply king over one nation or region; he is the eternal King above all things in existence. When Jesus comes for his own, creation's King will wear a victor's crown and will also dispense unfading crowns to all those who have believed (1Pe 5:4).

from the dens of lions,
from the mountains of leopards.

9 You have captivated my heart, my sister, my bride;
you have captivated my heart with one glance of your eyes,
with one jewel of your necklace.
10 How beautiful is your love, my sister, my bride!
How much better is your love than wine,
and the fragrance of your oils than any spice!
11 Your lips drip nectar, my bride;
honey and milk are under your tongue;
the fragrance of your garments is like the fragrance of
Lebanon.
12 A garden locked is my sister, my bride,
a spring locked, a fountain sealed.
13 Your shoots are an orchard of pomegranates
with all choicest fruits,
henna with nard,
14 nard and saffron, calamus and cinnamon,
with all trees of frankincense,
myrrh and aloes,
with all choice spices—
15 a garden fountain, a well of living water,
and flowing streams from Lebanon.

16 Awake, O north wind,
and come, O south wind!
Blow upon my garden,
let its spices flow.

Together in the Garden of Love

She

Let my beloved come to his garden,
and eat its choicest fruits.

He

5 I came to my garden, my sister, my bride,
I gathered my myrrh with my spice,
I ate my honeycomb with my honey,
I drank my wine with my milk.

Others

Eat, friends, drink,
and be drunk with love!

The Bride Searches for Her Beloved

She

2 I slept, but my heart was awake.
A sound! My beloved is knocking.
"Open to me, my sister, my love,
my dove, my perfect one,
for my head is wet with dew,
my locks with the drops of the night."
3 I had put off my garment;
how could I put it on?
I had bathed my feet;
how could I soil them?

4 My beloved put his hand to the latch,
and my heart was thrilled within me.
5 I arose to open to my beloved,
and my hands dripped with myrrh,
my fingers with liquid myrrh,
on the handles of the bolt.
6 I opened to my beloved,
but my beloved had turned and gone.
My soul failed me when he spoke.
I sought him, but found him not;
I called him, but he gave no answer.
7 The watchmen found me
as they went about in the city;
they beat me, they bruised me,
they took away my veil,
those watchmen of the walls.
8 I adjure you, O daughters of Jerusalem,
if you find my beloved,
that you tell him
I am sick with love.

Others

9 What is your beloved more than another beloved,
O most beautiful among women?
What is your beloved more than another beloved,
that you thus adjure us?

The Bride Praises Her Beloved

She

10 My beloved is radiant and ruddy,
distinguished among ten thousand.
11 His head is the finest gold;
his locks are wavy,
black as a raven.
12 His eyes are like doves
beside streams of water,
bathed in milk,
sitting beside a full pool.[1]
13 His cheeks are like beds of spices,
mounds of sweet-smelling herbs.
His lips are lilies,
dripping liquid myrrh.
14 His arms are rods of gold,
set with jewels.
His body is polished ivory,[2]
bedecked with sapphires.[3]
15 His legs are alabaster columns,
set on bases of gold.
His appearance is like Lebanon,
choice as the cedars.
16 His mouth[4] is most sweet,
and he is altogether desirable.
This is my beloved and this is my friend,
O daughters of Jerusalem.

[1]The meaning of the Hebrew is uncertain [2]The meaning of the Hebrew word is uncertain [3]Hebrew *lapis lazuli* [4]Hebrew *palate*

EMOTIONS

Every relationship experiences highs and lows, and the two lovers in Song of Solomon are no exception. In chapter 5, Solomon withdrew from the woman, and she quickly realized a gap had started to form between them. She cried for his return but heard no answer. The emotions of the two lovers are clear throughout the entire book, but most often they are emotions of great joy. Chapter 5 shows a severe emotional swing toward separation and sadness, as the woman's heart sank after being away from her lover.

The young bride is not unique in her experience of heavy emotions. Jesus showed he was capable of great emotional depth. He illustrated the joy a shepherd experiences when a lost sheep is found, pointing to his own happiness (Lk 15:5 – 6). Additionally, there were times when Jesus was filled with tremendous sorrow (Jn 11:35). One of Jesus' most emotional moments is recorded in Mark 14 while praying in the Garden of Gethsemane before his imminent arrest. Verse 34 says, "My soul is very sorrowful, even to death." He knew that he was on his way to the cross to die for the sins of humankind, and similar to the woman in Song of Solomon, his heart sank. Jesus' last words recorded in Matthew's Gospel are "*Eli, Eli, lema sabachthani?*" (which means "My God, my God, why have you forsaken me?") (Mt 27:46). Every past, present, and future sin was heaped upon Jesus at the moment when he cried out, and it was in that moment that Jesus experienced separation from God for the first time in all eternity.

It is important to know that Jesus' separation from God on the cross was only momentary. He died on the cross, atoning for sin, and he rose to life in victory over death (1Co 15:55 – 56). In Song of Solomon, the separation of the lovers was only temporary as well.

Others

6 Where has your beloved gone,
O most beautiful among women?
Where has your beloved turned,
that we may seek him with you?

Together in the Garden of Love

She

2 My beloved has gone down to his garden
to the beds of spices,
to graze[1] in the gardens
and to gather lilies.
3 I am my beloved's and my beloved is mine;
he grazes among the lilies.

Solomon and His Bride Delight in Each Other

He

4 You are beautiful as Tirzah, my love,
lovely as Jerusalem,
awesome as an army with banners.
5 Turn away your eyes from me,
for they overwhelm me—
Your hair is like a flock of goats
leaping down the slopes of Gilead.
6 Your teeth are like a flock of ewes
that have come up from the washing;
all of them bear twins;
not one among them has lost its young.
7 Your cheeks are like halves of a pomegranate
behind your veil.
8 There are sixty queens and eighty concubines,
and virgins without number.
9 My dove, my perfect one, is the only one,
the only one of her mother,
pure to her who bore her.
The young women saw her and called her blessed;
the queens and concubines also, and they praised her.

10 "Who is this who looks down like the dawn,
beautiful as the moon, bright as the sun,
awesome as an army with banners?"

She

11 I went down to the nut orchard
to look at the blossoms of the valley,
to see whether the vines had budded,
whether the pomegranates were in bloom.
12 Before I was aware, my desire set me
among the chariots of my kinsman, a prince.[2]

Others

13[3] Return, return, O Shulammite,
return, return, that we may look upon you.

[1]Or *to pasture his flock*; also verse 3 [2]Or *chariots of Ammi-Nadib* [3]Ch 7:1 in Hebrew

He

Why should you look upon the Shulammite,
as upon a dance before two armies?[1]

7 How beautiful are your feet in sandals,
O noble daughter!
Your rounded thighs are like jewels,
the work of a master hand.
2 Your navel is a rounded bowl
that never lacks mixed wine.
Your belly is a heap of wheat,
encircled with lilies.
3 Your two breasts are like two fawns,
twins of a gazelle.
4 Your neck is like an ivory tower.
Your eyes are pools in Heshbon,
by the gate of Bath-rabbim.
Your nose is like a tower of Lebanon,
which looks toward Damascus.
5 Your head crowns you like Carmel,
and your flowing locks are like purple;
a king is held captive in the tresses.

6 How beautiful and pleasant you are,
O loved one, with all your delights![2]
7 Your stature is like a palm tree,
and your breasts are like its clusters.
8 I say I will climb the palm tree
and lay hold of its fruit.
Oh may your breasts be like clusters of the vine,
and the scent of your breath like apples,
9 and your mouth[3] like the best wine.

She

It goes down smoothly for my beloved,
gliding over lips and teeth.[4]

10 I am my beloved's,
and his desire is for me.

The Bride Gives Her Love

11 Come, my beloved,
let us go out into the fields
and lodge in the villages;[5]
12 let us go out early to the vineyards
and see whether the vines have budded,
whether the grape blossoms have opened
and the pomegranates are in bloom.
There I will give you my love.
13 The mandrakes give forth fragrance,
and beside our doors are all choice fruits,
new as well as old,
which I have laid up for you, O my beloved.

[1]Or *dance of Mahanaim* [2]Or *among delights* [3]Hebrew *palate* [4]Septuagint, Syriac, Vulgate; Hebrew *causing the lips of sleepers to speak*, or *gliding over the lips of those who sleep* [5]Or *among the henna plants*

Longing for Her Beloved

8 Oh that you were like a brother to me
who nursed at my mother's breasts!
If I found you outside, I would kiss you,
and none would despise me.
2 I would lead you and bring you
into the house of my mother—
she who used to teach me.
I would give you spiced wine to drink,
the juice of my pomegranate.
3 His left hand is under my head,
and his right hand embraces me!
4 I adjure you, O daughters of Jerusalem,
that you not stir up or awaken love
until it pleases.

5 Who is that coming up from the wilderness,
leaning on her beloved?

Under the apple tree I awakened you.
There your mother was in labor with you;
there she who bore you was in labor.

6 Set me as a seal upon your heart,
as a seal upon your arm,
for love is strong as death,
jealousy[1] is fierce as the grave.[2]
Its flashes are flashes of fire,
the very flame of the LORD.
7 Many waters cannot quench love,
neither can floods drown it.
If a man offered for love
all the wealth of his house,
he[3] would be utterly despised.

Final Advice

Others

8 We have a little sister,
and she has no breasts.
What shall we do for our sister
on the day when she is spoken for?
9 If she is a wall,
we will build on her a battlement of silver,
but if she is a door,
we will enclose her with boards of cedar.

She

10 I was a wall,
and my breasts were like towers;
then I was in his eyes
as one who finds[4] peace.

11 Solomon had a vineyard at Baal-hamon;
he let out the vineyard to keepers;
each one was to bring for its fruit a thousand pieces
of silver.

[1]Or *ardor* [2]Hebrew *as Sheol* [3]Or *it* [4]Or *brings out*

LOVE AS STRONG AS DEATH

Song of Solomon describes the relationship between two people who are in love. But the book offers more than specific descriptions of a particular relationship. As the book concludes, the author shares a powerful reflection on the nature and essence of the love between husbands and wives. Love is not superficial in nature, but it is a strong bond that ties two individuals together.

"Love is strong as death." Nothing personifies love more than Jesus and his outrageous act of grace. He loves people so much that he was willing to die an undeserving death. Solomon's bride knew the depths of earthly love as an overwhelming force and unbreakable bond. Jesus defined the strength of love by dying for undeserving people (Ro 5:6 – 8).

The phrase "until death do us part" — a common wedding vow today — is another way of saying "our love is as strong as death." This phrase is a vow to a lifelong commitment to one's spouse, and it is not something to be said lightly. Jesus said that there was no greater love than the kind that makes one willing to lay down one's life for a friend, and he followed through (Jn 15:13).

In the same way that marriage begins with a profound and permanent commitment, beginning a relationship with God means committing to live one's entire life fully devoted to Jesus. Nothing can separate a Christian from God's strong love (Ro 8:37 – 39). Those who believe in Jesus cling to the promise that love endures beyond physical death because of the hope of eternal life.

12 My vineyard, my very own, is before me;
you, O Solomon, may have the thousand,
and the keepers of the fruit two hundred.

He

13 O you who dwell in the gardens,
with companions listening for your voice;
let me hear it.

She

14 Make haste, my beloved,
and be like a gazelle
or a young stag
on the mountains of spices.

SONG OF SOLOMON 8:14

JESUS' REUNION WITH HIS BRIDE

Secure and free in each other's love, the woman calls her beloved to her—longing for Solomon to overtake her in delight. She beckons him to rush to her, satisfying a long-anticipated togetherness.

Scripture here describes righteous desire—passion between a married man and woman. Their commitment to each other and their past experiences together fuel longing for new moments of intimacy. The calling and invitation in this text reflect the longing in the heart of the Christian to see Jesus face to face (Rev 19:7). One day, the anticipation of every believer will be satisfied. Until then, there is a calling back and forth between heaven and earth. "The Spirit and the Bride say, 'Come.' And let the one who hears say, 'Come.' And let the one who is thirsty come; let the one who desires take the water of life without price" (Rev 22:17). Jesus answers, "Surely I am coming soon" (Rev 22:20). Hallelujah!

JESUS: OUR SOVEREIGN SAVIOR

ISAIAH

ISAIAH

REIGN OF UZZIAH BEGINS *c. 792 BC*	PROPHETIC MINISTRY OF ISAIAH BEGINS *c. 740 BC*	FALL OF ISRAEL *c. 722 BC*

Isaiah's vision of God's glory (6:1 – 5) propelled his message and mission. The words he proclaimed were filled with warning, confrontation, and rebuke for God's people due to their spiritual unfaithfulness. As a result, Isaiah was opposed by his contemporaries, those who needed his message most.

Isaiah, Jeremiah, and Ezekiel are known as the "Major Prophets." This title does not denote the importance of these books compared to the "Minor Prophets," but rather refers to the length and the scope of their writings. All of the prophets were God-ordained spokespersons whom God called, appointed, and used to declare his word to his people.

Isaiah, like many of the prophets, warned a spiritually adulterous and morally corrupt people of the coming consequences for their waywardness. As God had promised, the disobedient nation of Israel would not be immune to God's wrath. As he had done to the nations before them, God would drive his people from the land if they did not turn to him in repentance and faith. The first portion of the book, chapters 1 – 39, describes the coming judgment at the hands of the Assyrians in the second half of the eighth century BC. The final portion of the book, chapters 40 – 66, looks forward more than a century to encourage the people of Judah who would be taken into exile in Babylon. In spite of the nation's rebellion, however, Isaiah pictured a coming day when God would demonstrate the majesty of his mercy and grace. Central to Isaiah's prophetic writings are the vivid images of the promised Messiah who would suffer and die for the sins of God's people (52:13 — 53:12). The images portray the coming

The Day of the LORD

6 For you have rejected your people,
the house of Jacob,
because they are full of things from the east
and of fortune-tellers like the Philistines,
and they strike hands with the children of foreigners.
7 Their land is filled with silver and gold,
and there is no end to their treasures;
their land is filled with horses,
and there is no end to their chariots.
8 Their land is filled with idols;
they bow down to the work of their hands,
to what their own fingers have made.
9 So man is humbled,
and each one is brought low—
do not forgive them!
10 Enter into the rock
and hide in the dust
from before the terror of the LORD,
and from the splendor of his majesty.
11 The haughty looks of man shall be brought low,
and the lofty pride of men shall be humbled,
and the LORD alone will be exalted in that day.

12 For the LORD of hosts has a day
against all that is proud and lofty,
against all that is lifted up—and it shall be brought low;
13 against all the cedars of Lebanon,
lofty and lifted up;
and against all the oaks of Bashan;
14 against all the lofty mountains,
and against all the uplifted hills;
15 against every high tower,
and against every fortified wall;
16 against all the ships of Tarshish,
and against all the beautiful craft.
17 And the haughtiness of man shall be humbled,
and the lofty pride of men shall be brought low,
and the LORD alone will be exalted in that day.
18 And the idols shall utterly pass away.
19 And people shall enter the caves of the rocks
and the holes of the ground,[1]
from before the terror of the LORD,
and from the splendor of his majesty,
when he rises to terrify the earth.

20 In that day mankind will cast away
their idols of silver and their idols of gold,
which they made for themselves to worship,
to the moles and to the bats,
21 to enter the caverns of the rocks
and the clefts of the cliffs,
from before the terror of the LORD,
and from the splendor of his majesty,
when he rises to terrify the earth.

[1]Hebrew *dust*

22 Stop regarding man
in whose nostrils is breath,
for of what account is he?

Judgment on Judah and Jerusalem

3 For behold, the Lord GOD of hosts
is taking away from Jerusalem and from Judah
support and supply,[1]
all support of bread,
and all support of water;
2 the mighty man and the soldier,
the judge and the prophet,
the diviner and the elder,
3 the captain of fifty
and the man of rank,
the counselor and the skillful magician
and the expert in charms.
4 And I will make boys their princes,
and infants[2] shall rule over them.
5 And the people will oppress one another,
every one his fellow
and every one his neighbor;
the youth will be insolent to the elder,
and the despised to the honorable.

6 For a man will take hold of his brother
in the house of his father, saying:
"You have a cloak;
you shall be our leader,
and this heap of ruins
shall be under your rule";
7 in that day he will speak out, saying:
"I will not be a healer;[3]
in my house there is neither bread nor cloak;
you shall not make me
leader of the people."
8 For Jerusalem has stumbled,
and Judah has fallen,
because their speech and their deeds are against the LORD,
defying his glorious presence.[4]

9 For the look on their faces bears witness against them;
they proclaim their sin like Sodom;
they do not hide it.
Woe to them!
For they have brought evil on themselves.
10 Tell the righteous that it shall be well with them,
for they shall eat the fruit of their deeds.
11 Woe to the wicked! It shall be ill with him,
for what his hands have dealt out shall be done to him.
12 My people—infants are their oppressors,
and women rule over them.
O my people, your guides mislead you
and they have swallowed up[5] the course of your paths.

[1]Hebrew *staff* [2]Or *caprice* [3]Hebrew *binder of wounds* [4]Hebrew *the eyes of his glory* [5]Or *they have confused*

13 The LORD has taken his place to contend;
he stands to judge peoples.
14 The LORD will enter into judgment
with the elders and princes of his people:
"It is you who have devoured[1] the vineyard,
the spoil of the poor is in your houses.
15 What do you mean by crushing my people,
by grinding the face of the poor?"
declares the Lord GOD of hosts.

16 The LORD said:
Because the daughters of Zion are haughty
and walk with outstretched necks,
glancing wantonly with their eyes,
mincing along as they go,
tinkling with their feet,
17 therefore the Lord will strike with a scab
the heads of the daughters of Zion,
and the LORD will lay bare their secret parts.

18 In that day the Lord will take away the finery of the anklets, the headbands,
and the crescents; 19 the pendants, the bracelets, and the scarves; 20 the headdress-
es, the armlets, the sashes, the perfume boxes, and the amulets; 21 the signet rings
and nose rings; 22 the festal robes, the mantles, the cloaks, and the handbags; 23 the
mirrors, the linen garments, the turbans, and the veils.

24 Instead of perfume there will be rottenness;
and instead of a belt, a rope;
and instead of well-set hair, baldness;
and instead of a rich robe, a skirt of sackcloth;
and branding instead of beauty.
25 Your men shall fall by the sword
and your mighty men in battle.
26 And her gates shall lament and mourn;
empty, she shall sit on the ground.

4 And seven women shall take hold of one man in that day, saying, "We will eat our own bread and wear our own clothes, only let us be called by your name; take away our reproach."

The Branch of the LORD Glorified

2 In that day the branch of the LORD shall be beautiful and glorious, and the
fruit of the land shall be the pride and honor of the survivors of Israel. 3 And he
who is left in Zion and remains in Jerusalem will be called holy, everyone who
has been recorded for life in Jerusalem, 4 when the Lord shall have washed away
the filth of the daughters of Zion and cleansed the bloodstains of Jerusalem from
its midst by a spirit of judgment and by a spirit of burning.[2] 5 Then the LORD will
create over the whole site of Mount Zion and over her assemblies a cloud by day,
and smoke and the shining of a flaming fire by night; for over all the glory there
will be a canopy. 6 There will be a booth for shade by day from the heat, and for a
refuge and a shelter from the storm and rain.

The Vineyard of the LORD Destroyed

5 Let me sing for my beloved
my love song concerning his vineyard:
My beloved had a vineyard
on a very fertile hill.

[1] Or *grazed over*; compare Exodus 22:5 [2] Or *purging*

ISAIAH 4:2

THE BRANCH

The image of the branch in this passage is used to represent both Judah and the coming Messiah. The word *branch* is derived from the Hebrew verb meaning "to sprout up" or "to come from death to life." In a literal sense, Isaiah is describing the prosperity and blessing that the people of Judah will one day experience following God's judgment for their unfaithfulness as described in Isaiah 3:1—4:1. However, the other important aspect of this section is the Messianic references that it contains. This is the first reference to the Messiah as the "Branch" of the Lord, yet there are several other mentions throughout Scripture (Isa 11:1; Jer 23:5; 33:15; Zec 3:8). The branch is an image for life and prosperity, and these verses point to the blessing that Jesus would one day bring to God's people. His blessing would allow fallen sinners to once again have fellowship and peace with God. This prophecy gives hope to the Israelites that the coming Messiah will bring life to the otherwise dying religion and law under which they were living. Jesus is not only the giver of life; he is life itself.

ISAIAH 5:1–7

THE SONG OF THE VINEYARD

In this song, Israel is a vineyard that has been planted by God. From this vineyard, he expects to receive fruit (v. 2). God established his people and positioned them in the promised land so that his glory might be seen throughout the world. The Law that he gave (and the sacrificial system he instituted) was God's appointed

(continued on next page)

(The Song of the Vineyard, continued)

way for his people to worship a God who was altogether different than the false gods of the surrounding nations. The fruit of the nation that God desired to see was worshipful obedience, but they failed in this task and would be judged as a result.

Jesus taught that God is the gardener who has established his people to bear fruit as well. As the gardener, Jesus said, God will prune branches that do not bear fruit (Jn 15:1–2). But he also taught that those who abide in him will bear fruit as a result of that connection: "I am the vine; you are the branches. Whoever abides in me and I in him, he it is that bears much fruit, for apart from me you can do nothing" (Jn 15:5).

2 He dug it and cleared it of stones,
and planted it with choice vines;
he built a watchtower in the midst of it,
and hewed out a wine vat in it;
and he looked for it to yield grapes,
but it yielded wild grapes.

3 And now, O inhabitants of Jerusalem
and men of Judah,
judge between me and my vineyard.
4 What more was there to do for my vineyard,
that I have not done in it?
When I looked for it to yield grapes,
why did it yield wild grapes?

5 And now I will tell you
what I will do to my vineyard.
I will remove its hedge,
and it shall be devoured;[1]
I will break down its wall,
and it shall be trampled down.
6 I will make it a waste;
it shall not be pruned or hoed,
and briers and thorns shall grow up;
I will also command the clouds
that they rain no rain upon it.

7 For the vineyard of the LORD of hosts
is the house of Israel,
and the men of Judah
are his pleasant planting;
and he looked for justice,
but behold, bloodshed;[2]
for righteousness,
but behold, an outcry![3]

Woe to the Wicked

8 Woe to those who join house to house,
who add field to field,
until there is no more room,
and you are made to dwell alone
in the midst of the land.
9 The LORD of hosts has sworn in my hearing:
"Surely many houses shall be desolate,
large and beautiful houses, without inhabitant.
10 For ten acres[4] of vineyard shall yield but one bath,
and a homer of seed shall yield but an ephah."[5]

11 Woe to those who rise early in the morning,
that they may run after strong drink,
who tarry late into the evening
as wine inflames them!
12 They have lyre and harp,
tambourine and flute and wine at their feasts,

[1]Or *grazed over*; compare Exodus 22:5 [2]The Hebrew words for *justice* and *bloodshed* sound alike [3]The Hebrew words for *righteous* and *outcry* sound alike [4]Hebrew *ten yoke*, the area ten yoke of oxen can plow in a day [5]A *bath* was about 6 gallons or 22 liters; a *homer* was about 6 bushels or 220 liters; an *ephah* was about 3/5 bushel or 22 liters

but they do not regard the deeds of the LORD,
or see the work of his hands.

13 Therefore my people go into exile
for lack of knowledge;[1]
their honored men go hungry,[2]
and their multitude is parched with thirst.
14 Therefore Sheol has enlarged its appetite
and opened its mouth beyond measure,
and the nobility of Jerusalem[3] and her multitude will go down,
her revelers and he who exults in her.
15 Man is humbled, and each one is brought low,
and the eyes of the haughty[4] are brought low.
16 But the LORD of hosts is exalted[5] in justice,
and the Holy God shows himself holy in righteousness.
17 Then shall the lambs graze as in their pasture,
and nomads shall eat among the ruins of the rich.

18 Woe to those who draw iniquity with cords of falsehood,
who draw sin as with cart ropes,
19 who say: "Let him be quick,
let him speed his work
that we may see it;
let the counsel of the Holy One of Israel draw near,
and let it come, that we may know it!"
20 Woe to those who call evil good
and good evil,
who put darkness for light
and light for darkness,
who put bitter for sweet
and sweet for bitter!
21 Woe to those who are wise in their own eyes,
and shrewd in their own sight!
22 Woe to those who are heroes at drinking wine,
and valiant men in mixing strong drink,
23 who acquit the guilty for a bribe,
and deprive the innocent of his right!

24 Therefore, as the tongue of fire devours the stubble,
and as dry grass sinks down in the flame,
so their root will be as rottenness,
and their blossom go up like dust;
for they have rejected the law of the LORD of hosts,
and have despised the word of the Holy One of Israel.
25 Therefore the anger of the LORD was kindled against his people,
and he stretched out his hand against them and struck them,
and the mountains quaked;
and their corpses were as refuse
in the midst of the streets.
For all this his anger has not turned away,
and his hand is stretched out still.

26 He will raise a signal for nations far away,
and whistle for them from the ends of the earth;
and behold, quickly, speedily they come!
27 None is weary, none stumbles,
none slumbers or sleeps,

[1]Or *without their knowledge* [2]Or *die of hunger* [3]Hebrew *her nobility* [4]Hebrew *high* [5]Hebrew *high*

ISAIAH 6:2–3

HOLY, HOLY, HOLY

The description of the seraphim provides an image that shows how one is supposed to act in the presence of God. God is holy—altogether pure and without blemish or sin. He is spotless and perfect, and as such is set apart from everything that is not as holy as he is. The seraphim cover their faces because even though they are supernatural beings, they are evidently unworthy to look on God. The fact that they humbly cover their feet implies that they are created beings. When one realizes the immensity of God's holiness, the only appropriate response is exactly what is described in this passage. (Read Isaiah's response in v. 5.)

Believers who read this passage can get a glimpse of how intense and pure God's holiness is. Likewise, God calls believers to be holy (1Pe 1:15–16). Once a person believes in God and who he says he is, they can begin to live a life empowered by the Holy Spirit, in accordance with his Word, and can join a community of imperfect people who have been set apart by God (1Pe 2:9). Although the struggle is real, believers can claim victory over sin through Christ's death and resurrection. And, by setting themselves apart from this world and the sin that entangles it, believers take steps to one day be united with God in holiness (Heb 12:1–3).

not a waistband is loose,
  not a sandal strap broken;
28 their arrows are sharp,
  all their bows bent,
their horses' hoofs seem like flint,
  and their wheels like the whirlwind.
29 Their roaring is like a lion,
  like young lions they roar;
they growl and seize their prey;
  they carry it off, and none can rescue.
30 They will growl over it on that day,
  like the growling of the sea.
And if one looks to the land,
  behold, darkness and distress;
and the light is darkened by its clouds.

Isaiah's Vision of the Lord

6 In the year that King Uzziah died I saw the Lord sitting upon a throne, high
and lifted up; and the train[1] of his robe filled the temple. 2 Above him stood
the seraphim. Each had six wings: with two he covered his face, and with two he
covered his feet, and with two he flew. 3 And one called to another and said:

"Holy, holy, holy is the LORD of hosts;
the whole earth is full of his glory!"[2]

4 And the foundations of the thresholds shook at the voice of him who called, and
the house was filled with smoke. 5 And I said: "Woe is me! For I am lost; for I am
a man of unclean lips, and I dwell in the midst of a people of unclean lips; for my
eyes have seen the King, the LORD of hosts!"

6 Then one of the seraphim flew to me, having in his hand a burning coal that
he had taken with tongs from the altar. 7 And he touched my mouth and said: "Behold, this has touched your lips; your guilt is taken away, and your sin atoned for."

Isaiah's Commission from the Lord

8 And I heard the voice of the Lord saying, "Whom shall I send, and who will
go for us?" Then I said, "Here I am! Send me." 9 And he said, "Go, and say to this
people:

"'Keep on hearing,[3] but do not understand;
keep on seeing,[4] but do not perceive.'
10 Make the heart of this people dull,[5]
  and their ears heavy,
  and blind their eyes;
lest they see with their eyes,
  and hear with their ears,
and understand with their hearts,
  and turn and be healed."
11 Then I said, "How long, O Lord?"
And he said:
"Until cities lie waste
  without inhabitant,
and houses without people,
  and the land is a desolate waste,
12 and the LORD removes people far away,
  and the forsaken places are many in the midst of
    the land.

[1]Or *hem* [2]Or *may his glory fill the whole earth* [3]Or *Hear indeed* [4]Or *see indeed* [5]Hebrew *fat*

PROPHECIES FULFILLED

God used Isaiah to speak his word, but God also told Isaiah that many people would not repent as they would be hardened in their unbelief. Moses faced a similar situation when he went before Pharaoh to demand the release of the Israelites. Before Moses even spoke to Pharaoh, God told him that he would harden Pharaoh's heart (Ex 7:3). In that instance, God used Pharaoh to show his sovereign power by freeing his people despite their oppressor's intentions. In both instances, the people on the receiving end had the opportunity to hear God's warnings and turn, but neither Pharaoh nor the Israelites chose to believe what they heard. As they chose to ignore God's prophets, their hearts only grew harder and more opposed to God.

God chose to use their hardened hearts for his glory. When Pharaoh's heart was hardened, God freed his people through many signs and acts of his greatness. When the Israelites refused to listen to Isaiah, they went into exile. Later, God sent his Son to the earth to fulfill many of Isaiah's prophecies and bring fruition to Isaiah's words. Even in justifying Isaiah, God brought mercy and a second chance for the people to hear what he had to say. However, just as before, their hearts remained hardened (Mt 13:14 – 15; Mk 4:12; Lk 8:10; Jn 12:37 – 41).

Jesus came and fulfilled many of the prophecies of Isaiah, and these verses are an example of how even the people around Jesus fulfilled Isaiah's prophecies (Ac 28:25 – 27). God knew that there would be people who heard Jesus' good news, yet failed to repent and adhere to what he said. God used those hardened hearts to orchestrate Jesus' crucifixion, and through his death on the cross he paid for the sins of the world.

13 And though a tenth remain in it,
it will be burned[1] again,
like a terebinth or an oak,
whose stump remains
when it is felled."
The holy seed[2] is its stump.

Isaiah Sent to King Ahaz

7 In the days of Ahaz the son of Jotham, son of Uzziah, king of Judah, Rezin the
king of Syria and Pekah the son of Remaliah the king of Israel came up to Jerusalem to wage war against it, but could not yet mount an attack against it. 2When
the house of David was told, "Syria is in league with[3] Ephraim," the heart of Ahaz[4]
and the heart of his people shook as the trees of the forest shake before the wind.
3And the LORD said to Isaiah, "Go out to meet Ahaz, you and Shear-jashub[5]
your son, at the end of the conduit of the upper pool on the highway to the
Washer's Field. 4And say to him, 'Be careful, be quiet, do not fear, and do not
let your heart be faint because of these two smoldering stumps of firebrands, at
the fierce anger of Rezin and Syria and the son of Remaliah. 5Because Syria, with
Ephraim and the son of Remaliah, has devised evil against you, saying, 6"Let us go
up against Judah and terrify it, and let us conquer it[6] for ourselves, and set up the
son of Tabeel as king in the midst of it," 7thus says the Lord GOD:

"'It shall not stand,
and it shall not come to pass.
8 For the head of Syria is Damascus,
and the head of Damascus is Rezin.
And within sixty-five years
Ephraim will be shattered from being a people.
9 And the head of Ephraim is Samaria,
and the head of Samaria is the son of Remaliah.
If you[7] are not firm in faith,
you will not be firm at all.'"

The Sign of Immanuel

10Again the LORD spoke to Ahaz: 11"Ask a sign of the LORD your[8] God; let it be
deep as Sheol or high as heaven." 12But Ahaz said, "I will not ask, and I will not
put the LORD to the test." 13And he[9] said, "Hear then, O house of David! Is it too
little for you to weary men, that you weary my God also? 14Therefore the Lord
himself will give you a sign. Behold, the virgin shall conceive and bear a son, and
shall call his name Immanuel.[10] 15He shall eat curds and honey when he knows
how to refuse the evil and choose the good. 16For before the boy knows how to
refuse the evil and choose the good, the land whose two kings you dread will be
deserted. 17The LORD will bring upon you and upon your people and upon your
father's house such days as have not come since the day that Ephraim departed
from Judah—the king of Assyria!"
18In that day the LORD will whistle for the fly that is at the end of the streams
of Egypt, and for the bee that is in the land of Assyria. 19And they will all come
and settle in the steep ravines, and in the clefts of the rocks, and on all the thornbushes, and on all the pastures.[11]
20In that day the Lord will shave with a razor that is hired beyond the River[12]—with the king of Assyria—the head and the hair of the feet, and it will sweep
away the beard also.
21In that day a man will keep alive a young cow and two sheep, 22and because

ISAIAH 7:14

IMMANUEL

Immanuel is a Hebrew word meaning "God with us," and it is a fitting name for the promised son in Isaiah's day and for Jesus, the One prophesied about in Isaiah. Because of the sin of mankind, a debt had to be paid in order to free humanity from living and dying in eternal separation from God. In order to pay this debt, God sent his Son Jesus to the earth to be born in desperately poor conditions, live a perfect life, die an undeserving death, and rise again so that humans may one day be united with God in heaven.

When Isaiah wrote about a child named Immanuel, he was referring to Jesus, who was "God with us" to the people he encountered while he was on earth. God the Son willingly laid aside his position in heaven and descended to the earth, taking on human form in order to save his sinful image-bearers (Php 2:5–11). God continues to be Immanuel, "God with us," through the indwelling presence of his Holy Spirit who fills believers, comforts them in a fallen world, and empowers them to live holy lives.

[1]Or *purged* [2]Or *offspring* [3]Hebrew *Syria has rested upon* [4]Hebrew *his heart* [5]*Shear-jashub* means *A remnant shall return* [6]Hebrew *let us split it open* [7]The Hebrew for *you* is plural in verses 9, 13, 14 [8]The Hebrew for *you* and *your* is singular in verses 11, 16, 17 [9]That is, Isaiah [10]*Immanuel* means *God is with us* [11]Or *watering holes*, or *brambles* [12]That is, the Euphrates

IMMANUEL IS COMING

As is true for many prophecies, here Isaiah portrays two coming events. First, during Ahaz's day, a child would be born who would witness the destruction of Judah's two prominent enemies — Israel and Syria. The word translated in English Bibles as *virgin* (*'almah*) is used to refer to an unmarried woman who is young (Ge 24:43; Pr 30:19). Some believe this is a prophecy that a child will be born to a young woman from the house of Ahaz who will marry and give birth to this promised son. Other writers feel that Isaiah's prophecy concerns a young woman who would become Isaiah's wife following the death of his first wife after she gave birth to Shear-jashub (Isa 7:3). In that case, the initial fulfillment of this prophecy is found in Isaiah 8:3. Regardless of the exact nature of this promised son, he would grow up during a time when God would crush the surrounding nations and fulfill his good promises to his people.

The second application of this prophecy was fulfilled by the coming of Jesus Christ, whose name *Immanuel* means "God with us." Born to a young virgin, Jesus was the promised Messiah which all Old Testament deliverers ultimately foreshadowed. What Ahaz lacked in vision and purpose, Jesus had — and more. He was the incarnate Son of God, miraculously born of a virgin, and with a mission to fulfill God's plan to save his people. Jesus would be the perfect King who would rule from a position of humility and grace, not tyranny and self-aggrandizement. Through God's miraculous provision, the coming Messiah would take on human flesh while retaining his full divinity. This promised Son would do far more than the son would accomplish or represent in Isaiah's day. Jesus would crush Satan, sin, and death through his sacrificial death and miraculous resurrection.

of the abundance of milk that they give, he will eat curds, for everyone who is left
in the land will eat curds and honey.
23 In that day every place where there used to be a thousand vines, worth a
thousand shekels[1] of silver, will become briers and thorns. 24 With bow and arrows a man will come there, for all the land will be briers and thorns. 25 And as
for all the hills that used to be hoed with a hoe, you will not come there for fear
of briers and thorns, but they will become a place where cattle are let loose and
where sheep tread.

The Coming Assyrian Invasion

8 Then the LORD said to me, "Take a large tablet and write on it in common
characters,[2] 'Belonging to Maher-shalal-hash-baz.'[3] 2 And I will get reliable
witnesses, Uriah the priest and Zechariah the son of Jeberechiah, to attest for
me."
3 And I went to the prophetess, and she conceived and bore a son. Then the
LORD said to me, "Call his name Maher-shalal-hash-baz; 4 for before the boy
knows how to cry 'My father' or 'My mother,' the wealth of Damascus and the
spoil of Samaria will be carried away before the king of Assyria."
5 The LORD spoke to me again: 6 "Because this people has refused the waters of
Shiloah that flow gently, and rejoice over Rezin and the son of Remaliah, 7 therefore, behold, the Lord is bringing up against them the waters of the River,[4] mighty
and many, the king of Assyria and all his glory. And it will rise over all its channels
and go over all its banks, 8 and it will sweep on into Judah, it will overflow and pass
on, reaching even to the neck, and its outspread wings will fill the breadth of your
land, O Immanuel."

9 Be broken,[5] you peoples, and be shattered;[6]
  give ear, all you far countries;
strap on your armor and be shattered;
  strap on your armor and be shattered.
10 Take counsel together, but it will come to nothing;
  speak a word, but it will not stand,
  for God is with us.[7]

Fear God, Wait for the LORD

11 For the LORD spoke thus to me with his strong hand upon me, and warned
me not to walk in the way of this people, saying: 12 "Do not call conspiracy all that
this people calls conspiracy, and do not fear what they fear, nor be in dread. 13 But
the LORD of hosts, him you shall honor as holy. Let him be your fear, and let him
be your dread. 14 And he will become a sanctuary and a stone of offense and a
rock of stumbling to both houses of Israel, a trap and a snare to the inhabitants
of Jerusalem. 15 And many shall stumble on it. They shall fall and be broken; they
shall be snared and taken."
16 Bind up the testimony; seal the teaching[8] among my disciples. 17 I will wait for
the LORD, who is hiding his face from the house of Jacob, and I will hope in him.
18 Behold, I and the children whom the LORD has given me are signs and portents
in Israel from the LORD of hosts, who dwells on Mount Zion. 19 And when they say
to you, "Inquire of the mediums and the necromancers who chirp and mutter,"
should not a people inquire of their God? Should they inquire of the dead on
behalf of the living? 20 To the teaching and to the testimony! If they will not speak
according to this word, it is because they have no dawn. 21 They will pass through
the land,[9] greatly distressed and hungry. And when they are hungry, they will be
enraged and will speak contemptuously against[10] their king and their God, and

[1] A *shekel* was about 2/5 ounce or 11 grams [2] Hebrew *with a man's stylus* [3] *Maher-shalal-hash-baz* means *The spoil speeds, the prey hastens* [4] That is, the Euphrates [5] Or *Be evil* [6] Or *dismayed* [7] The Hebrew for *God is with us* is *Immanuel* [8] Or *law*; also verse 20 [9] Hebrew *it* [10] Or *speak contemptuously by*

ISAIAH 8:14

SANCTUARY OR STUMBLING BLOCK?

Isaiah describes God as a sanctuary, which is a holy place for peace and refuge. But Isaiah also uses this image to portray God's sanctuary as a stumbling block leading to destruction for his people because his holy place would also expose the sin of those who entered.

Those who enter God's sanctuary, who earnestly seek after God, encounter God who is perfect. But because of their own imperfections and their inability to obey his commandments and follow him humbly, this same holy place that was meant for their good can also be the cause of stumbling. Paul wrote that pursuing God by works as opposed to faith is a similar stumbling block today (Ro 9:32–33). Faith is what brings believers into the holy place, and obedience to God's Word keeps believers from stumbling over the very thing that is meant to save them (1Pe 2:7–8).

turn their faces upward. [22]And they will look to the earth, but behold, distress
and darkness, the gloom of anguish. And they will be thrust into thick darkness.

For to Us a Child Is Born

9 [1] But there will be no gloom for her who was in anguish. In the former time he
brought into contempt the land of Zebulun and the land of Naphtali, but in
the latter time he has made glorious the way of the sea, the land beyond the Jordan, Galilee of the nations.[2]

2[3] The people who walked in darkness
have seen a great light;
those who dwelt in a land of deep darkness,
on them has light shone.
3 You have multiplied the nation;
you have increased its joy;
they rejoice before you
as with joy at the harvest,
as they are glad when they divide the spoil.
4 For the yoke of his burden,
and the staff for his shoulder,
the rod of his oppressor,
you have broken as on the day of Midian.
5 For every boot of the tramping warrior in battle tumult
and every garment rolled in blood
will be burned as fuel for the fire.
6 For to us a child is born,
to us a son is given;
and the government shall be upon[4] his shoulder,
and his name shall be called[5]
Wonderful Counselor, Mighty God,
Everlasting Father, Prince of Peace.
7 Of the increase of his government and of peace
there will be no end,
on the throne of David and over his kingdom,
to establish it and to uphold it
with justice and with righteousness
from this time forth and forevermore.
The zeal of the LORD of hosts will do this.

Judgment on Arrogance and Oppression

8 The Lord has sent a word against Jacob,
and it will fall on Israel;
9 and all the people will know,
Ephraim and the inhabitants of Samaria,
who say in pride and in arrogance of heart:
10 "The bricks have fallen,
but we will build with dressed stones;
the sycamores have been cut down,
but we will put cedars in their place."
11 But the LORD raises the adversaries of Rezin against him,
and stirs up his enemies.
12 The Syrians on the east and the Philistines on the west
devour Israel with open mouth.
For all this his anger has not turned away,
and his hand is stretched out still.

[1]Ch 8:23 in Hebrew [2]Or *of the Gentiles* [3]Ch 9:1 in Hebrew [4]Or *is upon* [5]Or *is called*

ISAIAH 9:1–2

A LIGHT HAS DAWNED

The light Isaiah describes in this passage is Jesus, the One who would bring salvation to the people of the world when he came to earth. Isaiah even specifically identified the region of Galilee as the place where the light would come, which was the place Jesus spent a majority of his time teaching and ministering (Mt 4:13–16). In verse 2, Isaiah shifts into the past tense, demonstrating the certainty of his prophecy, indicating that what was to happen in the future was as sure to happen as if it had already occurred. God would bring light to a people in darkness, and they would see that light dawning and bringing joy to their lives. Jesus fulfilled Isaiah's prophecy; he is the light of the world (Jn 8:12), and no one who trusts Jesus for salvation has to walk in the darkness of unforgiven sin ever again.

HOPE FOR PEACE

Isaiah portrays the eternal hope of God's people in this passage. Again, this prophecy refers directly to Jesus, the One who was to fulfill Isaiah's words (Lk 1:32–33). The coming of Jesus represented a new rule and a new King who would reign forever, and ultimately he will establish God's rule and reign forever (Rev 21:5–7). "Of the increase of his government and of peace there will be no end" (Isa 9:7). Earthly kingdoms advance through greed, war, and oppression. God's kingdom advances through righteousness and peace (Jn 14:27)—peace that will prevail forever in God's new heaven and new earth.

The people of God longed for this type of peace. Though the promised land was meant to be marked by God's provision and freedom from war, this had not been the case. Israel's persistent rebellion and idolatry prevented the kind of peaceful situation that God had promised, had they been obedient (Dt 6:3).

Isaiah encouraged the people to maintain hope that God's peace would prevail, but it would come in a future day inaugurated by the appearance of the Messiah. Believers today can have this hope as well. Though the world has been broken with strife and sin, Isaiah pictured a day when peace will cover the earth and all pain will cease (Isa 9:7; Rev 21:4). Jesus encouraged believers to have hope, for he overcame this world and is bringing about a new and better one (Jn 16:33). It is this hope that believers cling to, and it is their faith that makes hope possible. Jesus came to earth to seek and save those who were lost and wandering from him (Lk 19:10). He came to establish a way for people to enter into his kingdom and find the peace he offers. Believers find peace with God, knowing that their sins are forgiven and they can rely on the presence of a holy God, both now and forever. And they experience peace knowing that they will, one day, inhabit a world ruled by God himself that is free from violence, where peace reigns supreme.

13 The people did not turn to him who struck them,
nor inquire of the LORD of hosts.
14 So the LORD cut off from Israel head and tail,
palm branch and reed in one day—
15 the elder and honored man is the head,
and the prophet who teaches lies is the tail;
16 for those who guide this people have been leading them astray,
and those who are guided by them are swallowed up.
17 Therefore the Lord does not rejoice over their young men,
and has no compassion on their fatherless and widows;
for everyone is godless and an evildoer,
and every mouth speaks folly.[1]
For all this his anger has not turned away,
and his hand is stretched out still.

18 For wickedness burns like a fire;
it consumes briers and thorns;
it kindles the thickets of the forest,
and they roll upward in a column of smoke.
19 Through the wrath of the LORD of hosts
the land is scorched,
and the people are like fuel for the fire;
no one spares another.
20 They slice meat on the right, but are still hungry,
and they devour on the left, but are not satisfied;
each devours the flesh of his own arm,
21 Manasseh devours Ephraim, and Ephraim devours Manasseh;
together they are against Judah.
For all this his anger has not turned away,
and his hand is stretched out still.

10 Woe to those who decree iniquitous decrees,
and the writers who keep writing oppression,
2 to turn aside the needy from justice
and to rob the poor of my people of their right,
that widows may be their spoil,
and that they may make the fatherless their prey!
3 What will you do on the day of punishment,
in the ruin that will come from afar?
To whom will you flee for help,
and where will you leave your wealth?
4 Nothing remains but to crouch among the prisoners
or fall among the slain.
For all this his anger has not turned away,
and his hand is stretched out still.

Judgment on Arrogant Assyria

5 Woe to Assyria, the rod of my anger;
the staff in their hands is my fury!
6 Against a godless nation I send him,
and against the people of my wrath I command him,
to take spoil and seize plunder,
and to tread them down like the mire of the streets.
7 But he does not so intend,
and his heart does not so think;

[1] Or *speaks disgraceful things*

but it is in his heart to destroy,
and to cut off nations not a few;
8 for he says:
"Are not my commanders all kings?
9 Is not Calno like Carchemish?
Is not Hamath like Arpad?
Is not Samaria like Damascus?
10 As my hand has reached to the kingdoms of the idols,
whose carved images were greater than those of Jerusalem and Samaria,
11 shall I not do to Jerusalem and her idols
as I have done to Samaria and her images?"

12 When the Lord has finished all his work on Mount Zion and on Jerusalem,
he[1] will punish the speech[2] of the arrogant heart of the king of Assyria and the
boastful look in his eyes. 13 For he says:

"By the strength of my hand I have done it,
and by my wisdom, for I have understanding;
I remove the boundaries of peoples,
and plunder their treasures;
like a bull I bring down those who sit on thrones.
14 My hand has found like a nest
the wealth of the peoples;
and as one gathers eggs that have been forsaken,
so I have gathered all the earth;
and there was none that moved a wing
or opened the mouth or chirped."
15 Shall the axe boast over him who hews with it,
or the saw magnify itself against him who wields it?
As if a rod should wield him who lifts it,
or as if a staff should lift him who is not wood!
16 Therefore the Lord GOD of hosts
will send wasting sickness among his stout warriors,
and under his glory a burning will be kindled,
like the burning of fire.
17 The light of Israel will become a fire,
and his Holy One a flame,
and it will burn and devour
his thorns and briers in one day.
18 The glory of his forest and of his fruitful land
the LORD will destroy, both soul and body,
and it will be as when a sick man wastes away.
19 The remnant of the trees of his forest will be so few
that a child can write them down.

The Remnant of Israel Will Return

20 In that day the remnant of Israel and the survivors of the house of Jacob will
no more lean on him who struck them, but will lean on the LORD, the Holy One
of Israel, in truth. 21 A remnant will return, the remnant of Jacob, to the mighty
God. 22 For though your people Israel be as the sand of the sea, only a remnant of
them will return. Destruction is decreed, overflowing with righteousness. 23 For
the Lord GOD of hosts will make a full end, as decreed, in the midst of all the earth.
24 Therefore thus says the Lord GOD of hosts: "O my people, who dwell in Zion,
be not afraid of the Assyrians when they strike with the rod and lift up their staff
against you as the Egyptians did. 25 For in a very little while my fury will come to an

[1] Hebrew *I* [2] Hebrew *fruit*

ISAIAH 10:20–21

REMNANT

This passage is written in a tone of hope for the future. Though the Assyrian army had nearly conquered Judah in 701 BC, it was through that same invasion that God drew his people to himself. Later, a remnant would return to Judah after the destruction of Jerusalem by the Babylonians in 586 BC.

This passage demonstrates the fact that God always has a plan to bring people to the saving knowledge of himself. The Israelites would learn through God's judgment and his mercy that they should not trust in any earthly leader but rather trust in God alone. Despite the turmoil that surrounded Judah, Isaiah focused on the point of hope for the remnant, and he encouraged them to trust and believe that God was in control.

Believers should adhere to this same focus and encouragement today. God is ultimately in control; he sent Jesus as salvation for the lost, and he will one day return and redeem all of his people.

end, and my anger will be directed to their destruction. 26And the LORD of hosts
will wield against them a whip, as when he struck Midian at the rock of Oreb. And
his staff will be over the sea, and he will lift it as he did in Egypt. 27And in that day
his burden will depart from your shoulder, and his yoke from your neck; and the
yoke will be broken because of the fat."[1]

28 He has come to Aiath;
he has passed through Migron;
at Michmash he stores his baggage;
29 they have crossed over the pass;
at Geba they lodge for the night;
Ramah trembles;
Gibeah of Saul has fled.
30 Cry aloud, O daughter of Gallim!
Give attention, O Laishah!
O poor Anathoth!
31 Madmenah is in flight;
the inhabitants of Gebim flee for safety.
32 This very day he will halt at Nob;
he will shake his fist
at the mount of the daughter of Zion,
the hill of Jerusalem.

33 Behold, the Lord GOD of hosts
will lop the boughs with terrifying power;
the great in height will be hewn down,
and the lofty will be brought low.
34 He will cut down the thickets of the forest with an axe,
and Lebanon will fall by the Majestic One.

The Righteous Reign of the Branch

11 There shall come forth a shoot from the stump of Jesse,
and a branch from his roots shall bear fruit.
2 And the Spirit of the LORD shall rest upon him,
the Spirit of wisdom and understanding,
the Spirit of counsel and might,
the Spirit of knowledge and the fear of the LORD.
3 And his delight shall be in the fear of the LORD.
He shall not judge by what his eyes see,
or decide disputes by what his ears hear,
4 but with righteousness he shall judge the poor,
and decide with equity for the meek of the earth;
and he shall strike the earth with the rod of his mouth,
and with the breath of his lips he shall kill the wicked.
5 Righteousness shall be the belt of his waist,
and faithfulness the belt of his loins.

6 The wolf shall dwell with the lamb,
and the leopard shall lie down with the young goat,
and the calf and the lion and the fattened calf together;
and a little child shall lead them.
7 The cow and the bear shall graze;
their young shall lie down together;
and the lion shall eat straw like the ox.
8 The nursing child shall play over the hole of the cobra,
and the weaned child shall put his hand on the adder's den.

[1]The meaning of the Hebrew is uncertain

9 They shall not hurt or destroy
in all my holy mountain;
for the earth shall be full of the knowledge of the LORD
as the waters cover the sea.

10In that day the root of Jesse, who shall stand as a signal for the peoples—of
him shall the nations inquire, and his resting place shall be glorious.
11In that day the Lord will extend his hand yet a second time to recover the
remnant that remains of his people, from Assyria, from Egypt, from Pathros, from
Cush,[1] from Elam, from Shinar, from Hamath, and from the coastlands of the sea.

12 He will raise a signal for the nations
and will assemble the banished of Israel,
and gather the dispersed of Judah
from the four corners of the earth.
13 The jealousy of Ephraim shall depart,
and those who harass Judah shall be cut off;
Ephraim shall not be jealous of Judah,
and Judah shall not harass Ephraim.
14 But they shall swoop down on the shoulder of the Philistines in the west,
and together they shall plunder the people of the east.
They shall put out their hand against Edom and Moab,
and the Ammonites shall obey them.
15 And the LORD will utterly destroy[2]
the tongue of the Sea of Egypt,
and will wave his hand over the River[3]
with his scorching breath,[4]
and strike it into seven channels,
and he will lead people across in sandals.
16 And there will be a highway from Assyria
for the remnant that remains of his people,
as there was for Israel
when they came up from the land of Egypt.

The LORD Is My Strength and My Song

12 You[5] will say in that day:
"I will give thanks to you, O LORD,
for though you were angry with me,
your anger turned away,
that you might comfort me.

2 "Behold, God is my salvation;
I will trust, and will not be afraid;
for the LORD GOD[6] is my strength and my song,
and he has become my salvation."

3With joy you[7] will draw water from the wells of salvation. 4And you will say
in that day:

"Give thanks to the LORD,
call upon his name,
make known his deeds among the peoples,
proclaim that his name is exalted.

5 "Sing praises to the LORD, for he has done gloriously;
let this be made known[8] in all the earth.

[1]Probably *Nubia* [2]Hebrew *devote to destruction* [3]That is, the Euphrates [4]Or *wind* [5]The Hebrew for *you* is singular in verse 1 [6]Hebrew *for Yah, the LORD* [7]The Hebrew for *you* is plural in verses 3, 4 [8]Or *this is made known*

A BRANCH FROM JESSE

Isaiah again points Judah forward to the coming of the Messiah — this time emphasizing that he would come from the line of Jesse. Because the Jews during the time that Jesus lived studied Israel's prophets of old, they knew what they were looking for when it came to the Messiah. Matthew knew this truth, so he began his gospel witness by confirming that Jesus was from the line of Abraham, Isaac, Jacob, and David, as well as from David's father Jesse (Mt 1:1 – 6). Paul continued to confirm this truth in his letter to the Romans by pointing to the fact that Jesus was the One of whom Isaiah prophesied (Ro 15:12).

Isaiah used the images of a branch and a shoot to once again show that this coming One would be a source of life and blessing, removing the curse of disobedience, and setting things right in concern for justice. These images, combined with the prophecies found throughout Isaiah, provide a robust picture of the nature of God's chosen One and serve to confirm the truthfulness of God's Word from cover to cover.

The second verse of Isaiah 11 says that "the Spirit of the LORD shall rest upon him." In multiple Gospels, God's Spirit is described as resting on Jesus following his baptism (Mt 3:16; Mk 1:10; Lk 3:21 – 22). In each account, God's Spirit descends in the form of a dove, and God the Father confirms Jesus' identity as his beloved Son. Furthermore, Isaiah wrote that the coming Messiah would be given "the Spirit of wisdom and understanding, the Spirit of counsel and might, the Spirit of knowledge and the fear of the LORD" (Isa 11:2). In this Spirit, he would speak the wisdom of God and live in perfect conformity to it (Lk 2:52; 24:44; Heb 4:15). This branch from Jesse would embody the vibrant life of God's Spirit and demonstrate the life that could come to those who place their faith in his finished work. They could be born anew by the power of God's Spirit and live in the power of that same Spirit.

6 Shout, and sing for joy, O inhabitant of Zion,
for great in your[1] midst is the Holy One of Israel."

The Judgment of Babylon

13 The oracle concerning Babylon which Isaiah the son of Amoz saw.

2 On a bare hill raise a signal;
cry aloud to them;
wave the hand for them to enter
the gates of the nobles.
3 I myself have commanded my consecrated ones,
and have summoned my mighty men to execute my anger,
my proudly exulting ones.[2]

4 The sound of a tumult is on the mountains
as of a great multitude!
The sound of an uproar of kingdoms,
of nations gathering together!
The LORD of hosts is mustering
a host for battle.
5 They come from a distant land,
from the end of the heavens,
the LORD and the weapons of his indignation,
to destroy the whole land.[3]

6 Wail, for the day of the LORD is near;
as destruction from the Almighty[4] it will come!
7 Therefore all hands will be feeble,
and every human heart will melt.
8 They will be dismayed:
pangs and agony will seize them;
they will be in anguish like a woman in labor.
They will look aghast at one another;
their faces will be aflame.

9 Behold, the day of the LORD comes,
cruel, with wrath and fierce anger,
to make the land a desolation
and to destroy its sinners from it.
10 For the stars of the heavens and their constellations
will not give their light;
the sun will be dark at its rising,
and the moon will not shed its light.
11 I will punish the world for its evil,
and the wicked for their iniquity;
I will put an end to the pomp of the arrogant,
and lay low the pompous pride of the ruthless.
12 I will make people more rare than fine gold,
and mankind than the gold of Ophir.
13 Therefore I will make the heavens tremble,
and the earth will be shaken out of its place,
at the wrath of the LORD of hosts
in the day of his fierce anger.
14 And like a hunted gazelle,
or like sheep with none to gather them,

[1]The Hebrew for *your* in verse 6 is singular, referring to the *inhabitant of Zion* [2]Or *those who exult in my majesty* [3]Or *earth*; also verse 9 [4]The Hebrew words for *destruction* and *almighty* sound alike

JOY

Great joy and happiness come with knowing the Lord. One who is overjoyed and excited sings these two songs, and the verses describe someone who is completely and utterly amazed at what God has done for them. The fact that the Israelites could look forward to singing these songs is a testimony to the grace of God. Nothing about their current situation would occasion such rejoicing. Their moral and spiritual failure resulted in God's judgment, yet the future promise of hope remained.

Isaiah proclaimed a coming day when God's faithfulness would be seen clearly in the coming Messiah. On this day, God's people would shout for joy at the undeserved grace they had been shown. These songs of praise are for the remnant who will be gathered from the ends of the earth (11:12), and they can also be sung by believers today in celebration of the salvation that comes from Jesus. Joy-filled worship is indicative of intimate fellowship with God. To know God and be known by him is a source of great joy — in Isaiah's time and over the centuries to today.

Isaiah also describes the joy that comes from drawing water from "the wells of salvation" (12:3). While the task of drawing water from a well would have been arduous, water is a source of life. God's saving love would be like water — it would satisfy the thirst of his people forever. Those who drank from the water he provided would find life, delight, and joy. This joy described by Isaiah was symbolized at the Feast of Booths, or Tabernacles, in which all of Israel would come together and remember God's promise to deliver them out of slavery and into the promised land (Lev 23:39 – 43). One of the rituals on each of the seven days involved the priests taking water from the Pool of Siloam. There, they would draw the clear, cool water into their beautiful ceremonial golden vases. All the while, the trumpets blared and the people celebrated in remembrance of what God had done for them in the exodus.

When Jesus was at a well talking with a Samaritan woman, she was eager to learn how Jesus would offer her water that would allow her to never be thirsty again (Jn 4:10 – 11). Jesus provides his followers with much more than physical water from a normal well. Instead, what he offers is eternal life. Believers today can sing with the same joy and hope that the Israelites celebrated in their Feast of Booths because Jesus is the wellspring of salvation (Jn 7:37 – 38). The songs of praise in Isaiah 12 are intended to encourage believers to recognize this gift and to draw others to trust God for their salvation.

each will turn to his own people,
and each will flee to his own land.
15 Whoever is found will be thrust through,
and whoever is caught will fall by the sword.
16 Their infants will be dashed in pieces
before their eyes;
their houses will be plundered
and their wives ravished.

17 Behold, I am stirring up the Medes against them,
who have no regard for silver
and do not delight in gold.
18 Their bows will slaughter[1] the young men;
they will have no mercy on the fruit of the womb;
their eyes will not pity children.
19 And Babylon, the glory of kingdoms,
the splendor and pomp of the Chaldeans,
will be like Sodom and Gomorrah
when God overthrew them.
20 It will never be inhabited
or lived in for all generations;
no Arab will pitch his tent there;
no shepherds will make their flocks lie down there.
21 But wild animals will lie down there,
and their houses will be full of howling creatures;
there ostriches[2] will dwell,
and there wild goats will dance.
22 Hyenas[3] will cry in its towers,
and jackals in the pleasant palaces;
its time is close at hand
and its days will not be prolonged.

The Restoration of Jacob

14 For the LORD will have compassion on Jacob and will again choose Israel,
and will set them in their own land, and sojourners will join them and will
attach themselves to the house of Jacob. 2 And the peoples will take them and
bring them to their place, and the house of Israel will possess them in the LORD's
land as male and female slaves.[4] They will take captive those who were their captors, and rule over those who oppressed them.

Israel's Remnant Taunts Babylon

3 When the LORD has given you rest from your pain and turmoil and the hard
service with which you were made to serve, 4 you will take up this taunt against
the king of Babylon:

"How the oppressor has ceased,
the insolent fury[5] ceased!
5 The LORD has broken the staff of the wicked,
the scepter of rulers,
6 that struck the peoples in wrath
with unceasing blows,
that ruled the nations in anger
with unrelenting persecution.
7 The whole earth is at rest and quiet;
they break forth into singing.

[1]Hebrew *dash in pieces* [2]Or *owls* [3]Or *foxes* [4]Or *servants* [5]Dead Sea Scroll (compare Septuagint, Syriac, Vulgate); the meaning of the word in the Masoretic Text is uncertain

8 The cypresses rejoice at you,
the cedars of Lebanon, saying,
'Since you were laid low,
no woodcutter comes up against us.'
9 Sheol beneath is stirred up
to meet you when you come;
it rouses the shades to greet you,
all who were leaders of the earth;
it raises from their thrones
all who were kings of the nations.
10 All of them will answer
and say to you:
'You too have become as weak as we!
You have become like us!'
11 Your pomp is brought down to Sheol,
the sound of your harps;
maggots are laid as a bed beneath you,
and worms are your covers.

12 "How you are fallen from heaven,
O Day Star, son of Dawn!
How you are cut down to the ground,
you who laid the nations low!
13 You said in your heart,
'I will ascend to heaven;
above the stars of God
I will set my throne on high;
I will sit on the mount of assembly
in the far reaches of the north;[1]
14 I will ascend above the heights of the clouds;
I will make myself like the Most High.'
15 But you are brought down to Sheol,
to the far reaches of the pit.
16 Those who see you will stare at you
and ponder over you:
'Is this the man who made the earth tremble,
who shook kingdoms,
17 who made the world like a desert
and overthrew its cities,
who did not let his prisoners go home?'
18 All the kings of the nations lie in glory,
each in his own tomb;[2]
19 but you are cast out, away from your grave,
like a loathed branch,
clothed with the slain, those pierced by the sword,
who go down to the stones of the pit,
like a dead body trampled underfoot.
20 You will not be joined with them in burial,
because you have destroyed your land,
you have slain your people.

"May the offspring of evildoers
nevermore be named!
21 Prepare slaughter for his sons
because of the guilt of their fathers,

[1]Or *in the remote parts of Zaphon* [2]Hebrew *house*

ISAIAH 14:12–15

THE FALL OF THE PRIDEFUL

Isaiah wrote this passage promising that Israelites would one day use these words to taunt the king of Babylon who had brought destruction on them. Isaiah prophesies that arrogant Babylon, once powerful and mighty, will be thrown down.

How ironic that the thing that sets something or someone most in opposition to God is the desire to be God's equal. Some scholars suggest that although this text is directed at the ruler of Babylon, it also depicts the fall of Satan. Regardless of its target, the text makes clear that a desire to be on equal footing with God is a pride-generated desire that will result in destruction. God has no equal, and his greatness is beyond attainable. For believers, it is crucial to recognize the fact that the character of God is not something to be attained; rather it is something to be worshiped. True to the old adage, pride always comes before a fall, so it is best for believers to approach the unattainable greatness of God with sincere humility and respect.

lest they rise and possess the earth,
and fill the face of the world with cities."

22"I will rise up against them," declares the LORD of hosts, "and will cut off
from Babylon name and remnant, descendants and posterity," declares the LORD.
23"And I will make it a possession of the hedgehog,[1] and pools of water, and I will
sweep it with the broom of destruction," declares the LORD of hosts.

An Oracle Concerning Assyria

24 The LORD of hosts has sworn:
"As I have planned,
so shall it be,
and as I have purposed,
so shall it stand,
25 that I will break the Assyrian in my land,
and on my mountains trample him underfoot;
and his yoke shall depart from them,
and his burden from their shoulder."

26 This is the purpose that is purposed
concerning the whole earth,
and this is the hand that is stretched out
over all the nations.
27 For the LORD of hosts has purposed,
and who will annul it?
His hand is stretched out,
and who will turn it back?

An Oracle Concerning Philistia

28In the year that King Ahaz died came this oracle:

29 Rejoice not, O Philistia, all of you,
that the rod that struck you is broken,
for from the serpent's root will come forth an adder,
and its fruit will be a flying fiery serpent.
30 And the firstborn of the poor will graze,
and the needy lie down in safety;
but I will kill your root with famine,
and your remnant it will slay.
31 Wail, O gate; cry out, O city;
melt in fear, O Philistia, all of you!
For smoke comes out of the north,
and there is no straggler in his ranks.

32 What will one answer the messengers of the nation?
"The LORD has founded Zion,
and in her the afflicted of his people find refuge."

An Oracle Concerning Moab

15 An oracle concerning Moab.

Because Ar of Moab is laid waste in a night,
Moab is undone;
because Kir of Moab is laid waste in a night,
Moab is undone.
2 He has gone up to the temple,[2] and to Dibon,
to the high places[3] to weep;

[1]Possibly *porcupine*, or *owl* [2]Hebrew *the house* [3]Or *temple, even Dibon to the high places*

over Nebo and over Medeba
Moab wails.
On every head is baldness;
every beard is shorn;
3 in the streets they wear sackcloth;
on the housetops and in the squares
everyone wails and melts in tears.
4 Heshbon and Elealeh cry out;
their voice is heard as far as Jahaz;
therefore the armed men of Moab cry aloud;
his soul trembles.
5 My heart cries out for Moab;
her fugitives flee to Zoar,
to Eglath-shelishiyah.
For at the ascent of Luhith
they go up weeping;
on the road to Horonaim
they raise a cry of destruction;
6 the waters of Nimrim
are a desolation;
the grass is withered, the vegetation fails,
the greenery is no more.
7 Therefore the abundance they have gained
and what they have laid up
they carry away
over the Brook of the Willows.
8 For a cry has gone
around the land of Moab;
her wailing reaches to Eglaim;
her wailing reaches to Beer-elim.
9 For the waters of Dibon[1] are full of blood;
for I will bring upon Dibon even more,
a lion for those of Moab who escape,
for the remnant of the land.
16 Send the lamb to the ruler of the land,
from Sela, by way of the desert,
to the mount of the daughter of Zion.
2 Like fleeing birds,
like a scattered nest,
so are the daughters of Moab
at the fords of the Arnon.
3 "Give counsel;
grant justice;
make your shade like night
at the height of noon;
shelter the outcasts;
do not reveal the fugitive;
4 let the outcasts of Moab
sojourn among you;
be a shelter to them[2]
from the destroyer.
When the oppressor is no more,
and destruction has ceased,

[1]Dead Sea Scroll, Vulgate (compare Syriac); Masoretic Text *Dimon*; twice in this verse [2]Some Hebrew manuscripts, Septuagint, Syriac; Masoretic Text *let my outcasts sojourn among you; as for Moab, be a shelter to them*

and he who tramples underfoot has vanished from the land,
5 then a throne will be established in steadfast love,
and on it will sit in faithfulness
in the tent of David
one who judges and seeks justice
and is swift to do righteousness."

6 We have heard of the pride of Moab—
how proud he is!—
of his arrogance, his pride, and his insolence;
in his idle boasting he is not right.
7 Therefore let Moab wail for Moab,
let everyone wail.
Mourn, utterly stricken,
for the raisin cakes of Kir-hareseth.

8 For the fields of Heshbon languish,
and the vine of Sibmah;
the lords of the nations
have struck down its branches,
which reached to Jazer
and strayed to the desert;
its shoots spread abroad
and passed over the sea.
9 Therefore I weep with the weeping of Jazer
for the vine of Sibmah;
I drench you with my tears,
O Heshbon and Elealeh;
for over your summer fruit and your harvest
the shout has ceased.
10 And joy and gladness are taken away from the fruitful field,
and in the vineyards no songs are sung,
no cheers are raised;
no treader treads out wine in the presses;
I have put an end to the shouting.
11 Therefore my inner parts moan like a lyre for Moab,
and my inmost self for Kir-hareseth.

12 And when Moab presents himself, when he wearies himself on the high
place, when he comes to his sanctuary to pray, he will not prevail.
13 This is the word that the LORD spoke concerning Moab in the past. 14 But now
the LORD has spoken, saying, "In three years, like the years of a hired worker, the
glory of Moab will be brought into contempt, in spite of all his great multitude,
and those who remain will be very few and feeble."

An Oracle Concerning Damascus

17 An oracle concerning Damascus.

Behold, Damascus will cease to be a city
and will become a heap of ruins.
2 The cities of Aroer are deserted;
they will be for flocks,
which will lie down, and none will make them afraid.
3 The fortress will disappear from Ephraim,
and the kingdom from Damascus;
and the remnant of Syria will be
like the glory of the children of Israel,
declares the LORD of hosts.

4 And in that day the glory of Jacob will be brought low,
and the fat of his flesh will grow lean.
5 And it shall be as when the reaper gathers standing grain
and his arm harvests the ears,
and as when one gleans the ears of grain
in the Valley of Rephaim.
6 Gleanings will be left in it,
as when an olive tree is beaten—
two or three berries
in the top of the highest bough,
four or five
on the branches of a fruit tree,
declares the LORD God of Israel.

7In that day man will look to his Maker, and his eyes will look on the Holy One
of Israel. 8He will not look to the altars, the work of his hands, and he will not look
on what his own fingers have made, either the Asherim or the altars of incense.
9In that day their strong cities will be like the deserted places of the wooded
heights and the hilltops, which they deserted because of the children of Israel,
and there will be desolation.

10 For you have forgotten the God of your salvation
and have not remembered the Rock of your refuge;
therefore, though you plant pleasant plants
and sow the vine-branch of a stranger,
11 though you make them grow[1] on the day that you plant
them,
and make them blossom in the morning that you sow,
yet the harvest will flee away[2]
in a day of grief and incurable pain.

12 Ah, the thunder of many peoples;
they thunder like the thundering of the sea!
Ah, the roar of nations;
they roar like the roaring of mighty waters!
13 The nations roar like the roaring of many waters,
but he will rebuke them, and they will flee far away,
chased like chaff on the mountains before the wind
and whirling dust before the storm.
14 At evening time, behold, terror!
Before morning, they are no more!
This is the portion of those who loot us,
and the lot of those who plunder us.

An Oracle Concerning Cush

18 Ah, land of whirring wings
that is beyond the rivers of Cush,[3]
2 which sends ambassadors by the sea,
in vessels of papyrus on the waters!
Go, you swift messengers,
to a nation tall and smooth,
to a people feared near and far,
a nation mighty and conquering,
whose land the rivers divide.

3 All you inhabitants of the world,
you who dwell on the earth,

[1]Or *though you carefully fence them* [2]Or *will be a heap* [3]Probably *Nubia*

[3]Then the LORD said, "As my servant Isaiah has walked naked and barefoot for
three years as a sign and a portent against Egypt and Cush,[1] [4]so shall the king of
Assyria lead away the Egyptian captives and the Cushite exiles, both the young
and the old, naked and barefoot, with buttocks uncovered, the nakedness of
Egypt. [5]Then they shall be dismayed and ashamed because of Cush their hope
and of Egypt their boast. [6]And the inhabitants of this coastland will say in that
day, 'Behold, this is what has happened to those in whom we hoped and to whom
we fled for help to be delivered from the king of Assyria! And we, how shall we
escape?' "

Fallen, Fallen Is Babylon

21 The oracle concerning the wilderness of the sea.

As whirlwinds in the Negeb sweep on,
  it comes from the wilderness,
  from a terrible land.
2 A stern vision is told to me;
  the traitor betrays,
  and the destroyer destroys.
Go up, O Elam;
  lay siege, O Media;
all the sighing she has caused
  I bring to an end.
3 Therefore my loins are filled with anguish;
  pangs have seized me,
  like the pangs of a woman in labor;
I am bowed down so that I cannot hear;
  I am dismayed so that I cannot see.
4 My heart staggers; horror has appalled me;
  the twilight I longed for
  has been turned for me into trembling.
5 They prepare the table,
  they spread the rugs,[2]
  they eat, they drink.
Arise, O princes;
  oil the shield!
6 For thus the Lord said to me:
"Go, set a watchman;
  let him announce what he sees.
7 When he sees riders, horsemen in pairs,
  riders on donkeys, riders on camels,
let him listen diligently,
  very diligently."
8 Then he who saw cried out:[3]
"Upon a watchtower I stand, O Lord,
  continually by day,
and at my post I am stationed
  whole nights.
9 And behold, here come riders,
  horsemen in pairs!"
And he answered,
  "Fallen, fallen is Babylon;
and all the carved images of her gods
  he has shattered to the ground."

[1]Probably *Nubia* [2]Or *they set the watchman* [3]Dead Sea Scroll, Syriac; Masoretic Text *Then a lion cried out*, or *Then he cried out like a lion*

10 O my threshed and winnowed one,
what I have heard from the LORD of hosts,
the God of Israel, I announce to you.

11 The oracle concerning Dumah.

One is calling to me from Seir,
"Watchman, what time of the night?
Watchman, what time of the night?"
12 The watchman says:
"Morning comes, and also the night.
If you will inquire, inquire;
come back again."

13 The oracle concerning Arabia.

In the thickets in Arabia you will lodge,
O caravans of Dedanites.
14 To the thirsty bring water;
meet the fugitive with bread,
O inhabitants of the land of Tema.
15 For they have fled from the swords,
from the drawn sword,
from the bent bow,
and from the press of battle.

16 For thus the Lord said to me, "Within a year, according to the years of a hired
worker, all the glory of Kedar will come to an end. 17 And the remainder of the
archers of the mighty men of the sons of Kedar will be few, for the LORD, the God
of Israel, has spoken."

An Oracle Concerning Jerusalem

22 The oracle concerning the valley of vision.

What do you mean that you have gone up,
all of you, to the housetops,
2 you who are full of shoutings,
tumultuous city, exultant town?
Your slain are not slain with the sword
or dead in battle.
3 All your leaders have fled together;
without the bow they were captured.
All of you who were found were captured,
though they had fled far away.
4 Therefore I said:
"Look away from me;
let me weep bitter tears;
do not labor to comfort me
concerning the destruction of the daughter of my
people."

5 For the Lord GOD of hosts has a day
of tumult and trampling and confusion
in the valley of vision,
a battering down of walls
and a shouting to the mountains.
6 And Elam bore the quiver
with chariots and horsemen,
and Kir uncovered the shield.

7 Your choicest valleys were full of chariots,
and the horsemen took their stand at the gates.
8 He has taken away the covering of Judah.

In that day you looked to the weapons of the House of the Forest, 9and you
saw that the breaches of the city of David were many. You collected the waters of
the lower pool, 10and you counted the houses of Jerusalem, and you broke down
the houses to fortify the wall. 11You made a reservoir between the two walls for
the water of the old pool. But you did not look to him who did it, or see him who
planned it long ago.

12 In that day the Lord GOD of hosts
called for weeping and mourning,
for baldness and wearing sackcloth;
13 and behold, joy and gladness,
killing oxen and slaughtering sheep,
eating flesh and drinking wine.
"Let us eat and drink,
for tomorrow we die."
14 The LORD of hosts has revealed himself in my ears:
"Surely this iniquity will not be atoned for you until you die,"
says the Lord GOD of hosts.

15Thus says the Lord GOD of hosts, "Come, go to this steward, to Shebna, who
is over the household, and say to him: 16What have you to do here, and whom
have you here, that you have cut out here a tomb for yourself, you who cut out
a tomb on the height and carve a dwelling for yourself in the rock? 17Behold, the
LORD will hurl you away violently, O you strong man. He will seize firm hold on
you 18and whirl you around and around, and throw you like a ball into a wide land.
There you shall die, and there shall be your glorious chariots, you shame of your
master's house. 19I will thrust you from your office, and you will be pulled down
from your station. 20In that day I will call my servant Eliakim the son of Hilkiah,
21and I will clothe him with your robe, and will bind your sash on him, and will
commit your authority to his hand. And he shall be a father to the inhabitants of
Jerusalem and to the house of Judah. 22And I will place on his shoulder the key
of the house of David. He shall open, and none shall shut; and he shall shut, and
none shall open. 23And I will fasten him like a peg in a secure place, and he will
become a throne of honor to his father's house. 24And they will hang on him the
whole honor of his father's house, the offspring and issue, every small vessel,
from the cups to all the flagons. 25In that day, declares the LORD of hosts, the peg
that was fastened in a secure place will give way, and it will be cut down and fall,
and the load that was on it will be cut off, for the LORD has spoken."

An Oracle Concerning Tyre and Sidon

23 The oracle concerning Tyre.

Wail, O ships of Tarshish,
for Tyre is laid waste, without house or harbor!
From the land of Cyprus[1]
it is revealed to them.
2 Be still, O inhabitants of the coast;
the merchants of Sidon, who cross the sea, have filled you.
3 And on many waters
your revenue was the grain of Shihor,
the harvest of the Nile;
you were the merchant of the nations.

[1]Hebrew *Kittim*; also verse 12

THE OPEN DOOR

A steward is chiefly concerned with the affairs of his master. But here we find Shebna, identified as a steward in charge of the king's palace (a position second only to the king), more concerned with providing for himself than serving the king. While he should have been preparing the way for the siege that would come to the city, he was busy instead preparing a tomb for himself that was fit for a king. In this, Shebna represented Judah: he was more concerned with meeting his needs and pursuing the desires of his heart than he was in honoring God.

In contrast to the selfish intent of Shebna, Isaiah predicted that a new steward would rise up in his place. He would inherit the royal clothes and the authoritative seal. Unlike his self-serving predecessor, he would care for the people like a father, and he would put his own desires to the side for their good. He would inherit the keys to the kingdom and control who gets into the palace to see the king and who does not. Isaiah identifies this new steward as Eliakim, and yet we know that this compassionate and welcoming steward is just a shadow of the even greater One to come.

Jesus didn't only put aside his ambition for the sake of God's people; he gave up his life for their eternal benefit. Jesus holds not only the keys to an earthly palace, but also the keys to the kingdom of God. His servanthood stands in direct contrast to Shebna, in that Jesus took on the form of a servant, considered others as being more important than himself, and submitted himself to death on behalf of those whom he loved. He doesn't merely open the door for a one-time audience with a king; rather, through his own sacrifice he has provided complete access to the King of the universe for all who will believe. Through Jesus, the greatest door is freely opened to whoever will walk through it and accept his free gift of salvation. Those who believe in Jesus find him not only ready to open the door, but to actually *be* the door (Lk 13:22–29; Jn 10:9; 14:6), and through him to find unending and open access to God's throne room. It is through him, and only through him, that the door to God and the life he offers is open (Rev 3:7).

4 Be ashamed, O Sidon, for the sea has spoken,
the stronghold of the sea, saying:
"I have neither labored nor given birth,
I have neither reared young men
nor brought up young women."
5 When the report comes to Egypt,
they will be in anguish[1] over the report about
Tyre.
6 Cross over to Tarshish;
wail, O inhabitants of the coast!
7 Is this your exultant city
whose origin is from days of old,
whose feet carried her
to settle far away?
8 Who has purposed this
against Tyre, the bestower of crowns,
whose merchants were princes,
whose traders were the honored of the earth?
9 The LORD of hosts has purposed it,
to defile the pompous pride of all glory,[2]
to dishonor all the honored of the earth.
10 Cross over your land like the Nile,
O daughter of Tarshish;
there is no restraint anymore.
11 He has stretched out his hand over the sea;
he has shaken the kingdoms;
the LORD has given command concerning Canaan
to destroy its strongholds.
12 And he said:
"You will no more exult,
O oppressed virgin daughter of Sidon;
arise, cross over to Cyprus,
even there you will have no rest."

13Behold the land of the Chaldeans! This is the people that was not;[3] Assyria destined it for wild beasts. They erected their siege towers, they stripped her palaces bare, they made her a ruin.

14 Wail, O ships of Tarshish,
for your stronghold is laid waste.

15In that day Tyre will be forgotten for seventy years, like the days[4] of one king. At the end of seventy years, it will happen to Tyre as in the song of the prostitute:

16 "Take a harp;
go about the city,
O forgotten prostitute!
Make sweet melody;
sing many songs,
that you may be remembered."

17At the end of seventy years, the LORD will visit Tyre, and she will return to her wages and will prostitute herself with all the kingdoms of the world on the face of the earth. 18Her merchandise and her wages will be holy to the LORD. It will not be stored or hoarded, but her merchandise will supply abundant food and fine clothing for those who dwell before the LORD.

[1]Hebrew *they will have labor pains* [2]The Hebrew words for *glory* and *hosts* sound alike [3]Or *that has become nothing* [4]Or *lifetime*

Judgment on the Whole Earth

24 Behold, the LORD will empty the earth[1] and make it desolate,
and he will twist its surface and scatter its inhabitants.
2 And it shall be, as with the people, so with the priest;
as with the slave, so with his master;
as with the maid, so with her mistress;
as with the buyer, so with the seller;
as with the lender, so with the borrower;
as with the creditor, so with the debtor.
3 The earth shall be utterly empty and utterly plundered;
for the LORD has spoken this word.

4 The earth mourns and withers;
the world languishes and withers;
the highest people of the earth languish.
5 The earth lies defiled
under its inhabitants;
for they have transgressed the laws,
violated the statutes,
broken the everlasting covenant.
6 Therefore a curse devours the earth,
and its inhabitants suffer for their guilt;
therefore the inhabitants of the earth are scorched,
and few men are left.
7 The wine mourns,
the vine languishes,
all the merry-hearted sigh.
8 The mirth of the tambourines is stilled,
the noise of the jubilant has ceased,
the mirth of the lyre is stilled.
9 No more do they drink wine with singing;
strong drink is bitter to those who drink it.
10 The wasted city is broken down;
every house is shut up so that none can enter.
11 There is an outcry in the streets for lack of wine;
all joy has grown dark;
the gladness of the earth is banished.
12 Desolation is left in the city;
the gates are battered into ruins.
13 For thus it shall be in the midst of the earth
among the nations,
as when an olive tree is beaten,
as at the gleaning when the grape harvest is done.

14 They lift up their voices, they sing for joy;
over the majesty of the LORD they shout from the west.[2]
15 Therefore in the east[3] give glory to the LORD;
in the coastlands of the sea, give glory to the name of the LORD,
the God of Israel.
16 From the ends of the earth we hear songs of praise,
of glory to the Righteous One.
But I say, "I waste away,
I waste away. Woe is me!
For the traitors have betrayed,
with betrayal the traitors have betrayed."

[1]Or *land*; also throughout this chapter [2]Hebrew *from the sea* [3]Hebrew *in the realm of light*, or *with the fires*

17 Terror and the pit and the snare[1]
are upon you, O inhabitant of the earth!
18 He who flees at the sound of the terror
shall fall into the pit,
and he who climbs out of the pit
shall be caught in the snare.
For the windows of heaven are opened,
and the foundations of the earth tremble.
19 The earth is utterly broken,
the earth is split apart,
the earth is violently shaken.
20 The earth staggers like a drunken man;
it sways like a hut;
its transgression lies heavy upon it,
and it falls, and will not rise again.

21 On that day the LORD will punish
the host of heaven, in heaven,
and the kings of the earth, on the earth.
22 They will be gathered together
as prisoners in a pit;
they will be shut up in a prison,
and after many days they will be punished.
23 Then the moon will be confounded
and the sun ashamed,
for the LORD of hosts reigns
on Mount Zion and in Jerusalem,
and his glory will be before his elders.

God Will Swallow Up Death Forever

25 O LORD, you are my God;
I will exalt you; I will praise your name,
for you have done wonderful things,
plans formed of old, faithful and sure.
2 For you have made the city a heap,
the fortified city a ruin;
the foreigners' palace is a city no more;
it will never be rebuilt.
3 Therefore strong peoples will glorify you;
cities of ruthless nations will fear you.
4 For you have been a stronghold to the poor,
a stronghold to the needy in his distress,
a shelter from the storm and a shade from the heat;
for the breath of the ruthless is like a storm against a wall,
5 like heat in a dry place.
You subdue the noise of the foreigners;
as heat by the shade of a cloud,
so the song of the ruthless is put down.

6 On this mountain the LORD of hosts will make for all peoples
a feast of rich food, a feast of well-aged wine,
of rich food full of marrow, of aged wine well refined.
7 And he will swallow up on this mountain
the covering that is cast over all peoples,
the veil that is spread over all nations.
8 He will swallow up death forever;

[1]The Hebrew words for *terror*, *pit*, and *snare* sound alike

and the Lord GOD will wipe away tears from all faces,
and the reproach of his people he will take away from all the earth,
for the LORD has spoken.
9 It will be said on that day,
"Behold, this is our God; we have waited for him, that he might
save us.
This is the LORD; we have waited for him;
let us be glad and rejoice in his salvation."
10 For the hand of the LORD will rest on this mountain,
and Moab shall be trampled down in his place,
as straw is trampled down in a dunghill.[1]
11 And he will spread out his hands in the midst of it
as a swimmer spreads his hands out to swim,
but the LORD will lay low his pompous pride together with the skill[2]
of his hands.
12 And the high fortifications of his walls he will bring down,
lay low, and cast to the ground, to the dust.

You Keep Him in Perfect Peace

26 In that day this song will be sung in the land of Judah:

"We have a strong city;
he sets up salvation
as walls and bulwarks.
2 Open the gates,
that the righteous nation that keeps faith may enter in.
3 You keep him in perfect peace
whose mind is stayed on you,
because he trusts in you.
4 Trust in the LORD forever,
for the LORD GOD is an everlasting rock.
5 For he has humbled
the inhabitants of the height,
the lofty city.
He lays it low, lays it low to the ground,
casts it to the dust.
6 The foot tramples it,
the feet of the poor,
the steps of the needy."

7 The path of the righteous is level;
you make level the way of the righteous.
8 In the path of your judgments,
O LORD, we wait for you;
your name and remembrance
are the desire of our soul.
9 My soul yearns for you in the night;
my spirit within me earnestly seeks you.
For when your judgments are in the earth,
the inhabitants of the world learn righteousness.
10 If favor is shown to the wicked,
he does not learn righteousness;
in the land of uprightness he deals corruptly
and does not see the majesty of the LORD.

[1]The Hebrew words for *dunghill* and for the Moabite town *Madmen* (Jeremiah 48:2) sound alike [2]Or *in spite of the skill*

ISAIAH 26:4

THE EVERLASTING ROCK

This verse contains the simple imperative: "Trust." Though simple in word, trust is difficult to maintain in life. Most people have had negative life experiences that have taught them that trust is a commodity not to trade in easily, for anyone and everyone we fully trust will eventually fail. Many times failure is unintentional, but failure is inevitable. Humans, it seems, were not built to fully carry that kind of weight for each other.

But the Lord is the Rock. Unmovable. Unshakable. Unchangeable. His character stands more firmly than stone. Though any human will eventually crack under the pressure of the weight of carrying another's trust, the Lord is more than capable of carrying the trust of all who have faith in him. We know this is true because he has proven himself to be trustworthy time and time again—most of all through the life, death, and resurrection of Jesus. Jesus validates all of the trust that believers place in God; his saving work on our behalf proves that God, the Everlasting Rock, can bear that weight.

ISAIAH 26:8

WAITING

Isaiah describes those who waited and remained faithful to the Lord. As God's judgment on Judah unfolded around them, many waited patiently while remaining steadfast in their love for and devotion to the Lord. Waiting reflects a relinquishing of power, a trust in someone else for the future, and that is exactly

(continued on page 1051)

PROMISES

"It's better." That phrase can be applied to what waits for the people of God when they are fully with him someday — in comparison to almost anything in this life now. Every relationship, every emotion, every sense, every celebration — every aspect of what's good and right and joyful that believers experience in this life — is only a foretaste of what's coming.

Isaiah looks forward to a great banquet, a joyous celebration of God's rule by people from around the world. The kinds of things available at this banquet remind believers of God's extravagant generosity toward his people. At this banquet, the food will not be just good food; it will be the choicest of food. The wine will not be just good wine; it will be the choicest of wine. This is the unending and lavish celebration, the absolute fullness of joy, that waits for God's people in his presence (Ps 16:11). At this feast, all of God's people — those from every tribe, tongue, and nation, will gather together to celebrate the bountiful provision of God (Lk 13:29; 14:15).

Not only do believers see God's generosity on display in this passage, but they also see that the great shroud that hangs over humanity right now — that shadow that clouds over even the best of earthly celebrations — will one day be wiped out forever. Humans know that eventually birthdays will become memorials; that holidays will eventually be tinged with the sense of loss; that every celebration will eventually pass away as our loved ones do. Death is that cloud, that shroud, which hangs constantly in the background of the earthly experience reminding us that even the best of times on this earth have limitations and will eventually come to an end.

But one day that shroud will be no more. God will swallow up death forever, for the risen Christ has defeated it once and for all. Through him, death has died and been swallowed up in victory (Isa 25:8; 1Co 15:54). The punishment for sin has been paid, and all who trust in Jesus will live and celebrate forever.

This is the unshakable, unalterable, eternal Word of God. God will provide a feast for his people, even though they may find hunger and pain in this life. These promises are as sure as the eternal character of God. And God keeps his promises (Jos 23:14).

11 O LORD, your hand is lifted up,
but they do not see it.
Let them see your zeal for your people, and be ashamed.
Let the fire for your adversaries consume them.
12 O LORD, you will ordain peace for us,
for you have indeed done for us all our works.
13 O LORD our God,
other lords besides you have ruled over us,
but your name alone we bring to remembrance.
14 They are dead, they will not live;
they are shades, they will not arise;
to that end you have visited them with destruction
and wiped out all remembrance of them.
15 But you have increased the nation, O LORD,
you have increased the nation; you are glorified;
you have enlarged all the borders of the land.

16 O LORD, in distress they sought you;
they poured out a whispered prayer
when your discipline was upon them.
17 Like a pregnant woman
who writhes and cries out in her pangs
when she is near to giving birth,
so were we because of you, O LORD;
18 we were pregnant, we writhed,
but we have given birth to wind.
We have accomplished no deliverance in the earth,
and the inhabitants of the world have not fallen.
19 Your dead shall live; their bodies shall rise.
You who dwell in the dust, awake and sing for joy!
For your dew is a dew of light,
and the earth will give birth to the dead.

20 Come, my people, enter your chambers,
and shut your doors behind you;
hide yourselves for a little while
until the fury has passed by.
21 For behold, the LORD is coming out from his place
to punish the inhabitants of the earth for their iniquity,
and the earth will disclose the blood shed on it,
and will no more cover its slain.

The Redemption of Israel

27 In that day the LORD with his hard and great and strong sword will punish
Leviathan the fleeing serpent, Leviathan the twisting serpent, and he will
slay the dragon that is in the sea.

2 In that day,
"A pleasant vineyard,[1] sing of it!
3 I, the LORD, am its keeper;
every moment I water it.
Lest anyone punish it,
I keep it night and day;
4 I have no wrath.
Would that I had thorns and briers to battle!
I would march against them,
I would burn them up together.

[1]Many Hebrew manuscripts *A vineyard of wine*

(Waiting, continued)

how the people of Judah are pictured here. They know that God is ultimately the one in control, and they are content to wait for the ultimate blessing that God had promised them. To those who wait, God's names and his remembrance are the desire of our souls.

This kind of faith serves as an excellent example for how believers should continually carry themselves today. The people of God are waiting for Jesus to return and to bring justice to the earth. It is important to realize that there is nothing they can do to speed up his return. Instead, believers should ensure that God's name and his renown are the desire of their hearts, and in their waiting, remain patient in their praise and faithful to tell others about him.

5 Or let them lay hold of my protection,
let them make peace with me,
let them make peace with me."

6 In days to come[1] Jacob shall take root,
Israel shall blossom and put forth shoots
and fill the whole world with fruit.

7 Has he struck them as he struck those who struck them?
Or have they been slain as their slayers were slain?
8 Measure by measure,[2] by exile you contended with them;
he removed them with his fierce breath[3] in the day of the east wind.
9 Therefore by this the guilt of Jacob will be atoned for,
and this will be the full fruit of the removal of his sin:[4]
when he makes all the stones of the altars
like chalkstones crushed to pieces,
no Asherim or incense altars will remain standing.
10 For the fortified city is solitary,
a habitation deserted and forsaken, like the wilderness;
there the calf grazes;
there it lies down and strips its branches.
11 When its boughs are dry, they are broken;
women come and make a fire of them.
For this is a people without discernment;
therefore he who made them will not have compassion on them;
he who formed them will show them no favor.

12 In that day from the river Euphrates[5] to the Brook of Egypt the LORD will
thresh out the grain, and you will be gleaned one by one, O people of Israel. 13 And
in that day a great trumpet will be blown, and those who were lost in the land of
Assyria and those who were driven out to the land of Egypt will come and worship
the LORD on the holy mountain at Jerusalem.

Judgment on Ephraim and Jerusalem

28 Ah, the proud crown of the drunkards of Ephraim,
and the fading flower of its glorious beauty,
which is on the head of the rich valley of those overcome with wine!
2 Behold, the Lord has one who is mighty and strong;
like a storm of hail, a destroying tempest,
like a storm of mighty, overflowing waters,
he casts down to the earth with his hand.
3 The proud crown of the drunkards of Ephraim
will be trodden underfoot;
4 and the fading flower of its glorious beauty,
which is on the head of the rich valley,
will be like a first-ripe fig[6] before the summer:
when someone sees it, he swallows it
as soon as it is in his hand.

5 In that day the LORD of hosts will be a crown of glory,[7]
and a diadem of beauty, to the remnant of his people,
6 and a spirit of justice to him who sits in judgment,
and strength to those who turn back the battle at the gate.

7 These also reel with wine
and stagger with strong drink;

[1]Hebrew *In those to come* [2]Or *By driving her away*; the meaning of the Hebrew word is uncertain
[3]Or *wind* [4]Septuagint *and this is the blessing when I take away his sin* [5]Hebrew *from the River* [6]Or *fruit*
[7]The Hebrew words for *glory* and *hosts* sound alike

the priest and the prophet reel with strong drink,
they are swallowed by[1] wine,
they stagger with strong drink,
they reel in vision,
they stumble in giving judgment.
8 For all tables are full of filthy vomit,
with no space left.

9 "To whom will he teach knowledge,
and to whom will he explain the message?
Those who are weaned from the milk,
those taken from the breast?
10 For it is precept upon precept, precept upon precept,
line upon line, line upon line,
here a little, there a little."

11 For by people of strange lips
and with a foreign tongue
the LORD will speak to this people,
12 to whom he has said,
"This is rest;
give rest to the weary;
and this is repose";
yet they would not hear.
13 And the word of the LORD will be to them
precept upon precept, precept upon precept,
line upon line, line upon line,
here a little, there a little,
that they may go, and fall backward,
and be broken, and snared, and taken.

A Cornerstone in Zion

14 Therefore hear the word of the LORD, you scoffers,
who rule this people in Jerusalem!
15 Because you have said, "We have made a covenant with death,
and with Sheol we have an agreement,
when the overwhelming whip passes through
it will not come to us,
for we have made lies our refuge,
and in falsehood we have taken shelter";
16 therefore thus says the Lord GOD,
"Behold, I am the one who has laid[2] as a foundation in Zion,
a stone, a tested stone,
a precious cornerstone, of a sure foundation:
'Whoever believes will not be in haste.'
17 And I will make justice the line,
and righteousness the plumb line;
and hail will sweep away the refuge of lies,
and waters will overwhelm the shelter."
18 Then your covenant with death will be annulled,
and your agreement with Sheol will not stand;
when the overwhelming scourge passes through,
you will be beaten down by it.
19 As often as it passes through it will take you;
for morning by morning it will pass through,
by day and by night;

[1]Or *confused by* [2]Dead Sea Scroll *I am laying*

ISAIAH 28:14–16

A PRECIOUS CORNERSTONE

Because of their quickly changing political situation, the people of Isaiah's day were habitually looking for something sure and steadfast in which to find security and safety. Time and time again, their alliances and efforts to find such security and stability were thwarted. They foolishly made covenants that had deadly consequences and tried to secure themselves on less than firm footing. They should have turned to God to receive that sure foundation for which the people were searching.

The cornerstone was the first stone laid in building a structure; this single stone gave shape, security, and integrity to the rest of the structure; it was the stone off of which everything else about the structure was aligned. When it comes to the Christian faith, Jesus Christ is that precious cornerstone. When believers build their lives on Jesus and on him alone, they can know that on him, there is eternal integrity and security (1Pe 2:6). What is the basis for all hope? What stands at the cornerstone of life? What gives shape to every relationship, decision, and priority humans hold dear? If it's something other than Jesus, then people who are building their lives on that something else are building on sinking sand (Mt 7:26).

and it will be sheer terror to understand the message.
20 For the bed is too short to stretch oneself on,
and the covering too narrow to wrap oneself in.
21 For the LORD will rise up as on Mount Perazim;
as in the Valley of Gibeon he will be roused;
to do his deed—strange is his deed!
and to work his work—alien is his work!
22 Now therefore do not scoff,
lest your bonds be made strong;
for I have heard a decree of destruction
from the Lord GOD of hosts against the whole land.

23 Give ear, and hear my voice;
give attention, and hear my speech.
24 Does he who plows for sowing plow continually?
Does he continually open and harrow his ground?
25 When he has leveled its surface,
does he not scatter dill, sow cumin,
and put in wheat in rows
and barley in its proper place,
and emmer[1] as the border?
26 For he is rightly instructed;
his God teaches him.

27 Dill is not threshed with a threshing sledge,
nor is a cart wheel rolled over cumin,
but dill is beaten out with a stick,
and cumin with a rod.
28 Does one crush grain for bread?
No, he does not thresh it forever;[2]
when he drives his cart wheel over it
with his horses, he does not crush it.
29 This also comes from the LORD of hosts;
he is wonderful in counsel
and excellent in wisdom.

The Siege of Jerusalem

29 Ah, Ariel, Ariel,
the city where David encamped!
Add year to year;
let the feasts run their round.
2 Yet I will distress Ariel,
and there shall be moaning and lamentation,
and she shall be to me like an Ariel.[3]
3 And I will encamp against you all around,
and will besiege you with towers
and I will raise siegeworks against you.
4 And you will be brought low; from the earth you shall speak,
and from the dust your speech will be bowed down;
your voice shall come from the ground like the voice of a ghost,
and from the dust your speech shall whisper.

5 But the multitude of your foreign foes shall be like small dust,
and the multitude of the ruthless like passing chaff.
And in an instant, suddenly,
6 you will be visited by the LORD of hosts

[1]A type of wheat [2]Or *Grain is crushed for bread; he will surely thresh it, but not forever* [3]*Ariel* could mean *lion of God*, or *hero* (2 Samuel 23:20), or *altar hearth* (Ezekiel 43:15–16)

with thunder and with earthquake and great noise,
with whirlwind and tempest, and the flame of a devouring fire.
7 And the multitude of all the nations that fight against Ariel,
all that fight against her and her stronghold and distress her,
shall be like a dream, a vision of the night.
8 As when a hungry man dreams, and behold, he is eating,
and awakes with his hunger not satisfied,
or as when a thirsty man dreams, and behold, he is drinking,
and awakes faint, with his thirst not quenched,
so shall the multitude of all the nations be
that fight against Mount Zion.

9 Astonish yourselves[1] and be astonished;
blind yourselves and be blind!
Be drunk,[2] but not with wine;
stagger,[3] but not with strong drink!
10 For the LORD has poured out upon you
a spirit of deep sleep,
and has closed your eyes (the prophets),
and covered your heads (the seers).

11 And the vision of all this has become to you like the words of a book that
is sealed. When men give it to one who can read, saying, "Read this," he says, "I
cannot, for it is sealed." 12 And when they give the book to one who cannot read,
saying, "Read this," he says, "I cannot read."

13 And the Lord said:
"Because this people draw near with their mouth
and honor me with their lips,
while their hearts are far from me,
and their fear of me is a commandment taught by men,
14 therefore, behold, I will again
do wonderful things with this people,
with wonder upon wonder;
and the wisdom of their wise men shall perish,
and the discernment of their discerning men shall be hidden."

15 Ah, you who hide deep from the LORD your counsel,
whose deeds are in the dark,
and who say, "Who sees us? Who knows us?"
16 You turn things upside down!
Shall the potter be regarded as the clay,
that the thing made should say of its maker,
"He did not make me";
or the thing formed say of him who formed it,
"He has no understanding"?

17 Is it not yet a very little while
until Lebanon shall be turned into a fruitful field,
and the fruitful field shall be regarded as a forest?
18 In that day the deaf shall hear
the words of a book,
and out of their gloom and darkness
the eyes of the blind shall see.
19 The meek shall obtain fresh joy in the LORD,
and the poor among mankind shall exult in the Holy One
of Israel.

[1] Or *Linger awhile* [2] Or *They are drunk* [3] Or *they stagger*

ISAIAH 29:9–13

RELIGIOUSNESS

Idolatry takes many forms and is as insidious as it is destructive. While some might think of an idol as a form of something made of stone or wood, the human heart has a remarkable capacity to take even that which is good and twist it into something idolatrous. Because this is our tendency, believers must recognize that something as seemingly good and right as devotion to God can be twisted into a form to which they bow. Such was the case for the people in Isaiah's day.

Though they might not have worshiped a physical idol, the people of Judah were intoxicated with their own religiousness. They were devoted to their own devotion; committed to their own commitment. And in so doing, they were trusting and loving their own religious efforts to the point that they were blind and deaf to the true Word of God. Jesus fought the same tendency toward misdirected devotion in the Pharisees of his own day who loved the law not for the sake of God, but because it filled them with pride at their own accomplishments (Mt 15:8–9). Jesus, both then and now, desires the heart of a person, not merely their religious actions. He requires their genuine love, not a self-serving and ultimately empty form of devotion.

20 For the ruthless shall come to nothing
and the scoffer cease,
and all who watch to do evil shall be cut off,
21 who by a word make a man out to be an offender,
and lay a snare for him who reproves in the gate,
and with an empty plea turn aside him who is in the right.

22Therefore thus says the LORD, who redeemed Abraham, concerning the house of Jacob:

"Jacob shall no more be ashamed,
no more shall his face grow pale.
23 For when he sees his children,
the work of my hands, in his midst,
they will sanctify my name;
they will sanctify the Holy One of Jacob
and will stand in awe of the God of Israel.
24 And those who go astray in spirit will come to understanding,
and those who murmur will accept instruction."

Do Not Go Down to Egypt

30 "Ah, stubborn children," declares the LORD,
"who carry out a plan, but not mine,
and who make an alliance,[1] but not of my Spirit,
that they may add sin to sin;
2 who set out to go down to Egypt,
without asking for my direction,
to take refuge in the protection of Pharaoh
and to seek shelter in the shadow of Egypt!
3 Therefore shall the protection of Pharaoh turn to your shame,
and the shelter in the shadow of Egypt to your humiliation.
4 For though his officials are at Zoan
and his envoys reach Hanes,
5 everyone comes to shame
through a people that cannot profit them,
that brings neither help nor profit,
but shame and disgrace."

6An oracle on the beasts of the Negeb.

Through a land of trouble and anguish,
from where come the lioness and the lion,
the adder and the flying fiery serpent,
they carry their riches on the backs of donkeys,
and their treasures on the humps of camels,
to a people that cannot profit them.
7 Egypt's help is worthless and empty;
therefore I have called her
"Rahab who sits still."

A Rebellious People

8 And now, go, write it before them on a tablet
and inscribe it in a book,
that it may be for the time to come
as a witness forever.[2]

---

[1]Hebrew *who weave a web* [2]Some Hebrew manuscripts, Syriac, Targum, Vulgate, and Greek versions; Masoretic Text *forever and ever*

9 For they are a rebellious people,
lying children,
children unwilling to hear
the instruction of the LORD;
10 who say to the seers, "Do not see,"
and to the prophets, "Do not prophesy to us what is right;
speak to us smooth things,
prophesy illusions,
11 leave the way, turn aside from the path,
let us hear no more about the Holy One of Israel."
12 Therefore thus says the Holy One of Israel,
"Because you despise this word
and trust in oppression and perverseness
and rely on them,
13 therefore this iniquity shall be to you
like a breach in a high wall, bulging out and about to collapse,
whose breaking comes suddenly, in an instant;
14 and its breaking is like that of a potter's vessel
that is smashed so ruthlessly
that among its fragments not a shard is found
with which to take fire from the hearth,
or to dip up water out of the cistern."
15 For thus said the Lord GOD, the Holy One of Israel,
"In returning[1] and rest you shall be saved;
in quietness and in trust shall be your strength."
But you were unwilling, 16 and you said,
"No! We will flee upon horses";
therefore you shall flee away;
and, "We will ride upon swift steeds";
therefore your pursuers shall be swift.
17 A thousand shall flee at the threat of one;
at the threat of five you shall flee,
till you are left
like a flagstaff on the top of a mountain,
like a signal on a hill.

The LORD Will Be Gracious

18 Therefore the LORD waits to be gracious to you,
and therefore he exalts himself to show mercy to you.
For the LORD is a God of justice;
blessed are all those who wait for him.

19 For a people shall dwell in Zion, in Jerusalem; you shall weep no more. He
will surely be gracious to you at the sound of your cry. As soon as he hears it, he
answers you. 20 And though the Lord give you the bread of adversity and the water
of affliction, yet your Teacher will not hide himself anymore, but your eyes shall
see your Teacher. 21 And your ears shall hear a word behind you, saying, "This is
the way, walk in it," when you turn to the right or when you turn to the left. 22 Then
you will defile your carved idols overlaid with silver and your gold-plated metal
images. You will scatter them as unclean things. You will say to them, "Be gone!"
23 And he will give rain for the seed with which you sow the ground, and bread,
the produce of the ground, which will be rich and plenteous. In that day your livestock will graze in large pastures, 24 and the oxen and the donkeys that work the
ground will eat seasoned fodder, which has been winnowed with shovel and fork.

[1] Or *repentance*

ISAIAH 30:15

REST AND TRUST

There is something inside the heart of people that requires a human response to adversity. We demand action both from others and from ourselves when difficulties come. So the response God desires, as pictured in this verse, is counterintuitive. Quietness? Trust? Most people, whether now or in Isaiah's day, would say that these are not common ways to react in times of crisis. It's far easier to trust in horses and chariots than to rest and find strength in the Lord (v. 16; Ps 20:7). Nevertheless, when people know, understand, and believe in the character of the Holy One of Israel, they can fully and completely rest in him.

For the people of Isaiah's day, this trust was too much, and they felt as though they must take matters into their own hands. People who believe in and follow the gospel must fight the urge to do the same, taking up arms as a replacement for faith in God's ability to save completely. Walking in the way of Jesus means fully resting in him and his ability alone to fight on our behalf and win the battles his people experience (Jn 14:5–6).

25 And on every lofty mountain and every high hill there will be brooks running
with water, in the day of the great slaughter, when the towers fall. 26 Moreover,
the light of the moon will be as the light of the sun, and the light of the sun will
be sevenfold, as the light of seven days, in the day when the LORD binds up the
brokenness of his people, and heals the wounds inflicted by his blow.

27 Behold, the name of the LORD comes from afar,
burning with his anger, and in thick rising smoke;[1]
his lips are full of fury,
and his tongue is like a devouring fire;
28 his breath is like an overflowing stream
that reaches up to the neck;
to sift the nations with the sieve of destruction,
and to place on the jaws of the peoples a bridle that leads astray.

29 You shall have a song as in the night when a holy feast is kept, and gladness
of heart, as when one sets out to the sound of the flute to go to the mountain of
the LORD, to the Rock of Israel. 30 And the LORD will cause his majestic voice to
be heard and the descending blow of his arm to be seen, in furious anger and a
flame of devouring fire, with a cloudburst and storm and hailstones. 31 The Assyrians will be terror-stricken at the voice of the LORD, when he strikes with his rod.
32 And every stroke of the appointed staff that the LORD lays on them will be to
the sound of tambourines and lyres. Battling with brandished arm, he will fight
with them. 33 For a burning place[2] has long been prepared; indeed, for the king it
is made ready, its pyre made deep and wide, with fire and wood in abundance; the
breath of the LORD, like a stream of sulfur, kindles it.

Woe to Those Who Go Down to Egypt

31 Woe[3] to those who go down to Egypt for help
and rely on horses,
who trust in chariots because they are many
and in horsemen because they are very strong,
but do not look to the Holy One of Israel
or consult the LORD!
2 And yet he is wise and brings disaster;
he does not call back his words,
but will arise against the house of the evildoers
and against the helpers of those who work iniquity.
3 The Egyptians are man, and not God,
and their horses are flesh, and not spirit.
When the LORD stretches out his hand,
the helper will stumble, and he who is helped will fall,
and they will all perish together.

4 For thus the LORD said to me,
"As a lion or a young lion growls over his prey,
and when a band of shepherds is called out against him
he is not terrified by their shouting
or daunted at their noise,
so the LORD of hosts will come down
to fight[4] on Mount Zion and on its hill.
5 Like birds hovering, so the LORD of hosts
will protect Jerusalem;
he will protect and deliver it;
he will spare and rescue it."

[1] Hebrew *in weight of uplifted clouds* [2] Or *For Topheth* [3] Or *Ah,* [4] The Hebrew words for *hosts* and *to fight* sound alike

[6]Turn to him from whom people[1] have deeply revolted, O children of Israel.
[7]For in that day everyone shall cast away his idols of silver and his idols of gold,
which your hands have sinfully made for you.

8 "And the Assyrian shall fall by a sword, not of man;
and a sword, not of man, shall devour him;
and he shall flee from the sword,
and his young men shall be put to forced labor.
9 His rock shall pass away in terror,
and his officers desert the standard in panic,"
declares the LORD, whose fire is in Zion,
and whose furnace is in Jerusalem.

A King Will Reign in Righteousness

32 Behold, a king will reign in righteousness,
and princes will rule in justice.
2 Each will be like a hiding place from the wind,
a shelter from the storm,
like streams of water in a dry place,
like the shade of a great rock in a weary land.
3 Then the eyes of those who see will not be closed,
and the ears of those who hear will give attention.
4 The heart of the hasty will understand and know,
and the tongue of the stammerers will hasten to speak distinctly.
5 The fool will no more be called noble,
nor the scoundrel said to be honorable.
6 For the fool speaks folly,
and his heart is busy with iniquity,
to practice ungodliness,
to utter error concerning the LORD,
to leave the craving of the hungry unsatisfied,
and to deprive the thirsty of drink.
7 As for the scoundrel—his devices are evil;
he plans wicked schemes
to ruin the poor with lying words,
even when the plea of the needy is right.
8 But he who is noble plans noble things,
and on noble things he stands.

Complacent Women Warned of Disaster

9 Rise up, you women who are at ease, hear my voice;
you complacent daughters, give ear to my speech.
10 In little more than a year
you will shudder, you complacent women;
for the grape harvest fails,
the fruit harvest will not come.
11 Tremble, you women who are at ease,
shudder, you complacent ones;
strip, and make yourselves bare,
and tie sackcloth around your waist.
12 Beat your breasts for the pleasant fields,
for the fruitful vine,
13 for the soil of my people
growing up in thorns and briers,

[1]Hebrew *they*

ISAIAH 32:1–8

THE KINGDOM OF RIGHTEOUSNESS

The kingdom of God is an upside-down kingdom: it stands in direct opposition to the kingdom of the world into which we all have been born. For that reason, coming into the kingdom of God can have a whiplash kind of effect—it's a process of unlearning and relearning what is truly good and righteous and valuable in God's eyes.

Jesus told us about this dramatic reversal in his Sermon on the Mount (Mt 5–7). In this kingdom, the hungry are filled. The mourners rejoice. The poor are rich. God reverses the principles that lie at the foundation of the way we observe the world as we enter into his kingdom of righteousness. Here, God's prophet predicts this reversal in the coming kingdom when what is high will be brought low and what has been humiliated will be exalted. In this kingdom of righteousness, God's people will no longer know the hard work of seeking righteousness on their own merit but will instead know the quietness, assurance, and peace that can only come from a righteousness given through the sacrifice of Jesus.

yes, for all the joyous houses
in the exultant city.
14 For the palace is forsaken,
the populous city deserted;
the hill and the watchtower
will become dens forever,
a joy of wild donkeys,
a pasture of flocks;
15 until the Spirit is poured upon us from on high,
and the wilderness becomes a fruitful field,
and the fruitful field is deemed a forest.
16 Then justice will dwell in the wilderness,
and righteousness abide in the fruitful field.
17 And the effect of righteousness will be peace,
and the result of righteousness, quietness and trust[1]
forever.
18 My people will abide in a peaceful habitation,
in secure dwellings, and in quiet resting places.
19 And it will hail when the forest falls down,
and the city will be utterly laid low.
20 Happy are you who sow beside all waters,
who let the feet of the ox and the donkey range free.

O Lord, Be Gracious to Us

33 Ah, you destroyer,
who yourself have not been destroyed,
you traitor,
whom none has betrayed!
When you have ceased to destroy,
you will be destroyed;
and when you have finished betraying,
they will betray you.

2 O Lord, be gracious to us; we wait for you.
Be our arm every morning,
our salvation in the time of trouble.
3 At the tumultuous noise peoples flee;
when you lift yourself up, nations are scattered,
4 and your spoil is gathered as the caterpillar gathers;
as locusts leap, it is leapt upon.

5 The Lord is exalted, for he dwells on high;
he will fill Zion with justice and righteousness,
6 and he will be the stability of your times,
abundance of salvation, wisdom, and knowledge;
the fear of the Lord is Zion's[2] treasure.

7 Behold, their heroes cry in the streets;
the envoys of peace weep bitterly.
8 The highways lie waste;
the traveler ceases.
Covenants are broken;
cities[3] are despised;
there is no regard for man.
9 The land mourns and languishes;
Lebanon is confounded and withers away;

[1]Or *security* [2]Hebrew *his* [3]Masoretic Text; Dead Sea Scroll *witnesses*

Sharon is like a desert,
and Bashan and Carmel shake off their leaves.

10 "Now I will arise," says the LORD,
"now I will lift myself up;
now I will be exalted.
11 You conceive chaff; you give birth to stubble;
your breath is a fire that will consume you.
12 And the peoples will be as if burned to lime,
like thorns cut down, that are burned in the fire."

13 Hear, you who are far off, what I have done;
and you who are near, acknowledge my might.
14 The sinners in Zion are afraid;
trembling has seized the godless:
"Who among us can dwell with the consuming fire?
Who among us can dwell with everlasting burnings?"
15 He who walks righteously and speaks uprightly,
who despises the gain of oppressions,
who shakes his hands, lest they hold a bribe,
who stops his ears from hearing of bloodshed
and shuts his eyes from looking on evil,
16 he will dwell on the heights;
his place of defense will be the fortresses of rocks;
his bread will be given him; his water will be sure.

17 Your eyes will behold the king in his beauty;
they will see a land that stretches afar.
18 Your heart will muse on the terror:
"Where is he who counted, where is he who weighed the tribute?
Where is he who counted the towers?"
19 You will see no more the insolent people,
the people of an obscure speech that you cannot comprehend,
stammering in a tongue that you cannot understand.
20 Behold Zion, the city of our appointed feasts!
Your eyes will see Jerusalem,
an untroubled habitation, an immovable tent,
whose stakes will never be plucked up,
nor will any of its cords be broken.
21 But there the LORD in majesty will be for us
a place of broad rivers and streams,
where no galley with oars can go,
nor majestic ship can pass.
22 For the LORD is our judge; the LORD is our lawgiver;
the LORD is our king; he will save us.

23 Your cords hang loose;
they cannot hold the mast firm in its place
or keep the sail spread out.
Then prey and spoil in abundance will be divided;
even the lame will take the prey.
24 And no inhabitant will say, "I am sick";
the people who dwell there will be forgiven their iniquity.

Judgment on the Nations

34 Draw near, O nations, to hear,
and give attention, O peoples!
Let the earth hear, and all that fills it;
the world, and all that comes from it.

ISAIAH 33:13–17

THE BEAUTY OF THE KING

Judgment is a fearsome thing, and it is coming. God is a consuming fire (v. 14), and because he is, the prophet asked a somewhat rhetorical question in verse 14. Who indeed can live with God's consuming fire? Who can remain upright when the holiness of God burns away the hypocritical acts of righteousness along with the rebellious sin of humanity? Shockingly, after this we see in verse 17 a picture not of the fire of judgment from just a few verses earlier, but instead of the beauty of the King.

Such is the difference between the perspective of those who have, in humility, thrown themselves on the mercy of the King and those who, in arrogance, have presumed upon his patience. The fact that every human will bend their knee and give honor to Jesus is not a question of "if"; it's a question of "when." *Every* knee will bow. *Every* tongue will acknowledge. And it will be done to the glory of God the Father (Php 2:10–11). Some will bow in great joy at the beauty of the King; others will bow in terror at his judgment. But make no mistake—every person will bend their knee to Jesus.

2 For the LORD is enraged against all the nations,
and furious against all their host;
he has devoted them to destruction,[1] has given them over for slaughter.
3 Their slain shall be cast out,
and the stench of their corpses shall rise;
the mountains shall flow with their blood.
4 All the host of heaven shall rot away,
and the skies roll up like a scroll.
All their host shall fall,
as leaves fall from the vine,
like leaves falling from the fig tree.

5 For my sword has drunk its fill in the heavens;
behold, it descends for judgment upon Edom,
upon the people I have devoted to destruction.
6 The LORD has a sword; it is sated with blood;
it is gorged with fat,
with the blood of lambs and goats,
with the fat of the kidneys of rams.
For the LORD has a sacrifice in Bozrah,
a great slaughter in the land of Edom.
7 Wild oxen shall fall with them,
and young steers with the mighty bulls.
Their land shall drink its fill of blood,
and their soil shall be gorged with fat.

8 For the LORD has a day of vengeance,
a year of recompense for the cause of Zion.
9 And the streams of Edom[2] shall be turned into pitch,
and her soil into sulfur;
her land shall become burning pitch.
10 Night and day it shall not be quenched;
its smoke shall go up forever.
From generation to generation it shall lie waste;
none shall pass through it forever and ever.
11 But the hawk and the porcupine[3] shall possess it,
the owl and the raven shall dwell in it.
He shall stretch the line of confusion[4] over it,
and the plumb line of emptiness.
12 Its nobles—there is no one there to call it a kingdom,
and all its princes shall be nothing.

13 Thorns shall grow over its strongholds,
nettles and thistles in its fortresses.
It shall be the haunt of jackals,
an abode for ostriches.[5]
14 And wild animals shall meet with hyenas;
the wild goat shall cry to his fellow;
indeed, there the night bird[6] settles
and finds for herself a resting place.

15 There the owl nests and lays
and hatches and gathers her young in her shadow;
indeed, there the hawks are gathered,
each one with her mate.

[1]That is, set apart (devoted) as an offering to the Lord (for destruction); also verse 5 [2]Hebrew *her streams*
[3]The identity of the animals rendered *hawk* and *porcupine* is uncertain [4]Hebrew *formlessness* [5]Or *owls*
[6]Identity uncertain

16 Seek and read from the book of the LORD:
Not one of these shall be missing;
none shall be without her mate.
For the mouth of the LORD has commanded,
and his Spirit has gathered them.
17 He has cast the lot for them;
his hand has portioned it out to them with the line;
they shall possess it forever;
from generation to generation they shall dwell in it.

The Ransomed Shall Return

35 The wilderness and the dry land shall be glad;
the desert shall rejoice and blossom like the crocus;
2 it shall blossom abundantly
and rejoice with joy and singing.
The glory of Lebanon shall be given to it,
the majesty of Carmel and Sharon.
They shall see the glory of the LORD,
the majesty of our God.

3 Strengthen the weak hands,
and make firm the feeble knees.
4 Say to those who have an anxious heart,
"Be strong; fear not!
Behold, your God
will come with vengeance,
with the recompense of God.
He will come and save you."

5 Then the eyes of the blind shall be opened,
and the ears of the deaf unstopped;
6 then shall the lame man leap like a deer,
and the tongue of the mute sing for joy.
For waters break forth in the wilderness,
and streams in the desert;
7 the burning sand shall become a pool,
and the thirsty ground springs of water;
in the haunt of jackals, where they lie down,
the grass shall become reeds and rushes.
8 And a highway shall be there,
and it shall be called the Way of Holiness;
the unclean shall not pass over it.
It shall belong to those who walk on the way;
even if they are fools, they shall not go astray.[1]
9 No lion shall be there,
nor shall any ravenous beast come up on it;
they shall not be found there,
but the redeemed shall walk there.
10 And the ransomed of the LORD shall return
and come to Zion with singing;
everlasting joy shall be upon their heads;
they shall obtain gladness and joy,
and sorrow and sighing shall flee away.

[1]Or *if they are fools, they shall not wander in it*

POWER TO HEAL

God's plan, since the fall of the first humans in Genesis 3, has been to return all of creation to a restored and redeemed state. His ongoing work, exercised through the ministry of Jesus Christ, is to return all things to what they were. And this redemptive work goes beyond the scope of humanity. True, God's redemptive work will include the salvation of his people, who will be freed from the tyranny of sin forever. But God's plan also includes the salvation of a fallen world, which will be purged from the curse of sin and purified so that it radiates the very glory of God.

Isaiah 35 stands in contrast to the promise of divine judgment in Isaiah 34. This later chapter describes God's promises — his willingness, ability, and intent to bring healing to his creation. This healing will be all-encompassing as God transforms nature (vv. 1–2), broken humanity (vv. 3–6), and then eventually returns God's transformed creation and people to himself (vv. 6–10). Though the Israelites would certainly find hope in these verses as they looked forward to returning from their exile in foreign territory, we know that the greatest fulfillment of these verses, and of God's glory, will come when Jesus returns to the earth.

We might look on these promises about God's power to heal with cynicism when we see them in light of life as it stands today. Here, now, we see much evidence to the contrary as wars, violence, pain, disease, and famine define our current reality, and even believers find it difficult to envision that they are on the road to a fully and completely healed creation. In the New Testament, John the Baptist felt the same tension when he was imprisoned. In response to John's own questions about whether Jesus was the One to bring about this kind of holistic redemption, Jesus pointed his cousin back to this very passage (Mt 11:2–6).

By faith, we believe that Jesus can do what he promised. By faith, we trust that everything old and broken will be restored and made new again. By faith, we believe that not only our souls, but also our bodies and the rest of creation around us will be redeemed (Ro 8:18–23). Though today's surrounding circumstances might tell us otherwise, we trust not in what we visibly see but in the promises of the God who heals, restores, and makes everything new (Rev 21:5).

Sennacherib Invades Judah

36 In the fourteenth year of King Hezekiah, Sennacherib king of Assyria came up against all the fortified cities of Judah and took them. 2And the king of Assyria sent the Rabshakeh[1] from Lachish to King Hezekiah at Jerusalem, with a great army. And he stood by the conduit of the upper pool on the highway to the Washer's Field. 3And there came out to him Eliakim the son of Hilkiah, who was over the household, and Shebna the secretary, and Joah the son of Asaph, the recorder.

4And the Rabshakeh said to them, "Say to Hezekiah, 'Thus says the great king, the king of Assyria: On what do you rest this trust of yours? 5Do you think that mere words are strategy and power for war? In whom do you now trust, that you have rebelled against me? 6Behold, you are trusting in Egypt, that broken reed of a staff, which will pierce the hand of any man who leans on it. Such is Pharaoh king of Egypt to all who trust in him. 7But if you say to me, "We trust in the LORD our God," is it not he whose high places and altars Hezekiah has removed, saying to Judah and to Jerusalem, "You shall worship before this altar"? 8Come now, make a wager with my master the king of Assyria: I will give you two thousand horses, if you are able on your part to set riders on them. 9How then can you repulse a single captain among the least of my master's servants, when you trust in Egypt for chariots and for horsemen? 10Moreover, is it without the LORD that I have come up against this land to destroy it? The LORD said to me, "Go up against this land and destroy it."'"

11Then Eliakim, Shebna, and Joah said to the Rabshakeh, "Please speak to your servants in Aramaic, for we understand it. Do not speak to us in the language of Judah within the hearing of the people who are on the wall." 12But the Rabshakeh said, "Has my master sent me to speak these words to your master and to you, and not to the men sitting on the wall, who are doomed with you to eat their own dung and drink their own urine?"

13Then the Rabshakeh stood and called out in a loud voice in the language of Judah: "Hear the words of the great king, the king of Assyria! 14Thus says the king: 'Do not let Hezekiah deceive you, for he will not be able to deliver you. 15Do not let Hezekiah make you trust in the LORD by saying, "The LORD will surely deliver us. This city will not be given into the hand of the king of Assyria." 16Do not listen to Hezekiah. For thus says the king of Assyria: Make your peace with me[2] and come out to me. Then each one of you will eat of his own vine, and each one of his own fig tree, and each one of you will drink the water of his own cistern, 17until I come and take you away to a land like your own land, a land of grain and wine, a land of bread and vineyards. 18Beware lest Hezekiah mislead you by saying, "The LORD will deliver us." Has any of the gods of the nations delivered his land out of the hand of the king of Assyria? 19Where are the gods of Hamath and Arpad? Where are the gods of Sepharvaim? Have they delivered Samaria out of my hand? 20Who among all the gods of these lands have delivered their lands out of my hand, that the LORD should deliver Jerusalem out of my hand?'"

21But they were silent and answered him not a word, for the king's command was, "Do not answer him." 22Then Eliakim the son of Hilkiah, who was over the household, and Shebna the secretary, and Joah the son of Asaph, the recorder, came to Hezekiah with their clothes torn, and told him the words of the Rabshakeh.

Hezekiah Seeks Isaiah's Help

37 As soon as King Hezekiah heard it, he tore his clothes and covered himself with sackcloth and went into the house of the LORD. 2And he sent Eliakim, who was over the household, and Shebna the secretary, and the senior priests, covered with sackcloth, to the prophet Isaiah the son of Amoz. 3They said to him,

[1] *Rabshakeh* is the title of a high-ranking Assyrian military officer [2] Hebrew *Make a blessing with me*

"Thus says Hezekiah, 'This day is a day of distress, of rebuke, and of disgrace;
children have come to the point of birth, and there is no strength to bring them
forth. 4It may be that the LORD your God will hear the words of the Rabshakeh,
whom his master the king of Assyria has sent to mock the living God, and will
rebuke the words that the LORD your God has heard; therefore lift up your prayer
for the remnant that is left.'"

5When the servants of King Hezekiah came to Isaiah, 6Isaiah said to them,
"Say to your master, 'Thus says the LORD: Do not be afraid because of the words
that you have heard, with which the young men of the king of Assyria have reviled
me. 7Behold, I will put a spirit in him, so that he shall hear a rumor and return to
his own land, and I will make him fall by the sword in his own land.'"

8The Rabshakeh returned, and found the king of Assyria fighting against Libnah, for he had heard that the king had left Lachish. 9Now the king heard concerning Tirhakah king of Cush,[1] "He has set out to fight against you." And when
he heard it, he sent messengers to Hezekiah, saying, 10"Thus shall you speak to
Hezekiah king of Judah: 'Do not let your God in whom you trust deceive you by
promising that Jerusalem will not be given into the hand of the king of Assyria.
11Behold, you have heard what the kings of Assyria have done to all lands, devoting them to destruction. And shall you be delivered? 12Have the gods of the
nations delivered them, the nations that my fathers destroyed, Gozan, Haran,
Rezeph, and the people of Eden who were in Telassar? 13Where is the king of Hamath, the king of Arpad, the king of the city of Sepharvaim, the king of Hena, or
the king of Ivvah?'"

Hezekiah's Prayer for Deliverance

14Hezekiah received the letter from the hand of the messengers, and read it;
and Hezekiah went up to the house of the LORD, and spread it before the LORD.
15And Hezekiah prayed to the LORD: 16"O LORD of hosts, God of Israel, enthroned
above the cherubim, you are the God, you alone, of all the kingdoms of the earth;
you have made the heavens and the earth. 17Incline your ear, O LORD, and hear;
open your eyes, O LORD, and see; and hear all the words of Sennacherib, which
he has sent to mock the living God. 18Truly, O LORD, the kings of Assyria have laid
waste all the nations and their lands, 19and have cast their gods into the fire. For
they were no gods, but the work of men's hands, wood and stone. Therefore they
were destroyed. 20So now, O LORD our God, save us from his hand, that all the
kingdoms of the earth may know that you alone are the LORD."

Sennacherib's Fall

21Then Isaiah the son of Amoz sent to Hezekiah, saying, "Thus says the LORD,
the God of Israel: Because you have prayed to me concerning Sennacherib king of
Assyria, 22this is the word that the LORD has spoken concerning him:

"'She despises you, she scorns you—
the virgin daughter of Zion;
she wags her head behind you—
the daughter of Jerusalem.

23"'Whom have you mocked and reviled?
Against whom have you raised your voice
and lifted your eyes to the heights?
Against the Holy One of Israel!
24 By your servants you have mocked the Lord,
and you have said, With my many chariots
I have gone up the heights of the mountains,
to the far recesses of Lebanon,

1Probably *Nubia*

THE DANGER OF MOCKING GOD

Hezekiah and his people were facing an extreme threat. But up to this point, Hezekiah had failed to do the very thing he should have done at first. Instead of turning directly to the God who can save, he attempted to make an alliance with Egypt (Isa 30:1–2; 36:4–6) and probably with Babylon. Only when those alliances failed did he turn in desperation to the God who held Judah's future in his hands all along.

Hezekiah's appeal to the Lord was based not only on God's character, but also on the fact that Sennacherib had mocked God (37:9–13). He had called into question the reality and power of the Almighty. In their arrogance, the Assyrians had ruthlessly and mercilessly conquered all the nations before them, and in so doing had triumphed over their gods. Their victories had set the nation up to believe they were the captains of their destiny, the navigators of their own course, and that no one — neither God nor man — could stand in their way.

Hezekiah, though, knew better. Despite his attempts to form earthly alliances in the past, he was at this point aware that the true battle belonged to the Lord alone. God answered through his prophet to let Hezekiah know that he would defend his city from the Assyrians for his own sake and for the sake of his servant David (37:33–37). Here is another reminder that God delivers on his promises; that even in this desperate time, with a ruthless army standing in opposition to his people, against all reasonable human odds, he would continue to act on the promises he had previously made — to the honor of his own glory.

Like Hezekiah, we find ourselves in desperate situations. Like Hezekiah, we face a seemingly unbeatable foe in the prince of darkness. This is the fight behind the fight and the enemy behind all the other enemies. Whether we recognize it or not, we are all caught up in this broad, cosmic struggle that will not end until Jesus returns and brings final judgment. Like Hezekiah, we have the tendency to trust in our earthly alliances and weapons, but Paul would later write that in this fight we don't wage war like the world does. We do not use the weapons of the world, but instead we fight in the spiritual realm with spiritual weapons, and as we do, we demolish strongholds in that arena (2Co 10:3–5). For the Christian, the war is already won, though the battles rage on. For Christians, in the end we will see Jesus demonstrate his power against those who mock God just as God demonstrated his power on behalf of Hezekiah.

to cut down its tallest cedars,
  its choicest cypresses,
to come to its remotest height,
  its most fruitful forest.
25 I dug wells
  and drank waters,
to dry up with the sole of my foot
  all the streams of Egypt.

26“ ‘Have you not heard
  that I determined it long ago?
I planned from days of old
  what now I bring to pass,
that you should make fortified cities
  crash into heaps of ruins,
27 while their inhabitants, shorn of strength,
  are dismayed and confounded,
and have become like plants of the field
  and like tender grass,
like grass on the housetops,
  blighted[1] before it is grown.

28“ ‘I know your sitting down
  and your going out and coming in,
  and your raging against me.
29 Because you have raged against me
  and your complacency has come to my ears,
I will put my hook in your nose
  and my bit in your mouth,
and I will turn you back on the way
  by which you came.’

30“And this shall be the sign for you: this year you shall eat what grows of itself,
and in the second year what springs from that. Then in the third year sow and
reap, and plant vineyards, and eat their fruit. 31And the surviving remnant of the
house of Judah shall again take root downward and bear fruit upward. 32For out
of Jerusalem shall go a remnant, and out of Mount Zion a band of survivors. The
zeal of the LORD of hosts will do this.
33“Therefore thus says the LORD concerning the king of Assyria: He shall not
come into this city or shoot an arrow there or come before it with a shield or
cast up a siege mound against it. 34By the way that he came, by the same he shall
return, and he shall not come into this city, declares the LORD. 35For I will defend
this city to save it, for my own sake and for the sake of my servant David.”
36And the angel of the LORD went out and struck down 185,000 in the camp of
the Assyrians. And when people arose early in the morning, behold, these were
all dead bodies. 37Then Sennacherib king of Assyria departed and returned home
and lived at Nineveh. 38And as he was worshiping in the house of Nisroch his god,
Adrammelech and Sharezer, his sons, struck him down with the sword. And after
they escaped into the land of Ararat, Esarhaddon his son reigned in his place.

Hezekiah's Sickness and Recovery

38 In those days Hezekiah became sick and was at the point of death. And Isaiah the prophet the son of Amoz came to him, and said to him, “Thus says
the LORD: Set your house in order, for you shall die, you shall not recover.”[2] 2Then
Hezekiah turned his face to the wall and prayed to the LORD, 3and said, “Please,

[1]Some Hebrew manuscripts and 2 Kings 19:26; most Hebrew manuscripts *a field* [2]Or *live*; also verses 9, 21

O LORD, remember how I have walked before you in faithfulness and with a whole
heart, and have done what is good in your sight." And Hezekiah wept bitterly.
4Then the word of the LORD came to Isaiah: 5"Go and say to Hezekiah, Thus
says the LORD, the God of David your father: I have heard your prayer; I have seen
your tears. Behold, I will add fifteen years to your life.[1] 6I will deliver you and this
city out of the hand of the king of Assyria, and will defend this city.
7"This shall be the sign to you from the LORD, that the LORD will do this thing
that he has promised: 8Behold, I will make the shadow cast by the declining sun
on the dial of Ahaz turn back ten steps." So the sun turned back on the dial the
ten steps by which it had declined.[2]

9A writing of Hezekiah king of Judah, after he had been sick and had recovered
from his sickness:

10 I said, In the middle[3] of my days
  I must depart;
I am consigned to the gates of Sheol
  for the rest of my years.
11 I said, I shall not see the LORD,
  the LORD in the land of the living;
I shall look on man no more
  among the inhabitants of the world.
12 My dwelling is plucked up and removed from me
  like a shepherd's tent;
like a weaver I have rolled up my life;
  he cuts me off from the loom;
from day to night you bring me to an end;
13 I calmed myself[4] until morning;
like a lion he breaks all my bones;
  from day to night you bring me to an end.

14 Like a swallow or a crane I chirp;
  I moan like a dove.
My eyes are weary with looking upward.
  O Lord, I am oppressed; be my pledge of safety!
15 What shall I say? For he has spoken to me,
  and he himself has done it.
I walk slowly all my years
  because of the bitterness of my soul.

16 O Lord, by these things men live,
  and in all these is the life of my spirit.
  Oh restore me to health and make me live!
17 Behold, it was for my welfare
  that I had great bitterness;
but in love you have delivered my life
  from the pit of destruction,
for you have cast all my sins
  behind your back.
18 For Sheol does not thank you;
  death does not praise you;
those who go down to the pit do not hope
  for your faithfulness.
19 The living, the living, he thanks you,
  as I do this day;

[1]Hebrew *to your days* [2]The meaning of the Hebrew verse is uncertain [3]Or *In the quiet* [4]Or (with Targum) *I cried for help*

All flesh is grass,
and all its beauty[1] is like the flower of the field.
7 The grass withers, the flower fades
when the breath of the LORD blows on it;
surely the people are grass.
8 The grass withers, the flower fades,
but the word of our God will stand forever.

The Greatness of God

9 Go on up to a high mountain,
O Zion, herald of good news;[2]
lift up your voice with strength,
O Jerusalem, herald of good news;[3]
lift it up, fear not;
say to the cities of Judah,
"Behold your God!"
10 Behold, the Lord GOD comes with might,
and his arm rules for him;
behold, his reward is with him,
and his recompense before him.
11 He will tend his flock like a shepherd;
he will gather the lambs in his arms;
he will carry them in his bosom,
and gently lead those that are with young.

12 Who has measured the waters in the hollow of his hand
and marked off the heavens with a span,
enclosed the dust of the earth in a measure
and weighed the mountains in scales
and the hills in a balance?
13 Who has measured[4] the Spirit of the LORD,
or what man shows him his counsel?
14 Whom did he consult,
and who made him understand?
Who taught him the path of justice,
and taught him knowledge,
and showed him the way of understanding?
15 Behold, the nations are like a drop from a bucket,
and are accounted as the dust on the scales;
behold, he takes up the coastlands like fine dust.
16 Lebanon would not suffice for fuel,
nor are its beasts enough for a burnt offering.
17 All the nations are as nothing before him,
they are accounted by him as less than nothing and emptiness.

18 To whom then will you liken God,
or what likeness compare with him?
19 An idol! A craftsman casts it,
and a goldsmith overlays it with gold
and casts for it silver chains.
20 He who is too impoverished for an offering
chooses wood[5] that will not rot;
he seeks out a skillful craftsman
to set up an idol that will not move.

[1]Or *all its constancy* [2]Or *O herald of good news to Zion* [3]Or *O herald of good news to Jerusalem*
[4]Or *has directed* [5]Or *He chooses valuable wood*

21 Do you not know? Do you not hear?
Has it not been told you from the beginning?
Have you not understood from the foundations of the earth?
22 It is he who sits above the circle of the earth,
and its inhabitants are like grasshoppers;
who stretches out the heavens like a curtain,
and spreads them like a tent to dwell in;
23 who brings princes to nothing,
and makes the rulers of the earth as emptiness.

24 Scarcely are they planted, scarcely sown,
scarcely has their stem taken root in the earth,
when he blows on them, and they wither,
and the tempest carries them off like stubble.

25 To whom then will you compare me,
that I should be like him? says the Holy One.
26 Lift up your eyes on high and see:
who created these?
He who brings out their host by number,
calling them all by name;
by the greatness of his might
and because he is strong in power,
not one is missing.

27 Why do you say, O Jacob,
and speak, O Israel,
"My way is hidden from the LORD,
and my right is disregarded by my God"?
28 Have you not known? Have you not heard?
The LORD is the everlasting God,
the Creator of the ends of the earth.
He does not faint or grow weary;
his understanding is unsearchable.
29 He gives power to the faint,
and to him who has no might he increases strength.
30 Even youths shall faint and be weary,
and young men shall fall exhausted;
31 but they who wait for the LORD shall renew their strength;
they shall mount up with wings like eagles;
they shall run and not be weary;
they shall walk and not faint.

Fear Not, for I Am with You

41 Listen to me in silence, O coastlands;
let the peoples renew their strength;
let them approach, then let them speak;
let us together draw near for judgment.

2 Who stirred up one from the east
whom victory meets at every step?[1]
He gives up nations before him,
so that he tramples kings underfoot;
he makes them like dust with his sword,
like driven stubble with his bow.
3 He pursues them and passes on safely,
by paths his feet have not trod.

[1]Or *whom righteousness calls to follow?*

4 Who has performed and done this,
calling the generations from the beginning?
I, the LORD, the first,
and with the last; I am he.

5 The coastlands have seen and are afraid;
the ends of the earth tremble;
they have drawn near and come.
6 Everyone helps his neighbor
and says to his brother, "Be strong!"
7 The craftsman strengthens the goldsmith,
and he who smooths with the hammer him who strikes
the anvil,
saying of the soldering, "It is good";
and they strengthen it with nails so that it cannot be moved.

8 But you, Israel, my servant,
Jacob, whom I have chosen,
the offspring of Abraham, my friend;
9 you whom I took from the ends of the earth,
and called from its farthest corners,
saying to you, "You are my servant,
I have chosen you and not cast you off";
10 fear not, for I am with you;
be not dismayed, for I am your God;
I will strengthen you, I will help you,
I will uphold you with my righteous right hand.

11 Behold, all who are incensed against you
shall be put to shame and confounded;
those who strive against you
shall be as nothing and shall perish.
12 You shall seek those who contend with you,
but you shall not find them;
those who war against you
shall be as nothing at all.
13 For I, the LORD your God,
hold your right hand;
it is I who say to you, "Fear not,
I am the one who helps you."

14 Fear not, you worm Jacob,
you men of Israel!
I am the one who helps you, declares the LORD;
your Redeemer is the Holy One of Israel.
15 Behold, I make of you a threshing sledge,
new, sharp, and having teeth;
you shall thresh the mountains and crush them,
and you shall make the hills like chaff;
16 you shall winnow them, and the wind shall carry them away,
and the tempest shall scatter them.
And you shall rejoice in the LORD;
in the Holy One of Israel you shall glory.

17 When the poor and needy seek water,
and there is none,
and their tongue is parched with thirst,
I the LORD will answer them;
I the God of Israel will not forsake them.

ISAIAH 41:8–14

GOD'S CHOOSING

True security can only be found in the grace and mercy of God. This was the case for the Israelites. Though time and time again they had rebelled against their God, testing his patience with their consistent return to idolatry, he just as consistently reminded them that they were, and are, his chosen people.

The people of Israel did not earn this right; they did not pursue it on their own. Rather, God's choice of Israel was based on his good pleasure and will. For that reason, his choice of a people to be his favored nation is also to his great glory alone. Because God's choice of his people is based on himself, and for himself, security comes not in making a claim to personal righteousness, but rather in knowing and trusting that God keeps his promises to his people.

Like the Israelites then, we too can be free from fear. We can trust in his strength. We can know that ultimately God will be victorious, and that we will share in that victory. This is not because we can merit any such claim, but only because we have been chosen to be the recipients of God's grace in the sacrifice and resurrection of Jesus Christ.

18 I will open rivers on the bare heights,
and fountains in the midst of the valleys.
I will make the wilderness a pool of water,
and the dry land springs of water.
19 I will put in the wilderness the cedar,
the acacia, the myrtle, and the olive.
I will set in the desert the cypress,
the plane and the pine together,
20 that they may see and know,
may consider and understand together,
that the hand of the LORD has done this,
the Holy One of Israel has created it.

The Futility of Idols

21 Set forth your case, says the LORD;
bring your proofs, says the King of Jacob.
22 Let them bring them, and tell us
what is to happen.
Tell us the former things, what they are,
that we may consider them,
that we may know their outcome;
or declare to us the things to come.
23 Tell us what is to come hereafter,
that we may know that you are gods;
do good, or do harm,
that we may be dismayed and terrified.[1]
24 Behold, you are nothing,
and your work is less than nothing;
an abomination is he who chooses you.

25 I stirred up one from the north, and he has come,
from the rising of the sun, and he shall call upon
my name;
he shall trample on rulers as on mortar,
as the potter treads clay.
26 Who declared it from the beginning, that we might know,
and beforehand, that we might say, "He is right"?
There was none who declared it, none who proclaimed,
none who heard your words.
27 I was the first to say[2] to Zion, "Behold, here they are!"
and I give to Jerusalem a herald of good news.
28 But when I look, there is no one;
among these there is no counselor
who, when I ask, gives an answer.
29 Behold, they are all a delusion;
their works are nothing;
their metal images are empty wind.

The LORD's Chosen Servant

42 Behold my servant, whom I uphold,
my chosen, in whom my soul delights;
I have put my Spirit upon him;
he will bring forth justice to the nations.
2 He will not cry aloud or lift up his voice,
or make it heard in the street;

[1]Or *that we may both be dismayed and see* [2]Or *Formerly I said*

ISAIAH 42:1–4

HEALING THE BROKEN

Truth and justice can be wielded like a jackhammer: they can come with such force that even those who are eventual beneficiaries of these realities feel destroyed in their path. But this description of the servant of the Lord makes it clear that, though God's anointed one will indeed bring in these kingdom realities, he will not do so at the expense of the broken.

It is as true today as it was in Isaiah's day that in the world there are many people who are hanging on by a thread: it might be a thread of faith, a thread of fragile health, or a thread of hope. These people are bruised reeds, beaten down by their circumstances and their attempts at remaining faithful to God in their own broken world. God's chosen One is *for* these people: for those who know what it means to mourn, to hunger, to thirst, and to wait with patience. Consequently Jesus, this one whom God has chosen of whom Isaiah prophesied, did not withhold his power or compassion from those who were broken in body and spirit. Instead, he healed them. He brought—and still brings—justice to those who are overlooked and despised by the kingdom of this world.

3 a bruised reed he will not break,
and a faintly burning wick he will not quench;
he will faithfully bring forth justice.
4 He will not grow faint or be discouraged[1]
till he has established justice in the earth;
and the coastlands wait for his law.

5 Thus says God, the LORD,
who created the heavens and stretched them out,
who spread out the earth and what comes from it,
who gives breath to the people on it
and spirit to those who walk in it:
6 "I am the LORD; I have called you[2] in righteousness;
I will take you by the hand and keep you;
I will give you as a covenant for the people,
a light for the nations,
7 to open the eyes that are blind,
to bring out the prisoners from the dungeon,
from the prison those who sit in darkness.
8 I am the LORD; that is my name;
my glory I give to no other,
nor my praise to carved idols.
9 Behold, the former things have come to pass,
and new things I now declare;
before they spring forth
I tell you of them."

Sing to the LORD a New Song

10 Sing to the LORD a new song,
his praise from the end of the earth,
you who go down to the sea, and all that fills it,
the coastlands and their inhabitants.
11 Let the desert and its cities lift up their voice,
the villages that Kedar inhabits;
let the habitants of Sela sing for joy,
let them shout from the top of the mountains.
12 Let them give glory to the LORD,
and declare his praise in the coastlands.
13 The LORD goes out like a mighty man,
like a man of war he stirs up his zeal;
he cries out, he shouts aloud,
he shows himself mighty against his foes.

14 For a long time I have held my peace;
I have kept still and restrained myself;
now I will cry out like a woman in labor;
I will gasp and pant.
15 I will lay waste mountains and hills,
and dry up all their vegetation;
I will turn the rivers into islands,[3]
and dry up the pools.
16 And I will lead the blind
in a way that they do not know,
in paths that they have not known
I will guide them.

[1]Or *bruised* [2]The Hebrew for *you* is singular; four times in this verse [3]Or *into coastlands*

HUMBLE AND FAITHFUL SERVICE

Isaiah's prophecies would have filled God's people with encouragement and hope as they looked to God alone for strength and deliverance. God alone held their destiny in his hands, and he would not reject them as his people. But in Isaiah 42, we see the true greatness of the message: that God's special servant would be the very embodiment of God's help, deliverance, justice, and truth.

Though the original audience was no doubt primarily concerned about their nation and their destiny in particular, God wanted to expand the vision of his people to the entire world. The justice God was to establish would not only apply to Judah but also to all the nations of the earth; the coming kingdom would not just be made up of one nation but would rather spread throughout the world. This kingdom would be the fulfillment of all God's promises and the true hope of everyone who is defeated and hopeless. All of this is found in the person and work of Jesus Christ (Lk 2:25 – 32).

In addition to announcing this One who was to come, these verses also help pave the way for a different kind of ruler, a different kind of king. In his coming, he will not be marked by fanfare or military conquest, and his ministry will not be characterized by vanquishing his foes in earthly battle. Instead, this chosen One will lift up the low and make level all the places that had been rough (Isa 42:16). Eventually, all the ends of the earth will sing a song of praise to him (v. 10), for he will welcome all who are willing to follow him into this kingdom. He will not simply be the king of a particular nation; he will be the rightful king of the entire world who will gather together his subjects from all of the peoples of the earth.

Make no mistake — Isaiah's Spirit-inspired description of God's servant tells us that he will go out like a mighty warrior and destroy all his enemies (v. 13), but he will do so in a way that is unexpected. In fact, time would demonstrate that many in Israel would be so convinced of their own ideas about God's chosen One that they would actually miss the true Messiah who would come to serve in humbleness and faithfulness.

I will turn the darkness before them into light,
the rough places into level ground.
These are the things I do,
and I do not forsake them.
17 They are turned back and utterly put to shame,
who trust in carved idols,
who say to metal images,
"You are our gods."

Israel's Failure to Hear and See

18 Hear, you deaf,
and look, you blind, that you may see!
19 Who is blind but my servant,
or deaf as my messenger whom I send?
Who is blind as my dedicated one,[1]
or blind as the servant of the LORD?
20 He sees many things, but does not observe them;
his ears are open, but he does not hear.
21 The LORD was pleased, for his righteousness' sake,
to magnify his law and make it glorious.
22 But this is a people plundered and looted;
they are all of them trapped in holes
and hidden in prisons;
they have become plunder with none to rescue,
spoil with none to say, "Restore!"
23 Who among you will give ear to this,
will attend and listen for the time to come?
24 Who gave up Jacob to the looter,
and Israel to the plunderers?
Was it not the LORD, against whom we have sinned,
in whose ways they would not walk,
and whose law they would not obey?
25 So he poured on him the heat of his anger
and the might of battle;
it set him on fire all around, but he did not understand;
it burned him up, but he did not take it to heart.

Israel's Only Savior

43 But now thus says the LORD,
he who created you, O Jacob,
he who formed you, O Israel:
"Fear not, for I have redeemed you;
I have called you by name, you are mine.
2 When you pass through the waters, I will be with you;
and through the rivers, they shall not overwhelm you;
when you walk through fire you shall not be burned,
and the flame shall not consume you.
3 For I am the LORD your God,
the Holy One of Israel, your Savior.
I give Egypt as your ransom,
Cush and Seba in exchange for you.
4 Because you are precious in my eyes,
and honored, and I love you,
I give men in return for you,
peoples in exchange for your life.

[1]Or *as the one at peace with me*

ISAIAH 43:1

REDEMPTION

To *redeem* means literally "to buy back." Redemption is one of the key accomplishments of God's Son, Jesus. As this passage states, God's people were created and formed by God's own divine activity, and God himself through Jesus' sacrificial ministry would buy them back.

But the word *redeemed* itself begs the question: From what are God's people being bought back? The answer is that we all have willingly sold ourselves in slavery to sin; death is the cost of our disobedience. We are, both by nature and by our consistently sinful choices, rebels against God's kingdom. The consequence for that rebellion against the righteousness and holiness of God is death, and this price must be paid.

But God, in his mercy, has paid that price himself. He truly has redeemed those who trust in him, having paid the price for our sinful pride and rebellion. God has now the right not only as our Creator, but also as our Redeemer, to say that believers are his and to expect them to live lives that reflect gratitude for his gracious redemption.

5 Fear not, for I am with you;
I will bring your offspring from the east,
and from the west I will gather you.
6 I will say to the north, Give up,
and to the south, Do not withhold;
bring my sons from afar
and my daughters from the end of the earth,
7 everyone who is called by my name,
whom I created for my glory,
whom I formed and made."

8 Bring out the people who are blind, yet have eyes,
who are deaf, yet have ears!
9 All the nations gather together,
and the peoples assemble.
Who among them can declare this,
and show us the former things?
Let them bring their witnesses to prove them right,
and let them hear and say, It is true.
10 "You are my witnesses," declares the LORD,
"and my servant whom I have chosen,
that you may know and believe me
and understand that I am he.
Before me no god was formed,
nor shall there be any after me.
11 I, I am the LORD,
and besides me there is no savior.
12 I declared and saved and proclaimed,
when there was no strange god among you;
and you are my witnesses," declares the LORD, "and
I am God.
13 Also henceforth I am he;
there is none who can deliver from my hand;
I work, and who can turn it back?"

14 Thus says the LORD,
your Redeemer, the Holy One of Israel:
"For your sake I send to Babylon
and bring them all down as fugitives,
even the Chaldeans, in the ships in which they rejoice.
15 I am the LORD, your Holy One,
the Creator of Israel, your King."

16 Thus says the LORD,
who makes a way in the sea,
a path in the mighty waters,
17 who brings forth chariot and horse,
army and warrior;
they lie down, they cannot rise,
they are extinguished, quenched like a wick:
18 "Remember not the former things,
nor consider the things of old.
19 Behold, I am doing a new thing;
now it springs forth, do you not perceive it?
I will make a way in the wilderness
and rivers in the desert.
20 The wild beasts will honor me,
the jackals and the ostriches,

25 who frustrates the signs of liars
and makes fools of diviners,
who turns wise men back
and makes their knowledge foolish,
26 who confirms the word of his servant
and fulfills the counsel of his messengers,
who says of Jerusalem, 'She shall be inhabited,'
and of the cities of Judah, 'They shall be built,
and I will raise up their ruins';
27 who says to the deep, 'Be dry;
I will dry up your rivers';
28 who says of Cyrus, 'He is my shepherd,
and he shall fulfill all my purpose';
saying of Jerusalem, 'She shall be built,'
and of the temple, 'Your foundation shall be laid.'"

Cyrus, God's Instrument

45 Thus says the LORD to his anointed, to Cyrus,
whose right hand I have grasped,
to subdue nations before him
and to loose the belts of kings,
to open doors before him
that gates may not be closed:
2 "I will go before you
and level the exalted places,[1]
I will break in pieces the doors of bronze
and cut through the bars of iron,
3 I will give you the treasures of darkness
and the hoards in secret places,
that you may know that it is I, the LORD,
the God of Israel, who call you by your name.
4 For the sake of my servant Jacob,
and Israel my chosen,
I call you by your name,
I name you, though you do not know me.
5 I am the LORD, and there is no other,
besides me there is no God;
I equip you, though you do not know me,
6 that people may know, from the rising of the sun
and from the west, that there is none besides me;
I am the LORD, and there is no other.
7 I form light and create darkness;
I make well-being and create calamity;
I am the LORD, who does all these things.

8 "Shower, O heavens, from above,
and let the clouds rain down righteousness;
let the earth open, that salvation and righteousness may bear fruit;
let the earth cause them both to sprout;
I the LORD have created it.

9 "Woe to him who strives with him who formed him,
a pot among earthen pots!
Does the clay say to him who forms it, 'What are you making?'
or 'Your work has no handles'?

[1] Masoretic Text; Dead Sea Scroll, Septuagint *level the mountains*

10 Woe to him who says to a father, 'What are you begetting?'
or to a woman, 'With what are you in labor?'"

11 Thus says the LORD,
the Holy One of Israel, and the one who formed him:
"Ask me of things to come;
will you command me concerning my children and the work
of my hands?[1]
12 I made the earth
and created man on it;
it was my hands that stretched out the heavens,
and I commanded all their host.
13 I have stirred him up in righteousness,
and I will make all his ways level;
he shall build my city
and set my exiles free,
not for price or reward,"
says the LORD of hosts.

The LORD, the Only Savior

14 Thus says the LORD:
"The wealth of Egypt and the merchandise of Cush,
and the Sabeans, men of stature,
shall come over to you and be yours;
they shall follow you;
they shall come over in chains and bow down to you.
They will plead with you, saying:
'Surely God is in you, and there is no other,
no god besides him.'"

15 Truly, you are a God who hides himself,
O God of Israel, the Savior.
16 All of them are put to shame and confounded;
the makers of idols go in confusion together.
17 But Israel is saved by the LORD
with everlasting salvation;
you shall not be put to shame or confounded
to all eternity.

18 For thus says the LORD,
who created the heavens
(he is God!),
who formed the earth and made it
(he established it;
he did not create it empty,
he formed it to be inhabited!):
"I am the LORD, and there is no other.
19 *I did not speak in secret,*
in a land of darkness;
I did not say to the offspring of Jacob,
'Seek me in vain.'[2]
I the LORD speak the truth;
I declare what is right.

20 "Assemble yourselves and come;
draw near together,
you survivors of the nations!

[1]A slight emendation yields *will you question me about my children, or command me concerning the work of my hands?* [2]Hebrew *in emptiness*

They have no knowledge
who carry about their wooden idols,
and keep on praying to a god
that cannot save.
21 Declare and present your case;
let them take counsel together!
Who told this long ago?
Who declared it of old?
Was it not I, the LORD?
And there is no other god besides me,
a righteous God and a Savior;
there is none besides me.

22 "Turn to me and be saved,
all the ends of the earth!
For I am God, and there is no other.
23 By myself I have sworn;
from my mouth has gone out in righteousness
a word that shall not return:
'To me every knee shall bow,
every tongue shall swear allegiance.'[1]

24 "Only in the LORD, it shall be said of me,
are righteousness and strength;
to him shall come and be ashamed
all who were incensed against him.
25 In the LORD all the offspring of Israel
shall be justified and shall glory."

The Idols of Babylon and the One True God

46 Bel bows down; Nebo stoops;
their idols are on beasts and livestock;
these things you carry are borne
as burdens on weary beasts.
2 They stoop; they bow down together;
they cannot save the burden,
but themselves go into captivity.

3 "Listen to me, O house of Jacob,
all the remnant of the house of Israel,
who have been borne by me from before your birth,
carried from the womb;
4 even to your old age I am he,
and to gray hairs I will carry you.
I have made, and I will bear;
I will carry and will save.

5 "To whom will you liken me and make me equal,
and compare me, that we may be alike?
6 Those who lavish gold from the purse,
and weigh out silver in the scales,
hire a goldsmith, and he makes it into a god;
then they fall down and worship!
7 *They lift it* to their shoulders, they carry it,
they set it in its place, and it stands there;
it cannot move from its place.
If one cries to it, it does not answer
or save him from his trouble.

[1]Septuagint *every tongue shall confess to God*

ISAIAH 45:22–23

SWORN BY HIMSELF

Why would God swear by himself? The writer of Hebrews answers the question for us in the context of the promise God made to Abraham: God swore by himself because he could swear by no one greater (Heb 6:13). When God swears by himself, he is declaring once and for all that his word is good and unshakeable. Here we see God putting his stamp of absolute certitude on the fact that his word will accomplish its purposes, and that when it does, every tongue will confess its truth. This is an oath that God makes by himself, to himself, and for himself.

The oath will be fulfilled when every knee bows and every tongue confesses that Jesus Christ is Lord, all to the glory of God the Father (Php 2:10–11). This is not mere aspiration; it's not a pie-in-the-sky hope for God. Rather, it is so sure and certain that God has sealed the promise by himself. The question of Jesus' acknowledged reign in the universe is not in doubt; it's only a question of when it will be fully realized and acknowledged by all creation.

8 "Remember this and stand firm,
recall it to mind, you transgressors,
9 remember the former things of old;
for I am God, and there is no other;
I am God, and there is none like me,
10 declaring the end from the beginning
and from ancient times things not yet done,
saying, 'My counsel shall stand,
and I will accomplish all my purpose,'
11 calling a bird of prey from the east,
the man of my counsel from a far country.
I have spoken, and I will bring it to pass;
I have purposed, and I will do it.

12 "Listen to me, you stubborn of heart,
you who are far from righteousness:
13 I bring near my righteousness; it is not far off,
and my salvation will not delay;
I will put salvation in Zion,
for Israel my glory."

The Humiliation of Babylon

47 Come down and sit in the dust,
O virgin daughter of Babylon;
sit on the ground without a throne,
O daughter of the Chaldeans!
For you shall no more be called
tender and delicate.
2 Take the millstones and grind flour,
put off your veil,
strip off your robe, uncover your legs,
pass through the rivers.
3 Your nakedness shall be uncovered,
and your disgrace shall be seen.
I will take vengeance,
and I will spare no one.
4 Our Redeemer—the LORD of hosts is his name—
is the Holy One of Israel.

5 Sit in silence, and go into darkness,
O daughter of the Chaldeans;
for you shall no more be called
the mistress of kingdoms.
6 I was angry with my people;
I profaned my heritage;
I gave them into your hand;
you showed them no mercy;
on the aged you made your yoke exceedingly heavy.
7 You said, "I shall be mistress forever,"
so that you did not lay these things to heart
or remember their end.

8 Now therefore hear this, you lover of pleasures,
who sit securely,
who say in your heart,
"I am, and there is no one besides me;
I shall not sit as a widow
or know the loss of children":

ISAIAH 46:9–11

DECLARING THE END FROM THE BEGINNING

As the sovereign ruler of the cosmos, God can do anything he pleases. His word is not merely advice or a prediction: it is a declaration, even if humans do not yet see the visible evidence of that declaration in the world. He who knew the very end before the very beginning can be trusted to not only know what will transpire but to also bring it about in the way and time in which he sees fit.

As a prophet, Jesus too had the ability to declare what would and would not occur. Consider his declarations that he would rebuild the temple in three days, that Jerusalem would be destroyed, and even his straightforward declaration of his own suffering, death, and resurrection to come (Mt 16:21). Just as God declared his word through the prophet Isaiah, so also Jesus makes declarations as a prophet: words not born of his own opinion or logical deduction, but instead from the knowledge of God from the very beginning. As we trust the declarations of God the Father, so also can we trust in the declarations of Jesus, God's Son.

ISAIAH 47:12–15

WARNINGS ABOUT MAGIC

The Old Testament warned the people of Israel against practicing magic and sorcery (Lev 19:26,31; Dt 18:9–14). The breaking point for Saul, the first king of Israel, was his association with the medium at En-dor who conjured up the spirit of Samuel to solicit his counsel for the king. After that, the Lord removed Saul as king and gave the crown to David (1Sa 28:3–19). As with Saul's pursuit of a word from beyond, modern pursuit of magic and superstition represents misplaced human faith and confidence. When we choose to engage in and trust in processes like these, we show that we will not accept the Word of God and trust in him alone to guide us into his will.

In this passage, the prophet taunts the Babylonian effort to try to avert God's judgment through magic. He dares them to stand fast by their sorcery, knowing the foolishness of doing so. God alone holds true power, and anything else that people look to for guidance is a mere fabrication, a pathetic and blurry copy of what God provides. Believers in Christ have seen the power and glory of God displayed in the life, death, and resurrection of Jesus. Because of this, we no longer hold to meaningless superstitions and magic *incantations. All our faith is in him.*

9 These two things shall come to you
in a moment, in one day;
the loss of children and widowhood
shall come upon you in full measure,
in spite of your many sorceries
and the great power of your enchantments.

10 You felt secure in your wickedness;
you said, "No one sees me";
your wisdom and your knowledge led you astray,
and you said in your heart,
"I am, and there is no one besides me."
11 But evil shall come upon you,
which you will not know how to charm away;
disaster shall fall upon you,
for which you will not be able to atone;
and ruin shall come upon you suddenly,
of which you know nothing.

12 Stand fast in your enchantments
and your many sorceries,
with which you have labored from your youth;
perhaps you may be able to succeed;
perhaps you may inspire terror.
13 You are wearied with your many counsels;
let them stand forth and save you,
those who divide the heavens,
who gaze at the stars,
who at the new moons make known
what shall come upon you.

14 Behold, they are like stubble;
the fire consumes them;
they cannot deliver themselves
from the power of the flame.
No coal for warming oneself is this,
no fire to sit before!
15 Such to you are those with whom you have labored,
who have done business with you from your youth;
they wander about, each in his own direction;
there is no one to save you.

Israel Refined for God's Glory

48 Hear this, O house of Jacob,
who are called by the name of Israel,
and who came from the waters of Judah,
who swear by the name of the LORD
and confess the God of Israel,
but not in truth or right.
2 For they call themselves after the holy city,
and stay themselves on the God of Israel;
the LORD of hosts is his name.

3 "The former things I declared of old;
they went out from my mouth, and I announced them;
then suddenly I did them, and they came to pass.
4 Because I know that you are obstinate,
and your neck is an iron sinew
and your forehead brass,

5 I declared them to you from of old,
before they came to pass I announced them to you,
lest you should say, 'My idol did them,
my carved image and my metal image commanded them.'

6 "You have heard; now see all this;
and will you not declare it?
From this time forth I announce to you new things,
hidden things that you have not known.
7 They are created now, not long ago;
before today you have never heard of them,
lest you should say, 'Behold, I knew them.'
8 You have never heard, you have never known,
from of old your ear has not been opened.
For I knew that you would surely deal treacherously,
and that from before birth you were called a rebel.

9 "For my name's sake I defer my anger;
for the sake of my praise I restrain it for you,
that I may not cut you off.
10 Behold, I have refined you, but not as silver;
I have tried[1] you in the furnace of affliction.
11 For my own sake, for my own sake, I do it,
for how should my name[2] be profaned?
My glory I will not give to another.

The LORD's Call to Israel

12 "Listen to me, O Jacob,
and Israel, whom I called!
I am he; I am the first,
and I am the last.
13 My hand laid the foundation of the earth,
and my right hand spread out the heavens;
when I call to them,
they stand forth together.

14 "Assemble, all of you, and listen!
Who among them has declared these things?
The LORD loves him;
he shall perform his purpose on Babylon,
and his arm shall be against the Chaldeans.
15 I, even I, have spoken and called him;
I have brought him, and he will prosper in his way.
16 Draw near to me, hear this:
from the beginning I have not spoken in secret,
from the time it came to be I have been there."
And now the Lord GOD has sent me, and his Spirit.

17 Thus says the LORD,
your Redeemer, the Holy One of Israel:
"I am the LORD your God,
who teaches you to profit,
who leads you in the way you should go.
18 Oh that you had paid attention to my commandments!
Then your peace would have been like a river,
and your righteousness like the waves of the sea;

[1]Or *I have chosen* [2]Hebrew lacks *my name*

ISAIAH 48:12–15

THE FIRST AND THE LAST

Time is the great equalizer. Whether people are rich or poor, educated or not, prominent or lowly, time does not speed up or slow down for anyone. Each day offers the same amount of time for each of us, and not one of us knows when the present day could be our last. In contrast to our human limitations, God stands apart from time. He is the first and the last; he is the beginning and the ending.

Being both the first and the last is a unique claim that only God can make; in so doing, he separates himself from the supposed gods of the nations. Unlike these gods, who are fashioned from wood or stone, God has no beginning or ending. He has and will control every event from the beginning until the end of time. He laid the foundations of the earth, named the stars one by one, and will eventually redeem all of creation for his glory. In making this pronouncement, God reminded this Israelite audience that they would do well to listen to what he has to say, because the idols of the other nations are mute on any and every subject (v. 14).

Similarly, the risen Christ addressed the New Testament churches in Revelation, calling them to heed his words through the same pronouncement of his eternal nature. He is "the first and the last" (Rev 1:17; 2:8), and his Word is sure.

19 your offspring would have been like the sand,
and your descendants like its grains;
their name would never be cut off
or destroyed from before me."

20 Go out from Babylon, flee from Chaldea,
declare this with a shout of joy, proclaim it,
send it out to the end of the earth;
say, "The LORD has redeemed his servant Jacob!"
21 They did not thirst when he led them through the deserts;
he made water flow for them from the rock;
he split the rock and the water gushed out.

22 "There is no peace," says the LORD, "for the wicked."

The Servant of the LORD

49 Listen to me, O coastlands,
and give attention, you peoples from afar.
The LORD called me from the womb,
from the body of my mother he named my name.
2 He made my mouth like a sharp sword;
in the shadow of his hand he hid me;
he made me a polished arrow;
in his quiver he hid me away.
3 And he said to me, "You are my servant,
Israel, in whom I will be glorified."[1]
4 But I said, "I have labored in vain;
I have spent my strength for nothing and vanity;
yet surely my right is with the LORD,
and my recompense with my God."

5 And now the LORD says,
he who formed me from the womb to be his servant,
to bring Jacob back to him;
and that Israel might be gathered to him—
for I am honored in the eyes of the LORD,
and my God has become my strength—
6 he says:
"It is too light a thing that you should be my servant
to raise up the tribes of Jacob
and to bring back the preserved of Israel;
I will make you as a light for the nations,
that my salvation may reach to the end of the earth."

7 Thus says the LORD,
the Redeemer of Israel and his Holy One,
to one deeply despised, abhorred by the nation,
the servant of rulers:
"Kings shall see and arise;
princes, and they shall prostrate themselves;
because of the LORD, who is faithful,
the Holy One of Israel, who has chosen you."

The Restoration of Israel

8 Thus says the LORD:
"In a time of favor I have answered you;
in a day of salvation I have helped you;

[1]Or *I will display my beauty*

ISAIAH 49:6

A LIGHT FOR THE NATIONS

The greatness and glory of Jesus is meant to spread to every corner of the globe. This is what God promised through the prophet in this verse: that his coming servant would not be confined to the worship of a single nation.

Importantly, this intent has existed in the heart of God from the beginning of time; throughout redemptive history, he has been raising up a people for himself from every tribe, tongue, and nation. The expansion of the gospel was not initiated in the Great Commission of Jesus; in fact, it extends even further back in time than when the prophet Isaiah lived. When God chose Abraham as the father of his people, he did so not to the exclusion of all the other peoples of the earth, but for their sakes. God intended (and still intends) that his people will be a blessing to all the nations of the earth (Ge 12:2–3). This was fulfilled through the ministry of Jesus who then commissioned his followers to move past the traditional boundary lines of culture and bring the message of salvation to the furthest corners of the globe (Mt 28:18–20).

I will keep you and give you
as a covenant to the people,
to establish the land,
to apportion the desolate heritages,
9 saying to the prisoners, 'Come out,'
to those who are in darkness, 'Appear.'
They shall feed along the ways;
on all bare heights shall be their pasture;
10 they shall not hunger or thirst,
neither scorching wind nor sun shall strike them,
for he who has pity on them will lead them,
and by springs of water will guide them.
11 And I will make all my mountains a road,
and my highways shall be raised up.
12 Behold, these shall come from afar,
and behold, these from the north and from the west,[1]
and these from the land of Syene."[2]

13 Sing for joy, O heavens, and exult, O earth;
break forth, O mountains, into singing!
For the LORD has comforted his people
and will have compassion on his afflicted.

14 But Zion said, "The LORD has forsaken me;
my Lord has forgotten me."

15 "Can a woman forget her nursing child,
that she should have no compassion on the son of her womb?
Even these may forget,
yet I will not forget you.
16 Behold, I have engraved you on the palms of my hands;
your walls are continually before me.
17 Your builders make haste;[3]
your destroyers and those who laid you waste go out
from you.
18 Lift up your eyes around and see;
they all gather, they come to you.
As I live, declares the LORD,
you shall put them all on as an ornament;
you shall bind them on as a bride does.

19 "Surely your waste and your desolate places
and your devastated land—
surely now you will be too narrow for your inhabitants,
and those who swallowed you up will be far away.
20 The children of your bereavement
will yet say in your ears:
'The place is too narrow for me;
make room for me to dwell in.'
21 Then you will say in your heart:
'Who has borne me these?
I was bereaved and barren,
exiled and put away,
but who has brought up these?
Behold, I was left alone;
from where have these come?'"

[1]Hebrew *from the sea* [2]Dead Sea Scroll; Masoretic Text *Sinim* [3]Dead Sea Scroll; Masoretic Text *Your children make haste*

22 Thus says the Lord GOD:
"Behold, I will lift up my hand to the nations,
and raise my signal to the peoples;
and they shall bring your sons in their arms,[1]
and your daughters shall be carried on their shoulders.
23 Kings shall be your foster fathers,
and their queens your nursing mothers.
With their faces to the ground they shall bow down to you,
and lick the dust of your feet.
Then you will know that I am the LORD;
those who wait for me shall not be put to shame."

24 Can the prey be taken from the mighty,
or the captives of a tyrant[2] be rescued?
25 For thus says the LORD:
"Even the captives of the mighty shall be taken,
and the prey of the tyrant be rescued,
for I will contend with those who contend with you,
and I will save your children.
26 I will make your oppressors eat their own flesh,
and they shall be drunk with their own blood as with
wine.
Then all flesh shall know
that I am the LORD your Savior,
and your Redeemer, the Mighty One of Jacob."

Israel's Sin and the Servant's Obedience

50 Thus says the LORD:
"Where is your mother's certificate of divorce,
with which I sent her away?
Or which of my creditors is it
to whom I have sold you?
Behold, for your iniquities you were sold,
and for your transgressions your mother was sent away.
2 Why, when I came, was there no man;
why, when I called, was there no one to answer?
Is my hand shortened, that it cannot redeem?
Or have I no power to deliver?
Behold, by my rebuke I dry up the sea,
I make the rivers a desert;
their fish stink for lack of water
and die of thirst.
3 I clothe the heavens with blackness
and make sackcloth their covering."

4 The Lord GOD has given me
the tongue of those who are taught,
that I may know how to sustain with a word
him who is weary.
Morning by morning he awakens;
he awakens my ear
to hear as those who are taught.
5 The Lord GOD has opened my ear,
and I was not rebellious;
I turned not backward.

[1]Hebrew *in their bosom* [2]Dead Sea Scroll, Syriac, Vulgate (see also verse 25); Masoretic Text *of a righteous man*

6 I gave my back to those who strike,
and my cheeks to those who pull out the beard;
I hid not my face
from disgrace and spitting.

7 But the Lord God helps me;
therefore I have not been disgraced;
therefore I have set my face like a flint,
and I know that I shall not be put to shame.
8 He who vindicates me is near.
Who will contend with me?
Let us stand up together.
Who is my adversary?
Let him come near to me.
9 Behold, the Lord God helps me;
who will declare me guilty?
Behold, all of them will wear out like a garment;
the moth will eat them up.

10 Who among you fears the LORD
and obeys the voice of his servant?
Let him who walks in darkness
and has no light
trust in the name of the LORD
and rely on his God.
11 Behold, all you who kindle a fire,
who equip yourselves with burning torches!
Walk by the light of your fire,
and by the torches that you have kindled!
This you have from my hand:
you shall lie down in torment.

The LORD's Comfort for Zion

51 "Listen to me, you who pursue righteousness,
you who seek the LORD:
look to the rock from which you were hewn,
and to the quarry from which you were dug.
2 Look to Abraham your father
and to Sarah who bore you;
for he was but one when I called him,
that I might bless him and multiply him.
3 For the LORD comforts Zion;
he comforts all her waste places
and makes her wilderness like Eden,
her desert like the garden of the LORD;
joy and gladness will be found in her,
thanksgiving and the voice of song.

4 "Give attention to me, my people,
and give ear to me, my nation;
for a law[1] will go out from me,
and I will set my justice for a light to the peoples.
5 My righteousness draws near,
my salvation has gone out,
and my arms will judge the peoples;
the coastlands hope for me,
and for my arm they wait.

[1]Or *for teaching*; also verse 7

ISAIAH 51:4–6

SALVATION FOREVER

The prophet Isaiah spoke of the nearness of the righteousness and salvation of God. His arm, or his power, will go forth in judgment, but that same power will be used to deliver and save those who trust in him. Though the prophecy about God's righteousness drawing near speedily (v. 5) refers to the Israelites returning from exile in Babylon, the rest of this stanza (vv. 4–6) clearly looks beyond that event.

Just as judgment lies with God alone—he alone sets the standards of justice, righteousness, and holiness in the universe according to his good character—so too does salvation lie with him. God alone has the power to truly save, for he saves his people from the very judgment that he will execute in the world.

This text reminds readers that the entire cosmos is in a state of downward entropy: things are getting worse and worse and will continue to do so. Just as humans have been, so God's creation has also been mired and corrupted by sin. While the earth will pass away, God's salvation will stand forever. This salvation is accomplished through Jesus and Jesus alone; indeed, salvation was and is his mission on earth. God shows his eternal commitment to save those who trust in him through the life, death, and resurrection of Christ. Salvation, then, can only be had through Christ. This is why the New Testament echoes the fact that "salvation belongs to our God" (Rev 7:10).

VOLUNTARY SUFFERING

What would mark the coming of God's chosen One? The prophet foretold of songs of joy, glory, renown, and praise for his coming. But here we find another more surprising aspect of the Messiah's coming — that of suffering. The idea that the coming King would meet this kind of humiliation and hatred seems counterintuitive, but that's exactly what Isaiah's prophecy describes. While many Israelites expected the servant of God to be heralded as a king, conquering his enemies in triumph and riding into the city on a war horse, they would instead witness the rise of an inauspicious son of a tradesman — one who associated with the lowest and the least — riding into Jerusalem on the back of a donkey. Jesus Christ would be the King that no one expected, and he would receive brutal treatment that he did not deserve.

In ancient culture, people sometimes struck the back of a fool (Pr 19:29), and pulling someone's beard was a sign of contempt and disrespect (2Sa 10:4 – 5). Even today there is no greater insult than spitting in one's face, and yet Jesus willingly endured the mocking of his enemies (Mt 26:67 – 68; 27:26 – 31).

Note, however, the posture of the servant described in this verse: "I *gave* my back to those who strike" (emphasis added). Isaiah testified that these terrible things would not just be done to God's chosen One: they would be done with his permission. He would give them his back to strike, he would give them his cheeks, and they would mock him to his face. He would not turn away from the spit in his face.

We see in Matthew's crucifixion account that Jesus allowed all these things to happen. This is the great irony of the cross. The King of the universe who could, in a moment, defeat his enemies and free himself from their abuse, willingly submitted to the cross in order to satisfy the Father's wrath upon human sin. The King of kings became the suffering servant out of love for his chosen people.

Jesus, God's chosen servant, willingly took all these sufferings on himself even to the point of death. He did so not because his own life merited such suffering and humiliation, but because ours do. Jesus took that which we deserved so that we might accept what we do not deserve. Because of his willing suffering, we can be the recipients of his unmerited grace and favor.

6 Lift up your eyes to the heavens,
and look at the earth beneath;
for the heavens vanish like smoke,
the earth will wear out like a garment,
and they who dwell in it will die in like manner;[1]
but my salvation will be forever,
and my righteousness will never be dismayed.

7 "Listen to me, you who know righteousness,
the people in whose heart is my law;
fear not the reproach of man,
nor be dismayed at their revilings.
8 For the moth will eat them up like a garment,
and the worm will eat them like wool,
but my righteousness will be forever,
and my salvation to all generations."

9 Awake, awake, put on strength,
O arm of the LORD;
awake, as in days of old,
the generations of long ago.
Was it not you who cut Rahab in pieces,
who pierced the dragon?
10 Was it not you who dried up the sea,
the waters of the great deep,
who made the depths of the sea a way
for the redeemed to pass over?
11 And the ransomed of the LORD shall return
and come to Zion with singing;
everlasting joy shall be upon their heads;
they shall obtain gladness and joy,
and sorrow and sighing shall flee away.

12 "I, I am he who comforts you;
who are you that you are afraid of man who dies,
of the son of man who is made like grass,
13 and have forgotten the LORD, your Maker,
who stretched out the heavens
and laid the foundations of the earth,
and you fear continually all the day
because of the wrath of the oppressor,
when he sets himself to destroy?
And where is the wrath of the oppressor?
14 He who is bowed down shall speedily be released;
he shall not die and go down to the pit,
neither shall his bread be lacking.
15 I am the LORD your God,
who stirs up the sea so that its waves roar—
the LORD of hosts is his name.
16 And I have put my words in your mouth
and covered you in the shadow of my hand,
establishing[2] the heavens
and laying the foundations of the earth,
and saying to Zion, 'You are my people.'"

17 Wake yourself, wake yourself,
stand up, O Jerusalem,

[1]Or *will die like gnats* [2]Or *planting*

you who have drunk from the hand of the LORD
the cup of his wrath,
who have drunk to the dregs
the bowl, the cup of staggering.
18 There is none to guide her
among all the sons she has borne;
there is none to take her by the hand
among all the sons she has brought up.
19 These two things have happened to you—
who will console you?—
devastation and destruction, famine and sword;
who will comfort you?[1]
20 Your sons have fainted;
they lie at the head of every street
like an antelope in a net;
they are full of the wrath of the LORD,
the rebuke of your God.

21 Therefore hear this, you who are afflicted,
who are drunk, but not with wine:
22 Thus says your Lord, the LORD,
your God who pleads the cause of his people:
"Behold, I have taken from your hand the cup of staggering;
the bowl of my wrath you shall drink no more;
23 and I will put it into the hand of your tormentors,
who have said to you,
'Bow down, that we may pass over';
and you have made your back like the ground
and like the street for them to pass over."

The LORD's Coming Salvation

52 Awake, awake,
put on your strength, O Zion;
put on your beautiful garments,
O Jerusalem, the holy city;
for there shall no more come into you
the uncircumcised and the unclean.
2 Shake yourself from the dust and arise;
be seated, O Jerusalem;
loose the bonds from your neck,
O captive daughter of Zion.

3For thus says the LORD: "You were sold for nothing, and you shall be redeemed
without money." 4For thus says the Lord GOD: "My people went down at the first
into Egypt to sojourn there, and the Assyrian oppressed them for nothing.[2] 5Now
therefore what have I here," declares the LORD, "seeing that my people are taken
away for nothing? Their rulers wail," declares the LORD, "and continually all the
day my name is despised. 6Therefore my people shall know my name. Therefore
in that day they shall know that it is I who speak; here I am."

7 How beautiful upon the mountains
are the feet of him who brings good news,
who publishes peace, who brings good news of happiness,
who publishes salvation,
who says to Zion, "Your God reigns."

ISAIAH 52:7

BEAUTIFUL FEET

In the days of Isaiah, news of the outcome of a battle would be carried on foot by a messenger from the battle, bringing either good or bad news to the waiting population. In this case, the glorious message of this runner involved the announcement of the return from exile.

In the New Testament, the apostle Paul refers to this imagery for the sake of the gospel. He quotes this verse in Romans 10:15 to bolster his point about the importance of the proclamation of the Good News. There is no greater victory than that which God has won in Christ; this is the ultimate victory over the last and final enemy. Through Christ, the victory over sin and death has been fully accomplished, but the news of that victory must still be shared.

For those who follow Jesus, the task remains to herald that victory far and wide. It's the calling of every follower of Jesus to make this declaration until all have heard the Good News that people can, at long last, have peace with God because of the sacrifice of Jesus Christ.

[1]Dead Sea Scroll, Septuagint, Syriac, Vulgate; Masoretic Text *how shall I comfort you* [2]Or *the Assyrian has oppressed them of late*

8 The voice of your watchmen—they lift up their voice;
together they sing for joy;
for eye to eye they see
the return of the LORD to Zion.
9 Break forth together into singing,
you waste places of Jerusalem,
for the LORD has comforted his people;
he has redeemed Jerusalem.
10 The LORD has bared his holy arm
before the eyes of all the nations,
and all the ends of the earth shall see
the salvation of our God.

11 Depart, depart, go out from there;
touch no unclean thing;
go out from the midst of her; purify yourselves,
you who bear the vessels of the LORD.
12 For you shall not go out in haste,
and you shall not go in flight,
for the LORD will go before you,
and the God of Israel will be your rear guard.

He Was Pierced for Our Transgressions

13 Behold, my servant shall act wisely;[1]
he shall be high and lifted up,
and shall be exalted.
14 As many were astonished at you—
his appearance was so marred, beyond human
semblance,
and his form beyond that of the children of mankind—
15 so shall he sprinkle[2] many nations.
Kings shall shut their mouths because of him,
for that which has not been told them they see,
and that which they have not heard they understand.

53 Who has believed what he has heard from us?[3]
And to whom has the arm of the LORD been revealed?
2 For he grew up before him like a young plant,
and like a root out of dry ground;
he had no form or majesty that we should look at him,
and no beauty that we should desire him.
3 He was despised and rejected[4] by men,
a man of sorrows[5] and acquainted with[6] grief;[7]
and as one from whom men hide their faces[8]
he was despised, and we esteemed him not.

4 Surely he has borne our griefs
and carried our sorrows;
yet we esteemed him stricken,
smitten by God, and afflicted.
5 But he was pierced for our transgressions;
he was crushed for our iniquities;
upon him was the chastisement that brought us peace,
and with his wounds we are healed.
6 All we like sheep have gone astray;
we have turned—every one—to his own way;

[1]Or *shall prosper* [2]Or *startle* [3]Or *Who has believed what we have heard?* [4]Or *forsaken* [5]Or *pains*; also verse 4 [6]Or *and knowing* [7]Or *sickness*; also verse 4 [8]Or *as one who hides his face from us*

EXALTED SERVANT

Through his prophet Isaiah, the Lord promised that his servant would be exalted because of his obedience to his mission from God. We see in Jesus' exaltation a number of things about God's redemptive purposes in Christ.

Initially, we are reminded that the cross and resurrection of Jesus happened not by accident, but according to God's specific plan. People throughout history have sometimes considered the crucifixion of Jesus to be a tragic accident, a case of misappropriated justice and anger by the judicial system of the time. But this was no accident. Indeed, God was pleased by Jesus' sacrifice and even specifically sent him to offer himself up as that sacrifice (Gal 4:4 – 5; Eph 1:7 – 10). God orchestrated Jesus' life, death, and resurrection to happen in his predetermined time and according to his sovereign plan.

Because this was no accident, we must also conclude that this was not a secondary option to God. Others in history have seen the cross in this light, that God's initial plan was thwarted in the garden, and the crucifixion and resurrection of Jesus was God's last-ditch effort to save at least some of his creation. But God, who knows the beginning and the end, always knew that his one and only Son would be the required sacrifice to atone for humanity's sin.

Because of Christ's work, we also understand that it's only a matter of time before God's plan is completed and creation is redeemed. While God has exalted Jesus to the highest place (Ps 89:27; Php 2:9 – 10), eventually the rest of creation will follow suit. The recognition that God gave to Jesus after his resurrection will eventually be given by all of creation. Jesus will be recognized by Christian and non-Christian alike as the rightful King, and the honor that is due him because of his willing and obedient sacrifice will be paid. Every knee will bow and every tongue will acknowledge that Jesus is Lord, to the glory of God the Father (Php 2:10 – 11). Now, though the world is broken, Jesus the King sits on the throne, ruling and reigning at the right hand of the Father. He is worthy of all worship — in this life and the next (Rev 5:12).

and the LORD has laid on him
the iniquity of us all.

7 He was oppressed, and he was afflicted,
yet he opened not his mouth;
like a lamb that is led to the slaughter,
and like a sheep that before its shearers is silent,
so he opened not his mouth.
8 By oppression and judgment he was taken away;
and as for his generation, who considered
that he was cut off out of the land of the living,
stricken for the transgression of my people?
9 And they made his grave with the wicked
and with a rich man in his death,
although[1] he had done no violence,
and there was no deceit in his mouth.

10 Yet it was the will of the LORD to crush him;
he has put him to grief;[2]
when his soul makes[3] an offering for guilt,
he shall see his offspring; he shall prolong his days;
the will of the LORD shall prosper in his hand.
11 Out of the anguish of his soul he shall see[4] and be satisfied;
by his knowledge shall the righteous one, my servant,
make many to be accounted righteous,
and he shall bear their iniquities.
12 Therefore I will divide him a portion with the many,[5]
and he shall divide the spoil with the strong,[6]
because he poured out his soul to death
and was numbered with the transgressors;
yet he bore the sin of many,
and makes intercession for the transgressors.

The Eternal Covenant of Peace

54 "Sing, O barren one, who did not bear;
break forth into singing and cry aloud,
you who have not been in labor!
For the children of the desolate one will be more
than the children of her who is married," says the LORD.
2 "Enlarge the place of your tent,
and let the curtains of your habitations be stretched out;
do not hold back; lengthen your cords
and strengthen your stakes.
3 For you will spread abroad to the right and to the left,
and your offspring will possess the nations
and will people the desolate cities.

4 "Fear not, for you will not be ashamed;
be not confounded, for you will not be disgraced;
for you will forget the shame of your youth,
and the reproach of your widowhood you will remember no more.
5 For your Maker is your husband,
the LORD of hosts is his name;
and the Holy One of Israel is your Redeemer,
the God of the whole earth he is called.

[1]Or *because* [2]Or *he has made him sick* [3]Or *when you make his soul* [4]Masoretic Text; Dead Sea Scroll *he shall see light* [5]Or *with the great* [6]Or *with the numerous*

MAN OF SORROWS

There is perhaps no passage in the Old Testament that so clearly predicts and describes the character, life, and mission of Jesus Christ than this one. We see from this chapter as a whole that God's servant would be humiliated and disfigured by suffering (v. 3; Mk 15:17,19); he would be widely rejected (v. 3; Jn 12:37 – 38); he would bear our sins and suffering (Isa 53:4 – 6; Ro 4:25; 1Pe 2:24); he would make a blood atonement (Isa 53:7 – 8; Ro 3:25); he would become our substitute (Isa 53:7; 2Co 5:21); he would remain silent in the face of his enemies (Isa 53:7); he would voluntarily accept our guilt and punishment (v. 8; Jn 10:11); he would justify many from their sin (Isa 53:8,11; Ro 5:15 – 19); he would die with transgressors (Isa 53:9,12; Mk 15:27); and he would be buried in a rich man's tomb (Isa 53:9; Jn 19:38 – 42). And there are many more connections to be made in this chapter to the life of Jesus.

Isaiah 53 paints a stark picture of God's chosen One, but it does so in surprising ways. What we see here is the vivid picture of One who would be characterized by trial and suffering. No wonder Jesus is called the man of sorrows (v. 3), or suffering.

This title doesn't mean that Jesus lived a sad life or that he was incapable of humor. It does mean, though, that Jesus would be even more acquainted with sorrow than any of the rest of humanity would ever be. This is a startling statement given that so much suffering is possible for a single person. The world is — and, since the fall, always has been — riddled with disease, famine, injustice, and more; yet all of these things are the result of the condition of sin.

When sin entered the world, it not only corrupted the relationship between humankind and God: it flipped all of creation on its head. Sin is the condition of the universe, and as a result of that condition, there are not only acts of sin, but also natural disasters, disease, and all manner of negative and painful realities in the universe. While all of us are acquainted with sin because we all live in this sinful world, not one of us has had the experience with sin that Jesus has. He has felt it more deeply, suffered under its burden more completely, and ultimately triumphed over it fully.

The man of sorrows has experienced the worst the world has to offer and come out victorious on the other side. And for that, believers have reason to thank and praise him for all eternity.

YOUR MAKER, YOUR HUSBAND

One of the most beautiful images representative of the relationship between God and his people is that of marriage. Here God is seen as the husband with Israel as his bride. This image reminds us of the great love and compassion God has for his people. In the Bible, sin is often compared to adultery. Yet God demonstrates the profound nature of his love by pursuing his wayward, adulterous people, keeping his promises and loving them anyway. It further reminds us of the commitment God has to his people.

Like Gomer's unfaithfulness to Hosea (Hos 1:2; 3:1), Israel's past was riddled with infidelity to their covenant with God. But like Hosea's faithfulness to Gomer, the Lord steadfastly remained faithful to his people and even in their exile would not reject them (Isa 54:6 – 8). He is the husband who remained true, for his covenant was based on his own character.

In the same way that wedding vows include the commitment "for better, for worse," so God has joined himself to his people. This verse is meant to comfort the people in understanding that, no matter where they might find themselves in exile, God has not rejected them. Like a faithful spouse, he promised to continually pursue them in his love, call them with his kindness, and seek to restore them to right relationship with himself.

Along with the title of husband in this verse, we also see the title of "LORD of hosts." If the husband imagery reminds us of God's love and commitment, this second title speaks of his power. He is the Lord of hosts, commander of the armies of heaven, so there is nothing in all the universe that will prevent him from carrying out his will and protecting his own people. In the New Testament, Jesus is the husband of the church (Rev 19:7), who has the power to bring his people to himself. He is called "Faithful and True" (Rev 19:11), and we, as his bride, are secure in him. Despite our unfaithfulness, believers can rest assured that our keeping in God is based not on our own righteousness but instead on the strength of Jesus that God graciously credits to us.

6 For the LORD has called you
like a wife deserted and grieved in spirit,
like a wife of youth when she is cast off,
says your God.
7 For a brief moment I deserted you,
but with great compassion I will gather you.
8 In overflowing anger for a moment
I hid my face from you,
but with everlasting love I will have compassion on you,"
says the LORD, your Redeemer.

9 "This is like the days of Noah[1] to me:
as I swore that the waters of Noah
should no more go over the earth,
so I have sworn that I will not be angry with you,
and will not rebuke you.
10 For the mountains may depart
and the hills be removed,
but my steadfast love shall not depart from you,
and my covenant of peace shall not be removed,"
says the LORD, who has compassion on you.

11 "O afflicted one, storm-tossed and not comforted,
behold, I will set your stones in antimony,
and lay your foundations with sapphires.[2]
12 I will make your pinnacles of agate,[3]
your gates of carbuncles,[4]
and all your wall of precious stones.
13 All your children shall be taught by the LORD,
and great shall be the peace of your children.
14 In righteousness you shall be established;
you shall be far from oppression, for you shall not fear;
and from terror, for it shall not come near you.
15 If anyone stirs up strife,
it is not from me;
whoever stirs up strife with you
shall fall because of you.
16 Behold, I have created the smith
who blows the fire of coals
and produces a weapon for its purpose.
I have also created the ravager to destroy;
17 no weapon that is fashioned against you shall succeed,
and you shall refute every tongue that rises against you in judgment.
This is the heritage of the servants of the LORD
and their vindication[5] from me, declares the LORD."

The Compassion of the LORD

55 "Come, everyone who thirsts,
come to the waters;
and he who has no money,
come, buy and eat!
Come, buy wine and milk
without money and without price.
2 Why do you spend your money for that which is not bread,
and your labor for that which does not satisfy?

[1]Some manuscripts *For this is as the waters of Noah* [2]Or *lapis lazuli* [3]Or *jasper*, or *ruby* [4]Or *crystal*
[5]Or *righteousness*

ISAIAH 54:11–12

THE FUTURE GLORY OF ZION

These verses begin with the misery and affliction of the people of Jerusalem. The residents had been terrorized by an attack on the city, and God had not yet intervened to stop the invaders. But God, through Isaiah, detailed the bold plans he had to personally step into the city and gloriously transform it. This passage stunningly pictures everything from the foundation of the city to its ornamentation. The imagery described in terms of the jewels and precious stones is meant to help people visualize something beyond their wildest imagination.

Though Jerusalem has been destroyed and rebuilt many times throughout history, nothing has been erected by human hands that comes anywhere close to the glittering vision God presented in this passage. That's because the true fulfillment of the future glory of Zion is yet to come. The new Jerusalem is God's future city; it will be inhabited by his people from every tribe, tongue, and nation. United once and for all in his city, God's people will worship him in the splendor of his beauty and holiness. And Jesus, the Lamb of God, will be its centerpiece (Rev 21:18–23).

Listen diligently to me, and eat what is good,
and delight yourselves in rich food.
3 Incline your ear, and come to me;
hear, that your soul may live;
and I will make with you an everlasting covenant,
my steadfast, sure love for David.
4 Behold, I made him a witness to the peoples,
a leader and commander for the peoples.
5 Behold, you shall call a nation that you do not know,
and a nation that did not know you shall run to you,
because of the LORD your God, and of the Holy One of Israel,
for he has glorified you.

6 "Seek the LORD while he may be found;
call upon him while he is near;
7 let the wicked forsake his way,
and the unrighteous man his thoughts;
let him return to the LORD, that he may have compassion on him,
and to our God, for he will abundantly pardon.
8 For my thoughts are not your thoughts,
neither are your ways my ways, declares the LORD.
9 For as the heavens are higher than the earth,
so are my ways higher than your ways
and my thoughts than your thoughts.

10 "For as the rain and the snow come down from heaven
and do not return there but water the earth,
making it bring forth and sprout,
giving seed to the sower and bread to the eater,
11 so shall my word be that goes out from my mouth;
it shall not return to me empty,
but it shall accomplish that which I purpose,
and shall succeed in the thing for which I sent it.

12 "For you shall go out in joy
and be led forth in peace;
the mountains and the hills before you
shall break forth into singing,
and all the trees of the field shall clap their hands.
13 Instead of the thorn shall come up the cypress;
instead of the brier shall come up the myrtle;
and it shall make a name for the LORD,
an everlasting sign that shall not be cut off."

Salvation for Foreigners

56 Thus says the LORD:
"Keep justice, and do righteousness,
for soon my salvation will come,
and my righteousness be revealed.
2 Blessed is the man who does this,
and the son of man who holds it fast,
who keeps the Sabbath, not profaning it,
and keeps his hand from doing any evil."

3 Let not the foreigner who has joined himself to the LORD say,
"The LORD will surely separate me from his people";
and let not the eunuch say,
"Behold, I am a dry tree."

ISAIAH 55:3–5

AN INVITATION

It's staggering to consider that God, though wronged and rejected time and time again, actually extends an invitation of salvation to his sinful people. He did and does just that, inviting all people to consider the promises he made to David in his covenant. This invitation comes through God's Word to us; if we listen to it, we will find ourselves drawn to him over and over again. This is what the Word of God does; it engenders faith in sinners as they hear God's Word (Ro 10:17).

Years before Isaiah prophesied these words, God made David a promise that David would have a descendant who would reign on Israel's throne forever. This, of course, is Jesus Christ (Ac 13:32–39), through whom God continues to make his great invitation to sinners of every sort and origin. Through Jesus, the door is open to all who are willing to admit their need of cleansing and salvation in light of the holy standard of God, submitting themselves to that standard as revealed in God's Word and coming to him to accept this free gift.

INVITATION TO THE THIRSTY

God holds out his invitation in this passage to all who are willing to come, including Israel and the Gentile nations. God's invitation is not merely for the basic stuff of life; rather, he invites us to come to him to find that which is truly satisfying and fulfilling.

What do we find in God's presence? What can he alone give? These verses show us the futility we experience when we try to find satisfaction and joy apart from God. While we might spend a lifetime working hard to purchase things that will ultimately leave us frustrated and empty, God alone holds satisfaction in himself. In him, we can finally and ultimately be delighted (Ps 37:4), for God created us with a unique capacity to know and enjoy him for all eternity.

Remarkably, this great satisfaction is free to us. God made sure through his prophet Isaiah to emphasize that what is found in him cannot be purchased with money. There are no wells to be dug; there is no seed to be planted; there are no animals to tend. Instead, God's overwhelming bounty comes to us by grace alone, free to all who are willing to come. Though all the goodness of God is free, it is not without cost. Jesus himself paid that price on behalf of those who believe. Because of the death and resurrection of Jesus, God holds his arms open and says, "Come." The proper response to God's invitation is for all who hear it to "seek the LORD while he may be found" (Isa 55:6). Because he is the foundation of life, the fountain who won't run dry, the source of all human satisfaction, all people should willingly seek after and come to him.

When we "seek the LORD while he may be found," it means we agree with God's assessments of ourselves and the world around us. We no longer rebel against his calling us sinners but instead wholeheartedly accept his word to us. It's that word of God that issues his invitation, and it's through accepting the word that we actually find him. Jesus, as God's living Word (Jn 1:1), went out from him and accomplished the purposes God had for him. And it's through accepting the free gift of this living Word that we can ultimately return to God.

"I dwell in the high and holy place,
and also with him who is of a contrite and lowly spirit,
to revive the spirit of the lowly,
and to revive the heart of the contrite.
16 For I will not contend forever,
nor will I always be angry;
for the spirit would grow faint before me,
and the breath of life that I made.
17 Because of the iniquity of his unjust gain I was angry,
I struck him; I hid my face and was angry,
but he went on backsliding in the way of his own heart.
18 I have seen his ways, but I will heal him;
I will lead him and restore comfort to him and his mourners,
19 creating the fruit of the lips.
Peace, peace, to the far and to the near," says the LORD,
"and I will heal him.
20 But the wicked are like the tossing sea;
for it cannot be quiet,
and its waters toss up mire and dirt.
21 There is no peace," says my God, "for the wicked."

True and False Fasting

58 "Cry aloud; do not hold back;
lift up your voice like a trumpet;
declare to my people their transgression,
to the house of Jacob their sins.
2 Yet they seek me daily
and delight to know my ways,
as if they were a nation that did righteousness
and did not forsake the judgment of their God;
they ask of me righteous judgments;
they delight to draw near to God.
3 'Why have we fasted, and you see it not?
Why have we humbled ourselves, and you take no knowledge of it?'
Behold, in the day of your fast you seek your own pleasure,[1]
and oppress all your workers.
4 Behold, you fast only to quarrel and to fight
and to hit with a wicked fist.
Fasting like yours this day
will not make your voice to be heard on high.
5 Is such the fast that I choose,
a day for a person to humble himself?
Is it to bow down his head like a reed,
and to spread sackcloth and ashes under him?
Will you call this a fast,
and a day acceptable to the LORD?

6 "Is not this the fast that I choose:
to loose the bonds of wickedness,
to undo the straps of the yoke,
to let the oppressed[2] go free,
and to break every yoke?
7 Is it not to share your bread with the hungry
and bring the homeless poor into your house;

[1]Or *pursue your own business* [2]Or *bruised*

ISAIAH 58:3–9

FASTING THAT GOD ACCEPTS

Fasting is the intentional choice to deprive oneself of something, most often food, for a period of time. But fasting is also a spiritual discipline that can easily become corrupted and self-serving. The Israelites had fasted in times of national calamity and as a regular part of their liturgical calendar. While true fasting is done to heighten one's awareness of the things of God and move one toward holiness, the fasting Isaiah wrote about was largely hypocritical. It was focused on self-righteousness and not on the kind of justice for others that God desired. Ironically, the self-righteous were busy depriving themselves of food while others in their community and their nation went hungry because of their poverty. This, said the prophet, was not the fast that God desired.

Similarly, Jesus condemned the fasting he witnessed in his day. Fasting had become a way to publicly demonstrate one's righteousness, but Jesus pointed people back to the heart of the matter. This discipline was meant to be a private matter between the individual and God (Mt 6:16–18), with the goal of fostering greater commitment to God and a greater commitment to helping those in need.

when you see the naked, to cover him,
and not to hide yourself from your own flesh?
8 Then shall your light break forth like the dawn,
and your healing shall spring up speedily;
your righteousness shall go before you;
the glory of the LORD shall be your rear guard.
9 Then you shall call, and the LORD will answer;
you shall cry, and he will say, 'Here I am.'
If you take away the yoke from your midst,
the pointing of the finger, and speaking wickedness,
10 if you pour yourself out for the hungry
and satisfy the desire of the afflicted,
then shall your light rise in the darkness
and your gloom be as the noonday.
11 And the LORD will guide you continually
and satisfy your desire in scorched places
and make your bones strong;
and you shall be like a watered garden,
like a spring of water,
whose waters do not fail.
12 And your ancient ruins shall be rebuilt;
you shall raise up the foundations of many generations;
you shall be called the repairer of the breach,
the restorer of streets to dwell in.

13 "If you turn back your foot from the Sabbath,
from doing your pleasure[1] on my holy day,
and call the Sabbath a delight
and the holy day of the LORD honorable;
if you honor it, not going your own ways,
or seeking your own pleasure,[2] or talking idly;[3]
14 then you shall take delight in the LORD,
and I will make you ride on the heights of the earth;[4]
I will feed you with the heritage of Jacob your father,
for the mouth of the LORD has spoken."

Evil and Oppression

59 Behold, the LORD's hand is not shortened, that it cannot save,
or his ear dull, that it cannot hear;
2 but your iniquities have made a separation
between you and your God,
and your sins have hidden his face from you
so that he does not hear.
3 For your hands are defiled with blood
and your fingers with iniquity;
your lips have spoken lies;
your tongue mutters wickedness.
4 No one enters suit justly;
no one goes to law honestly;
they rely on empty pleas, they speak lies,
they conceive mischief and give birth to iniquity.
5 They hatch adders' eggs;
they weave the spider's web;
he who eats their eggs dies,
and from one that is crushed a viper is hatched.

[1]Or *business* [2]Or *pursuing your own business* [3]Hebrew *or speaking a word* [4]Or *of the land*

6 Their webs will not serve as clothing;
men will not cover themselves with what they make.
Their works are works of iniquity,
and deeds of violence are in their hands.
7 Their feet run to evil,
and they are swift to shed innocent blood;
their thoughts are thoughts of iniquity;
desolation and destruction are in their highways.
8 The way of peace they do not know,
and there is no justice in their paths;
they have made their roads crooked;
no one who treads on them knows peace.

9 Therefore justice is far from us,
and righteousness does not overtake us;
we hope for light, and behold, darkness,
and for brightness, but we walk in gloom.
10 We grope for the wall like the blind;
we grope like those who have no eyes;
we stumble at noon as in the twilight,
among those in full vigor we are like dead men.
11 We all growl like bears;
we moan and moan like doves;
we hope for justice, but there is none;
for salvation, but it is far from us.
12 For our transgressions are multiplied before you,
and our sins testify against us;
for our transgressions are with us,
and we know our iniquities:
13 transgressing, and denying the LORD,
and turning back from following our God,
speaking oppression and revolt,
conceiving and uttering from the heart lying words.

Judgment and Redemption

14 Justice is turned back,
and righteousness stands far away;
for truth has stumbled in the public squares,
and uprightness cannot enter.
15 Truth is lacking,
and he who departs from evil makes himself a prey.

The LORD saw it, and it displeased him[1]
that there was no justice.
16 He saw that there was no man,
and wondered that there was no one to intercede;
then his own arm brought him salvation,
and his righteousness upheld him.
17 He put on righteousness as a breastplate,
and a helmet of salvation on his head;
he put on garments of vengeance for clothing,
and wrapped himself in zeal as a cloak.
18 According to their deeds, so will he repay,
wrath to his adversaries, repayment to his enemies;
to the coastlands he will render repayment.

---

[1]Hebrew *and it was evil in his eyes*

19 So they shall fear the name of the LORD from the west,
and his glory from the rising of the sun;
for he will come like a rushing stream,[1]
which the wind of the LORD drives.

20 "And a Redeemer will come to Zion,
to those in Jacob who turn from transgression," declares the LORD.

21"And as for me, this is my covenant with them," says the LORD: "My Spirit that
is upon you, and my words that I have put in your mouth, shall not depart out of
your mouth, or out of the mouth of your offspring, or out of the mouth of your
children's offspring," says the LORD, "from this time forth and forevermore."

The Future Glory of Israel

60 Arise, shine, for your light has come,
and the glory of the LORD has risen upon you.
2 For behold, darkness shall cover the earth,
and thick darkness the peoples;
but the LORD will arise upon you,
and his glory will be seen upon you.
3 And nations shall come to your light,
and kings to the brightness of your rising.

4 Lift up your eyes all around, and see;
they all gather together, they come to you;
your sons shall come from afar,
and your daughters shall be carried on the hip.
5 Then you shall see and be radiant;
your heart shall thrill and exult,[2]
because the abundance of the sea shall be turned to you,
the wealth of the nations shall come to you.
6 A multitude of camels shall cover you,
the young camels of Midian and Ephah;
all those from Sheba shall come.
They shall bring gold and frankincense,
and shall bring good news, the praises of the LORD.
7 All the flocks of Kedar shall be gathered to you;
the rams of Nebaioth shall minister to you;
they shall come up with acceptance on my altar,
and I will beautify my beautiful house.

8 Who are these that fly like a cloud,
and like doves to their windows?
9 For the coastlands shall hope for me,
the ships of Tarshish first,
to bring your children from afar,
their silver and gold with them,
for the name of the LORD your God,
and for the Holy One of Israel,
because he has made you beautiful.

10 Foreigners shall build up your walls,
and their kings shall minister to you;
for in my wrath I struck you,
but in my favor I have had mercy on you.
11 Your gates shall be open continually;
day and night they shall not be shut,

[1]Hebrew *a narrow river* [2]Hebrew *your heart shall tremble and grow wide*

ISAIAH 60:1–3

LIGHT IN THE DARKNESS

In darkness there is wandering, apprehension, confusion, and fear. Conversely, light brings clarity, truth, understanding, and comfort. Isaiah spoke of the darkness that covered the whole earth. This description goes beyond the darkness that would come as the people were exiled to Babylon; this is the spiritual darkness that pervades a lost and broken world. It's the darkness into which all humanity has been born, blinded to the truth. But Jesus Christ is the light of the world (Jn 8:12). In him, we can know truth, life, and comfort, for Jesus alone shows us the true way to God.

In this context, it's beautiful to remember that on the night of Jesus' birth, a literal light from above pierced the darkness. The angel of the Lord, shining with "the glory of the Lord," surprised and frightened the shepherds. But the angel's message figuratively and literally pointed the way to the true light of the world, the One who would eliminate all darkness in the future (Lk 2:8–12). Because of Jesus, there is no longer any need to languish in spiritual darkness, for he himself is the light.

UNCONFESSED SIN

The land was filled with injustice during Isaiah's day. Though the people appeared to be very religious, their actions showed a shocking disregard for the needy around them. Instead of mercy and compassion, the land was filled with exploitation and hypocrisy. To this point, the people were unwilling to confess their sin to God, repent, and turn toward obedience.

This unconfessed sin might have seemed like a trivial matter; after all, the people might have argued, it was a private matter between themselves and God. Even worse, they might have been living in a web of self-deception, refusing to see the truth of their sin even when Isaiah confronted them. But unconfessed sin festers inside a person; it destroys one from the inside out.

Similarly, when believers are confronted by the Word of God which calls their sin exactly what it is, they have the choice about whether to agree with God or to continue in their obstinate pride. When they agree with God, they are acknowledging that God knows them better than they know themselves; indeed, that God will tell them the truth even when they are intentionally or unintentionally blind to it themselves. In this light, confession of sin is really simply agreeing with God, who is — lest believers fool themselves into thinking they're hiding anything — well aware of all sin.

Ultimately, the people's refusal to agree with God when he told them the truth resulted in his judgment. He raised up the Babylonians to destroy Judah and Jerusalem as a lasting reminder that God is right in his pronouncements. God's judgment on his people stands as a reminder today that in the future, every nation will be judged by the same God who raised up the Babylonians. Knowing this judgment is coming, the proper response is to agree with God and his Word.

Believers agree with God when they confess their sin; they agree with him when they repent of that sin; they agree with God when they look to the cross of Christ alone as the atoning sacrifice for their sin. Christians follow this pattern of agreement, repentance, and forgiveness time and time again as they look forward to the day when sin will be a thing of the past.

that people may bring to you the wealth of the nations,
with their kings led in procession.
12 For the nation and kingdom
that will not serve you shall perish;
those nations shall be utterly laid waste.
13 The glory of Lebanon shall come to you,
the cypress, the plane, and the pine,
to beautify the place of my sanctuary,
and I will make the place of my feet glorious.
14 The sons of those who afflicted you
shall come bending low to you,
and all who despised you
shall bow down at your feet;
they shall call you the City of the LORD,
the Zion of the Holy One of Israel.

15 Whereas you have been forsaken and hated,
with no one passing through,
I will make you majestic forever,
a joy from age to age.
16 You shall suck the milk of nations;
you shall nurse at the breast of kings;
and you shall know that I, the LORD, am your Savior
and your Redeemer, the Mighty One of Jacob.

17 Instead of bronze I will bring gold,
and instead of iron I will bring silver;
instead of wood, bronze,
instead of stones, iron.
I will make your overseers peace
and your taskmasters righteousness.
18 Violence shall no more be heard in your land,
devastation or destruction within your borders;
you shall call your walls Salvation,
and your gates Praise.

19 The sun shall be no more
your light by day,
nor for brightness shall the moon
give you light;[1]
but the LORD will be your everlasting light,
and your God will be your glory.[2]
20 Your sun shall no more go down,
nor your moon withdraw itself;
for the LORD will be your everlasting light,
and your days of mourning shall be ended.
21 Your people shall all be righteous;
they shall possess the land forever,
the branch of my planting, the work of my hands,
that I might be glorified.[3]
22 The least one shall become a clan,
and the smallest one a mighty nation;
I am the LORD;
in its time I will hasten it.

[1]Masoretic Text; Dead Sea Scroll, Septuagint, Targum add *by night* [2]Or *your beauty* [3]Or *that I might display my beauty*

The Year of the LORD's Favor

61 The Spirit of the Lord GOD is upon me,
because the LORD has anointed me
to bring good news to the poor;[1]
he has sent me to bind up the brokenhearted,
to proclaim liberty to the captives,
and the opening of the prison to those who are bound;[2]
2 to proclaim the year of the LORD's favor,
and the day of vengeance of our God;
to comfort all who mourn;
3 to grant to those who mourn in Zion—
to give them a beautiful headdress instead of ashes,
the oil of gladness instead of mourning,
the garment of praise instead of a faint spirit;
that they may be called oaks of righteousness,
the planting of the LORD, that he may be glorified.[3]
4 They shall build up the ancient ruins;
they shall raise up the former devastations;
they shall repair the ruined cities,
the devastations of many generations.

5 Strangers shall stand and tend your flocks;
foreigners shall be your plowmen and vinedressers;
6 but you shall be called the priests of the LORD;
they shall speak of you as the ministers of our God;
you shall eat the wealth of the nations,
and in their glory you shall boast.
7 Instead of your shame there shall be a double portion;
instead of dishonor they shall rejoice in their lot;
therefore in their land they shall possess a double portion;
they shall have everlasting joy.

8 For I the LORD love justice;
I hate robbery and wrong;[4]
I will faithfully give them their recompense,
and I will make an everlasting covenant with them.
9 Their offspring shall be known among the nations,
and their descendants in the midst of the peoples;
all who see them shall acknowledge them,
that they are an offspring the LORD has blessed.

10 I will greatly rejoice in the LORD;
my soul shall exult in my God,
for he has clothed me with the garments of salvation;
he has covered me with the robe of righteousness,
as a bridegroom decks himself like a priest with a beautiful headdress,
and as a bride adorns herself with her jewels.
11 For as the earth brings forth its sprouts,
and as a garden causes what is sown in it to sprout up,
so the Lord GOD will cause righteousness and praise
to sprout up before all the nations.

[1]Or *afflicted* [2]Or *the opening* [of the eyes] *to those who are blind*; Septuagint *and recovery of sight to the blind* [3]Or *that he may display his beauty* [4]Or *robbery with a burnt offering*

ISAIAH 61:1–2

YEAR OF JUBILEE

These verses describe the Year of Jubilee (Lev 25:8–55). According to the Levitical law, every seven years God's people were to observe not just a day of Sabbath, but a sabbatical year in which they allowed the land to lie unplowed. After seven sabbaticals, or forty-nine years, they were to celebrate the Year of Jubilee. During that year, the people were commanded to cancel all debts, return all land to the original owners, and free their fellow Israelites who had sold themselves as indentured servants. This Year of Jubilee signified a fresh start for God's people.

As Jesus was beginning his public ministry, he made a stop in his hometown of Nazareth. Upon visiting the synagogue, he stood up to read and chose this passage from Isaiah. When he concluded his reading, he boldly proclaimed that these verses had been fulfilled that day in the presence of the people (Lk 4:16–21).

Jesus is the one who will usher in the true Year of Jubilee. Through faith in him, the One who gives us his righteousness, we can be released from our debt to sin and truly start again.

ISAIAH 62:1–4

HEPHZIBAH AND BEULAH

In the biblical context, one's name carried great significance. Far from being a mere moniker, a person's name was the description of their character and identity, the summation of the very core of who they were. In these verses, we see that Jerusalem, or Zion, will go through a time when it will be called Forsaken and Desolate, but that time will not last forever. Though there would be years of exile and a great season of wandering and doubt, the Lord would one day, at the appropriate time, reconcile with his people, represented by the special city.

In that reconciliation, God would give the city a new name. *Hephzibah* means "my delight is in her." The old name Desolate would be replaced by *Beulah*, which means "married." Here stands another promise of God that he has not, and will not, abandon his people. His relationship with them and reconciliation with them is bound by his own character.

Similarly, through Christ alone we are given a new name. No matter who we were prior to our reconciliation with God through Christ, God has given us a new name as his own adopted sons and daughters (1Jn 3:1–2; Rev 2:17), and he will not revoke this name.

Zion's Coming Salvation

62 For Zion's sake I will not keep silent,
and for Jerusalem's sake I will not be quiet,
until her righteousness goes forth as brightness,
and her salvation as a burning torch.
2 The nations shall see your righteousness,
and all the kings your glory,
and you shall be called by a new name
that the mouth of the LORD will give.
3 You shall be a crown of beauty in the hand of the LORD,
and a royal diadem in the hand of your God.
4 You shall no more be termed Forsaken,[1]
and your land shall no more be termed Desolate,[2]
but you shall be called My Delight Is in Her,[3]
and your land Married;[4]
for the LORD delights in you,
and your land shall be married.
5 For as a young man marries a young woman,
so shall your sons marry you,
and as the bridegroom rejoices over the bride,
so shall your God rejoice over you.

6 On your walls, O Jerusalem,
I have set watchmen;
all the day and all the night
they shall never be silent.
You who put the LORD in remembrance,
take no rest,
7 and give him no rest
until he establishes Jerusalem
and makes it a praise in the earth.
8 The LORD has sworn by his right hand
and by his mighty arm:
"I will not again give your grain
to be food for your enemies,
and foreigners shall not drink your wine
for which you have labored;
9 but those who garner it shall eat it
and praise the LORD,
and those who gather it shall drink it
in the courts of my sanctuary."[5]

10 Go through, go through the gates;
prepare the way for the people;
build up, build up the highway;
clear it of stones;
lift up a signal over the peoples.
11 Behold, the LORD has proclaimed
to the end of the earth:
Say to the daughter of Zion,
"Behold, your salvation comes;
behold, his reward is with him,
and his recompense before him."
12 And they shall be called The Holy People,
The Redeemed of the LORD;

[1]Hebrew *Azubah* [2]Hebrew *Shemamah* [3]Hebrew *Hephzibah* [4]Hebrew *Beulah* [5]Or *in my holy courts*

and you shall be called Sought Out,
A City Not Forsaken.

The LORD's Day of Vengeance

63 Who is this who comes from Edom,
in crimsoned garments from Bozrah,
he who is splendid in his apparel,
marching in the greatness of his strength?
"It is I, speaking in righteousness,
mighty to save."

2 Why is your apparel red,
and your garments like his who treads in the winepress?

3 "I have trodden the winepress alone,
and from the peoples no one was with me;
I trod them in my anger
and trampled them in my wrath;
their lifeblood[1] spattered on my garments,
and stained all my apparel.
4 For the day of vengeance was in my heart,
and my year of redemption[2] had come.
5 I looked, but there was no one to help;
I was appalled, but there was no one to uphold;
so my own arm brought me salvation,
and my wrath upheld me.
6 I trampled down the peoples in my anger;
I made them drunk in my wrath,
and I poured out their lifeblood on the earth."

The LORD's Mercy Remembered

7 I will recount the steadfast love of the LORD,
the praises of the LORD,
according to all that the LORD has granted us,
and the great goodness to the house of Israel
that he has granted them according to his compassion,
according to the abundance of his steadfast love.
8 For he said, "Surely they are my people,
children who will not deal falsely."
And he became their Savior.
9 In all their affliction he was afflicted,[3]
and the angel of his presence saved them;
in his love and in his pity he redeemed them;
he lifted them up and carried them all the days of old.

10 But they rebelled
and grieved his Holy Spirit;
therefore he turned to be their enemy,
and himself fought against them.
11 Then he remembered the days of old,
of Moses and his people.[4]
Where is he who brought them up out of the sea
with the shepherds of his flock?
Where is he who put in the midst of them
his Holy Spirit,

[1]Or *their juice*; also verse 6 [2]Or *the year of my redeemed* [3]Or *he did not afflict* [4]Or *Then his people remembered the days of old, of Moses*

ISAIAH 63:1–6

GOD'S DAY OF VENGEANCE

Jesus came into the world the first time in an inauspicious way. Born in a stable in a backwater town, he inaugurated the year of true Jubilee, inviting all who are willing to repent and return to God to find true and lasting peace. When he comes the second time, it will not be with the message of peace but of vengeance and judgment. This second coming is described in Isaiah 63: God's day of vengeance.

The imagery in this chapter is vivid; among the most powerful images is that of the winepress. In those days, grapes were put into a large, hollowed rock for the people to tread on them. The juice of the grapes would run out of a hole in the rock to be caught, and as the grapes were crushed, some of the juice would stain the garments of the people. In this passage, the Lord's garments drip with the blood of his enemies as a result of his great victory.

Still, Isaiah concludes the chapter with a plea for God to demonstrate his power to his people before this great and terrible day. He asks the Lord for mercy so that people might trust in him before it is too late (63:15–19).

12 who caused his glorious arm
to go at the right hand of Moses,
who divided the waters before them
to make for himself an everlasting name,
13 who led them through the depths?
Like a horse in the desert,
they did not stumble.
14 Like livestock that go down into the valley,
the Spirit of the LORD gave them rest.
So you led your people,
to make for yourself a glorious name.

Prayer for Mercy

15 Look down from heaven and see,
from your holy and beautiful[1] habitation.
Where are your zeal and your might?
The stirring of your inner parts and your compassion
are held back from me.
16 For you are our Father,
though Abraham does not know us,
and Israel does not acknowledge us;
you, O LORD, are our Father,
our Redeemer from of old is your name.
17 O LORD, why do you make us wander from your ways
and harden our heart, so that we fear you not?
Return for the sake of your servants,
the tribes of your heritage.
18 Your holy people held possession for a little while;[2]
our adversaries have trampled down your sanctuary.
19 We have become like those over whom you have never ruled,
like those who are not called by your name.

64 Oh that you would rend the heavens and come down,
that the mountains might quake at your presence—
2[3] as when fire kindles brushwood
and the fire causes water to boil—
to make your name known to your adversaries,
and that the nations might tremble at your presence!
3 When you did awesome things that we did not look for,
you came down, the mountains quaked at your presence.
4 From of old no one has heard
or perceived by the ear,
no eye has seen a God besides you,
who acts for those who wait for him.
5 You meet him who joyfully works righteousness,
those who remember you in your ways.
Behold, you were angry, and we sinned;
in our sins we have been a long time, and shall we be saved?[4]
6 We have all become like one who is unclean,
and all our righteous deeds are like a polluted garment.
We all fade like a leaf,
and our iniquities, like the wind, take us away.
7 There is no one who calls upon your name,
who rouses himself to take hold of you;

ISAIAH 64:6–12

PUNISHMENT LEADING TO REPENTANCE

God's judgment on the world is a future reality. It's not a question of if it will come; rather, it's a question of when. But God is also patient; he desires that all people come to repentance (2Pe 3:9). Judgment is long in coming not because God is negligent, but because he is kind and generous.

These verses depict not only the reality of God's judgment, but also the apathy of the people. As it was in Isaiah's day, among unbelievers the judgment of God seems to be at best a distant reality, at worst a myth. We would do well to realize ourselves, and to help others see, the reality of what's to come. These promises are to us a warning so that we will not delay in our repentance. Because we have no righteousness to merit God's favor, our only choice is to throw ourselves at his feet asking for mercy and forgiveness. The time we have until God's great judgment and punishment for sin gives us and others an opportunity to repent and return to him (Ro 2:4). We must not neglect this chance, for we do not know when God's longsuffering patience will run out.

[1]Or *holy and glorious* [2]Or *They have dispossessed your holy people for a little while* [3]Ch 64:1 in Hebrew
[4]Or *in your ways is continuance, that we might be saved*

for you have hidden your face from us,
and have made us melt in[1] the hand of our iniquities.

8 But now, O LORD, you are our Father;
we are the clay, and you are our potter;
we are all the work of your hand.
9 Be not so terribly angry, O LORD,
and remember not iniquity forever.
Behold, please look, we are all your people.
10 Your holy cities have become a wilderness;
Zion has become a wilderness,
Jerusalem a desolation.
11 Our holy and beautiful[2] house,
where our fathers praised you,
has been burned by fire,
and all our pleasant places have become ruins.
12 Will you restrain yourself at these things, O LORD?
Will you keep silent, and afflict us so terribly?

Judgment and Salvation

65 I was ready to be sought by those who did not ask for me;
I was ready to be found by those who did not seek me.
I said, "Here I am, here I am,"
to a nation that was not called by[3] my name.
2 I spread out my hands all the day
to a rebellious people,
who walk in a way that is not good,
following their own devices;
3 a people who provoke me
to my face continually,
sacrificing in gardens
and making offerings on bricks;
4 who sit in tombs,
and spend the night in secret places;
who eat pig's flesh,
and broth of tainted meat is in their vessels;
5 who say, "Keep to yourself,
do not come near me, for I am too holy for you."
These are a smoke in my nostrils,
a fire that burns all the day.
6 Behold, it is written before me:
"I will not keep silent, but I will repay;
I will indeed repay into their lap
7 both your iniquities and your fathers' iniquities together,
says the LORD;
because they made offerings on the mountains
and insulted me on the hills,
I will measure into their lap
payment for their former deeds."[4]

8 Thus says the LORD:
"As the new wine is found in the cluster,
and they say, 'Do not destroy it,
for there is a blessing in it,'

[1]Masoretic Text; Septuagint, Syriac, Targum *have delivered us into* [2]Or *holy and glorious* [3]Or *that did not call upon* [4]Or *I will first measure their payment into their lap*

JUDGMENT AND SALVATION

God is waiting. As these verses tell us, God's desire is to receive those who come to him. Throughout history, he has implored all who hear his voice to respond and come to him. God has revealed his righteous character through nature (Ro 1:20), through the Law of Moses (Ro 2:12 – 13), and even through the human conscience that testifies to God's own righteousness and holiness (Ro 2:14 – 15). His hands are outstretched, and his invitation is open even though time and time again people have chosen to walk in the way that seems best to them.

Though God is and has been ready to receive all who come, people obstinately persist in their self-governance. They continue to go their own way so much so that Paul the apostle would echo the sentiment of Isaiah the prophet: "None is righteous, no, not one; no one understands; no one seeks for God. All have turned aside; together they have become worthless; no one does good, not even one" (Ro 3:10 – 12). But God's love is strong, and his desire to dwell with his people is lasting. He will save his people from judgment though they might not even be seeking after him (Isa 65:1). He is powerful to break the shackles of sin and open blind eyes to see the beauty of his love. All those who come to him are empowered to do so by the work of his Spirit, who convicts men and women of their sin, of the righteousness of Christ, and of their need for him.

This is the true peril of sin. Humanity is so blinded and so deeply corrupted by sin that all people must be awakened by the Spirit of God to even know that they are lost. Through the power of the Holy Spirit, God does this work, breaking through the blindness of sin to reveal the light of the gospel of Jesus Christ. Though we do not seek him, he has sought us. Though we have not called out to him, he has found us and brought us home. When God's judgment does come, then, there is no other option for those who have been saved but to revel completely in the grace alone that has saved them. Jesus alone will receive the honor of salvation even as he receives the honor that comes through judgment.

so I will do for my servants' sake,
and not destroy them all.
9 I will bring forth offspring from Jacob,
and from Judah possessors of my mountains;
my chosen shall possess it,
and my servants shall dwell there.
10 Sharon shall become a pasture for flocks,
and the Valley of Achor a place for herds to lie down,
for my people who have sought me.
11 But you who forsake the LORD,
who forget my holy mountain,
who set a table for Fortune
and fill cups of mixed wine for Destiny,
12 I will destine you to the sword,
and all of you shall bow down to the slaughter,
because, when I called, you did not answer;
when I spoke, you did not listen,
but you did what was evil in my eyes
and chose what I did not delight in."

13 Therefore thus says the Lord GOD:
"Behold, my servants shall eat,
but you shall be hungry;
behold, my servants shall drink,
but you shall be thirsty;
behold, my servants shall rejoice,
but you shall be put to shame;
14 behold, my servants shall sing for gladness of heart,
but you shall cry out for pain of heart
and shall wail for breaking of spirit.
15 You shall leave your name to my chosen for a curse,
and the Lord GOD will put you to death,
but his servants he will call by another name,
16 so that he who blesses himself in the land
shall bless himself by the God of truth,
and he who takes an oath in the land
shall swear by the God of truth;
because the former troubles are forgotten
and are hidden from my eyes.

New Heavens and a New Earth

17 "For behold, I create new heavens
and a new earth,
and the former things shall not be remembered
or come into mind.
18 But be glad and rejoice forever
in that which I create;
for behold, I create Jerusalem to be a joy,
and her people to be a gladness.
19 I will rejoice in Jerusalem
and be glad in my people;
no more shall be heard in it the sound of weeping
and the cry of distress.
20 No more shall there be in it
an infant who lives but a few days,
or an old man who does not fill out his days,

for the young man shall die a hundred years old,
and the sinner a hundred years old shall be accursed.
21 They shall build houses and inhabit them;
they shall plant vineyards and eat their fruit.
22 They shall not build and another inhabit;
they shall not plant and another eat;
for like the days of a tree shall the days of my people be,
and my chosen shall long enjoy[1] the work of their hands.
23 They shall not labor in vain
or bear children for calamity,[2]
for they shall be the offspring of the blessed of the LORD,
and their descendants with them.
24 Before they call I will answer;
while they are yet speaking I will hear.
25 The wolf and the lamb shall graze together;
the lion shall eat straw like the ox,
and dust shall be the serpent's food.
They shall not hurt or destroy
in all my holy mountain,"
says the LORD.

The Humble and Contrite in Spirit

66 Thus says the LORD:
"Heaven is my throne,
and the earth is my footstool;
what is the house that you would build for me,
and what is the place of my rest?
2 All these things my hand has made,
and so all these things came to be,
declares the LORD.
But this is the one to whom I will look:
he who is humble and contrite in spirit
and trembles at my word.

3 "He who slaughters an ox is like one who kills a man;
he who sacrifices a lamb, like one who breaks a dog's neck;
he who presents a grain offering, like one who offers pig's blood;
he who makes a memorial offering of frankincense, like one who blesses
an idol.
These have chosen their own ways,
and their soul delights in their abominations;
4 I also will choose harsh treatment for them
and bring their fears upon them,
because when I called, no one answered,
when I spoke, they did not listen;
but they did what was evil in my eyes
and chose that in which I did not delight."

5 Hear the word of the LORD,
you who tremble at his word:
"Your brothers who hate you
and cast you out for my name's sake
have said, 'Let the LORD be glorified,
that we may see your joy';
but it is they who shall be put to shame.

[1] Hebrew *shall wear out* [2] Or *for sudden terror*

6 "The sound of an uproar from the city!
A sound from the temple!
The sound of the LORD,
rendering recompense to his enemies!

Rejoice with Jerusalem

7 "Before she was in labor
she gave birth;
before her pain came upon her
she delivered a son.
8 Who has heard such a thing?
Who has seen such things?
Shall a land be born in one day?
Shall a nation be brought forth in one moment?
For as soon as Zion was in labor
she brought forth her children.
9 Shall I bring to the point of birth and not cause to bring forth?"
says the LORD;
"shall I, who cause to bring forth, shut the womb?"
says your God.

10 "Rejoice with Jerusalem, and be glad for her,
all you who love her;
rejoice with her in joy,
all you who mourn over her;
11 that you may nurse and be satisfied
from her consoling breast;
that you may drink deeply with delight
from her glorious abundance."[1]

12 For thus says the LORD:
"Behold, I will extend peace to her like a river,
and the glory of the nations like an overflowing stream;
and you shall nurse, you shall be carried upon her hip,
and bounced upon her knees.
13 As one whom his mother comforts,
so I will comfort you;
you shall be comforted in Jerusalem.
14 You shall see, and your heart shall rejoice;
your bones shall flourish like the grass;
and the hand of the LORD shall be known to his servants,
and he shall show his indignation against his enemies.

Final Judgment and Glory of the LORD

15 "For behold, the LORD will come in fire,
and his chariots like the whirlwind,
to render his anger in fury,
and his rebuke with flames of fire.
16 For by fire will the LORD enter into judgment,
and by his sword, with all flesh;
and those slain by the LORD shall be many.

17 "Those who sanctify and purify themselves to go into the gardens, following
one in the midst, eating pig's flesh and the abomination and mice, shall come to
an end together, declares the LORD.
18 "For I know[2] their works and their thoughts, and the time is coming[3] to

[1]Or *breast* [2]Septuagint, Syriac; Hebrew lacks *know* [3]Hebrew *and it is coming*

ISAIAH 66:18–24

FINAL WARNINGS

Isaiah's prophecy closes with the promise that God's Word will go out among the nations (v. 19). As a result, the kingdom of God will be filled with both the people of Israel and with those from the Gentile nations. Though in the past these idolatrous nations have attacked God and his people, they will one day come to worship and glorify their true King.

But there will also be those who do not come, those who do not receive God's Word in repentance and faith. Isaiah's prophecy closes with a vision of judgment, looking upon a scene filled with the corpses of rebels (v. 24). Jesus quoted this verse in picturing a grisly image of hell (Mk 9:48). These two descriptions define two alternatives for those who hear the message: they can either trust in the Lord and claim the salvation that comes through his servant Jesus and live, or they can continue in rebellion and die. The stark reality of these two alternatives shows people not only the greatness of the salvation that can only come through Jesus, but also the urgency with which believers must join Isaiah in proclaiming the message of God.

gather all nations and tongues. And they shall come and shall see my glory, 19and
I will set a sign among them. And from them I will send survivors to the nations,
to Tarshish, Pul, and Lud, who draw the bow, to Tubal and Javan, to the coastlands
far away, that have not heard my fame or seen my glory. And they shall declare
my glory among the nations. 20And they shall bring all your brothers from all the
nations as an offering to the LORD, on horses and in chariots and in litters and on
mules and on dromedaries, to my holy mountain Jerusalem, says the LORD, just as
the Israelites bring their grain offering in a clean vessel to the house of the LORD.
21And some of them also I will take for priests and for Levites, says the LORD.

22 "For as the new heavens and the new earth
    that I make
shall remain before me, says the LORD,
    so shall your offspring and your name remain.
23 From new moon to new moon,
    and from Sabbath to Sabbath,
all flesh shall come to worship before me,
declares the LORD.

24"And they shall go out and look on the dead bodies of the men who have rebelled against me. For their worm shall not die, their fire shall not be quenched, and they shall be an abhorrence to all flesh."

JESUS: OUR NEW COVENANT

JEREMIAH

JEREMIAH

PROPHETIC MINISTRY OF JEREMIAH BEGINS *c. 626 BC*	FALL OF JUDAH *c. 586 BC*	SOME JEWS FLEE TO EGYPT, TAKING JEREMIAH *c. 586 BC*

Jeremiah symbolized the overwhelming burden that God's spokespersons faced during the continual decline of the people of Israel. Called and appointed by God, Jeremiah undertook the daunting task of proclaiming a message of judgment against the Israelites and their removal from the land they had once received as a gift from God's hand. While overwhelming, Jeremiah's prophetic warnings came from God alone, and the prophet had no recourse but to share them with the people (Jer 20:9).

Jeremiah's words drip with anguish and grief over the spiritual state of Judah. In spite of their chosen status in God's eyes, the people had continually given themselves to idolatry and proven themselves incapable of keeping their covenant commitment to God. God had willingly bound himself to these people in covenant love, and the people were expected to respond with worshipful obedience. But they did not. As a result, God's coming judgment would be sure, swift, and severe.

At the time of Jeremiah's warnings, the nation of Judah was in its last days. Jeremiah warned that God would raise up the nation of Babylon to defeat God's people and haul them off into captivity. The fall of Jerusalem in 586 BC fulfilled the longstanding warnings of the prophets regarding the results of Judah's sinful rebellion.

Jeremiah's writings are not without a glimmer of hope. The prophet knew that God's character was unchanging and his mission was sure. God would secure a remnant of worshipers from among the exiled nation. Because of his faithful love for his people, God would bring the people back from captivity and into right relationship with himself (Jer 30:18 — 31:6; Eze 11:19). As a result, the people would once again sing for joy at the glory of God's salvation.

Through Jesus, the prophet's words still ring true today. These new covenant promises (Jer 31:31 – 34) are fulfilled in the person and work of Jesus Christ, who secured salvation through his righteous life, substitutionary death, and victorious resurrection. Through faith, God's people can be born again to a living hope that pulsates with life. Though sin is grotesque and the consequences painful, Jesus' work is altogether complete and provides the sure hope that God will fulfill his promises to his people.

FOR I KNOW THE PLANS I HAVE FOR YOU,
DECLARES THE LORD, PLANS FOR WELFARE
AND NOT FOR EVIL, TO GIVE YOU
A FUTURE AND A HOPE.

Jeremiah 29:11

JEREMIAH

1 The words of Jeremiah, the son of Hilkiah, one of the priests who were in Anathoth in the land of Benjamin, 2 to whom the word of the LORD came in the days
of Josiah the son of Amon, king of Judah, in the thirteenth year of his reign. 3 It
came also in the days of Jehoiakim the son of Josiah, king of Judah, and until the
end of the eleventh year of Zedekiah, the son of Josiah, king of Judah, until the
captivity of Jerusalem in the fifth month.

The Call of Jeremiah

4 Now the word of the LORD came to me, saying,

5 "Before I formed you in the womb I knew you,
and before you were born I consecrated you;
I appointed you a prophet to the nations."

6 Then I said, "Ah, Lord GOD! Behold, I do not know how to speak, for I am only a
youth." 7 But the LORD said to me,

"Do not say, 'I am only a youth';
for to all to whom I send you, you shall go,
and whatever I command you, you shall speak.
8 Do not be afraid of them,
for I am with you to deliver you,
declares the LORD."

9 Then the LORD put out his hand and touched my mouth. And the LORD said to
me,

"Behold, I have put my words in your mouth.
10 See, I have set you this day over nations and over
kingdoms,
to pluck up and to break down,
to destroy and to overthrow,
to build and to plant."

11 And the word of the LORD came to me, saying, "Jeremiah, what do you see?"
And I said, "I see an almond[1] branch." 12 Then the LORD said to me, "You have seen
well, for I am watching over my word to perform it."
13 The word of the LORD came to me a second time, saying, "What do you
see?" And I said, "I see a boiling pot, facing away from the north." 14 Then the
LORD said to me, "Out of the north disaster[2] shall be let loose upon all the inhabitants of the land. 15 For behold, I am calling all the tribes of the kingdoms of
the north, declares the LORD, and they shall come, and every one shall set his
throne at the entrance of the gates of Jerusalem, against all its walls all around
and against all the cities of Judah. 16 And I will declare my judgments against
them, for all their evil in forsaking me. They have made offerings to other
gods and worshiped the works of their own hands. 17 But you, dress yourself
for work;[3] arise, and say to them everything that I command you. Do not be
dismayed by them, lest I dismay you before them. 18 And I, behold, I make you
this day a fortified city, an iron pillar, and bronze walls, against the whole land,
against the kings of Judah, its officials, its priests, and the people of the land.
19 They will fight against you, but they shall not prevail against you, for I am with
you, declares the LORD, to deliver you."

[1] *Almond* sounds like the Hebrew for *watching* (compare verse 12) [2] The Hebrew word can mean *evil, harm,* or *disaster,* depending on the context; so throughout Jeremiah [3] Hebrew *gird up your loins*

JEREMIAH 1:5

BEFORE BIRTH

When God calls a person to fulfill a mission, that mission can seem overwhelming. Thoughts flood one's mind: "I'm not qualified," "I'm not good enough," "I'm not ready," or "What could I possibly have to offer?" Yet, for every assignment, God is faithful to provide an outpouring of grace, courage, and strength.

Jeremiah spent over 40 years as God's prophet to Judah. Even though he experienced many hardships, Jeremiah also experienced his ever-faithful God giving him the words and perseverance necessary to accomplish the work.

Like Jeremiah, Jesus was set apart for a divine mission. Jeremiah lived as a prophet sent to call the people back to God; Jesus, the fulfillment of over 300 prophesies, came as the living and literal *Way* back to God. Jeremiah revealed the grip of sin on the nation of Judah; Jesus came to deliver the people from their sin. As God called Jeremiah before he was born, the Father also knew how, when, and where the Messiah would be born and how he would redeem mankind.

Israel Forsakes the LORD

2 The word of the LORD came to me, saying, [2]"Go and proclaim in the hearing of
Jerusalem, Thus says the LORD,

"I remember the devotion of your youth,
your love as a bride,
how you followed me in the wilderness,
in a land not sown.
3 Israel was holy to the LORD,
the firstfruits of his harvest.
All who ate of it incurred guilt;
disaster came upon them,
declares the LORD."

[4]Hear the word of the LORD, O house of Jacob, and all the clans of the house of
Israel. [5]Thus says the LORD:

"What wrong did your fathers find in me
that they went far from me,
and went after worthlessness, and became worthless?
6 They did not say, 'Where is the LORD
who brought us up from the land of Egypt,
who led us in the wilderness,
in a land of deserts and pits,
in a land of drought and deep darkness,
in a land that none passes through,
where no man dwells?'
7 And I brought you into a plentiful land
to enjoy its fruits and its good things.
But when you came in, you defiled my land
and made my heritage an abomination.
8 The priests did not say, 'Where is the LORD?'
Those who handle the law did not know me;
the shepherds[1] transgressed against me;
the prophets prophesied by Baal
and went after things that do not profit.
9 "Therefore I still contend with you,
declares the LORD,
and with your children's children I will contend.
10 For cross to the coasts of Cyprus and see,
or send to Kedar and examine with care;
see if there has been such a thing.
11 Has a nation changed its gods,
even though they are no gods?
But my people have changed their glory
for that which does not profit.
12 Be appalled, O heavens, at this;
be shocked, be utterly desolate,
declares the LORD,
13 for my people have committed two evils:
they have forsaken me,
the fountain of living waters,
and hewed out cisterns for themselves,
broken cisterns that can hold no water.

[1]Or *rulers*

FOUNTAIN OF LIVING WATERS

God's pronouncement of judgment through Jeremiah likely carried a tone of raw emotion. God was livid — the enraged epitome of one betrayed. The Lord was not shocked at Judah's adultery as if he had suddenly become aware of it. Rather, he was stunned by what the people were willing to trade: "But my people have changed their glory for that which does not profit" (Jer 2:11).

The root sins of the people in Jeremiah 2:13 were forsaking him, "the fountain of living waters," and hewing out their own cisterns. The first charge against the people is that they abandoned God. They forgot his faithfulness and discarded their covenant obligations. The issue that's larger than the fact that they walked away is *who* they walked away *from* and *for what.* The key word in this part of verse 13 is "me," and the exchange is utterly irrational. God is incredulous — how could they reject the One who is always attentive, faithful, and sufficient? The very spring from which life-giving water originates?

The second charge against the people is they put faith in gods of their own design, trading God's living water for dead, dry, useless idols. Cisterns were receptacles for storing rain water to use during the dry season. Ancient peoples also used large pottery containers or, when possible, dug massive holding tanks into the rock face of a mountain or hill. It was a contingency of control, of supplying for one's own needs. God uses this metaphor to describe Judah's adoption of false gods. God describes himself as *the fountain of living waters* — always flowing, perpetually satisfying. His love and mercy are unfathomable, his power inexhaustible. His knowledge and wisdom are perfect and unrivaled. The Israelites' trade of their life-giving God for worthless idols was more than rebellion; it was utter foolishness. With the Lord, they had all that they would ever need. Their cisterns — the idols of wood and stone — would never answer a prayer, and they could never hold the people's hope.

During a conversation with a Samaritan woman, Jesus declared that he was, and is still today, the source of "a spring of water welling up to eternal life" (Jn 4:14). Men and women look to many things of human design for joy and satisfaction. None of them offer lasting hope. But if anyone believes in Christ, their soul's thirst is permanently quenched. Jesus is all that believers will ever need. He is the spring of living water — the constant source of abundant life, both now and throughout eternity.

14 "Is Israel a slave? Is he a homeborn servant?
Why then has he become a prey?
15 The lions have roared against him;
they have roared loudly.
They have made his land a waste;
his cities are in ruins, without inhabitant.
16 Moreover, the men of Memphis and Tahpanhes
have shaved[1] the crown of your head.
17 Have you not brought this upon yourself
by forsaking the LORD your God,
when he led you in the way?
18 And now what do you gain by going to Egypt
to drink the waters of the Nile?[2]
Or what do you gain by going to Assyria
to drink the waters of the Euphrates?[3]
19 Your evil will chastise you,
and your apostasy will reprove you.
Know and see that it is evil and bitter
for you to forsake the LORD your God;
the fear of me is not in you,
declares the Lord GOD of hosts.

20 "For long ago I broke your yoke
and burst your bonds;
but you said, 'I will not serve.'
Yes, on every high hill
and under every green tree
you bowed down like a whore.
21 Yet I planted you a choice vine,
wholly of pure seed.
How then have you turned degenerate
and become a wild vine?
22 Though you wash yourself with lye
and use much soap,
the stain of your guilt is still before me,
declares the Lord GOD.
23 How can you say, 'I am not unclean,
I have not gone after the Baals'?
Look at your way in the valley;
know what you have done—
a restless young camel running here and there,
24 a wild donkey used to the wilderness,
in her heat sniffing the wind!
Who can restrain her lust?
None who seek her need weary themselves;
in her month they will find her.
25 Keep your feet from going unshod
and your throat from thirst.
But you said, 'It is hopeless,
for I have loved foreigners,
and after them I will go.'

26 "As a thief is shamed when caught,
so the house of Israel shall be shamed:
they, their kings, their officials,
their priests, and their prophets,

[1]Hebrew *grazed* [2]Hebrew *Shihor* [3]Hebrew *the River*

27 who say to a tree, 'You are my father,'
and to a stone, 'You gave me birth.'
For they have turned their back to me,
and not their face.
But in the time of their trouble they say,
'Arise and save us!'
28 But where are your gods
that you made for yourself?
Let them arise, if they can save you,
in your time of trouble;
for as many as your cities
are your gods, O Judah.

29 "Why do you contend with me?
You have all transgressed against me,
declares the LORD.

30 In vain have I struck your children;
they took no correction;
your own sword devoured your prophets
like a ravening lion.
31 And you, O generation, behold the word of
the LORD.
Have I been a wilderness to Israel,
or a land of thick darkness?
Why then do my people say, 'We are free,
we will come no more to you'?
32 Can a virgin forget her ornaments,
or a bride her attire?
Yet my people have forgotten me
days without number.

33 "How well you direct your course
to seek love!
So that even to wicked women
you have taught your ways.
34 Also on your skirts is found
the lifeblood of the guiltless poor;
you did not find them breaking in.
Yet in spite of all these things
35 you say, 'I am innocent;
surely his anger has turned from me.'
Behold, I will bring you to judgment
for saying, 'I have not sinned.'
36 How much you go about,
changing your way!
You shall be put to shame by Egypt
as you were put to shame by Assyria.
37 From it too you will come away
with your hands on your head,
for the LORD has rejected those in whom you trust,
and you will not prosper by them.

3 "If[1] a man divorces his wife
and she goes from him
and becomes another man's wife,
will he return to her?

[1]Septuagint, Syriac; Hebrew *Saying, "If*

Would not that land be greatly polluted?
You have played the whore with many lovers;
and would you return to me?
declares the LORD.
2 Lift up your eyes to the bare heights, and see!
Where have you not been ravished?
By the waysides you have sat awaiting lovers
like an Arab in the wilderness.
You have polluted the land
with your vile whoredom.
3 Therefore the showers have been withheld,
and the spring rain has not come;
yet you have the forehead of a whore;
you refuse to be ashamed.
4 Have you not just now called to me,
'My father, you are the friend of my youth—
5 will he be angry forever,
will he be indignant to the end?'
Behold, you have spoken,
but you have done all the evil that you could."

Faithless Israel Called to Repentance

6The LORD said to me in the days of King Josiah: "Have you seen what she did,
that faithless one, Israel, how she went up on every high hill and under every
green tree, and there played the whore? 7And I thought, 'After she has done all
this she will return to me,' but she did not return, and her treacherous sister Judah
saw it. 8She saw that for all the adulteries of that faithless one, Israel, I had sent
her away with a decree of divorce. Yet her treacherous sister Judah did not fear,
but she too went and played the whore. 9Because she took her whoredom lightly,
she polluted the land, committing adultery with stone and tree. 10Yet for all this
her treacherous sister Judah did not return to me with her whole heart, but in
pretense, declares the LORD."
11And the LORD said to me, "Faithless Israel has shown herself more righteous
than treacherous Judah. 12Go, and proclaim these words toward the north, and
say,

"'Return, faithless Israel,
declares the LORD.
I will not look on you in anger,
for I am merciful,
declares the LORD;
I will not be angry forever.
13 Only acknowledge your guilt,
that you rebelled against the LORD your God
and scattered your favors among foreigners under
every green tree,
and that you have not obeyed my voice,
declares the LORD.
14 Return, O faithless children,
declares the LORD;
for I am your master;
I will take you, one from a city and two from a family,
and I will bring you to Zion.

15"'And I will give you shepherds after my own heart, who will feed you with
knowledge and understanding. 16And when you have multiplied and been fruitful in the land, in those days, declares the LORD, they shall no more say, "The

JEREMIAH 3:14

UNFAITHFUL MARRIAGE

Here God uses the human institution of marriage as a picture of his love relationship with Israel. He considers the unfaithfulness of Judah, along with her faithless "sister" Israel, as being equal to adultery (vv. 6–9). The people have betrayed their beloved—giving themselves over to idol worship. They have abandoned God, their provider and protector, spurning the One who chose them as the object of his affection and care. But God issues an astonishing call, an open-armed offer for the Israelites to return to him. He promises to take them back and live as their master if they will simply return to him (v. 14).

This invitation to grace reflects God's desire to save sinners through faith in Jesus. Even while humankind wandered in sin, Christ died for the ungodly (Ro 5:8). God's call to salvation is an offer to receive the opposite of what humanity deserves. Although he was betrayed, God paid the debt of human rebellion so he could be reconciled with the ones he loves.

JEREMIAH 4:4

CIRCUMCISION OF THE HEART

God sent Jeremiah to remind the people of Judah of their covenant with God. God had promised to lead and care for the Israelites, and they had pledged faithful obedience. Circumcision — removing a small part of the physical flesh — was a sign of this covenant, permanently marking a person's relationship with God as an outward sign of an inward reality. However, over time, most observances of the symbol became disconnected from the expression of an internal commitment. Jeremiah called the people to circumcise their hearts as an internal symbol of their honor and affection, declaring their allegiance, love, and commitment to obey God.

Jesus continued this emphasis on mankind's internal condition when he challenged the religious leaders of his day. He confronted the Pharisees about living lives that looked good on the outside while their hearts remained unclean (Mt 23:27–28). Salvation through Jesus results in a new kind of circumcision of the heart "by putting off the body of the flesh" (Col 2:11). And while Christians still continue to struggle with sin, they can also claim victory over it (1Co 15:56–57).

ark of the covenant of the LORD." It shall not come to mind or be remembered
or missed; it shall not be made again. 17 At that time Jerusalem shall be called the
throne of the LORD, and all nations shall gather to it, to the presence of the LORD
in Jerusalem, and they shall no more stubbornly follow their own evil heart. 18 In
those days the house of Judah shall join the house of Israel, and together they
shall come from the land of the north to the land that I gave your fathers for a
heritage.

19 " 'I said,
How I would set you among my sons,
and give you a pleasant land,
a heritage most beautiful of all nations.
And I thought you would call me, My Father,
and would not turn from following me.
20 Surely, as a treacherous wife leaves her husband,
so have you been treacherous to me, O house of Israel,
declares the LORD.' "

21 A voice on the bare heights is heard,
the weeping and pleading of Israel's sons
because they have perverted their way;
they have forgotten the LORD their God.
22 "Return, O faithless sons;
I will heal your faithlessness."
"Behold, we come to you,
for you are the LORD our God.
23 Truly the hills are a delusion,
the orgies[1] on the mountains.
Truly in the LORD our God
is the salvation of Israel.

24 "But from our youth the shameful thing has devoured all for which our fathers labored, their flocks and their herds, their sons and their daughters. 25 Let us
lie down in our shame, and let our dishonor cover us. For we have sinned against
the LORD our God, we and our fathers, from our youth even to this day, and we
have not obeyed the voice of the LORD our God."

4 "If you return, O Israel,
declares the LORD,
to me you should return.
If you remove your detestable things from my presence,
and do not waver,
2 and if you swear, 'As the LORD lives,'
in truth, in justice, and in righteousness,
then nations shall bless themselves in him,
and in him shall they glory."

3 For thus says the LORD to the men of Judah and Jerusalem:

"Break up your fallow ground,
and sow not among thorns.
4 Circumcise yourselves to the LORD;
remove the foreskin of your hearts,
O men of Judah and inhabitants of Jerusalem;
lest my wrath go forth like fire,
and burn with none to quench it,
because of the evil of your deeds."

[1]Hebrew *commotion*

FORGIVENESS OF SIN

God occasionally uses the metaphor of marriage in Scripture to portray his relationship with his people. He builds on this illustration in the book of Jeremiah by defining the worship of false gods as spiritual adultery and prostitution (v. 1). Adultery — sharing intimate physical affection with someone outside of marriage — cuts deep personal wounds. And God felt those same wounds: The Israelites had rebelled against God, disobeying his commands, and giving their intimate spiritual selves to idols.

Even though this breach of trust dishonored God and moved him to anger, he was willing to forgive their sin. He invited the people to return to him — to experience the end of his anger (v. 12). God implored the Israelites to return to him; he was eager to set them among his sons (v. 19). Though their sins were many, God's love never wavered. Above and beyond restoring the relationship, God even offered to do rehabilitating work on their souls — to cure their faithlessness (v. 22).

All people have sinned against God, violating his commands or worshiping other people and things in his place (Ro 3:23). Even so, God sent Jesus into the world — not to condemn it, but to make a way for sin to be forgiven (Jn 3:17). God did not forgive sin by decree, but he arranged for it to be paid for through the death of his own Son. Jesus sacrificed himself on a cross to pay the debt for every single sin against God. Believing in Christ's death and resurrection enables men and women to have all of their sins forgiven (Ac 13:38 – 39). Through faith, Christ's atoning sacrifice is applied to their lives; their guilt is exchanged for Christ's perfect righteousness (Php 3:9).

These spiritual realities support the relationship realities between people and God. Sins against him are betrayals, as ugly and as terrible as the adultery of the Israelites. Yet God, who is rich in mercy, is eager to forgive those who turn to him through repentance and faith in Jesus. Like God's offer to the Israelites, those who believe in Christ enter a process of sanctification, of becoming holy — a blessing and benefit on top of forgiveness. Because of Jesus' sacrifice on the cross, human sin is paid for. Because of his victorious resurrection, he still helps believers today, through the Holy Spirit, to transform his followers more and more into his own character.

Disaster from the North

5 Declare in Judah, and proclaim in Jerusalem, and say,

“Blow the trumpet through the land;
  cry aloud and say,
‘Assemble, and let us go
  into the fortified cities!’
6 Raise a standard toward Zion,
  flee for safety, stay not,
for I bring disaster from the north,
  and great destruction.
7 A lion has gone up from his thicket,
  a destroyer of nations has set out;
  he has gone out from his place
to make your land a waste;
  your cities will be ruins
  without inhabitant.
8 For this put on sackcloth,
  lament and wail,
for the fierce anger of the LORD
  has not turned back from us.”

9 “In that day, declares the LORD, courage shall fail both king and officials. The
priests shall be appalled and the prophets astounded.” 10 Then I said, “Ah, Lord
GOD, surely you have utterly deceived this people and Jerusalem, saying, ‘It shall
be well with you,’ whereas the sword has reached their very life.”
11 At that time it will be said to this people and to Jerusalem, “A hot wind from
the bare heights in the desert toward the daughter of my people, not to winnow
or cleanse, 12 a wind too full for this comes for me. Now it is I who speak in judgment upon them.”

13 Behold, he comes up like clouds;
  his chariots like the whirlwind;
his horses are swifter than eagles—
  woe to us, for we are ruined!
14 O Jerusalem, wash your heart from evil,
  that you may be saved.
How long shall your wicked thoughts
  lodge within you?
15 For a voice declares from Dan
  and proclaims trouble from Mount Ephraim.
16 Warn the nations that he is coming;
  announce to Jerusalem,
“Besiegers come from a distant land;
  they shout against the cities of Judah.
17 Like keepers of a field are they against her all around,
  because she has rebelled against me,
declares the LORD.
18 Your ways and your deeds
  have brought this upon you.
This is your doom, and it is bitter;
  it has reached your very heart.”

Anguish over Judah’s Desolation

19 My anguish, my anguish! I writhe in pain!
  Oh the walls of my heart!

My heart is beating wildly;
I cannot keep silent,
for I hear the sound of the trumpet,
the alarm of war.
20 Crash follows hard on crash;
the whole land is laid waste.
Suddenly my tents are laid waste,
my curtains in a moment.
21 How long must I see the standard
and hear the sound of the trumpet?

22 "For my people are foolish;
they know me not;
they are stupid children;
they have no understanding.
They are 'wise'—in doing evil!
But how to do good they know not."

23 I looked on the earth, and behold, it was without form and void;
and to the heavens, and they had no light.
24 I looked on the mountains, and behold, they were quaking,
and all the hills moved to and fro.
25 I looked, and behold, there was no man,
and all the birds of the air had fled.
26 I looked, and behold, the fruitful land was a desert,
and all its cities were laid in ruins
before the LORD, before his fierce anger.

27 For thus says the LORD, "The whole land shall be a desolation; yet I will not make a full end.

28 "For this the earth shall mourn,
and the heavens above be dark;
for I have spoken; I have purposed;
I have not relented, nor will I turn back."

29 At the noise of horseman and archer
every city takes to flight;
they enter thickets; they climb among rocks;
all the cities are forsaken,
and no man dwells in them.
30 And you, O desolate one,
what do you mean that you dress in scarlet,
that you adorn yourself with ornaments of gold,
that you enlarge your eyes with paint?
In vain you beautify yourself.
Your lovers despise you;
they seek your life.
31 For I heard a cry as of a woman in labor,
anguish as of one giving birth to her first child,
the cry of the daughter of Zion gasping for breath,
stretching out her hands,
"Woe is me! I am fainting before murderers."

Jerusalem Refused to Repent

5 Run to and fro through the streets of Jerusalem,
look and take note!
Search her squares to see
if you can find a man,

one who does justice
and seeks truth,
that I may pardon her.
2 Though they say, "As the LORD lives,"
yet they swear falsely.
3 O LORD, do not your eyes look for truth?
You have struck them down,
but they felt no anguish;
you have consumed them,
but they refused to take correction.
They have made their faces harder than rock;
they have refused to repent.

4 Then I said, "These are only the poor;
they have no sense;
for they do not know the way of the LORD,
the justice of their God.
5 I will go to the great
and will speak to them,
for they know the way of the LORD,
the justice of their God."
But they all alike had broken the yoke;
they had burst the bonds.

6 Therefore a lion from the forest shall strike them down;
a wolf from the desert shall devastate them.
A leopard is watching their cities;
everyone who goes out of them shall be torn in pieces,
because their transgressions are many,
their apostasies are great.

7 "How can I pardon you?
Your children have forsaken me
and have sworn by those who are no gods.
When I fed them to the full,
they committed adultery
and trooped to the houses of whores.
8 They were well-fed, lusty stallions,
each neighing for his neighbor's wife.
9 Shall I not punish them for these things?
declares the LORD;
and shall I not avenge myself
on a nation such as this?

10 "Go up through her vine rows and destroy,
but make not a full end;
strip away her branches,
for they are not the LORD's.
11 For the house of Israel and the house of Judah
have been utterly treacherous to me,
declares the LORD.
12 They have spoken falsely of the LORD
and have said, 'He will do nothing;
no disaster will come upon us,
nor shall we see sword or famine.
13 The prophets will become wind;
the word is not in them.
Thus shall it be done to them!' "

The LORD Proclaims Judgment

14 Therefore thus says the LORD, the God of hosts:
"Because you have spoken this word,
behold, I am making my words in your mouth a fire,
and this people wood, and the fire shall consume them.
15 Behold, I am bringing against you
a nation from afar, O house of Israel,
declares the LORD.
It is an enduring nation;
it is an ancient nation,
a nation whose language you do not know,
nor can you understand what they say.
16 Their quiver is like an open tomb;
they are all mighty warriors.
17 They shall eat up your harvest and your food;
they shall eat up your sons and your daughters;
they shall eat up your flocks and your herds;
they shall eat up your vines and your fig trees;
your fortified cities in which you trust
they shall beat down with the sword."

18 "But even in those days, declares the LORD, I will not make a full end of you.
19 And when your people say, 'Why has the LORD our God done all these things to
us?' you shall say to them, 'As you have forsaken me and served foreign gods in
your land, so you shall serve foreigners in a land that is not yours.'"

20 Declare this in the house of Jacob;
proclaim it in Judah:
21 "Hear this, O foolish and senseless people,
who have eyes, but see not,
who have ears, but hear not.
22 Do you not fear me? declares the LORD.
Do you not tremble before me?
I placed the sand as the boundary for the sea,
a perpetual barrier that it cannot pass;
though the waves toss, they cannot prevail;
though they roar, they cannot pass over it.
23 But this people has a stubborn and rebellious heart;
they have turned aside and gone away.
24 They do not say in their hearts,
'Let us fear the LORD our God,
who gives the rain in its season,
the autumn rain and the spring rain,
and keeps for us
the weeks appointed for the harvest.'
25 Your iniquities have turned these away,
and your sins have kept good from you.
26 For wicked men are found among my people;
they lurk like fowlers lying in wait.[1]
They set a trap;
they catch men.
27 Like a cage full of birds,
their houses are full of deceit;
therefore they have become great and rich;
28 they have grown fat and sleek.

[1]The meaning of the Hebrew is uncertain

They know no bounds in deeds of evil;
they judge not with justice
the cause of the fatherless, to make it prosper,
and they do not defend the rights of the needy.
29 Shall I not punish them for these things?
declares the LORD,
and shall I not avenge myself
on a nation such as this?"

30 An appalling and horrible thing
has happened in the land:
31 the prophets prophesy falsely,
and the priests rule at their direction;
my people love to have it so,
but what will you do when the end comes?

Impending Disaster for Jerusalem

6 Flee for safety, O people of Benjamin,
from the midst of Jerusalem!
Blow the trumpet in Tekoa,
and raise a signal on Beth-haccherem,
for disaster looms out of the north,
and great destruction.
2 The lovely and delicately bred I will destroy,
the daughter of Zion.[1]
3 Shepherds with their flocks shall come against her;
they shall pitch their tents around her;
they shall pasture, each in his place.
4 "Prepare war against her;
arise, and let us attack at noon!
Woe to us, for the day declines,
for the shadows of evening lengthen!
5 Arise, and let us attack by night
and destroy her palaces!"

6 For thus says the LORD of hosts:
"Cut down her trees;
cast up a siege mound against Jerusalem.
This is the city that must be punished;
there is nothing but oppression within her.
7 As a well keeps its water fresh,
so she keeps fresh her evil;
violence and destruction are heard within her;
sickness and wounds are ever before me.
8 Be warned, O Jerusalem,
lest I turn from you in disgust,
lest I make you a desolation,
an uninhabited land."

9 Thus says the LORD of hosts:
"They shall glean thoroughly as a vine
the remnant of Israel;
like a grape gatherer pass your hand again
over its branches."
10 To whom shall I speak and give warning,
that they may hear?

[1]Or *I have likened the daughter of Zion to the loveliest pasture*

AN APPALLING AND HORRIBLE THING

Jeremiah's was not the only voice in Jerusalem speaking about what God was about to do in response to the people's disobedience. The anointed priests and acknowledged prophets addressed the people — but they contradicted Jeremiah's warnings. Both priests and prophets had succumbed to the temptation of abusing their power, rejecting their responsibilities as messengers and servants of God. These official religious leaders provoked God by overtly lying, denying the truth of the imminent judgment. While Jeremiah sounded the alarm in an attempt to bring the Israelites to their senses, Jerusalem's spiritual leaders urged calm and confidence.

These false teachers asserted that God would not exert his discipline — that God would never initiate something so devastating to his chosen ones. The people were soothed by these words; they relaxed from their fear of the sword or famine (Jer 5:12). The priests and prophets did not rouse the people toward repentance. Instead, they offered words with neither substance nor weight, their speeches becoming like the sound of an empty wind. The "word" was not in them (v. 13). Perhaps the most shocking aspect of this predicament is seen in the people's contentment with compromised leaders. God observed, "My people love to have it so" (v. 31).

Centuries later, Jesus confronted the spiritual leaders of Jerusalem for their refusal to embrace the truth about what God was doing among them. Apparently they had abandoned all efforts to discern God's work in the world, spending their energies on preserving the institution of temple life. Jesus issued harsh rebukes against the teachers of the law and the religious leaders whose role should have included support for works performed to the glory of God. They failed to recognize Jesus as the promised Messiah (Lk 5:20–24), scoffing at his claims of authority, and dismissing his pronouncements about the kingdom of God. Eventually, they would resist Jesus to the point of arresting him, putting him on trial, and calling for his execution.

Clearly, these scholars had not learned the lessons of the exile, even though they should have known Jeremiah's prophecies. Despite their intentions, Jesus went to the cross as a willing sacrifice and not as a victim. Through his death and resurrection, Jesus accomplished the purpose and mission of his life (Mk 10:45).

Behold, their ears are uncircumcised,
they cannot listen;
behold, the word of the LORD is to them an object of scorn;
they take no pleasure in it.
11 Therefore I am full of the wrath of the LORD;
I am weary of holding it in.
"Pour it out upon the children in the street,
and upon the gatherings of young men, also;
both husband and wife shall be taken,
the elderly and the very aged.
12 Their houses shall be turned over to others,
their fields and wives together,
for I will stretch out my hand
against the inhabitants of the land,"
declares the LORD.
13 "For from the least to the greatest of them,
everyone is greedy for unjust gain;
and from prophet to priest,
everyone deals falsely.
14 They have healed the wound of my people lightly,
saying, 'Peace, peace,'
when there is no peace.
15 Were they ashamed when they committed abomination?
No, they were not at all ashamed;
they did not know how to blush.
Therefore they shall fall among those who fall;
at the time that I punish them, they shall be overthrown,"
says the LORD.

16 Thus says the LORD:
"Stand by the roads, and look,
and ask for the ancient paths,
where the good way is; and walk in it,
and find rest for your souls.
But they said, 'We will not walk in it.'
17 I set watchmen over you, saying,
'Pay attention to the sound of the trumpet!'
But they said, 'We will not pay attention.'
18 Therefore hear, O nations,
and know, O congregation, what will happen to them.
19 Hear, O earth; behold, I am bringing disaster upon this people,
the fruit of their devices,
because they have not paid attention to my words;
and as for my law, they have rejected it.
20 What use to me is frankincense that comes from Sheba,
or sweet cane from a distant land?
Your burnt offerings are not acceptable,
nor your sacrifices pleasing to me.
21 Therefore thus says the LORD:
'Behold, I will lay before this people
stumbling blocks against which they shall stumble;
fathers and sons together,
neighbor and friend shall perish.'"

22 Thus says the LORD:
"Behold, a people is coming from the north country,
a great nation is stirring from the farthest parts
of the earth.

JEREMIAH 6:19

JUDGMENT IS COMING

God invited the nations of the world to witness what was about to happen to his people. The impending disaster would result not from ambition in the hearts of foreign kings; rather, God himself would orchestrate the disaster. The Israelites earned God's judgment by disregarding his call to repentance and his clear warning of consequences for disobedience. Judah's rebellion altered their history. Jerusalem suffered ruin, and God allowed Judah's people to be killed or captured because they chose to act as if God's decrees did not matter—as if God would not actually hold them accountable.

On a day of God's choosing, Jesus will return to earth and administer judgment over all mankind (Heb 10:30–31). Those who have faith in Jesus will be saved, and those who do not believe will endure everlasting punishment. Similar to Jeremiah's announcements, the world needs to know that God is real and that a coming day of judgment is certain. But Jesus promised that those who believe would not be judged (Jn 5:24).

23 They lay hold on bow and javelin;
they are cruel and have no mercy;
the sound of them is like the roaring sea;
they ride on horses,
set in array as a man for battle,
against you, O daughter of Zion!"
24 We have heard the report of it;
our hands fall helpless;
anguish has taken hold of us,
pain as of a woman in labor.
25 Go not out into the field,
nor walk on the road,
for the enemy has a sword;
terror is on every side.
26 O daughter of my people, put on sackcloth,
and roll in ashes;
make mourning as for an only son,
most bitter lamentation,
for suddenly the destroyer
will come upon us.

27 "I have made you a tester of metals among my people,
that you may know and test their ways.
28 They are all stubbornly rebellious,
going about with slanders;
they are bronze and iron;
all of them act corruptly.
29 The bellows blow fiercely;
the lead is consumed by the fire;
in vain the refining goes on,
for the wicked are not removed.
30 Rejected silver they are called,
for the LORD has rejected them."

Evil in the Land

7 The word that came to Jeremiah from the LORD: 2"Stand in the gate of the
LORD's house, and proclaim there this word, and say, Hear the word of the
LORD, all you men of Judah who enter these gates to worship the LORD. 3Thus says
the LORD of hosts, the God of Israel: Amend your ways and your deeds, and I will
let you dwell in this place. 4Do not trust in these deceptive words: 'This is the
temple of the LORD, the temple of the LORD, the temple of the LORD.'
5"For if you truly amend your ways and your deeds, if you truly execute justice one with another, 6if you do not oppress the sojourner, the fatherless, or the
widow, or shed innocent blood in this place, and if you do not go after other gods
to your own harm, 7then I will let you dwell in this place, in the land that I gave of
old to your fathers forever.
8"Behold, you trust in deceptive words to no avail. 9Will you steal, murder,
commit adultery, swear falsely, make offerings to Baal, and go after other gods
that you have not known, 10and then come and stand before me in this house,
which is called by my name, and say, 'We are delivered!'—only to go on doing
all these abominations? 11Has this house, which is called by my name, become
a den of robbers in your eyes? Behold, I myself have seen it, declares the LORD.
12Go now to my place that was in Shiloh, where I made my name dwell at first,
and see what I did to it because of the evil of my people Israel. 13And now, because you have done all these things, declares the LORD, and when I spoke to
you persistently you did not listen, and when I called you, you did not answer,

JEREMIAH 7:9–11

REAL SECURITY

Long before the Law, the tabernacle, and the temple, God desired that his people love and follow him—joyfully reflecting his worth to the world. Disappointingly, the Israelites lost sight of the relationship's purpose and the very reason for their existence as a nation. They rejected an exclusive relationship with God yet continued to enter the temple gates to worship—going through the motions, treating the physical temple as a kind of good-luck charm. They missed the love story into which God invited them.

As they spiraled into following the same immoral and demonic practices of their ungodly neighbors, the community no longer resembled the one that God initially chose. Jeremiah used the blunt word picture of thieves hiding in a cave to confront Judah's broken moral compass and their false sense of security. Judah's association with the temple could not protect them. Even so God, in his covenant faithfulness, resolved to rescue them from themselves. He allowed Jerusalem and the temple to be utterly destroyed, arranging Babylon's invasion as a radical form of intervention for the sinful people he continued to love.

Jesus quoted part of this passage when he forcibly removed the buyers and sellers from the temple (Mt 21:13). He resented the man-made obstacles in the temple that prevented worshipers from drawing near to the Father. God will not ignore anything that hinders his people from following him wholeheartedly.

14 therefore I will do to the house that is called by my name, and in which you trust, and to the place that I gave to you and to your fathers, as I did to Shiloh. 15 And I will cast you out of my sight, as I cast out all your kinsmen, all the offspring of Ephraim.

16 "As for you, do not pray for this people, or lift up a cry or prayer for them, and do not intercede with me, for I will not hear you. 17 Do you not see what they are doing in the cities of Judah and in the streets of Jerusalem? 18 The children gather wood, the fathers kindle fire, and the women knead dough, to make cakes for the queen of heaven. And they pour out drink offerings to other gods, to provoke me to anger. 19 Is it I whom they provoke? declares the Lord. Is it not themselves, to their own shame? 20 Therefore thus says the Lord God: Behold, my anger and my wrath will be poured out on this place, upon man and beast, upon the trees of the field and the fruit of the ground; it will burn and not be quenched."

21 Thus says the Lord of hosts, the God of Israel: "Add your burnt offerings to your sacrifices, and eat the flesh. 22 For in the day that I brought them out of the land of Egypt, I did not speak to your fathers or command them concerning burnt offerings and sacrifices. 23 But this command I gave them: 'Obey my voice, and I will be your God, and you shall be my people. And walk in all the way that I command you, that it may be well with you.' 24 But they did not obey or incline their ear, but walked in their own counsels and the stubbornness of their evil hearts, and went backward and not forward. 25 From the day that your fathers came out of the land of Egypt to this day, I have persistently sent all my servants the prophets to them, day after day. 26 Yet they did not listen to me or incline their ear, but stiffened their neck. They did worse than their fathers.

27 "So you shall speak all these words to them, but they will not listen to you. You shall call to them, but they will not answer you. 28 And you shall say to them, 'This is the nation that did not obey the voice of the Lord their God, and did not accept discipline; truth has perished; it is cut off from their lips.

29 " 'Cut off your hair and cast it away;
raise a lamentation on the bare heights,
for the Lord has rejected and forsaken
the generation of his wrath.'

The Valley of Slaughter

30 "For the sons of Judah have done evil in my sight, declares the Lord. They have set their detestable things in the house that is called by my name, to defile it. 31 And they have built the high places of Topheth, which is in the Valley of the Son of Hinnom, to burn their sons and their daughters in the fire, which I did not command, nor did it come into my mind. 32 Therefore, behold, the days are coming, declares the Lord, when it will no more be called Topheth, or the Valley of the Son of Hinnom, but the Valley of Slaughter; for they will bury in Topheth, because there is no room elsewhere. 33 And the dead bodies of this people will be food for the birds of the air, and for the beasts of the earth, and none will frighten them away. 34 And I will silence in the cities of Judah and in the streets of Jerusalem the voice of mirth and the voice of gladness, the voice of the bridegroom and the voice of the bride, for the land shall become a waste.

8 "At that time, declares the Lord, the bones of the kings of Judah, the bones of its officials, the bones of the priests, the bones of the prophets, and the bones of the inhabitants of Jerusalem shall be brought out of their tombs. 2 And they shall be spread before the sun and the moon and all the host of heaven, which they have loved and served, which they have gone after, and which they have sought and worshiped. And they shall not be gathered or buried. They shall be as dung on the surface of the ground. 3 Death shall be preferred to life by all the remnant that remains of this evil family in all the places where I have driven them, declares the Lord of hosts.

Sin and Treachery

4 "You shall say to them, Thus says the LORD:
When men fall, do they not rise again?
If one turns away, does he not return?
5 Why then has this people turned away
in perpetual backsliding?
They hold fast to deceit;
they refuse to return.
6 I have paid attention and listened,
but they have not spoken rightly;
no man relents of his evil,
saying, 'What have I done?'
Everyone turns to his own course,
like a horse plunging headlong into battle.
7 Even the stork in the heavens
knows her times,
and the turtledove, swallow, and crane[1]
keep the time of their coming,
but my people know not
the rules[2] of the LORD.

8 "How can you say, 'We are wise,
and the law of the LORD is with us'?
But behold, the lying pen of the scribes
has made it into a lie.
9 The wise men shall be put to shame;
they shall be dismayed and taken;
behold, they have rejected the word of the LORD,
so what wisdom is in them?
10 Therefore I will give their wives to others
and their fields to conquerors,
because from the least to the greatest
everyone is greedy for unjust gain;
from prophet to priest,
everyone deals falsely.
11 They have healed the wound of my people lightly,
saying, 'Peace, peace,'
when there is no peace.
12 Were they ashamed when they committed abomination?
No, they were not at all ashamed;
they did not know how to blush.
Therefore they shall fall among the fallen;
when I punish them, they shall be overthrown,
says the LORD.

13 When I would gather them, declares the LORD,
there are no grapes on the vine,
nor figs on the fig tree;
even the leaves are withered,
and what I gave them has passed away from
them."[3]

14 Why do we sit still?
Gather together; let us go into the fortified cities
and perish there,

[1]The meaning of the Hebrew word is uncertain [2]Or *just decrees* [3]The meaning of the Hebrew is uncertain

SUPERFICIAL HEALING

Jerusalem's religious officials failed to lead the people to take God seriously regarding their sin and God's judgment, but God was not issuing an idle threat in response to the Israelites' compromise and idolatry. God likens this placating behavior to medical malpractice: "They have healed the wound of my people lightly" (v. 11).

There was a cruelty in the religious leaders' choice to be dishonest — to withhold truth because it would have been uncomfortable and unpopular in the ears of the people. The prognosis for Jerusalem should have included warnings that their condition was terminal. Given the clarity of Jeremiah's charges against the sinful nation, the priests and prophets grossly understated the situation. God had pronounced destruction for Jerusalem, and the leaders responded with the medical equivalent of a Band-Aid® on a severed limb. The people were living in the final days of God's judgment that would result in their exile to Babylon. The false hope proclaimed by the priests and prophets offered them no genuine peace.

During the years of Jesus' earthly ministry, the people of Jerusalem were similarly unaware of the coming destruction at the hands of the Romans in 70 AD. Jesus, as God, knew all things and alluded to the trouble that lay ahead (Lk 19:41 – 44). He taught the people with an aim toward giving them peace for all eternity — not just for the next few decades. As crowds listened to Jesus teach and watched his works of compassion, they marveled at the genuine concern he had for the poor, for children, for women, for the downtrodden — for people who truly needed lasting peace. They saw in his own life that the peace Jesus desired to give was of a superior quality to anything the world could offer. And Jesus himself promised as much (Jn 14:27).

Jesus never held back on the reality of the life-and-death crisis brought about by sin. He was clear about the need for personal repentance, and just as clear about his place as the exclusive path to the Father (Jn 14:6). Sent by God, Jesus proclaimed a message of good news (Ac 10:36). Christ's words and his actions did more than comfort; they are powerful enough to heal the condition of the sinful heart.

for the LORD our God has doomed us to perish
    and has given us poisoned water to drink,
    because we have sinned against the LORD.
15 We looked for peace, but no good came;
    for a time of healing, but behold, terror.

16 "The snorting of their horses is heard from Dan;
    at the sound of the neighing of their stallions
    the whole land quakes.
They come and devour the land and all that fills it,
    the city and those who dwell in it.
17 For behold, I am sending among you serpents,
    adders that cannot be charmed,
    and they shall bite you,"
declares the LORD.

Jeremiah Grieves for His People

18 My joy is gone; grief is upon me;[1]
    my heart is sick within me.
19 Behold, the cry of the daughter of my people
    from the length and breadth of the land:
"Is the LORD not in Zion?
    Is her King not in her?"
"Why have they provoked me to anger with their carved images
    and with their foreign idols?"
20 "The harvest is past, the summer is ended,
    and we are not saved."
21 For the wound of the daughter of my people is my heart wounded;
    I mourn, and dismay has taken hold on me.

22 Is there no balm in Gilead?
    Is there no physician there?
Why then has the health of the daughter of my people
    not been restored?
9[2] Oh that my head were waters,
    and my eyes a fountain of tears,
that I might weep day and night
    for the slain of the daughter of my people!
2[3] Oh that I had in the desert
    a travelers' lodging place,
that I might leave my people
    and go away from them!
For they are all adulterers,
    a company of treacherous men.
3 They bend their tongue like a bow;
    falsehood and not truth has grown strong[4] in the land;
for they proceed from evil to evil,
    and they do not know me, declares the LORD.

4 Let everyone beware of his neighbor,
    and put no trust in any brother,
for every brother is a deceiver,
    and every neighbor goes about as a slanderer.
5 Everyone deceives his neighbor,
    and no one speaks the truth;

[1]Compare Septuagint; the meaning of the Hebrew is uncertain [2]Ch 8:23 in Hebrew [3]Ch 9:1 in Hebrew
[4]Septuagint; Hebrew *and not for truth they have grown strong*

A BROKEN HEART

Jeremiah was undone, overwhelmed by the state of the relationship between God and his people. God had pronounced judgment and set in motion the wheels of destruction and captivity. The prophet's grief over his people went beyond mere dread of Babylonian invasion and the subsequent slaughter. He ached over the hard hearts that prevented repentance and reconciliation with the living God, knowing that the coming judgment could have been avoided. He lamented that God's hand was forced — the people must be disciplined. "For the wound of the daughter of my people is my heart wounded; I mourn, and dismay has taken hold on me" (Jer 8:21). The weeping prophet lived in a storm of emotions ranging from anger to sadness to shame.

Sin grips men and women in ways that make them forget who God is and what he has done. Lack of immediate retribution leads people to doubt that God will ever act in response to their rebellion. The world teems with young and old sinners, oblivious to their future judgment. Others remain so fixated on living everyday life on earth that death and eternity seem too far off to matter. Sin is so dark that it can lead people to reject the one true God for idols made of wood, stone, silver, or gold.

Jeremiah's tears mark the tragedy of a relationship wasted, of an invitation to repentance unaccepted. Jerusalem's people threw away the blessings of being chosen. They rejected the God who is infinite in glory and boundless in his desire to show love. God is worthy of unwavering faithfulness. Therefore, sin is an act of dishonor. For the people, for the Lord, for the loss and death that are to come — for all of these things, Jeremiah wept.

Jesus expressed sorrowful emotions over the way the teachers of the law misled and blinded the people to the truth. "O Jerusalem, Jerusalem, the city that kills the prophets and stones those who are sent to it! How often would I have gathered your children together as a hen gathers her brood under her wings, and you were not willing!" (Mt 23:37).

Heartbreak over sin is both appropriate and necessary if men and women are to find forgiveness in Jesus (Jas 4:9). Repentance — turning away from sinful ways — is the response that comes from a holy grief when a person realizes the magnitude of their offenses against God. When people confess their sin, God replaces the conviction of disobedience with forgiveness and a clean heart.

they have taught their tongue to speak lies;
they weary themselves committing iniquity.
6 Heaping oppression upon oppression, and deceit upon deceit,
they refuse to know me, declares the LORD.

7 Therefore thus says the LORD of hosts:
"Behold, I will refine them and test them,
for what else can I do, because of my people?
8 Their tongue is a deadly arrow;
it speaks deceitfully;
with his mouth each speaks peace to his neighbor,
but in his heart he plans an ambush for him.
9 Shall I not punish them for these things? declares the LORD,
and shall I not avenge myself
on a nation such as this?

10 "I will take up weeping and wailing for the mountains,
and a lamentation for the pastures of the wilderness,
because they are laid waste so that no one passes through,
and the lowing of cattle is not heard;
both the birds of the air and the beasts
have fled and are gone.
11 I will make Jerusalem a heap of ruins,
a lair of jackals,
and I will make the cities of Judah a desolation,
without inhabitant."

12Who is the man so wise that he can understand this? To whom has the
mouth of the LORD spoken, that he may declare it? Why is the land ruined and
laid waste like a wilderness, so that no one passes through? 13And the LORD says:
"Because they have forsaken my law that I set before them, and have not obeyed
my voice or walked in accord with it, 14but have stubbornly followed their own
hearts and have gone after the Baals, as their fathers taught them. 15Therefore
thus says the LORD of hosts, the God of Israel: Behold, I will feed this people with
bitter food, and give them poisonous water to drink. 16I will scatter them among
the nations whom neither they nor their fathers have known, and I will send the
sword after them, until I have consumed them."

17 Thus says the LORD of hosts:
"Consider, and call for the mourning women to come;
send for the skillful women to come;
18 let them make haste and raise a wailing over us,
that our eyes may run down with tears
and our eyelids flow with water.
19 For a sound of wailing is heard from Zion:
'How we are ruined!
We are utterly shamed,
because we have left the land,
because they have cast down our dwellings.'"
20 Hear, O women, the word of the LORD,
and let your ear receive the word of his mouth;
teach to your daughters a lament,
and each to her neighbor a dirge.
21 For death has come up into our windows;
it has entered our palaces,
cutting off the children from the streets
and the young men from the squares.

JEREMIAH 9:23–24

BOASTING

Human wisdom, strength, and wealth are not the highest reasons to boast. These three blessings, though significant, are fleeting and temporary. Their value is virtually nothing when compared with the undeserved honor of knowing the God of all.

The Lord led Jeremiah to encourage boasting as long as it glorifies God as the greatest of treasures. After all, God is the One whose very nature includes grace, even though he never compromises on justice. God is the only One whose every act is right and good. Knowing God, who delights in being God, is the greatest privilege and the only reason to boast.

Knowing certain facts about God is insufficient; truly knowing him requires having a relationship with him. This is only possible now through faith in Jesus and what he accomplished by his death and resurrection (Jn 14:6). The person made new in salvation should boast out of sheer gratitude (1Co 1:31), fully aware that nothing, compared to knowing Christ Jesus as Lord, amounts to anything (Php 3:7–8).

JEREMIAH 10:10

GOD IS IN CONTROL

The preceding verses point to the absurdity of worshiping idols of wood, silver, or gold. *Yahweh*—Judah's God, is the *true* God. He is real and full of power. He is alive and always has been—eternally existing, neither conceived nor crafted by anyone. He is the Creator of all things seen and unseen. As the eternal King, he is supreme with no rival

(continued on next page)

22 Speak: "Thus declares the LORD,
'The dead bodies of men shall fall
like dung upon the open field,
like sheaves after the reaper,
and none shall gather them.'"

23 Thus says the LORD: "Let not the wise man boast in his wisdom, let not the
mighty man boast in his might, let not the rich man boast in his riches, 24 but let
him who boasts boast in this, that he understands and knows me, that I am the
LORD who practices steadfast love, justice, and righteousness in the earth. For in
these things I delight, declares the LORD."

25 "Behold, the days are coming, declares the LORD, when I will punish all those
who are circumcised merely in the flesh— 26 Egypt, Judah, Edom, the sons of Ammon, Moab, and all who dwell in the desert who cut the corners of their hair, for
all these nations are uncircumcised, and all the house of Israel are uncircumcised
in heart."

Idols and the Living God

10 Hear the word that the LORD speaks to you, O house of Israel. 2 Thus says
the LORD:

"Learn not the way of the nations,
nor be dismayed at the signs of the heavens
because the nations are dismayed at them,
3 for the customs of the peoples are vanity.[1]
A tree from the forest is cut down
and worked with an axe by the hands of a craftsman.
4 They decorate it with silver and gold;
they fasten it with hammer and nails
so that it cannot move.
5 Their idols[2] are like scarecrows in a cucumber field,
and they cannot speak;
they have to be carried,
for they cannot walk.
Do not be afraid of them,
for they cannot do evil,
neither is it in them to do good."

6 There is none like you, O LORD;
you are great, and your name is great in might.
7 Who would not fear you, O King of the nations?
For this is your due;
for among all the wise ones of the nations
and in all their kingdoms
there is none like you.
8 They are both stupid and foolish;
the instruction of idols is but wood!
9 Beaten silver is brought from Tarshish,
and gold from Uphaz.
They are the work of the craftsman and of the hands of the goldsmith;
their clothing is violet and purple;
they are all the work of skilled men.
10 But the LORD is the true God;
he is the living God and the everlasting King.
At his wrath the earth quakes,
and the nations cannot endure his indignation.

[1] Or *vapor*, or *mist* [2] Hebrew *They*

11Thus shall you say to them: "The gods who did not make the heavens and the
earth shall perish from the earth and from under the heavens."[1]

12 It is he who made the earth by his power,
who established the world by his wisdom,
and by his understanding stretched out the heavens.
13 When he utters his voice, there is a tumult of waters in the heavens,
and he makes the mist rise from the ends of the earth.
He makes lightning for the rain,
and he brings forth the wind from his storehouses.
14 Every man is stupid and without knowledge;
every goldsmith is put to shame by his idols,
for his images are false,
and there is no breath in them.
15 They are worthless, a work of delusion;
at the time of their punishment they shall perish.
16 Not like these is he who is the portion of Jacob,
for he is the one who formed all things,
and Israel is the tribe of his inheritance;
the LORD of hosts is his name.

17 Gather up your bundle from the ground,
O you who dwell under siege!
18 For thus says the LORD:
"Behold, I am slinging out the inhabitants of the land
at this time,
and I will bring distress on them,
that they may feel it."

19 Woe is me because of my hurt!
My wound is grievous.
But I said, "Truly this is an affliction,
and I must bear it."
20 My tent is destroyed,
and all my cords are broken;
my children have gone from me,
and they are not;
there is no one to spread my tent again
and to set up my curtains.
21 For the shepherds are stupid
and do not inquire of the LORD;
therefore they have not prospered,
and all their flock is scattered.

22 A voice, a rumor! Behold, it comes!—
a great commotion out of the north country
to make the cities of Judah a desolation,
a lair of jackals.

23 I know, O LORD, that the way of man is not in himself,
that it is not in man who walks to direct his steps.
24 Correct me, O LORD, but in justice;
not in your anger, lest you bring me to nothing.

25 Pour out your wrath on the nations that know you not,
and on the peoples that call not on your name,
for they have devoured Jacob;
they have devoured him and consumed him,
and have laid waste his habitation.

[1]This verse is in Aramaic

(God Is in Control, continued)

and no place in existence where his authority is overridden. The idols are worse than powerless—they are false, not at all alive, completely devoid of any authority.

It is right and good to hope in and pray to the living God, the eternal King. God is in control of everything that happens, and he is absolutely worthy of trust. Jesus—who is the very image of God—is "the first-born of all creation" (Col 1:15). In him, all things—including the lives of every man and woman—hold together (Col 1:17).

JEREMIAH 11:1–17

COVENANT TERMS

Even though the entire earth belonged to him, God chose the nation of Israel to be in a relationship with him so he could put his goodness and greatness on display (Ex 19:4–6). He promised to be with them and to give them a land of their own. God's pledge to the people would endure even through the nation's most horrific betrayal. This covenant relationship was both unconditional and conditional: God maintained expectations for how the people would live, and the threshold for honoring the covenant was complete obedience. The benefit to Israel was astonishing—"So shall you be my people, and I will be your God" (Jer 11:4). When the Israelites obeyed the Lord, they enjoyed abundant blessings. When they resisted his leadership or defied his commands, consequences always followed. Jeremiah reminds the people about the clear terms of the covenant in chapter 11.

Jesus ushered in a new covenant relationship for men and women when he suffered death and arose again (Mt 26:28). Inspired by God, Jeremiah actually predicted this new covenant (Jer 31:31). Grace enables sinful people to receive adoption as God's chosen children (Eph 1:4–5). This new covenant relationship, like the old one, includes great blessings and expectations for believers to respond to Jesus' amazing love—with acts of love for others out of gratitude to him.

The Broken Covenant

11 The word that came to Jeremiah from the LORD: [2]"Hear the words of this covenant, and speak to the men of Judah and the inhabitants of Jerusalem. [3]You shall say to them, Thus says the LORD, the God of Israel: Cursed be the man who does not hear the words of this covenant [4]that I commanded your fathers when I brought them out of the land of Egypt, from the iron furnace, saying, Listen to my voice, and do all that I command you. So shall you be my people, and I will be your God, [5]that I may confirm the oath that I swore to your fathers, to give them a land flowing with milk and honey, as at this day." Then I answered, "So be it, LORD."

[6]And the LORD said to me, "Proclaim all these words in the cities of Judah and in the streets of Jerusalem: Hear the words of this covenant and do them. [7]For I solemnly warned your fathers when I brought them up out of the land of Egypt, warning them persistently, even to this day, saying, Obey my voice. [8]Yet they did not obey or incline their ear, but everyone walked in the stubbornness of his evil heart. Therefore I brought upon them all the words of this covenant, which I commanded them to do, but they did not."

[9]Again the LORD said to me, "A conspiracy exists among the men of Judah and the inhabitants of Jerusalem. [10]They have turned back to the iniquities of their forefathers, who refused to hear my words. They have gone after other gods to serve them. The house of Israel and the house of Judah have broken my covenant that I made with their fathers. [11]Therefore, thus says the LORD, Behold, I am bringing disaster upon them that they cannot escape. Though they cry to me, I will not listen to them. [12]Then the cities of Judah and the inhabitants of Jerusalem will go and cry to the gods to whom they make offerings, but they cannot save them in the time of their trouble. [13]For your gods have become as many as your cities, O Judah, and as many as the streets of Jerusalem are the altars you have set up to shame, altars to make offerings to Baal.

[14]"Therefore do not pray for this people, or lift up a cry or prayer on their behalf, for I will not listen when they call to me in the time of their trouble. [15]What right has my beloved in my house, when she has done many vile deeds? Can even sacrificial flesh avert your doom? Can you then exult? [16]The LORD once called you 'a green olive tree, beautiful with good fruit.' But with the roar of a great tempest he will set fire to it, and its branches will be consumed. [17]The LORD of hosts, who planted you, has decreed disaster against you, because of the evil that the house of Israel and the house of Judah have done, provoking me to anger by making offerings to Baal."

18 The LORD made it known to me and I knew;
then you showed me their deeds.
19 But I was like a gentle lamb
led to the slaughter.
I did not know it was against me
they devised schemes, saying,
"Let us destroy the tree with its fruit,
let us cut him off from the land of the living,
that his name be remembered no more."
20 But, O LORD of hosts, who judges righteously,
who tests the heart and the mind,
let me see your vengeance upon them,
for to you have I committed my cause.

[21]Therefore thus says the LORD concerning the men of Anathoth, who seek your life, and say, "Do not prophesy in the name of the LORD, or you will die by our hand"— [22]therefore thus says the LORD of hosts: "Behold, I will punish them. The young men shall die by the sword, their sons and their daughters shall die by

famine, [23]and none of them shall be left. For I will bring disaster upon the men of
Anathoth, the year of their punishment."

Jeremiah's Complaint

12 Righteous are you, O LORD,
when I complain to you;
yet I would plead my case before you.
Why does the way of the wicked prosper?
Why do all who are treacherous thrive?
2 You plant them, and they take root;
they grow and produce fruit;
you are near in their mouth
and far from their heart.
3 But you, O LORD, know me;
you see me, and test my heart toward you.
Pull them out like sheep for the slaughter,
and set them apart for the day of slaughter.
4 How long will the land mourn
and the grass of every field wither?
For the evil of those who dwell in it
the beasts and the birds are swept away,
because they said, "He will not see our latter end."

The LORD Answers Jeremiah

5 "If you have raced with men on foot, and they have wearied you,
how will you compete with horses?
And if in a safe land you are so trusting,
what will you do in the thicket of the Jordan?
6 For even your brothers and the house of your father,
even they have dealt treacherously with you;
they are in full cry after you;
do not believe them,
though they speak friendly words to you."

7 "I have forsaken my house;
I have abandoned my heritage;
I have given the beloved of my soul
into the hands of her enemies.
8 My heritage has become to me
like a lion in the forest;
she has lifted up her voice against me;
therefore I hate her.
9 Is my heritage to me like a hyena's lair?
Are the birds of prey against her all around?
Go, assemble all the wild beasts;
bring them to devour.
10 Many shepherds have destroyed my vineyard;
they have trampled down my portion;
they have made my pleasant portion
a desolate wilderness.
11 They have made it a desolation;
desolate, it mourns to me.
The whole land is made desolate,
but no man lays it to heart.
12 Upon all the bare heights in the desert
destroyers have come,

for the sword of the Lord devours
from one end of the land to the other;
no flesh has peace.
13 They have sown wheat and have reaped thorns;
they have tired themselves out but profit nothing.
They shall be ashamed of their[1] harvests
because of the fierce anger of the Lord."

14Thus says the Lord concerning all my evil neighbors who touch the heritage
that I have given my people Israel to inherit: "Behold, I will pluck them up from
their land, and I will pluck up the house of Judah from among them. 15And after
I have plucked them up, I will again have compassion on them, and I will bring
them again each to his heritage and each to his land. 16And it shall come to pass,
if they will diligently learn the ways of my people, to swear by my name, 'As the
Lord lives,' even as they taught my people to swear by Baal, then they shall be
built up in the midst of my people. 17But if any nation will not listen, then I will
utterly pluck it up and destroy it, declares the Lord."

The Ruined Loincloth

13 Thus says the Lord to me, "Go and buy a linen loincloth and put it around
your waist, and do not dip it in water." 2So I bought a loincloth according to
the word of the Lord, and put it around my waist. 3And the word of the Lord came
to me a second time, 4"Take the loincloth that you have bought, which is around
your waist, and arise, go to the Euphrates and hide it there in a cleft of the rock."
5So I went and hid it by the Euphrates, as the Lord commanded me. 6And after
many days the Lord said to me, "Arise, go to the Euphrates, and take from there
the loincloth that I commanded you to hide there." 7Then I went to the Euphrates, and dug, and I took the loincloth from the place where I had hidden it. And
behold, the loincloth was spoiled; it was good for nothing.

8Then the word of the Lord came to me: 9"Thus says the Lord: Even so will I
spoil the pride of Judah and the great pride of Jerusalem. 10This evil people, who
refuse to hear my words, who stubbornly follow their own heart and have gone
after other gods to serve them and worship them, shall be like this loincloth,
which is good for nothing. 11For as the loincloth clings to the waist of a man, so
I made the whole house of Israel and the whole house of Judah cling to me, declares the Lord, that they might be for me a people, a name, a praise, and a glory,
but they would not listen.

The Jars Filled with Wine

12"You shall speak to them this word: 'Thus says the Lord, the God of Israel,
"Every jar shall be filled with wine."' And they will say to you, 'Do we not indeed
know that every jar will be filled with wine?' 13Then you shall say to them, 'Thus
says the Lord: Behold, I will fill with drunkenness all the inhabitants of this land:
the kings who sit on David's throne, the priests, the prophets, and all the inhabitants of Jerusalem. 14And I will dash them one against another, fathers and sons
together, declares the Lord. I will not pity or spare or have compassion, that I
should not destroy them.'"

Exile Threatened

15 Hear and give ear; be not proud,
for the Lord has spoken.
16 Give glory to the Lord your God
before he brings darkness,
before your feet stumble
on the twilight mountains,

[1]Hebrew *your*

JEREMIAH 12:14–16

HOPE FOR THE GENTILES

God's promise to Abraham included a future when all peoples and nations would partake in the covenant blessings (Ge 12:2–3). God desired to show all nations what life could be like when led by the one true God; through his relationship with the Israelites, he demonstrated faithful provision, constant protection, and dependable intervention. Even the judgment announced and carried out in the book of Jeremiah points to the value that God placed on his relationship with Israel. The Lord would use the Babylonians to uproot both Judah and the nation's wicked neighbors. But he promised to bring exiles from each country back to their lands and to give the foreigners an opportunity to establish themselves among the Israelites (Jer 12:16).

Jesus came as Israel's Messiah, but he would also become the Savior for whoever chooses to turn to him in trust (Jn 3:16). This included the Gentiles—that is, anyone not born of Jewish descent (Lk 2:30–32). Through the Good News of salvation in Jesus Christ, men and women of every nation, tribe, and tongue can have a relationship with God.

and while you look for light
he turns it into gloom
and makes it deep darkness.
17 But if you will not listen,
my soul will weep in secret for your pride;
my eyes will weep bitterly and run down with tears,
because the LORD's flock has been taken captive.

18 Say to the king and the queen mother:
"Take a lowly seat,
for your beautiful crown
has come down from your head."
19 The cities of the Negeb are shut up,
with none to open them;
all Judah is taken into exile,
wholly taken into exile.

20 "Lift up your eyes and see
those who come from the north.
Where is the flock that was given you,
your beautiful flock?
21 What will you say when they set as head over you
those whom you yourself have taught to be friends to you?
Will not pangs take hold of you
like those of a woman in labor?
22 And if you say in your heart,
'Why have these things come upon me?'
it is for the greatness of your iniquity
that your skirts are lifted up
and you suffer violence.
23 Can the Ethiopian change his skin
or the leopard his spots?
Then also you can do good
who are accustomed to do evil.
24 I will scatter you[1] like chaff
driven by the wind from the desert.
25 This is your lot,
the portion I have measured out to you, declares the LORD,
because you have forgotten me
and trusted in lies.
26 I myself will lift up your skirts over your face,
and your shame will be seen.
27 I have seen your abominations,
your adulteries and neighings, your lewd whorings,
on the hills in the field.
Woe to you, O Jerusalem!
How long will it be before you are made clean?"

Famine, Sword, and Pestilence

14 The word of the LORD that came to Jeremiah concerning the drought:
2 "Judah mourns,
and her gates languish;
her people lament on the ground,
and the cry of Jerusalem goes up.

[1] Hebrew *them*

3 Her nobles send their servants for water;
they come to the cisterns;
they find no water;
they return with their vessels empty;
they are ashamed and confounded
and cover their heads.
4 Because of the ground that is dismayed,
since there is no rain on the land,
the farmers are ashamed;
they cover their heads.
5 Even the doe in the field forsakes her newborn fawn
because there is no grass.
6 The wild donkeys stand on the bare heights;
they pant for air like jackals;
their eyes fail
because there is no vegetation.

7 "Though our iniquities testify against us,
act, O LORD, for your name's sake;
for our backslidings are many;
we have sinned against you.
8 O you hope of Israel,
its savior in time of trouble,
why should you be like a stranger in the land,
like a traveler who turns aside to tarry for a night?
9 Why should you be like a man confused,
like a mighty warrior who cannot save?
Yet you, O LORD, are in the midst of us,
and we are called by your name;
do not leave us."

10 Thus says the LORD concerning this people:
"They have loved to wander thus;
they have not restrained their feet;
therefore the LORD does not accept them;
now he will remember their iniquity
and punish their sins."

11 The LORD said to me: "Do not pray for the welfare of this people. 12 Though
they fast, I will not hear their cry, and though they offer burnt offering and grain
offering, I will not accept them. But I will consume them by the sword, by famine,
and by pestilence."

Lying Prophets

13 Then I said: "Ah, Lord GOD, behold, the prophets say to them, 'You shall
not see the sword, nor shall you have famine, but I will give you assured peace
in this place.'" 14 And the LORD said to me: "The prophets are prophesying lies in
my name. I did not send them, nor did I command them or speak to them. They
are prophesying to you a lying vision, worthless divination, and the deceit of
their own minds. 15 Therefore thus says the LORD concerning the prophets who
prophesy in my name although I did not send them, and who say, 'Sword and
famine shall not come upon this land': By sword and famine those prophets shall
be consumed. 16 And the people to whom they prophesy shall be cast out in the
streets of Jerusalem, victims of famine and sword, with none to bury them—
them, their wives, their sons, and their daughters. For I will pour out their evil
upon them.

JEREMIAH 14:8

THE HOPE AND SAVIOR OF ISRAEL

Judah experienced a terrible drought that greatly affected both people and animals. Wells dried up and the land, parched and cracked, would not produce food. Jeremiah asked God to mercifully intervene even though the people had sinned (Jer 14:7). God's silence in their situation felt like God's absence from their lives. Jeremiah prayed with informed faith, acknowledging that God was the "hope of Israel" and "its savior in time of trouble" (v. 8). Many times before, God had proven his power by rescuing the people from trouble. Jeremiah asked him to do so again.

Between the days of the Old Testament and the era of the New Testament, some 400 years went by without a word from God. The people longed for the spiritual drought to end—they were desperate for God to speak or move (Lk 2:25). Jesus came into these dark and dry times to bring light and life (Jn 1:4). He was and is the answer to the hope of all nations; a Savior who brings the possibility of grace and eternal life to all people (2Ti 1:9–10).

17 "You shall say to them this word:
'Let my eyes run down with tears night and day,
and let them not cease,
for the virgin daughter of my people is shattered with a great wound,
with a very grievous blow.
18 If I go out into the field,
behold, those pierced by the sword!
And if I enter the city,
behold, the diseases of famine!
For both prophet and priest ply their trade through the land
and have no knowledge.'"

19 Have you utterly rejected Judah?
Does your soul loathe Zion?
Why have you struck us down
so that there is no healing for us?
We looked for peace, but no good came;
for a time of healing, but behold, terror.
20 We acknowledge our wickedness, O LORD,
and the iniquity of our fathers,
for we have sinned against you.
21 Do not spurn us, for your name's sake;
do not dishonor your glorious throne;
remember and do not break your covenant with us.
22 Are there any among the false gods of the nations that can bring rain?
Or can the heavens give showers?
Are you not he, O LORD our God?
We set our hope on you,
for you do all these things.

The LORD Will Not Relent

15 Then the LORD said to me, "Though Moses and Samuel stood before me,
yet my heart would not turn toward this people. Send them out of my sight,
and let them go! 2And when they ask you, 'Where shall we go?' you shall say to
them, 'Thus says the LORD:

"'Those who are for pestilence, to pestilence,
and those who are for the sword, to the sword;
those who are for famine, to famine,
and those who are for captivity, to captivity.'

3I will appoint over them four kinds of destroyers, declares the LORD: the sword
to kill, the dogs to tear, and the birds of the air and the beasts of the earth to devour and destroy. 4And I will make them a horror to all the kingdoms of the earth
because of what Manasseh the son of Hezekiah, king of Judah, did in Jerusalem.

5 "Who will have pity on you, O Jerusalem,
or who will grieve for you?
Who will turn aside
to ask about your welfare?
6 You have rejected me, declares the LORD;
you keep going backward,
so I have stretched out my hand against you and destroyed you—
I am weary of relenting.
7 I have winnowed them with a winnowing fork
in the gates of the land;
I have bereaved them; I have destroyed my people;
they did not turn from their ways.

JEREMIAH 15:18

STREAMS OF LIVING WATER?

God called Jeremiah to announce the coming judgment, and God protected his life. Yet the prophet was grieved by the message he had to proclaim, and he suffered under the hardship and rejection he experienced from the people (Jer 15:10). Jeremiah continually pleaded with God to relent from punishing his people — to forgive and to spare them. But God held his ground, intent on dispensing justice to those who had abandoned him to worship idols. Jeremiah's pain was a mixture of grief and frustration. He was sickened by the situation — he saw the inevitable disaster and knew that Judah deserved it, yet he still pleaded with God on behalf of the people. Jeremiah was disappointed that God would not change his mind; he compared God to a brook that fails to produce water.

In a conversation with a woman at a well, Jesus compared himself to a spring producing living water (Jn 4:10). While life as a disciple of Jesus includes a flow of many blessings, there are no guarantees that life will be free of hardship or suffering. Grace covers sin, and salvation through Jesus provides eternal life. But grace does not preclude dark and difficult days (Jn 16:33). Following Jesus requires faith in God's sovereign plan; this faith provides perspective on every event in life. Jesus offers an antidote to the frustration and disappointment believers might experience when some prayers go unanswered. He has promised to be with us wherever we go (Mt 28:20).

8 I have made their widows more in number
than the sand of the seas;
I have brought against the mothers of young men
a destroyer at noonday;
I have made anguish and terror
fall upon them suddenly.
9 She who bore seven has grown feeble;
she has fainted away;
her sun went down while it was yet day;
she has been shamed and disgraced.
And the rest of them I will give to the sword
before their enemies,
declares the LORD."

Jeremiah's Complaint

10Woe is me, my mother, that you bore me, a man of strife and contention to
the whole land! I have not lent, nor have I borrowed, yet all of them curse me.
11The LORD said, "Have I not[1] set you free for their good? Have I not pleaded for
you before the enemy in the time of trouble and in the time of distress? 12Can one
break iron, iron from the north, and bronze?
13"Your wealth and your treasures I will give as spoil, without price, for all your
sins, throughout all your territory. 14I will make you serve your enemies in a land
that you do not know, for in my anger a fire is kindled that shall burn forever."

15 O LORD, you know;
remember me and visit me,
and take vengeance for me on my persecutors.
In your forbearance take me not away;
know that for your sake I bear reproach.
16 Your words were found, and I ate them,
and your words became to me a joy
and the delight of my heart,
for I am called by your name,
O LORD, God of hosts.
17 I did not sit in the company of revelers,
nor did I rejoice;
I sat alone, because your hand was upon me,
for you had filled me with indignation.
18 Why is my pain unceasing,
my wound incurable,
refusing to be healed?
Will you be to me like a deceitful brook,
like waters that fail?

19 Therefore thus says the LORD:
"If you return, I will restore you,
and you shall stand before me.
If you utter what is precious, and not what is worthless,
you shall be as my mouth.
They shall turn to you,
but you shall not turn to them.
20 And I will make you to this people
a fortified wall of bronze;
they will fight against you,
but they shall not prevail over you,

[1]The meaning of the Hebrew is uncertain

for I am with you
to save you and deliver you,
declares the LORD.
21 I will deliver you out of the hand of the wicked,
and redeem you from the grasp of the ruthless."

Famine, Sword, and Death

16 The word of the LORD came to me: 2"You shall not take a wife, nor shall you
have sons or daughters in this place. 3For thus says the LORD concerning
the sons and daughters who are born in this place, and concerning the mothers
who bore them and the fathers who fathered them in this land: 4They shall die
of deadly diseases. They shall not be lamented, nor shall they be buried. They
shall be as dung on the surface of the ground. They shall perish by the sword and
by famine, and their dead bodies shall be food for the birds of the air and for the
beasts of the earth.
5"For thus says the LORD: Do not enter the house of mourning, or go to lament
or grieve for them, for I have taken away my peace from this people, my steadfast
love and mercy, declares the LORD. 6Both great and small shall die in this land.
They shall not be buried, and no one shall lament for them or cut himself or make
himself bald for them. 7No one shall break bread for the mourner, to comfort him
for the dead, nor shall anyone give him the cup of consolation to drink for his
father or his mother. 8You shall not go into the house of feasting to sit with them,
to eat and drink. 9For thus says the LORD of hosts, the God of Israel: Behold, I will
silence in this place, before your eyes and in your days, the voice of mirth and the
voice of gladness, the voice of the bridegroom and the voice of the bride.
10"And when you tell this people all these words, and they say to you, 'Why has
the LORD pronounced all this great evil against us? What is our iniquity? What is
the sin that we have committed against the LORD our God?' 11then you shall say to
them: 'Because your fathers have forsaken me, declares the LORD, and have gone
after other gods and have served and worshiped them, and have forsaken me and
have not kept my law, 12and because you have done worse than your fathers, for
behold, every one of you follows his stubborn, evil will, refusing to listen to me.
13Therefore I will hurl you out of this land into a land that neither you nor your
fathers have known, and there you shall serve other gods day and night, for I will
show you no favor.'

The LORD Will Restore Israel

14"Therefore, behold, the days are coming, declares the LORD, when it shall no
longer be said, 'As the LORD lives who brought up the people of Israel out of the
land of Egypt,' 15but 'As the LORD lives who brought up the people of Israel out of
the north country and out of all the countries where he had driven them.' For I
will bring them back to their own land that I gave to their fathers.
16"Behold, I am sending for many fishers, declares the LORD, and they shall
catch them. And afterward I will send for many hunters, and they shall hunt them
from every mountain and every hill, and out of the clefts of the rocks. 17For my
eyes are on all their ways. They are not hidden from me, nor is their iniquity concealed from my eyes. 18But first I will doubly repay their iniquity and their sin,
because they have polluted my land with the carcasses of their detestable idols,
and have filled my inheritance with their abominations."

19 O LORD, my strength and my stronghold,
my refuge in the day of trouble,
to you shall the nations come
from the ends of the earth and say:
"Our fathers have inherited nothing but lies,
worthless things in which there is no profit.

JEREMIAH 16:14–15

GATHERING THE SCATTERED

Just after God declared that he would exile Judah, he promised a future restoration. The Babylonian exile was a terrible and traumatic season—the people of Judah were scattered to foreign territory, enslaved and separated from worship. But God, through Jeremiah, assured the people that one day they would return and be restored to their land.

Those who know and follow Jesus cling to the promise that Christ will one day return to gather his people from this sin-corrupted earth (Mt 24:31). Jesus pledged that no matter how much his church suffered and regardless of how far they became scattered, he would one day call them to be with him. In the same way that God called his people out of exile to return to their land, Jesus will call his church out of exile in the world to enjoy him forever in heaven (1Th 4:16–17).

20 Can man make for himself gods?
Such are not gods!"

21 "Therefore, behold, I will make them know, this once I will make them know
my power and my might, and they shall know that my name is the LORD."

The Sin of Judah

17 "The sin of Judah is written with a pen of iron; with a point of diamond it is
engraved on the tablet of their heart, and on the horns of their altars, 2 while
their children remember their altars and their Asherim, beside every green tree
and on the high hills, 3 on the mountains in the open country. Your wealth and all
your treasures I will give for spoil as the price of your high places for sin throughout all your territory. 4 You shall loosen your hand from your heritage that I gave
to you, and I will make you serve your enemies in a land that you do not know, for
in my anger a fire is kindled that shall burn forever."

5 Thus says the LORD:
"Cursed is the man who trusts in man
and makes flesh his strength,[1]
whose heart turns away from the LORD.
6 He is like a shrub in the desert,
and shall not see any good come.
He shall dwell in the parched places of the wilderness,
in an uninhabited salt land.
7 "Blessed is the man who trusts in the LORD,
whose trust is the LORD.
8 He is like a tree planted by water,
that sends out its roots by the stream,
and does not fear when heat comes,
for its leaves remain green,
and is not anxious in the year of drought,
for it does not cease to bear fruit."

9 The heart is deceitful above all things,
and desperately sick;
who can understand it?
10 "I the LORD search the heart
and test the mind,[2]
to give every man according to his ways,
according to the fruit of his deeds."
11 Like the partridge that gathers a brood that she did not hatch,
so is he who gets riches but not by justice;
in the midst of his days they will leave him,
and at his end he will be a fool.
12 A glorious throne set on high from the beginning
is the place of our sanctuary.
13 O LORD, the hope of Israel,
all who forsake you shall be put to shame;
those who turn away from you[3] shall be written in the earth,
for they have forsaken the LORD, the fountain of living water.

Jeremiah Prays for Deliverance

14 Heal me, O LORD, and I shall be healed;
save me, and I shall be saved,
for you are my praise.

[1]Hebrew *arm* [2]Hebrew *kidneys* [3]Hebrew *me*

DECEITFUL HEARTS

Men and women were created in perfection with a pure heart to enjoy God. When Adam and Eve chose to defy God and to embrace sin, all that was perfect, including the human heart, became corrupted. This defiance of God separated people from their Creator, and the sin of Adam passed down to the whole human race. The root of this original sin is present at conception and leads to actual sin in the life of every man, woman, and child. All people have sinned against God, turning away from his laws and expectations (Ro 3:10).

God has been absolutely clear about what he requires. He has proclaimed warnings about disobedience. He has anointed prophets to remind people of what a life lived in obedience looks like as opposed to death through sin. Yet the human heart's default inclination is toward defiance and self-service.

The solution to a person's corrupted heart is not an attempt to try harder, to work toward a change of behavior. There is no hope for forced or natural improvement (Jer 17:9). Beyond simple selfishness or unkindness, sinful nature carries people to dark and wicked places far from God's life-giving paths (Mt 15:19). Men and women need a new nature — a new heart. The prophet Ezekiel announced that one day God would provide the cure for the sickness of sin: "And I will give you a new heart, and a new spirit I will put within you. And I will remove the heart of stone from your flesh and give you a heart of flesh" (Eze 36:26).

Jesus came into the world and lived a sinless life. He gave himself as a perfect sacrifice to pay in full the debt of humankind's sin. He rose from the dead to defeat the power of death for all time. Believing in him and trusting in his saving work secures forgiveness for any person. On top of this, faith in Jesus gives men and women what they desperately need — a new heart. Everyone who believes in him is made new (2Co 5:17). Through the power of the Holy Spirit, Christians can put off the old, corrupted self and put on the new self that is created through faith in Jesus.

15 Behold, they say to me,
"Where is the word of the LORD?
Let it come!"
16 I have not run away from being your shepherd,
nor have I desired the day of sickness.
You know what came out of my lips;
it was before your face.
17 Be not a terror to me;
you are my refuge in the day of disaster.
18 Let those be put to shame who persecute me,
but let me not be put to shame;
let them be dismayed,
but let me not be dismayed;
bring upon them the day of disaster;
destroy them with double destruction!

Keep the Sabbath Holy

19 Thus said the LORD to me: "Go and stand in the People's Gate, by which the
kings of Judah enter and by which they go out, and in all the gates of Jerusalem,
20 and say: 'Hear the word of the LORD, you kings of Judah, and all Judah, and all
the inhabitants of Jerusalem, who enter by these gates. 21 Thus says the LORD: Take
care for the sake of your lives, and do not bear a burden on the Sabbath day or
bring it in by the gates of Jerusalem. 22 And do not carry a burden out of your
houses on the Sabbath or do any work, but keep the Sabbath day holy, as I commanded your fathers. 23 Yet they did not listen or incline their ear, but stiffened
their neck, that they might not hear and receive instruction.
24 " 'But if you listen to me, declares the LORD, and bring in no burden by the
gates of this city on the Sabbath day, but keep the Sabbath day holy and do no
work on it, 25 then there shall enter by the gates of this city kings and princes who
sit on the throne of David, riding in chariots and on horses, they and their officials, the men of Judah and the inhabitants of Jerusalem. And this city shall be
inhabited forever. 26 And people shall come from the cities of Judah and the places
around Jerusalem, from the land of Benjamin, from the Shephelah, from the hill
country, and from the Negeb, bringing burnt offerings and sacrifices, grain offerings and frankincense, and bringing thank offerings to the house of the LORD.
27 But if you do not listen to me, to keep the Sabbath day holy, and not to bear a
burden and enter by the gates of Jerusalem on the Sabbath day, then I will kindle
a fire in its gates, and it shall devour the palaces of Jerusalem and shall not be
quenched.' "

The Potter and the Clay

18 The word that came to Jeremiah from the LORD: 2 "Arise, and go down to the
potter's house, and there I will let you hear[1] my words." 3 So I went down to
the potter's house, and there he was working at his wheel. 4 And the vessel he was
making of clay was spoiled in the potter's hand, and he reworked it into another
vessel, as it seemed good to the potter to do.
5 Then the word of the LORD came to me: 6 "O house of Israel, can I not do with
you as this potter has done? declares the LORD. Behold, like the clay in the potter's
hand, so are you in my hand, O house of Israel. 7 If at any time I declare concerning
a nation or a kingdom, that I will pluck up and break down and destroy it, 8 and if
that nation, concerning which I have spoken, turns from its evil, I will relent of
the disaster that I intended to do to it. 9 And if at any time I declare concerning a
nation or a kingdom that I will build and plant it, 10 and if it does evil in my sight,
not listening to my voice, then I will relent of the good that I had intended to do

[1] Or *will cause you to hear*

to it. [11]Now, therefore, say to the men of Judah and the inhabitants of Jerusalem:
'Thus says the LORD, Behold, I am shaping disaster against you and devising a
plan against you. Return, every one from his evil way, and amend your ways and
your deeds.'

[12]"But they say, 'That is in vain! We will follow our own plans, and will every
one act according to the stubbornness of his evil heart.'

13 "Therefore thus says the LORD:
Ask among the nations,
Who has heard the like of this?
The virgin Israel
has done a very horrible thing.
14 Does the snow of Lebanon leave
the crags of Sirion?[1]
Do the mountain waters run dry,[2]
the cold flowing streams?
15 But my people have forgotten me;
they make offerings to false gods;
they made them stumble in their ways,
in the ancient roads,
and to walk into side roads,
not the highway,
16 making their land a horror,
a thing to be hissed at forever.
Everyone who passes by it is horrified
and shakes his head.
17 Like the east wind I will scatter them
before the enemy.
I will show them my back, not my face,
in the day of their calamity."

[18]Then they said, "Come, let us make plots against Jeremiah, for the law shall
not perish from the priest, nor counsel from the wise, nor the word from the
prophet. Come, let us strike him with the tongue, and let us not pay attention to
any of his words."

19 Hear me, O LORD,
and listen to the voice of my adversaries.
20 Should good be repaid with evil?
Yet they have dug a pit for my life.
Remember how I stood before you
to speak good for them,
to turn away your wrath from them.
21 Therefore deliver up their children to famine;
give them over to the power of the sword;
let their wives become childless and widowed.
May their men meet death by pestilence,
their youths be struck down by the sword in battle.
22 May a cry be heard from their houses,
when you bring the plunderer suddenly upon them!
For they have dug a pit to take me
and laid snares for my feet.
23 Yet you, O LORD, know
all their plotting to kill me.
Forgive not their iniquity,
nor blot out their sin from your sight.

[1]Hebrew *of the field* [2]Hebrew *Are foreign waters plucked up*

GOD IS THE POTTER

God proposed the analogy of potter and clay as a picture of his power and sovereignty and to illustrate the futility of his people's stubbornness. At the Lord's instruction, Jeremiah observed the potter engaging the soft clay — determining its final form according to his pleasure and will (v. 4). The same lump of clay could end up as an oil lamp, a bowl, a vessel for water, or any other creation. The purpose in the mind of the artist determined the pull and pressure on the clay, combining with the speed of the wheel to spin out a desired shape. The potter was the sole determiner of the clay's destiny.

In the same way, the Lord alone controlled the Israelites' destiny. At any point, God could position Judah as a most-favored nation — thriving and advancing beyond all other peoples. At any point, the process of building could be halted and the form collapsed to begin something different (vv. 7 – 10). The Israelites attempted to resist God, but they did not succeed. They rejected the design he wanted for his people, pressing their own desires for going their own way. Over time, they abandoned their covenant with God to worship false gods. Faithful to his word, God arranged to discipline his children when they refused to repent.

The judgment of Judah through being conquered and exiled was a reminder that the clay was never free to determine its own form. Following a siege and the people's capture, the ruins of Jerusalem would become a monument to foolishness — of the people's attempt to defy the living God (vv. 16 – 17).

In his letter to the Romans, Paul asserted the same principle the Lord showed to Jeremiah: in the end, the fate of the clay is always dependent on the will of the potter (Ro 9:19 – 21). The rebel's resolve is irrelevant. God will not be mocked. People who sin never actually *get away* with defying him. At the cross of Christ, God demonstrated his justice to eventually punish previously unaddressed sin (Ro 3:25).

God invites all people to enjoy a relationship with him, to participate in abundant life through happy obedience to his ways. Jesus modeled the ideal of cooperating with God, demonstrating perfect obedience to the Father. On the night of his betrayal, completely aware of the horrors ahead, Jesus yielded to his Father's ultimate will (Mt 26:39).

Let them be overthrown before you;
deal with them in the time of your anger.

The Broken Flask

19 Thus says the LORD, "Go, buy a potter's earthenware flask, and take some of the elders of the people and some of the elders of the priests, 2and go out to the Valley of the Son of Hinnom at the entry of the Potsherd Gate, and proclaim there the words that I tell you. 3You shall say, 'Hear the word of the LORD, O kings of Judah and inhabitants of Jerusalem. Thus says the LORD of hosts, the God of Israel: Behold, I am bringing such disaster upon this place that the ears of everyone who hears of it will tingle. 4Because the people have forsaken me and have profaned this place by making offerings in it to other gods whom neither they nor their fathers nor the kings of Judah have known; and because they have filled this place with the blood of innocents, 5and have built the high places of Baal to burn their sons in the fire as burnt offerings to Baal, which I did not command or decree, nor did it come into my mind— 6therefore, behold, days are coming, declares the LORD, when this place shall no more be called Topheth, or the Valley of the Son of Hinnom, but the Valley of Slaughter. 7And in this place I will make void the plans of Judah and Jerusalem, and will cause their people to fall by the sword before their enemies, and by the hand of those who seek their life. I will give their dead bodies for food to the birds of the air and to the beasts of the earth. 8And I will make this city a horror, a thing to be hissed at. Everyone who passes by it will be horrified and will hiss because of all its wounds. 9And I will make them eat the flesh of their sons and their daughters, and everyone shall eat the flesh of his neighbor in the siege and in the distress, with which their enemies and those who seek their life afflict them.'

10"Then you shall break the flask in the sight of the men who go with you, 11and shall say to them, 'Thus says the LORD of hosts: So will I break this people and this city, as one breaks a potter's vessel, so that it can never be mended. Men shall bury in Topheth because there will be no place else to bury. 12Thus will I do to this place, declares the LORD, and to its inhabitants, making this city like Topheth. 13The houses of Jerusalem and the houses of the kings of Judah—all the houses on whose roofs offerings have been offered to all the host of heaven, and drink offerings have been poured out to other gods—shall be defiled like the place of Topheth.'"

14Then Jeremiah came from Topheth, where the LORD had sent him to prophesy, and he stood in the court of the LORD's house and said to all the people: 15"Thus says the LORD of hosts, the God of Israel, behold, I am bringing upon this city and upon all its towns all the disaster that I have pronounced against it, because they have stiffened their neck, refusing to hear my words."

Jeremiah Persecuted by Pashhur

20 Now Pashhur the priest, the son of Immer, who was chief officer in the house of the LORD, heard Jeremiah prophesying these things. 2Then Pashhur beat Jeremiah the prophet, and put him in the stocks that were in the upper Benjamin Gate of the house of the LORD. 3The next day, when Pashhur released Jeremiah from the stocks, Jeremiah said to him, "The LORD does not call your name Pashhur, but Terror on Every Side. 4For thus says the LORD: Behold, I will make you a terror to yourself and to all your friends. They shall fall by the sword of their enemies while you look on. And I will give all Judah into the hand of the king of Babylon. He shall carry them captive to Babylon, and shall strike them down with the sword. 5Moreover, I will give all the wealth of the city, all its gains, all its prized belongings, and all the treasures of the kings of Judah into the hand of their enemies, who shall plunder them and seize them and carry them to Babylon. 6And you, Pashhur, and all who dwell in your house, shall go into captivity. To Babylon you shall go, and there you shall die, and there you shall be buried, you and all your friends, to whom you have prophesied falsely."

7 O LORD, you have deceived me,
and I was deceived;
you are stronger than I,
and you have prevailed.
I have become a laughingstock all the day;
everyone mocks me.
8 For whenever I speak, I cry out,
I shout, "Violence and destruction!"
For the word of the LORD has become for me
a reproach and derision all day long.
9 If I say, "I will not mention him,
or speak any more in his name,"
there is in my heart as it were a burning fire
shut up in my bones,
and I am weary with holding it in,
and I cannot.
10 For I hear many whispering.
Terror is on every side!
"Denounce him! Let us denounce him!"
say all my close friends,
watching for my fall.
"Perhaps he will be deceived;
then we can overcome him
and take our revenge on him."
11 But the LORD is with me as a dread warrior;
therefore my persecutors will stumble;
they will not overcome me.
They will be greatly shamed,
for they will not succeed.
Their eternal dishonor
will never be forgotten.
12 O LORD of hosts, who tests the righteous,
who sees the heart and the mind,[1]
let me see your vengeance upon them,
for to you have I committed my cause.
13 Sing to the LORD;
praise the LORD!
For he has delivered the life of the needy
from the hand of evildoers.

14 Cursed be the day
on which I was born!
The day when my mother bore me,
let it not be blessed!
15 Cursed be the man who brought the news to my father,
"A son is born to you,"
making him very glad.
16 Let that man be like the cities
that the LORD overthrew without pity;
let him hear a cry in the morning
and an alarm at noon,

JEREMIAH 20:7–9

FIRED UP TO SHARE THE WORD

Jeremiah lamented that serving as the Lord's messenger of warning had brought him unending insult and rejection (Jer 20:7–8). Yet he could not physically withhold the news of God's impending judgment; the words were like a raging fire within him (v. 9). He could not remain silent about Judah's need to repent and return to the Lord, and the people needed to connect the coming tragedy to God's punishment for their disobedience and betrayal. Regardless of the resulting mistreatment, Jeremiah had no choice but to speak the words God put in his heart.

When John the Baptist saw Jesus approaching, he, like Jeremiah, found himself unable to remain silent. With joy John blurted out, "Behold, the Lamb of God, who takes away the sin of the world!" (Jn 1:29). Similarly, the apostle Paul's life was so radically changed by Christ that he could not keep the gospel to himself (Ac 26:19–20). Throughout history, Christ's true followers have experienced the same compelling desire: to tell others that God is real and that a relationship with him is possible through Jesus. Communicating a person's need for the Savior includes highlighting the reality of sin. This message can result in mistreatment when prideful people resist the notion of their sinfulness. Yet, the bad news about *sin and* the good news about grace through Jesus are too important for Christians to keep to themselves.

[1]Hebrew *kidneys*

17 because he did not kill me in the womb;
so my mother would have been my grave,
and her womb forever great.
18 Why did I come out from the womb
to see toil and sorrow,
and spend my days in shame?

Jerusalem Will Fall to Nebuchadnezzar

21 This is the word that came to Jeremiah from the LORD, when King Zedekiah
sent to him Pashhur the son of Malchiah and Zephaniah the priest, the son
of Maaseiah, saying, 2"Inquire of the LORD for us, for Nebuchadnezzar[1] king of
Babylon is making war against us. Perhaps the LORD will deal with us according to
all his wonderful deeds and will make him withdraw from us."
3Then Jeremiah said to them: "Thus you shall say to Zedekiah, 4'Thus says
the LORD, the God of Israel: Behold, I will turn back the weapons of war that are
in your hands and with which you are fighting against the king of Babylon and
against the Chaldeans who are besieging you outside the walls. And I will bring
them together into the midst of this city. 5I myself will fight against you with outstretched hand and strong arm, in anger and in fury and in great wrath. 6And I
will strike down the inhabitants of this city, both man and beast. They shall die
of a great pestilence. 7Afterward, declares the LORD, I will give Zedekiah king of
Judah and his servants and the people in this city who survive the pestilence,
sword, and famine into the hand of Nebuchadnezzar king of Babylon and into the
hand of their enemies, into the hand of those who seek their lives. He shall strike
them down with the edge of the sword. He shall not pity them or spare them or
have compassion.'
8"And to this people you shall say: 'Thus says the LORD: Behold, I set before
you the way of life and the way of death. 9He who stays in this city shall die by
the sword, by famine, and by pestilence, but he who goes out and surrenders to
the Chaldeans who are besieging you shall live and shall have his life as a prize of
war. 10For I have set my face against this city for harm and not for good, declares
the LORD: it shall be given into the hand of the king of Babylon, and he shall burn
it with fire.'

Message to the House of David

11"And to the house of the king of Judah say, 'Hear the word of the LORD,
12O house of David! Thus says the LORD:

"'Execute justice in the morning,
and deliver from the hand of the oppressor
him who has been robbed,
lest my wrath go forth like fire,
and burn with none to quench it,
because of your evil deeds.'"

13 "Behold, I am against you, O inhabitant of the valley,
O rock of the plain,
declares the LORD;
you who say, 'Who shall come down against us,
or who shall enter our habitations?'
14 I will punish you according to the fruit of your deeds,
declares the LORD;
I will kindle a fire in her forest,
and it shall devour all that is around her."

[1]Hebrew *Nebuchadrezzar*, an alternate spelling of *Nebuchadnezzar* (king of Babylon) occurring frequently from Jeremiah 21–52; this latter spelling is used throughout Jeremiah for consistency

22 Thus says the LORD: "Go down to the house of the king of Judah and
speak there this word, 2and say, 'Hear the word of the LORD, O king of
Judah, who sits on the throne of David, you, and your servants, and your people
who enter these gates. 3Thus says the LORD: Do justice and righteousness, and
deliver from the hand of the oppressor him who has been robbed. And do no
wrong or violence to the resident alien, the fatherless, and the widow, nor shed
innocent blood in this place. 4For if you will indeed obey this word, then there
shall enter the gates of this house kings who sit on the throne of David, riding
in chariots and on horses, they and their servants and their people. 5But if you
will not obey these words, I swear by myself, declares the LORD, that this house
shall become a desolation. 6For thus says the LORD concerning the house of the
king of Judah:

"'You are like Gilead to me,
like the summit of Lebanon,
yet surely I will make you a desert,
an uninhabited city.[1]
7 I will prepare destroyers against you,
each with his weapons,
and they shall cut down your choicest cedars
and cast them into the fire.

8"'And many nations will pass by this city, and every man will say to his neighbor, "Why has the LORD dealt thus with this great city?" 9And they will answer,
"Because they have forsaken the covenant of the LORD their God and worshiped
other gods and served them."'"

10 Weep not for him who is dead,
nor grieve for him,
but weep bitterly for him who goes away,
for he shall return no more
to see his native land.

Message to the Sons of Josiah

11For thus says the LORD concerning Shallum the son of Josiah, king of Judah,
who reigned instead of Josiah his father, and who went away from this place: "He
shall return here no more, 12but in the place where they have carried him captive,
there shall he die, and he shall never see this land again."

13 "Woe to him who builds his house by unrighteousness,
and his upper rooms by injustice,
who makes his neighbor serve him for nothing
and does not give him his wages,
14 who says, 'I will build myself a great house
with spacious upper rooms,'
who cuts out windows for it,
paneling it with cedar
and painting it with vermilion.
15 Do you think you are a king
because you compete in cedar?
Did not your father eat and drink
and do justice and righteousness?
Then it was well with him.
16 He judged the cause of the poor and needy;
then it was well.
Is not this to know me?
declares the LORD.

[1]Hebrew *cities*

THE LEAST OF THESE

Jeremiah delivered a word from the Lord to the king's court. In light of the Israelites' behavior, the Lord had a lot to say regarding their potential destruction. However, Jeremiah did not start out his prophetic word with destruction. Instead, he started with a command: "Do justice and righteousness" (v. 3). The verse continues on to command that those listening to Jeremiah rescue those who have been robbed; that they not violate the foreigner, the fatherless, or the widow; and that they avoid shedding innocent blood. Despite how far away the people drifted from the Lord, God gave them a few simple commands that gave them the opportunity to bring back the blessings they so strongly desired.

Jesus taught that whatever anyone does for "the least of these" they do for him (Mt 25:45). His teaching echoes the same commandments that God gave the people in Jeremiah 22:3. God deeply desires that his people care for those who need to be cared for the most; so much so that he considers it directly serving him when they serve someone in need. James 1:27 also says that pure and undefiled religion is "to visit orphans and widows in their affliction," and at the time when James wrote his letter, the idea of caring for those who were less fortunate was not a novel concept. God had been telling his people to care for and rescue those in need since the Law of Moses; Jesus told his followers the same thing, and James wrote to remind everyone of the same truth once more. God's pattern of urging his people to care for "the least of these" is crystal clear in Scripture.

The first five verses of Jeremiah 22 describe God's desires for King Zedekiah and his people: how they can obey him, and what will happen if they do. However, the next four verses give a tragic description of what was about to happen because they did not listen. For believers today, God has given his own word, Jesus' word, and James's word. Zedekiah and his court failed to listen to Jeremiah and they suffered for it, but the same does not have to be true of God's people today. God's desire is straightforward, and his commandment is clear: Love the least of these.

17 But you have eyes and heart
only for your dishonest gain,
for shedding innocent blood,
and for practicing oppression and violence."

18 Therefore thus says the LORD concerning Jehoiakim the son of Josiah, king
of Judah:

"They shall not lament for him, saying,
'Ah, my brother!' or 'Ah, sister!'
They shall not lament for him, saying,
'Ah, lord!' or 'Ah, his majesty!'
19 With the burial of a donkey he shall be buried,
dragged and dumped beyond the gates of Jerusalem."
20 "Go up to Lebanon, and cry out,
and lift up your voice in Bashan;
cry out from Abarim,
for all your lovers are destroyed.
21 I spoke to you in your prosperity,
but you said, 'I will not listen.'
This has been your way from your youth,
that you have not obeyed my voice.
22 The wind shall shepherd all your shepherds,
and your lovers shall go into captivity;
then you will be ashamed and confounded
because of all your evil.
23 O inhabitant of Lebanon,
nested among the cedars,
how you will be pitied when pangs come upon you,
pain as of a woman in labor!"

24 "As I live, declares the LORD, though Coniah the son of Jehoiakim, king of
Judah, were the signet ring on my right hand, yet I would tear you off 25 and give
you into the hand of those who seek your life, into the hand of those of whom
you are afraid, even into the hand of Nebuchadnezzar king of Babylon and into
the hand of the Chaldeans. 26 I will hurl you and the mother who bore you into
another country, where you were not born, and there you shall die. 27 But to the
land to which they will long to return, there they shall not return."

28 Is this man Coniah a despised, broken pot,
a vessel no one cares for?
Why are he and his children hurled and cast
into a land that they do not know?
29 O land, land, land,
hear the word of the LORD!
30 Thus says the LORD:
"Write this man down as childless,
a man who shall not succeed in his days,
for none of his offspring shall succeed
in sitting on the throne of David
and ruling again in Judah."

The Righteous Branch

23 "Woe to the shepherds who destroy and scatter the sheep of my pasture!"
declares the LORD. 2 Therefore thus says the LORD, the God of Israel, concerning the shepherds who care for my people: "You have scattered my flock and
have driven them away, and you have not attended to them. Behold, I will attend
to you for your evil deeds, declares the LORD. 3 Then I will gather the remnant of

my flock out of all the countries where I have driven them, and I will bring them
back to their fold, and they shall be fruitful and multiply. 4I will set shepherds
over them who will care for them, and they shall fear no more, nor be dismayed,
neither shall any be missing, declares the LORD.
5"Behold, the days are coming, declares the LORD, when I will raise up for David a righteous Branch, and he shall reign as king and deal wisely, and shall execute justice and righteousness in the land. 6In his days Judah will be saved, and
Israel will dwell securely. And this is the name by which he will be called: 'The
LORD is our righteousness.'
7"Therefore, behold, the days are coming, declares the LORD, when they shall
no longer say, 'As the LORD lives who brought up the people of Israel out of the
land of Egypt,' 8but 'As the LORD lives who brought up and led the offspring of the
house of Israel out of the north country and out of all the countries where he[1] had
driven them.' Then they shall dwell in their own land."

Lying Prophets

9Concerning the prophets:

My heart is broken within me;
all my bones shake;
I am like a drunken man,
like a man overcome by wine,
because of the LORD
and because of his holy words.
10 For the land is full of adulterers;
because of the curse the land mourns,
and the pastures of the wilderness are dried up.
Their course is evil,
and their might is not right.
11 "Both prophet and priest are ungodly;
even in my house I have found their evil,
declares the LORD.
12 Therefore their way shall be to them
like slippery paths in the darkness,
into which they shall be driven and fall,
for I will bring disaster upon them
in the year of their punishment,
declares the LORD.
13 In the prophets of Samaria
I saw an unsavory thing:
they prophesied by Baal
and led my people Israel astray.
14 But in the prophets of Jerusalem
I have seen a horrible thing:
they commit adultery and walk in lies;
they strengthen the hands of evildoers,
so that no one turns from his evil;
all of them have become like Sodom to me,
and its inhabitants like Gomorrah."
15 Therefore thus says the LORD of hosts concerning the
prophets:
"Behold, I will feed them with bitter food
and give them poisoned water to drink,
for from the prophets of Jerusalem
ungodliness has gone out into all the land."

[1]Septuagint; Hebrew *I*

OUR RIGHTEOUSNESS

The first two verses of Jeremiah 23 describe the Lord's lament at how poorly the kings took care of his people. He blamed the kings leading up to and including Zedekiah for leading the people away from God and into exile, for which he promised punishment. However, God's justice comes hand in hand with his mercy: while verse 3 promises punishment in exile, it also promises a united future back in the land. Not only did God promise to bring his people back to him, but he also said that they would one day no longer have to fear or worry because he himself would "set shepherds over them" to rule and protect them (v. 4).

Then Jeremiah described the ultimate ruler that God planned to raise up: a king from the line of David who would rule with wisdom, justice, and righteousness. The ruler is described as "a righteous Branch" of this family that God had blessed, a shepherd for his people who would be the ultimate ruler in every way: the Messiah, whom we know is Jesus. The people of Jeremiah's time were left to wonder about who God was promising through this passage, but believers today know the end of this particular story, having a different picture of the righteous and risen Savior.

Given the tumult of Jeremiah's time, the idea of a wise, just, and righteous ruler was undoubtedly appealing. Today, Jesus is the Savior of all who believe, but he is also the ruler over God's people as well. He is the Shepherd who is responsible for bringing God's people back from the nations where they were scattered, and he wears the crown under which all believers are able to unite. God's people have a ruler under which they can live safely and securely, and his name is Jesus.

16Thus says the LORD of hosts: "Do not listen to the words of the prophets
who prophesy to you, filling you with vain hopes. They speak visions of their
own minds, not from the mouth of the LORD. 17They say continually to those
who despise the word of the LORD, 'It shall be well with you'; and to everyone
who stubbornly follows his own heart, they say, 'No disaster shall come upon
you.'"

18 For who among them has stood in the council of the LORD
to see and to hear his word,
or who has paid attention to his word and listened?
19 Behold, the storm of the LORD!
Wrath has gone forth,
a whirling tempest;
it will burst upon the head of the wicked.
20 The anger of the LORD will not turn back
until he has executed and accomplished
the intents of his heart.
In the latter days you will understand it clearly.

21 "I did not send the prophets,
yet they ran;
I did not speak to them,
yet they prophesied.
22 But if they had stood in my council,
then they would have proclaimed my words to my people,
and they would have turned them from their evil way,
and from the evil of their deeds.

23"Am I a God at hand, declares the LORD, and not a God far away? 24Can a man
hide himself in secret places so that I cannot see him? declares the LORD. Do I not
fill heaven and earth? declares the LORD. 25I have heard what the prophets have
said who prophesy lies in my name, saying, 'I have dreamed, I have dreamed!'
26How long shall there be lies in the heart of the prophets who prophesy lies,
and who prophesy the deceit of their own heart, 27who think to make my people
forget my name by their dreams that they tell one another, even as their fathers
forgot my name for Baal? 28Let the prophet who has a dream tell the dream, but
let him who has my word speak my word faithfully. What has straw in common
with wheat? declares the LORD. 29Is not my word like fire, declares the LORD, and
like a hammer that breaks the rock in pieces? 30Therefore, behold, I am against
the prophets, declares the LORD, who steal my words from one another. 31Behold,
I am against the prophets, declares the LORD, who use their tongues and declare,
'declares the LORD.' 32Behold, I am against those who prophesy lying dreams, declares the LORD, and who tell them and lead my people astray by their lies and
their recklessness, when I did not send them or charge them. So they do not profit
this people at all, declares the LORD.

33"When one of this people, or a prophet or a priest asks you, 'What is the burden of the LORD?' you shall say to them, 'You are the burden,[1] and I will cast you
off, declares the LORD.' 34And as for the prophet, priest, or one of the people who
says, 'The burden of the LORD,' I will punish that man and his household. 35Thus
shall you say, every one to his neighbor and every one to his brother, 'What has
the LORD answered?' or 'What has the LORD spoken?' 36But 'the burden of the
LORD' you shall mention no more, for the burden is every man's own word, and
you pervert the words of the living God, the LORD of hosts, our God. 37Thus you
shall say to the prophet, 'What has the LORD answered you?' or 'What has the
LORD spoken?' 38But if you say, 'The burden of the LORD,' thus says the LORD, 'Because you have said these words, "The burden of the LORD," when I sent to you,

[1]Septuagint, Vulgate; Hebrew *What burden?*

JEREMIAH 23:25

TRUTH TELLERS

The Lord was aware that prophets were falsely claiming that they had dreams inspired by him. The people were misled and confused as to what God was actually saying. God has great disdain for those who teach falsely in his name and lead people astray.

In Matthew 7:15, Jesus warned his followers to beware of false prophets, comparing them to wolves disguised as sheep. How can believers tell the difference? Jesus answered that question: "You will recognize them by their fruits" (Mt 7:16). Look closely for the end results of their teachings. Are they bringing division rather than unity? Are they following the teachings of the Bible? And do these teachers personally exhibit the fruit of the Spirit (Gal 5:22–23)? False teachers will one day be brought to justice for leading God's people astray (2Pe 2), but until that day, it is the responsibility of believers to ensure that the teachers they follow are truly leading them closer to Jesus.

saying, "You shall not say, 'The burden of the LORD,'" 39 therefore, behold, I will surely lift you up[1] and cast you away from my presence, you and the city that I gave to you and your fathers. 40 And I will bring upon you everlasting reproach and perpetual shame, which shall not be forgotten.'"

The Good Figs and the Bad Figs

24 After Nebuchadnezzar king of Babylon had taken into exile from Jerusalem Jeconiah the son of Jehoiakim, king of Judah, together with the officials of Judah, the craftsmen, and the metal workers, and had brought them to Babylon, the LORD showed me this vision: behold, two baskets of figs placed before the temple of the LORD. 2 One basket had very good figs, like first-ripe figs, but the other basket had very bad figs, so bad that they could not be eaten. 3 And the LORD said to me, "What do you see, Jeremiah?" I said, "Figs, the good figs very good, and the bad figs very bad, so bad that they cannot be eaten."

4 Then the word of the LORD came to me: 5 "Thus says the LORD, the God of Israel: Like these good figs, so I will regard as good the exiles from Judah, whom I have sent away from this place to the land of the Chaldeans. 6 I will set my eyes on them for good, and I will bring them back to this land. I will build them up, and not tear them down; I will plant them, and not pluck them up. 7 I will give them a heart to know me, that I am the LORD, and they shall be my people and I will be their God, for they shall return to me with their whole heart.

8 "But thus says the LORD: Like the bad figs that are so bad they cannot be eaten, so will I treat Zedekiah the king of Judah, his officials, the remnant of Jerusalem who remain in this land, and those who dwell in the land of Egypt. 9 I will make them a horror[2] to all the kingdoms of the earth, to be a reproach, a byword, a taunt, and a curse in all the places where I shall drive them. 10 And I will send sword, famine, and pestilence upon them, until they shall be utterly destroyed from the land that I gave to them and their fathers."

Seventy Years of Captivity

25 The word that came to Jeremiah concerning all the people of Judah, in the fourth year of Jehoiakim the son of Josiah, king of Judah (that was the first year of Nebuchadnezzar king of Babylon), 2 which Jeremiah the prophet spoke to all the people of Judah and all the inhabitants of Jerusalem: 3 "For twenty-three years, from the thirteenth year of Josiah the son of Amon, king of Judah, to this day, the word of the LORD has come to me, and I have spoken persistently to you, but you have not listened. 4 You have neither listened nor inclined your ears to hear, although the LORD persistently sent to you all his servants the prophets, 5 saying, 'Turn now, every one of you, from his evil way and evil deeds, and dwell upon the land that the LORD has given to you and your fathers from of old and forever. 6 Do not go after other gods to serve and worship them, or provoke me to anger with the work of your hands. Then I will do you no harm.' 7 Yet you have not listened to me, declares the LORD, that you might provoke me to anger with the work of your hands to your own harm.

8 "Therefore thus says the LORD of hosts: Because you have not obeyed my words, 9 behold, I will send for all the tribes of the north, declares the LORD, and for Nebuchadnezzar the king of Babylon, my servant, and I will bring them against this land and its inhabitants, and against all these surrounding nations. I will devote them to destruction, and make them a horror, a hissing, and an everlasting desolation. 10 Moreover, I will banish from them the voice of mirth and the voice of gladness, the voice of the bridegroom and the voice of the bride, the grinding of the millstones and the light of the lamp. 11 This whole land shall become a ruin and a waste, and these nations shall serve the king of Babylon seventy years. 12 Then after seventy years are completed, I will punish the king of Babylon and that na-

[1] Or *surely forget you* [2] Compare Septuagint; Hebrew *horror for evil*

JEREMIAH 24:1–10

WORKING TOGETHER FOR GOD

This description of the good and bad figs is used to show that God had a purpose for sending some of his people away from their land. In allowing some of his people to be exiled, God was actually separating them from the influences of those who remained defiantly in Jerusalem with hardened hearts toward God. As Romans 8:28 says, "All things work together for good, for those who are called according to his purpose." Although exile may have seemed like a punishment, God was actually preparing and refining his people for when they would return.

God's good plan for his people is consistent throughout the Old Testament, and it continues to hold true for believers today. In John 10:28, Jesus said of his followers, "No one will snatch them out of my hand." Those who belong to Jesus cannot be removed from his hand, and God will always work toward the good of those who love him. These verses affirm Jeremiah's word to the people of his day that God would be with them. They also affirm Jesus' promise of care and concern for his followers today.

JEREMIAH 25:11–12

GOD'S TIMING

These verses describe God's timeline for allowing Jerusalem to fall under the rule of Babylon for 70 years. Despite the fact that the people had turned away from following him and felt the consequences of that disobedience, God promised deliverance and retribution for the oppression the people experienced under

(continued on next page)

tion, the land of the Chaldeans, for their iniquity, declares the LORD, making the land an everlasting waste. 13I will bring upon that land all the words that I have uttered against it, everything written in this book, which Jeremiah prophesied against all the nations. 14For many nations and great kings shall make slaves even of them, and I will recompense them according to their deeds and the work of their hands."

The Cup of the LORD's Wrath

15Thus the LORD, the God of Israel, said to me: "Take from my hand this cup of the wine of wrath, and make all the nations to whom I send you drink it. 16They shall drink and stagger and be crazed because of the sword that I am sending among them."

17So I took the cup from the LORD's hand, and made all the nations to whom the LORD sent me drink it: 18Jerusalem and the cities of Judah, its kings and officials, to make them a desolation and a waste, a hissing and a curse, as at this day; 19Pharaoh king of Egypt, his servants, his officials, all his people, 20and all the mixed tribes among them; all the kings of the land of Uz and all the kings of the land of the Philistines (Ashkelon, Gaza, Ekron, and the remnant of Ashdod); 21Edom, Moab, and the sons of Ammon; 22all the kings of Tyre, all the kings of Sidon, and the kings of the coastland across the sea; 23Dedan, Tema, Buz, and all who cut the corners of their hair; 24all the kings of Arabia and all the kings of the mixed tribes who dwell in the desert; 25all the kings of Zimri, all the kings of Elam, and all the kings of Media; 26all the kings of the north, far and near, one after another, and all the kingdoms of the world that are on the face of the earth. And after them the king of Babylon[1] shall drink.

27"Then you shall say to them, 'Thus says the LORD of hosts, the God of Israel: Drink, be drunk and vomit, fall and rise no more, because of the sword that I am sending among you.'

28"And if they refuse to accept the cup from your hand to drink, then you shall say to them, 'Thus says the LORD of hosts: You must drink! 29For behold, I begin to work disaster at the city that is called by my name, and shall you go unpunished? You shall not go unpunished, for I am summoning a sword against all the inhabitants of the earth, declares the LORD of hosts.'

30"You, therefore, shall prophesy against them all these words, and say to them:

"'The LORD will roar from on high,
    and from his holy habitation utter his voice;
he will roar mightily against his fold,
    and shout, like those who tread grapes,
    against all the inhabitants of the earth.
31 The clamor will resound to the ends of the earth,
    for the LORD has an indictment against the nations;
he is entering into judgment with all flesh,
    and the wicked he will put to the sword,
                declares the LORD.'

32 "Thus says the LORD of hosts:
Behold, disaster is going forth
    from nation to nation,
and a great tempest is stirring
    from the farthest parts of the earth!

33"And those pierced by the LORD on that day shall extend from one end of the earth to the other. They shall not be lamented, or gathered, or buried; they shall be dung on the surface of the ground.

[1]Hebrew *Sheshach*, a code name for Babylon

(God's Timing, continued)

Babylonian rule. God maintained a steadfast timeline for what would happen to them next, determined how long they would be punished, and promised that they would eventually be redeemed. Seventy years may seem like a long time, but there is no doubt that God had a very specific purpose for his timing.

In Mark 13:32, Jesus discussed the time and day of his return, and he made it clear that no one knows the day except for the Father. Neither the angels nor even Jesus himself knows the day and hour when he is to return, so Jesus warned his followers that it could be any day. Seventy years was God's timeline during the time of Jeremiah, but for believers today the only certainty regarding God's timing is that it is completely up to him. Therefore, remember these words of Jesus: "Be on guard, keep awake. For you do not know when the time will come" (Mk 13:33).

34 "Wail, you shepherds, and cry out,
and roll in ashes, you lords of the flock,
for the days of your slaughter and dispersion have come,
and you shall fall like a choice vessel.
35 No refuge will remain for the shepherds,
nor escape for the lords of the flock.
36 A voice—the cry of the shepherds,
and the wail of the lords of the flock!
For the LORD is laying waste their pasture,
37 and the peaceful folds are devastated
because of the fierce anger of the LORD.
38 Like a lion he has left his lair,
for their land has become a waste
because of the sword of the oppressor,
and because of his fierce anger."

Jeremiah Threatened with Death

26 In the beginning of the reign of Jehoiakim the son of Josiah, king of Judah,
this word came from the LORD: 2"Thus says the LORD: Stand in the court of
the LORD's house, and speak to all the cities of Judah that come to worship in the
house of the LORD all the words that I command you to speak to them; do not hold
back a word. 3It may be they will listen, and every one turn from his evil way, that
I may relent of the disaster that I intend to do to them because of their evil deeds.
4You shall say to them, 'Thus says the LORD: If you will not listen to me, to walk in
my law that I have set before you, 5and to listen to the words of my servants the
prophets whom I send to you urgently, though you have not listened, 6then I will
make this house like Shiloh, and I will make this city a curse for all the nations
of the earth.'"
7The priests and the prophets and all the people heard Jeremiah speaking
these words in the house of the LORD. 8And when Jeremiah had finished speaking
all that the LORD had commanded him to speak to all the people, then the priests
and the prophets and all the people laid hold of him, saying, "You shall die! 9Why
have you prophesied in the name of the LORD, saying, 'This house shall be like
Shiloh, and this city shall be desolate, without inhabitant'?" And all the people
gathered around Jeremiah in the house of the LORD.
10When the officials of Judah heard these things, they came up from the king's
house to the house of the LORD and took their seat in the entry of the New Gate
of the house of the LORD. 11Then the priests and the prophets said to the officials
and to all the people, "This man deserves the sentence of death, because he has
prophesied against this city, as you have heard with your own ears."
12Then Jeremiah spoke to all the officials and all the people, saying, "The LORD
sent me to prophesy against this house and this city all the words you have heard.
13Now therefore mend your ways and your deeds, and obey the voice of the LORD
your God, and the LORD will relent of the disaster that he has pronounced against
you. 14But as for me, behold, I am in your hands. Do with me as seems good and
right to you. 15Only know for certain that if you put me to death, you will bring innocent blood upon yourselves and upon this city and its inhabitants, for in truth
the LORD sent me to you to speak all these words in your ears."

Jeremiah Spared from Death

16Then the officials and all the people said to the priests and the prophets,
"This man does not deserve the sentence of death, for he has spoken to us in
the name of the LORD our God." 17And certain of the elders of the land arose and
spoke to all the assembled people, saying, 18"Micah of Moresheth prophesied in
the days of Hezekiah king of Judah, and said to all the people of Judah: 'Thus says
the LORD of hosts,

JEREMIAH 26:1–9

PERSECUTED FOR SPEAKING THE TRUTH

God was very clear with Jeremiah that he did not want him to edit anything out of the message God had for his people. And in return for speaking God's truth just as he was asked to, Jeremiah faced death threats from the very people he was trying to help.

In the same way, Jesus experienced persecution for the truth that he spoke. On multiple occasions people tried to kill Jesus because of something he said, but he never backed down from the truth that he proclaimed (Lk 4:29; Jn 8:59; 10:22–39). Jeremiah's treatment for speaking God's message foreshadowed the treatment Jesus would receive. Jesus warned that his followers were sure to face some level of persecution, but he taught that suffering should be regarded as a blessing (Mt 5:10–12)—a sign that God's countercultural message to a sinful world is having an impact.

"'Zion shall be plowed as a field;
Jerusalem shall become a heap of ruins,
and the mountain of the house a wooded height.'

19 Did Hezekiah king of Judah and all Judah put him to death? Did he not fear the LORD and entreat the favor of the LORD, and did not the LORD relent of the disaster that he had pronounced against them? But we are about to bring great disaster upon ourselves."

20 There was another man who prophesied in the name of the LORD, Uriah the son of Shemaiah from Kiriath-jearim. He prophesied against this city and against this land in words like those of Jeremiah. 21 And when King Jehoiakim, with all his warriors and all the officials, heard his words, the king sought to put him to death. But when Uriah heard of it, he was afraid and fled and escaped to Egypt. 22 Then King Jehoiakim sent to Egypt certain men, Elnathan the son of Achbor and others with him, 23 and they took Uriah from Egypt and brought him to King Jehoiakim, who struck him down with the sword and dumped his dead body into the burial place of the common people.

24 But the hand of Ahikam the son of Shaphan was with Jeremiah so that he was not given over to the people to be put to death.

The Yoke of Nebuchadnezzar

27 In the beginning of the reign of Zedekiah[1] the son of Josiah, king of Judah, this word came to Jeremiah from the LORD. 2 Thus the LORD said to me: "Make yourself straps and yoke-bars, and put them on your neck. 3 Send word[2] to the king of Edom, the king of Moab, the king of the sons of Ammon, the king of Tyre, and the king of Sidon by the hand of the envoys who have come to Jerusalem to Zedekiah king of Judah. 4 Give them this charge for their masters: 'Thus says the LORD of hosts, the God of Israel: This is what you shall say to your masters: 5 "It is I who by my great power and my outstretched arm have made the earth, with the men and animals that are on the earth, and I give it to whomever it seems right to me. 6 Now I have given all these lands into the hand of Nebuchadnezzar, the king of Babylon, my servant, and I have given him also the beasts of the field to serve him. 7 All the nations shall serve him and his son and his grandson, until the time of his own land comes. Then many nations and great kings shall make him their slave.

8 "'"But if any nation or kingdom will not serve this Nebuchadnezzar king of Babylon, and put its neck under the yoke of the king of Babylon, I will punish that nation with the sword, with famine, and with pestilence, declares the LORD, until I have consumed it by his hand. 9 So do not listen to your prophets, your diviners, your dreamers, your fortune-tellers, or your sorcerers, who are saying to you, 'You shall not serve the king of Babylon.' 10 For it is a lie that they are prophesying to you, with the result that you will be removed far from your land, and I will drive you out, and you will perish. 11 But any nation that will bring its neck under the yoke of the king of Babylon and serve him, I will leave on its own land, to work it and dwell there, declares the LORD."'"

12 To Zedekiah king of Judah I spoke in like manner: "Bring your necks under the yoke of the king of Babylon, and serve him and his people and live. 13 Why will you and your people die by the sword, by famine, and by pestilence, as the LORD has spoken concerning any nation that will not serve the king of Babylon? 14 Do not listen to the words of the prophets who are saying to you, 'You shall not serve the king of Babylon,' for it is a lie that they are prophesying to you. 15 I have not sent them, declares the LORD, but they are prophesying falsely in my name, with the result that I will drive you out and you will perish, you and the prophets who are prophesying to you."

16 Then I spoke to the priests and to all this people, saying, "Thus says the LORD:

[1] Or *Jehoiakim* [2] Hebrew *Send them*

JEREMIAH 27:21–22

PUNISHMENT AND REDEMPTION

These verses refer to valuable treasures and articles that decorated the house of the Lord and the palace of the king. No doubt these would be some of the first things that the Babylonians would take as they gained control of the city. However, even though God said he was going to allow Jerusalem to be overrun and the temple treasures removed, he also promised that these treasures would one day be returned.

This prophecy is similar to the parable of the lost coin in Luke 15:8–10. Although God allowed the valuable treasures of the temple to be taken, he assured the people that he would bring them back. God used the Babylonians to exact the justice that his people had brought upon themselves, but God also showed the greatness of his mercy by promising to one day bring the people, his true temple treasures, back to himself and to their land. No matter how far away from God a thing or person may seem to be, he is always capable of rescuing and redeeming that which belongs to him.

JEREMIAH 28:1–17

CONFRONTING FALSE PROPHETS

Here Jeremiah was forced to stand up to one of the false prophets that God had been warning his people against for so long. Jeremiah was told by God to wear a yoke around his neck—demonstrating that God would soon put the nations under the yoke of Nebuchadnezzar, king

(continued on next page)

Do not listen to the words of your prophets who are prophesying to you, saying, 'Behold, the vessels of the LORD's house will now shortly be brought back from Babylon,' for it is a lie that they are prophesying to you. 17Do not listen to them; serve the king of Babylon and live. Why should this city become a desolation? 18If they are prophets, and if the word of the LORD is with them, then let them intercede with the LORD of hosts, that the vessels that are left in the house of the LORD, in the house of the king of Judah, and in Jerusalem may not go to Babylon. 19For thus says the LORD of hosts concerning the pillars, the sea, the stands, and the rest of the vessels that are left in this city, 20which Nebuchadnezzar king of Babylon did not take away, when he took into exile from Jerusalem to Babylon Jeconiah the son of Jehoiakim, king of Judah, and all the nobles of Judah and Jerusalem— 21thus says the LORD of hosts, the God of Israel, concerning the vessels that are left in the house of the LORD, in the house of the king of Judah, and in Jerusalem: 22They shall be carried to Babylon and remain there until the day when I visit them, declares the LORD. Then I will bring them back and restore them to this place."

Hananiah the False Prophet

28 In that same year, at the beginning of the reign of Zedekiah king of Judah, in the fifth month of the fourth year, Hananiah the son of Azzur, the prophet from Gibeon, spoke to me in the house of the LORD, in the presence of the priests and all the people, saying, 2"Thus says the LORD of hosts, the God of Israel: I have broken the yoke of the king of Babylon. 3Within two years I will bring back to this place all the vessels of the LORD's house, which Nebuchadnezzar king of Babylon took away from this place and carried to Babylon. 4I will also bring back to this place Jeconiah the son of Jehoiakim, king of Judah, and all the exiles from Judah who went to Babylon, declares the LORD, for I will break the yoke of the king of Babylon."

5Then the prophet Jeremiah spoke to Hananiah the prophet in the presence of the priests and all the people who were standing in the house of the LORD, 6and the prophet Jeremiah said, "Amen! May the LORD do so; may the LORD make the words that you have prophesied come true, and bring back to this place from Babylon the vessels of the house of the LORD, and all the exiles. 7Yet hear now this word that I speak in your hearing and in the hearing of all the people. 8The prophets who preceded you and me from ancient times prophesied war, famine, and pestilence against many countries and great kingdoms. 9As for the prophet who prophesies peace, when the word of that prophet comes to pass, then it will be known that the LORD has truly sent the prophet."

10Then the prophet Hananiah took the yoke-bars from the neck of Jeremiah the prophet and broke them. 11And Hananiah spoke in the presence of all the people, saying, "Thus says the LORD: Even so will I break the yoke of Nebuchadnezzar king of Babylon from the neck of all the nations within two years." But Jeremiah the prophet went his way.

12Sometime after the prophet Hananiah had broken the yoke-bars from off the neck of Jeremiah the prophet, the word of the LORD came to Jeremiah: 13"Go, tell Hananiah, 'Thus says the LORD: You have broken wooden bars, but you have made in their place bars of iron. 14For thus says the LORD of hosts, the God of Israel: I have put upon the neck of all these nations an iron yoke to serve Nebuchadnezzar king of Babylon, and they shall serve him, for I have given to him even the beasts of the field.'" 15And Jeremiah the prophet said to the prophet Hananiah, "Listen, Hananiah, the LORD has not sent you, and you have made this people trust in a lie. 16Therefore thus says the LORD: 'Behold, I will remove you from the face of the earth. This year you shall die, because you have uttered rebellion against the LORD.'"

17In that same year, in the seventh month, the prophet Hananiah died.

Jeremiah's Letter to the Exiles

29 These are the words of the letter that Jeremiah the prophet sent from Jerusalem to the surviving elders of the exiles, and to the priests, the prophets, and all the people, whom Nebuchadnezzar had taken into exile from Jerusalem to Babylon. 2This was after King Jeconiah and the queen mother, the eunuchs, the officials of Judah and Jerusalem, the craftsmen, and the metal workers had departed from Jerusalem. 3The letter was sent by the hand of Elasah the son of Shaphan and Gemariah the son of Hilkiah, whom Zedekiah king of Judah sent to Babylon to Nebuchadnezzar king of Babylon. It said: 4"Thus says the LORD of hosts, the God of Israel, to all the exiles whom I have sent into exile from Jerusalem to Babylon: 5Build houses and live in them; plant gardens and eat their produce. 6Take wives and have sons and daughters; take wives for your sons, and give your daughters in marriage, that they may bear sons and daughters; multiply there, and do not decrease. 7But seek the welfare of the city where I have sent you into exile, and pray to the LORD on its behalf, for in its welfare you will find your welfare. 8For thus says the LORD of hosts, the God of Israel: Do not let your prophets and your diviners who are among you deceive you, and do not listen to the dreams that they dream,[1] 9for it is a lie that they are prophesying to you in my name; I did not send them, declares the LORD.

10"For thus says the LORD: When seventy years are completed for Babylon, I will visit you, and I will fulfill to you my promise and bring you back to this place. 11For I know the plans I have for you, declares the LORD, plans for welfare[2] and not for evil, to give you a future and a hope. 12Then you will call upon me and come and pray to me, and I will hear you. 13You will seek me and find me, when you seek me with all your heart. 14I will be found by you, declares the LORD, and I will restore your fortunes and gather you from all the nations and all the places where I have driven you, declares the LORD, and I will bring you back to the place from which I sent you into exile.

15"Because you have said, 'The LORD has raised up prophets for us in Babylon,' 16thus says the LORD concerning the king who sits on the throne of David, and concerning all the people who dwell in this city, your kinsmen who did not go out with you into exile: 17'Thus says the LORD of hosts, behold, I am sending on them sword, famine, and pestilence, and I will make them like vile figs that are so rotten they cannot be eaten. 18I will pursue them with sword, famine, and pestilence, and will make them a horror to all the kingdoms of the earth, to be a curse, a terror, a hissing, and a reproach among all the nations where I have driven them, 19because they did not pay attention to my words, declares the LORD, that I persistently sent to you by my servants the prophets, but you would not listen, declares the LORD.' 20Hear the word of the LORD, all you exiles whom I sent away from Jerusalem to Babylon: 21'Thus says the LORD of hosts, the God of Israel, concerning Ahab the son of Kolaiah and Zedekiah the son of Maaseiah, who are prophesying a lie to you in my name: Behold, I will deliver them into the hand of Nebuchadnezzar king of Babylon, and he shall strike them down before your eyes. 22Because of them this curse shall be used by all the exiles from Judah in Babylon: "The LORD make you like Zedekiah and Ahab, whom the king of Babylon roasted in the fire," 23because they have done an outrageous thing in Israel, they have committed adultery with their neighbors' wives, and they have spoken in my name lying words that I did not command them. I am the one who knows, and I am witness, declares the LORD.'"

Shemaiah's False Prophecy

24To Shemaiah of Nehelam you shall say: 25"Thus says the LORD of hosts, the God of Israel: You have sent letters in your name to all the people who are in

[1]Hebrew *your dreams, which you cause to dream* [2]Or *peace*

(Confronting False Prophets, continued)

of Babylon (Jer 27:2). Hananiah had been prophesying directly against everything that Jeremiah was saying, telling the people what they wanted to hear as opposed to the actual truth of God (Jer 28:1–11). Finally God told Jeremiah to go to Hananiah and condemn him for the lies that he had been spreading (vv. 12–14). Jeremiah did so, also prophesying that Hananiah would die within that same year (vv. 15–16).

In a similar way, Jesus constantly battled the Pharisees and other religious leaders who claimed to speak for God and undermined the message of Jesus (Jn 8:42–58). After his resurrection, Jesus was vindicated, and the religious leaders were exposed as frauds. Similarly, after Hananiah's death that same year (Jer 28:17) and the fulfillment of the rest of Jeremiah's prophecies, Jeremiah too was vindicated, and his word was proven as truth.

HOPE FOR THE FUTURE

Chapter 29 is Jeremiah's letter to those exiled in 597 BC, and it was written sometime between that deportation in 597 and the destruction of Jerusalem — and final exile — in 586. God told Jeremiah that he had allowed some of his people to be taken to Babylon and that he would one day bring them back to the city of Jerusalem. The idea of exile could hardly be seen as a blessing for Jeremiah's audience, a fact made even more difficult because not everyone had been taken away. Of the people who were still in Jerusalem, many remained defiant to God and lived with hardened hearts. Therefore, Jeremiah wrote this letter to the people who had been sent into exile to assure them that God had a plan for them and that everything was going to work out for their good. Verse 11 would have greatly encouraged these Israelites who were captives in foreign territory.

Taken in a broader context, this verse can also be seen as God's promise to all his people. The term "you" is plural, not singular, and we can expand it to point toward God's plan for anyone and everyone who follows him. Although believers may want to take this verse and apply it to their own lives as an assurance of God's individual plan for them, it is much bigger than the everyday decisions modern-day believers often apply it to: Deciding which college to attend, which job to take, and which city to move to are all trivial matters when compared to the future hope that God promises to all of his people.

Does God have plans for individuals? Absolutely, but this verse is so much more than a promise of personal benefit. This promise of redemption and salvation is brought about through the generous sovereignty of God. Jeremiah 29:11 was a future hope for the scattered people, and believers today can also see it as a future hope of eternal redemption and life with God — strong encouragement for those who endure serious hardship and trial. Then as now, God is the only reason for our hope for the future.

Jerusalem, and to Zephaniah the son of Maaseiah the priest, and to all the priests,
saying, 26"The LORD has made you priest instead of Jehoiada the priest, to have
charge in the house of the LORD over every madman who prophesies, to put him
in the stocks and neck irons. 27Now why have you not rebuked Jeremiah of Anathoth who is prophesying to you? 28For he has sent to us in Babylon, saying, "Your
exile will be long; build houses and live in them, and plant gardens and eat their
produce."'"

29Zephaniah the priest read this letter in the hearing of Jeremiah the prophet.
30Then the word of the LORD came to Jeremiah: 31"Send to all the exiles, saying,
'Thus says the LORD concerning Shemaiah of Nehelam: Because Shemaiah had
prophesied to you when I did not send him, and has made you trust in a lie,
32therefore thus says the LORD: Behold, I will punish Shemaiah of Nehelam and
his descendants. He shall not have anyone living among this people, and he shall
not see the good that I will do to my people, declares the LORD, for he has spoken
rebellion against the LORD.'"

Restoration for Israel and Judah

30 The word that came to Jeremiah from the LORD: 2"Thus says the LORD, the
God of Israel: Write in a book all the words that I have spoken to you. 3For
behold, days are coming, declares the LORD, when I will restore the fortunes of my
people, Israel and Judah, says the LORD, and I will bring them back to the land that
I gave to their fathers, and they shall take possession of it."

4These are the words that the LORD spoke concerning Israel and Judah:

5 "Thus says the LORD:
We have heard a cry of panic,
of terror, and no peace.
6 Ask now, and see,
can a man bear a child?
Why then do I see every man
with his hands on his stomach like a woman in labor?
Why has every face turned pale?
7 Alas! That day is so great
there is none like it;
it is a time of distress for Jacob;
yet he shall be saved out of it.

8"And it shall come to pass in that day, declares the LORD of hosts, that I will
break his yoke from off your neck, and I will burst your bonds, and foreigners
shall no more make a servant of him.[1] 9But they shall serve the LORD their God
and David their king, whom I will raise up for them.

10 "Then fear not, O Jacob my servant, declares the LORD,
nor be dismayed, O Israel;
for behold, I will save you from far away,
and your offspring from the land of their captivity.
Jacob shall return and have quiet and ease,
and none shall make him afraid.
11 For I am with you to save you,
declares the LORD;
I will make a full end of all the nations
among whom I scattered you,
but of you I will not make a full end.
I will discipline you in just measure,
and I will by no means leave you unpunished.

1Or *serve him*

12 "For thus says the LORD:
Your hurt is incurable,
and your wound is grievous.
13 There is none to uphold your cause,
no medicine for your wound,
no healing for you.
14 All your lovers have forgotten you;
they care nothing for you;
for I have dealt you the blow of an enemy,
the punishment of a merciless foe,
because your guilt is great,
because your sins are flagrant.
15 Why do you cry out over your hurt?
Your pain is incurable.
Because your guilt is great,
because your sins are flagrant,
I have done these things to you.
16 Therefore all who devour you shall be devoured,
and all your foes, every one of them, shall go into
captivity;
those who plunder you shall be plundered,
and all who prey on you I will make a prey.
17 For I will restore health to you,
and your wounds I will heal,
declares the LORD,
because they have called you an outcast:
'It is Zion, for whom no one cares!'

18 "Thus says the LORD:
Behold, I will restore the fortunes of the tents of Jacob
and have compassion on his dwellings;
the city shall be rebuilt on its mound,
and the palace shall stand where it used to be.
19 Out of them shall come songs of thanksgiving,
and the voices of those who celebrate.
I will multiply them, and they shall not be few;
I will make them honored, and they shall not be small.
20 Their children shall be as they were of old,
and their congregation shall be established before me,
and I will punish all who oppress them.
21 Their prince shall be one of themselves;
their ruler shall come out from their midst;
I will make him draw near, and he shall approach me,
for who would dare of himself to approach me?
declares the LORD.
22 And you shall be my people,
and I will be your God."

23 Behold the storm of the LORD!
Wrath has gone forth,
a whirling tempest;
it will burst upon the head of the wicked.
24 The fierce anger of the LORD will not turn back
until he has executed and accomplished
the intentions of his mind.
In the latter days you will understand this.

The LORD Will Turn Mourning to Joy

31 "At that time, declares the LORD, I will be the God of all the clans of Israel,
and they shall be my people."

2 Thus says the LORD:
"The people who survived the sword
found grace in the wilderness;
when Israel sought for rest,
3 the LORD appeared to him[1] from far away.
I have loved you with an everlasting love;
therefore I have continued my faithfulness to you.
4 Again I will build you, and you shall be built,
O virgin Israel!
Again you shall adorn yourself with tambourines
and shall go forth in the dance of the merrymakers.
5 Again you shall plant vineyards
on the mountains of Samaria;
the planters shall plant
and shall enjoy the fruit.
6 For there shall be a day when watchmen will call
in the hill country of Ephraim:
'Arise, and let us go up to Zion,
to the LORD our God.'"

7 For thus says the LORD:
"Sing aloud with gladness for Jacob,
and raise shouts for the chief of the nations;
proclaim, give praise, and say,
'O LORD, save your people,
the remnant of Israel.'
8 Behold, I will bring them from the north country
and gather them from the farthest parts of the earth,
among them the blind and the lame,
the pregnant woman and she who is in labor, together;
a great company, they shall return here.
9 With weeping they shall come,
and with pleas for mercy I will lead them back,
I will make them walk by brooks of water,
in a straight path in which they shall not stumble,
for I am a father to Israel,
and Ephraim is my firstborn.

10 "Hear the word of the LORD, O nations,
and declare it in the coastlands far away;
say, 'He who scattered Israel will gather him,
and will keep him as a shepherd keeps his flock.'
11 For the LORD has ransomed Jacob
and has redeemed him from hands too strong for him.
12 They shall come and sing aloud on the height of Zion,
and they shall be radiant over the goodness of the LORD,
over the grain, the wine, and the oil,
and over the young of the flock and the herd;
their life shall be like a watered garden,
and they shall languish no more.
13 Then shall the young women rejoice in the dance,
and the young men and the old shall be merry.

---

[1]Septuagint; Hebrew *me*

I will turn their mourning into joy;
I will comfort them, and give them gladness for sorrow.
14 I will feast the soul of the priests with abundance,
and my people shall be satisfied with my goodness,
declares the LORD."

15 Thus says the LORD:
"A voice is heard in Ramah,
lamentation and bitter weeping.
Rachel is weeping for her children;
she refuses to be comforted for her children,
because they are no more."

16 Thus says the LORD:
"Keep your voice from weeping,
and your eyes from tears,
for there is a reward for your work,
declares the LORD,
and they shall come back from the land of the enemy.
17 There is hope for your future,
declares the LORD,
and your children shall come back to their own country.
18 I have heard Ephraim grieving,
'You have disciplined me, and I was disciplined,
like an untrained calf;
bring me back that I may be restored,
for you are the LORD my God.
19 For after I had turned away, I relented,
and after I was instructed, I struck my thigh;
I was ashamed, and I was confounded,
because I bore the disgrace of my youth.'
20 Is Ephraim my dear son?
Is he my darling child?
For as often as I speak against him,
I do remember him still.
Therefore my heart[1] yearns for him;
I will surely have mercy on him,
declares the LORD.

21 "Set up road markers for yourself;
make yourself guideposts;
consider well the highway,
the road by which you went.
Return, O virgin Israel,
return to these your cities.
22 How long will you waver,
O faithless daughter?
For the LORD has created a new thing on the earth:
a woman encircles a man."

23 Thus says the LORD of hosts, the God of Israel: "Once more they shall use these words in the land of Judah and in its cities, when I restore their fortunes:

" 'The LORD bless you, O habitation of righteousness,
O holy hill!'

JEREMIAH 31:15

WEEPING FOR HER CHILDREN

In chapter 31, Jeremiah prophesies the future restoration of the people of God. From glowing predictions of grace and mercy, Jeremiah once again confronts the tragic conditions of his day. He speaks of Rachel at Ramah weeping over the loss of her children (v. 15). An ancestress of the people of God, Rachel was also weeping over the exile of God's people. The Lord invites Rachel to stop mourning because God would be faithful to restore his wayward people once again (vv. 16–17).

Matthew quotes Jeremiah 31:15 in Matthew 2:18 when Herod, in an attempt to kill the newborn Jesus, killed all of the infant boys born in Bethlehem. It is impossible to come to terms with the deaths of the infant boys in Matthew 2. But Jesus and his parents escaped this attempt on his life and went to Egypt for a time after having been warned in a dream. In the book of Jeremiah, God took his people through exile, but he eventually brought them back to their home country to live and worship him. Similarly, God brought his Son Jesus through attempted murder, both in Bethlehem and on the cross, to save and redeem the world so that people may live and worship him. In great darkness, there is great hope.

[1] Hebrew *bowels*

24 And Judah and all its cities shall dwell there together, and the farmers and those
who wander with their flocks. 25 For I will satisfy the weary soul, and every languishing soul I will replenish."
26 At this I awoke and looked, and my sleep was pleasant to me.
27 "Behold, the days are coming, declares the LORD, when I will sow the house
of Israel and the house of Judah with the seed of man and the seed of beast. 28 And
it shall come to pass that as I have watched over them to pluck up and break down,
to overthrow, destroy, and bring harm, so I will watch over them to build and to
plant, declares the LORD. 29 In those days they shall no longer say:

"'The fathers have eaten sour grapes,
and the children's teeth are set on edge.'

30 But everyone shall die for his own iniquity. Each man who eats sour grapes, his
teeth shall be set on edge.

The New Covenant

31 "Behold, the days are coming, declares the LORD, when I will make a new
covenant with the house of Israel and the house of Judah, 32 not like the covenant
that I made with their fathers on the day when I took them by the hand to bring
them out of the land of Egypt, my covenant that they broke, though I was their
husband, declares the LORD. 33 For this is the covenant that I will make with the
house of Israel after those days, declares the LORD: I will put my law within them,
and I will write it on their hearts. And I will be their God, and they shall be my
people. 34 And no longer shall each one teach his neighbor and each his brother,
saying, 'Know the LORD,' for they shall all know me, from the least of them to the
greatest, declares the LORD. For I will forgive their iniquity, and I will remember
their sin no more."

35 Thus says the LORD,
who gives the sun for light by day
and the fixed order of the moon and the stars for light by night,
who stirs up the sea so that its waves roar—
the LORD of hosts is his name:
36 "If this fixed order departs
from before me, declares the LORD,
then shall the offspring of Israel cease
from being a nation before me forever."

37 Thus says the LORD:
"If the heavens above can be measured,
and the foundations of the earth below can be explored,
then I will cast off all the offspring of Israel
for all that they have done,
declares the LORD."

38 "Behold, the days are coming, declares the LORD, when the city shall be
rebuilt for the LORD from the Tower of Hananel to the Corner Gate. 39 And the
measuring line shall go out farther, straight to the hill Gareb, and shall then
turn to Goah. 40 The whole valley of the dead bodies and the ashes, and all the
fields as far as the brook Kidron, to the corner of the Horse Gate toward the east,
shall be sacred to the LORD. It shall not be plucked up or overthrown anymore
forever."

Jeremiah Buys a Field During the Siege

32 The word that came to Jeremiah from the LORD in the tenth year of Zedekiah king of Judah, which was the eighteenth year of Nebuchadnezzar.
2 At that time the army of the king of Babylon was besieging Jerusalem, and Jeremiah the prophet was shut up in the court of the guard that was in the palace of

NEW COVENANT

In this passage, Jeremiah wrote of the new covenant that was to be later fulfilled by the Messiah. In Luke 22:20, when Jesus said, "This cup that is poured out for you is the new covenant in my blood," his reference to a new covenant echoed this passage from Jeremiah.

Writing during a time of great national turmoil, Jeremiah described what the people's relationship with their God would one day look like, and believers today can say that they now live in the time to which Jeremiah was referring. Jesus fulfilled this Scripture, and the lives of believers are today defined by the terms of this new covenant.

Hebrews 8 explains that God wrote this new covenant for his people, and in doing so, he made the old covenant "obsolete" (Heb 8:13). When Jesus came and sealed the new covenant between God and his people, he eliminated the covenant he had made with Israel at Sinai. This is why Christians are no longer required to live in accordance with much of the Old Testament law. Under the old covenant, the Israelites had a plethora of tangible requirements to perform to show their obedience to God. For example, they had to sacrifice animals to atone for their sins. However, under the new covenant, believers who recognize their need for a Savior joyfully accept Jesus as the Son of God and the perfect sacrifice for their sins, and they show their obedience by telling others about this great news. There is no longer a need to sacrifice animals because Jesus is the final and eternal sacrifice for sins.

Jeremiah's words showed why he had great reason to hope in what was yet to come. When he said "the days are coming," he pointed toward a time when the antiquated religion of the past was to be replaced with a greater one that better reflected God's close and personal relationship with his people. He looked forward to a time when everyone will know the Lord, "from the least of them to the greatest" (Jer 31:34). Jesus came to earth to offer salvation to everyone, both "the least" and "the greatest," and in doing so he fulfilled the new covenant between mankind and God that allows believers to know God and to have his law written on their hearts (vv. 33 – 34).

the king of Judah. 3For Zedekiah king of Judah had imprisoned him, saying, "Why do you prophesy and say, 'Thus says the LORD: Behold, I am giving this city into the hand of the king of Babylon, and he shall capture it; 4Zedekiah king of Judah shall not escape out of the hand of the Chaldeans, but shall surely be given into the hand of the king of Babylon, and shall speak with him face to face and see him eye to eye. 5And he shall take Zedekiah to Babylon, and there he shall remain until I visit him, declares the LORD. Though you fight against the Chaldeans, you shall not succeed'?"

6Jeremiah said, "The word of the LORD came to me: 7Behold, Hanamel the son of Shallum your uncle will come to you and say, 'Buy my field that is at Anathoth, for the right of redemption by purchase is yours.' 8Then Hanamel my cousin came to me in the court of the guard, in accordance with the word of the LORD, and said to me, 'Buy my field that is at Anathoth in the land of Benjamin, for the right of possession and redemption is yours; buy it for yourself.' Then I knew that this was the word of the LORD.

9"And I bought the field at Anathoth from Hanamel my cousin, and weighed out the money to him, seventeen shekels of silver. 10I signed the deed, sealed it, got witnesses, and weighed the money on scales. 11Then I took the sealed deed of purchase, containing the terms and conditions and the open copy. 12And I gave the deed of purchase to Baruch the son of Neriah son of Mahseiah, in the presence of Hanamel my cousin, in the presence of the witnesses who signed the deed of purchase, and in the presence of all the Judeans who were sitting in the court of the guard. 13I charged Baruch in their presence, saying, 14'Thus says the LORD of hosts, the God of Israel: Take these deeds, both this sealed deed of purchase and this open deed, and put them in an earthenware vessel, that they may last for a long time. 15For thus says the LORD of hosts, the God of Israel: Houses and fields and vineyards shall again be bought in this land.'

Jeremiah Prays for Understanding

16"After I had given the deed of purchase to Baruch the son of Neriah, I prayed to the LORD, saying: 17'Ah, Lord GOD! It is you who have made the heavens and the earth by your great power and by your outstretched arm! Nothing is too hard for you. 18You show steadfast love to thousands, but you repay the guilt of fathers to their children after them, O great and mighty God, whose name is the LORD of hosts, 19great in counsel and mighty in deed, whose eyes are open to all the ways of the children of man, rewarding each one according to his ways and according to the fruit of his deeds. 20You have shown signs and wonders in the land of Egypt, and to this day in Israel and among all mankind, and have made a name for yourself, as at this day. 21You brought your people Israel out of the land of Egypt with signs and wonders, with a strong hand and outstretched arm, and with great terror. 22And you gave them this land, which you swore to their fathers to give them, a land flowing with milk and honey. 23And they entered and took possession of it. But they did not obey your voice or walk in your law. They did nothing of all you commanded them to do. Therefore you have made all this disaster come upon them. 24Behold, the siege mounds have come up to the city to take it, and because of sword and famine and pestilence the city is given into the hands of the Chaldeans who are fighting against it. What you spoke has come to pass, and behold, you see it. 25Yet you, O Lord GOD, have said to me, "Buy the field for money and get witnesses"—though the city is given into the hands of the Chaldeans.'"

26The word of the LORD came to Jeremiah: 27"Behold, I am the LORD, the God of all flesh. Is anything too hard for me? 28Therefore, thus says the LORD: Behold, I am giving this city into the hands of the Chaldeans and into the hand of Nebuchadnezzar king of Babylon, and he shall capture it. 29The Chaldeans who are fighting against this city shall come and set this city on fire and burn it, with the houses on whose roofs offerings have been made to Baal and drink offerings

JEREMIAH 32:8–9

JUST WAIT

Jeremiah's opportunity to purchase land in this chapter tested whether or not he truly believed that the Lord would bring a remnant of Judah back home after the imminent exile. Jeremiah was imprisoned for his message when his cousin Hanamel gave him the opportunity to buy a piece of land from him. At this point, the Babylonians had already laid siege to Jerusalem, and the field at Anathoth that Hanamel wanted to sell him was already in enemy hands. Furthermore, once the Babylonians were in control of all of Judah, it was highly unlikely that they would recognize Jeremiah as the rightful owner of this property.

Despite all of the conventional wisdom that went against this purchase, Jeremiah obeyed God and bought the land from his cousin. He made a point to pay for the land, fill out the proper paperwork, and do everything publicly for others to see that he fully believed everything he had been preaching. In doing so, Jeremiah showed he was confident that God would be true to his promise and restore the land back to his people. Jeremiah had a literal investment in the fulfillment of God's word, and he showed he was willing to persevere (Jas 1:3) through anything and everything to stay true to what God had told him.

have been poured out to other gods, to provoke me to anger. 30 For the children of Israel and the children of Judah have done nothing but evil in my sight from their youth. The children of Israel have done nothing but provoke me to anger by the work of their hands, declares the LORD. 31 This city has aroused my anger and wrath, from the day it was built to this day, so that I will remove it from my sight 32 because of all the evil of the children of Israel and the children of Judah that they did to provoke me to anger—their kings and their officials, their priests and their prophets, the men of Judah and the inhabitants of Jerusalem. 33 They have turned to me their back and not their face. And though I have taught them persistently, they have not listened to receive instruction. 34 They set up their abominations in the house that is called by my name, to defile it. 35 They built the high places of Baal in the Valley of the Son of Hinnom, to offer up their sons and daughters to Molech, though I did not command them, nor did it enter into my mind, that they should do this abomination, to cause Judah to sin.

They Shall Be My People; I Will Be Their God

36 "Now therefore thus says the LORD, the God of Israel, concerning this city of which you say, 'It is given into the hand of the king of Babylon by sword, by famine, and by pestilence': 37 Behold, I will gather them from all the countries to which I drove them in my anger and my wrath and in great indignation. I will bring them back to this place, and I will make them dwell in safety. 38 And they shall be my people, and I will be their God. 39 I will give them one heart and one way, that they may fear me forever, for their own good and the good of their children after them. 40 I will make with them an everlasting covenant, that I will not turn away from doing good to them. And I will put the fear of me in their hearts, that they may not turn from me. 41 I will rejoice in doing them good, and I will plant them in this land in faithfulness, with all my heart and all my soul.

42 "For thus says the LORD: Just as I have brought all this great disaster upon this people, so I will bring upon them all the good that I promise them. 43 Fields shall be bought in this land of which you are saying, 'It is a desolation, without man or beast; it is given into the hand of the Chaldeans.' 44 Fields shall be bought for money, and deeds shall be signed and sealed and witnessed, in the land of Benjamin, in the places about Jerusalem, and in the cities of Judah, in the cities of the hill country, in the cities of the Shephelah, and in the cities of the Negeb; for I will restore their fortunes, declares the LORD."

The LORD Promises Peace

33 The word of the LORD came to Jeremiah a second time, while he was still shut up in the court of the guard: 2 "Thus says the LORD who made the earth,[1] the LORD who formed it to establish it—the LORD is his name: 3 Call to me and I will answer you, and will tell you great and hidden things that you have not known. 4 For thus says the LORD, the God of Israel, concerning the houses of this city and the houses of the kings of Judah that were torn down to make a defense against the siege mounds and against the sword: 5 They are coming in to fight against the Chaldeans and to fill them[2] with the dead bodies of men whom I shall strike down in my anger and my wrath, for I have hidden my face from this city because of all their evil. 6 Behold, I will bring to it health and healing, and I will heal them and reveal to them abundance of prosperity and security. 7 I will restore the fortunes of Judah and the fortunes of Israel, and rebuild them as they were at first. 8 I will cleanse them from all the guilt of their sin against me, and I will forgive all the guilt of their sin and rebellion against me. 9 And this city[3] shall be to me a name of joy, a praise and a glory before all the nations of the earth who shall hear of all the good that I do for them. They shall fear and tremble because of all the good and all the prosperity I provide for it.

[1] Septuagint; Hebrew *it* [2] That is, the torn-down houses [3] Hebrew *And it*

CALL TO ME

Throughout the book of Jeremiah, it is clear that the people had forsaken God and had completely wandered away from him. However, in spite of their sin, God promised to stay with them. All he desired was that they call to him and ask him for help. God sent the people into exile, but he also clearly promised that they would one day return to the land.

Chapter 33 includes a beautiful listing of the blessings God would shower on his people to show that he still wanted them back, despite their unfaithfulness. God only asked that they pray to him and simply ask for wisdom and direction. In Matthew 7:7, Jesus said, "Ask, and it will be given to you; seek, and you will find; knock, and it will be opened to you." Many people have misinterpreted this verse to mean that God will give believers whatever they ask for, but this is simply not true. Anyone who has prayed for a new car and found the same old car sitting in the driveway the next morning knows that God is not some sort of heavenly vending machine. He does not simply say yes to every prayer. However, for those who ask in faith and seek him, God will give them whatever it is he wants for them. Thankfully, the gifts and direction that God gives to his people are invariably better than what they ask for.

In times of hardship and turmoil, God wants his people to turn to him so that he can help them. Jeremiah 33:3 says that if God's people call to him, he will tell them "great and hidden things" that they have not known. The same is true for believers today who find themselves confused and in need. Through his Word, through his Son, and through his Spirit, God offers answers for his people's deepest life questions, no matter their circumstances.

10“Thus says the LORD: In this place of which you say, ‘It is a waste without man or beast,’ in the cities of Judah and the streets of Jerusalem that are desolate, without man or inhabitant or beast, there shall be heard again 11the voice of mirth and the voice of gladness, the voice of the bridegroom and the voice of the bride, the voices of those who sing, as they bring thank offerings to the house of the LORD:

“ ‘Give thanks to the LORD of hosts,
  for the LORD is good,
  for his steadfast love endures forever!’

For I will restore the fortunes of the land as at first, says the LORD.

12“Thus says the LORD of hosts: In this place that is waste, without man or beast, and in all of its cities, there shall again be habitations of shepherds resting their flocks. 13In the cities of the hill country, in the cities of the Shephelah, and in the cities of the Negeb, in the land of Benjamin, the places about Jerusalem, and in the cities of Judah, flocks shall again pass under the hands of the one who counts them, says the LORD.

The LORD’s Eternal Covenant with David

14“Behold, the days are coming, declares the LORD, when I will fulfill the promise I made to the house of Israel and the house of Judah. 15In those days and at that time I will cause a righteous Branch to spring up for David, and he shall execute justice and righteousness in the land. 16In those days Judah will be saved, and Jerusalem will dwell securely. And this is the name by which it will be called: ‘The LORD is our righteousness.’

17“For thus says the LORD: David shall never lack a man to sit on the throne of the house of Israel, 18and the Levitical priests shall never lack a man in my presence to offer burnt offerings, to burn grain offerings, and to make sacrifices forever.”

19The word of the LORD came to Jeremiah: 20“Thus says the LORD: If you can break my covenant with the day and my covenant with the night, so that day and night will not come at their appointed time, 21then also my covenant with David my servant may be broken, so that he shall not have a son to reign on his throne, and my covenant with the Levitical priests my ministers. 22As the host of heaven cannot be numbered and the sands of the sea cannot be measured, so I will multiply the offspring of David my servant, and the Levitical priests who minister to me.”

23The word of the LORD came to Jeremiah: 24“Have you not observed that these people are saying, ‘The LORD has rejected the two clans that he chose’? Thus they have despised my people so that they are no longer a nation in their sight. 25Thus says the LORD: If I have not established my covenant with day and night and the fixed order of heaven and earth, 26then I will reject the offspring of Jacob and David my servant and will not choose one of his offspring to rule over the offspring of Abraham, Isaac, and Jacob. For I will restore their fortunes and will have mercy on them.”

Zedekiah to Die in Babylon

34 The word that came to Jeremiah from the LORD, when Nebuchadnezzar king of Babylon and all his army and all the kingdoms of the earth under his dominion and all the peoples were fighting against Jerusalem and all of its cities: 2“Thus says the LORD, the God of Israel: Go and speak to Zedekiah king of Judah and say to him, ‘Thus says the LORD: Behold, I am giving this city into the hand of the king of Babylon, and he shall burn it with fire. 3You shall not escape from his hand but shall surely be captured and delivered into his hand. You shall see the king of Babylon eye to eye and speak with him face to face. And you shall go to Babylon.’ 4Yet hear the word of the LORD, O Zedekiah king of Judah! Thus

says the LORD concerning you: 'You shall not die by the sword. 5You shall die in peace. And as spices were burned for your fathers, the former kings who were before you, so people shall burn spices for you and lament for you, saying, "Alas, lord!"' For I have spoken the word, declares the LORD."

6Then Jeremiah the prophet spoke all these words to Zedekiah king of Judah, in Jerusalem, 7when the army of the king of Babylon was fighting against Jerusalem and against all the cities of Judah that were left, Lachish and Azekah, for these were the only fortified cities of Judah that remained.

8The word that came to Jeremiah from the LORD, after King Zedekiah had made a covenant with all the people in Jerusalem to make a proclamation of liberty to them, 9that everyone should set free his Hebrew slaves, male and female, so that no one should enslave a Jew, his brother. 10And they obeyed, all the officials and all the people who had entered into the covenant that everyone would set free his slave, male or female, so that they would not be enslaved again. They obeyed and set them free. 11But afterward they turned around and took back the male and female slaves they had set free, and brought them into subjection as slaves. 12The word of the LORD came to Jeremiah from the LORD: 13"Thus says the LORD, the God of Israel: I myself made a covenant with your fathers when I brought them out of the land of Egypt, out of the house of slavery, saying, 14'At the end of seven years each of you must set free the fellow Hebrew who has been sold to you and has served you six years; you must set him free from your service.' But your fathers did not listen to me or incline their ears to me. 15You recently repented and did what was right in my eyes by proclaiming liberty, each to his neighbor, and you made a covenant before me in the house that is called by my name, 16but then you turned around and profaned my name when each of you took back his male and female slaves, whom you had set free according to their desire, and you brought them into subjection to be your slaves.

17"Therefore, thus says the LORD: You have not obeyed me by proclaiming liberty, every one to his brother and to his neighbor; behold, I proclaim to you liberty to the sword, to pestilence, and to famine, declares the LORD. I will make you a horror to all the kingdoms of the earth. 18And the men who transgressed my covenant and did not keep the terms of the covenant that they made before me, I will make them like[1] the calf that they cut in two and passed between its parts— 19the officials of Judah, the officials of Jerusalem, the eunuchs, the priests, and all the people of the land who passed between the parts of the calf. 20And I will give them into the hand of their enemies and into the hand of those who seek their lives. Their dead bodies shall be food for the birds of the air and the beasts of the earth. 21And Zedekiah king of Judah and his officials I will give into the hand of their enemies and into the hand of those who seek their lives, into the hand of the army of the king of Babylon which has withdrawn from you. 22Behold, I will command, declares the LORD, and will bring them back to this city. And they will fight against it and take it and burn it with fire. I will make the cities of Judah a desolation without inhabitant."

The Obedience of the Rechabites

35 The word that came to Jeremiah from the LORD in the days of Jehoiakim the son of Josiah, king of Judah: 2"Go to the house of the Rechabites and speak with them and bring them to the house of the LORD, into one of the chambers; then offer them wine to drink." 3So I took Jaazaniah the son of Jeremiah, son of Habazziniah and his brothers and all his sons and the whole house of the Rechabites. 4I brought them to the house of the LORD into the chamber of the sons of Hanan the son of Igdaliah, the man of God, which was near the chamber of the officials, above the chamber of Maaseiah the son of Shallum, keeper of the threshold. 5Then I set before the Rechabites pitchers full of wine, and cups,

[1]Hebrew lacks *them like*

and I said to them, “Drink wine.” 6But they answered, “We will drink no wine,
for Jonadab the son of Rechab, our father, commanded us, ‘You shall not drink
wine, neither you nor your sons forever. 7You shall not build a house; you shall
not sow seed; you shall not plant or have a vineyard; but you shall live in tents
all your days, that you may live many days in the land where you sojourn.’ 8We
have obeyed the voice of Jonadab the son of Rechab, our father, in all that he
commanded us, to drink no wine all our days, ourselves, our wives, our sons, or
our daughters, 9and not to build houses to dwell in. We have no vineyard or field
or seed, 10but we have lived in tents and have obeyed and done all that Jonadab
our father commanded us. 11But when Nebuchadnezzar king of Babylon came up
against the land, we said, ‘Come, and let us go to Jerusalem for fear of the army of
the Chaldeans and the army of the Syrians.’ So we are living in Jerusalem.”

12Then the word of the LORD came to Jeremiah: 13“Thus says the LORD of hosts,
the God of Israel: Go and say to the people of Judah and the inhabitants of Jerusalem, Will you not receive instruction and listen to my words? declares the LORD.
14The command that Jonadab the son of Rechab gave to his sons, to drink no wine,
has been kept, and they drink none to this day, for they have obeyed their father’s
command. I have spoken to you persistently, but you have not listened to me. 15I
have sent to you all my servants the prophets, sending them persistently, saying,
‘Turn now every one of you from his evil way, and amend your deeds, and do not
go after other gods to serve them, and then you shall dwell in the land that I gave
to you and your fathers.’ But you did not incline your ear or listen to me. 16The
sons of Jonadab the son of Rechab have kept the command that their father gave
them, but this people has not obeyed me. 17Therefore, thus says the LORD, the God
of hosts, the God of Israel: Behold, I am bringing upon Judah and all the inhabitants of Jerusalem all the disaster that I have pronounced against them, because
I have spoken to them and they have not listened, I have called to them and they
have not answered.”

18But to the house of the Rechabites Jeremiah said, “Thus says the LORD of
hosts, the God of Israel: Because you have obeyed the command of Jonadab your
father and kept all his precepts and done all that he commanded you, 19therefore
thus says the LORD of hosts, the God of Israel: Jonadab the son of Rechab shall
never lack a man to stand before me.”

JEREMIAH 36:1–32

JEHOIAKIM AND REPENTANCE

Upon hearing a description of the wickedness of the people of Judah and God’s declarations of judgment, there were two ways King Jehoiakim could have responded. He could have either expressed great sorrow at what was written and led the nation in repenting of their actions, or he could have ignored the call to repent and continued living in sin. Jehoiakim went further than simply ignoring the scroll—he actually cut it up and burned it in the fire pot, as if that action would make God’s message go away.

Jeremiah saw the people sinning. He rebuked them, but they failed to repent. In Acts 3:19, Peter says that if people repent and turn to God, their sins will be wiped out. Jehoiakim had a chance to repent, but he ignored the rebuke of God through Jeremiah, and he now represents a perfect example of how people are not supposed to respond when they’re called to account for their sins.

Jehoiakim Burns Jeremiah’s Scroll

36 In the fourth year of Jehoiakim the son of Josiah, king of Judah, this word
came to Jeremiah from the LORD: 2“Take a scroll and write on it all the
words that I have spoken to you against Israel and Judah and all the nations,
from the day I spoke to you, from the days of Josiah until today. 3It may be that
the house of Judah will hear all the disaster that I intend to do to them, so that
every one may turn from his evil way, and that I may forgive their iniquity and
their sin.”

4Then Jeremiah called Baruch the son of Neriah, and Baruch wrote on a scroll
at the dictation of Jeremiah all the words of the LORD that he had spoken to him.
5And Jeremiah ordered Baruch, saying, “I am banned from going to the house of
the LORD, 6so you are to go, and on a day of fasting in the hearing of all the people
in the LORD’s house you shall read the words of the LORD from the scroll that you
have written at my dictation. You shall read them also in the hearing of all the
men of Judah who come out of their cities. 7It may be that their plea for mercy
will come before the LORD, and that every one will turn from his evil way, for great
is the anger and wrath that the LORD has pronounced against this people.” 8And
Baruch the son of Neriah did all that Jeremiah the prophet ordered him about
reading from the scroll the words of the LORD in the LORD’s house.

9In the fifth year of Jehoiakim the son of Josiah, king of Judah, in the ninth
month, all the people in Jerusalem and all the people who came from the cities of
Judah to Jerusalem proclaimed a fast before the LORD. 10Then, in the hearing of all

the people, Baruch read the words of Jeremiah from the scroll, in the house of the
LORD, in the chamber of Gemariah the son of Shaphan the secretary, which was
in the upper court, at the entry of the New Gate of the LORD's house.
11When Micaiah the son of Gemariah, son of Shaphan, heard all the words
of the LORD from the scroll, 12he went down to the king's house, into the secretary's chamber, and all the officials were sitting there: Elishama the secretary,
Delaiah the son of Shemaiah, Elnathan the son of Achbor, Gemariah the son
of Shaphan, Zedekiah the son of Hananiah, and all the officials. 13And Micaiah
told them all the words that he had heard, when Baruch read the scroll in the
hearing of the people. 14Then all the officials sent Jehudi the son of Nethaniah,
son of Shelemiah, son of Cushi, to say to Baruch, "Take in your hand the scroll
that you read in the hearing of the people, and come." So Baruch the son of
Neriah took the scroll in his hand and came to them. 15And they said to him, "Sit
down and read it." So Baruch read it to them. 16When they heard all the words,
they turned one to another in fear. And they said to Baruch, "We must report
all these words to the king." 17Then they asked Baruch, "Tell us, please, how did
you write all these words? Was it at his dictation?" 18Baruch answered them,
"He dictated all these words to me, while I wrote them with ink on the scroll."
19Then the officials said to Baruch, "Go and hide, you and Jeremiah, and let no
one know where you are."
20So they went into the court to the king, having put the scroll in the chamber
of Elishama the secretary, and they reported all the words to the king. 21Then the
king sent Jehudi to get the scroll, and he took it from the chamber of Elishama
the secretary. And Jehudi read it to the king and all the officials who stood beside
the king. 22It was the ninth month, and the king was sitting in the winter house,
and there was a fire burning in the fire pot before him. 23As Jehudi read three or
four columns, the king would cut them off with a knife and throw them into the
fire in the fire pot, until the entire scroll was consumed in the fire that was in the
fire pot. 24Yet neither the king nor any of his servants who heard all these words
was afraid, nor did they tear their garments. 25Even when Elnathan and Delaiah
and Gemariah urged the king not to burn the scroll, he would not listen to them.
26And the king commanded Jerahmeel the king's son and Seraiah the son of Azriel
and Shelemiah the son of Abdeel to seize Baruch the secretary and Jeremiah the
prophet, but the LORD hid them.
27Now after the king had burned the scroll with the words that Baruch wrote
at Jeremiah's dictation, the word of the LORD came to Jeremiah: 28"Take another
scroll and write on it all the former words that were in the first scroll, which Jehoiakim the king of Judah has burned. 29And concerning Jehoiakim king of Judah
you shall say, 'Thus says the LORD, You have burned this scroll, saying, "Why have
you written in it that the king of Babylon will certainly come and destroy this
land, and will cut off from it man and beast?" 30Therefore thus says the LORD concerning Jehoiakim king of Judah: He shall have none to sit on the throne of David,
and his dead body shall be cast out to the heat by day and the frost by night. 31And
I will punish him and his offspring and his servants for their iniquity. I will bring
upon them and upon the inhabitants of Jerusalem and upon the people of Judah
all the disaster that I have pronounced against them, but they would not hear.'"
32Then Jeremiah took another scroll and gave it to Baruch the scribe, the son
of Neriah, who wrote on it at the dictation of Jeremiah all the words of the scroll
that Jehoiakim king of Judah had burned in the fire. And many similar words were
added to them.

Jeremiah Warns Zedekiah

37 Zedekiah the son of Josiah, whom Nebuchadnezzar king of Babylon made
king in the land of Judah, reigned instead of Coniah the son of Jehoiakim.
2But neither he nor his servants nor the people of the land listened to the words
of the LORD that he spoke through Jeremiah the prophet.

[3]King Zedekiah sent Jehucal the son of Shelemiah, and Zephaniah the priest, the son of Maaseiah, to Jeremiah the prophet, saying, "Please pray for us to the LORD our God." [4]Now Jeremiah was still going in and out among the people, for he had not yet been put in prison. [5]The army of Pharaoh had come out of Egypt. And when the Chaldeans who were besieging Jerusalem heard news about them, they withdrew from Jerusalem.

[6]Then the word of the LORD came to Jeremiah the prophet: [7]"Thus says the LORD, God of Israel: Thus shall you say to the king of Judah who sent you to me to inquire of me, 'Behold, Pharaoh's army that came to help you is about to return to Egypt, to its own land. [8]And the Chaldeans shall come back and fight against this city. They shall capture it and burn it with fire. [9]Thus says the LORD, Do not deceive yourselves, saying, "The Chaldeans will surely go away from us," for they will not go away. [10]For even if you should defeat the whole army of Chaldeans who are fighting against you, and there remained of them only wounded men, every man in his tent, they would rise up and burn this city with fire.'"

Jeremiah Imprisoned

[11]Now when the Chaldean army had withdrawn from Jerusalem at the approach of Pharaoh's army, [12]Jeremiah set out from Jerusalem to go to the land of Benjamin to receive his portion there among the people. [13]When he was at the Benjamin Gate, a sentry there named Irijah the son of Shelemiah, son of Hananiah, seized Jeremiah the prophet, saying, "You are deserting to the Chaldeans." [14]And Jeremiah said, "It is a lie; I am not deserting to the Chaldeans." But Irijah would not listen to him, and seized Jeremiah and brought him to the officials. [15]And the officials were enraged at Jeremiah, and they beat him and imprisoned him in the house of Jonathan the secretary, for it had been made a prison.

[16]When Jeremiah had come to the dungeon cells and remained there many days, [17]King Zedekiah sent for him and received him. The king questioned him secretly in his house and said, "Is there any word from the LORD?" Jeremiah said, "There is." Then he said, "You shall be delivered into the hand of the king of Babylon." [18]Jeremiah also said to King Zedekiah, "What wrong have I done to you or your servants or this people, that you have put me in prison? [19]Where are your prophets who prophesied to you, saying, 'The king of Babylon will not come against you and against this land'? [20]Now hear, please, O my lord the king: let my humble plea come before you and do not send me back to the house of Jonathan the secretary, lest I die there." [21]So King Zedekiah gave orders, and they committed Jeremiah to the court of the guard. And a loaf of bread was given him daily from the bakers' street, until all the bread of the city was gone. So Jeremiah remained in the court of the guard.

Jeremiah Cast into the Cistern

38 Now Shephatiah the son of Mattan, Gedaliah the son of Pashhur, Jucal the son of Shelemiah, and Pashhur the son of Malchiah heard the words that Jeremiah was saying to all the people: [2]"Thus says the LORD: He who stays in this city shall die by the sword, by famine, and by pestilence, but he who goes out to the Chaldeans shall live. He shall have his life as a prize of war, and live. [3]Thus says the LORD: This city shall surely be given into the hand of the army of the king of Babylon and be taken." [4]Then the officials said to the king, "Let this man be put to death, for he is weakening the hands of the soldiers who are left in this city, and the hands of all the people, by speaking such words to them. For this man is not seeking the welfare of this people, but their harm." [5]King Zedekiah said, "Behold, he is in your hands, for the king can do nothing against you." [6]So they took Jeremiah and cast him into the cistern of Malchiah, the king's son, which was in the court of the guard, letting Jeremiah down by ropes. And there was no water in the cistern, but only mud, and Jeremiah sank in the mud.

JEREMIAH 37:16–21

SECRETLY SEEKING A WORD FROM GOD

Despite the fact that Jeremiah was imprisoned for his prophecies against Judah, Zedekiah still sought him out to hear if he had any word from the Lord. King Zedekiah clearly desired to hear the truth, but he risked serious retribution from his officials for consulting with this hated prophet. That led him to keep his conversations with Jeremiah secret (Jer 37:17; 38:14–27).

Nicodemus had a similar struggle in John 3. As a member of the Jewish ruling council, he took a great risk in meeting Jesus at night to discuss religious issues. What his actions showed is that he sought to discover who Jesus was. In the same way that Jeremiah spoke the truth from the Lord to Zedekiah, so Jesus spoke truth to Nicodemus about spiritual matters. While Jesus did not hesitate to speak strongly to religious hypocrites, he was always willing to answer anyone who was seeking truth.

Jeremiah Rescued from the Cistern

7When Ebed-melech the Ethiopian, a eunuch who was in the king's house,
heard that they had put Jeremiah into the cistern—the king was sitting in the
Benjamin Gate— 8Ebed-melech went from the king's house and said to the king,
9"My lord the king, these men have done evil in all that they did to Jeremiah the
prophet by casting him into the cistern, and he will die there of hunger, for there
is no bread left in the city." 10Then the king commanded Ebed-melech the Ethiopian, "Take thirty men with you from here, and lift Jeremiah the prophet out of
the cistern before he dies." 11So Ebed-melech took the men with him and went to
the house of the king, to a wardrobe in the storehouse, and took from there old
rags and worn-out clothes, which he let down to Jeremiah in the cistern by ropes.
12Then Ebed-melech the Ethiopian said to Jeremiah, "Put the rags and clothes
between your armpits and the ropes." Jeremiah did so. 13Then they drew Jeremiah
up with ropes and lifted him out of the cistern. And Jeremiah remained in the
court of the guard.

Jeremiah Warns Zedekiah Again

14King Zedekiah sent for Jeremiah the prophet and received him at the third
entrance of the temple of the LORD. The king said to Jeremiah, "I will ask you a
question; hide nothing from me." 15Jeremiah said to Zedekiah, "If I tell you, will
you not surely put me to death? And if I give you counsel, you will not listen to
me." 16Then King Zedekiah swore secretly to Jeremiah, "As the LORD lives, who
made our souls, I will not put you to death or deliver you into the hand of these
men who seek your life."

17Then Jeremiah said to Zedekiah, "Thus says the LORD, the God of hosts, the
God of Israel: If you will surrender to the officials of the king of Babylon, then
your life shall be spared, and this city shall not be burned with fire, and you and
your house shall live. 18But if you do not surrender to the officials of the king of
Babylon, then this city shall be given into the hand of the Chaldeans, and they
shall burn it with fire, and you shall not escape from their hand." 19King Zedekiah
said to Jeremiah, "I am afraid of the Judeans who have deserted to the Chaldeans,
lest I be handed over to them and they deal cruelly with me." 20Jeremiah said,
"You shall not be given to them. Obey now the voice of the LORD in what I say to
you, and it shall be well with you, and your life shall be spared. 21But if you refuse
to surrender, this is the vision which the LORD has shown to me: 22Behold, all the
women left in the house of the king of Judah were being led out to the officials of
the king of Babylon and were saying,

"'Your trusted friends have deceived you
    and prevailed against you;
now that your feet are sunk in the mud,
    they turn away from you.'

23All your wives and your sons shall be led out to the Chaldeans, and you yourself
shall not escape from their hand, but shall be seized by the king of Babylon, and
this city shall be burned with fire."

24Then Zedekiah said to Jeremiah, "Let no one know of these words, and you
shall not die. 25If the officials hear that I have spoken with you and come to you
and say to you, 'Tell us what you said to the king and what the king said to you;
hide nothing from us and we will not put you to death,' 26then you shall say
to them, 'I made a humble plea to the king that he would not send me back to
the house of Jonathan to die there.'" 27Then all the officials came to Jeremiah
and asked him, and he answered them as the king had instructed him. So they
stopped speaking with him, for the conversation had not been overheard. 28And
Jeremiah remained in the court of the guard until the day that Jerusalem was
taken.

JEREMIAH 38:14–18

PATIENCE AND PERSEVERANCE

Jeremiah had a very difficult time getting the people of Jerusalem to listen to him. He was imprisoned multiple times for his message and even thrown into a water cistern and left to die. However, King Zedekiah still asked this prophet of God to tell him the word of the Lord. In response, Jeremiah exclaimed his frustration and fear that Zedekiah would either put him to death or ignore him no matter what truth from God he shared.

Jesus had a similar moment to Jeremiah in Luke 9:41 in which he expressed frustration at the weak faith of the people around him. However, both Jesus and Jeremiah persevered through their frustration. Jeremiah told Zedekiah God's truth, and Jesus healed the boy that had been put in front of him. Both Jeremiah and Jesus showed great patience and shared God's truth, continuing the work they were called to do.

The Fall of Jerusalem

39 In the ninth year of Zedekiah king of Judah, in the tenth month, Nebuchadnezzar king of Babylon and all his army came against Jerusalem and besieged it. 2In the eleventh year of Zedekiah, in the fourth month, on the ninth day of the month, a breach was made in the city. 3Then all the officials of the king of Babylon came and sat in the middle gate: Nergal-sar-ezer of Samgar, Nebu-sar-sekim the Rab-saris, Nergal-sar-ezer the Rab-mag, with all the rest of the officers of the king of Babylon. 4When Zedekiah king of Judah and all the soldiers saw them, they fled, going out of the city at night by way of the king's garden through the gate between the two walls; and they went toward the Arabah. 5But the army of the Chaldeans pursued them and overtook Zedekiah in the plains of Jericho. And when they had taken him, they brought him up to Nebuchadnezzar king of Babylon, at Riblah, in the land of Hamath; and he passed sentence on him. 6The king of Babylon slaughtered the sons of Zedekiah at Riblah before his eyes, and the king of Babylon slaughtered all the nobles of Judah. 7He put out the eyes of Zedekiah and bound him in chains to take him to Babylon. 8The Chaldeans burned the king's house and the house of the people, and broke down the walls of Jerusalem. 9Then Nebuzaradan, the captain of the guard, carried into exile to Babylon the rest of the people who were left in the city, those who had deserted to him, and the people who remained. 10Nebuzaradan, the captain of the guard, left in the land of Judah some of the poor people who owned nothing, and gave them vineyards and fields at the same time.

The LORD Delivers Jeremiah

11Nebuchadnezzar king of Babylon gave command concerning Jeremiah through Nebuzaradan, the captain of the guard, saying, 12"Take him, look after him well, and do him no harm, but deal with him as he tells you." 13So Nebuzaradan the captain of the guard, Nebushazban the Rab-saris, Nergal-sar-ezer the Rab-mag, and all the chief officers of the king of Babylon 14sent and took Jeremiah from the court of the guard. They entrusted him to Gedaliah the son of Ahikam, son of Shaphan, that he should take him home. So he lived among the people.

15The word of the LORD came to Jeremiah while he was shut up in the court of the guard: 16"Go, and say to Ebed-melech the Ethiopian, 'Thus says the LORD of hosts, the God of Israel: Behold, I will fulfill my words against this city for harm and not for good, and they shall be accomplished before you on that day. 17But I will deliver you on that day, declares the LORD, and you shall not be given into the hand of the men of whom you are afraid. 18For I will surely save you, and you shall not fall by the sword, but you shall have your life as a prize of war, because you have put your trust in me, declares the LORD.'"

Jeremiah Remains in Judah

40 The word that came to Jeremiah from the LORD after Nebuzaradan the captain of the guard had let him go from Ramah, when he took him bound in chains along with all the captives of Jerusalem and Judah who were being exiled to Babylon. 2The captain of the guard took Jeremiah and said to him, "The LORD your God pronounced this disaster against this place. 3The LORD has brought it about, and has done as he said. Because you sinned against the LORD and did not obey his voice, this thing has come upon you. 4Now, behold, I release you today from the chains on your hands. If it seems good to you to come with me to Babylon, come, and I will look after you well, but if it seems wrong to you to come with me to Babylon, do not come. See, the whole land is before you; go wherever you think it good and right to go. 5If you remain,[1] then return to Gedaliah the son of Ahikam, son of Shaphan, whom the king of Babylon appointed governor of the cities of Judah, and dwell with him among the

JEREMIAH 40:1–4

SPIRITUAL TRUTH FROM AN UNBELIEVER

Despite the fact that the people of Judah ignored Jeremiah's prophecies, the Babylonians listened and believed what he had said. In chapter 40, the commander of the imperial guard spoke Jeremiah's words back to him and essentially confirmed what Jeremiah had been saying all along: that the Lord had brought about the destruction of Jerusalem because of the people's rebellion against the Lord. This instance was not the last time truth was to come from the mouth of an unbeliever.

When Jesus died on the cross, the Roman centurion who had supervised his crucifixion exclaimed, "Truly this man was the Son of God!" (Mk 15:39). The centurion's realization and the Babylonian commander's knowledge of Jeremiah's prophecies show how the truth of God is for anyone and everyone — believers and nonbelievers alike. Jesus came to save the lost (Lk 19:10), so no matter what unconventional manner the message may take, anyone can hear God's truth.

[1]Syriac; the meaning of the Hebrew phrase is uncertain

CONSEQUENCES

Despite all of Jeremiah's attempts to warn the people, chapter 39 depicts the fall of Jerusalem just as God's prophet had predicted it throughout this book. Through Jeremiah, God warned his people that their actions would have consequences, and their failure to ask for forgiveness and to repent from their wrongdoing sealed their fate. The Israelites sowed ignorance of God's truth, and they reaped destruction and exile (Gal 6:7). Verses 1 through 10 depict the horror of the punishment meted out against the people of the city for their disobedience.

True to Zedekiah's character, he tried to sneak out by night, but he was ultimately caught and taken as a prisoner to Babylon, where he was imprisoned until he died (Jer 52:11). God does not make empty promises in the Bible; he was not bluffing when he spoke words of judgment through Jeremiah.

For believers today, it is important to understand that everything God says in the Bible is his word, and his word has weight to it. Therefore, when Jesus said, "So everyone who acknowledges me before men, I also will acknowledge before my Father who is in heaven, but whoever denies me before men, I also will deny before my Father who is in heaven" (Mt 10:32 – 33), he was not bluffing either. These very words will come true on judgment day.

The people of Jerusalem chose to disown God, and they lived with the consequences of their disobedience. Yes, God brought some of the exiles back to their land, but that did not happen until 70 years after the first deportation in 605 BC. Most individuals died before the people were able to return to Jerusalem and experience God's mercy. Believers need to recognize who God is now and what he desires for them as citizens of his kingdom so that they may experience his grace when the time comes for him to return and give it to those who have been waiting.

people. Or go wherever you think it right to go." So the captain of the guard gave
him an allowance of food and a present, and let him go. 6Then Jeremiah went to
Gedaliah the son of Ahikam, at Mizpah, and lived with him among the people
who were left in the land.

7When all the captains of the forces in the open country and their men heard
that the king of Babylon had appointed Gedaliah the son of Ahikam governor
in the land and had committed to him men, women, and children, those of the
poorest of the land who had not been taken into exile to Babylon, 8they went to
Gedaliah at Mizpah—Ishmael the son of Nethaniah, Johanan the son of Kareah,
Seraiah the son of Tanhumeth, the sons of Ephai the Netophathite, Jezaniah the
son of the Maacathite, they and their men. 9Gedaliah the son of Ahikam, son of
Shaphan, swore to them and their men, saying, "Do not be afraid to serve the
Chaldeans. Dwell in the land and serve the king of Babylon, and it shall be well
with you. 10As for me, I will dwell at Mizpah, to represent you before the Chaldeans who will come to us. But as for you, gather wine and summer fruits and
oil, and store them in your vessels, and dwell in your cities that you have taken."
11Likewise, when all the Judeans who were in Moab and among the Ammonites
and in Edom and in other lands heard that the king of Babylon had left a remnant
in Judah and had appointed Gedaliah the son of Ahikam, son of Shaphan, as governor over them, 12then all the Judeans returned from all the places to which they
had been driven and came to the land of Judah, to Gedaliah at Mizpah. And they
gathered wine and summer fruits in great abundance.

13Now Johanan the son of Kareah and all the leaders of the forces in the open
country came to Gedaliah at Mizpah 14and said to him, "Do you know that Baalis
the king of the Ammonites has sent Ishmael the son of Nethaniah to take your
life?" But Gedaliah the son of Ahikam would not believe them. 15Then Johanan
the son of Kareah spoke secretly to Gedaliah at Mizpah, "Please let me go and
strike down Ishmael the son of Nethaniah, and no one will know it. Why should
he take your life, so that all the Judeans who are gathered about you would be
scattered, and the remnant of Judah would perish?" 16But Gedaliah the son of
Ahikam said to Johanan the son of Kareah, "You shall not do this thing, for you
are speaking falsely of Ishmael."

Gedaliah Murdered

41 In the seventh month, Ishmael the son of Nethaniah, son of Elishama, of
the royal family, one of the chief officers of the king, came with ten men to
Gedaliah the son of Ahikam, at Mizpah. As they ate bread together there at Mizpah, 2Ishmael the son of Nethaniah and the ten men with him rose up and struck
down Gedaliah the son of Ahikam, son of Shaphan, with the sword, and killed
him, whom the king of Babylon had appointed governor in the land. 3Ishmael also
struck down all the Judeans who were with Gedaliah at Mizpah, and the Chaldean
soldiers who happened to be there.

4On the day after the murder of Gedaliah, before anyone knew of it, 5eighty
men arrived from Shechem and Shiloh and Samaria, with their beards shaved and
their clothes torn, and their bodies gashed, bringing grain offerings and incense
to present at the temple of the LORD. 6And Ishmael the son of Nethaniah came out
from Mizpah to meet them, weeping as he came. As he met them, he said to them,
"Come in to Gedaliah the son of Ahikam." 7When they came into the city, Ishmael
the son of Nethaniah and the men with him slaughtered them and cast them into
a cistern. 8But there were ten men among them who said to Ishmael, "Do not
put us to death, for we have stores of wheat, barley, oil, and honey hidden in the
fields." So he refrained and did not put them to death with their companions.

9Now the cistern into which Ishmael had thrown all the bodies of the men
whom he had struck down along with[1] Gedaliah was the large cistern that King

[1]Hebrew *by the hand of*

Asa had made for defense against Baasha king of Israel; Ishmael the son of Nethaniah filled it with the slain. 10Then Ishmael took captive all the rest of the people
who were in Mizpah, the king's daughters and all the people who were left at Mizpah, whom Nebuzaradan, the captain of the guard, had committed to Gedaliah
the son of Ahikam. Ishmael the son of Nethaniah took them captive and set out
to cross over to the Ammonites.

11But when Johanan the son of Kareah and all the leaders of the forces with
him heard of all the evil that Ishmael the son of Nethaniah had done, 12they
took all their men and went to fight against Ishmael the son of Nethaniah. They
came upon him at the great pool that is in Gibeon. 13And when all the people
who were with Ishmael saw Johanan the son of Kareah and all the leaders of the
forces with him, they rejoiced. 14So all the people whom Ishmael had carried
away captive from Mizpah turned around and came back, and went to Johanan
the son of Kareah. 15But Ishmael the son of Nethaniah escaped from Johanan
with eight men, and went to the Ammonites. 16Then Johanan the son of Kareah
and all the leaders of the forces with him took from Mizpah all the rest of the
people whom he had recovered from Ishmael the son of Nethaniah, after he had
struck down Gedaliah the son of Ahikam—soldiers, women, children, and eunuchs, whom Johanan brought back from Gibeon. 17And they went and stayed
at Geruth Chimham near Bethlehem, intending to go to Egypt 18because of the
Chaldeans. For they were afraid of them, because Ishmael the son of Nethaniah
had struck down Gedaliah the son of Ahikam, whom the king of Babylon had
made governor over the land.

Warning Against Going to Egypt

42 Then all the commanders of the forces, and Johanan the son of Kareah
and Jezaniah the son of Hoshaiah, and all the people from the least
to the greatest, came near 2and said to Jeremiah the prophet, "Let our plea
for mercy come before you, and pray to the LORD your God for us, for all this
remnant—because we are left with but a few, as your eyes see us— 3that the
LORD your God may show us the way we should go, and the thing that we
should do." 4Jeremiah the prophet said to them, "I have heard you. Behold,
I will pray to the LORD your God according to your request, and whatever the
LORD answers you I will tell you. I will keep nothing back from you." 5Then they
said to Jeremiah, "May the LORD be a true and faithful witness against us if we
do not act according to all the word with which the LORD your God sends you
to us. 6Whether it is good or bad, we will obey the voice of the LORD our God to
whom we are sending you, that it may be well with us when we obey the voice
of the LORD our God."

7At the end of ten days the word of the LORD came to Jeremiah. 8Then he
summoned Johanan the son of Kareah and all the commanders of the forces who
were with him, and all the people from the least to the greatest, 9and said to
them, "Thus says the LORD, the God of Israel, to whom you sent me to present
your plea for mercy before him: 10If you will remain in this land, then I will build
you up and not pull you down; I will plant you, and not pluck you up; for I relent
of the disaster that I did to you. 11Do not fear the king of Babylon, of whom you
are afraid. Do not fear him, declares the LORD, for I am with you, to save you and
to deliver you from his hand. 12I will grant you mercy, that he may have mercy on
you and let you remain in your own land. 13But if you say, 'We will not remain in
this land,' disobeying the voice of the LORD your God 14and saying, 'No, we will go
to the land of Egypt, where we shall not see war or hear the sound of the trumpet or be hungry for bread, and we will dwell there,' 15then hear the word of the
LORD, O remnant of Judah. Thus says the LORD of hosts, the God of Israel: If you
set your faces to enter Egypt and go to live there, 16then the sword that you fear
shall overtake you there in the land of Egypt, and the famine of which you are
afraid shall follow close after you to Egypt, and there you shall die. 17All the men

JEREMIAH 42:1–22

WHEN WILL THEY LEARN?

After Jeremiah correctly prophesied the fall of Jerusalem, one would think that the people would have been more prone to listen to him and heed his message. Here a remnant that escaped death and exile asks Jeremiah to pray to the Lord and ask him what they should do. Jeremiah does so, telling them to stay where they are and not go to Egypt. The word of the Lord seems pretty straightforward, but what did the people do? They called Jeremiah a liar and went directly to Egypt in direct defiance of God's word (Jer 43:1–5).

Sometimes God's truth is obvious and explicit. For the Israelites, Jeremiah spelled out exactly what they should not do. For believers today, the truth revealed in Jesus Christ is written in Scripture. Everything that is necessary for life is found in Jesus. He can be trusted because his ways are perfect. Jesus says that he is "the way, and the truth, and the life" (Jn 14:6).

JEREMIAH 43:1–8

PERSECUTED FOR RIGHTEOUSNESS' SAKE

Despite Jeremiah's warning to those left behind in Jerusalem to not go to Egypt, the people completely ignored him. They left for Egypt, and even forced Jeremiah to go along with them (Jer 43:6). Jeremiah simply did what he did best and continued to preach the truth of God. In verse 8, Jeremiah heard the word of the Lord, and again he proclaimed it to the people. He did not hold back because of how poorly they had treated him in the past; rather, he remained obedient to his calling and passed along the truth that God gave him to share.

Jesus taught about being persecuted for the sake of righteousness (Mt 5:10–11), and few people experienced persecution like Jeremiah did. Almost every time he did what was right and shared God's truth, he received some sort of negative backlash. The story of Jeremiah can be encouraging to believers who experience persecution as a result of standing strong in the faith.

who set their faces to go to Egypt to live there shall die by the sword, by famine,
and by pestilence. They shall have no remnant or survivor from the disaster that
I will bring upon them.
18 "For thus says the LORD of hosts, the God of Israel: As my anger and my
wrath were poured out on the inhabitants of Jerusalem, so my wrath will be
poured out on you when you go to Egypt. You shall become an execration, a horror, a curse, and a taunt. You shall see this place no more. 19 The LORD has said to
you, O remnant of Judah, 'Do not go to Egypt.' Know for a certainty that I have
warned you this day 20 that you have gone astray at the cost of your lives. For
you sent me to the LORD your God, saying, 'Pray for us to the LORD our God, and
whatever the LORD our God says, declare to us and we will do it.' 21 And I have this
day declared it to you, but you have not obeyed the voice of the LORD your God
in anything that he sent me to tell you. 22 Now therefore know for a certainty that
you shall die by the sword, by famine, and by pestilence in the place where you
desire to go to live."

Jeremiah Taken to Egypt

43 When Jeremiah finished speaking to all the people all these words of the
LORD their God, with which the LORD their God had sent him to them,
2 Azariah the son of Hoshaiah and Johanan the son of Kareah and all the insolent
men said to Jeremiah, "You are telling a lie. The LORD our God did not send you
to say, 'Do not go to Egypt to live there,' 3 but Baruch the son of Neriah has set
you against us, to deliver us into the hand of the Chaldeans, that they may kill
us or take us into exile in Babylon." 4 So Johanan the son of Kareah and all the
commanders of the forces and all the people did not obey the voice of the LORD,
to remain in the land of Judah. 5 But Johanan the son of Kareah and all the commanders of the forces took all the remnant of Judah who had returned to live
in the land of Judah from all the nations to which they had been driven— 6 the
men, the women, the children, the princesses, and every person whom Nebuzaradan the captain of the guard had left with Gedaliah the son of Ahikam, son
of Shaphan; also Jeremiah the prophet and Baruch the son of Neriah. 7 And they
came into the land of Egypt, for they did not obey the voice of the LORD. And they
arrived at Tahpanhes.
8 Then the word of the LORD came to Jeremiah in Tahpanhes: 9 "Take in your
hands large stones and hide them in the mortar in the pavement that is at the
entrance to Pharaoh's palace in Tahpanhes, in the sight of the men of Judah, 10 and
say to them, 'Thus says the LORD of hosts, the God of Israel: Behold, I will send and
take Nebuchadnezzar the king of Babylon, my servant, and I will set his throne
above these stones that I have hidden, and he will spread his royal canopy over
them. 11 He shall come and strike the land of Egypt, giving over to the pestilence
those who are doomed to the pestilence, to captivity those who are doomed to
captivity, and to the sword those who are doomed to the sword. 12 I shall kindle a
fire in the temples of the gods of Egypt, and he shall burn them and carry them
away captive. And he shall clean the land of Egypt as a shepherd cleans his cloak
of vermin, and he shall go away from there in peace. 13 He shall break the obelisks
of Heliopolis, which is in the land of Egypt, and the temples of the gods of Egypt
he shall burn with fire.'"

Judgment for Idolatry

44 The word that came to Jeremiah concerning all the Judeans who lived in
the land of Egypt, at Migdol, at Tahpanhes, at Memphis, and in the land
of Pathros, 2 "Thus says the LORD of hosts, the God of Israel: You have seen all the
disaster that I brought upon Jerusalem and upon all the cities of Judah. Behold,
this day they are a desolation, and no one dwells in them, 3 because of the evil
that they committed, provoking me to anger, in that they went to make offerings
and serve other gods that they knew not, neither they, nor you, nor your fathers.

4Yet I persistently sent to you all my servants the prophets, saying, 'Oh, do not do this abomination that I hate!' 5But they did not listen or incline their ear, to turn from their evil and make no offerings to other gods. 6Therefore my wrath and my anger were poured out and kindled in the cities of Judah and in the streets of Jerusalem, and they became a waste and a desolation, as at this day. 7And now thus says the LORD God of hosts, the God of Israel: Why do you commit this great evil against yourselves, to cut off from you man and woman, infant and child, from the midst of Judah, leaving you no remnant? 8Why do you provoke me to anger with the works of your hands, making offerings to other gods in the land of Egypt where you have come to live, so that you may be cut off and become a curse and a taunt among all the nations of the earth? 9Have you forgotten the evil of your fathers, the evil of the kings of Judah, the evil of their[1] wives, your own evil, and the evil of your wives, which they committed in the land of Judah and in the streets of Jerusalem? 10They have not humbled themselves even to this day, nor have they feared, nor walked in my law and my statutes that I set before you and before your fathers.

11"Therefore thus says the LORD of hosts, the God of Israel: Behold, I will set my face against you for harm, to cut off all Judah. 12I will take the remnant of Judah who have set their faces to come to the land of Egypt to live, and they shall all be consumed. In the land of Egypt they shall fall; by the sword and by famine they shall be consumed. From the least to the greatest, they shall die by the sword and by famine, and they shall become an oath, a horror, a curse, and a taunt. 13I will punish those who dwell in the land of Egypt, as I have punished Jerusalem, with the sword, with famine, and with pestilence, 14so that none of the remnant of Judah who have come to live in the land of Egypt shall escape or survive or return to the land of Judah, to which they desire to return to dwell there. For they shall not return, except some fugitives."

15Then all the men who knew that their wives had made offerings to other gods, and all the women who stood by, a great assembly, all the people who lived in Pathros in the land of Egypt, answered Jeremiah: 16"As for the word that you have spoken to us in the name of the LORD, we will not listen to you. 17But we will do everything that we have vowed, make offerings to the queen of heaven and pour out drink offerings to her, as we did, both we and our fathers, our kings and our officials, in the cities of Judah and in the streets of Jerusalem. For then we had plenty of food, and prospered, and saw no disaster. 18But since we left off making offerings to the queen of heaven and pouring out drink offerings to her, we have lacked everything and have been consumed by the sword and by famine." 19And the women said,[2] "When we made offerings to the queen of heaven and poured out drink offerings to her, was it without our husbands' approval that we made cakes for her bearing her image and poured out drink offerings to her?"

20Then Jeremiah said to all the people, men and women, all the people who had given him this answer: 21"As for the offerings that you offered in the cities of Judah and in the streets of Jerusalem, you and your fathers, your kings and your officials, and the people of the land, did not the LORD remember them? Did it not come into his mind? 22The LORD could no longer bear your evil deeds and the abominations that you committed. Therefore your land has become a desolation and a waste and a curse, without inhabitant, as it is this day. 23It is because you made offerings and because you sinned against the LORD and did not obey the voice of the LORD or walk in his law and in his statutes and in his testimonies that this disaster has happened to you, as at this day."

24Jeremiah said to all the people and all the women, "Hear the word of the LORD, all you of Judah who are in the land of Egypt. 25Thus says the LORD of hosts, the God of Israel: You and your wives have declared with your mouths, and have

[1]Hebrew *his* [2]Compare Syriac; Hebrew lacks *And the women said*

JEREMIAH 44:14–18

RULER OF HEAVEN

God consistently warned his people throughout the Old Testament not to worship other gods. Yet many Israelites intermarried with people who practiced other religions, which often led the Israelites away from worshiping God. Unfortunately, the people did not understand that God was the true Ruler of heaven. Had they stopped worshiping false gods and instead listened to Jeremiah and followed the one true God, their circumstances could have been drastically different.

Jesus echoed Jeremiah's message when he was tempted by Satan in the wilderness: "You shall worship the Lord your God and him only shall you serve" (Mt 4:10). Even today believers worship false gods of money, pride, power, and other entities that promise rewards but don't deliver. While modern believers no longer offer sacrifices to the "queen of heaven," it is important for believers to be consistently aware of anything that may be distracting them from worshiping and obeying God.

fulfilled it with your hands, saying, 'We will surely perform our vows that we have
made, to make offerings to the queen of heaven and to pour out drink offerings to
her.' Then confirm your vows and perform your vows! 26Therefore hear the word
of the Lord, all you of Judah who dwell in the land of Egypt: Behold, I have sworn
by my great name, says the Lord, that my name shall no more be invoked by the
mouth of any man of Judah in all the land of Egypt, saying, 'As the Lord God lives.'
27Behold, I am watching over them for disaster and not for good. All the men of
Judah who are in the land of Egypt shall be consumed by the sword and by famine, until there is an end of them. 28And those who escape the sword shall return
from the land of Egypt to the land of Judah, few in number; and all the remnant of
Judah, who came to the land of Egypt to live, shall know whose word will stand,
mine or theirs. 29This shall be the sign to you, declares the Lord, that I will punish you in this place, in order that you may know that my words will surely stand
against you for harm: 30Thus says the Lord, Behold, I will give Pharaoh Hophra
king of Egypt into the hand of his enemies and into the hand of those who seek
his life, as I gave Zedekiah king of Judah into the hand of Nebuchadnezzar king of
Babylon, who was his enemy and sought his life."

Message to Baruch

45 The word that Jeremiah the prophet spoke to Baruch the son of Neriah,
when he wrote these words in a book at the dictation of Jeremiah, in the
fourth year of Jehoiakim the son of Josiah, king of Judah: 2"Thus says the Lord,
the God of Israel, to you, O Baruch: 3You said, 'Woe is me! For the Lord has added
sorrow to my pain. I am weary with my groaning, and I find no rest.' 4Thus shall
you say to him, Thus says the Lord: Behold, what I have built I am breaking down,
and what I have planted I am plucking up—that is, the whole land. 5And do you
seek great things for yourself? Seek them not, for behold, I am bringing disaster
upon all flesh, declares the Lord. But I will give you your life as a prize of war in
all places to which you may go."

Judgment on Egypt

46 The word of the Lord that came to Jeremiah the prophet concerning the
nations.
2About Egypt. Concerning the army of Pharaoh Neco, king of Egypt, which
was by the river Euphrates at Carchemish and which Nebuchadnezzar king of
Babylon defeated in the fourth year of Jehoiakim the son of Josiah, king of Judah:

3 "Prepare buckler and shield,
    and advance for battle!
4 Harness the horses;
    mount, O horsemen!
Take your stations with your helmets,
    polish your spears,
    put on your armor!
5 Why have I seen it?
They are dismayed
    and have turned backward.
Their warriors are beaten down
    and have fled in haste;
they look not back—
    terror on every side!
                                        declares the Lord.

6 "The swift cannot flee away,
    nor the warrior escape;
in the north by the river Euphrates
    they have stumbled and fallen.

7 "Who is this, rising like the Nile,
like rivers whose waters surge?
8 Egypt rises like the Nile,
like rivers whose waters surge.
He said, 'I will rise, I will cover the earth,
I will destroy cities and their inhabitants.'
9 Advance, O horses,
and rage, O chariots!
Let the warriors go out:
men of Cush and Put who handle the shield,
men of Lud, skilled in handling the bow.
10 That day is the day of the Lord GOD of hosts,
a day of vengeance,
to avenge himself on his foes.
The sword shall devour and be sated
and drink its fill of their blood.
For the Lord GOD of hosts holds a sacrifice
in the north country by the river Euphrates.
11 Go up to Gilead, and take balm,
O virgin daughter of Egypt!
In vain you have used many medicines;
there is no healing for you.
12 The nations have heard of your shame,
and the earth is full of your cry;
for warrior has stumbled against warrior;
they have both fallen together."

13The word that the LORD spoke to Jeremiah the prophet about the coming of Nebuchadnezzar king of Babylon to strike the land of Egypt:

14 "Declare in Egypt, and proclaim in Migdol;
proclaim in Memphis and Tahpanhes;
say, 'Stand ready and be prepared,
for the sword shall devour around you.'
15 Why are your mighty ones face down?
They do not stand[1]
because the LORD thrust them down.
16 He made many stumble, and they fell,
and they said one to another,
'Arise, and let us go back to our own people
and to the land of our birth,
because of the sword of the oppressor.'
17 Call the name of Pharaoh, king of Egypt,
'Noisy one who lets the hour go by.'

18 "As I live, declares the King,
whose name is the LORD of hosts,
like Tabor among the mountains
and like Carmel by the sea, shall one come.
19 Prepare yourselves baggage for exile,
O inhabitants of Egypt!
For Memphis shall become a waste,
a ruin, without inhabitant.

20 "A beautiful heifer is Egypt,
but a biting fly from the north has come upon her.

[1]Hebrew *He does not stand*

21 Even her hired soldiers in her midst
are like fattened calves;
yes, they have turned and fled together;
they did not stand,
for the day of their calamity has come upon them,
the time of their punishment.

22 "She makes a sound like a serpent gliding away;
for her enemies march in force
and come against her with axes
like those who fell trees.
23 They shall cut down her forest,
declares the LORD,
though it is impenetrable,
because they are more numerous than locusts;
they are without number.
24 The daughter of Egypt shall be put to shame;
she shall be delivered into the hand of a people from the north."

25The LORD of hosts, the God of Israel, said: "Behold, I am bringing punishment upon Amon of Thebes, and Pharaoh and Egypt and her gods and her kings,
upon Pharaoh and those who trust in him. 26I will deliver them into the hand of
those who seek their life, into the hand of Nebuchadnezzar king of Babylon and
his officers. Afterward Egypt shall be inhabited as in the days of old, declares the
LORD.

27 "But fear not, O Jacob my servant,
nor be dismayed, O Israel,
for behold, I will save you from far away,
and your offspring from the land of their captivity.
Jacob shall return and have quiet and ease,
and none shall make him afraid.
28 Fear not, O Jacob my servant,
declares the LORD,
for I am with you.
I will make a full end of all the nations
to which I have driven you,
but of you I will not make a full end.
I will discipline you in just measure,
and I will by no means leave you unpunished."

Judgment on the Philistines

47 The word of the LORD that came to Jeremiah the prophet concerning the Philistines, before Pharaoh struck down Gaza.

2 "Thus says the LORD:
Behold, waters are rising out of the north,
and shall become an overflowing torrent;
they shall overflow the land and all that fills it,
the city and those who dwell in it.
Men shall cry out,
and every inhabitant of the land shall wail.
3 At the noise of the stamping of the hoofs of his
stallions,
at the rushing of his chariots, at the rumbling of
their wheels,
the fathers look not back to their children,
so feeble are their hands,

4 because of the day that is coming to destroy
all the Philistines,
to cut off from Tyre and Sidon
every helper that remains.
For the LORD is destroying the Philistines,
the remnant of the coastland of Caphtor.
5 Baldness has come upon Gaza;
Ashkelon has perished.
O remnant of their valley,
how long will you gash yourselves?
6 Ah, sword of the LORD!
How long till you are quiet?
Put yourself into your scabbard;
rest and be still!
7 How can it[1] be quiet
when the LORD has given it a charge?
Against Ashkelon and against the seashore
he has appointed it."

Judgment on Moab

48 Concerning Moab.
Thus says the LORD of hosts, the God of Israel:

"Woe to Nebo, for it is laid waste!
Kiriathaim is put to shame, it is taken;
the fortress is put to shame and broken down;
2 the renown of Moab is no more.
In Heshbon they planned disaster against her:
'Come, let us cut her off from being a nation!'
You also, O Madmen, shall be brought to silence;
the sword shall pursue you.

3 "A voice! A cry from Horonaim,
'Desolation and great destruction!'
4 Moab is destroyed;
her little ones have made a cry.
5 For at the ascent of Luhith
they go up weeping;[2]
for at the descent of Horonaim
they have heard the distressed cry[3] of destruction.
6 Flee! Save yourselves!
You will be like a juniper in the desert!
7 For, because you trusted in your works and your treasures,
you also shall be taken;
and Chemosh shall go into exile
with his priests and his officials.
8 The destroyer shall come upon every city,
and no city shall escape;
the valley shall perish,
and the plain shall be destroyed,
as the LORD has spoken.

9 "Give wings to Moab,
for she would fly away;
her cities shall become a desolation,
with no inhabitant in them.

[1]Septuagint, Vulgate; Hebrew *you* [2]Hebrew *weeping goes up with weeping* [3]Septuagint (compare Isaiah 15:5) *heard the cry*

10"Cursed is he who does the work of the LORD with slackness, and cursed is
he who keeps back his sword from bloodshed.

11 "Moab has been at ease from his youth
and has settled on his dregs;
he has not been emptied from vessel to vessel,
nor has he gone into exile;
so his taste remains in him,
and his scent is not changed.

12"Therefore, behold, the days are coming, declares the LORD, when I shall
send to him pourers who will pour him, and empty his vessels and break his[1] jars
in pieces. 13Then Moab shall be ashamed of Chemosh, as the house of Israel was
ashamed of Bethel, their confidence.

14 "How do you say, 'We are heroes
and mighty men of war'?
15 The destroyer of Moab and his cities has come up,
and the choicest of his young men have gone down to slaughter,
declares the King, whose name is the LORD of hosts.
16 The calamity of Moab is near at hand,
and his affliction hastens swiftly.
17 Grieve for him, all you who are around him,
and all who know his name;
say, 'How the mighty scepter is broken,
the glorious staff.'

18 "Come down from your glory,
and sit on the parched ground,
O inhabitant of Dibon!
For the destroyer of Moab has come up against you;
he has destroyed your strongholds.
19 Stand by the way and watch,
O inhabitant of Aroer!
Ask him who flees and her who escapes;
say, 'What has happened?'
20 Moab is put to shame, for it is broken;
wail and cry!
Tell it beside the Arnon,
that Moab is laid waste.

21"Judgment has come upon the tableland, upon Holon, and Jahzah, and
Mephaath, 22and Dibon, and Nebo, and Beth-diblathaim, 23and Kiriathaim, and
Beth-gamul, and Beth-meon, 24and Kerioth, and Bozrah, and all the cities of the
land of Moab, far and near. 25The horn of Moab is cut off, and his arm is broken,
declares the LORD.

26"Make him drunk, because he magnified himself against the LORD, so that
Moab shall wallow in his vomit, and he too shall be held in derision. 27Was not
Israel a derision to you? Was he found among thieves, that whenever you spoke
of him you wagged your head?

28 "Leave the cities, and dwell in the rock,
O inhabitants of Moab!
Be like the dove that nests
in the sides of the mouth of a gorge.
29 We have heard of the pride of Moab—
he is very proud—

[1]Septuagint, Aquila; Hebrew *their*

of his loftiness, his pride, and his arrogance,
and the haughtiness of his heart.
30 I know his insolence, declares the LORD;
his boasts are false,
his deeds are false.
31 Therefore I wail for Moab;
I cry out for all Moab;
for the men of Kir-hareseth I mourn.
32 More than for Jazer I weep for you,
O vine of Sibmah!
Your branches passed over the sea,
reached to the Sea of Jazer;
on your summer fruits and your grapes
the destroyer has fallen.
33 Gladness and joy have been taken away
from the fruitful land of Moab;
I have made the wine cease from the winepresses;
no one treads them with shouts of joy;
the shouting is not the shout of joy.

34 "From the outcry at Heshbon even to Elealeh, as far as Jahaz they utter their
voice, from Zoar to Horonaim and Eglath-shelishiyah. For the waters of Nimrim
also have become desolate. 35 And I will bring to an end in Moab, declares the
LORD, him who offers sacrifice in the high place and makes offerings to his god.
36 Therefore my heart moans for Moab like a flute, and my heart moans like a flute
for the men of Kir-hareseth. Therefore the riches they gained have perished.

37 "For every head is shaved and every beard cut off. On all the hands are gash-
es, and around the waist is sackcloth. 38 On all the housetops of Moab and in the
squares there is nothing but lamentation, for I have broken Moab like a vessel for
which no one cares, declares the LORD. 39 How it is broken! How they wail! How
Moab has turned his back in shame! So Moab has become a derision and a horror
to all that are around him."

40 For thus says the LORD:
"Behold, one shall fly swiftly like an eagle
and spread his wings against Moab;
41 the cities shall be taken
and the strongholds seized.
The heart of the warriors of Moab shall be in
that day
like the heart of a woman in her birth pains;
42 Moab shall be destroyed and be no longer a people,
because he magnified himself against the LORD.
43 Terror, pit, and snare
are before you, O inhabitant of Moab!
declares the LORD.

44 He who flees from the terror
shall fall into the pit,
and he who climbs out of the pit
shall be caught in the snare.
For I will bring these things upon Moab,
the year of their punishment,
declares the LORD.

45 "In the shadow of Heshbon
fugitives stop without strength,
for fire came out from Heshbon,
flame from the house of Sihon;

it has destroyed the forehead of Moab,
the crown of the sons of tumult.
46 Woe to you, O Moab!
The people of Chemosh are undone,
for your sons have been taken captive,
and your daughters into captivity.
47 Yet I will restore the fortunes of Moab
in the latter days, declares the LORD."
Thus far is the judgment on Moab.

Judgment on Ammon

49 Concerning the Ammonites.
Thus says the LORD:

"Has Israel no sons?
Has he no heir?
Why then has Milcom[1] dispossessed Gad,
and his people settled in its cities?
2 Therefore, behold, the days are coming,
declares the LORD,
when I will cause the battle cry to be heard
against Rabbah of the Ammonites;
it shall become a desolate mound,
and its villages shall be burned with fire;
then Israel shall dispossess those who dispossessed him,
says the LORD.

3 "Wail, O Heshbon, for Ai is laid waste!
Cry out, O daughters of Rabbah!
Put on sackcloth,
lament, and run to and fro among the hedges!
For Milcom shall go into exile,
with his priests and his officials.
4 Why do you boast of your valleys,[2]
O faithless daughter,
who trusted in her treasures, saying,
'Who will come against me?'
5 Behold, I will bring terror upon you,
declares the Lord GOD of hosts,
from all who are around you,
and you shall be driven out, every man straight before him,
with none to gather the fugitives.

6 "But afterward I will restore the fortunes of the Ammonites, declares the LORD."

Judgment on Edom

7 Concerning Edom.
Thus says the LORD of hosts:

"Is wisdom no more in Teman?
Has counsel perished from the prudent?
Has their wisdom vanished?
8 Flee, turn back, dwell in the depths,
O inhabitants of Dedan!
For I will bring the calamity of Esau upon him,
the time when I punish him.

---

[1] Or *their king*; also verse 3 [2] Hebrew *boast of your valleys, your valley flows*

9 If grape gatherers came to you,
would they not leave gleanings?
If thieves came by night,
would they not destroy only enough for themselves?
10 But I have stripped Esau bare;
I have uncovered his hiding places,
and he is not able to conceal himself.
His children are destroyed, and his brothers,
and his neighbors; and he is no more.
11 Leave your fatherless children; I will keep them alive;
and let your widows trust in me."

12For thus says the Lord: "If those who did not deserve to drink the cup must
drink it, will you go unpunished? You shall not go unpunished, but you must
drink. 13For I have sworn by myself, declares the Lord, that Bozrah shall become
a horror, a taunt, a waste, and a curse, and all her cities shall be perpetual wastes."

14 I have heard a message from the Lord,
and an envoy has been sent among the nations:
"Gather yourselves together and come against her,
and rise up for battle!
15 For behold, I will make you small among the nations,
despised among mankind.
16 The horror you inspire has deceived you,
and the pride of your heart,
you who live in the clefts of the rock,[1]
who hold the height of the hill.
Though you make your nest as high as the eagle's,
I will bring you down from there,
declares the Lord.

17"Edom shall become a horror. Everyone who passes by it will be horrified
and will hiss because of all its disasters. 18As when Sodom and Gomorrah and
their neighboring cities were overthrown, says the Lord, no man shall dwell
there, no man shall sojourn in her. 19Behold, like a lion coming up from the jungle
of the Jordan against a perennial pasture, I will suddenly make him[2] run away
from her. And I will appoint over her whomever I choose. For who is like me?
Who will summon me? What shepherd can stand before me? 20Therefore hear the
plan that the Lord has made against Edom and the purposes that he has formed
against the inhabitants of Teman: Even the little ones of the flock shall be dragged
away. Surely their fold shall be appalled at their fate. 21At the sound of their fall the
earth shall tremble; the sound of their cry shall be heard at the Red Sea. 22Behold,
one shall mount up and fly swiftly like an eagle and spread his wings against Bozrah, and the heart of the warriors of Edom shall be in that day like the heart of a
woman in her birth pains."

Judgment on Damascus

23Concerning Damascus:

"Hamath and Arpad are confounded,
for they have heard bad news;
they melt in fear,
they are troubled like the sea that cannot be quiet.
24 Damascus has become feeble, she turned to flee,
and panic seized her;
anguish and sorrows have taken hold of her,
as of a woman in labor.

[1] Or *of Sela* [2] Septuagint, Syriac *them*

25 How is the famous city not forsaken,
the city of my joy?
26 Therefore her young men shall fall in her squares,
and all her soldiers shall be destroyed in that day,
declares the LORD of hosts.
27 And I will kindle a fire in the wall of Damascus,
and it shall devour the strongholds of Ben-hadad."

Judgment on Kedar and Hazor

28 Concerning Kedar and the kingdoms of Hazor that Nebuchadnezzar king of
Babylon struck down.

Thus says the LORD:
"Rise up, advance against Kedar!
Destroy the people of the east!
29 Their tents and their flocks shall be taken,
their curtains and all their goods;
their camels shall be led away from them,
and men shall cry to them: 'Terror on
every side!'
30 Flee, wander far away, dwell in the depths,
O inhabitants of Hazor!
declares the LORD.

For Nebuchadnezzar king of Babylon
has made a plan against you
and formed a purpose against you.
31 "Rise up, advance against a nation at ease,
that dwells securely,
declares the LORD,
that has no gates or bars,
that dwells alone.
32 Their camels shall become plunder,
their herds of livestock a spoil.
I will scatter to every wind
those who cut the corners of their hair,
and I will bring their calamity
from every side of them,
declares the LORD.
33 Hazor shall become a haunt of jackals,
an everlasting waste;
no man shall dwell there;
no man shall sojourn in her."

Judgment on Elam

34 The word of the LORD that came to Jeremiah the prophet concerning Elam,
in the beginning of the reign of Zedekiah king of Judah.
35 Thus says the LORD of hosts: "Behold, I will break the bow of Elam, the main-
stay of their might. 36 And I will bring upon Elam the four winds from the four
quarters of heaven. And I will scatter them to all those winds, and there shall be
no nation to which those driven out of Elam shall not come. 37 I will terrify Elam
before their enemies and before those who seek their life. I will bring disaster
upon them, my fierce anger, declares the LORD. I will send the sword after them,
until I have consumed them, 38 and I will set my throne in Elam and destroy their
king and officials, declares the LORD.
39 "But in the latter days I will restore the fortunes of Elam, declares the LORD."

Judgment on Babylon

50 The word that the LORD spoke concerning Babylon, concerning the land
of the Chaldeans, by Jeremiah the prophet:

2 "Declare among the nations and proclaim,
set up a banner and proclaim,
conceal it not, and say:
'Babylon is taken,
Bel is put to shame,
Merodach is dismayed.
Her images are put to shame,
her idols are dismayed.'

3 "For out of the north a nation has come up against her, which shall make her
land a desolation, and none shall dwell in it; both man and beast shall flee away.
4 "In those days and in that time, declares the LORD, the people of Israel and the
people of Judah shall come together, weeping as they come, and they shall seek
the LORD their God. 5 They shall ask the way to Zion, with faces turned toward it,
saying, 'Come, let us join ourselves to the LORD in an everlasting covenant that
will never be forgotten.'
6 "My people have been lost sheep. Their shepherds have led them astray, turning them away on the mountains. From mountain to hill they have gone. They
have forgotten their fold. 7 All who found them have devoured them, and their
enemies have said, 'We are not guilty, for they have sinned against the LORD, their
habitation of righteousness, the LORD, the hope of their fathers.'
8 "Flee from the midst of Babylon, and go out of the land of the Chaldeans,
and be as male goats before the flock. 9 For behold, I am stirring up and bringing
against Babylon a gathering of great nations, from the north country. And they
shall array themselves against her. From there she shall be taken. Their arrows
are like a skilled warrior who does not return empty-handed. 10 Chaldea shall be
plundered; all who plunder her shall be sated, declares the LORD.

11 "Though you rejoice, though you exult,
O plunderers of my heritage,
though you frolic like a heifer in the pasture,
and neigh like stallions,
12 your mother shall be utterly shamed,
and she who bore you shall be disgraced.
Behold, she shall be the last of the nations,
a wilderness, a dry land, and a desert.
13 Because of the wrath of the LORD she shall not be inhabited
but shall be an utter desolation;
everyone who passes by Babylon shall be appalled,
and hiss because of all her wounds.
14 Set yourselves in array against Babylon all around,
all you who bend the bow;
shoot at her, spare no arrows,
for she has sinned against the LORD.
15 Raise a shout against her all around;
she has surrendered;
her bulwarks have fallen;
her walls are thrown down.
For this is the vengeance of the LORD:
take vengeance on her;
do to her as she has done.
16 Cut off from Babylon the sower,
and the one who handles the sickle in time of harvest;

SCATTERED SHEEP

The Lord allowed Babylon to overtake Judah as punishment for the people's constant and consistent disobedience. However, God never intended for the nation of Babylon to remain in power over his people. This chapter describes the Lord's judgment on Babylon that would eventually come. Verses 4 – 5 speak of when the people of Israel and Judah together would seek the Lord and come and join themselves to the Lord in an everlasting covenant. Though this could refer to a remnant from both nations returning to the land of Judah after the Babylonian captivity, the ultimate fulfillment will be found in the Messianic age when God's divided people will be brought together and live in righteousness, peace, and unity.

In verse 6, Jeremiah compares his people to a flock of sheep that had wandered and been led astray. The false prophets and false gods acted as irresponsible and evil shepherds to the flock of Israel, and they caused the people to wander away from God and to forget from where they had come. The sheep of Israel needed to return to the one true Shepherd (Jn 10:11; Heb 13:20). In Luke 15:1 – 7, Jesus told the parable of the lost sheep and explained how a good shepherd will do everything within his power to keep his flock together. Even if 99 sheep are accounted for and one is missing, a good shepherd will go after the missing one and bring it back to the flock. Jeremiah pointed out that God, the Shepherd of the Israelites, was working to bring his flock back to him again.

These verses in Jeremiah provide great encouragement for believers today, for no matter how far someone may have wandered away from God, they are never fully out of his reach. The Israelites had wandered very far away from him, yet God continued to mercifully call for them to return to him. Psalm 51:17 says, "A broken and contrite heart, O God, you will not despise." God has a strong desire for his followers to stay near him, but even if they wander away, a broken heart of true repentance can always bring them back.

because of the sword of the oppressor,
every one shall turn to his own people,
and every one shall flee to his own land.

17"Israel is a hunted sheep driven away by lions. First the king of Assyria devoured him, and now at last Nebuchadnezzar king of Babylon has gnawed his
bones. 18Therefore, thus says the LORD of hosts, the God of Israel: Behold, I am
bringing punishment on the king of Babylon and his land, as I punished the king
of Assyria. 19I will restore Israel to his pasture, and he shall feed on Carmel and
in Bashan, and his desire shall be satisfied on the hills of Ephraim and in Gilead.
20In those days and in that time, declares the LORD, iniquity shall be sought in
Israel, and there shall be none, and sin in Judah, and none shall be found, for I will
pardon those whom I leave as a remnant.

21 "Go up against the land of Merathaim,[1]
and against the inhabitants of Pekod.[2]
Kill, and devote them to destruction,[3]
declares the LORD,
and do all that I have commanded you.
22 The noise of battle is in the land,
and great destruction!
23 How the hammer of the whole earth
is cut down and broken!
How Babylon has become
a horror among the nations!
24 I set a snare for you and you were taken,
O Babylon,
and you did not know it;
you were found and caught,
because you opposed the LORD.
25 The LORD has opened his armory
and brought out the weapons of his wrath,
for the Lord GOD of hosts has a work to do
in the land of the Chaldeans.
26 Come against her from every quarter;
open her granaries;
pile her up like heaps of grain, and devote her to
destruction;
let nothing be left of her.
27 Kill all her bulls;
let them go down to the slaughter.
Woe to them, for their day has come,
the time of their punishment.

28"A voice! They flee and escape from the land of Babylon, to declare in Zion
the vengeance of the LORD our God, vengeance for his temple.

29"Summon archers against Babylon, all those who bend the bow. Encamp
around her; let no one escape. Repay her according to her deeds; do to her according to all that she has done. For she has proudly defied the LORD, the Holy One
of Israel. 30Therefore her young men shall fall in her squares, and all her soldiers
shall be destroyed on that day, declares the LORD.

31 "Behold, I am against you, O proud one,
declares the Lord GOD of hosts,
for your day has come,
the time when I will punish you.

[1]*Merathaim* means *double rebellion* [2]*Pekod* means *punishment* [3]That is, set apart (devote) as an offering to the Lord (for destruction)

32 The proud one shall stumble and fall,
with none to raise him up,
and I will kindle a fire in his cities,
and it will devour all that is around him.

33"Thus says the LORD of hosts: The people of Israel are oppressed, and the
people of Judah with them. All who took them captive have held them fast; they
refuse to let them go. 34Their Redeemer is strong; the LORD of hosts is his name.
He will surely plead their cause, that he may give rest to the earth, but unrest to
the inhabitants of Babylon.

35 "A sword against the Chaldeans, declares the LORD,
and against the inhabitants of Babylon,
and against her officials and her wise men!
36 A sword against the diviners,
that they may become fools!
A sword against her warriors,
that they may be destroyed!
37 A sword against her horses and against her chariots,
and against all the foreign troops in her midst,
that they may become women!
A sword against all her treasures,
that they may be plundered!
38 A drought against her waters,
that they may be dried up!
For it is a land of images,
and they are mad over idols.

39"Therefore wild beasts shall dwell with hyenas in Babylon,[1] and ostriches
shall dwell in her. She shall never again have people, nor be inhabited for all generations. 40As when God overthrew Sodom and Gomorrah and their neighboring
cities, declares the LORD, so no man shall dwell there, and no son of man shall
sojourn in her.

41 "Behold, a people comes from the north;
a mighty nation and many kings
are stirring from the farthest parts of the earth.
42 They lay hold of bow and spear;
they are cruel and have no mercy.
The sound of them is like the roaring of the sea;
they ride on horses,
arrayed as a man for battle
against you, O daughter of Babylon!

43 "The king of Babylon heard the report of them,
and his hands fell helpless;
anguish seized him,
pain as of a woman in labor.

44"Behold, like a lion coming up from the thicket of the Jordan against a perennial pasture, I will suddenly make them run away from her, and I will appoint
over her whomever I choose. For who is like me? Who will summon me? What
shepherd can stand before me? 45Therefore hear the plan that the LORD has made
against Babylon, and the purposes that he has formed against the land of the
Chaldeans: Surely the little ones of their flock shall be dragged away; surely their
fold shall be appalled at their fate. 46At the sound of the capture of Babylon the
earth shall tremble, and her cry shall be heard among the nations."

[1]Hebrew lacks *in Babylon*

The Utter Destruction of Babylon

51 Thus says the LORD:
"Behold, I will stir up the spirit of a destroyer
against Babylon,
against the inhabitants of Leb-kamai,[1]
2 and I will send to Babylon winnowers,
and they shall winnow her,
and they shall empty her land,
when they come against her from every side
on the day of trouble.
3 Let not the archer bend his bow,
and let him not stand up in his armor.
Spare not her young men;
devote to destruction[2] all her army.
4 They shall fall down slain in the land of the Chaldeans,
and wounded in her streets.
5 For Israel and Judah have not been forsaken
by their God, the LORD of hosts,
but the land of the Chaldeans[3] is full of guilt
against the Holy One of Israel.

6 "Flee from the midst of Babylon;
let every one save his life!
Be not cut off in her punishment,
for this is the time of the LORD's vengeance,
the repayment he is rendering her.
7 Babylon was a golden cup in the LORD's hand,
making all the earth drunken;
the nations drank of her wine;
therefore the nations went mad.
8 Suddenly Babylon has fallen and been broken;
wail for her!
Take balm for her pain;
perhaps she may be healed.
9 We would have healed Babylon,
but she was not healed.
Forsake her, and let us go
each to his own country,
for her judgment has reached up to heaven
and has been lifted up even to the skies.
10 The LORD has brought about our vindication;
come, let us declare in Zion
the work of the LORD our God.

11 "Sharpen the arrows!
Take up the shields!

The LORD has stirred up the spirit of the kings of the Medes, because his purpose concerning Babylon is to destroy it, for that is the vengeance of the LORD, the vengeance for his temple.

12 "Set up a standard against the walls of Babylon;
make the watch strong;
set up watchmen;
prepare the ambushes;

---

[1]A code name for Chaldea [2]That is, set apart (devote) as an offering to the Lord (for destruction)
[3]Hebrew *their land*

for the LORD has both planned and done
what he spoke concerning the inhabitants of Babylon.
13 O you who dwell by many waters,
rich in treasures,
your end has come;
the thread of your life is cut.
14 The LORD of hosts has sworn by himself:
Surely I will fill you with men, as many as locusts,
and they shall raise the shout of victory over you.

15 "It is he who made the earth by his power,
who established the world by his wisdom,
and by his understanding stretched out the heavens.
16 When he utters his voice there is a tumult of waters in the heavens,
and he makes the mist rise from the ends of the earth.
He makes lightning for the rain,
and he brings forth the wind from his storehouses.
17 Every man is stupid and without knowledge;
every goldsmith is put to shame by his idols,
for his images are false,
and there is no breath in them.
18 They are worthless, a work of delusion;
at the time of their punishment they shall perish.
19 Not like these is he who is the portion of Jacob,
for he is the one who formed all things,
and Israel is the tribe of his inheritance;
the LORD of hosts is his name.

20 "You are my hammer and weapon of war:
with you I break nations in pieces;
with you I destroy kingdoms;
21 with you I break in pieces the horse and his rider;
with you I break in pieces the chariot and the charioteer;
22 with you I break in pieces man and woman;
with you I break in pieces the old man and the youth;
with you I break in pieces the young man and the young woman;
23 with you I break in pieces the shepherd and his flock;
with you I break in pieces the farmer and his team;
with you I break in pieces governors and commanders.

24 "I will repay Babylon and all the inhabitants of Chaldea before your very eyes
for all the evil that they have done in Zion, declares the LORD.

25 "Behold, I am against you, O destroying mountain,
declares the LORD,
which destroys the whole earth;
I will stretch out my hand against you,
and roll you down from the crags,
and make you a burnt mountain.
26 No stone shall be taken from you for a corner
and no stone for a foundation,
but you shall be a perpetual waste,
declares the LORD.

27 "Set up a standard on the earth;
blow the trumpet among the nations;
prepare the nations for war against her;
summon against her the kingdoms,
Ararat, Minni, and Ashkenaz;

appoint a marshal against her;
bring up horses like bristling locusts.
28 Prepare the nations for war against her,
the kings of the Medes, with their governors and deputies,
and every land under their dominion.
29 The land trembles and writhes in pain,
for the LORD's purposes against Babylon stand,
to make the land of Babylon a desolation,
without inhabitant.
30 The warriors of Babylon have ceased fighting;
they remain in their strongholds;
their strength has failed;
they have become women;
her dwellings are on fire;
her bars are broken.
31 One runner runs to meet another,
and one messenger to meet another,
to tell the king of Babylon
that his city is taken on every side;
32 the fords have been seized,
the marshes are burned with fire,
and the soldiers are in panic.
33 For thus says the LORD of hosts, the God of Israel:
The daughter of Babylon is like a threshing floor
at the time when it is trodden;
yet a little while
and the time of her harvest will come."

34 "Nebuchadnezzar the king of Babylon has devoured me;
he has crushed me;
he has made me an empty vessel;
he has swallowed me like a monster;
he has filled his stomach with my delicacies;
he has rinsed me out.[1]
35 The violence done to me and to my kinsmen be upon Babylon,"
let the inhabitant of Zion say.
"My blood be upon the inhabitants of Chaldea,"
let Jerusalem say.
36 Therefore thus says the LORD:
"Behold, I will plead your cause
and take vengeance for you.
I will dry up her sea
and make her fountain dry,
37 and Babylon shall become a heap of ruins,
the haunt of jackals,
a horror and a hissing,
without inhabitant.

38 "They shall roar together like lions;
they shall growl like lions' cubs.
39 While they are inflamed I will prepare them a feast
and make them drunk, that they may become merry,
then sleep a perpetual sleep
and not wake, declares the LORD.
40 I will bring them down like lambs to the slaughter,
like rams and male goats.

[1]Or *he has expelled me*

41 "How Babylon[1] is taken,
the praise of the whole earth seized!
How Babylon has become
a horror among the nations!
42 The sea has come up on Babylon;
she is covered with its tumultuous waves.
43 Her cities have become a horror,
a land of drought and a desert,
a land in which no one dwells,
and through which no son of man passes.
44 And I will punish Bel in Babylon,
and take out of his mouth what he has swallowed.
The nations shall no longer flow to him;
the wall of Babylon has fallen.

45 "Go out of the midst of her, my people!
Let every one save his life
from the fierce anger of the LORD!
46 Let not your heart faint, and be not fearful
at the report heard in the land,
when a report comes in one year
and afterward a report in another year,
and violence is in the land,
and ruler is against ruler.

47 "Therefore, behold, the days are coming
when I will punish the images of Babylon;
her whole land shall be put to shame,
and all her slain shall fall in the midst of her.
48 Then the heavens and the earth,
and all that is in them,
shall sing for joy over Babylon,
for the destroyers shall come against them out of the north,
declares the LORD.

49 Babylon must fall for the slain of Israel,
just as for Babylon have fallen the slain of all the earth.

50 "You who have escaped from the sword,
go, do not stand still!
Remember the LORD from far away,
and let Jerusalem come into your mind:
51 'We are put to shame, for we have heard reproach;
dishonor has covered our face,
for foreigners have come
into the holy places of the LORD's house.'

52 "Therefore, behold, the days are coming, declares the LORD,
when I will execute judgment upon her images,
and through all her land
the wounded shall groan.
53 Though Babylon should mount up to heaven,
and though she should fortify her strong height,
yet destroyers would come from me against her,
declares the LORD.

54 "A voice! A cry from Babylon!
The noise of great destruction from the land of the Chaldeans!

[1]Hebrew *Sheshach*, a code name for Babylon

55 For the LORD is laying Babylon waste
and stilling her mighty voice.
Their waves roar like many waters;
the noise of their voice is raised,
56 for a destroyer has come upon her,
upon Babylon;
her warriors are taken;
their bows are broken in pieces,
for the LORD is a God of recompense;
he will surely repay.
57 I will make drunk her officials and her wise men,
her governors, her commanders, and her warriors;
they shall sleep a perpetual sleep and not wake,
declares the King, whose name is the LORD of hosts.

58 "Thus says the LORD of hosts:
The broad wall of Babylon
shall be leveled to the ground,
and her high gates
shall be burned with fire.
The peoples labor for nothing,
and the nations weary themselves only for fire."

59The word that Jeremiah the prophet commanded Seraiah the son of Neriah,
son of Mahseiah, when he went with Zedekiah king of Judah to Babylon, in the
fourth year of his reign. Seraiah was the quartermaster. 60Jeremiah wrote in a
book all the disaster that should come upon Babylon, all these words that are
written concerning Babylon. 61And Jeremiah said to Seraiah: "When you come to
Babylon, see that you read all these words, 62and say, 'O LORD, you have said concerning this place that you will cut it off, so that nothing shall dwell in it, neither
man nor beast, and it shall be desolate forever.' 63When you finish reading this
book, tie a stone to it and cast it into the midst of the Euphrates, 64and say, 'Thus
shall Babylon sink, to rise no more, because of the disaster that I am bringing
upon her, and they shall become exhausted.'"
Thus far are the words of Jeremiah.

The Fall of Jerusalem Recounted

52 Zedekiah was twenty-one years old when he became king, and he reigned
eleven years in Jerusalem. His mother's name was Hamutal the daughter of
Jeremiah of Libnah. 2And he did what was evil in the sight of the LORD, according
to all that Jehoiakim had done. 3For because of the anger of the LORD it came to the
point in Jerusalem and Judah that he cast them out from his presence.
And Zedekiah rebelled against the king of Babylon. 4And in the ninth year of
his reign, in the tenth month, on the tenth day of the month, Nebuchadnezzar
king of Babylon came with all his army against Jerusalem, and laid siege to it.
And they built siegeworks all around it. 5So the city was besieged till the eleventh year of King Zedekiah. 6On the ninth day of the fourth month the famine
was so severe in the city that there was no food for the people of the land. 7Then
a breach was made in the city, and all the men of war fled and went out from the
city by night by the way of a gate between the two walls, by the king's garden,
and the Chaldeans were around the city. And they went in the direction of the
Arabah. 8But the army of the Chaldeans pursued the king and overtook Zedekiah in the plains of Jericho, and all his army was scattered from him. 9Then
they captured the king and brought him up to the king of Babylon at Riblah
in the land of Hamath, and he passed sentence on him. 10The king of Babylon
slaughtered the sons of Zedekiah before his eyes, and also slaughtered all the
officials of Judah at Riblah. 11He put out the eyes of Zedekiah, and bound him

JEREMIAH 52:1–34

ASSURANCE OF TRUTH

The text of Jeremiah ends with the fulfillment of the prophecy that Jeremiah had been preaching throughout the entire book. It details the fall of Jerusalem in 586 BC and reports how many people were sent into exile—all just as Jeremiah had said. Finally, it ends with the release of Jehoiachin, an earlier king of Judah, from prison.

Jehoiachin had been taken as one of the captives under Nebuchadnezzar in the deportation of 597 BC, but once Evil-merodach became king in 561, he released Jehoiachin from prison and gave him a regular allotment of provisions. The story of Jehoiachin's release ends the book of Jeremiah on a note of hope, and it also represents the story of the Israelites, which then points toward our ultimate hope for the future. Because everything that the Lord said through Jeremiah came true, believers today have an assurance that God will also deliver on his promise of eternal life for those who believe in Jesus Christ. God's Word held true in the past, it is true in the present, and it will remain true in the future.

in chains, and the king of Babylon took him to Babylon, and put him in prison till the day of his death.

The Temple Burned

12 In the fifth month, on the tenth day of the month—that was the nineteenth year of King Nebuchadnezzar, king of Babylon—Nebuzaradan the captain of the bodyguard, who served the king of Babylon, entered Jerusalem. 13 And he burned the house of the LORD, and the king's house and all the houses of Jerusalem; every great house he burned down. 14 And all the army of the Chaldeans, who were with the captain of the guard, broke down all the walls around Jerusalem. 15 And Nebuzaradan the captain of the guard carried away captive some of the poorest of the people and the rest of the people who were left in the city and the deserters who had deserted to the king of Babylon, together with the rest of the artisans. 16 But Nebuzaradan the captain of the guard left some of the poorest of the land to be vinedressers and plowmen.

17 And the pillars of bronze that were in the house of the LORD, and the stands and the bronze sea that were in the house of the LORD, the Chaldeans broke in pieces, and carried all the bronze to Babylon. 18 And they took away the pots and the shovels and the snuffers and the basins and the dishes for incense and all the vessels of bronze used in the temple service; 19 also the small bowls and the fire pans and the basins and the pots and the lampstands and the dishes for incense and the bowls for drink offerings. What was of gold the captain of the guard took away as gold, and what was of silver, as silver. 20 As for the two pillars, the one sea, the twelve bronze bulls that were under the sea,[1] and the stands, which Solomon the king had made for the house of the LORD, the bronze of all these things was beyond weight. 21 As for the pillars, the height of the one pillar was eighteen cubits,[2] its circumference was twelve cubits, and its thickness was four fingers, and it was hollow. 22 On it was a capital of bronze. The height of the one capital was five cubits. A network and pomegranates, all of bronze, were around the capital. And the second pillar had the same, with pomegranates. 23 There were ninety-six pomegranates on the sides; all the pomegranates were a hundred upon the network all around.

The People Exiled to Babylon

24 And the captain of the guard took Seraiah the chief priest, and Zephaniah the second priest and the three keepers of the threshold; 25 and from the city he took an officer who had been in command of the men of war, and seven men of the king's council, who were found in the city; and the secretary of the commander of the army, who mustered the people of the land; and sixty men of the people of the land, who were found in the midst of the city. 26 And Nebuzaradan the captain of the guard took them and brought them to the king of Babylon at Riblah. 27 And the king of Babylon struck them down and put them to death at Riblah in the land of Hamath. So Judah was taken into exile out of its land.

28 This is the number of the people whom Nebuchadnezzar carried away captive: in the seventh year, 3,023 Judeans; 29 in the eighteenth year of Nebuchadnezzar he carried away captive from Jerusalem 832 persons; 30 in the twenty-third year of Nebuchadnezzar, Nebuzaradan the captain of the guard carried away captive of the Judeans 745 persons; all the persons were 4,600.

Jehoiachin Released from Prison

31 And in the thirty-seventh year of the exile of Jehoiachin king of Judah, in the twelfth month, on the twenty-fifth day of the month, Evil-merodach king of Babylon, in the year that he began to reign, graciously freed[3] Jehoiachin king of Judah

[1] Hebrew lacks *the sea* [2] A *cubit* was about 18 inches or 45 centimeters [3] Hebrew *reign, lifted up the head of*

and brought him out of prison. 32And he spoke kindly to him and gave him a seat
above the seats of the kings who were with him in Babylon. 33So Jehoiachin put
off his prison garments. And every day of his life he dined regularly at the king's
table, 34and for his allowance, a regular allowance was given him by the king, according to his daily needs, until the day of his death, as long as he lived.

JESUS: OUR FAITHFUL LORD

LAMENTATIONS

LAMENTATIONS

PROPHETIC MINISTRY OF JEREMIAH BEGINS	FALL OF JUDAH	WRITING OF BOOK OF LAMENTATIONS
c. 626 BC	*c. 586 BC*	*Not long after 586 BC*

The aptly named book of Lamentations portrays the broken heart of its author, traditionally assumed to be the prophet Jeremiah, after the fall of Jerusalem to the Babylonians. This national tragedy was an unprecedented act of God's judgment for the people's unfaithfulness. Almost inconceivably, God had allowed the very center of worship for his people to be ransacked and demolished by a pagan nation.

Jeremiah's lament derived from his personal sorrow at the fate of those whom he dearly loved. Even more, he agonized over the people's unwillingness to turn from their sin when confronted by the prophet's clear and consistent warnings.

This short book is composed of five poems; specifically, laments. Chapters 1 and 5 summarize the siege and fall of Jerusalem at the hands of the Babylonians. The great city of Jerusalem was defeated, and with that the hopes of God's people faltered. Jeremiah begged God to remember his people and turn back to them in love once more. Chapters 2 and 4 focus on the destruction and devastation that resulted from God's judgment. The consequences of sin ravaged all segments of society, leaving no one untouched.

The third chapter functions as the climax and focal point of Jeremiah's writing. Jeremiah proclaimed the greatness of God's faithfulness in the face of his judgment (3:23). Though Judah was in shambles, God had not abandoned his people forever. His intention was to use Jerusalem's destruction to remind his people of the heinousness of their sin and draw them back to himself through his relentless grace. The circumstances of God's people may have obscured their view of God's faithfulness, but Jeremiah reminded the people that their sin had not irrevocably destroyed God's promises, and that God would certainly remain faithful. While the nation's rebellion was great, God's faithfulness was greater: "his mercies never come to an end" (3:22).

These never-ending mercies are seen most clearly in the life, death, and resurrection of Jesus Christ, who came to earth as the perfect embodiment of God's faithfulness. All those who have been defeated and destroyed by sin need to look no further than Jesus to see God's great faithfulness on display. They can turn to Christ and find the hope that all people so desperately need.

THE STEADFAST LOVE OF THE LORD NEVER CEASES;
HIS MERCIES NEVER COME TO AN END.

Lamentations 3:22

LAMENTATIONS

How Lonely Sits the City

1 How lonely sits the city
that was full of people!
How like a widow has she become,
she who was great among the nations!
She who was a princess among the provinces
has become a slave.

2 She weeps bitterly in the night,
with tears on her cheeks;
among all her lovers
she has none to comfort her;
all her friends have dealt treacherously with her;
they have become her enemies.

3 Judah has gone into exile because of affliction[1]
and hard servitude;
she dwells now among the nations,
but finds no resting place;
her pursuers have all overtaken her
in the midst of her distress.[2]

4 The roads to Zion mourn,
for none come to the festival;
all her gates are desolate;
her priests groan;
her virgins have been afflicted,[3]
and she herself suffers bitterly.

5 Her foes have become the head;
her enemies prosper,
because the LORD has afflicted her
for the multitude of her transgressions;
her children have gone away,
captives before the foe.

6 From the daughter of Zion
all her majesty has departed.
Her princes have become like deer
that find no pasture;
they fled without strength
before the pursuer.

7 Jerusalem remembers
in the days of her affliction and wandering
all the precious things
that were hers from days of old.
When her people fell into the hand of the foe,
and there was none to help her,
her foes gloated over her;
they mocked at her downfall.

8 Jerusalem sinned grievously;
therefore she became filthy;

[1]Or *under affliction* [2]Or *in the narrow passes* [3]Septuagint, Old Latin *dragged away*

LAMENTATIONS 1:1–10

THE TEMPLE

The first half of the first chapter of Lamentations describes the destruction of Jerusalem from the point of view of someone directly observing what has happened. The prophet Jeremiah shows, with extensive poetic language, how Jerusalem's sins have caused it to be completely desolated. Verse 10 shifts from the view of objective observer and makes the destruction of the city more personal for readers. By referring to "her sanctuary," Jeremiah pointed out that the pagan enemy has not just entered into any building. The congregation, or the temple, was a house of worship and a very important building for the people of Jerusalem to communicate with God. The author was saying it is not simply *a* building, it is *your* building, and furthermore it is a representation of one's relationship with God.

However, once Jesus arrived, the whole meaning and imagery of the temple changed. In John 2:19, Jesus said that he was going to destroy the temple and rebuild it in three days. What Jesus was saying is that he is now the temple, and with his crucifixion, the temple (his body) would be destroyed only to rise again (or be rebuilt) in three days. While the temple was the way God's people used to communicate with God, Jesus is the way Christians communicate with God today.

all who honored her despise her,
for they have seen her nakedness;
she herself groans
and turns her face away.

9 Her uncleanness was in her skirts;
she took no thought of her future;[1]
therefore her fall is terrible;
she has no comforter.
"O LORD, behold my affliction,
for the enemy has triumphed!"

10 The enemy has stretched out his hands
over all her precious things;
for she has seen the nations
enter her sanctuary,
those whom you forbade
to enter your congregation.

11 All her people groan
as they search for bread;
they trade their treasures for food
to revive their strength.
"Look, O LORD, and see,
for I am despised."

12 "Is it nothing to you, all you who pass by?
Look and see
if there is any sorrow like my sorrow,
which was brought upon me,
which the LORD inflicted
on the day of his fierce anger.

13 "From on high he sent fire;
into my bones[2] he made it descend;
he spread a net for my feet;
he turned me back;
he has left me stunned,
faint all the day long.

14 "My transgressions were bound[3] into a yoke;
by his hand they were fastened together;
they were set upon my neck;
he caused my strength to fail;
the Lord gave me into the hands
of those whom I cannot withstand.

15 "The Lord rejected
all my mighty men in my midst;
he summoned an assembly against me
to crush my young men;
the Lord has trodden as in a winepress
the virgin daughter of Judah.

16 "For these things I weep;
my eyes flow with tears;
for a comforter is far from me,
one to revive my spirit;
my children are desolate,
for the enemy has prevailed."

[1]Or *end* [2]Septuagint; Hebrew *bones and* [3]The meaning of the Hebrew is uncertain

17 Zion stretches out her hands,
but there is none to comfort her;
the LORD has commanded against Jacob
that his neighbors should be his foes;
Jerusalem has become
a filthy thing among them.

18 "The LORD is in the right,
for I have rebelled against his word;
but hear, all you peoples,
and see my suffering;
my young women and my young men
have gone into captivity.

19 "I called to my lovers,
but they deceived me;
my priests and elders
perished in the city,
while they sought food
to revive their strength.

20 "Look, O LORD, for I am in distress;
my stomach churns;
my heart is wrung within me,
because I have been very rebellious.
In the street the sword bereaves;
in the house it is like death.

21 "They heard[1] my groaning,
yet there is no one to comfort me.
All my enemies have heard of my trouble;
they are glad that you have done it.
You have brought[2] the day you announced;
now let them be as I am.

22 "Let all their evildoing come before you,
and deal with them
as you have dealt with me
because of all my transgressions;
for my groans are many,
and my heart is faint."

The Lord Has Destroyed Without Pity

2 How the Lord in his anger
has set the daughter of Zion under a cloud!
He has cast down from heaven to earth
the splendor of Israel;
he has not remembered his footstool
in the day of his anger.

2 The Lord has swallowed up without mercy
all the habitations of Jacob;
in his wrath he has broken down
the strongholds of the daughter of Judah;
he has brought down to the ground in dishonor
the kingdom and its rulers.

3 He has cut down in fierce anger
all the might of Israel;

[1]Septuagint, Syriac *Hear* [2]Syriac *Bring*

he has withdrawn from them his right hand
  in the face of the enemy;
he has burned like a flaming fire in Jacob,
  consuming all around.

4 He has bent his bow like an enemy,
  with his right hand set like a foe;
and he has killed all who were delightful in our eyes;
  in the tent of the daughter of Zion,
he has poured out his fury like fire.

5 The Lord has become like an enemy;
  he has swallowed up Israel;
he has swallowed up all its palaces;
  he has laid in ruins its strongholds,
and he has multiplied in the daughter of Judah
  mourning and lamentation.

6 He has laid waste his booth like a garden,
  laid in ruins his meeting place;
the LORD has made Zion forget
  festival and Sabbath,
and in his fierce indignation has spurned king and priest.

7 The Lord has scorned his altar,
  disowned his sanctuary;
he has delivered into the hand of the enemy
  the walls of her palaces;
they raised a clamor in the house of the LORD
  as on the day of festival.

8 The LORD determined to lay in ruins
  the wall of the daughter of Zion;
he stretched out the measuring line;
  he did not restrain his hand from destroying;
he caused rampart and wall to lament;
  they languished together.

9 Her gates have sunk into the ground;
  he has ruined and broken her bars;
her king and princes are among the nations;
  the law is no more,
and her prophets find
  no vision from the LORD.

10 The elders of the daughter of Zion
  sit on the ground in silence;
they have thrown dust on their heads
  and put on sackcloth;
the young women of Jerusalem
  have bowed their heads to the ground.

11 My eyes are spent with weeping;
  my stomach churns;
my bile is poured out to the ground
  because of the destruction of the daughter of my people,
because infants and babies faint
  in the streets of the city.

12 They cry to their mothers,
  "Where is bread and wine?"

as they faint like a wounded man
in the streets of the city,
as their life is poured out
on their mothers' bosom.

13 What can I say for you, to what compare you,
O daughter of Jerusalem?
What can I liken to you, that I may comfort you,
O virgin daughter of Zion?
For your ruin is vast as the sea;
who can heal you?

14 Your prophets have seen for you
false and deceptive visions;
they have not exposed your iniquity
to restore your fortunes,
but have seen for you oracles
that are false and misleading.

15 All who pass along the way
clap their hands at you;
they hiss and wag their heads
at the daughter of Jerusalem:
"Is this the city that was called
the perfection of beauty,
the joy of all the earth?"

16 All your enemies
rail against you;
they hiss, they gnash their teeth,
they cry: "We have swallowed her!
Ah, this is the day we longed for;
now we have it; we see it!"

17 The LORD has done what he purposed;
he has carried out his word,
which he commanded long ago;
he has thrown down without pity;
he has made the enemy rejoice over you
and exalted the might of your foes.

18 Their heart cried to the Lord.
O wall of the daughter of Zion,
let tears stream down like a torrent
day and night!
Give yourself no rest,
your eyes no respite!

19 "Arise, cry out in the night,
at the beginning of the night watches!
Pour out your heart like water
before the presence of the Lord!
Lift your hands to him
for the lives of your children,
who faint for hunger
at the head of every street."

20 Look, O LORD, and see!
With whom have you dealt thus?
Should women eat the fruit of their womb,
the children of their tender care?

Should priest and prophet be killed
in the sanctuary of the Lord?

21 In the dust of the streets
lie the young and the old;
my young women and my young men
have fallen by the sword;
you have killed them in the day of your anger,
slaughtering without pity.

22 You summoned as if to a festival day
my terrors on every side,
and on the day of the anger of the LORD
no one escaped or survived;
those whom I held and raised
my enemy destroyed.

Great Is Your Faithfulness

3 I am the man who has seen affliction
under the rod of his wrath;
2 he has driven and brought me
into darkness without any light;
3 surely against me he turns his hand
again and again the whole day long.

4 He has made my flesh and my skin waste away;
he has broken my bones;
5 he has besieged and enveloped me
with bitterness and tribulation;
6 he has made me dwell in darkness
like the dead of long ago.

7 He has walled me about so that I cannot escape;
he has made my chains heavy;
8 though I call and cry for help,
he shuts out my prayer;
9 he has blocked my ways with blocks of stones;
he has made my paths crooked.

10 He is a bear lying in wait for me,
a lion in hiding;
11 he turned aside my steps and tore me to pieces;
he has made me desolate;
12 he bent his bow and set me
as a target for his arrow.

13 He drove into my kidneys
the arrows of his quiver;
14 I have become the laughingstock of all my people,[1]
the object of their taunts all day long.
15 He has filled me with bitterness;
he has sated me with wormwood.

16 He has made my teeth grind on gravel,
and made me cower in ashes;
17 my soul is bereft of peace;
I have forgotten what happiness[2] is;
18 so I say, "My endurance has perished;
so has my hope from the LORD."

[1]Some manuscripts *all peoples* [2]Hebrew *good*

19 Remember my affliction and my wanderings,
the wormwood and the gall!
20 My soul continually remembers it
and is bowed down within me.
21 But this I call to mind,
and therefore I have hope:

22 The steadfast love of the LORD never ceases;[1]
his mercies never come to an end;
23 they are new every morning;
great is your faithfulness.
24 "The LORD is my portion," says my soul,
"therefore I will hope in him."

25 The LORD is good to those who wait for him,
to the soul who seeks him.
26 It is good that one should wait quietly
for the salvation of the LORD.
27 It is good for a man that he bear
the yoke in his youth.

28 Let him sit alone in silence
when it is laid on him;
29 let him put his mouth in the dust—
there may yet be hope;
30 let him give his cheek to the one who strikes,
and let him be filled with insults.

31 For the Lord will not
cast off forever,
32 for, though he cause grief, he will have compassion
according to the abundance of his steadfast love;
33 for he does not afflict from his heart
or grieve the children of men.

34 To crush underfoot
all the prisoners of the earth,
35 to deny a man justice
in the presence of the Most High,
36 to subvert a man in his lawsuit,
the Lord does not approve.

37 Who has spoken and it came to pass,
unless the Lord has commanded it?
38 Is it not from the mouth of the Most High
that good and bad come?
39 Why should a living man complain,
a man, about the punishment of his sins?

40 Let us test and examine our ways,
and return to the LORD!
41 Let us lift up our hearts and hands
to God in heaven:
42 "We have transgressed and rebelled,
and you have not forgiven.

43 "You have wrapped yourself with anger and pursued us,
killing without pity;

[1]Syriac, Targum; Hebrew *Because of the steadfast love of the LORD, we are not cut off*

GREAT IS HIS FAITHFULNESS

A complete shift in the prophet Jeremiah's tone and focus occurs in 3:21. While every verse up until this point has discussed the hardships of God's wrath, suddenly the prophet's hope is renewed and he proclaims God's love, compassion, and faithfulness. Despite all that has happened to Jerusalem and her people, verse 23 declares that God's compassions are "new every morning." It may not seem as though Jeremiah had much reason to declare praise for God, but he chose to remember that God had been faithful to his people all along.

God responds compassionately to his people's needs. One instance of such a response is in Exodus 16, when the Israelites were traveling through the desert and complaining of hunger. God heard their complaints and responded by raining manna (bread) from heaven every morning for the people to gather and eat. There was never a shortage of manna for the people, and they were able to live off of what God gave them.

In Matthew 6:11, Jesus referred to the manna that God gave the Israelites in his instructions regarding prayer. He told his followers to pray and ask God to "give us this day our daily bread." God met the daily needs of the Israelites, and he promises to do the same for his people today. Now, this does not mean that God will rain down from heaven whatever his people ask for, but it does show that he has compassion for his people's needs and responds to their cries.

Lamentations appeals to God's compassion and faithfulness. Even though those who survived the destruction of Jerusalem were facing incredible pain and hardship, Jeremiah reminded them that God had been faithful to his people in the past, and he would continue to be faithful to them in the future. While Lamentations is about difficulty and hardship, the central verses focus on the Lord's great love. Not only did Jeremiah remind readers of the goodness of God, but he also challenged his audience to remember God's love and live in it daily.

44 you have wrapped yourself with a cloud
so that no prayer can pass through.
45 You have made us scum and garbage
among the peoples.

46 "All our enemies
open their mouths against us;
47 panic and pitfall have come upon us,
devastation and destruction;
48 my eyes flow with rivers of tears
because of the destruction of the daughter of my people.

49 "My eyes will flow without ceasing,
without respite,
50 until the LORD from heaven
looks down and sees;
51 my eyes cause me grief
at the fate of all the daughters of my city.

52 "I have been hunted like a bird
by those who were my enemies without cause;
53 they flung me alive into the pit[1]
and cast stones on me;
54 water closed over my head;
I said, 'I am lost.'

55 "I called on your name, O LORD,
from the depths of the pit;
56 you heard my plea, 'Do not close
your ear to my cry for help!'
57 You came near when I called on you;
you said, 'Do not fear!'

58 "You have taken up my cause, O Lord;
you have redeemed my life.
59 You have seen the wrong done to me, O LORD;
judge my cause.
60 You have seen all their vengeance,
all their plots against me.

61 "You have heard their taunts, O LORD,
all their plots against me.
62 The lips and thoughts of my assailants
are against me all the day long.
63 Behold their sitting and their rising;
I am the object of their taunts.

64 "You will repay them,[2] O LORD,
according to the work of their hands.
65 You will give them[3] dullness of heart;
your curse will be[4] on them.
66 You will pursue them[5] in anger and destroy them
from under your heavens, O LORD."[6]

The Holy Stones Lie Scattered

4 How the gold has grown dim,
how the pure gold is changed!
The holy stones lie scattered
at the head of every street.

[1]Or *they end my life in the pit* [2]Or *Repay them* [3]Or *Give them* [4]Or *place your curse* [5]Or *Pursue them*
[6]Syriac (compare Septuagint, Vulgate); Hebrew *the heavens of the LORD*

LAMENTATIONS 3:64

THE LORD'S REVENGE

The third chapter of Lamentations displays a wide range of emotions. The entire chapter is written from the personal experience of the author, Jeremiah. In verses 1–20, Jeremiah describes his sorrows and despair, verses 21–39 provide reminders of God's faithfulness and the purpose of affliction, verses 40–47 are an encouragement to the Israelites to repent and return to God, and verses 48–66 represent the Israelites' prayer. The last section of chapter three specifically depicts the people's feelings toward their enemies who have attacked Jerusalem, and their injustices are provided in great detail. The prayer in verse 64 expresses the wish that God would "repay them ... according to the work of their hands." While this prayer may seem somewhat malicious, Jeremiah was simply asking God to follow through on what he had already promised to those who broke their covenant with him.

In Exodus 23:22, God said, "But if you carefully obey his voice and do all that I say, then I will be an enemy to your enemies and an adversary to your adversaries." In Lamentations, Jeremiah asked God to be an enemy to his enemies and to provide justice. Christians know now that God promises more than just justice on this earth, but that he offers eternal justice for the ultimate enemy. Revelation 20:10 says that "the devil who had deceived them was thrown into the lake of fire and sulfur" where he will be "tormented day and night forever and ever." Jesus' death on the cross and his resurrection were the first of many victories yet to come to achieve God's ultimate justice.

2 The precious sons of Zion,
worth their weight in fine gold,
how they are regarded as earthen pots,
the work of a potter's hands!

3 Even jackals offer the breast;
they nurse their young;
but the daughter of my people has become cruel,
like the ostriches in the wilderness.

4 The tongue of the nursing infant sticks
to the roof of its mouth for thirst;
the children beg for food,
but no one gives to them.

5 Those who once feasted on delicacies
perish in the streets;
those who were brought up in purple
embrace ash heaps.

6 For the chastisement[1] of the daughter of my people has been greater
than the punishment[2] of Sodom,
which was overthrown in a moment,
and no hands were wrung for her.[3]

7 Her princes were purer than snow,
whiter than milk;
their bodies were more ruddy than coral,
the beauty of their form[4] was like sapphire.[5]

8 Now their face is blacker than soot;
they are not recognized in the streets;
their skin has shriveled on their bones;
it has become as dry as wood.

9 Happier were the victims of the sword
than the victims of hunger,
who wasted away, pierced
by lack of the fruits of the field.

10 The hands of compassionate women
have boiled their own children;
they became their food
during the destruction of the daughter of my people.

11 The LORD gave full vent to his wrath;
he poured out his hot anger,
and he kindled a fire in Zion
that consumed its foundations.

12 The kings of the earth did not believe,
nor any of the inhabitants of the world,
that foe or enemy could enter
the gates of Jerusalem.

13 This was for the sins of her prophets
and the iniquities of her priests,
who shed in the midst of her
the blood of the righteous.

[1]Or *iniquity* [2]Or *sin* [3]The meaning of the Hebrew is uncertain [4]The meaning of the Hebrew is uncertain [5]Hebrew *lapis lazuli*

LAMENTATIONS 4:13

A JUST GOD

Lamentations may seem like a book that is full of strong sorrow and bitterness, and through most of the book, it is. The prophet Jeremiah continually complained about the plight of the city, and he was distraught at how the Lord had brought judgment upon his people. However, it is important to note that these complaints are never against God. Jeremiah was certainly upset about the situation, but there was no suggestion that God's judgment was somehow unjust. Lamentations 4:13 says, "This was for the sins of her prophets and the iniquities of her priests." The blame for the destruction of Jerusalem lay squarely on the shoulders of the prophets, priests, and people of the city. Never did the author lament about why God chose to destroy the city, nor did he ever wonder about why Jerusalem was facing such judgment. The people of the city had rebelled against God, and they were receiving their just reward.

Romans 6:23 says, "The wages of sin is death," which means someone had to die for sin. The wages had to be paid, and God did not simply remove the debt that was owed. Instead, he paid for the wages of sin himself with his perfect Son (Jn 3:16). Jesus fulfilled God's justice, so that believers may receive his mercy.

14 They wandered, blind, through the streets;
they were so defiled with blood
that no one was able to touch
their garments.

15 "Away! Unclean!" people cried at them.
"Away! Away! Do not touch!"
So they became fugitives and wanderers;
people said among the nations,
"They shall stay with us no longer."

16 The LORD himself[1] has scattered them;
he will regard them no more;
no honor was shown to the priests,
no favor to the elders.

17 Our eyes failed, ever watching
vainly for help;
in our watching we watched
for a nation which could not save.

18 They dogged our steps
so that we could not walk in our streets;
our end drew near; our days were numbered,
for our end had come.

19 Our pursuers were swifter
than the eagles in the heavens;
they chased us on the mountains;
they lay in wait for us in the wilderness.

20 The breath of our nostrils, the LORD's anointed,
was captured in their pits,
of whom we said, "Under his shadow
we shall live among the nations."

21 Rejoice and be glad, O daughter of Edom,
you who dwell in the land of Uz;
but to you also the cup shall pass;
you shall become drunk and strip yourself bare.

22 The punishment of your iniquity, O daughter of Zion, is accomplished;
he will keep you in exile no longer;[2]
but your iniquity, O daughter of Edom, he will punish;
he will uncover your sins.

Restore Us to Yourself, O LORD

5 Remember, O LORD, what has befallen us;
look, and see our disgrace!
2 Our inheritance has been turned over to strangers,
our homes to foreigners.
3 We have become orphans, fatherless;
our mothers are like widows.
4 We must pay for the water we drink;
the wood we get must be bought.
5 Our pursuers are at our necks;
we are weary; we are given no rest.
6 We have given the hand to Egypt, and to Assyria,
to get bread enough.

[1]Hebrew *The face of the LORD* [2]Or *he will not exile you again*

IS THERE HOPE?

Lamentations concludes with Jeremiah's desperate, tenacious hope against the backdrop of the recent destruction of Jerusalem. He summarized the hardships that he had described in great detail in the previous chapters. However, instead of Lamentations ending with mourning, it ends with a plea.

Just because God is faithful does not mean that everything is going to go perfectly. Chapters 4 and 5 vividly describe the suffering of the people of Jerusalem. Sovereignty does not eliminate calamity, and Jeremiah is fully aware of that. The writer realizes that the people deserve the judgment they are facing (4:13), but he also knows that God is in control over everything both good and bad (3:37).

Therefore, the book ends with a humble plea as the writer recognized the sovereign rule of God and begged that he not ignore the cries of his people. The final two verses ask that God restore his people unless he remains exceedingly angry. Does this mean that it is possible for God to be angered to the point where he remains separated from his people? In Romans 8:35 – 39, Paul wrote that nothing "will be able to separate us from the love of God in Christ Jesus our Lord." Before Moses died, he promised Joshua, "It is the Lord who goes before you. He will be with you; he will not leave you or forsake you" (Dt 31:8). And in Matthew, Jesus' last words are, "And behold, I am with you always, to the end of the age" (Mt 28:20).

Lamentations reminds us that there is always hope for God's people. Through the Old Testament, despite all of the calamities that the Israelites brought upon themselves, God stayed with them. In the New Testament, Jesus saved the world and sent the Holy Spirit to be with and lead those who believe. Nothing — whether the foolish acts of the Israelites, or ignorance of modern-day believers, or death, or life — can ever separate God's people from his love.

7 Our fathers sinned, and are no more;
and we bear their iniquities.
8 Slaves rule over us;
there is none to deliver us from their hand.
9 We get our bread at the peril of our lives,
because of the sword in the wilderness.
10 Our skin is hot as an oven
with the burning heat of famine.
11 Women are raped in Zion,
young women in the towns of Judah.
12 Princes are hung up by their hands;
no respect is shown to the elders.
13 Young men are compelled to grind at the mill,
and boys stagger under loads of wood.
14 The old men have left the city gate,
the young men their music.
15 The joy of our hearts has ceased;
our dancing has been turned to mourning.
16 The crown has fallen from our head;
woe to us, for we have sinned!
17 For this our heart has become sick,
for these things our eyes have grown dim,
18 for Mount Zion which lies desolate;
jackals prowl over it.
19 But you, O LORD, reign forever;
your throne endures to all generations.
20 Why do you forget us forever,
why do you forsake us for so many days?
21 Restore us to yourself, O LORD, that we may be restored!
Renew our days as of old—
22 unless you have utterly rejected us,
and you remain exceedingly angry with us.

JESUS: OUR TRUE TEMPLE

EZEKIEL

EZEKIEL

EZEKIEL EXILED TO BABYLON *c. 597 BC*	EZEKIEL'S VISIONS *c. 593 – 573 BC*	FALL OF JUDAH/TEMPLE DESTROYED *c. 586 BC*

God used Ezekiel to speak to God's people after their exile to Babylon. While Jeremiah warned the people in Jerusalem of the coming destruction, Ezekiel spoke to those who had already been taken captive. The messages of Jeremiah and Ezekiel are quite similar, though they spoke to people hundreds of miles away from one another who were facing differing stages of God's judgment.

Ezekiel knew the fate that awaited God's people. He knew of the similar deportation of the northern kingdom (Israel) at the hands of the Assyrians in 722 BC. The southern kingdom (Judah) remained faithful to God for about a century longer, but eventually they too became engrossed in the idolatry of the surrounding nations. God used the nation of Babylon to enact judgment on the southern kingdom of Judah, and Ezekiel was a part of that deportation to pagan Babylon.

In exile, Ezekiel experienced and shared with the people a number of visions. These were meant to remind God's people of their responsibility before God even though they were far away from the promised land. Ezekiel, a priest and a prophet, was well acquainted with God's Law and its covenant-keeping implications for God's people. Through Ezekiel, God called the people to return to follow him in worshipful obedience.

God, through Ezekiel, also reminded the exiles that God's judgment was purposeful and not vindictive. As God had used the years of wandering in the wilderness, so he was also using their exile to foster humility, remind them of their dependence, and bring about genuine repentance. Ultimately, God's purpose was that the people would know that he alone is Lord and deserving of their worship. This refrain echoes throughout the book, reminding the people of the glorious privilege of knowing God and their need for spiritual renewal.

Like other prophets, Ezekiel sounded a message of hope to accompany his warnings of judgment (Eze 33 – 48). He concluded his prophecy with the news of a coming day when God would restore proper worship in a new temple in a new, and better, city. There a renewed nation would one day worship their glorious King.

AND I WILL GIVE THEM ONE HEART, AND
A NEW SPIRIT I WILL PUT WITHIN THEM.
I WILL REMOVE THE HEART OF STONE FROM THEIR FLESH
AND GIVE THEM A HEART OF FLESH.

Ezekiel 11:19

EZEKIEL

Ezekiel in Babylon

1 In the thirtieth year, in the fourth month, on the fifth day of the month, as I was among the exiles by the Chebar canal, the heavens were opened, and I saw visions of God.[1] 2On the fifth day of the month (it was the fifth year of the exile of King Jehoiachin), 3the word of the LORD came to Ezekiel the priest, the son of Buzi, in the land of the Chaldeans by the Chebar canal, and the hand of the LORD was upon him there.

The Glory of the LORD

4As I looked, behold, a stormy wind came out of the north, and a great cloud, with brightness around it, and fire flashing forth continually, and in the midst of the fire, as it were gleaming metal.[2] 5And from the midst of it came the likeness of four living creatures. And this was their appearance: they had a human likeness, 6but each had four faces, and each of them had four wings. 7Their legs were straight, and the soles of their feet were like the sole of a calf's foot. And they sparkled like burnished bronze. 8Under their wings on their four sides they had human hands. And the four had their faces and their wings thus: 9their wings touched one another. Each one of them went straight forward, without turning as they went. 10As for the likeness of their faces, each had a human face. The four had the face of a lion on the right side, the four had the face of an ox on the left side, and the four had the face of an eagle. 11Such were their faces. And their wings were spread out above. Each creature had two wings, each of which touched the wing of another, while two covered their bodies. 12And each went straight forward. Wherever the spirit[3] would go, they went, without turning as they went. 13As for the likeness of the living creatures, their appearance was like burning coals of fire, like the appearance of torches moving to and fro among the living creatures. And the fire was bright, and out of the fire went forth lightning. 14And the living creatures darted to and fro, like the appearance of a flash of lightning.

15Now as I looked at the living creatures, I saw a wheel on the earth beside the living creatures, one for each of the four of them.[4] 16As for the appearance of the wheels and their construction: their appearance was like the gleaming of beryl. And the four had the same likeness, their appearance and construction being as it were a wheel within a wheel. 17When they went, they went in any of their four directions[5] without turning as they went. 18And their rims were tall and awesome, and the rims of all four were full of eyes all around. 19And when the living creatures went, the wheels went beside them; and when the living creatures rose from the earth, the wheels rose. 20Wherever the spirit wanted to go, they went, and the wheels rose along with them, for the spirit of the living creatures[6] was in the wheels. 21When those went, these went; and when those stood, these stood; and when those rose from the earth, the wheels rose along with them, for the spirit of the living creatures was in the wheels.

22Over the heads of the living creatures there was the likeness of an expanse, shining like awe-inspiring crystal, spread out above their heads. 23And under the expanse their wings were stretched out straight, one toward another. And each creature had two wings covering its body. 24And when they went, I heard the sound of their wings like the sound of many waters, like the sound of the Almighty, a sound of tumult like the sound of an army. When they stood still, they let down their wings. 25And there came a voice from above the expanse over their heads. When they stood still, they let down their wings.

[1]Or *from God* [2]Or *amber*; also verse 27 [3]Or *Spirit*; also twice in verse 20 and once in verse 21 [4]Hebrew *of their faces* [5]Hebrew *on their four sides* [6]Or *the spirit of life*; also verse 21

EZEKIEL 1:4–28

GOD'S GLORY

This book of prophecy opens with an incredible display of God's glory. This is important to recognize at the outset of a book that is full of prophecy from God, through God's prophet Ezekiel, to God's people Israel.

Through his prophet, God was delivering a firm word to his people. His people had lived in sin despite the fact that God had shown them so much grace. Sin has consequences, and God was preparing to tell them what their sin would cost. But before delivering that message, God showed his glory (v. 28); God's glory is the basis for everything that follows.

God is holy—completely pure and good. Humanity is not. As an expression of God's holiness, God disciplines his disobedient children. Reading the book of Ezekiel should lead people who are far from God to see his glory, hear of his grace, and draw near in repentance. This book should lead followers of Jesus to remember the perfect character of God—how he has already accomplished the gracious salvation this book looks forward to—and to depend on the Spirit of God to help them live for God in every area of life.

26And above the expanse over their heads there was the likeness of a throne, in appearance like sapphire;[1] and seated above the likeness of a throne was a likeness with a human appearance. 27And upward from what had the appearance of his waist I saw as it were gleaming metal, like the appearance of fire enclosed all around. And downward from what had the appearance of his waist I saw as it were the appearance of fire, and there was brightness around him.[2] 28Like the appearance of the bow that is in the cloud on the day of rain, so was the appearance of the brightness all around.

Such was the appearance of the likeness of the glory of the LORD. And when I saw it, I fell on my face, and I heard the voice of one speaking.

Ezekiel's Call

2 And he said to me, "Son of man,[3] stand on your feet, and I will speak with you." 2And as he spoke to me, the Spirit entered into me and set me on my feet, and I heard him speaking to me. 3And he said to me, "Son of man, I send you to the people of Israel, to nations of rebels, who have rebelled against me. They and their fathers have transgressed against me to this very day. 4The descendants also are impudent and stubborn: I send you to them, and you shall say to them, 'Thus says the Lord GOD.' 5And whether they hear or refuse to hear (for they are a rebellious house) they will know that a prophet has been among them. 6And you, son of man, be not afraid of them, nor be afraid of their words, though briers and thorns are with you and you sit on scorpions.[4] Be not afraid of their words, nor be dismayed at their looks, for they are a rebellious house. 7And you shall speak my words to them, whether they hear or refuse to hear, for they are a rebellious house.

8"But you, son of man, hear what I say to you. Be not rebellious like that rebellious house; open your mouth and eat what I give you." 9And when I looked, behold, a hand was stretched out to me, and behold, a scroll of a book was in it. 10And he spread it before me. And it had writing on the front and on the back, and there were written on it words of lamentation and mourning and woe.

3 And he said to me, "Son of man, eat whatever you find here. Eat this scroll, and go, speak to the house of Israel." 2So I opened my mouth, and he gave me this scroll to eat. 3And he said to me, "Son of man, feed your belly with this scroll that I give you and fill your stomach with it." Then I ate it, and it was in my mouth as sweet as honey.

4And he said to me, "Son of man, go to the house of Israel and speak with my words to them. 5For you are not sent to a people of foreign speech and a hard language, but to the house of Israel— 6not to many peoples of foreign speech and a hard language, whose words you cannot understand. Surely, if I sent you to such, they would listen to you. 7But the house of Israel will not be willing to listen to you, for they are not willing to listen to me: because all the house of Israel have a hard forehead and a stubborn heart. 8Behold, I have made your face as hard as their faces, and your forehead as hard as their foreheads. 9Like emery harder than flint have I made your forehead. Fear them not, nor be dismayed at their looks, for they are a rebellious house." 10Moreover, he said to me, "Son of man, all my words that I shall speak to you receive in your heart, and hear with your ears. 11And go to the exiles, to your people, and speak to them and say to them, 'Thus says the Lord GOD,' whether they hear or refuse to hear."

12Then the Spirit[5] lifted me up, and I heard behind me the voice[6] of a great earthquake: "Blessed be the glory of the LORD from its place!" 13It was the sound of the wings of the living creatures as they touched one another, and the sound of the wheels beside them, and the sound of a great earthquake. 14The Spirit lifted me up and took me away, and I went in bitterness in the heat of my spirit, the hand

[1]Or *lapis lazuli* [2]Or *it* [3]Or *Son of Adam*; so throughout Ezekiel [4]Or *on scorpion plants* [5]Or *the wind*; also verse 14 [6]Or *sound*

EZEKIEL 3:1–3

EAT A SCROLL?

Life as a prophet was often bittersweet, and painful experiences regularly outweighed the pleasant. The symbolic act of eating the scroll demonstrated that Ezekiel internalized God's message in preparation for speaking to the people. Eating a physical scroll does not seem appetizing, but in this case it tasted sweet like honey. At the same time, the message the scroll contained was full of mourning and woe (Eze 2:9–10).

This was not the only time God told one of his people to eat a scroll. In the New Testament, the apostle John prophesied about what God was going to do during the end times. God told John to eat that scroll as well— it was sweet to taste, but it made his stomach sour (Rev 10:9–11). It is a sweet thing to be empowered to speak God's truth, but at the same time it can be bitter when it contains a condemnation against sin.

God the Son spoke the same message as God the Father. Jesus came and preached the "sweet" news of God's love for all people and his offer to forgive their sins, but this message included the "bitter" news that people are sick and need to be healed (Mk 2:17), lost and in need of being found (Lk 15:1–32), in infinitely deep debt to God, and in desperate need of deliverance (Mt 18:21–35). God saves people who taste the bitterness of sin and cling to the sweet hope that only Jesus can save.

SON OF MAN

The phrase "son of man" is used as a title for Ezekiel the prophet 93 times throughout the book of Ezekiel. The name highlights the mortality of the prophet and places him at a distance from God. It is clear that Ezekiel is far from God and cannot compare to God. When Ezekiel stood in the presence of God, he noted that it was only possible with the help of God's Spirit (vv. 1–2).

Jesus used the title "Son of Man" to refer to himself more than any other name—more than 75 times through the Gospels. Whereas the phrase was used to refer to Ezekiel's distance from God, Jesus used it to refer to his nearness to us. Jesus is a "son of man" in the sense of being human in every way. Because Jesus is a member of the Trinity, the one true and holy God, he is not separated from God like the other prophets who had gone before him—Jesus is God.

There are many things that Jesus came to reveal to humanity. Although he is the eternal Word, he was made flesh to reveal God to the world (Jn 1:14). Jesus came to show the world God's love (Jn 3:16). Although he is God, Jesus relinquished the privileges of heaven so that he could seek and save the lost (Lk 19:10; Php 2:5–8). Jesus Christ lived the greatest life that anyone has ever lived. He was humble in character and mighty in word and deed. He came to fulfill God's Law and show himself to be Lord over it. He perfectly fulfilled the major offices of the Old Testament as he lived as the one true prophet, priest, and king. He died to atone for the sins of the world and rose from the dead, proving that he is God and that sin has been defeated. He will return as reigning royalty (Da 7:13–14), and all the nations will mourn their judgment. Until that day comes, he is with his church, guiding and nurturing them in every way.

Jesus is the only perfect person who ever lived. He was completely human and completely identified with the full range of human emotions, and yet he remained sinless. Hebrews 4:15 reads, "For we do not have a high priest who is unable to sympathize with our weaknesses, but one who in every respect has been tempted as we are, yet without sin." Jesus invites people to follow him. This involves casting off sin and the former sense of self and finding new identity in him. God is high above humanity in holiness and yet has drawn near to all people in Jesus.

of the LORD being strong upon me. 15And I came to the exiles at Tel-abib, who were dwelling by the Chebar canal, and I sat where they were dwelling.[1] And I sat there overwhelmed among them seven days.

A Watchman for Israel

16And at the end of seven days, the word of the LORD came to me: 17"Son of man, I have made you a watchman for the house of Israel. Whenever you hear a word from my mouth, you shall give them warning from me. 18If I say to the wicked, 'You shall surely die,' and you give him no warning, nor speak to warn the wicked from his wicked way, in order to save his life, that wicked person shall die for[2] his iniquity, but his blood I will require at your hand. 19But if you warn the wicked, and he does not turn from his wickedness, or from his wicked way, he shall die for his iniquity, but you will have delivered your soul. 20Again, if a righteous person turns from his righteousness and commits injustice, and I lay a stumbling block before him, he shall die. Because you have not warned him, he shall die for his sin, and his righteous deeds that he has done shall not be remembered, but his blood I will require at your hand. 21But if you warn the righteous person not to sin, and he does not sin, he shall surely live, because he took warning, and you will have delivered your soul."

22And the hand of the LORD was upon me there. And he said to me, "Arise, go out into the valley,[3] and there I will speak with you." 23So I arose and went out into the valley, and behold, the glory of the LORD stood there, like the glory that I had seen by the Chebar canal, and I fell on my face. 24But the Spirit entered into me and set me on my feet, and he spoke with me and said to me, "Go, shut yourself within your house. 25And you, O son of man, behold, cords will be placed upon you, and you shall be bound with them, so that you cannot go out among the people. 26And I will make your tongue cling to the roof of your mouth, so that you shall be mute and unable to reprove them, for they are a rebellious house. 27But when I speak with you, I will open your mouth, and you shall say to them, 'Thus says the Lord GOD.' He who will hear, let him hear; and he who will refuse to hear, let him refuse, for they are a rebellious house.

The Siege of Jerusalem Symbolized

4 "And you, son of man, take a brick and lay it before you, and engrave on it a city, even Jerusalem. 2And put siegeworks against it, and build a siege wall against it, and cast up a mound against it. Set camps also against it, and plant battering rams against it all around. 3And you, take an iron griddle, and place it as an iron wall between you and the city; and set your face toward it, and let it be in a state of siege, and press the siege against it. This is a sign for the house of Israel.

4"Then lie on your left side, and place the punishment[4] of the house of Israel upon it. For the number of the days that you lie on it, you shall bear their punishment. 5For I assign to you a number of days, 390 days, equal to the number of the years of their punishment. So long shall you bear the punishment of the house of Israel. 6And when you have completed these, you shall lie down a second time, but on your right side, and bear the punishment of the house of Judah. Forty days I assign you, a day for each year. 7And you shall set your face toward the siege of Jerusalem, with your arm bared, and you shall prophesy against the city. 8And behold, I will place cords upon you, so that you cannot turn from one side to the other, till you have completed the days of your siege.

9"And you, take wheat and barley, beans and lentils, millet and emmer,[5] and put them into a single vessel and make your bread from them. During the number of days that you lie on your side, 390 days, you shall eat it. 10And your food that you eat shall be by weight, twenty shekels[6] a day; from day to day[7] you shall eat

[1] Or *Chebar, and to where they dwelt* [2] Or *in*; also verses 19, 20 [3] Or *plain*; also verse 23 [4] Or *iniquity*; also verses 5, 6, 17 [5] A type of wheat [6] A *shekel* was about 2/5 ounce or 11 grams [7] Or *at a set time daily*; also verse 11

it. 11And water you shall drink by measure, the sixth part of a hin;[1] from day to day you shall drink. 12And you shall eat it as a barley cake, baking it in their sight on human dung." 13And the LORD said, "Thus shall the people of Israel eat their bread unclean, among the nations where I will drive them." 14Then I said, "Ah, Lord GOD! Behold, I have never defiled myself.[2] From my youth up till now I have never eaten what died of itself or was torn by beasts, nor has tainted meat come into my mouth." 15Then he said to me, "See, I assign to you cow's dung instead of human dung, on which you may prepare your bread." 16Moreover, he said to me, "Son of man, behold, I will break the supply[3] of bread in Jerusalem. They shall eat bread by weight and with anxiety, and they shall drink water by measure and in dismay. 17I will do this that they may lack bread and water, and look at one another in dismay, and rot away because of their punishment.

Jerusalem Will Be Destroyed

5 "And you, O son of man, take a sharp sword. Use it as a barber's razor and pass it over your head and your beard. Then take balances for weighing and divide the hair. 2A third part you shall burn in the fire in the midst of the city, when the days of the siege are completed. And a third part you shall take and strike with the sword all around the city. And a third part you shall scatter to the wind, and I will unsheathe the sword after them. 3And you shall take from these a small number and bind them in the skirts of your robe. 4And of these again you shall take some and cast them into the midst of the fire and burn them in the fire. From there a fire will come out into all the house of Israel.

5"Thus says the Lord GOD: This is Jerusalem. I have set her in the center of the nations, with countries all around her. 6And she has rebelled against my rules by doing wickedness more than the nations, and against my statutes more than the countries all around her; for they have rejected my rules and have not walked in my statutes. 7Therefore thus says the Lord GOD: Because you are more turbulent than the nations that are all around you, and have not walked in my statutes or obeyed my rules, and have not[4] even acted according to the rules of the nations that are all around you, 8therefore thus says the Lord GOD: Behold, I, even I, am against you. And I will execute judgments[5] in your midst in the sight of the nations. 9And because of all your abominations I will do with you what I have never yet done, and the like of which I will never do again. 10Therefore fathers shall eat their sons in your midst, and sons shall eat their fathers. And I will execute judgments on you, and any of you who survive I will scatter to all the winds. 11Therefore, as I live, declares the Lord GOD, surely, because you have defiled my sanctuary with all your detestable things and with all your abominations, therefore I will withdraw.[6] My eye will not spare, and I will have no pity. 12A third part of you shall die of pestilence and be consumed with famine in your midst; a third part shall fall by the sword all around you; and a third part I will scatter to all the winds and will unsheathe the sword after them.

13"Thus shall my anger spend itself, and I will vent my fury upon them and satisfy myself. And they shall know that I am the LORD—that I have spoken in my jealousy—when I spend my fury upon them. 14Moreover, I will make you a desolation and an object of reproach among the nations all around you and in the sight of all who pass by. 15You shall be[7] a reproach and a taunt, a warning and a horror, to the nations all around you, when I execute judgments on you in anger and fury, and with furious rebukes—I am the LORD; I have spoken— 16when I send against you[8] the deadly arrows of famine, arrows for destruction, which I will send to destroy you, and when I bring more and more famine upon you and break your

EZEKIEL 5:5–11

MORE ACCOUNTABLE

The entire Bible, from cover to cover, is the story of God's plan to create a people, choose a people, transform that people, and then work through his transformed people to change the world. God's people are supposed to be like a light that shines into the dark world, but this passage reveals that the Israelites literally outdid the world in sinning. While the other nations worshiped idols, Israel left the one true living God to turn to idols—a choice that brought dire consequences. God judged them, and his judgment was harsh because his mercy to them had been unfathomable. Of all the people in the world, God chose to love these people in a special way. For them to forsake that love was unthinkable.

The judgments of God are always relative based on the level of light people have received. All people will suffer if they never hear of God; this is why God's people are supposed to run to people with good news to share! At the same time, those who receive more are more accountable. Ezekiel 5:5–7 teaches about this enduring scriptural truth that Jesus repeated in his teaching: "From him to whom they entrusted much, they will demand the more" (Lk 12:48). If that was true for Israel, who spent their lives looking forward to Jesus' arrival, how much more true is it of believers today who have the Holy Spirit?

[1]A *hin* was about 4 quarts or 3.5 liters [2]Hebrew *my soul* (or *throat*) *has never been made unclean* [3]Hebrew *staff* [4]Some Hebrew manuscripts and Syriac lack *not* [5]The same Hebrew expression can mean *obey rules*, or *execute judgments*, depending on the context [6]Some Hebrew manuscripts *I will cut you down* [7]Dead Sea Scroll, Septuagint, Syriac, Vulgate, Targum; Masoretic Text *And it shall be* [8]Hebrew *them*

supply[1] of bread. 17 I will send famine and wild beasts against you, and they will rob you of your children. Pestilence and blood shall pass through you, and I will bring the sword upon you. I am the LORD; I have spoken."

Judgment Against Idolatry

6 The word of the LORD came to me: 2 "Son of man, set your face toward the mountains of Israel, and prophesy against them, 3 and say, You mountains of Israel, hear the word of the Lord GOD! Thus says the Lord GOD to the mountains and the hills, to the ravines and the valleys: Behold, I, even I, will bring a sword upon you, and I will destroy your high places. 4 Your altars shall become desolate, and your incense altars shall be broken, and I will cast down your slain before your idols. 5 And I will lay the dead bodies of the people of Israel before their idols, and I will scatter your bones around your altars. 6 Wherever you dwell, the cities shall be waste and the high places ruined, so that your altars will be waste and ruined,[2] your idols broken and destroyed, your incense altars cut down, and your works wiped out. 7 And the slain shall fall in your midst, and you shall know that I am the LORD.

8 "Yet I will leave some of you alive. When you have among the nations some who escape the sword, and when you are scattered through the countries, 9 then those of you who escape will remember me among the nations where they are carried captive, how I have been broken over their whoring heart that has departed from me and over their eyes that go whoring after their idols. And they will be loathsome in their own sight for the evils that they have committed, for all their abominations. 10 And they shall know that I am the LORD. I have not said in vain that I would do this evil to them."

11 Thus says the Lord GOD: "Clap your hands and stamp your foot and say, Alas, because of all the evil abominations of the house of Israel, for they shall fall by the sword, by famine, and by pestilence. 12 He who is far off shall die of pestilence, and he who is near shall fall by the sword, and he who is left and is preserved shall die of famine. Thus I will spend my fury upon them. 13 And you shall know that I am the LORD, when their slain lie among their idols around their altars, on every high hill, on all the mountaintops, under every green tree, and under every leafy oak, wherever they offered pleasing aroma to all their idols. 14 And I will stretch out my hand against them and make the land desolate and waste, in all their dwelling places, from the wilderness to Riblah.[3] Then they will know that I am the LORD."

The Day of the Wrath of the LORD

7 The word of the LORD came to me: 2 "And you, O son of man, thus says the Lord GOD to the land of Israel: An end! The end has come upon the four corners of the land.[4] 3 Now the end is upon you, and I will send my anger upon you; I will judge you according to your ways, and I will punish you for all your abominations. 4 And my eye will not spare you, nor will I have pity, but I will punish you for your ways, while your abominations are in your midst. Then you will know that I am the LORD.

5 "Thus says the Lord GOD: Disaster after disaster![5] Behold, it comes. 6 An end has come; the end has come; it has awakened against you. Behold, it comes. 7 Your doom[6] has come to you, O inhabitant of the land. The time has come; the day is near, a day of tumult, and not of joyful shouting on the mountains. 8 Now I will soon pour out my wrath upon you, and spend my anger against you, and judge you according to your ways, and I will punish you for all your abominations. 9 And my eye will not spare, nor will I have pity. I will punish you according to your ways, while your abominations are in your midst. Then you will know that I am the LORD, who strikes.

[1] Hebrew *staff* [2] Or *and punished* [3] Some Hebrew manuscripts; most Hebrew manuscripts *Diblah*
[4] Or *earth* [5] Some Hebrew manuscripts (compare Syriac, Targum); most Hebrew manuscripts *Disaster! A unique disaster!* [6] The meaning of the Hebrew word is uncertain; also verse 10

EZEKIEL 7:6

THE END HAS COME!

Predictions about the end of the world tend to get people's attention, as they have a natural tendency to wonder when the end will come. In the book of Ezekiel, God delivered a clear word to Judah not that the end of the world was coming, but that the end of this season of God's favor had come. Ezekiel told them they would experience punishment as their nation was conquered and they were sent away to live as exiles.

A few hundred years later, in the New Testament, Jesus' followers asked him how they could tell when the end would come. Jesus responded, "And you will hear of wars and rumors of wars. See that you are not alarmed, for this must take place, but the end is not yet. For nation will rise against nation, and kingdom against kingdom, and there will be famines and earthquakes in various places" (Mt 24:6–7). And then, Jesus went on to declare, "This gospel of the kingdom will be proclaimed throughout the whole world as a testimony to all nations, and then the end will come" (Mt 24:14).

God doesn't expect his people to know the exact time when his kingdom will come in fullness. He does, however, expect his church to be faithful and obedient in preparing for it.

YOU SHALL KNOW

One of the recurring themes of Ezekiel revolves around the phrase, "and you shall know that I am the LORD" (v. 7). The best way to experience God is through an encounter with his mercy. At the same time, it is possible to experience God through an encounter with his judgment. At this point, God's people had sinned so much that they were about to experience the judgment of God in an encounter they would never forget.

The recurring theme of "and you shall know" testifies to the God-centeredness of this book. God's sovereignty, glory, and love for his people converge in a powerful way. This combination of ideas is also found in Jeremiah's prophecy. It certainly seems that Ezekiel drew upon Jeremiah to develop these ideas further by focusing on the Babylonians' destruction of Jerusalem.

Ezekiel 6 is full of references to the theme of God's power and might for his people (vv. 7,10,13 – 14). In this case, God was dealing with a stiff-necked and rebellious people, who would discover that he was the Lord through judgment. The emphasis is not necessarily on the fact that God judges, though that is certainly true. The real goal is that people would know and experience the character of God. The emphasis is on getting to know God and experience God. Judgment is never for judgment's sake; its goal is for people to experience more truth about who God is.

Judgment is a critical way for people to experience the character of God. The most wonderful part of the idea of judgment is that God substituted Jesus for undeserving sinners. It was not until Jesus was "lifted up" via crucifixion that people could really get to know him and understand him in the fullest sense: "So Jesus said to them 'When you have lifted up the Son of Man, then you will know that I am he, and that I do nothing on my own authority, but speak just as the Father taught me.'" (Jn 8:28). It is only through seeing that God substituted Jesus for the sins of the world that people are able to see the truth that sets them free (Jn 8:32).

10“Behold, the day! Behold, it comes! Your doom has come; the rod has blossomed; pride has budded. 11Violence has grown up into a rod of wickedness. None
of them shall remain, nor their abundance, nor their wealth; neither shall there
be preeminence among them.[1] 12The time has come; the day has arrived. Let not
the buyer rejoice, nor the seller mourn, for wrath is upon all their multitude.[2]
13For the seller shall not return to what he has sold, while they live. For the vision
concerns all their multitude; it shall not turn back; and because of his iniquity,
none can maintain his life.[3]

14“They have blown the trumpet and made everything ready, but none goes to
battle, for my wrath is upon all their multitude. 15The sword is without; pestilence
and famine are within. He who is in the field dies by the sword, and him who is
in the city famine and pestilence devour. 16And if any survivors escape, they will
be on the mountains, like doves of the valleys, all of them moaning, each one
over his iniquity. 17All hands are feeble, and all knees turn to water. 18They put on
sackcloth, and horror covers them. Shame is on all faces, and baldness on all their
heads. 19They cast their silver into the streets, and their gold is like an unclean
thing. Their silver and gold are not able to deliver them in the day of the wrath
of the LORD. They cannot satisfy their hunger or fill their stomachs with it. For it
was the stumbling block of their iniquity. 20His beautiful ornament they used for
pride, and they made their abominable images and their detestable things of it.
Therefore I make it an unclean thing to them. 21And I will give it into the hands of
foreigners for prey, and to the wicked of the earth for spoil, and they shall profane
it. 22I will turn my face from them, and they shall profane my treasured[4] place.
Robbers shall enter and profane it.

23“Forge a chain![5] For the land is full of bloody crimes and the city is full
of violence. 24I will bring the worst of the nations to take possession of their
houses. I will put an end to the pride of the strong, and their holy places[6] shall
be profaned. 25When anguish comes, they will seek peace, but there shall be
none. 26Disaster comes upon disaster; rumor follows rumor. They seek a vision
from the prophet, while the law[7] perishes from the priest and counsel from the
elders. 27The king mourns, the prince is wrapped in despair, and the hands of
the people of the land are paralyzed by terror. According to their way I will do to
them, and according to their judgments I will judge them, and they shall know
that I am the LORD.”

Abominations in the Temple

8 In the sixth year, in the sixth month, on the fifth day of the month, as I sat
in my house, with the elders of Judah sitting before me, the hand of the Lord
GOD fell upon me there. 2Then I looked, and behold, a form that had the appearance of a man.[8] Below what appeared to be his waist was fire, and above his waist
was something like the appearance of brightness, like gleaming metal.[9] 3He put
out the form of a hand and took me by a lock of my head, and the Spirit lifted me
up between earth and heaven and brought me in visions of God to Jerusalem, to
the entrance of the gateway of the inner court that faces north, where was the seat
of the image of jealousy, which provokes to jealousy. 4And behold, the glory of the
God of Israel was there, like the vision that I saw in the valley.

5Then he said to me, “Son of man, lift up your eyes now toward the north.”
So I lifted up my eyes toward the north, and behold, north of the altar gate, in
the entrance, was this image of jealousy. 6And he said to me, “Son of man, do
you see what they are doing, the great abominations that the house of Israel are
committing here, to drive me far from my sanctuary? But you will see still greater
abominations.”

---

[1]The meaning of this last Hebrew sentence is uncertain [2]Or *abundance*; also verses 13, 14 [3]The meaning of this last Hebrew sentence is uncertain [4]Or *secret* [5]Probably refers to an instrument of captivity [6]By revocalization (compare Septuagint); Hebrew *and those who sanctify them* [7]Or *instruction* [8]By revocalization (compare Septuagint); Hebrew *of fire* [9]Or *amber*

[7]And he brought me to the entrance of the court, and when I looked, behold, there was a hole in the wall. [8]Then he said to me, "Son of man, dig in the wall." So I dug in the wall, and behold, there was an entrance. [9]And he said to me, "Go in, and see the vile abominations that they are committing here." [10]So I went in and saw. And there, engraved on the wall all around, was every form of creeping things and loathsome beasts, and all the idols of the house of Israel. [11]And before them stood seventy men of the elders of the house of Israel, with Jaazaniah the son of Shaphan standing among them. Each had his censer in his hand, and the smoke of the cloud of incense went up. [12]Then he said to me, "Son of man, have you seen what the elders of the house of Israel are doing in the dark, each in his room of pictures? For they say, 'The LORD does not see us, the LORD has forsaken the land.'" [13]He said also to me, "You will see still greater abominations that they commit."

[14]Then he brought me to the entrance of the north gate of the house of the LORD, and behold, there sat women weeping for Tammuz. [15]Then he said to me, "Have you seen this, O son of man? You will see still greater abominations than these."

[16]And he brought me into the inner court of the house of the LORD. And behold, at the entrance of the temple of the LORD, between the porch and the altar, were about twenty-five men, with their backs to the temple of the LORD, and their faces toward the east, worshiping the sun toward the east. [17]Then he said to me, "Have you seen this, O son of man? Is it too light a thing for the house of Judah to commit the abominations that they commit here, that they should fill the land with violence and provoke me still further to anger? Behold, they put the branch to their[1] nose. [18]Therefore I will act in wrath. My eye will not spare, nor will I have pity. And though they cry in my ears with a loud voice, I will not hear them."

Idolaters Killed

9 Then he cried in my ears with a loud voice, saying, "Bring near the executioners of the city, each with his destroying weapon in his hand." [2]And behold, six men came from the direction of the upper gate, which faces north, each with his weapon for slaughter in his hand, and with them was a man clothed in linen, with a writing case at his waist. And they went in and stood beside the bronze altar.

[3]Now the glory of the God of Israel had gone up from the cherub on which it rested to the threshold of the house. And he called to the man clothed in linen, who had the writing case at his waist. [4]And the LORD said to him, "Pass through the city, through Jerusalem, and put a mark on the foreheads of the men who sigh and groan over all the abominations that are committed in it." [5]And to the others he said in my hearing, "Pass through the city after him, and strike. Your eye shall not spare, and you shall show no pity. [6]Kill old men outright, young men and maidens, little children and women, but touch no one on whom is the mark. And begin at my sanctuary." So they began with the elders who were before the house. [7]Then he said to them, "Defile the house, and fill the courts with the slain. Go out." So they went out and struck in the city. [8]And while they were striking, and I was left alone, I fell upon my face, and cried, "Ah, Lord GOD! Will you destroy all the remnant of Israel in the outpouring of your wrath on Jerusalem?"

[9]Then he said to me, "The guilt of the house of Israel and Judah is exceedingly great. The land is full of blood, and the city full of injustice. For they say, 'The LORD has forsaken the land, and the LORD does not see.' [10]As for me, my eye will not spare, nor will I have pity; I will bring their deeds upon their heads."

[11]And behold, the man clothed in linen, with the writing case at his waist, brought back word, saying, "I have done as you commanded me."

---

[1]Or *my*

EZEKIEL 8:9–12

SIN OF THE PEOPLE

God's judgment was coming upon the Israelites because of their sin. This sin was not contained to a few lunatics on the fringes of their community; instead, the leaders of the community were committing it. In the temple, the very place where God's presence was meant to dwell with his people, they were committing wicked acts against God.

Like so many of the prophets, Ezekiel analyzed and spoke against the sins of the people. He focused especially on the sin of idolatry—the worship of other gods or other things in place of God. God's people were hiding in the dark and doing dark things. In his ministry, Jesus taught that what happens in the dark will eventually be brought into the light: "For nothing is hidden that will not be made manifest, nor is anything secret that will not be known and come to light. Take care then how you hear, for to the one who has, more will be given, and from the one who has not, even what he thinks that he has will be taken away" (Lk 8:17–18).

In Ezekiel, God's people were judged because they had so much favor from God and did so little with it. God gives great things to his people and then expects great things from his people. Sin keeps God's people from experiencing God's best for them.

The Glory of the LORD Leaves the Temple

10 Then I looked, and behold, on the expanse that was over the heads of the
cherubim there appeared above them something like a sapphire,[1] in appearance like a throne. 2 And he said to the man clothed in linen, "Go in among
the whirling wheels underneath the cherubim. Fill your hands with burning coals
from between the cherubim, and scatter them over the city."

And he went in before my eyes. 3 Now the cherubim were standing on the
south side of the house, when the man went in, and a cloud filled the inner
court. 4 And the glory of the LORD went up from the cherub to the threshold of
the house, and the house was filled with the cloud, and the court was filled with
the brightness of the glory of the LORD. 5 And the sound of the wings of the cherubim was heard as far as the outer court, like the voice of God Almighty when he
speaks.

6 And when he commanded the man clothed in linen, "Take fire from between
the whirling wheels, from between the cherubim," he went in and stood beside a
wheel. 7 And a cherub stretched out his hand from between the cherubim to the
fire that was between the cherubim, and took some of it and put it into the hands
of the man clothed in linen, who took it and went out. 8 The cherubim appeared
to have the form of a human hand under their wings.

9 And I looked, and behold, there were four wheels beside the cherubim, one
beside each cherub, and the appearance of the wheels was like sparkling beryl.
10 And as for their appearance, the four had the same likeness, as if a wheel were
within a wheel. 11 When they went, they went in any of their four directions[2] without turning as they went, but in whatever direction the front wheel[3] faced, the
others followed without turning as they went. 12 And their whole body, their rims,
and their spokes, their wings,[4] and the wheels were full of eyes all around—the
wheels that the four of them had. 13 As for the wheels, they were called in my hearing "the whirling wheels." 14 And every one had four faces: the first face was the
face of the cherub, and the second face was a human face, and the third the face
of a lion, and the fourth the face of an eagle.

15 And the cherubim mounted up. These were the living creatures that I saw by
the Chebar canal. 16 And when the cherubim went, the wheels went beside them.
And when the cherubim lifted up their wings to mount up from the earth, the
wheels did not turn from beside them. 17 When they stood still, these stood still,
and when they mounted up, these mounted up with them, for the spirit of the
living creatures[5] was in them.

18 Then the glory of the LORD went out from the threshold of the house, and
stood over the cherubim. 19 And the cherubim lifted up their wings and mounted
up from the earth before my eyes as they went out, with the wheels beside them.
And they stood at the entrance of the east gate of the house of the LORD, and the
glory of the God of Israel was over them.

20 These were the living creatures that I saw underneath the God of Israel by
the Chebar canal; and I knew that they were cherubim. 21 Each had four faces, and
each four wings, and underneath their wings the likeness of human hands. 22 And
as for the likeness of their faces, they were the same faces whose appearance I had
seen by the Chebar canal. Each one of them went straight forward.

Judgment on Wicked Counselors

11 The Spirit lifted me up and brought me to the east gate of the house of the
LORD, which faces east. And behold, at the entrance of the gateway there
were twenty-five men. And I saw among them Jaazaniah the son of Azzur, and
Pelatiah the son of Benaiah, princes of the people. 2 And he said to me, "Son of
man, these are the men who devise iniquity and who give wicked counsel in this

[1] Or *lapis lazuli* [2] Hebrew *to their four sides* [3] Hebrew *the head* [4] Or *their whole body, their backs, their hands, and their wings* [5] Or *spirit of life*

EZEKIEL 10:18–19

GLORY DEPARTING, GLORY COMING

God's glory in the temple was a manifestation of his presence, but since sin was happening in the temple, God removed his presence. Beginning with Ezekiel 9:3, the prophet recounts the steady withdrawal of God's presence from the temple. The removal of God's glory was a shocking reminder that God was not going to tolerate the Israelites' sin.

Thankfully, Jesus made a way for God's glory to remain with his people in a permanent way. Jesus was God's glory living on earth (Jn 17:24), but people did not see it. In time, Jesus' disciples realized that in Jesus' incarnation, death, and resurrection, they had witnessed the coming glory of God (Jn 1:14). Jesus came to live a perfect life and die as the perfect sacrifice for human sin.

When God took the sins of the entire world and heaped them on Jesus, sin was accounted for and punished. As a result, believers can experience God's glory and live because their sin is no longer an obstacle to them. Ezekiel taught about the removal of God's glory, and Jesus taught about the coming of God's glory (Mt 24:30; 25:31). Christians joyfully remember how gracious God is to save them and then dedicate their lives to loving and serving him wholeheartedly.

city; 3who say, 'The time is not near[1] to build houses. This city is the cauldron, and we are the meat.' 4Therefore prophesy against them; prophesy, O son of man."

5And the Spirit of the LORD fell upon me, and he said to me, "Say, Thus says the LORD: So you think, O house of Israel. For I know the things that come into your mind. 6You have multiplied your slain in this city and have filled its streets with the slain. 7Therefore thus says the Lord GOD: Your slain whom you have laid in the midst of it, they are the meat, and this city is the cauldron, but you shall be brought out of the midst of it. 8You have feared the sword, and I will bring the sword upon you, declares the Lord GOD. 9And I will bring you out of the midst of it, and give you into the hands of foreigners, and execute judgments upon you. 10You shall fall by the sword. I will judge you at the border of Israel, and you shall know that I am the LORD. 11This city shall not be your cauldron, nor shall you be the meat in the midst of it. I will judge you at the border of Israel, 12and you shall know that I am the LORD. For you have not walked in my statutes, nor obeyed my rules, but have acted according to the rules of the nations that are around you."

13And it came to pass, while I was prophesying, that Pelatiah the son of Benaiah died. Then I fell down on my face and cried out with a loud voice and said, "Ah, Lord GOD! Will you make a full end of the remnant of Israel?"

Israel's New Heart and Spirit

14And the word of the LORD came to me: 15"Son of man, your brothers, even your brothers, your kinsmen,[2] the whole house of Israel, all of them, are those of whom the inhabitants of Jerusalem have said, 'Go far from the LORD; to us this land is given for a possession.' 16Therefore say, 'Thus says the Lord GOD: Though I removed them far off among the nations, and though I scattered them among the countries, yet I have been a sanctuary to them for a while[3] in the countries where they have gone.' 17Therefore say, 'Thus says the Lord GOD: I will gather you from the peoples and assemble you out of the countries where you have been scattered, and I will give you the land of Israel.' 18And when they come there, they will remove from it all its detestable things and all its abominations. 19And I will give them one heart, and a new spirit I will put within them. I will remove the heart of stone from their flesh and give them a heart of flesh, 20that they may walk in my statutes and keep my rules and obey them. And they shall be my people, and I will be their God. 21But as for those whose heart goes after their detestable things and their abominations, I will[4] bring their deeds upon their own heads, declares the Lord GOD."

22Then the cherubim lifted up their wings, with the wheels beside them, and the glory of the God of Israel was over them. 23And the glory of the LORD went up from the midst of the city and stood on the mountain that is on the east side of the city. 24And the Spirit lifted me up and brought me in the vision by the Spirit of God into Chaldea, to the exiles. Then the vision that I had seen went up from me. 25And I told the exiles all the things that the LORD had shown me.

Judah's Captivity Symbolized

12 The word of the LORD came to me: 2"Son of man, you dwell in the midst of a rebellious house, who have eyes to see, but see not, who have ears to hear, but hear not, for they are a rebellious house. 3As for you, son of man, prepare for yourself an exile's baggage, and go into exile by day in their sight. You shall go like an exile from your place to another place in their sight. Perhaps they will understand, though[5] they are a rebellious house. 4You shall bring out your baggage by day in their sight, as baggage for exile, and you shall go out yourself at evening in their sight, as those do who must go into exile. 5In their sight dig through the wall,

[1] Or *Is not the time near . . . ?* [2] Hebrew *the men of your redemption* [3] Or *in small measure* [4] Hebrew *To the heart of their detestable things and their abominations their heart goes; I will* [5] Or *will see that*

WHERE GOD'S GLORY RESIDES

The word *glory* here literally means "weight" or "significance" and refers to the wonder and majesty of the living God. At times in the Old Testament, God's glory was displayed to his people to show that he was with them. When Moses set up the tabernacle, God's glory filled the tent and Moses was not able to enter it (Ex 40:34 – 35). Later, when Solomon built the temple, the cloud of God's glory appeared again (1Ki 8:10 – 12; 2Ch 7:1 – 2). But during Ezekiel's ministry, the prophet saw a vision of God's glory leaving the temple in Jerusalem.

God's glory left the presence of God's people because God's people were involved in unrelenting sin. Their idol worship permeated everything to the point that they went to the temple to pay homage to other idols instead of the one true and living God (Eze 8:3,14 – 16). They even painted images of idols and unclean animals on the walls of the temple (Eze 8:9 – 11). God's message to his people about their sin was clear: it was wrong. He told them to stop sinning. He warned them about its consequences. And he warned them that he would not tolerate it forever.

God took the most precious thing that he could have from his people: his presence. Regardless of what God's people valued, God's glory was the best reality they had ever experienced. It is interesting to note how God slowly removed his glory from his people. God's glory moved from above the cherubim in the Most Holy Place to the threshold of the house of God (Eze 9:3), then moved to the east gate of the house of the LORD (Eze 10:19), and then made one final stop above the Mount of Olives (Eze 11:23). God slowly and reluctantly removed himself from his people with a display that left no doubt as to what was happening. Not long after God removed his glory from Solomon's temple, the temple was destroyed, and God's glory never returned to that temple.

But God's glory did return to the world, and it returned in a way that was unlike anything the world had ever seen. John explains, "And the Word became flesh and dwelt among us, and we have seen his glory, glory as of the only Son from the Father, full of grace and truth" (Jn 1:14). Jesus fully embodied the glory of God. To see God, one only needs to look to Jesus (Heb 1:3). Following his short life, Jesus offered himself up as the perfect sacrifice for sin to end all other sacrifices. He gave parting words to his followers and departed to heaven from the Mount of Olives (Ac 1:7 – 12). His glory is with his people today because all who trust in Jesus possess his Spirit and live their lives reflecting God's glory in an ever-increasing way (2Co 3:18).

THE REBELLION

God's prophet had to speak to God's "rebellious house": a phrase the Lord used twice in this verse to describe the community of exiles in Babylon among whom Ezekiel ministered. They refused to listen to the prophet's words or heed his dramatizations of their coming judgments.

All people struggle with a rebellious heart toward God. The word *rebellious* is used all throughout Scripture to explain the condition of people's hearts as a result of sin. It depicts someone opposing an authority figure out of stubborn pride (Dt 21:18). Ezekiel described the Israelites as a rebellious people a dozen times, meaning they were willfully disobedient and persistent in their refusal to listen to God's message through Ezekiel (Eze 2:3 – 8). These people wanted nothing to do with God's authority in their lives.

Jesus was accused of being a rebel throughout his life. Religious leaders accused him of leading a rebellion (Lk 23:1 – 2,13 – 14). They had created an established system of religion to manage their relationship with God. Their man-made solution to their sin problem with God had no need of Jesus. When Jesus came preaching the gospel of repentance, the leaders hated it because it meant that their whole system was inadequate. Jesus was arrested, put on trial, and sentenced to death. As Jesus hung on the cross, he was crucified between two rebels (Mt 27:38,44).

The great irony is that Jesus was the ultimate example of someone who was not a rebel! Jesus obediently died as the substitute for sinners. He was not a sinner, but he willfully gave his life to die for everyone who has ever had a rebellious thought, season, or life. All people need to do is trust in him to claim the life that is truly life (1Ti 6:19). Jesus' life was perfectly aligned with God the Father in every way. In John 5:19, he stated that he would do only what he saw the Father doing. When teaching his followers to pray, he told them to say to the Father, "Your kingdom come, your will be done, on earth as it is in heaven" (Mt 6:10).

God sent both Ezekiel and Jesus to speak to a rebellious people. Jesus was a perfect man who lived a life of perfect obedience to God for undeserving people. Despite their rebellion, God launched a counter-rebellion against the defiance of his people. He has waged a war of love on the misplaced desires of human hearts.

and bring your baggage out through it. 6In their sight you shall lift the baggage upon your shoulder and carry it out at dusk. You shall cover your face that you may not see the land, for I have made you a sign for the house of Israel."

7And I did as I was commanded. I brought out my baggage by day, as baggage for exile, and in the evening I dug through the wall with my own hands. I brought out my baggage at dusk, carrying it on my shoulder in their sight.

8In the morning the word of the LORD came to me: 9"Son of man, has not the house of Israel, the rebellious house, said to you, 'What are you doing?' 10Say to them, 'Thus says the Lord GOD: This oracle concerns[1] the prince in Jerusalem and all the house of Israel who are in it.'[2] 11Say, 'I am a sign for you: as I have done, so shall it be done to them. They shall go into exile, into captivity.' 12And the prince who is among them shall lift his baggage upon his shoulder at dusk, and shall go out. They shall dig through the wall to bring him out through it. He shall cover his face, that he may not see the land with his eyes. 13And I will spread my net over him, and he shall be taken in my snare. And I will bring him to Babylon, the land of the Chaldeans, yet he shall not see it, and he shall die there. 14And I will scatter toward every wind all who are around him, his helpers and all his troops, and I will unsheathe the sword after them. 15And they shall know that I am the LORD, when I disperse them among the nations and scatter them among the countries. 16But I will let a few of them escape from the sword, from famine and pestilence, that they may declare all their abominations among the nations where they go, and may know that I am the LORD."

17And the word of the LORD came to me: 18"Son of man, eat your bread with quaking, and drink water with trembling and with anxiety. 19And say to the people of the land, Thus says the Lord GOD concerning the inhabitants of Jerusalem in the land of Israel: They shall eat their bread with anxiety, and drink water in dismay. In this way her land will be stripped of all it contains, on account of the violence of all those who dwell in it. 20And the inhabited cities shall be laid waste, and the land shall become a desolation; and you shall know that I am the LORD."

21And the word of the LORD came to me: 22"Son of man, what is this proverb that you[3] have about the land of Israel, saying, 'The days grow long, and every vision comes to nothing'? 23Tell them therefore, 'Thus says the Lord GOD: I will put an end to this proverb, and they shall no more use it as a proverb in Israel.' But say to them, The days are near, and the fulfillment[4] of every vision. 24For there shall be no more any false vision or flattering divination within the house of Israel. 25For I am the LORD; I will speak the word that I will speak, and it will be performed. It will no longer be delayed, but in your days, O rebellious house, I will speak the word and perform it, declares the Lord GOD."

26And the word of the LORD came to me: 27"Son of man, behold, they of the house of Israel say, 'The vision that he sees is for many days from now, and he prophesies of times far off.' 28Therefore say to them, Thus says the Lord GOD: None of my words will be delayed any longer, but the word that I speak will be performed, declares the Lord GOD."

False Prophets Condemned

13 The word of the LORD came to me: 2"Son of man, prophesy against the prophets of Israel, who are prophesying, and say to those who prophesy from their own hearts: 'Hear the word of the LORD!' 3Thus says the Lord GOD, Woe to the foolish prophets who follow their own spirit, and have seen nothing! 4Your prophets have been like jackals among ruins, O Israel. 5You have not gone up into the breaches, or built up a wall for the house of Israel, that it might stand in battle in the day of the LORD. 6They have seen false visions and lying divinations. They say, 'Declares the LORD,' when the LORD has not sent them, and yet

[1]Or *This burden is* [2]Hebrew *in the midst of them* [3]The Hebrew for *you* is plural [4]Hebrew *word*

they expect him to fulfill their word. 7Have you not seen a false vision and uttered a lying divination, whenever you have said, 'Declares the LORD,' although I have not spoken?"

8Therefore thus says the Lord GOD: "Because you have uttered falsehood and seen lying visions, therefore behold, I am against you, declares the Lord GOD. 9My hand will be against the prophets who see false visions and who give lying divinations. They shall not be in the council of my people, nor be enrolled in the register of the house of Israel, nor shall they enter the land of Israel. And you shall know that I am the Lord GOD. 10Precisely because they have misled my people, saying, 'Peace,' when there is no peace, and because, when the people build a wall, these prophets smear it with whitewash,[1] 11say to those who smear it with whitewash that it shall fall! There will be a deluge of rain, and you, O great hailstones, will fall, and a stormy wind break out. 12And when the wall falls, will it not be said to you, 'Where is the coating with which you smeared it?' 13Therefore thus says the Lord GOD: I will make a stormy wind break out in my wrath, and there shall be a deluge of rain in my anger, and great hailstones in wrath to make a full end. 14And I will break down the wall that you have smeared with whitewash, and bring it down to the ground, so that its foundation will be laid bare. When it falls, you shall perish in the midst of it, and you shall know that I am the LORD. 15Thus will I spend my wrath upon the wall and upon those who have smeared it with whitewash, and I will say to you, The wall is no more, nor those who smeared it, 16the prophets of Israel who prophesied concerning Jerusalem and saw visions of peace for her, when there was no peace, declares the Lord GOD.

17"And you, son of man, set your face against the daughters of your people, who prophesy out of their own hearts. Prophesy against them 18and say, Thus says the Lord GOD: Woe to the women who sew magic bands upon all wrists, and make veils for the heads of persons of every stature, in the hunt for souls! Will you hunt down souls belonging to my people and keep your own souls alive? 19You have profaned me among my people for handfuls of barley and for pieces of bread, putting to death souls who should not die and keeping alive souls who should not live, by your lying to my people, who listen to lies.

20"Therefore thus says the Lord GOD: Behold, I am against your magic bands with which you hunt the souls like birds, and I will tear them from your arms, and I will let the souls whom you hunt go free, the souls like birds. 21Your veils also I will tear off and deliver my people out of your hand, and they shall be no more in your hand as prey, and you shall know that I am the LORD. 22Because you have disheartened the righteous falsely, although I have not grieved him, and you have encouraged the wicked, that he should not turn from his evil way to save his life, 23therefore you shall no more see false visions nor practice divination. I will deliver my people out of your hand. And you shall know that I am the LORD."

Idolatrous Elders Condemned

14 Then certain of the elders of Israel came to me and sat before me. 2And the word of the LORD came to me: 3"Son of man, these men have taken their idols into their hearts, and set the stumbling block of their iniquity before their faces. Should I indeed let myself be consulted by them? 4Therefore speak to them and say to them, Thus says the Lord GOD: Any one of the house of Israel who takes his idols into his heart and sets the stumbling block of his iniquity before his face, and yet comes to the prophet, I the LORD will answer him as he comes with the multitude of his idols, 5that I may lay hold of the hearts of the house of Israel, who are all estranged from me through their idols.

6"Therefore say to the house of Israel, Thus says the Lord GOD: Repent and turn away from your idols, and turn away your faces from all your abominations. 7For any one of the house of Israel, or of the strangers who sojourn in Israel, who

[1] Or *plaster*; also verses 11, 14, 15

EZEKIEL 13:10–16

COVERING UP THE REAL PROBLEM

God's rage burned against Jerusalem's false prophets, and his message was clear: their city was going to be destroyed because of the sins of its inhabitants. Still these deceitful prophets gave God's people a false sense of hope. They reassured the people that their society's problems were not that bad, and they minimized the consequences of their sins. God spoke through Ezekiel to tell these prophets that they had "whitewashed" the sin problem in their city, covering over what was a deadly serious problem with whitewash paint. Because they covered up the problem of the people's sin but never really dealt with it, God would crush these false prophets under that same whitewashed stone wall when the city was destroyed.

Jesus warned the religious leaders during his day in a similar way, saying they were like "whitewashed tombs" (Mt 23:27–28). From the outside, their religious exterior looked good and presentable, but their empty religious practices were like rotting decay and dry bones on the inside. Sinful people will never be made whole until their problems are addressed all the way down to the core. Covering up the problem of sin never makes that sin go away. Only Jesus can heal the brokenness and restore relationships between people, and between believers and God (Ro 6:1–14).

IDOLS IN THE HEART

Loyalty is an important word; it has to do with what or whom a person relies on when a need arises, and it carries a sense of being dedicated and faithful to an idea or to a person. The elders here were double-minded men (1Ki 18:21). Outwardly, they came to the prophet Ezekiel in order to hear from God, but in their hearts their loyalty to God was divided. God told Ezekiel that he would not give revelatory guidance to these men who were not fully committed to worshiping him above all other gods. Loyalty to God means worshiping him alone. The religious leaders were not loyal to God because they had a heart problem.

Idolatry may sound primitive. Many people think of figures made from wood or stone to which people pray and offer sacrifices. When people engage in idolatrous practices they set the stumbling block for their iniquity before their faces (Eze 14:4). Idols are not only carved objects that sit in pagan temples; idols are the godless cravings and sinful commitments that rule people's hearts.

God's people during Ezekiel's day struggled with the same things that people struggle with today: idols in their hearts (vv. 3,4). Everyone struggled with this; it was not just a problem for a select few. Even the religious leaders were committed to godless purposes. Their hearts' divided loyalties manifested in mixing the worship of idols with the worship of the one true and living God. Their idols would fail when God's judgment came (vv. 4 – 5).

God announced his restorative purpose through loving rebuke and discipline of those he loves (Rev 3:19). Jesus came to rid the world of idols, and he accomplished this by focusing on the hearts of humanity. Jesus confronted people who struggled with idolatry in order to save them from their idolatry. He knew that idolatry was not a simple behavior problem but a deep and abiding heart problem.

God's work of salvation is "heart work." Humanity's idolatry is not a little issue that needs to be fixed but a path that will lead to judgment (Ro 2:5). God promised to give his people new hearts so they could worship him fully (Eze 11:19 – 20; 36:26). The resurrection of Jesus means that believers can have new life. As a promise of his love, God puts his Spirit in the hearts of his children; he has "put his seal on us and given us his Spirit in our hearts as a guarantee" (2Co 1:22).

separates himself from me, taking his idols into his heart and putting the stumbling block of his iniquity before his face, and yet comes to a prophet to consult
me through him, I the LORD will answer him myself. 8And I will set my face against
that man; I will make him a sign and a byword and cut him off from the midst of
my people, and you shall know that I am the LORD. 9And if the prophet is deceived
and speaks a word, I, the LORD, have deceived that prophet, and I will stretch out
my hand against him and will destroy him from the midst of my people Israel.
10And they shall bear their punishment[1]—the punishment of the prophet and the
punishment of the inquirer shall be alike— 11that the house of Israel may no more
go astray from me, nor defile themselves anymore with all their transgressions,
but that they may be my people and I may be their God, declares the Lord GOD."

Jerusalem Will Not Be Spared

12And the word of the LORD came to me: 13"Son of man, when a land sins
against me by acting faithlessly, and I stretch out my hand against it and break
its supply[2] of bread and send famine upon it, and cut off from it man and beast,
14even if these three men, Noah, Daniel, and Job, were in it, they would deliver but
their own lives by their righteousness, declares the Lord GOD.
15"If I cause wild beasts to pass through the land, and they ravage it, and it be
made desolate, so that no one may pass through because of the beasts, 16even if
these three men were in it, as I live, declares the Lord GOD, they would deliver
neither sons nor daughters. They alone would be delivered, but the land would
be desolate.
17"Or if I bring a sword upon that land and say, Let a sword pass through the
land, and I cut off from it man and beast, 18though these three men were in it, as
I live, declares the Lord GOD, they would deliver neither sons nor daughters, but
they alone would be delivered.
19"Or if I send a pestilence into that land and pour out my wrath upon it with
blood, to cut off from it man and beast, 20even if Noah, Daniel, and Job were in it,
as I live, declares the Lord GOD, they would deliver neither son nor daughter. They
would deliver but their own lives by their righteousness.
21"For thus says the Lord GOD: How much more when I send upon Jerusalem
my four disastrous acts of judgment, sword, famine, wild beasts, and pestilence,
to cut off from it man and beast! 22But behold, some survivors will be left in it,
sons and daughters who will be brought out; behold, when they come out to you,
and you see their ways and their deeds, you will be consoled for the disaster that
I have brought upon Jerusalem, for all that I have brought upon it. 23They will
console you, when you see their ways and their deeds, and you shall know that
I have not done without cause all that I have done in it, declares the Lord GOD."

Jerusalem, a Useless Vine

15 And the word of the LORD came to me: 2"Son of man, how does the wood of
the vine surpass any wood, the vine branch that is among the trees of the
forest? 3Is wood taken from it to make anything? Do people take a peg from it to
hang any vessel on it? 4Behold, it is given to the fire for fuel. When the fire has
consumed both ends of it, and the middle of it is charred, is it useful for anything?
5Behold, when it was whole, it was used for nothing. How much less, when the
fire has consumed it and it is charred, can it ever be used for anything! 6Therefore
thus says the Lord GOD: Like the wood of the vine among the trees of the forest,
which I have given to the fire for fuel, so have I given up the inhabitants of Jerusalem. 7And I will set my face against them. Though they escape from the fire, the
fire shall yet consume them, and you will know that I am the LORD, when I set my
face against them. 8And I will make the land desolate, because they have acted
faithlessly, declares the Lord GOD."

EZEKIEL 15:1–5

FRUITFUL VINE OR FIREWOOD?

The symbol of a vine is frequently used in the Bible to refer to God's people, Israel (Ge 49:22; Ps 80:8). God intended for his people to be a "vine" that would produce fruit, revealing to the surrounding nations who God is and how to be in relationship with him. In the book of Ezekiel, God described his people as a vine that was bearing no fruit—a vine that was useless except as firewood. In the New Testament, Jesus appears to compare the religious leaders of Jerusalem to a fig tree that failed to produce fruit. Desiring to eat the fruit from the tree and having none to eat, Jesus cursed the tree, and the tree withered (Mk 11:12–14,20–21).

Jesus encourages believers, saying that he is the true vine to whom we must be attached in order to be fruitful: "I am the true vine, and my Father is the vinedresser. Every branch in me that does not bear fruit he takes away, and every branch that does bear fruit he prunes, that it may bear more fruit" (Jn 15:1–2). In Ezekiel, God's people failed to depend on God, and they withered away. Today the evidence of real Christian growth is found in the fruit that God's people bear (Gal 5:22–23; Eph 5:9) so that others will see the hope that we have in Jesus and believe (1Pe 3:15–16).

---

[1]Or *iniquity*; three times in this verse [2]Hebrew *staff*

The LORD's Faithless Bride

16 Again the word of the LORD came to me: 2“Son of man, make known to Jerusalem her abominations, 3and say, Thus says the Lord GOD to Jerusalem:
Your origin and your birth are of the land of the Canaanites; your father was an
Amorite and your mother a Hittite. 4And as for your birth, on the day you were
born your cord was not cut, nor were you washed with water to cleanse you, nor
rubbed with salt, nor wrapped in swaddling cloths. 5No eye pitied you, to do any
of these things to you out of compassion for you, but you were cast out on the
open field, for you were abhorred, on the day that you were born.
6“And when I passed by you and saw you wallowing in your blood, I said to
you in your blood, ‘Live!’ I said to you in your blood, ‘Live!’ 7I made you flourish like a plant of the field. And you grew up and became tall and arrived at full
adornment. Your breasts were formed, and your hair had grown; yet you were
naked and bare.
8“When I passed by you again and saw you, behold, you were at the age for
love, and I spread the corner of my garment over you and covered your nakedness; I made my vow to you and entered into a covenant with you, declares the
Lord GOD, and you became mine. 9Then I bathed you with water and washed off
your blood from you and anointed you with oil. 10I clothed you also with embroidered cloth and shod you with fine leather. I wrapped you in fine linen and
covered you with silk.[1] 11And I adorned you with ornaments and put bracelets on
your wrists and a chain on your neck. 12And I put a ring on your nose and earrings
in your ears and a beautiful crown on your head. 13Thus you were adorned with
gold and silver, and your clothing was of fine linen and silk and embroidered
cloth. You ate fine flour and honey and oil. You grew exceedingly beautiful and
advanced to royalty. 14And your renown went forth among the nations because of
your beauty, for it was perfect through the splendor that I had bestowed on you,
declares the Lord GOD.
15“But you trusted in your beauty and played the whore[2] because of your renown and lavished your whorings[3] on any passerby; your beauty[4] became his.
16You took some of your garments and made for yourself colorful shrines, and
on them played the whore. The like has never been, nor ever shall be.[5] 17You also
took your beautiful jewels of my gold and of my silver, which I had given you, and
made for yourself images of men, and with them played the whore. 18And you
took your embroidered garments to cover them, and set my oil and my incense
before them. 19Also my bread that I gave you—I fed you with fine flour and oil
and honey—you set before them for a pleasing aroma; and so it was, declares the
Lord GOD. 20And you took your sons and your daughters, whom you had borne
to me, and these you sacrificed to them to be devoured. Were your whorings so
small a matter 21that you slaughtered my children and delivered them up as an
offering by fire to them? 22And in all your abominations and your whorings you
did not remember the days of your youth, when you were naked and bare, wallowing in your blood.
23“And after all your wickedness (woe, woe to you! declares the Lord GOD),
24you built yourself a vaulted chamber and made yourself a lofty place in every
square. 25At the head of every street you built your lofty place and made your
beauty an abomination, offering yourself[6] to any passerby and multiplying your
whoring. 26You also played the whore with the Egyptians, your lustful neighbors,
multiplying your whoring, to provoke me to anger. 27Behold, therefore, I stretched
out my hand against you and diminished your allotted portion and delivered you
to the greed of your enemies, the daughters of the Philistines, who were ashamed
of your lewd behavior. 28You played the whore also with the Assyrians, because
you were not satisfied; yes, you played the whore with them, and still you were

[1]Or *with rich fabric* [2]Or *were unfaithful*; also verses 16, 17, 26, 28 [3]Or *unfaithfulness*; also verses 20, 22, 25, 26, 29, 33, 34, 36 [4]Hebrew *it* [5]The meaning of this Hebrew sentence is uncertain [6]Hebrew *spreading your legs*

EZEKIEL 16:1–6

FORGETTING WHERE YOU COME FROM

God's people forgot all that God had done for them. They became proud and arrogant, and God loved them too much to let them remain in that pitiful condition. Sometimes hard words are required to break a hard heart, and that is exactly what God provided here.

God's people, living in Jerusalem, had forgotten where they came from. God reminded them of their hopeless past and all that he did for them to bring them to where they were: he had rescued them like an abandoned newborn child, unwashed and left exposed to the elements to die. A baby like that is utterly dependent upon the mercy of another to intervene and save, and God reminded them that he alone had rescued his people and given them life and blessing.

Centuries later Jesus spoke harsh words to the self-assured people living in Jerusalem. He warned them against the dangers of taking their right standing with God for granted. Jesus even went as far as to tell the religious leaders that they did not align themselves with God, but Satan (Jn 8:44)—harsh words for hard hearts. Because of their sin, the religious leaders in Jesus' day had once again become like a helpless infant, abandoned and at the mercy of the elements.

Believers today also do well to remember God's mercy to them in Jesus' work on the cross. Remembering where they came from and understanding where they are in Christ leads believers to humility and gratitude.

not satisfied. [29]You multiplied your whoring also with the trading land of Chaldea, and even with this you were not satisfied.

[30]"How sick is your heart,[1] declares the Lord God, because you did all these things, the deeds of a brazen prostitute, [31]building your vaulted chamber at the head of every street, and making your lofty place in every square. Yet you were not like a prostitute, because you scorned payment. [32]Adulterous wife, who receives strangers instead of her husband! [33]Men give gifts to all prostitutes, but you gave your gifts to all your lovers, bribing them to come to you from every side with your whorings. [34]So you were different from other women in your whorings. No one solicited you to play the whore, and you gave payment, while no payment was given to you; therefore you were different.

[35]"Therefore, O prostitute, hear the word of the Lord: [36]Thus says the Lord God, Because your lust was poured out and your nakedness uncovered in your whorings with your lovers, and with all your abominable idols, and because of the blood of your children that you gave to them, [37]therefore, behold, I will gather all your lovers with whom you took pleasure, all those you loved and all those you hated. I will gather them against you from every side and will uncover your nakedness to them, that they may see all your nakedness. [38]And I will judge you as women who commit adultery and shed blood are judged, and bring upon you the blood of wrath and jealousy. [39]And I will give you into their hands, and they shall throw down your vaulted chamber and break down your lofty places. They shall strip you of your clothes and take your beautiful jewels and leave you naked and bare. [40]They shall bring up a crowd against you, and they shall stone you and cut you to pieces with their swords. [41]And they shall burn your houses and execute judgments upon you in the sight of many women. I will make you stop playing the whore, and you shall also give payment no more. [42]So will I satisfy my wrath on you, and my jealousy shall depart from you. I will be calm and will no more be angry. [43]Because you have not remembered the days of your youth, but have enraged me with all these things, therefore, behold, I have returned your deeds upon your head, declares the Lord God. Have you not committed lewdness in addition to all your abominations?

[44]"Behold, everyone who uses proverbs will use this proverb about you: 'Like mother, like daughter.' [45]You are the daughter of your mother, who loathed her husband and her children; and you are the sister of your sisters, who loathed their husbands and their children. Your mother was a Hittite and your father an Amorite. [46]And your elder sister is Samaria, who lived with her daughters to the north of you; and your younger sister, who lived to the south of you, is Sodom with her daughters. [47]Not only did you walk in their ways and do according to their abominations; within a very little time you were more corrupt than they in all your ways. [48]As I live, declares the Lord God, your sister Sodom and her daughters have not done as you and your daughters have done. [49]Behold, this was the guilt of your sister Sodom: she and her daughters had pride, excess of food, and prosperous ease, but did not aid the poor and needy. [50]They were haughty and did an abomination before me. So I removed them, when I saw it. [51]Samaria has not committed half your sins. You have committed more abominations than they, and have made your sisters appear righteous by all the abominations that you have committed. [52]Bear your disgrace, you also, for you have intervened on behalf of your sisters. Because of your sins in which you acted more abominably than they, they are more in the right than you. So be ashamed, you also, and bear your disgrace, for you have made your sisters appear righteous.

[53]"I will restore their fortunes, both the fortunes of Sodom and her daughters, and the fortunes of Samaria and her daughters, and I will restore your own fortunes in their midst, [54]that you may bear your disgrace and be ashamed of all that you have done, becoming a consolation to them. [55]As for your sisters, Sodom and

[1]Revocalization yields *How I am filled with anger against you*

EZEKIEL 16:63

MAKING ATONEMENT

God made great promises to his people long before he spoke to them through Ezekiel. Centuries before, God made a covenant with Abraham; that covenant was God's promise to make his name great by blessing Abraham and Abraham's descendants (Ge 15:1–6). The covenant was based on God's character; God had made the promises and God would keep them.

In the midst of judging Israel for their sin, God never forgot that he had promises to keep. In the course of keeping the covenant, God's people would inevitably compare their unfaithfulness with God's unending faithfulness and feel shame. Yet God promised his people, through Ezekiel, that he would appropriately punish the sin of his people so that he could reestablish a relationship with them.

As the story of God's faithfulness to his people unfolded, it eventually became clear that Jesus' death would be the sacrifice that would restore sinners to God (Ro 5:18–19). All of God's promises are kept in Jesus, the living Savior of all who will believe in him.

BLAME SHIFTING

No one likes to accept blame. That is one of the hallmarks of the fallen nature of humanity. Sin makes people self-serving and self-protective. By nature, people are defensive against anyone or anything that threatens their well-being and reputation. People do not like blame because blame infers guilt, and guilt means imperfection. And people want to be seen as perfect — or at the very least, not the biggest part of the problem.

Ezekiel was careful to stress the themes of sin, judgment, and restoration not only for the nation as a whole, but especially for the individual. As Ezekiel spoke against the sins of the people, the people naturally tried to shift the blame to their ancestors who made mistakes that they were forced to live with. Ezekiel denounced this popular proverb conveying that children pay the penalty for their parents' actions. They wanted to shift the blame of their own sin to their parents so that they could not be held responsible for the coming judgment. To counter this, Ezekiel stressed individual sin and judgment, and individual righteousness and salvation. In Ezekiel 14:14 and 14:20, the prophet noted that even Noah, Daniel, and Job were able to save only themselves. A day was coming when Jesus would be the ultimate Deliverer, but even after his coming, people would be held individually accountable for the way they respond to him.

God's people were suffering from generations of sin and rebellion against God. They found it easier to blame their ancestors for the tough place their actions had put them in, rather than to accept responsibility for the sins they had committed that contributed to the situation. God reminded his people that experiencing hardship as a consequence of the sins of ancestors was not the same as being judged for one's own sins. Though it is unfortunate to suffer because of the sins that someone else has committed, God does not excuse willfully sinful behavior that occurs within that context.

God invites all people to accept responsibility, repent of sin, and have a full life. The prophet John the Baptist sounded a lot like the prophet Ezekiel: "Repent, for the kingdom of heaven is at hand" (Mt 3:2; compare with Eze 18:30). God meets repentance with the gift of a new heart and a new spirit (Eze 18:31). Ezekiel invited people to turn to God and live (v. 32). Jesus came so that people may have life and have it abundantly (Jn 10:10).

The righteousness of the righteous shall be upon himself, and the wickedness of the wicked shall be upon himself.

21 "But if a wicked person turns away from all his sins that he has committed and keeps all my statutes and does what is just and right, he shall surely live; he shall not die. 22 None of the transgressions that he has committed shall be remembered against him; for the righteousness that he has done he shall live. 23 Have I any pleasure in the death of the wicked, declares the Lord GOD, and not rather that he should turn from his way and live? 24 But when a righteous person turns away from his righteousness and does injustice and does the same abominations that the wicked person does, shall he live? None of the righteous deeds that he has done shall be remembered; for the treachery of which he is guilty and the sin he has committed, for them he shall die.

25 "Yet you say, 'The way of the Lord is not just.' Hear now, O house of Israel: Is my way not just? Is it not your ways that are not just? 26 When a righteous person turns away from his righteousness and does injustice, he shall die for it; for the injustice that he has done he shall die. 27 Again, when a wicked person turns away from the wickedness he has committed and does what is just and right, he shall save his life. 28 Because he considered and turned away from all the transgressions that he had committed, he shall surely live; he shall not die. 29 Yet the house of Israel says, 'The way of the Lord is not just.' O house of Israel, are my ways not just? Is it not your ways that are not just?

30 "Therefore I will judge you, O house of Israel, every one according to his ways, declares the Lord GOD. Repent and turn from all your transgressions, lest iniquity be your ruin.[1] 31 Cast away from you all the transgressions that you have committed, and make yourselves a new heart and a new spirit! Why will you die, O house of Israel? 32 For I have no pleasure in the death of anyone, declares the Lord GOD; so turn, and live."

A Lament for the Princes of Israel

19 And you, take up a lamentation for the princes of Israel, 2 and say:

What was your mother? A lioness!
  Among lions she crouched;
in the midst of young lions
  she reared her cubs.
3 And she brought up one of her cubs;
  he became a young lion,
and he learned to catch prey;
  he devoured men.
4 The nations heard about him;
  he was caught in their pit,
and they brought him with hooks
  to the land of Egypt.
5 When she saw that she waited in vain,
  that her hope was lost,
she took another of her cubs
  and made him a young lion.
6 He prowled among the lions;
  he became a young lion,
and he learned to catch prey;
  he devoured men,
7 and seized[2] their widows.
  He laid waste their cities,
and the land was appalled and all who were in it
  at the sound of his roaring.

[1] Or *lest iniquity be your stumbling block* [2] Hebrew *knew*

EZEKIEL 18:30

MAKING A U-TURN

Repentance involves conscious sorrow and regret over the former way of life and a change of course to a new direction. In short, it's like making a U-turn, a 180-degree about-face away from the path one has been following. Mere remorse over sin is not enough, and simply acknowledging sin without turning from it only leads to death. God requires this change in people because sin, without God's intervening grace, forcefully and destructively controls people's lives.

The first step of change is simply acknowledging the sin and fostering the desire to change—that is where repentance starts. God calls people to repentance, and the Bible contains some gripping examples of people who repented in prayer (Ezr 9–10; Ps 51). God's desire is that all people will repent of their sin and live a life in relationship with him. He issued this call to repentance through prophets such as Ezekiel, John the Baptist, Jesus, and Jesus' disciples. To those who confess their sin and turn to Jesus, God promises forgiveness and eternal life. The call to repentance is still given today, and those who heed it find God's grace and peace in this life.

EZEKIEL 19:1–9

BEHAVING LIKE A LION

The lion was a symbol of the tribe of Judah (Ge 49:9). Lions are known for their great strength, agility, and goose bump-raising roars. The lioness in Ezekiel's lament represents

(continued on next page)

8 Then the nations set against him
from provinces on every side;
they spread their net over him;
he was taken in their pit.
9 With hooks they put him in a cage[1]
and brought him to the king of Babylon;
they brought him into custody,
that his voice should no more be heard
on the mountains of Israel.

10 Your mother was like a vine in a vineyard[2]
planted by the water,
fruitful and full of branches
by reason of abundant water.
11 Its strong stems became
rulers' scepters;
it towered aloft
among the thick boughs;[3]
it was seen in its height
with the mass of its branches.
12 But the vine was plucked up in fury,
cast down to the ground;
the east wind dried up its fruit;
they were stripped off and withered.
As for its strong stem,
fire consumed it.
13 Now it is planted in the wilderness,
in a dry and thirsty land.
14 And fire has gone out from the stem of its shoots,
has consumed its fruit,
so that there remains in it no strong stem,
no scepter for ruling.

This is a lamentation and has become a lamentation.

Israel's Continuing Rebellion

20 In the seventh year, in the fifth month, on the tenth day of the month, certain of the elders of Israel came to inquire of the LORD, and sat before me.
2 And the word of the LORD came to me: 3 "Son of man, speak to the elders of Israel,
and say to them, Thus says the Lord GOD, Is it to inquire of me that you come?
As I live, declares the Lord GOD, I will not be inquired of by you. 4 Will you judge
them, son of man, will you judge them? Let them know the abominations of their
fathers, 5 and say to them, Thus says the Lord GOD: On the day when I chose Israel,
I swore[4] to the offspring of the house of Jacob, making myself known to them in
the land of Egypt; I swore to them, saying, I am the LORD your God. 6 On that day I
swore to them that I would bring them out of the land of Egypt into a land that I
had searched out for them, a land flowing with milk and honey, the most glorious
of all lands. 7 And I said to them, 'Cast away the detestable things your eyes feast
on, every one of you, and do not defile yourselves with the idols of Egypt; I am
the LORD your God.' 8 But they rebelled against me and were not willing to listen
to me. None of them cast away the detestable things their eyes feasted on, nor did
they forsake the idols of Egypt.

"Then I said I would pour out my wrath upon them and spend my anger
against them in the midst of the land of Egypt. 9 But I acted for the sake of my
name, that it should not be profaned in the sight of the nations among whom

[1] Or *in a wooden collar* [2] Some Hebrew manuscripts; most Hebrew manuscripts *in your blood* [3] Or *the clouds* [4] Hebrew *I lifted my hand*; twice in this verse; also verses 6, 15, 23, 28, 42

(Behaving Like a Lion, continued)

the nation or tribe of Judah, whose emblem was a lion (Ge 49:9). The first cub (Eze 19:3–4) stands for King Jehoahaz, whom Pharaoh Neco took in chains to Egypt. The second cub (vv. 5–9) symbolizes either King Jehoiachin or King Zedekiah, both of whom were carried off to Babylon. As the kings from David's tribe were expelled, the roar from the lion of Judah was silenced. God created his people to be a beautiful and a bold force in the world. Sin tames, tricks, and neutralizes the good things that God created his people to be about. Jesus was the sacrificial Lamb who died for the sins of the world and will return as the conquering Lion-King. Revelation 5:5 promises, "And one of the elders said to me, 'Weep no more; behold, the Lion of the tribe of Judah, the Root of David, has conquered, so that he can open the scroll and its seven seals.' " With the death and resurrection of Jesus, God's mighty Lion sprang to life and its roar shakes the silence.

EZEKIEL 20:4–29

A SIN HABIT

Old habits die hard. God spoke words of judgment through Ezekiel to his people. These words of judgment were not the first time God had spoken to his people in this way. Long before this time, God's people had habitually committed the same sins over and over again. Ezekiel had spoken to the people figuratively and in allegory, and now he spoke to the people plainly by simply retelling their story.

As Ezekiel rehearsed their history to them, he was careful to point out how their present sins were actually part of a long sin pattern that their

(continued on next page)

(A Sin Habit, continued)

ancestors struggled with as well. They forgot where they came from, they forgot God's exclusive claim on their lives through his covenant, and they became proud. In their pride, they thought they were good enough in God's eyes; they were surprised when God moved toward them in judgment.

God sent Jesus to deliver people from their sins (Mt 1:21). The way out of a sin pattern is to simply look to Jesus (Heb 12:1–2). God saves people from their sins to make them his special people, to purify them in every way, and to enable them to develop the new habit of doing good works (Titus 2:11–14).

they lived, in whose sight I made myself known to them in bringing them out of the land of Egypt. 10So I led them out of the land of Egypt and brought them into the wilderness. 11I gave them my statutes and made known to them my rules, by which, if a person does them, he shall live. 12Moreover, I gave them my Sabbaths, as a sign between me and them, that they might know that I am the LORD who sanctifies them. 13But the house of Israel rebelled against me in the wilderness. They did not walk in my statutes but rejected my rules, by which, if a person does them, he shall live; and my Sabbaths they greatly profaned.

"Then I said I would pour out my wrath upon them in the wilderness, to make a full end of them. 14But I acted for the sake of my name, that it should not be profaned in the sight of the nations, in whose sight I had brought them out. 15Moreover, I swore to them in the wilderness that I would not bring them into the land that I had given them, a land flowing with milk and honey, the most glorious of all lands, 16because they rejected my rules and did not walk in my statutes, and profaned my Sabbaths; for their heart went after their idols. 17Nevertheless, my eye spared them, and I did not destroy them or make a full end of them in the wilderness.

18"And I said to their children in the wilderness, 'Do not walk in the statutes of your fathers, nor keep their rules, nor defile yourselves with their idols. 19I am the LORD your God; walk in my statutes, and be careful to obey my rules, 20and keep my Sabbaths holy that they may be a sign between me and you, that you may know that I am the LORD your God.' 21But the children rebelled against me. They did not walk in my statutes and were not careful to obey my rules, by which, if a person does them, he shall live; they profaned my Sabbaths.

"Then I said I would pour out my wrath upon them and spend my anger against them in the wilderness. 22But I withheld my hand and acted for the sake of my name, that it should not be profaned in the sight of the nations, in whose sight I had brought them out. 23Moreover, I swore to them in the wilderness that I would scatter them among the nations and disperse them through the countries, 24because they had not obeyed my rules, but had rejected my statutes and profaned my Sabbaths, and their eyes were set on their fathers' idols. 25Moreover, I gave them statutes that were not good and rules by which they could not have life, 26and I defiled them through their very gifts in their offering up all their firstborn, that I might devastate them. I did it that they might know that I am the LORD.

27"Therefore, son of man, speak to the house of Israel and say to them, Thus says the Lord GOD: In this also your fathers blasphemed me, by dealing treacherously with me. 28For when I had brought them into the land that I swore to give them, then wherever they saw any high hill or any leafy tree, there they offered their sacrifices and there they presented the provocation of their offering; there they sent up their pleasing aromas, and there they poured out their drink offerings. 29(I said to them, 'What is the high place to which you go?' So its name is called Bamah[1] to this day.)

30"Therefore say to the house of Israel, Thus says the Lord GOD: Will you defile yourselves after the manner of your fathers and go whoring after their detestable things? 31When you present your gifts and offer up your children in fire,[2] you defile yourselves with all your idols to this day. And shall I be inquired of by you, O house of Israel? As I live, declares the Lord GOD, I will not be inquired of by you.

32"What is in your mind shall never happen—the thought, 'Let us be like the nations, like the tribes of the countries, and worship wood and stone.'

The LORD Will Restore Israel

33"As I live, declares the Lord GOD, surely with a mighty hand and an outstretched arm and with wrath poured out I will be king over you. 34I will bring you out from the peoples and gather you out of the countries where you are scattered,

[1] *Bamah* means *high place* [2] Hebrew *and make your children pass through the fire*

with a mighty hand and an outstretched arm, and with wrath poured out. 35And I
will bring you into the wilderness of the peoples, and there I will enter into judgment with you face to face. 36As I entered into judgment with your fathers in the
wilderness of the land of Egypt, so I will enter into judgment with you, declares
the Lord God. 37I will make you pass under the rod, and I will bring you into the
bond of the covenant. 38I will purge out the rebels from among you, and those
who transgress against me. I will bring them out of the land where they sojourn,
but they shall not enter the land of Israel. Then you will know that I am the Lord.
39"As for you, O house of Israel, thus says the Lord God: Go serve every one of
you his idols, now and hereafter, if you will not listen to me; but my holy name
you shall no more profane with your gifts and your idols.
40"For on my holy mountain, the mountain height of Israel, declares the Lord
God, there all the house of Israel, all of them, shall serve me in the land. There I
will accept them, and there I will require your contributions and the choicest of
your gifts, with all your sacred offerings. 41As a pleasing aroma I will accept you,
when I bring you out from the peoples and gather you out of the countries where
you have been scattered. And I will manifest my holiness among you in the sight
of the nations. 42And you shall know that I am the Lord, when I bring you into
the land of Israel, the country that I swore to give to your fathers. 43And there
you shall remember your ways and all your deeds with which you have defiled
yourselves, and you shall loathe yourselves for all the evils that you have committed. 44And you shall know that I am the Lord, when I deal with you for my
name's sake, not according to your evil ways, nor according to your corrupt deeds,
O house of Israel, declares the Lord God."
45[1]And the word of the Lord came to me: 46"Son of man, set your face toward
the southland;[2] preach against the south, and prophesy against the forest land in
the Negeb. 47Say to the forest of the Negeb, Hear the word of the Lord: Thus says
the Lord God, Behold, I will kindle a fire in you, and it shall devour every green
tree in you and every dry tree. The blazing flame shall not be quenched, and all
faces from south to north shall be scorched by it. 48All flesh shall see that I the
Lord have kindled it; it shall not be quenched." 49Then I said, "Ah, Lord God! They
are saying of me, 'Is he not a maker of parables?'"

The Lord Has Drawn His Sword

21 [3] The word of the Lord came to me: 2"Son of man, set your face toward Jerusalem and preach against the sanctuaries.[4] Prophesy against the land of
Israel 3and say to the land of Israel, Thus says the Lord: Behold, I am against you
and will draw my sword from its sheath and will cut off from you both righteous
and wicked. 4Because I will cut off from you both righteous and wicked, therefore
my sword shall be drawn from its sheath against all flesh from south to north.
5And all flesh shall know that I am the Lord. I have drawn my sword from its
sheath; it shall not be sheathed again.
6"As for you, son of man, groan; with breaking heart and bitter grief, groan
before their eyes. 7And when they say to you, 'Why do you groan?' you shall say,
'Because of the news that it is coming. Every heart will melt, and all hands will
be feeble; every spirit will faint, and all knees will be weak as water. Behold, it is
coming, and it will be fulfilled,'" declares the Lord God.
8And the word of the Lord came to me: 9"Son of man, prophesy and say, Thus
says the Lord, say:

"A sword, a sword is sharpened
and also polished,
10 sharpened for slaughter,
polished to flash like lightning!

[1]Ch 21:1 in Hebrew [2]Or *toward Teman* [3]Ch 21:6 in Hebrew [4]Some Hebrew manuscripts; compare Septuagint; Syriac *against their sanctuary*

EZEKIEL 21:1–5

PREACH AGAINST THE SANCTUARIES

Every religion has a place where one goes or a thing that one does to meet with God. For Israel, the place they went to was the temple, and the thing they did was to make sacrifices. People went to the temple to worship because that is the place where God's glory—his majesty and presence—lived. Ezekiel had terrible news to deliver to the people: Earlier he had communicated that they were so sinful that God had withdrawn his presence from the temple. And here the Lord stirred his prophet to "preach against the sanctuaries" (v. 2). The Most Holy Place was dark and empty instead of bright and the source of life. The sins of the people had pushed the glory of God out of their lives, and their punishment would be destruction and grief.

Centuries later, Jesus would preach against the empty practices of the Pharisees and religious leaders (Mt 23); he also predicted the destruction of that temple as well (Mt 24:1–2). Ezekiel and Jesus never spoke against the temple itself. Instead, they spoke against the way that God's people made little of the presence of God. Jesus rose from the grave so that people can experience the presence of God wherever they are. People were never meant to encounter God in a mere building. Instead, God is building a great temple called his church, person by person (1Pe 2:5). God doesn't live in a temple made with human hands (Ac 17:24–25) but chooses to live in his people through his Holy Spirit.

EZEKIEL 21:25–27

THE CROWN

Ezekiel spoke of the turban and the crown as a way of referencing the coming king who would rule over God's people. God's campaign against sin is severe, and nothing will remain after God's work is done. The current system would be wrecked and ruined. Israel never had a perfect king, though it seemed that several leaders would assume this role. They longed for a king. Yet, no mere human could ever perform the kingly role for which the people longed. They needed a kingly Messiah who would perfectly do what others had failed to accomplish.

The crown does not belong to any person but Jesus (Ge 49:10). Jesus is the ultimate King who sits on the throne (Lk 1:32–33). Jesus is worthy not only of the crown from God, but also of every measure of worth from the lives of his people. One day everyone who trusts in Jesus will be able to cast their glory and accomplishments at his feet and recognize him as the One who is worthy of all honor, because he and he alone has won salvation for those who believe in him.

(Or shall we rejoice? You have despised the rod, my son, with everything of wood.)[1] 11So the sword is given to be polished, that it may be grasped in the hand. It is sharpened and polished to be given into the hand of the slayer. 12Cry out and wail, son of man, for it is against my people. It is against all the princes of Israel. They are delivered over to the sword with my people. Strike therefore upon your thigh. 13For it will not be a testing—what could it do if you despise the rod?"[2] declares the Lord GOD.

14"As for you, son of man, prophesy. Clap your hands and let the sword come down twice, yes, three times,[3] the sword for those to be slain. It is the sword for the great slaughter, which surrounds them, 15that their hearts may melt, and many stumble.[4] At all their gates I have given the glittering sword. Ah, it is made like lightning; it is taken up[5] for slaughter. 16Cut sharply to the right; set yourself to the left, wherever your face is directed. 17I also will clap my hands, and I will satisfy my fury; I the LORD have spoken."

18The word of the LORD came to me again: 19"As for you, son of man, mark two ways for the sword of the king of Babylon to come. Both of them shall come from the same land. And make a signpost; make it at the head of the way to a city. 20Mark a way for the sword to come to Rabbah of the Ammonites and to Judah, into Jerusalem the fortified. 21For the king of Babylon stands at the parting of the way, at the head of the two ways, to use divination. He shakes the arrows; he consults the teraphim;[6] he looks at the liver. 22Into his right hand comes the divination for Jerusalem, to set battering rams, to open the mouth with murder, to lift up the voice with shouting, to set battering rams against the gates, to cast up mounds, to build siege towers. 23But to them it will seem like a false divination. They have sworn solemn oaths, but he brings their guilt to remembrance, that they may be taken.

24"Therefore thus says the Lord GOD: Because you have made your guilt to be remembered, in that your transgressions are uncovered, so that in all your deeds your sins appear—because you have come to remembrance, you shall be taken in hand. 25And you, O profane[7] wicked one, prince of Israel, whose day has come, the time of your final punishment, 26thus says the Lord GOD: Remove the turban and take off the crown. Things shall not remain as they are. Exalt that which is low, and bring low that which is exalted. 27A ruin, ruin, ruin I will make it. This also shall not be, until he comes, the one to whom judgment belongs, and I will give it to him.

28"And you, son of man, prophesy, and say, Thus says the Lord GOD concerning the Ammonites and concerning their reproach; say, A sword, a sword is drawn for the slaughter. It is polished to consume and to flash like lightning— 29while they see for you false visions, while they divine lies for you—to place you on the necks of the profane wicked, whose day has come, the time of their final punishment. 30Return it to its sheath. In the place where you were created, in the land of your origin, I will judge you. 31And I will pour out my indignation upon you; I will blow upon you with the fire of my wrath, and I will deliver you into the hands of brutish men, skillful to destroy. 32You shall be fuel for the fire. Your blood shall be in the midst of the land. You shall be no more remembered, for I the LORD have spoken."

Israel's Shedding of Blood

22 And the word of the LORD came to me, saying, 2"And you, son of man, will you judge, will you judge the bloody city? Then declare to her all her abominations. 3You shall say, Thus says the Lord GOD: A city that sheds blood in her midst, so that her time may come, and that makes idols to defile herself!

[1]Probable reading; Hebrew *The rod of my son despises everything of wood* [2]Or *For it is a testing; and what if even the rod despises? It shall not be!* [3]Hebrew *its third* [4]Hebrew *many stumbling blocks* [5]The meaning of the Hebrew word rendered *taken up* is uncertain [6]Or *household idols* [7]Or *slain*; also verse 29

4You have become guilty by the blood that you have shed, and defiled by the idols that you have made, and you have brought your days near, the appointed time of[1] your years has come. Therefore I have made you a reproach to the nations, and a mockery to all the countries. 5Those who are near and those who are far from you will mock you; your name is defiled; you are full of tumult.

6"Behold, the princes of Israel in you, every one according to his power, have been bent on shedding blood. 7Father and mother are treated with contempt in you; the sojourner suffers extortion in your midst; the fatherless and the widow are wronged in you. 8You have despised my holy things and profaned my Sabbaths. 9There are men in you who slander to shed blood, and people in you who eat on the mountains; they commit lewdness in your midst. 10In you men uncover their fathers' nakedness; in you they violate women who are unclean in their menstrual impurity. 11One commits abomination with his neighbor's wife; another lewdly defiles his daughter-in-law; another in you violates his sister, his father's daughter. 12In you they take bribes to shed blood; you take interest and profit[2] and make gain of your neighbors by extortion; but me you have forgotten, declares the Lord GOD.

13"Behold, I strike my hand at the dishonest gain that you have made, and at the blood that has been in your midst. 14Can your courage endure, or can your hands be strong, in the days that I shall deal with you? I the LORD have spoken, and I will do it. 15I will scatter you among the nations and disperse you through the countries, and I will consume your uncleanness out of you. 16And you shall be profaned by your own doing in the sight of the nations, and you shall know that I am the LORD."

17And the word of the LORD came to me: 18"Son of man, the house of Israel has become dross to me; all of them are bronze and tin and iron and lead in the furnace; they are dross of silver. 19Therefore thus says the Lord GOD: Because you have all become dross, therefore, behold, I will gather you into the midst of Jerusalem. 20As one gathers silver and bronze and iron and lead and tin into a furnace, to blow the fire on it in order to melt it, so I will gather you in my anger and in my wrath, and I will put you in and melt you. 21I will gather you and blow on you with the fire of my wrath, and you shall be melted in the midst of it. 22As silver is melted in a furnace, so you shall be melted in the midst of it, and you shall know that I am the LORD; I have poured out my wrath upon you."

23And the word of the LORD came to me: 24"Son of man, say to her, You are a land that is not cleansed or rained upon in the day of indignation. 25The conspiracy of her prophets in her midst is like a roaring lion tearing the prey; they have devoured human lives; they have taken treasure and precious things; they have made many widows in her midst. 26Her priests have done violence to my law and have profaned my holy things. They have made no distinction between the holy and the common, neither have they taught the difference between the unclean and the clean, and they have disregarded my Sabbaths, so that I am profaned among them. 27Her princes in her midst are like wolves tearing the prey, shedding blood, destroying lives to get dishonest gain. 28And her prophets have smeared whitewash for them, seeing false visions and divining lies for them, saying, 'Thus says the Lord GOD,' when the LORD has not spoken. 29The people of the land have practiced extortion and committed robbery. They have oppressed the poor and needy, and have extorted from the sojourner without justice. 30And I sought for a man among them who should build up the wall and stand in the breach before me for the land, that I should not destroy it, but I found none. 31Therefore I have poured out my indignation upon them. I have consumed them with the fire of my wrath. I have returned their way upon their heads, declares the Lord GOD."

[1]Some Hebrew manuscripts, Septuagint, Syriac, Vulgate, Targum; most Hebrew manuscripts *until* [2]That is, profit that comes from charging interest to the poor (compare Leviticus 25:36)

EZEKIEL 22:30

SOMEONE TO STAND IN THE GAP

God always follows through with both his warnings and his promises to his people. For generations, God had warned his people that he would destroy the nation of Judah because of their sin. They had had plenty of warnings and plenty of opportunities to turn to God before he acted in judgment. Before his judgment came, however, God gave Judah one final opportunity: If he could find one prophet to intercede to him on behalf of the nation, God would relent. Not a single person could be found in all the nation to fulfill this role, and consequently God's judgment fell upon the people.

Ezekiel 22:30 teaches that God desires to make things right with the world through a mediator, and thankfully, Jesus is that mediator (Ro 8:34; 1Ti 2:5–6). In his death he stood before the Father on behalf of his people and received punishment for their sins so that they could receive his righteousness (Heb 9:15; 1Jn 2:1). Because Jesus was and still is the means of grace for his church, his church is able to intercede on behalf of the nations for God to exercise mercy. Beyond this, his church is able to go to the nations to share the news of God's unrelenting love for them through Jesus.

Oholah and Oholibah

23 The word of the LORD came to me: 2"Son of man, there were two women, the daughters of one mother. 3They played the whore in Egypt; they played the whore in their youth; there their breasts were pressed and their virgin bosoms[1] handled. 4Oholah was the name of the elder and Oholibah the name of her sister. They became mine, and they bore sons and daughters. As for their names, Oholah is Samaria, and Oholibah is Jerusalem.

5"Oholah played the whore while she was mine, and she lusted after her lovers the Assyrians, warriors 6clothed in purple, governors and commanders, all of them desirable young men, horsemen riding on horses. 7She bestowed her whoring upon them, the choicest men of Assyria all of them, and she defiled herself with all the idols of everyone after whom she lusted. 8She did not give up her whoring that she had begun in Egypt; for in her youth men had lain with her and handled her virgin bosom and poured out their whoring lust upon her. 9Therefore I delivered her into the hands of her lovers, into the hands of the Assyrians, after whom she lusted. 10These uncovered her nakedness; they seized her sons and her daughters; and as for her, they killed her with the sword; and she became a byword among women, when judgment had been executed on her.

11"Her sister Oholibah saw this, and she became more corrupt than her sister[2] in her lust and in her whoring, which was worse than that of her sister. 12She lusted after the Assyrians, governors and commanders, warriors clothed in full armor, horsemen riding on horses, all of them desirable young men. 13And I saw that she was defiled; they both took the same way. 14But she carried her whoring further. She saw men portrayed on the wall, the images of the Chaldeans portrayed in vermilion, 15wearing belts on their waists, with flowing turbans on their heads, all of them having the appearance of officers, a likeness of Babylonians whose native land was Chaldea. 16When she saw them, she lusted after them and sent messengers to them in Chaldea. 17And the Babylonians came to her into the bed of love, and they defiled her with their whoring lust. And after she was defiled by them, she turned from them in disgust. 18When she carried on her whoring so openly and flaunted her nakedness, I turned in disgust from her, as I had turned in disgust from her sister. 19Yet she increased her whoring, remembering the days of her youth, when she played the whore in the land of Egypt 20and lusted after her lovers there, whose members were like those of donkeys, and whose issue was like that of horses. 21Thus you longed for the lewdness of your youth, when the Egyptians handled your bosom and pressed[3] your young breasts."

22Therefore, O Oholibah, thus says the Lord GOD: "Behold, I will stir up against you your lovers from whom you turned in disgust, and I will bring them against you from every side: 23the Babylonians and all the Chaldeans, Pekod and Shoa and Koa, and all the Assyrians with them, desirable young men, governors and commanders all of them, officers and men of renown, all of them riding on horses. 24And they shall come against you from the north[4] with chariots and wagons and a host of peoples. They shall set themselves against you on every side with buckler, shield, and helmet; and I will commit the judgment to them, and they shall judge you according to their judgments. 25And I will direct my jealousy against you, that they may deal with you in fury. They shall cut off your nose and your ears, and your survivors shall fall by the sword. They shall seize your sons and your daughters, and your survivors shall be devoured by fire. 26They shall also strip you of your clothes and take away your beautiful jewels. 27Thus I will put an end to your lewdness and your whoring begun in the land of Egypt, so that you shall not lift up your eyes to them or remember Egypt anymore.

28"For thus says the Lord GOD: Behold, I will deliver you into the hands of those whom you hate, into the hands of those from whom you turned in disgust, 29and

[1]Hebrew *nipples*; also verses 8, 21 [2]Hebrew *than she* [3]Vulgate, Syriac; Hebrew *bosom for the sake of*
[4]Septuagint; the meaning of the Hebrew word is uncertain

EZEKIEL 23:1–49

A TALE OF TWO CITIES

God's kingdom was torn in two because of sin: Israel, the northern kingdom, and Judah, the southern kingdom. In this chapter Ezekiel graphically depicts Israel and Judah, represented by their capital cities of Samaria and Jerusalem, as sisters who were guilty of political and spiritual prostitution—they had turned away from worshiping him and looked to other nations for security, and also adopted the idolatrous practices of their allies.

As the ultimate suitor to both Israel and Judah, God was furious at their betrayal. The imagery of prostitution represents the deep spiritual treason that God's people had committed against him. Jesus used similar language to talk about his contemporaries in calling them "an evil and adulterous generation" (Mt 12:39). God was outraged because the culture shapers in Israel and Judah had led the people of these nations away from him. But Jesus died for the idolatrous rebellion of all of humanity. His atoning death provided forgiveness for the sins of his people who, like the cities of Samaria and Jerusalem, rebelled against God.

they shall deal with you in hatred and take away all the fruit of your labor and
leave you naked and bare, and the nakedness of your whoring shall be uncovered. Your lewdness and your whoring 30have brought this upon you, because you
played the whore with the nations and defiled yourself with their idols. 31You have
gone the way of your sister; therefore I will give her cup into your hand. 32Thus
says the Lord GOD:

"You shall drink your sister's cup
  that is deep and large;
you shall be laughed at and held in derision,
  for it contains much;
33 you will be filled with drunkenness and sorrow.
A cup of horror and desolation,
  the cup of your sister Samaria;
34 you shall drink it and drain it out,
  and gnaw its shards,
  and tear your breasts;

for I have spoken, declares the Lord GOD. 35Therefore thus says the Lord GOD:
Because you have forgotten me and cast me behind your back, you yourself must
bear the consequences of your lewdness and whoring."

36The LORD said to me: "Son of man, will you judge Oholah and Oholibah?
Declare to them their abominations. 37For they have committed adultery, and
blood is on their hands. With their idols they have committed adultery, and they
have even offered up[1] to them for food the children whom they had borne to me.
38Moreover, this they have done to me: they have defiled my sanctuary on the
same day and profaned my Sabbaths. 39For when they had slaughtered their children in sacrifice to their idols, on the same day they came into my sanctuary to
profane it. And behold, this is what they did in my house. 40They even sent for
men to come from afar, to whom a messenger was sent; and behold, they came.
For them you bathed yourself, painted your eyes, and adorned yourself with ornaments. 41You sat on a stately couch, with a table spread before it on which you
had placed my incense and my oil. 42The sound of a carefree multitude was with
her; and with men of the common sort, drunkards[2] were brought from the wilderness; and they put bracelets on the hands of the women, and beautiful crowns
on their heads.

43"Then I said of her who was worn out by adultery, 'Now they will continue
to use her for a whore, even her!'[3] 44For they have gone in to her, as men go in to
a prostitute. Thus they went in to Oholah and to Oholibah, lewd women! 45But
righteous men shall pass judgment on them with the sentence of adulteresses,
and with the sentence of women who shed blood, because they are adulteresses,
and blood is on their hands."

46For thus says the Lord GOD: "Bring up a vast host against them, and make
them an object of terror and a plunder. 47And the host shall stone them and cut
them down with their swords. They shall kill their sons and their daughters, and
burn up their houses. 48Thus will I put an end to lewdness in the land, that all
women may take warning and not commit lewdness as you have done. 49And they
shall return your lewdness upon you, and you shall bear the penalty for your sinful idolatry, and you shall know that I am the Lord GOD."

The Siege of Jerusalem

24 In the ninth year, in the tenth month, on the tenth day of the month, the
word of the LORD came to me: 2"Son of man, write down the name of this
day, this very day. The king of Babylon has laid siege to Jerusalem this very day.
3And utter a parable to the rebellious house and say to them, Thus says the Lord
GOD:

[1]Or *have even made pass through the fire* [2]Or *Sabeans* [3]The meaning of the Hebrew verse is uncertain

"Set on the pot, set it on;
  pour in water also;
4 put in it the pieces of meat,
  all the good pieces, the thigh and the shoulder;
  fill it with choice bones.
5 Take the choicest one of the flock;
  pile the logs[1] under it;
boil it well;
  seethe also its bones in it.

6"Therefore thus says the Lord God: Woe to the bloody city, to the pot whose corrosion is in it, and whose corrosion has not gone out of it! Take out of it piece after piece, without making any choice.[2] 7For the blood she has shed is in her midst; she put it on the bare rock; she did not pour it out on the ground to cover it with dust. 8To rouse my wrath, to take vengeance, I have set on the bare rock the blood she has shed, that it may not be covered. 9Therefore thus says the Lord God: Woe to the bloody city! I also will make the pile great. 10Heap on the logs, kindle the fire, boil the meat well, mix in the spices,[3] and let the bones be burned up. 11Then set it empty upon the coals, that it may become hot, and its copper may burn, that its uncleanness may be melted in it, its corrosion consumed. 12She has wearied herself with toil;[4] its abundant corrosion does not go out of it. Into the fire with its corrosion! 13On account of your unclean lewdness, because I would have cleansed you and you were not cleansed from your uncleanness, you shall not be cleansed anymore till I have satisfied my fury upon you. 14I am the Lord. I have spoken; it shall come to pass; I will do it. I will not go back; I will not spare; I will not relent; according to your ways and your deeds you will be judged, declares the Lord God."

Ezekiel's Wife Dies

15The word of the Lord came to me: 16"Son of man, behold, I am about to take the delight of your eyes away from you at a stroke; yet you shall not mourn or weep, nor shall your tears run down. 17Sigh, but not aloud; make no mourning for the dead. Bind on your turban, and put your shoes on your feet; do not cover your lips, nor eat the bread of men." 18So I spoke to the people in the morning, and at evening my wife died. And on the next morning I did as I was commanded.

19And the people said to me, "Will you not tell us what these things mean for us, that you are acting thus?" 20Then I said to them, "The word of the Lord came to me: 21'Say to the house of Israel, Thus says the Lord God: Behold, I will profane my sanctuary, the pride of your power, the delight of your eyes, and the yearning of your soul, and your sons and your daughters whom you left behind shall fall by the sword. 22And you shall do as I have done; you shall not cover your lips, nor eat the bread of men. 23Your turbans shall be on your heads and your shoes on your feet; you shall not mourn or weep, but you shall rot away in your iniquities and groan to one another. 24Thus shall Ezekiel be to you a sign; according to all that he has done you shall do. When this comes, then you will know that I am the Lord God.'

25"As for you, son of man, surely on the day when I take from them their stronghold, their joy and glory, the delight of their eyes and their soul's desire, and also their sons and daughters, 26on that day a fugitive will come to you to report to you the news. 27On that day your mouth will be opened to the fugitive, and you shall speak and be no longer mute. So you will be a sign to them, and they will know that I am the Lord."

[1]Compare verse 10; Hebrew *the bones* [2]Hebrew *no lot has fallen upon it* [3]Or *empty out the broth*
[4]The meaning of the Hebrew is uncertain

EZEKIEL 24:21

JUDGMENT

Sin always leads to judgment. God's people had opposed God for some time, despite God's multiple warnings and opportunities to repent. Their hearts were stubborn, and they did not want to change, so God moved in to judge them because what God says he will do, he will do.

God told the people that Jerusalem would fall, that the temple of God would be desecrated, and that the people would be either destroyed or carried off into exile. Ezekiel reserved the harshest words of judgment for the leaders of God's people. All of this might sound severe, but it was just. God's chosen people had disobeyed their infinitely holy God in the face of his persistent pleas for them to stop.

This was a judgment day of sorts; God's judgment was coming down upon his people because of their disobedience. At the cross, another judgment day occurred: God sacrificed Jesus because of the sins of his people. The city of Jerusalem railed against him. His body was beaten and bloodied; he died, and was exiled to the grave. Then he arose from the grave in victory so that all who look to him for salvation can escape judgment.

UNABLE TO GRIEVE

God wanted to show his people how much their sin hurt his heart. To do this, God told Ezekiel that he was going to take his wife, "the delight of your eyes," in order to illustrate for the people how great a loss God felt over the loss of Jerusalem. Though the nation of Israel had been warned, their grief over the fall of Jerusalem would be unimaginable. The conventional means of expressing grief would be insufficient for the great pain the exiles would feel.

People express sorrow in different ways. A long period of mourning was a normal response to the death of a loved one in the ancient Near East (Mic 1:8). There were certain things that mourners would do to illustrate their sorrow: weep, take off their turbans and put dust on their heads, and fast or eat the "bread of men" (Eze 24:17) — Ezekiel was to do none of those things. Ezekiel's apparent indifference to the death of his beloved wife was a powerful object lesson to God's people about how they would feel in the future when they learned about the fall of Israel (Eze 33:21).

Ezekiel reveals that God was about to administer a far greater calamity than the death of a wife. Jerusalem was going to fall, and the temple — the delight of the people's eyes — was going to fall as well. After this the people who weren't killed were going to be taken to Babylon, joining Ezekiel and the other Israelites already in exile. What made this worse was that many of the sons and daughters of those Ezekiel spoke to were going to be murdered in the process.

The death of Ezekiel's wife points the reader to the death of the only truly innocent person who ever lived — Jesus Christ. People may be tempted to look to the death of Ezekiel's wife and call it unfair. Yet, if anything in the Bible is unfair, it is that Jesus died for people who did not deserve it. Paul explained what God intended through the death of his Son: "God shows his love for us in that while we were still sinners, Christ died for us" (Ro 5:8). Jesus' death was a necessary death; no one can be saved without it. God the Father allowed his Son to die to show us the depth of the love he has for his children. God is not heartless toward human pain. People may not always understand his ways (Isa 55:9), but his children can trust that he is working things for good for those who love him (Ro 8:28).

Prophecy Against Ammon

25 The word of the LORD came to me: 2"Son of man, set your face toward the Ammonites and prophesy against them. 3Say to the Ammonites, Hear the word of the Lord GOD: Thus says the Lord GOD, Because you said, 'Aha!' over my sanctuary when it was profaned, and over the land of Israel when it was made desolate, and over the house of Judah when they went into exile, 4therefore behold, I am handing you over to the people of the East for a possession, and they shall set their encampments among you and make their dwellings in your midst. They shall eat your fruit, and they shall drink your milk. 5I will make Rabbah a pasture for camels and Ammon[1] a fold for flocks. Then you will know that I am the LORD. 6For thus says the Lord GOD: Because you have clapped your hands and stamped your feet and rejoiced with all the malice within your soul against the land of Israel, 7therefore, behold, I have stretched out my hand against you, and will hand you over as plunder to the nations. And I will cut you off from the peoples and will make you perish out of the countries; I will destroy you. Then you will know that I am the LORD.

Prophecy Against Moab and Seir

8"Thus says the Lord GOD: Because Moab and Seir[2] said, 'Behold, the house of Judah is like all the other nations,' 9therefore I will lay open the flank of Moab from the cities, from its cities on its frontier, the glory of the country, Beth-jeshimoth, Baal-meon, and Kiriathaim. 10I will give it along with the Ammonites to the people of the East as a possession, that the Ammonites may be remembered no more among the nations, 11and I will execute judgments upon Moab. Then they will know that I am the LORD.

Prophecy Against Edom

12"Thus says the Lord GOD: Because Edom acted revengefully against the house of Judah and has grievously offended in taking vengeance on them, 13therefore thus says the Lord GOD, I will stretch out my hand against Edom and cut off from it man and beast. And I will make it desolate; from Teman even to Dedan they shall fall by the sword. 14And I will lay my vengeance upon Edom by the hand of my people Israel, and they shall do in Edom according to my anger and according to my wrath, and they shall know my vengeance, declares the Lord GOD.

Prophecy Against Philistia

15"Thus says the Lord GOD: Because the Philistines acted revengefully and took vengeance with malice of soul to destroy in never-ending enmity, 16therefore thus says the Lord GOD, Behold, I will stretch out my hand against the Philistines, and I will cut off the Cherethites and destroy the rest of the seacoast. 17I will execute great vengeance on them with wrathful rebukes. Then they will know that I am the LORD, when I lay my vengeance upon them."

Prophecy Against Tyre

26 In the eleventh year, on the first day of the month, the word of the LORD came to me: 2"Son of man, because Tyre said concerning Jerusalem, 'Aha, the gate of the peoples is broken; it has swung open to me. I shall be replenished, now that she is laid waste,' 3therefore thus says the Lord GOD: Behold, I am against you, O Tyre, and will bring up many nations against you, as the sea brings up its waves. 4They shall destroy the walls of Tyre and break down her towers, and I will scrape her soil from her and make her a bare rock. 5She shall be in the midst of the sea a place for the spreading of nets, for I have spoken, declares the Lord GOD. And she shall become plunder for the nations, 6and her daughters on the mainland shall be killed by the sword. Then they will know that I am the LORD.

[1]Hebrew *and the Ammonites* [2]Septuagint lacks *and Seir*

EZEKIEL 26:1–21

PREYING ON GOD'S PEOPLE

Tyre was a Phoenician city off the coast of Lebanon, north of Israel. The city was known for shipping and commerce as it exercised great influence throughout the ancient Mediterranean world. The king of Tyre was once a friend to David and Solomon and assisted them in the construction of God's temple.

During the days of Ezekiel, Tyre was a pagan commercial city that had completely forgotten about God. God judged this city in the midst of judging his own people because Tyre was opposed to God's purposes. The people of Tyre didn't lead God's people deeper into God's purposes for them, but further away. Furthermore, the greedy and materialistic people of Tyre saw a vulnerable Jerusalem as their opportunity to serve themselves (v. 2).

God's judgment against Tyre teaches that God is fiercely committed to his purposes. All who do not stand with God are against God and will face his judgment. Interestingly, God in his grace was not done with Tyre forever. Jesus ministered in "the region of Tyre," one of the few places outside of Israel he traveled, and there he healed the demon-possessed daughter of a woman from Syrian Phoenicia (Mk 7:24–30).

TRAGICALLY MISSING THE POINT

God's actions may sometimes be mysterious to his children. But God's enemies face a very different difficulty when confronted by God's actions: they fail to see him working at all. This was true for the nations of Moab and Edom, which were enemies of God's people Israel. As they watched God's judgment play out from a distance, they did not recognize it as such. When they saw the people of Judah being captured and their city and temple being destroyed, they concluded that the God of Israel was powerless in this situation. These nations taunted the Israelite people because they thought their God had failed them. In so doing, they taunted God.

But God was certainly present and active and was carrying out his great plan to punish, purify, and prepare his people for their coming Deliverer. God was at work; the fact that the Moabites and the Edomites could not see God's activity did not change the reality.

The Jewish religious leaders taunted Jesus in a way that echoed the Moabites and Edomites. The situation was more complex than even the one referred to in Ezekiel. Jesus came preaching the gospel of the kingdom of God. He was gathering a following, challenging the status quo, and talking about how different the future was going to be. Then the unthinkable happened: he was crucified. In ignorance, people taunted him by jeering, "You who would destroy the temple and rebuild it in three days, save yourself! If you are the Son of God, come down from the cross" (Mt 27:40). They could not see the bigger picture. They said, "He saved others; he cannot save himself. He is the King of Israel; let him come down now from the cross, and we will believe in him" (Mt 27:42).

Tragically, they missed the point. The fact that Jesus did not come down from the cross demonstrated the magnitude of his power. In his sacrifice, Jesus displayed his power over sin, over death, over Satan, and over hell. In that moment, as people taunted him, they assumed he lacked power. In reality, they were witnessing the greatest power the world has ever seen. They simply did not have the spiritual "eyes" to see it.

7"For thus says the Lord GOD: Behold, I will bring against Tyre from the north Nebuchadnezzar[1] king of Babylon, king of kings, with horses and chariots, and with horsemen and a host of many soldiers. 8He will kill with the sword your daughters on the mainland. He will set up a siege wall against you and throw up a mound against you, and raise a roof of shields against you. 9He will direct the shock of his battering rams against your walls, and with his axes he will break down your towers. 10His horses will be so many that their dust will cover you. Your walls will shake at the noise of the horsemen and wagons and chariots, when he enters your gates as men enter a city that has been breached. 11With the hoofs of his horses he will trample all your streets. He will kill your people with the sword, and your mighty pillars will fall to the ground. 12They will plunder your riches and loot your merchandise. They will break down your walls and destroy your pleasant houses. Your stones and timber and soil they will cast into the midst of the waters. 13And I will stop the music of your songs, and the sound of your lyres shall be heard no more. 14I will make you a bare rock. You shall be a place for the spreading of nets. You shall never be rebuilt, for I am the LORD; I have spoken, declares the Lord GOD.

15"Thus says the Lord GOD to Tyre: Will not the coastlands shake at the sound of your fall, when the wounded groan, when slaughter is made in your midst? 16Then all the princes of the sea will step down from their thrones and remove their robes and strip off their embroidered garments. They will clothe themselves with trembling; they will sit on the ground and tremble every moment and be appalled at you. 17And they will raise a lamentation over you and say to you,

"'How you have perished,
you who were inhabited from the seas,
O city renowned,
who was mighty on the sea;
she and her inhabitants imposed their terror
on all her inhabitants!
18 Now the coastlands tremble
on the day of your fall,
and the coastlands that are on the sea
are dismayed at your passing.'

19"For thus says the Lord GOD: When I make you a city laid waste, like the cities that are not inhabited, when I bring up the deep over you, and the great waters cover you, 20then I will make you go down with those who go down to the pit, to the people of old, and I will make you to dwell in the world below, among ruins from of old, with those who go down to the pit, so that you will not be inhabited; but I will set beauty in the land of the living. 21I will bring you to a dreadful end, and you shall be no more. Though you be sought for, you will never be found again, declares the Lord GOD."

A Lament for Tyre

27 The word of the LORD came to me: 2"Now you, son of man, raise a lamentation over Tyre, 3and say to Tyre, who dwells at the entrances to the sea, merchant of the peoples to many coastlands, thus says the Lord GOD:

"O Tyre, you have said,
'I am perfect in beauty.'
4 Your borders are in the heart of the seas;
your builders made perfect your beauty.
5 They made all your planks
of fir trees from Senir;
they took a cedar from Lebanon
to make a mast for you.

[1]Hebrew *Nebuchadrezzar*; so throughout Ezekiel

6 Of oaks of Bashan
they made your oars;
they made your deck of pines
from the coasts of Cyprus,
inlaid with ivory.
7 Of fine embroidered linen from Egypt
was your sail,
serving as your banner;
blue and purple from the coasts of Elishah
was your awning.
8 The inhabitants of Sidon and Arvad
were your rowers;
your skilled men, O Tyre, were in you;
they were your pilots.
9 The elders of Gebal and her skilled men were in you,
caulking your seams;
all the ships of the sea with their mariners were in you
to barter for your wares.

10"Persia and Lud and Put were in your army as your men of war. They hung
the shield and helmet in you; they gave you splendor. 11Men of Arvad and Helech
were on your walls all around, and men of Gamad were in your towers. They hung
their shields on your walls all around; they made perfect your beauty.

12"Tarshish did business with you because of your great wealth of every kind;
silver, iron, tin, and lead they exchanged for your wares. 13Javan, Tubal, and
Meshech traded with you; they exchanged human beings and vessels of bronze
for your merchandise. 14From Beth-togarmah they exchanged horses, war
horses, and mules for your wares. 15The men of Dedan[1] traded with you. Many
coastlands were your own special markets; they brought you in payment ivory
tusks and ebony. 16Syria did business with you because of your abundant goods;
they exchanged for your wares emeralds, purple, embroidered work, fine linen,
coral, and ruby. 17Judah and the land of Israel traded with you; they exchanged
for your merchandise wheat of Minnith, meal,[2] honey, oil, and balm. 18Damascus
did business with you for your abundant goods, because of your great wealth of
every kind; wine of Helbon and wool of Sahar 19and casks of wine[3] from Uzal
they exchanged for your wares; wrought iron, cassia, and calamus were bartered
for your merchandise. 20Dedan traded with you in saddlecloths for riding. 21Ara-
bia and all the princes of Kedar were your favored dealers in lambs, rams, and
goats; in these they did business with you. 22The traders of Sheba and Raamah
traded with you; they exchanged for your wares the best of all kinds of spices and
all precious stones and gold. 23Haran, Canneh, Eden, traders of Sheba, Asshur,
and Chilmad traded with you. 24In your market these traded with you in choice
garments, in clothes of blue and embroidered work, and in carpets of colored
material, bound with cords and made secure. 25The ships of Tarshish traveled
for you with your merchandise. So you were filled and heavily laden in the heart
of the seas.

26 "Your rowers have brought you out
into the high seas.
The east wind has wrecked you
in the heart of the seas.
27 Your riches, your wares, your merchandise,
your mariners and your pilots,
your caulkers, your dealers in merchandise,
and all your men of war who are in you,

[1]Hebrew; Septuagint *Rhodes* [2]The meaning of the Hebrew word is uncertain [3]Probable reading; Hebrew *wool of Sahar* [19]*and Dan and Javan*

with all your crew
    that is in your midst,
sink into the heart of the seas
    on the day of your fall.
28 At the sound of the cry of your pilots
    the countryside shakes,
29 and down from their ships
    come all who handle the oar.
The mariners and all the pilots of the sea
    stand on the land
30 and shout aloud over you
    and cry out bitterly.
They cast dust on their heads
    and wallow in ashes;
31 they make themselves bald for you
    and put sackcloth on their waist,
and they weep over you in bitterness of soul,
    with bitter mourning.
32 In their wailing they raise a lamentation for you
    and lament over you:
'Who is like Tyre,
    like one destroyed in the midst of the sea?
33 When your wares came from the seas,
    you satisfied many peoples;
with your abundant wealth and merchandise
    you enriched the kings of the earth.
34 Now you are wrecked by the seas,
    in the depths of the waters;
your merchandise and all your crew in your midst
    have sunk with you.
35 All the inhabitants of the coastlands
    are appalled at you,
and the hair of their kings bristles with horror;
    their faces are convulsed.
36 The merchants among the peoples hiss at you;
    you have come to a dreadful end
    and shall be no more forever.'"

Prophecy Against the Prince of Tyre

28 The word of the LORD came to me: 2 "Son of man, say to the prince of Tyre,
Thus says the Lord GOD:

"Because your heart is proud,
    and you have said, 'I am a god,
I sit in the seat of the gods,
    in the heart of the seas,'
yet you are but a man, and no god,
    though you make your heart like the heart of a god—
3 you are indeed wiser than Daniel;
    no secret is hidden from you;
4 by your wisdom and your understanding
    you have made wealth for yourself,
and have gathered gold and silver
    into your treasuries;
5 by your great wisdom in your trade
    you have increased your wealth,
    and your heart has become proud in your wealth—

6 therefore thus says the Lord GOD:
Because you make your heart
like the heart of a god,
7 therefore, behold, I will bring foreigners upon you,
the most ruthless of the nations;
and they shall draw their swords against the beauty of your wisdom
and defile your splendor.
8 They shall thrust you down into the pit,
and you shall die the death of the slain
in the heart of the seas.
9 Will you still say, 'I am a god,'
in the presence of those who kill you,
though you are but a man, and no god,
in the hands of those who slay you?
10 You shall die the death of the uncircumcised
by the hand of foreigners;
for I have spoken, declares the Lord GOD."

A Lament over the King of Tyre

11Moreover, the word of the LORD came to me: 12"Son of man, raise a lamentation over the king of Tyre, and say to him, Thus says the Lord GOD:

"You were the signet of perfection,[1]
full of wisdom and perfect in beauty.
13 You were in Eden, the garden of God;
every precious stone was your covering,
sardius, topaz, and diamond,
beryl, onyx, and jasper,
sapphire,[2] emerald, and carbuncle;
and crafted in gold were your settings
and your engravings.[3]
On the day that you were created
they were prepared.
14 You were an anointed guardian cherub.
I placed you;[4] you were on the holy mountain of God;
in the midst of the stones of fire you walked.
15 You were blameless in your ways
from the day you were created,
till unrighteousness was found in you.
16 In the abundance of your trade
you were filled with violence in your midst, and you sinned;
so I cast you as a profane thing from the mountain of God,
and I destroyed you,[5] O guardian cherub,
from the midst of the stones of fire.
17 Your heart was proud because of your beauty;
you corrupted your wisdom for the sake of your splendor.
I cast you to the ground;
I exposed you before kings,
to feast their eyes on you.
18 By the multitude of your iniquities,
in the unrighteousness of your trade
you profaned your sanctuaries;
so I brought fire out from your midst;
it consumed you,

[1]The meaning of the Hebrew phrase is uncertain [2]Or *lapis lazuli* [3]The meaning of the Hebrew phrase is uncertain [4]The meaning of the Hebrew phrase is uncertain [5]Or *banished you*

and I turned you to ashes on the earth
in the sight of all who saw you.
19 All who know you among the peoples
are appalled at you;
you have come to a dreadful end
and shall be no more forever."

Prophecy Against Sidon

20The word of the LORD came to me: 21"Son of man, set your face toward Sidon,
and prophesy against her 22and say, Thus says the Lord GOD:

"Behold, I am against you, O Sidon,
and I will manifest my glory in your midst.
And they shall know that I am the LORD
when I execute judgments in her
and manifest my holiness in her;
23 for I will send pestilence into her,
and blood into her streets;
and the slain shall fall in her midst,
by the sword that is against her on every side.
Then they will know that I am the LORD.

24"And for the house of Israel there shall be no more a brier to prick or a thorn
to hurt them among all their neighbors who have treated them with contempt.
Then they will know that I am the Lord GOD.

Israel Gathered in Security

25"Thus says the Lord GOD: When I gather the house of Israel from the peoples
among whom they are scattered, and manifest my holiness in them in the sight
of the nations, then they shall dwell in their own land that I gave to my servant
Jacob. 26And they shall dwell securely in it, and they shall build houses and plant
vineyards. They shall dwell securely, when I execute judgments upon all their
neighbors who have treated them with contempt. Then they will know that I am
the LORD their God."

Prophecy Against Egypt

29 In the tenth year, in the tenth month, on the twelfth day of the month, the
word of the LORD came to me: 2"Son of man, set your face against Pharaoh
king of Egypt, and prophesy against him and against all Egypt; 3speak, and say,
Thus says the Lord GOD:

"Behold, I am against you,
Pharaoh king of Egypt,
the great dragon that lies
in the midst of his streams,
that says, 'My Nile is my own;
I made it for myself.'
4 I will put hooks in your jaws,
and make the fish of your streams stick to your
scales;
and I will draw you up out of the midst of your
streams,
with all the fish of your streams
that stick to your scales.
5 And I will cast you out into the wilderness,
you and all the fish of your streams;
you shall fall on the open field,
and not be brought together or gathered.

EZEKIEL 28:25–26

SCATTERED AND THEN GATHERED

God is the gathering and scattering God. He gathers his people together to give them a new purpose and then scatters them out in order to live for that purpose. His ultimate purpose is to bring his people to a place where they will dwell with him forever and he will be their God. All of God's gathering and scattering finds its unity in that one great purpose of eventually having God's people live in perfect communion with each other and with God.

In this particular instance, God had scattered his people because they did not trust him in faith. But God also promised his people that he would one day gather them from their dispersion among the nations and return them to live with him in their own land.

This promise reflects God's previous promise to their forefathers Abraham and Isaac (Ge 26:3). While not a direct reference, this "gathering" provides another illustration of Jesus' promise to prepare places for his followers and then bring believers one day to be with him (Jn 14:2–3).

To the beasts of the earth and to the birds of the heavens
I give you as food.

6 Then all the inhabitants of Egypt shall know that I am the LORD.
"Because you[1] have been a staff of reed to the house of Israel, 7 when they
grasped you with the hand, you broke and tore all their shoulders; and when they
leaned on you, you broke and made all their loins to shake.[2] 8 Therefore thus says
the Lord GOD: Behold, I will bring a sword upon you, and will cut off from you man
and beast, 9 and the land of Egypt shall be a desolation and a waste. Then they will
know that I am the LORD.
"Because you[3] said, 'The Nile is mine, and I made it,' 10 therefore, behold, I am
against you and against your streams, and I will make the land of Egypt an utter
waste and desolation, from Migdol to Syene, as far as the border of Cush. 11 No
foot of man shall pass through it, and no foot of beast shall pass through it; it
shall be uninhabited forty years. 12 And I will make the land of Egypt a desolation
in the midst of desolated countries, and her cities shall be a desolation forty years
among cities that are laid waste. I will scatter the Egyptians among the nations,
and disperse them through the countries.
13 "For thus says the Lord GOD: At the end of forty years I will gather the Egyptians from the peoples among whom they were scattered, 14 and I will restore the
fortunes of Egypt and bring them back to the land of Pathros, the land of their
origin, and there they shall be a lowly kingdom. 15 It shall be the most lowly of the
kingdoms, and never again exalt itself above the nations. And I will make them so
small that they will never again rule over the nations. 16 And it shall never again be
the reliance of the house of Israel, recalling their iniquity, when they turn to them
for aid. Then they will know that I am the Lord GOD."
17 In the twenty-seventh year, in the first month, on the first day of the month,
the word of the LORD came to me: 18 "Son of man, Nebuchadnezzar king of Babylon made his army labor hard against Tyre. Every head was made bald, and every
shoulder was rubbed bare, yet neither he nor his army got anything from Tyre to
pay for the labor that he had performed against her. 19 Therefore thus says the Lord
GOD: Behold, I will give the land of Egypt to Nebuchadnezzar king of Babylon;
and he shall carry off its wealth[4] and despoil it and plunder it; and it shall be the
wages for his army. 20 I have given him the land of Egypt as his payment for which
he labored, because they worked for me, declares the Lord GOD.
21 "On that day I will cause a horn to spring up for the house of Israel, and I will
open your lips among them. Then they will know that I am the LORD."

A Lament for Egypt

30 The word of the LORD came to me: 2 "Son of man, prophesy, and say, Thus
says the Lord GOD:

"Wail, 'Alas for the day!'
3 For the day is near,
the day of the LORD is near;
it will be a day of clouds,
a time of doom for[5] the nations.
4 A sword shall come upon Egypt,
and anguish shall be in Cush,
when the slain fall in Egypt,
and her wealth[6] is carried away,
and her foundations are torn down.

5 Cush, and Put, and Lud, and all Arabia, and Libya,[7] and the people of the land
that is in league,[8] shall fall with them by the sword.

[1]Hebrew *they* [2]Syriac (compare Psalm 69:23); Hebrew *to stand* [3]Hebrew *he* [4]Or *multitude* [5]Hebrew lacks *doom for* [6]Or *multitude*; also verse 10 [7]With Septuagint; Hebrew *Cub* [8]Hebrew *and the sons of the land of the covenant*

EZEKIEL 29:16

MISPLACED HOPE

People are created to have hope. Be it a person, a place, a thing, a status, or a destination—everyone hopes in something or someone. God's people, the Israelites, were supposed to hope in God, but they frequently struggled to do so and instead placed their security in alliances with foreign nations.

God promised to bring down the neighboring nation of Egypt, and then Judah would no longer look to them as a source of hope and help. God took seriously his people's tendency to misplace their trust and hope. Jesus rebuked those who trusted in anything other than God—those who trusted in riches (Mt 6:19–21), in religious heritage (Mt 3:9), or in their religious activities (Mk 13:1–2). Confidence in anyone or anything other than God is an issue of misplaced hope. Like the Israelites before, all of God's people must learn to trust him today.

EZEKIEL 30:1–3

THE DAY OF THE LORD

Throughout the prophetic books of the Old Testament and parts of the New Testament, "the day of the LORD" is a common expression for God's judgment, especially his future judgment. This is a comforting concept for those who follow God and are weary of the injustice of the world, those who long for God to set things right as he has promised to do in Scripture. God will come near to a sin-soaked world and make all things right. But those who oppose God will have to deal with Jesus on

(continued on next page)

(The Day of the Lord, continued)

that day. Jesus taught that he would ultimately act as the final judge for all humanity (Mt 25:31–46; Jn 5:22). He came to provide people with a chance to escape the future judgment that is surely coming to all people. Jesus already paid the debt of sin, and all people are encouraged to cry out to him for mercy in order to escape the coming judgment on their sin.

6 "Thus says the LORD:
Those who support Egypt shall fall,
and her proud might shall come down;
from Migdol to Syene
they shall fall within her by the sword,
declares the Lord GOD.
7 And they shall be desolated in the midst of desolated
countries,
and their cities shall be in the midst of cities that are
laid waste.
8 Then they will know that I am the LORD,
when I have set fire to Egypt,
and all her helpers are broken.

9 "On that day messengers shall go out from me in ships to terrify the unsuspecting people of Cush, and anguish shall come upon them on the day of Egypt's
doom;[1] for, behold, it comes!
10 "Thus says the Lord GOD:

"I will put an end to the wealth of Egypt,
by the hand of Nebuchadnezzar king of Babylon.
11 He and his people with him, the most ruthless of nations,
shall be brought in to destroy the land,
and they shall draw their swords against Egypt
and fill the land with the slain.
12 And I will dry up the Nile
and will sell the land into the hand of evildoers;
I will bring desolation upon the land and everything in it,
by the hand of foreigners;
I am the LORD; I have spoken.

13 "Thus says the Lord GOD:

"I will destroy the idols
and put an end to the images in Memphis;
there shall no longer be a prince from the land of Egypt;
so I will put fear in the land of Egypt.
14 I will make Pathros a desolation
and will set fire to Zoan
and will execute judgments on Thebes.
15 And I will pour out my wrath on Pelusium,
the stronghold of Egypt,
and cut off the multitude[2] of Thebes.
16 And I will set fire to Egypt;
Pelusium shall be in great agony;
Thebes shall be breached,
and Memphis shall face enemies[3] by day.
17 The young men of On and of Pi-beseth shall fall by the
sword,
and the women[4] shall go into captivity.
18 At Tehaphnehes the day shall be dark,
when I break there the yoke bars of Egypt,
and her proud might shall come to an end in her;
she shall be covered by a cloud,
and her daughters shall go into captivity.
19 Thus I will execute judgments on Egypt.
Then they will know that I am the LORD."

[1]Hebrew *the day of Egypt* [2]Or *wealth* [3]Or *distress* [4]Or *the cities*; Hebrew *they*

Egypt Shall Fall to Babylon

[20]In the eleventh year, in the first month, on the seventh day of the month, the
word of the LORD came to me: [21]"Son of man, I have broken the arm of Pharaoh
king of Egypt, and behold, it has not been bound up, to heal it by binding it with
a bandage, so that it may become strong to wield the sword. [22]Therefore thus says
the Lord GOD: Behold, I am against Pharaoh king of Egypt and will break his arms,
both the strong arm and the one that was broken, and I will make the sword fall
from his hand. [23]I will scatter the Egyptians among the nations and disperse them
through the countries. [24]And I will strengthen the arms of the king of Babylon and
put my sword in his hand, but I will break the arms of Pharaoh, and he will groan
before him like a man mortally wounded. [25]I will strengthen the arms of the king
of Babylon, but the arms of Pharaoh shall fall. Then they shall know that I am the
LORD, when I put my sword into the hand of the king of Babylon and he stretches
it out against the land of Egypt. [26]And I will scatter the Egyptians among the nations and disperse them throughout the countries. Then they will know that I am
the LORD."

Pharaoh to Be Slain

31 In the eleventh year, in the third month, on the first day of the month, the
word of the LORD came to me: [2]"Son of man, say to Pharaoh king of Egypt
and to his multitude:

"Whom are you like in your greatness?
3 Behold, Assyria was a cedar in Lebanon,
with beautiful branches and forest shade,
and of towering height,
its top among the clouds.[1]
4 The waters nourished it;
the deep made it grow tall,
making its rivers flow
around the place of its planting,
sending forth its streams
to all the trees of the field.
5 So it towered high
above all the trees of the field;
its boughs grew large
and its branches long
from abundant water in its shoots.
6 All the birds of the heavens
made their nests in its boughs;
under its branches all the beasts of the field
gave birth to their young,
and under its shadow
lived all great nations.
7 It was beautiful in its greatness,
in the length of its branches;
for its roots went down
to abundant waters.
8 The cedars in the garden of God could not rival it,
nor the fir trees equal its boughs;
neither were the plane trees
like its branches;
no tree in the garden of God
was its equal in beauty.

[1]Or *its top went through the thick boughs*

EZEKIEL 31:3–17

PRIDE GOES BEFORE A FALL

The bigger they are, the harder they fall. The powerful nations in the Bible can seem as if they are untouchable or immoveable. Ezekiel compared Assyria to a massive tree. This tree had its roots deep in the earth and the top branches in the clouds and was higher and mightier than all the trees of the earth (vv. 3–7). It was the greatest and overlord of the nations, but the great tree of Assyria fell because it became proud (Pr 16:18).

Assyria never recognized that her lofty status came from God. The Lord had elevated her to such a great status, but she considered her attainments something of which to be proud (Eze 31:10). As great as Assyria was, the Lord easily cast her down.

Jesus came to save people from the terrible sin of pride. Jesus was full of humility, and he showed this by giving his life for others (Php 2:5–11). Jesus taught that the humble would be exalted (Mt 23:12). And so, Jesus turns the values of the world on their head: the way to earn glory in God's kingdom is to be humble.

9 I made it beautiful
in the mass of its branches,
and all the trees of Eden envied it,
that were in the garden of God.

10 "Therefore thus says the Lord GOD: Because it[1] towered high and set its top
among the clouds,[2] and its heart was proud of its height, 11 I will give it into the
hand of a mighty one of the nations. He shall surely deal with it as its wickedness
deserves. I have cast it out. 12 Foreigners, the most ruthless of nations, have cut it
down and left it. On the mountains and in all the valleys its branches have fallen,
and its boughs have been broken in all the ravines of the land, and all the peoples
of the earth have gone away from its shadow and left it. 13 On its fallen trunk dwell
all the birds of the heavens, and on its branches are all the beasts of the field. 14 All
this is in order that no trees by the waters may grow to towering height or set
their tops among the clouds,[3] and that no trees that drink water may reach up to
them in height. For they are all given over to death, to the world below, among the
children of man,[4] with those who go down to the pit.
15 "Thus says the Lord GOD: On the day the cedar[5] went down to Sheol I caused
mourning; I closed the deep over it, and restrained its rivers, and many waters
were stopped. I clothed Lebanon in gloom for it, and all the trees of the field
fainted because of it. 16 I made the nations quake at the sound of its fall, when I
cast it down to Sheol with those who go down to the pit. And all the trees of Eden,
the choice and best of Lebanon, all that drink water, were comforted in the world
below. 17 They also went down to Sheol with it, to those who are slain by the sword;
yes, those who were its arm, who lived under its shadow among the nations.
18 "Whom are you thus like in glory and in greatness among the trees of Eden?
You shall be brought down with the trees of Eden to the world below. You shall lie
among the uncircumcised, with those who are slain by the sword.
"This is Pharaoh and all his multitude, declares the Lord GOD."

A Lament over Pharaoh and Egypt

32 In the twelfth year, in the twelfth month, on the first day of the month,
the word of the LORD came to me: 2 "Son of man, raise a lamentation over
Pharaoh king of Egypt and say to him:

"You consider yourself a lion of the nations,
but you are like a dragon in the seas;
you burst forth in your rivers,
trouble the waters with your feet,
and foul their rivers.
3 Thus says the Lord GOD:
I will throw my net over you
with a host of many peoples,
and they will haul you up in my dragnet.
4 And I will cast you on the ground;
on the open field I will fling you,
and will cause all the birds of the heavens to settle on you,
and I will gorge the beasts of the whole earth with you.
5 I will strew your flesh upon the mountains
and fill the valleys with your carcass.[6]
6 I will drench the land even to the mountains
with your flowing blood,
and the ravines will be full of you.
7 When I blot you out, I will cover the heavens
and make their stars dark;

[1]Syriac, Vulgate; Hebrew *you* [2]Or *its top through the thick boughs* [3]Or *their tops through the thick boughs*
[4]Or *of Adam* [5]Hebrew *it* [6]Hebrew *your height*

I will cover the sun with a cloud,
    and the moon shall not give its light.
8 All the bright lights of heaven
    will I make dark over you,
    and put darkness on your land,
        declares the Lord GOD.

9"I will trouble the hearts of many peoples, when I bring your destruction
among the nations, into the countries that you have not known. 10I will make
many peoples appalled at you, and the hair of their kings shall bristle with horror
because of you, when I brandish my sword before them. They shall tremble every
moment, every one for his own life, on the day of your downfall.
11"For thus says the Lord GOD: The sword of the king of Babylon shall come
upon you. 12I will cause your multitude to fall by the swords of mighty ones, all of
them most ruthless of nations.

"They shall bring to ruin the pride of Egypt,
    and all its multitude[1] shall perish.
13 I will destroy all its beasts
    from beside many waters;
and no foot of man shall trouble them anymore,
    nor shall the hoofs of beasts trouble them.
14 Then I will make their waters clear,
    and cause their rivers to run like oil,
        declares the Lord GOD.
15 When I make the land of Egypt desolate,
    and when the land is desolate of all that fills it,
when I strike down all who dwell in it,
    then they will know that I am the LORD.

16This is a lamentation that shall be chanted; the daughters of the nations shall
chant it; over Egypt, and over all her multitude, shall they chant it, declares the
Lord GOD."
17In the twelfth year, in the twelfth month,[2] on the fifteenth day of the month,
the word of the LORD came to me: 18"Son of man, wail over the multitude of Egypt,
and send them down, her and the daughters of majestic nations, to the world
below, to those who have gone down to the pit:
19 'Whom do you surpass in beauty?
    Go down and be laid to rest with the uncircumcised.'

20They shall fall amid those who are slain by the sword. Egypt[3] is delivered to the
sword; drag her away, and all her multitudes. 21The mighty chiefs shall speak of
them, with their helpers, out of the midst of Sheol: 'They have come down, they
lie still, the uncircumcised, slain by the sword.'
22"Assyria is there, and all her company, its graves all around it, all of them
slain, fallen by the sword, 23whose graves are set in the uttermost parts of the pit;
and her company is all around her grave, all of them slain, fallen by the sword,
who spread terror in the land of the living.
24"Elam is there, and all her multitude around her grave; all of them slain,
fallen by the sword, who went down uncircumcised into the world below, who
spread their terror in the land of the living; and they bear their shame with
those who go down to the pit. 25They have made her a bed among the slain
with all her multitude, her graves all around it, all of them uncircumcised, slain
by the sword; for terror of them was spread in the land of the living, and they
bear their shame with those who go down to the pit; they are placed among
the slain.

[1]Or *wealth* [2]Hebrew lacks *in the twelfth month* [3]Hebrew *She*

26“Meshech-Tubal is there, and all her multitude, her graves all around it, all of them uncircumcised, slain by the sword; for they spread their terror in the land of the living. 27And they do not lie with the mighty, the fallen from among the uncircumcised, who went down to Sheol with their weapons of war, whose swords were laid under their heads, and whose iniquities are upon their bones; for the terror of the mighty men was in the land of the living. 28But as for you, you shall be broken and lie among the uncircumcised, with those who are slain by the sword.

29“Edom is there, her kings and all her princes, who for all their might are laid with those who are killed by the sword; they lie with the uncircumcised, with those who go down to the pit.

30“The princes of the north are there, all of them, and all the Sidonians, who have gone down in shame with the slain, for all the terror that they caused by their might; they lie uncircumcised with those who are slain by the sword, and bear their shame with those who go down to the pit.

31“When Pharaoh sees them, he will be comforted for all his multitude, Pharaoh and all his army, slain by the sword, declares the Lord GOD. 32For I spread terror in the land of the living; and he shall be laid to rest among the uncircumcised, with those who are slain by the sword, Pharaoh and all his multitude, declares the Lord GOD.”

Ezekiel Is Israel’s Watchman

33 The word of the LORD came to me: 2“Son of man, speak to your people and say to them, If I bring the sword upon a land, and the people of the land take a man from among them, and make him their watchman, 3and if he sees the sword coming upon the land and blows the trumpet and warns the people, 4then if anyone who hears the sound of the trumpet does not take warning, and the sword comes and takes him away, his blood shall be upon his own head. 5He heard the sound of the trumpet and did not take warning; his blood shall be upon himself. But if he had taken warning, he would have saved his life. 6But if the watchman sees the sword coming and does not blow the trumpet, so that the people are not warned, and the sword comes and takes any one of them, that person is taken away in his iniquity, but his blood I will require at the watchman’s hand.

7“So you, son of man, I have made a watchman for the house of Israel. Whenever you hear a word from my mouth, you shall give them warning from me. 8If I say to the wicked, O wicked one, you shall surely die, and you do not speak to warn the wicked to turn from his way, that wicked person shall die in his iniquity, but his blood I will require at your hand. 9But if you warn the wicked to turn from his way, and he does not turn from his way, that person shall die in his iniquity, but you will have delivered your soul.

Why Will You Die, Israel?

10“And you, son of man, say to the house of Israel, Thus have you said: ‘Surely our transgressions and our sins are upon us, and we rot away because of them. How then can we live?’ 11Say to them, As I live, declares the Lord GOD, I have no pleasure in the death of the wicked, but that the wicked turn from his way and live; turn back, turn back from your evil ways, for why will you die, O house of Israel?

12“And you, son of man, say to your people, The righteousness of the righteous shall not deliver him when he transgresses, and as for the wickedness of the wicked, he shall not fall by it when he turns from his wickedness, and the righteous shall not be able to live by his righteousness[1] when he sins. 13Though I say to the righteous that he shall surely live, yet if he trusts in his righteousness

[1]Hebrew *by it*

WATCH AND WARN

In the ancient world, a watchman was an official military title. The person was to watch in anticipation and be on the lookout for opposition and attacks. Watchmen were positioned on the city wall and were responsible for spotting approaching armies and sounding the alarm to alert the city to their approach (1Sa 14:16; 2Sa 18:24).

God used the title "watchman" here to assign Ezekiel the role of reporting to the people the things that God showed him. This was not the only time God assigned the role of watchman to a prophet (Hos 9:8; Hab 2:1). Like a military watchman, Ezekiel's task was to alert God's people at the sight of alarm so that they could respond in repentance. The watchman was an important role to fulfill, and failure to report to the people meant punishment by death (Eze 33:8).

Jesus taught his disciples to be watchful as well so that they could be ready for his return (Mt 24:42–43). His disciples were to look to Jesus as the great model and to be ready to respond when they saw God at work.

God is gracious to provide elders to "watch" and oversee his church today. Their role is similar to the prophets and disciples who came before them. The apostle Paul reminded the Ephesian elders of how he served as a watchman when he said, "Therefore be alert, remembering that for three years I did not cease night or day to admonish every one with tears" (Ac 20:31). The author of Hebrews later encouraged God's people to "obey your leaders and submit to them, for they are keeping watch over your souls, as those who will have to give an account. Let them do this with joy and not with groaning, for that would be of no advantage to you" (Heb 13:17).

God's best for his people is to lead them and guide them through the lives of other people. Only Jesus is able to give people the humility to submit to others in authority, and to grant those in authority the compassion to lead well (1Pe 5:1–4).

and does injustice, none of his righteous deeds shall be remembered, but in his injustice that he has done he shall die. 14Again, though I say to the wicked, 'You shall surely die,' yet if he turns from his sin and does what is just and right, 15if the wicked restores the pledge, gives back what he has taken by robbery, and walks in the statutes of life, not doing injustice, he shall surely live; he shall not die. 16None of the sins that he has committed shall be remembered against him. He has done what is just and right; he shall surely live.

17"Yet your people say, 'The way of the Lord is not just,' when it is their own way that is not just. 18When the righteous turns from his righteousness and does injustice, he shall die for it. 19And when the wicked turns from his wickedness and does what is just and right, he shall live by this. 20Yet you say, 'The way of the Lord is not just.' O house of Israel, I will judge each of you according to his ways."

Jerusalem Struck Down

21In the twelfth year of our exile, in the tenth month, on the fifth day of the month, a fugitive from Jerusalem came to me and said, "The city has been struck down." 22Now the hand of the LORD had been upon me the evening before the fugitive came; and he had opened my mouth by the time the man came to me in the morning, so my mouth was opened, and I was no longer mute.

23The word of the LORD came to me: 24"Son of man, the inhabitants of these waste places in the land of Israel keep saying, 'Abraham was only one man, yet he got possession of the land; but we are many; the land is surely given us to possess.' 25Therefore say to them, Thus says the Lord GOD: You eat flesh with the blood and lift up your eyes to your idols and shed blood; shall you then possess the land? 26You rely on the sword, you commit abominations, and each of you defiles his neighbor's wife; shall you then possess the land? 27Say this to them, Thus says the Lord GOD: As I live, surely those who are in the waste places shall fall by the sword, and whoever is in the open field I will give to the beasts to be devoured, and those who are in strongholds and in caves shall die by pestilence. 28And I will make the land a desolation and a waste, and her proud might shall come to an end, and the mountains of Israel shall be so desolate that none will pass through. 29Then they will know that I am the LORD, when I have made the land a desolation and a waste because of all their abominations that they have committed.

30"As for you, son of man, your people who talk together about you by the walls and at the doors of the houses say to one another, each to his brother, 'Come, and hear what the word is that comes from the LORD.' 31And they come to you as people come, and they sit before you as my people, and they hear what you say but they will not do it; for with lustful talk in their mouths they act; their heart is set on their gain. 32And behold, you are to them like one who sings lustful songs with a beautiful voice and plays[1] well on an instrument, for they hear what you say, but they will not do it. 33When this comes—and come it will!—then they will know that a prophet has been among them."

Prophecy Against the Shepherds of Israel

34 The word of the LORD came to me: 2"Son of man, prophesy against the shepherds of Israel; prophesy, and say to them, even to the shepherds, Thus says the Lord GOD: Ah, shepherds of Israel who have been feeding yourselves! Should not shepherds feed the sheep? 3You eat the fat, you clothe yourselves with the wool, you slaughter the fat ones, but you do not feed the sheep. 4The weak you have not strengthened, the sick you have not healed, the injured you have not bound up, the strayed you have not brought back, the lost you have not sought, and with force and harshness you have ruled them. 5So they were scattered, because there was no shepherd, and they became food for all the wild beasts. My sheep were scattered; 6they wandered over all the mountains and on

[1]Hebrew *like the singing of lustful songs with a beautiful voice and one who plays*

every high hill. My sheep were scattered over all the face of the earth, with none to search or seek for them.

7"Therefore, you shepherds, hear the word of the LORD: 8As I live, declares the Lord GOD, surely because my sheep have become a prey, and my sheep have become food for all the wild beasts, since there was no shepherd, and because my shepherds have not searched for my sheep, but the shepherds have fed themselves, and have not fed my sheep, 9therefore, you shepherds, hear the word of the LORD: 10Thus says the Lord GOD, Behold, I am against the shepherds, and I will require my sheep at their hand and put a stop to their feeding the sheep. No longer shall the shepherds feed themselves. I will rescue my sheep from their mouths, that they may not be food for them.

The Lord GOD Will Seek Them Out

11"For thus says the Lord GOD: Behold, I, I myself will search for my sheep and will seek them out. 12As a shepherd seeks out his flock when he is among his sheep that have been scattered, so will I seek out my sheep, and I will rescue them from all places where they have been scattered on a day of clouds and thick darkness. 13And I will bring them out from the peoples and gather them from the countries, and will bring them into their own land. And I will feed them on the mountains of Israel, by the ravines, and in all the inhabited places of the country. 14I will feed them with good pasture, and on the mountain heights of Israel shall be their grazing land. There they shall lie down in good grazing land, and on rich pasture they shall feed on the mountains of Israel. 15I myself will be the shepherd of my sheep, and I myself will make them lie down, declares the Lord GOD. 16I will seek the lost, and I will bring back the strayed, and I will bind up the injured, and I will strengthen the weak, and the fat and the strong I will destroy.[1] I will feed them in justice.

17"As for you, my flock, thus says the Lord GOD: Behold, I judge between sheep and sheep, between rams and male goats. 18Is it not enough for you to feed on the good pasture, that you must tread down with your feet the rest of your pasture; and to drink of clear water, that you must muddy the rest of the water with your feet? 19And must my sheep eat what you have trodden with your feet, and drink what you have muddied with your feet?

20"Therefore, thus says the Lord GOD to them: Behold, I, I myself will judge between the fat sheep and the lean sheep. 21Because you push with side and shoulder, and thrust at all the weak with your horns, till you have scattered them abroad, 22I will rescue[2] my flock; they shall no longer be a prey. And I will judge between sheep and sheep. 23And I will set up over them one shepherd, my servant David, and he shall feed them: he shall feed them and be their shepherd. 24And I, the LORD, will be their God, and my servant David shall be prince among them. I am the LORD; I have spoken.

The LORD's Covenant of Peace

25"I will make with them a covenant of peace and banish wild beasts from the land, so that they may dwell securely in the wilderness and sleep in the woods. 26And I will make them and the places all around my hill a blessing, and I will send down the showers in their season; they shall be showers of blessing. 27And the trees of the field shall yield their fruit, and the earth shall yield its increase, and they shall be secure in their land. And they shall know that I am the LORD, when I break the bars of their yoke, and deliver them from the hand of those who enslaved them. 28They shall no more be a prey to the nations, nor shall the beasts of the land devour them. They shall dwell securely, and none shall make them afraid. 29And I will provide for them a renowned place for planting so that they shall no more be consumed with hunger in the land, and no longer suffer the reproach

---

[1]Septuagint, Syriac, Vulgate *I will watch over* [2]Or *save*

THE GREAT SHEPHERD

Shepherds are important. Sheep lack common-sense intelligence. Therefore, they are constantly getting into trouble, eating things that are bad for them, and unknowingly endangering their own lives. Sheep need a shepherd, someone who would give his very life to care for the sheep and find those that wander.

God acknowledges that his people are like sheep: careless, helpless, easily led astray, and yet so precious to the shepherd. God called his people to care for others as a way of reflecting his goodness; that was his desire for his people Israel. But God's leaders ended up caring for themselves a lot more than they cared for others. As a result, God got involved. God became the personal Shepherd of his people and tended to their needs himself.

God makes many promises to his sheep: He will search for and rescue them in times of trouble (vv. 11 – 12); he will lead them to good grass that will allow for flourishing (vv. 13 – 14); he will tend to their needs and give them strength when they are hurting and weak (vv. 15 – 16).

Jesus is the Good Shepherd (Jn 10:11). He personally leads his sheep (Jn 10:3 – 4) and delivers them from danger when they stray (Jn 10:11 – 13). Many good shepherds care for their sheep, but Jesus uniquely gave his life to save his sheep. Jesus' sacrificial death entitles him to be called the Great Shepherd (Heb 13:20).

Jesus' example allows "under-shepherds" to lead God's people well. Paul did not mince words in describing how pastors are supposed to shepherd God's flock: "Pay careful attention to yourselves and to all the flock, in which the Holy Spirit has made you overseers, to care for the church of God, which he obtained with his own blood. I know that after my departure fierce wolves will come in among you, not sparing the flock" (Ac 20:28 – 29).

While it is good to hold God's under-shepherds in great respect as they lead God's church, there is a sense in which all of God's people are under-shepherds: they reflect the caring character of God in how they love and look after one another.

of the nations. 30And they shall know that I am the LORD their God with them, and that they, the house of Israel, are my people, declares the Lord GOD. 31And you are my sheep, human sheep of my pasture, and I am your God, declares the Lord GOD."

Prophecy Against Mount Seir

35 The word of the LORD came to me: 2"Son of man, set your face against Mount Seir, and prophesy against it, 3and say to it, Thus says the Lord GOD: Behold, I am against you, Mount Seir, and I will stretch out my hand against you, and I will make you a desolation and a waste. 4I will lay your cities waste, and you shall become a desolation, and you shall know that I am the LORD. 5Because you cherished perpetual enmity and gave over the people of Israel to the power of the sword at the time of their calamity, at the time of their final punishment, 6therefore, as I live, declares the Lord GOD, I will prepare you for blood, and blood shall pursue you; because you did not hate bloodshed, therefore blood shall pursue you. 7I will make Mount Seir a waste and a desolation, and I will cut off from it all who come and go. 8And I will fill its mountains with the slain. On your hills and in your valleys and in all your ravines those slain with the sword shall fall. 9I will make you a perpetual desolation, and your cities shall not be inhabited. Then you will know that I am the LORD.

10"Because you said, 'These two nations and these two countries shall be mine, and we will take possession of them'—although the LORD was there— 11therefore, as I live, declares the Lord GOD, I will deal with you according to the anger and envy that you showed because of your hatred against them. And I will make myself known among them, when I judge you. 12And you shall know that I am the LORD.

"I have heard all the revilings that you uttered against the mountains of Israel, saying, 'They are laid desolate; they are given us to devour.' 13And you magnified yourselves against me with your mouth, and multiplied your words against me; I heard it. 14Thus says the Lord GOD: While the whole earth rejoices, I will make you desolate. 15As you rejoiced over the inheritance of the house of Israel, because it was desolate, so I will deal with you; you shall be desolate, Mount Seir, and all Edom, all of it. Then they will know that I am the LORD.

Prophecy to the Mountains of Israel

36 "And you, son of man, prophesy to the mountains of Israel, and say, O mountains of Israel, hear the word of the LORD. 2Thus says the Lord GOD: Because the enemy said of you, 'Aha!' and, 'The ancient heights have become our possession,' 3therefore prophesy, and say, Thus says the Lord GOD: Precisely because they made you desolate and crushed you from all sides, so that you became the possession of the rest of the nations, and you became the talk and evil gossip of the people, 4therefore, O mountains of Israel, hear the word of the Lord GOD: Thus says the Lord GOD to the mountains and the hills, the ravines and the valleys, the desolate wastes and the deserted cities, which have become a prey and derision to the rest of the nations all around, 5therefore thus says the Lord GOD: Surely I have spoken in my hot jealousy against the rest of the nations and against all Edom, who gave my land to themselves as a possession with wholehearted joy and utter contempt, that they might make its pasturelands a prey. 6Therefore prophesy concerning the land of Israel, and say to the mountains and hills, to the ravines and valleys, Thus says the Lord GOD: Behold, I have spoken in my jealous wrath, because you have suffered the reproach of the nations. 7Therefore thus says the Lord GOD: I swear that the nations that are all around you shall themselves suffer reproach.

8"But you, O mountains of Israel, shall shoot forth your branches and yield your fruit to my people Israel, for they will soon come home. 9For behold, I am for you, and I will turn to you, and you shall be tilled and sown. 10And I will multiply

EZEKIEL 35:1–4

EDOM

The people of Israel and the people of Edom (referred to as Mount Seir here) were longtime enemies. Edom had a heritage of not only wanting bad things for the Israelites but also celebrating when things went badly for them (Eze 35:12–15). When Judah lost their city of Jerusalem, the Edomites swarmed to loot the city, and they also handed over those who fled to their attackers (Ob 12–14). Their attitude went beyond contempt for the people of Judah; they spurned the work of God and God's decision to choose and love the people of Judah.

Their problem was not merely with another group of people; their problem was with the God who loved these people and acted on their behalf. Because of their continued hatred of the Israelites, God gave them over to devastation and spiritual barrenness. So it will be with everyone who denies God's lordship and the work of Jesus toward salvation.

people on you, the whole house of Israel, all of it. The cities shall be inhabited and the waste places rebuilt. 11And I will multiply on you man and beast, and they shall multiply and be fruitful. And I will cause you to be inhabited as in your former times, and will do more good to you than ever before. Then you will know that I am the LORD. 12I will let people walk on you, even my people Israel. And they shall possess you, and you shall be their inheritance, and you shall no longer bereave them of children. 13Thus says the Lord GOD: Because they say to you, 'You devour people, and you bereave your nation of children,' 14therefore you shall no longer devour people and no longer bereave your nation of children, declares the Lord GOD. 15And I will not let you hear anymore the reproach of the nations, and you shall no longer bear the disgrace of the peoples and no longer cause your nation to stumble, declares the Lord GOD."

The LORD's Concern for His Holy Name

16The word of the LORD came to me: 17"Son of man, when the house of Israel lived in their own land, they defiled it by their ways and their deeds. Their ways before me were like the uncleanness of a woman in her menstrual impurity. 18So I poured out my wrath upon them for the blood that they had shed in the land, for the idols with which they had defiled it. 19I scattered them among the nations, and they were dispersed through the countries. In accordance with their ways and their deeds I judged them. 20But when they came to the nations, wherever they came, they profaned my holy name, in that people said of them, 'These are the people of the LORD, and yet they had to go out of his land.' 21But I had concern for my holy name, which the house of Israel had profaned among the nations to which they came.

I Will Put My Spirit Within You

22"Therefore say to the house of Israel, Thus says the Lord GOD: It is not for your sake, O house of Israel, that I am about to act, but for the sake of my holy name, which you have profaned among the nations to which you came. 23And I will vindicate the holiness of my great name, which has been profaned among the nations, and which you have profaned among them. And the nations will know that I am the LORD, declares the Lord GOD, when through you I vindicate my holiness before their eyes. 24I will take you from the nations and gather you from all the countries and bring you into your own land. 25I will sprinkle clean water on you, and you shall be clean from all your uncleannesses, and from all your idols I will cleanse you. 26And I will give you a new heart, and a new spirit I will put within you. And I will remove the heart of stone from your flesh and give you a heart of flesh. 27And I will put my Spirit within you, and cause you to walk in my statutes and be careful to obey my rules.[1] 28You shall dwell in the land that I gave to your fathers, and you shall be my people, and I will be your God. 29And I will deliver you from all your uncleannesses. And I will summon the grain and make it abundant and lay no famine upon you. 30I will make the fruit of the tree and the increase of the field abundant, that you may never again suffer the disgrace of famine among the nations. 31Then you will remember your evil ways, and your deeds that were not good, and you will loathe yourselves for your iniquities and your abominations. 32It is not for your sake that I will act, declares the Lord GOD; let that be known to you. Be ashamed and confounded for your ways, O house of Israel.

33"Thus says the Lord GOD: On the day that I cleanse you from all your iniquities, I will cause the cities to be inhabited, and the waste places shall be rebuilt. 34And the land that was desolate shall be tilled, instead of being the desolation that it was in the sight of all who passed by. 35And they will say, 'This land that was desolate has become like the garden of Eden, and the waste and

[1]Or *my just decrees*

desolate and ruined cities are now fortified and inhabited.' 36Then the nations that are left all around you shall know that I am the LORD; I have rebuilt the ruined places and replanted that which was desolate. I am the LORD; I have spoken, and I will do it.

37"Thus says the Lord GOD: This also I will let the house of Israel ask me to do for them: to increase their people like a flock. 38Like the flock for sacrifices,[1] like the flock at Jerusalem during her appointed feasts, so shall the waste cities be filled with flocks of people. Then they will know that I am the LORD."

The Valley of Dry Bones

37 The hand of the LORD was upon me, and he brought me out in the Spirit of the LORD and set me down in the middle of the valley;[2] it was full of bones. 2And he led me around among them, and behold, there were very many on the surface of the valley, and behold, they were very dry. 3And he said to me, "Son of man, can these bones live?" And I answered, "O Lord GOD, you know." 4Then he said to me, "Prophesy over these bones, and say to them, O dry bones, hear the word of the LORD. 5Thus says the Lord GOD to these bones: Behold, I will cause breath[3] to enter you, and you shall live. 6And I will lay sinews upon you, and will cause flesh to come upon you, and cover you with skin, and put breath in you, and you shall live, and you shall know that I am the LORD."

7So I prophesied as I was commanded. And as I prophesied, there was a sound, and behold, a rattling,[4] and the bones came together, bone to its bone. 8And I looked, and behold, there were sinews on them, and flesh had come upon them, and skin had covered them. But there was no breath in them. 9Then he said to me, "Prophesy to the breath; prophesy, son of man, and say to the breath, Thus says the Lord GOD: Come from the four winds, O breath, and breathe on these slain, that they may live." 10So I prophesied as he commanded me, and the breath came into them, and they lived and stood on their feet, an exceedingly great army.

11Then he said to me, "Son of man, these bones are the whole house of Israel. Behold, they say, 'Our bones are dried up, and our hope is lost; we are indeed cut off.' 12Therefore prophesy, and say to them, Thus says the Lord GOD: Behold, I will open your graves and raise you from your graves, O my people. And I will bring you into the land of Israel. 13And you shall know that I am the LORD, when I open your graves, and raise you from your graves, O my people. 14And I will put my Spirit within you, and you shall live, and I will place you in your own land. Then you shall know that I am the LORD; I have spoken, and I will do it, declares the LORD."

I Will Be Their God; They Shall Be My People

15The word of the LORD came to me: 16"Son of man, take a stick[5] and write on it, 'For Judah, and the people of Israel associated with him'; then take another stick and write on it, 'For Joseph (the stick of Ephraim) and all the house of Israel associated with him.' 17And join them one to another into one stick, that they may become one in your hand. 18And when your people say to you, 'Will you not tell us what you mean by these?' 19say to them, Thus says the Lord GOD: Behold, I am about to take the stick of Joseph (that is in the hand of Ephraim) and the tribes of Israel associated with him. And I will join with it the stick of Judah,[6] and make them one stick, that they may be one in my hand. 20When the sticks on which you write are in your hand before their eyes, 21then say to them, Thus says the Lord GOD: Behold, I will take the people of Israel from the nations among which they have gone, and will gather them from all around, and bring them to their own land. 22And I will make them one nation in the land, on the mountains of Israel. And one king shall be king over them all, and they shall be no longer two nations,

[1]Hebrew *flock of holy things* [2]Or *plain*; also verse 2 [3]Or *spirit*; also verses 6, 8, 9, 10 [4]Or *an earthquake* (compare 3:12, 13) [5]Or *one piece of wood*; also verses 17, 19, 20 [6]Hebrew *And I will place them on it, the stick of Judah*

HEART TRANSPLANT

God loves to send his message of hope into situations of despair. God was clear that his people's sin broke his heart. As a result of their sin they were sent into exile, many of their children were murdered, their city was overtaken, and their temple was destroyed. In the midst of this hopelessness, God sent a message of hope: he would give his people a new heart, a new start, and most importantly a new spirit (v. 26).

God's people had a fundamental problem: they could not change themselves because they had hearts that were full of sin (Jer 17:9). To change their problem, God was going to have to change their hearts.

God is a heart surgeon of incomparable skill. He does not simply fix a small problem in the hearts of his people; he gives them brand-new spiritual hearts. The problem with the sinful heart is that it is hard and unresponsive to correction and warning. For those who trust in him, God removes that old heart and replaces it with a new one that is soft, tender, and responsive to God's leading and guiding (Eze 36:26). The new heart won't resist in the same way the old one did. The old one was dead, and this new one is alive.

To accompany the new heart, God promises to fill his people with the very Spirit of God (v. 27). In the Old Testament, the Spirit of God would come upon people from time to time, but in the New Testament, because of what Jesus accomplished, the Spirit comes to live in people. The change in how the Spirit would be given under this new covenant would make all the difference. Jesus made this same promise to his people: that his Spirit would live in them and guide them into all truth (Jn 16:12–15).

Jesus made it clear that people speak from the overflow of their hearts (Mt 12:34). God gave his people the Law in order to expose the sinful tendencies of their hearts so that they would cry out to God for help. Jesus gives his people a new heart so that they may finally love him fully and completely. To tell if God's love is reigning in the hearts of his children, one needs only to look at the lives his people are living.

THE VALLEY OF DRY BONES

God can put the pieces back together. God can reassemble what was once beautiful in people's lives, relationships, and circumstances. More importantly, God can put his people's hearts back together. To prove this, God took Ezekiel on an amazing journey around a valley full of dry bones.

God asked Ezekiel a simple question: "Son of man, can these bones live?" (v. 3). When asked to reply, Ezekiel really had to think about it: to deny that the bones could live would mean that Ezekiel doubted God's power; to agree that the bones could live would mean that Ezekiel was embracing a human impossibility. The prophet responded with the safest answer: "O Lord GOD, you know" (v. 3).

Then God gave Ezekiel an unthinkable directive. God told him to prophesy to the bones so that the bones would come to life. It is one thing for God to bring the dead to life; it is quite another thing for God to involve mere mortals in the process. Ezekiel began to speak to the bones, and God worked through Ezekiel's words: The bones started to come back together. Tendons and skin appeared, and Ezekiel marveled as a resurrection took place. At the end of the process, an entire army stood before Ezekiel awaiting God's command. God did this miracle to remind Ezekiel that his word is powerful and effective. God is the Lord, and his promises are powerful and true (vv. 13 – 14).

God's Word has incredible effects; it brings the dead to life. As God's Word is proclaimed, the Spirit of God uses the Word of God to revitalize the people of God. Jesus told his followers that their only hope was to depend on him in every way (Jn 15:5). God's Word always does what he intends: "So shall my word be that goes out from my mouth; it shall not return to me empty, but it shall accomplish that which I purpose, and shall succeed in the thing for which I sent it" (Isa 55:11). God's Word can bring light into darkness and life into dead places. People are encouraged to read and listen to the Word of God to live.

God is building an army to tell the world who he is and what he has done. His army is totally dependent on the Word of God to accomplish the mission of God. When believing in God's ability is hard, Ezekiel 37:1 – 14 is a wonderful reminder of the great things God has done and is capable of doing.

and no longer divided into two kingdoms. 23They shall not defile themselves anymore with their idols and their detestable things, or with any of their transgressions. But I will save them from all the backslidings[1] in which they have sinned, and will cleanse them; and they shall be my people, and I will be their God.

24"My servant David shall be king over them, and they shall all have one shepherd. They shall walk in my rules and be careful to obey my statutes. 25They shall dwell in the land that I gave to my servant Jacob, where your fathers lived. They and their children and their children's children shall dwell there forever, and David my servant shall be their prince forever. 26I will make a covenant of peace with them. It shall be an everlasting covenant with them. And I will set them in their land[2] and multiply them, and will set my sanctuary in their midst forevermore. 27My dwelling place shall be with them, and I will be their God, and they shall be my people. 28Then the nations will know that I am the LORD who sanctifies Israel, when my sanctuary is in their midst forevermore."

Prophecy Against Gog

38 The word of the LORD came to me: 2"Son of man, set your face toward Gog, of the land of Magog, the chief prince of Meshech[3] and Tubal, and prophesy against him 3and say, Thus says the Lord GOD: Behold, I am against you, O Gog, chief prince of Meshech[4] and Tubal. 4And I will turn you about and put hooks into your jaws, and I will bring you out, and all your army, horses and horsemen, all of them clothed in full armor, a great host, all of them with buckler and shield, wielding swords. 5Persia, Cush, and Put are with them, all of them with shield and helmet; 6Gomer and all his hordes; Beth-togarmah from the uttermost parts of the north with all his hordes—many peoples are with you.

7"Be ready and keep ready, you and all your hosts that are assembled about you, and be a guard for them. 8After many days you will be mustered. In the latter years you will go against the land that is restored from war, the land whose people were gathered from many peoples upon the mountains of Israel, which had been a continual waste. Its people were brought out from the peoples and now dwell securely, all of them. 9You will advance, coming on like a storm. You will be like a cloud covering the land, you and all your hordes, and many peoples with you.

10"Thus says the Lord GOD: On that day, thoughts will come into your mind, and you will devise an evil scheme 11and say, 'I will go up against the land of unwalled villages. I will fall upon the quiet people who dwell securely, all of them dwelling without walls, and having no bars or gates,' 12to seize spoil and carry off plunder, to turn your hand against the waste places that are now inhabited, and the people who were gathered from the nations, who have acquired livestock and goods, who dwell at the center of the earth. 13Sheba and Dedan and the merchants of Tarshish and all its leaders[5] will say to you, 'Have you come to seize spoil? Have you assembled your hosts to carry off plunder, to carry away silver and gold, to take away livestock and goods, to seize great spoil?'

14"Therefore, son of man, prophesy, and say to Gog, Thus says the Lord GOD: On that day when my people Israel are dwelling securely, will you not know it? 15You will come from your place out of the uttermost parts of the north, you and many peoples with you, all of them riding on horses, a great host, a mighty army. 16You will come up against my people Israel, like a cloud covering the land. In the latter days I will bring you against my land, that the nations may know me, when through you, O Gog, I vindicate my holiness before their eyes.

17"Thus says the Lord GOD: Are you he of whom I spoke in former days by my servants the prophets of Israel, who in those days prophesied for years that I would bring you against them? 18But on that day, the day that Gog shall come

[1]Many Hebrew manuscripts; other Hebrew manuscripts *dwellings* [2]Hebrew lacks *in their land*
[3]Or *Magog, the prince of Rosh, Meshech* [4]Or *Gog, prince of Rosh, Meshech* [5]Hebrew *young lions*

against the land of Israel, declares the Lord GOD, my wrath will be roused in my anger. 19For in my jealousy and in my blazing wrath I declare, On that day there shall be a great earthquake in the land of Israel. 20The fish of the sea and the birds of the heavens and the beasts of the field and all creeping things that creep on the ground, and all the people who are on the face of the earth, shall quake at my presence. And the mountains shall be thrown down, and the cliffs shall fall, and every wall shall tumble to the ground. 21I will summon a sword against Gog[1] on all my mountains, declares the Lord GOD. Every man's sword will be against his brother. 22With pestilence and bloodshed I will enter into judgment with him, and I will rain upon him and his hordes and the many peoples who are with him torrential rains and hailstones, fire and sulfur. 23So I will show my greatness and my holiness and make myself known in the eyes of many nations. Then they will know that I am the LORD.

39 "And you, son of man, prophesy against Gog and say, Thus says the Lord GOD: Behold, I am against you, O Gog, chief prince of Meshech[2] and Tubal. 2And I will turn you about and drive you forward,[3] and bring you up from the uttermost parts of the north, and lead you against the mountains of Israel. 3Then I will strike your bow from your left hand, and will make your arrows drop out of your right hand. 4You shall fall on the mountains of Israel, you and all your hordes and the peoples who are with you. I will give you to birds of prey of every sort and to the beasts of the field to be devoured. 5You shall fall in the open field, for I have spoken, declares the Lord GOD. 6I will send fire on Magog and on those who dwell securely in the coastlands, and they shall know that I am the LORD.

7"And my holy name I will make known in the midst of my people Israel, and I will not let my holy name be profaned anymore. And the nations shall know that I am the LORD, the Holy One in Israel. 8Behold, it is coming and it will be brought about, declares the Lord GOD. That is the day of which I have spoken.

9"Then those who dwell in the cities of Israel will go out and make fires of the weapons and burn them, shields and bucklers, bow and arrows, clubs[4] and spears; and they will make fires of them for seven years, 10so that they will not need to take wood out of the field or cut down any out of the forests, for they will make their fires of the weapons. They will seize the spoil of those who despoiled them, and plunder those who plundered them, declares the Lord GOD.

11"On that day I will give to Gog a place for burial in Israel, the Valley of the Travelers, east of the sea. It will block the travelers, for there Gog and all his multitude will be buried. It will be called the Valley of Hamon-gog.[5] 12For seven months the house of Israel will be burying them, in order to cleanse the land. 13All the people of the land will bury them, and it will bring them renown on the day that I show my glory, declares the Lord GOD. 14They will set apart men to travel through the land regularly and bury those travelers remaining on the face of the land, so as to cleanse it. At[6] the end of seven months they will make their search. 15And when these travel through the land and anyone sees a human bone, then he shall set up a sign by it, till the buriers have buried it in the Valley of Hamon-gog. 16(Hamonah[7] is also the name of the city.) Thus shall they cleanse the land.

17"As for you, son of man, thus says the Lord GOD: Speak to the birds of every sort and to all beasts of the field: 'Assemble and come, gather from all around to the sacrificial feast that I am preparing for you, a great sacrificial feast on the mountains of Israel, and you shall eat flesh and drink blood. 18You shall eat the flesh of the mighty, and drink the blood of the princes of the earth—of rams, of lambs, and of he-goats, of bulls, all of them fat beasts of Bashan. 19And you shall eat fat till you are filled, and drink blood till you are drunk, at the sacrificial feast that I am preparing for you. 20And you shall be filled at my table with horses and charioteers, with mighty men and all kinds of warriors,' declares the Lord GOD.

[1]Hebrew *against him* [2]Or *Gog, prince of Rosh, Meshech* [3]Or *and drag you along* [4]Or *javelins*
[5]*Hamon-gog* means *the multitude of Gog* [6]Or *Until* [7]*Hamonah* means *multitude*

21“And I will set my glory among the nations, and all the nations shall see my judgment that I have executed, and my hand that I have laid on them. 22The house of Israel shall know that I am the LORD their God, from that day forward. 23And the nations shall know that the house of Israel went into captivity for their iniquity, because they dealt so treacherously with me that I hid my face from them and gave them into the hand of their adversaries, and they all fell by the sword. 24I dealt with them according to their uncleanness and their transgressions, and hid my face from them.

The LORD Will Restore Israel

25“Therefore thus says the Lord GOD: Now I will restore the fortunes of Jacob and have mercy on the whole house of Israel, and I will be jealous for my holy name. 26They shall forget their shame and all the treachery they have practiced against me, when they dwell securely in their land with none to make them afraid, 27when I have brought them back from the peoples and gathered them from their enemies' lands, and through them have vindicated my holiness in the sight of many nations. 28Then they shall know that I am the LORD their God, because I sent them into exile among the nations and then assembled them into their own land. I will leave none of them remaining among the nations anymore. 29And I will not hide my face anymore from them, when I pour out my Spirit upon the house of Israel, declares the Lord GOD.”

Vision of the New Temple

40 In the twenty-fifth year of our exile, at the beginning of the year, on the tenth day of the month, in the fourteenth year after the city was struck down, on that very day, the hand of the LORD was upon me, and he brought me to the city.[1] 2In visions of God he brought me to the land of Israel, and set me down on a very high mountain, on which was a structure like a city to the south. 3When he brought me there, behold, there was a man whose appearance was like bronze, with a linen cord and a measuring reed in his hand. And he was standing in the gateway. 4And the man said to me, “Son of man, look with your eyes, and hear with your ears, and set your heart upon all that I shall show you, for you were brought here in order that I might show it to you. Declare all that you see to the house of Israel.”

The East Gate to the Outer Court

5And behold, there was a wall all around the outside of the temple area, and the length of the measuring reed in the man's hand was six long cubits, each being a cubit and a handbreadth[2] in length. So he measured the thickness of the wall, one reed; and the height, one reed. 6Then he went into the gateway facing east, going up its steps, and measured the threshold of the gate, one reed deep.[3] 7And the side rooms, one reed long and one reed broad; and the space between the side rooms, five cubits; and the threshold of the gate by the vestibule of the gate at the inner end, one reed. 8Then he measured the vestibule of the gateway, on the inside, one reed. 9Then he measured the vestibule of the gateway, eight cubits; and its jambs, two cubits; and the vestibule of the gate was at the inner end. 10And there were three side rooms on either side of the east gate. The three were of the same size, and the jambs on either side were of the same size. 11Then he measured the width of the opening of the gateway, ten cubits; and the length of the gateway, thirteen cubits. 12There was a barrier before the side rooms, one cubit on either side. And the side rooms were six cubits on either side. 13Then he measured the gate from the ceiling of the one side room to the ceiling of the other, a breadth of twenty-five cubits; the openings faced each other. 14He measured also the vestibule, sixty cubits. And around the vestibule of the gateway was the

[1]Hebrew *brought me there* [2]A *cubit* was about 18 inches or 45 centimeters; a *handbreadth* was about 3 inches or 7.5 centimeters [3]Hebrew *deep, and one threshold, one reed deep*

GLORY AMONG THE NATIONS

God's ultimate purpose is to make his glory known in all parts of the earth. God made this promise to Abraham (Ge 12:2 – 3) and has been working for its fulfillment ever since. Here Ezekiel joins the sweeping prophetic voice of Scripture that God is working to make his glory known among all peoples in general and among the people of Israel in particular.

All of this is good news for a book that is filled with so much prophecy about judgment. The Israelites had disobeyed God, and God made it absolutely clear that they would suffer for their disobedience. Yet in the midst of his prophecies of God's judgment against the nations, Ezekiel focused on the wonderful, unexpected outcome: that one day when his glory is revealed to the nations, Israel would know that God is the Lord.

God's desire is for all people to know him and love him. When this does not happen, God's heart breaks. Jesus longed for the people of Jerusalem to know him as well, though he lamented that they were not willing to do so. He said, "O Jerusalem, Jerusalem, the city that kills the prophets and stones those who are sent to it! How often would I have gathered your children together as a hen gathers her brood under her wings, and you were not willing!" (Mt 23:37). God's desire is for all people, including all of Israel, to repent and believe the gospel (Ro 11:25 – 27), though some will refuse to believe.

While we don't know all that God will do in the last days, we know this truth: people are saved when they confess that Jesus is Lord and believe in their hearts that God raised him from the dead (Ro 10:9 – 10). So, in his grace, God plans to do something in the end times that will turn Israel toward Jesus as Lord. And one day people from all nations will surround the throne of God in worship (Rev 15:4; 21:26).

God's church ought to see God's plan for the world, which is clearly revealed in his Word, and join God in his redemptive purposes. The fact that God's throne will be surrounded with representatives from all nations (Rev 5) should propel believers to approach all people with the confidence that they may repent and believe after hearing the good news of the gospel.

court.[1] [15]From the front of the gate at the entrance to the front of the inner vestibule of the gate was fifty cubits. [16]And the gateway had windows all around, narrowing inwards toward the side rooms and toward their jambs, and likewise the vestibule had windows all around inside, and on the jambs were palm trees.

The Outer Court

[17]Then he brought me into the outer court. And behold, there were chambers and a pavement, all around the court. Thirty chambers faced the pavement. [18]And the pavement ran along the side of the gates, corresponding to the length of the gates. This was the lower pavement. [19]Then he measured the distance from the inner front of the lower gate to the outer front of the inner court,[2] a hundred cubits on the east side and on the north side.[3]

The North Gate

[20]As for the gate that faced toward the north, belonging to the outer court, he measured its length and its breadth. [21]Its side rooms, three on either side, and its jambs and its vestibule were of the same size as those of the first gate. Its length was fifty cubits, and its breadth twenty-five cubits. [22]And its windows, its vestibule, and its palm trees were of the same size as those of the gate that faced toward the east. And by seven steps people would go up to it, and find its vestibule before them. [23]And opposite the gate on the north, as on the east, was a gate to the inner court. And he measured from gate to gate, a hundred cubits.

The South Gate

[24]And he led me toward the south, and behold, there was a gate on the south. And he measured its jambs and its vestibule; they had the same size as the others. [25]Both it and its vestibule had windows all around, like the windows of the others. Its length was fifty cubits, and its breadth twenty-five cubits. [26]And there were seven steps leading up to it, and its vestibule was before them, and it had palm trees on its jambs, one on either side. [27]And there was a gate on the south of the inner court. And he measured from gate to gate toward the south, a hundred cubits.

The Inner Court

[28]Then he brought me to the inner court through the south gate, and he measured the south gate. It was of the same size as the others. [29]Its side rooms, its jambs, and its vestibule were of the same size as the others, and both it and its vestibule had windows all around. Its length was fifty cubits, and its breadth twenty-five cubits. [30]And there were vestibules all around, twenty-five cubits long and five cubits broad. [31]Its vestibule faced the outer court, and palm trees were on its jambs, and its stairway had eight steps.

[32]Then he brought me to the inner court on the east side, and he measured the gate. It was of the same size as the others. [33]Its side rooms, its jambs, and its vestibule were of the same size as the others, and both it and its vestibule had windows all around. Its length was fifty cubits, and its breadth twenty-five cubits. [34]Its vestibule faced the outer court, and it had palm trees on its jambs, on either side, and its stairway had eight steps.

[35]Then he brought me to the north gate, and he measured it. It had the same size as the others. [36]Its side rooms, its jambs, and its vestibule were of the same size as the others,[4] and it had windows all around. Its length was fifty cubits, and its breadth twenty-five cubits. [37]Its vestibule[5] faced the outer court, and it had palm trees on its jambs, on either side, and its stairway had eight steps.

---

[1]Text uncertain; Hebrew *And he made the jambs sixty cubits, and to the jamb of the court was the gateway all around* [2]Hebrew *distance from before the low gate before the inner court to the outside* [3]Or *cubits. So far the eastern gate; now to the northern gate* [4]One manuscript (compare verses 29 and 33); most manuscripts lack *were of the same size as the others* [5]Septuagint, Vulgate (compare verses 26, 31, 34); Hebrew *jambs*

38 There was a chamber with its door in the vestibule of the gate,[1] where the
burnt offering was to be washed. 39 And in the vestibule of the gate were two tables
on either side, on which the burnt offering and the sin offering and the guilt offering were to be slaughtered. 40 And off to the side, on the outside as one goes up to
the entrance of the north gate, were two tables; and off to the other side of the vestibule of the gate were two tables. 41 Four tables were on either side of the gate, eight
tables, on which to slaughter. 42 And there were four tables of hewn stone for the
burnt offering, a cubit and a half long, and a cubit and a half broad, and one cubit
high, on which the instruments were to be laid with which the burnt offerings and
the sacrifices were slaughtered. 43 And hooks,[2] a handbreadth long, were fastened
all around within. And on the tables the flesh of the offering was to be laid.

Chambers for the Priests

44 On the outside of the inner gateway there were two chambers[3] in the inner
court, one[4] at the side of the north gate facing south, the other at the side of the
south[5] gate facing north. 45 And he said to me, "This chamber that faces south is
for the priests who have charge of the temple, 46 and the chamber that faces north
is for the priests who have charge of the altar. These are the sons of Zadok, who
alone[6] among the sons of Levi may come near to the LORD to minister to him."
47 And he measured the court, a hundred cubits long and a hundred cubits broad,
a square. And the altar was in front of the temple.

The Vestibule of the Temple

48 Then he brought me to the vestibule of the temple and measured the jambs
of the vestibule, five cubits on either side. And the breadth of the gate was fourteen cubits, and the sidewalls of the gate[7] were three cubits on either side. 49 The
length of the vestibule was twenty cubits, and the breadth twelve[8] cubits, and
people would go up to it by ten steps.[9] And there were pillars beside the jambs,
one on either side.

The Inner Temple

41 Then he brought me to the nave and measured the jambs. On each side six
cubits[10] was the breadth of the jambs.[11] 2 And the breadth of the entrance
was ten cubits, and the sidewalls of the entrance were five cubits on either side.
And he measured the length of the nave,[12] forty cubits, and its breadth, twenty
cubits. 3 Then he went into the inner room and measured the jambs of the entrance, two cubits; and the entrance, six cubits; and the sidewalls on either side[13]
of the entrance, seven cubits. 4 And he measured the length of the room, twenty
cubits, and its breadth, twenty cubits, across the nave. And he said to me, "This
is the Most Holy Place."

5 Then he measured the wall of the temple, six cubits thick, and the breadth
of the side chambers, four cubits, all around the temple. 6 And the side chambers
were in three stories, one over another, thirty in each story. There were offsets[14]
all around the wall of the temple to serve as supports for the side chambers, so
that they should not be supported by the wall of the temple. 7 And it became
broader as it wound upward to the side chambers, because the temple was enclosed upward all around the temple. Thus the temple had a broad area upward,
and so one went up from the lowest story to the top story through the middle
story. 8 I saw also that the temple had a raised platform all around; the foundations
of the side chambers measured a full reed of six long cubits. 9 The thickness of the

EZEKIEL 40:38–43

ONCE AND FOR ALL

No sacrifice before or after Jesus can accomplish salvation. They only point to him, the one true Lamb who takes away sin. Jesus is the one-time sacrifice to make things right forever: "But when Christ had offered for all time a single sacrifice for sins, he sat down at the right hand of God, waiting from that time until his enemies should be made a footstool for his feet. For by a single offering he has perfected for all time those who are being sanctified" (Heb 10:12–14). Throughout all time, Jesus is the Lamb of God who takes away the sin of the world (Jn 1:29). Only through Jesus are all the wrong things made right.

[1] Hebrew *at the jambs, the gates* [2] Or *shelves* [3] Septuagint; Hebrew *were chambers for singers* [4] Hebrew lacks *one* [5] Septuagint; Hebrew *east* [6] Hebrew lacks *alone* [7] Septuagint; Hebrew lacks *was fourteen cubits, and the sidewalls of the gate* [8] Septuagint; Hebrew *eleven* [9] Septuagint; Hebrew *and by steps that would go up to it* [10] A *cubit* was about 18 inches or 45 centimeters; a *long cubit* (see 40:5) was about 21 inches or 53 centimeters [11] Compare Septuagint; Hebrew *tent* [12] Hebrew *its length* [13] Septuagint; Hebrew *and the breadth* [14] Septuagint, compare 1 Kings 6:6; the meaning of the Hebrew word is uncertain

outer wall of the side chambers was five cubits. The free space between the side chambers of the temple 10and the other chambers was a breadth of twenty cubits all around the temple on every side. 11And the doors of the side chambers opened on the free space, one door toward the north, and another door toward the south. And the breadth of the free space was five cubits all around.

12The building that was facing the separate yard on the west side was seventy cubits broad, and the wall of the building was five cubits thick all around, and its length ninety cubits.

13Then he measured the temple, a hundred cubits long; and the yard and the building with its walls, a hundred cubits long; 14also the breadth of the east front of the temple and the yard, a hundred cubits.

15Then he measured the length of the building facing the yard that was at the back and its galleries[1] on either side, a hundred cubits.

The inside of the nave and the vestibules of the court, 16the thresholds and the narrow windows and the galleries all around the three of them, opposite the threshold, were paneled with wood all around, from the floor up to the windows (now the windows were covered), 17to the space above the door, even to the inner room, and on the outside. And on all the walls all around, inside and outside, was a measured pattern.[2] 18It was carved of cherubim and palm trees, a palm tree between cherub and cherub. Every cherub had two faces: 19a human face toward the palm tree on the one side, and the face of a young lion toward the palm tree on the other side. They were carved on the whole temple all around. 20From the floor to above the door, cherubim and palm trees were carved; similarly the wall of the nave.

21The doorposts of the nave were squared, and in front of the Holy Place was something resembling 22an altar of wood, three cubits high, two cubits long, and two cubits broad.[3] Its corners, its base,[4] and its walls were of wood. He said to me, "This is the table that is before the LORD." 23The nave and the Holy Place had each a double door. 24The double doors had two leaves apiece, two swinging leaves for each door. 25And on the doors of the nave were carved cherubim and palm trees, such as were carved on the walls. And there was a canopy[5] of wood in front of the vestibule outside. 26And there were narrow windows and palm trees on either side, on the sidewalls of the vestibule, the side chambers of the temple, and the canopies.

The Temple's Chambers

42 Then he led me out into the outer court, toward the north, and he brought me to the chambers that were opposite the separate yard and opposite the building on the north. 2The length of the building whose door faced north was a hundred cubits,[6] and the breadth fifty cubits. 3Facing the twenty cubits that belonged to the inner court, and facing the pavement that belonged to the outer court, was gallery[7] against gallery in three stories. 4And before the chambers was a passage inward, ten cubits wide and a hundred cubits long,[8] and their doors were on the north. 5Now the upper chambers were narrower, for the galleries took more away from them than from the lower and middle chambers of the building. 6For they were in three stories, and they had no pillars like the pillars of the courts. Thus the upper chambers were set back from the ground more than the lower and the middle ones. 7And there was a wall outside parallel to the chambers, toward the outer court, opposite the chambers, fifty cubits long. 8For the chambers on the outer court were fifty cubits long, while those opposite the nave[9] were a hundred cubits long. 9Below these chambers was an entrance on the east side, as one enters them from the outer court.

10In the thickness of the wall of the court, on the south[10] also, opposite the yard

[1]The meaning of the Hebrew term is uncertain; also verse 16 [2]Hebrew *were measurements* [3]Septuagint; Hebrew lacks *two cubits broad* [4]Septuagint; Hebrew *length* [5]The meaning of the Hebrew word is uncertain; also verse 26 [6]A *cubit* was about 18 inches or 45 centimeters; a *long cubit* (see 40:5) was about 21 inches or 53 centimeters [7]The meaning of the Hebrew word is uncertain; also verse 5 [8]Septuagint, Syriac; Hebrew *and a way of one cubit* [9]Or *temple* [10]Septuagint; Hebrew *east*

and opposite the building, there were chambers 11with a passage in front of them.
They were similar to the chambers on the north, of the same length and breadth,
with the same exits[1] and arrangements and doors, 12as were the entrances of the
chambers on the south. There was an entrance at the beginning of the passage, the
passage before the corresponding wall on the east as one enters them.[2]

13Then he said to me, "The north chambers and the south chambers opposite
the yard are the holy chambers, where the priests who approach the LORD shall eat
the most holy offerings. There they shall put the most holy offerings—the grain
offering, the sin offering, and the guilt offering—for the place is holy. 14When the
priests enter the Holy Place, they shall not go out of it into the outer court without
laying there the garments in which they minister, for these are holy. They shall
put on other garments before they go near to that which is for the people."

15Now when he had finished measuring the interior of the temple area, he
led me out by the gate that faced east, and measured the temple area all around.
16He measured the east side with the measuring reed, 500 cubits by the measuring reed all around. 17He measured the north side, 500 cubits by the measuring
reed all around. 18He measured the south side, 500 cubits by the measuring reed.
19Then he turned to the west side and measured, 500 cubits by the measuring
reed. 20He measured it on the four sides. It had a wall around it, 500 cubits long
and 500 cubits broad, to make a separation between the holy and the common.

The Glory of the LORD Fills the Temple

43 Then he led me to the gate, the gate facing east. 2And behold, the glory of
the God of Israel was coming from the east. And the sound of his coming
was like the sound of many waters, and the earth shone with his glory. 3And the
vision I saw was just like the vision that I had seen when he[3] came to destroy the
city, and just like the vision that I had seen by the Chebar canal. And I fell on my
face. 4As the glory of the LORD entered the temple by the gate facing east, 5the
Spirit lifted me up and brought me into the inner court; and behold, the glory of
the LORD filled the temple.

6While the man was standing beside me, I heard one speaking to me out of the
temple, 7and he said to me, "Son of man, this is the place of my throne and the
place of the soles of my feet, where I will dwell in the midst of the people of Israel
forever. And the house of Israel shall no more defile my holy name, neither they,
nor their kings, by their whoring and by the dead bodies[4] of their kings at their
high places,[5] 8by setting their threshold by my threshold and their doorposts beside my doorposts, with only a wall between me and them. They have defiled my
holy name by their abominations that they have committed, so I have consumed
them in my anger. 9Now let them put away their whoring and the dead bodies of
their kings far from me, and I will dwell in their midst forever.

10"As for you, son of man, describe to the house of Israel the temple, that they
may be ashamed of their iniquities; and they shall measure the plan. 11And if they
are ashamed of all that they have done, make known to them the design of the
temple, its arrangement, its exits and its entrances, that is, its whole design; and
make known to them as well all its statutes and its whole design and all its laws, and
write it down in their sight, so that they may observe all its laws and all its statutes
and carry them out. 12This is the law of the temple: the whole territory on the top
of the mountain all around shall be most holy. Behold, this is the law of the temple.

The Altar

13"These are the measurements of the altar by cubits (the cubit being a cubit
and a handbreadth):[6] its base shall be one cubit high[7] and one cubit broad, with a

EZEKIEL 43:1–12

THE GLORY RETURNS TO THE TEMPLE

The vision of the return of God's glory to the temple is one of the high points of the book of Ezekiel. On its return, the glory of God not only fills the temple, but it even causes the earth itself to shine (v. 2). Without the presence of God at the heart of a community, there can be no life at all; there will simply be a collection of dry bones.

Ezekiel's vision of the return of God's glory is a picture of what must happen before people can be restored. God's presence must arrive for healing to take place. This vision gives readers a picture of the future city of God, when his glory will be revealed and there will be no need for the sun (Rev 22:5); it also points toward the time when God himself would live inside his people and reside in the temples that he has made them to be. In both the present and future, God dwells with his people. By dwelling with them, God will make all things new. He lives within his believers today through his Spirit; he will gather all people who love him to himself one day in the future.

[1]Hebrew *and all their exits* [2]The meaning of the Hebrew verse is uncertain [3]Some Hebrew manuscripts and Vulgate; most Hebrew manuscripts *when I* [4]Or *the monuments*; also verse 9 [5]Or *at their deaths*
[6]A *cubit* was about 18 inches or 45 centimeters; a *handbreadth* was about 3 inches or 7.5 centimeters
[7]Or *its gutter shall be one cubit deep*

rim of one span[1] around its edge. And this shall be the height of the altar: 14from the base on the ground to the lower ledge, two cubits, with a breadth of one cubit; and from the smaller ledge to the larger ledge, four cubits, with a breadth of one cubit; 15and the altar hearth, four cubits; and from the altar hearth projecting upward, four horns. 16The altar hearth shall be square, twelve cubits long by twelve broad. 17The ledge also shall be square, fourteen cubits long by fourteen broad, with a rim around it half a cubit broad, and its base one cubit all around. The steps of the altar shall face east."

18And he said to me, "Son of man, thus says the Lord GOD: These are the ordinances for the altar: On the day when it is erected for offering burnt offerings upon it and for throwing blood against it, 19you shall give to the Levitical priests of the family of Zadok, who draw near to me to minister to me, declares the Lord GOD, a bull from the herd for a sin offering. 20And you shall take some of its blood and put it on the four horns of the altar and on the four corners of the ledge and upon the rim all around. Thus you shall purify the altar and make atonement for it. 21You shall also take the bull of the sin offering, and it shall be burned in the appointed place belonging to the temple, outside the sacred area. 22And on the second day you shall offer a male goat without blemish for a sin offering; and the altar shall be purified, as it was purified with the bull. 23When you have finished purifying it, you shall offer a bull from the herd without blemish and a ram from the flock without blemish. 24You shall present them before the LORD, and the priests shall sprinkle salt on them and offer them up as a burnt offering to the LORD. 25For seven days you shall provide daily a male goat for a sin offering; also, a bull from the herd and a ram from the flock, without blemish, shall be provided. 26Seven days shall they make atonement for the altar and cleanse it, and so consecrate it.[2] 27And when they have completed these days, then from the eighth day onward the priests shall offer on the altar your burnt offerings and your peace offerings, and I will accept you, declares the Lord GOD."

The Gate for the Prince

44 Then he brought me back to the outer gate of the sanctuary, which faces east. And it was shut. 2And the LORD said to me, "This gate shall remain shut; it shall not be opened, and no one shall enter by it, for the LORD, the God of Israel, has entered by it. Therefore it shall remain shut. 3Only the prince may sit in it to eat bread before the LORD. He shall enter by way of the vestibule of the gate, and shall go out by the same way."

4Then he brought me by way of the north gate to the front of the temple, and I looked, and behold, the glory of the LORD filled the temple of the LORD. And I fell on my face. 5And the LORD said to me, "Son of man, mark well, see with your eyes, and hear with your ears all that I shall tell you concerning all the statutes of the temple of the LORD and all its laws. And mark well the entrance to the temple and all the exits from the sanctuary. 6And say to the rebellious house,[3] to the house of Israel, Thus says the Lord GOD: O house of Israel, enough of all your abominations, 7in admitting foreigners, uncircumcised in heart and flesh, to be in my sanctuary, profaning my temple, when you offer to me my food, the fat and the blood. You[4] have broken my covenant, in addition to all your abominations. 8And you have not kept charge of my holy things, but you have set others to keep my charge for you in my sanctuary.

9"Thus says the Lord GOD: No foreigner, uncircumcised in heart and flesh, of all the foreigners who are among the people of Israel, shall enter my sanctuary. 10But the Levites who went far from me, going astray from me after their idols when Israel went astray, shall bear their punishment.[5] 11They shall be ministers in my sanctuary, having oversight at the gates of the temple and ministering in the

[1] A *span* was about 9 inches or 22 centimeters [2] Hebrew *fill its hand* [3] Septuagint; Hebrew lacks *house*
[4] Septuagint, Syriac, Vulgate; Hebrew *They* [5] Or *iniquity*; also verse 12

temple. They shall slaughter the burnt offering and the sacrifice for the people, and they shall stand before the people, to minister to them. 12Because they ministered to them before their idols and became a stumbling block of iniquity to the house of Israel, therefore I have sworn concerning them, declares the Lord GOD, and they shall bear their punishment. 13They shall not come near to me, to serve me as priest, nor come near any of my holy things and the things that are most holy, but they shall bear their shame and the abominations that they have committed. 14Yet I will appoint them to keep charge of the temple, to do all its service and all that is to be done in it.

Rules for Levitical Priests

15"But the Levitical priests, the sons of Zadok, who kept the charge of my sanctuary when the people of Israel went astray from me, shall come near to me to minister to me. And they shall stand before me to offer me the fat and the blood, declares the Lord GOD. 16They shall enter my sanctuary, and they shall approach my table, to minister to me, and they shall keep my charge. 17When they enter the gates of the inner court, they shall wear linen garments. They shall have nothing of wool on them, while they minister at the gates of the inner court, and within. 18They shall have linen turbans on their heads, and linen undergarments around their waists. They shall not bind themselves with anything that causes sweat. 19And when they go out into the outer court to the people, they shall put off the garments in which they have been ministering and lay them in the holy chambers. And they shall put on other garments, lest they transmit holiness to the people with their garments. 20They shall not shave their heads or let their locks grow long; they shall surely trim the hair of their heads. 21No priest shall drink wine when he enters the inner court. 22They shall not marry a widow or a divorced woman, but only virgins of the offspring of the house of Israel, or a widow who is the widow of a priest. 23They shall teach my people the difference between the holy and the common, and show them how to distinguish between the unclean and the clean. 24In a dispute, they shall act as judges, and they shall judge it according to my judgments. They shall keep my laws and my statutes in all my appointed feasts, and they shall keep my Sabbaths holy. 25They shall not defile themselves by going near to a dead person. However, for father or mother, for son or daughter, for brother or unmarried sister they may defile themselves. 26After he[1] has become clean, they shall count seven days for him. 27And on the day that he goes into the Holy Place, into the inner court, to minister in the Holy Place, he shall offer his sin offering, declares the Lord GOD.

28"This shall be their inheritance: I am their inheritance: and you shall give them no possession in Israel; I am their possession. 29They shall eat the grain offering, the sin offering, and the guilt offering, and every devoted thing in Israel shall be theirs. 30And the first of all the firstfruits of all kinds, and every offering of all kinds from all your offerings, shall belong to the priests. You shall also give to the priests the first of your dough, that a blessing may rest on your house. 31The priests shall not eat of anything, whether bird or beast, that has died of itself or is torn by wild animals.

The Holy District

45 "When you allot the land as an inheritance, you shall set apart for the LORD a portion of the land as a holy district, 25,000 cubits[2] long and 20,000[3] cubits broad. It shall be holy throughout its whole extent. 2Of this a square plot of 500 by 500 cubits shall be for the sanctuary, with fifty cubits for an open space around it. 3And from this measured district you shall measure off a section 25,000 cubits long and 10,000 broad, in which shall be the sanctuary, the Most Holy Place. 4It shall be the holy portion of the land. It shall be for the

[1]That is, a priest [2]A *cubit* was about 18 inches or 45 centimeters; a *long cubit* (see 40:5) was about 21 inches or 53 centimeters [3]Septuagint; Hebrew *10,000*

priests, who minister in the sanctuary and approach the LORD to minister to him, and it shall be a place for their houses and a holy place for the sanctuary. 5Another section, 25,000 cubits long and 10,000 cubits broad, shall be for the Levites who minister at the temple, as their possession for cities to live in.[1]

6"Alongside the portion set apart as the holy district you shall assign for the property of the city an area 5,000 cubits broad and 25,000 cubits long. It shall belong to the whole house of Israel.

The Portion for the Prince

7"And to the prince shall belong the land on both sides of the holy district and the property of the city, alongside the holy district and the property of the city, on the west and on the east, corresponding in length to one of the tribal portions, and extending from the western to the eastern boundary 8of the land. It is to be his property in Israel. And my princes shall no more oppress my people, but they shall let the house of Israel have the land according to their tribes.

9"Thus says the Lord GOD: Enough, O princes of Israel! Put away violence and oppression, and execute justice and righteousness. Cease your evictions of my people, declares the Lord GOD.

10"You shall have just balances, a just ephah, and a just bath.[2] 11The ephah and the bath shall be of the same measure, the bath containing one tenth of a homer,[3] and the ephah one tenth of a homer; the homer shall be the standard measure. 12The shekel shall be twenty gerahs;[4] twenty shekels plus twenty-five shekels plus fifteen shekels shall be your mina.[5]

13"This is the offering that you shall make: one sixth of an ephah from each homer of wheat, and one sixth of an ephah from each homer of barley, 14and as the fixed portion of oil, measured in baths, one tenth of a bath from each cor[6] (the cor, like the homer, contains ten baths).[7] 15And one sheep from every flock of two hundred, from the watering places of Israel for grain offering, burnt offering, and peace offerings, to make atonement for them, declares the Lord GOD. 16All the people of the land shall be obliged to give this offering to the prince in Israel. 17It shall be the prince's duty to furnish the burnt offerings, grain offerings, and drink offerings, at the feasts, the new moons, and the Sabbaths, all the appointed feasts of the house of Israel: he shall provide the sin offerings, grain offerings, burnt offerings, and peace offerings, to make atonement on behalf of the house of Israel.

18"Thus says the Lord GOD: In the first month, on the first day of the month, you shall take a bull from the herd without blemish, and purify the sanctuary. 19The priest shall take some of the blood of the sin offering and put it on the doorposts of the temple, the four corners of the ledge of the altar, and the posts of the gate of the inner court. 20You shall do the same on the seventh day of the month for anyone who has sinned through error or ignorance; so you shall make atonement for the temple.

21"In the first month, on the fourteenth day of the month, you shall celebrate the Feast of the Passover, and for seven days unleavened bread shall be eaten. 22On that day the prince shall provide for himself and all the people of the land a young bull for a sin offering. 23And on the seven days of the festival he shall provide as a burnt offering to the LORD seven young bulls and seven rams without blemish, on each of the seven days; and a male goat daily for a sin offering. 24And he shall provide as a grain offering an ephah for each bull, an ephah for each ram, and a hin[8] of oil to each ephah. 25In the seventh month, on the fifteenth day of the month and for the seven days of the feast, he shall make the same provision for sin offerings, burnt offerings, and grain offerings, and for the oil.

---

[1]Septuagint; Hebrew *as their possession, twenty chambers* [2]An *ephah* was about 3/5 of a bushel or 22 liters; a *bath* was about 6 gallons or 22 liters [3]A *homer* was about 6 bushels or 220 liters [4]A *shekel* was about 2/5 ounce or 11 grams; a *gerah* was about 1/50 ounce or 0.6 gram [5]A *mina* was about 1 1/4 pounds or 0.6 kilogram [6]A *cor* was about 6 bushels or 220 liters [7]See Vulgate; Hebrew *(ten baths are a homer, for ten baths are a homer)* [8]A *hin* was about 4 quarts or 3.5 liters

The Prince and the Feasts

46 "Thus says the Lord GOD: The gate of the inner court that faces east shall be shut on the six working days, but on the Sabbath day it shall be opened, and on the day of the new moon it shall be opened. 2The prince shall enter by the vestibule of the gate from outside, and shall take his stand by the post of the gate. The priests shall offer his burnt offering and his peace offerings, and he shall worship at the threshold of the gate. Then he shall go out, but the gate shall not be shut until evening. 3The people of the land shall bow down at the entrance of that gate before the LORD on the Sabbaths and on the new moons. 4The burnt offering that the prince offers to the LORD on the Sabbath day shall be six lambs without blemish and a ram without blemish. 5And the grain offering with the ram shall be an ephah,[1] and the grain offering with the lambs shall be as much as he is able, together with a hin[2] of oil to each ephah. 6On the day of the new moon he shall offer a bull from the herd without blemish, and six lambs and a ram, which shall be without blemish. 7As a grain offering he shall provide an ephah with the bull and an ephah with the ram, and with the lambs as much as he is able, together with a hin of oil to each ephah. 8When the prince enters, he shall enter by the vestibule of the gate, and he shall go out by the same way.

9"When the people of the land come before the LORD at the appointed feasts, he who enters by the north gate to worship shall go out by the south gate, and he who enters by the south gate shall go out by the north gate: no one shall return by way of the gate by which he entered, but each shall go out straight ahead. 10When they enter, the prince shall enter with them, and when they go out, he shall go out.

11"At the feasts and the appointed festivals, the grain offering with a young bull shall be an ephah, and with a ram an ephah, and with the lambs as much as one is able to give, together with a hin of oil to an ephah. 12When the prince provides a freewill offering, either a burnt offering or peace offerings as a freewill offering to the LORD, the gate facing east shall be opened for him. And he shall offer his burnt offering or his peace offerings as he does on the Sabbath day. Then he shall go out, and after he has gone out the gate shall be shut.

13"You shall provide a lamb a year old without blemish for a burnt offering to the LORD daily; morning by morning you shall provide it. 14And you shall provide a grain offering with it morning by morning, one sixth of an ephah, and one third of a hin of oil to moisten the flour, as a grain offering to the LORD. This is a perpetual statute. 15Thus the lamb and the meal offering and the oil shall be provided, morning by morning, for a regular burnt offering.

16"Thus says the Lord GOD: If the prince makes a gift to any of his sons as his inheritance, it shall belong to his sons. It is their property by inheritance. 17But if he makes a gift out of his inheritance to one of his servants, it shall be his to the year of liberty. Then it shall revert to the prince; surely it is his inheritance—it shall belong to his sons. 18The prince shall not take any of the inheritance of the people, thrusting them out of their property. He shall give his sons their inheritance out of his own property, so that none of my people shall be scattered from his property."

Boiling Places for Offerings

19Then he brought me through the entrance, which was at the side of the gate, to the north row of the holy chambers for the priests, and behold, a place was there at the extreme western end of them. 20And he said to me, "This is the place where the priests shall boil the guilt offering and the sin offering, and where they shall bake the grain offering, in order not to bring them out into the outer court and so transmit holiness to the people."

21Then he brought me out to the outer court and led me around to the four corners of the court. And behold, in each corner of the court there was another

[1] An *ephah* was about 3/5 bushel or 22 liters [2] A *hin* was about 4 quarts or 3.5 liters

court— 22in the four corners of the court were small[1] courts, forty cubits[2] long and thirty broad; the four were of the same size. 23On the inside, around each of the four courts was a row of masonry, with hearths made at the bottom of the rows all around. 24Then he said to me, "These are the kitchens where those who minister at the temple shall boil the sacrifices of the people."

Water Flowing from the Temple

47 Then he brought me back to the door of the temple, and behold, water was issuing from below the threshold of the temple toward the east (for the temple faced east). The water was flowing down from below the south end of the threshold of the temple, south of the altar. 2Then he brought me out by way of the north gate and led me around on the outside to the outer gate that faces toward the east; and behold, the water was trickling out on the south side.

3Going on eastward with a measuring line in his hand, the man measured a thousand cubits,[3] and then led me through the water, and it was ankle-deep. 4Again he measured a thousand, and led me through the water, and it was knee-deep. Again he measured a thousand, and led me through the water, and it was waist-deep. 5Again he measured a thousand, and it was a river that I could not pass through, for the water had risen. It was deep enough to swim in, a river that could not be passed through. 6And he said to me, "Son of man, have you seen this?"

Then he led me back to the bank of the river. 7As I went back, I saw on the bank of the river very many trees on the one side and on the other. 8And he said to me, "This water flows toward the eastern region and goes down into the Arabah, and enters the sea;[4] when the water flows into the sea, the water will become fresh.[5] 9And wherever the river goes,[6] every living creature that swarms will live, and there will be very many fish. For this water goes there, that the waters of the sea[7] may become fresh; so everything will live where the river goes. 10Fishermen will stand beside the sea. From Engedi to Eneglaim it will be a place for the spreading of nets. Its fish will be of very many kinds, like the fish of the Great Sea.[8] 11But its swamps and marshes will not become fresh; they are to be left for salt. 12And on the banks, on both sides of the river, there will grow all kinds of trees for food. Their leaves will not wither, nor their fruit fail, but they will bear fresh fruit every month, because the water for them flows from the sanctuary. Their fruit will be for food, and their leaves for healing."

Division of the Land

13Thus says the Lord GOD: "This is the boundary[9] by which you shall divide the land for inheritance among the twelve tribes of Israel. Joseph shall have two portions. 14And you shall divide equally what I swore to give to your fathers. This land shall fall to you as your inheritance.

15"This shall be the boundary of the land: On the north side, from the Great Sea by way of Hethlon to Lebo-hamath, and on to Zedad,[10] 16Berothah, Sibraim (which lies on the border between Damascus and Hamath), as far as Hazer-hatticon, which is on the border of Hauran. 17So the boundary shall run from the sea to Hazar-enan, which is on the northern border of Damascus, with the border of Hamath to the north.[11] This shall be the north side.[12]

18"On the east side, the boundary shall run between Hauran and Damascus; along the Jordan between Gilead and the land of Israel; to the eastern sea and as far as Tamar.[13] This shall be the east side.

EZEKIEL 47:1–12

THE RIVER OF LIFE

The Dead Sea is the saltiest body of water on the planet. It is presently unable to support life of any kind. Ezekiel 47 tells of a wonderful moment that is coming in the future when the Dead Sea will one day teem with all kinds of life. This will happen when God's restoring salvation starts to make its way through every sphere of life.

Ezekiel foretells a time when God's restoring presence will flow out from the temple and into every part of life. The progress of his presence will leave nothing but restoration and new life in its wake. This is pictured as a river flowing from the temple and to the Dead Sea. Much later, the apostle John saw a similar vision. He saw a river flowing from the throne of God. On the banks of this river was the tree of life whose leaves were for the "healing of the nations" (Rev 22:2). Both visions peer into the future in which God's presence and provision for his people are unmistakably central. Jesus likened himself to the river of life when he said, "Everyone who drinks of this water will be thirsty again, but whoever drinks of the water that I will give him will never be thirsty again. The water that I will give him will become in him a spring of water welling up to eternal life" (Jn 4:13–14).

[1]Septuagint, Syriac, Vulgate; the meaning of the Hebrew word is uncertain [2]A *cubit* was about 18 inches or 45 centimeters; a *long cubit* (see 40:5) was about 21 inches or 53 centimeters [3]A *cubit* was about 18 inches or 45 centimeters; a *long cubit* (see 40:5) was about 21 inches or 53 centimeters [4]That is, the Dead Sea [5]Hebrew *will be healed*; also verses 9, 11 [6]Septuagint, Syriac, Vulgate, Targum; Hebrew *the two rivers go* [7]Hebrew lacks *the waters of the sea* [8]That is, the Mediterranean Sea; also verses 15, 19, 20 [9]Probable reading; Hebrew *The valley of the boundary* [10]Septuagint; Hebrew *the entrance of Zedad, Hamath* [11]The meaning of the Hebrew is uncertain [12]Probable reading; Hebrew *and as for the north side* [13]Compare Syriac; Hebrew *to the eastern sea you shall measure*

ALL OF LIFE IS HOLY

Holy places are incredibly important for the world's major religions. For many people, the concept of holy places brings to mind cities, cathedrals, and temples. It would be easy to think of holiness as simply something that happens in such a place, especially when there are so many references to these kinds of "holy places" in the Old Testament.

The description of holy places continues with Ezekiel's vision of the new temple. But despite the fact that holiness has often been attached to certain places, holiness is less about places and more about how God's people ought to live. Jesus' work and teaching redefines everything. Instead of inhabiting a holy temple as the exclusive place of worship, Jesus makes his home in the life of every believer and promises to be with them whenever they get together (Mt 18:20). Instead of people trying to work hard to do good and earn Jesus' acceptance, Jesus' own righteous life is applied to sinners, who only need to look to him in order to be made right with God (2Co 5:17).

Jesus redefines what it means to be holy. All of life is to be holy, no matter where one is. Ezekiel pinpoints some very practical and even mundane aspects of holiness that are all made possible because of Jesus: God's people are supposed to stop the use of violence and oppression (Eze 45:9); they are to conduct their business and entrepreneurial ventures with integrity and trust (45:10 – 12); they are also to live with a sense of purposeful balance, working six days and taking one day to be refreshed and rejuvenated (46:1 – 15).

All of life is meant to be holy. There is nothing wrong with being more reverent in certain places and on certain occasions, but worshiping in particular holy places or undertaking certain rituals to symbolize holiness is no longer necessary for one to be made right with God. Jesus Christ has already provided his people access to the most holy place possible, and he did that by giving his life as a sacrifice for sin (Heb 9:11 – 15). As people who already have unprecedented access to him, God's people are now free to live for God in all of life: "Let us hold fast the confession of our hope without wavering, for he who promised is faithful. And let us consider how to stir up one another to love and good works, not neglecting to meet together, as is the habit of some, but encouraging one another, and all the more as you see the Day drawing near" (Heb 10:23 – 25).

19 "On the south side, it shall run from Tamar as far as the waters of Meribah-kadesh, from there along the Brook of Egypt[1] to the Great Sea. This shall be the south side.

20 "On the west side, the Great Sea shall be the boundary to a point opposite Lebo-hamath. This shall be the west side.

21 "So you shall divide this land among you according to the tribes of Israel. 22 You shall allot it as an inheritance for yourselves and for the sojourners who reside among you and have had children among you. They shall be to you as native-born children of Israel. With you they shall be allotted an inheritance among the tribes of Israel. 23 In whatever tribe the sojourner resides, there you shall assign him his inheritance, declares the Lord God.

48 "These are the names of the tribes: Beginning at the northern extreme, beside the way of Hethlon to Lebo-hamath, as far as Hazar-enan (which is on the northern border of Damascus over against Hamath), and extending[2] from the east side to the west,[3] Dan, one portion. 2 Adjoining the territory of Dan, from the east side to the west, Asher, one portion. 3 Adjoining the territory of Asher, from the east side to the west, Naphtali, one portion. 4 Adjoining the territory of Naphtali, from the east side to the west, Manasseh, one portion. 5 Adjoining the territory of Manasseh, from the east side to the west, Ephraim, one portion. 6 Adjoining the territory of Ephraim, from the east side to the west, Reuben, one portion. 7 Adjoining the territory of Reuben, from the east side to the west, Judah, one portion.

8 "Adjoining the territory of Judah, from the east side to the west, shall be the portion which you shall set apart, 25,000 cubits[4] in breadth, and in length equal to one of the tribal portions, from the east side to the west, with the sanctuary in the midst of it. 9 The portion that you shall set apart for the Lord shall be 25,000 cubits in length, and 20,000[5] in breadth. 10 These shall be the allotments of the holy portion: the priests shall have an allotment measuring 25,000 cubits on the northern side, 10,000 cubits in breadth on the western side, 10,000 in breadth on the eastern side, and 25,000 in length on the southern side, with the sanctuary of the Lord in the midst of it. 11 This shall be for the consecrated priests, the sons of Zadok, who kept my charge, who did not go astray when the people of Israel went astray, as the Levites did. 12 And it shall belong to them as a special portion from the holy portion of the land, a most holy place, adjoining the territory of the Levites. 13 And alongside the territory of the priests, the Levites shall have an allotment 25,000 cubits in length and 10,000 in breadth. The whole length shall be 25,000 cubits and the breadth 20,000.[6] 14 They shall not sell or exchange any of it. They shall not alienate this choice portion of the land, for it is holy to the Lord.

15 "The remainder, 5,000 cubits in breadth and 25,000 in length, shall be for common use for the city, for dwellings and for open country. In the midst of it shall be the city, 16 and these shall be its measurements: the north side 4,500 cubits, the south side 4,500, the east side 4,500, and the west side 4,500. 17 And the city shall have open land: on the north 250 cubits, on the south 250, on the east 250, and on the west 250. 18 The remainder of the length alongside the holy portion shall be 10,000 cubits to the east, and 10,000 to the west, and it shall be alongside the holy portion. Its produce shall be food for the workers of the city. 19 And the workers of the city, from all the tribes of Israel, shall till it. 20 The whole portion that you shall set apart shall be 25,000 cubits square, that is, the holy portion together with the property of the city.

21 "What remains on both sides of the holy portion and of the property of the city shall belong to the prince. Extending from the 25,000 cubits of the holy portion to the east border, and westward from the 25,000 cubits to the west border, parallel to the tribal portions, it shall belong to the prince. The holy portion with

[1] Hebrew lacks *of Egypt* [2] Probable reading; Hebrew *and they shall be his* [3] Septuagint (compare verses 2–8); Hebrew *the east side the west* [4] A *cubit* was about 18 inches or 45 centimeters; a *long cubit* (see 40:5) was about 21 inches or 53 centimeters [5] Compare 45:1; Hebrew *10,000* [6] Septuagint; Hebrew *10,000*

the sanctuary of the temple shall be in its midst. [22]It shall be separate from the property of the Levites and the property of the city, which are in the midst of that which belongs to the prince. The portion of the prince shall lie between the territory of Judah and the territory of Benjamin.

[23]"As for the rest of the tribes: from the east side to the west, Benjamin, one portion. [24]Adjoining the territory of Benjamin, from the east side to the west, Simeon, one portion. [25]Adjoining the territory of Simeon, from the east side to the west, Issachar, one portion. [26]Adjoining the territory of Issachar, from the east side to the west, Zebulun, one portion. [27]Adjoining the territory of Zebulun, from the east side to the west, Gad, one portion. [28]And adjoining the territory of Gad to the south, the boundary shall run from Tamar to the waters of Meribah-kadesh, from there along the Brook of Egypt[1] to the Great Sea.[2] [29]This is the land that you shall allot as an inheritance among the tribes of Israel, and these are their portions, declares the Lord GOD.

The Gates of the City

[30]"These shall be the exits of the city: On the north side, which is to be 4,500 cubits by measure, [31]three gates, the gate of Reuben, the gate of Judah, and the gate of Levi, the gates of the city being named after the tribes of Israel. [32]On the east side, which is to be 4,500 cubits, three gates, the gate of Joseph, the gate of Benjamin, and the gate of Dan. [33]On the south side, which is to be 4,500 cubits by measure, three gates, the gate of Simeon, the gate of Issachar, and the gate of Zebulun. [34]On the west side, which is to be 4,500 cubits, three gates,[3] the gate of Gad, the gate of Asher, and the gate of Naphtali. [35]The circumference of the city shall be 18,000 cubits. And the name of the city from that time on shall be, The LORD Is There."

[1]Hebrew lacks *of Egypt* [2]That is, the Mediterranean Sea [3]One Hebrew manuscript, Syriac (compare Septuagint); most Hebrew manuscripts *their gates three*

EZEKIEL 48:30–35

THE GATES OF THE CITY

From the very beginning, God's plan has been to have a pure and permanent relationship with his people. Ezekiel's final vision is one of the city in which this will happen, and the name of the city is literally "The Lord Is There." The prophet saw 12 gates surrounding the city, representing the 12 tribes of Israel. The apostle John later saw similar gates in his vision of the new Jerusalem (Rev 21:12–14). Both visions foreshadow the physical presence of the Lord in the future, perfect city where God and his people will live in eternal harmony.

Revelation 21:3 summarizes this theme wonderfully, "And I heard a loud voice from the throne saying, 'Behold, the dwelling place of God is with man. He will dwell with them, and they will be his people, and God himself will be with them as their God.'" God has always desired a permanent relationship with his people, and God will have it. Jesus Christ made that relationship with God possible by dying on the cross to remove the sin barrier that separated people from God (Eph 2:13–14). Jesus then secured the presence of God for his people by rising from the dead to bring his people to God (1Pe 3:18).

JESUS: OUR GREAT KING

DANIEL

DANIEL

DANIEL EXILED TO BABYLON	BABYLONIANS DESTROY JERUSALEM	DECREE OF CYRUS ALLOWING JEWS TO RETURN
c. 605 BC	*c. 586 BC*	*c. 538 BC*

The book of Daniel is a unique combination of two types of literature: first, it presents a historical narrative about the people of God in exile in Babylon; second, it details prophetic visions of the coming rule and reign of God. Daniel, a Jewish exile in Babylon, provided an insider's perspective on the plight of God's people during this critical stage in God's mission. As a well-educated Jew and adviser to the Babylonian king Nebuchadnezzar, God used Daniel to model faithfulness in a pagan culture and to testify to God's faithfulness in a time of judgment.

Later, through his influential relationship with the Persian king Cyrus, Daniel was in another unique position. Cyrus had defeated the Babylonians and enacted a number of new policies — one of which was to allow exiled peoples to return to their homelands. Under Cyrus, the Jews returned to their homeland as well to rebuild their capital city and their temple. Perhaps God used Daniel to influence the king so that God's people could return to the promised land and seek to rebuild their life under leaders such as Zerubbabel, Haggai, and Zechariah initially, and later Nehemiah and Ezra.

In his writings, Daniel reminded God's people of two main themes. First, God is in control of all things — even mighty pagan nations are pawns in God's hand. God had used these nations to judge his people, and whenever and however he wanted to, God could restore the fortunes of his people. In due time, God would destroy the other nations; Daniel pictured a coming day when the Babylonian and Persian Empires, as well as others in the distant future, would come to an end. History would continue to see empires rise and fall, all according to God's will and under his control.

Second, Daniel reminded the people that God was faithful and would not forget them. Though they would suffer under these empires for a lengthy period, their time under punishment would one day come to a close. God would preserve his people despite the exile and reestablish them at the time of his choosing.

With Daniel's encouragement, the hope of God's people rested on the fact that God is a great king and is far more powerful than any king of this earth. In Jesus, God will usher in his divine kingdom on earth and invite anyone who will trust in him into the realm of his benevolent rule and reign. In his eternal kingdom, peace will reign forever.

AND IN THE DAYS OF THOSE KINGS THE GOD OF HEAVEN WILL SET UP A KINGDOM THAT SHALL NEVER BE DESTROYED, NOR SHALL THE KINGDOM BE LEFT TO ANOTHER PEOPLE. IT SHALL BREAK IN PIECES ALL THESE KINGDOMS AND BRING THEM TO AN END, AND IT SHALL STAND FOREVER.

Daniel 2:44

DANIEL

Daniel Taken to Babylon

1 In the third year of the reign of Jehoiakim king of Judah, Nebuchadnezzar king of Babylon came to Jerusalem and besieged it. 2And the Lord gave Jehoiakim king of Judah into his hand, with some of the vessels of the house of God. And he brought them to the land of Shinar, to the house of his god, and placed the vessels in the treasury of his god. 3Then the king commanded Ashpenaz, his chief eunuch, to bring some of the people of Israel, both of the royal family[1] and of the nobility, 4youths without blemish, of good appearance and skillful in all wisdom, endowed with knowledge, understanding learning, and competent to stand in the king's palace, and to teach them the literature and language of the Chaldeans. 5The king assigned them a daily portion of the food that the king ate, and of the wine that he drank. They were to be educated for three years, and at the end of that time they were to stand before the king. 6Among these were Daniel, Hananiah, Mishael, and Azariah of the tribe of Judah. 7And the chief of the eunuchs gave them names: Daniel he called Belteshazzar, Hananiah he called Shadrach, Mishael he called Meshach, and Azariah he called Abednego.

Daniel's Faithfulness

8But Daniel resolved that he would not defile himself with the king's food, or with the wine that he drank. Therefore he asked the chief of the eunuchs to allow him not to defile himself. 9And God gave Daniel favor and compassion in the sight of the chief of the eunuchs, 10and the chief of the eunuchs said to Daniel, "I fear my lord the king, who assigned your food and your drink; for why should he see that you were in worse condition than the youths who are of your own age? So you would endanger my head with the king." 11Then Daniel said to the steward whom the chief of the eunuchs had assigned over Daniel, Hananiah, Mishael, and Azariah, 12"Test your servants for ten days; let us be given vegetables to eat and water to drink. 13Then let our appearance and the appearance of the youths who eat the king's food be observed by you, and deal with your servants according to what you see." 14So he listened to them in this matter, and tested them for ten days. 15At the end of ten days it was seen that they were better in appearance and fatter in flesh than all the youths who ate the king's food. 16So the steward took away their food and the wine they were to drink, and gave them vegetables.

17As for these four youths, God gave them learning and skill in all literature and wisdom, and Daniel had understanding in all visions and dreams. 18At the end of the time, when the king had commanded that they should be brought in, the chief of the eunuchs brought them in before Nebuchadnezzar. 19And the king spoke with them, and among all of them none was found like Daniel, Hananiah, Mishael, and Azariah. Therefore they stood before the king. 20And in every matter of wisdom and understanding about which the king inquired of them, he found them ten times better than all the magicians and enchanters that were in all his kingdom. 21And Daniel was there until the first year of King Cyrus.

Nebuchadnezzar's Dream

2 In the second year of the reign of Nebuchadnezzar, Nebuchadnezzar had dreams; his spirit was troubled, and his sleep left him. 2Then the king commanded that the magicians, the enchanters, the sorcerers, and the Chaldeans be summoned to tell the king his dreams. So they came in and stood before the king. 3And the king said to them, "I had a dream, and my spirit is troubled to know the dream." 4Then the Chaldeans said to the king in Aramaic,[2] "O king, live

[1]Hebrew *of the seed of the kingdom* [2]The text from this point to the end of chapter 7 is in Aramaic

forever! Tell your servants the dream, and we will show the interpretation." [5]The
king answered and said to the Chaldeans, "The word from me is firm: if you do
not make known to me the dream and its interpretation, you shall be torn limb
from limb, and your houses shall be laid in ruins. [6]But if you show the dream and
its interpretation, you shall receive from me gifts and rewards and great honor.
Therefore show me the dream and its interpretation." [7]They answered a second
time and said, "Let the king tell his servants the dream, and we will show its interpretation." [8]The king answered and said, "I know with certainty that you are
trying to gain time, because you see that the word from me is firm— [9]if you do
not make the dream known to me, there is but one sentence for you. You have
agreed to speak lying and corrupt words before me till the times change. Therefore tell me the dream, and I shall know that you can show me its interpretation."
[10]The Chaldeans answered the king and said, "There is not a man on earth who
can meet the king's demand, for no great and powerful king has asked such a
thing of any magician or enchanter or Chaldean. [11]The thing that the king asks
is difficult, and no one can show it to the king except the gods, whose dwelling
is not with flesh."

[12]Because of this the king was angry and very furious, and commanded that all
the wise men of Babylon be destroyed. [13]So the decree went out, and the wise men
were about to be killed; and they sought Daniel and his companions, to kill them.
[14]Then Daniel replied with prudence and discretion to Arioch, the captain of the
king's guard, who had gone out to kill the wise men of Babylon. [15]He declared[1] to
Arioch, the king's captain, "Why is the decree of the king so urgent?" Then Arioch
made the matter known to Daniel. [16]And Daniel went in and requested the king to
appoint him a time, that he might show the interpretation to the king.

God Reveals Nebuchadnezzar's Dream

[17]Then Daniel went to his house and made the matter known to Hananiah,
Mishael, and Azariah, his companions, [18]and told them to seek mercy from the
God of heaven concerning this mystery, so that Daniel and his companions might
not be destroyed with the rest of the wise men of Babylon. [19]Then the mystery was
revealed to Daniel in a vision of the night. Then Daniel blessed the God of heaven.
[20]Daniel answered and said:

"Blessed be the name of God forever and ever,
  to whom belong wisdom and might.
21 He changes times and seasons;
  he removes kings and sets up kings;
he gives wisdom to the wise
  and knowledge to those who have understanding;
22 he reveals deep and hidden things;
  he knows what is in the darkness,
  and the light dwells with him.
23 To you, O God of my fathers,
  I give thanks and praise,
for you have given me wisdom and might,
  and have now made known to me what we asked of you,
  for you have made known to us the king's matter."

[24]Therefore Daniel went in to Arioch, whom the king had appointed to destroy
the wise men of Babylon. He went and said thus to him: "Do not destroy the wise
men of Babylon; bring me in before the king, and I will show the king the interpretation."

[25]Then Arioch brought in Daniel before the king in haste and said thus to
him: "I have found among the exiles from Judah a man who will make known

[1]Aramaic *answered and said*; also verse 26

to the king the interpretation." 26The king declared to Daniel, whose name was
Belteshazzar, "Are you able to make known to me the dream that I have seen and
its interpretation?" 27Daniel answered the king and said, "No wise men, enchanters, magicians, or astrologers can show to the king the mystery that the king has
asked, 28but there is a God in heaven who reveals mysteries, and he has made
known to King Nebuchadnezzar what will be in the latter days. Your dream and
the visions of your head as you lay in bed are these: 29To you, O king, as you lay
in bed came thoughts of what would be after this, and he who reveals mysteries
made known to you what is to be. 30But as for me, this mystery has been revealed
to me, not because of any wisdom that I have more than all the living, but in order
that the interpretation may be made known to the king, and that you may know
the thoughts of your mind.

Daniel Interprets the Dream

31"You saw, O king, and behold, a great image. This image, mighty and of exceeding brightness, stood before you, and its appearance was frightening. 32The
head of this image was of fine gold, its chest and arms of silver, its middle and
thighs of bronze, 33its legs of iron, its feet partly of iron and partly of clay. 34As you
looked, a stone was cut out by no human hand, and it struck the image on its feet
of iron and clay, and broke them in pieces. 35Then the iron, the clay, the bronze,
the silver, and the gold, all together were broken in pieces, and became like the
chaff of the summer threshing floors; and the wind carried them away, so that not
a trace of them could be found. But the stone that struck the image became a great
mountain and filled the whole earth.

36"This was the dream. Now we will tell the king its interpretation. 37You,
O king, the king of kings, to whom the God of heaven has given the kingdom,
the power, and the might, and the glory, 38and into whose hand he has given,
wherever they dwell, the children of man, the beasts of the field, and the birds of
the heavens, making you rule over them all—you are the head of gold. 39Another
kingdom inferior to you shall arise after you, and yet a third kingdom of bronze,
which shall rule over all the earth. 40And there shall be a fourth kingdom, strong
as iron, because iron breaks to pieces and shatters all things. And like iron that
crushes, it shall break and crush all these. 41And as you saw the feet and toes,
partly of potter's clay and partly of iron, it shall be a divided kingdom, but some
of the firmness of iron shall be in it, just as you saw iron mixed with the soft clay.
42And as the toes of the feet were partly iron and partly clay, so the kingdom shall
be partly strong and partly brittle. 43As you saw the iron mixed with soft clay, so
they will mix with one another in marriage,[1] but they will not hold together, just
as iron does not mix with clay. 44And in the days of those kings the God of heaven
will set up a kingdom that shall never be destroyed, nor shall the kingdom be left
to another people. It shall break in pieces all these kingdoms and bring them to
an end, and it shall stand forever, 45just as you saw that a stone was cut from a
mountain by no human hand, and that it broke in pieces the iron, the bronze, the
clay, the silver, and the gold. A great God has made known to the king what shall
be after this. The dream is certain, and its interpretation sure."

Daniel Is Promoted

46Then King Nebuchadnezzar fell upon his face and paid homage to Daniel,
and commanded that an offering and incense be offered up to him. 47The king
answered and said to Daniel, "Truly, your God is God of gods and Lord of kings,
and a revealer of mysteries, for you have been able to reveal this mystery." 48Then
the king gave Daniel high honors and many great gifts, and made him ruler over
the whole province of Babylon and chief prefect over all the wise men of Babylon.
49Daniel made a request of the king, and he appointed Shadrach, Meshach, and

[1]Aramaic *by the seed of men*

DANIEL 2:44–45

THE STONE

Daniel interpreted King Nebuchadnezzar's dream about the giant statue (Da 2:31–32). The dream showed what would take place in the future, and Daniel explained that the statue stood for four kingdoms which would succeed one another. Daniel 7 describes another vision that parallels this one. Daniel explains the main point of Nebuchadnezzar's dream: The kingdoms of the world would fall, and the kingdom of God would topple them as God would establish his eternal kingdom.

This vision would have been unthinkable in Daniel's day. The kingdoms of this earth were vast. Surely these kingdoms would stand forever. Yet, God promised that these kingdoms would come to an end. The image of a stone is later used by the apostle Paul to describe the person and work of Jesus (Eph 2:20). He is the cornerstone the builders rejected but is the means by which God will establish his kingdom forever. He has been given the throne of David (Lk 1:32). Jesus taught about the kingdom of God—how the kingdom would start small and seemingly insignificant but grow like the stone of Daniel 2:34–35 (Mt 13:31–32). And Revelation 11:15 promises that the kingdom of the world will "become the kingdom of our Lord and of his Christ, and he shall reign forever and ever."

Abednego over the affairs of the province of Babylon. But Daniel remained at the king's court.

Nebuchadnezzar's Golden Image

3 King Nebuchadnezzar made an image of gold, whose height was sixty cubits[1] and its breadth six cubits. He set it up on the plain of Dura, in the province of Babylon. 2Then King Nebuchadnezzar sent to gather the satraps, the prefects, and the governors, the counselors, the treasurers, the justices, the magistrates, and all the officials of the provinces to come to the dedication of the image that King Nebuchadnezzar had set up. 3Then the satraps, the prefects, and the governors, the counselors, the treasurers, the justices, the magistrates, and all the officials of the provinces gathered for the dedication of the image that King Nebuchadnezzar had set up. And they stood before the image that Nebuchadnezzar had set up. 4And the herald proclaimed aloud, "You are commanded, O peoples, nations, and languages, 5that when you hear the sound of the horn, pipe, lyre, trigon, harp, bagpipe, and every kind of music, you are to fall down and worship the golden image that King Nebuchadnezzar has set up. 6And whoever does not fall down and worship shall immediately be cast into a burning fiery furnace." 7Therefore, as soon as all the peoples heard the sound of the horn, pipe, lyre, trigon, harp, bagpipe, and every kind of music, all the peoples, nations, and languages fell down and worshiped the golden image that King Nebuchadnezzar had set up.

The Fiery Furnace

8Therefore at that time certain Chaldeans came forward and maliciously accused the Jews. 9They declared[2] to King Nebuchadnezzar, "O king, live forever! 10You, O king, have made a decree, that every man who hears the sound of the horn, pipe, lyre, trigon, harp, bagpipe, and every kind of music, shall fall down and worship the golden image. 11And whoever does not fall down and worship shall be cast into a burning fiery furnace. 12There are certain Jews whom you have appointed over the affairs of the province of Babylon: Shadrach, Meshach, and Abednego. These men, O king, pay no attention to you; they do not serve your gods or worship the golden image that you have set up."

13Then Nebuchadnezzar in furious rage commanded that Shadrach, Meshach, and Abednego be brought. So they brought these men before the king. 14Nebuchadnezzar answered and said to them, "Is it true, O Shadrach, Meshach, and Abednego, that you do not serve my gods or worship the golden image that I have set up? 15Now if you are ready when you hear the sound of the horn, pipe, lyre, trigon, harp, bagpipe, and every kind of music, to fall down and worship the image that I have made, well and good.[3] But if you do not worship, you shall immediately be cast into a burning fiery furnace. And who is the god who will deliver you out of my hands?"

16Shadrach, Meshach, and Abednego answered and said to the king, "O Nebuchadnezzar, we have no need to answer you in this matter. 17If this be so, our God whom we serve is able to deliver us from the burning fiery furnace, and he will deliver us out of your hand, O king.[4] 18But if not, be it known to you, O king, that we will not serve your gods or worship the golden image that you have set up."

19Then Nebuchadnezzar was filled with fury, and the expression of his face was changed against Shadrach, Meshach, and Abednego. He ordered the furnace heated seven times more than it was usually heated. 20And he ordered some of the mighty men of his army to bind Shadrach, Meshach, and Abednego, and to cast them into the burning fiery furnace. 21Then these men were bound in their cloaks, their tunics,[5] their hats, and their other garments, and they were thrown

[1]A *cubit* was about 18 inches or 45 centimeters [2]Aramaic *answered and said*; also verses 24, 26
[3]Aramaic lacks *well and good* [4]Or *If our God whom we serve is able to deliver us, he will deliver us from the burning fiery furnace and out of your hand, O king* [5]The meaning of the Aramaic words rendered *cloaks* and *tunics* is uncertain; also verse 27

into the burning fiery furnace. 22Because the king's order was urgent and the furnace overheated, the flame of the fire killed those men who took up Shadrach,
Meshach, and Abednego. 23And these three men, Shadrach, Meshach, and Abednego, fell bound into the burning fiery furnace.

24Then King Nebuchadnezzar was astonished and rose up in haste. He declared to his counselors, "Did we not cast three men bound into the fire?" They
answered and said to the king, "True, O king." 25He answered and said, "But I see
four men unbound, walking in the midst of the fire, and they are not hurt; and the
appearance of the fourth is like a son of the gods."

26Then Nebuchadnezzar came near to the door of the burning fiery furnace;
he declared, "Shadrach, Meshach, and Abednego, servants of the Most High God,
come out, and come here!" Then Shadrach, Meshach, and Abednego came out
from the fire. 27And the satraps, the prefects, the governors, and the king's counselors gathered together and saw that the fire had not had any power over the
bodies of those men. The hair of their heads was not singed, their cloaks were not
harmed, and no smell of fire had come upon them. 28Nebuchadnezzar answered
and said, "Blessed be the God of Shadrach, Meshach, and Abednego, who has sent
his angel and delivered his servants, who trusted in him, and set aside[1] the king's
command, and yielded up their bodies rather than serve and worship any god except their own God. 29Therefore I make a decree: Any people, nation, or language
that speaks anything against the God of Shadrach, Meshach, and Abednego shall
be torn limb from limb, and their houses laid in ruins, for there is no other god
who is able to rescue in this way." 30Then the king promoted Shadrach, Meshach,
and Abednego in the province of Babylon.

Nebuchadnezzar Praises God

4 [2] King Nebuchadnezzar to all peoples, nations, and languages, that dwell in
all the earth: Peace be multiplied to you! 2It has seemed good to me to show
the signs and wonders that the Most High God has done for me.

3 How great are his signs,
  how mighty his wonders!
His kingdom is an everlasting kingdom,
  and his dominion endures from generation to generation.

Nebuchadnezzar's Second Dream

4[3]I, Nebuchadnezzar, was at ease in my house and prospering in my palace. 5I
saw a dream that made me afraid. As I lay in bed the fancies and the visions of my
head alarmed me. 6So I made a decree that all the wise men of Babylon should be
brought before me, that they might make known to me the interpretation of the
dream. 7Then the magicians, the enchanters, the Chaldeans, and the astrologers
came in, and I told them the dream, but they could not make known to me its
interpretation. 8At last Daniel came in before me—he who was named Belteshazzar after the name of my god, and in whom is the spirit of the holy gods[4]—and
I told him the dream, saying, 9"O Belteshazzar, chief of the magicians, because I
know that the spirit of the holy gods is in you and that no mystery is too difficult
for you, tell me the visions of my dream that I saw and their interpretation. 10The
visions of my head as I lay in bed were these: I saw, and behold, a tree in the midst
of the earth, and its height was great. 11The tree grew and became strong, and its
top reached to heaven, and it was visible to the end of the whole earth. 12Its leaves
were beautiful and its fruit abundant, and in it was food for all. The beasts of the
field found shade under it, and the birds of the heavens lived in its branches, and
all flesh was fed from it.

13"I saw in the visions of my head as I lay in bed, and behold, a watcher, a holy

[1]Aramaic *and changed* [2]Ch 3:31 in Aramaic [3]Ch 4:1 in Aramaic [4]Or *Spirit of the holy God*; also verses 9, 18

THE NEW EXODUS AND GREAT COMMISSION

Shadrach, Meshach, and Abednego trusted in the Lord and refused to bow down to the statue King Nebuchadnezzar made. As a result, the king had them thrown into a blazing furnace. It is important to remember the context for this event. The Babylonian exile was not the first time that God's people had been captives in a foreign country. They had been slaves in Egypt, and God miraculously brought them out. Deuteronomy 4:20 describes the exodus in this way: "But the LORD has taken you and brought you out of the iron furnace, out of Egypt, to be a people of his own inheritance, as you are this day." God had rescued his people from a powerful empire and a fiery furnace before, and in Daniel 3 he did it again, which is exactly what these three Hebrews trusted God could do. Amazingly, when the men were thrown into the furnace, the king saw four men instead of three, and the additional man looked like "a son of the gods." Some believe this fourth figure was an angel, while others believe it was a pre-incarnate appearance of Jesus, the second person of the Trinity. Regardless of the exact nature of this person, the words of the prophet Isaiah ring true: "When you pass through the waters, I will be with you … when you walk through fire you shall not be burned, and the flame shall not consume you" (Isa 43:2).

After seeing the men walk out of the furnace unharmed, King Nebuchadnezzar exclaimed that no other god is able to save like this, and that was a true statement. There is no other god who walks through the fire *with* his people. God, through Jesus Christ, took on the suffering and death of his people at the cross to rescue them, ultimately, from suffering and death. Like these three Hebrews, Jesus was held captive under a pagan world empire, Rome. He was handed over to die, and then he emerged from death three days later.

When Jesus emerged from his death, he commissioned his disciples to take the gospel to the ends of the earth because his blood was spilled to redeem people for God from every tribe, language, people, and nation (Rev 5:9; 7:9). In Daniel 3, the pagan king praised the Hebrews' God and prohibited the people of any nation or language from speaking against him. God's deliverance and his message of salvation are always meant to be declared among all nations.

one, came down from heaven. 14He proclaimed aloud and said thus: 'Chop down the tree and lop off its branches, strip off its leaves and scatter its fruit. Let the beasts flee from under it and the birds from its branches. 15But leave the stump of its roots in the earth, bound with a band of iron and bronze, amid the tender grass of the field. Let him be wet with the dew of heaven. Let his portion be with the beasts in the grass of the earth. 16Let his mind be changed from a man's, and let a beast's mind be given to him; and let seven periods of time pass over him. 17The sentence is by the decree of the watchers, the decision by the word of the holy ones, to the end that the living may know that the Most High rules the kingdom of men and gives it to whom he will and sets over it the lowliest of men.' 18This dream I, King Nebuchadnezzar, saw. And you, O Belteshazzar, tell me the interpretation, because all the wise men of my kingdom are not able to make known to me the interpretation, but you are able, for the spirit of the holy gods is in you."

Daniel Interprets the Second Dream

19Then Daniel, whose name was Belteshazzar, was dismayed for a while, and his thoughts alarmed him. The king answered and said, "Belteshazzar, let not the dream or the interpretation alarm you." Belteshazzar answered and said, "My lord, may the dream be for those who hate you and its interpretation for your enemies! 20The tree you saw, which grew and became strong, so that its top reached to heaven, and it was visible to the end of the whole earth, 21whose leaves were beautiful and its fruit abundant, and in which was food for all, under which beasts of the field found shade, and in whose branches the birds of the heavens lived— 22it is you, O king, who have grown and become strong. Your greatness has grown and reaches to heaven, and your dominion to the ends of the earth. 23And because the king saw a watcher, a holy one, coming down from heaven and saying, 'Chop down the tree and destroy it, but leave the stump of its roots in the earth, bound with a band of iron and bronze, in the tender grass of the field, and let him be wet with the dew of heaven, and let his portion be with the beasts of the field, till seven periods of time pass over him,' 24this is the interpretation, O king: It is a decree of the Most High, which has come upon my lord the king, 25that you shall be driven from among men, and your dwelling shall be with the beasts of the field. You shall be made to eat grass like an ox, and you shall be wet with the dew of heaven, and seven periods of time shall pass over you, till you know that the Most High rules the kingdom of men and gives it to whom he will. 26And as it was commanded to leave the stump of the roots of the tree, your kingdom shall be confirmed for you from the time that you know that Heaven rules. 27Therefore, O king, let my counsel be acceptable to you: break off your sins by practicing righteousness, and your iniquities by showing mercy to the oppressed, that there may perhaps be a lengthening of your prosperity."

Nebuchadnezzar's Humiliation

28All this came upon King Nebuchadnezzar. 29At the end of twelve months he was walking on the roof of the royal palace of Babylon, 30and the king answered and said, "Is not this great Babylon, which I have built by my mighty power as a royal residence and for the glory of my majesty?" 31While the words were still in the king's mouth, there fell a voice from heaven, "O King Nebuchadnezzar, to you it is spoken: The kingdom has departed from you, 32and you shall be driven from among men, and your dwelling shall be with the beasts of the field. And you shall be made to eat grass like an ox, and seven periods of time shall pass over you, until you know that the Most High rules the kingdom of men and gives it to whom he will." 33Immediately the word was fulfilled against Nebuchadnezzar. He was driven from among men and ate grass like an ox, and his body was wet with the dew of heaven till his hair grew as long as eagles' feathers, and his nails were like birds' claws.

DANIEL 4:17

GOD IS SOVEREIGN

King Nebuchadnezzar had a dream about a tree that grew and provided food and protection for the whole earth. It was cut down, but the roots were preserved for the future. Inspired by God, Daniel interpreted the dream as being about the king himself. In essence, Daniel says that because of King Nebuchadnezzar's pride in his kingdom and his accomplishments, God would humble him to show that God alone gives power and takes it away. In this act God would show that his kingdom reigns supreme over all. The dream came true when the most powerful man on earth began to crawl on the ground and eat grass like an ox.

Ultimately God determines who is or isn't in positions of authority and influence. The vision of Daniel 7 continued the point that God made here in Daniel 4. The powerful empires of the world (represented by four beasts) would eventually fall, and "one like a son of man" (referring to the Messiah, Jesus) would be given an eternal kingdom (Da 7:13–14). Who is this "one like a son of man"? He is the One who humbled himself and then was exalted (Php 2:8–9). He is the One who receives and transforms the kingdom of the world (Rev 11:15). Daniel 4 encouraged God's people that eventually he would flip the tables on the world's kingdoms and establish his kingdom. This promise was spoken after the fall (Ge 3:15) and began through the choice of Israel as God's people; it blossomed in the person and work of Jesus Christ and will ultimately be fulfilled in the future—in God's perfect timing (1Th 5:2).

Nebuchadnezzar Restored

34At the end of the days I, Nebuchadnezzar, lifted my eyes to heaven, and my
reason returned to me, and I blessed the Most High, and praised and honored him
who lives forever,

for his dominion is an everlasting dominion,
and his kingdom endures from generation to generation;
35 all the inhabitants of the earth are accounted as nothing,
and he does according to his will among the host of heaven
and among the inhabitants of the earth;
and none can stay his hand
or say to him, "What have you done?"

36At the same time my reason returned to me, and for the glory of my kingdom, my
majesty and splendor returned to me. My counselors and my lords sought me, and
I was established in my kingdom, and still more greatness was added to me. 37Now
I, Nebuchadnezzar, praise and extol and honor the King of heaven, for all his works
are right and his ways are just; and those who walk in pride he is able to humble.

The Handwriting on the Wall

5 King Belshazzar made a great feast for a thousand of his lords and drank wine
in front of the thousand.
2Belshazzar, when he tasted the wine, commanded that the vessels of gold and
of silver that Nebuchadnezzar his father[1] had taken out of the temple in Jerusalem
be brought, that the king and his lords, his wives, and his concubines might drink
from them. 3Then they brought in the golden vessels that had been taken out of
the temple, the house of God in Jerusalem, and the king and his lords, his wives,
and his concubines drank from them. 4They drank wine and praised the gods of
gold and silver, bronze, iron, wood, and stone.
5Immediately the fingers of a human hand appeared and wrote on the plaster
of the wall of the king's palace, opposite the lampstand. And the king saw the
hand as it wrote. 6Then the king's color changed, and his thoughts alarmed him;
his limbs gave way, and his knees knocked together. 7The king called loudly to
bring in the enchanters, the Chaldeans, and the astrologers. The king declared[2]
to the wise men of Babylon, "Whoever reads this writing, and shows me its interpretation, shall be clothed with purple and have a chain of gold around his neck
and shall be the third ruler in the kingdom." 8Then all the king's wise men came
in, but they could not read the writing or make known to the king the interpretation. 9Then King Belshazzar was greatly alarmed, and his color changed, and his
lords were perplexed.
10The queen,[3] because of the words of the king and his lords, came into the
banqueting hall, and the queen declared, "O king, live forever! Let not your
thoughts alarm you or your color change. 11There is a man in your kingdom in
whom is the spirit of the holy gods.[4] In the days of your father, light and understanding and wisdom like the wisdom of the gods were found in him, and King
Nebuchadnezzar, your father—your father the king—made him chief of the
magicians, enchanters, Chaldeans, and astrologers, 12because an excellent spirit,
knowledge, and understanding to interpret dreams, explain riddles, and solve
problems were found in this Daniel, whom the king named Belteshazzar. Now let
Daniel be called, and he will show the interpretation."

Daniel Interprets the Handwriting

13Then Daniel was brought in before the king. The king answered and said to
Daniel, "You are that Daniel, one of the exiles of Judah, whom the king my father

[1]Or *predecessor*; also verses 11, 13, 18 [2]Aramaic *answered and said*; also verse 10 [3]Or *queen mother*; twice in this verse [4]Or *Spirit of the holy God*

brought from Judah. 14 I have heard of you that the spirit of the gods[1] is in you, and that light and understanding and excellent wisdom are found in you. 15 Now the wise men, the enchanters, have been brought in before me to read this writing and make known to me its interpretation, but they could not show the interpretation of the matter. 16 But I have heard that you can give interpretations and solve problems. Now if you can read the writing and make known to me its interpretation, you shall be clothed with purple and have a chain of gold around your neck and shall be the third ruler in the kingdom."

17 Then Daniel answered and said before the king, "Let your gifts be for yourself, and give your rewards to another. Nevertheless, I will read the writing to the king and make known to him the interpretation. 18 O king, the Most High God gave Nebuchadnezzar your father kingship and greatness and glory and majesty. 19 And because of the greatness that he gave him, all peoples, nations, and languages trembled and feared before him. Whom he would, he killed, and whom he would, he kept alive; whom he would, he raised up, and whom he would, he humbled. 20 But when his heart was lifted up and his spirit was hardened so that he dealt proudly, he was brought down from his kingly throne, and his glory was taken from him. 21 He was driven from among the children of mankind, and his mind was made like that of a beast, and his dwelling was with the wild donkeys. He was fed grass like an ox, and his body was wet with the dew of heaven, until he knew that the Most High God rules the kingdom of mankind and sets over it whom he will. 22 And you his son,[2] Belshazzar, have not humbled your heart, though you knew all this, 23 but you have lifted up yourself against the Lord of heaven. And the vessels of his house have been brought in before you, and you and your lords, your wives, and your concubines have drunk wine from them. And you have praised the gods of silver and gold, of bronze, iron, wood, and stone, which do not see or hear or know, but the God in whose hand is your breath, and whose are all your ways, you have not honored.

24 "Then from his presence the hand was sent, and this writing was inscribed. 25 And this is the writing that was inscribed: MENE, MENE, TEKEL, and PARSIN. 26 This is the interpretation of the matter: MENE, God has numbered[3] the days of your kingdom and brought it to an end; 27 TEKEL, you have been weighed[4] in the balances and found wanting; 28 PERES, your kingdom is divided and given to the Medes and Persians."[5]

29 Then Belshazzar gave the command, and Daniel was clothed with purple, a chain of gold was put around his neck, and a proclamation was made about him, that he should be the third ruler in the kingdom.

30 That very night Belshazzar the Chaldean king was killed. 31[6] And Darius the Mede received the kingdom, being about sixty-two years old.

Daniel and the Lions' Den

6 It pleased Darius to set over the kingdom 120 satraps, to be throughout the whole kingdom; 2 and over them three high officials, of whom Daniel was one, to whom these satraps should give account, so that the king might suffer no loss. 3 Then this Daniel became distinguished above all the other high officials and satraps, because an excellent spirit was in him. And the king planned to set him over the whole kingdom. 4 Then the high officials and the satraps sought to find a ground for complaint against Daniel with regard to the kingdom, but they could find no ground for complaint or any fault, because he was faithful, and no error or fault was found in him. 5 Then these men said, "We shall not find any ground for complaint against this Daniel unless we find it in connection with the law of his God."

6 Then these high officials and satraps came by agreement[7] to the king and

[1] Or *Spirit of God* [2] Or *successor* [3] *MENE* sounds like the Aramaic for *numbered* [4] *TEKEL* sounds like the Aramaic for *weighed* [5] *PERES* (the singular of *Parsin*) sounds like the Aramaic for *divided* and for *Persia* [6] Ch 6:1 in Aramaic [7] Or *came thronging*; also verses 11, 15

said to him, "O King Darius, live forever! 7All the high officials of the kingdom,
the prefects and the satraps, the counselors and the governors are agreed that
the king should establish an ordinance and enforce an injunction, that whoever
makes petition to any god or man for thirty days, except to you, O king, shall be
cast into the den of lions. 8Now, O king, establish the injunction and sign the
document, so that it cannot be changed, according to the law of the Medes and
the Persians, which cannot be revoked." 9Therefore King Darius signed the document and injunction.

10When Daniel knew that the document had been signed, he went to his
house where he had windows in his upper chamber open toward Jerusalem. He
got down on his knees three times a day and prayed and gave thanks before his
God, as he had done previously. 11Then these men came by agreement and found
Daniel making petition and plea before his God. 12Then they came near and said
before the king, concerning the injunction, "O king! Did you not sign an injunction, that anyone who makes petition to any god or man within thirty days except
to you, O king, shall be cast into the den of lions?" The king answered and said,
"The thing stands fast, according to the law of the Medes and Persians, which
cannot be revoked." 13Then they answered and said before the king, "Daniel, who
is one of the exiles from Judah, pays no attention to you, O king, or the injunction
you have signed, but makes his petition three times a day."

14Then the king, when he heard these words, was much distressed and set
his mind to deliver Daniel. And he labored till the sun went down to rescue him.
15Then these men came by agreement to the king and said to the king, "Know,
O king, that it is a law of the Medes and Persians that no injunction or ordinance
that the king establishes can be changed."

16Then the king commanded, and Daniel was brought and cast into the den of
lions. The king declared[1] to Daniel, "May your God, whom you serve continually,
deliver you!" 17And a stone was brought and laid on the mouth of the den, and the
king sealed it with his own signet and with the signet of his lords, that nothing
might be changed concerning Daniel. 18Then the king went to his palace and spent
the night fasting; no diversions were brought to him, and sleep fled from him.

19Then, at break of day, the king arose and went in haste to the den of lions.
20As he came near to the den where Daniel was, he cried out in a tone of anguish.
The king declared to Daniel, "O Daniel, servant of the living God, has your God,
whom you serve continually, been able to deliver you from the lions?" 21Then
Daniel said to the king, "O king, live forever! 22My God sent his angel and shut the
lions' mouths, and they have not harmed me, because I was found blameless before him; and also before you, O king, I have done no harm." 23Then the king was
exceedingly glad, and commanded that Daniel be taken up out of the den. So Daniel was taken up out of the den, and no kind of harm was found on him, because
he had trusted in his God. 24And the king commanded, and those men who had
maliciously accused Daniel were brought and cast into the den of lions—they,
their children, and their wives. And before they reached the bottom of the den,
the lions overpowered them and broke all their bones in pieces.

25Then King Darius wrote to all the peoples, nations, and languages that dwell
in all the earth: "Peace be multiplied to you. 26I make a decree, that in all my royal
dominion people are to tremble and fear before the God of Daniel,

for he is the living God,
  enduring forever;
his kingdom shall never be destroyed,
  and his dominion shall be to the end.
27 He delivers and rescues;
  he works signs and wonders
  in heaven and on earth,

[1]Aramaic *answered and said*; also verse 20

DANIEL 6:17–23

THE STONE AND THE PIT

When the Medo-Persian Empire toppled the Babylonian Empire and King Darius reigned, Daniel—who had served under Babylon's defeated King Nebuchadnezzar—rose in the government ranks, which made other officials jealous. Their devious plot to bolster the king's self-image and entrap Daniel is well known—as is their fate when God intervened to save Daniel from the lions.

This episode points to Jesus. Like Daniel, Jesus was unjustly condemned by his enemies. The pagan ruler, Pontius Pilate, though he knew Jesus was innocent, agreed to send him to his death. He was placed in a pit—a tomb—and had a sealed stone rolled over it. Both rose victoriously from the pit; however, Daniel didn't experience death, but Jesus did. Daniel didn't defeat death in his own power, but Jesus did. Daniel and Jesus were both faithful to God, but Jesus conquered death so that all believers can have victory over sin and death through him.

he who has saved Daniel
from the power of the lions."

28So this Daniel prospered during the reign of Darius and the reign of Cyrus
the Persian.

Daniel's Vision of the Four Beasts

7 In the first year of Belshazzar king of Babylon, Daniel saw a dream and visions of his head as he lay in his bed. Then he wrote down the dream and told
the sum of the matter. 2Daniel declared,[1] "I saw in my vision by night, and behold,
the four winds of heaven were stirring up the great sea. 3And four great beasts
came up out of the sea, different from one another. 4The first was like a lion and
had eagles' wings. Then as I looked its wings were plucked off, and it was lifted
up from the ground and made to stand on two feet like a man, and the mind of
a man was given to it. 5And behold, another beast, a second one, like a bear. It
was raised up on one side. It had three ribs in its mouth between its teeth; and
it was told, 'Arise, devour much flesh.' 6After this I looked, and behold, another,
like a leopard, with four wings of a bird on its back. And the beast had four heads,
and dominion was given to it. 7After this I saw in the night visions, and behold,
a fourth beast, terrifying and dreadful and exceedingly strong. It had great iron
teeth; it devoured and broke in pieces and stamped what was left with its feet.
It was different from all the beasts that were before it, and it had ten horns. 8I
considered the horns, and behold, there came up among them another horn,
a little one, before which three of the first horns were plucked up by the roots.
And behold, in this horn were eyes like the eyes of a man, and a mouth speaking
great things.

The Ancient of Days Reigns

9"As I looked,
thrones were placed,
and the Ancient of Days took his seat;
his clothing was white as snow,
and the hair of his head like pure wool;
his throne was fiery flames;
its wheels were burning fire.
10 A stream of fire issued
and came out from before him;
a thousand thousands served him,
and ten thousand times ten thousand stood before him;
the court sat in judgment,
and the books were opened.

11"I looked then because of the sound of the great words that the horn was
speaking. And as I looked, the beast was killed, and its body destroyed and given
over to be burned with fire. 12As for the rest of the beasts, their dominion was
taken away, but their lives were prolonged for a season and a time.

The Son of Man Is Given Dominion

13"I saw in the night visions,

and behold, with the clouds of heaven
there came one like a son of man,
and he came to the Ancient of Days
and was presented before him.
14 And to him was given dominion
and glory and a kingdom,

[1] Aramaic *answered and said*

DANIEL 7:13–14

SON OF MAN

The promise of Daniel 7 is that "one like a son of man" will come with the clouds of heaven and be given authority. People speaking every language on the planet will worship him, and his kingdom will last forever.

While Jesus walked the earth, he repeatedly called himself "Son of Man" (Mk 2:27–28; 9:11–13; 10:45; Lk 9:58), a title used at least 29 times in the Gospel of Matthew alone. At his trial, Jesus alluded to Daniel 7:13 to identify himself as the Son of Man: "You will see the Son of Man seated at the right hand of Power, and coming with the clouds of heaven" (Mk 14:62). Stephen saw this at his martyrdom and proclaimed, "Behold, I see the heavens opened, and the Son of Man standing at the right hand of God" (Ac 7:56). And this promise will be fulfilled when Jesus returns at the end of the age to establish his eternal kingdom, which will be made up of people from every nation and language on the earth (Rev 7:9).

BEASTS FROM THE SEA

Daniel's prophetic vision was of four beasts coming out of the sea, which stand symbolically for pagan kings or kingdoms. Who were they? Since the visions and dreams of Daniel 2, 7, and 8 are parallel, three of the four beasts were actually named in Daniel.

The first beast was Babylon, as named by Daniel when he said to Nebuchadnezzar, "You are the head of gold" (2:38). The second beast was the Medo-Persian Empire, which was made clear in Daniel 8:20: "The ram that you saw with the two horns, these are the kings of Media and Persia." The third beast was the Greek Empire, which was named in Daniel 8:21: "The goat is the king of Greece." The reader can surmise that the shaggy goat is parallel to the third beast in the vision of Daniel 7:6, which was a leopard with four heads, because the shaggy goat had a "horn that was broken, in place of which four others arose" (8:22). When Alexander the Great — the king who spread Greek culture across the known world in the fourth century BC — died, his kingdom broke into four kingdoms. The fourth beast was not named in the book, but it appears to symbolize every evil empire that would succeed these others, beginning with the Roman Empire and continuing until the antichrist's final empire. In the end, the good news of the gospel is that Jesus will defeat evil and rule over an eternal kingdom (Rev 19:19–21).

Daniel demonstrates that the greatest kingdoms on earth are no match for the sovereign King of the universe. All earthly kingdoms will crumble. History has already testified to this reality as numerous mighty kingdoms have collapsed already. The same will ultimately be true for all earthly kingdoms. Only one kingdom will last in the end — the great and glorious kingdom of our God and Savior, Jesus Christ.

that all peoples, nations, and languages
should serve him;
his dominion is an everlasting dominion,
which shall not pass away,
and his kingdom one
that shall not be destroyed.

Daniel's Vision Interpreted

15"As for me, Daniel, my spirit within me[1] was anxious, and the visions of my
head alarmed me. 16I approached one of those who stood there and asked him the
truth concerning all this. So he told me and made known to me the interpretation
of the things. 17'These four great beasts are four kings who shall arise out of the
earth. 18But the saints of the Most High shall receive the kingdom and possess the
kingdom forever, forever and ever.'

19"Then I desired to know the truth about the fourth beast, which was different from all the rest, exceedingly terrifying, with its teeth of iron and claws
of bronze, and which devoured and broke in pieces and stamped what was left
with its feet, 20and about the ten horns that were on its head, and the other horn
that came up and before which three of them fell, the horn that had eyes and a
mouth that spoke great things, and that seemed greater than its companions. 21As
I looked, this horn made war with the saints and prevailed over them, 22until the
Ancient of Days came, and judgment was given for the saints of the Most High,
and the time came when the saints possessed the kingdom.

23"Thus he said: 'As for the fourth beast,

there shall be a fourth kingdom on earth,
which shall be different from all the kingdoms,
and it shall devour the whole earth,
and trample it down, and break it to pieces.
24 As for the ten horns,
out of this kingdom ten kings shall arise,
and another shall arise after them;
he shall be different from the former ones,
and shall put down three kings.
25 He shall speak words against the Most High,
and shall wear out the saints of the Most High,
and shall think to change the times and the law;
and they shall be given into his hand
for a time, times, and half a time.
26 But the court shall sit in judgment,
and his dominion shall be taken away,
to be consumed and destroyed to the end.
27 And the kingdom and the dominion
and the greatness of the kingdoms under the whole heaven
shall be given to the people of the saints of the Most High;
his kingdom shall be an everlasting kingdom,
and all dominions shall serve and obey him.'[2]

28"Here is the end of the matter. As for me, Daniel, my thoughts greatly
alarmed me, and my color changed, but I kept the matter in my heart."

Daniel's Vision of the Ram and the Goat

8 In the third year of the reign of King Belshazzar a vision appeared to me, Daniel, after that which appeared to me at the first. 2And I saw in the vision; and
when I saw, I was in Susa the citadel, which is in the province of Elam. And I saw

[1]Aramaic *within its sheath* [2]Or *their kingdom shall be an everlasting kingdom, and all dominions shall serve and obey them*

in the vision, and I was at the Ulai canal. [3]I raised my eyes and saw, and behold,
a ram standing on the bank of the canal. It had two horns, and both horns were
high, but one was higher than the other, and the higher one came up last. [4]I saw
the ram charging westward and northward and southward. No beast could stand
before him, and there was no one who could rescue from his power. He did as he
pleased and became great.

[5]As I was considering, behold, a male goat came from the west across the face
of the whole earth, without touching the ground. And the goat had a conspicuous
horn between his eyes. [6]He came to the ram with the two horns, which I had seen
standing on the bank of the canal, and he ran at him in his powerful wrath. [7]I saw
him come close to the ram, and he was enraged against him and struck the ram
and broke his two horns. And the ram had no power to stand before him, but he
cast him down to the ground and trampled on him. And there was no one who
could rescue the ram from his power. [8]Then the goat became exceedingly great,
but when he was strong, the great horn was broken, and instead of it there came
up four conspicuous horns toward the four winds of heaven.

[9]Out of one of them came a little horn, which grew exceedingly great toward
the south, toward the east, and toward the glorious land. [10]It grew great, even to
the host of heaven. And some of the host and some[1] of the stars it threw down
to the ground and trampled on them. [11]It became great, even as great as the
Prince of the host. And the regular burnt offering was taken away from him, and
the place of his sanctuary was overthrown. [12]And a host will be given over to it
together with the regular burnt offering because of transgression,[2] and it will
throw truth to the ground, and it will act and prosper. [13]Then I heard a holy one
speaking, and another holy one said to the one who spoke, "For how long is the
vision concerning the regular burnt offering, the transgression that makes desolate, and the giving over of the sanctuary and host to be trampled underfoot?"
[14]And he said to me,[3] "For 2,300 evenings and mornings. Then the sanctuary
shall be restored to its rightful state."

The Interpretation of the Vision

[15]When I, Daniel, had seen the vision, I sought to understand it. And behold,
there stood before me one having the appearance of a man. [16]And I heard a man's
voice between the banks of the Ulai, and it called, "Gabriel, make this man understand the vision." [17]So he came near where I stood. And when he came, I was
frightened and fell on my face. But he said to me, "Understand, O son of man, that
the vision is for the time of the end."

[18]And when he had spoken to me, I fell into a deep sleep with my face to the
ground. But he touched me and made me stand up. [19]He said, "Behold, I will make
known to you what shall be at the latter end of the indignation, for it refers to
the appointed time of the end. [20]As for the ram that you saw with the two horns,
these are the kings of Media and Persia. [21]And the goat[4] is the king of Greece.
And the great horn between his eyes is the first king. [22]As for the horn that was
broken, in place of which four others arose, four kingdoms shall arise from his[5]
nation, but not with his power. [23]And at the latter end of their kingdom, when the
transgressors have reached their limit, a king of bold face, one who understands
riddles, shall arise. [24]His power shall be great—but not by his own power; and he
shall cause fearful destruction and shall succeed in what he does, and destroy
mighty men and the people who are the saints. [25]By his cunning he shall make
deceit prosper under his hand, and in his own mind he shall become great. Without warning he shall destroy many. And he shall even rise up against the Prince
of princes, and he shall be broken—but by no human hand. [26]The vision of the
evenings and the mornings that has been told is true, but seal up the vision, for it
refers to many days from now."

[1]Or *host, that is, some* [2]Or *in an act of rebellion* [3]Hebrew; Septuagint, Theodotion, Vulgate *to him*
[4]Or *the shaggy goat* [5]Theodotion, Septuagint, Vulgate; Hebrew *a*

27And I, Daniel, was overcome and lay sick for some days. Then I rose and went about the king's business, but I was appalled by the vision and did not understand it.

Daniel's Prayer for His People

9 In the first year of Darius the son of Ahasuerus, by descent a Mede, who was made king over the realm of the Chaldeans— 2in the first year of his reign, I, Daniel, perceived in the books the number of years that, according to the word of the LORD to Jeremiah the prophet, must pass before the end of the desolations of Jerusalem, namely, seventy years.

3Then I turned my face to the Lord God, seeking him by prayer and pleas for mercy with fasting and sackcloth and ashes. 4I prayed to the LORD my God and made confession, saying, "O Lord, the great and awesome God, who keeps covenant and steadfast love with those who love him and keep his commandments, 5we have sinned and done wrong and acted wickedly and rebelled, turning aside from your commandments and rules. 6We have not listened to your servants the prophets, who spoke in your name to our kings, our princes, and our fathers, and to all the people of the land. 7To you, O Lord, belongs righteousness, but to us open shame, as at this day, to the men of Judah, to the inhabitants of Jerusalem, and to all Israel, those who are near and those who are far away, in all the lands to which you have driven them, because of the treachery that they have committed against you. 8To us, O LORD, belongs open shame, to our kings, to our princes, and to our fathers, because we have sinned against you. 9To the Lord our God belong mercy and forgiveness, for we have rebelled against him 10and have not obeyed the voice of the LORD our God by walking in his laws, which he set before us by his servants the prophets. 11All Israel has transgressed your law and turned aside, refusing to obey your voice. And the curse and oath that are written in the Law of Moses the servant of God have been poured out upon us, because we have sinned against him. 12He has confirmed his words, which he spoke against us and against our rulers who ruled us,[1] by bringing upon us a great calamity. For under the whole heaven there has not been done anything like what has been done against Jerusalem. 13As it is written in the Law of Moses, all this calamity has come upon us; yet we have not entreated the favor of the LORD our God, turning from our iniquities and gaining insight by your truth. 14Therefore the LORD has kept ready the calamity and has brought it upon us, for the LORD our God is righteous in all the works that he has done, and we have not obeyed his voice. 15And now, O Lord our God, who brought your people out of the land of Egypt with a mighty hand, and have made a name for yourself, as at this day, we have sinned, we have done wickedly.

16"O Lord, according to all your righteous acts, let your anger and your wrath turn away from your city Jerusalem, your holy hill, because for our sins, and for the iniquities of our fathers, Jerusalem and your people have become a byword among all who are around us. 17Now therefore, O our God, listen to the prayer of your servant and to his pleas for mercy, and for your own sake, O Lord,[2] make your face to shine upon your sanctuary, which is desolate. 18O my God, incline your ear and hear. Open your eyes and see our desolations, and the city that is called by your name. For we do not present our pleas before you because of our righteousness, but because of your great mercy. 19O Lord, hear; O Lord, forgive. O Lord, pay attention and act. Delay not, for your own sake, O my God, because your city and your people are called by your name."

Gabriel Brings an Answer

20While I was speaking and praying, confessing my sin and the sin of my people Israel, and presenting my plea before the LORD my God for the holy hill of my

[1]Or *our judges who judged us* [2]Hebrew *for the Lord's sake*

God, 21 while I was speaking in prayer, the man Gabriel, whom I had seen in the
vision at the first, came to me in swift flight at the time of the evening sacrifice.
22 He made me understand, speaking with me and saying, "O Daniel, I have now
come out to give you insight and understanding. 23 At the beginning of your pleas
for mercy a word went out, and I have come to tell it to you, for you are greatly
loved. Therefore consider the word and understand the vision.

The Seventy Weeks

24 "Seventy weeks[1] are decreed about your people and your holy city, to finish the transgression, to put an end to sin, and to atone for iniquity, to bring in
everlasting righteousness, to seal both vision and prophet, and to anoint a most
holy place.[2] 25 Know therefore and understand that from the going out of the word
to restore and build Jerusalem to the coming of an anointed one, a prince, there
shall be seven weeks. And for sixty-two weeks it shall be built again[3] with squares
and moat, but in a troubled time. 26 And after the sixty-two weeks, an anointed
one shall be cut off and shall have nothing. And the people of the prince who is
to come shall destroy the city and the sanctuary. Its[4] end shall come with a flood,
and to the end there shall be war. Desolations are decreed. 27 And he shall make
a strong covenant with many for one week,[5] and for half of the week he shall put
an end to sacrifice and offering. And on the wing of abominations shall come one
who makes desolate, until the decreed end is poured out on the desolator."

Daniel's Terrifying Vision of a Man

10 In the third year of Cyrus king of Persia a word was revealed to Daniel, who
was named Belteshazzar. And the word was true, and it was a great conflict.[6] And he understood the word and had understanding of the vision.

2 In those days I, Daniel, was mourning for three weeks. 3 I ate no delicacies,
no meat or wine entered my mouth, nor did I anoint myself at all, for the full
three weeks. 4 On the twenty-fourth day of the first month, as I was standing on
the bank of the great river (that is, the Tigris) 5 I lifted up my eyes and looked,
and behold, a man clothed in linen, with a belt of fine gold from Uphaz around
his waist. 6 His body was like beryl, his face like the appearance of lightning, his
eyes like flaming torches, his arms and legs like the gleam of burnished bronze,
and the sound of his words like the sound of a multitude. 7 And I, Daniel, alone
saw the vision, for the men who were with me did not see the vision, but a great
trembling fell upon them, and they fled to hide themselves. 8 So I was left alone
and saw this great vision, and no strength was left in me. My radiant appearance
was fearfully changed,[7] and I retained no strength. 9 Then I heard the sound of his
words, and as I heard the sound of his words, I fell on my face in deep sleep with
my face to the ground.

10 And behold, a hand touched me and set me trembling on my hands and
knees. 11 And he said to me, "O Daniel, man greatly loved, understand the words
that I speak to you, and stand upright, for now I have been sent to you." And
when he had spoken this word to me, I stood up trembling. 12 Then he said to me,
"Fear not, Daniel, for from the first day that you set your heart to understand
and humbled yourself before your God, your words have been heard, and I have
come because of your words. 13 The prince of the kingdom of Persia withstood me
twenty-one days, but Michael, one of the chief princes, came to help me, for I was
left there with the kings of Persia, 14 and came to make you understand what is to
happen to your people in the latter days. For the vision is for days yet to come."

15 When he had spoken to me according to these words, I turned my face toward the ground and was mute. 16 And behold, one in the likeness of the children
of man touched my lips. Then I opened my mouth and spoke. I said to him who

[1] Or *sevens*; also twice in verse 25 and once in verse 26 [2] Or *thing*, or *one* [3] Or *there shall be seven weeks and sixty-two weeks. It shall be built again* [4] Or *His* [5] Or *seven*; twice in this verse [6] Or *and it was about a great conflict* [7] Hebrew *My splendor was changed to ruin*

DANIEL 9:23–27

SEVENTY SEVENS

When Daniel was reading Jeremiah's writings — specifically 25:11–12 and 29:10 — he realized the exile would only last seventy years (Da 9:2). That realization sparked a prayer of repentance to prepare the Israelites to reenter the promised land. Daniel's prayer prompted God to send Gabriel with a vision to explain more about the exile to Daniel. Gabriel said, "Seventy weeks are decreed about your people." This prophecy is complex, but many scholars agree that the word "weeks" refers to seven-year periods.

While many point to this timeline as predicting the arrival of the Messiah (the "anointed one"), the dates themselves are debatable. What is important to note is that Daniel affirmed that this One will be cut off from his people and have nothing (v. 26). Though he will be the promised provision of God, he would be rejected. Years later, Jesus' death fulfilled this promise as the anointed one was cut off from his people in order to accomplish a far greater exile for sinful humans — making it possible for them to return to God himself.

stood before me, "O my lord, by reason of the vision pains have come upon me, and I retain no strength. 17How can my lord's servant talk with my lord? For now no strength remains in me, and no breath is left in me."

18Again one having the appearance of a man touched me and strengthened me. 19And he said, "O man greatly loved, fear not, peace be with you; be strong and of good courage." And as he spoke to me, I was strengthened and said, "Let my lord speak, for you have strengthened me." 20Then he said, "Do you know why I have come to you? But now I will return to fight against the prince of Persia; and when I go out, behold, the prince of Greece will come. 21But I will tell you what is inscribed in the book of truth: there is none who contends by my side against these except Michael, your prince.

The Kings of the South and the North

11 "And as for me, in the first year of Darius the Mede, I stood up to confirm and strengthen him.

2"And now I will show you the truth. Behold, three more kings shall arise in Persia, and a fourth shall be far richer than all of them. And when he has become strong through his riches, he shall stir up all against the kingdom of Greece. 3Then a mighty king shall arise, who shall rule with great dominion and do as he wills. 4And as soon as he has arisen, his kingdom shall be broken and divided toward the four winds of heaven, but not to his posterity, nor according to the authority with which he ruled, for his kingdom shall be plucked up and go to others besides these.

5"Then the king of the south shall be strong, but one of his princes shall be stronger than he and shall rule, and his authority shall be a great authority. 6After some years they shall make an alliance, and the daughter of the king of the south shall come to the king of the north to make an agreement. But she shall not retain the strength of her arm, and he and his arm shall not endure, but she shall be given up, and her attendants, he who fathered her, and he who supported[1] her in those times.

7"And from a branch from her roots one shall arise in his place. He shall come against the army and enter the fortress of the king of the north, and he shall deal with them and shall prevail. 8He shall also carry off to Egypt their gods with their metal images and their precious vessels of silver and gold, and for some years he shall refrain from attacking the king of the north. 9Then the latter shall come into the realm of the king of the south but shall return to his own land.

10"His sons shall wage war and assemble a multitude of great forces, which shall keep coming and overflow and pass through, and again shall carry the war as far as his fortress. 11Then the king of the south, moved with rage, shall come out and fight against the king of the north. And he shall raise a great multitude, but it shall be given into his hand. 12And when the multitude is taken away, his heart shall be exalted, and he shall cast down tens of thousands, but he shall not prevail. 13For the king of the north shall again raise a multitude, greater than the first. And after some years[2] he shall come on with a great army and abundant supplies.

14"In those times many shall rise against the king of the south, and the violent among your own people shall lift themselves up in order to fulfill the vision, but they shall fail. 15Then the king of the north shall come and throw up siegeworks and take a well-fortified city. And the forces of the south shall not stand, or even his best troops, for there shall be no strength to stand. 16But he who comes against him shall do as he wills, and none shall stand before him. And he shall stand in the glorious land, with destruction in his hand. 17He shall set his face to come with the strength of his whole kingdom, and he shall bring terms of an agreement and perform them. He shall give him the daughter of women to destroy the kingdom,[3] but it shall not stand or be to his advantage. 18Afterward he shall turn his face to

[1]Or *obtained* [2]Hebrew *at the end of the times* [3]Hebrew *her*, or *it*

the coastlands and shall capture many of them, but a commander shall put an end to his insolence. Indeed,[1] he shall turn his insolence back upon him. 19Then he shall turn his face back toward the fortresses of his own land, but he shall stumble and fall, and shall not be found.

20"Then shall arise in his place one who shall send an exactor of tribute for the glory of the kingdom. But within a few days he shall be broken, neither in anger nor in battle. 21In his place shall arise a contemptible person to whom royal majesty has not been given. He shall come in without warning and obtain the kingdom by flatteries. 22Armies shall be utterly swept away before him and broken, even the prince of the covenant. 23And from the time that an alliance is made with him he shall act deceitfully, and he shall become strong with a small people. 24Without warning he shall come into the richest parts[2] of the province, and he shall do what neither his fathers nor his fathers' fathers have done, scattering among them plunder, spoil, and goods. He shall devise plans against strongholds, but only for a time. 25And he shall stir up his power and his heart against the king of the south with a great army. And the king of the south shall wage war with an exceedingly great and mighty army, but he shall not stand, for plots shall be devised against him. 26Even those who eat his food shall break him. His army shall be swept away, and many shall fall down slain. 27And as for the two kings, their hearts shall be bent on doing evil. They shall speak lies at the same table, but to no avail, for the end is yet to be at the time appointed. 28And he shall return to his land with great wealth, but his heart shall be set against the holy covenant. And he shall work his will and return to his own land.

29"At the time appointed he shall return and come into the south, but it shall not be this time as it was before. 30For ships of Kittim shall come against him, and he shall be afraid and withdraw, and shall turn back and be enraged and take action against the holy covenant. He shall turn back and pay attention to those who forsake the holy covenant. 31Forces from him shall appear and profane the temple and fortress, and shall take away the regular burnt offering. And they shall set up the abomination that makes desolate. 32He shall seduce with flattery those who violate the covenant, but the people who know their God shall stand firm and take action. 33And the wise among the people shall make many understand, though for some days they shall stumble by sword and flame, by captivity and plunder. 34When they stumble, they shall receive a little help. And many shall join themselves to them with flattery, 35and some of the wise shall stumble, so that they may be refined, purified, and made white, until the time of the end, for it still awaits the appointed time.

36"And the king shall do as he wills. He shall exalt himself and magnify himself above every god, and shall speak astonishing things against the God of gods. He shall prosper till the indignation is accomplished; for what is decreed shall be done. 37He shall pay no attention to the gods of his fathers, or to the one beloved by women. He shall not pay attention to any other god, for he shall magnify himself above all. 38He shall honor the god of fortresses instead of these. A god whom his fathers did not know he shall honor with gold and silver, with precious stones and costly gifts. 39He shall deal with the strongest fortresses with the help of a foreign god. Those who acknowledge him he shall load with honor. He shall make them rulers over many and shall divide the land for a price.[3]

40"At the time of the end, the king of the south shall attack[4] him, but the king of the north shall rush upon him like a whirlwind, with chariots and horsemen, and with many ships. And he shall come into countries and shall overflow and pass through. 41He shall come into the glorious land. And tens of thousands shall fall, but these shall be delivered out of his hand: Edom and Moab and the main part of the Ammonites. 42He shall stretch out his hand against the countries, and the land of Egypt shall not escape. 43He shall become ruler of the treasures of gold

[1]The meaning of the Hebrew is uncertain [2]Or *among the richest men* [3]Or *land as payment* [4]Hebrew *thrust at*

and of silver, and all the precious things of Egypt, and the Libyans and the Cushites shall follow in his train. 44But news from the east and the north shall alarm him, and he shall go out with great fury to destroy and devote many to destruction. 45And he shall pitch his palatial tents between the sea and the glorious holy mountain. Yet he shall come to his end, with none to help him.

The Time of the End

12 "At that time shall arise Michael, the great prince who has charge of your people. And there shall be a time of trouble, such as never has been since there was a nation till that time. But at that time your people shall be delivered, everyone whose name shall be found written in the book. 2And many of those who sleep in the dust of the earth shall awake, some to everlasting life, and some to shame and everlasting contempt. 3And those who are wise shall shine like the brightness of the sky above;[1] and those who turn many to righteousness, like the stars forever and ever. 4But you, Daniel, shut up the words and seal the book, until the time of the end. Many shall run to and fro, and knowledge shall increase."

5Then I, Daniel, looked, and behold, two others stood, one on this bank of the stream and one on that bank of the stream. 6And someone said to the man clothed in linen, who was above the waters of the stream,[2] "How long shall it be till the end of these wonders?" 7And I heard the man clothed in linen, who was above the waters of the stream; he raised his right hand and his left hand toward heaven and swore by him who lives forever that it would be for a time, times, and half a time, and that when the shattering of the power of the holy people comes to an end all these things would be finished. 8I heard, but I did not understand. Then I said, "O my lord, what shall be the outcome of these things?" 9He said, "Go your way, Daniel, for the words are shut up and sealed until the time of the end. 10Many shall purify themselves and make themselves white and be refined, but the wicked shall act wickedly. And none of the wicked shall understand, but those who are wise shall understand. 11And from the time that the regular burnt offering is taken away and the abomination that makes desolate is set up, there shall be 1,290 days. 12Blessed is he who waits and arrives at the 1,335 days. 13But go your way till the end. And you shall rest and shall stand in your allotted place at the end of the days."

DANIEL 12:1–3

THE RESURRECTION

Daniel 12 looks to the end of the world. The great distress caused by the beastly empires would end as God would judge evil and vindicate the righteous. Some would be raised from the dead to everlasting life and others to everlasting shame.

In the New Testament, God did pour out his final judgment on sin when Jesus submitted by giving his life on the cross so that sinners could be made right with God. And God vindicated Jesus—the only righteous human to ever walk the earth—in his resurrection from the dead.

Paul made this truth clear in 1 Corinthians 15:20–23 when he wrote, "But in fact Christ has been raised from the dead, the firstfruits of those who have fallen asleep. For as by a man came death, by a man has come also the resurrection of the dead. For as in Adam all die, so also in Christ shall all be made alive. But each in his own order: Christ the firstfruits, then at his coming those who belong to Christ."

When Jesus returns to judge the nations, those who are in Christ will be raised to everlasting life. Those who reject Jesus' gracious offer of salvation will be raised to everlasting shame. God's judgment on sin and death has already happened; how each person responds to Jesus' work makes an eternal difference in how each will be regarded by him at the end of this age.

[1]Hebrew *the expanse*; compare Genesis 1:6–8 [2]Or *who was upstream*; also verse 7

JESUS: OUR PURSUING SPOUSE

HOSEA

HOSEA

REIGN OF JEROBOAM II *c. 793 – 753 BC*	PROPHETIC MINISTRY OF HOSEA *c. 753 – 715 BC*	FALL OF ISRAEL *c. 722 BC*

Hosea was the only writing prophet to come from the northern kingdom of Israel, and his messages were primarily directed to that kingdom. Like others before him, Hosea experienced firsthand the challenges that come from being a prophet. God often used the prophets to do more than proclaim the word of God; at times they were also asked to provide living object lessons for the people to see and experience the ramifications of their sin.

Hosea was asked to do just that. At the outset of his ministry, God told Hosea to marry a woman whose adultery God would use to illustrate Israel's spiritual adultery. Hosea obeyed God and took Gomer as his wife. Together they had three children, who each received a name that symbolized the sin of the people. The first child, a son named Jezreel, was a reminder of the calamity that occurred in that city and a foreshadowing of ensuing judgment. The second, a daughter whose name meant "no mercy," forced the people to consider the consequences of God temporarily removing his love from them. The final child, "not my people," foreshadowed the consequences of Israel's sin on their relationship with God.

Throughout the Bible, marriage serves as a tangible picture of God's love for his beloved people. The intimacy, fidelity, and love seen between a husband and wife in a committed marriage are meant to vividly portray God's deep passion for his people. For this reason, adultery paints an equally profound picture of disobedience to God. The unfaithfulness, treachery, and rejection demonstrated through an adulterous and promiscuous relationship highlights the detestable nature of sin.

Hosea's life and ministry were meant to shock the Israelites and awaken them from spiritual adultery before it was too late. Their sin was put on display as they heard from Hosea about his wife's adultery. Israel proved, time and again, to be unfaithful to their covenant commitments to God. As a jealous spouse, God longed for the singular love of his people.

More importantly, however, God demonstrated his faithful love for Israel in Hosea's ongoing pursuit of his wayward bride. Though Israel suffered under God's judgment, God remained loyal to his people. Like a faithful spouse, God continued to demonstrate a faithfulness to his covenant promise regardless of the ongoing adultery of his people. God's love for his people was — and is — not based on their faithfulness, but on his faithfulness to his word. He would never give up on his people, even though his love would come at the cost of his Son. Jesus perfectly and finally pursued, and now claims, his wayward bride.

FOR I DESIRE STEADFAST LOVE AND NOT SACRIFICE,
THE KNOWLEDGE OF GOD RATHER
THAN BURNT OFFERINGS.

Hosea 6:6

HOSEA

1 The word of the LORD that came to Hosea, the son of Beeri, in the days of Uzziah, Jotham, Ahaz, and Hezekiah, kings of Judah, and in the days of Jeroboam
the son of Joash, king of Israel.

Hosea's Wife and Children

2 When the LORD first spoke through Hosea, the LORD said to Hosea, "Go, take
to yourself a wife of whoredom and have children of whoredom, for the land commits great whoredom by forsaking the LORD." 3 So he went and took Gomer, the
daughter of Diblaim, and she conceived and bore him a son.
4 And the LORD said to him, "Call his name Jezreel, for in just a little while I
will punish the house of Jehu for the blood of Jezreel, and I will put an end to the
kingdom of the house of Israel. 5 And on that day I will break the bow of Israel in
the Valley of Jezreel."
6 She conceived again and bore a daughter. And the LORD said to him, "Call her
name No Mercy,[1] for I will no more have mercy on the house of Israel, to forgive
them at all. 7 But I will have mercy on the house of Judah, and I will save them by
the LORD their God. I will not save them by bow or by sword or by war or by horses
or by horsemen."
8 When she had weaned No Mercy, she conceived and bore a son. 9 And the
LORD said, "Call his name Not My People,[2] for you are not my people, and I am
not your God."[3]
10[4] Yet the number of the children of Israel shall be like the sand of the sea,
which cannot be measured or numbered. And in the place where it was said to
them, "You are not my people," it shall be said to them, "Children[5] of the living
God." 11 And the children of Judah and the children of Israel shall be gathered together, and they shall appoint for themselves one head. And they shall go up from
the land, for great shall be the day of Jezreel.

Israel's Unfaithfulness Punished

2 [6] Say to your brothers, "You are my people,"[7] and to your sisters, "You have
received mercy."[8]

2 "Plead with your mother, plead—
for she is not my wife,
and I am not her husband—
that she put away her whoring from her face,
and her adultery from between her breasts;
3 lest I strip her naked
and make her as in the day she was born,
and make her like a wilderness,
and make her like a parched land,
and kill her with thirst.
4 Upon her children also I will have no mercy,
because they are children of whoredom.
5 For their mother has played the whore;
she who conceived them has acted shamefully.
For she said, 'I will go after my lovers,
who give me my bread and my water,
my wool and my flax, my oil and my drink.'

[1] Hebrew *Lo-ruhama*, which means *she has not received mercy* [2] Hebrew *Lo-ammi*, which means *not my people* [3] Hebrew *I am not yours* [4] Ch 2:1 in Hebrew [5] Or *Sons* [6] Ch 2:3 in Hebrew [7] Hebrew *ammi*, which means *my people* [8] Hebrew *ruhama*, which means *she has received mercy*

HOSEA 1:2

AN UNFAITHFUL SPOUSE

The opening chapter of Hosea unveils a clear problem between God and his people: they had been unfaithful. God commanded Hosea to take a wife who would be unfaithful to him. Hosea and Gomer's ensuing relationship symbolized the way the people of Israel had departed from God to pursue the Canaanites' false gods. Hosea was instructed to love Gomer despite her promiscuous actions and knowing she would continue to be unfaithful.

Unfaithfulness is not just a character flaw reserved for the Israelites of the Old Testament; it is a problem for all of humanity. Sin by definition is forsaking God's way and going one's own way, resulting in a broken relationship between humans and God. This is the very foundation of why Jesus came. Isaiah 53:6 beautifully says it this way: "All we like sheep have gone astray; we have turned—every one—to his own way; and the LORD has laid on him the iniquity of us all." With the heart of humanity bent on pursuing false gods, or going "his own way," all people would have been utterly lost and separated from God forever if not for the pursuit of God sending his Son to bring humanity back to himself (1Pe 3:18). Those who believe and follow Christ are invited into the perfect love Christ has for the church, his bride, for whom he gave his life (Eph 5:25–27).

AN OBEDIENT SON

In the Old Testament, God carefully outlined the blessings of obedience and the punishments that would follow in the wake of disobedience (Hos 4:1 – 6). Hosea 1:9 presents a living picture of this principle when God told Hosea to name one of his children Lo-ammi, meaning "not my people." Though Israel was always in covenant relationship with God, their rebellion kept them from experiencing their rights and privileges as dearly loved children. Yet even in their disobedience, God promised restoration (v. 10). Throughout all of Hosea, God is pictured as Israel's steadfast pursuer despite the nation's continued unfaithfulness and rebellion.

The fullness of this illustration was not realized until the coming of Jesus, God's perfect Son, the One who refused to rebel against his Father. Through his perfect obedience and sinless death, he would absorb the wrath rightfully incurred by God's disobedient son, Israel, as well as the whole world. Jesus came from God, and as John 1:1 – 2 notes, he "was God" and "was in the beginning with God." Matthew 2:15 helps us to see Jesus' early exile in Egypt as an infant as the fulfillment of the prophecy from Hosea 11:1: "When Israel was a child, I loved him, and out of Egypt I called my son." Matthew applies to Christ what Hosea spoke about the Israelites in Moses' time.

Through his death and resurrection, Jesus made a way for the deliverance and restoration of the original children of God, the Jews, and of all those outside the nation of Israel as well. This salvation occurs for both groups by believing and trusting Jesus as Savior. Through faith, the promise of Hosea 1:10 applies to believers today: "And in the place where it was said to them, 'You are not my people,' it shall be said to them, 'Children of the living God.' " By trusting and believing in the Son, all people can become children of the living God.

6 Therefore I will hedge up her[1] way with thorns,
and I will build a wall against her,
so that she cannot find her paths.
7 She shall pursue her lovers
but not overtake them,
and she shall seek them
but shall not find them.
Then she shall say,
'I will go and return to my first husband,
for it was better for me then than now.'
8 And she did not know
that it was I who gave her
the grain, the wine, and the oil,
and who lavished on her silver and gold,
which they used for Baal.
9 Therefore I will take back
my grain in its time,
and my wine in its season,
and I will take away my wool and my flax,
which were to cover her nakedness.
10 Now I will uncover her lewdness
in the sight of her lovers,
and no one shall rescue her out of my hand.
11 And I will put an end to all her mirth,
her feasts, her new moons, her Sabbaths,
and all her appointed feasts.
12 And I will lay waste her vines and her fig trees,
of which she said,
'These are my wages,
which my lovers have given me.'
I will make them a forest,
and the beasts of the field shall devour them.
13 And I will punish her for the feast days of the Baals
when she burned offerings to them
and adorned herself with her ring and jewelry,
and went after her lovers
and forgot me, declares the LORD.

The LORD's Mercy on Israel

14 "Therefore, behold, I will allure her,
and bring her into the wilderness,
and speak tenderly to her.
15 And there I will give her her vineyards
and make the Valley of Achor[2] a door of hope.
And there she shall answer as in the days of her youth,
as at the time when she came out of the land of Egypt.

16 "And in that day, declares the LORD, you will call me 'My Husband,' and no
longer will you call me 'My Baal.' 17 For I will remove the names of the Baals from her
mouth, and they shall be remembered by name no more. 18 And I will make for them
a covenant on that day with the beasts of the field, the birds of the heavens, and the
creeping things of the ground. And I will abolish[3] the bow, the sword, and war from
the land, and I will make you lie down in safety. 19 And I will betroth you to me forever. I will betroth you to me in righteousness and in justice, in steadfast love and
in mercy. 20 I will betroth you to me in faithfulness. And you shall know the LORD.

[1]Hebrew *your* [2]*Achor* means *trouble*; compare Joshua 7:26 [3]Hebrew *break*

21 "And in that day I will answer, declares the LORD,
I will answer the heavens,
and they shall answer the earth,
22 and the earth shall answer the grain, the wine, and the oil,
and they shall answer Jezreel,[1]
23 and I will sow her for myself in the land.
And I will have mercy on No Mercy,[2]
and I will say to Not My People,[3] 'You are my people';
and he shall say, 'You are my God.'"

Hosea Redeems His Wife

3 And the LORD said to me, "Go again, love a woman who is loved by another
man and is an adulteress, even as the LORD loves the children of Israel, though
they turn to other gods and love cakes of raisins." 2 So I bought her for fifteen
shekels of silver and a homer and a lethech[4] of barley. 3 And I said to her, "You
must dwell as mine for many days. You shall not play the whore, or belong to
another man; so will I also be to you." 4 For the children of Israel shall dwell many
days without king or prince, without sacrifice or pillar, without ephod or household gods. 5 Afterward the children of Israel shall return and seek the LORD their
God, and David their king, and they shall come in fear to the LORD and to his
goodness in the latter days.

The LORD Accuses Israel

4 Hear the word of the LORD, O children of Israel,
for the LORD has a controversy with the inhabitants of the land.
There is no faithfulness or steadfast love,
and no knowledge of God in the land;
2 there is swearing, lying, murder, stealing, and committing adultery;
they break all bounds, and bloodshed follows bloodshed.
3 Therefore the land mourns,
and all who dwell in it languish,
and also the beasts of the field
and the birds of the heavens,
and even the fish of the sea are taken away.

4 Yet let no one contend,
and let none accuse,
for with you is my contention, O priest.[5]
5 You shall stumble by day;
the prophet also shall stumble with you by night;
and I will destroy your mother.
6 My people are destroyed for lack of knowledge;
because you have rejected knowledge,
I reject you from being a priest to me.
And since you have forgotten the law of your God,
I also will forget your children.

7 The more they increased,
the more they sinned against me;
I will change their glory into shame.
8 They feed on the sin[6] of my people;
they are greedy for their iniquity.
9 And it shall be like people, like priest;
I will punish them for their ways
and repay them for their deeds.

[1] *Jezreel* means *God will sow* [2] Hebrew *Lo-ruhama* [3] Hebrew *Lo-ammi* [4] A *shekel* was about 2/5 ounce or 11 grams; a *homer* was about 6 bushels or 220 liters; a *lethech* was about 3 bushels or 110 liters [5] Or *for your people are like those who contend with the priest* [6] Or *sin offering*

A DIVINE LOVE

Since names in the Old Testament often held great meaning and purpose, the people of Hosea's day would have recognized the special significance God intended when he instructed the prophet to name his children Jezreel ("God scatters"), Lo-ruhama ("no mercy"), and Lo-ammi ("not my people") (1:4,6,9). In Hosea's culture, unrepentant idolatry infected the land, and as symbolized by these names, Israel was poised to reap the consequences of their disobedience and waywardness. Yet, even as they experienced God's discipline, he indicated that his divine love and mercy would ultimately triumph over judgment (2:19–23; Jas 2:13). In fact, in Hosea 2:22, Jezreel is used in the reversed sense: "God will sow" rather than "God scatters."

By pursuing and restoring Gomer to her rightful place as his wife (Hos 3:1–3), Hosea paralleled (though imperfectly) God's unrelenting desire for fellowship with his people and the high price he was willing to pay to purchase his people back from their slavery to sin. Hosea highlighted not only God's original covenant with his people, but also his unending commitment that continued despite Israel's superficial claims to faithfulness. Carrying forward the theme of restoration, he reminded them that it is he alone who could provide comfort, companionship, fruitfulness, and the hope that they would eventually be called his people once again (2:14–16).

Just as Hosea pursued an unfaithful wife, God pursues an unfaithful people, based solely in his own unchanging love, faithfulness, and glory. With the redemption plan of Jesus in play before the beginning of the world (Eph 1:4), God declared his intention even before people became aware of their need. Humanity was chosen as the unlikely recipient of unmerited favor, an extravagant grace.

While God's heart has always desired relationship with his people, the coming of Christ revealed the fullness of the promise. All people were once cut off from mercy and could not attain it through personal effort, but now all can possess it through faith in Jesus and stand in his righteousness, being fully redeemed by his blood (Eph 2:11–13). Fulfilling the prophecy of Hosea, Jesus alone makes it possible for all believers to be the mercy-lavished children of God. Peter wrote triumphantly: "Once you were not a people, but now you are God's people; once you had not received mercy, but now you have received mercy" (1Pe 2:10). The people of God are loved by a divine love pictured most perfectly in Jesus, who would pursue all of humanity through his life, death, and resurrection. "Greater love has no one than this, that someone lay down his life for his friends" (Jn 15:13).

HOSEA 3:1 – 3

REDEEMED

Redemption is a primary theme in Hosea, as evidenced by the way the prophet's personal story mirrors the love and redemption of God Almighty. In Hosea 3:1, God said to him, "Go again, love a woman who is loved by another man and is an adulteress, even as the LORD loves the children of Israel, though they turn to other gods." Through her illicit lifestyle, Hosea's wife, Gomer, became enslaved to her passions and eventually found herself in a state of literal slavery. Despite the heartbreak he must have felt, Hosea honored God's command to pursue and rescue her from her own folly.

Hosea's experience mirrored the devastating betrayal God felt from his own people. Despite his people's rebellious wandering, God's deep affection for them manifested itself in a constant quest to show them his unconditional love. Hosea took Gomer back to live with him, paralleling the way God's heart is bent toward his people with an everlasting devotion.

Just as Hosea was steadfast in his desire to restore his relationship with his wife despite her unfaithfulness, so also God persists in pursuing his people and graciously bringing them back to their proper (though undeserved) place with him.

The account of Hosea's rescue of his unfaithful wife beautifully prefigures the way God went to the utmost lengths to pursue an adulterous people and win them back by sending his own Son Jesus to pay their ransom. Hosea's story is but a shadow image of God's perfect love for the people of Israel and also for all people through Jesus Christ. Now, believers in Christ can express a genuine love relationship with God since, as 1 John 4:19 reminds Christians, "We love because he first loved us."

God fully expressed his love to his people by purchasing them with the precious blood of Christ (1Pe 1:18 – 19). As a result of this redemption, those who were called "not my people" now are embraced fully as "God's chosen ones, holy and beloved" (Col 3:12). Quoting Hosea twice, Paul declares that all people, whether Jew or Gentile, have the opportunity to become children of God (Ro 9:22 – 26). By looking at Hosea in light of what Jesus has done, it is clear that despite sinful choices or deliberate rebellion, God is always at work redeeming his people with the end goal of full recovery and restoration for those who will claim that redemption in Jesus.

10 They shall eat, but not be satisfied;
they shall play the whore, but not multiply,
because they have forsaken the LORD
to cherish [11]whoredom, wine, and new wine,
which take away the understanding.
12 My people inquire of a piece of wood,
and their walking staff gives them oracles.
For a spirit of whoredom has led them astray,
and they have left their God to play the whore.
13 They sacrifice on the tops of the mountains
and burn offerings on the hills,
under oak, poplar, and terebinth,
because their shade is good.
Therefore your daughters play the whore,
and your brides commit adultery.
14 I will not punish your daughters when they play the whore,
nor your brides when they commit adultery;
for the men themselves go aside with prostitutes
and sacrifice with cult prostitutes,
and a people without understanding shall come to ruin.

15 Though you play the whore, O Israel,
let not Judah become guilty.
Enter not into Gilgal,
nor go up to Beth-aven,
and swear not, "As the LORD lives."
16 Like a stubborn heifer,
Israel is stubborn;
can the LORD now feed them
like a lamb in a broad pasture?

17 Ephraim is joined to idols;
leave him alone.
18 When their drink is gone, they give themselves to whoring;
their rulers[1] dearly love shame.
19 A wind has wrapped them[2] in its wings,
and they shall be ashamed because of their sacrifices.

Punishment Coming for Israel and Judah

5 Hear this, O priests!
Pay attention, O house of Israel!
Give ear, O house of the king!
For the judgment is for you;
for you have been a snare at Mizpah
and a net spread upon Tabor.
2 And the revolters have gone deep into slaughter,
but I will discipline all of them.

3 I know Ephraim,
and Israel is not hidden from me;
for now, O Ephraim, you have played the whore;
Israel is defiled.
4 Their deeds do not permit them
to return to their God.
For the spirit of whoredom is within them,
and they know not the LORD.

[1]Hebrew *shields* [2]Hebrew *her*

HOSEA 4:12–13

ADULTERY

The religious practices associated with Baal worship included worshiping wooden idols made by human hands and engaging in sexual fertility rituals. The Israelites got tangled up in both of these activities, as many were corrupted by the surrounding pagan religious practices and led astray from the one true God. Instead of worshiping the Lord and trusting in him alone for their provision, they were offering their bodies to prostitutes as a way of appealing to other gods (Hos 4:14).

This provides a sobering picture of the heart of humanity and what happens when people stray from God — whether literally committing adultery or being unfaithful in heart or word. It also describes the condition of a heart before being redeemed by God through Jesus' work on the cross — a heart divided and eyes that prize created things over the Creator. Pondering the saving work of Jesus at the cross through the filter of personal unfaithfulness to God highlights the incredible lengths God went to for the sake of winning back each one of his adulterous people.

TIME OF JUDGMENT

By the time Hosea prophesied in the land, these religious and civic leaders had abandoned their prime responsibilities of inspiring faithfulness and leading the people to worship only God. Instead, they often encouraged and supported blatant idolatry and led the people to worship false gods. Chapter 5 opens with a strong word of impending judgment against three groups of people: the priests, the nation of Israel, and the royal family. The ongoing rebellion of each of these groups was such that God should, and surely would, judge them for their sin.

Chapter 6 breathes some hope into this desperate situation, reminding Israel that divine justice is always delivered against a backdrop of divine love and the promise of coming redemption (Hos 6:1 – 3). Whether the consequences are imminent (as Israel was soon to experience at the hands of a conquering nation) or delayed (as all can expect at the end of time), judgment from a perfect and holy God on human unfaithfulness and rampant wickedness is sure and certain. Because even the best effort and most consistent faithfulness still fail to live up to God's righteous standards, the rightful and impending consequence that awaits humanity is separation, wrath, and ultimately death.

But that is not the end of the story. Even though it's definitely true that "the wages of sin is death," God stepped in to provide the only payment that could satisfy his righteous standards and offer to all his free alternative: "eternal life in Christ Jesus" (Ro 6:23). Jesus didn't come to make bad people good, but rather to give spiritually dead people life "abundantly" when they place their trust in him (Jn 10:10).

The prophecies in Hosea represented judgments that would happen for Israel's idolatrous rebellion and also future judgment for all people. The ultimate Judge, the Son of God, Jesus Christ himself, will one day determine rewards for service by faithful followers or just punishment for rebellion and unbelief. He himself will "repay each person according to what he has done" (Mt 16:27). Since Christ satisfied the sentence of death by offering his life on the cross, when the day of the Lord comes, those who have trusted him will find their sins covered and not counted against them (Ro 4:7 – 8).

5 The pride of Israel testifies to his face;[1]
Israel and Ephraim shall stumble in his guilt;
Judah also shall stumble with them.
6 With their flocks and herds they shall go
to seek the LORD,
but they will not find him;
he has withdrawn from them.
7 They have dealt faithlessly with the LORD;
for they have borne alien children.
Now the new moon shall devour them with their fields.

8 Blow the horn in Gibeah,
the trumpet in Ramah.
Sound the alarm at Beth-aven;
we follow you,[2] O Benjamin!
9 Ephraim shall become a desolation
in the day of punishment;
among the tribes of Israel
I make known what is sure.
10 The princes of Judah have become
like those who move the landmark;
upon them I will pour out
my wrath like water.
11 Ephraim is oppressed, crushed in judgment,
because he was determined to go after filth.[3]
12 But I am like a moth to Ephraim,
and like dry rot to the house of Judah.

13 When Ephraim saw his sickness,
and Judah his wound,
then Ephraim went to Assyria,
and sent to the great king.[4]
But he is not able to cure you
or heal your wound.
14 For I will be like a lion to Ephraim,
and like a young lion to the house of Judah.
I, even I, will tear and go away;
I will carry off, and no one shall rescue.
15 I will return again to my place,
until they acknowledge their guilt and seek my face,
and in their distress earnestly seek me.

Israel and Judah Are Unrepentant

6 "Come, let us return to the LORD;
for he has torn us, that he may heal us;
he has struck us down, and he will bind us up.
2 After two days he will revive us;
on the third day he will raise us up,
that we may live before him.
3 Let us know; let us press on to know the LORD;
his going out is sure as the dawn;
he will come to us as the showers,
as the spring rains that water the earth."

4 What shall I do with you, O Ephraim?
What shall I do with you, O Judah?

[1]Or *in his presence* [2]Or *after you* [3]Or *to follow human precepts* [4]Or *to King Jareb*

Your love is like a morning cloud,
like the dew that goes early away.
5 Therefore I have hewn them by the prophets;
I have slain them by the words of my mouth,
and my judgment goes forth as the light.
6 For I desire steadfast love[1] and not sacrifice,
the knowledge of God rather than burnt offerings.

7 But like Adam they transgressed the covenant;
there they dealt faithlessly with me.
8 Gilead is a city of evildoers,
tracked with blood.
9 As robbers lie in wait for a man,
so the priests band together;
they murder on the way to Shechem;
they commit villainy.
10 In the house of Israel I have seen a horrible thing;
Ephraim's whoredom is there; Israel is defiled.

11 For you also, O Judah, a harvest is appointed.

When I restore the fortunes of my people,
7 when I would heal Israel,
the iniquity of Ephraim is revealed,
and the evil deeds of Samaria,
for they deal falsely;
the thief breaks in,
and the bandits raid outside.
2 But they do not consider
that I remember all their evil.
Now their deeds surround them;
they are before my face.
3 By their evil they make the king glad,
and the princes by their treachery.
4 They are all adulterers;
they are like a heated oven
whose baker ceases to stir the fire,
from the kneading of the dough
until it is leavened.
5 On the day of our king, the princes
became sick with the heat of wine;
he stretched out his hand with mockers.
6 For with hearts like an oven they approach their
intrigue;
all night their anger smolders;
in the morning it blazes like a flaming fire.
7 All of them are hot as an oven,
and they devour their rulers.
All their kings have fallen,
and none of them calls upon me.

8 Ephraim mixes himself with the peoples;
Ephraim is a cake not turned.
9 Strangers devour his strength,
and he knows it not;
gray hairs are sprinkled upon him,
and he knows it not.

[1]Septuagint *mercy*

HOSEA 6:6

THE HEART OF THE LAW

The heart of the Law was concerned with just that: the heart. God's rules were always for the benefit of his people, intended to draw their hearts toward him so that they would be transformed and so they would lean on him completely (Pr 3:5). It is clear in Hosea 6:6 that God desires "steadfast love," or loyal hearts that are wholly devoted to him and compassionate toward others, over lives filled with lip service and empty sacrifices. God desires people actually to know him, not just know about him while ignoring what God considers important. Living a life of obedience and love is the hallmark of a worshiping heart, which stands in stark contrast to a life of going through the motions: outwardly sacrificing and saying the right things, yet inwardly remaining far from God.

Jesus gave himself as the final sacrifice to satisfy God, to be both the mercy *and* the sacrifice. As Jesus emphatically asserted, "Do not think that I have come to abolish the Law or the Prophets; I have not come to abolish them but to fulfill them" (Mt 5:17). Worship is made possible through a relationship with Jesus, and it happens as one increasingly devotes one's entire life to God (Ro 12:1). When believers joyfully surrender every day to Jesus, with loyal hearts and expectant obedience and with compassion toward others, they are actually living, breathing representations of proper worship toward God.

HOSEA 8:7

SOWING THE WIND

Hosea 8 references sowing and reaping. It is used as an image of judgment: the people have rebelled ("sow the wind") and will therefore experience judgment ("reap the whirlwind"). Under the law, Israel was to repent and follow God's every command in order to receive his blessing. But the never-ending cycle of failure and repentance persisted, for who could perfectly live up to the law? What is done in selfishness and sin will always reap death and ruin.

But Christ's work on the cross enables all people to choose to live, or "sow," Spirit-filled lives. Galatians 6:7–8 outlines this principle: "For whatever one sows, that will he also reap. For the one who sows to his own flesh will from the flesh reap corruption, but the one who sows to the Spirit will from the Spirit reap eternal life." When followers of Jesus walk with the Holy Spirit and live intentional lives for God, the natural overflow will be lives that yield a righteous and blessed harvest and impact God's kingdom for all eternity.

10 The pride of Israel testifies to his face;[1]
yet they do not return to the LORD their God,
nor seek him, for all this.

11 Ephraim is like a dove,
silly and without sense,
calling to Egypt, going to Assyria.
12 As they go, I will spread over them my net;
I will bring them down like birds of the heavens;
I will discipline them according to the report made to
their congregation.
13 Woe to them, for they have strayed from me!
Destruction to them, for they have rebelled against me!
I would redeem them,
but they speak lies against me.

14 They do not cry to me from the heart,
but they wail upon their beds;
for grain and wine they gash themselves;
they rebel against me.
15 Although I trained and strengthened their arms,
yet they devise evil against me.
16 They return, but not upward;[2]
they are like a treacherous bow;
their princes shall fall by the sword
because of the insolence of their tongue.
This shall be their derision in the land of Egypt.

Israel Will Reap the Whirlwind

8 Set the trumpet to your lips!
One like a vulture is over the house of the LORD,
because they have transgressed my covenant
and rebelled against my law.
2 To me they cry,
"My God, we—Israel—know you."
3 Israel has spurned the good;
the enemy shall pursue him.

4 They made kings, but not through me.
They set up princes, but I knew it not.
With their silver and gold they made idols
for their own destruction.
5 I have[3] spurned your calf, O Samaria.
My anger burns against them.
How long will they be incapable of innocence?
6 For it is from Israel;
a craftsman made it;
it is not God.
The calf of Samaria
shall be broken to pieces.[4]

7 For they sow the wind,
and they shall reap the whirlwind.
The standing grain has no heads;
it shall yield no flour;
if it were to yield,
strangers would devour it.

[1]Or *in his presence* [2]Or *to the Most High* [3]Hebrew *He has* [4]Or *shall go up in flames*

8 Israel is swallowed up;
already they are among the nations
as a useless vessel.
9 For they have gone up to Assyria,
a wild donkey wandering alone;
Ephraim has hired lovers.
10 Though they hire allies among the nations,
I will soon gather them up.
And the king and princes shall soon writhe
because of the tribute.

11 Because Ephraim has multiplied altars for sinning,
they have become to him altars for sinning.
12 Were I to write for him my laws by the ten thousands,
they would be regarded as a strange thing.
13 As for my sacrificial offerings,
they sacrifice meat and eat it,
but the LORD does not accept them.
Now he will remember their iniquity
and punish their sins;
they shall return to Egypt.
14 For Israel has forgotten his Maker
and built palaces,
and Judah has multiplied fortified cities;
so I will send a fire upon his cities,
and it shall devour her strongholds.

The LORD Will Punish Israel

9 Rejoice not, O Israel!
Exult not like the peoples;
for you have played the whore, forsaking your God.
You have loved a prostitute's wages
on all threshing floors.
2 Threshing floor and wine vat shall not feed them,
and the new wine shall fail them.
3 They shall not remain in the land of the LORD,
but Ephraim shall return to Egypt,
and they shall eat unclean food in Assyria.

4 They shall not pour drink offerings of wine to the LORD,
and their sacrifices shall not please him.
It shall be like mourners' bread to them;
all who eat of it shall be defiled;
for their bread shall be for their hunger only;
it shall not come to the house of the LORD.
5 What will you do on the day of the appointed festival,
and on the day of the feast of the LORD?
6 For behold, they are going away from destruction;
but Egypt shall gather them;
Memphis shall bury them.
Nettles shall possess their precious things of silver;
thorns shall be in their tents.

7 The days of punishment have come;
the days of recompense have come;
Israel shall know it.
The prophet is a fool;
the man of the spirit is mad,

because of your great iniquity
and great hatred.
8 The prophet is the watchman of Ephraim with my God;
yet a fowler's snare is on all his ways,
and hatred in the house of his God.
9 They have deeply corrupted themselves
as in the days of Gibeah:
he will remember their iniquity;
he will punish their sins.

10 Like grapes in the wilderness,
I found Israel.
Like the first fruit on the fig tree
in its first season,
I saw your fathers.
But they came to Baal-peor
and consecrated themselves to the thing of shame,
and became detestable like the thing they loved.
11 Ephraim's glory shall fly away like a bird—
no birth, no pregnancy, no conception!
12 Even if they bring up children,
I will bereave them till none is left.
Woe to them
when I depart from them!
13 Ephraim, as I have seen, was like a young palm[1] planted in a meadow;
but Ephraim must lead his children out to slaughter.[2]
14 Give them, O LORD—
what will you give?
Give them a miscarrying womb
and dry breasts.

15 Every evil of theirs is in Gilgal;
there I began to hate them.
Because of the wickedness of their deeds
I will drive them out of my house.
I will love them no more;
all their princes are rebels.

16 Ephraim is stricken;
their root is dried up;
they shall bear no fruit.
Even though they give birth,
I will put their beloved children to death.
17 My God will reject them
because they have not listened to him;
they shall be wanderers among the nations.

10 Israel is a luxuriant vine
that yields its fruit.
The more his fruit increased,
the more altars he built;
as his country improved,
he improved his pillars.
2 Their heart is false;
now they must bear their guilt.
The LORD[3] will break down their altars
and destroy their pillars.

[1]Or *like Tyre* [2]Hebrew *to him who slaughters* [3]Hebrew *He*

3 For now they will say:
"We have no king,
for we do not fear the LORD;
and a king—what could he do for us?"
4 They utter mere words;
with empty[1] oaths they make covenants;
so judgment springs up like poisonous weeds
in the furrows of the field.
5 The inhabitants of Samaria tremble
for the calf[2] of Beth-aven.
Its people mourn for it, and so do its idolatrous priests—
those who rejoiced over it and over its glory—
for it has departed[3] from them.
6 The thing itself shall be carried to Assyria
as tribute to the great king.[4]
Ephraim shall be put to shame,
and Israel shall be ashamed of his idol.[5]

7 Samaria's king shall perish
like a twig on the face of the waters.
8 The high places of Aven, the sin of Israel,
shall be destroyed.
Thorn and thistle shall grow up
on their altars,
and they shall say to the mountains, "Cover us,"
and to the hills, "Fall on us."

9 From the days of Gibeah, you have sinned, O Israel;
there they have continued.
Shall not the war against the unjust[6] overtake them in Gibeah?
10 When I please, I will discipline them,
and nations shall be gathered against them
when they are bound up for their double iniquity.

11 Ephraim was a trained calf
that loved to thresh,
and I spared her fair neck;
but I will put Ephraim to the yoke;
Judah must plow;
Jacob must harrow for himself.
12 Sow for yourselves righteousness;
reap steadfast love;
break up your fallow ground,
for it is the time to seek the LORD,
that he may come and rain righteousness upon you.

13 You have plowed iniquity;
you have reaped injustice;
you have eaten the fruit of lies.
Because you have trusted in your own way
and in the multitude of your warriors,
14 therefore the tumult of war shall arise among your people,
and all your fortresses shall be destroyed,
as Shalman destroyed Beth-arbel on the day of battle;
mothers were dashed in pieces with their children.
15 Thus it shall be done to you, O Bethel,
because of your great evil.

[1]Or *vain* (see Exodus 20:7) [2]Or *calves* [3]Or *has gone into exile* [4]Or *to King Jareb* [5]Or *counsel*
[6]Hebrew *the children of injustice*

HOSEA 10:5

IN SPIRIT AND TRUTH

In Hosea 10:5, "Beth-aven" means "house of wickedness," a derogatory name for "Bethel," which means "house of God." Years earlier, the schism following Solomon's reign had resulted in two kingdoms. Jeroboam I, the first king of the northern kingdom (Israel), moved worship from Jerusalem by establishing golden calves in the towns of Bethel and Dan (1Ki 12:28–30). Under this king and nearly all of his successors, the people of Israel went further and further astray. They intermingled worship of the one true God with worship of foreign gods. Eventually the city of Samaria became the capital of the northern kingdom, and "Samaria" became another name for the entire nation.

By the time of Jesus, a bitter hostility existed between the Jews and Samaritans. When Jesus passed through Samaria and spoke with a woman at a well, she was living with the difficult history between Jews and Samaritans every single day. This outcast among outcasts challenged Jesus with a question about worship in John 4:20: "Our fathers worshiped on this mountain, but you say that in Jerusalem is the place where people ought to worship." Jesus explained that ultimately it was not going to be about the location of where a person worships, but, because of the Messiah, a time was coming—and indeed, "is now here"—when God's people would worship "in spirit and truth" (Jn 4:23). He revealed that he was, in fact, the Messiah. Jesus made returning to God a reality with his life, death, and resurrection. Now, through faith in Jesus, people can worship God in the Spirit and in truth.

At dawn the king of Israel
shall be utterly cut off.

The LORD's Love for Israel

11 When Israel was a child, I loved him,
and out of Egypt I called my son.
2 The more they were called,
the more they went away;
they kept sacrificing to the Baals
and burning offerings to idols.
3 Yet it was I who taught Ephraim to walk;
I took them up by their arms,
but they did not know that I healed them.
4 I led them with cords of kindness,[1]
with the bands of love,
and I became to them as one who eases the yoke on their jaws,
and I bent down to them and fed them.
5 They shall not[2] return to the land of Egypt,
but Assyria shall be their king,
because they have refused to return to me.
6 The sword shall rage against their cities,
consume the bars of their gates,
and devour them because of their own counsels.
7 My people are bent on turning away from me,
and though they call out to the Most High,
he shall not raise them up at all.
8 How can I give you up, O Ephraim?
How can I hand you over, O Israel?
How can I make you like Admah?
How can I treat you like Zeboiim?
My heart recoils within me;
my compassion grows warm and tender.
9 I will not execute my burning anger;
I will not again destroy Ephraim;
for I am God and not a man,
the Holy One in your midst,
and I will not come in wrath.[3]
10 They shall go after the LORD;
he will roar like a lion;
when he roars,
his children shall come trembling from the west;
11 they shall come trembling like birds from Egypt,
and like doves from the land of Assyria,
and I will return them to their homes, declares the LORD.
12[4] Ephraim has surrounded me with lies,
and the house of Israel with deceit,
but Judah still walks with God
and is faithful to the Holy One.

12 Ephraim feeds on the wind
and pursues the east wind all day long;
they multiply falsehood and violence;
they make a covenant with Assyria,
and oil is carried to Egypt.

HOSEA 11:1

EXODUS FROM EGYPT

In Hosea 11:1, God spoke through Hosea of his great love for his people, a promised love that was deep and parental. God regarded Israel as a child, and the Israelites were often referred to as God's children. When God said he called his people out of Egypt, he was referring to how he redeemed his people from slavery and bondage in Egypt during the exodus. This great act was *the* act of redemption the Israelites associated with God as Redeemer of his people. This was the event that exemplified true redemption for the people of Israel in Old Testament times.

Now, living in the shadow of the cross, followers of Jesus can see how God is always redeeming, and just like he brought his people out of Egypt and out of slavery, he has now brought all people out of slavery to sin through the life, death, and resurrection of Jesus Christ, giving them the title "sons of God." In Romans 8:14–15, the promise is clear: "All who are led by the Spirit of God are sons of God. For you did not receive the spirit of slavery to fall back into fear, but you have received the Spirit of adoption as sons." As the Israelites walked out of slavery, so also people today can make their exodus from fear and death into the freedom and life found in Christ.

[1]Or *humaneness*; Hebrew *man* [2]Or *surely* [3]Or *into the city* [4]Ch 12:1 in Hebrew

A REBELLIOUS SON

Scripture records the unique relationship that God established between himself and Israel. Referred to as God's child or son (Hos 11:1), God deeply loved the people of Israel and gifted them with special rights, privileges, promises, and an inheritance corresponding to that which is reserved for children by their fathers. Grasping this foundational bond helps the reader to understand the great heartbreak God felt when the Israelites rejected his affection and chose to go their own way. It also points to the steadfast character of God as a loving Father to his people.

Jesus told a parable about a lost son in Luke 15:11–32 in which a son decided to go his own way and leave his father's house in rebellion. Jesus described the son's downward spiral as he tried to find fulfillment in worldly things. When the son came to the end of himself and realized his terrible error in judgment, he decided to return home. Before he could even get the full apology out of his mouth, the father had run to embrace him in his repentance with open arms and a joyful celebration. The father also had an older son who never left his side, yet this son held both his father and brother in contempt when the father accepted his brother so easily. Despite the actions of and the conflict between the sons, the true heart of the story is the extravagant grace of the father toward both of the sons.

Israel and the sons in Jesus' parable had in common their disobedience and their quest to find satisfaction apart from God, either in outright rebellion or through moral performance. A person can be near the things of God without recognizing the grace of God — saying and doing the right things without actually knowing God (Hos 6:6). Rebellion separates people from God, but both Hosea and the parable of the lost son reveal that God's heart is full of abundant grace and a kindness that leads to repentance (Ro 2:4). When Jesus came, he came as the true and perfect Son, a ransom for Israel, and the Savior for all people who will trust in him. And he displayed the heart of God as the perfect Father who welcomes all those who call upon Christ into his family.

The LORD's Indictment of Israel and Judah

2 The LORD has an indictment against Judah
and will punish Jacob according to his ways;
he will repay him according to his deeds.
3 In the womb he took his brother by the heel,
and in his manhood he strove with God.
4 He strove with the angel and prevailed;
he wept and sought his favor.
He met God[1] at Bethel,
and there God spoke with us—
5 the LORD, the God of hosts,
the LORD is his memorial name:
6 "So you, by the help of your God, return,
hold fast to love and justice,
and wait continually for your God."

7 A merchant, in whose hands are false balances,
he loves to oppress.
8 Ephraim has said, "Ah, but I am rich;
I have found wealth for myself;
in all my labors they cannot find in me iniquity or sin."
9 I am the LORD your God
from the land of Egypt;
I will again make you dwell in tents,
as in the days of the appointed feast.

10 I spoke to the prophets;
it was I who multiplied visions,
and through the prophets gave parables.
11 If there is iniquity in Gilead,
they shall surely come to nothing:
in Gilgal they sacrifice bulls;
their altars also are like stone heaps
on the furrows of the field.
12 Jacob fled to the land of Aram;
there Israel served for a wife,
and for a wife he guarded sheep.
13 By a prophet the LORD brought Israel up from Egypt,
and by a prophet he was guarded.
14 Ephraim has given bitter provocation;
so his Lord will leave his bloodguilt on him
and will repay him for his disgraceful deeds.

The LORD's Relentless Judgment on Israel

13 When Ephraim spoke, there was trembling;
he was exalted in Israel,
but he incurred guilt through Baal and died.
2 And now they sin more and more,
and make for themselves metal images,
idols skillfully made of their silver,
all of them the work of craftsmen.
It is said of them,
"Those who offer human sacrifice kiss calves!"
3 Therefore they shall be like the morning mist
or like the dew that goes early away,
like the chaff that swirls from the threshing floor
or like smoke from a window.

[1]Hebrew *him*

4 But I am the LORD your God
from the land of Egypt;
you know no God but me,
and besides me there is no savior.
5 It was I who knew you in the wilderness,
in the land of drought;
6 but when they had grazed,[1] they became full,
they were filled, and their heart was lifted up;
therefore they forgot me.
7 So I am to them like a lion;
like a leopard I will lurk beside the way.
8 I will fall upon them like a bear robbed of her cubs;
I will tear open their breast,
and there I will devour them like a lion,
as a wild beast would rip them open.

9 He destroys[2] you, O Israel,
for you are against me, against your helper.
10 Where now is your king, to save you in all your cities?
Where are all your rulers—
those of whom you said,
"Give me a king and princes"?
11 I gave you a king in my anger,
and I took him away in my wrath.

12 The iniquity of Ephraim is bound up;
his sin is kept in store.
13 The pangs of childbirth come for him,
but he is an unwise son,
for at the right time he does not present himself
at the opening of the womb.

14 I shall ransom them from the power of Sheol;
I shall redeem them from Death.[3]
O Death, where are your plagues?
O Sheol, where is your sting?
Compassion is hidden from my eyes.

15 Though he may flourish among his brothers,
the east wind, the wind of the LORD, shall come,
rising from the wilderness,
and his fountain shall dry up;
his spring shall be parched;
it shall strip his treasury
of every precious thing.
16[4] Samaria shall bear her guilt,
because she has rebelled against her God;
they shall fall by the sword;
their little ones shall be dashed in pieces,
and their pregnant women ripped open.

A Plea to Return to the LORD

14 Return, O Israel, to the LORD your God,
for you have stumbled because of your iniquity.
2 Take with you words
and return to the LORD;

[1]Hebrew *according to their pasture* [2]Or *I will destroy* [3]Or *Shall I ransom them from the power of Sheol? Shall I redeem them from Death?* [4]Ch 14:1 in Hebrew

HOSEA 13:14

RANSOM AND REDEMPTION

Relentless judgment seems to be rampant throughout the pages of Hosea. But God's love is revealed to be even more unstoppable than divine judgment when readers view this Scripture through the lens of love personified—that is, through Jesus Christ. The extensive judgment in this text is followed by rhetorical questions that point toward redemption and ransom: God seems to be asking himself, "Will I ransom my people?" and, "Will I redeem them from death?" The unfaithfulness of the people has incited extreme judgment and wrath, yet God still holds out a promise of hope (Hos 14:4–8).

Despite their sin, God was faithful and loving to save his people. There is no more beautiful expression of this love than when Jesus arrived on the scene hundreds of years later, leaving heaven to walk on earth with the primary purpose of ransoming his people and defeating death once and for all. Hosea 13:14 is mentioned in 1 Corinthians 15:55–57, in what is perhaps one of the most triumphant and victorious exclamations of the finished work of Jesus: "'O death, where is your victory? O death, where is your sting?' The sting of death is sin, and the power of sin is the law. But thanks be to God, who gives us the victory through our Lord Jesus Christ." God's people are redeemed from punishment into glorious life both now and forever.

HOSEA 14:4–8

HOPE FOR A FUTURE

In the stunning conclusion to the book of Hosea, God puts the exclamation mark on his intention for his people, the chosen ones of God: he has chosen to redeem them despite their blatant rebellion. When Israel returns to God, he will not turn away from them as they deserve, but will rather provide healing and a home for them with him, allowing them to once again belong to him; they will put their roots down in him and be fruitful because of his care and compassion to them. Instead of cutting them off forever, God will give them a beautiful future with him as his people.

There is perhaps no better parallel than one that comes from the prophet Jeremiah, although it came over a century later. It also reveals God's heart and purpose for his people in the midst of their struggle, and reminds them of the hope only he can provide: "For I know the plans I have for you, declares the LORD, plans for welfare and not for evil, to give you a future and a hope" (Jer 29:11). God reminded his people continually of his love throughout their trials, assuring them that when they repented and sought him, he would bring them back to him. This is shown in the ultimate way through Jesus—who is "the way, and the truth, and the life" (Jn 14:6). Jesus gives those who will trust in him the best hope: everlasting life with him.

say to him,
"Take away all iniquity;
accept what is good,
and we will pay with bulls
the vows[1] of our lips.
3 Assyria shall not save us;
we will not ride on horses;
and we will say no more, 'Our God,'
to the work of our hands.
In you the orphan finds mercy."

4 I will heal their apostasy;
I will love them freely,
for my anger has turned from them.
5 I will be like the dew to Israel;
he shall blossom like the lily;
he shall take root like the trees of Lebanon;
6 his shoots shall spread out;
his beauty shall be like the olive,
and his fragrance like Lebanon.
7 They shall return and dwell beneath my[2] shadow;
they shall flourish like the grain;
they shall blossom like the vine;
their fame shall be like the wine of Lebanon.

8 O Ephraim, what have I to do with idols?
It is I who answer and look after you.[3]
I am like an evergreen cypress;
from me comes your fruit.

9 Whoever is wise, let him understand these things;
whoever is discerning, let him know them;
for the ways of the LORD are right,
and the upright walk in them,
but transgressors stumble in them.

[1]Septuagint, Syriac *pay the fruit* [2]Hebrew *his* [3]Hebrew *him*

JESUS: OUR BLESSED HOPE

JOEL

JOEL

ELISHA SUCCEEDS ELIJAH *c. 848 BC*	ESTIMATED DATE FOR THE PROPHETIC MINISTRY OF JOEL *c. 830 BC*	FALL OF ISRAEL *c. 722 BC*

Joel used the image of a natural disaster to picture God's forthcoming judgment. Floods, earthquakes, famine, and other calamities provoke fear and dread among all people. They are usually unexpected and often unexplained — leaving a wake of destruction, despair, and confusion in their path.

This time, however, the disaster would have a clear cause. Joel began with a terrifying image — a plague of ravenous locusts that would wreak havoc on the people, their land, and their crops. Nothing would escape the locusts' devastating work. This plague, like those God used to release the Israelites from slavery in Egypt, was meant to demonstrate the all-surpassing power of the one true God and provoke repentance from all those who witnessed the stunning devastation. Joel called the people of Judah to return to God based on their experience of his judgment in the locust plague (2:12 – 14). He warned that, should they continue in their rebellion, a greater and more devastating judgment would soon come. The intervening time between the plague of locusts and the forthcoming judgment of God would allow space for the people to return humbly to God.

Joel knew that the people's propensity to sin would unleash the coming acts of judgment as well. God's patience would be tested again, as there seemed to be no end to the people's rebellion and recklessness against God. Would he finally give up on his people forever? Had they finally crossed the line and gone too far for the love of God?

The answer, once again, is a resounding, no! A day would come when God would pour out his Spirit on his people (2:28 – 32). This coming day, known only by God, would restore the fortunes of God's people and demonstrate God's faithfulness. God would restore the prosperity of the land, destroy the pagan nations, and once again dwell in Zion.

Following the sending of the Spirit at Pentecost, Peter proclaimed that the prophet Joel's words had been fulfilled in their day (Ac 2:16 – 21). The Spirit would serve as an ever-present reminder of the faithfulness of God to fulfill his promises to restore his people and "restore to you the years that the swarming locust has eaten" (Joel 2:25).

RETURN TO THE LORD YOUR GOD, FOR HE IS GRACIOUS AND MERCIFUL, SLOW TO ANGER, AND ABOUNDING IN STEADFAST LOVE; AND HE RELENTS OVER DISASTER.

Joel 2:13

JOEL

1 The word of the LORD that came to Joel, the son of Pethuel:

An Invasion of Locusts

2 Hear this, you elders;
give ear, all inhabitants of the land!
Has such a thing happened in your days,
or in the days of your fathers?
3 Tell your children of it,
and let your children tell their children,
and their children to another generation.
4 What the cutting locust left,
the swarming locust has eaten.
What the swarming locust left,
the hopping locust has eaten,
and what the hopping locust left,
the destroying locust has eaten.

5 Awake, you drunkards, and weep,
and wail, all you drinkers of wine,
because of the sweet wine,
for it is cut off from your mouth.
6 For a nation has come up against my land,
powerful and beyond number;
its teeth are lions' teeth,
and it has the fangs of a lioness.
7 It has laid waste my vine
and splintered my fig tree;
it has stripped off their bark and thrown it down;
their branches are made white.

8 Lament like a virgin[1] wearing sackcloth
for the bridegroom of her youth.
9 The grain offering and the drink offering are cut off
from the house of the LORD.
The priests mourn,
the ministers of the LORD.
10 The fields are destroyed,
the ground mourns,
because the grain is destroyed,
the wine dries up,
the oil languishes.

11 Be ashamed,[2] O tillers of the soil;
wail, O vinedressers,
for the wheat and the barley,
because the harvest of the field has perished.
12 The vine dries up;
the fig tree languishes.
Pomegranate, palm, and apple,
all the trees of the field are dried up,
and gladness dries up
from the children of man.

---

[1]Or *young woman* [2]The Hebrew words for *dry up* and *be ashamed* in verses 10–12, 17 sound alike

A Call to Repentance

13 Put on sackcloth and lament, O priests;
wail, O ministers of the altar.
Go in, pass the night in sackcloth,
O ministers of my God!
Because grain offering and drink offering
are withheld from the house of your God.

14 Consecrate a fast;
call a solemn assembly.
Gather the elders
and all the inhabitants of the land
to the house of the LORD your God,
and cry out to the LORD.

15 Alas for the day!
For the day of the LORD is near,
and as destruction from the Almighty[1] it comes.
16 Is not the food cut off
before our eyes,
joy and gladness
from the house of our God?

17 The seed shrivels under the clods;[2]
the storehouses are desolate;
the granaries are torn down
because the grain has dried up.
18 How the beasts groan!
The herds of cattle are perplexed
because there is no pasture for them;
even the flocks of sheep suffer.[3]

19 To you, O LORD, I call.
For fire has devoured
the pastures of the wilderness,
and flame has burned
all the trees of the field.
20 Even the beasts of the field pant for you
because the water brooks are dried up,
and fire has devoured
the pastures of the wilderness.

The Day of the LORD

2 Blow a trumpet in Zion;
sound an alarm on my holy mountain!
Let all the inhabitants of the land tremble,
for the day of the LORD is coming; it is near,
2 a day of darkness and gloom,
a day of clouds and thick darkness!
Like blackness there is spread upon the mountains
a great and powerful people;
their like has never been before,
nor will be again after them
through the years of all generations.

3 Fire devours before them,
and behind them a flame burns.

---

[1] *Destruction* sounds like the Hebrew for *Almighty* [2] The meaning of the Hebrew line is uncertain
[3] Or *are made desolate*

The land is like the garden of Eden before them,
but behind them a desolate wilderness,
and nothing escapes them.

4 Their appearance is like the appearance of horses,
and like war horses they run.
5 As with the rumbling of chariots,
they leap on the tops of the mountains,
like the crackling of a flame of fire
devouring the stubble,
like a powerful army
drawn up for battle.

6 Before them peoples are in anguish;
all faces grow pale.
7 Like warriors they charge;
like soldiers they scale the wall.
They march each on his way;
they do not swerve from their paths.
8 They do not jostle one another;
each marches in his path;
they burst through the weapons
and are not halted.
9 They leap upon the city,
they run upon the walls,
they climb up into the houses,
they enter through the windows like a thief.

10 The earth quakes before them;
the heavens tremble.
The sun and the moon are darkened,
and the stars withdraw their shining.
11 The LORD utters his voice
before his army,
for his camp is exceedingly great;
he who executes his word is powerful.
For the day of the LORD is great and very awesome;
who can endure it?

Return to the LORD

12 "Yet even now," declares the LORD,
"return to me with all your heart,
with fasting, with weeping, and with mourning;
13 and rend your hearts and not your garments."
Return to the LORD your God,
for he is gracious and merciful,
slow to anger, and abounding in steadfast love;
and he relents over disaster.
14 Who knows whether he will not turn and relent,
and leave a blessing behind him,
a grain offering and a drink offering
for the LORD your God?

15 Blow the trumpet in Zion;
consecrate a fast;
call a solemn assembly;
16 gather the people.
Consecrate the congregation;
assemble the elders;

gather the children,
even nursing infants.
Let the bridegroom leave his room,
and the bride her chamber.

17 Between the vestibule and the altar
let the priests, the ministers of the LORD, weep
and say, "Spare your people, O LORD,
and make not your heritage a reproach,
a byword among the nations.[1]
Why should they say among the peoples,
'Where is their God?'"

The LORD Had Pity

18 Then the LORD became jealous for his land
and had pity on his people.
19 The LORD answered and said to his people,
"Behold, I am sending to you
grain, wine, and oil,
and you will be satisfied;
and I will no more make you
a reproach among the nations.

20 "I will remove the northerner far from you,
and drive him into a parched and desolate land,
his vanguard[2] into the eastern sea,
and his rear guard[3] into the western sea;
the stench and foul smell of him will rise,
for he has done great things.

21 "Fear not, O land;
be glad and rejoice,
for the LORD has done great things!
22 Fear not, you beasts of the field,
for the pastures of the wilderness are green;
the tree bears its fruit;
the fig tree and vine give their full yield.

23 "Be glad, O children of Zion,
and rejoice in the LORD your God,
for he has given the early rain for your vindication;
he has poured down for you abundant rain,
the early and the latter rain, as before.

24 "The threshing floors shall be full of grain;
the vats shall overflow with wine and oil.
25 I will restore[4] to you the years
that the swarming locust has eaten,
the hopper, the destroyer, and the cutter,
my great army, which I sent among you.

26 "You shall eat in plenty and be satisfied,
and praise the name of the LORD your God,
who has dealt wondrously with you.
And my people shall never again be put to shame.
27 You shall know that I am in the midst of Israel,
and that I am the LORD your God and there is none else.
And my people shall never again be put to shame.

[1]Or *reproach, that the nations should rule over them* [2]Hebrew *face* [3]Hebrew *his end* [4]Or *pay back*

JOEL 2:28–32

CALLING ON JESUS' NAME

Joel began his prophecy by declaring God's judgment on the people of Judah for their sins. He urged his listeners to repent and to return to God. This was Joel's core message: repentance brings about salvation. He promised that as the people repented and sought after God (Joel 1:13–14; 2:12–13), God would answer them and come to their rescue (2:25–27).

Joel 2:28–32 details that God not only wanted to rescue his people, he also wanted to bring his people to a place of complete and future restoration. The Lord promised that he would place his Spirit on all people. He desired to make a way for his presence to dwell within humankind. He also promised that anyone who would call on the name of the Lord would be saved. Later, in Acts 2:14–41, Peter preached the same message as Joel. He called the people to repent from their sins and call on the name of Jesus to be forgiven and to receive the gift of the Holy Spirit of God. Since that day, the Holy Spirit has been fueling and building the church.

JOEL 3:17–21

A FUTURE HOPE

Joel prophesied that God would judge other nations for how they treated his people. On the day of the Lord, this future judgment would come; however, on that terrible day, the Lord promised to be a refuge for his people. In this passage, God promised to be the God of his people and live among them in Jerusalem.

(continued on page 1362)

The LORD Will Pour Out His Spirit

28[1] "And it shall come to pass afterward,
that I will pour out my Spirit on all flesh;
your sons and your daughters shall prophesy,
your old men shall dream dreams,
and your young men shall see visions.
29 Even on the male and female servants
in those days I will pour out my Spirit.

30 "And I will show wonders in the heavens and on the earth, blood and fire and
columns of smoke. 31 The sun shall be turned to darkness, and the moon to blood,
before the great and awesome day of the LORD comes. 32 And it shall come to pass
that everyone who calls on the name of the LORD shall be saved. For in Mount
Zion and in Jerusalem there shall be those who escape, as the LORD has said, and
among the survivors shall be those whom the LORD calls.

The LORD Judges the Nations

3[2] "For behold, in those days and at that time, when I restore the fortunes of
Judah and Jerusalem, 2 I will gather all the nations and bring them down to
the Valley of Jehoshaphat. And I will enter into judgment with them there, on
behalf of my people and my heritage Israel, because they have scattered them
among the nations and have divided up my land, 3 and have cast lots for my people, and have traded a boy for a prostitute, and have sold a girl for wine and have
drunk it.

4 "What are you to me, O Tyre and Sidon, and all the regions of Philistia?
Are you paying me back for something? If you are paying me back, I will return
your payment on your own head swiftly and speedily. 5 For you have taken my
silver and my gold, and have carried my rich treasures into your temples.[3] 6 You
have sold the people of Judah and Jerusalem to the Greeks in order to remove
them far from their own border. 7 Behold, I will stir them up from the place to
which you have sold them, and I will return your payment on your own head.
8 I will sell your sons and your daughters into the hand of the people of Judah,
and they will sell them to the Sabeans, to a nation far away, for the LORD has
spoken."

9 Proclaim this among the nations:
Consecrate for war;[4]
stir up the mighty men.
Let all the men of war draw near;
let them come up.
10 Beat your plowshares into swords,
and your pruning hooks into spears;
let the weak say, "I am a warrior."

11 Hasten and come,
all you surrounding nations,
and gather yourselves there.
Bring down your warriors, O LORD.
12 Let the nations stir themselves up
and come up to the Valley of Jehoshaphat;
for there I will sit to judge
all the surrounding nations.

13 Put in the sickle,
for the harvest is ripe.
Go in, tread,
for the winepress is full.

[1] Ch 3:1 in Hebrew [2] Ch 4:1 in Hebrew [3] Or *palaces* [4] Or *Consecrate a war*

THE SIGNIFICANCE OF PENTECOST

The outpouring of the Holy Spirit was an extraordinary event that happened on the day of Pentecost. After the crucifixion, Jesus' disciples had seen him alive and risen from the dead. Before Jesus ascended to heaven, he told them to remain in Jerusalem and wait for the gift of the Holy Spirit. They were all gathered in one room when "suddenly there came from heaven a sound like a mighty rushing wind, and it filled the entire house where they were sitting" (Ac 2:2). Then "divided tongues as of fire appeared to them and rested on each one of them" (v. 3). They were all "filled with the Holy Spirit and began to speak in other tongues" (v. 4), declaring "the mighty works of God" in different languages (v. 11).

Because of the festival of Pentecost (the ancient Jewish Feast of Harvest; Ex 23:16), people from many nations were gathered in Jerusalem. As a crowd gathered around the disciples, many were bewildered to hear Galileans speaking in their native language. Peter stood up and preached to the crowd, proclaiming that the prophecy in Joel 2:28–32 had been fulfilled (Ac 2:14–21): the Holy Spirit had come to be with God's people. The disciples were filled with, and empowered to speak in other languages by, the Holy Spirit of God. Peter declared that Jesus was the way to salvation and anyone who put their faith in him could have eternal life. As Joel prophesied, "Everyone who calls on the name of the Lord shall be saved" (Joel 2:32). On that day of Pentecost, three thousand people were added to the church (Ac 2:41).

Jesus was the one who made possible the indwelling of the Holy Spirit. Because sin separated humans from God, God's presence could not live inside of his people. Jesus' atoning sacrifice made a way for the Holy Spirit to come and make his home in the hearts and lives of believers (Ro 8:1–4).

The Holy Spirit is one member of the Trinity, along with the Son and the Father. His role is to reveal and magnify Jesus (Jn 14:26; 15:26; 16:13–14; Ac 1:8), to restore and refine his people into the image of Christ (Ro 8:5–13), and to unite and lead the church (1Co 12:12–31).

The day of Pentecost ushered in a new era of history. The church was born, and God's Spirit became accessible for everybody. Today, the Holy Spirit is still at work in the lives of those who trust in Jesus alone for salvation and surrender to the Spirit's leading.

(A Future Hope, continued)

As a result of God's presence among the people, the land would be blessed, fruitful, and safe from foreign invasion.

This blessing points believers to the day referenced in Revelation 22:1–2, where in the new heaven and the new earth, the river of life will flow from the throne of God and bring life to all the city—including the tree of life, which will continually bear fruit. The people of God can take part in this beautiful blessing because of the work of Jesus on the cross. When Jesus died on the cross, he took on the guilt of all who will trust in him for salvation, and he became the one way that God would pardon human sin.

Jesus, then, is the ultimate refuge for the people of God. He not only protects them from their enemies, but he has also absorbed the wrath of God on their behalf. This is what makes it possible for God to dwell within his people. Now, the people of God, with the indwelling of the Holy Spirit, live each day of their lives with the hope of a great future and wait for this promise of eternal blessing to be realized.

The vats overflow,
for their evil is great.

14 Multitudes, multitudes,
in the valley of decision!
For the day of the LORD is near
in the valley of decision.
15 The sun and the moon are darkened,
and the stars withdraw their shining.

16 The LORD roars from Zion,
and utters his voice from Jerusalem,
and the heavens and the earth quake.
But the LORD is a refuge to his people,
a stronghold to the people of Israel.

The Glorious Future of Judah

17 "So you shall know that I am the LORD your God,
who dwells in Zion, my holy mountain.
And Jerusalem shall be holy,
and strangers shall never again pass through it.

18 "And in that day
the mountains shall drip sweet wine,
and the hills shall flow with milk,
and all the streambeds of Judah
shall flow with water;
and a fountain shall come forth from the house of the LORD
and water the Valley of Shittim.

19 "Egypt shall become a desolation
and Edom a desolate wilderness,
for the violence done to the people of Judah,
because they have shed innocent blood in their land.
20 But Judah shall be inhabited forever,
and Jerusalem to all generations.
21 I will avenge their blood,
blood I have not avenged,[1]
for the LORD dwells in Zion."

[1]Or *I will acquit their bloodguilt that I have not acquitted*

JESUS: OUR JUSTICE BEARER

AMOS

AMOS

REIGN OF UZZIAH OF JUDAH	REIGN OF JEROBOAM II OF ISRAEL	PROPHETIC MINISTRY OF AMOS
c. 792 – 740 BC	*c. 793 – 753 BC*	*c. 760 – 750 BC*

The striking metaphors and dynamic themes of the book of Amos make it one of the most familiar of all of the Minor Prophets. Amos, a shepherd, prophesied during the reigns of Uzziah king of Judah and Jeroboam II king of Israel. Though his home was in Judah, Amos was sent to announce God's judgment on the northern kingdom of Israel. His familiarity with the needs of the people of Israel prompted the remarkable clarity of his prophetic call.

Amos's words contain a different tone than many of the other prophets. His main concern was justice among God's people. Their spiritual failures resulted in ongoing injustice within the nation of Israel itself.

Justice is meant to be tangible. Injustice fosters hostility, hatred, jealousy, and rage. Justice, on the other hand, fosters loving-kindness, care, and service. God's people are to be marked by justice because God acts justly toward his people.

God's bountiful provision to the nation of Israel produced a spirit of superiority between the wealthy and those whom they were called to love. The upper class, bolstered by the prosperity brought about under the rule of Jeroboam II, neglected their social responsibility to care for their own countrymen. As in many societies in our world today, people of means marginalized and exploited people who were poor in order to advance their selfish pursuits.

God, through Amos, warns that such divisiveness is unfit for his people. God's law demanded that his people care for the downtrodden and marginalized and supply their needs — even if they were outsiders and sojourners living among the nation of

Israel. If there was ever a place where social inequity and injustice should not have been found, it should have been among the people of Israel.

Yet injustice was pervasive in the hearts of the Israelites. Amos warned Israel's leaders to repent, to lead the people to right the inequality and to restore justice in the land. He longed for Israel to "let justice roll down like waters, and righteousness like an ever-flowing stream" (5:24). These days would fully come only when God ushered in his kingdom through the work of his Son, Jesus Christ, who would come to seek and save all those who were lost — poor and rich, weak and strong, marginalized and powerful. Today all who come to him, regardless of their social status, can become children of God and be part of his family, the church, where all people can find love, acceptance and care.

BUT LET JUSTICE ROLL DOWN LIKE WATERS,
AND RIGHTEOUSNESS LIKE AN EVER-FLOWING STREAM.

Amos 5:24

AMOS

1 The words of Amos, who was among the shepherds[1] of Tekoa, which he saw concerning Israel in the days of Uzziah king of Judah and in the days of Jeroboam the son of Joash, king of Israel, two years[2] before the earthquake.

Judgment on Israel's Neighbors

2 And he said:

"The LORD roars from Zion
and utters his voice from Jerusalem;
the pastures of the shepherds mourn,
and the top of Carmel withers."

3 Thus says the LORD:

"For three transgressions of Damascus,
and for four, I will not revoke the punishment,[3]
because they have threshed Gilead
with threshing sledges of iron.
4 So I will send a fire upon the house of Hazael,
and it shall devour the strongholds of Ben-hadad.
5 I will break the gate-bar of Damascus,
and cut off the inhabitants from the Valley of Aven,[4]
and him who holds the scepter from Beth-eden;
and the people of Syria shall go into exile to Kir,"
says the LORD.

6 Thus says the LORD:

"For three transgressions of Gaza,
and for four, I will not revoke the punishment,
because they carried into exile a whole people
to deliver them up to Edom.
7 So I will send a fire upon the wall of Gaza,
and it shall devour her strongholds.
8 I will cut off the inhabitants from Ashdod,
and him who holds the scepter from Ashkelon;
I will turn my hand against Ekron,
and the remnant of the Philistines shall perish,"
says the Lord GOD.

9 Thus says the LORD:

"For three transgressions of Tyre,
and for four, I will not revoke the punishment,
because they delivered up a whole people to Edom,
and did not remember the covenant of brotherhood.
10 So I will send a fire upon the wall of Tyre,
and it shall devour her strongholds."

11 Thus says the LORD:

"For three transgressions of Edom,
and for four, I will not revoke the punishment,
because he pursued his brother with the sword
and cast off all pity,

[1] Or *sheep breeders* [2] Or *during two years* [3] Hebrew *I will not turn it back*; also verses 6, 9, 11, 13 [4] Or *On*

and his anger tore perpetually,
and he kept his wrath forever.
12 So I will send a fire upon Teman,
and it shall devour the strongholds of Bozrah."

13Thus says the LORD:

"For three transgressions of the Ammonites,
and for four, I will not revoke the punishment,
because they have ripped open pregnant women in Gilead,
that they might enlarge their border.
14 So I will kindle a fire in the wall of Rabbah,
and it shall devour her strongholds,
with shouting on the day of battle,
with a tempest in the day of the whirlwind;
15 and their king shall go into exile,
he and his princes[1] together,"
says the LORD.

2 Thus says the LORD:

"For three transgressions of Moab,
and for four, I will not revoke the punishment,[2]
because he burned to lime
the bones of the king of Edom.
2 So I will send a fire upon Moab,
and it shall devour the strongholds of Kerioth,
and Moab shall die amid uproar,
amid shouting and the sound of the trumpet;
3 I will cut off the ruler from its midst,
and will kill all its princes[3] with him,"
says the LORD.

Judgment on Judah

4Thus says the LORD:

"For three transgressions of Judah,
and for four, I will not revoke the punishment,
because they have rejected the law of the LORD,
and have not kept his statutes,
but their lies have led them astray,
those after which their fathers walked.
5 So I will send a fire upon Judah,
and it shall devour the strongholds of Jerusalem."

Judgment on Israel

6Thus says the LORD:

"For three transgressions of Israel,
and for four, I will not revoke the punishment,
because they sell the righteous for silver,
and the needy for a pair of sandals—
7 those who trample the head of the poor into the dust of
the earth
and turn aside the way of the afflicted;
a man and his father go in to the same girl,
so that my holy name is profaned;

[1]Or *officials* [2]Hebrew *I will not turn it back*; also verses 4, 6 [3]Or *officials*

AMOS 2:6–16

JUDGMENT COMES

From the time he established the Mosaic covenant at Mount Sinai (Ex 19:1–8), God had clearly laid out his expectation that his people would treat others fairly. In this portion of Amos, God told the people of Israel that they would be judged severely for continually oppressing others—including selling people, mistreating the poor, and persisting in the practice of sexual immorality.

Similarly, Jesus told the people of his day that judgment would soon come because they also had continued to oppress others. When confronted by a temple system that valued the pocketbooks of merchants more than providing an opportunity for non-Jews to worship the true God, he literally turned the tables on the money changers (Mk 11:15–17).

Jesus refused to tolerate the mistreatment of others. In Matthew 23:13–39, Jesus made it clear that God would soon judge Israel's religious leaders who spiritually oppressed others, saying they had "neglected the weightier matters of the law: justice and mercy and faithfulness" (v. 23).

HAPPY TO JUDGE OTHERS

God's call on our lives is rarely easy, and Amos's call was no exception. The Lord told this shepherd of Tekoa (a town about six miles south of Bethlehem) to leave his home in the southern kingdom of Judah to preach divine judgment to the people of the northern kingdom of Israel. Yet Amos's unflinching prophetic message didn't begin with Israel, but instead with her neighbors.

Imagine the smiles on the faces of the Israelites as Amos systematically proclaimed God's judgment on Syria and its capital city Damascus (1:3 – 5), Philistia and its major cities (1:6 – 8), Phoenicia and its principal city Tyre (1:9 – 10), Edom (1:11 – 12), Ammon (1:13 – 15), Moab (2:1 – 3), and even Judah (2:4 – 5). These countries (with the exception of Phoenicia) had been Israel's enemies for generations.

However, God reserved most of Amos's prophetic message for Israel. The people of Israel may have been cheering the beginning of Amos's message, but they likely didn't appreciate the rest of his message.

Jesus had strong words for religious leaders in his day who were quick to pile judgment upon others without looking at themselves first. Jesus said, "Judge not, that you be not judged. For with the judgment you pronounce you will be judged, and with the measure you use it will be measured to you" (Mt 7:1 – 2). Jesus went on to make his famous analogy urging his listeners not to look at the speck in their brother's eye and ignore the plank in their own (Mt 7:3 – 5).

Jesus never celebrated the sin of others, nor did he celebrate the impending judgment of that sin. Instead, he mourned the coming judgment of God. In Matthew 23, Jesus lamented the impending devastation of Jerusalem that he knew was coming; its residents had killed the prophets and stoned those whom God had sent to warn the city (vv. 37 – 39), and so they were marked for judgment. Jesus modeled a truly broken heart when confronted with God's impending judgment on sin-stained humanity.

Jesus wasn't suggesting that the sins of others be ignored — far from it. Jesus always took sin seriously. Rather he instructed his followers to deal first with their own rebellious hearts before they concerned themselves with the challenges that others faced. Amos's message to the people of Israel was similar, as he called them to face their own sin rather than judging the sins of the surrounding nations.

8 they lay themselves down beside every altar
on garments taken in pledge,
and in the house of their God they drink
the wine of those who have been fined.

9 "Yet it was I who destroyed the Amorite before them,
whose height was like the height of the cedars
and who was as strong as the oaks;
I destroyed his fruit above
and his roots beneath.
10 Also it was I who brought you up out of the land
of Egypt
and led you forty years in the wilderness,
to possess the land of the Amorite.
11 And I raised up some of your sons for prophets,
and some of your young men for Nazirites.
Is it not indeed so, O people of Israel?"
declares the LORD.

12 "But you made the Nazirites drink wine,
and commanded the prophets,
saying, 'You shall not prophesy.'
13 "Behold, I will press you down in your place,
as a cart full of sheaves presses down.
14 Flight shall perish from the swift,
and the strong shall not retain his strength,
nor shall the mighty save his life;
15 he who handles the bow shall not stand,
and he who is swift of foot shall not save himself,
nor shall he who rides the horse save his life;
16 and he who is stout of heart among the mighty
shall flee away naked in that day,"
declares the LORD.

Israel's Guilt and Punishment

3 Hear this word that the LORD has spoken against you, O people of Israel,
against the whole family that I brought up out of the land of Egypt:

2 "You only have I known
of all the families of the earth;
therefore I will punish you
for all your iniquities.

3 "Do two walk together,
unless they have agreed to meet?
4 Does a lion roar in the forest,
when he has no prey?
Does a young lion cry out from his den,
if he has taken nothing?
5 Does a bird fall in a snare on the earth,
when there is no trap for it?
Does a snare spring up from the ground,
when it has taken nothing?
6 Is a trumpet blown in a city,
and the people are not afraid?
Does disaster come to a city,
unless the LORD has done it?

7 "For the Lord GOD does nothing
without revealing his secret
to his servants the prophets.
8 The lion has roared;
who will not fear?
The Lord GOD has spoken;
who can but prophesy?"

9 Proclaim to the strongholds in Ashdod
and to the strongholds in the land of Egypt,
and say, "Assemble yourselves on the mountains of Samaria,
and see the great tumults within her,
and the oppressed in her midst."
10 "They do not know how to do right," declares the LORD,
"those who store up violence and robbery in their strongholds."

11 Therefore thus says the Lord GOD:

"An adversary shall surround the land
and bring down[1] your defenses from you,
and your strongholds shall be plundered."

12 Thus says the LORD: "As the shepherd rescues from the mouth of the lion
two legs, or a piece of an ear, so shall the people of Israel who dwell in Samaria be
rescued, with the corner of a couch and part[2] of a bed.

13 "Hear, and testify against the house of Jacob,"
declares the Lord GOD, the God of hosts,
14 "that on the day I punish Israel for his transgressions,
I will punish the altars of Bethel,
and the horns of the altar shall be cut off
and fall to the ground.
15 I will strike the winter house along with the summer house,
and the houses of ivory shall perish,
and the great houses[3] shall come to an end,"
declares the LORD.

4 "Hear this word, you cows of Bashan,
who are on the mountain of Samaria,
who oppress the poor, who crush the needy,
who say to your husbands, 'Bring, that we may drink!'
2 The Lord GOD has sworn by his holiness
that, behold, the days are coming upon you,
when they shall take you away with hooks,
even the last of you with fishhooks.
3 And you shall go out through the breaches,
each one straight ahead;
and you shall be cast out into Harmon,"
declares the LORD.

4 "Come to Bethel, and transgress;
to Gilgal, and multiply transgression;
bring your sacrifices every morning,
your tithes every three days;
5 offer a sacrifice of thanksgiving of that which is leavened,
and proclaim freewill offerings, publish them;
for so you love to do, O people of Israel!"
declares the Lord GOD.

[1] Hebrew *An adversary, one who surrounds the land—he shall bring down* [2] The meaning of the Hebrew word is uncertain [3] Or *and many houses*

DEMOLISHING STRONGHOLDS

Concerned that citizens of the northern kingdom might return their allegiance to the house of David, Jeroboam had, after his revolt against Judah (1Ki 12:1 – 24), built sanctuaries in Bethel and Dan where his people could go and worship. These convenient places of worship quickly drifted into outright false worship: Like his pagan neighbors, Jeroboam established high places for worship; he then enrolled people into the priesthood who were not a part of Levitical families, and he altered the Hebrew religious calendar. Jeroboam even had two golden calves built (1Ki 12:25 – 30), which were a key part of Canaanite Baal worship — and eerily similar to the idols the people built at the base of Mount Sinai when Moses was on the mountain receiving the Ten Commandments (Ex 32:1,4).

Amos's message was clear: God would judge the nation for their apostasy by destroying the altars of Bethel. Jeroboam and the people of the northern kingdom had practiced their religion within these structures of false worship without considering the inevitable judgment that God would bring.

Throughout the Bible, God consistently judges spiritual strongholds that keep people in bondage to false religions. The good news is that the Bible gives us the battle plan we need as we set about to demolish the spiritual strongholds that seek to dethrone King Jesus in our world. Paul said that we must "take every thought captive to obey Christ" (2Co 10:5), following Christ's example of complete devotion to his Father.

Jeroboam tried to "protect" Israel by setting up an intricate yet false system of religion that kept the people from drifting back to the house of David. Yet he didn't realize that he had become a pawn in a cosmic battle — one in which Jesus had already been declared the winner.

Israel Has Not Returned to the LORD

6 "I gave you cleanness of teeth in all your cities,
and lack of bread in all your places,
yet you did not return to me,"
declares the LORD.

7 "I also withheld the rain from you
when there were yet three months to the harvest;
I would send rain on one city,
and send no rain on another city;
one field would have rain,
and the field on which it did not rain would wither;
8 so two or three cities would wander to another city
to drink water, and would not be satisfied;
yet you did not return to me,"
declares the LORD.

9 "I struck you with blight and mildew;
your many gardens and your vineyards,
your fig trees and your olive trees the locust devoured;
yet you did not return to me,"
declares the LORD.

10 "I sent among you a pestilence after the manner of Egypt;
I killed your young men with the sword,
and carried away your horses,[1]
and I made the stench of your camp go up into your nostrils;
yet you did not return to me,"
declares the LORD.

11 "I overthrew some of you,
as when God overthrew Sodom and Gomorrah,
and you were as a brand[2] plucked out of the burning;
yet you did not return to me,"
declares the LORD.

12 "Therefore thus I will do to you, O Israel;
because I will do this to you,
prepare to meet your God, O Israel!"

13 For behold, he who forms the mountains and creates the wind,
and declares to man what is his thought,
who makes the morning darkness,
and treads on the heights of the earth—
the LORD, the God of hosts, is his name!

Seek the LORD and Live

5 Hear this word that I take up over you in lamentation, O house of Israel:

2 "Fallen, no more to rise,
is the virgin Israel;
forsaken on her land,
with none to raise her up."

3 For thus says the Lord GOD:

"The city that went out a thousand
shall have a hundred left,

[1] Hebrew *along with the captivity of your horses* [2] That is, a burning stick

---

AMOS 4:12

PREPARE TO MEET YOUR GOD

Amos told the Israelites that they would need to "prepare to meet your God," as the nation would soon be held accountable for its ongoing mistreatment of others and its broken religious system. This language recalls God's encounter with Israel at Mount Sinai (Ex 19:10–19), but instead of founding a new covenant, this meeting would be to institute firm discipline for Israel's failure to follow the covenant. Since Israel would soon meet their all-powerful Creator, they had to prepare themselves.

Jesus frequently told his followers to prepare to meet him when he returned. He told a parable about ten virgins who took lamps to go out and meet the bridegroom (Mt 25:1–13). Five of the virgins were unwise and left the house unprepared without enough oil to keep the lamps going. When their lamps went out, these unwise young women had to leave to find more. While they were gone, the groom came.

Jesus urged the people of his day not to be unprepared for his return. Instead, as Amos warned the people of Israel, and as Jesus warned his followers—including believers today—we are always to be prepared to meet our God.

and that which went out a hundred
shall have ten left
to the house of Israel."

4 For thus says the LORD to the house of Israel:

"Seek me and live;
5 but do not seek Bethel,
and do not enter into Gilgal
or cross over to Beersheba;
for Gilgal shall surely go into exile,
and Bethel shall come to nothing."

6 Seek the LORD and live,
lest he break out like fire in the house of Joseph,
and it devour, with none to quench it for Bethel,
7 O you who turn justice to wormwood[1]
and cast down righteousness to the earth!

8 He who made the Pleiades and Orion,
and turns deep darkness into the morning
and darkens the day into night,
who calls for the waters of the sea
and pours them out on the surface of the earth,
the LORD is his name;
9 who makes destruction flash forth against the strong,
so that destruction comes upon the fortress.

10 They hate him who reproves in the gate,
and they abhor him who speaks the truth.
11 Therefore because you trample on[2] the poor
and you exact taxes of grain from him,
you have built houses of hewn stone,
but you shall not dwell in them;
you have planted pleasant vineyards,
but you shall not drink their wine.
12 For I know how many are your transgressions
and how great are your sins—
you who afflict the righteous, who take a bribe,
and turn aside the needy in the gate.
13 Therefore he who is prudent will keep silent in such a time,
for it is an evil time.

14 Seek good, and not evil,
that you may live;
and so the LORD, the God of hosts, will be with you,
as you have said.
15 Hate evil, and love good,
and establish justice in the gate;
it may be that the LORD, the God of hosts,
will be gracious to the remnant of Joseph.

16 Therefore thus says the LORD, the God of hosts, the Lord:

"In all the squares there shall be wailing,
and in all the streets they shall say, 'Alas! Alas!'
They shall call the farmers to mourning
and to wailing those who are skilled in lamentation,

[1]Or *to bitter fruit* [2]Or *you tax*

AMOS 5:18–20

THE DAY OF THE LORD

Apparently a popular theory in Amos's day was that the coming day of the Lord would be a positive development for Israel as God would restore her military, political, and economic status. But God through Amos warned the people that their expectations were severely misdirected, as that day would be one of "darkness, and not light." Instead of restoring Israel's greatness, God's judgment would fall on the nation for its generational disobedience.

Jesus, too, told the people of his day that many people would be surprised at his return. In fact, some would say that they had done many wonderful things in Jesus' name, yet he would declare that he did not know them (Mt 7:21–23). True conversion is necessary for one to know God and await his coming. Those who are truly saved will await the coming of Jesus like a bride waits for her groom (Mt 25:1–13). The love of God's people for their Savior prompts expectant hearts that long for his coming, knowing they will be spared his judgment and granted the joy of living forever in his presence.

17 and in all vineyards there shall be wailing,
for I will pass through your midst,"
says the LORD.

Let Justice Roll Down

18 Woe to you who desire the day of the LORD!
Why would you have the day of the LORD?
It is darkness, and not light,
19 as if a man fled from a lion,
and a bear met him,
or went into the house and leaned his hand against the wall,
and a serpent bit him.
20 Is not the day of the LORD darkness, and not light,
and gloom with no brightness in it?

21 "I hate, I despise your feasts,
and I take no delight in your solemn assemblies.
22 Even though you offer me your burnt offerings and grain offerings,
I will not accept them;
and the peace offerings of your fattened animals,
I will not look upon them.
23 Take away from me the noise of your songs;
to the melody of your harps I will not listen.
24 But let justice roll down like waters,
and righteousness like an ever-flowing stream.

25 "Did you bring to me sacrifices and offerings during the forty years in the
wilderness, O house of Israel? 26 You shall take up Sikkuth your king, and Kiyyun
your star-god—your images that you made for yourselves, 27 and I will send you
into exile beyond Damascus," says the LORD, whose name is the God of hosts.

Woe to Those at Ease in Zion

6 "Woe to those who are at ease in Zion,
and to those who feel secure on the mountain of Samaria,
the notable men of the first of the nations,
to whom the house of Israel comes!
2 Pass over to Calneh, and see,
and from there go to Hamath the great;
then go down to Gath of the Philistines.
Are you better than these kingdoms?
Or is their territory greater than your territory,
3 O you who put far away the day of disaster
and bring near the seat of violence?

4 "Woe to those who lie on beds of ivory
and stretch themselves out on their couches,
and eat lambs from the flock
and calves from the midst of the stall,
5 who sing idle songs to the sound of the harp
and like David invent for themselves instruments of music,
6 who drink wine in bowls
and anoint themselves with the finest oils,
but are not grieved over the ruin of Joseph!
7 Therefore they shall now be the first of those who go into exile,
and the revelry of those who stretch themselves out shall pass away."

FALSE CONFIDENCE

Though Amos's primary calling was to proclaim God's judgment upon the northern kingdom of Israel, represented here by its fortress on the "mountain of Samaria," he also pronounced woe upon Judah, represented here by "Zion" (Jerusalem). Both Israel and Judah had great confidence in their own military strength and their ability to overcome the challenge of outside invaders. But at God's direction, foreign powers eventually conquered both nations, and their people were taken into exile.

When Jesus began his earthly ministry hundreds of years later, he did so with the descendants of those two nations, and it's clear they hadn't yet learned their lesson. Even under Roman occupation, the people of Jesus' day felt secure in their situation and proud of their temple and ever-expanding system of worship. They thought they had no reason to expect that their way of life would soon come to an end. God would judge their misplaced priorities and hard hearts with swift and decisive action. Still, the people did not listen — and God's judgment came.

God's decisive judgment on people and nations never comes without consistent warnings, yet there's no doubt that Scripture presents that judgment as something people do not expect. Jesus compared the people of his day to those in Noah's day, who "were eating and drinking, marrying and giving in marriage, until the day when Noah entered the ark, and they were unaware until the flood came and swept them all away" (Mt 24:38 – 39). Yet judgment, Jesus said again, was coming quickly, as "the Son of Man is coming at an hour you do not expect" (Mt 24:44).

Spiritual complacency and false confidence are themes of at least two of Jesus' letters to the seven churches in Revelation 2 and 3. He told the church in Ephesus that although he appreciated their hard work and perseverance, those works did not replace a relationship with him. Jesus said they had "abandoned the love you had at first" (Rev 2:4). The church in Laodicea also seemed to have an overconfidence that drew them away from Jesus, yet theirs was based upon an abundance of material possessions. Though they had much wealth and prosperity, Jesus said they had also grown "lukewarm" (Rev 3:16). As believers anticipate the day of Jesus' return, they can expect to be surprised. But they are also called to keep watch in anticipation of that day that is sure to come (Mt 25:13).

AMOS 7:7–9

THE PLUMB LINE

To help illustrate the message of God's judgment upon Israel, Amos described a vision that he had of a plumb line. A plumb line is a string with a weight attached to the end. As the string is held against a wall, the weight is allowed to hang freely. Using this device, it soon becomes clear whether the wall is precisely vertical ("plumb") or not. God, through Amos, was telling the people of Israel that their lives simply didn't line up with God's standards.

Jesus clarified this plumb line concept in his conversation with a rich young man (Mt 19:16–24). This man saw himself as blameless when compared to the law, yet Jesus told him there was more to God's standards than merely outward behavior. God cares more about the heart and motivation of a person than he does about their outward appearances or actions. Jesus presented this wealthy young man with an opportunity to see his life in terms of God's plumb line and to repent. Unfortunately the young man—like so many others in Jesus' day and in our modern day as well—thought he was already aligned with God's standards. He went away confused and sorrowful. May this never be the case for seekers who ask Jesus' followers about the hope that they have in him (1Pe 3:15).

8 The Lord GOD has sworn by himself, declares the LORD, the God of hosts:

"I abhor the pride of Jacob
and hate his strongholds,
and I will deliver up the city and all that is in it."

9 And if ten men remain in one house, they shall die. 10 And when one's relative,
the one who anoints him for burial, shall take him up to bring the bones out of the
house, and shall say to him who is in the innermost parts of the house, "Is there
still anyone with you?" he shall say, "No"; and he shall say, "Silence! We must not
mention the name of the LORD."

11 For behold, the LORD commands,
and the great house shall be struck down into fragments,
and the little house into bits.
12 Do horses run on rocks?
Does one plow there[1] with oxen?
But you have turned justice into poison
and the fruit of righteousness into wormwood[2]—
13 you who rejoice in Lo-debar,[3]
who say, "Have we not by our own strength
captured Karnaim[4] for ourselves?"
14 "For behold, I will raise up against you a nation,
O house of Israel," declares the LORD, the God of hosts;
"and they shall oppress you from Lebo-hamath
to the Brook of the Arabah."

Warning Visions

7 This is what the Lord GOD showed me: behold, he was forming locusts when
the latter growth was just beginning to sprout, and behold, it was the latter
growth after the king's mowings. 2 When they had finished eating the grass of the
land, I said,

"O Lord GOD, please forgive!
How can Jacob stand?
He is so small!"
3 The LORD relented concerning this:
"It shall not be," said the LORD.

4 This is what the Lord GOD showed me: behold, the Lord GOD was calling for
a judgment by fire, and it devoured the great deep and was eating up the land.
5 Then I said,

"O Lord GOD, please cease!
How can Jacob stand?
He is so small!"
6 The LORD relented concerning this:
"This also shall not be," said the Lord GOD.

7 This is what he showed me: behold, the Lord was standing beside a wall built
with a plumb line, with a plumb line in his hand. 8 And the LORD said to me, "Amos,
what do you see?" And I said, "A plumb line." Then the Lord said,

"Behold, I am setting a plumb line
in the midst of my people Israel;
I will never again pass by them;
9 the high places of Isaac shall be made desolate,
and the sanctuaries of Israel shall be laid waste,
and I will rise against the house of Jeroboam with the sword."

[1] Or *the sea* [2] Or *into bitter fruit* [3] *Lo-debar* means *nothing* [4] *Karnaim* means *horns* (a symbol of strength)

Amos Accused

10 Then Amaziah the priest of Bethel sent to Jeroboam king of Israel, saying,
"Amos has conspired against you in the midst of the house of Israel. The land is
not able to bear all his words. 11 For thus Amos has said,

"'Jeroboam shall die by the sword,
and Israel must go into exile
away from his land.'"

12 And Amaziah said to Amos, "O seer, go, flee away to the land of Judah, and eat
bread there, and prophesy there, 13 but never again prophesy at Bethel, for it is the
king's sanctuary, and it is a temple of the kingdom."

14 Then Amos answered and said to Amaziah, "I was[1] no prophet, nor a prophet's son, but I was a herdsman and a dresser of sycamore figs. 15 But the LORD took
me from following the flock, and the LORD said to me, 'Go, prophesy to my people
Israel.' 16 Now therefore hear the word of the LORD.

"You say, 'Do not prophesy against Israel,
and do not preach against the house of Isaac.'

17 Therefore thus says the LORD:

"'Your wife shall be a prostitute in the city,
and your sons and your daughters shall fall by the sword,
and your land shall be divided up with a measuring line;
you yourself shall die in an unclean land,
and Israel shall surely go into exile away from its land.'"

The Coming Day of Bitter Mourning

8 This is what the Lord GOD showed me: behold, a basket of summer fruit. 2 And
he said, "Amos, what do you see?" And I said, "A basket of summer fruit."
Then the LORD said to me,

"The end[2] has come upon my people Israel;
I will never again pass by them.
3 The songs of the temple[3] shall become wailings[4] in that day,"
declares the Lord GOD.
"So many dead bodies!"
"They are thrown everywhere!"
"Silence!"

4 Hear this, you who trample on the needy
and bring the poor of the land to an end,
5 saying, "When will the new moon be over,
that we may sell grain?
And the Sabbath,
that we may offer wheat for sale,
that we may make the ephah small and the shekel[5] great
and deal deceitfully with false balances,
6 that we may buy the poor for silver
and the needy for a pair of sandals
and sell the chaff of the wheat?"

7 The LORD has sworn by the pride of Jacob:
"Surely I will never forget any of their deeds.
8 Shall not the land tremble on this account,
and everyone mourn who dwells in it,

---

[1]Or *am*; twice in this verse [2]The Hebrew words for *end* and *summer fruit* sound alike [3]Or *palace*
[4]Or *The singing women of the palace shall wail* [5]An *ephah* was about 3/5 bushel or 22 liters; a *shekel* was about 2/5 ounce or 11 grams

and all of it rise like the Nile,
and be tossed about and sink again, like the Nile of Egypt?"

9 "And on that day," declares the Lord GOD,
"I will make the sun go down at noon
and darken the earth in broad daylight.
10 I will turn your feasts into mourning
and all your songs into lamentation;
I will bring sackcloth on every waist
and baldness on every head;
I will make it like the mourning for an only son
and the end of it like a bitter day.

11 "Behold, the days are coming," declares the Lord GOD,
"when I will send a famine on the land—
not a famine of bread, nor a thirst for water,
but of hearing the words of the LORD.
12 They shall wander from sea to sea,
and from north to east;
they shall run to and fro, to seek the word of the LORD,
but they shall not find it.

13 "In that day the lovely virgins and the young men
shall faint for thirst.
14 Those who swear by the Guilt of Samaria,
and say, 'As your god lives, O Dan,'
and, 'As the Way of Beersheba lives,'
they shall fall, and never rise again."

AMOS 8:11–13

A FAMINE OF GOD'S WORD

The people of Amos's day desperately feared famine, disease, and plagues. These were among the most devastating disasters in the known world at the time. Yet Israel's history pointed to a more desperate situation—a dearth of hearing a word from God. They saw this in the downfall of their first king, Saul (1Sa 14:37; 28:6).

Micah expressed the possibility of the loss of the word of the Lord in the bleakest terms: "Therefore it shall be night to you, without vision, and darkness to you, without divination. The sun shall go down on the prophets, and the day shall be black over them; the seers shall be disgraced, and the diviners put to shame; they shall all cover their lips, for there is no answer from God" (Mic 3:6–7).

Jesus, too, knew that it was better to lack food than to be deprived of the word of God. He reminded Satan of this when he was tempted in the wilderness (Mt 4:4). Praise God that he sent Jesus to be the living Word and living bread for those who will believe in him (Jn 6:51). When people trust in Jesus alone for their salvation, he tells them that they will live forever.

The Destruction of Israel

9 I saw the Lord standing beside[1] the altar, and he said:

"Strike the capitals until the thresholds shake,
and shatter them on the heads of all the people;[2]
and those who are left of them I will kill with the sword;
not one of them shall flee away;
not one of them shall escape.

2 "If they dig into Sheol,
from there shall my hand take them;
if they climb up to heaven,
from there I will bring them down.
3 If they hide themselves on the top of Carmel,
from there I will search them out and take them;
and if they hide from my sight at the bottom of the sea,
there I will command the serpent, and it shall bite them.
4 And if they go into captivity before their enemies,
there I will command the sword, and it shall kill them;
and I will fix my eyes upon them
for evil and not for good."

5 The Lord GOD of hosts,
he who touches the earth and it melts,
and all who dwell in it mourn,
and all of it rises like the Nile,
and sinks again, like the Nile of Egypt;
6 who builds his upper chambers in the heavens
and founds his vault upon the earth;

[1]Or *on* [2]Hebrew *all of them*

who calls for the waters of the sea
and pours them out upon the surface of the earth—
the LORD is his name.

7 "Are you not like the Cushites to me,
O people of Israel?" declares the LORD.
"Did I not bring up Israel from the land of Egypt,
and the Philistines from Caphtor and the Syrians from Kir?
8 Behold, the eyes of the Lord GOD are upon the sinful kingdom,
and I will destroy it from the surface of the ground,
except that I will not utterly destroy the house of Jacob,"
declares the LORD.

9 "For behold, I will command,
and shake the house of Israel among all the nations
as one shakes with a sieve,
but no pebble shall fall to the earth.
10 All the sinners of my people shall die by the sword,
who say, 'Disaster shall not overtake or meet us.'

The Restoration of Israel

11 "In that day I will raise up
the booth of David that is fallen
and repair its breaches,
and raise up its ruins
and rebuild it as in the days of old,
12 that they may possess the remnant of Edom
and all the nations who are called by my name,"[1]
declares the LORD who does this.

13 "Behold, the days are coming," declares the LORD,
"when the plowman shall overtake the reaper
and the treader of grapes him who sows the seed;
the mountains shall drip sweet wine,
and all the hills shall flow with it.
14 I will restore the fortunes of my people Israel,
and they shall rebuild the ruined cities and inhabit them;
they shall plant vineyards and drink their wine,
and they shall make gardens and eat their fruit.
15 I will plant them on their land,
and they shall never again be uprooted
out of the land that I have given them,"
says the LORD your God.

AMOS 9:11–15

SALVATION FOR THE GENTILES

At the Council of Jerusalem, James quoted the first two verses of this passage from the Septuagint (a Greek translation of the Old Testament completed between 250 and 150 BC). The early church leader quoted the following words from the Greek translation of Amos to make a case for Gentile inclusion in the church: "After this I will return, and I will rebuild the tent of David that has fallen; I will rebuild its ruins, and I will restore it, that the remnant of mankind may seek the Lord, and all the Gentiles who are called by my name" (Ac 15:16–17).

James's quote was spoken at a pivotal moment in likely the most significant event in the history of the post-Pentecost church. The letter that resulted from the council clarified that Gentiles would no longer be required to follow traditional Jewish customs either before or after becoming Christians. Jesus himself predicted this unconditional enfolding of the Gentiles into the church in John 10:16 when he said, "I have other sheep that are not of this fold"—sheep that he would bring into a united movement of his followers. Praise God that his vision for salvation expands to all people of the world, Jews and Gentiles alike.

[1]Hebrew; Septuagint (compare Acts 15:17) *that the remnant of mankind and all the nations who are called by my name may seek the Lord*

JESUS: OUR RIGHTEOUS JUDGE

OBADIAH

OBADIAH

BABYLONIAN INVASIONS OF JUDAH	FALL OF JERUSALEM	WRITING OF BOOK OF OBADIAH
c. 605, 597 and 586 BC	*c. 586 BC*	*Shortly after 586 BC*

Obadiah announced God's judgment on the nation of Edom. His prophetic ministry is unusual in the Old Testament because it was not addressed primarily to either Israel or Judah. Rather, Obadiah wrote to the descendants of Esau, the nation of Edom, in light of the ongoing feud between them and the descendants of Esau's brother Jacob, the people of Israel.

Though some scholars believe the historical setting of this book takes place around 850 BC, it is more likely that the context is the fall of Judah in 586 BC. When King Nebuchadnezzar's army demolished Jerusalem and deported the survivors to Babylon, the people of Edom watched with delight. Because the Edomites were related to the Israelites, they should have rallied in support of the people of Judah and offered them refuge in their land. Instead, the Edomites handed God's people over to the Babylonians, killing some of the refugees in the process. And they went into Jerusalem and looted the Israelites' possessions.

The Edomites' prideful self-sufficiency led to their demise, as God allowed them to fall prey to their Arab neighbors. Eventually the Edomites disappeared from history.

The nation about whom Obadiah wrote his prophecy likely never heard or read his words. The prophecy was primarily meant to encourage the people of Judah: even though it appeared that the pagan nations were going unpunished and often emerging victorious over God's people, their fate was sealed. They would not go unpunished. God would care for his people in spite of the rejection they faced at the hands of the Edomites and ultimately bring them back as a remnant to the land he had promised.

This little-known prophet declares a message of resounding familiarity throughout the history of God's people: God is in control of all things, even pagan nations, and will use them to accomplish his sovereign purposes and judge them in due time. Nothing escapes the reach of an all-powerful God, and nothing is hidden from his eyes. Through Christ, God rules and reigns as a righteous judge. Those who turn to him in faith and repentance will escape his just wrath. Those who do not, like the nation of Edom, will face the consequences of their rejection.

FOR THE DAY OF THE LORD IS NEAR UPON ALL THE NATIONS.
AS YOU HAVE DONE, IT SHALL BE DONE TO YOU;
YOUR DEEDS SHALL RETURN ON YOUR OWN HEAD.

Obadiah 15

OBADIAH

[1]The vision of Obadiah.

Edom Will Be Humbled

Thus says the Lord God concerning Edom:
We have heard a report from the Lord,
and a messenger has been sent among the nations:
"Rise up! Let us rise against her for battle!"
2 Behold, I will make you small among the nations;
you shall be utterly despised.[1]
3 The pride of your heart has deceived you,
you who live in the clefts of the rock,[2]
in your lofty dwelling,
who say in your heart,
"Who will bring me down to the ground?"
4 Though you soar aloft like the eagle,
though your nest is set among the stars,
from there I will bring you down,
declares the Lord.

5 If thieves came to you,
if plunderers came by night—
how you have been destroyed!—
would they not steal only enough for themselves?
If grape gatherers came to you,
would they not leave gleanings?
6 How Esau has been pillaged,
his treasures sought out!
7 All your allies have driven you to your border;
those at peace with you have deceived you;
they have prevailed against you;
those who eat your bread[3] have set a trap beneath you—
you have[4] no understanding.

8 Will I not on that day, declares the Lord,
destroy the wise men out of Edom,
and understanding out of Mount Esau?
9 And your mighty men shall be dismayed, O Teman,
so that every man from Mount Esau will be cut off by slaughter.

Edom's Violence Against Jacob

10 Because of the violence done to your brother Jacob,
shame shall cover you,
and you shall be cut off forever.
11 On the day that you stood aloof,
on the day that strangers carried off his wealth
and foreigners entered his gates
and cast lots for Jerusalem,
you were like one of them.
12 But do not gloat over the day of your brother
in the day of his misfortune;

[1]Or *Behold, I have made you small among the nations; you are utterly despised* [2]Or *of Sela* [3]Hebrew lacks *those who eat* [4]Hebrew *he has*

JUDGMENT DAY

God used Obadiah to stand up for Judah and speak a stern warning against its brotherly enemy, Edom. The two nations had a contentious past that started with the twin brothers Jacob and Esau (Ge 25:21 – 34; 27:1 – 41), continued after the exodus of Israel (Nu 20:14 – 21), and persisted until Israel's exile. In fact, in 586 BC, when Nebuchadnezzar's army devastated Jerusalem, the Edomites handed fleeing refugees over to the Babylonians instead of coming to their aid. In God's message through the prophet Obadiah, he makes it clear that Edom will pay for its history of mistreating the people of Israel.

In verse 10 Obadiah says, "Because of the violence done to your brother Jacob, shame shall cover you, and you shall be cut off forever." Although at times it may seem as if God ignores the pain and suffering of his people, the Bible is crystal clear that the sovereign God of Scripture will not overlook evil forever.

Scripture says one day God will decisively judge evil and make right all that is wrong in the world. Obadiah speaks of this day throughout his prophecy but addresses it specifically in verse 15 when he declares that "the day of the LORD is near upon all the nations," not just Edom. On this day Edom will finally pay a price for its treachery against Judah.

Called by multiple names (such as "the day of the LORD/Lord," "the day of wrath," and "the day of the Lord Jesus"), the foreshadowing of the last judgment permeates much of the story of Scripture. Jesus, too, speaks of a day when all people on the planet will be judged. Even careless words will be judged on this day (Mt 12:36 – 37). The activities of our lives — and the lives of all who have ever walked the earth — will be judged then (2Co 5:10).

Scripture says that Jesus himself is the Judge who will preside over that monumental day (Ac 10:42). Not only was Jesus present and active in creation (Col 1:16) and made the payment for believers' sin (Jn 1:29), but he is also the satisfaction of God's judgment (Ro 3:25). The Bible teaches that Jesus' death on the cross satisfies the wrath and judgment of God for any and all who believe in him.

do not rejoice over the people of Judah
in the day of their ruin;
do not boast[1]
in the day of distress.
13 Do not enter the gate of my people
in the day of their calamity;
do not gloat over his disaster
in the day of his calamity;
do not loot his wealth
in the day of his calamity.
14 Do not stand at the crossroads
to cut off his fugitives;
do not hand over his survivors
in the day of distress.

The Day of the Lord Is Near

15 For the day of the Lord is near upon all the nations.
As you have done, it shall be done to you;
your deeds shall return on your own head.
16 For as you have drunk on my holy mountain,
so all the nations shall drink continually;
they shall drink and swallow,
and shall be as though they had never been.
17 But in Mount Zion there shall be those who escape,
and it shall be holy,
and the house of Jacob shall possess their own possessions.
18 The house of Jacob shall be a fire,
and the house of Joseph a flame,
and the house of Esau stubble;
they shall burn them and consume them,
and there shall be no survivor for the house of Esau,
for the Lord has spoken.

The Kingdom of the Lord

19 Those of the Negeb shall possess Mount Esau,
and those of the Shephelah shall possess the land of the Philistines;
they shall possess the land of Ephraim and the land of Samaria,
and Benjamin shall possess Gilead.
20 The exiles of this host of the people of Israel
shall possess the land of the Canaanites as far as Zarephath,
and the exiles of Jerusalem who are in Sepharad
shall possess the cities of the Negeb.
21 Saviors shall go up to Mount Zion
to rule Mount Esau,
and the kingdom shall be the Lord's.

[1]Hebrew *do not enlarge your mouth*

JESUS: OUR MISSIONARY GOD

JONAH

JONAH

REIGN OF JEROBOAM II *c. 793 – 753 BC*	PROPHETIC MINISTRY OF JONAH *c. 800 – 750 BC*	FALL OF NINEVEH *c. 612 BC*

God called Jonah to a difficult and intimidating mission. He commissioned Jonah to go to "Nineveh, that great city" in Assyria and preach against it (1:2), warning this militarily brutal and spiritually pagan nation of God's coming judgment, should the inhabitants fail to repent.

Instead, Jonah boarded a ship heading in the opposite direction. What follows is a very well-known story: God raised a powerful storm, enlightened an insightful crew, and delivered a great fish to thwart Jonah's rebellion. Jonah cried out to God for deliverance, proclaiming his faith in God and his belief that "salvation belongs to the LORD" (2:9). God heard Jonah's prayer and once again called him to go to Nineveh and proclaim God's warning. This time Jonah obeyed and warned the people of God's coming judgment and the city's impending destruction.

Much to Jonah's chagrin, the king of Nineveh and the city's inhabitants responded to his message by believing God and repenting of their sin (3:7 – 10). Their response revealed Jonah's initial motive for disobeying God: Assyria was Israel's hated enemy, and Jonah firmly believed that God's judgment and punishment on this nation was richly deserved. He further erroneously believed that God's saving work should be limited to the chosen people of Israel. Their superiority, in Jonah's mind, came from God's unique call on the nation and his promises to Abraham, Isaac, and Jacob. While God continued to demonstrate patience and persistent love toward Israel, Jonah failed to appreciate the fact that God may do the same for other nations.

Yet God's mission includes all the nations of the world. He is the rightful King who can do with the nations as he sees fit — even choosing to bless those who turn to him for salvation. God is free to show mercy to any person and any nation at any time that he wills. Jonah's sorrow over Nineveh's repentance shows his narrow view of God's kindness.

While the book of Jonah contains no specific prophecies, its narrative structure demonstrates God's passion to bring salvation to the nations. All those who turn to him, even residents of a pagan city at the heart of an evil empire, can find God's mercy (Jer 29:13).

Jesus' stated mission makes this point clear. His mission focused on the Jews first, but extended to graft in Gentile believers who turned to him (Mt 15:21 – 28). Following his resurrection, the church was commissioned, like Jonah, to take the message of the gospel to Gentiles everywhere and invite them to trust in the One who holds salvation in his hands.

WHEN MY LIFE WAS FAINTING AWAY,
I REMEMBERED THE LORD, AND MY PRAYER CAME
TO YOU, INTO YOUR HOLY TEMPLE.

Jonah 2:7

JONAH

Jonah Flees the Presence of the Lord

1 Now the word of the Lord came to Jonah the son of Amittai, saying, 2“Arise, go to Nineveh, that great city, and call out against it, for their evil[1] has come up before me.” 3But Jonah rose to flee to Tarshish from the presence of the Lord. He went down to Joppa and found a ship going to Tarshish. So he paid the fare and went down into it, to go with them to Tarshish, away from the presence of the Lord.

4But the Lord hurled a great wind upon the sea, and there was a mighty tempest on the sea, so that the ship threatened to break up. 5Then the mariners were afraid, and each cried out to his god. And they hurled the cargo that was in the ship into the sea to lighten it for them. But Jonah had gone down into the inner part of the ship and had lain down and was fast asleep. 6So the captain came and said to him, “What do you mean, you sleeper? Arise, call out to your god! Perhaps the god will give a thought to us, that we may not perish.”

Jonah Is Thrown into the Sea

7And they said to one another, “Come, let us cast lots, that we may know on whose account this evil has come upon us.” So they cast lots, and the lot fell on Jonah. 8Then they said to him, “Tell us on whose account this evil has come upon us. What is your occupation? And where do you come from? What is your country? And of what people are you?” 9And he said to them, “I am a Hebrew, and I fear the Lord, the God of heaven, who made the sea and the dry land.” 10Then the men were exceedingly afraid and said to him, “What is this that you have done!” For the men knew that he was fleeing from the presence of the Lord, because he had told them.

11Then they said to him, “What shall we do to you, that the sea may quiet down for us?” For the sea grew more and more tempestuous. 12He said to them, “Pick me up and hurl me into the sea; then the sea will quiet down for you, for I know it is because of me that this great tempest has come upon you.” 13Nevertheless, the men rowed hard[2] to get back to dry land, but they could not, for the sea grew more and more tempestuous against them. 14Therefore they called out to the Lord, “O Lord, let us not perish for this man’s life, and lay not on us innocent blood, for you, O Lord, have done as it pleased you.” 15So they picked up Jonah and hurled him into the sea, and the sea ceased from its raging. 16Then the men feared the Lord exceedingly, and they offered a sacrifice to the Lord and made vows.

A Great Fish Swallows Jonah

17[3]And the Lord appointed[4] a great fish to swallow up Jonah. And Jonah was in the belly of the fish three days and three nights.

Jonah’s Prayer

2 Then Jonah prayed to the Lord his God from the belly of the fish, 2saying,

“I called out to the Lord, out of my distress,
and he answered me;
out of the belly of Sheol I cried,
and you heard my voice.
3 For you cast me into the deep,
into the heart of the seas,
and the flood surrounded me;

[1]The same Hebrew word can mean *evil* or *disaster*, depending on the context; so throughout Jonah
[2]Hebrew *the men dug in* [their oars] [3]Ch 2:1 in Hebrew [4]Or *had appointed*

JONAH 1:12

WATER AS JUDGMENT

When Jonah fled from the Lord’s call and booked passage on a ship headed toward Tarshish, God sent a mighty storm that threatened the lives of everyone in the boat. Jonah knew the wind and the waves were God’s judgment on his decision, and that the only solution to this problem was for them to throw him into the waters.

Throughout the Old Testament, water is a sign of God’s judgment. Jesus also uses water imagery to characterize his crucifixion (Lk 12:50). All of humanity has sinned, and the wages of that sin is death (Ro 6:23), but the good news is that Jesus drowned under God’s overwhelming wrath against sin at the cross and walked away alive three days later so that all who believe on him could be forgiven.

In fact, we picture this gospel story in the sacrament of baptism. The baptismal waters symbolize judgment and salvation, death and resurrection. In baptism, the church announces to the individual in the water, “You have already died, been buried, and walked away from death to new life in Christ.” Baptism replays Noah’s flood, the Red Sea crossing, and Jonah’s rescue from the fish. It tells the story over and over again of a God who rescues his people through the water of judgment.

COMPARING JESUS AND JONAH

Jesus clearly linked his life with the prophet Jonah. When some of the Pharisees challenged Jesus to give them a sign that he was the Messiah, Jesus rebuked them and said that they would only receive the sign of Jonah (Mt 12:38–39). He went on to make this comparison: "For just as Jonah was three days and three nights in the belly of the great fish, so will the Son of Man be three days and three nights in the heart of the earth" (12:40).

Though there are similarities in Jesus' and Jonah's stories, Jesus is much greater! Jonah was a disobedient prophet who ran from his mission to proclaim judgment on the lost people of Nineveh; Jesus was the true, obedient prophet who came to seek and save the lost people of the entire world. When faced with a storm that raged and threatened the lives of the crew, both Jonah and Jesus slept deeply in the boat they were in and had to be awakened. However, while Jonah's crew threw him into the sea to calm the wind and the waves, Jesus told the wind and the waves to be still, and they obeyed his voice (Mk 4:35–41)!

Ultimately Jonah experienced punishment for his own sin, and by his punishment the sailors were saved. Jesus lived a life that was without sin, but at his death he experienced judgment for the sins of the world in order to save others.

In Matthew 12, Jesus essentially told the Pharisees, "I'll give you a sign, but it's not the kind of sign you want. It's a sign of judgment for your resistance toward God." Whether it's the flood of Noah's day, or the Red Sea crashing in on the Egyptian army, or a reluctant prophet thrown overboard into the sea, water consistently represents judgment in the Old Testament. That is why Jesus referred to his cross as a "baptism" (Lk 12:50). That is the sign of Jonah. Jonah almost drowned under the wrath of God, spent three days in the belly of the fish, and then he was brought out alive on the other side to carry out his commission to go to Nineveh. But Jesus, the true and better Jonah, was engulfed under God's complete wrath at Calvary's cross, spent three days in the belly of the earth, then came out alive on the other side to carry out his commission to the nations through his followers (Mt 28:18–20).

Jesus gives the Jewish leaders the sign of Jonah to reveal his identity and mission. They longed for a sign they could see, and Jesus pointed them to the faithfulness of God in history.

JONAH 2:4 – 6

EVERYONE WHO CALLS ON THE NAME OF THE LORD

As he was sinking into the depths of the Mediterranean, Jonah cried out to God. After he was swallowed into the belly of the huge fish, he lifted up a prayer of thanksgiving for God's deliverance. He proclaimed his faith in God and his belief that "salvation belongs to the LORD!" (2:9). Jonah spent three days and three nights in the belly of that fish before being vomited onto the shore. According to Jonah, those who look to God's dwelling will be saved.

The New Testament reveals to us that the temple is no longer a building made with stone and mortar; the new temple is a person—Jesus Christ himself (Jn 2:21; Rev 21:22). All who look to him in trust and repentance and call on his name will be delivered (Ro 10:13).

JONAH 4:1 – 3

JONAH AND THE OLDER BROTHER

Instead of celebrating God's salvation of the people of Nineveh, Jonah became very angry that God would show mercy to the Ninevites. The story of Jonah is similar to a parable that Jesus told about a lost son (Lk 15:11 – 32). The younger of two sons, violating every cultural norm, demanded his inheritance from his father and wasted it all in wild living in a foreign country. When the younger son ran out of resources and returned home, the father showed mercy to him, embracing him and throwing a party. But instead of

(continued on page 1394)

all your breakers and your waves
passed over me.
4 Then I said, 'I am driven away
from your sight;
yet I shall again look
upon your holy temple.'
5 The waters closed in over me to take my life;
the deep surrounded me;
weeds were wrapped about my head.
6 To the roots of the mountains I went down,
to the land whose bars closed upon me forever.
Yet you brought up my life from the pit,
O LORD my God.
7 When my life was fainting away,
I remembered the LORD,
and my prayer came to you,
into your holy temple.
8 Those who pay regard to vain idols
forsake their hope of steadfast love.
9 But I with the voice of thanksgiving
will sacrifice to you;
what I have vowed I will pay.
Salvation belongs to the LORD!"

10 And the LORD spoke to the fish, and it vomited Jonah out upon the dry land.

Jonah Goes to Nineveh

3 Then the word of the LORD came to Jonah the second time, saying, 2 "Arise, go
to Nineveh, that great city, and call out against it the message that I tell you."
3 So Jonah arose and went to Nineveh, according to the word of the LORD. Now
Nineveh was an exceedingly great city,[1] three days' journey in breadth.[2] 4 Jonah
began to go into the city, going a day's journey. And he called out, "Yet forty days,
and Nineveh shall be overthrown!" 5 And the people of Nineveh believed God.
They called for a fast and put on sackcloth, from the greatest of them to the least
of them.

The People of Nineveh Repent

6 The word reached[3] the king of Nineveh, and he arose from his throne, removed his robe, covered himself with sackcloth, and sat in ashes. 7 And he issued
a proclamation and published through Nineveh, "By the decree of the king and
his nobles: Let neither man nor beast, herd nor flock, taste anything. Let them
not feed or drink water, 8 but let man and beast be covered with sackcloth, and
let them call out mightily to God. Let everyone turn from his evil way and from
the violence that is in his hands. 9 Who knows? God may turn and relent and turn
from his fierce anger, so that we may not perish."

10 When God saw what they did, how they turned from their evil way, God
relented of the disaster that he had said he would do to them, and he did not do it.

Jonah's Anger and the LORD's Compassion

4 But it displeased Jonah exceedingly,[4] and he was angry. 2 And he prayed to the
LORD and said, "O LORD, is not this what I said when I was yet in my country?
That is why I made haste to flee to Tarshish; for I knew that you are a gracious God
and merciful, slow to anger and abounding in steadfast love, and relenting from

[1] Hebrew *a great city to God* [2] Or *a visit was a three days' journey* [3] Or *had reached* [4] Hebrew *it was exceedingly evil to Jonah*

GOD'S HEART FOR THE NATIONS

Jonah resisted God's call to bring his word to the Ninevites because he hated the people of Nineveh and did not want them to be saved. In some ways, his disposition was understandable. After all, Nineveh was known as the Assyrian Empire's "great city" (Jnh 1:2). Because they were a militarily ruthless people, the Assyrians were the most feared threat in that era.

Jonah ran from his mission not because he was scared of what the Ninevites might do to him; rather, he was afraid of what God would do for the Ninevites. He knew that God's mercy is an intimate part of God's revealed character (Jnh 4:2), and he wanted judgment for Nineveh, not forgiveness. True to form, throughout the book of Jonah God repeatedly shows mercy: not only to the Ninevites, but also to the sailors and especially to his rebellious prophet Jonah.

Jonah does not share God's heart for the nations. But from the beginning of Israel's history, the divinely chosen people of Israel were meant to be a light to the nations. When God chose Abraham, God said that he would bless all the peoples of the earth through this family (Ge 12:3). The book of Jonah is not just an indictment on God's runaway prophet; it's also a condemnation of the people of Israel, who failed to be a light to the nations.

And yet, God loves Nineveh so much that he will not allow Jonah to fail. Through the fish, he transports Jonah to shore, giving him a second chance to preach the message so that the people of Nineveh can repent. Jonah walks away from death, then walks many miles to the gates of the city to fulfill his commission. Upon hearing God's pronouncement, the king and the people of Nineveh repent and the city is saved.

Believers must be reminded that Paul says that Jesus is the seed of Abraham who will bring salvation to the world (Gal 3:16). Jesus also walked away from death to give the Great Commission to the church. Corporately, we as the church are commanded to go to all nations — regardless of our cultural, political, or ideological differences with those nations — to make disciples. Why? Because the God who loves the entire world has saved us. God has a heart for and a plan to save all people who will come to him in faith and trust; in his goodness, he allows us to be part of that plan: "The Lord is not slow to fulfill his promise as some count slowness, but is patient toward you, not wishing that any should perish, but that all should reach repentance" (2Pe 3:9).

(Jonah and the Older Brother, continued)

celebrating, the father's older son—like Jonah—got angry and protested the unfairness of the father's decision.

These stories are similar in that they end with Jonah and the older brother being corrected for their anger. The stories are also open-ended, because God hopes the reader will get the point that those who struggle to show mercy to the lost need to repent. After all, God is a "gracious God and merciful, slow to anger and abounding in steadfast love, and relenting from disaster" (Jnh 4:2). Isn't it right that a gracious God would seek out the lost and show mercy to them?

The book of Jonah is in the Old Testament to teach us that lesson; the parable of the lost son is in the New Testament to teach us that seeking out and saving the lost is perfectly in line with Jesus' character and his plan of salvation for all who will believe in him.

disaster. 3Therefore now, O LORD, please take my life from me, for it is better for
me to die than to live." 4And the LORD said, "Do you do well to be angry?"
5Jonah went out of the city and sat to the east of the city and made a booth
for himself there. He sat under it in the shade, till he should see what would become of the city. 6Now the LORD God appointed a plant[1] and made it come up over
Jonah, that it might be a shade over his head, to save him from his discomfort.[2]
So Jonah was exceedingly glad because of the plant. 7But when dawn came up
the next day, God appointed a worm that attacked the plant, so that it withered.
8When the sun rose, God appointed a scorching east wind, and the sun beat down
on the head of Jonah so that he was faint. And he asked that he might die and said,
"It is better for me to die than to live." 9But God said to Jonah, "Do you do well to
be angry for the plant?" And he said, "Yes, I do well to be angry, angry enough to
die." 10And the LORD said, "You pity the plant, for which you did not labor, nor did
you make it grow, which came into being in a night and perished in a night. 11And
should not I pity Nineveh, that great city, in which there are more than 120,000
persons who do not know their right hand from their left, and also much cattle?"

[1]Hebrew *qiqayon*, probably the castor oil plant; also verses 7, 9, 10 [2]Or *his evil*

JESUS: OUR COMPASSIONATE KING

MICAH

MICAH

PROPHETIC MINISTRY OF MICAH *c. 735 – 700 BC*	FALL OF ISRAEL *c. 722 BC*	FALL OF JUDAH *c. 586 BC*

Micah, who was from a town in southern Judah, prophesied mostly to the southern kingdom of Judah, though he also spoke to the northern kingdom of Israel. Micah's hope-filled message was meant to encourage God's people in the face of God's judgment. This message did not minimize the impending destruction; in fact, Micah went to great lengths to demonstrate the severity of the punishment God would unleash on the people for their sin.

Micah countered their self-assurance that they would be protected because of their unique covenant relationship with God. Ignoring the warnings of the prophets, many within Judah felt that Jerusalem was impenetrable because it was the site of God's temple — his dwelling place among his people. Surely God would not allow the destruction of the holy city, regardless of how wicked the nation became. Micah sternly warned Judah against such prideful thinking and flawed logic. God would protect his name among the nations. He would not allow the Israelites to defame his glory or tarnish his reputation through their bold-faced idol worship in the very heart of the promised land. Micah assured them that God would purge the people from the land if they did not quickly repent. In kindness, God spared Jerusalem from destruction for over a hundred years after Micah's prophecies. But because of the people's ongoing sin, he finally acted in judgment in 586 BC when the Babylonians captured Jerusalem, destroyed the temple, and led the people into exile.

But Micah weaved threads of hope into his dire warnings for the people of God. Micah pointed back to God's covenant promises as the basis for his ongoing faithfulness to those whom he loves, assuring them that, because God is intent on keeping his promises to Abraham, he will always act to sustain a remnant of his people. Micah also pointed to a future day when a true King would rule over God's people (4:2 – 3). This King would reign in peace and would bring justice to the earth once more. Hundreds of years before Jesus' birth, Micah prophesied that this King would be born in Bethlehem and would one day rule over all Israel (5:2).

The twin themes of judgment and mercy that characterize the prophetic writings derive from God's perfect nature and character. He is a God of holy judgment for sin who, at the same time, shows merciful compassion to his people. God put these characteristics on display time and again for the people of Israel. Micah's writings, and the glorious and specific promises of God's compassionate Messiah, Jesus Christ, provide hope that God will indeed show compassion to his chosen ones once more.

HE HAS TOLD YOU, O MAN, WHAT IS GOOD;
AND WHAT DOES THE LORD REQUIRE OF YOU
BUT TO DO JUSTICE, AND TO LOVE KINDNESS,
AND TO WALK HUMBLY WITH YOUR GOD?

Micah 6:8

MICAH

1 The word of the LORD that came to Micah of Moresheth in the days of Jotham, Ahaz, and Hezekiah, kings of Judah, which he saw concerning Samaria and Jerusalem.

The Coming Destruction

2 Hear, you peoples, all of you;[1]
pay attention, O earth, and all that is in it,
and let the Lord GOD be a witness against you,
the Lord from his holy temple.
3 For behold, the LORD is coming out of his place,
and will come down and tread upon the high places of the earth.
4 And the mountains will melt under him,
and the valleys will split open,
like wax before the fire,
like waters poured down a steep place.
5 All this is for the transgression of Jacob
and for the sins of the house of Israel.
What is the transgression of Jacob?
Is it not Samaria?
And what is the high place of Judah?
Is it not Jerusalem?
6 Therefore I will make Samaria a heap in the open country,
a place for planting vineyards,
and I will pour down her stones into the valley
and uncover her foundations.
7 All her carved images shall be beaten to pieces,
all her wages shall be burned with fire,
and all her idols I will lay waste,
for from the fee of a prostitute she gathered them,
and to the fee of a prostitute they shall return.

8 For this I will lament and wail;
I will go stripped and naked;
I will make lamentation like the jackals,
and mourning like the ostriches.
9 For her wound is incurable,
and it has come to Judah;
it has reached to the gate of my people,
to Jerusalem.

10 Tell it not in Gath;
weep not at all;
in Beth-le-aphrah
roll yourselves in the dust.
11 Pass on your way,
inhabitants of Shaphir,
in nakedness and shame;
the inhabitants of Zaanan
do not come out;
the lamentation of Beth-ezel
shall take away from you its standing place.

[1] Hebrew *all of them*

12 For the inhabitants of Maroth
wait anxiously for good,
because disaster has come down from the LORD
to the gate of Jerusalem.
13 Harness the steeds to the chariots,
inhabitants of Lachish;
it was the beginning of sin
to the daughter of Zion,
for in you were found
the transgressions of Israel.
14 Therefore you shall give parting gifts[1]
to Moresheth-gath;
the houses of Achzib shall be a deceitful thing
to the kings of Israel.
15 I will again bring a conqueror to you,
inhabitants of Mareshah;
the glory of Israel
shall come to Adullam.
16 Make yourselves bald and cut off your hair,
for the children of your delight;
make yourselves as bald as the eagle,
for they shall go from you into exile.

Woe to the Oppressors

2 Woe to those who devise wickedness
and work evil on their beds!
When the morning dawns, they perform it,
because it is in the power of their hand.
2 They covet fields and seize them,
and houses, and take them away;
they oppress a man and his house,
a man and his inheritance.
3 Therefore thus says the LORD:
behold, against this family I am devising disaster,[2]
from which you cannot remove your necks,
and you shall not walk haughtily,
for it will be a time of disaster.
4 In that day they shall take up a taunt song against you
and moan bitterly,
and say, "We are utterly ruined;
he changes the portion of my people;
how he removes it from me!
To an apostate he allots our fields."
5 Therefore you will have none to cast the line by lot
in the assembly of the LORD.

6 "Do not preach"—thus they preach—
"one should not preach of such things;
disgrace will not overtake us."
7 Should this be said, O house of Jacob?
Has the LORD grown impatient?[3]
Are these his deeds?
Do not my words do good
to him who walks uprightly?

[1]Or *give dowry* [2]The same Hebrew word can mean *evil* or *disaster*, depending on the context [3]Hebrew *Has the spirit of the LORD grown short?*

8 But lately my people have risen up as an enemy;
you strip the rich robe from those who pass by trustingly
with no thought of war.[1]
9 The women of my people you drive out
from their delightful houses;
from their young children you take away
my splendor forever.
10 Arise and go,
for this is no place to rest,
because of uncleanness that destroys
with a grievous destruction.
11 If a man should go about and utter wind and lies,
saying, "I will preach to you of wine and strong
drink,"
he would be the preacher for this people!
12 I will surely assemble all of you, O Jacob;
I will gather the remnant of Israel;
I will set them together
like sheep in a fold,
like a flock in its pasture,
a noisy multitude of men.
13 He who opens the breach goes up before them;
they break through and pass the gate,
going out by it.
Their king passes on before them,
the LORD at their head.

MICAH 2:12

THE GOOD SHEPHERD

God, through the prophet Micah, emphatically demonstrates his fierce determination to gather his people from wherever they are scattered, to bring them back to him and to shepherd them to the place where they belong (Mic 2:12). Like a good shepherd, God promised to lead and protect his sheep at all costs; Jesus, God's Son, spoke of himself as the good shepherd who would lay down his very life for his sheep (Jn 10:11).

The people of Israel in Micah's day walked the path of all sinners: As sheep without a shepherd, they were lost, helpless, and doomed to wander aimlessly. God's promise to draw his wayward sheep back was accomplished in Jesus, who, through his work on the cross, leads believers beside quiet waters and restores their souls (Ps 23:1–3).

Rulers and Prophets Denounced

3 And I said:
Hear, you heads of Jacob
and rulers of the house of Israel!
Is it not for you to know justice?—
2 you who hate the good and love the evil,
who tear the skin from off my people[2]
and their flesh from off their bones,
3 who eat the flesh of my people,
and flay their skin from off them,
and break their bones in pieces
and chop them up like meat in a pot,
like flesh in a cauldron.

4 Then they will cry to the LORD,
but he will not answer them;
he will hide his face from them at that time,
because they have made their deeds evil.

5 Thus says the LORD concerning the prophets
who lead my people astray,
who cry "Peace"
when they have something to eat,
but declare war against him
who puts nothing into their mouths.
6 Therefore it shall be night to you, without vision,
and darkness to you, without divination.
The sun shall go down on the prophets,
and the day shall be black over them;

[1]Or *returning from war* [2]Hebrew *from off them*

7 the seers shall be disgraced,
and the diviners put to shame;
they shall all cover their lips,
for there is no answer from God.
8 But as for me, I am filled with power,
with the Spirit of the LORD,
and with justice and might,
to declare to Jacob his transgression
and to Israel his sin.

9 Hear this, you heads of the house of Jacob
and rulers of the house of Israel,
who detest justice
and make crooked all that is straight,
10 who build Zion with blood
and Jerusalem with iniquity.
11 Its heads give judgment for a bribe;
its priests teach for a price;
its prophets practice divination for money;
yet they lean on the LORD and say,
"Is not the LORD in the midst of us?
No disaster shall come upon us."
12 Therefore because of you
Zion shall be plowed as a field;
Jerusalem shall become a heap of ruins,
and the mountain of the house a wooded height.

The Mountain of the LORD

4 It shall come to pass in the latter days
that the mountain of the house of the LORD
shall be established as the highest of the mountains,
and it shall be lifted up above the hills;
and peoples shall flow to it,
2 and many nations shall come, and say:
"Come, let us go up to the mountain of the LORD,
to the house of the God of Jacob,
that he may teach us his ways
and that we may walk in his paths."
For out of Zion shall go forth the law,[1]
and the word of the LORD from Jerusalem.
3 He shall judge between many peoples,
and shall decide disputes for strong nations far
away;
and they shall beat their swords into plowshares,
and their spears into pruning hooks;
nation shall not lift up sword against nation,
neither shall they learn war anymore;
4 but they shall sit every man under his vine and under his
fig tree,
and no one shall make them afraid,
for the mouth of the LORD of hosts has spoken.
5 For all the peoples walk
each in the name of its god,
but we will walk in the name of the LORD our God
forever and ever.

[1]Or *teaching*

MICAH 4:1–5

IN THE LAST DAYS

Micah and Isaiah were contemporaries, and Micah 4:1–3 is a nearly identical echo of Isaiah 2:2–4. Both prophets knew that there would be a time in the last days when a Savior King would rule the nations. Although the people of God would experience hardship in the days before, they would, in this day, live under the protection of the Lord their God, and no one would be able to make them afraid (Mic 4:4–5).

Believers in Christ hold this to be true as well today. Jesus tells his followers, "In the world you will have tribulation. But take heart; I have overcome the world" (Jn 16:33). When Jesus comes again, he will come to judge the people (Jn 5:22), and God will wipe away every tear from every eye of every believer (Rev 21:4). Those who follow Jesus will never be put to shame (Ro 10:11), for they have received by the Spirit a hope that does not disappoint (Ro 5:5). A person who abides in Christ through the Holy Spirit can live a God-glorifying life, since Jesus provides life and peace and salvation both now and forever. And for that, believers will eternally praise "God, our Savior" (Jude 24–25).

The Lord Shall Rescue Zion

6 In that day, declares the Lord,
I will assemble the lame
and gather those who have been driven away
and those whom I have afflicted;
7 and the lame I will make the remnant,
and those who were cast off, a strong nation;
and the Lord will reign over them in Mount Zion
from this time forth and forevermore.

8 And you, O tower of the flock,
hill of the daughter of Zion,
to you shall it come,
the former dominion shall come,
kingship for the daughter of Jerusalem.

9 Now why do you cry aloud?
Is there no king in you?
Has your counselor perished,
that pain seized you like a woman in labor?
10 Writhe and groan,[1] O daughter of Zion,
like a woman in labor,
for now you shall go out from the city
and dwell in the open country;
you shall go to Babylon.
There you shall be rescued;
there the Lord will redeem you
from the hand of your enemies.

11 Now many nations
are assembled against you,
saying, "Let her be defiled,
and let our eyes gaze upon Zion."
12 But they do not know
the thoughts of the Lord;
they do not understand his plan,
that he has gathered them as sheaves to the threshing floor.
13 Arise and thresh,
O daughter of Zion,
for I will make your horn iron,
and I will make your hoofs bronze;
you shall beat in pieces many peoples;
and shall devote[2] their gain to the Lord,
their wealth to the Lord of the whole earth.

The Ruler to Be Born in Bethlehem

5 [3] Now muster your troops, O daughter[4] of troops;
siege is laid against us;
with a rod they strike the judge of Israel
on the cheek.
2[5] But you, O Bethlehem Ephrathah,
who are too little to be among the clans of Judah,
from you shall come forth for me
one who is to be ruler in Israel,
whose coming forth is from of old,
from ancient days.

[1]Or *push* [2]Hebrew *devote to destruction* [3]Ch 4:14 in Hebrew [4]That is, city [5]Ch 5:1 in Hebrew

3 Therefore he shall give them up until the time
when she who is in labor has given birth;
then the rest of his brothers shall return
to the people of Israel.
4 And he shall stand and shepherd his flock in the strength
of the LORD,
in the majesty of the name of the LORD his God.
And they shall dwell secure, for now he shall be great
to the ends of the earth.
5 And he shall be their peace.

When the Assyrian comes into our land
and treads in our palaces,
then we will raise against him seven shepherds
and eight princes of men;
6 they shall shepherd the land of Assyria with the sword,
and the land of Nimrod at its entrances;
and he shall deliver us from the Assyrian
when he comes into our land
and treads within our border.

A Remnant Shall Be Delivered

7 Then the remnant of Jacob shall be
in the midst of many peoples
like dew from the LORD,
like showers on the grass,
which delay not for a man
nor wait for the children of man.
8 And the remnant of Jacob shall be among the nations,
in the midst of many peoples,
like a lion among the beasts of the forest,
like a young lion among the flocks of sheep,
which, when it goes through, treads down
and tears in pieces, and there is none to deliver.
9 Your hand shall be lifted up over your adversaries,
and all your enemies shall be cut off.

10 And in that day, declares the LORD,
I will cut off your horses from among you
and will destroy your chariots;
11 and I will cut off the cities of your land
and throw down all your strongholds;
12 and I will cut off sorceries from your hand,
and you shall have no more tellers of fortunes;
13 and I will cut off your carved images
and your pillars from among you,
and you shall bow down no more
to the work of your hands;
14 and I will root out your Asherah images from among you
and destroy your cities.
15 And in anger and wrath I will execute vengeance
on the nations that did not obey.

The Indictment of the LORD

6 Hear what the LORD says:
Arise, plead your case before the mountains,
and let the hills hear your voice.

A PROMISED RULER FROM BETHLEHEM

God prophesied through the prophet Micah that the Savior of the world — the Davidic king who would rule forever — would come from a small, obscure town called Bethlehem (Mic 5:2). He would shepherd God's people and be their peace (vv. 4 – 5). Bethlehem had its fair share of lows, such as times of moral decay during the judges (Jdg 19). However, the chief priests and teachers of the law confirmed Bethlehem as the birthplace of the Messiah when Herod questioned them, citing Micah as their source of information (Mt 2:1 – 6).

Bethlehem means "house of bread." Bread was critical in ancient times as it signified economic stability and sustained physical life. In a spiritual sense, it also represented provision from God, who had provided manna, which was actual "bread from heaven" (Ex 16:4), in the desert, demonstrating his willingness and power to supply his people with all that they needed.

At one point in his ministry, Jesus reminded the Jewish crowd listening to him that although God provided for their forefathers by giving them manna in the wilderness, there was now a new picture of provision: Jesus himself (Jn 6:31 – 35). The true bread from heaven was standing in front of them as the One who came down from heaven to give life to the world (Jn 6:33). Jesus is the true "bread of life," and anyone who comes to him will never go hungry (Jn 6:35).

Micah also described this Messianic shepherd as one whose greatness will reach "to the ends of the earth" (Mic 5:4) and defines him as one who "shall be their peace" (5:5). Paul encourages Christians in the church at Ephesus that Jesus "himself is our peace" (Eph 2:14). Bethlehem is significant — both as a sweet promise for the people of Israel in Micah's time and also for all who follow Jesus. Believers can point back to this city as the birthplace of their Savior, their peace, the fulfillment of God's prophecy through Micah, which is perfectly and completely satisfied in Christ.

2 Hear, you mountains, the indictment of the LORD,
and you enduring foundations of the earth,
for the LORD has an indictment against his people,
and he will contend with Israel.

3 "O my people, what have I done to you?
How have I wearied you? Answer me!
4 For I brought you up from the land of Egypt
and redeemed you from the house of slavery,
and I sent before you Moses,
Aaron, and Miriam.
5 O my people, remember what Balak king of Moab devised,
and what Balaam the son of Beor answered him,
and what happened from Shittim to Gilgal,
that you may know the righteous acts of the LORD."

What Does the LORD Require?

6 "With what shall I come before the LORD,
and bow myself before God on high?
Shall I come before him with burnt offerings,
with calves a year old?
7 Will the LORD be pleased with[1] thousands of rams,
with ten thousands of rivers of oil?
Shall I give my firstborn for my transgression,
the fruit of my body for the sin of my soul?"
8 He has told you, O man, what is good;
and what does the LORD require of you
but to do justice, and to love kindness,[2]
and to walk humbly with your God?

Destruction of the Wicked

9 The voice of the LORD cries to the city—
and it is sound wisdom to fear your name:
"Hear of the rod and of him who appointed it![3]
10 Can I forget any longer the treasures[4] of wickedness in the house
of the wicked,
and the scant measure that is accursed?
11 Shall I acquit the man with wicked scales
and with a bag of deceitful weights?
12 Your[5] rich men are full of violence;
your inhabitants speak lies,
and their tongue is deceitful in their mouth.
13 Therefore I strike you with a grievous blow,
making you desolate because of your sins.
14 You shall eat, but not be satisfied,
and there shall be hunger within you;
you shall put away, but not preserve,
and what you preserve I will give to the sword.
15 You shall sow, but not reap;
you shall tread olives, but not anoint yourselves with oil;
you shall tread grapes, but not drink wine.
16 For you have kept the statutes of Omri,[6]
and all the works of the house of Ahab;
and you have walked in their counsels,

[1]Or *Will the LORD accept* [2]Or *steadfast love* [3]The meaning of the Hebrew is uncertain [4]Or *Are there still treasures* [5]Hebrew *whose* [6]Hebrew *For the statutes of Omri are kept*

MICAH 6:8

WHAT DOES GOD REQUIRE OF US?

These beautiful, famous words of the prophet Micah outline God's simple expectations of his people: "To do justice, and to love kindness, and to walk humbly" with God (Mic 6:8). These qualities of the heart that lead to a God-pleasing life have stood the test of time because they reflect the heart of God himself. Throughout the history of his interaction with his people, God has longed for them to remember his goodness and generosity to his people and to live in response to all they know about the Lord.

Jesus confronted the religious leaders of his day, the teachers of the law and Pharisees, for turning worship into drudgery and for outwardly doing all the right things but inwardly neglecting to show justice and mercy. He harshly criticized them, calling them "hypocrites" and "blind guides" (Mt 23:23–24). God desires that his people walk humbly with him, for as they walk with him, they become more like him. Jesus is the way (Jn 14:6). He is the One who came to serve, not to be served (Mk 10:45). When a crowd asked him what kind of works God requires, he simply answered, "This is the work of God, that you believe in him whom he has sent" (Jn 6:28–29). When Jesus' people follow him with their whole hearts, they develop hearts like his—hearts that are compassionate and swift to do justice.

that I may make you a desolation, and your[1] inhabitants a hissing;
so you shall bear the scorn of my people."

Wait for the God of Salvation

7 Woe is me! For I have become
as when the summer fruit has been gathered,
as when the grapes have been gleaned:
there is no cluster to eat,
no first-ripe fig that my soul desires.
2 The godly has perished from the earth,
and there is no one upright among mankind;
they all lie in wait for blood,
and each hunts the other with a net.
3 Their hands are on what is evil, to do it well;
the prince and the judge ask for a bribe,
and the great man utters the evil desire of his soul;
thus they weave it together.
4 The best of them is like a brier,
the most upright of them a thorn hedge.
The day of your watchmen, of your punishment, has come;
now their confusion is at hand.
5 Put no trust in a neighbor;
have no confidence in a friend;
guard the doors of your mouth
from her who lies in your arms;[2]
6 for the son treats the father with contempt,
the daughter rises up against her mother,
the daughter-in-law against her mother-in-law;
a man's enemies are the men of his own house.
7 But as for me, I will look to the LORD;
I will wait for the God of my salvation;
my God will hear me.

8 Rejoice not over me, O my enemy;
when I fall, I shall rise;
when I sit in darkness,
the LORD will be a light to me.
9 I will bear the indignation of the LORD
because I have sinned against him,
until he pleads my cause
and executes judgment for me.
He will bring me out to the light;
I shall look upon his vindication.
10 Then my enemy will see,
and shame will cover her who said to me,
"Where is the LORD your God?"
My eyes will look upon her;
now she will be trampled down
like the mire of the streets.

11 A day for the building of your walls!
In that day the boundary shall be far extended.
12 In that day they[3] will come to you,
from Assyria and the cities of Egypt,
and from Egypt to the River,[4]
from sea to sea and from mountain to mountain.

[1]Hebrew *its* [2]Hebrew *bosom* [3]Hebrew *he* [4]That is, the Euphrates

FORGIVENESS

Forgiveness and compassion are at the very heart of who God is: a God who casts "all our sins into the depths of the sea" (Mic 7:19). What a beautiful exclamation point with which to finish out the book of Micah. As his prophecy comes to a close, Micah ends with this vivid picture of the forgiveness God offers. This promise recalls a similar promise made to the people of Israel through Moses at Mount Sinai (Ex 34:6–9).

God's promise unfolds as his people confess their sin earlier in the chapter (Mic 7:9). Micah likens it to sitting in darkness, yet holding onto the hope that through God's grace the people will be brought into the light (7:8). The prophet goes on to explain that the people will experience God's wrath as a consequence of their sin, until there is someone to plead their case (7:9). Incredibly, Jesus came to do just that.

The divine verdict against human sin is "guilty," and its consequence is death (Ro 6:23). But God delights to show mercy (Mic 7:18), and his own arm works salvation (Isa 59:16). Before Jesus, no one else could satisfy God's wrath against sin. No one in history was righteous — not even one person (Ro 3:10)! Yet God's promise of forgiveness remained. That's why God "made him to be sin who knew no sin, so that in him we might become the righteousness of God" (2Co 5:21). Because Jesus is the Righteous One, followers of Christ now have an Advocate who will stand at their side before the Father — that Advocate is the Son, Jesus Christ (1Jn 2:1).

There is now a responsibility on the forgiven to extend forgiveness to the world around them. Jesus clearly calls his followers to a higher standard by telling them to forgive others just as their heavenly Father has forgiven them. He warns them that if forgiveness is withheld, God will withhold it from them as well (Mt 6:14–15). Paul exhorts the church at Ephesus in the same way, encouraging them to be kind and compassionate, "forgiving one another, as God in Christ forgave you" (Eph 4:32). This type of forgiveness should mark God's church throughout all generations as well.

13 But the earth will be desolate
because of its inhabitants,
for the fruit of their deeds.

14 Shepherd your people with your staff,
the flock of your inheritance,
who dwell alone in a forest
in the midst of a garden land;[1]
let them graze in Bashan and Gilead
as in the days of old.
15 As in the days when you came out of the land of Egypt,
I will show them[2] marvelous things.
16 The nations shall see and be ashamed of all their might;
they shall lay their hands on their mouths;
their ears shall be deaf;
17 they shall lick the dust like a serpent,
like the crawling things of the earth;
they shall come trembling out of their strongholds;
they shall turn in dread to the LORD our God,
and they shall be in fear of you.

God's Steadfast Love and Compassion

18 Who is a God like you, pardoning iniquity
and passing over transgression
for the remnant of his inheritance?
He does not retain his anger forever,
because he delights in steadfast love.
19 He will again have compassion on us;
he will tread our iniquities underfoot.
You will cast all our[3] sins
into the depths of the sea.
20 You will show faithfulness to Jacob
and steadfast love to Abraham,
as you have sworn to our fathers
from the days of old.

[1]Hebrew *of Carmel* [2]Hebrew *him* [3]Hebrew *their*

JESUS: OUR WRATH BEARER

NAHUM

NAHUM

ASSYRIA CONQUERS ISRAEL	WRITING OF BOOK OF NAHUM	FALL OF NINEVEH
c. 722 BC	*Probably shortly before 612 BC*	*c. 612 BC*

Nahum, like Jonah, addressed the city of Nineveh. During the century or more in between these two prophets, King Sennacherib made Nineveh the capital of Assyria. In Jonah's day, the Ninevites heeded the prophet's warning and appeared to repent of their sin. Not long after that, however, Nineveh returned to its extremely wicked, cruel, and prideful ways. Rather than extending another warning to Nineveh, God called Nahum to announce a message of doom. Though most of his prophecies are addressed to Nineveh — representing the entire nation of Assyria — Nahum wrote this book to comfort and encourage the people of Judah.

God had used the Assyrians to execute judgment against his own people. By 722 BC, Assyria had routed Samaria and deported many Israelites into exile. Diabolical and cruel, the Assyrian regime enacted swift and severe punishment upon their enemies. Nineveh earned a reputation for bloodthirsty and deplorable acts of terror and war. These atrocities, wrote Nahum, had not escaped God's notice (Na 1:3).

Even though God used the Assyrians to accomplish his purposes, they were not excused from their own guilt before God. God could, at the same time, use them and judge them. God would surely do to them what they had done to the Israelites. However, God's judgment (unlike Assyria's) would be righteous and pure. He would not dole out punishment in a capricious manner; rather, he would rightly judge these rebellious people.

Nineveh's judgment serves as a prototype of the wrath of God that comes to all those who scorn his mercy and rebelliously pursue their wicked ways. Because he is omniscient, God sees and knows everything that humanity does. Because he is sovereign, he can act at any time to crush any form of evil. And because he is just, he will perfectly judge evildoers in due time.

The people of Judah, and subsequent believers, can find hope in the fact that while this life is filled with evil and pain, God will ultimately right all wrongs. Because of Jesus, believers can take joy in the fact that the wrath of God that was due them as a result of their sin has been poured out on Christ. They will not suffer in the coming day of God's wrath; until God ushers in his new heaven and new earth, believers must cry out to the nations to turn from their sin and turn to Christ for salvation. Jesus' followers must tell their friends, family members, coworkers, and the nations about the salvation that's freely available before they, like Nineveh, face the judgment of a holy and just Judge.

THE LORD IS SLOW TO ANGER AND GREAT IN POWER,
AND THE LORD WILL BY NO MEANS CLEAR THE GUILTY.
HIS WAY IS IN WHIRLWIND AND STORM, AND
THE CLOUDS ARE THE DUST OF HIS FEET.

Nahum 1:3

NAHUM

1 An oracle concerning Nineveh. The book of the vision of Nahum of Elkosh.

God's Wrath Against Nineveh

2 The LORD is a jealous and avenging God;
the LORD is avenging and wrathful;
the LORD takes vengeance on his adversaries
and keeps wrath for his enemies.
3 The LORD is slow to anger and great in power,
and the LORD will by no means clear the guilty.
His way is in whirlwind and storm,
and the clouds are the dust of his feet.
4 He rebukes the sea and makes it dry;
he dries up all the rivers;
Bashan and Carmel wither;
the bloom of Lebanon withers.
5 The mountains quake before him;
the hills melt;
the earth heaves before him,
the world and all who dwell in it.

6 Who can stand before his indignation?
Who can endure the heat of his anger?
His wrath is poured out like fire,
and the rocks are broken into pieces by him.
7 The LORD is good,
a stronghold in the day of trouble;
he knows those who take refuge in him.
8 But with an overflowing flood
he will make a complete end of the adversaries,[1]
and will pursue his enemies into darkness.
9 What do you plot against the LORD?
He will make a complete end;
trouble will not rise up a second time.
10 For they are like entangled thorns,
like drunkards as they drink;
they are consumed like stubble fully dried.
11 From you came one
who plotted evil against the LORD,
a worthless counselor.

12 Thus says the LORD,
"Though they are at full strength and many,
they will be cut down and pass away.
Though I have afflicted you,
I will afflict you no more.
13 And now I will break his yoke from off you
and will burst your bonds apart."

14 The LORD has given commandment about you:
"No more shall your name be perpetuated;
from the house of your gods I will cut off
the carved image and the metal image.
I will make your grave, for you are vile."

[1] Hebrew *of her place*

A GOSPEL CASE STUDY

The people of Israel and Judah had suffered because of the evil actions of the people of Nineveh. Yet as Nahum waited in hope, he affirmed that God is good all the time, providing a refuge in times of trouble. Rather than faltering in faith, Nahum declared that God cares for those who trust in him.

Years earlier, God had commanded the prophet Jonah to travel to Nineveh and warn the people of God's coming wrath if they did not repent (Jnh 1:1 – 2; 3:1 – 2). In spite of Jonah's efforts and hopes to the contrary, the people of Nineveh repented and God withheld his judgment (Jnh 3:10). Unfortunately, as the years passed their commitment faded, and the people of Nineveh returned to their evil ways. Knowing the impact of Nineveh's short-lived repentance, Nahum prophesied God's coming judgment. In a message filled with gospel truth, Nahum extolled God's patience and mercy, but also God's judgment.

The people of Nineveh became an Old Testament case study of the gospel story. They lived in the destructive power of sin, yet Nineveh experienced God's inexplicable mercy through the reluctant prophet Jonah, who brought them the minimum possible warning to repent (Jnh 3:4). Nineveh's reprieve from judgment proclaimed for all times the extent of God's love. Yet Nineveh's return to sin and its turning away from the one true God clarifies to all who read the book of Nahum that sin brings profound consequences. The wages of sin is death (Ro 6:23), so the people of Nineveh died rejecting his mercy.

Ultimately, Jesus exemplified the truth that Nahum's experience foreshadowed. Jesus came preaching a gospel of repentance, declaring that people need to turn from sin and toward God (Mt 4:17). Jesus led people who took sin seriously to realize that sin pervaded their lives to a degree they had never imagined (Mt 5:27 – 28). To those trapped in sin and assumed to be lost by the religious elite, Jesus extended the hope of forgiveness through the full extent of God's love. In the end, Jesus quantified the high price of sin when he, the only perfect One, died for all who would never be truly good, much less perfect. Then, through his resurrection and resounding defeat of death itself, Jesus punctuated all that he had previously promised.

Nahum had declared that God is good, a refuge in times of trouble. Jesus embodied the goodness of God; the good news about Jesus offers refuge to all who will respond in faith.

15[1] Behold, upon the mountains, the feet of him
who brings good news,
who publishes peace!
Keep your feasts, O Judah;
fulfill your vows,
for never again shall the worthless pass through you;
he is utterly cut off.

The Destruction of Nineveh

2 The scatterer has come up against you.
Man the ramparts;
watch the road;
dress for battle;[2]
collect all your strength.

2 For the LORD is restoring the majesty of Jacob
as the majesty of Israel,
for plunderers have plundered them
and ruined their branches.

3 The shield of his mighty men is red;
his soldiers are clothed in scarlet.
The chariots come with flashing metal
on the day he musters them;
the cypress spears are brandished.
4 The chariots race madly through the streets;
they rush to and fro through the squares;
they gleam like torches;
they dart like lightning.
5 He remembers his officers;
they stumble as they go,
they hasten to the wall;
the siege tower[3] is set up.
6 The river gates are opened;
the palace melts away;
7 its mistress[4] is stripped;[5] she is carried off,
her slave girls lamenting,
moaning like doves
and beating their breasts.
8 Nineveh is like a pool
whose waters run away.[6]
"Halt! Halt!" they cry,
but none turns back.
9 Plunder the silver,
plunder the gold!
There is no end of the treasure
or of the wealth of all precious things.

10 Desolate! Desolation and ruin!
Hearts melt and knees tremble;
anguish is in all loins;
all faces grow pale!
11 Where is the lions' den,
the feeding place of the young lions,

[1]Ch 2:1 in Hebrew [2]Hebrew *gird your loins* [3]Or *the mantelet* [4]The meaning of the Hebrew word rendered *its mistress* is uncertain [5]Or *exiled* [6]Compare Septuagint; the meaning of the Hebrew is uncertain

NAHUM 2:2

RESTORING WHAT WAS LOST

For years, the people of Israel had suffered under the onslaught of the nation of Assyria and its flagship city, Nineveh. Earlier, the Assyrians had crushed the northern kingdom of Israel, and now the southern kingdom of Judah was subject to Assyria. Having fallen from their days of glory under David and Solomon, the Israelites heard the offer of restoration and a return to splendor through the prophet Nahum: everything that sin had destroyed could be rebuilt through God's strength. Years earlier Moses had affirmed a similar promise, telling the people that even if they were exiled among the nations God would reclaim and restore them to himself (Dt 30:1–3). Later Isaiah expanded this promise to include the gospel purpose for which Israel existed: to become a light to the Gentiles so that all nations could experience his salvation (Isa 49:6).

Ultimately, Jesus offered the promise of restoration. Lives devastated by sin's brutal attack could be made new. The people in Nahum's day likely struggled to believe such good news could be true. Yet the tide changed; Nineveh faltered and failed. The Israelites experienced temporary relief, but Jesus now offers complete restoration from sin's domination. Through faith, Jesus transforms lives so thoroughly that those impacted can best be described as new creations (2Co 5:17).

where the lion and lioness went,
where his cubs were, with none to disturb?
12 The lion tore enough for his cubs
and strangled prey for his lionesses;
he filled his caves with prey
and his dens with torn flesh.

13 Behold, I am against you, declares the LORD of hosts, and I will burn your[1] chariots in smoke, and the sword shall devour your young lions. I will cut off your prey from the earth, and the voice of your messengers shall no longer be heard.

Woe to Nineveh

3 Woe to the bloody city,
all full of lies and plunder—
no end to the prey!
2 The crack of the whip, and rumble of the wheel,
galloping horse and bounding chariot!
3 Horsemen charging,
flashing sword and glittering spear,
hosts of slain,
heaps of corpses,
dead bodies without end—
they stumble over the bodies!
4 And all for the countless whorings of the prostitute,
graceful and of deadly charms,
who betrays nations with her whorings,
and peoples with her charms.

5 Behold, I am against you,
declares the LORD of hosts,
and will lift up your skirts over your face;
and I will make nations look at your nakedness
and kingdoms at your shame.
6 I will throw filth at you
and treat you with contempt
and make you a spectacle.
7 And all who look at you will shrink from you and say,
"Wasted is Nineveh; who will grieve for her?"
Where shall I seek comforters for you?

8 Are you better than Thebes[2]
that sat by the Nile,
with water around her,
her rampart a sea,
and water her wall?
9 Cush was her strength;
Egypt too, and that without limit;
Put and the Libyans were her[3] helpers.

10 Yet she became an exile;
she went into captivity;
her infants were dashed in pieces
at the head of every street;
for her honored men lots were cast,
and all her great men were bound in chains.
11 You also will be drunken;
you will go into hiding;
you will seek a refuge from the enemy.

[1]Hebrew *her* [2]Hebrew *No-amon* [3]Hebrew *your*

NAHUM 3:5

WHEN GOD IS AGAINST YOU

Once the people of Nineveh rejected God's mercy and returned to their pattern of sin, they experienced God's wrath through judgment. For a short season, Assyria and its "great city" of Nineveh had glimpsed the grace that flowed when God was acting mercifully on their behalf (Jnh 3:10; 4:10–11). Yet as their pride swelled and they flexed their military might once again, Nineveh encountered the practical implications of rejecting God. Nahum's declaration against Nineveh lays out in graphic detail the ramifications of their choices. As they stood for themselves, God stood against them. God's perfect holiness requires that he stand against sin. As a result God stands against all people, since all people sin and fall short of the glory of God (Ro 3:23). The gospel offers an elegant escape from inevitable judgment: Jesus took on the death penalty for the sin of all who would believe in him.

With sin's debt paid in full, those who place their faith in Jesus enter a new reality, an eternally altered standing with God. This right standing with God is so complete that it doesn't matter if anyone or anything else stands against the believer (Ro 8:31–32). In the end, only two options exist: God standing against or God standing for. Jesus makes the second option possible through the good news of the gospel, and that option changes eternity for those who trust in him for salvation.

12 All your fortresses are like fig trees
with first-ripe figs—
if shaken they fall
into the mouth of the eater.
13 Behold, your troops
are women in your midst.
The gates of your land
are wide open to your enemies;
fire has devoured your bars.

14 Draw water for the siege;
strengthen your forts;
go into the clay;
tread the mortar;
take hold of the brick mold!
15 There will the fire devour you;
the sword will cut you off.
It will devour you like the locust.
Multiply yourselves like the locust;
multiply like the grasshopper!
16 You increased your merchants
more than the stars of the heavens.
The locust spreads its wings and flies away.

17 Your princes[1] are like grasshoppers,
your scribes[2] like clouds of locusts
settling on the fences
in a day of cold—
when the sun rises, they fly away;
no one knows where they are.

18 Your shepherds are asleep,
O king of Assyria;
your nobles slumber.
Your people are scattered on the mountains
with none to gather them.
19 There is no easing your hurt;
your wound is grievous.
All who hear the news about you
clap their hands over you.
For upon whom has not come
your unceasing evil?

[1]Or *guards* [2]Or *marshals*

JESUS: OUR JOYFUL SALVATION

HABAKKUK

HABAKKUK

BABYLONIANS ATTACK JUDAH	WRITING OF BOOK OF HABAKKUK	BABYLONIANS CONQUER JUDAH
c. 605 and 597 BC	*c. 605 BC*	*c. 586 BC*

The prophet Habakkuk was filled with questions for God. Unlike many other God-appointed spokesmen, Habakkuk publicly expressed his inner frustration at evil and at God's perceived lack of response to it. The prophet pleaded, "How long shall I cry for help, and you will not hear?" (1:2). Habakkuk's longing for answers and his cries for deliverance match the fervor of many of the psalms that David wrote during a similarly treacherous time in his own life.

The tone of Habakkuk's questions reveals two central frustrations. First, he did not understand why evil ran unchecked among the people of God; it seemed as if God left the sins of Judah unpunished. Second, Habakkuk watched as the pagan Babylonians (Chaldeans) prospered and were even used as God's instrument to conquer his own people. How could God bless a nation that so obviously stood in opposition to God's commands?

God graciously responded to Habakkuk's laments, and he pronounced five woes on the Babylonians because of their evil deeds (2:6 – 19). While it may seem that the Babylonians prospered while the people of God perished, God would see to it that all would be made right in the end: God would judge — and judge perfectly.

Habakkuk concluded this brief book with a prayer of praise to God (3:17 – 19). In it, he beautifully captured the deep-rooted faith that is sustained by a high view of God's control in the world. Though outwardly it may seem that evil is winning and the righteous are perishing, God will judge justly and set things right. Habakkuk called Judah to not lose hope, even if external signs of blessing from God's hand were scarce.

With the prophet, God's people "will take joy in the God of my salvation" (3:18), knowing that he is good and his perfect purposes will prevail.

Ultimately, such joyful hope is only possible because of the work of Jesus Christ. He is God's perfect answer to the evil that pervades our fallen world. God took the greatest act of evil in human history — the murder of his innocent Son — and used it to open the way of salvation for all who will trust in Jesus' saving work. And God, through Christ, will one day purge the world of evil, sin, and death forever and prove once again to be the God who saves.

YET I WILL REJOICE IN THE LORD;
I WILL TAKE JOY IN THE GOD OF MY SALVATION.
GOD, THE LORD, IS MY STRENGTH;
HE MAKES MY FEET LIKE THE DEER'S;
HE MAKES ME TREAD ON MY HIGH PLACES.

Habakkuk 3:18 – 19

HABAKKUK

1 The oracle that Habakkuk the prophet saw.

Habakkuk's Complaint

2 O LORD, how long shall I cry for help,
and you will not hear?
Or cry to you "Violence!"
and you will not save?
3 Why do you make me see iniquity,
and why do you idly look at wrong?
Destruction and violence are before me;
strife and contention arise.
4 So the law is paralyzed,
and justice never goes forth.
For the wicked surround the righteous;
so justice goes forth perverted.

The LORD's Answer

5 "Look among the nations, and see;
wonder and be astounded.
For I am doing a work in your days
that you would not believe if told.
6 For behold, I am raising up the Chaldeans,
that bitter and hasty nation,
who march through the breadth of the earth,
to seize dwellings not their own.
7 They are dreaded and fearsome;
their justice and dignity go forth from themselves.
8 Their horses are swifter than leopards,
more fierce than the evening wolves;
their horsemen press proudly on.
Their horsemen come from afar;
they fly like an eagle swift to devour.
9 They all come for violence,
all their faces forward.
They gather captives like sand.
10 At kings they scoff,
and at rulers they laugh.
They laugh at every fortress,
for they pile up earth and take it.
11 Then they sweep by like the wind and go on,
guilty men, whose own might is their god!"

Habakkuk's Second Complaint

12 Are you not from everlasting,
O LORD my God, my Holy One?
We shall not die.
O LORD, you have ordained them as a judgment,
and you, O Rock, have established them for
reproof.
13 You who are of purer eyes than to see evil
and cannot look at wrong,

HABAKKUK 1:5–6

DON'T BE FOOLISH

Habakkuk questioned how a loving God could surrender his chosen people to defeat by the cruel and pagan Babylonians. While Judah had sinned, most of the people continued to assume that they were automatically entitled to God's blessing, yet God had consistently communicated that their physical and emotional comfort were not his top priority. In fact, he promised through the prophet Habakkuk that he would do things in their day that they would not believe, even if they were told what was coming. While some could have interpreted this as good news, it was not. God would call the wicked nation of Babylon to bring judgment to his people.

Years later, the apostle Paul quoted Habakkuk 1:5 while speaking to a congregation in a Jewish synagogue. He encouraged his hearers not to allow religious tradition to prevent them from accepting Jesus as God's Messiah (Ac 13:38–41). God had instructed Habakkuk and his people that he would punish evil and establish righteousness, and in the end redeem his people in an amazing way. Paul pointed his hearers to the fulfillment of this prophecy: the work of Jesus Christ on their behalf. He exhorted them that they would be foolish not to see God at work through this amazing Messiah, Jesus, to whose saving work the prophet Habakkuk and others had pointed.

why do you idly look at traitors
and remain silent when the wicked swallows up
the man more righteous than he?
14 You make mankind like the fish of the sea,
like crawling things that have no ruler.
15 He[1] brings all of them up with a hook;
he drags them out with his net;
he gathers them in his dragnet;
so he rejoices and is glad.
16 Therefore he sacrifices to his net
and makes offerings to his dragnet;
for by them he lives in luxury,[2]
and his food is rich.
17 Is he then to keep on emptying his net
and mercilessly killing nations forever?

2 I will take my stand at my watchpost
and station myself on the tower,
and look out to see what he will say to me,
and what I will answer concerning my complaint.

The Righteous Shall Live by His Faith

2 And the LORD answered me:

"Write the vision;
make it plain on tablets,
so he may run who reads it.
3 For still the vision awaits its appointed time;
it hastens to the end—it will not lie.
If it seems slow, wait for it;
it will surely come; it will not delay.

4 "Behold, his soul is puffed up; it is not upright within him,
but the righteous shall live by his faith.[3]

5 "Moreover, wine[4] is a traitor,
an arrogant man who is never at rest.[5]
His greed is as wide as Sheol;
like death he has never enough.
He gathers for himself all nations
and collects as his own all peoples."

Woe to the Chaldeans

6 Shall not all these take up their taunt against him, with scoffing and riddles
for him, and say,

"Woe to him who heaps up what is not his own—
for how long?—
and loads himself with pledges!"
7 Will not your debtors suddenly arise,
and those awake who will make you tremble?
Then you will be spoil for them.
8 Because you have plundered many nations,
all the remnant of the peoples shall plunder you,
for the blood of man and violence to the earth,
to cities and all who dwell in them.

[1]That is, the wicked foe [2]Hebrew *his portion is fat* [3]Or *faithfulness* [4]Masoretic Text; Dead Sea Scroll *wealth* [5]The meaning of the Hebrew of these two lines is uncertain

HABAKKUK 2:1–3

MAKE IT CLEAR

God instructed Habakkuk to write down the revelation and make it plain on tablets so that a herald could run with it (Hab 2:2). He wanted the people to understand, without any room for misinterpretation or doubt, what he was saying, and he wanted to make certain that everyone had the opportunity to respond. The message was about what would happen in the future—initially in God's judgment of the Babylonians and ultimately in the earth being filled with the knowledge of God's glory (2:14).

In the New Testament, God gave the apostle John a more complete vision, which compelled John to refer to the message as "the revelation of Jesus Christ" (Rev 1:1). Through time, God has communicated in different ways (Heb 1:1) but has spoken with ultimate clarity through Jesus (Jn 1:17; Heb 1:2). God's Word, and all that God has revealed, works like a surgeon's knife in human hearts—penetrating and dividing as it exposes the truth (Heb 4:12). In Habakkuk's day, God communicated because he expected people to respond. Because of his crystal-clear communication in Jesus, God desires that those who hear his Word today choose life's most important response—turning to Jesus for the forgiveness of their sin and accepting God's free gift of new life as his adopted children.

HABAKKUK 3:1–2

IN WRATH REMEMBER MERCY

In the midst of his confusion about God's revealed ways and plans, Habakkuk expressed his faith through prayer. He affirmed that he had heard of God's fame and stood in awe of God's deeds, and he pleaded with God to renew his work in the past so it would be known in the present. Yet, since God had clearly communicated his plans to judge Judah, Habakkuk asked God to remember mercy even as he poured out his wrath.

What Habakkuk could not understand at the time was that God's mercy was woven through all that was to come. Without having mercy, God would have completely destroyed the people of Judah. Without God's mercy, the nation would never return from exile to rebuild Jerusalem and the temple. Without his mercy, God would not send Jesus into the world to die. Without his mercy, God would not offer Jesus' perfect payment for sin to a hopelessly sinful world so that people who deserved only judgment could experience only grace.

Even as Habakkuk prayed, God continued the work he had started. This work encompassed all that would happen to Judah through Babylon, but it continued purposefully through the death, resurrection and ascension of Jesus. Jesus now reigns forever in heaven, surrounded by all those who did not get what they deserved but rather received what they could never have hoped to earn: complete forgiveness, utter peace, and eternal life with God.

9 "Woe to him who gets evil gain for his house,
to set his nest on high,
to be safe from the reach of harm!
10 You have devised shame for your house
by cutting off many peoples;
you have forfeited your life.
11 For the stone will cry out from the wall,
and the beam from the woodwork respond.

12 "Woe to him who builds a town with blood
and founds a city on iniquity!
13 Behold, is it not from the LORD of hosts
that peoples labor merely for fire,
and nations weary themselves for nothing?
14 For the earth will be filled
with the knowledge of the glory of the LORD
as the waters cover the sea.

15 "Woe to him who makes his neighbors drink—
you pour out your wrath and make them drunk,
in order to gaze at their nakedness!
16 You will have your fill of shame instead of glory.
Drink, yourself, and show your uncircumcision!
The cup in the LORD's right hand
will come around to you,
and utter shame will come upon your glory!
17 The violence done to Lebanon will overwhelm you,
as will the destruction of the beasts that terrified
them,
for the blood of man and violence to the earth,
to cities and all who dwell in them.

18 "What profit is an idol
when its maker has shaped it,
a metal image, a teacher of lies?
For its maker trusts in his own creation
when he makes speechless idols!
19 Woe to him who says to a wooden thing, Awake;
to a silent stone, Arise!
Can this teach?
Behold, it is overlaid with gold and silver,
and there is no breath at all in it.
20 But the LORD is in his holy temple;
let all the earth keep silence before him."

Habakkuk's Prayer

3 A prayer of Habakkuk the prophet, according to Shigionoth.

2 O LORD, I have heard the report of you,
and your work, O LORD, do I fear.
In the midst of the years revive it;
in the midst of the years make it known;
in wrath remember mercy.
3 God came from Teman,
and the Holy One from Mount Paran. *Selah*
His splendor covered the heavens,
and the earth was full of his praise.

4 His brightness was like the light;
rays flashed from his hand;
and there he veiled his power.
5 Before him went pestilence,
and plague followed at his heels.[1]
6 He stood and measured the earth;
he looked and shook the nations;
then the eternal mountains were scattered;
the everlasting hills sank low.
His were the everlasting ways.
7 I saw the tents of Cushan in affliction;
the curtains of the land of Midian did tremble.
8 Was your wrath against the rivers, O LORD?
Was your anger against the rivers,
or your indignation against the sea,
when you rode on your horses,
on your chariot of salvation?
9 You stripped the sheath from your bow,
calling for many arrows.[2] *Selah*
You split the earth with rivers.
10 The mountains saw you and writhed;
the raging waters swept on;
the deep gave forth its voice;
it lifted its hands on high.
11 The sun and moon stood still in their place
at the light of your arrows as they sped,
at the flash of your glittering spear.
12 You marched through the earth in fury;
you threshed the nations in anger.
13 You went out for the salvation of your people,
for the salvation of your anointed.
You crushed the head of the house of the wicked,
laying him bare from thigh to neck.[3] *Selah*
14 You pierced with his own arrows the heads of his warriors,
who came like a whirlwind to scatter me,
rejoicing as if to devour the poor in secret.
15 You trampled the sea with your horses,
the surging of mighty waters.
16 I hear, and my body trembles;
my lips quiver at the sound;
rottenness enters into my bones;
my legs tremble beneath me.
Yet I will quietly wait for the day of trouble
to come upon people who invade us.

Habakkuk Rejoices in the LORD

17 Though the fig tree should not blossom,
nor fruit be on the vines,
the produce of the olive fail
and the fields yield no food,
the flock be cut off from the fold
and there be no herd in the stalls,

[1]Hebrew *feet* [2]The meaning of the Hebrew line is uncertain [3]The meaning of the Hebrew line is uncertain

YET I WILL REJOICE

Habakkuk saw the sin of his day, its impact on the people of Judah, and the collective corrosion of the nation. Seeking to frame what he saw with a lens of faith, he waited on God, calling out for divine help. But Habakkuk struggled when God told him his plan to punish evilness with more evilness. Would God actually use the wicked nation of Babylon (Chaldea) to punish the (relatively less wicked) nation of Judah (Hab 1:6)?

Habakkuk waited for God to answer his questions (1:2 – 3; 2:1). He listened as God explained that the righteous would live by faith (2:4) and marveled as God promised that, in time, the earth would be filled with the knowledge of the glory of the Lord as the waters cover the sea (2:3,14).

As Habakkuk reflected on all that was happening in Judah and the devastation to come, he turned to God in prayer. He poured out his praise, his questions, his longing, and his confusion. He recalled Israel's past, the era when God's glory covered the heavens and his praise filled the earth (3:3). He reveled in the memory of how God had chastened Israel's enemies and delivered Israel from those who sought to devour them (3:13 – 15).

Habakkuk acted in faith during this dark and difficult time. He thought about the future and imagined fig trees no longer budding, vines without grapes, olive crops failing, fields with no food, pens with no sheep, and stalls with no cattle (3:17).

Centuries later, as Jesus walked into Jerusalem, he knew he would soon be crucified. Like Habakkuk, he knew the Father's will and acknowledged that horrific events were coming that he would have to endure. Unlike Habakkuk, Jesus could have altered the course of his life on earth and traveled the easier path. Yet no other path would make Jesus the way, the truth, and the life through which every person would be able to gain access to the Father (Jn 14:6).

On earth, Jesus was a real person, experiencing life as we all do, yet without sin. In his humanity, like the prophet Habakkuk, he experienced a troubled heart. He knew he could ask to be saved from that dark hour to come. But he also fully knew that the brutal path of crucifixion was the reason he had come to the world (Jn 12:27). So in this intense hour he prayed, "Father, glorify your name" (Jn 12:28). In that moment Jesus, the Son of God, lived by faith and perfectly modeled for us complete reliance on God.

18 yet I will rejoice in the LORD;
    I will take joy in the God of my salvation.
19 GOD, the Lord, is my strength;
    he makes my feet like the deer's;
    he makes me tread on my high places.

To the choirmaster: with stringed[1] instruments.

[1]Hebrew *my stringed*

JESUS: OUR MIGHTY ONE

ZEPHANIAH

ZEPHANIAH

REIGN OF JOSIAH *c. 640 – 609 BC*	WRITING OF BOOK OF ZEPHANIAH *Probably between 640 and 627 BC*	FALL OF JUDAH *c. 586 BC*

Zephaniah wrote to warn God's people of the coming day of the Lord. Certainly, he was not the only prophet to use this theme, though the looming judgment of this day featured more prominently in Zephaniah's ministry than in some of the other prophets' writings.

He began with a stern word of warning to his fellow Israelites in Judah. Instead of following God's commands, they had modeled the pagan ways of the surrounding nations. They disregarded God's law, engaged in idolatrous worship, and lived without remorse. Zephaniah begged the people to repent and turn back to God before it was too late.

History records that they did heed Zephaniah's warning, at least for a time. The southern kingdom, Judah, had watched as Assyria destroyed the northern kingdom, Israel. It had seemed that the same fate was imminent for Judah as well. Under the evil reign of Manasseh, the people had engaged in deplorable acts of wickedness. But God used godly King Josiah to foster a revival in the nation. Under Josiah's leadership, the people heard the Book of the Law and were broken by their sin. Their repentance led to a number of reforms, which promoted worship and obedience among the people once again (2Ki 22:1 — 23:25). Zephaniah ministered during Josiah's reign (Zep 1:1), and this prophecy was likely delivered early in Josiah's reign — helping to spur Josiah on in his reforms. This spiritual transformation, though short-lived, prevented an Assyrian invasion and the destruction of Jerusalem for a time.

God's judgment on his appointed day — through the Babylonians — would certainly come. Zephaniah knew that the people's obedience was a faulty basis for confidence; they were sinful through and through. Yet, Zephaniah's conclusion expressed hope based not on the moral uprightness of the people but on the power of God. He is "a mighty one" who would save a remnant of his people from the coming judgment (3:17). Zephaniah encouraged the people that God "will rejoice over you with gladness; he will quiet you by his love; he will exult over you with loud singing" (3:17). These poetic refrains depict an astonishing act of God's grace. In the person and work of Jesus, God's mighty power and tender affections meet. Jesus proves that God is mighty to save his people through the sacrifice of his Son.

THE LORD WITHIN HER IS RIGHTEOUS;
HE DOES NO INJUSTICE; EVERY MORNING
HE SHOWS FORTH HIS JUSTICE;
EACH DAWN HE DOES NOT FAIL;
BUT THE UNJUST KNOWS NO SHAME.

Zephaniah 3:5

ZEPHANIAH

1 The word of the LORD that came to Zephaniah the son of Cushi, son of Gedaliah, son of Amariah, son of Hezekiah, in the days of Josiah the son of Amon,
king of Judah.

The Coming Judgment on Judah

2 "I will utterly sweep away everything
from the face of the earth," declares the LORD.
3 "I will sweep away man and beast;
I will sweep away the birds of the heavens
and the fish of the sea,
and the rubble[1] with the wicked.
I will cut off mankind
from the face of the earth," declares the LORD.
4 "I will stretch out my hand against Judah
and against all the inhabitants of Jerusalem;
and I will cut off from this place the remnant of Baal
and the name of the idolatrous priests along with the priests,
5 those who bow down on the roofs
to the host of the heavens,
those who bow down and swear to the LORD
and yet swear by Milcom,[2]
6 those who have turned back from following the LORD,
who do not seek the LORD or inquire of him."

The Day of the LORD Is Near

7 Be silent before the Lord GOD!
For the day of the LORD is near;
the LORD has prepared a sacrifice
and consecrated his guests.
8 And on the day of the LORD's sacrifice—
"I will punish the officials and the king's sons
and all who array themselves in foreign attire.
9 On that day I will punish
everyone who leaps over the threshold,
and those who fill their master's[3] house
with violence and fraud.

10 "On that day," declares the LORD,
"a cry will be heard from the Fish Gate,
a wail from the Second Quarter,
a loud crash from the hills.
11 Wail, O inhabitants of the Mortar!
For all the traders[4] are no more;
all who weigh out silver are cut off.
12 At that time I will search Jerusalem with lamps,
and I will punish the men
who are complacent,[5]
those who say in their hearts,
'The LORD will not do good,
nor will he do ill.'

[1]Or *stumbling blocks* (that is, idols) [2]Or *their king* [3]Or *their Lord's* [4]Or *all the people of Canaan*
[5]Hebrew *are thickening on the dregs* [of their wine]

13 Their goods shall be plundered,
and their houses laid waste.
Though they build houses,
they shall not inhabit them;
though they plant vineyards,
they shall not drink wine from them."

14 The great day of the LORD is near,
near and hastening fast;
the sound of the day of the LORD is bitter;
the mighty man cries aloud there.
15 A day of wrath is that day,
a day of distress and anguish,
a day of ruin and devastation,
a day of darkness and gloom,
a day of clouds and thick darkness,
16 a day of trumpet blast and battle cry
against the fortified cities
and against the lofty battlements.

17 I will bring distress on mankind,
so that they shall walk like the blind,
because they have sinned against the LORD;
their blood shall be poured out like dust,
and their flesh like dung.
18 Neither their silver nor their gold
shall be able to deliver them
on the day of the wrath of the LORD.
In the fire of his jealousy,
all the earth shall be consumed;
for a full and sudden end
he will make of all the inhabitants of the earth.

Judgment on Judah's Enemies

2 Gather together, yes, gather,
O shameless nation,
2 before the decree takes effect[1]
—before the day passes away like chaff—
before there comes upon you
the burning anger of the LORD,
before there comes upon you
the day of the anger of the LORD.
3 Seek the LORD, all you humble of the land,
who do his just commands;[2]
seek righteousness; seek humility;
perhaps you may be hidden
on the day of the anger of the LORD.
4 For Gaza shall be deserted,
and Ashkelon shall become a desolation;
Ashdod's people shall be driven out at noon,
and Ekron shall be uprooted.

5 Woe to you inhabitants of the seacoast,
you nation of the Cherethites!
The word of the LORD is against you,
O Canaan, land of the Philistines;
and I will destroy you until no inhabitant is left.

[1]Hebrew *gives birth* [2]Or *who carry out his judgment*

ZEPHANIAH 2:3

SEEK HUMILITY

Zephaniah—the prophet to Judah—devoted the early part of his manuscript to warning Judah and Jerusalem of the coming day of the Lord (1:4–7). For those who continued to sin against the Lord, this day's approach only meant the increasing proximity of God's judgment. Though the northern kingdom of Israel experienced destruction nearly 100 years earlier—something these readers knew well—the southern kingdom of Judah continued to stiffen its neck against the Lord's warnings.

In mercy, God sent Zephaniah to call them to repentance once again. He commanded them to seek the Lord, particularly in a spirit of humility. It is evident that pride had contributed to their rebellion in some sense, as the author referred to humility twice in 2:3.

Paul wrote about the day of the Lord in a letter to the Thessalonian church, describing it as coming "like a thief in the night" (1Th 5:2). Paul describes two categories of people in that text as well. Those who are in the *darkness* will not escape the coming destruction (1Th 5:4). However, Christ died so that children of the *light* might be sheltered from the coming wrath of God (1Th 5:5,9). While God opposes pride, his grace and favor await the humble (1Pe 5:5).

6 And you, O seacoast, shall be pastures,
with meadows[1] for shepherds
and folds for flocks.
7 The seacoast shall become the possession
of the remnant of the house of Judah,
on which they shall graze,
and in the houses of Ashkelon
they shall lie down at evening.
For the LORD their God will be mindful of them
and restore their fortunes.

8 "I have heard the taunts of Moab
and the revilings of the Ammonites,
how they have taunted my people
and made boasts against their territory.
9 Therefore, as I live," declares the LORD of hosts,
the God of Israel,
"Moab shall become like Sodom,
and the Ammonites like Gomorrah,
a land possessed by nettles and salt pits,
and a waste forever.
The remnant of my people shall plunder them,
and the survivors of my nation shall possess them."
10 This shall be their lot in return for their pride,
because they taunted and boasted
against the people of the LORD of hosts.
11 The LORD will be awesome against them;
for he will famish all the gods of the earth,
and to him shall bow down,
each in its place,
all the lands of the nations.

12 You also, O Cushites,
shall be slain by my sword.

13 And he will stretch out his hand against the north
and destroy Assyria,
and he will make Nineveh a desolation,
a dry waste like the desert.
14 Herds shall lie down in her midst,
all kinds of beasts;[2]
even the owl and the hedgehog[3]
shall lodge in her capitals;
a voice shall hoot in the window;
devastation will be on the threshold;
for her cedar work will be laid bare.
15 This is the exultant city
that lived securely,
that said in her heart,
"I am, and there is no one else."
What a desolation she has become,
a lair for wild beasts!
Everyone who passes by her
hisses and shakes his fist.

[1]Or *caves* [2]Hebrew *beasts of every nation* [3]The identity of the animals rendered *owl* and *hedgehog* is uncertain

Judgment on Jerusalem and the Nations

3 Woe to her who is rebellious and defiled,
the oppressing city!
2 She listens to no voice;
she accepts no correction.
She does not trust in the LORD;
she does not draw near to her God.

3 Her officials within her
are roaring lions;
her judges are evening wolves
that leave nothing till the morning.
4 Her prophets are fickle, treacherous men;
her priests profane what is holy;
they do violence to the law.
5 The LORD within her is righteous;
he does no injustice;
every morning he shows forth his justice;
each dawn he does not fail;
but the unjust knows no shame.

6 "I have cut off nations;
their battlements are in ruins;
I have laid waste their streets
so that no one walks in them;
their cities have been made desolate,
without a man, without an inhabitant.
7 I said, 'Surely you will fear me;
you will accept correction.
Then your[1] dwelling would not be cut off
according to all that I have appointed against you.'[2]
But all the more they were eager
to make all their deeds corrupt.

8 "Therefore wait for me," declares the LORD,
"for the day when I rise up to seize the prey.
For my decision is to gather nations,
to assemble kingdoms,
to pour out upon them my indignation,
all my burning anger;
for in the fire of my jealousy
all the earth shall be consumed.

The Conversion of the Nations

9 "For at that time I will change the speech of the peoples
to a pure speech,
that all of them may call upon the name of the LORD
and serve him with one accord.
10 From beyond the rivers of Cush
my worshipers, the daughter of my dispersed ones,
shall bring my offering.

11 "On that day you shall not be put to shame
because of the deeds by which you have rebelled against me;
for then I will remove from your midst
your proudly exultant ones,

[1]Hebrew *her* [2]Hebrew *her*

ZEPHANIAH 3:5

JUSTICE

Zephaniah began this chapter describing the city of Jerusalem. God's image-bearers—living inside the walls of God's city—continued to reject God's word. An oppressing and rebellious metropolis, the corruption within this city knew no bounds. Zephaniah described the officials and rulers as bloodthirsty animals; the prophets and priests he labeled treacherous and perverse (vv. 3–4).

However, the Lord of the city remained righteous, having never done wrong. He had no trouble meeting the standard of justice he maintained. In fact, the prophet portrayed each morning as fresh evidence of the Lord's faithfulness (v. 5).

As the pages of the Gospels reveal, Jesus puts this perfect justice on display, even declaring, "I always do the things that are pleasing to him [God]" (Jn 8:29). Jesus always did what was right. Therefore, he proved to be the only one who could rightly judge the world. God's ways are perfect, and in his grace he provides a way, through Jesus, for people to come to him.

HE WILL REJOICE OVER YOU WITH GLADNESS

Zephaniah closed his book by pointing his audience to the coming day of the Lord. The impending judgment will be extensive, as the jealous anger of the Lord removes all prideful people from his city, Jerusalem (3:7–8,11). On that day, God's wrath will leave no rebel untouched.

However, within his city, God will leave people who are humble—his remnant (vv. 12–13). As a foreshadowing of later teaching (Mt 5:5), the meek will inherit Jerusalem. In an appropriate response to the swift and decisive judgment on their enemies, Zephaniah called upon believers to rejoice (Zep 3:14–15). Their God—the "mighty one"—was with them (vv. 16–17).

Their rejoicing is reflective of another's rejoicing. Zephaniah goes on to detail the Lord's affections toward his people. Zephaniah does not portray God as indifferent to his people. Rather, God delights in those whom he delivers. In fact, the One who created music—soaring melodies and resonant harmonies—actually sings over his people (v. 17).

Though God sees his people this way, God's people often fail to see God this way—as one who enthusiastically rejoices over them. The apostle Paul, knowing the calloused human heart, prayed that believers' eyes would be enlightened to see God's joy in the redeemed. His prayer for the Ephesian church included a request that they might see the "riches of his glorious inheritance in the saints" (Eph 1:18). The inheritance Paul described does not appear to be one awaiting God's people; rather, the inheritance is one that awaits God. God sees a diverse body of believers, united in and clothed with Christ's righteousness. The meek inherit the earth; God inherits the meek.

Zephaniah described a mighty-to-save God who would be with his people (3:17). In the Gospel of Matthew, an angel appeared to Joseph to tell him to name his soon-to-arrive son "Jesus, for he will save his people from their sins" (Mt 1:21). Matthew goes on to interpret this as a fulfillment of another name, Immanuel, meaning "God with us" (Mt 1:22–23). This saving God dwells with—and *delights in*—his people. God rejoices over those who choose to trust him.

and you shall no longer be haughty
in my holy mountain.
12 But I will leave in your midst
a people humble and lowly.
They shall seek refuge in the name of the LORD,
13 those who are left in Israel;
they shall do no injustice
and speak no lies,
nor shall there be found in their mouth
a deceitful tongue.
For they shall graze and lie down,
and none shall make them afraid."

Israel's Joy and Restoration

14 Sing aloud, O daughter of Zion;
shout, O Israel!
Rejoice and exult with all your heart,
O daughter of Jerusalem!
15 The LORD has taken away the judgments against you;
he has cleared away your enemies.
The King of Israel, the LORD, is in your midst;
you shall never again fear evil.
16 On that day it shall be said to Jerusalem:
"Fear not, O Zion;
let not your hands grow weak.
17 The LORD your God is in your midst,
a mighty one who will save;
he will rejoice over you with gladness;
he will quiet you by his love;
he will exult over you with loud singing.
18 I will gather those of you who mourn for the festival,
so that you will no longer suffer reproach.[1]
19 Behold, at that time I will deal
with all your oppressors.
And I will save the lame
and gather the outcast,
and I will change their shame into praise
and renown in all the earth.
20 At that time I will bring you in,
at the time when I gather you together;
for I will make you renowned and praised
among all the peoples of the earth,
when I restore your fortunes
before your eyes," says the LORD.

[1]The meaning of the Hebrew is uncertain

JESUS: OUR MAIN PRIORITY

HAGGAI

HAGGAI

FALL OF JUDAH/TEMPLE DESTROYED *c. 586 BC*	HAGGAI PROPHESIES/ WORK ON TEMPLE RENEWED *c. 520 BC*	TEMPLE COMPLETED *c. 516 BC*

Haggai proclaimed the word of God to the Jews who had returned from exile in Babylon and were attempting to rebuild their lives in the promised land. After conquering the Babylonians, in 538 BC King Cyrus of Persia allowed the Jews to go back to their homeland. Led by Zerubbabel, about 50,000 Jews made the long journey and began working to restore God-centered worship among their people by rebuilding Jerusalem and the temple.

But the zeal that should have marked the people of God for this work was lacking. The extent of the work combined with criticism from hostile neighbors produced a defeated spirit among the remnant who returned. More than that, they focused on their own selfish desires and abandoned God's work in favor of their own individual pursuits. Claiming that it was not yet the right time to begin work on God's house, they were passionately building their own houses (1:2 – 4).

Haggai directed the people's attention to the problems of their day — namely, the challenging economic times and the infertility of the land. These factors were not the result of poor planning or strategy on the part of the people, but were rather the direct result of their spiritual lethargy. God himself withheld rain and brought about economic turmoil to demonstrate the folly of the people's priorities. They had willingly chosen to prioritize their own desires over the explicit commands of God (1:5 – 11).

As a result, the temple remained in ruins. The place where God chose to dwell among his people was still in shambles, and to make matters worse, the people seemingly didn't care. The ruined temple site served as a tangible symbol of the ruined spiritual state of God's people.

Thankfully, the people heeded Haggai's message and promptly began work on the temple. Haggai followed with another simple yet profound message of hope. He assured them that God was with them in their work and would continue to dwell in their midst. "Be strong ... Work, for I am with you, declares the Lord of hosts" (2:4). Though the people would continue to falter, God's full and final dwelling among his people would find its fulfillment in "God with us," Immanuel (Mt 1:23) — Jesus the Christ, who would rightly receive his people's worship forever.

NOW, THEREFORE, THUS SAYS THE LORD OF HOSTS:
CONSIDER YOUR WAYS.

Haggai 1:5

HAGGAI

The Command to Rebuild the Temple

1 In the second year of Darius the king, in the sixth month, on the first day of
the month, the word of the LORD came by the hand of Haggai the prophet
to Zerubbabel the son of Shealtiel, governor of Judah, and to Joshua the son of
Jehozadak, the high priest: 2"Thus says the LORD of hosts: These people say the
time has not yet come to rebuild the house of the LORD." 3Then the word of the
LORD came by the hand of Haggai the prophet, 4"Is it a time for you yourselves to
dwell in your paneled houses, while this house lies in ruins? 5Now, therefore, thus
says the LORD of hosts: Consider your ways. 6You have sown much, and harvested
little. You eat, but you never have enough; you drink, but you never have your fill.
You clothe yourselves, but no one is warm. And he who earns wages does so to
put them into a bag with holes.

7"Thus says the LORD of hosts: Consider your ways. 8Go up to the hills and
bring wood and build the house, that I may take pleasure in it and that I may
be glorified, says the LORD. 9You looked for much, and behold, it came to little.
And when you brought it home, I blew it away. Why? declares the LORD of hosts.
Because of my house that lies in ruins, while each of you busies himself with his
own house. 10Therefore the heavens above you have withheld the dew, and the
earth has withheld its produce. 11And I have called for a drought on the land and
the hills, on the grain, the new wine, the oil, on what the ground brings forth, on
man and beast, and on all their labors."

The People Obey the LORD

12Then Zerubbabel the son of Shealtiel, and Joshua the son of Jehozadak, the
high priest, with all the remnant of the people, obeyed the voice of the LORD their
God, and the words of Haggai the prophet, as the LORD their God had sent him.
And the people feared the LORD. 13Then Haggai, the messenger of the LORD, spoke
to the people with the LORD's message, "I am with you, declares the LORD." 14And
the LORD stirred up the spirit of Zerubbabel the son of Shealtiel, governor of Judah, and the spirit of Joshua the son of Jehozadak, the high priest, and the spirit
of all the remnant of the people. And they came and worked on the house of the
LORD of hosts, their God, 15on the twenty-fourth day of the month, in the sixth
month, in the second year of Darius the king.

The Coming Glory of the Temple

2 In the seventh month, on the twenty-first day of the month, the word of the
LORD came by the hand of Haggai the prophet: 2"Speak now to Zerubbabel
the son of Shealtiel, governor of Judah, and to Joshua the son of Jehozadak, the
high priest, and to all the remnant of the people, and say, 3'Who is left among you
who saw this house in its former glory? How do you see it now? Is it not as nothing in your eyes? 4Yet now be strong, O Zerubbabel, declares the LORD. Be strong,
O Joshua, son of Jehozadak, the high priest. Be strong, all you people of the land,
declares the LORD. Work, for I am with you, declares the LORD of hosts, 5according
to the covenant that I made with you when you came out of Egypt. My Spirit remains in your midst. Fear not. 6For thus says the LORD of hosts: Yet once more, in
a little while, I will shake the heavens and the earth and the sea and the dry land.
7And I will shake all nations, so that the treasures of all nations shall come in, and
I will fill this house with glory, says the LORD of hosts. 8The silver is mine, and the
gold is mine, declares the LORD of hosts. 9The latter glory of this house shall be
greater than the former, says the LORD of hosts. And in this place I will give peace,
declares the LORD of hosts.'"

HAGGAI 1:5–6

THE DISCIPLINE OF A SMALL HARVEST

For agrarian societies like those of the ancient world, harvest was a cultural event that was central to the lives of most of the people. Israel celebrated feast days three times a year (Firstfruits, Weeks, and Booths), with each one tied to a harvest. As God's people celebrated the feast days, plentiful harvests assured them that God was with them and cared for them.

Unfortunately, those who returned to Judah from exile prioritized building their own houses over rebuilding God's temple (Hag 1:2–4). In response, God disciplined his people with a drought (v. 11). Though they have "sown much," they "harvested little" (v. 6). After receiving the discipline of a small harvest and hearing Haggai's message, God's people began to rebuild the temple.

Christians today experience God's discipline as a form of protection, a reminder that they belong to a loving Father (Heb 12:5–10). Such discipline "yields the peaceful fruit of righteousness" in believers' lives (Heb 12:11). Jesus used the imagery of harvest to teach spiritual truths about his mission. He described people who needed to hear the gospel as a field ripe for harvest, and he exhorted his disciples to pray for more laborers to be sent to gather the harvest (Mt 9:35–38). In Haggai's day, God was ready to bless his people with a plentiful harvest when they prioritized the building of the temple.

(continued on page 1442)

HAGGAI 2:7

PRESENT AND FUTURE HOPE IN CHRIST

In different seasons of life, the people of God face the possibility of discouragement. Discouragement can hold believers back from fulfilling God's plans for their lives. This is exactly where those who had returned from exile were when God, through Haggai, brought them a message of hope.

Through Haggai's ministry, this remnant renewed their passion for God and began to rebuild the temple, the place where God's people gathered for worship. When the temple was in shambles, the Israelites' relationship with God suffered. God had disciplined his people through drought (1:11); when they listened to Haggai's message, they were ready to get to work on rebuilding the temple (1:14 – 15). However, discouragement quickly began to creep in as they remembered the glory of the former temple. How could they ever restore the temple to its former beauty and majesty? Yet, this was exactly what God promised.

God spoke directly to the people's discouragement with hope. He told them to be strong; he told them he was with them (2:4). He reminded them of his covenant with them, he assured them that his Spirit was with them, and he admonished them not to fear (2:5).

These are the same words of hope that God gives Christians today. He exhorts believers to be strong (1Co 16:13). God has promised never to leave his people (Heb 13:5). Jesus has told his followers not to fear (Jn 14:27).

The temple was completed in Haggai's day, yet without the ark of the covenant, it lacked the former glory. Still, hope remained. The Messiah was still to come to his temple (Mal 3:1). Haggai pointed to the appearance of that which "will shake all nations" (Hag 2:7); both of these prophecies likely found their fulfillment in Jesus Christ. Jesus would fill the temple with the greatest glory it had ever known when he came to Jerusalem and taught in it (Hag 2:9). Jesus personified the rebuilding of the temple with a greater glory through his death, burial, and resurrection (Jn 2:19 – 22). Even now, Jesus is drawing all nations to himself, and God's people wait with great hope for the final fulfillment of Haggai 2:7, when those from "every nation, from all tribes and peoples and languages" will gather around the throne to worship Jesus Christ (Rev 7:9 – 10).

(The Discipline of a Small Harvest, continued)

In Jesus' death, the need for the temple as a conduit for salvation was eliminated (Mk 15:38). Today, believers participate in the building of the church as they share the good news of Jesus with the people around them. The church that Jesus is building (unlike the temple in Haggai's time) will be indestructible and serves as a living sign of the kingdom of God until Christ's return (Mt 16:18).

Blessings for a Defiled People

10On the twenty-fourth day of the ninth month, in the second year of Darius, the word of the LORD came by Haggai the prophet, 11"Thus says the LORD of hosts: Ask the priests about the law: 12'If someone carries holy meat in the fold of his garment and touches with his fold bread or stew or wine or oil or any kind of food, does it become holy?'" The priests answered and said, "No." 13Then Haggai said, "If someone who is unclean by contact with a dead body touches any of these, does it become unclean?" The priests answered and said, "It does become unclean." 14Then Haggai answered and said, "So is it with this people, and with this nation before me, declares the LORD, and so with every work of their hands. And what they offer there is unclean. 15Now then, consider from this day onward.[1] Before stone was placed upon stone in the temple of the LORD, 16how did you fare? When[2] one came to a heap of twenty measures, there were but ten. When one came to the wine vat to draw fifty measures, there were but twenty. 17I struck you and all the products of your toil with blight and with mildew and with hail, yet you did not turn to me, declares the LORD. 18Consider from this day onward, from the twenty-fourth day of the ninth month. Since the day that the foundation of the LORD's temple was laid, consider: 19Is the seed yet in the barn? Indeed, the vine, the fig tree, the pomegranate, and the olive tree have yielded nothing. But from this day on I will bless you."

Zerubbabel Chosen as a Signet

20The word of the LORD came a second time to Haggai on the twenty-fourth day of the month, 21"Speak to Zerubbabel, governor of Judah, saying, I am about to shake the heavens and the earth, 22and to overthrow the throne of kingdoms. I am about to destroy the strength of the kingdoms of the nations, and overthrow the chariots and their riders. And the horses and their riders shall go down, every one by the sword of his brother. 23On that day, declares the LORD of hosts, I will take you, O Zerubbabel my servant, the son of Shealtiel, declares the LORD, and make you like a[3] signet ring, for I have chosen you, declares the LORD of hosts."

[1]Or *backward*; also verse 18 [2]Probable reading (compare Septuagint); Hebrew *LORD, since they were. When* [3]Hebrew *the*

JESUS: OUR HUMBLE KING

ZECHARIAH

ZECHARIAH

DECREE OF CYRUS ALLOWING JEWS TO RETURN *c. 538 BC*	ZECHARIAH'S PROPHECIES *c. 520 – 480 BC*	WORK ON TEMPLE RENEWED AND COMPLETED *c. 520 – 516 BC*

Zechariah, whose name means "the LORD remembers," testified about God's faithfulness to the remnant of Jews who returned to rebuild Jerusalem. Along with Haggai, Zechariah served to enliven the faith and confidence of God's people as they rebuilt the temple.

Of primary importance for Zechariah was encouraging the people's loyalty to God and faithfulness to his word throughout their labors. Encouraging them to avoid the sins of their predecessors, Zechariah reminded the people to stay true to God, forsake all idolatry, and maintain their covenant promises to God (1:2 – 6). Zechariah also encouraged the people by assuring them of God's faithfulness to bless their work and restore their fortunes.

These promises were based on a coming anointed one who would rule and reign as God's Messiah from Zion, ushering in a desperately longed-for era of peace. Zechariah employed a number of images to refer to this Messiah: God's servant (3:8), the Branch (3:8), a stone (3:9), and God's shepherd (13:7). He would serve both as a king, ruling over God's people with righteousness, and a priest, caring for the people with loving-kindness.

Zechariah's clear message also revealed a number of fascinating details about this coming One: He would enter Jerusalem on a donkey colt (9:9), he would be betrayed for 30 pieces of silver (11:12 – 13), and his body would be pierced (12:10). Most importantly, Zechariah spoke of the forgiveness of sins that would come through the Messiah's death (13:1). The prophet's writings provide striking parallels with the writings of the New Testament authors. Zechariah also looked forward to the second coming of Christ, when he would ultimately save his people (12:10 — 13:1), vanquish their enemies (14:3,12 – 15), and reign in the new Jerusalem (14:9,16).

Zechariah detailed God's clear plan for salvation: they need only to repent, turn to him, and trust in the provision he offers. These decisions make it possible for fallen, sinful humans to have a restored relationship with God and live a life of worshipful obedience. Because Jesus, as God's anointed one, fulfilled the prophecies of Zechariah and other Old Testament prophets, he alone provides the purification and righteousness all people so desperately need.

THEREFORE SAY TO THEM, THUS DECLARES
THE LORD OF HOSTS: RETURN TO ME,
SAYS THE LORD OF HOSTS, AND I WILL
RETURN TO YOU, SAYS THE LORD OF HOSTS.

Zechariah 1:3

ZECHARIAH

A Call to Return to the LORD

1 In the eighth month, in the second year of Darius, the word of the LORD came to the prophet Zechariah, the son of Berechiah, son of Iddo, saying, 2"The LORD was very angry with your fathers. 3Therefore say to them, Thus declares the LORD of hosts: Return to me, says the LORD of hosts, and I will return to you, says the LORD of hosts. 4Do not be like your fathers, to whom the former prophets cried out, 'Thus says the LORD of hosts, Return from your evil ways and from your evil deeds.' But they did not hear or pay attention to me, declares the LORD. 5Your fathers, where are they? And the prophets, do they live forever? 6But my words and my statutes, which I commanded my servants the prophets, did they not overtake your fathers? So they repented and said, 'As the LORD of hosts purposed to deal with us for our ways and deeds, so has he dealt with us.'"

A Vision of a Horseman

7On the twenty-fourth day of the eleventh month, which is the month of Shebat, in the second year of Darius, the word of the LORD came to the prophet Zechariah, the son of Berechiah, son of Iddo, saying, 8"I saw in the night, and behold, a man riding on a red horse! He was standing among the myrtle trees in the glen, and behind him were red, sorrel, and white horses. 9Then I said, 'What are these, my lord?' The angel who talked with me said to me, 'I will show you what they are.' 10So the man who was standing among the myrtle trees answered, 'These are they whom the LORD has sent to patrol the earth.' 11And they answered the angel of the LORD who was standing among the myrtle trees, and said, 'We have patrolled the earth, and behold, all the earth remains at rest.' 12Then the angel of the LORD said, 'O LORD of hosts, how long will you have no mercy on Jerusalem and the cities of Judah, against which you have been angry these seventy years?' 13And the LORD answered gracious and comforting words to the angel who talked with me. 14So the angel who talked with me said to me, 'Cry out, Thus says the LORD of hosts: I am exceedingly jealous for Jerusalem and for Zion. 15And I am exceedingly angry with the nations that are at ease; for while I was angry but a little, they furthered the disaster. 16Therefore, thus says the LORD, I have returned to Jerusalem with mercy; my house shall be built in it, declares the LORD of hosts, and the measuring line shall be stretched out over Jerusalem. 17Cry out again, Thus says the LORD of hosts: My cities shall again overflow with prosperity, and the LORD will again comfort Zion and again choose Jerusalem.'"

A Vision of Horns and Craftsmen

18[1]And I lifted my eyes and saw, and behold, four horns! 19And I said to the angel who talked with me, "What are these?" And he said to me, "These are the horns that have scattered Judah, Israel, and Jerusalem." 20Then the LORD showed me four craftsmen. 21And I said, "What are these coming to do?" He said, "These are the horns that scattered Judah, so that no one raised his head. And these have come to terrify them, to cast down the horns of the nations who lifted up their horns against the land of Judah to scatter it."

A Vision of a Man with a Measuring Line

2 [2] And I lifted my eyes and saw, and behold, a man with a measuring line in his hand! 2Then I said, "Where are you going?" And he said to me, "To measure Jerusalem, to see what is its width and what is its length." 3And behold, the angel

---

ZECHARIAH 1:8–17

THE MAN AMONG THE MYRTLE TREES

The book of Zechariah finds the Israelites back in the promised land after exile, though the temple remained in ruins. The Lord used the prophet Haggai to begin spurring the people of God to take on this construction project. A couple of months later, Zechariah joined with Haggai in calling Judah to return to their God and rebuild the temple.

The book of Zechariah contains eight visions; this is the first. During this vision, the conversation between the man on a horse and the angel of the Lord came to this conclusion: the world seemed to be at peace (v. 11).

However, the Lord's anger was kindled against the nations who had added atrocity to the punishment that God allowed his people to experience in exile (vv. 12–15). As a result, God would turn again with favor toward his people and celebrate his renewed presence in Jerusalem and the surrounding towns (vv. 16–17). This beautiful picture of God's blessing and care points believers today toward the city that will be fully established when Jesus comes again (Rev 21:2–10).

---

[1]Ch 2:1 in Hebrew [2]Ch 2:5 in Hebrew

who talked with me came forward, and another angel came forward to meet him
[4]and said to him, "Run, say to that young man, 'Jerusalem shall be inhabited as
villages without walls, because of the multitude of people and livestock in it. [5]And
I will be to her a wall of fire all around, declares the LORD, and I will be the glory
in her midst.'"

[6]Up! Up! Flee from the land of the north, declares the LORD. For I have spread
you abroad as the four winds of the heavens, declares the LORD. [7]Up! Escape to
Zion, you who dwell with the daughter of Babylon. [8]For thus said the LORD of
hosts, after his glory sent me[1] to the nations who plundered you, for he who
touches you touches the apple of his eye: [9]"Behold, I will shake my hand over
them, and they shall become plunder for those who served them. Then you will
know that the LORD of hosts has sent me. [10]Sing and rejoice, O daughter of Zion,
for behold, I come and I will dwell in your midst, declares the LORD. [11]And many
nations shall join themselves to the LORD in that day, and shall be my people. And
I will dwell in your midst, and you shall know that the LORD of hosts has sent me
to you. [12]And the LORD will inherit Judah as his portion in the holy land, and will
again choose Jerusalem."

[13]Be silent, all flesh, before the LORD, for he has roused himself from his holy
dwelling.

A Vision of Joshua the High Priest

3 Then he showed me Joshua the high priest standing before the angel of the
LORD, and Satan[2] standing at his right hand to accuse him. [2]And the LORD said
to Satan, "The LORD rebuke you, O Satan! The LORD who has chosen Jerusalem
rebuke you! Is not this a brand[3] plucked from the fire?" [3]Now Joshua was standing
before the angel, clothed with filthy garments. [4]And the angel said to those who
were standing before him, "Remove the filthy garments from him." And to him he
said, "Behold, I have taken your iniquity away from you, and I will clothe you with
pure vestments." [5]And I said, "Let them put a clean turban on his head." So they
put a clean turban on his head and clothed him with garments. And the angel of
the LORD was standing by.

[6]And the angel of the LORD solemnly assured Joshua, [7]"Thus says the LORD
of hosts: If you will walk in my ways and keep my charge, then you shall rule my
house and have charge of my courts, and I will give you the right of access among
those who are standing here. [8]Hear now, O Joshua the high priest, you and your
friends who sit before you, for they are men who are a sign: behold, I will bring
my servant the Branch. [9]For behold, on the stone that I have set before Joshua, on
a single stone with seven eyes,[4] I will engrave its inscription, declares the LORD of
hosts, and I will remove the iniquity of this land in a single day. [10]In that day, declares the LORD of hosts, every one of you will invite his neighbor to come under
his vine and under his fig tree."

A Vision of a Golden Lampstand

4 And the angel who talked with me came again and woke me, like a man who
is awakened out of his sleep. [2]And he said to me, "What do you see?" I said,
"I see, and behold, a lampstand all of gold, with a bowl on the top of it, and seven
lamps on it, with seven lips on each of the lamps that are on the top of it. [3]And
there are two olive trees by it, one on the right of the bowl and the other on its
left." [4]And I said to the angel who talked with me, "What are these, my lord?"
[5]Then the angel who talked with me answered and said to me, "Do you not know
what these are?" I said, "No, my lord." [6]Then he said to me, "This is the word of the
LORD to Zerubbabel: Not by might, nor by power, but by my Spirit, says the LORD
of hosts. [7]Who are you, O great mountain? Before Zerubbabel you shall become a
plain. And he shall bring forward the top stone amid shouts of 'Grace, grace to it!'"

[1]Or *he sent me after glory* [2]Hebrew *the Accuser* or *the Adversary* [3]That is, a burning stick [4]Or *facets*

ZECHARIAH 3:1–2

OUR DEFENDER

This text details the fourth of eight visions, and this vision appears to be located in a courtroom in the heavens. Verse 1 sets the scene. The angel of the Lord sat as judge. The high priest Joshua, here representing the sinful nation, stood in the room as the defendant. The fallen angel, Satan, opposed and accused Joshua.

Scripture records other such scenes where an accuser points a finger at God's people. Job 1:1–12 records the classic scene where Satan accuses Job of only giving lip service to God because he's been blessed and protected by God. Revelation 12:7–12 details a vision of Satan, "the accuser of our brothers" (v. 10), losing a future battle. In each of these scenes, the accuser loses his argument under the defense of One who advocates for fallen humans.

In a precursor to later revelation, the Lord defended his people before Satan (Zec 3:2). And believers today have One who still stands as our advocate before the Father (1Jn 2:1). The book of Revelation reveals the Lord's power over the accuser. Out of the fire, God snatched Joshua; through the person and work of the living Savior, Jesus Christ, he still does the same today.

ZECHARIAH 3:3–5

CLEAN CLOTHES

As the courtroom scene of verses 1 and 2 continued, Zechariah revealed that Joshua wore filthy clothes, indicating Satan's case was not entirely without merit. Tragically, the high priest—an intermediary for

(continued on page 1449)

GOD LAYS THE FOUNDATION

Haggai charged Judah's high priest Joshua and governor Zerubbabel to rebuild the temple. In the face of construction obstacles, the Lord's angel gave Zechariah a message to encourage Zerubbabel in the work. Though it might have seemed natural to the Israelites to depend upon their own strength or ingenuity for this project, God said the temple would only be built by depending upon his Spirit (v. 6).

With the Spirit's aid, Zechariah revealed that the obstacles the people faced were not as insurmountable as they seemed. Using metaphoric language, the prophet asserted that mighty mountains would become like level ground (v. 7). Though opposition slowed the process, Zerubbabel would indeed complete the construction (v. 9). Then, as the capstone was set, the people would shout in praise (v. 7). These promises proved to be true in the days that followed.

The New Testament calls the church the temple of God (Eph 2:21). Christ himself serves as the chosen and precious cornerstone (1Pe 2:6). Like the prophetic vision in Zechariah 4 says of the building of the temple, the building of this New Testament temple depends entirely upon the Spirit (1Co 12:13). Similarly, apparent obstacles — even the gates of hell — will not prevail against it (Mt 16:18). The construction will be completed (1Pe 2:5). Nothing thwarts God's purposes in building his church.

The purposes of the New Testament church reflect the temple's purposes as well. God dwelled with his people at the temple. By his Spirit, God dwells with his people in the church (Eph 2:22). The praises of God filled the temple. God builds his church so the people might declare his praises (1Pe 2:9).

Viable buildings depend upon viable foundations. However, God's people always face the temptation of attempting to build the church without the Spirit. God's people might endeavor to create pseudo-community, devoid of essential unity in Christ. God's people might attempt to live on mission, while missing God entirely. Paul wrote, "No one can lay a foundation other than that which is laid, which is Jesus Christ" (1Co 3:11). Therefore, each one should be careful how they build. One day, all will be brought to light (1Co 3:10,12–13).

8Then the word of the LORD came to me, saying, 9"The hands of Zerubbabel have laid the foundation of this house; his hands shall also complete it. Then you will know that the LORD of hosts has sent me to you. 10For whoever has despised the day of small things shall rejoice, and shall see the plumb line in the hand of Zerubbabel.

"These seven are the eyes of the LORD, which range through the whole earth." 11Then I said to him, "What are these two olive trees on the right and the left of the lampstand?" 12And a second time I answered and said to him, "What are these two branches of the olive trees, which are beside the two golden pipes from which the golden oil[1] is poured out?" 13He said to me, "Do you not know what these are?" I said, "No, my lord." 14Then he said, "These are the two anointed ones[2] who stand by the Lord of the whole earth."

A Vision of a Flying Scroll

5 Again I lifted my eyes and saw, and behold, a flying scroll! 2And he said to me, "What do you see?" I answered, "I see a flying scroll. Its length is twenty cubits, and its width ten cubits."[3] 3Then he said to me, "This is the curse that goes out over the face of the whole land. For everyone who steals shall be cleaned out according to what is on one side, and everyone who swears falsely[4] shall be cleaned out according to what is on the other side. 4I will send it out, declares the LORD of hosts, and it shall enter the house of the thief, and the house of him who swears falsely by my name. And it shall remain in his house and consume it, both timber and stones."

A Vision of a Woman in a Basket

5Then the angel who talked with me came forward and said to me, "Lift your eyes and see what this is that is going out." 6And I said, "What is it?" He said, "This is the basket[5] that is going out." And he said, "This is their iniquity[6] in all the land." 7And behold, the leaden cover was lifted, and there was a woman sitting in the basket! 8And he said, "This is Wickedness." And he thrust her back into the basket, and thrust down the leaden weight on its opening.

9Then I lifted my eyes and saw, and behold, two women coming forward! The wind was in their wings. They had wings like the wings of a stork, and they lifted up the basket between earth and heaven. 10Then I said to the angel who talked with me, "Where are they taking the basket?" 11He said to me, "To the land of Shinar, to build a house for it. And when this is prepared, they will set the basket down there on its base."

A Vision of Four Chariots

6 Again I lifted my eyes and saw, and behold, four chariots came out from between two mountains. And the mountains were mountains of bronze. 2The first chariot had red horses, the second black horses, 3the third white horses, and the fourth chariot dappled horses—all of them strong.[7] 4Then I answered and said to the angel who talked with me, "What are these, my lord?" 5And the angel answered and said to me, "These are going out to the four winds of heaven,[8] after presenting themselves before the Lord of all the earth. 6The chariot with the black horses goes toward the north country, the white ones go after them, and the dappled ones go toward the south country." 7When the strong horses came out, they were impatient to go and patrol the earth. And he said, "Go, patrol the earth." So they patrolled the earth. 8Then he cried to me, "Behold, those who go toward the north country have set my Spirit at rest in the north country."

[1]Hebrew lacks *oil* [2]Hebrew *two sons of new oil* [3]A *cubit* was about 18 inches or 45 centimeters [4]Hebrew lacks *falsely* (supplied from verse 4) [5]Hebrew *ephah*; also verses 7–11. An *ephah* was about 3/5 bushel or 22 liters [6]One Hebrew manuscript, Septuagint, Syriac; most Hebrew manuscripts *eye* [7]Or *and the fourth chariot strong dappled horses* [8]Or *These are the four winds of heaven going out*

(Clean Clothes, continued)

the defiled—was himself defiled. The angel ordered Joshua's filthy clothes to be removed, interpreting that action as sin being taken away (v. 4). While this certainly served as evidence of God's grace, clearing humanity's debt only keeps the believer from sin's punishment. A neutral position does not give the believer access to a righteous and holy God.

The book of Zechariah pictured the other aspect of salvation. Not only did the angel have the filthy garments removed, but Joshua also received fine, clean garments in their place. To be reconciled to a holy God, believers must claim the righteousness of Christ as their own. Paul puts in clear terms what Zechariah pictured: "He [God] made him to be sin who knew no sin, so that in him we might become the righteousness of God" (2Co 5:21). In Revelation 3:5, the risen Christ similarly talks about believers being dressed in new garments in heaven, using courtroom language as well: "The one who conquers will be clothed thus in white garments, and I will never blot his name out of the book of life. I will confess his name before my Father and before his angels."

ZECHARIAH 4:1–14

SEEKING ANSWERS

Zechariah asked the Lord three times what the meaning of the two olive trees and branches was (vv. 4,11,12). At first, the Lord does not answer him directly. He is wanting Zechariah to trust him and seek him in a deeper way.

God will oftentimes speak indirectly with his children. This is not because he does not care for them

(continued on next page)

(Seeking Answers, continued)

or that he does not want to answer them, but he is wanting them to seek in a deeper way and to trust that his actions are perfect.

Zechariah was persistent in his questioning about the identity of the two olive trees. Finally, the Lord through an angel responded, indicating that the two olive trees represented two anointed men. The vision, according to many interpreters, referred to Zerubbabel and Joshua. Joshua served the Lord as high priest; Zerubbabel, a descendant of King David, served the Lord as the governor. The Lord anointed these men for his purposes.

These anointed offices point the reader toward one who is to come. In fact, the terms "Messiah" and "Christ" come from Hebrew and Greek words that mean "anointed one."

God anointed Zerubbabel and Joshua to serve Israel. The anointed one — Jesus Christ — "came not to be served but to serve, and to give his life as a ransom for many" (Mt 20:28).

ZECHARIAH 6:9–15

KING AND PRIEST

In mercy, the Lord continued to reveal his purposes and plans. The word of the Lord came to Zechariah, instructing him to get silver and gold from a few of the exiles for the purpose of making a crown.

Typically, a crown was reserved for a king. However, the Lord told Zechariah in this text to place it upon the high priest's head. Joshua took on some kingly symbolism in this vision, showing his significant role in the rebuilding of the temple (v. 12).

(continued on next page)

The Crown and the Temple

9And the word of the LORD came to me: 10"Take from the exiles Heldai, Tobijah, and Jedaiah, who have arrived from Babylon, and go the same day to the house of Josiah, the son of Zephaniah. 11Take from them silver and gold, and make a crown, and set it on the head of Joshua, the son of Jehozadak, the high priest. 12And say to him, 'Thus says the LORD of hosts, "Behold, the man whose name is the Branch: for he shall branch out from his place, and he shall build the temple of the LORD. 13It is he who shall build the temple of the LORD and shall bear royal honor, and shall sit and rule on his throne. And there[1] shall be a priest on his throne, and the counsel of peace shall be between them both."' 14And the crown shall be in the temple of the LORD as a reminder to Helem,[2] Tobijah, Jedaiah, and Hen the son of Zephaniah.

15"And those who are far off shall come and help to build the temple of the LORD. And you shall know that the LORD of hosts has sent me to you. And this shall come to pass, if you will diligently obey the voice of the LORD your God."

A Call for Justice and Mercy

7 In the fourth year of King Darius, the word of the LORD came to Zechariah on the fourth day of the ninth month, which is Chislev. 2Now the people of Bethel had sent Sharezer and Regem-melech and their men to entreat the favor of the LORD, 3saying to the priests of the house of the LORD of hosts and the prophets, "Should I weep and abstain in the fifth month, as I have done for so many years?"

4Then the word of the LORD of hosts came to me: 5"Say to all the people of the land and the priests, 'When you fasted and mourned in the fifth month and in the seventh, for these seventy years, was it for me that you fasted? 6And when you eat and when you drink, do you not eat for yourselves and drink for yourselves? 7Were not these the words that the LORD proclaimed by the former prophets, when Jerusalem was inhabited and prosperous, with her cities around her, and the South and the lowland were inhabited?'"

8And the word of the LORD came to Zechariah, saying, 9"Thus says the LORD of hosts, Render true judgments, show kindness and mercy to one another, 10do not oppress the widow, the fatherless, the sojourner, or the poor, and let none of you devise evil against another in your heart." 11But they refused to pay attention and turned a stubborn shoulder and stopped their ears that they might not hear.[3] 12They made their hearts diamond-hard lest they should hear the law and the words that the LORD of hosts had sent by his Spirit through the former prophets. Therefore great anger came from the LORD of hosts. 13"As I[4] called, and they would not hear, so they called, and I would not hear," says the LORD of hosts, 14"and I scattered them with a whirlwind among all the nations that they had not known. Thus the land they left was desolate, so that no one went to and fro, and the pleasant land was made desolate."

The Coming Peace and Prosperity of Zion

8 And the word of the LORD of hosts came, saying, 2"Thus says the LORD of hosts: I am jealous for Zion with great jealousy, and I am jealous for her with great wrath. 3Thus says the LORD: I have returned to Zion and will dwell in the midst of Jerusalem, and Jerusalem shall be called the faithful city, and the mountain of the LORD of hosts, the holy mountain. 4Thus says the LORD of hosts: Old men and old women shall again sit in the streets of Jerusalem, each with staff in hand because of great age. 5And the streets of the city shall be full of boys and girls playing in its streets. 6Thus says the LORD of hosts: If it is marvelous in the sight of the remnant of this people in those days, should it also be marvelous in my sight, declares the LORD of hosts? 7Thus says the LORD of hosts: Behold, I will

[1]Or *he* [2]An alternate spelling of *Heldai* (verse 10) [3]Hebrew *and made their ears too heavy to hear*
[4]Hebrew *he*

save my people from the east country and from the west country, 8and I will bring
them to dwell in the midst of Jerusalem. And they shall be my people, and I will
be their God, in faithfulness and in righteousness."

9Thus says the LORD of hosts: "Let your hands be strong, you who in these
days have been hearing these words from the mouth of the prophets who were
present on the day that the foundation of the house of the LORD of hosts was
laid, that the temple might be built. 10For before those days there was no wage
for man or any wage for beast, neither was there any safety from the foe for him
who went out or came in, for I set every man against his neighbor. 11But now I
will not deal with the remnant of this people as in the former days, declares the
LORD of hosts. 12For there shall be a sowing of peace. The vine shall give its fruit,
and the ground shall give its produce, and the heavens shall give their dew. And
I will cause the remnant of this people to possess all these things. 13And as you
have been a byword of cursing among the nations, O house of Judah and house
of Israel, so will I save you, and you shall be a blessing. Fear not, but let your
hands be strong."

14For thus says the LORD of hosts: "As I purposed to bring disaster to you when
your fathers provoked me to wrath, and I did not relent, says the LORD of hosts,
15so again have I purposed in these days to bring good to Jerusalem and to the
house of Judah; fear not. 16These are the things that you shall do: Speak the truth
to one another; render in your gates judgments that are true and make for peace;
17do not devise evil in your hearts against one another, and love no false oath, for
all these things I hate, declares the LORD."

18And the word of the LORD of hosts came to me, saying, 19"Thus says the LORD
of hosts: The fast of the fourth month and the fast of the fifth and the fast of the
seventh and the fast of the tenth shall be to the house of Judah seasons of joy and
gladness and cheerful feasts. Therefore love truth and peace.

20"Thus says the LORD of hosts: Peoples shall yet come, even the inhabitants
of many cities. 21The inhabitants of one city shall go to another, saying, 'Let us
go at once to entreat the favor of the LORD and to seek the LORD of hosts; I myself
am going.' 22Many peoples and strong nations shall come to seek the LORD of
hosts in Jerusalem and to entreat the favor of the LORD. 23Thus says the LORD of
hosts: In those days ten men from the nations of every tongue shall take hold
of the robe of a Jew, saying, 'Let us go with you, for we have heard that God is
with you.'"

Judgment on Israel's Enemies

9 The oracle of the word of the LORD is against the land of Hadrach
and Damascus is its resting place.
For the LORD has an eye on mankind
and on all the tribes of Israel,[1]
2 and on Hamath also, which borders on it,
Tyre and Sidon, though they are very wise.
3 Tyre has built herself a rampart
and heaped up silver like dust,
and fine gold like the mud of the streets.
4 But behold, the Lord will strip her of her possessions
and strike down her power on the sea,
and she shall be devoured by fire.

5 Ashkelon shall see it, and be afraid;
Gaza too, and shall writhe in anguish;
Ekron also, because its hopes are confounded.
The king shall perish from Gaza;
Ashkelon shall be uninhabited;

[1]Or *For the eye of mankind, especially of all the tribes of Israel, is toward the LORD*

(King and Priest, continued)

As the passage continues, it details a certain harmony between these two offices (v. 13). The people needed governance to build the temple; yet the temple needed priests to offer sacrifices.

The degree of unity between these offices depicted in Zechariah foreshadowed a perfect harmony to come. While Zerubbabel and Joshua served individually, Jesus — the Branch of Jesse (Isa 11:1) — would come to unite the offices; he would rule as King and intercede as Priest. He now sits at the right hand of God and governs perfectly while also interceding for the imperfect.

God instructed the people to store this crown as a reminder that God acted on their behalf (v. 14). The people of God must not forget his gracious actions toward them.

ZECHARIAH 8:20 – 23

ONE JEW, MANY NATIONS

The Old Testament focused upon God's choice of Israel. However, God saved Israel not for their sake alone, but for the good of the nations. This passage defines the mission of God as one that will compel the nations to come to Jerusalem to seek the Lord (v. 22). The inhabitants of many cities will flock to the city of God (v. 20). In fact, residents of each city will share the good news with one another (v. 21).

Verse 23 pointed to a future day when a diverse group of people — ten people from all languages and nations — will take hold of one Jew. Grabbing him by the hem of his robe indicates that they desire his company and presence.

(continued on next page)

(One Jew, Many Nations, continued)

In Genesis 11, the nations of the world were scattered among the world. However, as we start to see in Zechariah, God ultimately desires for the nations of the world to be united. This unity will come in the person of Jesus. In Acts 2:9–11, one of the first acts of the Holy Spirit is to begin unifying the nations of the world so that they are able to understand the "mighty works of God" in a common language. Paul asserted that Jesus' death and resurrection transformed two divided groups—Jew and Gentile—into one new humanity (Eph 2:14–16).

All people from every nation who grasp at Jesus' robe, who desire a relationship with him, will certainly find God.

6 a mixed people[1] shall dwell in Ashdod,
and I will cut off the pride of Philistia.
7 I will take away its blood from its mouth,
and its abominations from between its teeth;
it too shall be a remnant for our God;
it shall be like a clan in Judah,
and Ekron shall be like the Jebusites.
8 Then I will encamp at my house as a guard,
so that none shall march to and fro;
no oppressor shall again march over them,
for now I see with my own eyes.

The Coming King of Zion

9 Rejoice greatly, O daughter of Zion!
Shout aloud, O daughter of Jerusalem!
Behold, your king is coming to you;
righteous and having salvation is he,
humble and mounted on a donkey,
on a colt, the foal of a donkey.
10 I will cut off the chariot from Ephraim
and the war horse from Jerusalem;
and the battle bow shall be cut off,
and he shall speak peace to the nations;
his rule shall be from sea to sea,
and from the River[2] to the ends of the earth.
11 As for you also, because of the blood of my covenant
with you,
I will set your prisoners free from the waterless pit.
12 Return to your stronghold, O prisoners of hope;
today I declare that I will restore to you double.
13 For I have bent Judah as my bow;
I have made Ephraim its arrow.
I will stir up your sons, O Zion,
against your sons, O Greece,
and wield you like a warrior's sword.

The LORD Will Save His People

14 Then the LORD will appear over them,
and his arrow will go forth like lightning;
the Lord GOD will sound the trumpet
and will march forth in the whirlwinds of the south.
15 The LORD of hosts will protect them,
and they shall devour, and tread down the sling
stones,
and they shall drink and roar as if drunk with wine,
and be full like a bowl,
drenched like the corners of the altar.

16 On that day the LORD their God will save them,
as the flock of his people;
for like the jewels of a crown
they shall shine on his land.
17 For how great is his goodness, and how great his beauty!
Grain shall make the young men flourish,
and new wine the young women.

---

[1]Or *a foreign people*; Hebrew *a bastard* [2]That is, the Euphrates

HUMBLE AND MOUNTED ON A DONKEY

Zechariah points toward a coming king. While the first part of this chapter concerns God's judgment on Judah's enemies, it goes on to declare that true peace ultimately comes through this coming King, the Messiah.

Zechariah announced his imminent arrival, admonishing Zion, or Jerusalem, to rejoice and shout. According to verse 9, this king proves to be righteous. Furthermore, his arrival brings salvation.

In a typical ancient Near Eastern context, a king's arrival to a city would be marked by conspicuous pomp and pageantry. In this honor- and shame-based culture, anything less would be an affront to the king's rule. Royalty traveled with an entourage. Here Zechariah's royal prophecy pointed to the well-known ancient practice of kings who came in peace, riding into town on a donkey rather than a war horse.

Entering the final week of Jesus' earthly ministry, he asked his disciples to run an errand. If anyone asked the disciples what they sought, they were to respond that the Lord required it (Mt 21:2–3).

More than anyone else, Jesus knew who he was. He knew — in fact he inspired — the prophecy in Zechariah. So, in what many now call the Triumphal Entry, Jesus rode into Jerusalem on the back of a humble colt, the foal of a donkey; the symbol of a king arriving in peace. The whole city, Matthew records, wondered about the identity of this man (Mt 21:10). However, Jesus was not confused. As he rode in on the donkey, he claimed — in visible terms — to be the Messiah that this prophecy foretold.

Though Zechariah told them this was to come, the Jews failed to connect the prophetic dots. In tragic ways, they misunderstood Jesus. They celebrated him as a king on Sunday; they crucified him as a criminal the next Friday.

While the palm branches and shouting were appropriate, so was the donkey. This King ruled perfectly, including the attitudes with which he ruled. Deserving of all honor, he humbled himself, even to the point of death on a cross (Php 2:8). No one had ever seen a King like this. The next Sunday proved it.

ZECHARIAH 10:4

THE CORNERSTONE

While the Lord's anger burned against Judah's shepherds, he promised to care for the flock. In this verse, he used metaphoric language to describe how he planned to tend to those who were ultimately *his* people.

He assured them, initially, that a cornerstone would soon come. As any builder knows, the cornerstone determines the position of the rest of the foundation; furthermore, the foundation is vital to the structural integrity of the building. From the Lord would come the tent peg as well, referring to a certain capability to carry weight (Isa 22:20–23), and the battle bow, an image representing military power.

Though each of these images could be elaborated upon, Jesus employed the cornerstone image most frequently in his teaching. In the parable of the wicked tenants, he called himself the stone the builders rejected that has become the cornerstone (Mt 21:42). In Zechariah's day, the Jewish leaders hindered the people's relationship with their God. In Jesus' day, the Jewish leaders rejected the cornerstone, God in the flesh. In fact, they sought his arrest (Mt 21:46), plotted to kill him (Mt 26:4), and eventually influenced Pilate to crucify him.

God replaced the leaders of Old Testament Israel, providing faithfully for his people. For New Testament believers, the stone that the leaders rejected became the cornerstone. Once again, God took care of his people, as he still does today.

The Restoration for Judah and Israel

10 Ask rain from the LORD
in the season of the spring rain,
from the LORD who makes the storm clouds,
and he will give them showers of rain,
to everyone the vegetation in the field.
2 For the household gods utter nonsense,
and the diviners see lies;
they tell false dreams
and give empty consolation.
Therefore the people wander like sheep;
they are afflicted for lack of a shepherd.

3 "My anger is hot against the shepherds,
and I will punish the leaders;[1]
for the LORD of hosts cares for his flock, the house of Judah,
and will make them like his majestic steed in battle.
4 From him shall come the cornerstone,
from him the tent peg,
from him the battle bow,
from him every ruler—all of them together.
5 They shall be like mighty men in battle,
trampling the foe in the mud of the streets;
they shall fight because the LORD is with them,
and they shall put to shame the riders on horses.

6 "I will strengthen the house of Judah,
and I will save the house of Joseph.
I will bring them back because I have compassion on them,
and they shall be as though I had not rejected them,
for I am the LORD their God and I will answer them.
7 Then Ephraim shall become like a mighty warrior,
and their hearts shall be glad as with wine.
Their children shall see it and be glad;
their hearts shall rejoice in the LORD.

8 "I will whistle for them and gather them in,
for I have redeemed them,
and they shall be as many as they were before.
9 Though I scattered them among the nations,
yet in far countries they shall remember me,
and with their children they shall live and return.
10 I will bring them home from the land of Egypt,
and gather them from Assyria,
and I will bring them to the land of Gilead and to Lebanon,
till there is no room for them.
11 He shall pass through the sea of troubles
and strike down the waves of the sea,
and all the depths of the Nile shall be dried up.
The pride of Assyria shall be laid low,
and the scepter of Egypt shall depart.
12 I will make them strong in the LORD,
and they shall walk in his name,"
declares the LORD.

[1]Hebrew *the male goats*

The Flock Doomed to Slaughter

11 Open your doors, O Lebanon,
that the fire may devour your cedars!
2 Wail, O cypress, for the cedar has fallen,
for the glorious trees are ruined!
Wail, oaks of Bashan,
for the thick forest has been felled!
3 The sound of the wail of the shepherds,
for their glory is ruined!
The sound of the roar of the lions,
for the thicket of the Jordan is ruined!

4Thus said the LORD my God: "Become shepherd of the flock doomed to
slaughter. 5Those who buy them slaughter them and go unpunished, and those
who sell them say, 'Blessed be the LORD, I have become rich,' and their own shepherds have no pity on them. 6For I will no longer have pity on the inhabitants of
this land, declares the LORD. Behold, I will cause each of them to fall into the hand
of his neighbor, and each into the hand of his king, and they shall crush the land,
and I will deliver none from their hand."

7So I became the shepherd of the flock doomed to be slaughtered by the sheep
traders. And I took two staffs, one I named Favor, the other I named Union. And
I tended the sheep. 8In one month I destroyed the three shepherds. But I became
impatient with them, and they also detested me. 9So I said, "I will not be your
shepherd. What is to die, let it die. What is to be destroyed, let it be destroyed.
And let those who are left devour the flesh of one another." 10And I took my staff
Favor, and I broke it, annulling the covenant that I had made with all the peoples.
11So it was annulled on that day, and the sheep traders, who were watching me,
knew that it was the word of the LORD. 12Then I said to them, "If it seems good to
you, give me my wages; but if not, keep them." And they weighed out as my wages
thirty pieces of silver. 13Then the LORD said to me, "Throw it to the potter"—the
lordly price at which I was priced by them. So I took the thirty pieces of silver and
threw them into the house of the LORD, to the potter. 14Then I broke my second
staff Union, annulling the brotherhood between Judah and Israel.

15Then the LORD said to me, "Take once more the equipment of a foolish
shepherd. 16For behold, I am raising up in the land a shepherd who does not care
for those being destroyed, or seek the young or heal the maimed or nourish the
healthy, but devours the flesh of the fat ones, tearing off even their hoofs.

17 "Woe to my worthless shepherd,
who deserts the flock!
May the sword strike his arm
and his right eye!
Let his arm be wholly withered,
his right eye utterly blinded!"

The LORD Will Give Salvation

12 The oracle of the word of the LORD concerning Israel: Thus declares the
LORD, who stretched out the heavens and founded the earth and formed
the spirit of man within him: 2"Behold, I am about to make Jerusalem a cup of
staggering to all the surrounding peoples. The siege of Jerusalem will also be
against Judah. 3On that day I will make Jerusalem a heavy stone for all the peoples.
All who lift it will surely hurt themselves. And all the nations of the earth will
gather against it. 4On that day, declares the LORD, I will strike every horse with
panic, and its rider with madness. But for the sake of the house of Judah I will
keep my eyes open, when I strike every horse of the peoples with blindness. 5Then
the clans of Judah shall say to themselves, 'The inhabitants of Jerusalem have
strength through the LORD of hosts, their God.'

ZECHARIAH 11:12–13

THIRTY PIECES OF SILVER

In these latter chapters, Judah's situation escalated quickly. Zechariah got rid of three prominent shepherds, assuming their leadership role. However, he quickly tired of the people; they, in turn, detested him (v. 8). He, presumably to leave them to their sinful ways, promptly resigned from leadership (v. 9).

Zechariah's severance package had not been made clear, so Zechariah gave them the option to pay him or not (v. 12). In a most inadequate middle ground, they sent him off for the price of a slave—thirty pieces of silver. He rejected this devaluation, hurling the coins to the potter at the house of the Lord as the Lord directed him (v. 13).

The flock underestimated the worth of Zechariah's leadership, assigning him a value the Lord found insufficient. However, this pales in comparison to the narrative in Matthew's Gospel, which reports history's worst appraisal of worth. God incarnate came to dwell with humanity. Humanity promptly sold him for thirty pieces of silver (Mt 27:1–10).

ZECHARIAH 13:7

SHEPHERD STRUCK, SHEEP SCATTERED

Sheep are not the smartest creatures on the planet. In fact, their survival largely depends upon the care of their shepherd. In the final sections of Zechariah's book, God described the leaders of Israel as cruel shepherds and the people as oppressed sheep.

Nevertheless, when a good shepherd finally began to care for the people of God, the sheep rejected him as well. Zechariah quoted these words: "Strike the shepherd, and the sheep will be scattered" (v. 7). God's good shepherd would die, the flock would scatter, and many would perish (v. 8). However, the Lord indicated that through that testing he would refine his remaining people (v. 9).

Jesus quoted this prophecy on the evening of Judas' betrayal. With the disciples gathered, he told them they would *all* scatter that night (Mt 26:31). And, just as Jesus foretold, the Gospels reveal that all the disciples soon fled (Mt 26:56).

Soon after, the Good Shepherd laid down his life for his wandering sheep (Jn 10:14–15). Though the shepherd would be struck, Jesus assured his disciples this would not be the end. He comforted them, saying, "After I am raised up, I will go before you to Galilee" (Mt 26:32). The rest of Matthew's Gospel relates the fulfillment of this promise.

The balance of the New Testament details the full restoration of all of God's people. Ultimately, Jesus' death did not scatter his sheep. When the Good Shepherd was struck, God gathered them together (Jn 10:27).

6“On that day I will make the clans of Judah like a blazing pot in the midst of
wood, like a flaming torch among sheaves. And they shall devour to the right and
to the left all the surrounding peoples, while Jerusalem shall again be inhabited
in its place, in Jerusalem.
7“And the LORD will give salvation to the tents of Judah first, that the glory of
the house of David and the glory of the inhabitants of Jerusalem may not surpass
that of Judah. 8On that day the LORD will protect the inhabitants of Jerusalem, so
that the feeblest among them on that day shall be like David, and the house of
David shall be like God, like the angel of the LORD, going before them. 9And on that
day I will seek to destroy all the nations that come against Jerusalem.

Him Whom They Have Pierced

10“And I will pour out on the house of David and the inhabitants of Jerusalem
a spirit of grace and pleas for mercy, so that, when they look on me, on him whom
they have pierced, they shall mourn for him, as one mourns for an only child, and
weep bitterly over him, as one weeps over a firstborn. 11On that day the mourning in
Jerusalem will be as great as the mourning for Hadad-rimmon in the plain of Megiddo. 12The land shall mourn, each family[1] by itself: the family of the house of David by
itself, and their wives by themselves; the family of the house of Nathan by itself, and
their wives by themselves; 13the family of the house of Levi by itself, and their wives
by themselves; the family of the Shimeites by itself, and their wives by themselves;
14and all the families that are left, each by itself, and their wives by themselves.

13 “On that day there shall be a fountain opened for the house of David and
the inhabitants of Jerusalem, to cleanse them from sin and uncleanness.

Idolatry Cut Off

2“And on that day, declares the LORD of hosts, I will cut off the names of the
idols from the land, so that they shall be remembered no more. And also I will
remove from the land the prophets and the spirit of uncleanness. 3And if anyone
again prophesies, his father and mother who bore him will say to him, ‘You shall
not live, for you speak lies in the name of the LORD.’ And his father and mother
who bore him shall pierce him through when he prophesies.
4“On that day every prophet will be ashamed of his vision when he prophesies. He will not put on a hairy cloak in order to deceive, 5but he will say, ‘I am
no prophet, I am a worker of the soil, for a man sold me in my youth.’[2] 6And if
one asks him, ‘What are these wounds on your back?’[3] he will say, ‘The wounds I
received in the house of my friends.’

The Shepherd Struck

7 “Awake, O sword, against my shepherd,
against the man who stands next to me,”
declares the LORD of hosts.
“Strike the shepherd, and the sheep will be scattered;
I will turn my hand against the little ones.
8 In the whole land, declares the LORD,
two thirds shall be cut off and perish,
and one third shall be left alive.
9 And I will put this third into the fire,
and refine them as one refines silver,
and test them as gold is tested.
They will call upon my name,
and I will answer them.
I will say, ‘They are my people’;
and they will say, ‘The LORD is my God.’ ”

[1]Or *clan*; throughout verses 12–14 [2]Or *for the land has been my possession since my youth* [3]Or *on your chest*; Hebrew *wounds between your hands*

SEEING THE ONE WHOM THEY HAVE PIERCED

A number of centuries before Christ, the Word of God alluded to crucifixion as a form of execution — specifically, what would happen to the Messiah in his death. Immediately after sharing God's promise to pour out a "spirit of grace" on his people, Zechariah mentioned the people looking upon "him whom they have pierced" (Zec 12:10). Hundreds of years after the time Zechariah wrote, the Romans utilized crucifixion as a way to discourage subversive activity. In a crucifixion, authorities nailed the criminal to a cross where they often hung in agony for days until they died of multiple traumas (Ps 22:16).

The cross signified the deepest shame — the convicted criminal died, naked and suffering, in front of a public audience whose jeering or sheer horror at the sight only made it worse. Incredibly, almost impossibly, the One who spoke creation into existence submitted to this horrible form of death. On the cross, he sacrificed himself for the sins of all humanity; he hung on a cross between two criminals to forge a new pathway for people to find their way to God.

On the day of Jesus' execution, the Jewish leaders asked that his legs be broken so death would occur more quickly; they wanted the bodies down before the Sabbath. Pilate agreed. But after the soldiers broke the legs of the two rebels, they found Jesus already dead. Rather than breaking Jesus' legs, one of the soldiers pierced Jesus' side with a spear (Jn 19:33 – 34). John, knowing well the book of Zechariah, saw these events with his own eyes (Jn 19:35). In his Gospel, he made clear that nothing about Jesus' crucifixion happened by chance. When he watched the spear pierce Jesus' side, he remembered Zechariah's prophecy. God continued to fulfill his Word, even in the death of God's Son (Jn 19:37).

Of course, Jesus did not remain dead. John went on to tell God's people much more about the Jesus who lived *after* the cross. When John described the return of this risen Christ, he used these words: "Behold, he is coming with the clouds, and every eye will see him, even those who *pierced* him" (Rev 1:7, emphasis added). The pierced, crucified and risen Christ will return to rule over his people forever.

The Coming Day of the Lord

14 Behold, a day is coming for the LORD, when the spoil taken from you will
be divided in your midst. 2For I will gather all the nations against Jerusalem
to battle, and the city shall be taken and the houses plundered and the women
raped. Half of the city shall go out into exile, but the rest of the people shall not be
cut off from the city. 3Then the LORD will go out and fight against those nations as
when he fights on a day of battle. 4On that day his feet shall stand on the Mount
of Olives that lies before Jerusalem on the east, and the Mount of Olives shall be
split in two from east to west by a very wide valley, so that one half of the Mount
shall move northward, and the other half southward. 5And you shall flee to the
valley of my mountains, for the valley of the mountains shall reach to Azal. And
you shall flee as you fled from the earthquake in the days of Uzziah king of Judah.
Then the LORD my God will come, and all the holy ones with him.[1]

6On that day there shall be no light, cold, or frost.[2] 7And there shall be a
unique[3] day, which is known to the LORD, neither day nor night, but at evening
time there shall be light.

8On that day living waters shall flow out from Jerusalem, half of them to the
eastern sea[4] and half of them to the western sea.[5] It shall continue in summer as
in winter.

9And the LORD will be king over all the earth. On that day the LORD will be one
and his name one.

10The whole land shall be turned into a plain from Geba to Rimmon south of
Jerusalem. But Jerusalem shall remain aloft on its site from the Gate of Benjamin
to the place of the former gate, to the Corner Gate, and from the Tower of Hananel
to the king's winepresses. 11And it shall be inhabited, for there shall never again be
a decree of utter destruction.[6] Jerusalem shall dwell in security.

12And this shall be the plague with which the LORD will strike all the peoples
that wage war against Jerusalem: their flesh will rot while they are still standing
on their feet, their eyes will rot in their sockets, and their tongues will rot in their
mouths.

13And on that day a great panic from the LORD shall fall on them, so that each
will seize the hand of another, and the hand of the one will be raised against the
hand of the other. 14Even Judah will fight at Jerusalem.[7] And the wealth of all the
surrounding nations shall be collected, gold, silver, and garments in great abundance. 15And a plague like this plague shall fall on the horses, the mules, the camels, the donkeys, and whatever beasts may be in those camps.

16Then everyone who survives of all the nations that have come against Jerusalem shall go up year after year to worship the King, the LORD of hosts, and to
keep the Feast of Booths. 17And if any of the families of the earth do not go up to
Jerusalem to worship the King, the LORD of hosts, there will be no rain on them.
18And if the family of Egypt does not go up and present themselves, then on them
there shall be no rain;[8] there shall be the plague with which the LORD afflicts the
nations that do not go up to keep the Feast of Booths. 19This shall be the punishment to Egypt and the punishment to all the nations that do not go up to keep the
Feast of Booths.

20And on that day there shall be inscribed on the bells of the horses, "Holy to
the LORD." And the pots in the house of the LORD shall be as the bowls before the
altar. 21And every pot in Jerusalem and Judah shall be holy to the LORD of hosts,
so that all who sacrifice may come and take of them and boil the meat of the
sacrifice in them. And there shall no longer be a trader[9] in the house of the LORD
of hosts on that day.

---

[1]Other Hebrew manuscripts *you* [2]Compare Septuagint, Syriac, Vulgate, Targum; the meaning of the Hebrew is uncertain [3]Hebrew *one* [4]That is, the Dead Sea [5]That is, the Mediterranean Sea [6]The Hebrew term rendered *decree of utter destruction* refers to things devoted (or set apart) to the Lord (or by the Lord) for destruction [7]Or *against Jerusalem* [8]Hebrew lacks *rain* [9]Or *Canaanite*

ZECHARIAH 14:20–21

SET APART AS HOLY

Scripture describes the God of creation as holy (Isa 6:3). Holiness, a much-used term that is seldom carefully defined, necessitates the idea of separation. In fact, to the degree that God is holy, he expects his people to be holy (Lev 19:2). God called the people of Israel, and he calls his church today, to be set apart from the world: visibly and demonstrably different as a reflection of his holiness.

After the Lord delivered the Israelites from slavery, he labeled this newly formed people a *holy* nation (Ex 19:5–6). Much of the Old Testament outlined in specific terms how the Israelites were to relate to one another as well as to God. This careful instruction was intended to distinguish Israel from other pagan nations, just as God was distinguished from their false gods. Israel's conduct before the world was intended to show God's intent for all human life.

The purity of God's people serves as a recurring theme in the final chapters of Zechariah's prophecy. In this passage, Zechariah looked forward to a time when normal cooking pots would be considered holy—like the bowls used before the altar (Zec 14:20–21). Even the bells of horses were to include the inscription "Holy to the LORD," a phrase usually reserved for the high priest's turban (Ex 28:36–38). The extensiveness of these descriptions indicated that nothing lay outside God's purview. Israel's relationship to God was to infuse every aspect of their lives.

Through his chosen people, God intended to put on display his holy character before the world. He chose and set apart Israel not only for privilege but also for missionary responsibility.

As any cursory reading of the Scripture reveals, the Old Testament people of God failed to embody God's holy standard. But rather than judging all of humanity irrevocably, God sent his Son to be that which he intended for Israel. In every detail of his life, Jesus perfectly embodied holiness.

Jesus' holy life makes possible a holy people today. The New Testament uses the term "saints" or "holy people" (Ro 1:7) to describe the people of God for this reason. The Holy Spirit applies Christ's holy work to each believer's heart.

To truly understand holiness, today's people of God look to Jesus as their standard. In seeing the impossibility of perfectly imitating Christ's perfect life, they continue looking to him as their present and future hope.

JESUS: OUR COMING MESSIAH

MALACHI

MALACHI

COMPLETION OF REBUILT TEMPLE *c. 516 BC*	RECONSTRUCTION OF JERUSALEM'S WALL *c. 444 BC*	WRITING OF BOOK OF MALACHI *c. 430 BC*

The final prophecy of the Old Testament challenges Israel to remember the glorious nature of God's love.

The theme of forgetfulness was prominent throughout the Old Testament. When the nation prepared to cross the Jordan River and possess the land, Moses warned them of the danger of forgetting God (Dt 8:10 – 20). Their years in the wilderness had taught the people to depend on God, quite literally, for their daily bread. Once they entered the land, however, they found ample provision, just as God had promised. But rather than prompting the people to worship, this surplus often caused them to forget God and trust in their own resources.

In a similar fashion, the Jews who lived in Judah in Malachi's day, about a century after the Babylonian exile, were prone to forget God. They were blessed by the fact that they were established in the land, enjoying a rebuilt temple and wall around Jerusalem and thus given the chance to restore united worship among God's people. But their hopes for the glory that the prophets had promised flagged in the face of their low political status and the lack of a visible symbol of God's presence in the temple. Their worship became listless and rote rather than being inspiring.

Malachi reminded the people that rightly remembering God comes about by proper worship; but the priests, who offered blemished animals and were otherwise negligent about worship, offered a poor example that resulted in lackluster worship practices among God's people. The spillover effect of this faulty worship was broken social relationships; especially the relationships between husbands and wives

(Mal 2:10 – 16). Rather than modeling God's covenant love, marriages among the people of God were broken by divorce. Also, Malachi chided the nation for robbing God by withholding tithes and offerings meant for the needy and to fund worship.

At the end of his prophecy, Malachi pointed forward to a coming messenger who would both speak the word of God and model conformity to his message (4:5). This messenger would minister "in the spirit and power of Elijah" (Lk 1:17) and point the way to the Messiah, who would worship God perfectly and give his very life on behalf of his people. Malachi's prophecy culminated the ministry of the prophets before God's Word came in the flesh, centuries later, as Jesus Christ, God's promised Messiah.

THEY SHALL BE MINE, SAYS THE LORD OF HOSTS, IN THE DAY WHEN I MAKE UP MY TREASURED POSSESSION, AND I WILL SPARE THEM AS A MAN SPARES HIS SON WHO SERVES HIM.

Malachi 3:17

MALACHI

1 The oracle of the word of the LORD to Israel by Malachi.[1]

The LORD's Love for Israel

2"I have loved you," says the LORD. But you say, "How have you loved us?" "Is not Esau Jacob's brother?" declares the LORD. "Yet I have loved Jacob 3but Esau I have hated. I have laid waste his hill country and left his heritage to jackals of the desert." 4If Edom says, "We are shattered but we will rebuild the ruins," the LORD of hosts says, "They may build, but I will tear down, and they will be called 'the wicked country,' and 'the people with whom the LORD is angry forever.' " 5Your own eyes shall see this, and you shall say, "Great is the LORD beyond the border of Israel!"

The Priests' Polluted Offerings

6"A son honors his father, and a servant his master. If then I am a father, where is my honor? And if I am a master, where is my fear? says the LORD of hosts to you, O priests, who despise my name. But you say, 'How have we despised your name?' 7By offering polluted food upon my altar. But you say, 'How have we polluted you?' By saying that the LORD's table may be despised. 8When you offer blind animals in sacrifice, is that not evil? And when you offer those that are lame or sick, is that not evil? Present that to your governor; will he accept you or show you favor? says the LORD of hosts. 9And now entreat the favor of God, that he may be gracious to us. With such a gift from your hand, will he show favor to any of you? says the LORD of hosts. 10Oh that there were one among you who would shut the doors, that you might not kindle fire on my altar in vain! I have no pleasure in you, says the LORD of hosts, and I will not accept an offering from your hand. 11For from the rising of the sun to its setting my name will be[2] great among the nations, and in every place incense will be offered to my name, and a pure offering. For my name will be great among the nations, says the LORD of hosts. 12But you profane it when you say that the Lord's table is polluted, and its fruit, that is, its food, may be despised. 13But you say, 'What a weariness this is,' and you snort at it, says the LORD of hosts. You bring what has been taken by violence or is lame or sick, and this you bring as your offering! Shall I accept that from your hand? says the LORD. 14Cursed be the cheat who has a male in his flock, and vows it, and yet sacrifices to the Lord what is blemished. For I am a great King, says the LORD of hosts, and my name will be feared among the nations.

The LORD Rebukes the Priests

2 "And now, O priests, this command is for you. 2If you will not listen, if you will not take it to heart to give honor to my name, says the LORD of hosts, then I will send the curse upon you and I will curse your blessings. Indeed, I have already cursed them, because you do not lay it to heart. 3Behold, I will rebuke your offspring,[3] and spread dung on your faces, the dung of your offerings, and you shall be taken away with it.[4] 4So shall you know that I have sent this command to you, that my covenant with Levi may stand, says the LORD of hosts. 5My covenant with him was one of life and peace, and I gave them to him. It was a covenant of fear, and he feared me. He stood in awe of my name. 6True instruction[5] was in his mouth, and no wrong was found on his lips. He walked with me in peace and uprightness, and he turned many from iniquity. 7For the lips of a priest should guard knowledge, and people[6] should seek instruction from his mouth, for he

[1] *Malachi* means *my messenger* [2] Or *is* (three times in verse 11; also verse 14) [3] Hebrew *seed* [4] Or *to it*
[5] Or *law*; also verses 7, 8, 9 [6] Hebrew *they*

is the messenger of the LORD of hosts. 8But you have turned aside from the way.
You have caused many to stumble by your instruction. You have corrupted the
covenant of Levi, says the LORD of hosts, 9and so I make you despised and abased
before all the people, inasmuch as you do not keep my ways but show partiality
in your instruction."

Judah Profaned the Covenant

10Have we not all one Father? Has not one God created us? Why then are we
faithless to one another, profaning the covenant of our fathers? 11Judah has been
faithless, and abomination has been committed in Israel and in Jerusalem. For Judah has profaned the sanctuary of the LORD, which he loves, and has married the
daughter of a foreign god. 12May the LORD cut off from the tents of Jacob any descendant[1] of the man who does this, who brings an offering to the LORD of hosts!
13And this second thing you do. You cover the LORD's altar with tears, with
weeping and groaning because he no longer regards the offering or accepts it with
favor from your hand. 14But you say, "Why does he not?" Because the LORD was
witness between you and the wife of your youth, to whom you have been faithless, though she is your companion and your wife by covenant. 15Did he not make
them one, with a portion of the Spirit in their union?[2] And what was the one
God[3] seeking?[4] Godly offspring. So guard yourselves[5] in your spirit, and let none
of you be faithless to the wife of your youth. 16"For the man who does not love
his wife but divorces her,[6] says the LORD, the God of Israel, covers[7] his garment
with violence, says the LORD of hosts. So guard yourselves in your spirit, and do
not be faithless."

The Messenger of the LORD

17You have wearied the LORD with your words. But you say, "How have we wearied him?" By saying, "Everyone who does evil is good in the sight of the LORD, and
he delights in them." Or by asking, "Where is the God of justice?"
3 "Behold, I send my messenger, and he will prepare the way before me. And
the Lord whom you seek will suddenly come to his temple; and the messenger of the covenant in whom you delight, behold, he is coming, says the LORD of
hosts. 2But who can endure the day of his coming, and who can stand when he
appears? For he is like a refiner's fire and like fullers' soap. 3He will sit as a refiner
and purifier of silver, and he will purify the sons of Levi and refine them like gold
and silver, and they will bring offerings in righteousness to the LORD.[8] 4Then the
offering of Judah and Jerusalem will be pleasing to the LORD as in the days of old
and as in former years.
5"Then I will draw near to you for judgment. I will be a swift witness against
the sorcerers, against the adulterers, against those who swear falsely, against
those who oppress the hired worker in his wages, the widow and the fatherless,
against those who thrust aside the sojourner, and do not fear me, says the LORD
of hosts.

Robbing God

6"For I the LORD do not change; therefore you, O children of Jacob, are not consumed. 7From the days of your fathers you have turned aside from my statutes and
have not kept them. Return to me, and I will return to you, says the LORD of hosts.
But you say, 'How shall we return?' 8Will man rob God? Yet you are robbing me.
But you say, 'How have we robbed you?' In your tithes and contributions. 9You are
cursed with a curse, for you are robbing me, the whole nation of you. 10Bring the

[1]Hebrew *any who wakes and answers* [2]Hebrew *in it* [3]Hebrew *the one* [4]Or *And not one has done this who has a portion of the Spirit. And what was that one seeking?* [5]Or *So take care*; also verse 16 [6]Hebrew *who hates and divorces* [7]Probable meaning (compare Septuagint and Deuteronomy 24:1–4); or *"The LORD, the God of Israel, says that he hates divorce, and him who covers* [8]Or *and they will belong to the LORD, bringers of an offering in righteousness*

MALACHI 2:16

DIVORCE MATTERS

God's verdict concerning divorce was severe, noting that the one who pursues divorce acts violently and shows hatred for their spouse.

The fact that Malachi singled out marriage in his prophecy shows the significance God places on marriage. The nation's spiritual regression was demonstrated in their inability to keep their marriage commitments and in their open embrace of pagan immorality. Therefore, God said, his people should "guard yourselves in your spirit, and do not be faithless."

These commands are rooted in the nature and character of God, who is always faithful to his covenant promises. The fact that God always keeps his word to his people is seen throughout the Old Testament. Time and time again, God sought out his wayward people and loved them in spite of their sin (Hos 3:1). Since marriage is a picture of God's relationship with his church, his people should keep their promises to one another — especially the covenant promises of marriage vows (Eph 5:32).

MALACHI 3:1

PREPARE THE WAY

Malachi prophesied of a coming messenger who would prepare the way for the Messiah (called "the Lord" in this passage). Matthew's and Luke's Gospels identify this messenger as John the Baptist, the forerunner of Jesus Christ (Mt 11:10; Mk 1:2–3). John's ministry did not look like what one might expect for one chosen to prepare the way

(continued on page 1467)

THE DAY OF THE LORD

The book of Malachi concludes the Old Testament in a somewhat cryptic way. After encouraging his audience to turn from their spiritual apathy and return to God, Malachi pointed to a righteous remnant of people who would hold fast to God and fear his name. To these faithful ones, God promised to send healing; they would find joy and gladness and leap "like calves from the stall" (v. 2). To the unfaithful, he promised his coming judgment (vv. 1,3).

Before this day comes, Malachi said, the prophet Elijah would return. Elijah's story appears in 1 Kings 17 through 2 Kings 2. During a dreadful time in Israel's history, Elijah was faithful to the Lord and called people to repent and return to God. But Malachi said that he would come again. There are three commonly identified possibilities in which this prophecy has been or will be fulfilled.

First, the Gospel writers identify John the Baptist with Elijah (Mt 11:14; 17:10 – 12; Mk 9:11 – 13; Lk 1:17). Elijah and John share much in common, including their message of the need for repentance, their ascetic lifestyles, and the rejection they faced at the hands of the people of their respective cultures.

Second, two leading Old Testament figures appeared with Jesus at his transfiguration — Moses and Elijah (Mt 17:1 – 8). Clearly, those in Jesus' day were looking for Elijah to come as a precursor to the establishment of the kingdom of God. The transfiguration radically demonstrated that Jesus was the Son of God who had come to do the very things Malachi described in this text.

Finally, some believe that an Elijah-like figure will come before Jesus' second coming. This person may, like Elijah, call down fire from heaven and bring the judgment of God upon those who reject the gospel message (Rev 11:3 – 6).

Malachi's concluding statement portrays the twin themes of the character of God that have been seen throughout the Old Testament: On the one hand, he is a God of judgment. He will curse those who live and die in their sin and who never turn to him in repentance and faith. But he is also a God who gives grace. Because of Jesus' work on the cross, all people have the opportunity to seek and find the Lord before it is too late.

full tithe into the storehouse, that there may be food in my house. And thereby
put me to the test, says the LORD of hosts, if I will not open the windows of heaven
for you and pour down for you a blessing until there is no more need. 11I will rebuke the devourer[1] for you, so that it will not destroy the fruits of your soil, and
your vine in the field shall not fail to bear, says the LORD of hosts. 12Then all nations will call you blessed, for you will be a land of delight, says the LORD of hosts.
13"Your words have been hard against me, says the LORD. But you say, 'How
have we spoken against you?' 14You have said, 'It is vain to serve God. What is the
profit of our keeping his charge or of walking as in mourning before the LORD of
hosts? 15And now we call the arrogant blessed. Evildoers not only prosper but
they put God to the test and they escape.'"

The Book of Remembrance

16Then those who feared the LORD spoke with one another. The LORD paid attention and heard them, and a book of remembrance was written before him of
those who feared the LORD and esteemed his name. 17"They shall be mine, says the
LORD of hosts, in the day when I make up my treasured possession, and I will spare
them as a man spares his son who serves him. 18Then once more you shall see the
distinction between the righteous and the wicked, between one who serves God
and one who does not serve him.

The Great Day of the LORD

4 [2] "For behold, the day is coming, burning like an oven, when all the arrogant and all evildoers will be stubble. The day that is coming shall set them
ablaze, says the LORD of hosts, so that it will leave them neither root nor branch.
2But for you who fear my name, the sun of righteousness shall rise with healing in
its wings. You shall go out leaping like calves from the stall. 3And you shall tread
down the wicked, for they will be ashes under the soles of your feet, on the day
when I act, says the LORD of hosts.
4"Remember the law of my servant Moses, the statutes and rules[3] that I commanded him at Horeb for all Israel.
5"Behold, I will send you Elijah the prophet before the great and awesome day
of the LORD comes. 6And he will turn the hearts of fathers to their children and
the hearts of children to their fathers, lest I come and strike the land with a decree
of utter destruction."[4]

(Prepare the Way, continued)

for the King of the universe. John's unique lifestyle and prophetic message countered the culture of his day (Mk 1:4–8).

Like John, those who declare the message of Jesus today will often be shunned. The "aroma of Christ" will be compelling to some and lead them to repentance and faith, but to others it will be "a fragrance from death to death" and they will reject the gospel message (2Co 2:15–16). God's people should find confidence in knowing that God has commissioned them to proclaim his message until Jesus returns.

[1]Probably a name for some crop-destroying pest or pests [2]Ch 4:1–6 is ch 3:19–24 in Hebrew [3]Or *and just decrees* [4]The Hebrew term rendered *decree of utter destruction* refers to things devoted (or set apart) to the Lord (or by the Lord) for destruction

INTERTESTAMENTAL PERIOD

Approximately 400 years lie between the time of Malachi, the final prophetic book of the Old Testament, and the birth of Jesus Christ. During this time, God was "silent" — the Bible records no revelation from God to his people during this period. The absence of God's written word through his prophets was surely a fearful reality for his people. Had God finally given up on them? Had their sin caused him to reject them forever?

God's four-hundred-year silence stands in stark contrast to his previous interaction with humanity. He had a close relationship with Adam and Eve and was quick to call out to Adam when he hid from God's presence in the garden (Ge 3:9). When corruption filled the earth and God regretted even making humans because of the darkness of their hearts, he still called to Noah and protected him and his family from the coming destruction (Ge 6:13). After the debacle at Babel, God called Abram and chose him to be the father of his people (Ge 12:1 – 3). And God led his people, powerfully and visibly, out of Egypt and through their wilderness wanderings (Dt 1:1 — 2:3). From the beginning of time, God had been a speaking God, always calling out to his people, inviting them to repentance and faith, and assuring them of his love.

For years he spoke through his prophets. Some — such as Hosea, Amos, and Micah — warned the nation of Israel of God's coming judgment prior to the exile. They called the people to spiritual reform and renewal, warning them of the consequences of disobedience. God's people did not listen, but God continued to speak. During the exile, prophets such as Ezekiel and Daniel reminded the people of the reason for their punishment and continued to encourage them to return to God and live faithful lives, even though they were now scattered throughout the pagan world. Finally, the prophets Haggai, Zechariah, and Malachi spoke God's word to his people as they began to return to the land to rebuild the city of Jerusalem and the temple of God. Through it all, God spoke clearly and often.

But then he did stop — for over 400 years. The people were left to hope that the prophets' words of restoration and redemption would come true one day. They longed for God to send his promised One, his Messiah, to save his people and usher in his rule and reign forever. However, with each passing year it must have been more and more difficult for the people to maintain their hope that the promised One would ever come.

Those who held out hope had all sorts of notions as to what the Messiah would be like. Some likely expected a military ruler who would rid the world of those who oppressed God's people and would bring God's kingdom to preeminence through military might. Others likely expected a political king who would enact justice in the land and lead God's people into the peace and stability foreshadowed by King

David's rule. The people's perspectives, hopes, and dreams about the coming Messiah differed widely during this period, which we now know as the intertestamental period. (Some also refer to this time as the "Second Temple" period, due to the fact that a remnant of Jews was allowed to rebuild the temple that was destroyed during the exile.)

Throughout the world, various nations such as the Greeks and the Romans rose to power through this time. These nations continued to influence the people of God and shape the spiritual vitality (or lack thereof) of God's people. Roman rule and Greek influence also greatly impacted the cultural milieu into which Jesus was born.

Throughout Israel and Judah, various factions also developed between the time when the Old and New Testaments were written. The Pharisees, Sadducees, Essenes, and Zealots each maintained differing understandings of God's Law and the promises related to the coming of his Messiah. These groups also had varying ideas regarding how God's people should live obedient lives in light of the wickedness of the surrounding society. By the time of Jesus, these different entities exerted influence over the religious practices of God's people and shaped the way in which the people understood Jesus' life and ministry.

God's apparent silence, compounded by the pagan culture, ongoing moral depravity, and internal factionalism, created a dark world indeed for the chosen people of God. Those who still held out hope of the coming of the Messiah longed for a word from God. But "when the fullness of time had come" (Gal 4:4), when God chose to reveal more of himself and his plan to redeem his people, Israel did not merely get *a* word from God, they got *the* Word from God.

The New Testament opens with the announcement that God's word took on flesh and made his dwelling among a sin-darkened world (Jn 1:14). The birth of Jesus, his redeeming work and ministry, and his sacrifice and resurrection confirm for his people — believers in the distant past, now, and in the future — that though God may at times seem silent, he will never forget his people.

BEGINNINGS	REVOLT	PEOPLE	INTERTESTAMENTAL PERIOD	SAVIOR	CHURCH	FOREVER
GENESIS 1–2 (pg. 10)	GENESIS 3–11 (pg. 24)	GENESIS 12 to MALACHI (pg. 256)	(pg. 1468)	GOSPELS to ACTS 1 (pg. 1518)	ACTS 2 to REVELATION 20 (pg. 1686)	REVELATION 21–22 (pg. 1938)

NEW TESTAMENT

JESUS: OUR PROMISED KING

MATTHEW

MATTHEW

BIRTH OF JESUS *c. 5 BC*	HEROD ANTIPAS RULES GALILEE AND PEREA *4 BC – AD 39*	JESUS' MINISTRY, DEATH, RESURRECTION *c. AD 27 – 30*

Kings came and went throughout the Old Testament. With each successive king, the hope of the people of God continued to fade. Israel longed for the promised king who would usher in God's peace and deliverance. With their own eyes, they witnessed the failure of even the best kings, the demise of the nation, and the exile of God's people. Though the prophets spoke of a coming day when God would prove faithful, the lengthy silence after Malachi's writing left the fate of God's people seemingly in question.

Matthew's Gospel proclaims Jesus to be the long-awaited King of kings — the one to whom the entire Old Testament points. Matthew, a Jewish believer, began his summary of Jesus' life and ministry with a lengthy genealogy that served to connect the Lord's coming to the promises God made to David so long ago. He was a king like David, but one who would succeed where David failed and accomplish what David had been incapable of doing in his life. At the conclusion of the book, the sign that hung above Jesus' head on the cross ironically makes the same claim: "This is Jesus, the King of the Jews" (27:37). Between these two bookends, Matthew makes a clear and compelling argument for the divine origin of Jesus and his kingly role among his people.

Though many Jews in Jesus' day were blind to his identity, Matthew anchors Jesus' life and mission in the Old Testament promises of God. Using more than 70 quotations or allusions from the Old Testament, Matthew demonstrates that Jesus is the promised king who came to fulfill the hope of his people. Matthew invites his readers to embrace the rightful king through faith and repentance and submit to life in "the kingdom of heaven" or "the kingdom of God."

Those who come under the rule and reign of the King find this king to be a righteous and loving ruler who humbly serves his beloved kingdom citizens. This king invites his people to participate in his mission to the world and the establishment of his kingdom on earth as it is in heaven (28:18 – 20). In his kingdom, Jews and Gentiles alike find forgiveness of sin, peace with God, and hope for this life and the next.

BUT SEEK FIRST THE KINGDOM OF GOD
AND HIS RIGHTEOUSNESS,
AND ALL THESE THINGS
WILL BE ADDED TO YOU.

Matthew 6:33

MATTHEW

MATTHEW 1:1–17

THE GENEALOGY OF JESUS

Part of Matthew's goal in writing his Gospel was to show Jesus as the true Messiah for whom the Jews had been waiting. Because the Messiah had to come from the line of David, it was important for Matthew to show Jesus' legitimacy by connecting him not only to David, but all the way back to Abraham (v. 2; Ge 12:3). Another interesting point in Matthew's genealogy is the mention of five women, especially Tamar (Mt 1:3), Rahab (v. 5), and Bathsheba (simply called "the wife of Uriah" in v. 6). Tamar had deceitfully posed as a prostitute to bear her children (Ge 38), Rahab was a prostitute in the city of Jericho (Jos 2), and Bathsheba was the woman with whom David committed adultery (2Sa 11). Not only was it unusual for women to be mentioned in genealogies, but it was even stranger that Matthew decided to list three women of relatively low moral standing. The inclusion of Tamar, Rahab, and Bathsheba shows that God is able to use anyone to accomplish his plan. God could have handpicked anyone to be in the genealogy of Jesus, but he included these and many other imperfect people to comprise the line that would eventually bring his Son into the world. These women are an incredible image of God's sovereign desire to take what is broken and make it new. Matthew begins his Gospel by showing the legitimacy of Jesus and the redemptive power of God.

The Genealogy of Jesus Christ

1 The book of the genealogy of Jesus Christ, the son of David, the son of Abraham.

2 Abraham was the father of Isaac, and Isaac the father of Jacob, and Jacob the father of Judah and his brothers, 3 and Judah the father of Perez and Zerah by Tamar, and Perez the father of Hezron, and Hezron the father of Ram,[1] 4 and Ram the father of Amminadab, and Amminadab the father of Nahshon, and Nahshon the father of Salmon, 5 and Salmon the father of Boaz by Rahab, and Boaz the father of Obed by Ruth, and Obed the father of Jesse, 6 and Jesse the father of David the king.

And David was the father of Solomon by the wife of Uriah, 7 and Solomon the father of Rehoboam, and Rehoboam the father of Abijah, and Abijah the father of Asaph,[2] 8 and Asaph the father of Jehoshaphat, and Jehoshaphat the father of Joram, and Joram the father of Uzziah, 9 and Uzziah the father of Jotham, and Jotham the father of Ahaz, and Ahaz the father of Hezekiah, 10 and Hezekiah the father of Manasseh, and Manasseh the father of Amos,[3] and Amos the father of Josiah, 11 and Josiah the father of Jechoniah and his brothers, at the time of the deportation to Babylon.

12 And after the deportation to Babylon: Jechoniah was the father of Shealtiel,[4] and Shealtiel the father of Zerubbabel, 13 and Zerubbabel the father of Abiud, and Abiud the father of Eliakim, and Eliakim the father of Azor, 14 and Azor the father of Zadok, and Zadok the father of Achim, and Achim the father of Eliud, 15 and Eliud the father of Eleazar, and Eleazar the father of Matthan, and Matthan the father of Jacob, 16 and Jacob the father of Joseph the husband of Mary, of whom Jesus was born, who is called Christ.

17 So all the generations from Abraham to David were fourteen generations, and from David to the deportation to Babylon fourteen generations, and from the deportation to Babylon to the Christ fourteen generations.

The Birth of Jesus Christ

18 Now the birth of Jesus Christ[5] took place in this way. When his mother Mary had been betrothed[6] to Joseph, before they came together she was found to be with child from the Holy Spirit. 19 And her husband Joseph, being a just man and unwilling to put her to shame, resolved to divorce her quietly. 20 But as he considered these things, behold, an angel of the Lord appeared to him in a dream, saying, "Joseph, son of David, do not fear to take Mary as your wife, for that which is conceived in her is from the Holy Spirit. 21 She will bear a son, and you shall call his name Jesus, for he will save his people from their sins." 22 All this took place to fulfill what the Lord had spoken by the prophet:

23 "Behold, the virgin shall conceive and bear a son,
and they shall call his name Immanuel"

(which means, God with us). 24 When Joseph woke from sleep, he did as the angel of the Lord commanded him: he took his wife, 25 but knew her not until she had given birth to a son. And he called his name Jesus.

The Visit of the Wise Men

2 Now after Jesus was born in Bethlehem of Judea in the days of Herod the king, behold, wise men[7] from the east came to Jerusalem, 2 saying, "Where is he who has been born king of the Jews? For we saw his star when it rose[8] and have come

[1] Greek *Aram*; also verse 4 [2] *Asaph* is probably an alternate spelling of *Asa*; some manuscripts *Asa*; also verse 8 [3] *Amos* is probably an alternate spelling of *Amon*; some manuscripts *Amon*; twice in this verse [4] Greek *Salathiel*; twice in this verse [5] Some manuscripts *of the Christ* [6] That is, legally pledged to be married [7] Greek *magi*; also verses 7, 16 [8] Or *in the east*; also verse 9

to worship him." 3When Herod the king heard this, he was troubled, and all Jerusalem with him; 4and assembling all the chief priests and scribes of the people, he
inquired of them where the Christ was to be born. 5They told him, "In Bethlehem
of Judea, for so it is written by the prophet:

6 "'And you, O Bethlehem, in the land of Judah,
are by no means least among the rulers of Judah;
for from you shall come a ruler
who will shepherd my people Israel.'"

7Then Herod summoned the wise men secretly and ascertained from them
what time the star had appeared. 8And he sent them to Bethlehem, saying, "Go
and search diligently for the child, and when you have found him, bring me word,
that I too may come and worship him." 9After listening to the king, they went
on their way. And behold, the star that they had seen when it rose went before
them until it came to rest over the place where the child was. 10When they saw
the star, they rejoiced exceedingly with great joy. 11And going into the house, they
saw the child with Mary his mother, and they fell down and worshiped him. Then,
opening their treasures, they offered him gifts, gold and frankincense and myrrh.
12And being warned in a dream not to return to Herod, they departed to their own
country by another way.

The Flight to Egypt

13Now when they had departed, behold, an angel of the Lord appeared to Joseph in a dream and said, "Rise, take the child and his mother, and flee to Egypt,
and remain there until I tell you, for Herod is about to search for the child, to destroy him." 14And he rose and took the child and his mother by night and departed
to Egypt 15and remained there until the death of Herod. This was to fulfill what
the Lord had spoken by the prophet, "Out of Egypt I called my son."

Herod Kills the Children

16Then Herod, when he saw that he had been tricked by the wise men, became
furious, and he sent and killed all the male children in Bethlehem and in all that
region who were two years old or under, according to the time that he had ascertained from the wise men. 17Then was fulfilled what was spoken by the prophet
Jeremiah:

18 "A voice was heard in Ramah,
weeping and loud lamentation,
Rachel weeping for her children;
she refused to be comforted, because they are no more."

The Return to Nazareth

19But when Herod died, behold, an angel of the Lord appeared in a dream to
Joseph in Egypt, 20saying, "Rise, take the child and his mother and go to the land
of Israel, for those who sought the child's life are dead." 21And he rose and took
the child and his mother and went to the land of Israel. 22But when he heard that
Archelaus was reigning over Judea in place of his father Herod, he was afraid to go
there, and being warned in a dream he withdrew to the district of Galilee. 23And
he went and lived in a city called Nazareth, so that what was spoken by the prophets might be fulfilled, that he would be called a Nazarene.

John the Baptist Prepares the Way

3 In those days John the Baptist came preaching in the wilderness of Judea,
2"Repent, for the kingdom of heaven is at hand."[1] 3For this is he who was spoken of by the prophet Isaiah when he said,

[1]Or *the kingdom of heaven has come near*

MATTHEW 3:1–2

JOHN'S BAPTISM OF REPENTANCE

John the Baptist was the son of Zechariah and Elizabeth and was a cousin of Jesus (Lk 1). His birth was a signal of the coming of the Messiah, and Jesus himself said that there was none "greater than John the Baptist" (Mt 11:11). John called his followers to repent from their wrongdoing because of the nearness of the kingdom of heaven. In order for people to repent, they had to recognize and acknowledge the fact that they were not living lives that glorified God. In Matthew 4:17, Jesus echoes John's call as he preaches the same message of repentance. Believers are expected to live lives that honor and glorify God. Throughout Jesus' ministry, he explained what it means to live according to the standard that God has set—in a way that mirrors the Father's heart—and he also lived a life that believers are meant to imitate. Obviously it is impossible to be completely like Jesus; after all, he was perfect. But the first step for anyone to begin to live according to Scripture is to repent and turn away from that which is wrong or sinful.

"The voice of one crying in the wilderness:
'Prepare[1] the way of the Lord;
make his paths straight.'"

4 Now John wore a garment of camel's hair and a leather belt around his waist, and
his food was locusts and wild honey. 5 Then Jerusalem and all Judea and all the
region about the Jordan were going out to him, 6 and they were baptized by him in
the river Jordan, confessing their sins.

7 But when he saw many of the Pharisees and Sadducees coming to his baptism, he said to them, "You brood of vipers! Who warned you to flee from the
wrath to come? 8 Bear fruit in keeping with repentance. 9 And do not presume to
say to yourselves, 'We have Abraham as our father,' for I tell you, God is able from
these stones to raise up children for Abraham. 10 Even now the axe is laid to the
root of the trees. Every tree therefore that does not bear good fruit is cut down
and thrown into the fire.

11 "I baptize you with water for repentance, but he who is coming after me is
mightier than I, whose sandals I am not worthy to carry. He will baptize you with
the Holy Spirit and fire. 12 His winnowing fork is in his hand, and he will clear his
threshing floor and gather his wheat into the barn, but the chaff he will burn with
unquenchable fire."

The Baptism of Jesus

13 Then Jesus came from Galilee to the Jordan to John, to be baptized by him.
14 John would have prevented him, saying, "I need to be baptized by you, and do
you come to me?" 15 But Jesus answered him, "Let it be so now, for thus it is fitting for us to fulfill all righteousness." Then he consented. 16 And when Jesus was
baptized, immediately he went up from the water, and behold, the heavens were
opened to him,[2] and he saw the Spirit of God descending like a dove and coming
to rest on him; 17 and behold, a voice from heaven said, "This is my beloved Son,[3]
with whom I am well pleased."

The Temptation of Jesus

4 Then Jesus was led up by the Spirit into the wilderness to be tempted by the
devil. 2 And after fasting forty days and forty nights, he was hungry. 3 And the
tempter came and said to him, "If you are the Son of God, command these stones
to become loaves of bread." 4 But he answered, "It is written,

"'Man shall not live by bread alone,
but by every word that comes from the mouth of God.'"

5 Then the devil took him to the holy city and set him on the pinnacle of the temple
6 and said to him, "If you are the Son of God, throw yourself down, for it is written,

"'He will command his angels concerning you,'

and

"'On their hands they will bear you up,
lest you strike your foot against a stone.'"

7 Jesus said to him, "Again it is written, 'You shall not put the Lord your God to the
test.'" 8 Again, the devil took him to a very high mountain and showed him all the
kingdoms of the world and their glory. 9 And he said to him, "All these I will give
you, if you will fall down and worship me." 10 Then Jesus said to him, "Be gone,
Satan! For it is written,

"'You shall worship the Lord your God
and him only shall you serve.'"

11 Then the devil left him, and behold, angels came and were ministering to him.

MATTHEW 4:1–11

THE TEMPTATION OF THE SON OF GOD

As a human, Jesus experienced everything that any other human has experienced, including temptation. Matthew 4 describes Jesus' experience of being tempted by the devil for 40 days and 40 nights. Jesus was tempted by the opportunity to use his power to meet his own needs rather than relying on God (v. 3), to put God to the test in order to win a large following (v. 5), and to compromise with Satan to win the kingdoms of the world, thereby avoiding the cross (v. 9). Jesus' experience was no less real than any sort of temptation that other people experience. However, the difference is that Jesus did not give in to the temptation he faced (Heb 4:15). Jesus boldly and convincingly refuted with Scripture each of the temptations he faced. Jesus defeated Satan by using a weapon that every believer has at their disposal: "the sword of the Spirit, which is the word of God" (Eph 6:17).

[1] Or *crying: Prepare in the wilderness* [2] Some manuscripts omit *to him* [3] Or *my Son, my* (or *the*) *Beloved*

MY BELOVED SON

The Father confirmed the identity of the Son at his baptism. Though Jesus had no sin, he willingly submitted to John's baptism. This action further identified him with those he came to save. As the author of Hebrews writes, "Since therefore the children share in flesh and blood, he himself likewise partook of the same things" (Heb 2:14). His association with frail humans allowed him to understand their pain, sympathize with their weakness, and enter into their suffering.

It is fitting that God spoke from the heavens upon this significant event. Jesus knew his identity as the preexistent Son of God, who was the central agent of God's created handiwork at the dawn of creation (Col 1:15 – 20). Yet, God the Father publicly proclaimed that Jesus was his beloved Son before he fully inaugurated his earthly mission. This statement was certainly a source of encouragement to Jesus, but it was also a public testimony to all those who heard that Jesus was, in fact, God's Messiah — the One who was promised so long ago (Ge 3:15).

The same motive lies at the heart of the Gospel writers, who sought to demonstrate that Jesus was the Son of God. Matthew, writing to a Jewish audience, established that Jesus was the fulfillment of both the Abrahamic and Davidic covenants (Mt 1:17). Mark used Jesus' miracles and message to show that he was "the Son of God" (Mk 1:1). Luke compiled an orderly account of the life and ministry of Jesus — focused on his death, burial, and resurrection — in order to prove the validity of the message concerning Jesus the Christ (Lk 1:1 – 4). John focuses on Christ as the *logos*. Jesus reveals the Father to God's people in a way that is reminiscent of, but much clearer than, the Word of God that had revealed him throughout the Old Testament (Jn 1:1 – 14). Though the contextual realities differed, each Gospel story sought to affirm Jesus' identity and convince the original hearers, and all subsequent humanity, "that Jesus is the Christ, the Son of God, and that by believing you may have life in his name" (Jn 20:31). The Father's pronouncement at Jesus' baptism is affirmed whenever a person repents of their sins and trusts in Christ.

Jesus Begins His Ministry

12Now when he heard that John had been arrested, he withdrew into Galilee.
13And leaving Nazareth he went and lived in Capernaum by the sea, in the territory of Zebulun and Naphtali, 14so that what was spoken by the prophet Isaiah
might be fulfilled:

15 "The land of Zebulun and the land of Naphtali,
the way of the sea, beyond the Jordan, Galilee of the
Gentiles—
16 the people dwelling in darkness
have seen a great light,
and for those dwelling in the region and shadow of death,
on them a light has dawned."

17From that time Jesus began to preach, saying, "Repent, for the kingdom of heav-
en is at hand."[1]

Jesus Calls the First Disciples

18While walking by the Sea of Galilee, he saw two brothers, Simon (who is
called Peter) and Andrew his brother, casting a net into the sea, for they were fishermen. 19And he said to them, "Follow me, and I will make you fishers of men."[2]
20Immediately they left their nets and followed him. 21And going on from there
he saw two other brothers, James the son of Zebedee and John his brother, in the
boat with Zebedee their father, mending their nets, and he called them. 22Imme-
diately they left the boat and their father and followed him.

Jesus Ministers to Great Crowds

23And he went throughout all Galilee, teaching in their synagogues and proclaiming the gospel of the kingdom and healing every disease and every affliction
among the people. 24So his fame spread throughout all Syria, and they brought
him all the sick, those afflicted with various diseases and pains, those oppressed
by demons, those having seizures, and paralytics, and he healed them. 25And
great crowds followed him from Galilee and the Decapolis, and from Jerusalem
and Judea, and from beyond the Jordan.

The Sermon on the Mount

5 Seeing the crowds, he went up on the mountain, and when he sat down, his
disciples came to him.

The Beatitudes

2And he opened his mouth and taught them, saying:
3"Blessed are the poor in spirit, for theirs is the kingdom of heaven.
4"Blessed are those who mourn, for they shall be comforted.
5"Blessed are the meek, for they shall inherit the earth.
6"Blessed are those who hunger and thirst for righteousness, for they shall
be satisfied.
7"Blessed are the merciful, for they shall receive mercy.
8"Blessed are the pure in heart, for they shall see God.
9"Blessed are the peacemakers, for they shall be called sons[3] of God.
10"Blessed are those who are persecuted for righteousness' sake, for theirs is
the kingdom of heaven.
11"Blessed are you when others revile you and persecute you and utter all kinds
of evil against you falsely on my account. 12Rejoice and be glad, for your reward is
great in heaven, for so they persecuted the prophets who were before you.

[1]Or *the kingdom of heaven has come near* [2]The Greek word *anthropoi* refers here to both men and women
[3]Greek *huioi*; see Preface

MATTHEW 5:2

JESUS AND THE LAW

The Sermon on the Mount includes Jesus' explanation of how he is the fulfillment of the law. This discourse was not meant to replace Old Testament law, but rather it points to the ultimate fulfillment of the spiritual intention of the law. Jesus explained the true meaning and purpose of the Old Testament law. The law was designed not to confine people to their own futile efforts but rather to show complete dependence on God.

Here in the book of Matthew, Jesus created a standard that no human can fully achieve. He did not preach such a high standard of law in order to discourage his followers from obeying it, but rather he taught it in such a way as to show how necessary is human dependence on the Spirit of God. Jesus expects his followers to give their fullest effort to obey his commandments, yet he knows they will fall short. He gives them his Spirit to empower them whenever they ask.

Salt and Light

13“You are the salt of the earth, but if salt has lost its taste, how shall its saltiness be restored? It is no longer good for anything except to be thrown out and trampled under people’s feet.

14“You are the light of the world. A city set on a hill cannot be hidden. 15Nor do people light a lamp and put it under a basket, but on a stand, and it gives light to all in the house. 16In the same way, let your light shine before others, so that[1] they may see your good works and give glory to your Father who is in heaven.

Christ Came to Fulfill the Law

17“Do not think that I have come to abolish the Law or the Prophets; I have not come to abolish them but to fulfill them. 18For truly, I say to you, until heaven and earth pass away, not an iota, not a dot, will pass from the Law until all is accomplished. 19Therefore whoever relaxes one of the least of these commandments and teaches others to do the same will be called least in the kingdom of heaven, but whoever does them and teaches them will be called great in the kingdom of heaven. 20For I tell you, unless your righteousness exceeds that of the scribes and Pharisees, you will never enter the kingdom of heaven.

Anger

21“You have heard that it was said to those of old, ‘You shall not murder; and whoever murders will be liable to judgment.’ 22But I say to you that everyone who is angry with his brother[2] will be liable to judgment; whoever insults[3] his brother will be liable to the council; and whoever says, ‘You fool!’ will be liable to the hell[4] of fire. 23So if you are offering your gift at the altar and there remember that your brother has something against you, 24leave your gift there before the altar and go. First be reconciled to your brother, and then come and offer your gift. 25Come to terms quickly with your accuser while you are going with him to court, lest your accuser hand you over to the judge, and the judge to the guard, and you be put in prison. 26Truly, I say to you, you will never get out until you have paid the last penny.[5]

Lust

27“You have heard that it was said, ‘You shall not commit adultery.’ 28But I say to you that everyone who looks at a woman with lustful intent has already committed adultery with her in his heart. 29If your right eye causes you to sin, tear it out and throw it away. For it is better that you lose one of your members than that your whole body be thrown into hell. 30And if your right hand causes you to sin, cut it off and throw it away. For it is better that you lose one of your members than that your whole body go into hell.

Divorce

31“It was also said, ‘Whoever divorces his wife, let him give her a certificate of divorce.’ 32But I say to you that everyone who divorces his wife, except on the ground of sexual immorality, makes her commit adultery, and whoever marries a divorced woman commits adultery.

Oaths

33“Again you have heard that it was said to those of old, ‘You shall not swear falsely, but shall perform to the Lord what you have sworn.’ 34But I say to you, Do not take an oath at all, either by heaven, for it is the throne of God, 35or by the earth, for it is his footstool, or by Jerusalem, for it is the city of the great King. 36And do not take an oath by your head, for you cannot make one hair white or

[1]Or *house*. 16*Let your light so shine before others that* [2]Some manuscripts insert *without cause* [3]Greek *says Raca to* (a term of abuse) [4]Greek *Gehenna*; also verses 29, 30 [5]Greek *kodrantes*, Roman copper coin (Latin *quadrans*) worth about 1/64 of a *denarius* (which was a day’s wage for a laborer)

black. 37 Let what you say be simply 'Yes' or 'No'; anything more than this comes
from evil.[1]

Retaliation

38 "You have heard that it was said, 'An eye for an eye and a tooth for a tooth.'
39 But I say to you, Do not resist the one who is evil. But if anyone slaps you on the
right cheek, turn to him the other also. 40 And if anyone would sue you and take
your tunic,[2] let him have your cloak as well. 41 And if anyone forces you to go one
mile, go with him two miles. 42 Give to the one who begs from you, and do not
refuse the one who would borrow from you.

Love Your Enemies

43 "You have heard that it was said, 'You shall love your neighbor and hate your
enemy.' 44 But I say to you, Love your enemies and pray for those who persecute
you, 45 so that you may be sons of your Father who is in heaven. For he makes his
sun rise on the evil and on the good, and sends rain on the just and on the unjust.
46 For if you love those who love you, what reward do you have? Do not even the
tax collectors do the same? 47 And if you greet only your brothers,[3] what more are
you doing than others? Do not even the Gentiles do the same? 48 You therefore
must be perfect, as your heavenly Father is perfect.

Giving to the Needy

6 "Beware of practicing your righteousness before other people in order to be
seen by them, for then you will have no reward from your Father who is in
heaven.

2 "Thus, when you give to the needy, sound no trumpet before you, as the
hypocrites do in the synagogues and in the streets, that they may be praised by
others. Truly, I say to you, they have received their reward. 3 But when you give to
the needy, do not let your left hand know what your right hand is doing, 4 so that
your giving may be in secret. And your Father who sees in secret will reward you.

The Lord's Prayer

5 "And when you pray, you must not be like the hypocrites. For they love to
stand and pray in the synagogues and at the street corners, that they may be seen
by others. Truly, I say to you, they have received their reward. 6 But when you pray,
go into your room and shut the door and pray to your Father who is in secret. And
your Father who sees in secret will reward you.

7 "And when you pray, do not heap up empty phrases as the Gentiles do, for
they think that they will be heard for their many words. 8 Do not be like them, for
your Father knows what you need before you ask him. 9 Pray then like this:

"Our Father in heaven,
hallowed be your name.[4]
10 Your kingdom come,
your will be done,[5]
on earth as it is in heaven.
11 Give us this day our daily bread,[6]
12 and forgive us our debts,
as we also have forgiven our debtors.
13 And lead us not into temptation,
but deliver us from evil.[7]

[1] Or *the evil one* [2] Greek *chiton*, a long garment worn under the cloak next to the skin [3] Or *brothers and sisters*. In New Testament usage, depending on the context, the plural Greek word *adelphoi* (translated "brothers") may refer either to *brothers* or to *brothers and sisters* [4] Or *Let your name be kept holy*, or *Let your name be treated with reverence* [5] Or *Let your kingdom come, let your will be done* [6] Or *our bread for tomorrow* [7] Or *the evil one*; some manuscripts add *For yours is the kingdom and the power and the glory, forever. Amen*

14 For if you forgive others their trespasses, your heavenly Father will also forgive you, 15 but if you do not forgive others their trespasses, neither will your Father forgive your trespasses.

Fasting

16 “And when you fast, do not look gloomy like the hypocrites, for they disfigure their faces that their fasting may be seen by others. Truly, I say to you, they have received their reward. 17 But when you fast, anoint your head and wash your face, 18 that your fasting may not be seen by others but by your Father who is in secret. And your Father who sees in secret will reward you.

Lay Up Treasures in Heaven

19 “Do not lay up for yourselves treasures on earth, where moth and rust[1] destroy and where thieves break in and steal, 20 but lay up for yourselves treasures in heaven, where neither moth nor rust destroys and where thieves do not break in and steal. 21 For where your treasure is, there your heart will be also.

22 “The eye is the lamp of the body. So, if your eye is healthy, your whole body will be full of light, 23 but if your eye is bad, your whole body will be full of darkness. If then the light in you is darkness, how great is the darkness!

24 “No one can serve two masters, for either he will hate the one and love the other, or he will be devoted to the one and despise the other. You cannot serve God and money.[2]

Do Not Be Anxious

25 “Therefore I tell you, do not be anxious about your life, what you will eat or what you will drink, nor about your body, what you will put on. Is not life more than food, and the body more than clothing? 26 Look at the birds of the air: they neither sow nor reap nor gather into barns, and yet your heavenly Father feeds them. Are you not of more value than they? 27 And which of you by being anxious can add a single hour to his span of life?[3] 28 And why are you anxious about clothing? Consider the lilies of the field, how they grow: they neither toil nor spin, 29 yet I tell you, even Solomon in all his glory was not arrayed like one of these. 30 But if God so clothes the grass of the field, which today is alive and tomorrow is thrown into the oven, will he not much more clothe you, O you of little faith? 31 Therefore do not be anxious, saying, ‘What shall we eat?’ or ‘What shall we drink?’ or ‘What shall we wear?’ 32 For the Gentiles seek after all these things, and your heavenly Father knows that you need them all. 33 But seek first the kingdom of God and his righteousness, and all these things will be added to you.

34 “Therefore do not be anxious about tomorrow, for tomorrow will be anxious for itself. Sufficient for the day is its own trouble.

Judging Others

7 “Judge not, that you be not judged. 2 For with the judgment you pronounce you will be judged, and with the measure you use it will be measured to you. 3 Why do you see the speck that is in your brother’s eye, but do not notice the log that is in your own eye? 4 Or how can you say to your brother, ‘Let me take the speck out of your eye,’ when there is the log in your own eye? 5 You hypocrite, first take the log out of your own eye, and then you will see clearly to take the speck out of your brother’s eye.

6 “Do not give dogs what is holy, and do not throw your pearls before pigs, lest they trample them underfoot and turn to attack you.

Ask, and It Will Be Given

7 “Ask, and it will be given to you; seek, and you will find; knock, and it will be opened to you. 8 For everyone who asks receives, and the one who seeks finds,

[1] Or *worm*; also verse 20 [2] Greek *mammon*, a Semitic word for money or possessions [3] Or *a single cubit to his stature*; a *cubit* was about 18 inches or 45 centimeters

and to the one who knocks it will be opened. 9Or which one of you, if his son
asks him for bread, will give him a stone? 10Or if he asks for a fish, will give him a
serpent? 11If you then, who are evil, know how to give good gifts to your children,
how much more will your Father who is in heaven give good things to those who
ask him!

The Golden Rule

12"So whatever you wish that others would do to you, do also to them, for this
is the Law and the Prophets.

13"Enter by the narrow gate. For the gate is wide and the way is easy[1] that leads
to destruction, and those who enter by it are many. 14For the gate is narrow and
the way is hard that leads to life, and those who find it are few.

A Tree and Its Fruit

15"Beware of false prophets, who come to you in sheep's clothing but inwardly
are ravenous wolves. 16You will recognize them by their fruits. Are grapes gathered
from thornbushes, or figs from thistles? 17So, every healthy tree bears good fruit,
but the diseased tree bears bad fruit. 18A healthy tree cannot bear bad fruit, nor
can a diseased tree bear good fruit. 19Every tree that does not bear good fruit is
cut down and thrown into the fire. 20Thus you will recognize them by their fruits.

I Never Knew You

21"Not everyone who says to me, 'Lord, Lord,' will enter the kingdom of heav-
en, but the one who does the will of my Father who is in heaven. 22On that day
many will say to me, 'Lord, Lord, did we not prophesy in your name, and cast out
demons in your name, and do many mighty works in your name?' 23And then will
I declare to them, 'I never knew you; depart from me, you workers of lawlessness.'

Build Your House on the Rock

24"Everyone then who hears these words of mine and does them will be like
a wise man who built his house on the rock. 25And the rain fell, and the floods
came, and the winds blew and beat on that house, but it did not fall, because it
had been founded on the rock. 26And everyone who hears these words of mine
and does not do them will be like a foolish man who built his house on the sand.
27And the rain fell, and the floods came, and the winds blew and beat against that
house, and it fell, and great was the fall of it."

The Authority of Jesus

28And when Jesus finished these sayings, the crowds were astonished at his
teaching, 29for he was teaching them as one who had authority, and not as their
scribes.

Jesus Cleanses a Leper

8 When he came down from the mountain, great crowds followed him. 2And
behold, a leper[2] came to him and knelt before him, saying, "Lord, if you will,
you can make me clean." 3And Jesus[3] stretched out his hand and touched him,
saying, "I will; be clean." And immediately his leprosy was cleansed. 4And Jesus
said to him, "See that you say nothing to anyone, but go, show yourself to the
priest and offer the gift that Moses commanded, for a proof to them."

The Faith of a Centurion

5When he had entered Capernaum, a centurion came forward to him, appealing to him, 6"Lord, my servant is lying paralyzed at home, suffering terribly." 7And
he said to him, "I will come and heal him." 8But the centurion replied, "Lord, I am

MATTHEW 7:13–14

THE WIDE AND THE NARROW GATES

Jesus explained that the roads to life and destruction are roads guarded by narrow and wide gates, respectively. In doing so, he taught that many people walk down the road that leads to destruction, while few people choose to walk down the road that leads to life. The road that leads to destruction is easy to find (Pr 14:12). Anyone who chases after the cares of the world without the mind of the Spirit (Php 2:1–11) walks along the broad road that leads to destruction, and they do so with many other people. In contrast, the narrow road is smaller, and fewer people travel upon it. In John 14:6, Jesus said, "I am the way, and the truth, and the life. No one comes to the Father except through me." Jesus is the narrow gate, and by following him and living in his power, believers are able to walk upon the path of life.

[1]Some manuscripts *For the way is wide and easy* [2]*Leprosy* was a term for several skin diseases; see Leviticus 13 [3]Greek *he*

not worthy to have you come under my roof, but only say the word, and my servant will be healed. [9]For I too am a man under authority, with soldiers under me. And I say to one, 'Go,' and he goes, and to another, 'Come,' and he comes, and to my servant,[1] 'Do this,' and he does it." [10]When Jesus heard this, he marveled and said to those who followed him, "Truly, I tell you, with no one in Israel[2] have I found such faith. [11]I tell you, many will come from east and west and recline at table with Abraham, Isaac, and Jacob in the kingdom of heaven, [12]while the sons of the kingdom will be thrown into the outer darkness. In that place there will be weeping and gnashing of teeth." [13]And to the centurion Jesus said, "Go; let it be done for you as you have believed." And the servant was healed at that very moment.

Jesus Heals Many

[14]And when Jesus entered Peter's house, he saw his mother-in-law lying sick with a fever. [15]He touched her hand, and the fever left her, and she rose and began to serve him. [16]That evening they brought to him many who were oppressed by demons, and he cast out the spirits with a word and healed all who were sick. [17]This was to fulfill what was spoken by the prophet Isaiah: "He took our illnesses and bore our diseases."

The Cost of Following Jesus

[18]Now when Jesus saw a crowd around him, he gave orders to go over to the other side. [19]And a scribe came up and said to him, "Teacher, I will follow you wherever you go." [20]And Jesus said to him, "Foxes have holes, and birds of the air have nests, but the Son of Man has nowhere to lay his head." [21]Another of the disciples said to him, "Lord, let me first go and bury my father." [22]And Jesus said to him, "Follow me, and leave the dead to bury their own dead."

Jesus Calms a Storm

[23]And when he got into the boat, his disciples followed him. [24]And behold, there arose a great storm on the sea, so that the boat was being swamped by the waves; but he was asleep. [25]And they went and woke him, saying, "Save us, Lord; we are perishing." [26]And he said to them, "Why are you afraid, O you of little faith?" Then he rose and rebuked the winds and the sea, and there was a great calm. [27]And the men marveled, saying, "What sort of man is this, that even winds and sea obey him?"

Jesus Heals Two Men with Demons

[28]And when he came to the other side, to the country of the Gadarenes,[3] two demon-possessed[4] men met him, coming out of the tombs, so fierce that no one could pass that way. [29]And behold, they cried out, "What have you to do with us, O Son of God? Have you come here to torment us before the time?" [30]Now a herd of many pigs was feeding at some distance from them. [31]And the demons begged him, saying, "If you cast us out, send us away into the herd of pigs." [32]And he said to them, "Go." So they came out and went into the pigs, and behold, the whole herd rushed down the steep bank into the sea and drowned in the waters. [33]The herdsmen fled, and going into the city they told everything, especially what had happened to the demon-possessed men. [34]And behold, all the city came out to meet Jesus, and when they saw him, they begged him to leave their region.

Jesus Heals a Paralytic

9 And getting into a boat he crossed over and came to his own city. [2]And behold, some people brought to him a paralytic, lying on a bed. And when Jesus saw their faith, he said to the paralytic, "Take heart, my son; your sins are forgiven."

[1]Or *bondservant* [2]Some manuscripts *not even in Israel* [3]Some manuscripts *Gergesenes*; some *Gerasenes*
[4]Greek *daimonizomai* (demonized); also verse 33; elsewhere rendered *oppressed by demons*

JESUS' POWER OVER DISEASE

Matthew 8 begins with three stories of Jesus' healing miracles. Throughout the Gospels, Jesus healed many people; in doing so, he fulfilled the Old Testament prophecy of Isaiah 53:4: "He has borne our griefs and carried our sorrows." Not only did Jesus heal physical infirmities while he was on earth, but he also healed all infirmities, physical and spiritual, through his death on the cross. The stories of Jesus' healing miracles are precursors to his ultimate healing miracle on the cross.

The key phrase worth noting in the story of the man with leprosy is "Lord, if you will" (Mt 8:2). As a leper, this man was a social outcast because leprosy was thought to be highly contagious. This man was incredibly bold even to approach Jesus in light of his disease, yet he did so confidently. He knew that having faith was no guarantee that Jesus *would* heal him, but he knew Jesus *could* heal him (Da 3:17 – 18).

The next story shows, for the first time in the Gospels, Jesus interacting with someone who was not Jewish. As a Gentile, the centurion had little reason to interact with, let alone believe in, Jesus. However, he showed faith similar to that of the leper in asking Jesus to heal his servant. The centurion, a man in charge of roughly 80 to 100 soldiers, rebuffed Jesus' offer to come into his home. He knew that if Jesus would only say the word, his servant would be healed, which even further showed his confidence in Jesus' power. Jesus was astonished at the faith of the centurion: "Truly, I tell you, with no one in Israel have I found such faith" (Mt 8:10).

These two stories are remarkable in Scripture specifically because they tell stories of two individuals' great faith despite the supposed odds against Jesus acting on their behalf. The social outcast and the Gentile showed more faith in Jesus than he had seen before, and they reaped the rewards of their faith and trust.

3 And behold, some of the scribes said to themselves, "This man is blaspheming."
4 But Jesus, knowing[1] their thoughts, said, "Why do you think evil in your hearts?
5 For which is easier, to say, 'Your sins are forgiven,' or to say, 'Rise and walk'? 6 But
that you may know that the Son of Man has authority on earth to forgive sins"—
he then said to the paralytic—"Rise, pick up your bed and go home." 7 And he rose
and went home. 8 When the crowds saw it, they were afraid, and they glorified
God, who had given such authority to men.

Jesus Calls Matthew

9 As Jesus passed on from there, he saw a man called Matthew sitting at the tax
booth, and he said to him, "Follow me." And he rose and followed him.
10 And as Jesus[2] reclined at table in the house, behold, many tax collectors
and sinners came and were reclining with Jesus and his disciples. 11 And when the
Pharisees saw this, they said to his disciples, "Why does your teacher eat with tax
collectors and sinners?" 12 But when he heard it, he said, "Those who are well have
no need of a physician, but those who are sick. 13 Go and learn what this means: 'I
desire mercy, and not sacrifice.' For I came not to call the righteous, but sinners."

A Question About Fasting

14 Then the disciples of John came to him, saying, "Why do we and the Pharisees fast,[3] but your disciples do not fast?" 15 And Jesus said to them, "Can the wedding guests mourn as long as the bridegroom is with them? The days will come
when the bridegroom is taken away from them, and then they will fast. 16 No one
puts a piece of unshrunk cloth on an old garment, for the patch tears away from
the garment, and a worse tear is made. 17 Neither is new wine put into old wineskins. If it is, the skins burst and the wine is spilled and the skins are destroyed.
But new wine is put into fresh wineskins, and so both are preserved."

A Girl Restored to Life and a Woman Healed

18 While he was saying these things to them, behold, a ruler came in and knelt
before him, saying, "My daughter has just died, but come and lay your hand on
her, and she will live." 19 And Jesus rose and followed him, with his disciples. 20 And
behold, a woman who had suffered from a discharge of blood for twelve years
came up behind him and touched the fringe of his garment, 21 for she said to herself, "If I only touch his garment, I will be made well." 22 Jesus turned, and seeing
her he said, "Take heart, daughter; your faith has made you well." And instantly[4]
the woman was made well. 23 And when Jesus came to the ruler's house and saw
the flute players and the crowd making a commotion, 24 he said, "Go away, for the
girl is not dead but sleeping." And they laughed at him. 25 But when the crowd had
been put outside, he went in and took her by the hand, and the girl arose. 26 And
the report of this went through all that district.

Jesus Heals Two Blind Men

27 And as Jesus passed on from there, two blind men followed him, crying
aloud, "Have mercy on us, Son of David." 28 When he entered the house, the blind
men came to him, and Jesus said to them, "Do you believe that I am able to do
this?" They said to him, "Yes, Lord." 29 Then he touched their eyes, saying, "According to your faith let it be done to you." 30 And their eyes were opened. And
Jesus sternly warned them, "See that no one knows about it." 31 But they went away
and spread his fame through all that district.

Jesus Heals a Man Unable to Speak

32 As they were going away, behold, a demon-oppressed man who was mute
was brought to him. 33 And when the demon had been cast out, the mute man

[1] Some manuscripts *perceiving* [2] Greek *he* [3] Some manuscripts add *much*, or *often* [4] Greek *from that hour*

THE SON OF MAN HAS AUTHORITY TO FORGIVE SINS

This story has been a favorite of children and adults over the centuries. The image of these concerned and loving friends breaking through every obstacle to get their friend to the Lord is endearing — a very physical, material story of faith and persistence. Yet in the midst of this story, Jesus redirects those who read this story as he redirected the men who believed that their friend would be healed. What must they have been thinking as they heard this great healer, who had performed many healing and other miracles in the region, declare that their friend's sins were forgiven?

Imagine their puzzlement. This is not what they were expecting. Yet Jesus decided to use this very public forum to demonstrate his power to forgive sins as well as his power to heal this man's body.

Jesus had performed other miracles before this one, yet this is the first instance in which he claimed to forgive someone's sins. Jesus wanted to prove that his ministry did not only involve healing people of their illnesses; his ministry was so much more than that, and in this instance he gave further notice of what he truly came to earth to accomplish. How easy would it have been to merely *say* that the man who was paralyzed was forgiven of his sins, yet Jesus showed that he was able to back up everything he claimed: that not only could he provide physical healing, but that he could provide spiritual healing as well. His words and this miracle point to the ultimate purpose of Jesus' ministry on earth: "But he was pierced for our transgressions; he was crushed for our iniquities; upon him was the chastisement that brought us peace, and with his wounds we are healed" (Isa 53:5). Through Jesus' ministry in his life, death, and resurrection, we are completely and gloriously healed.

spoke. And the crowds marveled, saying, "Never was anything like this seen in
Israel." 34But the Pharisees said, "He casts out demons by the prince of demons."

The Harvest Is Plentiful, the Laborers Few

35And Jesus went throughout all the cities and villages, teaching in their synagogues and proclaiming the gospel of the kingdom and healing every disease and
every affliction. 36When he saw the crowds, he had compassion for them, because
they were harassed and helpless, like sheep without a shepherd. 37Then he said to
his disciples, "The harvest is plentiful, but the laborers are few; 38therefore pray
earnestly to the Lord of the harvest to send out laborers into his harvest."

The Twelve Apostles

10 And he called to him his twelve disciples and gave them authority over
unclean spirits, to cast them out, and to heal every disease and every affliction. 2The names of the twelve apostles are these: first, Simon, who is called
Peter, and Andrew his brother; James the son of Zebedee, and John his brother;
3Philip and Bartholomew; Thomas and Matthew the tax collector; James the son
of Alphaeus, and Thaddaeus;[1] 4Simon the Zealot,[2] and Judas Iscariot, who betrayed him.

Jesus Sends Out the Twelve Apostles

5These twelve Jesus sent out, instructing them, "Go nowhere among the Gentiles and enter no town of the Samaritans, 6but go rather to the lost sheep of the
house of Israel. 7And proclaim as you go, saying, 'The kingdom of heaven is at
hand.'[3] 8Heal the sick, raise the dead, cleanse lepers,[4] cast out demons. You received without paying; give without pay. 9Acquire no gold or silver or copper for
your belts, 10no bag for your journey, or two tunics[5] or sandals or a staff, for the
laborer deserves his food. 11And whatever town or village you enter, find out who
is worthy in it and stay there until you depart. 12As you enter the house, greet
it. 13And if the house is worthy, let your peace come upon it, but if it is not worthy, let your peace return to you. 14And if anyone will not receive you or listen to
your words, shake off the dust from your feet when you leave that house or town.
15Truly, I say to you, it will be more bearable on the day of judgment for the land
of Sodom and Gomorrah than for that town.

Persecution Will Come

16"Behold, I am sending you out as sheep in the midst of wolves, so be wise as
serpents and innocent as doves. 17Beware of men, for they will deliver you over to
courts and flog you in their synagogues, 18and you will be dragged before governors and kings for my sake, to bear witness before them and the Gentiles. 19When
they deliver you over, do not be anxious how you are to speak or what you are to
say, for what you are to say will be given to you in that hour. 20For it is not you who
speak, but the Spirit of your Father speaking through you. 21Brother will deliver
brother over to death, and the father his child, and children will rise against parents and have them put to death, 22and you will be hated by all for my name's sake.
But the one who endures to the end will be saved. 23When they persecute you in
one town, flee to the next, for truly, I say to you, you will not have gone through
all the towns of Israel before the Son of Man comes.

24"A disciple is not above his teacher, nor a servant[6] above his master. 25It is
enough for the disciple to be like his teacher, and the servant like his master. If
they have called the master of the house Beelzebul, how much more will they
malign[7] those of his household.

[1]Some manuscripts *Lebbaeus*, or *Lebbaeus called Thaddaeus* [2]Greek *kananaios*, meaning *zealot* [3]Or *The kingdom of heaven has come near* [4]*Leprosy* was a term for several skin diseases; see Leviticus 13 [5]Greek *chiton*, a long garment worn under the cloak next to the skin [6]Or *bondservant*; also verse 25 [7]Greek lacks *will they malign*

Have No Fear

26"So have no fear of them, for nothing is covered that will not be revealed, or hidden that will not be known. 27What I tell you in the dark, say in the light, and what you hear whispered, proclaim on the housetops. 28And do not fear those who kill the body but cannot kill the soul. Rather fear him who can destroy both soul and body in hell.[1] 29Are not two sparrows sold for a penny?[2] And not one of them will fall to the ground apart from your Father. 30But even the hairs of your head are all numbered. 31Fear not, therefore; you are of more value than many sparrows. 32So everyone who acknowledges me before men, I also will acknowledge before my Father who is in heaven, 33but whoever denies me before men, I also will deny before my Father who is in heaven.

Not Peace, but a Sword

34"Do not think that I have come to bring peace to the earth. I have not come to bring peace, but a sword. 35For I have come to set a man against his father, and a daughter against her mother, and a daughter-in-law against her mother-in-law. 36And a person's enemies will be those of his own household. 37Whoever loves father or mother more than me is not worthy of me, and whoever loves son or daughter more than me is not worthy of me. 38And whoever does not take his cross and follow me is not worthy of me. 39Whoever finds his life will lose it, and whoever loses his life for my sake will find it.

Rewards

40"Whoever receives you receives me, and whoever receives me receives him who sent me. 41The one who receives a prophet because he is a prophet will receive a prophet's reward, and the one who receives a righteous person because he is a righteous person will receive a righteous person's reward. 42And whoever gives one of these little ones even a cup of cold water because he is a disciple, truly, I say to you, he will by no means lose his reward."

Messengers from John the Baptist

11 When Jesus had finished instructing his twelve disciples, he went on from there to teach and preach in their cities.

2Now when John heard in prison about the deeds of the Christ, he sent word by his disciples 3and said to him, "Are you the one who is to come, or shall we look for another?" 4And Jesus answered them, "Go and tell John what you hear and see: 5the blind receive their sight and the lame walk, lepers[3] are cleansed and the deaf hear, and the dead are raised up, and the poor have good news preached to them. 6And blessed is the one who is not offended by me."

7As they went away, Jesus began to speak to the crowds concerning John: "What did you go out into the wilderness to see? A reed shaken by the wind? 8What then did you go out to see? A man[4] dressed in soft clothing? Behold, those who wear soft clothing are in kings' houses. 9What then did you go out to see? A prophet?[5] Yes, I tell you, and more than a prophet. 10This is he of whom it is written,

"'Behold, I send my messenger before your face,
who will prepare your way before you.'

11Truly, I say to you, among those born of women there has arisen no one greater than John the Baptist. Yet the one who is least in the kingdom of heaven is greater than he. 12From the days of John the Baptist until now the kingdom of heaven has suffered violence,[6] and the violent take it by force. 13For all the Prophets and the

MATTHEW 11:2–3

THE CHRIST

Today, the title "Christ" naturally follows the name of Jesus. However, during the time that the Gospels were written, people sparingly and carefully used the word "Christ," the Greek form of the Hebrew word "Messiah," which literally means "anointed one." In the Old Testament, the three types of people who were anointed were prophets (1Ki 19:16), priests (Ex 28:41), and kings (1Sa 16:13). In the New Testament, Jesus is God's preeminent anointed one who was anointed by God to be the ultimate prophet, priest, and king (Mt 27:11; Heb 6:20; cf. Isa 61:1). The Pharisees and religious leaders during that time viewed such a claim as blasphemous and punishable by death. However, the word "Christ" is used to refer to Jesus 470 times throughout the New Testament. When the word "Christ" was used anywhere in the New Testament, the author was very aware of the implications of his use of that word—what it meant for him as an author, and what it said about his Savior.

[1]Greek *Gehenna* [2]Greek *assarion*, Roman copper coin worth about 1/16 of a *denarius* (which was a day's wage for a laborer) [3]*Leprosy* was a term for several skin diseases; see Leviticus 13 [4]Or *Why then did you go out? To see a man* [5]Some manuscripts *Why then did you go out? To see a prophet?* [6]Or *has been coming violently*

JESUS SENDS OUT THE TWELVE

Matthew 10 is the first place where Jesus referred to the twelve disciples as "apostles." The word "apostle" is a derivative of the Greek word *apostello*, which means "to send." Here Jesus gave the apostles the authority to drive out evil spirits and heal the sick, which up until this point only Jesus had been able to do. He then sent them to go into other towns and preach the message that "the kingdom of heaven is at hand" (v. 7).

It is one thing that Jesus was able to heal and cast out demons himself, but the fact that he was able to give the same authority to his disciples only further shows the strength of his divine nature and power. To represent the fact that these apostles did not act in their own strength, but fully relied on God's provision, Jesus told them not to take provisions for themselves (vv. 9–10). Jesus instructed them to rely solely on God. His power was enough to sustain their entire journey.

Jesus also warned them that they would face opposition. Verses 16 through 23 of this chapter have been both a warning and a comfort to believers in Jesus around the world for centuries. As the apostles found out, some will not accept the message that believers in Jesus have to bring to a broken and fallen world. Millions have faced the opposition that Jesus was describing in these verses and have faithfully withstood persecution of many types, even to the point of death, relying on the Holy Spirit to give them the words to say in the face of persecution. Jesus told the apostles not to worry when they were arrested, and notice he said "when" and not "if" (v. 19). Later each of the disciples, with the exception of Judas, experienced the opposition that Jesus described. They were called to a gritty, physical, desperate, minute-by-minute faith and reliance on the person and work of Jesus to be manifested in their lives.

The authority that Jesus gave to each disciple was enough to get them through any hardship that they might have faced upon their journey, and the same is true for believers today.

Law prophesied until John, 14and if you are willing to accept it, he is Elijah who is to come. 15He who has ears to hear,[1] let him hear.

16"But to what shall I compare this generation? It is like children sitting in the marketplaces and calling to their playmates,

17 "'We played the flute for you, and you did not dance;
we sang a dirge, and you did not mourn.'

18For John came neither eating nor drinking, and they say, 'He has a demon.' 19The Son of Man came eating and drinking, and they say, 'Look at him! A glutton and a drunkard, a friend of tax collectors and sinners!' Yet wisdom is justified by her deeds."[2]

Woe to Unrepentant Cities

20Then he began to denounce the cities where most of his mighty works had been done, because they did not repent. 21"Woe to you, Chorazin! Woe to you, Bethsaida! For if the mighty works done in you had been done in Tyre and Sidon, they would have repented long ago in sackcloth and ashes. 22But I tell you, it will be more bearable on the day of judgment for Tyre and Sidon than for you. 23And you, Capernaum, will you be exalted to heaven? You will be brought down to Hades. For if the mighty works done in you had been done in Sodom, it would have remained until this day. 24But I tell you that it will be more tolerable on the day of judgment for the land of Sodom than for you."

Come to Me, and I Will Give You Rest

25At that time Jesus declared, "I thank you, Father, Lord of heaven and earth, that you have hidden these things from the wise and understanding and revealed them to little children; 26yes, Father, for such was your gracious will.[3] 27All things have been handed over to me by my Father, and no one knows the Son except the Father, and no one knows the Father except the Son and anyone to whom the Son chooses to reveal him. 28Come to me, all who labor and are heavy laden, and I will give you rest. 29Take my yoke upon you, and learn from me, for I am gentle and lowly in heart, and you will find rest for your souls. 30For my yoke is easy, and my burden is light."

Jesus Is Lord of the Sabbath

12 At that time Jesus went through the grainfields on the Sabbath. His disciples were hungry, and they began to pluck heads of grain and to eat. 2But when the Pharisees saw it, they said to him, "Look, your disciples are doing what is not lawful to do on the Sabbath." 3He said to them, "Have you not read what David did when he was hungry, and those who were with him: 4how he entered the house of God and ate the bread of the Presence, which it was not lawful for him to eat nor for those who were with him, but only for the priests? 5Or have you not read in the Law how on the Sabbath the priests in the temple profane the Sabbath and are guiltless? 6I tell you, something greater than the temple is here. 7And if you had known what this means, 'I desire mercy, and not sacrifice,' you would not have condemned the guiltless. 8For the Son of Man is lord of the Sabbath."

A Man with a Withered Hand

9He went on from there and entered their synagogue. 10And a man was there with a withered hand. And they asked him, "Is it lawful to heal on the Sabbath?"—so that they might accuse him. 11He said to them, "Which one of you who has a sheep, if it falls into a pit on the Sabbath, will not take hold of it and lift it out? 12Of how much more value is a man than a sheep! So it is lawful to do good on the Sabbath." 13Then he said to the man, "Stretch out your hand." And the man stretched

[1] Some manuscripts omit *to hear* [2] Some manuscripts *children* (compare Luke 7:35) [3] Or *for so it pleased you well*

it out, and it was restored, healthy like the other. 14But the Pharisees went out and conspired against him, how to destroy him.

God's Chosen Servant

15Jesus, aware of this, withdrew from there. And many followed him, and he healed them all 16and ordered them not to make him known. 17This was to fulfill what was spoken by the prophet Isaiah:

18 "Behold, my servant whom I have chosen,
my beloved with whom my soul is well pleased.
I will put my Spirit upon him,
and he will proclaim justice to the Gentiles.
19 He will not quarrel or cry aloud,
nor will anyone hear his voice in the streets;
20 a bruised reed he will not break,
and a smoldering wick he will not quench,
until he brings justice to victory;
21 and in his name the Gentiles will hope."

Blasphemy Against the Holy Spirit

22Then a demon-oppressed man who was blind and mute was brought to him, and he healed him, so that the man spoke and saw. 23And all the people were amazed, and said, "Can this be the Son of David?" 24But when the Pharisees heard it, they said, "It is only by Beelzebul, the prince of demons, that this man casts out demons." 25Knowing their thoughts, he said to them, "Every kingdom divided against itself is laid waste, and no city or house divided against itself will stand. 26And if Satan casts out Satan, he is divided against himself. How then will his kingdom stand? 27And if I cast out demons by Beelzebul, by whom do your sons cast them out? Therefore they will be your judges. 28But if it is by the Spirit of God that I cast out demons, then the kingdom of God has come upon you. 29Or how can someone enter a strong man's house and plunder his goods, unless he first binds the strong man? Then indeed he may plunder his house. 30Whoever is not with me is against me, and whoever does not gather with me scatters. 31Therefore I tell you, every sin and blasphemy will be forgiven people, but the blasphemy against the Spirit will not be forgiven. 32And whoever speaks a word against the Son of Man will be forgiven, but whoever speaks against the Holy Spirit will not be forgiven, either in this age or in the age to come.

A Tree Is Known by Its Fruit

33"Either make the tree good and its fruit good, or make the tree bad and its fruit bad, for the tree is known by its fruit. 34You brood of vipers! How can you speak good, when you are evil? For out of the abundance of the heart the mouth speaks. 35The good person out of his good treasure brings forth good, and the evil person out of his evil treasure brings forth evil. 36I tell you, on the day of judgment people will give account for every careless word they speak, 37for by your words you will be justified, and by your words you will be condemned."

The Sign of Jonah

38Then some of the scribes and Pharisees answered him, saying, "Teacher, we wish to see a sign from you." 39But he answered them, "An evil and adulterous generation seeks for a sign, but no sign will be given to it except the sign of the prophet Jonah. 40For just as Jonah was three days and three nights in the belly of the great fish, so will the Son of Man be three days and three nights in the heart of the earth. 41The men of Nineveh will rise up at the judgment with this generation and condemn it, for they repented at the preaching of Jonah, and behold, something greater than Jonah is here. 42The queen of the South will rise up at

MATTHEW 12:38–42

JONAH AND THE RESURRECTION

Jesus referred to those who asked for a sign as proof of Jesus' identity as an "evil and adulterous generation" (Mt 12:39), saying that the only sign they would receive was the sign of Jonah. But what did this mean? Jonah had spent three days and three nights in the belly of a fish; in the same way, Jesus said he would spend three days and three nights in "the heart of the earth" (v. 40). Jesus was clearly foreshadowing his death, burial, and resurrection; yet it is doubtful that the Pharisees understood what he was saying. In John 20:29, Jesus said, "Blessed are those who have not seen and yet have believed"; Jesus' frustration with the Pharisees stemmed from the fact that they saw and heard him and yet still did not believe. They were the opposite of the "blessed" he referred to in John 20:29. His purpose in referring to Jonah, however, was twofold: to give a picture of his death and resurrection and to call those who heard these words to repentance, in imitation of the people of Nineveh now that One greater than Jonah had come.

the judgment with this generation and condemn it, for she came from the ends
of the earth to hear the wisdom of Solomon, and behold, something greater than
Solomon is here.

Return of an Unclean Spirit

43“When the unclean spirit has gone out of a person, it passes through waterless places seeking rest, but finds none. 44Then it says, ‘I will return to my house
from which I came.’ And when it comes, it finds the house empty, swept, and put
in order. 45Then it goes and brings with it seven other spirits more evil than itself,
and they enter and dwell there, and the last state of that person is worse than the
first. So also will it be with this evil generation.”

Jesus’ Mother and Brothers

46While he was still speaking to the people, behold, his mother and his brothers[1] stood outside, asking to speak to him.[2] 48But he replied to the man who
told him, “Who is my mother, and who are my brothers?” 49And stretching out
his hand toward his disciples, he said, “Here are my mother and my brothers!
50For whoever does the will of my Father in heaven is my brother and sister and
mother.”

The Parable of the Sower

13 That same day Jesus went out of the house and sat beside the sea. 2And
great crowds gathered about him, so that he got into a boat and sat down.
And the whole crowd stood on the beach. 3And he told them many things in parables, saying: “A sower went out to sow. 4And as he sowed, some seeds fell along the
path, and the birds came and devoured them. 5Other seeds fell on rocky ground,
where they did not have much soil, and immediately they sprang up, since they
had no depth of soil, 6but when the sun rose they were scorched. And since they
had no root, they withered away. 7Other seeds fell among thorns, and the thorns
grew up and choked them. 8Other seeds fell on good soil and produced grain,
some a hundredfold, some sixty, some thirty. 9He who has ears,[3] let him hear.”

The Purpose of the Parables

10Then the disciples came and said to him, “Why do you speak to them in
parables?” 11And he answered them, “To you it has been given to know the secrets
of the kingdom of heaven, but to them it has not been given. 12For to the one who
has, more will be given, and he will have an abundance, but from the one who has
not, even what he has will be taken away. 13This is why I speak to them in parables,
because seeing they do not see, and hearing they do not hear, nor do they understand. 14Indeed, in their case the prophecy of Isaiah is fulfilled that says:

“ ‘ “You will indeed hear but never understand,
and you will indeed see but never perceive.”
15 For this people’s heart has grown dull,
and with their ears they can barely hear,
and their eyes they have closed,
lest they should see with their eyes
and hear with their ears
and understand with their heart
and turn, and I would heal them.’

16But blessed are your eyes, for they see, and your ears, for they hear. 17For truly, I
say to you, many prophets and righteous people longed to see what you see, and
did not see it, and to hear what you hear, and did not hear it.

[1]Or *brothers and sisters*; also verses 48, 49 [2]Some manuscripts insert verse 47: *Someone told him, “Your mother and your brothers are standing outside, asking to speak to you”* [3]Some manuscripts add here and in verse 43 *to hear*

The Parable of the Sower Explained

18“Hear then the parable of the sower: 19When anyone hears the word of the
kingdom and does not understand it, the evil one comes and snatches away what
has been sown in his heart. This is what was sown along the path. 20As for what
was sown on rocky ground, this is the one who hears the word and immediately
receives it with joy, 21yet he has no root in himself, but endures for a while, and
when tribulation or persecution arises on account of the word, immediately he
falls away.[1] 22As for what was sown among thorns, this is the one who hears the
word, but the cares of the world and the deceitfulness of riches choke the word,
and it proves unfruitful. 23As for what was sown on good soil, this is the one who
hears the word and understands it. He indeed bears fruit and yields, in one case a
hundredfold, in another sixty, and in another thirty.”

The Parable of the Weeds

24He put another parable before them, saying, “The kingdom of heaven
may be compared to a man who sowed good seed in his field, 25but while his
men were sleeping, his enemy came and sowed weeds[2] among the wheat and
went away. 26So when the plants came up and bore grain, then the weeds appeared also. 27And the servants[3] of the master of the house came and said to
him, ‘Master, did you not sow good seed in your field? How then does it have
weeds?’ 28He said to them, ‘An enemy has done this.’ So the servants said to
him, ‘Then do you want us to go and gather them?’ 29But he said, ‘No, lest in
gathering the weeds you root up the wheat along with them. 30Let both grow
together until the harvest, and at harvest time I will tell the reapers, “Gather
the weeds first and bind them in bundles to be burned, but gather the wheat
into my barn.”’”

The Mustard Seed and the Leaven

31He put another parable before them, saying, “The kingdom of heaven is like a
grain of mustard seed that a man took and sowed in his field. 32It is the smallest of
all seeds, but when it has grown it is larger than all the garden plants and becomes
a tree, so that the birds of the air come and make nests in its branches.”

33He told them another parable. “The kingdom of heaven is like leaven that a
woman took and hid in three measures of flour, till it was all leavened.”

Prophecy and Parables

34All these things Jesus said to the crowds in parables; indeed, he said nothing
to them without a parable. 35This was to fulfill what was spoken by the prophet:[4]

“I will open my mouth in parables;
I will utter what has been hidden since the foundation of the world.”

The Parable of the Weeds Explained

36Then he left the crowds and went into the house. And his disciples came to
him, saying, “Explain to us the parable of the weeds of the field.” 37He answered,
“The one who sows the good seed is the Son of Man. 38The field is the world, and
the good seed is the sons of the kingdom. The weeds are the sons of the evil one,
39and the enemy who sowed them is the devil. The harvest is the end of the age,
and the reapers are angels. 40Just as the weeds are gathered and burned with fire,
so will it be at the end of the age. 41The Son of Man will send his angels, and they
will gather out of his kingdom all causes of sin and all law-breakers, 42and throw
them into the fiery furnace. In that place there will be weeping and gnashing of
teeth. 43Then the righteous will shine like the sun in the kingdom of their Father.
He who has ears, let him hear.

[1]Or *stumbles* [2]Probably *darnel*, a wheat-like weed [3]Or *bondservants*; also verse 28 [4]Some manuscripts *Isaiah the prophet*

The Parable of the Hidden Treasure

44“The kingdom of heaven is like treasure hidden in a field, which a man found and covered up. Then in his joy he goes and sells all that he has and buys that field.

The Parable of the Pearl of Great Value

45“Again, the kingdom of heaven is like a merchant in search of fine pearls, 46who, on finding one pearl of great value, went and sold all that he had and bought it.

The Parable of the Net

47“Again, the kingdom of heaven is like a net that was thrown into the sea and gathered fish of every kind. 48When it was full, men drew it ashore and sat down and sorted the good into containers but threw away the bad. 49So it will be at the end of the age. The angels will come out and separate the evil from the righteous 50and throw them into the fiery furnace. In that place there will be weeping and gnashing of teeth.

New and Old Treasures

51“Have you understood all these things?” They said to him, “Yes.” 52And he said to them, “Therefore every scribe who has been trained for the kingdom of heaven is like a master of a house, who brings out of his treasure what is new and what is old.”

Jesus Rejected at Nazareth

53And when Jesus had finished these parables, he went away from there, 54and coming to his hometown he taught them in their synagogue, so that they were astonished, and said, “Where did this man get this wisdom and these mighty works? 55Is not this the carpenter's[1] son? Is not his mother called Mary? And are not his brothers James and Joseph and Simon and Judas? 56And are not all his sisters with us? Where then did this man get all these things?” 57And they took offense at him. But Jesus said to them, “A prophet is not without honor except in his hometown and in his own household.” 58And he did not do many mighty works there, because of their unbelief.

The Death of John the Baptist

14 At that time Herod the tetrarch heard about the fame of Jesus, 2and he said to his servants, “This is John the Baptist. He has been raised from the dead; that is why these miraculous powers are at work in him.” 3For Herod had seized John and bound him and put him in prison for the sake of Herodias, his brother Philip's wife,[2] 4because John had been saying to him, “It is not lawful for you to have her.” 5And though he wanted to put him to death, he feared the people, because they held him to be a prophet. 6But when Herod's birthday came, the daughter of Herodias danced before the company and pleased Herod, 7so that he promised with an oath to give her whatever she might ask. 8Prompted by her mother, she said, “Give me the head of John the Baptist here on a platter.” 9And the king was sorry, but because of his oaths and his guests he commanded it to be given. 10He sent and had John beheaded in the prison, 11and his head was brought on a platter and given to the girl, and she brought it to her mother. 12And his disciples came and took the body and buried it, and they went and told Jesus.

Jesus Feeds the Five Thousand

13Now when Jesus heard this, he withdrew from there in a boat to a desolate place by himself. But when the crowds heard it, they followed him on foot from

[1]Or *builder's* [2]Some manuscripts *his brother's wife*

MATTHEW 14:13–21

FEEDING THE FIVE THOUSAND

Jesus' feeding of the five thousand is the only pre-crucifixion miracle recorded in all four Gospels, and it is significant for a multitude of reasons. Through this miracle, Jesus fulfilled the expectation of those looking forward to a new prophet after Moses (Jn 1:21; Ac 3:22; 7:37). While Moses was their prophet-leader, the Israelites received manna from heaven. Jesus' provision of bread parallels the miracle that the Israelites experienced under Moses and thus fulfills Deuteronomy 18:15 (quoted twice in Acts, referred to above). Also, Jesus showed that he could supply both the physical and the spiritual “daily bread” requested in the prayer in Matthew 6:11. Finally, Jesus showed that he is the Messiah who will provide the coming Messianic banquet (Ps 132:15; Isa 25:6; Mt 22:1–14; 26:29). Not only does the feeding of the five thousand preview that kingdom banquet, but it also provides a wholesome contrast to the degenerate banquet held by Herod in Matthew 14:1–12. In giving the people physical bread, Jesus showed that he was the compassionate provider that his people needed.

JESUS AND HIS PARABLES

Jesus commonly taught the crowds and his followers through parables, which are stories that illustrate a moral or spiritual truth. In Matthew 13, Jesus told parables relating to soil, weeds, a mustard seed, yeast, hidden treasure, a pearl, and a fishing net. Jesus' parables cover a spectrum of topics and truths, and they also represent the confirmation of a Messianic prophecy from Isaiah 6:9 – 10: "Go, and say to this people: 'Keep on hearing, but do not understand; keep on seeing, but do not perceive.' Make the heart of this people dull, and their ears heavy, and blind their eyes; lest they see with their eyes, and hear with their ears, and understand with their hearts, and turn and be healed."

Jesus told parables to teach God's truth to those who were ready and willing to hear it, but he also knew there were people in his audience who would not understand his words because their hearts were calloused. At times, parables were Jesus' tools to reveal truth to the faithful and to conceal it from those who would object to it and seek to stop his ministry and mission.

Jesus used six of the seven parables in this chapter to describe the nature of the kingdom of heaven. The people who rejected Jesus' teaching because of their inability to understand it, including the Jewish religious leaders, only further blinded themselves to the spiritual nature of the kingdom of God. On the other hand, those who had ears to hear received a great blessing in knowing and understanding Jesus' truth — as do believers who read these stories today.

As to the parables themselves, notice that even Jesus' disciples, the men who had left their jobs, businesses, and families for the sake of this amazing teacher, misunderstood some of Jesus' parables (Mt 13:36). Jesus carefully and patiently explained to the disciples who sought to learn more. They asked for wisdom, and Jesus provided it (Jas 1:5) along with meaningful word pictures of the coming kingdom loaded with meaning and nuance. For believers today, these parables and teachings provide a rich picture of the kingdom as it exists and also as it is to come.

the towns. 14 When he went ashore he saw a great crowd, and he had compassion
on them and healed their sick. 15 Now when it was evening, the disciples came to
him and said, "This is a desolate place, and the day is now over; send the crowds
away to go into the villages and buy food for themselves." 16 But Jesus said, "They
need not go away; you give them something to eat." 17 They said to him, "We have
only five loaves here and two fish." 18 And he said, "Bring them here to me." 19 Then
he ordered the crowds to sit down on the grass, and taking the five loaves and the
two fish, he looked up to heaven and said a blessing. Then he broke the loaves
and gave them to the disciples, and the disciples gave them to the crowds. 20 And
they all ate and were satisfied. And they took up twelve baskets full of the broken pieces left over. 21 And those who ate were about five thousand men, besides
women and children.

Jesus Walks on the Water

22 Immediately he made the disciples get into the boat and go before him to
the other side, while he dismissed the crowds. 23 And after he had dismissed the
crowds, he went up on the mountain by himself to pray. When evening came,
he was there alone, 24 but the boat by this time was a long way[1] from the land,[2]
beaten by the waves, for the wind was against them. 25 And in the fourth watch of
the night[3] he came to them, walking on the sea. 26 But when the disciples saw him
walking on the sea, they were terrified, and said, "It is a ghost!" and they cried
out in fear. 27 But immediately Jesus spoke to them, saying, "Take heart; it is I. Do
not be afraid."

28 And Peter answered him, "Lord, if it is you, command me to come to you on
the water." 29 He said, "Come." So Peter got out of the boat and walked on the water and came to Jesus. 30 But when he saw the wind,[4] he was afraid, and beginning
to sink he cried out, "Lord, save me." 31 Jesus immediately reached out his hand
and took hold of him, saying to him, "O you of little faith, why did you doubt?"
32 And when they got into the boat, the wind ceased. 33 And those in the boat worshiped him, saying, "Truly you are the Son of God."

Jesus Heals the Sick in Gennesaret

34 And when they had crossed over, they came to land at Gennesaret. 35 And
when the men of that place recognized him, they sent around to all that region
and brought to him all who were sick 36 and implored him that they might only
touch the fringe of his garment. And as many as touched it were made well.

Traditions and Commandments

15 Then Pharisees and scribes came to Jesus from Jerusalem and said, 2 "Why
do your disciples break the tradition of the elders? For they do not wash
their hands when they eat." 3 He answered them, "And why do you break the commandment of God for the sake of your tradition? 4 For God commanded, 'Honor
your father and your mother,' and, 'Whoever reviles father or mother must surely
die.' 5 But you say, 'If anyone tells his father or his mother, "What you would have
gained from me is given to God,"[5] 6 he need not honor his father.' So for the sake
of your tradition you have made void the word[6] of God. 7 You hypocrites! Well did
Isaiah prophesy of you, when he said:

8 " 'This people honors me with their lips,
but their heart is far from me;
9 in vain do they worship me,
teaching as doctrines the commandments
of men.' "

MATTHEW 15:1–9

TRADITIONS OF THE ELDERS

The tradition of the elders referred to in verse 2 was not the Law of Moses. It was the oral tradition that had been built up over the centuries and was based on human interpretations of the law. But these rules were not of God; rather they were simply traditions invented by humans. Jesus used this opportunity to expose these men and the hypocritical way in which they lived their lives. They cared more about the ceremonial washing of hands than they did about faithfully obeying God's commands. God cares more about the hearts of his followers than any human tradition (1Sa 16:7).

[1] Greek *many stadia*, a *stadion* was about 607 feet or 185 meters [2] Some manuscripts *was out on the sea* [3] That is, between 3 A.M. and 6 A.M. [4] Some manuscripts *strong wind* [5] Or *is an offering* [6] Some manuscripts *law*

What Defiles a Person

10 And he called the people to him and said to them, "Hear and understand:
11 it is not what goes into the mouth that defiles a person, but what comes out of
the mouth; this defiles a person." 12 Then the disciples came and said to him, "Do
you know that the Pharisees were offended when they heard this saying?" 13 He
answered, "Every plant that my heavenly Father has not planted will be rooted up.
14 Let them alone; they are blind guides.[1] And if the blind lead the blind, both will fall
into a pit." 15 But Peter said to him, "Explain the parable to us." 16 And he said, "Are
you also still without understanding? 17 Do you not see that whatever goes into the
mouth passes into the stomach and is expelled?[2] 18 But what comes out of the mouth
proceeds from the heart, and this defiles a person. 19 For out of the heart come evil
thoughts, murder, adultery, sexual immorality, theft, false witness, slander. 20 These
are what defile a person. But to eat with unwashed hands does not defile anyone."

The Faith of a Canaanite Woman

21 And Jesus went away from there and withdrew to the district of Tyre and Sidon.
22 And behold, a Canaanite woman from that region came out and was crying, "Have
mercy on me, O Lord, Son of David; my daughter is severely oppressed by a demon."
23 But he did not answer her a word. And his disciples came and begged him, saying,
"Send her away, for she is crying out after us." 24 He answered, "I was sent only to
the lost sheep of the house of Israel." 25 But she came and knelt before him, saying,
"Lord, help me." 26 And he answered, "It is not right to take the children's bread and
throw it to the dogs." 27 She said, "Yes, Lord, yet even the dogs eat the crumbs that
fall from their masters' table." 28 Then Jesus answered her, "O woman, great is your
faith! Let it be done for you as you desire." And her daughter was healed instantly.[3]

Jesus Heals Many

29 Jesus went on from there and walked beside the Sea of Galilee. And he went
up on the mountain and sat down there. 30 And great crowds came to him, bringing with them the lame, the blind, the crippled, the mute, and many others, and
they put them at his feet, and he healed them, 31 so that the crowd wondered,
when they saw the mute speaking, the crippled healthy, the lame walking, and
the blind seeing. And they glorified the God of Israel.

Jesus Feeds the Four Thousand

32 Then Jesus called his disciples to him and said, "I have compassion on the
crowd because they have been with me now three days and have nothing to eat.
And I am unwilling to send them away hungry, lest they faint on the way." 33 And
the disciples said to him, "Where are we to get enough bread in such a desolate
place to feed so great a crowd?" 34 And Jesus said to them, "How many loaves do
you have?" They said, "Seven, and a few small fish." 35 And directing the crowd to
sit down on the ground, 36 he took the seven loaves and the fish, and having given
thanks he broke them and gave them to the disciples, and the disciples gave them
to the crowds. 37 And they all ate and were satisfied. And they took up seven baskets full of the broken pieces left over. 38 Those who ate were four thousand men,
besides women and children. 39 And after sending away the crowds, he got into the
boat and went to the region of Magadan.

The Pharisees and Sadducees Demand Signs

16 And the Pharisees and Sadducees came, and to test him they asked him to
show them a sign from heaven. 2 He answered them,[4] "When it is evening,
you say, 'It will be fair weather, for the sky is red.' 3 And in the morning, 'It will be
stormy today, for the sky is red and threatening.' You know how to interpret the

---

[1] Some manuscripts add *of the blind* [2] Greek *is expelled into the latrine* [3] Greek *from that hour* [4] Some manuscripts omit the following words to the end of verse 3

appearance of the sky, but you cannot interpret the signs of the times. 4An evil
and adulterous generation seeks for a sign, but no sign will be given to it except
the sign of Jonah." So he left them and departed.

The Leaven of the Pharisees and Sadducees

5When the disciples reached the other side, they had forgotten to bring any
bread. 6Jesus said to them, "Watch and beware of the leaven of the Pharisees
and Sadducees." 7And they began discussing it among themselves, saying, "We
brought no bread." 8But Jesus, aware of this, said, "O you of little faith, why are
you discussing among yourselves the fact that you have no bread? 9Do you not
yet perceive? Do you not remember the five loaves for the five thousand, and how
many baskets you gathered? 10Or the seven loaves for the four thousand, and how
many baskets you gathered? 11How is it that you fail to understand that I did not
speak about bread? Beware of the leaven of the Pharisees and Sadducees." 12Then
they understood that he did not tell them to beware of the leaven of bread, but of
the teaching of the Pharisees and Sadducees.

Peter Confesses Jesus as the Christ

13Now when Jesus came into the district of Caesarea Philippi, he asked his disciples, "Who do people say that the Son of Man is?" 14And they said, "Some say
John the Baptist, others say Elijah, and others Jeremiah or one of the prophets."
15He said to them, "But who do you say that I am?" 16Simon Peter replied, "You are
the Christ, the Son of the living God." 17And Jesus answered him, "Blessed are you,
Simon Bar-Jonah! For flesh and blood has not revealed this to you, but my Father
who is in heaven. 18And I tell you, you are Peter, and on this rock[1] I will build my
church, and the gates of hell[2] shall not prevail against it. 19I will give you the keys
of the kingdom of heaven, and whatever you bind on earth shall be bound in
heaven, and whatever you loose on earth shall be loosed[3] in heaven." 20Then he
strictly charged the disciples to tell no one that he was the Christ.

Jesus Foretells His Death and Resurrection

21From that time Jesus began to show his disciples that he must go to Jerusalem and suffer many things from the elders and chief priests and scribes, and be
killed, and on the third day be raised. 22And Peter took him aside and began to rebuke him, saying, "Far be it from you, Lord![4] This shall never happen to you." 23But
he turned and said to Peter, "Get behind me, Satan! You are a hindrance[5] to me.
For you are not setting your mind on the things of God, but on the things of man."

Take Up Your Cross and Follow Jesus

24Then Jesus told his disciples, "If anyone would come after me, let him deny
himself and take up his cross and follow me. 25For whoever would save his life[6]
will lose it, but whoever loses his life for my sake will find it. 26For what will it
profit a man if he gains the whole world and forfeits his soul? Or what shall a man
give in return for his soul? 27For the Son of Man is going to come with his angels
in the glory of his Father, and then he will repay each person according to what
he has done. 28Truly, I say to you, there are some standing here who will not taste
death until they see the Son of Man coming in his kingdom."

The Transfiguration

17 And after six days Jesus took with him Peter and James, and John his brother, and led them up a high mountain by themselves. 2And he was transfigured before them, and his face shone like the sun, and his clothes became white

---

[1]The Greek words for *Peter* and *rock* sound similar [2]Greek *the gates of Hades* [3]Or *shall have been bound . . . shall have been loosed* [4]Or "[May God be] *merciful to you, Lord!*" [5]Greek *stumbling block* [6]The same Greek word can mean either *soul* or *life*, depending on the context; twice in this verse and twice in verse 26

WHO DO YOU SAY THAT I AM?

A critically important question Jesus asks his followers is: "Who do you say that I am?" (Mt 16:15). Jesus knew that a proper understanding of who he is would lead to a right relationship with God. He first asked the disciples to tell him who other people thought he was, then who they thought he was. Peter answered by professing what millions have come to acknowledge throughout the centuries: "You are the Christ, the Son of the living God" (v. 16). This answer could not be a more accurate description of who Jesus is. And Peter was only beginning to find out what his statement of belief would mean not only to his life, but to the life of the church that Jesus would establish on the basis of his testimony (v. 18).

The faith of any believer today can be determined by their answer to this question. True believers are those who say that Jesus is the Christ and the Son of God, and anyone who says otherwise does not fully understand the character and nature of Jesus. Some say that Jesus was simply a great moral teacher or a prophet, but Jesus never claimed to be anything other than the Son of God. When theories abounded about who he might be, he acknowledged that Peter alone had a correct understanding of who he was.

For believers today, it is crucial that they understand the power and truth of Peter's proclamation of Jesus as the Son of God. To say that Jesus was, and is, the Son of God is to say that he is the truth and the one way to enter into a right relationship with God. Through Jesus, believers are able to experience everything that comes with knowing God and having a relationship with his Son — grace, peace, mercy in this life, and eternity with him in the next.

as light. 3And behold, there appeared to them Moses and Elijah, talking with him. 4And Peter said to Jesus, “Lord, it is good that we are here. If you wish, I will make three tents here, one for you and one for Moses and one for Elijah.” 5He was still speaking when, behold, a bright cloud overshadowed them, and a voice from the cloud said, “This is my beloved Son,[1] with whom I am well pleased; listen to him.” 6When the disciples heard this, they fell on their faces and were terrified. 7But Jesus came and touched them, saying, “Rise, and have no fear.” 8And when they lifted up their eyes, they saw no one but Jesus only.

9And as they were coming down the mountain, Jesus commanded them, “Tell no one the vision, until the Son of Man is raised from the dead.” 10And the disciples asked him, “Then why do the scribes say that first Elijah must come?” 11He answered, “Elijah does come, and he will restore all things. 12But I tell you that Elijah has already come, and they did not recognize him, but did to him whatever they pleased. So also the Son of Man will certainly suffer at their hands.” 13Then the disciples understood that he was speaking to them of John the Baptist.

Jesus Heals a Boy with a Demon

14And when they came to the crowd, a man came up to him and, kneeling before him, 15said, “Lord, have mercy on my son, for he has seizures and he suffers terribly. For often he falls into the fire, and often into the water. 16And I brought him to your disciples, and they could not heal him.” 17And Jesus answered, “O faithless and twisted generation, how long am I to be with you? How long am I to bear with you? Bring him here to me.” 18And Jesus rebuked the demon,[2] and it[3] came out of him, and the boy was healed instantly.[4] 19Then the disciples came to Jesus privately and said, “Why could we not cast it out?” 20He said to them, “Because of your little faith. For truly, I say to you, if you have faith like a grain of mustard seed, you will say to this mountain, ‘Move from here to there,’ and it will move, and nothing will be impossible for you.”[5]

Jesus Again Foretells Death, Resurrection

22As they were gathering[6] in Galilee, Jesus said to them, “The Son of Man is about to be delivered into the hands of men, 23and they will kill him, and he will be raised on the third day.” And they were greatly distressed.

The Temple Tax

24When they came to Capernaum, the collectors of the two-drachma tax went up to Peter and said, “Does your teacher not pay the tax?” 25He said, “Yes.” And when he came into the house, Jesus spoke to him first, saying, “What do you think, Simon? From whom do kings of the earth take toll or tax? From their sons or from others?” 26And when he said, “From others,” Jesus said to him, “Then the sons are free. 27However, not to give offense to them, go to the sea and cast a hook and take the first fish that comes up, and when you open its mouth you will find a shekel.[7] Take that and give it to them for me and for yourself.”

Who Is the Greatest?

18 At that time the disciples came to Jesus, saying, “Who is the greatest in the kingdom of heaven?” 2And calling to him a child, he put him in the midst of them 3and said, “Truly, I say to you, unless you turn and become like children, you will never enter the kingdom of heaven. 4Whoever humbles himself like this child is the greatest in the kingdom of heaven.

5“Whoever receives one such child in my name receives me, 6but whoever causes one of these little ones who believe in me to sin,[8] it would be better for

[1]Or *my Son, my* (or *the*) *Beloved* [2]Greek *it* [3]Greek *the demon* [4]Greek *from that hour* [5]Some manuscripts insert verse 21: *But this kind never comes out except by prayer and fasting* [6]Some manuscripts *remained* [7]Greek *stater*, a silver coin worth four drachmas or approximately one shekel [8]Greek *causes . . . to stumble*; also verses 8, 9

MATTHEW 17:24–27

PAYING THE TEMPLE TAX

The temple tax was paid annually by every adult Jewish male over 20 years old to fund maintenance of the temple. This tax was based on Exodus 30:13 and amounted to two days' wages for a common laborer. Evidently, Jesus had not yet paid the tax, and the temple tax collector was following up. However, instead of speaking to Jesus, the tax collector spoke to Peter regarding his teacher's payment. Through the resulting conversation, Jesus showed that he (and his followers) are a part of a different kingdom, a heavenly kingdom. He does not live by the rules set by mankind but by the will of God the Father. However, not wanting to "give offense," Jesus paid the temple tax, but he delivered it in a way that showed that he was the Son of God.

him to have a great millstone fastened around his neck and to be drowned in the
depth of the sea.

Temptations to Sin

7“Woe to the world for temptations to sin![1] For it is necessary that temptations
come, but woe to the one by whom the temptation comes! 8And if your hand or
your foot causes you to sin, cut it off and throw it away. It is better for you to enter
life crippled or lame than with two hands or two feet to be thrown into the eternal
fire. 9And if your eye causes you to sin, tear it out and throw it away. It is better for
you to enter life with one eye than with two eyes to be thrown into the hell[2] of fire.

The Parable of the Lost Sheep

10“See that you do not despise one of these little ones. For I tell you that in
heaven their angels always see the face of my Father who is in heaven.[3] 12What do
you think? If a man has a hundred sheep, and one of them has gone astray, does
he not leave the ninety-nine on the mountains and go in search of the one that
went astray? 13And if he finds it, truly, I say to you, he rejoices over it more than
over the ninety-nine that never went astray. 14So it is not the will of my[4] Father
who is in heaven that one of these little ones should perish.

If Your Brother Sins Against You

15“If your brother sins against you, go and tell him his fault, between you and
him alone. If he listens to you, you have gained your brother. 16But if he does not
listen, take one or two others along with you, that every charge may be established by the evidence of two or three witnesses. 17If he refuses to listen to them,
tell it to the church. And if he refuses to listen even to the church, let him be to
you as a Gentile and a tax collector. 18Truly, I say to you, whatever you bind on
earth shall be bound in heaven, and whatever you loose on earth shall be loosed[5]
in heaven. 19Again I say to you, if two of you agree on earth about anything they
ask, it will be done for them by my Father in heaven. 20For where two or three are
gathered in my name, there am I among them.”

The Parable of the Unforgiving Servant

21Then Peter came up and said to him, “Lord, how often will my brother sin
against me, and I forgive him? As many as seven times?” 22Jesus said to him, “I do
not say to you seven times, but seventy-seven times.[6]

23“Therefore the kingdom of heaven may be compared to a king who wished
to settle accounts with his servants.[7] 24When he began to settle, one was brought
to him who owed him ten thousand talents.[8] 25And since he could not pay, his
master ordered him to be sold, with his wife and children and all that he had, and
payment to be made. 26So the servant[9] fell on his knees, imploring him, ‘Have patience with me, and I will pay you everything.’ 27And out of pity for him, the master of that servant released him and forgave him the debt. 28But when that same
servant went out, he found one of his fellow servants who owed him a hundred
denarii,[10] and seizing him, he began to choke him, saying, ‘Pay what you owe.’
29So his fellow servant fell down and pleaded with him, ‘Have patience with me,
and I will pay you.’ 30He refused and went and put him in prison until he should
pay the debt. 31When his fellow servants saw what had taken place, they were
greatly distressed, and they went and reported to their master all that had taken
place. 32Then his master summoned him and said to him, ‘You wicked servant!
I forgave you all that debt because you pleaded with me. 33And should not you
have had mercy on your fellow servant, as I had mercy on you?’ 34And in anger

[1]Greek *stumbling blocks* [2]Greek *Gehenna* [3]Some manuscripts add verse 11: *For the Son of Man came to save the lost* [4]Some manuscripts *your* [5]Or *shall have been bound . . . shall have been loosed* [6]Or *seventy times seven* [7]Or *bondservants*; also verses 28, 31 [8]A *talent* was a monetary unit worth about twenty years' wages for a laborer [9]Or *bondservant*; also verses 27, 28, 29, 32, 33 [10]A *denarius* was a day's wage for a laborer

his master delivered him to the jailers,[1] until he should pay all his debt. 35 So also my heavenly Father will do to every one of you, if you do not forgive your brother from your heart."

Teaching About Divorce

19 Now when Jesus had finished these sayings, he went away from Galilee and entered the region of Judea beyond the Jordan. 2 And large crowds followed him, and he healed them there.

3 And Pharisees came up to him and tested him by asking, "Is it lawful to divorce one's wife for any cause?" 4 He answered, "Have you not read that he who created them from the beginning made them male and female, 5 and said, 'Therefore a man shall leave his father and his mother and hold fast to his wife, and the two shall become one flesh'? 6 So they are no longer two but one flesh. What therefore God has joined together, let not man separate." 7 They said to him, "Why then did Moses command one to give a certificate of divorce and to send her away?" 8 He said to them, "Because of your hardness of heart Moses allowed you to divorce your wives, but from the beginning it was not so. 9 And I say to you: whoever divorces his wife, except for sexual immorality, and marries another, commits adultery."[2]

10 The disciples said to him, "If such is the case of a man with his wife, it is better not to marry." 11 But he said to them, "Not everyone can receive this saying, but only those to whom it is given. 12 For there are eunuchs who have been so from birth, and there are eunuchs who have been made eunuchs by men, and there are eunuchs who have made themselves eunuchs for the sake of the kingdom of heaven. Let the one who is able to receive this receive it."

Let the Children Come to Me

13 Then children were brought to him that he might lay his hands on them and pray. The disciples rebuked the people, 14 but Jesus said, "Let the little children come to me and do not hinder them, for to such belongs the kingdom of heaven." 15 And he laid his hands on them and went away.

The Rich Young Man

16 And behold, a man came up to him, saying, "Teacher, what good deed must I do to have eternal life?" 17 And he said to him, "Why do you ask me about what is good? There is only one who is good. If you would enter life, keep the commandments." 18 He said to him, "Which ones?" And Jesus said, "You shall not murder, You shall not commit adultery, You shall not steal, You shall not bear false witness, 19 Honor your father and mother, and, You shall love your neighbor as yourself." 20 The young man said to him, "All these I have kept. What do I still lack?" 21 Jesus said to him, "If you would be perfect, go, sell what you possess and give to the poor, and you will have treasure in heaven; and come, follow me." 22 When the young man heard this he went away sorrowful, for he had great possessions.

23 And Jesus said to his disciples, "Truly, I say to you, only with difficulty will a rich person enter the kingdom of heaven. 24 Again I tell you, it is easier for a camel to go through the eye of a needle than for a rich person to enter the kingdom of God." 25 When the disciples heard this, they were greatly astonished, saying, "Who then can be saved?" 26 But Jesus looked at them and said, "With man this is impossible, but with God all things are possible." 27 Then Peter said in reply, "See, we have left everything and followed you. What then will we have?" 28 Jesus said to them, "Truly, I say to you, in the new world,[3] when the Son of Man will sit on his glorious throne, you who have followed me will also sit on twelve thrones, judging the twelve tribes of Israel. 29 And everyone who has left houses or brothers or

MATTHEW 19:16–26

WEALTH AND THE KINGDOM OF GOD

This story's application is not to imply that believers need to give away all of their possessions in order to get into heaven. Rather, it is intended to show that Jesus cared about the hearts of those who were following him. Knowing all things, he knew that this rich young man's heart was preoccupied with his wealth. So when he asked about eternal life, Jesus showed him that right standing with God flows from a pure heart. It is not enough merely to follow external standards. That sort of life tends to foster a spirit of self-righteousness. Followers of Jesus are expected to rely on Jesus alone as the one and only way to heaven, and to have a heart for God and his kingdom before all else (Mt 6:33).

[1] Greek *torturers* [2] Some manuscripts add *and whoever marries a divorced woman commits adultery;* other manuscripts *except for sexual immorality, makes her commit adultery, and whoever marries a divorced woman commits adultery* [3] Greek *in the regeneration*

sisters or father or mother or children or lands, for my name's sake, will receive
a hundredfold[1] and will inherit eternal life. 30But many who are first will be last,
and the last first.

Laborers in the Vineyard

20 "For the kingdom of heaven is like a master of a house who went out early
in the morning to hire laborers for his vineyard. 2After agreeing with the
laborers for a denarius[2] a day, he sent them into his vineyard. 3And going out
about the third hour he saw others standing idle in the marketplace, 4and to them
he said, 'You go into the vineyard too, and whatever is right I will give you.' 5So
they went. Going out again about the sixth hour and the ninth hour, he did the
same. 6And about the eleventh hour he went out and found others standing. And
he said to them, 'Why do you stand here idle all day?' 7They said to him, 'Because
no one has hired us.' He said to them, 'You go into the vineyard too.' 8And when
evening came, the owner of the vineyard said to his foreman, 'Call the laborers
and pay them their wages, beginning with the last, up to the first.' 9And when
those hired about the eleventh hour came, each of them received a denarius.
10Now when those hired first came, they thought they would receive more, but
each of them also received a denarius. 11And on receiving it they grumbled at the
master of the house, 12saying, 'These last worked only one hour, and you have
made them equal to us who have borne the burden of the day and the scorching
heat.' 13But he replied to one of them, 'Friend, I am doing you no wrong. Did you
not agree with me for a denarius? 14Take what belongs to you and go. I choose to
give to this last worker as I give to you. 15Am I not allowed to do what I choose
with what belongs to me? Or do you begrudge my generosity?'[3] 16So the last will
be first, and the first last."

Jesus Foretells His Death a Third Time

17And as Jesus was going up to Jerusalem, he took the twelve disciples aside,
and on the way he said to them, 18"See, we are going up to Jerusalem. And the
Son of Man will be delivered over to the chief priests and scribes, and they will
condemn him to death 19and deliver him over to the Gentiles to be mocked and
flogged and crucified, and he will be raised on the third day."

A Mother's Request

20Then the mother of the sons of Zebedee came up to him with her sons, and
kneeling before him she asked him for something. 21And he said to her, "What do
you want?" She said to him, "Say that these two sons of mine are to sit, one at your
right hand and one at your left, in your kingdom." 22Jesus answered, "You do not
know what you are asking. Are you able to drink the cup that I am to drink?" They
said to him, "We are able." 23He said to them, "You will drink my cup, but to sit at
my right hand and at my left is not mine to grant, but it is for those for whom it has
been prepared by my Father." 24And when the ten heard it, they were indignant
at the two brothers. 25But Jesus called them to him and said, "You know that the
rulers of the Gentiles lord it over them, and their great ones exercise authority
over them. 26It shall not be so among you. But whoever would be great among
you must be your servant,[4] 27and whoever would be first among you must be your
slave,[5] 28even as the Son of Man came not to be served but to serve, and to give his
life as a ransom for many."

Jesus Heals Two Blind Men

29And as they went out of Jericho, a great crowd followed him. 30And behold,
there were two blind men sitting by the roadside, and when they heard that Jesus

[1]Some manuscripts *manifold* [2]A *denarius* was a day's wage for a laborer [3]Or *is your eye bad because I am good?* [4]Greek *diakonos* [5]Or *bondservant*, or *servant* (for the contextual rendering of the Greek word *doulos*, see Preface)

MATTHEW 20:20–28

SERVANTHOOD

This exchange provides an interesting view on Jesus' perception of what it takes to be able to sit in the seat of power. Here, two disciples were seeking to advance their own status. James and John were the ones asking, but the other ten were indignant as well, so all of the disciples' attitudes are on display in this story. Each of the twelve wanted to occupy seats of authority and power in heaven. However, they did not understand that those seats required partnership in suffering (v. 22). Jesus' "cup" was not only that he, as God, allowed himself to become human, but also that he was to be crucified on the cross as the perfect, sinless sacrifice for the sins of humankind (Php 2:6–9). The "cup" for James and John would be one of suffering for the kingdom. As Jesus often did, he was emphasizing that one must be willing to sacrifice their own comfort and livelihood in order to follow him.

was passing by, they cried out, "Lord,[1] have mercy on us, Son of David!" [31]The crowd rebuked them, telling them to be silent, but they cried out all the more, "Lord, have mercy on us, Son of David!" [32]And stopping, Jesus called them and said, "What do you want me to do for you?" [33]They said to him, "Lord, let our eyes be opened." [34]And Jesus in pity touched their eyes, and immediately they recovered their sight and followed him.

The Triumphal Entry

21 Now when they drew near to Jerusalem and came to Bethphage, to the Mount of Olives, then Jesus sent two disciples, [2]saying to them, "Go into the village in front of you, and immediately you will find a donkey tied, and a colt with her. Untie them and bring them to me. [3]If anyone says anything to you, you shall say, 'The Lord needs them,' and he will send them at once." [4]This took place to fulfill what was spoken by the prophet, saying,

[5] "Say to the daughter of Zion,
'Behold, your king is coming to you,
humble, and mounted on a donkey,
on a colt,[2] the foal of a beast of burden.'"

[6]The disciples went and did as Jesus had directed them. [7]They brought the donkey and the colt and put on them their cloaks, and he sat on them. [8]Most of the crowd spread their cloaks on the road, and others cut branches from the trees and spread them on the road. [9]And the crowds that went before him and that followed him were shouting, "Hosanna to the Son of David! Blessed is he who comes in the name of the Lord! Hosanna in the highest!" [10]And when he entered Jerusalem, the whole city was stirred up, saying, "Who is this?" [11]And the crowds said, "This is the prophet Jesus, from Nazareth of Galilee."

Jesus Cleanses the Temple

[12]And Jesus entered the temple[3] and drove out all who sold and bought in the temple, and he overturned the tables of the money-changers and the seats of those who sold pigeons. [13]He said to them, "It is written, 'My house shall be called a house of prayer,' but you make it a den of robbers."

[14]And the blind and the lame came to him in the temple, and he healed them. [15]But when the chief priests and the scribes saw the wonderful things that he did, and the children crying out in the temple, "Hosanna to the Son of David!" they were indignant, [16]and they said to him, "Do you hear what these are saying?" And Jesus said to them, "Yes; have you never read,

"'Out of the mouth of infants and nursing babies
you have prepared praise'?"

[17]And leaving them, he went out of the city to Bethany and lodged there.

Jesus Curses the Fig Tree

[18]In the morning, as he was returning to the city, he became hungry. [19]And seeing a fig tree by the wayside, he went to it and found nothing on it but only leaves. And he said to it, "May no fruit ever come from you again!" And the fig tree withered at once.

[20]When the disciples saw it, they marveled, saying, "How did the fig tree wither at once?" [21]And Jesus answered them, "Truly, I say to you, if you have faith and do not doubt, you will not only do what has been done to the fig tree, but even if you say to this mountain, 'Be taken up and thrown into the sea,' it will happen. [22]And whatever you ask in prayer, you will receive, if you have faith."

The Authority of Jesus Challenged

[23]And when he entered the temple, the chief priests and the elders of the people came up to him as he was teaching, and said, "By what authority are you

[1]Some manuscripts omit *Lord* [2]Or *donkey, and on a colt* [3]Some manuscripts add *of God*

JESUS COMES TO JERUSALEM AS KING

Jesus' coming to Jerusalem riding on a donkey, to the accolades and praise of the gathered crowd, fulfilled the Old Testament prophecies of Jesus as King. Isaiah 62:11 calls for the "daughter of Zion" to watch for this King, and Zechariah 9:9 depicts the King "humble and mounted on a donkey, on a colt, the foal of a donkey." While most royal processions feature incredible extravagance, Jesus humbly entered town on a simple donkey. While horses were ridden during times of war, rulers rode donkeys during times of peace as a sign of humility toward the people (1Ki 1:38 – 40). Here, Jesus exemplified the peaceful return of a king to Jerusalem. By riding on a donkey, he showed that he came to bring grace and not judgment. Also, it is significant that Jesus rode a colt, which is a young and untrained donkey. Normally, it would be incredibly difficult for someone to ride an unbroken animal through a crowded and chaotic scene with an unfamiliar burden on its back. But this was Jesus, Creator of the world!

This scene was nothing less than a royal procession (2Ki 9:13), yet up until this point, Jesus had consistently avoided such displays (Mt 8:4; 9:30; 12:16). However, he was now ready to present himself publicly as the Messiah and King. This was Jesus' last trip to Jerusalem, and he chose to enter in such a way as to leave no doubt that he was the promised Messiah who had come to save the nation. No one in the city could possibly miss the procession or the prophecy-fulfilling reference Jesus' entry conveyed.

doing these things, and who gave you this authority?" 24Jesus answered them, "I
also will ask you one question, and if you tell me the answer, then I also will tell
you by what authority I do these things. 25The baptism of John, from where did
it come? From heaven or from man?" And they discussed it among themselves,
saying, "If we say, 'From heaven,' he will say to us, 'Why then did you not believe
him?' 26But if we say, 'From man,' we are afraid of the crowd, for they all hold that
John was a prophet." 27So they answered Jesus, "We do not know." And he said to
them, "Neither will I tell you by what authority I do these things.

The Parable of the Two Sons

28"What do you think? A man had two sons. And he went to the first and said,
'Son, go and work in the vineyard today.' 29And he answered, 'I will not,' but afterward he changed his mind and went. 30And he went to the other son and said
the same. And he answered, 'I will, sir,' but did not go. 31Which of the two did the
will of his father?" They said, "The first." Jesus said to them, "Truly, I say to you,
the tax collectors and the prostitutes go into the kingdom of God before you. 32For
John came to you in the way of righteousness, and you did not believe him, but the
tax collectors and the prostitutes believed him. And even when you saw it, you did
not afterward change your minds and believe him.

The Parable of the Tenants

33"Hear another parable. There was a master of a house who planted a vineyard and put a fence around it and dug a winepress in it and built a tower and
leased it to tenants, and went into another country. 34When the season for fruit
drew near, he sent his servants[1] to the tenants to get his fruit. 35And the tenants
took his servants and beat one, killed another, and stoned another. 36Again he
sent other servants, more than the first. And they did the same to them. 37Finally
he sent his son to them, saying, 'They will respect my son.' 38But when the tenants
saw the son, they said to themselves, 'This is the heir. Come, let us kill him and
have his inheritance.' 39And they took him and threw him out of the vineyard and
killed him. 40When therefore the owner of the vineyard comes, what will he do
to those tenants?" 41They said to him, "He will put those wretches to a miserable
death and let out the vineyard to other tenants who will give him the fruits in
their seasons."

42Jesus said to them, "Have you never read in the Scriptures:

"'The stone that the builders rejected
    has become the cornerstone;[2]
this was the Lord's doing,
    and it is marvelous in our eyes'?

43Therefore I tell you, the kingdom of God will be taken away from you and given
to a people producing its fruits. 44And the one who falls on this stone will be broken to pieces; and when it falls on anyone, it will crush him."[3]

45When the chief priests and the Pharisees heard his parables, they perceived
that he was speaking about them. 46And although they were seeking to arrest him,
they feared the crowds, because they held him to be a prophet.

The Parable of the Wedding Feast

22 And again Jesus spoke to them in parables, saying, 2"The kingdom of
heaven may be compared to a king who gave a wedding feast for his son,
3and sent his servants[4] to call those who were invited to the wedding feast, but
they would not come. 4Again he sent other servants, saying, 'Tell those who are
invited, "See, I have prepared my dinner, my oxen and my fat calves have been
slaughtered, and everything is ready. Come to the wedding feast."' 5But they paid

[1] Or *bondservants*; also verses 35, 36 [2] Greek *the head of the corner* [3] Some manuscripts omit verse 44
[4] Or *bondservants*; also verses 4, 6, 8, 10

no attention and went off, one to his farm, another to his business, [6]while the rest
seized his servants, treated them shamefully, and killed them. [7]The king was angry, and he sent his troops and destroyed those murderers and burned their city.
[8]Then he said to his servants, 'The wedding feast is ready, but those invited were
not worthy. [9]Go therefore to the main roads and invite to the wedding feast as
many as you find.' [10]And those servants went out into the roads and gathered all
whom they found, both bad and good. So the wedding hall was filled with guests.

[11]"But when the king came in to look at the guests, he saw there a man who
had no wedding garment. [12]And he said to him, 'Friend, how did you get in here
without a wedding garment?' And he was speechless. [13]Then the king said to the
attendants, 'Bind him hand and foot and cast him into the outer darkness. In that
place there will be weeping and gnashing of teeth.' [14]For many are called, but few
are chosen."

Paying Taxes to Caesar

[15]Then the Pharisees went and plotted how to entangle him in his words.
[16]And they sent their disciples to him, along with the Herodians, saying, "Teacher,
we know that you are true and teach the way of God truthfully, and you do not
care about anyone's opinion, for you are not swayed by appearances.[1] [17]Tell us,
then, what you think. Is it lawful to pay taxes to Caesar, or not?" [18]But Jesus, aware
of their malice, said, "Why put me to the test, you hypocrites? [19]Show me the
coin for the tax." And they brought him a denarius.[2] [20]And Jesus said to them,
"Whose likeness and inscription is this?" [21]They said, "Caesar's." Then he said
to them, "Therefore render to Caesar the things that are Caesar's, and to God the
things that are God's." [22]When they heard it, they marveled. And they left him
and went away.

Sadducees Ask About the Resurrection

[23]The same day Sadducees came to him, who say that there is no resurrection, and they asked him a question, [24]saying, "Teacher, Moses said, 'If a man dies
having no children, his brother must marry the widow and raise up offspring for
his brother.' [25]Now there were seven brothers among us. The first married and
died, and having no offspring left his wife to his brother. [26]So too the second and
third, down to the seventh. [27]After them all, the woman died. [28]In the resurrection, therefore, of the seven, whose wife will she be? For they all had her."

[29]But Jesus answered them, "You are wrong, because you know neither the
Scriptures nor the power of God. [30]For in the resurrection they neither marry nor
are given in marriage, but are like angels in heaven. [31]And as for the resurrection
of the dead, have you not read what was said to you by God: [32]'I am the God of
Abraham, and the God of Isaac, and the God of Jacob'? He is not God of the dead,
but of the living." [33]And when the crowd heard it, they were astonished at his
teaching.

The Great Commandment

[34]But when the Pharisees heard that he had silenced the Sadducees, they
gathered together. [35]And one of them, a lawyer, asked him a question to test him.
[36]"Teacher, which is the great commandment in the Law?" [37]And he said to him,
"You shall love the Lord your God with all your heart and with all your soul and
with all your mind. [38]This is the great and first commandment. [39]And a second is
like it: You shall love your neighbor as yourself. [40]On these two commandments
depend all the Law and the Prophets."

Whose Son Is the Christ?

[41]Now while the Pharisees were gathered together, Jesus asked them a question, [42]saying, "What do you think about the Christ? Whose son is he?" They said

[1]Greek *for you do not look at people's faces* [2]A *denarius* was a day's wage for a laborer

MATTHEW 22:1–14

THE WEDDING FEAST

When families planned Jewish weddings, they sent out two invitations (similar to our "save-the-date" mailings that sometimes come before the actual invitation). In this instance, the first invitation portrays the ministry of John the Baptist. He told people to repent and prepare, for the kingdom of God was coming (Mt 3:2). The indifferent response describes Israel—specifically, the religious authorities—at the time of Jesus' earthly ministry. They ignored John's call to repent, and they opposed the arrival of the second invitation as well in the ministry of Jesus. But God is in the business of drawing people to himself, so the king in the story still instructs his servants to invite others to attend his wedding. Those who accept these gracious invitations and are truly prepared to engage in this banquet as citizens of the kingdom (which the religious leaders were not, 22:11–13) are welcomed in. The point of this parable is to portray how God shows grace in extending invitations to his kingdom while at the same time mandating requirements for entrance.

MATTHEW 23:1–39

HYPOCRISY

Throughout his ministry, Jesus consistently confronted hypocrisy, especially in the Jewish religious leaders of his day. Chapter 23 includes Jesus' angry condemnation of those who were much more concerned about securing their power base than they were about bringing their followers closer to God. The rules that they forced on others were man-made responses to their study of the law, and while they required strict adherence to those rules, they themselves did not practice what they preached (v. 4). Notice the language with which the perfect, sinless Son of God addressed them: lazy (v. 4), prideful (v. 6), hypocrites (vv. 25,27,29), blind (v. 26), "full of hypocrisy and lawlessness" (v. 28), deluded (v. 30), self-incriminating (v. 31), hell-bound vipers (v. 33), murderers (v. 34), and condemned because of their blood-guilt (v. 35). Jesus' righteous indignation burned against these self-important men who were leading others astray. Their devotion was not to God but to a set of rules they held over the people beneath them, and Jesus was not shy to point out the contradiction that manifested itself in their daily lives. In contrast, Jesus lived without any misalignment between his heart and his actions. He lived with perfect integrity in service to God, and believers are called to desire to be like him and share his mindset (1Co 2:16).

to him, "The son of David." 43 He said to them, "How is it then that David, in the Spirit, calls him Lord, saying,

44 "'The Lord said to my Lord,
"Sit at my right hand,
until I put your enemies under your feet"'?

45 If then David calls him Lord, how is he his son?" 46 And no one was able to answer him a word, nor from that day did anyone dare to ask him any more questions.

Seven Woes to the Scribes and Pharisees

23 Then Jesus said to the crowds and to his disciples, 2 "The scribes and the Pharisees sit on Moses' seat, 3 so do and observe whatever they tell you, but not the works they do. For they preach, but do not practice. 4 They tie up heavy burdens, hard to bear,[1] and lay them on people's shoulders, but they themselves are not willing to move them with their finger. 5 They do all their deeds to be seen by others. For they make their phylacteries broad and their fringes long, 6 and they love the place of honor at feasts and the best seats in the synagogues 7 and greetings in the marketplaces and being called rabbi[2] by others. 8 But you are not to be called rabbi, for you have one teacher, and you are all brothers.[3] 9 And call no man your father on earth, for you have one Father, who is in heaven. 10 Neither be called instructors, for you have one instructor, the Christ. 11 The greatest among you shall be your servant. 12 Whoever exalts himself will be humbled, and whoever humbles himself will be exalted.

13 "But woe to you, scribes and Pharisees, hypocrites! For you shut the kingdom of heaven in people's faces. For you neither enter yourselves nor allow those who would enter to go in.[4] 15 Woe to you, scribes and Pharisees, hypocrites! For you travel across sea and land to make a single proselyte, and when he becomes a proselyte, you make him twice as much a child of hell[5] as yourselves.

16 "Woe to you, blind guides, who say, 'If anyone swears by the temple, it is nothing, but if anyone swears by the gold of the temple, he is bound by his oath.' 17 You blind fools! For which is greater, the gold or the temple that has made the gold sacred? 18 And you say, 'If anyone swears by the altar, it is nothing, but if anyone swears by the gift that is on the altar, he is bound by his oath.' 19 You blind men! For which is greater, the gift or the altar that makes the gift sacred? 20 So whoever swears by the altar swears by it and by everything on it. 21 And whoever swears by the temple swears by it and by him who dwells in it. 22 And whoever swears by heaven swears by the throne of God and by him who sits upon it.

23 "Woe to you, scribes and Pharisees, hypocrites! For you tithe mint and dill and cumin, and have neglected the weightier matters of the law: justice and mercy and faithfulness. These you ought to have done, without neglecting the others. 24 You blind guides, straining out a gnat and swallowing a camel!

25 "Woe to you, scribes and Pharisees, hypocrites! For you clean the outside of the cup and the plate, but inside they are full of greed and self-indulgence. 26 You blind Pharisee! First clean the inside of the cup and the plate, that the outside also may be clean.

27 "Woe to you, scribes and Pharisees, hypocrites! For you are like whitewashed tombs, which outwardly appear beautiful, but within are full of dead people's bones and all uncleanness. 28 So you also outwardly appear righteous to others, but within you are full of hypocrisy and lawlessness.

29 "Woe to you, scribes and Pharisees, hypocrites! For you build the tombs of the prophets and decorate the monuments of the righteous, 30 saying, 'If we had

[1] Some manuscripts omit *hard to bear* [2] *Rabbi* means *my teacher*, or *my master*; also verse 8 [3] Or *brothers and sisters* [4] Some manuscripts add here (or after verse 12) verse 14: *Woe to you, scribes and Pharisees, hypocrites! For you devour widows' houses and for a pretense you make long prayers; therefore you will receive the greater condemnation* [5] Greek *Gehenna*; also verse 33

lived in the days of our fathers, we would not have taken part with them in shedding the blood of the prophets.' [31]Thus you witness against yourselves that you
are sons of those who murdered the prophets. [32]Fill up, then, the measure of your
fathers. [33]You serpents, you brood of vipers, how are you to escape being sentenced to hell? [34]Therefore I send you prophets and wise men and scribes, some
of whom you will kill and crucify, and some you will flog in your synagogues and
persecute from town to town, [35]so that on you may come all the righteous blood
shed on earth, from the blood of righteous Abel to the blood of Zechariah the son
of Barachiah,[1] whom you murdered between the sanctuary and the altar. [36]Truly,
I say to you, all these things will come upon this generation.

Lament over Jerusalem

[37]"O Jerusalem, Jerusalem, the city that kills the prophets and stones those
who are sent to it! How often would I have gathered your children together as
a hen gathers her brood under her wings, and you were not willing! [38]See, your
house is left to you desolate. [39]For I tell you, you will not see me again, until you
say, 'Blessed is he who comes in the name of the Lord.'"

Jesus Foretells Destruction of the Temple

24 Jesus left the temple and was going away, when his disciples came to point
out to him the buildings of the temple. [2]But he answered them, "You see
all these, do you not? Truly, I say to you, there will not be left here one stone upon
another that will not be thrown down."

Signs of the End of the Age

[3]As he sat on the Mount of Olives, the disciples came to him privately, saying,
"Tell us, when will these things be, and what will be the sign of your coming and
of the end of the age?" [4]And Jesus answered them, "See that no one leads you
astray. [5]For many will come in my name, saying, 'I am the Christ,' and they will
lead many astray. [6]And you will hear of wars and rumors of wars. See that you
are not alarmed, for this must take place, but the end is not yet. [7]For nation will
rise against nation, and kingdom against kingdom, and there will be famines and
earthquakes in various places. [8]All these are but the beginning of the birth pains.

[9]"Then they will deliver you up to tribulation and put you to death, and you
will be hated by all nations for my name's sake. [10]And then many will fall away[2]
and betray one another and hate one another. [11]And many false prophets will
arise and lead many astray. [12]And because lawlessness will be increased, the love
of many will grow cold. [13]But the one who endures to the end will be saved. [14]And
this gospel of the kingdom will be proclaimed throughout the whole world as a
testimony to all nations, and then the end will come.

The Abomination of Desolation

[15]"So when you see the abomination of desolation spoken of by the prophet
Daniel, standing in the holy place (let the reader understand), [16]then let those
who are in Judea flee to the mountains. [17]Let the one who is on the housetop not
go down to take what is in his house, [18]and let the one who is in the field not turn
back to take his cloak. [19]And alas for women who are pregnant and for those who
are nursing infants in those days! [20]Pray that your flight may not be in winter or
on a Sabbath. [21]For then there will be great tribulation, such as has not been from
the beginning of the world until now, no, and never will be. [22]And if those days
had not been cut short, no human being would be saved. But for the sake of the
elect those days will be cut short. [23]Then if anyone says to you, 'Look, here is the
Christ!' or 'There he is!' do not believe it. [24]For false christs and false prophets will
arise and perform great signs and wonders, so as to lead astray, if possible, even

[1]Some manuscripts omit *the son of Barachiah* [2]Or *stumble*

MATTHEW 24:1–14,36–42

THE SECOND COMING (PART 1)

Here Jesus described the second coming by using symbolic language. While these words and various proposed timelines have been interpreted differently by committed Christians over the centuries, we do know that Jesus' second coming will be preceded by persecution and opposition (vv. 9–10), marked by false prophets claiming to be the Messiah (v. 5), and will include a time of testing for believers whose persistence and commitment will be rewarded (v. 14). Above all, the second coming of Christ will be sudden (v. 36). Altogether, Jesus made it clear that there will be no mistaking the second coming when it happens, and it is important for his followers to be prepared, each and every day, for that day.

MATTHEW 25:1–46

THE SECOND COMING (PART 2)

The final section of this discourse involves judgment, which is not a new theme in the Gospel of Matthew (3:12; 6:2; 13:30; 18:23–35; 21:33–43; 22:1–14). Because Matthew spent a significant portion of his Gospel focusing on the coming of the kingdom, he also needed to discuss the judgment that comes with it. In the first two parables in this chapter, Jesus spoke about the judgment that will come upon those who are not prepared for his return, and in the last parable he focuses on all of the nations of the earth. To fully understand Jesus, it is important to see not only his love but also the reality that his coming will be accompanied by judgment. With the opportunity for people to accept his sacrifice and the grace and forgiveness that come with it, there also is an opportunity for people to reject that same sacrifice. Jesus came so that those who love God may devote their lives to following him, but his offer has another side: judgment on those who willfully choose to turn their backs on God.

the elect. [25]See, I have told you beforehand. [26]So, if they say to you, ‘Look, he is in the wilderness,’ do not go out. If they say, ‘Look, he is in the inner rooms,’ do not believe it. [27]For as the lightning comes from the east and shines as far as the west, so will be the coming of the Son of Man. [28]Wherever the corpse is, there the vultures will gather.

The Coming of the Son of Man

[29]“Immediately after the tribulation of those days the sun will be darkened, and the moon will not give its light, and the stars will fall from heaven, and the powers of the heavens will be shaken. [30]Then will appear in heaven the sign of the Son of Man, and then all the tribes of the earth will mourn, and they will see the Son of Man coming on the clouds of heaven with power and great glory. [31]And he will send out his angels with a loud trumpet call, and they will gather his elect from the four winds, from one end of heaven to the other.

The Lesson of the Fig Tree

[32]“From the fig tree learn its lesson: as soon as its branch becomes tender and puts out its leaves, you know that summer is near. [33]So also, when you see all these things, you know that he is near, at the very gates. [34]Truly, I say to you, this generation will not pass away until all these things take place. [35]Heaven and earth will pass away, but my words will not pass away.

No One Knows That Day and Hour

[36]“But concerning that day and hour no one knows, not even the angels of heaven, nor the Son,[1] but the Father only. [37]For as were the days of Noah, so will be the coming of the Son of Man. [38]For as in those days before the flood they were eating and drinking, marrying and giving in marriage, until the day when Noah entered the ark, [39]and they were unaware until the flood came and swept them all away, so will be the coming of the Son of Man. [40]Then two men will be in the field; one will be taken and one left. [41]Two women will be grinding at the mill; one will be taken and one left. [42]Therefore, stay awake, for you do not know on what day your Lord is coming. [43]But know this, that if the master of the house had known in what part of the night the thief was coming, he would have stayed awake and would not have let his house be broken into. [44]Therefore you also must be ready, for the Son of Man is coming at an hour you do not expect.

[45]“Who then is the faithful and wise servant,[2] whom his master has set over his household, to give them their food at the proper time? [46]Blessed is that servant whom his master will find so doing when he comes. [47]Truly, I say to you, he will set him over all his possessions. [48]But if that wicked servant says to himself, ‘My master is delayed,’ [49]and begins to beat his fellow servants[3] and eats and drinks with drunkards, [50]the master of that servant will come on a day when he does not expect him and at an hour he does not know [51]and will cut him in pieces and put him with the hypocrites. In that place there will be weeping and gnashing of teeth.

The Parable of the Ten Virgins

25 “Then the kingdom of heaven will be like ten virgins who took their lamps[4] and went to meet the bridegroom.[5] [2]Five of them were foolish, and five were wise. [3]For when the foolish took their lamps, they took no oil with them, [4]but the wise took flasks of oil with their lamps. [5]As the bridegroom was delayed, they all became drowsy and slept. [6]But at midnight there was a cry, ‘Here is the bridegroom! Come out to meet him.’ [7]Then all those virgins rose and trimmed their lamps. [8]And the foolish said to the wise, ‘Give us some of your oil, for our lamps are going out.’ [9]But the wise answered, saying, ‘Since there will not be enough for us and for you, go rather to the dealers and buy for yourselves.’ [10]And

[1]Some manuscripts omit *nor the Son* [2]Or *bondservant*; also verses 46, 48, 50 [3]Or *bondservants*
[4]Or *torches* [5]Some manuscripts add *and the bride*

while they were going to buy, the bridegroom came, and those who were ready
went in with him to the marriage feast, and the door was shut. 11Afterward the
other virgins came also, saying, 'Lord, lord, open to us.' 12But he answered, 'Truly,
I say to you, I do not know you.' 13Watch therefore, for you know neither the day
nor the hour.

The Parable of the Talents

14"For it will be like a man going on a journey, who called his servants[1] and
entrusted to them his property. 15To one he gave five talents,[2] to another two, to
another one, to each according to his ability. Then he went away. 16He who had
received the five talents went at once and traded with them, and he made five
talents more. 17So also he who had the two talents made two talents more. 18But he
who had received the one talent went and dug in the ground and hid his master's
money. 19Now after a long time the master of those servants came and settled
accounts with them. 20And he who had received the five talents came forward,
bringing five talents more, saying, 'Master, you delivered to me five talents; here,
I have made five talents more.' 21His master said to him, 'Well done, good and
faithful servant.[3] You have been faithful over a little; I will set you over much.
Enter into the joy of your master.' 22And he also who had the two talents came
forward, saying, 'Master, you delivered to me two talents; here, I have made two
talents more.' 23His master said to him, 'Well done, good and faithful servant. You
have been faithful over a little; I will set you over much. Enter into the joy of your
master.' 24He also who had received the one talent came forward, saying, 'Master, I knew you to be a hard man, reaping where you did not sow, and gathering
where you scattered no seed, 25so I was afraid, and I went and hid your talent in
the ground. Here, you have what is yours.' 26But his master answered him, 'You
wicked and slothful servant! You knew that I reap where I have not sown and
gather where I scattered no seed? 27Then you ought to have invested my money
with the bankers, and at my coming I should have received what was my own with
interest. 28So take the talent from him and give it to him who has the ten talents.
29For to everyone who has will more be given, and he will have an abundance.
But from the one who has not, even what he has will be taken away. 30And cast
the worthless servant into the outer darkness. In that place there will be weeping
and gnashing of teeth.'

The Final Judgment

31"When the Son of Man comes in his glory, and all the angels with him, then
he will sit on his glorious throne. 32Before him will be gathered all the nations,
and he will separate people one from another as a shepherd separates the sheep
from the goats. 33And he will place the sheep on his right, but the goats on the left.
34Then the King will say to those on his right, 'Come, you who are blessed by my
Father, inherit the kingdom prepared for you from the foundation of the world.
35For I was hungry and you gave me food, I was thirsty and you gave me drink, I
was a stranger and you welcomed me, 36I was naked and you clothed me, I was
sick and you visited me, I was in prison and you came to me.' 37Then the righteous will answer him, saying, 'Lord, when did we see you hungry and feed you,
or thirsty and give you drink? 38And when did we see you a stranger and welcome
you, or naked and clothe you? 39And when did we see you sick or in prison and
visit you?' 40And the King will answer them, 'Truly, I say to you, as you did it to
one of the least of these my brothers,[4] you did it to me.'

41"Then he will say to those on his left, 'Depart from me, you cursed, into the
eternal fire prepared for the devil and his angels. 42For I was hungry and you gave
me no food, I was thirsty and you gave me no drink, 43I was a stranger and you did

[1]Or *bondservants*; also verse 19 [2]A *talent* was a monetary unit worth about twenty years' wages for a laborer [3]Or *bondservant*; also verses 23, 26, 30 [4]Or *brothers and sisters*

not welcome me, naked and you did not clothe me, sick and in prison and you did not visit me.' [44]Then they also will answer, saying, 'Lord, when did we see you hungry or thirsty or a stranger or naked or sick or in prison, and did not minister to you?' [45]Then he will answer them, saying, 'Truly, I say to you, as you did not do it to one of the least of these, you did not do it to me.' [46]And these will go away into eternal punishment, but the righteous into eternal life."

The Plot to Kill Jesus

26 When Jesus had finished all these sayings, he said to his disciples, [2]"You know that after two days the Passover is coming, and the Son of Man will be delivered up to be crucified."

[3]Then the chief priests and the elders of the people gathered in the palace of the high priest, whose name was Caiaphas, [4]and plotted together in order to arrest Jesus by stealth and kill him. [5]But they said, "Not during the feast, lest there be an uproar among the people."

Jesus Anointed at Bethany

[6]Now when Jesus was at Bethany in the house of Simon the leper,[1] [7]a woman came up to him with an alabaster flask of very expensive ointment, and she poured it on his head as he reclined at table. [8]And when the disciples saw it, they were indignant, saying, "Why this waste? [9]For this could have been sold for a large sum and given to the poor." [10]But Jesus, aware of this, said to them, "Why do you trouble the woman? For she has done a beautiful thing to me. [11]For you always have the poor with you, but you will not always have me. [12]In pouring this ointment on my body, she has done it to prepare me for burial. [13]Truly, I say to you, wherever this gospel is proclaimed in the whole world, what she has done will also be told in memory of her."

Judas to Betray Jesus

[14]Then one of the twelve, whose name was Judas Iscariot, went to the chief priests [15]and said, "What will you give me if I deliver him over to you?" And they paid him thirty pieces of silver. [16]And from that moment he sought an opportunity to betray him.

The Passover with the Disciples

[17]Now on the first day of Unleavened Bread the disciples came to Jesus, saying, "Where will you have us prepare for you to eat the Passover?" [18]He said, "Go into the city to a certain man and say to him, 'The Teacher says, My time is at hand. I will keep the Passover at your house with my disciples.'" [19]And the disciples did as Jesus had directed them, and they prepared the Passover.

[20]When it was evening, he reclined at table with the twelve.[2] [21]And as they were eating, he said, "Truly, I say to you, one of you will betray me." [22]And they were very sorrowful and began to say to him one after another, "Is it I, Lord?" [23]He answered, "He who has dipped his hand in the dish with me will betray me. [24]The Son of Man goes as it is written of him, but woe to that man by whom the Son of Man is betrayed! It would have been better for that man if he had not been born." [25]Judas, who would betray him, answered, "Is it I, Rabbi?" He said to him, "You have said so."

Institution of the Lord's Supper

[26]Now as they were eating, Jesus took bread, and after blessing it broke it and gave it to the disciples, and said, "Take, eat; this is my body." [27]And he took a cup, and when he had given thanks he gave it to them, saying, "Drink of it, all of you, [28]for this is my blood of the[3] covenant, which is poured out for many for the for-

---

[1] *Leprosy* was a term for several skin diseases; see Leviticus 13 [2]Some manuscripts add *disciples* [3]Some manuscripts insert *new*

giveness of sins. 29 I tell you I will not drink again of this fruit of the vine until that day when I drink it new with you in my Father's kingdom."

Jesus Foretells Peter's Denial

30 And when they had sung a hymn, they went out to the Mount of Olives. 31 Then Jesus said to them, "You will all fall away because of me this night. For it is written, 'I will strike the shepherd, and the sheep of the flock will be scattered.' 32 But after I am raised up, I will go before you to Galilee." 33 Peter answered him, "Though they all fall away because of you, I will never fall away." 34 Jesus said to him, "Truly, I tell you, this very night, before the rooster crows, you will deny me three times." 35 Peter said to him, "Even if I must die with you, I will not deny you!" And all the disciples said the same.

Jesus Prays in Gethsemane

36 Then Jesus went with them to a place called Gethsemane, and he said to his disciples, "Sit here, while I go over there and pray." 37 And taking with him Peter and the two sons of Zebedee, he began to be sorrowful and troubled. 38 Then he said to them, "My soul is very sorrowful, even to death; remain here, and watch[1] with me." 39 And going a little farther he fell on his face and prayed, saying, "My Father, if it be possible, let this cup pass from me; nevertheless, not as I will, but as you will." 40 And he came to the disciples and found them sleeping. And he said to Peter, "So, could you not watch with me one hour? 41 Watch and pray that you may not enter into temptation. The spirit indeed is willing, but the flesh is weak." 42 Again, for the second time, he went away and prayed, "My Father, if this cannot pass unless I drink it, your will be done." 43 And again he came and found them sleeping, for their eyes were heavy. 44 So, leaving them again, he went away and prayed for the third time, saying the same words again. 45 Then he came to the disciples and said to them, "Sleep and take your rest later on.[2] See, the hour is at hand, and the Son of Man is betrayed into the hands of sinners. 46 Rise, let us be going; see, my betrayer is at hand."

Betrayal and Arrest of Jesus

47 While he was still speaking, Judas came, one of the twelve, and with him a great crowd with swords and clubs, from the chief priests and the elders of the people. 48 Now the betrayer had given them a sign, saying, "The one I will kiss is the man; seize him." 49 And he came up to Jesus at once and said, "Greetings, Rabbi!" And he kissed him. 50 Jesus said to him, "Friend, do what you came to do."[3] Then they came up and laid hands on Jesus and seized him. 51 And behold, one of those who were with Jesus stretched out his hand and drew his sword and struck the servant[4] of the high priest and cut off his ear. 52 Then Jesus said to him, "Put your sword back into its place. For all who take the sword will perish by the sword. 53 Do you think that I cannot appeal to my Father, and he will at once send me more than twelve legions of angels? 54 But how then should the Scriptures be fulfilled, that it must be so?" 55 At that hour Jesus said to the crowds, "Have you come out as against a robber, with swords and clubs to capture me? Day after day I sat in the temple teaching, and you did not seize me. 56 But all this has taken place that the Scriptures of the prophets might be fulfilled." Then all the disciples left him and fled.

Jesus Before Caiaphas and the Council

57 Then those who had seized Jesus led him to Caiaphas the high priest, where the scribes and the elders had gathered. 58 And Peter was following him at a distance, as far as the courtyard of the high priest, and going inside he sat with the guards to see the end. 59 Now the chief priests and the whole council[5] were seeking

[1] Or *keep awake*; also verses 40, 41 [2] Or *Are you still sleeping and taking your rest?* [3] Or *Friend, why are you here?* [4] Or *bondservant* [5] Greek *Sanhedrin*

OLD TESTAMENT FULFILLMENTS

The events that led up to the crucifixion of Jesus directly parallel what was prophesied about the Messiah as the suffering servant in the Old Testament. But not only did Jesus fulfill Old Testament prophecy; others around Jesus did as well.

Judas betrayed Jesus for 30 pieces of silver (v. 14), which was the equivalent to the price of a slave (Ex 21:32). Zechariah wrote about this exact price in his Messianic foreshadowing (Zec 11:12–13). Thirty pieces of silver was not a very large sum of money in that era, and in Matthew, Judas' story provides a stark contrast to the verses preceding his betrayal (Mt 26:6–13). While Mary went to great expense to anoint Jesus with precious oil, giving to Jesus what was probably her entire dowry (and therefore her entire future), Judas turned against Jesus for a relatively small price. Great is the cost of devotion, but cheap is the price of betrayal.

After the description of Judas' betrayal, Matthew transitioned to the preparations of the Passover meal. The Passover was celebrated in remembrance of God freeing his people from Egypt (Nu 9:2). However, for believers, Jesus completely transformed the way the meal was celebrated. It is now in remembrance of God freeing his people from sin and death through Jesus. In honoring old traditions, Jesus also created new traditions for believers to follow today. During this Passover celebration, Jesus represented the very fulfillment of the Passover's promise of deliverance from sin, ushering in a new covenant to replace the old covenant. This new covenant had been promised in the Old Testament multiple times (Jer 31:31–34; Eze 34:25–31; 37:26–28), and Jesus finally fulfilled it.

In addition to Judas and Jesus, Peter and the rest of the disciples also fulfilled Old Testament prophecies. While Peter's denial was a blatant betrayal of Jesus, it is important to remember that Peter was not the only disciple to avoid being associated with Jesus after his arrest. None of the other disciples had the courage to follow Jesus on that night; they all hid, which Jesus referred to by quoting Zechariah 13:7 (Mt 26:31). After Jesus' resurrection, ever the Good Shepherd, Jesus brought his flock back together (28:16–20), as he will again in the last days (Ac 2:17–21).

false testimony against Jesus that they might put him to death, [60]but they found none, though many false witnesses came forward. At last two came forward [61]and said, "This man said, 'I am able to destroy the temple of God, and to rebuild it in three days.'" [62]And the high priest stood up and said, "Have you no answer to make? What is it that these men testify against you?"[1] [63]But Jesus remained silent. And the high priest said to him, "I adjure you by the living God, tell us if you are the Christ, the Son of God." [64]Jesus said to him, "You have said so. But I tell you, from now on you will see the Son of Man seated at the right hand of Power and coming on the clouds of heaven." [65]Then the high priest tore his robes and said, "He has uttered blasphemy. What further witnesses do we need? You have now heard his blasphemy. [66]What is your judgment?" They answered, "He deserves death." [67]Then they spit in his face and struck him. And some slapped him, [68]saying, "Prophesy to us, you Christ! Who is it that struck you?"

Peter Denies Jesus

[69]Now Peter was sitting outside in the courtyard. And a servant girl came up to him and said, "You also were with Jesus the Galilean." [70]But he denied it before them all, saying, "I do not know what you mean." [71]And when he went out to the entrance, another servant girl saw him, and she said to the bystanders, "This man was with Jesus of Nazareth." [72]And again he denied it with an oath: "I do not know the man." [73]After a little while the bystanders came up and said to Peter, "Certainly you too are one of them, for your accent betrays you." [74]Then he began to invoke a curse on himself and to swear, "I do not know the man." And immediately the rooster crowed. [75]And Peter remembered the saying of Jesus, "Before the rooster crows, you will deny me three times." And he went out and wept bitterly.

Jesus Delivered to Pilate

27 When morning came, all the chief priests and the elders of the people took counsel against Jesus to put him to death. [2]And they bound him and led him away and delivered him over to Pilate the governor.

Judas Hangs Himself

[3]Then when Judas, his betrayer, saw that Jesus[2] was condemned, he changed his mind and brought back the thirty pieces of silver to the chief priests and the elders, [4]saying, "I have sinned by betraying innocent blood." They said, "What is that to us? See to it yourself." [5]And throwing down the pieces of silver into the temple, he departed, and he went and hanged himself. [6]But the chief priests, taking the pieces of silver, said, "It is not lawful to put them into the treasury, since it is blood money." [7]So they took counsel and bought with them the potter's field as a burial place for strangers. [8]Therefore that field has been called the Field of Blood to this day. [9]Then was fulfilled what had been spoken by the prophet Jeremiah, saying, "And they took the thirty pieces of silver, the price of him on whom a price had been set by some of the sons of Israel, [10]and they gave them for the potter's field, as the Lord directed me."

Jesus Before Pilate

[11]Now Jesus stood before the governor, and the governor asked him, "Are you the King of the Jews?" Jesus said, "You have said so." [12]But when he was accused by the chief priests and elders, he gave no answer. [13]Then Pilate said to him, "Do you not hear how many things they testify against you?" [14]But he gave him no answer, not even to a single charge, so that the governor was greatly amazed.

The Crowd Chooses Barabbas

[15]Now at the feast the governor was accustomed to release for the crowd any one prisoner whom they wanted. [16]And they had then a notorious prisoner called

[1]Or *Have you no answer to what these men testify against you?* [2]Greek *he*

SAVIOR

SEEING IS BELIEVING

GOSPELS TO ACTS 1

From the time my four children were very young, the legend of Disney World ran wild in their heads. Through the magic of cinema, they were transported to the magical world of Arendelle, where they dreamed of climbing the North Mountain. Through storybooks they have been "Under the Sea" with Ariel and Flounder. They each could see it all in their mind's eye. However, the reality was, they had not been there. They had only seen Disney through the eyes of others, but they had not seen it for themselves.

Then one Christmas, everything changed. We surprised them with a trip to Disney. We loaded the minivan and off we went. The ten-hour drive from our home felt like a thousand. The anticipation and excitement were on a whole other level. When we arrived, we went straight to meet the princesses. What had been only fairytales became real when Elsa, Anna, Snow White, Belle, and Tiana were standing in front of them.

The stories had been great. The movies were phenomenal, but when their faith had become sight, everything changed. Because seeing is believing.

The ancient Greeks believed that all the deep questions in the world could be explained in the *Logos*. Heraclitus and Aristotle used the *Logos* as a foundation in their philosophical works. By the time of John's Gospel the *Logos* had become the prevailing way of understanding the "higher power" that exists. However, John, under the inspiration of God, used the opening stanzas of his account to shed more light on this *Logos*. He began by acknowledging the eternality of the *Logos* by saying that it had been from the beginning. Thus, he was validating what his audience had understood for centuries. However, he then took it further by helping them understand that the *Logos* (word) is connected to the *Theos* (God). In fact, the *Logos* (word) is *Theos* (God). He was clarifying that the *Logos* is more than a "higher power." He is more than an "all knowing" spirit. The *Logos* is God.

John was not finished providing clarity. He takes his readers into a deeper understanding of who the *Logos* is by saying, "He was with God in the beginning." (See Jn 1:1.)

Who is this he? Where did *he* come from? John tells us that "in him was life, and the life was the light of men" (1:4). In using the personal pronoun, the Gospel writer helps us understand that God is not some far-off "being," unable to identify with humanity. No, he has definition and is knowable. The *Logos* has substance and character and is not a mysterious force. However, John had one more significant qualifier to add to help his readers understand the identity of the *Logos*. The *Logos* (Word) became flesh and dwelt among us!

The God of the universe who had, up to this point in history resided in his celestial home, had now taken up residence with humanity on earth. What was mystery is now reality. What was spirit is now flesh and blood. What had been experienced only by faith had now become sight. Seeing is believing.

The fact that sets the Christian gospel apart from all other belief systems is that God "gave his only Son" by sending him to earth (Jn 3:16). Jesus "did not count equality with God a thing to be grasped, but emptied himself, by taking the form of a servant, being born in the likeness of men" (Php 2:6–7). God, in his grace, sent Jesus to earth so that we could see him and therefore believe him.

God knew that humanity would need to tangibly see him, to experience him, so that we could identify with him. He stepped out of cosmic glory for 33 years. He walked the earth, living in a physical place and time. He had human emotion and was able to identify with humanity's struggles. He modeled what living in the kingdom of God should look like. Ultimately, he stood in humanity's place. The place where all of humankind, because of our sin, deserved to be.

We have a Savior who was seen and therefore can be believed.

Jesus Lived in a Real Time and Place

Our Savior was born in Bethlehem, lived in Nazareth, worked in Galilee, died and then rose from the grave in Jerusalem. These are real places in the Near East Mediterranean region of earth. Anyone today can visit these exact sites. You can walk the grounds, touch the dirt, and smell the aromas.

A few years ago I had the opportunity to be in the Holy Land. While driving along the western shore of the Sea of Galilee, we came to the town of Magdala. Magdala was the home of Mary *Magdalene*, who played an integral role in Jesus' earthly ministry.

Modern-day Magdala is a small resort community north of the town of Tiberias referenced in John 6:23 and east of Mount Arbel. In recent years, a major archaeological discovery was made here. As the ancient ruins of the city were uncovered, among the discoveries were many homes, a marketplace, and a synagogue. In the synagogue a remnant of the mosaic tile floor was discovered. The archaeological experts date the floor to the time of Jesus, making it highly likely that the floor I saw was the same one he walked on 2,000 years ago. My faith was bolstered by knowing that the stories I read in the Bible about Jesus' encounters with Mary Magdalene happened in a real place, a place I could visit.

SAVIOR

(CONTINUED)

GOSPELS TO ACTS 1

For Christians, throughout the centuries, being able to see the places of Jesus' ministry has provided a foundation to our beliefs.

Jesus Fulfilled the Old Testament Prophecies about Himself

Not only did Jesus live in a real time and place, but also the most significant aspects of his ministry had been prophesied about in the Old Testament, thousands of years prior. Many of the movements during his 33-year life were foretold by the prophets Micah, Zechariah, Isaiah, Malachi, and many others.

The prophet Micah described that the Messiah would be born in Bethlehem (Mic 5:2). The book of Malachi tells us that a "messenger," who ended up being John the Baptist, would prepare the way for Jesus and announce the coming of his ministry (Mal 3:1). Zechariah foretells that Jesus would be sold out for 30 pieces of silver (Zec 11:13). Psalm 22:16–18 tells us that not only would Jesus be crucified, but also that his robe would be divided.

Imagine, if before you were born, your parents wrote a book predicting whom you would marry, where you would live, and how many children you would have. You would be blown away at their ability to correctly guess those handful of milestones about your life. However, the reality is, even for the people who know you best, it is not very likely that they would even get a few things right about how your life was going to turn out.

In Jesus' case, scholars point to the fact that Jesus fulfilled over 400 Old Testament prophecies about the coming Messiah. Thousands of years before he walked the earth, people were foretelling intimate details of his life and ministry. To get a few details right might be chalked up to coincidence, but to get hundreds right makes it a miraculous revelation about the Son of God.

Seeing the prophecies of the Old Testament come to fruition gave the early Christians, and gives Christians today, the confidence to believe that Jesus is the Messiah, the Savior.

Jesus Identifies with Us

Our Savior, because he walked the earth as God in human flesh, can relate to the joys and struggles that humankind faces. He was not a God who only knew about human weakness in theoretical terms. He knew about them in practical terms because he lived through them. The writer of Hebrews says, "For we do not have a high priest who is unable to sympathize with our weaknesses, but one who in every respect has been tempted as we are, yet without sin" (Heb 4:15). In Jesus, God came near to his people, so he could relate to them in a tangible way.

Jesus Celebrated

All throughout the New Testament we see instances where Jesus displays the humanity in his divinity. At the wedding feast at Cana, Jesus celebrated. In his divinity, the wedding at Cana was Jesus' first recorded miracle. It is where he turned water into choice wine (see Jn 2:10). However, in his humanity, Jesus was at this wedding as an invited guest.

It is not hard to imagine that Jesus had the same emotion that anyone has when attending a wedding—joy for the couple. Jesus identifies with human celebration.

Jesus Wept

Conversely, Jesus mourned with those who were mourning. After Mary and Martha's brother (and Jesus' friend) died, Jesus was there. He was brokenhearted for their agony. He saw their pain, and he "wept" (Jn 11:35) with them. He did not rush to fix the problem. (He would get to that later.) No, he met Mary and Martha where they were. He identified with them in their suffering.

Jesus is not a cosmic overlord who is unable to understand the plight of humans. Quite the opposite. He can identify with humanity because he was human and knows our exact emotions. Seeing Jesus put his emotions on display helps us believe that empathy for others is possible.

Jesus Modeled Kingdom Living

Kings do not willingly give up power. They hold onto it with everything they have. However, Jesus modeled the upside-down nature of God's kingdom by living out the reality that the most powerful people are the ones who hold their position loosely. He showed that kingdom living is contrary to the way humans are inclined to live.

Jesus, though divine, did not wield the power of his divinity over humanity. He did the exact opposite. He became a servant to humanity by taking on its likeness. He literally was willing to do anything to serve other humans. He was even willing to die for them (see Php 2:6–8).

Jesus modeled kingdom thinking by showing that if a person was willing to lose their life for another person, then literally they would be willing to do anything for them. On the surface when Scripture instructs us, "Bless those who persecute you," it sounds radical. But it is not radical if you were willing to give your life for them.

Seeing Jesus model the upside-down nature of the kingdom makes us believe that the radical serving of others is possible.

Jesus Stood in Our Place

Jesus had to come to earth because, ultimately, he would have to physically stand in our place through his death on the cross.

SAVIOR

(CONTINUED)

GOSPELS TO ACTS 1

In the Old Testament, the way that the people of God restored their relationship to him was through a physical sacrifice. The system required a blood sacrifice. Saying "I am sorry" would not do the trick. No, a living creature without blemish had to stand in for the guilty party. Blood was the currency of forgiveness.

This is why Jesus had to be both divine and human. In his divinity, he would lead a perfect life without sin. In his humanity, he would physically stand in for sinful humanity. "For our sake he [God] made him to be sin who knew no sin, so that in him we might become the righteousness of God" (2Co 5:21). One of the Protestant Reformers said, "The Son of God, though spotlessly pure, took upon him the disgrace and ignominy of our iniquities, and in return clothes us with his purity."

Jesus was our substitute. Theologians use the word *propitiation* to describe what Jesus has done on our behalf. However, that is just a big word that means Jesus took the place where we were meant to stand. Because of our sin, we deserved death. We deserved wrath. We deserved judgment, but Jesus physically took that upon himself.

Seeing Jesus stand in our place helps us to believe that he is our Savior.

Today, when my kids talk about Disney World, they are talking from firsthand experience. They are no longer trying to describe something in the abstract. They can describe it in concrete detail that only firsthand experience can provide. They are confident Disney exists because they have seen Disney.

Jesus did not live in the realm of the abstract. He came to earth. He embraced our messiness all the way to death, and in the end overcame death by rising from the grave. This would all sound like a fairytale if not for the fact that it all happened in a real time and place—a place we can visit today—and happened among real people who provided their eyewitness accounts.

We can see the places where Jesus lived. We can read firsthand accounts of the miraculous nature of his 33 years on earth, and, therefore, we can believe that everything about him is true, because seeing is believing.

BEGINNINGS	REVOLT	PEOPLE	INTERTESTAMENTAL PERIOD	SAVIOR	CHURCH	FOREVER
GENESIS 1–2 (pg. 10)	GENESIS 3–11 (pg. 24)	GENESIS 12 to MALACHI (pg. 256)	(pg. 1468)	GOSPELS to ACTS 1 (pg. 1518)	ACTS 2 to REVELATION 20 (pg. 1686)	REVELATION 21–22 (pg. 1938)

Barabbas. 17So when they had gathered, Pilate said to them, "Whom do you want me to release for you: Barabbas, or Jesus who is called Christ?" 18For he knew that it was out of envy that they had delivered him up. 19Besides, while he was sitting on the judgment seat, his wife sent word to him, "Have nothing to do with that righteous man, for I have suffered much because of him today in a dream." 20Now the chief priests and the elders persuaded the crowd to ask for Barabbas and destroy Jesus. 21The governor again said to them, "Which of the two do you want me to release for you?" And they said, "Barabbas." 22Pilate said to them, "Then what shall I do with Jesus who is called Christ?" They all said, "Let him be crucified!" 23And he said, "Why? What evil has he done?" But they shouted all the more, "Let him be crucified!"

Pilate Delivers Jesus to Be Crucified

24So when Pilate saw that he was gaining nothing, but rather that a riot was beginning, he took water and washed his hands before the crowd, saying, "I am innocent of this man's blood;[1] see to it yourselves." 25And all the people answered, "His blood be on us and on our children!" 26Then he released for them Barabbas, and having scourged[2] Jesus, delivered him to be crucified.

Jesus Is Mocked

27Then the soldiers of the governor took Jesus into the governor's headquarters,[3] and they gathered the whole battalion[4] before him. 28And they stripped him and put a scarlet robe on him, 29and twisting together a crown of thorns, they put it on his head and put a reed in his right hand. And kneeling before him, they mocked him, saying, "Hail, King of the Jews!" 30And they spit on him and took the reed and struck him on the head. 31And when they had mocked him, they stripped him of the robe and put his own clothes on him and led him away to crucify him.

The Crucifixion

32As they went out, they found a man of Cyrene, Simon by name. They compelled this man to carry his cross. 33And when they came to a place called Golgotha (which means Place of a Skull), 34they offered him wine to drink, mixed with gall, but when he tasted it, he would not drink it. 35And when they had crucified him, they divided his garments among them by casting lots. 36Then they sat down and kept watch over him there. 37And over his head they put the charge against him, which read, "This is Jesus, the King of the Jews." 38Then two robbers were crucified with him, one on the right and one on the left. 39And those who passed by derided him, wagging their heads 40and saying, "You who would destroy the temple and rebuild it in three days, save yourself! If you are the Son of God, come down from the cross." 41So also the chief priests, with the scribes and elders, mocked him, saying, 42"He saved others; he cannot save himself. He is the King of Israel; let him come down now from the cross, and we will believe in him. 43He trusts in God; let God deliver him now, if he desires him. For he said, 'I am the Son of God.'" 44And the robbers who were crucified with him also reviled him in the same way.

The Death of Jesus

45Now from the sixth hour[5] there was darkness over all the land[6] until the ninth hour.[7] 46And about the ninth hour Jesus cried out with a loud voice, saying, "Eli, Eli, lema sabachthani?" that is, "My God, my God, why have you forsaken me?" 47And some of the bystanders, hearing it, said, "This man is calling Elijah." 48And one of them at once ran and took a sponge, filled it with sour wine, and

[1]Some manuscripts *this righteous blood*, or *this righteous man's blood* [2]A Roman judicial penalty, consisting of a severe beating with a multi-lashed whip containing embedded pieces of bone and metal [3]Greek *the praetorium* [4]Greek *cohort*; a tenth of a Roman legion, usually about 600 men [5]That is, noon [6]Or *earth* [7]That is, 3 P.M.

MATTHEW 27:62–66

WORRIED ABOUT A RESURRECTION

Matthew made sure to emphasize the fact that the tomb was sealed in order to show that there was no possible way for the disciples to steal the body. The Jewish leaders and the guard were instructed to "make it as secure as you can" (v. 65), and they did so by placing a seal on the stone that was rolled in front of the tomb and also by placing a guard there. After the grave was reported empty and the disciples began telling others about the resurrection, those who opposed Jesus attempted to spread the rumor that the disciples had stolen the body (Mt 28:11–15). However, Matthew made it clear in his Gospel that the religious leaders had sealed the tomb specifically for the purpose of preventing anyone from stealing the body and faking a resurrection, which directly contradicts the false narrative they attempted to spread. There is no way the disciples could have stolen the body of Christ, and Matthew did well to show that despite the chief priests and Pharisees' attempts to guard the tomb, there was nothing they could do to prevent Jesus' actual, physical resurrection from the dead.

put it on a reed and gave it to him to drink. 49But the others said, "Wait, let us see
whether Elijah will come to save him." 50And Jesus cried out again with a loud
voice and yielded up his spirit.
51And behold, the curtain of the temple was torn in two, from top to bottom.
And the earth shook, and the rocks were split. 52The tombs also were opened.
And many bodies of the saints who had fallen asleep were raised, 53and coming
out of the tombs after his resurrection they went into the holy city and appeared
to many. 54When the centurion and those who were with him, keeping watch over
Jesus, saw the earthquake and what took place, they were filled with awe and said,
"Truly this was the Son[1] of God!"
55There were also many women there, looking on from a distance, who had
followed Jesus from Galilee, ministering to him, 56among whom were Mary Magdalene and Mary the mother of James and Joseph and the mother of the sons of
Zebedee.

Jesus Is Buried

57When it was evening, there came a rich man from Arimathea, named Joseph,
who also was a disciple of Jesus. 58He went to Pilate and asked for the body of
Jesus. Then Pilate ordered it to be given to him. 59And Joseph took the body and
wrapped it in a clean linen shroud 60and laid it in his own new tomb, which he
had cut in the rock. And he rolled a great stone to the entrance of the tomb and
went away. 61Mary Magdalene and the other Mary were there, sitting opposite
the tomb.

The Guard at the Tomb

62The next day, that is, after the day of Preparation, the chief priests and the
Pharisees gathered before Pilate 63and said, "Sir, we remember how that impos-
tor said, while he was still alive, 'After three days I will rise.' 64Therefore order the
tomb to be made secure until the third day, lest his disciples go and steal him away
and tell the people, 'He has risen from the dead,' and the last fraud will be worse
than the first." 65Pilate said to them, "You have a guard[2] of soldiers. Go, make it
as secure as you can." 66So they went and made the tomb secure by sealing the
stone and setting a guard.

The Resurrection

28 Now after the Sabbath, toward the dawn of the first day of the week, Mary
Magdalene and the other Mary went to see the tomb. 2And behold, there
was a great earthquake, for an angel of the Lord descended from heaven and came
and rolled back the stone and sat on it. 3His appearance was like lightning, and
his clothing white as snow. 4And for fear of him the guards trembled and became
like dead men. 5But the angel said to the women, "Do not be afraid, for I know
that you seek Jesus who was crucified. 6He is not here, for he has risen, as he said.
Come, see the place where he[3] lay. 7Then go quickly and tell his disciples that
he has risen from the dead, and behold, he is going before you to Galilee; there
you will see him. See, I have told you." 8So they departed quickly from the tomb
with fear and great joy, and ran to tell his disciples. 9And behold, Jesus met them
and said, "Greetings!" And they came up and took hold of his feet and worshiped
him. 10Then Jesus said to them, "Do not be afraid; go and tell my brothers to go to
Galilee, and there they will see me."

The Report of the Guard

11While they were going, behold, some of the guard went into the city and told
the chief priests all that had taken place. 12And when they had assembled with
the elders and taken counsel, they gave a sufficient sum of money to the soldiers

[1]Or *a son* [2]Or *Take a guard* [3]Some manuscripts *the Lord*

JESUS' ASSIGNMENT TO HIS DISCIPLES

The Great Commission (vv. 19–20) is a command that rests on the authority of Christ described in the preceding verse. The phrase "Go ... make disciples" is commonly spoken among believers, but it is important to note the word "therefore" that comes between. Followers of Jesus are expected to *go and make disciples* solely because of who Jesus is and with the power and authority that he has been given (v. 18). Jesus has all authority in heaven and earth, and he doesn't give this command without empowering his followers to go and tell others about who he is.

The Great Commission is not the first call for world evangelism in the Bible. In fact, Genesis 12:1–3 describes God's promise that Abraham and his descendants would be a blessing to all nations. Jesus was simply building on what God had already told his people long before. Believers are expected to share the true and life-giving story of Jesus to every nation far and wide; this command has always been true for people who follow Jesus.

Jesus' command involves a simple three-step process; go, baptize, and teach. Within this phrase, Jesus clarified exactly what he expects of his followers. They are to first go and tell others about him so that others can know and understand his story. Then they are to baptize those who have heard the story so that they can publicly declare their belief in who he is. Finally, believers need to teach and encourage one another (Col 3:16). Believers will never stop teaching each other and learning about the nature of God. The command to go, baptize, and teach was Jesus' last command in the book of Matthew, and it is of the utmost importance for followers of Christ.

However, Jesus did not ask his disciples to do so alone. He promised that although he was leaving them physically he would always be with them through his Spirit. As long as believers hold fast to Jesus and rely on the Holy Spirit, the pathway is open for his followers to do what they have been called to do (Php 4:13).

13 and said, "Tell people, 'His disciples came by night and stole him away while we
were asleep.' 14 And if this comes to the governor's ears, we will satisfy him and
keep you out of trouble." 15 So they took the money and did as they were directed.
And this story has been spread among the Jews to this day.

The Great Commission

16 Now the eleven disciples went to Galilee, to the mountain to which Jesus had
directed them. 17 And when they saw him they worshiped him, but some doubted.
18 And Jesus came and said to them, "All authority in heaven and on earth has been
given to me. 19 Go therefore and make disciples of all nations, baptizing them in[1]
the name of the Father and of the Son and of the Holy Spirit, 20 teaching them to
observe all that I have commanded you. And behold, I am with you always, to the
end of the age."

---

[1] Or *into*

JESUS: OUR TRUE GOD

MARK

MARK

BIRTH OF JESUS *c. 5 BC*	PONTIUS PILATE GOVERNS JUDEA *c. AD 26 – 36*	JESUS' MINISTRY, DEATH, RESURRECTION *c. AD 27 – 30*

Jesus is the Son of God. This is the message of Mark's Gospel, which contains an action-packed summary of the life and accomplishments of God's Son, Jesus Christ. Mark provides his readers with vivid, compelling, and emotional descriptions of many of Jesus' greatest works. Informed by eyewitness accounts, especially by the disciple Peter, Mark wrote with the clarity and precision of one who knew the life-transforming implications of Jesus' life, death, and resurrection.

The shortest of the Gospels, Mark's Gospel is written to Gentile believers, especially Romans, in an effort to show that Jesus' might and miracles prove that he is God in the flesh. Jesus' birth and baptism are covered in the span of only 13 verses, with Mark's main focus being the ministry of the second person of the Trinity.

Mark selected critical episodes and interactions from Jesus' ministry and often arranged them in thematic order to show that Jesus is "the Son of God" (1:1). The status is validated through Jesus' breathtaking power over all of his creation. He is powerful over the wind and the waves, the demonic kingdom, and even sickness and death. For Mark, there was no denying the fact that these miracles prove Jesus is who he says he is and that all people owe him their supreme allegiance.

Mark invites his readers to hear and respond to the invitation offered by the Son of God. Since Jesus is God, his words are the word of God. This message is good news for those who have ears to hear the gracious call of God through Jesus. The kingdom of God has come on earth in the person of Jesus. The throne of David is occupied by the true anointed one, the King of kings, who rules and reigns with perfect justice and righteousness. Of his kingdom, there will be no end.

Kingdom citizens are sent to declare and demonstrate this gospel message to the world. Disciples are sent in the power of God to do the work of God. Their passionate zeal spreads the message of the availability of the kingdom and plants the seeds for the development of the church. Mark himself gave his life to this mission by serving as a travel companion to Paul and Barnabas as they established the church throughout the book of Acts. These churches would continue to proclaim the message: Jesus is the Son of God.

A VOICE CAME FROM HEAVEN,
"YOU ARE MY BELOVED SON;
WITH YOU I AM WELL PLEASED."

Mark 1:11

MARK

John the Baptist Prepares the Way

1 The beginning of the gospel of Jesus Christ, the Son of God.[1]
2As it is written in Isaiah the prophet,[2]

"Behold, I send my messenger before your face,
who will prepare your way,
3 the voice of one crying in the wilderness:
'Prepare[3] the way of the Lord,
make his paths straight,'"

4John appeared, baptizing in the wilderness and proclaiming a baptism of repentance for the forgiveness of sins. 5And all the country of Judea and all Jerusalem
were going out to him and were being baptized by him in the river Jordan, confessing their sins. 6Now John was clothed with camel's hair and wore a leather belt
around his waist and ate locusts and wild honey. 7And he preached, saying, "After
me comes he who is mightier than I, the strap of whose sandals I am not worthy
to stoop down and untie. 8I have baptized you with water, but he will baptize you
with the Holy Spirit."

The Baptism of Jesus

9In those days Jesus came from Nazareth of Galilee and was baptized by John
in the Jordan. 10And when he came up out of the water, immediately he saw the
heavens being torn open and the Spirit descending on him like a dove. 11And a
voice came from heaven, "You are my beloved Son;[4] with you I am well pleased."

The Temptation of Jesus

12The Spirit immediately drove him out into the wilderness. 13And he was in
the wilderness forty days, being tempted by Satan. And he was with the wild animals, and the angels were ministering to him.

Jesus Begins His Ministry

14Now after John was arrested, Jesus came into Galilee, proclaiming the gospel
of God, 15and saying, "The time is fulfilled, and the kingdom of God is at hand;[5]
repent and believe in the gospel."

Jesus Calls the First Disciples

16Passing alongside the Sea of Galilee, he saw Simon and Andrew the brother
of Simon casting a net into the sea, for they were fishermen. 17And Jesus said to
them, "Follow me, and I will make you become fishers of men."[6] 18And immediately they left their nets and followed him. 19And going on a little farther, he saw
James the son of Zebedee and John his brother, who were in their boat mending
the nets. 20And immediately he called them, and they left their father Zebedee in
the boat with the hired servants and followed him.

Jesus Heals a Man with an Unclean Spirit

21And they went into Capernaum, and immediately on the Sabbath he entered
the synagogue and was teaching. 22And they were astonished at his teaching, for
he taught them as one who had authority, and not as the scribes. 23And immediately there was in their synagogue a man with an unclean spirit. And he cried

MARK 1:14

THE GOOD NEWS

The world is full of bad news, and all of the bad news the world has ever known can be traced back to the Garden of Eden when Adam and Eve disobeyed God (Ge 3:1–24). Disobeying God's Word always leads to pain and suffering. Thankfully, God doesn't leave people in their pain. As soon as Adam and Eve brought chaos into God's good world, God promised to one day make everything right again (Ge 3:15). Humanity's fall corrupted God's perfect world and brought all of this bad news. But God comes to people with the gospel, the "Good News" that God has covered believers' sins through the work of Jesus and will one day make all things right through him. The gospel is not the news of what people must do in order to get to God; rather, the gospel is the news of what God has done to make a bridge to people. With Jesus, the reign and presence of God came into the world in a special way. Jesus came to fix the wrongs by going to the cross and by being broken for the sin of the world. God is in the business of "making all things new" (Rev 21:5). This is the Good News that Jesus came to share, and this is the news his people can tell their friends, family, and others throughout the world as well.

[1]Some manuscripts omit *the Son of God* [2]Some manuscripts *in the prophets* [3]Or *crying: Prepare in the wilderness* [4]Or *my Son, my* (or *the*) *Beloved* [5]Or *the kingdom of God has come near* [6]The Greek word *anthropoi* refers here to both men and women

out, 24“What have you to do with us, Jesus of Nazareth? Have you come to destroy
us? I know who you are—the Holy One of God.” 25But Jesus rebuked him, saying, “Be silent, and come out of him!” 26And the unclean spirit, convulsing him
and crying out with a loud voice, came out of him. 27And they were all amazed,
so that they questioned among themselves, saying, “What is this? A new teaching with authority! He commands even the unclean spirits, and they obey him.”
28And at once his fame spread everywhere throughout all the surrounding region
of Galilee.

Jesus Heals Many

29And immediately he[1] left the synagogue and entered the house of Simon
and Andrew, with James and John. 30Now Simon’s mother-in-law lay ill with a
fever, and immediately they told him about her. 31And he came and took her by
the hand and lifted her up, and the fever left her, and she began to serve them.

32That evening at sundown they brought to him all who were sick or oppressed by demons. 33And the whole city was gathered together at the door. 34And
he healed many who were sick with various diseases, and cast out many demons.
And he would not permit the demons to speak, because they knew him.

Jesus Preaches in Galilee

35And rising very early in the morning, while it was still dark, he departed and
went out to a desolate place, and there he prayed. 36And Simon and those who
were with him searched for him, 37and they found him and said to him, “Everyone
is looking for you.” 38And he said to them, “Let us go on to the next towns, that I
may preach there also, for that is why I came out.” 39And he went throughout all
Galilee, preaching in their synagogues and casting out demons.

Jesus Cleanses a Leper

40And a leper[2] came to him, imploring him, and kneeling said to him, “If you
will, you can make me clean.” 41Moved with pity, he stretched out his hand and
touched him and said to him, “I will; be clean.” 42And immediately the leprosy
left him, and he was made clean. 43And Jesus[3] sternly charged him and sent him
away at once, 44and said to him, “See that you say nothing to anyone, but go, show
yourself to the priest and offer for your cleansing what Moses commanded, for a
proof to them.” 45But he went out and began to talk freely about it, and to spread
the news, so that Jesus could no longer openly enter a town, but was out in desolate places, and people were coming to him from every quarter.

Jesus Heals a Paralytic

2 And when he returned to Capernaum after some days, it was reported that he
was at home. 2And many were gathered together, so that there was no more
room, not even at the door. And he was preaching the word to them. 3And they
came, bringing to him a paralytic carried by four men. 4And when they could
not get near him because of the crowd, they removed the roof above him, and
when they had made an opening, they let down the bed on which the paralytic lay.
5And when Jesus saw their faith, he said to the paralytic, “Son, your sins are forgiven.” 6Now some of the scribes were sitting there, questioning in their hearts,
7“Why does this man speak like that? He is blaspheming! Who can forgive sins
but God alone?” 8And immediately Jesus, perceiving in his spirit that they thus
questioned within themselves, said to them, “Why do you question these things
in your hearts? 9Which is easier, to say to the paralytic, ‘Your sins are forgiven,’ or
to say, ‘Rise, take up your bed and walk’? 10But that you may know that the Son of
Man has authority on earth to forgive sins”—he said to the paralytic— 11“I say to
you, rise, pick up your bed, and go home.” 12And he rose and immediately picked

---

1 Some manuscripts *they* 2 *Leprosy* was a term for several skin diseases; see Leviticus 13 3 Greek *he*; also verse 45

up his bed and went out before them all, so that they were all amazed and glorified God, saying, "We never saw anything like this!"

Jesus Calls Levi

13He went out again beside the sea, and all the crowd was coming to him, and
he was teaching them. 14And as he passed by, he saw Levi the son of Alphaeus sitting at the tax booth, and he said to him, "Follow me." And he rose and followed
him.

15And as he reclined at table in his house, many tax collectors and sinners
were reclining with Jesus and his disciples, for there were many who followed
him. 16And the scribes of[1] the Pharisees, when they saw that he was eating with
sinners and tax collectors, said to his disciples, "Why does he eat[2] with tax collectors and sinners?" 17And when Jesus heard it, he said to them, "Those who are
well have no need of a physician, but those who are sick. I came not to call the
righteous, but sinners."

A Question About Fasting

18Now John's disciples and the Pharisees were fasting. And people came and
said to him, "Why do John's disciples and the disciples of the Pharisees fast, but
your disciples do not fast?" 19And Jesus said to them, "Can the wedding guests fast
while the bridegroom is with them? As long as they have the bridegroom with
them, they cannot fast. 20The days will come when the bridegroom is taken away
from them, and then they will fast in that day. 21No one sews a piece of unshrunk
cloth on an old garment. If he does, the patch tears away from it, the new from the
old, and a worse tear is made. 22And no one puts new wine into old wineskins. If
he does, the wine will burst the skins—and the wine is destroyed, and so are the
skins. But new wine is for fresh wineskins."[3]

Jesus Is Lord of the Sabbath

23One Sabbath he was going through the grainfields, and as they made their
way, his disciples began to pluck heads of grain. 24And the Pharisees were saying
to him, "Look, why are they doing what is not lawful on the Sabbath?" 25And he
said to them, "Have you never read what David did, when he was in need and was
hungry, he and those who were with him: 26how he entered the house of God, in
the time of[4] Abiathar the high priest, and ate the bread of the Presence, which it
is not lawful for any but the priests to eat, and also gave it to those who were with
him?" 27And he said to them, "The Sabbath was made for man, not man for the
Sabbath. 28So the Son of Man is lord even of the Sabbath."

A Man with a Withered Hand

3 Again he entered the synagogue, and a man was there with a withered hand.
2And they watched Jesus,[5] to see whether he would heal him on the Sabbath,
so that they might accuse him. 3And he said to the man with the withered hand,
"Come here." 4And he said to them, "Is it lawful on the Sabbath to do good or to
do harm, to save life or to kill?" But they were silent. 5And he looked around at
them with anger, grieved at their hardness of heart, and said to the man, "Stretch
out your hand." He stretched it out, and his hand was restored. 6The Pharisees
went out and immediately held counsel with the Herodians against him, how to
destroy him.

A Great Crowd Follows Jesus

7Jesus withdrew with his disciples to the sea, and a great crowd followed, from
Galilee and Judea 8and Jerusalem and Idumea and from beyond the Jordan and
from around Tyre and Sidon. When the great crowd heard all that he was doing,

---

MARK 2:13–17

TAX COLLECTORS AND SINNERS

Religion that leaves Jesus out of the equation teaches that people can do enough good to earn God's love and acceptance. This kind of religion manipulates the system by putting God in your debt. Religious people have difficulty with Jesus because he challenges their understanding of God and salvation. Too often people believe they can earn their way to heaven, but Jesus came to save people who will never be good enough to save themselves. For people who think too highly of themselves, the free gift of salvation that Jesus offers is offensive. Tragically, people who think they are good enough don't see any need for a Savior. During Jesus' ministry, the people who knew they had problems flocked to him: tax collectors, women of questionable character, and others who saw their own desperate need. The religious leaders of his day didn't understand how or why a good, moral religious teacher like Jesus could spend time with such bad people. But Jesus knew that all people, without exception, need saving. As the Good Shepherd, Jesus came to seek and to save the lost (Lk 19:10).

---

[1]Some manuscripts *and* [2]Some manuscripts add *and drink* [3]Some manuscripts omit *But new wine is for fresh wineskins* [4]Or *in the passage about* [5]Greek *him*

they came to him. [9]And he told his disciples to have a boat ready for him because of the crowd, lest they crush him, [10]for he had healed many, so that all who had diseases pressed around him to touch him. [11]And whenever the unclean spirits saw him, they fell down before him and cried out, "You are the Son of God." [12]And he strictly ordered them not to make him known.

The Twelve Apostles

[13]And he went up on the mountain and called to him those whom he desired, and they came to him. [14]And he appointed twelve (whom he also named apostles) so that they might be with him and he might send them out to preach [15]and have authority to cast out demons. [16]He appointed the twelve: Simon (to whom he gave the name Peter); [17]James the son of Zebedee and John the brother of James (to whom he gave the name Boanerges, that is, Sons of Thunder); [18]Andrew, and Philip, and Bartholomew, and Matthew, and Thomas, and James the son of Alphaeus, and Thaddaeus, and Simon the Zealot,[1] [19]and Judas Iscariot, who betrayed him.

[20]Then he went home, and the crowd gathered again, so that they could not even eat. [21]And when his family heard it, they went out to seize him, for they were saying, "He is out of his mind."

Blasphemy Against the Holy Spirit

[22]And the scribes who came down from Jerusalem were saying, "He is possessed by Beelzebul," and "by the prince of demons he casts out the demons." [23]And he called them to him and said to them in parables, "How can Satan cast out Satan? [24]If a kingdom is divided against itself, that kingdom cannot stand. [25]And if a house is divided against itself, that house will not be able to stand. [26]And if Satan has risen up against himself and is divided, he cannot stand, but is coming to an end. [27]But no one can enter a strong man's house and plunder his goods, unless he first binds the strong man. Then indeed he may plunder his house.

[28]"Truly, I say to you, all sins will be forgiven the children of man, and whatever blasphemies they utter, [29]but whoever blasphemes against the Holy Spirit never has forgiveness, but is guilty of an eternal sin"— [30]for they were saying, "He has an unclean spirit."

Jesus' Mother and Brothers

[31]And his mother and his brothers came, and standing outside they sent to him and called him. [32]And a crowd was sitting around him, and they said to him, "Your mother and your brothers[2] are outside, seeking you." [33]And he answered them, "Who are my mother and my brothers?" [34]And looking about at those who sat around him, he said, "Here are my mother and my brothers! [35]For whoever does the will of God, he is my brother and sister and mother."

The Parable of the Sower

4 Again he began to teach beside the sea. And a very large crowd gathered about him, so that he got into a boat and sat in it on the sea, and the whole crowd was beside the sea on the land. [2]And he was teaching them many things in parables, and in his teaching he said to them: [3]"Listen! Behold, a sower went out to sow. [4]And as he sowed, some seed fell along the path, and the birds came and devoured it. [5]Other seed fell on rocky ground, where it did not have much soil, and immediately it sprang up, since it had no depth of soil. [6]And when the sun rose, it was scorched, and since it had no root, it withered away. [7]Other seed fell among thorns, and the thorns grew up and choked it, and it yielded no grain. [8]And other seeds fell into good soil and produced grain, growing up and increasing and

[1]Greek *kananaios*, meaning *zealot* [2]Other manuscripts add *and your sisters*

MARK 3:13–19

THE TWELVE APOSTLES

Jesus' strategy to influence the world was to invest in people and then unleash them to be his ambassadors.

Note several characteristics of the men he chose as his disciples. First, he chose ordinary people. One might think a global strategy would include people of global influence; however, Jesus chose the ordinary. He picked fishermen and tax collectors and others of humble routine, those we would consider "blue-collar" status. They were no-names. Nobodies.

Second, Jesus' disciples were invited. Discipleship for these men began with an invitation. He invited them to eat with him, talk with him, travel with him, and learn from him. He cared for them personally. He instilled in them everything that they would need to preach and cast out demons (vv. 14–15). His instruction over their lives came not through lecture but through life. These men observed Jesus in the good moments and the bad, and in so doing learned how to emulate his life.

Third, some of the disciples received new names. Jesus gave James and John the moniker "Sons of Thunder." We know he also gave Simon the name Peter, meaning "rock." Through the Bible we see instances of God changing the names of people when something significant happened in their lives. God changed the name of Abram ("exalted father") to Abraham ("father of a multitude") (Ge 17:3–5), and Jacob ("deceiver") became Israel ("he strives with God") (Ge 32:28). Individuals in the Bible receive new names as a sign of the new purpose that God intends. Their lives were once headed in a particular direction, and now, under divine authority, they are headed in a completely new trajectory.

Jesus' leadership model and strategy to influence the world is one that his followers today can use. Paul implemented this model himself by personally investing his life into Timothy. To Timothy he wrote, "And what you have heard from me in the presence of many witnesses entrust to faithful men, who will be able to teach others also" (2Ti 2:2). Likewise, followers of Jesus should spend their lives inviting a few people into an intentional and life-giving relationship, just like Jesus did.

yielding thirtyfold and sixtyfold and a hundredfold." [9]And he said, "He who has ears to hear, let him hear."

The Purpose of the Parables

[10]And when he was alone, those around him with the twelve asked him about the parables. [11]And he said to them, "To you has been given the secret of the kingdom of God, but for those outside everything is in parables, [12]so that

"'they may indeed see but not perceive,
    and may indeed hear but not understand,
  lest they should turn and be forgiven.'"

[13]And he said to them, "Do you not understand this parable? How then will you understand all the parables? [14]The sower sows the word. [15]And these are the ones along the path, where the word is sown: when they hear, Satan immediately comes and takes away the word that is sown in them. [16]And these are the ones sown on rocky ground: the ones who, when they hear the word, immediately receive it with joy. [17]And they have no root in themselves, but endure for a while; then, when tribulation or persecution arises on account of the word, immediately they fall away.[1] [18]And others are the ones sown among thorns. They are those who hear the word, [19]but the cares of the world and the deceitfulness of riches and the desires for other things enter in and choke the word, and it proves unfruitful. [20]But those that were sown on the good soil are the ones who hear the word and accept it and bear fruit, thirtyfold and sixtyfold and a hundredfold."

A Lamp Under a Basket

[21]And he said to them, "Is a lamp brought in to be put under a basket, or under a bed, and not on a stand? [22]For nothing is hidden except to be made manifest; nor is anything secret except to come to light. [23]If anyone has ears to hear, let him hear." [24]And he said to them, "Pay attention to what you hear: with the measure you use, it will be measured to you, and still more will be added to you. [25]For to the one who has, more will be given, and from the one who has not, even what he has will be taken away."

The Parable of the Seed Growing

[26]And he said, "The kingdom of God is as if a man should scatter seed on the ground. [27]He sleeps and rises night and day, and the seed sprouts and grows; he knows not how. [28]The earth produces by itself, first the blade, then the ear, then the full grain in the ear. [29]But when the grain is ripe, at once he puts in the sickle, because the harvest has come."

The Parable of the Mustard Seed

[30]And he said, "With what can we compare the kingdom of God, or what parable shall we use for it? [31]It is like a grain of mustard seed, which, when sown on the ground, is the smallest of all the seeds on earth, [32]yet when it is sown it grows up and becomes larger than all the garden plants and puts out large branches, so that the birds of the air can make nests in its shade."

[33]With many such parables he spoke the word to them, as they were able to hear it. [34]He did not speak to them without a parable, but privately to his own disciples he explained everything.

Jesus Calms a Storm

[35]On that day, when evening had come, he said to them, "Let us go across to the other side." [36]And leaving the crowd, they took him with them in the boat, just

[1]Or *stumble*

MARK 4:11

THE SECRET OF THE KINGDOM

Jesus' parables were like wrapped gifts given for people to enjoy. Jesus taught people about the kingdom by using these short stories that contained deeper meanings. Like all packages, the wrapping can either distract or captivate, and unless the package is opened, the gift remains unseen and not yet enjoyed. In the same way, Jesus' parables have to be unwrapped in order to uncover the application and understand the intent. Jesus said that even those who had physical sight and hearing might not understand what was presented to them (4:12, quoting Isa 6:9). Isaiah's words point to the fact that people's hardness of heart is created by sin. Those who seek the wisdom of God need to humble themselves, soften their hearts, and honestly seek truth in order to find it. The religious leaders in this account were unwilling to give up their pride, humble themselves, and learn from Jesus.

God is the One who fills us with understanding and gives wisdom (Col 1:9). All of this happens through Jesus, of whom John wrote, "And we know that the Son of God has come and has given us understanding, so that we may know him who is true; and we are in him who is true, in his Son Jesus Christ. He is the true God and eternal life" (1Jn 5:20).

as he was. And other boats were with him. 37And a great windstorm arose, and the waves were breaking into the boat, so that the boat was already filling. 38But he was in the stern, asleep on the cushion. And they woke him and said to him, "Teacher, do you not care that we are perishing?" 39And he awoke and rebuked the wind and said to the sea, "Peace! Be still!" And the wind ceased, and there was a great calm. 40He said to them, "Why are you so afraid? Have you still no faith?" 41And they were filled with great fear and said to one another, "Who then is this, that even the wind and the sea obey him?"

Jesus Heals a Man with a Demon

5 They came to the other side of the sea, to the country of the Gerasenes.[1] 2And when Jesus[2] had stepped out of the boat, immediately there met him out of the tombs a man with an unclean spirit. 3He lived among the tombs. And no one could bind him anymore, not even with a chain, 4for he had often been bound with shackles and chains, but he wrenched the chains apart, and he broke the shackles in pieces. No one had the strength to subdue him. 5Night and day among the tombs and on the mountains he was always crying out and cutting himself with stones. 6And when he saw Jesus from afar, he ran and fell down before him. 7And crying out with a loud voice, he said, "What have you to do with me, Jesus, Son of the Most High God? I adjure you by God, do not torment me." 8For he was saying to him, "Come out of the man, you unclean spirit!" 9And Jesus asked him, "What is your name?" He replied, "My name is Legion, for we are many." 10And he begged him earnestly not to send them out of the country. 11Now a great herd of pigs was feeding there on the hillside, 12and they begged him, saying, "Send us to the pigs; let us enter them." 13So he gave them permission. And the unclean spirits came out and entered the pigs; and the herd, numbering about two thousand, rushed down the steep bank into the sea and drowned in the sea.

14The herdsmen fled and told it in the city and in the country. And people came to see what it was that had happened. 15And they came to Jesus and saw the demon-possessed[3] man, the one who had had the legion, sitting there, clothed and in his right mind, and they were afraid. 16And those who had seen it described to them what had happened to the demon-possessed man and to the pigs. 17And they began to beg Jesus[4] to depart from their region. 18As he was getting into the boat, the man who had been possessed with demons begged him that he might be with him. 19And he did not permit him but said to him, "Go home to your friends and tell them how much the Lord has done for you, and how he has had mercy on you." 20And he went away and began to proclaim in the Decapolis how much Jesus had done for him, and everyone marveled.

Jesus Heals a Woman and Jairus's Daughter

21And when Jesus had crossed again in the boat to the other side, a great crowd gathered about him, and he was beside the sea. 22Then came one of the rulers of the synagogue, Jairus by name, and seeing him, he fell at his feet 23and implored him earnestly, saying, "My little daughter is at the point of death. Come and lay your hands on her, so that she may be made well and live." 24And he went with him.

And a great crowd followed him and thronged about him. 25And there was a woman who had had a discharge of blood for twelve years, 26and who had suffered much under many physicians, and had spent all that she had, and was no better but rather grew worse. 27She had heard the reports about Jesus and came up behind him in the crowd and touched his garment. 28For she said, "If I touch even his garments, I will be made well." 29And immediately the flow of blood dried up, and she felt in her body that she was healed of her disease. 30And Jesus, perceiving

[1]Some manuscripts *Gergesenes*; some *Gadarenes* [2]Greek *he*; also verse 9 [3]Greek *daimonizomai* (demonized); also verses 16, 18; elsewhere rendered *oppressed by demons* [4]Greek *him*

MARK 5:24–34

FAITH AND UNBELIEF

Faith is different from feelings. Feelings are based on circumstances, and they change like the weather. Faith involves acting, trusting, and believing that God is real, at work, and working for believers' good—regardless of what one may happen to feel at the moment. In fact, sometimes faith leads believers in the opposite direction of feelings.

The woman in this passage had been suffering for a long time. As her disorder involved blood, she was perpetually "unclean" (according to Jewish law), and as a result had likely been ostracized by her community. When she heard about the healing power of Jesus, she boldly braved the large crowd and reached out to him in faith. His response: "Daughter, your faith has made you well" (Mk 5:34).

God invites people to faithfully trust him for all of life (Pr 3:5–6). The way of Jesus is the way of trust. All throughout his life on earth, Jesus demonstrated absolute faith in his Father and challenged his followers to exercise the same kind of faith.

For many reasons, people are prone to doubt. Modern western culture is fraught with skepticism. The contemporary search for truth says, "Understand in order to believe." And against this thinking, Jesus has always maintained, "Believe in order to understand." In the struggle with doubt and unbelief, Jesus encourages people: "Do not fear, only believe" (Mk 5:36). The way of Jesus is the way of trusting God every day, for this life and the next.

in himself that power had gone out from him, immediately turned about in the
crowd and said, "Who touched my garments?" 31And his disciples said to him,
"You see the crowd pressing around you, and yet you say, 'Who touched me?'"
32And he looked around to see who had done it. 33But the woman, knowing what
had happened to her, came in fear and trembling and fell down before him and
told him the whole truth. 34And he said to her, "Daughter, your faith has made you
well; go in peace, and be healed of your disease."
35While he was still speaking, there came from the ruler's house some who
said, "Your daughter is dead. Why trouble the Teacher any further?" 36But over-
hearing[1] what they said, Jesus said to the ruler of the synagogue, "Do not fear,
only believe." 37And he allowed no one to follow him except Peter and James
and John the brother of James. 38They came to the house of the ruler of the
synagogue, and Jesus[2] saw a commotion, people weeping and wailing loudly.
39And when he had entered, he said to them, "Why are you making a commotion and weeping? The child is not dead but sleeping." 40And they laughed at
him. But he put them all outside and took the child's father and mother and
those who were with him and went in where the child was. 41Taking her by
the hand he said to her, "Talitha cumi," which means, "Little girl, I say to you,
arise." 42And immediately the girl got up and began walking (for she was twelve
years of age), and they were immediately overcome with amazement. 43And he
strictly charged them that no one should know this, and told them to give her
something to eat.

Jesus Rejected at Nazareth

6 He went away from there and came to his hometown, and his disciples followed him. 2And on the Sabbath he began to teach in the synagogue, and
many who heard him were astonished, saying, "Where did this man get these
things? What is the wisdom given to him? How are such mighty works done by
his hands? 3Is not this the carpenter,[3] the son of Mary and brother of James and
Joses and Judas and Simon? And are not his sisters here with us?" And they took
offense at him. 4And Jesus said to them, "A prophet is not without honor, except in
his hometown and among his relatives and in his own household." 5And he could
do no mighty work there, except that he laid his hands on a few sick people and
healed them. 6And he marveled because of their unbelief.

And he went about among the villages teaching.

Jesus Sends Out the Twelve Apostles

7And he called the twelve and began to send them out two by two, and gave
them authority over the unclean spirits. 8He charged them to take nothing for
their journey except a staff—no bread, no bag, no money in their belts— 9but to
wear sandals and not put on two tunics.[4] 10And he said to them, "Whenever you
enter a house, stay there until you depart from there. 11And if any place will not
receive you and they will not listen to you, when you leave, shake off the dust that
is on your feet as a testimony against them." 12So they went out and proclaimed
that people should repent. 13And they cast out many demons and anointed with
oil many who were sick and healed them.

The Death of John the Baptist

14King Herod heard of it, for Jesus'[5] name had become known. Some[6] said,
"John the Baptist[7] has been raised from the dead. That is why these miraculous
powers are at work in him." 15But others said, "He is Elijah." And others said,
"He is a prophet, like one of the prophets of old." 16But when Herod heard of
it, he said, "John, whom I beheaded, has been raised." 17For it was Herod who
had sent and seized John and bound him in prison for the sake of Herodias, his

[1]Or *ignoring*; some manuscripts *hearing* [2]Greek *he* [3]Or *builder* [4]Greek *chiton*, a long garment worn under the cloak next to the skin [5]Greek *his* [6]Some manuscripts *He* [7]Greek *baptizer*; also verse 24

MIRACLES: A FORESHADOWING OF THE RESTORED CREATION

In his model prayer, Jesus prayed that the kingdom of God would come "on earth as it is in heaven" (Mt 6:10). In praying for this, he recognized the effects that sin has on the earth, pointing to God's much greater kingdom plans. When we pray this prayer, we look forward to the kingdom of God, where creation will be made new and the effects of sin completely removed. What a day that will be!

Mark 5 shows three people who had been deeply impacted by the imperfection of this physical world and the terrors of the spiritual world. The first was a man "with an unclean spirit." This spirit caused him to do many destructive things to others and to himself. He was a social outcast, banished to live in the tombs because no one in his community could manage his demon possession. Scripture says that he tried to deal with his pain by crying out and cutting himself with stones (5:5). These behaviors are a far cry from the peace and flourishing life that God desires for people, so Jesus stepped into the man's reality and saved him. He restored the possessed man to "his right mind" (5:15). In bringing the man back to his right mind, Jesus pointed to the way things will be in the kingdom of God, when all things will someday be made right.

The next encounters were with a woman who was sick and a girl who had died. In both instances, Jesus stepped into their reality and restored their lives. Death and sickness are not a part of the kingdom of God; therefore as a sign of that coming kingdom, Jesus healed both of these people.

The accounts of Jesus' miracles give believers a look in three directions. First, miracles cause believers to look back to God's original intention for creation to see how things were meant to be. Second, miracles cause believers to look inward to consider the pervasive effects of sin in the world and to cry out to God for deliverance. Finally, miracles are also a glimpse ahead to the kingdom of God in its fullness, where we eagerly anticipate the complete restoration of creation.

brother Philip's wife, because he had married her. 18For John had been saying to
Herod, "It is not lawful for you to have your brother's wife." 19And Herodias had
a grudge against him and wanted to put him to death. But she could not, 20for
Herod feared John, knowing that he was a righteous and holy man, and he kept
him safe. When he heard him, he was greatly perplexed, and yet he heard him
gladly.

21But an opportunity came when Herod on his birthday gave a banquet for
his nobles and military commanders and the leading men of Galilee. 22For when
Herodias's daughter came in and danced, she pleased Herod and his guests. And
the king said to the girl, "Ask me for whatever you wish, and I will give it to you."
23And he vowed to her, "Whatever you ask me, I will give you, up to half of my
kingdom." 24And she went out and said to her mother, "For what should I ask?"
And she said, "The head of John the Baptist." 25And she came in immediately with
haste to the king and asked, saying, "I want you to give me at once the head of
John the Baptist on a platter." 26And the king was exceedingly sorry, but because
of his oaths and his guests he did not want to break his word to her. 27And immediately the king sent an executioner with orders to bring John's[1] head. He went
and beheaded him in the prison 28and brought his head on a platter and gave it to
the girl, and the girl gave it to her mother. 29When his disciples heard of it, they
came and took his body and laid it in a tomb.

Jesus Feeds the Five Thousand

30The apostles returned to Jesus and told him all that they had done and
taught. 31And he said to them, "Come away by yourselves to a desolate place and
rest a while." For many were coming and going, and they had no leisure even to
eat. 32And they went away in the boat to a desolate place by themselves. 33Now
many saw them going and recognized them, and they ran there on foot from all
the towns and got there ahead of them. 34When he went ashore he saw a great
crowd, and he had compassion on them, because they were like sheep without
a shepherd. And he began to teach them many things. 35And when it grew late,
his disciples came to him and said, "This is a desolate place, and the hour is now
late. 36Send them away to go into the surrounding countryside and villages and
buy themselves something to eat." 37But he answered them, "You give them something to eat." And they said to him, "Shall we go and buy two hundred denarii[2]
worth of bread and give it to them to eat?" 38And he said to them, "How many
loaves do you have? Go and see." And when they had found out, they said, "Five,
and two fish." 39Then he commanded them all to sit down in groups on the green
grass. 40So they sat down in groups, by hundreds and by fifties. 41And taking the
five loaves and the two fish, he looked up to heaven and said a blessing and broke
the loaves and gave them to the disciples to set before the people. And he divided
the two fish among them all. 42And they all ate and were satisfied. 43And they took
up twelve baskets full of broken pieces and of the fish. 44And those who ate the
loaves were five thousand men.

Jesus Walks on the Water

45Immediately he made his disciples get into the boat and go before him to the
other side, to Bethsaida, while he dismissed the crowd. 46And after he had taken
leave of them, he went up on the mountain to pray. 47And when evening came,
the boat was out on the sea, and he was alone on the land. 48And he saw that they
were making headway painfully, for the wind was against them. And about the
fourth watch of the night[3] he came to them, walking on the sea. He meant to pass
by them, 49but when they saw him walking on the sea they thought it was a ghost,
and cried out, 50for they all saw him and were terrified. But immediately he spoke
to them and said, "Take heart; it is I. Do not be afraid." 51And he got into the boat

[1]Greek *his* [2]A *denarius* was a day's wage for a laborer [3]That is, between 3 A.M. and 6 A.M.

with them, and the wind ceased. And they were utterly astounded, 52for they did
not understand about the loaves, but their hearts were hardened.

Jesus Heals the Sick in Gennesaret

53When they had crossed over, they came to land at Gennesaret and moored to
the shore. 54And when they got out of the boat, the people immediately recognized
him 55and ran about the whole region and began to bring the sick people on their
beds to wherever they heard he was. 56And wherever he came, in villages, cities, or
countryside, they laid the sick in the marketplaces and implored him that they might
touch even the fringe of his garment. And as many as touched it were made well.

Traditions and Commandments

7 Now when the Pharisees gathered to him, with some of the scribes who had
come from Jerusalem, 2they saw that some of his disciples ate with hands that
were defiled, that is, unwashed. 3(For the Pharisees and all the Jews do not eat unless they wash their hands properly,[1] holding to the tradition of the elders, 4and
when they come from the marketplace, they do not eat unless they wash.[2] And
there are many other traditions that they observe, such as the washing of cups
and pots and copper vessels and dining couches.[3]) 5And the Pharisees and the
scribes asked him, "Why do your disciples not walk according to the tradition of
the elders, but eat with defiled hands?" 6And he said to them, "Well did Isaiah
prophesy of you hypocrites, as it is written,

"'This people honors me with their lips,
but their heart is far from me;
7 in vain do they worship me,
teaching as doctrines the commandments of men.'

8You leave the commandment of God and hold to the tradition of men."
9And he said to them, "You have a fine way of rejecting the commandment
of God in order to establish your tradition! 10For Moses said, 'Honor your father
and your mother'; and, 'Whoever reviles father or mother must surely die.' 11But
you say, 'If a man tells his father or his mother, "Whatever you would have gained
from me is Corban"' (that is, given to God)[4]— 12then you no longer permit him to
do anything for his father or mother, 13thus making void the word of God by your
tradition that you have handed down. And many such things you do."

What Defiles a Person

14And he called the people to him again and said to them, "Hear me, all of you,
and understand: 15There is nothing outside a person that by going into him can defile him, but the things that come out of a person are what defile him."[5] 17And when
he had entered the house and left the people, his disciples asked him about the
parable. 18And he said to them, "Then are you also without understanding? Do you
not see that whatever goes into a person from outside cannot defile him, 19since
it enters not his heart but his stomach, and is expelled?"[6] (Thus he declared all
foods clean.) 20And he said, "What comes out of a person is what defiles him. 21For
from within, out of the heart of man, come evil thoughts, sexual immorality, theft,
murder, adultery, 22coveting, wickedness, deceit, sensuality, envy, slander, pride,
foolishness. 23All these evil things come from within, and they defile a person."

The Syrophoenician Woman's Faith

24And from there he arose and went away to the region of Tyre and Sidon.[7]
And he entered a house and did not want anyone to know, yet he could not

---

MARK 7:24–30

"MEAN" JESUS?

During dinner, a local woman sought Jesus' attention and care. Jesus responded in a way that could be misinterpreted as mean or rude (v. 27). But Jesus was not attempting to insult the woman with this metaphor. In fact, he was testing her faith. He wanted the woman to consider what she felt about him: whether she thought he was merely another religious guru or he was the only way her daughter could be healed.

Matthew, one of the other Gospel writers, records Jesus' response to this hopeful mother in this way: "Then Jesus answered her, 'O woman, great is your faith! Be it done for you as you desire.' And her daughter was healed instantly" (Mt 15:28). This wise woman understood the test and persisted in seeking Jesus' help. Believers today can learn a valuable lesson from the faith and practice of this mother who cared enough to push the envelope, in faith.

---

[1]Greek *unless they wash the hands with a fist*, probably indicating a kind of ceremonial washing [2]Greek *unless they baptize*; some manuscripts *unless they purify themselves* [3]Some manuscripts omit *and dining couches* [4]Or *an offering* [5]Some manuscripts add verse 16: *If anyone has ears to hear, let him hear* [6]Greek *goes out into the latrine* [7]Some manuscripts omit *and Sidon*

be hidden. 25But immediately a woman whose little daughter had an unclean spirit heard of him and came and fell down at his feet. 26Now the woman was a Gentile, a Syrophoenician by birth. And she begged him to cast the demon out of her daughter. 27And he said to her, "Let the children be fed first, for it is not right to take the children's bread and throw it to the dogs." 28But she answered him, "Yes, Lord; yet even the dogs under the table eat the children's crumbs." 29And he said to her, "For this statement you may go your way; the demon has left your daughter." 30And she went home and found the child lying in bed and the demon gone.

Jesus Heals a Deaf Man

31Then he returned from the region of Tyre and went through Sidon to the Sea of Galilee, in the region of the Decapolis. 32And they brought to him a man who was deaf and had a speech impediment, and they begged him to lay his hand on him. 33And taking him aside from the crowd privately, he put his fingers into his ears, and after spitting touched his tongue. 34And looking up to heaven, he sighed and said to him, "Ephphatha," that is, "Be opened." 35And his ears were opened, his tongue was released, and he spoke plainly. 36And Jesus[1] charged them to tell no one. But the more he charged them, the more zealously they proclaimed it. 37And they were astonished beyond measure, saying, "He has done all things well. He even makes the deaf hear and the mute speak."

Jesus Feeds the Four Thousand

8 In those days, when again a great crowd had gathered, and they had nothing to eat, he called his disciples to him and said to them, 2"I have compassion on the crowd, because they have been with me now three days and have nothing to eat. 3And if I send them away hungry to their homes, they will faint on the way. And some of them have come from far away." 4And his disciples answered him, "How can one feed these people with bread here in this desolate place?" 5And he asked them, "How many loaves do you have?" They said, "Seven." 6And he directed the crowd to sit down on the ground. And he took the seven loaves, and having given thanks, he broke them and gave them to his disciples to set before the people; and they set them before the crowd. 7And they had a few small fish. And having blessed them, he said that these also should be set before them. 8And they ate and were satisfied. And they took up the broken pieces left over, seven baskets full. 9And there were about four thousand people. And he sent them away. 10And immediately he got into the boat with his disciples and went to the district of Dalmanutha.[2]

The Pharisees Demand a Sign

11The Pharisees came and began to argue with him, seeking from him a sign from heaven to test him. 12And he sighed deeply in his spirit and said, "Why does this generation seek a sign? Truly, I say to you, no sign will be given to this generation." 13And he left them, got into the boat again, and went to the other side.

The Leaven of the Pharisees and Herod

14Now they had forgotten to bring bread, and they had only one loaf with them in the boat. 15And he cautioned them, saying, "Watch out; beware of the leaven of the Pharisees and the leaven of Herod."[3] 16And they began discussing with one another the fact that they had no bread. 17And Jesus, aware of this, said to them, "Why are you discussing the fact that you have no bread? Do you not yet perceive or understand? Are your hearts hardened? 18Having eyes do you not see, and having ears do you not hear? And do you not remember? 19When I broke the five loaves for the five thousand, how many baskets full of broken pieces did you

---

[1] Greek *he* [2] Some manuscripts *Magadan*, or *Magdala* [3] Some manuscripts *the Herodians*

take up?" They said to him, "Twelve." 20"And the seven for the four thousand,
how many baskets full of broken pieces did you take up?" And they said to him,
"Seven." 21And he said to them, "Do you not yet understand?"

Jesus Heals a Blind Man at Bethsaida

22And they came to Bethsaida. And some people brought to him a blind man
and begged him to touch him. 23And he took the blind man by the hand and led
him out of the village, and when he had spit on his eyes and laid his hands on him,
he asked him, "Do you see anything?" 24And he looked up and said, "I see people,
but they look like trees, walking." 25Then Jesus[1] laid his hands on his eyes again;
and he opened his eyes, his sight was restored, and he saw everything clearly.
26And he sent him to his home, saying, "Do not even enter the village."

Peter Confesses Jesus as the Christ

27And Jesus went on with his disciples to the villages of Caesarea Philippi. And
on the way he asked his disciples, "Who do people say that I am?" 28And they told
him, "John the Baptist; and others say, Elijah; and others, one of the prophets."
29And he asked them, "But who do you say that I am?" Peter answered him, "You
are the Christ." 30And he strictly charged them to tell no one about him.

Jesus Foretells His Death and Resurrection

31And he began to teach them that the Son of Man must suffer many things
and be rejected by the elders and the chief priests and the scribes and be killed,
and after three days rise again. 32And he said this plainly. And Peter took him
aside and began to rebuke him. 33But turning and seeing his disciples, he rebuked
Peter and said, "Get behind me, Satan! For you are not setting your mind on the
things of God, but on the things of man."
34And calling the crowd to him with his disciples, he said to them, "If anyone
would come after me, let him deny himself and take up his cross and follow me.
35For whoever would save his life[2] will lose it, but whoever loses his life for my
sake and the gospel's will save it. 36For what does it profit a man to gain the whole
world and forfeit his soul? 37For what can a man give in return for his soul? 38For
whoever is ashamed of me and of my words in this adulterous and sinful generation, of him will the Son of Man also be ashamed when he comes in the glory of
his Father with the holy angels."

9 And he said to them, "Truly, I say to you, there are some standing here who
will not taste death until they see the kingdom of God after it has come with
power."

The Transfiguration

2And after six days Jesus took with him Peter and James and John, and led
them up a high mountain by themselves. And he was transfigured before them,
3and his clothes became radiant, intensely white, as no one[3] on earth could
bleach them. 4And there appeared to them Elijah with Moses, and they were
talking with Jesus. 5And Peter said to Jesus, "Rabbi,[4] it is good that we are here.
Let us make three tents, one for you and one for Moses and one for Elijah." 6For
he did not know what to say, for they were terrified. 7And a cloud overshadowed
them, and a voice came out of the cloud, "This is my beloved Son;[5] listen to
him." 8And suddenly, looking around, they no longer saw anyone with them
but Jesus only.
9And as they were coming down the mountain, he charged them to tell no
one what they had seen, until the Son of Man had risen from the dead. 10So they
kept the matter to themselves, questioning what this rising from the dead might

[1]Greek *he* [2]The same Greek word can mean either *soul* or *life*, depending on the context; twice in this verse and once in verse 36 and once in verse 37 [3]Greek *launderer* (*gnapheus*) [4]*Rabbi* means *my teacher*, or *my master* [5]Or *my Son, my* (or *the*) *Beloved*

MARK 9:7

SON OF GOD

In the Old Testament, Moses asked God to show him his glory to confirm his calling on Moses' life (Ex 33:18–23). God could not fully reveal his glory to a mere man, so God showed Moses only a shielded portion of his glory. It was so intense that Moses reflected that glory on his face for a couple of days (Ge 34:29–32)!

In the episode of the transfiguration, God the Father showed his glory in a special way to Jesus in front of a few of his disciples. God revealed his glory in his Son to prove that Jesus is the Son of God, a title that is used often through the Gospel of Mark (3:11; 5:7; 13:32).

Both the sun and the moon give light so that people can see, but the moon only reflects the sun's light and shines just a fraction of it into the world. In a similar way, Moses was like the moon, but Jesus, the Son of God and the full revelation of God himself, reflects God's brilliant and blazing presence: "He [Jesus] is the radiance of the glory of God and the exact imprint of his nature" (Heb 1:3).

mean. 11And they asked him, "Why do the scribes say that first Elijah must come?"
12And he said to them, "Elijah does come first to restore all things. And how is it
written of the Son of Man that he should suffer many things and be treated with
contempt? 13But I tell you that Elijah has come, and they did to him whatever they
pleased, as it is written of him."

Jesus Heals a Boy with an Unclean Spirit

14And when they came to the disciples, they saw a great crowd around them,
and scribes arguing with them. 15And immediately all the crowd, when they saw
him, were greatly amazed and ran up to him and greeted him. 16And he asked
them, "What are you arguing about with them?" 17And someone from the crowd
answered him, "Teacher, I brought my son to you, for he has a spirit that makes
him mute. 18And whenever it seizes him, it throws him down, and he foams and
grinds his teeth and becomes rigid. So I asked your disciples to cast it out, and
they were not able." 19And he answered them, "O faithless generation, how long
am I to be with you? How long am I to bear with you? Bring him to me." 20And
they brought the boy to him. And when the spirit saw him, immediately it convulsed the boy, and he fell on the ground and rolled about, foaming at the mouth.
21And Jesus asked his father, "How long has this been happening to him?" And
he said, "From childhood. 22And it has often cast him into fire and into water, to
destroy him. But if you can do anything, have compassion on us and help us."
23And Jesus said to him, "'If you can'! All things are possible for one who believes."
24Immediately the father of the child cried out[1] and said, "I believe; help my unbelief!" 25And when Jesus saw that a crowd came running together, he rebuked
the unclean spirit, saying to it, "You mute and deaf spirit, I command you, come
out of him and never enter him again." 26And after crying out and convulsing him
terribly, it came out, and the boy was like a corpse, so that most of them said, "He
is dead." 27But Jesus took him by the hand and lifted him up, and he arose. 28And
when he had entered the house, his disciples asked him privately, "Why could
we not cast it out?" 29And he said to them, "This kind cannot be driven out by
anything but prayer."[2]

Jesus Again Foretells Death, Resurrection

30They went on from there and passed through Galilee. And he did not want
anyone to know, 31for he was teaching his disciples, saying to them, "The Son of
Man is going to be delivered into the hands of men, and they will kill him. And
when he is killed, after three days he will rise." 32But they did not understand the
saying, and were afraid to ask him.

Who Is the Greatest?

33And they came to Capernaum. And when he was in the house he asked
them, "What were you discussing on the way?" 34But they kept silent, for on the
way they had argued with one another about who was the greatest. 35And he sat
down and called the twelve. And he said to them, "If anyone would be first, he
must be last of all and servant of all." 36And he took a child and put him in the
midst of them, and taking him in his arms, he said to them, 37"Whoever receives
one such child in my name receives me, and whoever receives me, receives not
me but him who sent me."

Anyone Not Against Us Is for Us

38John said to him, "Teacher, we saw someone casting out demons in your
name,[3] and we tried to stop him, because he was not following us." 39But Jesus
said, "Do not stop him, for no one who does a mighty work in my name will be

[1] Some manuscripts add *with tears* [2] Some manuscripts add *and fasting* [3] Some manuscripts add *who does not follow us*

able soon afterward to speak evil of me. 40 For the one who is not against us is for us. 41 For truly, I say to you, whoever gives you a cup of water to drink because[1] you belong to Christ will by no means lose his reward.

Temptations to Sin

42 "Whoever causes one of these little ones who believe in me to sin,[2] it would be better for him if a great millstone were hung around his neck and he were thrown into the sea. 43 And if your hand causes you to sin, cut it off. It is better for you to enter life crippled than with two hands to go to hell,[3] to the unquenchable fire.[4] 45 And if your foot causes you to sin, cut it off. It is better for you to enter life lame than with two feet to be thrown into hell. 47 And if your eye causes you to sin, tear it out. It is better for you to enter the kingdom of God with one eye than with two eyes to be thrown into hell, 48 'where their worm does not die and the fire is not quenched.' 49 For everyone will be salted with fire.[5] 50 Salt is good, but if the salt has lost its saltiness, how will you make it salty again? Have salt in yourselves, and be at peace with one another."

Teaching About Divorce

10 And he left there and went to the region of Judea and beyond the Jordan, and crowds gathered to him again. And again, as was his custom, he taught them.

2 And Pharisees came up and in order to test him asked, "Is it lawful for a man to divorce his wife?" 3 He answered them, "What did Moses command you?" 4 They said, "Moses allowed a man to write a certificate of divorce and to send her away." 5 And Jesus said to them, "Because of your hardness of heart he wrote you this commandment. 6 But from the beginning of creation, 'God made them male and female.' 7 'Therefore a man shall leave his father and mother and hold fast to his wife,[6] 8 and the two shall become one flesh.' So they are no longer two but one flesh. 9 What therefore God has joined together, let not man separate."

10 And in the house the disciples asked him again about this matter. 11 And he said to them, "Whoever divorces his wife and marries another commits adultery against her, 12 and if she divorces her husband and marries another, she commits adultery."

Let the Children Come to Me

13 And they were bringing children to him that he might touch them, and the disciples rebuked them. 14 But when Jesus saw it, he was indignant and said to them, "Let the children come to me; do not hinder them, for to such belongs the kingdom of God. 15 Truly, I say to you, whoever does not receive the kingdom of God like a child shall not enter it." 16 And he took them in his arms and blessed them, laying his hands on them.

The Rich Young Man

17 And as he was setting out on his journey, a man ran up and knelt before him and asked him, "Good Teacher, what must I do to inherit eternal life?" 18 And Jesus said to him, "Why do you call me good? No one is good except God alone. 19 You know the commandments: 'Do not murder, Do not commit adultery, Do not steal, Do not bear false witness, Do not defraud, Honor your father and mother.'" 20 And he said to him, "Teacher, all these I have kept from my youth." 21 And Jesus, looking at him, loved him, and said to him, "You lack one thing: go, sell all that you have and give to the poor, and you will have treasure in heaven; and come, follow me." 22 Disheartened by the saying, he went away sorrowful, for he had great possessions.

---

[1] Greek *in name that* [2] Greek *to stumble*; also verses 43, 45, 47 [3] Greek *Gehenna*; also verse 47 [4] Some manuscripts add verses 44 and 46 (which are identical with verse 48) [5] Some manuscripts add *and every sacrifice will be salted with salt* [6] Some manuscripts omit *and hold fast to his wife*

[23]And Jesus looked around and said to his disciples, "How difficult it will be
for those who have wealth to enter the kingdom of God!" [24]And the disciples were
amazed at his words. But Jesus said to them again, "Children, how difficult it is[1]
to enter the kingdom of God! [25]It is easier for a camel to go through the eye of a
needle than for a rich person to enter the kingdom of God." [26]And they were exceedingly
astonished, and said to him,[2] "Then who can be saved?" [27]Jesus looked
at them and said, "With man it is impossible, but not with God. For all things are
possible with God." [28]Peter began to say to him, "See, we have left everything
and followed you." [29]Jesus said, "Truly, I say to you, there is no one who has left
house or brothers or sisters or mother or father or children or lands, for my sake
and for the gospel, [30]who will not receive a hundredfold now in this time, houses
and brothers and sisters and mothers and children and lands, with persecutions,
and in the age to come eternal life. [31]But many who are first will be last, and the
last first."

Jesus Foretells His Death a Third Time

[32]And they were on the road, going up to Jerusalem, and Jesus was walking
ahead of them. And they were amazed, and those who followed were afraid. And
taking the twelve again, he began to tell them what was to happen to him, [33]saying,
"See, we are going up to Jerusalem, and the Son of Man will be delivered
over to the chief priests and the scribes, and they will condemn him to death and
deliver him over to the Gentiles. [34]And they will mock him and spit on him, and
flog him and kill him. And after three days he will rise."

The Request of James and John

[35]And James and John, the sons of Zebedee, came up to him and said to him,
"Teacher, we want you to do for us whatever we ask of you." [36]And he said to
them, "What do you want me to do for you?" [37]And they said to him, "Grant us to
sit, one at your right hand and one at your left, in your glory." [38]Jesus said to them,
"You do not know what you are asking. Are you able to drink the cup that I drink,
or to be baptized with the baptism with which I am baptized?" [39]And they said to
him, "We are able." And Jesus said to them, "The cup that I drink you will drink,
and with the baptism with which I am baptized, you will be baptized, [40]but to sit
at my right hand or at my left is not mine to grant, but it is for those for whom
it has been prepared." [41]And when the ten heard it, they began to be indignant
at James and John. [42]And Jesus called them to him and said to them, "You know
that those who are considered rulers of the Gentiles lord it over them, and their
great ones exercise authority over them. [43]But it shall not be so among you. But
whoever would be great among you must be your servant,[3] [44]and whoever would
be first among you must be slave[4] of all. [45]For even the Son of Man came not to be
served but to serve, and to give his life as a ransom for many."

Jesus Heals Blind Bartimaeus

[46]And they came to Jericho. And as he was leaving Jericho with his disciples
and a great crowd, Bartimaeus, a blind beggar, the son of Timaeus, was sitting by
the roadside. [47]And when he heard that it was Jesus of Nazareth, he began to cry
out and say, "Jesus, Son of David, have mercy on me!" [48]And many rebuked him,
telling him to be silent. But he cried out all the more, "Son of David, have mercy on
me!" [49]And Jesus stopped and said, "Call him." And they called the blind man, saying
to him, "Take heart. Get up; he is calling you." [50]And throwing off his cloak, he
sprang up and came to Jesus. [51]And Jesus said to him, "What do you want me to do
for you?" And the blind man said to him, "Rabbi, let me recover my sight." [52]And
Jesus said to him, "Go your way; your faith has made you well." And immediately
he recovered his sight and followed him on the way.

[1]Some manuscripts add *for those who trust in riches* [2]Some manuscripts *to one another* [3]Greek *diakonos*
[4]Or *bondservant*, or *servant* (for the contextual rendering of the Greek word *doulos*, see Preface)

The Triumphal Entry

11 Now when they drew near to Jerusalem, to Bethphage and Bethany, at the Mount of Olives, Jesus[1] sent two of his disciples 2 and said to them, "Go into the village in front of you, and immediately as you enter it you will find a colt tied, on which no one has ever sat. Untie it and bring it. 3 If anyone says to you, 'Why are you doing this?' say, 'The Lord has need of it and will send it back here immediately.'" 4 And they went away and found a colt tied at a door outside in the street, and they untied it. 5 And some of those standing there said to them, "What are you doing, untying the colt?" 6 And they told them what Jesus had said, and they let them go. 7 And they brought the colt to Jesus and threw their cloaks on it, and he sat on it. 8 And many spread their cloaks on the road, and others spread leafy branches that they had cut from the fields. 9 And those who went before and those who followed were shouting, "Hosanna! Blessed is he who comes in the name of the Lord! 10 Blessed is the coming kingdom of our father David! Hosanna in the highest!"

11 And he entered Jerusalem and went into the temple. And when he had looked around at everything, as it was already late, he went out to Bethany with the twelve.

Jesus Curses the Fig Tree

12 On the following day, when they came from Bethany, he was hungry. 13 And seeing in the distance a fig tree in leaf, he went to see if he could find anything on it. When he came to it, he found nothing but leaves, for it was not the season for figs. 14 And he said to it, "May no one ever eat fruit from you again." And his disciples heard it.

Jesus Cleanses the Temple

15 And they came to Jerusalem. And he entered the temple and began to drive out those who sold and those who bought in the temple, and he overturned the tables of the money-changers and the seats of those who sold pigeons. 16 And he would not allow anyone to carry anything through the temple. 17 And he was teaching them and saying to them, "Is it not written, 'My house shall be called a house of prayer for all the nations'? But you have made it a den of robbers." 18 And the chief priests and the scribes heard it and were seeking a way to destroy him, for they feared him, because all the crowd was astonished at his teaching. 19 And when evening came they[2] went out of the city.

The Lesson from the Withered Fig Tree

20 As they passed by in the morning, they saw the fig tree withered away to its roots. 21 And Peter remembered and said to him, "Rabbi, look! The fig tree that you cursed has withered." 22 And Jesus answered them, "Have faith in God. 23 Truly, I say to you, whoever says to this mountain, 'Be taken up and thrown into the sea,' and does not doubt in his heart, but believes that what he says will come to pass, it will be done for him. 24 Therefore I tell you, whatever you ask in prayer, believe that you have received[3] it, and it will be yours. 25 And whenever you stand praying, forgive, if you have anything against anyone, so that your Father also who is in heaven may forgive you your trespasses."[4]

The Authority of Jesus Challenged

27 And they came again to Jerusalem. And as he was walking in the temple, the chief priests and the scribes and the elders came to him, 28 and they said to him, "By what authority are you doing these things, or who gave you this authority to do them?" 29 Jesus said to them, "I will ask you one question; answer

[1] Greek *he* [2] Some manuscripts *he* [3] Some manuscripts *are receiving* [4] Some manuscripts add verse 26: *But if you do not forgive, neither will your Father who is in heaven forgive your trespasses*

me, and I will tell you by what authority I do these things. 30Was the baptism of John from heaven or from man? Answer me." 31And they discussed it with one another, saying, "If we say, 'From heaven,' he will say, 'Why then did you not believe him?' 32But shall we say, 'From man'?"—they were afraid of the people, for they all held that John really was a prophet. 33So they answered Jesus, "We do not know." And Jesus said to them, "Neither will I tell you by what authority I do these things."

The Parable of the Tenants

12 And he began to speak to them in parables. "A man planted a vineyard and put a fence around it and dug a pit for the winepress and built a tower, and leased it to tenants and went into another country. 2When the season came, he sent a servant[1] to the tenants to get from them some of the fruit of the vineyard. 3And they took him and beat him and sent him away empty-handed. 4Again he sent to them another servant, and they struck him on the head and treated him shamefully. 5And he sent another, and him they killed. And so with many others: some they beat, and some they killed. 6He had still one other, a beloved son. Finally he sent him to them, saying, 'They will respect my son.' 7But those tenants said to one another, 'This is the heir. Come, let us kill him, and the inheritance will be ours.' 8And they took him and killed him and threw him out of the vineyard. 9What will the owner of the vineyard do? He will come and destroy the tenants and give the vineyard to others. 10Have you not read this Scripture:

"'The stone that the builders rejected
has become the cornerstone;[2]
11 this was the Lord's doing,
and it is marvelous in our eyes'?"

12And they were seeking to arrest him but feared the people, for they perceived that he had told the parable against them. So they left him and went away.

Paying Taxes to Caesar

13And they sent to him some of the Pharisees and some of the Herodians, to trap him in his talk. 14And they came and said to him, "Teacher, we know that you are true and do not care about anyone's opinion. For you are not swayed by appearances,[3] but truly teach the way of God. Is it lawful to pay taxes to Caesar, or not? Should we pay them, or should we not?" 15But, knowing their hypocrisy, he said to them, "Why put me to the test? Bring me a denarius[4] and let me look at it." 16And they brought one. And he said to them, "Whose likeness and inscription is this?" They said to him, "Caesar's." 17Jesus said to them, "Render to Caesar the things that are Caesar's, and to God the things that are God's." And they marveled at him.

The Sadducees Ask About the Resurrection

18And Sadducees came to him, who say that there is no resurrection. And they asked him a question, saying, 19"Teacher, Moses wrote for us that if a man's brother dies and leaves a wife, but leaves no child, the man[5] must take the widow and raise up offspring for his brother. 20There were seven brothers; the first took a wife, and when he died left no offspring. 21And the second took her, and died, leaving no offspring. And the third likewise. 22And the seven left no offspring. Last of all the woman also died. 23In the resurrection, when they rise again, whose wife will she be? For the seven had her as wife."

24Jesus said to them, "Is this not the reason you are wrong, because you know neither the Scriptures nor the power of God? 25For when they rise from the dead, they neither marry nor are given in marriage, but are like angels in heaven. 26And

[1]Or *bondservant;* also verse 4 [2]Greek *the head of the corner* [3]Greek *you do not look at people's faces*
[4]A *denarius* was a day's wage for a laborer [5]Greek *his brother*

MARK 12:9–11

THE CORNERSTONE

Jesus, as a trained carpenter and possibly also a stonemason, knew that building requires precision. In biblical times, buildings were often made of cut stones that were squared together, side by side. To keep the entire building "plumb," the builders would establish a "cornerstone" and work off that. The cornerstone would help align the two intersecting walls of the building and would serve to show if another stone was out of line. Appropriately, at various points in the New Testament, Jesus is referred to as the "cornerstone" (Ac 4:10,11; Eph 2:20). He is the stone that the builders rejected (Ps 118:22). Some people, in their pride, trip and stumble over Jesus' teaching. Thus, Jesus is a stumbling block for some and the source of life for others.

Jesus is the chief cornerstone of the church because "there is salvation in no one else, for there is no other name under heaven given among men by which we must be saved" (Ac 4:12). God continues to build his church—a throng of people who will exist as his temple in the world and will help others encounter God. The church is all about Jesus, because in him "the whole structure, being joined together, grows into a holy temple in the Lord" (Eph 2:21).

as for the dead being raised, have you not read in the book of Moses, in the passage about the bush, how God spoke to him, saying, 'I am the God of Abraham, and the God of Isaac, and the God of Jacob'? 27He is not God of the dead, but of the living. You are quite wrong."

The Great Commandment

28And one of the scribes came up and heard them disputing with one another, and seeing that he answered them well, asked him, "Which commandment is the most important of all?" 29Jesus answered, "The most important is, 'Hear, O Israel: The Lord our God, the Lord is one. 30And you shall love the Lord your God with all your heart and with all your soul and with all your mind and with all your strength.' 31The second is this: 'You shall love your neighbor as yourself.' There is no other commandment greater than these." 32And the scribe said to him, "You are right, Teacher. You have truly said that he is one, and there is no other besides him. 33And to love him with all the heart and with all the understanding and with all the strength, and to love one's neighbor as oneself, is much more than all whole burnt offerings and sacrifices." 34And when Jesus saw that he answered wisely, he said to him, "You are not far from the kingdom of God." And after that no one dared to ask him any more questions.

Whose Son Is the Christ?

35And as Jesus taught in the temple, he said, "How can the scribes say that the Christ is the son of David? 36David himself, in the Holy Spirit, declared,

"'The Lord said to my Lord,
"Sit at my right hand,
until I put your enemies under your feet."'

37David himself calls him Lord. So how is he his son?" And the great throng heard him gladly.

Beware of the Scribes

38And in his teaching he said, "Beware of the scribes, who like to walk around in long robes and like greetings in the marketplaces 39and have the best seats in the synagogues and the places of honor at feasts, 40who devour widows' houses and for a pretense make long prayers. They will receive the greater condemnation."

The Widow's Offering

41And he sat down opposite the treasury and watched the people putting money into the offering box. Many rich people put in large sums. 42And a poor widow came and put in two small copper coins, which make a penny.[1] 43And he called his disciples to him and said to them, "Truly, I say to you, this poor widow has put in more than all those who are contributing to the offering box. 44For they all contributed out of their abundance, but she out of her poverty has put in everything she had, all she had to live on."

Jesus Foretells Destruction of the Temple

13 And as he came out of the temple, one of his disciples said to him, "Look, Teacher, what wonderful stones and what wonderful buildings!" 2And Jesus said to him, "Do you see these great buildings? There will not be left here one stone upon another that will not be thrown down."

Signs of the End of the Age

3And as he sat on the Mount of Olives opposite the temple, Peter and James and John and Andrew asked him privately, 4"Tell us, when will these things be,

[1]Greek *two lepta*, which make a *kodrantes*; a *kodrantes* (Latin *quadrans*) was a Roman copper coin worth about 1/64 of a *denarius* (which was a day's wage for a laborer)

and what will be the sign when all these things are about to be accomplished?"
5And Jesus began to say to them, "See that no one leads you astray. 6Many will
come in my name, saying, 'I am he!' and they will lead many astray. 7And when
you hear of wars and rumors of wars, do not be alarmed. This must take place, but
the end is not yet. 8For nation will rise against nation, and kingdom against kingdom. There will be earthquakes in various places; there will be famines. These are
but the beginning of the birth pains.

9"But be on your guard. For they will deliver you over to councils, and you will
be beaten in synagogues, and you will stand before governors and kings for my
sake, to bear witness before them. 10And the gospel must first be proclaimed to all
nations. 11And when they bring you to trial and deliver you over, do not be anxious beforehand what you are to say, but say whatever is given you in that hour,
for it is not you who speak, but the Holy Spirit. 12And brother will deliver brother
over to death, and the father his child, and children will rise against parents and
have them put to death. 13And you will be hated by all for my name's sake. But the
one who endures to the end will be saved.

The Abomination of Desolation

14"But when you see the abomination of desolation standing where he ought
not to be (let the reader understand), then let those who are in Judea flee to the
mountains. 15Let the one who is on the housetop not go down, nor enter his
house, to take anything out, 16and let the one who is in the field not turn back
to take his cloak. 17And alas for women who are pregnant and for those who are
nursing infants in those days! 18Pray that it may not happen in winter. 19For in
those days there will be such tribulation as has not been from the beginning of the
creation that God created until now, and never will be. 20And if the Lord had not
cut short the days, no human being would be saved. But for the sake of the elect,
whom he chose, he shortened the days. 21And then if anyone says to you, 'Look,
here is the Christ!' or 'Look, there he is!' do not believe it. 22For false christs and
false prophets will arise and perform signs and wonders, to lead astray, if possible,
the elect. 23But be on guard; I have told you all things beforehand.

The Coming of the Son of Man

24"But in those days, after that tribulation, the sun will be darkened, and the
moon will not give its light, 25and the stars will be falling from heaven, and the
powers in the heavens will be shaken. 26And then they will see the Son of Man
coming in clouds with great power and glory. 27And then he will send out the
angels and gather his elect from the four winds, from the ends of the earth to the
ends of heaven.

The Lesson of the Fig Tree

28"From the fig tree learn its lesson: as soon as its branch becomes tender and
puts out its leaves, you know that summer is near. 29So also, when you see these
things taking place, you know that he is near, at the very gates. 30Truly, I say to
you, this generation will not pass away until all these things take place. 31Heaven
and earth will pass away, but my words will not pass away.

No One Knows That Day or Hour

32"But concerning that day or that hour, no one knows, not even the angels in
heaven, nor the Son, but only the Father. 33Be on guard, keep awake.[1] For you do
not know when the time will come. 34It is like a man going on a journey, when he
leaves home and puts his servants[2] in charge, each with his work, and commands
the doorkeeper to stay awake. 35Therefore stay awake—for you do not know when
the master of the house will come, in the evening, or at midnight, or when the

[1]Some manuscripts add *and pray* [2]Or *bondservants*

MARK 13:32–36

JESUS: GOD INCARNATE

Jesus is unlike any man who ever lived. He was at the same time both fully God and fully human, and he is able to identify with us as humans in every way. When Jesus came to earth, he never stopped being anything less than God. Yet he set aside his divine power in order to live as a human being (Php 2:7). Jesus' ability to heal, knowledge of the unknowable, and command over demonic spirits and nature alike came from his anointing by the Holy Spirit at his baptism.

This mystery illustrates the wonder of the incarnation: "For God so loved the world, that he gave his only Son, that whoever believes in him should not perish but have eternal life" (Jn 3:16). Jesus' life represented the love of God. He testified to the fact that he is the only way that people can come to God (Jn 14:6). He knew that he must give his life for others to have life, and Jesus willingly gave his earthly life so that others could live eternally (Mk 10:45).

rooster crows,[1] or in the morning— 36lest he come suddenly and find you asleep. 37And what I say to you I say to all: Stay awake."

The Plot to Kill Jesus

14 It was now two days before the Passover and the Feast of Unleavened Bread. And the chief priests and the scribes were seeking how to arrest him by stealth and kill him, 2for they said, "Not during the feast, lest there be an uproar from the people."

Jesus Anointed at Bethany

3And while he was at Bethany in the house of Simon the leper,[2] as he was reclining at table, a woman came with an alabaster flask of ointment of pure nard, very costly, and she broke the flask and poured it over his head. 4There were some who said to themselves indignantly, "Why was the ointment wasted like that? 5For this ointment could have been sold for more than three hundred denarii[3] and given to the poor." And they scolded her. 6But Jesus said, "Leave her alone. Why do you trouble her? She has done a beautiful thing to me. 7For you always have the poor with you, and whenever you want, you can do good for them. But you will not always have me. 8She has done what she could; she has anointed my body beforehand for burial. 9And truly, I say to you, wherever the gospel is proclaimed in the whole world, what she has done will be told in memory of her."

Judas to Betray Jesus

10Then Judas Iscariot, who was one of the twelve, went to the chief priests in order to betray him to them. 11And when they heard it, they were glad and promised to give him money. And he sought an opportunity to betray him.

The Passover with the Disciples

12And on the first day of Unleavened Bread, when they sacrificed the Passover lamb, his disciples said to him, "Where will you have us go and prepare for you to eat the Passover?" 13And he sent two of his disciples and said to them, "Go into the city, and a man carrying a jar of water will meet you. Follow him, 14and wherever he enters, say to the master of the house, 'The Teacher says, Where is my guest room, where I may eat the Passover with my disciples?' 15And he will show you a large upper room furnished and ready; there prepare for us." 16And the disciples set out and went to the city and found it just as he had told them, and they prepared the Passover.

17And when it was evening, he came with the twelve. 18And as they were reclining at table and eating, Jesus said, "Truly, I say to you, one of you will betray me, one who is eating with me." 19They began to be sorrowful and to say to him one after another, "Is it I?" 20He said to them, "It is one of the twelve, one who is dipping bread into the dish with me. 21For the Son of Man goes as it is written of him, but woe to that man by whom the Son of Man is betrayed! It would have been better for that man if he had not been born."

Institution of the Lord's Supper

22And as they were eating, he took bread, and after blessing it broke it and gave it to them, and said, "Take; this is my body." 23And he took a cup, and when he had given thanks he gave it to them, and they all drank of it. 24And he said to them, "This is my blood of the[4] covenant, which is poured out for many. 25Truly, I say to you, I will not drink again of the fruit of the vine until that day when I drink it new in the kingdom of God."

---

[1]That is, the third watch of the night, between midnight and 3 A.M. [2]*Leprosy* was a term for several skin diseases; see Leviticus 13 [3]A *denarius* was a day's wage for a laborer [4]Some manuscripts insert *new*

Jesus Foretells Peter's Denial

[26]And when they had sung a hymn, they went out to the Mount of Olives.
[27]And Jesus said to them, "You will all fall away, for it is written, 'I will strike the
shepherd, and the sheep will be scattered.' [28]But after I am raised up, I will go
before you to Galilee." [29]Peter said to him, "Even though they all fall away, I will
not." [30]And Jesus said to him, "Truly, I tell you, this very night, before the rooster
crows twice, you will deny me three times." [31]But he said emphatically, "If I must
die with you, I will not deny you." And they all said the same.

Jesus Prays in Gethsemane

[32]And they went to a place called Gethsemane. And he said to his disciples,
"Sit here while I pray." [33]And he took with him Peter and James and John, and began to be greatly distressed and troubled. [34]And he said to them, "My soul is very
sorrowful, even to death. Remain here and watch."[1] [35]And going a little farther, he
fell on the ground and prayed that, if it were possible, the hour might pass from
him. [36]And he said, "Abba, Father, all things are possible for you. Remove this cup
from me. Yet not what I will, but what you will." [37]And he came and found them
sleeping, and he said to Peter, "Simon, are you asleep? Could you not watch one
hour? [38]Watch and pray that you may not enter into temptation. The spirit indeed
is willing, but the flesh is weak." [39]And again he went away and prayed, saying the
same words. [40]And again he came and found them sleeping, for their eyes were
very heavy, and they did not know what to answer him. [41]And he came the third
time and said to them, "Are you still sleeping and taking your rest? It is enough;
the hour has come. The Son of Man is betrayed into the hands of sinners. [42]Rise,
let us be going; see, my betrayer is at hand."

Betrayal and Arrest of Jesus

[43]And immediately, while he was still speaking, Judas came, one of the
twelve, and with him a crowd with swords and clubs, from the chief priests and
the scribes and the elders. [44]Now the betrayer had given them a sign, saying,
"The one I will kiss is the man. Seize him and lead him away under guard." [45]And
when he came, he went up to him at once and said, "Rabbi!" And he kissed him.
[46]And they laid hands on him and seized him. [47]But one of those who stood by
drew his sword and struck the servant[2] of the high priest and cut off his ear.
[48]And Jesus said to them, "Have you come out as against a robber, with swords
and clubs to capture me? [49]Day after day I was with you in the temple teaching,
and you did not seize me. But let the Scriptures be fulfilled." [50]And they all left
him and fled.

A Young Man Flees

[51]And a young man followed him, with nothing but a linen cloth about his
body. And they seized him, [52]but he left the linen cloth and ran away naked.

Jesus Before the Council

[53]And they led Jesus to the high priest. And all the chief priests and the elders and the scribes came together. [54]And Peter had followed him at a distance,
right into the courtyard of the high priest. And he was sitting with the guards
and warming himself at the fire. [55]Now the chief priests and the whole council[3]
were seeking testimony against Jesus to put him to death, but they found none.
[56]For many bore false witness against him, but their testimony did not agree.
[57]And some stood up and bore false witness against him, saying, [58]"We heard
him say, 'I will destroy this temple that is made with hands, and in three days I
will build another, not made with hands.'" [59]Yet even about this their testimony
did not agree. [60]And the high priest stood up in the midst and asked Jesus, "Have

[1]Or *keep awake*; also verses 37, 38 [2]Or *bondservant* [3]Greek *Sanhedrin*

MARK 14:35–36

ABBA, FATHER

Jesus was a Son. Understanding Jesus' relationship to his Father is essential to understanding who Jesus is. When Jesus prayed in this passage, he used the word "Abba," which is the Aramaic word for "dad." When Jesus uttered his Father's name in both terms, it revealed a love both in his heart language and in the common language of the day, and it represents Jesus talking to God in the most personal of terms. Jesus talked to his Father as a loving son would talk to his dad.

The circumstances of this conversation were dire. Jesus was talking about "this cup" he was to drink, which foreshadowed his impending death (Mk 10:38). Figuratively, the cup held God's judgment for the sin of the world. Jesus knew that he had to drink it in order to fulfill the Father's plan for his life, for the redemption of his people.

In Jesus' suffering, we discover a wonderful truth about God's love. Our heavenly Father works everything together for the greatest good in the long run, even if that good requires difficult seasons for his children in the short run. The presence of pain and suffering does not negate the goodness of God as a Father to his children. Instead, God's presence is what helps carry his people through pain and suffering. Believers can look to God and call him "dad" as well: "For you did not receive the spirit of slavery to fall back into fear, but you have received the Spirit of adoption as sons, by whom we cry, 'Abba! Father!'" (Ro 8:15).

you no answer to make? What is it that these men testify against you?"[1] 61 But he remained silent and made no answer. Again the high priest asked him, "Are you the Christ, the Son of the Blessed?" 62 And Jesus said, "I am, and you will see the Son of Man seated at the right hand of Power, and coming with the clouds of heaven." 63 And the high priest tore his garments and said, "What further witnesses do we need? 64 You have heard his blasphemy. What is your decision?" And they all condemned him as deserving death. 65 And some began to spit on him and to cover his face and to strike him, saying to him, "Prophesy!" And the guards received him with blows.

Peter Denies Jesus

66 And as Peter was below in the courtyard, one of the servant girls of the high priest came, 67 and seeing Peter warming himself, she looked at him and said, "You also were with the Nazarene, Jesus." 68 But he denied it, saying, "I neither know nor understand what you mean." And he went out into the gateway[2] and the rooster crowed.[3] 69 And the servant girl saw him and began again to say to the bystanders, "This man is one of them." 70 But again he denied it. And after a little while the bystanders again said to Peter, "Certainly you are one of them, for you are a Galilean." 71 But he began to invoke a curse on himself and to swear, "I do not know this man of whom you speak." 72 And immediately the rooster crowed a second time. And Peter remembered how Jesus had said to him, "Before the rooster crows twice, you will deny me three times." And he broke down and wept.[4]

Jesus Delivered to Pilate

15 And as soon as it was morning, the chief priests held a consultation with the elders and scribes and the whole council. And they bound Jesus and led him away and delivered him over to Pilate. 2 And Pilate asked him, "Are you the King of the Jews?" And he answered him, "You have said so." 3 And the chief priests accused him of many things. 4 And Pilate again asked him, "Have you no answer to make? See how many charges they bring against you." 5 But Jesus made no further answer, so that Pilate was amazed.

Pilate Delivers Jesus to Be Crucified

6 Now at the feast he used to release for them one prisoner for whom they asked. 7 And among the rebels in prison, who had committed murder in the insurrection, there was a man called Barabbas. 8 And the crowd came up and began to ask Pilate to do as he usually did for them. 9 And he answered them, saying, "Do you want me to release for you the King of the Jews?" 10 For he perceived that it was out of envy that the chief priests had delivered him up. 11 But the chief priests stirred up the crowd to have him release for them Barabbas instead. 12 And Pilate again said to them, "Then what shall I do with the man you call the King of the Jews?" 13 And they cried out again, "Crucify him." 14 And Pilate said to them, "Why? What evil has he done?" But they shouted all the more, "Crucify him." 15 So Pilate, wishing to satisfy the crowd, released for them Barabbas, and having scourged[5] Jesus, he delivered him to be crucified.

Jesus Is Mocked

16 And the soldiers led him away inside the palace (that is, the governor's headquarters),[6] and they called together the whole battalion.[7] 17 And they clothed him in a purple cloak, and twisting together a crown of thorns, they put it on him. 18 And they began to salute him, "Hail, King of the Jews!" 19 And they were striking his head with a reed and spitting on him and kneeling down in homage to him.

[1] Or *Have you no answer to what these men testify against you?* [2] Or *forecourt* [3] Some manuscripts omit *and the rooster crowed* [4] Or *And when he had thought about it, he wept* [5] A Roman judicial penalty, consisting of a severe beating with a multi-lashed whip containing embedded pieces of bone and metal [6] Greek *the praetorium* [7] Greek *cohort*; a tenth of a Roman legion, usually about 600 men

20 And when they had mocked him, they stripped him of the purple cloak and put
his own clothes on him. And they led him out to crucify him.

The Crucifixion

21 And they compelled a passerby, Simon of Cyrene, who was coming in from
the country, the father of Alexander and Rufus, to carry his cross. 22 And they
brought him to the place called Golgotha (which means Place of a Skull). 23 And
they offered him wine mixed with myrrh, but he did not take it. 24 And they crucified him and divided his garments among them, casting lots for them, to decide
what each should take. 25 And it was the third hour[1] when they crucified him.
26 And the inscription of the charge against him read, "The King of the Jews." 27 And
with him they crucified two robbers, one on his right and one on his left.[2] 29 And
those who passed by derided him, wagging their heads and saying, "Aha! You who
would destroy the temple and rebuild it in three days, 30 save yourself, and come
down from the cross!" 31 So also the chief priests with the scribes mocked him to
one another, saying, "He saved others; he cannot save himself. 32 Let the Christ,
the King of Israel, come down now from the cross that we may see and believe."
Those who were crucified with him also reviled him.

The Death of Jesus

33 And when the sixth hour[3] had come, there was darkness over the whole land
until the ninth hour.[4] 34 And at the ninth hour Jesus cried with a loud voice, "Eloi,
Eloi, lema sabachthani?" which means, "My God, my God, why have you forsaken
me?" 35 And some of the bystanders hearing it said, "Behold, he is calling Elijah."
36 And someone ran and filled a sponge with sour wine, put it on a reed and gave
it to him to drink, saying, "Wait, let us see whether Elijah will come to take him
down." 37 And Jesus uttered a loud cry and breathed his last. 38 And the curtain of
the temple was torn in two, from top to bottom. 39 And when the centurion, who
stood facing him, saw that in this way he[5] breathed his last, he said, "Truly this
man was the Son[6] of God!"

40 There were also women looking on from a distance, among whom were
Mary Magdalene, and Mary the mother of James the younger and of Joses, and
Salome. 41 When he was in Galilee, they followed him and ministered to him, and
there were also many other women who came up with him to Jerusalem.

Jesus Is Buried

42 And when evening had come, since it was the day of Preparation, that is, the
day before the Sabbath, 43 Joseph of Arimathea, a respected member of the council, who was also himself looking for the kingdom of God, took courage and went
to Pilate and asked for the body of Jesus. 44 Pilate was surprised to hear that he
should have already died.[7] And summoning the centurion, he asked him whether
he was already dead. 45 And when he learned from the centurion that he was dead,
he granted the corpse to Joseph. 46 And Joseph[8] bought a linen shroud, and taking
him down, wrapped him in the linen shroud and laid him in a tomb that had been
cut out of the rock. And he rolled a stone against the entrance of the tomb. 47 Mary
Magdalene and Mary the mother of Joses saw where he was laid.

The Resurrection

16 When the Sabbath was past, Mary Magdalene, Mary the mother of James,
and Salome bought spices, so that they might go and anoint him. 2 And very
early on the first day of the week, when the sun had risen, they went to the tomb.
3 And they were saying to one another, "Who will roll away the stone for us from
the entrance of the tomb?" 4 And looking up, they saw that the stone had been

[1]That is, 9 A.M. [2]Some manuscripts insert verse 28: *And the Scripture was fulfilled that says, "He was numbered with the transgressors"* [3]That is, noon [4]That is, 3 P.M. [5]Some manuscripts insert *cried out and* [6]*Or a son* [7]*Or Pilate wondered whether he had already died* [8]Greek *he*

UNDEFEATED

Living in this broken world, people know defeat all too well. Everyone has experienced a relationship where someone let them down, or a situation that didn't work out the way they hoped. These moments of disappointment or frustration reveal the tragic fact that this world is deeply flawed. Even though believers live in the hope of the resurrection and the victorious life that Jesus promises through his Spirit, he still calls us to live in this world, where we experience death, brokenness, mourning, and pain (in contrast to the coming kingdom: Rev 21:4).

Jesus' resurrection reveals to believers the true way to life. Those who think that the abundant life consists of finding one's way around suffering and hardship have a misguided perception of what Jesus promised. Jesus' life and example teach that the way to a full life consists of service, hardship, opposition, pain, and suffering. Believers look at Jesus' life and see that God's best plan for his Son was to stay close to him through the most unimaginable of circumstances. The New Testament shows many times over that God was with his Son until the end, when Jesus took our sin upon himself and suffered on the cross.

But the good news is God didn't leave his Son in the grave! Because Jesus submitted to the point of death, and then defeated death, he paved the way for all people to find eternal life. By submitting himself to death, Jesus found life. "For whoever would save his life will lose it, but whoever loses his life for my sake and the gospel's will save it" (Mk 8:35). It's only in surrendering to his will and his way that believers actually find the fullness of life as God intended it. Giving is the key to gaining.

In all of this, Jesus is victorious. He was, is, and will always be undefeated by sin, by death, and by the grave. His victory is found in the fact that he was, and is, a selfless servant. In graciously giving his life, he also created a pathway to the life that is truly life eternal.

rolled back—it was very large. 5And entering the tomb, they saw a young man sitting on the right side, dressed in a white robe, and they were alarmed. 6And he said to them, "Do not be alarmed. You seek Jesus of Nazareth, who was crucified. He has risen; he is not here. See the place where they laid him. 7But go, tell his disciples and Peter that he is going before you to Galilee. There you will see him, just as he told you." 8And they went out and fled from the tomb, for trembling and astonishment had seized them, and they said nothing to anyone, for they were afraid.

[SOME OF THE EARLIEST MANUSCRIPTS DO NOT INCLUDE 16:9–20.][1]

Jesus Appears to Mary Magdalene

[[9Now when he rose early on the first day of the week, he appeared first to Mary Magdalene, from whom he had cast out seven demons. 10She went and told those who had been with him, as they mourned and wept. 11But when they heard that he was alive and had been seen by her, they would not believe it.

Jesus Appears to Two Disciples

12After these things he appeared in another form to two of them, as they were walking into the country. 13And they went back and told the rest, but they did not believe them.

The Great Commission

14Afterward he appeared to the eleven themselves as they were reclining at table, and he rebuked them for their unbelief and hardness of heart, because they had not believed those who saw him after he had risen. 15And he said to them, "Go into all the world and proclaim the gospel to the whole creation. 16Whoever believes and is baptized will be saved, but whoever does not believe will be condemned. 17And these signs will accompany those who believe: in my name they will cast out demons; they will speak in new tongues; 18they will pick up serpents with their hands; and if they drink any deadly poison, it will not hurt them; they will lay their hands on the sick, and they will recover."

19So then the Lord Jesus, after he had spoken to them, was taken up into heaven and sat down at the right hand of God. 20And they went out and preached everywhere, while the Lord worked with them and confirmed the message by accompanying signs.]]

[1]Some manuscripts end the book with 16:8; others include verses 9–20 immediately after verse 8. At least one manuscript inserts additional material after verse 14; some manuscripts include after verse 8 the following: *But they reported briefly to Peter and those with him all that they had been told. And after this, Jesus himself sent out by means of them, from east to west, the sacred and imperishable proclamation of eternal salvation.* These manuscripts then continue with verses 9–20

JESUS: OUR GRACIOUS SAVIOR

LUKE

LUKE

TIBERIUS CAESAR IS ROMAN EMPEROR *c. AD 14 – 37*	JOHN THE BAPTIST'S MINISTRY *c. AD 25 – 27*	JESUS' MINISTRY, DEATH, RESURRECTION *c. AD 27 – 30*

Jesus was sent by God to save sinners. Luke was one such sinner saved by the perfect life and substitutionary death of Jesus, the Messiah. Though Luke never met Jesus personally, it is clear that his life was radically transformed by the message he received from those who had.

Luke, a physician by trade, compiled information concerning the Christ from eyewitnesses to his life, death, and resurrection. The letter is addressed to Theophilus, presumably a Gentile convert who served among the Christian community established through Jesus' work. This neophyte church was facing persecution, and Luke sought to reassure Theophilus of God's faithfulness throughout history, seen most clearly in the sending of Jesus Christ. God would surely not abandon his people in the face of persecution when he had already gone to such great lengths to secure their salvation through Christ.

Luke's Gospel is the only one with a sequel — the book of Acts. There Luke continues to describe the ongoing acts of God through the power of the Holy Spirit as the church spread throughout the known world of the first century. Through the church's proclamation of Jesus, God continues to seek and save sinners.

This mission is vividly portrayed in the life of Christ seen throughout Luke's Gospel. Jesus was sent by God to fulfill his pledge to save his people from their sins. Though many would fail to trust him, Jesus relentlessly pursued them in his love. This passionate, gracious love is portrayed in the three stories found in Luke 15 — a lost sheep, a lost coin, and two lost sons. There Jesus is pictured as a loving Savior who will go to any length to find what belongs to him.

The message of salvation is available to all through Christ's work. But, as Luke shows, few will accept this gracious offer. Even his own people, the Jews, turn their backs on him and reject Jesus and his disciples. The brutal execution of the Son of God shows the widening gulf between followers of Jesus and those hardened in rebellion. Yet, the grace of God would overcome the height of human folly. In God's wisdom, the death of Jesus was God's perfect plan to defeat Satan, sin, and death once and for all. Through this sacrifice, the lost could be saved. Not only the Jews, but also Gentiles could receive the priceless gift of salvation. God's people could then give their lives for the sake of God's mission, the world — a mission that continues through the founding of the church in the book of Acts.

THE SPIRIT OF THE LORD IS UPON ME,
BECAUSE HE HAS ANOINTED ME TO PROCLAIM
GOOD NEWS TO THE POOR. HE HAS SENT ME
TO PROCLAIM LIBERTY TO THE CAPTIVES
AND RECOVERING OF SIGHT TO THE BLIND,
TO SET AT LIBERTY THOSE WHO ARE OPPRESSED.

Luke 4:18

LUKE

Dedication to Theophilus

1 Inasmuch as many have undertaken to compile a narrative of the things that have been accomplished among us, 2just as those who from the beginning were eyewitnesses and ministers of the word have delivered them to us, 3it seemed good to me also, having followed all things closely for some time past, to write an orderly account for you, most excellent Theophilus, 4that you may have certainty concerning the things you have been taught.

Birth of John the Baptist Foretold

5In the days of Herod, king of Judea, there was a priest named Zechariah,[1] of the division of Abijah. And he had a wife from the daughters of Aaron, and her name was Elizabeth. 6And they were both righteous before God, walking blamelessly in all the commandments and statutes of the Lord. 7But they had no child, because Elizabeth was barren, and both were advanced in years.

8Now while he was serving as priest before God when his division was on duty, 9according to the custom of the priesthood, he was chosen by lot to enter the temple of the Lord and burn incense. 10And the whole multitude of the people were praying outside at the hour of incense. 11And there appeared to him an angel of the Lord standing on the right side of the altar of incense. 12And Zechariah was troubled when he saw him, and fear fell upon him. 13But the angel said to him, "Do not be afraid, Zechariah, for your prayer has been heard, and your wife Elizabeth will bear you a son, and you shall call his name John. 14And you will have joy and gladness, and many will rejoice at his birth, 15for he will be great before the Lord. And he must not drink wine or strong drink, and he will be filled with the Holy Spirit, even from his mother's womb. 16And he will turn many of the children of Israel to the Lord their God, 17and he will go before him in the spirit and power of Elijah, to turn the hearts of the fathers to the children, and the disobedient to the wisdom of the just, to make ready for the Lord a people prepared."

18And Zechariah said to the angel, "How shall I know this? For I am an old man, and my wife is advanced in years." 19And the angel answered him, "I am Gabriel. I stand in the presence of God, and I was sent to speak to you and to bring you this good news. 20And behold, you will be silent and unable to speak until the day that these things take place, because you did not believe my words, which will be fulfilled in their time." 21And the people were waiting for Zechariah, and they were wondering at his delay in the temple. 22And when he came out, he was unable to speak to them, and they realized that he had seen a vision in the temple. And he kept making signs to them and remained mute. 23And when his time of service was ended, he went to his home.

24After these days his wife Elizabeth conceived, and for five months she kept herself hidden, saying, 25"Thus the Lord has done for me in the days when he looked on me, to take away my reproach among people."

Birth of Jesus Foretold

26In the sixth month the angel Gabriel was sent from God to a city of Galilee named Nazareth, 27to a virgin betrothed[2] to a man whose name was Joseph, of the house of David. And the virgin's name was Mary. 28And he came to her and said, "Greetings, O favored one, the Lord is with you!"[3] 29But she was greatly troubled at the saying, and tried to discern what sort of greeting this might be.

[1]Greek *Zacharias* [2]That is, legally pledged to be married [3]Some manuscripts add *Blessed are you among women!*

30 And the angel said to her, "Do not be afraid, Mary, for you have found favor
with God. 31 And behold, you will conceive in your womb and bear a son, and
you shall call his name Jesus. 32 He will be great and will be called the Son of the
Most High. And the Lord God will give to him the throne of his father David,
33 and he will reign over the house of Jacob forever, and of his kingdom there
will be no end."

34 And Mary said to the angel, "How will this be, since I am a virgin?"[1]

35 And the angel answered her, "The Holy Spirit will come upon you, and the
power of the Most High will overshadow you; therefore the child to be born[2] will
be called holy—the Son of God. 36 And behold, your relative Elizabeth in her old
age has also conceived a son, and this is the sixth month with her who was called
barren. 37 For nothing will be impossible with God." 38 And Mary said, "Behold, I
am the servant[3] of the Lord; let it be to me according to your word." And the angel
departed from her.

Mary Visits Elizabeth

39 In those days Mary arose and went with haste into the hill country, to a town
in Judah, 40 and she entered the house of Zechariah and greeted Elizabeth. 41 And
when Elizabeth heard the greeting of Mary, the baby leaped in her womb. And
Elizabeth was filled with the Holy Spirit, 42 and she exclaimed with a loud cry,
"Blessed are you among women, and blessed is the fruit of your womb! 43 And
why is this granted to me that the mother of my Lord should come to me? 44 For
behold, when the sound of your greeting came to my ears, the baby in my womb
leaped for joy. 45 And blessed is she who believed that there would be[4] a fulfillment
of what was spoken to her from the Lord."

Mary's Song of Praise: The Magnificat

46 And Mary said,

"My soul magnifies the Lord,
47 and my spirit rejoices in God my Savior,
48 for he has looked on the humble estate of his servant.
For behold, from now on all generations will call me blessed;
49 for he who is mighty has done great things for me,
and holy is his name.
50 And his mercy is for those who fear him
from generation to generation.
51 He has shown strength with his arm;
he has scattered the proud in the thoughts of their hearts;
52 he has brought down the mighty from their thrones
and exalted those of humble estate;
53 he has filled the hungry with good things,
and the rich he has sent away empty.
54 He has helped his servant Israel,
in remembrance of his mercy,
55 as he spoke to our fathers,
to Abraham and to his offspring forever."

56 And Mary remained with her about three months and returned to her home.

The Birth of John the Baptist

57 Now the time came for Elizabeth to give birth, and she bore a son. 58 And
her neighbors and relatives heard that the Lord had shown great mercy to her,
and they rejoiced with her. 59 And on the eighth day they came to circumcise
the child. And they would have called him Zechariah after his father, 60 but his

[1] Greek *since I do not know a man* [2] Some manuscripts add *of you* [3] Greek *bondservant*; also verse 48
[4] Or *believed, for there will be*

SON OF THE MOST HIGH

When Gabriel announced to Mary that she would have a son, the angel invoked a promise that had echoed throughout the Old Testament. Her son would be called the Son of the Most High and would reign on the throne of his father, David. Those familiar with the Law and the Prophets, including Mary herself, would have quickly begun to connect the prophetic dots.

God had picked David, a young shepherd boy, from among an entire family of brothers and made him the ruler over Israel. God promised to make David's name great. In addition, God promised that after David died, God would raise up one of his offspring to establish the throne of his kingdom forever (2Sa 7:8 – 16).

During his life, as David faced enemies and conspiracy, he sang songs of praise to God for protecting him as God's anointed (Ps 2:1 – 12) and for establishing his line for as long as the heavens endure (Ps 89:19 – 29). David intoned a psalm of praise that contained a phrase that Jesus later quoted to confound his critics: "The LORD says to my lord ..." (Ps 110:1; Mt 22:44). Another psalm affirmed that God, in his promise to David about the duration of his throne, had sworn an oath that could not be revoked (Ps 132:11 – 12).

The prophet Isaiah continued to prophesy the fulfillment of God's promise to David. He wrote that to his people a child would be born, a son would be given, and the government would be on his shoulders (Isa 9:6 – 7). Isaiah also affirmed that a shoot would come up from the stump of Jesse, David's father, and from its roots a Branch (referring to Jesus) would bear fruit (Isa 11:1 – 15).

In time, God's plan became clear: he would fulfill this promise through his Son, Jesus. When the angel appeared to Mary, God provided the ultimate update on God's plan to keep his promise. The baby in Mary's womb, conceived by the Holy Spirit though Mary was a virgin, was God's Son who would reign eternally (Lk 1:31 – 33). As a capstone to the astounding declaration, the angel reminded Mary that no word from God would ever fail (v. 37).

The intricate history of God's initial promise realized so fully at Jesus' first coming increases confidence that the rest of God's promises will be fulfilled at Jesus' second coming and after that, into eternity.

mother answered, "No; he shall be called John." 61And they said to her, "None
of your relatives is called by this name." 62And they made signs to his father,
inquiring what he wanted him to be called. 63And he asked for a writing tablet
and wrote, "His name is John." And they all wondered. 64And immediately his
mouth was opened and his tongue loosed, and he spoke, blessing God. 65And
fear came on all their neighbors. And all these things were talked about through
all the hill country of Judea, 66and all who heard them laid them up in their
hearts, saying, "What then will this child be?" For the hand of the Lord was
with him.

Zechariah's Prophecy

67And his father Zechariah was filled with the Holy Spirit and prophesied, saying,

68 "Blessed be the Lord God of Israel,
for he has visited and redeemed his people
69 and has raised up a horn of salvation for us
in the house of his servant David,
70 as he spoke by the mouth of his holy prophets from of old,
71 that we should be saved from our enemies
and from the hand of all who hate us;
72 to show the mercy promised to our fathers
and to remember his holy covenant,
73 the oath that he swore to our father Abraham, to grant us
74 that we, being delivered from the hand of our enemies,
might serve him without fear,
75 in holiness and righteousness before him all our days.
76 And you, child, will be called the prophet of the Most High;
for you will go before the Lord to prepare his ways,
77 to give knowledge of salvation to his people
in the forgiveness of their sins,
78 because of the tender mercy of our God,
whereby the sunrise shall visit us[1] from on high
79 to give light to those who sit in darkness and in the shadow of death,
to guide our feet into the way of peace."

80And the child grew and became strong in spirit, and he was in the wilderness
until the day of his public appearance to Israel.

The Birth of Jesus Christ

2 In those days a decree went out from Caesar Augustus that all the world
should be registered. 2This was the first registration when[2] Quirinius was
governor of Syria. 3And all went to be registered, each to his own town. 4And Joseph also went up from Galilee, from the town of Nazareth, to Judea, to the city
of David, which is called Bethlehem, because he was of the house and lineage
of David, 5to be registered with Mary, his betrothed,[3] who was with child. 6And
while they were there, the time came for her to give birth. 7And she gave birth to
her firstborn son and wrapped him in swaddling cloths and laid him in a manger,
because there was no place for them in the inn.[4]

The Shepherds and the Angels

8And in the same region there were shepherds out in the field, keeping watch
over their flock by night. 9And an angel of the Lord appeared to them, and the
glory of the Lord shone around them, and they were filled with great fear. 10And
the angel said to them, "Fear not, for behold, I bring you good news of great joy

---

[1] Or *when the sunrise shall dawn upon us*; some manuscripts *since the sunrise has visited us* [2] Or *This was the registration before* [3] That is, one legally pledged to be married [4] Or *guest room*

LUKE 2:11

SAVIOR, CHRIST, LORD

The three titles "Savior," "Christ," and "Lord" summarize the work of the Messiah to save. What God was called in 1:47 ("Savior"), Jesus is called here. This description includes the related meanings of deliverer, protector, or preserver. The word "Christ" means "anointed one," referring to Jesus' royal position, the One who was promised and long expected. The word "Lord" is the title of a ruler. The use of "Lord" throughout the New Testament is also significant because, out of reverence for God's covenant name, the Greek word for "Lord" stood in place of *Yahweh* in the Greek translation of the Old Testament.

Peter elaborated on the meaning of these words in Acts 2:30–36 where Jesus is pictured as sitting on a throne and distributing the gift of salvation from God's side, ruling with the Father. In this way, Peter connected Jesus with God's promises to give David an everlasting kingdom. To refer to Jesus as a good man or a good teacher falls immeasurably short of reality. Jesus came to save people from their sin, as promised. He came to minister, to suffer and die, to rise again, and rule and reign forever as Lord. This was the outworking of God's grand plan, what the writer of Hebrews would call "such a great salvation" (Heb 2:3).

that will be for all the people. 11For unto you is born this day in the city of David
a Savior, who is Christ the Lord. 12And this will be a sign for you: you will find a
baby wrapped in swaddling cloths and lying in a manger." 13And suddenly there
was with the angel a multitude of the heavenly host praising God and saying,

14 "Glory to God in the highest,
  and on earth peace among those with whom he is pleased!"[1]

15When the angels went away from them into heaven, the shepherds said
to one another, "Let us go over to Bethlehem and see this thing that has happened, which the Lord has made known to us." 16And they went with haste and
found Mary and Joseph, and the baby lying in a manger. 17And when they saw
it, they made known the saying that had been told them concerning this child.
18And all who heard it wondered at what the shepherds told them. 19But Mary
treasured up all these things, pondering them in her heart. 20And the shepherds
returned, glorifying and praising God for all they had heard and seen, as it had
been told them.

21And at the end of eight days, when he was circumcised, he was called Jesus,
the name given by the angel before he was conceived in the womb.

Jesus Presented at the Temple

22And when the time came for their purification according to the Law of Moses, they brought him up to Jerusalem to present him to the Lord 23(as it is written
in the Law of the Lord, "Every male who first opens the womb shall be called
holy to the Lord") 24and to offer a sacrifice according to what is said in the Law of
the Lord, "a pair of turtledoves, or two young pigeons." 25Now there was a man
in Jerusalem, whose name was Simeon, and this man was righteous and devout,
waiting for the consolation of Israel, and the Holy Spirit was upon him. 26And it
had been revealed to him by the Holy Spirit that he would not see death before he
had seen the Lord's Christ. 27And he came in the Spirit into the temple, and when
the parents brought in the child Jesus, to do for him according to the custom of
the Law, 28he took him up in his arms and blessed God and said,

29 "Lord, now you are letting your servant[2] depart in peace,
  according to your word;
30 for my eyes have seen your salvation
31   that you have prepared in the presence of all peoples,
32 a light for revelation to the Gentiles,
  and for glory to your people Israel."

33And his father and his mother marveled at what was said about him. 34And
Simeon blessed them and said to Mary his mother, "Behold, this child is appointed for the fall and rising of many in Israel, and for a sign that is opposed 35(and a
sword will pierce through your own soul also), so that thoughts from many hearts
may be revealed."

36And there was a prophetess, Anna, the daughter of Phanuel, of the tribe of
Asher. She was advanced in years, having lived with her husband seven years
from when she was a virgin, 37and then as a widow until she was eighty-four.[3] She
did not depart from the temple, worshiping with fasting and prayer night and day.
38And coming up at that very hour she began to give thanks to God and to speak
of him to all who were waiting for the redemption of Jerusalem.

The Return to Nazareth

39And when they had performed everything according to the Law of the Lord,
they returned into Galilee, to their own town of Nazareth. 40And the child grew
and became strong, filled with wisdom. And the favor of God was upon him.

[1]Some manuscripts *peace, good will among men* [2]Or *bondservant* [3]Or *as a widow for eighty-four years*

The Boy Jesus in the Temple

41 Now his parents went to Jerusalem every year at the Feast of the Passover. 42 And when he was twelve years old, they went up according to custom. 43 And when the feast was ended, as they were returning, the boy Jesus stayed behind in Jerusalem. His parents did not know it, 44 but supposing him to be in the group they went a day's journey, but then they began to search for him among their relatives and acquaintances, 45 and when they did not find him, they returned to Jerusalem, searching for him. 46 After three days they found him in the temple, sitting among the teachers, listening to them and asking them questions. 47 And all who heard him were amazed at his understanding and his answers. 48 And when his parents[1] saw him, they were astonished. And his mother said to him, "Son, why have you treated us so? Behold, your father and I have been searching for you in great distress." 49 And he said to them, "Why were you looking for me? Did you not know that I must be in my Father's house?"[2] 50 And they did not understand the saying that he spoke to them. 51 And he went down with them and came to Nazareth and was submissive to them. And his mother treasured up all these things in her heart.

52 And Jesus increased in wisdom and in stature[3] and in favor with God and man.

John the Baptist Prepares the Way

3 In the fifteenth year of the reign of Tiberius Caesar, Pontius Pilate being governor of Judea, and Herod being tetrarch of Galilee, and his brother Philip tetrarch of the region of Ituraea and Trachonitis, and Lysanias tetrarch of Abilene, 2 during the high priesthood of Annas and Caiaphas, the word of God came to John the son of Zechariah in the wilderness. 3 And he went into all the region around the Jordan, proclaiming a baptism of repentance for the forgiveness of sins. 4 As it is written in the book of the words of Isaiah the prophet,

"The voice of one crying in the wilderness:
'Prepare the way of the Lord,[4]
make his paths straight.
5 Every valley shall be filled,
and every mountain and hill shall be made low,
and the crooked shall become straight,
and the rough places shall become level ways,
6 and all flesh shall see the salvation of God.'"

7 He said therefore to the crowds that came out to be baptized by him, "You brood of vipers! Who warned you to flee from the wrath to come? 8 Bear fruits in keeping with repentance. And do not begin to say to yourselves, 'We have Abraham as our father.' For I tell you, God is able from these stones to raise up children for Abraham. 9 Even now the axe is laid to the root of the trees. Every tree therefore that does not bear good fruit is cut down and thrown into the fire."

10 And the crowds asked him, "What then shall we do?" 11 And he answered them, "Whoever has two tunics[5] is to share with him who has none, and whoever has food is to do likewise." 12 Tax collectors also came to be baptized and said to him, "Teacher, what shall we do?" 13 And he said to them, "Collect no more than you are authorized to do." 14 Soldiers also asked him, "And we, what shall we do?" And he said to them, "Do not extort money from anyone by threats or by false accusation, and be content with your wages."

15 As the people were in expectation, and all were questioning in their hearts concerning John, whether he might be the Christ, 16 John answered them all, saying, "I baptize you with water, but he who is mightier than I is coming, the strap

[1] Greek *they* [2] Or *about my Father's business* [3] Or *years* [4] Or *crying, Prepare in the wilderness the way of the Lord* [5] Greek *chiton*, a long garment worn under the cloak next to the skin

LUKE 2:49

MY FATHER'S BUSINESS

The Bible provides limited information about Jesus' life as a child. We know his parents took him to the temple when he was eight days old to present him to the Lord, to circumcise him, and to offer a sacrifice as prescribed by the law (Lk 2:21–24). Then when Jesus was age 12, he and his family returned to the temple. There Jesus demonstrated an understanding of the work God had commissioned him to accomplish. This evocative statement in the Greek text is an elliptical clause that leaves out a key word. It reads, "I must be in the ... of my Father," without specifying a place or activity. So what young Jesus proclaimed here is that either he must be in the house of God discussing God's truth as the translation suggests, or he must be busy with the Father's work in another context. In the end, the two possibilities are not very different. Over time, it became clear that Jesus understood fully the work he had to do—preaching the Good News while traveling to Jerusalem to be killed and to rise on the third day (Lk 9:22). In anticipation of the day he would begin his earthly ministry, he "increased in wisdom and in stature and in favor with God and man" (Lk 2:52).

of whose sandals I am not worthy to untie. He will baptize you with the Holy Spirit and fire. [17]His winnowing fork is in his hand, to clear his threshing floor and to gather the wheat into his barn, but the chaff he will burn with unquenchable fire."

[18]So with many other exhortations he preached good news to the people. [19]But Herod the tetrarch, who had been reproved by him for Herodias, his brother's wife, and for all the evil things that Herod had done, [20]added this to them all, that he locked up John in prison.

[21]Now when all the people were baptized, and when Jesus also had been baptized and was praying, the heavens were opened, [22]and the Holy Spirit descended on him in bodily form, like a dove; and a voice came from heaven, "You are my beloved Son;[1] with you I am well pleased."[2]

The Genealogy of Jesus Christ

[23]Jesus, when he began his ministry, was about thirty years of age, being the son (as was supposed) of Joseph, the son of Heli, [24]the son of Matthat, the son of Levi, the son of Melchi, the son of Jannai, the son of Joseph, [25]the son of Mattathias, the son of Amos, the son of Nahum, the son of Esli, the son of Naggai, [26]the son of Maath, the son of Mattathias, the son of Semein, the son of Josech, the son of Joda, [27]the son of Joanan, the son of Rhesa, the son of Zerubbabel, the son of Shealtiel,[3] the son of Neri, [28]the son of Melchi, the son of Addi, the son of Cosam, the son of Elmadam, the son of Er, [29]the son of Joshua, the son of Eliezer, the son of Jorim, the son of Matthat, the son of Levi, [30]the son of Simeon, the son of Judah, the son of Joseph, the son of Jonam, the son of Eliakim, [31]the son of Melea, the son of Menna, the son of Mattatha, the son of Nathan, the son of David, [32]the son of Jesse, the son of Obed, the son of Boaz, the son of Sala, the son of Nahshon, [33]the son of Amminadab, the son of Admin, the son of Arni, the son of Hezron, the son of Perez, the son of Judah, [34]the son of Jacob, the son of Isaac, the son of Abraham, the son of Terah, the son of Nahor, [35]the son of Serug, the son of Reu, the son of Peleg, the son of Eber, the son of Shelah, [36]the son of Cainan, the son of Arphaxad, the son of Shem, the son of Noah, the son of Lamech, [37]the son of Methuselah, the son of Enoch, the son of Jared, the son of Mahalaleel, the son of Cainan, [38]the son of Enos, the son of Seth, the son of Adam, the son of God.

The Temptation of Jesus

4 And Jesus, full of the Holy Spirit, returned from the Jordan and was led by the Spirit in the wilderness [2]for forty days, being tempted by the devil. And he ate nothing during those days. And when they were ended, he was hungry. [3]The devil said to him, "If you are the Son of God, command this stone to become bread." [4]And Jesus answered him, "It is written, 'Man shall not live by bread alone.'" [5]And the devil took him up and showed him all the kingdoms of the world in a moment of time, [6]and said to him, "To you I will give all this authority and their glory, for it has been delivered to me, and I give it to whom I will. [7]If you, then, will worship me, it will all be yours." [8]And Jesus answered him, "It is written,

"'You shall worship the Lord your God,
and him only shall you serve.'"

[9]And he took him to Jerusalem and set him on the pinnacle of the temple and said to him, "If you are the Son of God, throw yourself down from here, [10]for it is written,

"'He will command his angels concerning you,
to guard you,'

[1]Or *my Son, my* (or *the*) *Beloved* [2]Some manuscripts *beloved Son; today I have begotten you*
[3]Greek *Salathiel*

LUKE 4:1–13

TEMPTATION AND SCRIPTURE

In his humanity, Jesus experienced every temptation that humans do, yet he was without sin (Heb 4:15). When Satan tempted Jesus in the wilderness, Jesus demonstrated his ability to resist the devil and declared his allegiance to God. What Adam failed to do in the garden, Jesus did in the wilderness. When Satan challenged Jesus' identity and authority, Jesus responded by quoting Scripture (Dt 8:3), a succinct way to demonstrate his refusal to live independently from his Father. Next, when Satan enticed Jesus to avoid the cross and gain power in an easier way, Jesus confronted Satan's exaggerated claims about power and authority with another scriptural quote (Dt 6:13). Finally, Satan suggested that Jesus jump from the highest point on the temple, fighting fire with fire and bolstering this temptation with a Scripture passage (Ps 91:11–12). Refusing to put God to a test, Jesus withstood this last temptation by quoting Scripture once again (Dt 6:16). Satan retreated, defeated for the moment by Jesus, who resisted his advances by submitting humbly to God (Jas 4:7). Using the sword of the Spirit, which is the Word of God, Jesus demonstrated how to defeat the devil's schemes and extinguish the flaming arrows directed at God's children (Eph 6:10–17).

LUKE 3:15 – 18

ONE MORE POWERFUL

When John began to preach in the wilderness, crowds flocked to see him. He baptized those who confessed their sins but rebuked the pious religious leaders for their self-reliance (Mt 3:7 – 10). After 400 years without a prophet, people rushed to John, wondering if he might be the Christ, the one for whom they as a people had been waiting for centuries. John pointed them to one more powerful than himself who was to come — Jesus. While John baptized with water as a sign of repentance, Jesus would baptize with the Holy Spirit and fire (Mt 3:11).

The power Jesus demonstrated in his baptism differed from John's to an infinite degree. To observers, their physical actions looked similar. While both used water, Jesus' baptism pointed to an imminent change, the time when God would take up residence in the lives of believers through the person of the Holy Spirit. Each of the Gospel writers reference this distinctive element of Jesus' work (Mt 3:11; Mk 1:8; Jn 1:33), foreshadowing the nature of the Trinity: one God in three persons — Father, Son, and Holy Spirit.

During Jesus' earthly ministry, his disciples experienced power for immediate tasks in Jesus' name (Lk 10:17 – 20). While the disciples relished these experiences, Jesus knew they would soon experience a substantively different reality — something that could only happen when he returned to his Father (Jn 16:7). Before he ascended into heaven after his resurrection, Jesus commanded his disciples not to leave Jerusalem but to wait for the gift his Father had promised, the Holy Spirit (Ac 1:4 – 5). Once the Spirit came in fullness, the Holy Spirit's filling became the confirmation that God had accepted people by grace through faith in Jesus. This grace extended even to Gentiles who had not kept the Law of Moses (Ac 11:15 – 17).

Throughout his ministry, John stated firmly that Jesus must become greater while he became less (Jn 3:30). John understood that he was responsible for preparing the way for Jesus, calling people to repentance. Jesus affirmed this role, stating that John was a great man (Mt 11:10 – 11) who had faithfully fulfilled his purpose. During his life, John never confused his role or ministry with that of Jesus. He knew Jesus was the Lamb of God who would take away the sin of the world — one who was more powerful than himself and greater in all possible ways (Jn 1:36).

11and

"'On their hands they will bear you up,
lest you strike your foot against a stone.'"

12And Jesus answered him, "It is said, 'You shall not put the Lord your God to the test.'" 13And when the devil had ended every temptation, he departed from him until an opportune time.

Jesus Begins His Ministry

14And Jesus returned in the power of the Spirit to Galilee, and a report about him went out through all the surrounding country. 15And he taught in their synagogues, being glorified by all.

Jesus Rejected at Nazareth

16And he came to Nazareth, where he had been brought up. And as was his custom, he went to the synagogue on the Sabbath day, and he stood up to read. 17And the scroll of the prophet Isaiah was given to him. He unrolled the scroll and found the place where it was written,

18 "The Spirit of the Lord is upon me,
because he has anointed me
to proclaim good news to the poor.
He has sent me to proclaim liberty to the captives
and recovering of sight to the blind,
to set at liberty those who are oppressed,
19 to proclaim the year of the Lord's favor."

20And he rolled up the scroll and gave it back to the attendant and sat down. And the eyes of all in the synagogue were fixed on him. 21And he began to say to them, "Today this Scripture has been fulfilled in your hearing." 22And all spoke well of him and marveled at the gracious words that were coming from his mouth. And they said, "Is not this Joseph's son?" 23And he said to them, "Doubtless you will quote to me this proverb, '"Physician, heal yourself." What we have heard you did at Capernaum, do here in your hometown as well.'" 24And he said, "Truly, I say to you, no prophet is acceptable in his hometown. 25But in truth, I tell you, there were many widows in Israel in the days of Elijah, when the heavens were shut up three years and six months, and a great famine came over all the land, 26and Elijah was sent to none of them but only to Zarephath, in the land of Sidon, to a woman who was a widow. 27And there were many lepers[1] in Israel in the time of the prophet Elisha, and none of them was cleansed, but only Naaman the Syrian." 28When they heard these things, all in the synagogue were filled with wrath. 29And they rose up and drove him out of the town and brought him to the brow of the hill on which their town was built, so that they could throw him down the cliff. 30But passing through their midst, he went away.

Jesus Heals a Man with an Unclean Demon

31And he went down to Capernaum, a city of Galilee. And he was teaching them on the Sabbath, 32and they were astonished at his teaching, for his word possessed authority. 33And in the synagogue there was a man who had the spirit of an unclean demon, and he cried out with a loud voice, 34"Ha![2] What have you to do with us, Jesus of Nazareth? Have you come to destroy us? I know who you are—the Holy One of God." 35But Jesus rebuked him, saying, "Be silent and come out of him!" And when the demon had thrown him down in their midst, he came out of him, having done him no harm. 36And they were all amazed and said to one another, "What is this word? For with authority and power he commands the

---

[1]*Leprosy* was a term for several skin diseases; see Leviticus 13 [2]Or *Leave us alone*

unclean spirits, and they come out!" 37 And reports about him went out into every
place in the surrounding region.

Jesus Heals Many

38 And he arose and left the synagogue and entered Simon's house. Now Simon's mother-in-law was ill with a high fever, and they appealed to him on her
behalf. 39 And he stood over her and rebuked the fever, and it left her, and immediately she rose and began to serve them.

40 Now when the sun was setting, all those who had any who were sick with
various diseases brought them to him, and he laid his hands on every one of them
and healed them. 41 And demons also came out of many, crying, "You are the Son
of God!" But he rebuked them and would not allow them to speak, because they
knew that he was the Christ.

Jesus Preaches in Synagogues

42 And when it was day, he departed and went into a desolate place. And the
people sought him and came to him, and would have kept him from leaving them,
43 but he said to them, "I must preach the good news of the kingdom of God to the
other towns as well; for I was sent for this purpose." 44 And he was preaching in
the synagogues of Judea.[1]

Jesus Calls the First Disciples

5 On one occasion, while the crowd was pressing in on him to hear the word
of God, he was standing by the lake of Gennesaret, 2 and he saw two boats by
the lake, but the fishermen had gone out of them and were washing their nets.
3 Getting into one of the boats, which was Simon's, he asked him to put out a little
from the land. And he sat down and taught the people from the boat. 4 And when
he had finished speaking, he said to Simon, "Put out into the deep and let down
your nets for a catch." 5 And Simon answered, "Master, we toiled all night and took
nothing! But at your word I will let down the nets." 6 And when they had done this,
they enclosed a large number of fish, and their nets were breaking. 7 They signaled
to their partners in the other boat to come and help them. And they came and
filled both the boats, so that they began to sink. 8 But when Simon Peter saw it, he
fell down at Jesus' knees, saying, "Depart from me, for I am a sinful man, O Lord."
9 For he and all who were with him were astonished at the catch of fish that they
had taken, 10 and so also were James and John, sons of Zebedee, who were partners
with Simon. And Jesus said to Simon, "Do not be afraid; from now on you will be
catching men."[2] 11 And when they had brought their boats to land, they left everything and followed him.

Jesus Cleanses a Leper

12 While he was in one of the cities, there came a man full of leprosy.[3] And
when he saw Jesus, he fell on his face and begged him, "Lord, if you will, you can
make me clean." 13 And Jesus[4] stretched out his hand and touched him, saying,
"I will; be clean." And immediately the leprosy left him. 14 And he charged him
to tell no one, but "go and show yourself to the priest, and make an offering
for your cleansing, as Moses commanded, for a proof to them." 15 But now even
more the report about him went abroad, and great crowds gathered to hear him
and to be healed of their infirmities. 16 But he would withdraw to desolate places
and pray.

Jesus Heals a Paralytic

17 On one of those days, as he was teaching, Pharisees and teachers of the law
were sitting there, who had come from every village of Galilee and Judea and from

---

[1] Some manuscripts *Galilee* [2] The Greek word *anthropoi* refers here to both men and women [3] *Leprosy* was a term for several skin diseases; see Leviticus 13 [4] Greek *he*

Jerusalem. And the power of the Lord was with him to heal.[1] 18And behold, some men were bringing on a bed a man who was paralyzed, and they were seeking to bring him in and lay him before Jesus, 19but finding no way to bring him in, because of the crowd, they went up on the roof and let him down with his bed through the tiles into the midst before Jesus. 20And when he saw their faith, he said, "Man, your sins are forgiven you." 21And the scribes and the Pharisees began to question, saying, "Who is this who speaks blasphemies? Who can forgive sins but God alone?" 22When Jesus perceived their thoughts, he answered them, "Why do you question in your hearts? 23Which is easier, to say, 'Your sins are forgiven you,' or to say, 'Rise and walk'? 24But that you may know that the Son of Man has authority on earth to forgive sins"—he said to the man who was paralyzed—"I say to you, rise, pick up your bed and go home." 25And immediately he rose up before them and picked up what he had been lying on and went home, glorifying God. 26And amazement seized them all, and they glorified God and were filled with awe, saying, "We have seen extraordinary things today."

Jesus Calls Levi

27After this he went out and saw a tax collector named Levi, sitting at the tax booth. And he said to him, "Follow me." 28And leaving everything, he rose and followed him.

29And Levi made him a great feast in his house, and there was a large company of tax collectors and others reclining at table with them. 30And the Pharisees and their scribes grumbled at his disciples, saying, "Why do you eat and drink with tax collectors and sinners?" 31And Jesus answered them, "Those who are well have no need of a physician, but those who are sick. 32I have not come to call the righteous but sinners to repentance."

A Question About Fasting

33And they said to him, "The disciples of John fast often and offer prayers, and so do the disciples of the Pharisees, but yours eat and drink." 34And Jesus said to them, "Can you make wedding guests fast while the bridegroom is with them? 35The days will come when the bridegroom is taken away from them, and then they will fast in those days." 36He also told them a parable: "No one tears a piece from a new garment and puts it on an old garment. If he does, he will tear the new, and the piece from the new will not match the old. 37And no one puts new wine into old wineskins. If he does, the new wine will burst the skins and it will be spilled, and the skins will be destroyed. 38But new wine must be put into fresh wineskins. 39And no one after drinking old wine desires new, for he says, 'The old is good.'"[2]

Jesus Is Lord of the Sabbath

6 On a Sabbath,[3] while he was going through the grainfields, his disciples plucked and ate some heads of grain, rubbing them in their hands. 2But some of the Pharisees said, "Why are you doing what is not lawful to do on the Sabbath?" 3And Jesus answered them, "Have you not read what David did when he was hungry, he and those who were with him: 4how he entered the house of God and took and ate the bread of the Presence, which is not lawful for any but the priests to eat, and also gave it to those with him?" 5And he said to them, "The Son of Man is lord of the Sabbath."

A Man with a Withered Hand

6On another Sabbath, he entered the synagogue and was teaching, and a man was there whose right hand was withered. 7And the scribes and the Pharisees watched him, to see whether he would heal on the Sabbath, so that they might

[1]Some manuscripts *was present to heal them* [2]Some manuscripts *better* [3]Some manuscripts *On the second first Sabbath* (that is, on the second Sabbath after the first)

LUKE 5:24

SON OF MAN

The religious leaders watched to see if Jesus would heal on the Sabbath. Jesus increased the stakes by stating that he, as the Son of Man, had the power and authority to forgive sin. The phrase "Son of Man" was an Aramaic idiom that referred to a human being, meaning "someone" or "I." But in this situation, Jesus referenced a title from Daniel 7:13, something he did regularly during his ministry, especially when he wanted to emphasize the nature of his relationship to the Father (Lk 21:27; 22:69). Daniel used the title "son of man" to describe one who shared authority with the Ancient of Days, a powerful reference to the one true God. By invoking this image, Jesus tapped into the supernatural impression of this figure, for only God rides the clouds (Ex 14:20; Ps 104:3).

The question Jesus posed to the religious leaders was whether he had the authority to forgive sin. By referring to himself as the Son of Man in that context, Jesus claimed the authority to forgive sins with the full understanding that such authority was limited only to God.

find a reason to accuse him. [8]But he knew their thoughts, and he said to the man
with the withered hand, "Come and stand here." And he rose and stood there.
[9]And Jesus said to them, "I ask you, is it lawful on the Sabbath to do good or to
do harm, to save life or to destroy it?" [10]And after looking around at them all he
said to him, "Stretch out your hand." And he did so, and his hand was restored.
[11]But they were filled with fury and discussed with one another what they might
do to Jesus.

The Twelve Apostles

[12]In these days he went out to the mountain to pray, and all night he continued in prayer to God. [13]And when day came, he called his disciples and chose
from them twelve, whom he named apostles: [14]Simon, whom he named Peter,
and Andrew his brother, and James and John, and Philip, and Bartholomew, [15]and
Matthew, and Thomas, and James the son of Alphaeus, and Simon who was called
the Zealot, [16]and Judas the son of James, and Judas Iscariot, who became a traitor.

Jesus Ministers to a Great Multitude

[17]And he came down with them and stood on a level place, with a great crowd
of his disciples and a great multitude of people from all Judea and Jerusalem and
the seacoast of Tyre and Sidon, [18]who came to hear him and to be healed of their
diseases. And those who were troubled with unclean spirits were cured. [19]And
all the crowd sought to touch him, for power came out from him and healed
them all.

The Beatitudes

[20]And he lifted up his eyes on his disciples, and said:
"Blessed are you who are poor, for yours is the kingdom of God.
[21]"Blessed are you who are hungry now, for you shall be satisfied.
"Blessed are you who weep now, for you shall laugh.
[22]"Blessed are you when people hate you and when they exclude you and revile you and spurn your name as evil, on account of the Son of Man! [23]Rejoice in
that day, and leap for joy, for behold, your reward is great in heaven; for so their
fathers did to the prophets.

Jesus Pronounces Woes

[24]"But woe to you who are rich, for you have received your consolation.
[25]"Woe to you who are full now, for you shall be hungry.
"Woe to you who laugh now, for you shall mourn and weep.
[26]"Woe to you, when all people speak well of you, for so their fathers did to
the false prophets.

Love Your Enemies

[27]"But I say to you who hear, Love your enemies, do good to those who hate
you, [28]bless those who curse you, pray for those who abuse you. [29]To one who
strikes you on the cheek, offer the other also, and from one who takes away your
cloak do not withhold your tunic[1] either. [30]Give to everyone who begs from you,
and from one who takes away your goods do not demand them back. [31]And as you
wish that others would do to you, do so to them.
[32]"If you love those who love you, what benefit is that to you? For even sinners
love those who love them. [33]And if you do good to those who do good to you, what
benefit is that to you? For even sinners do the same. [34]And if you lend to those
from whom you expect to receive, what credit is that to you? Even sinners lend to
sinners, to get back the same amount. [35]But love your enemies, and do good, and
lend, expecting nothing in return, and your reward will be great, and you will be

[1]Greek *chiton*, a long garment worn under the cloak next to the skin

JESUS AND THE POOR

Many, if not most, of the people who listened to Jesus' words that day were poor. The difficulties and hardships of their lives drove them to listen to this prophet, Jesus. As those who lacked material wealth, they may have hoped Jesus would tell them more about the kingdom of God — the day when the righteous Messiah and not the cruel Romans would govern them.

From his initial statement, Jesus launched into a series of statements that turned the crowd's perceptions upside down. Jesus' speech contrasted possessions and values with those that flow from a heavenly perspective. In a few sentences, Jesus affirmed that things in this world are not always what they seem and certainly are not what they will one day be.

At face value, it seemed as though Jesus was making a blanket promise of salvation and blessing to everyone who was poor materially. Based on this interpretation, some have viewed the poor as God's chosen people — those who suffer in this world but can expect immeasurable blessings in the next. Those holding this view often advocate that God's people, the church, should prioritize ministry to the poor and in this way advance the kingdom of God.

Others view Jesus' statement as an insight into spiritual poverty, referencing a similar sermon in which Jesus talked about the "poor in spirit" (Mt 5:3). In their view, Jesus was offering great blessing to those who recognize their spiritual poverty before God. Because they acknowledge that nothing they do can enhance their spiritual standing, these people, the poor in spirit, receive God's unmerited favor. So, in this second view, Jesus is not affirming the value of being poor materially but warning against the profound danger of being self-sufficient spiritually.

Since Jesus referenced both the "poor" and the "poor in spirit," the implications of his words can be intertwined. Throughout his ministry on earth, Jesus met the practical needs of the poor — feeding, healing, and honoring them. In spite of this emphasis, Jesus refused to place a higher priority on meeting physical needs than on meeting spiritual needs. Through his words and his actions, Jesus demonstrated the divine balance — pay attention to those with physical needs but never forget the priority of spiritual needs.

sons of the Most High, for he is kind to the ungrateful and the evil. 36Be merciful, even as your Father is merciful.

Judging Others

37"Judge not, and you will not be judged; condemn not, and you will not be condemned; forgive, and you will be forgiven; 38give, and it will be given to you. Good measure, pressed down, shaken together, running over, will be put into your lap. For with the measure you use it will be measured back to you."

39He also told them a parable: "Can a blind man lead a blind man? Will they not both fall into a pit? 40A disciple is not above his teacher, but everyone when he is fully trained will be like his teacher. 41Why do you see the speck that is in your brother's eye, but do not notice the log that is in your own eye? 42How can you say to your brother, 'Brother, let me take out the speck that is in your eye,' when you yourself do not see the log that is in your own eye? You hypocrite, first take the log out of your own eye, and then you will see clearly to take out the speck that is in your brother's eye.

A Tree and Its Fruit

43"For no good tree bears bad fruit, nor again does a bad tree bear good fruit, 44for each tree is known by its own fruit. For figs are not gathered from thornbushes, nor are grapes picked from a bramble bush. 45The good person out of the good treasure of his heart produces good, and the evil person out of his evil treasure produces evil, for out of the abundance of the heart his mouth speaks.

Build Your House on the Rock

46"Why do you call me 'Lord, Lord,' and not do what I tell you? 47Everyone who comes to me and hears my words and does them, I will show you what he is like: 48he is like a man building a house, who dug deep and laid the foundation on the rock. And when a flood arose, the stream broke against that house and could not shake it, because it had been well built.[1] 49But the one who hears and does not do them is like a man who built a house on the ground without a foundation. When the stream broke against it, immediately it fell, and the ruin of that house was great."

Jesus Heals a Centurion's Servant

7 After he had finished all his sayings in the hearing of the people, he entered Capernaum. 2Now a centurion had a servant[2] who was sick and at the point of death, who was highly valued by him. 3When the centurion[3] heard about Jesus, he sent to him elders of the Jews, asking him to come and heal his servant. 4And when they came to Jesus, they pleaded with him earnestly, saying, "He is worthy to have you do this for him, 5for he loves our nation, and he is the one who built us our synagogue." 6And Jesus went with them. When he was not far from the house, the centurion sent friends, saying to him, "Lord, do not trouble yourself, for I am not worthy to have you come under my roof. 7Therefore I did not presume to come to you. But say the word, and let my servant be healed. 8For I too am a man set under authority, with soldiers under me: and I say to one, 'Go,' and he goes; and to another, 'Come,' and he comes; and to my servant, 'Do this,' and he does it." 9When Jesus heard these things, he marveled at him, and turning to the crowd that followed him, said, "I tell you, not even in Israel have I found such faith." 10And when those who had been sent returned to the house, they found the servant well.

Jesus Raises a Widow's Son

11Soon afterward[4] he went to a town called Nain, and his disciples and a great crowd went with him. 12As he drew near to the gate of the town, behold, a man

LUKE 7:1–10

AUTHORITY

A Roman soldier who was a centurion demonstrated insight into Jesus' authority. After asking Jesus to heal his servant, the soldier exhorted Jesus not to travel to him; Jesus needed only to issue the command for the request to be granted. The centurion reasoned that since he exercised authority over the soldiers he led, Jesus could exercise far greater authority. Upon hearing what the centurion said, Jesus affirmed his great faith (Lk 7:9–10).

This Roman discerned what the spiritual leaders of the day missed as they questioned Jesus repeatedly about his authority (Mt 21:23–27; Lk 20:2). The centurion and the common people recognized Jesus' authority, contrasting his powerful teaching with that of the teachers of the law (Mt 7:29). Before his ascension into heaven, Jesus explained to his disciples that all authority in heaven and on earth had been given to him (Mt 28:18). Years later, the apostle Paul would proclaim that God the Father had placed everything in the present age and the age to come under Jesus' feet (Eph 1:19–21). As a result, acknowledging or denying Jesus' absolute authority changes people's eternal destinies, as well as their lives now.

[1]Some manuscripts *founded upon the rock* [2]Or *bondservant*; also verses 3, 8, 10 [3]Greek *he* [4]Some manuscripts *The next day*

who had died was being carried out, the only son of his mother, and she was a widow, and a considerable crowd from the town was with her. 13And when the Lord saw her, he had compassion on her and said to her, "Do not weep." 14Then he came up and touched the bier, and the bearers stood still. And he said, "Young man, I say to you, arise." 15And the dead man sat up and began to speak, and Jesus[1] gave him to his mother. 16Fear seized them all, and they glorified God, saying, "A great prophet has arisen among us!" and "God has visited his people!" 17And this report about him spread through the whole of Judea and all the surrounding country.

Messengers from John the Baptist

18The disciples of John reported all these things to him. And John, 19calling two of his disciples to him, sent them to the Lord, saying, "Are you the one who is to come, or shall we look for another?" 20And when the men had come to him, they said, "John the Baptist has sent us to you, saying, 'Are you the one who is to come, or shall we look for another?' " 21In that hour he healed many people of diseases and plagues and evil spirits, and on many who were blind he bestowed sight. 22And he answered them, "Go and tell John what you have seen and heard: the blind receive their sight, the lame walk, lepers[2] are cleansed, and the deaf hear, the dead are raised up, the poor have good news preached to them. 23And blessed is the one who is not offended by me."

24When John's messengers had gone, Jesus[3] began to speak to the crowds concerning John: "What did you go out into the wilderness to see? A reed shaken by the wind? 25What then did you go out to see? A man dressed in soft clothing? Behold, those who are dressed in splendid clothing and live in luxury are in kings' courts. 26What then did you go out to see? A prophet? Yes, I tell you, and more than a prophet. 27This is he of whom it is written,

" 'Behold, I send my messenger before your face,
who will prepare your way before you.'

28I tell you, among those born of women none is greater than John. Yet the one who is least in the kingdom of God is greater than he." 29(When all the people heard this, and the tax collectors too, they declared God just,[4] having been baptized with the baptism of John, 30but the Pharisees and the lawyers rejected the purpose of God for themselves, not having been baptized by him.)

31"To what then shall I compare the people of this generation, and what are they like? 32They are like children sitting in the marketplace and calling to one another,

" 'We played the flute for you, and you did not dance;
we sang a dirge, and you did not weep.'

33For John the Baptist has come eating no bread and drinking no wine, and you say, 'He has a demon.' 34The Son of Man has come eating and drinking, and you say, 'Look at him! A glutton and a drunkard, a friend of tax collectors and sinners!' 35Yet wisdom is justified by all her children."

A Sinful Woman Forgiven

36One of the Pharisees asked him to eat with him, and he went into the Pharisee's house and reclined at table. 37And behold, a woman of the city, who was a sinner, when she learned that he was reclining at table in the Pharisee's house, brought an alabaster flask of ointment, 38and standing behind him at his feet, weeping, she began to wet his feet with her tears and wiped them with the hair of her head and kissed his feet and anointed them with the ointment. 39Now when the Pharisee who had invited him saw this, he said to himself, "If this man were a

[1]Greek *he* [2]*Leprosy* was a term for several skin diseases; see Leviticus 13 [3]Greek *he* [4]Greek *they justified God*

prophet, he would have known who and what sort of woman this is who is touching him, for she is a sinner." 40And Jesus answering said to him, "Simon, I have something to say to you." And he answered, "Say it, Teacher."

41"A certain moneylender had two debtors. One owed five hundred denarii, and the other fifty. 42When they could not pay, he cancelled the debt of both. Now which of them will love him more?" 43Simon answered, "The one, I suppose, for whom he cancelled the larger debt." And he said to him, "You have judged rightly." 44Then turning toward the woman he said to Simon, "Do you see this woman? I entered your house; you gave me no water for my feet, but she has wet my feet with her tears and wiped them with her hair. 45You gave me no kiss, but from the time I came in she has not ceased to kiss my feet. 46You did not anoint my head with oil, but she has anointed my feet with ointment. 47Therefore I tell you, her sins, which are many, are forgiven—for she loved much. But he who is forgiven little, loves little." 48And he said to her, "Your sins are forgiven." 49Then those who were at table with him began to say among[1] themselves, "Who is this, who even forgives sins?" 50And he said to the woman, "Your faith has saved you; go in peace."

Women Accompanying Jesus

8 Soon afterward he went on through cities and villages, proclaiming and bringing the good news of the kingdom of God. And the twelve were with him, 2and also some women who had been healed of evil spirits and infirmities: Mary, called Magdalene, from whom seven demons had gone out, 3and Joanna, the wife of Chuza, Herod's household manager, and Susanna, and many others, who provided for them[2] out of their means.

The Parable of the Sower

4And when a great crowd was gathering and people from town after town came to him, he said in a parable, 5"A sower went out to sow his seed. And as he sowed, some fell along the path and was trampled underfoot, and the birds of the air devoured it. 6And some fell on the rock, and as it grew up, it withered away, because it had no moisture. 7And some fell among thorns, and the thorns grew up with it and choked it. 8And some fell into good soil and grew and yielded a hundredfold." As he said these things, he called out, "He who has ears to hear, let him hear."

The Purpose of the Parables

9And when his disciples asked him what this parable meant, 10he said, "To you it has been given to know the secrets of the kingdom of God, but for others they are in parables, so that 'seeing they may not see, and hearing they may not understand.' 11Now the parable is this: The seed is the word of God. 12The ones along the path are those who have heard; then the devil comes and takes away the word from their hearts, so that they may not believe and be saved. 13And the ones on the rock are those who, when they hear the word, receive it with joy. But these have no root; they believe for a while, and in time of testing fall away. 14And as for what fell among the thorns, they are those who hear, but as they go on their way they are choked by the cares and riches and pleasures of life, and their fruit does not mature. 15As for that in the good soil, they are those who, hearing the word, hold it fast in an honest and good heart, and bear fruit with patience.

A Lamp Under a Jar

16"No one after lighting a lamp covers it with a jar or puts it under a bed, but puts it on a stand, so that those who enter may see the light. 17For nothing is

[1]Or *to* [2]Some manuscripts *him*

hidden that will not be made manifest, nor is anything secret that will not be known and come to light. 18 Take care then how you hear, for to the one who has, more will be given, and from the one who has not, even what he thinks that he has will be taken away."

Jesus' Mother and Brothers

19 Then his mother and his brothers[1] came to him, but they could not reach him because of the crowd. 20 And he was told, "Your mother and your brothers are standing outside, desiring to see you." 21 But he answered them, "My mother and my brothers are those who hear the word of God and do it."

Jesus Calms a Storm

22 One day he got into a boat with his disciples, and he said to them, "Let us go across to the other side of the lake." So they set out, 23 and as they sailed he fell asleep. And a windstorm came down on the lake, and they were filling with water and were in danger. 24 And they went and woke him, saying, "Master, Master, we are perishing!" And he awoke and rebuked the wind and the raging waves, and they ceased, and there was a calm. 25 He said to them, "Where is your faith?" And they were afraid, and they marveled, saying to one another, "Who then is this, that he commands even winds and water, and they obey him?"

Jesus Heals a Man with a Demon

26 Then they sailed to the country of the Gerasenes,[2] which is opposite Galilee. 27 When Jesus[3] had stepped out on land, there met him a man from the city who had demons. For a long time he had worn no clothes, and he had not lived in a house but among the tombs. 28 When he saw Jesus, he cried out and fell down before him and said with a loud voice, "What have you to do with me, Jesus, Son of the Most High God? I beg you, do not torment me." 29 For he had commanded the unclean spirit to come out of the man. (For many a time it had seized him. He was kept under guard and bound with chains and shackles, but he would break the bonds and be driven by the demon into the desert.) 30 Jesus then asked him, "What is your name?" And he said, "Legion," for many demons had entered him. 31 And they begged him not to command them to depart into the abyss. 32 Now a large herd of pigs was feeding there on the hillside, and they begged him to let them enter these. So he gave them permission. 33 Then the demons came out of the man and entered the pigs, and the herd rushed down the steep bank into the lake and drowned.

34 When the herdsmen saw what had happened, they fled and told it in the city and in the country. 35 Then people went out to see what had happened, and they came to Jesus and found the man from whom the demons had gone, sitting at the feet of Jesus, clothed and in his right mind, and they were afraid. 36 And those who had seen it told them how the demon-possessed[4] man had been healed. 37 Then all the people of the surrounding country of the Gerasenes asked him to depart from them, for they were seized with great fear. So he got into the boat and returned. 38 The man from whom the demons had gone begged that he might be with him, but Jesus sent him away, saying, 39 "Return to your home, and declare how much God has done for you." And he went away, proclaiming throughout the whole city how much Jesus had done for him.

Jesus Heals a Woman and Jairus's Daughter

40 Now when Jesus returned, the crowd welcomed him, for they were all waiting for him. 41 And there came a man named Jairus, who was a ruler of the

[1] Or *brothers and sisters*. In New Testament usage, depending on the context, the plural Greek word *adelphoi* (translated "brothers") may refer either to *brothers* or to *brothers and sisters*; also verses 20, 21 [2] Some manuscripts *Gadarenes*; others *Gergesenes*; also verse 37 [3] Greek *he*; also verses 38, 42 [4] Greek *daimonizomai* (demonized); elsewhere rendered *oppressed by demons*

LUKE 8:19–21

JESUS' FAMILY

One of the mysteries of the incarnation (Jesus' coming to earth as a human being without ceasing to be God), is the fact that Jesus had a flesh-and-blood family—a mother, father, and siblings (Mt 13:55–56). While many if not all of his family members ultimately became his disciples, the Gospels demonstrate that they did not follow him initially. On one occasion they traveled "to seize him" because they believed he was out of his mind (Mk 3:21). Another time, his brothers taunted that he should travel to Jerusalem so his disciples could see his works there. "No one works in secret if he seeks to be known openly. If you do these things, show yourself to the world" (Jn 7:2–4).

Through his life and teachings, Jesus framed the context of family in terms of the kingdom of God. He expanded the concept of family to include all who did the will of his Father in heaven (Mt 12:50). While he rebuked religious leaders who failed to honor their parents for the sake of their traditions, he called his disciples to love him more than all else, including their families (Mt 10:37). Yet from the cross, Jesus assigned his disciple John to care for Mary, his mother, demonstrating his love and concern for her (Jn 19:26–27). For Jesus, family remained important but not ultimate, aligning with his mandate to seek God's kingdom first so that all other realities in life could align correctly (Mt 6:33).

synagogue. And falling at Jesus' feet, he implored him to come to his house, 42for
he had an only daughter, about twelve years of age, and she was dying.
As Jesus went, the people pressed around him. 43And there was a woman who
had had a discharge of blood for twelve years, and though she had spent all her
living on physicians,[1] she could not be healed by anyone. 44She came up behind
him and touched the fringe of his garment, and immediately her discharge of
blood ceased. 45And Jesus said, "Who was it that touched me?" When all denied it,
Peter[2] said, "Master, the crowds surround you and are pressing in on you!" 46But
Jesus said, "Someone touched me, for I perceive that power has gone out from
me." 47And when the woman saw that she was not hidden, she came trembling,
and falling down before him declared in the presence of all the people why she
had touched him, and how she had been immediately healed. 48And he said to
her, "Daughter, your faith has made you well; go in peace."
49While he was still speaking, someone from the ruler's house came and said,
"Your daughter is dead; do not trouble the Teacher any more." 50But Jesus on hearing this answered him, "Do not fear; only believe, and she will be well." 51And
when he came to the house, he allowed no one to enter with him, except Peter and
John and James, and the father and mother of the child. 52And all were weeping
and mourning for her, but he said, "Do not weep, for she is not dead but sleeping." 53And they laughed at him, knowing that she was dead. 54But taking her by
the hand he called, saying, "Child, arise." 55And her spirit returned, and she got
up at once. And he directed that something should be given her to eat. 56And her
parents were amazed, but he charged them to tell no one what had happened.

Jesus Sends Out the Twelve Apostles

9 And he called the twelve together and gave them power and authority over all
demons and to cure diseases, 2and he sent them out to proclaim the kingdom
of God and to heal. 3And he said to them, "Take nothing for your journey, no staff,
nor bag, nor bread, nor money; and do not have two tunics.[3] 4And whatever house
you enter, stay there, and from there depart. 5And wherever they do not receive
you, when you leave that town shake off the dust from your feet as a testimony
against them." 6And they departed and went through the villages, preaching the
gospel and healing everywhere.

Herod Is Perplexed by Jesus

7Now Herod the tetrarch heard about all that was happening, and he was perplexed, because it was said by some that John had been raised from the dead, 8by
some that Elijah had appeared, and by others that one of the prophets of old had
risen. 9Herod said, "John I beheaded, but who is this about whom I hear such
things?" And he sought to see him.

Jesus Feeds the Five Thousand

10On their return the apostles told him all that they had done. And he took
them and withdrew apart to a town called Bethsaida. 11When the crowds learned
it, they followed him, and he welcomed them and spoke to them of the kingdom
of God and cured those who had need of healing. 12Now the day began to wear
away, and the twelve came and said to him, "Send the crowd away to go into the
surrounding villages and countryside to find lodging and get provisions, for we
are here in a desolate place." 13But he said to them, "You give them something to
eat." They said, "We have no more than five loaves and two fish—unless we are to
go and buy food for all these people." 14For there were about five thousand men.
And he said to his disciples, "Have them sit down in groups of about fifty each."
15And they did so, and had them all sit down. 16And taking the five loaves and the
two fish, he looked up to heaven and said a blessing over them. Then he broke

[1]Some manuscripts omit *and though she had spent all her living on physicians* [2]Some manuscripts add *and those who were with him* [3]Greek *chiton*, a long garment worn under the cloak next to the skin

the loaves and gave them to the disciples to set before the crowd. 17And they all ate and were satisfied. And what was left over was picked up, twelve baskets of broken pieces.

Peter Confesses Jesus as the Christ

18Now it happened that as he was praying alone, the disciples were with him. And he asked them, "Who do the crowds say that I am?" 19And they answered, "John the Baptist. But others say, Elijah, and others, that one of the prophets of old has risen." 20Then he said to them, "But who do you say that I am?" And Peter answered, "The Christ of God."

Jesus Foretells His Death

21And he strictly charged and commanded them to tell this to no one, 22saying, "The Son of Man must suffer many things and be rejected by the elders and chief priests and scribes, and be killed, and on the third day be raised."

Take Up Your Cross and Follow Jesus

23And he said to all, "If anyone would come after me, let him deny himself and take up his cross daily and follow me. 24For whoever would save his life will lose it, but whoever loses his life for my sake will save it. 25For what does it profit a man if he gains the whole world and loses or forfeits himself? 26For whoever is ashamed of me and of my words, of him will the Son of Man be ashamed when he comes in his glory and the glory of the Father and of the holy angels. 27But I tell you truly, there are some standing here who will not taste death until they see the kingdom of God."

The Transfiguration

28Now about eight days after these sayings he took with him Peter and John and James and went up on the mountain to pray. 29And as he was praying, the appearance of his face was altered, and his clothing became dazzling white. 30And behold, two men were talking with him, Moses and Elijah, 31who appeared in glory and spoke of his departure,[1] which he was about to accomplish at Jerusalem. 32Now Peter and those who were with him were heavy with sleep, but when they became fully awake they saw his glory and the two men who stood with him. 33And as the men were parting from him, Peter said to Jesus, "Master, it is good that we are here. Let us make three tents, one for you and one for Moses and one for Elijah"—not knowing what he said. 34As he was saying these things, a cloud came and overshadowed them, and they were afraid as they entered the cloud. 35And a voice came out of the cloud, saying, "This is my Son, my Chosen One;[2] listen to him!" 36And when the voice had spoken, Jesus was found alone. And they kept silent and told no one in those days anything of what they had seen.

Jesus Heals a Boy with an Unclean Spirit

37On the next day, when they had come down from the mountain, a great crowd met him. 38And behold, a man from the crowd cried out, "Teacher, I beg you to look at my son, for he is my only child. 39And behold, a spirit seizes him, and he suddenly cries out. It convulses him so that he foams at the mouth, and shatters him, and will hardly leave him. 40And I begged your disciples to cast it out, but they could not." 41Jesus answered, "O faithless and twisted generation, how long am I to be with you and bear with you? Bring your son here." 42While he was coming, the demon threw him to the ground and convulsed him. But Jesus rebuked the unclean spirit and healed the boy, and gave him back to his father. 43And all were astonished at the majesty of God.

[1]Greek *exodus* [2]Some manuscripts *my Beloved*

LUKE 9:21

JESUS' SECRET

After Simon Peter affirmed that Jesus was God's Messiah, Jesus "strictly charged" his disciples not to tell anyone. This was not the first time Jesus cautioned against sharing his identity. After healing a man from leprosy, he said, "See that you say nothing to anyone" (Mt 8:4). When Jesus came down from the mountain after Peter, James, and John had seen him transfigured, Jesus told them, "Tell no one the vision, until the Son of Man is raised from the dead" (Mt 17:9).

Scholars have pondered this "Messianic secret," seeking to understand why Jesus commanded his disciples not to share what they knew. The problem was not that the disciples knew too much; it was that they knew too little. For example, on the way to Jerusalem where Jesus would be crucified, James and John became indignant by the way a village of Samaritans treated them. "Lord, do you want us to tell fire to come down from heaven and consume them?" they asked (Lk 9:54). At that moment, they were prepared to kill those for whom Jesus came to die. Clearly, they needed to know more, to experience more: Jesus' trial, torture, crucifixion, death, resurrection, and ascension to heaven. After that, Jesus commanded them to go to the whole world and make disciples, teaching them to obey everything he had commanded them (Mt 28:19–20). Only then, after their understanding had increased, would the disciples be ready and free to share the Good News.

Jesus Again Foretells His Death

But while they were all marveling at everything he was doing, Jesus[1] said to his
disciples, 44“Let these words sink into your ears: The Son of Man is about to be
delivered into the hands of men.” 45But they did not understand this saying, and it
was concealed from them, so that they might not perceive it. And they were afraid
to ask him about this saying.

Who Is the Greatest?

46An argument arose among them as to which of them was the greatest. 47But
Jesus, knowing the reasoning of their hearts, took a child and put him by his side
48and said to them, “Whoever receives this child in my name receives me, and
whoever receives me receives him who sent me. For he who is least among you
all is the one who is great.”

Anyone Not Against Us Is For Us

49John answered, “Master, we saw someone casting out demons in your name,
and we tried to stop him, because he does not follow with us.” 50But Jesus said to
him, “Do not stop him, for the one who is not against you is for you.”

A Samaritan Village Rejects Jesus

51When the days drew near for him to be taken up, he set his face to go to Jerusalem. 52And he sent messengers ahead of him, who went and entered a village
of the Samaritans, to make preparations for him. 53But the people did not receive
him, because his face was set toward Jerusalem. 54And when his disciples James
and John saw it, they said, “Lord, do you want us to tell fire to come down from
heaven and consume them?”[2] 55But he turned and rebuked them.[3] 56And they
went on to another village.

The Cost of Following Jesus

57As they were going along the road, someone said to him, “I will follow
you wherever you go.” 58And Jesus said to him, “Foxes have holes, and birds
of the air have nests, but the Son of Man has nowhere to lay his head.” 59To
another he said, “Follow me.” But he said, “Lord, let me first go and bury my
father.” 60And Jesus[4] said to him, “Leave the dead to bury their own dead. But
as for you, go and proclaim the kingdom of God.” 61Yet another said, “I will follow you, Lord, but let me first say farewell to those at my home.” 62Jesus said
to him, “No one who puts his hand to the plow and looks back is fit for the
kingdom of God.”

Jesus Sends Out the Seventy-Two

10 After this the Lord appointed seventy-two[5] others and sent them on ahead
of him, two by two, into every town and place where he himself was about
to go. 2And he said to them, “The harvest is plentiful, but the laborers are few.
Therefore pray earnestly to the Lord of the harvest to send out laborers into his
harvest. 3Go your way; behold, I am sending you out as lambs in the midst of
wolves. 4Carry no moneybag, no knapsack, no sandals, and greet no one on the
road. 5Whatever house you enter, first say, ‘Peace be to this house!’ 6And if a son
of peace is there, your peace will rest upon him. But if not, it will return to you.
7And remain in the same house, eating and drinking what they provide, for the
laborer deserves his wages. Do not go from house to house. 8Whenever you enter
a town and they receive you, eat what is set before you. 9Heal the sick in it and say
to them, ‘The kingdom of God has come near to you.’ 10But whenever you enter

---

[1]Greek *he* [2]Some manuscripts add *as Elijah did* [3]Some manuscripts add *And he said, “You do not know what manner of spirit you are of;* 56*for the Son of Man came not to destroy people’s lives but to save them”*
[4]Greek *he* [5]Some manuscripts *seventy*; also verse 17

a town and they do not receive you, go into its streets and say, 11‘Even the dust of your town that clings to our feet we wipe off against you. Nevertheless know this, that the kingdom of God has come near.’ 12I tell you, it will be more bearable on that day for Sodom than for that town.

Woe to Unrepentant Cities

13“Woe to you, Chorazin! Woe to you, Bethsaida! For if the mighty works done in you had been done in Tyre and Sidon, they would have repented long ago, sitting in sackcloth and ashes. 14But it will be more bearable in the judgment for Tyre and Sidon than for you. 15And you, Capernaum, will you be exalted to heaven? You shall be brought down to Hades.

16“The one who hears you hears me, and the one who rejects you rejects me, and the one who rejects me rejects him who sent me.”

The Return of the Seventy-Two

17The seventy-two returned with joy, saying, “Lord, even the demons are subject to us in your name!” 18And he said to them, “I saw Satan fall like lightning from heaven. 19Behold, I have given you authority to tread on serpents and scorpions, and over all the power of the enemy, and nothing shall hurt you. 20Nevertheless, do not rejoice in this, that the spirits are subject to you, but rejoice that your names are written in heaven.”

Jesus Rejoices in the Father’s Will

21In that same hour he rejoiced in the Holy Spirit and said, “I thank you, Father, Lord of heaven and earth, that you have hidden these things from the wise and understanding and revealed them to little children; yes, Father, for such was your gracious will.[1] 22All things have been handed over to me by my Father, and no one knows who the Son is except the Father, or who the Father is except the Son and anyone to whom the Son chooses to reveal him.”

23Then turning to the disciples he said privately, “Blessed are the eyes that see what you see! 24For I tell you that many prophets and kings desired to see what you see, and did not see it, and to hear what you hear, and did not hear it.”

The Parable of the Good Samaritan

25And behold, a lawyer stood up to put him to the test, saying, “Teacher, what shall I do to inherit eternal life?” 26He said to him, “What is written in the Law? How do you read it?” 27And he answered, “You shall love the Lord your God with all your heart and with all your soul and with all your strength and with all your mind, and your neighbor as yourself.” 28And he said to him, “You have answered correctly; do this, and you will live.”

29But he, desiring to justify himself, said to Jesus, “And who is my neighbor?” 30Jesus replied, “A man was going down from Jerusalem to Jericho, and he fell among robbers, who stripped him and beat him and departed, leaving him half dead. 31Now by chance a priest was going down that road, and when he saw him he passed by on the other side. 32So likewise a Levite, when he came to the place and saw him, passed by on the other side. 33But a Samaritan, as he journeyed, came to where he was, and when he saw him, he had compassion. 34He went to him and bound up his wounds, pouring on oil and wine. Then he set him on his own animal and brought him to an inn and took care of him. 35And the next day he took out two denarii[2] and gave them to the innkeeper, saying, ‘Take care of him, and whatever more you spend, I will repay you when I come back.’ 36Which of these three, do you think, proved to be a neighbor to the man who fell among the robbers?” 37He said, “The one who showed him mercy.” And Jesus said to him, “You go, and do likewise.”

---

[1]Or *for so it pleased you well* [2]A *denarius* was a day’s wage for a laborer

Martha and Mary

38 Now as they went on their way, Jesus[1] entered a village. And a woman named
Martha welcomed him into her house. 39 And she had a sister called Mary, who
sat at the Lord's feet and listened to his teaching. 40 But Martha was distracted
with much serving. And she went up to him and said, "Lord, do you not care that
my sister has left me to serve alone? Tell her then to help me." 41 But the Lord answered her, "Martha, Martha, you are anxious and troubled about many things,
42 but one thing is necessary.[2] Mary has chosen the good portion, which will not
be taken away from her."

The Lord's Prayer

11 Now Jesus[3] was praying in a certain place, and when he finished, one of his
disciples said to him, "Lord, teach us to pray, as John taught his disciples."
2 And he said to them, "When you pray, say:

"Father, hallowed be your name.
Your kingdom come.
3 Give us each day our daily bread,[4]
4 and forgive us our sins,
for we ourselves forgive everyone who is indebted to us.
And lead us not into temptation."

5 And he said to them, "Which of you who has a friend will go to him at midnight and say to him, 'Friend, lend me three loaves, 6 for a friend of mine has arrived on a journey, and I have nothing to set before him'; 7 and he will answer from
within, 'Do not bother me; the door is now shut, and my children are with me in
bed. I cannot get up and give you anything'? 8 I tell you, though he will not get up
and give him anything because he is his friend, yet because of his impudence[5] he
will rise and give him whatever he needs. 9 And I tell you, ask, and it will be given
to you; seek, and you will find; knock, and it will be opened to you. 10 For everyone
who asks receives, and the one who seeks finds, and to the one who knocks it will
be opened. 11 What father among you, if his son asks for[6] a fish, will instead of a
fish give him a serpent; 12 or if he asks for an egg, will give him a scorpion? 13 If you
then, who are evil, know how to give good gifts to your children, how much more
will the heavenly Father give the Holy Spirit to those who ask him!"

Jesus and Beelzebul

14 Now he was casting out a demon that was mute. When the demon had gone
out, the mute man spoke, and the people marveled. 15 But some of them said, "He
casts out demons by Beelzebul, the prince of demons," 16 while others, to test
him, kept seeking from him a sign from heaven. 17 But he, knowing their thoughts,
said to them, "Every kingdom divided against itself is laid waste, and a divided
household falls. 18 And if Satan also is divided against himself, how will his kingdom stand? For you say that I cast out demons by Beelzebul. 19 And if I cast out
demons by Beelzebul, by whom do your sons cast them out? Therefore they will
be your judges. 20 But if it is by the finger of God that I cast out demons, then the
kingdom of God has come upon you. 21 When a strong man, fully armed, guards
his own palace, his goods are safe; 22 but when one stronger than he attacks him
and overcomes him, he takes away his armor in which he trusted and divides his
spoil. 23 Whoever is not with me is against me, and whoever does not gather with
me scatters.

Return of an Unclean Spirit

24 "When the unclean spirit has gone out of a person, it passes through waterless places seeking rest, and finding none it says, 'I will return to my house from

[1]Greek *he* [2]Some manuscripts *few things are necessary, or only one* [3]Greek *he* [4]Or *our bread for tomorrow* [5]Or *persistence* [6]Some manuscripts insert *bread, will give him a stone; or if he asks for*

LUKE 11:20

THE KINGDOM OF GOD

Jesus proclaimed and explained the kingdom of God — God's rule over all things. In the Old Testament, God established his kingdom politically under David. When the Babylonians destroyed Jerusalem, the prophets continued to speak of the reestablishment of the kingdom of God under the coming Messiah (Isa 9:6 – 7). When Jesus came to earth, he preached that the kingdom of God had arrived (Mt 4:17; 5:3; Lk 11:20). With Jesus' coming, God's redemptive rule has freed men and women from Satan's power. When Jesus cast out demons, he demonstrated the reality of the kingdom. And through his parables, Jesus described what the kingdom was like (Mt 25).

What we know from Jesus' own accounts of the kingdom is that, from an earthly perspective, it turns worldly values and priorities upside down. In God's kingdom, the poor are rich; those who mourn will be comforted; the meek are powerful; and seekers, mercy-givers, peacemakers, and those who are persecuted are the ones who will inherit the kingdom (Mt 5:3 – 12). Jesus' ministry on earth ushered in the kingdom; the coming of the Spirit (Ac 2:1 – 13) brought it into a new phase; and someday, when the dead in Christ are raised and Jesus comes again to establish his earthly kingdom, it will be fully realized in all of its splendor, justice, and perfection (Rev 22:1 – 5).

JESUS AND THE HOLY SPIRIT

One of the cautions in studying exclusively about Jesus is the implication that Jesus was and is separate from the Father and the Holy Spirit. While the truth remains mysterious, the Bible clearly teaches that God exists in three persons, the Trinity. The Bible does not use that term, but it is impossible to understand the Bible's teaching without embracing this reality. Luke, in his writings (Luke and Acts), focused on the Holy Spirit to provide insight into Jesus and the Holy Spirit. Here's an overview:

The Holy Spirit filled John the Baptist in his mother's womb (Lk 1:15 – 17).

The Holy Spirit was the agent of divine conception with Mary, the mother of Jesus (Lk 1:35).

The Holy Spirit filled Mary's relative, Elizabeth, the mother of John the Baptist, and empowered her to encourage Mary (Lk 1:41 – 45).

The Holy Spirit filled Zacharias, John's father, so he could prophesy about the Messiah (Lk 1:67 – 75).

At Jesus' baptism, the Holy Spirit descended in bodily form like a dove as God the Father spoke (Lk 3:22).

The Holy Spirit led Jesus into the wilderness to be tempted by the devil (Lk 4:1 – 13).

The Holy Spirit empowered Jesus as he began his earthly ministry (Lk 4:14 – 21).

Jesus spoke of the Father giving the Holy Spirit as he taught his disciples about prayer (Lk 11:1 – 4,13).

The Holy Spirit filled Jesus' disciples at Pentecost and empowered them to preach the Good News (Ac 2:1 – 21).

Before his crucifixion, Jesus encouraged his disciples with deep spiritual realities about the Father and the Holy Spirit. He said, "If you love me, you will keep my commandments. And I will ask the Father, and he will give you another Helper, to be with you forever, even the Spirit of truth" (Jn 14:15 – 17). Then, as the disciples struggled to understand, Jesus said, "I will not leave you as orphans; I will come to you. Yet a little while and the world will see me no more, but you will see me. Because I live, you also will live. In that day you will know that I am in my Father, and you in me, and I in you" (Jn 14:18 – 20).

which I came.' 25And when it comes, it finds the house swept and put in order. 26Then it goes and brings seven other spirits more evil than itself, and they enter and dwell there. And the last state of that person is worse than the first."

True Blessedness

27As he said these things, a woman in the crowd raised her voice and said to him, "Blessed is the womb that bore you, and the breasts at which you nursed!" 28But he said, "Blessed rather are those who hear the word of God and keep it!"

The Sign of Jonah

29When the crowds were increasing, he began to say, "This generation is an evil generation. It seeks for a sign, but no sign will be given to it except the sign of Jonah. 30For as Jonah became a sign to the people of Nineveh, so will the Son of Man be to this generation. 31The queen of the South will rise up at the judgment with the men of this generation and condemn them, for she came from the ends of the earth to hear the wisdom of Solomon, and behold, something greater than Solomon is here. 32The men of Nineveh will rise up at the judgment with this generation and condemn it, for they repented at the preaching of Jonah, and behold, something greater than Jonah is here.

The Light in You

33"No one after lighting a lamp puts it in a cellar or under a basket, but on a stand, so that those who enter may see the light. 34Your eye is the lamp of your body. When your eye is healthy, your whole body is full of light, but when it is bad, your body is full of darkness. 35Therefore be careful lest the light in you be darkness. 36If then your whole body is full of light, having no part dark, it will be wholly bright, as when a lamp with its rays gives you light."

Woes to the Pharisees and Lawyers

37While Jesus[1] was speaking, a Pharisee asked him to dine with him, so he went in and reclined at table. 38The Pharisee was astonished to see that he did not first wash before dinner. 39And the Lord said to him, "Now you Pharisees cleanse the outside of the cup and of the dish, but inside you are full of greed and wickedness. 40You fools! Did not he who made the outside make the inside also? 41But give as alms those things that are within, and behold, everything is clean for you.

42"But woe to you Pharisees! For you tithe the mint and rue and every herb, and neglect justice and the love of God. These you ought to have done, without neglecting the others. 43Woe to you Pharisees! For you love the best seat in the synagogues and greetings in the marketplaces. 44Woe to you! For you are like unmarked graves, and people walk over them without knowing it."

45One of the lawyers answered him, "Teacher, in saying these things you insult us also." 46And he said, "Woe to you lawyers also! For you load people with burdens hard to bear, and you yourselves do not touch the burdens with one of your fingers. 47Woe to you! For you build the tombs of the prophets whom your fathers killed. 48So you are witnesses and you consent to the deeds of your fathers, for they killed them, and you build their tombs. 49Therefore also the Wisdom of God said, 'I will send them prophets and apostles, some of whom they will kill and persecute,' 50so that the blood of all the prophets, shed from the foundation of the world, may be charged against this generation, 51from the blood of Abel to the blood of Zechariah, who perished between the altar and the sanctuary. Yes, I tell you, it will be required of this generation. 52Woe to you lawyers! For you have taken away the key of knowledge. You did not enter yourselves, and you hindered those who were entering."

53As he went away from there, the scribes and the Pharisees began to press

[1]Greek *he*

him hard and to provoke him to speak about many things, 54 lying in wait for him,
to catch him in something he might say.

Beware of the Leaven of the Pharisees

12 In the meantime, when so many thousands of the people had gathered
together that they were trampling one another, he began to say to his disciples first, "Beware of the leaven of the Pharisees, which is hypocrisy. 2 Nothing is
covered up that will not be revealed, or hidden that will not be known. 3 Therefore
whatever you have said in the dark shall be heard in the light, and what you have
whispered in private rooms shall be proclaimed on the housetops.

Have No Fear

4 "I tell you, my friends, do not fear those who kill the body, and after that have
nothing more that they can do. 5 But I will warn you whom to fear: fear him who,
after he has killed, has authority to cast into hell.[1] Yes, I tell you, fear him! 6 Are
not five sparrows sold for two pennies?[2] And not one of them is forgotten before
God. 7 Why, even the hairs of your head are all numbered. Fear not; you are of more
value than many sparrows.

Acknowledge Christ Before Men

8 "And I tell you, everyone who acknowledges me before men, the Son of Man
also will acknowledge before the angels of God, 9 but the one who denies me before men will be denied before the angels of God. 10 And everyone who speaks
a word against the Son of Man will be forgiven, but the one who blasphemes
against the Holy Spirit will not be forgiven. 11 And when they bring you before the
synagogues and the rulers and the authorities, do not be anxious about how you
should defend yourself or what you should say, 12 for the Holy Spirit will teach you
in that very hour what you ought to say."

The Parable of the Rich Fool

13 Someone in the crowd said to him, "Teacher, tell my brother to divide the
inheritance with me." 14 But he said to him, "Man, who made me a judge or arbitrator over you?" 15 And he said to them, "Take care, and be on your guard against all
covetousness, for one's life does not consist in the abundance of his possessions."
16 And he told them a parable, saying, "The land of a rich man produced plentifully, 17 and he thought to himself, 'What shall I do, for I have nowhere to store
my crops?' 18 And he said, 'I will do this: I will tear down my barns and build larger
ones, and there I will store all my grain and my goods. 19 And I will say to my soul,
"Soul, you have ample goods laid up for many years; relax, eat, drink, be merry."'
20 But God said to him, 'Fool! This night your soul is required of you, and the things
you have prepared, whose will they be?' 21 So is the one who lays up treasure for
himself and is not rich toward God."

Do Not Be Anxious

22 And he said to his disciples, "Therefore I tell you, do not be anxious about
your life, what you will eat, nor about your body, what you will put on. 23 For life
is more than food, and the body more than clothing. 24 Consider the ravens: they
neither sow nor reap, they have neither storehouse nor barn, and yet God feeds
them. Of how much more value are you than the birds! 25 And which of you by
being anxious can add a single hour to his span of life?[3] 26 If then you are not able
to do as small a thing as that, why are you anxious about the rest? 27 Consider the
lilies, how they grow: they neither toil nor spin, yet I tell you, even Solomon in
all his glory was not arrayed like one of these. 28 But if God so clothes the grass,

LUKE 12:10

BLASPHEMY

Jesus' critics accused him of blasphemy, the act of showing contempt or lack of reverence for God. In the Old Testament, blaspheming God was a crime punishable by death (Lev 24:15–16). Blasphemy violated the third of the Ten Commandments, which required people to uphold the name and reputation of the Lord (Ex 20:7). The unbelieving Jewish leaders of Jesus' day charged Jesus with blasphemy since, in their view, he was a man who falsely claimed to be God's Son (Mt 9:3).

Actually, the Jewish leaders' own lawlessness and hypocrisy caused God's name to be blasphemed among the Gentiles (Ro 2:24). Also, their bitter opposition to Jesus and his gospel blasphemed God (Ac 18:6), and Jesus confronted their blasphemy as they attributed the work of the Holy Spirit to Satan (Mt 12:31–32). In the Scripture, Christians are commanded to avoid words or actions that blaspheme the Lord's name and teaching (1Ti 6:1). Rejecting Jesus' gracious gift of salvation remains the ultimate form of blasphemy, one with eternal repercussions.

[1] Greek *Gehenna* [2] Greek *two assaria*; an *assarion* was a Roman copper coin worth about 1/16 of a *denarius* (which was a day's wage for a laborer) [3] Or *a single cubit to his stature*; a *cubit* was about 18 inches or 45 centimeters

which is alive in the field today, and tomorrow is thrown into the oven, how much more will he clothe you, O you of little faith! 29And do not seek what you are to eat and what you are to drink, nor be worried. 30For all the nations of the world seek after these things, and your Father knows that you need them. 31Instead, seek his[1] kingdom, and these things will be added to you.

32"Fear not, little flock, for it is your Father's good pleasure to give you the kingdom. 33Sell your possessions, and give to the needy. Provide yourselves with moneybags that do not grow old, with a treasure in the heavens that does not fail, where no thief approaches and no moth destroys. 34For where your treasure is, there will your heart be also.

You Must Be Ready

35"Stay dressed for action[2] and keep your lamps burning, 36and be like men who are waiting for their master to come home from the wedding feast, so that they may open the door to him at once when he comes and knocks. 37Blessed are those servants[3] whom the master finds awake when he comes. Truly, I say to you, he will dress himself for service and have them recline at table, and he will come and serve them. 38If he comes in the second watch, or in the third, and finds them awake, blessed are those servants! 39But know this, that if the master of the house had known at what hour the thief was coming, he[4] would not have left his house to be broken into. 40You also must be ready, for the Son of Man is coming at an hour you do not expect."

41Peter said, "Lord, are you telling this parable for us or for all?" 42And the Lord said, "Who then is the faithful and wise manager, whom his master will set over his household, to give them their portion of food at the proper time? 43Blessed is that servant[5] whom his master will find so doing when he comes. 44Truly, I say to you, he will set him over all his possessions. 45But if that servant says to himself, 'My master is delayed in coming,' and begins to beat the male and female servants, and to eat and drink and get drunk, 46the master of that servant will come on a day when he does not expect him and at an hour he does not know, and will cut him in pieces and put him with the unfaithful. 47And that servant who knew his master's will but did not get ready or act according to his will, will receive a severe beating. 48But the one who did not know, and did what deserved a beating, will receive a light beating. Everyone to whom much was given, of him much will be required, and from him to whom they entrusted much, they will demand the more.

Not Peace, but Division

49"I came to cast fire on the earth, and would that it were already kindled! 50I have a baptism to be baptized with, and how great is my distress until it is accomplished! 51Do you think that I have come to give peace on earth? No, I tell you, but rather division. 52For from now on in one house there will be five divided, three against two and two against three. 53They will be divided, father against son and son against father, mother against daughter and daughter against mother, mother-in-law against her daughter-in-law and daughter-in-law against mother-in-law."

Interpreting the Time

54He also said to the crowds, "When you see a cloud rising in the west, you say at once, 'A shower is coming.' And so it happens. 55And when you see the south wind blowing, you say, 'There will be scorching heat,' and it happens. 56You hypocrites! You know how to interpret the appearance of earth and sky, but why do you not know how to interpret the present time?

[1]Some manuscripts *God's* [2]Greek *Let your loins stay girded*; compare Exodus 12:11 [3]Or *bondservants*
[4]Some manuscripts add *would have stayed awake and* [5]Or *bondservant*; also verses 45, 46, 47

Settle with Your Accuser

[57]"And why do you not judge for yourselves what is right? [58]As you go with your accuser before the magistrate, make an effort to settle with him on the way, lest he drag you to the judge, and the judge hand you over to the officer, and the officer put you in prison. [59]I tell you, you will never get out until you have paid the very last penny."[1]

Repent or Perish

13 There were some present at that very time who told him about the Galileans whose blood Pilate had mingled with their sacrifices. [2]And he answered them, "Do you think that these Galileans were worse sinners than all the other Galileans, because they suffered in this way? [3]No, I tell you; but unless you repent, you will all likewise perish. [4]Or those eighteen on whom the tower in Siloam fell and killed them: do you think that they were worse offenders than all the others who lived in Jerusalem? [5]No, I tell you; but unless you repent, you will all likewise perish."

The Parable of the Barren Fig Tree

[6]And he told this parable: "A man had a fig tree planted in his vineyard, and he came seeking fruit on it and found none. [7]And he said to the vinedresser, 'Look, for three years now I have come seeking fruit on this fig tree, and I find none. Cut it down. Why should it use up the ground?' [8]And he answered him, 'Sir, let it alone this year also, until I dig around it and put on manure. [9]Then if it should bear fruit next year, well and good; but if not, you can cut it down.'"

A Woman with a Disabling Spirit

[10]Now he was teaching in one of the synagogues on the Sabbath. [11]And behold, there was a woman who had had a disabling spirit for eighteen years. She was bent over and could not fully straighten herself. [12]When Jesus saw her, he called her over and said to her, "Woman, you are freed from your disability." [13]And he laid his hands on her, and immediately she was made straight, and she glorified God. [14]But the ruler of the synagogue, indignant because Jesus had healed on the Sabbath, said to the people, "There are six days in which work ought to be done. Come on those days and be healed, and not on the Sabbath day." [15]Then the Lord answered him, "You hypocrites! Does not each of you on the Sabbath untie his ox or his donkey from the manger and lead it away to water it? [16]And ought not this woman, a daughter of Abraham whom Satan bound for eighteen years, be loosed from this bond on the Sabbath day?" [17]As he said these things, all his adversaries were put to shame, and all the people rejoiced at all the glorious things that were done by him.

The Mustard Seed and the Leaven

[18]He said therefore, "What is the kingdom of God like? And to what shall I compare it? [19]It is like a grain of mustard seed that a man took and sowed in his garden, and it grew and became a tree, and the birds of the air made nests in its branches."

[20]And again he said, "To what shall I compare the kingdom of God? [21]It is like leaven that a woman took and hid in three measures of flour, until it was all leavened."

The Narrow Door

[22]He went on his way through towns and villages, teaching and journeying toward Jerusalem. [23]And someone said to him, "Lord, will those who are saved be

[1]Greek *lepton*, a Jewish bronze or copper coin worth about 1/128 of a *denarius* (which was a day's wage for a laborer)

few?" And he said to them, [24]"Strive to enter through the narrow door. For many, I tell you, will seek to enter and will not be able. [25]When once the master of the house has risen and shut the door, and you begin to stand outside and to knock at the door, saying, 'Lord, open to us,' then he will answer you, 'I do not know where you come from.' [26]Then you will begin to say, 'We ate and drank in your presence, and you taught in our streets.' [27]But he will say, 'I tell you, I do not know where you come from. Depart from me, all you workers of evil!' [28]In that place there will be weeping and gnashing of teeth, when you see Abraham and Isaac and Jacob and all the prophets in the kingdom of God but you yourselves cast out. [29]And people will come from east and west, and from north and south, and recline at table in the kingdom of God. [30]And behold, some are last who will be first, and some are first who will be last."

Lament over Jerusalem

[31]At that very hour some Pharisees came and said to him, "Get away from here, for Herod wants to kill you." [32]And he said to them, "Go and tell that fox, 'Behold, I cast out demons and perform cures today and tomorrow, and the third day I finish my course. [33]Nevertheless, I must go on my way today and tomorrow and the day following, for it cannot be that a prophet should perish away from Jerusalem.' [34]O Jerusalem, Jerusalem, the city that kills the prophets and stones those who are sent to it! How often would I have gathered your children together as a hen gathers her brood under her wings, and you were not willing! [35]Behold, your house is forsaken. And I tell you, you will not see me until you say, 'Blessed is he who comes in the name of the Lord!'"

Healing of a Man on the Sabbath

14 One Sabbath, when he went to dine at the house of a ruler of the Pharisees, they were watching him carefully. [2]And behold, there was a man before him who had dropsy. [3]And Jesus responded to the lawyers and Pharisees, saying, "Is it lawful to heal on the Sabbath, or not?" [4]But they remained silent. Then he took him and healed him and sent him away. [5]And he said to them, "Which of you, having a son[1] or an ox that has fallen into a well on a Sabbath day, will not immediately pull him out?" [6]And they could not reply to these things.

The Parable of the Wedding Feast

[7]Now he told a parable to those who were invited, when he noticed how they chose the places of honor, saying to them, [8]"When you are invited by someone to a wedding feast, do not sit down in a place of honor, lest someone more distinguished than you be invited by him, [9]and he who invited you both will come and say to you, 'Give your place to this person,' and then you will begin with shame to take the lowest place. [10]But when you are invited, go and sit in the lowest place, so that when your host comes he may say to you, 'Friend, move up higher.' Then you will be honored in the presence of all who sit at table with you. [11]For everyone who exalts himself will be humbled, and he who humbles himself will be exalted."

The Parable of the Great Banquet

[12]He said also to the man who had invited him, "When you give a dinner or a banquet, do not invite your friends or your brothers[2] or your relatives or rich neighbors, lest they also invite you in return and you be repaid. [13]But when you give a feast, invite the poor, the crippled, the lame, the blind, [14]and you will be blessed, because they cannot repay you. For you will be repaid at the resurrection of the just."

[15]When one of those who reclined at table with him heard these things, he

[1]Some manuscripts *a donkey* [2]Or *your brothers and sisters*

LUKE 13:31–35

PROPHETS DYING IN JERUSALEM

Near the end of Jesus' earthly ministry, he moved purposefully toward Jerusalem knowing that he would be mocked, flogged, and crucified in that city (Mt 20:18–20). Jesus followed a long line of prophets who were executed in the nation's capital (1Ki 18:4; 2Ch 24:21). During the last week before his death, Jesus looked out over the city and cried, "Jerusalem, Jerusalem" (Lk 13:34). Repeating the name twice was a sign of intense sorrow, like one mourning the loss of a child (2Sa 18:33). Jesus' emotion expressed his love for the people despite the bitter experience that he knew was coming by way of their hands. In the end, like the prophets of old, Jesus issued a declaration of judgment on the city, calling it a house that would be forsaken (Lk 13:35). Unlike the prophets of old who died as martyrs, Jesus' death and resurrection brought everlasting life—life that would explode in resurrection power (Php 3:10).

JESUS AND THE SABBATH

Jesus clashed with the religious leaders of his day over many issues: religious traditions, associating with sinners, spiritual authority, and more. On one issue in particular — the Sabbath — these leaders monitored Jesus' actions scrupulously. The Ten Commandments prohibited work on the Sabbath since it was a holy day set apart (Ex 20:8 – 11). Just as the Israelites were commanded to tithe part of their earnings to God, they were to give him their time as well. Breaking the Sabbath was a grave matter, for God's law demanded death for those who ignored it (Ex 31:14 – 15).

The question, though, was what activities constituted "work." In the years after the temple was rebuilt following the exile (515 BC – AD 70), scribes and rabbis studied the words of Scripture, interpreting every detail. What kinds of work could be allowed on the Sabbath within the Law? For example, according to the Law, no work was to be done on the Sabbath, so that meant burdens were not to be carried on that day. So scholars debated what constituted a "burden." On the surface, the scribes had good reasons for interpreting the Law carefully since they did not want anyone to break it inadvertently. But their interpretations increasingly emphasized external adherence to the Law rather than cultivating an attitude of submission before God. Obeying their own interpretations became a source of pride instead of an expression of love for God. By Jesus' day, the rabbis and scribes had become so strict that they accused Jesus' disciples of breaking the Sabbath because they picked some grain and ate it as they walked through a field on the Sabbath (Lk 6:1 – 2).

Jesus' healings on the Sabbath enraged the religious teachers who classified healing as "work" and therefore prohibited it (Dt 5:15). He revealed the rabbis' hypocrisy with his response.

God had given the Law to encourage the Israelites to love him and to love others (Mk 12:30 – 31). He had never prohibited doing good on the Sabbath. The Pharisees acted as if God had created people so that he would have someone to keep the Sabbath, but Jesus clarified that God had given the Sabbath as a gift to the people he had created (Mk 2:27). For the Pharisees, the Ten Commandments provided great restrictions punishable by death. For Jesus, the Law outlined great freedoms that led to real life (Mt 5:17).

said to him, "Blessed is everyone who will eat bread in the kingdom of God!"
16But he said to him, "A man once gave a great banquet and invited many. 17And
at the time for the banquet he sent his servant[1] to say to those who had been
invited, 'Come, for everything is now ready.' 18But they all alike began to make
excuses. The first said to him, 'I have bought a field, and I must go out and see
it. Please have me excused.' 19And another said, 'I have bought five yoke of oxen,
and I go to examine them. Please have me excused.' 20And another said, 'I have
married a wife, and therefore I cannot come.' 21So the servant came and reported
these things to his master. Then the master of the house became angry and said
to his servant, 'Go out quickly to the streets and lanes of the city, and bring in
the poor and crippled and blind and lame.' 22And the servant said, 'Sir, what you
commanded has been done, and still there is room.' 23And the master said to the
servant, 'Go out to the highways and hedges and compel people to come in, that
my house may be filled. 24For I tell you,[2] none of those men who were invited
shall taste my banquet.'"

The Cost of Discipleship

25Now great crowds accompanied him, and he turned and said to them, 26"If
anyone comes to me and does not hate his own father and mother and wife and
children and brothers and sisters, yes, and even his own life, he cannot be my
disciple. 27Whoever does not bear his own cross and come after me cannot be
my disciple. 28For which of you, desiring to build a tower, does not first sit down
and count the cost, whether he has enough to complete it? 29Otherwise, when he
has laid a foundation and is not able to finish, all who see it begin to mock him,
30saying, 'This man began to build and was not able to finish.' 31Or what king,
going out to encounter another king in war, will not sit down first and deliberate
whether he is able with ten thousand to meet him who comes against him with
twenty thousand? 32And if not, while the other is yet a great way off, he sends a
delegation and asks for terms of peace. 33So therefore, any one of you who does
not renounce all that he has cannot be my disciple.

Salt Without Taste Is Worthless

34"Salt is good, but if salt has lost its taste, how shall its saltiness be restored?
35It is of no use either for the soil or for the manure pile. It is thrown away. He who
has ears to hear, let him hear."

The Parable of the Lost Sheep

15 Now the tax collectors and sinners were all drawing near to hear him. 2And
the Pharisees and the scribes grumbled, saying, "This man receives sinners
and eats with them."
3So he told them this parable: 4"What man of you, having a hundred sheep,
if he has lost one of them, does not leave the ninety-nine in the open country,
and go after the one that is lost, until he finds it? 5And when he has found it, he
lays it on his shoulders, rejoicing. 6And when he comes home, he calls together
his friends and his neighbors, saying to them, 'Rejoice with me, for I have found
my sheep that was lost.' 7Just so, I tell you, there will be more joy in heaven over
one sinner who repents than over ninety-nine righteous persons who need no
repentance.

The Parable of the Lost Coin

8"Or what woman, having ten silver coins,[3] if she loses one coin, does not light
a lamp and sweep the house and seek diligently until she finds it? 9And when she
has found it, she calls together her friends and neighbors, saying, 'Rejoice with

[1]Or *bondservant*; also verses 21 (twice), 22, 23 [2]The Greek word for *you* here is plural [3]Greek *ten drachmas*; a *drachma* was a Greek coin approximately equal in value to a Roman *denarius*, worth about a day's wage for a laborer

LUKE 14:25–34

THE COST OF DISCIPLESHIP

Jesus paid an incalculable price for the salvation of sinners. As the Romans executed him on trumped-up charges (Lk 23:22), the Father substituted the death of his innocent Son for the lives of all believers, who are justly charged with the capital offense of sinning against a holy God. This substitution made it possible for a just God to forgive guilty sinners. This divine pardon cannot be bought or earned but only received by grace through faith (Eph 2:8). The miracle of the gospel is that God would accept sinners because of what Jesus did through his life, death, and resurrection.

The high cost Jesus paid for salvation demands a high price for discipleship. Jesus clarified this truth when he said that whoever wanted to be his disciples must take up their cross and follow him (Lk 9:23). Jesus' disciples were to surrender completely to God and his will, just as Jesus submitted completely to his Father's will (Jn 5:19). Then, as now, the ones who desire to follow Jesus must obey him (Jn 14:15).

Robust discipleship reflects a realistic understanding of salvation: the price paid, the pain borne, and the great gift delivered. Those who seek to follow Jesus casually have failed to think deeply about his death on the cross. While God gives sinners salvation freely, living a life of discipleship costs everything, as what is required is daily and complete surrender to God and his will.

me, for I have found the coin that I had lost.' 10Just so, I tell you, there is joy before the angels of God over one sinner who repents."

The Parable of the Prodigal Son

11And he said, "There was a man who had two sons. 12And the younger of them said to his father, 'Father, give me the share of property that is coming to me.' And he divided his property between them. 13Not many days later, the younger son gathered all he had and took a journey into a far country, and there he squandered his property in reckless living. 14And when he had spent everything, a severe famine arose in that country, and he began to be in need. 15So he went and hired himself out to[1] one of the citizens of that country, who sent him into his fields to feed pigs. 16And he was longing to be fed with the pods that the pigs ate, and no one gave him anything.

17"But when he came to himself, he said, 'How many of my father's hired servants have more than enough bread, but I perish here with hunger! 18I will arise and go to my father, and I will say to him, "Father, I have sinned against heaven and before you. 19I am no longer worthy to be called your son. Treat me as one of your hired servants."' 20And he arose and came to his father. But while he was still a long way off, his father saw him and felt compassion, and ran and embraced him and kissed him. 21And the son said to him, 'Father, I have sinned against heaven and before you. I am no longer worthy to be called your son.'[2] 22But the father said to his servants,[3] 'Bring quickly the best robe, and put it on him, and put a ring on his hand, and shoes on his feet. 23And bring the fattened calf and kill it, and let us eat and celebrate. 24For this my son was dead, and is alive again; he was lost, and is found.' And they began to celebrate.

25"Now his older son was in the field, and as he came and drew near to the house, he heard music and dancing. 26And he called one of the servants and asked what these things meant. 27And he said to him, 'Your brother has come, and your father has killed the fattened calf, because he has received him back safe and sound.' 28But he was angry and refused to go in. His father came out and entreated him, 29but he answered his father, 'Look, these many years I have served you, and I never disobeyed your command, yet you never gave me a young goat, that I might celebrate with my friends. 30But when this son of yours came, who has devoured your property with prostitutes, you killed the fattened calf for him!' 31And he said to him, 'Son, you are always with me, and all that is mine is yours. 32It was fitting to celebrate and be glad, for this your brother was dead, and is alive; he was lost, and is found.'"

The Parable of the Dishonest Manager

16 He also said to the disciples, "There was a rich man who had a manager, and charges were brought to him that this man was wasting his possessions. 2And he called him and said to him, 'What is this that I hear about you? Turn in the account of your management, for you can no longer be manager.' 3And the manager said to himself, 'What shall I do, since my master is taking the management away from me? I am not strong enough to dig, and I am ashamed to beg. 4I have decided what to do, so that when I am removed from management, people may receive me into their houses.' 5So, summoning his master's debtors one by one, he said to the first, 'How much do you owe my master?' 6He said, 'A hundred measures[4] of oil.' He said to him, 'Take your bill, and sit down quickly and write fifty.' 7Then he said to another, 'And how much do you owe?' He said, 'A hundred measures[5] of wheat.' He said to him, 'Take your bill, and write eighty.' 8The master commended the dishonest manager for his shrewdness. For the sons of this world[6] are more shrewd in dealing with their own generation than the sons

[1] Greek *joined himself to* [2] Some manuscripts add *treat me as one of your hired servants* [3] Or *bondservants*
[4] About 875 gallons or 3,200 liters [5] Between 1,000 and 1,200 bushels or 37,000 to 45,000 liters
[6] Greek *age*

CELEBRATING WHEN THE LOST ARE FOUND

Throughout his earthly ministry, Jesus' association with sinners chafed his religious critics, but Jesus consistently explained that he had come to seek and save the lost (Lk 19:10). To reinforce this truth, Jesus told three stories about a search for lost things.

With each story, Jesus confronted the religious leaders with the truth they kept missing — God is in the business of restoration and celebration (Lk 15:7). These leaders failed to listen with discernment as Jesus confronted them with the fact that they were like the older brother in the third story who had stayed home, served his father grudgingly, judged his brother unfairly, then distanced himself from his father without leaving home (Lk 15:25 – 30).

Jesus came to earth to launch a search-and-rescue mission, seeking and saving those who were spiritually lost. The sinners of his day loved to invite Jesus to their gatherings (Lk 5:29). The Pharisees stood by, scowled, and judged. They complained to Jesus' disciples about his eating and drinking with tax collectors and sinners. Jesus responded that it was not the healthy who needed a doctor but rather those who were sick (Mt 9:12).

The Pharisees and other religious leaders loved the trappings of their offices — respectful greetings, sitting in the most important seats, and having the opportunity to load others with religious burdens they personally had no intention of carrying (Lk 11:46). In contrast, Jesus did not come to be served but to serve and give his life as a ransom for many (Mt 20:28). The Pharisees thanked God that they were not needy like the sinners around them. Jesus rebuked them with a story about a tax collector who cried out to God in his spiritual poverty and found salvation (Lk 18:9 – 14).

Earthly concerns clouded the judgment of the religious leaders and caused them to disregard the spiritual truths Jesus taught. Confident that they knew God's will and that God was pleased with them, they resisted Jesus. As Jesus submitted to the grand plan of the gospel, the religious leaders manipulated the political system to ensure Jesus' death. Unwittingly, their actions set in motion all that was required for the lost to be found and for celebration to erupt in heaven.

of light. [9]And I tell you, make friends for yourselves by means of unrighteous wealth,[1] so that when it fails they may receive you into the eternal dwellings.

[10]"One who is faithful in a very little is also faithful in much, and one who is dishonest in a very little is also dishonest in much. [11]If then you have not been faithful in the unrighteous wealth, who will entrust to you the true riches? [12]And if you have not been faithful in that which is another's, who will give you that which is your own? [13]No servant can serve two masters, for either he will hate the one and love the other, or he will be devoted to the one and despise the other. You cannot serve God and money."

The Law and the Kingdom of God

[14]The Pharisees, who were lovers of money, heard all these things, and they ridiculed him. [15]And he said to them, "You are those who justify yourselves before men, but God knows your hearts. For what is exalted among men is an abomination in the sight of God.

[16]"The Law and the Prophets were until John; since then the good news of the kingdom of God is preached, and everyone forces his way into it.[2] [17]But it is easier for heaven and earth to pass away than for one dot of the Law to become void.

Divorce and Remarriage

[18]"Everyone who divorces his wife and marries another commits adultery, and he who marries a woman divorced from her husband commits adultery.

The Rich Man and Lazarus

[19]"There was a rich man who was clothed in purple and fine linen and who feasted sumptuously every day. [20]And at his gate was laid a poor man named Lazarus, covered with sores, [21]who desired to be fed with what fell from the rich man's table. Moreover, even the dogs came and licked his sores. [22]The poor man died and was carried by the angels to Abraham's side.[3] The rich man also died and was buried, [23]and in Hades, being in torment, he lifted up his eyes and saw Abraham far off and Lazarus at his side. [24]And he called out, 'Father Abraham, have mercy on me, and send Lazarus to dip the end of his finger in water and cool my tongue, for I am in anguish in this flame.' [25]But Abraham said, 'Child, remember that you in your lifetime received your good things, and Lazarus in like manner bad things; but now he is comforted here, and you are in anguish. [26]And besides all this, between us and you a great chasm has been fixed, in order that those who would pass from here to you may not be able, and none may cross from there to us.' [27]And he said, 'Then I beg you, father, to send him to my father's house— [28]for I have five brothers—so that he may warn them, lest they also come into this place of torment.' [29]But Abraham said, 'They have Moses and the Prophets; let them hear them.' [30]And he said, 'No, father Abraham, but if someone goes to them from the dead, they will repent.' [31]He said to him, 'If they do not hear Moses and the Prophets, neither will they be convinced if someone should rise from the dead.'"

Temptations to Sin

17 And he said to his disciples, "Temptations to sin[4] are sure to come, but woe to the one through whom they come! [2]It would be better for him if a millstone were hung around his neck and he were cast into the sea than that he should cause one of these little ones to sin.[5] [3]Pay attention to yourselves! If your brother sins, rebuke him, and if he repents, forgive him, [4]and if he sins against you seven times in the day, and turns to you seven times, saying, 'I repent,' you must forgive him."

---

[1]Greek *mammon*, a Semitic word for money or possessions; also verse 11; rendered *money* in verse 13
[2]Or *everyone is forcefully urged into it* [3]Greek *bosom*; also verse 23 [4]Greek *Stumbling blocks* [5]Greek *stumble*

LUKE 16:19–31

JESUS AND HELL

Jesus taught more about hell than he taught about heaven. Through the parable of the rich man and a poor man named Lazarus, Jesus provided unforgettable insights into life now and the life to come.

While they lived on earth, a great economic chasm separated the rich man from Lazarus. While the rich man feasted, Lazarus starved. While the rich man lived in pleasure, Lazarus lived in pain. If Jesus had asked his disciples which of these men God favored, they would not have faltered: their answer would have been "the rich man." That's why the disciples were so surprised when Jesus explained that it was easier for a camel to go through the eye of a needle than for a rich man to go to heaven. They exclaimed, "Who then can be saved?" Jesus responded, "With man this is impossible, but with God all things are possible" (Mt 19:25–26).

In the parable, after the rich man and Lazarus died, a great spiritual chasm separated them. While Lazarus enjoyed comfort, the rich man writhed in torment. For these two men, eternity brought about a great reversal. Jesus' story teaches that there is an unbridgeable divide between heaven and hell; no one can travel from one to the other. The good news is that eternity in hell is not inevitable. Choices made in this life impact what happens after death.

The Pharisees and other religious leaders listened that day but clearly missed the point. Later, Jesus raised another man, Lazarus, from the dead. Only God could perform such a miracle. Some placed their faith in Jesus, but others, especially the religious leaders, left and began plotting how and when to kill Jesus (Jn 11:38–53). Jesus had enough power to raise Lazarus from the dead, yet the religious elite pooled their political power to trap, accuse, bring to trial, and then crucify Jesus. Jesus confronted them with the truth that they were in league with their father, the devil, and working to carry out his murderous desires (Jn 8:44).

Jesus graciously explained the reality of hell so that people would understand the consequences of their choices. Because of the gospel, everyone can call on the name of the Lord before they die and be saved (Ac 2:21).

Increase Our Faith

5The apostles said to the Lord, "Increase our faith!" 6And the Lord said, "If you had faith like a grain of mustard seed, you could say to this mulberry tree, 'Be uprooted and planted in the sea,' and it would obey you.

Unworthy Servants

7"Will any one of you who has a servant[1] plowing or keeping sheep say to him when he has come in from the field, 'Come at once and recline at table'? 8Will he not rather say to him, 'Prepare supper for me, and dress properly,[2] and serve me while I eat and drink, and afterward you will eat and drink'? 9Does he thank the servant because he did what was commanded? 10So you also, when you have done all that you were commanded, say, 'We are unworthy servants;[3] we have only done what was our duty.'"

Jesus Cleanses Ten Lepers

11On the way to Jerusalem he was passing along between Samaria and Galilee. 12And as he entered a village, he was met by ten lepers,[4] who stood at a distance 13and lifted up their voices, saying, "Jesus, Master, have mercy on us." 14When he saw them he said to them, "Go and show yourselves to the priests." And as they went they were cleansed. 15Then one of them, when he saw that he was healed, turned back, praising God with a loud voice; 16and he fell on his face at Jesus' feet, giving him thanks. Now he was a Samaritan. 17Then Jesus answered, "Were not ten cleansed? Where are the nine? 18Was no one found to return and give praise to God except this foreigner?" 19And he said to him, "Rise and go your way; your faith has made you well."[5]

The Coming of the Kingdom

20Being asked by the Pharisees when the kingdom of God would come, he answered them, "The kingdom of God is not coming in ways that can be observed, 21nor will they say, 'Look, here it is!' or 'There!' for behold, the kingdom of God is in the midst of you."[6]

22And he said to the disciples, "The days are coming when you will desire to see one of the days of the Son of Man, and you will not see it. 23And they will say to you, 'Look, there!' or 'Look, here!' Do not go out or follow them. 24For as the lightning flashes and lights up the sky from one side to the other, so will the Son of Man be in his day.[7] 25But first he must suffer many things and be rejected by this generation. 26Just as it was in the days of Noah, so will it be in the days of the Son of Man. 27They were eating and drinking and marrying and being given in marriage, until the day when Noah entered the ark, and the flood came and destroyed them all. 28Likewise, just as it was in the days of Lot—they were eating and drinking, buying and selling, planting and building, 29but on the day when Lot went out from Sodom, fire and sulfur rained from heaven and destroyed them all— 30so will it be on the day when the Son of Man is revealed. 31On that day, let the one who is on the housetop, with his goods in the house, not come down to take them away, and likewise let the one who is in the field not turn back. 32Remember Lot's wife. 33Whoever seeks to preserve his life will lose it, but whoever loses his life will keep it. 34I tell you, in that night there will be two in one bed. One will be taken and the other left. 35There will be two women grinding together. One will be taken and the other left."[8] 37And they said to him, "Where, Lord?" He said to them, "Where the corpse[9] is, there the vultures[10] will gather."

[1]Or *bondservant*; also verse 9 [2]Greek *gird yourself* [3]Or *bondservants* [4]*Leprosy* was a term for several skin diseases; see Leviticus 13 [5]Or *has saved you* [6]Or *within you*, or *within your grasp* [7]Some manuscripts omit *in his day* [8]Some manuscripts add verse 36: *Two men will be in the field; one will be taken and the other left* [9]Greek *body* [10]Or *eagles*

LUKE 17:20–21

THE KINGDOM OF GOD IN YOUR MIDST

In Jesus' day, people wanted to know about the kingdom of God, and they asked Jesus about it. Jesus confounded their assumptions by asserting that the kingdom of God was already in their midst. Clearly, an aspect of the kingdom promise was fulfilled in Jesus' first coming. The kingdom of God operates among earthly kingdoms today, but one day, God's kingdom will swallow up all rival kingdoms (Rev 11:15).

The kingdom of God is not the same as the church, though the church is part of the kingdom. The kingdom now is the presence of God alongside earthly kingdoms. The power of God is shown now in the distribution and work of the Holy Spirit (Heb 2:4). One day, however, Jesus will rule over all, and he will share that rule with his people (Rev 5:9–10). Until then, believers wait in anticipation for God's kingdom rule to be complete.

The Parable of the Persistent Widow

18 And he told them a parable to the effect that they ought always to pray and
not lose heart. 2He said, "In a certain city there was a judge who neither
feared God nor respected man. 3And there was a widow in that city who kept
coming to him and saying, 'Give me justice against my adversary.' 4For a while he
refused, but afterward he said to himself, 'Though I neither fear God nor respect
man, 5yet because this widow keeps bothering me, I will give her justice, so that
she will not beat me down by her continual coming.'" 6And the Lord said, "Hear
what the unrighteous judge says. 7And will not God give justice to his elect, who
cry to him day and night? Will he delay long over them? 8I tell you, he will give
justice to them speedily. Nevertheless, when the Son of Man comes, will he find
faith on earth?"

The Pharisee and the Tax Collector

9He also told this parable to some who trusted in themselves that they were
righteous, and treated others with contempt: 10"Two men went up into the temple
to pray, one a Pharisee and the other a tax collector. 11The Pharisee, standing by
himself, prayed[1] thus: 'God, I thank you that I am not like other men, extortioners,
unjust, adulterers, or even like this tax collector. 12I fast twice a week; I give tithes
of all that I get.' 13But the tax collector, standing far off, would not even lift up
his eyes to heaven, but beat his breast, saying, 'God, be merciful to me, a sinner!'
14I tell you, this man went down to his house justified, rather than the other. For
everyone who exalts himself will be humbled, but the one who humbles himself
will be exalted."

Let the Children Come to Me

15Now they were bringing even infants to him that he might touch them. And
when the disciples saw it, they rebuked them. 16But Jesus called them to him, saying, "Let the children come to me, and do not hinder them, for to such belongs
the kingdom of God. 17Truly, I say to you, whoever does not receive the kingdom
of God like a child shall not enter it."

The Rich Ruler

18And a ruler asked him, "Good Teacher, what must I do to inherit eternal
life?" 19And Jesus said to him, "Why do you call me good? No one is good except
God alone. 20You know the commandments: 'Do not commit adultery, Do not
murder, Do not steal, Do not bear false witness, Honor your father and mother.'"
21And he said, "All these I have kept from my youth." 22When Jesus heard this, he
said to him, "One thing you still lack. Sell all that you have and distribute to the
poor, and you will have treasure in heaven; and come, follow me." 23But when he
heard these things, he became very sad, for he was extremely rich. 24Jesus, seeing
that he had become sad, said, "How difficult it is for those who have wealth to
enter the kingdom of God! 25For it is easier for a camel to go through the eye of a
needle than for a rich person to enter the kingdom of God." 26Those who heard
it said, "Then who can be saved?" 27But he said, "What is impossible with man is
possible with God." 28And Peter said, "See, we have left our homes and followed
you." 29And he said to them, "Truly, I say to you, there is no one who has left
house or wife or brothers[2] or parents or children, for the sake of the kingdom
of God, 30who will not receive many times more in this time, and in the age to
come eternal life."

Jesus Foretells His Death a Third Time

31And taking the twelve, he said to them, "See, we are going up to Jerusalem,
and everything that is written about the Son of Man by the prophets will be

[1] Or *standing, prayed to himself* [2] Or *wife or brothers and sisters*

LUKE 18:9–14

JESUS AND MERCY

The Greek word translated "have mercy" can also mean "to be favorably inclined." This word is used only one other time in the New Testament, and there it describes how Christ made reconciliation possible between God and humanity by his sacrifice on the cross (Heb 2:17). The noun form appears in 1 John 2:2 and 4:10; in both places, Jesus is called the atoning sacrifice for our sins. Jesus, as our sacrifice, paid the price our sins required, thereby making it possible for God to turn aside his righteous wrath.

The tax collector in Jesus' story understood his sinful condition and asked God for mercy. Thankfully, God does not save people because of their righteous acts but solely through his rich mercy (Eph 2:4–5; Titus 3:5). Later, the apostle Peter would write that in God's great mercy, he has given believers new birth into a living hope through the resurrection of Jesus Christ from the dead (1Pe 1:3). When people cry out to God for mercy, God's merciful response is Jesus.

accomplished. 32For he will be delivered over to the Gentiles and will be mocked
and shamefully treated and spit upon. 33And after flogging him, they will kill him,
and on the third day he will rise." 34But they understood none of these things. This
saying was hidden from them, and they did not grasp what was said.

Jesus Heals a Blind Beggar

35As he drew near to Jericho, a blind man was sitting by the roadside begging.
36And hearing a crowd going by, he inquired what this meant. 37They told him,
"Jesus of Nazareth is passing by." 38And he cried out, "Jesus, Son of David, have
mercy on me!" 39And those who were in front rebuked him, telling him to be silent. But he cried out all the more, "Son of David, have mercy on me!" 40And Jesus
stopped and commanded him to be brought to him. And when he came near, he
asked him, 41"What do you want me to do for you?" He said, "Lord, let me recover
my sight." 42And Jesus said to him, "Recover your sight; your faith has made you
well." 43And immediately he recovered his sight and followed him, glorifying God.
And all the people, when they saw it, gave praise to God.

Jesus and Zacchaeus

19 He entered Jericho and was passing through. 2And behold, there was a man
named Zacchaeus. He was a chief tax collector and was rich. 3And he was
seeking to see who Jesus was, but on account of the crowd he could not, because
he was small in stature. 4So he ran on ahead and climbed up into a sycamore tree
to see him, for he was about to pass that way. 5And when Jesus came to the place,
he looked up and said to him, "Zacchaeus, hurry and come down, for I must stay
at your house today." 6So he hurried and came down and received him joyfully.
7And when they saw it, they all grumbled, "He has gone in to be the guest of a man
who is a sinner." 8And Zacchaeus stood and said to the Lord, "Behold, Lord, the
half of my goods I give to the poor. And if I have defrauded anyone of anything,
I restore it fourfold." 9And Jesus said to him, "Today salvation has come to this
house, since he also is a son of Abraham. 10For the Son of Man came to seek and
to save the lost."

The Parable of the Ten Minas

11As they heard these things, he proceeded to tell a parable, because he was near
to Jerusalem, and because they supposed that the kingdom of God was to appear
immediately. 12He said therefore, "A nobleman went into a far country to receive
for himself a kingdom and then return. 13Calling ten of his servants,[1] he gave them
ten minas,[2] and said to them, 'Engage in business until I come.' 14But his citizens
hated him and sent a delegation after him, saying, 'We do not want this man to
reign over us.' 15When he returned, having received the kingdom, he ordered these
servants to whom he had given the money to be called to him, that he might know
what they had gained by doing business. 16The first came before him, saying, 'Lord,
your mina has made ten minas more.' 17And he said to him, 'Well done, good servant![3] Because you have been faithful in a very little, you shall have authority over
ten cities.' 18And the second came, saying, 'Lord, your mina has made five minas.'
19And he said to him, 'And you are to be over five cities.' 20Then another came, saying, 'Lord, here is your mina, which I kept laid away in a handkerchief; 21for I was
afraid of you, because you are a severe man. You take what you did not deposit, and
reap what you did not sow.' 22He said to him, 'I will condemn you with your own
words, you wicked servant! You knew that I was a severe man, taking what I did not
deposit and reaping what I did not sow? 23Why then did you not put my money in
the bank, and at my coming I might have collected it with interest?' 24And he said
to those who stood by, 'Take the mina from him, and give it to the one who has
the ten minas.' 25And they said to him, 'Lord, he has ten minas!' 26'I tell you that to

[1]Or *bondservants*; also verse 15 [2]A *mina* was about three months' wages for a laborer [3]Or *bondservant*; also verse 22

everyone who has, more will be given, but from the one who has not, even what he has will be taken away. 27But as for these enemies of mine, who did not want me to reign over them, bring them here and slaughter them before me.'"

The Triumphal Entry

28And when he had said these things, he went on ahead, going up to Jerusalem. 29When he drew near to Bethphage and Bethany, at the mount that is called Olivet, he sent two of the disciples, 30saying, "Go into the village in front of you, where on entering you will find a colt tied, on which no one has ever yet sat. Untie it and bring it here. 31If anyone asks you, 'Why are you untying it?' you shall say this: 'The Lord has need of it.'" 32So those who were sent went away and found it just as he had told them. 33And as they were untying the colt, its owners said to them, "Why are you untying the colt?" 34And they said, "The Lord has need of it." 35And they brought it to Jesus, and throwing their cloaks on the colt, they set Jesus on it. 36And as he rode along, they spread their cloaks on the road. 37As he was drawing near—already on the way down the Mount of Olives—the whole multitude of his disciples began to rejoice and praise God with a loud voice for all the mighty works that they had seen, 38saying, "Blessed is the King who comes in the name of the Lord! Peace in heaven and glory in the highest!" 39And some of the Pharisees in the crowd said to him, "Teacher, rebuke your disciples." 40He answered, "I tell you, if these were silent, the very stones would cry out."

Jesus Weeps over Jerusalem

41And when he drew near and saw the city, he wept over it, 42saying, "Would that you, even you, had known on this day the things that make for peace! But now they are hidden from your eyes. 43For the days will come upon you, when your enemies will set up a barricade around you and surround you and hem you in on every side 44and tear you down to the ground, you and your children within you. And they will not leave one stone upon another in you, because you did not know the time of your visitation."

Jesus Cleanses the Temple

45And he entered the temple and began to drive out those who sold, 46saying to them, "It is written, 'My house shall be a house of prayer,' but you have made it a den of robbers."

47And he was teaching daily in the temple. The chief priests and the scribes and the principal men of the people were seeking to destroy him, 48but they did not find anything they could do, for all the people were hanging on his words.

The Authority of Jesus Challenged

20 One day, as Jesus[1] was teaching the people in the temple and preaching the gospel, the chief priests and the scribes with the elders came up 2and said to him, "Tell us by what authority you do these things, or who it is that gave you this authority." 3He answered them, "I also will ask you a question. Now tell me, 4was the baptism of John from heaven or from man?" 5And they discussed it with one another, saying, "If we say, 'From heaven,' he will say, 'Why did you not believe him?' 6But if we say, 'From man,' all the people will stone us to death, for they are convinced that John was a prophet." 7So they answered that they did not know where it came from. 8And Jesus said to them, "Neither will I tell you by what authority I do these things."

The Parable of the Wicked Tenants

9And he began to tell the people this parable: "A man planted a vineyard and let it out to tenants and went into another country for a long while. 10When the

[1]Greek *he*

LUKE 19:28–44

THE TRIUMPHAL ENTRY

Jesus' entry into Jerusalem bears the unmistakable marks of a royal procession—the arrival of a king greeted by his people with celebration and joy. In the space of a few verses, Luke deftly weaves together historical allusions and nods to prophecy to emphasize that Jesus was indeed Israel's promised king. The ride on the colt strongly resembles Solomon's journey to Gihon where he was to be proclaimed king (1Ki 1:33–35). The description of people eagerly spreading their outer garments to create a pathway for Jesus (roughly equivalent to "rolling out the red carpet" today) recalls the scene of Jehu's coronation (2Ki 9:13). Luke's account of Christ's triumphal entry culminates with a citation from Psalm 118:26, adding the title of "King" so as to leave no doubt: Jesus was the long-awaited King who would bring peace between people and God.

time came, he sent a servant[1] to the tenants, so that they would give him some of the fruit of the vineyard. But the tenants beat him and sent him away empty-handed. 11And he sent another servant. But they also beat and treated him shamefully, and sent him away empty-handed. 12And he sent yet a third. This one also they wounded and cast out. 13Then the owner of the vineyard said, 'What shall I do? I will send my beloved son; perhaps they will respect him.' 14But when the tenants saw him, they said to themselves, 'This is the heir. Let us kill him, so that the inheritance may be ours.' 15And they threw him out of the vineyard and killed him. What then will the owner of the vineyard do to them? 16He will come and destroy those tenants and give the vineyard to others." When they heard this, they said, "Surely not!" 17But he looked directly at them and said, "What then is this that is written:

"'The stone that the builders rejected
has become the cornerstone'?[2]

18Everyone who falls on that stone will be broken to pieces, and when it falls on anyone, it will crush him."

Paying Taxes to Caesar

19The scribes and the chief priests sought to lay hands on him at that very hour, for they perceived that he had told this parable against them, but they feared the people. 20So they watched him and sent spies, who pretended to be sincere, that they might catch him in something he said, so as to deliver him up to the authority and jurisdiction of the governor. 21So they asked him, "Teacher, we know that you speak and teach rightly, and show no partiality,[3] but truly teach the way of God. 22Is it lawful for us to give tribute to Caesar, or not?" 23But he perceived their craftiness, and said to them, 24"Show me a denarius.[4] Whose likeness and inscription does it have?" They said, "Caesar's." 25He said to them, "Then render to Caesar the things that are Caesar's, and to God the things that are God's." 26And they were not able in the presence of the people to catch him in what he said, but marveling at his answer they became silent.

Sadducees Ask About the Resurrection

27There came to him some Sadducees, those who deny that there is a resurrection, 28and they asked him a question, saying, "Teacher, Moses wrote for us that if a man's brother dies, having a wife but no children, the man[5] must take the widow and raise up offspring for his brother. 29Now there were seven brothers. The first took a wife, and died without children. 30And the second 31and the third took her, and likewise all seven left no children and died. 32Afterward the woman also died. 33In the resurrection, therefore, whose wife will the woman be? For the seven had her as wife."

34And Jesus said to them, "The sons of this age marry and are given in marriage, 35but those who are considered worthy to attain to that age and to the resurrection from the dead neither marry nor are given in marriage, 36for they cannot die anymore, because they are equal to angels and are sons of God, being sons[6] of the resurrection. 37But that the dead are raised, even Moses showed, in the passage about the bush, where he calls the Lord the God of Abraham and the God of Isaac and the God of Jacob. 38Now he is not God of the dead, but of the living, for all live to him." 39Then some of the scribes answered, "Teacher, you have spoken well." 40For they no longer dared to ask him any question.

Whose Son Is the Christ?

41But he said to them, "How can they say that the Christ is David's son? 42For David himself says in the Book of Psalms,

---

LUKE 20:19–26

"WHOSE LIKENESS?"

Jesus and his teachings posed a direct challenge to Jewish religious leaders. Yet, because of Jesus' popularity, the chief priests and scribes remained wary of taking direct action against either Jesus or his teachings. Instead, they watched and waited, hoping Jesus' words would be his own downfall. In this passage, the religious leaders set a subtle trap for Jesus by asking a question for which there was no easy answer: Should Jews pay a citizenship tax to Caesar? If Jesus said yes, this would indicate his acceptance of foreign rule and undermine his standing with the people. If Jesus said no, he would sound like a political revolutionary.

But Jesus knew their hearts and risked neither losing the support of the people or being handed over to the Roman governor for sedition. Jesus sidestepped the trap—and set a trap of his own. When Jesus asked for a coin, the Pharisees produced a Roman denarius, proving that they already recognized Roman sovereignty. Jesus pointed out that since this coin bore the image of Caesar, it belonged to Caesar. Caesar had the right to require taxes, and the Jews were not exempt. But Jesus went a step further, taking the opportunity to turn a political debate into a spiritual lesson. Alluding to the fact that human beings are "stamped" with the image of God (Ge 1:26–27), Jesus reminded the religious leaders of the vital importance of giving to God what is due to him. God's people, as bearers of God's image, belong to him alone.

---

[1]Or *bondservant*; also verse 11 [2]Greek *the head of the corner* [3]Greek *and do not receive a face*
[4]A *denarius* was a day's wage for a laborer [5]Greek *his brother* [6]Greek *huioi*; see Preface

"'The Lord said to my Lord,
"Sit at my right hand,
43 until I make your enemies your footstool."'

44David thus calls him Lord, so how is he his son?"

Beware of the Scribes

45And in the hearing of all the people he said to his disciples, 46"Beware of the scribes, who like to walk around in long robes, and love greetings in the marketplaces and the best seats in the synagogues and the places of honor at feasts, 47who devour widows' houses and for a pretense make long prayers. They will receive the greater condemnation."

The Widow's Offering

21 Jesus[1] looked up and saw the rich putting their gifts into the offering box, 2and he saw a poor widow put in two small copper coins.[2] 3And he said, "Truly, I tell you, this poor widow has put in more than all of them. 4For they all contributed out of their abundance, but she out of her poverty put in all she had to live on."

Jesus Foretells Destruction of the Temple

5And while some were speaking of the temple, how it was adorned with noble stones and offerings, he said, 6"As for these things that you see, the days will come when there will not be left here one stone upon another that will not be thrown down." 7And they asked him, "Teacher, when will these things be, and what will be the sign when these things are about to take place?" 8And he said, "See that you are not led astray. For many will come in my name, saying, 'I am he!' and, 'The time is at hand!' Do not go after them. 9And when you hear of wars and tumults, do not be terrified, for these things must first take place, but the end will not be at once."

Jesus Foretells Wars and Persecution

10Then he said to them, "Nation will rise against nation, and kingdom against kingdom. 11There will be great earthquakes, and in various places famines and pestilences. And there will be terrors and great signs from heaven. 12But before all this they will lay their hands on you and persecute you, delivering you up to the synagogues and prisons, and you will be brought before kings and governors for my name's sake. 13This will be your opportunity to bear witness. 14Settle it therefore in your minds not to meditate beforehand how to answer, 15for I will give you a mouth and wisdom, which none of your adversaries will be able to withstand or contradict. 16You will be delivered up even by parents and brothers[3] and relatives and friends, and some of you they will put to death. 17You will be hated by all for my name's sake. 18But not a hair of your head will perish. 19By your endurance you will gain your lives.

Jesus Foretells Destruction of Jerusalem

20"But when you see Jerusalem surrounded by armies, then know that its desolation has come near. 21Then let those who are in Judea flee to the mountains, and let those who are inside the city depart, and let not those who are out in the country enter it, 22for these are days of vengeance, to fulfill all that is written. 23Alas for women who are pregnant and for those who are nursing infants in those days! For there will be great distress upon the earth and wrath against this people. 24They will fall by the edge of the sword and be led captive among all nations, and Jerusalem will be trampled underfoot by the Gentiles, until the times of the Gentiles are fulfilled.

[1]Greek *He* [2]Greek *two lepta*; a *lepton* was a Jewish bronze or copper coin worth about 1/128 of a *denarius* (which was a day's wage for a laborer) [3]Or *parents and brothers and sisters*

LUKE 21:5–6

FULFILLED PROPHECY

When Jesus prophesied the destruction of the temple, he was standing on the grounds of that magnificently adorned place of worship. The temple was at the heart of Israel's religious life, and Herod the Great had initiated an extravagant refurbishing process. Residents and tourists saw gold- and silver-plated gates, golden grapevine clusters that decorated the courtyard, and ornate Babylonian linen tapestries that hung from the temple veil. Even a Roman historian, Tacitus, was impressed, declaring it to be an "immensely opulent temple."

Jesus' prediction must have seemed unlikely, even unthinkable, to the people listening. Not only was the temple itself impressive, but Jesus lived during a time when Judaism was experiencing great Messianic fervor, with high expectations of national deliverance from Roman rule. How could it be that this building that stood at the center of Jewish life and hope would be reduced to a heap of rubble? But just a few short decades later, in AD 70, Roman forces attacked the city of Jerusalem and ransacked, demolished, and burned the temple.

Despite the tragic nature of this episode in history, it highlights a great truth: Jesus' words are reliable. As God's people now live in the hope of Jesus' return, the final resurrection, and all the other promises of Jesus that have yet to come to pass, they can find reassurance in knowing that Jesus' prophecies have proven reliable time and time again. Christian hope is well founded on the One who does not change (Mal 3:6; Jas 1:17).

The Coming of the Son of Man

25“And there will be signs in sun and moon and stars, and on the earth distress of nations in perplexity because of the roaring of the sea and the waves, 26people fainting with fear and with foreboding of what is coming on the world. For the powers of the heavens will be shaken. 27And then they will see the Son of Man coming in a cloud with power and great glory. 28Now when these things begin to take place, straighten up and raise your heads, because your redemption is drawing near.”

The Lesson of the Fig Tree

29And he told them a parable: “Look at the fig tree, and all the trees. 30As soon as they come out in leaf, you see for yourselves and know that the summer is already near. 31So also, when you see these things taking place, you know that the kingdom of God is near. 32Truly, I say to you, this generation will not pass away until all has taken place. 33Heaven and earth will pass away, but my words will not pass away.

Watch Yourselves

34“But watch yourselves lest your hearts be weighed down with dissipation and drunkenness and cares of this life, and that day come upon you suddenly like a trap. 35For it will come upon all who dwell on the face of the whole earth. 36But stay awake at all times, praying that you may have strength to escape all these things that are going to take place, and to stand before the Son of Man.”

37And every day he was teaching in the temple, but at night he went out and lodged on the mount called Olivet. 38And early in the morning all the people came to him in the temple to hear him.

The Plot to Kill Jesus

22 Now the Feast of Unleavened Bread drew near, which is called the Passover. 2And the chief priests and the scribes were seeking how to put him to death, for they feared the people.

Judas to Betray Jesus

3Then Satan entered into Judas called Iscariot, who was of the number of the twelve. 4He went away and conferred with the chief priests and officers how he might betray him to them. 5And they were glad, and agreed to give him money. 6So he consented and sought an opportunity to betray him to them in the absence of a crowd.

The Passover with the Disciples

7Then came the day of Unleavened Bread, on which the Passover lamb had to be sacrificed. 8So Jesus[1] sent Peter and John, saying, “Go and prepare the Passover for us, that we may eat it.” 9They said to him, “Where will you have us prepare it?” 10He said to them, “Behold, when you have entered the city, a man carrying a jar of water will meet you. Follow him into the house that he enters 11and tell the master of the house, ‘The Teacher says to you, Where is the guest room, where I may eat the Passover with my disciples?’ 12And he will show you a large upper room furnished; prepare it there.” 13And they went and found it just as he had told them, and they prepared the Passover.

Institution of the Lord’s Supper

14And when the hour came, he reclined at table, and the apostles with him. 15And he said to them, “I have earnestly desired to eat this Passover with you before I suffer. 16For I tell you I will not eat it[2] until it is fulfilled in the kingdom of

[1]Greek *he* [2]Some manuscripts *never eat it again*

God." [17]And he took a cup, and when he had given thanks he said, "Take this, and divide it among yourselves. [18]For I tell you that from now on I will not drink of the fruit of the vine until the kingdom of God comes." [19]And he took bread, and when he had given thanks, he broke it and gave it to them, saying, "This is my body, which is given for you. Do this in remembrance of me." [20]And likewise the cup after they had eaten, saying, "This cup that is poured out for you is the new covenant in my blood.[1] [21]But behold, the hand of him who betrays me is with me on the table. [22]For the Son of Man goes as it has been determined, but woe to that man by whom he is betrayed!" [23]And they began to question one another, which of them it could be who was going to do this.

Who Is the Greatest?

[24]A dispute also arose among them, as to which of them was to be regarded as the greatest. [25]And he said to them, "The kings of the Gentiles exercise lordship over them, and those in authority over them are called benefactors. [26]But not so with you. Rather, let the greatest among you become as the youngest, and the leader as one who serves. [27]For who is the greater, one who reclines at table or one who serves? Is it not the one who reclines at table? But I am among you as the one who serves.

[28]"You are those who have stayed with me in my trials, [29]and I assign to you, as my Father assigned to me, a kingdom, [30]that you may eat and drink at my table in my kingdom and sit on thrones judging the twelve tribes of Israel.

Jesus Foretells Peter's Denial

[31]"Simon, Simon, behold, Satan demanded to have you,[2] that he might sift you like wheat, [32]but I have prayed for you that your faith may not fail. And when you have turned again, strengthen your brothers." [33]Peter[3] said to him, "Lord, I am ready to go with you both to prison and to death." [34]Jesus[4] said, "I tell you, Peter, the rooster will not crow this day, until you deny three times that you know me."

Scripture Must Be Fulfilled in Jesus

[35]And he said to them, "When I sent you out with no moneybag or knapsack or sandals, did you lack anything?" They said, "Nothing." [36]He said to them, "But now let the one who has a moneybag take it, and likewise a knapsack. And let the one who has no sword sell his cloak and buy one. [37]For I tell you that this Scripture must be fulfilled in me: 'And he was numbered with the transgressors.' For what is written about me has its fulfillment." [38]And they said, "Look, Lord, here are two swords." And he said to them, "It is enough."

Jesus Prays on the Mount of Olives

[39]And he came out and went, as was his custom, to the Mount of Olives, and the disciples followed him. [40]And when he came to the place, he said to them, "Pray that you may not enter into temptation." [41]And he withdrew from them about a stone's throw, and knelt down and prayed, [42]saying, "Father, if you are willing, remove this cup from me. Nevertheless, not my will, but yours, be done." [43]And there appeared to him an angel from heaven, strengthening him. [44]And being in agony he prayed more earnestly; and his sweat became like great drops of blood falling down to the ground.[5] [45]And when he rose from prayer, he came to the disciples and found them sleeping for sorrow, [46]and he said to them, "Why are you sleeping? Rise and pray that you may not enter into temptation."

[1]Some manuscripts omit, in whole or in part, verses 19b–20 (*which is given . . . in my blood*) [2]The Greek word for *you* (twice in this verse) is plural; in verse 32, all four instances are singular [3]Greek *He* [4]Greek *He* [5]Some manuscripts omit verses 43 and 44

Betrayal and Arrest of Jesus

[47]While he was still speaking, there came a crowd, and the man called Judas, one of the twelve, was leading them. He drew near to Jesus to kiss him, [48]but Jesus said to him, "Judas, would you betray the Son of Man with a kiss?" [49]And when those who were around him saw what would follow, they said, "Lord, shall we strike with the sword?" [50]And one of them struck the servant[1] of the high priest and cut off his right ear. [51]But Jesus said, "No more of this!" And he touched his ear and healed him. [52]Then Jesus said to the chief priests and officers of the temple and elders, who had come out against him, "Have you come out as against a robber, with swords and clubs? [53]When I was with you day after day in the temple, you did not lay hands on me. But this is your hour, and the power of darkness."

Peter Denies Jesus

[54]Then they seized him and led him away, bringing him into the high priest's house, and Peter was following at a distance. [55]And when they had kindled a fire in the middle of the courtyard and sat down together, Peter sat down among them. [56]Then a servant girl, seeing him as he sat in the light and looking closely at him, said, "This man also was with him." [57]But he denied it, saying, "Woman, I do not know him." [58]And a little later someone else saw him and said, "You also are one of them." But Peter said, "Man, I am not." [59]And after an interval of about an hour still another insisted, saying, "Certainly this man also was with him, for he too is a Galilean." [60]But Peter said, "Man, I do not know what you are talking about." And immediately, while he was still speaking, the rooster crowed. [61]And the Lord turned and looked at Peter. And Peter remembered the saying of the Lord, how he had said to him, "Before the rooster crows today, you will deny me three times." [62]And he went out and wept bitterly.

Jesus Is Mocked

[63]Now the men who were holding Jesus in custody were mocking him as they beat him. [64]They also blindfolded him and kept asking him, "Prophesy! Who is it that struck you?" [65]And they said many other things against him, blaspheming him.

Jesus Before the Council

[66]When day came, the assembly of the elders of the people gathered together, both chief priests and scribes. And they led him away to their council, and they said, [67]"If you are the Christ, tell us." But he said to them, "If I tell you, you will not believe, [68]and if I ask you, you will not answer. [69]But from now on the Son of Man shall be seated at the right hand of the power of God." [70]So they all said, "Are you the Son of God, then?" And he said to them, "You say that I am." [71]Then they said, "What further testimony do we need? We have heard it ourselves from his own lips."

Jesus Before Pilate

23 Then the whole company of them arose and brought him before Pilate. [2]And they began to accuse him, saying, "We found this man misleading our nation and forbidding us to give tribute to Caesar, and saying that he himself is Christ, a king." [3]And Pilate asked him, "Are you the King of the Jews?" And he answered him, "You have said so." [4]Then Pilate said to the chief priests and the crowds, "I find no guilt in this man." [5]But they were urgent, saying, "He stirs up the people, teaching throughout all Judea, from Galilee even to this place."

Jesus Before Herod

[6]When Pilate heard this, he asked whether the man was a Galilean. [7]And when he learned that he belonged to Herod's jurisdiction, he sent him over to Herod,

[1]Or *bondservant*

LUKE 23:1–25

JESUS' TRIAL

Jesus' multistage trial—from the Jewish religious council, to the initial hearing before the Roman governor Pilate, to Herod's court, and finally back to Pilate for sentencing—marked the culmination of a lengthy plot by certain religious leaders to trap and condemn Jesus. After various unsuccessful attempts to undermine Jesus' popularity or frame him for sedition, the elders, chief priests, and scribes finally had Jesus in their clutches. They were not about to waste the opportunity. Outraged at Jesus' claim to be the Son of God (Lk 22:70–71), these religious leaders brought Jesus before Pilate and leveled three accusations (23:2), each designed to frame Jesus as a threat to Roman authority. The first charge, "misleading our nation," was a general complaint implying that Jesus was disturbing the peace and stirring up civil unrest. The second and third charges were more directly related to Roman rule: Jesus, they claimed, forbade paying taxes to Caesar (a blatant fabrication; Lk 20:25) and had declared himself to be the king over Israel. The final charge had an element of truth, but the religious leaders deliberately twisted Jesus' claim into one that usurped Caesar's earthly reign. Pilate himself saw through the unjust accusations, but his repeated attempts to set Jesus free were to no avail. The farcical nature of the trial is just one more indication that Jesus' suffering and death were those of an innocent and righteous man (Lk 23:47).

who was himself in Jerusalem at that time. 8When Herod saw Jesus, he was very glad, for he had long desired to see him, because he had heard about him, and he was hoping to see some sign done by him. 9So he questioned him at some length, but he made no answer. 10The chief priests and the scribes stood by, vehemently accusing him. 11And Herod with his soldiers treated him with contempt and mocked him. Then, arraying him in splendid clothing, he sent him back to Pilate. 12And Herod and Pilate became friends with each other that very day, for before this they had been at enmity with each other.

13Pilate then called together the chief priests and the rulers and the people, 14and said to them, "You brought me this man as one who was misleading the people. And after examining him before you, behold, I did not find this man guilty of any of your charges against him. 15Neither did Herod, for he sent him back to us. Look, nothing deserving death has been done by him. 16I will therefore punish and release him."[1]

Pilate Delivers Jesus to Be Crucified

18But they all cried out together, "Away with this man, and release to us Barabbas"— 19a man who had been thrown into prison for an insurrection started in the city and for murder. 20Pilate addressed them once more, desiring to release Jesus, 21but they kept shouting, "Crucify, crucify him!" 22A third time he said to them, "Why? What evil has he done? I have found in him no guilt deserving death. I will therefore punish and release him." 23But they were urgent, demanding with loud cries that he should be crucified. And their voices prevailed. 24So Pilate decided that their demand should be granted. 25He released the man who had been thrown into prison for insurrection and murder, for whom they asked, but he delivered Jesus over to their will.

The Crucifixion

26And as they led him away, they seized one Simon of Cyrene, who was coming in from the country, and laid on him the cross, to carry it behind Jesus. 27And there followed him a great multitude of the people and of women who were mourning and lamenting for him. 28But turning to them Jesus said, "Daughters of Jerusalem, do not weep for me, but weep for yourselves and for your children. 29For behold, the days are coming when they will say, 'Blessed are the barren and the wombs that never bore and the breasts that never nursed!' 30Then they will begin to say to the mountains, 'Fall on us,' and to the hills, 'Cover us.' 31For if they do these things when the wood is green, what will happen when it is dry?"

32Two others, who were criminals, were led away to be put to death with him. 33And when they came to the place that is called The Skull, there they crucified him, and the criminals, one on his right and one on his left. 34And Jesus said, "Father, forgive them, for they know not what they do."[2] And they cast lots to divide his garments. 35And the people stood by, watching, but the rulers scoffed at him, saying, "He saved others; let him save himself, if he is the Christ of God, his Chosen One!" 36The soldiers also mocked him, coming up and offering him sour wine 37and saying, "If you are the King of the Jews, save yourself!" 38There was also an inscription over him,[3] "This is the King of the Jews."

39One of the criminals who were hanged railed at him,[4] saying, "Are you not the Christ? Save yourself and us!" 40But the other rebuked him, saying, "Do you not fear God, since you are under the same sentence of condemnation? 41And we indeed justly, for we are receiving the due reward of our deeds; but this man has done nothing wrong." 42And he said, "Jesus, remember me when you come into your kingdom." 43And he said to him, "Truly, I say to you, today you will be with me in paradise."

---

[1]Here, or after verse 19, some manuscripts add verse 17: *Now he was obliged to release one man to them at the festival* [2]Some manuscripts omit the sentence *And Jesus . . . what they do* [3]Some manuscripts add *in letters of Greek and Latin and Hebrew* [4]Or *blasphemed him*

LUKE 23:33

CRUCIFIXION

At the time of Jesus' death, crucifixion was the Roman Empire's most brutal and degrading form of capital punishment — a death so horrible it was reserved for slaves and the vilest of criminals. No Roman citizen could be subjected to crucifixion. Indeed, church tradition indicates that while the Jewish apostle Peter eventually was crucified for following Christ, the apostle Paul, who was a Roman citizen, suffered the relatively humane fate of being beheaded.

Crucifixion seems to have taken various forms throughout the Roman Empire, but biblical and historical sources reveal a pattern. First, the condemned person usually was scourged with a flagellum, a whip constructed of leather thongs interwoven with bits of metal or bone. Greatly weakened by the scourging, the victim then carried the crossbeam through a crowd of people to the place of execution, enduring their taunts and jeers along the way. Sometimes a sign specifying the crime was hung around the criminal's neck. At the place of execution, the condemned was forced to lie on the ground with the crossbeam under his shoulders. Adding degradation to suffering, the executioners stripped the victim naked before nailing or binding him with ropes to the crossbeam.

After the condemned had been nailed or tied to the crossbeam, executioners lifted the crossbeam and secured it to a post, with the person's feet hanging above the ground. Archaeological evidence indicates that sometimes a pin or wooden block was placed halfway up the post to provide a seat for the body — allowing the prisoner to rest periodically, further prolonging the agony — and preventing the nails from tearing open the wounds and allowing the body to fall. The feet were also nailed or tied to the post. Finally, as in the case of the two criminals crucified with Jesus, executioners would sometimes break the legs of the crucified. This last brutal tactic sped up death for those lingering on the cross by causing massive shock, loss of circulation, and heart failure.

Jesus, completely innocent of all sin and wrongdoing, suffered the ancient world's most horrific and disgraceful punishment. But this was no ordinary case of wrongful condemnation. This perfect man was also the Son of God, and what appeared to be his defeat gave way to the most glorious victory the world has ever known. After suffering and dying for the sins of the world, Jesus Christ rose from the dead three days later. Jesus' glorious resurrection broke the power of sin and death and empowered his disciples to preach the Good News. Through his suffering on the cross and his resurrection, Jesus offers salvation to all who believe in him.

The Death of Jesus

44It was now about the sixth hour,[1] and there was darkness over the whole land until the ninth hour,[2] 45while the sun's light failed. And the curtain of the temple was torn in two. 46Then Jesus, calling out with a loud voice, said, "Father, into your hands I commit my spirit!" And having said this he breathed his last. 47Now when the centurion saw what had taken place, he praised God, saying, "Certainly this man was innocent!" 48And all the crowds that had assembled for this spectacle, when they saw what had taken place, returned home beating their breasts. 49And all his acquaintances and the women who had followed him from Galilee stood at a distance watching these things.

Jesus Is Buried

50Now there was a man named Joseph, from the Jewish town of Arimathea. He was a member of the council, a good and righteous man, 51who had not consented to their decision and action; and he was looking for the kingdom of God. 52This man went to Pilate and asked for the body of Jesus. 53Then he took it down and wrapped it in a linen shroud and laid him in a tomb cut in stone, where no one had ever yet been laid. 54It was the day of Preparation, and the Sabbath was beginning.[3] 55The women who had come with him from Galilee followed and saw the tomb and how his body was laid. 56Then they returned and prepared spices and ointments.

On the Sabbath they rested according to the commandment.

The Resurrection

24 But on the first day of the week, at early dawn, they went to the tomb, taking the spices they had prepared. 2And they found the stone rolled away from the tomb, 3but when they went in they did not find the body of the Lord Jesus. 4While they were perplexed about this, behold, two men stood by them in dazzling apparel. 5And as they were frightened and bowed their faces to the ground, the men said to them, "Why do you seek the living among the dead? 6He is not here, but has risen. Remember how he told you, while he was still in Galilee, 7that the Son of Man must be delivered into the hands of sinful men and be crucified and on the third day rise." 8And they remembered his words, 9and returning from the tomb they told all these things to the eleven and to all the rest. 10Now it was Mary Magdalene and Joanna and Mary the mother of James and the other women with them who told these things to the apostles, 11but these words seemed to them an idle tale, and they did not believe them. 12But Peter rose and ran to the tomb; stooping and looking in, he saw the linen cloths by themselves; and he went home marveling at what had happened.

On the Road to Emmaus

13That very day two of them were going to a village named Emmaus, about seven miles[4] from Jerusalem, 14and they were talking with each other about all these things that had happened. 15While they were talking and discussing together, Jesus himself drew near and went with them. 16But their eyes were kept from recognizing him. 17And he said to them, "What is this conversation that you are holding with each other as you walk?" And they stood still, looking sad. 18Then one of them, named Cleopas, answered him, "Are you the only visitor to Jerusalem who does not know the things that have happened there in these days?" 19And he said to them, "What things?" And they said to him, "Concerning Jesus of Nazareth, a man who was a prophet mighty in deed and word before God and all the people, 20and how our chief priests and rulers delivered him up to be condemned to death, and crucified him. 21But we had hoped that he was the one to redeem

[1]That is, noon [2]That is, 3 P.M. [3]Greek *was dawning* [4]Greek *sixty stadia*; a *stadion* was about 607 feet or 185 meters

Israel. Yes, and besides all this, it is now the third day since these things happened.
22Moreover, some women of our company amazed us. They were at the tomb early in the morning, 23and when they did not find his body, they came back saying
that they had even seen a vision of angels, who said that he was alive. 24Some of
those who were with us went to the tomb and found it just as the women had
said, but him they did not see." 25And he said to them, "O foolish ones, and slow
of heart to believe all that the prophets have spoken! 26Was it not necessary that
the Christ should suffer these things and enter into his glory?" 27And beginning
with Moses and all the Prophets, he interpreted to them in all the Scriptures the
things concerning himself.

28So they drew near to the village to which they were going. He acted as if
he were going farther, 29but they urged him strongly, saying, "Stay with us, for
it is toward evening and the day is now far spent." So he went in to stay with
them. 30When he was at table with them, he took the bread and blessed and
broke it and gave it to them. 31And their eyes were opened, and they recognized
him. And he vanished from their sight. 32They said to each other, "Did not our
hearts burn within us while he talked to us on the road, while he opened to us
the Scriptures?" 33And they rose that same hour and returned to Jerusalem. And
they found the eleven and those who were with them gathered together, 34say-
ing, "The Lord has risen indeed, and has appeared to Simon!" 35Then they told
what had happened on the road, and how he was known to them in the breaking
of the bread.

Jesus Appears to His Disciples

36As they were talking about these things, Jesus himself stood among them,
and said to them, "Peace to you!" 37But they were startled and frightened and
thought they saw a spirit. 38And he said to them, "Why are you troubled, and why
do doubts arise in your hearts? 39See my hands and my feet, that it is I myself.
Touch me, and see. For a spirit does not have flesh and bones as you see that I
have." 40And when he had said this, he showed them his hands and his feet. 41And
while they still disbelieved for joy and were marveling, he said to them, "Have
you anything here to eat?" 42They gave him a piece of broiled fish,[1] 43and he took
it and ate before them.

44Then he said to them, "These are my words that I spoke to you while I was
still with you, that everything written about me in the Law of Moses and the
Prophets and the Psalms must be fulfilled." 45Then he opened their minds to understand the Scriptures, 46and said to them, "Thus it is written, that the Christ
should suffer and on the third day rise from the dead, 47and that repentance for[2]
the forgiveness of sins should be proclaimed in his name to all nations, beginning
from Jerusalem. 48You are witnesses of these things. 49And behold, I am sending
the promise of my Father upon you. But stay in the city until you are clothed with
power from on high."

The Ascension

50And he led them out as far as Bethany, and lifting up his hands he blessed
them. 51While he blessed them, he parted from them and was carried up into
heaven. 52And they worshiped him and returned to Jerusalem with great joy, 53and
were continually in the temple blessing God.

[1]Some manuscripts add *and some honeycomb* [2]Some manuscripts *and*

LUKE 24:46–47

FORGIVENESS OF SINS

Jesus' power over sin had been called into question early in his ministry. Witnessing the faith of a group of people who made an extraordinary effort to bring their paralyzed friend to him for healing, Jesus said, "Man, your sins are forgiven you" (Lk 5:20). The Pharisees and teachers of the law recognized that only God could forgive sins—and not believing that Jesus was indeed God, they accused him of blasphemy. After Jesus' resurrection, there was no longer room for questioning or doubt. In defeating death, Jesus proved he was neither a pretender nor a blasphemer but the very Son of God. This victory over death signaled his divine authority to forgive sin.

Luke connects the preaching of the life-changing, sin-defeating gospel with Christ's resurrection. The Good News of repentance and remission of sins, which the disciples began preaching following Jesus' ascension and the coming of the Holy Spirit in power, is rooted in this fundamental truth: In fulfillment of God's promises in Scripture, Christ suffered and died and was raised to life on the third day. Death is defeated; sin's power is broken. The remission of sins is now available to all who believe in the powerful name of Jesus.

JESUS: OUR GREAT I AM

JOHN

JOHN

BIRTH OF JESUS *c. 5 BC*	JESUS' MINISTRY, DEATH, RESURRECTION *c. AD 27 – 30*	JOHN'S GOSPEL WRITTEN *c. AD 90*

John writes with one clear purpose: to show that Jesus is the path to eternal life (20:31). There is no other way to peace with God, in this life or the next, apart from having a saving faith in Jesus. For salvation to happen, a person who is dead in sin must be born again by the power of God's Spirit (3:1 – 21). John invites his readers to do just that — to be born again — to a living hope made possible by Jesus' work.

John did not write as a detached observer to these truths; rather he was one who trusted and followed after Jesus personally. The beloved disciple, John, knew firsthand the joy found in a loving relationship with God's Son. He longed to see others respond in faith and repentance to the good news that had transformed his life.

This good news is based on God's plans and promises throughout history. In John's Gospel, Jesus is described as the Word made flesh, the dwelling of God among men, the true light of the world. These images serve to connect readers with powerful ideas found throughout the Old Testament — ideas related to the coming of God's promised Savior. These images also remind readers of the all-encompassing scope of Jesus' mission.

The most prominent feature of John's Gospel is his repeated use of Jesus' "I am" statements, which communicate his identity to his hearers. Jesus is the bread of life (6:35,48), the light of the world (8:12), the door (10:7,9), the good shepherd (10:11,14), the resurrection and the life (11:25), the way, the truth, and the life (14:6), and the true vine (15:1). Jesus uses these images to communicate his offer of salvation, but more importantly to communicate that he is the same God who told

Moses "I AM" so long ago (Ex 3:14). Jesus boldly proclaims: "Before Abraham was, I am" (Jn 8:58). His eternal status as the God who was, who is, and who will always be is seen in the perfect fulfillment of his plans in the coming of Jesus. God perfectly executed his plan to send his Son, at just the right time, to secure the salvation of his people. Throughout all generations, those who look to him in faith will be saved because he is the only One powerful enough to save.

JESUS SAID TO HIM, "I AM THE WAY, AND THE TRUTH, AND THE LIFE. NO ONE COMES TO THE FATHER EXCEPT THROUGH ME."

John 14:6

JOHN

The Word Became Flesh

1 In the beginning was the Word, and the Word was with God, and the Word was God. 2 He was in the beginning with God. 3 All things were made through him, and without him was not any thing made that was made. 4 In him was life,[1] and the life was the light of men. 5 The light shines in the darkness, and the darkness has not overcome it.

6 There was a man sent from God, whose name was John. 7 He came as a witness, to bear witness about the light, that all might believe through him. 8 He was not the light, but came to bear witness about the light.

9 The true light, which gives light to everyone, was coming into the world. 10 He was in the world, and the world was made through him, yet the world did not know him. 11 He came to his own,[2] and his own people[3] did not receive him. 12 But to all who did receive him, who believed in his name, he gave the right to become children of God, 13 who were born, not of blood nor of the will of the flesh nor of the will of man, but of God.

14 And the Word became flesh and dwelt among us, and we have seen his glory, glory as of the only Son[4] from the Father, full of grace and truth. 15 (John bore witness about him, and cried out, "This was he of whom I said, 'He who comes after me ranks before me, because he was before me.'") 16 For from his fullness we have all received, grace upon grace.[5] 17 For the law was given through Moses; grace and truth came through Jesus Christ. 18 No one has ever seen God; God the only Son, who[6] is at the Father's side,[7] he has made him known.

The Testimony of John the Baptist

19 And this is the testimony of John, when the Jews sent priests and Levites from Jerusalem to ask him, "Who are you?" 20 He confessed, and did not deny, but confessed, "I am not the Christ." 21 And they asked him, "What then? Are you Elijah?" He said, "I am not." "Are you the Prophet?" And he answered, "No." 22 So they said to him, "Who are you? We need to give an answer to those who sent us. What do you say about yourself?" 23 He said, "I am the voice of one crying out in the wilderness, 'Make straight[8] the way of the Lord,' as the prophet Isaiah said."

24 (Now they had been sent from the Pharisees.) 25 They asked him, "Then why are you baptizing, if you are neither the Christ, nor Elijah, nor the Prophet?" 26 John answered them, "I baptize with water, but among you stands one you do not know, 27 even he who comes after me, the strap of whose sandal I am not worthy to untie." 28 These things took place in Bethany across the Jordan, where John was baptizing.

Behold, the Lamb of God

29 The next day he saw Jesus coming toward him, and said, "Behold, the Lamb of God, who takes away the sin of the world! 30 This is he of whom I said, 'After me comes a man who ranks before me, because he was before me.' 31 I myself did not know him, but for this purpose I came baptizing with water, that he might be revealed to Israel." 32 And John bore witness: "I saw the Spirit descend from heaven like a dove, and it remained on him. 33 I myself did not know him, but he who sent me to baptize with water said to me, 'He on whom you see the Spirit descend and remain, this is he who baptizes with the Holy Spirit.' 34 And I have seen and have borne witness that this is the Son[9] of God."

[1] Or *was not any thing made. That which has been made was life in him* [2] Greek *to his own things*; that is, to his own domain, or to his own people [3] *People* is implied in Greek [4] Or *only One*, or *unique One* [5] Or *grace in place of grace* [6] Or *seen God; the only God who*; some manuscripts *seen God; the only Son, who* (see verse 14) [7] Greek *in the bosom of the Father* [8] Or *crying out, 'In the wilderness make straight* [9] Some manuscripts *the Chosen One*

THE WORD OF GOD

From the very beginning of creation, God has been making himself known to people by his revealed word. In Genesis 1 we read the account of God speaking the world into existence, then speaking relationally to Adam (Ge 1:27 – 30). In Exodus 3, God spoke to Moses from a burning bush, calling him to be his agent to liberate Israel from slavery in Egypt. Throughout the Torah (the first five books of the Bible), God gave instructions to his chosen people so that they would know the glories of his righteousness and the wonders of his love.

God taught his people how to worship through the words of the psalmists, and he reminded them of their coming hope through the words of the prophets. But God gave his greatest revelation when Jesus, the Son and the very "Word" of God, came to earth. The author of Hebrews explains this well (Heb 1:1 – 3).

From the beginning, Jesus, the Word, was with God and was God (Jn 1:1). In this verse, John is making a very important Trinitarian statement: Jesus is not just *like* God; rather, Jesus actually *is* God. But Jesus is also *with* God, meaning that Jesus is separate from God. This mystery is explained through the Christian doctrine of the Trinity. This biblical doctrine explains that God exists in three persons, being of one substance, power, and eternity. This doctrine is clear in Scripture, and without it, the message of the gospel falls apart. For example, in delivering the Great Commission, Jesus commands his church to baptize his disciples "in the name of the Father and of the Son and of the Holy Spirit" (Mt 28:19), the three members of the Trinity. This doctrine has been affirmed throughout church history.

Jesus is the eternal "Word of the Father." Therefore we understand his powerful role in creation, for "all things were made through him" (Jn 1:3). But the great mystery of the gospel is that Jesus came to live with us; he left his position as Creator and ruler of the universe to become human and endure all of the miseries of this life. He came to earth to completely identify with us in order that we might in turn identify with him and receive him as our Savior and Lord. And to those who receive him, he gives the amazing promise that they will be the very children of God (v. 12), not simply permitted into the presence of God as servants or guests. Rather, they are eternally welcomed into the house of God as his own sons and daughters, heirs of all of God's promised blessings (Gal 4:4 – 7).

Jesus Calls the First Disciples

35The next day again John was standing with two of his disciples, 36and he looked at Jesus as he walked by and said, "Behold, the Lamb of God!" 37The two disciples heard him say this, and they followed Jesus. 38Jesus turned and saw them following and said to them, "What are you seeking?" And they said to him, "Rabbi" (which means Teacher), "where are you staying?" 39He said to them, "Come and you will see." So they came and saw where he was staying, and they stayed with him that day, for it was about the tenth hour.[1] 40One of the two who heard John speak and followed Jesus[2] was Andrew, Simon Peter's brother. 41He first found his own brother Simon and said to him, "We have found the Messiah" (which means Christ). 42He brought him to Jesus. Jesus looked at him and said, "You are Simon the son of John. You shall be called Cephas" (which means Peter[3]).

Jesus Calls Philip and Nathanael

43The next day Jesus decided to go to Galilee. He found Philip and said to him, "Follow me." 44Now Philip was from Bethsaida, the city of Andrew and Peter. 45Philip found Nathanael and said to him, "We have found him of whom Moses in the Law and also the prophets wrote, Jesus of Nazareth, the son of Joseph." 46Nathanael said to him, "Can anything good come out of Nazareth?" Philip said to him, "Come and see." 47Jesus saw Nathanael coming toward him and said of him, "Behold, an Israelite indeed, in whom there is no deceit!" 48Nathanael said to him, "How do you know me?" Jesus answered him, "Before Philip called you, when you were under the fig tree, I saw you." 49Nathanael answered him, "Rabbi, you are the Son of God! You are the King of Israel!" 50Jesus answered him, "Because I said to you, 'I saw you under the fig tree,' do you believe? You will see greater things than these." 51And he said to him, "Truly, truly, I say to you,[4] you will see heaven opened, and the angels of God ascending and descending on the Son of Man."

The Wedding at Cana

2 On the third day there was a wedding at Cana in Galilee, and the mother of Jesus was there. 2Jesus also was invited to the wedding with his disciples. 3When the wine ran out, the mother of Jesus said to him, "They have no wine." 4And Jesus said to her, "Woman, what does this have to do with me? My hour has not yet come." 5His mother said to the servants, "Do whatever he tells you."

6Now there were six stone water jars there for the Jewish rites of purification, each holding twenty or thirty gallons.[5] 7Jesus said to the servants, "Fill the jars with water." And they filled them up to the brim. 8And he said to them, "Now draw some out and take it to the master of the feast." So they took it. 9When the master of the feast tasted the water now become wine, and did not know where it came from (though the servants who had drawn the water knew), the master of the feast called the bridegroom 10and said to him, "Everyone serves the good wine first, and when people have drunk freely, then the poor wine. But you have kept the good wine until now." 11This, the first of his signs, Jesus did at Cana in Galilee, and manifested his glory. And his disciples believed in him.

12After this he went down to Capernaum, with his mother and his brothers[6] and his disciples, and they stayed there for a few days.

Jesus Cleanses the Temple

13The Passover of the Jews was at hand, and Jesus went up to Jerusalem. 14In the temple he found those who were selling oxen and sheep and pigeons, and the money-changers sitting there. 15And making a whip of cords, he drove them all out

[1]That is, about 4 P.M. [2]Greek *him* [3]*Cephas* and *Peter* are from the word for *rock* in Aramaic and Greek, respectively [4]The Greek for *you* is plural; twice in this verse [5]Greek *two or three measures* (*metrētas*); a *metrētēs* was about 10 gallons or 35 liters [6]Or *brothers and sisters*. In New Testament usage, depending on the context, the plural Greek word *adelphoi* (translated "brothers") may refer either to *brothers* or to *brothers and sisters*

JOHN 2:1–12

THE HOUR OF CHRIST

At first glance, Jesus' response to his mother at the wedding in Cana can be confusing or even troubling: "Woman, what does this have to do with me? My hour has not yet come." But then he proceeds to perform his first miracle, producing somewhere between 120 and 180 gallons of wine.

When considering Jesus' evident change of heart, it is important to remember the setting of this miracle: a wedding. Whenever people attend a wedding, they inevitably entertain thoughts about their own wedding. This is true for married people, but many single people as well long for their wedding day, when it will be their "hour"—when they will be the bride or groom, finally joined to the one they love.

So in this moment, as Jesus looked on at the bride and groom in Cana, perhaps he too was longing for his "hour," when he would be joined with his bride, his church. Perhaps he looked forward to the wedding banquet that is to come, when men and women from every tribe and language will be joined with him at the marriage supper of the Lamb in the new heavens and new earth (Rev 19:6–9). How utterly appropriate that Jesus' first sign pointed toward the ultimate celebration and the ultimate wedding: his own with his church.

of the temple, with the sheep and oxen. And he poured out the coins of the money-changers and overturned their tables. 16And he told those who sold the pigeons, "Take these things away; do not make my Father's house a house of trade." 17His disciples remembered that it was written, "Zeal for your house will consume me."

18So the Jews said to him, "What sign do you show us for doing these things?" 19Jesus answered them, "Destroy this temple, and in three days I will raise it up." 20The Jews then said, "It has taken forty-six years to build this temple,[1] and will you raise it up in three days?" 21But he was speaking about the temple of his body. 22When therefore he was raised from the dead, his disciples remembered that he had said this, and they believed the Scripture and the word that Jesus had spoken.

Jesus Knows What Is in Man

23Now when he was in Jerusalem at the Passover Feast, many believed in his name when they saw the signs that he was doing. 24But Jesus on his part did not entrust himself to them, because he knew all people 25and needed no one to bear witness about man, for he himself knew what was in man.

You Must Be Born Again

3 Now there was a man of the Pharisees named Nicodemus, a ruler of the Jews. 2This man came to Jesus[2] by night and said to him, "Rabbi, we know that you are a teacher come from God, for no one can do these signs that you do unless God is with him." 3Jesus answered him, "Truly, truly, I say to you, unless one is born again[3] he cannot see the kingdom of God." 4Nicodemus said to him, "How can a man be born when he is old? Can he enter a second time into his mother's womb and be born?" 5Jesus answered, "Truly, truly, I say to you, unless one is born of water and the Spirit, he cannot enter the kingdom of God. 6That which is born of the flesh is flesh, and that which is born of the Spirit is spirit.[4] 7Do not marvel that I said to you, 'You[5] must be born again.' 8The wind[6] blows where it wishes, and you hear its sound, but you do not know where it comes from or where it goes. So it is with everyone who is born of the Spirit."

9Nicodemus said to him, "How can these things be?" 10Jesus answered him, "Are you the teacher of Israel and yet you do not understand these things? 11Truly, truly, I say to you, we speak of what we know, and bear witness to what we have seen, but you[7] do not receive our testimony. 12If I have told you earthly things and you do not believe, how can you believe if I tell you heavenly things? 13No one has ascended into heaven except he who descended from heaven, the Son of Man.[8] 14And as Moses lifted up the serpent in the wilderness, so must the Son of Man be lifted up, 15that whoever believes in him may have eternal life.[9]

For God So Loved the World

16"For God so loved the world,[10] that he gave his only Son, that whoever believes in him should not perish but have eternal life. 17For God did not send his Son into the world to condemn the world, but in order that the world might be saved through him. 18Whoever believes in him is not condemned, but whoever does not believe is condemned already, because he has not believed in the name of the only Son of God. 19And this is the judgment: the light has come into the world, and people loved the darkness rather than the light because their works were evil. 20For everyone who does wicked things hates the light and does not come to the light, lest his works should be exposed. 21But whoever does what is true comes to the light, so that it may be clearly seen that his works have been carried out in God."

---

[1] Or *This temple was built forty-six years ago* [2] Greek *him* [3] Or *from above*; the Greek is purposely ambiguous and can mean both *again* and *from above*; also verse 7 [4] The same Greek word means both *wind* and *spirit* [5] The Greek for *you* is plural here [6] The same Greek word means both *wind* and *spirit* [7] The Greek for *you* is plural here; also four times in verse 12 [8] Some manuscripts add *who is in heaven* [9] Some interpreters hold that the quotation ends at verse 15 [10] Or *For this is how God loved the world*

JOHN 3:1–21

THE NEW BIRTH

Throughout his ministry, Jesus taught about God's kingdom. He preached about the kingdom to crowds, to small groups, and to individuals like Nicodemus. Nicodemus was a teacher of the Hebrew Scriptures and must have been taken aback when Jesus said, "Unless one is born again he cannot see the kingdom of God" (v. 3).

Nicodemus, like most teachers of the Hebrew law, would have expected the Jewish Messiah to come and establish his kingdom in a very forceful and very visible way. As Alexander the Great and Julius Caesar had come and ushered in their kingdoms by force, the Jewish people expected a messiah to come with authoritative power to reestablish the Jewish kingdom. But when Jesus, the true Messiah, came, he did not rule with an iron fist or crush his enemies; rather, he came in humility to serve and to lay down his life for other people (Mk 10:45). In his first coming, Jesus did establish his authority over men and women — not externally, but internally in their hearts (Mt 9:8; Mk 1:27; Lk 4:36).

That authority is absolute. So the allegiance of a Christian is not ultimately with Caesar, or with Rome, or with any king or country (Mk 12:17); the allegiance of a Christian is rather with Jesus, and a believer's citizenship is in his eternal kingdom (Php 3:20). Therefore, followers of Christ are born again — not as citizens of any earthly country, but as Christians born with Christ and born into his kingdom.

How does this new birth occur? How does Jesus establish his authority in our hearts? Again, unlike the kingdoms of this world, Jesus does not establish his present rule with an army or by force; rather, he establishes his rule with love. His kingdom is not of this world (Jn 18:36). "For God so loved the world, that he gave his only Son, that whoever believes in him should not perish but have eternal life. For God did not send his Son into the world to condemn the world, but in order that the world might be saved through him" (3:16 – 17). When, with the help of the Holy Spirit, individuals see their own sin and need for a Savior, and when they see Jesus for all that he is and realize how deep his sacrifice was and how deep his love is, then the believer is "captured" by the love and beauty of Christ. When his followers see how deeply God has loved his people in Christ, then they are inspired, by their own desire for him, to surrender to his lordship. Such an experience is salvation, the new birth.

John the Baptist Exalts Christ

[22]After this Jesus and his disciples went into the Judean countryside, and he
remained there with them and was baptizing. [23]John also was baptizing at Aenon
near Salim, because water was plentiful there, and people were coming and being
baptized [24](for John had not yet been put in prison).

[25]Now a discussion arose between some of John's disciples and a Jew over purification. [26]And they came to John and said to him, "Rabbi, he who was with you
across the Jordan, to whom you bore witness—look, he is baptizing, and all are
going to him." [27]John answered, "A person cannot receive even one thing unless it
is given him from heaven. [28]You yourselves bear me witness, that I said, 'I am not
the Christ, but I have been sent before him.' [29]The one who has the bride is the
bridegroom. The friend of the bridegroom, who stands and hears him, rejoices
greatly at the bridegroom's voice. Therefore this joy of mine is now complete. [30]He
must increase, but I must decrease."[1]

[31]He who comes from above is above all. He who is of the earth belongs to the
earth and speaks in an earthly way. He who comes from heaven is above all. [32]He
bears witness to what he has seen and heard, yet no one receives his testimony.
[33]Whoever receives his testimony sets his seal to this, that God is true. [34]For he
whom God has sent utters the words of God, for he gives the Spirit without measure. [35]The Father loves the Son and has given all things into his hand. [36]Whoever
believes in the Son has eternal life; whoever does not obey the Son shall not see
life, but the wrath of God remains on him.

Jesus and the Woman of Samaria

4 Now when Jesus learned that the Pharisees had heard that Jesus was making and baptizing more disciples than John [2](although Jesus himself did not
baptize, but only his disciples), [3]he left Judea and departed again for Galilee. [4]And
he had to pass through Samaria. [5]So he came to a town of Samaria called Sychar,
near the field that Jacob had given to his son Joseph. [6]Jacob's well was there; so
Jesus, wearied as he was from his journey, was sitting beside the well. It was about
the sixth hour.[2]

[7]A woman from Samaria came to draw water. Jesus said to her, "Give me a
drink." [8](For his disciples had gone away into the city to buy food.) [9]The Samaritan
woman said to him, "How is it that you, a Jew, ask for a drink from me, a woman of
Samaria?" (For Jews have no dealings with Samaritans.) [10]Jesus answered her, "If
you knew the gift of God, and who it is that is saying to you, 'Give me a drink,' you
would have asked him, and he would have given you living water." [11]The woman
said to him, "Sir, you have nothing to draw water with, and the well is deep. Where
do you get that living water? [12]Are you greater than our father Jacob? He gave us
the well and drank from it himself, as did his sons and his livestock." [13]Jesus said
to her, "Everyone who drinks of this water will be thirsty again, [14]but whoever
drinks of the water that I will give him will never be thirsty again.[3] The water that I
will give him will become in him a spring of water welling up to eternal life." [15]The
woman said to him, "Sir, give me this water, so that I will not be thirsty or have to
come here to draw water."

[16]Jesus said to her, "Go, call your husband, and come here." [17]The woman answered him, "I have no husband." Jesus said to her, "You are right in saying, 'I have
no husband'; [18]for you have had five husbands, and the one you now have is not
your husband. What you have said is true." [19]The woman said to him, "Sir, I perceive that you are a prophet. [20]Our fathers worshiped on this mountain, but you
say that in Jerusalem is the place where people ought to worship." [21]Jesus said to
her, "Woman, believe me, the hour is coming when neither on this mountain nor
in Jerusalem will you worship the Father. [22]You worship what you do not know;

[1]Some interpreters hold that the quotation continues through verse 36 [2]That is, about noon
[3]Greek *forever*

JOHN 4:1–26

THE FIRST REVELATION

Throughout his ministry, Jesus revealed himself to the most unlikely people in the most unlikely places; his encounter with the Samaritan woman is no exception. Centuries of bitterness and disagreement divided the Jewish people and the Samaritans. Though they lived near one another and had a common heritage, the Samaritans were of mixed race—Hebrew people whose ancestors had intermarried with the Assyrians, a pagan enemy nation. They had developed a different culture and a different place of worship, at Mount Gerizim (4:20). No respectable Jewish man would have lowered himself to interact with a Samaritan, much less a Samaritan *woman*, as Jewish culture dictated strict social division between men and women who were not married or close relatives.

But there's even more to Jesus' surprising choice: this woman was an outcast even among her own people. She had been married five times and was living with a man who was not her husband; in a very conservative and traditional culture, Jesus' conversation with her is doubly puzzling. Still, Jesus, a Jewish rabbi, engages in conversation with this woman. He speaks to her with love and offers her salvation (v. 14). More than that, she is the first person to whom Jesus reveals his identity as the Messiah (vv. 25–26). By revealing his identity first to this woman, Jesus emphasized his interest in outcasts. Jesus seeks out those who are broken and poor in spirit (Mt 5:3), and he offers himself as living water to all who thirst for him.

JOHN 5:1–15

SALVATION THROUGH JESUS

Before and while Jesus walked the earth, the people of Israel had been given to systems and superstitions in trying to know and experience God. The meticulous laws of the Sabbath, as shown in this story, were a prime example of such a Hebrew system; the pool of Bethesda is a prime example of a Hebrew superstition.

Evidently the pool would stir or bubble periodically, and allegedly this bubbling brought healing to the first person to jump in the pool after it began. Jesus came across a man who, in 38 years, had not been able to get into the pool first. Coincidentally, 38 years is the same amount of time that the people of Israel wandered in the wilderness from Kadesh Barnea to the Zered Valley (Dt 2:14); and he, the man who at 38 years was an invalid, was just as depressed and helpless as they were. But Jesus looked beyond the man's excuses and superstition. He looked beyond this man's depression and his poor theology. Jesus looked beyond all this, and he showed him grace and brought him healing.

Such is the salvation of Jesus; it cannot be earned by obedience to a system, good theological knowledge, a good attitude, or familial connections. Salvation is a gift of God; it is only by his grace that we are saved (Eph 2:8–9). It is appropriate that Jesus asked this man if he *wanted* to be healed; it's the same question he asks of those who would believe in him today.

we worship what we know, for salvation is from the Jews. 23But the hour is coming, and is now here, when the true worshipers will worship the Father in spirit and truth, for the Father is seeking such people to worship him. 24God is spirit, and those who worship him must worship in spirit and truth." 25The woman said to him, "I know that Messiah is coming (he who is called Christ). When he comes, he will tell us all things." 26Jesus said to her, "I who speak to you am he."

27Just then his disciples came back. They marveled that he was talking with a woman, but no one said, "What do you seek?" or, "Why are you talking with her?" 28So the woman left her water jar and went away into town and said to the people, 29"Come, see a man who told me all that I ever did. Can this be the Christ?" 30They went out of the town and were coming to him.

31Meanwhile the disciples were urging him, saying, "Rabbi, eat." 32But he said to them, "I have food to eat that you do not know about." 33So the disciples said to one another, "Has anyone brought him something to eat?" 34Jesus said to them, "My food is to do the will of him who sent me and to accomplish his work. 35Do you not say, 'There are yet four months, then comes the harvest'? Look, I tell you, lift up your eyes, and see that the fields are white for harvest. 36Already the one who reaps is receiving wages and gathering fruit for eternal life, so that sower and reaper may rejoice together. 37For here the saying holds true, 'One sows and another reaps.' 38I sent you to reap that for which you did not labor. Others have labored, and you have entered into their labor."

39Many Samaritans from that town believed in him because of the woman's testimony, "He told me all that I ever did." 40So when the Samaritans came to him, they asked him to stay with them, and he stayed there two days. 41And many more believed because of his word. 42They said to the woman, "It is no longer because of what you said that we believe, for we have heard for ourselves, and we know that this is indeed the Savior of the world."

43After the two days he departed for Galilee. 44(For Jesus himself had testified that a prophet has no honor in his own hometown.) 45So when he came to Galilee, the Galileans welcomed him, having seen all that he had done in Jerusalem at the feast. For they too had gone to the feast.

Jesus Heals an Official's Son

46So he came again to Cana in Galilee, where he had made the water wine. And at Capernaum there was an official whose son was ill. 47When this man heard that Jesus had come from Judea to Galilee, he went to him and asked him to come down and heal his son, for he was at the point of death. 48So Jesus said to him, "Unless you[1] see signs and wonders you will not believe." 49The official said to him, "Sir, come down before my child dies." 50Jesus said to him, "Go; your son will live." The man believed the word that Jesus spoke to him and went on his way. 51As he was going down, his servants[2] met him and told him that his son was recovering. 52So he asked them the hour when he began to get better, and they said to him, "Yesterday at the seventh hour[3] the fever left him." 53The father knew that was the hour when Jesus had said to him, "Your son will live." And he himself believed, and all his household. 54This was now the second sign that Jesus did when he had come from Judea to Galilee.

The Healing at the Pool on the Sabbath

5 After this there was a feast of the Jews, and Jesus went up to Jerusalem. 2Now there is in Jerusalem by the Sheep Gate a pool, in Aramaic[4] called Bethesda,[5] which has five roofed colonnades. 3In these lay a multitude of invalids—blind, lame, and paralyzed.[6] 5One man was there who had been an in-

[1]The Greek for *you* is plural; twice in this verse [2]Or *bondservants* [3]That is, at 1 P.M. [4]Or *Hebrew*
[5]Some manuscripts *Bethsaida* [6]Some manuscripts insert, wholly or in part, *waiting for the moving of the water; 4for an angel of the Lord went down at certain seasons into the pool, and stirred the water: whoever stepped in first after the stirring of the water was healed of whatever disease he had*

valid for thirty-eight years. 6When Jesus saw him lying there and knew that he had already been there a long time, he said to him, "Do you want to be healed?" 7The sick man answered him, "Sir, I have no one to put me into the pool when the water is stirred up, and while I am going another steps down before me." 8Jesus said to him, "Get up, take up your bed, and walk." 9And at once the man was healed, and he took up his bed and walked.

Now that day was the Sabbath. 10So the Jews[1] said to the man who had been healed, "It is the Sabbath, and it is not lawful for you to take up your bed." 11But he answered them, "The man who healed me, that man said to me, 'Take up your bed, and walk.'" 12They asked him, "Who is the man who said to you, 'Take up your bed and walk'?" 13Now the man who had been healed did not know who it was, for Jesus had withdrawn, as there was a crowd in the place. 14Afterward Jesus found him in the temple and said to him, "See, you are well! Sin no more, that nothing worse may happen to you." 15The man went away and told the Jews that it was Jesus who had healed him. 16And this was why the Jews were persecuting Jesus, because he was doing these things on the Sabbath. 17But Jesus answered them, "My Father is working until now, and I am working."

Jesus Is Equal with God

18This was why the Jews were seeking all the more to kill him, because not only was he breaking the Sabbath, but he was even calling God his own Father, making himself equal with God.

The Authority of the Son

19So Jesus said to them, "Truly, truly, I say to you, the Son can do nothing of his own accord, but only what he sees the Father doing. For whatever the Father[2] does, that the Son does likewise. 20For the Father loves the Son and shows him all that he himself is doing. And greater works than these will he show him, so that you may marvel. 21For as the Father raises the dead and gives them life, so also the Son gives life to whom he will. 22For the Father judges no one, but has given all judgment to the Son, 23that all may honor the Son, just as they honor the Father. Whoever does not honor the Son does not honor the Father who sent him. 24Truly, truly, I say to you, whoever hears my word and believes him who sent me has eternal life. He does not come into judgment, but has passed from death to life.

25"Truly, truly, I say to you, an hour is coming, and is now here, when the dead will hear the voice of the Son of God, and those who hear will live. 26For as the Father has life in himself, so he has granted the Son also to have life in himself. 27And he has given him authority to execute judgment, because he is the Son of Man. 28Do not marvel at this, for an hour is coming when all who are in the tombs will hear his voice 29and come out, those who have done good to the resurrection of life, and those who have done evil to the resurrection of judgment.

Witnesses to Jesus

30"I can do nothing on my own. As I hear, I judge, and my judgment is just, because I seek not my own will but the will of him who sent me. 31If I alone bear witness about myself, my testimony is not true. 32There is another who bears witness about me, and I know that the testimony that he bears about me is true. 33You sent to John, and he has borne witness to the truth. 34Not that the testimony that I receive is from man, but I say these things so that you may be saved. 35He was a burning and shining lamp, and you were willing to rejoice for a while in his light. 36But the testimony that I have is greater than that of John. For the works that the Father has given me to accomplish, the very works that I am doing, bear witness about me that the Father has sent me. 37And the Father who sent me has himself borne witness about me. His voice you have never heard, his form you have never

[1]The Greek word *Ioudaioi* refers specifically here to Jewish religious leaders, and others under their influence, who opposed Jesus in that time; also verses 15, 16, 18 [2]Greek *he*

seen, 38and you do not have his word abiding in you, for you do not believe the
one whom he has sent. 39You search the Scriptures because you think that in them
you have eternal life; and it is they that bear witness about me, 40yet you refuse
to come to me that you may have life. 41I do not receive glory from people. 42But
I know that you do not have the love of God within you. 43I have come in my Father's name, and you do not receive me. If another comes in his own name, you
will receive him. 44How can you believe, when you receive glory from one another
and do not seek the glory that comes from the only God? 45Do not think that I
will accuse you to the Father. There is one who accuses you: Moses, on whom
you have set your hope. 46For if you believed Moses, you would believe me; for
he wrote of me. 47But if you do not believe his writings, how will you believe my
words?"

Jesus Feeds the Five Thousand

6 After this Jesus went away to the other side of the Sea of Galilee, which is the
Sea of Tiberias. 2And a large crowd was following him, because they saw the
signs that he was doing on the sick. 3Jesus went up on the mountain, and there he
sat down with his disciples. 4Now the Passover, the feast of the Jews, was at hand.
5Lifting up his eyes, then, and seeing that a large crowd was coming toward him,
Jesus said to Philip, "Where are we to buy bread, so that these people may eat?"
6He said this to test him, for he himself knew what he would do. 7Philip answered
him, "Two hundred denarii[1] worth of bread would not be enough for each of them
to get a little." 8One of his disciples, Andrew, Simon Peter's brother, said to him,
9"There is a boy here who has five barley loaves and two fish, but what are they
for so many?" 10Jesus said, "Have the people sit down." Now there was much grass
in the place. So the men sat down, about five thousand in number. 11Jesus then
took the loaves, and when he had given thanks, he distributed them to those who
were seated. So also the fish, as much as they wanted. 12And when they had eaten
their fill, he told his disciples, "Gather up the leftover fragments, that nothing
may be lost." 13So they gathered them up and filled twelve baskets with fragments
from the five barley loaves left by those who had eaten. 14When the people saw
the sign that he had done, they said, "This is indeed the Prophet who is to come
into the world!"

15Perceiving then that they were about to come and take him by force to make
him king, Jesus withdrew again to the mountain by himself.

Jesus Walks on Water

16When evening came, his disciples went down to the sea, 17got into a boat, and
started across the sea to Capernaum. It was now dark, and Jesus had not yet come
to them. 18The sea became rough because a strong wind was blowing. 19When
they had rowed about three or four miles,[2] they saw Jesus walking on the sea and
coming near the boat, and they were frightened. 20But he said to them, "It is I; do
not be afraid." 21Then they were glad to take him into the boat, and immediately
the boat was at the land to which they were going.

I Am the Bread of Life

22On the next day the crowd that remained on the other side of the sea saw
that there had been only one boat there, and that Jesus had not entered the boat
with his disciples, but that his disciples had gone away alone. 23Other boats from
Tiberias came near the place where they had eaten the bread after the Lord had
given thanks. 24So when the crowd saw that Jesus was not there, nor his disciples,
they themselves got into the boats and went to Capernaum, seeking Jesus.

25When they found him on the other side of the sea, they said to him, "Rabbi,
when did you come here?" 26Jesus answered them, "Truly, truly, I say to you, you

[1] A *denarius* was a day's wage for a laborer [2] Greek *twenty-five or thirty stadia*; a *stadion* was about 607 feet or 185 meters

JOHN 6:1–15

KING FOR A DAY

On this enormously notable day in the life of Jesus, the people tried to make him king. Yet, rather than accepting their praise and love, he escaped the crowd in order to go experience the praise and love of his Father. After Jesus miraculously multiplied the fish and loaves, many people believed that he was the promised Messiah and wanted him to establish his earthly rule. Jesus had his sights set on a different throne and a different kingdom.

God the Father had sent Jesus to earth not to be exalted but to be humbled. Throughout Jesus' ministry, even when he was standing atop a hill in Galilee, he had his sights set on another hill—one just outside of Jerusalem, where he would give his life as a ransom payment for many (Mk 10:45). In this instance, as always, Jesus did not consider his power and eternal equality with God something to be used for his own advantage. He could have taken the glory for this miracle, but he refused. Instead, he took "the form of a servant" and "humbled himself by becoming obedient to the point of death, even death on a cross" (Php 2:6–9). Because of his complete obedience, God the Father raised him from the dead and exalted him to the highest place in heaven, giving him the name that is above every name.

Jesus understood that earthly accolades are empty and fickle. He remained obedient to God's plan. The throne where Jesus now sits is infinitely higher than any earthly throne.

are seeking me, not because you saw signs, but because you ate your fill of the
loaves. 27 Do not work for the food that perishes, but for the food that endures to
eternal life, which the Son of Man will give to you. For on him God the Father has
set his seal." 28 Then they said to him, "What must we do, to be doing the works of
God?" 29 Jesus answered them, "This is the work of God, that you believe in him
whom he has sent." 30 So they said to him, "Then what sign do you do, that we may
see and believe you? What work do you perform? 31 Our fathers ate the manna in
the wilderness; as it is written, 'He gave them bread from heaven to eat.'" 32 Jesus
then said to them, "Truly, truly, I say to you, it was not Moses who gave you the
bread from heaven, but my Father gives you the true bread from heaven. 33 For
the bread of God is he who comes down from heaven and gives life to the world."
34 They said to him, "Sir, give us this bread always."

35 Jesus said to them, "I am the bread of life; whoever comes to me shall not
hunger, and whoever believes in me shall never thirst. 36 But I said to you that you
have seen me and yet do not believe. 37 All that the Father gives me will come to
me, and whoever comes to me I will never cast out. 38 For I have come down from
heaven, not to do my own will but the will of him who sent me. 39 And this is the
will of him who sent me, that I should lose nothing of all that he has given me,
but raise it up on the last day. 40 For this is the will of my Father, that everyone who
looks on the Son and believes in him should have eternal life, and I will raise him
up on the last day."

41 So the Jews grumbled about him, because he said, "I am the bread that came
down from heaven." 42 They said, "Is not this Jesus, the son of Joseph, whose
father and mother we know? How does he now say, 'I have come down from
heaven'?" 43 Jesus answered them, "Do not grumble among yourselves. 44 No one
can come to me unless the Father who sent me draws him. And I will raise him
up on the last day. 45 It is written in the Prophets, 'And they will all be taught
by God.' Everyone who has heard and learned from the Father comes to me—
46 not that anyone has seen the Father except he who is from God; he has seen
the Father. 47 Truly, truly, I say to you, whoever believes has eternal life. 48 I am
the bread of life. 49 Your fathers ate the manna in the wilderness, and they died.
50 This is the bread that comes down from heaven, so that one may eat of it and
not die. 51 I am the living bread that came down from heaven. If anyone eats of
this bread, he will live forever. And the bread that I will give for the life of the
world is my flesh."

52 The Jews then disputed among themselves, saying, "How can this man give
us his flesh to eat?" 53 So Jesus said to them, "Truly, truly, I say to you, unless
you eat the flesh of the Son of Man and drink his blood, you have no life in you.
54 Whoever feeds on my flesh and drinks my blood has eternal life, and I will
raise him up on the last day. 55 For my flesh is true food, and my blood is true
drink. 56 Whoever feeds on my flesh and drinks my blood abides in me, and I in
him. 57 As the living Father sent me, and I live because of the Father, so whoever
feeds on me, he also will live because of me. 58 This is the bread that came down
from heaven, not like the bread[1] the fathers ate, and died. Whoever feeds on this
bread will live forever." 59 Jesus[2] said these things in the synagogue, as he taught
at Capernaum.

The Words of Eternal Life

60 When many of his disciples heard it, they said, "This is a hard saying; who
can listen to it?" 61 But Jesus, knowing in himself that his disciples were grumbling
about this, said to them, "Do you take offense at this? 62 Then what if you were to
see the Son of Man ascending to where he was before? 63 It is the Spirit who gives
life; the flesh is no help at all. The words that I have spoken to you are spirit and
life. 64 But there are some of you who do not believe." (For Jesus knew from the

[1] Greek lacks *the bread* [2] Greek *He*

beginning who those were who did not believe, and who it was who would betray
him.) 65And he said, "This is why I told you that no one can come to me unless it
is granted him by the Father."
66After this many of his disciples turned back and no longer walked with him.
67So Jesus said to the twelve, "Do you want to go away as well?" 68Simon Peter answered him, "Lord, to whom shall we go? You have the words of eternal life, 69and
we have believed, and have come to know, that you are the Holy One of God."
70Jesus answered them, "Did I not choose you, the twelve? And yet one of you is
a devil." 71He spoke of Judas the son of Simon Iscariot, for he, one of the twelve,
was going to betray him.

Jesus at the Feast of Booths

7 After this Jesus went about in Galilee. He would not go about in Judea, because
the Jews[1] were seeking to kill him. 2Now the Jews' Feast of Booths was at hand.
3So his brothers[2] said to him, "Leave here and go to Judea, that your disciples also
may see the works you are doing. 4For no one works in secret if he seeks to be
known openly. If you do these things, show yourself to the world." 5For not even
his brothers believed in him. 6Jesus said to them, "My time has not yet come, but
your time is always here. 7The world cannot hate you, but it hates me because I
testify about it that its works are evil. 8You go up to the feast. I am not[3] going up
to this feast, for my time has not yet fully come." 9After saying this, he remained
in Galilee.
10But after his brothers had gone up to the feast, then he also went up, not
publicly but in private. 11The Jews were looking for him at the feast, and saying,
"Where is he?" 12And there was much muttering about him among the people.
While some said, "He is a good man," others said, "No, he is leading the people
astray." 13Yet for fear of the Jews no one spoke openly of him.
14About the middle of the feast Jesus went up into the temple and began teaching. 15The Jews therefore marveled, saying, "How is it that this man has learning,[4]
when he has never studied?" 16So Jesus answered them, "My teaching is not mine,
but his who sent me. 17If anyone's will is to do God's[5] will, he will know whether
the teaching is from God or whether I am speaking on my own authority. 18The
one who speaks on his own authority seeks his own glory; but the one who seeks
the glory of him who sent him is true, and in him there is no falsehood. 19Has not
Moses given you the law? Yet none of you keeps the law. Why do you seek to kill
me?" 20The crowd answered, "You have a demon! Who is seeking to kill you?"
21Jesus answered them, "I did one work, and you all marvel at it. 22Moses gave you
circumcision (not that it is from Moses, but from the fathers), and you circumcise
a man on the Sabbath. 23If on the Sabbath a man receives circumcision, so that
the law of Moses may not be broken, are you angry with me because on the Sabbath I made a man's whole body well? 24Do not judge by appearances, but judge
with right judgment."

Can This Be the Christ?

25Some of the people of Jerusalem therefore said, "Is not this the man whom
they seek to kill? 26And here he is, speaking openly, and they say nothing to him!
Can it be that the authorities really know that this is the Christ? 27But we know
where this man comes from, and when the Christ appears, no one will know
where he comes from." 28So Jesus proclaimed, as he taught in the temple, "You
know me, and you know where I come from. But I have not come of my own
accord. He who sent me is true, and him you do not know. 29I know him, for I
come from him, and he sent me." 30So they were seeking to arrest him, but no one
laid a hand on him, because his hour had not yet come. 31Yet many of the people

[1]Or *Judeans*; Greek *Ioudaioi* probably refers here to Jewish religious leaders, and others under their influence, in that time [2]Or *brothers and sisters*; also verses 5, 10 [3]Some manuscripts add *yet* [4]Or *this man knows his letters* [5]Greek *his*

believed in him. They said, "When the Christ appears, will he do more signs than
this man has done?"

Officers Sent to Arrest Jesus

32The Pharisees heard the crowd muttering these things about him, and the
chief priests and Pharisees sent officers to arrest him. 33Jesus then said, "I will be
with you a little longer, and then I am going to him who sent me. 34You will seek
me and you will not find me. Where I am you cannot come." 35The Jews said to
one another, "Where does this man intend to go that we will not find him? Does
he intend to go to the Dispersion among the Greeks and teach the Greeks? 36What
does he mean by saying, 'You will seek me and you will not find me,' and, 'Where
I am you cannot come'?"

Rivers of Living Water

37On the last day of the feast, the great day, Jesus stood up and cried out, "If
anyone thirsts, let him come to me and drink. 38Whoever believes in me, as[1] the
Scripture has said, 'Out of his heart will flow rivers of living water.'" 39Now this he
said about the Spirit, whom those who believed in him were to receive, for as yet
the Spirit had not been given, because Jesus was not yet glorified.

Division Among the People

40When they heard these words, some of the people said, "This really is the
Prophet." 41Others said, "This is the Christ." But some said, "Is the Christ to come
from Galilee? 42Has not the Scripture said that the Christ comes from the offspring of David, and comes from Bethlehem, the village where David was?" 43So
there was a division among the people over him. 44Some of them wanted to arrest
him, but no one laid hands on him.

45The officers then came to the chief priests and Pharisees, who said to them,
"Why did you not bring him?" 46The officers answered, "No one ever spoke like
this man!" 47The Pharisees answered them, "Have you also been deceived? 48Have
any of the authorities or the Pharisees believed in him? 49But this crowd that does
not know the law is accursed." 50Nicodemus, who had gone to him before, and
who was one of them, said to them, 51"Does our law judge a man without first
giving him a hearing and learning what he does?" 52They replied, "Are you from
Galilee too? Search and see that no prophet arises from Galilee."

[THE EARLIEST MANUSCRIPTS DO NOT INCLUDE 7:53–8:11.][2]

The Woman Caught in Adultery

8 [[53They went each to his own house, 1but Jesus went to the Mount of Olives.
2Early in the morning he came again to the temple. All the people came to
him, and he sat down and taught them. 3The scribes and the Pharisees brought a
woman who had been caught in adultery, and placing her in the midst 4they said
to him, "Teacher, this woman has been caught in the act of adultery. 5Now in the
Law, Moses commanded us to stone such women. So what do you say?" 6This they
said to test him, that they might have some charge to bring against him. Jesus bent
down and wrote with his finger on the ground. 7And as they continued to ask him,
he stood up and said to them, "Let him who is without sin among you be the first
to throw a stone at her." 8And once more he bent down and wrote on the ground.
9But when they heard it, they went away one by one, beginning with the older
ones, and Jesus was left alone with the woman standing before him. 10Jesus stood
up and said to her, "Woman, where are they? Has no one condemned you?" 11She
said, "No one, Lord." And Jesus said, "Neither do I condemn you; go, and from
now on sin no more."]]

[1]Or *let him come to me, and let him who believes in me drink. As* [2]Some manuscripts do not include 7:53–8:11; others add the passage here or after 7:36 or after 21:25 or after Luke 21:38, with variations in the text

I Am the Light of the World

[12]Again Jesus spoke to them, saying, "I am the light of the world. Whoever follows me will not walk in darkness, but will have the light of life." [13]So the Pharisees said to him, "You are bearing witness about yourself; your testimony is not true." [14]Jesus answered, "Even if I do bear witness about myself, my testimony is true, for I know where I came from and where I am going, but you do not know where I come from or where I am going. [15]You judge according to the flesh; I judge no one. [16]Yet even if I do judge, my judgment is true, for it is not I alone who judge, but I and the Father[1] who sent me. [17]In your Law it is written that the testimony of two people is true. [18]I am the one who bears witness about myself, and the Father who sent me bears witness about me." [19]They said to him therefore, "Where is your Father?" Jesus answered, "You know neither me nor my Father. If you knew me, you would know my Father also." [20]These words he spoke in the treasury, as he taught in the temple; but no one arrested him, because his hour had not yet come.

[21]So he said to them again, "I am going away, and you will seek me, and you will die in your sin. Where I am going, you cannot come." [22]So the Jews said, "Will he kill himself, since he says, 'Where I am going, you cannot come'?" [23]He said to them, "You are from below; I am from above. You are of this world; I am not of this world. [24]I told you that you would die in your sins, for unless you believe that I am he you will die in your sins." [25]So they said to him, "Who are you?" Jesus said to them, "Just what I have been telling you from the beginning. [26]I have much to say about you and much to judge, but he who sent me is true, and I declare to the world what I have heard from him." [27]They did not understand that he had been speaking to them about the Father. [28]So Jesus said to them, "When you have lifted up the Son of Man, then you will know that I am he, and that I do nothing on my own authority, but speak just as the Father taught me. [29]And he who sent me is with me. He has not left me alone, for I always do the things that are pleasing to him." [30]As he was saying these things, many believed in him.

The Truth Will Set You Free

[31]So Jesus said to the Jews who had believed him, "If you abide in my word, you are truly my disciples, [32]and you will know the truth, and the truth will set you free." [33]They answered him, "We are offspring of Abraham and have never been enslaved to anyone. How is it that you say, 'You will become free'?"

[34]Jesus answered them, "Truly, truly, I say to you, everyone who practices sin is a slave[2] to sin. [35]The slave does not remain in the house forever; the son remains forever. [36]So if the Son sets you free, you will be free indeed. [37]I know that you are offspring of Abraham; yet you seek to kill me because my word finds no place in you. [38]I speak of what I have seen with my Father, and you do what you have heard from your father."

You Are of Your Father the Devil

[39]They answered him, "Abraham is our father." Jesus said to them, "If you were Abraham's children, you would be doing the works Abraham did, [40]but now you seek to kill me, a man who has told you the truth that I heard from God. This is not what Abraham did. [41]You are doing the works your father did." They said to him, "We were not born of sexual immorality. We have one Father—even God." [42]Jesus said to them, "If God were your Father, you would love me, for I came from God and I am here. I came not of my own accord, but he sent me. [43]Why do you not understand what I say? It is because you cannot bear to hear my word. [44]You are of your father the devil, and your will is to do your father's desires. He was a murderer from the beginning, and does not stand in the truth, because there is no truth in him. When he lies, he speaks out of his own character, for he is a

---

[1]Some manuscripts *he* [2]For the contextual rendering of the Greek word *doulos*, see Preface; also verse 35

THE "I AM" STATEMENTS OF CHRIST

A defining mark of the Gospel of John is Jesus' seven "I am" statements. The statements are all revelations from Jesus that he is the promised Messiah, the anointed one for which Israel had been waiting for centuries.

I am the bread of life—Jn 6:35,48. In identifying himself as such, Jesus references the bread from heaven that the people of Israel ate in the wilderness; yet, eventually, they still died. Jesus says believers will have endless life if they eat him (6:51), meaning, believe in and follow him.

I am the light of the world—Jn 8:12. Again Jesus references the people of ancient Israel and the pillar of fire that they followed through the wilderness (Ex 13:21). It is fitting that Jesus makes this statement in the temple courts during the Feast of Booths, which commemorates Israel's sojourn in the desert with a display of bright lights. Jesus is a better and eternal light; whoever follows him will never walk in darkness, but will have the light of life (Jn 8:12).

I am the door of the sheep—Jn 10:7,9 and I am the good shepherd—v. 11. In these statements Jesus is likely referencing Jerusalem's Sheep Gate (Ne 3:1,32) and the shepherd of Psalm 23. The sacrificial sheep and lambs were brought through the Sheep Gate to the temple for sacrifice, providing a way for the sins of the people of Israel to be covered. But Jesus is a better gate and a better shepherd; he is the gateway to eternal forgiveness and salvation for all people, and he is the ultimate Good Shepherd who restores the souls of everyone who believes in him.

I am the resurrection and the life—Jn 11:25. Jesus' words follow Martha's reference to the final resurrection of the body that Daniel prophesied (Da 12:2). Jesus explains that the resurrection and life is found in more than just an event; it is found in a person—more specifically, in him.

I am the way, and the truth, and the life—Jn 14:6. As the only sinless human ever to walk the earth, only Jesus was able to keep all of the decrees, commands, and laws of God and thus walk in the way and truth of God that leads to life (Dt 26:17).

I am the true vine—Jn 15:1,5. Jesus drew on the many Old Testament references to Israel as a vine (Ps 80:8–16; Isa 5:1–7; Jer 2:21; Eze 15:1–8; 17:5–10; 19:10–14; Hos 10:1). Though Israel was the vine God transplanted from Egypt and planted on a hillside, it became a vine that was cut down (Ps 80:16), corrupt (Jer 2:21), and ultimately destroyed (Isa 5:5). Jesus, however, is the true vine. He fulfills Israel's promise to obey the commands of God and bear fruit on Israel's behalf. Whoever is connected to him will have life and bear much fruit (Jn 15:5).

liar and the father of lies. 45But because I tell the truth, you do not believe me. 46Which one of you convicts me of sin? If I tell the truth, why do you not believe me? 47Whoever is of God hears the words of God. The reason why you do not hear them is that you are not of God."

Before Abraham Was, I Am

48The Jews answered him, "Are we not right in saying that you are a Samaritan and have a demon?" 49Jesus answered, "I do not have a demon, but I honor my Father, and you dishonor me. 50Yet I do not seek my own glory; there is One who seeks it, and he is the judge. 51Truly, truly, I say to you, if anyone keeps my word, he will never see death." 52The Jews said to him, "Now we know that you have a demon! Abraham died, as did the prophets, yet you say, 'If anyone keeps my word, he will never taste death.' 53Are you greater than our father Abraham, who died? And the prophets died! Who do you make yourself out to be?" 54Jesus answered, "If I glorify myself, my glory is nothing. It is my Father who glorifies me, of whom you say, 'He is our God.'[1] 55But you have not known him. I know him. If I were to say that I do not know him, I would be a liar like you, but I do know him and I keep his word. 56Your father Abraham rejoiced that he would see my day. He saw it and was glad." 57So the Jews said to him, "You are not yet fifty years old, and have you seen Abraham?"[2] 58Jesus said to them, "Truly, truly, I say to you, before Abraham was, I am." 59So they picked up stones to throw at him, but Jesus hid himself and went out of the temple.

Jesus Heals a Man Born Blind

9 As he passed by, he saw a man blind from birth. 2And his disciples asked him, "Rabbi, who sinned, this man or his parents, that he was born blind?" 3Jesus answered, "It was not that this man sinned, or his parents, but that the works of God might be displayed in him. 4We must work the works of him who sent me while it is day; night is coming, when no one can work. 5As long as I am in the world, I am the light of the world." 6Having said these things, he spit on the ground and made mud with the saliva. Then he anointed the man's eyes with the mud 7and said to him, "Go, wash in the pool of Siloam" (which means Sent). So he went and washed and came back seeing.

8The neighbors and those who had seen him before as a beggar were saying, "Is this not the man who used to sit and beg?" 9Some said, "It is he." Others said, "No, but he is like him." He kept saying, "I am the man." 10So they said to him, "Then how were your eyes opened?" 11He answered, "The man called Jesus made mud and anointed my eyes and said to me, 'Go to Siloam and wash.' So I went and washed and received my sight." 12They said to him, "Where is he?" He said, "I do not know."

13They brought to the Pharisees the man who had formerly been blind. 14Now it was a Sabbath day when Jesus made the mud and opened his eyes. 15So the Pharisees again asked him how he had received his sight. And he said to them, "He put mud on my eyes, and I washed, and I see." 16Some of the Pharisees said, "This man is not from God, for he does not keep the Sabbath." But others said, "How can a man who is a sinner do such signs?" And there was a division among them. 17So they said again to the blind man, "What do you say about him, since he has opened your eyes?" He said, "He is a prophet."

18The Jews[3] did not believe that he had been blind and had received his sight, until they called the parents of the man who had received his sight 19and asked them, "Is this your son, who you say was born blind? How then does he now see?" 20His parents answered, "We know that this is our son and that he was born blind. 21But how he now sees we do not know, nor do we know who opened his eyes. Ask

[1]Some manuscripts *your God* [2]Some manuscripts *has Abraham seen you?* [3]Greek *Ioudaioi* probably refers here to Jewish religious leaders, and others under their influence, in that time; also verse 22

JOHN 9:1–12

NOW I SEE

Christians will be plumbing the depths of God's truth for all of eternity. We will learn all about the nature and the work of God and how he is meticulously working all things together for his glory. The more we learn about him, the more we will be amazed at his power, character, and love.

But becoming a Christian does not require deep knowledge of God. It simply requires recognition of our brokenness and an experience with Jesus that causes us to follow him. The man in this story did not know who Jesus was, where he came from, or what he was like. All he knew was that he had been born blind, and that Jesus had caused him to see (9:25). That was all he needed to know to begin following Jesus.

In the same way, when we really encounter Jesus, he heals us of our spiritual blindness. When we understand his work, we are able to see our sin and our need for him, which draws us to his free gift of salvation. When we are drawn to him, we begin to follow him. This man who had been born blind first saw the light because of Jesus' gracious work on his behalf. So also for believers who seek him—in Jesus' light, everything else begins to make sense.

him; he is of age. He will speak for himself." 22(His parents said these things because they feared the Jews, for the Jews had already agreed that if anyone should
confess Jesus[1] to be Christ, he was to be put out of the synagogue. 23Therefore his
parents said, "He is of age; ask him.")
24So for the second time they called the man who had been blind and said
to him, "Give glory to God. We know that this man is a sinner." 25He answered,
"Whether he is a sinner I do not know. One thing I do know, that though I was
blind, now I see." 26They said to him, "What did he do to you? How did he open
your eyes?" 27He answered them, "I have told you already, and you would not listen. Why do you want to hear it again? Do you also want to become his disciples?"
28And they reviled him, saying, "You are his disciple, but we are disciples of Moses.
29We know that God has spoken to Moses, but as for this man, we do not know
where he comes from." 30The man answered, "Why, this is an amazing thing! You
do not know where he comes from, and yet he opened my eyes. 31We know that
God does not listen to sinners, but if anyone is a worshiper of God and does his
will, God listens to him. 32Never since the world began has it been heard that
anyone opened the eyes of a man born blind. 33If this man were not from God, he
could do nothing." 34They answered him, "You were born in utter sin, and would
you teach us?" And they cast him out.
35Jesus heard that they had cast him out, and having found him he said, "Do
you believe in the Son of Man?"[2] 36He answered, "And who is he, sir, that I may
believe in him?" 37Jesus said to him, "You have seen him, and it is he who is speaking to you." 38He said, "Lord, I believe," and he worshiped him. 39Jesus said, "For
judgment I came into this world, that those who do not see may see, and those
who see may become blind." 40Some of the Pharisees near him heard these things,
and said to him, "Are we also blind?" 41Jesus said to them, "If you were blind, you
would have no guilt;[3] but now that you say, 'We see,' your guilt remains.

I Am the Good Shepherd

10 "Truly, truly, I say to you, he who does not enter the sheepfold by the door
but climbs in by another way, that man is a thief and a robber. 2But he who
enters by the door is the shepherd of the sheep. 3To him the gatekeeper opens.
The sheep hear his voice, and he calls his own sheep by name and leads them
out. 4When he has brought out all his own, he goes before them, and the sheep
follow him, for they know his voice. 5A stranger they will not follow, but they will
flee from him, for they do not know the voice of strangers." 6This figure of speech
Jesus used with them, but they did not understand what he was saying to them.
7So Jesus again said to them, "Truly, truly, I say to you, I am the door of the
sheep. 8All who came before me are thieves and robbers, but the sheep did not
listen to them. 9I am the door. If anyone enters by me, he will be saved and
will go in and out and find pasture. 10The thief comes only to steal and kill and
destroy. I came that they may have life and have it abundantly. 11I am the good
shepherd. The good shepherd lays down his life for the sheep. 12He who is a
hired hand and not a shepherd, who does not own the sheep, sees the wolf coming and leaves the sheep and flees, and the wolf snatches them and scatters
them. 13He flees because he is a hired hand and cares nothing for the sheep. 14I
am the good shepherd. I know my own and my own know me, 15just as the Father knows me and I know the Father; and I lay down my life for the sheep. 16And
I have other sheep that are not of this fold. I must bring them also, and they will
listen to my voice. So there will be one flock, one shepherd. 17For this reason the
Father loves me, because I lay down my life that I may take it up again. 18No one
takes it from me, but I lay it down of my own accord. I have authority to lay it
down, and I have authority to take it up again. This charge I have received from
my Father."

[1]Greek *him* [2]Some manuscripts *the Son of God* [3]Greek *you would not have sin*

19There was again a division among the Jews because of these words. 20Many
of them said, "He has a demon, and is insane; why listen to him?" 21Others said,
"These are not the words of one who is oppressed by a demon. Can a demon open
the eyes of the blind?"

I and the Father Are One

22At that time the Feast of Dedication took place at Jerusalem. It was winter,
23and Jesus was walking in the temple, in the colonnade of Solomon. 24So the Jews
gathered around him and said to him, "How long will you keep us in suspense?
If you are the Christ, tell us plainly." 25Jesus answered them, "I told you, and you
do not believe. The works that I do in my Father's name bear witness about me,
26but you do not believe because you are not among my sheep. 27My sheep hear
my voice, and I know them, and they follow me. 28I give them eternal life, and they
will never perish, and no one will snatch them out of my hand. 29My Father, who
has given them to me,[1] is greater than all, and no one is able to snatch them out of
the Father's hand. 30I and the Father are one."

31The Jews picked up stones again to stone him. 32Jesus answered them, "I have
shown you many good works from the Father; for which of them are you going to
stone me?" 33The Jews answered him, "It is not for a good work that we are going
to stone you but for blasphemy, because you, being a man, make yourself God."
34Jesus answered them, "Is it not written in your Law, 'I said, you are gods'? 35If he
called them gods to whom the word of God came—and Scripture cannot be broken— 36do you say of him whom the Father consecrated and sent into the world,
'You are blaspheming,' because I said, 'I am the Son of God'? 37If I am not doing
the works of my Father, then do not believe me; 38but if I do them, even though
you do not believe me, believe the works, that you may know and understand that
the Father is in me and I am in the Father." 39Again they sought to arrest him, but
he escaped from their hands.

40He went away again across the Jordan to the place where John had been baptizing at first, and there he remained. 41And many came to him. And they said,
"John did no sign, but everything that John said about this man was true." 42And
many believed in him there.

The Death of Lazarus

11 Now a certain man was ill, Lazarus of Bethany, the village of Mary and
her sister Martha. 2It was Mary who anointed the Lord with ointment and
wiped his feet with her hair, whose brother Lazarus was ill. 3So the sisters sent
to him, saying, "Lord, he whom you love is ill." 4But when Jesus heard it he said,
"This illness does not lead to death. It is for the glory of God, so that the Son of
God may be glorified through it."

5Now Jesus loved Martha and her sister and Lazarus. 6So, when he heard that
Lazarus[2] was ill, he stayed two days longer in the place where he was. 7Then after this he said to the disciples, "Let us go to Judea again." 8The disciples said to
him, "Rabbi, the Jews were just now seeking to stone you, and are you going there
again?" 9Jesus answered, "Are there not twelve hours in the day? If anyone walks
in the day, he does not stumble, because he sees the light of this world. 10But if
anyone walks in the night, he stumbles, because the light is not in him." 11After
saying these things, he said to them, "Our friend Lazarus has fallen asleep, but I
go to awaken him." 12The disciples said to him, "Lord, if he has fallen asleep, he
will recover." 13Now Jesus had spoken of his death, but they thought that he meant
taking rest in sleep. 14Then Jesus told them plainly, "Lazarus has died, 15and for
your sake I am glad that I was not there, so that you may believe. But let us go to
him." 16So Thomas, called the Twin,[3] said to his fellow disciples, "Let us also go,
that we may die with him."

JOHN 10:22–30

I AND THE FATHER ARE ONE

Throughout his ministry, Jesus regularly made bold claims that the Jewish leaders either didn't like or didn't understand. His claim to be one with the Father (Jn 10:30) might have been the boldest, most disliked, and most misunderstood of all his claims. The Jewish leaders and the crowd charged him with blasphemy and tried to stone him.

For a man to claim to be one with God was unthinkable. This is the great miracle of Christ, the miracle of the incarnation: that Jesus is fully God and as such is utterly holy, yet also fully man and completely human. Christians believe that the divinity of Christ is fully present in the person of Jesus but is veiled in flesh (Jn 1:14). Because of his miraculous incarnation, people can identify with Christ. He is a man, but he simultaneously has the power to save since he is also fully God.

The amazing truth of the gospel is that Jesus left the power, peace, and love of his Father to endure the miseries of this life and to willingly take the guilt of human sin upon himself, bearing the brunt of God's wrath on the cross. Now, in exchange for our sin, he offers us his righteousness. This righteousness is so complete that when we are clothed in it, we become united with Christ and one with God the Father (Jn 17:11,21).

[1]Some manuscripts *What my Father has given to me* [2]Greek *he*; also verse 17 [3]Greek *Didymus*

I Am the Resurrection and the Life

[17]Now when Jesus came, he found that Lazarus had already been in the tomb four days. [18]Bethany was near Jerusalem, about two miles[1] off, [19]and many of the Jews had come to Martha and Mary to console them concerning their brother. [20]So when Martha heard that Jesus was coming, she went and met him, but Mary remained seated in the house. [21]Martha said to Jesus, "Lord, if you had been here, my brother would not have died. [22]But even now I know that whatever you ask from God, God will give you." [23]Jesus said to her, "Your brother will rise again." [24]Martha said to him, "I know that he will rise again in the resurrection on the last day." [25]Jesus said to her, "I am the resurrection and the life.[2] Whoever believes in me, though he die, yet shall he live, [26]and everyone who lives and believes in me shall never die. Do you believe this?" [27]She said to him, "Yes, Lord; I believe that you are the Christ, the Son of God, who is coming into the world."

Jesus Weeps

[28]When she had said this, she went and called her sister Mary, saying in private, "The Teacher is here and is calling for you." [29]And when she heard it, she rose quickly and went to him. [30]Now Jesus had not yet come into the village, but was still in the place where Martha had met him. [31]When the Jews who were with her in the house, consoling her, saw Mary rise quickly and go out, they followed her, supposing that she was going to the tomb to weep there. [32]Now when Mary came to where Jesus was and saw him, she fell at his feet, saying to him, "Lord, if you had been here, my brother would not have died." [33]When Jesus saw her weeping, and the Jews who had come with her also weeping, he was deeply moved[3] in his spirit and greatly troubled. [34]And he said, "Where have you laid him?" They said to him, "Lord, come and see." [35]Jesus wept. [36]So the Jews said, "See how he loved him!" [37]But some of them said, "Could not he who opened the eyes of the blind man also have kept this man from dying?"

Jesus Raises Lazarus

[38]Then Jesus, deeply moved again, came to the tomb. It was a cave, and a stone lay against it. [39]Jesus said, "Take away the stone." Martha, the sister of the dead man, said to him, "Lord, by this time there will be an odor, for he has been dead four days." [40]Jesus said to her, "Did I not tell you that if you believed you would see the glory of God?" [41]So they took away the stone. And Jesus lifted up his eyes and said, "Father, I thank you that you have heard me. [42]I knew that you always hear me, but I said this on account of the people standing around, that they may believe that you sent me." [43]When he had said these things, he cried out with a loud voice, "Lazarus, come out." [44]The man who had died came out, his hands and feet bound with linen strips, and his face wrapped with a cloth. Jesus said to them, "Unbind him, and let him go."

The Plot to Kill Jesus

[45]Many of the Jews therefore, who had come with Mary and had seen what he did, believed in him, [46]but some of them went to the Pharisees and told them what Jesus had done. [47]So the chief priests and the Pharisees gathered the council and said, "What are we to do? For this man performs many signs. [48]If we let him go on like this, everyone will believe in him, and the Romans will come and take away both our place and our nation." [49]But one of them, Caiaphas, who was high priest that year, said to them, "You know nothing at all. [50]Nor do you understand that it is better for you that one man should die for the people, not that the whole nation should perish." [51]He did not say this of his own accord, but being high priest that year he prophesied that Jesus would die for the nation, [52]and not for

[1]Greek *fifteen stadia*; a *stadion* was about 607 feet or 185 meters [2]Some manuscripts omit *and the life*
[3]Or *was indignant*; also verse 38

THE HOPE OF LIFE

Of the many miracles in the Gospel of John, one of the most dramatic is Jesus' raising of Lazarus. Not only is this sign one of the most vivid, it also tells us the most about the ministry and purpose of Jesus. From the very beginning of time God could have certainly kept sin, pain, and even death out of the world that he created. However, God allowed sin to enter into his good creation through the serpent's temptation and the man and woman's disobedience, so that through the power of redemption, God's glory might be displayed. Similarly, Jesus allowed Lazarus to die "so that the Son of God may be glorified through it" (Jn 11:4).

God sent that redemption through his own Son, Jesus, who came to earth to sympathize with us in every way. We see that sympathy in this story as he goes to comfort Mary and Martha, Lazarus's sisters and his dear friends (11:35). We understand from Scripture that Jesus can sympathize with us in our weaknesses and in our temptations (Heb 4:15). Jesus even identified with us to the point of becoming our sin and dying the death that we should have died because of our rebellion against God (2Co 5:21; Php 2:8). But Jesus is the resurrection and the life (Jn 11:25), and by the power of God he overcame death, was raised to eternal life, and now reigns forever in his eternal kingdom.

As Lazarus was undeniably physically dead, so we are spiritually dead and separated from God in our own sins. Like Lazarus, any hope of life is gone, and the stench of our spiritual decomposition is pungent. As Paul explained, we "were dead in the trespasses and sins ... and were by nature children of wrath" (Eph 2:1–3). But just as Jesus raised Lazarus from his physical death, if we believe that Jesus is the resurrection and the life, he promises to raise us from our spiritual death and gives us the promise of a physical resurrection on the last day.

Understand that last statement: Just as Jesus physically raised Lazarus from the dead, so he will one day do that with each of us who believe in and trust him alone for our salvation. In fact, we will do one better: our bodies will be reinvigorated, but not to their old, imperfect state; instead, in that day we will be like him (1Jn 3:2).

the nation only, but also to gather into one the children of God who are scattered abroad. 53So from that day on they made plans to put him to death.

54Jesus therefore no longer walked openly among the Jews, but went from there to the region near the wilderness, to a town called Ephraim, and there he stayed with the disciples.

55Now the Passover of the Jews was at hand, and many went up from the country to Jerusalem before the Passover to purify themselves. 56They were looking for[1] Jesus and saying to one another as they stood in the temple, "What do you think? That he will not come to the feast at all?" 57Now the chief priests and the Pharisees had given orders that if anyone knew where he was, he should let them know, so that they might arrest him.

Mary Anoints Jesus at Bethany

12 Six days before the Passover, Jesus therefore came to Bethany, where Lazarus was, whom Jesus had raised from the dead. 2So they gave a dinner for him there. Martha served, and Lazarus was one of those reclining with him at table. 3Mary therefore took a pound[2] of expensive ointment made from pure nard, and anointed the feet of Jesus and wiped his feet with her hair. The house was filled with the fragrance of the perfume. 4But Judas Iscariot, one of his disciples (he who was about to betray him), said, 5"Why was this ointment not sold for three hundred denarii[3] and given to the poor?" 6He said this, not because he cared about the poor, but because he was a thief, and having charge of the moneybag he used to help himself to what was put into it. 7Jesus said, "Leave her alone, so that she may keep it[4] for the day of my burial. 8For the poor you always have with you, but you do not always have me."

The Plot to Kill Lazarus

9When the large crowd of the Jews learned that Jesus[5] was there, they came, not only on account of him but also to see Lazarus, whom he had raised from the dead. 10So the chief priests made plans to put Lazarus to death as well, 11because on account of him many of the Jews were going away and believing in Jesus.

The Triumphal Entry

12The next day the large crowd that had come to the feast heard that Jesus was coming to Jerusalem. 13So they took branches of palm trees and went out to meet him, crying out, "Hosanna! Blessed is he who comes in the name of the Lord, even the King of Israel!" 14And Jesus found a young donkey and sat on it, just as it is written,

15 "Fear not, daughter of Zion;
behold, your king is coming,
sitting on a donkey's colt!"

16His disciples did not understand these things at first, but when Jesus was glorified, then they remembered that these things had been written about him and had been done to him. 17The crowd that had been with him when he called Lazarus out of the tomb and raised him from the dead continued to bear witness. 18The reason why the crowd went to meet him was that they heard he had done this sign. 19So the Pharisees said to one another, "You see that you are gaining nothing. Look, the world has gone after him."

Some Greeks Seek Jesus

20Now among those who went up to worship at the feast were some Greeks. 21So these came to Philip, who was from Bethsaida in Galilee, and asked him,

---

[1]Greek *were seeking for* [2]Greek *litra;* a *litra* (or Roman pound) was equal to about 11 1/2 ounces or 327 grams [3]A *denarius* was a day's wage for a laborer [4]Or *Leave her alone; she intended to keep it* [5]Greek *he*

JOHN 12:37–43

THE PRAISE OF GOD

One of the most haunting stories in the Bible is this story of the Jews who were fearful of following Jesus. Jesus, the Messiah, the one whom the people of Israel had been expecting for generations, was standing right in front of them. Jesus had spoken the truth about God's kingdom, had given them many miraculous signs and had just raised Lazarus from the dead. Many believed that Jesus was the Messiah, but they were too afraid to acknowledge him and follow him because "they loved the glory that comes from man more than the glory that comes from God" (Jn 12:43).

This is a great warning to all. Following Jesus is not always convenient or popular. Often, the call to follow Christ is a call to forsake comfort, wealth, status, and the approval of others; in some contexts, following Jesus is quite literally a call to die. Those who follow Jesus may forsake human praise, but in return they gain praise from God.

Christ promises that believers will one day see the incredible riches of God's grace (Eph 2:7) and sit with Jesus on his eternal throne (Rev 3:21). These fearful Jewish people traded the eternal throne of Christ for the temporal praise of humans. Believers today reject this bad trade, choosing rather by God's grace to forsake the small things of this world for the eternal things of God.

"Sir, we wish to see Jesus." [22]Philip went and told Andrew; Andrew and Philip
went and told Jesus. [23]And Jesus answered them, "The hour has come for the
Son of Man to be glorified. [24]Truly, truly, I say to you, unless a grain of wheat
falls into the earth and dies, it remains alone; but if it dies, it bears much fruit.
[25]Whoever loves his life loses it, and whoever hates his life in this world will
keep it for eternal life. [26]If anyone serves me, he must follow me; and where I
am, there will my servant be also. If anyone serves me, the Father will honor
him.

The Son of Man Must Be Lifted Up

[27]"Now is my soul troubled. And what shall I say? 'Father, save me from this
hour'? But for this purpose I have come to this hour. [28]Father, glorify your name."
Then a voice came from heaven: "I have glorified it, and I will glorify it again."
[29]The crowd that stood there and heard it said that it had thundered. Others said,
"An angel has spoken to him." [30]Jesus answered, "This voice has come for your
sake, not mine. [31]Now is the judgment of this world; now will the ruler of this
world be cast out. [32]And I, when I am lifted up from the earth, will draw all people
to myself." [33]He said this to show by what kind of death he was going to die. [34]So
the crowd answered him, "We have heard from the Law that the Christ remains
forever. How can you say that the Son of Man must be lifted up? Who is this Son
of Man?" [35]So Jesus said to them, "The light is among you for a little while longer.
Walk while you have the light, lest darkness overtake you. The one who walks in
the darkness does not know where he is going. [36]While you have the light, believe
in the light, that you may become sons of light."

The Unbelief of the People

When Jesus had said these things, he departed and hid himself from them.
[37]Though he had done so many signs before them, they still did not believe in
him, [38]so that the word spoken by the prophet Isaiah might be fulfilled:

"Lord, who has believed what he heard from us,
and to whom has the arm of the Lord been revealed?"

[39]Therefore they could not believe. For again Isaiah said,

[40] "He has blinded their eyes
and hardened their heart,
lest they see with their eyes,
and understand with their heart, and turn,
and I would heal them."

[41]Isaiah said these things because he saw his glory and spoke of him. [42]Neverthe-
less, many even of the authorities believed in him, but for fear of the Pharisees
they did not confess it, so that they would not be put out of the synagogue; [43]for
they loved the glory that comes from man more than the glory that comes from
God.

Jesus Came to Save the World

[44]And Jesus cried out and said, "Whoever believes in me, believes not in me
but in him who sent me. [45]And whoever sees me sees him who sent me. [46]I have
come into the world as light, so that whoever believes in me may not remain in
darkness. [47]If anyone hears my words and does not keep them, I do not judge him;
for I did not come to judge the world but to save the world. [48]The one who rejects
me and does not receive my words has a judge; the word that I have spoken will
judge him on the last day. [49]For I have not spoken on my own authority, but the
Father who sent me has himself given me a commandment—what to say and
what to speak. [50]And I know that his commandment is eternal life. What I say,
therefore, I say as the Father has told me."

Jesus Washes the Disciples' Feet

13 Now before the Feast of the Passover, when Jesus knew that his hour had come to depart out of this world to the Father, having loved his own who were in the world, he loved them to the end. 2During supper, when the devil had already put it into the heart of Judas Iscariot, Simon's son, to betray him, 3Jesus, knowing that the Father had given all things into his hands, and that he had come from God and was going back to God, 4rose from supper. He laid aside his outer garments, and taking a towel, tied it around his waist. 5Then he poured water into a basin and began to wash the disciples' feet and to wipe them with the towel that was wrapped around him. 6He came to Simon Peter, who said to him, "Lord, do you wash my feet?" 7Jesus answered him, "What I am doing you do not understand now, but afterward you will understand." 8Peter said to him, "You shall never wash my feet." Jesus answered him, "If I do not wash you, you have no share with me." 9Simon Peter said to him, "Lord, not my feet only but also my hands and my head!" 10Jesus said to him, "The one who has bathed does not need to wash, except for his feet,[1] but is completely clean. And you[2] are clean, but not every one of you." 11For he knew who was to betray him; that was why he said, "Not all of you are clean."

12When he had washed their feet and put on his outer garments and resumed his place, he said to them, "Do you understand what I have done to you? 13You call me Teacher and Lord, and you are right, for so I am. 14If I then, your Lord and Teacher, have washed your feet, you also ought to wash one another's feet. 15For I have given you an example, that you also should do just as I have done to you. 16Truly, truly, I say to you, a servant[3] is not greater than his master, nor is a messenger greater than the one who sent him. 17If you know these things, blessed are you if you do them. 18I am not speaking of all of you; I know whom I have chosen. But the Scripture will be fulfilled,[4] 'He who ate my bread has lifted his heel against me.' 19I am telling you this now, before it takes place, that when it does take place you may believe that I am he. 20Truly, truly, I say to you, whoever receives the one I send receives me, and whoever receives me receives the one who sent me."

One of You Will Betray Me

21After saying these things, Jesus was troubled in his spirit, and testified, "Truly, truly, I say to you, one of you will betray me." 22The disciples looked at one another, uncertain of whom he spoke. 23One of his disciples, whom Jesus loved, was reclining at table at Jesus' side,[5] 24so Simon Peter motioned to him to ask Jesus[6] of whom he was speaking. 25So that disciple, leaning back against Jesus, said to him, "Lord, who is it?" 26Jesus answered, "It is he to whom I will give this morsel of bread when I have dipped it." So when he had dipped the morsel, he gave it to Judas, the son of Simon Iscariot. 27Then after he had taken the morsel, Satan entered into him. Jesus said to him, "What you are going to do, do quickly." 28Now no one at the table knew why he said this to him. 29Some thought that, because Judas had the moneybag, Jesus was telling him, "Buy what we need for the feast," or that he should give something to the poor. 30So, after receiving the morsel of bread, he immediately went out. And it was night.

A New Commandment

31When he had gone out, Jesus said, "Now is the Son of Man glorified, and God is glorified in him. 32If God is glorified in him, God will also glorify him in himself, and glorify him at once. 33Little children, yet a little while I am with you. You will seek me, and just as I said to the Jews, so now I also say to you, 'Where I am going you cannot come.' 34A new commandment I give to you, that you love

JOHN 13:1–17,34–35

A NEW COMMANDMENT

During the Passover meal, Jesus, the master and teacher of the twelve disciples, got up, wrapped a towel around his waist and began to wash the disciples' feet. This was a dirty job normally reserved for a lowly servant. But Jesus, the obvious leader of this group, decided to wash feet to serve his disciples and make a profound point. While it's true that the disciples had dirty feet, Jesus' motive was far beyond the circumstances. The disciples knew this was an important night, yet none of them had bothered to wash their own, much less one another's, feet. Jesus realized this was the perfect opportunity to show them that the way of his kingdom is very different from the way of earthly kingdoms.

Jesus came to serve and love, and so he gave his disciples a new command: "Love one another"; he then went on to say, "By this all people will know that you are my disciples, if you have love for one another" (13:34–35). It's this kind of aspiration that Jesus wanted his disciples to pursue; its countercultural nature is just as radical today. God's love in believers' lives is to be evident as they show his love to a lost and broken world today, pointing toward a kingdom that is not of this world (Jn 18:36).

[1]Some manuscripts omit *except for his feet* [2]The Greek words for *you* in this verse are plural [3]Or *bondservant*, or *slave* (for the contextual rendering of the Greek word *doulos*, see Preface) [4]Greek *But in order that the Scripture may be fulfilled* [5]Greek *in the bosom of Jesus* [6]Greek lacks *Jesus*

one another: just as I have loved you, you also are to love one another. 35By this
all people will know that you are my disciples, if you have love for one another."

Jesus Foretells Peter's Denial

36Simon Peter said to him, "Lord, where are you going?" Jesus answered him,
"Where I am going you cannot follow me now, but you will follow afterward."
37Peter said to him, "Lord, why can I not follow you now? I will lay down my life
for you." 38Jesus answered, "Will you lay down your life for me? Truly, truly, I say
to you, the rooster will not crow till you have denied me three times.

I Am the Way, and the Truth, and the Life

14 "Let not your hearts be troubled. Believe in God;[1] believe also in me. 2In
my Father's house are many rooms. If it were not so, would I have told you
that I go to prepare a place for you?[2] 3And if I go and prepare a place for you, I will
come again and will take you to myself, that where I am you may be also. 4And
you know the way to where I am going."[3] 5Thomas said to him, "Lord, we do not
know where you are going. How can we know the way?" 6Jesus said to him, "I am
the way, and the truth, and the life. No one comes to the Father except through
me. 7If you had known me, you would have known my Father also.[4] From now on
you do know him and have seen him."

8Philip said to him, "Lord, show us the Father, and it is enough for us." 9Jesus
said to him, "Have I been with you so long, and you still do not know me, Philip?
Whoever has seen me has seen the Father. How can you say, 'Show us the Father'?
10Do you not believe that I am in the Father and the Father is in me? The words
that I say to you I do not speak on my own authority, but the Father who dwells in
me does his works. 11Believe me that I am in the Father and the Father is in me, or
else believe on account of the works themselves.

12"Truly, truly, I say to you, whoever believes in me will also do the works that
I do; and greater works than these will he do, because I am going to the Father.
13Whatever you ask in my name, this I will do, that the Father may be glorified in
the Son. 14If you ask me[5] anything in my name, I will do it.

Jesus Promises the Holy Spirit

15"If you love me, you will keep my commandments. 16And I will ask the Father,
and he will give you another Helper,[6] to be with you forever, 17even the Spirit of
truth, whom the world cannot receive, because it neither sees him nor knows
him. You know him, for he dwells with you and will be[7] in you.

18"I will not leave you as orphans; I will come to you. 19Yet a little while and the
world will see me no more, but you will see me. Because I live, you also will live.
20In that day you will know that I am in my Father, and you in me, and I in you.
21Whoever has my commandments and keeps them, he it is who loves me. And he
who loves me will be loved by my Father, and I will love him and manifest myself
to him." 22Judas (not Iscariot) said to him, "Lord, how is it that you will manifest
yourself to us, and not to the world?" 23Jesus answered him, "If anyone loves me,
he will keep my word, and my Father will love him, and we will come to him and
make our home with him. 24Whoever does not love me does not keep my words.
And the word that you hear is not mine but the Father's who sent me.

25"These things I have spoken to you while I am still with you. 26But the Helper,
the Holy Spirit, whom the Father will send in my name, he will teach you all things
and bring to your remembrance all that I have said to you. 27Peace I leave with you;
my peace I give to you. Not as the world gives do I give to you. Let not your hearts

---

[1] Or *You believe in God* [2] Or *In my Father's house are many rooms; if it were not so, I would have told you; for I go to prepare a place for you* [3] Some manuscripts *Where I am going you know, and the way you know*
[4] Or *If you know me, you will know my Father also*, or *If you have known me, you will know my Father also*
[5] Some manuscripts omit *me* [6] Or *Advocate*, or *Counselor*; also 14:26; 15:26; 16:7 [7] Some manuscripts *and is*

be troubled, neither let them be afraid. 28You heard me say to you, 'I am going
away, and I will come to you.' If you loved me, you would have rejoiced, because I
am going to the Father, for the Father is greater than I. 29And now I have told you
before it takes place, so that when it does take place you may believe. 30I will no
longer talk much with you, for the ruler of this world is coming. He has no claim
on me, 31but I do as the Father has commanded me, so that the world may know
that I love the Father. Rise, let us go from here.

I Am the True Vine

15 "I am the true vine, and my Father is the vinedresser. 2Every branch in me
that does not bear fruit he takes away, and every branch that does bear fruit
he prunes, that it may bear more fruit. 3Already you are clean because of the word
that I have spoken to you. 4Abide in me, and I in you. As the branch cannot bear
fruit by itself, unless it abides in the vine, neither can you, unless you abide in
me. 5I am the vine; you are the branches. Whoever abides in me and I in him, he
it is that bears much fruit, for apart from me you can do nothing. 6If anyone does
not abide in me, he is thrown away like a branch and withers; and the branches
are gathered, thrown into the fire, and burned. 7If you abide in me, and my words
abide in you, ask whatever you wish, and it will be done for you. 8By this my Father is glorified, that you bear much fruit and so prove to be my disciples. 9As
the Father has loved me, so have I loved you. Abide in my love. 10If you keep my
commandments, you will abide in my love, just as I have kept my Father's commandments and abide in his love. 11These things I have spoken to you, that my joy
may be in you, and that your joy may be full.

12"This is my commandment, that you love one another as I have loved you.
13Greater love has no one than this, that someone lay down his life for his friends.
14You are my friends if you do what I command you. 15No longer do I call you servants,[1] for the servant does not know what his master is doing; but I have called
you friends, for all that I have heard from my Father I have made known to you.
16You did not choose me, but I chose you and appointed you that you should go
and bear fruit and that your fruit should abide, so that whatever you ask the
Father in my name, he may give it to you. 17These things I command you, so that
you will love one another.

The Hatred of the World

18"If the world hates you, know that it has hated me before it hated you. 19If
you were of the world, the world would love you as its own; but because you are
not of the world, but I chose you out of the world, therefore the world hates you.
20Remember the word that I said to you: 'A servant is not greater than his master.'
If they persecuted me, they will also persecute you. If they kept my word, they will
also keep yours. 21But all these things they will do to you on account of my name,
because they do not know him who sent me. 22If I had not come and spoken to
them, they would not have been guilty of sin,[2] but now they have no excuse for
their sin. 23Whoever hates me hates my Father also. 24If I had not done among
them the works that no one else did, they would not be guilty of sin, but now they
have seen and hated both me and my Father. 25But the word that is written in their
Law must be fulfilled: 'They hated me without a cause.'

26"But when the Helper comes, whom I will send to you from the Father, the
Spirit of truth, who proceeds from the Father, he will bear witness about me.
27And you also will bear witness, because you have been with me from the beginning.

16 "I have said all these things to you to keep you from falling away. 2They will
put you out of the synagogues. Indeed, the hour is coming when whoever
kills you will think he is offering service to God. 3And they will do these things

[1]Or *bondservants*, or *slaves* (for the contextual rendering of the Greek word *doulos*, see Preface); likewise for *servant* later in this verse and in verse 20 [2]Greek *they would not have sin*; also verse 24

JOHN 15:1–8

THE VINE AND THE BRANCHES

Jesus here draws on Old Testament "vine" language (Isa 5:1) in his final "I am" statement to declare that all of the prophecies and laws of Israel are fulfilled in him (Mt 5:17). By this statement, believers discover that the secret of staying connected to God is to stay connected to Christ.

When his followers are connected to Jesus, they will "bear much fruit" (Jn 15:8), but apart from him they can do "nothing" (v. 5). Practically then, to remain in the "vine of Christ," believers must be faithful to pursue God on a regular basis. Regular worship, prayer, and Bible study are essential in the life of a believer. The more disciplined they are in pursuing God through these disciplines, the more fruit they will bear.

because they have not known the Father, nor me. 4But I have said these things to you, that when their hour comes you may remember that I told them to you.

The Work of the Holy Spirit

"I did not say these things to you from the beginning, because I was with you. 5But now I am going to him who sent me, and none of you asks me, 'Where are you going?' 6But because I have said these things to you, sorrow has filled your heart. 7Nevertheless, I tell you the truth: it is to your advantage that I go away, for if I do not go away, the Helper will not come to you. But if I go, I will send him to you. 8And when he comes, he will convict the world concerning sin and righteousness and judgment: 9concerning sin, because they do not believe in me; 10concerning righteousness, because I go to the Father, and you will see me no longer; 11concerning judgment, because the ruler of this world is judged.

12"I still have many things to say to you, but you cannot bear them now. 13When the Spirit of truth comes, he will guide you into all the truth, for he will not speak on his own authority, but whatever he hears he will speak, and he will declare to you the things that are to come. 14He will glorify me, for he will take what is mine and declare it to you. 15All that the Father has is mine; therefore I said that he will take what is mine and declare it to you.

Your Sorrow Will Turn into Joy

16"A little while, and you will see me no longer; and again a little while, and you will see me." 17So some of his disciples said to one another, "What is this that he says to us, 'A little while, and you will not see me, and again a little while, and you will see me'; and, 'because I am going to the Father'?" 18So they were saying, "What does he mean by 'a little while'? We do not know what he is talking about." 19Jesus knew that they wanted to ask him, so he said to them, "Is this what you are asking yourselves, what I meant by saying, 'A little while and you will not see me, and again a little while and you will see me'? 20Truly, truly, I say to you, you will weep and lament, but the world will rejoice. You will be sorrowful, but your sorrow will turn into joy. 21When a woman is giving birth, she has sorrow because her hour has come, but when she has delivered the baby, she no longer remembers the anguish, for joy that a human being has been born into the world. 22So also you have sorrow now, but I will see you again, and your hearts will rejoice, and no one will take your joy from you. 23In that day you will ask nothing of me. Truly, truly, I say to you, whatever you ask of the Father in my name, he will give it to you. 24Until now you have asked nothing in my name. Ask, and you will receive, that your joy may be full.

I Have Overcome the World

25"I have said these things to you in figures of speech. The hour is coming when I will no longer speak to you in figures of speech but will tell you plainly about the Father. 26In that day you will ask in my name, and I do not say to you that I will ask the Father on your behalf; 27for the Father himself loves you, because you have loved me and have believed that I came from God.[1] 28I came from the Father and have come into the world, and now I am leaving the world and going to the Father."

29His disciples said, "Ah, now you are speaking plainly and not using figurative speech! 30Now we know that you know all things and do not need anyone to question you; this is why we believe that you came from God." 31Jesus answered them, "Do you now believe? 32Behold, the hour is coming, indeed it has come, when you will be scattered, each to his own home, and will leave me alone. Yet I am not alone, for the Father is with me. 33I have said these things to you, that in me you may have peace. In the world you will have tribulation. But take heart; I have overcome the world."

[1]Some manuscripts *from the Father*

THE HELPER

While the Gospel of John covers most of the significant events in Jesus' ministry, nearly a third of the book covers the events of just one night. This night was, of course, one of the most important nights of his life: his last night with his disciples before he was betrayed and arrested. On this night he comforted his disciples by promising them the greatest gift they could ever receive: the indwelling power of the Holy Spirit of God.

The Holy Spirit is the third person of the holy Trinity; he is fully God, and his will is always in line with God the Father and God the Son. The Holy Spirit was present at creation (Ge 1:2) and was with the people of Israel in the tabernacle (Ex 40:34 – 35) and the temple (1Ki 8:6 – 13). This same Spirit had led Jesus throughout his earthly ministry (Mt 3:16), but on this final night of Jesus' life, he promised his disciples that the Holy Spirit would be present with each one of them: "I will ask the Father, and he will give you another Helper, to be with you forever, even the Spirit of truth" (Jn 14:16 – 17).

The disciples, like many believers throughout history, did not understand what Jesus was promising; they undoubtedly would have preferred for Jesus to stay with them. But Jesus emphasized the benefits of the Spirit's indwelling when he said, "It is to your advantage that I go away, for if I do not go away, the Helper will not come to you. But if I go, I will send him to you" (Jn 16:7). After the Spirit came at Pentecost (Ac 2:1 – 18), the disciples must have remembered Jesus' teaching about the ministry of the Holy Spirit: "When he comes, he will convict the world concerning sin and righteousness and judgment" (Jn 16:8). "He will guide you into all the truth" (16:13).

The Holy Spirit teaches Christians that sin is wrong, and when believers surrender to him, he begins to take away their desire for sin. The Spirit reminds Christians of Christ's righteousness. Jesus has gone to the Father to advocate for those who believe (16:10). Since we no longer have Jesus to show us righteousness through his earthly life, believers now have the Holy Spirit to lead us into what is good, right, and true. Finally, the Holy Spirit reminds believers of the coming judgment (16:11): that one day Jesus will return to condemn all evil and reward all good. He will settle all accounts, bring justice to the world, and will renew his creation (Isa 43:18 – 19; Rev 21:5).

JOHN 17:1–26

THE PRAYER OF CHRIST

One of the great blessings of being a follower of Jesus is knowing that right now he is interceding for his people before the Father (Ro 8:34; Heb 7:25). While we do not know exactly what Jesus says to the Father, we do have an example of Jesus' prayer here in John 17.

First, Jesus prays that the Father would protect his church. He not only prays for physical protection, but even more he prays for spiritual protection—that the church's faith would stay strong after Jesus left them to return to his Father (17:11).

Second, Jesus prays for his church to be sanctified, that they would be made holy; that they would know the truth of God and reflect the glory of God on earth (17:17,19).

Third, Jesus prays for those who will believe through the message of the disciples (17:20). Jesus prays that his church will grow and that many people in all the earth will come to know him through the faithful ministry of all his disciples.

What an amazing gift to believers today to be able to read this prayer and know that Jesus was, and still is, going to God—directly and personally—on their behalf.

The High Priestly Prayer

17 When Jesus had spoken these words, he lifted up his eyes to heaven, and
said, "Father, the hour has come; glorify your Son that the Son may glorify you, 2since you have given him authority over all flesh, to give eternal life
to all whom you have given him. 3And this is eternal life, that they know you,
the only true God, and Jesus Christ whom you have sent. 4I glorified you on
earth, having accomplished the work that you gave me to do. 5And now, Father,
glorify me in your own presence with the glory that I had with you before the
world existed.

6"I have manifested your name to the people whom you gave me out of the
world. Yours they were, and you gave them to me, and they have kept your word.
7Now they know that everything that you have given me is from you. 8For I have
given them the words that you gave me, and they have received them and have
come to know in truth that I came from you; and they have believed that you sent
me. 9I am praying for them. I am not praying for the world but for those whom
you have given me, for they are yours. 10All mine are yours, and yours are mine,
and I am glorified in them. 11And I am no longer in the world, but they are in the
world, and I am coming to you. Holy Father, keep them in your name, which you
have given me, that they may be one, even as we are one. 12While I was with them,
I kept them in your name, which you have given me. I have guarded them, and not
one of them has been lost except the son of destruction, that the Scripture might
be fulfilled. 13But now I am coming to you, and these things I speak in the world,
that they may have my joy fulfilled in themselves. 14I have given them your word,
and the world has hated them because they are not of the world, just as I am not
of the world. 15I do not ask that you take them out of the world, but that you keep
them from the evil one.[1] 16They are not of the world, just as I am not of the world.
17Sanctify them[2] in the truth; your word is truth. 18As you sent me into the world,
so I have sent them into the world. 19And for their sake I consecrate myself,[3] that
they also may be sanctified[4] in truth.

20"I do not ask for these only, but also for those who will believe in me through
their word, 21that they may all be one, just as you, Father, are in me, and I in you,
that they also may be in us, so that the world may believe that you have sent me.
22The glory that you have given me I have given to them, that they may be one
even as we are one, 23I in them and you in me, that they may become perfectly
one, so that the world may know that you sent me and loved them even as you
loved me. 24Father, I desire that they also, whom you have given me, may be with
me where I am, to see my glory that you have given me because you loved me
before the foundation of the world. 25O righteous Father, even though the world
does not know you, I know you, and these know that you have sent me. 26I made
known to them your name, and I will continue to make it known, that the love
with which you have loved me may be in them, and I in them."

Betrayal and Arrest of Jesus

18 When Jesus had spoken these words, he went out with his disciples across
the brook Kidron, where there was a garden, which he and his disciples
entered. 2Now Judas, who betrayed him, also knew the place, for Jesus often met
there with his disciples. 3So Judas, having procured a band of soldiers and some
officers from the chief priests and the Pharisees, went there with lanterns and
torches and weapons. 4Then Jesus, knowing all that would happen to him, came
forward and said to them, "Whom do you seek?" 5They answered him, "Jesus of
Nazareth." Jesus said to them, "I am he."[5] Judas, who betrayed him, was standing
with them. 6When Jesus[6] said to them, "I am he," they drew back and fell to the

[1] Or *from evil* [2] Greek *Set them apart* (for holy service to God) [3] Or *I sanctify myself*; or *I set myself apart* (for holy service to God) [4] Greek *may be set apart* (for holy service to God) [5] Greek *I am*; also verses 6, 8 [6] Greek *he*

ground. 7So he asked them again, "Whom do you seek?" And they said, "Jesus of Nazareth." 8Jesus answered, "I told you that I am he. So, if you seek me, let these men go." 9This was to fulfill the word that he had spoken: "Of those whom you gave me I have lost not one." 10Then Simon Peter, having a sword, drew it and struck the high priest's servant[1] and cut off his right ear. (The servant's name was Malchus.) 11So Jesus said to Peter, "Put your sword into its sheath; shall I not drink the cup that the Father has given me?"

Jesus Faces Annas and Caiaphas

12So the band of soldiers and their captain and the officers of the Jews[2] arrested Jesus and bound him. 13First they led him to Annas, for he was the father-in-law of Caiaphas, who was high priest that year. 14It was Caiaphas who had advised the Jews that it would be expedient that one man should die for the people.

Peter Denies Jesus

15Simon Peter followed Jesus, and so did another disciple. Since that disciple was known to the high priest, he entered with Jesus into the courtyard of the high priest, 16but Peter stood outside at the door. So the other disciple, who was known to the high priest, went out and spoke to the servant girl who kept watch at the door, and brought Peter in. 17The servant girl at the door said to Peter, "You also are not one of this man's disciples, are you?" He said, "I am not." 18Now the servants[3] and officers had made a charcoal fire, because it was cold, and they were standing and warming themselves. Peter also was with them, standing and warming himself.

The High Priest Questions Jesus

19The high priest then questioned Jesus about his disciples and his teaching. 20Jesus answered him, "I have spoken openly to the world. I have always taught in synagogues and in the temple, where all Jews come together. I have said nothing in secret. 21Why do you ask me? Ask those who have heard me what I said to them; they know what I said." 22When he had said these things, one of the officers standing by struck Jesus with his hand, saying, "Is that how you answer the high priest?" 23Jesus answered him, "If what I said is wrong, bear witness about the wrong; but if what I said is right, why do you strike me?" 24Annas then sent him bound to Caiaphas the high priest.

Peter Denies Jesus Again

25Now Simon Peter was standing and warming himself. So they said to him, "You also are not one of his disciples, are you?" He denied it and said, "I am not." 26One of the servants of the high priest, a relative of the man whose ear Peter had cut off, asked, "Did I not see you in the garden with him?" 27Peter again denied it, and at once a rooster crowed.

Jesus Before Pilate

28Then they led Jesus from the house of Caiaphas to the governor's headquarters.[4] It was early morning. They themselves did not enter the governor's headquarters, so that they would not be defiled, but could eat the Passover. 29So Pilate went outside to them and said, "What accusation do you bring against this man?" 30They answered him, "If this man were not doing evil, we would not have delivered him over to you." 31Pilate said to them, "Take him yourselves and judge him by your own law." The Jews said to him, "It is not lawful for us to put anyone to death." 32This was to fulfill the word that Jesus had spoken to show by what kind of death he was going to die.

---

[1]Or *bondservant*; twice in this verse [2]Greek *Ioudaioi* probably refers here to Jewish religious leaders, and others under their influence, in that time; also verses 14, 31, 36, 38 [3]Or *bondservants*; also verse 26
[4]Greek *the praetorium*

My Kingdom Is Not of This World

33 So Pilate entered his headquarters again and called Jesus and said to him, "Are you the King of the Jews?" 34 Jesus answered, "Do you say this of your own accord, or did others say it to you about me?" 35 Pilate answered, "Am I a Jew? Your own nation and the chief priests have delivered you over to me. What have you done?" 36 Jesus answered, "My kingdom is not of this world. If my kingdom were of this world, my servants would have been fighting, that I might not be delivered over to the Jews. But my kingdom is not from the world." 37 Then Pilate said to him, "So you are a king?" Jesus answered, "You say that I am a king. For this purpose I was born and for this purpose I have come into the world—to bear witness to the truth. Everyone who is of the truth listens to my voice." 38 Pilate said to him, "What is truth?"

After he had said this, he went back outside to the Jews and told them, "I find no guilt in him. 39 But you have a custom that I should release one man for you at the Passover. So do you want me to release to you the King of the Jews?" 40 They cried out again, "Not this man, but Barabbas!" Now Barabbas was a robber.[1]

Jesus Delivered to Be Crucified

19 Then Pilate took Jesus and flogged him. 2 And the soldiers twisted together a crown of thorns and put it on his head and arrayed him in a purple robe. 3 They came up to him, saying, "Hail, King of the Jews!" and struck him with their hands. 4 Pilate went out again and said to them, "See, I am bringing him out to you that you may know that I find no guilt in him." 5 So Jesus came out, wearing the crown of thorns and the purple robe. Pilate said to them, "Behold the man!" 6 When the chief priests and the officers saw him, they cried out, "Crucify him, crucify him!" Pilate said to them, "Take him yourselves and crucify him, for I find no guilt in him." 7 The Jews[2] answered him, "We have a law, and according to that law he ought to die because he has made himself the Son of God." 8 When Pilate heard this statement, he was even more afraid. 9 He entered his headquarters again and said to Jesus, "Where are you from?" But Jesus gave him no answer. 10 So Pilate said to him, "You will not speak to me? Do you not know that I have authority to release you and authority to crucify you?" 11 Jesus answered him, "You would have no authority over me at all unless it had been given you from above. Therefore he who delivered me over to you has the greater sin."

12 From then on Pilate sought to release him, but the Jews cried out, "If you release this man, you are not Caesar's friend. Everyone who makes himself a king opposes Caesar." 13 So when Pilate heard these words, he brought Jesus out and sat down on the judgment seat at a place called The Stone Pavement, and in Aramaic[3] Gabbatha. 14 Now it was the day of Preparation of the Passover. It was about the sixth hour.[4] He said to the Jews, "Behold your King!" 15 They cried out, "Away with him, away with him, crucify him!" Pilate said to them, "Shall I crucify your King?" The chief priests answered, "We have no king but Caesar." 16 So he delivered him over to them to be crucified.

The Crucifixion

So they took Jesus, 17 and he went out, bearing his own cross, to the place called The Place of a Skull, which in Aramaic is called Golgotha. 18 There they crucified him, and with him two others, one on either side, and Jesus between them. 19 Pilate also wrote an inscription and put it on the cross. It read, "Jesus of Nazareth, the King of the Jews." 20 Many of the Jews read this inscription, for the place where Jesus was crucified was near the city, and it was written in Aramaic, in Latin, and in Greek. 21 So the chief priests of the Jews said to Pilate, "Do not write, 'The King of the Jews,' but rather, 'This man said, I am King of the Jews.'" 22 Pilate answered, "What I have written I have written."

---

[1] Or *an insurrectionist* [2] Greek *Ioudaioi* probably refers here to Jewish religious leaders, and others under their influence, in that time; also verses 12, 14, 31, 38 [3] Or *Hebrew*; also verses 17, 20 [4] That is, about noon

23When the soldiers had crucified Jesus, they took his garments and divided them into four parts, one part for each soldier; also his tunic.[1] But the tunic was seamless, woven in one piece from top to bottom, 24so they said to one another, "Let us not tear it, but cast lots for it to see whose it shall be." This was to fulfill the Scripture which says,

"They divided my garments among them,
and for my clothing they cast lots."

So the soldiers did these things, 25but standing by the cross of Jesus were his mother and his mother's sister, Mary the wife of Clopas, and Mary Magdalene. 26When Jesus saw his mother and the disciple whom he loved standing nearby, he said to his mother, "Woman, behold, your son!" 27Then he said to the disciple, "Behold, your mother!" And from that hour the disciple took her to his own home.

The Death of Jesus

28After this, Jesus, knowing that all was now finished, said (to fulfill the Scripture), "I thirst." 29A jar full of sour wine stood there, so they put a sponge full of the sour wine on a hyssop branch and held it to his mouth. 30When Jesus had received the sour wine, he said, "It is finished," and he bowed his head and gave up his spirit.

Jesus' Side Is Pierced

31Since it was the day of Preparation, and so that the bodies would not remain on the cross on the Sabbath (for that Sabbath was a high day), the Jews asked Pilate that their legs might be broken and that they might be taken away. 32So the soldiers came and broke the legs of the first, and of the other who had been crucified with him. 33But when they came to Jesus and saw that he was already dead, they did not break his legs. 34But one of the soldiers pierced his side with a spear, and at once there came out blood and water. 35He who saw it has borne witness—his testimony is true, and he knows that he is telling the truth—that you also may believe. 36For these things took place that the Scripture might be fulfilled: "Not one of his bones will be broken." 37And again another Scripture says, "They will look on him whom they have pierced."

Jesus Is Buried

38After these things Joseph of Arimathea, who was a disciple of Jesus, but secretly for fear of the Jews, asked Pilate that he might take away the body of Jesus, and Pilate gave him permission. So he came and took away his body. 39Nicodemus also, who earlier had come to Jesus[2] by night, came bringing a mixture of myrrh and aloes, about seventy-five pounds[3] in weight. 40So they took the body of Jesus and bound it in linen cloths with the spices, as is the burial custom of the Jews. 41Now in the place where he was crucified there was a garden, and in the garden a new tomb in which no one had yet been laid. 42So because of the Jewish day of Preparation, since the tomb was close at hand, they laid Jesus there.

The Resurrection

20 Now on the first day of the week Mary Magdalene came to the tomb early, while it was still dark, and saw that the stone had been taken away from the tomb. 2So she ran and went to Simon Peter and the other disciple, the one whom Jesus loved, and said to them, "They have taken the Lord out of the tomb, and we do not know where they have laid him." 3So Peter went out with the other disciple, and they were going toward the tomb. 4Both of them were running together, but the other disciple outran Peter and reached the tomb first. 5And stooping to look in, he saw the linen cloths lying there, but he did not go in. 6Then Simon Peter came, following him, and went into the tomb. He saw the linen cloths

[1]Greek *chiton*, a long garment worn under the cloak next to the skin [2]Greek *him* [3]Greek *one hundred litras*; a *litra* (or Roman pound) was equal to about 11 1/2 ounces or 327 grams

JOHN 19:30

IT IS FINISHED

"It is finished"—a simple sentence, made of only three simple words, but the significance of this sentence has eternal consequences for billions of people. When Jesus declared, "It is finished," he indicated that his work of salvation was finished; that he had paid the full price for our sins. The cross is about so much more than a man enduring pain and suffering; it is about so much more than a man being abandoned by his friends and family. The cross is about Jesus, the eternal Son of God, being forsaken by his Father. Jesus, who had forever been one with the Father, was willing to come to earth and identify with sinners like us. He was even willing to become our sin (2Co 5:21), so that on the cross he could die in our place. On the cross, the hellish punishment that we deserved was placed on him; he willingly endured God's wrath in order to set us free.

The prophet Isaiah says of him, "You who have drunk from the hand of the LORD the cup of his wrath, who have drunk to the dregs the bowl, the cup of staggering" (Isa 51:17)—this is what Jesus did on the cross for everyone who believes in him. Our sins have been paid for, and the work of redemption is, gloriously, "finished"!

lying there, 7and the face cloth, which had been on Jesus'[1] head, not lying with the linen cloths but folded up in a place by itself. 8Then the other disciple, who had reached the tomb first, also went in, and he saw and believed; 9for as yet they did not understand the Scripture, that he must rise from the dead. 10Then the disciples went back to their homes.

Jesus Appears to Mary Magdalene

11But Mary stood weeping outside the tomb, and as she wept she stooped to look into the tomb. 12And she saw two angels in white, sitting where the body of Jesus had lain, one at the head and one at the feet. 13They said to her, "Woman, why are you weeping?" She said to them, "They have taken away my Lord, and I do not know where they have laid him." 14Having said this, she turned around and saw Jesus standing, but she did not know that it was Jesus. 15Jesus said to her, "Woman, why are you weeping? Whom are you seeking?" Supposing him to be the gardener, she said to him, "Sir, if you have carried him away, tell me where you have laid him, and I will take him away." 16Jesus said to her, "Mary." She turned and said to him in Aramaic,[2] "Rabboni!" (which means Teacher). 17Jesus said to her, "Do not cling to me, for I have not yet ascended to the Father; but go to my brothers and say to them, 'I am ascending to my Father and your Father, to my God and your God.'" 18Mary Magdalene went and announced to the disciples, "I have seen the Lord"—and that he had said these things to her.

Jesus Appears to the Disciples

19On the evening of that day, the first day of the week, the doors being locked where the disciples were for fear of the Jews,[3] Jesus came and stood among them and said to them, "Peace be with you." 20When he had said this, he showed them his hands and his side. Then the disciples were glad when they saw the Lord. 21Jesus said to them again, "Peace be with you. As the Father has sent me, even so I am sending you." 22And when he had said this, he breathed on them and said to them, "Receive the Holy Spirit. 23If you forgive the sins of any, they are forgiven them; if you withhold forgiveness from any, it is withheld."

Jesus and Thomas

24Now Thomas, one of the twelve, called the Twin,[4] was not with them when Jesus came. 25So the other disciples told him, "We have seen the Lord." But he said to them, "Unless I see in his hands the mark of the nails, and place my finger into the mark of the nails, and place my hand into his side, I will never believe."

26Eight days later, his disciples were inside again, and Thomas was with them. Although the doors were locked, Jesus came and stood among them and said, "Peace be with you." 27Then he said to Thomas, "Put your finger here, and see my hands; and put out your hand, and place it in my side. Do not disbelieve, but believe." 28Thomas answered him, "My Lord and my God!" 29Jesus said to him, "Have you believed because you have seen me? Blessed are those who have not seen and yet have believed."

The Purpose of This Book

30Now Jesus did many other signs in the presence of the disciples, which are not written in this book; 31but these are written so that you may believe that Jesus is the Christ, the Son of God, and that by believing you may have life in his name.

Jesus Appears to Seven Disciples

21 After this Jesus revealed himself again to the disciples by the Sea of Tiberias, and he revealed himself in this way. 2Simon Peter, Thomas (called the Twin), Nathanael of Cana in Galilee, the sons of Zebedee, and two others of his

[1]Greek *his* [2]Or *Hebrew* [3]Greek *Ioudaioi* probably refers here to Jewish religious leaders, and others under their influence, in that time [4]Greek *Didymus*

THE POWER OF THE RESURRECTION

In many of the accounts of Jesus' resurrection, people who saw him had a difficult time recognizing him. Before he spoke her name (v. 16), Mary thought Jesus was the gardener (vv. 14 – 15); the disciples had difficulty recognizing Jesus on the shore (Jn 21:4); and the men on the road to Emmaus did not realize they were talking to Jesus (Lk 24:15 – 16). In these resurrection accounts, all of the people ultimately do recognize Jesus. Yet there is something different about him, some new quality that makes his appearance different from what it was before his arrest and crucifixion. This is helpful for us as we seek to understand our own resurrection in Christ.

The ultimate hope of the believer is not heaven, but the new heavens and new earth, of which Jesus emphatically says, "I am making all things new" (Rev 21:5). The essence of the word "new" in that phrase is not "different," or "new" in terms of time, but rather "new" in terms of quality. One day Jesus will make all things that do exist new or better, fuller, more complete; this is certainly resurrection language.

In other words, the ultimate hope of the believer is the resurrection — when God will do for us and for all creation what he did for Jesus on Easter. The resurrected Jesus was still the same Jesus who had lived for more than thirty-three years and worked among the disciples for more than three years, but he was changed; he was "new," he was more, he was resurrected.

Paul gives us an exciting glimpse of this coming reality (1Co 15:42 – 44,49 – 54). God's plans for his people in Christ are so good. The sure hope that believers have is that, one day, the whole creation will be made new, and all will be made right. God himself will dwell among his people, and he will wipe every tear from their eyes. More than that, there will be no more death or mourning or crying or pain (Rev 21:4).

In the new heavens and new earth, Jesus will reign fully and forever, and everything will be as it should be. There will be no sin and no possibility of sin, and believers will finally live the lives God had designed them to live from the beginning of time. So as believers think back to the glorious resurrection of Christ, it also becomes a reminder of the future resurrection in Christ.

disciples were together. 3 Simon Peter said to them, "I am going fishing." They said to him, "We will go with you." They went out and got into the boat, but that night they caught nothing.

4 Just as day was breaking, Jesus stood on the shore; yet the disciples did not know that it was Jesus. 5 Jesus said to them, "Children, do you have any fish?" They answered him, "No." 6 He said to them, "Cast the net on the right side of the boat, and you will find some." So they cast it, and now they were not able to haul it in, because of the quantity of fish. 7 That disciple whom Jesus loved therefore said to Peter, "It is the Lord!" When Simon Peter heard that it was the Lord, he put on his outer garment, for he was stripped for work, and threw himself into the sea. 8 The other disciples came in the boat, dragging the net full of fish, for they were not far from the land, but about a hundred yards[1] off.

9 When they got out on land, they saw a charcoal fire in place, with fish laid out on it, and bread. 10 Jesus said to them, "Bring some of the fish that you have just caught." 11 So Simon Peter went aboard and hauled the net ashore, full of large fish, 153 of them. And although there were so many, the net was not torn. 12 Jesus said to them, "Come and have breakfast." Now none of the disciples dared ask him, "Who are you?" They knew it was the Lord. 13 Jesus came and took the bread and gave it to them, and so with the fish. 14 This was now the third time that Jesus was revealed to the disciples after he was raised from the dead.

Jesus and Peter

15 When they had finished breakfast, Jesus said to Simon Peter, "Simon, son of John, do you love me more than these?" He said to him, "Yes, Lord; you know that I love you." He said to him, "Feed my lambs." 16 He said to him a second time, "Simon, son of John, do you love me?" He said to him, "Yes, Lord; you know that I love you." He said to him, "Tend my sheep." 17 He said to him the third time, "Simon, son of John, do you love me?" Peter was grieved because he said to him the third time, "Do you love me?" and he said to him, "Lord, you know everything; you know that I love you." Jesus said to him, "Feed my sheep. 18 Truly, truly, I say to you, when you were young, you used to dress yourself and walk wherever you wanted, but when you are old, you will stretch out your hands, and another will dress you and carry you where you do not want to go." 19 (This he said to show by what kind of death he was to glorify God.) And after saying this he said to him, "Follow me."

Jesus and the Beloved Apostle

20 Peter turned and saw the disciple whom Jesus loved following them, the one who also had leaned back against him during the supper and had said, "Lord, who is it that is going to betray you?" 21 When Peter saw him, he said to Jesus, "Lord, what about this man?" 22 Jesus said to him, "If it is my will that he remain until I come, what is that to you? You follow me!" 23 So the saying spread abroad among the brothers[2] that this disciple was not to die; yet Jesus did not say to him that he was not to die, but, "If it is my will that he remain until I come, what is that to you?"

24 This is the disciple who is bearing witness about these things, and who has written these things, and we know that his testimony is true.

25 Now there are also many other things that Jesus did. Were every one of them to be written, I suppose that the world itself could not contain the books that would be written.

JOHN 21:15–19

TRUE LOVE

Even though the disciples had seen the resurrected Jesus, they did not really know what they were supposed to do next. For three years they had been following Jesus and carrying out his ministry, but now Jesus was not with them on a regular basis. That being the case, it only made sense for the disciples to return to what they knew: fishing.

Peter, in particular, had not seen Jesus for more than a few moments since he had denied knowing him three times in Jesus' hour of greatest need (Mt 26:69–75; Lk 22:54–62; Jn 18:15–27). Usually when a person knows that they have hurt someone, or done something to wrong someone, they are not eager to see that person. Yet Peter was so confident in Jesus' love and forgiveness that as soon as he realized it was Jesus standing on the shore, he jumped from the boat and swam to shore so that he could be face to face with his Lord. There Jesus lovingly and gently reinstated his bold disciple and went on to use him greatly for the sake of his kingdom. This story reminds all believers that those who repent of the pain they have caused Jesus and others in the past can have full confidence that his arms of grace are open to all who are willing to run into them.

[1] Greek *two hundred cubits*; a *cubit* was about 18 inches or 45 centimeters [2] Or *brothers and sisters*

JESUS: OUR CONTINUED MISSION

ACTS

ACTS

PENTECOST c. *AD 30 – 35*	PAUL'S MISSIONARY JOURNEYS c. *AD 47 – 57*	PAUL IMPRISONED IN ROME c. *AD 60 – 62*

The news of Jesus cannot be stopped. Beginning with a fledgling band of disciples, the transforming message of hope offered by Jesus would spread from Jerusalem to Rome in less than 35 years. The leaders of Jesus' day assumed his death would forever stamp out his claims. In God-sized irony, Jesus' death only fueled the spread of this message because he did not remain dead but defeated death through his glorious resurrection.

The resurrected Christ forever changed those who witnessed these events. They trusted that he would send them his Spirit to empower them for the mission that lay ahead (2:1 – 4). At Pentecost, the Spirit came in might and power and established the church that will prevail over the gates of Hades for all time (Mt 16:18). Peter's sermon following the sending of the Spirit made it clear that this miracle was the fulfillment of God's promises and further validated the claims of Jesus to be God's Messiah and the Savior of the world.

Luke provides Theophilus and all subsequent readers with a glimpse into the culture of this young church. Those who trusted Jesus gathered together in teaching, singing, prayer, fellowship, and shared meals. By the power of God, many placed their faith in Christ and were added to the church (Ac 2:42 – 47).

The church would never permanently escape the fires of persecution, but through this opposition the church would continue to spread. The stoning of Stephen in Acts 8 scattered believers throughout the known world, and with them went God's Spirit and the message of the gospel. These displaced believers established churches and invited the inhabitants of new cities to place their faith in Christ.

A primary catalyst for the spread of the gospel was the conversion of Saul, a vehement persecutor of the church (9:1 – 22). God revealed himself in a blinding flash of light and altered Saul's fate forever. Saul began to be called Paul (Ac 13:9). Paul's subsequent mission work focused on the Gentiles and is central to the later portion of Luke's writing in the book of Acts. Luke describes Paul's three chief missionary journeys, his labor among the churches, and the countless obstacles he faced in his mission. Through it all, however, God continued to show himself faithful to his promise to build his church and use his people in that grand mission.

BUT YOU WILL RECEIVE POWER WHEN
THE HOLY SPIRIT HAS COME UPON YOU,
AND YOU WILL BE MY WITNESSES IN JERUSALEM
AND IN ALL JUDEA AND SAMARIA,
AND TO THE END OF THE EARTH.

Acts 1:8

ACTS

The Promise of the Holy Spirit

1 In the first book, O Theophilus, I have dealt with all that Jesus began to do
and teach, 2until the day when he was taken up, after he had given commands
through the Holy Spirit to the apostles whom he had chosen. 3He presented himself alive to them after his suffering by many proofs, appearing to them during
forty days and speaking about the kingdom of God.
4And while staying[1] with them he ordered them not to depart from Jerusalem,
but to wait for the promise of the Father, which, he said, "you heard from me; 5for
John baptized with water, but you will be baptized with[2] the Holy Spirit not many
days from now."

The Ascension

6So when they had come together, they asked him, "Lord, will you at this time
restore the kingdom to Israel?" 7He said to them, "It is not for you to know times
or seasons that the Father has fixed by his own authority. 8But you will receive
power when the Holy Spirit has come upon you, and you will be my witnesses in
Jerusalem and in all Judea and Samaria, and to the end of the earth." 9And when
he had said these things, as they were looking on, he was lifted up, and a cloud
took him out of their sight. 10And while they were gazing into heaven as he went,
behold, two men stood by them in white robes, 11and said, "Men of Galilee, why
do you stand looking into heaven? This Jesus, who was taken up from you into
heaven, will come in the same way as you saw him go into heaven."

Matthias Chosen to Replace Judas

12Then they returned to Jerusalem from the mount called Olivet, which is near
Jerusalem, a Sabbath day's journey away. 13And when they had entered, they went
up to the upper room, where they were staying, Peter and John and James and Andrew, Philip and Thomas, Bartholomew and Matthew, James the son of Alphaeus
and Simon the Zealot and Judas the son of James. 14All these with one accord were
devoting themselves to prayer, together with the women and Mary the mother of
Jesus, and his brothers.[3]
15In those days Peter stood up among the brothers (the company of persons
was in all about 120) and said, 16"Brothers, the Scripture had to be fulfilled, which
the Holy Spirit spoke beforehand by the mouth of David concerning Judas, who
became a guide to those who arrested Jesus. 17For he was numbered among us and
was allotted his share in this ministry." 18(Now this man acquired a field with the
reward of his wickedness, and falling headlong[4] he burst open in the middle and
all his bowels gushed out. 19And it became known to all the inhabitants of Jerusalem, so that the field was called in their own language Akeldama, that is, Field of
Blood.) 20"For it is written in the Book of Psalms,

"'May his camp become desolate,
and let there be no one to dwell in it';

and

"'Let another take his office.'

21So one of the men who have accompanied us during all the time that the Lord
Jesus went in and out among us, 22beginning from the baptism of John until the

---

ACTS 1:5–8

EMPOWERED BY THE SPIRIT

Central to the book of Acts is the role the Holy Spirit plays in advancing the church. Prior to beginning their earthly mission, Jesus instructed his followers to wait until he sent his Spirit, who would supply the power behind the task that lay ahead. This mission would necessitate such power. It was massive—this small group of disciples were instructed to take the good news of Jesus to the very ends of the earth. One wonders what thoughts played in the minds of these first followers of Jesus. Were they afraid? Certainly. Did they understand all that was ahead? Certainly not. Yet they trusted God. Verse 8 serves as an outline of the book of Acts, as Luke describes the faith-filled mission of this group to spread the gospel in Jerusalem, then Judea and Samaria, and then to the ends of the known world of that day. The very same Spirit that empowered the disciples for this great mission is the Spirit who indwells all followers of Jesus (Lk 11:13; Gal 3:14; Eph 1:13–14). He propels ordinary disciples to do extraordinary things through the power only God can supply.

---

[1]Or *eating* [2]Or *in* [3]Or *brothers and sisters*. In New Testament usage, depending on the context, the plural Greek word *adelphoi* (translated "brothers") may refer either to *brothers* or to *brothers and sisters*; also verse 15 [4]Or *swelling up*

day when he was taken up from us—one of these men must become with us a witness to his resurrection." 23And they put forward two, Joseph called Barsabbas, who was also called Justus, and Matthias. 24And they prayed and said, "You, Lord, who know the hearts of all, show which one of these two you have chosen 25to take the place in this ministry and apostleship from which Judas turned aside to go to his own place." 26And they cast lots for them, and the lot fell on Matthias, and he was numbered with the eleven apostles.

The Coming of the Holy Spirit

2 When the day of Pentecost arrived, they were all together in one place. 2And suddenly there came from heaven a sound like a mighty rushing wind, and it filled the entire house where they were sitting. 3And divided tongues as of fire appeared to them and rested[1] on each one of them. 4And they were all filled with the Holy Spirit and began to speak in other tongues as the Spirit gave them utterance.

5Now there were dwelling in Jerusalem Jews, devout men from every nation under heaven. 6And at this sound the multitude came together, and they were bewildered, because each one was hearing them speak in his own language. 7And they were amazed and astonished, saying, "Are not all these who are speaking Galileans? 8And how is it that we hear, each of us in his own native language? 9Parthians and Medes and Elamites and residents of Mesopotamia, Judea and Cappadocia, Pontus and Asia, 10Phrygia and Pamphylia, Egypt and the parts of Libya belonging to Cyrene, and visitors from Rome, 11both Jews and proselytes, Cretans and Arabians—we hear them telling in our own tongues the mighty works of God." 12And all were amazed and perplexed, saying to one another, "What does this mean?" 13But others mocking said, "They are filled with new wine."

Peter's Sermon at Pentecost

14But Peter, standing with the eleven, lifted up his voice and addressed them: "Men of Judea and all who dwell in Jerusalem, let this be known to you, and give ear to my words. 15For these people are not drunk, as you suppose, since it is only the third hour of the day.[2] 16But this is what was uttered through the prophet Joel:

17 " 'And in the last days it shall be, God declares,
that I will pour out my Spirit on all flesh,
and your sons and your daughters shall prophesy,
and your young men shall see visions,
and your old men shall dream dreams;
18 even on my male servants and female servants
in those days I will pour out my Spirit, and they shall prophesy.
19 And I will show wonders in the heavens above
and signs on the earth below,
blood, and fire, and vapor of smoke;
20 the sun shall be turned to darkness
and the moon to blood,
before the day of the Lord comes, the great and magnificent day.
21 And it shall come to pass that everyone who calls upon the name of the Lord
shall be saved.'

22"Men of Israel, hear these words: Jesus of Nazareth, a man attested to you by God with mighty works and wonders and signs that God did through him in your midst, as you yourselves know— 23this Jesus,[3] delivered up according to the definite plan and foreknowledge of God, you crucified and killed by the hands of

[1]Or *And tongues as of fire appeared to them, distributed among them, and rested* [2]That is, 9 A.M.
[3]Greek *this one*

ACTS 2:14–21

THE SPIRIT AND THE OLD TESTAMENT

Peter quoted the prophet Joel to explain the supernatural phenomenon of Pentecost. Joel predicted that an outpouring of God's Spirit would come on the young and the old, on men and women alike, as a sign of God's commitment to deliver those "who [call] on the name of the LORD" (Joel 2:32). Joel explained that those who oppressed God's people and those who refused to repent would be judged, yet the opportunity to be saved was—and still is—clearly offered. Given the context of Joel's proclamation then, it seems that the author (Luke) also uses this passage to underscore the assuring message of salvation for those who believe. In sum, Peter's speech makes clear the idea that Jesus is the long-awaited Messiah who fulfills the prophecies of old, who issues the anticipated outpouring of God's Spirit on his people, and who offers salvation from judgment to any and all who will repent and follow Christ.

lawless men. 24God raised him up, loosing the pangs of death, because it was not
possible for him to be held by it. 25For David says concerning him,

"'I saw the Lord always before me,
for he is at my right hand that I may not be shaken;
26 therefore my heart was glad, and my tongue rejoiced;
my flesh also will dwell in hope.
27 For you will not abandon my soul to Hades,
or let your Holy One see corruption.
28 You have made known to me the paths of life;
you will make me full of gladness with your presence.'

29"Brothers, I may say to you with confidence about the patriarch David that
he both died and was buried, and his tomb is with us to this day. 30Being therefore a prophet, and knowing that God had sworn with an oath to him that he
would set one of his descendants on his throne, 31he foresaw and spoke about
the resurrection of the Christ, that he was not abandoned to Hades, nor did his
flesh see corruption. 32This Jesus God raised up, and of that we all are witnesses.
33Being therefore exalted at the right hand of God, and having received from the
Father the promise of the Holy Spirit, he has poured out this that you yourselves
are seeing and hearing. 34For David did not ascend into the heavens, but he himself says,

"'The Lord said to my Lord,
"Sit at my right hand,
35 until I make your enemies your footstool."'

36Let all the house of Israel therefore know for certain that God has made him
both Lord and Christ, this Jesus whom you crucified."
37Now when they heard this they were cut to the heart, and said to Peter
and the rest of the apostles, "Brothers, what shall we do?" 38And Peter said to
them, "Repent and be baptized every one of you in the name of Jesus Christ for
the forgiveness of your sins, and you will receive the gift of the Holy Spirit. 39For
the promise is for you and for your children and for all who are far off, everyone whom the Lord our God calls to himself." 40And with many other words he
bore witness and continued to exhort them, saying, "Save yourselves from this
crooked generation." 41So those who received his word were baptized, and there
were added that day about three thousand souls.

The Fellowship of the Believers

42And they devoted themselves to the apostles' teaching and the fellowship,
to the breaking of bread and the prayers. 43And awe[1] came upon every soul, and
many wonders and signs were being done through the apostles. 44And all who
believed were together and had all things in common. 45And they were selling
their possessions and belongings and distributing the proceeds to all, as any had
need. 46And day by day, attending the temple together and breaking bread in their
homes, they received their food with glad and generous hearts, 47praising God
and having favor with all the people. And the Lord added to their number day by
day those who were being saved.

The Lame Beggar Healed

3 Now Peter and John were going up to the temple at the hour of prayer, the
ninth hour.[2] 2And a man lame from birth was being carried, whom they laid
daily at the gate of the temple that is called the Beautiful Gate to ask alms of those
entering the temple. 3Seeing Peter and John about to go into the temple, he asked
to receive alms. 4And Peter directed his gaze at him, as did John, and said, "Look
at us." 5And he fixed his attention on them, expecting to receive something from

[1]Or *fear* [2]That is, 3 P.M.

ACTS 3:1–26

BEARING WITNESS TO JESUS

In Acts 3, Luke focuses on the importance of Jesus' name by documenting the disciples' empowerment to heal people "in the name of Jesus Christ of Nazareth" (3:6). This theme is seen throughout the book as the disciples continue to perform miracles and baptize in Jesus' name, as well as witnessing to and suffering "dishonor for the name" (5:41; 9:16; 10:48; 21:13). Not only is their power to do these things directly sourced from Jesus himself, but also their *purpose* is, unquestionably, to proclaim Jesus' name. The core of discipleship is always centered on the person of Christ, nothing else. The mission is always to know Jesus and to make him known. Jesus' disciples give, serve, heal, witness, are empowered, and live for Jesus—not for their own glory, but to bring glory and honor to his name above all others (Ac 4:12; Php 2:9–11; Rev 15:4).

them. 6But Peter said, "I have no silver and gold, but what I do have I give to you.
In the name of Jesus Christ of Nazareth, rise up and walk!" 7And he took him by
the right hand and raised him up, and immediately his feet and ankles were made
strong. 8And leaping up, he stood and began to walk, and entered the temple with
them, walking and leaping and praising God. 9And all the people saw him walking
and praising God, 10and recognized him as the one who sat at the Beautiful Gate
of the temple, asking for alms. And they were filled with wonder and amazement
at what had happened to him.

Peter Speaks in Solomon's Portico

11While he clung to Peter and John, all the people, utterly astounded, ran together to them in the portico called Solomon's. 12And when Peter saw it he addressed the people: "Men of Israel, why do you wonder at this, or why do you
stare at us, as though by our own power or piety we have made him walk? 13The
God of Abraham, the God of Isaac, and the God of Jacob, the God of our fathers,
glorified his servant[1] Jesus, whom you delivered over and denied in the presence
of Pilate, when he had decided to release him. 14But you denied the Holy and Righteous One, and asked for a murderer to be granted to you, 15and you killed the
Author of life, whom God raised from the dead. To this we are witnesses. 16And
his name—by faith in his name—has made this man strong whom you see and
know, and the faith that is through Jesus[2] has given the man this perfect health in
the presence of you all.

17"And now, brothers, I know that you acted in ignorance, as did also your
rulers. 18But what God foretold by the mouth of all the prophets, that his Christ
would suffer, he thus fulfilled. 19Repent therefore, and turn back, that your sins
may be blotted out, 20that times of refreshing may come from the presence of the
Lord, and that he may send the Christ appointed for you, Jesus, 21whom heaven
must receive until the time for restoring all the things about which God spoke by
the mouth of his holy prophets long ago. 22Moses said, 'The Lord God will raise up
for you a prophet like me from your brothers. You shall listen to him in whatever
he tells you. 23And it shall be that every soul who does not listen to that prophet
shall be destroyed from the people.' 24And all the prophets who have spoken,
from Samuel and those who came after him, also proclaimed these days. 25You
are the sons of the prophets and of the covenant that God made with your fathers,
saying to Abraham, 'And in your offspring shall all the families of the earth be
blessed.' 26God, having raised up his servant, sent him to you first, to bless you by
turning every one of you from your wickedness."

Peter and John Before the Council

4 And as they were speaking to the people, the priests and the captain of the
temple and the Sadducees came upon them, 2greatly annoyed because they
were teaching the people and proclaiming in Jesus the resurrection from the dead.
3And they arrested them and put them in custody until the next day, for it was
already evening. 4But many of those who had heard the word believed, and the
number of the men came to about five thousand.

5On the next day their rulers and elders and scribes gathered together in
Jerusalem, 6with Annas the high priest and Caiaphas and John and Alexander,
and all who were of the high-priestly family. 7And when they had set them in
the midst, they inquired, "By what power or by what name did you do this?"
8Then Peter, filled with the Holy Spirit, said to them, "Rulers of the people
and elders, 9if we are being examined today concerning a good deed done to
a crippled man, by what means this man has been healed, 10let it be known
to all of you and to all the people of Israel that by the name of Jesus Christ of
Nazareth, whom you crucified, whom God raised from the dead—by him this

[1]Or *child*; also verse 26 [2]Greek *him*

man is standing before you well. 11This Jesus[1] is the stone that was rejected by
you, the builders, which has become the cornerstone.[2] 12And there is salvation
in no one else, for there is no other name under heaven given among men[3] by
which we must be saved."
13Now when they saw the boldness of Peter and John, and perceived that they
were uneducated, common men, they were astonished. And they recognized that
they had been with Jesus. 14But seeing the man who was healed standing beside
them, they had nothing to say in opposition. 15But when they had commanded
them to leave the council, they conferred with one another, 16saying, "What shall
we do with these men? For that a notable sign has been performed through them
is evident to all the inhabitants of Jerusalem, and we cannot deny it. 17But in order
that it may spread no further among the people, let us warn them to speak no
more to anyone in this name." 18So they called them and charged them not to
speak or teach at all in the name of Jesus. 19But Peter and John answered them,
"Whether it is right in the sight of God to listen to you rather than to God, you
must judge, 20for we cannot but speak of what we have seen and heard." 21And
when they had further threatened them, they let them go, finding no way to punish them, because of the people, for all were praising God for what had happened.
22For the man on whom this sign of healing was performed was more than forty
years old.

The Believers Pray for Boldness

23When they were released, they went to their friends and reported what the
chief priests and the elders had said to them. 24And when they heard it, they lifted
their voices together to God and said, "Sovereign Lord, who made the heaven and
the earth and the sea and everything in them, 25who through the mouth of our
father David, your servant,[4] said by the Holy Spirit,

"'Why did the Gentiles rage,
    and the peoples plot in vain?
26 The kings of the earth set themselves,
    and the rulers were gathered together,
    against the Lord and against his Anointed'[5]—

27for truly in this city there were gathered together against your holy servant
Jesus, whom you anointed, both Herod and Pontius Pilate, along with the Gentiles
and the peoples of Israel, 28to do whatever your hand and your plan had predestined to take place. 29And now, Lord, look upon their threats and grant to your
servants to continue to speak your word with all boldness, 30while you stretch
out your hand to heal, and signs and wonders are performed through the name
of your holy servant Jesus." 31And when they had prayed, the place in which they
were gathered together was shaken, and they were all filled with the Holy Spirit
and continued to speak the word of God with boldness.

They Had Everything in Common

32Now the full number of those who believed were of one heart and soul, and
no one said that any of the things that belonged to him was his own, but they
had everything in common. 33And with great power the apostles were giving their
testimony to the resurrection of the Lord Jesus, and great grace was upon them all.
34There was not a needy person among them, for as many as were owners of lands
or houses sold them and brought the proceeds of what was sold 35and laid it at the
apostles' feet, and it was distributed to each as any had need. 36Thus Joseph, who
was also called by the apostles Barnabas (which means son of encouragement),
a Levite, a native of Cyprus, 37sold a field that belonged to him and brought the
money and laid it at the apostles' feet.

[1]Greek *This one* [2]Greek *the head of the corner* [3]The Greek word *anthropoi* refers here to both men and women [4]Or *child*; also verses 27, 30 [5]Or *Christ*

ACTS 4:32

UNITY

It is difficult to overstate the importance of unity among believers. Unity was one of the most obvious characteristics of the early church (Ac 2:42), and at least in part led to the remarkably effective spread of the gospel. And, as this verse indicates, unity played an important role in providing holistic provision for all the believers' needs. Jesus himself emphasized the importance of unity when he said, "By this all people will know that you are my disciples, if you have love for one another" (Jn 13:35).

Still today believers must consistently and intentionally prioritize unity. It is the most obvious means to meet each other's needs (spiritually, economically, and socially), to demonstrate God's love to an unbelieving world, and to facilitate harmony and peace. Psalm 133:1 says it best: "How good and pleasant it is when brothers dwell in unity!"

SALVATION IN NO ONE ELSE

God created the world to display his glory to all creation. The Garden of Eden was the first temple of God, where God showed his glory and lived with his people. The first humans, Adam and Eve, rebelled against God, even after he gave them directives about what would harm them. They chose to doubt God's goodness, failed to trust him, and acted against God in disobedience, but God showed his glory by being patient with them. He provided consequences for their sin, but he promised deliverance as well. Immediately after their punishment was enacted, God promised to send a Savior to fix the relationship between himself and his people (Ge 3:15). He would have been justified in letting his creation degrade in its sin and collapse into confusion. And yet, he showed his glory in being patient with his people.

As part of his eternal, perfect nature, God makes and keeps his promises. Time and time again throughout the Old Testament, God made promises to his people and delivered on those promises (Jos 21:45). Whenever God's people fell into trouble, God's heart was to bring them out, restore them, and commission them to live as his people once again.

The great saving event of the Old Testament was the exodus. God's people were bound in physical slavery in Egypt, and God sent a deliverer named Moses to bring them out. Once they were set free, God himself, not some ill-defined deity that operated in obscurity, renewed the covenant promises he had made with Israel's ancestors Abram (Ge 15:1 – 20), Isaac (Ge 26:2 – 5), and Jacob (Ge 28:13 – 15) and gave them his law and taught them how to live.

God wants to show his glory in this world by saving sinners. The entire Bible, from cover to cover, tells the one story of God's desire to save sinners from their sin. God kept all of his promises by sending Jesus to die for sinners and then rise again from the dead. Jesus was the true and better Moses, the ultimate liberator who broke people out of the ultimate form of bondage — slavery to sin and death.

Ananias and Sapphira

5 But a man named Ananias, with his wife Sapphira, sold a piece of property, 2 and with his wife's knowledge he kept back for himself some of the proceeds and brought only a part of it and laid it at the apostles' feet. 3 But Peter said, "Ananias, why has Satan filled your heart to lie to the Holy Spirit and to keep back for yourself part of the proceeds of the land? 4 While it remained unsold, did it not remain your own? And after it was sold, was it not at your disposal? Why is it that you have contrived this deed in your heart? You have not lied to man but to God." 5 When Ananias heard these words, he fell down and breathed his last. And great fear came upon all who heard of it. 6 The young men rose and wrapped him up and carried him out and buried him.

7 After an interval of about three hours his wife came in, not knowing what had happened. 8 And Peter said to her, "Tell me whether you[1] sold the land for so much." And she said, "Yes, for so much." 9 But Peter said to her, "How is it that you have agreed together to test the Spirit of the Lord? Behold, the feet of those who have buried your husband are at the door, and they will carry you out." 10 Immediately she fell down at his feet and breathed her last. When the young men came in they found her dead, and they carried her out and buried her beside her husband. 11 And great fear came upon the whole church and upon all who heard of these things.

Many Signs and Wonders Done

12 Now many signs and wonders were regularly done among the people by the hands of the apostles. And they were all together in Solomon's Portico. 13 None of the rest dared join them, but the people held them in high esteem. 14 And more than ever believers were added to the Lord, multitudes of both men and women, 15 so that they even carried out the sick into the streets and laid them on cots and mats, that as Peter came by at least his shadow might fall on some of them. 16 The people also gathered from the towns around Jerusalem, bringing the sick and those afflicted with unclean spirits, and they were all healed.

The Apostles Arrested and Freed

17 But the high priest rose up, and all who were with him (that is, the party of the Sadducees), and filled with jealousy 18 they arrested the apostles and put them in the public prison. 19 But during the night an angel of the Lord opened the prison doors and brought them out, and said, 20 "Go and stand in the temple and speak to the people all the words of this Life." 21 And when they heard this, they entered the temple at daybreak and began to teach.

Now when the high priest came, and those who were with him, they called together the council, all the senate of the people of Israel, and sent to the prison to have them brought. 22 But when the officers came, they did not find them in the prison, so they returned and reported, 23 "We found the prison securely locked and the guards standing at the doors, but when we opened them we found no one inside." 24 Now when the captain of the temple and the chief priests heard these words, they were greatly perplexed about them, wondering what this would come to. 25 And someone came and told them, "Look! The men whom you put in prison are standing in the temple and teaching the people." 26 Then the captain with the officers went and brought them, but not by force, for they were afraid of being stoned by the people.

27 And when they had brought them, they set them before the council. And the high priest questioned them, 28 saying, "We strictly charged you not to teach in this name, yet here you have filled Jerusalem with your teaching, and you intend to bring this man's blood upon us." 29 But Peter and the apostles answered, "We must obey God rather than men. 30 The God of our fathers raised Jesus, whom you killed by hanging him on a tree. 31 God exalted him at his right hand as Leader and Savior,

[1] The Greek for *you* is plural here

ACTS 5:1–11

GIVING OUR ALL TO JESUS

The sudden deaths of Ananias and Sapphira are jarring at first glance. After all, the couple voluntarily gave up part of their profits to the church, so what could possibly warrant their deaths? The problem was that they lied about their gift and withheld money for themselves, desiring the status of the large donation and the appearance of radical generosity in the eyes of the apostles and the other members of the church. Furthermore, Peter says that they allowed Satan to fill their hearts (5:3). They lied to the Holy Spirit (5:4), who had filled their community of believers. In the midst of the church's miraculous growth, remarkable unity, and amazing gospel message, Ananias and Sapphira's deceitful plan stood as the antithesis of the church's faith-filled generosity and brotherly love.

The Good Shepherd refuses to tolerate wolves roaming freely among his sheep. In contrast, the preceding story of Barnabas (4:36–37) reveals the greater truth that authentic allegiance to Jesus is characterized by the kind of cheerful generosity that both honors God and cares for his people. May those who follow Jesus be so struck by his worth, so confident of his care, and so committed to his ways that they likewise "seek first the kingdom of God and his righteousness" (Mt 6:33).

to give repentance to Israel and forgiveness of sins. 32And we are witnesses to these things, and so is the Holy Spirit, whom God has given to those who obey him."

33When they heard this, they were enraged and wanted to kill them. 34But a Pharisee in the council named Gamaliel, a teacher of the law held in honor by all the people, stood up and gave orders to put the men outside for a little while. 35And he said to them, "Men of Israel, take care what you are about to do with these men. 36For before these days Theudas rose up, claiming to be somebody, and a number of men, about four hundred, joined him. He was killed, and all who followed him were dispersed and came to nothing. 37After him Judas the Galilean rose up in the days of the census and drew away some of the people after him. He too perished, and all who followed him were scattered. 38So in the present case I tell you, keep away from these men and let them alone, for if this plan or this undertaking is of man, it will fail; 39but if it is of God, you will not be able to overthrow them. You might even be found opposing God!" So they took his advice, 40and when they had called in the apostles, they beat them and charged them not to speak in the name of Jesus, and let them go. 41Then they left the presence of the council, rejoicing that they were counted worthy to suffer dishonor for the name. 42And every day, in the temple and from house to house, they did not cease teaching and preaching that the Christ is Jesus.

Seven Chosen to Serve

6 Now in these days when the disciples were increasing in number, a complaint by the Hellenists[1] arose against the Hebrews because their widows were being neglected in the daily distribution. 2And the twelve summoned the full number of the disciples and said, "It is not right that we should give up preaching the word of God to serve tables. 3Therefore, brothers,[2] pick out from among you seven men of good repute, full of the Spirit and of wisdom, whom we will appoint to this duty. 4But we will devote ourselves to prayer and to the ministry of the word." 5And what they said pleased the whole gathering, and they chose Stephen, a man full of faith and of the Holy Spirit, and Philip, and Prochorus, and Nicanor, and Timon, and Parmenas, and Nicolaus, a proselyte of Antioch. 6These they set before the apostles, and they prayed and laid their hands on them.

7And the word of God continued to increase, and the number of the disciples multiplied greatly in Jerusalem, and a great many of the priests became obedient to the faith.

Stephen Is Seized

8And Stephen, full of grace and power, was doing great wonders and signs among the people. 9Then some of those who belonged to the synagogue of the Freedmen (as it was called), and of the Cyrenians, and of the Alexandrians, and of those from Cilicia and Asia, rose up and disputed with Stephen. 10But they could not withstand the wisdom and the Spirit with which he was speaking. 11Then they secretly instigated men who said, "We have heard him speak blasphemous words against Moses and God." 12And they stirred up the people and the elders and the scribes, and they came upon him and seized him and brought him before the council, 13and they set up false witnesses who said, "This man never ceases to speak words against this holy place and the law, 14for we have heard him say that this Jesus of Nazareth will destroy this place and will change the customs that Moses delivered to us." 15And gazing at him, all who sat in the council saw that his face was like the face of an angel.

Stephen's Speech

7 And the high priest said, "Are these things so?" 2And Stephen said:

"Brothers and fathers, hear me. The God of glory appeared to our father Abraham when he was in Mesopotamia, before he lived in Haran, 3and said to him, 'Go

[1]That is, Greek-speaking Jews [2]Or *brothers and sisters*

ACTS 7:1–53

STEPHEN'S SPEECH

Having been falsely accused of blasphemy, Stephen replied to his accusers by speaking to them about that which they "knew"—the prophecies and teachings of the Old Testament. The crowd was filled with experts on Jewish history and law, yet they failed to understand the significance of the *whole* story. Stephen deftly highlighted what they had long since overlooked: Israel's long history of rejecting God and his prophets, despite God's repeated provision of clear, specific messages through his spokespeople.

Here is a classic example of history forgotten becoming history repeated. What the Jewish leaders had done in the past, they had done again by rejecting Jesus, the ultimate deliverer. This tendency to forget how God has been faithful is all too common among his people. Christians today remember God's goodness by faithfully reading the Scriptures and gathering with other believers. Stephen faithfully bore witness to Jesus as the first Christian martyr because he had this awareness of redemptive history, the embracing presence of Christ, and a personal commitment to remain sensitive to the Holy Spirit.

out from your land and from your kindred and go into the land that I will show
you.’ 4Then he went out from the land of the Chaldeans and lived in Haran. And
after his father died, God removed him from there into this land in which you
are now living. 5Yet he gave him no inheritance in it, not even a foot’s length, but
promised to give it to him as a possession and to his offspring after him, though
he had no child. 6And God spoke to this effect—that his offspring would be sojourners in a land belonging to others, who would enslave them and afflict them
four hundred years. 7‘But I will judge the nation that they serve,’ said God, ‘and
after that they shall come out and worship me in this place.’ 8And he gave him the
covenant of circumcision. And so Abraham became the father of Isaac, and circumcised him on the eighth day, and Isaac became the father of Jacob, and Jacob
of the twelve patriarchs.

9“And the patriarchs, jealous of Joseph, sold him into Egypt; but God was with
him 10and rescued him out of all his afflictions and gave him favor and wisdom
before Pharaoh, king of Egypt, who made him ruler over Egypt and over all his
household. 11Now there came a famine throughout all Egypt and Canaan, and
great affliction, and our fathers could find no food. 12But when Jacob heard that
there was grain in Egypt, he sent out our fathers on their first visit. 13And on the
second visit Joseph made himself known to his brothers, and Joseph’s family became known to Pharaoh. 14And Joseph sent and summoned Jacob his father and
all his kindred, seventy-five persons in all. 15And Jacob went down into Egypt, and
he died, he and our fathers, 16and they were carried back to Shechem and laid in
the tomb that Abraham had bought for a sum of silver from the sons of Hamor
in Shechem.

17“But as the time of the promise drew near, which God had granted to Abraham, the people increased and multiplied in Egypt 18until there arose over Egypt
another king who did not know Joseph. 19He dealt shrewdly with our race and
forced our fathers to expose their infants, so that they would not be kept alive.
20At this time Moses was born; and he was beautiful in God’s sight. And he was
brought up for three months in his father’s house, 21and when he was exposed,
Pharaoh’s daughter adopted him and brought him up as her own son. 22And Moses was instructed in all the wisdom of the Egyptians, and he was mighty in his
words and deeds.

23“When he was forty years old, it came into his heart to visit his brothers, the
children of Israel. 24And seeing one of them being wronged, he defended the oppressed man and avenged him by striking down the Egyptian. 25He supposed that
his brothers would understand that God was giving them salvation by his hand,
but they did not understand. 26And on the following day he appeared to them as
they were quarreling and tried to reconcile them, saying, ‘Men, you are brothers.
Why do you wrong each other?’ 27But the man who was wronging his neighbor
thrust him aside, saying, ‘Who made you a ruler and a judge over us? 28Do you
want to kill me as you killed the Egyptian yesterday?’ 29At this retort Moses fled
and became an exile in the land of Midian, where he became the father of two
sons.

30“Now when forty years had passed, an angel appeared to him in the wilderness of Mount Sinai, in a flame of fire in a bush. 31When Moses saw it, he was
amazed at the sight, and as he drew near to look, there came the voice of the
Lord: 32‘I am the God of your fathers, the God of Abraham and of Isaac and of
Jacob.’ And Moses trembled and did not dare to look. 33Then the Lord said to him,
‘Take off the sandals from your feet, for the place where you are standing is holy
ground. 34I have surely seen the affliction of my people who are in Egypt, and have
heard their groaning, and I have come down to deliver them. And now come, I will
send you to Egypt.’

35“This Moses, whom they rejected, saying, ‘Who made you a ruler and a
judge?’—this man God sent as both ruler and redeemer by the hand of the angel
who appeared to him in the bush. 36This man led them out, performing wonders

and signs in Egypt and at the Red Sea and in the wilderness for forty years. [37]This
is the Moses who said to the Israelites, 'God will raise up for you a prophet like me
from your brothers.' [38]This is the one who was in the congregation in the wilderness with the angel who spoke to him at Mount Sinai, and with our fathers. He
received living oracles to give to us. [39]Our fathers refused to obey him, but thrust
him aside, and in their hearts they turned to Egypt, [40]saying to Aaron, 'Make for
us gods who will go before us. As for this Moses who led us out from the land of
Egypt, we do not know what has become of him.' [41]And they made a calf in those
days, and offered a sacrifice to the idol and were rejoicing in the works of their
hands. [42]But God turned away and gave them over to worship the host of heaven,
as it is written in the book of the prophets:

"'Did you bring to me slain beasts and sacrifices,
during the forty years in the wilderness, O house of Israel?
43 You took up the tent of Moloch
and the star of your god Rephan,
the images that you made to worship;
and I will send you into exile beyond Babylon.'

[44]"Our fathers had the tent of witness in the wilderness, just as he who spoke
to Moses directed him to make it, according to the pattern that he had seen. [45]Our
fathers in turn brought it in with Joshua when they dispossessed the nations that
God drove out before our fathers. So it was until the days of David, [46]who found
favor in the sight of God and asked to find a dwelling place for the God of Jacob.[1]
[47]But it was Solomon who built a house for him. [48]Yet the Most High does not
dwell in houses made by hands, as the prophet says,

49 "'Heaven is my throne,
and the earth is my footstool.
What kind of house will you build for me, says the Lord,
or what is the place of my rest?
50 Did not my hand make all these things?'

[51]"You stiff-necked people, uncircumcised in heart and ears, you always resist the Holy Spirit. As your fathers did, so do you. [52]Which of the prophets did
your fathers not persecute? And they killed those who announced beforehand
the coming of the Righteous One, whom you have now betrayed and murdered,
[53]you who received the law as delivered by angels and did not keep it."

The Stoning of Stephen

[54]Now when they heard these things they were enraged, and they ground their
teeth at him. [55]But he, full of the Holy Spirit, gazed into heaven and saw the glory
of God, and Jesus standing at the right hand of God. [56]And he said, "Behold, I see
the heavens opened, and the Son of Man standing at the right hand of God." [57]But
they cried out with a loud voice and stopped their ears and rushed together[2] at
him. [58]Then they cast him out of the city and stoned him. And the witnesses laid
down their garments at the feet of a young man named Saul. [59]And as they were
stoning Stephen, he called out, "Lord Jesus, receive my spirit." [60]And falling to his
knees he cried out with a loud voice, "Lord, do not hold this sin against them."
And when he had said this, he fell asleep.

Saul Ravages the Church

8 And Saul approved of his execution.
And there arose on that day a great persecution against the church in Jerusalem, and they were all scattered throughout the regions of Judea and Samaria,
except the apostles. [2]Devout men buried Stephen and made great lamentation

[1]Some manuscripts *for the house of Jacob* [2]Or *rushed with one mind*

ACTS 8:4

PROCLAIMING THE MESSAGE

The early church is well known for caring for one another (i.e., "They were selling their possessions and belongings and distributing the proceeds to all" [2:45]; "There was not a needy person among them" [4:34]), but it is also known for its commitment to boldly preaching the Good News.

Both deeds *and* words defined the early church. But what was the main message? Looking at three of the sermons in Acts (2:14–36; 4:8–22; 13:16–41), the primary points can be summarized as: (1) Through Jesus, the Scriptures are fulfilled. (2) Jesus is the long-awaited Messiah, Savior, and Lord who lived, died, and rose again to new life. (3) Jesus is able to forgive sin and will return again as judge. (4) Repent, believe, and be baptized.

The responsibility for all Christians remains the same: to live in a Christ-like manner, which includes the call to preach the Good News of Jesus to the world (Mt 28:19–20; Mk 16:15; Ac 1:8; 2Co 5:20).

ACTS 8:26–40

USING THE OLD TESTAMENT TO REVEAL JESUS

Because God is unchanging, his plan of salvation has been steadfast since the beginning. The Old Testament is thus the firm foundation for all of redemptive history; it provides the framework for understanding Jesus, which is why the New Testament

(continued on next page)

over him. [3]But Saul was ravaging the church, and entering house after house, he dragged off men and women and committed them to prison.

Philip Proclaims Christ in Samaria

[4]Now those who were scattered went about preaching the word. [5]Philip went down to the city[1] of Samaria and proclaimed to them the Christ. [6]And the crowds with one accord paid attention to what was being said by Philip, when they heard him and saw the signs that he did. [7]For unclean spirits, crying out with a loud voice, came out of many who had them, and many who were paralyzed or lame were healed. [8]So there was much joy in that city.

Simon the Magician Believes

[9]But there was a man named Simon, who had previously practiced magic in the city and amazed the people of Samaria, saying that he himself was somebody great. [10]They all paid attention to him, from the least to the greatest, saying, "This man is the power of God that is called Great." [11]And they paid attention to him because for a long time he had amazed them with his magic. [12]But when they believed Philip as he preached good news about the kingdom of God and the name of Jesus Christ, they were baptized, both men and women. [13]Even Simon himself believed, and after being baptized he continued with Philip. And seeing signs and great miracles[2] performed, he was amazed.

[14]Now when the apostles at Jerusalem heard that Samaria had received the word of God, they sent to them Peter and John, [15]who came down and prayed for them that they might receive the Holy Spirit, [16]for he had not yet fallen on any of them, but they had only been baptized in the name of the Lord Jesus. [17]Then they laid their hands on them and they received the Holy Spirit. [18]Now when Simon saw that the Spirit was given through the laying on of the apostles' hands, he offered them money, [19]saying, "Give me this power also, so that anyone on whom I lay my hands may receive the Holy Spirit." [20]But Peter said to him, "May your silver perish with you, because you thought you could obtain the gift of God with money! [21]You have neither part nor lot in this matter, for your heart is not right before God. [22]Repent, therefore, of this wickedness of yours, and pray to the Lord that, if possible, the intent of your heart may be forgiven you. [23]For I see that you are in the gall[3] of bitterness and in the bond of iniquity." [24]And Simon answered, "Pray for me to the Lord, that nothing of what you have said may come upon me."

[25]Now when they had testified and spoken the word of the Lord, they returned to Jerusalem, preaching the gospel to many villages of the Samaritans.

Philip and the Ethiopian Eunuch

[26]Now an angel of the Lord said to Philip, "Rise and go toward the south[4] to the road that goes down from Jerusalem to Gaza." This is a desert place. [27]And he rose and went. And there was an Ethiopian, a eunuch, a court official of Candace, queen of the Ethiopians, who was in charge of all her treasure. He had come to Jerusalem to worship [28]and was returning, seated in his chariot, and he was reading the prophet Isaiah. [29]And the Spirit said to Philip, "Go over and join this chariot." [30]So Philip ran to him and heard him reading Isaiah the prophet and asked, "Do you understand what you are reading?" [31]And he said, "How can I, unless someone guides me?" And he invited Philip to come up and sit with him. [32]Now the passage of the Scripture that he was reading was this:

"Like a sheep he was led to the slaughter
 and like a lamb before its shearer is silent,
 so he opens not his mouth.

[1]Some manuscripts *a city* [2]Greek *works of power* [3]That is, a bitter fluid secreted by the liver; bile
[4]Or *go at about noon*

33 In his humiliation justice was denied him.
Who can describe his generation?
For his life is taken away from the earth."

34And the eunuch said to Philip, "About whom, I ask you, does the prophet say
this, about himself or about someone else?" 35Then Philip opened his mouth, and
beginning with this Scripture he told him the good news about Jesus. 36And as
they were going along the road they came to some water, and the eunuch said,
"See, here is water! What prevents me from being baptized?"[1] 38And he commanded the chariot to stop, and they both went down into the water, Philip and the eunuch, and he baptized him. 39And when they came up out of the water, the Spirit
of the Lord carried Philip away, and the eunuch saw him no more, and went on his
way rejoicing. 40But Philip found himself at Azotus, and as he passed through he
preached the gospel to all the towns until he came to Caesarea.

The Conversion of Saul

9 But Saul, still breathing threats and murder against the disciples of the
Lord, went to the high priest 2and asked him for letters to the synagogues
at Damascus, so that if he found any belonging to the Way, men or women,
he might bring them bound to Jerusalem. 3Now as he went on his way, he approached Damascus, and suddenly a light from heaven shone around him.
4And falling to the ground, he heard a voice saying to him, "Saul, Saul, why are
you persecuting me?" 5And he said, "Who are you, Lord?" And he said, "I am
Jesus, whom you are persecuting. 6But rise and enter the city, and you will be
told what you are to do." 7The men who were traveling with him stood speechless, hearing the voice but seeing no one. 8Saul rose from the ground, and although his eyes were opened, he saw nothing. So they led him by the hand
and brought him into Damascus. 9And for three days he was without sight, and
neither ate nor drank.

10Now there was a disciple at Damascus named Ananias. The Lord said to him
in a vision, "Ananias." And he said, "Here I am, Lord." 11And the Lord said to him,
"Rise and go to the street called Straight, and at the house of Judas look for a man
of Tarsus named Saul, for behold, he is praying, 12and he has seen in a vision a
man named Ananias come in and lay his hands on him so that he might regain
his sight." 13But Ananias answered, "Lord, I have heard from many about this man,
how much evil he has done to your saints at Jerusalem. 14And here he has authority from the chief priests to bind all who call on your name." 15But the Lord said
to him, "Go, for he is a chosen instrument of mine to carry my name before the
Gentiles and kings and the children of Israel. 16For I will show him how much
he must suffer for the sake of my name." 17So Ananias departed and entered the
house. And laying his hands on him he said, "Brother Saul, the Lord Jesus who appeared to you on the road by which you came has sent me so that you may regain
your sight and be filled with the Holy Spirit." 18And immediately something like
scales fell from his eyes, and he regained his sight. Then he rose and was baptized;
19and taking food, he was strengthened.

Saul Proclaims Jesus in Synagogues

For some days he was with the disciples at Damascus. 20And immediately he
proclaimed Jesus in the synagogues, saying, "He is the Son of God." 21And all who
heard him were amazed and said, "Is not this the man who made havoc in Jerusalem of those who called upon this name? And has he not come here for this
purpose, to bring them bound before the chief priests?" 22But Saul increased all
the more in strength, and confounded the Jews who lived in Damascus by proving
that Jesus was the Christ.

[1]Some manuscripts add all or most of verse 37: *And Philip said, "If you believe with all your heart, you may." And he replied, "I believe that Jesus Christ is the Son of God."*

(Using the Old Testament to Reveal Jesus, continued)

authors took such great pains to quote, allude to, echo, and interpret the Old Testament in their writings. These authors recognized that Jesus' birth and ministry confirmed his identity as the Davidic Messiah in fulfillment of Old Testament prophecy. Furthermore, since many of the early Christians had a strong Jewish background, the New Testament writers were careful to honor their audience as they addressed Jesus' fulfillment of the law and readily drew typological connections between Jesus and Old Testament characters.

Through this rigorous method of harkening back to the ancient Scriptures, the writers highlighted the good news that God has always been faithful to his people, and Jesus has always been the pinnacle of his plan.

SAUL'S CONVERSION

Saul's conversion teaches many truths about how people come to God and what it means to live for God.

As a member of the religious leadership, Saul was actively and vehemently opposed to the work of Jesus and his disciples. He was a staunch follower of the traditions of the Pharisees, which had been developed over time to supplement God's direct revelations to Israel's ancestors. Although many of the rules taught by the Pharisees were intended to help God's people honor God, they very often had the opposite effect: alienating the lowest of society and fostering religious pride. This religious spirit could not accept a crucified Messiah, so Saul refused to believe that Jesus was who he had claimed to be. Therefore, Saul "persecuted the church" violently (Gal 1:13–15) and opposed Christianity with all he had. But even Saul was not beyond God's reach.

Up until the day that God saved him, Saul believed he was advancing God's cause and doing work that would please the Lord. He wasn't scared, and he didn't feel guilty. On the surface, it appeared that he had it all together. He had the right education from the right teachers and was part of the right family (Php 3:1–9). He was on his way, ascending the ranks of the Jewish hierarchy — and then, suddenly, God broke through to him.

God saved Saul by grace, through faith, in Christ. Jesus, who was completely sovereign over Saul's conversion, confronted Saul in his sin. He showed up in a blinding light (Ac 9:3–4), then simply told this suddenly former persecutor what city to go to and what to do (vv. 5–6).

Saul's conversion teaches that the gospel message isn't only for "the right kind of person." Saul was deeply opposed to Jesus and deeply committed to his own path, but none of that stopped God's plan. God works through all kinds of people and situations to bring people to him.

Saul's conversion teaches that coming to Christ is personal and absolutely possible even in the most unlikely situations. Saul was personally changed; he saw his past differently, and he understood his present situation with new eyes. After Jesus' revelation, Saul looked at the future with a changed perspective. For many throughout the centuries and still today, conversion means a radical U-turn, and Jesus Christ himself is the turning point.

Saul Escapes from Damascus

23When many days had passed, the Jews[1] plotted to kill him, 24but their plot became known to Saul. They were watching the gates day and night in order to kill him, 25but his disciples took him by night and let him down through an opening in the wall,[2] lowering him in a basket.

Saul in Jerusalem

26And when he had come to Jerusalem, he attempted to join the disciples. And they were all afraid of him, for they did not believe that he was a disciple. 27But Barnabas took him and brought him to the apostles and declared to them how on the road he had seen the Lord, who spoke to him, and how at Damascus he had preached boldly in the name of Jesus. 28So he went in and out among them at Jerusalem, preaching boldly in the name of the Lord. 29And he spoke and disputed against the Hellenists.[3] But they were seeking to kill him. 30And when the brothers learned this, they brought him down to Caesarea and sent him off to Tarsus.

31So the church throughout all Judea and Galilee and Samaria had peace and was being built up. And walking in the fear of the Lord and in the comfort of the Holy Spirit, it multiplied.

The Healing of Aeneas

32Now as Peter went here and there among them all, he came down also to the saints who lived at Lydda. 33There he found a man named Aeneas, bedridden for eight years, who was paralyzed. 34And Peter said to him, "Aeneas, Jesus Christ heals you; rise and make your bed." And immediately he rose. 35And all the residents of Lydda and Sharon saw him, and they turned to the Lord.

Dorcas Restored to Life

36Now there was in Joppa a disciple named Tabitha, which, translated, means Dorcas.[4] She was full of good works and acts of charity. 37In those days she became ill and died, and when they had washed her, they laid her in an upper room. 38Since Lydda was near Joppa, the disciples, hearing that Peter was there, sent two men to him, urging him, "Please come to us without delay." 39So Peter rose and went with them. And when he arrived, they took him to the upper room. All the widows stood beside him weeping and showing tunics[5] and other garments that Dorcas made while she was with them. 40But Peter put them all outside, and knelt down and prayed; and turning to the body he said, "Tabitha, arise." And she opened her eyes, and when she saw Peter she sat up. 41And he gave her his hand and raised her up. Then, calling the saints and widows, he presented her alive. 42And it became known throughout all Joppa, and many believed in the Lord. 43And he stayed in Joppa for many days with one Simon, a tanner.

Peter and Cornelius

10 At Caesarea there was a man named Cornelius, a centurion of what was known as the Italian Cohort, 2a devout man who feared God with all his household, gave alms generously to the people, and prayed continually to God. 3About the ninth hour of the day[6] he saw clearly in a vision an angel of God come in and say to him, "Cornelius." 4And he stared at him in terror and said, "What is it, Lord?" And he said to him, "Your prayers and your alms have ascended as a memorial before God. 5And now send men to Joppa and bring one Simon who is called Peter. 6He is lodging with one Simon, a tanner, whose house is by the sea." 7When the angel who spoke to him had departed, he called two of his servants

[1]The Greek word *Ioudaioi* refers specifically here to Jewish religious leaders, and others under their influence, who opposed the Christian faith in that time [2]Greek *through the wall* [3]That is, Greek-speaking Jews [4]The Aramaic name *Tabitha* and the Greek name *Dorcas* both mean *gazelle* [5]Greek *chiton*, a long garment worn under the cloak next to the skin [6]That is, 3 P.M.

ACTS 10:1–23

BREAKING BARRIERS

Ethnic divides were deeply ingrained in the culture of first-century Israel. Even Jewish Christians such as Peter thought of themselves as being among God's favorites. This is why a thorough reading of the New Testament, especially noting the literary structure of many of the books, reveals a careful progression in thought to lead the audience out of their biases and into the truth that Jesus came for *all* people. For example, the author (Luke) hints at God's work in non-Jewish nations when he records Stephen's references to God showing up in Mesopotamia (7:2), Haran (7:4), Egypt (7:9), and Sinai (7:38). And it's why the first half of the book of Acts is focused on Peter's ministry to the Jews before widening the lens to incorporate Paul's ministry to the Gentiles.

Quite tactfully, Luke aims to help the eyes of his audience to adjust as he slowly turns one light on at a time, ultimately illuminating the good news that Jesus brought the Gentiles into the kingdom. Luke's choice to repeat the episode of Peter's dream in both chapters 10 and 11, as well as to explain the interaction between Peter and Cornelius, serves to cement the truths that God shows no partiality and that God desires that people from all nations be welcomed into his kingdom (Mt 28:19; Ro 2:11; Gal 3:8; 1Ti 2:4; Rev 15:4).

and a devout soldier from among those who attended him, 8and having related everything to them, he sent them to Joppa.

Peter's Vision

9The next day, as they were on their journey and approaching the city, Peter went up on the housetop about the sixth hour[1] to pray. 10And he became hungry and wanted something to eat, but while they were preparing it, he fell into a trance 11and saw the heavens opened and something like a great sheet descending, being let down by its four corners upon the earth. 12In it were all kinds of animals and reptiles and birds of the air. 13And there came a voice to him: "Rise, Peter; kill and eat." 14But Peter said, "By no means, Lord; for I have never eaten anything that is common or unclean." 15And the voice came to him again a second time, "What God has made clean, do not call common." 16This happened three times, and the thing was taken up at once to heaven.

17Now while Peter was inwardly perplexed as to what the vision that he had seen might mean, behold, the men who were sent by Cornelius, having made inquiry for Simon's house, stood at the gate 18and called out to ask whether Simon who was called Peter was lodging there. 19And while Peter was pondering the vision, the Spirit said to him, "Behold, three men are looking for you. 20Rise and go down and accompany them without hesitation,[2] for I have sent them." 21And Peter went down to the men and said, "I am the one you are looking for. What is the reason for your coming?" 22And they said, "Cornelius, a centurion, an upright and God-fearing man, who is well spoken of by the whole Jewish nation, was directed by a holy angel to send for you to come to his house and to hear what you have to say." 23So he invited them in to be his guests.

The next day he rose and went away with them, and some of the brothers from Joppa accompanied him. 24And on the following day they entered Caesarea. Cornelius was expecting them and had called together his relatives and close friends. 25When Peter entered, Cornelius met him and fell down at his feet and worshiped him. 26But Peter lifted him up, saying, "Stand up; I too am a man." 27And as he talked with him, he went in and found many persons gathered. 28And he said to them, "You yourselves know how unlawful it is for a Jew to associate with or to visit anyone of another nation, but God has shown me that I should not call any person common or unclean. 29So when I was sent for, I came without objection. I ask then why you sent for me."

30And Cornelius said, "Four days ago, about this hour, I was praying in my house at the ninth hour,[3] and behold, a man stood before me in bright clothing 31and said, 'Cornelius, your prayer has been heard and your alms have been remembered before God. 32Send therefore to Joppa and ask for Simon who is called Peter. He is lodging in the house of Simon, a tanner, by the sea.' 33So I sent for you at once, and you have been kind enough to come. Now therefore we are all here in the presence of God to hear all that you have been commanded by the Lord."

Gentiles Hear the Good News

34So Peter opened his mouth and said: "Truly I understand that God shows no partiality, 35but in every nation anyone who fears him and does what is right is acceptable to him. 36As for the word that he sent to Israel, preaching good news of peace through Jesus Christ (he is Lord of all), 37you yourselves know what happened throughout all Judea, beginning from Galilee after the baptism that John proclaimed: 38how God anointed Jesus of Nazareth with the Holy Spirit and with power. He went about doing good and healing all who were oppressed by the devil, for God was with him. 39And we are witnesses of all that he did both in the country of the Jews and in Jerusalem. They put him to death by hanging him on

[1]That is, noon [2]Or *accompany them, making no distinction* [3]That is, 3 P.M.

a tree, 40but God raised him on the third day and made him to appear, 41not to all
the people but to us who had been chosen by God as witnesses, who ate and drank
with him after he rose from the dead. 42And he commanded us to preach to the
people and to testify that he is the one appointed by God to be judge of the living
and the dead. 43To him all the prophets bear witness that everyone who believes
in him receives forgiveness of sins through his name."

The Holy Spirit Falls on the Gentiles

44While Peter was still saying these things, the Holy Spirit fell on all who heard
the word. 45And the believers from among the circumcised who had come with
Peter were amazed, because the gift of the Holy Spirit was poured out even on the
Gentiles. 46For they were hearing them speaking in tongues and extolling God.
Then Peter declared, 47"Can anyone withhold water for baptizing these people,
who have received the Holy Spirit just as we have?" 48And he commanded them
to be baptized in the name of Jesus Christ. Then they asked him to remain for
some days.

Peter Reports to the Church

11 Now the apostles and the brothers[1] who were throughout Judea heard that
the Gentiles also had received the word of God. 2So when Peter went up to
Jerusalem, the circumcision party[2] criticized him, saying, 3"You went to uncircumcised men and ate with them." 4But Peter began and explained it to them in
order: 5"I was in the city of Joppa praying, and in a trance I saw a vision, something
like a great sheet descending, being let down from heaven by its four corners, and
it came down to me. 6Looking at it closely, I observed animals and beasts of prey
and reptiles and birds of the air. 7And I heard a voice saying to me, 'Rise, Peter;
kill and eat.' 8But I said, 'By no means, Lord; for nothing common or unclean has
ever entered my mouth.' 9But the voice answered a second time from heaven,
'What God has made clean, do not call common.' 10This happened three times,
and all was drawn up again into heaven. 11And behold, at that very moment three
men arrived at the house in which we were, sent to me from Caesarea. 12And the
Spirit told me to go with them, making no distinction. These six brothers also
accompanied me, and we entered the man's house. 13And he told us how he had
seen the angel stand in his house and say, 'Send to Joppa and bring Simon who
is called Peter; 14he will declare to you a message by which you will be saved, you
and all your household.' 15As I began to speak, the Holy Spirit fell on them just as
on us at the beginning. 16And I remembered the word of the Lord, how he said,
'John baptized with water, but you will be baptized with the Holy Spirit.' 17If then
God gave the same gift to them as he gave to us when we believed in the Lord
Jesus Christ, who was I that I could stand in God's way?" 18When they heard these
things they fell silent. And they glorified God, saying, "Then to the Gentiles also
God has granted repentance that leads to life."

The Church in Antioch

19Now those who were scattered because of the persecution that arose over
Stephen traveled as far as Phoenicia and Cyprus and Antioch, speaking the
word to no one except Jews. 20But there were some of them, men of Cyprus and
Cyrene, who on coming to Antioch spoke to the Hellenists[3] also, preaching the
Lord Jesus. 21And the hand of the Lord was with them, and a great number who
believed turned to the Lord. 22The report of this came to the ears of the church in
Jerusalem, and they sent Barnabas to Antioch. 23When he came and saw the grace
of God, he was glad, and he exhorted them all to remain faithful to the Lord with
steadfast purpose, 24for he was a good man, full of the Holy Spirit and of faith.
And a great many people were added to the Lord. 25So Barnabas went to Tarsus

[1]Or *brothers and sisters* [2]Or *Jerusalem, those of the circumcision* [3]Or *Greeks* (that is, Greek-speaking non-Jews)

to look for Saul, 26and when he had found him, he brought him to Antioch. For a whole year they met with the church and taught a great many people. And in Antioch the disciples were first called Christians.

27Now in these days prophets came down from Jerusalem to Antioch. 28And one of them named Agabus stood up and foretold by the Spirit that there would be a great famine over all the world (this took place in the days of Claudius). 29So the disciples determined, every one according to his ability, to send relief to the brothers[1] living in Judea. 30And they did so, sending it to the elders by the hand of Barnabas and Saul.

James Killed and Peter Imprisoned

12 About that time Herod the king laid violent hands on some who belonged to the church. 2He killed James the brother of John with the sword, 3and when he saw that it pleased the Jews, he proceeded to arrest Peter also. This was during the days of Unleavened Bread. 4And when he had seized him, he put him in prison, delivering him over to four squads of soldiers to guard him, intending after the Passover to bring him out to the people. 5So Peter was kept in prison, but earnest prayer for him was made to God by the church.

Peter Is Rescued

6Now when Herod was about to bring him out, on that very night, Peter was sleeping between two soldiers, bound with two chains, and sentries before the door were guarding the prison. 7And behold, an angel of the Lord stood next to him, and a light shone in the cell. He struck Peter on the side and woke him, saying, "Get up quickly." And the chains fell off his hands. 8And the angel said to him, "Dress yourself and put on your sandals." And he did so. And he said to him, "Wrap your cloak around you and follow me." 9And he went out and followed him. He did not know that what was being done by the angel was real, but thought he was seeing a vision. 10When they had passed the first and the second guard, they came to the iron gate leading into the city. It opened for them of its own accord, and they went out and went along one street, and immediately the angel left him. 11When Peter came to himself, he said, "Now I am sure that the Lord has sent his angel and rescued me from the hand of Herod and from all that the Jewish people were expecting."

12When he realized this, he went to the house of Mary, the mother of John whose other name was Mark, where many were gathered together and were praying. 13And when he knocked at the door of the gateway, a servant girl named Rhoda came to answer. 14Recognizing Peter's voice, in her joy she did not open the gate but ran in and reported that Peter was standing at the gate. 15They said to her, "You are out of your mind." But she kept insisting that it was so, and they kept saying, "It is his angel!" 16But Peter continued knocking, and when they opened, they saw him and were amazed. 17But motioning to them with his hand to be silent, he described to them how the Lord had brought him out of the prison. And he said, "Tell these things to James and to the brothers."[2] Then he departed and went to another place.

18Now when day came, there was no little disturbance among the soldiers over what had become of Peter. 19And after Herod searched for him and did not find him, he examined the sentries and ordered that they should be put to death. Then he went down from Judea to Caesarea and spent time there.

The Death of Herod

20Now Herod was angry with the people of Tyre and Sidon, and they came to him with one accord, and having persuaded Blastus, the king's chamberlain,[3] they asked for peace, because their country depended on the king's country for

[1]Or *brothers and sisters* [2]Or *brothers and sisters* [3]That is, trusted personal attendant

---

ACTS 11:26

CHRISTIANS

Given the marked diversity in religious backgrounds, social status, economic power, age, and ethnicity among the early Christians, it's a miracle that the young church ever gained its footing. What was it that unified and identified believers despite all these differences? In short, Christians were known by what they said and did. They preached about Jesus and they acted like Jesus. They were originally called "followers of the Way," but the term "Christians" was eventually coined, likely by nonbelievers, to mean "ones who are like Christ." Paul says that God "leads us [Christians] in triumphal procession, and through us spreads the fragrance of the knowledge of him everywhere. For we are the aroma of Christ to God among those who are being saved and among those who are perishing" (2Co 2:14–15). The descriptions of the church in Acts are distinctive and profound, painting Christians as compassionate, prophetic, selfless, committed, and loving followers of Christ. True Christians have always been committed to more than a set of ideas and beliefs; they are active, giving people who reach out to others in service, joyfully telling them about their relationship with Jesus. In short, they are "ones who are like Christ," devoted to their King who makes a way for all who will repent and be saved (2Pe 3:9).

UNJUST PERSECUTION

The early church experienced intense persecution. Herod saw some political advantage in persecuting the fledgling church, yet those who are in opposition to God's ways and his plan to redeem the world through Jesus Christ cite many other reasons for persecuting the church. The Jewish leadership during the time of the early church perpetuated this persecution. Their historical lineage included being God's chosen people, Israel. But they presumed upon God's kindness and didn't really trust God in their hearts. They were proud. They believed that their outward actions as defined by their ancestors earned God's favor, and this showed in how they lived their lives. Many Jews persecuted the church with incredible vigor. They saw Jesus as a blasphemer and a rebel, and they actively tried to stop what the early church was doing in and around Jerusalem.

Jesus was persecuted, and he promised that his followers would also endure persecution (Jn 16:33). In their own pride, the Jewish leaders believed they were doing what was required to please God and earn his favor, but Jesus represented a radically different perspective. Jesus came to fulfill the law that they so closely followed (Mt 5:17), but they could not see that the entire Old Testament had pointed to him all along (Lk 24:27).

Jesus taught his followers that persecution was real and was coming. "If the world hates you, know that it has hated me before it hated you. If you were of the world, the world would love you as its own; but because you are not of the world, but I chose you out of the world, therefore the world hates you. Remember the word that I said to you: 'A servant is not greater than his master.' If they persecuted me, they will also persecute you. If they kept my word, they will also keep yours. But all these things they will do to you on account of my name, because they do not know him who sent me" (Jn 15:18 – 21).

Jesus' promise still stands today as the worldwide church experiences opposition and persecution. The persecuted can "take heart" that Jesus voluntarily endured brutal persecution and died on the cross so that, regardless of the "tribulation" they experience, Jesus has indeed "overcome the world" (Jn 16:33). Inspired by Jesus' example under persecution, the church continues to bring the message of God's unending love to a lost world.

food. 21On an appointed day Herod put on his royal robes, took his seat upon the throne, and delivered an oration to them. 22And the people were shouting, "The voice of a god, and not of a man!" 23Immediately an angel of the Lord struck him down, because he did not give God the glory, and he was eaten by worms and breathed his last.

24But the word of God increased and multiplied.

25And Barnabas and Saul returned from[1] Jerusalem when they had completed their service, bringing with them John, whose other name was Mark.

Barnabas and Saul Sent Off

13 Now there were in the church at Antioch prophets and teachers, Barnabas, Simeon who was called Niger,[2] Lucius of Cyrene, Manaen a lifelong friend of Herod the tetrarch, and Saul. 2While they were worshiping the Lord and fasting, the Holy Spirit said, "Set apart for me Barnabas and Saul for the work to which I have called them." 3Then after fasting and praying they laid their hands on them and sent them off.

Barnabas and Saul on Cyprus

4So, being sent out by the Holy Spirit, they went down to Seleucia, and from there they sailed to Cyprus. 5When they arrived at Salamis, they proclaimed the word of God in the synagogues of the Jews. And they had John to assist them. 6When they had gone through the whole island as far as Paphos, they came upon a certain magician, a Jewish false prophet named Bar-Jesus. 7He was with the proconsul, Sergius Paulus, a man of intelligence, who summoned Barnabas and Saul and sought to hear the word of God. 8But Elymas the magician (for that is the meaning of his name) opposed them, seeking to turn the proconsul away from the faith. 9But Saul, who was also called Paul, filled with the Holy Spirit, looked intently at him 10and said, "You son of the devil, you enemy of all righteousness, full of all deceit and villainy, will you not stop making crooked the straight paths of the Lord? 11And now, behold, the hand of the Lord is upon you, and you will be blind and unable to see the sun for a time." Immediately mist and darkness fell upon him, and he went about seeking people to lead him by the hand. 12Then the proconsul believed, when he saw what had occurred, for he was astonished at the teaching of the Lord.

Paul and Barnabas at Antioch in Pisidia

13Now Paul and his companions set sail from Paphos and came to Perga in Pamphylia. And John left them and returned to Jerusalem, 14but they went on from Perga and came to Antioch in Pisidia. And on the Sabbath day they went into the synagogue and sat down. 15After the reading from the Law and the Prophets, the rulers of the synagogue sent a message to them, saying, "Brothers, if you have any word of encouragement for the people, say it." 16So Paul stood up, and motioning with his hand said:

"Men of Israel and you who fear God, listen. 17The God of this people Israel chose our fathers and made the people great during their stay in the land of Egypt, and with uplifted arm he led them out of it. 18And for about forty years he put up with[3] them in the wilderness. 19And after destroying seven nations in the land of Canaan, he gave them their land as an inheritance. 20All this took about 450 years. And after that he gave them judges until Samuel the prophet. 21Then they asked for a king, and God gave them Saul the son of Kish, a man of the tribe of Benjamin, for forty years. 22And when he had removed him, he raised up David to be their king, of whom he testified and said, 'I have found in David the son of Jesse a man after my heart, who will do all my will.' 23Of this man's offspring God has brought to Israel a Savior, Jesus, as he promised. 24Before his coming,

[1]Some manuscripts *to* [2]*Niger* is a Latin word meaning *black*, or *dark* [3]Some manuscripts *he carried* (compare Deuteronomy 1:31)

THE ACTS OF THE HOLY SPIRIT

The Holy Spirit is the power that God has provided to move his kingdom mission forward. God's mission has always been to work through his people to show his glory to the world: first through the nation of Israel, and now through his Christian church. But God doesn't leave his people without help. Thankfully, God sent the Holy Spirit to be our Helper and Advocate (Jn 14:15 – 17,25 – 27).

The book of Acts tells about many functions of the Holy Spirit: giving boldness and power to preach the gospel (Ac 6:10), inspiring people to prophesy (2:18), and directing ministry activity (13:2). Ultimately, the Spirit leads the church through the proper exercise of the people's different ministry offices and gifts.

God creates a unique unity in believers through the Holy Spirit. This unity is unlike anything that can be found anywhere else in the world. An example of this is found in Acts 13:1 – 3. The church in Antioch sent missionaries to other locations at an incredible rate. Interestingly, the church in Antioch was birthed by ordinary believers who had traveled to the city to escape persecution (11:19 – 21). The greatest local congregation in the world at the time was started by everyday people living for God in their everyday lives.

From what we know of it, the church in Antioch was also diverse, which gives us another picture of the Spirit's unifying work. Barnabas was a bicultural Hellenistic Jew, and he was one of the leaders of the church. Simeon, who was called Niger, was a leader in the church — no one knows his background. Another leader was Lucius of Cyrene in North Africa. Manaen used to keep terrible company; he was a lifelong friend of the man who had John the Baptist beheaded. And finally there was Paul, the Jewish Pharisee and persecutor-turned-evangelist. This was the group of people who came together to advance the message of Jesus as the Messiah. They were empowered by the Holy Spirit of God leading and guiding them.

The Spirit of Jesus created unity in the past through unthinkable combinations of diverse people coming together to advance one cause in the world: the kingdom of God. And the same Spirit still works in and through believers to do the same today.

John had proclaimed a baptism of repentance to all the people of Israel. 25 And
as John was finishing his course, he said, 'What do you suppose that I am? I am
not he. No, but behold, after me one is coming, the sandals of whose feet I am
not worthy to untie.'

26 "Brothers, sons of the family of Abraham, and those among you who fear
God, to us has been sent the message of this salvation. 27 For those who live in
Jerusalem and their rulers, because they did not recognize him nor understand
the utterances of the prophets, which are read every Sabbath, fulfilled them by
condemning him. 28 And though they found in him no guilt worthy of death, they
asked Pilate to have him executed. 29 And when they had carried out all that was
written of him, they took him down from the tree and laid him in a tomb. 30 But
God raised him from the dead, 31 and for many days he appeared to those who had
come up with him from Galilee to Jerusalem, who are now his witnesses to the
people. 32 And we bring you the good news that what God promised to the fathers,
33 this he has fulfilled to us their children by raising Jesus, as also it is written in
the second Psalm,

"'You are my Son,
today I have begotten you.'

34 And as for the fact that he raised him from the dead, no more to return to corruption, he has spoken in this way,

"'I will give you the holy and sure blessings of David.'

35 Therefore he says also in another psalm,

"'You will not let your Holy One see corruption.'

36 For David, after he had served the purpose of God in his own generation, fell
asleep and was laid with his fathers and saw corruption, 37 but he whom God
raised up did not see corruption. 38 Let it be known to you therefore, brothers,
that through this man forgiveness of sins is proclaimed to you, 39 and by him everyone who believes is freed[1] from everything from which you could not be freed
by the law of Moses. 40 Beware, therefore, lest what is said in the Prophets should
come about:

41 "'Look, you scoffers,
be astounded and perish;
for I am doing a work in your days,
a work that you will not believe, even if one tells it to you.'"

42 As they went out, the people begged that these things might be told them the
next Sabbath. 43 And after the meeting of the synagogue broke up, many Jews and
devout converts to Judaism followed Paul and Barnabas, who, as they spoke with
them, urged them to continue in the grace of God.

44 The next Sabbath almost the whole city gathered to hear the word of the
Lord. 45 But when the Jews[2] saw the crowds, they were filled with jealousy and began to contradict what was spoken by Paul, reviling him. 46 And Paul and Barnabas
spoke out boldly, saying, "It was necessary that the word of God be spoken first to
you. Since you thrust it aside and judge yourselves unworthy of eternal life, behold, we are turning to the Gentiles. 47 For so the Lord has commanded us, saying,

"'I have made you a light for the Gentiles,
that you may bring salvation to the ends of the earth.'"

48 And when the Gentiles heard this, they began rejoicing and glorifying the
word of the Lord, and as many as were appointed to eternal life believed. 49 And
the word of the Lord was spreading throughout the whole region. 50 But the Jews

[1] Or *justified*; twice in this verse [2] Greek *Ioudaioi* probably refers here to Jewish religious leaders, and others under their influence, in that time; also verse 50

incited the devout women of high standing and the leading men of the city, stirred
up persecution against Paul and Barnabas, and drove them out of their district.
51But they shook off the dust from their feet against them and went to Iconium.
52And the disciples were filled with joy and with the Holy Spirit.

Paul and Barnabas at Iconium

14 Now at Iconium they entered together into the Jewish synagogue and spoke
in such a way that a great number of both Jews and Greeks believed. 2But
the unbelieving Jews stirred up the Gentiles and poisoned their minds against the
brothers.[1] 3So they remained for a long time, speaking boldly for the Lord, who
bore witness to the word of his grace, granting signs and wonders to be done by
their hands. 4But the people of the city were divided; some sided with the Jews
and some with the apostles. 5When an attempt was made by both Gentiles and
Jews, with their rulers, to mistreat them and to stone them, 6they learned of it and
fled to Lystra and Derbe, cities of Lycaonia, and to the surrounding country, 7and
there they continued to preach the gospel.

Paul and Barnabas at Lystra

8Now at Lystra there was a man sitting who could not use his feet. He was crippled from birth and had never walked. 9He listened to Paul speaking. And Paul,
looking intently at him and seeing that he had faith to be made well,[2] 10said in a
loud voice, "Stand upright on your feet." And he sprang up and began walking.
11And when the crowds saw what Paul had done, they lifted up their voices, saying
in Lycaonian, "The gods have come down to us in the likeness of men!" 12Barnabas
they called Zeus, and Paul, Hermes, because he was the chief speaker. 13And the
priest of Zeus, whose temple was at the entrance to the city, brought oxen and
garlands to the gates and wanted to offer sacrifice with the crowds. 14But when the
apostles Barnabas and Paul heard of it, they tore their garments and rushed out
into the crowd, crying out, 15"Men, why are you doing these things? We also are
men, of like nature with you, and we bring you good news, that you should turn
from these vain things to a living God, who made the heaven and the earth and
the sea and all that is in them. 16In past generations he allowed all the nations to
walk in their own ways. 17Yet he did not leave himself without witness, for he did
good by giving you rains from heaven and fruitful seasons, satisfying your hearts
with food and gladness." 18Even with these words they scarcely restrained the
people from offering sacrifice to them.

Paul Stoned at Lystra

19But Jews came from Antioch and Iconium, and having persuaded the crowds,
they stoned Paul and dragged him out of the city, supposing that he was dead.
20But when the disciples gathered about him, he rose up and entered the city, and
on the next day he went on with Barnabas to Derbe. 21When they had preached
the gospel to that city and had made many disciples, they returned to Lystra and
to Iconium and to Antioch, 22strengthening the souls of the disciples, encouraging them to continue in the faith, and saying that through many tribulations
we must enter the kingdom of God. 23And when they had appointed elders for
them in every church, with prayer and fasting they committed them to the Lord
in whom they had believed.

Paul and Barnabas Return to Antioch in Syria

24Then they passed through Pisidia and came to Pamphylia. 25And when they
had spoken the word in Perga, they went down to Attalia, 26and from there they
sailed to Antioch, where they had been commended to the grace of God for the
work that they had fulfilled. 27And when they arrived and gathered the church

[1]Or *brothers and sisters* [2]Or *be saved*

ACTS 14:19–20

SUFFERING FOR JESUS

Paul was well acquainted with suffering. He was imprisoned, stoned, beaten, flogged, shipwrecked, starved, exhausted, and endangered throughout his life as a follower of Christ (2Co 11:16–33). Because of his experiences, throughout his letters Paul was intent on reminding Christians that hardship is to be *expected.* He said it quite clearly in Philippians: "For it has been granted to you that for the sake of Christ you should not only believe in him but also suffer for his sake" (Php 1:29).

Though the typical human response is to avoid pain at all costs, Paul calls Christians to accept their trials in light of the fact that God suffers with us and because God causes good things to come from our difficulties (Ps 34:18; Ro 8:28). He says, "We rejoice in our sufferings, knowing that suffering produces endurance, and endurance produces character, and character produces hope" (Ro 5:3–4). Furthermore, suffering is part of being united with Jesus (Php 3:10–11) and, thankfully, it is temporary: "So we do not lose heart. Though our outer self is wasting away, our inner self is being renewed day by day. For this light momentary affliction is preparing for us an eternal weight of glory beyond all comparison" (2Co 4:16–17).

together, they declared all that God had done with them, and how he had opened a door of faith to the Gentiles. 28And they remained no little time with the disciples.

The Jerusalem Council

15 But some men came down from Judea and were teaching the brothers, "Unless you are circumcised according to the custom of Moses, you cannot be saved." 2And after Paul and Barnabas had no small dissension and debate with them, Paul and Barnabas and some of the others were appointed to go up to Jerusalem to the apostles and the elders about this question. 3So, being sent on their way by the church, they passed through both Phoenicia and Samaria, describing in detail the conversion of the Gentiles, and brought great joy to all the brothers.[1] 4When they came to Jerusalem, they were welcomed by the church and the apostles and the elders, and they declared all that God had done with them. 5But some believers who belonged to the party of the Pharisees rose up and said, "It is necessary to circumcise them and to order them to keep the law of Moses."

6The apostles and the elders were gathered together to consider this matter. 7And after there had been much debate, Peter stood up and said to them, "Brothers, you know that in the early days God made a choice among you, that by my mouth the Gentiles should hear the word of the gospel and believe. 8And God, who knows the heart, bore witness to them, by giving them the Holy Spirit just as he did to us, 9and he made no distinction between us and them, having cleansed their hearts by faith. 10Now, therefore, why are you putting God to the test by placing a yoke on the neck of the disciples that neither our fathers nor we have been able to bear? 11But we believe that we will be saved through the grace of the Lord Jesus, just as they will."

12And all the assembly fell silent, and they listened to Barnabas and Paul as they related what signs and wonders God had done through them among the Gentiles. 13After they finished speaking, James replied, "Brothers, listen to me. 14Simeon has related how God first visited the Gentiles, to take from them a people for his name. 15And with this the words of the prophets agree, just as it is written,

16 "'After this I will return,
and I will rebuild the tent of David that has fallen;
I will rebuild its ruins,
and I will restore it,
17 that the remnant[2] of mankind may seek the Lord,
and all the Gentiles who are called by my name,
says the Lord, who makes these things 18known from of old.'

19Therefore my judgment is that we should not trouble those of the Gentiles who turn to God, 20but should write to them to abstain from the things polluted by idols, and from sexual immorality, and from what has been strangled, and from blood. 21For from ancient generations Moses has had in every city those who proclaim him, for he is read every Sabbath in the synagogues."

The Council's Letter to Gentile Believers

22Then it seemed good to the apostles and the elders, with the whole church, to choose men from among them and send them to Antioch with Paul and Barnabas. They sent Judas called Barsabbas, and Silas, leading men among the brothers, 23with the following letter: "The brothers, both the apostles and the elders, to the brothers[3] who are of the Gentiles in Antioch and Syria and Cilicia, greetings. 24Since we have heard that some persons have gone out from us and troubled you[4]

[1]Or *brothers and sisters*; also verse 22 [2]Or *rest* [3]Or *brothers and sisters*; also verses 32, 33, 36 [4]Some manuscripts *some persons from us have troubled you*

ACTS 15:24–29

JESUS IS EVERYTHING

At the heart of what it means to be fallen human beings, people are proud and want to do things for themselves. Even Christians, after God saves them, struggle with trying to earn their way to God. Yet people who have surrendered their life to Christ grow with God the same way they were saved by God: by grace, through faith, in Christ.

Some of the first converts to Christianity struggled with this same issue of wanting to contribute in some way to their salvation. A group of Jewish Christians believed that to be Christians, Gentile converts must follow the Old Testament laws and traditions. In contrast to this, Peter and others argued that Christians did not need to follow the law in the same way—because Jesus had already fulfilled the law for everyone (Mt 5:17).

Even today there is a danger that well-meaning Christians will burden themselves and others with "add-ons" to the core of the gospel message, which is simply that Jesus is enough. As people try to add good works and other requirements to that message, the message of salvation by grace is lost: "For by grace you have been saved through faith. And this is not your own doing; it is the gift of God, not a result of works, so that no one may boast. For we are his workmanship, created in Christ Jesus for good works, which God prepared beforehand, that we should walk in them" (Eph 2:8–10).

with words, unsettling your minds, although we gave them no instructions, 25it
has seemed good to us, having come to one accord, to choose men and send them
to you with our beloved Barnabas and Paul, 26men who have risked their lives for
the name of our Lord Jesus Christ. 27We have therefore sent Judas and Silas, who
themselves will tell you the same things by word of mouth. 28For it has seemed
good to the Holy Spirit and to us to lay on you no greater burden than these requirements: 29that you abstain from what has been sacrificed to idols, and from
blood, and from what has been strangled, and from sexual immorality. If you keep
yourselves from these, you will do well. Farewell."

30So when they were sent off, they went down to Antioch, and having gathered the congregation together, they delivered the letter. 31And when they had
read it, they rejoiced because of its encouragement. 32And Judas and Silas, who
were themselves prophets, encouraged and strengthened the brothers with
many words. 33And after they had spent some time, they were sent off in peace
by the brothers to those who had sent them.[1] 35But Paul and Barnabas remained
in Antioch, teaching and preaching the word of the Lord, with many others
also.

Paul and Barnabas Separate

36And after some days Paul said to Barnabas, "Let us return and visit the brothers in every city where we proclaimed the word of the Lord, and see how they are."
37Now Barnabas wanted to take with them John called Mark. 38But Paul thought
best not to take with them one who had withdrawn from them in Pamphylia and
had not gone with them to the work. 39And there arose a sharp disagreement, so
that they separated from each other. Barnabas took Mark with him and sailed
away to Cyprus, 40but Paul chose Silas and departed, having been commended
by the brothers to the grace of the Lord. 41And he went through Syria and Cilicia,
strengthening the churches.

Timothy Joins Paul and Silas

16 Paul[2] came also to Derbe and to Lystra. A disciple was there, named Timothy, the son of a Jewish woman who was a believer, but his father was
a Greek. 2He was well spoken of by the brothers[3] at Lystra and Iconium. 3Paul
wanted Timothy to accompany him, and he took him and circumcised him because of the Jews who were in those places, for they all knew that his father was
a Greek. 4As they went on their way through the cities, they delivered to them
for observance the decisions that had been reached by the apostles and elders
who were in Jerusalem. 5So the churches were strengthened in the faith, and they
increased in numbers daily.

The Macedonian Call

6And they went through the region of Phrygia and Galatia, having been forbidden by the Holy Spirit to speak the word in Asia. 7And when they had come up
to Mysia, they attempted to go into Bithynia, but the Spirit of Jesus did not allow
them. 8So, passing by Mysia, they went down to Troas. 9And a vision appeared to
Paul in the night: a man of Macedonia was standing there, urging him and saying,
"Come over to Macedonia and help us." 10And when Paul[4] had seen the vision,
immediately we sought to go on into Macedonia, concluding that God had called
us to preach the gospel to them.

The Conversion of Lydia

11So, setting sail from Troas, we made a direct voyage to Samothrace, and
the following day to Neapolis, 12and from there to Philippi, which is a leading
city of the[5] district of Macedonia and a Roman colony. We remained in this city

[1]Some manuscripts insert verse 34: *But it seemed good to Silas to remain there* [2]Greek *He* [3]Or *brothers and sisters*; also verse 40 [4]Greek *he* [5]Or *that*

ACTS 16:24–34

"WHAT MUST I DO TO BE SAVED?"

Faith is about trusting in Jesus regardless of daily circumstances. Paul and Silas had been beaten, stripped, and thrown in jail for following Jesus (16:22–23), but the real test of their faith came in how they responded to their imprisonment. They didn't seek legal action or resort to grumbling; they didn't question God's plan. Instead, they decided to pray and sing to God (v. 25). This activity and their attitude must have seemed strange to the other prisoners—and to the jailer!

To show his glory through Paul and Silas's circumstances, God sent an earthquake to shake things up. The jailer thought the prisoners had escaped; desperate, he prepared to take his own life. He knew he would be sentenced to death if the prisoners escaped under his watch. Instead of seeking their own welfare, Paul and Silas stayed in the prison and ministered to the jailer. It had to be mind-boggling to see two prisoners respond to his cruelty in such a tender way.

He asked the question that is "The Question" for people who have seen God and his people at work: "What must I do to be saved?" (v. 30). The answer is simple because the message is clear: "Believe in the Lord Jesus, and you will be saved" (v. 31). Paul was a brilliant theologian, but he also knew that the message of Jesus was beautifully simple, and he was ready to share it clearly in a moment of openness and opportunity.

some days. 13And on the Sabbath day we went outside the gate to the riverside,
where we supposed there was a place of prayer, and we sat down and spoke to
the women who had come together. 14One who heard us was a woman named
Lydia, from the city of Thyatira, a seller of purple goods, who was a worshiper of
God. The Lord opened her heart to pay attention to what was said by Paul. 15And
after she was baptized, and her household as well, she urged us, saying, "If you
have judged me to be faithful to the Lord, come to my house and stay." And she
prevailed upon us.

Paul and Silas in Prison

16As we were going to the place of prayer, we were met by a slave girl who had
a spirit of divination and brought her owners much gain by fortune-telling. 17She
followed Paul and us, crying out, "These men are servants of the Most High God,
who proclaim to you the way of salvation." 18And this she kept doing for many
days. Paul, having become greatly annoyed, turned and said to the spirit, "I command you in the name of Jesus Christ to come out of her." And it came out that
very hour.

19But when her owners saw that their hope of gain was gone, they seized Paul
and Silas and dragged them into the marketplace before the rulers. 20And when
they had brought them to the magistrates, they said, "These men are Jews, and
they are disturbing our city. 21They advocate customs that are not lawful for us
as Romans to accept or practice." 22The crowd joined in attacking them, and the
magistrates tore the garments off them and gave orders to beat them with rods.
23And when they had inflicted many blows upon them, they threw them into
prison, ordering the jailer to keep them safely. 24Having received this order, he
put them into the inner prison and fastened their feet in the stocks.

The Philippian Jailer Converted

25About midnight Paul and Silas were praying and singing hymns to God, and
the prisoners were listening to them, 26and suddenly there was a great earthquake, so that the foundations of the prison were shaken. And immediately all
the doors were opened, and everyone's bonds were unfastened. 27When the jailer
woke and saw that the prison doors were open, he drew his sword and was about
to kill himself, supposing that the prisoners had escaped. 28But Paul cried with a
loud voice, "Do not harm yourself, for we are all here." 29And the jailer[1] called for
lights and rushed in, and trembling with fear he fell down before Paul and Silas.
30Then he brought them out and said, "Sirs, what must I do to be saved?" 31And
they said, "Believe in the Lord Jesus, and you will be saved, you and your household." 32And they spoke the word of the Lord to him and to all who were in his
house. 33And he took them the same hour of the night and washed their wounds;
and he was baptized at once, he and all his family. 34Then he brought them up
into his house and set food before them. And he rejoiced along with his entire
household that he had believed in God.

35But when it was day, the magistrates sent the police, saying, "Let those men
go." 36And the jailer reported these words to Paul, saying, "The magistrates have
sent to let you go. Therefore come out now and go in peace." 37But Paul said to
them, "They have beaten us publicly, uncondemned, men who are Roman citizens, and have thrown us into prison; and do they now throw us out secretly?
No! Let them come themselves and take us out." 38The police reported these
words to the magistrates, and they were afraid when they heard that they were
Roman citizens. 39So they came and apologized to them. And they took them
out and asked them to leave the city. 40So they went out of the prison and visited Lydia. And when they had seen the brothers, they encouraged them and
departed.

[1]Greek *he*

Paul and Silas in Thessalonica

17 Now when they had passed through Amphipolis and Apollonia, they came to Thessalonica, where there was a synagogue of the Jews. 2 And Paul went in, as was his custom, and on three Sabbath days he reasoned with them from the Scriptures, 3 explaining and proving that it was necessary for the Christ to suffer and to rise from the dead, and saying, "This Jesus, whom I proclaim to you, is the Christ." 4 And some of them were persuaded and joined Paul and Silas, as did a great many of the devout Greeks and not a few of the leading women. 5 But the Jews[1] were jealous, and taking some wicked men of the rabble, they formed a mob, set the city in an uproar, and attacked the house of Jason, seeking to bring them out to the crowd. 6 And when they could not find them, they dragged Jason and some of the brothers before the city authorities, shouting, "These men who have turned the world upside down have come here also, 7 and Jason has received them, and they are all acting against the decrees of Caesar, saying that there is another king, Jesus." 8 And the people and the city authorities were disturbed when they heard these things. 9 And when they had taken money as security from Jason and the rest, they let them go.

Paul and Silas in Berea

10 The brothers[2] immediately sent Paul and Silas away by night to Berea, and when they arrived they went into the Jewish synagogue. 11 Now these Jews were more noble than those in Thessalonica; they received the word with all eagerness, examining the Scriptures daily to see if these things were so. 12 Many of them therefore believed, with not a few Greek women of high standing as well as men. 13 But when the Jews from Thessalonica learned that the word of God was proclaimed by Paul at Berea also, they came there too, agitating and stirring up the crowds. 14 Then the brothers immediately sent Paul off on his way to the sea, but Silas and Timothy remained there. 15 Those who conducted Paul brought him as far as Athens, and after receiving a command for Silas and Timothy to come to him as soon as possible, they departed.

Paul in Athens

16 Now while Paul was waiting for them at Athens, his spirit was provoked within him as he saw that the city was full of idols. 17 So he reasoned in the synagogue with the Jews and the devout persons, and in the marketplace every day with those who happened to be there. 18 Some of the Epicurean and Stoic philosophers also conversed with him. And some said, "What does this babbler wish to say?" Others said, "He seems to be a preacher of foreign divinities"—because he was preaching Jesus and the resurrection. 19 And they took him and brought him to the Areopagus, saying, "May we know what this new teaching is that you are presenting? 20 For you bring some strange things to our ears. We wish to know therefore what these things mean." 21 Now all the Athenians and the foreigners who lived there would spend their time in nothing except telling or hearing something new.

Paul Addresses the Areopagus

22 So Paul, standing in the midst of the Areopagus, said: "Men of Athens, I perceive that in every way you are very religious. 23 For as I passed along and observed the objects of your worship, I found also an altar with this inscription: 'To the unknown god.' What therefore you worship as unknown, this I proclaim to you. 24 The God who made the world and everything in it, being Lord of heaven and earth, does not live in temples made by man,[3] 25 nor is he served by human hands, as though he needed anything, since he himself gives to all mankind life

[1]Greek *Ioudaioi* probably refers here to Jewish religious leaders, and others under their influence, in that time; also verse 13 [2]Or *brothers and sisters*; also verse 14 [3]Greek *made by hands*

ACTS 17:23

AN UNKNOWN GOD

Sharing the story of Jesus begins with understanding the story people are living. Paul traveled the then-known world planting churches and sharing the story of Jesus. As he did, he shared the story in different ways, depending on people's life experiences. He looked for a simple way to connect with the people he met in order to talk about Jesus, "the way, and the truth, and the life" (Jn 14:6). As Paul looked around Athens to uncover the residents' story, he saw many idols to artificial gods that the people worshiped. Just in case they missed a god, they also had an altar set up with the inscription, "To the unknown god" (Ac 17:23). Paul knew this was his opportunity.

Paul did not ridicule the Athenians for their struggle with sin, nor did he blindly approve of it. Instead, Paul engaged their idolatry as an essential part of their story and turned their attention to Jesus. Since Mars Hill was directly opposite the Acropolis with its temples, it was clear to everyone that the people were very religious. Paul points out this reality and directs their attention to the true and living God.

Christians need to have a similar posture with the great cities of the world today. The church is a group of people who look for brokenness, connect with others on that basis, and then bring the story of Jesus into the conversation.

and breath and everything. 26And he made from one man every nation of mankind to live on all the face of the earth, having determined allotted periods and
the boundaries of their dwelling place, 27that they should seek God, and perhaps
feel their way toward him and find him. Yet he is actually not far from each one
of us, 28for

"'In him we live and move and have our being';[1]

as even some of your own poets have said,

"'For we are indeed his offspring.'[2]

29Being then God's offspring, we ought not to think that the divine being is like
gold or silver or stone, an image formed by the art and imagination of man. 30The
times of ignorance God overlooked, but now he commands all people everywhere
to repent, 31because he has fixed a day on which he will judge the world in righteousness by a man whom he has appointed; and of this he has given assurance
to all by raising him from the dead."

32Now when they heard of the resurrection of the dead, some mocked. But
others said, "We will hear you again about this." 33So Paul went out from their
midst. 34But some men joined him and believed, among whom also were Diony-
sius the Areopagite and a woman named Damaris and others with them.

Paul in Corinth

18 After this Paul[3] left Athens and went to Corinth. 2And he found a Jew
named Aquila, a native of Pontus, recently come from Italy with his wife
Priscilla, because Claudius had commanded all the Jews to leave Rome. And he
went to see them, 3and because he was of the same trade he stayed with them and
worked, for they were tentmakers by trade. 4And he reasoned in the synagogue
every Sabbath, and tried to persuade Jews and Greeks.

5When Silas and Timothy arrived from Macedonia, Paul was occupied with
the word, testifying to the Jews that the Christ was Jesus. 6And when they opposed
and reviled him, he shook out his garments and said to them, "Your blood be on
your own heads! I am innocent. From now on I will go to the Gentiles." 7And he
left there and went to the house of a man named Titius Justus, a worshiper of God.
His house was next door to the synagogue. 8Crispus, the ruler of the synagogue,
believed in the Lord, together with his entire household. And many of the Corinthians hearing Paul believed and were baptized. 9And the Lord said to Paul one
night in a vision, "Do not be afraid, but go on speaking and do not be silent, 10for I
am with you, and no one will attack you to harm you, for I have many in this city
who are my people." 11And he stayed a year and six months, teaching the word of
God among them.

12But when Gallio was proconsul of Achaia, the Jews[4] made a united attack
on Paul and brought him before the tribunal, 13saying, "This man is persuading
people to worship God contrary to the law." 14But when Paul was about to open his
mouth, Gallio said to the Jews, "If it were a matter of wrongdoing or vicious crime,
O Jews, I would have reason to accept your complaint. 15But since it is a matter of
questions about words and names and your own law, see to it yourselves. I refuse
to be a judge of these things." 16And he drove them from the tribunal. 17And they
all seized Sosthenes, the ruler of the synagogue, and beat him in front of the tribunal. But Gallio paid no attention to any of this.

Paul Returns to Antioch

18After this, Paul stayed many days longer and then took leave of the brothers[5] and set sail for Syria, and with him Priscilla and Aquila. At Cenchreae he

[1]Probably from Epimenides of Crete [2]From Aratus's poem "Phainomena" [3]Greek *he* [4]Greek *Ioudaioi* probably refers here to Jewish religious leaders, and others under their influence, in that time; also verses 14 (twice), 28 [5]Or *brothers and sisters*; also verse 27

had cut his hair, for he was under a vow. 19 And they came to Ephesus, and he left them there, but he himself went into the synagogue and reasoned with the Jews. 20 When they asked him to stay for a longer period, he declined. 21 But on taking leave of them he said, "I will return to you if God wills," and he set sail from Ephesus.

22 When he had landed at Caesarea, he went up and greeted the church, and then went down to Antioch. 23 After spending some time there, he departed and went from one place to the next through the region of Galatia and Phrygia, strengthening all the disciples.

Apollos Speaks Boldly in Ephesus

24 Now a Jew named Apollos, a native of Alexandria, came to Ephesus. He was an eloquent man, competent in the Scriptures. 25 He had been instructed in the way of the Lord. And being fervent in spirit,[1] he spoke and taught accurately the things concerning Jesus, though he knew only the baptism of John. 26 He began to speak boldly in the synagogue, but when Priscilla and Aquila heard him, they took him aside and explained to him the way of God more accurately. 27 And when he wished to cross to Achaia, the brothers encouraged him and wrote to the disciples to welcome him. When he arrived, he greatly helped those who through grace had believed, 28 for he powerfully refuted the Jews in public, showing by the Scriptures that the Christ was Jesus.

Paul in Ephesus

19 And it happened that while Apollos was at Corinth, Paul passed through the inland[2] country and came to Ephesus. There he found some disciples. 2 And he said to them, "Did you receive the Holy Spirit when you believed?" And they said, "No, we have not even heard that there is a Holy Spirit." 3 And he said, "Into what then were you baptized?" They said, "Into John's baptism." 4 And Paul said, "John baptized with the baptism of repentance, telling the people to believe in the one who was to come after him, that is, Jesus." 5 On hearing this, they were baptized in[3] the name of the Lord Jesus. 6 And when Paul had laid his hands on them, the Holy Spirit came on them, and they began speaking in tongues and prophesying. 7 There were about twelve men in all.

8 And he entered the synagogue and for three months spoke boldly, reasoning and persuading them about the kingdom of God. 9 But when some became stubborn and continued in unbelief, speaking evil of the Way before the congregation, he withdrew from them and took the disciples with him, reasoning daily in the hall of Tyrannus.[4] 10 This continued for two years, so that all the residents of Asia heard the word of the Lord, both Jews and Greeks.

The Sons of Sceva

11 And God was doing extraordinary miracles by the hands of Paul, 12 so that even handkerchiefs or aprons that had touched his skin were carried away to the sick, and their diseases left them and the evil spirits came out of them. 13 Then some of the itinerant Jewish exorcists undertook to invoke the name of the Lord Jesus over those who had evil spirits, saying, "I adjure you by the Jesus whom Paul proclaims." 14 Seven sons of a Jewish high priest named Sceva were doing this. 15 But the evil spirit answered them, "Jesus I know, and Paul I recognize, but who are you?" 16 And the man in whom was the evil spirit leaped on them, mastered all[5] of them and overpowered them, so that they fled out of that house naked and wounded. 17 And this became known to all the residents of Ephesus, both Jews and Greeks. And fear fell upon them all, and the name of the Lord Jesus was extolled. 18 Also many of those who were now believers came, confessing and divulging their practices. 19 And a number of those who had practiced magic arts brought

[1]Or *in the Spirit* [2]Greek *upper* (that is, highland) [3]Or *into* [4]Some manuscripts add *from the fifth hour to the tenth* (that is, from 11 A.M. to 4 P.M.) [5]Or *both*

ACTS 19:13–17

"JESUS I KNOW . . . BUT WHO ARE YOU?"

Throughout history, religious practitioners and those who are involved in the occult have attempted to co-opt the name of Jesus, and the results are never good.

The Ephesian participants in these dark arts were aware of the apostle Paul and the incredible miracles that he was doing in the name of Jesus. Recognizing the power that came when the name was used, they attempted to use it as well. The demon's verbal response is chilling, and these men paid the physical price for their misuse of Jesus' name (Ac 19:15–16).

The Bible tells us that demons have a great respect for Jesus. James says, "You believe that God is one; you do well. Even the demons believe—and shudder!" (Jas 2:19). Even though they do not love God, they know about and tremble at the thought of him. The would-be exorcists had a weak theology compared to the demons. They tried to use Jesus' name without really identifying with him or following him in their own lives.

The name of Jesus is never to be used to enhance one's status. Instead, it is a gift that should be upheld with reverence and used to honor God. Jesus has rescued his people from the dominion of darkness so that they can live as his agents of light (Col 1:13–15).

their books together and burned them in the sight of all. And they counted the value of them and found it came to fifty thousand pieces of silver. 20 So the word of the Lord continued to increase and prevail mightily.

A Riot at Ephesus

21 Now after these events Paul resolved in the Spirit to pass through Macedonia and Achaia and go to Jerusalem, saying, "After I have been there, I must also see Rome." 22 And having sent into Macedonia two of his helpers, Timothy and Erastus, he himself stayed in Asia for a while.

23 About that time there arose no little disturbance concerning the Way. 24 For a man named Demetrius, a silversmith, who made silver shrines of Artemis, brought no little business to the craftsmen. 25 These he gathered together, with the workmen in similar trades, and said, "Men, you know that from this business we have our wealth. 26 And you see and hear that not only in Ephesus but in almost all of Asia this Paul has persuaded and turned away a great many people, saying that gods made with hands are not gods. 27 And there is danger not only that this trade of ours may come into disrepute but also that the temple of the great goddess Artemis may be counted as nothing, and that she may even be deposed from her magnificence, she whom all Asia and the world worship."

28 When they heard this they were enraged and were crying out, "Great is Artemis of the Ephesians!" 29 So the city was filled with the confusion, and they rushed together into the theater, dragging with them Gaius and Aristarchus, Macedonians who were Paul's companions in travel. 30 But when Paul wished to go in among the crowd, the disciples would not let him. 31 And even some of the Asiarchs,[1] who were friends of his, sent to him and were urging him not to venture into the theater. 32 Now some cried out one thing, some another, for the assembly was in confusion, and most of them did not know why they had come together. 33 Some of the crowd prompted Alexander, whom the Jews had put forward. And Alexander, motioning with his hand, wanted to make a defense to the crowd. 34 But when they recognized that he was a Jew, for about two hours they all cried out with one voice, "Great is Artemis of the Ephesians!"

35 And when the town clerk had quieted the crowd, he said, "Men of Ephesus, who is there who does not know that the city of the Ephesians is temple keeper of the great Artemis, and of the sacred stone that fell from the sky?[2] 36 Seeing then that these things cannot be denied, you ought to be quiet and do nothing rash. 37 For you have brought these men here who are neither sacrilegious nor blasphemers of our goddess. 38 If therefore Demetrius and the craftsmen with him have a complaint against anyone, the courts are open, and there are proconsuls. Let them bring charges against one another. 39 But if you seek anything further,[3] it shall be settled in the regular assembly. 40 For we really are in danger of being charged with rioting today, since there is no cause that we can give to justify this commotion." 41 And when he had said these things, he dismissed the assembly.

Paul in Macedonia and Greece

20 After the uproar ceased, Paul sent for the disciples, and after encouraging them, he said farewell and departed for Macedonia. 2 When he had gone through those regions and had given them much encouragement, he came to Greece. 3 There he spent three months, and when a plot was made against him by the Jews[4] as he was about to set sail for Syria, he decided to return through Macedonia. 4 Sopater the Berean, son of Pyrrhus, accompanied him; and of the Thessalonians, Aristarchus and Secundus; and Gaius of Derbe, and Timothy; and the Asians, Tychicus and Trophimus. 5 These went on ahead and

[1] That is, high-ranking officers of the province of Asia [2] The meaning of the Greek is uncertain [3] Some manuscripts *seek about other matters* [4] Greek *Ioudaioi* probably refers here to Jewish religious leaders, and others under their influence, in that time; also verse 19

PAUL'S THIRD MISSIONARY JOURNEY

We see from Paul's life that God's people are sometimes called to be mobile. Paul took three major missionary journeys. Each of these trips had a different strategy, but all of them had the same goal: spreading God's glory by planting and strengthening churches among the unreached parts of the Greco-Roman world.

Paul fostered many close relationships during his journeys, spending three full years in Ephesus that were especially formative periods in his ministry. He maintained contact with the church in Corinth, a church that actually sent people to Paul to update him on what was happening in the life of their congregation (1Co 1:11; 16:17). Paul wrote at least two letters to those believers in Corinth while in Ephesus, and he visited Corinth on his missionary journeys.

During Paul's missionary journeys, the Holy Spirit created extraordinary gospel unity. We see this in the networking that Paul did with other churches during his journeys. As Paul was passing through Macedonia, he received a substantial financial gift to take to the poorer Christians living in Jerusalem. He also asked the believers in Corinth to contribute, and they did as well. These were largely Gentile believers raising support for their Jewish brothers and sisters.

Finally, Paul found opportunity to write letters during his journeys. During the three months that Paul was in Corinth, before he left for Jerusalem, Paul wrote his letter to the church in Rome. God worked through Paul to lay out a masterful exposition of theology in order to foster understanding in the church and to motivate believers in Rome to support his missionary efforts.

As believers read about Paul's example, they see him taking God's Word to the ends of what was the known world at the time. They can take that as inspiration to follow Jesus' call, as Paul did, to teach, baptize, and tell others about Jesus — whether that be in the family, in the neighborhood, or on the other side of the world.

were waiting for us at Troas, 6but we sailed away from Philippi after the days of Unleavened Bread, and in five days we came to them at Troas, where we stayed for seven days.

Eutychus Raised from the Dead

7On the first day of the week, when we were gathered together to break bread, Paul talked with them, intending to depart on the next day, and he prolonged his speech until midnight. 8There were many lamps in the upper room where we were gathered. 9And a young man named Eutychus, sitting at the window, sank into a deep sleep as Paul talked still longer. And being overcome by sleep, he fell down from the third story and was taken up dead. 10But Paul went down and bent over him, and taking him in his arms, said, "Do not be alarmed, for his life is in him." 11And when Paul had gone up and had broken bread and eaten, he conversed with them a long while, until daybreak, and so departed. 12And they took the youth away alive, and were not a little comforted.

13But going ahead to the ship, we set sail for Assos, intending to take Paul aboard there, for so he had arranged, intending himself to go by land. 14And when he met us at Assos, we took him on board and went to Mitylene. 15And sailing from there we came the following day opposite Chios; the next day we touched at Samos; and[1] the day after that we went to Miletus. 16For Paul had decided to sail past Ephesus, so that he might not have to spend time in Asia, for he was hastening to be at Jerusalem, if possible, on the day of Pentecost.

Paul Speaks to the Ephesian Elders

17Now from Miletus he sent to Ephesus and called the elders of the church to come to him. 18And when they came to him, he said to them:

"You yourselves know how I lived among you the whole time from the first day that I set foot in Asia, 19serving the Lord with all humility and with tears and with trials that happened to me through the plots of the Jews; 20how I did not shrink from declaring to you anything that was profitable, and teaching you in public and from house to house, 21testifying both to Jews and to Greeks of repentance toward God and of faith in our Lord Jesus Christ.[2] 22And now, behold, I am going to Jerusalem, constrained by[3] the Spirit, not knowing what will happen to me there, 23except that the Holy Spirit testifies to me in every city that imprisonment and afflictions await me. 24But I do not account my life of any value nor as precious to myself, if only I may finish my course and the ministry that I received from the Lord Jesus, to testify to the gospel of the grace of God. 25And now, behold, I know that none of you among whom I have gone about proclaiming the kingdom will see my face again. 26Therefore I testify to you this day that I am innocent of the blood of all, 27for I did not shrink from declaring to you the whole counsel of God. 28Pay careful attention to yourselves and to all the flock, in which the Holy Spirit has made you overseers, to care for the church of God,[4] which he obtained with his own blood.[5] 29I know that after my departure fierce wolves will come in among you, not sparing the flock; 30and from among your own selves will arise men speaking twisted things, to draw away the disciples after them. 31Therefore be alert, remembering that for three years I did not cease night or day to admonish every one with tears. 32And now I commend you to God and to the word of his grace, which is able to build you up and to give you the inheritance among all those who are sanctified. 33I coveted no one's silver or gold or apparel. 34You yourselves know that these hands ministered to my necessities and to those who were with me. 35In all things I have shown you that by working hard in this way we must help the weak and remember the words of the Lord Jesus, how he himself said, 'It is more blessed to give than to receive.'"

[1]Some manuscripts add *after remaining at Trogyllium* [2]Some manuscripts omit *Christ* [3]Or *bound in*
[4]Some manuscripts *of the Lord* [5]Or *with the blood of his Own*

ACTS 20:24

THE GOOD NEWS OF GOD'S GRACE

Telling people about Jesus is a joy for those who realize what God has saved them from and what God has saved them to do. Paul laid out the single ambition of his life: to testify to the good news of God's grace. Grace refers to the love God shows to us through Jesus. We don't deserve it, and we could never earn it. Every person who ever lived is responsible for the death of Jesus (Ro 4:25; 5:8). Our sin made the cross necessary. Each of us is guilty and deserving of punishment forever. But God pursues people in his love (Lk 19:10) and freely forgives people when they turn to Jesus in repentance (Heb 9:14).

Paul invited the church to join him in sharing about the grace of God: "Share in suffering for the gospel by the power of God, who saved us and called us to a holy calling, not because of our works but because of his own purpose and grace, which he gave us in Christ Jesus before the ages began" (2Ti 1:8–9). God has saved his people from eternal punishment by his generous and merciful grace. For those who remember that they are saved to new life in Jesus by his grace alone, sharing about this Good News is an incredible joy!

36And when he had said these things, he knelt down and prayed with them all.
37And there was much weeping on the part of all; they embraced Paul and kissed
him, 38being sorrowful most of all because of the word he had spoken, that they
would not see his face again. And they accompanied him to the ship.

Paul Goes to Jerusalem

21 And when we had parted from them and set sail, we came by a straight
course to Cos, and the next day to Rhodes, and from there to Patara.[1] 2And
having found a ship crossing to Phoenicia, we went aboard and set sail. 3When we
had come in sight of Cyprus, leaving it on the left we sailed to Syria and landed
at Tyre, for there the ship was to unload its cargo. 4And having sought out the
disciples, we stayed there for seven days. And through the Spirit they were telling
Paul not to go on to Jerusalem. 5When our days there were ended, we departed
and went on our journey, and they all, with wives and children, accompanied us
until we were outside the city. And kneeling down on the beach, we prayed 6and
said farewell to one another. Then we went on board the ship, and they returned
home.

7When we had finished the voyage from Tyre, we arrived at Ptolemais, and
we greeted the brothers[2] and stayed with them for one day. 8On the next day we
departed and came to Caesarea, and we entered the house of Philip the evangelist,
who was one of the seven, and stayed with him. 9He had four unmarried daughters, who prophesied. 10While we were staying for many days, a prophet named
Agabus came down from Judea. 11And coming to us, he took Paul's belt and bound
his own feet and hands and said, "Thus says the Holy Spirit, 'This is how the Jews[3]
at Jerusalem will bind the man who owns this belt and deliver him into the hands
of the Gentiles.'" 12When we heard this, we and the people there urged him not
to go up to Jerusalem. 13Then Paul answered, "What are you doing, weeping and
breaking my heart? For I am ready not only to be imprisoned but even to die in
Jerusalem for the name of the Lord Jesus." 14And since he would not be persuaded,
we ceased and said, "Let the will of the Lord be done."

15After these days we got ready and went up to Jerusalem. 16And some of the
disciples from Caesarea went with us, bringing us to the house of Mnason of Cyprus, an early disciple, with whom we should lodge.

Paul Visits James

17When we had come to Jerusalem, the brothers received us gladly. 18On the
following day Paul went in with us to James, and all the elders were present. 19Af-
ter greeting them, he related one by one the things that God had done among
the Gentiles through his ministry. 20And when they heard it, they glorified God.
And they said to him, "You see, brother, how many thousands there are among
the Jews of those who have believed. They are all zealous for the law, 21and they
have been told about you that you teach all the Jews who are among the Gentiles
to forsake Moses, telling them not to circumcise their children or walk according
to our customs. 22What then is to be done? They will certainly hear that you have
come. 23Do therefore what we tell you. We have four men who are under a vow;
24take these men and purify yourself along with them and pay their expenses, so
that they may shave their heads. Thus all will know that there is nothing in what
they have been told about you, but that you yourself also live in observance of
the law. 25But as for the Gentiles who have believed, we have sent a letter with our
judgment that they should abstain from what has been sacrificed to idols, and
from blood, and from what has been strangled,[4] and from sexual immorality."
26Then Paul took the men, and the next day he purified himself along with them

[1]Some manuscripts add *and Myra* [2]Or *brothers and sisters*; also verse 17 [3]Greek *Ioudaioi* probably refers here to Jewish religious leaders, and others under their influence, in that time [4]Some manuscripts omit *and from what has been strangled*

PETER AND PAUL

The Bible tells the story of God's mission to heal the world through Jesus. Through the book of Acts, the focus of God's advancing of this mission narrows to the lives of two people in the early church: Peter and Paul. In these two men we find many similarities, but also some deep contrasts.

Peter was one of Jesus' original disciples. He followed Jesus through his entire ministry and experienced Jesus' miracles and teachings firsthand. Yet Peter also struggled with his belief in and loyalty to Jesus. As such, Peter is a comforting character for many Christians today. One might expect Peter to have had a clear picture of Jesus as the Messiah, as he professed (Mt 16:16). And yet, like the other disciples, he struggled with Jesus' teachings (Jn 16:17–18); Jesus even had to rebuke him several times during their ministry together (Mt 26:31–35; Mk 8:32–33; 14:37). Peter is an example of someone who took a long time to "get it." Nevertheless, Jesus was faithful to Peter even when Peter struggled to be faithful to him.

Paul was an opponent of the church and an enemy of God — by all human accounts, he was the last kind of person one would expect to become a Christian. Paul was caught up in his own way of life, in his own way of practicing religion. But Jesus broke through to Paul, rocked his world to its foundations, and saved him. Paul's life changed dramatically. He went from being a great opponent of Jesus to a great leader in the church within a few years. Unlike Peter, Paul's understanding of Jesus' identity and mission seemed instantaneous.

The author of Acts records many parallel events involving Peter and Paul to show that they were both effective servants of God. They both had direct encounters with Jesus (Peter, Mt 14:22–34; Paul, Ac 9:1–19), and they repented of their sins and trusted in him. Each man pronounced judgment against a sorcerer (Peter, Ac 8:20–23; Paul, Ac 13:9–11), healed men who had been disabled from birth (Peter, Ac 3:6; Paul, Ac 14:8–10), and exhibited amazing Spirit-empowered healing (Peter, Ac 5:15; Paul, Ac 19:12).

Peter and Paul represent different extremes of the same process. Peter's path to ministry was one of following Jesus up close for a season and then becoming a builder of the church after Jesus' ascension. Paul, on the other hand, took a different path. But both men's lives were transformed by Jesus, and their ministries were Spirit-empowered. No matter what one's spiritual heritage is, Jesus can transform any life, and the Spirit is available to empower a life of ministry.

and went into the temple, giving notice when the days of purification would be
fulfilled and the offering presented for each one of them.

Paul Arrested in the Temple

27When the seven days were almost completed, the Jews from Asia, seeing
him in the temple, stirred up the whole crowd and laid hands on him, 28crying
out, "Men of Israel, help! This is the man who is teaching everyone everywhere
against the people and the law and this place. Moreover, he even brought Greeks
into the temple and has defiled this holy place." 29For they had previously seen
Trophimus the Ephesian with him in the city, and they supposed that Paul had
brought him into the temple. 30Then all the city was stirred up, and the people
ran together. They seized Paul and dragged him out of the temple, and at once
the gates were shut. 31And as they were seeking to kill him, word came to the tribune of the cohort that all Jerusalem was in confusion. 32He at once took soldiers
and centurions and ran down to them. And when they saw the tribune and the
soldiers, they stopped beating Paul. 33Then the tribune came up and arrested him
and ordered him to be bound with two chains. He inquired who he was and what
he had done. 34Some in the crowd were shouting one thing, some another. And as
he could not learn the facts because of the uproar, he ordered him to be brought
into the barracks. 35And when he came to the steps, he was actually carried by
the soldiers because of the violence of the crowd, 36for the mob of the people followed, crying out, "Away with him!"

Paul Speaks to the People

37As Paul was about to be brought into the barracks, he said to the tribune,
"May I say something to you?" And he said, "Do you know Greek? 38Are you not
the Egyptian, then, who recently stirred up a revolt and led the four thousand
men of the Assassins out into the wilderness?" 39Paul replied, "I am a Jew, from
Tarsus in Cilicia, a citizen of no obscure city. I beg you, permit me to speak to the
people." 40And when he had given him permission, Paul, standing on the steps,
motioned with his hand to the people. And when there was a great hush, he addressed them in the Hebrew language,[1] saying:

22 "Brothers and fathers, hear the defense that I now make before you."
2And when they heard that he was addressing them in the Hebrew language,[2] they became even more quiet. And he said:
3"I am a Jew, born in Tarsus in Cilicia, but brought up in this city, educated at
the feet of Gamaliel[3] according to the strict manner of the law of our fathers, being zealous for God as all of you are this day. 4I persecuted this Way to the death,
binding and delivering to prison both men and women, 5as the high priest and the
whole council of elders can bear me witness. From them I received letters to the
brothers, and I journeyed toward Damascus to take those also who were there and
bring them in bonds to Jerusalem to be punished.
6"As I was on my way and drew near to Damascus, about noon a great light
from heaven suddenly shone around me. 7And I fell to the ground and heard a
voice saying to me, 'Saul, Saul, why are you persecuting me?' 8And I answered,
'Who are you, Lord?' And he said to me, 'I am Jesus of Nazareth, whom you are
persecuting.' 9Now those who were with me saw the light but did not understand[4]
the voice of the one who was speaking to me. 10And I said, 'What shall I do, Lord?'
And the Lord said to me, 'Rise, and go into Damascus, and there you will be told
all that is appointed for you to do.' 11And since I could not see because of the
brightness of that light, I was led by the hand by those who were with me, and
came into Damascus.
12"And one Ananias, a devout man according to the law, well spoken of by all

[1]Or *the Hebrew dialect* (probably Aramaic) [2]Or *the Hebrew dialect* (probably Aramaic) [3]Or *city at the feet of Gamaliel, educated* [4]Or *hear with understanding*

ACTS 22:6–10

THE PERSONAL GOSPEL

Many kinds of people, living all around the world and down through the centuries, have believed the truth of Christianity. Though the scope of Christianity is universal, Christianity is a very personal religion for those who trust in God. Before Paul was a follower of Jesus, he was an enemy of Jesus and his cause. He spent his early years trying to stop God's redemptive work in the world through his Messiah. When Jesus confronted Saul, he said, "Saul, Saul, why are you persecuting me?" (Ac 22:7). Jesus took Saul's persecution of the church personally.

In addition to this, the implications of Christianity are personal as well. Jesus is not simply an idea to be thought about; rather, he is a person who invites us into relationship with him. When Paul became a follower of Jesus, he learned that his Savior had a specific assignment for him (Ac 22:10). Jesus took Saul's opposition personally. And after he confronted Paul, this former enemy took the implications of that call just as personally. Every single believer in the church has a joyful responsibility to do the same—to take Jesus' call to heart and to play their own unique role in God's mission to show his glory to the world.

the Jews who lived there, [13]came to me, and standing by me said to me, 'Brother
Saul, receive your sight.' And at that very hour I received my sight and saw him.
[14]And he said, 'The God of our fathers appointed you to know his will, to see the
Righteous One and to hear a voice from his mouth; [15]for you will be a witness for
him to everyone of what you have seen and heard. [16]And now why do you wait?
Rise and be baptized and wash away your sins, calling on his name.'

[17]"When I had returned to Jerusalem and was praying in the temple, I fell into
a trance [18]and saw him saying to me, 'Make haste and get out of Jerusalem quickly,
because they will not accept your testimony about me.' [19]And I said, 'Lord, they
themselves know that in one synagogue after another I imprisoned and beat
those who believed in you. [20]And when the blood of Stephen your witness was
being shed, I myself was standing by and approving and watching over the garments of those who killed him.' [21]And he said to me, 'Go, for I will send you far
away to the Gentiles.'"

Paul and the Roman Tribune

[22]Up to this word they listened to him. Then they raised their voices and
said, "Away with such a fellow from the earth! For he should not be allowed to
live." [23]And as they were shouting and throwing off their cloaks and flinging
dust into the air, [24]the tribune ordered him to be brought into the barracks, saying that he should be examined by flogging, to find out why they were shouting
against him like this. [25]But when they had stretched him out for the whips,[1] Paul
said to the centurion who was standing by, "Is it lawful for you to flog a man
who is a Roman citizen and uncondemned?" [26]When the centurion heard this,
he went to the tribune and said to him, "What are you about to do? For this
man is a Roman citizen." [27]So the tribune came and said to him, "Tell me, are
you a Roman citizen?" And he said, "Yes." [28]The tribune answered, "I bought
this citizenship for a large sum." Paul said, "But I am a citizen by birth." [29]So
those who were about to examine him withdrew from him immediately, and
the tribune also was afraid, for he realized that Paul was a Roman citizen and
that he had bound him.

Paul Before the Council

[30]But on the next day, desiring to know the real reason why he was being accused by the Jews, he unbound him and commanded the chief priests and all the
council to meet, and he brought Paul down and set him before them.

23 And looking intently at the council, Paul said, "Brothers, I have lived my
life before God in all good conscience up to this day." [2]And the high priest
Ananias commanded those who stood by him to strike him on the mouth. [3]Then
Paul said to him, "God is going to strike you, you whitewashed wall! Are you sit-
ting to judge me according to the law, and yet contrary to the law you order me to
be struck?" [4]Those who stood by said, "Would you revile God's high priest?" [5]And
Paul said, "I did not know, brothers, that he was the high priest, for it is written,
'You shall not speak evil of a ruler of your people.'"

[6]Now when Paul perceived that one part were Sadducees and the other Pharisees, he cried out in the council, "Brothers, I am a Pharisee, a son of Pharisees.
It is with respect to the hope and the resurrection of the dead that I am on trial."
[7]And when he had said this, a dissension arose between the Pharisees and the
Sadducees, and the assembly was divided. [8]For the Sadducees say that there is
no resurrection, nor angel, nor spirit, but the Pharisees acknowledge them all.
[9]Then a great clamor arose, and some of the scribes of the Pharisees' party stood
up and contended sharply, "We find nothing wrong in this man. What if a spirit
or an angel spoke to him?" [10]And when the dissension became violent, the tribune, afraid that Paul would be torn to pieces by them, commanded the soldiers

[1]Or *when they had tied him up with leather strips*

to go down and take him away from among them by force and bring him into the barracks.

11The following night the Lord stood by him and said, "Take courage, for as you have testified to the facts about me in Jerusalem, so you must testify also in Rome."

A Plot to Kill Paul

12When it was day, the Jews made a plot and bound themselves by an oath neither to eat nor drink till they had killed Paul. 13There were more than forty who made this conspiracy. 14They went to the chief priests and elders and said, "We have strictly bound ourselves by an oath to taste no food till we have killed Paul. 15Now therefore you, along with the council, give notice to the tribune to bring him down to you, as though you were going to determine his case more exactly. And we are ready to kill him before he comes near."

16Now the son of Paul's sister heard of their ambush, so he went and entered the barracks and told Paul. 17Paul called one of the centurions and said, "Take this young man to the tribune, for he has something to tell him." 18So he took him and brought him to the tribune and said, "Paul the prisoner called me and asked me to bring this young man to you, as he has something to say to you." 19The tribune took him by the hand, and going aside asked him privately, "What is it that you have to tell me?" 20And he said, "The Jews have agreed to ask you to bring Paul down to the council tomorrow, as though they were going to inquire somewhat more closely about him. 21But do not be persuaded by them, for more than forty of their men are lying in ambush for him, who have bound themselves by an oath neither to eat nor drink till they have killed him. And now they are ready, waiting for your consent." 22So the tribune dismissed the young man, charging him, "Tell no one that you have informed me of these things."

Paul Sent to Felix the Governor

23Then he called two of the centurions and said, "Get ready two hundred soldiers, with seventy horsemen and two hundred spearmen to go as far as Caesarea at the third hour of the night.[1] 24Also provide mounts for Paul to ride and bring him safely to Felix the governor." 25And he wrote a letter to this effect:

26"Claudius Lysias, to his Excellency the governor Felix, greetings. 27This man was seized by the Jews and was about to be killed by them when I came upon them with the soldiers and rescued him, having learned that he was a Roman citizen. 28And desiring to know the charge for which they were accusing him, I brought him down to their council. 29I found that he was being accused about questions of their law, but charged with nothing deserving death or imprisonment. 30And when it was disclosed to me that there would be a plot against the man, I sent him to you at once, ordering his accusers also to state before you what they have against him."

31So the soldiers, according to their instructions, took Paul and brought him by night to Antipatris. 32And on the next day they returned to the barracks, letting the horsemen go on with him. 33When they had come to Caesarea and delivered the letter to the governor, they presented Paul also before him. 34On reading the letter, he asked what province he was from. And when he learned that he was from Cilicia, 35he said, "I will give you a hearing when your accusers arrive." And he commanded him to be guarded in Herod's praetorium.

Paul Before Felix at Caesarea

24 And after five days the high priest Ananias came down with some elders and a spokesman, one Tertullus. They laid before the governor their case against Paul. 2And when he had been summoned, Tertullus began to accuse him, saying:

[1]That is, 9 P.M.

ACTS 23:11

PERSONAL SAVIOR

Jesus is a personal Savior. He came to save the world, and he does that by saving people individually as they trust in him. Jesus is not a distant cosmic deity, unaware of what is happening in his world. Instead, Jesus is intensely and personally aware of and concerned about every detail of our lives.

Paul was on trial in front of the Jewish religious leadership of his day. A near-riot broke out, and Paul suffered because of it. These leaders wanted to kill Paul because of the message he shared. In the midst of this hardship, Jesus showed up personally to care for his apostle. Our living Savior physically appeared to Paul and gave him his next assignment.

As he wrote in his letter to the Romans (Ro 8:38–39), nothing could keep Paul from Jesus. Paul was in a difficult circumstance, but Jesus was aware of it and chose to interact with him personally. While such interactions are not common, they are real. Jesus' awareness and concern for individuals continues today. He is the great God of the universe who has come near to love people individually.

"Since through you we enjoy much peace, and since by your foresight, most
excellent Felix, reforms are being made for this nation, 3in every way and everywhere we accept this with all gratitude. 4But, to detain[1] you no further, I beg you
in your kindness to hear us briefly. 5For we have found this man a plague, one
who stirs up riots among all the Jews throughout the world and is a ringleader
of the sect of the Nazarenes. 6He even tried to profane the temple, but we seized
him.[2] 8By examining him yourself you will be able to find out from him about
everything of which we accuse him."

9The Jews also joined in the charge, affirming that all these things were so.

10And when the governor had nodded to him to speak, Paul replied:

"Knowing that for many years you have been a judge over this nation, I
cheerfully make my defense. 11You can verify that it is not more than twelve days
since I went up to worship in Jerusalem, 12and they did not find me disputing
with anyone or stirring up a crowd, either in the temple or in the synagogues or
in the city. 13Neither can they prove to you what they now bring up against me.
14But this I confess to you, that according to the Way, which they call a sect, I
worship the God of our fathers, believing everything laid down by the Law and
written in the Prophets, 15having a hope in God, which these men themselves
accept, that there will be a resurrection of both the just and the unjust. 16So I
always take pains to have a clear conscience toward both God and man. 17Now
after several years I came to bring alms to my nation and to present offerings.
18While I was doing this, they found me purified in the temple, without any
crowd or tumult. But some Jews from Asia— 19they ought to be here before you
and to make an accusation, should they have anything against me. 20Or else let
these men themselves say what wrongdoing they found when I stood before
the council, 21other than this one thing that I cried out while standing among
them: 'It is with respect to the resurrection of the dead that I am on trial before
you this day.' "

Paul Kept in Custody

22But Felix, having a rather accurate knowledge of the Way, put them off, saying, "When Lysias the tribune comes down, I will decide your case." 23Then he
gave orders to the centurion that he should be kept in custody but have some
liberty, and that none of his friends should be prevented from attending to his
needs.

24After some days Felix came with his wife Drusilla, who was Jewish, and he
sent for Paul and heard him speak about faith in Christ Jesus. 25And as he reasoned about righteousness and self-control and the coming judgment, Felix was
alarmed and said, "Go away for the present. When I get an opportunity I will summon you." 26At the same time he hoped that money would be given him by Paul.
So he sent for him often and conversed with him. 27When two years had elapsed,
Felix was succeeded by Porcius Festus. And desiring to do the Jews a favor, Felix
left Paul in prison.

Paul Appeals to Caesar

25 Now three days after Festus had arrived in the province, he went up to
Jerusalem from Caesarea. 2And the chief priests and the principal men of
the Jews laid out their case against Paul, and they urged him, 3asking as a favor
against Paul[3] that he summon him to Jerusalem—because they were planning an
ambush to kill him on the way. 4Festus replied that Paul was being kept at Caesarea and that he himself intended to go there shortly. 5"So," said he, "let the men
of authority among you go down with me, and if there is anything wrong about
the man, let them bring charges against him."

[1]Or *weary* [2]Some manuscripts add *and we would have judged him according to our law. 7But the chief captain Lysias came and with great violence took him out of our hands, 8commanding his accusers to come before you.* [3]Greek *him*

ACTS 24:14–16

THE WAY

The entire Bible is the story of how people gain access to God. In the first part of the Bible, God established the Law as a way for people to atone for their sins. In the second part, God called prophets to mediate the relationship between God and his people. Finally, God sent Jesus to be the fulfillment of the Law and the Prophets and to personally give people eternal access to God.

Jesus is the only way to God; he said, "I am the way, and the truth, and the life. No one comes to the Father except through me" (Jn 14:6). Human sin has created an impassable canyon between God and his people. Paul testified that Jesus is "the Way" back to God and believed that Jesus' claims were consistent with the Law and the Prophets.

The Old Testament provides a rich and detailed backdrop for Jesus' life and helps people see Jesus more clearly. In a sense, viewing Jesus against the backdrop of the Old Testament is like seeing a movie in 3-D. Three-dimensional movies accomplish depth by adding different visual dimensions on the screen. In a similar way, our relationship with Jesus becomes more vivid when we understand him within the story of the Bible as the fulfillment of the Law. Jesus taught his followers to read the whole Bible in reference to him: "And beginning with Moses and all the Prophets, he interpreted to them in all the Scriptures the things concerning himself" (Lk 24:27).

[6]After he stayed among them not more than eight or ten days, he went down to Caesarea. And the next day he took his seat on the tribunal and ordered Paul to be brought. [7]When he had arrived, the Jews who had come down from Jerusalem stood around him, bringing many and serious charges against him that they could not prove. [8]Paul argued in his defense, "Neither against the law of the Jews, nor against the temple, nor against Caesar have I committed any offense." [9]But Festus, wishing to do the Jews a favor, said to Paul, "Do you wish to go up to Jerusalem and there be tried on these charges before me?" [10]But Paul said, "I am standing before Caesar's tribunal, where I ought to be tried. To the Jews I have done no wrong, as you yourself know very well. [11]If then I am a wrongdoer and have committed anything for which I deserve to die, I do not seek to escape death. But if there is nothing to their charges against me, no one can give me up to them. I appeal to Caesar." [12]Then Festus, when he had conferred with his council, answered, "To Caesar you have appealed; to Caesar you shall go."

Paul Before Agrippa and Bernice

[13]Now when some days had passed, Agrippa the king and Bernice arrived at Caesarea and greeted Festus. [14]And as they stayed there many days, Festus laid Paul's case before the king, saying, "There is a man left prisoner by Felix, [15]and when I was at Jerusalem, the chief priests and the elders of the Jews laid out their case against him, asking for a sentence of condemnation against him. [16]I answered them that it was not the custom of the Romans to give up anyone before the accused met the accusers face to face and had opportunity to make his defense concerning the charge laid against him. [17]So when they came together here, I made no delay, but on the next day took my seat on the tribunal and ordered the man to be brought. [18]When the accusers stood up, they brought no charge in his case of such evils as I supposed. [19]Rather they had certain points of dispute with him about their own religion and about a certain Jesus, who was dead, but whom Paul asserted to be alive. [20]Being at a loss how to investigate these questions, I asked whether he wanted to go to Jerusalem and be tried there regarding them. [21]But when Paul had appealed to be kept in custody for the decision of the emperor, I ordered him to be held until I could send him to Caesar." [22]Then Agrippa said to Festus, "I would like to hear the man myself." "Tomorrow," said he, "you will hear him."

[23]So on the next day Agrippa and Bernice came with great pomp, and they entered the audience hall with the military tribunes and the prominent men of the city. Then, at the command of Festus, Paul was brought in. [24]And Festus said, "King Agrippa and all who are present with us, you see this man about whom the whole Jewish people petitioned me, both in Jerusalem and here, shouting that he ought not to live any longer. [25]But I found that he had done nothing deserving death. And as he himself appealed to the emperor, I decided to go ahead and send him. [26]But I have nothing definite to write to my lord about him. Therefore I have brought him before you all, and especially before you, King Agrippa, so that, after we have examined him, I may have something to write. [27]For it seems to me unreasonable, in sending a prisoner, not to indicate the charges against him."

Paul's Defense Before Agrippa

26 So Agrippa said to Paul, "You have permission to speak for yourself." Then Paul stretched out his hand and made his defense:

[2]"I consider myself fortunate that it is before you, King Agrippa, I am going to make my defense today against all the accusations of the Jews, [3]especially because you are familiar with all the customs and controversies of the Jews. Therefore I beg you to listen to me patiently.

[4]"My manner of life from my youth, spent from the beginning among my own nation and in Jerusalem, is known by all the Jews. [5]They have known for a long

ACTS 25:1–27

TURNING THE WORLD UPSIDE DOWN

In the book of Acts, God's people caused great trouble for the government and religious establishments of their day. That's what living according to the values of the coming kingdom does — it's countercultural; it's disruptive; it challenges the status quo.

The kingdom of God operates according to values that are antithetical to the world. The world values self-advancement by stepping on or over other people; in God's kingdom, true reward is found in humility and in service to others. The world sees hard work and status as the key identifiers of success; in God's kingdom, the only way to find your life is to lose it for the sake of the gospel, surrendering yourself in the interest of advancing the cause of Jesus in the world. When God's people live according to the values of the kingdom, it causes trouble because God is in the business of turning the ways of the world upside down.

Acts 25 details Paul's confrontations with the authorities of his day; Jesus caused trouble for the Roman authorities as well (Mk 15:1 – 15). Also following Jesus' lead (Mk 14:53 – 65), Paul caused trouble and was opposed by Jewish religious leaders for his beliefs.

In the eyes of the prevailing religious and political authorities, Paul was a troublemaker. He was completely devoted to Jesus, and Jesus was turning the world upside down through him. The authorities couldn't stop him. If they put Paul on trial, then he simply shared the gospel. If they put Paul in prison, then he would befriend and disciple everyone there. Paul was causing trouble because he refused to settle for anything less than advancing the values of Christ's kingdom. Paul knew that the way of Jesus would mean suffering at times (Ac 9:15 – 16). Therefore, he was not alarmed when he found himself in prison. God continued to use him wherever he found himself. And God does the same for believers today. Around the dinner table, in the workplace, or in a remote corner of the world, they can represent kingdom values, no matter where they find themselves.

Jesus came to bring God's kingdom — a kingdom set on turning the values of the world upside down through the mission of the church. Then as now, any attempts to stop the church only propel it forward. God's work will not be stopped. He is using his followers, his own children, to bring about an entirely new world and way of life.

time, if they are willing to testify, that according to the strictest party of our religion I have lived as a Pharisee. 6And now I stand here on trial because of my hope
in the promise made by God to our fathers, 7to which our twelve tribes hope to
attain, as they earnestly worship night and day. And for this hope I am accused by
Jews, O king! 8Why is it thought incredible by any of you that God raises the dead?
9"I myself was convinced that I ought to do many things in opposing the name
of Jesus of Nazareth. 10And I did so in Jerusalem. I not only locked up many of the
saints in prison after receiving authority from the chief priests, but when they
were put to death I cast my vote against them. 11And I punished them often in all
the synagogues and tried to make them blaspheme, and in raging fury against
them I persecuted them even to foreign cities.

Paul Tells of His Conversion

12"In this connection I journeyed to Damascus with the authority and commission of the chief priests. 13At midday, O king, I saw on the way a light from
heaven, brighter than the sun, that shone around me and those who journeyed
with me. 14And when we had all fallen to the ground, I heard a voice saying to me
in the Hebrew language,[1] 'Saul, Saul, why are you persecuting me? It is hard for
you to kick against the goads.' 15And I said, 'Who are you, Lord?' And the Lord
said, 'I am Jesus whom you are persecuting. 16But rise and stand upon your feet,
for I have appeared to you for this purpose, to appoint you as a servant and witness to the things in which you have seen me and to those in which I will appear
to you, 17delivering you from your people and from the Gentiles—to whom I am
sending you 18to open their eyes, so that they may turn from darkness to light and
from the power of Satan to God, that they may receive forgiveness of sins and a
place among those who are sanctified by faith in me.'
19"Therefore, O King Agrippa, I was not disobedient to the heavenly vision,
20but declared first to those in Damascus, then in Jerusalem and throughout all
the region of Judea, and also to the Gentiles, that they should repent and turn to
God, performing deeds in keeping with their repentance. 21For this reason the
Jews seized me in the temple and tried to kill me. 22To this day I have had the
help that comes from God, and so I stand here testifying both to small and great,
saying nothing but what the prophets and Moses said would come to pass: 23that
the Christ must suffer and that, by being the first to rise from the dead, he would
proclaim light both to our people and to the Gentiles."
24And as he was saying these things in his defense, Festus said with a loud
voice, "Paul, you are out of your mind; your great learning is driving you out of
your mind." 25But Paul said, "I am not out of my mind, most excellent Festus, but
I am speaking true and rational words. 26For the king knows about these things,
and to him I speak boldly. For I am persuaded that none of these things has escaped his notice, for this has not been done in a corner. 27King Agrippa, do you
believe the prophets? I know that you believe." 28And Agrippa said to Paul, "In a
short time would you persuade me to be a Christian?"[2] 29And Paul said, "Whether
short or long, I would to God that not only you but also all who hear me this day
might become such as I am—except for these chains."
30Then the king rose, and the governor and Bernice and those who were sitting with them. 31And when they had withdrawn, they said to one another, "This
man is doing nothing to deserve death or imprisonment." 32And Agrippa said to
Festus, "This man could have been set free if he had not appealed to Caesar."

Paul Sails for Rome

27 And when it was decided that we should sail for Italy, they delivered Paul
and some other prisoners to a centurion of the Augustan Cohort named
Julius. 2And embarking in a ship of Adramyttium, which was about to sail to the

[1]Or *the Hebrew dialect* (probably Aramaic) [2]Or *In a short time you would persuade me to act like a Christian!*

ACTS 26:24–29

SHARING OUR STORY

Paul was once a highly educated religious leader in the Jewish faith. He found his identity in that expertise; because of his deep knowledge, after Jesus confronted him, Paul could make all of the connections between Jesus and the prophets. He was so convinced and his life changed so dramatically that Paul couldn't help but tell people the gospel story no matter where he was.

As Jesus promised (Ac 23:11), Paul found himself before the most influential rulers of the day. Even in that situation, Paul wasn't concerned about self-preservation. Instead of defending himself, Paul shared about his background, his encounter with Jesus, and his subsequent change of heart. Quite simply, Paul shared his story because it was all about Jesus. The rulers responded with shock and ridicule, but they listened and considered what he said against the charges that were levied against him (Ac 26:31–32). This encounter between Paul and the secular leaders of his day teaches that the message of Jesus always runs counter to the culture. Paul taught with his teaching and modeled with his life how to share the story of Jesus with others (2Ti 2:2). The church's story of God's radical grace in the face of consistent human sin should draw a similar reaction from the surrounding culture. Believers need only to plant the seed and let the Spirit do the rest (1Co 3:6).

CHURCH

JESUS ON DISPLAY TO THE WORLD

ACTS 2 TO REVELATION 20

A short time after his resurrection, Jesus appeared to his followers and proclaimed, "You will receive power when the Holy Spirit has come upon you, and you will be my witnesses in Jerusalem and in all Judea and Samaria, and to the end of the earth" (Ac 1:8).

A powerful witness. This is what Jesus intends the church to be.

This powerful witness shows the world what transformed lives look like. Not perfect lives, mind you, but lives testifying to what is possible when Jesus is at the center of our lives.

What was the mightiest miracle of the New Testament church? As you think about the early days of the church, what stands out as the most powerful moment? Mentally thumb through the book of Acts and consider the greatest events:

- The falling of the Holy Spirit on the apostles in the upper room.
- The baptism of three thousand people on the day of Pentecost.
- The healing of the lame man at the temple gate.
- The conversion of Saul. The deliverance of Peter. The vision of Stephen.

These are all amazing and miraculous events. If you were to list any one of them as the greatest of the New Testament church, I wouldn't blame you. But I wouldn't agree with you. As stunning as these are, I feel there is one even greater. One that is often overlooked, easily neglected, yet absolutely amazing. What was this mighty event? Unity. This church loved each other, and this is what set it apart as an amazing display of God's grace to the world.

"And all who believed were together and had all things in common. And they were selling their possessions and belongings and distributing the proceeds to all, as any had need. And day by day, attending the temple together and breaking bread in their homes, they received their food with glad and generous hearts, praising God and having favor with all the people. And the Lord added to their number day by day those who were being saved" (Ac 2:44 – 47).

The charter members of Jesus Christ's church were Jews who had come to Jerusalem to celebrate the Passover. "Those who received his word were baptized, and there were added that day about three thousand souls" (Ac 2:41).

The church exploded. Membership went from zero to three thousand overnight! "The Lord added to their number day by day those who were being saved" (Ac 2:47). Every meeting had more faces. Every service had new members. The Jerusalem 101 class was bursting at the seams. This was a dynamic church.

And this was a diverse church! They were from different places: Parthia, Media, Elam, Mesopotamia, Judea, Cappadocia, Pontus, Asia, Phrygia, Pamphylia, Egypt, the areas of Libya near Cyrene, Rome (both Jews and those who had become Jews), Crete, and Arabia (Ac 2:8 – 11).

Fifteen different regions were represented! The Parthians came from the east. The Egyptians came from the south. The Romans were from the north. They had different cultures and spoke different languages; they ate different types of food. They came to be a part of the Passover. They stayed to be a part of the church.

Within a short time, the church grew to as many as 20,000 men, women, and children (Ac 4:4).* What was the church's strategy? They had no buildings. They were not affiliated with any denomination. No mention is made of a budget or program. What enabled them to increase in number and deepen in faith? It was simple: "They devoted themselves to the apostles' teaching and the fellowship, to the breaking of bread and the prayers" (Ac 2:42).

The verb "devoted" means *steadfast determination*. They were steadfastly determined to grow in four areas: teaching, fellowship, the breaking of bread (likely communion), and prayer. Three of the four activities are done with others. We may pray alone, but teaching, the breaking of bread, and fellowship require community. The church was devoted to develop this community.

Could the world use such community today?

Conflicts rage on every continent. Loneliness stalks our streets. Neighbors live next door to each other without sharing a word. Our world is hungry for community.

The church is God's way of giving it. The church is a community of saved sinners. No economic level required. No education level expected. If you call God your Father and Jesus your Savior then I call you brother or sister. Period.

We:

"Are one body in Christ, and individually members one of another" (Ro 12:5).

We are told to:

"Welcome one another" (Ro 15:7).

"Instruct one another" (Ro 15:14).

"Greet one another" (Ro 16:16).

*The reference of 5,000 men implies that, with women and children, the church could have numbered 20,000 people.

CHURCH

(CONTINUED)

ACTS 2 TO REVELATION 20

"Serve one another" (Gal 5:13).

"Bear one another's burdens" (Gal 6:2).

"Encourage one another and build one another up" (1Th 5:11)

What would happen if we took these verses seriously? What if we truly devoted ourselves to one another?

I spoke at each Good Friday service of a nearby Episcopal church for many years. On one occasion, I shared the responsibility with the bishop of the diocese of West Texas. He wore a robe and a large gold cross around his neck. My church background didn't make me too keen on preachers wearing religious jewelry. So, I was less than impressed. And, I confess, even a bit judgmental.

But as he shared the story behind his gold cross, my attitude began to change. In order to assume his role as bishop, he had to leave behind St. Mark's Episcopal, a church where he was loved dearly. The people tried to talk him into staying, but he felt it was God's will to leave. The members, then, expressed their gratitude by making him this cross. Two hundred and forty-two households contributed gold pieces which were melted down and forged together. Some of the gold provided was from the wedding bands of widows and widowers. Three couples who had divorced and then reconciled each gave a set of wedding rings to the cross. One friend of the bishop was a bachelor who was rejected by "the love of his life" just days before the ceremony and contributed her ring to the cross as a symbolic surrendering of the pain of his lost love. The cross includes a college ring as well as the bridge from a fellow bishop's mouth. One mom donated some gold beads. When her son was four, he found them on a dresser, thought they were toys, and damaged them. He died soon thereafter in an accident. She donated them on the day before what would have been his seventh birthday.

Two hundred and forty-two stories. Stories of celebration, stories of sorrow. Stories of peace, stories of pain. But when forged together they form the cross of Christ.

What happened literally with the bishop's cross happens spiritually in every church that devotes itself to fellowship. When your story intermingles with mine, and our stories interweave with others, the cross is formed. When one hand holds another in a hospital, the cross is lifted up. When a conservative loves a liberal; when an Anglo seeks to understand a Hispanic; when the redneck and the tree-hugger stand side by side at the communion table, the cross is lifted up.

When Jesus is at the center of the church:

- People with a diversity of backgrounds serve and love each other.
- Prejudices and biases are replaced with love and grace.
- Peace, not conflict, is the goal of all of our relationships.

This is what was on display in the first church. Those early believers were a powerful testimony of what is possible in Jesus. This same possibility is available for us today. May we, through the example of Jesus and the power of the Holy Spirit, strive to pattern our lives after theirs.

BEGINNINGS GENESIS 1–2 (pg. 10)	**REVOLT** GENESIS 3–11 (pg. 24)	**PEOPLE** GENESIS 12 to MALACHI (pg. 256)	**INTERTESTAMENTAL PERIOD** (pg. 1468)	**SAVIOR** GOSPELS to ACTS 1 (pg. 1518)	**CHURCH** ACTS 2 to REVELATION 20 (pg. 1686)	**FOREVER** REVELATION 21–22 (pg. 1938)

ports along the coast of Asia, we put to sea, accompanied by Aristarchus, a Macedonian from Thessalonica. [3]The next day we put in at Sidon. And Julius treated Paul kindly and gave him leave to go to his friends and be cared for. [4]And putting out to sea from there we sailed under the lee of Cyprus, because the winds were against us. [5]And when we had sailed across the open sea along the coast of Cilicia and Pamphylia, we came to Myra in Lycia. [6]There the centurion found a ship of Alexandria sailing for Italy and put us on board. [7]We sailed slowly for a number of days and arrived with difficulty off Cnidus, and as the wind did not allow us to go farther, we sailed under the lee of Crete off Salmone. [8]Coasting along it with difficulty, we came to a place called Fair Havens, near which was the city of Lasea.

[9]Since much time had passed, and the voyage was now dangerous because even the Fast[1] was already over, Paul advised them, [10]saying, "Sirs, I perceive that the voyage will be with injury and much loss, not only of the cargo and the ship, but also of our lives." [11]But the centurion paid more attention to the pilot and to the owner of the ship than to what Paul said. [12]And because the harbor was not suitable to spend the winter in, the majority decided to put out to sea from there, on the chance that somehow they could reach Phoenix, a harbor of Crete, facing both southwest and northwest, and spend the winter there.

The Storm at Sea

[13]Now when the south wind blew gently, supposing that they had obtained their purpose, they weighed anchor and sailed along Crete, close to the shore. [14]But soon a tempestuous wind, called the northeaster, struck down from the land. [15]And when the ship was caught and could not face the wind, we gave way to it and were driven along. [16]Running under the lee of a small island called Cauda,[2] we managed with difficulty to secure the ship's boat. [17]After hoisting it up, they used supports to undergird the ship. Then, fearing that they would run aground on the Syrtis, they lowered the gear,[3] and thus they were driven along. [18]Since we were violently storm-tossed, they began the next day to jettison the cargo. [19]And on the third day they threw the ship's tackle overboard with their own hands. [20]When neither sun nor stars appeared for many days, and no small tempest lay on us, all hope of our being saved was at last abandoned.

[21]Since they had been without food for a long time, Paul stood up among them and said, "Men, you should have listened to me and not have set sail from Crete and incurred this injury and loss. [22]Yet now I urge you to take heart, for there will be no loss of life among you, but only of the ship. [23]For this very night there stood before me an angel of the God to whom I belong and whom I worship, [24]and he said, 'Do not be afraid, Paul; you must stand before Caesar. And behold, God has granted you all those who sail with you.' [25]So take heart, men, for I have faith in God that it will be exactly as I have been told. [26]But we must run aground on some island."

[27]When the fourteenth night had come, as we were being driven across the Adriatic Sea, about midnight the sailors suspected that they were nearing land. [28]So they took a sounding and found twenty fathoms.[4] A little farther on they took a sounding again and found fifteen fathoms.[5] [29]And fearing that we might run on the rocks, they let down four anchors from the stern and prayed for day to come. [30]And as the sailors were seeking to escape from the ship, and had lowered the ship's boat into the sea under pretense of laying out anchors from the bow, [31]Paul said to the centurion and the soldiers, "Unless these men stay in the ship, you cannot be saved." [32]Then the soldiers cut away the ropes of the ship's boat and let it go.

[33]As day was about to dawn, Paul urged them all to take some food, saying,

[1]That is, the Day of Atonement [2]Some manuscripts *Clauda* [3]That is, the sea-anchor (or possibly the mainsail) [4]About 120 feet; a fathom (Greek *orguia*) was about 6 feet or 2 meters [5]About 90 feet (see previous note)

"Today is the fourteenth day that you have continued in suspense and without
food, having taken nothing. 34Therefore I urge you to take some food. For it will
give you strength,[1] for not a hair is to perish from the head of any of you." 35And
when he had said these things, he took bread, and giving thanks to God in the
presence of all he broke it and began to eat. 36Then they all were encouraged and
ate some food themselves. 37(We were in all 276[2] persons in the ship.) 38And when
they had eaten enough, they lightened the ship, throwing out the wheat into the
sea.

The Shipwreck

39Now when it was day, they did not recognize the land, but they noticed a
bay with a beach, on which they planned if possible to run the ship ashore. 40So
they cast off the anchors and left them in the sea, at the same time loosening the
ropes that tied the rudders. Then hoisting the foresail to the wind they made for
the beach. 41But striking a reef,[3] they ran the vessel aground. The bow stuck and
remained immovable, and the stern was being broken up by the surf. 42The soldiers' plan was to kill the prisoners, lest any should swim away and escape. 43But
the centurion, wishing to save Paul, kept them from carrying out their plan. He ordered those who could swim to jump overboard first and make for the land, 44and
the rest on planks or on pieces of the ship. And so it was that all were brought
safely to land.

Paul on Malta

28 After we were brought safely through, we then learned that the island was
called Malta. 2The native people[4] showed us unusual kindness, for they
kindled a fire and welcomed us all, because it had begun to rain and was cold.
3When Paul had gathered a bundle of sticks and put them on the fire, a viper came
out because of the heat and fastened on his hand. 4When the native people saw
the creature hanging from his hand, they said to one another, "No doubt this man
is a murderer. Though he has escaped from the sea, Justice[5] has not allowed him
to live." 5He, however, shook off the creature into the fire and suffered no harm.
6They were waiting for him to swell up or suddenly fall down dead. But when they
had waited a long time and saw no misfortune come to him, they changed their
minds and said that he was a god.

7Now in the neighborhood of that place were lands belonging to the chief man
of the island, named Publius, who received us and entertained us hospitably for
three days. 8It happened that the father of Publius lay sick with fever and dysen-
tery. And Paul visited him and prayed, and putting his hands on him, healed him.
9And when this had taken place, the rest of the people on the island who had
diseases also came and were cured. 10They also honored us greatly,[6] and when we
were about to sail, they put on board whatever we needed.

Paul Arrives at Rome

11After three months we set sail in a ship that had wintered in the island, a
ship of Alexandria, with the twin gods[7] as a figurehead. 12Putting in at Syracuse,
we stayed there for three days. 13And from there we made a circuit and arrived at
Rhegium. And after one day a south wind sprang up, and on the second day we
came to Puteoli. 14There we found brothers[8] and were invited to stay with them
for seven days. And so we came to Rome. 15And the brothers there, when they
heard about us, came as far as the Forum of Appius and Three Taverns to meet
us. On seeing them, Paul thanked God and took courage. 16And when we came
into Rome, Paul was allowed to stay by himself, with the soldier who guarded him.

[1]Or *For it is for your deliverance* [2]Some manuscripts *seventy-six*, or *about seventy-six* [3]Or *sandbank*, or *crosscurrent*; Greek *place between two seas* [4]Greek *barbaroi* (that is, non–Greek speakers); also verse 4
[5]Or *justice* [6]Greek *honored us with many honors* [7]That is, the Greek gods Castor and Pollux
[8]Or *brothers and sisters*; also verses 15, 21

Paul in Rome

17 After three days he called together the local leaders of the Jews, and when
they had gathered, he said to them, "Brothers, though I had done nothing against
our people or the customs of our fathers, yet I was delivered as a prisoner from
Jerusalem into the hands of the Romans. 18 When they had examined me, they
wished to set me at liberty, because there was no reason for the death penalty in
my case. 19 But because the Jews objected, I was compelled to appeal to Caesar—
though I had no charge to bring against my nation. 20 For this reason, therefore, I
have asked to see you and speak with you, since it is because of the hope of Israel
that I am wearing this chain." 21 And they said to him, "We have received no letters from Judea about you, and none of the brothers coming here has reported or
spoken any evil about you. 22 But we desire to hear from you what your views are,
for with regard to this sect we know that everywhere it is spoken against."

23 When they had appointed a day for him, they came to him at his lodging in
greater numbers. From morning till evening he expounded to them, testifying to
the kingdom of God and trying to convince them about Jesus both from the Law
of Moses and from the Prophets. 24 And some were convinced by what he said,
but others disbelieved. 25 And disagreeing among themselves, they departed after
Paul had made one statement: "The Holy Spirit was right in saying to your fathers
through Isaiah the prophet:

26 " 'Go to this people, and say,
"You will indeed hear but never understand,
and you will indeed see but never perceive."
27 For this people's heart has grown dull,
and with their ears they can barely hear,
and their eyes they have closed;
lest they should see with their eyes
and hear with their ears
and understand with their heart
and turn, and I would heal them.'

28 Therefore let it be known to you that this salvation of God has been sent to the
Gentiles; they will listen."[1]

30 He lived there two whole years at his own expense,[2] and welcomed all who
came to him, 31 proclaiming the kingdom of God and teaching about the Lord Jesus
Christ with all boldness and without hindrance.

---

[1] Some manuscripts add verse 29: *And when he had said these words, the Jews departed, having much dispute among themselves* [2] Or *in his own hired dwelling*

JESUS: OUR ETERNAL SALVATION

ROMANS

ROMANS

THE JERUSALEM COUNCIL *c. AD 50*	PAUL WRITES ROMANS *c. AD 57*	PAUL MARTYRED IN ROME *c. AD 67 – 68*

The letter to the church at Rome is one of Paul's most magisterial books. At the time of writing, Paul had never visited the vibrant church at Rome, though he clearly held the church in high regard and longed to visit the people soon (1:8 – 15). He wrote this theological treatise in order to summarize the message of the gospel for a church at such a critical cultural nexus in the world of that day.

Paul began with a formal introduction of himself and his calling as a slave or servant of Jesus (1:1 – 7). Paul then described the plight of sinners living in a fallen world, who willingly chose to worship created things rather than the Creator (1:25). All human sin is explained by this foolish exchange.

God must judge human sin. His holiness cannot dwell in the presence of sin, and his justice necessitates a proper punishment for all wickedness. Death is the only just wage for sin (6:23) and all people — Jew and Gentile alike — should receive their just condemnation (3:23).

But God graciously made a way for salvation through Jesus. God poured out his punishment for human sin on Christ, who served as God's appointed wrath-bearing substitute (5:6 – 11). Those who place their faith in Christ are forgiven because of Jesus' work on the cross. Jesus pays for their sin. In addition, God's people are given the righteousness that Christ earned through his perfect life. They can now know peace and fellowship with God (5:12 – 20). This is true for Jews, though most will scorn Jesus' offer of salvation, and for Gentiles, who can now be grafted into God's family tree (chs. 9 – 11). Nothing in all of creation can take God's love away from those he has saved because salvation is of God, from God, and for God.

Those whom God saves offer up their lives as "living sacrifice[s]" to God, which is their act of spiritual worship (12:1). Paul ends his letter by demonstrating the scope of the transformation that the gospel should produce. Christians should worship God through their gifts in service to the church, by loving what is good, by rejoicing in all things, by serving one another in love, by submitting to governmental leaders, by making wise decisions, and by bearing one another's burdens. These actions, and a host of others like them, demonstrate God's work of salvation in a person's life and produce in them hope, joy, and peace that can never be taken away.

FOR THE WAGES OF SIN IS DEATH,
BUT THE FREE GIFT OF GOD IS ETERNAL LIFE
IN CHRIST JESUS OUR LORD.

Romans 6:23

ROMANS

Greeting

1 Paul, a servant[1] of Christ Jesus, called to be an apostle, set apart for the gospel of God, 2which he promised beforehand through his prophets in the holy
Scriptures, 3concerning his Son, who was descended from David[2] according to the
flesh 4and was declared to be the Son of God in power according to the Spirit of
holiness by his resurrection from the dead, Jesus Christ our Lord, 5through whom
we have received grace and apostleship to bring about the obedience of faith for
the sake of his name among all the nations, 6including you who are called to belong to Jesus Christ,

7To all those in Rome who are loved by God and called to be saints:

Grace to you and peace from God our Father and the Lord Jesus Christ.

Longing to Go to Rome

8First, I thank my God through Jesus Christ for all of you, because your faith is
proclaimed in all the world. 9For God is my witness, whom I serve with my spirit in
the gospel of his Son, that without ceasing I mention you 10always in my prayers,
asking that somehow by God's will I may now at last succeed in coming to you.
11For I long to see you, that I may impart to you some spiritual gift to strengthen
you— 12that is, that we may be mutually encouraged by each other's faith, both
yours and mine. 13I do not want you to be unaware, brothers,[3] that I have often intended to come to you (but thus far have been prevented), in order that I may reap
some harvest among you as well as among the rest of the Gentiles. 14I am under
obligation both to Greeks and to barbarians,[4] both to the wise and to the foolish.
15So I am eager to preach the gospel to you also who are in Rome.

The Righteous Shall Live by Faith

16For I am not ashamed of the gospel, for it is the power of God for salvation to
everyone who believes, to the Jew first and also to the Greek. 17For in it the righteousness of God is revealed from faith for faith,[5] as it is written, "The righteous
shall live by faith."[6]

God's Wrath on Unrighteousness

18For the wrath of God is revealed from heaven against all ungodliness and
unrighteousness of men, who by their unrighteousness suppress the truth. 19For
what can be known about God is plain to them, because God has shown it to
them. 20For his invisible attributes, namely, his eternal power and divine nature,
have been clearly perceived, ever since the creation of the world,[7] in the things
that have been made. So they are without excuse. 21For although they knew God,
they did not honor him as God or give thanks to him, but they became futile in
their thinking, and their foolish hearts were darkened. 22Claiming to be wise, they
became fools, 23and exchanged the glory of the immortal God for images resembling mortal man and birds and animals and creeping things.

24Therefore God gave them up in the lusts of their hearts to impurity, to the
dishonoring of their bodies among themselves, 25because they exchanged the
truth about God for a lie and worshiped and served the creature rather than the
Creator, who is blessed forever! Amen.

26For this reason God gave them up to dishonorable passions. For their women

---

[1]For the contextual rendering of the Greek word *doulos*, see Preface [2]Or *who came from the offspring of David* [3]Or *brothers and sisters*. In New Testament usage, depending on the context, the plural Greek word *adelphoi* (translated "brothers") may refer either to *brothers* or to *brothers and sisters* [4]That is, non-Greeks [5]Or *beginning and ending in faith* [6]Or *The one who by faith is righteous shall live* [7]Or *clearly perceived from the creation of the world*

SALVATION

The letter to the church in Rome contains a comprehensive, clear, and detailed explanation of the gospel message. Paul's thesis statement — not only of this letter, but also, in many ways, of his entire ministry — can be summed up by Romans 1:16 – 17: "For I am not ashamed of the gospel, for it is the power of God for salvation to everyone who believes, to the Jew first and also to the Greek. For in it the righteousness of God is revealed from faith for faith, as it is written, 'The righteous shall live by faith.' "

Paul and the other New Testament writers portray Jesus Christ as the author and provider of salvation on the basis of his sacrificial death on the cross in the place of sinners. This salvation is by grace alone and through faith in Jesus alone. Through faith, the righteousness of Christ is credited to sinners, who are declared righteous on the basis of that faith.

The word *salvation* itself implies rescue. Paul makes it clear in Romans 1 – 3 that all humanity is desperately lost in sin. The just punishment from a holy God for that sin is death. Salvation, then, is not only rescue from our sin, but it is also rescue from the justified punishment of God. God is perfect in his justice, and because of that, is justified in his wrath toward those who don't trust him. However, the rescue that comes through faith in Jesus completely erases the eternal separation between a holy God and imperfect humanity.

What is the result of this great salvation that comes by grace and through faith? The answer is a reconciled relationship with God (Ro 5:1). The fact that stands at the heart of the gospel is that God desires to be in relationship with his people. Rebellious people are reconciled with their holy God through the cross. Ultimately, all who come to Jesus in faith and trust are saved to the great glory of God. Because salvation is by grace alone, apart from good works, God alone receives the credit for this complete and astonishing deliverance.

exchanged natural relations for those that are contrary to nature; 27and the men likewise gave up natural relations with women and were consumed with passion for one another, men committing shameless acts with men and receiving in themselves the due penalty for their error.

28And since they did not see fit to acknowledge God, God gave them up to a debased mind to do what ought not to be done. 29They were filled with all manner of unrighteousness, evil, covetousness, malice. They are full of envy, murder, strife, deceit, maliciousness. They are gossips, 30slanderers, haters of God, insolent, haughty, boastful, inventors of evil, disobedient to parents, 31foolish, faithless, heartless, ruthless. 32Though they know God's righteous decree that those who practice such things deserve to die, they not only do them but give approval to those who practice them.

God's Righteous Judgment

2 Therefore you have no excuse, O man, every one of you who judges. For in passing judgment on another you condemn yourself, because you, the judge, practice the very same things. 2We know that the judgment of God rightly falls on those who practice such things. 3Do you suppose, O man—you who judge those who practice such things and yet do them yourself—that you will escape the judgment of God? 4Or do you presume on the riches of his kindness and forbearance and patience, not knowing that God's kindness is meant to lead you to repentance? 5But because of your hard and impenitent heart you are storing up wrath for yourself on the day of wrath when God's righteous judgment will be revealed.

6He will render to each one according to his works: 7to those who by patience in well-doing seek for glory and honor and immortality, he will give eternal life; 8but for those who are self-seeking[1] and do not obey the truth, but obey unrighteousness, there will be wrath and fury. 9There will be tribulation and distress for every human being who does evil, the Jew first and also the Greek, 10but glory and honor and peace for everyone who does good, the Jew first and also the Greek. 11For God shows no partiality.

God's Judgment and the Law

12For all who have sinned without the law will also perish without the law, and all who have sinned under the law will be judged by the law. 13For it is not the hearers of the law who are righteous before God, but the doers of the law who will be justified. 14For when Gentiles, who do not have the law, by nature do what the law requires, they are a law to themselves, even though they do not have the law. 15They show that the work of the law is written on their hearts, while their conscience also bears witness, and their conflicting thoughts accuse or even excuse them 16on that day when, according to my gospel, God judges the secrets of men by Christ Jesus.

17But if you call yourself a Jew and rely on the law and boast in God 18and know his will and approve what is excellent, because you are instructed from the law; 19and if you are sure that you yourself are a guide to the blind, a light to those who are in darkness, 20an instructor of the foolish, a teacher of children, having in the law the embodiment of knowledge and truth— 21you then who teach others, do you not teach yourself? While you preach against stealing, do you steal? 22You who say that one must not commit adultery, do you commit adultery? You who abhor idols, do you rob temples? 23You who boast in the law dishonor God by breaking the law. 24For, as it is written, "The name of God is blasphemed among the Gentiles because of you."

25For circumcision indeed is of value if you obey the law, but if you break the law, your circumcision becomes uncircumcision. 26So, if a man who is

[1] Or *contentious*

ROMANS 2:1–4

WITHOUT EXCUSE

Paul's description of sin throughout the book of Romans is cosmic in scope. Not only is the whole of creation itself broken by sin, but also all people—Jew and Gentile alike—are dead in sin. Though Paul seems to focus his attention on the Gentiles at the outset of the book of Romans, he turns his attention to the Jews starting in chapter 2. These people had every opportunity to live by faith. Instead of taking full advantage of being the recipients of the revelation and blessing of being God's chosen people, the Jews had become self-righteous, focusing on outward symbols related to God's standards while neglecting the heart behind those standards. In the process, they underestimated their own sinfulness.

One can almost imagine the self-righteous audience of Jewish Christians in Rome, full of their own religiosity, at first reading with a smug smile on their faces about the sinfulness of the Gentiles, only to read a bit further and find their own guilt exposed. In the end, whether someone has a religious pedigree, hears the gospel early in life, or has access to clear explanations of the gospel only late in life, they still stand guilty before a holy God. Both the religious and the nonreligious alike stand condemned before him, so the ground is completely level when it comes to our own sinfulness. Each person must decide whether or not they will turn to Jesus Christ and trust him alone for their salvation.

uncircumcised keeps the precepts of the law, will not his uncircumcision be
regarded[1] as circumcision? 27Then he who is physically[2] uncircumcised but
keeps the law will condemn you who have the written code[3] and circumcision
but break the law. 28For no one is a Jew who is merely one outwardly, nor is circumcision outward and physical. 29But a Jew is one inwardly, and circumcision
is a matter of the heart, by the Spirit, not by the letter. His praise is not from
man but from God.

God's Righteousness Upheld

3 Then what advantage has the Jew? Or what is the value of circumcision?
2Much in every way. To begin with, the Jews were entrusted with the oracles
of God. 3What if some were unfaithful? Does their faithlessness nullify the faithfulness of God? 4By no means! Let God be true though every one were a liar, as
it is written,

"That you may be justified in your words,
  and prevail when you are judged."

5But if our unrighteousness serves to show the righteousness of God, what shall
we say? That God is unrighteous to inflict wrath on us? (I speak in a human way.)
6By no means! For then how could God judge the world? 7But if through my lie
God's truth abounds to his glory, why am I still being condemned as a sinner?
8And why not do evil that good may come?—as some people slanderously charge
us with saying. Their condemnation is just.

No One Is Righteous

9What then? Are we Jews[4] any better off?[5] No, not at all. For we have already
charged that all, both Jews and Greeks, are under sin, 10as it is written:

"None is righteous, no, not one;
11 no one understands;
  no one seeks for God.
12 All have turned aside; together they have become worthless;
  no one does good,
  not even one."
13 "Their throat is an open grave;
  they use their tongues to deceive."
"The venom of asps is under their lips."
14 "Their mouth is full of curses and bitterness."
15 "Their feet are swift to shed blood;
16 in their paths are ruin and misery,
17 and the way of peace they have not known."
18 "There is no fear of God before their eyes."

19Now we know that whatever the law says it speaks to those who are under
the law, so that every mouth may be stopped, and the whole world may be held
accountable to God. 20For by works of the law no human being[6] will be justified
in his sight, since through the law comes knowledge of sin.

The Righteousness of God Through Faith

21But now the righteousness of God has been manifested apart from the law,
although the Law and the Prophets bear witness to it— 22the righteousness of
God through faith in Jesus Christ for all who believe. For there is no distinction:
23for all have sinned and fall short of the glory of God, 24and are justified by his
grace as a gift, through the redemption that is in Christ Jesus, 25whom God put
forward as a propitiation by his blood, to be received by faith. This was to show
God's righteousness, because in his divine forbearance he had passed over former

[1]Or *counted* [2]Or *is by nature* [3]Or *the letter* [4]Greek *Are we* [5]Or *at any disadvantage?* [6]Greek *flesh*

sins. 26It was to show his righteousness at the present time, so that he might be just and the justifier of the one who has faith in Jesus.

27Then what becomes of our boasting? It is excluded. By what kind of law? By a law of works? No, but by the law of faith. 28For we hold that one is justified by faith apart from works of the law. 29Or is God the God of Jews only? Is he not the God of Gentiles also? Yes, of Gentiles also, 30since God is one—who will justify the circumcised by faith and the uncircumcised through faith. 31Do we then overthrow the law by this faith? By no means! On the contrary, we uphold the law.

Abraham Justified by Faith

4 What then shall we say was gained by Abraham, our forefather according to the flesh? 2For if Abraham was justified by works, he has something to boast about, but not before God. 3For what does the Scripture say? "Abraham believed God, and it was counted to him as righteousness." 4Now to the one who works, his wages are not counted as a gift but as his due. 5And to the one who does not work but believes in[1] him who justifies the ungodly, his faith is counted as righteousness, 6just as David also speaks of the blessing of the one to whom God counts righteousness apart from works:

7 "Blessed are those whose lawless deeds are forgiven,
and whose sins are covered;
8 blessed is the man against whom the Lord will not count his sin."

9Is this blessing then only for the circumcised, or also for the uncircumcised? For we say that faith was counted to Abraham as righteousness. 10How then was it counted to him? Was it before or after he had been circumcised? It was not after, but before he was circumcised. 11He received the sign of circumcision as a seal of the righteousness that he had by faith while he was still uncircumcised. The purpose was to make him the father of all who believe without being circumcised, so that righteousness would be counted to them as well, 12and to make him the father of the circumcised who are not merely circumcised but who also walk in the footsteps of the faith that our father Abraham had before he was circumcised.

The Promise Realized Through Faith

13For the promise to Abraham and his offspring that he would be heir of the world did not come through the law but through the righteousness of faith. 14For if it is the adherents of the law who are to be the heirs, faith is null and the promise is void. 15For the law brings wrath, but where there is no law there is no transgression.

16That is why it depends on faith, in order that the promise may rest on grace and be guaranteed to all his offspring—not only to the adherent of the law but also to the one who shares the faith of Abraham, who is the father of us all, 17as it is written, "I have made you the father of many nations"—in the presence of the God in whom he believed, who gives life to the dead and calls into existence the things that do not exist. 18In hope he believed against hope, that he should become the father of many nations, as he had been told, "So shall your offspring be." 19He did not weaken in faith when he considered his own body, which was as good as dead (since he was about a hundred years old), or when he considered the barrenness[2] of Sarah's womb. 20No unbelief made him waver concerning the promise of God, but he grew strong in his faith as he gave glory to God, 21fully convinced that God was able to do what he had promised. 22That is why his faith was "counted to him as righteousness." 23But the words "it was counted to him" were not written for his sake alone, 24but for ours also. It will be counted to us who believe in him who raised from the dead Jesus our Lord, 25who was delivered up for our trespasses and raised for our justification.

[1]Or *but trusts*; compare verse 24 [2]Greek *deadness*

ROMANS 4:3

ABRAHAM: SAVED THROUGH FAITH

The gospel is not only the central message of the New Testament, it's also the storyline of the entire Bible. For Paul in Romans 4, Abraham is the case study of salvation by faith. By the time Paul wrote this letter, Jewish belief was that Abraham was justified because of his circumcision and his willingness to sacrifice Isaac. If that were the case, Abraham would have earned righteousness with his works. As he builds his argument for salvation by faith in Jesus alone, Paul's concern is that his audience understand that there is only one way a person is made righteous before God—through faith.

In verses 9–16, Paul confronts the issue of Abraham's righteousness with the simple issue of chronology. God declared Abraham righteous prior to his obedience and hundreds of years before God gave the Law to Moses. Therefore Abraham's faith saved him, just as today God's people are only saved through the same kind of faith.

THE RIGHTEOUSNESS OF GOD

Righteousness is a core component of the gospel message. The holy and eternal God expects the people who are in relationship with him to be without sin. This is, as we all know, a requirement that is utterly impossible for any of us to meet on our own! However, in the gospel, God delivers his righteousness to unrighteous people without sacrificing his own righteousness in the process.

Paul spends the opening chapters of this book making his case that all people are guilty of sin, regardless of their supposed morality or their association with the things of God. There is no wiggle room in this argument (3:23) — all people have sinned; all have fallen short of God's righteous standard. The only hope for humanity, then, is the gift of righteousness that comes not by works of the law but instead through faith alone.

This righteousness by faith is not a departure from God's work in the Old Testament; then as now, no one can live up to God's righteous standard. The only way men and women have ever come into righteousness is through faith. But before Jesus came to earth, there was in the air a lingering question of cosmic importance: how could a righteous God, perfect in every way, freely forgive and justify sinful and guilty human beings? Because God is perfectly holy and perfectly righteous, there must be punishment for sin. Otherwise, God's perfect character would be compromised.

This pivotal moment in universal history, the day when Jesus took away the sin of the world, was not only about the souls of men and women; it was about the very character of God. The cross is the answer to the question above; the crucifixion is the apex of God's love and mercy but also of his justice and righteousness. At the cross, God not only provided the ultimate answer for how a person can be made righteous by faith, but he also dispensed his justice. At the cross, God poured out his wrath on his own Son so that sinful human beings might be forgiven and granted the righteousness of Jesus' life. At the cross, the God of righteousness both demonstrates and grants righteousness, for he is both just and the One who justifies.

ROMANS 5:1

JUSTIFIED

The word *justify* is a legal term. Behind that word is a courtroom setting, and in this case, God is the judge who has on the docket before him the guilt or innocence of every person ever born. Paul has already in chapters 1–3 made it clear that the guilt of all humanity is not in question. But here is an amazing declaration: despite our clear guilt, God the Judge declares his people righteous. This happens not only because of God's great love, but because God has demonstrated his justice through the death of Jesus. When someone believes in Jesus, God gives that person the righteousness of Christ and in so doing declares them to be right before God. In other words, God declaring our innocence is not an exception to justice because justice was fully dispensed on Jesus instead of on the sinner who repents. This is truly amazing grace. Because God's people have been justified by faith, they have eternal life and peace with God. Of course, if someone can only have peace with God through faith, then the opposite is also true. Outside of a personal faith commitment, all people stand in eternal conflict with God.

ROMANS 5:10

RECONCILIATION

Could there be anything more terrifying than to be considered an enemy of God? But apart from Christ, that's the status of all people. This is not a relationship of neutrality, but instead of hostility, for all people are born under God's just judgment for sin. However, through Jesus and the gospel the unthinkable happens:

(continued on page 1704)

Peace with God Through Faith

5 Therefore, since we have been justified by faith, we[1] have peace with God
through our Lord Jesus Christ. 2Through him we have also obtained access by
faith[2] into this grace in which we stand, and we[3] rejoice[4] in hope of the glory of
God. 3Not only that, but we rejoice in our sufferings, knowing that suffering produces endurance, 4and endurance produces character, and character produces
hope, 5and hope does not put us to shame, because God's love has been poured
into our hearts through the Holy Spirit who has been given to us.

6For while we were still weak, at the right time Christ died for the ungodly. 7For
one will scarcely die for a righteous person—though perhaps for a good person
one would dare even to die— 8but God shows his love for us in that while we were
still sinners, Christ died for us. 9Since, therefore, we have now been justified by
his blood, much more shall we be saved by him from the wrath of God. 10For if
while we were enemies we were reconciled to God by the death of his Son, much
more, now that we are reconciled, shall we be saved by his life. 11More than that,
we also rejoice in God through our Lord Jesus Christ, through whom we have now
received reconciliation.

Death in Adam, Life in Christ

12Therefore, just as sin came into the world through one man, and death
through sin, and so death spread to all men[5] because all sinned— 13for sin indeed
was in the world before the law was given, but sin is not counted where there is no
law. 14Yet death reigned from Adam to Moses, even over those whose sinning was
not like the transgression of Adam, who was a type of the one who was to come.

15But the free gift is not like the trespass. For if many died through one man's
trespass, much more have the grace of God and the free gift by the grace of that
one man Jesus Christ abounded for many. 16And the free gift is not like the result
of that one man's sin. For the judgment following one trespass brought condemnation, but the free gift following many trespasses brought justification. 17For if,
because of one man's trespass, death reigned through that one man, much more
will those who receive the abundance of grace and the free gift of righteousness
reign in life through the one man Jesus Christ.

18Therefore, as one trespass[6] led to condemnation for all men, so one act of
righteousness[7] leads to justification and life for all men. 19For as by the one man's
disobedience the many were made sinners, so by the one man's obedience the
many will be made righteous. 20Now the law came in to increase the trespass,
but where sin increased, grace abounded all the more, 21so that, as sin reigned
in death, grace also might reign through righteousness leading to eternal life
through Jesus Christ our Lord.

Dead to Sin, Alive to God

6 What shall we say then? Are we to continue in sin that grace may abound? 2By
no means! How can we who died to sin still live in it? 3Do you not know that
all of us who have been baptized into Christ Jesus were baptized into his death?
4We were buried therefore with him by baptism into death, in order that, just as
Christ was raised from the dead by the glory of the Father, we too might walk in
newness of life.

5For if we have been united with him in a death like his, we shall certainly be
united with him in a resurrection like his. 6We know that our old self[8] was crucified with him in order that the body of sin might be brought to nothing, so that we
would no longer be enslaved to sin. 7For one who has died has been set free[9] from
sin. 8Now if we have died with Christ, we believe that we will also live with him.
9We know that Christ, being raised from the dead, will never die again; death no

[1]Some manuscripts *let us* [2]Some manuscripts omit *by faith* [3]Or *let us*; also verse 3 [4]Or *boast*; also verses 3, 11 [5]The Greek word *anthropoi* refers here to both men and women; also twice in verse 18 [6]Or *the trespass of one* [7]Or *the act of righteousness of one* [8]Greek *man* [9]Greek *has been justified*

JESUS AS THE LAST ADAM

It has been said that those who fail to learn the lessons of history are doomed to repeat them. To reinterpret this quote in light of redemptive history, one might say that believers who fail to understand where they have come from will also fail to understand where humanity has been, where they themselves, as followers of Christ, are now, and where they are going.

Paul helps his readers see the overwhelming consequence of Adam's sin. When the "one man" of verse 12 disobeyed God's direct command, sin and death entered the world. Adam represented all future humanity. He was, in many ways, the first and best hope of humanity: There was and never would be a more idyllic situation in which to have perfect and unbroken fellowship with God, and yet he fell. With Adam's choice to sin came the inherited implications to every person born into Adam's race: namely, that all people have a sinful nature at their core. All people are born into sin; all are under the curse of disobedience that came from the Garden of Eden. Any parent can testify to the truth that they never taught their toddlers how to be selfish; they came by that inclination naturally.

But Jesus Christ is the new and last Adam. Adam faced temptation in the garden under the best of circumstances; Jesus Christ faced temptation in another garden under the worst of circumstances. Adam bent to his selfish pride and desire to be like God. Jesus withstood temptation and submitted himself to the will of God. "Therefore, as one trespass led to condemnation for all men, so one act of righteousness leads to justification and life for all men" (Ro 5:18). But there's even more.

As Paul wrote, although the disobedience that brought about condemnation and alienation was purely evil, the work of Jesus did more good. Through the cross, Jesus overcame sin and death and is now able to bring sons and daughters of God into glory. Where Adam failed, Jesus won.

(Reconciliation, continued)

God grants reconciliation to those who turn to Jesus in repentance and trust. The word *reconciliation* means "change" or "exchange," but it's important to remember that true reconciliation involves a change in the attitudes of both parties who had been previously estranged or at odds. Through Christ, sinners are not left as beggars on the doorstep of heaven, hoping God will somehow open the door. Instead, his attitude toward those who believe has been wholly changed because of Jesus Christ's sacrifice. His wrath and justice have been satisfied, and his people are made right with him based on the righteousness of Christ. God sees his people not as former enemies, but as dearly beloved and adopted children. Like the father in the story of the lost son, God's people are welcomed home—not as slaves, but with celebration as returning sons and daughters (Lk 15:11–32).

ROMANS 6:22–23

GIFT OF ETERNAL LIFE

Workers are paid for the work they do, and while at times that wage is merited on the quality of the work performed, quite often it is static based on economic realities—especially in entry-level jobs. Similarly, Paul notes that all sin, no matter how seemingly innocuous, has earned every person who has ever lived a single and eternal wage from the hand of a just God: death. The gift of God's grace, however, stands in stark contrast to the wages of sin. God gives eternal life not because sinners merit it, but because his Son earned it. Eternal life is a gracious gift from a loving God

(continued on page 1706)

longer has dominion over him. 10For the death he died he died to sin, once for all,
but the life he lives he lives to God. 11So you also must consider yourselves dead to
sin and alive to God in Christ Jesus.
12Let not sin therefore reign in your mortal body, to make you obey its passions. 13Do not present your members to sin as instruments for unrighteousness,
but present yourselves to God as those who have been brought from death to life,
and your members to God as instruments for righteousness. 14For sin will have no
dominion over you, since you are not under law but under grace.

Slaves to Righteousness

15What then? Are we to sin because we are not under law but under grace? By
no means! 16Do you not know that if you present yourselves to anyone as obedient slaves,[1] you are slaves of the one whom you obey, either of sin, which leads
to death, or of obedience, which leads to righteousness? 17But thanks be to God,
that you who were once slaves of sin have become obedient from the heart to the
standard of teaching to which you were committed, 18and, having been set free
from sin, have become slaves of righteousness. 19I am speaking in human terms,
because of your natural limitations. For just as you once presented your members
as slaves to impurity and to lawlessness leading to more lawlessness, so now present your members as slaves to righteousness leading to sanctification.
20For when you were slaves of sin, you were free in regard to righteousness.
21But what fruit were you getting at that time from the things of which you are
now ashamed? For the end of those things is death. 22But now that you have been
set free from sin and have become slaves of God, the fruit you get leads to sanctification and its end, eternal life. 23For the wages of sin is death, but the free gift of
God is eternal life in Christ Jesus our Lord.

Released from the Law

7 Or do you not know, brothers[2]—for I am speaking to those who know the
law—that the law is binding on a person only as long as he lives? 2For a married woman is bound by law to her husband while he lives, but if her husband
dies she is released from the law of marriage.[3] 3Accordingly, she will be called
an adulteress if she lives with another man while her husband is alive. But if her
husband dies, she is free from that law, and if she marries another man she is not
an adulteress.
4Likewise, my brothers, you also have died to the law through the body of
Christ, so that you may belong to another, to him who has been raised from the
dead, in order that we may bear fruit for God. 5For while we were living in the
flesh, our sinful passions, aroused by the law, were at work in our members to
bear fruit for death. 6But now we are released from the law, having died to that
which held us captive, so that we serve in the new way of the Spirit and not in the
old way of the written code.[4]

The Law and Sin

7What then shall we say? That the law is sin? By no means! Yet if it had not
been for the law, I would not have known sin. For I would not have known what it
is to covet if the law had not said, "You shall not covet." 8But sin, seizing an opportunity through the commandment, produced in me all kinds of covetousness. For
apart from the law, sin lies dead. 9I was once alive apart from the law, but when the
commandment came, sin came alive and I died. 10The very commandment that
promised life proved to be death to me. 11For sin, seizing an opportunity through
the commandment, deceived me and through it killed me. 12So the law is holy, and
the commandment is holy and righteous and good.

[1]For the contextual rendering of the Greek word *doulos*, see Preface; twice in this verse; also verses 17, 19 (twice), 20 [2]Or *brothers and sisters*; also verse 4 [3]Greek *law concerning the husband* [4]Greek *of the letter*

FIGHTING SIN

Paul the apostle was a realist. He knew that though conversion and justification might happen in a moment, the process of sanctification, or becoming more and more like Christ, is a progression that happens over time for the Christian. In fact, as believers come closer and closer in relationship with Christ, they will find not that they are more confident of their own holiness, but less so; in coming closer to Christ, they find more and more corners of their dark hearts exposed in his light. For the Christian, then, fighting sin is a part of life — it's a battle in which they must fully engage to take up the work God has done and is doing in their lives.

The key difference in this battle for the Christian is that in Christ, a person is no longer fighting *for* victory; he or she is fighting *from* victory. Because one's position in respect to salvation has changed and God has initiated an irrevocable change in the heart, this person is no longer under the dominion of sin. Take a moment to let this thought sink in: *sin is no longer in control.* That person now has access to the power of the Holy Spirit, who aids in the ongoing everyday fight for holiness. This is why Paul can speak in such definite terms here — that Christians have died and been raised to life in Christ. This death and resurrection is a reference to one's eternal position of salvation in Jesus.

In light of that position, believers are to "consider," or "reckon," themselves dead to sin (vv. 10 – 11). This counting and reckoning involves reminding oneself of what has been done for us and in us through Christ, and then bringing the truth of our position in him to bear on any given situation. When Christians count themselves dead to sin, they remind themselves that they are the blood-bought children of God. Then they allow that truth to impact their daily choices as they "abide" in Jesus throughout the course of their everyday life (Jn 15:5 – 8).

The process of sanctification requires that Christians continually rely on Jesus' teachings and the Holy Spirit, time and time again, as they "take every thought captive to obey Christ" (2Co 10:5). As they do, believers are offering daily actions, thoughts, and attitudes as worship to God because of his glory. Christians no longer give themselves over to the old desires they had before their new life in Christ, but instead they align more and more with the work of the Holy Spirit to become more like Jesus to their families, friends, and coworkers.

(Gift of Eternal Life, continued)

to his people who repent and trust in his salvation.

This gift of eternal life is not static; it's not something that will only be actualized upon physical death. Rather, eternal life is a dynamic relationship that believers enter into through faith in Jesus Christ and experience right here and now. Jesus promised his followers that they could have life abundantly while living on this earth (Jn 10:10). This joyful, victorious life is possible through a deep and abiding relationship with God (Jn 15:4–6). Eternal life in heaven and on the new earth is, then, the glorious and unimaginably awe-inspiring extension of the believer's dynamic and growing relationship with God on earth.

ROMANS 7:25

THANKS BE TO GOD, WHO DELIVERS ME

Romans 7 is nothing if not a verbal picture of struggle. In this chapter, readers get a firsthand glimpse into the inner thoughts of the apostle, which can either be uplifting and encouraging or crushing and discouraging depending on one's perspective.

It might be discouraging to know that even Paul—who had experienced Jesus in a personal way and had seen the explosive growth of the early church—still struggled so violently with his own heart. But this chapter can also be encouraging for the same reason. When the weight of sin is particularly oppressive, Christians can take heart, knowing that all people struggle; even the apostle Paul battled mightily with sin. The New Testament never char-

(continued on next page)

13 Did that which is good, then, bring death to me? By no means! It was sin, producing death in me through what is good, in order that sin might be shown to be sin, and through the commandment might become sinful beyond measure. 14 For we know that the law is spiritual, but I am of the flesh, sold under sin. 15 For I do not understand my own actions. For I do not do what I want, but I do the very thing I hate. 16 Now if I do what I do not want, I agree with the law, that it is good. 17 So now it is no longer I who do it, but sin that dwells within me. 18 For I know that nothing good dwells in me, that is, in my flesh. For I have the desire to do what is right, but not the ability to carry it out. 19 For I do not do the good I want, but the evil I do not want is what I keep on doing. 20 Now if I do what I do not want, it is no longer I who do it, but sin that dwells within me.

21 So I find it to be a law that when I want to do right, evil lies close at hand. 22 For I delight in the law of God, in my inner being, 23 but I see in my members another law waging war against the law of my mind and making me captive to the law of sin that dwells in my members. 24 Wretched man that I am! Who will deliver me from this body of death? 25 Thanks be to God through Jesus Christ our Lord! So then, I myself serve the law of God with my mind, but with my flesh I serve the law of sin.

Life in the Spirit

8 There is therefore now no condemnation for those who are in Christ Jesus.[1] 2 For the law of the Spirit of life has set you[2] free in Christ Jesus from the law of sin and death. 3 For God has done what the law, weakened by the flesh, could not do. By sending his own Son in the likeness of sinful flesh and for sin,[3] he condemned sin in the flesh, 4 in order that the righteous requirement of the law might be fulfilled in us, who walk not according to the flesh but according to the Spirit. 5 For those who live according to the flesh set their minds on the things of the flesh, but those who live according to the Spirit set their minds on the things of the Spirit. 6 For to set the mind on the flesh is death, but to set the mind on the Spirit is life and peace. 7 For the mind that is set on the flesh is hostile to God, for it does not submit to God's law; indeed, it cannot. 8 Those who are in the flesh cannot please God.

9 You, however, are not in the flesh but in the Spirit, if in fact the Spirit of God dwells in you. Anyone who does not have the Spirit of Christ does not belong to him. 10 But if Christ is in you, although the body is dead because of sin, the Spirit is life because of righteousness. 11 If the Spirit of him who raised Jesus from the dead dwells in you, he who raised Christ Jesus[4] from the dead will also give life to your mortal bodies through his Spirit who dwells in you.

Heirs with Christ

12 So then, brothers,[5] we are debtors, not to the flesh, to live according to the flesh. 13 For if you live according to the flesh you will die, but if by the Spirit you put to death the deeds of the body, you will live. 14 For all who are led by the Spirit of God are sons[6] of God. 15 For you did not receive the spirit of slavery to fall back into fear, but you have received the Spirit of adoption as sons, by whom we cry, "Abba! Father!" 16 The Spirit himself bears witness with our spirit that we are children of God, 17 and if children, then heirs—heirs of God and fellow heirs with Christ, provided we suffer with him in order that we may also be glorified with him.

Future Glory

18 For I consider that the sufferings of this present time are not worth comparing with the glory that is to be revealed to us. 19 For the creation waits with eager

[1] Some manuscripts add *who walk not according to the flesh (but according to the Spirit)* [2] Some manuscripts *me* [3] Or *and as a sin offering* [4] Some manuscripts lack *Jesus* [5] Or *brothers and sisters*; also verse 29 [6] See discussion on "sons" in the Preface

longing for the revealing of the sons of God. [20]For the creation was subjected to futility, not willingly, but because of him who subjected it, in hope [21]that the creation itself will be set free from its bondage to corruption and obtain the freedom of the glory of the children of God. [22]For we know that the whole creation has been groaning together in the pains of childbirth until now. [23]And not only the creation, but we ourselves, who have the firstfruits of the Spirit, groan inwardly as we wait eagerly for adoption as sons, the redemption of our bodies. [24]For in this hope we were saved. Now hope that is seen is not hope. For who hopes for what he sees? [25]But if we hope for what we do not see, we wait for it with patience.

[26]Likewise the Spirit helps us in our weakness. For we do not know what to pray for as we ought, but the Spirit himself intercedes for us with groanings too deep for words. [27]And he who searches hearts knows what is the mind of the Spirit, because[1] the Spirit intercedes for the saints according to the will of God. [28]And we know that for those who love God all things work together for good,[2] for those who are called according to his purpose. [29]For those whom he foreknew he also predestined to be conformed to the image of his Son, in order that he might be the firstborn among many brothers. [30]And those whom he predestined he also called, and those whom he called he also justified, and those whom he justified he also glorified.

God's Everlasting Love

[31]What then shall we say to these things? If God is for us, who can be[3] against us? [32]He who did not spare his own Son but gave him up for us all, how will he not also with him graciously give us all things? [33]Who shall bring any charge against God's elect? It is God who justifies. [34]Who is to condemn? Christ Jesus is the one who died—more than that, who was raised—who is at the right hand of God, who indeed is interceding for us.[4] [35]Who shall separate us from the love of Christ? Shall tribulation, or distress, or persecution, or famine, or nakedness, or danger, or sword? [36]As it is written,

> "For your sake we are being killed all the day long;
> we are regarded as sheep to be slaughtered."

[37]No, in all these things we are more than conquerors through him who loved us. [38]For I am sure that neither death nor life, nor angels nor rulers, nor things present nor things to come, nor powers, [39]nor height nor depth, nor anything else in all creation, will be able to separate us from the love of God in Christ Jesus our Lord.

God's Sovereign Choice

9 I am speaking the truth in Christ—I am not lying; my conscience bears me witness in the Holy Spirit— [2]that I have great sorrow and unceasing anguish in my heart. [3]For I could wish that I myself were accursed and cut off from Christ for the sake of my brothers,[5] my kinsmen according to the flesh. [4]They are Israelites, and to them belong the adoption, the glory, the covenants, the giving of the law, the worship, and the promises. [5]To them belong the patriarchs, and from their race, according to the flesh, is the Christ, who is God over all, blessed forever. Amen.

[6]But it is not as though the word of God has failed. For not all who are descended from Israel belong to Israel, [7]and not all are children of Abraham because they are his offspring, but "Through Isaac shall your offspring be named." [8]This means that it is not the children of the flesh who are the children of God, but the children of the promise are counted as offspring. [9]For this is what the promise said: "About this time next year I will return, and Sarah shall have a son." [10]And not only so,

[1]Or *that* [2]Some manuscripts *God works all things together for good,* or *God works in all things for the good*
[3]Or *who is* [4]Or *Is it Christ Jesus who died . . . for us?* [5]Or *brothers and sisters*

(Thanks Be To God, Who Delivers Me, continued)

acterizes Christians as those who do not struggle with sin; rather, they are those who stay in the fight.

When Christians feel the weight of sin's burden; when they're torn between righteousness and unrighteousness, between the desires of the Spirit and the desires of the flesh, then the only solution is Jesus. He is the only One who can deliver those who are dead in sin and, through the Holy Spirit, help his followers to resist sin. The Christian needs the gospel as much as the non-Christian does, for it is by the gospel God's people were saved from their slavery to sin. It is the same gospel that reminds believers that they are "more than conquerors through him who loved us" (Ro 8:37).

ROMANS 8:1–2

NO CONDEMNATION

God did not give the law to his people as the means of their salvation, for he knew that no sinful person could ever perfectly keep the law. Instead, the law both exposes the sinfulness of the human heart and displays the perfect holiness of God's character. In both cases, the law reminds all people that apart from Christ, there is only condemnation.

But in Christ, there is no condemnation. None. In Christ, believers have been given the gift of his hard-won righteousness. This gift comes by faith in Jesus, who fulfilled the law on their behalf. Along with the imputed righteousness of Christ comes the gift of the Holy Spirit, who gives Christians the power to live for Jesus every day. Rather than having a law written on tablets of stone, the Holy

(continued on page 1709)

ELECTION

Throughout the ages, theologians have debated the doctrine of election that Paul brings into consideration in these verses. This doctrine is more than a matter of theological debate; in this context, it is one of the reasons for the great assurance Christians have of God's love that is available in Christ.

There are two main opinions that have arisen over the ages in regard to this doctrine. The first opinion is that God's foreknowledge involves his future knowledge of the people who will respond to him by faith and those who will not. Those who accept Christ and the gospel are the elect, for they were predestined according to the choice God knew they would make. Those who take this position find that it reconciles well with the fact that God desires that all people come to a saving knowledge of him (1Ti 2:3–4; 2Pe 3:9) and that salvation is universally available to all who will claim this free gift. It is a "whosoever will come" kind of call, in which people have the real choice to either accept or reject God's offer of salvation.

The other viewpoint understands God's foreknowledge as an unconditional choice. Anyone who is saved, according to this view, is saved only because God chose some that they would believe; indeed, apart from God's active choosing of individuals, all people are so lost in sin that not one would actively choose Christ if left to themselves to decide. Supporting this position is the doctrine of absolute human depravity (Eph 2:1–10), which holds that sinners are dead in their trespasses and incapable of responding to God apart from his divine intervention. God changes the human heart, removes the scales from the eyes of some, and gives them the gift of faith that allows them to believe the gospel message.

Where these two views come together is that every person, apart from God's intervening grace in sending Jesus, is hopelessly lost, and the only way to salvation is through his grace and mercy. Furthermore, each understanding of the doctrine, when rightly applied, results in the glory of God alone rather than human pride. Regardless of where we land on the particulars of the doctrine of election, in the end it inspires our worship because we are directed back to the gospel of Jesus Christ, our only hope.

but also when Rebekah had conceived children by one man, our forefather Isaac,
11though they were not yet born and had done nothing either good or bad—in
order that God's purpose of election might continue, not because of works but
because of him who calls— 12she was told, "The older will serve the younger." 13As
it is written, "Jacob I loved, but Esau I hated."

14What shall we say then? Is there injustice on God's part? By no means! 15For
he says to Moses, "I will have mercy on whom I have mercy, and I will have compassion on whom I have compassion." 16So then it depends not on human will or
exertion,[1] but on God, who has mercy. 17For the Scripture says to Pharaoh, "For
this very purpose I have raised you up, that I might show my power in you, and
that my name might be proclaimed in all the earth." 18So then he has mercy on
whomever he wills, and he hardens whomever he wills.

19You will say to me then, "Why does he still find fault? For who can resist his
will?" 20But who are you, O man, to answer back to God? Will what is molded say
to its molder, "Why have you made me like this?" 21Has the potter no right over
the clay, to make out of the same lump one vessel for honorable use and another
for dishonorable use? 22What if God, desiring to show his wrath and to make
known his power, has endured with much patience vessels of wrath prepared
for destruction, 23in order to make known the riches of his glory for vessels of
mercy, which he has prepared beforehand for glory— 24even us whom he has
called, not from the Jews only but also from the Gentiles? 25As indeed he says
in Hosea,

"Those who were not my people I will call 'my people,'
  and her who was not beloved I will call 'beloved.'"
26 "And in the very place where it was said to them, 'You are not my people,'
  there they will be called 'sons of the living God.'"

27And Isaiah cries out concerning Israel: "Though the number of the sons of
Israel[2] be as the sand of the sea, only a remnant of them will be saved, 28for the
Lord will carry out his sentence upon the earth fully and without delay." 29And
as Isaiah predicted,

"If the Lord of hosts had not left us offspring,
  we would have been like Sodom
  and become like Gomorrah."

Israel's Unbelief

30What shall we say, then? That Gentiles who did not pursue righteousness
have attained it, that is, a righteousness that is by faith; 31but that Israel who pursued a law that would lead to righteousness[3] did not succeed in reaching that law.
32Why? Because they did not pursue it by faith, but as if it were based on works.
They have stumbled over the stumbling stone, 33as it is written,

"Behold, I am laying in Zion a stone of stumbling, and a rock of offense;
  and whoever believes in him will not be put to shame."

10 Brothers,[4] my heart's desire and prayer to God for them is that they may
be saved. 2For I bear them witness that they have a zeal for God, but not
according to knowledge. 3For, being ignorant of the righteousness of God, and
seeking to establish their own, they did not submit to God's righteousness. 4For
Christ is the end of the law for righteousness to everyone who believes.[5]

The Message of Salvation to All

5For Moses writes about the righteousness that is based on the law, that the
person who does the commandments shall live by them. 6But the righteousness

[1]Greek *not of him who wills or runs* [2]Or *children of Israel* [3]Greek *a law of righteousness* [4]Or *Brothers and sisters* [5]Or *end of the law, that everyone who believes may be justified*

(No Condemnation, continued)

Spirit writes the law on the hearts of God's people. It's only through the Spirit, and his power, that his people can bring glory to God and help to build his kingdom.

ROMANS 9:33

STUMBLING

Expectation is a powerful thing. When it comes to God, people can easily convince themselves of what God *should* do in a given situation and end up missing what God is actually doing. Such were the tragic ironies of many Jews in Paul's day. Though they had for centuries looked with longing toward a day when God would send a deliverer, a Messiah, they were so committed to their expectations of what that Messiah should do and be that many missed the reality of God's work in Jesus Christ.

The prophet Isaiah said it would be so—he said that Israel would reject their own Messiah (Isa 8:14; 28:16) in prophecies echoed here by the apostle Paul. Many Jews were busy looking for a political leader like King David of old; they were focused on deliverance from the Roman oppression and so they neglected the greater King who was sent and the greater deliverance he offered. Jesus, the cornerstone for all Christian faith and righteousness, was—and still is—a stumbling block for many.

RIGHTEOUSNESS

One of the predominant themes in both the Old and New Testaments is that of righteousness. Paul's understanding of this word is not that it is an extensive list of rules to keep, but rather something that Jesus earned through his perfectly obedient life and credits to believers by faith. For Paul, righteousness is not so much a *description* of conduct as it is a *condition* of a proper relationship between God and a person.

In the Old Testament, righteousness is established fundamentally as a characteristic of God. He alone is truly righteous. Because this is true, God always kept his promises, even when his people, Israel, were not faithful to theirs. Time and time again, the people abandoned God through their pursuit of idols and their unfaithfulness to the covenant God had made with them, but time and time again, God remained faithful and restored his people. However, eventually God took drastic measures to discipline his people, raising up the pagan nations of Assyria and Babylon to conquer Israel and Judah and bring them into exile in foreign lands. When Judah returned, the people returned with the understanding that their unrighteousness and idolatry had led to God's judgment.

Because they realized this, their leaders encouraged the people of Judah to foster a new zeal for the law; they were determined never to let what happened in the exile happen again. Unfortunately, though, the people confused this external and rule-based adherence to the law with true righteousness. True righteousness goes well beyond external compliance to a set of rules; true righteousness comes from a heart that is bent toward loving God and participating in joyful worship.

This is why true righteousness can only come about through faith and through the gospel. Jesus alone is fully righteous, inside and out; the only way in which a person can become righteous is by faith in him. When a person believes in Jesus, that person's sin is laid upon Jesus and is paid for by his sacrifice. Meanwhile, the believer in exchange receives the perfect righteousness of Christ. By faith, a person can at long last not only act in a righteous way, but can actually become more and more righteous as their heart is changed by the continual influence of the Holy Spirit.

based on faith says, “Do not say in your heart, ‘Who will ascend into heaven?’ ”
(that is, to bring Christ down) 7“or ‘Who will descend into the abyss?’ ” (that is,
to bring Christ up from the dead). 8But what does it say? “The word is near you,
in your mouth and in your heart” (that is, the word of faith that we proclaim);
9because, if you confess with your mouth that Jesus is Lord and believe in your
heart that God raised him from the dead, you will be saved. 10For with the heart
one believes and is justified, and with the mouth one confesses and is saved. 11For
the Scripture says, “Everyone who believes in him will not be put to shame.” 12For
there is no distinction between Jew and Greek; for the same Lord is Lord of all,
bestowing his riches on all who call on him. 13For “everyone who calls on the
name of the Lord will be saved.”

14How then will they call on him in whom they have not believed? And how
are they to believe in him of whom they have never heard?[1] And how are they to
hear without someone preaching? 15And how are they to preach unless they are
sent? As it is written, “How beautiful are the feet of those who preach the good
news!” 16But they have not all obeyed the gospel. For Isaiah says, “Lord, who has
believed what he has heard from us?” 17So faith comes from hearing, and hearing
through the word of Christ.

18But I ask, have they not heard? Indeed they have, for

“Their voice has gone out to all the earth,
 and their words to the ends of the world.”

19But I ask, did Israel not understand? First Moses says,

“I will make you jealous of those who are not a nation;
 with a foolish nation I will make you angry.”

20Then Isaiah is so bold as to say,

“I have been found by those who did not seek me;
 I have shown myself to those who did not ask for me.”

21But of Israel he says, “All day long I have held out my hands to a disobedient and
contrary people.”

The Remnant of Israel

11 I ask, then, has God rejected his people? By no means! For I myself am an
Israelite, a descendant of Abraham,[2] a member of the tribe of Benjamin.
2God has not rejected his people whom he foreknew. Do you not know what the
Scripture says of Elijah, how he appeals to God against Israel? 3“Lord, they have
killed your prophets, they have demolished your altars, and I alone am left, and
they seek my life.” 4But what is God’s reply to him? “I have kept for myself seven
thousand men who have not bowed the knee to Baal.” 5So too at the present time
there is a remnant, chosen by grace. 6But if it is by grace, it is no longer on the basis
of works; otherwise grace would no longer be grace.

7What then? Israel failed to obtain what it was seeking. The elect obtained it,
but the rest were hardened, 8as it is written,

“God gave them a spirit of stupor,
 eyes that would not see
 and ears that would not hear,
down to this very day.”

9And David says,

“Let their table become a snare and a trap,
 a stumbling block and a retribution for them;
10 let their eyes be darkened so that they cannot see,
 and bend their backs forever.”

[1]Or *him whom they have never heard* [2]Or *one of the offspring of Abraham*

ROMANS 11:33–36

DOXOLOGY

Paul's pattern of writing letters was broadly the same—he built his convincing arguments by explaining doctrine, but then brought it to a more practical level by discussing behavior. This holds true in the book of Romans. Having spent 11 chapters extrapolating the gravity of sin, the necessity of faith, and the profound grace of the gospel, Paul is ready to turn the corner into the practical implications of behavior in Romans 12. As he closes the first section of his letter, he erupts in praise for who God is and for what he has done.

In this passage, Paul acknowledges the mysterious and incomparable nature of God and his plan. The gospel, which Paul has explained in detail in the previous pages, was not something any human could have devised. Rather, it took God's great and unsearchable wisdom to provide the solution for the terrible and universal problem of sin. He acted in history in such a way that men and women could be made righteous.

Because the foundation of the gospel is not humanity but God, God alone can and should receive the glory and honor he is due. The gospel, as with all things, begins and ends with God, for he is the center of all things.

Gentiles Grafted In

11 So I ask, did they stumble in order that they might fall? By no means! Rather,
through their trespass salvation has come to the Gentiles, so as to make Israel jealous. 12 Now if their trespass means riches for the world, and if their failure means
riches for the Gentiles, how much more will their full inclusion[1] mean!
13 Now I am speaking to you Gentiles. Inasmuch then as I am an apostle to
the Gentiles, I magnify my ministry 14 in order somehow to make my fellow Jews
jealous, and thus save some of them. 15 For if their rejection means the reconciliation of the world, what will their acceptance mean but life from the dead? 16 If the
dough offered as firstfruits is holy, so is the whole lump, and if the root is holy,
so are the branches.
17 But if some of the branches were broken off, and you, although a wild olive
shoot, were grafted in among the others and now share in the nourishing root[2] of
the olive tree, 18 do not be arrogant toward the branches. If you are, remember it
is not you who support the root, but the root that supports you. 19 Then you will
say, "Branches were broken off so that I might be grafted in." 20 That is true. They
were broken off because of their unbelief, but you stand fast through faith. So do
not become proud, but fear. 21 For if God did not spare the natural branches, neither will he spare you. 22 Note then the kindness and the severity of God: severity
toward those who have fallen, but God's kindness to you, provided you continue
in his kindness. Otherwise you too will be cut off. 23 And even they, if they do not
continue in their unbelief, will be grafted in, for God has the power to graft them
in again. 24 For if you were cut from what is by nature a wild olive tree, and grafted,
contrary to nature, into a cultivated olive tree, how much more will these, the
natural branches, be grafted back into their own olive tree.

The Mystery of Israel's Salvation

25 Lest you be wise in your own sight, I do not want you to be unaware of this
mystery, brothers:[3] a partial hardening has come upon Israel, until the fullness of
the Gentiles has come in. 26 And in this way all Israel will be saved, as it is written,

"The Deliverer will come from Zion,
he will banish ungodliness from Jacob";
27 "and this will be my covenant with them
when I take away their sins."

28 As regards the gospel, they are enemies for your sake. But as regards election,
they are beloved for the sake of their forefathers. 29 For the gifts and the calling of
God are irrevocable. 30 For just as you were at one time disobedient to God but now
have received mercy because of their disobedience, 31 so they too have now been
disobedient in order that by the mercy shown to you they also may now[4] receive
mercy. 32 For God has consigned all to disobedience, that he may have mercy on all.
33 Oh, the depth of the riches and wisdom and knowledge of God! How unsearchable are his judgments and how inscrutable his ways!

34 "For who has known the mind of the Lord,
or who has been his counselor?"
35 "Or who has given a gift to him
that he might be repaid?"

36 For from him and through him and to him are all things. To him be glory forever.
Amen.

A Living Sacrifice

12 I appeal to you therefore, brothers,[5] by the mercies of God, to present your
bodies as a living sacrifice, holy and acceptable to God, which is your spiritual worship.[6] 2 Do not be conformed to this world,[7] but be transformed by the

[1] Greek *their fullness* [2] Greek *root of richness*; some manuscripts *richness* [3] Or *brothers and sisters* [4] Some manuscripts omit *now* [5] Or *brothers and sisters* [6] Or *your rational service* [7] Greek *age*

renewal of your mind, that by testing you may discern what is the will of God, what is good and acceptable and perfect.[1]

Gifts of Grace

3For by the grace given to me I say to everyone among you not to think of himself more highly than he ought to think, but to think with sober judgment, each according to the measure of faith that God has assigned. 4For as in one body we have many members,[2] and the members do not all have the same function, 5so we, though many, are one body in Christ, and individually members one of another. 6Having gifts that differ according to the grace given to us, let us use them: if prophecy, in proportion to our faith; 7if service, in our serving; the one who teaches, in his teaching; 8the one who exhorts, in his exhortation; the one who contributes, in generosity; the one who leads,[3] with zeal; the one who does acts of mercy, with cheerfulness.

Marks of the True Christian

9Let love be genuine. Abhor what is evil; hold fast to what is good. 10Love one another with brotherly affection. Outdo one another in showing honor. 11Do not be slothful in zeal, be fervent in spirit,[4] serve the Lord. 12Rejoice in hope, be patient in tribulation, be constant in prayer. 13Contribute to the needs of the saints and seek to show hospitality.

14Bless those who persecute you; bless and do not curse them. 15Rejoice with those who rejoice, weep with those who weep. 16Live in harmony with one another. Do not be haughty, but associate with the lowly.[5] Never be wise in your own sight. 17Repay no one evil for evil, but give thought to do what is honorable in the sight of all. 18If possible, so far as it depends on you, live peaceably with all. 19Beloved, never avenge yourselves, but leave it[6] to the wrath of God, for it is written, "Vengeance is mine, I will repay, says the Lord." 20To the contrary, "if your enemy is hungry, feed him; if he is thirsty, give him something to drink; for by so doing you will heap burning coals on his head." 21Do not be overcome by evil, but overcome evil with good.

Submission to the Authorities

13 Let every person be subject to the governing authorities. For there is no authority except from God, and those that exist have been instituted by God. 2Therefore whoever resists the authorities resists what God has appointed, and those who resist will incur judgment. 3For rulers are not a terror to good conduct, but to bad. Would you have no fear of the one who is in authority? Then do what is good, and you will receive his approval, 4for he is God's servant for your good. But if you do wrong, be afraid, for he does not bear the sword in vain. For he is the servant of God, an avenger who carries out God's wrath on the wrongdoer. 5Therefore one must be in subjection, not only to avoid God's wrath but also for the sake of conscience. 6For because of this you also pay taxes, for the authorities are ministers of God, attending to this very thing. 7Pay to all what is owed to them: taxes to whom taxes are owed, revenue to whom revenue is owed, respect to whom respect is owed, honor to whom honor is owed.

Fulfilling the Law Through Love

8Owe no one anything, except to love each other, for the one who loves another has fulfilled the law. 9For the commandments, "You shall not commit adultery, You shall not murder, You shall not steal, You shall not covet," and any other commandment, are summed up in this word: "You shall love your neighbor as yourself." 10Love does no wrong to a neighbor; therefore love is the fulfilling of the law.

11Besides this you know the time, that the hour has come for you to wake from

[1]Or *what is the good and acceptable and perfect will of God* [2]Greek *parts*; also verse 5 [3]Or *gives aid* [4]Or *fervent in the Spirit* [5]Or *give yourselves to humble tasks* [6]Greek *give place*

ROMANS 12:3–8

MEMBERS OF ONE BODY

Christian unity is one of the imperatives of the gospel. When someone is born again, he or she is born into a family of faith for all eternity. This family, God's people, is the church. Unlike any other earthly entity, the church is not divided according to physical boundary, race, culture, education, or any other reality. Instead, the church is unified because of its members' common experience with the grace of Jesus Christ.

Unity, however, does not mean uniformity or a lack of diversity. Indeed, the great diversity of the church's members is one of its unique aspects. Though each member is gifted differently, every member comes together to form the whole church. Furthermore, because of the variety of gifts possessed, every member is integral to the church's healthy functioning. There is, then, no member greater than another, just as there is no part of the body that would boast over its position. The proper response of the Christian is to love and value the other members of the church because of their essential contributions to the health and well-being of the church worldwide.

KEY TERMS OF SALVATION

The more one understands the key terms Paul chose to explain the gospel, the deeper one's experience will be with the gospel.

Atonement/propitiation (3:25): "The satisfaction of God's holy wrath against sin." The consequence of our sin is the righteous judgment that God will exercise on sinners. By dying in our place and taking our sins on himself, Jesus is the propitiation for our sin: he satisfies God's righteous anger against all who believe.

Faith (1:17): Meaning "belief" or "trust," faith is the means by which sinful people come into right standing with God. It is a complete and active trust in Jesus alone for salvation.

Gospel (1:16): Literally means "good news" and is the word Paul uses to refer to the message of forgiveness, eternal life, and the lordship of Christ.

Grace (6:14): "The unmerited favor of God." This refers to God's inexplicable and unwarranted giving of good things (especially salvation) to those who could never earn it. There is power for holy living in the grace of God.

Justification (5:18): A legal term that means "the act of being declared righteous." This exchange happens at salvation when God the Judge declares righteous those who trust in Christ and his work at the cross. Christ took on the punishment for the sins of those who believe.

Law (13:8): "The commandments given by God." The law is good, yet sinful people are incapable of fully keeping it. The law then serves to fully expose our sin. That's why Paul emphasizes the law in comparison with God's grace (5:20; 6:14–15).

Redemption (3:23–24): What we experience when we are saved. This is "the act of freeing someone by paying a price," an economic term Paul employed to show how God buys us back with the blood of his own Son.

Righteousness (1:17): As God buys us back, he gifts us with righteousness, "God's standard of purity" or "God's own truthfulness and faithfulness." Amazingly, in the gospel we are not only forgiven, but we are also granted perfect purity in Christ.

Salvation (1:16): Means "deliverance" or "healing" and is the word Paul most often uses to denote deliverance from sin and its deadly consequences.

Sin (3:20): Means "missing the mark" or "disobedience to God's law." Sin is more than an action; it's a condition that leads to disobedient action. Broadly defined, it's the tendency of humans to rebel against God, which leads to any action or attitude that opposes God's character and will.

Paul uses these terms throughout the book of Romans to describe the free gift of salvation and eternal transformation that is available to all who will believe and trust in Jesus for the forgiveness of their sin.

sleep. For salvation is nearer to us now than when we first believed. 12The night
is far gone; the day is at hand. So then let us cast off the works of darkness and
put on the armor of light. 13Let us walk properly as in the daytime, not in orgies
and drunkenness, not in sexual immorality and sensuality, not in quarreling and
jealousy. 14But put on the Lord Jesus Christ, and make no provision for the flesh,
to gratify its desires.

Do Not Pass Judgment on One Another

14 As for the one who is weak in faith, welcome him, but not to quarrel over
opinions. 2One person believes he may eat anything, while the weak person
eats only vegetables. 3Let not the one who eats despise the one who abstains, and
let not the one who abstains pass judgment on the one who eats, for God has
welcomed him. 4Who are you to pass judgment on the servant of another? It is
before his own master[1] that he stands or falls. And he will be upheld, for the Lord
is able to make him stand.

5One person esteems one day as better than another, while another esteems
all days alike. Each one should be fully convinced in his own mind. 6The one who
observes the day, observes it in honor of the Lord. The one who eats, eats in honor
of the Lord, since he gives thanks to God, while the one who abstains, abstains in
honor of the Lord and gives thanks to God. 7For none of us lives to himself, and none
of us dies to himself. 8For if we live, we live to the Lord, and if we die, we die to the
Lord. So then, whether we live or whether we die, we are the Lord's. 9For to this end
Christ died and lived again, that he might be Lord both of the dead and of the living.

10Why do you pass judgment on your brother? Or you, why do you despise
your brother? For we will all stand before the judgment seat of God; 11for it is
written,

> "As I live, says the Lord, every knee shall bow to me,
> and every tongue shall confess[2] to God."

12So then each of us will give an account of himself to God.

Do Not Cause Another to Stumble

13Therefore let us not pass judgment on one another any longer, but rather
decide never to put a stumbling block or hindrance in the way of a brother. 14I
know and am persuaded in the Lord Jesus that nothing is unclean in itself, but
it is unclean for anyone who thinks it unclean. 15For if your brother is grieved by
what you eat, you are no longer walking in love. By what you eat, do not destroy
the one for whom Christ died. 16So do not let what you regard as good be spoken
of as evil. 17For the kingdom of God is not a matter of eating and drinking but of
righteousness and peace and joy in the Holy Spirit. 18Whoever thus serves Christ
is acceptable to God and approved by men. 19So then let us pursue what makes for
peace and for mutual upbuilding.

20Do not, for the sake of food, destroy the work of God. Everything is indeed
clean, but it is wrong for anyone to make another stumble by what he eats. 21It
is good not to eat meat or drink wine or do anything that causes your brother to
stumble.[3] 22The faith that you have, keep between yourself and God. Blessed is the
one who has no reason to pass judgment on himself for what he approves. 23But
whoever has doubts is condemned if he eats, because the eating is not from faith.
For whatever does not proceed from faith is sin.[4]

The Example of Christ

15 We who are strong have an obligation to bear with the failings of the weak,
and not to please ourselves. 2Let each of us please his neighbor for his
good, to build him up. 3For Christ did not please himself, but as it is written, "The

[1]Or *lord* [2]Or *shall give praise* [3]Some manuscripts add *or be hindered or be weakened* [4]Some manuscripts insert here 16:25–27

ROMANS 15:1–4

AN UNSELFISH ATTITUDE

The Bible does not speak clearly about every specific issue people encounter in this life. Paul recognized this and penned for his readers a key principle to follow in those matters not specifically addressed. In Romans 14, Paul laid out the law of liberty in which the Christian chooses not to exercise all the freedom at their disposal, but instead processes decisions about debatable matters based on what's best for their brothers and sisters. The first four verses of chapter 15 summarize and close out that section of the book and provide the true fuel for such an attitude.

When a Christian faces a questionable matter, one in which they are not constrained by their conscience or guided by a clear biblical mandate, they should be willing to forgo their personal freedom for the sake of a brother or sister. This is what Jesus modeled for us. He did not live to benefit himself, but instead willingly and unselfishly gave himself over to insult and injury for the sake of others (1Pe 2:23). For those who follow Jesus, the same attitude is expected—being willing to give up our freedom for the edification of another.

reproaches of those who reproached you fell on me." 4For whatever was written in
former days was written for our instruction, that through endurance and through
the encouragement of the Scriptures we might have hope. 5May the God of endurance and encouragement grant you to live in such harmony with one another, in
accord with Christ Jesus, 6that together you may with one voice glorify the God
and Father of our Lord Jesus Christ. 7Therefore welcome one another as Christ has
welcomed you, for the glory of God.

Christ the Hope of Jews and Gentiles

8For I tell you that Christ became a servant to the circumcised to show God's
truthfulness, in order to confirm the promises given to the patriarchs, 9and in
order that the Gentiles might glorify God for his mercy. As it is written,

> "Therefore I will praise you among the Gentiles,
> and sing to your name."

10And again it says,

> "Rejoice, O Gentiles, with his people."

11And again,

> "Praise the Lord, all you Gentiles,
> and let all the peoples extol him."

12And again Isaiah says,

> "The root of Jesse will come,
> even he who arises to rule the Gentiles;
> in him will the Gentiles hope."

13May the God of hope fill you with all joy and peace in believing, so that by the
power of the Holy Spirit you may abound in hope.

Paul the Minister to the Gentiles

14I myself am satisfied about you, my brothers,[1] that you yourselves are full
of goodness, filled with all knowledge and able to instruct one another. 15But on
some points I have written to you very boldly by way of reminder, because of
the grace given me by God 16to be a minister of Christ Jesus to the Gentiles in the
priestly service of the gospel of God, so that the offering of the Gentiles may be
acceptable, sanctified by the Holy Spirit. 17In Christ Jesus, then, I have reason to
be proud of my work for God. 18For I will not venture to speak of anything except
what Christ has accomplished through me to bring the Gentiles to obedience—by
word and deed, 19by the power of signs and wonders, by the power of the Spirit of
God—so that from Jerusalem and all the way around to Illyricum I have fulfilled
the ministry of the gospel of Christ; 20and thus I make it my ambition to preach
the gospel, not where Christ has already been named, lest I build on someone
else's foundation, 21but as it is written,

> "Those who have never been told of him will see,
> and those who have never heard will understand."

Paul's Plan to Visit Rome

22This is the reason why I have so often been hindered from coming to you.
23But now, since I no longer have any room for work in these regions, and since I
have longed for many years to come to you, 24I hope to see you in passing as I go
to Spain, and to be helped on my journey there by you, once I have enjoyed your
company for a while. 25At present, however, I am going to Jerusalem bringing aid
to the saints. 26For Macedonia and Achaia have been pleased to make some contribution for the poor among the saints at Jerusalem. 27For they were pleased to do

[1] Or *brothers and sisters*; also verse 30

it, and indeed they owe it to them. For if the Gentiles have come to share in their spiritual blessings, they ought also to be of service to them in material blessings. 28 When therefore I have completed this and have delivered to them what has been collected,[1] I will leave for Spain by way of you. 29 I know that when I come to you I will come in the fullness of the blessing[2] of Christ.

30 I appeal to you, brothers, by our Lord Jesus Christ and by the love of the Spirit, to strive together with me in your prayers to God on my behalf, 31 that I may be delivered from the unbelievers in Judea, and that my service for Jerusalem may be acceptable to the saints, 32 so that by God's will I may come to you with joy and be refreshed in your company. 33 May the God of peace be with you all. Amen.

Personal Greetings

16 I commend to you our sister Phoebe, a servant[3] of the church at Cenchreae, 2 that you may welcome her in the Lord in a way worthy of the saints, and help her in whatever she may need from you, for she has been a patron of many and of myself as well.

3 Greet Prisca and Aquila, my fellow workers in Christ Jesus, 4 who risked their necks for my life, to whom not only I give thanks but all the churches of the Gentiles give thanks as well. 5 Greet also the church in their house. Greet my beloved Epaenetus, who was the first convert[4] to Christ in Asia. 6 Greet Mary, who has worked hard for you. 7 Greet Andronicus and Junia,[5] my kinsmen and my fellow prisoners. They are well known to the apostles,[6] and they were in Christ before me. 8 Greet Ampliatus, my beloved in the Lord. 9 Greet Urbanus, our fellow worker in Christ, and my beloved Stachys. 10 Greet Apelles, who is approved in Christ. Greet those who belong to the family of Aristobulus. 11 Greet my kinsman Herodion. Greet those in the Lord who belong to the family of Narcissus. 12 Greet those workers in the Lord, Tryphaena and Tryphosa. Greet the beloved Persis, who has worked hard in the Lord. 13 Greet Rufus, chosen in the Lord; also his mother, who has been a mother to me as well. 14 Greet Asyncritus, Phlegon, Hermes, Patrobas, Hermas, and the brothers[7] who are with them. 15 Greet Philologus, Julia, Nereus and his sister, and Olympas, and all the saints who are with them. 16 Greet one another with a holy kiss. All the churches of Christ greet you.

Final Instructions and Greetings

17 I appeal to you, brothers, to watch out for those who cause divisions and create obstacles contrary to the doctrine that you have been taught; avoid them. 18 For such persons do not serve our Lord Christ, but their own appetites,[8] and by smooth talk and flattery they deceive the hearts of the naive. 19 For your obedience is known to all, so that I rejoice over you, but I want you to be wise as to what is good and innocent as to what is evil. 20 The God of peace will soon crush Satan under your feet. The grace of our Lord Jesus Christ be with you.

21 Timothy, my fellow worker, greets you; so do Lucius and Jason and Sosipater, my kinsmen.

22 I Tertius, who wrote this letter, greet you in the Lord.

23 Gaius, who is host to me and to the whole church, greets you. Erastus, the city treasurer, and our brother Quartus, greet you.[9]

Doxology

25 Now to him who is able to strengthen you according to my gospel and the preaching of Jesus Christ, according to the revelation of the mystery that was kept secret for long ages 26 but has now been disclosed and through the prophetic writings has been made known to all nations, according to the command of the eternal God, to bring about the obedience of faith— 27 to the only wise God be glory forevermore through Jesus Christ! Amen.

[1] Greek *sealed to them this fruit* [2] Some manuscripts insert *of the gospel* [3] Or *deaconess* [4] Greek *firstfruit* [5] Or *Junias* [6] Or *messengers* [7] Or *brothers and sisters*; also verse 17 [8] Greek *their own belly* [9] Some manuscripts insert verse 24: *The grace of our Lord Jesus Christ be with you all. Amen*

ROMANS 16:25–27

BENEDICTION

How does one conclude the greatest theological treatise ever written? For Paul, the answer was to refer back to what he had already said. Indeed, this is what Paul's ministry was, as he was committed to preaching only Christ and Christ crucified time and time again (1Co 2:2). This good-news message is the only lasting hope for humanity.

In his final benediction to the letter of Romans, Paul again reminds readers of the great and mysterious gospel of Jesus Christ, which is immensely available to all who believe, whether Jew or Gentile. This is the central storyline of all Scripture, and now through the work of Jesus, God's plans are fulfilled. Appropriately, this letter ends in the same way that all of history will end: on bended knee, eyes on Christ alone, with Paul—and by extension, us as well—giving glory to God for what he has done and what he will surely do in the future.

JESUS: OUR HOPE FOR CHANGE

1 CORINTHIANS

1 CORINTHIANS

PAUL'S MISSIONARY JOURNEYS	PAUL PLANTS CHURCH AT CORINTH	PAUL WRITES 1 CORINTHIANS
c. AD 47 – 57	*c. AD 51*	*c. AD 54*

The New Testament church was far from perfect. The idyllic pictures of the church found in small sections of the book of Acts might lead one to believe that all the churches of the first century were permeated by purity and holiness. The church in Corinth dispels that faulty belief due to its gross immorality and wickedness.

In Acts 18:1 – 18, Luke records the founding of the church in Corinth. Paul was well acquainted with this church, having visited it on his second mission journey. Paul served the church for a year and a half, seeking to establish the predominately Gentile believers in the ways of the Lord. This work was vital since Corinth was an important cosmopolitan city in ancient Greece. Believers in that region were faced with constant temptation to succumb to the idolatry of the pagans living throughout the region.

The Corinthian letters differ in style from Paul's other writings. Rather than his typical pattern of first describing the Good News of Jesus, followed by a summary of the ethical implications of this message, Paul uses the Corinthian letters to respond to particular issues facing the young church after his departure. Paul received troubling reports about the church and their ongoing proclivity toward waywardness, and he wrote to address the issues that continued to plague the church, such as divisions, abuse of liberty, sexual immorality, drunkenness, and the influence of false teaching.

As he wrote, Paul demonstrated the holistic and communal effects of the gospel. Every facet of life is shaped by Jesus' work, and all decisions can and should be informed by what was accomplished in his death and resurrection. Also, the gospel is pervasive among the people of God as the church gathers in worship and scatters in mission. The hope of the gospel is not merely a means of personal salvation, but it transforms the corporate life of God's people.

While the overall tone of this book is forceful and passionate, Paul ends with a reminder of the great hope that the gospel brings. Satan, sin, and death are defeated, and as a result, God's people can experience victory over Satan, sin, and death themselves. At the appointed time, God will vindicate himself before the watching world and prove, once and for all, that he has accomplished his plan of redeeming the world (15:50–58).

YET FOR US THERE IS ONE GOD,
THE FATHER, FROM WHOM ARE ALL THINGS
AND FOR WHOM WE EXIST, AND
ONE LORD, JESUS CHRIST,
THROUGH WHOM ARE ALL THINGS
AND THROUGH WHOM WE EXIST.

---

1 Corinthians 8:6

1 CORINTHIANS

Greeting

1 Paul, called by the will of God to be an apostle of Christ Jesus, and our brother
Sosthenes,
2 To the church of God that is in Corinth, to those sanctified in Christ Jesus,
called to be saints together with all those who in every place call upon the name
of our Lord Jesus Christ, both their Lord and ours:
3 Grace to you and peace from God our Father and the Lord Jesus Christ.

Thanksgiving

4 I give thanks to my God always for you because of the grace of God that
was given you in Christ Jesus, 5 that in every way you were enriched in him in all
speech and all knowledge— 6 even as the testimony about Christ was confirmed
among you— 7 so that you are not lacking in any gift, as you wait for the revealing
of our Lord Jesus Christ, 8 who will sustain you to the end, guiltless in the day of
our Lord Jesus Christ. 9 God is faithful, by whom you were called into the fellowship of his Son, Jesus Christ our Lord.

Divisions in the Church

10 I appeal to you, brothers,[1] by the name of our Lord Jesus Christ, that all of
you agree, and that there be no divisions among you, but that you be united in
the same mind and the same judgment. 11 For it has been reported to me by Chloe's
people that there is quarreling among you, my brothers. 12 What I mean is that
each one of you says, "I follow Paul," or "I follow Apollos," or "I follow Cephas,"
or "I follow Christ." 13 Is Christ divided? Was Paul crucified for you? Or were you
baptized in the name of Paul? 14 I thank God that I baptized none of you except
Crispus and Gaius, 15 so that no one may say that you were baptized in my name.
16 (I did baptize also the household of Stephanas. Beyond that, I do not know
whether I baptized anyone else.) 17 For Christ did not send me to baptize but to
preach the gospel, and not with words of eloquent wisdom, lest the cross of Christ
be emptied of its power.

Christ the Wisdom and Power of God

18 For the word of the cross is folly to those who are perishing, but to us who
are being saved it is the power of God. 19 For it is written,

> "I will destroy the wisdom of the wise,
> and the discernment of the discerning I will thwart."

20 Where is the one who is wise? Where is the scribe? Where is the debater of this
age? Has not God made foolish the wisdom of the world? 21 For since, in the wisdom of God, the world did not know God through wisdom, it pleased God through
the folly of what we preach[2] to save those who believe. 22 For Jews demand signs
and Greeks seek wisdom, 23 but we preach Christ crucified, a stumbling block to
Jews and folly to Gentiles, 24 but to those who are called, both Jews and Greeks,
Christ the power of God and the wisdom of God. 25 For the foolishness of God is
wiser than men, and the weakness of God is stronger than men.
26 For consider your calling, brothers: not many of you were wise according
to worldly standards,[3] not many were powerful, not many were of noble birth.
27 But God chose what is foolish in the world to shame the wise; God chose what

---

[1] Or *brothers and sisters*. In New Testament usage, depending on the context, the plural Greek word *adelphoi* (translated "brothers") may refer either to *brothers* or to *brothers and sisters*; also verses 11, 26
[2] Or *the folly of preaching* [3] Greek *according to the flesh*

UNITY IN CHRIST

Paul challenged this newly formed Corinthian church based on a troubling report he received (v. 11). Because of pervasive pride, these new believers were cultivating a disruptive spirit. Some championed Paul, others Apollos, and some Cephas (v. 12). Teaching preference divided the church.

In response to this division, Paul exhorted the church to unite around the person and work of Jesus Christ, not those who are used by him to lead the church. Paul asked, "Is Christ divided?" (v. 13). The implied and obvious answer is a clear "no." A unified Christ works to unify believers one with another. Therefore, Paul appealed to them, asking "that all of you agree, and that there be no divisions among you, but that you be united in the same mind and the same judgment" (v. 10). One Christ necessitates one united church.

Few divisions marked this New Testament era as much as the chasm between Jews and Greeks (Gentiles). However, this chapter makes it clear that for those God called from among both Jews and Gentiles, Christ is both the power and the wisdom of God (v. 24). In the gospel, these two groups become one (Eph 2:15). That which sin divides, Christ gathers together.

Therefore, any division that remains among God's people repudiates the gospel. Elsewhere, Paul admonishes the church to maintain the unity created by Christ (Eph 4:3). Jesus prayed that this unity might further God's mission (Jn 17:20–26). Inasmuch as the church becomes a single community, it portrays to the world the unifying work of the gospel (Jn 17:21). So Christians should be marked by unity, regardless of what earthly barriers threaten to divide them, be they racial, socioeconomic, or cultural.

Christ unites a divided people, purchasing unity rather than uniformity. In the beginning, God created a united humanity of worshipers. In the end, God will restore a united humanity of diverse worshipers under the banner of his crucified and risen Son (Rev 5:9). In fact, this diversity on display will only magnify the glory of the unifier. Christ unites Christians in his church, for this life and for all eternity.

1 CORINTHIANS 2:2

JESUS CHRIST AND HIM CRUCIFIED

Paul told the Corinthians that he decided to know *nothing* but "Jesus Christ and him crucified." This immediately raises the question: Did Paul mean he intended cognitively to forget all other knowledge, such as the alphabet, the direction to Corinth, or how to make a tent? Of course not. The thrust of the language pointed instead to a surpassing knowledge; the other information in his brain paled in comparison to the message about Jesus and his work. Furthermore, the balance of the New Testament makes plain that the crucified Jesus informs and directs all other knowledge.

Believers never graduate from the cross. Though some teach that the crucifixion and resurrection of Jesus only inform initial conversion, the New Testament describes the entirety of a Christian's life as a working out of salvation (Php 2:12). A well-educated man like Paul — never to be confused with an intellectual slouch — spoke of the cross as if he was always moving into a deeper understanding of it, continually seeing new facets of this inexhaustible gospel. He did not intend to move on to lesser pursuits. Neither should the church.

1 CORINTHIANS 3:1–9

INFANTS IN CHRIST

No adult likes to be called a baby. However, Paul refused to sugarcoat his words to the toddling Corinthian church. While it is acceptable to be a baby for a season — in fact, unavoidable — a 30-year-old

(continued on next page)

is weak in the world to shame the strong; 28God chose what is low and despised in the world, even things that are not, to bring to nothing things that are, 29so that no human being[1] might boast in the presence of God. 30And because of him[2] you are in Christ Jesus, who became to us wisdom from God, righteousness and sanctification and redemption, 31so that, as it is written, "Let the one who boasts, boast in the Lord."

Proclaiming Christ Crucified

2 And I, when I came to you, brothers,[3] did not come proclaiming to you the testimony[4] of God with lofty speech or wisdom. 2For I decided to know nothing among you except Jesus Christ and him crucified. 3And I was with you in weakness and in fear and much trembling, 4and my speech and my message were not in plausible words of wisdom, but in demonstration of the Spirit and of power, 5so that your faith might not rest in the wisdom of men[5] but in the power of God.

Wisdom from the Spirit

6Yet among the mature we do impart wisdom, although it is not a wisdom of this age or of the rulers of this age, who are doomed to pass away. 7But we impart a secret and hidden wisdom of God, which God decreed before the ages for our glory. 8None of the rulers of this age understood this, for if they had, they would not have crucified the Lord of glory. 9But, as it is written,

"What no eye has seen, nor ear heard,
  nor the heart of man imagined,
what God has prepared for those who love him"—

10these things God has revealed to us through the Spirit. For the Spirit searches everything, even the depths of God. 11For who knows a person's thoughts except the spirit of that person, which is in him? So also no one comprehends the thoughts of God except the Spirit of God. 12Now we have received not the spirit of the world, but the Spirit who is from God, that we might understand the things freely given us by God. 13And we impart this in words not taught by human wisdom but taught by the Spirit, interpreting spiritual truths to those who are spiritual.[6]

14The natural person does not accept the things of the Spirit of God, for they are folly to him, and he is not able to understand them because they are spiritually discerned. 15The spiritual person judges all things, but is himself to be judged by no one. 16"For who has understood the mind of the Lord so as to instruct him?" But we have the mind of Christ.

Divisions in the Church

3 But I, brothers,[7] could not address you as spiritual people, but as people of the flesh, as infants in Christ. 2I fed you with milk, not solid food, for you were not ready for it. And even now you are not yet ready, 3for you are still of the flesh. For while there is jealousy and strife among you, are you not of the flesh and behaving only in a human way? 4For when one says, "I follow Paul," and another, "I follow Apollos," are you not being merely human?

5What then is Apollos? What is Paul? Servants through whom you believed, as the Lord assigned to each. 6I planted, Apollos watered, but God gave the growth. 7So neither he who plants nor he who waters is anything, but only God who gives the growth. 8He who plants and he who waters are one, and each will receive his wages according to his labor. 9For we are God's fellow workers. You are God's field, God's building.

10According to the grace of God given to me, like a skilled[8] master builder I

[1]Greek *no flesh* [2]Greek *And from him* [3]Or *brothers and sisters* [4]Some manuscripts *mystery* (or *secret*) [5]The Greek word *anthropoi* can refer to both men and women [6]Or *interpreting spiritual truths in spiritual language*, or *comparing spiritual things with spiritual* [7]Or *brothers and sisters* [8]Or *wise*

laid a foundation, and someone else is building upon it. Let each one take care
how he builds upon it. 11For no one can lay a foundation other than that which
is laid, which is Jesus Christ. 12Now if anyone builds on the foundation with
gold, silver, precious stones, wood, hay, straw— 13each one's work will become
manifest, for the Day will disclose it, because it will be revealed by fire, and the
fire will test what sort of work each one has done. 14If the work that anyone has
built on the foundation survives, he will receive a reward. 15If anyone's work
is burned up, he will suffer loss, though he himself will be saved, but only as
through fire.

16Do you not know that you[1] are God's temple and that God's Spirit dwells in
you? 17If anyone destroys God's temple, God will destroy him. For God's temple is
holy, and you are that temple.

18Let no one deceive himself. If anyone among you thinks that he is wise in
this age, let him become a fool that he may become wise. 19For the wisdom of this
world is folly with God. For it is written, "He catches the wise in their craftiness,"
20and again, "The Lord knows the thoughts of the wise, that they are futile." 21So
let no one boast in men. For all things are yours, 22whether Paul or Apollos or
Cephas or the world or life or death or the present or the future—all are yours,
23and you are Christ's, and Christ is God's.

The Ministry of Apostles

4 This is how one should regard us, as servants of Christ and stewards of the
mysteries of God. 2Moreover, it is required of stewards that they be found
faithful. 3But with me it is a very small thing that I should be judged by you or by
any human court. In fact, I do not even judge myself. 4For I am not aware of anything against myself, but I am not thereby acquitted. It is the Lord who judges me.
5Therefore do not pronounce judgment before the time, before the Lord comes,
who will bring to light the things now hidden in darkness and will disclose the
purposes of the heart. Then each one will receive his commendation from God.

6I have applied all these things to myself and Apollos for your benefit, brothers,[2] that you may learn by us not to go beyond what is written, that none of you
may be puffed up in favor of one against another. 7For who sees anything different
in you? What do you have that you did not receive? If then you received it, why do
you boast as if you did not receive it?

8Already you have all you want! Already you have become rich! Without us
you have become kings! And would that you did reign, so that we might share
the rule with you! 9For I think that God has exhibited us apostles as last of all,
like men sentenced to death, because we have become a spectacle to the world,
to angels, and to men. 10We are fools for Christ's sake, but you are wise in Christ.
We are weak, but you are strong. You are held in honor, but we in disrepute. 11To
the present hour we hunger and thirst, we are poorly dressed and buffeted and
homeless, 12and we labor, working with our own hands. When reviled, we bless;
when persecuted, we endure; 13when slandered, we entreat. We have become, and
are still, like the scum of the world, the refuse of all things.

14I do not write these things to make you ashamed, but to admonish you as my
beloved children. 15For though you have countless[3] guides in Christ, you do not
have many fathers. For I became your father in Christ Jesus through the gospel.
16I urge you, then, be imitators of me. 17That is why I sent[4] you Timothy, my beloved and faithful child in the Lord, to remind you of my ways in Christ,[5] as I teach
them everywhere in every church. 18Some are arrogant, as though I were not coming to you. 19But I will come to you soon, if the Lord wills, and I will find out not
the talk of these arrogant people but their power. 20For the kingdom of God does
not consist in talk but in power. 21What do you wish? Shall I come to you with a
rod, or with love in a spirit of gentleness?

[1]The Greek for *you* is plural in verses 16 and 17 [2]Or *brothers and sisters* [3]Greek *you have ten thousand*
[4]Or *am sending* [5]Some manuscripts add *Jesus*

(Infants in Christ, continued)

depending entirely upon his mother needs to be admonished. Such is the nature of Paul's rebuke in this text.

To continue the imagery Paul employed, no one teaches a baby the intricacies of selfishness. Infants only pursue what makes them happy at all times. The Corinthians' sinful pride seems to have perpetuated this selfishness into full adulthood. They continued to be jealous of and quarrel with one another, demonstrating attitudes and actions that were at odds with mature Christian living.

Not only did Paul call these believers infants, but he also went on to rebuke them for modeling the pagan ways of nonbelievers. In the Corinthian context—alluding back to chapter 1—a spirit of favoritism led individuals to place an undue emphasis upon their preferred teacher. This kind of behavior resembled the prevailing worldly patterns more than it resembled Christ. So Paul quickly reminded these believers of the role he and Apollos played. Human teachers merely plant and water; God gives the growth. Contrary to some teaching, Paul did not indicate that there were two acceptable kinds of Christians in this text. Rather, he called upon the immature to grow up and to trust that God would be faithful to do his part.

1 CORINTHIANS 4:1

SERVANTS OF CHRIST

The Corinthian church admired celebrities. Prizing lofty rhetoric, they focused upon the teacher more than the teaching. And once they elevated their teacher of choice—branding and marketing him—they chose a

(continued on next page)

(Servants of Christ, continued)

tribe to which they would belong. In response to the Corinthian climate, Paul wrote plainly: "Let no one boast in men" (1Co 3:21).

Paul penned an image he wanted the believers to keep in mind as they considered their teachers. Rather than viewing their teachers as rhetoricians waxing eloquent upon their pedestals, the Corinthians should envision teachers as *servants*, Paul said. The word used in this passage refers often to the rower on a ship, listening to and obeying the orders of a supervisor. As long as the rowers listened and obeyed, the ship moved smoothly toward its destination. With that humble language, Paul made clear that he, Apollos, and Cephas were merely servants of the true teacher: Jesus Christ.

These teachers—actually servants—stewarded the mysteries of God. When Paul used the term *mystery*, he did not mean to imply something that cannot be figured out. *Mystery* refers instead to truths that God knew before time and has now revealed to his people. In this case, Paul used mystery language to describe the gospel of Jesus Christ. God entrusted his servants with the faithful stewardship of this mystery as they taught the glorious gospel of Jesus.

Sexual Immorality Defiles the Church

5 It is actually reported that there is sexual immorality among you, and of a kind that is not tolerated even among pagans, for a man has his father's wife. 2And you are arrogant! Ought you not rather to mourn? Let him who has done this be removed from among you.

3For though absent in body, I am present in spirit; and as if present, I have already pronounced judgment on the one who did such a thing. 4When you are assembled in the name of the Lord Jesus and my spirit is present, with the power of our Lord Jesus, 5you are to deliver this man to Satan for the destruction of the flesh, so that his spirit may be saved in the day of the Lord.[1]

6Your boasting is not good. Do you not know that a little leaven leavens the whole lump? 7Cleanse out the old leaven that you may be a new lump, as you really are unleavened. For Christ, our Passover lamb, has been sacrificed. 8Let us therefore celebrate the festival, not with the old leaven, the leaven of malice and evil, but with the unleavened bread of sincerity and truth.

9I wrote to you in my letter not to associate with sexually immoral people—10not at all meaning the sexually immoral of this world, or the greedy and swindlers, or idolaters, since then you would need to go out of the world. 11But now I am writing to you not to associate with anyone who bears the name of brother if he is guilty of sexual immorality or greed, or is an idolater, reviler, drunkard, or swindler—not even to eat with such a one. 12For what have I to do with judging outsiders? Is it not those inside the church[2] whom you are to judge? 13God judges[3] those outside. "Purge the evil person from among you."

Lawsuits Against Believers

6 When one of you has a grievance against another, does he dare go to law before the unrighteous instead of the saints? 2Or do you not know that the saints will judge the world? And if the world is to be judged by you, are you incompetent to try trivial cases? 3Do you not know that we are to judge angels? How much more, then, matters pertaining to this life! 4So if you have such cases, why do you lay them before those who have no standing in the church? 5I say this to your shame. Can it be that there is no one among you wise enough to settle a dispute between the brothers, 6but brother goes to law against brother, and that before unbelievers? 7To have lawsuits at all with one another is already a defeat for you. Why not rather suffer wrong? Why not rather be defrauded? 8But you yourselves wrong and defraud—even your own brothers![4]

9Or do you not know that the unrighteous[5] will not inherit the kingdom of God? Do not be deceived: neither the sexually immoral, nor idolaters, nor adulterers, nor men who practice homosexuality,[6] 10nor thieves, nor the greedy, nor drunkards, nor revilers, nor swindlers will inherit the kingdom of God. 11And such were some of you. But you were washed, you were sanctified, you were justified in the name of the Lord Jesus Christ and by the Spirit of our God.

Flee Sexual Immorality

12"All things are lawful for me," but not all things are helpful. "All things are lawful for me," but I will not be dominated by anything. 13"Food is meant for the stomach and the stomach for food"—and God will destroy both one and the other. The body is not meant for sexual immorality, but for the Lord, and the Lord for the body. 14And God raised the Lord and will also raise us up by his power. 15Do you not know that your bodies are members of Christ? Shall I then take the members of Christ and make them members of a prostitute? Never! 16Or do you not know that he who is joined[7] to a prostitute becomes one body with her? For,

[1]Some manuscripts add *Jesus* [2]Greek *those inside* [3]Or *will judge* [4]Or *brothers and sisters*
[5]Or *wrongdoers* [6]The two Greek terms translated by this phrase refer to the passive and active partners in consensual homosexual acts [7]Or *who holds fast* (compare Genesis 2:24 and Deuteronomy 10:20); also verse 17

CHRIST, THE PASSOVER LAMB

The Corinthian believers seemed to misunderstand what Paul meant when he described the church as those who were "called to be saints" (1Co 1:2). Preceding this letter, Paul received word that a man living in open immorality continued to fellowship with the rest of the Corinthian church. Responding in this passage, Paul addressed not only this man's culpability, but the corporate body's as well.

It seemed that rather than the church being sorrowful over the sin in their midst, they boasted. Rather than rebuking this man corporately, they continued to worship and fellowship as if nothing was amiss. The absence of corporate grief grieved Paul.

Paul consistently connected the church's conduct with the gospel, calling believers to live in a way that reflected their new life in Christ (Ro 12:1 – 2; Gal 2:14; 5:1 – 26; Eph 4 – 6; Col 3). As an implication of the gospel's power, God expects his people to live in a manner distinct from the mindsets and practices of the world.

Paul recognized that an unbeliever might do exactly what the immoral man did, though God does not call believers to judge those outside the church. But when this sort of behavior occurs within the body of Christ, the church must act (1Co 5:12). Though some might consider this instruction harsh, Paul admonished the Corinthians to put the man living in sin out of their fellowship (v. 13).

The apostle connected the Corinthians' conduct with the Israelites' preparation for the Passover. Before Passover, the Jewish family would make sure no yeast remained in their home, as even a little yeast leavened the whole lump (v. 6). The analogy Paul used here implies that this individual's sin affected the corporate body, though their approval was only implicit.

Paul goes on to reason that if the Israelites showed this amount of care in preparation for Passover, how much more should the church deal with sin in light of the cross? At Passover, the Israelites sacrificed an unknowing lamb so others might live (Ex 12:1 – 30). However, the Corinthians' Passover Lamb was not an ignorant sheep. Nor did he die unwillingly. The precious Lamb of God died in the Corinthians' place so they might live a life of obedience out of gratitude to him.

as it is written, "The two will become one flesh." 17But he who is joined to the Lord becomes one spirit with him. 18Flee from sexual immorality. Every other sin[1] a person commits is outside the body, but the sexually immoral person sins against his own body. 19Or do you not know that your body is a temple of the Holy Spirit within you, whom you have from God? You are not your own, 20for you were bought with a price. So glorify God in your body.

Principles for Marriage

7 Now concerning the matters about which you wrote: "It is good for a man not to have sexual relations with a woman." 2But because of the temptation to sexual immorality, each man should have his own wife and each woman her own husband. 3The husband should give to his wife her conjugal rights, and likewise the wife to her husband. 4For the wife does not have authority over her own body, but the husband does. Likewise the husband does not have authority over his own body, but the wife does. 5Do not deprive one another, except perhaps by agreement for a limited time, that you may devote yourselves to prayer; but then come together again, so that Satan may not tempt you because of your lack of self-control.

6Now as a concession, not a command, I say this.[2] 7I wish that all were as I myself am. But each has his own gift from God, one of one kind and one of another.

8To the unmarried and the widows I say that it is good for them to remain single, as I am. 9But if they cannot exercise self-control, they should marry. For it is better to marry than to burn with passion.

10To the married I give this charge (not I, but the Lord): the wife should not separate from her husband 11(but if she does, she should remain unmarried or else be reconciled to her husband), and the husband should not divorce his wife.

12To the rest I say (I, not the Lord) that if any brother has a wife who is an unbeliever, and she consents to live with him, he should not divorce her. 13If any woman has a husband who is an unbeliever, and he consents to live with her, she should not divorce him. 14For the unbelieving husband is made holy because of his wife, and the unbelieving wife is made holy because of her husband. Otherwise your children would be unclean, but as it is, they are holy. 15But if the unbelieving partner separates, let it be so. In such cases the brother or sister is not enslaved. God has called you[3] to peace. 16For how do you know, wife, whether you will save your husband? Or how do you know, husband, whether you will save your wife?

Live as You Are Called

17Only let each person lead the life[4] that the Lord has assigned to him, and to which God has called him. This is my rule in all the churches. 18Was anyone at the time of his call already circumcised? Let him not seek to remove the marks of circumcision. Was anyone at the time of his call uncircumcised? Let him not seek circumcision. 19For neither circumcision counts for anything nor uncircumcision, but keeping the commandments of God. 20Each one should remain in the condition in which he was called. 21Were you a bondservant[5] when called? Do not be concerned about it. (But if you can gain your freedom, avail yourself of the opportunity.) 22For he who was called in the Lord as a bondservant is a freedman of the Lord. Likewise he who was free when called is a bondservant of Christ. 23You were bought with a price; do not become bondservants of men. 24So, brothers,[6] in whatever condition each was called, there let him remain with God.

The Unmarried and the Widowed

25Now concerning[7] the betrothed,[8] I have no command from the Lord, but I give my judgment as one who by the Lord's mercy is trustworthy. 26I think

[1]Or *Every sin* [2]Or *I say this:* [3]Some manuscripts *us* [4]Or *each person walk in the way* [5]For the contextual rendering of the Greek word *doulos*, see Preface; also verses 22 (twice), 23 [6]Or *brothers and sisters*; also verse 29 [7]The expression *Now concerning* introduces a reply to a question in the Corinthians' letter; see 7:1 [8]Greek *virgins*

1 CORINTHIANS 6:19–20

MEMBERS OF CHRIST

Though some draw a sharp distinction between the spiritual and the physical, God made humanity neither a soulless body nor a bodiless soul. Instead, God made humans as spiritual and physical creatures, integrating both in a complex whole that cannot be divided. Therefore, that which a human being does physically directly affects their spirituality, and vice versa.

While the fall of humanity in Genesis 3 perverted every aspect of creation, the created order should never be described as evil in its essence. If the Bible considered creation evil, Jesus could not have become human in the incarnation. Jesus did not come as a mirage, but instead he took on human flesh (Jn 1:14). Coming as a man, Jesus reconciled all things—the spiritual and the physical—to himself on the cross (Col 1:20). Because of this, the physical aspects of creation—including our bodies—can be directed toward good or evil (Ro 6:5–7).

This passage indicates that salvation created unity to such a degree that believers actually become members of Christ himself (1Co 6:15). Paul described the corporate body of Christ as a temple of the Holy Spirit. God did not purchase the believer's body at a discount store for a small price; he purchased each person on the cross at the cost of his Son's life. Therefore, the Christian is to honor God spiritually with their physical body (v. 20).

1 CORINTHIANS 7:19

OBEDIENCE

Though many see obedience as being opposed to their personal freedom,

(continued on next page)

that in view of the present[1] distress it is good for a person to remain as he is.
27Are you bound to a wife? Do not seek to be free. Are you free from a wife? Do
not seek a wife. 28But if you do marry, you have not sinned, and if a betrothed
woman[2] marries, she has not sinned. Yet those who marry will have worldly
troubles, and I would spare you that. 29This is what I mean, brothers: the appointed time has grown very short. From now on, let those who have wives
live as though they had none, 30and those who mourn as though they were not
mourning, and those who rejoice as though they were not rejoicing, and those
who buy as though they had no goods, 31and those who deal with the world
as though they had no dealings with it. For the present form of this world is
passing away.

32I want you to be free from anxieties. The unmarried man is anxious about
the things of the Lord, how to please the Lord. 33But the married man is anxious
about worldly things, how to please his wife, 34and his interests are divided. And
the unmarried or betrothed woman is anxious about the things of the Lord, how
to be holy in body and spirit. But the married woman is anxious about worldly
things, how to please her husband. 35I say this for your own benefit, not to lay
any restraint upon you, but to promote good order and to secure your undivided
devotion to the Lord.

36If anyone thinks that he is not behaving properly toward his betrothed,[3]
if his[4] passions are strong, and it has to be, let him do as he wishes: let them
marry—it is no sin. 37But whoever is firmly established in his heart, being under no necessity but having his desire under control, and has determined this
in his heart, to keep her as his betrothed, he will do well. 38So then he who
marries his betrothed does well, and he who refrains from marriage will do
even better.

39A wife is bound to her husband as long as he lives. But if her husband dies,
she is free to be married to whom she wishes, only in the Lord. 40Yet in my judgment she is happier if she remains as she is. And I think that I too have the Spirit
of God.

Food Offered to Idols

8 Now concerning[5] food offered to idols: we know that "all of us possess knowledge." This "knowledge" puffs up, but love builds up. 2If anyone imagines that
he knows something, he does not yet know as he ought to know. 3But if anyone
loves God, he is known by God.[6]

4Therefore, as to the eating of food offered to idols, we know that "an idol has
no real existence," and that "there is no God but one." 5For although there may be
so-called gods in heaven or on earth—as indeed there are many "gods" and many
"lords"— 6yet for us there is one God, the Father, from whom are all things and
for whom we exist, and one Lord, Jesus Christ, through whom are all things and
through whom we exist.

7However, not all possess this knowledge. But some, through former association with idols, eat food as really offered to an idol, and their conscience, being
weak, is defiled. 8Food will not commend us to God. We are no worse off if we do
not eat, and no better off if we do. 9But take care that this right of yours does not
somehow become a stumbling block to the weak. 10For if anyone sees you who
have knowledge eating[7] in an idol's temple, will he not be encouraged,[8] if his conscience is weak, to eat food offered to idols? 11And so by your knowledge this weak
person is destroyed, the brother for whom Christ died. 12Thus, sinning against
your brothers[9] and wounding their conscience when it is weak, you sin against
Christ. 13Therefore, if food makes my brother stumble, I will never eat meat, lest I
make my brother stumble.

[1]Or *impending* [2]Greek *virgin*; also verse 34 [3]Greek *virgin*; also verses 37, 38 [4]Or *her* [5]The expression *Now concerning* introduces a reply to a question in the Corinthians' letter; see 7:1 [6]Greek *him* [7]Greek *reclining at table* [8]Or *fortified*; Greek *built up* [9]Or *brothers and sisters*

(Obedience, continued)

individuals find true freedom in embracing the right restrictions. Any relationship based on absolute freedom quickly erodes. One need only ask the abandoned spouse. Paul—in the middle of a complex section on marriage—argues for the necessity of obedience.

Disobedience to God's Word often stems from a misunderstanding of God's character. Deceived by their own deceptive hearts, believers often wonder whether God intends to do them harm. However, as God's commands reflect his flawless character, believers can assuredly trust in God's directives. The One who created all things knows perfectly how believers should live. In fact, in obedience the believer finds true joy (Jn 15:10–11).

In this context, some Corinthian believers wanted to blame their circumstances for their lack of Christian growth. It seemed that a few of them even wanted to be circumcised for some perceived spiritual benefit. However, Paul pointedly rebuked that desire: "Neither circumcision counts for anything nor uncircumcision" (1Co 7:19). Paul made clear that the believer must continue to faithfully follow the Lord whatever their circumstances (vv. 17,20). God not only carefully wrote his Word and gave us a perfect example of faithfulness in the life of Jesus Christ, but he also carefully orchestrates the circumstances in which the believer lives and in which God's Word is to be obeyed.

SINNING AGAINST JESUS

The Bible often outlines broad principles that guide behavior, rather than telling the believer explicitly what he or she can or cannot do. In other words, the Bible does not detail a particular style of music one must enjoy, as if eighteenth-century harpsichord sonatas please the Lord's ears more than modern worship led with an acoustic guitar. Instead, the Bible tells the believer what kinds of things to think about and meditate upon (Php 4:8). This principle helps guide the believer's choices.

If the Scriptures do not condemn a particular activity, and the believer's conscience is not convicted by the Spirit's application of a biblical principle, then God gives the believer liberty to engage in it. Legalism goes beyond what the Scriptures teach, requiring more in the way of rules and regulations than Jesus did. Libertinism, conversely, believes the Bible requires almost nothing of the believer. Scripture, however, opposes both views and the lifestyles that proceed from them.

Nevertheless, believers regularly abuse their liberty in Christ. Just as we do today, the Corinthians found this balance to be elusive. It seems that some in the Corinthian church prioritized their personal liberty over love for their neighbor. In this text, the details involved some Corinthians eating meat that had been sacrificed to idols, an issue a mature follower might have long ago settled in their hearts. However, someone with a weaker conscience — for example, one recently converted out of paganism — may have continued to struggle with this complicated issue.

Paul pointed out that if the mature believer ate this meat in front of the newer or weaker believer, the new believer might stumble spiritually (1Co 8:10). In essence, Paul confronted the individualistic liberty so often prized in Corinth. Contrary to today's more popular notions, one's personal liberties do not trump everyone else's. Paul emphasized love over liberty. The controlling factor in the believer's decision to do something or act in a certain way is not whether they have the liberty, but whether love motivates their action.

Furthermore, when the stronger believer refuses to consider the weaker, he sins against Christ (v. 12). Paul knew this truth well. As a former persecutor of believers in Christ, Paul (known as Saul at the time) met the God of those martyrs. On the road to Damascus, Jesus did not ask Paul why he persecuted God's people. Instead, he asked Paul why he persecuted him personally (Ac 9:4). To sin against the body of Christ is to sin against Christ.

Paul Surrenders His Rights

9 Am I not free? Am I not an apostle? Have I not seen Jesus our Lord? Are not you my workmanship in the Lord? 2If to others I am not an apostle, at least I am to you, for you are the seal of my apostleship in the Lord.

3This is my defense to those who would examine me. 4Do we not have the right to eat and drink? 5Do we not have the right to take along a believing wife,[1] as do the other apostles and the brothers of the Lord and Cephas? 6Or is it only Barnabas and I who have no right to refrain from working for a living? 7Who serves as a soldier at his own expense? Who plants a vineyard without eating any of its fruit? Or who tends a flock without getting some of the milk?

8Do I say these things on human authority? Does not the Law say the same? 9For it is written in the Law of Moses, "You shall not muzzle an ox when it treads out the grain." Is it for oxen that God is concerned? 10Does he not certainly speak for our sake? It was written for our sake, because the plowman should plow in hope and the thresher thresh in hope of sharing in the crop. 11If we have sown spiritual things among you, is it too much if we reap material things from you? 12If others share this rightful claim on you, do not we even more? Nevertheless, we have not made use of this right, but we endure anything rather than put an obstacle in the way of the gospel of Christ.

13Do you not know that those who are employed in the temple service get their food from the temple, and those who serve at the altar share in the sacrificial offerings? 14In the same way, the Lord commanded that those who proclaim the gospel should get their living by the gospel.

15But I have made no use of any of these rights, nor am I writing these things to secure any such provision. For I would rather die than have anyone deprive me of my ground for boasting. 16For if I preach the gospel, that gives me no ground for boasting. For necessity is laid upon me. Woe to me if I do not preach the gospel! 17For if I do this of my own will, I have a reward, but if not of my own will, I am still entrusted with a stewardship. 18What then is my reward? That in my preaching I may present the gospel free of charge, so as not to make full use of my right in the gospel.

19For though I am free from all, I have made myself a servant to all, that I might win more of them. 20To the Jews I became as a Jew, in order to win Jews. To those under the law I became as one under the law (though not being myself under the law) that I might win those under the law. 21To those outside the law I became as one outside the law (not being outside the law of God but under the law of Christ) that I might win those outside the law. 22To the weak I became weak, that I might win the weak. I have become all things to all people, that by all means I might save some. 23I do it all for the sake of the gospel, that I may share with them in its blessings.

24Do you not know that in a race all the runners run, but only one receives the prize? So run that you may obtain it. 25Every athlete exercises self-control in all things. They do it to receive a perishable wreath, but we an imperishable. 26So I do not run aimlessly; I do not box as one beating the air. 27But I discipline my body and keep it under control,[2] lest after preaching to others I myself should be disqualified.

Warning Against Idolatry

10 For I do not want you to be unaware, brothers,[3] that our fathers were all under the cloud, and all passed through the sea, 2and all were baptized into Moses in the cloud and in the sea, 3and all ate the same spiritual food, 4and all drank the same spiritual drink. For they drank from the spiritual Rock that followed them, and the Rock was Christ. 5Nevertheless, with most of them God was not pleased, for they were overthrown[4] in the wilderness.

[1]Greek *a sister as wife* [2]Greek *I pummel my body and make it a slave* [3]Or *brothers and sisters* [4]Or *were laid low*

---

1 CORINTHIANS 9:12

EXERCISING RIGHTS

To illustrate the emphasis in chapter 8 on love's priority over liberty, in this text the apostle Paul described one of his own rights he personally curtailed. As Paul served the Corinthians with the gospel, it may have been appropriate to receive some form of financial compensation (v. 11); however, Paul chose not to demand this right (v. 12).

Paul intended his refusal of this personal liberty as a means to further the gospel. The Corinthians likely encountered traveling charlatans—preachers who proclaimed a message for the express purpose of receiving compensation. With that context in mind, Paul refused to exercise his right so that no one would accuse him of the same. Rather than hinder the gospel's message, he worked while he was among them so to provide for his own financial needs.

Paul considered the integrity of the message to be bound up in the integrity of the messenger. If false accusations about Paul gained traction, the gospel's credibility would be undermined. Though the gospel might offend, Paul endeavored to make sure his actions would not. Paul taught a love that trumped liberty (1Co 8; 13). He also modeled it.

---

1 CORINTHIANS 10:4

JESUS: THE ROCK

God's provision does not always mean life will be easy. Citing Israel's experience in the wilderness, Paul warned the Corinthians of this reality. Though God delivered these Israelites from bondage in Egypt, turned

(continued on next page)

(Jesus: The Rock, continued)

the Red Sea into dry land, and led them by a cloud through the wilderness, miraculous intervention did not necessarily indicate God's approval (v. 5). Out of the thousands of first-generation Israelites who left Egypt, only Joshua and Caleb made it to the promised land. In the wilderness, funerals were a very common activity.

However, neither does humankind's faithlessness demonstrate God's distance. Paul said that despite the Israelites' rebellion, God stayed near to them. When their throats were parched, the Israelites drank from a rock (Ex 17). Though God judged them temporarily, he did not leave them.

Using this well-known Exodus narrative—as a clear display of God's nearness—Paul points to an unseen character. Along with a literal rock, a spiritual Rock accompanied the Israelites throughout the wilderness (1Co 10:4). In plain language, Paul identifies this spiritual Rock. Though he remained invisible in Moses' narrative, Jesus Christ provided the miracle and made water pour from the rock. As they wandered, Christ remained their compass and their provision.

This episode in Israel's history serves as a warning to idolaters (v. 6). Without qualification, God's image-bearers benefit from God's provision. In gratitude, the proper response is to flee from idolatry, preferring instead the pleasure of God (v. 14).

6 Now these things took place as examples for us, that we might not desire
evil as they did. 7 Do not be idolaters as some of them were; as it is written, "The
people sat down to eat and drink and rose up to play." 8 We must not indulge in
sexual immorality as some of them did, and twenty-three thousand fell in a single
day. 9 We must not put Christ[1] to the test, as some of them did and were destroyed
by serpents, 10 nor grumble, as some of them did and were destroyed by the Destroyer. 11 Now these things happened to them as an example, but they were written down for our instruction, on whom the end of the ages has come. 12 Therefore
let anyone who thinks that he stands take heed lest he fall. 13 No temptation has
overtaken you that is not common to man. God is faithful, and he will not let you
be tempted beyond your ability, but with the temptation he will also provide the
way of escape, that you may be able to endure it.

14 Therefore, my beloved, flee from idolatry. 15 I speak as to sensible people;
judge for yourselves what I say. 16 The cup of blessing that we bless, is it not a participation in the blood of Christ? The bread that we break, is it not a participation
in the body of Christ? 17 Because there is one bread, we who are many are one body,
for we all partake of the one bread. 18 Consider the people of Israel:[2] are not those
who eat the sacrifices participants in the altar? 19 What do I imply then? That food
offered to idols is anything, or that an idol is anything? 20 No, I imply that what
pagans sacrifice they offer to demons and not to God. I do not want you to be
participants with demons. 21 You cannot drink the cup of the Lord and the cup
of demons. You cannot partake of the table of the Lord and the table of demons.
22 Shall we provoke the Lord to jealousy? Are we stronger than he?

Do All to the Glory of God

23 "All things are lawful," but not all things are helpful. "All things are lawful,"
but not all things build up. 24 Let no one seek his own good, but the good of his
neighbor. 25 Eat whatever is sold in the meat market without raising any question on the ground of conscience. 26 For "the earth is the Lord's, and the fullness
thereof." 27 If one of the unbelievers invites you to dinner and you are disposed
to go, eat whatever is set before you without raising any question on the ground
of conscience. 28 But if someone says to you, "This has been offered in sacrifice,"
then do not eat it, for the sake of the one who informed you, and for the sake of
conscience— 29 I do not mean your conscience, but his. For why should my liberty
be determined by someone else's conscience? 30 If I partake with thankfulness,
why am I denounced because of that for which I give thanks?

31 So, whether you eat or drink, or whatever you do, do all to the glory of God.
32 Give no offense to Jews or to Greeks or to the church of God, 33 just as I try to
please everyone in everything I do, not seeking my own advantage, but that of
many, that they may be saved.

11 Be imitators of me, as I am of Christ.

Head Coverings

2 Now I commend you because you remember me in everything and maintain the traditions even as I delivered them to you. 3 But I want you to understand
that the head of every man is Christ, the head of a wife[3] is her husband,[4] and the
head of Christ is God. 4 Every man who prays or prophesies with his head covered
dishonors his head, 5 but every wife[5] who prays or prophesies with her head uncovered dishonors her head, since it is the same as if her head were shaven. 6 For
if a wife will not cover her head, then she should cut her hair short. But since it is
disgraceful for a wife to cut off her hair or shave her head, let her cover her head.
7 For a man ought not to cover his head, since he is the image and glory of God,

[1] Some manuscripts *the Lord* [2] Greek *Consider Israel according to the flesh* [3] Greek *gunē*. This term may refer to a *woman* or a *wife*, depending on the context [4] Greek *anēr*. This term may refer to a *man* or a *husband*, depending on the context [5] In verses 5–13, the Greek word *gunē* is translated *wife* in verses that deal with wearing a veil, a sign of being married in first-century culture

but woman is the glory of man. 8For man was not made from woman, but woman from man. 9Neither was man created for woman, but woman for man. 10That is why a wife ought to have a symbol of authority on her head, because of the angels.[1] 11Nevertheless, in the Lord woman is not independent of man nor man of woman; 12for as woman was made from man, so man is now born of woman. And all things are from God. 13Judge for yourselves: is it proper for a wife to pray to God with her head uncovered? 14Does not nature itself teach you that if a man wears long hair it is a disgrace for him, 15but if a woman has long hair, it is her glory? For her hair is given to her for a covering. 16If anyone is inclined to be contentious, we have no such practice, nor do the churches of God.

The Lord's Supper

17But in the following instructions I do not commend you, because when you come together it is not for the better but for the worse. 18For, in the first place, when you come together as a church, I hear that there are divisions among you. And I believe it in part,[2] 19for there must be factions among you in order that those who are genuine among you may be recognized. 20When you come together, it is not the Lord's supper that you eat. 21For in eating, each one goes ahead with his own meal. One goes hungry, another gets drunk. 22What! Do you not have houses to eat and drink in? Or do you despise the church of God and humiliate those who have nothing? What shall I say to you? Shall I commend you in this? No, I will not.

23For I received from the Lord what I also delivered to you, that the Lord Jesus on the night when he was betrayed took bread, 24and when he had given thanks, he broke it, and said, "This is my body, which is for[3] you. Do this in remembrance of me."[4] 25In the same way also he took the cup, after supper, saying, "This cup is the new covenant in my blood. Do this, as often as you drink it, in remembrance of me." 26For as often as you eat this bread and drink the cup, you proclaim the Lord's death until he comes.

27Whoever, therefore, eats the bread or drinks the cup of the Lord in an unworthy manner will be guilty concerning the body and blood of the Lord. 28Let a person examine himself, then, and so eat of the bread and drink of the cup. 29For anyone who eats and drinks without discerning the body eats and drinks judgment on himself. 30That is why many of you are weak and ill, and some have died.[5] 31But if we judged[6] ourselves truly, we would not be judged. 32But when we are judged by the Lord, we are disciplined[7] so that we may not be condemned along with the world.

33So then, my brothers,[8] when you come together to eat, wait for[9] one another— 34if anyone is hungry, let him eat at home—so that when you come together it will not be for judgment. About the other things I will give directions when I come.

Spiritual Gifts

12 Now concerning[10] spiritual gifts,[11] brothers,[12] I do not want you to be uninformed. 2You know that when you were pagans you were led astray to mute idols, however you were led. 3Therefore I want you to understand that no one speaking in the Spirit of God ever says "Jesus is accursed!" and no one can say "Jesus is Lord" except in the Holy Spirit.

4Now there are varieties of gifts, but the same Spirit; 5and there are varieties of service, but the same Lord; 6and there are varieties of activities, but it is the same God who empowers them all in everyone. 7To each is given the manifestation of

[1]Or *messengers*, that is, people sent to observe and report [2]Or *I believe a certain report* [3]Some manuscripts *broken for* [4]Or *as my memorial*; also verse 25 [5]Greek *have fallen asleep* (as in 15:6, 20) [6]Or *discerned* [7]Or *when we are judged we are being disciplined by the Lord* [8]Or *brothers and sisters* [9]Or *share with* [10]The expression *Now concerning* introduces a reply to a question in the Corinthians' letter; see 7:1 [11]Or *spiritual persons* [12]Or *brothers and sisters*

1 CORINTHIANS 11:17–34

THE LORD'S SUPPER

This passage outlines some of the clearest instruction concerning the church's worship gatherings. While diverse understandings of the Lord's Supper often separate churches from one another, the Lord's Supper is intended to be a visible display of the unity of the church. In Paul's instruction, the church as a whole is to proclaim Christ's death (v. 26).

Although the exact role and function the Lord's Supper is to play in a believers' life remains a matter of debate among Christians, Paul makes it very clear that the Lord's Supper can be taken incorrectly (v. 27). Paul wrote that those who celebrate the meal should examine their lives prior to partaking of the bread and the cup (v. 28). This examination includes both personal and corporate elements. The recognition of "the body" in this passage (v. 29) included both Jesus' body *and* the church, outlined in the chapter that follows (1Co 12:12–27). Therefore, at the Supper believers are to examine their lives concerning sin toward Christ and any offense toward one another.

At the communion table, believers celebrate with other believers their unity in Christ, renewing their commitment to God, his people, and his mission.

the Spirit for the common good. 8 For to one is given through the Spirit the utterance of wisdom, and to another the utterance of knowledge according to the same Spirit, 9 to another faith by the same Spirit, to another gifts of healing by the one Spirit, 10 to another the working of miracles, to another prophecy, to another the ability to distinguish between spirits, to another various kinds of tongues, to another the interpretation of tongues. 11 All these are empowered by one and the same Spirit, who apportions to each one individually as he wills.

One Body with Many Members

12 For just as the body is one and has many members, and all the members of the body, though many, are one body, so it is with Christ. 13 For in one Spirit we were all baptized into one body—Jews or Greeks, slaves[1] or free—and all were made to drink of one Spirit.

14 For the body does not consist of one member but of many. 15 If the foot should say, "Because I am not a hand, I do not belong to the body," that would not make it any less a part of the body. 16 And if the ear should say, "Because I am not an eye, I do not belong to the body," that would not make it any less a part of the body. 17 If the whole body were an eye, where would be the sense of hearing? If the whole body were an ear, where would be the sense of smell? 18 But as it is, God arranged the members in the body, each one of them, as he chose. 19 If all were a single member, where would the body be? 20 As it is, there are many parts,[2] yet one body.

21 The eye cannot say to the hand, "I have no need of you," nor again the head to the feet, "I have no need of you." 22 On the contrary, the parts of the body that seem to be weaker are indispensable, 23 and on those parts of the body that we think less honorable we bestow the greater honor, and our unpresentable parts are treated with greater modesty, 24 which our more presentable parts do not require. But God has so composed the body, giving greater honor to the part that lacked it, 25 that there may be no division in the body, but that the members may have the same care for one another. 26 If one member suffers, all suffer together; if one member is honored, all rejoice together.

27 Now you are the body of Christ and individually members of it. 28 And God has appointed in the church first apostles, second prophets, third teachers, then miracles, then gifts of healing, helping, administrating, and various kinds of tongues. 29 Are all apostles? Are all prophets? Are all teachers? Do all work miracles? 30 Do all possess gifts of healing? Do all speak with tongues? Do all interpret? 31 But earnestly desire the higher gifts.

And I will show you a still more excellent way.

The Way of Love

13 If I speak in the tongues of men and of angels, but have not love, I am a noisy gong or a clanging cymbal. 2 And if I have prophetic powers, and understand all mysteries and all knowledge, and if I have all faith, so as to remove mountains, but have not love, I am nothing. 3 If I give away all I have, and if I deliver up my body to be burned,[3] but have not love, I gain nothing.

4 Love is patient and kind; love does not envy or boast; it is not arrogant 5 or rude. It does not insist on its own way; it is not irritable or resentful;[4] 6 it does not rejoice at wrongdoing, but rejoices with the truth. 7 Love bears all things, believes all things, hopes all things, endures all things.

8 Love never ends. As for prophecies, they will pass away; as for tongues, they will cease; as for knowledge, it will pass away. 9 For we know in part and we prophesy in part, 10 but when the perfect comes, the partial will pass away. 11 When I was a child, I spoke like a child, I thought like a child, I reasoned like a child. When I became a man, I gave up childish ways. 12 For now we see in a mirror dimly, but

[1] For the contextual rendering of the Greek word *doulos*, see Preface [2] Or *members*; also verse 22
[3] Some manuscripts *deliver up my body* [to death] *that I may boast* [4] Greek *irritable and does not count up wrongdoing*

1 CORINTHIANS 12:12–30

THE BODY OF CHRIST

Many of the three-year-olds in Corinth could probably have comprehended Paul's main point in this passage. He essentially wrote: "The body is one. And the body has many parts." Even most toddlers understand that a person who has two ears and two eyes is still one body and, thus, one person.

Paul used the human body as an analogy to describe the church as the body of Christ. While elsewhere this image points to the headship of Jesus Christ, in this passage Paul emphasizes unity within diversity. At salvation, God baptizes by his Spirit both Jews and Gentiles into one body (v. 13).

Paul laid out two aspects of the diversity. For those troubled with a sense of inferiority, he reminded them that the foot is no less part of the body than the hand (v. 15). For those convinced of their superiority, Paul reminded them that the rest of the body would be limited without feet (v. 21). God composed the body just as he saw fit (v. 18). God created this unity to such a degree that whatever happens to one, happens to all, whether joy or pain (v. 26).

Paul taught simple truths in this text, though the church's application continues to be far from simple. People tend to surround themselves with people just like them—those who share the same hobbies, possess the same ethnicity, or have similar jobs. But the body of Christ crosses every racial, cultural, and social barrier, uniting people under one umbrella alone: the Christ of the gospel.

LOVE

In recent history, few Christian women have worn a wedding dress and not heard this passage. While it certainly can be applied to the marriage relationship, Paul originally wrote it to describe a love that was to characterize the Corinthians' relationships with one another. However, Paul did not command the church to do anything the Lord Jesus had not already done perfectly. While this chapter is famous for its description of love, the Gospels provide further insight about the characteristics of genuine love by holding up the example of Christ's own life. For instance, Jesus embodied patience (v. 4). Consider the passage in the Gospel of Mark in which James and John asked Jesus to do whatever they asked of him. They boldly asked — maybe even with a hint of demand — to sit on either side of him in glory. However, rather than chiding them for such brashness, Jesus spoke to them patiently (Mk 10:35 – 40).

Jesus' patience was matched by his kindness. While his disciples thought he would not have the time or the inclination to visit with children, Jesus welcomed little children to come to him, laying his hands on them graciously (Mt 19:14). In the upper room, he took on the role of a servant, washing his disciples' feet (Jn 13:5). Love is not proud (1Co 13:4).

Jesus was not easily angered, either. The careful reader might immediately think of the Lord driving out the money-changers in the temple. Clearly, these people angered the Lord. However, Jesus' anger was not an easily triggered rage over something insignificant. Instead, love for his Father's house consumed him (Jn 2:17). Rather than delighting in evil, Jesus rejoiced in the truth. In fact, before Pilate he declared, "I was born and for this purpose I have come into the world — to bear witness to the truth" (Jn 18:37). Jesus would not back down nor compromise truth, though it would ultimately lead to his crucifixion. He chose not to protect himself so that others might be protected. That's what perfect love does (1Co 13:7).

Jesus died believing the Father would raise him from the dead. Love always perseveres (v. 7). Scorning the shame, he endured the cross for his people (Heb 12:2). This patient, kind, truth-rejoicing, protecting, trusting, and persevering love kept no record of wrongs (1Co 13:5). Because of Jesus' death, the amassed wrongs committed by the people of God were forgiven. The love demonstrated on the cross will forever remain unmatched (1Jn 4:10). First Corinthians 13 certainly applies to marriage, but it's more about a loving Groom who died for his bride, the church (Eph 5:25).

then face to face. Now I know in part; then I shall know fully, even as I have been fully known.

13So now faith, hope, and love abide, these three; but the greatest of these is love.

Prophecy and Tongues

14 Pursue love, and earnestly desire the spiritual gifts, especially that you may prophesy. 2For one who speaks in a tongue speaks not to men but to God; for no one understands him, but he utters mysteries in the Spirit. 3On the other hand, the one who prophesies speaks to people for their upbuilding and encouragement and consolation. 4The one who speaks in a tongue builds up himself, but the one who prophesies builds up the church. 5Now I want you all to speak in tongues, but even more to prophesy. The one who prophesies is greater than the one who speaks in tongues, unless someone interprets, so that the church may be built up.

6Now, brothers,[1] if I come to you speaking in tongues, how will I benefit you unless I bring you some revelation or knowledge or prophecy or teaching? 7If even lifeless instruments, such as the flute or the harp, do not give distinct notes, how will anyone know what is played? 8And if the bugle gives an indistinct sound, who will get ready for battle? 9So with yourselves, if with your tongue you utter speech that is not intelligible, how will anyone know what is said? For you will be speaking into the air. 10There are doubtless many different languages in the world, and none is without meaning, 11but if I do not know the meaning of the language, I will be a foreigner to the speaker and the speaker a foreigner to me. 12So with yourselves, since you are eager for manifestations of the Spirit, strive to excel in building up the church.

13Therefore, one who speaks in a tongue should pray that he may interpret. 14For if I pray in a tongue, my spirit prays but my mind is unfruitful. 15What am I to do? I will pray with my spirit, but I will pray with my mind also; I will sing praise with my spirit, but I will sing with my mind also. 16Otherwise, if you give thanks with your spirit, how can anyone in the position of an outsider[2] say "Amen" to your thanksgiving when he does not know what you are saying? 17For you may be giving thanks well enough, but the other person is not being built up. 18I thank God that I speak in tongues more than all of you. 19Nevertheless, in church I would rather speak five words with my mind in order to instruct others, than ten thousand words in a tongue.

20Brothers, do not be children in your thinking. Be infants in evil, but in your thinking be mature. 21In the Law it is written, "By people of strange tongues and by the lips of foreigners will I speak to this people, and even then they will not listen to me, says the Lord." 22Thus tongues are a sign not for believers but for unbelievers, while prophecy is a sign[3] not for unbelievers but for believers. 23If, therefore, the whole church comes together and all speak in tongues, and outsiders or unbelievers enter, will they not say that you are out of your minds? 24But if all prophesy, and an unbeliever or outsider enters, he is convicted by all, he is called to account by all, 25the secrets of his heart are disclosed, and so, falling on his face, he will worship God and declare that God is really among you.

Orderly Worship

26What then, brothers? When you come together, each one has a hymn, a lesson, a revelation, a tongue, or an interpretation. Let all things be done for building up. 27If any speak in a tongue, let there be only two or at most three, and each in turn, and let someone interpret. 28But if there is no one to interpret, let each of them keep silent in church and speak to himself and to God. 29Let two or three prophets speak, and let the others weigh what is said. 30If a revelation is made

[1]Or *brothers and sisters*; also verses 20, 26, 39 [2]Or *of him that is without gifts* [3]Greek lacks *a sign*

to another sitting there, let the first be silent. 31For you can all prophesy one by one, so that all may learn and all be encouraged, 32and the spirits of prophets are subject to prophets. 33For God is not a God of confusion but of peace.

As in all the churches of the saints, 34the women should keep silent in the churches. For they are not permitted to speak, but should be in submission, as the Law also says. 35If there is anything they desire to learn, let them ask their husbands at home. For it is shameful for a woman to speak in church.

36Or was it from you that the word of God came? Or are you the only ones it has reached? 37If anyone thinks that he is a prophet, or spiritual, he should acknowledge that the things I am writing to you are a command of the Lord. 38If anyone does not recognize this, he is not recognized. 39So, my brothers, earnestly desire to prophesy, and do not forbid speaking in tongues. 40But all things should be done decently and in order.

The Resurrection of Christ

15 Now I would remind you, brothers,[1] of the gospel I preached to you, which you received, in which you stand, 2and by which you are being saved, if you hold fast to the word I preached to you—unless you believed in vain.

3For I delivered to you as of first importance what I also received: that Christ died for our sins in accordance with the Scriptures, 4that he was buried, that he was raised on the third day in accordance with the Scriptures, 5and that he appeared to Cephas, then to the twelve. 6Then he appeared to more than five hundred brothers at one time, most of whom are still alive, though some have fallen asleep. 7Then he appeared to James, then to all the apostles. 8Last of all, as to one untimely born, he appeared also to me. 9For I am the least of the apostles, unworthy to be called an apostle, because I persecuted the church of God. 10But by the grace of God I am what I am, and his grace toward me was not in vain. On the contrary, I worked harder than any of them, though it was not I, but the grace of God that is with me. 11Whether then it was I or they, so we preach and so you believed.

The Resurrection of the Dead

12Now if Christ is proclaimed as raised from the dead, how can some of you say that there is no resurrection of the dead? 13But if there is no resurrection of the dead, then not even Christ has been raised. 14And if Christ has not been raised, then our preaching is in vain and your faith is in vain. 15We are even found to be misrepresenting God, because we testified about God that he raised Christ, whom he did not raise if it is true that the dead are not raised. 16For if the dead are not raised, not even Christ has been raised. 17And if Christ has not been raised, your faith is futile and you are still in your sins. 18Then those also who have fallen asleep in Christ have perished. 19If in Christ we have hope[2] in this life only, we are of all people most to be pitied.

20But in fact Christ has been raised from the dead, the firstfruits of those who have fallen asleep. 21For as by a man came death, by a man has come also the resurrection of the dead. 22For as in Adam all die, so also in Christ shall all be made alive. 23But each in his own order: Christ the firstfruits, then at his coming those who belong to Christ. 24Then comes the end, when he delivers the kingdom to God the Father after destroying every rule and every authority and power. 25For he must reign until he has put all his enemies under his feet. 26The last enemy to be destroyed is death. 27For "God[3] has put all things in subjection under his feet." But when it says, "all things are put in subjection," it is plain that he is excepted who put all things in subjection under him. 28When all things are subjected to him, then the Son himself will also be subjected to him who put all things in subjection under him, that God may be all in all.

---

[1]Or *brothers and sisters*; also verses 6, 31, 50, 58 [2]Or *we have hoped* [3]Greek *he*

29 Otherwise, what do people mean by being baptized on behalf of the dead? If
the dead are not raised at all, why are people baptized on their behalf? 30 Why are
we in danger every hour? 31 I protest, brothers, by my pride in you, which I have
in Christ Jesus our Lord, I die every day! 32 What do I gain if, humanly speaking, I
fought with beasts at Ephesus? If the dead are not raised, "Let us eat and drink,
for tomorrow we die." 33 Do not be deceived: "Bad company ruins good morals."[1]
34 Wake up from your drunken stupor, as is right, and do not go on sinning. For
some have no knowledge of God. I say this to your shame.

The Resurrection Body

35 But someone will ask, "How are the dead raised? With what kind of body do
they come?" 36 You foolish person! What you sow does not come to life unless it
dies. 37 And what you sow is not the body that is to be, but a bare kernel, perhaps
of wheat or of some other grain. 38 But God gives it a body as he has chosen, and
to each kind of seed its own body. 39 For not all flesh is the same, but there is one
kind for humans, another for animals, another for birds, and another for fish.
40 There are heavenly bodies and earthly bodies, but the glory of the heavenly is
of one kind, and the glory of the earthly is of another. 41 There is one glory of the
sun, and another glory of the moon, and another glory of the stars; for star differs
from star in glory.

42 So is it with the resurrection of the dead. What is sown is perishable; what
is raised is imperishable. 43 It is sown in dishonor; it is raised in glory. It is sown in
weakness; it is raised in power. 44 It is sown a natural body; it is raised a spiritual
body. If there is a natural body, there is also a spiritual body. 45 Thus it is written,
"The first man Adam became a living being";[2] the last Adam became a life-giving
spirit. 46 But it is not the spiritual that is first but the natural, and then the spiritual. 47 The first man was from the earth, a man of dust; the second man is from
heaven. 48 As was the man of dust, so also are those who are of the dust, and as is
the man of heaven, so also are those who are of heaven. 49 Just as we have borne
the image of the man of dust, we shall[3] also bear the image of the man of heaven.

Mystery and Victory

50 I tell you this, brothers: flesh and blood cannot inherit the kingdom of God,
nor does the perishable inherit the imperishable. 51 Behold! I tell you a mystery.
We shall not all sleep, but we shall all be changed, 52 in a moment, in the twinkling
of an eye, at the last trumpet. For the trumpet will sound, and the dead will be
raised imperishable, and we shall be changed. 53 For this perishable body must put
on the imperishable, and this mortal body must put on immortality. 54 When the
perishable puts on the imperishable, and the mortal puts on immortality, then
shall come to pass the saying that is written:

"Death is swallowed up in victory."
55 "O death, where is your victory?
O death, where is your sting?"

56 The sting of death is sin, and the power of sin is the law. 57 But thanks be to God,
who gives us the victory through our Lord Jesus Christ.

58 Therefore, my beloved brothers, be steadfast, immovable, always abounding
in the work of the Lord, knowing that in the Lord your labor is not in vain.

The Collection for the Saints

16 Now concerning[4] the collection for the saints: as I directed the churches of
Galatia, so you also are to do. 2 On the first day of every week, each of you is
to put something aside and store it up, as he may prosper, so that there will be no
collecting when I come. 3 And when I arrive, I will send those whom you accredit

[1] Probably from Menander's comedy *Thais* [2] Greek *a living soul* [3] Some manuscripts *let us* [4] The expression *Now concerning* introduces a reply to a question in the Corinthians' letter; see 7:1; also verse 12

1 CORINTHIANS 15:1 – 58

RESURRECTION FACTS

To be a Christian, one must affirm the resurrection of Jesus Christ from the dead. Paul argues in this key chapter that any alternative to the resurrection of Jesus results in a dismantling of every other aspect of the faith. In other words, Christianity hinges on whether or not Jesus rose from the dead. If he did not, Christianity is irrelevant. If he did, then faith in Christ is all that matters. The following points outline Paul's explanation of the significance of Jesus' resurrection:

1 Corinthians 15:4: There are Old Testament prophesies about Christ's resurrection (Ps 16:10). Peter made this claim in his sermon at Pentecost (Ac 2:25 – 31).

1 Corinthians 15:5 – 8: The resurrected Jesus appeared to more than 500 witnesses. The Gospels describe some of those who saw him (Mt 28:1 – 10,16 – 17). Paul mentioned the reality of witnesses in part to challenge those who doubted the resurrection to ask one of the witnesses themselves. Most of the witnesses were still alive at the time of Paul's writing.

1 Corinthians 15:14 – 15: If Jesus did not rise, the believer's faith is empty and void, and the believer proves to be nothing more than a liar.

1 Corinthians 15:17 – 19: Jesus' resurrection assures believers that God accepted Jesus' sacrifice for sins. Paul mentioned the alternative in this verse; namely, that if Jesus had not been raised, there would have been no assurance that God accepted his sacrifice. If that were true, then individuals would remain under sin's punishment, and those who died would have truly perished without hope.

1 Corinthians 15:20 – 26: However, Jesus did rise. His resurrection foreshadows the resurrection of all those who would trust in him. Paul described Jesus as the "firstfruits." If he lives, so will those who believe in him (v. 22). Adam's sin infected the entire human race, resulting in spiritual death. Christ represented all those who would believe in him, and his resurrected life becomes theirs.

1 Corinthians 15:50: Bodies marked by corruption cannot inherit the kingdom of God.

1 Corinthians 15:52: At the resurrection, perishable bodies will become imperishable. For those who believe in Christ, what is now mortal will put on immortality.

1 Corinthians 15:55 – 58: Jesus' resurrection conquered death, the final enemy. In light of that truth, believers can and should give thanks to God, who gives them victory. Furthermore, the resurrection gives the believer confidence that their labor is not void of purpose, and it strengthens their resolve to give themselves fully to God's work.

by letter to carry your gift to Jerusalem. 4If it seems advisable that I should go also, they will accompany me.

Plans for Travel

5I will visit you after passing through Macedonia, for I intend to pass through Macedonia, 6and perhaps I will stay with you or even spend the winter, so that you may help me on my journey, wherever I go. 7For I do not want to see you now just in passing. I hope to spend some time with you, if the Lord permits. 8But I will stay in Ephesus until Pentecost, 9for a wide door for effective work has opened to me, and there are many adversaries.

10When Timothy comes, see that you put him at ease among you, for he is doing the work of the Lord, as I am. 11So let no one despise him. Help him on his way in peace, that he may return to me, for I am expecting him with the brothers.

Final Instructions

12Now concerning our brother Apollos, I strongly urged him to visit you with the other brothers, but it was not at all his will[1] to come now. He will come when he has opportunity.

13Be watchful, stand firm in the faith, act like men, be strong. 14Let all that you do be done in love.

15Now I urge you, brothers[2]—you know that the household[3] of Stephanas were the first converts[4] in Achaia, and that they have devoted themselves to the service of the saints— 16be subject to such as these, and to every fellow worker and laborer. 17I rejoice at the coming of Stephanas and Fortunatus and Achaicus, because they have made up for your absence, 18for they refreshed my spirit as well as yours. Give recognition to such people.

Greetings

19The churches of Asia send you greetings. Aquila and Prisca, together with the church in their house, send you hearty greetings in the Lord. 20All the brothers send you greetings. Greet one another with a holy kiss.

21I, Paul, write this greeting with my own hand. 22If anyone has no love for the Lord, let him be accursed. Our Lord, come![5] 23The grace of the Lord Jesus be with you. 24My love be with you all in Christ Jesus. Amen.

[1]Or *God's will for him* [2]Or *brothers and sisters*; also verse 20 [3]Greek *house* [4]Greek *the firstfruits*
[5]Greek *Maranatha* (a transliteration of Aramaic)

JESUS: OUR INVITATION TO REPENTANCE

2 CORINTHIANS

2 CORINTHIANS

PAUL'S MISSIONARY JOURNEYS	PAUL PLANTS CHURCH AT CORINTH	PAUL WRITES 2 CORINTHIANS
c. AD 47 – 57	*c. AD 51*	*c. AD 54*

God loves his church and desires that its worshipful obedience proclaims his glory to the watching world. The rampant sin in the Corinthian church harmed not only those engaged in such sin, but also sabotaged the church's witness. Paul's passionate challenge in the first letter to the Corinthian church was designed to awaken them from their sin-induced spiritual stupor and remind them of the necessity of obedience motivated by God's grace.

Some disregarded Paul's appeal and continued to scorn the grace of God. False teachers led many in the church to question Paul's authority as an apostle and thus to ignore his message. As a result, 2 Corinthians reads like an autobiography in which Paul defends his life's mission and the truthfulness of his message. These personal reflections reveal the trials, problems, and suffering Paul faced as a traveling minister in the first century. Through his letter, Paul models the hope that only comes to those who find their comfort in Christ alone (1:5). All Christians should embrace suffering, like Paul, as a way of following after the suffering servant, who gave his life as a ransom for many.

Paul's ongoing interaction with the church fostered a personal tone throughout the correspondence in which Paul was both forceful yet gracious, stern yet hopeful, realistic yet joyful. He was also able to speak with specificity to the problems within the church — many of which he already addressed in his first letter to the church. He also cautions all people, particularly false teachers, that they will stand before the judgment seat of God and be called to account for their actions.

The church, according to Paul, faces the continual onslaught of Satan's opposition and the disastrous effects of sin. Believers must fight Satan and sin with the power afforded to them by virtue of Christ's resurrection and his indwelling Spirit. Should they genuinely repent, they will find a merciful and gracious God who will grant forgiveness and empower them to live holy lives that are pleasing to God. Paul longs for the church in Corinth to turn from their sin and joyfully submit to God's good purposes for their individual lives and the corporate life of the church.

THEREFORE, WE ARE AMBASSADORS FOR CHRIST,
GOD MAKING HIS APPEAL THROUGH US.
WE IMPLORE YOU ON BEHALF OF CHRIST,
BE RECONCILED TO GOD.

---

2 Corinthians 5:20

2 CORINTHIANS

Greeting

1 Paul, an apostle of Christ Jesus by the will of God, and Timothy our brother,
To the church of God that is at Corinth, with all the saints who are in the whole of Achaia:

2Grace to you and peace from God our Father and the Lord Jesus Christ.

God of All Comfort

3Blessed be the God and Father of our Lord Jesus Christ, the Father of mercies and God of all comfort, 4who comforts us in all our affliction, so that we may be able to comfort those who are in any affliction, with the comfort with which we ourselves are comforted by God. 5For as we share abundantly in Christ's sufferings, so through Christ we share abundantly in comfort too.[1] 6If we are afflicted, it is for your comfort and salvation; and if we are comforted, it is for your comfort, which you experience when you patiently endure the same sufferings that we suffer. 7Our hope for you is unshaken, for we know that as you share in our sufferings, you will also share in our comfort.

8For we do not want you to be unaware, brothers,[2] of the affliction we experienced in Asia. For we were so utterly burdened beyond our strength that we despaired of life itself. 9Indeed, we felt that we had received the sentence of death. But that was to make us rely not on ourselves but on God who raises the dead. 10He delivered us from such a deadly peril, and he will deliver us. On him we have set our hope that he will deliver us again. 11You also must help us by prayer, so that many will give thanks on our behalf for the blessing granted us through the prayers of many.

Paul's Change of Plans

12For our boast is this, the testimony of our conscience, that we behaved in the world with simplicity[3] and godly sincerity, not by earthly wisdom but by the grace of God, and supremely so toward you. 13For we are not writing to you anything other than what you read and understand and I hope you will fully understand—14just as you did partially understand us—that on the day of our Lord Jesus you will boast of us as we will boast of you.

15Because I was sure of this, I wanted to come to you first, so that you might have a second experience of grace. 16I wanted to visit you on my way to Macedonia, and to come back to you from Macedonia and have you send me on my way to Judea. 17Was I vacillating when I wanted to do this? Do I make my plans according to the flesh, ready to say "Yes, yes" and "No, no" at the same time? 18As surely as God is faithful, our word to you has not been Yes and No. 19For the Son of God, Jesus Christ, whom we proclaimed among you, Silvanus and Timothy and I, was not Yes and No, but in him it is always Yes. 20For all the promises of God find their Yes in him. That is why it is through him that we utter our Amen to God for his glory. 21And it is God who establishes us with you in Christ, and has anointed us, 22and who has also put his seal on us and given us his Spirit in our hearts as a guarantee.[4]

23But I call God to witness against me—it was to spare you that I refrained from coming again to Corinth. 24Not that we lord it over your faith, but we work with you for your joy, for you stand firm in your faith.

---

[1]Or *For as the sufferings of Christ abound for us, so also our comfort abounds through Christ* [2]Or *brothers and sisters*. In New Testament usage, depending on the context, the plural Greek word *adelphoi* (translated "brothers") may refer either to *brothers* or to *brothers and sisters* [3]Some manuscripts *holiness* [4]Or *down payment*

---

2 CORINTHIANS 1:3–11

SUFFERING WITH PURPOSE

Paul understood the reality of suffering as well as anyone. His troubles extended to the point that he "despaired of life itself" (v. 8). But Paul recognized that "through Christ we share abundantly in comfort too" (v. 5). Knowing this, Paul found joy in his own sufferings and encouraged the believers in Corinth to do the same. Further, Paul recognized that Christ comforts believers in their sufferings so that they, in turn, can bring comfort to others. Paul used his own times of suffering as opportunities to bless those around him. Even when all seemed lost, Paul knew that his suffering occurred so that he would learn to rely less on himself and more fully on God. Having seen Christ work in his own trials in the past, Paul had even greater confidence that God would continue to deliver him so that he might, in turn, continue to minister to the young church.

Just as Paul did, believers today can view struggles and suffering as opportunities to bless those around them. Just as he did not abandon Paul, Jesus will be faithful to his people in all circumstances.

2 For I made up my mind not to make another painful visit to you. 2For if I cause
you pain, who is there to make me glad but the one whom I have pained?
3And I wrote as I did, so that when I came I might not suffer pain from those who
should have made me rejoice, for I felt sure of all of you, that my joy would be the
joy of you all. 4For I wrote to you out of much affliction and anguish of heart and
with many tears, not to cause you pain but to let you know the abundant love
that I have for you.

Forgive the Sinner

5Now if anyone has caused pain, he has caused it not to me, but in some
measure—not to put it too severely—to all of you. 6For such a one, this punishment by the majority is enough, 7so you should rather turn to forgive and comfort
him, or he may be overwhelmed by excessive sorrow. 8So I beg you to reaffirm
your love for him. 9For this is why I wrote, that I might test you and know whether
you are obedient in everything. 10Anyone whom you forgive, I also forgive. Indeed, what I have forgiven, if I have forgiven anything, has been for your sake in
the presence of Christ, 11so that we would not be outwitted by Satan; for we are
not ignorant of his designs.

Triumph in Christ

12When I came to Troas to preach the gospel of Christ, even though a door was
opened for me in the Lord, 13my spirit was not at rest because I did not find my
brother Titus there. So I took leave of them and went on to Macedonia.
14But thanks be to God, who in Christ always leads us in triumphal procession,
and through us spreads the fragrance of the knowledge of him everywhere. 15For
we are the aroma of Christ to God among those who are being saved and among
those who are perishing, 16to one a fragrance from death to death, to the other a
fragrance from life to life. Who is sufficient for these things? 17For we are not, like
so many, peddlers of God's word, but as men of sincerity, as commissioned by
God, in the sight of God we speak in Christ.

Ministers of the New Covenant

3 Are we beginning to commend ourselves again? Or do we need, as some do,
letters of recommendation to you, or from you? 2You yourselves are our letter
of recommendation, written on our[1] hearts, to be known and read by all. 3And
you show that you are a letter from Christ delivered by us, written not with ink
but with the Spirit of the living God, not on tablets of stone but on tablets of human hearts.[2]
4Such is the confidence that we have through Christ toward God. 5Not that
we are sufficient in ourselves to claim anything as coming from us, but our sufficiency is from God, 6who has made us sufficient to be ministers of a new covenant, not of the letter but of the Spirit. For the letter kills, but the Spirit gives life.
7Now if the ministry of death, carved in letters on stone, came with such
glory that the Israelites could not gaze at Moses' face because of its glory, which
was being brought to an end, 8will not the ministry of the Spirit have even more
glory? 9For if there was glory in the ministry of condemnation, the ministry of
righteousness must far exceed it in glory. 10Indeed, in this case, what once had
glory has come to have no glory at all, because of the glory that surpasses it. 11For
if what was being brought to an end came with glory, much more will what is
permanent have glory.
12Since we have such a hope, we are very bold, 13not like Moses, who would
put a veil over his face so that the Israelites might not gaze at the outcome of what
was being brought to an end. 14But their minds were hardened. For to this day,
when they read the old covenant, that same veil remains unlifted, because only

[1]Some manuscripts *your* [2]Greek *fleshly hearts*

2 CORINTHIANS 3:13–18

FREEDOM

Moses' face physically glowed when he spent time in the presence of God (Ex 34:29–30). The Israelites were so disturbed by his otherworldly appearance that Moses actually had to wear a veil for their benefit (Ex 34:33–35). The veil shielded the people from the remaining reflection of the glory of God on Moses' face, for which their hearts and minds were not prepared.

Paul compared the physical veil worn by Moses with the spiritual veil covering the hearts and minds of the Israelites who did not believe in Jesus. He explained that the spiritual veil could be removed only through faith in Christ.

As long as the veil remains, it is impossible to completely understand the old covenant. "But when one turns to the Lord, the veil is removed" (2Co 3:16). Through faith in Christ, believers are able not only to understand the law itself, but also to revel in the freedom that comes through Christ's fulfillment of the law. Indeed, when the veil is removed from the hearts of those who come to faith in Christ, their lives are freed to reflect God's glory. Just as the glory of the Lord was evident on Moses' face, Jesus' glory should be unmistakably evident in the lives of his followers when they experience freedom in Christ.

THE VICTORY PARADE

After great victories, triumphant armies often conduct massive parades to revel in the glory of the victory won. This has been true throughout history. In ancient times, soldiers from victorious armies would march in parade to receive the adulation of the masses. In addition, the surviving soldiers from the defeated armies were often forced to participate in the parade as humiliated captives to demonstrate the power and the glory of the conquering heroes.

Ever aware of his own prior violent hostility toward the gospel, Paul now envisioned himself and the host of believers as those captives. Those who were formerly adversarial to the cause of Christ were now joyfully able to participate in Christ's victory parade. Rather than being humiliated by being Christ's captive, Paul found great honor in that position.

As part of these victory parades, conquering generals would often have their attendants carry censers of incense, the fragrance of which became, quite literally, the "smell of victory." Paul declared that Christ similarly uses his people to spread "the fragrance of the knowledge of him everywhere" (v. 14). Christ's followers are to carry the gospel to the nations so that the knowledge of Christ and his great victory over sin and death can be spread far and wide.

But Paul recognized that the scent of Jesus' victory would not be pleasing to all. There are unbelievers to whom the smell of Christ in believers' lives serves as a reminder of the darkness in which they live. It may be jealousy of the freedom believers have found in Jesus' victory or merely the fundamental repulsion between light and darkness, life and death. Sadly, the light of Christ in his followers will be violently rejected by some.

Regardless of the reception, followers of Christ have the amazing opportunity to participate in his victory procession throughout the world. While all people, like Paul, once rebelled against the gospel, Christians now revel in the incredible privilege and honor of raising his banner and spreading his glory with their lives and their words.

2 CORINTHIANS 3:1–3

THE SOURCE OF PAUL'S CONFIDENCE

Paul here responded directly to his opponents in Corinth. He outlined two questions in verse 1, presumably rhetorical, to frame the apparent objections to the authority of his ministry. First he asked if he was bragging about himself and his credentials, and second if he needed some sort of recommendation to the believers at Corinth from a higher authority.

The answer to both questions was a resounding "No!" Paul's ministry stood in contrast to the itinerant preachers and philosophers referenced in chapter 2 whom Paul described as "peddlers of God's word" (v. 17). Paul wanted to be very clear with the Corinthian believers that he was not like this crowd, but that his only interest was their continued maturity in Christ.

In the early church, it was not uncommon for a visiting preacher or believer to take to the believers in a new locale a letter of recommendation or introduction from a leader known to them (Ac 18:27). The letter served as a voucher of the sincerity and credibility of the visiting preacher and acknowledged his status in the church. Paul wasn't opposed to the use of such letters. Paul's letter to Philemon is, to some extent, just such a letter and Paul references such letters in his other writings (1Co 16:3).

However, Paul in this passage argues that the only letter of recommendation that he needs at this point is the Corinthian believers themselves. Their new lives in Christ were testimony enough of the validity of Paul's ministry. Significantly, just as traditional letters of recommendation were written in ink, the old covenant was written on stone tablets. In stark contrast, the new covenant was written "not on tablets of stone but on tablets of human hearts" (2Co 3:3). Remarkably, this covenant was etched on the lives of the first-century believers.

Speaking in the confidence of the new covenant, Paul recognized and proclaimed that his authority was validated not by adherence to the old covenant but by the glory directed to God as a result of the power of Jesus Christ manifested in the lives of the Corinthian believers. The power and authority of this new covenant continues today in the lives of believers everywhere.

through Christ is it taken away. 15Yes, to this day whenever Moses is read a veil lies over their hearts. 16But when one[1] turns to the Lord, the veil is removed. 17Now the Lord[2] is the Spirit, and where the Spirit of the Lord is, there is freedom. 18And we all, with unveiled face, beholding the glory of the Lord,[3] are being transformed into the same image from one degree of glory to another.[4] For this comes from the Lord who is the Spirit.

The Light of the Gospel

4 Therefore, having this ministry by the mercy of God,[5] we do not lose heart. 2But we have renounced disgraceful, underhanded ways. We refuse to practice[6] cunning or to tamper with God's word, but by the open statement of the truth we would commend ourselves to everyone's conscience in the sight of God. 3And even if our gospel is veiled, it is veiled to those who are perishing. 4In their case the god of this world has blinded the minds of the unbelievers, to keep them from seeing the light of the gospel of the glory of Christ, who is the image of God. 5For what we proclaim is not ourselves, but Jesus Christ as Lord, with ourselves as your servants[7] for Jesus' sake. 6For God, who said, "Let light shine out of darkness," has shone in our hearts to give the light of the knowledge of the glory of God in the face of Jesus Christ.

Treasure in Jars of Clay

7But we have this treasure in jars of clay, to show that the surpassing power belongs to God and not to us. 8We are afflicted in every way, but not crushed; perplexed, but not driven to despair; 9persecuted, but not forsaken; struck down, but not destroyed; 10always carrying in the body the death of Jesus, so that the life of Jesus also may be manifested in our bodies. 11For we who live are always being given over to death for Jesus' sake, so that the life of Jesus also may be manifested in our mortal flesh. 12So death is at work in us, but life in you.

13Since we have the same spirit of faith according to what has been written, "I believed, and so I spoke," we also believe, and so we also speak, 14knowing that he who raised the Lord Jesus will raise us also with Jesus and bring us with you into his presence. 15For it is all for your sake, so that as grace extends to more and more people it may increase thanksgiving, to the glory of God.

16So we do not lose heart. Though our outer self[8] is wasting away, our inner self is being renewed day by day. 17For this light momentary affliction is preparing for us an eternal weight of glory beyond all comparison, 18as we look not to the things that are seen but to the things that are unseen. For the things that are seen are transient, but the things that are unseen are eternal.

Our Heavenly Dwelling

5 For we know that if the tent that is our earthly home is destroyed, we have a building from God, a house not made with hands, eternal in the heavens. 2For in this tent we groan, longing to put on our heavenly dwelling, 3if indeed by putting it on[9] we may not be found naked. 4For while we are still in this tent, we groan, being burdened—not that we would be unclothed, but that we would be further clothed, so that what is mortal may be swallowed up by life. 5He who has prepared us for this very thing is God, who has given us the Spirit as a guarantee.[10]

6So we are always of good courage. We know that while we are at home in the body we are away from the Lord, 7for we walk by faith, not by sight. 8Yes, we are of good courage, and we would rather be away from the body and at home with the Lord. 9So whether we are at home or away, we make it our aim to please him. 10For we must all appear before the judgment seat of Christ, so that each one may receive what is due for what he has done in the body, whether good or evil.

[1]Greek *he* [2]Or *this Lord* [3]Or *reflecting the glory of the Lord* [4]Greek *from glory to glory* [5]Greek *having this ministry as we have received mercy* [6]Greek *to walk in* [7]Or *slaves* (for the contextual rendering of the Greek word *doulos*, see Preface) [8]Greek *man* [9]Some manuscripts *putting it off* [10]Or *down payment*

MINISTRY THROUGH JARS OF CLAY

Paul described his ministry fully in this letter to the Corinthian church. In this passage, he explained that he had this ministry because of God's mercy and because he was being transformed into God's likeness.

Paul explained that the message of his ministry was focused on the glory of God as revealed through Jesus Christ and mediated through the Spirit. This focus on God's glory required Paul's singular focus and devotion, just as it requires the same of believers today.

The joy of carrying this message was not without challenges for Paul. Few before or since have faced the kind of suffering Paul experienced on a regular basis in his ministry. And yet, despite the incredible suffering he endured for the sake of the gospel, Paul rejoiced because his own weakness revealed the incredible power of God. Indeed, he continued by explaining that the glory of the gospel is carried by believers in "jars of clay" (v. 7). Believers themselves are those fragile jars — ordinary and common creatures. Despite this, or even because of this, God has chosen believers to take the unsurpassed glory of his name to the world, to proclaim reconciliation and freedom to the broken and lost so that they might find new life in Jesus.

Paul acknowledged the persecution that would come to believers as they spread the good news of Jesus Christ. But in every circumstance, he explained, there is victory. Jesus' followers may be "afflicted in every way, but not crushed; perplexed, but not driven to despair; persecuted, but not forsaken; struck down, but not destroyed" (vv. 8–9). No matter one's circumstances, it is never too late and no one is ever too far gone for Christ to bring victory into their lives. Paul knew that Jesus Christ had overcome the grave, and as a result he can overcome any and every situation and circumstance that threatens to defeat his followers.

Even today, believers around the world experience all kinds of suffering and persecution because they carry the gospel message of reconciliation to others. Just like Paul, believers today can find joy in knowing that their weakness and suffering reveal the awe-inspiring power of God on display in the gospel of Jesus Christ.

THE JUDGMENT SEAT

At the judgment seat, Jesus will evaluate the faithfulness and work of each believer as Paul explained in 1 Corinthians 3:13 – 15. One must be careful to recognize that the works evaluated at the judgment seat do not determine an individual's eternal salvation. That issue is resolved solely by the redeeming work of Jesus Christ at the moment the believer places their faith in Christ, and it is validated at the great white throne as believers' names are found written in the book of life (Rev 20:15). In contrast, the judgment seat provides opportunity for Christ to evaluate the faithfulness of each believer. Those who invested in the kingdom of God will receive rewards from Christ, while believers who wasted their opportunities will "suffer loss" (1Co 3:15).

While Scripture is not specific about the timing of the judgment seat, it does indicate that believers will be judged and rewarded at the time of Christ's second coming and the resurrection of the dead (Lk 14:14; 1Co 4:5).

The nature of the rewards distributed at the judgment seat is not clear. The New Testament refers to crowns as rewards (1Pe 5:4). Revelation 4:10 explains that these crowns will ultimately be laid at the feet of Jesus. The parable of the minas in Luke 19:11 – 27 suggests that the rewards could also include the opportunity to serve and to govern in eternity. In any event, the Bible indicates that eternal benefit will be bestowed at the judgment seat.

In light of the knowledge that believers will one day stand before the judgment seat of Christ and be rewarded for their faithfulness in life, it is important for all of those who call Jesus Lord to be diligent to their calling to bring him glory in all things, including their efforts to invest in the kingdom of God on earth. It is a privilege not to be ignored.

The Ministry of Reconciliation

[11]Therefore, knowing the fear of the Lord, we persuade others. But what we
are is known to God, and I hope it is known also to your conscience. [12]We are not
commending ourselves to you again but giving you cause to boast about us, so
that you may be able to answer those who boast about outward appearance and
not about what is in the heart. [13]For if we are beside ourselves, it is for God; if we
are in our right mind, it is for you. [14]For the love of Christ controls us, because we
have concluded this: that one has died for all, therefore all have died; [15]and he
died for all, that those who live might no longer live for themselves but for him
who for their sake died and was raised.

[16]From now on, therefore, we regard no one according to the flesh. Even
though we once regarded Christ according to the flesh, we regard him thus no
longer. [17]Therefore, if anyone is in Christ, he is a new creation.[1] The old has
passed away; behold, the new has come. [18]All this is from God, who through
Christ reconciled us to himself and gave us the ministry of reconciliation;
[19]that is, in Christ God was reconciling[2] the world to himself, not counting their
trespasses against them, and entrusting to us the message of reconciliation.
[20]Therefore, we are ambassadors for Christ, God making his appeal through
us. We implore you on behalf of Christ, be reconciled to God. [21]For our sake
he made him to be sin who knew no sin, so that in him we might become the
righteousness of God.

6 Working together with him, then, we appeal to you not to receive the grace of
God in vain. [2]For he says,

"In a favorable time I listened to you,
and in a day of salvation I have helped you."

Behold, now is the favorable time; behold, now is the day of salvation. [3]We put no
obstacle in anyone's way, so that no fault may be found with our ministry, [4]but
as servants of God we commend ourselves in every way: by great endurance, in
afflictions, hardships, calamities, [5]beatings, imprisonments, riots, labors, sleepless nights, hunger; [6]by purity, knowledge, patience, kindness, the Holy Spirit,
genuine love; [7]by truthful speech, and the power of God; with the weapons of
righteousness for the right hand and for the left; [8]through honor and dishonor,
through slander and praise. We are treated as impostors, and yet are true; [9]as
unknown, and yet well known; as dying, and behold, we live; as punished, and
yet not killed; [10]as sorrowful, yet always rejoicing; as poor, yet making many rich;
as having nothing, yet possessing everything.

[11]We have spoken freely to you,[3] Corinthians; our heart is wide open. [12]You are
not restricted by us, but you are restricted in your own affections. [13]In return (I
speak as to children) widen your hearts also.

The Temple of the Living God

[14]Do not be unequally yoked with unbelievers. For what partnership has righteousness with lawlessness? Or what fellowship has light with darkness? [15]What
accord has Christ with Belial?[4] Or what portion does a believer share with an
unbeliever? [16]What agreement has the temple of God with idols? For we are the
temple of the living God; as God said,

"I will make my dwelling among them and walk among them,
and I will be their God,
and they shall be my people.
17 Therefore go out from their midst,
and be separate from them, says the Lord,
and touch no unclean thing;
then I will welcome you,

[1]Or *creature* [2]Or *God was in Christ, reconciling* [3]Greek *Our mouth is open to you* [4]Greek *Beliar*

2 CORINTHIANS 5:18–20

RECONCILIATION

Reconciliation happens when two parties at odds with one another are brought back together. It occurs when one party reaches out to the other and seeks to establish peace in the conflict.

Sin brought war between God and humanity. As created beings, men and women were powerless to reconcile with their Creator. Recognizing this, God sent his Son, Jesus Christ, as the ultimate peace offering, laying down his life so that those who would accept his forgiveness of sin could be reconciled to him.

In turn, God is "entrusting to [his followers] the message of reconciliation" (v. 19). This offer of reconciliation is for the whole world. Because God has reached out to believers, they are instructed to take this message of reconciliation to the world. Christ's followers must share the good news of Jesus everywhere they go.

2 CORINTHIANS 7:8–13

GODLY GRIEF

How often do people in today's culture express sorrow for their actions once they are confronted and the consequences of their actions are manifested? The expressed "sorrow" is really disappointment that they were caught in their misdeeds, not true regret over the underlying actions. Sadly, this is often true for believers and nonbelievers alike.

In the case of the Corinthian church, Paul had sent an earlier letter calling out the inappropriate behavior in the church. This letter, now lost, was written between the letters now canonized as 1 and 2 Corinthians. This intermediate letter may have caused the Corinthians sorrow, but this sorrow led to true repentance.

Paul contrasts "godly grief," which leads to repentance, with "worldly grief," which leads to death (v. 10). Being confronted with one's sin can be painful. However, it can be a powerful and productive exercise when it leads to repentance and spiritual growth—a genuine turning from the sinful behavior. Christ's followers must be receptive to godly confrontation and must be ready and willing to alter their own behavior in order to grow in their relationship with Christ. In their repentance, the Corinthian believers set an example that can still be followed today.

2 CORINTHIANS 8:9

TRADING PLACES

Christ's grace to us was manifested when he became poor, according to Paul. While his earthly life was certainly austere, there is no evidence to suggest that Jesus was any poorer

(continued on page 1754)

18 and I will be a father to you,
  and you shall be sons and daughters to me,
says the Lord Almighty."

7 Since we have these promises, beloved, let us cleanse ourselves from every defilement of body[1] and spirit, bringing holiness to completion in the fear of God.

Paul's Joy

2 Make room in your hearts[2] for us. We have wronged no one, we have corrupted no one, we have taken advantage of no one. 3 I do not say this to condemn you, for I said before that you are in our hearts, to die together and to live together. 4 I am acting with great boldness toward you; I have great pride in you; I am filled with comfort. In all our affliction, I am overflowing with joy.

5 For even when we came into Macedonia, our bodies had no rest, but we were afflicted at every turn—fighting without and fear within. 6 But God, who comforts the downcast, comforted us by the coming of Titus, 7 and not only by his coming but also by the comfort with which he was comforted by you, as he told us of your longing, your mourning, your zeal for me, so that I rejoiced still more. 8 For even if I made you grieve with my letter, I do not regret it—though I did regret it, for I see that that letter grieved you, though only for a while. 9 As it is, I rejoice, not because you were grieved, but because you were grieved into repenting. For you felt a godly grief, so that you suffered no loss through us.

10 For godly grief produces a repentance that leads to salvation without regret, whereas worldly grief produces death. 11 For see what earnestness this godly grief has produced in you, but also what eagerness to clear yourselves, what indignation, what fear, what longing, what zeal, what punishment! At every point you have proved yourselves innocent in the matter. 12 So although I wrote to you, it was not for the sake of the one who did the wrong, nor for the sake of the one who suffered the wrong, but in order that your earnestness for us might be revealed to you in the sight of God. 13 Therefore we are comforted.

And besides our own comfort, we rejoiced still more at the joy of Titus, because his spirit has been refreshed by you all. 14 For whatever boasts I made to him about you, I was not put to shame. But just as everything we said to you was true, so also our boasting before Titus has proved true. 15 And his affection for you is even greater, as he remembers the obedience of you all, how you received him with fear and trembling. 16 I rejoice, because I have complete confidence in you.

Encouragement to Give Generously

8 We want you to know, brothers,[3] about the grace of God that has been given among the churches of Macedonia, 2 for in a severe test of affliction, their abundance of joy and their extreme poverty have overflowed in a wealth of generosity on their part. 3 For they gave according to their means, as I can testify, and beyond their means, of their own accord, 4 begging us earnestly for the favor[4] of taking part in the relief of the saints— 5 and this, not as we expected, but they gave themselves first to the Lord and then by the will of God to us. 6 Accordingly, we urged Titus that as he had started, so he should complete among you this act of grace. 7 But as you excel in everything—in faith, in speech, in knowledge, in all earnestness, and in our love for you[5]—see that you excel in this act of grace also.

8 I say this not as a command, but to prove by the earnestness of others that your love also is genuine. 9 For you know the grace of our Lord Jesus Christ, that though he was rich, yet for your sake he became poor, so that you by his poverty might become rich. 10 And in this matter I give my judgment: this benefits you, who a year ago started not only to do this work but also to desire to do it. 11 So

[1] Greek *flesh* [2] Greek lacks *in your hearts* [3] Or *brothers and sisters* [4] The Greek word *charis* can mean *favor* or *grace* or *thanks*, depending on the context [5] Some manuscripts *in your love for us*

BE SEPARATE

A prosperous metropolitan center, Corinth was a seaport and hub of art and industry in the Roman world. It was also a center for immorality and materialism, which was the context in which the church in Corinth was planted. And it was in this environment that the Corinthian church struggled with understanding how to relate to the surrounding culture.

This is the background for Paul's admonition in verse 17 to "go out from their midst, and be separate." Paul phrased this as a directive from God that quoted Old Testament prophecy. This command also closely mirrors John's prophecy in Revelation 18:4. With this instruction, Paul called out the church in Corinth to stop imitating the immoral practices of their pagan neighbors.

Paul's charge to "be separate" has been interpreted in many ways throughout the centuries. Some believers segregate themselves from the world (in whole or in part), and refuse to participate as members of the larger society outside of their circle of belief and practice. Some groups shun modern conveniences as basic as electricity and live in cloistered seclusion from the world. Other groups refuse to build relationships of any significance with nonbelievers for fear of becoming entangled with the world.

But rather than requiring believers to live in isolation from the world, Paul called the Corinthian believers — and by extension, all believers throughout history — to be set apart in their lifestyles. Instead of participating in the base and immoral activities of the people around them, the Corinthian believers were to come out of that pagan lifestyle and pursue holiness. In so doing, they would draw attention to Jesus.

Paul's admonition follows closely with Jesus' call to be salt and light in Matthew 5:13 – 16. Just as salt loses its value if it loses its saltiness, so too if a believer has patterns and behaviors that mimic the sinfulness of the world, the believer's spiritual value in reaching others is lost. Instead, like a light on a lampstand, believers are to live in such a way as to shine in the darkness. This can only occur when the believer chooses a life of holiness and purity, standing in contrast to the sinful behavior of the surrounding culture.

(Trading Places, continued)

than most first-century Galileans. However, when viewed through an eternal lens, it is clear that Christ laid down riches beyond measure in order to enter time and history on behalf of those who would follow him. Even though he possessed all the wealth of heaven, Jesus chose to set aside his own glory and become a man so that his followers could ultimately share in his glory.

The believer's relationship with God is based on this incredible juxtaposition. Jesus gave up his wealth of glory so that his followers, in their own spiritual poverty, could share in his relationship with God the Father—a relationship of more value than anything earthly. Because Jesus was willing to become poor, his followers are able to become rich beyond measure if they merely accept the grace he offers.

2 CORINTHIANS 9:6–8

GIVING

Christ's followers have received the most incredible gift imaginable in the love, grace, and mercy of God. It costs them nothing, but it cost Jesus everything. Not only has Christ given his followers life and breath, but by his death and resurrection, he has defeated sin and death.

Because of this, when it comes to giving, strict percentages are a thing of the past and Christians do not live under the weight of obligation. Instead, Paul makes it clear that believers are to give generously and may enjoy a generous return. What is more, the attitude of the giver is more important than the size of their gift.

Giving is intended to be an act of worship—the believer's opportunity

(continued on next page)

now finish doing it as well, so that your readiness in desiring it may be matched by your completing it out of what you have. 12For if the readiness is there, it is acceptable according to what a person has, not according to what he does not have. 13For I do not mean that others should be eased and you burdened, but that as a matter of fairness 14your abundance at the present time should supply their need, so that their abundance may supply your need, that there may be fairness. 15As it is written, "Whoever gathered much had nothing left over, and whoever gathered little had no lack."

Commendation of Titus

16But thanks be to God, who put into the heart of Titus the same earnest care I have for you. 17For he not only accepted our appeal, but being himself very earnest he is going[1] to you of his own accord. 18With him we are sending[2] the brother who is famous among all the churches for his preaching of the gospel. 19And not only that, but he has been appointed by the churches to travel with us as we carry out this act of grace that is being ministered by us, for the glory of the Lord himself and to show our good will. 20We take this course so that no one should blame us about this generous gift that is being administered by us, 21for we aim at what is honorable not only in the Lord's sight but also in the sight of man. 22And with them we are sending our brother whom we have often tested and found earnest in many matters, but who is now more earnest than ever because of his great confidence in you. 23As for Titus, he is my partner and fellow worker for your benefit. And as for our brothers, they are messengers[3] of the churches, the glory of Christ. 24So give proof before the churches of your love and of our boasting about you to these men.

The Collection for Christians in Jerusalem

9 Now it is superfluous for me to write to you about the ministry for the saints, 2for I know your readiness, of which I boast about you to the people of Macedonia, saying that Achaia has been ready since last year. And your zeal has stirred up most of them. 3But I am sending[4] the brothers so that our boasting about you may not prove empty in this matter, so that you may be ready, as I said you would be. 4Otherwise, if some Macedonians come with me and find that you are not ready, we would be humiliated—to say nothing of you—for being so confident. 5So I thought it necessary to urge the brothers to go on ahead to you and arrange in advance for the gift[5] you have promised, so that it may be ready as a willing gift, not as an exaction.[6]

The Cheerful Giver

6The point is this: whoever sows sparingly will also reap sparingly, and whoever sows bountifully[7] will also reap bountifully. 7Each one must give as he has decided in his heart, not reluctantly or under compulsion, for God loves a cheerful giver. 8And God is able to make all grace abound to you, so that having all sufficiency[8] in all things at all times, you may abound in every good work. 9As it is written,

> "He has distributed freely, he has given to the poor;
> his righteousness endures forever."

10He who supplies seed to the sower and bread for food will supply and multiply your seed for sowing and increase the harvest of your righteousness. 11You will be enriched in every way to be generous in every way, which through us will produce thanksgiving to God. 12For the ministry of this service is not only supplying the needs of the saints but is also overflowing in many thanksgivings to God.

[1]Or *he went* [2]Or *we sent*; also verse 22 [3]Greek *apostles* [4]Or *I have sent* [5]Greek *blessing*; twice in this verse [6]Or *a gift expecting something in return*; Greek *greed* [7]Greek *with blessings*; twice in this verse [8]Or *all contentment*

13By their approval of this service, they[1] will glorify God because of your submission that comes from your confession of the gospel of Christ, and the generosity
of your contribution for them and for all others, 14while they long for you and pray
for you, because of the surpassing grace of God upon you. 15Thanks be to God for
his inexpressible gift!

Paul Defends His Ministry

10 I, Paul, myself entreat you, by the meekness and gentleness of Christ—I
who am humble when face to face with you, but bold toward you when I
am away!— 2I beg of you that when I am present I may not have to show boldness with such confidence as I count on showing against some who suspect us
of walking according to the flesh. 3For though we walk in the flesh, we are not
waging war according to the flesh. 4For the weapons of our warfare are not of the
flesh but have divine power to destroy strongholds. 5We destroy arguments and
every lofty opinion raised against the knowledge of God, and take every thought
captive to obey Christ, 6being ready to punish every disobedience, when your
obedience is complete.

7Look at what is before your eyes. If anyone is confident that he is Christ's, let
him remind himself that just as he is Christ's, so also are we. 8For even if I boast a
little too much of our authority, which the Lord gave for building you up and not
for destroying you, I will not be ashamed. 9I do not want to appear to be frightening you with my letters. 10For they say, "His letters are weighty and strong, but his
bodily presence is weak, and his speech of no account." 11Let such a person understand that what we say by letter when absent, we do when present. 12Not that
we dare to classify or compare ourselves with some of those who are commending themselves. But when they measure themselves by one another and compare
themselves with one another, they are without understanding.

13But we will not boast beyond limits, but will boast only with regard to the
area of influence God assigned to us, to reach even to you. 14For we are not over-
extending ourselves, as though we did not reach you. For we were the first to
come all the way to you with the gospel of Christ. 15We do not boast beyond limit
in the labors of others. But our hope is that as your faith increases, our area of
influence among you may be greatly enlarged, 16so that we may preach the gospel
in lands beyond you, without boasting of work already done in another's area
of influence. 17"Let the one who boasts, boast in the Lord." 18For it is not the one
who commends himself who is approved, but the one whom the Lord commends.

Paul and the False Apostles

11 I wish you would bear with me in a little foolishness. Do bear with me! 2For
I feel a divine jealousy for you, since I betrothed you to one husband, to
present you as a pure virgin to Christ. 3But I am afraid that as the serpent deceived
Eve by his cunning, your thoughts will be led astray from a sincere and pure devotion to Christ. 4For if someone comes and proclaims another Jesus than the one
we proclaimed, or if you receive a different spirit from the one you received, or if
you accept a different gospel from the one you accepted, you put up with it readily enough. 5Indeed, I consider that I am not in the least inferior to these super-
apostles. 6Even if I am unskilled in speaking, I am not so in knowledge; indeed, in
every way we have made this plain to you in all things.

7Or did I commit a sin in humbling myself so that you might be exalted, because I preached God's gospel to you free of charge? 8I robbed other churches by
accepting support from them in order to serve you. 9And when I was with you and
was in need, I did not burden anyone, for the brothers who came from Macedonia
supplied my need. So I refrained and will refrain from burdening you in any way.
10As the truth of Christ is in me, this boasting of mine will not be silenced in the
regions of Achaia. 11And why? Because I do not love you? God knows I do!

[1] Or *you*

(Giving, continued)

to respond to the extravagant grace and glory of God. God generously meets the needs of his people, both physical and spiritual. Giving is an opportunity for his people to use those gifts to return honor and glory to him. Just as he was extravagant in his giving, so too Christ's followers have the opportunity to be extravagant in their gifts back to him.

2 CORINTHIANS 10:17

BOASTING

Paul circled back in this passage to the same issue he addressed at the end of chapter 2 and the beginning of chapter 3. Specifically, he again argued the legitimacy of his own authority in the gospel. In doing so, he started by summarizing the prophet's admonition in Jeremiah 9:23–24.

Given his education in the law of the Old Testament through his training as a Pharisee, Paul was well versed in the idea that one should not boast about himself. And yet, in this single letter he felt compelled to defend himself and his ministry repeatedly.

Paul's motive is of utmost importance in this matter. His purposes in establishing his authority were not to bring honor to himself. Instead, his intent was to distinguish the authority of his ministry from the deceptive influence of the false leaders who wanted to build themselves up at the expense of the Corinthian church.

In any event, Paul concluded his own defense by pointing out that the approval of humans should not be the goal of believers, but instead they should seek the approval of God. He who created everything knows the

(continued on next page)

(Boasting, continued)

hearts and motives of those who follow him. It is his glory and his approval that his followers should seek.

2 CORINTHIANS 11:21–29

SUFFERING

Jesus' followers are not promised a life of comfort and wealth. Indeed, Jesus himself warned his followers of the suffering they should expect (Mt 10:16–39). Paul's own experience certainly confirms that the earthly life of a believer will not be easy.

In this passage, Paul recounted for the church at Corinth his own struggles. He experienced prison, beatings, and was near death with remarkable regularity. Danger seemed to have become a lifestyle for him. Hunger, thirst, exposure to the elements, and sleeplessness all became a part of Paul's experience when he began using his life to lift up the name of Jesus.

Suffering this extreme may seem foreign to believers who have found lives of relative comfort in many parts of the world in the twenty-first century. However, the reality of suffering for the cause of Christ continues today. Whether in cultures where the worship of Jesus is outlawed or in nations where Christianity is embraced, the possibility of suffering for one's faith remains. Believers should not be surprised when they face suffering of any kind but should recognize that their suffering places them in good company.

2 CORINTHIANS 12:7–10

THORN IN THE FLESH

Paul recognized his inclination to become conceited because of his

(continued on next page)

12And what I am doing I will continue to do, in order to undermine the claim
of those who would like to claim that in their boasted mission they work on the
same terms as we do. 13For such men are false apostles, deceitful workmen, disguising themselves as apostles of Christ. 14And no wonder, for even Satan disguises himself as an angel of light. 15So it is no surprise if his servants, also, disguise
themselves as servants of righteousness. Their end will correspond to their deeds.

Paul's Sufferings as an Apostle

16I repeat, let no one think me foolish. But even if you do, accept me as a fool,
so that I too may boast a little. 17What I am saying with this boastful confidence, I
say not as the Lord would[1] but as a fool. 18Since many boast according to the flesh,
I too will boast. 19For you gladly bear with fools, being wise yourselves! 20For you
bear it if someone makes slaves of you, or devours you, or takes advantage of you,
or puts on airs, or strikes you in the face. 21To my shame, I must say, we were too
weak for that!

But whatever anyone else dares to boast of—I am speaking as a fool—I also
dare to boast of that. 22Are they Hebrews? So am I. Are they Israelites? So am I. Are
they offspring of Abraham? So am I. 23Are they servants of Christ? I am a better
one—I am talking like a madman—with far greater labors, far more imprisonments, with countless beatings, and often near death. 24Five times I received at
the hands of the Jews the forty lashes less one. 25Three times I was beaten with
rods. Once I was stoned. Three times I was shipwrecked; a night and a day I was
adrift at sea; 26on frequent journeys, in danger from rivers, danger from robbers,
danger from my own people, danger from Gentiles, danger in the city, danger in
the wilderness, danger at sea, danger from false brothers; 27in toil and hardship,
through many a sleepless night, in hunger and thirst, often without food,[2] in cold
and exposure. 28And, apart from other things, there is the daily pressure on me of
my anxiety for all the churches. 29Who is weak, and I am not weak? Who is made
to fall, and I am not indignant?

30If I must boast, I will boast of the things that show my weakness. 31The God
and Father of the Lord Jesus, he who is blessed forever, knows that I am not lying.
32At Damascus, the governor under King Aretas was guarding the city of Damascus in order to seize me, 33but I was let down in a basket through a window in the
wall and escaped his hands.

Paul's Visions and His Thorn

12 I must go on boasting. Though there is nothing to be gained by it, I will
go on to visions and revelations of the Lord. 2I know a man in Christ who
fourteen years ago was caught up to the third heaven—whether in the body or
out of the body I do not know, God knows. 3And I know that this man was caught
up into paradise—whether in the body or out of the body I do not know, God
knows— 4and he heard things that cannot be told, which man may not utter. 5On
behalf of this man I will boast, but on my own behalf I will not boast, except of my
weaknesses— 6though if I should wish to boast, I would not be a fool, for I would
be speaking the truth; but I refrain from it, so that no one may think more of me
than he sees in me or hears from me. 7So to keep me from becoming conceited
because of the surpassing greatness of the revelations,[3] a thorn was given me in
the flesh, a messenger of Satan to harass me, to keep me from becoming conceited. 8Three times I pleaded with the Lord about this, that it should leave me.
9But he said to me, "My grace is sufficient for you, for my power is made perfect
in weakness." Therefore I will boast all the more gladly of my weaknesses, so that
the power of Christ may rest upon me. 10For the sake of Christ, then, I am content
with weaknesses, insults, hardships, persecutions, and calamities. For when I am
weak, then I am strong.

[1]Greek *not according to the Lord* [2]Or *often in fasting* [3]Or *hears from me, even because of the surpassing greatness of the revelations. So to keep me from becoming conceited*

Concern for the Corinthian Church

[11]I have been a fool! You forced me to it, for I ought to have been commended by you. For I was not at all inferior to these super-apostles, even though I am nothing. [12]The signs of a true apostle were performed among you with utmost patience, with signs and wonders and mighty works. [13]For in what were you less favored than the rest of the churches, except that I myself did not burden you? Forgive me this wrong!

[14]Here for the third time I am ready to come to you. And I will not be a burden, for I seek not what is yours but you. For children are not obligated to save up for their parents, but parents for their children. [15]I will most gladly spend and be spent for your souls. If I love you more, am I to be loved less? [16]But granting that I myself did not burden you, I was crafty, you say, and got the better of you by deceit. [17]Did I take advantage of you through any of those whom I sent to you? [18]I urged Titus to go, and sent the brother with him. Did Titus take advantage of you? Did we not act in the same spirit? Did we not take the same steps?

[19]Have you been thinking all along that we have been defending ourselves to you? It is in the sight of God that we have been speaking in Christ, and all for your upbuilding, beloved. [20]For I fear that perhaps when I come I may find you not as I wish, and that you may find me not as you wish—that perhaps there may be quarreling, jealousy, anger, hostility, slander, gossip, conceit, and disorder. [21]I fear that when I come again my God may humble me before you, and I may have to mourn over many of those who sinned earlier and have not repented of the impurity, sexual immorality, and sensuality that they have practiced.

Final Warnings

13 This is the third time I am coming to you. Every charge must be established by the evidence of two or three witnesses. [2]I warned those who sinned before and all the others, and I warn them now while absent, as I did when present on my second visit, that if I come again I will not spare them— [3]since you seek proof that Christ is speaking in me. He is not weak in dealing with you, but is powerful among you. [4]For he was crucified in weakness, but lives by the power of God. For we also are weak in him, but in dealing with you we will live with him by the power of God.

[5]Examine yourselves, to see whether you are in the faith. Test yourselves. Or do you not realize this about yourselves, that Jesus Christ is in you?—unless indeed you fail to meet the test! [6]I hope you will find out that we have not failed the test. [7]But we pray to God that you may not do wrong—not that we may appear to have met the test, but that you may do what is right, though we may seem to have failed. [8]For we cannot do anything against the truth, but only for the truth. [9]For we are glad when we are weak and you are strong. Your restoration is what we pray for. [10]For this reason I write these things while I am away from you, that when I come I may not have to be severe in my use of the authority that the Lord has given me for building up and not for tearing down.

Final Greetings

[11]Finally, brothers,[1] rejoice. Aim for restoration, comfort one another,[2] agree with one another, live in peace; and the God of love and peace will be with you. [12]Greet one another with a holy kiss. [13]All the saints greet you.

[14]The grace of the Lord Jesus Christ and the love of God and the fellowship of the Holy Spirit be with you all.

(Thorn in the Flesh, continued)

own apostolic authority and impressive spiritual credentials. To keep Paul humble and maximize the glory given to God through Paul's ministry, God gave Paul "a thorn ... in the flesh" (v. 7).

Paul referred to this thorn as "a messenger of Satan" (v. 7), and therefore it may have been that God allowed the devil to attack Paul in some limited way in order to serve the Lord's own good purposes (Job 2:1). Beyond this, however, Scripture is not clear as to the precise nature of Paul's struggle. Some have speculated that it was an issue related to his eyesight based on his comments in Galatians 4:13–15. In any event, it is clear that the issue was chronic and debilitating and was a hindrance to his work and ministry.

Regardless of the nature of Paul's thorn, two things are clear. First, God's grace was sufficient to sustain Paul through his struggle. And second, because of the disability in Paul's life, God received even more glory through Paul's ministry. It is for this reason that Paul was able to rejoice in his own suffering and delight in his own weakness.

The same principles apply to believers today. While God uses the strengths and skills of his people, even more glory can be attributed to God when his people rely on him, serve him, and make themselves available despite their weaknesses and struggles.

[1]Or *brothers and sisters* [2]Or *listen to my appeal*

JESUS: OUR JUSTIFICATION BY FAITH

GALATIANS

GALATIANS

PAUL'S MISSIONARY JOURNEYS	PAUL VISITS, WRITES TO GALATIANS	PAUL MARTYRED IN ROME
c. AD 47 – 57	*c. AD 48*	*c. AD 67 – 68*

How can sinful people be made right with a holy God? This question is central to understanding Paul's letter to the churches of Galatia, and also the entirety of the Bible.

The churches in this region were established by Paul on either his first or second missionary journey. Since his departure, false teachers had perverted the gospel he proclaimed. These teachers led many to conclude erroneously that keeping the law, especially practicing circumcision, was essential for salvation.

Paul did not mince words in countering this heresy, which Paul argued had fundamentally altered the message of the gospel. Salvation is found through faith in Jesus Christ alone (2:16; 3:11 – 12). The law was used by God to reveal the extent of human sin and point forward to the coming of Christ. It was, as it had always been, a response to the grace of God. Those who try to earn salvation by keeping the law will find themselves cursed by God because they cannot obey it perfectly (3:10).

With fatherly affection, Paul writes to his "little children" (4:19) in the faith and hope that they would not abandon the gospel he proclaimed. Works-based salvation is not good news. It is crushing, burdensome, and condemning. The good news is that God pursued his people in love, knowing full well the extent of their sinfulness. Jesus lived a life of perfect conformity to the law and gives his righteous standing before God as a gift to his people. On the cross, Jesus became a curse on behalf of believers so they would never face the condemnation sin deserves (3:13). These gifts — right standing before God and freedom from the wrath of God — are given apart from the works of the law. They are a gift of grace.

God then indwells believers by means of his Holy Spirit, who empowers them to live the lives for which God created them. The Spirit produces in them what the law never could (5:22 – 23). Those who are saved by faith will find this faith working in them to produce lives marked by love of God and of one another (5:5 – 6). Jesus alone is the basis for the church's hope — both for their salvation and their ongoing sanctification.

I HAVE BEEN CRUCIFIED WITH CHRIST.
IT IS NO LONGER I WHO LIVE, BUT CHRIST WHO
LIVES IN ME. AND THE LIFE I NOW LIVE IN THE FLESH
I LIVE BY FAITH IN THE SON OF GOD,
WHO LOVED ME AND GAVE HIMSELF FOR ME.

Galatians 2:20

GALATIANS

Greeting

1 Paul, an apostle—not from men nor through man, but through Jesus Christ and God the Father, who raised him from the dead— 2and all the brothers[1] who are with me,

To the churches of Galatia:

3Grace to you and peace from God our Father and the Lord Jesus Christ, 4who gave himself for our sins to deliver us from the present evil age, according to the will of our God and Father, 5to whom be the glory forever and ever. Amen.

No Other Gospel

6I am astonished that you are so quickly deserting him who called you in the grace of Christ and are turning to a different gospel— 7not that there is another one, but there are some who trouble you and want to distort the gospel of Christ. 8But even if we or an angel from heaven should preach to you a gospel contrary to the one we preached to you, let him be accursed. 9As we have said before, so now I say again: If anyone is preaching to you a gospel contrary to the one you received, let him be accursed.

10For am I now seeking the approval of man, or of God? Or am I trying to please man? If I were still trying to please man, I would not be a servant[2] of Christ.

Paul Called by God

11For I would have you know, brothers, that the gospel that was preached by me is not man's gospel.[3] 12For I did not receive it from any man, nor was I taught it, but I received it through a revelation of Jesus Christ. 13For you have heard of my former life in Judaism, how I persecuted the church of God violently and tried to destroy it. 14And I was advancing in Judaism beyond many of my own age among my people, so extremely zealous was I for the traditions of my fathers. 15But when he who had set me apart before I was born,[4] and who called me by his grace, 16was pleased to reveal his Son to[5] me, in order that I might preach him among the Gentiles, I did not immediately consult with anyone;[6] 17nor did I go up to Jerusalem to those who were apostles before me, but I went away into Arabia, and returned again to Damascus.

18Then after three years I went up to Jerusalem to visit Cephas and remained with him fifteen days. 19But I saw none of the other apostles except James the Lord's brother. 20(In what I am writing to you, before God, I do not lie!) 21Then I went into the regions of Syria and Cilicia. 22And I was still unknown in person to the churches of Judea that are in Christ. 23They only were hearing it said, "He who used to persecute us is now preaching the faith he once tried to destroy." 24And they glorified God because of me.

Paul Accepted by the Apostles

2 Then after fourteen years I went up again to Jerusalem with Barnabas, taking Titus along with me. 2I went up because of a revelation and set before them (though privately before those who seemed influential) the gospel that I proclaim among the Gentiles, in order to make sure I was not running or had not run in vain. 3But even Titus, who was with me, was not forced to be circumcised, though he was a Greek. 4Yet because of false brothers secretly brought in—who slipped in to spy out our freedom that we have in Christ Jesus, so that they might bring

GALATIANS 1:6–7

AMAZING GRACE

Often believers find it difficult to rest in the undeserved, amazing grace of Jesus. With gratitude and good intentions, believers look to prove themselves worthy of their unearned position. In this letter, Paul confronts the church of Galatia on this point. They had become confused and were trying to work out their salvation by suggesting they should add the rules and legalism of Jewish laws to the saving grace God the Father offered through Jesus' death and resurrection. Paul reasoned that if believers were required to keep the law in order to be saved, a savior wasn't necessary (v. 7).

[1]Or *brothers and sisters*. In New Testament usage, depending on the context, the plural Greek word *adelphoi* (translated "brothers") may refer either to *brothers* or to *brothers and sisters*; also verse 11
[2]For the contextual rendering of the Greek word *doulos*, see Preface [3]Greek *not according to man*
[4]Greek *set me apart from my mother's womb* [5]Greek *in* [6]Greek *with flesh and blood*

us into slavery— 5to them we did not yield in submission even for a moment, so
that the truth of the gospel might be preserved for you. 6And from those who
seemed to be influential (what they were makes no difference to me; God shows
no partiality)—those, I say, who seemed influential added nothing to me. 7On
the contrary, when they saw that I had been entrusted with the gospel to the uncircumcised, just as Peter had been entrusted with the gospel to the circumcised
8(for he who worked through Peter for his apostolic ministry to the circumcised
worked also through me for mine to the Gentiles), 9and when James and Cephas
and John, who seemed to be pillars, perceived the grace that was given to me, they
gave the right hand of fellowship to Barnabas and me, that we should go to the
Gentiles and they to the circumcised. 10Only, they asked us to remember the poor,
the very thing I was eager to do.

Paul Opposes Peter

11But when Cephas came to Antioch, I opposed him to his face, because he
stood condemned. 12For before certain men came from James, he was eating with
the Gentiles; but when they came he drew back and separated himself, fearing
the circumcision party.[1] 13And the rest of the Jews acted hypocritically along with
him, so that even Barnabas was led astray by their hypocrisy. 14But when I saw that
their conduct was not in step with the truth of the gospel, I said to Cephas before
them all, "If you, though a Jew, live like a Gentile and not like a Jew, how can you
force the Gentiles to live like Jews?"

Justified by Faith

15We ourselves are Jews by birth and not Gentile sinners; 16yet we know that a
person is not justified[2] by works of the law but through faith in Jesus Christ, so we
also have believed in Christ Jesus, in order to be justified by faith in Christ and not
by works of the law, because by works of the law no one will be justified.

17But if, in our endeavor to be justified in Christ, we too were found to be sinners, is Christ then a servant of sin? Certainly not! 18For if I rebuild what I tore
down, I prove myself to be a transgressor. 19For through the law I died to the law,
so that I might live to God. 20I have been crucified with Christ. It is no longer I
who live, but Christ who lives in me. And the life I now live in the flesh I live by
faith in the Son of God, who loved me and gave himself for me. 21I do not nullify
the grace of God, for if righteousness[3] were through the law, then Christ died for
no purpose.

By Faith, or by Works of the Law?

3 O foolish Galatians! Who has bewitched you? It was before your eyes that
Jesus Christ was publicly portrayed as crucified. 2Let me ask you only this:
Did you receive the Spirit by works of the law or by hearing with faith? 3Are you
so foolish? Having begun by the Spirit, are you now being perfected by[4] the flesh?
4Did you suffer[5] so many things in vain—if indeed it was in vain? 5Does he who
supplies the Spirit to you and works miracles among you do so by works of the
law, or by hearing with faith— 6just as Abraham "believed God, and it was counted to him as righteousness"?

7Know then that it is those of faith who are the sons of Abraham. 8And the
Scripture, foreseeing that God would justify[6] the Gentiles by faith, preached the
gospel beforehand to Abraham, saying, "In you shall all the nations be blessed."
9So then, those who are of faith are blessed along with Abraham, the man of faith.

The Righteous Shall Live by Faith

10For all who rely on works of the law are under a curse; for it is written,
"Cursed be everyone who does not abide by all things written in the Book of the

[1] Or *fearing those of the circumcision* [2] Or *counted righteous* (three times in verse 16); also verse 17
[3] Or *justification* [4] Or *now ending with* [5] Or *experience* [6] Or *count righteous*; also verses 11, 24

CRUCIFIED WITH CHRIST

To truly appreciate the claim Paul makes in Galatians 2:20, "I have been crucified with Christ," first consider the symbol of the cross in Jesus' day. An excruciating, shameful death by crucifixion was reserved for society's worst criminal offenders. So why would Paul choose to align himself with the cross? The gospel flips everything on its head. Not until his conversion did Paul really see what the cross stood for. Only God could turn a horrible death on a cross into something beautiful. On the cross, Jesus exchanged the punishment we deserved for his grace — a gift so profound and so complete that nothing could be added to it.

So Paul couldn't understand why the church leaders would want to make symbols of righteousness through Jewish law requirements for salvation. He stood firm in his belief: Either salvation was through faith alone or it wasn't (v. 15)! For the believer, works are not a *prerequisite* for salvation; rather, they are a *response* to salvation. Paul's identity with Christ's crucifixion symbolized the reality that Jesus removed the stain of his sin once and for all and brought life, grace, and freedom to this former persecutor of the church. His letter to the Galatians reinforces the completeness of this transformation to convince them that nothing needed to be added to their faith to assure their salvation.

In their first meeting together after Paul's conversion (vv. 1 – 10), Paul and Peter confirmed the unity and oneness they shared in the gospel and affirmed each other's unique call. However, when the two met again in Antioch, Paul called Peter out for acting one way around Gentiles and another way around those who still practiced the Jewish law. Paul was concerned that Peter's behavior could be perceived by the Gentiles as showing that there must be something more that believers have to do to continue in God's grace after salvation. Paul fiercely protected the freedom that grace offers (v. 21).

With Jesus, the entire concept of "the cross" was changed to the point that Paul would "boast ... in the cross of ... Christ" (6:14). He would never belittle the cross by adding elements of the Jewish law to it — elements that fell short of true righteousness before God. Christianity centers on complete change — a change in our status before God, in our view of the present world, and even in the way we think about the cross. Paul emphasized that Christ's one sacrifice covers all of our sin completely; we need not add even one more thing to that sacrifice to somehow earn more favor with God.

Law, and do them." 11Now it is evident that no one is justified before God by the law, for "The righteous shall live by faith."[1] 12But the law is not of faith, rather "The one who does them shall live by them." 13Christ redeemed us from the curse of the law by becoming a curse for us—for it is written, "Cursed is everyone who is hanged on a tree"— 14so that in Christ Jesus the blessing of Abraham might come to the Gentiles, so that we might receive the promised Spirit[2] through faith.

The Law and the Promise

15To give a human example, brothers:[3] even with a man-made covenant, no one annuls it or adds to it once it has been ratified. 16Now the promises were made to Abraham and to his offspring. It does not say, "And to offsprings," referring to many, but referring to one, "And to your offspring," who is Christ. 17This is what I mean: the law, which came 430 years afterward, does not annul a covenant previously ratified by God, so as to make the promise void. 18For if the inheritance comes by the law, it no longer comes by promise; but God gave it to Abraham by a promise.

19Why then the law? It was added because of transgressions, until the offspring should come to whom the promise had been made, and it was put in place through angels by an intermediary. 20Now an intermediary implies more than one, but God is one.

21Is the law then contrary to the promises of God? Certainly not! For if a law had been given that could give life, then righteousness would indeed be by the law. 22But the Scripture imprisoned everything under sin, so that the promise by faith in Jesus Christ might be given to those who believe.

23Now before faith came, we were held captive under the law, imprisoned until the coming faith would be revealed. 24So then, the law was our guardian until Christ came, in order that we might be justified by faith. 25But now that faith has come, we are no longer under a guardian, 26for in Christ Jesus you are all sons of God, through faith. 27For as many of you as were baptized into Christ have put on Christ. 28There is neither Jew nor Greek, there is neither slave[4] nor free, there is no male and female, for you are all one in Christ Jesus. 29And if you are Christ's, then you are Abraham's offspring, heirs according to promise.

Sons and Heirs

4 I mean that the heir, as long as he is a child, is no different from a slave,[5] though he is the owner of everything, 2but he is under guardians and managers until the date set by his father. 3In the same way we also, when we were children, were enslaved to the elementary principles[6] of the world. 4But when the fullness of time had come, God sent forth his Son, born of woman, born under the law, 5to redeem those who were under the law, so that we might receive adoption as sons. 6And because you are sons, God has sent the Spirit of his Son into our hearts, crying, "Abba! Father!" 7So you are no longer a slave, but a son, and if a son, then an heir through God.

Paul's Concern for the Galatians

8Formerly, when you did not know God, you were enslaved to those that by nature are not gods. 9But now that you have come to know God, or rather to be known by God, how can you turn back again to the weak and worthless elementary principles of the world, whose slaves you want to be once more? 10You observe days and months and seasons and years! 11I am afraid I may have labored over you in vain.

12Brothers,[7] I entreat you, become as I am, for I also have become as you

[1]Or *The one who by faith is righteous will live* [2]Greek *receive the promise of the Spirit* [3]Or *brothers and sisters* [4]For the contextual rendering of the Greek word *doulos*, see Preface [5]For the contextual rendering of the Greek word *doulos*, see Preface; also verse 7 [6]Or *elemental spirits*; also verse 9 [7]Or *Brothers and sisters*; also verses 28, 31

GALATIANS 4:4–5

CHILDREN OF GOD'S PROMISE

The law was given as a guardian, a steward of the relationship between God and his people until the promise of the coming Messiah was fulfilled. It was established by God to uphold a standard of holiness and make a way for people to temporarily atone for their sins. God determined the time between the giving of the law and the fulfillment of the promise for our benefit. Not a moment of what went on before Jesus came was wasted.

The Israelites of the Old Testament lived with expectation, waiting for God to fulfill his promises. Like underage heirs, they were subject to their guardian, the law—and that arrangement made them no better off than slaves. But Jesus came "to redeem those who were under the law, so that we might receive adoption as sons" (v. 5). He was the fulfilled promise that made adoption into God's eternal family possible.

Believers are children of God. And they share in the mind-blowingly abundant inheritance of the Lord himself! There is no more uncertainty: God calls believers his beloved and they walk in the close, deeply affectionate, committed love of their heavenly Father.

GRACE VERSUS THE LAW

Paul didn't waste words. He saw that his Galatian brothers and sisters were headed down a dangerous path. They may or may not have been ready for a heavyweight theological match, but Paul was ready to throw down. While the Galatians were led astray by those who wanted to add such Jewish traditions as circumcision to the requirements for salvation, Paul stood firm on the issue of righteousness gained through faith alone. Paul considered this a hill worth dying on; Jesus did too. Salvation by grace alone centers on the cross of Christ, and any human law, Jewish or otherwise, centers on submitting to human requirements. Paul is clear: the enemy wants Christ-followers to believe that faith in Jesus alone is not sufficient for salvation.

Faith is a matter of trust, not a pursuit of perfection. These believers were mistakenly trying to achieve perfection through their own efforts. Sound familiar? Paul emphasized that the law is based on works and depends on human effort, whereas grace is based on faith and depends on the power of the Holy Spirit. Paul challenged his audience, "Having begun by the Spirit, are you now being perfected by the flesh?" (v. 3). Does the Spirit come to believers because they perfectly keep all the rules? Of course not. "But God shows his love for us in that while we were still sinners, Christ died for us" (Ro 5:8).

The Holy Spirit frees us from the rule of law and empowers us, changing our desires so that we want to live holy, godly lives. This reality moves believers away from being "sanctified scorekeepers" to people who live joyfully for Jesus: "But you are a chosen race, a royal priesthood, a holy nation, a people for his own possession, *that you may* proclaim the excellencies of him who called you out of darkness into his marvelous light" (1Pe 2:9, emphasis added). This "that you may" attitude involves a complete mind shift: Believers don't *have* to ... they *get* to respond to Jesus' love by showing love to others in return.

Children of God don't live to keep all the rules and then concern themselves with how they rank as compared to others. Life under the law is motivated by pride. Life under grace is motivated by love. To support his argument, Paul points out that it can't go both ways. Even if some believed they could keep parts of the law, they were essentially condemning themselves to keep the whole law. James taught similarly (Jas 2:10). Paul wrote to convince the Galatians — and us as well — that living under the law, or even part of the law, brings bondage. But grace brings liberty.

are. You did me no wrong. 13You know it was because of a bodily ailment that I preached the gospel to you at first, 14and though my condition was a trial to you, you did not scorn or despise me, but received me as an angel of God, as Christ Jesus. 15What then has become of your blessedness? For I testify to you that, if possible, you would have gouged out your eyes and given them to me. 16Have I then become your enemy by telling you the truth?[1] 17They make much of you, but for no good purpose. They want to shut you out, that you may make much of them. 18It is always good to be made much of for a good purpose, and not only when I am present with you, 19my little children, for whom I am again in the anguish of childbirth until Christ is formed in you! 20I wish I could be present with you now and change my tone, for I am perplexed about you.

Example of Hagar and Sarah

21Tell me, you who desire to be under the law, do you not listen to the law? 22For it is written that Abraham had two sons, one by a slave woman and one by a free woman. 23But the son of the slave was born according to the flesh, while the son of the free woman was born through promise. 24Now this may be interpreted allegorically: these women are two covenants. One is from Mount Sinai, bearing children for slavery; she is Hagar. 25Now Hagar is Mount Sinai in Arabia;[2] she corresponds to the present Jerusalem, for she is in slavery with her children. 26But the Jerusalem above is free, and she is our mother. 27For it is written,

"Rejoice, O barren one who does not bear;
break forth and cry aloud, you who are not in labor!
For the children of the desolate one will be more
than those of the one who has a husband."

28Now you,[3] brothers, like Isaac, are children of promise. 29But just as at that time he who was born according to the flesh persecuted him who was born according to the Spirit, so also it is now. 30But what does the Scripture say? "Cast out the slave woman and her son, for the son of the slave woman shall not inherit with the son of the free woman." 31So, brothers, we are not children of the slave but of the free woman.

Christ Has Set Us Free

5 For freedom Christ has set us free; stand firm therefore, and do not submit again to a yoke of slavery.

2Look: I, Paul, say to you that if you accept circumcision, Christ will be of no advantage to you. 3I testify again to every man who accepts circumcision that he is obligated to keep the whole law. 4You are severed from Christ, you who would be justified[4] by the law; you have fallen away from grace. 5For through the Spirit, by faith, we ourselves eagerly wait for the hope of righteousness. 6For in Christ Jesus neither circumcision nor uncircumcision counts for anything, but only faith working through love.

7You were running well. Who hindered you from obeying the truth? 8This persuasion is not from him who calls you. 9A little leaven leavens the whole lump. 10I have confidence in the Lord that you will take no other view, and the one who is troubling you will bear the penalty, whoever he is. 11But if I, brothers,[5] still preach[6] circumcision, why am I still being persecuted? In that case the offense of the cross has been removed. 12I wish those who unsettle you would emasculate themselves!

13For you were called to freedom, brothers. Only do not use your freedom as an opportunity for the flesh, but through love serve one another. 14For the whole law is fulfilled in one word: "You shall love your neighbor as yourself." 15But if you bite and devour one another, watch out that you are not consumed by one another.

[1]Or *by dealing truthfully with you* [2]Some manuscripts *For Sinai is a mountain in Arabia* [3]Some manuscripts *we* [4]Or *counted righteous* [5]Or *brothers and sisters*; also verse 13 [6]Greek *proclaim*

Keep in Step with the Spirit

16 But I say, walk by the Spirit, and you will not gratify the desires of the flesh. 17 For the desires of the flesh are against the Spirit, and the desires of the Spirit are against the flesh, for these are opposed to each other, to keep you from doing the things you want to do. 18 But if you are led by the Spirit, you are not under the law. 19 Now the works of the flesh are evident: sexual immorality, impurity, sensuality, 20 idolatry, sorcery, enmity, strife, jealousy, fits of anger, rivalries, dissensions, divisions, 21 envy,[1] drunkenness, orgies, and things like these. I warn you, as I warned you before, that those who do[2] such things will not inherit the kingdom of God. 22 But the fruit of the Spirit is love, joy, peace, patience, kindness, goodness, faithfulness, 23 gentleness, self-control; against such things there is no law. 24 And those who belong to Christ Jesus have crucified the flesh with its passions and desires.

25 If we live by the Spirit, let us also keep in step with the Spirit. 26 Let us not become conceited, provoking one another, envying one another.

Bear One Another's Burdens

6 Brothers,[3] if anyone is caught in any transgression, you who are spiritual should restore him in a spirit of gentleness. Keep watch on yourself, lest you too be tempted. 2 Bear one another's burdens, and so fulfill the law of Christ. 3 For if anyone thinks he is something, when he is nothing, he deceives himself. 4 But let each one test his own work, and then his reason to boast will be in himself alone and not in his neighbor. 5 For each will have to bear his own load.

6 Let the one who is taught the word share all good things with the one who teaches. 7 Do not be deceived: God is not mocked, for whatever one sows, that will he also reap. 8 For the one who sows to his own flesh will from the flesh reap corruption, but the one who sows to the Spirit will from the Spirit reap eternal life. 9 And let us not grow weary of doing good, for in due season we will reap, if we do not give up. 10 So then, as we have opportunity, let us do good to everyone, and especially to those who are of the household of faith.

Final Warning and Benediction

11 See with what large letters I am writing to you with my own hand. 12 It is those who want to make a good showing in the flesh who would force you to be circumcised, and only in order that they may not be persecuted for the cross of Christ. 13 For even those who are circumcised do not themselves keep the law, but they desire to have you circumcised that they may boast in your flesh. 14 But far be it from me to boast except in the cross of our Lord Jesus Christ, by which[4] the world has been crucified to me, and I to the world. 15 For neither circumcision counts for anything, nor uncircumcision, but a new creation. 16 And as for all who walk by this rule, peace and mercy be upon them, and upon the Israel of God.

17 From now on let no one cause me trouble, for I bear on my body the marks of Jesus.

18 The grace of our Lord Jesus Christ be with your spirit, brothers. Amen.

GALATIANS 5:22–23

FRUIT OF THE SPIRIT

As Christians begin to live lives that are transformed more and more into the image of Christ, certain character traits begin to show up: love, joy, peace, kindness, and the like. Paul tells his audience that as a person's heart changes, their outward disposition, demeanor, and actions will also change. This "fruit" comes as the Holy Spirit works and changes the way believers live. This passage tells us that the words, actions, character, and values of a believer will increasingly align with the behavior Jesus modeled during his earthly ministry. Paul's preview to the fruit describes how the process works: "But I say, walk by the Spirit, and you will not gratify the desires of the flesh" (v. 16).

All believers have days when love or joy is less evident. But overall, the transformational nature of salvation—when a believer's eternal status is converted once and for all time—can't help but begin to change their daily attitudes and actions.

---

[1] Some manuscripts add *murder* [2] Or *make a practice of doing* [3] Or *Brothers and sisters*; also verse 18
[4] Or *through whom*

JESUS: OUR PEACE WITH GOD

EPHESIANS

EPHESIANS

PAUL PLANTS EPHESIAN CHURCH	PAUL'S EXTENDED STAY IN EPHESUS	PAUL IMPRISONED, WRITES EPHESIANS
c. AD 53	*c. AD 54 – 56*	*c. AD 60 – 62*

The depth of the gospel's message is unfathomable. Since the beginning of the church, pastors and scholars have written countless books attempting to address the nature and implications of Jesus' work. There is perhaps no greater and more succinct summary of the gospel message, however, than the book of Ephesians.

Ephesus was the capital of the Roman province of Asia and was a major thoroughfare in the Roman Empire. Its location made it a multicultural, cosmopolitan city, bustling with activity and influence.

Paul visited Ephesus on his second missionary journey and witnessed the birth of the church in that region. He then returned on his third missionary journey and spent three years working to establish the church (Ac 18:18 – 21; 19:1 – 41). God used the inhabitants' spiritual fervor and the strategic location of the city to make the church a center for evangelism and mission to the surrounding region (Ac 19:18 – 20). Upon leaving, Paul warned the church that fierce wolves would attack the church from inside and outside (Ac 20:17 – 38).

Years later, Paul wrote from a Roman prison to his beloved friends in Ephesus. He wanted to remind them of the gospel he proclaimed, spur them on to perseverance in the face of suffering and encourage them with the blessed hope the gospel brings. There is evidence to suggest that Ephesians may also have been a circular letter that was used to instruct and encourage believers in the broader world. The first three chapters explore many of the central doctrines of the Christian faith to show that Jesus' work brings peace with God and peace with others. The grace of God lies at the heart of Paul's letter (Eph 2:8 – 9). This grace saves God's people apart from their works so that, through salvation, God gets all the glory.

In light of Jesus' work, then, Paul discusses the "good works" that naturally flow from a high view of God's grace and a proper understanding of the peace he brings (2:10). The peace God provides transforms every aspect of life — especially the relationships Christians have with one another. As the head of his church, Jesus shapes human relationships to model and display the love, grace, and mercy he demonstrated through his death and resurrection. Dynamic, countercultural love for God and one another was to distinguish the church, in Ephesus and throughout all history, as God's people.

BUT GOD, BEING RICH IN MERCY, BECAUSE OF THE GREAT LOVE WITH WHICH HE LOVED US, EVEN WHEN WE WERE DEAD IN OUR TRESPASSES, MADE US ALIVE TOGETHER WITH CHRIST — BY GRACE YOU HAVE BEEN SAVED.

Ephesians 2:4 – 5

EPHESIANS

EPHESIANS 2:1–10

DEATH TO LIFE

There is a stark contrast between death and life. Ephesians 2:1–3 explores the terrible reality for unbelievers. Using such words as "trespasses," "disobedience," "passions of our flesh," and "wrath," these verses communicate that there is something dreadfully wrong with the identity and life experience of people who are not followers of Christ. What an appalling description! There is no worse condition than spiritual death.

But hope emerges from the ashes of death (vv. 4–5). Those who are in Christ are God's "workmanship" (v. 10), meaning he has crafted something beautiful. But how could beauty come from desperation, ugliness and complete destruction? It seems unfathomable that life could come from death and despair. The apostle Paul communicated this stark contrast to teach believers where ultimate praise and glory belong. Christians have nothing to offer for their salvation—it comes about only by God's rich mercy (v. 4), kindness (v. 7), grace (v. 8), and gift (v. 8).

A Christian has no grounds for boasting about their status as a child of God (v. 9): not their wisdom, effort to obey, morality . . . nothing! Every ounce of the believer's being must therefore give absolute adoration to the Lord God, thus fulfilling the first great commandment (Mt 22:37). Closely flowing from this praise is the second great commandment (Mt 22:39). God's handiwork of recreating Christians from

(continued on page 1774)

Greeting

1 Paul, an apostle of Christ Jesus by the will of God,
To the saints who are in Ephesus, and are faithful[1] in Christ Jesus:
2 Grace to you and peace from God our Father and the Lord Jesus Christ.

Spiritual Blessings in Christ

3 Blessed be the God and Father of our Lord Jesus Christ, who has blessed us in
Christ with every spiritual blessing in the heavenly places, 4 even as he chose us
in him before the foundation of the world, that we should be holy and blameless
before him. In love 5 he predestined us[2] for adoption to himself as sons through
Jesus Christ, according to the purpose of his will, 6 to the praise of his glorious
grace, with which he has blessed us in the Beloved. 7 In him we have redemption
through his blood, the forgiveness of our trespasses, according to the riches of his
grace, 8 which he lavished upon us, in all wisdom and insight 9 making known[3] to
us the mystery of his will, according to his purpose, which he set forth in Christ[4]
10 as a plan for the fullness of time, to unite all things in Christ, things in heaven
and things on earth in him.
11 In him we have obtained an inheritance, having been predestined according to the purpose of him who works all things according to the counsel of his
will, 12 so that we who were the first to hope in Christ might be to the praise of
his glory. 13 In him you also, when you heard the word of truth, the gospel of your
salvation, and believed in him, were sealed with the promised Holy Spirit, 14 who
is the guarantee[5] of our inheritance until we acquire possession of it,[6] to the praise
of his glory.

Thanksgiving and Prayer

15 For this reason, because I have heard of your faith in the Lord Jesus and your
love[7] toward all the saints, 16 I do not cease to give thanks for you, remembering
you in my prayers, 17 that the God of our Lord Jesus Christ, the Father of glory, may
give you the Spirit of wisdom and of revelation in the knowledge of him, 18 having
the eyes of your hearts enlightened, that you may know what is the hope to which
he has called you, what are the riches of his glorious inheritance in the saints,
19 and what is the immeasurable greatness of his power toward us who believe,
according to the working of his great might 20 that he worked in Christ when he
raised him from the dead and seated him at his right hand in the heavenly places,
21 far above all rule and authority and power and dominion, and above every name
that is named, not only in this age but also in the one to come. 22 And he put all
things under his feet and gave him as head over all things to the church, 23 which
is his body, the fullness of him who fills all in all.

By Grace Through Faith

2 And you were dead in the trespasses and sins 2 in which you once walked, following the course[8] of this world, following the prince of the power of the air,
the spirit that is now at work in the sons of disobedience— 3 among whom we all
once lived in the passions of our flesh, carrying out the desires of the flesh and
the mind, and were by nature children of wrath, like the rest of mankind.[9] 4 But[10]
God, being rich in mercy, because of the great love with which he loved us, 5 even

[1] Some manuscripts *saints who are also faithful* (omitting *in Ephesus*) [2] Or *before him in love, 5having predestined us* [3] Or *he lavished upon us in all wisdom and insight, making known . . .* [4] Greek *him* [5] Or *down payment* [6] Or *until God redeems his possession* [7] Some manuscripts omit *your love* [8] Or *age* [9] Greek *like the rest* [10] Or *And*

A DOXOLOGY OF PRAISE

This text relates the ultimate purpose for which all creation exists and to which all human activity should lead: the praise and glory of God. As seen throughout these verses, God acts according to the purpose of his will (v. 5) and glorious grace (v. 6). The richness of God's grace toward his children is not an obligation. It is, instead, a free act of God that dumbfounds all rational explanation — it is completely awe-inspiring. What reason could God possibly have to redeem sinful humanity? For Adam and his descendants, nothing but condemnation should be expected (Ro 5:12 – 19). There is nothing good in humankind that warrants redemption. In fact, all people have turned aside, choosing to revolt against God's way (Ro 3:9 – 20). In light of humanity's complete rebellion, the idea that God would offer a gift as magnificent as redemption is truly astonishing. And yet, shortly after Adam and Eve first sinned, God promised that he would bring about that redemption (Ge 3:15). He reaffirmed this promise to his servant David (2Sa 7:12 – 17) and at many other times throughout Old Testament history.

The Lord's promises are never empty words. Our triune God has carried out his plan of redemption through specific acts. Knowing that humanity would sin and ruin his creation and bring about the need for redemption, God the Father crafted a plan before the creation of the world (Eph 1:4). He would not leave his precious creation without hope, so he provided a way out of the mess produced by humanity's father, Adam. God the Father's plan required the "God-man" to pay the ultimate penalty for human rebellion. It was a penalty that was too much for humans to pay; only God could do it. Yet, a human had to pay it because it was the failure of Adam that brought about the curses of Genesis 3. Thus, only someone who was fully God and fully human could satisfy the justice due to all of fallen creation.

Jesus, being completely God and also fully human, was the one whose sacrifice provided the necessary redemption. This plan, laid out by the Father and secured by the Son, is now guaranteed by the indwelling of the Spirit (vv. 13 – 14). The Holy Spirit is the seal, or guarantee, of these promises to Christians for all eternity. The word "guarantee" in this text conveys the same idea as that of a wedding ring — a mark of belonging, which reflects God's unbreakable relationship with his people. Thus, the God of glory initiated, secured, and guaranteed a promise that forms a doxology of praise due to the Father, Son, and Holy Spirit.

(Death to Life, continued)

death to life, according to Ephesians 2:10, is meant to result in good works toward one's neighbors out of sheer gratitude to God.

EPHESIANS 3:14–19

THE FULLNESS OF GOD

Paul prayed for God to grant something to his Ephesian readers, something that all Christians should desire with the very essence of their beings: the "fullness of God" (v. 19). As opposed to the emptiness offered by the fleeting—and often unattainable—pleasures of this world, experiencing the fullness of God is much preferred.

Simply surveying the descriptive words Paul used to describe God's fullness is impressive: "riches of his glory," "rooted and grounded in love," "breadth and length and height and depth," "knowledge," and "fullness." Rather than scarcity, Christ's love offers us great riches. In contrast to humiliating embarrassment, Jesus is glorious. Whereas some promises and hopes go unfulfilled or abandoned, Christ's everlasting love and presence are rooted and dwell in the believer. Rather than having limits or strict parameters, God's fullness is boundless. In Christ, believers can know a love beyond any other relationship or possession, something that is unimaginably satisfying. In fact, the reality Paul conveyed so shatters human categories that he said it "surpasses knowledge." Jesus' essence is defined not by emptiness but by completeness. Nothing and no one can separate a believer from the full height and depth of God's love in Christ (Ro 8:38–39).

when we were dead in our trespasses, made us alive together with Christ—by grace you have been saved— 6and raised us up with him and seated us with him in the heavenly places in Christ Jesus, 7so that in the coming ages he might show the immeasurable riches of his grace in kindness toward us in Christ Jesus. 8For by grace you have been saved through faith. And this is not your own doing; it is the gift of God, 9not a result of works, so that no one may boast. 10For we are his workmanship, created in Christ Jesus for good works, which God prepared beforehand, that we should walk in them.

One in Christ

11Therefore remember that at one time you Gentiles in the flesh, called "the uncircumcision" by what is called the circumcision, which is made in the flesh by hands— 12remember that you were at that time separated from Christ, alienated from the commonwealth of Israel and strangers to the covenants of promise, having no hope and without God in the world. 13But now in Christ Jesus you who once were far off have been brought near by the blood of Christ. 14For he himself is our peace, who has made us both one and has broken down in his flesh the dividing wall of hostility 15by abolishing the law of commandments expressed in ordinances, that he might create in himself one new man in place of the two, so making peace, 16and might reconcile us both to God in one body through the cross, thereby killing the hostility. 17And he came and preached peace to you who were far off and peace to those who were near. 18For through him we both have access in one Spirit to the Father. 19So then you are no longer strangers and aliens,[1] but you are fellow citizens with the saints and members of the household of God, 20built on the foundation of the apostles and prophets, Christ Jesus himself being the cornerstone, 21in whom the whole structure, being joined together, grows into a holy temple in the Lord. 22In him you also are being built together into a dwelling place for God by[2] the Spirit.

The Mystery of the Gospel Revealed

3 For this reason I, Paul, a prisoner of Christ Jesus on behalf of you Gentiles— 2assuming that you have heard of the stewardship of God's grace that was given to me for you, 3how the mystery was made known to me by revelation, as I have written briefly. 4When you read this, you can perceive my insight into the mystery of Christ, 5which was not made known to the sons of men in other generations as it has now been revealed to his holy apostles and prophets by the Spirit. 6This mystery is[3] that the Gentiles are fellow heirs, members of the same body, and partakers of the promise in Christ Jesus through the gospel.

7Of this gospel I was made a minister according to the gift of God's grace, which was given me by the working of his power. 8To me, though I am the very least of all the saints, this grace was given, to preach to the Gentiles the unsearchable riches of Christ, 9and to bring to light for everyone what is the plan of the mystery hidden for ages in[4] God, who created all things, 10so that through the church the manifold wisdom of God might now be made known to the rulers and authorities in the heavenly places. 11This was according to the eternal purpose that he has realized in Christ Jesus our Lord, 12in whom we have boldness and access with confidence through our faith in him. 13So I ask you not to lose heart over what I am suffering for you, which is your glory.

Prayer for Spiritual Strength

14For this reason I bow my knees before the Father, 15from whom every family[5] in heaven and on earth is named, 16that according to the riches of his glory he may grant you to be strengthened with power through his Spirit in your inner being, 17so that Christ may dwell in your hearts through faith—that you, being

[1]Or *sojourners* [2]Or *in* [3]The words *This mystery is* are inferred from verse 4 [4]Or *by* [5]Or *from whom all fatherhood*; the Greek word *patria* in verse 15 is closely related to the word for *Father* in verse 14

rooted and grounded in love, 18may have strength to comprehend with all the
saints what is the breadth and length and height and depth, 19and to know the
love of Christ that surpasses knowledge, that you may be filled with all the fullness of God.
20Now to him who is able to do far more abundantly than all that we ask or
think, according to the power at work within us, 21to him be glory in the church
and in Christ Jesus throughout all generations, forever and ever. Amen.

Unity in the Body of Christ

4 I therefore, a prisoner for the Lord, urge you to walk in a manner worthy of
the calling to which you have been called, 2with all humility and gentleness,
with patience, bearing with one another in love, 3eager to maintain the unity of
the Spirit in the bond of peace. 4There is one body and one Spirit—just as you
were called to the one hope that belongs to your call— 5one Lord, one faith, one
baptism, 6one God and Father of all, who is over all and through all and in all.
7But grace was given to each one of us according to the measure of Christ's gift.
8Therefore it says,

> "When he ascended on high he led a host of captives,
> and he gave gifts to men."[1]

9(In saying, "He ascended," what does it mean but that he had also descended into
the lower regions, the earth?[2] 10He who descended is the one who also ascended
far above all the heavens, that he might fill all things.) 11And he gave the apostles,
the prophets, the evangelists, the shepherds[3] and teachers,[4] 12to equip the saints
for the work of ministry, for building up the body of Christ, 13until we all attain
to the unity of the faith and of the knowledge of the Son of God, to mature manhood,[5] to the measure of the stature of the fullness of Christ, 14so that we may
no longer be children, tossed to and fro by the waves and carried about by every
wind of doctrine, by human cunning, by craftiness in deceitful schemes. 15Rather,
speaking the truth in love, we are to grow up in every way into him who is the
head, into Christ, 16from whom the whole body, joined and held together by every
joint with which it is equipped, when each part is working properly, makes the
body grow so that it builds itself up in love.

The New Life

17Now this I say and testify in the Lord, that you must no longer walk as the
Gentiles do, in the futility of their minds. 18They are darkened in their understanding, alienated from the life of God because of the ignorance that is in them,
due to their hardness of heart. 19They have become callous and have given themselves up to sensuality, greedy to practice every kind of impurity. 20But that is
not the way you learned Christ!— 21assuming that you have heard about him and
were taught in him, as the truth is in Jesus, 22to put off your old self,[6] which belongs to your former manner of life and is corrupt through deceitful desires, 23and
to be renewed in the spirit of your minds, 24and to put on the new self, created
after the likeness of God in true righteousness and holiness.
25Therefore, having put away falsehood, let each one of you speak the truth
with his neighbor, for we are members one of another. 26Be angry and do not sin;
do not let the sun go down on your anger, 27and give no opportunity to the devil.
28Let the thief no longer steal, but rather let him labor, doing honest work with his
own hands, so that he may have something to share with anyone in need. 29Let no
corrupting talk come out of your mouths, but only such as is good for building up,
as fits the occasion, that it may give grace to those who hear. 30And do not grieve
the Holy Spirit of God, by whom you were sealed for the day of redemption. 31Let
all bitterness and wrath and anger and clamor and slander be put away from you,

---

[1]The Greek word *anthropoi* can refer to both men and women [2]Or *the lower parts of the earth?*
[3]Or *pastors* [4]Or *the shepherd-teachers* [5]Greek *to a full-grown man* [6]Greek *man*; also verse 24

BLESSINGS AND RESPONSIBILITIES OF BELIEVERS

These verses speak of a stark contrast between believers and unbelievers as Paul encouraged the Ephesian church to live according to their status as God's children. Christians have been enlightened, awakened from the darkness and the ignorant pursuits that consume non-Christians. According to the apostle Paul, nonbelievers walk in futility (v. 17), have darkened understanding (v. 18), are "alienated from the life of God" (v. 18), are ignorant (v. 18), are impure (v. 19), and are "greedy" (v. 19). Not so with a child of God. These descriptions apply to the believer's "old self" and have nothing to do with Christ (vv. 21–22).

The believer's status has completely shifted—from old to new, from death and blindness to life and light. Yet this beautiful gift of the believer's new identity is not simply meant to benefit the individual. This new standing before God also entails obligations as stated in verse 28: Paul commanded the believing thief to steal no longer but rather work with their own hands in order to have means to bless others. In short, the former thief received the blessing of redemption and was therefore obligated to become a blessing to others.

The following list shows the blessing of new life along with certain responsibilities associated with the believer's new status as a child of God.

Blessings Christians Enjoy

- Chosen by God; election (1:4)
- Adoption into God's family (1:5; 2:19)
- Acceptance before God (1:6)
- Forgiveness of sins (1:7)
- Insight into God's will (1:9)
- An eternal inheritance (1:11)
- The seal of the Spirit (1:13; 2:18)
- God's mercy and love (2:4; 3:17–19)
- Wisdom and knowledge (1:17)
- Divine power (1:19–20; 3:16,20)
- Spiritual life (2:1,5)
- The promise of eternal kindness (2:7)
- The knowledge that God's plan for believers is good (2:10)
- Unity and peace with all believers (2:11–18; 3:6)
- Heavenly citizenship (2:19)
- Access to God through Christ (3:12)

Responsibilities of Believers

- To keep the unity of the Spirit (4:3–6)
- To use one's gifts for the church's benefit (4:7–13)
- To keep growing and maturing (4:14–15)
- To put away old, sinful ways (4:17–24; 5:2–14)
- To speak honestly and purely (4:25,29)
- To do what the Spirit leads us to do (4:30)
- To imitate God (5:1)
- To walk in love (5:2)
- To know what is acceptable to the Lord (5:10)
- To make the most of our time (5:16)
- To be filled with the Spirit (5:18)
- To submit to one another (5:21)
- To have marriages that honor God (5:22–33)
- To honor God in family contexts (6:1–4)
- To demonstrate integrity before those who have authority over us, including in the workplace (6:5–9)
- To stand strong against the forces of evil (6:10–18)

along with all malice. 32Be kind to one another, tenderhearted, forgiving one another, as God in Christ forgave you.

Walk in Love

5 Therefore be imitators of God, as beloved children. 2And walk in love, as
Christ loved us and gave himself up for us, a fragrant offering and sacrifice
to God.
3But sexual immorality and all impurity or covetousness must not even be
named among you, as is proper among saints. 4Let there be no filthiness nor foolish talk nor crude joking, which are out of place, but instead let there be thanksgiving. 5For you may be sure of this, that everyone who is sexually immoral or
impure, or who is covetous (that is, an idolater), has no inheritance in the kingdom of Christ and God. 6Let no one deceive you with empty words, for because of
these things the wrath of God comes upon the sons of disobedience. 7Therefore
do not become partners with them; 8for at one time you were darkness, but now
you are light in the Lord. Walk as children of light 9(for the fruit of light is found
in all that is good and right and true), 10and try to discern what is pleasing to the
Lord. 11Take no part in the unfruitful works of darkness, but instead expose them.
12For it is shameful even to speak of the things that they do in secret. 13But when
anything is exposed by the light, it becomes visible, 14for anything that becomes
visible is light. Therefore it says,

"Awake, O sleeper,
    and arise from the dead,
and Christ will shine on you."

15Look carefully then how you walk, not as unwise but as wise, 16making the
best use of the time, because the days are evil. 17Therefore do not be foolish, but
understand what the will of the Lord is. 18And do not get drunk with wine, for that
is debauchery, but be filled with the Spirit, 19addressing one another in psalms
and hymns and spiritual songs, singing and making melody to the Lord with your
heart, 20giving thanks always and for everything to God the Father in the name
of our Lord Jesus Christ, 21submitting to one another out of reverence for Christ.

Wives and Husbands

22Wives, submit to your own husbands, as to the Lord. 23For the husband is the
head of the wife even as Christ is the head of the church, his body, and is himself
its Savior. 24Now as the church submits to Christ, so also wives should submit in
everything to their husbands.
25Husbands, love your wives, as Christ loved the church and gave himself up
for her, 26that he might sanctify her, having cleansed her by the washing of water with the word, 27so that he might present the church to himself in splendor,
without spot or wrinkle or any such thing, that she might be holy and without
blemish.[1] 28In the same way husbands should love their wives as their own bodies.
He who loves his wife loves himself. 29For no one ever hated his own flesh, but
nourishes and cherishes it, just as Christ does the church, 30because we are members of his body. 31"Therefore a man shall leave his father and mother and hold
fast to his wife, and the two shall become one flesh." 32This mystery is profound,
and I am saying that it refers to Christ and the church. 33However, let each one of
you love his wife as himself, and let the wife see that she respects her husband.

Children and Parents

6 Children, obey your parents in the Lord, for this is right. 2"Honor your father
and mother" (this is the first commandment with a promise), 3"that it may go
well with you and that you may live long in the land." 4Fathers, do not provoke your
children to anger, but bring them up in the discipline and instruction of the Lord.

---

[1]Or *holy and blameless*

CHRISTIAN BAPTISM

In the Jewish tradition, ceremonial washing and baptism are key elements of faith. Gentiles receive baptism when they embrace the religion of the Jews, and some Jewish sects regularly practice baptism as a symbol of purification. Serving as an early example of this practice, John the Baptist emphasized baptism as a foundational part of his ministry, calling his listeners to repent and receive baptism as an expression of their sincere faith. At least for part of his ministry, Jesus offered baptism to his followers, though it seems his disciples performed the baptisms rather than Jesus himself (Jn 4:1 – 2). We also know that he received baptism personally (Mk 1:9 – 11). And Paul stated that Jesus' disciples baptized people "into Christ" (Gal 3:27).

A clear shift from Jewish baptism to a distinctively Christian understanding of baptism is recorded in texts such as Acts 18:26 – 27 when Priscilla and Aquila redirected Apollos's understanding of the act. The early church understood baptism in various ways — as a symbol of a person's death to sin (Ro 6:4), of the cleansing from sin (Eph 5:26; Ac 22:16), and of the new life in Christ (Ac 2:41; Ro 6:3).

Throughout church history, the Christian understanding of the command to baptize has been linked to evangelism and making disciples. For instance, Matthew 28:19 has a clear mandate to make disciples, which is the command of this passage that ties together the other three commands — to go, evangelize, and baptize. These three words describe how to make disciples. Specific traditions within the Christian faith have understood the relationship of these three words to making disciples in different ways. When someone is baptized, they join the fellowship of Jesus' disciples, so it makes sense that the Great Commission links evangelism with baptism. Evangelism invites lost people into the community of saints; baptism is a sign of their membership within that community.

Despite the different interpretations of these questions in the Christian faith, one issue is clear: the New Testament modification of Jewish baptism was distinct. For Christians, baptism is linked directly to redemption and being a disciple. In baptism, believers carry out this rite as an act of obedience to genuine faith, signifying a change in the person by burying the Christian's "old Adam" and being raised to life in Christ (Ro 5:12 – 18; 1Co 15:20 – 22; Col 2:11 – 12).

Bondservants and Masters

5Bondservants,[1] obey your earthly masters[2] with fear and trembling, with a sincere heart, as you would Christ, 6not by the way of eye-service, as people-pleasers, but as bondservants of Christ, doing the will of God from the heart, 7rendering service with a good will as to the Lord and not to man, 8knowing that whatever good anyone does, this he will receive back from the Lord, whether he is a bondservant or is free. 9Masters, do the same to them, and stop your threatening, knowing that he who is both their Master[3] and yours is in heaven, and that there is no partiality with him.

The Whole Armor of God

10Finally, be strong in the Lord and in the strength of his might. 11Put on the whole armor of God, that you may be able to stand against the schemes of the devil. 12For we do not wrestle against flesh and blood, but against the rulers, against the authorities, against the cosmic powers over this present darkness, against the spiritual forces of evil in the heavenly places. 13Therefore take up the whole armor of God, that you may be able to withstand in the evil day, and having done all, to stand firm. 14Stand therefore, having fastened on the belt of truth, and having put on the breastplate of righteousness, 15and, as shoes for your feet, having put on the readiness given by the gospel of peace. 16In all circumstances take up the shield of faith, with which you can extinguish all the flaming darts of the evil one; 17and take the helmet of salvation, and the sword of the Spirit, which is the word of God, 18praying at all times in the Spirit, with all prayer and supplication. To that end, keep alert with all perseverance, making supplication for all the saints, 19and also for me, that words may be given to me in opening my mouth boldly to proclaim the mystery of the gospel, 20for which I am an ambassador in chains, that I may declare it boldly, as I ought to speak.

Final Greetings

21So that you also may know how I am and what I am doing, Tychicus the beloved brother and faithful minister in the Lord will tell you everything. 22I have sent him to you for this very purpose, that you may know how we are, and that he may encourage your hearts.

23Peace be to the brothers,[4] and love with faith, from God the Father and the Lord Jesus Christ. 24Grace be with all who love our Lord Jesus Christ with love incorruptible.

EPHESIANS 6:12

SPIRITUAL WARFARE

Ephesians offers a window into the spiritual realities that underlie the struggles and difficulties of life many people face. Sins that people commit against God, themselves, and others spring from a deeper well than simple bad choices or mere circumstances. Believers are engaged in spiritual warfare.

Second Corinthians 10:1–6 (particularly vv. 4–5) offers a helpful addition to Paul's teachings here concerning spiritual warfare. These passages combined offer a picture of the spiritual battle taking place behind the scenes of many human experiences. Arguments against the gospel, failures of biblical morality and lines of unbiblical thinking are not merely the skewed actions and beliefs of humans. According to Paul's teachings, these issues come from the intentional activity of an enemy who influences people each and every day. When a Christian faces overwhelming trials and oppressive circumstances, the evil one may be intimately involved.

Yet, believers must not despair. The Christian has every reason to be confident as he takes up the approach to spiritual warfare prescribed by God. The means of success are the spiritual disciplines commanded by God in Ephesians 6. Using the familiar image of Roman armor, this passage reveals how to do battle against spiritual enemies and outlines the rules of engagement for this specific fight. The end goal of spiritual warfare is to make every thought captive to Christ (2Co 10:5).

[1]For the contextual rendering of the Greek word *doulos*, see Preface; also verse 6; likewise for *bondservant* in verse 8 [2]Or *your masters according to the flesh* [3]Greek *Lord* [4]Or *brothers and sisters*

JESUS: OUR JOY IN SUFFERING

PHILIPPIANS

PHILIPPIANS

PAUL PLANTS PHILIPPIAN CHURCH	PAUL REVISITS PHILIPPI	PAUL IMPRISONED, WRITES PHILIPPIANS
c. AD 50	*c. AD 56*	*c. AD 60 – 62*

Christians can have joy in all circumstances, even in the face of immense suffering. Paul's life testified to the truthfulness of this claim, and he wrote the letter of Philippians to remind the church in Philippi that they, too, could find joy in suffering.

The church in Philippi was established during Paul's second missionary journey, in response to a vision from God instructing Paul to travel to Macedonia and proclaim the gospel. As the first church in Europe, the Philippian church represented a mixture of races, classes, and cultures. Paul wrote to remind the church of the hope they have by virtue of Christ's work.

Throughout the letter, Paul spends considerable time thanking the church for their partnership in the gospel. Clearly, the church has been an encouragement to Paul — through their prayers and financial support. In their generosity, the believers in Philippi became partakers in the missionary advance of the church.

The continued spread of the gospel, however, faced considerable opposition — both in Paul's ministry and in the ongoing work of the church at Philippi. Therefore, Paul reminded the church that suffering should not be seen as evidence of God's lack of care and concern for his church. In fact, suffering is a God-ordained means of spreading the message of salvation. As Christians suffer with joy and find contentment in all things, they have the privilege of modeling a hope that this world cannot provide. This type of joy is only possible if the church has a deep understanding of the gospel and continues to grow in knowledge and discernment of God's will and ways.

The Philippian church needed to look no further than Paul for their example. By the time Paul wrote Philippians, he had suffered greatly for his faith in Jesus and his work to spread the message of the gospel. Writing from a Roman prison, Paul reminds the church that he can find joy in all things. His hope and confidence is not based on his circumstances but is firmly rooted in the inalterable truth of Jesus' work. All people, including believers today, can look to this letter to find encouragement to face life with pervasive joy, even in a fallen world.

I KNOW HOW TO BE BROUGHT LOW, AND I KNOW HOW TO ABOUND. IN ANY AND EVERY CIRCUMSTANCE, I HAVE LEARNED THE SECRET OF FACING PLENTY AND HUNGER, ABUNDANCE AND NEED. I CAN DO ALL THINGS THROUGH HIM WHO STRENGTHENS ME.

Philippians 4:12 – 13

PHILIPPIANS

Greeting

1 Paul and Timothy, servants[1] of Christ Jesus,
To all the saints in Christ Jesus who are at Philippi, with the overseers[2] and
deacons:[3]
2 Grace to you and peace from God our Father and the Lord Jesus Christ.

Thanksgiving and Prayer

3 I thank my God in all my remembrance of you, 4 always in every prayer of
mine for you all making my prayer with joy, 5 because of your partnership in the
gospel from the first day until now. 6 And I am sure of this, that he who began
a good work in you will bring it to completion at the day of Jesus Christ. 7 It is
right for me to feel this way about you all, because I hold you in my heart, for
you are all partakers with me of grace,[4] both in my imprisonment and in the
defense and confirmation of the gospel. 8 For God is my witness, how I yearn for
you all with the affection of Christ Jesus. 9 And it is my prayer that your love may
abound more and more, with knowledge and all discernment, 10 so that you may
approve what is excellent, and so be pure and blameless for the day of Christ,
11 filled with the fruit of righteousness that comes through Jesus Christ, to the
glory and praise of God.

The Advance of the Gospel

12 I want you to know, brothers,[5] that what has happened to me has really
served to advance the gospel, 13 so that it has become known throughout the
whole imperial guard[6] and to all the rest that my imprisonment is for Christ. 14 And
most of the brothers, having become confident in the Lord by my imprisonment,
are much more bold to speak the word[7] without fear.

15 Some indeed preach Christ from envy and rivalry, but others from good will.
16 The latter do it out of love, knowing that I am put here for the defense of the
gospel. 17 The former proclaim Christ out of selfish ambition, not sincerely but
thinking to afflict me in my imprisonment. 18 What then? Only that in every way,
whether in pretense or in truth, Christ is proclaimed, and in that I rejoice.

To Live Is Christ

Yes, and I will rejoice, 19 for I know that through your prayers and the help of
the Spirit of Jesus Christ this will turn out for my deliverance, 20 as it is my eager
expectation and hope that I will not be at all ashamed, but that with full courage
now as always Christ will be honored in my body, whether by life or by death. 21 For
to me to live is Christ, and to die is gain. 22 If I am to live in the flesh, that means
fruitful labor for me. Yet which I shall choose I cannot tell. 23 I am hard pressed
between the two. My desire is to depart and be with Christ, for that is far better.
24 But to remain in the flesh is more necessary on your account. 25 Convinced of
this, I know that I will remain and continue with you all, for your progress and
joy in the faith, 26 so that in me you may have ample cause to glory in Christ Jesus,
because of my coming to you again.

27 Only let your manner of life be worthy[8] of the gospel of Christ, so that
whether I come and see you or am absent, I may hear of you that you are standing

---

[1] For the contextual rendering of the Greek word *doulos*, see Preface [2] Or *bishops*; Greek *episkopoi* [3] Or *servants*, or *ministers*; Greek *diakonoi* [4] Or *you all have fellowship with me in grace* [5] Or *brothers and sisters*. In New Testament usage, depending on the context, the plural Greek word *adelphoi* (translated "brothers") may refer either to *brothers* or to *brothers and sisters*; also verse 14 [6] Greek *in the whole praetorium* [7] Some manuscripts add *of God* [8] Greek *Only behave as citizens worthy*

firm in one spirit, with one mind striving side by side for the faith of the gospel, 28and not frightened in anything by your opponents. This is a clear sign to them of their destruction, but of your salvation, and that from God. 29For it has been granted to you that for the sake of Christ you should not only believe in him but also suffer for his sake, 30engaged in the same conflict that you saw I had and now hear that I still have.

Christ's Example of Humility

2 So if there is any encouragement in Christ, any comfort from love, any participation in the Spirit, any affection and sympathy, 2complete my joy by being of the same mind, having the same love, being in full accord and of one mind. 3Do nothing from selfish ambition or conceit, but in humility count others more significant than yourselves. 4Let each of you look not only to his own interests, but also to the interests of others. 5Have this mind among yourselves, which is yours in Christ Jesus,[1] 6who, though he was in the form of God, did not count equality with God a thing to be grasped,[2] 7but emptied himself, by taking the form of a servant,[3] being born in the likeness of men. 8And being found in human form, he humbled himself by becoming obedient to the point of death, even death on a cross. 9Therefore God has highly exalted him and bestowed on him the name that is above every name, 10so that at the name of Jesus every knee should bow, in heaven and on earth and under the earth, 11and every tongue confess that Jesus Christ is Lord, to the glory of God the Father.

Lights in the World

12Therefore, my beloved, as you have always obeyed, so now, not only as in my presence but much more in my absence, work out your own salvation with fear and trembling, 13for it is God who works in you, both to will and to work for his good pleasure.

14Do all things without grumbling or disputing, 15that you may be blameless and innocent, children of God without blemish in the midst of a crooked and twisted generation, among whom you shine as lights in the world, 16holding fast to the word of life, so that in the day of Christ I may be proud that I did not run in vain or labor in vain. 17Even if I am to be poured out as a drink offering upon the sacrificial offering of your faith, I am glad and rejoice with you all. 18Likewise you also should be glad and rejoice with me.

Timothy and Epaphroditus

19I hope in the Lord Jesus to send Timothy to you soon, so that I too may be cheered by news of you. 20For I have no one like him, who will be genuinely concerned for your welfare. 21For they all seek their own interests, not those of Jesus Christ. 22But you know Timothy's[4] proven worth, how as a son[5] with a father he has served with me in the gospel. 23I hope therefore to send him just as soon as I see how it will go with me, 24and I trust in the Lord that shortly I myself will come also.

25I have thought it necessary to send to you Epaphroditus my brother and fellow worker and fellow soldier, and your messenger and minister to my need, 26for he has been longing for you all and has been distressed because you heard that he was ill. 27Indeed he was ill, near to death. But God had mercy on him, and not only on him but on me also, lest I should have sorrow upon sorrow. 28I am the more eager to send him, therefore, that you may rejoice at seeing him again, and that I may be less anxious. 29So receive him in the Lord with all joy, and honor such men, 30for he nearly died[6] for the work of Christ, risking his life to complete what was lacking in your service to me.

[1]Or *which was also in Christ Jesus* [2]Or *a thing to be held on to for advantage* [3]Or *slave* (for the contextual rendering of the Greek word *doulos*, see Preface) [4]Greek *his* [5]Greek *child* [6]Or *he drew near to the point of death*; compare verse 8

PHILIPPIANS 2:6–11

TRUE HUMILITY

The words of this beloved passage may have existed as a hymn for the early church. Paul's description of Jesus is quite lyrical — a crescendo of praise for the matchless Son of God. Jesus is celebrated as the One worthy to receive the highest place because he chose to become a servant. He is the epitome of true humility.

Jesus did not stop being God, but he willfully released the glorious entitlements of his position and power. He laid aside his deserved privilege as God's Son in order to accomplish the will of his Father. Believers begin to appreciate the magnitude of Jesus' choice to empty himself when they contrast it to the immeasurable honor due his name. The One worthy of the finest throne began life on earth by being placed in a manger. The Word became flesh and lived among humans (Jn 1:14). The eternal King became a servant.

Jesus served humankind by yielding to God's plan for atonement on the gruesome cross of Calvary. Christ sacrificed himself to redeem humanity from the debt of sin. Though Jesus never sinned, he took the place of the guilty, absorbing punishment that he did not deserve (2Co 5:21). Mocked and exposed, Jesus experienced the shame and humiliation of public execution. Death by crucifixion was agonizing, yet Jesus endured it with a vision of greater purposes. He willingly endured the cross because of the "joy that was set before him" (Heb 12:2).

Jesus served the Father by making a way for people to be reconciled with their Creator (2Co 5:18). God gave Jesus to the world because he loved people and desired a relationship with them. Jesus bridged the separation between God and humankind. At the same time, the cross provided a public declaration of God's unwavering commitment to his Word — finally dealing with sin long passed over (Ro 3:25). Christ's sacrifice and victorious resurrection also won worshipers for God — those who believe and find new life and joy in him.

In recognition of Jesus' obedience through restraint and suffering, the Father gave him the highest place, establishing his name above every other name. And a day is coming when every person in all of history will bow to the Son who served. All will humble themselves to exalt and praise Christ the Lord (Php 2:10–11).

Righteousness Through Faith in Christ

3 Finally, my brothers,[1] rejoice in the Lord. To write the same things to you is no trouble to me and is safe for you.

2 Look out for the dogs, look out for the evildoers, look out for those who mutilate the flesh. 3 For we are the circumcision, who worship by the Spirit of God[2] and glory in Christ Jesus and put no confidence in the flesh— 4 though I myself have reason for confidence in the flesh also. If anyone else thinks he has reason for confidence in the flesh, I have more: 5 circumcised on the eighth day, of the people of Israel, of the tribe of Benjamin, a Hebrew of Hebrews; as to the law, a Pharisee; 6 as to zeal, a persecutor of the church; as to righteousness under the law,[3] blameless. 7 But whatever gain I had, I counted as loss for the sake of Christ. 8 Indeed, I count everything as loss because of the surpassing worth of knowing Christ Jesus my Lord. For his sake I have suffered the loss of all things and count them as rubbish, in order that I may gain Christ 9 and be found in him, not having a righteousness of my own that comes from the law, but that which comes through faith in Christ, the righteousness from God that depends on faith— 10 that I may know him and the power of his resurrection, and may share his sufferings, becoming like him in his death, 11 that by any means possible I may attain the resurrection from the dead.

Straining Toward the Goal

12 Not that I have already obtained this or am already perfect, but I press on to make it my own, because Christ Jesus has made me his own. 13 Brothers, I do not consider that I have made it my own. But one thing I do: forgetting what lies behind and straining forward to what lies ahead, 14 I press on toward the goal for the prize of the upward call of God in Christ Jesus. 15 Let those of us who are mature think this way, and if in anything you think otherwise, God will reveal that also to you. 16 Only let us hold true to what we have attained.

17 Brothers, join in imitating me, and keep your eyes on those who walk according to the example you have in us. 18 For many, of whom I have often told you and now tell you even with tears, walk as enemies of the cross of Christ. 19 Their end is destruction, their god is their belly, and they glory in their shame, with minds set on earthly things. 20 But our citizenship is in heaven, and from it we await a Savior, the Lord Jesus Christ, 21 who will transform our lowly body to be like his glorious body, by the power that enables him even to subject all things to himself.

4 Therefore, my brothers,[4] whom I love and long for, my joy and crown, stand firm thus in the Lord, my beloved.

Exhortation, Encouragement, and Prayer

2 I entreat Euodia and I entreat Syntyche to agree in the Lord. 3 Yes, I ask you also, true companion,[5] help these women, who have labored[6] side by side with me in the gospel together with Clement and the rest of my fellow workers, whose names are in the book of life.

4 Rejoice in the Lord always; again I will say, rejoice. 5 Let your reasonableness[7] be known to everyone. The Lord is at hand; 6 do not be anxious about anything, but in everything by prayer and supplication with thanksgiving let your requests be made known to God. 7 And the peace of God, which surpasses all understanding, will guard your hearts and your minds in Christ Jesus.

8 Finally, brothers, whatever is true, whatever is honorable, whatever is just, whatever is pure, whatever is lovely, whatever is commendable, if there is any excellence, if there is anything worthy of praise, think about these things. 9 What you have learned[8] and received and heard and seen in me—practice these things, and the God of peace will be with you.

---

[1] Or *brothers and sisters*; also verses 13, 17 [2] Some manuscripts *God in spirit* [3] Greek *in the law* [4] Or *brothers and sisters*; also verses 8, 21 [5] Or *loyal Syzygus*; Greek *true yokefellow* [6] Or *strived* (see 1:27) [7] Or *gentleness* [8] Or *these things—*[9] *which things you have also learned*

PHILIPPIANS 3:8–9

KNOWING CHRIST

The apostle Paul's standard summary of a Christian is one who is "in Christ." All of salvation takes place in Christ. Before the creation, believers were chosen in him (Eph 1:4). Through faith, Christians are justified in him (Ro 5:1) and sealed in him (Eph 1:13). Throughout life, believers are sanctified in him (2Co 3:18).

Chapter 3 of Philippians highlights Paul's intense desire to be found in Christ when his life comes to an end (Php 3:8–9). To be "in Christ" is to trust in his work on the cross as the basis for salvation. Noah survived judgment in the ark that God provided (Ge 6:17–18). In a similar way, sinful people can pass through the coming judgment by believing in Christ, the one and only Savior. For Christians, their present experience of life is in Christ. When death comes, they will die in Christ. When God initiates the return of Christ, those who believe will be made alive in him and reign with him (2Ti 2:12).

God's Provision

10I rejoiced in the Lord greatly that now at length you have revived your concern for me. You were indeed concerned for me, but you had no opportunity. 11Not
that I am speaking of being in need, for I have learned, in whatever situation I am,
to be content. 12I know how to be brought low, and I know how to abound. In any
and every circumstance, I have learned the secret of facing plenty and hunger,
abundance and need. 13I can do all things through him who strengthens me.
14Yet it was kind of you to share[1] my trouble. 15And you Philippians yourselves
know that in the beginning of the gospel, when I left Macedonia, no church entered into partnership with me in giving and receiving, except you only. 16Even in
Thessalonica you sent me help for my needs once and again. 17Not that I seek the
gift, but I seek the fruit that increases to your credit.[2] 18I have received full payment, and more. I am well supplied, having received from Epaphroditus the gifts
you sent, a fragrant offering, a sacrifice acceptable and pleasing to God. 19And my
God will supply every need of yours according to his riches in glory in Christ Jesus.
20To our God and Father be glory forever and ever. Amen.

Final Greetings

21Greet every saint in Christ Jesus. The brothers who are with me greet you.
22All the saints greet you, especially those of Caesar's household.
23The grace of the Lord Jesus Christ be with your spirit.

PHILIPPIANS 4:19

ALL WE NEED

Humans are fundamentally needy creatures—newborns instinctively gasp for oxygen, kids hunger for afternoon snacks, high schoolers seek friends and popularity, young adults chase careers, and so on. People are needy by design—physically, socially, emotionally, and most importantly, spiritually. God is intimately acquainted with the needs of his people. As all-knowing God, he anticipates his people's needs; as a loving Father, he tenderly provides (Mt 7:7–11).

Having a laugh with friends or grabbing a bite to eat cannot result in lasting satisfaction. The deepest needs are of the soul, not the body. Thankfully, this passage proclaims that these needs can be satisfied through Jesus, who is rich in glory. The more we grow in our faith in Christ, the more our needs are satisfied by the riches he offers. Paul confirmed that the God of the universe is able: the One who created humans will also be their continuing resource. God can be trusted to take care of those who believe in Christ and who follow him with their lives. His supply of mercy is endless—flowing from the glory that is in Christ Jesus, who left heaven to show love and mercy to rebels. The God whom believers trust for provision is the same God with the power to conquer sin and death. He can meet any need.

[1]Or *have fellowship in* [2]Or *I seek the profit that accrues to your account*

JESUS: OUR HEAD OF ALL THINGS

COLOSSIANS

COLOSSIANS

PAUL EVANGELIZES COLOSSAE *c. AD 54–56*	PAUL IMPRISONED, WRITES COLOSSIANS *c. AD 60–62*	PAUL MARTYRED IN ROME *c. AD 67–68*

Jesus is the supreme head of all things (2:10). As the image of the invisible God, Jesus shows the world what God is like. He also demonstrates the scope of the rule and reign of God. God is not some ill-defined deity, unseen and unknowable. In his grace, God has made himself known in the person of Christ.

These truths lie at the heart of Paul's letter to the church at Colossae. This church, located about a hundred miles east of Ephesus, was likely evangelized during Paul's three-year stay in that region. Like many of the churches Paul established, false teachers wreaked havoc on the church after his departure. Some apparently taught that the works of the law were vital for salvation. Others seemingly promoted a form of mysticism that affirmed Jesus as a higher being but not God.

While in prison in Rome, Paul wrote this letter to confront these two errors. This letter mirrors a similar one Paul sent to the church at Ephesus, leading many to presume that they were written around the same time. Both follow the classic outline common to many of Paul's writings. They begin with an introduction and word of encouragement, followed by a summary of the gospel, and conclude with the way these truths should shape all of life.

Colossians is unique in its emphasis on the cosmic rule of Christ. Jesus is the head of his people, the church. He leads them as a benevolent king, who rules over his beloved people with sacrificial love. But his reign does not stop with the church. He is the head over all of creation — with authority over the natural world and also over the principalities and authorities of the unseen world. He is the head of all and the one to whom all allegiance is due (2:10).

Since Jesus is the head of all things, the church at Colossae can depend on him alone for salvation. Works of the flesh do not save — only the singular work of Christ in the flesh can save. Paul reminds the church to seek the things that are above and worship God alone because he is their life and only hope (3:1 – 4). This worship should permeate every aspect of the life of the church. As Paul does elsewhere, he called the church's attention to the various implications of the gospel message. This includes that Jesus, as the head of all things, deserves all worship and praise (3:1 — 4:6).

FOR BY HIM ALL THINGS WERE CREATED, IN HEAVEN AND ON EARTH, VISIBLE AND INVISIBLE, WHETHER THRONES OR DOMINIONS OR RULERS OR AUTHORITIES — ALL THINGS WERE CREATED THROUGH HIM AND FOR HIM.

Colossians 1:16

COLOSSIANS

Greeting

1 Paul, an apostle of Christ Jesus by the will of God, and Timothy our brother,
2 To the saints and faithful brothers[1] in Christ at Colossae:
Grace to you and peace from God our Father.

Thanksgiving and Prayer

3 We always thank God, the Father of our Lord Jesus Christ, when we pray
for you, 4 since we heard of your faith in Christ Jesus and of the love that you
have for all the saints, 5 because of the hope laid up for you in heaven. Of this
you have heard before in the word of the truth, the gospel, 6 which has come to
you, as indeed in the whole world it is bearing fruit and increasing—as it also
does among you, since the day you heard it and understood the grace of God in
truth, 7 just as you learned it from Epaphras our beloved fellow servant.[2] He is
a faithful minister of Christ on your[3] behalf 8 and has made known to us your
love in the Spirit.

9 And so, from the day we heard, we have not ceased to pray for you, asking
that you may be filled with the knowledge of his will in all spiritual wisdom and
understanding, 10 so as to walk in a manner worthy of the Lord, fully pleasing to
him: bearing fruit in every good work and increasing in the knowledge of God;
11 being strengthened with all power, according to his glorious might, for all endurance and patience with joy; 12 giving thanks[4] to the Father, who has qualified you[5]
to share in the inheritance of the saints in light. 13 He has delivered us from the
domain of darkness and transferred us to the kingdom of his beloved Son, 14 in
whom we have redemption, the forgiveness of sins.

The Preeminence of Christ

15 He is the image of the invisible God, the firstborn of all creation. 16 For
by[6] him all things were created, in heaven and on earth, visible and invisible,
whether thrones or dominions or rulers or authorities—all things were created
through him and for him. 17 And he is before all things, and in him all things hold
together. 18 And he is the head of the body, the church. He is the beginning, the
firstborn from the dead, that in everything he might be preeminent. 19 For in him
all the fullness of God was pleased to dwell, 20 and through him to reconcile to
himself all things, whether on earth or in heaven, making peace by the blood of
his cross.

21 And you, who once were alienated and hostile in mind, doing evil deeds,
22 he has now reconciled in his body of flesh by his death, in order to present you
holy and blameless and above reproach before him, 23 if indeed you continue in
the faith, stable and steadfast, not shifting from the hope of the gospel that you
heard, which has been proclaimed in all creation[7] under heaven, and of which I,
Paul, became a minister.

Paul's Ministry to the Church

24 Now I rejoice in my sufferings for your sake, and in my flesh I am filling up
what is lacking in Christ's afflictions for the sake of his body, that is, the church,
25 of which I became a minister according to the stewardship from God that was
given to me for you, to make the word of God fully known, 26 the mystery hidden

[1] Or *brothers and sisters*. In New Testament usage, depending on the context, the plural Greek word *adelphoi* (translated "brothers") may refer either to *brothers* or to *brothers and sisters* [2] For the contextual rendering of the Greek word *sundoulos*, see Preface [3] Some manuscripts *our* [4] Or *patience, with joy giving thanks* [5] Some manuscripts *us* [6] That is, by means of; or *in* [7] Or *to every creature*

THE PREEMINENCE OF CHRIST

Everyone worships someone or something. All people give someone or something first place in their lives. The apostle Paul was determined that the church at Colossae give Jesus Christ preeminence in everything. Paul used what is most likely an early Christian hymn to explain how Jesus is preeminent in the entire universe and worthy of the church's allegiance and affection.

The beginning of the hymn explains that when people see Jesus, they see God. Remarkably, even in his human form, Jesus is God. Jesus himself affirmed this when he said, "I and the Father are one" (Jn 10:30). Jesus' deity displays his preeminence. Paul then used a phrase that has often been misunderstood. He said Jesus is the "firstborn of all creation" (Col 1:15). At times, people have mistakenly taken this to mean that God the Father created the Son. The immediate context reveals otherwise, describing Jesus as the Creator of all things, who existed "before all things" (vv. 16–17). Additionally, John affirmed that Jesus was in existence with the Father at the very beginning: "In the beginning was the Word, and the Word was with God, and the Word was God. He was in the beginning with God" (Jn 1:1–2). The description of Jesus as "firstborn" points to his exalted position. In the Jewish context, "firstborn" implied the highest rank and value.

Paul then pointed to the fact that Jesus created the universe. He hoped to stretch his readers' minds by leading them to think about invisible things that Jesus created, including the unseen angelic realm. When Christians ponder all of creation, galaxies upon galaxies, unexplored oceans, and the complexity of the human body, they only begin to understand the majesty and power of Jesus. All of creation exists to bring glory to God.

Jesus is preeminent in his church. Jesus creates, sustains, and leads his church as its head. Every church has its challenges and problems; however, because the church belongs to Jesus, Christians should have a heart to build up the church rather than tear it down. Jesus' preeminence shines brightly through his work of reconciling all things through his death on the cross. Jesus' death and resurrection are among the ultimate displays of his preeminence. Jesus is greater than humanity's sin. Jesus is greater than death. Jesus is greater than the devil. Indeed, in a world that often feels out of control, Christians can rejoice and take hope that Jesus Christ is reconciling all things to the Father and will bring peace to the cosmos.

for ages and generations but now revealed to his saints. 27To them God chose to make known how great among the Gentiles are the riches of the glory of this mystery, which is Christ in you, the hope of glory. 28Him we proclaim, warning everyone and teaching everyone with all wisdom, that we may present everyone mature in Christ. 29For this I toil, struggling with all his energy that he powerfully works within me.

2 For I want you to know how great a struggle I have for you and for those at Laodicea and for all who have not seen me face to face, 2that their hearts may be encouraged, being knit together in love, to reach all the riches of full assurance of understanding and the knowledge of God's mystery, which is Christ, 3in whom are hidden all the treasures of wisdom and knowledge. 4I say this in order that no one may delude you with plausible arguments. 5For though I am absent in body, yet I am with you in spirit, rejoicing to see your good order and the firmness of your faith in Christ.

Alive in Christ

6Therefore, as you received Christ Jesus the Lord, so walk in him, 7rooted and built up in him and established in the faith, just as you were taught, abounding in thanksgiving.

8See to it that no one takes you captive by philosophy and empty deceit, according to human tradition, according to the elemental spirits[1] of the world, and not according to Christ. 9For in him the whole fullness of deity dwells bodily, 10and you have been filled in him, who is the head of all rule and authority. 11In him also you were circumcised with a circumcision made without hands, by putting off the body of the flesh, by the circumcision of Christ, 12having been buried with him in baptism, in which you were also raised with him through faith in the powerful working of God, who raised him from the dead. 13And you, who were dead in your trespasses and the uncircumcision of your flesh, God made alive together with him, having forgiven us all our trespasses, 14by canceling the record of debt that stood against us with its legal demands. This he set aside, nailing it to the cross. 15He disarmed the rulers and authorities[2] and put them to open shame, by triumphing over them in him.[3]

Let No One Disqualify You

16Therefore let no one pass judgment on you in questions of food and drink, or with regard to a festival or a new moon or a Sabbath. 17These are a shadow of the things to come, but the substance belongs to Christ. 18Let no one disqualify you, insisting on asceticism and worship of angels, going on in detail about visions,[4] puffed up without reason by his sensuous mind, 19and not holding fast to the Head, from whom the whole body, nourished and knit together through its joints and ligaments, grows with a growth that is from God.

20If with Christ you died to the elemental spirits of the world, why, as if you were still alive in the world, do you submit to regulations— 21"Do not handle, Do not taste, Do not touch" 22(referring to things that all perish as they are used)— according to human precepts and teachings? 23These have indeed an appearance of wisdom in promoting self-made religion and asceticism and severity to the body, but they are of no value in stopping the indulgence of the flesh.

Put On the New Self

3 If then you have been raised with Christ, seek the things that are above, where Christ is, seated at the right hand of God. 2Set your minds on things that are above, not on things that are on earth. 3For you have died, and your life is hidden with Christ in God. 4When Christ who is your[5] life appears, then you also will appear with him in glory.

[1]Or *elementary principles*; also verse 20 [2]Probably demonic rulers and authorities [3]Or *in it* (that is, the cross) [4]Or *about the things he has seen* [5]Some manuscripts *our*

COLOSSIANS 2:11–14

SALVATION IS A MIRACULOUS ACT

Salvation is a miracle. Scripture paints a bleak picture of humanity's spiritual condition. The problem is not just that people are bad. The problem is that people are spiritually dead. Every person needs a spiritual resurrection to be able to know God and live for him. The good news is that Jesus Christ provides spiritual resurrection.

In the Bible, circumcision usually refers to the practice of cutting away the foreskin of males on the eighth day after birth, signifying the child's entrance into the Old Testament community of faith. Paul picked up on this well-known imagery when he wrote, "in him also you were circumcised with a circumcision made without hands" to describe the miraculous act of being made alive spiritually in Christ (v. 11). This echoes the promise made by God in Ezekiel 36:26: "And I will give you a new heart, and a new spirit I will put within you. And I will remove the heart of stone from your flesh and give you a heart of flesh." It is only because Jesus died and rose again that people can experience life today, and the resurrection of their bodies in the future. Anyone can experience spiritual resurrection by placing their faith in Jesus Christ. Jesus does not just help people become better people; he raises people from spiritual death to new life. Salvation is at the hands of God alone. Mankind cannot do any level of work that would bring approval in the sight of God. No ritual, whether ancient or modern, can replace the gracious work of God in the salvation of humanity.

5Put to death therefore what is earthly in you:[1] sexual immorality, impurity, passion, evil desire, and covetousness, which is idolatry. 6On account of these the wrath of God is coming.[2] 7In these you too once walked, when you were living in them. 8But now you must put them all away: anger, wrath, malice, slander, and obscene talk from your mouth. 9Do not lie to one another, seeing that you have put off the old self[3] with its practices 10and have put on the new self, which is being renewed in knowledge after the image of its creator. 11Here there is not Greek and Jew, circumcised and uncircumcised, barbarian, Scythian, slave,[4] free; but Christ is all, and in all.

12Put on then, as God's chosen ones, holy and beloved, compassionate hearts, kindness, humility, meekness, and patience, 13bearing with one another and, if one has a complaint against another, forgiving each other; as the Lord has forgiven you, so you also must forgive. 14And above all these put on love, which binds everything together in perfect harmony. 15And let the peace of Christ rule in your hearts, to which indeed you were called in one body. And be thankful. 16Let the word of Christ dwell in you richly, teaching and admonishing one another in all wisdom, singing psalms and hymns and spiritual songs, with thankfulness in your hearts to God. 17And whatever you do, in word or deed, do everything in the name of the Lord Jesus, giving thanks to God the Father through him.

Rules for Christian Households

18Wives, submit to your husbands, as is fitting in the Lord. 19Husbands, love your wives, and do not be harsh with them. 20Children, obey your parents in everything, for this pleases the Lord. 21Fathers, do not provoke your children, lest they become discouraged. 22Bondservants, obey in everything those who are your earthly masters,[5] not by way of eye-service, as people-pleasers, but with sincerity of heart, fearing the Lord. 23Whatever you do, work heartily, as for the Lord and not for men, 24knowing that from the Lord you will receive the inheritance as your reward. You are serving the Lord Christ. 25For the wrongdoer will be paid back for the wrong he has done, and there is no partiality.

4 Masters, treat your bondservants[6] justly and fairly, knowing that you also have a Master in heaven.

Further Instructions

2Continue steadfastly in prayer, being watchful in it with thanksgiving. 3At the same time, pray also for us, that God may open to us a door for the word, to declare the mystery of Christ, on account of which I am in prison— 4that I may make it clear, which is how I ought to speak.

5Walk in wisdom toward outsiders, making the best use of the time. 6Let your speech always be gracious, seasoned with salt, so that you may know how you ought to answer each person.

Final Greetings

7Tychicus will tell you all about my activities. He is a beloved brother and faithful minister and fellow servant[7] in the Lord. 8I have sent him to you for this very purpose, that you may know how we are and that he may encourage your hearts, 9and with him Onesimus, our faithful and beloved brother, who is one of you. They will tell you of everything that has taken place here.

10Aristarchus my fellow prisoner greets you, and Mark the cousin of Barnabas (concerning whom you have received instructions—if he comes to you, welcome him), 11and Jesus who is called Justus. These are the only men of the circumcision

[1]Greek *therefore your members that are on the earth* [2]Some manuscripts add *upon the sons of disobedience* [3]Greek *man*; also as supplied in verse 10 [4]For the contextual rendering of the Greek word *doulos*, see Preface; likewise for *Bondservants* in verse 22 [5]Or *your masters according to the flesh* [6]For the contextual rendering of the Greek word *doulos*, see Preface; likewise for *servant* in verse 12 [7]For the contextual rendering of the Greek word *sundoulos*, see Preface

COLOSSIANS 4:2–6

DEVOTED TO PRAYER

Almost every Christian knows that prayer is important. Even many unbelievers think prayer is a good thing. Devoting oneself to prayer, however, is a challenge for many people. Nevertheless, this is exactly what Paul instructed the church at Colossae to do as he concluded his letter. Paul gave an immediate explanation of what he meant by "continue steadfastly in prayer," when he followed up with "being watchful . . . with thanksgiving" (v. 2). Remaining watchful for the "flaming darts of the evil one" (Eph 6:16) keeps believers in a posture of prayerful dependence upon God.

Paul then directed the church to pray for his proclamation of Jesus. Specifically, he needed opportunities (open doors) and God's help in making sure he proclaimed the mystery of Jesus with clarity.

Jesus is the very One who makes prayer possible. Jesus paved the way for prayer to be possible by removing the sin barrier between God and humanity through his death, burial, and resurrection. The author of Hebrews said it this way: "Since we have a great priest over the house of God, let us draw near with a true heart in full assurance of faith, with our hearts sprinkled clean from an evil conscience and our bodies washed with pure water" (Heb 10:21–22). Jesus makes prayer possible, allowing Christians to draw near to God with the confidence that God will hear and act according to his will.

RENEWAL IN THE IMAGE OF GOD

Humanity has been blessed with the unique privilege of being created in the image of God. People alone enjoy the special blessing of reflecting the image of God like a mirror. Unfortunately, sin has changed the reflection of God in humanity, twisting and distorting his reflection like a fun-house mirror. His image is still there, yet it is not in focus. Indeed, sin has darkened the hearts and minds of all of humanity. Out of these darkened hearts flow all kinds of sins: "sexual immorality, impurity, passion, evil desire, and covetousness, which is idolatry ... anger, wrath, malice, slander, and obscene talk" (vv. 5,8). Paul warned that the wrath of God is coming because of sins like these. But Jesus changes everything.

Jesus offers forgiveness of sin and the removal of God's wrath. In his grace, God sent Jesus to rescue people from their sin. When people become believers by repenting of their sin and trusting in Jesus Christ, God's Spirit comes to dwell inside them. The Holy Spirit then begins to transform believers from the inside out, helping them to repent of further sin and to walk in holiness. Paul described these radical changes as "putting to death" the old self and "putting on" the new self. The old self consists of the attitudes and lifestyles that are governed by sin. The new self consists of the new attitude and lifestyle that are governed by Jesus and empowered by the indwelling of the Holy Spirit. The result of putting off the old self and putting on the new self is a renewed reflection of the image of God. As believers are increasingly renewed in the image of God, the beauty, love, and holiness of God shines through and becomes visible to other people.

Essentially, Paul's challenge to Christians is to become who they are. Paul wrote, "Therefore, if anyone is in Christ, he is a new creation. The old has passed away; behold, the new has come" (2Co 5:17). For the Christian, recognizing that Jesus has already made him or her new is foundational to the daily process of putting on the new self.

among my fellow workers for the kingdom of God, and they have been a comfort
to me. 12 Epaphras, who is one of you, a servant of Christ Jesus, greets you, always
struggling on your behalf in his prayers, that you may stand mature and fully assured in all the will of God. 13 For I bear him witness that he has worked hard for
you and for those in Laodicea and in Hierapolis. 14 Luke the beloved physician
greets you, as does Demas. 15 Give my greetings to the brothers[1] at Laodicea, and
to Nympha and the church in her house. 16 And when this letter has been read
among you, have it also read in the church of the Laodiceans; and see that you
also read the letter from Laodicea. 17 And say to Archippus, "See that you fulfill the
ministry that you have received in the Lord."

18 I, Paul, write this greeting with my own hand. Remember my chains. Grace
be with you.

[1] Or *brothers and sisters*

JESUS: OUR SOURCE OF COMFORT

1 THESSALONIANS

1 THESSALONIANS

THESSALONIAN CHURCH IS STARTED	PAUL WRITES 1 THESSALONIANS	PAUL MARTYRED IN ROME
c. AD 51	*c. AD 51*	*c. AD 67 – 68*

Lives were changed everywhere the gospel message was proclaimed. Paul and Silas saw many converted to faith in Jesus Christ in Thessalonica, a wealthy trade center on the continent of Europe. The church that developed from these converts was filled with young believers who needed grounding in their newly formed faith. After leaving Thessalonica, Paul sent his protégé Timothy back to the church to assess their health and spiritual vitality. Timothy rejoined Paul in Corinth and brought with him an encouraging report about the faithfulness of the church, even in the face of continued persecution. As with all new converts, however, they were filled with questions concerning the nature of the gospel and particularly the second coming of Jesus. Paul wrote his first letter to the church to answer these questions and to encourage the church to continue to grow, mature, and persevere as they await the coming of Christ.

The hope in Christ's return intensified due to the death of a number of believers in the church. Some may have believed that Jesus would return during their lifetimes and usher in his full and total reign on earth. This had not yet happened, and some in the church had begun to doubt that it would.

Paul wrote to encourage the church that they should not be dismayed by the delay in Christ's second coming. He will return, as he had promised; he will give his people renewed, resurrected bodies, and they will reign with him forever (4:13 – 18). This promise was meant to comfort the church in their mourning and motivate them to keep watch for his return (5:1 – 11).

Paul exhorts the church to live godly lives in the meantime, as they anticipate this coming. They should not lose heart in light of the persecution they were facing or doubt the truthfulness of Paul's message because of the influence of false teachers. The church must persevere, knowing that nothing they face in this world can take away the hope they have in Christ. The One who made these promises is faithful, as he has been throughout history, and he will surely accomplish all that he sets out to do (5:24).

GIVE THANKS IN ALL CIRCUMSTANCES;
FOR THIS IS THE WILL OF GOD
IN CHRIST JESUS FOR YOU.

---

1 Thessalonians 5:18

1 THESSALONIANS

Greeting

1 Paul, Silvanus, and Timothy,
To the church of the Thessalonians in God the Father and the Lord Jesus Christ:
Grace to you and peace.

The Thessalonians' Faith and Example

2We give thanks to God always for all of you, constantly[1] mentioning you in
our prayers, 3remembering before our God and Father your work of faith and
labor of love and steadfastness of hope in our Lord Jesus Christ. 4For we know,
brothers[2] loved by God, that he has chosen you, 5because our gospel came to you
not only in word, but also in power and in the Holy Spirit and with full conviction. You know what kind of men we proved to be among you for your sake. 6And
you became imitators of us and of the Lord, for you received the word in much
affliction, with the joy of the Holy Spirit, 7so that you became an example to all
the believers in Macedonia and in Achaia. 8For not only has the word of the Lord
sounded forth from you in Macedonia and Achaia, but your faith in God has gone
forth everywhere, so that we need not say anything. 9For they themselves report
concerning us the kind of reception we had among you, and how you turned to
God from idols to serve the living and true God, 10and to wait for his Son from
heaven, whom he raised from the dead, Jesus who delivers us from the wrath to
come.

Paul's Ministry to the Thessalonians

2 For you yourselves know, brothers,[3] that our coming to you was not in vain.
2But though we had already suffered and been shamefully treated at Philippi,
as you know, we had boldness in our God to declare to you the gospel of God in
the midst of much conflict. 3For our appeal does not spring from error or impurity or any attempt to deceive, 4but just as we have been approved by God to be
entrusted with the gospel, so we speak, not to please man, but to please God who
tests our hearts. 5For we never came with words of flattery,[4] as you know, nor with
a pretext for greed—God is witness. 6Nor did we seek glory from people, whether
from you or from others, though we could have made demands as apostles of
Christ. 7But we were gentle[5] among you, like a nursing mother taking care of her
own children. 8So, being affectionately desirous of you, we were ready to share
with you not only the gospel of God but also our own selves, because you had
become very dear to us.

9For you remember, brothers, our labor and toil: we worked night and day, that
we might not be a burden to any of you, while we proclaimed to you the gospel
of God. 10You are witnesses, and God also, how holy and righteous and blameless
was our conduct toward you believers. 11For you know how, like a father with his
children, 12we exhorted each one of you and encouraged you and charged you to
walk in a manner worthy of God, who calls you into his own kingdom and glory.

13And we also thank God constantly[6] for this, that when you received the word
of God, which you heard from us, you accepted it not as the word of men[7] but as
what it really is, the word of God, which is at work in you believers. 14For you,
brothers, became imitators of the churches of God in Christ Jesus that are in Judea. For you suffered the same things from your own countrymen as they did

---

1 THESSALONIANS 1:10

HOPE

The people to whom Paul wrote as part of the church in Thessalonica were new followers of Jesus. They had many questions and challenges in the midst of severe opposition from the Jews. Therefore it seems natural that Paul would inject hope into every chapter of 1 Thessalonians. In much of the book, Jesus is pictured as the hope of salvation—both for this life and when he returns to earth. This message was especially vital to this audience since the gospel originally came to them amidst great suffering and affliction (1Th 1:6).

Paul encouraged the Thessalonians to hope, or "wait for" Jesus, who would rescue them from the coming wrath (v. 10). This phrase "wait for" implies looking forward, eagerly and expectantly, to the return of the Lord. This hope is a confident waiting and not a wishful thinking. Those who believe in and follow Christ can face life confidently despite their surrounding circumstances, and they can most assuredly wait in joyful expectation for his second coming.

---

[1]Or *without ceasing* [2]Or *brothers and sisters*. In New Testament usage, depending on the context, the plural Greek word *adelphoi* (translated "brothers") may refer either to *brothers* or to *brothers and sisters* [3]Or *brothers and sisters*; also verses 9, 14, 17 [4]Or *with a flattering speech* [5]Some manuscripts *infants* [6]Or *without ceasing* [7]The Greek word *anthropoi* can refer to both men and women

from the Jews,[1] 15 who killed both the Lord Jesus and the prophets, and drove us out, and displease God and oppose all mankind 16 by hindering us from speaking to the Gentiles that they might be saved—so as always to fill up the measure of their sins. But wrath has come upon them at last![2]

Paul's Longing to See Them Again

17 But since we were torn away from you, brothers, for a short time, in person not in heart, we endeavored the more eagerly and with great desire to see you face to face, 18 because we wanted to come to you—I, Paul, again and again—but Satan hindered us. 19 For what is our hope or joy or crown of boasting before our Lord Jesus at his coming? Is it not you? 20 For you are our glory and joy.

3 Therefore when we could bear it no longer, we were willing to be left behind at Athens alone, 2 and we sent Timothy, our brother and God's coworker[3] in the gospel of Christ, to establish and exhort you in your faith, 3 that no one be moved by these afflictions. For you yourselves know that we are destined for this. 4 For when we were with you, we kept telling you beforehand that we were to suffer affliction, just as it has come to pass, and just as you know. 5 For this reason, when I could bear it no longer, I sent to learn about your faith, for fear that somehow the tempter had tempted you and our labor would be in vain.

Timothy's Encouraging Report

6 But now that Timothy has come to us from you, and has brought us the good news of your faith and love and reported that you always remember us kindly and long to see us, as we long to see you— 7 for this reason, brothers,[4] in all our distress and affliction we have been comforted about you through your faith. 8 For now we live, if you are standing fast in the Lord. 9 For what thanksgiving can we return to God for you, for all the joy that we feel for your sake before our God, 10 as we pray most earnestly night and day that we may see you face to face and supply what is lacking in your faith?

11 Now may our God and Father himself, and our Lord Jesus, direct our way to you, 12 and may the Lord make you increase and abound in love for one another and for all, as we do for you, 13 so that he may establish your hearts blameless in holiness before our God and Father, at the coming of our Lord Jesus with all his saints.

A Life Pleasing to God

4 Finally, then, brothers,[5] we ask and urge you in the Lord Jesus, that as you received from us how you ought to walk and to please God, just as you are doing, that you do so more and more. 2 For you know what instructions we gave you through the Lord Jesus. 3 For this is the will of God, your sanctification:[6] that you abstain from sexual immorality; 4 that each one of you know how to control his own body[7] in holiness and honor, 5 not in the passion of lust like the Gentiles who do not know God; 6 that no one transgress and wrong his brother in this matter, because the Lord is an avenger in all these things, as we told you beforehand and solemnly warned you. 7 For God has not called us for impurity, but in holiness. 8 Therefore whoever disregards this, disregards not man but God, who gives his Holy Spirit to you.

9 Now concerning brotherly love you have no need for anyone to write to you, for you yourselves have been taught by God to love one another, 10 for that indeed is what you are doing to all the brothers throughout Macedonia. But we urge you, brothers, to do this more and more, 11 and to aspire to live quietly, and to mind your own affairs, and to work with your hands, as we instructed you, 12 so that you may walk properly before outsiders and be dependent on no one.

1 THESSALONIANS 4:3–8

SANCTIFICATION

Sanctification is simply the process of becoming more like God. Believers become more like him in holiness out of gratitude to God for what he's done in their lives. The Greek word "sanctify" means "to set apart" for God's special plans. Paul urged the new believers in Thessalonica to live this kind of life, outlining that it was God's will for them to walk with Jesus, thus pleasing God with their lives (vv. 1,3). He expressed that holy living is very practical and that rejecting the instruction of God brings consequences (v. 8). God has called his people to make daily choices through a different lens: the lens of gospel truth.

When someone puts their faith in Christ, he or she has "been sanctified," or made holy through the sacrifice of Jesus Christ once and for all (Heb 10:10). Sin is completely wiped away, death is defeated, and eternal life is at hand. This is the good news! At the same time, the believer enters into a lifelong process of being purified and becoming more like God through the power of the Holy Spirit (1Th 4:8). Paul echoes this reality, declaring that God would sanctify the Thessalonians "completely," and keep them "blameless at the coming of our Lord Jesus Christ" (1Th 5:23).

Followers of Jesus today can hold on to that promise, for "he who calls you is faithful; he will surely do it" (1Th 5:24).

[1]The Greek word *Ioudaioi* can refer to Jewish religious leaders, and others under their influence, who opposed the Christian faith in that time [2]Or *completely*, or *forever* [3]Some manuscripts *servant*
[4]Or *brothers and sisters* [5]Or *brothers and sisters*; also verses 10, 13 [6]Or *your holiness* [7]Or *how to take a wife for himself*; Greek *how to possess his own vessel*

SUFFERING

Paul was no stranger to trouble and suffering. He experienced escape after harrowing escape (2Co 11:23). He was beaten, imprisoned, shipwrecked, stoned, and left for dead (Ac 14:19; 2Co 11:24–27). In addition to the physical suffering he faced, he carried the emotional strain and stress of caring for the churches he planted (2Co 11:28). Similarly, he and Timothy faced turbulent opposition from the Jews when they began to preach the gospel message to the Thessalonians. This came on the heels of the mistreatment that they had endured at Philippi. Yet Paul said their work with this church was not in vain (1Th 2:1). Paul's life exemplifies following God in hard times and in "the midst of much conflict" (v. 2).

Jesus himself said, "In the world you will have tribulation. But take heart; I have overcome the world" (Jn 16:33). Jesus taught that any who would be his disciples would have to "deny himself and take up his cross daily and follow me" (Lk 9:23). It should be no surprise to the disciple of Christ when he or she experiences resistance, pressure, trials, or suffering as he or she spiritually matures. But the glorious, and seemingly paradoxical, result of this suffering is "all joy" (Jas 1:2). The Thessalonians experienced this firsthand as they had received the gospel with great joy amidst "much affliction" (1Th 1:6). Their joyful faith was contagious. Their steadfast faith in the midst of suffering made them an example to all the believers and had "gone forth everywhere" (1:8).

The Christ-follower is called to this "all joy" faith. It is in looking to Jesus, "the founder and perfecter of our faith," that the Christian can rest in times of trouble and hardship, because Jesus, "for the joy that was set before him endured the cross" (Heb 12:2). In the same way, because we have eternal life in Christ, we can endure our "light momentary affliction," trusting that it is achieving "an eternal weight of glory beyond all comparison" (2Co 4:17). Jesus is a beacon of hope and a light in the midst of trial and suffering; Christ is alive and has defeated death through his own suffering, bringing peace both now and forever and eternal victory to those who follow him.

The Coming of the Lord

13But we do not want you to be uninformed, brothers, about those who are
asleep, that you may not grieve as others do who have no hope. 14For since we
believe that Jesus died and rose again, even so, through Jesus, God will bring with
him those who have fallen asleep. 15For this we declare to you by a word from
the Lord,[1] that we who are alive, who are left until the coming of the Lord, will
not precede those who have fallen asleep. 16For the Lord himself will descend
from heaven with a cry of command, with the voice of an archangel, and with the
sound of the trumpet of God. And the dead in Christ will rise first. 17Then we who
are alive, who are left, will be caught up together with them in the clouds to meet
the Lord in the air, and so we will always be with the Lord. 18Therefore encourage
one another with these words.

The Day of the Lord

5 Now concerning the times and the seasons, brothers,[2] you have no need to
have anything written to you. 2For you yourselves are fully aware that the day
of the Lord will come like a thief in the night. 3While people are saying, "There is
peace and security," then sudden destruction will come upon them as labor pains
come upon a pregnant woman, and they will not escape. 4But you are not in darkness, brothers, for that day to surprise you like a thief. 5For you are all children[3] of
light, children of the day. We are not of the night or of the darkness. 6So then let us
not sleep, as others do, but let us keep awake and be sober. 7For those who sleep,
sleep at night, and those who get drunk, are drunk at night. 8But since we belong
to the day, let us be sober, having put on the breastplate of faith and love, and for a
helmet the hope of salvation. 9For God has not destined us for wrath, but to obtain
salvation through our Lord Jesus Christ, 10who died for us so that whether we are
awake or asleep we might live with him. 11Therefore encourage one another and
build one another up, just as you are doing.

Final Instructions and Benediction

12We ask you, brothers, to respect those who labor among you and are over
you in the Lord and admonish you, 13and to esteem them very highly in love because of their work. Be at peace among yourselves. 14And we urge you, brothers,
admonish the idle,[4] encourage the fainthearted, help the weak, be patient with
them all. 15See that no one repays anyone evil for evil, but always seek to do good
to one another and to everyone. 16Rejoice always, 17pray without ceasing, 18give
thanks in all circumstances; for this is the will of God in Christ Jesus for you. 19Do
not quench the Spirit. 20Do not despise prophecies, 21but test everything; hold fast
what is good. 22Abstain from every form of evil.

23Now may the God of peace himself sanctify you completely, and may your
whole spirit and soul and body be kept blameless at the coming of our Lord Jesus
Christ. 24He who calls you is faithful; he will surely do it.

25Brothers, pray for us.

26Greet all the brothers with a holy kiss.

27I put you under oath before the Lord to have this letter read to all the brothers.

28The grace of our Lord Jesus Christ be with you.

1 THESSALONIANS 5:1–8

THIEF IN THE NIGHT

In the Old Testament, the prophets spoke repeatedly of a "day of the LORD" which was to be a day of much judgment, yet also a day of blessing and restoration for the people of God (Joel 2:28; 3:14,18). Paul refers to this "day of the Lord" as the day Jesus returns and describes it as one that will come "like a thief in the night" (1Th 5:2). Jesus himself made clear that no one knows the time or date, "not even the angels of heaven, nor the Son, but the Father only" (Mt 24:36).

It is not for believers to know the hour or day that Jesus will come again, but rather for them to be awake and ready at any time (1Th 5:6). Paul describes Christ-followers as those who "belong to the day" as a stark contrast to the night, where people do sinful things and are unaware of Christ and his pending return (vv. 5,8). The Jesus-follower, therefore, should be living with eyes wide open to the things of God, full of faith, love, and the hope of salvation — not caught off guard when Jesus returns.

1Or *by the word of the Lord* 2Or *brothers and sisters;* also verses 4, 12, 14, 25, 26, 27 3Or *sons;* twice in this verse 4Or *disorderly,* or *undisciplined*

JESUS: OUR COMING KING

2 THESSALONIANS

2 THESSALONIANS

THESSALONIAN CHURCH IS STARTED *c. AD 51*	PAUL WRITES 1 THESSALONIANS *c. AD 51*	PAUL WRITES 2 THESSALONIANS *c. AD 51 – 52*

The day of the Lord's return will come suddenly (1Th 5:2). This reality was meant to encourage the church to persevere in the face of suffering and not lose heart when members of the church died prior to Christ's return.

Apparently, some in the church twisted Paul's words and distorted the truthfulness of his message. False teachers had deceived the church into believing that the day of the Lord was already at hand. As a result, some in the church had stopped working altogether and were waiting passively for Christ's return.

Paul wrote his second letter to counter this theology and compel the church to active obedience as they wait for the day of the Lord. While Christ will return, his second coming will be preceded by a number of signs that had not yet taken place (2Th 2:1 – 12). Therefore, the church should continue to anticipate Christ's coming, though there would be an intervening period of time before the end would come.

The faithfulness of God would guard his people during this time of lawlessness that would precede Christ's second coming. God had done the work to save his people, and he would continue to demonstrate his faithfulness by protecting them from the evil one. Thus, the church could live with confidence, knowing that while suffering and pain awaited, God's purposes would ultimately prevail.

This confidence should embolden the church to steward their gifts and the time allotted to them to bring God glory. Rather than squandering the days in idleness, God's people should redeem the time in prayerfulness, worship, and meaningful service to one another. They should not grow weary in these good works because they know that God has called them by his grace, transformed them by his Spirit, and entrusted them with a mission to declare his glory to all mankind. Paul challenged the church to follow his model of missionary zeal, passionate proclamation, and fervent prayer in the time between the first and second comings of Christ. In so doing, they would be found faithful on that glorious day when Christ fulfills his promise to come again and, with his people, rule and reign over a new heaven and new earth where righteousness dwells forever.

WHEN HE COMES ON THAT DAY TO BE GLORIFIED IN HIS SAINTS, AND TO BE MARVELED AT AMONG ALL WHO HAVE BELIEVED, BECAUSE OUR TESTIMONY TO YOU WAS BELIEVED.

---

2 Thessalonians 1:10

2 THESSALONIANS

Greeting

1 Paul, Silvanus, and Timothy,
To the church of the Thessalonians in God our Father and the Lord Jesus Christ:
2 Grace to you and peace from God our Father and the Lord Jesus Christ.

Thanksgiving

3 We ought always to give thanks to God for you, brothers,[1] as is right, because your faith is growing abundantly, and the love of every one of you for one another is increasing. 4 Therefore we ourselves boast about you in the churches of God for your steadfastness and faith in all your persecutions and in the afflictions that you are enduring.

The Judgment at Christ's Coming

5 This is evidence of the righteous judgment of God, that you may be considered worthy of the kingdom of God, for which you are also suffering— 6 since indeed God considers it just to repay with affliction those who afflict you, 7 and to grant relief to you who are afflicted as well as to us, when the Lord Jesus is revealed from heaven with his mighty angels 8 in flaming fire, inflicting vengeance on those who do not know God and on those who do not obey the gospel of our Lord Jesus. 9 They will suffer the punishment of eternal destruction, away from[2] the presence of the Lord and from the glory of his might, 10 when he comes on that day to be glorified in his saints, and to be marveled at among all who have believed, because our testimony to you was believed. 11 To this end we always pray for you, that our God may make you worthy of his calling and may fulfill every resolve for good and every work of faith by his power, 12 so that the name of our Lord Jesus may be glorified in you, and you in him, according to the grace of our God and the Lord Jesus Christ.

The Man of Lawlessness

2 Now concerning the coming of our Lord Jesus Christ and our being gathered together to him, we ask you, brothers,[3] 2 not to be quickly shaken in mind or alarmed, either by a spirit or a spoken word, or a letter seeming to be from us, to the effect that the day of the Lord has come. 3 Let no one deceive you in any way. For that day will not come, unless the rebellion comes first, and the man of lawlessness[4] is revealed, the son of destruction,[5] 4 who opposes and exalts himself against every so-called god or object of worship, so that he takes his seat in the temple of God, proclaiming himself to be God. 5 Do you not remember that when I was still with you I told you these things? 6 And you know what is restraining him now so that he may be revealed in his time. 7 For the mystery of lawlessness is already at work. Only he who now restrains it will do so until he is out of the way. 8 And then the lawless one will be revealed, whom the Lord Jesus will kill with the breath of his mouth and bring to nothing by the appearance of his coming. 9 The coming of the lawless one is by the activity of Satan with all power and false signs and wonders, 10 and with all wicked deception for those who are perishing, because they refused to love the truth and so be saved. 11 Therefore God sends them a strong delusion, so that they may believe what is false, 12 in order that all may be condemned who did not believe the truth but had pleasure in unrighteousness.

[1] Or *brothers and sisters*. In New Testament usage, depending on the context, the plural Greek word *adelphoi* (translated "brothers") may refer either to *brothers* or to *brothers and sisters* [2] Or *destruction that comes from* [3] Or *brothers and sisters*; also verses 13, 15 [4] Some manuscripts *sin* [5] Greek *the son of perdition* (a Hebrew idiom)

2 THESSALONIANS 1:4–12

THE NAME OF JESUS GLORIFIED IN YOU

Steeped in suffering and opposition, the Thessalonians were steadfast in their faith as they persevered through the trials they encountered (vv. 4–5). It is against this backdrop that Paul wrote his second letter to the believers in Thessalonica. Paul reminded the church that God is triumphant over evil, and that their faith in him and obedience to Jesus is more than enough for them to hold on to, even and especially in times of trouble (vv. 6–10). In the midst of great trial, their enduring trust in Jesus demonstrated the hope they had in Christ.

The same holds true for Christians today. The watching world should see in Christians a joyful and compelling hope, even in the midst of trials. God's power in each believer is at work in both good and bad circumstances, as "all things work together for good, for those who are called according to his purpose" (Ro 8:28). God has called, justified, and glorified every Christian through Christ (Ro 8:30). Thus, in every season, circumstance, and relationship, Christ-followers are enabled to love and serve those around them. Through the Holy Spirit's power, the believer can live a life "worthy of his calling": a life that makes a difference for the kingdom and magnifies Jesus' name (2Th 1:11).

BUSY WAITING

How is the Christian to live until Jesus returns? This question has confronted every generation of Jesus' followers. Throughout history some people have lived as they please, as though Christ will not return. Others have tried to figure out the date and time of Jesus' coming, even though Scripture says that day will come "like a thief in the night" (1Th 5:2), and no one will know "neither the day nor the hour" (Mt 25:13). Believers in Christ are to live expecting that he will return at any time, never tiring of doing good works, continually abiding in Christ and in God's purpose for their lives (Gal 6:9).

In the second letter to the believers at Thessalonica, Paul addressed this young church and encouraged them to stand firm by living a life "worthy of his calling" that they had received (2Th 1:11). Some of the believers had become lazy "busybodies" (3:11), and he strongly warned the church against this kind of idle and disruptive behavior (3:6,11,14). Paul reminded them that they weren't called to simply wait around for Jesus' return or to take advantage of their fellow Christians in the meantime. Paul knew that such people could easily hide under a guise of spirituality or a misguided logic that assumed if Christ was coming back at any moment, working hard was not necessary. Paul exhorted them, rather, to "work quietly," "earn their own living," and to "not grow weary in doing good" (3:12 – 13).

Jesus taught a parable about ten virgins who were to put oil in their lamps and wait for the return of the bridegroom (Mt 25:1 – 13). Five of them were wise, keeping enough oil on hand to light their lamps at any time; five were foolish, not possessing enough oil to keep their lamps lit when the bridegroom arrived (Mt 25:2,7 – 9). Jesus commanded those listening to keep watch since they didn't know the day or hour of his return (Mt 25:13).

Followers of Jesus are to have their "oil" with them at all times; in other words, they are to be ready, keeping busy with the works prepared in advance for them (Eph 2:10). They are to work hard and ardently pursue the things of God, building his kingdom and bringing heaven to earth (Mt 6:10). Although Christians are still awaiting the return of Christ, they are to be "busy waiting," not tiring in doing good works and holding fast to the hope of Christ's return.

Stand Firm

13 But we ought always to give thanks to God for you, brothers beloved by the Lord, because God chose you as the firstfruits[1] to be saved, through sanctification by the Spirit and belief in the truth. 14 To this he called you through our gospel, so that you may obtain the glory of our Lord Jesus Christ. 15 So then, brothers, stand firm and hold to the traditions that you were taught by us, either by our spoken word or by our letter.

16 Now may our Lord Jesus Christ himself, and God our Father, who loved us and gave us eternal comfort and good hope through grace, 17 comfort your hearts and establish them in every good work and word.

Pray for Us

3 Finally, brothers,[2] pray for us, that the word of the Lord may speed ahead and be honored,[3] as happened among you, 2 and that we may be delivered from wicked and evil men. For not all have faith. 3 But the Lord is faithful. He will establish you and guard you against the evil one.[4] 4 And we have confidence in the Lord about you, that you are doing and will do the things that we command. 5 May the Lord direct your hearts to the love of God and to the steadfastness of Christ.

Warning Against Idleness

6 Now we command you, brothers, in the name of our Lord Jesus Christ, that you keep away from any brother who is walking in idleness and not in accord with the tradition that you received from us. 7 For you yourselves know how you ought to imitate us, because we were not idle when we were with you, 8 nor did we eat anyone's bread without paying for it, but with toil and labor we worked night and day, that we might not be a burden to any of you. 9 It was not because we do not have that right, but to give you in ourselves an example to imitate. 10 For even when we were with you, we would give you this command: If anyone is not willing to work, let him not eat. 11 For we hear that some among you walk in idleness, not busy at work, but busybodies. 12 Now such persons we command and encourage in the Lord Jesus Christ to do their work quietly and to earn their own living.[5]

13 As for you, brothers, do not grow weary in doing good. 14 If anyone does not obey what we say in this letter, take note of that person, and have nothing to do with him, that he may be ashamed. 15 Do not regard him as an enemy, but warn him as a brother.

Benediction

16 Now may the Lord of peace himself give you peace at all times in every way. The Lord be with you all.

17 I, Paul, write this greeting with my own hand. This is the sign of genuineness in every letter of mine; it is the way I write. 18 The grace of our Lord Jesus Christ be with you all.

---

[1] Some manuscripts *chose you from the beginning* [2] Or *brothers and sisters*; also verses 6, 13 [3] Or *glorified*
[4] Or *evil* [5] Greek *to eat their own bread*

JESUS: OUR ONE MEDIATOR

1 TIMOTHY

1 TIMOTHY

TIMOTHY JOINS PAUL'S SECOND JOURNEY *c. AD 50*	TIMOTHY JOINS PAUL'S THIRD JOURNEY *c. AD 54*	PAUL IN ROME, WRITES 1 TIMOTHY *c. AD 62*

Paul lived the message he proclaimed. God radically saved Paul and called him to spread God's message to those who had not yet heard it. Along the way, Paul saw many come to saving faith in Jesus and was a vital catalyst for the planting of churches throughout Asia Minor. Timothy was one such convert who came to faith during Paul's first missionary journey. The strong paternal language Paul uses to speak of Timothy leads many to surmise that Timothy was converted directly under Paul's teaching.

Whatever the case, Timothy's newfound faith was evident to those in his hometown, and when Paul returned to the region, Timothy was a clear choice to take along for his ongoing missionary labors. For many years, Timothy accompanied Paul in his travels — often venturing out on his own to work among the churches that Paul could not visit himself. Paul's trust in Timothy allowed him to send him to difficult churches in the hopes that Timothy could root the believers there in gospel fidelity and faithful worship.

The church in Ephesus was one such church. The church faced numerous threats in the forms of satanic attack, false teaching, impoverished leadership, and internal divisiveness. Timothy was sent by Paul to lead the church during a critical season in the life of the newly formed congregation.

Paul wrote 1 Timothy to his young protégé from Macedonia in an effort to encourage him in this daunting work. He reminded Timothy of his great love for him and the clear call God had placed on Timothy's life. Now, in Ephesus, Timothy should apply theological acumen and the leadership savvy he had observed from Paul through the years. Paul gave instructions for the appointment of godly leaders (3:1 – 13) and conduct in Christian worship (3:15). Timothy would also have to consider how to provide care for church members, such as widows who would need special consideration by the leaders of the church (5:1 – 16).

While Timothy was a young pastor and the leadership of the church was complex, Paul reminded Timothy that his confidence was not in his wisdom or ability but in the Lord. He must not let others look down on him because of his age, but set an example to others for godly living and maturity (4:12). He could do this because of Jesus, who served as his mediator and advocate with the Father (2:5). What Timothy lacked in age and experience, he could find in dependence on the wisdom that comes from God above.

FOR THERE IS ONE GOD, AND THERE IS
ONE MEDIATOR BETWEEN GOD AND MEN,
THE MAN CHRIST JESUS.

---

1 Timothy 2:5

1 TIMOTHY

1 TIMOTHY 1:12–17

THE FOREMOST SINNER

Although he was one of the most devout and influential Christians to ever live, Paul described himself as "the foremost" sinner. While this statement might at first appear hyperbolic, Paul believed it to be an accurate self-assessment because he knew his own heart. Paul knew not only every sinful action he had committed, but also his sinful thoughts and motivations that were hidden from everyone else. When he examined himself, he saw the depths of his personal battle with sin (Ro 7:13–25).

Likewise, if we are honest with ourselves, we will assess our lives the same way: we are the worst of sinners. While we might make a futile guess at the sinful thoughts and motivations in others, we know the depths of our own sinful hearts. Jesus referenced this reality when he told his hearers to mind the log in their own eye before removing the speck in another's (Mt 7:3).

Yet, the recognition of this truth should not lead to depression but worship. Jesus came to seek and save the lost; Paul knew this meant that Jesus came to save *him*. This fueled his passionate desire to spend his life spreading the gospel. In the same way, our honest recognition of the depths of our own sinfulness should lead us to praise Jesus for the mercy he has shown us. And as a gesture of gratitude for our salvation, we are to share this message of grace with all who will listen, just as Paul did.

Greeting

1 Paul, an apostle of Christ Jesus by command of God our Savior and of Christ
Jesus our hope,
2To Timothy, my true child in the faith:
Grace, mercy, and peace from God the Father and Christ Jesus our Lord.

Warning Against False Teachers

3As I urged you when I was going to Macedonia, remain at Ephesus so that you
may charge certain persons not to teach any different doctrine, 4nor to devote
themselves to myths and endless genealogies, which promote speculations rather
than the stewardship[1] from God that is by faith. 5The aim of our charge is love that
issues from a pure heart and a good conscience and a sincere faith. 6Certain persons, by swerving from these, have wandered away into vain discussion, 7desiring
to be teachers of the law, without understanding either what they are saying or
the things about which they make confident assertions.
8Now we know that the law is good, if one uses it lawfully, 9understanding
this, that the law is not laid down for the just but for the lawless and disobedient,
for the ungodly and sinners, for the unholy and profane, for those who strike
their fathers and mothers, for murderers, 10the sexually immoral, men who practice homosexuality, enslavers,[2] liars, perjurers, and whatever else is contrary to
sound[3] doctrine, 11in accordance with the gospel of the glory of the blessed God
with which I have been entrusted.

Christ Jesus Came to Save Sinners

12I thank him who has given me strength, Christ Jesus our Lord, because he
judged me faithful, appointing me to his service, 13though formerly I was a blasphemer, persecutor, and insolent opponent. But I received mercy because I had
acted ignorantly in unbelief, 14and the grace of our Lord overflowed for me with
the faith and love that are in Christ Jesus. 15The saying is trustworthy and deserving of full acceptance, that Christ Jesus came into the world to save sinners, of
whom I am the foremost. 16But I received mercy for this reason, that in me, as the
foremost, Jesus Christ might display his perfect patience as an example to those
who were to believe in him for eternal life. 17To the King of the ages, immortal,
invisible, the only God, be honor and glory forever and ever.[4] Amen.
18This charge I entrust to you, Timothy, my child, in accordance with the
prophecies previously made about you, that by them you may wage the good
warfare, 19holding faith and a good conscience. By rejecting this, some have made
shipwreck of their faith, 20among whom are Hymenaeus and Alexander, whom I
have handed over to Satan that they may learn not to blaspheme.

Pray for All People

2 First of all, then, I urge that supplications, prayers, intercessions, and thanksgivings be made for all people, 2for kings and all who are in high positions,
that we may lead a peaceful and quiet life, godly and dignified in every way. 3This
is good, and it is pleasing in the sight of God our Savior, 4who desires all people
to be saved and to come to the knowledge of the truth. 5For there is one God, and
there is one mediator between God and men, the man[5] Christ Jesus, 6who gave
himself as a ransom for all, which is the testimony given at the proper time. 7For

[1]Or *good order* [2]That is, those who take someone captive in order to sell him into slavery [3]Or *healthy* [4]Greek *to the ages of ages* [5]*men* and *man* render the same Greek word that is translated *people* in verses 1 and 4

APPOINTED TO HIS SERVICE

After coming to know Christ, Paul was consumed by a desire to share the good news of Christ's work with as many people as possible. Not only that, but Paul felt especially burdened to preach the gospel where it had never been shared (Ro 15:20). We know from Acts 13:1 — 21:16 that Paul went on three missionary journeys, planting churches in Asia Minor and Macedonia before his arrest in Jerusalem (Ac 21:27 – 36) and eventual transportation to Rome to stand trial (Ac 27:1 — 28:31).

These travels brought immense suffering into Paul's life. He was the constant target of hostility from those around him (Ac 13:45; 14:5; 18:12; 26:24; 27:9 – 11). He was repeatedly arrested (Ac 16:23; 21:33; 22:24; 23:35) and beaten (Ac 16:22; 21:30 – 32; 23:2). He was once even stoned and left for dead (Ac 14:19).

Despite these trials, Paul remained steadfast in his commitment to preach Christ where there were not yet any churches. The beauty of the gospel captivated him to the point that he willingly sacrificed his own safety that others might hear.

In addition to these three journeys, it is possible Paul made a fourth journey after his release from the Roman imprisonment recorded in Acts 28:16. The conclusion that such a journey did indeed take place is based on Paul's declared intention to go to Spain (Ro 15:24,28) and statements in early Christian literature that indicate that Paul took the gospel as far as Spain.

Whether or not Paul was able to make an additional journey, believers today should seek to emulate his passion for the spread of the gospel. After his resurrection, Jesus charged his followers to take the gospel to the ends of the globe (Mt 28:19 – 20). This Great Commission, as it is known, motivated Paul and should motivate us to make sacrifices so others might hear the message of Jesus. Just as the spread of the gospel was Paul's primary concern until the end of his life (2Ti 2:1 – 13), so believers today should also seek to discover how their lives can be leveraged to spread the good news of Jesus Christ to the nations.

this I was appointed a preacher and an apostle (I am telling the truth, I am not lying), a teacher of the Gentiles in faith and truth.

8I desire then that in every place the men should pray, lifting holy hands without anger or quarreling; 9likewise also that women should adorn themselves in respectable apparel, with modesty and self-control, not with braided hair and gold or pearls or costly attire, 10but with what is proper for women who profess godliness—with good works. 11Let a woman learn quietly with all submissiveness. 12I do not permit a woman to teach or to exercise authority over a man; rather, she is to remain quiet. 13For Adam was formed first, then Eve; 14and Adam was not deceived, but the woman was deceived and became a transgressor. 15Yet she will be saved through childbearing—if they continue in faith and love and holiness, with self-control.

Qualifications for Overseers

3 The saying is trustworthy: If anyone aspires to the office of overseer, he desires a noble task. 2Therefore an overseer[1] must be above reproach, the husband of one wife,[2] sober-minded, self-controlled, respectable, hospitable, able to teach, 3not a drunkard, not violent but gentle, not quarrelsome, not a lover of money. 4He must manage his own household well, with all dignity keeping his children submissive, 5for if someone does not know how to manage his own household, how will he care for God's church? 6He must not be a recent convert, or he may become puffed up with conceit and fall into the condemnation of the devil. 7Moreover, he must be well thought of by outsiders, so that he may not fall into disgrace, into a snare of the devil.

Qualifications for Deacons

8Deacons likewise must be dignified, not double-tongued,[3] not addicted to much wine, not greedy for dishonest gain. 9They must hold the mystery of the faith with a clear conscience. 10And let them also be tested first; then let them serve as deacons if they prove themselves blameless. 11Their wives likewise[4] must be dignified, not slanderers, but sober-minded, faithful in all things. 12Let deacons each be the husband of one wife, managing their children and their own households well. 13For those who serve well as deacons gain a good standing for themselves and also great confidence in the faith that is in Christ Jesus.

The Mystery of Godliness

14I hope to come to you soon, but I am writing these things to you so that, 15if I delay, you may know how one ought to behave in the household of God, which is the church of the living God, a pillar and buttress of the truth. 16Great indeed, we confess, is the mystery of godliness:

He[5] was manifested in the flesh,
  vindicated[6] by the Spirit,[7]
    seen by angels,
proclaimed among the nations,
  believed on in the world,
    taken up in glory.

Some Will Depart from the Faith

4 Now the Spirit expressly says that in later times some will depart from the faith by devoting themselves to deceitful spirits and teachings of demons, 2through the insincerity of liars whose consciences are seared, 3who forbid marriage and require abstinence from foods that God created to be received with thanksgiving by those who believe and know the truth. 4For everything created

[1]Or *bishop*; Greek *episkopos*; a similar term occurs in verse 1 [2]Or *a man of one woman*; also verse 12 [3]Or *devious in speech* [4]Or *Wives likewise*, or *Women likewise* [5]Greek *Who*; some manuscripts *God*; others *Which* [6]Or *justified* [7]Or *vindicated in spirit*

1 TIMOTHY 2:5

MEDIATOR

If you asked someone to list the titles of Jesus in the Bible, it would likely be a while before they said "mediator." Yet this often-overlooked title is of critical importance for believers. A mediator enters into a dispute between two parties and brings about a resolution. According to the Bible, sin has placed every human being in conflict with the perfectly righteous God of the universe (Ro 3:10). There is nothing a person can do to bridge this chasm that sin creates between himself or herself and God.

Despite this problem originating because of human sin, God took it upon himself to resolve the conflict. Instead of letting people experience the just result of their rebellion against him, God sent Jesus, his own Son, to act as a mediator of his new covenant of grace (Heb 9:15). For those who place their faith in him, the Bible says Jesus bore their sin so that they could become the righteousness of God (2Co 5:21). Now Jesus sits at the right hand of the Father, interceding on their behalf (Ro 8:34).

If we are in Christ, he paid the penalty for our sin, and his perfect obedience is credited to us. Because of Jesus' work, we are no longer in conflict with God and we have been adopted as children and co-heirs with Christ (Ro 8:17). With Jesus as our mediator, we partake in God's amazing grace!

1 TIMOTHY 4:1–2

DO NOT ABANDON THE FAITH

Paul warned Timothy to guard against false teachers who lead

(continued on next page)

by God is good, and nothing is to be rejected if it is received with thanksgiving, 5for it is made holy by the word of God and prayer.

A Good Servant of Christ Jesus

6If you put these things before the brothers,[1] you will be a good servant of Christ Jesus, being trained in the words of the faith and of the good doctrine that you have followed. 7Have nothing to do with irreverent, silly myths. Rather train yourself for godliness; 8for while bodily training is of some value, godliness is of value in every way, as it holds promise for the present life and also for the life to come. 9The saying is trustworthy and deserving of full acceptance. 10For to this end we toil and strive,[2] because we have our hope set on the living God, who is the Savior of all people, especially of those who believe.

11Command and teach these things. 12Let no one despise you for your youth, but set the believers an example in speech, in conduct, in love, in faith, in purity. 13Until I come, devote yourself to the public reading of Scripture, to exhortation, to teaching. 14Do not neglect the gift you have, which was given you by prophecy when the council of elders laid their hands on you. 15Practice these things, immerse yourself in them,[3] so that all may see your progress. 16Keep a close watch on yourself and on the teaching. Persist in this, for by so doing you will save both yourself and your hearers.

Instructions for the Church

5 Do not rebuke an older man but encourage him as you would a father, younger men as brothers, 2older women as mothers, younger women as sisters, in all purity.

3Honor widows who are truly widows. 4But if a widow has children or grandchildren, let them first learn to show godliness to their own household and to make some return to their parents, for this is pleasing in the sight of God. 5She who is truly a widow, left all alone, has set her hope on God and continues in supplications and prayers night and day, 6but she who is self-indulgent is dead even while she lives. 7Command these things as well, so that they may be without reproach. 8But if anyone does not provide for his relatives, and especially for members of his household, he has denied the faith and is worse than an unbeliever.

9Let a widow be enrolled if she is not less than sixty years of age, having been the wife of one husband,[4] 10and having a reputation for good works: if she has brought up children, has shown hospitality, has washed the feet of the saints, has cared for the afflicted, and has devoted herself to every good work. 11But refuse to enroll younger widows, for when their passions draw them away from Christ, they desire to marry 12and so incur condemnation for having abandoned their former faith. 13Besides that, they learn to be idlers, going about from house to house, and not only idlers, but also gossips and busybodies, saying what they should not. 14So I would have younger widows marry, bear children, manage their households, and give the adversary no occasion for slander. 15For some have already strayed after Satan. 16If any believing woman has relatives who are widows, let her care for them. Let the church not be burdened, so that it may care for those who are truly widows.

17Let the elders who rule well be considered worthy of double honor, especially those who labor in preaching and teaching. 18For the Scripture says, "You shall not muzzle an ox when it treads out the grain," and, "The laborer deserves his wages." 19Do not admit a charge against an elder except on the evidence of two or three witnesses. 20As for those who persist in sin, rebuke them in the presence of all, so that the rest may stand in fear. 21In the presence of God and of Christ Jesus and of the elect angels I charge you to keep these rules without prejudging,

[1]Or *brothers and sisters*. In New Testament usage, depending on the context, the plural Greek word *adelphoi* (translated "brothers") may refer either to *brothers* or to *brothers and sisters* [2]Some manuscripts *and suffer reproach* [3]Greek *be in them* [4]Or *a woman of one man*

(Do Not Abandon the Faith, continued)

people astray. For Paul, false teachers represented a serious danger to the church, prompting him to frequently warn those under his care about them. He wrote to other churches about false teachers (2Th 2:3–12), warning the elders several years earlier at the church in Ephesus, where Timothy ministered (Ac 20:29–30). He focused on this subject extensively in his final letter to Timothy.

Paul was not alone in his concern. Peter wrote about false teachers (2Pe 2:1–3), as did John (1Jn 2:18–19; 4:3; 2Jn 7–11) and Jude (Jude 18). The author of Hebrews repeatedly warned about falling away from the faith (Heb 3:12; 5:11—6:8; 10:26–31). Throughout the New Testament epistles, one finds frequent warnings that in the last days—from the time of the life of Jesus until his return (Eph 5:6; Col 2:4; 2Th 2:3,10)—deceivers would pose a threat to the church.

How did these authors come to share this concern? From Jesus himself. He told his disciples to beware of false teachers—"in sheep's clothing but inwardly are ravenous wolves" (Mt 7:15)—who would come and attempt to deceive people with their message (Mt 24:4–12). It is clear the apostles of Jesus took these words to heart as they sought to remind the early church, and us today, of the dangers that accepting the ideas of false teachers can have on our faith.

1 TIMOTHY 6:13–16

LIGHT

The Bible often speaks of God in connection with light. Here Paul uses this imagery to communicate an important truth: God is concealed from us. This is not because God is hiding in the shadows, but rather because our human eyes are too weak to perceive him due to the brightness of the light in which he dwells. This metaphoric picture reveals the spiritual reality of sinful humanity. Instead of walking with God in close relationship (Ge 2:4–25), sin has rendered humanity utterly unable to approach God (Ex 33:20).

Thankfully, the story does not end there. At Jesus' incarnation, the light of God came into the world so that we might be given the ability to see God (Jn 12:46; 14:9). Because of what Jesus accomplished on our behalf, we have the ability to see some of God's light (Ps 36:9). However, even after we come to know God through Christ, we cannot know him fully in this life (1Co 13:9–12). Christians look forward to a time when this will not still be the case. The Bible teaches that there will come a time when God will make all things new and once again dwell face-to-face with his people. When describing that day, the Bible again speaks of the light of God, as it will illuminate the new Jerusalem like the sun (Rev 21:23), and believers will live in the glory of that light for eternity.

doing nothing from partiality. 22 Do not be hasty in the laying on of hands, nor take part in the sins of others; keep yourself pure. 23 No longer drink only water, but use a little wine for the sake of your stomach and your frequent ailments. 24 The sins of some people are conspicuous, going before them to judgment, but the sins of others appear later. 25 So also good works are conspicuous, and even those that are not cannot remain hidden.

6 Let all who are under a yoke as bondservants[1] regard their own masters as worthy of all honor, so that the name of God and the teaching may not be reviled. 2 Those who have believing masters must not be disrespectful on the ground that they are brothers; rather they must serve all the better since those who benefit by their good service are believers and beloved.

False Teachers and True Contentment

Teach and urge these things. 3 If anyone teaches a different doctrine and does not agree with the sound[2] words of our Lord Jesus Christ and the teaching that accords with godliness, 4 he is puffed up with conceit and understands nothing. He has an unhealthy craving for controversy and for quarrels about words, which produce envy, dissension, slander, evil suspicions, 5 and constant friction among people who are depraved in mind and deprived of the truth, imagining that godliness is a means of gain. 6 But godliness with contentment is great gain, 7 for we brought nothing into the world, and[3] we cannot take anything out of the world. 8 But if we have food and clothing, with these we will be content. 9 But those who desire to be rich fall into temptation, into a snare, into many senseless and harmful desires that plunge people into ruin and destruction. 10 For the love of money is a root of all kinds of evils. It is through this craving that some have wandered away from the faith and pierced themselves with many pangs.

Fight the Good Fight of Faith

11 But as for you, O man of God, flee these things. Pursue righteousness, godliness, faith, love, steadfastness, gentleness. 12 Fight the good fight of the faith. Take hold of the eternal life to which you were called and about which you made the good confession in the presence of many witnesses. 13 I charge you in the presence of God, who gives life to all things, and of Christ Jesus, who in his testimony before[4] Pontius Pilate made the good confession, 14 to keep the commandment unstained and free from reproach until the appearing of our Lord Jesus Christ, 15 which he will display at the proper time—he who is the blessed and only Sovereign, the King of kings and Lord of lords, 16 who alone has immortality, who dwells in unapproachable light, whom no one has ever seen or can see. To him be honor and eternal dominion. Amen.

17 As for the rich in this present age, charge them not to be haughty, nor to set their hopes on the uncertainty of riches, but on God, who richly provides us with everything to enjoy. 18 They are to do good, to be rich in good works, to be generous and ready to share, 19 thus storing up treasure for themselves as a good foundation for the future, so that they may take hold of that which is truly life.

20 O Timothy, guard the deposit entrusted to you. Avoid the irreverent babble and contradictions of what is falsely called "knowledge," 21 for by professing it some have swerved from the faith.

Grace be with you.[5]

[1] For the contextual rendering of the Greek word *doulos*, see Preface [2] Or *healthy* [3] Greek *for*; some manuscripts insert [it is] *certain* [that] [4] Or *in the time of* [5] The Greek for *you* is plural

JESUS: OUR SOURCE OF STRENGTH

2 TIMOTHY

2 TIMOTHY

PAUL IN ROME, WRITES 1 TIMOTHY	PAUL IMPRISONED, WRITES 2 TIMOTHY	PAUL MARTYRED IN ROME
c. AD 62	*c. AD 64 – 67*	*c. AD 67 – 68*

The faithful transmission of the gospel message from one generation to the next is at the heart of the mission of God's people. Paul, the foremost missionary of the Christian faith, spent his life investing in others in the hopes that the message he proclaimed would continue to resound throughout the world long after his death.

Paul knew that his death was imminent as he wrote his second letter to pastor Timothy in Ephesus. Imprisoned in a hole in the ground in Rome, Paul penned a passionate letter to his son in the faith. By this time, it was clear that Paul's life would soon end and, though he longed to see Timothy again, he knew that might never be possible.

Second Timothy drips with emotion as the aging Paul begged his beloved Timothy to stay true to the faith in an age of apostasy. Paul knew that the life of a pastor is fraught with dangers and challenges and that Timothy would face overwhelming burdens in the days ahead. He compared the Christian life, and ministry in particular, to the work of a soldier, an athlete, and a farmer — since each job requires diligent perseverance in the face of obstacles in order to accomplish their objectives (2:1 – 13). As a pastor, Timothy would need to tirelessly labor and not give up in order to properly care for God's people.

Central to his pastoral duties is the preaching of the Word of God (2:12 – 26; 4:1 – 5). He needed to handle this responsibility with all seriousness — guarding the proper content of the gospel message and protecting the church from aberrant teaching and heretical doctrine. Paul's life and mission served as an example to Timothy of the type of persecution that would await those who continue to boldly proclaim the Word of God. Yet Paul reminded Timothy of the great reward that awaits those who keep their focus fixed on Christ and persevere to the end (4:8). Timothy must not lose heart, though the world is broken and marred by sin and his mentor would soon be gone. Jesus was a sufficient source of strength to faithfully fulfill the ministry with which Timothy was entrusted. Just as Timothy did, all of God's people will find in 2 Timothy a reminder of the glorious privilege of representing God to others and the need to continue in this work, even in the face of opposition.

FOR GOD GAVE US A SPIRIT
NOT OF FEAR BUT OF POWER AND LOVE
AND SELF-CONTROL.

---

2 Timothy 1:7

2 TIMOTHY

Greeting

1 Paul, an apostle of Christ Jesus by the will of God according to the promise of
the life that is in Christ Jesus,
2To Timothy, my beloved child:
Grace, mercy, and peace from God the Father and Christ Jesus our Lord.

Guard the Deposit Entrusted to You

3I thank God whom I serve, as did my ancestors, with a clear conscience,
as I remember you constantly in my prayers night and day. 4As I remember
your tears, I long to see you, that I may be filled with joy. 5I am reminded of
your sincere faith, a faith that dwelt first in your grandmother Lois and your
mother Eunice and now, I am sure, dwells in you as well. 6For this reason I
remind you to fan into flame the gift of God, which is in you through the laying
on of my hands, 7for God gave us a spirit not of fear but of power and love and
self-control.

8Therefore do not be ashamed of the testimony about our Lord, nor of me his
prisoner, but share in suffering for the gospel by the power of God, 9who saved us
and called us to[1] a holy calling, not because of our works but because of his own
purpose and grace, which he gave us in Christ Jesus before the ages began,[2] 10and
which now has been manifested through the appearing of our Savior Christ Jesus,
who abolished death and brought life and immortality to light through the gospel,
11for which I was appointed a preacher and apostle and teacher, 12which is why I
suffer as I do. But I am not ashamed, for I know whom I have believed, and I am
convinced that he is able to guard until that day what has been entrusted to me.[3]
13Follow the pattern of the sound[4] words that you have heard from me, in the faith
and love that are in Christ Jesus. 14By the Holy Spirit who dwells within us, guard
the good deposit entrusted to you.

15You are aware that all who are in Asia turned away from me, among whom
are Phygelus and Hermogenes. 16May the Lord grant mercy to the household of
Onesiphorus, for he often refreshed me and was not ashamed of my chains, 17but
when he arrived in Rome he searched for me earnestly and found me— 18may the
Lord grant him to find mercy from the Lord on that day!—and you well know all
the service he rendered at Ephesus.

A Good Soldier of Christ Jesus

2 You then, my child, be strengthened by the grace that is in Christ Jesus, 2and
what you have heard from me in the presence of many witnesses entrust to
faithful men,[5] who will be able to teach others also. 3Share in suffering as a good
soldier of Christ Jesus. 4No soldier gets entangled in civilian pursuits, since his
aim is to please the one who enlisted him. 5An athlete is not crowned unless he
competes according to the rules. 6It is the hard-working farmer who ought to have
the first share of the crops. 7Think over what I say, for the Lord will give you understanding in everything.

8Remember Jesus Christ, risen from the dead, the offspring of David, as
preached in my gospel, 9for which I am suffering, bound with chains as a criminal.
But the word of God is not bound! 10Therefore I endure everything for the sake
of the elect, that they also may obtain the salvation that is in Christ Jesus with
eternal glory. 11The saying is trustworthy, for:

---

[1]Or *with* [2]Greek *before times eternal* [3]Or *what I have entrusted to him*; Greek *my deposit* [4]Or *healthy*
[5]The Greek word *anthropoi* can refer to both men and women, depending on the context

2 TIMOTHY 2:1 – 26

HANDBOOK FOR THE CHRISTIAN LIFE

In this his final letter to Timothy, his "child" in the faith, Paul summarizes the essential elements of faithful Christian ministry based on the good news of Jesus. All believers, not just pastors like Timothy, can have an eternal impact on the world if they follow Paul's timeless advice.

First, Paul tells Timothy to find his strength in the grace of God (v. 1). A Christian's relationship with God begins with grace, not works. God freely gives salvation, forgiveness, and the indwelling of the Holy Spirit to everyone who believes the good news about Jesus (1:5 – 6,9 – 10; 3:15). These are gifts; they are not something earned. Therefore, Timothy would find the strength he needed to weather life's storms by clinging in faith to the gifts he had already received from God.

Second, faithful ministry is built upon the inspired Word of God. The Bible is no mere book; it contains God's very words recorded without error, capable of equipping Christians for every good deed (3:16 – 17). Therefore, Timothy needed to hold fast to the essential truths revealed in Scripture (1:13 – 14; 2:2 – 8; 3:14 – 15). Any drifting away from these truths would have jeopardized both his public ministry and personal walk with the Lord. So Paul challenged Timothy to continue studying and teaching God's Word (4:1 – 5). Only then would he be able to stand before God as a "worker who has no need to be ashamed" (2:15). Furthermore, as Timothy entrusted the truths he learned from the Word of God to other believers who would, in turn, entrust those truths to others, he would ensure that his ministry would last long after his life ended (2:2). The secret to building a ministry that honors God for decades to come is keeping God's Word at the center.

Third, character matters in ministry. It is not enough to simply know and teach the Word of God. One must live it. In particular, all those who wish to follow Timothy's example must flee from youthful lusts and pointless arguments and instead pursue righteousness, faith, love, and peace (2:22 – 24).

Finally, faithful ministry requires endurance in the midst of suffering. Anyone who desires to serve the Lord faithfully will face persecution in this life (3:12). Timothy needed to accept suffering as an unavoidable part of a faithful life. He had to learn to look beyond the pain and see the reward that God has in store for those who endure persecution because of their allegiance to Jesus (1:8,12; 2:3 – 6,12; 3:1; 4:5 – 8).

If we have died with him, we will also live with him;
12 if we endure, we will also reign with him;
if we deny him, he also will deny us;
13 if we are faithless, he remains faithful—
for he cannot deny himself.

A Worker Approved by God

14Remind them of these things, and charge them before God[1] not to quarrel about words, which does no good, but only ruins the hearers. 15Do your best
to present yourself to God as one approved,[2] a worker who has no need to be
ashamed, rightly handling the word of truth. 16But avoid irreverent babble, for it
will lead people into more and more ungodliness, 17and their talk will spread like
gangrene. Among them are Hymenaeus and Philetus, 18who have swerved from
the truth, saying that the resurrection has already happened. They are upsetting
the faith of some. 19But God's firm foundation stands, bearing this seal: "The Lord
knows those who are his," and, "Let everyone who names the name of the Lord
depart from iniquity."

20Now in a great house there are not only vessels of gold and silver but also
of wood and clay, some for honorable use, some for dishonorable. 21Therefore, if
anyone cleanses himself from what is dishonorable,[3] he will be a vessel for honorable use, set apart as holy, useful to the master of the house, ready for every
good work.

22So flee youthful passions and pursue righteousness, faith, love, and peace,
along with those who call on the Lord from a pure heart. 23Have nothing to do
with foolish, ignorant controversies; you know that they breed quarrels. 24And
the Lord's servant[4] must not be quarrelsome but kind to everyone, able to teach,
patiently enduring evil, 25correcting his opponents with gentleness. God may perhaps grant them repentance leading to a knowledge of the truth, 26and they may
come to their senses and escape from the snare of the devil, after being captured
by him to do his will.

Godlessness in the Last Days

3 But understand this, that in the last days there will come times of difficulty.
2For people will be lovers of self, lovers of money, proud, arrogant, abusive,
disobedient to their parents, ungrateful, unholy, 3heartless, unappeasable, slan-
derous, without self-control, brutal, not loving good, 4treacherous, reckless, swol-
len with conceit, lovers of pleasure rather than lovers of God, 5having the appearance of godliness, but denying its power. Avoid such people. 6For among them
are those who creep into households and capture weak women, burdened with
sins and led astray by various passions, 7always learning and never able to arrive
at a knowledge of the truth. 8Just as Jannes and Jambres opposed Moses, so these
men also oppose the truth, men corrupted in mind and disqualified regarding the
faith. 9But they will not get very far, for their folly will be plain to all, as was that
of those two men.

All Scripture Is Breathed Out by God

10You, however, have followed my teaching, my conduct, my aim in life, my
faith, my patience, my love, my steadfastness, 11my persecutions and sufferings
that happened to me at Antioch, at Iconium, and at Lystra—which persecutions I
endured; yet from them all the Lord rescued me. 12Indeed, all who desire to live a
godly life in Christ Jesus will be persecuted, 13while evil people and impostors will
go on from bad to worse, deceiving and being deceived. 14But as for you, continue
in what you have learned and have firmly believed, knowing from whom[5] you

[1]Some manuscripts *the Lord* [2]That is, one approved after being tested [3]Greek *from these things*
[4]For the contextual rendering of the Greek word *doulos*, see Preface [5]The Greek for *whom* is plural

2 TIMOTHY 4:1 – 8

DESCRIPTIONS OF THE CHRISTIAN LIFE

In describing how Christians should live, Paul and other New Testament writers often used analogies or metaphors. These word pictures help believers to understand more clearly God's expectations for his people. This article lists some of the metaphors of the Christian life found in the New Testament.

Soldiers (2Ti 2:3 – 4). Like good soldiers, we should accept hardships and keep our lives focused on the mission that our commander, Jesus, has given us.

Athletes (2Ti 4:6 – 8). Just as athletes follow strict rules and train hard to win their races, so we must follow the Lord's commands (2:1 – 3) to receive our reward from him.

Farmers (2Ti 2:6). Like farmers who work ceaselessly to reap a fruitful harvest, so we must also work hard in ministry to receive our reward from Jesus.

Workers (2Ti 2:15). As a craftsman is honored for his skillful construction, so the Lord honors believers for their skillful use of his Word.

Vessels/Dishes (2Ti 2:20 – 21). Like a dish kept clean and ready for use, so we must keep our lives pure and righteous to be useful to the Lord.

Fishers of men (Mt 4:19). We are called to "catch" people for God's kingdom with God's good news, the gospel.

Salt (Mt 5:13). Like salt, we can act as a godly preservative in an evil society if we remain righteous.

Light (Mt 5:14 – 16). If we obey God's Word we will shine brightly in the midst of a dark world and attract others to know and follow God.

Branches (Jn 15:5). As branches, we bear godly fruit so long as we abide in the vine, Jesus, by obeying and surrendering to him.

Servants (1Co 4:1 – 2). Like household servants entrusted with resources and responsibilities, we will be evaluated by our Master based on our faithfulness to his commands.

Ambassadors (2Co 5:20). We are representatives of God's kingdom to the lost citizens of this world.

Living stones (1Pe 2:5). In the Old Testament, God's presence dwelled in a physical temple. Now he dwells within his people, the church.

Priests (1Pe 2:9). Like priests, we have the privilege of drawing near to God and the responsibility of helping others find reconciliation with God.

Sojourners and Exiles (1Pe 2:11). As children of God, we do not belong to this world. It is not our home; we await our true home, which is being in the presence of God for eternity.

learned it 15and how from childhood you have been acquainted with the sacred
writings, which are able to make you wise for salvation through faith in Christ
Jesus. 16All Scripture is breathed out by God and profitable for teaching, for reproof, for correction, and for training in righteousness, 17that the man of God[1] may
be complete, equipped for every good work.

Preach the Word

4 I charge you in the presence of God and of Christ Jesus, who is to judge the living and the dead, and by his appearing and his kingdom: 2preach the word; be
ready in season and out of season; reprove, rebuke, and exhort, with complete patience and teaching. 3For the time is coming when people will not endure sound[2]
teaching, but having itching ears they will accumulate for themselves teachers to
suit their own passions, 4and will turn away from listening to the truth and wander off into myths. 5But as for you, always be sober-minded, endure suffering, do
the work of an evangelist, fulfill your ministry.

6For I am already being poured out as a drink offering, and the time of my
departure has come. 7I have fought the good fight, I have finished the race, I have
kept the faith. 8Henceforth there is laid up for me the crown of righteousness,
which the Lord, the righteous judge, will award to me on that day, and not only to
me but also to all who have loved his appearing.

Personal Instructions

9Do your best to come to me soon. 10For Demas, in love with this present
world, has deserted me and gone to Thessalonica. Crescens has gone to Galatia,[3]
Titus to Dalmatia. 11Luke alone is with me. Get Mark and bring him with you, for
he is very useful to me for ministry. 12Tychicus I have sent to Ephesus. 13When you
come, bring the cloak that I left with Carpus at Troas, also the books, and above
all the parchments. 14Alexander the coppersmith did me great harm; the Lord
will repay him according to his deeds. 15Beware of him yourself, for he strongly
opposed our message. 16At my first defense no one came to stand by me, but all
deserted me. May it not be charged against them! 17But the Lord stood by me and
strengthened me, so that through me the message might be fully proclaimed and
all the Gentiles might hear it. So I was rescued from the lion's mouth. 18The Lord
will rescue me from every evil deed and bring me safely into his heavenly kingdom. To him be the glory forever and ever. Amen.

Final Greetings

19Greet Prisca and Aquila, and the household of Onesiphorus. 20Erastus remained at Corinth, and I left Trophimus, who was ill, at Miletus. 21Do your best to
come before winter. Eubulus sends greetings to you, as do Pudens and Linus and
Claudia and all the brothers.[4]

22The Lord be with your spirit. Grace be with you.[5]

2 TIMOTHY 3:15–17

A GOD-BREATHED BOOK

In 2 Timothy 3:16, Paul declares that Scripture is "breathed out by God," a concept that combines the Greek words *theos* meaning "God" with *pneo* meaning "to breathe." Paul's point is that the Bible is not a man-made book. All sixty-six of the Bible's books were "breathed out" by God through the unique writing style and vocabulary of each biblical author. Since God is always truthful (Nu 23:19; Titus 1:2; Heb 6:18) and since the Bible is his own word, then the Bible must therefore be completely true. Theologians call it "inerrant," meaning "without error." So while our understanding of Scripture may be fallible, the Bible itself is as true as God himself is true.

Furthermore, because the Bible comes from God, it carries his own authority. The authoritative Word, the One who spoke all things into existence and brought the dead to life during his ministry on earth—Jesus himself—continues to exert the same power over God's people today through the Scripture, God's revelation to his people. Scripture defines our values, directs our lives, and commands our obedience. It is, therefore, useful "for teaching, for reproof, for correction, and for training in righteousness" (2Ti 3:16). It can lead a person to salvation (v. 15) and equip a believer to face every opportunity and challenge in life (v. 17).

[1]That is, a messenger of God (the phrase echoes a common Old Testament expression) [2]Or *healthy*
[3]Some manuscripts *Gaul* [4]Or *brothers and sisters*. In New Testament usage, depending on the context, the plural Greek word *adelphoi* (translated "brothers") may refer either to *brothers* or to *brothers and sisters*
[5]The Greek for *you* is plural

JESUS: OUR GREAT GOD AND SAVIOR

TITUS

TITUS

TITUS MINISTERS WITH PAUL *c. AD 53 – 57*	PAUL WRITES TITUS *c. AD 63*	PAUL MARTYRED IN ROME *c. AD 67 – 68*

The work of the church is central to God's plan. Paul invested his life in the establishment of the church and wrote a number of letters to these churches in order to encourage their ongoing faithfulness and gospel fidelity. Two pastors, Timothy and Titus, received personal letters instructing them in how to lead their respective churches — Timothy in Ephesus and Titus on the island of Crete. Together these letters form what are commonly known as the Pastoral Epistles, due to the recipient's task in each letter and the instructions they contain regarding leadership in the church. The church at Crete, a large island near Greece, was a newly formed congregation located among a radically pagan culture. Paul left Titus to lead the church and bring order to the young church (1:5). This challenge was made all the more difficult due to the fact that Crete had a reputation for wickedness that was known throughout the region (1:12).

Titus was an appropriate choice for this challenging role since he had been discipled personally under the apostle Paul. Like Timothy, Titus traveled with Paul on numerous missionary journeys, received personal training in doctrine and theology under his care, and was sent by Paul to minister among the churches they established.

The organization of the church was central to Paul's instructions in this short letter. He instructed Titus on the role and qualifications of elders and deacons, which contrasted sharply with the false teachers that were pervasive in that day (1:5 – 16). As in the letters to Timothy, Paul exhorted Titus to proclaim the Word of God with boldness and confidence because it was the God-ordained means of bringing transformation to God's people (2:1).

Paul concluded his letter with the motive for such challenging work. The grace of God compels leaders to invest their lives in God's church. Because of Jesus, all people should live godly, honorable lives as they await his second coming (2:11). They can shun immorality and idolatry, knowing that the worship of Jesus far surpasses anything this world has to offer. And they can run the race God has given them, knowing that they are heirs to the abundant riches of God through our great God and Savior, Jesus Christ (2:13).

HE SAVED US, NOT BECAUSE OF WORKS
DONE BY US IN RIGHTEOUSNESS, BUT
ACCORDING TO HIS OWN MERCY,
BY THE WASHING OF REGENERATION AND
RENEWAL OF THE HOLY SPIRIT.

Titus 3:5

TITUS

TITUS 2:2–3

MULTIGENERATIONAL MINISTRY

Too often, generations struggle to understand and appreciate one another. In a church context, such conflict can result in a weakened church or even a church split. The biblical vision of community, however, has always been multigenerational. Some of the earliest biblical instruction to parents is about passing on God's Word to their children (Dt 6:4–9). Multigenerational ministry is championed in Psalm 145:4: "One generation shall commend your works to another, and shall declare your mighty acts."

In Titus, Paul commended multigenerational ministry because he knew how it could strengthen the church and advance its mission. He knew younger generations need to see examples of older godly men and women that they can emulate. By looking to their elders, young people can find a wealth of wisdom and experience, such as how to honor God in their marriages and vocations. This kind of multigenerational ministry requires the younger generation to display humility and a teachable attitude.

Jesus modeled humility when he visited the temple as a 12-year-old boy to learn and ask questions from those who were older and wiser (Lk 2:46). Christians today should follow Jesus' example. They should remain teachable and open to mentoring by older, mature believers. If they do this, the church will experience the blessing of increased unity and will grow stronger and healthier.

Greeting

1 Paul, a servant[1] of God and an apostle of Jesus Christ, for the sake of the faith of God's elect and their knowledge of the truth, which accords with godliness, 2in hope of eternal life, which God, who never lies, promised before the ages began[2] 3and at the proper time manifested in his word[3] through the preaching with which I have been entrusted by the command of God our Savior;

4To Titus, my true child in a common faith:

Grace and peace from God the Father and Christ Jesus our Savior.

Qualifications for Elders

5This is why I left you in Crete, so that you might put what remained into order, and appoint elders in every town as I directed you— 6if anyone is above reproach, the husband of one wife,[4] and his children are believers[5] and not open to the charge of debauchery or insubordination. 7For an overseer,[6] as God's steward, must be above reproach. He must not be arrogant or quick-tempered or a drunkard or violent or greedy for gain, 8but hospitable, a lover of good, self-controlled, upright, holy, and disciplined. 9He must hold firm to the trustworthy word as taught, so that he may be able to give instruction in sound[7] doctrine and also to rebuke those who contradict it.

10For there are many who are insubordinate, empty talkers and deceivers, especially those of the circumcision party.[8] 11They must be silenced, since they are upsetting whole families by teaching for shameful gain what they ought not to teach. 12One of the Cretans,[9] a prophet of their own, said, "Cretans are always liars, evil beasts, lazy gluttons."[10] 13This testimony is true. Therefore rebuke them sharply, that they may be sound in the faith, 14not devoting themselves to Jewish myths and the commands of people who turn away from the truth. 15To the pure, all things are pure, but to the defiled and unbelieving, nothing is pure; but both their minds and their consciences are defiled. 16They profess to know God, but they deny him by their works. They are detestable, disobedient, unfit for any good work.

Teach Sound Doctrine

2 But as for you, teach what accords with sound[11] doctrine. 2Older men are to be sober-minded, dignified, self-controlled, sound in faith, in love, and in steadfastness. 3Older women likewise are to be reverent in behavior, not slanderers or slaves to much wine. They are to teach what is good, 4and so train the young women to love their husbands and children, 5to be self-controlled, pure, working at home, kind, and submissive to their own husbands, that the word of God may not be reviled. 6Likewise, urge the younger men to be self-controlled. 7Show yourself in all respects to be a model of good works, and in your teaching show integrity, dignity, 8and sound speech that cannot be condemned, so that an opponent may be put to shame, having nothing evil to say about us. 9Bondservants[12] are to be submissive to their own masters in everything; they are to be well-pleasing, not argumentative, 10not pilfering, but showing all good faith, so that in everything they may adorn the doctrine of God our Savior.

11For the grace of God has appeared, bringing salvation for all people, 12training us to renounce ungodliness and worldly passions, and to live self-controlled,

[1]For the contextual rendering of the Greek word *doulos*, see Preface [2]Greek *before times eternal* [3]Or *manifested his word* [4]Or *a man of one woman* [5]Or *are faithful* [6]Or *bishop*; Greek *episkopos* [7]Or *healthy*; also verse 13 [8]Or *especially those of the circumcision* [9]Greek *One of them* [10]Probably from Epimenides of Crete [11]Or *healthy*; also verses 2, 8 [12]For the contextual rendering of the Greek word *doulos*, see Preface

THE GOSPEL TO ALL PEOPLE

Titus was part of a band of early Christians who were gripped with a passion to spread the gospel of Jesus Christ to unreached peoples. He did not end up in Crete randomly. He was sent by Paul to make disciples of all nations, following God's desire from the beginning for all nations to know and worship him. In Genesis 12:1 – 3, God promised Abram that all of the peoples of the earth would be blessed through him. After his resurrection, Jesus commissioned his followers to make disciples of all nations (Mt 28:18 – 20), and John wrote in Revelation 7:9 – 12 about a vision of the future that God gave him. This future included people from every nation, tribe, and language around the throne worshiping Jesus. Titus' very presence in Crete is evidence that his passion for Jesus translated into action for Jesus. That is also what is needed from the church today: passion wedded to action.

Today there are multiple thousands of unreached people groups around the world. A "people group" is an *ethnolinguistic group* (a group with a common culture and language) with a common self-identity. A people group is considered to be unreached when evangelical Christians make up less than two percent of the population. Jesus is calling his followers today to leverage their lives to spread the gospel to unreached people groups. In order to reach these people, the church needs people like Paul and Titus — those who will give of their lives to take the gospel into uncharted territory and those who will build on the work God has started in these infant churches and labor to build them in a healthy, God-honoring, manner (Titus 1:5).

Yet the challenge of spreading the gospel to unreached people groups is sobering. New languages, new cultures, and new contexts await those who answer the call. Throughout history, believers have made innumerable sacrifices to get the gospel to unreached people groups. Many Christians make financial sacrifices, fast, and pray for these efforts. Some people work to translate Scripture into new languages. Many have lost their lives spreading the gospel.

Despite the challenges, the church must get the gospel to unreached people groups. A passion for God's glory naturally propels the church around the world to reach the nations. The church should be discontent with a world where God is not receiving the worship of which he is worthy. Titus' presence in Crete should encourage every believer that reaching unreached people is possible. May the Spirit give his church compassion, and may he motivate his church to spread the gospel to all nations.

upright, and godly lives in the present age, 13waiting for our blessed hope, the appearing of the glory of our great God and Savior Jesus Christ, 14who gave himself
for us to redeem us from all lawlessness and to purify for himself a people for his
own possession who are zealous for good works.
15Declare these things; exhort and rebuke with all authority. Let no one disregard you.

Be Ready for Every Good Work

3 Remind them to be submissive to rulers and authorities, to be obedient, to be
ready for every good work, 2to speak evil of no one, to avoid quarreling, to be
gentle, and to show perfect courtesy toward all people. 3For we ourselves were
once foolish, disobedient, led astray, slaves to various passions and pleasures,
passing our days in malice and envy, hated by others and hating one another.
4But when the goodness and loving kindness of God our Savior appeared, 5he
saved us, not because of works done by us in righteousness, but according to his
own mercy, by the washing of regeneration and renewal of the Holy Spirit, 6whom
he poured out on us richly through Jesus Christ our Savior, 7so that being justified
by his grace we might become heirs according to the hope of eternal life. 8The
saying is trustworthy, and I want you to insist on these things, so that those who
have believed in God may be careful to devote themselves to good works. These
things are excellent and profitable for people. 9But avoid foolish controversies,
genealogies, dissensions, and quarrels about the law, for they are unprofitable
and worthless. 10As for a person who stirs up division, after warning him once
and then twice, have nothing more to do with him, 11knowing that such a person
is warped and sinful; he is self-condemned.

Final Instructions and Greetings

12When I send Artemas or Tychicus to you, do your best to come to me at
Nicopolis, for I have decided to spend the winter there. 13Do your best to speed
Zenas the lawyer and Apollos on their way; see that they lack nothing. 14And let
our people learn to devote themselves to good works, so as to help cases of urgent
need, and not be unfruitful.
15All who are with me send greetings to you. Greet those who love us in the
faith.

Grace be with you all.

TITUS 3:3–7

THE LOVING-KINDNESS OF GOD OUR SAVIOR

God's love is not blind. He knows the depths and details of every person's sin. Here in the third chapter of Titus, he describes humanity as being "foolish, disobedient, led astray, slaves to various passions and pleasures" and continues by describing how people envy and hate one another. Yet, God loves sinners. He is kind and showed great mercy by sending a Savior for sinful people who can never save themselves. This Savior is Jesus Christ.

When Jesus came to this earth, he arrived as the clearest picture of God's kindness and love. Jesus is described as "the radiance of the glory of God and the exact imprint of his nature" (Heb 1:3). Jesus befriended sinners and showed compassion to the outcasts of society. In love, Jesus sacrificially laid down his life for sinners. God's love and kindness are plain for all to see in the person of Jesus Christ.

All of God's people can find freedom in not trying to hide their sin and brokenness. Instead, people can fall freely on the mercy of God and experience his kindness and love through the forgiveness that Jesus provides. God gives the gift of the Holy Spirit to dwell inside everyone who turns to him in faith. God's children need not doubt the lovingkindness of the Father—they can receive his love by faith and find joy through the knowledge that their sins have been forgiven.

JESUS: OUR SOURCE OF RECONCILIATION

PHILEMON

PHILEMON

PAUL'S EXTENDED STAY IN EPHESUS	PAUL IMPRISONED, WRITES PHILEMON	PAUL MARTYRED IN ROME
c. AD 54 – 56	*c. AD 60 – 62*	*c. AD 67 – 68*

The gospel radically affects a person's relationship with God and all people, since they have been created in his image. In his letter to Philemon, Paul invites his brother in Christ to demonstrate love, mercy, and grace that could only be possible because of the work of Jesus.

Philemon, like many in his day, was a slave owner, but he had come to faith during Paul's missionary travels. A resident of Colossae, Philemon owned a slave named Onesimus, who had apparently run away from his master and had taken some of his possessions in the process. In God's providence, Onesimus fled to Rome, met Paul, and came to faith in Christ. Following his conversion, Onesimus served Paul while he was in prison. However, the two men agreed that full restitution and restoration were needed between Onesimus and his former master, Philemon. Paul wrote this brief letter and sent it with the letter to the church at Colossae. In it, he asked Philemon to demonstrate Christian love toward Onesimus and receive him back, not as a slave, but as a beloved brother (vv. 16 – 17).

It was a life-threatening risk for Onesimus to seek to be restored to a right relationship with Philemon. Typically, a rebellious, treacherous slave would be subject to death should he be caught. For Onesimus to willingly pursue Philemon was unheard of. Philemon, however, was given a monumental opportunity to demonstrate the change that faith in Jesus could produce. Jesus provided the model of one who sought out his enemy and willingly laid down his life in order to bring his people into right relationship with God. Reconciliation with God was only possible because of Jesus, who can make God's enemies his friends. As a loving master, he can restore sinful humans into a right relationship with him out of the sheer abundance of his grace. Now Philemon was given a chance to model this type of love. Their relationship could demonstrate the reality that, in Christ, all dividing walls that separate humanity are rendered obsolete. Only in Christ can masters and slaves be brothers. God's people, reborn into his family, can follow Paul's encouragement and demonstrate the unity that comes to all people regardless of gender, race, class, or life history.

FOR I HAVE DERIVED MUCH JOY AND COMFORT FROM YOUR LOVE, MY BROTHER, BECAUSE THE HEARTS OF THE SAINTS HAVE BEEN REFRESHED THROUGH YOU.

Philemon 7

PHILEMON

Greeting

1 Paul, a prisoner for Christ Jesus, and Timothy our brother,

To Philemon our beloved fellow worker 2 and Apphia our sister and Archippus our fellow soldier, and the church in your house:

3 Grace to you and peace from God our Father and the Lord Jesus Christ.

Philemon's Love and Faith

4 I thank my God always when I remember you in my prayers, 5 because I hear of your love and of the faith that you have toward the Lord Jesus and for all the saints, 6 and I pray that the sharing of your faith may become effective for the full knowledge of every good thing that is in us for the sake of Christ.[1] 7 For I have derived much joy and comfort from your love, my brother, because the hearts of the saints have been refreshed through you.

Paul's Plea for Onesimus

8 Accordingly, though I am bold enough in Christ to command you to do what is required, 9 yet for love's sake I prefer to appeal to you—I, Paul, an old man and now a prisoner also for Christ Jesus— 10 I appeal to you for my child, Onesimus,[2] whose father I became in my imprisonment. 11 (Formerly he was useless to you, but now he is indeed useful to you and to me.) 12 I am sending him back to you, sending my very heart. 13 I would have been glad to keep him with me, in order that he might serve me on your behalf during my imprisonment for the gospel, 14 but I preferred to do nothing without your consent in order that your goodness might not be by compulsion but of your own accord. 15 For this perhaps is why he was parted from you for a while, that you might have him back forever, 16 no longer as a bondservant[3] but more than a bondservant, as a beloved brother—especially to me, but how much more to you, both in the flesh and in the Lord.

17 So if you consider me your partner, receive him as you would receive me. 18 If he has wronged you at all, or owes you anything, charge that to my account. 19 I, Paul, write this with my own hand: I will repay it—to say nothing of your owing me even your own self. 20 Yes, brother, I want some benefit from you in the Lord. Refresh my heart in Christ.

21 Confident of your obedience, I write to you, knowing that you will do even more than I say. 22 At the same time, prepare a guest room for me, for I am hoping that through your prayers I will be graciously given to you.

Final Greetings

23 Epaphras, my fellow prisoner in Christ Jesus, sends greetings to you, 24 and so do Mark, Aristarchus, Demas, and Luke, my fellow workers.

25 The grace of the Lord Jesus Christ be with your spirit.

---

[1] Or *for Christ's service* [2] *Onesimus* means *useful* (see verse 11) or *beneficial* (see verse 20) [3] For the contextual rendering of the Greek word *doulos*, see Preface; twice in this verse

THE SLAVE IS OUR BROTHER

The issue of slavery was very real and present under the rule of the Roman Empire. Paul wrote to slaves: "Obey your earthly masters with fear and trembling, with a sincere heart, as you would Christ" (Eph 6:5). He also commanded the masters of slaves to treat their slaves well (Eph 6:9). While he did not advocate for the outright abolition of slavery as an institution, he instead argued for the gospel truth to be infused into every layer of the socio-economic system.

In Philemon, Paul addressed the idea of slavery and introduced a new, revolutionary perspective. This book is a personal letter from Paul to Philemon about a runaway slave named Onesimus. Paul had crossed paths with Onesimus in Rome and led him to become a believer in Jesus. Paul, respecting Philemon's legal right to Onesimus, sent him back to Colossae. In Philemon 10 – 16, Paul referred to Onesimus as his son and asked Philemon to regard Onesimus as his brother. Because slaves were considered property, this request was very countercultural. Paul advocated that Onesimus be treated the same way he himself would be treated.

The essence of the gospel is freedom. Jesus was anointed by the Holy Spirit to "bind up the brokenhearted, to proclaim liberty to the captives, and the opening of the prison to those who are bound" (Isa 61:1). Jesus came to bring the dead to life. This gospel transcends any socioeconomic status. Without Christ, everyone is lost and enslaved to sin (Ro 6:17 – 18). No one can earn or attain their freedom. Everyone needs Jesus and to embrace his finished work on the cross. Because of the cross, the slave can be set free.

The power of the gospel can exist in every context and at every human level. Paul's words to Philemon help the church understand that in Christ there is a new value system. People are no longer defined by who they once were but rather by their status as children of God. When the church sees people the way that God sees them, it is empowered and emboldened to stand for slaves' freedom. Humans are not property and should never be devalued in any way. Because every person bears the image of God, the church is called to be a voice for those who do not have a voice.

JESUS: OUR GREATER SACRIFICE

HEBREWS

HEBREWS

JESUS' MINISTRY, DEATH, RESURRECTION *c. AD 27 – 30*	HEBREWS WRITTEN *c. AD 68*	JERUSALEM AND THE TEMPLE DESTROYED *c. AD 70*

All of the Old Testament is fulfilled in the person of Christ. To a modern reader, this claim may seem clear. Yet, to the early converts of the Christian faith, the relationship between Jesus and the Old Testament law, sacrificial system, and priesthood required careful explanation.

Some of the first Christians were Jewish and understood that Jesus was the one who embodied the ceremonies, sacrifices, and laws they held dear. Others were Gentiles who may not have been familiar with the significance of the Jewish faith for the coming of the Christ. The author of Hebrews wrote to connect the Christian faith with all that God had done to reveal himself and his promises throughout the Old Testament.

This task was vital because many of the recipients of the book of Hebrews were questioning their faith in Christ and considering returning to their former ways of life in Judaism. Though the author of the book is unknown, he wrote to exhort these believers not to fall away, but to persevere in Christ.

He systematically considers various facets of life for the Old Testament people of God and shows that Jesus is their fulfillment. He wrote to show that Jesus is greater than everything that came before him. He is greater than the towering figures of the Old Testament — men like the inimitable Moses (3:1 – 6). He is a greater Sabbath rest because he can truly provide long-term rest for his people (3:7 – 19). He is a better priest than those who mediated between the people and God in the Old Testament (4:14 – 16). He is greater than the tabernacle because God does not dwell in a temple built with human hands (8:1 — 9:11). He is a better sacrifice because his substitutionary death was a once-and-for-all offering to God that does not have to be repeated year after year (9:11 – 28). He offers a better covenant between God and mankind, one established on the basis of Christ's blood (8:1 – 13).

Because Jesus is greater, the people would be foolish to neglect such a great salvation and return to lesser forms of worship. The author gives five dire warnings throughout the book on the implications of neglecting the salvation provided in Christ (2:1 – 4; 4:12 – 13; 6:4 – 8; 10:26 – 31; 12:25 – 29). These warnings, combined with the author's testimony to the greatness of Christ, were meant to protect these first Christians from apostasy and to foster their passionate worship of the One who is greater.

WE HAVE BEEN SANCTIFIED THROUGH
THE OFFERING OF THE BODY
OF JESUS CHRIST ONCE FOR ALL.

Hebrews 10:10

HEBREWS

The Supremacy of God's Son

1 Long ago, at many times and in many ways, God spoke to our fathers by the
prophets, 2but in these last days he has spoken to us by his Son, whom he appointed the heir of all things, through whom also he created the world. 3He is the
radiance of the glory of God and the exact imprint of his nature, and he upholds
the universe by the word of his power. After making purification for sins, he sat
down at the right hand of the Majesty on high, 4having become as much superior
to angels as the name he has inherited is more excellent than theirs.
5For to which of the angels did God ever say,

"You are my Son,
today I have begotten you"?

Or again,

"I will be to him a father,
and he shall be to me a son"?

6And again, when he brings the firstborn into the world, he says,

"Let all God's angels worship him."

7Of the angels he says,

"He makes his angels winds,
and his ministers a flame of fire."

8But of the Son he says,

"Your throne, O God, is forever and ever,
the scepter of uprightness is the scepter of your kingdom.
9 You have loved righteousness and hated wickedness;
therefore God, your God, has anointed you
with the oil of gladness beyond your companions."

10And,

"You, Lord, laid the foundation of the earth in the beginning,
and the heavens are the work of your hands;
11 they will perish, but you remain;
they will all wear out like a garment,
12 like a robe you will roll them up,
like a garment they will be changed.[1]
But you are the same,
and your years will have no end."

13And to which of the angels has he ever said,

"Sit at my right hand
until I make your enemies a footstool for your feet"?

14Are they not all ministering spirits sent out to serve for the sake of those who
are to inherit salvation?

Warning Against Neglecting Salvation

2 Therefore we must pay much closer attention to what we have heard, lest we
drift away from it. 2For since the message declared by angels proved to be
reliable, and every transgression or disobedience received a just retribution, 3how

[1]Some manuscripts omit *like a garment*

JESUS IS GREATER

Jesus is greater. This is one of the major themes in the book of Hebrews. Jesus is greater than every person, practice, policy, and procedure in the Old Testament. The fact that Jesus is unquestionably greater than the people and practices in the Old Testament is not just an abstract idea with little bearing on life today. Rather, it demonstrates the fact that God's plan to redeem his people has moved forward in the person and work of Jesus. The author of Hebrews drives home the greatness of Jesus by comparing him to a number of people and events from the Old Testament.

Jesus is greater than every person in the Old Testament. Jesus is the Son of God who represents the Father perfectly (v. 3). As a result, Jesus is greater than the angels, and he is greater than Moses (Heb 3:3). Further, Jesus is the ultimate "apostle" and leader of God's people (Heb 3:1). He is the ultimate high priest whom all the other high priests merely foreshadowed (Heb 4:14). Because of all these things, Jesus and Jesus alone is the only person who can serve as an "anchor of the soul" (Heb 6:19). No one in the Old Testament comes close to Jesus in terms of importance; he is greater than all of them.

Jesus is greater than every event in the Old Testament. Animal sacrifices in the Old Testament were never intended to be an end in themselves; the covering they provided was only temporary. Instead, God designed the entire sacrificial system as a means of pointing people to the ultimate sacrifice for sins: Jesus' work on the cross. Jesus' death established a permanent path by which sinful people could have a relationship with the holy God (Heb 7:24). God promised a day when he would give his people the ability to obey him, a day when he would live in harmony with his people. With this in view, Jesus made a "new covenant" between people and God (Heb 9:15).

Finally, Jesus is the "founder and perfecter of our faith," which means that he is where people first encounter God and keep encountering God (Heb 12:1–2). Jesus never changes, unlike so many patterns and seasons of life (Heb 13:8). To encounter God, people simply need to go to Jesus and trust in his sacrificial work to cover their sins.

shall we escape if we neglect such a great salvation? It was declared at first by the
Lord, and it was attested to us by those who heard, 4while God also bore witness
by signs and wonders and various miracles and by gifts of the Holy Spirit distributed according to his will.

The Founder of Salvation

5For it was not to angels that God subjected the world to come, of which we
are speaking. 6It has been testified somewhere,

"What is man, that you are mindful of him,
   or the son of man, that you care for him?
7 You made him for a little while lower than the angels;
   you have crowned him with glory and honor,[1]
8   putting everything in subjection under his feet."

Now in putting everything in subjection to him, he left nothing outside his control. At present, we do not yet see everything in subjection to him. 9But we see him
who for a little while was made lower than the angels, namely Jesus, crowned with
glory and honor because of the suffering of death, so that by the grace of God he
might taste death for everyone.

10For it was fitting that he, for whom and by whom all things exist, in bringing
many sons to glory, should make the founder of their salvation perfect through
suffering. 11For he who sanctifies and those who are sanctified all have one
source.[2] That is why he is not ashamed to call them brothers,[3] 12saying,

"I will tell of your name to my brothers;
   in the midst of the congregation I will sing your praise."

13And again,

"I will put my trust in him."

And again,

"Behold, I and the children God has given me."

14Since therefore the children share in flesh and blood, he himself likewise
partook of the same things, that through death he might destroy the one who has
the power of death, that is, the devil, 15and deliver all those who through fear of
death were subject to lifelong slavery. 16For surely it is not angels that he helps,
but he helps the offspring of Abraham. 17Therefore he had to be made like his
brothers in every respect, so that he might become a merciful and faithful high
priest in the service of God, to make propitiation for the sins of the people. 18For
because he himself has suffered when tempted, he is able to help those who are
being tempted.

Jesus Greater Than Moses

3 Therefore, holy brothers,[4] you who share in a heavenly calling, consider Jesus,
the apostle and high priest of our confession, 2who was faithful to him who
appointed him, just as Moses also was faithful in all God's[5] house. 3For Jesus has
been counted worthy of more glory than Moses—as much more glory as the
builder of a house has more honor than the house itself. 4(For every house is
built by someone, but the builder of all things is God.) 5Now Moses was faithful
in all God's house as a servant, to testify to the things that were to be spoken later,
6but Christ is faithful over God's house as a son. And we are his house, if indeed
we hold fast our confidence and our boasting in our hope.[6]

HEBREWS 3:1–4

APOSTLE AND HIGH PRIEST

In the Old Testament, the office of high priest was critical to the religious life of the Jewish people. The high priest had the important role of representing God to the people and making sacrifices for sin on their behalf to God (Nu 18:1–7). In the New Testament, the office of apostle was critical to the early Christian church. God sent apostles to declare his message of salvation from sin.

Hebrews points out that Jesus is both the greatest high priest and the greatest apostle who ever lived. No one is greater than Jesus, and no one holds a more significant office than he, for he holds the highest position in both the Old and New Testaments. Once and for all, Jesus made the sacrifice for sin that is sufficient for all who would trust him in faith (Heb 10:1–4). Jesus was sent from the Father (Mt 10:40; Mk 9:37), and he sends his church to preach the gospel to the whole world (Jn 20:21).

---

[1]Some manuscripts insert *and set him over the works of your hands* [2]Greek *all are of one* [3]Or *brothers and sisters*. In New Testament usage, depending on the context, the plural Greek word *adelphoi* (translated "brothers") may refer either to *brothers* or to *brothers and sisters*; also verse 12 [4]Or *brothers and sisters*; also verse 12 [5]Greek *his*; also verses 5, 6 [6]Some manuscripts insert *firm to the end*

A Rest for the People of God

7Therefore, as the Holy Spirit says,

"Today, if you hear his voice,
8 do not harden your hearts as in the rebellion,
on the day of testing in the wilderness,
9 where your fathers put me to the test
and saw my works for forty years.
10 Therefore I was provoked with that generation,
and said, 'They always go astray in their heart;
they have not known my ways.'
11 As I swore in my wrath,
'They shall not enter my rest.'"

12Take care, brothers, lest there be in any of you an evil, unbelieving heart, leading
you to fall away from the living God. 13But exhort one another every day, as long as
it is called "today," that none of you may be hardened by the deceitfulness of sin.
14For we have come to share in Christ, if indeed we hold our original confidence
firm to the end. 15As it is said,

"Today, if you hear his voice,
do not harden your hearts as in the rebellion."

16For who were those who heard and yet rebelled? Was it not all those who left
Egypt led by Moses? 17And with whom was he provoked for forty years? Was it not
with those who sinned, whose bodies fell in the wilderness? 18And to whom did
he swear that they would not enter his rest, but to those who were disobedient?
19So we see that they were unable to enter because of unbelief.

4 Therefore, while the promise of entering his rest still stands, let us fear lest
any of you should seem to have failed to reach it. 2For good news came to us
just as to them, but the message they heard did not benefit them, because they
were not united by faith with those who listened.[1] 3For we who have believed
enter that rest, as he has said,

"As I swore in my wrath,
'They shall not enter my rest,'"

although his works were finished from the foundation of the world. 4For he has
somewhere spoken of the seventh day in this way: "And God rested on the seventh
day from all his works." 5And again in this passage he said,

"They shall not enter my rest."

6Since therefore it remains for some to enter it, and those who formerly received
the good news failed to enter because of disobedience, 7again he appoints a certain day, "Today," saying through David so long afterward, in the words already
quoted,

"Today, if you hear his voice,
do not harden your hearts."

8For if Joshua had given them rest, God[2] would not have spoken of another day
later on. 9So then, there remains a Sabbath rest for the people of God, 10for whoever has entered God's rest has also rested from his works as God did from his.

11Let us therefore strive to enter that rest, so that no one may fall by the same
sort of disobedience. 12For the word of God is living and active, sharper than any
two-edged sword, piercing to the division of soul and of spirit, of joints and of
marrow, and discerning the thoughts and intentions of the heart. 13And no creature is hidden from his sight, but all are naked and exposed to the eyes of him to
whom we must give account.

[1]Some manuscripts *it did not meet with faith in the hearers* [2]Greek *he*

Jesus the Great High Priest

14Since then we have a great high priest who has passed through the heavens,
Jesus, the Son of God, let us hold fast our confession. 15For we do not have a high
priest who is unable to sympathize with our weaknesses, but one who in every
respect has been tempted as we are, yet without sin. 16Let us then with confidence
draw near to the throne of grace, that we may receive mercy and find grace to help
in time of need.

5 For every high priest chosen from among men is appointed to act on behalf
of men in relation to God, to offer gifts and sacrifices for sins. 2He can deal
gently with the ignorant and wayward, since he himself is beset with weakness.
3Because of this he is obligated to offer sacrifice for his own sins just as he does
for those of the people. 4And no one takes this honor for himself, but only when
called by God, just as Aaron was.

5So also Christ did not exalt himself to be made a high priest, but was appointed by him who said to him,

"You are my Son,
today I have begotten you";

6as he says also in another place,

"You are a priest forever,
after the order of Melchizedek."

7In the days of his flesh, Jesus[1] offered up prayers and supplications, with loud
cries and tears, to him who was able to save him from death, and he was heard
because of his reverence. 8Although he was a son, he learned obedience through
what he suffered. 9And being made perfect, he became the source of eternal salvation to all who obey him, 10being designated by God a high priest after the order
of Melchizedek.

Warning Against Apostasy

11About this we have much to say, and it is hard to explain, since you have
become dull of hearing. 12For though by this time you ought to be teachers, you
need someone to teach you again the basic principles of the oracles of God. You
need milk, not solid food, 13for everyone who lives on milk is unskilled in the word
of righteousness, since he is a child. 14But solid food is for the mature, for those
who have their powers of discernment trained by constant practice to distinguish
good from evil.

6 Therefore let us leave the elementary doctrine of Christ and go on to maturity, not laying again a foundation of repentance from dead works and of
faith toward God, 2and of instruction about washings,[2] the laying on of hands,
the resurrection of the dead, and eternal judgment. 3And this we will do if God
permits. 4For it is impossible, in the case of those who have once been enlightened, who have tasted the heavenly gift, and have shared in the Holy Spirit, 5and
have tasted the goodness of the word of God and the powers of the age to come,
6and then have fallen away, to restore them again to repentance, since they are
crucifying once again the Son of God to their own harm and holding him up to
contempt. 7For land that has drunk the rain that often falls on it, and produces a
crop useful to those for whose sake it is cultivated, receives a blessing from God.
8But if it bears thorns and thistles, it is worthless and near to being cursed, and
its end is to be burned.

9Though we speak in this way, yet in your case, beloved, we feel sure of better
things—things that belong to salvation. 10For God is not unjust so as to overlook
your work and the love that you have shown for his name in serving the saints,
as you still do. 11And we desire each one of you to show the same earnestness to

[1]Greek *he* [2]Or *baptisms* (that is, cleansing rites)

HEBREWS 5:1–10

COMPASSIONATE HIGH PRIEST

Old Testament priests had many rules to follow. God was not one to be approached flippantly; the priests had to go through certain steps in order to prepare themselves to encounter God (Lev 16; Heb 5:1–3). Only on specific occasions could the high priest enter the Most Holy Place to intercede between God and his people.

Jesus is superior to every high priest in the Old Testament priesthood (Heb 4:14—7:28). He came to be both the sin sacrifice and the high priest who presided over the atonement. Jesus is fully human—he is able to empathize with the people for whom he makes atonement. And Jesus is fully God—he is able to atone for the sins of people fully and completely. Jesus is also the only high priest who can usher believers directly into the presence of the Father. When he died on the cross for the sins of his people, the curtain of the temple was torn in two from top to bottom (Mk 15:38). This signified that God was no longer unapproachable and that people now have direct access to God through Jesus instead of having to go through an intermediary (Heb 4:16).

Most major religions of the world teach that God dwells at a great distance from people and that he can only be approached with great apprehension. Christianity teaches that Jesus has made a way for God to be with his people.

HEBREWS 6:1

MATURITY

Having faith in Jesus is all it takes to be made right with God. However,

(continued on page 1850)

HEBREWS 4:16

THE MAJESTY OF CHRIST

"Christology" is simply the study of who Jesus is and what that implies for the lives of those who believe in him for their salvation. The book of Hebrews provides an especially robust Christology, describing who Jesus is, detailing his many roles in relation to Old Testament Scriptures, and outlining what all of this means for each Christian.

Jesus is heir of all things (1:2), which means that as God's "firstborn" Son, Christ will inherit infinite glory and honor.

He is the One through whom God made the world (1:2), the creative agent behind the universe and the One who still stewards his creation.

He is the radiance of God's glory and the exact imprint of God's person (1:3), the One who perfectly reflects the majesty of God and is himself God in the flesh.

Jesus sustains the world by his power and sits at the right hand of God (1:3). He is the living, ruling Savior who provides for his creation on a daily basis and who also superintends the universe.

Because he is one with God, Jesus is better than the angels (1:4) — no matter how glorious and awe-inspiring they are — and is also better than Moses (3:3) and all the prophets.

He is the founder of our salvation (2:10), the pioneer of the effort to bring "many sons to glory."

He is the destroyer of the devil (2:14), overcoming death and Satan through his resurrection.

As a merciful high priest (2:17), Jesus presented his own blood as the perfect sacrifice for human sin.

Also as the believers' high priest, he can sympathize with our weaknesses (4:15) because he experienced life as a human on earth.

As an eternal priest, Jesus always makes intercession before God for his people (7:25).

Jesus is the mediator of a better covenant (8:6), superseding the old covenant with its earthly tabernacle and need for animal sacrifices.

He is our model for enduring hostility from sinful people (12:2 – 3). When we are discouraged, we can find great strength and inspiration in Christ's willingness to persevere under persecution.

Jesus is the Great Shepherd of the sheep (13:20), the One who cares for us and who will ultimately lead us to our eternal home.

(Maturity, continued)

this first step alone is not enough to grow into all of the good things that God desires for his people. The author of Hebrews encouraged his readers to grow in their faith until they reached maturity. To illustrate what this was going to require, the author appealed to the way physical growth relies on nourishment acquired through right eating.

Growth cannot be dependent on "milk" alone—the "elementary doctrine of Christ." Instead, growth takes place through "solid food"—the study of God's Word and the daily pursuit of holy living. All of this is possible only by depending on Jesus. Therefore, the writer of Hebrews instructs people in how to strengthen their faith and live a morally acceptable life before God.

The Christian life is a life of progress. It begins with simply trusting in Jesus, and it ends with an eternity of coming to know more about God as one continually grows in both knowledge about God and experiences with God. The life of a Christian is a life that seeks these heavenly realities here and now by growing to maturity by grace, through faith, in Christ.

have the full assurance of hope until the end, 12so that you may not be sluggish,
but imitators of those who through faith and patience inherit the promises.

The Certainty of God's Promise

13For when God made a promise to Abraham, since he had no one greater by
whom to swear, he swore by himself, 14saying, "Surely I will bless you and multiply you." 15And thus Abraham,[1] having patiently waited, obtained the promise.
16For people swear by something greater than themselves, and in all their disputes
an oath is final for confirmation. 17So when God desired to show more convincingly to the heirs of the promise the unchangeable character of his purpose, he
guaranteed it with an oath, 18so that by two unchangeable things, in which it is
impossible for God to lie, we who have fled for refuge might have strong encouragement to hold fast to the hope set before us. 19We have this as a sure and steadfast anchor of the soul, a hope that enters into the inner place behind the curtain,
20where Jesus has gone as a forerunner on our behalf, having become a high priest
forever after the order of Melchizedek.

The Priestly Order of Melchizedek

7 For this Melchizedek, king of Salem, priest of the Most High God, met Abraham returning from the slaughter of the kings and blessed him, 2and to him
Abraham apportioned a tenth part of everything. He is first, by translation of his
name, king of righteousness, and then he is also king of Salem, that is, king of
peace. 3He is without father or mother or genealogy, having neither beginning of
days nor end of life, but resembling the Son of God he continues a priest forever.
4See how great this man was to whom Abraham the patriarch gave a tenth of
the spoils! 5And those descendants of Levi who receive the priestly office have a
commandment in the law to take tithes from the people, that is, from their brothers,[2] though these also are descended from Abraham. 6But this man who does not
have his descent from them received tithes from Abraham and blessed him who
had the promises. 7It is beyond dispute that the inferior is blessed by the superior.
8In the one case tithes are received by mortal men, but in the other case, by one
of whom it is testified that he lives. 9One might even say that Levi himself, who
receives tithes, paid tithes through Abraham, 10for he was still in the loins of his
ancestor when Melchizedek met him.

Jesus Compared to Melchizedek

11Now if perfection had been attainable through the Levitical priesthood (for
under it the people received the law), what further need would there have been
for another priest to arise after the order of Melchizedek, rather than one named
after the order of Aaron? 12For when there is a change in the priesthood, there is
necessarily a change in the law as well. 13For the one of whom these things are
spoken belonged to another tribe, from which no one has ever served at the altar.
14For it is evident that our Lord was descended from Judah, and in connection
with that tribe Moses said nothing about priests.
15This becomes even more evident when another priest arises in the likeness
of Melchizedek, 16who has become a priest, not on the basis of a legal requirement
concerning bodily descent, but by the power of an indestructible life. 17For it is
witnessed of him,

> "You are a priest forever,
> after the order of Melchizedek."

18For on the one hand, a former commandment is set aside because of its weakness and uselessness 19(for the law made nothing perfect); but on the other hand,
a better hope is introduced, through which we draw near to God.

---

[1]Greek *he* [2]Or *brothers and sisters*

20And it was not without an oath. For those who formerly became priests were made such without an oath, 21but this one was made a priest with an oath by the one who said to him:

"The Lord has sworn
 and will not change his mind,
'You are a priest forever.' "

22This makes Jesus the guarantor of a better covenant.

23The former priests were many in number, because they were prevented by death from continuing in office, 24but he holds his priesthood permanently, because he continues forever. 25Consequently, he is able to save to the uttermost[1] those who draw near to God through him, since he always lives to make intercession for them.

26For it was indeed fitting that we should have such a high priest, holy, innocent, unstained, separated from sinners, and exalted above the heavens. 27He has no need, like those high priests, to offer sacrifices daily, first for his own sins and then for those of the people, since he did this once for all when he offered up himself. 28For the law appoints men in their weakness as high priests, but the word of the oath, which came later than the law, appoints a Son who has been made perfect forever.

Jesus, High Priest of a Better Covenant

8 Now the point in what we are saying is this: we have such a high priest, one who is seated at the right hand of the throne of the Majesty in heaven, 2a minister in the holy places, in the true tent[2] that the Lord set up, not man. 3For every high priest is appointed to offer gifts and sacrifices; thus it is necessary for this priest also to have something to offer. 4Now if he were on earth, he would not be a priest at all, since there are priests who offer gifts according to the law. 5They serve a copy and shadow of the heavenly things. For when Moses was about to erect the tent, he was instructed by God, saying, "See that you make everything according to the pattern that was shown you on the mountain." 6But as it is, Christ[3] has obtained a ministry that is as much more excellent than the old as the covenant he mediates is better, since it is enacted on better promises. 7For if that first covenant had been faultless, there would have been no occasion to look for a second.

8For he finds fault with them when he says:[4]

"Behold, the days are coming, declares the Lord,
 when I will establish a new covenant with the house of Israel
 and with the house of Judah,
9 not like the covenant that I made with their fathers
 on the day when I took them by the hand to bring them out
  of the land of Egypt.
For they did not continue in my covenant,
 and so I showed no concern for them, declares the Lord.
10 For this is the covenant that I will make with the house
  of Israel
 after those days, declares the Lord:
I will put my laws into their minds,
 and write them on their hearts,
and I will be their God,
 and they shall be my people.
11 And they shall not teach, each one his neighbor
 and each one his brother, saying, 'Know the Lord,'

[1]That is, completely; or *at all times* [2]Or *tabernacle*; also verse 5 [3]Greek *he* [4]Some manuscripts *For finding fault with it he says to them*

HEBREWS 8:1–2

OLD TESTAMENT CONNECTION

People broke the relationship with God that he had established. The creation and the Creator were once tethered together by a life-giving relationship, and humanity broke the bond by sinning against their Creator. Since that moment, life has been filled with pain and frustration because it has not had the life-giving power of God flowing through it. But God loves people too much to leave them in this condition, so he made a series of promises to bring his people out of it.

The Bible speaks of a "new covenant" that God makes with his people. This covenant does not depend on people's ability to fulfill it by loving and being faithful to God. Instead, this covenant depends on God. In this covenant, God promises to help his people obey his law (Jer 31:31–34). God also promises to bring his people from death to life and to care for them forever (Eze 37:24–26). The author of Hebrews declared that God has fulfilled and accomplished that covenant through Jesus. The sacrifice of the great high priest Jesus supersedes all Old Testament rituals. Jesus, therefore, fulfilled the Old Testament laws. He fulfilled the terms of the covenant by being the priest who presides over the covenant. He is the priest who brings his people into the presence of God (Heb 10:19).

THE SUPERIORITY OF JESUS

The book of Hebrews was written to a group of people in the midst of a great struggle. The original audience was a group of Jewish Christians. Life was difficult as followers of Jesus. These believers faced persecution and hardship. They had their doubts about the gospel and whether their salvation depended only on Jesus. Some were even tempted to give up and turn away from the faith. To these people God sent a clear message: look to Jesus.

More than a prophet, Jesus is God in the flesh (1:2–3). More than a man, Jesus is the Creator and Sustainer of all that exists (1:3,10–12). More than a high priest who works on behalf of God, Jesus is the great high priest who is God and serves people as God (2:10–11).

Many Christians look at their circumstances and settle for superficial spirituality. They look for religious practices to improve their lives without truly turning to Jesus to provide what they really need. They major on minor points and don't take Jesus' offer of a better life seriously. Many other Christians are tempted to be overwhelmed by the weight and worry of life and give up on asking Jesus for help. These kinds of Christians suffer in a different way as they allow negativity and difficulty to dominate their lives. For both types of people, God sends the message of Hebrews, which is the message of the gospel: Jesus Christ comes to people and gives his life to them. For every situation that followers of Jesus face, the message of the book is to simply look to Jesus, who is better than any person or experience they have ever encountered before. Jesus is the perfect example of perseverance and is also the One who actively provides for and cares for his people.

Jesus has provided forgiveness of sins. This means that people can go to him and find eternal life. Eternal life is not just about where we go when we die (though that is certainly important); it is also about the fullness of life. Life with Jesus is about having a full and rich experience of life now; this is God's word of hope to people who struggle with their circumstances. When people look to Jesus, they receive from God the assurance that they do not need to look anywhere else or settle for anything less (13:20–21).

for they shall all know me,
from the least of them to the greatest.
12 For I will be merciful toward their iniquities,
and I will remember their sins no more."

13 In speaking of a new covenant, he makes the first one obsolete. And what is
becoming obsolete and growing old is ready to vanish away.

The Earthly Holy Place

9 Now even the first covenant had regulations for worship and an earthly
place of holiness. 2 For a tent[1] was prepared, the first section, in which were
the lampstand and the table and the bread of the Presence.[2] It is called the Holy
Place. 3 Behind the second curtain was a second section[3] called the Most Holy
Place, 4 having the golden altar of incense and the ark of the covenant covered
on all sides with gold, in which was a golden urn holding the manna, and Aaron's
staff that budded, and the tablets of the covenant. 5 Above it were the cherubim
of glory overshadowing the mercy seat. Of these things we cannot now speak in
detail.

6 These preparations having thus been made, the priests go regularly into the
first section, performing their ritual duties, 7 but into the second only the high
priest goes, and he but once a year, and not without taking blood, which he offers
for himself and for the unintentional sins of the people. 8 By this the Holy Spirit
indicates that the way into the holy places is not yet opened as long as the first
section is still standing 9 (which is symbolic for the present age).[4] According to this
arrangement, gifts and sacrifices are offered that cannot perfect the conscience of
the worshiper, 10 but deal only with food and drink and various washings, regulations for the body imposed until the time of reformation.

Redemption Through the Blood of Christ

11 But when Christ appeared as a high priest of the good things that have come,[5]
then through the greater and more perfect tent (not made with hands, that is,
not of this creation) 12 he entered once for all into the holy places, not by means
of the blood of goats and calves but by means of his own blood, thus securing
an eternal redemption. 13 For if the blood of goats and bulls, and the sprinkling
of defiled persons with the ashes of a heifer, sanctify[6] for the purification of the
flesh, 14 how much more will the blood of Christ, who through the eternal Spirit
offered himself without blemish to God, purify our[7] conscience from dead works
to serve the living God.

15 Therefore he is the mediator of a new covenant, so that those who are called
may receive the promised eternal inheritance, since a death has occurred that
redeems them from the transgressions committed under the first covenant.[8] 16 For
where a will is involved, the death of the one who made it must be established.
17 For a will takes effect only at death, since it is not in force as long as the one who
made it is alive. 18 Therefore not even the first covenant was inaugurated without
blood. 19 For when every commandment of the law had been declared by Moses to
all the people, he took the blood of calves and goats, with water and scarlet wool
and hyssop, and sprinkled both the book itself and all the people, 20 saying, "This
is the blood of the covenant that God commanded for you." 21 And in the same
way he sprinkled with the blood both the tent and all the vessels used in worship.
22 Indeed, under the law almost everything is purified with blood, and without the
shedding of blood there is no forgiveness of sins.

23 Thus it was necessary for the copies of the heavenly things to be purified
with these rites, but the heavenly things themselves with better sacrifices than

[1] Or *tabernacle*; also verses 11, 21 [2] Greek *the presentation of the loaves* [3] Greek *tent*; also verses 6, 8
[4] Or *which is symbolic for the age then present* [5] Some manuscripts *good things to come* [6] Or *For if the sprinkling of defiled persons with the blood of goats and bulls and with the ashes of a heifer sanctifies* [7] Some manuscripts *your* [8] The Greek word means both *covenant* and *will*; also verses 16, 17

HEBREWS 9:11–15

THE BLOOD THAT CLEANSES

Some things can easily be removed or fixed with minor adjustments. Sin is not one of those things. Sin separates people from God because God is holy (1Pe 1:16). From creation, God has spoken clearly about the fact that sin leads to death (Ge 2:17). Therefore, sin will always lead to the shedding of blood. Sin is costly.

God set up a temporary sacrificial system to provide relief and cover the sins of people—sin payment from the blood of animals (Lev 4; 16). This system was only temporary because the blood of animals cannot cover the sins of people forever (Heb 9:12,14). The animals functioned as substitutes for people, and they died so that the people could live.

In dramatic fashion, God sent Jesus to be the sacrificial Lamb who would die for the sins of the world. Jesus was "without blemish," meaning that his relationship with God was not broken because of sin. This means that Jesus did not deserve to die, but chose to die for sinners as their substitute. Therefore, Jesus' blood cleanses people from their sins. Unlike Old Testament priests who entered into a man-made temple, God admitted Jesus into his very presence (v. 24). When Jesus returns to earth, it will not be "to deal with sin but to save those who are eagerly waiting for him" (v. 28). His offer of forgiveness must be accepted in faith (1Pe 1:18–21).

these. 24For Christ has entered, not into holy places made with hands, which are
copies of the true things, but into heaven itself, now to appear in the presence
of God on our behalf. 25Nor was it to offer himself repeatedly, as the high priest
enters the holy places every year with blood not his own, 26for then he would have
had to suffer repeatedly since the foundation of the world. But as it is, he has appeared once for all at the end of the ages to put away sin by the sacrifice of himself.
27And just as it is appointed for man to die once, and after that comes judgment,
28so Christ, having been offered once to bear the sins of many, will appear a second time, not to deal with sin but to save those who are eagerly waiting for him.

Christ's Sacrifice Once for All

10 For since the law has but a shadow of the good things to come instead of
the true form of these realities, it can never, by the same sacrifices that are
continually offered every year, make perfect those who draw near. 2Otherwise,
would they not have ceased to be offered, since the worshipers, having once been
cleansed, would no longer have any consciousness of sins? 3But in these sacrifices
there is a reminder of sins every year. 4For it is impossible for the blood of bulls
and goats to take away sins.

5Consequently, when Christ[1] came into the world, he said,

"Sacrifices and offerings you have not desired,
  but a body have you prepared for me;
6 in burnt offerings and sin offerings
  you have taken no pleasure.
7 Then I said, 'Behold, I have come to do your will, O God,
  as it is written of me in the scroll of the book.'"

8When he said above, "You have neither desired nor taken pleasure in sacrifices
and offerings and burnt offerings and sin offerings" (these are offered according
to the law), 9then he added, "Behold, I have come to do your will." He does away
with the first in order to establish the second. 10And by that will we have been
sanctified through the offering of the body of Jesus Christ once for all.

11And every priest stands daily at his service, offering repeatedly the same sacrifices, which can never take away sins. 12But when Christ[2] had offered for all time
a single sacrifice for sins, he sat down at the right hand of God, 13waiting from that
time until his enemies should be made a footstool for his feet. 14For by a single
offering he has perfected for all time those who are being sanctified.

15And the Holy Spirit also bears witness to us; for after saying,

16 "This is the covenant that I will make with them
  after those days, declares the Lord:
I will put my laws on their hearts,
  and write them on their minds,"

17then he adds,

"I will remember their sins and their lawless deeds no more."

18Where there is forgiveness of these, there is no longer any offering for sin.

The Full Assurance of Faith

19Therefore, brothers,[3] since we have confidence to enter the holy places by
the blood of Jesus, 20by the new and living way that he opened for us through
the curtain, that is, through his flesh, 21and since we have a great priest over the
house of God, 22let us draw near with a true heart in full assurance of faith, with
our hearts sprinkled clean from an evil conscience and our bodies washed with
pure water. 23Let us hold fast the confession of our hope without wavering, for
he who promised is faithful. 24And let us consider how to stir up one another to

---

[1] Greek *he* [2] Greek *this one* [3] Or *brothers and sisters*

love and good works, 25not neglecting to meet together, as is the habit of some,
but encouraging one another, and all the more as you see the Day drawing near.
26For if we go on sinning deliberately after receiving the knowledge of the
truth, there no longer remains a sacrifice for sins, 27but a fearful expectation of
judgment, and a fury of fire that will consume the adversaries. 28Anyone who has
set aside the law of Moses dies without mercy on the evidence of two or three witnesses. 29How much worse punishment, do you think, will be deserved by the one
who has trampled underfoot the Son of God, and has profaned the blood of the
covenant by which he was sanctified, and has outraged the Spirit of grace? 30For
we know him who said, "Vengeance is mine; I will repay." And again, "The Lord
will judge his people." 31It is a fearful thing to fall into the hands of the living God.
32But recall the former days when, after you were enlightened, you endured
a hard struggle with sufferings, 33sometimes being publicly exposed to reproach
and affliction, and sometimes being partners with those so treated. 34For you
had compassion on those in prison, and you joyfully accepted the plundering of
your property, since you knew that you yourselves had a better possession and an
abiding one. 35Therefore do not throw away your confidence, which has a great
reward. 36For you have need of endurance, so that when you have done the will of
God you may receive what is promised. 37For,

"Yet a little while,
    and the coming one will come and will not delay;
38 but my righteous one shall live by faith,
    and if he shrinks back,
my soul has no pleasure in him."

39But we are not of those who shrink back and are destroyed, but of those who
have faith and preserve their souls.

By Faith

11 Now faith is the assurance of things hoped for, the conviction of things not
seen. 2For by it the people of old received their commendation. 3By faith we
understand that the universe was created by the word of God, so that what is seen
was not made out of things that are visible.
4By faith Abel offered to God a more acceptable sacrifice than Cain, through
which he was commended as righteous, God commending him by accepting his
gifts. And through his faith, though he died, he still speaks. 5By faith Enoch was
taken up so that he should not see death, and he was not found, because God had
taken him. Now before he was taken he was commended as having pleased God.
6And without faith it is impossible to please him, for whoever would draw near
to God must believe that he exists and that he rewards those who seek him. 7By
faith Noah, being warned by God concerning events as yet unseen, in reverent
fear constructed an ark for the saving of his household. By this he condemned the
world and became an heir of the righteousness that comes by faith.
8By faith Abraham obeyed when he was called to go out to a place that he was
to receive as an inheritance. And he went out, not knowing where he was going.
9By faith he went to live in the land of promise, as in a foreign land, living in tents
with Isaac and Jacob, heirs with him of the same promise. 10For he was looking
forward to the city that has foundations, whose designer and builder is God. 11By
faith Sarah herself received power to conceive, even when she was past the age,
since she considered him faithful who had promised. 12Therefore from one man,
and him as good as dead, were born descendants as many as the stars of heaven
and as many as the innumerable grains of sand by the seashore.
13These all died in faith, not having received the things promised, but having
seen them and greeted them from afar, and having acknowledged that they were
strangers and exiles on the earth. 14For people who speak thus make it clear that
they are seeking a homeland. 15If they had been thinking of that land from which

HEBREWS 10:35–39

PERSEVERANCE

Newton's third law states that "For every action, there is an equal and opposite reaction." When an object is pushed, there will always be movement of some sort. In a similar way, the Christian life is full of pressures that God allows to happen in order to push his people into deeper dependence on him.

One of the reasons that God gave his church the book of Hebrews is to encourage his people to endure in the midst of persecution. The Christian life will have moments, perhaps even seasons, of opposition. This should not surprise followers of Christ. Jesus himself even warned his disciples that they would experience hardships (Mt 24:9–10). Yet, this warning is followed by an encouragement: some people will continue to believe, all people will have an opportunity to believe, and Jesus will come back to save his people (Mt 24:11–14).

The author of Hebrews twice told his audience to hang on and endure, and in between those exhortations he highlights Jesus as the hope for people who are in the midst of difficult situations. When the pressure increases, Christians are encouraged to remember those who endured faithfully. Among those who lived lives worthy of imitation, Jesus is the greatest example. Jesus won victory through suffering and lives to give strength in every moment.

HEBREWS 12:1–3

LOOKING TO JESUS

Perception is a powerful thing. The author of Hebrews encouraged Christians to stare obsessively at Jesus in the face of their circumstances. While remembering Jesus in everything is a wonderful idea, it is difficult actually to do. Life is full of needs and demands, and people can easily become distracted by things that are inconsequential; they become burdened by things that are beyond their ability to control.

Despite the problems of life, God wants people to look to Jesus. When people get a glimpse of who God really is, they then see themselves for what they really are, and life comes into focus. God tells people to look to Jesus because doing so actually has a transformative effect on life. Paul spoke of this as well when writing to encourage the church to be faithful to Jesus. He told them that as they beheld God's glory, God would transform them and change their lives (2Co 3:18). Put simply, people become what they behold.

they had gone out, they would have had opportunity to return. 16But as it is, they
desire a better country, that is, a heavenly one. Therefore God is not ashamed to
be called their God, for he has prepared for them a city.

17By faith Abraham, when he was tested, offered up Isaac, and he who had
received the promises was in the act of offering up his only son, 18of whom it
was said, "Through Isaac shall your offspring be named." 19He considered that
God was able even to raise him from the dead, from which, figuratively speaking, he did receive him back. 20By faith Isaac invoked future blessings on Jacob
and Esau. 21By faith Jacob, when dying, blessed each of the sons of Joseph, bowing in worship over the head of his staff. 22By faith Joseph, at the end of his life,
made mention of the exodus of the Israelites and gave directions concerning
his bones.

23By faith Moses, when he was born, was hidden for three months by his parents, because they saw that the child was beautiful, and they were not afraid of
the king's edict. 24By faith Moses, when he was grown up, refused to be called the
son of Pharaoh's daughter, 25choosing rather to be mistreated with the people
of God than to enjoy the fleeting pleasures of sin. 26He considered the reproach
of Christ greater wealth than the treasures of Egypt, for he was looking to the
reward. 27By faith he left Egypt, not being afraid of the anger of the king, for he endured as seeing him who is invisible. 28By faith he kept the Passover and sprinkled
the blood, so that the Destroyer of the firstborn might not touch them.

29By faith the people crossed the Red Sea as on dry land, but the Egyptians,
when they attempted to do the same, were drowned. 30By faith the walls of Jericho fell down after they had been encircled for seven days. 31By faith Rahab the
prostitute did not perish with those who were disobedient, because she had given
a friendly welcome to the spies.

32And what more shall I say? For time would fail me to tell of Gideon, Barak,
Samson, Jephthah, of David and Samuel and the prophets— 33who through faith
conquered kingdoms, enforced justice, obtained promises, stopped the mouths
of lions, 34quenched the power of fire, escaped the edge of the sword, were made
strong out of weakness, became mighty in war, put foreign armies to flight.
35Women received back their dead by resurrection. Some were tortured, refusing
to accept release, so that they might rise again to a better life. 36Others suffered
mocking and flogging, and even chains and imprisonment. 37They were stoned,
they were sawn in two,[1] they were killed with the sword. They went about in skins
of sheep and goats, destitute, afflicted, mistreated— 38of whom the world was
not worthy—wandering about in deserts and mountains, and in dens and caves
of the earth.

39And all these, though commended through their faith, did not receive what
was promised, 40since God had provided something better for us, that apart from
us they should not be made perfect.

Jesus, Founder and Perfecter of Our Faith

12 Therefore, since we are surrounded by so great a cloud of witnesses, let us
also lay aside every weight, and sin which clings so closely, and let us run
with endurance the race that is set before us, 2looking to Jesus, the founder and
perfecter of our faith, who for the joy that was set before him endured the cross,
despising the shame, and is seated at the right hand of the throne of God.

Do Not Grow Weary

3Consider him who endured from sinners such hostility against himself, so
that you may not grow weary or fainthearted. 4In your struggle against sin you
have not yet resisted to the point of shedding your blood. 5And have you forgotten
the exhortation that addresses you as sons?

[1]Some manuscripts add *they were tempted*

HEBREWS 11:1–40

FAITH

Faith is an intense form of trust, and people's relationship with God has always operated on the basis of faith. Time and time again, all throughout the Bible, salvation is found in the same way: trusting God's promises by faith, and then following God's commands. Hebrews 11 looks at faith through the lens of the stories of people who lived their lives by faith in God. Faith is "the assurance of things hoped for, the conviction of things not seen" (v. 1), and these biblical characters were commended for having such faith, understanding that faith was necessary to please God (v. 6). In faith, Abel offered a costly sacrifice (v. 4); Enoch lived in a way that pleased God (v. 5); Noah obeyed divine warnings and built a giant ark (v. 7), having never seen a drop of rain; Abraham left his hometown of Ur and went out, not knowing where God was leading (v. 8); Sarah bore Isaac in her old age (v. 11), and the stories continue.

The writer of Hebrews makes the point that many Old Testament people of faith trusted God for power and victory, and they refused to compromise their faith in God, even in the midst of life-threatening circumstances (vv. 32–38). Some of these faithful people died without having received what God had promised (v. 13); some had to find consolation in the fact that they would not realize the full blessings of God until they entered heaven (vv. 14–16). Other people powerfully experienced God's strength and deliverance (vv. 33–35), and their testimony of deliverance still stands. But many others, despite their implicit trust in God, experienced torture, mocking, beatings, imprisonment, stoning, destitution, and affliction (vv. 35–38). These are the people of whom the world was not worthy (v. 38).

Because of the example of these faithful ones, we should be motivated to lay aside every weight that threatens to slow us down in our pursuit of God's kingdom. When we do, we'll be much better able to "run with endurance the race that is set before us" (12:1), looking to Jesus as our ultimate example of determination and faithfulness.

All of God's promises are kept in Jesus. Every promise that God made to these people in the Old Testament looked ahead to Jesus. By believing the promise, these people were made right with God. Every promise God makes to people in the New Testament also looks to Jesus, whose work enables the blessings of God to come to people. In every case, God's promises are kept in Jesus, the "founder and perfecter of our faith" (12:2).

"My son, do not regard lightly the discipline of the Lord,
nor be weary when reproved by him.
6 For the Lord disciplines the one he loves,
and chastises every son whom he receives."

7It is for discipline that you have to endure. God is treating you as sons. For what son is there whom his father does not discipline? 8If you are left without discipline, in which all have participated, then you are illegitimate children and not sons. 9Besides this, we have had earthly fathers who disciplined us and we respected them. Shall we not much more be subject to the Father of spirits and live? 10For they disciplined us for a short time as it seemed best to them, but he disciplines us for our good, that we may share his holiness. 11For the moment all discipline seems painful rather than pleasant, but later it yields the peaceful fruit of righteousness to those who have been trained by it.

12Therefore lift your drooping hands and strengthen your weak knees, 13and make straight paths for your feet, so that what is lame may not be put out of joint but rather be healed. 14Strive for peace with everyone, and for the holiness without which no one will see the Lord. 15See to it that no one fails to obtain the grace of God; that no "root of bitterness" springs up and causes trouble, and by it many become defiled; 16that no one is sexually immoral or unholy like Esau, who sold his birthright for a single meal. 17For you know that afterward, when he desired to inherit the blessing, he was rejected, for he found no chance to repent, though he sought it with tears.

A Kingdom That Cannot Be Shaken

18For you have not come to what may be touched, a blazing fire and darkness and gloom and a tempest 19and the sound of a trumpet and a voice whose words made the hearers beg that no further messages be spoken to them. 20For they could not endure the order that was given, "If even a beast touches the mountain, it shall be stoned." 21Indeed, so terrifying was the sight that Moses said, "I tremble with fear." 22But you have come to Mount Zion and to the city of the living God, the heavenly Jerusalem, and to innumerable angels in festal gathering, 23and to the assembly[1] of the firstborn who are enrolled in heaven, and to God, the judge of all, and to the spirits of the righteous made perfect, 24and to Jesus, the mediator of a new covenant, and to the sprinkled blood that speaks a better word than the blood of Abel.

25See that you do not refuse him who is speaking. For if they did not escape when they refused him who warned them on earth, much less will we escape if we reject him who warns from heaven. 26At that time his voice shook the earth, but now he has promised, "Yet once more I will shake not only the earth but also the heavens." 27This phrase, "Yet once more," indicates the removal of things that are shaken—that is, things that have been made—in order that the things that cannot be shaken may remain. 28Therefore let us be grateful for receiving a kingdom that cannot be shaken, and thus let us offer to God acceptable worship, with reverence and awe, 29for our God is a consuming fire.

Sacrifices Pleasing to God

13 Let brotherly love continue. 2Do not neglect to show hospitality to strangers, for thereby some have entertained angels unawares. 3Remember those who are in prison, as though in prison with them, and those who are mistreated, since you also are in the body. 4Let marriage be held in honor among all, and let the marriage bed be undefiled, for God will judge the sexually immoral and adulterous. 5Keep your life free from love of money, and be content with what you have, for he has said, "I will never leave you nor forsake you." 6So we can confidently say,

---

[1]Or *church*

"The Lord is my helper;
I will not fear;
what can man do to me?"

7 Remember your leaders, those who spoke to you the word of God. Consider
the outcome of their way of life, and imitate their faith. 8 Jesus Christ is the same
yesterday and today and forever. 9 Do not be led away by diverse and strange
teachings, for it is good for the heart to be strengthened by grace, not by foods,
which have not benefited those devoted to them. 10 We have an altar from which
those who serve the tent[1] have no right to eat. 11 For the bodies of those animals
whose blood is brought into the holy places by the high priest as a sacrifice for sin
are burned outside the camp. 12 So Jesus also suffered outside the gate in order to
sanctify the people through his own blood. 13 Therefore let us go to him outside
the camp and bear the reproach he endured. 14 For here we have no lasting city,
but we seek the city that is to come. 15 Through him then let us continually offer
up a sacrifice of praise to God, that is, the fruit of lips that acknowledge his name.
16 Do not neglect to do good and to share what you have, for such sacrifices are
pleasing to God.

17 Obey your leaders and submit to them, for they are keeping watch over your
souls, as those who will have to give an account. Let them do this with joy and not
with groaning, for that would be of no advantage to you.

18 Pray for us, for we are sure that we have a clear conscience, desiring to act
honorably in all things. 19 I urge you the more earnestly to do this in order that I
may be restored to you the sooner.

Benediction

20 Now may the God of peace who brought again from the dead our Lord Jesus,
the great shepherd of the sheep, by the blood of the eternal covenant, 21 equip you
with everything good that you may do his will, working in us[2] that which is pleasing in his sight, through Jesus Christ, to whom be glory forever and ever. Amen.

Final Greetings

22 I appeal to you, brothers,[3] bear with my word of exhortation, for I have written to you briefly. 23 You should know that our brother Timothy has been released,
with whom I shall see you if he comes soon. 24 Greet all your leaders and all the
saints. Those who come from Italy send you greetings. 25 Grace be with all of you.

---

[1] Or *tabernacle* [2] Some manuscripts *you* [3] Or *brothers and sisters*

JESUS: OUR PERFECT EXAMPLE

JAMES

JAMES

JAMES WRITES HIS LETTER *c. AD 46 – 61*	JAMES LEADS JERUSALEM COUNCIL *c. AD 50*	JAMES MARTYRED IN JERUSALEM *c. AD 62 – 69*

Jesus transforms every aspect of life. All of the New Testament letters describe the transformation that the Good News brings to those who embrace it by faith. The book of James is unique in its singular focus on this theme. James, the half brother of Jesus, is thought to be the author of this book bearing his name. He wrote to the believers scattered abroad who were undoubtedly facing persecution for their faith in Christ (1:1).

James begins his letter by challenging believers to find joy in the midst of their suffering. They can find comfort in the knowledge that God is using these trials to make his people holy (1:2 – 4). Though they were a scattered, persecuted minority living among idolatrous nations, believers could have hope that God was at work.

Christians today also can seek wisdom from the Lord and find guidance for faithful living (1:5 – 7). God provides wisdom to his people through his Spirit and his Word, and believers honor God when they listen to the voice of God and obey what he says (1:19 – 27). James connects one's faith in God with their obedience to his commands. He wrote that one who professes faith in Christ but lives in rebellion to his commands is a liar (2:14 – 26). The connection between faith and obedience, according to James, should be seen in the way a Christian loves and serves others (2:1 – 13), guards their speech from sin (3:1 – 12), and rejects worldly forms of wickedness and rebellion from God (4:1 – 10). James bookends his letter with another reminder of patient suffering in light of the coming return of Christ (5:7 – 11). Endurance under this kind of intense suffering requires Christian community — other believers who are given by God to pray, love, and serve one another, as they together seek to obey God.

Though James does not speak at great length about Jesus, it is clear that the principles he outlines in his letter follow the model set forth by Jesus during his earthly ministry. As the perfect Son of God, he patiently suffered with an awareness that he was fulfilling the Father's perfect plan. All the while, he modeled virtues that James calls the church to embody. By fixing their gaze and affections on Christ, they could be doers of the Word and not merely hearers only.

COUNT IT ALL JOY, MY BROTHERS,
WHEN YOU MEET TRIALS
OF VARIOUS KINDS.

James 1:2

JAMES

Greeting

1 James, a servant[1] of God and of the Lord Jesus Christ,
To the twelve tribes in the Dispersion:
Greetings.

Testing of Your Faith

2 Count it all joy, my brothers,[2] when you meet trials of various kinds, 3 for
you know that the testing of your faith produces steadfastness. 4 And let steadfastness have its full effect, that you may be perfect and complete, lacking in
nothing.
5 If any of you lacks wisdom, let him ask God, who gives generously to all without reproach, and it will be given him. 6 But let him ask in faith, with no doubting,
for the one who doubts is like a wave of the sea that is driven and tossed by the
wind. 7 For that person must not suppose that he will receive anything from the
Lord; 8 he is a double-minded man, unstable in all his ways.
9 Let the lowly brother boast in his exaltation, 10 and the rich in his humiliation,
because like a flower of the grass[3] he will pass away. 11 For the sun rises with its
scorching heat and withers the grass; its flower falls, and its beauty perishes. So
also will the rich man fade away in the midst of his pursuits.
12 Blessed is the man who remains steadfast under trial, for when he has stood
the test he will receive the crown of life, which God has promised to those who
love him. 13 Let no one say when he is tempted, "I am being tempted by God,"
for God cannot be tempted with evil, and he himself tempts no one. 14 But each
person is tempted when he is lured and enticed by his own desire. 15 Then desire
when it has conceived gives birth to sin, and sin when it is fully grown brings
forth death.
16 Do not be deceived, my beloved brothers. 17 Every good gift and every perfect gift is from above, coming down from the Father of lights, with whom
there is no variation or shadow due to change.[4] 18 Of his own will he brought
us forth by the word of truth, that we should be a kind of firstfruits of his
creatures.

Hearing and Doing the Word

19 Know this, my beloved brothers: let every person be quick to hear, slow to
speak, slow to anger; 20 for the anger of man does not produce the righteousness
of God. 21 Therefore put away all filthiness and rampant wickedness and receive
with meekness the implanted word, which is able to save your souls.
22 But be doers of the word, and not hearers only, deceiving yourselves. 23 For if
anyone is a hearer of the word and not a doer, he is like a man who looks intently
at his natural face in a mirror. 24 For he looks at himself and goes away and at once
forgets what he was like. 25 But the one who looks into the perfect law, the law of
liberty, and perseveres, being no hearer who forgets but a doer who acts, he will
be blessed in his doing.
26 If anyone thinks he is religious and does not bridle his tongue but deceives
his heart, this person's religion is worthless. 27 Religion that is pure and undefiled
before God the Father is this: to visit orphans and widows in their affliction, and
to keep oneself unstained from the world.

JAMES 1:19–27

LIVING FOR JESUS

The book of James is filled with practical commands for authentic Christian living. In his letter, James, the brother of Jesus, instructed Christians to control their tongues, be slow to anger, and fight selfish ambition. But James was not interested in simply sharing a list of things Christians *should not* do—he also included a number of positive commands for believers.

Just as Jesus spent much of his ministry among those neglected by society, followers of Jesus are commanded to care for and show concern for people who are orphans and widows, the underprivileged, and for sinning brothers and sisters. James placed a specific emphasis on believers emulating the everyday ministry of Jesus within their own lives by showing compassion toward the brokenhearted and poor and by avoiding sin.

The disciples of Jesus should not merely listen to the words of Jesus; they should actively seek opportunities to engage the world with his life-changing message. Just as with Jesus, a believer's relationships with others—be it family, friends, coworkers, or a person who is begging on the street—should be defined by love, mercy, patience, and grace.

[1] For the contextual rendering of the Greek word *doulos*, see Preface [2] Or *brothers and sisters*. In New Testament usage, depending on the context, the plural Greek word *adelphoi* (translated "brothers") may refer either to *brothers* or to *brothers and sisters*; also verses 16, 19 [3] Or *a wild flower* [4] Some manuscripts *variation due to a shadow of turning*

The Sin of Partiality

2 My brothers,[1] show no partiality as you hold the faith in our Lord Jesus Christ, the Lord of glory. 2For if a man wearing a gold ring and fine clothing comes into your assembly, and a poor man in shabby clothing also comes in, 3and if you pay attention to the one who wears the fine clothing and say, "You sit here in a good place," while you say to the poor man, "You stand over there," or, "Sit down at my feet," 4have you not then made distinctions among yourselves and become judges with evil thoughts? 5Listen, my beloved brothers, has not God chosen those who are poor in the world to be rich in faith and heirs of the kingdom, which he has promised to those who love him? 6But you have dishonored the poor man. Are not the rich the ones who oppress you, and the ones who drag you into court? 7Are they not the ones who blaspheme the honorable name by which you were called?

8If you really fulfill the royal law according to the Scripture, "You shall love your neighbor as yourself," you are doing well. 9But if you show partiality, you are committing sin and are convicted by the law as transgressors. 10For whoever keeps the whole law but fails in one point has become guilty of all of it. 11For he who said, "Do not commit adultery," also said, "Do not murder." If you do not commit adultery but do murder, you have become a transgressor of the law. 12So speak and so act as those who are to be judged under the law of liberty. 13For judgment is without mercy to one who has shown no mercy. Mercy triumphs over judgment.

Faith Without Works Is Dead

14What good is it, my brothers, if someone says he has faith but does not have works? Can that faith save him? 15If a brother or sister is poorly clothed and lacking in daily food, 16and one of you says to them, "Go in peace, be warmed and filled," without giving them the things needed for the body, what good[2] is that? 17So also faith by itself, if it does not have works, is dead.

18But someone will say, "You have faith and I have works." Show me your faith apart from your works, and I will show you my faith by my works. 19You believe that God is one; you do well. Even the demons believe—and shudder! 20Do you want to be shown, you foolish person, that faith apart from works is useless? 21Was not Abraham our father justified by works when he offered up his son Isaac on the altar? 22You see that faith was active along with his works, and faith was completed by his works; 23and the Scripture was fulfilled that says, "Abraham believed God, and it was counted to him as righteousness"—and he was called a friend of God. 24You see that a person is justified by works and not by faith alone. 25And in the same way was not also Rahab the prostitute justified by works when she received the messengers and sent them out by another way? 26For as the body apart from the spirit is dead, so also faith apart from works is dead.

Taming the Tongue

3 Not many of you should become teachers, my brothers, for you know that we who teach will be judged with greater strictness. 2For we all stumble in many ways. And if anyone does not stumble in what he says, he is a perfect man, able also to bridle his whole body. 3If we put bits into the mouths of horses so that they obey us, we guide their whole bodies as well. 4Look at the ships also: though they are so large and are driven by strong winds, they are guided by a very small rudder wherever the will of the pilot directs. 5So also the tongue is a small member, yet it boasts of great things.

How great a forest is set ablaze by such a small fire! 6And the tongue is a fire, a world of unrighteousness. The tongue is set among our members, staining the whole body, setting on fire the entire course of life,[3] and set on fire by hell.[4]

[1]Or *brothers and sisters*; also verses 5, 14 [2]Or *benefit* [3]Or *wheel of birth* [4]Greek *Gehenna*

FAITH AND WORKS

At first glance, James's statements concerning justification seem to contradict the message of the apostle Paul. In 2:24, James declared that "a person is justified by works and not by faith alone." But in Romans 3:28, Paul wrote that "one is justified by faith apart from works of the law." This raises a critical question: Are Christians saved by faith in Jesus alone or by faith combined with their own efforts? It is important to note that these men were not as far apart as the above quotes seem. James and Paul knew each other. They were both major contributors at the first church council in Jerusalem, which assembled specifically to address the relationship between faith and works. As recorded in Acts 15, they arrived at a consensus.

Paul preached that a person is declared to be in a right relationship with God by grace alone, through faith alone in the finished work of Jesus, with no basis whatsoever in works (Ro 3:28; Gal 2:16; Eph 2:8–9). At the moment of conversion, God sends his Spirit into the new believer (Gal 3:26; 4:6). Paul describes this as a new birth. The Spirit then works within the Christian to manifest good works. Paul said that true saving faith expresses itself through love (Gal 5:6). Loving deeds display outwardly the inward change that has occurred by grace through faith.

James also declared that a person enters a right relationship with God by the grace of God alone. Like Jesus (Jn 3:3–8), James used birth imagery to describe conversion. James stated that God "brought us forth by the word of truth" and then planted that word in the souls of believers (Jas 1:18,21). James then went to great lengths to explain that this kind of faith manifests itself in loving acts toward those in need (Jas 1:27). According to James, acts of love toward God and others display the inward faith of the believer. This stands in complete agreement with Paul.

Tensions in the verses quoted at the outset are resolved when one understands that Paul and James used the word "justified" in different ways. The word can mean "declared to be in right standing" or "displayed to be right standing." Paul used the first sense. God declares an individual to be in right standing with him upon the basis of faith alone, as occurred with Abraham in Genesis 15:6. James used the second sense. A person's faith is shown to be legitimate when their outward works display the inward change that has taken place as a result of their conversion. Faith alone saves, but the faith that saves is never alone.

7For every kind of beast and bird, of reptile and sea creature, can be tamed and has been tamed by mankind, 8but no human being can tame the tongue. It is a restless evil, full of deadly poison. 9With it we bless our Lord and Father, and with it we curse people who are made in the likeness of God. 10From the same mouth come blessing and cursing. My brothers,[1] these things ought not to be so. 11Does a spring pour forth from the same opening both fresh and salt water? 12Can a fig tree, my brothers, bear olives, or a grapevine produce figs? Neither can a salt pond yield fresh water.

Wisdom from Above

13Who is wise and understanding among you? By his good conduct let him show his works in the meekness of wisdom. 14But if you have bitter jealousy and selfish ambition in your hearts, do not boast and be false to the truth. 15This is not the wisdom that comes down from above, but is earthly, unspiritual, demonic. 16For where jealousy and selfish ambition exist, there will be disorder and every vile practice. 17But the wisdom from above is first pure, then peaceable, gentle, open to reason, full of mercy and good fruits, impartial and sincere. 18And a harvest of righteousness is sown in peace by those who make peace.

Warning Against Worldliness

4 What causes quarrels and what causes fights among you? Is it not this, that your passions[2] are at war within you?[3] 2You desire and do not have, so you murder. You covet and cannot obtain, so you fight and quarrel. You do not have, because you do not ask. 3You ask and do not receive, because you ask wrongly, to spend it on your passions. 4You adulterous people![4] Do you not know that friendship with the world is enmity with God? Therefore whoever wishes to be a friend of the world makes himself an enemy of God. 5Or do you suppose it is to no purpose that the Scripture says, "He yearns jealously over the spirit that he has made to dwell in us"? 6But he gives more grace. Therefore it says, "God opposes the proud but gives grace to the humble." 7Submit yourselves therefore to God. Resist the devil, and he will flee from you. 8Draw near to God, and he will draw near to you. Cleanse your hands, you sinners, and purify your hearts, you double-minded. 9Be wretched and mourn and weep. Let your laughter be turned to mourning and your joy to gloom. 10Humble yourselves before the Lord, and he will exalt you.

11Do not speak evil against one another, brothers.[5] The one who speaks against a brother or judges his brother, speaks evil against the law and judges the law. But if you judge the law, you are not a doer of the law but a judge. 12There is only one lawgiver and judge, he who is able to save and to destroy. But who are you to judge your neighbor?

Boasting About Tomorrow

13Come now, you who say, "Today or tomorrow we will go into such and such a town and spend a year there and trade and make a profit"— 14yet you do not know what tomorrow will bring. What is your life? For you are a mist that appears for a little time and then vanishes. 15Instead you ought to say, "If the Lord wills, we will live and do this or that." 16As it is, you boast in your arrogance. All such boasting is evil. 17So whoever knows the right thing to do and fails to do it, for him it is sin.

Warning to the Rich

5 Come now, you rich, weep and howl for the miseries that are coming upon you. 2Your riches have rotted and your garments are moth-eaten. 3Your gold and silver have corroded, and their corrosion will be evidence against you and will eat your flesh like fire. You have laid up treasure in the last days. 4Behold, the

[1]Or *brothers and sisters*; also verse 12 [2]Greek *pleasures*; also verse 3 [3]Greek *in your members* [4]Or *You adulteresses!* [5]Or *brothers and sisters*

JAMES 3:9–12

HYPOCRISY

James demanded that believers display a changed life. His letter seems to pack more commands per square inch than any other book in the Bible. Yet James does not call Christians to alter their behavior in order to earn God's approval. Rather, he calls for consistency.

According to James, God "brought us forth by the word of truth" (1:18). An individual becomes a child of God entirely by the grace of God. But when the gospel of Jesus Christ renovates a person's heart, changes in activity should naturally result. New identity results in new activity. James called his audience to evaluate the way they deal with hardship, handle money, use words, and plan for the future in light of their allegiance to the Lord. James confronted the inconsistency of claiming to belong to Jesus, yet making decisions that are incompatible with that confession—in other words, saying one thing and doing another. James did not advocate throwing a garment of religious activity over an unconverted heart. Rather, he called for the Christian to live a consistent life. Everything in the world produces something according to its own nature. Fig trees produce figs. Grapevines produce grapes. In the same way, James asserted that Christian people should naturally produce Christ-honoring activity. In doing so, he simply restated Jesus' illustration from Matthew 7:15–20: As a good tree produces good fruit, so a Christian produces a life that honors Christ.

wages of the laborers who mowed your fields, which you kept back by fraud, are crying out against you, and the cries of the harvesters have reached the ears of the Lord of hosts. 5You have lived on the earth in luxury and in self-indulgence. You have fattened your hearts in a day of slaughter. 6You have condemned and murdered the righteous person. He does not resist you.

Patience in Suffering

7Be patient, therefore, brothers,[1] until the coming of the Lord. See how the farmer waits for the precious fruit of the earth, being patient about it, until it receives the early and the late rains. 8You also, be patient. Establish your hearts, for the coming of the Lord is at hand. 9Do not grumble against one another, brothers, so that you may not be judged; behold, the Judge is standing at the door. 10As an example of suffering and patience, brothers, take the prophets who spoke in the name of the Lord. 11Behold, we consider those blessed who remained steadfast. You have heard of the steadfastness of Job, and you have seen the purpose of the Lord, how the Lord is compassionate and merciful.

12But above all, my brothers, do not swear, either by heaven or by earth or by any other oath, but let your "yes" be yes and your "no" be no, so that you may not fall under condemnation.

The Prayer of Faith

13Is anyone among you suffering? Let him pray. Is anyone cheerful? Let him sing praise. 14Is anyone among you sick? Let him call for the elders of the church, and let them pray over him, anointing him with oil in the name of the Lord. 15And the prayer of faith will save the one who is sick, and the Lord will raise him up. And if he has committed sins, he will be forgiven. 16Therefore, confess your sins to one another and pray for one another, that you may be healed. The prayer of a righteous person has great power as it is working.[2] 17Elijah was a man with a nature like ours, and he prayed fervently that it might not rain, and for three years and six months it did not rain on the earth. 18Then he prayed again, and heaven gave rain, and the earth bore its fruit.

19My brothers, if anyone among you wanders from the truth and someone brings him back, 20let him know that whoever brings back a sinner from his wandering will save his soul from death and will cover a multitude of sins.

JAMES 4:13–17

GOD'S WILL

The will of God has two meanings in the Bible—first, God's law, or the way he wants us to live; second, the events God allows in history, including pain and suffering. It appears James used both meanings in his instruction on how Christians should view and approach their lives. James was not encouraging an apathetic attitude toward events that may appear outside of humanity's control. To the contrary, James was actually pointing Christians toward the example set by Jesus.

Jesus is the only person in history who perfectly fulfilled the will of God. Not only did Jesus live a perfect life by following God's law, but he also accepted God's will for his life—the unimaginable suffering of crucifixion and separation from God that paid for human sin. It is because of Jesus' example that the Christian can joyfully submit to God's will in this life.

The Son of God is not a far-off deity who sits idly and toys with humanity's fate. He is intimately present as his people struggle to obey his commands, and he walks with believers through the painful suffering of life's darkest valleys. This is the Lord who guides a Christian's future—a God who empathizes with, relates to, and loves his people. Accepting the will of God is not a burden. Instead, it should be regarded with all the reverence and joy that comes with following in the footsteps of God himself.

1Or *brothers and sisters*; also verses 9, 10, 12, 19 2Or *The effective prayer of a righteous person has great power*

JESUS: OUR ETERNAL REWARD

1 PETER

1 PETER

PETER LEADS THE CHURCH AFTER PENTECOST *c. AD 30*	PETER WRITES FIRST LETTER *c. AD 62 – 64*	PETER MARTYRED IN ROME *c. AD 67 – 68*

Suffering is a vital part of the Christian life. The recipients of Peter's letter knew this reality firsthand. Asia Minor was a difficult place to live in obedience to Christ's commands and to proclaim the gospel. Christians were often persecuted by their pagan neighbors and by the governing authorities of the day. Most likely, Peter wrote his first letter during the sporadic persecutions that occurred before the severe, official persecutions under Kings Nero, Domitian, and Trajan at the end of the first century and the beginning of the second.

Peter wrote to prepare the church for the ongoing reality of suffering. He did not want them to lose heart or think that God had abandoned them during these trials. God was using their sufferings, first and foremost, to shape their character and conform them to the image of Christ (1:6 – 7; 3:14; 4:12 – 14). Suffering is a primary tool that God uses to refine his people. Peter also reminded the church that God was with them in their suffering and would, by the power of his Spirit, empower them to live holy lives (1:13 – 16). Though it can be tempting, believers must not return evil for evil but entrust themselves to God in the face of hostility from others (2:23). God sees the plight of believers, knows their burdens, and will reward his people for their faithfulness (2:9; 3:16 – 17; 4:15 – 19). Life in a fallen world brings great trouble, but Christians can trust that they will receive their eternal reward that will far surpass temporary pain.

Persecuted believers must pursue harmonious relationships with other people in order to suffer well (2:13 – 19). The church community is the God-given context where Christ is worshiped, believers are reminded of the truths of the gospel, and people are encouraged to persevere (4:7 – 11; 5:1 – 7). The fires of persecution purify the church from hypocrisy and false converts, leaving true believers to band together in faithfulness and holiness. Peter concluded with the hope that awaits all true believers: "The God of all grace, who has called you to his eternal glory in Christ, will himself restore, confirm, strengthen, and establish you" (5:10).

SO THAT THE TESTED GENUINENESS OF YOUR FAITH — MORE PRECIOUS THAN GOLD THAT PERISHES THOUGH IT IS TESTED BY FIRE — MAY BE FOUND TO RESULT IN PRAISE AND GLORY AND HONOR AT THE REVELATION OF JESUS CHRIST.

---

1 Peter 1:7

1 PETER

Greeting

1 Peter, an apostle of Jesus Christ,

To those who are elect exiles of the Dispersion in Pontus, Galatia, Cappadocia, Asia, and Bithynia, [2]according to the foreknowledge of God the Father, in the sanctification of the Spirit, for obedience to Jesus Christ and for sprinkling with his blood:

May grace and peace be multiplied to you.

Born Again to a Living Hope

[3]Blessed be the God and Father of our Lord Jesus Christ! According to his great mercy, he has caused us to be born again to a living hope through the resurrection of Jesus Christ from the dead, [4]to an inheritance that is imperishable, undefiled, and unfading, kept in heaven for you, [5]who by God's power are being guarded through faith for a salvation ready to be revealed in the last time. [6]In this you rejoice, though now for a little while, if necessary, you have been grieved by various trials, [7]so that the tested genuineness of your faith—more precious than gold that perishes though it is tested by fire—may be found to result in praise and glory and honor at the revelation of Jesus Christ. [8]Though you have not seen him, you love him. Though you do not now see him, you believe in him and rejoice with joy that is inexpressible and filled with glory, [9]obtaining the outcome of your faith, the salvation of your souls.

[10]Concerning this salvation, the prophets who prophesied about the grace that was to be yours searched and inquired carefully, [11]inquiring what person or time[1] the Spirit of Christ in them was indicating when he predicted the sufferings of Christ and the subsequent glories. [12]It was revealed to them that they were serving not themselves but you, in the things that have now been announced to you through those who preached the good news to you by the Holy Spirit sent from heaven, things into which angels long to look.

Called to Be Holy

[13]Therefore, preparing your minds for action,[2] and being sober-minded, set your hope fully on the grace that will be brought to you at the revelation of Jesus Christ. [14]As obedient children, do not be conformed to the passions of your former ignorance, [15]but as he who called you is holy, you also be holy in all your conduct, [16]since it is written, "You shall be holy, for I am holy." [17]And if you call on him as Father who judges impartially according to each one's deeds, conduct yourselves with fear throughout the time of your exile, [18]knowing that you were ransomed from the futile ways inherited from your forefathers, not with perishable things such as silver or gold, [19]but with the precious blood of Christ, like that of a lamb without blemish or spot. [20]He was foreknown before the foundation of the world but was made manifest in the last times for the sake of you [21]who through him are believers in God, who raised him from the dead and gave him glory, so that your faith and hope are in God.

[22]Having purified your souls by your obedience to the truth for a sincere brotherly love, love one another earnestly from a pure heart, [23]since you have been born again, not of perishable seed but of imperishable, through the living and abiding word of God; [24]for

"All flesh is like grass
    and all its glory like the flower of grass.

[1]Or *what time or circumstances* [2]Greek *girding up the loins of your mind*

HOLINESS

People who believe in Christ Jesus have been made holy through faith — set apart and dedicated strictly to God (Heb 10:10). Therefore, believers live as claimed and purchased people (1Co 6:20). Christians do not live in purity in order to become holy — they live this way because they *are* holy. Peter affirmed this reality with a call to a lifestyle of holiness. God expects Christians to live distinctive lives among people who do not know Jesus. By observing Christians' lives, the culture learns how God cares for those he loves and how believers care for each other. The abundant Christian life dedicated to the teachings of Scripture shows the world a contrast to an empty life spent in the service of sin.

Holiness requires a separation from certain parts of culture in order to pursue purity and obedience out of reverence for God. This separation refers to choices that honor God's Word — not a separation that prohibits engaging with and showing love to those who need to give their lives to Christ. Pleasing God while remaining winsome to the culture is a challenge for all Christians. When one is fully satisfied in Christ — with no need for the sinful pleasures of earth — one becomes a light in the darkness. This is in keeping with what Jesus desires for those who love and follow him: "Let your light shine before others, so that they may see your good works and give glory to your Father who is in heaven" (Mt 5:16).

Believers who read Peter's letter can clearly understand that there is a cost associated with the choice to live a godly life. Internally, they experience the tug-of-war between the Spirit and their flesh. Holiness requires discipline and self-denial. Externally, Christ-followers risk persecution and rejection from the people around them. Choosing to honor God rather than adopt the unholy practices of the culture will most often result in persecution (2Ti 3:12).

A relationship with Jesus brings overflowing joy and lasting satisfaction (Jn 17:3). Following him in discipleship leads to an abundant life (Jn 10:10). Every day Jesus' presence, provision, and plan for a believer are sufficient. He is *enough*. Holiness for Christians is evidence that satisfaction in life does not require the fleeting and empty pleasures of sin.

The grass withers,
  and the flower falls,
25 but the word of the Lord remains forever."

And this word is the good news that was preached to you.

A Living Stone and a Holy People

2 So put away all malice and all deceit and hypocrisy and envy and all slander.
2 Like newborn infants, long for the pure spiritual milk, that by it you may
grow up into salvation— 3 if indeed you have tasted that the Lord is good.
4 As you come to him, a living stone rejected by men but in the sight of God
chosen and precious, 5 you yourselves like living stones are being built up as a
spiritual house, to be a holy priesthood, to offer spiritual sacrifices acceptable to
God through Jesus Christ. 6 For it stands in Scripture:

"Behold, I am laying in Zion a stone,
  a cornerstone chosen and precious,
and whoever believes in him will not be put to shame."

7 So the honor is for you who believe, but for those who do not believe,

"The stone that the builders rejected
  has become the cornerstone,"[1]

8 and

"A stone of stumbling,
  and a rock of offense."

They stumble because they disobey the word, as they were destined to do.
9 But you are a chosen race, a royal priesthood, a holy nation, a people for his
own possession, that you may proclaim the excellencies of him who called you
out of darkness into his marvelous light. 10 Once you were not a people, but now
you are God's people; once you had not received mercy, but now you have received mercy.
11 Beloved, I urge you as sojourners and exiles to abstain from the passions
of the flesh, which wage war against your soul. 12 Keep your conduct among the
Gentiles honorable, so that when they speak against you as evildoers, they may
see your good deeds and glorify God on the day of visitation.

Submission to Authority

13 Be subject for the Lord's sake to every human institution,[2] whether it be
to the emperor[3] as supreme, 14 or to governors as sent by him to punish those
who do evil and to praise those who do good. 15 For this is the will of God, that
by doing good you should put to silence the ignorance of foolish people. 16 Live
as people who are free, not using your freedom as a cover-up for evil, but living
as servants[4] of God. 17 Honor everyone. Love the brotherhood. Fear God. Honor
the emperor.
18 Servants, be subject to your masters with all respect, not only to the good
and gentle but also to the unjust.[5] 19 For this is a gracious thing, when, mindful
of God, one endures sorrows while suffering unjustly. 20 For what credit is it if,
when you sin and are beaten for it, you endure? But if when you do good and suffer for it you endure, this is a gracious thing in the sight of God. 21 For to this you
have been called, because Christ also suffered for you, leaving you an example,
so that you might follow in his steps. 22 He committed no sin, neither was deceit
found in his mouth. 23 When he was reviled, he did not revile in return; when
he suffered, he did not threaten, but continued entrusting himself to him who
judges justly. 24 He himself bore our sins in his body on the tree, that we might die

[1]Greek *the head of the corner* [2]Or *every institution ordained for people* [3]Or *king*; also verse 17 [4]For the contextual rendering of the Greek word *doulos*, see Preface [5]Or *crooked*

1 PETER 2:4–7

LIVING TEMPLE

Peter, whose name means "rock" (Jn 1:42), reminded his readers that God sent Jesus to build a spiritual temple. During the reigns of King David and his heir Solomon, God arranged for a physical structure to be built where his presence would dwell. Now, because of Jesus and the indwelling of the Holy Spirit, all believers comprise God's temple. His presence lives in people all over the world, not just in one building made of stone.

The ancient temple was spectacular in design and detail. The church—the community of believers in Jesus—is equally beautiful. Men and women who are alive in Christ gather to worship God, to proclaim and practice his Word, mobilizing to carry the gospel to those who do not yet believe in Jesus.

In ancient construction, the first stone set in place was called the cornerstone, and all subsequent work was built upon this key foundational element. Jesus is the cornerstone of the church, precious to those who believe. He is first in importance and the source of the church's power, direction, and purpose. He is a strong foundation—those who build their lives on the rock of Christ will endure (Mt 7:24–29).

to sin and live to righteousness. By his wounds you have been healed. 25For you were straying like sheep, but have now returned to the Shepherd and Overseer of your souls.

Wives and Husbands

3 Likewise, wives, be subject to your own husbands, so that even if some do not obey the word, they may be won without a word by the conduct of their wives, 2when they see your respectful and pure conduct. 3Do not let your adorning be external—the braiding of hair and the putting on of gold jewelry, or the clothing you wear— 4but let your adorning be the hidden person of the heart with the imperishable beauty of a gentle and quiet spirit, which in God's sight is very precious. 5For this is how the holy women who hoped in God used to adorn themselves, by submitting to their own husbands, 6as Sarah obeyed Abraham, calling him lord. And you are her children, if you do good and do not fear anything that is frightening.

7Likewise, husbands, live with your wives in an understanding way, showing honor to the woman as the weaker vessel, since they are heirs with you[1] of the grace of life, so that your prayers may not be hindered.

Suffering for Righteousness' Sake

8Finally, all of you, have unity of mind, sympathy, brotherly love, a tender heart, and a humble mind. 9Do not repay evil for evil or reviling for reviling, but on the contrary, bless, for to this you were called, that you may obtain a blessing. 10For

"Whoever desires to love life
 and see good days,
let him keep his tongue from evil
 and his lips from speaking deceit;
11 let him turn away from evil and do good;
 let him seek peace and pursue it.
12 For the eyes of the Lord are on the righteous,
 and his ears are open to their prayer.
But the face of the Lord is against those who
 do evil."

13Now who is there to harm you if you are zealous for what is good? 14But even if you should suffer for righteousness' sake, you will be blessed. Have no fear of them, nor be troubled, 15but in your hearts honor Christ the Lord as holy, always being prepared to make a defense to anyone who asks you for a reason for the hope that is in you; yet do it with gentleness and respect, 16having a good conscience, so that, when you are slandered, those who revile your good behavior in Christ may be put to shame. 17For it is better to suffer for doing good, if that should be God's will, than for doing evil.

18For Christ also suffered[2] once for sins, the righteous for the unrighteous, that he might bring us to God, being put to death in the flesh but made alive in the spirit, 19in which[3] he went and proclaimed[4] to the spirits in prison, 20because[5] they formerly did not obey, when God's patience waited in the days of Noah, while the ark was being prepared, in which a few, that is, eight persons, were brought safely through water. 21Baptism, which corresponds to this, now saves you, not as a removal of dirt from the body but as an appeal to God for a good conscience, through the resurrection of Jesus Christ, 22who has gone into heaven and is at the right hand of God, with angels, authorities, and powers having been subjected to him.

[1]Some manuscripts *since you are joint heirs* [2]Some manuscripts *died* [3]Or *the Spirit, in whom*
[4]Or *preached* [5]Or *when*

1 PETER 3:18–22

WATER

Water was featured prominently at various times in God's relationship with his people. In the time of Noah, God used water to flood the earth as an act of judgment, yet preserved a faithful man and his family (Ge 6:13–18). Water ceremonially cleansed the one made unclean by sin or contamination (Lev 14:8). God demonstrated love, protection, and power by parting the waters of the Red Sea (Ex 14:21), destroying those who pursued the Israelites and performing a miracle to be forever remembered. Water satisfies thirst, and God graciously provided water after desperate days in the desert (Dt 8:15).

In the New Testament, the water of baptism symbolizes spiritual cleansing through the blood of Jesus Christ that washes away sin (1Pe 3:21). The Holy Spirit is living water for all who believe (Jn 4:10–14). He is capable of satisfying the deepest thirsts of the soul and the simplest needs of daily life.

Stewards of God's Grace

4 Since therefore Christ suffered in the flesh,[1] arm yourselves with the same way of thinking, for whoever has suffered in the flesh has ceased from sin, 2so as to live for the rest of the time in the flesh no longer for human passions but for the will of God. 3For the time that is past suffices for doing what the Gentiles want to do, living in sensuality, passions, drunkenness, orgies, drinking parties, and lawless idolatry. 4With respect to this they are surprised when you do not join them in the same flood of debauchery, and they malign you; 5but they will give account to him who is ready to judge the living and the dead. 6For this is why the gospel was preached even to those who are dead, that though judged in the flesh the way people are, they might live in the spirit the way God does.

7The end of all things is at hand; therefore be self-controlled and sober-minded for the sake of your prayers. 8Above all, keep loving one another earnestly, since love covers a multitude of sins. 9Show hospitality to one another without grumbling. 10As each has received a gift, use it to serve one another, as good stewards of God's varied grace: 11whoever speaks, as one who speaks oracles of God; whoever serves, as one who serves by the strength that God supplies—in order that in everything God may be glorified through Jesus Christ. To him belong glory and dominion forever and ever. Amen.

Suffering as a Christian

12Beloved, do not be surprised at the fiery trial when it comes upon you to test you, as though something strange were happening to you. 13But rejoice insofar as you share Christ's sufferings, that you may also rejoice and be glad when his glory is revealed. 14If you are insulted for the name of Christ, you are blessed, because the Spirit of glory[2] and of God rests upon you. 15But let none of you suffer as a murderer or a thief or an evildoer or as a meddler. 16Yet if anyone suffers as a Christian, let him not be ashamed, but let him glorify God in that name. 17For it is time for judgment to begin at the household of God; and if it begins with us, what will be the outcome for those who do not obey the gospel of God? 18And

"If the righteous is scarcely saved,
what will become of the ungodly and the sinner?"[3]

19Therefore let those who suffer according to God's will entrust their souls to a faithful Creator while doing good.

Shepherd the Flock of God

5 So I exhort the elders among you, as a fellow elder and a witness of the sufferings of Christ, as well as a partaker in the glory that is going to be revealed: 2shepherd the flock of God that is among you, exercising oversight,[4] not under compulsion, but willingly, as God would have you;[5] not for shameful gain, but eagerly; 3not domineering over those in your charge, but being examples to the flock. 4And when the chief Shepherd appears, you will receive the unfading crown of glory. 5Likewise, you who are younger, be subject to the elders. Clothe yourselves, all of you, with humility toward one another, for "God opposes the proud but gives grace to the humble."

6Humble yourselves, therefore, under the mighty hand of God so that at the proper time he may exalt you, 7casting all your anxieties on him, because he cares for you. 8Be sober-minded; be watchful. Your adversary the devil prowls around like a roaring lion, seeking someone to devour. 9Resist him, firm in your faith, knowing that the same kinds of suffering are being experienced by your brotherhood throughout the world. 10And after you have suffered a little while, the

[1]Some manuscripts add *for us*; some *for you* [2]Some manuscripts insert *and of power* [3]Greek *where will the ungodly and sinner appear?* [4]Some manuscripts omit *exercising oversight* [5]Some manuscripts omit *as God would have you*

CHURCH LEADERS

Peter concluded his first letter with an exhortation for church leaders to be shepherds of "the flock of God" (v. 2). This image of leadership assumes both vigilance and tenderness. Shepherds cannot become passive, for if they do, the sheep suffer. And God desires his leaders to exercise gentle guidance rather than kingly rule. The fact that the people are *God's flock* reminds leaders that the foundation of their role is caretaking — their primary responsibility is to lead them as God would.

Those who are called to lead God's people must meet a higher standard — they hold positions of authority over willing followers, and they will eventually give an account to God (Jas 3:1). The Greek word *presbuteros* means "elder," "bishop," or "overseer" (1Pe 5:2–4; 1Ti 3:1–7; 5:17–18; Titus 1:6–9). Overseers are responsible for leading, guiding, and nurturing a local church. They administrate governance, teach and preach, represent the church, and pray for the sick. These are the qualifications listed in the book of 1 Timothy for the office of elder: he must be above reproach, faithful to his wife, temperate, self-controlled, respectable, hospitable, able to teach, not a drunkard, not violent but gentle, not quarrelsome, not a lover of money, a good manager of his family, not a recent convert, and he must have a good reputation with outsiders. The book of Titus adds that an elder must be self-controlled, upright, holy, disciplined, and one who loves what is good and holds firmly to the gospel.

Likewise, the Greek word *diakonos* means "servant" (Ac 6:1–6; 1Ti 3:8–13). Servants are responsible for tending to physical needs among the believers so that overseers are released to minister through teaching and prayer. These are the qualifications for deacons, as listed in the book of 1 Timothy: they must be dignified, sincere, not addicted to much wine, not greedy for dishonest gain, holding doctrine with a clear conscience, and tested for approval. And they must be faithful spouses and parents, managing their households well.

Leaders in the church represent God to all those who come together to worship, but also to all those they meet in their everyday lives. That's why the New Testament is careful to outline these stringent guidelines.

God of all grace, who has called you to his eternal glory in Christ, will himself
restore, confirm, strengthen, and establish you. [11]To him be the dominion forever
and ever. Amen.

Final Greetings

[12]By Silvanus, a faithful brother as I regard him, I have written briefly to you,
exhorting and declaring that this is the true grace of God. Stand firm in it. [13]She
who is at Babylon, who is likewise chosen, sends you greetings, and so does Mark,
my son. [14]Greet one another with the kiss of love.

Peace to all of you who are in Christ.

JESUS: OUR LORD OF SALVATION

2 PETER

2 PETER

PETER SPEAKS AT JERUSALEM COUNCIL *c. AD 50*	NERO BEGINS REIGN IN ROME *c. AD 54*	PETER WRITES SECOND LETTER, THEN MARTYRED *c. AD 64 – 68*

The enemy seeks to destroy God's people. From the beginning of the book of Genesis, Satan has been bent on distorting God's Word and leading people away from God to their sure and certain deaths. Satan's plan does not change throughout the Bible — he is still at work, bringing great harm to God's people and his church.

Peter's second letter addressed believers facing a steady onslaught of attacks from the enemy. As he warned in his first letter, Satan is prowling around like a roaring lion seeking to devour as many people as he can (1Pe 5:8). Without constant vigilance, the church could have been deceived and destroyed. By the time of the writing of 2 Peter, the believers scattered throughout Asia Minor needed encouragement to continue to fight — and fight hard against Satan's advances.

Peter knew that his life was soon coming to a close (2Pe 1:12 – 15). He, like Paul, proclaimed the gospel message and fulfilled the mission that God had given him. He wrote to those he had been given to serve. He had a desire that they not stumble and fall away once he was gone.

Foremost in Peter's mind was the deceptive nature of false teaching that continually oppresses the church (2:1 – 3). False teaching is one of the primary ways Satan breeds destruction in the church, and Peter knew that believers scattered among the pagan nations must be on their guard against distorting the gospel message. He reminded believers that false teachers are doomed to destruction (2:4 – 22) and that God will see to it that they face the just consequences of their deception (3:1 – 9).

God's church must resist the devil and false teachers and hold fast to the gospel message Peter proclaimed. The day of the Lord's return will come, as Jesus had promised, and the earth will be purified from all ungodliness (3:10 – 13). Christians should focus not on Satan and his advances, but on the future coming of the Lord Jesus Christ when all wrongs will be made right and righteousness will reign upon the earth forever. Jesus has given salvation to his people, and those who have received this gift should see to it that they remain steadfast in the face of great suffering. His church can take heart that he has already defeated Satan on the cross, and one day this truth will be seen clearly by all of the world.

BUT ACCORDING TO HIS PROMISE WE ARE WAITING FOR NEW HEAVENS AND A NEW EARTH IN WHICH RIGHTEOUSNESS DWELLS. THEREFORE, BELOVED, SINCE YOU ARE WAITING FOR THESE, BE DILIGENT TO BE FOUND BY HIM WITHOUT SPOT OR BLEMISH, AND AT PEACE. AND COUNT THE PATIENCE OF OUR LORD AS SALVATION, JUST AS OUR BELOVED BROTHER PAUL ALSO WROTE TO YOU ACCORDING TO THE WISDOM GIVEN HIM.

---

2 Peter 3:13 – 15

2 PETER

Greeting

1 Simeon[1] Peter, a servant[2] and apostle of Jesus Christ,
To those who have obtained a faith of equal standing with ours by the righteousness of our God and Savior Jesus Christ:

2 May grace and peace be multiplied to you in the knowledge of God and of Jesus our Lord.

Confirm Your Calling and Election

3 His divine power has granted to us all things that pertain to life and godliness, through the knowledge of him who called us to[3] his own glory and excellence,[4] 4 by which he has granted to us his precious and very great promises, so that through them you may become partakers of the divine nature, having escaped from the corruption that is in the world because of sinful desire. 5 For this very reason, make every effort to supplement your faith with virtue,[5] and virtue with knowledge, 6 and knowledge with self-control, and self-control with steadfastness, and steadfastness with godliness, 7 and godliness with brotherly affection, and brotherly affection with love. 8 For if these qualities[6] are yours and are increasing, they keep you from being ineffective or unfruitful in the knowledge of our Lord Jesus Christ. 9 For whoever lacks these qualities is so nearsighted that he is blind, having forgotten that he was cleansed from his former sins. 10 Therefore, brothers,[7] be all the more diligent to confirm your calling and election, for if you practice these qualities you will never fall. 11 For in this way there will be richly provided for you an entrance into the eternal kingdom of our Lord and Savior Jesus Christ.

12 Therefore I intend always to remind you of these qualities, though you know them and are established in the truth that you have. 13 I think it right, as long as I am in this body,[8] to stir you up by way of reminder, 14 since I know that the putting off of my body will be soon, as our Lord Jesus Christ made clear to me. 15 And I will make every effort so that after my departure you may be able at any time to recall these things.

Christ's Glory and the Prophetic Word

16 For we did not follow cleverly devised myths when we made known to you the power and coming of our Lord Jesus Christ, but we were eyewitnesses of his majesty. 17 For when he received honor and glory from God the Father, and the voice was borne to him by the Majestic Glory, "This is my beloved Son,[9] with whom I am well pleased," 18 we ourselves heard this very voice borne from heaven, for we were with him on the holy mountain. 19 And we have the prophetic word more fully confirmed, to which you will do well to pay attention as to a lamp shining in a dark place, until the day dawns and the morning star rises in your hearts, 20 knowing this first of all, that no prophecy of Scripture comes from someone's own interpretation. 21 For no prophecy was ever produced by the will of man, but men spoke from God as they were carried along by the Holy Spirit.

False Prophets and Teachers

2 But false prophets also arose among the people, just as there will be false teachers among you, who will secretly bring in destructive heresies, even denying the Master who bought them, bringing upon themselves swift destruction.

[1]Some manuscripts *Simon* [2]For the contextual rendering of the Greek word *doulos*, see Preface [3]Or *by* [4]Or *virtue* [5]Or *excellence*; twice in this verse [6]Greek *these things*; also verses 9, 10, 12 [7]Or *brothers and sisters*. In New Testament usage, depending on the context, the plural Greek word *adelphoi* (translated "brothers") may refer either to *brothers* or to *brothers and sisters* [8]Greek *tent*; also verse 14 [9]Or *my Son, my* (or *the*) *Beloved*

---

2 PETER 1:1–8

KNOWING GOD

In the Old Testament, the people of Israel were continually reminded of their separation from God due to sin. The people knew the Most Holy Place in the temple of the Lord was forbidden to everyone except the high priest who himself only entered it once a year (Lev 16). They were taught the story of the unapproachable smoking mountain of God (Ex 19:16–25) and were told of the tragedy of Uzzah, who was struck dead after irreverently reaching out to steady the ark of God (2Sa 6:6–8). They had learned that God was unapproachable in his holiness. Only a complex system of sacrifices and priestly mediators allowed the people to relate to God.

But when Jesus came to earth, God reached down and made himself available to his people in a previously unimaginable way. While God will always remain holy and does not excuse or ignore sin, Jesus' work as the ultimate and final mediator allows his followers to draw near to the Father in freedom and intimacy. And as God in the flesh, Jesus assures his followers that "whoever has seen me has seen the Father" (Jn 14:9). So to know the Father essentially means knowing Christ; in fact, no one can bypass Jesus and truly know God at all. Jesus came to show the world what his Father was like, but more importantly, his sacrifice on the cross established the one and only path to fellowship with him (Jn 14:6).

TRUSTWORTHY AND TRUE

History records many religious figures who have claimed exclusive spiritual knowledge. From Egyptian pharaohs who were once hailed as divine to modern-day advisers who present themselves as spokespersons for God, leaders such as these attempt to exert control over their followers by proclaiming their words infallible. So when Scripture is held up as the only reliable source of truth, how can one be sure that this claim is authoritative against the backdrop of so many other voices? The apostle Paul wrote the definitive statement on the veracity of Scripture, reminding readers that the verses penned by its authors are more than ordinary literature or historical accounts. They are "breathed out by God" (2Ti 3:16). The Lord himself took an active role in birthing these manuscripts, and through them equips people with an unparalleled foundation for right thinking and living. The approximately 40 writers of the 66 books that form the biblical text composed their contributions in three languages in a variety of literary genres (poetry, history, narrative, correspondence, exposition, parable, and apocalyptic) over the span of many hundreds of years. And yet, remarkably, they contain a unified story of creation, revolt, redemption, and restoration. Compelling evidence for the reliability of Scripture lies also in its many incidences of fulfilled prophecy. For example, centuries before the event itself, the prophet Ezekiel accurately predicted the cataclysmic fate of the city of Tyre (Eze 26); the book of Psalms described crucifixion as a capital punishment more than 400 years before it was used (Ps 22); and, as one of hundreds of Messianic prophecies, Micah identified Bethlehem (Mic 5:2) as the birthplace of the Christ 600 years before Jesus arrived on earth in that exact spot.

In addition to Scripture's internal consistencies, archaeology continues to provide convincing evidence that supports Scripture. Findings pointing to biblical people groups, places, and customs greatly increase textual credibility. Most significantly, the Dead Sea Scrolls — discovered in caves outside Jerusalem in the 1940s and 50s — contain over 800 ancient Jewish documents that include at least fragments of every book of the Old Testament except Esther. These scrolls, estimated to have been written between 150 BC and AD 70, clearly establish the high degree of fidelity between the modern texts and the original source material and serve as strong evidence of the authenticity and trustworthiness of the entire scriptural record. The more that readers examine the evidence for the accuracy of God's Word, the more they can be assured that "his divine power has granted to us all things that pertain to life and godliness, through the knowledge of him who called us to his own glory and excellence" (2Pe 1:3).

[2]And many will follow their sensuality, and because of them the way of truth will be blasphemed. [3]And in their greed they will exploit you with false words. Their condemnation from long ago is not idle, and their destruction is not asleep.

[4]For if God did not spare angels when they sinned, but cast them into hell[1] and committed them to chains[2] of gloomy darkness to be kept until the judgment; [5]if he did not spare the ancient world, but preserved Noah, a herald of righteousness, with seven others, when he brought a flood upon the world of the ungodly; [6]if by turning the cities of Sodom and Gomorrah to ashes he condemned them to extinction, making them an example of what is going to happen to the ungodly;[3] [7]and if he rescued righteous Lot, greatly distressed by the sensual conduct of the wicked [8](for as that righteous man lived among them day after day, he was tormenting his righteous soul over their lawless deeds that he saw and heard); [9]then the Lord knows how to rescue the godly from trials,[4] and to keep the unrighteous under punishment until the day of judgment, [10]and especially those who indulge[5] in the lust of defiling passion and despise authority.

Bold and willful, they do not tremble as they blaspheme the glorious ones, [11]whereas angels, though greater in might and power, do not pronounce a blasphemous judgment against them before the Lord. [12]But these, like irrational animals, creatures of instinct, born to be caught and destroyed, blaspheming about matters of which they are ignorant, will also be destroyed in their destruction, [13]suffering wrong as the wage for their wrongdoing. They count it pleasure to revel in the daytime. They are blots and blemishes, reveling in their deceptions,[6] while they feast with you. [14]They have eyes full of adultery,[7] insatiable for sin. They entice unsteady souls. They have hearts trained in greed. Accursed children! [15]Forsaking the right way, they have gone astray. They have followed the way of Balaam, the son of Beor, who loved gain from wrongdoing, [16]but was rebuked for his own transgression; a speechless donkey spoke with human voice and restrained the prophet's madness.

[17]These are waterless springs and mists driven by a storm. For them the gloom of utter darkness has been reserved. [18]For, speaking loud boasts of folly, they entice by sensual passions of the flesh those who are barely escaping from those who live in error. [19]They promise them freedom, but they themselves are slaves[8] of corruption. For whatever overcomes a person, to that he is enslaved. [20]For if, after they have escaped the defilements of the world through the knowledge of our Lord and Savior Jesus Christ, they are again entangled in them and overcome, the last state has become worse for them than the first. [21]For it would have been better for them never to have known the way of righteousness than after knowing it to turn back from the holy commandment delivered to them. [22]What the true proverb says has happened to them: "The dog returns to its own vomit, and the sow, after washing herself, returns to wallow in the mire."

The Day of the Lord Will Come

3 This is now the second letter that I am writing to you, beloved. In both of them I am stirring up your sincere mind by way of reminder, [2]that you should remember the predictions of the holy prophets and the commandment of the Lord and Savior through your apostles, [3]knowing this first of all, that scoffers will come in the last days with scoffing, following their own sinful desires. [4]They will say, "Where is the promise of his coming? For ever since the fathers fell asleep, all things are continuing as they were from the beginning of creation." [5]For they deliberately overlook this fact, that the heavens existed long ago, and the earth was formed out of water and through water by the word of God, [6]and that by means of these the world that then existed was deluged with water and perished. [7]But by the same word the heavens and earth that now exist are stored up for fire, being kept until the day of judgment and destruction of the ungodly.

[1]Greek *Tartarus* [2]Some manuscripts *pits* [3]Some manuscripts *an example to those who were to be ungodly* [4]Or *temptations* [5]Greek *who go after the flesh* [6]Some manuscripts *love feasts* [7]Or *eyes full of an adulteress* [8]For the contextual rendering of the Greek word *doulos*, see Preface

DEMONIC ACTIVITY

Demons — these unseen wicked forces are common subjects of popular movies, fantasy games, and literature. While those depictions are largely the stuff of imagination, one cannot accept the Word of God as authentic without acknowledging the existence of a spiritual dimension populated with malicious adversaries. Scripture is not abundantly clear on demonic origins, but it does suggest they were once servants of the Most High God but who engaged in a doomed rebellion and were cast from his presence.

In the book of Revelation, John used bold imagery and symbolic language to describe Satan's ill-fated revolt, and he attested to the outcome of the "war" that "arose in heaven" (Rev 12:7): "The great dragon ... called the devil and Satan ... was thrown down to the earth, and his angels ... with him" (Rev 12:9). At present, it appears that not all of these fallen angels have free reign upon the earth. The New Testament refers to some of these beings as kept in darkness and bound with everlasting chains until their final judgment (2Pe 2:4; Jude 6). But whatever their current state, Jesus assured his followers that these evil entities are destined for unending torment of "eternal fire" in a "lake of fire and sulfur" (Mt 25:41; Rev 20:10). However, until their judgment is meted out, the devil and his cohorts continue to lead a calculated effort to thwart God, deceive humanity, and lead the whole world astray (Rev 12:9). Their tactics include temptation to sin (Ge 3:1 – 6; Mt 4:1 – 4; Lk 4:1 – 2; Eph 2:1 – 2), physical ailments (Job 2:7; Mt 12:22; Mk 9:25; Lk 13:11; Ac 10:37 – 38; 2Co 12:7), deceitful miraculous signs (Rev 16:14), manipulation of the environment (Job 1:16 – 19), mental/emotional distress (Mt 8:28; Eph 4:26 – 27), spiritual possession/oppression (Mt 12:22 – 28; 17:18; Lk 4:33 – 35), confusion and false teaching (Lk 22:31; 1Ti 4:1; 1Jn 4:1 – 3), and issues of self-control and moral compromise (1Co 7:4 – 5; Rev 2:20).

Although the devil is called "the prince of the power of the air" (Eph 2:2) and, along with his legions, seems to have much influence, believers have no reason to fear. Demonic activity is sovereignly limited by God's power. Colossians 2:15 points to the certain victory over these spiritual enemies already achieved by Christ: "He disarmed the rulers and authorities and put them to open shame, by triumphing over them in him."

WHAT KIND OF PEOPLE OUGHT YOU BE?

A right relationship with God begins by accepting Christ's forgiveness of sins by grace through faith (Eph 2:8–9). But that is only the launching point of a journey that should be marked by ongoing spiritual development. Peter's second letter challenged new believers to make a lifelong investment in growing "in the grace and knowledge of our Lord and Savior Jesus Christ" (2Pe 3:18). With a strong emphasis on correct doctrine, he stressed the importance of a deep commitment to Christ that should result in holy living. Instead of recommending outward actions to effect inward change, Peter pointed to the urgent need for believers to root their relationship with Jesus deeply in the Scriptures. God's "precious and very great promises" and union with Christ serve as the foundation for a life of godliness and as protection from the corrupting influence of an ungodly world system with its perverse and selfish desires (1:2–4). Since God has made such a vast supply of divine resources available, believers must participate actively in applying them. Resting on the solid underpinning of faith, disciplines such as goodness, knowledge, self-control, perseverance, godliness, mutual affection, and love ought to be evident and obvious in the lives of those who claim Jesus as their Savior (1:5–7).

In addition, diligent study and application of the truth form a solid shield against "destructive heresies" that are continually introduced into Christian fellowships by false teachers (2:1). Often approving of lustful indulgences, aberrant philosophies can appear persuasive, but their empty promises (ironically, championed by those who are themselves enslaved to fleshly passions) provide no real freedom or stability (2:18–19). Warnings against false prophets appear first in the Law of Moses (Dt 13:1–4; 18:20–22) and are reiterated throughout the New Testament (2Pe 2:1–22; Ro 16:17–18; 2Co 11:13–15; Gal 1:6–9; 1Jn 4:1–6; Jude 3–4). Jesus warned that a proliferation of these teachers would be a sign of the end of the age and of his eventual return (Mt 24:5,11).

While the fate of those who lead others astray is fixed (2Pe 2:1–22), Christians must vigilantly guard against their infiltration into the church. Though scoffers, mockers, and those who twist the truth will always exist (3:3), Peter encouraged his audience to remain resolutely rooted in the promises of God, knowing that the Lord has set a firm date at which time he will bring about cleansing and final justice (3:10). In the meantime, he was also clear about a believer's personal responsibility: to live "lives of holiness and godliness" (3:11–12).

8But do not overlook this one fact, beloved, that with the Lord one day is as a
thousand years, and a thousand years as one day. 9The Lord is not slow to fulfill
his promise as some count slowness, but is patient toward you,[1] not wishing that
any should perish, but that all should reach repentance. 10But the day of the Lord
will come like a thief, and then the heavens will pass away with a roar, and the
heavenly bodies[2] will be burned up and dissolved, and the earth and the works
that are done on it will be exposed.[3]

11Since all these things are thus to be dissolved, what sort of people ought you
to be in lives of holiness and godliness, 12waiting for and hastening the coming of
the day of God, because of which the heavens will be set on fire and dissolved, and
the heavenly bodies will melt as they burn! 13But according to his promise we are
waiting for new heavens and a new earth in which righteousness dwells.

Final Words

14Therefore, beloved, since you are waiting for these, be diligent to be found
by him without spot or blemish, and at peace. 15And count the patience of our
Lord as salvation, just as our beloved brother Paul also wrote to you according to
the wisdom given him, 16as he does in all his letters when he speaks in them of
these matters. There are some things in them that are hard to understand, which
the ignorant and unstable twist to their own destruction, as they do the other
Scriptures. 17You therefore, beloved, knowing this beforehand, take care that you
are not carried away with the error of lawless people and lose your own stability.
18But grow in the grace and knowledge of our Lord and Savior Jesus Christ. To him
be the glory both now and to the day of eternity. Amen.

---

[1]Some manuscripts *on your account* [2]Or *elements*; also verse 12 [3]Greek *found*; some manuscripts *will be burned up*

JESUS: OUR WORD OF LIFE AND LOVE

1 JOHN

1 JOHN

JESUS CALLS JOHN *c. AD 27*	TEMPLE DESTROYED, CHURCH SCATTERS *c. AD 70*	JOHN WRITES HIS GOSPEL AND LETTERS *c. AD 90*

A restored relationship with God produces a right relationship with others. The two cannot be separated. When asked about the greatest commandments, Jesus made this point clearly. He said, "You shall love the Lord your God with all your heart and with all your soul and with all your mind. This is the great and first commandment. And a second is like it: You shall love your neighbor as yourself" (Mt 22:37 – 39). A true Christian cannot profess to love God without pursuing authentic and enduring relationships with others.

John knew that the fellowship of the church was vital for the perseverance of Christians living near the end of the first century. But the love of Christians for one another does not merely serve a practical purpose of accountability and support. The love of the church models the love of God. The trinitarian God — Father, Son, and Holy Spirit — exists in loving harmony. The nature of the Godhead serves as a model for the communal nature of God's people (1Jn 1:5; 2:29; 4:7 – 8). They are to love one another in a way that models the love of the Trinity. Genuine love is an indication of the authenticity of their relationship with God (4:7 – 16; 4:20 — 5:5) and provides believers with assurance that their salvation is indeed genuine (4:17 – 19). Love also has a missionary purpose — others see mature, self-sacrificial love between God's people and have a picture of the way that God loves his people.

Those who do not truly know Christ will not fulfill this law of love. False teachers were continuing to deceive the church — failing to model the love of God for his people. Their teaching consisted of an early form of Gnosticism that falsely divided one's spiritual life from their physical existence. Many false teachers went so far as to teach the heresy that Jesus was a spiritual being but lacked a physical body. John countered this claim, arguing that Jesus Christ was a physical being who, in his body, accomplished the plan of God (1:1 – 4). Those who follow the Word made flesh should live out the gospel message in real, tangible, and concrete ways that can be observed by all people — primarily through their love and service to one another. Love, not mystical experiences, is meant to be the defining mark of God's people.

BY THIS WE KNOW LOVE,
THAT HE LAID DOWN HIS LIFE FOR US,
AND WE OUGHT TO LAY DOWN OUR LIVES
FOR THE BROTHERS.

---

1 John 3:16

1 JOHN

The Word of Life

1 That which was from the beginning, which we have heard, which we have seen with our eyes, which we looked upon and have touched with our hands, concerning the word[1] of life— 2 the life was made manifest, and we have seen it, and testify to it and proclaim to you the eternal life, which was with the Father and was made manifest to us— 3 that which we have seen and heard we proclaim also to you, so that you too may have fellowship with us; and indeed our fellowship is with the Father and with his Son Jesus Christ. 4 And we are writing these things so that our[2] joy may be complete.

Walking in the Light

5 This is the message we have heard from him and proclaim to you, that God is light, and in him is no darkness at all. 6 If we say we have fellowship with him while we walk in darkness, we lie and do not practice the truth. 7 But if we walk in the light, as he is in the light, we have fellowship with one another, and the blood of Jesus his Son cleanses us from all sin. 8 If we say we have no sin, we deceive ourselves, and the truth is not in us. 9 If we confess our sins, he is faithful and just to forgive us our sins and to cleanse us from all unrighteousness. 10 If we say we have not sinned, we make him a liar, and his word is not in us.

Christ Our Advocate

2 My little children, I am writing these things to you so that you may not sin. But if anyone does sin, we have an advocate with the Father, Jesus Christ the righteous. 2 He is the propitiation for our sins, and not for ours only but also for the sins of the whole world. 3 And by this we know that we have come to know him, if we keep his commandments. 4 Whoever says "I know him" but does not keep his commandments is a liar, and the truth is not in him, 5 but whoever keeps his word, in him truly the love of God is perfected. By this we may know that we are in him: 6 whoever says he abides in him ought to walk in the same way in which he walked.

The New Commandment

7 Beloved, I am writing you no new commandment, but an old commandment that you had from the beginning. The old commandment is the word that you have heard. 8 At the same time, it is a new commandment that I am writing to you, which is true in him and in you, because[3] the darkness is passing away and the true light is already shining. 9 Whoever says he is in the light and hates his brother is still in darkness. 10 Whoever loves his brother abides in the light, and in him[4] there is no cause for stumbling. 11 But whoever hates his brother is in the darkness and walks in the darkness, and does not know where he is going, because the darkness has blinded his eyes.

12 I am writing to you, little children,
because your sins are forgiven for his name's sake.
13 I am writing to you, fathers,
because you know him who is from the beginning.
I am writing to you, young men,
because you have overcome the evil one.
I write to you, children,
because you know the Father.

[1]Or *Word* [2]Some manuscripts *your* [3]Or *that* [4]Or *it*

1 JOHN 1:1–3

LOGOS: THE WORD

John's reference to Jesus as "the word" (Greek *logos,* v. 1) carried great significance to his Jewish readers. They clearly understood the power and authority that was present when the Lord spoke: to create the world (Ge 1:1—2:25; Ps 33:6), to enter into his covenant with Abraham (Ge 15:1–8), and to deliver his Law to Moses on Mount Sinai (Ex 24:1–18; Dt 9:9–10). Greek readers also acknowledged the concept of "logos" as the fundamental commanding force that gave order and form to the universe. So when John ascribed this designation to Jesus (1Jn 1:1; Jn 1:1–2; Rev 19:13), he clearly pointed to Christ as the embodiment of God's creative, sustaining power and as the final word to humanity. His eyewitness account went beyond simply recording that a mere mortal named Jesus lived, but that this man whom he had "heard," "seen" and "touched" (1Jn 1:1) was none other than the author of eternal life (v. 2). Christ's entrance into the world replaced the concept of God as distant with a clarified one showing him as personal and involved, as a God who, through faith in the death and resurrection of his Son, believers can know and love (v. 3).

FATHER, SON, AND HOLY SPIRIT

A time-honored hymn entitled "Holy, Holy, Holy" declares, "God in three persons, blessed Trinity." *Trinity* is a term coined between the second and fourth centuries to describe a fundamental doctrine of the Christian faith. This doctrine states that simultaneously and individually, the Father, Son, and Holy Spirit are wholly God. While the word itself does not occur in Scripture, there is ample evidence to support God's triune nature throughout the Bible (Ge 1:26; 3:22; Isa 48:16; 61:1; Mt 3:13–17; 22:43–46; 28:19; 2Co 13:14; 1Pe 1:2). However, it is in the writings of John that Christians find the most nuanced view of the divine relationship.

In a very straightforward way, John opened by proclaiming the most important thing his readers needed to know: Jesus is God. Jesus has always existed, from the beginning, and he is not a subservient being as the heavenly hosts are. Rather Jesus was, is, and will always be of the same nature as the Father (Jn 1:1–4). Jesus himself attested to this unique relationship when he laid claim to the revered name of God revealed to Moses at the burning bush (Jn 8:58; cf. Ex 3:14) and later reiterated this truth by stating "I and the Father are one" (Jn 10:30).

John also delivered key insight into the special unity Jesus shares with the Holy Spirit. While the word "advocate" (Greek *parakletos*) appears other places in Scripture, the form of the word used to describe a person appears only twice in the New Testament writings and uniquely in John's letters. He once used *parakletos* to identify the "advocate with the Father" to be "Jesus Christ the righteous" (1Jn 2:1). And in Christ's last discourse with his disciples, John's Gospel recorded Jesus' words that gave this same designation to the promised Holy Spirit, calling him another advocate, or Helper (Jn 14:16,26; 15:26; 16:7). John also taught that the Spirit and Christ interchangeably serve as companion (Jn 14:26–28), teacher (Jn 14:26; 2Jn 9), judge (Jn 5:22–23; 16:8), Guide (Jn 10:3–4; 16:13), and truth (1Jn 5:6–8; Jn 14:6).

Throughout his letters, John encourages all believers to be confident in the certainty of their salvation that is initiated, completed, and secured by the harmonious work of the Father, Son, and Spirit. "By this we know that we abide in him and he in us, because he has given us of his Spirit. And we have seen and testify that the Father has sent his Son to be the Savior of the world" (1Jn 4:13–14).

14 I write to you, fathers,
because you know him who is from the beginning.
I write to you, young men,
because you are strong,
and the word of God abides in you,
and you have overcome the evil one.

Do Not Love the World

15 Do not love the world or the things in the world. If anyone loves the world, the love of the Father is not in him. 16 For all that is in the world—the desires of the flesh and the desires of the eyes and pride of life[1]—is not from the Father but is from the world. 17 And the world is passing away along with its desires, but whoever does the will of God abides forever.

Warning Concerning Antichrists

18 Children, it is the last hour, and as you have heard that antichrist is coming, so now many antichrists have come. Therefore we know that it is the last hour. 19 They went out from us, but they were not of us; for if they had been of us, they would have continued with us. But they went out, that it might become plain that they all are not of us. 20 But you have been anointed by the Holy One, and you all have knowledge.[2] 21 I write to you, not because you do not know the truth, but because you know it, and because no lie is of the truth. 22 Who is the liar but he who denies that Jesus is the Christ? This is the antichrist, he who denies the Father and the Son. 23 No one who denies the Son has the Father. Whoever confesses the Son has the Father also. 24 Let what you heard from the beginning abide in you. If what you heard from the beginning abides in you, then you too will abide in the Son and in the Father. 25 And this is the promise that he made to us[3]—eternal life.

26 I write these things to you about those who are trying to deceive you. 27 But the anointing that you received from him abides in you, and you have no need that anyone should teach you. But as his anointing teaches you about everything, and is true, and is no lie—just as it has taught you, abide in him.

Children of God

28 And now, little children, abide in him, so that when he appears we may have confidence and not shrink from him in shame at his coming. 29 If you know that he is righteous, you may be sure that everyone who practices righteousness has been born of him.

3 See what kind of love the Father has given to us, that we should be called children of God; and so we are. The reason why the world does not know us is that it did not know him. 2 Beloved, we are God's children now, and what we will be has not yet appeared; but we know that when he appears[4] we shall be like him, because we shall see him as he is. 3 And everyone who thus hopes in him purifies himself as he is pure.

4 Everyone who makes a practice of sinning also practices lawlessness; sin is lawlessness. 5 You know that he appeared in order to take away sins, and in him there is no sin. 6 No one who abides in him keeps on sinning; no one who keeps on sinning has either seen him or known him. 7 Little children, let no one deceive you. Whoever practices righteousness is righteous, as he is righteous. 8 Whoever makes a practice of sinning is of the devil, for the devil has been sinning from the beginning. The reason the Son of God appeared was to destroy the works of the devil. 9 No one born of God makes a practice of sinning, for God's[5] seed abides in him; and he cannot keep on sinning, because he has been born of God. 10 By this it is evident who are the children of God, and who are the children of the devil:

[1] Or *pride in possessions* [2] Some manuscripts *you know everything* [3] Some manuscripts *you* [4] Or *when it appears* [5] Greek *his*

1 JOHN 2:18–27

SPIRIT OF ANTICHRIST

The word *antichrist* is often associated only with the powerful and influential leader who will come into the spotlight to deceive the masses during the world's last days. While the Bible certainly does refer to this "man of lawlessness" who will emerge in the future (2Th 2:3), John's letter alerted believers to the danger of false teachers in the church and warned them to be aware that "many antichrists have come" (1Jn 2:18; 4:3). As the simple definition of the term indicates, this force encompasses any attitude or action that is generally "anti" (or against) Christ, and it especially includes any viewpoint that opposes belief in Jesus as fully God and the promised Messiah (2:22; 4:2–3).

Those who know scriptural truth but neglect to apply it to their lives easily fall prey to corrupt teachings that sound attractive but, in reality, are only myths that appeal to fleshly desires and satisfy "itching ears" (2Ti 4:3). Christians are not powerless against these deceptions. John reminded readers that God has equipped them with two key defenses against those who attempt to distort the gospel: first, a commitment to consistent study and application of the Word of truth (2Ti 2:15; 1Jn 2:24–25) and second, the indwelling guidance given by the Spirit of truth (Jn 16:13; 1Jn 2:27; 4:6). Both of these teach discernment and form a solid shield of protection against any falsehood.

whoever does not practice righteousness is not of God, nor is the one who does
not love his brother.

Love One Another

11For this is the message that you have heard from the beginning, that we
should love one another. 12We should not be like Cain, who was of the evil one
and murdered his brother. And why did he murder him? Because his own deeds
were evil and his brother's righteous. 13Do not be surprised, brothers,[1] that the
world hates you. 14We know that we have passed out of death into life, because
we love the brothers. Whoever does not love abides in death. 15Everyone who
hates his brother is a murderer, and you know that no murderer has eternal life
abiding in him.

16By this we know love, that he laid down his life for us, and we ought to lay
down our lives for the brothers. 17But if anyone has the world's goods and sees
his brother in need, yet closes his heart against him, how does God's love abide
in him? 18Little children, let us not love in word or talk but in deed and in truth.

19By this we shall know that we are of the truth and reassure our heart before
him; 20for whenever our heart condemns us, God is greater than our heart, and
he knows everything. 21Beloved, if our heart does not condemn us, we have confidence before God; 22and whatever we ask we receive from him, because we keep
his commandments and do what pleases him. 23And this is his commandment,
that we believe in the name of his Son Jesus Christ and love one another, just as
he has commanded us. 24Whoever keeps his commandments abides in God,[2] and
God[3] in him. And by this we know that he abides in us, by the Spirit whom he has
given us.

Test the Spirits

4 Beloved, do not believe every spirit, but test the spirits to see whether they
are from God, for many false prophets have gone out into the world. 2By this
you know the Spirit of God: every spirit that confesses that Jesus Christ has come
in the flesh is from God, 3and every spirit that does not confess Jesus is not from
God. This is the spirit of the antichrist, which you heard was coming and now is in
the world already. 4Little children, you are from God and have overcome them, for
he who is in you is greater than he who is in the world. 5They are from the world;
therefore they speak from the world, and the world listens to them. 6We are from
God. Whoever knows God listens to us; whoever is not from God does not listen
to us. By this we know the Spirit of truth and the spirit of error.

God Is Love

7Beloved, let us love one another, for love is from God, and whoever loves has
been born of God and knows God. 8Anyone who does not love does not know
God, because God is love. 9In this the love of God was made manifest among us,
that God sent his only Son into the world, so that we might live through him. 10In
this is love, not that we have loved God but that he loved us and sent his Son to be
the propitiation for our sins. 11Beloved, if God so loved us, we also ought to love
one another. 12No one has ever seen God; if we love one another, God abides in us
and his love is perfected in us.

13By this we know that we abide in him and he in us, because he has given
us of his Spirit. 14And we have seen and testify that the Father has sent his Son
to be the Savior of the world. 15Whoever confesses that Jesus is the Son of God,
God abides in him, and he in God. 16So we have come to know and to believe the
love that God has for us. God is love, and whoever abides in love abides in God,
and God abides in him. 17By this is love perfected with us, so that we may have

---

[1]Or *brothers and sisters*. In New Testament usage, depending on the context, the plural Greek word *adelphoi* (translated "brothers") may refer either to *brothers* or to *brothers and sisters*; also verses 14, 16
[2]Greek *him* [3]Greek *he*

confidence for the day of judgment, because as he is so also are we in this world.
18There is no fear in love, but perfect love casts out fear. For fear has to do with
punishment, and whoever fears has not been perfected in love. 19We love because
he first loved us. 20If anyone says, "I love God," and hates his brother, he is a liar;
for he who does not love his brother whom he has seen cannot[1] love God whom
he has not seen. 21And this commandment we have from him: whoever loves God
must also love his brother.

Overcoming the World

5 Everyone who believes that Jesus is the Christ has been born of God, and everyone who loves the Father loves whoever has been born of him. 2By this
we know that we love the children of God, when we love God and obey his commandments. 3For this is the love of God, that we keep his commandments. And
his commandments are not burdensome. 4For everyone who has been born of
God overcomes the world. And this is the victory that has overcome the world—
our faith. 5Who is it that overcomes the world except the one who believes that
Jesus is the Son of God?

Testimony Concerning the Son of God

6This is he who came by water and blood—Jesus Christ; not by the water only
but by the water and the blood. And the Spirit is the one who testifies, because
the Spirit is the truth. 7For there are three that testify: 8the Spirit and the water
and the blood; and these three agree. 9If we receive the testimony of men, the
testimony of God is greater, for this is the testimony of God that he has borne
concerning his Son. 10Whoever believes in the Son of God has the testimony in
himself. Whoever does not believe God has made him a liar, because he has not
believed in the testimony that God has borne concerning his Son. 11And this is the
testimony, that God gave us eternal life, and this life is in his Son. 12Whoever has
the Son has life; whoever does not have the Son of God does not have life.

That You May Know

13I write these things to you who believe in the name of the Son of God, that
you may know that you have eternal life. 14And this is the confidence that we have
toward him, that if we ask anything according to his will he hears us. 15And if we
know that he hears us in whatever we ask, we know that we have the requests that
we have asked of him.

16If anyone sees his brother committing a sin not leading to death, he shall ask,
and God[2] will give him life—to those who commit sins that do not lead to death.
There is sin that leads to death; I do not say that one should pray for that. 17All
wrongdoing is sin, but there is sin that does not lead to death.

18We know that everyone who has been born of God does not keep on sinning,
but he who was born of God protects him, and the evil one does not touch him.

19We know that we are from God, and the whole world lies in the power of
the evil one.

20And we know that the Son of God has come and has given us understanding,
so that we may know him who is true; and we are in him who is true, in his Son
Jesus Christ. He is the true God and eternal life. 21Little children, keep yourselves
from idols.

[1] Some manuscripts *how can he* [2] Greek *he*

JESUS: OUR GOD IN THE FLESH

2 JOHN

2 JOHN

JOHN LEADS IN THE EARLY CHURCH *c. AD 30*	TEMPLE DESTROYED, CHURCH SCATTERS *c. AD 70*	JOHN WRITES HIS GOSPEL AND LETTERS *c. AD 90*

Followers of Jesus must be on their guard against deception. The recurring theme of false teaching is pervasive throughout the New Testament epistles and is the central focus of John's second letter. Little is known about the recipient of John's letter: "to the elect lady and her children," though it is clear that the apostle John has deep love for those to whom he writes (v. 1).

This love is seen most clearly in his desire to protect them from harmful false teaching. An abundance of false views regarding God's nature and his work through Jesus had infiltrated God's people. One such view, Docetism, taught that Jesus had not come in the flesh. False teachers deceived many with the notion that Jesus did not have a physical body but only appeared to have one. Thus, his death on the cross and resurrection were not physical realities.

John warns true believers to beware of such heresy. The physical life, actual death, and bodily resurrection of Jesus are vital components of the Christian faith. Someone had to actually live the perfect life that God desired in order to give God's people the gift of a righteous standing before God. Someone had to die a physical death and endure the spiritual weight of humanity's sin in order to satisfy the wrath of God for that sin. Someone had to overcome death in a physical body in order to demonstrate that Satan, sin, and death had been defeated.

For this reason, John wrote that the false teachers were not peddling a minor distortion to the truth. They were teaching rank heresy and had to be silenced. The same law of love he established in his first letter motivated John's challenge to the church.

False teachers must be silenced out of love and protection for God's people. Elders and church members alike must see to it that they protect one another from the harm that Satan brings through false teaching. Together, they must hold to the truth of the gospel, which was handed down by God to the apostles and protected by the careful leadership of the church. Throughout all generations, though the nature of the false teaching may change, churches must fight for the truth of the gospel.

AND THIS IS LOVE, THAT WE WALK
ACCORDING TO HIS COMMANDMENTS;
THIS IS THE COMMANDMENT, JUST AS YOU
HAVE HEARD FROM THE BEGINNING,
SO THAT YOU SHOULD WALK IN IT.

---

2 John 6

2 JOHN

Greeting

1 The elder to the elect lady and her children, whom I love in truth, and not only I, but also all who know the truth, 2 because of the truth that abides in us and will be with us forever:

3 Grace, mercy, and peace will be with us, from God the Father and from Jesus Christ the Father's Son, in truth and love.

Walking in Truth and Love

4 I rejoiced greatly to find some of your children walking in the truth, just as we were commanded by the Father. 5 And now I ask you, dear lady—not as though I were writing you a new commandment, but the one we have had from the beginning—that we love one another. 6 And this is love, that we walk according to his commandments; this is the commandment, just as you have heard from the beginning, so that you should walk in it. 7 For many deceivers have gone out into the world, those who do not confess the coming of Jesus Christ in the flesh. Such a one is the deceiver and the antichrist. 8 Watch yourselves, so that you may not lose what we[1] have worked for, but may win a full reward. 9 Everyone who goes on ahead and does not abide in the teaching of Christ, does not have God. Whoever abides in the teaching has both the Father and the Son. 10 If anyone comes to you and does not bring this teaching, do not receive him into your house or give him any greeting, 11 for whoever greets him takes part in his wicked works.

Final Greetings

12 Though I have much to write to you, I would rather not use paper and ink. Instead I hope to come to you and talk face to face, so that our joy may be complete.

13 The children of your elect sister greet you.

2 JOHN 6

TRUTH AND LOVE

In the latter half of the first century, the young church faced many new problems. At the command of Emperor Nero, the Roman government launched a structured campaign to persecute Christians that included some of the most atrocious forms of torture and execution ever devised. Historians believe that both Peter, Christ's boldest disciple and preacher at Pentecost, and Paul, the greatest church planter and missionary of the first century, were martyred under Nero's brutal reign. And while attacks from outside the church escalated, deceptive philosophies from false teachers proliferated and began to erode it from the inside. This confusion caused many ungrounded believers to embrace aberrant ideas about the person and work of Christ.

Into this troubling atmosphere, John ("the elder" [v. 1] and the last of Jesus' twelve disciples to survive) wrote this short letter to remind the early church of the importance of holding fast to the truth of the gospel (as recorded in the pages of Scripture) and of walking in love. Instead of defining love in situational or emotional terms, he gave believers a clear understanding of the meaning of genuine love: to walk according to Jesus' commands (v. 6). And that love is exhibited most genuinely by a life lived in consistency with the teachings of Christ.

[1] Some manuscripts *you*

JESUS: OUR BOND OF FELLOWSHIP

3 JOHN

3 JOHN

JOHN RESIDES IN EPHESUS *c. AD 67*	TEMPLE DESTROYED, CHURCH SCATTERS *c. AD 70*	JOHN WRITES HIS GOSPEL AND LETTERS *c. AD 90*

Internal conflict is divisive for the church of Jesus Christ. In his first two letters, John warned the church against false teachers who were deceiving the church from the outside. Their heresy was leading many astray and contaminating their understanding of the truthfulness of the gospel. In 3 John, the church is facing another destructive influence. Diotrephes, a church leader, was exerting control over his congregation by barring other ministers from serving his congregation. Even worse, Diotrephes was disassociating from members of the congregation who demonstrated kindness to these ministers. In so doing, he was violating John's challenge for the church to model the love of Christ in their relationships with all believers.

Diotrephes' arrogance was harming the church, and it needed to be stopped. John was planning a visit to the church to address this issue, but in the meantime he wrote to challenge this moral failure of its leader.

John's letter is addressed to a member of the church, Gaius, who had the resources to show care to these itinerant ministers. John encouraged Gaius in his support of these fellow workers "for the truth" (v. 8). They were fellow ministers of the gospel, doing faithful ministry among the Gentiles. The church, according to John, had a responsibility to support, encourage, and equip these gospel workers. Diotrephes' actions were hindering the good work these laborers were doing. Apparently, John felt that Gaius had the confidence, strength, and ability to counter Diotrephes' actions and continue to lead the church to support and send workers.

The sending of missionaries and ministers of the gospel should mark the church.

Established churches, founded on the true claims of Jesus Christ, must see to it that they invest time, effort, and energy in the advancement of the gospel around the world. Missionaries such as Paul, Barnabas, John Mark, and others throughout the book of Acts are examples of the faithfulness of God's church in sending gospel ministers and the way God uses these leaders to build up his church around the world. Faithful leaders should follow John's exhortation in this brief letter and empower their churches to love, serve, and send those taking the name of Jesus around the world.

FOR I REJOICED GREATLY WHEN THE BROTHERS
CAME AND TESTIFIED TO YOUR TRUTH,
AS INDEED YOU ARE WALKING IN THE TRUTH.

---

3 John 3

3 JOHN

3 JOHN 2

HAVE OR HAVE NOT

In John's greeting to Gaius, he prayed that his friend would find balance between the spiritual and physical world (v. 2). While much is written in the Bible about material possessions, there is little written to indicate that either worldly prosperity or poverty are reliable indicators of God's approval or disapproval. Scripture records that some of God's key servants possessed significant material means, including Abraham (Ge 13:2), Isaac (Ge 26:12–14), Jacob (Ge 36:6–7), David (1Ch 28:1), Solomon (2Ch 9:22), Jehoshaphat (2Ch 17:5) and Joseph of Arimathea (Mt 27:57). Conversely, the lives of others such as Elijah (1Ki 17:1–14), Naomi (Ru 1:1–21), Jeremiah (Jer 37:1–21), John the Baptist (Mt 3:4; Lk 1:80), and Paul (Ac 16:16–36; 28:16–31; Php 1:12–14) bear witness that others had to endure want, imprisonment, and unjust punishment. Though there's no indication that Jesus lacked for food or clothing, it is likely that he accumulated very little, if anything, in the way of material belongings during his time on earth (Mt 8:20).

Living as Jesus' disciples today does not guarantee health and financial success nor lead necessarily to a life of poverty. It does, however, promise believers the opportunity to flourish spiritually and be assured of God's enduring prosperity that will not fail when they are careful to set their eyes and hearts on things above rather than earthly things (Col 3:1–2) and are vigilant to lay up "treasures in heaven" that will not wear out (Mt 6:20).

Greeting

1The elder to the beloved Gaius, whom I love in truth.
2Beloved, I pray that all may go well with you and that you may be in good
health, as it goes well with your soul. 3For I rejoiced greatly when the brothers[1]
came and testified to your truth, as indeed you are walking in the truth. 4I have no
greater joy than to hear that my children are walking in the truth.

Support and Opposition

5Beloved, it is a faithful thing you do in all your efforts for these brothers,
strangers as they are, 6who testified to your love before the church. You will do
well to send them on their journey in a manner worthy of God. 7For they have
gone out for the sake of the name, accepting nothing from the Gentiles. 8There-
fore we ought to support people like these, that we may be fellow workers for the
truth.
9I have written something to the church, but Diotrephes, who likes to put himself first, does not acknowledge our authority. 10So if I come, I will bring up what
he is doing, talking wicked nonsense against us. And not content with that, he
refuses to welcome the brothers, and also stops those who want to and puts them
out of the church.
11Beloved, do not imitate evil but imitate good. Whoever does good is from
God; whoever does evil has not seen God. 12Demetrius has received a good testimony from everyone, and from the truth itself. We also add our testimony, and
you know that our testimony is true.

Final Greetings

13I had much to write to you, but I would rather not write with pen and ink. 14I
hope to see you soon, and we will talk face to face.
15Peace be to you. The friends greet you. Greet the friends, each by name.

[1]Or *brothers and sisters*. In New Testament usage, depending on the context, the plural Greek word *adelphoi* (translated "brothers") may refer either to *brothers* or to *brothers and sisters*; also verses 5, 10

JESUS: OUR SUSTAINING GRACE

JUDE

JUDE

REIGN OF NERO *c. AD 54 – 68*	JUDE WRITES HIS LETTER *c. AD 60 – 64*	TEMPLE DESTROYED, CHURCH SCATTERS *c. AD 70*

God will judge and punish all evil. From cover to cover, the Bible testifies to this fact. At times, however, it may appear that evil prospers and wickedness prevails. Evildoers include the false teachers who were battling the church during the first century of its existence.

Jude earnestly wrote to the church "to contend for the faith that was once for all delivered to the saints" (v. 3). The gospel message is irrevocable and true. God, in his kindness, gave his Word to the apostles, which testified to the nature of God and his work through Jesus Christ. False teachers undermined this message — distorting its meaning and leading the church astray.

Jude reminds the church that God will judge these deceivers. God has already demonstrated his judgment in the condemnation of the devil — the chief deceiver himself. Since God has judged Satan, he will also pour out his wrath on all those who deceived God's people (vv. 5 – 11).

The church, however, should not be surprised when these false teachers continue to harm the church. And, they should expect that some will be led astray (vv. 12 – 19). They will follow after their own passions, rebel against God's Word, and bring upon themselves the condemnation of God.

In contrast, God's church will be sustained by the grace of God. Believers should build one another up in Christ and keep themselves in the love of God (vv. 20 – 21). The mercy of God protects those who truly know Christ and sustains them in the gospel message and faithful obedience in the face of outward hostility

(v. 21). Jesus keeps his people from stumbling and will present them faultless one day (v. 24).

Jude's message is an encouragement that truth will prevail. The deception of false teachers will be exposed, and they will be judged — in God's time and in God's way. The hypocrisy of false converts will also be exposed. They will leave the church and prove they were never truly converted. And the true church will be sustained by the grace of God. Those who truly have been saved by his might will be kept by his power until the time when the earth is purified from all falsehood forever.

NOW TO HIM WHO IS ABLE TO KEEP YOU FROM STUMBLING AND TO PRESENT YOU BLAMELESS BEFORE THE PRESENCE OF HIS GLORY WITH GREAT JOY, TO THE ONLY GOD, OUR SAVIOR, THROUGH JESUS CHRIST OUR LORD, BE GLORY, MAJESTY, DOMINION, AND AUTHORITY, BEFORE ALL TIME AND NOW AND FOREVER. AMEN.

Jude 24 – 25

JUDE

Greeting

1 Jude, a servant[1] of Jesus Christ and brother of James,

To those who are called, beloved in God the Father and kept for[2] Jesus Christ:

2 May mercy, peace, and love be multiplied to you.

Judgment on False Teachers

3 Beloved, although I was very eager to write to you about our common salvation, I found it necessary to write appealing to you to contend for the faith that was once for all delivered to the saints. 4 For certain people have crept in unnoticed who long ago were designated for this condemnation, ungodly people, who pervert the grace of our God into sensuality and deny our only Master and Lord, Jesus Christ.

5 Now I want to remind you, although you once fully knew it, that Jesus, who saved[3] a people out of the land of Egypt, afterward destroyed those who did not believe. 6 And the angels who did not stay within their own position of authority, but left their proper dwelling, he has kept in eternal chains under gloomy darkness until the judgment of the great day— 7 just as Sodom and Gomorrah and the surrounding cities, which likewise indulged in sexual immorality and pursued unnatural desire,[4] serve as an example by undergoing a punishment of eternal fire.

8 Yet in like manner these people also, relying on their dreams, defile the flesh, reject authority, and blaspheme the glorious ones. 9 But when the archangel Michael, contending with the devil, was disputing about the body of Moses, he did not presume to pronounce a blasphemous judgment, but said, "The Lord rebuke you." 10 But these people blaspheme all that they do not understand, and they are destroyed by all that they, like unreasoning animals, understand instinctively. 11 Woe to them! For they walked in the way of Cain and abandoned themselves for the sake of gain to Balaam's error and perished in Korah's rebellion. 12 These are hidden reefs[5] at your love feasts, as they feast with you without fear, shepherds feeding themselves; waterless clouds, swept along by winds; fruitless trees in late autumn, twice dead, uprooted; 13 wild waves of the sea, casting up the foam of their own shame; wandering stars, for whom the gloom of utter darkness has been reserved forever.

14 It was also about these that Enoch, the seventh from Adam, prophesied, saying, "Behold, the Lord comes with ten thousands of his holy ones, 15 to execute judgment on all and to convict all the ungodly of all their deeds of ungodliness that they have committed in such an ungodly way, and of all the harsh things that ungodly sinners have spoken against him." 16 These are grumblers, malcontents, following their own sinful desires; they are loud-mouthed boasters, showing favoritism to gain advantage.

A Call to Persevere

17 But you must remember, beloved, the predictions of the apostles of our Lord Jesus Christ. 18 They[6] said to you, "In the last time there will be scoffers, following their own ungodly passions." 19 It is these who cause divisions, worldly people, devoid of the Spirit. 20 But you, beloved, building yourselves up in your most holy faith and praying in the Holy Spirit, 21 keep yourselves in the love of God, waiting for the mercy of our Lord Jesus Christ that leads to eternal life. 22 And have mercy

---

[1] For the contextual rendering of the Greek word *doulos*, see Preface [2] Or *by* [3] Some manuscripts *although you fully knew it, that the Lord who once saved* [4] Greek *different flesh* [5] Or *are blemishes* [6] Or *Christ, because they*

on those who doubt; [23]save others by snatching them out of the fire; to others
show mercy with fear, hating even the garment[1] stained by the flesh.

Doxology

[24]Now to him who is able to keep you from stumbling and to present you
blameless before the presence of his glory with great joy, [25]to the only God, our
Savior, through Jesus Christ our Lord, be glory, majesty, dominion, and authority,
before all time[2] and now and forever. Amen.

JUDE 24–25

TO HIM

Jude concluded his book with a beautiful doxology, inviting readers throughout history to join him in ascribing glory to God. In this passage, Jude took human weakness into account as something God can easily overcome. He also reaffirmed human destiny, that one day all people will stand before the Lord.

These verses read like a song that grows into a shout of triumphant praise—all for God our Savior (v. 25). God arranged for believers to be saved through faith in Jesus (Jn 3:16). He showed mercy to those who deserved to be crushed. God sacrificed his own Son to purchase pardon for the whole world—for all who will believe the gospel (1Jn 2:2).

Jesus' work makes it possible for believers to know and praise their holy God. Jesus gives believers hope and assurance that they will someday stand before God in righteousness, without blame (Php 3:9), and with great joy. Jesus is the difference-maker for all mankind: He is the Lamb (Rev 5:6), the Branch (Isa 4:2; 11:1), the Redeemer (Isa 44:24), the Savior (1Jn 4:14), the door (Jn 10:9), the way (Jn 14:6), the living water (Jn 4:10), the light of the world (Jn 9:5), and the bread of life (Jn 6:35). He offers salvation to all who will accept it, and he is worthy of resounding praise forever!

[1]Greek *chiton*, a long garment worn under the cloak next to the skin [2]Or *before any age*

JESUS: OUR WORSHIP FOREVER

REVELATION

REVELATION

JOHN WRITES HIS GOSPEL AND LETTERS *c. AD 90*	JOHN EXILED TO ISLAND OF PATMOS *c. AD 93*	JOHN WRITES REVELATION *c. AD 95*

Christ's promised return was the hope of the church. In the first century, the church faced ongoing persecution, spiritual warfare, internal divisions, and heretical doctrine. These factors caused the faithful believers to look forward to the second coming of Christ with great anticipation, though they were still filled with questions regarding the timing and nature of his return.

John wrote to encourage the church with the hope of the coming of Christ and to challenge them to ongoing faithfulness in the meantime. While exiled on the island of Patmos, John was given a vision of the return of Christ, and he recorded this vision for the churches of his day — particularly the seven churches in Asia Minor.

John's vision is vivid and beautiful. The reigning King, the lion of Judah, the worthy Lamb of God would return and reign as the victorious King (5:8 – 13; 12:5). Through symbolic imagery, John captured the climactic stages of God's redemptive plan to restore his kingdom on earth and rule and reign with his chosen people forever. His return will mark the final destruction of all wickedness — both those who failed to repent and place their faith in Christ and all forms of brokenness and destruction that have plagued the earth since the fall. Believers will be saved from the coming destruction and given the glorious privilege of dwelling with God, worshiping him as King, and serving him in a new, purified world (21:1 – 8). John seemingly grasps for words to describe the glorious splendor of the coming kingdom and the beauty of the spotless Lamb of God who sits on the throne. In light of these sure promises, the church should not cower in the midst of persecution. Should they falter, God will remove his presence from them (2:1 — 3:22).

Though many questions remain about the exact nature of John's prophecy concerning the second coming, one thing is sure — God wins, and Jesus reigns. Worship today is a mere shadow of the magnificent scenes of worship around the throne of God (4:1 – 11; 5:8 – 14). There, believers of every tribe, tongue, and nation will gather together to proclaim the glory of Jesus Christ. Throughout the generations, the church has longed and continues to long for that day, begging God to hasten his coming (22:20 – 21).

HE WILL WIPE AWAY EVERY TEAR FROM THEIR EYES, AND DEATH SHALL BE NO MORE, NEITHER SHALL THERE BE MOURNING, NOR CRYING, NOR PAIN ANYMORE, FOR THE FORMER THINGS HAVE PASSED AWAY.

Revelation 21:4

REVELATION

Prologue

1 The revelation of Jesus Christ, which God gave him to show to his servants[1] the things that must soon take place. He made it known by sending his angel to his servant John, [2]who bore witness to the word of God and to the testimony of Jesus Christ, even to all that he saw. [3]Blessed is the one who reads aloud the words of this prophecy, and blessed are those who hear, and who keep what is written in it, for the time is near.

Greeting to the Seven Churches

[4]John to the seven churches that are in Asia:

Grace to you and peace from him who is and who was and who is to come, and from the seven spirits who are before his throne, [5]and from Jesus Christ the faithful witness, the firstborn of the dead, and the ruler of kings on earth.

To him who loves us and has freed us from our sins by his blood [6]and made us a kingdom, priests to his God and Father, to him be glory and dominion forever and ever. Amen. [7]Behold, he is coming with the clouds, and every eye will see him, even those who pierced him, and all tribes of the earth will wail[2] on account of him. Even so. Amen.

[8]"I am the Alpha and the Omega," says the Lord God, "who is and who was and who is to come, the Almighty."

Vision of the Son of Man

[9]I, John, your brother and partner in the tribulation and the kingdom and the patient endurance that are in Jesus, was on the island called Patmos on account of the word of God and the testimony of Jesus. [10]I was in the Spirit on the Lord's day, and I heard behind me a loud voice like a trumpet [11]saying, "Write what you see in a book and send it to the seven churches, to Ephesus and to Smyrna and to Pergamum and to Thyatira and to Sardis and to Philadelphia and to Laodicea."

[12]Then I turned to see the voice that was speaking to me, and on turning I saw seven golden lampstands, [13]and in the midst of the lampstands one like a son of man, clothed with a long robe and with a golden sash around his chest. [14]The hairs of his head were white, like white wool, like snow. His eyes were like a flame of fire, [15]his feet were like burnished bronze, refined in a furnace, and his voice was like the roar of many waters. [16]In his right hand he held seven stars, from his mouth came a sharp two-edged sword, and his face was like the sun shining in full strength.

[17]When I saw him, I fell at his feet as though dead. But he laid his right hand on me, saying, "Fear not, I am the first and the last, [18]and the living one. I died, and behold I am alive forevermore, and I have the keys of Death and Hades. [19]Write therefore the things that you have seen, those that are and those that are to take place after this. [20]As for the mystery of the seven stars that you saw in my right hand, and the seven golden lampstands, the seven stars are the angels of the seven churches, and the seven lampstands are the seven churches.

To the Church in Ephesus

2 "To the angel of the church in Ephesus write: 'The words of him who holds the seven stars in his right hand, who walks among the seven golden lampstands.

[2]" 'I know your works, your toil and your patient endurance, and how you cannot bear with those who are evil, but have tested those who call themselves

---

[1]For the contextual rendering of the Greek word *doulos*, see Preface; likewise for *servant* later in this verse
[2]Or *mourn*

A PICTURE OF JESUS

The first chapter of Revelation provides an introduction to the rest of the book, and it also provides three critical depictions of Jesus.

In verse 5, John wrote that Jesus is "the faithful witness," which is to say that he is a prophet who came to earth as a witness to the truth. Not only did Jesus remain faithful to God's message throughout his life, but he also remained steadfast to God's truth, even to the point of death (Lk 22:42). He encouraged believers to do the same (Rev 2:10). John also referred to Jesus as "the firstborn of the dead" (1:5) because in his resurrection, Jesus was the first one to overcome death by his own power (Jn 2:19). He is the only person to die, to physically rise from the dead, and to continue to live forever (Ro 8:34; 6:9 – 11). Lastly, John called Jesus "the ruler of kings on earth" (Rev 1:5) because Jesus is the one to whom God gave the throne of David forever, as the angel attested when he announced his upcoming birth to Mary (Lk 1:31 – 33).

Between these three descriptions, John confirmed Jesus' threefold office as prophet (Dt 18:18 – 19), priest (Ps 110:1 – 4), and king (Ps 2:4 – 9). Because Jesus filled each of these roles on earth, he was qualified to be the "Anointed" (Ac 4:26; cf. Lk 4:18), and John's vision reaffirms each of these positions that Jesus fulfilled to further confirm that he is the Son of God.

After establishing Jesus' elevated position, John wrote a vivid description of the exalted Jesus. John observed that the one "like a son of man" wears a robe and sash (Rev 1:13), which is similar to what a priest would typically wear (Ex 28:4). His hair is "white, like white wool, like snow" (Rev 1:14), which is a symbol of wisdom and dignity (Lev 19:32; Pr 16:31). John described Jesus' voice as "like the roar of many waters" (Rev 1:15), which is a description that is also used to describe what God sounds like (Eze 43:2). Also, John depicts a "sharp two-edged sword" (Rev 1:16) coming out of his mouth, which is to show both how precise Jesus' Word is (Heb 4:12) and that what he says is meant for judgment (Mt 10:34).

John's description of Jesus in the first chapter of Revelation is incredibly vivid, and it is meant to set the scene for the rest of the book. John started by confirming that Jesus is who he claimed to be during his earthly ministry (Rev 1:5), and also confirmed that, when Jesus returns, it will be clear to all people that he is the Son of God (v. 7).

apostles and are not, and found them to be false. 3 I know you are enduring patiently and bearing up for my name's sake, and you have not grown weary. 4 But
I have this against you, that you have abandoned the love you had at first. 5 Remember therefore from where you have fallen; repent, and do the works you did
at first. If not, I will come to you and remove your lampstand from its place, unless
you repent. 6 Yet this you have: you hate the works of the Nicolaitans, which I also
hate. 7 He who has an ear, let him hear what the Spirit says to the churches. To the
one who conquers I will grant to eat of the tree of life, which is in the paradise of
God.'

To the Church in Smyrna

8 "And to the angel of the church in Smyrna write: 'The words of the first and
the last, who died and came to life.

9 " 'I know your tribulation and your poverty (but you are rich) and the slander[1]
of those who say that they are Jews and are not, but are a synagogue of Satan. 10 Do
not fear what you are about to suffer. Behold, the devil is about to throw some of
you into prison, that you may be tested, and for ten days you will have tribulation.
Be faithful unto death, and I will give you the crown of life. 11 He who has an ear,
let him hear what the Spirit says to the churches. The one who conquers will not
be hurt by the second death.'

To the Church in Pergamum

12 "And to the angel of the church in Pergamum write: 'The words of him who
has the sharp two-edged sword.

13 " 'I know where you dwell, where Satan's throne is. Yet you hold fast my
name, and you did not deny my faith[2] even in the days of Antipas my faithful
witness, who was killed among you, where Satan dwells. 14 But I have a few things
against you: you have some there who hold the teaching of Balaam, who taught
Balak to put a stumbling block before the sons of Israel, so that they might eat
food sacrificed to idols and practice sexual immorality. 15 So also you have some
who hold the teaching of the Nicolaitans. 16 Therefore repent. If not, I will come
to you soon and war against them with the sword of my mouth. 17 He who has an
ear, let him hear what the Spirit says to the churches. To the one who conquers I
will give some of the hidden manna, and I will give him a white stone, with a new
name written on the stone that no one knows except the one who receives it.'

To the Church in Thyatira

18 "And to the angel of the church in Thyatira write: 'The words of the Son of
God, who has eyes like a flame of fire, and whose feet are like burnished bronze.

19 " 'I know your works, your love and faith and service and patient endurance,
and that your latter works exceed the first. 20 But I have this against you, that you
tolerate that woman Jezebel, who calls herself a prophetess and is teaching and
seducing my servants to practice sexual immorality and to eat food sacrificed to
idols. 21 I gave her time to repent, but she refuses to repent of her sexual immorality. 22 Behold, I will throw her onto a sickbed, and those who commit adultery
with her I will throw into great tribulation, unless they repent of her works, 23 and
I will strike her children dead. And all the churches will know that I am he who
searches mind and heart, and I will give to each of you according to your works.
24 But to the rest of you in Thyatira, who do not hold this teaching, who have not
learned what some call the deep things of Satan, to you I say, I do not lay on you
any other burden. 25 Only hold fast what you have until I come. 26 The one who
conquers and who keeps my works until the end, to him I will give authority over
the nations, 27 and he will rule[3] them with a rod of iron, as when earthen pots are
broken in pieces, even as I myself have received authority from my Father. 28 And

[1]Greek *blasphemy* [2]Or *your faith in me* [3]Greek *shepherd*

REVELATION 2:7

HE WHO HAS AN EAR, LET HIM HEAR

In the first chapters of Revelation, Jesus ended each of his addresses to the seven churches with the phrase, "He who has an ear, let him hear" (vv. 7,11,17,29; 3:6,13,22). Jesus used this same phrase in Matthew 11:15 prior to his message of warning to unrepentant cities. In Revelation, Jesus gives one final warning to each of the seven major churches, telling them that it is important for them to heed what he is saying while there is still time.

Isaiah 6:10 described how the ears of the people would be closed when Jesus came, and this prophecy was fulfilled by the many people who did not understand his teachings and in the actions of the Jewish leaders who openly opposed him. However, Isaiah 32:3 also promises that the eyes and ears of the people will one day be opened, and that many will accept the words of Jesus.

Believers and nonbelievers alike have the choice to be the people described in Isaiah 6 or the people described in Isaiah 32. Revelation 2–3 begins Jesus' last appeal for people to follow Isaiah 32—to listen to and heed his words. These chapters are also a warning that one day it will be too late; that those who chose to hear and repent will be saved and those who chose to keep their ears and hearts closed to the gospel will be subject to judgment.

I will give him the morning star. 29He who has an ear, let him hear what the Spirit says to the churches.'

To the Church in Sardis

3 "And to the angel of the church in Sardis write: 'The words of him who has the seven spirits of God and the seven stars.

"'I know your works. You have the reputation of being alive, but you are dead. 2Wake up, and strengthen what remains and is about to die, for I have not found your works complete in the sight of my God. 3Remember, then, what you received and heard. Keep it, and repent. If you will not wake up, I will come like a thief, and you will not know at what hour I will come against you. 4Yet you have still a few names in Sardis, people who have not soiled their garments, and they will walk with me in white, for they are worthy. 5The one who conquers will be clothed thus in white garments, and I will never blot his name out of the book of life. I will confess his name before my Father and before his angels. 6He who has an ear, let him hear what the Spirit says to the churches.'

To the Church in Philadelphia

7"And to the angel of the church in Philadelphia write: 'The words of the holy one, the true one, who has the key of David, who opens and no one will shut, who shuts and no one opens.

8"'I know your works. Behold, I have set before you an open door, which no one is able to shut. I know that you have but little power, and yet you have kept my word and have not denied my name. 9Behold, I will make those of the synagogue of Satan who say that they are Jews and are not, but lie—behold, I will make them come and bow down before your feet, and they will learn that I have loved you. 10Because you have kept my word about patient endurance, I will keep you from the hour of trial that is coming on the whole world, to try those who dwell on the earth. 11I am coming soon. Hold fast what you have, so that no one may seize your crown. 12The one who conquers, I will make him a pillar in the temple of my God. Never shall he go out of it, and I will write on him the name of my God, and the name of the city of my God, the new Jerusalem, which comes down from my God out of heaven, and my own new name. 13He who has an ear, let him hear what the Spirit says to the churches.'

To the Church in Laodicea

14"And to the angel of the church in Laodicea write: 'The words of the Amen, the faithful and true witness, the beginning of God's creation.

15"'I know your works: you are neither cold nor hot. Would that you were either cold or hot! 16So, because you are lukewarm, and neither hot nor cold, I will spit you out of my mouth. 17For you say, "I am rich, I have prospered, and I need nothing," not realizing that you are wretched, pitiable, poor, blind, and naked. 18I counsel you to buy from me gold refined by fire, so that you may be rich, and white garments so that you may clothe yourself and the shame of your nakedness may not be seen, and salve to anoint your eyes, so that you may see. 19Those whom I love, I reprove and discipline, so be zealous and repent. 20Behold, I stand at the door and knock. If anyone hears my voice and opens the door, I will come in to him and eat with him, and he with me. 21The one who conquers, I will grant him to sit with me on my throne, as I also conquered and sat down with my Father on his throne. 22He who has an ear, let him hear what the Spirit says to the churches.'"

The Throne in Heaven

4 After this I looked, and behold, a door standing open in heaven! And the first voice, which I had heard speaking to me like a trumpet, said, "Come up here, and I will show you what must take place after this." 2At once I was in the Spirit,

---

REVELATION 3:1–6

SPIRITUAL DEATH

John recorded Jesus' address to the church in Sardis in which he admonishes the church for having a reputation for being alive, yet being dead all the while (v. 1). Jesus implores the people of Sardis to wake up and reinvigorate their deeds, which are incomplete before God.

John's writing is reminiscent of James 2:14–26, in which James challenges believers by saying that "faith by itself, if it does not have works, is dead." The church in Sardis is an example of a group of Christians who had deeds without faith. They were going through the motions and doing what they thought was right, but Jesus warned them that God had seen their works and found them to be lacking. In the same way that faith without works is dead, works without faith are also dead.

Believers today can take note: faith and works should go hand in hand. The relationship between faith and works is natural, and neither one should be overemphasized at the expense of the other. Jesus taught that God clearly sees into the hearts of people (Lk 16:15), and this is exactly what he demonstrated in Revelation 3:1–6. The church of Sardis was spiritually dead, but Jesus reminded them that it was not too late for them to change their hearts—nor is it too late for those who are alive today.

and behold, a throne stood in heaven, with one seated on the throne. 3And he
who sat there had the appearance of jasper and carnelian, and around the throne
was a rainbow that had the appearance of an emerald. 4Around the throne were
twenty-four thrones, and seated on the thrones were twenty-four elders, clothed
in white garments, with golden crowns on their heads. 5From the throne came
flashes of lightning, and rumblings[1] and peals of thunder, and before the throne
were burning seven torches of fire, which are the seven spirits of God, 6and before
the throne there was as it were a sea of glass, like crystal.

And around the throne, on each side of the throne, are four living creatures,
full of eyes in front and behind: 7the first living creature like a lion, the second
living creature like an ox, the third living creature with the face of a man, and the
fourth living creature like an eagle in flight. 8And the four living creatures, each
of them with six wings, are full of eyes all around and within, and day and night
they never cease to say,

"Holy, holy, holy, is the Lord God Almighty,
who was and is and is to come!"

9And whenever the living creatures give glory and honor and thanks to him who
is seated on the throne, who lives forever and ever, 10the twenty-four elders fall
down before him who is seated on the throne and worship him who lives forever
and ever. They cast their crowns before the throne, saying,

11 "Worthy are you, our Lord and God,
to receive glory and honor and power,
for you created all things,
and by your will they existed and were created."

The Scroll and the Lamb

5 Then I saw in the right hand of him who was seated on the throne a scroll
written within and on the back, sealed with seven seals. 2And I saw a mighty
angel proclaiming with a loud voice, "Who is worthy to open the scroll and break
its seals?" 3And no one in heaven or on earth or under the earth was able to open
the scroll or to look into it, 4and I began to weep loudly because no one was found
worthy to open the scroll or to look into it. 5And one of the elders said to me,
"Weep no more; behold, the Lion of the tribe of Judah, the Root of David, has
conquered, so that he can open the scroll and its seven seals."

6And between the throne and the four living creatures and among the elders
I saw a Lamb standing, as though it had been slain, with seven horns and with
seven eyes, which are the seven spirits of God sent out into all the earth. 7And he
went and took the scroll from the right hand of him who was seated on the throne.
8And when he had taken the scroll, the four living creatures and the twenty-four
elders fell down before the Lamb, each holding a harp, and golden bowls full of
incense, which are the prayers of the saints. 9And they sang a new song, saying,

"Worthy are you to take the scroll
and to open its seals,
for you were slain, and by your blood you ransomed people for God
from every tribe and language and people and nation,
10 and you have made them a kingdom and priests to our God,
and they shall reign on the earth."

11Then I looked, and I heard around the throne and the living creatures and the
elders the voice of many angels, numbering myriads of myriads and thousands of
thousands, 12saying with a loud voice,

"Worthy is the Lamb who was slain,
to receive power and wealth and wisdom and might
and honor and glory and blessing!"

[1] Or *voices*, or *sounds*

REVELATION 5:11–12

WORTHY OF ALL

The second half of Revelation 5 vividly portrays the worship in heaven as the heavenly throng gathers around the throne on which the King of kings sits. In verse 6, John describes the Lamb as slain yet standing between the throne and the elders. The Lamb pictured here is Jesus, the one who overcame death. Jesus sacrificed himself for the sins of humankind, so that believers can stand before the throne of God and accept for themselves Jesus' sacrifice, which takes away the wrath that they deserve.

Verse 9 says that the Lamb is worthy of praise because he has "ransomed people for God from every tribe and language and people and nation" with his blood. Jesus' sacrifice makes it possible for humans to be made right with God, and this verse refers to what Jesus' blood purchased. The praise continues in verse 12, which lists seven things that the Lamb is worthy of: power, wealth, wisdom, might, honor, glory, and blessing. Jesus deserves all these things and more by virtue of what he accomplished on the cross and through the empty tomb. The Lamb who is worthy of all praise gives the angels, and his people, a reason to sing.

NAMES AND TITLES OF JESUS IN REVELATION

John described God as he "who is and who was and who is to come" (Rev 1:4; cf. 4:8). His vision of heaven includes an image of four creatures who worship God day and night, and they also refer to God as him "who is and who was and who is to come" (v. 8). This phrase echoes Exodus 3:14–15, where God spoke of himself as "I AM" as he revealed his name to Moses. Jesus also referred to himself as "I am" (Jn 8:58) and thereby declared himself to be God. John reinforces this reality by declaring that not only is God who he says he is now, but he is also the same God he was throughout history, and he will continue to be the same God in the future. With this eternal consistency in mind, let's look at the names for Jesus revealed throughout John's book.

Jesus is the Christ (Rev 1:1; 20:4); the faithful witness, the firstborn of the dead, the and ruler of kings on earth (1:5); the Alpha and Omega (1:8–13); like a son of man (1:13) who holds a sharp two-edged sword (1:16); the first and the last (1:17); the living one who lives and was dead (1:18; 2:8); the one who holds the keys of Death and Hades (1:18); the one who holds the seven stars and who walks among the seven golden lampstands (2:1); the Son of God (2:18); the one who searches the mind and heart (2:23); the one who has the seven spirits of God and the seven stars (3:1); the one who is holy and true and who has the key of David (3:7); the Amen, the faithful and true witness, the beginning of God's creation (3:14); the Lord, who is worthy to receive glory and honor and power (4:11); the Lion of the tribe of Judah and the Root of David (5:5); the Lamb that has been slain (5:6–7); the Lamb who is worthy (5:8–9); the Lord of lords and King of kings (17:14; 19:16); the just Judge who is Faithful and True and the warrior on the white horse (19:11); the Word of God (19:13–16); the Lord, the God who inspires the prophets (22:6); the Alpha and the Omega (22:13); and the bright morning star (22:16).

This list may be a little overwhelming, but this quick look presents Jesus as the promised Messiah, the one who died and was raised to life again to defeat death, and the eternally consistent and powerful ruler who loves his people — yesterday, today, and forever.

13And I heard every creature in heaven and on earth and under the earth and in the sea, and all that is in them, saying,

> "To him who sits on the throne and to the Lamb
> be blessing and honor and glory and might forever and ever!"

14And the four living creatures said, "Amen!" and the elders fell down and worshiped.

The Seven Seals

6 Now I watched when the Lamb opened one of the seven seals, and I heard one of the four living creatures say with a voice like thunder, "Come!" 2And I looked, and behold, a white horse! And its rider had a bow, and a crown was given to him, and he came out conquering, and to conquer.

3When he opened the second seal, I heard the second living creature say, "Come!" 4And out came another horse, bright red. Its rider was permitted to take peace from the earth, so that people should slay one another, and he was given a great sword.

5When he opened the third seal, I heard the third living creature say, "Come!" And I looked, and behold, a black horse! And its rider had a pair of scales in his hand. 6And I heard what seemed to be a voice in the midst of the four living creatures, saying, "A quart[1] of wheat for a denarius,[2] and three quarts of barley for a denarius, and do not harm the oil and wine!"

7When he opened the fourth seal, I heard the voice of the fourth living creature say, "Come!" 8And I looked, and behold, a pale horse! And its rider's name was Death, and Hades followed him. And they were given authority over a fourth of the earth, to kill with sword and with famine and with pestilence and by wild beasts of the earth.

9When he opened the fifth seal, I saw under the altar the souls of those who had been slain for the word of God and for the witness they had borne. 10They cried out with a loud voice, "O Sovereign Lord, holy and true, how long before you will judge and avenge our blood on those who dwell on the earth?" 11Then they were each given a white robe and told to rest a little longer, until the number of their fellow servants and their brothers[3] should be complete, who were to be killed as they themselves had been.

12When he opened the sixth seal, I looked, and behold, there was a great earthquake, and the sun became black as sackcloth, the full moon became like blood, 13and the stars of the sky fell to the earth as the fig tree sheds its winter fruit when shaken by a gale. 14The sky vanished like a scroll that is being rolled up, and every mountain and island was removed from its place. 15Then the kings of the earth and the great ones and the generals and the rich and the powerful, and everyone, slave[4] and free, hid themselves in the caves and among the rocks of the mountains, 16calling to the mountains and rocks, "Fall on us and hide us from the face of him who is seated on the throne, and from the wrath of the Lamb, 17for the great day of their wrath has come, and who can stand?"

The 144,000 of Israel Sealed

7 After this I saw four angels standing at the four corners of the earth, holding back the four winds of the earth, that no wind might blow on earth or sea or against any tree. 2Then I saw another angel ascending from the rising of the sun, with the seal of the living God, and he called with a loud voice to the four angels who had been given power to harm earth and sea, 3saying, "Do not harm the earth or the sea or the trees, until we have sealed the servants of our God on

---

[1]Greek *choinix*, a dry measure equal to about a quart [2]A *denarius* was a day's wage for a laborer
[3]Or *brothers and sisters*. In New Testament usage, depending on the context, the plural Greek word *adelphoi* (translated "brothers") may refer either to *brothers* or to *brothers and sisters* [4]For the contextual rendering of the Greek word *doulos*, see Preface

their foreheads." [4]And I heard the number of the sealed, 144,000, sealed from
every tribe of the sons of Israel:

5 12,000 from the tribe of Judah were sealed,
12,000 from the tribe of Reuben,
12,000 from the tribe of Gad,
6 12,000 from the tribe of Asher,
12,000 from the tribe of Naphtali,
12,000 from the tribe of Manasseh,
7 12,000 from the tribe of Simeon,
12,000 from the tribe of Levi,
12,000 from the tribe of Issachar,
8 12,000 from the tribe of Zebulun,
12,000 from the tribe of Joseph,
12,000 from the tribe of Benjamin were sealed.

A Great Multitude from Every Nation

[9]After this I looked, and behold, a great multitude that no one could number,
from every nation, from all tribes and peoples and languages, standing before the
throne and before the Lamb, clothed in white robes, with palm branches in their
hands, [10]and crying out with a loud voice, "Salvation belongs to our God who sits
on the throne, and to the Lamb!" [11]And all the angels were standing around the
throne and around the elders and the four living creatures, and they fell on their
faces before the throne and worshiped God, [12]saying, "Amen! Blessing and glory
and wisdom and thanksgiving and honor and power and might be to our God
forever and ever! Amen."

[13]Then one of the elders addressed me, saying, "Who are these, clothed in
white robes, and from where have they come?" [14]I said to him, "Sir, you know."
And he said to me, "These are the ones coming out of the great tribulation. They
have washed their robes and made them white in the blood of the Lamb.

15 "Therefore they are before the throne of God,
and serve him day and night in his temple;
and he who sits on the throne will shelter them with his presence.
16 They shall hunger no more, neither thirst anymore;
the sun shall not strike them,
nor any scorching heat.
17 For the Lamb in the midst of the throne will be their shepherd,
and he will guide them to springs of living water,
and God will wipe away every tear from their eyes."

The Seventh Seal and the Golden Censer

8 When the Lamb opened the seventh seal, there was silence in heaven for
about half an hour. [2]Then I saw the seven angels who stand before God, and
seven trumpets were given to them. [3]And another angel came and stood at the altar with a golden censer, and he was given much incense to offer with the prayers
of all the saints on the golden altar before the throne, [4]and the smoke of the incense, with the prayers of the saints, rose before God from the hand of the angel.
[5]Then the angel took the censer and filled it with fire from the altar and threw
it on the earth, and there were peals of thunder, rumblings,[1] flashes of lightning,
and an earthquake.

The Seven Trumpets

[6]Now the seven angels who had the seven trumpets prepared to blow them.
[7]The first angel blew his trumpet, and there followed hail and fire, mixed with

[1]Or *voices*, or *sounds*

REVELATION 7:17

THE LAMB AS SHEPHERD

In Luke 15:1–7 Jesus told the parable of the lost sheep, recounting the joy that a shepherd experiences when he finds one lost sheep. Revelation 7 infinitely multiplies this as it depicts all of God's lost sheep being found, and Jesus is shown as both Lamb and shepherd. John describes great worship and praise in verses 10 and 12, which recalls the rejoicing that Jesus described in Luke 15:6–7.

Furthermore, John wrote here that this Lamb will shepherd his people "to springs of living water." Jesus promised this living water in John 4:14, where he declared that anyone who follows him will be given water that leads to eternal life. It is this exact water to which the Lamb is leading the great multitude of people in Revelation 7. No longer will there be sadness or tears (v. 17), but there will only be cause for rejoicing as the Lamb leads his sheep into eternal refreshment and rejoicing.

REVELATION 8:2

TRUMPETS AND TIMING

In Old Testament times, trumpets were used to signify important events, to give signals during war, and to warn people of something that was coming (Eze 33:4–5). In Revelation 8:6, the angels prepare to sound the trumpets to warn people of the coming judgment—these are the same trumpets that Jesus described in Matthew 24:31.

Furthermore, the seven trumpets are reminiscent of the seven trumpets

(continued on next page)

blood, and these were thrown upon the earth. And a third of the earth was burned up, and a third of the trees were burned up, and all green grass was burned up.

8 The second angel blew his trumpet, and something like a great mountain, burning with fire, was thrown into the sea, and a third of the sea became blood. 9 A third of the living creatures in the sea died, and a third of the ships were destroyed.

10 The third angel blew his trumpet, and a great star fell from heaven, blazing like a torch, and it fell on a third of the rivers and on the springs of water. 11 The name of the star is Wormwood.[1] A third of the waters became wormwood, and many people died from the water, because it had been made bitter.

12 The fourth angel blew his trumpet, and a third of the sun was struck, and a third of the moon, and a third of the stars, so that a third of their light might be darkened, and a third of the day might be kept from shining, and likewise a third of the night.

13 Then I looked, and I heard an eagle crying with a loud voice as it flew directly overhead, "Woe, woe, woe to those who dwell on the earth, at the blasts of the other trumpets that the three angels are about to blow!"

9 And the fifth angel blew his trumpet, and I saw a star fallen from heaven to earth, and he was given the key to the shaft of the bottomless pit.[2] 2 He opened the shaft of the bottomless pit, and from the shaft rose smoke like the smoke of a great furnace, and the sun and the air were darkened with the smoke from the shaft. 3 Then from the smoke came locusts on the earth, and they were given power like the power of scorpions of the earth. 4 They were told not to harm the grass of the earth or any green plant or any tree, but only those people who do not have the seal of God on their foreheads. 5 They were allowed to torment them for five months, but not to kill them, and their torment was like the torment of a scorpion when it stings someone. 6 And in those days people will seek death and will not find it. They will long to die, but death will flee from them.

7 In appearance the locusts were like horses prepared for battle: on their heads were what looked like crowns of gold; their faces were like human faces, 8 their hair like women's hair, and their teeth like lions' teeth; 9 they had breastplates like breastplates of iron, and the noise of their wings was like the noise of many chariots with horses rushing into battle. 10 They have tails and stings like scorpions, and their power to hurt people for five months is in their tails. 11 They have as king over them the angel of the bottomless pit. His name in Hebrew is Abaddon, and in Greek he is called Apollyon.[3]

12 The first woe has passed; behold, two woes are still to come.

13 Then the sixth angel blew his trumpet, and I heard a voice from the four horns of the golden altar before God, 14 saying to the sixth angel who had the trumpet, "Release the four angels who are bound at the great river Euphrates." 15 So the four angels, who had been prepared for the hour, the day, the month, and the year, were released to kill a third of mankind. 16 The number of mounted troops was twice ten thousand times ten thousand; I heard their number. 17 And this is how I saw the horses in my vision and those who rode them: they wore breastplates the color of fire and of sapphire[4] and of sulfur, and the heads of the horses were like lions' heads, and fire and smoke and sulfur came out of their mouths. 18 By these three plagues a third of mankind was killed, by the fire and smoke and sulfur coming out of their mouths. 19 For the power of the horses is in their mouths and in their tails, for their tails are like serpents with heads, and by means of them they wound.

20 The rest of mankind, who were not killed by these plagues, did not repent of the works of their hands nor give up worshiping demons and idols of gold and silver

(Trumpets and Timing, continued)

that Israel's priests sounded when God defeated Jericho (Jos 6). In Joshua, God called the people to march around the city once a day for six days, while the priests blew their trumpets. Then on the seventh day, they marched around the city seven times, but this time when the priests blew the trumpets, the people gave a war cry, and God pulled down the walls of that great city.

The sound of the trumpets served not only to announce the coming of the Lord in Joshua's victory, but also here in Revelation. As God toppled those walls, so he will also topple those people and institutions and other entities that stand in rebellion against him and refuse to heed the good news of the gospel. Once the angels sound the trumpets, the judgment of the Lord is coming. His judgment, and his timing, will be perfect.

[1] *Wormwood* is the name of a plant and of the bitter-tasting extract derived from it [2] Greek *the abyss*; also verses 2, 11 [3] *Abaddon* means *destruction*; *Apollyon* means *destroyer* [4] Greek *hyacinth*

HUMAN STUBBORNNESS

This chapter represents God's judgment as swift, severe, and just, with an intensity that no human would want to confront. John's vision of the end times includes multiple beasts released by angels to wreak havoc on the earth in response to human sin. The devastation that he describes is shocking. However, these verses record that some people who will not be killed by the plagues will fail to repent and will continue living in their sin (Rev 9:20 – 21). How incredible that, even though God will continue to offer people the opportunity to repent throughout the entire period of judgment, there will still be people who choose their own sinful ways over God's way!

These verses serve as a warning concerning the sure judgment that is to come, and a reminder of the ultimate depravity of humanity and its need for a Savior. The people who will remain in their rebellion shock us, but Jesus came to die for these same people. In fact, they're representative of all people who become believers (Ro 5:8). Jesus' sacrifice was not merely for some of the sin that exists in the world; it was for *all* of the sin — past, present, and future. People who refuse to recognize their own sin and accept Jesus' free gift of salvation scorn Christ's work and run swiftly to their own demise.

It is easy for believers to compare themselves to those described in these verses and think, "Well, that's not me," but the truth is that, apart from Christ, every human is rebellious at their core and is therefore capable of being that far away from God. The most devout saint was once a sinner destined for hell until God awakened their spirit to new life. The message here is that it is important for Christians to continually surrender their lives and their circumstances to God so that they can be found to be walking in humility with the Lord (Mic 6:8) when he comes again.

Also, these verses are a challenge to believers to tell others about the good news so that there are fewer people who will choose to remain stubborn in the face of God's judgment. Believers live in a broken world filled with broken people, but God's redemptive power is enough to overcome all of the evil that has infiltrated this world. Those who accept Jesus' saving work on their behalf, in gratitude for the grace that they have received, should do everything in their power to share that grace with others so that the number of those who remain stubbornly rebellious in their sin may be few.

and bronze and stone and wood, which cannot see or hear or walk, 21 nor did they repent of their murders or their sorceries or their sexual immorality or their thefts.

The Angel and the Little Scroll

10 Then I saw another mighty angel coming down from heaven, wrapped in a cloud, with a rainbow over his head, and his face was like the sun, and his legs like pillars of fire. 2 He had a little scroll open in his hand. And he set his right foot on the sea, and his left foot on the land, 3 and called out with a loud voice, like a lion roaring. When he called out, the seven thunders sounded. 4 And when the seven thunders had sounded, I was about to write, but I heard a voice from heaven saying, "Seal up what the seven thunders have said, and do not write it down." 5 And the angel whom I saw standing on the sea and on the land raised his right hand to heaven 6 and swore by him who lives forever and ever, who created heaven and what is in it, the earth and what is in it, and the sea and what is in it, that there would be no more delay, 7 but that in the days of the trumpet call to be sounded by the seventh angel, the mystery of God would be fulfilled, just as he announced to his servants the prophets.

8 Then the voice that I had heard from heaven spoke to me again, saying, "Go, take the scroll that is open in the hand of the angel who is standing on the sea and on the land." 9 So I went to the angel and told him to give me the little scroll. And he said to me, "Take and eat it; it will make your stomach bitter, but in your mouth it will be sweet as honey." 10 And I took the little scroll from the hand of the angel and ate it. It was sweet as honey in my mouth, but when I had eaten it my stomach was made bitter. 11 And I was told, "You must again prophesy about many peoples and nations and languages and kings."

The Two Witnesses

11 Then I was given a measuring rod like a staff, and I was told, "Rise and measure the temple of God and the altar and those who worship there, 2 but do not measure the court outside the temple; leave that out, for it is given over to the nations, and they will trample the holy city for forty-two months. 3 And I will grant authority to my two witnesses, and they will prophesy for 1,260 days, clothed in sackcloth."

4 These are the two olive trees and the two lampstands that stand before the Lord of the earth. 5 And if anyone would harm them, fire pours from their mouth and consumes their foes. If anyone would harm them, this is how he is doomed to be killed. 6 They have the power to shut the sky, that no rain may fall during the days of their prophesying, and they have power over the waters to turn them into blood and to strike the earth with every kind of plague, as often as they desire. 7 And when they have finished their testimony, the beast that rises from the bottomless pit[1] will make war on them and conquer them and kill them, 8 and their dead bodies will lie in the street of the great city that symbolically[2] is called Sodom and Egypt, where their Lord was crucified. 9 For three and a half days some from the peoples and tribes and languages and nations will gaze at their dead bodies and refuse to let them be placed in a tomb, 10 and those who dwell on the earth will rejoice over them and make merry and exchange presents, because these two prophets had been a torment to those who dwell on the earth. 11 But after the three and a half days a breath of life from God entered them, and they stood up on their feet, and great fear fell on those who saw them. 12 Then they heard a loud voice from heaven saying to them, "Come up here!" And they went up to heaven in a cloud, and their enemies watched them. 13 And at that hour there was a great earthquake, and a tenth of the city fell. Seven thousand people were killed in the earthquake, and the rest were terrified and gave glory to the God of heaven.

14 The second woe has passed; behold, the third woe is soon to come.

[1]Or *the abyss* [2]Greek *spiritually*

REVELATION 10:11

THE WHOLE WORLD

It is important to note that the book of Revelation is written for the entire world. The book does not prophesy to one people, nation, language, or king, but rather to all of them. John's writing makes clear that judgment is not coming only to parts of our planet, but it is coming to the entire world. When Satan is mentioned, John said that he is "the deceiver of the whole world" (12:9). John said that "all who dwell on earth" who have not followed the gospel will worship the beast out of the sea (13:8), and the actions of the beast out of the earth will affect "all, both small and great, both rich and poor, both free and slave" (13:16). The multiple tribulations foretold in Revelation involve everybody on earth, and this serves as a reminder of the universal scope of God's judgment.

However, not only does judgment come to all parts of the earth, but redemption will also come to all parts of the world as well, as people "from every nation, from all tribes and peoples and languages" turn to him in faith (7:9). When the seventh trumpet is sounded, the angels declare, "The kingdom of the world has become the kingdom of our Lord and of his Christ" (11:15). When Jesus returns, he will return with justice and salvation for those who follow him and will establish his kingdom, both throughout the world and for eternity.

THE CHALLENGE OF INTERPRETING REVELATION

Scholars generally espouse one of four main views on how to interpret the book of Revelation:

The preterist view says that most of what is depicted in Revelation happened during John's lifetime while the Roman Empire was in power.

The historicist view believes that most of the prophecies in Revelation have been fulfilled throughout history and are continuing to be fulfilled today.

The futurist view believes that everything after chapter 3 of Revelation is going to happen sometime in the future.

The spiritual (or symbolic) view argues that Revelation is a symbolic interpretation of the ongoing cosmic conflict, which has had, and will continue to have, many fulfillments throughout history.

While these views have their differences, it is important for Christians not to get distracted in continuous debates over which view is more accurate. No matter what view one takes on the book of Revelation, the dominant idea is that Christ will return sometime in the future and that his return will be a welcome sight to his people. Regardless of when, where, and how God's judgment occurs, Jesus promised he would one day return (Jn 14:3), and it is this promise to which believers should hold fast, repeating John's closing prayer: "Come, Lord Jesus!" (Rev 22:20).

Also, no matter how one interprets Revelation, the book is intended to be a reminder and warning that when Jesus comes, he will be coming for those who trust in him for salvation. Many people in the world do not believe that Jesus is who he said he is, and the future of those people is tragic. Believers who have a secure future in Christ should be challenged by Revelation to tell as many people as they can about Jesus, so that more people can share in the joy that believers will experience at the return of Christ.

REVELATION 11:15

JESUS' VICTORY

This verse marks the declaration of Christ's complete victory over the kingdom of the world. Jesus foretold this event in John 12:31–32, and in Revelation his promise is manifested. After Jesus' victory was declared, the 24 elders "fell on their faces and worshiped God" (Rev 11:16). Five times in the book of Revelation the elders similarly demonstrate with their bodies the posture of their hearts (5:8,14; 7:11; 11:16; 19:4).

This absolute victory should cause those who rebel against Christ to shudder. Their doom is promised and assured. They will face the tribulation and punishment described in John's vision. Yet, Jesus' ultimate victory is a great hope for his followers. Though the world is in chaos, believers can be assured that Jesus has already won the victory over sin and death, and that the whole earth will soon see this victory. The kingdom of God will fully and finally come on earth as it has been in heaven (Mt 6:9–13). At the end of time, God's promise from Genesis 3:15 will come true as the offspring of the woman will crush the serpent's head forever.

REVELATION 12:11

OVERCOMING THE ENEMY

The first half of chapter 12 describes the battle that takes place between Satan and the angels in heaven, which ends with Satan being thrown down to earth in utter defeat. John said that this victory comes by virtue of the blood of the Lamb, and that, while Michael and his angels fight

(continued on next page)

The Seventh Trumpet

15Then the seventh angel blew his trumpet, and there were loud voices in heaven, saying, "The kingdom of the world has become the kingdom of our Lord and of his Christ, and he shall reign forever and ever." 16And the twenty-four elders who sit on their thrones before God fell on their faces and worshiped God, 17saying,

"We give thanks to you, Lord God Almighty,
  who is and who was,
for you have taken your great power
  and begun to reign.
18 The nations raged,
  but your wrath came,
  and the time for the dead to be judged,
and for rewarding your servants, the prophets and saints,
  and those who fear your name,
  both small and great,
and for destroying the destroyers of the earth."

19Then God's temple in heaven was opened, and the ark of his covenant was seen within his temple. There were flashes of lightning, rumblings,[1] peals of thunder, an earthquake, and heavy hail.

The Woman and the Dragon

12 And a great sign appeared in heaven: a woman clothed with the sun, with the moon under her feet, and on her head a crown of twelve stars. 2She was pregnant and was crying out in birth pains and the agony of giving birth. 3And another sign appeared in heaven: behold, a great red dragon, with seven heads and ten horns, and on his heads seven diadems. 4His tail swept down a third of the stars of heaven and cast them to the earth. And the dragon stood before the woman who was about to give birth, so that when she bore her child he might devour it. 5She gave birth to a male child, one who is to rule[2] all the nations with a rod of iron, but her child was caught up to God and to his throne, 6and the woman fled into the wilderness, where she has a place prepared by God, in which she is to be nourished for 1,260 days.

Satan Thrown Down to Earth

7Now war arose in heaven, Michael and his angels fighting against the dragon. And the dragon and his angels fought back, 8but he was defeated, and there was no longer any place for them in heaven. 9And the great dragon was thrown down, that ancient serpent, who is called the devil and Satan, the deceiver of the whole world—he was thrown down to the earth, and his angels were thrown down with him. 10And I heard a loud voice in heaven, saying, "Now the salvation and the power and the kingdom of our God and the authority of his Christ have come, for the accuser of our brothers[3] has been thrown down, who accuses them day and night before our God. 11And they have conquered him by the blood of the Lamb and by the word of their testimony, for they loved not their lives even unto death. 12Therefore, rejoice, O heavens and you who dwell in them! But woe to you, O earth and sea, for the devil has come down to you in great wrath, because he knows that his time is short!"

13And when the dragon saw that he had been thrown down to the earth, he pursued the woman who had given birth to the male child. 14But the woman was given the two wings of the great eagle so that she might fly from the serpent into the wilderness, to the place where she is to be nourished for a time, and times, and half a time. 15The serpent poured water like a river out of his mouth after the

[1]Or *voices*, or *sounds* [2]Greek *shepherd* [3]Or *brothers and sisters*

woman, to sweep her away with a flood. 16But the earth came to the help of the
woman, and the earth opened its mouth and swallowed the river that the dragon
had poured from his mouth. 17Then the dragon became furious with the woman
and went off to make war on the rest of her offspring, on those who keep the
commandments of God and hold to the testimony of Jesus. And he stood[1] on the
sand of the sea.

The First Beast

13 And I saw a beast rising out of the sea, with ten horns and seven heads,
with ten diadems on its horns and blasphemous names on its heads. 2And
the beast that I saw was like a leopard; its feet were like a bear's, and its mouth
was like a lion's mouth. And to it the dragon gave his power and his throne and
great authority. 3One of its heads seemed to have a mortal wound, but its mortal
wound was healed, and the whole earth marveled as they followed the beast.
4And they worshiped the dragon, for he had given his authority to the beast,
and they worshiped the beast, saying, "Who is like the beast, and who can fight
against it?"

5And the beast was given a mouth uttering haughty and blasphemous words,
and it was allowed to exercise authority for forty-two months. 6It opened its
mouth to utter blasphemies against God, blaspheming his name and his dwelling,[2] that is, those who dwell in heaven. 7Also it was allowed to make war on the
saints and to conquer them.[3] And authority was given it over every tribe and people and language and nation, 8and all who dwell on earth will worship it, everyone
whose name has not been written from the foundation of the world in the book of
life of the Lamb who was slain. 9If anyone has an ear, let him hear:

10 If anyone is to be taken captive,
 to captivity he goes;
if anyone is to be slain with the sword,
 with the sword must he be slain.

Here is a call for the endurance and faith of the saints.

The Second Beast

11Then I saw another beast rising out of the earth. It had two horns like a lamb
and it spoke like a dragon. 12It exercises all the authority of the first beast in its
presence,[4] and makes the earth and its inhabitants worship the first beast, whose
mortal wound was healed. 13It performs great signs, even making fire come down
from heaven to earth in front of people, 14and by the signs that it is allowed to
work in the presence of[5] the beast it deceives those who dwell on earth, telling
them to make an image for the beast that was wounded by the sword and yet
lived. 15And it was allowed to give breath to the image of the beast, so that the image of the beast might even speak and might cause those who would not worship
the image of the beast to be slain. 16Also it causes all, both small and great, both
rich and poor, both free and slave,[6] to be marked on the right hand or the forehead, 17so that no one can buy or sell unless he has the mark, that is, the name of
the beast or the number of its name. 18This calls for wisdom: let the one who has
understanding calculate the number of the beast, for it is the number of a man,
and his number is 666.[7]

The Lamb and the 144,000

14 Then I looked, and behold, on Mount Zion stood the Lamb, and with him
144,000 who had his name and his Father's name written on their foreheads. 2And I heard a voice from heaven like the roar of many waters and like the

[1]Some manuscripts *And I stood,* connecting the sentence with 13:1 [2]Or *tabernacle* [3]Some manuscripts omit this sentence [4]Or *on its behalf* [5]Or *on behalf of* [6]For the contextual rendering of the Greek word *doulos*, see Preface [7]Some manuscripts *616*

(Overcoming the Enemy, continued)

in the heavenly realm, the people also triumph over their accuser by the word of their testimony and their willingness to obey to the point of death.

The blood of Jesus is the means by which God's people are spared the wrath of God and kept from the hand of the enemy. They testify to the truth that God is who he says he is and that Jesus accomplished what he said he would, and they have accepted his gift by faith. Finally, these individuals "loved not their lives even unto death" (Rev 12:11). God sustains his children, even in the face of great suffering, thus proving that they are in fact his.

REVELATION 14:1–20

PERFECT AND COMPLETE

Chapter 14 of Revelation is divided into seven parts: the Lamb with his glorious company (vv. 1–5), the angel proclaims the eternal gospel (vv. 6–7), another angel declares the fall of Babylon (v. 8), the threat against worshiping the beast (vv. 9–12), the blessing for those who die in the Lord (v. 13), the harvest (vv. 14–16), and the gathering of grapes into the winepress (vv. 17–20).

The number seven, thought to be the number of perfection, appears thirty-six times in Revelation to symbolize the finality and brilliance of God's saving work. John writes of seven messages to seven churches, seven seals, seven trumpets, and seven bowls of God's wrath. Furthermore, Jesus is represented with multiple sets of seven to show his perfection and completion under

(continued on next page)

(Perfect and Complete, continued)

God. In Chapter 1, Jesus has seven stars in his right hand, which show his complete authority over the church, represented by seven lampstands (1:12). In chapter 5, the Lamb has seven horns and seven eyes, which show his power and omniscience (5:6). And the many other mentions of this symbolic number in Revelation make it clear that, at the end of creation, God's plan and his judgment will be perfectly and completely realized.

REVELATION 15:1–4

THE LAST EXODUS

This portion of Revelation is reminiscent of God freeing the Israelites from Egypt (Ex 1–14). Just as God used plagues against Egypt, he will also use plagues against those who stand against him during the tribulation.

In the first exodus the people of God sang a song of deliverance, praising God for his faithfulness in leading them out of Egypt (Ex 15:1–21). Now, in the second exodus, God's people will also sing praises to God because they have been spared from his judgment. While the Israelites sang to God after they had witnessed the plagues and had been delivered from the Egyptian army, the singing in Revelation precedes the seven plagues because God's people have already been saved and know they are spared from God's wrath as described in chapter 16.

In both cases, there is great singing and shouts of praise to God because of his faithfulness in saving his people. Throughout history, God's salvation has caused his people to sing, and they will continue to do so for all eternity.

sound of loud thunder. The voice I heard was like the sound of harpists playing on their harps, 3and they were singing a new song before the throne and before the four living creatures and before the elders. No one could learn that song except the 144,000 who had been redeemed from the earth. 4It is these who have not defiled themselves with women, for they are virgins. It is these who follow the Lamb wherever he goes. These have been redeemed from mankind as firstfruits for God and the Lamb, 5and in their mouth no lie was found, for they are blameless.

The Messages of the Three Angels

6Then I saw another angel flying directly overhead, with an eternal gospel to proclaim to those who dwell on earth, to every nation and tribe and language and people. 7And he said with a loud voice, "Fear God and give him glory, because the hour of his judgment has come, and worship him who made heaven and earth, the sea and the springs of water."

8Another angel, a second, followed, saying, "Fallen, fallen is Babylon the great, she who made all nations drink the wine of the passion[1] of her sexual immorality."

9And another angel, a third, followed them, saying with a loud voice, "If anyone worships the beast and its image and receives a mark on his forehead or on his hand, 10he also will drink the wine of God's wrath, poured full strength into the cup of his anger, and he will be tormented with fire and sulfur in the presence of the holy angels and in the presence of the Lamb. 11And the smoke of their torment goes up forever and ever, and they have no rest, day or night, these worshipers of the beast and its image, and whoever receives the mark of its name."

12Here is a call for the endurance of the saints, those who keep the commandments of God and their faith in Jesus.[2]

13And I heard a voice from heaven saying, "Write this: Blessed are the dead who die in the Lord from now on." "Blessed indeed," says the Spirit, "that they may rest from their labors, for their deeds follow them!"

The Harvest of the Earth

14Then I looked, and behold, a white cloud, and seated on the cloud one like a son of man, with a golden crown on his head, and a sharp sickle in his hand. 15And another angel came out of the temple, calling with a loud voice to him who sat on the cloud, "Put in your sickle, and reap, for the hour to reap has come, for the harvest of the earth is fully ripe." 16So he who sat on the cloud swung his sickle across the earth, and the earth was reaped.

17Then another angel came out of the temple in heaven, and he too had a sharp sickle. 18And another angel came out from the altar, the angel who has authority over the fire, and he called with a loud voice to the one who had the sharp sickle, "Put in your sickle and gather the clusters from the vine of the earth, for its grapes are ripe." 19So the angel swung his sickle across the earth and gathered the grape harvest of the earth and threw it into the great winepress of the wrath of God. 20And the winepress was trodden outside the city, and blood flowed from the winepress, as high as a horse's bridle, for 1,600 stadia.[3]

The Seven Angels with Seven Plagues

15 Then I saw another sign in heaven, great and amazing, seven angels with seven plagues, which are the last, for with them the wrath of God is finished.

2And I saw what appeared to be a sea of glass mingled with fire—and also those who had conquered the beast and its image and the number of its name, standing beside the sea of glass with harps of God in their hands. 3And they sing the song of Moses, the servant of God, and the song of the Lamb, saying,

[1]Or *wrath* [2]Greek *and the faith of Jesus* [3]About 184 miles; a *stadion* was about 607 feet or 185 meters

"Great and amazing are your deeds,
O Lord God the Almighty!
Just and true are your ways,
O King of the nations![1]
4 Who will not fear, O Lord,
and glorify your name?
For you alone are holy.
All nations will come
and worship you,
for your righteous acts have been revealed."

5After this I looked, and the sanctuary of the tent[2] of witness in heaven was
opened, 6and out of the sanctuary came the seven angels with the seven plagues,
clothed in pure, bright linen, with golden sashes around their chests. 7And one of
the four living creatures gave to the seven angels seven golden bowls full of the
wrath of God who lives forever and ever, 8and the sanctuary was filled with smoke
from the glory of God and from his power, and no one could enter the sanctuary
until the seven plagues of the seven angels were finished.

The Seven Bowls of God's Wrath

16 Then I heard a loud voice from the temple telling the seven angels, "Go and
pour out on the earth the seven bowls of the wrath of God."
2So the first angel went and poured out his bowl on the earth, and harmful
and painful sores came upon the people who bore the mark of the beast and worshiped its image.
3The second angel poured out his bowl into the sea, and it became like the
blood of a corpse, and every living thing died that was in the sea.
4The third angel poured out his bowl into the rivers and the springs of
water, and they became blood. 5And I heard the angel in charge of the waters[3]
say,

"Just are you, O Holy One, who is and who was,
for you brought these judgments.
6 For they have shed the blood of saints and prophets,
and you have given them blood to drink.
It is what they deserve!"

7And I heard the altar saying,

"Yes, Lord God the Almighty,
true and just are your judgments!"

8The fourth angel poured out his bowl on the sun, and it was allowed to scorch
people with fire. 9They were scorched by the fierce heat, and they cursed[4] the
name of God who had power over these plagues. They did not repent and give
him glory.
10The fifth angel poured out his bowl on the throne of the beast, and its kingdom was plunged into darkness. People gnawed their tongues in anguish 11and
cursed the God of heaven for their pain and sores. They did not repent of their
deeds.
12The sixth angel poured out his bowl on the great river Euphrates, and its
water was dried up, to prepare the way for the kings from the east. 13And I saw,
coming out of the mouth of the dragon and out of the mouth of the beast and out
of the mouth of the false prophet, three unclean spirits like frogs. 14For they are
demonic spirits, performing signs, who go abroad to the kings of the whole world,
to assemble them for battle on the great day of God the Almighty. 15("Behold, I am

[1]Some manuscripts *the ages* [2]Or *tabernacle* [3]Greek *angel of the waters* [4]Greek *blasphemed*; also verses 11, 21

JESUS IN JUDGMENT

The first time Jesus came to earth he came to seek and to save the lost (Lk 19:10). He came in peace with the intention of redeeming and saving God's people. The second time will be much different from the first. While he once rode into Jerusalem on a colt as a sign of peace (Mt 21:7), he will ride on a white horse as a sign of war during his second coming (Rev 19:11). Jesus is the same yesterday, today, and forever. He will not change between his first and second coming, but his purpose in coming will. He first came to save; he will one day come again to judge.

The mercy and justice of God may seem like two incompatible characteristics. On the one hand, God will bring righteous judgment and pour out his wrath on those who refuse to trust in his saving grace. On the other hand, he is merciful and compassionate toward humanity, not wanting any to be lost (2Pe 3:9). God is unique in that his mercy is shown through his justice. Because of sin, humans deserve death and eternal separation from God (Ro 6:23). However, Jesus died on the cross and his perfect sacrifice was both an act of justice against the sin in the world and an act of mercy toward mankind. The cross is the symbol of the perfect integration of God's justice and mercy.

Standing as we are between Jesus' first and second coming, the world is now living in a state of peace and mercy. God's compassion and patience are extended to everyone on earth, and his mercies are new every morning (La 3:22 – 23). However, soon the justice of God will come, and Jesus will be the judge of all mankind. In Revelation 16, the angels praise God for exacting justice in the wrath that he pours out. The reason the angels are able to praise God is that justice is finally coming for every sin ever committed. God is glorified in his judgment because he is perfectly just. But he is also merciful. He poured out his wrath on Christ so that any who believe in him could be forgiven, once and for all. But sin is always punished — either at Calvary or in eternity — because God is a righteous judge.

coming like a thief! Blessed is the one who stays awake, keeping his garments on,
that he may not go about naked and be seen exposed!") 16And they assembled
them at the place that in Hebrew is called Armageddon.

The Seventh Bowl

17The seventh angel poured out his bowl into the air, and a loud voice came
out of the temple, from the throne, saying, "It is done!" 18And there were flashes
of lightning, rumblings,[1] peals of thunder, and a great earthquake such as there
had never been since man was on the earth, so great was that earthquake. 19The
great city was split into three parts, and the cities of the nations fell, and God
remembered Babylon the great, to make her drain the cup of the wine of the fury
of his wrath. 20And every island fled away, and no mountains were to be found.
21And great hailstones, about one hundred pounds[2] each, fell from heaven on
people; and they cursed God for the plague of the hail, because the plague was
so severe.

The Great Prostitute and the Beast

17 Then one of the seven angels who had the seven bowls came and said to
me, "Come, I will show you the judgment of the great prostitute who is seated on many waters, 2with whom the kings of the earth have committed sexual
immorality, and with the wine of whose sexual immorality the dwellers on earth
have become drunk." 3And he carried me away in the Spirit into a wilderness, and
I saw a woman sitting on a scarlet beast that was full of blasphemous names, and
it had seven heads and ten horns. 4The woman was arrayed in purple and scarlet,
and adorned with gold and jewels and pearls, holding in her hand a golden cup
full of abominations and the impurities of her sexual immorality. 5And on her
forehead was written a name of mystery: "Babylon the great, mother of prostitutes and of earth's abominations." 6And I saw the woman, drunk with the blood
of the saints, the blood of the martyrs of Jesus.[3]

When I saw her, I marveled greatly. 7But the angel said to me, "Why do you
marvel? I will tell you the mystery of the woman, and of the beast with seven
heads and ten horns that carries her. 8The beast that you saw was, and is not,
and is about to rise from the bottomless pit[4] and go to destruction. And the
dwellers on earth whose names have not been written in the book of life from
the foundation of the world will marvel to see the beast, because it was and
is not and is to come. 9This calls for a mind with wisdom: the seven heads are
seven mountains on which the woman is seated; 10they are also seven kings,
five of whom have fallen, one is, the other has not yet come, and when he does
come he must remain only a little while. 11As for the beast that was and is not,
it is an eighth but it belongs to the seven, and it goes to destruction. 12And the
ten horns that you saw are ten kings who have not yet received royal power,
but they are to receive authority as kings for one hour, together with the beast.
13These are of one mind, and they hand over their power and authority to the
beast. 14They will make war on the Lamb, and the Lamb will conquer them, for
he is Lord of lords and King of kings, and those with him are called and chosen
and faithful."

15And the angel[5] said to me, "The waters that you saw, where the prostitute
is seated, are peoples and multitudes and nations and languages. 16And the ten
horns that you saw, they and the beast will hate the prostitute. They will make
her desolate and naked, and devour her flesh and burn her up with fire, 17for God
has put it into their hearts to carry out his purpose by being of one mind and
handing over their royal power to the beast, until the words of God are fulfilled.
18And the woman that you saw is the great city that has dominion over the kings
of the earth."

---

[1]Or *voices*, or *sounds* [2]Greek *a talent in weight* [3]Greek *the witnesses to Jesus* [4]Greek *the abyss*
[5]Greek *he*

The Fall of Babylon

18 After this I saw another angel coming down from heaven, having great authority, and the earth was made bright with his glory. 2And he called out
with a mighty voice,

"Fallen, fallen is Babylon the great!
She has become a dwelling place for demons,
a haunt for every unclean spirit,
a haunt for every unclean bird,
a haunt for every unclean and detestable beast.
3 For all nations have drunk[1]
the wine of the passion of her sexual immorality,
and the kings of the earth have committed immorality
with her,
and the merchants of the earth have grown rich from the
power of her luxurious living."

4Then I heard another voice from heaven saying,

"Come out of her, my people,
lest you take part in her sins,
lest you share in her plagues;
5 for her sins are heaped high as heaven,
and God has remembered her iniquities.
6 Pay her back as she herself has paid back others,
and repay her double for her deeds;
mix a double portion for her in the cup she mixed.
7 As she glorified herself and lived in luxury,
so give her a like measure of torment and mourning,
since in her heart she says,
'I sit as a queen,
I am no widow,
and mourning I shall never see.'
8 For this reason her plagues will come in a single day,
death and mourning and famine,
and she will be burned up with fire;
for mighty is the Lord God who has judged her."

9And the kings of the earth, who committed sexual immorality and lived in
luxury with her, will weep and wail over her when they see the smoke of her burning. 10They will stand far off, in fear of her torment, and say,

"Alas! Alas! You great city,
you mighty city, Babylon!
For in a single hour your judgment has come."

11And the merchants of the earth weep and mourn for her, since no one buys
their cargo anymore, 12cargo of gold, silver, jewels, pearls, fine linen, purple cloth,
silk, scarlet cloth, all kinds of scented wood, all kinds of articles of ivory, all kinds
of articles of costly wood, bronze, iron and marble, 13cinnamon, spice, incense,
myrrh, frankincense, wine, oil, fine flour, wheat, cattle and sheep, horses and
chariots, and slaves, that is, human souls.[2]

14 "The fruit for which your soul longed
has gone from you,
and all your delicacies and your splendors
are lost to you,
never to be found again!"

[1]Some manuscripts *fallen by* [2]Or *and slaves, and human lives*

REVELATION 18:2

GOD'S GUARANTEE

The repetition of the word "fallen" in verse two points to the fact that God has already predicted the destruction of Babylon, and his promise is coming true (Isa 21:9; Jer 51:8; Rev 14:8). The prophecies made long ago by Ezekiel and Daniel have now come true (Eze 38–39; Da 7; 11). Babylon, a vivid picture of a world system broken by sin, is now destroyed forever. Through God's eternal power, sin and death are destroyed, including all the broken systems and structures that define this sinful world.

As with Jesus' first coming, his second coming will usher in the fulfillment of the prophecies that involve his final work. Though no one knows the timing of Jesus' return, God uses John's words to continually remind this people that they have nothing to fear. Sin will not run amok forever. God will defeat it and destroy Babylon the great and all it represents, once and for all time.

15The merchants of these wares, who gained wealth from her, will stand far off, in
fear of her torment, weeping and mourning aloud,

16 "Alas, alas, for the great city
that was clothed in fine linen,
in purple and scarlet,
adorned with gold,
with jewels, and with pearls!
17 For in a single hour all this wealth has been laid waste."

And all shipmasters and seafaring men, sailors and all whose trade is on the
sea, stood far off 18and cried out as they saw the smoke of her burning,

"What city was like the great city?"

19And they threw dust on their heads as they wept and mourned, crying out,

"Alas, alas, for the great city
where all who had ships at sea
grew rich by her wealth!
For in a single hour she has been laid waste.
20 Rejoice over her, O heaven,
and you saints and apostles and prophets,
for God has given judgment for you against her!"

21Then a mighty angel took up a stone like a great millstone and threw it into
the sea, saying,

"So will Babylon the great city be thrown down with violence,
and will be found no more;
22 and the sound of harpists and musicians, of flute players
and trumpeters,
will be heard in you no more,
and a craftsman of any craft
will be found in you no more,
and the sound of the mill
will be heard in you no more,
23 and the light of a lamp
will shine in you no more,
and the voice of bridegroom and bride
will be heard in you no more,
for your merchants were the great ones of the earth,
and all nations were deceived by your sorcery.
24 And in her was found the blood of prophets and of saints,
and of all who have been slain on earth."

Rejoicing in Heaven

19 After this I heard what seemed to be the loud voice of a great multitude in
heaven, crying out,

"Hallelujah!
Salvation and glory and power belong to our God,
2 for his judgments are true and just;
for he has judged the great prostitute
who corrupted the earth with her immorality,
and has avenged on her the blood of his servants."

3Once more they cried out,

"Hallelujah!
The smoke from her goes up forever and ever."

4 And the twenty-four elders and the four living creatures fell down and worshiped God who was seated on the throne, saying, "Amen. Hallelujah!" 5 And from
the throne came a voice saying,

"Praise our God,
all you his servants,
you who fear him,
small and great."

The Marriage Supper of the Lamb

6 Then I heard what seemed to be the voice of a great multitude, like the roar of
many waters and like the sound of mighty peals of thunder, crying out,

"Hallelujah!
For the Lord our God
the Almighty reigns.
7 Let us rejoice and exult
and give him the glory,
for the marriage of the Lamb has come,
and his Bride has made herself ready;
8 it was granted her to clothe herself
with fine linen, bright and pure"—

for the fine linen is the righteous deeds of the saints.
9 And the angel said[1] to me, "Write this: Blessed are those who are invited to
the marriage supper of the Lamb." And he said to me, "These are the true words
of God." 10 Then I fell down at his feet to worship him, but he said to me, "You must
not do that! I am a fellow servant with you and your brothers who hold to the testimony of Jesus. Worship God." For the testimony of Jesus is the spirit of prophecy.

The Rider on a White Horse

11 Then I saw heaven opened, and behold, a white horse! The one sitting on it is
called Faithful and True, and in righteousness he judges and makes war. 12 His eyes are
like a flame of fire, and on his head are many diadems, and he has a name written that
no one knows but himself. 13 He is clothed in a robe dipped in[2] blood, and the name
by which he is called is The Word of God. 14 And the armies of heaven, arrayed in fine
linen, white and pure, were following him on white horses. 15 From his mouth comes
a sharp sword with which to strike down the nations, and he will rule[3] them with a
rod of iron. He will tread the winepress of the fury of the wrath of God the Almighty.
16 On his robe and on his thigh he has a name written, King of kings and Lord of lords.
17 Then I saw an angel standing in the sun, and with a loud voice he called to all
the birds that fly directly overhead, "Come, gather for the great supper of God, 18 to
eat the flesh of kings, the flesh of captains, the flesh of mighty men, the flesh of
horses and their riders, and the flesh of all men, both free and slave,[4] both small and
great." 19 And I saw the beast and the kings of the earth with their armies gathered to
make war against him who was sitting on the horse and against his army. 20 And the
beast was captured, and with it the false prophet who in its presence[5] had done the
signs by which he deceived those who had received the mark of the beast and those
who worshiped its image. These two were thrown alive into the lake of fire that
burns with sulfur. 21 And the rest were slain by the sword that came from the mouth
of him who was sitting on the horse, and all the birds were gorged with their flesh.

The Thousand Years

20 Then I saw an angel coming down from heaven, holding in his hand the
key to the bottomless pit[6] and a great chain. 2 And he seized the dragon,
that ancient serpent, who is the devil and Satan, and bound him for a thousand

[1] Greek *he said* [2] Some manuscripts *sprinkled with* [3] Greek *shepherd* [4] For the contextual rendering of the Greek word *doulos*, see Preface [5] Or *on its behalf* [6] Greek *the abyss*; also verse 3

REVELATION 19:11

JESUS AND HIS WHITE HORSE

In the era when Rome was the dominant world power, a Roman general riding on a white horse after a battle was symbolic of victory in that battle; it showed that the captives and spoils of war belonged to Rome. In ancient cultures the white horse was considered a symbol of dominant rule and royalty, and that's the image in this passage as well.

John recorded Jesus riding a white horse *into* battle (v. 11), demonstrating that he has already won the war. What might have been considered an arrogant gesture in ancient culture is, for Jesus, a symbol that this battle is over before it even begins. He will not come to earth to struggle against the enemy; he will come to destroy the enemy. The captives and the spoils of war already belong to Jesus: he is superior, and the victory is already won.

years, [3]and threw him into the pit, and shut it and sealed it over him, so that he
might not deceive the nations any longer, until the thousand years were ended.
After that he must be released for a little while.
[4]Then I saw thrones, and seated on them were those to whom the authority to
judge was committed. Also I saw the souls of those who had been beheaded for
the testimony of Jesus and for the word of God, and those who had not worshiped
the beast or its image and had not received its mark on their foreheads or their
hands. They came to life and reigned with Christ for a thousand years. [5]The rest of
the dead did not come to life until the thousand years were ended. This is the first
resurrection. [6]Blessed and holy is the one who shares in the first resurrection!
Over such the second death has no power, but they will be priests of God and of
Christ, and they will reign with him for a thousand years.

The Defeat of Satan

[7]And when the thousand years are ended, Satan will be released from his prison [8]and will come out to deceive the nations that are at the four corners of the
earth, Gog and Magog, to gather them for battle; their number is like the sand of
the sea. [9]And they marched up over the broad plain of the earth and surrounded
the camp of the saints and the beloved city, but fire came down from heaven[1] and
consumed them, [10]and the devil who had deceived them was thrown into the lake
of fire and sulfur where the beast and the false prophet were, and they will be
tormented day and night forever and ever.

Judgment Before the Great White Throne

[11]Then I saw a great white throne and him who was seated on it. From his presence earth and sky fled away, and no place was found for them. [12]And I saw the
dead, great and small, standing before the throne, and books were opened. Then
another book was opened, which is the book of life. And the dead were judged
by what was written in the books, according to what they had done. [13]And the
sea gave up the dead who were in it, Death and Hades gave up the dead who were
in them, and they were judged, each one of them, according to what they had
done. [14]Then Death and Hades were thrown into the lake of fire. This is the second
death, the lake of fire. [15]And if anyone's name was not found written in the book
of life, he was thrown into the lake of fire.

The New Heaven and the New Earth

21 Then I saw a new heaven and a new earth, for the first heaven and the
first earth had passed away, and the sea was no more. [2]And I saw the holy
city, new Jerusalem, coming down out of heaven from God, prepared as a bride
adorned for her husband. [3]And I heard a loud voice from the throne saying, "Behold, the dwelling place[2] of God is with man. He will dwell with them, and they
will be his people,[3] and God himself will be with them as their God.[4] [4]He will
wipe away every tear from their eyes, and death shall be no more, neither shall
there be mourning, nor crying, nor pain anymore, for the former things have
passed away."
[5]And he who was seated on the throne said, "Behold, I am making all things
new." Also he said, "Write this down, for these words are trustworthy and true."
[6]And he said to me, "It is done! I am the Alpha and the Omega, the beginning
and the end. To the thirsty I will give from the spring of the water of life without
payment. [7]The one who conquers will have this heritage, and I will be his God
and he will be my son. [8]But as for the cowardly, the faithless, the detestable,
as for murderers, the sexually immoral, sorcerers, idolaters, and all liars, their
portion will be in the lake that burns with fire and sulfur, which is the second
death."

---

[1]Some manuscripts *from God, out of heaven*, or *out of heaven from God* [2]Or *tabernacle* [3]Some manuscripts *peoples* [4]Some manuscripts omit *as their God*

GOD AND THE PROBLEM OF EVIL

The presence of evil in the world makes many people doubt the existence or the goodness of God. Critics have argued that if God were perfect and loving, then he would not allow the presence of evil in the world. However, this argument does not account for the multiple ways God has worked to deal with evil and sin.

The first and most basic way that God brings justice to evil is through natural consequences. In this imperfect world, all people experience the natural consequences of their sin. On a larger scale, the story of the cities of Sodom and Gomorrah provide us with an example of God's judgment coming about as a consequence of people's rebellion (Ge 19). In a similar way, the book of Revelation as a whole shows the consequences that will come as a result of the world's sin.

Second, God dealt with sin on the cross. Jesus' death, though it did not eliminate evil from the world, dealt a deathblow to its permanent presence in the world. While the world today is obviously still plagued with evil, Jesus' sacrifice and resurrection made it possible for the world to one day be free from evil. By giving Jesus over to be crucified and raising him from the dead, God defeated death and made it possible for his children to be made right with him. Jesus served as a perfect sacrifice for the evil of mankind; the judgment of sin was carried out against him as he hung on the cross in humanity's place.

Third, Revelation depicts God's ultimate elimination of evil from the world. The judgment day is his final act of justice and retribution against the evil that humans have brought upon themselves. God is perfect and therefore cannot be associated with anything that is evil or sinful, and so he will one day completely eliminate the existence of evil from the world when his kingdom is perfectly realized in the new earth (Isa 65:17; Rev 21:1 – 4).

While it may look to us as if sin goes unchecked, God will surely right all wrongs in his time. The consequences of sin, Jesus' death on the cross, and the final judgment day are three parts of God's plan to ultimately defeat evil and to fully establish his kingdom. While people may wonder why God does things the way he does, it is important to remember that his plan is perfect; it has been and will continue to be fulfilled, and it will lead to a good and perfect kingdom that believers will share with him.

THE ALPHA AND THE OMEGA

Alpha and *Omega* are the first and last letters of the Greek alphabet, and together they also comprise one of the names for God. The name "the first and the last" appears in multiple places in the Old Testament as a representation for God's eternal existence (see Isa 41:4; 44:6; 48:12). God is the Alpha and the Omega because he is responsible for both the beginning and end of everything that has ever existed. Jesus had no beginning; he was present for the creation of the world (Jn 1:3), and he will be present for the end of the world (Rev 21:6), after which he will reign over the universe for eternity.

Jesus is the beginning and the end in many ways. Hebrews 12:2 says that he is the "founder and perfecter" of faith, which signifies that he initiated faith and he will bring it to completion. He is the summation of and the actual Word of God (Jn 1:1,14); he is the fulfillment of the Law (Mt 5:17); and he is the beginning of the gospel of grace through faith, not works (Eph 2:8–9).

Jesus is there in the first verse of Genesis and the last verse of Revelation, and he is present in every Bible verse, story, and teaching in between. To say that Jesus is the Alpha and the Omega is to say that he is God, a declaration that is reinforced as true in the Gospels and throughout the entire New Testament. The book of Revelation never wavers from proclaiming that Jesus and God are one, and that together they bring about the creation and culmination of everything.

The Bible paints an astonishing picture of how everything began and how everything will end. And the best part about the beginning, the end, and everything in between is that Jesus is the backbone, the central thread, the main theme, and the summation of all of it. Not a single second in history has or will escape God's watchful eye; there is no part of the story where Jesus was not, is not, or will not be present and perfectly sovereign. That's the hopeful message of God's Word, his revelation to all who will believe.

Believers can be confident that the God they trust in is fully in control of everything that was, everything that is, and everything that will be. The name "the Alpha and the Omega" succinctly defines who God is and what he has done. From the beginning and to the end, God is eternal, God is in control, God is gracious and loving, God is just, and GOD WINS.

FOREVER

MADE FOR A DIFFERENT PLACE

REVELATION 21 – 22

We were made for a person and a place. Jesus is the person. Heaven is the place.

God promises that all his children — whoever places their faith in Jesus to rescue them from sin and eternal death — will live *forever* with him in heaven (Lk 24:23 – 24; Jn 1:12; 3:16; 1Th 5:10).

But what exactly will eternal life with Jesus in heaven be like?

Heaven is God's central dwelling place. God is everywhere-present, yet heaven is the special location from which he rules the universe; it's where his throne is (1Ki 22:19).

When God's children die, we immediately go to heaven to be with Christ (Lk 23:43). But when we carefully read Scripture, we find that one day God will permanently relocate the present heaven to the newly transformed earth, which then will become the "forever heaven."

We normally think death ushers us into heaven to live with God in his place. That's in fact what happens when Christ-followers die (2Co 5:8). But the ultimate promise is that *God will come down to live with us in our place.* He says of the new earth, "Behold, the dwelling place of God is with man. He will dwell with them, and they will be his people, and God himself will be with them as their God" (Rev 21:3). Three times in this one verse God says he will live "with" us! So the ultimate heaven, on the new earth, will not be "us with God" but "God with us."

While the throne of God is now in the present heaven, when God descends to live on the new earth, "The throne of God and of the Lamb will be in it [the city]" (Rev 22:3). Where God's throne is, that is heaven, his central dwelling place. So the new earth will literally be "heaven on earth."

A WHOLE NEW WORLD!

God created the entire physical universe for his glory and our good. But humanity rebelled and the universe fell under the weight of our sin. Yet Adam and Eve's seduction by the serpent didn't catch God off guard. He had a plan in place for humanity's redemption — and the restoration of creation, forever rescuing it from sin, corruption, and death. Just as he promises to make humankind new, he promises to renew earth itself.

> "Behold, I create new heavens and a new earth" (Isa 65:17).
>
> "For as the new heavens and the new earth that I make shall remain before me, says the LORD, so shall your offspring and your name remain" (Isa 66:22).
>
> "According to his promise we are waiting for

"new heavens and a new earth in which righteousness dwells" (2Pe 3:13).

"Then I saw a new heaven and a new earth, for the first heaven and the first earth had passed away" (Rev 21:1).

Imagine how delighted Jesus' disciples were when he said to them, "In *the new world,* when the Son of Man will sit on his glorious throne, you who have followed me will also sit on twelve thrones, judging the twelve tribes of Israel" (Mt 19:28, italics added).

Christ didn't speak of the *destruction* or *abandonment* of all things but "the new world." God designed humans to live on earth to his glory. Christ's incarnation, life, death, and resurrection secured the new earth's eternal future, where life will be lived in complete fulfillment and without sin, the way God always intended.

So never think Satan beat God and thwarted his plans by tempting Adam and Eve in Eden. Rather, unwittingly his attempts to sabotage God's plans were used by the sovereign Creator as a part of his redemptive story that includes the incarnation, life, death, resurrection, and return of Jesus, as well as the devil's final destruction (Ge 3:15; Rev 20:10).

Similarly, Peter preached that Christ must remain in heaven "until the time for *restoring all the things* about which God spoke by the mouth of his holy prophets long ago" (Ac 3:21, italics added).

This cosmic restoration will not consist of God bringing disembodied angel-like people to fellowship with him in a spirit realm. Rather, God will bring humankind to something greater than even his original design in Eden. The entire physical universe won't go back to its pre-fall glory but forward to something still more magnificent.

THE FUTURE HEAVEN, WHERE WE'LL LIVE FOREVER

The exact location of the present heaven is unknown. It seems likely that it's not in our physical universe, but it exists in another dimension that we can't see. But we do know it is a wonderful place to live between the time the followers of Jesus die and our future resurrection.

Life in the present heaven (which theologians call the "intermediate" heaven) "is far better" than living here on earth under the curse (Php 1:23). But it's not our final destination.

Many understand Revelation 20:1 – 10 to teach that after we're raised, we will live on the original earth for a thousand years. After that will come the final judgment and end of the old earth, followed by its resurrection in the form of the new earth, where we will live with God and each other forever.

FOREVER

(CONTINUED)

REVELATION 21 – 22

When the New Jerusalem comes down out of heaven from God, it will descend to the new earth. From that time on, God's dwelling place will be with his redeemed people on *earth*. This means the new earth will literally be heaven on earth!

Jesus says of those who would be his disciple, "My Father will love him, and we will come to him and make our home with him" (Jn 14:23). This is a picture of God's ultimate plan. Think about this: God could have taken Adam and Eve up to heaven to visit with him — but he didn't. Instead, he walked with them here in their own world (Ge 3:8). And that's what he will do with us forever!

The idea of the new earth as a physical place isn't an invention of shortsighted human imagination. It's the invention of our infinitely resourceful Creator, who made physical human beings to live on a physical earth, *and* who chose to become a man himself on that same earth. He wanted to redeem mankind *and* earth. Why? In order to glorify himself and enjoy forever the company of men and women in a world he's made for us.

JESUS: THE PRIME EXAMPLE OF OUR RESURRECTED LIVES

When Jesus Christ came to earth, one of his names was Immanuel, which means "God with us" (Mt 1:23). Jesus' ascension to heaven in his resurrected body demonstrated the permanence of the incarnation. This has great bearing on where God chooses for us to dwell together. The new earth will be heaven incarnate, just as Jesus Christ is God incarnate. It will not be strange for Jesus to live on the new earth, since like all of us, he first lived on the original earth!

In the forty days between Christ's resurrection and ascension, he walked, talked, ate, and drank with his disciples. They saw a preview of the resurrected life reminding us that we will be both spiritual *and* physical beings forever.

It's fascinating to compare the first three and last three chapters of the Bible. In both we see the "tree of life," a great river or rivers, a bride and a bridegroom. In Genesis, paradise is lost; in Revelation, paradise is regained. In Genesis, Satan wins his first victory; in Revelation, he experiences his final defeat. In Genesis, God hides his face from sinful man; in Revelation, it's said of God's children "they will see his face" (Rev 22:4).

In Genesis, the curse is pronounced; in Revelation, it's removed. In Genesis, the gates of paradise are shut; in Revelation, the heavenly city's gates are open. In Genesis, death appears; in Revelation, death is finally destroyed. It's the Lamb of God, Jesus Christ, the second Adam, who is given full credit for his sweeping victory over sin and death and his dramatic rescue of his people. By his incredible grace, those who believe in him will live forever in heaven rather than in hell.

UNITING HEAVEN AND EARTH

"The saints of the Most High shall receive the kingdom and possess the kingdom forever, forever and ever" (Da 7:18). What is "the kingdom"? Earth. God's people will reign over it not just for a thousand years but forever. God never abandoned his original plan for righteous humans to rule the earth — and through Jesus he will yet fulfill that plan in glorious ways. Earth is unique. It's the one planet — perhaps among billions — where God chose to act out the unfolding drama of redemption and reveal the wonders of his grace.

If the new Jerusalem will be capital city of the new earth, the new earth will be capital planet of the new universe. There God will establish an eternal kingdom where he will "unite all things in him, things in heaven and things on earth" (Eph 1:10). "All things" is inclusive — neither animals nor trees nor flowers nor mountains nor valleys will be left out. This verse corresponds precisely to the culmination of history we see enacted in Revelation 21, the merging together of previously separate realms of heaven and earth, fully under Christ's lordship.

As God and humankind are reconciled and united in Jesus, so too the dwellings of God and humankind — heaven and earth — will be reconciled and united in Jesus. The prayer of the ages, "your will be done, on earth as it is in heaven" (Mt 6:10) will at last be fully answered! Heaven is God's home. Earth is our home. Jesus Christ, as the God-man, forever links God and humankind, and thereby forever links heaven and earth. As Ephesians 1:10 demonstrates, this idea of earth and heaven becoming one is explicitly biblical. Just as the veil that separated God from humankind was torn in two at Christ's death (Mt 27:51), so the veil that separates heaven and earth will be forever split. The gulf between the spiritual and physical worlds will be removed. No divided realms or divided loyalties to different homelands. Just one cosmos, one universe united under one Lord — forever. This is the unstoppable plan of God. This is history's destination, the culmination of the greatest story ever told, a Jesus-centered story with a happy ending that will never end.

When God walked with Adam and Eve in the Garden of Eden, earth was heaven's backyard. The new earth will be heaven itself. And those who know Jesus will have the privilege of living there.

OUR FOREVER HOME

God paints a compelling picture of the coming world: "'For behold, I create new heavens and a new earth ... But be glad and rejoice forever in that which I create; for behold, I create Jerusalem to be a joy, and her people to be a gladness. I will rejoice in Jerusalem and be glad in my people; no more shall be heard in it the sound of weeping and the cry of distress ...

FOREVER
(CONTINUED)

REVELATION 21 – 22

They shall build houses and inhabit them; they shall plant vineyards and eat their fruit ... The wolf and the lamb shall graze together; the lion shall eat straw like the ox, and dust shall be the serpent's food. They shall not hurt or destroy in all my holy mountain,' says the LORD" (Isa 65:17 – 19,21,25).

Although Isaiah 60 doesn't contain the term *new earth* (as do nearby chapters 65 and 66), we know much of the chapter describes that place, since John applied the prophet's words directly to the new earth in Revelation 21 – 22.

This will be a time of unprecedented rejoicing: "Then you shall see and be radiant; your heart shall thrill and exult." On the renewed earth, the nations will bring their greatest treasures into this glorified city: "The abundance of the sea shall be turned to you, the wealth of the nations shall come to you" (Isa 60:5).

There will be animals from various nations on the new earth: "A multitude of camels shall cover you, the young camels of Midian and Ephah" (Isa 60:6). Redeemed people will travel from far places to the glorified Jerusalem: "All those from Sheba shall come. They shall bring gold and frankincense, and shall bring good news" (v. 6). People who dwell on islands will worship God, and ships will come from "Tarshish first, to bring your children from afar, their silver and gold with them, for the name of the LORD your God, and for the Holy One of Israel, because he has made you beautiful" (v. 9).

Most of us are unaccustomed to thinking of nations, rulers, civilizations, and culture (as well as animals) in heaven, but Isaiah 60 is one of many passages demonstrating the new earth's true earthiness.

THE WONDERS OF THE HOLY CITY

John applied Isaiah 60:11 directly to the new Jerusalem: "By its light will the nations walk, and the kings of the earth will bring their glory into it, and its gates will never be shut by day — and there will be no night there. They will bring into it the glory and the honor of the nations" (Rev 21:24 – 26).

The references to splendor of kings and glory of nations give us biblical basis to suppose that the best history, culture, art, music, and the languages of the old earth will be redeemed, purified, and restored to the new earth. Even now in heaven there are people "from every tribe and language and people and nation" (Rev 5:9). It appears God's people will forever be multicultural!

God promises something that has never yet been true of the present Jerusalem: "I will make your overseers peace and your taskmasters righteousness. Violence shall no more be heard in your land, devastation or destruction within your borders; you shall call your walls Salvation, and your gates Praise" (Isa 60:17 – 18).

Isaiah then describes another scene that John

connects directly to the new earth in Revelation 21:23; 22:5: "The sun shall be no more your light by day, nor for brightness shall the moon give you light; but the LORD will be your everlasting light, and your God will be your glory. Your sun shall no more go down, nor your moon withdraw itself; for the LORD will be your everlasting light, and your days of mourning shall be ended" (Isa 60:19 – 20).

Of the new Jerusalem, we're told, "Nothing unclean will ever enter it, nor anyone who does what is detestable or false, but only those who are written in the Lamb's book of life" (Rev 21:27). Likewise, Isaiah uses inclusive language that could not apply to the old earth under the curse: "Your people shall all be righteous" (Isa 60:21). Verse 21 continues, "They shall possess the land [in the Hebrew, literally *earth*] forever." The earth will be theirs — not for a glorious decade or century or millennium, but *forever.*

ANYTHING BUT BORING!

A pastor once told me he dreaded heaven. Why? "I can't stand the thought of endless tedium. To float around in the clouds with nothing to do but strum a harp ... it's all so terribly boring. Heaven doesn't sound much better than hell. I'd rather be annihilated than spend eternity in a place like that."

Jesus said of the devil, "When he lies, he speaks out of his own character, for he is a liar and the father of lies" (Jn 8:44). Our enemy slanders three things: God's person, God's people, and God's place — namely, heaven. Satan need not convince us that heaven doesn't exist, only that heaven is a place of boring, unearthly existence. What an insult to the infinitely fascinating Maker of the universe, whose creative wonders will never cease!

Believing Satan's lies robs us of our joy and anticipation. We set our minds on this life — not the next — and lose motivation to share our faith. Why should we share the "good news" that people can spend eternity in a boring, ghostly place that *even we* don't look forward to?

The new Jerusalem will be a new Eden, a huge garden city of startling beauty. Heaven won't be filled with hammocks — with nothing to do but rest (though some rest will be great for a while). We'll honor God by enjoying him through enjoying his creation. We'll always get to do what we want to do, and we'll always want to do what brings joy to God and to us.

On the new earth, we're told "his servants will worship him" (Rev 22:3). Servants of a King — especially his children who are royalty themselves — have important things to do, places to go, people to see. It's said of God's children "they will reign forever and ever" (Rev 22:5). Servants work and rulers work. But on the new earth, with a totally righteous and loving Father, our work will be a privilege — refreshing work

FOREVER
(CONTINUED)

REVELATION 21–22

without the curse — similar to work done by Adam and Eve in the Garden of Eden.

ANTICIPATING LIFE ON THE NEW EARTH

The Westminster Shorter Catechism, completed in 1647, begins, "Man's chief end is to glorify God and to enjoy him forever." What will we do forever? Enjoy God! Will we use the arts to praise God? Since the new earth will supersede and surpass the present earth, then surely the greatest books, dramas, and poems have yet to be written. Just as we can use our voices and musical instruments to worship God, we can also dance to honor him.

What about sports? Picture yourself enjoying your favorite sport (which may be a new one you haven't yet played) when you live on the new earth with a perfectly healthy body. Olympic champion Eric Liddell said, "God made me fast. And when I run I feel his pleasure."

After our resurrection, Matthew 8:11 and several other Scriptures say we'll enjoy feasts with Jesus "in the kingdom of heaven." But that heavenly kingdom is depicted in a very tangible, earthly way. What do people do at a feast? Eat and drink, tell stories, celebrate, and laugh. God will be the host and Christ the guest of honor, and all stories and laughter will honor him.

We'll never know everything — we're not God. But as resurrected beings, we'll certainly be capable of learning and growing, discovering and exploring. God tells us "in the coming ages" he'll "show the immeasurable riches of his grace in kindness toward us in Christ Jesus" (Eph 2:6–7). We may learn exactly how God fulfilled his promise to work all things, even the hardest things in our lives, together for our good (Ro 8:28).

THE OLD EARTH MADE NEW AND FAR BETTER

The whole creation groans and, implicitly, awaits with us the redemption of our bodies in the resurrection (Ro 8:22–23). This suggests that animals, which experience suffering due to our sin, will likewise experience new life on the new earth. The creation that fell on our coattails will rise on our coattails. Perhaps God will bring even extinct animals back to life. Since he's a kind Father and the giver of all good gifts, if having your pets on the new earth would please you, God might well bring them back.

Though the splendor of creation that remains testifies to God's greatness (Ro 1:20), the curse removed much of the world's beauty. But Revelation 22:3 says, "No longer will there be anything accursed." God will make all his children beautiful and whole and happy.

When God brings heaven down to the new earth, "he will wipe away every tear from their eyes" (Rev 21:4). What an intimate picture — God's hands will touch the face of each individual child, removing every tear. The same verse says, "Death shall be no more, neither shall there be mourning, nor crying, nor pain anymore." As Thomas Moore put it, "Earth has no sorrow that heaven cannot heal."

There'll be no diseases, no disabilities, no tragic accidents. No hospitals. No cemeteries. No sin. No evil. No fear. No abuse, rape, murder, drugs, drunkenness, bombs, shootings, or terrorism.

The disabled, liberated from ravaged bodies and minds, and the sick and elderly, free from pains and restrictions, will deeply appreciate heaven. They'll walk and run and see and hear, some for the first time. Hymn writer Fanny Crosby said, "Don't pity me for my blindness, for the first face I ever see will be the face of my Lord Jesus."

The promise of the resurrection means that none of God's children will pass our peak in this life. We won't have to look back with regret, pining away for an earlier time when we were at our best. The resurrection means not simply taking us back to the best we once were, but moving us forward to a new best, beyond our wildest dreams! Our peaks are yet to come, and we will never pass them!

OUR BEST RELATIONSHIPS ARE AHEAD OF US

Crowds followed Jesus because they loved him and wanted to be near him. The best part of heaven will be spending time with Jesus.

While Jesus will be our best friend, God understands our need and desire for friendships to continue in heaven. He made us that way. In heaven we'll have our old friends who know Jesus and many new friends as well. Every time we sit together at feasts we will meet new people and hear new stories!

Married couples needn't fear the words of Jesus concerning human marriage discontinuing in heaven (Mt 22:30). Scripture does *not* teach there will be no marriage in heaven. Instead there'll be *one* marriage, between Christ and his bride — and we'll all be part of it. Our marriage to Christ will be so completely satisfying that even the most wonderful earthly marriage couldn't compete.

But Christ never suggested an end to deep relationships between couples. I fully expect my wife, Nanci, and I will be closer friends than ever. We'll remember fondly the lives we forged together on the old earth, our children and grandchildren and friends. All of us together will be part of the same unbreakable marriage to Jesus.

The most ordinary moment in heaven will far surpass the best moments of this life. In that day we'll all agree with the apostle Paul: "The sufferings of this present time are not worth comparing with the glory that is to be revealed to us" (Ro 8:18).

FOREVER

(CONTINUED)

REVELATION 21 – 22

GET A HEAD START ON KINGDOM LIVING

"Seek the things that are above, where Christ is, seated at the right hand of God. Set your minds on things that are above, not on the things that are on earth" (Col 3:1 – 2). If we understand what "new heavens and a new earth" means, we'll look forward to and focus on our forever home.

Knowing where we're going and what rewards we'll receive for serving Christ directly affects how we live today. Our choices make an indelible mark on eternity — including our choices of personal holiness and how we act toward others. After saying "we are waiting for new heavens and a new earth in which righteousness dwells," Peter immediately adds, "Therefore, beloved ... be diligent to be found by him without spot or blemish, and at peace" (2Pe 3:13 – 14).

When this is true of us, we can face death with an eternal perspective. Calvin Miller, in the *Divine Symphony* prayed,

> I once scorned ev'ry fearful thought of death,
> When it was but the end of pulse and breath,
> But now my eyes have seen that past the pain
> There is a world that's waiting to be claimed.
> Earthmaker, Holy, let me now depart,
> For living's such a temporary art.
> And dying is but getting dressed for God,
> Our graves are merely doorways cut in sod.

C. S. Lewis said, "I must keep alive in myself the desire for my true country, which I shall not find till after death; I must never let it get snowed under or turned aside; I must make it the main object of life to press on to that other country and to help others to do the same."

If you know Jesus, we'll live together on that resurrected world. With the Lord we love and with friends we cherish, we'll embark together on the ultimate adventure, in a spectacular new universe. Jesus will be the center of all things, and joy will be the air we breathe. And we really will live "happily ever after."

And right when we think, "It can't get any better than this" ... it will!

BEGINNINGS	REVOLT	PEOPLE	INTERTESTAMENTAL PERIOD	SAVIOR	CHURCH	FOREVER
GENESIS 1–2 (pg. 10)	GENESIS 3–11 (pg. 24)	GENESIS 12 to MALACHI (pg. 256)	(pg. 1468)	GOSPELS to ACTS 1 (pg. 1518)	ACTS 2 to REVELATION 20 (pg. 1686)	REVELATION 21–22 (pg. 1938)

The New Jerusalem

9Then came one of the seven angels who had the seven bowls full of the seven
last plagues and spoke to me, saying, "Come, I will show you the Bride, the wife
of the Lamb." 10And he carried me away in the Spirit to a great, high mountain,
and showed me the holy city Jerusalem coming down out of heaven from God,
11having the glory of God, its radiance like a most rare jewel, like a jasper, clear
as crystal. 12It had a great, high wall, with twelve gates, and at the gates twelve
angels, and on the gates the names of the twelve tribes of the sons of Israel were
inscribed— 13on the east three gates, on the north three gates, on the south three
gates, and on the west three gates. 14And the wall of the city had twelve foundations, and on them were the twelve names of the twelve apostles of the Lamb.
15And the one who spoke with me had a measuring rod of gold to measure
the city and its gates and walls. 16The city lies foursquare, its length the same as
its width. And he measured the city with his rod, 12,000 stadia.[1] Its length and
width and height are equal. 17He also measured its wall, 144 cubits[2] by human
measurement, which is also an angel's measurement. 18The wall was built of jasper, while the city was pure gold, like clear glass. 19The foundations of the wall of
the city were adorned with every kind of jewel. The first was jasper, the second
sapphire, the third agate, the fourth emerald, 20the fifth onyx, the sixth carnelian,
the seventh chrysolite, the eighth beryl, the ninth topaz, the tenth chrysoprase,
the eleventh jacinth, the twelfth amethyst. 21And the twelve gates were twelve
pearls, each of the gates made of a single pearl, and the street of the city was pure
gold, like transparent glass.
22And I saw no temple in the city, for its temple is the Lord God the Almighty
and the Lamb. 23And the city has no need of sun or moon to shine on it, for the
glory of God gives it light, and its lamp is the Lamb. 24By its light will the nations
walk, and the kings of the earth will bring their glory into it, 25and its gates will
never be shut by day—and there will be no night there. 26They will bring into it
the glory and the honor of the nations. 27But nothing unclean will ever enter it,
nor anyone who does what is detestable or false, but only those who are written
in the Lamb's book of life.

The River of Life

22 Then the angel[3] showed me the river of the water of life, bright as crystal,
flowing from the throne of God and of the Lamb 2through the middle of
the street of the city; also, on either side of the river, the tree of life[4] with its twelve
kinds of fruit, yielding its fruit each month. The leaves of the tree were for the
healing of the nations. 3No longer will there be anything accursed, but the throne
of God and of the Lamb will be in it, and his servants will worship him. 4They will
see his face, and his name will be on their foreheads. 5And night will be no more.
They will need no light of lamp or sun, for the Lord God will be their light, and
they will reign forever and ever.

Jesus Is Coming

6And he said to me, "These words are trustworthy and true. And the Lord, the
God of the spirits of the prophets, has sent his angel to show his servants what
must soon take place."
7"And behold, I am coming soon. Blessed is the one who keeps the words of
the prophecy of this book."
8I, John, am the one who heard and saw these things. And when I heard and saw
them, I fell down to worship at the feet of the angel who showed them to me, 9but
he said to me, "You must not do that! I am a fellow servant with you and your brothers the prophets, and with those who keep the words of this book. Worship God."

[1]About 1,380 miles; a *stadion* was about 607 feet or 185 meters [2]A *cubit* was about 18 inches or 45 centimeters [3]Greek *he* [4]Or *the Lamb. In the midst of the street of the city, and on either side of the river, was the tree of life*

REVELATION 22:1–2

PARADISE REGAINED

The river and tree pictured here are reminiscent of the Garden of Eden, and rightly so (Ge 2:8–10; 3:22–24). In the garden, people could have perfect fellowship with God, though they chose to rebel against him and broke that fellowship. In heaven, the relationship between God and his people will be free of sin; therefore, it will embody God's created design.

The great hope of believers is that they will one day be able to worship God and find joy in his presence forever. John must have grappled for words to describe the glory of heaven: All that sin has destroyed will be no more. The relationship between God and his people will be made right, as will the entire world. Since his ascension, Jesus, the Creator of the world, has been preparing this paradise for all of his people who will dwell with him and revel in his glory forever (Jn 14:3). In fact, after all of these events come to pass, all of God's creation will proclaim his glory, which will fill the earth as the waters cover the sea (Hab 2:14).

10And he said to me, "Do not seal up the words of the prophecy of this book,
for the time is near. 11Let the evildoer still do evil, and the filthy still be filthy, and
the righteous still do right, and the holy still be holy."
12"Behold, I am coming soon, bringing my recompense with me, to repay each
one for what he has done. 13I am the Alpha and the Omega, the first and the last,
the beginning and the end."
14Blessed are those who wash their robes,[1] so that they may have the right
to the tree of life and that they may enter the city by the gates. 15Outside are the
dogs and sorcerers and the sexually immoral and murderers and idolaters, and
everyone who loves and practices falsehood.
16"I, Jesus, have sent my angel to testify to you about these things for the
churches. I am the root and the descendant of David, the bright morning star."
17The Spirit and the Bride say, "Come." And let the one who hears say, "Come."
And let the one who is thirsty come; let the one who desires take the water of life
without price.
18I warn everyone who hears the words of the prophecy of this book: if anyone
adds to them, God will add to him the plagues described in this book, 19and if anyone takes away from the words of the book of this prophecy, God will take away
his share in the tree of life and in the holy city, which are described in this book.
20He who testifies to these things says, "Surely I am coming soon." Amen.
Come, Lord Jesus!
21The grace of the Lord Jesus be with all.[2] Amen.

---

[1]Some manuscripts *do his commandments* [2]Some manuscripts *all the saints*

TABLE OF
WEIGHTS AND MEASURES
AND MONETARY UNITS

The following table is based on the best generally accepted information available for biblical weights, measures, and monetary units. All equivalents are approximate. Weights and measures also varied somewhat in different times and places in the ancient world. Most weights, measures, and monetary units are also explained in footnotes on the pages where they occur in the ESV text.

Biblical Unit	Approximate American and Metric Equivalents	Biblical Equivalent
bath	A *bath* was about 6 gallons or 22 liters	1 ephah
beka	A *beka* was about 1/5 ounce or 5.5 grams	10 gerahs
cor	A *cor* was about 6 bushels or 220 liters	10 ephahs
cubit	A *cubit* was about 18 inches or 45 centimeters	6 handbreadths
daric	A *daric* was a coin of about 1/4 ounce or 8.5 grams	
denarius	A *denarius* was a day's wage for a laborer	
ephah	An *ephah* was about 3/5 bushel or 22 liters	10 omers
gerah	A *gerah* was about 1/50 ounce or 0.6 gram	1/10 beka
handbreadth	A *handbreadth* was about 3 inches or 7.5 centimeters	1/6 cubit
hin	A *hin* was about 4 quarts or 3.5 liters	1/6 bath
homer	A *homer* was about 6 bushels or 220 liters	10 ephahs
kab	A *kab* was about 1 quart or 1 liter	1/22 ephah
lethech	A *lethech* was about 3 bushels or 110 liters	5 ephahs
log	A *log* was about 1/3 quart or 0.3 liter	1/72 bath
mina	A *mina* was about 1 1/4 pounds or 0.6 kilogram	50 shekels
omer	An *omer* was about 2 quarts or 2 liters	1/10 ephah
pim	A *pim* was about 1/3 ounce or 7.5 grams	2/3 shekel
seah	A *seah* was about 7 quarts or 7.3 liters	1/3 ephah
shekel	A *shekel* was about 2/5 ounce or 11 grams	2 bekas
span	A *span* was about 9 inches or 22 centimeters	3 handbreadths
stadion	A *stadion* was about 607 feet or 185 meters	
talent	A *talent* was about 75 pounds or 34 kilograms	60 minas

CONCORDANCE

As an essentially literal translation, the ESV Bible is ideally suited for use with a concordance, as the ESV seeks to use the same English word, as far as possible and where appropriate to the meaning in each context, to translate important recurring words in the original languages. However, with a total of more than 757,000 words appearing in the ESV Bible, a shorter concordance such as this must be selective in the words it includes.

In choosing which words to list, the guiding principles were importance, familiarity, and breadth of coverage. Since the ESV is within the stream of English Bible translations that began with the King James Version of 1611, there was a special effort to include references to as many familiar Bible passages as possible. As to breadth of coverage, the goal has been to list key references for many different words rather than more lengthy listings for fewer words.

Passages appearing in more than one of the Synoptic Gospels usually have only one reference, most often to the book of Matthew.

Those desiring a more complete concordance for the ESV Bible should consult *The Crossway Comprehensive Concordance*, which has more than 300,000 verse listings for nearly 14,000 different words. Readers with internet access will find optimal word-search capability with the search engine at the ESV web site, www.esv.org.

ABBREVIATIONS

Abbreviations for the books of the Bible as used in the concordance

OLD TESTAMENT

Genesis	Gn	2 Chronicles	2 Chr	Daniel	Dn
Exodus	Ex	Ezra	Ezr	Hosea	Hos
Leviticus	Lv	Nehemiah	Neh	Joel	Jl
Numbers	Nm	Esther	Est	Amos	Am
Deuteronomy	Dt	Job	Jb	Obadiah	Ob
Joshua	Jos	Psalms	Ps	Jonah	Jon
Judges	Jgs	Proverbs	Prv	Micah	Mi
Ruth	Ru	Ecclesiastes	Eccl	Nahum	Na
1 Samuel	1 Sm	Song of Solomon	Sg	Habakkuk	Hb
2 Samuel	2 Sm	Isaiah	Is	Zephaniah	Zep
1 Kings	1 Kgs	Jeremiah	Jer	Haggai	Hg
2 Kings	2 Kgs	Lamentations	Lam	Zechariah	Zec
1 Chronicles	1 Chr	Ezekiel	Ez	Malachi	Mal

NEW TESTAMENT

Matthew	Mt	Ephesians	Eph	Hebrews	Heb
Mark	Mk	Philippians	Phil	James	Jas
Luke	Lk	Colossians	Col	1 Peter	1 Pt
John	Jn	1 Thessalonians	1 Thes	2 Peter	2 Pt
Acts	Acts	2 Thessalonians	2 Thes	1 John	1 Jn
Romans	Rom	1 Timothy	1 Tm	2 John	2 Jn
1 Corinthians	1 Cor	2 Timothy	2 Tm	3 John	3 Jn
2 Corinthians	2 Cor	Titus	Ti	Jude	Jude
Galatians	Gal	Philemon	Phlm	Revelation	Rv

ABANDON
For you will not **a** my soul to............Ps 16:10
he will not **a** his heritage;.................Ps 94:14
For you will not **a** my soul to............Acts 2:27

ABANDONED
'Because they **a** the LORD.................1 Kgs 9:9
that you have **a** the love you..................Rv 2:4

ABBA
"**A**, Father, all things are.................Mk 14:36
whom we cry, "**A**! Father!"...............Rom 8:15
crying, "**A**! Father!"............................Gal 4:6

ABHOR
and my soul will **a** you......................Lv 26:30
You shall utterly detest and **a**............Dt 7:26
I hate and **a** falsehood, but...........Ps 119:163

ABIDE
"My Spirit shall not **a** in man..............Gn 6:3
of the Most High will **a**.......................Ps 91:1
A in me, and I in you. As the...............Jn 15:4

ABIDES
be moved, but **a** forever....................Ps 125:1
flesh and drinks my blood **a**................Jn 6:56
No one who **a** in him keeps.................1 Jn 3:6

ABIDING
shadow, and there is no **a**...........1 Chr 29:15
do not have his word **a** in you.............Jn 5:38
through the living and **a** word.........1 Pt 1:23

ABILITY
have given to all able men **a**,..............Ex 31:6
to each according to his **a**.................Mt 25:15
tempted beyond your **a**,...............1 Cor 10:13

ABLE
Moses chose **a** men out of all............Ex 18:25
man shall give as he is **a**,.................Dt 16:17
silver and gold are not **a**.....................Ez 7:19
our God whom we serve is **a**...............Dn 3:17
Are you **a** to drink the cup.................Mt 20:22
will be **a** to separate us from...........Rom 8:39

ABODE
strength to your holy **a**......................Ex 15:13
His **a** has been established in.............Ps 76:2
From your lofty **a** you water.............Ps 104:13

ABOMINABLE
And you shall not bring an **a**..............Dt 7:26
doing **a** iniquity; there is none............Ps 53:1

ABOMINATION
as with a woman; it is an **a**..............Lv 18:22
does these things is an **a**..................Dt 18:12
seven that are an **a** to him:................Prv 6:16
are both alike an **a**..........................Prv 17:15
the scoffer is an **a** to mankind...........Prv 24:9
when they committed **a**?.......................Jer 6:15
And they shall set up the **a**..............Dn 11:31
is taken away and the **a**...................Dn 12:11
"So when you see the **a**......................Mt 24:15

ABOUND
in sin that grace may **a**?....................Rom 6:1

ABOUNDING
a in steadfast love and faithfulness... Ex 34:6
LORD is slow to anger and **a**............Nm 14:18
slow to anger and **a** in.......................Ps 86:15
and **a** in steadfast love; and he...........Jl 2:13
slow to anger and **a** in.........................Jon 4:2
taught, **a** in thanksgiving....................Col 2:7

ABRAHAM
but your name shall be **A**,.................Gn 17:5
"**A** believed God, and it was..............Rom 4:3
By faith **A** obeyed when he...............Heb 11:8

ABUNDANCE
bread from heaven in **a**...................Ps 105:40
contributed out of their **a**,...............Mk 12:44
for out of the **a** of the heart...............Lk 6:45

ABUNDANT
according to your **a** mercy blot............Ps 51:1
Lord, and **a** in power; his..................Ps 147:5

ABUNDANTLY
God, for he will **a** pardon......................Is 55:7
may have life and have it **a**..............Jn 10:10
your faith is growing **a**,.................2 Thes 1:3

ABYSS
them to depart into the **a**...................Lk 8:31
into the **a**?'" (that is, to bring.........Rom 10:7

ACCEPTANCE
but the upright enjoy **a**.......................Prv 14:9
and deserving of full **a**,..................1 Tm 1:15

ACCEPTED
to be **a** it must be perfect;................Lv 22:21
and the LORD **a** Job's prayer..................Jb 42:9
and their sacrifices will be **a**...............Is 56:7

ACCESS
him we have also obtained **a**.............Rom 5:2
him we both have **a**..........................Eph 2:18
we have boldness and **a**....................Eph 3:12

ACCOMPLISH
and I will **a** all my purpose,'...............Is 46:10
of him who sent me and to **a**..............Jn 4:34

ACCOMPLISHED
from the Law until all is **a**..................Mt 5:18
having **a** the work that you.................Jn 17:4
except what Christ has **a**..............Rom 15:18

ACCORD
the prophets with one **a**..............1 Kgs 22:13
and serve him with one **a**...................Zep 3:9
I lay it down of my own **a**.................Jn 10:18

ACCOUNT
"You will not call to **a**"?...................Ps 10:13
against you falsely on my **a**................Mt 5:11
On **a** of these the wrath of God............Col 3:6
but they will give **a** to him.................1 Pt 4:5

ACCOUNTABLE
whole world may be held **a**..............Rom 3:19

ACCURSED
God ever says "Jesus is **a**!"...........1 Cor 12:3

ACCUSATION
"What **a** do you bring against...........Jn 18:29
you and to make an **a**,...................Acts 24:19

ACCUSE
so that they might **a** him...................Mt 12:10
And they began to **a** him,....................Lk 23:2

ACCUSER
appeal for mercy to my **a**....................Jb 9:15
lest your **a** hand you over to...............Mt 5:25
for the **a** of our brothers has............Rv 12:10

ACKNOWLEDGE
In all your ways **a** him, and he............Prv 3:6
Only **a** your guilt, that you..................Jer 3:13
the fruit of lips that **a** his name......Heb 13:15

ACQUIRE
Do not toil to **a** wealth; be.................Prv 23:4
our inheritance until we **a**................Eph 1:14

ACQUIT
for I will not **a** the wicked....................Ex 23:7
who **a** the guilty for a bribe,.................Is 5:23

ACQUITTED
and I would be **a** forever by................Jb 23:7
but I am not thereby **a**.....................1 Cor 4:4

ACT
place and forgive and **a**................1 Kgs 8:39
trust in him, and he will **a**..................Ps 37:5

ACTED
We have **a** very corruptly....................Neh 1:7
I know that you **a** in ignorance,........Acts 3:17

ACTS
of the land of Egypt by great **a**.............Ex 7:4
repays the one who **a** in pride..........Ps 31:23

ADAM
Thus all the days that **A** lived..............Gn 5:5
For as in **A** all die, so also...........1 Cor 15:22

ADD
You shall not **a** to the word that...........Dt 4:2
Do not **a** to his words, lest he............Prv 30:6
them, God will **a** to him the..............Rv 22:18

ADDED
and all these things will be **a**.............Mt 6:33
And the Lord **a** to their....................Acts 2:47
law? It was **a** because of....................Gal 3:19

ADMINISTERED
he **a** justice and equity................1 Chr 18:14
gift that is being **a** by us...............2 Cor 8:20

ADMONISH
while I **a** you! O Israel, if you..............Ps 81:8
a the idle, encourage the............1 Thes 5:14

ADOPTION
received the Spirit of **a**....................Rom 8:15
that we might receive **a** as sons.........Gal 4:5

ADULTERERS
They are all **a**; they are like a.............Hos 7:4
a, or even like this tax collector........Lk 18:11
nor **a**, nor men who practice............1 Cor 6:9

ADULTEROUS
me and of my words in this **a**............Mk 8:38
the sexually immoral and **a**..............Heb 13:4
You **a** people! Do you not know............Jas 4:4

ADULTERY
“You shall not commit **a**. ... Ex 20:14
He who commits **a** lacks ... Prv 6:32
already committed **a** with her ... Mt 5:28
marries another commits **a**, ... Lk 16:18

ADVANTAGE
and man has no **a** over the ... Eccl 3:19
it is to your **a** that I go away, ... Jn 16:7
Christ will be of no **a** to you. ... Gal 5:2
for that would be of no **a** ... Heb 13:17
favoritism to gain **a**. ... Jude 1:16

ADVERSARY
and give the **a** no occasion ... 1 Tm 5:14
Your **a** the devil prowls ... 1 Pt 5:8

ADVERSITY
and opens their ear by **a**. ... Jb 36:15
and a brother is born for **a**. ... Prv 17:17
and in the day of **a** consider: ... Eccl 7:14

ADVICE
but a wise man listens to **a**. ... Prv 12:15
Listen to **a** and accept ... Prv 19:20

AFFAIRS
who conducts his **a** with justice. ... Ps 112:5
and to mind your own **a**, ... 1 Thes 4:11

AFFECTION
another with brotherly **a**. ... Rom 12:10
and brotherly **a** with love. ... 2 Pt 1:7

AFFLICT
taskmasters over them to **a** ... Ex 1:11
And I will **a** the offspring ... 1 Kgs 11:39

AFFLICTED
He delivers the **a** by their ... Jb 36:15
your hand; forget not the **a**. ... Ps 10:12

AFFLICTION
Lord has listened to your **a**. ... Gn 16:11
tried you in the furnace of **a**. ... Is 48:10
momentary **a** is preparing ... 2 Cor 4:17

AFFLICTIONS
Many are the **a** of the ... Ps 34:19
what is lacking in Christ’s **a** ... Col 1:24

AFRAID
and I was **a**, because I was ... Gn 3:10
Do not be **a** and do not be ... 1 Chr 28:20
it is I. Do not be **a**.” ... Mt 14:27

AGE
and of the end of the **a**?” ... Mt 24:3
he is of **a**. He will speak for ... Jn 9:21

AGES
O Lord, throughout all **a**. ... Ps 135:13
God decreed before the **a** ... 1 Cor 2:7
for all at the end of the **a** ... Heb 9:26

AGONY
pangs and **a** will seize them; ... Is 13:8
And being in **a** he prayed ... Lk 22:44

AGREE
their testimony did not **a**. ... Mk 14:56
a with one another, live ... 2 Cor 13:11
the blood; and these three **a**. ... 1 Jn 5:8

AGREEMENT
except perhaps by **a** for a ... 1 Cor 7:5
What **a** has the temple of ... 2 Cor 6:16

AIM
who **a** bitter words like arrows, ... Ps 64:3
A for restoration, comfort ... 2 Cor 13:11

AIR
prince of the power of the **a**, ... Eph 2:2
to meet the Lord in the **a**, ... 1 Thes 4:17

ALARM
I had said in my **a**, “I am cut ... Ps 31:22
Let not your thoughts **a** you ... Dn 5:10

ALARMED
See that you are not **a**, for this ... Mt 24:6
“Do not be **a**. You seek Jesus ... Mk 16:6

ALERT
Therefore be **a**, remembering ... Acts 20:31
To that end, keep **a** with all ... Eph 6:18

ALIEN
or violence to the resident **a**, ... Jer 22:3

ALIVE
is **a**; he was lost, and is found.’” ... Lk 15:32
dead to sin and **a** ... Rom 6:11
in the flesh but made **a** ... 1 Pt 3:18

ALLEGIANCE
of Canaan and swear **a** ... Is 19:18
every tongue shall swear **a**.’ ... Is 45:23

ALLOWED
no evil shall be **a** to befall ... Ps 91:10
Also it was **a** to make war on ... Rv 13:7

ALMIGHTY
“I am God **A**: be fruitful and ... Gn 35:11
contend with the **A**? ... Jb 40:2
and who is to come, the **A**.” ... Rv 1:8
is the Lord God the **A** ... Rv 21:22

ALMS
But give as **a** those things ... Lk 11:41
the Beautiful Gate to ask **a** ... Acts 3:2

ALONE
that the man should be **a**; ... Gn 2:18
O Lord, are God **a**.” ... 2 Kgs 19:19
shall not live by bread **a**.’” ... Lk 4:4
can forgive sins but God **a**?” ... Lk 5:21
Yet I am not **a**, for the Father ... Jn 16:32
by works and not by faith **a**. ... Jas 2:24

ALPHA
“I am the **A** and the Omega,” ... Rv 1:8
I am the **A** and the Omega, ... Rv 22:13

ALTAR
Then Noah built an **a** to the ... Gn 8:20
So he built there an **a** to the ... Gn 12:7
make atonement for the **a** ... Ex 29:37
And Saul built an **a** to the ... 1 Sm 14:35
David built there an **a** ... 2 Sm 24:25
He erected an **a** for Baal ... 1 Kgs 16:32
And he repaired the **a** ... 1 Kgs 18:30
up his son Isaac on the **a**? ... Jas 2:21

ALTARS
You shall tear down their **a** ... Dt 12:3
And he built **a** in the house ... 2 Kgs 21:4
will break down their **a** ... Hos 10:2

ALWAYS
and his commandments **a**. ... Dt 11:1
For you **a** have the poor with ... Mk 14:7

AMAZED
And the disciples were **a** ... Mk 10:24
so that Pilate was **a**. ... Mk 15:5
come with Peter were **a**, ... Acts 10:45

AMBUSH
Lay an **a** against the city, ... Jos 8:2
us **a** the innocent without reason; ... Prv 1:11
they were planning an **a** ... Acts 25:3

AMEN
shall answer and say, ‘**A**.’ ... Dt 27:15
to everlasting! **A** and **A**. ... Ps 41:13
him that we utter our **A** ... 2 Cor 1:20
Lord Jesus be with all. **A**. ... Rv 22:21

ANCHOR
as a sure and steadfast **a** ... Heb 6:19

ANCIENT
and the **A** of Days took ... Dn 7:9
until the **A** of Days came, and ... Dn 7:22

ANGEL
The **a** of the Lord found her ... Gn 16:7
And the **a** of the Lord appeared ... Ex 3:2
Now the **a** of the Lord came ... Jgs 6:11
The **a** of the Lord encamps ... Ps 34:7
My God sent his **a** and shut ... Dn 6:22
And the **a** said to them, “Fear ... Lk 2:10
Now an **a** of the Lord said to ... Acts 8:26
disguises himself as an **a** ... 2 Cor 11:14
But even if we or an **a** from ... Gal 1:8

ANGELS
The two **a** came to Sodom in ... Gn 19:1
the **a** of God were ascending ... Gn 28:12
and all the **a** with him, then ... Mt 25:31
the **a** were ministering to him. ... Mk 1:13
some have entertained **a** ... Heb 13:2
things into which **a** long to look ... 1 Pt 1:12
And the **a** who did not stay ... Jude 1:6
Michael and his **a** fighting ... Rv 12:7

ANGER
And the **a** of the Lord burned ... Jos 7:1
rebuke me not in your **a**, nor ... Ps 6:1
slow to **a** and abounding in ... Ps 86:15
but a harsh word stirs up **a**. ... Prv 15:1
Therefore the **a** of the Lord ... Is 5:25
Why do you provoke me to **a** ... Jer 44:8
He does not retain his **a** ... Mi 7:18
provoke your children to **a**, ... Eph 6:4
lifting holy hands without **a** ... 1 Tm 2:8
slow to speak, slow to **a**; ... Jas 1:19

ANGRY
“Why are you **a**, and why has ... Gn 4:6
And the Lord was so **a** with ... Dt 9:20
And the Lord was **a** with ... 1 Kgs 11:9
Be **a**, and do not sin; ponder in ... Ps 4:4

I will not be **a** forever.......................... Jer 3:12
you that everyone who is **a**..................Mt 5:22
Be **a** and do not sin; do not..............Eph 4:26

ANGUISH
I will speak in the **a** of my................... Jb 7:11
My heart is in **a** within me; the...........Ps 55:4
When **a** comes, they will seek............. Ez 7:25
for I am in **a** in this flame.'.............. Lk 16:24

ANOINT
and shall **a** them and ordain............ Ex 28:41
You did not **a** my head with................. Lk 7:46

ANOINTED
And the priest who is **a**.................... Lv 16:32
could; she has **a** my body.................. Mk 14:8
It was Mary who **a** the Lord .... Jn 11:2
has **a** you with the oil of.....................Heb 1:9

ANOINTING
Then you shall take the **a** oil .... Ex 40:9
But the **a** that you received............. 1 Jn 2:27

ANSWER
A me, O Lord, **a** me,..................... 1 Kgs 18:37
A soft **a** turns away wrath, ...Prv 15:1
"And in that day I will **a**,..................Hos 2:21
that you may be able to **a**.............. 2 Cor 5:12

ANTICHRIST
a is coming, so now many............... 1 Jn 2:18
This is the spirit of the **a**,................... 1 Jn 4:3
is the deceiver and the **a**.................... 2 Jn 1:7

ANXIETIES
you to be free from **a**. .... 1 Cor 7:32
casting all your **a** on him, ... 1 Pt 5:7

ANXIETY
A in a man's heart weighs................Prv 12:25
bread by weight and with **a**,................ Ez 4:16
pressure on me of my **a**............... 2 Cor 11:28

ANXIOUS
Say to those who have an **a**.................Is 35:4
do not be **a** beforehand what .... Mk 13:11
do not be **a** about your life, ... Lk 12:22
do not be **a** about anything, ...Phil 4:6

APOLLOS
Now a Jew named **A**, a...................Acts 18:24
or "I follow **A**," or "I follow............. 1 Cor 1:12

APOSTLE
Am I not an **a**? Have I not................ 1 Cor 9:1
The signs of a true **a**................... 2 Cor 12:12
a and high priest of our confession,....Heb 3:1

APOSTLES
The names of the twelve **a**..................Mt 10:2
with the eleven **a**..............................Acts 1:26
that God has exhibited us **a**............ 1 Cor 4:9
in the church first **a**,.................... 1 Cor 12:28
on the foundation of the **a**................Eph 2:20
And he gave the **a**, the prophets, ...Eph 4:11

APOSTLESHIP
have received grace and **a**.................Rom 1:5
for you are the seal of my **a**............. 1 Cor 9:2

APPEAL
you think that I cannot **a**...................Mt 26:53
God making his **a** through............. 2 Cor 5:20
from the body but as an **a**............... 1 Pt 3:21

APPEAR
and let the dry land **a**." And it............. Gn 1:9
When shall I come and **a**....................Ps 42:2
Then will **a** in heaven the..................Mt 24:30

APPEARANCES
for you are not swayed by **a**..............Mt 22:16
Do not judge by **a**, but judge.............. Jn 7:24

APPEARED
But the glory of the Lord **a**.............. Nm 14:10
of King Belshazzar a vision **a**.............. Dn 8:1
And a great sign **a** in heaven: ....Rv 12:1

APPEARS
but we know that when he **a** .... 1 Jn 3:2

APPOINT
"You shall **a** judges and................... Dt 16:18
whom we will **a** to this duty...............Acts 6:3

APPOINTED
but I chose you and **a** you................. Jn 15:16
And just as it is **a** for man to ....Heb 9:27

APPROVAL
not only do them but give **a**.............Rom 1:32
For am I now seeking the **a** .... Gal 1:10

APPROVE
yet after them people **a** of.................Ps 49:13
and know his will and **a**..................Rom 2:18

ARCHANGEL
with the voice of an **a**,................. 1 Thes 4:16
But when the **a** Michael, ...Jude 1:9

ARISE
A, walk through the length.............. Gn 13:17
"**A**, go to Nineveh, that great...............Jon 1:2
I say to you, **a**." .... Mk 5:41
a." And she opened her eyes, ...Acts 9:40
and **a** from the dead, and.................Eph 5:14

ARK
Make yourself an **a** of gopher............ Gn 6:14
"They shall make an **a** of .... Ex 25:10
"As soon as you see the **a** ....Jos 3:3
and the **a** of his covenant ....Rv 11:19

ARM
you with an outstretched **a**.................... Ex 6:6
You with your **a** redeemed ....Ps 77:15

ARMAGEDDON
that in Hebrew is called **A**. ....Rv 16:16

ARMOR
strap on your **a** and be shattered...........Is 8:9
Put on the whole **a** of God, ...Eph 6:11

ARMS
are the everlasting **a**........................ Dt 33:27
strength and makes her **a**...............Prv 31:17
gather the lambs in his **a**;..................Is 40:11

ARROGANCE
let not **a** come from your ....1 Sm 2:3
Pride and **a** and the way of ....Prv 8:13
who say in pride and in **a** of heart:.........Is 9:9

ARROGANT
Everyone who is **a** in heart is.............Prv 16:5
do not be **a** toward the...................Rom 11:18
envy or boast; it is not **a**................ 1 Cor 13:4

ASCEND
If I **a** to heaven, you are.....................Ps 139:8
For David did not **a** into the.............Acts 2:34
'Who will **a** into heaven?'"................Rom 10:6

ASCENDED
You **a** on high, leading a host............Ps 68:18
for I have not yet **a** to the .... Jn 20:17
"When he **a** on high he led a ....Eph 4:8

ASCENDING
the angels of God were **a**................. Gn 28:12
and the angels of God **a** and............... Jn 1:51
were to see the Son of Man **a** .... Jn 6:62

ASCRIBE
Lord; **a** greatness to our God!............. Dt 32:3
knowledge from afar and **a**................ Jb 36:3
A to the Lord, O heavenly......................Ps 29:1
A power to God, whose ....Ps 68:34
A to the Lord, O families of the...........Ps 96:7

ASHAMED
All my enemies shall be **a** ....Ps 6:10
For whoever is **a** of me and of .... Lk 9:26
For I am not **a** of the gospel, ...Rom 1:16

ASHES
I who am but dust and **a**................. Gn 18:27
with sackcloth, and sat in **a**................Jon 3:6
long ago in sackcloth and **a**.............Mt 11:21

ASIDE
You shall not turn **a** to the.................. Dt 5:32
They have all turned **a**;........................Ps 14:3
Let not your heart turn **a** ....Prv 7:25
But you have turned **a** from................Mal 2:8

ASLEEP
or perhaps he is **a** and .... 1 Kgs 18:27
friend Lazarus has fallen **a**, ... Jn 11:11
about those who are **a**,................ 1 Thes 4:13

ASSEMBLY
day you shall hold a holy **a**,.............. Ex 12:16
It is a solemn **a**; you shall .... Lv 23:36
his praise in the **a** of the godly! ....Ps 149:1
a fast; call a solemn **a**; .... Jl 2:15

ASSIGNED
as my Father **a** to me, a kingdom,..... Lk 22:29
as the Lord **a** to each. .... 1 Cor 3:5
area of influence God **a**............... 2 Cor 10:13

ASSOCIATE
therefore do not **a** with a.................Prv 20:19
but **a** with the lowly. Never............Rom 12:16
not to **a** with sexually immoral......... 1 Cor 5:9

ASSURANCE
and of this he has given **a** ....Acts 17:31
with a true heart in full **a**..............Heb 10:22
Now faith is the **a** of things..............Heb 11:1

ASTONISHED
passing by it will be **a**..................... 1 Kgs 9:8
the crowds were **a** at his teaching, ...Mt 7:28
they were amazed and **a**, ...Acts 2:7

ASTRAY
they go **a** from birth, speaking lies......Ps 58:3
and whoever is led **a** by it is..............Prv 20:1
we like sheep have gone **a**; ....Is 53:6
to lead **a**, if possible, the elect......... Mk 13:22

ATE
she took of its fruit and **a**,................... Gn 3:6
and he **a**; and he brought................ Gn 27:25
Then I **a** it, and it was in my................. Ez 3:3
And they all **a** and were satisfied....... Mk 6:42

ATHLETE
Every **a** exercises self-control......... 1 Cor 9:25
An **a** is not crowned unless ....2 Tm 2:5

ATONE
you will not be able to **a**; ....Is 47:11

ATONED
so that their blood guilt be **a**.............. Dt 21:8
and faithfulness iniquity is **a**............Prv 16:6
away, and your sin **a** for." ....Is 6:7
this iniquity will not be **a** for you........Is 22:14

ATONEMENT
a bull as a sin offering for **a**. .... Ex 29:36
And the priest shall make **a**................ Lv 4:20
month is the Day of **A**....................... Lv 23:27
days shall they make **a** .... Ez 43:26

ATTAINED
righteousness have **a**......................Rom 9:30
true to what we have **a**....................Phil 3:16

ATTENTIVE
be open and your ears **a**................2 Chr 6:40
Let your ears be **a** to the....................Ps 130:2
be **a** to the words of my mouth...........Prv 7:24

AUTHORITIES
many even of the **a** believed............. Jn 12:42
subject to the governing **a**. ....Rom 13:1

AUTHORITY
"All **a** in heaven and on....................Mt 28:18
A new teaching with **a**! He .... Mk 1:27
"Tell us by what **a** you do .... Lk 20:2
to teach or to exercise **a** over...........1 Tm 2:12
exhort and rebuke with all **a**................ Ti 2:15

AVENGE
and shall I not **a** myself on a............... Jer 5:9
I will **a** their blood, blood...................... Jl 3:21
never **a** yourselves, but ....Rom 12:19

AVENGER
to still the enemy and the **a**. ....Ps 8:2
an **a** who carries out God's..............Rom 13:4
because the Lord is an **a**................ 1 Thes 4:6

AVOID
But **a** irreverent babble, for............2 Tm 2:16
to **a** quarreling, to be gentle,................. Ti 3:2

AWAKE
a and sing for joy! For your ....Is 26:19
Therefore stay **a** — for you .... Mk 13:35
"**A**, O sleeper, and arise from ....Eph 5:14

AWE
the ends of the earth are in **a**.............Ps 65:8
of Jacob and will stand in **a**..............Is 29:23
they were filled with **a** and...............Mt 27:54

AWESOME
the great and **a** God who.....................Neh 1:5
"How **a** are your deeds! So ....Ps 66:3
them praise your great and **a**.............Ps 99:3
Holy and **a** is his name! ....Ps 111:9

AXE
his **a** head fell into the.....................2 Kgs 6:5
Even now the **a** is laid to the................. Lk 3:9

BABEL
of his kingdom was **B**,...................... Gn 10:10
Therefore its name was called **B**,....... Gn 11:9

BABY
the **b** leaped in her womb.................... Lk 1:41
you will find a **b** wrapped in................ Lk 2:12
she has delivered the **b**,.................... Jn 16:21

BABYLON
Nebuchadnezzar the king of **B**............. Ezr 2:1
fallen is **B**; and all the carved.............Is 21:9
"I will repay **B** and all the .... Jer 51:24
fallen is **B** the great! She has ....Rv 18:2

BAD
good for **b**, or **b** for good;................... Lv 27:10
nothing either good or **b**.................Rom 9:11

BAG
would be sealed up in a **b**,................ Jb 14:17
he took a **b** of money with ....Prv 7:20

BAKER
cupbearer and the chief **b**,................ Gn 40:2
like a heated oven whose **b**................Hos 7:4

BALANCE
me be weighed in a just **b**,................. Jb 31:6
A false **b** is an abomination to...........Prv 11:1

BALANCES
You shall have just **b**, just................ Lv 19:36
have been weighed in the **b** .... Dn 5:27

BALDNESS
cut yourselves or make any **b**............. Dt 14:1
and **b** on all their heads...................... Ez 7:18

BALM
a little **b** and a little honey,............. Gn 43:11
Is there no **b** in Gilead? Is .... Jer 8:22

BAND
I pursue after this **b**? ....1 Sm 30:8
leader of a marauding **b**, ...1 Kgs 11:24
They **b** together against the ....Ps 94:21

BANK
by the other cows on the **b** .... Gn 41:3
Stand on the **b** of the Nile to .... Ex 7:15
not put my money in the **b**,............... Lk 19:23

BANNER
of it, The LORD Is My **B**,..................... Ex 17:15
You have set up a **b** for those.............Ps 60:4
and his **b** over me was love....................Sg 2:4

BAPTISM
The **b** of John, from where ....Mt 21:25
and with the **b** with which I.............. Mk 10:39
he knew only the **b** ....Acts 18:25
one Lord, one faith, one **b**,..................Eph 4:5
been buried with him in **b**, ...Col 2:12

BAPTIST
In those days John the **B** came..............Mt 3:1
"John the **B** has been raised .... Mk 6:14
For John the **B** has come .... Lk 7:33

BAPTIZE
but he will **b** you with the.................... Mk 1:8
He will **b** you with the Holy .... Lk 3:16
did not send me to **b** .... 1 Cor 1:17

BAPTIZED
just, having been **b** with the .... Lk 7:29
were coming and being **b**.................... Jn 3:23
"Repent and be **b** every one ....Acts 2:38
were **b**, both men and women. ....Acts 8:12
Rise and be **b** and wash................Acts 22:16
into Christ Jesus were **b**...................Rom 6:3
one Spirit we were all **b**............... 1 Cor 12:13

BAPTIZING
b them in the name of the.................Mt 28:19
but for this purpose I came **b**............. Jn 1:31
withhold water for **b**......................Acts 10:47

BARE
of the world were laid **b**,................2 Sm 22:16
and the LORD will lay **b** their ....Is 3:17

BARLEY
a cake of **b** bread tumbled into ....Jgs 7:13
is a boy here who has five **b**................. Jn 6:9

BARN
gather his wheat into the **b**,...............Mt 3:12
the wheat into my **b**.'"" ....Mt 13:30
neither storehouse nor **b**, ... Lk 12:24

BARNS
the blessing on you in your **b**.............. Dt 28:8
then your **b** will be filled....................Prv 3:10
nor reap nor gather into **b**, ...Mt 6:26

BARREN
Sarai was **b**; she had no child.......... Gn 11:30
He gives the **b** woman a...................Ps 113:9
because Elizabeth was **b**, and.............. Lk 1:7

BASKET
One **b** had very good figs, like .... Jer 24:2
a lamp and put it under a **b**,...............Mt 5:15
wall, lowering him in a **b**.................Acts 9:25

BATHE
of Pharaoh came down to **b**.................. Ex 2:5
shave off all his hair and **b**................ Lv 14:8

BATHING
from the roof a woman **b**;...............2 Sm 11:2

BATTLE
the **b** is not yours but God's.......... 2 Chr 20:15
the LORD, mighty in **b**! ....Ps 24:8
nor the **b** to the strong, nor .... Eccl 9:11

BEAM
was like a weaver's **b**, ...1 Sm 17:7
a **b** shall be pulled out of his ....Ezr 6:11
b from the woodwork respond. .... Hb 2:11

BEAR
The cow and the **b** shall graze;.............Is 11:7
will fall upon them like a **b** .... Hos 13:8
She will **b** a son, and you ....Mt 1:21
we shall also **b** the image .... 1 Cor 15:49

BIRDS
the **b** of the heavens, and the ... Ps 8:8
Look at the **b** of the air: they ... Mt 6:26

BIRTH
go astray from **b**, speaking lies. ... Ps 58:3
And she gave **b** to her firstborn ... Lk 2:7
it has conceived gives **b** ... Jas 1:15

BIRTHRIGHT
said, "Sell me your **b** now." ... Gn 25:31
firstborn according to his **b** ... Gn 43:33
who sold his **b** for a single meal. ... Heb 12:16

BITTERLY
She weeps **b** in the night, ... Lam 1:2
he went out and wept **b** ... Mt 26:75

BITTERNESS
The heart knows its own **b**, ... Prv 14:10
Let all **b** and wrath and ... Eph 4:31
that no "root of **b**" springs ... Heb 12:15

BLACK
and the day shall be **b** over them; ... Mi 3:6
the sun became **b** as sackcloth, ... Rv 6:12

BLAMELESS
walk before me, and be **b**, ... Gn 17:1
May my heart be **b** in your ... Ps 119:80
to present you holy and **b** ... Col 1:22

BLAMELESSLY
He who walks **b** and does ... Ps 15:2
God, walking **b** in all the ... Lk 1:6

BLASPHEMED
"The name of God is **b** ... Rom 2:24
the way of truth will be **b**. ... 2 Pt 2:2

BLASPHEMES
Whoever **b** the name of the ... Lv 24:16
but the one who **b** against ... Lk 12:10

BLEMISH
lamb shall be without **b**, ... Ex 12:5
offered himself without **b** ... Heb 9:14
like that of a lamb without **b** ... 1 Pt 1:19

BLESS
The LORD **b** you and keep you; ... Nm 6:24
I will **b** the LORD at all times; ... Ps 34:1
LORD, **b** his name; tell of his ... Ps 96:2
B the LORD, O my soul, and all ... Ps 103:1
him, that I might **b** him and ... Is 51:2
b those who curse you, pray ... Lk 6:28
we **b**; when persecuted, we ... 1 Cor 4:12

BLESSED
For the LORD your God has **b** ... Dt 2:7
B is the man who walks not in ... Ps 1:1
B be the LORD forever! Amen ... Ps 89:52
B is he who comes in the ... Ps 118:26
And **b** is the one who is not ... Mt 11:6
more **b** to give than to receive. ... Acts 20:35
shall all the nations be **b**." ... Gal 3:8
who has **b** us in Christ with ... Eph 1:3

BLESSING
so that you will be a **b**. ... Gn 12:2
turned the curse into a **b** ... Neh 13:2
and after **b** it broke it and ... Mt 26:26

BLIND
LORD opens the eyes of the **b** ... Ps 146:8
Then the eyes of the **b** shall be ... Is 35:5
the **b** receive their sight and ... Mt 11:5
"Can a **b** man lead a **b** man? ... Lk 6:39

BLOOD
Whoever sheds the **b** of man, ... Gn 9:6
in the Nile turned into **b**. ... Ex 7:20
I do not delight in the **b** of ... Is 1:11
on my flesh and drinks my **b** ... Jn 6:54
as a propitiation by his **b**, ... Rom 3:25
now been justified by his **b**, ... Rom 5:9
redemption through his **b**, ... Eph 1:7
peace by the **b** of his cross ... Col 1:20
freed us from our sins by his **b** ... Rv 1:5

BLOODGUILT
has restrained you from **b** ... 1 Sm 25:26
so his Lord will leave his **b** ... Hos 12:14

BLOODSHED
because you did not hate **b**, ... Ez 35:6
and **b** follows **b**. ... Hos 4:2

BLOSSOM
and may people **b** in the ... Ps 72:16
Israel shall **b** and put forth ... Is 27:6
the fig tree should not **b**, ... Hb 3:17

BLOT
that I have made I will **b** ... Gn 7:4

BLOW
And God made a wind **b** over ... Gn 8:1
the priests shall **b** the trumpets ... Jos 6:4
He caused the east wind to **b** ... Ps 78:26

BOAST
Do not **b** about tomorrow, for ... Prv 27:1
but let him who boasts **b** ... Jer 9:24
boasts, **b** in the Lord." ... 1 Cor 1:31
Therefore I will **b** all the ... 2 Cor 12:9
works, so that no one may **b** ... Eph 2:9

BOASTING
gives me no ground for **b**. ... 1 Cor 9:16
without **b** of work already ... 2 Cor 10:16
arrogance. All such **b** is evil. ... Jas 4:16

BODIES
the dishonoring of their **b** ... Rom 1:24
to present your **b** as a living ... Rom 12:1
be manifested in our **b**. ... 2 Cor 4:10

BODILY
Spirit descended on him in **b** ... Lk 3:22
fullness of deity dwells **b**, ... Col 2:9
for while **b** training is of ... 1 Tm 4:8

BODY
with him in order that the **b** ... Rom 6:6
will deliver me from this **b** ... Rom 7:24
For as in one **b** we have ... Rom 12:4
members of the same **b**, and ... Eph 3:6
There is one **b** and one Spirit ... Eph 4:4
will transform our lowly **b** ... Phil 3:21
has now reconciled in his **b** ... Col 1:22
the offering of the **b** of Jesus ... Heb 10:10
bore our sins in his **b** ... 1 Pt 2:24

BOLD
but the righteous are **b** as a lion. ... Prv 28:1
a hope, we are very **b**, ... 2 Cor 3:12

BOLDLY
He began to speak **b** in the ... Acts 18:26
that I may declare it **b**, as I ... Eph 6:20

BOND
I will bring you into the **b** ... Ez 20:37
unity of the Spirit in the **b** ... Eph 4:3

BONDAGE
out of the house of **b**, saying, ... Jer 34:13
will be set free from its **b** ... Rom 8:21

BONE
"This at last is **b** of my bones ... Gn 2:23
"Surely you are my **b** and ... Gn 29:14
also that I am your **b** ... Jgs 9:2

BONES
He keeps all his **b**; not one of ... Ps 34:20
dry **b**, hear the word of the LORD. ... Ez 37:4
Not one of his **b** will be broken. ... Jn 19:36

BOOK
This **B** of the Law shall not ... Jos 1:8
blot his name out of the **b** ... Rv 3:5

BORN
For to us a child is **b**, to us a son ... Is 9:6
unless one is **b** again he cannot ... Jn 3:3
he has caused us to be **b** ... 1 Pt 1:3
because he has been **b** ... 1 Jn 3:9

BORNE
Surely he has **b** our griefs and ... Is 53:4
And I have seen and have **b** ... Jn 1:34

BOW
let us worship and **b** down; let ... Ps 95:6
Jesus every knee should **b**, ... Phil 2:10

BRANCH
In that day the **b** of the LORD ... Is 4:2
up for David a righteous **B**, ... Jer 23:5
and every **b** that does bear ... Jn 15:2

BREAD
I am about to rain **b** from ... Ex 16:4
that man does not live by **b** ... Dt 8:3
Man ate of the **b** of the ... Ps 78:25
"I am the **b** of life; whoever ... Jn 6:35
breaking of **b** and the prayers. ... Acts 2:42

BREAKING
sins that people commit by **b** ... Nm 5:6
the law dishonor God by **b** ... Rom 2:23

BREASTPLATE
put on righteousness as a **b**, ... Is 59:17
having put on the **b** of faith ... 1 Thes 5:8

BREATH
everything that has the **b** ... Gn 1:30
Man is like a **b**; his days are ... Ps 144:4
Let everything that has **b** ... Ps 150:6

BREATHED
of dust from the ground and **b** ... Gn 2:7

BRIBE
And you shall take no **b**, ... Ex 23:8
and a **b** corrupts the heart. ... Eccl 7:7

BRIDE
and as a **b** adorns herself with ....Is 61:10
I will show you the **B**, the ....Rv 21:9

BROKEN
sacrifices of God are a **b** spirit....Ps 51:17
and Scripture cannot be **b**....Jn 10:35
made us both one and has **b**....Eph 2:14

BROKENHEARTED
The LORD is near to the **b** ....Ps 34:18
He heals the **b** and binds up ....Ps 147:3
has sent me to bind up the **b**, ...Is 61:1

BROTHER
and a **b** is born for adversity. ....Prv 17:17
who sticks closer than a **b**. ....Prv 18:24
First be reconciled to your **b**, ...Mt 5:24
"If your **b** sins against you, ...Mt 18:15
if food makes my **b** stumble, ... 1 Cor 8:13
Whoever loves his **b** abides .... 1 Jn 2:10

BROTHERHOOD
Love the **b**. Fear God. Honor.... 1 Pt 2:17
being experienced by your **b** .... 1 Pt 5:9

BROTHERLY
Now concerning **b** love you .... 1 Thes 4:9

BROTHERS
and pleasant it is when **b** ....Ps 133:1
and who are my **b**?" ....Mt 12:48

BUILD
let us **b** ourselves a city and a .... Gn 11:4
and in three days I will **b**....Mk 14:58

BUILDER
like a skilled master **b**.... 1 Cor 3:10
more glory as the **b** of a ....Heb 3:3
whose designer and **b** is God. ....Heb 11:10

BUILDING
he is like a man **b** a house, ...Lk 6:48
to excel in **b** up the church.... 1 Cor 14:12
for **b** up the body of Christ, ...Eph 4:12

BUILDS
Unless the LORD **b** the house, ...Ps 127:1
"Woe to him who **b** his ....Jer 22:13
puffs up, but love **b** up.... 1 Cor 8:1

BUILT
By wisdom a house is **b**, ...Prv 24:3
be like a wise man who **b**....Mt 7:24
that the church may be **b**.... 1 Cor 14:5

BURDEN
Cast your **b** on the LORD, and ....Ps 55:22
is easy, and my **b** is light." ....Mt 11:30

BURNED
thrown into the fire, and **b**. ....Jn 15:6
heavenly bodies will be **b** up .... 2 Pt 3:10

BURNING
bush was **b**, yet it was not consumed ... Ex 3:2
and keep your lamps **b**, ...Lk 12:35

BUSINESS
It is an unhappy **b** that God .... Eccl 1:13
and went about the king's **b**, ...Dn 8:27
'Engage in **b** until I come.' ....Lk 19:13

BYWORD
and a **b** among all the peoples....Dt 28:37
You have made us a **b** among ....Ps 44:14
And as you have been a **b** .... Zec 8:13

CALF
tool and made a golden **c**. ....Ex 32:4
And bring the fattened **c** ....Lk 15:23

CALL
to all who **c** on him in truth....Ps 145:18
Then all nations will **c** you ....Mal 3:12
No longer do I **c** you....Jn 15:15
hope that belongs to your **c**....Eph 4:4

CALLED
the hope to which he has **c** ....Eph 1:18
To this he **c** you through .... 2 Thes 2:14
life to which you were **c**.... 1 Tm 6:12

CALLING
your sins, **c** on his name.' ....Acts 22:16
For consider your **c**, ... 1 Cor 1:26

CALLS
and he **c** his own sheep by....Jn 10:3
For "everyone who **c** on the ....Rom 10:13
He who **c** you is faithful; .... 1 Thes 5:24

CAMEL
a gnat and swallowing a **c**! ....Mt 23:24
It is easier for a **c** to go....Mk 10:25

CAPTIVE
died to that which held us **c**, ...Rom 7:6
and take every thought **c** .... 2 Cor 10:5
we were held **c** under the ....Gal 3:23

CAPTIVES
to proclaim liberty to the **c**....Lk 4:18
on high he led a host of **c**, ...Eph 4:8

CAREFUL
and be **c** to do them, that it may....Dt 6:3
and be **c** to obey my rules, ...Ez 20:19

CARES
When the **c** of my heart are ....Ps 94:19
but the **c** of the world and....Mt 13:22
him, because he **c** for you.... 1 Pt 5:7

CAST
Why are you **c** down, O my....Ps 42:11
by the Spirit of God that I **c** ....Mt 12:28

CAUSE
and defend my **c** against an ....Ps 43:1
I will **c** your name to be....Ps 45:17
divorce one's wife for any **c**?" ....Mt 19:3

CEASE
before my eyes; **c** to do evil, ...Is 1:16
they will **c**; as for knowledge,.... 1 Cor 13:8

CENTURION
And when the **c**, who stood .... Mk 15:39
When the **c** heard about Jesus, ...Lk 7:3
a **c** of what was known as....Acts 10:1

CHAFF
but are like **c** that the wind....Ps 1:4
but the **c** he will burn with....Mt 3:12

CHAINS
I am an ambassador in **c**, ...Eph 6:20
Remember my **c**. Grace be ....Col 4:18
bound with **c** as a criminal. .... 2 Tm 2:9

CHANGE
that he should **c** his mind. ....Nm 23:19
"For I the LORD do not **c**; ....Mal 3:6

CHARACTER
he speaks out of his own **c**, ...Jn 8:44
and endurance produces **c**, ...Rom 5:4
promise the unchangeable **c**....Heb 6:17

CHARGE
Who shall bring any **c** ....Rom 8:33
present the gospel free of **c**, ... 1 Cor 9:18
Every **c** must be established.... 2 Cor 13:1

CHARIOTS
returned and covered the **c** ....Ex 14:28
c of fire and horses of fire.... 2 Kgs 2:11

CHEEK
strike all my enemies on the **c**; ....Ps 3:7
slaps you on the right **c**, ...Mt 5:39

CHEER
sad face, and be of good **c**,' .... Jb 9:27
your consolations **c** my soul. ....Ps 94:19
and let your heart **c** you in .... Eccl 11:9

CHEERFUL
A glad heart makes a **c** face, ...Prv 15:13
for God loves a **c** giver.... 2 Cor 9:7
Is anyone **c**? Let him sing praise....Jas 5:13

CHERUBIM
of Eden he placed the **c** .... Gn 3:24
The **c** spread out their wings.... 2 Chr 5:8
He sits enthroned upon the **c**; ....Ps 99:1
Above it were the **c** of glory ....Heb 9:5

CHILD
Train up a **c** in the way he....Prv 22:6
For to us a **c** is born, to us a son ....Is 9:6
When I was a **c**, I spoke.... 1 Cor 13:11

CHILDREN
teach them diligently to your **c**, ... Dt 6:7
c are a heritage from the ....Ps 127:3
blessed are his **c** after him!....Prv 20:7
he gave the right to become **c**.... Jn 1:12
our spirit that we are **c** ....Rom 8:16
of God, as beloved **c**....Eph 5:1
C, obey your parents in....Col 3:20

CHOOSE
Therefore **c** life, that you and ....Dt 30:19
c this day whom you will....Jos 24:15
You did not **c** me, but I chose.... Jn 15:16

CHOSE
Moses **c** able men out of all .... Ex 18:25
he **c**, he shortened the days.... Mk 13:20
even as he **c** us in him before ....Eph 1:4
because God **c** you as the .... 2 Thes 2:13

CHOSEN
The LORD your God has **c** you to....Dt 7:6
made a covenant with my **c** ....Ps 89:3
A good name is to be **c** rather....Prv 22:1
and Israel my **c**, I call you by....Is 45:4

CHRIST
"You are the **C**, the Son of ....Mt 16:16
of the gospel of Jesus **C**, ...Mk 1:1
a Savior, who is **C** the Lord. ....Lk 2:11
that the **C** should suffer and............ Lk 24:46
truth came through Jesus **C**. .... Jn 1:17
I believe that you are the **C**, ... Jn 11:27
that by the name of Jesus **C**............Acts 4:10
of peace through Jesus **C**.............Acts 10:36
have been baptized into **C**.................Rom 6:3
but we preach **C** crucified................1 Cor 1:23
bodies are members of **C**?............. 1 Cor 6:15
that **C** died for our sins in .... 1 Cor 15:3
For we are the aroma of **C** .... 2 Cor 2:15
For the love of **C** controls............... 2 Cor 5:14
C redeemed us from the..................... Gal 3:13
created in **C** Jesus for good ....Eph 2:10
When **C** who is your life ....Col 3:4
Jesus **C** is the same ....Heb 13:8

CHRIST'S
We are fools for **C** sake, but .... 1 Cor 4:10
we share abundantly in **C** .... 2 Cor 1:5
up what is lacking in **C** ....Col 1:24

CHRISTIAN
persuade me to be a **C**?"..............Acts 26:28
Yet if anyone suffers as a **C**, ... 1 Pt 4:16

CHRISTIANS
were first called **C**..........................Acts 11:26

CHURCH
this rock I will build my **c**,.................Mt 16:18
to care for the **c** of God, ...Acts 20:28
Christ is the head of the **c**, ...Eph 5:23
the **c**. He is the beginning,................Col 1:18
will he care for God's **c**? ....1 Tm 3:5

CHURCHES
So the **c** were strengthened.............Acts 16:5
John to the seven **c** that are in.............Rv 1:4
about these things for the **c**.............Rv 22:16

CIRCUMCISED
male among you shall be **c**. .... Gn 17:10

CIRCUMCISION
For neither **c** counts for...................... Gal 6:15
the flesh, by the **c** of Christ,...............Col 2:11

CITY
A **c** set on a hill cannot be hidden.......Mt 5:14
And I saw the holy **c**, new...................Rv 21:2

CLAP
C your hands, all peoples! ....Ps 47:1
Let the rivers **c** their hands; let...........Ps 98:8
the trees of the field shall **c**...............Is 55:12

CLAY
Does the **c** say to him who ....Is 45:9
we are the **c**, and you are our..............Is 64:8
like the **c** in the potter's hand, ... Jer 18:6
potter no right over the **c**, ...Rom 9:21

CLEAN
make yourselves **c**; remove the ....Is 1:16
be **c**." And immediately the.................Lk 5:13

CLEANSE
and **c** me from my sin!.......................Ps 51:2
let us **c** ourselves from every........... 2 Cor 7:1

CLEANSED
having **c** their hearts by faith. ....Acts 15:9
having **c** her by the washing..............Eph 5:26

CLINGS
My soul **c** to you; your right ....Ps 63:8

CLOAK
you take your neighbor's **c**................. Ex 22:26
let him have your **c** as well. ....Mt 5:40
stripped him of the purple **c** .... Mk 15:20

CLOSE
right, evil lies **c** at hand..................Rom 7:21
Keep a **c** watch on yourself ....1 Tm 4:16

CLOTHED
wife garments of skins and **c**............ Gn 3:21
I was naked and you **c** me, I..............Mt 25:36
in the city until you are **c** .... Lk 24:49

CLOTHING
are you anxious about **c**? ....Mt 6:28
But if we have food and **c**, ...1 Tm 6:8

CLOUD
them by day in a pillar of **c** .... Ex 13:21
Son of Man coming in a **c** ....Lk 21:27
a **c** took him out of their sight............Acts 1:9

CLOUDS
he makes the **c** his chariot; he...........Ps 104:3
coming with the **c** of heaven." .... Mk 14:62

COINS
put in two small copper **c**, ... Mk 12:42
having ten silver **c**, if she loses .... Lk 15:8
And he poured out the **c** of the........... Jn 2:15

COLD
love of many will grow **c**....................Mt 24:12
Would that you were either **c**...............Rv 3:15

COLT
on a **c**, the foal of a donkey. .... Zec 9:9
sitting on a donkey's **c**!" .... Jn 12:15

COMFORT
rod and your staff, they **c** me. ....Ps 23:4
C, **c** my people, says ....Is 40:1
c one another, agree with............ 2 Cor 13:11
Christ, any **c** from love, any ....Phil 2:1

COMFORTED
mourn, for they shall be **c**. ....Mt 5:4
affliction we have been **c**.............. 1 Thes 3:7

COMFORTS
I am he who **c** you; who are..............Is 51:12
who **c** us in all our affliction, ... 2 Cor 1:4
God, who **c** the downcast, ... 2 Cor 7:6

COMMAND
You shall speak all that I **c** .... Ex 7:2
"'He will **c** his angels............................ Lk 4:10
C and teach these things.................1 Tm 4:11

COMMANDED
And the LORD God **c** the man,.............. Gn 2:16
to observe all that I have **c** ....Mt 28:20
but I do as the Father has **c**............. Jn 14:31

COMMANDMENT
very careful to observe the **c** ....Jos 22:5
For the **c** is a lamp and the...............Prv 6:23
A new **c** I give to you, that................ Jn 13:34

COMMANDMENTS
of the covenant, the Ten **C**................ Ex 34:28
wise of heart will receive **c**,..............Prv 10:8
Fear God and keep his **c**,...................Eccl 12:13
On these two **c** depend all...................Mt 22:40
And his **c** are not burdensome. .... 1 Jn 5:3

COMMENDED
A man is **c** according to his ....Prv 12:8
though **c** through their.....................Heb 11:39

COMMIT
C your way to the LORD; trust ....Ps 37:5
'You shall not **c** adultery.'......................Mt 5:27
into your hands I **c** my....................... Lk 23:46

COMMITTED
He **c** no sin, neither was................... 1 Pt 2:22

COMMON
between the holy and the **c**, ... Lv 10:10
and had all things in **c**. ....Acts 2:44
made clean, do not call **c**.'..............Acts 11:9

COMPANION
who forsakes the **c** of her...................Prv 2:17
the **c** of fools will suffer harm..........Prv 13:20
though she is your **c** and.................Mal 2:14

COMPARE
none can **c** with you! I will ....Ps 40:5
nothing you desire can **c**....................Prv 3:15

COMPASSION
As a father shows **c** to his..............Ps 103:13
everlasting love I will have **c**................Is 54:8
he will have **c** according to ....Lam 3:32
my **c** grows warm and tender..........Hos 11:8
and he had **c** on them,........................ Mk 6:34
and I will have **c** on whom ....Rom 9:15

COMPASSIONATE
I will hear, for I am **c**......................... Ex 22:27
being **c**, atoned for their ....Ps 78:38
how the Lord is **c** and merciful..........Jas 5:11

COMPLAINT
I pour out my **c** before him; I ....Ps 142:2
and, if one has a **c** against................Col 3:13

COMPLETE
c my joy by being of the same.............Phil 2:2
the man of God may be **c**, ... 2 Tm 3:17
that you may be perfect and **c**, ...Jas 1:4
so that our joy may be **c**..................... 1 Jn 1:4

COMPLETION
bringing holiness to **c** in the .... 2 Cor 7:1
work in you will bring it to **c**................Phil 1:6

CONCEAL
he will **c** me under the cover ....Ps 27:5
It is the glory of God to **c**..................Prv 25:2

CONCEIT
Do nothing from selfish ambition
or **c**, ...Phil 2:3
he is puffed up with **c** and.................1 Tm 6:4

CONCEIVED
for that which is **c** in her is...............Mt 1:20

CROOKED
The way of the guilty is **c**, ...Prv 21:8
and the **c** shall become straight, ... Lk 3:5
blemish in the midst of a **c**..............Phil 2:15

CROSS
himself and take up his **c**.................. Lk 9:23
boast except in the **c** of our Lord....... Gal 6:14
peace by the blood of his **c**. ....Col 1:20

CROWN
An excellent wife is the **c**..................Prv 12:4
Grandchildren are the **c**.....................Prv 17:6
wearing the **c** of thorns and............... Jn 19:5
there is laid up for me the **c**.............2 Tm 4:8
the test he will receive the **c**.............Jas 1:12
receive the unfading **c** of glory.......... 1 Pt 5:4
and I will give you the **c** of life. ....Rv 2:10

CROWNED
the heavenly beings and **c**....................Ps 8:5
An athlete is not **c** unless he............2 Tm 2:5
you have **c** him with glory ....Heb 2:7

CRUCIFIED
but we preach Christ **c**.................. 1 Cor 1:23
For he was **c** in weakness, ... 2 Cor 13:4

CRUCIFY
of whom you will kill and **c**,..............Mt 23:34
they kept shouting, "**C**, **c** him!" .... Lk 23:21
"Shall I **c** your King?" The................ Jn 19:15

CRUSHED
and saves the **c** in spirit. ....Ps 34:18
he was **c** for our iniquities; ....Is 53:5
but not **c**; perplexed, but not........... 2 Cor 4:8

CRY
to me and heard my **c**. ....Ps 40:1
the very stones would **c** out." .... Lk 19:40

CUNNING
deceived Eve by his **c**,................... 2 Cor 11:3
by human **c**, by craftiness in............Eph 4:14

CUP
with oil; my **c** overflows.......................Ps 23:5
let this **c** pass from me;...................Mt 26:39
"This **c** is the new covenant........ 1 Cor 11:25

CURSE
"I will never again **c** the..................... Gn 8:21
you today a blessing and a **c**: .... Dt 11:26
bless those who **c** you, pray .... Lk 6:28
bless and do not **c** them. ....Rom 12:14

CURSED
c is the ground because of................ Gn 3:17
"'**C** be the man who makes a .... Dt 27:15

CURTAIN
the **c** of the temple was torn ....Mt 27:51
inner place behind the **c**,.................Heb 6:19

DAGON
it into the house of **D**.......................1 Sm 5:2

DAILY
and take up his cross **d**...................... Lk 9:23
examining the Scriptures **d**...........Acts 17:11

DANCE
to mourn, and a time to **d**; .... Eccl 3:4
and you did not **d**; we sang a ....Mt 11:17

DANCING
for me my mourning into **d**;...............Ps 30:11
praise his name with **d**, ...Ps 149:3

DANGER
The prudent sees **d** and...................Prv 27:12
nakedness, or **d**, or sword?.............Rom 8:35

DARK
you have said in the **d**......................... Lk 12:3
as to a lamp shining in a **d**............. 2 Pt 1:19

DARKENED
They are **d** in their...........................Eph 4:18

DARKNESS
separated the light from the **d**. .... Gn 1:4
follows me will not walk in **d**,............. Jn 8:12
and in him is no **d** at all....................... 1 Jn 1:5
hates his brother is still in **d**............. 1 Jn 2:9
chains under gloomy **d**......................Jude 1:6
kingdom was plunged into **d**............Rv 16:10

DAUGHTERS
your sons and your **d** shall .... Jl 2:28
you shall be sons and **d** .... 2 Cor 6:18

DAVID
D took the lyre and played............1 Sm 16:23
and there they anointed **D**................2 Sm 2:4
D said to Nathan, "I have.............2 Sm 12:13
D said to Solomon, "My................. 1 Chr 22:7
to the city of **D**, which is called .... Lk 2:4
Son of **D**, have mercy on me!" .... Lk 18:38
comes from the offspring of **D**,........... Jn 7:42

DAWN
righteous is like the light of **d**, ...Prv 4:18
at early **d**, they went to the................. Lk 24:1

DAY
God called the light **D**, and the .... Gn 1:5
for it is a **D** of Atonement, to............ Lv 23:28
in a pillar of cloud by **d**.................. Nm 14:14
This is the **d** that the LORD..............Ps 118:24
Give us this **d** our daily bread, ...Mt 6:11
you do not know on what **d**...............Mt 24:42
the **d** is at hand. So then let...........Rom 13:12
when he comes on that **d**............ 2 Thes 1:10

DAYS
his **d** shall be 120 years." .... Gn 6:3
So teach us to number our **d**............Ps 90:12
also your Creator in the **d**................ Eccl 12:1
and female servants in those **d**........... Jl 2:29
but in these last **d** he has ....Heb 1:2

DEACONS
with the overseers and **d**:...................Phil 1:1
D likewise must be dignified,............1 Tm 3:8
then let them serve as **d** ....1 Tm 3:10

DEAD
that he has risen from the **d**, ...Mt 28:7
him who raised from the **d**..............Rom 4:24
And you were **d** in the..........................Eph 2:1
the resurrection from the **d**. ....Phil 3:11
judge the living and the **d**,...............2 Tm 4:1
and him as good as **d**, were ....Heb 11:12

DEATH
murderer shall be put to **d**. .... Nm 35:16
He will swallow up **d** forever....................Is 25:8
he poured out his soul to **d**....................Is 53:12
but has passed from **d** to life................. Jn 5:24
reconciled to God by the **d**...............Rom 5:10
point of **d**, even **d** on a cross. ....Phil 2:8
is fully grown brings forth **d**..................Jas 1:15
And its rider's name was **D**, ...Rv 6:8
Over such the second **d** has no ....Rv 20:6

DEBT
I forgave you all that **d**......................Mt 18:32
by canceling the record of **d**..............Col 2:14

DEBTORS
we also have forgiven our **d**. ....Mt 6:12
we are **d**, not to the flesh, to ....Rom 8:12

DECEIT
D is in the heart of those.................Prv 12:20

DECEITFUL
The heart is **d** above all...................... Jer 17:9
d workmen, disguising................. 2 Cor 11:13

DECEITFULNESS
cares of the world and the **d** .... Mk 4:19
may be hardened by the **d**..............Heb 3:13

DECEIVE
Let no one **d** himself. If .... 1 Cor 3:18
Let no one **d** you with empty...............Eph 5:6
let no one **d** you. Whoever.................. 1 Jn 3:7

DECEIVED
"The serpent **d** me, and I ate." .... Gn 3:13
care lest your heart be **d**, ... Dt 11:16
d me and through it killed me.........Rom 7:11
Do not be **d**: God is not mocked,.......... Gal 6:7
Do not be **d**, my beloved brothers.......Jas 1:16

DECEIVER
the **d** of the whole world — ....Rv 12:9

DECEIVERS
empty talkers and **d**, especially............ Ti 1:10
For many **d** have gone out................. 2 Jn 1:7

DECLARE
The heavens **d** the glory of ....Ps 19:1
and new things I now **d**;.........................Is 42:9
D these things; exhort and .... Ti 2:15

DEED
was a prophet mighty in **d** .... Lk 24:19
in word or talk but in **d**.................. 1 Jn 3:18

DEEDS
in glorious **d**, doing wonders? .... Ex 15:11
performing **d** in keeping................Acts 26:20
in mind, doing evil **d**, ...Col 1:21
according to each one's **d**, ... 1 Pt 1:17

DEFEND
d your cause; remember how.............Ps 74:22
d the rights of the poor and ....Prv 31:9

DEFILE
resolved that he would not **d**................ Dn 1:8
These are what **d** a person. ....Mt 15:20

DELAY
will surely come; it will not **d**. ... Hb 2:3
there would be no more **d**, ... Rv 10:6

DELIGHT
D yourself in the Lord, and he ... Ps 37:4
I **d** to do your will, O my God; ... Ps 40:8
For you will not **d** in ... Ps 51:16
to me a joy and the **d** ... Jer 15:16
For I **d** in the law of God, in ... Rom 7:22

DELIGHTS
rescue him, for he **d** in him!" ... Ps 22:8
drink from the river of your **d**. ... Ps 36:8
because he **d** in steadfast love. ... Mi 7:18

DELIVER
In your righteousness **d** me ... Ps 71:2
but **d** us from evil. ... Mt 6:13

DELIVERED
who was **d** up for our ... Rom 4:25
He has **d** us from the domain ... Col 1:13

DELIVERER
the Lord raised up a **d** for the ... Jgs 3:9
and my fortress and my **d**, ... Ps 18:2
my stronghold and my **d**, ... Ps 144:2
"The **D** will come from ... Rom 11:26

DELIVERS
the Lord hears and **d** them ... Ps 34:17
but righteousness **d** from death. ... Prv 10:2
when he **d** the kingdom to ... 1 Cor 15:24

DEMON
the spirit of an unclean **d**, ... Lk 4:33
"I do not have a **d**, but I honor ... Jn 8:49

DEMON-OPPRESSED
a **d** man who was mute was ... Mt 9:32
Then a **d** man who was blind ... Mt 12:22

DEMON-POSSESSED
came to Jesus and saw the **d** ... Mk 5:15
seen it told them how the **d** ... Lk 8:36

DEMONIC
but is earthly, unspiritual, **d**. ... Jas 3:15
For they are **d** spirits, ... Rv 16:14

DEMONS
And if I cast out **d** by ... Mt 12:27
And they cast out many **d** ... Mk 6:13
spirits and teachings of **d**, ... 1 Tm 4:1

DEN
become a **d** of robbers in your ... Jer 7:11
brought and cast into the **d** ... Dn 6:16
but you make it a **d** of robbers." ... Mt 21:13

DENIED
Peter again **d** it, and at once a ... Jn 18:27
he has **d** the faith and is ... 1 Tm 5:8

DENIES
but whoever **d** me before ... Mt 10:33
No one who **d** the Son has ... 1 Jn 2:23

DENY
let him **d** himself and take up ... Lk 9:23
you will **d** me three times." ... Lk 22:61

DENYING
and **d** the Lord, and turning ... Is 59:13
d its power. Avoid such people. ... 2 Tm 3:5
even **d** the Master who bought ... 2 Pt 2:1

DEPART
The scepter shall not **d** from ... Gn 49:10
when he is old he will not **d**. ... Prv 22:6
'**D** from me, you cursed, into ... Mt 25:41

DEPARTED
"The glory has **d** from Israel, ... 1 Sm 4:22
nor have our steps **d** from ... Ps 44:18

DEPRIVE
partial to the wicked or to **d** ... Prv 18:5
and **d** the innocent of his right! ... Is 5:23
and to **d** the thirsty of drink. ... Is 32:6

DEPTH
nor height nor **d**, nor ... Rom 8:39
Oh, the **d** of the riches and ... Rom 11:33
length and height and **d**, ... Eph 3:18

DEPTHS
from the **d** of the earth you ... Ps 71:20
even the **d** of God. ... 1 Cor 2:10

DESCEND
"I saw the Spirit **d** from ... Jn 1:32
the Lord himself will **d** ... 1 Thes 4:16

DESCENDED
because the Lord had **d**. ... Ex 19:18
for an angel of the Lord **d** ... Mt 28:2
For not all who are **d** from ... Rom 9:6

DESERT
He turns a **d** into pools of ... Ps 107:35
make straight in the **d** a ... Is 40:3

DESERVE
to the proud what they **d**! ... Ps 94:2
practice such things **d** to die, ... Rom 1:32

DESERVES
of you less than your guilt **d**. ... Jb 11:6
for the laborer **d** his wages. Do ... Lk 10:7

DESIRE
Your **d** shall be contrary to your ... Gn 3:16
Its **d** is contrary to you, but you ... Gn 4:7
For I **d** steadfast love and not ... Hos 6:6
'I **d** mercy, and not sacrifice.' ... Mt 9:13
My **d** is to depart and be with ... Phil 1:23
they **d** a better country, that ... Heb 11:16

DESIRED
More to be **d** are they than ... Ps 19:10
And whatever my eyes **d** ... Eccl 2:10
many prophets and kings **d** ... Lk 10:24

DESIRES
will is to do your father's **d**. ... Jn 8:44
who **d** all people to be saved ... 1 Tm 2:4
following their own sinful **d**. ... 2 Pt 3:3
their own sinful **d**; ... Jude 1:16

DESOLATE
For the children of the **d** one ... Is 54:1
went away in the boat to a **d** ... Mk 6:32

DESOLATION
see the abomination of **d** ... Mt 24:15
then know that its **d** has ... Lk 21:20

DESPAIR
but not driven to **d**; ... 2 Cor 4:8

DESPISE
therefore I **d** myself, and ... Jb 42:6

DESPISED
Thus Esau **d** his birthright. ... Gn 25:34
scorned by mankind and **d** ... Ps 22:6
chose what is low and **d** ... 1 Cor 1:28

DESTINED
know that we are **d**. ... 1 Thes 3:3
For God has not **d** us for ... 1 Thes 5:9
word, as they were **d** to do. ... 1 Pt 2:8

DESTITUTE
regards the prayer of the **d** ... Ps 102:17
the rights of all who are **d**. ... Prv 31:8
d, afflicted, mistreated — ... Heb 11:37

DESTROY
fear him who can **d** both soul ... Mt 10:28
only to steal and kill and **d**. ... Jn 10:10
through death he might **d** ... Heb 2:14

DESTROYED
My people are **d** for lack of ... Hos 4:6
is **d**, we have a building ... 2 Cor 5:1
who shrink back and are **d**, ... Heb 10:39

DESTRUCTION
way is easy that leads to **d**, ... Mt 7:13
of wrath prepared for **d**, ... Rom 9:22
upon themselves swift **d**. ... 2 Pt 2:1

DETERMINED
Since his days are **d**, and the ... Jb 14:5
having **d** allotted periods ... Acts 17:26

DEVIL
And yet one of you is a **d**." ... Jn 6:70
give no opportunity to the **d**. ... Eph 4:27
and the **d** who had deceived ... Rv 20:10

DEVOTE
But we will **d** ourselves to ... Acts 6:4
d yourself to the public ... 1 Tm 4:13
And let our people learn to **d** ... Ti 3:14

DEVOUT
d men are taken away, while ... Is 57:1
man was righteous and **d**, ... Lk 2:25

DIE
integrity? Curse God and **d**." ... Jb 2:9
and a time to **d**; a time to ... Eccl 3:2
is Christ, and to **d** is gain. ... Phil 1:21
it is appointed for man to **d** ... Heb 9:27
that we might **d** to sin and ... 1 Pt 2:24

DIED
at the right time Christ **d** ... Rom 5:6
that Christ **d** for our sins in ... 1 Cor 15:3
If we have **d** with him, we ... 2 Tm 2:11

DIES
When the wicked **d**, his hope ... Prv 11:7
but if it **d**, it bears much fruit. ... Jn 12:24

DIFFERENT
because he has a **d** spirit .... Nm 14:24
Christ and are turning to a **d** .... Gal 1:6
If anyone teaches a **d** .... 1 Tm 6:3

DIGNITY
Strength and **d** are her .... Prv 31:25
teaching show integrity, **d**, ... Ti 2:7

DILIGENT
The plans of the **d** lead surely .... Prv 21:5
be **d** to be found by him .... 2 Pt 3:14

DIRECT
God will **d** you, you will be .... Ex 18:23
and **d** your heart in the way. .... Prv 23:19
May the Lord **d** your hearts .... 2 Thes 3:5

DISASTER
D pursues sinners, but the .... Prv 13:21
love, and relenting from **d**. .... Jon 4:2

DISCERN
Who can **d** his errors? .... Ps 19:12
you **d** my thoughts from afar. .... Ps 139:2
and try to **d** what is pleasing .... Eph 5:10

DISCIPLE
cold water because he is a **d**, ... Mt 10:42
life, he cannot be my **d**. .... Lk 14:26

DISCIPLES
Go therefore and make **d** .... Mt 28:19
my word, you are truly my **d**, ... Jn 8:31
know that you are my **d**, ... Jn 13:35

DISCIPLINE
therefore despise not the **d** .... Jb 5:17
do not despise the LORD's **d** .... Prv 3:11
Do not withhold **d** from a .... Prv 23:13
D your son, and he will give .... Prv 29:17
But I **d** my body and keep it .... 1 Cor 9:27
but bring them up in the **d** .... Eph 6:4
I reprove and **d**, so be zealous .... Rv 3:19

DISCIPLINED
The LORD has **d** me severely, ... Ps 118:18
we are **d** so that we may .... 1 Cor 11:32
had earthly fathers who **d** .... Heb 12:9

DISCOURAGED
He will not grow faint or be **d** .... Is 42:4
lest they become **d**. .... Col 3:21

DISCRETION
may the LORD grant you **d** .... 1 Chr 22:12
knowledge and **d** to the youth — .... Prv 1:4
that you may keep **d**, and your .... Prv 5:2

DISGRACE
honor, but fools get **d**. .... Prv 3:35
that he may not fall into **d**, ... 1 Tm 3:7

DISHONOR
counted worthy to suffer **d** .... Acts 5:41
You who boast in the law **d** .... Rom 2:23
It is sown in **d**; it is raised .... 1 Cor 15:43

DISHONORABLE
God gave them up to **d** .... Rom 1:26
honorable use, some for **d**. .... 2 Tm 2:20

DISOBEDIENCE
by the one man's **d** the many .... Rom 5:19
ready to punish every **d**, ... 2 Cor 10:6
every transgression or **d** received .... Heb 2:2

DISOBEDIENT
as you were at one time **d** .... Rom 11:30
d to their parents, ungrateful, ... 2 Tm 3:2
d, unfit for any good work. .... Ti 1:16

DISORDER
gossip, conceit, and **d**. .... 2 Cor 12:20
will be **d** and every vile practice. .... Jas 3:16

DISPERSED
of the whole earth were **d**. .... Gn 9:19
So the LORD **d** them from .... Gn 11:8

DISPERSION
of your slaughter and **d** .... Jer 25:34
Does he intend to go to the **D** .... Jn 7:35
who are elect exiles of the **D** .... 1 Pt 1:1

DISQUALIFIED
corrupted in mind and **d** .... 2 Tm 3:8

DISTINCTION
and he made no **d** between .... Acts 15:9
For there is no **d** between .... Rom 10:12

DISTINGUISH
You are to **d** between the .... Lv 10:10
to another the ability to **d** .... 1 Cor 12:10
by constant practice to **d** .... Heb 5:14

DISTRESS
In my **d** I called upon the .... Ps 18:6
out of my **d**, and he answered .... Jon 2:2
or **d**, or persecution, or .... Rom 8:35

DISTRIBUTED
by gifts of the Holy Spirit **d** .... Heb 2:4

DIVIDED
and a **d** household falls. .... Lk 11:17
Is Christ **d**? Was Paul crucified ...... 1 Cor 1:13

DIVINE
his eternal power and **d** .... Rom 1:20
because in his **d** forbearance .... Rom 3:25
become partakers of the **d** .... 2 Pt 1:4

DIVISION
I tell you, but rather **d**. .... Lk 12:51
that there may be no **d** .... 1 Cor 12:25

DIVISIONS
out for those who cause **d** .... Rom 16:17
and that there be no **d** .... 1 Cor 1:10
It is these who cause **d**, ... Jude 1:19

DIVORCE
He may not **d** her all his days. .... Dt 22:19
the husband should not **d** .... 1 Cor 7:11

DIVORCES
does not love his wife but **d** .... Mal 2:16
whoever **d** his wife, except for .... Mt 19:9
"Everyone who **d** his wife .... Lk 16:18

DOCTRINE
'My **d** is pure, and I am clean .... Jb 11:4
about by every wind of **d**, ... Eph 4:14
to give instruction in sound **d** .... Ti 1:9

DOERS
but the **d** of the law who .... Rom 2:13
But be **d** of the word, and not .... Jas 1:22

DOMINION
and subdue it and have **d** .... Gn 1:28
his **d** is an everlasting **d**, ... Dn 4:34

DOOR
sin is crouching at the **d**. Its .... Gn 4:7
I am the **d**. If anyone enters .... Jn 10:9
I stand at the **d** and knock. If .... Rv 3:20

DOUBLE-MINDED
I hate the **d**, but I love .... Ps 119:113
he is a **d** man, unstable in all .... Jas 1:8

DOUBT
little faith, why did you **d**?" .... Mt 14:31
and does not **d** in his heart, ... Mk 11:23
mercy on those who **d**; .... Jude 1:22

DOVE
And the **d** came back to him .... Gn 8:11
of God descending like a **d** .... Mt 3:16

DOWNCAST
"Why are your faces **d** today?" .... Gn 40:7
God, who comforts the **d**, ... 2 Cor 7:6

DRAGON
and he will slay the **d** that is .... Is 27:1
a great red **d**, with seven .... Rv 12:3

DREAD
Whom did you **d** and fear, ... Is 57:11
they shall turn in **d** to the .... Mi 7:17

DREAM
Now Joseph had a **d**, and .... Gn 37:5
Therefore show me the **d** .... Dn 2:6
your old men shall **d** dreams, ... Jl 2:28
appeared to Joseph in a **d** .... Mt 2:13

DRINK
D water from your own .... Prv 5:15
let him come to me and **d**. .... Jn 7:37
you eat this bread and **d** .... 1 Cor 11:26
being poured out as a **d** offering .... 2 Tm 4:6

DRUNK
Be **d**, but not with wine; .... Is 29:9
For these people are not **d**, ... Acts 2:15
And do not get **d** with wine, ... Eph 5:18

DRUNKARD
for the **d** and the glutton .... Prv 23:21
not a **d**, not violent but .... 1 Tm 3:3

DRUNKENNESS
down with dissipation and **d** .... Lk 21:34
d, orgies, and things like .... Gal 5:21

DRY
God called the **d** land Earth, ... Gn 1:10
plant, and like a root out of **d** .... Is 53:2
O **d** bones, hear the word of .... Ez 37:4

DUE
in themselves the **d** .... Rom 1:27
one may receive what is **d** .... 2 Cor 5:10
d to their hardness of heart. .... Eph 4:18

DUST
Lord God formed the man of **d**............ Gn 2:7
remembers that we are **d**. ....Ps 103:14
All are from the **d**, and to ....Eccl 3:20

DUTY
for this is the whole **d** .... Eccl 12:13

DWELL
"But will God indeed **d** .... 2 Chr 6:18
so that Christ may **d** in your.............Eph 3:17

DWELLING
"I will make my **d** among .... 2 Cor 6:16
the **d** place of God is with ....Rv 21:3

DWELLS
God's Spirit **d** in you?..................... 1 Cor 3:16
Holy Spirit who **d** within us,............2 Tm 1:14

EAGER
So I am **e** to preach the gospel.........Rom 1:15

EAGERLY
by faith, we ourselves **e** wait.............. Gal 5:5
but to save those who are **e** ....Heb 9:28

EAR
Incline your **e**, and hear ....Prv 22:17
And if the **e** should say,............... 1 Cor 12:16
He who has an **e**, let him hear ....Rv 2:7

EARNESTLY
Therefore pray **e** to the Lord .... Lk 10:2
Pursue love, and **e** desire.............. 1 Cor 14:1
keep loving one another **e**, ... 1 Pt 4:8

EARTH
is your name in all the **e**! .... Ps 8:1
The **e** is the Lord's and the..................Ps 24:1
I made the **e** and created..................Is 45:12
come, your will be done, on **e** ....Mt 6:10
authority in heaven and on **e** ....Mt 28:18
I am lifted up from the **e**,................. Jn 12:32
and to the end of the **e**." ....Acts 1:8
a new heaven and a new **e**,...................Rv 21:1

EARTHLY
if the tent that is our **e**..................... 2 Cor 5:1
shame, with minds set on **e**..............Phil 3:19
to death therefore what is **e** ....Col 3:5

EASIER
For which is **e**, to say, 'Your..................Mt 9:5
Again I tell you, it is **e** for a ....Mt 19:24

EAST
a garden in Eden, in the **e**,.................... Gn 2:8
as far as the **e** is from the ....Ps 103:12
behold, wise men from the **e**.................Mt 2:1

EASY
gate is wide and the way is **e**..............Mt 7:13
For my yoke is **e**, and my...................Mt 11:30

EAT
give him bread to **e**, and if he..........Prv 25:21
disciples, and said, "Take, **e**;............Mt 26:26
as often as you **e** this bread......... 1 Cor 11:26

EDEN
God planted a garden in **E**, ... Gn 2:8
makes her wilderness like **E**, ...Is 51:3
You were in **E**, the garden................. Ez 28:13

EFFECT
And the **e** of righteousness ....Is 32:17
For a will takes **e** only at ....Heb 9:17
steadfastness have its full **e**, ...Jas 1:4

ELDERS
Let the **e** who rule well be .... 1 Tm 5:17
So I exhort the **e** among you, ... 1 Pt 5:1

ELECT
But for the sake of the **e** ....Mt 24:22
for the sake of the **e**,.......................2 Tm 2:10

ELECTION
that God's purpose of **e** ....Rom 9:11
But as regards **e**, they are............Rom 11:28
to confirm your calling and **e**, ... 2 Pt 1:10

ELIJAH
Now **E** the Tishbite, of.................... 1 Kgs 17:1
"Behold, I will send you **E**..................Mal 4:5
But I tell you that **E** has ....Mt 17:12
E was a man with a nature ....Jas 5:17

ELISHA
spirit of Elijah rests on **E**." ....2 Kgs 2:15

ELOQUENT
"Oh, my Lord, I am not **e**, ... Ex 4:10
He was an **e** man, ...Acts 18:24
and not with words of **e** .... 1 Cor 1:17

EMMAUS
going to a village named **E**, ... Lk 24:13

EMPTY
it shall not return to me **e**, ...Is 55:11
no one deceive you with **e** words, ...Eph 5:6
by philosophy and **e** deceit,..................Col 2:8

ENCOURAGE
Therefore **e** one another .... 1 Thes 5:11
rebuke an older man but **e**................ 1 Tm 5:1

ENCOURAGED
that we may be mutually **e**...............Rom 1:12
may learn and all be **e**, ... 1 Cor 14:31
that their hearts may be **e**, ...Col 2:2

ENCOURAGEMENT
and through the **e** ....Rom 15:4
refuge might have strong **e**..............Heb 6:18

END
right to a man, but its **e**..................Prv 16:25
endures to the **e** will be saved. ....Mt 10:22
Then comes the **e**, when.............. 1 Cor 15:24
once for all at the **e**.........................Heb 9:26

ENDURANCE
your **e** you will gain your lives. .... Lk 21:19
that suffering produces **e**, ...Rom 5:3
his glorious might, for all **e**................Col 1:11
Here is a call for the **e** and................Rv 13:10

ENDURE
May his name **e** forever, his ....Ps 72:17
But who can **e** the day of his..............Mal 3:2
if we **e**, we will also reign...............2 Tm 2:12

ENDURES
for his steadfast love **e** .... 1 Chr 16:34
good, for his steadfast love **e**...........Ps 106:1
his righteousness **e** forever;..............Ps 112:9
But the one who **e** to the end ....Mt 24:13
things, hopes all things, **e**........... 1 Cor 13:7

ENDURING
for he is the living God, **e**.................. Dn 6:26
I know you are **e** patiently and ....Rv 2:3

ENEMIES
But love your **e**, and do good,............. Lk 6:35
I make your **e** your footstool.' .... Lk 20:43
For if while we were **e**.......................Rom 5:10

ENEMY
Do not rejoice when your **e** ....Prv 24:17
If your **e** is hungry, give...................Prv 25:21
the world makes himself an **e**.............Jas 4:4

ENJOY
E life with the wife whom .... Eccl 9:9
us with everything to **e**.................. 1 Tm 6:17
the people of God than to **e**............Heb 11:25

ENLIGHTENED
those who have once been **e**, ...Heb 6:4
when, after you were **e**, ...Heb 10:32

ENSLAVED
we would no longer be **e**....................Rom 6:6
we were children, were **e**..................... Gal 4:3

ENTANGLED
No soldier gets **e** in civilian..............2 Tm 2:4
Christ, they are again **e** .... 2 Pt 2:20

ENTER
Pharisees, you will never **e**.................Mt 5:20
of life and that they may **e**...............Rv 22:14

ENTERS
since it **e** not his heart but................ Mk 7:19
If anyone **e** by me, he will be.............. Jn 10:9

ENTHRONED
the Lord of hosts, who is **e** .... 1 Sm 4:4
hosts, God of Israel, **e** above.............Is 37:16

ENTICE
My son, if sinners **e** you, do................Prv 1:10
They **e** unsteady souls. They............ 2 Pt 2:14

ENTRUSTED
approved by God to be **e**................ 1 Thes 2:4
with which I have been **e**. .... 1 Tm 1:11
guard the deposit **e** to you. .... 1 Tm 6:20

ENVY
e, slander, pride, foolishness. .... Mk 7:22
love does not **e** or boast; it............ 1 Cor 13:4

EPHESUS
hear that not only in **E**.....................Acts 19:26
fought with beasts at **E**?............. 1 Cor 15:32
the angel of the church in **E**..................Rv 2:1

EQUAL
But it is you, a man, my **e**, ...Ps 55:13
because they are **e** to angels .... Lk 20:36
Father, making himself **e** .... Jn 5:18

EQUALITY
form of God, did not count **e** ....Phil 2:6

EQUIPPED
the God who **e** me with......................Ps 18:32

FAITHFULNESS
A God of **f** and without ... Dt 32:4
LORD are steadfast love and **f**, ... Ps 25:10
his **f** is a shield and buckler. ... Ps 91:4
be the belt of his waist, and **f** ... Is 11:5
morning; great is your **f**. ... Lam 3:23
kindness, goodness, **f**, ... Gal 5:22

FAITHLESS
I look at the **f** with disgust, ... Ps 119:158
Return, O **f** children, declares ... Jer 3:14
if we are **f**, he remains ... 2 Tm 2:13

FALL
a haughty spirit before a **f**. ... Prv 16:18
For if they **f**, one will lift up ... Eccl 4:10
And not one of them will **f** ... Mt 10:29
for all have sinned and **f** ... Rom 3:23

FALLEN
How the mighty have **f**! ... 2 Sm 1:19
"How you are **f** from heaven, ... Is 14:12
him those who have **f** ... 1 Thes 4:14

FALLS
rejoice when your enemy **f**, ... Prv 24:17
unless a grain of wheat **f** ... Jn 12:24

FALSE
"You shall not bear **f** witness ... Ex 20:16
A **f** witness will not go ... Prv 19:5
"Beware of **f** prophets, who ... Mt 7:15
does what is detestable or **f**, ... Rv 21:27

FALSEHOOD
Remove far from me **f** and ... Prv 30:8
having put away **f**, let each ... Eph 4:25

FAMILIES
curse, and in you all the **f** ... Gn 12:3
to the LORD, and all the **f** ... Ps 22:27

FAMINE
will arise seven years of **f**, ... Gn 41:30
not a **f** of bread, nor a thirst ... Am 8:11

FAR
their lips, but their heart is **f** ... Mt 15:8
Jesus you who once were **f** ... Eph 2:13

FAST
shall serve him and hold **f** ... Dt 13:4
"And when you **f**, do not look ... Mt 6:16

FATHER
a man shall leave his **f** ... Gn 2:24
you, and you shall be the **f** ... Gn 17:4
"'Honor your **f** and your ... Dt 5:16
him whom he loves, as a **f** ... Prv 3:12
A wise son makes a glad **f**, ... Prv 10:1
Everlasting **F**, Prince of Peace. ... Is 9:6
acknowledge before my **F** ... Mt 10:32
a man shall leave his **f** ... Mt 19:5
And Jesus said, "**F**, forgive ... Lk 23:34
As the **F** has sent me, even ... Jn 20:21
was to make him the **f** ... Rom 4:11
For I became your **f** in ... 1 Cor 4:15
access in one Spirit to the **F**. ... Eph 2:18
coming down from the **F** ... Jas 1:17
See what kind of love the **F** ... 1 Jn 3:1

FATHER'S
to snatch them out of the **F**. ... Jn 10:29

FATHERLESS
He executes justice for the **f** ... Dt 10:18
the **f**, and the widow, ... Dt 24:19
Father of the **f** and protector of ... Ps 68:5
the widow and the **f**, ... Ps 146:9

FAVOR
the LORD bestows **f** and ... Ps 84:11
And the **f** of God was upon him. ... Lk 2:40
and in stature and in **f** ... Lk 2:52

FEAR
God require of you, but to **f** ... Dt 10:12
the **f** of the LORD is clean, ... Ps 19:9
whom shall I **f**? The LORD is ... Ps 27:1
The **f** of the LORD is the ... Ps 111:10
heard. **F** God and keep his ... Eccl 12:13
his delight shall be in the **f** ... Is 11:3
f not, for I am with you; be ... Is 41:10
And do not **f** those who kill ... Mt 10:28
to completion in the **f** ... 2 Cor 7:1
God gave us a spirit not of **f** ... 2 Tm 1:7
F God. Honor the emperor. ... 1 Pt 2:17
Do not **f** what you are about to ... Rv 2:10

FEARS
and upright man, who **f** God ... Jb 1:8
Blessed is the one who **f** ... Prv 28:14

FEED
f them and be their shepherd ... Ez 34:23
He said to him, "**F** my lambs." ... Jn 21:15
your enemy is hungry, **f** ... Rom 12:20

FEET
have put all things under his **f**, ... Ps 8:6
have pierced my hands and **f** ... Ps 22:16
of the miry bog, and set my **f** ... Ps 40:2
word is a lamp to my **f** ... Ps 119:105
upon the mountains are the **f** ... Is 52:7

FELLOW
fall, one will lift up his **f** ... Eccl 4:10
heirs of God and **f** heirs with ... Rom 8:17
For we are God's **f** workers ... 1 Cor 3:9

FELLOWSHIP
the apostles' teaching and the **f**, ... Acts 2:42
they gave the right hand of **f** ... Gal 2:9

FEMALE
male and **f** he created them. ... Gn 1:27
'God made them male and **f**.' ... Mk 10:6
there is no male and **f**, ... Gal 3:28

FEW
let your words be **f**. ... Eccl 5:2
called, but **f** are chosen. ... Mt 22:14
but the laborers are **f**. ... Lk 10:2

FIELD
Consider the lilies of the **f**, ... Mt 6:28
The **f** is the world, and the ... Mt 13:38
You are God's **f**, God's ... 1 Cor 3:9

FIG
And they sewed **f** leaves ... Gn 3:7
And seeing a **f** tree by the ... Mt 21:19

FIGHT
The LORD will **f** for you, and ... Ex 14:14
goes before you will himself **f** ... Dt 1:30

FILL
May the God of hope **f** ... Rom 15:13
the heavens, that he might **f** ... Eph 4:10

FILLED
may the whole earth be **f** ... Ps 72:19
the glory of the LORD **f** the temple. ... Ez 43:5
For the earth will be **f** with ... Hb 2:14
And the disciples were **f** ... Acts 13:52
f with the fruit of righteousness ... Phil 1:11

FILTHINESS
Let there be no **f** nor foolish ... Eph 5:4
Therefore put away all **f** ... Jas 1:21

FIND
and be sure your sin will **f** ... Nm 32:23
for I **f** my delight in your ... Ps 119:47
excellent wife who can **f**? ... Prv 31:10
all the promises of God **f** ... 2 Cor 1:20

FINDS
and the one who seeks **f**, ... Mt 7:8
Whoever **f** his life will lose ... Mt 10:39

FINISH
build and was not able to **f**.' ... Lk 14:30
to myself, if only I may **f** ... Acts 20:24
So now **f** doing it as well, ... 2 Cor 8:11

FINISHED
And on the seventh day God **f** ... Gn 2:2
"It is **f**," and he bowed his ... Jn 19:30
the good fight, I have **f** the ... 2 Tm 4:7

FIRE
dark, behold, a smoking **f** pot ... Gn 15:17
appeared to him in a flame of **f** ... Ex 3:2
and by night in a pillar of **f** ... Ex 13:21
your God is a consuming **f**, ... Dt 4:24
Is not my word like **f**, ... Jer 23:29
walking in the midst of the **f**, ... Dn 3:25
the Holy Spirit and **f**. ... Mt 3:11
hell, to the unquenchable **f**. ... Mk 9:43
And divided tongues as of **f** ... Acts 2:3
revealed by **f**, and the **f** will test ... 1 Cor 3:13
second death, the lake of **f** ... Rv 20:14

FIRM
people, "Fear not, stand **f**, ... Ex 14:13
my covenant will stand **f** ... Ps 89:28
his heart is **f**, trusting in the ... Ps 112:7
Be watchful, stand **f** in the ... 1 Cor 16:13
having done all, to stand **f**. ... Eph 6:13
So then, brothers, stand **f** ... 2 Thes 2:15

FIRST
"I am the **f** and I am the last; ... Is 44:6
But many who are **f** will be ... Mt 19:30
And the gospel must **f** be ... Mk 13:10

FIRSTBORN
and every **f** in the land of ... Ex 11:5
of the invisible God, the **f** ... Col 1:15

FIRSTFRUITS
ourselves, who have the **f** ... Rom 8:23
that we should be a kind of **f** ... Jas 1:18

FITTING
and a song of praise is **f**. ... Ps 147:1
in harvest, so honor is not **f** ... Prv 26:1
For it was **f** that he, for ... Heb 2:10

FIXED
because he has **f** a day on ... Acts 17:31

FLAME
a fire, and his Holy One a **f**, ... Is 10:17
I remind you to fan into **f** ... 2 Tm 1:6
His eyes were like a **f** of fire, ... Rv 1:14

FLAMING
placed the cherubim and a **f** ... Gn 3:24
you can extinguish all the **f** ... Eph 6:16

FLATTERS
For he **f** himself in his own ... Ps 36:2
more favor than he who **f** ... Prv 28:23
A man who **f** his neighbor ... Prv 29:5

FLATTERY
and by smooth talk and **f** ... Rom 16:18
came with words of **f**, ... 1 Thes 2:5

FLEE
as for you, O man of God, **f**. ... 1 Tm 6:11
So **f** youthful passions and ... 2 Tm 2:22
Resist the devil, and he will **f** ... Jas 4:7

FLEETING
let me know how **f** I am! ... Ps 39:4
by a lying tongue is a **f** ... Prv 21:6
of God than to enjoy the **f** ... Heb 11:25

FLESH
and they shall become one **f**. ... Gn 2:24
thus destroyed, yet in my **f** ... Jb 19:26
and give you a heart of **f**. ... Ez 36:26
are no longer two but one **f**. ... Mt 19:6
and all **f** shall see the salvation ... Lk 3:6
And the Word became **f** and ... Jn 1:14
we were living in the **f**, ... Rom 7:5
no provision for the **f**, ... Rom 13:14
for the destruction of the **f**, ... 1 Cor 5:5
gratify the desires of the **f** ... Gal 5:16
not wrestle against **f** and blood, ... Eph 6:12
put no confidence in the **f** ... Phil 3:3
from the passions of the **f**, ... 1 Pt 2:11
Christ has come in the **f** ... 1 Jn 4:2

FLOCK
a shepherd seeks out his **f** ... Ez 34:12
sheep of the **f** will be scattered.' ... Mt 26:31
keeping watch over their **f** ... Lk 2:8
shepherd the **f** of God that is ... 1 Pt 5:2

FLOG
him and spit on him, and **f** ... Mk 10:34
"Is it lawful for you to **f** ... Acts 22:25

FLOOD
shall never again become a **f** ... Gn 9:15
every night I **f** my bed with ... Ps 6:6
others, when he brought a **f** ... 2 Pt 2:5

FLOURISH
The righteous **f** like the palm ... Ps 92:12
but the righteous will **f** ... Prv 11:28

FLOWER
The grass withers, the **f** fades, ... Is 40:8
The grass withers, and the **f** ... 1 Pt 1:24

FOLLOW
You shall **f** my rules and keep ... Lv 18:4
he said to him, "**F** me." ... Mt 9:9
before them, and the sheep **f** ... Jn 10:4
so that you might **f** in his steps. ... 1 Pt 2:21

FOLLY
rather than a fool in his **f**. ... Prv 17:12
the word of the cross is **f** ... 1 Cor 1:18

FOOD
that the tree was good for **f**, ... Gn 3:6
himself with the king's **f**, ... Dn 1:8
Is not life more than **f**, and ... Mt 6:25
hungry and you gave me **f**, ... Mt 25:35
But if we have **f** and ... 1 Tm 6:8

FOODS
(Thus he declared all **f** clean.) ... Mk 7:19
require abstinence from **f** ... 1 Tm 4:3

FOOL
The **f** says in his heart, "There ... Ps 53:1
in his own mind is a **f**, ... Prv 28:26
whoever says, 'You **f**!' will ... Mt 5:22
But God said to him, '**F**! ... Lk 12:20

FOOLISH
Five of them were **f**, and five ... Mt 25:2
But God chose what is **f** ... 1 Cor 1:27

FOOLS
f despise wisdom and instruction. ... Prv 1:7
to be wise, they became **f**, ... Rom 1:22
We are **f** for Christ's sake, ... 1 Cor 4:10

FOOT
He will not let your **f** be ... Ps 121:3
And if your **f** causes you to ... Mk 9:45
If the **f** should say, ... 1 Cor 12:15

FORCES
And if anyone **f** you to go one ... Mt 5:41
against the spiritual **f** of evil ... Eph 6:12

FOREKNOWLEDGE
to the definite plan and **f** ... Acts 2:23
according to the **f** of God the ... 1 Pt 1:2

FOREVER
Remember his covenant **f**, ... 1 Chr 16:15
But the LORD sits enthroned **f**; ... Ps 9:7
Your throne, O God, is **f** and ... Ps 45:6
You are a priest **f** after the order ... Ps 110:4
place, "You are a priest **f**, ... Heb 5:6

FORGAVE
to the LORD," and you **f** the ... Ps 32:5
You **f** the iniquity of your ... Ps 85:2
servant released him and **f** ... Mt 18:27
another, as God in Christ **f** ... Eph 4:32

FORGET
then take care lest you **f** the ... Dt 6:12
does not **f** the cry of the afflicted. ... Ps 9:12
I will never **f** your precepts, ... Ps 119:93

FORGIVE
from heaven and will **f** ... 2 Chr 7:14
For I will **f** their iniquity, ... Jer 31:34
Who can **f** sins but God alone?" ... Mk 2:7
he is faithful and just to **f** ... 1 Jn 1:9

FORGIVEN
one whose transgression is **f**, ... Ps 32:1
our debts, as we also have **f** ... Mt 6:12
sins, which are many, are **f** ... Lk 7:47
committed sins, he will be **f**. ... Jas 5:15

FORGIVENESS
But with you there is **f**, that ... Ps 130:4
out for many for the **f** ... Mt 26:28
believes in him receives **f** ... Acts 10:43
through his blood, the **f** of our ... Eph 1:7

FORGIVING
you, O Lord, are good and **f**, ... Ps 86:5
complaint against another, **f** ... Col 3:13

FORM
himself nothing, taking the **f** ... Phil 2:7

FORMED
then the LORD God **f** the man of ... Gn 2:7
For you **f** my inward parts; ... Ps 139:13
"Before I **f** you in the womb ... Jer 1:5

FORMER
which belongs to your **f** manner ... Eph 4:22
passions of your **f** ignorance ... 1 Pt 1:14

FORSAKE
He will not leave you or **f** ... Dt 31:6
I will not leave you or **f** you. ... Jos 1:5
For the LORD will not **f** his ... Ps 94:14
will never leave you nor **f** ... Heb 13:5

FORSAKEN
not seen the righteous **f** ... Ps 37:25
my God, why have you **f** me? ... Mk 15:34

FOUND
you seek him, he will be **f** ... 2 Chr 15:2
the LORD while he may be **f**; ... Is 55:6
he was lost, and is **f**.'" ... Lk 15:32

FOUNDATION
cornerstone, of a sure **f**: ... Is 28:16
For no one can lay a **f** ... 1 Cor 3:11
was foreknown before the **f** ... 1 Pt 1:20

FREE
LORD sets the prisoners **f**; ... Ps 146:7
and the truth will set you **f**." ... Jn 8:32
there is neither slave nor **f**, ... Gal 3:28

FREEDOM
to corruption and obtain the **f** ... Rom 8:21
For **f** Christ has set us free; ... Gal 5:1

FRIEND
as a man speaks to his **f** ... Ex 33:11
to ruin, but there is a **f** ... Prv 18:24
Do not forsake your **f** and ... Prv 27:10

FRIENDS
whisperer separates close **f**. ... Prv 16:28
in the house of my **f**.' ... Zec 13:6
lay down his life for his **f** ... Jn 15:13

FRIENDSHIP
The **f** of the LORD is for those ... Ps 25:14
Make no **f** with a man given ... Prv 22:24

GOAT
one male **g** for a sin offering; ... Nm 7:16
lie down with the young **g**, ... Is 11:6

GOATS
the sheep from the **g**. ... Mt 25:32
by means of the blood of **g** ... Heb 9:12

GOD
In the beginning, **G** created the ... Gn 1:1
Enoch walked with **G** after he ... Gn 5:22
Abraham said, "**G** will provide ... Gn 22:8
evil against me, but **G** meant ... Gn 50:20
no one like the LORD our **G**. ... Ex 8:10
"I am the LORD your **G**, who ... Ex 20:2
G is not man, that he should ... Nm 23:19
LORD your **G** is a consuming fire, ... Dt 4:24
You shall love the LORD your **G** ... Dt 6:5
A **G** of faithfulness and ... Dt 32:4
dismayed, for the LORD your **G** ... Jos 1:9
things that the LORD your **G** ... Jos 23:14
LORD and said, "O Lord **G**, ... Jgs 16:28
be my people, and your **G** ... Ru 1:16
there is no rock like our **G**. ... 1 Sm 2:2
But **G** will not take away ... 2 Sm 14:14
And **G** gave Solomon ... 1 Kgs 4:29
of Israel, there is no **G** ... 1 Kgs 8:23
If the LORD is **G**, follow ... 1 Kgs 18:21
"O LORD, the **G** of Israel, ... 2 Kgs 19:15
for the footstool of our **G**, ... 1 Chr 28:2
LORD filled the house of **G**. ... 2 Chr 5:14
He set himself to seek **G** ... 2 Chr 26:5
king, "The hand of our **G** ... Ezr 8:22
But you are a **G** ready to ... Neh 9:17
yet in my flesh I shall see **G**, ... Jb 19:26
my deliverer, my **G**, my rock, ... Ps 18:2
heavens declare the glory of **G**, ... Ps 19:1
My **G**, my **G**, why have you ... Ps 22:1
still, and know that I am **G**. ... Ps 46:10
Your way, O **G**, is holy. ... Ps 77:13
should set their hope in **G** ... Ps 78:7
O **G**, do not keep silence; do ... Ps 83:1
sing for joy to the living **G**. ... Ps 84:2
Every word of **G** proves true; ... Prv 30:5
Mighty **G**, Everlasting Father, ... Is 9:6
LORD is the everlasting **G**, ... Is 40:28
And I will be their **G**, and ... Jer 31:33
If this be so, our **G** whom we ... Dn 3:17
that are Caesar's, and to **G** ... Mt 22:21
The Lord our **G**, the Lord is ... Mk 12:29
will be impossible with **G**." ... Lk 1:37
shall love the Lord your **G** ... Lk 10:27
No one is good except **G** ... Lk 18:19
"For **G** so loved the world, that ... Jn 3:16
him, "My Lord and my **G**!" ... Jn 20:28
not lied to men but to **G**." ... Acts 5:4
'To the unknown **g**.' What ... Acts 17:23
but **G** shows his love for us in ... Rom 5:8
If **G** is for us, who can be ... Rom 8:31
Therefore be imitators of **G**, ... Eph 5:1
And my **G** will supply every ... Phil 4:19
For there is one **G**, and the ... 1 Tm 2:5
lacks wisdom, let him ask **G**, ... Jas 1:5
You believe that **G** is one; you ... Jas 2:19
holy, holy, is the Lord **G** ... Rv 4:8
For the Lord our **G** the ... Rv 19:6

GODLINESS
truth, which accords with **g**, ... Ti 1:1
that pertain to life and **g**, ... 2 Pt 1:3
be in lives of holiness and **g**, ... 2 Pt 3:11

GODLY
the LORD has set apart the **g** ... Ps 4:3
a peaceful and quiet life, **g** ... 1 Tm 2:2
all who desire to live a **g** ... 2 Tm 3:12

GODS
you, O LORD, among the **g**? ... Ex 15:11
shall have no other **g** before me. ... Ex 20:3
You shall not make **g** of silver ... Ex 20:23

GOLD
is better than silver or **g**. ... Prv 22:1
For which is greater, the **g** ... Mt 23:17
said, "I have no silver and **g**, ... Acts 3:6
more precious than **g** that ... 1 Pt 1:7

GOLIATH
a champion named **G** of Gath, ... 1 Sm 17:4

GOOD
and behold, it was very **g**. ... Gn 1:31
me, but God meant it for **g**, ... Gn 50:20
there is none who does **g**. ... Ps 14:1
No **g** thing does he withhold ... Ps 84:11
Woe to those who call evil **g** ... Is 5:20
The LORD is **g**, a stronghold in ... Na 1:7
said to him, 'Well done, **g** ... Mt 25:21
"Why do you call me **g**? ... Mk 10:18
Love your enemies, do **g** to ... Lk 6:27
are evil, know how to give **g** ... Lk 11:13
things work together for **g**, ... Rom 8:28
but overcome evil with **g**. ... Rom 12:21
us not grow weary of doing **g**, ... Gal 6:9
he who began a **g** work in you ... Phil 1:6
they may see your **g** deeds ... 1 Pt 2:12

GOODNESS
Surely **g** and mercy shall ... Ps 23:6
For how great is his **g**, and ... Zec 9:17
kindness, **g**, faithfulness, ... Gal 5:22

GOSPEL
and proclaiming the **g** ... Mt 4:23
the **g** must first be proclaimed ... Mk 13:10
it all for the sake of the **g**, ... 1 Cor 9:23
that we may preach the **g** ... 2 Cor 10:16
is preaching to you a **g** contrary ... Gal 1:9
from the hope of the **g** ... Col 1:23
to be entrusted with the **g**, ... 1 Thes 2:4
share in suffering for the **g** ... 2 Tm 1:8
overhead, with an eternal **g** ... Rv 14:6

GOSSIPS
maliciousness. They are **g**, ... Rom 1:29
not only idlers, but also **g** ... 1 Tm 5:13

GRACE
full of **g** and truth. ... Jn 1:14
and are justified by his **g** ... Rom 3:24
not under law but under **g**. ... Rom 6:14
But he said to me, "My **g** ... 2 Cor 12:9
you have fallen away from **g**. ... Gal 5:4
But **g** was given to each one ... Eph 4:7
The **g** of our Lord Jesus ... 2 Thes 3:18
For the **g** of God has appeared, ... Ti 2:11
near to the throne of **g**, ... Heb 4:16
set your hope fully on the **g** ... 1 Pt 1:13
stewards of God's varied **g**: ... 1 Pt 4:10
But grow in the **g** and ... 2 Pt 3:18

GRACIOUS
And I will be **g** to whom I ... Ex 33:19
to shine upon you and be **g** ... Nm 6:25
But the LORD was **g** to ... 2 Kgs 13:23
are a God merciful and **g**, ... Ps 86:15
The LORD is merciful and **g**, ... Ps 103:8
G is the LORD, and righteous; ... Ps 116:5
the LORD waits to be **g** ... Is 30:18
the God of hosts, will be **g** ... Am 5:15
Let your speech always be **g**, ... Col 4:6

GRAIN
brothers went down to buy **g** ... Gn 42:3
And the **g** offering with it ... Lv 23:13
The firstfruits of your **g**, of ... Dt 18:4
you provide their **g**, for so ... Ps 65:9
on good soil and produced **g**, ... Mt 13:8
choked it, and it yielded no **g**. ... Mk 4:7

GRASS
for man, his days are like **g**; ... Ps 103:15
But if God so clothes the **g**, ... Lk 12:28
for "All flesh is like **g** and all ... 1 Pt 1:24

GRAVE
their throat is an open **g**; they ... Ps 5:9
And they made his **g** with the ... Is 53:9
"Their throat is an open **g**; ... Rom 3:13

GREAT
And I will make of you a **g** ... Gn 12:2
How **g** are your works, O LORD! ... Ps 92:5
For your steadfast love is **g** ... Ps 108:4
G is the LORD, and greatly to ... Ps 145:3
is the **g** and first commandment ... Mt 22:38
But whoever would be **g** ... Mk 10:43
you all is the one who is **g**." ... Lk 9:48
in a cloud with power and **g** ... Lk 21:27
Now there is **g** gain in ... 1 Tm 6:6
escape if we neglect such a **g** ... Heb 2:3

GREATER
G love has no one than this, ... Jn 15:13
for he who is in you is **g** ... 1 Jn 4:4
I have no **g** joy than to hear ... 3 Jn 1:4

GREATEST
himself like this child is the **g** ... Mt 18:4
to which of them was the **g**. ... Lk 9:46
but the **g** of these is love. ... 1 Cor 13:13

GREATNESS
according to his excellent **g**! ... Ps 150:2
apparel, marching in the **g** ... Is 63:1

GREED
but inside they are full of **g** ... Mt 23:25
nor with a pretext for **g** ... 1 Thes 2:5

GREEDY
Whoever is **g** for unjust ... Prv 15:27
nor thieves, nor the **g**, ... 1 Cor 6:10
up to sensuality, **g** to practice ... Eph 4:19

GREEK
Jew first and also to the **G** ... Rom 1:16
There is neither Jew nor **G**, ... Gal 3:28

GREEN
will flourish like a **g** ... Prv 11:28

GREW
For he **g** up before him ... Is 53:2
And the child **g** and became ... Lk 2:40

GRIEF
g is upon me; my heart is sick ... Jer 8:18
but, though he cause **g**, ... Lam 3:32
For you felt a godly **g**, so ... 2 Cor 7:9

GRIEFS
Surely he has borne our **g** ... Is 53:4

GRIEVE
And do not **g** the Holy Spirit ... Eph 4:30
that you may not **g** as ... 1 Thes 4:13

GRIEVED
man on the earth, and it **g** ... Gn 6:6
Peter was **g** because he said ... Jn 21:17
you have been **g** by various trials, ... 1 Pt 1:6

GROAN
because the needy **g**, I will ... Ps 12:5
I **g** because of the tumult of ... Ps 38:8
land the wounded shall **g** ... Jer 51:52
For in this tent we **g**, ... 2 Cor 5:2

GROANING
And God heard their **g**, and ... Ex 2:24
me, from the words of my **g**? ... Ps 22:1
creation has been **g** together ... Rom 8:22
with joy and not with **g**, ... Heb 13:17

GROUND
not eat of it,' cursed is the **g** ... Gn 3:17
will never again curse the **g** ... Gn 8:21
of water into thirsty **g**, ... Ps 107:33

GROW
truth in love, we are to **g** ... Eph 4:15
But **g** in the grace and ... 2 Pt 3:18

GRUMBLE
nor **g**, as some of them ... 1 Cor 10:10
Do not **g** against one another, ... Jas 5:9

GRUMBLED
And the people **g** against ... Ex 15:24
all the people of Israel **g** ... Nm 14:2
Pharisees and their scribes **g** ... Lk 5:30

GRUMBLING
because he has heard your **g** ... Ex 16:7
Do all things without **g** ... Phil 2:14
to one another without **g**. ... 1 Pt 4:9

GUARANTEE
given us the Spirit as a **g**. ... 2 Cor 5:5
who is the **g** of our inheritance ... Eph 1:14

GUARANTEED
may rest on grace and be **g** ... Rom 4:16
of his purpose, he **g** it with ... Heb 6:17

GUARD
Oh, **g** my soul, and deliver ... Ps 25:20
So **g** yourselves in your ... Mal 2:15
all understanding, will **g** ... Phil 4:7
O Timothy, **g** the deposit ... 1 Tm 6:20

GUIDANCE
He did not seek **g** from the ... 1 Chr 10:14
who understands obtain **g**, ... Prv 1:5
Where there is no **g**, a people ... Prv 11:14

GUIDE
You **g** me with your counsel, ... Ps 73:24
And the LORD will **g** you ... Is 58:11
of truth comes, he will **g** ... Jn 16:13

GUIDED
you have **g** them by your ... Ex 15:13
his people like sheep and **g** ... Ps 78:52

GUILT
and Aaron shall bear any **g** ... Ex 28:38
pardon my **g**, for it is great. ... Ps 25:11
they acknowledge their **g** ... Hos 5:15
they found in him no **g** ... Acts 13:28

GUILTY
will by no means clear the **g**, ... Ex 34:7
name of brother if he is **g** ... 1 Cor 5:11
manner will be **g** concerning ... 1 Cor 11:27

HADES
will be brought down to **H**. ... Mt 11:23
and in **H**, being in torment, ... Lk 16:23
the keys of Death and **H**. ... Rv 1:18

HAGAR
servant whose name was **H** ... Gn 16:1

HAIR
not a **h** of your head will perish. ... Lk 21:18
wiped his feet with her **h**, ... Jn 11:2

HALLELUJAH
in heaven, crying out, "**H**! ... Rv 19:1

HAND
because he is at my right **h**, ... Ps 16:8
"Sit at my right **h**, until I ... Ps 110:1
Whatever your **h** finds to do, ... Eccl 9:10
needy, do not let your left **h** ... Mt 6:3
"Because I am not a **h**, ... 1 Cor 12:15

HANDS
He who has clean **h** and a pure ... Ps 24:4
Clap your **h**, all peoples! ... Ps 47:1
a little folding of the **h** to rest, ... Prv 6:10
and to work with your **h**, ... 1 Thes 4:11
should pray, lifting holy **h** ... 1 Tm 2:8
washings, the laying on of **h**, ... Heb 6:2

HARD
Is anything too **h** for the LORD? ... Gn 18:14
is narrow and the way is **h** ... Mt 7:14
they said, "This is a **h** saying; ... Jn 6:60

HARDEN
it was the LORD's doing to **h** ... Jos 11:20
do not **h** your hearts, as at ... Ps 95:8
do not **h** your hearts as in the ... Heb 3:8

HARDENED
has blinded their eyes and **h** ... Jn 12:40
it, but the rest were **h**, ... Rom 11:7
But their minds were **h** ... 2 Cor 3:14

HARDNESS
to them, "Because of your **h** ... Mt 19:8
with anger, grieved at their **h** ... Mk 3:5
in them, due to their **h** of heart. ... Eph 4:18

HARM
does him good, and not **h**, ... Prv 31:12
Son of God to their own **h** ... Heb 6:6
Now who is there to **h** you if ... 1 Pt 3:13

HARMONY
Live in **h** with one ... Rom 12:16
together in perfect **h**. ... Col 3:14

HARVEST
And he said to them, "The **h** ... Lk 10:2
that the fields are white for **h**. ... Jn 4:35
And a **h** of righteousness is ... Jas 3:18

HASTY
but he who has a **h** temper ... Prv 14:29
Do not be **h** in the laying ... 1 Tm 5:22

HATE
"You shall not **h** your ... Lv 19:17
your eyes; you **h** all evildoers. ... Ps 5:5
Do I not **h** those who **h** you, ... Ps 139:21
all who **h** me love death." ... Prv 8:36
H evil, and love good, and ... Am 5:15
do good to those who **h** you, ... Lk 6:27
but I do the very thing I **h**. ... Rom 7:15

HATED
our days in malice and envy, **h** ... Ti 3:3

HATES
six things that the LORD **h**, ... Prv 6:16
who does wicked things **h** ... Jn 3:20
says he is in the light and **h** ... 1 Jn 2:9

HATRED
The fear of the LORD is **h** of evil ... Prv 8:13
H stirs up strife, but love ... Prv 10:12

HEAD
he shall bruise your **h**, and ... Gn 3:15
burning coals on his **h**, ... Prv 25:22
helmet of salvation on his **h**; ... Is 59:17
has nowhere to lay his **h**." ... Mt 8:20
For the husband is the **h** ... Eph 5:23

HEAL
me; **h** me, for I have sinned ... Ps 41:4
H the sick, raise the dead, ... Mt 10:8
and turn, and I would **h** ... Acts 28:27

HEALED
you for help, and you have **h** ... Ps 30:2
another, that you may be **h** ... Jas 5:16
his wounds you have been **h**. ... 1 Pt 2:24

HEALING
shall rise with **h** in its wings ... Mal 4:2
gospel of the kingdom and **h** ... Mt 4:23
then gifts of **h**, helping, ... 1 Cor 12:28
of the tree were for the **h** ... Rv 22:2

HEALS
all your iniquity, who **h** ... Ps 103:3
He **h** the brokenhearted and ... Ps 147:3

HEALTH
you restore him to full **h**. ... Ps 41:3

sweetness to the soul and **h**.............Prv 16:24
Oh restore me to **h** and make.............Is 38:16

HEAR
In that day the deaf shall **h**................Is 29:18
And how are they to **h**.................Rom 10:14

HEARD
I had **h** of you by the hearing.............. Jb 42:5
Who has **h** such a thing? Who.............Is 66:8
"You have **h** that it was said to...........Mt 5:21
no eye has seen, nor ear **h**,............... 1 Cor 2:9
of God, which you **h** from............. 1 Thes 2:13

HEART
LORD your God with all your **h**................. Dt 6:5
to him freely, and your **h**.................... Dt 15:10
to serve him with all your **h**................Jos 22:5
a man after his own **h**,..................1 Sm 13:14
the LORD looks on the **h**."................1 Sm 16:7
My eyes and my **h** will be................ 2 Chr 7:16
give you the desires of your **h**.............Ps 37:4
Create in me a clean **h**, O God,..........Ps 51:10
cherished iniquity in my **h**,................Ps 66:18
in the LORD with all your **h**,....................Prv 3:5
A joyful **h** is good medicine, ...Prv 17:22
A wise man's **h** inclines him............ Eccl 10:2
The **h** is deceitful above all .... Jer 17:9
I will give you a new **h**,..................... Ez 36:26
treasure is, there your **h** will be..........Mt 6:21
this they were cut to the **h**,..............Acts 2:37
draw near with a true **h**..................Heb 10:22
he who searches mind and **h**, ...Rv 2:23

HEARTS
that he may incline our **h**............... 1 Kgs 8:58
for the LORD searches all **h**............ 1 Chr 28:9
"Let not your **h** be troubled................. Jn 14:1
having cleansed their **h**..................Acts 15:9
law is written on their **h**,.................Rom 2:15
but on tablets of human **h**. .... 2 Cor 3:3
Christ may dwell in your **h**.................Eph 3:17

HEAVEN
"How you are fallen from **h**,................Is 14:12
behold, with the clouds of **h**............... Dn 7:13
enter the kingdom of **h**......................Mt 19:23
to them, "All authority in **h**................Mt 28:18
But our citizenship is in **h**, ...Phil 3:20
and unfading, kept in **h** for you,......... 1 Pt 1:4

HEAVENLY
him a little lower than the **h** beings......Ps 8:5
can you believe if I tell you **h**............... Jn 3:12
seated us with him in the **h**................Eph 2:6
better country, that is, a **h**..............Heb 11:16

HEAVENS
The **h** declare the glory of God,...........Ps 19:1
The **h** declare his righteousness..........Ps 50:6
love is great above the **h**;..................Ps 108:4
we are waiting for new **h**................. 2 Pt 3:13

HEAVY
and night your hand was **h**.................Ps 32:4
like a **h** burden, they are too................Ps 38:4
all who labor and are **h**....................Mt 11:28

HEIR
own son shall be your **h**."................... Gn 15:4
a son, and if a son, then an **h**............ Gal 4:7
whom he appointed the **h**....................Heb 1:2
the world and became an **h**..............Heb 11:7

HEIRS
vessel, since they are **h** with .... 1 Pt 3:7

HELL
will be liable to the **h** of fire. ....Mt 5:22
both soul and body in **h**....................Mt 10:28
of life, and set on fire by **h**. ....Jas 3:6

HELMET
as a breastplate, and a **h**...................Is 59:17
faith and love, and for a **h**............ 1 Thes 5:8

HELP
is none like you to **h**, ... 2 Chr 14:11
to my God I cried for **h**. From ....Ps 18:6
strength, a very present **h**...................Ps 46:1
H us, O God of our salvation,...............Ps 79:9
From where does my **h** come?...........Ps 121:1
will strengthen you, I will **h**................Is 41:10
"I believe; **h** my unbelief!" ....Mk 9:24

HELPER
I will make him a **h** fit for him."........ Gn 2:18
have been the **h** of the fatherless......Ps 10:14
say, "The Lord is my **h**; I will.............Heb 13:6

HID
and the man and his wife **h**................ Gn 3:8
And Moses **h** his face, for he................ Ex 3:6
shall live, because she **h**....................Jos 6:17

HIDDEN
and search for it as for **h**.....................Prv 2:4
to you new things, **h** things..................Is 48:6
God, and your sins have **h**....................Is 59:2
the mystery **h** for ages and................Col 1:26

HIDE
h me in the shadow of your wings,......Ps 17:8
H your face from my sins, and.............Ps 51:9
And I will not **h** my face any............. Ez 39:29

HIDING
You are a **h** place for me; you ....Ps 32:7
You are my **h** place and my ....Ps 119:114

HIGH
name of the LORD, the Most **H**. ....Ps 7:17
called the Son of the Most **H**. .... Lk 1:32

HILL
shall dwell on your holy **h**? ....Ps 15:1
city set on a **h** cannot be hidden. ....Mt 5:14

HILLS
the cattle on a thousand **h**. ....Ps 50:10
I lift up my eyes to the **h**....................Ps 121:1

HINDER
for us, for nothing can **h** ....1 Sm 14:6
come to me and do not **h**...................Mt 19:14

HOLD
Keep **h** of instruction; do not ....Prv 4:13
For I, the LORD your God, **h** ....Is 41:13
who, hearing the word, **h**..................... Lk 8:15

HOLINESS
the LORD in the splendor of **h**. ....Ps 29:2
bringing **h** to completion.................. 2 Cor 7:1
in true righteousness and **h**. ....Eph 4:24
and for the **h** without which............Heb 12:14

HOME
come **h** with shouts of joy,....................Ps 126:6
come to him and make our **h**............. Jn 14:23
pure, working at **h**, kind, ... Ti 2:5

HOMES
"See, we have left our **h**.................... Lk 18:28
breaking bread in their **h**, ...Acts 2:46

HOMOSEXUALITY
nor men who practice **h**,.................. 1 Cor 6:9
men who practice **h**, enslavers........ 1 Tm 1:10

HONEST
speaks the truth gives **h**.................Prv 12:17
Whoever gives an **h** answer..............Prv 24:26

HONEY
land flowing with milk and **h**, ... Ex 3:8
sweeter also than **h** and.....................Ps 19:10
my taste, sweeter than **h**..............Ps 119:103

HONOR
"**H** your father and your..................... Ex 20:12
crowned him with glory and **h**. ....Ps 8:5
humility comes before **h**....................Prv 15:33
For God commanded, '**H** your..............Mt 15:4
that a prophet has no **h**....................... Jn 4:44
"**H** your father and mother"................Eph 6:2
worthy of double **h**,......................... 1 Tm 5:17
Let marriage be held in **h**.................Heb 13:4
creatures give glory and **h**.....................Rv 4:9

HONORABLE
is true, whatever is **h**, ...Phil 4:8
wood and clay, some for **h**.............. 2 Tm 2:20

HONORS
person is despised, but who **h**............Ps 15:4
is generous to the needy **h** ....Prv 14:31

HOPE
do I wait? My **h** is in you.......................Ps 39:7
H in God; for I shall again ....Ps 42:5
I **h** in your word. ....Ps 119:81
H deferred makes the heart.............Prv 13:12
We set our **h** on you, for you............. Jer 14:22
Rejoice in **h**, be patient in ....Rom 12:12
So now faith, **h**, and love............. 1 Cor 13:13
On him we have set our **h**.............. 2 Cor 1:10
eagerly wait for the **h**........................ Gal 5:5
and our boasting in our **h**..................Heb 3:6
to be born again to a living **h**............ 1 Pt 1:3

HORSE
the **h** and his rider he has................... Ex 15:1
not in the strength of the **h**, ...Ps 147:10
A whip for the **h**, a bridle....................Prv 26:3
a man riding on a red **h**! He................ Zec 1:8
looked, and behold, a white **h**! ....Rv 6:2
and behold, a white **h**! The ....Rv 19:11

HOSANNA
the Lord! **H** in the highest!" ....Mt 21:9

HOSPITABLE
respectable, **h**, able to teach,............1 Tm 3:2
but **h**, a lover of good,............................Ti 1:8

HOSPITALITY
saints and seek to show **h**.............Rom 12:13
up children, has shown **h**,...............1 Tm 5:10

HOST
were finished, and all the **h** .... Gn 2:1
As the **h** of heaven cannot............... Jer 33:22
multitude of the heavenly **h** .... Lk 2:13

HOSTILE
that is set on the flesh is **h** ....Rom 8:7
once were alienated and **h** ....Col 1:21
from sinners such **h** ....Heb 12:3

HOUR
anxious can add a single **h** ....Mt 6:27
But the **h** is coming, and is................ Jn 4:23

HOUSE
But as for me and my **h**,...................Jos 24:15
and I shall dwell in the **h** ....Ps 23:6
the LORD builds the **h**,.........................Ps 127:1
By wisdom a **h** is built, and by...........Prv 24:3
h shall be called a **h** of prayer.............Is 56:7
divided against itself, that **h** .... Mk 3:25
In my Father's **h** are many.................. Jn 14:2

HOUSEHOLD
will be those of his own **h**.................Mt 10:36
He must manage his own **h**..............1 Tm 3:4

HUMAN
"Whoever takes a **h** life shall .... Lv 24:17
a stone was cut out by no **h** .... Dn 2:34

HUMBLE
are called by my name **h** .... 2 Chr 7:14
he adorns the **h** with salvation..........Ps 149:4
he who is **h** and contrite in...................Is 66:2
walk in pride he is able to **h**.............. Dn 4:37
but gives grace to the **h**." ....Jas 4:6
H yourselves before the Lord, ...Jas 4:10
H yourselves, therefore,...................... 1 Pt 5:6

HUMBLED
exalts himself will be **h**, ...Mt 23:12
he **h** himself by becoming ....Phil 2:8

HUMILITY
in wisdom, and **h** comes ....Prv 15:33
h, meekness, and patience, ...Col 3:12
yourselves, all of you, with **h** .... 1 Pt 5:5

HUNGER
they shall not **h** or thirst,.....................Is 49:10
"Blessed are those who **h** and..............Mt 5:6
comes to me shall not **h**,..................... Jn 6:35
They shall **h** no more, neither ....Rv 7:16

HUNGRY
the longing soul, and the **h** ....Ps 107:9
who gives food to the **h**. ....Ps 146:7
If your enemy is **h**, give ....Prv 25:21
gives his bread to the **h** and .... Ez 18:7
"Blessed are you who are **h**..................Lk 6:21
if your enemy is **h**, feed him ....Rom 12:20

HURT
the fire, and they are not **h**;............... Dn 3:25
who conquers will not be **h**.................Rv 2:11

HUSBAND
shall be contrary to your **h**,................ Gn 3:16
wife is the crown of her **h**,..................Prv 12:4
I betrothed you to one **h**,.............. 2 Cor 11:2

HUSBANDS
H, love your wives, as......................Eph 5:25
young women to love their **h**.................. Ti 2:4
Likewise, **h**, live with your ....1 Pt 3:7

HYMN
when they had sung a **h**,..................Mt 26:30
each one has a **h**, a lesson,.......... 1 Cor 14:26

HYMNS
praying and singing **h**...................Acts 16:25
singing psalms and **h** and ....Col 3:16

HYPOCRISY
but within you are full of **h**..............Mt 23:28
of the Pharisees, which is **h**. .... Lk 12:1
malice and all deceit and **h** .... 1 Pt 2:1

HYPOCRITE
You **h**, first take the log out of..............Mt 7:5

HYPOCRITES
nor do I consort with **h**. ....Ps 26:4
you must not be like the **h**.....................Mt 6:5
put me to the test, you **h**? ....Mt 22:18

IDLE
brothers, admonish the **i**,............ 1 Thes 5:14
because we were not **i**.................. 2 Thes 3:7
from long ago is not **i**,........................ 2 Pt 2:3

IDOL
it he makes into a god, his **i**,..............Is 44:17
"an **i** has no real existence,"........... 1 Cor 8:4
is anything, or that an **i** .... 1 Cor 10:19

IDOLATER
or greed, or is an **i**, reviler, ... 1 Cor 5:11
an **i**), has no inheritance in................Eph 5:5

IDOLATRY
my beloved, flee from **i**................ 1 Cor 10:14
i, sorcery, enmity, strife,.................... Gal 5:20
and covetousness, which is **i**. ....Col 3:5

IDOLS
concerning food offered to **i**: .... 1 Cor 8:1
you turned to God from **i**................ 1 Thes 1:9
keep yourselves from **i**...................... 1 Jn 5:21

IGNORANT
being **i** of the righteousness...............Rom 10:3
with foolish, **i** controversies; ....2 Tm 2:23

IGNORES
at once, but the prudent **i** ....Prv 12:16
disgrace come to him who **i** ....Prv 13:18
Whoever **i** instruction ....Prv 15:32

IMAGE
make for yourself a carved **i**,.............. Ex 20:4
the glory of God for the **i**.................Ps 106:20
conformed to the **i** of his Son, ...Rom 8:29
we shall also bear the **i**...............1 Cor 15:49
He is the **i** of the invisible ....Col 1:15

IMITATE
ourselves an example to **i**............... 2 Thes 3:9
of their way of life, and **i** ....Heb 13:7
do not **i** evil but **i** good .... 3 Jn 1:11

IMITATORS
And you became **i** of us and .... 1 Thes 1:6
may not be sluggish, but **i** ....Heb 6:12

IMMANUEL
and shall call his name **I**. ....Is 7:14
call his name **I**" (which means, ...Mt 1:23

IMMORAL
everyone who is sexually **i** ....Eph 5:5
the sexually **i**, men who..................1 Tm 1:10
the sexually **i**, sorcerers,......................Rv 21:8

IMMORALITY
evident: sexual **i**, impurity, ... Gal 5:19
you abstain from sexual **i**;............. 1 Thes 4:3

IMMORTAL
exchanged the glory of the **i** God ......Rom 1:23
To the King of ages, **i**,........................1 Tm 1:17

IMMORTALITY
for glory and honor and **i**,...................Rom 2:7
who alone has **i**, who........................1 Tm 6:16
and brought life and **i** ....2 Tm 1:10

IMPERISHABLE
wreath, but we an **i**. .... 1 Cor 9:25
body must put on the **i**, ... 1 Cor 15:53
of perishable seed but of **i**, ... 1 Pt 1:23

IMPORTANT
commandment is the most **i** .... Mk 12:28

IMPOSSIBLE
propose to do will now be **i**................. Gn 11:6
move, and nothing will be **i**...............Mt 17:20

IMPURITY
not repented of the **i**,.................. 2 Cor 12:21
God has not called us for **i**, ... 1 Thes 4:7

INCENSE
put the golden altar for **i**..................... Ex 40:5
my prayer be counted as **i**...................Ps 141:2
having the golden altar of **i**..................Heb 9:4

INCOME
trouble befalls the **i** of the wicked......Prv 15:6
who loves wealth with his **i**;............. Eccl 5:10

INCREASE
if riches **i**, set not your ....Ps 62:10
said to the Lord, "**I** our faith!" .... Lk 17:5
He must **i**, but I must .... Jn 3:30

INCREASED
And Jesus **i** in wisdom and in.............. Lk 2:52
word of God **i** and multiplied.........Acts 12:24
trespass, but where sin **i**,.................Rom 5:20

INCREASING
the disciples were **i** in number, ...Acts 6:1
in every good work and **i**....................Col 1:10
of you for one another is **i**.............. 2 Thes 1:3

INEXPRESSIBLE
Thanks be to God for his **i** .... 2 Cor 9:15
and rejoice with joy that is **i**.............. 1 Pt 1:8

INFANTS
of the mouth of babies and **i**, Ps 8:2
read, "'Out of the mouth of **i** Mt 21:16
Be **i** in evil, but in your 1 Cor 14:20
Like newborn **i**, long for the 1 Pt 2:2

INHERIT
But the meek shall **i** the land Ps 37:11
are the meek, for they shall **i** Mt 5:5

INHERITANCE
that I may glory with your **i** Ps 106:5
the riches of his glorious **i** Eph 1:18
you to share in the **i** Col 1:12
the promised eternal **i**, Heb 9:15

INIQUITIES
repay us according to our **i** Ps 103:10
he was crushed for our **i**; Is 53:5
be merciful toward their **i**, Heb 8:12

INIQUITY
of faithfulness and without **i**, Dt 32:4
me thoroughly from my **i**, Ps 51:2
of the Lord depart from **i**." 2 Tm 2:19

INJUSTICE
you do, for there is no **i** 2 Chr 19:7
Is there **i** on God's part? By Rom 9:14

INNOCENT
I shall be blameless, and **i** Ps 19:13
so be wise as serpents and **i** Mt 10:16
you may be blameless and **i**, Phil 2:15
priest, holy, **i**, unstained, Heb 7:26

INSOLENT
slanderers, haters of God, **i**, Rom 1:30
persecutor, and **i** opponent 1 Tm 1:13

INSTRUCT
I will **i** you and teach you in Ps 32:8
knowledge and able to **i** Rom 15:14
mind of the Lord so as to **i** 1 Cor 2:16

INSTRUCTION
Hear, O sons, a father's **i**, and Prv 4:1
so that he may be able to give **i** Ti 1:9

INSTRUMENTS
play my music on stringed **i** Is 38:20
If even lifeless **i**, such as 1 Cor 14:7

INSULT
who has avenged the **i** 1 Sm 25:39
the prudent ignores an **i** Prv 12:16
in saying these things you **i** Lk 11:45

INSULTS
whoever **i** his brother will be Mt 5:22
weaknesses, **i**, hardships, 2 Cor 12:10

INTEGRITY
your father walked, with **i** 1 Kgs 9:4
I die I will not put away my **i** Jb 27:5
I will walk with **i** of heart Ps 101:2
and in your teaching show **i**, Ti 2:7

INTELLIGENCE
of God, with ability and **i**, Ex 31:3
listens to reproof gains **i**. Prv 15:32

INTERCESSION
the sin of many, and makes **i** Is 53:12
he always lives to make **i** Heb 7:25

INTERESTS
and his **i** are divided. And 1 Cor 7:34
look not only to his own **i**, Phil 2:4

INTERPRET
You know how to **i** the Mt 16:3
if there is no one to **i**, 1 Cor 14:28

INTERPRETATION
tongues, to another the **i** 1 Cor 12:10
from someone's own **i**. 2 Pt 1:20

INVITE
But when you give a feast, **i** Lk 14:13

IRON
I sharpens **i**, and one man Prv 27:17
rule them with a rod of **i**. Rv 19:15

IRREVERENT
Have nothing to do with **i**, 1 Tm 4:7
But avoid **i** babble, for it 2 Tm 2:16

ISAAC
she tells you, for through **I** Gn 21:12
he was tested, offered up **I**, Heb 11:17

ISHMAEL
You shall call his name **I**, Gn 16:11

ISRAEL
spoke thus to the people of **I**, Ex 6:9
I was holy to the LORD, the Jer 2:3
lost sheep of the house of **I**. Mt 10:6
I failed to obtain what it Rom 11:7

JACOB
so his name was called **J**. Gn 25:26
Now the sons of **J** were twelve. Gn 35:22

JEALOUS
I the LORD your God am a **j** Ex 20:5
I am exceedingly **j** for Jerusalem Zec 1:14
to make my fellow Jews **j**, Rom 11:14

JEALOUSY
they moved him to **j**. Ps 78:58
For while there is **j** and 1 Cor 3:3

JERICHO
When Joshua was by **J**, he Jos 5:13
By faith the walls of **J** fell Heb 11:30

JERUSALEM
the ark of God back to **J**, 2 Sm 15:29
desired to build in **J**, 1 Kgs 9:19
He carried away all **J** 2 Kgs 24:14
So I went to **J** and was Neh 2:11
I create **J** to be a joy, and her Is 65:18
"O **J**, **J**, the city that Mt 23:37
boy Jesus stayed behind in **J**. Lk 2:43
the heavenly **J**, and to Heb 12:22
the new **J**, which comes down Rv 3:12

JESUS
and you shall call his name **J**, Mt 1:21
Then **J** was led up by the Spirit Mt 4:1
But **J** remained silent. And Mt 26:63
beginning of the gospel of **J** Mk 1:1
And at the ninth hour **J** Mk 15:34
and truth came through **J**. Jn 1:17
"I am **J**, whom you are persecuting. Acts 9:5
"Believe in the Lord **J**, Acts 16:31
"This **J**, whom I proclaim to Acts 17:3
"**J** I know, and Paul Acts 19:15
J himself being the cornerstone, Eph 2:20
so that at the name of **J** Phil 2:10
in the name of the Lord **J**, Col 3:17
of our great God and Savior **J** Ti 2:13
J, the Son of God, let us hold Heb 4:14
and coming of our Lord **J** 2 Pt 1:16
The revelation of **J** Christ, Rv 1:1
soon." Amen. Come, Lord **J**! Rv 22:20

JEW
the **J** first and also to the Greek. Rom 1:16
the Jews I became as a **J**, 1 Cor 9:20
There is neither **J** nor Greek, Gal 3:28

JEWELS
She is more precious than **j**, Prv 3:15
adorns herself with her **j**. Is 61:10
for like the **j** of a crown they Zec 9:16

JEWS
has been born king of the **J**? Mt 2:2
"Are you the King of the **J**?" Mt 27:11
for salvation is from the **J**. Jn 4:22
For **J** demand signs and 1 Cor 1:22

JOIN
and do not **j** with those who Prv 24:21
j in imitating me, and keep Phil 3:17
surprised when you do not **j** 1 Pt 4:4

JOINED
What therefore God has **j** Mt 19:6
But he who is **j** to the Lord 1 Cor 6:17
being **j** together, grows into a Eph 2:21

JOY
the **j** of the LORD is your strength Neh 8:10
You have put more **j** in my Ps 4:7
you make him glad with the **j** Ps 21:6
to God my exceeding **j**, and I Ps 43:4
Shout for **j** to God, all the earth; Ps 66:1
take **j** in the God of my salvation Hb 3:18
in my womb leaped for **j**. Lk 1:44
you good news of great **j** Lk 2:10
j, peace, patience, kindness, Gal 5:22
with the **j** of the Holy Spirit, 1 Thes 1:6
Count it all **j**, my brothers, Jas 1:2
in him and rejoice with **j** 1 Pt 1:8

JOYFUL
Make a **j** noise to the LORD, all Ps 98:4

JUDGE
for he comes to **j** the earth. 1 Chr 16:33
God is a righteous **j**, and a God Ps 7:11
he will **j** the peoples with equity Ps 96:10
for there I will sit to **j** all the Jl 3:12
for I did not come to **j** the Jn 12:47
a day on which he will **j** Acts 17:31

JUDGED
under the law will be **j** Rom 2:12
But if we **j** ourselves 1 Cor 11:31
that we who teach will be **j** Jas 3:1

JUDGES
Then the LORD raised up **j**, ... Jgs 2:16
surely there is a God who **j** .... Ps 58:11
call on him as Father who **j** .... 1 Pt 1:17

JUDGMENT
but it is God who executes **j**, ... Ps 75:7
bring every deed into **j**, ... Eccl 12:14
will the LORD enter into **j**, ... Is 66:16
but has given all **j** to the Son, ... Jn 5:22
a fearful expectation of **j**, ... Heb 10:27
Mercy triumphs over **j**. .... Jas 2:13
For it is time for **j** to begin at .... 1 Pt 4:17

JUST
iniquity, **j** and upright is he. .... Dt 32:4
his hands are faithful and **j**; .... Ps 111:7
so that he might be **j** and .... Rom 3:26

JUSTICE
He executes **j** for the .... Dt 10:18
You shall not pervert **j**. You .... Dt 16:19
j and abundant righteousness .... Jb 37:23
sing of steadfast love and **j**; .... Ps 101:1
are they who observe **j**, ... Ps 106:3
When **j** is done, it is a joy to .... Prv 21:15
men do not understand **j**, ... Prv 28:5
seek **j**, correct oppression; .... Is 1:17
And I will make **j** the line, ... Is 28:17
For I the LORD love **j**; I hate .... Is 61:8
and establish **j** in the gate; it .... Am 5:15
But let **j** roll down like .... Am 5:24
LORD require of you but to do **j**, ... Mi 6:8
j and mercy and faithfulness. .... Mt 23:23
enforced **j**, obtained .... Heb 11:33

JUSTIFICATION
and raised for our **j**. .... Rom 4:25
many trespasses brought **j**. .... Rom 5:16

JUSTIFIED
so that you may be **j** in your .... Ps 51:4
you were **j** in the name of .... 1 Cor 6:11
it is evident that no one is **j** .... Gal 3:11
so that being **j** by his grace we .... Ti 3:7

JUSTIFIES
He who **j** the wicked and he .... Prv 17:15
work but believes in him who **j** .... Rom 4:5
elect? It is God who **j**. .... Rom 8:33

KEEP
of Eden to work it and **k** it. .... Gn 2:15
The LORD bless you and **k** .... Nm 6:24
to fear me and to **k** all my .... Dt 5:29
all evil; he will **k** your life. .... Ps 121:7
to **k** you from stumbling .... Jude 1:24

KEEPS
the faithful God who **k** .... Dt 7:9
commandments and **k** them, ... Jn 14:21

KEPT
For when I **k** silent, my .... Ps 32:3
k in heaven for you, ... 1 Pt 1:4

KEYS
I will give you the **k** of the .... Mt 16:19
and I have the **k** of Death .... Rv 1:18

KILL
a time to **k**, and a time to .... Eccl 3:3
and they will **k** him, and he .... Mt 17:23

KILLED
and you **k** the Author of .... Acts 3:15
we are being **k** all the day .... Rom 8:36

KILLS
and whoever **k** a person .... Lv 24:21
For the letter **k**, but the .... 2 Cor 3:6

KIND
his words and **k** in all his .... Ps 145:13
for he is **k** to the ungrateful .... Lk 6:35
Love is patient and **k**; love .... 1 Cor 13:4
pure, working at home, **k**, ... Ti 2:5

KINDNESS
"He who withholds **k** from a .... Jb 6:14
I led them with cords of **k**, ... Hos 11:4
but to do justice, and to love **k**, ... Mi 6:8
of his **k** and forbearance and .... Rom 2:4
fallen, but God's **k** to you, ... Rom 11:22
k, goodness, faithfulness, ... Gal 5:22
k, humility, meekness, ... Col 3:12

KINDS
produced in me all **k** of .... Rom 7:8
is a root of all **k** of evils. .... 1 Tm 6:10

KING
In those days there was no **k**. .... Jgs 17:6
your God was your **k**. .... 1 Sm 12:12
that the **K** of glory may come. .... Ps 24:7
the LORD sits enthroned as **k** .... Ps 29:10
has been born **k** of the Jews? .... Mt 2:2
your **k** is coming to you, ... Mt 21:5
he himself is Christ, a **k**." .... Lk 23:2
You are the **K** of Israel!" .... Jn 1:49
"You say that I am a **k**. For .... Jn 18:37
"We have no **k** but Caesar." .... Jn 19:15
K of kings and Lord of lords. .... Rv 19:16

KINGDOM
and you shall be to me a **k** of .... Ex 19:6
Yours is the **k**, O LORD, ... 1 Chr 29:11
His **k** is an everlasting .... Dn 4:3
"Repent, for the **k** of heaven is .... Mt 3:2
Your **k** come, your will be .... Mt 6:10
But seek first the **k** of God .... Mt 6:33
And this gospel of the **k** .... Mt 24:14
inherit the **k** prepared for .... Mt 25:34
for to such belongs the **k** of .... Mk 10:14
for behold, the **k** of God is .... Lk 17:21
he cannot enter the **k** of God. .... Jn 3:5
a **k** that cannot be shaken, ... Heb 12:28

KINGS
May all **k** fall down before .... Ps 72:11
and all the **k** of the earth .... Ps 102:15
is God of gods and Lord of **k**, ... Dn 2:47
for **k** and all who are in .... 1 Tm 2:2
and the ruler of **k** on earth. .... Rv 1:5

KISS
K the Son, lest he be angry, ... Ps 2:12
righteousness and peace **k** .... Ps 85:10
the Son of Man with a **k**?" .... Lk 22:48

KNEE
'To me every **k** shall bow, ... Is 45:23
not bowed the **k** to Baal." .... Rom 11:4
every **k** shall bow to me, ... Rom 14:11
Jesus every **k** should bow, ... Phil 2:10

KNEES
For this reason I bow my **k** .... Eph 3:14

KNEW
you in the womb I **k** you, ... Jer 1:5
For although they **k** God, ... Rom 1:21

KNOCK
seek, and you will find; **k**, and it .... Mt 7:7
I stand at the door and **k**. .... Rv 3:20

KNOW
K then in your heart that, ... Dt 8:5
For I **k** that my Redeemer .... Jb 19:25
"I **k** that you can do all .... Jb 42:2
still, and **k** that I am God. .... Ps 46:10
And I applied my heart to **k** .... Eccl 1:17
saying, '**K** the LORD,' for they .... Jer 31:34
do not let your left hand **k** .... Mt 6:3
yet the world did not **k** him. .... Jn 1:10
therefore **k** for certain that .... Acts 2:36
part; then I shall **k** fully, ... 1 Cor 13:12
that I may **k** him and the .... Phil 3:10
yet you do not **k** what .... Jas 4:14

KNOWLEDGE
counsel by words without **k**? .... Jb 38:2
Such **k** is too wonderful for .... Ps 139:6
LORD is the beginning of **k**; .... Prv 1:7
loves discipline loves **k**, ... Prv 12:1
Desire without **k** is not good, ... Prv 19:2
be full of the **k** of the LORD .... Is 11:9
the **k** of him everywhere. .... 2 Cor 2:14
of Christ that surpasses **k**, ... Eph 3:19
treasures of wisdom and **k** .... Col 2:3
what is falsely called "**k**," .... 1 Tm 6:20

KNOWN
Make them **k** to your children .... Dt 4:9
You make **k** to me the path .... Ps 16:11
or hidden that will not be **k**. .... Mt 10:26
"For who has **k** the mind .... Rom 11:34

KNOWS
But he **k** the way that I take; .... Jb 23:10
For he **k** the secrets of the .... Ps 44:21
he **k** those who take refuge in .... Na 1:7
"The Lord **k** those who are .... 2 Tm 2:19

LABOR
Six days you shall **l**, and do .... Ex 20:9
not run in vain or **l** in vain. .... Phil 2:16

LABORER
Sweet is the sleep of a **l**, ... Eccl 5:12
"The **l** deserves his wages." .... 1 Tm 5:18

LACK
the LORD **l** no good thing. .... Ps 34:10
of your **l** of self-control. .... 1 Cor 7:5

LACKS
worthless pursuits **l** sense. .... Prv 12:11
If any of you **l** wisdom, let .... Jas 1:5

LAMB
and kill the Passover l. .... Ex 12:21
said, "Behold, the **L** of God, ... Jn 1:29
like a l before its shearer ....Acts 8:32
like that of a l without..................... 1 Pt 1:19
the elders I saw a **L** standing, ...Rv 5:6
"Worthy is the **L** who was ....Rv 5:12

LAMBS
I am sending you out as l in .... Lk 10:3
He said to him, "Feed my l." .... Jn 21:15

LAME
their sight and the l walk, ...Mt 11:5
to enter life l than with two................ Mk 9:45
so that what is l may not ....Heb 12:13

LAMP
For you are my l, O LORD, ...2 Sm 22:29
Your word is a l to my....................Ps 119:105
For the commandment is a l ....Prv 6:23
Nor do people light a l and ....Mt 5:15
light, and its l is the Lamb................Rv 21:23

LAMPS
who took their l and went to................Mt 25:1
and keep your l burning, ... Lk 12:35

LAND
and let the dry l appear." And .... Gn 1:9
offspring I will give this l." .... Gn 12:7
You shall not pollute the l .... Nm 35:33
their sin and heal their l. .... 2 Chr 7:14
LORD in the l of the living...................Ps 116:9
upright will inhabit the l, ...Prv 2:21
off out of the l of the living, ...Is 53:8
bring you into your own l. .... Ez 36:24

LANGUAGE
had one l and the same .... Gn 11:1
them speak in his own l. ....Acts 2:6
tribe and l and people and....................Rv 5:9

LAST
first, and with the l; I am he. ....Is 41:4
"I am the first and I am the l; ....Is 44:6
raise him up on the l day."................... Jn 6:40

LAUGH
time to weep, and a time to l; .... Eccl 3:4
weep now, for you shall l. .... Lk 6:21

LAUGHS
He who sits in the heavens l; ....Ps 2:4
but the Lord l at the wicked, ...Ps 37:13

LAUGHTER
said, "God has made l for me; .... Gn 21:6
our mouth was filled with l, ...Ps 126:2
Let your l be turned to ....Jas 4:9

LAW
do all the words of this l. .... Dt 29:29
from the **L** of God, clearly, ...Neh 8:8
but his delight is in the l of.....................Ps 1:2
for a l will go out from me, ...Is 51:4
I will put my l within them, ... Jer 31:33
abolish the **L** or the Prophets; ....Mt 5:17
for this is the **L** and the.........................Mt 7:12
For the l was given through................. Jn 1:17
For the l brings wrath,......................Rom 4:15
is the fulfilling of the l. ....Rom 13:10
the power of sin is the l................ 1 Cor 15:56
of the l but through faith ....Gal 2:16
For the whole l is fulfilled...................Gal 5:14
by abolishing the l of ....Eph 2:15
own that comes from the l, ...Phil 3:9
keeps the whole l but fails in.................Jas 2:10

LAWLESSNESS
us from all l and to purify ....Ti 2:14
of sinning also practices l; .... 1 Jn 3:4

LAYING
I am l in Zion a stone of ....Rom 9:33
Do not be hasty in the l .... 1 Tm 5:22
not l again a foundation of ....Heb 6:1

LEAD
of cloud to l them along the .... Ex 13:21
L me, O LORD, in your ....Ps 5:8
L me in your truth and teach...................Ps 25:5
and a little child shall l them...............Is 11:6
and gently l those that are.................Is 40:11
And if the blind l the blind, ...Mt 15:14
that we may l a peaceful................... 1 Tm 2:2

LEADS
He l me beside still waters..................Ps 23:2
the way is hard that l to life, ...Mt 7:14
There is sin that l to death; .... 1 Jn 5:16

LEARN
l to do good; seek justice, ...Is 1:17
upon you, and l from me, ...Mt 11:29

LEARNED
What you have l and............................Phil 4:9
you have l and have firmly ....2 Tm 3:14

LEAST
Yet the one who is l in the ....Mt 11:11
For I am the l of the..................... 1 Cor 15:9
from the l of them to the ....Heb 8:11

LEAVE
Peace I l with you; my peace .... Jn 14:27
"I will never l you nor ....Heb 13:5

LED
like a lamb that is l to the.......................Is 53:7
I l them with cords of ....Hos 11:4
For all who are l by the....................Rom 8:14
But if you are l by the Spirit, ... Gal 5:18

LEND
to him and l him sufficient for............ Dt 15:8
And if you l to those from .... Lk 6:34

LENDS
to the poor l to the LORD, ...Prv 19:17

LENGTH
l of days forever and ever. ....Ps 21:4
for l of days and years of life...............Prv 3:2
and l and height and ....Eph 3:18

LETTER
by the Spirit, not by the l. ....Rom 2:29
For the l kills, but the....................... 2 Cor 3:6
what we say in this l, ... 2 Thes 3:14

LETTERS
For they say, "His l are .... 2 Cor 10:10
as he does in all his l when............ 2 Pt 3:16

LEVEL
My foot stands on l ground; ....Ps 26:12
The path of the righteous is l; ....Is 26:7
places shall become l ways, ... Lk 3:5

LIAR
poor man is better than a l. ....Prv 19:22
for he is a l and the father of............. Jn 8:44
hates his brother, he is a l; .... 1 Jn 4:20

LIBERTY
to proclaim l to the captives, ...Is 61:1
For why should my l be................ 1 Cor 10:29
the law of l, and perseveres, ...Jas 1:25

LIE
you shall not l to one......................... Lv 19:11
not man, that he should l, ... Nm 23:19
He makes me l down in ....Ps 23:2
for a l and worshiped and ....Rom 1:25
Do not l to one another, ...Col 3:9

LIFE
his nostrils the breath of l, ... Gn 2:7
the way to the tree of l. .... Gn 3:24
then you shall pay l for l, ... Ex 21:23
For the l of the flesh is in .... Lv 17:11
known to me the path of l; ....Ps 16:11
me finds l and obtains favor..............Prv 8:35
and kindness will find l, ...Prv 21:21
delivered my l from the pit ....Is 38:17
not be anxious about your l, ...Mt 6:25
and to give his l as a ....Mt 20:28
It is better for you to enter l............... Mk 9:43
down his l for the sheep. .... Jn 10:11
way, and the truth, and the l. .... Jn 14:6
you may have l in his name.............. Jn 20:31
to eternal l believed. ....Acts 13:48
lead the l that the Lord .... 1 Cor 7:17
kills, but the Spirit gives l. .... 2 Cor 3:6

LIFT
the LORD l up his .... Nm 6:26
I l up my eyes to the hills. ....Ps 121:1
Let us l up our hearts and................Lam 3:41

LIFTED
he shall be high and l up, ...Is 52:13
And I, when I am l up from .... Jn 12:32

LIGHT
And God said, "Let there be l,"............ Gn 1:3
The LORD is my l and my ....Ps 27:1
I will make you as a l for the ....Is 49:6
"You are the l of the world......................Mt 5:14
the l has come into the world, ... Jn 3:19
"I am the l of the world. .... Jn 8:12
"'I have made you a l for...............Acts 13:47
and put on the armor of l. ....Rom 13:12
himself as an angel of l. .... 2 Cor 11:14
the Lord God will be their l, ...Rv 22:5

LIGHTNING
face like the appearance of l, ... Dn 10:6
For as the l comes from the..............Mt 24:27
His appearance was like l, ...Mt 28:3

LIKENESS
in our image, after our l. .... Gn 1:26
or any l of anything that is.................. Ex 20:4

MILK
a land flowing with **m** and .... Ex 3:8
I fed you with **m**, not solid .... 1 Cor 3:2

MILLSTONE
great **m** fastened around his .... Mt 18:6

MIND
he should change his **m**. .... Nm 23:19
and will not change his **m**, ... Ps 110:4
peace whose **m** is stayed on .... Is 26:3
soul and with all your **m** .... Mt 22:37
by the renewal of your **m**, ... Rom 12:2
my spirit prays but my **m** .... 1 Cor 14:14
and will not change his **m**, ... Heb 7:21
have unity of **m**, sympathy, ... 1 Pt 3:8

MINDS
you who test the **m** and hearts, ... Ps 7:9
put my laws into their **m**, ... Heb 8:10

MINISTERING
and the angels were **m** to .... Mk 1:13
Are they not all **m** spirits .... Heb 1:14

MINISTRY
and to the **m** of the word." .... Acts 6:4
us the **m** of reconciliation; .... 2 Cor 5:18
an evangelist, fulfill your **m**. .... 2 Tm 4:5
Christ has obtained a **m** that .... Heb 8:6

MIRACLES
his **m** and the judgments .... 1 Chr 16:12
the working of **m**, ... 1 Cor 12:10
and various **m** and by gifts .... Heb 2:4

MIRROR
For now we see in a **m** .... 1 Cor 13:12

MISERY
over the **m** of Israel. .... Jgs 10:16
their paths are ruin and **m**, ... Rom 3:16

MISLEADS
"'Cursed be anyone who **m** .... Dt 27:18
Whoever **m** the upright .... Prv 28:10

MIST
and a **m** was going up from .... Gn 2:6
a cloud and your sins like **m**; .... Is 44:22
For you are a **m** that .... Jas 4:14

MOCK
All who see me **m** me; they .... Ps 22:7
And they will **m** him and .... Mk 10:34

MOCKED
And at noon Elijah **m** .... 1 Kgs 18:27
they **m** him, saying, "Hail, ... Mt 27:29
not be deceived: God is not **m**, ... Gal 6:7

MODESTY
treated with greater **m**, ... 1 Cor 12:23
with **m** and self-control, ... 1 Tm 2:9

MOMENT
joy of the godless but for a **m**? .... Jb 20:5
For his anger is but for a **m**, ... Ps 30:5
in a **m**, in the twinkling .... 1 Cor 15:52

MONEY
and he who has no **m**, come, ... Is 55:1
nor bag, nor bread, nor **m**; .... Lk 9:3
the gift of God with **m**! .... Acts 8:20
For the love of **m** is a root .... 1 Tm 6:10

MOON
fingers, the **m** and the stars, ... Ps 8:3
and the **m** will not give its .... Mt 24:29
and the **m** to blood, ... Acts 2:20

MORNING
evening and there was **m**, ... Gn 1:5
in the **m** you hear my voice; .... Ps 5:3
they are new every **m**; .... Lam 3:23
of David, the bright **m** star." .... Rv 22:16

MORTAL
'Can **m** man be in the right .... Jb 4:17
and the **m** puts on .... 1 Cor 15:54

MOSES
Now **M** was keeping the flock .... Ex 3:1
while **M** went up to God. .... Ex 19:3
just as **M** also was faithful in .... Heb 3:2
And they sing the song of **M**, ... Rv 15:3

MOTHER
and his **m** and hold fast .... Gn 2:24
because she was the **m** of all .... Gn 3:20
cursed his father or his **m**; .... Lv 20:9
foolish man despises his **m**. .... Prv 15:20
As one whom his **m** comforts, ... Is 66:13
When his **m** Mary had been .... Mt 1:18

MOTHER'S
my **m** womb, and naked shall .... Jb 1:21

MOUNTAIN
came to Horeb, the **m** of God. .... Ex 3:1
city of our God! His holy **m**, ... Ps 48:1
the Spirit to a great, high **m**, ... Rv 21:10

MOUNTAINS
How beautiful upon the **m** .... Is 52:7
the **m** and the hills before .... Is 55:12
faith, so as to remove **m**, ... 1 Cor 13:2

MOURN
and those who **m** are lifted to .... Jb 5:11
a time to laugh; a time to **m**, ... Eccl 3:4
God; to comfort all who **m**; .... Is 61:2
"Blessed are those who **m**, ... Mt 5:4

MOURNING
and your days of **m** shall be .... Is 60:20
I will turn their **m** into joy; .... Jer 31:13
neither shall there be **m**, nor .... Rv 21:4

MOUTH
shall not depart from your **m**, ... Jos 1:8
Let the words of my **m** and .... Ps 19:14
He put a new song in my **m**, ... Ps 40:3
in your **m** and covered you .... Is 51:16
of the heart the **m** speaks. .... Mt 12:34

MULTIPLY
"Be fruitful and **m** and fill .... Gn 1:22
they shall be fruitful and **m**. .... Jer 23:3
I will bless you and **m** you." .... Heb 6:14

MULTITUDE
and will cover a **m** of sins. .... Jas 5:20
since love covers a **m** of sins. .... 1 Pt 4:8
a great **m** that no one could .... Rv 7:9

MURDER
"You shall not **m**. .... Ex 20:13
those of old, 'You shall not **m**; .... Mt 5:21
adultery, You shall not **m**, ... Rom 13:9

MURDERER
The **m** shall be put to death. .... Nm 35:16
you suffer as a **m** or a thief .... 1 Pt 4:15
hates his brother is a **m**, ... 1 Jn 3:15

MURDERERS
fathers and mothers, for **m**, ... 1 Tm 1:9
the detestable, as for **m**, ... Rv 21:8

MUSIC
you, O Lord, I will make **m**. .... Ps 101:1
and we will play my **m** on .... Is 38:20

MUSTARD
like a grain of **m** seed that a .... Mt 13:31
faith like a grain of **m** seed, ... Mt 17:20

MYSTERY
you to understand this **m**, ... Rom 11:25
I tell you a **m**. We shall .... 1 Cor 15:51

MYTHS
truth and wander off into **m**. .... 2 Tm 4:4
Jewish **m** and the commands .... Ti 1:14
devised **m** when we made .... 2 Pt 1:16

NAKED
were both **n** and were not .... Gn 2:25
And he said, "**N** I came from .... Jb 1:21
house; when you see the **n**, ... Is 58:7

NAME
This is my **n** forever, and .... Ex 3:15
"You shall not take the **n** of .... Ex 20:7
to put his **n** and make his .... Dt 12:5
build the house for my **n**.' .... 1 Kgs 5:5
A good **n** is to be chosen .... Prv 22:1
my people shall know my **n**. .... Is 52:6
had concern for my holy **n**, ... Ez 36:21
everyone whose **n** shall be .... Dn 12:1
him, who believed in his **n**, ... Jn 1:12
Whatever you ask in my **n**, ... Jn 14:13
you may have life in his **n**. .... Jn 20:31
for there is no other **n** .... Acts 4:12
do everything in the **n** of .... Col 3:17
as the **n** he has inherited .... Heb 1:4
And if anyone's **n** was not .... Rv 20:15

NAME'S
for my **n** sake, and you have .... Rv 2:3

NAMES
but rejoice that your **n** are .... Lk 10:20
earth whose **n** have not been .... Rv 17:8

NATION
I will make of you a great **n**, ... Gn 12:2
Blessed is the **n** whose God .... Ps 33:12
a royal priesthood, a holy **n**, ... 1 Pt 2:9

NATIONS
father of a multitude of **n** .... Gn 17:4
He makes **n** great, and he .... Jb 12:23
Behold, the **n** are like a drop .... Is 40:15
And the **n** will know that I .... Ez 36:23
kingdom, that all peoples, **n**, ... Dn 7:14

and make disciples of all **n**, ... Mt 28:19
first be proclaimed to all **n**. ... Mk 13:10
proclaimed among the **n**, ... 1 Tm 3:16

NATURAL
n relations for those ... Rom 1:26
not spare the **n** branches, ... Rom 11:21
The **n** person does not ... 1 Cor 2:14
If there is a **n** body, ... 1 Cor 15:44

NATURE
by **n** do what the law ... Rom 2:14
the exact imprint of his **n**, ... Heb 1:3

NEED
lend him sufficient for his **n**, ... Dt 15:8
to share with anyone in **n**. ... Eph 4:28
every **n** of yours according ... Phil 4:19
grace to help in time of **n**. ... Heb 4:16

NEEDY
out her hands to the **n**. ... Prv 31:20

NEGLECT
and be wise, and do not **n** it. ... Prv 8:33
Do not **n** to show hospitality ... Heb 13:2

NEIGHBOR
but you shall love your **n** ... Lv 19:18
Whoever despises his **n** is ... Prv 14:21
Better is a **n** who is near ... Prv 27:10
Let each of us please his **n** ... Rom 15:2
"You shall love your **n** as ... Gal 5:14
speak the truth with his **n**, ... Eph 4:25
each one his **n** and each ... Heb 8:11

NEIGHBOR'S
your **n** wife, or his male ... Ex 20:17
n landmark, which the men ... Dt 19:14
your **n** house, lest he have ... Prv 25:17

NEW
Sing to him a **n** song; play ... Ps 33:3
He put a **n** song in my mouth, ... Ps 40:3
and there is nothing **n**. ... Eccl 1:9
"For behold, I create **n** ... Is 65:17
And I will give you a **n** ... Ez 36:26
Neither is **n** wine put into ... Mt 9:17
A **n** teaching with authority! ... Mk 1:27
you is the **n** covenant in my ... Lk 22:20
Christ, he is a **n** creation. ... 2 Cor 5:17
uncircumcision, but a **n** creation. ... Gal 6:15
and have put on the **n** self, ... Col 3:10

NEWS
and the poor have good **n** ... Mt 11:5
I bring you good **n** of great ... Lk 2:10
And this word is the good **n**. ... 1 Pt 1:25

NIGHT
and the darkness he called **N**. ... Gn 1:5
But the **n** is long, and I am ... Jb 7:4
law he meditates day and **n**. ... Ps 1:2
my covenant with the **n**, ... Jer 33:20
come like a thief in the **n**. ... 1 Thes 5:2
And **n** will be no more. They ... Rv 22:5

NOAH
Then the LORD said to **N**, "Go ... Gn 7:1
For as were the days of **N**, so ... Mt 24:37
By faith **N**, being warned by ... Heb 11:7

NOBLE
for I will speak **n** things, ... Prv 8:6
not many were of **n** birth. ... 1 Cor 1:26
he desires a **n** task. ... 1 Tm 3:1

NOTHING
strong drink, and eat **n** unclean, ... Jgs 13:4
there is **n** on earth that I desire ... Ps 73:25
shall take **n** for his toil that he ... Eccl 5:15
All who fashion idols are **n**, ... Is 44:9
arm! **N** is too hard for you. ... Jer 32:17
for apart from me you can do **n**. ... Jn 15:5
know that **n** good dwells in me, ... Rom 7:18
made himself **n**, taking the form ... Phil 2:7
we brought **n** into the world, ... 1 Tm 6:7

NUMBER
if you are able to **n** them." ... Gn 15:5
So teach us to **n** our days ... Ps 90:12
brings out their host by **n**, ... Is 40:26
multitude that no one could **n**, ... Rv 7:9
of a man, and his **n** is 666. ... Rv 13:18

OATH
is keeping the **o** that he swore ... Dt 7:8
you, Do not take an **o** at all, ... Mt 5:34
by earth or by any other **o**, ... Jas 5:12

OBEDIENCE
and to him shall be the **o** of ... Gn 49:10
so by the one man's **o** the ... Rom 5:19
he learned **o** through what ... Heb 5:8

OBEDIENT
priests became **o** to the faith. ... Acts 6:7
become **o** from the heart ... Rom 6:17
you are **o** in everything. ... 2 Cor 2:9

OBEY
"But if you carefully **o** his ... Ex 23:22
who will not **o** the voice of ... Dt 21:18
If you **o** the commandments ... Dt 30:16
Behold, to **o** is better than ... 1 Sm 15:22
"We must **o** God rather ... Acts 5:29
Children, **o** your parents in ... Col 3:20
who do not **o** the gospel of ... 2 Thes 1:8
who do not **o** the gospel of ... 1 Pt 4:17

OBTAINED
The elect **o** it, but the rest ... Rom 11:7
In him we have **o** an ... Eph 1:11
But as it is, Christ has **o** a ... Heb 8:6

OFFENDED
A brother **o** is more ... Prv 18:19
the one who is not **o** by me." ... Mt 11:6

OFFENSE
stumbling, and a rock of **o**; ... Rom 9:33
In that case the **o** of the cross ... Gal 5:11

OFFERING
the lamb for a burnt **o**, ... Gn 22:8
sacrifice and **o** you have not ... Ps 40:6
be pleased with a burnt **o**. ... Ps 51:16
So if you are **o** your gift at ... Mt 5:23

OFFERINGS
burnt **o** and sacrifices." ... Mk 12:33
"Sacrifices and **o** you have ... Heb 10:5

OFFSPRING
and between your **o** and her ... Gn 3:15
I will make your **o** as the ... Gn 13:16
then you are Abraham's **o**, ... Gal 3:29

OIL
you anoint my head with **o**; ... Ps 23:5
the **o** of gladness instead of ... Is 61:3
anointing him with **o** in the ... Jas 5:14

OLD
The **o** has passed away; ... 2 Cor 5:17
than the **o** as the covenant ... Heb 8:6

OLIVE
although a wild **o** shoot, ... Rom 11:17
These are the two **o** trees ... Rv 11:4

OMEGA
I am the Alpha and the **O**, ... Rv 21:6

OPEN
I have set before you an **o** ... Rv 3:8
"Who is worthy to **o** the scroll ... Rv 5:2

OPENED
eat of it your eyes will be **o**, ... Gn 3:5
yet he **o** not his mouth; ... Is 53:7
I see the heavens **o**, ... Acts 7:56

OPENS
the LORD **o** the eyes of the ... Ps 146:8
my voice and **o** the door, ... Rv 3:20

OPINIONS
between two different **o**? ... 1 Kgs 18:21
but not to quarrel over **o**. ... Rom 14:1

OPPORTUNITY
But sin, seizing an **o** ... Rom 7:8
So then, as we have **o**, let us ... Gal 6:10
and give no **o** to the devil ... Eph 4:27

OPPRESS
wrong a sojourner or **o** him, ... Ex 22:21
do not **o** the widow, the ... Zec 7:10

OPPRESSED
executes justice for the **o**, ... Ps 146:7
He was **o**, and he was afflicted ... Is 53:7

ORGIES
the **o** on the mountains. Truly ... Jer 3:23
not in **o** and drunkenness, ... Rom 13:13

ORPHANS
"I will not leave you as **o**; ... Jn 14:18
to visit **o** and widows in ... Jas 1:27

OUTSIDERS
I to do with judging **o**? ... 1 Cor 5:12
Walk in wisdom toward **o**, ... Col 4:5
be well thought of by **o**, ... 1 Tm 3:7

OVERCOME
and the darkness has not **o** it. ... Jn 1:5
Do not be **o** by evil, but ... Rom 12:21

OVERCOMES
For whatever **o** a person, ... 2 Pt 2:19
born of God **o** the world. ... 1 Jn 5:4

OVERSEER
aspires to the office of **o**, ... 1 Tm 3:1
For an **o**, as God's steward, ... Ti 1:7
and **O** of your souls. ... 1 Pt 2:25

PHILOSOPHY
captive by **p** and empty deceit, ...Col 2:8

PIERCED
they have **p** my hands and ....Ps 22:16
on him whom they have **p**, ... Zec 12:10

PILATE
him over to **P** the governor. ....Mt 27:2
P answered, "What I have................ Jn 19:22

PILLAR
and she became a **p** of salt............. Gn 19:26
by day in a **p** of cloud to.................... Ex 13:21
a **p** and buttress of the truth..........1 Tm 3:15

PIT
He drew me up from the **p** of..............Ps 40:2
your life from the **p**,..........................Ps 103:4
and threw him into the **p**,...................Rv 20:3

PLACES
blessing in the heavenly **p**, ...Eph 1:3
once for all into the holy **p**,...............Heb 9:12

PLAGUE
"Yet one **p** more I will bring................ Ex 11:1
earth with every kind of **p**,...................Rv 11:6

PLAN
Do not **p** evil against your ....Prv 3:29
p and foreknowledge of...................Acts 2:23
as a **p** for the fullness of..................Eph 1:10

PLANNED
I **p** from days of old ....2 Kgs 19:25
"As I have **p**, so shall it be, ...Is 14:24

PLANS
desire and fulfill all your **p**! ....Ps 20:4
the **p** of his heart to all ....Ps 33:11
P are established by ....Prv 20:18
But he who is noble **p** noble ....Is 32:8

PLANTS
vegetation, **p** yielding seed, ... Gn 1:11
So neither he who **p** nor................... 1 Cor 3:7
Who **p** a vineyard without................ 1 Cor 9:7

PLAYED
"'We **p** the flute for you, ... Lk 7:32
anyone know what is **p**? .... 1 Cor 14:7

PLEAD
If you will seek God and **p** .... Jb 8:5
and to the Lord I **p** for mercy: ....Ps 30:8

PLEASANT
tree that is **p** to the sight .... Gn 2:9
Behold, how good and **p** it is............Ps 133:1
How beautiful and **p** you are, ...Sg 7:6

PLEASE
This will **p** the LORD more...................Ps 69:31
but to **p** God who tests our............ 1 Thes 2:4
since his aim is to **p** the one............2 Tm 2:4

PLEASED
with whom I am well **p**." ....Mt 3:17
commended as having **p** God...........Heb 11:5

PLEASES
for this **p** the Lord. ....Col 3:20
and do what **p** him.......................... 1 Jn 3:22

PLEASING
May my meditation be **p** to.............Ps 104:34
of the Lord, fully **p** to him:..................Col 1:10
for such sacrifices are **p** to ....Heb 13:16

PLEASURE
but the LORD takes **p** in...................Ps 147:11
lovers of **p** rather than ....2 Tm 3:4

PLEASURES
cares and riches and **p** of life, ... Lk 8:14

POLLUTED
And they **p** the house of............... 2 Chr 36:14
spring or a **p** fountain is a ....Prv 25:26
from the things **p** by idols, ...Acts 15:20

POOR
But there will be no **p** among .... Dt 15:4
The LORD makes **p** and......................1 Sm 2:7
and the hope of the **p** shall ....Ps 9:18
delivering the **p** from him.................Ps 35:10
who is generous to the **p**. ....Prv 14:21
Better is a **p** person who ....Prv 19:1
defend the rights of the **p** ....Prv 31:9
"Blessed are the **p** in spirit, ...Mt 5:3
possess and give to the **p**, ...Mt 19:21
For you always have the **p**................Mt 26:11
for your sake he became **p**, ... 2 Cor 8:9
those who are **p** in the world ....Jas 2:5

PORTION
my heart and my **p** forever................Ps 73:26
they shall possess a double **p**; ....Is 61:7
"The LORD is my **p**," says ....Lam 3:24

POSSESS
to give you this land to **p**." .... Gn 15:7
the land to you to **p** it...................... Nm 33:53
and **p** the kingdom forever, ... Dn 7:18

POSSESSION
I will give it to you for a **p**..................... Ex 6:8
a better **p** and an abiding ....Heb 10:34
a people for his own **p**,...................... 1 Pt 2:9

POSSESSIONS
in the abundance of his **p**." .... Lk 12:15

POSSIBLE
with God all things are **p**." ....Mt 19:26
that by any means **p** I may...............Phil 3:11

POTTER
Shall the **p** be regarded as................Is 29:16
as it seemed good to the **p** to............ Jer 18:4
Has the **p** no right over the..............Rom 9:21

POURED
Spirit was **p** out even on................Acts 10:45
has been **p** into our hearts ....Rom 5:5
For I am already being **p** ....2 Tm 4:6

POVERTY
sleep, lest you come to **p**;................Prv 20:13
give me neither **p** nor riches;..............Prv 30:8
but she out of her **p** has put............ Mk 12:44
p have overflowed in .... 2 Cor 8:2
so that you by his **p** might................. 2 Cor 8:9

POWER
God is exalted in his **p**;..................... Jb 36:22
He gives **p** to the faint, and................Is 40:29
Scriptures nor the **p** of God. ....Mt 22:29
God after it has come with **p**." .... Mk 9:1
And the **p** of the Lord was .... Lk 5:17
But you will receive **p** when................Acts 1:8
surpassing **p** belongs to God........... 2 Cor 4:7
with **p** through his Spirit ....Eph 3:16
the **p** of his resurrection,....................Phil 3:10
being strengthened with all **p**, ...Col 1:11
godliness, but denying its **p**..............2 Tm 3:5
by the word of his **p**..............................Heb 1:3
the second death has no **p**,.................Rv 20:6

POWERFUL
The voice of the LORD is **p**; ....Ps 29:4
not many were **p**,........................... 1 Cor 1:26
in the **p** working of God, ...Col 2:12

POWERS
nor things to come, nor **p**, ...Rom 8:38
against the cosmic **p** over.................Eph 6:12
and **p** having been subjected........... 1 Pt 3:22

PRACTICE
P these things, immerse .... 1 Tm 4:15
for if you **p** these qualities .... 2 Pt 1:10
of God makes a **p** of sinning, ... 1 Jn 3:9

PRAISE
is my God, and I will **p** him,................ Ex 15:2
LORD and **p** him in holy .... 2 Chr 20:21
his **p** shall continually be in................Ps 34:1
and his courts with **p**! Give..............Ps 100:4
Let my soul live and **p**................Ps 119:175
Let another **p** you, and not ....Prv 27:2
and **p** the name of the LORD................. Jl 2:26
you have prepared **p**'?" ....Mt 21:16
I will sing **p** with my.................... 1 Cor 14:15
cheerful? Let him sing **p**. ....Jas 5:13

PRAISING
p and giving thanks to the................Ezr 3:11
glorifying and **p** God for all .... Lk 2:20
p God and having favor....................Acts 2:47

PRAY
by ceasing to **p** for you, ...1 Sm 12:23
and my God, for to you do I **p**................Ps 5:2
P for the peace of Jerusalem! ....Ps 122:6
"And when you **p**, you must..................Mt 6:5
P then like this: "Our Father ....Mt 6:9
therefore **p** earnestly to the ....Mt 9:38
know what to **p** for as we ....Rom 8:26
should **p** for the power .... 1 Cor 14:13

PRAYER
plea; the LORD accepts my **p**. ....Ps 6:9
a house of **p** for all peoples." ....Is 56:7
house of **p**,' but you make it.............Mt 21:13
devoting themselves to **p**, ...Acts 1:14
but in everything by **p** and ....Phil 4:6
And the **p** of faith will save ....Jas 5:15
his ears are open to their **p**. .... 1 Pt 3:12

PRAYERS
breaking of bread and the **p**.........Acts 2:42
supplications, **p**, intercessions, ...1 Tm 2:1

SELF-CONTROL
A man without **s** is like a.................Prv 25:28
gentleness, **s**; against such............. Gal 5:23
apparel, with modesty and **s**,............1 Tm 2:9

SELF-CONTROLLED
a lover of good, **s**, upright, holy,............ Ti 1:8
therefore be **s** and............................ 1 Pt 4:7

SELF-INDULGENCE
they are full of greed and **s**. ....Mt 23:25
the earth in luxury and in **s**. ....Jas 5:5

SELFISH
and not to **s** gain! ....Ps 119:36
and **s** ambition in your......................Jas 3:14

SEND
"Here am I! **S** me."................................Is 6:8
For God did not **s** his Son .... Jn 3:17
if I go, I will **s** him to you.................... Jn 16:7

SENDING
"Behold, I am **s** you out as ....Mt 10:16
me, even so I am **s** you." .... Jn 20:21
By **s** his own Son in the ....Rom 8:3

SENT
preach unless they are **s**? ....Rom 10:15
come, God **s** forth his Son, ... Gal 4:4
loved us and **s** his Son to .... 1 Jn 4:10

SEPARATE
Who shall **s** us from the ....Rom 8:35
the wife should not **s** from .... 1 Cor 7:10

SEPARATED
at that time **s** from Christ, ...Eph 2:12
unstained, **s** from sinners, ...Heb 7:26

SEPARATES
and a whisperer **s** close ....Prv 16:28
a shepherd **s** the sheep from............Mt 25:32
the unbelieving partner **s**,............. 1 Cor 7:15

SERPENT
Now the **s** was more crafty.................. Gn 3:1
And as Moses lifted up the **s**.............. Jn 3:14
the dragon, that ancient **s**, ...Rv 20:2

SERVANT
among you must be your **s**, ...Mt 20:26
done, good and faithful **s**..................Mt 25:21
No **s** can serve two masters, ... Lk 16:13
I have made myself a **s** to .... 1 Cor 9:19
taking the form of a **s**, ...Phil 2:7
And the Lord's **s** must not ....2 Tm 2:24

SERVANTS
say, 'We are unworthy **s**;.................... Lk 17:10
but as **s** of God we commend .... 2 Cor 6:4
evil, but living as **s** of God. .... 1 Pt 2:16

SERVE
to **s** the LORD your God with............... Dt 10:12
this day whom you will **s**, ...Jos 24:15
and him only shall you **s**.'" ....Mt 4:10
not to be served but to **s**, ...Mt 20:28
so that we **s** in the new way ....Rom 7:6
rather they must **s** all the................. 1 Tm 6:2

SEVEN
march around the city **s** times, ...Jos 6:4
s that are an abomination to ....Prv 6:16
him? As many as **s** times?" ....Mt 18:21
"I have kept for myself **s** ....Rom 11:4
who holds the **s** stars in his ....Rv 2:1
opened one of the **s** seals,.....................Rv 6:1
and **s** trumpets were given to................Rv 8:2
And when the **s** thunders ....Rv 10:4
angels **s** golden bowls full ....Rv 15:7

SEVENTH
And on the **s** day God .... Gn 2:2
but on the **s** day you shall .... Ex 23:12

SEXUAL
except on the ground of **s**...................Mt 5:32
Flee from **s** immorality................... 1 Cor 6:18
that you abstain from **s**................. 1 Thes 4:3

SEXUALLY
with **s** immoral people — .... 1 Cor 5:9
that everyone who is **s**........................Eph 5:5

SHADOW
the valley of the **s** of death,...................Ps 23:4
refuge in the **s** of your wings................Ps 36:7
These are a **s** of the things................Col 2:17

SHADRACH
Hananiah he called **S**,.......................... Dn 1:7

SHAME
Then I shall not be put to **s**, ...Ps 119:6
the cross, despising the **s**, ...Heb 12:2

SHARE
word must **s** all good things................ Gal 6:6
to **s** with anyone in..........................Eph 4:28
But rejoice insofar as you **s**............. 1 Pt 4:13

SHEEP
and the **s** of his pasture....................Ps 100:3
All we like **s** have gone.........................Is 53:6
for my **s** and will seek .... Ez 34:11
I am sending you out as **s** ....Mt 10:16
The **s** hear his voice, and he............... Jn 10:3
He said to him, "Tend my **s**."............ Jn 21:16

SHELTER
under the **s** of your wings! ....Ps 61:4
He who dwells in the **s** of the ....Ps 91:1

SHEOL
he brings down to **S** and ....1 Sm 2:6
not abandon my soul to **S**,.................Ps 16:10
her steps follow the path to **S**; ....Prv 5:5
to the gates of **S** for the rest ....Is 38:10
them from the power of **S**;..............Hos 13:14

SHEPHERD
'You shall be **s** of my...................... 1 Chr 11:2
and will keep him as a **s**................. Jer 31:10
And he shall stand and **s** his ....Mi 5:4
I am the good **s**. The good .... Jn 10:11
the great **s** of the sheep, ...Heb 13:20
of the throne will be their **s**, ...Rv 7:17

SHEPHERDS
Should not **s** feed the sheep? .... Ez 34:2
region there were **s** out in the............... Lk 2:8
evangelists, the **s** and teachers ....Eph 4:11

SHIELD
"Fear not, Abram, I am your **s**; .... Gn 15:1
LORD is my strength and my **s**;.............Ps 28:7

SHINE
the LORD make his face to **s**.............. Nm 6:25
make his face to **s** upon us, ...Ps 67:1
Arise, **s**, for your light has ....Is 60:1

SHINES
of beauty, God **s** forth.........................Ps 50:2
The light **s** in the darkness,................... Jn 1:5

SHONE
of his face **s** because he had .... Ex 34:29
and his face **s** like the sun,.................Mt 17:2
and the glory of the Lord **s** .... Lk 2:9

SHORT
those days will be cut **s**....................Mt 24:22
and fall **s** of the glory of God,...........Rom 3:23

SHOW
s the immeasurable riches..................Eph 2:7
S me your faith apart from.................Jas 2:18
S hospitality to one another .... 1 Pt 4:9

SICK
deferred makes the heart **s**, ...Prv 13:12
but those who are **s**............................Mt 9:12
s and in prison and you did..............Mt 25:43

SIGHT
Precious in the **s** of the ....Ps 116:15
we walk by faith, not by **s**................ 2 Cor 5:7
and it is pleasing in the **s** of ....1 Tm 2:3
which in God's **s** is very...................... 1 Pt 3:4

SIGN
The blood shall be a **s** for.................. Ex 12:13
You shall bind them as a **s** on.............. Dt 6:8
He received the **s** of..........................Rom 4:11
This is the **s** of genuineness......... 2 Thes 3:17
Then I saw another **s** in.......................Rv 15:1

SIGNS
Now Jesus did many other **s**............. Jn 20:30
above and **s** on the earth ....Acts 2:19
by **s** and wonders and ....Heb 2:4

SILENCE
time to sew; a time to keep **s**, ... Eccl 3:7
put to **s** the ignorance of................. 1 Pt 2:15
there was **s** in heaven for......................Rv 8:1

SILENT
Even a fool who keeps **s** is ....Prv 17:28
that before its shearers is **s**, ...Is 53:7
Be **s** before the Lord GOD! ....Zep 1:7

SILVER
if you seek it like **s** and ....Prv 2:4
The **s** is mine, and the gold is .... Hg 2:8
said, "I have no **s** and gold, ...Acts 3:6
things such as **s** or gold,.................. 1 Pt 1:18

SIN
s is crouching at the door..................... Gn 4:7
he shall confess his **s** that he .... Nm 5:7
their **s** and heal their .... 2 Chr 7:14
in my bones because of my **s**. ....Ps 38:3
and cleanse me from my **s**!................Ps 51:2

you covered all their **s**. Selah .... Ps 85:2
that I might not **s** against .... Ps 119:11
away, and your **s** atoned for." .... Is 6:7
ones who believe in me to **s**, ... Mt 18:6
"Temptations to **s** are sure to .... Lk 17:1
who takes away the **s** of the .... Jn 1:29
but where **s** increased, ... Rom 5:20
For the wages of **s** is death, ... Rom 6:23
him to be **s** who knew no .... 2 Cor 5:21
for those who persist in **s**, ... 1 Tm 5:20
conceived gives birth to **s**, ... Jas 1:15
fails to do it, for him it is **s**. .... Jas 4:17
He committed no **s**, neither .... 1 Pt 2:22
Son cleanses us from all **s**. .... 1 Jn 1:7

SINFUL
the world because of **s** desire .... 2 Pt 1:4
following their own **s** desires; .... Jude 1:16

SING
I will **s** and make melody to .... Ps 27:6
S to the Lord with thanksgiving; .... Ps 147:7
cheerful? Let him **s** praise .... Jas 5:13

SINGING
into his presence with **s**! .... Ps 100:2
s psalms and hymns and .... Col 3:16

SINGLE
them to remain **s**, as I am .... 1 Cor 7:8

SINNED
have I **s** and done what is .... Ps 51:4
for all have **s** and fall short .... Rom 3:23

SINNER
but one **s** destroys much .... Eccl 9:18
over one **s** who repents." .... Lk 15:10

SINNERS
Let not your heart envy **s**, ... Prv 23:17
to call the righteous, but **s**." .... Mt 9:13
into the world to save **s**, ... 1 Tm 1:15

SINNING
Thus, **s** against your .... 1 Cor 8:12
of God does not keep on **s**, ... 1 Jn 5:18

SINS
are my iniquities and my **s**? .... Jb 13:23
our secret **s** in the light of .... Ps 90:8
for you have cast all my **s** .... Is 38:17
save his people from their **s**." .... Mt 1:21
for the forgiveness of **s**. .... Mt 26:28
once to bear the **s** of many, ... Heb 9:28
Therefore, confess your **s** to .... Jas 5:16
also suffered once for **s**, ... 1 Pt 3:18
cleansed from his former **s**. .... 2 Pt 1:9
If we confess our **s**, he is .... 1 Jn 1:9

SIT
Lord: "**S** at my right hand, ... Ps 110:1
to give light to those who **s** .... Lk 1:79

SKIN
and I have escaped by the **s** .... Jb 19:20
change his **s** or the leopard .... Jer 13:23
and **s** had covered them. But .... Ez 37:8

SLANDER
who does not **s** with his .... Ps 15:3
and whoever utters **s** is a .... Prv 10:18
hypocrisy and envy and all **s**. .... 1 Pt 2:1

SLANDERED
when **s**, we entreat. We .... 1 Cor 4:13
so that, when you are **s**, ... 1 Pt 3:16

SLAVE
among you must be your **s**, ... Mt 20:27
who practices sin is a **s** to sin .... Jn 8:34
there is neither **s** nor free, ... Gal 3:28

SLAVERY
the spirit of **s** to fall back .... Rom 8:15
submit again to a yoke of **s**. .... Gal 5:1
were subject to lifelong **s**. .... Heb 2:15

SLAVES
you are **s** of the one whom .... Rom 6:16
s to various passions and .... Ti 3:3

SLEEP
caused a deep **s** to fall upon .... Gn 2:21
will neither slumber nor **s**. .... Ps 121:4
Sweet is the **s** of a laborer, ... Eccl 5:12

SLOW
and gracious, **s** to anger, ... Ex 34:6
s to anger and abounding in .... Ps 103:8
Whoever is **s** to anger has .... Prv 14:29
The Lord is **s** to anger and .... Na 1:3
If it seems **s**, wait for it; it will .... Hb 2:3
The Lord is not **s** to fulfill .... 2 Pt 3:9

SNARE
which became a **s** to them. .... Ps 106:36
fall into temptation, into a **s**, ... 1 Tm 6:9
from the **s** of the devil, ... 2 Tm 2:26

SNOW
and I shall be whiter than **s**. .... Ps 51:7
they shall be as white as **s**; .... Is 1:18
and his clothing white as **s**. .... Mt 28:3

SOBER
but to think with **s** .... Rom 12:3
us keep awake and be **s**. .... 1 Thes 5:6

SOBER-MINDED
one wife, **s**, self-controlled, ... 1 Tm 3:2
Older men are to be **s**, ... Ti 2:2
for action, and being **s**, ... 1 Pt 1:13

SOLDIER
Who serves as a **s** at his .... 1 Cor 9:7
fellow worker and fellow **s**, ... Phil 2:25
as a good **s** of Christ Jesus. .... 2 Tm 2:3

SON
He said, "Take your **s**, your .... Gn 22:2
said to me, "You are my **S**; .... Ps 2:7
and the **s** of man that you care .... Ps 8:4
A wise **s** hears his father's .... Prv 13:1
shall conceive and bear a **s**, ... Is 7:14
child is born, to us a **s** is given; .... Is 9:6
out of Egypt I called my **s**. .... Hos 11:1
said, "This is my beloved **S**, ... Mt 17:5
firstborn **s** and wrapped him .... Lk 2:7
that he gave his only **S**, ... Jn 3:16
his own **S** but gave him .... Rom 8:32
a slave, but a **s**, and if a **s**, ... Gal 4:7
and this life is in his **S**. .... 1 Jn 5:11

SONG
is my strength and my **s**, ... Ex 15:2
He put a new **s** in my mouth, ... Ps 40:3

SONGS
who gives **s** in the night, ... Jb 35:10
Shout to God with loud **s** of .... Ps 47:1
and hymns and spiritual **s**, ... Eph 5:19

SONS
your **s** and your daughters .... Jl 2:28
that is, **S** of Thunder); .... Mk 3:17
that you may become **s** of .... Jn 12:36
and you shall be **s** and .... 2 Cor 6:18
God is treating you as **s**. .... Heb 12:7

SOON
The God of peace will **s** .... Rom 16:20
things that must **s** take place. .... Rv 1:1
"Surely I am coming **s**." .... Rv 22:20

SORROW
knowledge increases **s**. .... Eccl 1:18
give them gladness for **s**. .... Jer 31:13
but your **s** will turn into joy. .... Jn 16:20

SORROWS
rejected by men, a man of **s** .... Is 53:3
one endures **s** while suffering .... 1 Pt 2:19

SOUL
heart and with all your **s**." .... Jos 22:5
He restores my **s**. He leads me .... Ps 23:3
so pants my **s** for you, O God. .... Ps 42:1
The **s** who sins shall die. .... Ez 18:20
with all your **s** and with all .... Mt 22:37
piercing to the division of **s** .... Heb 4:12

SOULS
in it, and find rest for your **s**. .... Jer 6:16
faith, the salvation of your **s**. .... 1 Pt 1:9

SOUND
heaven a **s** like a mighty .... Acts 2:2
be able to give instruction in **s** .... Ti 1:9

SOVEREIGN
to God and said, "**S** Lord, ... Acts 4:24
is the blessed and only **S**, ... 1 Tm 6:15
"O **S** Lord, holy and true, ... Rv 6:10

SOW
Those who **s** in tears shall .... Ps 126:5
"A sower went out to **s**. .... Mt 13:3

SOWS
but one who **s** righteousness .... Prv 11:18
'One **s** and another reaps.' .... Jn 4:37

SPARE
For if God did not **s** the .... Rom 11:21
For if God did not **s** angels .... 2 Pt 2:4

SPEECH
understand one another's **s**." .... Gn 11:7
Day to day pours out **s**, and .... Ps 19:2
Let your **s** always be gracious, ... Col 4:6

SPIRIT
And the **S** of God was .... Gn 1:2
And the **S** of God came .... Nm 24:2
The **S** of the Lord was upon .... Jgs 3:10
Now the **S** of the Lord .... 1 Sm 16:14

TEMPER
A man of quick **t** acts ... Prv 14:17
but he who has a hasty **t** ... Prv 14:29

TEMPEST
from the raging wind and **t**." ... Ps 55:8
and no small **t** lay on us, ... Acts 27:20

TEMPLE
of the LORD filled the **t**. ... 2 Chr 7:1
The LORD is in his holy **t**; the ... Ps 11:4
But the LORD is in his holy **t**; ... Hb 2:20
grows into a holy **t** in the ... Eph 2:21
for its **t** is the Lord God the ... Rv 21:22

TEMPTATION
And lead us not into **t**, but ... Mt 6:13
you may not enter into **t**. ... Mt 26:41
desire to be rich fall into **t**, ... 1 Tm 6:9

TEMPTED
on yourself, lest you too be **t**. ... Gal 6:1
help those who are being **t**. ... Heb 2:18
Let no one say when he is **t**, ... Jas 1:13

TEMPTER
And the **t** came and said to ... Mt 4:3
the **t** had tempted you ... 1 Thes 3:5

TEN
covenant, the **T** Commandments ... Ex 34:28
that is, the **T** Commandments, ... Dt 4:13

TENDER
because of the **t** mercy of our ... Lk 1:78
brotherly love, a **t** heart, ... 1 Pt 3:8

TENT
about in a **t** for my dwelling. ... 2 Sm 7:6

TERROR
You will not fear the **t** of the ... Ps 91:5
For rulers are not a **t** to ... Rom 13:3

TEST
me; **t** my heart and my mind. ... Ps 26:2
the Lord your God to the **t**.'" ... Mt 4:7
T yourselves. Or do you not ... 2 Cor 13:5
it comes upon you to **t** you, ... 1 Pt 4:12

TESTED
After these things God **t** ... Gn 22:1
For you, O God, have **t** us; ... Ps 66:10
and a man is **t** by his praise. ... Prv 27:21

TESTIMONY
world as a **t** to all nations, ... Mt 24:14
And this is the **t**, that God ... 1 Jn 5:11

TESTING
For the LORD your God is **t** ... Dt 13:3
that by **t** you may discern ... Rom 12:2

TESTS
The LORD **t** the righteous, ... Ps 11:5
gold, and the LORD **t** hearts ... Prv 17:3

THANK
Let them **t** the LORD for his ... Ps 107:8
First, I **t** my God through ... Rom 1:8

THANKFULNESS
If I partake with **t**, why ... 1 Cor 10:30
with **t** in your hearts to God. ... Col 3:16

THANKS
will give **t** to you forever; ... Ps 79:13
But **t** be to God, who in ... 2 Cor 2:14
give **t** in all circumstances ... 1 Thes 5:18

THANKSGIVING
a sacrifice of **t** to the LORD, ... Lv 22:29
I will magnify him with **t**. ... Ps 69:30
Enter his gates with **t**, and ... Ps 100:4
But I with the voice of **t** will ... Jon 2:9
but instead let there be **t**. ... Eph 5:4
wisdom and **t** and honor and ... Rv 7:12

THIEF
the Lord will come like a **t**, ... 2 Pt 3:10
I am coming like a **t**! Blessed ... Rv 16:15

THIEVES
and where **t** do not break ... Mt 6:20
nor **t**, nor the greedy, nor ... 1 Cor 6:10

THINK
you not to **t** of himself more ... Rom 12:3
praise, **t** about these things. ... Phil 4:8
T over what I say, for the ... 2 Tm 2:7

THINKING
became futile in their **t**, ... Rom 1:21
not be children in your **t**. ... 1 Cor 14:20
with the same way of **t**, ... 1 Pt 4:1

THINKS
If anyone **t** he is religious ... Jas 1:26

THIRST
and for my **t** they gave me ... Ps 69:21
and **t** for righteousness, ... Mt 5:6
believes in me shall never **t**. ... Jn 6:35

THIRSTS
My soul **t** for God, for the ... Ps 42:2
"Come, everyone who **t**, come ... Is 55:1

THIRSTY
hungry and **t**, their soul ... Ps 107:5
I was **t** and you gave me ... Mt 25:35
feed him; if he is **t**, give ... Rom 12:20
And let the one who is **t** ... Rv 22:17

THOUGHT
but the prudent gives **t** to ... Prv 14:15
and take every **t** captive to ... 2 Cor 10:5

THOUGHTS
intention of the **t** of his heart ... Gn 6:5
knows the **t** of man, that ... Ps 94:11
Try me and know my **t**! ... Ps 139:23

THREE
'After **t** days I will rise.' ... Mt 27:63
and love abide, these **t**; ... 1 Cor 13:13
of two or **t** witnesses. ... 2 Cor 13:1
For there are **t** that testify: ... 1 Jn 5:7

THRONE
Your **t** shall be established ... 2 Sm 7:16
Your **t**, O God, is forever and ... Ps 45:6
then a **t** will be established in ... Is 16:5
cast their crowns before the **t**, ... Rv 4:10
Then I saw a great white **t** ... Rv 20:11

TIME
for such a **t** as this?" ... Est 4:14
to you at a **t** when you may ... Ps 32:6
everything beautiful in its **t**. ... Eccl 3:11
for it is the **t** to seek the ... Hos 10:12
making the best use of the **t**, ... Eph 5:16
for all **t** a single sacrifice ... Heb 10:12
For it is **t** for judgment to ... 1 Pt 4:17

TIMES
I will bless the LORD at all **t**; ... Ps 34:1
"It is not for you to know **t** ... Acts 1:7
will come **t** of difficulty ... 2 Tm 3:1

TITHE
"Every **t** of the land, whether ... Lv 27:30
towns the **t** of your grain ... Dt 12:17
Bring the full **t** into the ... Mal 3:10

TODAY
as long as it is called "**t**," ... Heb 3:13
yesterday and **t** and forever ... Heb 13:8
Come now, you who say, "**T** ... Jas 4:13

TOMB
Therefore order the **t** to be ... Mt 27:64
stone rolled away from the **t**, ... Lk 24:2
and his **t** is with us to this ... Acts 2:29

TOMORROW
Do not boast about **t**, for you ... Prv 27:1
eat and drink, for **t** we die." ... Is 22:13
do not be anxious about **t**, ... Mt 6:34

TONGUE
and every **t** confess that ... Phil 2:11
let him keep his **t** from evil ... 1 Pt 3:10

TONGUES
to gather all nations and **t**. ... Is 66:18
And divided **t** as of fire ... Acts 2:3
in **t** and extolling God. ... Acts 10:46
various kinds of **t**, ... 1 Cor 12:10
not forbid speaking in **t**. ... 1 Cor 14:39

TOOTH
eye for eye, **t** for **t**, hand ... Ex 21:24
'An eye for an eye and a **t**. ... Mt 5:38

TOUCH
"**T** not my anointed ones, ... Ps 105:15

TOUCHED
whose hearts God had **t**. ... 1 Sm 10:26
And as many as **t** it were ... Mt 14:36

TOWER
a city and a **t** with its top ... Gn 11:4
of the LORD is a strong **t**; ... Prv 18:10

TRADITION
So for the sake of your **t** you ... Mt 15:6
deceit, according to human **t**, ... Col 2:8

TRADITIONS
maintain the **t** even as I ... 1 Cor 11:2
to the **t** that you were ... 2 Thes 2:15

TRAIN
T up a child in the way he ... Prv 22:6
Rather **t** yourself for ... 1 Tm 4:7

TRANCE
and in a **t** I saw a vision, ... Acts 11:5
the temple, I fell into a **t** ... Acts 22:17

TRANSFIGURED
And he was **t** before them, ...Mt 17:2

TRANSFORMED
but be **t** by the renewal of ....Rom 12:2
are being **t** into the same.............. 2 Cor 3:18

TRANSGRESSION
forgiving iniquity and **t** and .... Ex 34:7
Blessed is the one whose **t** is ....Ps 32:1
if anyone is caught in any **t**,................ Gal 6:1

TRANSGRESSIONS
Deliver me from all my **t**.....................Ps 39:8
so far does he remove our **t**.............Ps 103:12
It was added because of **t**,................ Gal 3:19

TRANSGRESSORS
Then I will teach **t** your......................Ps 51:13
was numbered with the **t**; ....Is 53:12

TREASURE
and you will have **t** in........................Mt 19:21
But we have this **t** in jars................. 2 Cor 4:7
thus storing up **t** for........................1 Tm 6:19

TREASURED
a people for his **t** possession,................ Dt 7:6
But Mary **t** up all these........................ Lk 2:19

TREASURES
but lay up for yourselves **t** in...............Mt 6:20
in whom are hidden all the **t**................Col 2:3

TREE
The **t** of life was in the midst .... Gn 2:9
but of the **t** of the knowledge .... Gn 2:17
He is like a **t** planted by ....Ps 1:3
Every **t** therefore that does ....Mt 3:10
for the **t** is known by its.....................Mt 12:33
who is hanged on a **t**" — .... Gal 3:13
the right to the **t** of life and..............Rv 22:14

TREMBLING
with fear, and rejoice with **t**. ....Ps 2:11
salvation with fear and **t**,..................Phil 2:12

TRESPASSES
And you were dead in the **t**..................Eph 2:1
having forgiven us all our **t**,...............Col 2:13

TRIAL
remains steadfast under **t**, ...Jas 1:12
at the fiery **t** when it comes............. 1 Pt 4:12
the hour of **t** that is coming ....Rv 3:10

TRIALS
been grieved by various **t**, ... 1 Pt 1:6
to rescue the godly from **t**, ... 2 Pt 2:9

TRIBES
All these are the twelve **t**................. Gn 49:28
from all **t** and peoples and....................Rv 7:9

TRIBULATION
then there will be great **t**,..................Mt 24:21
Shall **t**, or distress, or.......................Rom 8:35

TROUBLE
is few of days and full of **t**. .... Jb 14:1
a very present help in **t**. ....Ps 46:1
although man's **t** lies heavy .... Eccl 8:6
a stronghold in the day of **t**;................. Na 1:7

TRUE
not come to pass or come **t**,............. Dt 18:22
word of the LORD proves **t**;..............2 Sm 22:31
"I am the **t** vine, and my .... Jn 15:1
serve the living and **t** God, ... 1 Thes 1:9
it is called Faithful and **T**,.................Rv 19:11

TRUMPET
For the **t** will sound, ... 1 Cor 15:52
the sound of the **t** of God............. 1 Thes 4:16

TRUST
am afraid, I put my **t** in you................Ps 56:3
LORD, whose **t** is the LORD. .... Jer 17:7

TRUSTED
But I have **t** in your steadfast.............Ps 13:5
his servants, who **t** in him,................ Dn 3:28

TRUSTS
"He **t** in the LORD; let him.....................Ps 22:8
Whoever **t** in his riches....................Prv 11:28
but whoever **t** in the LORD ....Prv 29:25

TRUSTWORTHY
Your decrees are very **t**; ....Ps 93:5
just; all his precepts are **t**;................Ps 111:7
"These words are **t** and true.................Rv 22:6

TRUTH
Lead me in your **t** and teach...............Ps 25:5
the Father in spirit and **t**, ... Jn 4:23
and the **t** will set you free." .... Jn 8:32
way, and the **t**, and the life. .... Jn 14:6
in the **t**; your word is **t**. .... Jn 17:17
said to him, "What is **t**?" .... Jn 18:38
the **t** about God for.........................Rom 1:25
so that the **t** of the gospel.................. Gal 2:5
fastened on the belt of **t**,...................Eph 6:14
the knowledge of the **t**,..................Heb 10:26

TRUTHFUL
T lips endure forever, but a ....Prv 12:19
A **t** witness saves lives,....................Prv 14:25
by **t** speech, and the power .... 2 Cor 6:7

TURN
You shall not **t** aside to the .... Dt 5:32
Do not **t** from it to the right ....Jos 1:7
You **t** things upside down! ....Is 29:16
And he will **t** the hearts of..................Mal 4:6
let him **t** away from evil .... 1 Pt 3:11

TWELVE
All these are the **t** tribes of.............. Gn 49:28
And he called to him his **t**...................Mt 10:1

UNBELIEF
marveled because of their **u**................. Mk 6:6
off because of their **u**,....................Rom 11:20
had acted ignorantly in **u**, ...1 Tm 1:13

UNBELIEVER
has a wife who is an **u**, ... 1 Cor 7:12
believer share with an **u**?............. 2 Cor 6:15

UNBELIEVERS
brother, and that before **u**? .... 1 Cor 6:6
blinded the minds of the **u**,............. 2 Cor 4:4

UNBELIEVING
For the **u** husband is .... 1 Cor 7:14

pure, but to the defiled and **u**, ... Ti 1:15
any of you an evil, **u** heart,...............Heb 3:12

UNBORN
to a people yet **u**,...............................Ps 22:31
them, the children yet **u**, ...Ps 78:6

UNCHANGEABLE
But he is **u**, and who can .... Jb 23:13
the **u** character of his..........................Heb 6:17

UNCIRCUMCISED
with the gospel to the **u**, ... Gal 2:7
and Jew, circumcised and **u**, ...Col 3:11

UNCLEAN
lost; for I am a man of **u** lips,................Is 6:5
that nothing is **u** in itself, ...Rom 14:14
and touch no **u** thing;................... 2 Cor 6:17

UNDERSTAND
uttered what I did not **u**, ... Jb 42:3
but **u** what the will of the.................Eph 5:17
in them that are hard to **u**,.............. 2 Pt 3:16

UNDERSTANDING
do not lean on your own **u**. ....Prv 3:5
he who keeps **u** will.............................Prv 19:8
and **u** to interpret dreams, ... Dn 5:12
Who is wise and **u** among ....Jas 3:13

UNDERSTANDS
no one **u**; no one seeks for................Rom 3:11
with conceit and **u** nothing. .... 1 Tm 6:4

UNFRUITFUL
Take no part in the **u** ....Eph 5:11

UNGODLINESS
u and unrighteousness of ....Rom 1:18
into more and more **u**,.....................2 Tm 2:16

UNGODLY
him who justifies the **u**, ...Rom 4:5
time Christ died for the **u**..................Rom 5:6
what will become of the **u** .... 1 Pt 4:18

UNITE
u my heart to fear your......................Ps 86:11
time, to **u** all things in him, ...Eph 1:10

UNITED
For if we have been **u** with ....Rom 6:5
but that you be **u** in the................. 1 Cor 1:10
because they were not **u** by ....Heb 4:2

UNITY
is when brothers dwell in **u**!.............Ps 133:1
eager to maintain the **u** of ....Eph 4:3
until we all attain to the **u** ....Eph 4:13
have **u** of mind, sympathy, ... 1 Pt 3:8

UNIVERSE
and he upholds the **u** by the...............Heb 1:3
that the **u** was created by ....Heb 11:3

UNJUST
rain on the just and on the **u**..............Mt 5:45
of both the just and the **u**. ....Acts 24:15

UNLEAVENED
observe the Feast of **U** Bread, ... Ex 12:17

UNPUNISHED
evil person will not go **u**, ...Prv 11:21
false witness will not go **u**, ...Prv 19:5

UNRIGHTEOUSNESS
But if our **u** serves to show................Rom 3:5
but had pleasure in **u**.................. 2 Thes 2:12

UNSEARCHABLE
How **u** are his judgments ....Rom 11:33
the **u** riches of Christ, ...Eph 3:8

UNWORTHY
say, 'We are **u** servants; .... Lk 17:10
in an **u** manner will be .... 1 Cor 11:27

UPHOLD
and **u** me with a willing ....Ps 51:12
U me according to your.................Ps 119:116
the contrary, we **u** the law. ....Rom 3:31

UPRIGHT
that man was blameless and **u**,............ Jb 1:1
For the word of the Lord is **u**,...............Ps 33:4
but the prayer of the **u** is..................Prv 15:8
and to live self-controlled, **u**, ... Ti 2:12

URGE
u you to walk in a manner..................Eph 4:1
Teach and **u** these things.................1 Tm 6:2
Beloved, I **u** you as .... 1 Pt 2:11

UTTERANCE
as the Spirit gave them **u**..................Acts 2:4
the Spirit the **u** of wisdom,............ 1 Cor 12:8

VAIN
of the Lord your God in **v**, ... Ex 20:7
unless you believed in **v**. .... 1 Cor 15:2
did not run in **v** or labor in ....Phil 2:16

VALLEY
through the **v** of the shadow ....Ps 23:4
is near in the **v** of decision.................. Jl 3:14
Every **v** shall be filled, and.................... Lk 3:5

VEIL
And the **v** shall separate for............. Ex 26:33
he put a **v** over his face..................... Ex 34:33
that same **v** remains...................... 2 Cor 3:14

VENGEANCE
For the Lord has a day of **v**,..................Is 34:8
"**V** is mine, I will repay, ...Rom 12:19

VESSEL
lump one **v** for honorable use...........Rom 9:21
he will be a **v** for honorable............2 Tm 2:21

VICTORY
until he brings justice to **v**; ....Mt 12:20
is swallowed up in **v**." .... 1 Cor 15:54
And this is the **v** that has.................. 1 Jn 5:4

VINE
"I am the true **v**, and my.................... Jn 15:1

VIOLENCE
V shall no more be heard in ....Is 60:18
Put away **v** and oppression, ... Ez 45:9

VIRGIN
Behold, the **v** shall conceive................Is 7:14
to a **v** betrothed to a man.................. Lk 1:27
to present you as a pure **v**............. 2 Cor 11:2

VISIONS
your young men shall see **v**. .... Jl 2:28

VOICE
Today, if you hear his **v**,......................Ps 95:7
The sheep hear his **v**, and he .... Jn 10:3
"Today, if you hear his **v**, ...Heb 3:7

VOW
If a man vows a **v** to the................... Nm 30:2
When you **v** a **v** to God, ... Eccl 5:4

WAGES
the laborer deserves his **w**. .... Lk 10:7
For the **w** of sin is death,..................Rom 6:23
laborer deserves his **w**.".................1 Tm 5:18

WAIT
I **w** for your salvation, O .... Gn 49:18
Be still before the Lord and **w** ....Ps 37:7
groan inwardly as we **w**..................Rom 8:23
to eat, **w** for one another .... 1 Cor 11:33

WAITED
I **w** patiently for the Lord; ....Ps 40:1
when God's patience **w** in................. 1 Pt 3:20

WALK
You shall **w** in all the way................... Dt 5:33
from those who **w** uprightly. ....Ps 84:11
the good way is; and **w** in it, ... Jer 6:16
But I say, **w** by the Spirit, ... Gal 5:16
carefully then how you **w**, ...Eph 5:15
But if we **w** in the light,...................... 1 Jn 1:7

WALKED
Enoch **w** with God, and he................. Gn 5:24
Noah **w** with God. .... Gn 6:9
the boat and **w** on the water ....Mt 14:29

WALKING
the Lord God **w** in the garden .... Gn 3:8
w blamelessly in all the .... Lk 1:6
you are no longer **w** in ....Rom 14:15

WALKS
your God **w** in the midst .... Dt 23:14
Whoever **w** in uprightness ....Prv 14:2
Let him who **w** in darkness................Is 50:10
The one who **w** in the....................... Jn 12:35

WALL
and the **w** fell down flat, ...Jos 6:20
Come, let us build the **w** of ....Neh 2:17
the dividing **w** of hostility.................Eph 2:14
It had a great, high **w**, with..............Rv 21:12

WANT
is my shepherd; I shall not **w**. ....Ps 23:1
For I do not do what I **w**,..................Rom 7:15

WAR
a time to hate; a time for **w**,.............. Eccl 3:8
neither shall they learn **w**......................Is 2:4
to the end there shall be **w**................ Dn 9:26

WARFARE
For the weapons of our **w** .... 2 Cor 10:4
you may wage the good **w**, ...1 Tm 1:18

WARN
But if you **w** the wicked, and .... Ez 3:19
I **w** you, as I warned you .... Gal 5:21
but **w** him as a brother................ 2 Thes 3:15

WARNED
by them is your servant **w**; ....Ps 19:11
him who **w** them on earth,.............Heb 12:25

WARS
He makes **w** cease to the end.............Ps 46:9
And you will hear of **w** and ....Mt 24:6

WASH
W me thoroughly from my ....Ps 51:2
and **w** away your sins,...................Acts 22:16
Blessed are those who **w**..................Rv 22:14

WASHED
But you were **w**, you were .... 1 Cor 6:11
bodies **w** with pure water. ....Heb 10:22
They have **w** their robes and................Rv 7:14

WASHING
her by the **w** of water with................Eph 5:26
by the **w** of regeneration and................. Ti 3:5

WATCH
W therefore, for you know.................Mt 25:13
Keep **w** on yourself, lest you .... Gal 6:1
Keep a close **w** on yourself ....1 Tm 4:16

WATCHFUL
Be **w**, stand firm in the .... 1 Cor 16:13
being **w** in it with ....Col 4:2
Be sober-minded; be **w**. Your............. 1 Pt 5:8

WATER
I am poured out like **w**,......................Ps 22:14
give him **w** to drink, ...Prv 25:21
is like a tree planted by **w**, ... Jer 17:8
"I baptize you with **w** for ....Mt 3:11
cup of cold **w** because he is ....Mt 10:42
unless one is born of **w** and .... Jn 3:5
will flow rivers of living **w**.'" .... Jn 7:38
formed out of **w** and through **w**......... 2 Pt 3:5
them to springs of living **w**, ...Rv 7:17

WATERED
waters will himself be **w**. ....Prv 11:25
I planted, Apollos **w**, but .... 1 Cor 3:6

WATERS
over the face of the **w**.......................... Gn 1:2
He leads me beside still **w**. ....Ps 23:2
water, whose **w** do not fail..................Is 58:11
the fountain of living **w**,...................... Jer 2:13

WAY
the **w** of the wicked will perish..............Ps 1:6
Teach me your **w**, O Lord, that I ....Ps 86:11
young man keep his **w** pure?............Ps 119:9
there be any grievous **w** in me,........Ps 139:24
There is a **w** that seems right ....Prv 16:25
Train up a child in the **w** he ....Prv 22:6
do not know the **w** the spirit............ Eccl 11:5
shall be called the **W** of Holiness;........Is 35:8
— every one — to his own **w**; ....Is 53:6
'Prepare the **w** of the Lord; ....Mt 3:3
but truly teach the **w** of God............. Lk 20:21
Jesus said to him, "I am the **w**, ... Jn 14:6
you, that according to the **W**, ...Acts 24:14
hindrance in the **w** of a brother......Rom 14:13
you a still more excellent **w**. .... 1 Cor 12:31
We are afflicted in every **w**, ... 2 Cor 4:8
godliness is of value in every **w**,........ 1 Tm 4:8

WAYS
teach transgressors your w, … Ps 51:13
neither are your w my w, … Is 55:8
for the w of the Lord are … Hos 14:9
how inscrutable his w! … Rom 11:33

WEAK
willing, but the flesh is w." … Mt 26:41
God chose what is w in … 1 Cor 1:27
To the w I became w, … 1 Cor 9:22
For when I am w, then … 2 Cor 12:10
strengthen your w knees, … Heb 12:12

WEAKER
be w are indispensable, … 1 Cor 12:22
the woman as the w vessel, … 1 Pt 3:7

WEAKNESS
Spirit helps us in our w. … Rom 8:26
he himself is beset with w. … Heb 5:2

WEAKNESSES
not boast, except of my w. … 2 Cor 12:5
to sympathize with our w, … Heb 4:15

WEALTH
Honor the Lord with your w … Prv 3:9
who have w to enter the … Mk 10:23

WEAPONS
with the w of righteousness … 2 Cor 6:7
For the w of our warfare … 2 Cor 10:4

WEARY
they shall run and not be w; … Is 40:31
And let us not grow w of … Gal 6:9

WEDDING
who had no w garment … Mt 22:11
Jesus also was invited to the w … Jn 2:2

WEEP
a time to w, and a time to … Eccl 3:4
"Blessed are you who w now, … Lk 6:21
w with those who w. … Rom 12:15

WEEPING
W may tarry for the night, … Ps 30:5
In that place there will be w … Mt 8:12

WEPT
When I w and humbled my … Ps 69:10
Jesus w. … Jn 11:35

WHIRLWIND
Elijah up to heaven by a w, … 2 Kgs 2:1
Job out of the w and said: … Jb 38:1
His way is in w and storm, … Na 1:3

WHITE
they shall be as w as snow; … Is 1:18
his clothing was w as snow, … Dn 7:9
The hairs of his head were w, … Rv 1:14

WHOLE
who seek him with their w … Ps 119:2
you the w counsel of God … Acts 20:27
For whoever keeps the w … Jas 2:10

WICKED
Therefore the w will not stand … Ps 1:5
the w will be no more; … Ps 37:10
let the w forsake his way, … Is 55:7
nor speak to warn the w … Ez 3:18
in the death of the w, … Ez 18:23
though I say to the w, … Ez 33:14
For everyone who does w … Jn 3:20

WIDOW
for the fatherless and the w, … Dt 10:18
and he saw a poor w put in … Lk 21:2

WIDOWS
Honor w who are truly … 1 Tm 5:3
to visit orphans and w in … Jas 1:27

WIFE
and hold fast to his w, … Gn 2:24
and rejoice in the w of your … Prv 5:18
An excellent w is the crown … Prv 12:4
a quarrelsome w are alike; … Prv 27:15
An excellent w who can … Prv 31:10
everyone who divorces his w, … Mt 5:32
own w and each woman … 1 Cor 7:2
should not divorce his w. … 1 Cor 7:11
of the w even as Christ … Eph 5:23
Bride, the w of the Lamb." … Rv 21:9

WILL
the w of the Lord to crush him; … Is 53:10
kingdom come, your w be done, … Mt 6:10
does the w of my Father … Mt 12:50
anyone's w is to do God's w, … Jn 7:17
who works in you, both to w … Phil 2:13
captured by him to do his w. … 2 Tm 2:26
and by your w they existed … Rv 4:11

WILLING
and uphold me with a w … Ps 51:12
The spirit indeed is w, but … Mt 26:41

WILLS
mercy on whomever he w, … Rom 9:18
ought to say, "If the Lord w, … Jas 4:15

WIN
that I might w more of … 1 Cor 9:19
but may w a full reward. … 2 Jn 1:8

WIND
like a mighty rushing w, … Acts 2:2
by every w of doctrine, … Eph 4:14
is driven and tossed by the w. … Jas 1:6

WINE
W is a mocker, strong drink … Prv 20:1
For your love is better than w; … Sg 1:2
the water now become w, … Jn 2:9
do not get drunk with w, … Eph 5:18
but use a little w for the … 1 Tm 5:23

WINGS
me in the shadow of your w, … Ps 17:8
they shall mount up with w … Is 40:31
her brood under her w, … Lk 13:34

WIPE
and the Lord God will w … Is 25:8
He will w away every tear … Rv 21:4

WISDOM
And God gave Solomon w … 1 Kgs 4:29
Lord is the beginning of w; … Ps 111:10
Lord is the beginning of w, … Prv 9:10
Yet w is justified by her … Mt 11:19
For the w of this world is … 1 Cor 3:19
If any of you lacks w, let him … Jas 1:5
But the w from above is first … Jas 3:17

WISE
is sure, making w the simple; … Ps 19:7
Be not w in your own eyes; … Prv 3:7
A w son makes a glad father, … Prv 10:1
silent is considered w; … Prv 17:28
w men from the east came to … Mt 2:1
Claiming to be w, they … Rom 1:22
Never be w in your own … Rom 12:16
the world to shame the w; … 1 Cor 1:27

WITNESS
"You shall not bear false w … Ex 20:16
A truthful w saves lives, … Prv 14:25
conscience also bears w, … Rom 2:15
Jesus Christ the faithful w, … Rv 1:5

WITNESSES
of two w or of three … Dt 19:15
and you will be my w in … Acts 1:8
of two or three w. … 1 Tm 5:19
by so great a cloud of w, … Heb 12:1

WIVES
W, submit to your own … Eph 5:22

WOLF
The w shall dwell with the … Is 11:6
sees the w coming and … Jn 10:12

WOMAN
into a w and brought her … Gn 2:22
that you are a worthy w. … Ru 3:11
but a w who fears the Lord … Prv 31:30
at a w with lustful intent … Mt 5:28
For a married w is bound … Rom 7:2
but w is the glory of man. … 1 Cor 11:7
sent forth his Son, born of w, … Gal 4:4
Let a w learn quietly with … 1 Tm 2:11
showing honor to the w as … 1 Pt 3:7

WOMB
I came from my mother's w, … Jb 1:21
together in my mother's w. … Ps 139:13
his mother's w he shall go … Eccl 5:15

WOMEN
"Blessed are you among w, … Lk 1:42
likewise also that w should … 1 Tm 2:9
Older w likewise are to be … Ti 2:3

WONDERFUL
I will recount all of your w … Ps 9:1
and his name shall be called W … Is 9:6
for you have done w things, … Is 25:1

WONDERS
who alone does great w, … Ps 136:4
"And I will show w in the … Jl 2:30
And I will show w in the … Acts 2:19

WOOD
down before a block of w?" … Is 44:19
stones, w, hay, straw — … 1 Cor 3:12

WORD
After these things the w of … Gn 15:1

NOTES

NOTES

NOTES

NOTES

NOTES